Contemporary Authors

Contemporary Authors

A Bio-Bibliographical Guide to
Current Writers in Fiction, General Nonfiction,
Poetry, Journalism, Drama, Motion Pictures,
Television, and Other Fields

FRANCES C. LOCHER
Editor

MARTHA G. CONWAY
B. HAL MAY
DAVID VERSICAL
Associate Editors

volume 106

GALE RESEARCH COMPANY • THE BOOK TOWER • DETROIT, MICHIGAN 48226

EDITORIAL STAFF

Christine Nasso, *General Editor, Contemporary Authors*

Frances C. Locher, *Editor, Original Volumes*

Martha G. Conway, B. Hal May, and David Versical, *Associate Editors*

Charity Anne Dorgan, Anne M. Guerrini, Les Stone,
and Mary Sullivan, *Senior Assistant Editors*

Tim Connor, Diane L. Dupuis, Susan D. Finley, Nancy S. Gearhart,
Debra G. Jones, Michael L. LaBlanc, Nancy Pear, Lillian S. Sims,
and Susan M. Trosky, *Assistant Editors*

Dean D. Dauphinais, Shirley Kuenz, Timothy P. Loszewski,
Christine J. May, Barbara Rutkowski, Norma Sawaya,
and Shirley Seip, *Editorial Assistants*

Linda Metzger, *Index Coordinator*

Adele Sarkissian, *Contributing Editor*

Ann Bardach, Peter Benjaminson, Barbara Braun, C. H. Gervais,
Trisha Gorman, Jean W. Ross, and Judith Spiegelman, *Interviewers*

Eunice Bergin, *Copy Editor*

Special recognition is given to the staff of
Young People's Literature Department, Gale Research Company

Frederick G. Ruffner, *Publisher*　　　　　　　　　　James M. Ethridge, *Editorial Director*

Copyright © 1982 by
GALE RESEARCH COMPANY

Library of Congress Catalog Card Number 62-52046
ISBN 0-8103-1906-3
ISSN 0010-7468

Authors and Media People
Featured in This Volume

Berenice Abbott—American photographer; author of several books on the subject, including *Changing New York;* recognized as one of the foremost photographers of this century.

Kenneth Anger—Avant-garde American underground filmmaker; best-known films include "Fireworks," "Scorpio Rising," and "Lucifer Rising"; considered an authority on scandals in the motion picture industry, the subject of his book *Hollywood Babylon.* (Sketch includes interview.)

Walter Bernstein—American screenwriter best known for his scripts for "Fail Safe," "The Front," and "Semi-Tough." (Sketch includes interview.)

Bernardo Bertolucci—Award-winning Italian screenwriter and motion picture director; "Before the Revolution," "The Conformist," and "Last Tango in Paris" are among his best-known works.

Barry Bingham, Jr.—American newspaper executive; editor and publisher of the *Louisville Courier-Journal* and *Louisville Times.* (Sketch includes interview.)

Malcolm J. Bosse—American novelist; author of several award-winning books, including *The Journey of Tao Kim Nam, The Seventy-nine Squares,* and *Ganesh.*

Antonio Buero Vallejo—Award-winning Spanish painter and playwright; leading figure in Spain's Theatre of Commitment; author of many tragedies and historical plays, notably "El sueno de la razon."

Douglas Crase—American poet; his book of poems, *The Revisionist,* was nominated for the 1981 National Book Critics Circle Award in poetry

R. Crumb—First American underground cartoonist to have his work issued by a trade publisher; *R. Crumb's Fritz the Cat,* published by Ballantine, remains one of Crumb's best-known and most popular creations.

Richard M. Dorson—American folklorist who died in 1981; author of well-received works in his field, notably *Jonathan Draws the Long Bow, America Begins,* and *America Rebels.*

Tess Gallagher—Award-winning American poet; best known for her collection of poems *Instructions to the Double.*

Emily Genauer—Well-known American art journalist and critic; only individual ever to win a Pulitzer Prize for art criticism; in addition to her newspaper work, Genauer has written a number of books in her field, including *Modern Interiors Today and Tomorrow.* (Sketch includes interview.)

Peter Gzowski—Canadian journalist; hosted "This Country in the Morning" for radio and "90 Minutes Live" for television. (Sketch includes interview.)

Paavo Juhani Haavikko—Prize-winning Finnish author, recognized as a major contributor to Finland's post-World War II modernist revival; author of fiction, essays, and poetry, including the nine-cycle poem *Talvipalatsi* ("The Winter Palace"), considered a landmark of modern Finnish literature.

David J. Hagberg—American novelist; author of "Nick Carter" and "Flash Gordon" series in addition to several other books, notably *The Kremlin Conspiracy,* published under his Sean Flannery pseudonym.

Ian Hamilton—British poet and poetry critic; founder and editor of *Review* (now *New Review*); among his books are *A Poetry Chronicle: Essays and Reviews* and *The Little Magazines: A Study of Six Editors.*

John Hammond—Well-known American record producer; discoverer of some of jazz's most influential talents, including Teddy Wilson, Billie Holiday, and the Count Basie Band; a lifelong activist for racial equality, Hammond wrote articles exposing discrimination in the record industry; also author of his autobiography, *John Hammond on Record.*

Alfred Hayes—American novelist and screenwriter; best-known works include *The Girl on the Via Flaminia* and such screen adaptations as "The Left Hand of God," "Island in the Sun," and "A Hatful of Rain." (Sketch includes interview.)

Bohumil Hrabal—Czechoslovakian writer; books in English translation include *The Death of Mr. Baltisberger* and *Closely Watched Trains;* his screen adaptation of the latter work received an Academy Award for best foreign language film in 1967.

B. Kliban—American cartoonist and painter best known for his cat cartoons; among his books of cartoons are *Cat, Never Eat Anything Bigger Than Your Head, and Other Drawings,* and *Two Guys Fooling Around With the Moon.*

Alfred A. Knopf—American publishing executive; founder, in 1915, of his own publishing company; known for having "set and maintained the highest standards in American publishing."

John Korty—American filmmaker; notable achievements include "The Autobiography of Miss Jane Pittman" and "Who Are the DeBolts? And Where Did They Get Nineteen Kids?"

Frederick Leboyer—French obstetrician who advocates gentle childbirthing procedures; author of well-known book *Birth Without Violence.*

Harold A. Loeb—American novelist and editor who died in 1974; founder and chief editor of *Broom: An International Magazine of the Arts,* which featured the writing of Hart Crane, William Carlos Williams, and Gertrude Stein, among others; author of three novels, several economics texts, and his autobiography, *The Way It Was;* served as the prototype for the character Robert Cohn in Ernest Hemingway's novel *The Sun Also Rises.*

John E. Mack—American psychiatrist and biographer; Mack's biography of Lawrence of Arabia, *Prince of Our Disorder: The*

Life of T.E. Lawrence, was awarded the 1976 Pulitzer Prize in biography. (Sketch includes interview.)

Mary McGrory—Pulitzer Prize-winning American journalist; author of syndicated political column. (Sketch includes interview.)

Bette Midler—American recording artist and stage personality well known for earthy performances; author of *View From a Broad,* recounting her 1978 international tour.

Jane Pauley—Award-winning American broadcast journalist; co-anchor of NBC-TV's "Today" show.

Stephen Poliakoff—British playwright of the New Left; "Strawberry Fields," "City Sugar," "Hitting Town," and "American Days" are among his works.

Leon Radzinowicz—Internationally known Polish-born British criminologist; author of works in his field, including the multi-volume classic, *A History of English Criminal Law and Its Administration From 1750.*

Bob Randall—American playwright, television writer, and novelist; among his works are the award-winning play "6 Rms Riv Vu" and *The Fan,* a novel.

James Fowler Ridgeway—American investigative journalist and political columnist for the *Village Voice;* author of *The Politics of Ecology, The Closed Corporation: American Universities in Crisis,* and other exposes.

Robert Scheer—American free-lance writer and journalist; noted practitioner, during the 1960's, of what he calls "counter-journalism"; served as managing editor and editor in chief of *Ramparts* and West Coast editor of *New Times;* author of *How the United States Got Involved in Vietnam, America After Nixon,* and other books.

George Davis Snell—American scientist specializing in mice genetics; co-recipient of 1980 Nobel Prize in physiology and medicine; author of works in his field.

Paolo Soleri—Italian-born architect; founder of Cosanti Foundation in Scottsdale, Ariz.; architect of Arcosanti, a visionary city in the Arizona desert begun in 1970; his books include *Arcology: The City in the Image of Man* and *The Bridge Between Matter and Spirit Is Matter Becoming Spirit.*

Benjamin Stein—American writer and syndicated columnist; former television scriptwriter, political speechwriter, and Federal Trade Commission lawyer; author of both nonfiction books and novels, including *Moneypower* and *On the Brink,* as well as his memoir, *Dreemz.* (Sketch includes interview.)

Herbert Stein—American economist and educator who served as chairman of President Richard M. Nixon's Council of Economic Advisers in the early 1970's; author of syndicated column for *Wall Street Journal* as well as numerous economics texts; co-author with son, Benjamin Stein, of the novel *On the Brink.*

Arkadii Strugatskii—Soviet science fiction author who has collaborated with his brother Boris on such novels as *The Ugly Swan, Roadside Picnic,* and *Definitely Maybe.*

Boris Strugatskii—Soviet science fiction novelist and short story writer; co-author with brother Arkadii of numerous science fiction works; the Strugatskiis are considered "among the most Westernized sources of Eastern SF."

Harry S. Truman—Thirty-third American president who died in 1972; author of his memoirs, *Years of Decisions* and *Years of Trial and Hope.*

Pamela Zekman—Award-winning American investigative journalist; won several national awards, including two Pulitzer Prizes, for her newspaper series on voting fraud, hospital abuses, slum landlords, and other issues. (Sketch includes interview.)

Preface

The over 1,400 entries in *Contemporary Authors,* Volume 106, bring to more than 70,000 the number of authors now represented in the *Contemporary Authors* series. *CA* includes nontechnical writers in all genres—fiction, nonfiction, poetry, drama, etc.—whose books are issued by commercial, risk publishers or by university presses. Authors of books published only by known vanity or author-subsidized firms are ordinarily not included. Since native language and nationality have no bearing on inclusion in *CA,* authors who write in languages other than English are included in *CA* if their works have been published in the United States or translated into English.

Although *CA* focuses primarily on authors of published books, the series also encompasses prominent persons in communications: newspaper and television reporters and correspondents, columnists, newspaper and magazine editors, photojournalists, syndicated cartoonists, screenwriters, television scriptwriters, and other media people.

Starting with Volume 104, the editors of *CA* began to broaden the series' scope to encompass authors deceased since 1900 whose works are still of interest to today's readers. (Previously, *CA* covered only living writers and authors deceased 1960 or later.) Since the great poets, novelists, short story writers, and playwrights of the early twentieth century are popular writers for study in today's high school and college curriculums, and since their writings continue to be analyzed by today's literary critics, these writers are in many ways as contemporary as the authors *CA* has featured up to this point.

Therefore, future volumes of *CA* will contain full-length sketches on important authors who lived and wrote between 1900 and 1959. To begin providing information on authors from this period, most of whom will receive longer treatment later, we are including in *CA* volumes brief, one-paragraph entries on such authors. These brief entries are further explained in the section of the preface below headed "Brief Entries."

No charge or obligation is attached to a *CA* listing. Authors are included in the series solely on the basis of the above criteria and their interest to *CA* users.

Compilation Methods

The editors make every effort to secure information directly from the authors through questionnaires and personal correspondence. If authors of special interest to *CA* users are deceased or fail to reply to requests for information, material is gathered from other reliable sources. Biographical dictionaries are checked (a task made easier through the use of Gale's *Biography and Genealogy Master Index* and other volumes in the "Gale Biographical Index Series"), as are bibliographical sources, such as *Cumulative Book Index* and *The National Union Catalog.* Published interviews, feature stories, and book reviews are examined, and often material is supplied by the authors' publishers. All sketches, whether prepared from questionnaires or through extensive research, are sent to the authors for review prior to publication.Sketches on recently deceased authors are sent to family members, agents, etc., if possible, for a similar review.

Brief Entries

CA users have indicated that having some information, however brief, on authors not yet in the series would be preferable to waiting until full-length sketches can be prepared as outlined above under "Compilation Methods." Since Volume 104, therefore, *CA* has included one-paragraph entries on both early twentieth-century and current writers who presently do not have sketches in *CA.* These short listings, identified by the heading *BRIEF ENTRY,* highlight the author's career and writings and often provide a few sources where additional information can be found.

Brief entries are not intended to replace sketches. Instead, they are designed to increase *CA*'s comprehensiveness and thus better serve *CA* users by providing pertinent information about a large number of authors, many of whom will be the subjects of full sketches in forthcoming volumes.

This volume, for example, includes brief entries on living authors, such as Pope John Paul II, economist Robert Lekachman, journalist and former presidential press secretary Ron Nessen, and U.S. Senator John

Tower. As noted earlier in the preface, Volume 106 also contains a substantial number of brief entries on authors deceased since 1900 who are still of interest to today's readers. Among the early twentieth-century authors in this volume who are slated for full sketch treatment in the future are Theodore Dreiser, Anatole France, and John Reed.

Informative Sidelights

Numerous *CA* sketches contain Sidelights, which provide a personal dimension to the listing, supply information about the critical reception the authors' works have received, or both. Some authors work closely with *CA*'s editors to develop lengthy, incisive Sidelights, as in the case of romance novelist Marguerite Lazarus, who remarks, "I am interested in the contrast between the surface of civilized society and the more primitive impulses it conceals, and in the exploitation of gentle and generous people by their opposites." In such works as *The Look of Innocence* and *Flowers for Lilian,* she explains, the stories "revolve around close-knit, claustrophobic relationships," often bearing the "tension [that] arises from some element of mystery: secrecy, deception, and illusion, and the gradual accumulation of detail leading to its disclosure." The author, too, encounters a similar process of disclosure, she suggests: "One finds a pattern of images emerging, and similar themes recur in stories which seemed in their inception quite different....It isn't so much a matter of creating another world as of being admitted to it. The story is there. One finds it."

Victoria Mauricio, a spiritualist who possesses both psychic and healing powers, informs *CA*'s editors of the unusual circumstances behind her first book, *The Return of Chief Black Foot:* "It has been said that [my book] is fifty years ahead of its time. It is absolute proof of communication between the so-called dead and the living. It is incredible when one realizes that a spirit [Black Foot] came to me and told me that he wanted to be brought back to his own tribe.... His people (the Crow Indians) were led to his burial place through visions and dreams he brought to me." According to Mauricio, her role in the return of Black Foot was foretold in a prophecy more than two hundred years old, which predicted "that a great chief would be brought back to his tribe, that an outsider would bring him back and that the outsider would have healing powers."

CA's editors compile equally incisive Sidelights when authors and media people of particular interest to *CA* readers do not supply Sidelights material, or when demand for information about the critical reception their works have received is especially high. For instance, in his Sidelights on Italian director Bernardo Bertolucci, senior assistant editor Les Stone reports on the critical debate inspired by such films as "Last Tango in Paris," "1900," and "Luna." *Time*'s Frank Rich declares, "If Bertolucci irritates as much as he dazzles, he never bores: his extravagant failure has greater staying power than most other director's triumphs," but reviewer Stanley Kauffmann strongly disagrees: "[Bertolucci] is a monstrous and disgusting artist, not a failed authentic one."

John Hammond has long been regarded as a virtuoso among record producers. In his concise review of Hammond's special place in the recording industry, assistant editor Tim Connor outlines a career that spans the "golden age" of jazz and the contemporary world of rock music. Numbering Teddy Wilson, Billie Holiday, Count Basie, Bob Dylan, and Bruce Springsteen among his discoveries, Hammond announces in his autobiography, "I still expect to hear, if not today then tomorrow, a voice or sound I have never heard, with something to say which has never been said before."

In her Sidelights for Paavo Haavikko, assistant editor Susan M. Trosky describes a major figure in Finland's modernist revival. A versatile and prolific writer, Haavikko is the author of the nine-cycle poem *Talvipalatsi* ("The Winter Palace"), which "firmly established Haavikko as the most original voice in postwar Finnish poetry" and became "one of the landmarks of modern Finnish literature." This single work, observes critic Richard Dauenhauer, convinced younger Finnish poets "to redefine their conception of lyric poetry."

Architect Paolo Soleri's Sidelights, by assistant editor Nancy Pear, surveys the work of a man "better known for what he has not built than for what he has." Since 1970 Soleri has pursued his vision of a "melding of architecture and ecology" in the Arizona desert city known as Arcosanti. Although only 2 percent complete, it represents, in one critic's view, "a mystical vision in concrete."

And senior assistant editor Charity Anne Dorgan writes about investigative journalist James Fowler Ridgeway, author of *The Closed Corporation: American Universities in Crisis.* The "idea that the university is a community of scholars is a myth," Ridgeway contends. "The charming elitism of the professors has long since given way to the greed of the social and political scientists whose manipulative theories aim only at political power."

These sketches, as well as others with Sidelights compiled by *CA*'s editors, provide informative and enjoyable reading.

Writers of Special Interest

CA's editors make every effort to include a substantial number of entries in each volume on active authors and media people of special interest to *CA*'s readers. Since *CA* also includes sketches on noteworthy deceased writers, a significant amount of work on the part of *CA*'s editors goes into the compilation of full-length entries on important deceased authors. Some of the prominent writers, both living and deceased, whose sketches are contained in this volume are noted in the list headed "Authors and Media People Featured in This Volume" immediately preceding the preface.

Exclusive Interviews

CA provides exclusive, primary information on certain authors in the form of interviews. Prepared specifically for *CA,* the never-before-published conversations presented in the section of the sketch headed *CA INTERVIEW* give *CA* users the opportunity to learn the authors' thoughts, in depth, about their craft. Subjects chosen for interviews are, the editors feel, authors who hold special interest for *CA*'s readers.

Authors and journalists in this volume whose sketches include interviews are Kenneth Anger, Walter Bernstein, Barry Bingham, Jr., Emily Genauer, Peter Gzowski, Alfred Hayes, John E. Mack, Mary McGrory, Benjamin Stein, and Pamela Zekman.

Obituary Notices Make *CA* Timely and Comprehensive

To be as timely and comprehensive as possible, *CA* publishes brief, one-paragraph obituary notices on deceased authors within the scope of the series. These notices provide date and place of birth and death, highlight the author's career and writings, and list other sources where additional biographical information and obituaries may be found. To distinguish them from full-length sketches, obituaries are identified with the heading *OBITUARY NOTICE.*

CA includes obituary notices for authors who already have full-length entries in earlier *CA* volumes—35 percent of the obituary notices in this volume are for such authors—as well as for authors who do not yet have sketches in the series. Deceased authors of special interest presently represented only by obituary notices are scheduled for full-length sketch treatment in forthcoming *CA* volumes.

Contemporary Authors New Revision Series

A major change in the preparation of *CA* revision volumes began with the first volume of the newly titled *Contemporary Authors New Revision Series.* No longer are all of the sketches in a given *CA* volume updated and published together as a revision volume. Instead, sketches from a number of volumes are assessed, and only those sketches requiring *significant change* are revised and published in a *New Revision Series* volume. This change enables us to provide *CA* users with updated information about active writers on a more timely basis and avoids printing sketches in which there has been little or no change. As always, the most recent *CA* cumulative index continues to be the user's guide to the location of an individual author's revised listing.

Retaining *CA* Volumes

As new volumes in the series are published, users often ask which *CA* volumes, if any, can be discarded. Since the *New Revision Series* does not supersede any specific volumes of *CA,* all of the following must be retained in order to have information on all authors in the series:

- all revised volumes
- the two *Contemporary Authors Permanent Series* volumes
- *CA* Volumes 45-48 and subsequent original volumes

The chart following the preface is designed to assist users in keeping their collections as complete as possible.

Cumulative Index Should Always Be Consulted

The key to locating an individual author's listing is the *CA* cumulative index bound into the back of alternate original volumes (and available separately as an offprint). Since the *CA* cumulative index provides access to *all* entries in the *CA* series, the latest cumulative index should always be consulted to find the specific volume containing an author's original or most recently revised sketch.

For the convenience of *CA* users, the *CA* cumulative index also includes references to all entries in three related Gale series—*Contemporary Literary Criticism* (CLC), which is devoted entirely to current criticism of the works of today's novelists, poets, playwrights, short story writers, filmmakers, screenwriters, and other creative writers, *Something About the Author* (SATA), a series of heavily illustrated sketches on authors and illustrators of books for young people, and *Authors in the News* (AITN), a compilation of news stories and feature articles from American newspapers and magazines covering writers and other members of the communciations media.

As always, suggestions from users about any aspect of *CA* will be welcomed.

IF YOU HAVE:	YOU MAY DISCARD:
1-4 First Revision (1967)	1 (1962) 2 (1963) 3 (1963) 4 (1963)
5-8 First Revision (1969)	5-6 (1963) 7-8 (1963)

Both 9-12 First Revision (1974)
    AND *Contemporary Authors Permanent Series,*
    Volume 1 (1975)
	9-10 (1964)
	11-12 (1965)

Both 13-16 First Revision (1975)
    AND *Contemporary Authors Permanent Series,*
    Volumes 1 and 2 (1975, 1978)
	13-14 (1965)
	15-16 (1966)

Both 17-20 First Revision (1976)
    AND *Contemporary Authors Permanent Series,*
    Volumes 1 and 2 (1975, 1978)
	17-18 (1967)
	19-20 (1968)

Both 21-24 First Revision (1977)
    AND *Contemporary Authors Permanent Series,*
    Volumes 1 and 2 (1975, 1978)
	21-22 (1969)
	23-24 (1970)

Both 25-28 First Revision (1977)
    AND *Contemporary Authors Permanent Series,*
    Volume 2 (1978)
	25-28 (1971)

Both 29-32 First Revision (1978)
    AND *Contemporary Authors Permanent Series,*
    Volume 2 (1978)
	29-32 (1972)

Both 33-36 First Revision (1978)
    AND *Contemporary Authors Permanent Series,*
    Volume 2 (1978)
	33-36 (1973)

37-40 First Revision (1979)	37-40 (1973)
41-44 First Revision (1979)	41-44 (1974)
45-48 (1974) 49-52 (1975) 53-56 (1975) 57-60 (1976) ↓ ↓ 106 (1982)	NONE: These volumes will not be super-seded by corresponding revised vol-umes. Individual entries from these and all other volumes appearing in the left column of this chart will be revised and included in the *New Revision Series*.
Volumes in the *Contemporary Authors New Revision Series*	NONE: The *New Revision Series* does not replace any single volume of *CA*. All volumes appearing in the left column of this chart must be retained to have in-formation on all authors in the series.

Contemporary Authors

*Indicates that a listing has been compiled from secondary sources believed to be reliable, but has not been personally verified for this edition by the author sketched.

AARONS, Slim 1916-

BRIEF ENTRY: American photojournalist. A free-lance photographer since 1939, Aarons also worked as a combat photographer during World War II. His work has appeared in major national magazines, including *Harper's, Life,* and *Look.* Aarons wrote *A Wonderful Time: An Intimate Portrait of the Good Life* (Harper, 1974). *Address:* Old Cross River Rd., Katonah, N.Y. 10536. *Biographical/critical sources: Saturday Review,* November 30, 1974.

* * *

AASENG, Nate
See AASENG, Nathan

* * *

AASENG, Nathan 1953-
(Nate Aaseng)

PERSONAL: Born July 7, 1953, in Park Rapids, Minn.; son of Rolf E. and Viola (Anderson) Aaseng; married Linda Jansen, December 20, 1975; children: Jay, Maury. *Education:* Luther College, B.A., 1975. *Home and office:* 2450 Cavell Ave. S., St. Louis Park, Minn. 55426.

CAREER: Bio-Tech Resources, Manitowoc, Wis., microbiologist, 1975-79; writer, 1979—.

WRITINGS—For young people; all published by Lerner, except as noted: *Bruce Jenner: Decathlon Winner,* 1979; *Football's Fierce Defenses,* 1980; *Basketball's High Flyers,* 1980; *Little Giants of Pro Sports,* 1980; *Winners Never Quit,* 1980; *Baseball's Finest Pitchers,* 1980; *Football's Winning Quarterbacks,* 1980; *Football's Breakaway Backs,* 1980; *Football's Sure-Handed Receivers,* 1980; *Eric Heiden: Winner in Gold,* 1980; *Winning Men of Tennis,* 1981; *Winning Women of Tennis,* 1981; *Track's Magnificent Milers,* 1981; *Football's Cunning Coaches,* 1981; *Football's Steadiest Kickers,* 1981; *Football's Toughest Tight Ends,* 1981; *Pete Rose: Baseball's Charlie Hustle,* 1981; (under name Nate Aaseng) *I'm Learning, Lord, but I Still Need Help,* Augsburg, 1981; *Football's Crushing Blockers,* 1982; *World-Class Marathoners,* 1982; *Superstars Stopped Short,* 1982.

WORK IN PROGRESS: Sport books; juvenile fiction.

SIDELIGHTS: Aaseng wrote: "I took a chance on a writing career because I couldn't see myself in any other vocation. I don't consider myself a children's writer or a sportswriter, even though that is what I have written so far. I write what I have the opportunity to write. Aiming at a younger audience requires more effort because a writer has fewer tools (words) to use in communicating."

* * *

ABARBANEL, Sam X. 1914-

BRIEF ENTRY: Born March 17, 1914, in Jersey City, N.J. American producer, publicist, and writer. Abarbanel has been an independent film producer and publicist since World War II. His productions include "Golden Mistress" (United Artists), "Gunfighters of Casa Grande" (Metro-Goldwyn-Mayer), and "Narco Men." His writing credits include the screenplays "Prehistoric Women" (United Artists, 1950), "Last Day of War," and "Summertime Killer" (Avco, 1972).

* * *

ABBOTT, Berenice 1898-

PERSONAL: Born July 17, 1898, in Springfield, Ohio; daughter of Charles E. and Alice (Bunn) Abbott. *Education:* Attended Ohio State University, 1917-18; studied painting and sculpture in New York City, 1918-21, in Paris under Bourdelle and Brancusi, and at Kunstschule, Berlin. *Home:* 50 Commerce St., New York, N.Y. 10014.

CAREER: Photographic assistant to Man Ray, Paris, 1923-25; portrait photographer in Paris, 1926-29; portrait and free-lance magazine photographer in New York City, 1929-35; Federal Art Project, New York City, photographer, 1935-39. Teacher at New School for Social Research, New York City; lecturer, broadcaster of radio presentations. Photographs have been exhibited at one-woman shows in Paris, 1926, at the Museum of Modern Art, 1939, 1970, at Art Institute of Chicago, 1951, and at Smithsonian Institution, 1969.

WRITINGS: A Guide to Better Photography, Crown, 1941, revised edition pubished as *New Guide to Better Photography,* 1953; *The View Camera Made Simple,* Ziff-Davis, 1948; *The World of Atget,* Horizon Press, 1964; *Photographs,* Horizon Press, 1970.

Photographer: Elizabeth McCausland, *Changing New York,* Dutton, 1939, published as *New York in the Thirties,* Dover, 1973; Henry W. Lanier, *Greenwich Village: Today and Yes-*

terday, Harper, 1949; Evans G. Valens, *Magnet* (juvenile), World Publishing, 1964; Valens, *Motion* (juvenile), World Publishing, 1965; Chenoweth Hall, *A Portrait of Maine,* Macmillan, 1968; Valens, *The Attractive Universe: Gravity and the Shape of Space* (juvenile), World Publishing, 1969.

SIDELIGHTS: Berenice Abbott is recognized as one of the foremost photographers of this century and is credited with influencing the development of photography by shifting its early emphasis on pictorialism or "artiness" to an appreciation for realism.

Abbott began taking pictures in the early 1920's while living in Paris among other artists and writers. Initially a portraitist, she became famous for her straightforward photographs of Jean Cocteau, Andre Gide, and James Joyce, to name a few. In an interview with *Art in America,* Abbott revealed the factors that contributed to her success as a portrait photographer. "Each person was extremely important to me," she said. "I wasn't trying to make a still life of them, but a person. It's kind of an exchange between people—it has to be—and I enjoyed it."

This attitude, critics claimed, carried over into Abbott's later work and shaped her "realistic style." According to Abbott, her idea of the "realistic image" referred to the early style of photography which expected photographs to imitate paintings, emphasizing simulation. Holding this to be inevitable and unfortunate, Abbott believed that the view formed by a camera's lens should be the final "reality" presented to the public, making the rearrangement and distortion of what the camera sees unnecessary.

Instead, she submitted, the photographer must rely on his own instincts. "A photographer," Abbott maintained, "explores and discovers and reacts to the world he lives in. There's also the matter of discernment—the way you interpret things, see things and relate them; the way you bring your subjects together. . . . The challenge for me is to see things as they are. I have tried to be, in other words, objective. What I mean by objectivity is the objectivity not of a machine but of a sensible human being, with the mystery of personal selection at the heart of it. The second challenge has been to impose order on the things seen and to supply the visual context and the intellectual framework. That to me is the art of photography."

Commenting on Abbott's style as well as on the photographs she contributed to *Changing New York,* perhaps her best known book, a writer for the *New York Times Book Review* noted that "the value of (this series of photographs on New York City in the early 1930's) lies in its 'straight photography.'"

AVOCATIONAL INTERESTS: Travel, playing the concertina.

BIOGRAPHICAL/CRITICAL SOURCES: Popular Photographer, September, 1938, May, 1939, February, 1940; *Springfield Republican,* April 9, 1939, July 6, 1941; *New York Times Book Review,* April 16, 1939, September 28, 1941; *Nation,* April 29, 1939; *New Republic,* May 17, 1939; *Modern Photography,* September, 1976; *Art in America,* November/December, 1976; Margaretta K. Mitchell, *Recollections: Ten Women of Photography,* Viking, 1979.*

*   *   *

ABBOTT, Philip R.   1944-

BRIEF ENTRY: Born October 18, 1944, in Philadelphia, Pa. American educator and author. Abbott has taught political science at Wayne State University since 1970. His writings include *Reflections in American Political Thought: Readings From Past and Present* (Chandler Publishing, 1973), *The Shotgun Behind the Door: Liberalism and the Problem of Political Ob-*

ligation (University of Georgia Press, 1975), and *Furious Fancies: American Political Thought in the Post-Liberal Era* (Greenwood Press, 1980). *Address:* Department of Political Science, Wayne State University, 888 MacKenzie Hall, 5950 Cass Ave., Detroit, Mich. 48202. *Biographical/critical sources: Virginia Quarterly Review,* summer, 1976; *American Political Science Review,* March, 1978.

*   *   *

ACE, Goodman   1899-1982

OBITUARY NOTICE—See index for *CA* sketch: Born January 15, 1899, in Kansas City, Mo.; died March 25, 1982, in Manhattan, N.Y. Journalist, radio broadcaster, producer, comedy writer, columnist, reviewer, and author. Best known as a humorist, Ace was once called the "utility man of comic writers, one who can bunt for the smile on demand, or swing for the belly laugh." He supplied jokes and skits to several comedians, including Milton Berle, Sid Caesar, Bob Newhart, and Danny Kaye. Beginning his career as a journalist with the *Kansas City Post* and the *Kansas City Journal-Post,* Ace became a broadcaster and comedy writer by chance. In 1928 he started moonlighting as a film critic on radio. One day after his regular fifteen-minute broadcast, a desperate station manager asked him to ad lib on the air until the next scheduled performers showed up. Ace and his wife, Jane, then improvised an amusing chat about a bridge game. The station was so impressed that it hired the couple to do two such programs each week. Their show, "Easy Aces," was noted for Jane Ace's use of humorous malapropisms written for her by her husband. Sporting such lines as "He's a ragged individualist," "Up at the crank of dawn," and "Familiarity breeds attempt," the show became popular and remained on the air for more than fifteen years. In 1945 the program ended due to a squabble between Ace and his sponsors. The couple returned to radio with "Mr. Ace and Jane," but the show was unsuccessful and ended after a year. Ace wrote for various comics for the remainder of his career. He was also a columnist for the *Saturday Review* and wrote a book, *Ladies and Gentlemen: Easy Aces,* published in 1970. Obituaries and other sources: *Chicago Tribune,* March 27, 1982; *New York Times,* March 27, 1982; *Washington Post,* March 28, 1982; *Newsweek,* April 5, 1982; *Time,* April 5, 1982.

*   *   *

ACETO, Vincent J(ohn)   1932-

PERSONAL: Born February 2, 1932, in Schenectady, N.Y.; son of Henry (a foundry worker) and Gilda (Maietta) Aceto; divorced, 1979; children: David Henry, Paul Vincent, Andrew Harry. *Education:* State University of New York at Albany, A.B., 1953, M.A., 1954, M.L.S., 1959. *Home:* 950 Madison Ave., Albany, N.Y. 12208. *Office:* School of Library and Information Science, State University of New York at Albany, Albany, N.Y. 12222.

CAREER: History teacher in public schools in Scotia, N.Y., 1956-57; houseparent-counselor in girls school in Burnt Hills, N.Y.; 1956-58; high school librarian in Burnt Hills, 1957-59; Town of Ballston Community Library, Burnt Hills, library director, 1958-60; State University of New York at Albay, assistant professor, 1959-63, associate professor, 1963-69, professor of library science, 1969—. Visiting lecturer at University of Dacca, East Pakistan (now Bangladesh) 1964-65, and Case Western Reserve University, 1966. Consultant to New York State Education Department and various public school districts. *Military service:* U.S. Army, radio chief, 1954-56.

MEMBER: American Society of Information Science, Association of American Library Schools, American Society of Indexers, American Library Association, American Film Institute, American Association of School Librarians, Association of Educational Communications and Technology, Educational Film Library Association, Film Library Information Council, University Film Association, Bangladesh Library Association, Pakistan Library Association, New York Library Association, Hudson-Mohawk Library Association (vice-president, 1964-66), Phi Delta Kappa. *Awards, honors:* Grants from U.S. Office of Education, 1967-68, New York State Council on the Arts, 1971-72, National Endowment for the Arts, 1979, and National Endowment for the Humanities, 1979-81.

WRITINGS: Film Literature Index, 1973, Bowker, 1975; *Film Literature Index, 1974,* Bowker, 1975; *Film Literature Index, 1975,* Bowker, 1977; *Film Literature: Current,* Filmdex, 1979. Contributor to library journals.

WORK IN PROGRESS: Research on bibliographic control of film and television literature and on information use patterns of film and television scholars.

*   *   *

ADAMS, Douglas Noel   1952-

PERSONAL: Born March 11, 1952, in Cambridge, England; son of Christopher Douglas (a management consultant) and Janet (Donovan) Adams. *Education:* St. John's College, Cambridge, B.A. (with honors). *Agent:* Ed Victor Ltd., 162 Wardour St., London W1, England.

CAREER: British Broadcasting Corporation (BBC), London, England, radio producer and scriptwriter for "Hitchhiker's Guide to the Galaxy" radio and television series, 1978—, script editor for television series "Doctor Who," 1978-80; writer, 1978—.

WRITINGS: The Hitchhiker's Guide to the Galaxy (novel), Pan Books, 1979; *The Restaurant at the End of the Universe* (novel), Pan Books, 1980; *Life, the Universe and Everything* (novel), Harmony, 1982. Also author of episodes of "Doctor Who" for BBC-TV.

SIDELIGHTS: Described by David N. Samuelson of the *Los Angeles Times Book Review* as "'Monty Python in Outer Space,'" Adams's first novel, *The Hitchhiker's Guide to the Galaxy,* is a humorous science fiction work. Based on the hit BBC radio and television series of the same name, the book chronicles the adventures of Arthur Dent, an Englishman, and alien Ford Prefect, Dent's friend who has been posing as an unemployed actor for fifteen years. When Ford warns Arthur that Earth is minutes away from destruction, the two hitch a ride on a space vehicle, narrowly escaping the calamity. Traveling through the galaxy, Prefect and Dent encounter a motley array of characters, including Marvin, a robot; Zaphod Beeblebrox, the three-armed, two-headed galaxy president; and Veet Voojagig, a man bewildered over the disappearance of his ballpoint pens.

Adams told James Brown of the *Los Angeles Times* that the characters are based on people Adams knows. "Arthur Dent is to a certain extent autobiographical," the novelist said. "He moves from one astonishing event to another without fully comprehending what's going on. He's the Everyman character—an ordinary person caught up in some extraordinary events. . . . As for Ford Prefect," Adams added, "well, he's the sort of guy who, when faced with saving the world from destruction or going to a good party, will choose the party every time."

The Hitchhiker's Guide to the Galaxy elicited favorable critical reviews. Noting that "humorous science fiction novels have notoriously limited audiences," Gerald Jonas of the *New York Times Book Review* declared: "The 'Hitchhiker's Guide' is a delightful exception." And Samuelson suggested: "If you've had it with people imputing philosophical depth to 'Star Wars' and the like, and just want to get off on silliness for its own sake, this may be the book for you."

Adams's second effort, *The Restaurant at the End of the Universe,* is a sequel to his first novel. *Restaurant* inspired *Washington Post Book World*'s Ron Goulart to write: "[Adams] has a gift for sending up the sacred precepts of sf and those who took his vastly successful *The Hitchhiker's Guide to the Galaxy* to their hearts will want to perform similar acts with this sequel."

Adams told *CA:* "I first started writing novels inadvertently. I never set out to be a novelist, because I thought I was just a scriptwriter. When I was asked by Pan Books to turn my radio scripts of 'The Hitchhiker's Guide to the Galaxy' into a book, I thought that there were two ways of doing it. I could either do the normal script-novelization hack job, which involves going through the script putting 'he said' or 'she said' (and in the case of my books, 'it said' as well) at the end of each line, or I could have a go at doing it properly. I decided to see if I could do it properly.

"I'm not a science fiction writer, but a comedy writer who happens to be using the conventions of science fiction for this particular thing. I used to hitch a lot when I was a student and loved it. You can't take the slow boat to China anymore as people with wanderlust and no money used to do. So you hitch. Unfortunately it's something you can only do for real, you can't do it as an affectation. I occasionally think it would be great to do some hitching again, but since I can afford to go by car or plane or whatever, it would not work. I'd feel a complete fraud.

"*The Hitchhiker's Guide to the Galaxy* was originally intended to consist of a lot of things that I associated with real hitchhiking transferred up on the cosmic scale, but somehow that never materialized, and there is very little about hitching in it in the end. Still, what you end up with tends to be a by-product of your failure to write whatever it was you set out to write."

The American Broadcasting Company (ABC-TV) holds the rights to release *Hitchhiker's Guide* as a television series in the United States.

BIOGRAPHICAL/CRITICAL SOURCES: Chicago Tribune Book World, October 12, 1980; *Los Angeles Times Book Review,* December 7, 1980; *New York Times Book Review,* January 25, 1981; *Washington Post Book World,* December 27, 1981.

*   *   *

ADAMS, Harriet S(tratemeyer)   1894-1982
(Victor W. Appleton II, Franklin W. Dixon, Laura Lee Hope, Carolyn Keene)

OBITUARY NOTICE—See index for *CA* sketch: Born December 6, 1894, in Newark, N.J.; died of a heart attack, March 27, 1982, in Pottersville, N.J. Business executive and author. Although best known for writing the "Nancy Drew" mystery series, Adams wrote hundreds of other books for children. As head of the Stratemeyer Syndicate, she supervised and often helped in writing stories for such adventure series as "The Hardy Boys," "Tom Swift, Jr.," and "The Bobbsey Twins." Adams began managing the Stratemeyer Syndicate in 1930, when its founder, her father, Edward L. Stratemeyer, died.

Stratemeyer had created most of the series, and after his death Adams continued his work. All of the syndicate's books feature a safe and pleasant world in which curious children had various adventures without the threat of danger. The villains were restricted to the crimes of thievery and arson and were always brought to justice. Good triumphed over evil. Each series was written under one pseudonym used by several authors. The syndicate's books appear in more than one dozen countries around the world, numbering over 250 million copies. At the time of her death, Adams was developing a new ghost story series. She suffered a heart attack while viewing "The Wizard of Oz" on television for the first time. Adams's books include *Clue of the Whistling Bagpipes, Phantom of Pine Hill,* and *Secret of the Forgotten City.* Obituaries and other sources: *New York Times,* March 29, 1982; *London Times,* March 30, 1982; *Washington Post,* March 30, 1982; *Detroit Free Press,* March 30, 1982, March 31, 1982; *Chicago Tribune,* March 30, 1982; *Newsweek,* April 5, 1982; *Publishers Weekly,* April 9, 1982; *AB Bookman's Weekly,* April 12, 1982; *Time,* April 12, 1982; *School Library Journal,* May, 1982.

*   *   *

ADAMS, Harry Baker   1924-

BRIEF ENTRY: Born October 13, 1924, in Stanford, Ky. American educator, minister, and author. An ordained minister of the Christian Church (Disciples of Christ) since 1950, Adams has been a professor of pastoral theology at Yale University's Divinity School since 1956. His writings include *The Life of Faith in God: A Study Course for Adults* (Christian Board of Publication, 1965), *Seeking the Christian Way: The Meaning of Church Membership for Senior Youth and Adults* (Christian Board of Publication, 1965), *God Confronts Man: Adult Leader's Guide* (American Baptist Board of Education and Publication, 1969), and *Priorities and People* (Bethany Press, 1975). *Address:* 228 Crescent Circle, Cheshire, Conn. 06410; and 409 Prospect St., New Haven, Conn. 06510; and Department of Pastoral Theology, Yale University, New Haven, Conn. 06250. *Biographical/critical sources: Who's Who in Religion,* Marquis, 1977.

*   *   *

ADAMS, Ramona Shepherd   1921-

PERSONAL: Born December 17, 1921, in Paris, Idaho; daughter of Earl Budge (a banker) and Jhoun (a real estate broker; maiden name, Chugg) Shepherd; married Wendell Ellison Adams (a company vice-president), December 26, 1941; children: Graig Shepherd (deceased), Stanley Shepherd, John Shepherd, Ann Shepherd (Mrs. H. Brent Whitney), Douglas Shepherd, Richard Shepherd, Wendy Shepherd Adams Mendenhall, Kathryn Shepherd Adams Sidwell. *Education:* San Mateo Junior College, A.A., 1941; University of California, Berkeley, B.A., 1943; University of Utah, M.S.W., 1964, Ph.D., 1969. *Home:* 1727 Countryside Dr., Salt Lake City, Utah 84106. *Office:* 270 Union Building, University of Utah, Salt Lake City, Utah 84112.

CAREER: Henry J. Kaiser Co., Richmond, Calif., assistant director of public relations, 1943-45; Salt Lake City Board of Education, Salt Lake City, Utah, member of social work staff, 1964-65; University of Utah, Salt Lake City, senior staff member at Counseling Center, 1965-69, member of staff at Marriage and Family Therapy Clinic, 1969-70, and School on Alcoholism and Other Drug Dependencies, 1969—, associate professor of social work, 1970—, associate dean of students, 1970—. Private practice in marriage and family counseling. Member

of advisory board of Community Mental Health, Salt Lake City, 1970-72.

MEMBER: American Association of Marriage and Family Therapists, American Personnel and Guidance Association, American Psychological Association, National Association of Social Workers, National Association of Women Deans, Administrators, and Counselors, Academy of Certified Social Workers, Virginia Satirs Avunta Network, Utah Personnel and Guidance Association, Phi Beta Kappa, Alpha Gamma Sigma, Phi Kappa Phi, Delta Kappa Gamma, Mortar Board.

WRITINGS: Letting Go: Uncomplicating Your Life, Macmillan, 1980.

WORK IN PROGRESS: Relationships: The Fourth R, with A. S. Cowley.

SIDELIGHTS: Adams commented: "My career in public relations lasted three years. Then I had eight children and stayed at home to care for them until 1962. I have only begun writing since 1979. I have had some valuable experience in the area of human relations and would like to summarize these experiences through my writings."

*   *   *

ADAMS, Richard E(dward) W(ood)   1931-

PERSONAL: Birth-given name, Richard Edward Wood; name legally changed in 1936; born July 17, 1931, in Kansas City, Mo.; son of Luther E. (a stockbroker) and Hallie (Reece) Wood; married Jane Haven Jackson, December 22, 1955; children: Richard, Katherine, Joseph (deceased), Samuel. *Education:* Attended University of Kansas, 1948-50, University of Pennsylvania, 1950-51, and Kansas City University, 1951; University of New Mexico, B.A., 1953; attended Escuela Nacional de Antropologia e Historia de Mexico and Universidad Autonoma de Mexico, both 1953; Harvard University, M.A., 1960, Ph.D., 1963. *Religion:* Episcopalian. *Home:* 14070 Mint Trail, San Antonio, Tex. 78232. *Office:* College of Humanities and Social Sciences, University of Texas, San Antonio, Tex. 78285.

CAREER: University of Pennsylvania, Museum, Philadelphia, archaeologist on Tikal Project, 1958; in sales, 1958-59; University of Minnesota, Minneapolis, assistant professor, 1963-67, associate professor, 1967-71, professor of anthropology, 1971-72, director of Cotzal Valley Project in Guatemala, 1965-66; University of Texas, San Antonio, professor of anthropology, 1972—, dean of College of Humanities and Social Science, 1972-78. Field director of National Geographic Society's Becan excavations in Mexico, 1970; lecturer for Archaeological Institute of America; conference organizer. *Military service:* U.S. Marine Corps, 1954-57. U.S. Marine Corps Reserve, 1957-67; became captain. *Member:* Society for American Archaeology (president, 1981-83), American Anthropological Association, Sociedad Mexicana de Antropologia, Seminario de Cultura Maya, Mexico. *Awards, honors:* National Science Foundation grant, 1965-66; grants from McMillan Fund, 1968, and Minnesota Foundation (for Yucatan), 1970.

WRITINGS: (Contributor) William R. Bullard, Jr., editor, *Monographs and Essays in Maya Archaeology,* Peabody Museum of Archaeology and Ethnology, Harvard University, 1970; *The Ceramics of Altar de Sacrificios,* Peabody Museum of Archaeology and Ethnology, Harvard University, 1971; *Prehistoric Mesoamerica,* Little, Brown, 1976. Contributor of articles and reviews to archaeology journals. Co-editor of

Handbook of Latin American Studies of the Library of Congress.

WORK IN PROGRESS: Editing *The Archaeology and Ethnohistory of San Juan Batista, Coahuila, Mexico.*

* * *

ADAMSON, Gareth   1925-1982(?)

OBITUARY NOTICE—See index for *CA* sketch: Born May 10, 1925, in Liverpool, England; died c. 1982 in Cambridge, England. Illustrator and author. Adamson wrote more than one hundred children's books during his career. With his wife, Jean Adamson, he produced numerous volumes for the "Topsy and Tim" series. Before devoting himself entirely to writing and illustrating, Adamson worked as a research designer with Hunt Partners Ltd. and as a creative chief with Cravens Advertising Ltd. His works include *Topsy and Tim's Snowy Day, Harold, the Happy Handyman,* and *People at Home.* Obituaries and other sources: *AB Bookman's Weekly,* April 12, 1982.

* * *

ADCOCK, Frank Ezra   1886-1968

OBITUARY NOTICE: Born April 15, 1886, in Desford, England; died February 22, 1968. Educator and author. Adcock was a professor of ancient history at Cambridge University from 1925 to 1951. His writings include *The Character of the Romans in Their History and Their Literature* and *Diplomacy in Ancient Greece.* Obituaries and other sources: *Who Was Who,* Volume VI: *1961-1970,* A. & C. Black, 1972; *Who Was Who Among English and European Authors, 1931-1949,* Gale, 1978.

* * *

ADRIAN, Rhys

BRIEF ENTRY: Playwright. Adrian has written numerous radio and television plays since the 1950's. "Evelyn" (1969) earned him the Italia Prize in 1970. Adrian's writings include "No Charge for Extra Service" (1971), "A Chance Encounter" (1972), "Tea at Four" (1975), and "Buffet" (1976), as well as adaptations of several works by Thomas Hardy and Isaac Bashevis Singer. *Biographical/critical sources: Contemporary Dramatists,* 2nd edition, St. Martin's, 1977.

* * *

AIKEN, Henry David   1912-1982

OBITUARY NOTICE—See index for *CA* sketch: Born July 3, 1912, in Portland, Ore.; died March 30, 1982, in Cambridge, Mass. Educator, editor, and author. An authority on ethics and aesthetics, Aiken taught philosophy at several schools, including Harvard University, Columbia University, and the universities of Washington, Michigan, and California at Los Angeles. He became the Charles Goldman Professor of Philosophy at Brandeis University in 1967, a position he held for more than twelve years. Aiken wrote several books in his field, such as *Reason and Conduct* and *Problems in Aesthetics.* He also edited a number of works, including *Dialogues Concerning Natural Religion, The Age of Ideology,* and *Hume's Moral and Political Philosophy.* Obituaries and other sources: *New York Times,* April 2, 1982.

* * *

ALAN, Sandy
See ULLMAN, Allan

ALBRIGHT, Roger (Lynch)   1922-

PERSONAL: Born November 5, 1922, in Evanston, Ill.; son of Charles Rogers (an educator) and Laura Virginia (a writer; maiden name, Lynch) Albright; married Nina Penelope Lee (an artist and illustrator); children: Elizabeth, Stephen, Andrew, David, Joanna, Nina, Daisy. *Education:* Allegheny College, B.A., 1944; graduate study at Boston University, 1944-45. *Home and office address:* Hanksville Schoolhouse, Starksboro, Vt. 05487. *Agent:* Richard Curtis Associates, Inc., 156 East 52nd St., New York, N.Y. 10022.

CAREER: Student pastor of Methodist churches in East Conneaut, Ohio, 1942-43, and Vernon, Ohio, 1943-44; Fairchild Aircraft, Hagerstown, Md., editor of *Fad,* writer and producer of weekly radio program, and director of special events, 1946-49; WJEJ, Hagerstown, Md., announcer and salesman, 1949-50; WENT, Gloversville, N.Y., station manager, 1950-51; WJW, Cleveland, Ohio, director of advertising, 1951-52; associated with Gregory & House, Cleveland, 1952-53, McCann-Erickson, Cleveland, 1953-55, and Marcus Advertising, Cleveland, 1955-56; *Rutland Daily Herald,* Rutland, Vt., director of advertising and community public relations departments, 1956-65; ordained minister of United Church of Christ, 1963; Vermont Council of Churches, Burlington, executive minister, 1965-68; founder, editor, and publisher of *Vermont Freeman,* 1968-74; Garden Way Publishing Co., Charlotte, Vt., editor, 1974-76; free-lance writer, 1977-79; community artist with Vermont Council on the Arts, 1979-80; WEZF-Radio, Burlington, creative director, 1980—. Instructor at Cleveland College, 1955; visiting lecturer at Goddard College, 1969-70; lecturer at colleges and universities, including Case Western Reserve University, State University of New York at Albany, University of Vermont, and Middlebury College. Pastor of Methodist church in Cleveland, 1955-66, United Church of Christ in West Rutland, Vt., 1957-65, and Methodist church in Mendon, Vt., 1963-65; chaplain of Cuyahoga County Juvenile Detention Home, 1952-55; designed and produced "Prayer Meeting," a weekly program on WEWS-TV, 1953-56; founding member of development council of Burlington Ecumenical Action Ministry, 1967-69.

Town moderator of Mendon, 1958-62; first chairman of Vermont Commission on Human Rights, 1967-70; delegate to Democratic National Convention, 1972. Director and member of professional advisory board of Rutland County Counseling Service, 1962-65; drug, abortion, career, and marriage counselor, 1966—; drug abuse prevention counselor at Kornerstone, 1972-74. Member of Vermont Educational Television Advisory Board, 1973-75. Member of Rutland Community Chorus and Potomac Playmakers. *Military service:* U.S. Army, 13th and 82nd Airborne Division, in journalism, public relations, and radio production, 1945-46; became staff sergeant. U.S. Air Force Reserve, 1946-55; became second lieutenant. *Awards, honors:* First honors from Maryland Association of Industrial Editors, 1948, for *Fad;* annual award citation from Cleveland Advertising Club, 1954, for radio commercials for Sohio; honor certificate from Freedoms Foundation, 1977, for radio program, "Day by Day."

WRITINGS: Five Hundred Forty-seven Easy Ways to Save Energy in Your Home, Garden Way Publishing, 1978; (with Larry Gay) *The Complete Book of Insulating,* Stephen Greene, 1980; *Old Houses, New Homes,* Stephen Greene, 1981.

Writer and producer of "Polly Pickens," a live daytime serial on WXEL-TV, 1952-53; writer and producer of "Day by Day," a daily radio series distributed by Garden Way Broadcasting, 1974-76; writer and producer for "A Home of Your Own," a daily radio program syndicated nationally by Sunbelt Network, 1981—. Also author of "Cyrus Prior" (television play), first broadcast by WEW-TV, 1955.

Contributor of articles and poems to magazines and newspapers, including *Ladies Home Journal.* Editor of *Franklin County Weeklies,* 1970-71.

WORK IN PROGRESS: Volodya's Vision, a biography of Vladimir Zworykin, inventor of television; *Partners,* nonfiction on "contemporary partnering patterns."

SIDELIGHTS: "I have been a wordsmith all my adult life," Albright told *CA.* "I was an English major in college and wrote for the college literary magazine; I was editor of *Paraglide* for the 82nd Airborne Division at the end of World War II, and went to work for the people who made the planes we had been jumping from, as editor of the company's internal house organ. I began working in radio while in the 82nd and continued part time for a local station, then became manager of a small radio station in New York State. In radio I have been an announcer, copywriter, newswriter, newscaster, program director, station manager, and creative director.

"My next step was Cleveland, directing advertising and public relations for a network station there, then on to advertising agencies, ultimately as director of the radio and television department of a local agency. I have written literally tens of thousands of pieces of radio and television copy, and other advertising material for newspapers, magazines, and direct mail. I believe it is good discipline if you can avoid getting mired down in it.

"In whatever job I have had, there has always been a typewriter at my desk. For thirty years I have had an office at home as well as where I was employed, and today I work principally at home in an unusual arrangement I have with WEZF-Radio, whereby I am salaried as creative director for the station, but do it principally on the phone from my home office.

"At the Hanksville Schoolhouse, where I live, I have a reasonably well-equipped business office and a small recording studio. I am writing radio advertising campaigns and a syndicated radio program. I am recording radio advertising and program continuity, the daily program, and occasional film narrations and other special voice parts. I learn every day.

"I came to have a degree of disgust for myself writing advertising copy at the national agency level; the quotient of scam and dishonesty became too high for my tender conscience to cope with. Writing advertising copy for local newspapers and radio stations is work of a different order; one is making a reasonably straightforward persuasive presentation for, principally, individual small-business people whose style of enterprise I applaud.

"The form of the radio commercial is as rigid and structured a discipline as the classical sonnet, which I also write, and very few do it well, leaving an open field for one who chooses to master the form and can find an employer who appreciates and is willing to pay for excellence. I am fortunate in having such an employer. There are many notable writers who have served an apprenticeship in advertising. It is an excellent workshop for building vocabulary, for learning flexibility within form in phrasing and sentence structure; in radio copy, for learning to write lean prose. In advertising writing there is also a degree of feedback that lets the writer know if he said what he wanted to say.

"Writing for the voice is, or should be considered, quite different from writing for the eye. Well-written broadcast material is sometimes good to read, sometimes looks silly, is often ungrammatical. Well-written print material frequently is impossible to read aloud. Writing radio material can be fascinating, because one is sometimes attempting to draw pictures in the mind, in the manner of a skillful novelist, but within a most compressed compass, wherein, quite literally, every word must count."

*   *   *

ALCALA-GALIANO, Juan Valera y
See VALERA y ALCALA-GALIANO, Juan

*   *   *

ALCIBIADE
See PRAZ, Mario

*   *   *

ALEXANDER, Eric   1910(?)-1982

OBITUARY NOTICE: Born c. 1910; died April 10, 1982, in Chilston Park, Maidstone, England. Third viscount Chilston and author of two biographies, including *Chief Whip,* an account of the first viscount Chilston. A member of the Royal Air Force during World War II, Alexander was responsible for the recovery and evaluation of key enemy documents after Germany surrendered. He was renowned for his interest in nature and the gardens he maintained in Kentish parkland. Obituaries and other sources: *London Times,* April 17, 1982.

*   *   *

ALLAN, Robert Alexander   1914-1979

OBITUARY NOTICE: Born in 1914; died April 4, 1979, in Australia. Public servant and publisher. Allan served in the British Parliament from 1951 to 1966. He was chairman of Longman Penguin publishers from 1972 until his death. In 1939 he wrote *The Open Door Policy in China.* (Date of death provided by Mrs. Hazel Thame, secretary to T. J. Rix, chief executive of Longman Group Ltd.)

*   *   *

ALLISON, A(ntony) F(rancis)   1916-

PERSONAL: Born February 3, 1916, in Bognor Regis, England; son of Francis Dominic and Adeline Cecile (Procter) Allison; married Marion Forbes Wilkinson, December 13, 1941; children: Marion Forbes, Rosemary Anthea, Richard Francis. *Education:* University of London, B.A. (general), 1936, B.A. (English language and literature; with honors), 1938. *Home:* Kinnordy, Welcomes Rd., Kenley, Surrey CR2 5HD, England.

CAREER: British Library, London, England, assistant keeper in department of printed books, 1946-72; Catholic Record Society, London, general editor, 1963—. *Military service:* British Army, 1940-46; became major.

WRITINGS: (With D. M. Rogers) *A Catalogue of Catholic Books in English Printed Abroad or Secretly in England, 1558-1640,* Arundel Press, 1956, reprinted, Dawson, 1972; *Thomas Dekker: A Bibliographical Catalogue of the Early Editions,* Dawson, 1972; *Four Metaphysical Poets, George Herbert, Richard Crashaw, Henry Vaughan, Andrew Marvell: A Bibliographical Catalogue of the Early Editions of Their Poetry and Prose,* Dawson, 1973; *Thomas Lodge: A Bibliographical*

Catalogue of the Early Editions, Dawson, 1973; *English Translations From the Spanish and Portuguese to the Year 1700: An Annotated Catalogue of the Extant Printed Versions,* Dawson, 1974; *Robert Greene: A Bibliographical Catalogue of the Early Editions,* Dawson, 1975; (with V. F. Goldsmith) *Titles of English Books: An Alphabetical Finding List,* Dawson, Volume I: *1475-1640,* 1976, Volume II: *1641-1700,* 1977. Co-editor of *Recusant History,* 1951—.

WORK IN PROGRESS: An extended supplement to *Catalogue of Catholic Books,* with D. M. Rogers, completion expected in 1983 or 1984; *The English Counter-Reformation: An Annotated Catalogue of the Printed Material, to 1640,* with Rogers.

SIDELIGHTS: Allison told *CA:* "The aim of the Counter-Reformation catalogue, now in progress, as is that of much of my other bibliographical work, is to provide a solid basis for historical research. The importance of bibliography for literary scholars is well enough understood, but for historians less so. Concentration on manuscripts has tended to obscure the fact that much primary material has survived in early printed tracts and leaflets (and sometimes *only* in these). My object is to locate and analyze all the material of this kind in the field chosen and within the terms of reference adopted. *The English Counter-Reformation* will take several years to complete."

* * *

ALLRED, Ruel A(cord)   1929-

PERSONAL: Born March 30, 1929, in Spring City, Utah; son of Reid H. (a teacher) and Anna E. (Acord) Allred; married Betty B. Best, September 3, 1954; children: Anita, Chad, Lynette, Eileen, Brent, Marie, Reid. *Education:* Received degree from Snow Junior College, 1949; Brigham Young University, B.S., 1954, M.S., 1958; University of Oregon, D.Ed., 1965. *Religion:* Church of Jesus Christ of Latter-day Saints (Mormons). *Residence:* Provo, Utah 84601. *Office:* College of Education, Brigham Young University, 204 McKay Building, Provo, Utah 84602.

CAREER: Test administrator for public schools in Provo, Utah, 1958, teacher at elementary schools, 1958-61; Brigham Young University, Provo, elementary teacher at laboratory school, 1961-62, writer of curriculum material at laboratory school, 1962-63, principal, 1963-64, clinical instructor at university, 1965-66, assistant professor, 1966-68, associate professor, 1968-73, professor of education, 1973—. Visiting assistant professor at University of Missouri, St. Louis, summer, 1966; visiting professor at University of Alaska, Anchorage, 1974; conducts workshops. *Military service:* U.S. Air Force, jet fighter pilot, 1955-57. *Member:* International Reading Association, Phi Kappa Phi, Phi Delta Phi.

WRITINGS: (With Floyd Sucher) *Screening Students for Placement in Reading,* Brigham Young University Press, 1971; (with Louise O. Baird and Edwin A. Read) *Continuous Progress in Spelling: An Individualized Spelling Program,* Economy Co., 1972, revised edition published as *Continuous Progress in Spelling (CPS) Readiness,* 1977; (with Sucher) *Sucher-Allred Reading Placement Inventory,* Economy Co., 1973; (with Sucher) *Word Analysis Competency Skill Tests for Keys to Independence in Reading,* Economy Co., 1974; (with Baird and Read) *Continuous Progress in Spelling Variety Day Kit,* Economy Co., 1975; *Spelling: The Application of Research Findings,* National Education Association, 1977. Contributor to education journals.

AVOCATIONAL INTERESTS: Travel (Western Europe, South Seas islands, Japan, Mexico, South America).

ALTIERI, Charles F(rancis)   1942-

PERSONAL: Born November 11, 1942, in New York, N.Y.; son of Francis (a construction supervisor) and Ida (Picciotti) Altieri; married Joanne Smith (a lecturer in English), 1966; children: two. *Education:* LeMoyne College, A.B., 1964; University of North Carolina at Chapel Hill, Ph.D., 1969. *Home:* 907 11th Ave. E., Seattle, Wash, 98102. *Office:* Department of English, University of Washington, Seattle, Wash. 98195.

CAREER: State University of New York at Buffalo, assistant professor, 1968-75, associate professor of English, 1975-77; University of Washington, Seattle, professor of English, 1977—. Consultant, National Endowment for Humanities Fellowships and Grants, 1974-75 and 1978. *Member:* International Association for Study of Philosophy and Literature, Modern Language Association of America, Society of Critical Exchange.

WRITINGS: Enlarging the Temple: New Directions in American Poetry During the 1960's, Bucknell University Press, 1979; (compiler) *Modern Poetry,* AHM Publishing, 1979; *Act and Quality: A Theory of Literary Meaning and Humanistic Understanding,* University of Massachusetts Press, 1981. Contributor to literary journals and magazines, including *Boundary 2, Iowa Review, Modern Language Notes,* and *Publications of the Modern Language Association.*

WORK IN PROGRESS: Self and Sensibility in Contemporary Poetry; Abstraction in Modern Painting and Modern Poetry; The Ends of Literary Criticism: How to Talk About Values in the Wake of Foundationalism.

SIDELIGHTS: In his first book, *Enlarging the Temple: New Directions in American Poetry of the 1960's,* Altieri develops what Robert Kern of *Criticism* describes as "Altieri's basic assumption as a critic—that literary style itself necessarily has philosophical implications . . . demonstrat[ing] the extent to which poems themselves are often the best manifestations of their underlying poetics." Altieri contends in his theory of contemporary poetry that certain poets of the 1960's, including Charles Olson, Robert Duncan, Robert Bly, and Denise Levertov, thought that the dominant modes of poetry in their time constituted an enervated version of the Eliot-Pound tradition. In reaction, these poets reassessed, and consequently redefined, literary issues such as the relationship between the poem and its author, the relationship between the poem and its audience, and the functions of language in poetry. Their reassessment reflected the times in which they lived, and they launched a "postmodern" period which Altieri feels can be viewed as a historical period in its own right.

According to Altieri's theory, the decade of the 1960's can be viewed as a unique historical moment, separate as a unit of poetic history. Nonetheless, the decade was linked to the past in both its reaction to the modernist literary period prior to the decade and in its renewal of the nineteenth-century poetic tradition of Wordsworth. Altieri's philosophical approach to poetry, described by Kern as a "theoretical map of the period," locates these contemporary poets in the context of literary theoretical history while allowing that postmodernist poetry may not always reflect a conscious theory on the part of the poet.

Altieri's purpose in this book is to probe alternate theories of literary meaning; consequently, the book is largely theoretical with limited analysis of individual poems. Altieri is hindered by the highly theoretical nature of the material, J. D. McClatchy of the *Yale Review* observed, at times regressing into a style characterized as "windy," "boring," "gibberish."

Despite some objections to Altieri's heavily academic style, critics tend to agree that this book is an important contribution to the field of poetics. As McClatchy himself concluded, Altieri's "insistence on bringing philosophical weight to bear on critical method is commendable; . . . he boldly raises the intellectual level of discourse about contemporary poetry."

Altieri told *CA:* "*Act and Quality* presents a dramatistic account of meaning as an alternative to deconstruction. Literary works offer acts in situations which we assess in terms of qualities. One man's gibberish may, just may, be a form of situating qualities for the less effete and linguistically fastidious."

BIOGRAPHICAL/CRITICAL SOURCES: Criticism: A Quarterly for Literature and Arts, summer, 1980; *Yale Review,* winter, 1980.

* * *

AMANN, Richard 1945-

PERSONAL: Born November 2, 1945, in New York, N.Y.; son of William (a sailmaker) and Gwendolyn (a nurse and writer; maiden name, Champion) Amann; married Barbara Ferrara (a publisher and literary agent), July 4, 1968; children: Robert. *Education:* University of Missouri, B.S.E.E., 1968; State University of New York, M.S., 1971; further graduate study at Boston University, 1972-75. *Politics:* "Individual freedom must be primary." *Religion:* "Searching." *Home and office address:* Adams Dr., Stow, Mass. 01775.

CAREER: Worked in electronics and relay logic design at Bell Laboratories, N.J., at General Electric Co., New York City, and at RCA Corp., New York City, 1961-71; Digital Equipment Corp. (computers), Maynard, Mass., 1971-77, began as manager of marketing for militarized computers, became manager and founder of component engineering department. *Member:* Society of Manufacturing Engineers (senior member), Committee of Small Magazine Editors and Publishers, Lions Club.

WRITINGS: How to Make the Purchased Part Cycle Work to Your Company's Advantage, Programmed Studies, 1977; *Forgotten Women of Computer History,* Programmed Studies, 1977; *The Technological Level of Soviet Industry,* Yale University Press, 1977. Editor of Digital Equipment Corporation's *Engineering Newsletter* and *Component Engineering Newsletter.*

WORK IN PROGRESS: Caribbean Trip Planner: A Looseleaf Guide to the Caribbean.

SIDELIGHTS: Amann commented: "The concepts discussed in *How to Make the Purchased Part Cycle Work to Your Company's Advantage* were actually put into practice at Digital Equipment Corporation and General Electric Company with amazing results. Both companies saved many millions of dollars, and General Electric won a major contract. The concepts have never been available in print before, but they are so controversial and off-beat that many companies that need them (and much of the business media) dismiss the book with little thought."

* * *

AMDUR, Neil 1939-

PERSONAL: Born December 19, 1939, in Wilkes-Barre, Pa.; son of Daniel (in sales) and Sarah (a merchant; maiden name, Siegel) Amdur; married Marilyn Falk (a real estate agent), January 29, 1967; children: Michael, David. *Education:* University of Missouri, B.J., 1961. *Politics:* Independent. *Religion:* Jewish. *Home:* 135 Spring St., Harrington Park, N.J. 07640. *Agent:* Edward J. Acton, Inc., 17 Grove St., New York, N.Y. 10014. *Office: New York Times,* 229 West 43rd St., New York, N.Y. 10036.

CAREER: Miami Herald, Miami, Fla., sports reporter, 1961-67; *New York Times,* New York City, sports reporter, 1967-75; Columbia Broadcasting System (CBS-TV), New York City, producer of "CBS Sports," 1975-76; *New York Times,* sports reporter, 1976—. *Military service:* U.S. Coast Guard Reserve, 1961-67. *Member:* U.S. Tennis Writers Association (past president; vice-president, 1980-81), Track and Field Writers of America, Pro Football Writers Association of America, Baseball Writers Association, Sigma Delta Chi. *Awards, honors:* Sportswriting award from Associated Press, 1966, for series on Steve Spurrier; Jesse Abramson Memorial Award from Track and Field Writers of America, 1980, for excellence in track and field journalism; named writer of the year by Women's Tennis Association, 1981.

WRITINGS: The Fifth Down, Coward, 1971; (with Vincent Matthews) *My Race Be Won,* Charterhouse, 1974; (with Arthur Ashe) *Off the Court,* New American Library, 1981; (with Chris Evert Lloyd) *Chrissie,* Simon & Schuster, 1982. Contributing editor of *World Tennis, Runner,* and *Running Guide.*

WORK IN PROGRESS: The One-Hundred-Mile War, a novel, for Bantam; "Balls and Strikes," a television play, with Murray Chass.

SIDELIGHTS: Amdur has covered the Olympic Games since 1968.

Amdur told *CA:* "I was the first reporter to be hijacked—on a flight from Allentown, Pennsylvania, to Washington, in May, 1972; I filed accounts for the *New York Times.* I also spent ten days in Cuba in August, 1971, with the U.S. volleyball team trying to qualify for the Olympics."

AVOCATIONAL INTERESTS: Tennis, running, reading, travel.

BIOGRAPHICAL/CRITICAL SOURCES: Jewish Standard, November 20, 1981; *New York Times Book Review,* November 22, 1981.

* * *

AMES, Walter Lansing 1946-

PERSONAL: Born August 17, 1946, in Long Beach, Calif.; son of Bill Chester (a civil servant) and Frances (Armor) Ames; married Evelyn Hinton, September 6, 1969; children: Kimberly, Byron, Darren, Spencer. *Education:* Brigham Young University, B.S. (magna cum laude), 1971; University of Michigan, M.A., 1972, Ph.D., 1976; Harvard University Law School, J.D., 1979. *Politics:* Independent. *Religion:* Church of Jesus Christ of Latter-day Saints (Mormons). *Home:* 4-6-12 Higashi-cho, Kichijoji, Mushashino-shi, Tokyo 180, Japan. *Office:* Bain & Co., Azabu Heights 515, 1-5-10 Roppongi, Minato-ku, Tokyo 106, Japan.

CAREER: Bain & Co., Boston, Mass., consultant in Menlo Park, Calif., and Tokyo, Japan, offices, 1979—. Summer associate of Mori & Ota (law firm), Los Angeles, Calif., and Fenwick, Stone, Davis & West (law firm), Palo Alto, Calif., 1978. Assistant to director of East Asian legal studies at Harvard University, 1976-79. Lecturer at Shikoku Regional Police College, Keio University, and University of Michigan, 1975, Stanford University, 1978, University of California, Berkeley, 1980, and University of Tokyo, 1982. *Member:* American Bar Association, Association for Asian Studies, Japanese American Society for Legal Studies, Asiatic Society of Japan, American

Chamber of Commerce in Japan, Japan Society of New York, California Bar Association, Phi Kappa Phi. *Awards, honors:* National Science Foundation fellow, 1971-74; foreign area fellow of Social Science Research Council and American Council of Learned Societies, 1974-76.

WRITINGS: Police and Community in Japan, University of California Press, 1981. Contributor to *Encyclopedia of Japan.* Contributor to Asian studies and police science journals. Editor of *Asia: Journal of the Society for Asian Studies,* 1971.

WORK IN PROGRESS: Research on Japanese business and law in societal perspective, comparative concepts of law, and police and gangster organizations.

SIDELIGHTS: Ames told *CA:* "I am an anthropologist interested in Japanese society and social organization, particularly in the applied areas of government (for example, police), law, and business. My work as a management consultant allows me in-depth access to Japanese business organizations, which, as an anthropologist, I plan to write about in the near future. To understand Japan-U.S. interactions, it helps to have a grasp of the role of government and law in Japan, the organization and functioning of Japanese business, and the pervasive impact of culture in all Japanese transactions."

AVOCATIONAL INTERESTS: Guitar, singing, racquetball.

*   *   *

AMMER, Christine (Parker)   1931-

PERSONAL: Born May 25, 1931, in Vienna, Austria; came to the United States in 1938, naturalized citizen, 1943; daughter of Herbert (in business) and Helen (a pathologist; maiden name, Reitmann) Pollak; married Dean S. Ammer (an economist); children: Karen, John, David. *Education:* Swarthmore College, B.A., 1952. *Residence:* Lexington, Mass. *Agent:* Helen Rees, 655 Boylston St., Boston, Mass. 02116.

CAREER: Editor with National Lexicographic Board, Physicians Publications, and Parents Magazine Press in New York, N.Y., 1953-62; free-lance editor in Massachusetts, 1962-66; Harvard University Press, Cambridge, Mass., editor, 1966-68; free-lance writer, 1968—. Editor and publisher with Hospital Purchasing Institute in Boston, Mass., 1976-79. *Member:* International League of Women Composers, National Organization for Women, National Women's Health Network, Phi Beta Kappa.

WRITINGS: Riches of the Animal World, Doubleday, 1961; *Musician's Handbook of Foreign Terms,* G. Schirmer, 1971; *Harper's Dictionary of Music,* Harper, 1972; (with husband, Dean S. Ammer) *Dictionary of Business and Economics,* Free Press, 1977; *Unsung: A History of Women in American Music,* Greenwood Press, 1980; (with Nathan T. Sidley) *A Common Sense Guide to Mental Health Care,* Lewis, 1982; *The A to Z of Women's Health: A Concise Encyclopedia,* Everest, 1982.

Associate editor of *Illustrated Encyclopedia of Knowledge,* National Lexicographic Board, 1954; executive editor of *Cultural Library,* ten volumes, Parents Magazine Press, 1959-68, and *Harvard Dictionary of Music,* 2nd edition (Ammer was not associated with first edition), Harvard University Press, 1969.

WORK IN PROGRESS: Dictionary of Business and Economics, 2nd edition, with husband, Dean S. Ammer, publication by Free Press expected in 1984; another book on women in music; a cookbook; a humor book.

SIDELIGHTS: Christine Ammer commented: "I prefer to remain a 'generalist,' rather than confine myself to a single field

and will continue to write about whatever interests me deeply." *Avocational interests:* Travel, hiking, tennis, choral singing.

*   *   *

ANDERSEN, Kurt   1954-

PERSONAL: Born August 22, 1954, in Omaha, Neb.; son of Robert Keith (a lawyer) and Jean (Swarr) Andersen; married Anne Kreamer (a television executive), May 9, 1981. *Education:* Harvard University, A.B. (magna cum laude), 1976. *Politics:* Democrat. *Religion:* Unitarian-Universalist. *Home:* 343 East Ninth St., New York, N.Y. 10003. *Agent:* Wendy Weil, Julian Bach Literary Agency, Inc., 747 Third Ave., New York, N.Y. 10017. *Office: Time,* 1271 Sixth Ave., New York, N.Y. 10020.

CAREER: National Broadcasting Co. (NBC-TV), New York City, writer (including work on "Today Show"), 1976-81; *Time,* New York City, staff writer, 1981—.

WRITINGS—Nonfiction: *The Real Thing,* Doubleday, 1980; (with Mark O'Donnell and Roger Parloff) *Tools of Power,* Viking, 1980. Writer for "Daytime Television Drama," a comedy special broadcast by WCVB-TV, Boston, Mass., May, 1975. Contributor to magazines and newspapers, including *Sport,* and *New York Times.* Past editor of *Harvard Lampoon.*

WORK IN PROGRESS: A theatre piece based on the life of an eighteenth-century American eccentric.

SIDELIGHTS: The Real Thing is Andersen's humorous guide to the quintessential attributes and artifacts of American life. He examines a wide range of subjects, including consumer products, weapons, human feelings, art forms, places, and even the animal world. His second book, *Tools of Power,* is a satirical dissection of the corporate ethos and its most ferocious devotees.

He wrote: "It may be that the keys to literary success, artistic and otherwise, are good luck and a scrupulous patience. I've been blessed with more than enough of the first, and I'm groping now to achieve some of the second."

BIOGRAPHICAL/CRITICAL SOURCES: Soho News, November 12, 1980; *New York Daily News,* December 18, 1980; *Chicago Tribune Book World,* April 11, 1982.

*   *   *

ANDERSON, A(rthur) J(ames)   1933-

PERSONAL: Born October 29, 1933. *Education:* Bishop's University, B.A., 1956; Simmons College, M.S., 1967; Boston University, D.Ed., 1979. *Home:* 134 High Plain Rd., Andover, Mass. 01810. *Office:* School of Library Science, Simmons College, Boston, Mass. 02115.

CAREER: Director of Memorial Hall Public Library, Andover, Mass.; associate professor of library science at Simmons College, Boston, Mass.

WRITINGS: Problems in Intellectual Freedom and Censorship, Bowker, 1974; *Lin Yutang: The Best of an Old Friend,* Mason/ Charter, 1975; *E. B. White: A Bibliography,* Scarecrow, 1978; *Problems in Library Management,* Libraries Unlimited, 1981. Contributor of articles and reviews to library journals.

*   *   *

ANDERSON, Brad(ley Jay)   1924-

PERSONAL: Born May 14, 1924, in Jamestown, N.Y.; son

of Perle J. (a machinist) and Jennie (Solomonson) Anderson; married Barbara Marie Jones, September 8, 1945; children: Christine Dorothy (Mrs. Ruben Castaneda, Jr.), Craig Bradley, Paul Richard, Mark Stephen. *Education:* Syracuse University, B.F.A., 1951. *Home:* 1439 Pebble Beach, Yuma, Ariz. 85364.

CAREER: Free-lance cartoonist, 1950—; Ball & Grier (public relations firm), Utica, N.Y., art director, 1952-53; author and cartoonist, syndicated newspaper features "Marmaduke," 1954—, and "Grandpa's Boy." Work has been included in several exhibitions, including *Punch* magazine's British-American Exhibition, 1954, Selected Cartoons of Fourteen Saturday Evening Post Cartoonists, 1958, and San Francisco Museum of Fine Arts exhibit, 1977; cartoons are also represented in permanent collections at Albert T. Reid College, William Allen White Foundation (University of Kansas), and Syracuse University Manuscripts Library. *Wartime Service:* U.S. Naval Reserve, 1943-46. *Member:* National Cartoonists Society, Magazine Cartoonists Guild, Newspaper Comics Council, Masons, Sigma Delta Chi.

WRITINGS: (With Phil Leeming) *Marmaduke*, Gilbert Press, 1955; (with Leeming) *Marmaduke: An Amusing Collection of Dog Cartoons*, Popular Library, 1957; *Marmaduke!*, Associated Newspapers (London), 1967: (with Leeming) *Marmaduke Rides Again*, Scholastic Book Services, 1972; *More Marmaduke*, Scholastic Book Services, 1974; *Marmaduke . . . Again?*, Scholastic Book Services, 1977; *Down, Marmaduke*, Scholastic Book Services, 1978; *The Marmaduke Treasury*, introduction by Charles M. Schulz, Sheed, Andrews, 1978; *Marmaduke on the Loose*, Scholastic Book Services, 1982. Has contributed cartoons to periodicals, including *Saturday Evening Post* and *Look*.

* * *

ANDERSON, Eric (Douglas)   1949-

PERSONAL: Born October 5, 1949, in Columbus, Ohio; son of Charles Landis (a physician) and Elizabeth (Caviness) Anderson; married Loretta Tallios, May 31, 1970; children: Matthew Tallios, Seth Eric. *Education:* Andrews University, B.A. (with honors), 1970; University of Chicago, M.A., 1972, Ph.D., 1978. *Religion:* Seventh-day Adventist. *Home:* 1425 Howell Mountain Rd. N., Angwin, Calif. 94508. *Office:* Department of History, Pacific Union College, Angwin, Calif. 94508.

CAREER: Volunteer teacher at high school near Serian, Sarawak (Malaysia), 1970-71; Pacific Union College, Angwin, Calif., instructor, 1975-77, assistant professor, 1977-80, associate professor of history, 1980—. *Member:* American Historical Association, Southern Historical Association. *Awards, honors:* Ford Foundation fellow, 1982.

WRITINGS: Race and Politics in North Carolina, 1872-1901: The Black Second, Louisiana State University Press, 1981; (contributor) Howard Rabinowitz, editor, *Southern Black Leaders of the Reconstruction Era*, University of Illinois Press, 1982. Contributor to journals in the social sciences. Assistant editor of *Adventist Heritage;* contributing editor of *Spectrum*.

WORK IN PROGRESS: Research on the role of private giving in the development of black education.

SIDELIGHTS: Anderson commented: "My research interests grow out of the conviction that Afro-American history is central to an accurate understanding of the American experience." *Avocational interests:* Growing grapes, old guns.

* * *

ANDERSON, Raymond L(loyd)   1927-

PERSONAL: Born March 1, 1927, in Beloit, Wis.; son of

Elmer A. (a farmer) and Mae (Howell) Anderson; married Betty Echegon, July 9, 1952; children: Jeff, Jennifer, Jerry. *Education:* University of Minnesota, B.S., 1951, M.S., 1955; University of Wisconsin—Madison, Ph.D., 1959. *Home:* 1301 Luke St., Fort Collins, Colo. 80521. *Office:* Department of Economics, Colorado State University, Fort Collins, Colo. 80521.

CAREER: U.S. Department of Agriculture, Washington, D.C., agricultural economist at Economic Research Service in Bozeman, Mont., 1955-57, research economist at Economic Research Service in Fort Collins, Colo., 1959—. Faculty affiliate at Colorado State University, 1959—. Member of International Commission on Irrigation and Drainage. *Military service:* U.S. Army Air Forces, 1945-47. *Member:* American Agricultural Economics Association, Western Agricultural Economics Association.

WRITINGS: And the Desert Shall Rejoice: Conflict, Growth, and Justice in Arid Environments, M.I.T. Press, 1978. Contributor of more than twenty articles to technical journals.

WORK IN PROGRESS: A book on irrigation in China.

* * *

ANDERSON, Sydney   1927-

PERSONAL: Born January 11, 1927, in Topeka, Kan.; son of Robert Grant and Evelyn Fern (Hunt) Anderson; married Ratia Justine Klusmire, August 5, 1951; children: Evelyn Lee (Mrs. Stephen Randall Wheelhouse), Charles Sydney, Laura Lynette (Mrs. Thomas Patrick Dooley). *Education:* Attended Baker University, 1944-49; University of Kansas, B.A., 1950, M.A., 1952, Ph.D., 1959. *Home:* 98 Wainwright Ave., Closter, N.J. 07624. *Office:* American Museum of Natural History, Central Park W. at 79th St., New York, N.Y. 10024.

CAREER: Museum of Natural History, Lawrence, Kan., assistant curator of mammals, 1954-59; American Museum of Natural History, New York, N.Y., assistant curator, 1960-64, associate curator, 1964-69, curator, 1969—, chairman of department of mammalogy, 1974-81. Instructor in zoology, University of Kansas, 1954-59; adjunct professor, City University of New York, 1969—; adjunct professor, New York University, 1973; technical consultant, Time-Life Book Co. and C.S. Hammond, Inc. *Member:* American Association for the Advancement of Science (fellow), American Society of Mammalogists (director, 1964—, secretary, 1968-74, president, 1974-76), Ecological Society of America, Society for the Study of Evolution, Society of Systematic Zoology, Closter Nature Center Association (trustee, 1967—, president, 1973-79), Bergen Community Museum of Arts and Science (trustee, 1981—).

WRITINGS: The Lives of Animals (juvenile), Creative Education, 1966; (editor with J. Knox Jones, Jr.) *Recent Mammals of the World: A Synopsis of Families*, Wiley, 1967, revised edition, Ronald, 1983; (editor with Jones) *Readings in Mammalogy*, Museum of Natural History, University of Kansas, 1970, published as *Selected Readings in Mammalogy* (revised and expanded; with Jones and Robert S. Hoffmann), 1976. Contributor to books on mammals. Contributor of monographs to American Museum "Novitates" series, *Bulletin of the American Museum of Natural History*, and to Museum of Natural History Publications, University of Kansas. Editor of *Mammalian Species*, 1969—, and *Recent Literature of Mammalogy*, 1968-74.

BIOGRAPHICAL/CRITICAL SOURCES: Science Books, December, 1966; *Science*, September 22, 1967.

ANDREWS, Benny 1930-

PERSONAL: Born November 13, 1930, in Madison, Ga.; married Mary Ellen Jones Smith; children: Christopher, Thomas Michael, Julia Rachael. *Education:* Attended Fort Valley State College, 1948-50; University of Chicago, 1956-58; Chicago Art Institute, B.F.A., 1958.

CAREER: Artist and illustrator. New School for Social Research, New York City, instructor in art, 1967-68; Queens College of the City University of New York, New York City, instructor in art, 1968—. Visiting artist at California State College, Hayward, 1969. Has participated in numerous exhibits, including those at Detroit Institute of Arts, 1959, Brooklyn Museum of Art, 1963, Carnegie Institute, 1969, Museum of Modern Art, 1969, San Francisco Museum of Art, 1969, and Boston Museum of Fine Arts, 1971. Work represented in permanent collections at numerous galleries, including Museum of African Art, Washington, D.C., Slater Memorial Museum, Norwich, Conn., Museum of Modern Art, New York City, and Norfolk Museum, Norfolk, Va. *Military service:* U.S. Air Force, 1950-54. *Awards, honors:* John Hay Whitney fellowship, 1965; New York State Council Creative Arts Program award, 1971; Negro Art Collection award, Atlanta University, 1971, for "Educational Arts."

WRITINGS: (Editor with Rudolf Baranik) *Attica Book,* Custom Communications Systems, c.1972; *Between the Lines: Seventy Drawings and Seven Essays,* Pella Publishing, 1978.

Illustrator: Arnold Adoff, editor, *I Am the Darker Brother: An Anthology of Modern Poems by Negro Americans,* Macmillan, 1968.

Contributor of articles on black art and culture to professional journals.

BIOGRAPHICAL/CRITICAL SOURCES: New York Times Book Review, November 3, 1968; *Art News,* April, 1971, October, 1975.

*   *   *

ANDREYEV, Nikolay Efremych 1908-1982

OBITUARY NOTICE: Born March 13, 1908, in St. Petersburg, Russia (now Leningrad, U.S.S.R.); died February 25, 1982. Educator, scholar in Slavic studies, and author of numerous works in his field. Andreyev lectured at the Russian Free University in Prague during the 1930's and 1940's. When World War II ended, he was abducted by Russian troops and sent to a prison in East Germany, where he was incarcerated for three years. Later, Andreyev procured a position as lecturer at Cambridge University. Throughout the 1960's and 1970's he distinguished himself at Magdalene College as an authority on Russian culture. Obituaries and other sources: *London Times,* February 26, 1982, March 8, 1982.

*   *   *

ANGER, Kenneth 1930-

PERSONAL: Born February 3, 1930, in Santa Monica, Calif. *Education:* Educated in California. *Residence:* New York, N.Y.

CAREER: Filmmaker and writer. Actor in motion pictures, including "A Midsummer Night's Dream," 1935, and "Fireworks," 1947.

WRITINGS: Hollywood Babylone (nonfiction), J. F. Pauvert (Paris), 1959, published as *Hollywood Babylon,* Associated Professional Services, 1965, revised edition, Simon & Schuster, 1975.

Screenplays; also director: "Who Has Been Rocking My Dream Boat?," 1941; "Tinsel Tree," 1942; "Prisoner of Mars," 1942; "The Nest," 1943; "Escape Episode," 1944, revised edition, 1946; "Drastic Demise," 1945; "Fireworks," 1947; "Puce Moment," 1949; "La Lune des lapins" (title means "Rabbit's Moon"), 1950; "Eaux d'Artifice," 1953; "Inauguration of the Pleasure Dome/Lord Shiva's Dream," 1954, revised edition, 1958; "Thelema Abbey," 1955; "Scorpio Rising," 1963; "Invocation of My Demon Brother," 1969; "Lucifer Rising," 1980. Also author and director of unfinished motion picture, "Kustom Kar Kommandos."

WORK IN PROGRESS: A collection of memorabilia, *Kenneth Anger's Autographs;* a photo-biography of Marilyn Monroe, *Private Marilyn; Hollywood Babylon II.*

SIDELIGHTS: Anger is among the best known avant-garde filmmakers in the United States. His films reveal obsessions with the occult and fetishism, thus making him one of the most intriguing yet oblique artists of the underground cinema. His first well-known film, "Fireworks," is a surprisingly graphic depiction of a sado-masochistic homosexual encounter between a young man and several sailors. It impressed French poet and filmmaker Jean Cocteau so much that he invited Anger to France. Anger then met Anais Nin, whom he featured in later films.

Returning to the United States as penniless as he'd departed, Anger nonetheless continued to make accomplished films with special effects that rivaled those of Hollywood's polished products. In 1963, he released "Scorpio Rising," probably his best known film, which details the fanatical devotion cyclists have for their motorbikes. To a soundtrack of popular rock songs, Anger shows the cyclists shining their machines and adjusting their leather clothing. The film also reveals parallels between the behavior of the outcast cyclists and cinematic equivalents James Dean and Marlon Brando.

Most of Anger's films are rooted in the rituals and symbols of the occult. A disciple of Aleister Crowley, Anger used that mystic figure's teachings as inspiration for films such as "Invocation of My Demon Brother" and "Lucifer Rising." The latter was ten years in the making, and culminates in a spectacular celebration of occultism featuring an extra-terrestrial spacecraft passing over the pyramids. Though Anger's symbols and sources are often obscure, his mastery of special effects and ability to evoke an awe of his subject has enabled him to develop a following and thus continue working in film.

Anger is also considered an authority on scandals in the film industry. His book *Hollywood Babylon* is a recounting of several controversies that raged in Hollywood, including the death of Tom Ince, the trial of "Fatty" Arbuckle, and the secret diary of Mary Astor. "Dope, rape, murder, suicide, madness: the litany pounds throughout Anger's book," wrote Jack Kroll. Peter Andrews called it "a book you read with the same morbid fascination that you look at a bad automobile accident." He also praised Anger as "a man who knows the territory" and called him "a master of the quick anecdote."

CA INTERVIEW

Kenneth Anger was interviewed on May 10, 1979.

CA: Was your childhood relatively normal?

ANGER: For Hollywood puritans, yes. Very odd family. Presbyterians. No smoking or drinking. Also no comic books; I wasn't supposed to have them. They tried to bring me up on Tennyson, things like that. I was a Depression baby. I arrived with bad news about the stock market, February 3, 1930.

CA: When did you become interested in films?

ANGER: I think I started seeing my first movies when I was three or four years old. I was in dance school already: expressive dancing. My parents were both university graduates. They had definite ideas about what I could and could not do. Everyone thinks that everyone in Hollywood is throwing wild parties and carrying on; they aren't. My parents were puritanical; they looked down on it.

CA: When did you decide to enter the film world?

ANGER: When I was selected by Warner Brothers to play the changeling prince in Max Reinhardt's "A Midsummer Night's Dream" in 1934. I was a little kid about three feet tall. The part was not a speaking part; it was a dancing and mime part. It is a beautiful film.

The thing that I really remember about working on "A Midsummer Night's Dream" at four years old was the day the cellophane moon beam caught on fire. Because to me that was sort of magical. The arc lights were too close to the stretched cellophane that the children were supposed to run down. There were steel steps hidden beneath the cellophane, and the little fairy kids, who also had on cellophane costumes, had to scamper up and down the moon beams. There was a little panic, but it looked beautiful. It puffed with smoke and it all started to go. The kids scattered. A couple of them got singed a little bit, no damage really. But it was so beautiful. I loved it.

When I first saw Warner Brothers—all those trees painted silver on the set, the costumes, everything—I was completely bowled over. I wanted a studio all my own. And I never had one because in a way I really had a very scratchy career in the movies. It was strictly a one-shot deal. One movie, this one part, then my family put me back in school. There was no question of following the path of other child actors of the time.

CA: After the film was completed, did you resume your traditional childhood?

ANGER: Sort of. I was always a rather rebellious child. I wouldn't go to Sunday school. I did go to Beverly Hills High School, which at that time was kind of like a private club. It was pretty nice and there were a lot of the children of people in films; the girl who used to help me get through chemistry was Groucho Marx's daughter.

CA: Did you work in films again?

ANGER: Not in the industry, no. My father wanted me to go to California Tech and become an aeronautical engineer like my brother because the whole family was in aviation. It wasn't my trip; I wasn't going to do it. When I graduated from high school my grandmother gave me the money to go to Paris to meet Jean Cocteau. She had been there and had told me stories about it.

CA: Then you met Cocteau.

ANGER: Yes. I sent the film "Fireworks" to a festival called "The Festival of Damned Films." These were films that could never be shown publicly for censorship reasons or whatever. He was the chairman of the jury, and the film won a prize. He sent me just an honor, no money (which would have been

welcomed). He also sent me a little fan letter and invited me to see his ballet "Le Jeune Homme de la mort."

CA: Do you still have the letter?

ANGER: Yes I do; I'm very careful. I have a collection of autographs, too. I was staying in Paris through the 1950's, where I wrote the first version of *Hollywood Babylon*. I wrote it to get some money to stay on in Paris. It was part of the trivia cinema thing. I expanded it in 1959 and came back to America to make "Scorpio Rising" in 1963. It was a little like visiting a foreign country. I had been away almost ten years. Brooklyn was as strange to me as darkest Africa.

CA: Were you successful in Paris?

ANGER: Yeah, I guess so. *Hollywood Babylon* was done strictly because I needed some money to work on my movie. Well, I'm a collector. I grew up in Hollywood and I've been collecting Hollywood memorabilia of all kinds since I was a child. A lot of things were given to me. I expressed an interest in film since I was five. At that time, since I had a few "ins" in the studio through my grandmother's friends, particularly at Warner Brothers, they would say, "Here kid, take the whole set," and they would give me a key book with a still from each scene in the movie. I still have them. I had an interest in collecting the history of Hollywood, not the corporate history, but the human stuff. And the human side is scandal, you know, the people in conflict with the mores of the time. Hollywood has always been a reflection of America in the sense of what goes, what won't go, what will wash, what they get away with, what they can't get away with. I think people talked because I was a kid. I was interested in the stuff and I was keeping notebooks on it from my childhood on, like a hobby.

CA: What inspired you to make "Scorpio Rising"?

ANGER: It came about out of a blue summer sky. I went to Coney Island, as I was wont to do in those days around 1963. Around the Cyclone there was this friendly gang of motorcyclists. Not Hell's Angels but a little Brooklyn gang of Italians who worked in the Fulton Fish Market. And they were showing off these incredible surrealist machines that they had built with ten tail fins and twenty exhaust pipes and fifty headlights at least.

I was really flipped out over these things and they let me photograph their parties, their private lives, their rooms. Working completely alone. I think if I had had a crew of even one or two people I never could have done what I did. Like going into their little garages and rooms and into their private lives, and they respected me as being a kind of a camera nut. You know the kind. It was more that me being around made them a little more exhibitionistic than they would ordinarily be. But it turned into "Scorpio Rising" and it was fun. I enjoyed making the film even though I was not emotionally involved. I always wanted to be a director. My childhood fantasy was having my own studio. I wanted to have a little Warner Brothers.

CA: Did you think you were making an underground film or a studio film?

ANGER: I gave up that idea years ago. I knew that I would never have an actual building that would be a studio. I was just doing it for myself. Even then, I had a certain audience. My films were distributed. But I never thought that I could do this because I'd be going to certain reach markets. Actually,

"Scorpio Rising," of all my movies, was called "box-office" by Pauline Kael. It's had the widest screenings and it has made more money for me.

CA: When "Scorpio Rising" came out and did so well, did you get offers from studios?

ANGER: I had a little talk. I never went down to actually see them. But at that time things like "Easy Rider" were being made also.

CA: Dennis Hopper, [director of "Easy Rider"] was a fan of yours.

ANGER: So was Jack Nicholson, but they never said, "You should be making a big film." They never said, "Gee, you've got to meet this American International Pictures guy," you know. None of those things ever happened. And I am a little diffident about it, because I had this connection with Hollywood studios when I was a kid. I mean I never went hustling *ever*. I said, "If something comes my way and someone wants to talk to me, fine." But it just never happened.

CA: "Scorpio Rising" contains associations between violence and sex. Do you always do this?

ANGER: "Scorpio Rising" was a documentary. I was filming a phenomenon that happened. I didn't direct the phenomenon. I didn't add anything to the scene that was not there already. The only thing that I did add was my participation with the camera. And the fact that I believe quite strongly that with a camera in their presence, people act differently than when the camera isn't present. People exaggerate a little and show off. They were sweet innocent kids. They weren't vicious and nasty. They stole a few things. They weren't really bad. 1962 was the beginning of the Vietnam War. Several of them went off and got killed in the war.

CA: But earlier films had similar imagery.

ANGER: I mean the fact that I would make it. I was attracted to "Scorpio Rising" but I wasn't emotionally involved with it. Other films, like "Inauguration of the Pleasure Dome," I was emotionally involved with the people in the film. People like Anais Nin, whom I'd known since I was a teenager. It overlapped into her circle of people who also used to be interested in black magic, writers, sculptors. It was not the Hollywood crowd.

CA: Who are your favorite filmmakers today?

ANGER: Leni Riefenstahl is the only living hero I know. She is a fantastic woman. She is incredibly talented. She is an incredible survivor. She makes still photographs now. She was one of the greatest filmmakers of the twentieth century. Films like "Blue Light," "Olympia," and "Triumph of the Will" are some of the greatest works. Whether they are selling Nazis or selling automobiles has absolutely nothing to do with it. They are gorgeous works of art. It has nothing to do with the ideology that she had then. She doesn't have it now. She said she had to do it. It was glamorous, powerful. Hitler was very puritanical.

Puritans are very dangerous people. I don't go to see modern movies. The only thing I liked about living in New York was that you can see good prints of beautiful old pictures more than anywhere else. The Museum of Modern Art shows thirty-five millimeter original nitrate prints of gorgeous things from the late 1920's and 1930's. They have a special fire permit. The film is very explosive. People see an old silent film and say, "That's so ugly. How could anyone have ever thought that was any good?" They are seeing a fifth-generation duplicate which has been copied five or six times. So it loses the sensuous glamour that the image had.

CA: How can you write Hollywood Babylon II *if you don't go to any movies now?*

ANGER: It's not a book about movies. It's a book about the people that make them.

CA: If you don't see the stars' and directors' work, how can you really have a sense of what they're about?

ANGER: I pick it up by osmosis. The last big Hollywood film I saw was "Close Encounters of the Third Kind." [Director] Steven Spielberg mailed me the monkey from the film afterwards. He got the idea from "Scorpio Rising," that's why he did it.

CA: What about Japanese films like "In the Realm of the Senses?"

ANGER: Maybe I'm missing something. But I have my life structured in such a way that I would prefer to go see an early RKO "B" picture.

CA: Did you see "Star Wars"?

ANGER: I liked some of the special effects. But the actors: I didn't like any of them. It would have been better as a comic strip.

CA: Do you have any blatant dislikes?

ANGER: I am a loner. My name when I was in grade school was "The Lone Anger," like "The Lone Ranger" only dropping the "r." I used to sing ranger songs. In other words I am totally disconnected with political parties. They're all bluffs. Everyone is a rip-off. The ones that talk ideals are the worst.

CA: So you've kept the same friends over the years?

ANGER: Friends? Who said anything about friends? I don't have any friends. Truly. I am very proud of the fact that I have no friends. If someone says that they are Kenneth Anger's friend, watch out! Maybe they will say that after I've died, but you better check with me. I don't believe in friends.

CA: What about Anais Nin?

ANGER: She was an associate, but I would never say that she was a friend. In other words, friendship is something that I feel very strongly about because it's a swamp. I see more people disappear with just a few little bubbles over so-called friendships. Jesus Christ learned about friends. He had twelve friends and one of them turned out to be Judas. I feel that every disciple is a potential Judas. Magicians say that as long as you have twelve people together, one of them is going to betray you. I work alone. I'm independent.

AVOCATIONAL INTERESTS: Collecting Hollywood memorabilia, the occult.

BIOGRAPHICAL/CRITICAL SOURCES: Film Culture, summer, 1960, winter, 1963-64, spring, 1964, spring, 1967, winter-spring, 1967; *Spider,* April, 1965; *Village Voice,* April 21,

1966, August 21, 1969, May 17, 1973, October 13, 1975, October 18, 1976; *Take One,* August, 1967; *Cinema,* October, 1969; *Variety,* May 9, 1973; *Film Quarterly,* summer, 1974; *Newsweek,* July 16, 1975; *New York Times Book Review,* August 31, 1975; *American Film,* April, 1976; *Avant-Scene,* October 15, 1976.*

—Interview by Ann Bardach

* * *

ANGREMY, Jean-Pierre 1937-
(Raymond Marlot, Pierre-Jean Remy)

PERSONAL: Born March 21, 1937, in Angouleme, France; son of Pierre (a commercial agent) and Alice (Collebrans) Angremy; married Odile Cail (a publisher), June 4, 1963; children: Antoine, Berenice. *Education:* Attended Institut d'Etudes Politiques, 1955-60, Brandeis University, 1958-59, and Ecole Nationale d'Administration, 1960-63. *Home:* 100 rue de l'Universite, 75007 Paris, France. *Agent:* Georges Beaume, 3 quai Malaquais, 75006 Paris, France. *Office:* Ministry for Culture, Maison Opera-Bastille, 3 Rue de Valois, 75001 Paris, France.

CAREER: Served in French diplomatic corps, with positions including vice-counsul archivist, Hong Kong, 1963-64, second secretary, Peking, China, 1964-66, second secretary, London, England, 1966-69, first secretary, London, 1969-70, counselor of foreign affairs, second class, 1970-71, Department of cultural, scientific, and technical relations, Paris, France, adjunct to the chief of artistic exchange service, 1971-72, cultural counselor, London, 1975-79, counselor of foreign affairs, first class, 1977; Office de Radiodiffusion Television Francaise, Paris, adjunct director in charge of programming, 1972-75; Ministry of Culture, Paris, director of theatre and entertainment, 1979-81; Nouvel Opera de la Bastille, Paris, artistic director, 1982—. *Member:* P.E.N. Club, Society of Writers. *Awards, honors:* Prix Theophaste Renaudot, 1971, for *Le Sac du Palais d'Ete;* Prix Alexandre Dumas, 1981, for *Pandora;* Chevalier in French Order of Merit; Commander of Arts and Letters.

WRITINGS—Under pseudonym Pierre-Jean Remy, except as noted: (Under name Jean-Pierre Angremy) *Et Gulliver mourut de sommeil* (novel; title means "Gulliver Died of Sleepiness"), Julliard, 1962; *Midi; ou, L'Attentat* (novel; title means "Noon; or, The Attempt"), Julliard, 1963; (under pseudonym Raymond Marlot) *Gauguin a gogo* (title means "Too Many Gauguins"), Denoel, 1971; *Le Sac du Palais d'Ete* (novel; title means "The Sacking of the Summer Palace"), Gallimard, 1971; *Urbanisme* (poems; title means "Urbanism"), Gallimard, 1972; (under pseudonym Raymond Marlot) *Les Suicides du printemps* (novel; title means "Suicides in the Spring"), Denoel, 1972; *La Vie d'Adrien Putney, poete* (novel; title means "The Life of Adrien Putney, Poet"), La Table Ronde, 1973; *Une Mort sale* (novel; title means "A Dirty Death"), Gallimard, 1973; *Ava* (novel), Gallimard, 1974; *La Mort de Floria Tosca* (essay; title means "The Death of Floria Tosca"), Mercure de France, 1974; *Memoires secrets pour servir a l'histoire de ce siecle* (novel; title means "Secret Diaries Concerning the History of This Century"), Gallimard, 1974.

Rever de la vie (novel; title means "To Dream One's Life"), Gallimard, 1975; (with others) *L'Amerique des stars: L'Histoire, la mythologie, et le reve* (essays; title means "America of Stars: History, Mythology, and Dream"), Film Editions, 1976; *La Figure dans la pierre* (novel; title means "The Figure in the Stone"), Gallimard, 1976; *Callas: Une Vie,* Ramsay, 1977, translation by Catherine Atthill published as *Maria Callas: A Tribute,* Macdonald and Jane's, 1978, St. Martin's,

1980; *Chine: Un Itineraire* (essay; title means "China: An Itinerary"), Orban, 1977; *Les Enfants du parc* (novel; title means "The Children of the Park"), Gallimard, 1977; *Si j'etais romancier: On se mettrait a cent pour ecrire mille romans qui auraient cent mille pages* (essay; title means "If I Were a Novelist: We Would Be One Hundred Writers Writing One Thousand Novels of One Hundred Thousand Pages"), Garnier, 1977.

Les Nouvelles Aventures du chevalier de La Barre (novel; title means "New Adventures of Chevalier de La Barre"), Gallimard, 1978; *Cordelia: ou, L'Angleterre* (title means "Cordelia: Images of England"), Gallimard, 1979; *Don Giovanni: Mozart, Losey* (title means "Don Giovanni: According to Mozart and Losey"), A. Michel, 1979; *Orient-express: Roman* (novel), A. Michel, 1979, translation by St. John Field published as *Compartment East: Love and Adventure on the Orient Express,* Morrow, 1980; *Pandora* (novel), A. Michel, 1980; *Les Memoires de la petite comtesse* (essay; title means "The Memoirs of the Little Countess"), Le Signe, 1980; *Salue pour moi le monde* (novel; title means "Greet the World for Me"), Gallimard, 1980; *Un Voyage d'hiver* (novel; title means "A Winter Journey"), Gallimard, 1981.

Author of television script "Orient Express" (based on own novel) for French television.

WORK IN PROGRESS: A novel and television series based on the life of Mata-Hari; a novel based on Don Giovanni.

SIDELIGHTS: Jean-Pierre Angremy maintains dual careers as a diplomat and author. He published two novels before entering French diplomatic service in 1963, and from 1971 produced more than twenty works of fiction, nonfiction, and poetry, covering a wide range of topics. Angremy's personal interest in opera led to *Callas: Une Vie,* his 1977 tribute to opera star Maria Callas. The book, written under the pseudonym Pierre-Jean Remy, presents Callas as a great singer who was also a great tragic actress, and as an innovator who, recognizing opera as theatre, changed the development of opera presentation.

"Remy also has a special idea about the Callas phenomenon: for him this is to be construed as a myth of woman's destruction by man," explains *New York Review of Books* critic Joseph Kerman. "Off stage he sees her victimized by her husband, her agent Bagarozy, Bing, Onassis, Visconti, columnists, audiences, Remy himself; on stage she ritually reenacts her destruction in the personae of doomed heroines such as Violetta and Tosca." *Washington Post Book World* reviewer Joseph McLellan praised Angremy's discussion of Callas's vocal art, but joined other critics in questioning the book's accuracy in other areas: "Remy, an intelligent and perceptive writer and fine stylist, . . . is unfortunately inclined to be a little hazy at times (in the grand old style of French journalism) about hard facts."

Angremy's 1977 novel *Les Enfants du parc* details the scenes and dreams of youth as recalled by a man in his sixties, a man in his late thirties, and a young man of eighteen. The episodes described often involve sexual encounters, prompting *French Review* critic Allan H. Pasco to conclude: "In Remy's curious world, sex, the apparent key to human brotherhood, matters more than anything else." Pasco, impressed with the author's cultural background, noted that *Les Enfants du parc* contains many references to literature, cinema, opera, and music. While citing the novel's "convincing dialogue and frequently evocative descriptions," Pasco observed that the "characters, motivated by shallow cliches, remain uncomplicated silhouettes."

Based on an eighteenth-century Frenchman who was executed at age nineteen for desecrating a crucifix, Angremy's novel

Les Nouvelles Aventures du chevalier de La Barre fabricates for the historical character an escape from execution. He magically remains young, reappearing in England throughout the eighteenth and nineteenth centuries. Critics praised Angremy's evocation of past eras as he describes the character's various sexual adventures. Themes of the past and love are also central to Angremy's 1980 novel *Compartment East: Love and Adventure on the Orient Express*. In this book a young woman sets out to record the memoirs of a retired diplomat. Rather than recounting historical events, the former French Ambassador tells of six women who influenced him between the years 1913 and 1939. Each of the stories involves travel on the Orient Express, and together they offer mystery, passion, and tragedy. Critics found the characters captivating and the exotic stories romantically satisfying. Angremy wrote a screenplay based on *Orient Express* that was broadcast as a six-hour series on French television.

Angremy told *CA:* "A stay of two years in China, seven years spent in London, and a deep interest in French eighteenth-century literature have been, up to now, the main influences in my writing, together with a passionate love for theatre and, above all, opera. I have been collecting eighteenth-century French literature, mainly novels, for many years."

BIOGRAPHICAL/CRITICAL SOURCES: Times Literary Supplement, February 25, 1972, September 10, 1976; *World Literature Today,* summer, 1978, autumn, 1979; *French Review,* March, 1979; *Los Angeles Times Book Review,* July 6, 1980; *Washington Post Book World,* February 22, 1981; *New York Review of Books,* April 2, 1981.

* * *

ANTHONY, Julie 1948-

PERSONAL: Born January 13, 1948, in Los Angeles, Calif.; daughter of Thomas C. (an architect) and Emolyn (a secretary; maiden name, Hyndman) Anthony; married Richard Butera (in real estate), December 28, 1976. *Education:* Stanford University, A.B., 1969; University of California, Los Angeles, M.A., 1971, Ph.D., 1979. *Home:* 15 L Valley Forge Towers, King of Prussia, Pa. 19406. *Agent:* Mel Berger, William Morris Agency, 1350 Avenue of the Americas, New York, N.Y. 10019. *Office:* Philadelphia Flyers, Broad & Pattison, Philadelphia, Pa. 19148.

CAREER: Professional tennis player, 1969-78; television tennis commentator, 1975-81; Philadelphia Flyers (professional hockey team), Philadelphia, Pa., psychologist, 1981—.

WRITINGS: A Winning Combination (psychological guide), Scribner, 1980.

* * *

APPLETON, Victor W. II
  See ADAMS, Harriet S(tratemeyer)

* * *

APPLEWHITE, Harriet Branson 1940-

PERSONAL: Born June 5, 1940, in Cleveland, Ohio; daughter of Robert Lees (a manufacturer's agent) and Eleanor (Verdier) Branson; married Philip B. Applewhite (a biologist), August 10, 1963; children: Eleanor Verdier, Kate Maria, Douglas Robert. *Education:* Smith College, B.A. (magna cum laude), 1962; Stanford University, M.A., 1964, Ph.D., 1972. *Residence:* Hamden, Conn. *Office:* Department of Political Science, Southern Connecticut State College, New Haven, Conn. 06515.

CAREER: Smith College, Northampton, Mass., lecturer in political science, 1965-66; Southern Connecticut State College, New Haven, assistant professor, 1967-76, associate professor of political science, 1976—. *Member:* American Association of University Professors, Ameican Political Science Association, Phi Beta Kappa. *Awards, honors:* Fellow of National Endowment for the Humanities, 1973-74.

WRITINGS: Women in Revolutionary Paris, 1784-1795, University of Illinois Press, 1979; (contributor) Carol Berkin and Clara Maria Lovett, editors, *Women, War, and Revolution,* Holmes & Meier, 1980. Contributor to history journals.

WORK IN PROGRESS: Political Culture in Revolutionary France.

* * *

ARBEITER, Jean S(onkin) 1937-

PERSONAL: Born January 13, 1937, in New York, N.Y.; daughter of Daniel (a writer) and Clara (a teacher; maiden name, Paley) Sonkin; married Solomon Arbeiter, December 26, 1964; children: Daniel, Peter, Claire. *Education:* Vassar College, A.B., 1958; New York University, A.M., 1964. *Politics:* Democrat. *Religion:* Jewish. *Home:* 329 Park Ave., Leonia, N.J. 07605. *Agent:* Carole Abel, 160 West 87th St., New York, N.Y. 10024.

CAREER: Funk & Wagnalls, New York City, promotion director, 1959-61; World Publishing Co., New York City, promotion director, 1961-63; Family Service Association of America, New York City, 1963-65; National Association of Social Workers, Washington, D.C., promotion director, 1974-78. *Member:* Leonia Democratic Club (president).

WRITINGS: (With Marjorie P. Katz) *Pegs to Hang Ideas On,* M. Evans, 1972; (with Marjorie P. Weiser) *Woman List,* Atheneum, 1981; (with Linda Cerino Cirius) *Permanent Addresses,* Fawcett, 1982. Contributor to magazines and newspapers.

* * *

ARCHER HOUBLON, Doreen (Lindsay) 1899-1977

PERSONAL: Born June 29, 1899, in Dublin, Ireland; died December 1, 1977; daughter of Walter (a military colonel) and Lady Kathleen (Butler) Lindsay; married Richard Archer Houblon (a major in Royal Horse Artillery of British Army), October 12, 1929. *Education:* Attended private school in Sussex, England. *Religion:* Church of Ireland.

CAREER: Farmer, and breeder of horses, ponies, and dairy short horn and Aberdeen Angus cattle. Commander of Victorian Order. *Member:* Soil Association, Bio-Dynamic Agriculture Association, English-Speaking Union.

WRITINGS: Side-Saddle, foreword by C. C. Lucas, Scribner, 1938, reprinted as *Side Saddle Riding,* J. A. Allen, 1972.

* * *

ARMER, J(ohn) Michael 1937-

PERSONAL: Born June 27, 1937, in Phoenix, Ariz.; children: two. *Education:* Whittier College, B.A., 1959; University of Wisconsin—Madison, M.A., 1962, Ph.D., 1964. *Office:* Department of Sociology, Florida State University, Tallahassee, Fla. 32306.

CAREER: University of Oregon, Eugene, assistant professor of sociology, 1965-70; Indiana University, Bloomington, associate professor of sociology beginning in 1970—; Currently member of faculty of Florida State University; Tallahassee, Fla. Visiting associate professor at Northwestern University, 1968-69. *Member:* American Sociological Association, African Studies Association. *Awards, honors:* National Science Foundation grant, 1966-70.

WRITINGS: (Editor with Allen D. Grimshaw) *Comparative Social Research: Methodological Problems and Strategies,* Robert E. Krieger, 1973; (editor) *African Social Psychology: Review and Annotated Bibliography,* Holmes & Meier, 1975. Contributor to *Sport, Play, and Leisure,* Also contributor to sociology journals.*

* * *

ARNESON, D(on) J(on)   1935-

PERSONAL: Born August 15, 1935, in Montevideo, Minn.; married wife, Beatrice in 1958; children: Leif Eric, Marc Antony. *Education:* Mexico City College, B.A., 1959. *Address:* Box 141, Southbury, Conn. 06488.

CAREER: Dell Publishing Co., Inc., New York, N.Y., editor, 1962-69; free-lance writer. *Military service:* U.S. Army, 1954-56, served with counterintelligence.

WRITINGS: (With Jack Sparling) *Instant Candidate '64: Pick Your Politician, Pose, Platform,* Pocket Books, 1964; *The Great Society Comic Book,* illustrations by Tony Tallarico, Parallax Press, 1966; *The Most Famous Ghost of All and Other Ghost Stories* (juvenile), Young Reader's Press, 1971; *Secret Places* (juvenile) photographs by Peter Arnold, Holt, 1971; *Creature Reader* (juvenile), Young Reader's Press, 1972; *Jokes and Riddles Roundup* (juvenile), illustrations by Jim Kersell, Xerox Education Publications, 1972. Also author of *A Friend Indeed,* F. Watts, and *Walk to Survival,* Ace Books.

WORK IN PROGRESS: Books for young adults, including *The Night of the Wolves, The Bogman,* and *The Alien Link.*

SIDELIGHTS: D. J. Arneson commented to *CA:* "I perceive all 'being' as a unified, simultaneous experience and write from that position."

* * *

AROUT, Gabriel   1909-1982

OBITUARY NOTICE: Born January 28, 1909, in Armenia; died in 1982 in Paris, France. Author. Arout wrote his first novel, in Russian, at age fourteen. After graduating from the Sorbonne, he wrote two novels in French. None of the books, however, were published, and Arout was forced to work in France as a manual laborer. In 1943 a revision of his first play, "Orphee," was staged by Louis Ducreux, and Arout was able to once again devote his full attention to writing. He adapted many novels for the French stage, including Patrick Hamilton's *Rope* and Dostoevsky's *Crime and Punishment* and *The Idiot.* He also wrote the screenplay for Luis Bunuel's "La Mort en ce jardin." In 1981 Arout received an award from the French Academy. Obituaries and other sources: *London Times,* March 4, 1982.

* * *

ARTHURS, Peter   1933-

PERSONAL: Born November 1, 1933, in Dundalk, County Louth, Ireland; son of Peter Joseph and Margaret (a dietician; maiden name, Brady) Arthurs. *Education:* Attended Christian Brothers Schools of Ireland. *Politics:* "Staunch believer in democracy." *Home:* 246 East 74th St., New York, N.Y. 10021. *Agent:* Scott Meredith Literary Agency, Inc., 845 Third Ave., New York, N.Y. 10022. *Office address:* Box 70, 15 State St., New York, N.Y. 10004.

CAREER: Merchant seaman, 1948—, stowaway on S.S. *Black Sod,* 1948, served on S.S. *Beryl,* 1949. Worked as actor, sparring partner for boxers, saloon keeper, doorman, gravedigger, and bodyguard. *Member:* Seafarers International Union of North America, Alcoholics Anonymous.

WRITINGS: With Brendan Behan: A Personal Memoir (biography), St. Martin's, 1981; *The Last Roominghouse* (autobiographical novel), St. Martin's, 1983.

WORK IN PROGRESS: A novel, *Urchin in the Chain Locker;* "The Couch," a tragi-comedy in two acts.

SIDELIGHTS: Arthurs was chauffeur, companion, and occasional lover of Brendan Behan in the last three years before the legendary Irish poet and playwright died of alcoholism and diabetes. In *With Brendan Behan: A Personal Memoir,* Arthurs documents the details of Behan's sexual and alcoholic excesses. Arthurs felt that he had been exploited by Behan in their years together, and the spirit of vengeance which permeates the work caused Seymour Krim of the *Chicago Tribune Book World* to label it "subjective" and "self-serving." Even so, Krim praised Arthurs because he "transcends his own pettiness to give us a true picture of a man of desperate genius. . . . [H]e makes us see and feel Brendan Behan as he must have been, and to admire him even when he was at his most cruel and destructive." All told, Krim assessed the book as "the most graphic picture of Behan ever published."

Arthurs told *CA:* "Good writing is usually—at least in part—autobiographical. Reading the works of others, only leisurely, verified my own thoughts, enhanced my writing vocabulary, and enabled me to write on a higher literary plane. The telling of a good story should be a form of personal purging, an exorcism of the soul. A true writer should be interested in all subjects. Malamud is a perfect example of what it takes to be a great writer."

"I now have some fifty reviews," he continued, "most of which are excellent. Almost all of the leading U.S. papers (mostly Sunday editions), with the exception of the *New York Times,* have highly praised my book."

BIOGRAPHICAL/CRITICAL SOURCES: Chicago Tribune Book World, August 9, 1981.

* * *

ASHLEY, Jack   1922-

PERSONAL: Born December 6, 1922, in England; son of John and Isabella (Bridge) Ashley; married Pauline Kay Crispin in 1951; children: Jacqueline, Jane, Carolyn. *Education:* Attended Ruskin College, Oxford, 1946-48; and Caius College, Cambridge, 1948-51. *Office:* House of Commons, London S.W.1, England.

CAREER: Laborer and crane operator, 1936-46; British Broadcasting Corp., London, England, radio producer, 1951-59, senior television producer, 1960-66, member of general advisory council, 1967-69 and 1970-74; House of Commons, London, Labour member of Parliament for Stoke-on-Trent South, 1966—, Parliamentary Private Secretary to Department of Health and Social Security, 1974, member of Privy Council, 1981—. Member of Widnes Borough Council, 1946-47. Member of general advisory council of British Broadcasting Corp., 1967-69 and 1970-74. *Awards, honors:* Companion of Honor.

WRITINGS: Journey Into Silence (autobiography), Bodley Head, 1973.

* * *

ASHMOLE, Bernard 1894-

PERSONAL: Born June 22, 1894, in Ilford, England; son of William (an estate agent) and Caroline Wharton (Tiver) Ashmole; married Dorothy De Peyer, October 12, 1920; children: Stella (Mrs. Peter Ring), Silvia (Mrs. Peter Ebert), Philip. *Education:* Hertford College, Oxford, M.A., 1921, B.Litt., 1924. *Home:* 5 Tweed Green, Peebles, Scotland.

CAREER: Oxford University, Oxford, England, assistant curator of coins at Ashmolean Museum, 1923-25; British School at Rome, Rome, Italy, director, 1925-28; University of London, London, England, Yates Professor of Classical Archaeology, 1929-48; British Museum, London, keeper of Greek and Roman antiquities, 1939-56; Oxford University, Lincoln Professor of Classical Archaeology and Art, 1956-61; University of Aberdeen, Aberdeen, Scotland, Geddes-Harrower Professor of Greek Archaeology and Art, 1961-62; writer and researcher, 1962—. Visiting professor at Yale University, 1964; fellow of Lincoln College, Oxford, Hertford College, Oxford, and University College, London. *Military service:* British Army, Royal Fusiliers, 1914-18; became captain; received Military Cross. Royal Air Force, 1941-45; became wing commander; received Hellenic Flying Cross.

MEMBER: British Academy (fellow), Royal Institute of British Architects (fellow), Archaeological Institute of America (fellow), Archaeological Society of Athens (fellow). *Awards, honors:* Commander of the Order of the British Empire, 1957; LL.D. from University of Aberdeen, 1968; Kenyon Medal from British Academy, 1979, for *Architect and Sculptor in Classical Greece;* Cassano Medal from Convegno di Studio sulla Magna Grecia, 1979, for articles on the art of Greece in its western colonies.

WRITINGS: Catalogue of Ancient Marbles at Ince Blundell Hall, Clarendon Press, 1929; (with J. D. Beazley) *Greek Sculpture and Painting,* Cambridge University Press, 1932, reprinted, 1966; (with Nicholas Yalouris and Alison Frantz) *Olympia: The Sculpture of the Temple of Zeus,* Phaidon, 1967; (with H. A. Groenewegen) *Art of the Ancient World,* Volume I, Prentice-Hall, 1967; *Architect and Sculptor in Classical Greece,* New York University Press, 1972. Contributor to learned journals.

SIDELIGHTS: Ashmole wrote: "I specialize in Greek sculpture, chiefly in the practical problems facing sculptors and architects in obtaining, transporting, and using their materials."

* * *

ASHMORE, Owen 1920-

PERSONAL: Born November 7, 1920, in Disley, Cheshire, England; son of Frank Owen (a buyer) and Beatrice Maud (a teacher; maiden name, Swindells) Ashmore; married Sheila Latimer Parker, August 10, 1948; children: Geoffrey Owen, Anne, Matthew, David. *Education:* Peterhouse, Cambridge, M.A., 1948. *Religion:* Church of England. *Home:* Flowery Field, Woodsmoor, Stockport, Cheshire SK2 7ED, England. *Office:* Extra-Mural Department, Victoria University of Manchester, Manchester M13 9PL, England.

CAREER: Assistant history teacher at grammar school in New Mills, Derbyshire, England, 1948-50; Victoria University of Manchester, Manchester, England, resident staff tutor, 1950-62, deputy director of extra-mural studies, 1962-69, associate director, 1969-73, acting director, 1973-76, director, 1976—. *Military service:* British Army, Royal Artillery, 1942-46; became lieutenant. *Member:* Historical Association, Association for Industrial Archaeology, Association of University Teachers, Society of Antiquaries.

WRITINGS: The Development of Power in Britain, Macmillan, 1967; *Industrial Archaeology of Lancashire,* David & Charles, 1969; *The Industrial Archaeology of Stockport,* Extra-Mural Department, Victoria University of Manchester, 1975; (editor) *Historic Industries of Marple and Mellor,* Stockport Metropolitan Borough Council, 1977; *Industrial Archaeology in North West England,* Manchester University Press, 1982. Contributor to history journals.

* * *

AUBRY, Claude B. 1914-

PERSONAL: Born October 23, 1914, in Morin Heights, Quebec, Canada; son of Ernest and Augustine (Lafleur) Aubry. *Education:* University of Montreal, B.A., 1936; McGill University, B.L.S., 1945. *Home:* 14 Claver St., Ottawa, Ontario K1J 6W7, Canada. *Office:* Ottawa Public Library, 120 Metcalfe St., Ottawa, Ontario K1P 5M2, Canada.

CAREER: Worked as accountant, 1936-44; Montreal Civil Library (also called Montreal Municipal Library), Montreal, Quebec, chief of personnel, 1945-49; Ottawa Public Library, Ottawa, Ontario, assistant chief librarian, 1949-53, director, 1953—; Eastern Ontario Regional Library System, director, 1965-76. Member of board, Montfort Hospital Corp.; vice-president, Canadian Film Institute, 1974-76. *Member:* Canadian Authors Association, Canadian Library Association, Society of Canadian Writers, Ontario Library Association, Ontario Provincial Library Council, Alliance Francaise (vice-president of Ottawa chapter), Association France-Canada. *Awards, honors:* Association Canadienne des Bibliothecaires de Langue Francaise award, for *Les Iles du roi Maha Maha II,* 1962; Book of the Year for Children medal from Canadian Library Association, 1962, for *Le Loup de Noel,* 1965; decorated, Order of Canada, 1974; appointed Officier de l'Ordre International du Bien Public, 1975; Quebec Provincial Government award, for *Le Loup de Noel.*

*WRITINGS—*In English translation: *Les Iles du roi Maha Maha II: Conte fantaisiste canadien* (juvenile), illustrations by Edouard Perret, Pelican (Quebec), 1960, translation by Alice Kane published as *The King of the Thousand Islands: A Canadian Fairy Tale,* McClelland & Stewart (Toronto), 1963, another edition translated by Harvey Swados, illustrations by Grey Cohoe, Doubleday, 1971; *Le Loup de Noel* (juvenile), illustrations by Perret, Editions Centre de Psychologie et de Pedagogie (Montreal), 1962, translation by Kane published as *The Christmas Wolf,* McClelland & Stewart, 1965; *Le Violon magique et autres legendes du Canada francais,* illustrations by Saul Field, Editions des Deux Rives (Ottawa), 1968, translation by Kane published as *The Magic Fiddler and Other Legends of French Canada,* Peter Martin (Toronto), 1968; *Agouhanna* (juvenile), illustrations by Julie Brinckloe, translation by Swados, Doubleday, 1972, French edition published in 1974.

Other: *Miroirs deformants,* Fides, 1945; (with Laurent G. Denis) *Rapport de l'etude des bibliotheques publiques de la region de Montreal,* Ministere des affaires culturelles, 1976; *Legendes du Canada francais,* Les Editions de l'Espoir, 1977.

Member of library consultants board of *Encyclopedia Canadiana* and of editorial board of *Canadian Children's Literature.**

AYCOCK, Don M(ilton) 1951-

PERSONAL: Born December 10, 1951, in El Campo, Tex.; son of Dewey (an oil field worker) and Mabel (Stout) Aycock; married Carla Ricketts (a high school mathematics teacher), November 17, 1973; children: Christopher Carl and Ryan Don (twins). *Education:* Louisiana College, B.A., 1974; Southern Baptist Theological Seminary, Louisville, Ky., M.Div., 1976, Th.M., 1978; attended Mansfield College, Oxford, 1979; doctoral study at New Orleans Baptist Seminary, 1982—. *Politics:* Democrat. *Address:* Box 402 NOBTS, 3939 Gentilly Blvd., New Orleans, La.

CAREER: Ordained Southern Baptist minister, 1974; West Side-Portland Baptist Church, Louisville, Ky., pastor, 1977-82. Founder of literary agency for writers of Christian books. Member of Portland Area Council and Portland Area Churches Together.

WRITINGS: The E. Y. Mullins Lectures on Preaching, University Press of America, 1980; (with wife, Carla Aycock) *Not Quite Heaven,* C.S.S. Publishing, 1981; (editor) *Preaching With Purpose and Power,* Mercer University Press, 1982; *Symbols of Salvation,* Broadman, 1982.

WORK IN PROGRESS: Writing Nonfiction Religious Books: A Beginner's Guide; editing and contributing to *Apathy in the Pew;* research on Christian theology, the religious imagination, and the business side of the writing industry.

SIDELIGHTS: Aycock told *CA:* "I compiled *Apathy in the Pew* when I discovered there was very little material available dealing with the psychological and sociological reasons for which people stay out of church. My book on writing religious books and my literary agency were created because agents do not like to handle authors of religious books.

"My ministry during the past five years has been in a small, inner-city church. We see many of the 'raw' needs of people here, so we concentrate on helping to provide basic necessities of food and clothing. We also work on what I call 'preventative religion'—and a healthy self-understanding in the light of the Christian gospel.

"While working on the book *Apathy in the Pew,* I found many reasons why even people with a religious orientation do not attend church. Catalogued briefly, these reasons include general resistance to authority; anger at people within the church or at God; boredom; a general moratorium on anything other than the basic necessities of living; insecurity (fear of being around other people); guilt; inadequate understanding of their responsibilities to the church (we call this an inadequate contract in our book); basic conflict between the personality of the individual and the church (this we call mismarriage); life fatigue; heavy-handed church leadership; a reaction to the work ethic; reaction to the gospel; church coldness; and family dynamics.

"As to Christian book writing, this field is on the growing edge of the publishing industry. *Publishers Weekly* estimates that by 1983 this will be a $300 million per year industry. In my opinion, this is both good and bad. It is good because the area has been stifled too long. But it is bad because some of what is being published is inferior material. An editor recently told me that, in his opinion, only about 10 percent of the religious books published last year were worth the effort of bringing them out.

"Personally, I would ultimately like to teach on the college or seminary level and to continue my work as a literary agent for Christian book writers. I will begin work in the fall of 1982 on a Doctor of Theology degree in the field of systematic theology. I want to write my dissertation in the area of religious imagination and creativity."

AVOCATIONAL INTERESTS: Hunting, fishing, photography, music, travel.

* * *

AYLESWORTH, Jim 1943-

PERSONAL: Born February 21, 1943; married wife, Donna (an interior designer); children: John, Daniel. *Education:* Miami University, Oxford, Ohio, B.A., 1965; Concordia College, River Forest, Ill., M.A., 1979. *Home:* 213 North Elm, Hinsdale, Ill. 60521.

CAREER: Hatch School, Oak Park, Ill., teacher of first grade, 1971—. *Awards, honors:* Award for excellence from Illinois Office of Education, 1975.

WRITINGS: Hush Up! (juvenile), Holt, 1980; *Tonight's the Night* (juvenile), Whitman Publishing, 1981; *Mary's Mirror* (juvenile), Holt, 1982.

B

BABA, Meher 1894-1969
(Merwan S. Irani)

OBITUARY NOTICE: Born in 1894 in Poona, India; died January 31, 1969. Mystic and author of several volumes of journals. Baba was a devotee of Sufi mysticism. Much of his life was spent informally instructing his disciples and leading them on obscure pilgrimages. In 1925 Baba ceased speaking. He remained silent to his death in 1969. He wrote *God Speaks: The Theme of Creation and Its Purpose* and *God to Man and Man to God: The Discourses of Meher Baba.* Obituaries and other sources: *Encyclopedia of Occultism and Parapsychology,* Gale, 1978.

*   *   *

BABCOCK, Leland S. 1922-

BRIEF ENTRY: Born April 24, 1922, in Sacramento, Calif. American educator and author. Babcock has taught at Occidental College since 1952 and has been a professor of German since 1967. He wrote *German and Germany in Review* (Van Nostrand, 1972). *Address:* Department of German, Occidental College, 1600 Campus Rd., Los Angeles, Calif. 90041. *Biographical/critical sources: Directory of American Scholars,* Volume III: *Foreign Languages, Linguistics, and Philology,* 7th edition, Bowker, 1978.

*   *   *

BACON, Margaret

PERSONAL: Born in Leeds, England; daughter of Reginald Kingsley (a journalist and biographer) and Maud (Davison) Bacon; married Richard E. Tuckwell (a civil engineer), September 23, 1955; children: Penelope Jane, Caroline Ann. *Education:* St. Anne's College, Oxford, B.A., 1952, M.A., 1955. *Politics:* Liberal. *Home:* Hill House, Shrivenham Rd., Highworth, near Swindon, Wiltshire, England. *Agent:* Bolt & Watson Ltd., 26 Charing Cross Rd., Suite 8, London WC2H 0DG, England.

CAREER: History teacher and department head at private school in Limpsfield, England, 1952-55; teacher at secondary schools in London, England, 1957-59, high school English teacher in Georgetown, Guyana, 1959-61; writer, 1961—. Broadcaster for British Broadcasting Corp.

WRITINGS—Published by Dobson, except as noted: *Journey to Guyana* (travel book), 1970; *The Episode* (novel), 1971;

Kitty (novel), 1972; *The Unentitled* (novel), 1974; *A Packetful of Trouble* (juvenile novel), 1974; *The Package* (novel), 1975; *Snow in Winter* (novel), Collins, 1978. Also author of *The Kingdom of the Rose,* a fictional biography, 1982.

WORK IN PROGRESS: "I prefer not to talk about work in progress, as I never know exactly how it is going to turn out. I can only say that it is going to be a shorter and lighter book than my last."

SIDELIGHTS: Margaret Bacon commented: "*The Kingdom of the Rose* is a fictional biography of Eglantine Thorpe (1896-1976), who appeared in *Snow in Winter.* My training as a historian was helpful to me when I wrote it, since it covers nearly a hundred years of political and social history. Economic knowledge provided useful background for writing *Journey to Guyana.* For my novels, I think the driving force has been my interest in relationships, particularly within the family."

*   *   *

BAILEY, James H(enry) 1919-

PERSONAL: Born November 1, 1919, in Petersburg, Va.; son of John Henry (a public official) and Elizabeth (Beasley) Bailey. *Education:* Attended University of Virginia, 1935-37, M.A., 1942; College of William and Mary, A.B., 1939; Georgetown University, D.Phil., 1953. *Politics:* Independent. *Religion:* Roman Catholic. *Home:* 110 Marshall St., Petersburg, Va. 23803.

CAREER: Medical College of Virginia, Richmond, assistant professor of history, 1959-60, 1962-67; Brenau College, Gainesville, Ga., professor of history and chairman of department of history and political science, 1967-71; Petersburg Department of Tourism, Petersburg, Va., historical adviser, 1974—. Member of board of directors of Southside Virginia Community Concerts. *Military service:* U.S. Army, 1942-46; became second lieutenant. *Member:* American Historical Association, American Catholic Historical Association, American Association of University Professors, English-Speaking Union, National Council of Catholic Men, Society for the Prevention of Cruelty to Animals, Sons of Confederate Veterans, Royal Stuart Society, Irish Georgian Society, Virginia Historical Society, Association for the Preservation of Virginia Antiquities (director, Fort Henry branch), Jamestowne Society, Downtown Churches United (president, 1979), Phi Alpha Theta, Pi Sigma Alpha.

WRITINGS: A History of the Diocese of Richmond: The Formative Years, Whittet & Shepperson, 1956; (editor) *Henrico Home Front,* Whittet & Shepperson, 1963; *Old Petersburg,* Hale, 1976; *The Miracle of Jesus for Today,* Abingdon, 1977; *Petersburg in the Revolution: 1781,* Petersburg Bicentennial Commission, 1981. Contributor to *New Catholic Encyclopedia* and *Catholic Youth Encyclopedia.* Contributor of articles and reviews to magazines, including *Virginia Cavalcade.*

WORK IN PROGRESS: A History of the Diocese of Richmond: The Middle Years, completion expected in 1983.

SIDELIGHTS: Bailey told *CA:* "I strongly feel that one is expected to employ whatever gifts one may have in the service of the giver of those gifts and of his fellow man. With regard to my interests, I enjoy history and biography, classical and semi-classical music, the theatre (I have done quite a bit of amateur acting), and I am supportive of the humane treatment of animals."

AVOCATIONAL INTERESTS: Acting, genealogical research, preservation and restoration of old buildings.

*   *   *

BAILEY, Stephen Kemp 1916-1982

OBITUARY NOTICE—See index for *CA* sketch: Born May 14, 1916, in Newton, Mass.; died after a brief illness, March 27, 1982, in Lincoln, Mass. Educator, public administrator, and author. Bailey taught political science at Princeton and Syracuse universities before joining Harvard University as the Francis Keppel Professor of Educational Policy and Administration. He held a number of public offices, including that of mayor of Middletown, Connecticut, and member of the New York State Board of Regents. Bailey also served as vice-president of the American Council on Education and as staff associate for the Hoover Commission's study on the presidency. His works include *Congress Makes a Law, The Purposes of Education,* and *Education Interest Groups in the Nation's Capital.* Obituaries and other sources: *New York Times,* March 30, 1982; *Chicago Tribune,* March 31, 1982.

*   *   *

BAINES, Jocelyn 1925-1973

PERSONAL: Born October 28, 1925, in London, England; died December, 1973, in London, England; son of Patrick and Joyce (Bevan) Baines; married (Marjorie) Claire Schiff, November 11, 1955; children: Camilla, Ivan. *Education:* Received B.A., Christ Church, Oxford.

CAREER: Antiquarian and editor at Longmans, Green & Co. Ltd. (now Longman Group; publishers), London, England; bookseller at Sotheran's, London; managing editor of Thomas Nelson & Sons Ltd. (publishers), London; managing director of Bernard Quaritch (rare book sellers), London. *Military service:* served as captain in army. *Awards, honors:* Duff Cooper Memorial Prize, 1961, for *Joseph Conrad: A Critical Biography.*

WRITINGS: Joseph Conrad: A Critical Biography, Weidenfeld & Nicholson, 1959, McGraw, 1960; (with Katherine Key) *The ABC of Indoor Plants,* Knopf, 1973 (published in England as *The ABC of House and Conservatory Plants,* M. Joseph, 1973).

SIDELIGHTS: In 1960, Baines's *Joseph Conrad: A Critical Biography* was hailed by many critics as the definitive study of its subject. The reviewers were especially impressed with the documentation of Conrad's childhood in Poland, his years at sea, and his cognizance of the English language in his twen-

ties. "Little can have escaped Mr. Baines's intelligent and tenacious search," declared Douglas Hewitt in the *Guardian.* Similarly, a reviewer for the *Times Literary Supplement* stated, "It is hard to imagine a more thorough or reliable or readable book on a subject as full of complexities and pitfalls as this is." The reviewer added that the volume was "candid, lucid, and unpretentious."

Despite the general acclaim, Baines's work was met with some reservations from critics assessing its critical value. Writing in the *New Yorker,* Anthony West charged that "while [Baines] is as solemn as an owl he has nothing much to say." A. J. Guerard, however, hailed the book as "the indispensable biography" despite his objections to its "inadequacy as literary criticism."

The biographical elements of *Joseph Conrad* excited several reviewers. Kenneth Millar wrote in the *San Francisco Chronicle* that "Baines' account of [Conrad's] career at sea is almost as interesting as one of Conrad's own sea stories." And David Daiches, in a review for the *New York Times Book Review,* noted that Baines "has gone through all the available evidence about Conrad's life and . . . presents us with a full and persuasive account of it." Daiches added that "the biographical side is splendid."

Baines's *The ABC of Indoor Plants,* co-written with Katherine Key, details the wide variety of houseplants available to plant growers. A reviewer for the *Times Literary Supplement* noted that "a series of symbols has been devised which will be a useful guide for amateurs, summarizing the main characteristics and requirements of each plant."

BIOGRAPHICAL/CRITICAL SOURCES: New Statesman, January 30, 1960; *Guardian,* February 5, 1960; *Spectator,* February 5, 1960; *Times Literary Supplement,* February 5, 1960, November 23, 1973; *Christian Science Monitor,* March 31, 1960; *New York Herald Tribune,* April 3, 1960; *New York Times Book Review,* April 3, 1960; *New Republic,* April 18, 1960; *Nation,* April 30, 1960; *New Yorker,* May 28, 1960; *San Francisco Chronicle,* May 29, 1960.

[Sketch verified by wife, Claire Baines]

*   *   *

BAIRD, Bil 1904-

PERSONAL: Given name William Britton Baird; born August 15, 1904, in Grand Island, Neb.; son of William Hull (a chemical engineer and playwright) and Louise (Hetzel) Baird; married Evelyn Schwartz, 1932 (divorced, 1934); married Cora Burlar (an actress and puppeteer), January 13, 1937 (died December 7, 1967); married Patricia Courtleigh, June, 1969 (marriage ended); married Susanna Lloyd, December 29, 1974; children: (second marriage) Peter Britton, Laura Jenne; (fourth marriage) Madeleine. *Education:* State University of Iowa, B.A., 1926; graduated from Chicago Academy of Fine Arts, 1927. *Home:* 59 Barrow St., New York, N.Y. 10014.

CAREER: Tony Sarg Marionettes, puppeteer, 1928-32, writer, director, and builder, 1933; creator and producer for Bil Baird's Marionettes, appearing at the Chicago World's Fair, 1934, and in industrial shows, 1935-40; teamed with wife Cora Baird and opened the Fire Horse Manor, a puppet warehouse and workshop, 1937; presented puppet shows in vaudeville, for nightclubs, and Broadway, including performances for Ziegfeld's Follies, 1943-59; produced the Baird series for Columbia Broadcasting System (CBS-TV), including "Life With Snarky Parker," 1949-50, "The Whistling Wizard," 1952-53, and "The Bil Baird Show," 1953; toured the United States, India,

Nepal, Afghanistan, and Soviet Union with his marionette production of ''Davy Jones' Locker,'' 1959-63; worked in New York productions, including the Broadway musical ''Baker Street,'' 1963-65; performed for the New York World's Fair, 1964-65; opened (with wife) Bil Baird Theatre and presented several original productions and revivals, including ''Winnie the Pooh,'' ''The Wizard of Oz,'' and ''The Magic Onion,'' 1966—; appeared in ''L'Histoire du soldat'' with the New York Philharmonic, 1969; toured India and Turkey for U.S. AID, 1970; has worked with Cartonella, his puppet cow, explaining nutritional labeling for the Milk Packaging Group of the Paperboard Packaging Council, 1975—. Producer of more than four hundred commercials, the simulations for the Apollo and Gemini spaceflights, and several films, including government films during World War II and films for the Social Security Administration; appeared with his puppets in the motion picture ''The Sound of Music.''

MEMBER: International Alliance of Theatrical Stage Employees, International Puppet Federation (director), American Federation of Musicians, American Federation of Television and Radio Artists, American Guild of Musical Artists, American Guild of Variety Artists, National Academy of Television Arts and Sciences, Screen Actors Guild, Sigma Chi Fraternity (Alpha Eta Chapter), Omicron Delta Kappa.

AWARDS, HONORS: Nominated for Emmy Award from the National Academy of Television Arts and Sciences, 1958, for television special ''Art Carney Meets Peter and the Wolf''; Outer Circle Award (with wife Cora Baird), 1967, for founding a permanent puppet theatre; Jennie Heiden Award from American Theatre Association, 1974, for excellence in professional children's theatre.

WRITINGS: The Art of the Puppet (young adult), Macmillan, 1965; *Schnitzel, the Yodeling Goat* (juvenile), Nelson, 1965; *Puppets and Population,* World Education, 1971.

SIDELIGHTS: Bil Baird's involvement with puppetry is more to him than an occupation or trade; the art of building puppets has spanned generations of the Baird family. As Baird commented: ''I think about my grandfather—the farmer, toolmaker, miller—and my father—the engineer, builder. Each made puppets for his son. My son is now making puppets.'' Bil Baird met his late wife, Cora, when he was designing puppets for the Orson Welles Mercury Theatre. Together they started the world-renowned Bil and Cora Baird Marionettes, working as a team throughout their thirty-year marriage. Besides their stage, television, and filmed puppet work, the Bairds began the award-winning Bil Baird Theatre and the Fire Horse Manor. An off-Broadway theatre in Greenwich Village, the Bil Baird Theatre is now run by the nonprofit American Puppets Arts Council. Bil and Cora Baird's first home, the Fire Horse Manor, located on the Hudson River, is now a workshop and warehouse for over twenty-five hundred puppets. Baird has been involved with every aspect of puppetry, including building, staging, filming, choreographing, writing music, and promoting the value of marionettes for adults and children through his television specials and books.

BIOGRAPHICAL/CRITICAL SOURCES: Alan Stern and Rupert Pray, *Bil Baird's Whistling Wizard,* Simon & Schuster, 1952; Carlyle Wood, *TV Personalities Biographical Sketch Book,* TV Personalities, 1954; *Time,* December 29, 1958; *Life,* February 1, 1963; *Biography News,* Gale, December, 1974.

* * *

BAIRD, William Britton
    See BAIRD, Bil

BAKER, John C(hester)   1909-

PERSONAL: Born April 1, 1909, in Indiana; son of John Emery (an osteopath) and Edith (Kidd) Baker; married Mary Kleckner, July 25, 1931; children: John Louis, Mary Jo Baker Long. *Education:* Purdue University, B.S.A., 1930. *Home:* 4301 Columbia Pike, Arlington, Va. 22204.

CAREER: Massachusetts Extension Service, Amherst, extension editor, 1931-35; WLS-Radio, Chicago, Ill., writer and broadcaster, 1935-38; U.S. Department of Agriculture, Washington, D.C., writer and broadcaster, 1938-42, 1945-46; information officer for War Relocation Authority, 1942-44; WLS-Radio, writer and broadcaster, 1947-49; U.S. Department of Agriculture, information specialist in Chicago, 1950-61, writer and broadcaster in Washington, D.C., 1961-63; U.S. Bureau of the Census, Washington, D.C., public information officer, 1963-70; free-lance writer and speech teacher, 1970—. *Military service:* U.S. Marine Corps, 1944-45; became first lieutenant. *Member:* Society of Professional Journalists, Association of Farm Broadcasters, National Association of Government Communicators.

WRITINGS: Farm Broadcasting: The First Sixty Years, Iowa State University Press, 1981. Also author of *Profile, U.S.A.,* 1970, *Writing for Listeners,* 1974, and *How to Talk Plainly,* 1976.

WORK IN PROGRESS: Magazine articles and short stories.

SIDELIGHTS: Baker wrote: ''*Farm Broadcasting* is a tribute to former colleagues in the profession, a profession in which I was one of the early participants. *How to Talk Plainly* and *Writing for Listeners* were prepared as texts for courses which I taught at the U.S. Department of Agriculture Graduate School. *Profile, U.S.A.* is a study unit for high school students, reflecting results of the 1970 Census of Population.''

* * *

BAKKEN, Dick   1941-

PERSONAL: Born August 24, 1941, in Miles City, Mont.; son of Richard Leo (in sales) and Dorothy Lillian (a secretary; maiden name, Virtue) Bakken; married Pamela Sue Rachford (a nurse), August 31, 1963 (divorced); children: Eric Michael, Cresey de Donne. *Education:* Pacific Lutheran University, B.A., 1963, M.A., 1966. *Home address:* P.O. Box BT, Old Bisbee, Ariz. 85603.

CAREER: Pacific Lutheran University, Tacoma, Wash., instructor in English, 1965-66; Portland State University, Portland, Ore., assistant professor of English, 1966-70; writer and lecturer, 1970—. Poet-in-residence at Thomas Jefferson College, 1975, field studies supervisor, 1975-77; poet-in-residence at St. Andrews Presbyterian College, 1976-78; instructor at Cochise College, 1981; gives readings, workshops, and lectures. Co-founder of Portland Poetry Center and Portland Oregon Poets, 1968-69; co-founder and coordinator of Portland Poetry Festival, 1973-74, member of board of directors, 1978-80; coordinator of Windmill Festival, 1975; co-organizer of Grand Valley State College National Poetry Festival, 1975; co-founder of Third Coast Poetry Center, 1975.

WRITINGS: (Editor) *Hungry!* (poems), Salted Feathers, 1967; (editor with Philip Dow, Gwen Head, Sandra McPherson, and others) *Miracle Finger* (works by children), Salted Feathers, 1975; *Here I Am* (long poem), St. Andrews, 1979; *Grand Opening* (poems), Trask House, 1981; *Feet With the Jesus* (poems), Lynx, 1981.

Contributor of poems to magazines, including *Poetry Now, Poetry Northwest, Iron Country, Abraxis, Human Voice,* and *Matrix.* Editor and publisher of *Salted Feathers,* 1964—.

WORK IN PROGRESS: Book of the Cur, poems; *Pinch Ass,* short poems; *Origin of the Valentine,* ten poems; *Brute Faith,* poems.

BIOGRAPHICAL/CRITICAL SOURCES: Poetry Flash, April, 1980; *Willamette Week,* April 15, 1980; *Artspace: Southwestern Contemporary Arts Quarterly,* April, 1981.

*   *   *

BALL, Desmond (John)   1947-

PERSONAL: Born May 20, 1947, in Nyah West, Australia; son of John Selwyn and Dorothy Louisa (Cook) Ball. *Education:* Australian National University, B.Ec. (with first class honors), 1969, Ph.D., 1972. *Politics:* Labor. *Religion:* None. *Home:* 5 Gormanston Cres., Deakin, Australian Capital Territory, Australia. *Office:* Strategic and Defence Studies Centre, Australian National University, Canberra, Australian Capital Territory 2600, Australia.

CAREER: University of Sydney, Sydney, Australia, lecturer in international relations, 1972-74; Australian National University, Canberra, research fellow at Strategic and Defence Studies Centre, 1974-78, senior research fellow, 1978-79; International Institute for Strategic Studies, London, England, research associate, 1979-80; Australian National University, fellow at Strategic and Defence Studies Centre, 1980—. Visiting scholar at Institute of War and Peace Studies, Columbia University, 1970; fellow at Center for International Affairs, Harvard University, 1972-73; lecturer at Australian universities and military staff colleges, including Australian Staff College, Royal Australian Air Force Staff College, and Joint Services Staff College, and at American and British institutions, including University of California, Los Angeles, National War College, and Oxford University. Conducted field research in the United States, Belgium, Canada, Norway, Sweden, Finland, the Soviet Union, West Germany, France, the United Kingdom, India, Italy, Sri Lanka, the Philippines, South Korea, Pakistan, and Thailand; consultant to RAND Corp. *Military service:* Australian Army, 1965-66. *Member:* United Services Institute, Returned Services League.

WRITINGS: (Editor and contributor) *The Future of Tactical Airpower in the Defence of Australia,* Australian National University, 1977; (with J. O. Langtry, Robert J. O'Neill, and Ross Babbage) *The Development of Australian Army Officers for the 1980's* (monograph), Strategic and Defence Studies Centre, Australian National University, 1978; (with Langtry) *Controlling Australia's Threat Environment: A Methodology for Planning Australian Defence Force Development,* Australian National University, 1979; *Politics and Force Levels: The Strategic Missile Program of the Kennedy Administration,* University of California Press, 1980; *A Suitable Piece of Real Estate: American Installations in Australia,* Hale & Iremonger, 1980; (editor with Langtry, and contributor) *Problems of Mobilisation in Defence of Australia,* Phoenix Defence Publications, 1980; *Can Nuclear War Be Controlled?* (monograph), International Institute for Strategic Studies, 1981; (editor) *Strategy and Defence: Australian Essays,* Allen & Unwin [Sydney], 1982; (editor with Langtry, and contributor) *Civil Defense and Australia's Security,* Australian National University, 1982; *The Politics of Australian Defence Decision-Making,* University of Queensland Press, in press; (editor with Jeffrey T. Richelson) *Strategic Nuclear Targeting,* Center for International and Strategic Affairs, University of California, Los Angeles, in press; *Secret Satellites Over Australia,* Hale & Iremonger, in press.

Contributor: O'Neill, editor, *The Strategic Nuclear Balance,* Australian National University, 1975; Roger Scott and J. L. Richardson, editors, *The First Thousand Days of Labor,* Canberra College of Advanced Education, 1975; H. G. Gelber, editor, *The Strategic Nuclear Balance,* University of Tasmania, 1976; O'Neill, editor, *The Defence of Australia: Fundamental New Aspects,* Australian National University, 1977; Fedor Mediansky, editor, *The Military and Australia's Defence,* Longman Cheshire, 1979; Jae Kyu Park, editor, *Prospects for Nuclear Proliferation in Developing Countries,* Institute for Far Eastern Studies, Kyungnam University, 1979; Coral Bell, editor, *Agenda for the Eighties,* Australian National University Press, 1980; J. M. Roherty, editor, *Defence Policy Formation: Towards Comparative Analysis,* Carolina Academic Press, 1980; Lawrence S. Hagen, editor, *The Crisis in Western Security,* Croom Helm, 1982; O'Neill and D. M. Horner, editors, *Australia's Defence in the 1980's,* University of Queensland Press, 1982; Bernard Brodie, Michael D. Intriligator and Roman Kolkowicz, editors, *National Security and International Stability,* Center for International and Strategic Affairs, University of California, Los Angeles, in press. Contributor to scholarly journals.

SIDELIGHTS: Ball told *CA:* "I believe very strongly that information on such critical public policy issues as strategy and defence should be much more accessible to the general public and that there should be much greater public debate on these issues. Information on defense matters is often unnecessarily cloaked in secrecy, while the academic literature is frequently filled with jargon and available only in specialized journals. Granted that defense is a highly technical subject, I believe that it remains possible to write about developments in national strategic policies and military capabilities in a way that is accessible to any interested person. Such accessibility on defense matters, no less than on other matters of public policy, is essential to the proper functioning of democracy."

*   *   *

BALL, Zachary
See JANAS, Frankie-Lee

*   *   *

BALLANTINE, Bill
See BALLANTINE, William (Oliver)

*   *   *

BALLANTINE, William (Oliver)   1911-
(Bill Ballantine)

PERSONAL: Born August 26, 1911, in Millvale, Pa.; son of William and Marie Eva (Paulisch) Ballantine; married Roberta Louise Light, September 8, 1948; children: Toby Circus, Bridget Mamie, Tia Clara, Tim Joey, Lulu Suzanne. *Education:* Attended the Art Institute of Pittsburgh, 1937-39. *Office:* Ringling Brothers Barnum and Baily Circus, Box 967, Venice, Fla. 33595.

CAREER: Freelance illustrator, 1939-43; free-lance writer and commercial artist, New York, N.Y., 1943—. Ringling Brothers Barnum and Bailey Circus, performer, 1946-48, special representative to the executive director, 1952-54, director of Clown College and coordinator of clowns, 1968—. *Wartime service:* U.S. Office of Wartime Information, propaganda graphics artist, 1944; U.S. Army, Psychological Warfare Division, 1945-46.

WRITINGS—All under name Bill Ballantine; all juveniles, except as noted: (Self-illustrated) *Wild Tigers and Tame Fleas*, Holt, 1958; (self-illustrated) *Horses and Their Bosses*, Lippincott, 1963; *Nobody Loves a Cockroach* (illustrated by daughter Toby Ballantine), Little, Brown, 1968; (and photographer) *High West* (adult nonfiction), Rand McNally, 1969; *The Flute*, F. Watts, 1971; *The Piano*, F. Watts, 1971; *The Violin*, F. Watts, 1971.

Illustrator: Juniper Sage, *The Man in the Manhole and the Fix-It Men*, W. R. Scott, 1946; Herman Schneider and Nina Schneider, *Now Try This*, W. R. Scott, 1947, reprinted as *Now Try This to Move a Heavy Load*, 1963; H. Schneider and N. Schneider, *More Power to You: A Short History of Power From the Windmill to the Atom*, W. R. Scott, 1953; H. Schneider and N. Schneider, *Let's Look Under the City*, W. R. Scott, 1954.

Contributor of articles and illustrations to periodicals, including *Collier's*, *Saturday Evening Post*, *Reader's Digest*, *Holiday*, *American Artist*, and *Cosmopolitan*.*

* * *

BALTHASAR, Hans Urs von
See von BALTHASAR, Hans Urs

* * *

BANDEL, Betty 1912-

PERSONAL: Born July 28, 1912, in Washington, D.C.; daughter of George Edwin (with U.S. Postal Service) and Emma Louise (an actress; maiden name, Frederick) Bandel. *Education:* University of Arizona, B. Mus., 1933; Columbia University, M.A., 1947, Ph.D., 1951. *Politics:* Democrat. *Religion:* Congregational. *Home:* Cheese Factory Rd., South Burlington, Vt. 05401.

CAREER: *Arizona Daily Star*, Tucson, Ariz., reporter and women's page editor, 1935-42; University of Vermont, Burlington, 1947-75, began as instructor, became professor of English, professor emeritus, 1975—. Visiting lecturer at University of Southern California, summer, 1962, and University of Arizona. Member of National Committee for Celebration of Shakespeare Quadri-Centenary, 1964; member of college evaluation inspection team, New England Association of Colleges and Universities. *Military service:* U.S. Army Air Forces, 1942-46; became lieutenant colonel; received Legion of Merit. *Member:* National Council of Teachers of English, College English Association, Modern Language Association of America, Shakespeare Association of America, Vermont Historical Society, Phi Kappa Phi, Chittendon County Historical Society. *Awards, honors:* Grant-in-aid from University of Vermont, 1956, for study of Ethan Allen.

WRITINGS: (Editor) Daniel Clarke Sanders, *A Lost Chapter From "A History of The Indian Wars" (1812)*, privately printed, 1953; *Margaret Lane Cooper* (novel), Exposition Press, 1958; (editor) *Walk Into My Parlor* (juvenile anthology), Tuttle, 1972; *Sing the Lord's Song in a Strange Land: The Life of Justin Morgan*, Fairleigh Dickinson University Press, 1981.

Plays: "Viva Mexico" (one-act), included in *Twenty Short Plays on a Royalty Holiday*, edited by Margaret Mayorga, Samuel French, 1947; "The Merits of the Case" (one-act), first produced before the Vermont state legislature, February, 1951; "John Bull's Other Playwright" (three-act), first produced in Burlington at the University of Vermont, April 23, 1964; "Amanda," first produced in Burlington at the University of Vermont, May, 1967.

Contributor of articles to professional journals, including *Vermont History*, *Theatre Survey*, *Journal of the History of Ideas*, and *New England Historical and Genealogical Register;* also author of program notes for several recordings by the University of Vermont Choral Union.

WORK IN PROGRESS: Biographical sketches of eight early Vermont composers of church-related music.

* * *

BANGS, Lester 1949(?)-1982

OBITUARY NOTICE: Born c. 1949; died April 30, 1982, in New York, N.Y. Rock performer and critic best known for his flamboyant coverage of musicians, such as Lou Reed, Brian Eno, and Blondie in several publications, including *Rolling Stone*, *Village Voice*, *Creem*, and *New Musical Express*. In 1981 Bangs recorded a rock album entitled "Juke Savages on the Brazos." Obituaries and other sources: *New York Times*, May 3, 1982; *Chicago Tribune*, May 4, 1982; *Time*, May 17, 1982; *Publishers Weekly*, May 28, 1982.

* * *

BANNER, Charla Ann Leibenguth 1942-
(Charla Ann Leibenguth)

PERSONAL: Born February 6, 1942, in Lafayette, Ind.; daughter of Charles Aaron (a utility storekeeper) and Myrtle (Cooley) Leibenguth; married Glen E. Banner (a newspaper editor), June 23, 1979. *Education:* Purdue University, B.S., 1965, M.S., 1966. *Politics:* Independent. *Religion:* Roman Catholic. *Home:* 1609 South Lafountain, Kokomo, Ind. 46902.

CAREER: Butler University, Indianapolis, Ind., instructor in pharmacy and pharmacy librarian, 1968-73, science librarian, 1973-81, instructor in pharmaceutical literature, 1981; freelance writer, 1981—. Partner of Features Unlimited. *Member:* American Auto Racing Writers and Broadcasters Association, Rho Chi, Kappa Epsilon.

WRITINGS: (Under name Charla Ann Leibenguth) *Motorsports: A Guide to Information Sources*, Gale, 1979. Author of "Wine and Wedges," a column in *Zionsville Times*, 1980, and in *Community Messenger*, 1981—, and "Above the Maddening Noise," a column in *Community Messenger*, 1981—. Contributor of articles and reviews to magazines, including *Motor Trend*, *Health*, *Grit*, *Science Digest*, and *Modern People*, sometimes under name Charla Ann Leibenguth. Contributing editor of *Auto Racing News*.

WORK IN PROGRESS: A gothic novel; a book on survival living; "Annotated Bibliography of Unusual Energy Sources," to be included in *American Reference Book Annual*.

SIDELIGHTS: Charla Banner commented: "I enjoy the horror genre of writing and wish there was a better market for stories of this type. I have been influenced by Lovecraft, Bradbury, and Rod Serling. I am also greatly interested in automobile racing and animal conservation, and write on these topics when it is feasible."

* * *

BARACKS, Barbara 1951-

PERSONAL: Born July 7, 1951, in New York, N.Y.; daughter of Clarence A. and Alice (Feinberg) Baracks. *Education:* University of California, Berkeley, A.B., 1973. *Politics:* "Politically progressive lesbian-feminist." *Office address:* P.O. Box 830, Peter Stuyvesant Station, New York, N.Y. 10009.

CAREER: Teachers and Writers Collaborative, New York, N.Y., teacher, 1979—. Literature consultant to New York State Council on the Arts, 1980. *Member:* Poets and Writers, New York Area Media Alliance. *Awards, honors:* Creative Artists Public Service fellowship, 1978.

WRITINGS: No Sleep, Tuumba Press, 1978; (editor with Kent Jarratt) *Sage Writings,* Teachers and Writers Collaborative, 1980. Contributor of articles and reviews to periodicals, including *Artforum* and *New Women's Times Feminist Review.* Editor of *Big Deal,* 1973-77.

WORK IN PROGRESS: Pleasure, a novel.

SIDELIGHTS: Barbara Baracks wrote: "My central concern is unifying my work as a fiction writer, journalist, and teacher. I am now writing about gay teachers and gay students, and about older adults."

*   *   *

BARKER, Graham H(arold)   1949-

PERSONAL: Born January 11, 1949, in Cambridge, England; son of Harold George (an engineer) and Dorothy (Speechley) Barker; married Esther Louise Farrow (a nurse), September 23, 1978. *Education:* Attended King's College, London; received M.B. and B.S. from George's Hospital Medical School. *Politics:* "Just right of center." *Religion:* Church of England. *Home:* Trinity Lodge, Arterberry Rd., Wimbledon, London, S.W.20, England.

CAREER: Registrar at Queen Charlotte's Maternity Hospital, 1976-80; currently in department of obstetrics and gynecology at Middlesex Hospitals, London, England. Past Johnson-Matthey-Rustenberg fellow in gynecological malignancy at Royal Marsden Hospital. *Military service:* British Army, Territorial Army, Medical Corps, 1972—; present rank, major. *Member:* Royal College of Obstetricians and Gynaecologists, Royal College of Surgeons (Edinburgh; fellow).

WRITINGS: Family Health and Medical Guide, Hearst Books, 1978; *Your Search for Fertility,* Morrow, 1980. Author of a column in *World Medicine.* Contributor to medical journals.

WORK IN PROGRESS: Drugs in Pregnancy; Chemotherapy of Gynaecological Malignancy.

SIDELIGHTS: Barker wrote: "I am anxious to explain medical problems to an intelligent 'lay' public: hence, my fertility book. I am currently correlating worldwide knowledge concerning the chemotherapy of gynecological malignancy for the medical profession. My *World Medicine* articles are mainly humorous. I enjoy laughing at medical matters—it relieves the tension. When doctors start laughing at themselves they become human again!"

*   *   *

BARMAN, Charles R(oy)   1945-

PERSONAL: Born November 17, 1945, in Two Rivers, Wis.; son of Charles P. and Norma (Naidl) Barman; married Natalie Sue Schofield, March 25, 1972; children: Tania Marie, Stephanie Sue. *Education:* Wisconsin State University—Oshkosh (now University of Wisconsin—Oshkosh), B.S., 1968; University of Wisconsin—Superior, M.S.T., 1972, postdoctoral study, 1979-80; University of Northern Colorado, Ed.D., 1974. *Home:* 815 West Sixth St., Storm Lake, Iowa 50588. *Office:* Department of Education, Buena Vista College, Storm Lake, Iowa 50588.

CAREER: High school biology teacher in West Allis, Wis., 1968-74; University of Wisconsin—Superior, assistant profes-

sor, 1974-79, associate professor of science education, 1979-80; Buena Vista College, Storm Lake, Iowa, associate professor of education, 1980—. Guest lecturer at University of Iowa, 1980—. *Member:* Association for the Education of Teachers in Science, Institute of Society, Ethics, and the Life Sciences, National Association of Biology Teachers, National Science Teachers Association, School, Science and Mathematics Association, Iowa Educational Media Association, Iowa State Science Teachers Association. *Awards, honors:* Gustav-Ohaus Award from National Science Teachers Association, 1977; National Science Foundation grant, 1976-77.

WRITINGS: (With John J. Rusch, Myron O. Schneiderwent, and Wendy M. Hinden) *Physical Science,* Silver Burdett, 1979; *Introductory Biology: A Self-Paced and Competency-Based Course,* University of Wisconsin—Superior, 1979; (with Rusch and Timothy M. Cooney) *Science and Societal Issues: A Guide for Science Teachers,* Iowa State University Press, 1981; (with Rusch, Virginia R. Johnson, and Michael B. Leyden) *Teaching Science: Grades Five to Nine,* Silver Burdett, 1982. Contributor of more than twenty articles and reviews to science and education journals. "Projector Center" department editor of *American Biology Teacher.*

WORK IN PROGRESS: Developing material for pre-service and in-service teachers dealing with practical applications of Piaget's and Kohlberg's theories.

SIDELIGHTS: Barman told *CA:* "My main professional goal is to assist in the improvement of education at all levels. Writing is one way in which I can work toward this objective. It allows me to share some of my ideas with a large number of colleagues."

*   *   *

BARNES, Kenneth Charles   1903-

PERSONAL: Born September 17, 1903, in London, England; son of Charles Henry and Katherine (MacInnes) Barnes; married Frances Jackson, August 15, 1927 (died May 25, 1969); married Eleanor Mary Spray (a social worker), November 12, 1969; children: Rosalind Barnes Phillips, Roger. *Education:* King's College, London, B.Sc. (with honors), 1924. *Religion:* Society of Friends (Quakers). *Home:* Ingsway, Bolton Percy, Yorkshire YO5 7BA, England.

CAREER: Science teacher and department head at independent boarding school in Petersfield, England, 1930-40; Wennington School, Wetherby, England, founder and head of school, 1940-68; writer, 1968—. Radio and television broadcaster for British Broadcasting Corp., 1948—.

WRITINGS: Sex, Friendship and Marriage, Allen & Unwin, 1938; *He and She,* Penguin, 1958, 3rd edition, 1970; *The Creative Imagination,* Allen & Unwin, 1960; *The Involved Man,* Allen & Unwin, 1966, revised edition, 1969; (with others) *What I Believe,* Allen & Unwin, 1966; (with Maurice Ash and others) *Who Are the Progressives Now?,* Routledge & Kegan Paul, 1969; *Making Judgments and Decisions,* Edward Arnold, 1971; *A Vast Bundle of Opportunities,* Allen & Unwin, 1974; *Has Science Exploded God?,* National Christian Education Council, 1976; *Energy Unbound,* Sessions of York, 1980. Contributor to Quaker journals and *Listener.*

WORK IN PROGRESS: Editing an anthology of the writings of John Macmurray; research on Macmurray's philosophy.

SIDELIGHTS: Barnes commented: "I am concerned about the quality of personal relationships (emphasized in the philosophy of John Macmurray and Martin Buber) in relation to sex, education, and industrial problems. In this connection I am also interested in Ivan Illich and Fritz Schumacher, who wrote *Small Is Beautiful.*"

Barnes's work with the Quakers took him around the world in 1970 and 1971, and included a six-month visit in the United States. He has also traveled extensively in Africa.

AVOCATIONAL INTERESTS: Painting, crafts.

*   *   *

BARNETT, Joe R(ichard) 1933-

PERSONAL: Born March 11, 1933, in San Angelo, Tex.; son of John W. (in sales) and Jewel (King) Barnett; married Alyce Gaines, September 8, 1955; children: John Hugh, Douglas Richard. *Education:* Abilene Christian College, B.S., 1955. *Religion:* Church of Christ. *Home:* 5419 27th St., Lubbock, Tex. 79407. *Office:* Broadway Church of Christ, 1924 Broadway, Lubbock, Tex. 79401.

CAREER: Minister at Churches of Christ in Evant, Tex., 1954-56, Anton, Tex., 1956-58, Levelland, Tex., 1958-64, and Amarillo, Tex., 1964-68; Broadway Church of Christ, Lubbock, Tex., minister, 1968—. Host of television program, "A Better Life." Founder and president of Pathway Evangelism, Inc., 1970-75. Member of board of trustees of Lubbock Christian College and Pepperdine University and of alumni board of Abilene Christian College; speaker at Christian colleges. Member of Lubbock Civic Centers Board and Civic Lubbock, Inc. *Member:* Rotary International. *Awards, honors:* LL.D. from Pepperdine University, 1973.

WRITINGS: (With John Gipson) *Happiness Day and Night,* Pathway Publishing, 1968; (with Gipson) *Paths to Peace,* Pathway Publishing, 1969; (editor) *Just for Today,* Pathway Publishing, 1974; *Live With Peace, Power, and Purpose,* Biblical Research Press, 1978; *The People Who Tested God,* Sweet Publishing, *Some Quiet Place,* Brownlow, 1980; (with Batsell Baxter and Harold Hazlip) *Anchors in Troubled Waters,* Baker, 1981. Staff writer for *Power for Today* and *Action.* Associate editor of *Twentieth-Century Christian.*

*   *   *

BARR, Stringfellow 1897-1982

OBITUARY NOTICE—See index for *CA* sketch: Born January 15, 1897, in Suffolk, Va.; died of pneumonia, February 3, 1982, in Alexandria, Va. Educator, lecturer, historian, and author. Barr taught history at the University of Virginia for more than a decade before becoming president of St. John's College. At St. John's he instituted a "great books" curriculum that required the reading of "the 100 best books of European thought in all fields" in place of normal course work. Barr also taught at Rutgers University, the University of Chicago, and Hofstra University. His several works include *Mazzini: Portrait of an Exile, The Will of Zeus: A History of Greece From the Origins of Hellenic Culture to the Death of Alexander,* and *Voices That Endured: The Great Books and the Active Life.* Obituaries and other sources: *Newsweek,* February 15, 1982; *Time,* February 15, 1982; *AB Bookman's Weekly,* February 22, 1982.

*   *   *

BARROW, Harold M(arion) 1909-

PERSONAL: Born August 8, 1909. *Education:* Westminster College, Fulton, Mo., A.B., 1936; University of Missouri, M.A., 1942; Indiana University, Pe.D., 1953. *Office:* Department of Physical Education, Wake Forest University, Winston-Salem, N.C. 27109.

CAREER: Elementary school teacher in New Bloomfield, Mo., 1930-34; high school athletic coach and director of physical education in Owensville, Mo., 1936-37, and Fulton, Mo., 1937-43; Eureka College, Eureka, Ill., head coach of football and basketball and director of athletics and physical education, 1945-48; Wake Forest University, Winston-Salem, N.C., professor of physical education, 1948-57, chairman of department, 1957—. Visiting professor at University of Toledo, summer, 1958, Oregon State University, summer, 1969, and Indiana University, summers, 1971-72. Member of National Foundation for Health, Physical Education, and Recreation. Member of advisory committee of North Carolina Youth Fitness Commission; chairman of Committee on Articulation Between Junior and Senior Colleges in North Carolina; member of Winston-Salem Recreation Commission. *Military service:* U.S. Navy, specialist in athletics and rehabilitation, 1943-45.

MEMBER: American Association for Health, Physical Education, Recreation and Dance (member of general division council; chairman of measurement and evaluation section; chairman of winter sports section; president of southern district, 1971-73), American Academy of Physical Education (fellow), National College Physical Education Association for Men, North Carolina Association for Health, Physical Education and Recreation (president; chairman of fitness committee), Phi Delta Kappa, Phi Epsilon Kappa (national vice-president, 1958-60).

AWARDS, HONORS: Honor award from Kingdom of Callaway, 1958; distinguished service awards from North Carolina Association for Health, Physical Education, and Recreation, 1964, and from southern district of American Association for Health, Physical Education, and Recreation, 1970; excellence award from Pi Lambda Theta, 1971, for *Man and His Movement.*

WRITINGS: Motor Ability Testing for College Men, Burgess, 1957; (with James W. Long and Marjorie Crisp) *Physical Education Syllabus,* Burgess, 1961, revised edition (with Tommy Boone), 1979; (co-author) *North Carolina Fitness Test,* Burgess, 1961; (with Rosemary A. McGee) *A Practical Approach to Measurement in Physical Education,* Lea & Febiger, 1967, revised edition, 1970; *Man and His Movement: Principles of His Physical Education,* Lea & Febiger, 1971, 2nd edition, 1977; (co-editor) *Professional Preparation in Dance, Physical Education, Recreation Education, Safety Education, and School Health Education,* American Association for Health, Physical Education, and Recreation, 1974. Contributor of more than one dozen articles to physical education journals. Member of editorial board of *Journal of the American Association of Health, Physical Education, and Recreation* and *Physical Educator.*

*   *   *

BARRY, Margaret Stuart 1927-

PERSONAL: Born December 7, 1927, in Darlington, County Durham, England; daughter of Edward (a bank manager) and Elizabeth (Tait) Bell; married Pierce Barry (an electrical engineer), February 3, 1957; children: Jane, Philip, Helen. *Education:* Teacher Training College, Liverpool, England, teaching diploma, 1947. *Politics:* None. *Religion:* Roman Catholic. *Home:* 5 Belvidere Rd., Liverpool, Lancashire L8 3TF, England. *Agent:* Curtis Brown Group Ltd., 1 Craven Hill, London W2 3EW, England.

CAREER: Teacher at Lindisfarne Convent Preparatory School, Essex, England, 1947-49, and Woolten College, 1950-52; art teacher in Huyton, Lancashire, England; teacher at Alder Hey Children's Hospital, 1957-58; part-time teacher at inner-city schools in Liverpool, England.

WRITINGS—All juveniles: *Boffy and the Teacher Eater*, illustrations by George W. Adamson, Harrap, 1971; *Tommy Mac*, illustrations by Dinah Dryhurst, Longman, 1972; "Bill Books" Readers, twelve books, illustrations by Gwen Fulton, Collins, 1973; *The Woozies Go to School*, illustrations by John Castle, Harrap, 1973; *The Woozies on Television*, illustrations by Castle, Harrap, 1973; *Woozy*, illustrations by Castle, Harrap, 1973; *Woozy Gets Lost*, illustrations by Castle, Harrap, 1973; *Boffy and the Mumford Ghosts* [and] *Boffy and the Terrasaurus*, illustrations by Adamson, Harrap, 1974; *Tommy Mac Battles On*, illustrations by Dryhurst, Kestrel Books, 1974; *Tommy Mac on Safari*, illustrations by Rosemary Evans, Kestrel Books, 1975; *Simon and the Witch*, illustrations by Linda Birch, Collins, 1976; *The Monster in Woozy Garden*, illustrations by Andrea Smith, Harrap, 1977; *The Woozies Go Visiting*, illustrations by Smith, Harrap, 1977; *The Woozies Hold a Frubarb Week*, illustrations by Smith, Harrap, 1977; *Woozy and the Weight Watchers*, illustrations by Smith, Harrap, 1977; *The Return of the Witch*, illustrations by Birch, Collins, 1978; *Maggie Gumption*, illustrations by Gunvor Edwards, Hutchinson, 1979; *Witch of Monopoly Manor*, illustrations by Birch, Collins, 1980; *Maggie Gumption Flies High*, illustrations by Edwards, Hutchinson, 1981; *The Witch on Holiday*, Collins, in press.

WORK IN PROGRESS: Writing scripts and preparing slides in an attempt to break into the comic strip business.

SIDELIGHTS: "I was a tomboy," Margaret Stuart Barry told *CA*, "and roamed the countryside with my brother, Stuart. Together, we learned more about nature than we ever learned in school. We caught tadpoles and when they turned into tiny frogs, my sister, Pat, made miniature desks and chairs for them. We were quite determined to train the baby frogs to read and write. We reckoned it was merely a matter of patience—but like ourselves, the young frogs wouldn't behave!

"It was teaching that led me into writing," Barry continued. "I felt sorry for the children who had the misfortune to be thrown into my care. I felt duty-bound to alleviate their boredom by making them laugh.

"After forty-two rejections, I had my first book, *Boffy and the Teacher Eater*, published. My next book, *Tommy Mac*, more or less wrote itself. Tommy was an actual boy in a downtown Liverpool school and he fairly and squarely gave me my comeuppance! All I really had to do was record his awful activities, and then exaggerate them. To this day, I am criticized for grossly exaggerating the most mundane situations. But I believe that is what writing is all about.

"I think it is every author's experience that writing about the known is the only way to succeed. Up until the acceptance of my first book, I aped my favorite writers: Lewis Carroll, A. A. Milne, and the Brothers Grimm. Consequently, I failed. It was only when I relaxed and vigorously threw the rules out of the window that I met with any sort of success. In short, I wrote about things that appealed to me and totally disregarded everything else.''

Barry's "Woozie" and "Tommy Mac" books have been adapted for television.

AVOCATIONAL INTERESTS: Photography.

* * *

BARSKY, Arthur   1900(?)-1982(?)

OBITUARY NOTICE: Born c. 1900; died c. 1982 near Le Beausset, France. Plastic surgeon and author of textbooks in his field. Barsky treated survivors of the atomic bomb that fell on Hiroshima in 1945. During the Vietnam War he treated more than seven thousand young burn victims in Saigon. Obituaries and other sources: *Time*, February 22, 1982.

* * *

BARTH, Peter S.   1937-

PERSONAL: Born November 21, 1937, in Karlsruhe, Germany (now West Germany); came to the United States in 1938, U.S. citizen; son of Lazarus (a stockbroker) and Olga (Bergmann) Barth; married Nancy J. Boor, August 12, 1962; children: Sara Elizabeth. *Education:* Columbia University, B.A., 1958; University of Michigan, Ph.D., 1965. *Address:* c/o MIT Press, 28 Carleton St., Cambridge, Mass. 02142.

CAREER: University of Michigan, Ann Arbor, teaching fellow in economics, 1963-65; Ohio State University, Columbus, assistant professor, 1965-68, associate professor of economics, 1969-71, research associate at Center for Human Resource Research, beginning in 1965; executive director of National Commission on State Workman's Compensation Laws, 1971-72; U.S. Department of Labor, Washington, D.C., director of Office of Research, beginning in 1972. Visiting assistant professor at University of Chicago, 1968; seminar lecturer. Economic policy fellow at Brookings Institution, 1970-71. Member of small grants panel of Manpower Administration, 1968-71. Consultant to U.S. Agency for International Development and the governments of Bolivia and Ecuador. *Military service:* U.S. Army, 1958-59; National Guard, 1959-64. *Member:* Industrial Relations Research Association.

WRITINGS: (Co-author) *Ecuador: A National Plan for Economic and Human Resource Development*, Ohio State University Press, 1969; (with Micha Gisser) *Basic Economics*, International Textbook Co., 1970; (with H. Allan Hunt) *Workers: Compensation and Work Related Illnesses and Diseases*, MIT Press, 1980. Contributor to economic and business journals.

* * *

BASKIN, Leonard   1922-

PERSONAL: Born August 15, 1922, in New Brunswick, N.J.; son of Samuel (a rabbi) and May (Guss) Baskin; married Esther Tane (a writer), November 26, 1946; married Lisa Unger, October 29, 1957; children: (first marriage) Tobias Isaac; (second marriage) Hosea Thomas, Lucretia Manya. *Education:* Attended New York University, 1939-41, and Yale University, 1941-43; New School for Social Research, A.B., 1949; graduate study at Academie de la Grande Chaumiere, 1950, and Academia di Belle Arti, 1951. *Home:* Lurley Manor, Lurley near Tiverton, Devon, England.

CAREER: Graphic artist and sculptor, professor, illustrator, and printer. Worcester Museum, Worcester, Mass., art teacher, 1952; Smith College, Northampton, Mass., 1953-74, began as instructor, became professor of sculpture and graphic arts; Gehenna Press, Northampton, Mass., operator and co-owner, 1962-74. Numerous one-man shows, including those at Glickman Studio, New York City, 1939, Numero Galleria d'Arte, Florence, Italy, 1951, Museum Boymans-van Beuningen, Rotterdam, Holland, 1961, Royal Watercolor Society, London, England, 1962, National Collection of Fine Arts, Washington, D.C., 1970, Jewish Museum, New York City, 1974, and Kennedy Gallery, New York City, 1975. Contributor to retrospective and group shows, and to permanent collections in numerous institutions, including Bezalel Museum (Jerusalem), Brandeis University, the Chase Manhattan Bank, Detroit Institute of Art, Harvard University, Metropolitan Museum of Art, National Gallery, Pennsylvania Academy of Fine Arts, and Princeton University. *Military service:* U.S. Naval Reserves, 1943-46. *Member:* American Academy of Arts and Sciences, American Institute of Graphic Artists, National Institute of Arts and Letters.

AWARDS, HONORS—Art: Louis Comfort Tiffany Foundation Fellowship, 1947, for sculpture; award from International Society of Wood Engravers exhibition in Zurich, 1953, for graphic art; Guggenheim fellowship, 1953, for sculpture and print making; Mrs. A. W. Erickson Prize from Society of American Graphic Artists, 1953; Ohara Museum Prize in Tokyo biennial of prints at Japanese National Museum, 1957, for graphic art; international prize from Sao Paulo Biennial in Brazil, 1961, for engraving; Alonzo C. Mather Prize from Art Institute of Chicago, 1961; medal of merit from American Institute of Graphic Arts, 1965; gold medal from Pennsylvania Academy of Fine Arts, 1965; medal of merit from American Academy of Arts and Letters, 1968; gold medal from National Institute of Arts and Letters, 1969.

Literary: American Institute of Graphic Arts Children's Book Show selection, 1971-72, American Institute of Graphic Arts fifty books of the year selection, 1972, *New York Times* choice of best illustrated children's books of the year, 1972, Caldecott honor book, 1973, and Brooklyn Art Books for Children citation from Brooklyn Museum and Brooklyn Public Library, 1975, all for *Hosie's Alphabet;* Children's Book Showcase selection from Children's Book Council, 1976, for illustration of Ted Hughes's *Season Songs;* L.H.D. from Clark University, 1966; D.F.A. from New School for Social Research, 1966, and University of Massachusetts, 1968.

WRITINGS: Figures of Dead Men, preface by Archibald MacLeish, University of Massachusetts Press, 1968; *Baskin: Sculpture, Drawings, and Prints,* Braziller, 1970; *The Graphic Work, 1950-1970,* Far Gallery, 1970; *Leonard Baskin's Natural History,* Pantheon, 1983.

Illustrator: Esther Baskin, *Creatures of Darkness,* Little, Brown, 1962; *The Iliad of Homer,* translated by Richard Lattimore, University of Chicago Press, 1962; Aristotle, *Politics and Poetics,* translated by Benjamin Jowett and S. H. Butcher, Stinehour Press (limited edition), 1964, Heritage Press, 1964; Joseph Pulitzer, *A Tradition of Conscience: Proposals for Journalism,* St. Louis, 1965; E. Baskin, *The Poppy and Other Deadly Plants,* Delacorte, 1967; Jonathan Swift, *A Modest Proposal,* Grossman, 1969; *Beowulf,* translated by Burton Raffel, University of Massachusetts Press, 1971; Hosea, Tobias, and Lisa Baskin, *Hosie's Alphabet* (juvenile), Viking, 1972; William Shakespeare, *Othello,* Gehenna Press, 1973; Shakespeare, *Titus Andronicus,* Gehenna Press, 1973; Fitz-James O'Brien, *What Was It?,* Oliphant, 1974; *A Passover Haggadah,* edited by Herbert Bronstein, Grossman, 1974, revised edition, Penguin, 1978; Ted Hughes, *Cave Birds: Poems,* Scholar Press, 1975, Viking, 1978; Hughes, *Season Songs,* Viking, 1975; Apollodorus, *Gods and Heroes of the Greeks: The Library of Apollodorus,* translated by Michael Simpson, University of Massachusetts Press, 1976; Hughes, *Moon Whales and Other Poems,* Viking, 1976; United States National Park Service, *The Framing of the Federal Constitution,* text by R. B. Morris, U.S. Government Printing Office, 1979; Tobias, Lucretia, Hosie, and Lisa Baskin, *Hosie's Aviary* (juvenile), Viking, 1979; Tobias, Lucretia, Hosie, and Lisa Baskin, *Hosie's Zoo,* Viking, 1981.

Also author and illustrator of over thirty-five limited art edition pamphlets, and illustrator of booklets by such authors as Conrad Aiken, William Blake, Marianne Moore, Alfred Tennyson, and Sylvia Plath.

SIDELIGHTS: Leonard Baskin is a popular artist who became a success at children's book illustrating with his first attempt, *Hosie's Alphabet.* Already experienced as an adult book illustrator, Baskin received praise for his work in *The Iliad. Hosie's Alphabet,* the result of a Baskin family project, was a new beginning for the well-established artist. His wife, Lisa, and children, Hosie, Tobias, and Lucretia, are credited with the text of the book. Together the family has produced a second book and Baskin's most recent, *Hosie's Aviary.*

Baskin was internationally known for his sculpture, drawings, and engravings for many years before his work appeared in a book designed for children. As an artist, particularly as a sculptor, he brought attention to humanism in modern art. Characteristic of Baskin's work is his mastery of the old techniques in wood engraving and sculpturing, and his focus on themes of death and weakness. He was described in *American Artist* by Alfred Werner as "a philosopher who chooses wood, bronze, and other media to express what he thinks and feels about man's battle to preserve and cultivate his individual soul in the brief interlude between birth and death. . . . For him the most important subject matter is anxiety-ridden man, imprisoned in his ungainly self. Whatever Baskin does or says, he knows that he belongs in a world that found its spokesmen in Freud and Kafka, Sartre and Camus, in Faulkner and Tennessee Williams. In him, we have an artist preoccupied with the theme of mortality, and oblivious to all that is exclusively decorative, predominantly private (there are 'thorny passages' in his mildest, least 'aggressive' works)."

Indeed Baskin's "thorny passages" do enter into his children's books, as James R. Mellow, a reviewer for the *New York Times,* states: "I have never been a great admirer of the work of Leonard Baskin, the prize-winning artist and illustrator. His illustrations of heroes and authors, bogeymen and demons . . . have always seemed to me routinely spooky and unrewarding. His illustrations of the smaller feathered creatures in *Hosie's Aviary,* however, are certainly charming. . . . In its understated way, the present volume seems even better than his earlier Caldecott Honor Award book, *Hosie's Alphabet.* The soft pen and watercolor drawings of hummingbirds in flight, of a cluster of brightly colored finches, and an unassuming city sparrow, ought to delight the eye of any beholder, child or adult."

BIOGRAPHICAL/CRITICAL SOURCES: Time, January 18, 1960; *Life,* January 24, 1964; *American Artist,* November, 1964; *Newsweek,* June 29, 1970; *Art and Artists,* October, 1976; *New York Times Book Review,* April 29, 1979.

* * *

BASU, Asoke (Kumar) 1940-

PERSONAL: Born April 26, 1940, in Calcutta, India; came to the United States in 1958; son of Sudhir (a clerk) and Ila (Dutta) Basu; married Mollie Pope (a Montessori teacher), January 26, 1966; children: Melissa. *Education:* West Virginia University, A.B., 1961; University of Oklahoma, M.A., 1963, Ph.D., 1966. *Residence:* Hayward, Calif. *Office:* Department of Sociology, California State University, Hayward, Calif. 94542.

CAREER: University of Oklahoma, Norman, part-time instructor in sociology, autumn, 1965; University of Southern California, Los Angeles, assistant professor of political science,

1966-68; California State University, Hayward, assistant professor, 1968-70, associate professor, 1970-75, professor of sociology, 1975—, director of Asian-American Cultural Center, 1969-71, director of Asian-American studies, 1972—. University of California, Berkeley, visiting lecturer, 1969, research associate at Center for South and Southeast Asia Studies, 1971-79; visiting scholar at Harvard University, 1973, and Hoover Institution on War, Revolution, and Peace, 1981-82. Conference organizer; testified before U.S. Senate.

MEMBER: International Sociological Association (member of executive committee), American Association for the Advancement of Science (fellow; divisional president, 1982-84), American Sociological Association, American Association for the Advancement of the Humanities, Society for the Study of Social Problems. *Awards, honors:* Liberty Fund fellow at Reason Foundation, summer, 1981.

WRITINGS: (Contributor) Lewis Coser, editor, *The Idea of Social Structures: Papers in Honor of Robert K. Merton*, Harcourt, 1975; *Elementary Statistical Theory*, E. J. Brill, 1976; (with Ralph Segalman) *Poverty in America: The Welfare Dilemma*, Greenwood Press, 1981; *Culture, Politics, and Critical Academics*, Archana Publications, 1981.

Editor of "International Monograph Series on Sociology of Education," International Sociological Association, 1980-83. Contributor of more than a dozen articles and reviews to sociology journals. Member of editorial board of *Journal of Sociology and Social Welfare*, 1973— (editor, November, 1977), and *Social Welfare, Social Planning, and Social Development: An International Data Base.*

WORK IN PROGRESS: *Welfare Poor*, with Ralph Segalman; research on public policy and higher education.

SIDELIGHTS: Basu told *CA:* "When I was growing up in India, my father earned less than thirty-two dollars a month in wages. He believed earnestly in the value of education and encouraged and supported me through the early school years. Education has improved the intellectual content of my life and has provided me with a rewarding and challenging career. My advice to students who aspire to higher education is not to be intimidated by one's background; excellence is achieved through disciplined creativity and undogmatic persistence to seek reason in nature and society."

*   *   *

BATTEN, Jean (Gardner) 1909-

PERSONAL: Born September 15, 1909, in Rotorua, New Zealand; daughter of Frederick Harold (a dental surgeon) and Ellen (an artist; maiden name, Blackmore) Batten. *Education:* Attended secondary school in Auckland, New Zealand. *Politics:* Conservative. *Religion:* Anglican. *Address:* c/o Barclay's Bank Ltd., 25 Charing Cross Rd., London WC2H 0HZ, England.

CAREER: Aviator. Earned private pilot's license, 1930, commercial pilot's license, 1932; made solo flights from England to India, 1933, England to Australia (women's record), 1934, Australia to England (first woman to complete flight), 1935, England to Argentina and Brazil (world record time; first woman to fly across the South Atlantic Ocean and make an England-to-South-America flight), 1935, England to Auckland, New Zealand (world record time from England to New Zealand; first direct flight to Auckland), 1936, England to Australia (solo record time), 1937, Australia to New Zealand (record time across Tasman Sea), 1937, and Australia to England (record solo time), 1937. Writer and lecturer. *Member:* Royal Aero Club of Great Britain, British Women Pilots Association, Guild of Air Pilots and Air Navigators (liveryman), London Aeroplane Club.

AWARDS, HONORS: Challenge Trophy (United States) from Women's International Association of Aeronautics, 1934, 1935, and 1936; officer of Order of the Southern Cross (Brazil); chevalier of Legion of Honor (France), 1935; Britannia Trophy from Royal Aero Club, 1935 and 1936; Harmon Trophy (United States), awarded by international vote, 1935, 1936, and 1937; Johnston Memorial Air Navigation Trophy, 1935; Segrave Trophy, awarded by vote of representatives from flying and motoring organizations and the press, 1936; commander of Order of the British Empire, 1936; Coupe de Sibour, 1937; Royal Air Force Museum in Hendon, England, established a Jean Batten Archive, 1972; Jean Batten Commemorative Cover issued by Royal Air Force Museum, 1976; named freeman of city of London, 1978; Britannia Airways named an airliner "Jean Batten," 1981; gold medals from Federation Aeronautique Internationale, Royal Aero Club, Aero Club de France, Belgian Royal Aero Club, Academie des Sports, Royal Swedish Aero Club, Ligue International des Aviateurs, Aero Club of Argentine, Royal Danish Aeronautical Society, Royal Norwegian Aero Club, Aero Club of Finland, and city of Paris.

WRITINGS: *Solo Flight*, O'Sullivan and Co., 1934; *My Life*, Harrap, 1938, reprinted as *Alone in the Sky*, Airlife Publishing, 1979.

SIDELIGHTS: Jean Batten was about twenty-one years old when she earned her private pilot's license. A few years later she made her first long distance flight, and it was followed by solo flights between England, India, and Australia. She earned her first world speed record in 1935, when she flew her Percival Gull monoplane from England to Brazil in less than sixty-two hours.

Batten continued her record-setting career, flying from England to New Zealand and Australia, breaking records that had been set by men. She was the first woman to receive the medal of the Federation Aeronautique International, and the first woman to fly solo to South America and New Zealand, across the South Atlantic Ocean and the Tasman Sea. In 1980 Britannia Airways christened a Boeing 737 the "Jean Batten."

Batten told *CA:* "Seventy years ago New Zealand was a very remote country indeed, and it is not surprising that I grew up with the conviction that transport and communication were of paramount importance. I went to London at the age of nineteen and, after learning to fly in 1930, became one of a small band of pilots who demonstrated the possibilities of the airplane as a normal method of transport over long distances, as a vehicle able to compete successfully over the shipping routes of the world at a time when most people traveled by ship.

"Fifty years ago flying great distances was very different from what it is today, when one consideres the speed and comfort enjoyed by the modern air traveler. In his foreword to *Alone in the Sky*, Michael Ramsden wrote, 'The full significance of Jean Batten's achievements is almost impossible to grasp today, sitting in a jet, listening to stereo and trying not to eat too much. Imagine flying alone for almost six days in a wood and fabric aeroplane with one engine, no navigation-aids and only the most primitive servicing facilities, and all the time, just one piston-beat away from death by shark or wild animal.'"

BIOGRAPHICAL/CRITICAL SOURCES: Herve Lauwick, *Heroines of the Sky*, Muller, 1960; Graham Paton, editor, *Great Men and Women of Modern Times*, Purnell, 1968; Jean Batten, *Alone in the Sky*, Airlife Publishing, 1979.

BATTERSBY, Martin 1914(?)-1982

OBITUARY NOTICE: Born c. 1914; died April 3, 1982, in Lewes, Sussex, England. Painter, designer, and author. Battersby's optical-illusion art made him a popular painter among European and American collectors, and his historically detailed stage sets and costumes placed him in demand at such theatres as Stratford-upon-Avon. Through his writings, including *Art Nouveau* and *The Decorative Twenties,* Battersby also helped revive interest in decorative arts of the late nineteenth and early twentieth centuries. Obituaries and other sources: *London Times,* April 7, 1982.

* * *

BATTLE, Lois 1942-

PERSONAL: Born October 10, 1942, in Australia; daughter of John H. (in U.S. Navy) and Doreen (White) Battle. *Education:* University of California, Los Angeles, B.A., 1961. *Agent:* Jane Rotrosen Agency, 318 East 51st St., New York, N.Y. 10022.

CAREER: Writer. Worked as actress and director, nursery school teacher, probation officer, and dance instructor. *Member:* American Federation of Television and Radio Artists, Authors Guild, Actors' Equity Association, Screen Actors Guild.

WRITINGS: Season of Change, St. Martin's, 1980; *War Brides,* St. Martin's, 1982.

* * *

BATTLE, Richard John Vulliamy 1907-1982

OBITUARY NOTICE: Born January 21, 1907; died May 26, 1982. Plastic surgeon and author of *Plastic Surgery.* During World War II Battle served England as a surgical specialist in France and Italy. Afterwards, he worked at both St. Thomas's Hospital and King Edward VII Hospital for Officers. From 1955 to 1971, Battle was consultant in plastic surgery to the British army. Obituaries and other sources: *Who's Who,* 134th edition, St. Martin's, 1982; *London Times,* May 28, 1982.

* * *

BAUMAN, Edward Walter 1927-

PERSONAL: Born January 22, 1927, in East St. Louis, Ill.; son of Edward Walter (a civil engineer) and Dorothy (Woodruff) Bauman; married Audree Miller (president of "Bauman Bible Telecast"), December 24, 1946; children: Deborah, Kathleen, Mark. *Education:* DePauw University, A.B., 1948; Boston University, S.T.B., 1951, Ph.D., 1954. *Home:* 5214 Wehawken Rd., Washington, D.C. 20016. *Office:* Foundry United Methodist Church, 1500 16th St. N.W., Washington, D.C. 20036.

CAREER: Ordained Methodist minister, 1954; pastor of Methodist church in Utica, Ohio, 1954-57; American University, Washington, D.C., associate professor of philosophy and religion, 1957-59; Wesley Theological Seminary, Washington, D.C., professor of theology and Christian ethics, 1959-64; Foundry United Methodist Church, Washington, D.C., senior minister, 1964—. Adjunct professor at Wesley Theological Seminary, 1964—. Writer, producer, and teacher on "Bauman Bible Telecasts," a television series syndicated by Bauman Bible Telecasts, 1957—; presented a weekly program on WMAL-Radio, 1967—. *Military service:* U.S. Navy, 1945-46. *Awards,*

honors: L.H.D. from DePauw University, 1964; Emmy Awards from Washington Academy of Television Arts and Sciences, 1963, for "Introduction to the Old Testament," and 1967, for "Go Down Death"; mass media award from American Association of University Women, 1972, for "Introduction to the New Testament"; D.D. from MacMurray College, 1978.

WRITINGS: Intercessory Prayer, Westminster, 1959; *The Life and Teaching of Jesus,* Westminster, 1960; *An Introduction to the New Testament,* Westminster, 1961; *Beyond Belief,* Westminster, 1964; *God's Presence in My Life,* Abingdon, 1981.

* * *

BAYER, Ronald 1943-

PERSONAL: Born January 16, 1943, in New York, N.Y.; son of Max and Adelle (Kressel) Bayer; married Jane Alexander (a psychiatric social worker), November 10, 1979; children: Alessandra Stapleford, Julian Stapleford. *Education:* State University of New York at Binghamton, B.A., 1964; University of Chicago, M.A., 1967, Ph.D., 1976. *Politics:* Democratic socialist. *Home:* 215 West 88th St., New York, N.Y. 10024. *Office:* Hastings Center, 360 Broadway, Hastings-on-Hudson, N.Y. 10706.

CAREER: Greenwich House Counseling Center, New York, N.Y., research associate, 1971-76; Hastings Center, Hastings-on-Hudson, N.Y., associate for policy studies, 1978—. *Awards, honors:* Fellow of Albert Einstein College of Medicine, 1976-78, and Hastings Center, 1978—.

WRITINGS: Homosexuality and American Psychiatry: The Politics of Diagnosis, Basic Books, 1981. Contributor to law, sociology, and drug abuse journals.

WORK IN PROGRESS: Psychoanalysis and the American West; Reproductive Hazards in the Workplace.

BIOGRAPHICAL/CRITICAL SOURCES: Los Angeles Times Book Review, May 10, 1981.

* * *

BAYLEY, Stephen 1951-

PERSONAL: Born October 13, 1951, in Cardiff, Wales; son of Donald (a management consultant) and Anne Bayley; married Flo Fothergill (a graphic designer), September 29, 1981. *Education:* Victoria University of Manchester, B.A., 1972; University of Liverpool, M.A., 1974. *Politics:* None. *Religion:* None. *Home:* 5B Harbledown Rd., London SW6 5TW, England. *Agent:* Andrew Best, Curtis Brown Ltd., 1 Craven Hill, London W2 3E, England. *Office:* Boilerhouse Project, Victoria and Albert Museum, London SW7 2RL, England.

CAREER: Liverpool Polytechnic, Liverpool, England, lecturer in art history, 1972-74; Open University, Milton Keynes, England, lecturer in art history, 1974-76; University of Kent at Canterbury, Canterbury, England, lecturer in art history, 1976-80; Victoria and Albert Museum, London, England, director of Conran Foundation, 1981—. *Member:* Savile Club.

WRITINGS: In Good Shape: Style in Industrial Products, 1900-1960, Van Nostrand, 1979; *The Albert Memorial,* Scolar Press, 1981; *Dreams That Money Can Buy: American Society and Design,* Thames & Hudson, 1983. Contributor to newspapers.

WORK IN PROGRESS: A Dictionary of Modern Design, publication by Harper expected in 1983 or 1984.

SIDELIGHTS: Bayley told *CA:* "What interests me most is how, in recent years, technology and popular culture have outpaced the traditional arts in their ability to astonish and delight us.'' *Avocational interests:* Food, drink, furniture, travel, popular culture.

*   *   *

BAZLEY, Margaret C. 1938-

PERSONAL: Born January 23, 1938, in New Zealand. *Education:* Received N.Z.R.N., N.Z.R.P.N., N.Z.R.M.N., and diploma of nursing. *Office:* Office of the Matron-in-Chief, Waikato Hospital Board, Hamilton, New Zealand.

CAREER: Sunnyside Hospital, Christchurch, New Zealand, matron, 1965-73; Auckland Hospital Board, Auckland, New Zealand, deputy matron-in-chief, 1974-75; Waikato Hospital Board, Hamilton, New Zealand, matron-in-chief, 1975—. *Member:* New Zealand Nurses Association (national president, 1972-74). *Awards, honors:* Scholarship from British Commonwealth Nurses War Memorial Fund, 1969.

WRITINGS: (With N. C. Cakman, John H. W. Kyle, and Lyall B. Thomas) *The Nurse and the Psychiatric Patient,* International Publications Service, 1973. Contributor to New Zealand nursing journals.

*   *   *

BEALL, Karen F(riedmann) 1938-

PERSONAL: Born April 15, 1938, in Washington, D.C. *Education:* American University, B.A., 1959, graduate study, 1960-61; further graduate study at Johns Hopkins University, 1965-66. *Office:* Office of the Curator of Fine Prints, Library of Congress, Washington, D.C. 20540.

CAREER: National Gallery of Art, Washington, D.C., summer intern, 1957-58, museum aide, 1959-60, slide librarian, 1960-64; Library of Congress, Washington, D.C., cataloger of fine prints, 1964-67, specialist in fine prints, 1967-68, curator of fine prints, 1968—, coordinator of exhibitions with National Collection of Fine Prints at Smithsonian Institution, 1973-77. Member of competition juries. *Member:* Print Council of America, College Art Association, Shillelagh Air Travel Club (trip director, 1974-79; member of board of directors, 1977-79). *Awards, honors:* Outstanding service award from National Gallery of Art, 1962; American Philosophical Society grant, 1966.

WRITINGS: (Editor) *American Prints in the Library of Congress,* Johns Hopkins Press, 1970; *Cries and Itinerant Trades,* Gale, 1975; (contributor) *The Graphic Sampler,* Library of Congress, 1979. Contributor to museum and art journals.

AVOCATIONAL INTERESTS: Travel (Africa, South America, Eastern and Western Europe).

*   *   *

BEAR, David 1949-

PERSONAL: Born January 14, 1949, in Lawrence, Kan.; son of William George and Pauline (a travel agent; maiden name, Silver) Bear; married Adria A. Fredericks, March 25, 1978 (divorced); children: Zachary Thompson. *Education:* Princeton University, B.A., 1970. *Home address:* P.O. Box 25, Whitesville, N.Y. 14897. *Agent:* Maria Carvainis Agency, 235 West End Ave., New York, N.Y. 10023.

CAREER: K. D. German Rhine Lines, New York, N.Y., vice-president, 1970-75; free-lance writer, 1975-81; Ketchum, Macleod & Grove (public relations firm), Pittsburgh, Pa., account supervisor, 1981—.

WRITINGS: Keeping Time (novel), St. Martin's, 1979. Contributor of articles and stories to magazines, including *East-West Review, Country Journal,* and *New Shelter.*

WORK IN PROGRESS: Opalescence, an adventure novel; *The Coming.*

*   *   *

BEATTIE, Edward J(ames), Jr. 1918-

PERSONAL: Born June 30, 1918, in Philadelphia, Pa.; son of Edward James Beattie; married wife, Nicole-Mary; children: Bruce Stewart. *Education:* Princeton University, B.A. (cum laude), 1939; Harvard University, M.D. (cum laude), 1943. *Politics:* Republican. *Home:* 430 East 67th St., New York, N.Y. 10021. *Office:* 1275 York Ave., New York, N.Y. 10021.

CAREER: Peter Bent Brigham Hospital, Boston, Mass., surgical house officer, 1942-43, assistant resident, 1944, resident in surgery, 1944-45, Harvey Cushing research fellow, 1945-46, junior associate in surgery, 1945-47; George Washington University, Washington, D.C., instructor and surgical fellow, 1947-48, research associate and Markle scholar, 1948-50, assistant professor of surgery, 1950-52, director of surgical research, 1948-52; University of Illinois, Urbana-Champaign, assistant professor, 1952-54, associate professor, 1954-56, professor of surgery, 1956-65; Cornell University, Ithaca, N.Y., professor of surgery, 1965—. Instructor at Harvard University, 1945-47. Chief of thoracic surgery at George Washington Service of Gallinger Municipal Hospital, 1948-52; Presbyterian St. Luke's Hospital, chief of thoracic service, 1952-54, attending surgeon, 1953-55, director of surgical research, 1953-55, chairman of department of surgery, 1954-65; visiting surgeon at James Ewing Hospital, 1965-68; Memorial Hospital, New York, N.Y., attending surgeon, 1965—, chief of thoracic service, 1965-75, chairman of department of surgery, 1966-78, chief medical officer, 1966—, general director, 1974—, chief executive officer, 1974-80, chief operating officer, 1980—.

American Board of Thoracic Surgery, diplomate, 1960, vice-chairman, 1965-67, and chairman, 1967-69. Disaster chairman of Chicago chapter of American Red Cross, 1960-65. Director of National Intern and Residency Matching Program, 1969-73. Consultant to Walter Reed Hospital. Member of executive committee of Advisory Board for Medical Specialties, 1964-68; member of boards of trustees of Lawrence Armour Day Schools, 1964-65, and of Sloan-Kettering Institute, 1973-78; Memorial Sloan-Kettering Cancer Center, member of board of trustees, 1967, board of overseers, 1978—, and board of managers, 1978—; American Board for Medical Specialties, member of surgical council, 1971-73, and chairman of basic surgical examination committee, 1973-75. *Military service:* U.S. Army Reserve, Medical Corps, 1942-45; became first lieutenant.

MEMBER: International Association for the Study of Lung Cancer, International Society of Surgery, American Academy of Pediatrics, American Association for Thoracic Surgery (member of council, 1976-77), American Association for the Advancement of Science, American Broncho-Esophageal Association, American Cancer Society (member of New York board of directors, 1967-76), American College of Chest Physicians (state vice-president, 1977-79; state president, 1979—), American College of Surgeons (fellow), American Federation of Clinical Research, American Heart Association (member of council on cardiovascular surgery, 1966-70), American Medical Association, American Radium Society (second vice-president and member of executive committee, 1973-74), American Society of Clinical Oncology, American Surgical Association.

American Thoracic Society, Association of American Cancer Institutes (member of board of directors, 1975-77; chairman of policy and programs committee, 1976-77), Association of American Medical Colleges, Pan-American Medical Association (chairman of North American section on thoracic surgery, 1977—), Pan-Pacific Surgical Association, Physician's Scientific Society, Society of Clinical Surgery, Society of Surgical Oncology, Society of Thoracic Surgeons, Society of Vascular Surgeons, Transplantation Society, James Ewing Society, Western Surgical Association, Central Surgical Association, New York Academy of Medicine, New York Cancer Society, New York Medical Society, New York Society for Cardiovascular Surgery, New York Surgical Society, New York Society for Thoracic Surgery (vice-president, 1973-74; president, 1974-75; member of council, 1977-80), Medical Society of the County of New York, Metropolitan Breast Cancer Group, Harvard Medical Society (New York president, 1971-72), Memorial Hospital Alumni Society, Center Alumni Council of New York Hospital-Cornell Medical Center (founding member), Sigma Xi, Alpha Omega Alpha.

AWARDS, HONORS: Mosely fellowship from Harvard University for University of London, 1946-47; Ben Park Medal from Medical Center at Cornell University, 1974; LL.D. from Hampden-Sydney College, 1978; meritorious honorary diploma from Liga Nacional contra el Cancer de El Salvador, 1980.

WRITINGS: (With Steven G. Economou) *An Atlas of Advanced Surgical Techniques,* Saunders, 1968; (editor) *Problems in Surgical Oncology,* Saunders, 1969; (with Stuart D. Cowan) *Toward the Conquest of Cancer,* Crown, 1980.

Contributor: Joseph Nash, editor, *Nash's Surgical Physiology,* 2nd edition, C. C Thomas, 1953; J. H. Schneewind, editor, *Emergency Service Manual,* Year Book Medical Publishers, 1963; Brian Blades, editor, *Surgical Diseases of the Chest,* Mosby, 1961, 2nd edition, 1966; Schneewind, editor, *Medical and Surgical Emergencies,* 2nd edition, Year Book Medical Publishers, 1968; Richard H. Egdahl and John A. Mannick, editors, *Modern Surgery,* Grune, 1970; Cranston W. Holman and Carl Muschenheim, editors, *Bronchopulmonary Diseases and Related Disorders,* Volume II, Harper, 1972; Thomas W. Shields, editor, *General Thoracic Surgery,* Lea & Febiger, 1972; Basil S. Hilaris, editor, *Handbook of Interstitial Brachytherapy,* Publishing Sciences Group, 1975; H. D. Flad and M. Betzler, editors, *Immunodiagnosis and Immunotherapy of Malignant Tumors: Relevance to Surgery,* Springer-Verlag, 1979; Stephen K. Carter, editor, *Principles of Cancer Treatment,* McGraw, 1981.

Contributor of more than two hundred articles to medical journals. Member of editorial boards of *Pediatrics Digest,* 1962—, *Journal of Thoracic and Cardiovascular Surgery,* 1962-81, *Journal of Surgical Oncology,* 1972—, *Cancer Clinical Trials,* 1977—, and *Acta Oncologica Brasileira,* 1979—. *International Advances in Surgical Oncology,* member of editorial advisory committee, 1977-78, and of editorial board, 1978—.

* * *

BECKWITH, Yvonne

PERSONAL: Born in Ashtabula, Ohio; daughter of Clare Flint and Isabelle Alice (Kaehler) Beckwith; children: Anthony Hobart. *Education:* Ohio State University, B.F.A., 1958.

CAREER: R. H. Donnelley Co., Chicago, Ill., assistant art director, 1960-62; Child's World, Elgin, Ill., children's book editor, 1962-68; Standard Educational Corp., Chicago, art director, beginning 1968. *Member:* Artists Guild of Chicago.

WRITINGS: (With Harry Bricker) *Words to Know* (juvenile), illustrated by Dan Siculan, Standard Education Corp., 1969; (editor) *People and Great Deeds* (juvenile), Standard Educational Corp., 1971; (editor) *Child's World,* eight volumes, Standard Educational Corp., 1971. Also editor of *Countries and Their Children,* 1971, and *The World and Its Wonders,* 1971.*

* * *

BEEGLE, Charles William 1928-

PERSONAL: Born May 19, 1928, in Charleston, W.Va.; married Jean Rittenour; children: one son, two daughters. *Education:* Ohio State University, B.S. in Ed., 1951, M.A., 1956, Ph.D., 1969. *Office:* Department of Education, University of Virginia, Charlottesville, Va. 22903.

CAREER: Teacher of preschool and elementary school children at day-care center in Galion, Ohio, 1951-52, 1954-55; high school teacher of fine arts in Ashtabula, Ohio, 1956-57, and Marion, Ohio, 1957-59; principal of public schools in Gahanna, Ohio, 1959-62; junior high school counselor and audiovisual director in Franklin County, Ohio, 1962-65, coordinator of instruction, 1965-67; coordinator of federal planning grant for public schools in Brookville, Ohio, 1967-68; Ohio State University, Columbus, instructor in education, 1968-69; University of Virginia, Charlottesville, associate professor of education, 1969—. Chairman of advisory board of Mid-Atlantic Community Education Center. Plenary session representative to University Council for Educational Administration. *Military service:* U.S. Marine Corps, 1952-54; and U.S. Marine Corps Reserve, 1954-58.

MEMBER: American Association of School Administrators, American Education Research Association, National Community School Education Association, Association for Supervision and Curriculum Development (chairman of staff development working group, 1972-74), Charlottesville Albermarle Oratorio (member of board of directors), Ivy Creek Foundation (member of board of directors), Phi Delta Kappa, Kappa Delta Pi, Farmington Hunt Club.

WRITINGS: (Contributor) Bill Pinar, editor, *Proceedings of the University of Rochester Curriculum Seminar,* McCutchan, 1971; (editor with Richard M. Brandt) *Observational Methods in the Classroom,* Association for Supervision and Curriculum Development, 1973; (editor with R. A. Edelfelt) *Staff Development: Staff Liberation,* Association for Supervision and Curriculum Development, 1977. Contributor to *Educational Considerations.* Contributor to education journals.

AVOCATIONAL INTERESTS: Farming, fox hunting, showing and training horses, painting, ceramics, music, antiques.

* * *

BEHRSTOCK, Barry 1948-

PERSONAL: Surname is pronounced *Bear*-stock; born July 12, 1948, in Los Angeles, Calif.; son of Victor (an attorney) and Sophia (a secretary; maiden name, Waisblum) Behrstock; married Gwen Hochman (a counselor), June 9, 1976; children: Jason, Jennifer. *Education:* University of California, Berkeley, A.B., 1970, and San Francisco, M.D., 1974. *Home:* 1830 Port Stanhope, Newport Beach, Calif. 92660. *Office:* 275 Victoria St., Suite 20, Costa Mesa, Calif. 92627.

CAREER: Children's Hospital, Los Angeles, Calif., pediatric residency, 1974-77; in private pediatric practice in Newport Beach and Costa Mesa, Calif., 1977—. Assistant clinical professor of pediatrics at University of California, Irvine, 1981—. Diplomat of American Board of Pediatrics, 1979; designer of patented pediatric resusitation device, 1981. *Member:* American Academy of Pediatrics (fellow), California Medical Association, Orange County Medical Association, Phi Beta Kappa.

WRITINGS: (With Richard Trubo) *The Parent's When-Not-to-Worry Book: Straight Talk About All Those Myths You've Learned From Your Parents, Friends, and Even Doctors,* Harper, 1981. Contributor of articles to *Time Teletext Project Cable* (magazine). Author of daily column, "Infant and Child Care," in *Time Teletext TV Magazine.*

SIDELIGHTS: Behrstock told *CA:* "My writings to date have centered around disseminating current pediatric knowledge to the general public. My primary work, *The Parent's When-Not-to-Worry Book,* was prompted by the unjustified worries so many new parents are subjected to." *Avocational interests:* New physics, woodworking, oriental cooking.

*   *   *

BELDEN, Wilanne Schneider 1925-

PERSONAL: Born October 14, 1925, in Pittsburgh, Pa.; daughter of W. (a salesman) and Ida Mary (a teacher; maiden name, Hood) Schneider; married Robert Adams Belden (a business consultant and college lecturer), August 14, 1948; children: Leigh Schneider. *Education:* State University of Iowa, B.F.A., 1946; San Diego State College (now California State University, San Diego), teacher's certificate, 1958; California Western University (now United States International University), M.A., 1963; further graduate study at various universities. *Politics:* Republican. *Religion:* Episcopalian. *Home:* 1029 Santa Barbara St., San Diego, Calif. 92107. *Office:* Torrey Pines Elementary School, La Jolla, Calif. 92037.

CAREER: Erie Playhouse, Erie, Pa., director of children's theatre, 1948; San Diego Chamber of Commerce, San Diego, Calif., corresponding secretary, 1955-58; San Diego Unified School District, San Diego, teacher, 1958—; playwright, director, and producer of musical productions. Teacher of animated filmmaking at University of California, San Diego, 1973; staff teacher in filmmaking at La Jolla Museum of Contemporary Art, La Jolla, Calif.; supervisor of student teachers. Lecturer. Founding director of San Diego Gilbert & Sullivan Repertory Company, 1970. *Member:* National Education Association, Authors Guild, California Teachers' Association, California Association for the Gifted, San Diego Teachers' Association, Association of San Diego Educators of the Gifted, Delta Kappa Gamma (past president, Theta Beta chapter), University Women's Club (London, England), Information Film Producers Association.

WRITINGS: Mind-Call (modern fantasy; juvenile), Atheneum, 1981; *Rescue of Ranor* (juvenile), Atheneum, 1983.

WORK IN PROGRESS—Juveniles: Another title in the *Rescue of Ranor* series; three titles in the *Mind-Call* series; a three-book series of legendary fantasy.

SIDELIGHTS: The writings of Wilanne Schneider Belden form an integral part of her larger concern, the nurturing and guidance of highly intelligent children. As Belden told *CA:* "Somehow, to be different in this way is to be other-than-human. The kids I teach have to face this. And they aren't nonhuman. They are the best the human race has yet developed. I want other children to meet such young people, to accept that having intellectual gifts makes a person only as different from others as all others are from each other."

Mind-Call, Belden's first published book, was a direct result of the shortage she perceived in literature that "faced squarely and without equivocation the almost insurmountable problem of being very highly intelligent." She continued: "I write what my editor calls science fiction and what I call modern fantasy because I read it and always have. The most interesting, exciting, mind-stretching books I read as a child and young person were in those categories." Belden named MacDonald, Tolkien, Lang, Norton, Bradbury, Burroughs, and LeGuinn among those who influenced her writing.

Underlying Belden's personal philosophy is a belief that every child is gifted in some way. She summed up her views on the writer's craft by saying: "While a story is written with a specific target audience in mind, the book is enjoyed by people of all ages who retain the attributes of childhood—the ability to wonder, to explore, to greet each new thing with delight."

AVOCATIONAL INTERESTS: Drama, dance, animated filmmaking, photography, music, handcrafts, travel.

*   *   *

BELL, Elizabeth Rose 1912-

PERSONAL: Born October 12, 1912, in Montpelier, Idaho; daughter of William C. and Helen (Carnes) Furchner; married Leslie Curtis Bell, August 25, 1933 (deceased); children: Nicholas Alan. *Education:* San Jose State College (now San Jose State University), A.B., 1940; University of Southern California, M.S.L.S., 1967. *Home:* 1351 Jacobsen Blvd., Bremerton, Wash. 98310.

CAREER: Teacher at elementary schools in Orange County, Calif., 1942-69; Nicolas Junior High, Fullerton, Calif., librarian, 1953-69. Part-time librarian in Bremerton, Wash., 1981—. Instructor in weaving; has exhibited weaving at art shows. *Member:* National Association of Retired Teachers, California Retired Teachers, Pacific Northwest Writers' Conference (member of board of directors), Northwest Weavers Association (chairman).

WRITINGS—For children: *Magic-Go-Round* (illustrated by Cher Slater), Childrens Press, 1974.

Contributor of articles to periodicals, including *Seattle Sunday Magazine, Scenic Idaho,* and *Orange County Journal.*

WORK IN PROGRESS: What's It Like Beyond?, a fictional book for children; *Adam's Cove,* a novel.

*   *   *

BELLOC, (Joseph) Hilaire (Pierre) 1870-1953

BRIEF ENTRY: Born July 27, 1870, in St. Cloud, France; died of burns, July 16, 1953, in Guildford, England. British author. Belloc was one of the most prolific writers of the early twentieth century, with about one hundred fifty books to his credit. His earliest and most lasting successes were in verse, such as *The Bad Child's Book of Beasts* (1896). He wrote histories, notably the biography *Danton* (1899), and travel books, such as *The Path to Rome* (1902), which was acclaimed by some critics as his best book. After serving as a Liberal member of Parliament, Belloc developed strong antipathy to the British party system of government and to socialist theories then prevalent in England. He expressed his political views as well as his strong devotion to Roman Catholicism in his essays and other writings. He also collaborated with G. K. Chesterton. Both authors shared and expressed their political and religious beliefs in satirical novels that prompted their opponent George Bernard Shaw to create the mythical monster "Chesterbelloc." Though much of Belloc's writing was well received in his lifetime, its place in British letters is based on the medieval simplicity and empathy for children which is displayed in his light verse and collected in *Cautionary Tales* (1908). *Biographical/critical sources: Cyclopedia of World Authors,* Harper, 1958; *Renascence,* spring, 1965; *Meanjin Quarterly,* March, 1965; *Longman Companion to Twentieth Century Literature,* Longman, 1970; Herbert Van Thal, editor, *Belloc: A Biographical Anthology,* Knopf, 1970.

* * *

BELLOC, Joseph Peter Rene Hilaire
  See BELLOC, (Joseph) Hilaire (Pierre)

* * *

BELLOC, Joseph Pierre Hilaire
  See BELLOC, (Joseph) Hilaire (Pierre)

* * *

BELLONE, Enrico 1938-

PERSONAL: Born August 14, 1938, in Tortona, Italy. *Education:* Istituto di Fisica, degree in physics, 1962. *Home:* Via Leonardo da Vinci 19, Tortona, Italy. *Office:* Istituto di Fisica, via Benedetto XV, Genova, Italy.

CAREER: Istituto di Fisica, Genova, Italy, professor of science, 1981—.

WRITINGS—In English translation: *Il mondo di carta: Ricerche sulla seconda rivoluzione scientifica* (nonfiction), Mondadori, 1976, translation by Mirella Giacconi and Riccardo Giacconi published as *The World on Paper: Studies on the Second Scientific Revolution,* MIT Press, 1980.

In Italian; nonfiction: *Aspetti dell' approccio statistico alla meccanica: 1849-1905,* G. Barbera, 1972; *I modelli e la concezione del mondo nella fisica moderna da Laplace a Bohr,* Feltrinelli, 1973; (with others) *Attualita del materialismo dialettico* (essays), Editori Riuniti, 1974; *Il logno di Galileo,* Il Mulino, 1980.

* * *

BELOFF, Nora 1919-

PERSONAL: Born January 24, 1919, in London, England; daughter of Simon and Marie (Spivak) Beloff; married Clifford Makins, March 7, 1977. *Education:* Lady Margaret Hall, Oxford, B.A., 1940. *Religion:* Agnostic. *Home:* 11 Belsize Rd., London NW6 4RX, England. *Agent:* Curtis Brown, 1 Craven Hill, London W2 3EW, England.

CAREER: Worked as journalist for Reuters News Agency, 1945-46, and for *Economist* (newspaper), 1946-48; *Observer,* London, England, began as editorial leader writer, became correspondent in Paris, France, and Washington, D.C., 1948-62, and U.S.S.R., 1962-64, political correspondent, 1964-76, correspondent in Washington, D.C., 1977. *Awards, honors:* Grant from Institute for Educational Affairs for research on Yugoslavia.

WRITINGS: The General Says No, Penguin, 1963; *Transit of Britain,* Collins, 1973; *Freedom Under Foot: The Battle Over the Closed Shop in British Journalism,* Temple Smith, 1976; *No Travel Like Russian Travel,* Allen & Unwin, 1979, published as *Inside the Soviet Empire: The Myth, the Reality,* New York Times Books, 1980. Contributor of articles to American

and British periodicals, including *Daily Telegraph, Atlantic Monthly,* and *Encounter.*

WORK IN PROGRESS: Writing on the Soviet bloc and Yugoslavia.

SIDELIGHTS: Beloff's *Inside the Soviet Empire* is a travelogue account of her experiences and observations as a correspondent for the *Observer.* The *Washington Post Book World*'s S. Frederick Starr wrote: "Like countless Europeans over the centuries [Beloff] chose the loose form of the travel account as a vehicle for presenting her observations. It was a happy choice. Beloff combines a keen eye with a feisty temperament. . . . Like many British intellectuals of her generation, she is not one to flinch from underscoring the Soviet Union's shortcomings. Yet she is fair. . . . As a result, hers is a book worth reading."

Beloff told *CA:* "I have just returned from a tour of Eastern Europe which has been sponsored by the *Daily Telegraph.* (I shall also be writing for American magazines.) One of the most encouraging incidents was meeting, at the U.S. embassy in East Berlin, a group of senior army officers who had been given a reprint of my piece in the *Atlantic Monthly* as background reading. In it I used the experiences of a young defector from an international institute in Moscow to illuminate Soviet attitudes.

"I have just received a grant from the Institute for Educational Affairs to proceed with my research on Yugoslavia. If the investigation succeeds, I hope to publish another book. So far, I have done a piece in the British monthly *Encounter,* which was the basis on which I requested further support.

"I became interested in writing because I am a naturally inquisitive person who wants to know what is really going on in the world. This led me first to journalism and later, when I discovered I had more to say than would fit into the confines of a newspaper, to authorship. I recently had my entry in the British *Who's Who* changed from 'journalist and author' to 'author and journalist.' In my view, free-lance journalism only makes sense after a writer has established a world-wide reputation and can claim to be known in the country he or she visits. This is not, of course, true of descriptive travel writers or war correspondents, but it applies to people like myself who need to know what is happening and who care to talk to someone they have reason to believe they can trust."

BIOGRAPHICAL/CRITICAL SOURCES: Washington Post Book World, May 25, 1980.

* * *

BELUSHI, John 1949-1982

OBITUARY NOTICE: Born January 24, 1949, in Chicago, Ill.; died March 5, 1982, in Los Angeles, Calif., of an accidental drug overdose. Actor, singer, and writer. Belushi broke into the entertainment profession as an actor and writer with the improvisatory Second City comedy group in Chicago. He then appeared on "The National Lampoon Radio Hour" and the touring "National Lampoon Show." In the mid-1970's, he achieved popularity on the acclaimed television show "Saturday Night Live." Among his most outrageous characterizations for the series were a contemporary samurai, a volatile "bee person," and a foreign cook in a New York diner. His best-known portrayal, however, was probably as Joliet Jake, the acrobatic vocalist of the Blues Brothers musical group, which Belushi created with fellow performer Dan Ayckroyd. While Ayckroyd danced and intoned the blues on his harmonica, Belushi did cartwheels and howled lyrics to classic tunes, such as "I'm a Soul Man" and "Hold On, I'm Comin'." In

1978 Belushi acted in the popular film "Animal House." As Bluto Blutarski, the grotesque but puckish leader of an outcast fraternity, Belushi exhilarated audiences with his phenomenal powers of consumption and acrobatics. In 1979 Belushi and Ayckroyd abandoned television to reprise the Blues Brothers on film and in concert, and their rendition of "I'm a Soul Man" became one of the most popular songs on American radio. By 1981 Belushi was expanding his acting range with a semi-dramatic performance as a Chicago journalist who falls in love with a conservationist in "Continental Divide." He also appeared as a complacent suburbanite in the surreal film "Neighbors." Belushi's death at age thirty-three shocked his fans, many of whom believed his greatest performances were still to come. Obituaries and other sources: *Who's Who in America*, 42nd edition, Marquis, 1982; *Newsweek*, March 15, 1982, March 22, 1982; *Time*, March 15, 1982; *People*, March 22, 1982.

* * *

BENAVENTE (y MARTINEZ), Jacinto 1866-1954

BRIEF ENTRY: Born August 12, 1866, in Madrid, Spain; died July 14, 1954, in Madrid, Spain. Spanish playwright, translator, essayist, poet, and short story writer. Author of nearly two hundred dramatic works, Benavente won the Nobel Prize for literature in 1922. His plays, noted for their subtle satire, artful dialogue, and lucid philosophical reflection, present the theme of good and evil at war in human nature. Benavente's dramatic style differed greatly from that of his predecessors and introduced the realist movement to the Spanish theatre. Popular in his lifetime, Benavente was awarded membership in the Academia Espanola in 1912. Many of his most celebrated works have been collected in English translation, including *Plays* (1917; contains "His Widow's Husband," "The Bonds of Interest," "The Evil Doers of Good," and "La Malquerida"), *Plays: Second Series* (1919; contains "No Smoking," "Princess Bebe," "The Governor's Wife," and "Autumnal Roses"), *Plays: Third Series* (1923; contains "The Prince Who Learned Everything Out of Books," "Saturday Night," "In the Clouds," and "The Truth"), and *Plays: Fourth Series* (1924; contains "The School of Princesses," "A Lady," "The Magic of an Hour," and "Field of Ermine"). *Biographical/ critical sources:* Walter Starkie, *Jacinto Benavente*, Oxford University Press, 1924; *Columbia Dictionary of Modern European Literature*, Columbia University Press, 1947; *Encyclopedia of World Literature in the Twentieth Century*, updated edition, Ungar, 1967; *Twentieth Century Writing: A Reader's Guide to Contemporary Literature*, Transatlantic, 1969; *Twentieth-Century Literary Criticism*, Volume 3, Gale, 1980.

* * *

BENN, Gottfried 1886-1956

BRIEF ENTRY: Born May 2, 1886, in Mansfield, Brandenburg, Germany (now East Germany); died July 7, 1956, in Bad Slangenbad, Germany; buried in the Neue Waldfriedhof in Berlin, Germany. German physician, poet, essayist, critic, and short story writer. With the publication of his first two collections of poems, *Morgue* (1912) and *Soehne* (1913), Benn established himself as an influential voice in the expressionist literary movement. In both theme and style Benn's poems reflect the nihilistic convictions of his era, presenting human agony and corporeality in the light of the ultimate isolation and disintegration of the self. In many of his writings Benn proposed artistic creation as a means of defying the void of isolation between individuals. Benn also thought that a return to tribal primitivism would reestablish human bonds; it was this

line of thought that led him to an initial acceptance of the Nazi regime, which he later renounced. A practicing physician specializing in dermatology and venereal diseases, Benn often included scientific terms and pathological images in his writings. Among his other works are *Gehirne* (1916), *Fleisch* (1917), *Spaltung* (1925), and *Dopelleben: Zwei Selbstdarstellungen* (1950). A selection of Benn's poetry, essays, dramatic sketches, and short stories in English translation appeared as *Primal Vision: Selected Writings of Gottfried Benn* (1960). *Biographical/critical sources: Encyclopedia of World Literature in the Twentieth Century*, updated edition, Ungar, 1967; Marion Adams, *Gottfried Benn's Critique of Substance*, Van Gorcum, 1969; J. M. Ritchie, *Gottfried Benn: The Unreconstructed Expressionist*, Oswald Wolff, 1972; *World Authors, 1950-1970*, H. W. Wilson, 1975; *Twentieth-Century Literary Criticism*, Volume 3, Gale, 1980.

* * *

BENNETT, (Enoch) Arnold 1867-1931
(Gwendolyn, Jacob Tonson)

BRIEF ENTRY: Born May 25, 1867, in Hanley, Staffordshire, England; died of typhoid fever, March 27, 1931, in London, England. English journalist, editor, essayist, short story writer, playwright, and novelist. Influenced by the French naturalists of the 1800's, Bennett wrote realistically and unromantically about middle-class life and values. A prolific writer, he wrote a novel a year from 1898 until his death, as well as almost as many plays, more than one thousand short stories and essays, and an extensive journal. Nevertheless, Bennett is best remembered for his stories set in the "Five Towns" of Staffordshire, his home district. His novel *The Old Wives' Tale* (1908), a story of two sisters from Bursley, one of the Five Towns, is often regarded as the best example of English realism of its time. Other "Five Towns" novels include *Anna of the Five Towns* (1902) and the "Clayhanger Family" series, a trilogy consisting of *Clayhanger* (1910), *Hilda Lessways* (1911), and *These Twain* (1915). After collaborating with Edward Knoblock on a play, "Milestones" (1912), Bennett gained popularity as a playwright, and in 1913 he dramatized his own comic novel *Buried Alive* (1908) as "The Great Adventure." He also achieved note as a journalist for his "Books and Persons" articles, which appeared in the *New Age* under the pen name Jacob Tonson from 1908 to 1910 and in the *Evening Standard* from 1926 until his death. The three volumes of *The Journals of Arnold Bennett* (1932-1933) are recognized as both a personal record and a chronicle of the author's age. Bennett's novel *Riceman Steps* (1923) won the James Tait Black Memorial Prize in 1924. *Biographical/critical sources: Cyclopedia of World Authors*, Harper, 1958; *The Concise Encyclopedia of Modern World Literature*, Hutchinson, 1963; *Encyclopedia of World Literature in the Twentieth Century*, updated edition, Ungar, 1967; *Twentieth-Century Writing: A Reader's Guide to Contemporary Literature*, Transatlantic, 1969.

* * *

BENNETT, James Thomas 1942-

PERSONAL: Born October 19, 1942, in Memphis, Tenn.; son of Louie Edward (a surgeon) and Carrie (a dancer; maiden name, Tunnell) Bennett; married Sara Ellen Dorman (an executive), September 2, 1967. *Education:* Case Institute of Technology (now Case Western Reserve University), B.S., 1964, M.S., 1966, Ph.D., 1970. *Politics:* Libertarian. *Religion:* Presbyterian. *Home:* 5011 Gadsden Dr., Fairfax, Va. 22032. *Office:* Department of Economics, George Mason University, Fairfax, Va. 22030.

CAREER: Ford Motor Co., Dearborn, Mich., operations research analyst on finance central staff, 1964-65; Cleveland State University, Cleveland, Ohio, assistant professor of industrial management, 1967-70; George Washington University, Washington, D.C., began as assistant professor, became associate professor of economics, 1970-75; George Mason University, Fairfax, Va., professor of economics, 1975—, senior staff scientist with program in logistics. Research fellow at Federal Reserve Bank, Cleveland, 1969-70; member of board of trustees of Ohio Epsilon Corp.; consultant to Chesapeake & Ohio Railway and Cleveland Transit System. *Member:* American Economic Association, American Statistical Association, Contemporary Economics and Business Association, Econometric Society, Phi Kappa Psi, Tau Beta Pi.

WRITINGS: *The Political Economy of Federal Government Growth*, Texas A & M University Press, 1980; *Deregulating Labor Relations*, Fisher Institute, 1981; *Better Government at Half the Price*, Caroline House, 1981. Editor of *Journal of Labor Research.*

WORK IN PROGRESS: *Political Economics of Off-Budget Government; Labor Unions, Political Spending, and Public Policy.*

*   *   *

BENNETT, Jill 1947-

PERSONAL: Born February 1, 1947, in Karachi, Pakistan; daughter of Donald Leonard (an airline executive) and Audrey (Isaacks) Winn; married Colin Bennett (a chartered surveyor), March 30, 1968. *Education:* Furzedown College of Education, London, Teacher's Diploma, 1970; Institute of Education, London, Advanced Diploma in Education, 1981. *Home:* 50 Queens Ave., Hanworth, Feltham, Middlesex, England.

CAREER: Sparrow Farm (infants' school), Feltham, Middlesex, England, teacher, 1970-79; *Child Education,* London, England, literary editor, 1977—. Director of school Bookshop Association, 1977—; support service teacher of reading and language in Southall, Middlesex, England.

WRITINGS: *Learning to Read With Picture Books,* Thimble Press, 1979; (compiler) *Skylark Short Stories,* Book Club Associates, 1979; *Reaching Out: Stories for Six- to Eight-Year-Olds,* Thimble Press, 1980; (compiler) *Roger Was a Razor Fish and Other Poems,* illustrated by Maureen Roffey, Bodley Head, 1980, Morrow, 1981; (compiler) *Skylark Ghost and Monster Stories,* Book Club Associates, 1980; (compiler) *Skylark Science Fiction Stories,* Book Club Associates, 1980; (compiler) *Tiny Tim* (poems), illustrated by Helen Oxenbury, Heinemann, 1981; (compiler) *Days Are Where We Live,* Bodley Head, 1981; (compiler) *A Packet of Poems* (poems), Oxford University Press, 1982; *A Choice of Stories* (educational materials guide), School Library Association, 1982.

Advisory editor to Oxford University Press's children's book series. Contributor of book reviews and articles to periodicals, including *Books for Keeps* and *Horn Book.*

SIDELIGHTS: Jill Bennett told *CA:* "As a teacher of four- to seven-year-olds my primary concern is to help children to become committed readers, rather than just teaching them to read. This aim has directed all my literary activities."

*   *   *

BERGMAN, David 1950-

PERSONAL: Born March 13, 1950, in Fitchburg, Mass.; son of Stanley S. (an artist) and Rita (a teacher; maiden name, Fergonson) Bergman. *Education:* Kenyon College, B.A., 1972; Johns Hopkins University, M.A., 1974, Ph.D., 1977. *Home:* 18 North Carey St., Baltimore, Md. 21223. *Agent:* Robert Cornfield Literary Agency, 145 West 79th St., New York, N.Y. 10024. *Office:* Department of English, Towson State University, Towson, Md. 21204.

CAREER: Towson State University, Towson, Md., assistant professor of English, 1978—.

WRITINGS: (Editor of adaptation with Patricia Plante) *The Turtle and the Two Ducks: Selected Fables of La Fontaine,* Crowell, 1981; (with Daniel Mark Epstein) *The Heath Guide to Poetry,* Heath, 1982; (with Epstein) *The Heath Guide to Literature,* Heath, 1983.

Work represented in anthologies, including *A Sampling of Poems,* edited by Eric Cheyfitz, 1977; *The Anthology of Magazine Verse and Yearbook of American Poetry,* Monitor Book, 1980.

Contributor of nearly fifty articles, poems, and reviews to magazines, including *Mouth of the Dragon, Arnoldian: A Review of Mid-Victorian Culture, Cimarron Review, Shenandoah, Kenyon Review,* and *Paris Review.*

WORK IN PROGRESS: Adapting French classics with Patricia Plante.

SIDELIGHTS: Bergman told *CA:* "I like trying my hand at all sorts of writing: poetry, drama, criticism, children's literature, journalism. I do not like to be pinned down as a writer or an intellect."

*   *   *

BERKE, Roberta 1943-

PERSONAL: Born March 16, 1943, in Elyria, Ohio; daughter of Robert Sterling (in business) and Meriam Leota (in business; maiden name, Roller) Elzey; married Joseph H. Berke (a psychiatrist and writer), May 18, 1968; children: Joshua Damien, Deborah Melissa. *Education:* Bennington College, B.A., 1965. *Home and office:* 9 Regent's Park Ter., London NW1 7EE, England. *Agent:* Victoria Gould Pryor, Literistic Ltd., 32 West 40th St., New York, N.Y. 10018.

CAREER: Pitman College, London, England, instructor in English, 1966-67; Family Service Units, London, caseworker, 1967-68; writer. Guest lecturer at University of Copenhagen and Kent State University. Gives readings at schools and theatres and on BBC-Radio. Founding member of Arbours Association (operates crisis center and half-way houses for the emotionally distressed). *Member:* Society of Authors. *Awards, honors:* Glascock Memorial Prize for Poetry from Mount Holyoke College, 1965, for *Sphere of Light.*

WRITINGS: *Sphere of Light* (poems), Trigram Press, 1972; *Bounds Out of Bounds: A Compass for Recent American and British Poetry,* Oxford University Press, 1981. Author of "Backwards Through the Funhouse," a poem sequence broadcast by BBC-Radio 3, April, 1982. Contributing feature writer for BBC-Radio 3. Contributor of poems and articles to magazines in the United States and England.

WORK IN PROGRESS: *Backwards Through the Funhouse,* poems; a novel about a young poet who disrupts a university campus.

SIDELIGHTS: Roberta Berke wrote: "My early poems were relatively short lyrics, often nature studies, which aimed for precision and clarity. In *Sphere of Light,* eight interlocked sequences of poems reflected each other in a complex circular form which was amplified by my symbolic woodcuts. Sequences continue to attract me: the poems in *Backwards Through the Funhouse* are less formal, considerably longer and almost all are concerned with human dilemmas and human speech. At the moment, I am working with actors and sound effects on radio, hoping to add another dimension to my poetry, as I did earlier with graphics.

"In my literary criticism, I write for literate but nonspecialist readers. My critical touchstone is: 'Does this poem intensify our experience?' I believe the critic's primary purpose is to serve the writer and the reader, not to promote esoteric theories. The aspect of criticism I find most exciting is discovering new or neglected poets. I write in a variety of forms, my choice being determined by the nature of the idea nagging me at the time.

"I keep in close contact with the United States and many of my values and priorities are American ones, though I have lived in London since 1966."

AVOCATIONAL INTERESTS: "Riding on bridlepaths through the English countryside, exploring old towns."

BIOGRAPHICAL/CRITICAL SOURCES: London Sunday Times, July 15, 1973; *Directions,* April, 1981; *Booklist,* April 1, 1981; *Choice,* May 14, 1981; *Grand Rapids Press,* June 7, 1981.

*   *   *

BERKOVE, Lawrence Ivan 1930-

PERSONAL: Born January 8, 1930, in Rochester, N.Y.; son of Harry (a podiatrist) and Sally (Berkowitz) Berkove; married Gail Roberta Feldman (a psychologist), July 2, 1967; children: Ethan Jacob, Naomi Susannah, Daniel Reuben. *Education:* Attended University of Montana, 1947-48; University of Illinois, A.B., 1951; University of Minnesota, M.A., 1953; University of Pennsylvania, Ph.D., 1962. *Politics:* Independent. *Religion:* Jewish. *Residence:* Southfield, Mich. *Office:* Department of Humanities, University of Michigan—Dearborn, Dearborn, Mich. 48128.

CAREER: Skidmore College, Saratoga Springs, N.Y., instructor, 1958-60; DePaul University, Chicago, Ill., instructor, 1961-62; Colorado College, Colorado Springs, Colo., instructor, 1962-63, assistant professor, 1963-64; University of Michigan, Dearborn, assistant professor, 1964-67, associate professor, 1967-74, professor of English and American literature, 1974—, chairman of humanities department, 1968-70, director of American studies program, 1978—. Visiting professor at Rikkyo University, Tokyo, 1982-83. Member of boards of directors of United Hebrew Schools of Metropolitan Detroit, 1979-82, and Friends of Southfield Public Library, 1979-82. *Military service:* U.S. Army, 1953-56. *Member:* Modern Language Association of America, American Studies Association, American Association of University Professors, College English Association, Michigan Academy. *Awards, honors:* Grant from National Endowment for the Humanities, 1975-76; *Skepticism and Dissent* was selected an outstanding academic book of 1980 by *Choice* magazine.

WRITINGS: (Editor and author of introduction) Ambrose Bierce, *Skepticism and Dissent: Selected Journalism from 1898-1901,* Delmas, 1980. Contributor of articles to more than ten literary journals, including *Huntington Library Quarterly, American Literary Realism, Southern Quarterly, Studies in Scottish Literature,* and *Mark Twain Journal.*

WORK IN PROGRESS: A critical study of Ambrose Bierce's fiction, completion expected in 1982; continuing research on late nineteenth- and early twentieth-century American authors,

including Ambrose Bierce, Mark Twain (Samuel Clemens), Dan DeQuille (William Wright), and Edith Wharton.

SIDELIGHTS: Berkove told *CA:* "I am particularly interested in the way literature embodies and reflects the religious and ethical values of authors. I do not regard literature as a substitute for religion or ethics, but as a superior means of extending and applying values already in place to new situations. Hence, the study of literature becomes an important index of the ethical vitality and imagination of authors and their cultural milieu."

BIOGRAPHICAL/CRITICAL SOURCES: Nation, March 1, 1980; *Journalism History,* summer, 1980; *National Review,* September 5, 1980; *American Literary Realism,* autumn, 1980.

*   *   *

BERMAN, Ed 1941-
(Otto Premier Check, Professor R. L. Dogg, Super Santa)

PERSONAL: Born March 8, 1941, in Lewiston, Maine; son of Jack and Ida (Webber) Berman. *Education:* Harvard University, B.A., 1962; attended Exeter College, Oxford, 1962-65 and 1978-80. *Politics:* "Beneath." *Religion:* None. *Home:* Inter-Action Housing Co-operative, 81 Willes Rd., London N.W.5, England. *Office:* Inter-Action Trust, 15 Wilkin St., London N.W.5, England.

CAREER: Theatrical director and producer, 1967—; Inter-Action Trust, London, England, founder and artistic director, 1968—. Actor under pseudonyms Otto Premier Check, Professor R. L. Dogg, and Super Santa. Resident dramatist and director of International Theatre Club at Mercury Theatre, 1967; founder and company director of Other Company, 1968, Ambiance Lunch-Hour Theatre Club, 1968, Professor Dogg's Troupe for Children, 1968, Community Arts Workshop (Chalk Farm), 1968, Labrys Trust, 1969, Inter-Action Advisory Service, 1970, Infilms, 1970, Inter-Action Housing Trust Ltd., 1970, Almost Free Theatre, 1971, Inprint Publishing Unit, 1972, City Farm One, 1972, Neighbourhood Use of Buildings and Space (Community Design Centre), 1974, Town and Country Inter-Action (Milton Keynes) Ltd., 1975, Ambiance Inter-Action, Inc. (New York, N.Y.), 1976, Talacre Centre Ltd., 1977, Beginners Books Ltd., 1978, Inter-Action Housing Co-operative, 1978, and British-American Repertory Company, 1978. Created "Inter-Action Game Method," 1967, "Super Santa, Father Christmas Union," 1969-79, Fun Art Bus, 1972, Community Media Van, 1973, Fun Art Loo, 1975, and Community Cameos, 1977.

Chairman of Save Piccadilly Campaign, 1971-79, and Talacre Action Group, 1972 (life president, 1974—); co-founder of Fair Play for Children Campaign, 1975; founder of City Farm Movement and Sport-Space, 1976; director of International Institute for Social Enterprise; member of board of directors of Islington Bus Co., 1974-76. *Member:* British Actors Equity, Society of Directors and Choreographers, National Association of Arts Centres (chairman, 1975-77), Father Christmas Trade Union (chairman). *Awards, honors:* Rhodes scholar at Oxford University, 1962-65; member of Order of the British Empire, 1979.

WRITINGS: Fun Art Bus (coloring book for children), edited by Justin Wintle, Eyre Methuen, 1973, Inprint, 1974; *Homosexual Acts: Five Short Plays From the Gay Season at the Almost Free Theatre,* Inter-Action Imprint, 1975. Also author of *Professor R. L. Dogg's Zoo's Who I and II,* 1975, and *The Creative Game,* 1979.

Plays: "Freeze," 1966; "Stamp," 1967; "Super Santa," 1967; "Sagittarius," 1968; "Virgo," 1968; "The Nudist Campers Grow and Grow," 1968; "The Alien Singer," 1978.

Educational films: "The Head," 1971; "Two Wheeler"; "The Dogg's Troupe Hamlet," Infilms, 1976; "Farm in the City," Mary Glasgow Publications, 1977; "Marx for Beginners" (animated), 1978.

Also editor of *Print: How to Do It Yourself, Community Newspapers, Community Bookshops, Basic Video and Community Work,* and *Converting a Bus.*

WORK IN PROGRESS: Participation, Theatre, and Reality; Street Theatre; The Creative Game; The Fourth "R"; How to Save the World While You're Still Young Enough to Enjoy It; "Hancock's First Half Hour," a one-act play on the life of Tony Hancock.

SIDELIGHTS: Berman's record albums include "Newfoundland" and "The Dogg's Troupe Hamlet."

Berman commented that his work "has emphasized participatory theatre, group work (in addition to experimental and integrated art work), and the social application of the arts." "I pioneered," he said, "a variety of film and television experiments and the use of video with children. At present I am mainly concerned with community action and the changing role of the artist in society."

*   *   *

BERNSTEIN, Walter   1919-

PERSONAL: Born August 20, 1919, in New York, N.Y.; son of Lewis and Hanna (Bistrong) Bernstein; married third wife, Judith Braun, 1961; children: Joan, Peter, Nicholas, Andrew, Jacob. *Education:* Dartmouth College, B.A., 1940. *Politics:* Socialist. *Religion:* Jewish. *Home:* 320 Central Park W., New York, N.Y. 10025. *Agent:* Sam Cohen, International Creative Management, 40 West 57th St., New York, N.Y. 10019.

CAREER: Screenwriter. Associated with *New Yorker,* c. 1946. Appeared in the motion picture "Annie Hall," 1977. *Military service:* U.S. Army, 1941-45; reporter for *Yank. Awards, honors:* Nomination for Academy Award for best original screenplay from Academy of Motion Picture Arts and Sciences and award from Writers Guild, both 1976, both for "The Front"; nomination for award from Writers Guild, 1977, for "Semi-Tough."

WRITINGS: Keep Your Head Down (columns), Viking, 1945.

Screenplays: "That Kind of Woman," Paramount, 1958; (with Dudley Nichols) "Heller in Pink Tights" (adapted from the novel by Louis L'Amour, *Heller With a Gun*), Paramount, 1960; (with Jack Sher and Irene Kamp) "Paris Blues" (adapted from the novel by Harold Flender), United Artists, 1961; "The Money Trap" (adapted from the novel by Lionel White), Metro-Goldwyn-Mayer (MGM), 1961; "Fail Safe" (adapted from the novel by Eugene Burdick and Harvey Wheeler), Columbia, 1964; "The Molly Maguires," Paramount, 1969; "The Front," Columbia, 1976; "Semi-Tough" (adapted from the novel by Dan Jenkins), United Artists, 1977; (with Don Petersen) "An Almost Perfect Affair," Paramount, 1979; (with Colin Welland) "Yanks," Universal, 1979; (and director) "Little Miss Marker" (adapted from the short story by Damon Runyon), Universal, 1980. Also adapter, with Ben Maddow, of "Kiss the Blood Off My Hands," Universal, 1948.

Author of column "Reporter at Large" for *New Yorker,* 1941-45. Contributor to periodicals, including *New Yorker, Colliers, Argosy,* and *Esquire.*

WORK IN PROGRESS: Directing a contemporary comedy.

SIDELIGHTS: Bernstein has proven himself an extremely diverse screenwriter. Among his best-known scripts are "Fail Safe," which dealt with the threat of nuclear war, "The Front," a treatise on the blacklisting that occurred in the film industry during Senator Joe McCarthy's Un-American Activities hearings, and "Semi-Tough," a spoof on chic self-improvement movements set in the world of professional football. Bernstein also wrote "Yanks," a film Gary Arnold of the *Washington Post* called "a sincere, engrossing, skillful anachronism" that is "a more effective 'anti-war'" film than "Apocalypse Now." Bernstein was especially successful at intertwining the film's three separate romances against the background of World War II.

In 1980 Bernstein made his directorial debut with "Little Miss Marker, a film many critics deemed inconsistent though entertaining. Janet Maslin, for example, cited the film's frequently "listless" pacing, but conceded that "the movie has a number of winning gags." She also found special praise for actor Walter Matthau, whom she credited with making the film "reasonably funny and appealing."

CA INTERVIEW

Bernstein was interviewed by *CA* on November 5, 1980, during lunch at his apartment.

Bernstein's career as a writer was launched when, as a junior at Dartmouth College, he sold his first story to *New Yorker.* "It was the first fiction piece in the issue," he recalled. "I felt I had reached the summit of achievement in having a story in *New Yorker.*" That was the beginning of Bernstein's long association with the magazine. During World War II, he wrote "Reporter at Large," a column detailing his experiences while serving as a staff sergeant in the army. His European tour of duty was highlighted by two-and-one-half years on the staff of *Yank,* where he worked with writers Marion Hargrove and Merle Miller. As a correspondent, Bernstein was also the first person to interview Marshal Tito.

Returning home after the war, Bernstein worked for *New Yorker,* then left to try screenwriting in Hollywood. "I'd always wanted to go to Hollywood," he said, "and on the strength of my book, *Keep Your Head Down* [a collection of "Reporter at Large" columns], I got a job on Robert Rossen's 'All the King's Men.'" Bernstein then worked on a draft of Burt Lancaster's independently produced "Kiss the Blood Off My Hands."

Bernstein went back to New York in 1947 to work in television. "It was an exciting time and we were creating a whole new form," he noted. Victimized by the Un-American Activities hearings that scandalized the film industry during the early 1950's, Bernstein found himself unable to receive credit for much of his television writing. He was, however, able to use his own by-line in magazines such as *Colliers, Argosy,* and *New Yorker,* because he "knew the editors personally, and they were willing to stick their necks out for me."

Producer Carlo Ponti was responsible for Bernstein's reinstatement in 1958, when he hired Sidney Lumet to direct "That Kind of Woman" and agreed to Lumet's choice of Bernstein as screenwriter. Other moguls at Paramount Pictures agreed with the hiring of Bernstein, then disagreed, and ultimately hired, fired, and rehired him. "I've been writing ever since," Bernstein acknowledged.

Bernstein considers himself "well disciplined" and writes from early morning to mid-afternoon six or seven days each week.

He types quickly using just two fingers on an old manual typewriter. "My first draft is equivalent to others' second or third drafts," he said, "so I rewrite less." His favorite screenplays include "The Front," "The Molly Maguires," "Fail Safe," and "Yanks." Of these films, only "Fail Safe" has been a great commercial success. "I still get checks for about six dollars each time it is shown on television," he added. Bernstein's other commercial and critical success, "Semi-Tough," was "a spoof of the human potential movement" set in the world of professional football.

Asked to name his favorite screenwriters, Bernstein cited Robert Towne, author of "Chinatown," "Shampoo," and "The Last Detail"; Waldo Salt, who wrote "Midnight Cowboy" and "Coming Home"; and Alvin Sargent, of "Ordinary People" fame. But, Bernstein admitted, "it is a measure of the medium that you think of directors rather than screenwriters." Seeking "final control on a picture," Bernstein entered the directing profession in 1980. "I'd wanted to direct for some time," he revealed, "but was neither twenty-four years old nor possessor of a big hit. Then Universal approached me to write the script for 'Little Miss Marker,' and I agreed on the condition that I would direct."

According to Bernstein, the difference between the writer and the director can be observed by assessing how each would handle the idea, "And now the Indians take the town." Bernstein declared that "a director has to spend three weeks on it; a writer, one sentence." He added: "I loved directing. It's the closest thing to being a dictator. Directors are control freaks. You're the captain of a ship going from here to there, and you're the only one responsible for that cargo. Everyone is there to help you in a technical sense. Moviemaking is a co-operative enterprise; scriptwriting isn't."

Bernstein was pleased with his first directorial effort. "'Little Miss Marker' is a nice picture even though not successful. I hope to do it again with the next one." He was only mildly disturbed by some critics' negative responses to the film. "I pay far too much attention to criticism, but you don't learn anything from it, and for the most part it is irrelevant," he said. "Critics are not creative." A pet theory of Bernstein's is that "everybody sees two movies—the one on the screen and the one in his head. The two have nothing to do with one another."

Bernstein plans on directing more of his own scripts. Among his projects is a comedy. "I've always liked comedy," he noted, "and haven't done too much until recently. I mean comedy with a serious subject. The best comedy is the sort of situation that can be played straight as well."

BIOGRAPHICAL/CRITICAL SOURCES: New York Times, April 29, 1979, September 19, 1979, March 21, 1980; *Washington Post,* October 26, 1979; *Chicago Tribune,* March 21, 1980.

—*Interview by Barbara Braun*

*   *   *

BERRY, Don (George) 1932-

PERSONAL: Born January 23, 1932. *Agent:* Barthold Fles Literary Agency, 501 Fifth Ave., New York, N.Y. 10017.

CAREER: Writer.

WRITINGS: Trask, Viking, 1960; *Majority of Scoundrels,* Harper, 1961; *Moontrap,* Comstock, 1976; *To Build a Ship,* Comstock, 1977.

BERTOLUCCI, Bernardo 1940-

PERSONAL: Born March 16, 1940, in Parma, Italy; son of Attilio (a poet, film critic, and teacher) and Ninetta Bertolucci. *Education:* Attended University of Rome, 1960-62. *Politics:* Communist. *Home:* Via del Babuino 51, Rome, Italy.

CAREER: Screenwriter and director of motion pictures. Worked as assistant director for Pier Paolo Pasolini on the motion picture "Accatone," 1961. Lecturer at Museum of Modern Art, 1969.

AWARDS, HONORS: Premio Viareggio, 1962, for *In cerca del mistero;* Critics' Award from Cannes Film Festival and Max Ophuls Prize, both 1964, both for "Prima della revoluzione"; best director award from National Society of Film Critics and Academy Award ("Oscar") nomination for best foreign language film from Academy of Motion Picture Arts and Sciences, both 1971, both for "Il conformista"; Raoul Levy Prize and Silver Ribbon, both 1973, both for "Last Tango in Paris"; and other filmmaking awards.

WRITINGS: In cerca del mistero (poetry; title means "In Search of Mystery"), Longanesi, 1962.

Published screenplays; and director: (With Pier Paolo Pasolini and Sergio Citti) *La commare secca* (released by Cinematografica Cervi, 1962; title means "The Grim Reaper"; adapted from the story by Pasolini), G. Zibetti, 1962; (with Franco Arcalli, Pauline Kael, and Norman Mailer) *Bernardo Bertolucci's "Last Tango in Paris"* (contains the screenplay by Bertolucci and Arcalli [United Artists, 1973], and essays by Kael and Mailer), Delacorte, 1973; (with Arcalli and brother, Giuseppe Bertolucci) *Novecento* (two volumes; released in the United States as "1900," Paramount, 1977), Einaudi, 1976.

Unpublished screenplays; and director: (With Gianni Amico) "Prima della rivoluzione" (released in the U.S. as "Before the Revolution"), Iride Cinematografica, 1964; "Il fico infruttuoso" (included in the omnibus motion picture "Vangela 70"), Castoro Films, 1967; (with Amico) "Partner" (adapted from the novel by Fyodor Dostoevski, *The Double*), Red Films, 1968; (with Marilu Parolini and Edoardo De Gregorio) "La strategia del ragno" (released in the U.S. as "The Spider's Strategy"; adapted from the story by Jorge Luis Borges, "Theme of the Traitor and the Hero"), Red Films, 1970; "Il conformista" (released in the U.S. as "The Conformist"; adapted from the novel by Alberto Moravia), Mars Film/Marianne Productions/Maran Film, 1970; (with Arcalli and G. Bertolucci) "La luna" (released in the U.S. as "Luna"; title means "The Moon"), Twentieth Century-Fox, 1979; "Tragedio dell uomo ridiculo" (released in the U.S. as "Tragedy of a Ridiculous Man," Ladd, 1982), Fiction Cinematografica, 1981.

Also writer and director of "La via del petrolio" (contains "Le origini," "Il viaggio," and "Attraverso L'Europe"), for RAI-TV, 1965-66, and the documentary "I poveri muoino prima," 1971. Co-author of screen story for "Once Upon a Time in the West," Rafran-San Marco, 1969.

Contributor of poems to Italian periodicals.

SIDELIGHTS: "Who can tell the dancer from the dance?" Bertolucci—paraphrasing Yeats during an interview—thus refuses to separate himself from his art. As a self-described "desperately autobiographical" artist, Bertolucci creates films that are alternately obscure and overt in their expressions of subconscious fears and anxieties. "Movies are made of the same stuff as dreams," he contends, adding that it is the act of self-expression that makes "the irrational become lucid."

The act of filmmaking then becomes a process of self-liberation for Bertolucci. "Self-liberation . . . is a first step towards living better," he told an interviewer in 1972, "towards the finding of an equilibrium with your subconscious, towards the finding of a peaceful relationship towards the subconscious."

But Bertolucci also wants his films to be popular, and he unites the violent with the sentimental and the melodramatic with the realistic in an effort to engage audiences. "What I want to make today must be very popular," he said in 1975. "A cinema that goes back to popular forms. A cinema . . . that not only wishes to be popular inasmuch as it addresses itself to a large, popular audience, but also in that which it has to offer that audience." And because Bertolucci tries to engage audiences with relevent subjects, he considers his films to be "political." He believes that "no film ever has a direct political effect," but contends that it "*can* have a direct effect on the level of emotions."

Bertolucci's ability to sustain an audience is largely dependent on his skill at depicting sexuality, particularly in its most controversial forms, such as lesbianism and incest. In "The Conformist" lesbianism serves as background to a tale of treachery and murder; "Last Tango in Paris" embraces sadomasochistic elements; "1900" similarly delves into such sexual bizarreness as a *menage a trois* with a convulsing epileptic, and child molestation; and "Luna" melodramatically renders the psychological implications of mother-son incest.

Such pessimistic depictions have inspired wildly conflicting reactions from Bertolucci's critics. Pauline Kael hailed the "primitive force, the . . . thrusting, jabbing eroticism" of "Last Tango in Paris" as perhaps "the most liberating movie ever made," while other reviewers characterized the numerous acts of male dominance as a celebration of chauvinism. Similarly, the intimations of incest in "Luna" prompted *Rolling Stone*'s Jonathan Cott to praise the filmmaker for "reawakening . . . the possibilities of the cinema." The same film, however, inspired *New Republic*'s Stanley Kauffmann to declare that Bertolucci is "a clever, cheap exploiter of everything that comes to his hand, including the talent he began with."

But Bertolucci trusts his audience to appreciate and understand even what the critics condemn. "The audience, being more innocent, is so much more close to the truth of the movie than the critic," he believes. Accusing critics of a preference for evaluation over comprehension, Bertolucci contends that "movie critics are quite irresponsible," and adds that "they should side with different movies; instead, they want to destroy different movies." He also thinks that critics have something to learn from the other spectators, noting that "the audience is part of the movie, really—the last touch of a movie is the tears of the audience."

Bertolucci's art was largely inspired by his father's own poetry and enthusiasm for films. "He made us aware of reality, its ugliness and its beauty," Bertolucci recalled. The father encouraged his son's poetic and filmmaking endeavors. At twelve young Bernardo had already published his poems; at fifteen he completed his second sixteen-millimeter film. When he entered the University of Rome in 1960, Bertolucci was already steeped in film lore culled from viewing as many as four motion pictures per day, and his familiarity with English-language literature included the writers of the "Lost Generation" as well as poets such as Emily Dickinson and Dylan Thomas.

During his second year at the university, Bertolucci met Pier Paolo Pasolini, an eminent writer and friend to Bertolucci's father. Pasolini was preparing to direct "Accatone," his first film, and he engaged Bertolucci as his assistant director. Work-ing with Pasolini thrilled Bertolucci, and when the film—detailing the actions of pimps and prostitutes in Roman slums—was applauded by critics for its grueling and unflinching style, Bertolucci decided to quit school and direct his own films.

In 1962 Bertolucci visited Paris, where he frequented cinemas that featured the work of "New Wave" directors such as Francois Truffaut and Jean-Luc Godard. Stimulated by Godard's unconventional techniques, especially the jump-cutting and freewheeling camerawork of "Breathless," Bertolucci returned to Italy and accepted an offer from Pasolini to direct "The Grim Reaper." The novice filmmaker overcame severe budget restrictions by completely rewriting Pasolini's original script, then produced a film that was both a thriller and a tale of budding political consciousness. Reviewers cited Bertolucci's affinity with Godard and praised his disdain for sentimentality. "Bertolucci's style establishes itself as a passionate romanticism," declared *Film Quarterly*'s Henry Heifetz; "he uses a restless, widely moving camera, with jump-cuts derived from Godard but without Godard's elegance or his watered emotion."

While awaiting the premiere of "The Grim Reaper," Bertolucci was awarded the prestigious Premio Viareggio for a collection of his poetry, *In Search of Mystery,* most of which recalled his childhood and life in the Italian countryside. Bertolucci had already abandoned verse, however, in favor of filmmaking, calling cinema "the true poetic language."

Most critics considered Bertolucci's next film, "Before the Revolution," precisely poetic. It concerns a young intellectual's flirtation with Marxism before succumbing to the bourgeois life, and most reviewers were amazed by the twenty-four-year-old Bertolucci's skill in fashioning a film that was both political and intimate. "Astonishingly, he has managed to assimilate a high degree of filmic and literary erudition into a distinctively personal visual approach," contended Eugene Archer in *New Yorker.* He called Bertolucci "a new talent of outstanding promise." John Thomas of *Film Quarterly* agreed, noting that "Bertolucci tries something new in every scene; like Godard, often fails; like Godard, sometimes succeeds spectacularly."

After the success of "Before the Revolution," Bertolucci turned to several small projects. He directed a series of short films and documentaries for television, then contributed "The Infertile Fig Tree" to the omnibus "Vangelo 70" that also featured works of Pasolini and Godard. The influence of these two filmmakers was also evident in "Partner," which marked Bertolucci's return to the feature-length format in 1968. The film details the schizophrenic nature of a radical professor whose obsession with Antonin Artaud's "Theatre of Cruelty" compels him towards violence—he drowns a girl in a washing machine—that repulses his passive personality. Most critics expressed dissatisfaction with the use of Godardian devices, such as discontinuity and gyroscopic camerawork, that frequently obscured the narrative. Peter Cowie found the film "confusing in its effort to equate art with politics and to distinguish revolutionary theory from practice." In a 1974 review for *New Republic,* Stanley Kauffmann called "Partner" "heavily dated" and added, "cinematically it's redolent of high sixties Godard; politically it's full of late sixties rhetoric and gesture. Bertolucci was also displeased with the work. He deemed it "sadomasochistic" to the audience and himself and later explained, "In the sixties, when I was making a dolly shot, I used to think the audience had to understand that the camera was on wheels—it was like every movie was asking the great question of what cinema is." He also admitted that he "tried to hide the emotions behind any kind of alibi—like existential characters or political statements."

Bertolucci's next film, "The Spider's Strategy," marked a departure from the pyrotechnics and explicit politics of his previous work. The film is a meticulously crafted account of a young man's efforts to discover the killers of his martyred, war-hero father. After returning to the site of his father's death, the son learns that his father had actually turned against his fellow anti-Fascists during World War II and had consented to his own murder as a means of rectifying his betrayal. The subdued quality of "The Spider's Strategy" impressed critics as an improvement over the flashy technique of "Partner." A reviewer in *New York* deemed the film Bertolucci's "simplest and most glowing work." Vincent Canby noted it's "premeditated elegance" and called it "a handsome film."

For Bertolucci "The Spider's Strategy" was also a vehicle of atonement for the flourishing camerawork and explicit politics of "Partner." "I had arrived at a point of departure when I made *Partner,* the film in which I most violently went against my own nature of being a showman," he acknowledged. "Besides the fact that this film caused me a tremendous psychological trauma, because nobody, almost nobody, accepted it." In "The Spider's Strategy" he toned down the camerawork and concentrated on the psychological and sociological implications of the young man's discovery. Some critics have attributed these changes to Bertolucci's decision to undergo psychoanalysis after directing "Partner," and Bertolucci admitted that the self-confidence he gained from analysis allowed him to engage audiences instead of antagonize them. "I was terrified by the audience when I was younger," he recalled in 1980. "In the sixties I made some movies almost against the audience, really, because I was terrified. Now I really need an audience. I changed the same way in my private life. I was much more closed. Now I'm much more open."

With "The Conformist," Bertolucci's other work of 1970, he clinched his separation from the excessive experimentation that marred "Partner." "The Conformist" did feature Bertolucci's signature, the floating camerawork, but most of the work subordinated flashy technique to the plot: young Marcello shoots his sexual assailant, matures into an opportunist willing to murder his old professor to please his fellow Fascists, and learns that his assailant from childhood survived the shooting. The film ends with Mussolini's fall, after which Marcello exposes the other Fascists to curry favor with the new regime.

Most reviewers hailed "The Conformist" as Bertolucci's finest work, and several critics accorded special attention to his recreation and portrayal of the decadent Fascist society. Canby called the film "a superior chronicle" and cited "scenes of . . . unusual beauty and vitality" such as Marcello's visit to a mental hospital and a portentuous tango between the professor's wife and her lesbian lover. In *Film* Ruth Kreitzman wrote: "From start to finish ['The Conformist'] has been immaculately conceived and constructed. Bertolucci's keen eye for architecture here reaches its most perfect synthesis yet, and each shot is constructed as though traced from a drawing-board." And Bill Nichols, writing in *Cineaste,* cited Bertolucci's fusion of sumptuous cinematography and camerawork with such topics as lesbianism and fascism. "Bertolucci avoids the melodramatic pitfalls that claim many socially conscious films," Nichols declared, "crafting a work of considerable polish and remarkable unity." He added that the film's "greatest value is in the beauty of its own, unique appearance."

The popularity of "The Conformist" at film festivals in Cannes and New York City led Bertolucci to an increased awareness of his purpose as an artist. He now felt capable of being both an experimenter and an entertainer, and he intended to fuse both aspects in his next work. "Now that I have fully accepted my showman role I find I can return safely to a whole series of questions, obsessions, discussions over the meaning of the camera," he told an interviewer. To engage an audience, he decided to make a film exploring the present nature of sexuality. "All my previous films in a sense were in the past," he noted. "The erotic act is what is most present in today's life."

But Bertolucci's erotic film brought him even more attention than he had anticipated. When "Last Tango in Paris" premiered at the New York Film Festival in 1972, audiences were shocked by the fairly explicit sexuality in Bertolucci's tale of two people meeting for brutally sexual purposes. Kael acclaimed the premier as "a landmark in movie history" and declared, "This must be the most powerfully erotic movie ever made." Canby deemed the sexual encounters "extraordinary" and mused, "It's anything but pornographic, but the candor of its love scenes is such that a number of right-thinking people are certain to become outraged—and very noisy in their outrage."

Many viewers did voice their discontent with the film. In Italy Bertolucci and actors Marlon Brando and Maria Schneider were accused of promoting obscenity, and charges were filed (though later dropped). And some critics decried the film's potentially sexist characterization of the woman played by Schneider; Joan Mellen, who considered the work a "brilliant" indictment of bourgeois values, nonetheless objected to the film's "narrow . . . conception of what human beings can give to each other." Even Brando expressed dissatisfaction with the work. "It was too calculated," he contended, "designed to make an impact rather than a statement."

It was Brando's character, Paul, in "Last Tango in Paris" that some observers found particularly outrageous. As a profane American widower whose sole diversion from despair is his position as caretaker of a flophouse, Paul indulges in several monologues on humiliation and cruelty. In many of their encounters, he forces Jeanne, his nubile partner, into unwilling sodomy and other, more psychically jarring, acts. "The excitement of Brando's performance here is in the revelation of how creative screen acting can be," wrote Kael. She attributed much of the film's success to Brando's performance and claimed that both Brando and Bertolucci "have altered the face of an art form."

Equally unnerving to audiences were the unexpected moments of sorrow and romance that precede the film's violent climax. Angered by his wife's suicide, Paul uses his base relationship with Jeanne as an outlet for his hostility. After accepting his wife's death, Paul confesses his affection for Jeanne and suggests they adopt a more conventional lifestyle together. Jeanne, who is planning her marriage to a fanatical filmmaker despite her relationship with Paul, is repulsed by Paul's revelations of his squalid past. After masturbating him in a tango parlor, Jeanne declares that their relationship has ended. She flees home with Paul giving chase. Then, after finally revealing her name to Paul, Jeanne shoots him with her father's pistol and begins formulating an explanation for the police.

Despite critical appraisal to the contrary, Bertolucci insists that "Last Tango in Paris" is not "an erotic film, only a film *about* eroticism." He attributes the film's erotic aspects to the initial sexual nature of the relationship between Paul and Jeanne. "It is almost always like this," he told Gideon Bachmann, "that things are 'erotic' only before relationships develop; the strongest erotic moments in a relationship are always at the beginning." For Bertolucci, the relationship evolves from eroticism to "dependence." He claims that "every sexual relationship is condemned. It is condemned to lose its purity, its animal nature; sex becomes an instrument for saying other things.''

In a 1973 interview in *Film Quarterly,* Bertolucci also maintained that ''Last Tango in Paris'' recalled ''Partner'' in its intensely cinematic nature. ''Last Tango in Paris'' is full of references to other films and filmmakers, including former inspiration Godard, and reveals Bertolucci's interest in both showmanship and technique. ''I find *Tango* very close to *Partner*,'' he revealed, ''because in *Tango* there is a continual enquiry in filmic terms, a research on the use of the camera, an attempt to question the structures of cinema.'' Kael agreed, according particular attention to the cinematography. ''The colors in this movie are late-afternoon orange-beige-browns and pink—the pink of flesh drained of blood, corpse blood,'' she asserted. ''They are so delicately modulated . . . that romance and rot are one.'' She added: ''The film is utterly beautiful to look at. The virtuosity of Bertolucci's gliding camera style is such that he can show you the hype of the tango-contest scene (with its own echo of *The Conformist*) by stylizing it . . . and still make it work.''

Buoyed by the overwhelming critical and popular success of ''Last Tango in Paris,'' Bertolucci undertook his most ambitious project, ''1900.'' ''I want this to become a film about the agony of the culture of the land,'' he related to Bachmann, ''of peasant culture, of a civilization that lasted thousands of years and has practically died in only 50-70 years of industrial 'progress.''' To fashion this epic, Bertolucci procured $5 million from producer Alberto Grimaldi, thus making ''1900'' one of Italy's most expensive productions.

Once filming began, unfortunately, Bertolucci's original conception of ''1900'' was superceded by an explicit—and, according to some critics, ''naive''—recounting of events culminating in the rise of communism in Italy in 1945. Adjusting to seasonal and multilingual logistics, as well as to his own improvisatory nature, Bertolucci compromised the initial premise with a less ''nostalgic'' approach. ''I had started out on the classic trip of nostalgia,'' he recounted. ''It was the nostalgia for a peasant culture I had known in childhood, and which I had thought dead.'' But when he commenced filming, Bertolucci contended, ''I began to suspect that I had been wrong, and that I wasn't, after all, going to make a film about a vanished world. . . . My prejudices were transformed under my own eyes, day by day, and so I am making a different film.''

Bachmann spent two weeks with the crew of ''1900.'' He reported that the experience was ''not pleasant.'' ''Bertolucci has become very big, very famous, very quickly,'' Bachmann wrote in *Film Quarterly*. He also noted that ''the intuition that the story being put into images was only partly based on reality and that the other part was hope . . . created in all of us a feeling of tension.'' But Bertolucci remained undaunted. ''The film becomes something different than planned, as soon as the cameras start digging into reality,'' he observed. He added that improvisation was necessary ''to let the film go into the direction that it must go, even if that turns out a different direction than the one I plan at the beginning.'' Even Bachmann was forced to note that, despite the tremendous difficulties of filmmaking, Bertolucci ''never seems to doubt the pleasure of final victory.''

Bertolucci persevered with ''1900'' for more than three years before filming was completed in 1976. But his difficulties with the film were not over. After enduring escalated budgets and expanded filming schedules, Grimaldi was under pressure to repay almost $2 million in funds he had borrowed to underwrite Bertolucci's work. The money, from Paramount Pictures, was

for distribution rights for a version of not more than three hours and ten minutes. Therefore, Grimaldi was immensely dissatisfied when Bertolucci deemed the film complete at more than five hours. Grimaldi protested and Paramount threatened to abandon the film, but Bertolucci was adamant. ''I will not cut one frame,'' he told Grimaldi. Paramount then rejected the film, and Grimaldi began pursuing other distributors. He negotiated with Twentieth Century-Fox for distribution of a four-hour version, and the studio accepted his terms. But again Bertolucci warned Grimaldi that no additional editing was forthcoming. Successful screenings of ''1900'' at film festivals in Cannes and Venice—where it was shown in its five-hour, two-part, version—assured Bertolucci that his stubbornness was justified. *Newsweek* reported that the film was considered ''controversial, but incomparably beautiful and rich in texture'' by privileged audiences.

Finally, in autumn of 1977, Grimaldi negotiated another deal with Paramount for distribution of a four-hour version of ''1900.'' ''We must compromise,'' he conceded. ''The main thing is to get the picture released.'' Bertolucci agreed, and after re-editing the film, he announced the new version as definitive. Later, Bertolucci withdrew his preference for the four-hour film, contending that the first edition was better despite ''the smell of megalomania.''

Few reviewers believed that the missing ninety minutes ultimately impaired the quality of ''1900.'' As a tale of two men—landowner Alfredo and one of his peasant workers, Olmo—spanning the first half of the twentieth century, ''1900,'' according to most viewers, exhausted its appeal in the first two hours. The film begins with Alfredo's birth in 1900, continues with the death of the two men's grandparents, details the conflicts between the peasants and the landowners, completely omits World War I, and concludes its first half with premonitions of fascism. ''By the end of 'Act One,''' wrote Jack Kroll, ''most viewers will be dazzled and excited by two hours of almost relentless beauty and power.''

The film's second half, however, was faulted by *Time*'s Frank Rich as ''good-guys *v.* bad-guys melodrama.'' The rise of Fascist leader Attila, an employee of Alfredo's family, precipitates several ghoulish murders, including the impaling of a woman on a spiked fence. After Alfredo slaughters several peasants in retaliation for his own public humiliation—they bombarded him with horse manure—Olmo leads a revolt against the Fascists and the wealthy landowners. The action culminates in Alfredo's death and a renunciation of Italy's class society. ''The *padrone* [landowner] is dead,'' the peasants announce during an elaborate celebration of communism. Rich called the finale a ''propagandistic pageant'' and asserted, ''By the time *1900* reaches its flag-waving Liberation Day climax, the sloganeering and confusion are almost unbearable.''

But despite reservations regarding the film's political slant, many reviewers still found much to praise in ''1900.'' Rich hailed its ''voluptuous emotional texture'' and conceded, ''If Bertolucci irritates as much as he dazzles, he never bores: his extravagant failure has greater staying power than most other director's triumphs.'' Kroll agreed, acknowledging the acting and cinematography as ''marvelous'' and contending, ''It's a huge work and its faults are the excesses of a huge talent.'' Perhaps the film's most exuberant acclaim came from Kael. She recognized flaws in some of the characterizations, but charged that ''it's like a course to be enrolled in'' and added, ''The film is appalling, yet it has the grandeur of a classic visionary folly. Next to it, all other new movies are like something you hold up at the end of a toothpick.''

In Bertolucci's next film, ''Luna,'' he returned to the sexual sensationalism of ''Last Tango in Paris.'' ''Luna,'' according to Bertolucci, is a ''symbolic and melodramatic'' account of a potentially incestuous relationship between an opera diva, Caterina, and her son, Joe. Following the death of her second husband, Caterina returns to Italy with Joe to resume her musical career. What follows is a harrowing tale of drug addiction and perversity, as Caterina tries to cope with Joe's heroin use. Their relationship culminates in a series of violent encounters: after witnessing Joe's initial withdrawal symptoms, Caterina gives him the necessary heroin but reveals that she has disposed of his syringe. Enraged, Joe tries to pierce his vein with a fork, then collapses against Caterina, who proceeds to suckle and masturbate him. Later, Joe abandons his mother after she has changed a flat tire on their car. They rendezvous at an inn, whereupon Caterina tries to seduce Joe. He resists, however, and begins searching for his father. The quest ends with Joe and his father reunited as they watch Caterina rehearse. Moments before, she had reached an oblique understanding, if not reconciliation, with Joe.

The critical reception for ''Luna'' was mixed. Rich called it ''perfect,'' and Cott noted its ''intensity and cinematic brilliance.'' But other viewers were appalled by Bertolucci's unabashed exploitation of incest. John Simon deemed it ''a dreadfully poseurish film,'' and Kauffmann called it ''ludicrously bad.'' He added, ''When the film isn't being portentously symbolic, it's being empty—one or the other.'' Kauffmann concluded that Bertolucci ''is a monstrous and disgusting artist, not a failed authentic one.''

In response to the negative reviews, Bertolucci charged the critics with ''irresponsibility.'' ''I've been through very hard times with critics on *Luna*,'' he told *American Film*. ''I've read things almost personally offensive, like 'There is not a second in this movie that is acceptable.' It's a very experimental movie.'' In an interview with Cott, Bertolucci also explained that ''Luna'' was actually ''autobiographical'' and that he may have been using the film to psychoanalyze himself. Of the film's prologue he said, ''You see the baby in a basket on a bicycle. It's night and his mother is riding the bicycle. . . . The face of the mother is young, the face of the moon is ageless. . . . This is one of my first memories—the bicycle and the moon—and I wanted to find out why I remembered it, and to discover something about the relationship between the son and the mother.'' He also conceded that ''the movie gravitates between melodrama and psychoanalysis,'' but insisted that both elements were necessary because ''the characters are either epical-lyrical or determined by their own subconsciouses.''

Bertolucci's style was more subdued in his following film, ''The Tragedy of a Ridiculous Man.'' Departing from the sensationalized sex and violence that marked ''Last Tango in Paris,'' ''1900,'' and ''Luna,'' he fashioned, according to Canby, ''a distant meditation on Italian politics'' in the manner of ''The Spider's Strategy.'' The ''ridiculous man'' of the film's title is Primo, a factory owner faced with ransom demands from his son's kidnappers. After learning of his son's possible murder, Primo nonetheless continues compiling the ransom for business purposes. Canby was especially impressed with Bertolucci's attention to characterization in the film. ''' Tragedy of a Ridiculous Man' is sometimes poetic and warm-hearted, then cooly satiric and finally surreal,'' he observed. ''The reality of the characters, however, is never in doubt.'' He added, ''It's Mr. Bertolucci's most rewarding, most invigorating film since 'Last Tango.'''

''The Tragedy of a Ridiculous Man'' also reveals Bertolucci's willingness to engage audiences without relying on sensation-

alism. ''The reasons why people continue to go to the cinema are horrible, foul,'' he once told Bachmann. ''They are publicity-type reasons . . . , brainwashing reasons. . . . It's wrong to think too much about this. It's a question of liberty, really. The cinema, in this respect, is far behind literature, and today, making films instead of writing novels . . . , I want to obtain the same liberty I would have enjoyed if I was writing novels. Only through liberty of expression can the relationship with the spectator be improved.''

AVOCATIONAL INTERESTS: Literature, opera.

BIOGRAPHICAL/CRITICAL SOURCES: New York Times, September 25, 1964, September 18, 1970, September 19, 1970, October 16, 1972, February 2, 1973, February 11, 1973, February 12, 1982; *Film Quarterly,* fall, 1966, winter, 1966-67, summer, 1972, spring, 1973, fall, 1975; *Cineaste,* spring, 1971; *Film,* spring, 1971; *Sight and Sound,* spring, 1971, spring, 1973, autumn, 1973, spring, 1978; *New Yorker,* October 28, 1972, October 31, 1972; Peter Cowie, editor, *International Film Guide,* A. S. Barnes, 1972; *Time,* January 22, 1973, May 24, 1976, October 17, 1977, October 8, 1979; *New York Post,* February 3, 1973; *New Republic,* March 3, 1973, February 9, 1974, October 20, 1979; *Guardian,* March 14, 1973; *New York Review of Books,* May 17, 1973; *Film Comment,* May-June, 1974, November-December, 1979; *Newsweek,* November 18, 1974, September 27, 1976, October 17, 1977, October 28, 1979; *Massachusetts Review,* autumn, 1975; *Film Heritage,* summer, 1976; *New Times,* November 11, 1977; *Commonweal,* December 23, 1977; *Village Voice,* October 8, 1979; *Detroit Free Press,* October 26, 1979, October 30, 1979; *Rolling Stone,* November 15, 1979; *National Review,* December 21, 1979; *Observer,* January 6, 1980; *American Film,* January-February, 1980; *Contemporary Literary Criticism,* Volume 16, Gale, 1981.*

—Sketch by Les Stone

*   *   *

BEST, Marshall A.   1901(?)-1982

OBITUARY NOTICE: Born c. 1901; died March 14, 1982, in Great Barrington, Mass. Editor. Best was associated with Viking Press from 1925 until his death. In 1928 he became a director and in 1935 he worked as general manager. During World War II Best performed a variety of roles, including editor-in-chief, production manager, and artistic director. He also helped create the Viking Portable Library, whose first volumes were *As You Were,* an anthology devised for servicemen, and *The Portable John Steinbeck.* Obituaries and other sources: *New York Times,* March 16, 1982; *Publishers Weekly,* April 2, 1982.

*   *   *

BETHEL, Elizabeth Rauh   1942-

PERSONAL: Born August 27, 1942, in Grosse Pointe, Mich.; daughter of Edward Martin (a petroleum engineer) and Esther Ruth (Jones) Rauh; children: Edward Wesley, Charles Burton. *Education:* Oklahoma City University, B.A., 1969; University of Oklahoma, M.A., 1971, Ph.D., 1974. *Office:* Department of Sociology, Lander College, Greenwood, S.C. 29646.

CAREER: Oklahoma City University, Oklahoma City, Okla., instructor in sociology, 1971-73; Lander College, Greenwood, S.C., assistant professor, 1973-76, associate professor, 1977—. *Member:* American Sociological Association, Social Science History Association, Speech Communication Association.

WRITINGS: Promiseland: A Century of Life in a Negro Community, Temple University Press, 1981.

WORK IN PROGRESS: In an Unlikely Time and Place, research on women's friendship networks.

SIDELIGHTS: Promiseland is a historical study of an all-black farming community founded in the fear and violence of Reconstruction in post-Civil War South Carolina. Emancipated blacks, finding themselves in direct competition with disenfranchised whites and fearing terrorist action by the Ku Klux Klan, established communities in a segregated society. Bethel's study follows the community of Promised Land from its inception in 1870 to its evolved form one century later.

New York Times Book Review critic David Bradley thought the book "stimulating and important" and commended Bethel's "impressively abundant raw data" and use of living informants to create a "rich blend." Bradley felt that one flaw in the book is that "Bethel seems to view the kinship structure of Promised Land as a variation of the white middle-class norm, although her own descriptions make it obvious that it is something far different, quite possibly a survival of ancient African patterns." Even though Bradley disagreed with Bethel's analysis, he praised her for her "diligent and caring" presentation of the study.

BIOGRAPHICAL/CRITICAL SOURCES: New York Times Book Review, July 19, 1981.

*   *   *

BETTS, John (Edward)   1939-

PERSONAL: Born April 12, 1939, in London, England; son of Percy W. and Jessie M. (Baker) Betts; married Ursule M. Gauthier, April 6, 1963; children: Jessica, Teresa, Christine. *Education:* Chelmsford Technical College, General Certificate of Education, 1957; attended Vancouver City College, 1964-65; Simon Fraser University, B.Sc. (with first class honors), 1968; University of Toronto, M.Sc., 1969. *Home:* 4886 West Saanich Rd., Victoria, British Columbia, Canada V8Z 3H7. *Office:* Camosun College, 1950 Lansdowne Rd., Victoria, British Columbia, Canada V8P 5J2.

CAREER: Mohawk College, Hamilton, Ontario, instructor in physics, 1969-71; Camosun College, Victoria, British Columbia, instructor in physics, 1971-78, coordinator of physics, 1978—. Trustee, Saanich school board, 1979— (vice-chairman, 1982—). *Military service:* Royal Canadian Air Force, navigator, 1957-64; became flying officer. *Member:* American Association of Physics Teachers.

WRITINGS: Physics for Technology, Reston, 1976, 2nd edition, 1981. Also author, with N. K. Preston, of *Foundations of Elementary Physics,* 1978.

WORK IN PROGRESS: Elements of Applied Physics, for Reston.

AVOCATIONAL INTERESTS: Photography, tennis, golf, gardening.

*   *   *

BEVAN, Aneurin   1897-1960

OBITUARY NOTICE: Born November 15, 1897, in Tredegar, Monmouthshire, South Wales; died July 6, 1960. Labor leader, public servant, and editor. As leader of the South Wales miners' union and editor of the left-wing *Tribune* during the 1940's, Bevan was often outspoken in his criticism of Prime Minister Winston Churchill and of his own Labour party. Bevan accused the governing conservative party of lacking "spirit and militancy" and protested against the electoral truce that prohibited labour candidates from challenging Conservative candidates during the war. Bevan served in the British Parliament for more than thirty years. Obituaries and other sources: *Current Biography,* Wilson, 1943, October, 1960; *New York Times,* July 7, 1960.

*   *   *

BEVAN, James (Stuart)   1930-

PERSONAL: Born September 28, 1930, in London, England; son of Peter James Stuart (a barrister) and Phyllis Marjorie (Enthoven) Bevan; married Rosemary Mendus, April 28, 1962; children: Richard Stuart, Katharine. *Education:* Cambridge University, M.A., 1952; St. Mary's Hospital Medical School, London, M.B., B.Chir., 1955. *Home:* 9 Hill Rd., London NW8 9QE, England.

CAREER: St. Mary's Hospital, London, England, house physician in professorial unit of medicine and in departments of neurology, dermatology, and venerealogy, 1955-77, deputy medical superintendent, 1977—; private practice of medicine in London, 1960—. Addenbrooke's Hospital, Cambridge, England, house surgeon, 1977. Diplomate of Royal College of Obstetricians and Gynaecologists. Medical adviser to London College of Music; senior medical consultant to Automobile Association; consultant to computer and engineering companies. *Military service:* British Army, Royal Army Medical Corps, junior specialist in medicine, 1977-79; served in Malaya; became captain. *Member:* Royal College of General Practitioners, British Medical Association, Medical Society of London, St. Albans Medical Club.

WRITINGS: State Final Questions and Answers for Nurses, Faber, 1962, 5th edition, 1971; *Preliminary Questions and Answers for Nurses,* Faber, 1966; *Sex: The Plain Facts,* Faber, 1966; *The Simon & Schuster Handbook of Anatomy and Physiology,* Simon & Schuster, 1979 (published in England as *A Pictorial Handbook of Anatomy and Physiology,* Mitchell Beazley, 1979); *The Pocket Medical Encyclopedia and First Aid Guide,* Simon & Schuster, 1979 (published in England as *The Pocket Medical and First Aid Guide,* Mitchell Beazley, 1979); *The World Book Illustrated Home Medical Encyclopedia,* World Book, 1980 (published in England as *Your Family Doctor,* Mitchell Beazley, 1980). Contributor to *Illustrated London News.*

SIDELIGHTS: Bevan told *CA:* "I work outside the National Health Service in a fee-paying, private practice independent of insurance companies and am mainly concerned with family medicine. I have two partners and split the day between office consultations and visits to patients in their homes and in the hospital."

*   *   *

BEVERIDGE, William (Ian Beardmore)   1908-

PERSONAL: Born April 23, 1908, in Junee, Australia; son of James (a pastoralist) and Ada (Beardmore) Beveridge; married Patricia Thomson, May 30, 1935; children: John. *Education:* University of Sydney, B.V.Sc., 1930, D.V.Sc., 1940; Cambridge University, Sc.D., 1974. *Home:* University House, P.O. Box 1535, Canberra, Australian Capital Territory 2601, Australia.

CAREER: McMaster Laboratory, Sydney, Australia, research officer, 1930-38; Rockefeller Institute, Princeton, N.J., Harkness fellow, 1938-39; Walter and Eliza Hall Institute, Melbourne, Australia, research officer, 1940-44; Pasteur Institute, Paris, France, visiting scientist, 1945-46; Cambridge University, Cambridge, England, professor of animal pathology, 1947-75; writer, 1975—. Wesley W. Spink Lecturer at University of Minnesota; visiting fellow at Australian National University, Canberra, 1979-82. Consultant to World Health Organization and Bureau of Animal Health, Canberra.

MEMBER: World Veterinary Association (president, 1957-75), British Veterinary Association (honorary member), American Veterinary Medical Association (honorary member), Australian College of Veterinary Scientists (life fellow), Academie Royale de Medicine de Belgique (honorary member), German Academy for Scientific Research (honorary member), Hungarian Micro Association (honorary member). *Awards, honors:* K. Meyer gold-headed cane from American Veterinary Epidemiological Society, 1971; Gamgee Gold Medal from World Veterinary Association, 1975, for services to veterinary science.

WRITINGS: Foot-Rot in Sheep: A Transmissible Disease Due to Infection With Fusiformis Nodosus—Studies on Its Cause, Epidemiology, and Control, H. E. Daw, 1941; (with F. M. Burnet) *The Cultivation of Viruses and Rickettsiae in the Chick Embryo,* H.M.S.O., 1946; *The Art of Scientific Investigation: An Entirely Fresh Approach to the Intellectual Adventure of Scientific Research,* Norton, 1950, revised edition, 1957; *Frontiers in Comparative Medicine,* University of Minnesota Press, 1972; *Influenza: The Last Great Plague,* Prodist, 1977, revised edition, 1978; *Seeds of Discovery,* Norton, 1980; *Viral Diseases of Farm Livestock,* Australia Government Publishing Service, 1981; *Bacterial Diseases of Ruminants,* Australian Government Publishing Service, 1982.

Editor: *Using Primates in Medical Research,* S. Karger, 1969; *Infections and Immunosuppression in Subhuman Primates,* Williams & Wilkins, 1970; *Breeding Primates,* S. Karger, 1972.

Contributor of about one hundred articles to scientific journals.

SIDELIGHTS: Beveridge wrote: "My main interests, apart from my professional work as a virologist, have been the ways in which discoveries are made and research is done, which are different from the so-called 'scientific method' as portrayed by philosophers with only second-hand knowledge of scientific research."

* * *

BIDDLE, Wayne 1948-

PERSONAL: Born March 27, 1948, in Baltimore, Md.; son of George Arthur (an engineer) and Irene (Woodward) Biddle. *Education:* Cornell University, B.S.E.E., 1970. *Home and office:* 265 Water St., New York, N.Y. 10038. *Agent:* Harriet Wasserman, 230 East 48th St., New York, N.Y. 10017.

CAREER: Cornell University, Ithaca, N.Y., founding associate editor of *Cornell Review,* 1976-79; *Harper's,* New York, N.Y., contributing editor, 1980—. *Awards, honors:* Fellow of National Endowment for the Arts, 1980.

WRITINGS: Coming to Terms (science dictionary), Viking, 1981.

Work represented in anthologies, including *Intro Six,* Doubleday, 1974, and *Best American Short Stories of 1975,* Hart-Davis, Mac Gibbon, 1975. Contributor of about thirty stories, articles, and reviews to magazines, including *New Society, New Scientist, Epoch,* and *TriQuarterly,* and newspapers.

WORK IN PROGRESS: No Joy Yet, a novel; *U.S. Arabia,* a study of American technology in Saudi Arabia.

SIDELIGHTS: Biddle told *CA:* "The urge to write came out of my own naivete and I continue to be terrified by the extent of it."

* * *

BIEMILLER, Carl Ludwig 1912-1979

OBITUARY NOTICE: Born in 1912 in Haddonfield, N.J.; died October 2, 1979, in Monmouth, N.J. Editor and writer. Biemiller began his literary career as an assistant publisher of the *Philadelphia Daily News.* From 1945 to 1957 he serve as executive editor of *Holiday* magazine. Among his numerous writings for young adults is a science fiction trilogy that includes *The Hydronauts, Follow the Whales,* and *Escape From the Crater.* Obituaries and other sources: *Authors of Books for Young People,* 2nd edition supplement, Scarecrow, 1979; *New York Times,* October 3, 1979.

* * *

BIENENFELD, Florence L(ucille) 1929-

PERSONAL: Born December 29, 1929, in Los Angeles, Calif.; daughter of Jack (a sign painter) and Gertrude (Lewis) Gottlieb; married Milton Bienenfeld (a business executive), September 7, 1952; children: Ruth Bienenfeld Barrett, Joel, Daniel. *Education:* California State University, B.A., 1950; University of California, Los Angeles, M.A., 1968; doctoral study at University of Southern California, 1972-73; Columbia Pacific University, Ph.D., 1981. *Politics:* Democrat. *Religion:* Jewish. *Residence:* Marina del Rey, Calif. *Office:* Conciliation Court of Los Angeles County, 1725 Main St., Room 225, Santa Monica, Calif. 90401.

CAREER: Montebello Unified School District, Montebello, Calif., elementary school teacher, 1949-51; educational therapist and private practitioner in marriage and family counseling, 1968-74; Conciliation Court of Los Angeles County, Santa Monica, Calif., senior marriage and family counselor, 1974-76; Superior Court of Los Angeles County, Los Angeles, Calif., child custody investigator, 1977; Conciliation Court of Los Angeles County, senior marriage and family counselor, 1977—. Workshop leader; lecturer; guest on radio and television programs. *Member:* American Association for Marriage and Family Therapy (clinical member), Association of Family Conciliation Courts. *Awards, honors:* Award of merit from Association of Family Conciliation Courts, 1980, for outstanding service to victims of divorce.

WRITINGS: My Mom and Dad Are Getting a Divorce (juvenile), EMC Corp., 1980; (contributor) H. Norman Wright, editor, *Marital Counseling: A Biblically Based Cognitive Approach,* Christian Marriage Enrichment, 1981. Author of "Family Matters," a column syndicated by Community Features. Contributor to counseling journals.

WORK IN PROGRESS: Divorce Without Child-Abuse: A Model for Counseling and Mediating Custody Disputes.

SIDELIGHTS: Florence Bienenfeld commented: "I want to ease tension and pain for children involved in marital or post-marital conflicts. Most children take divorce very hard and they take custody battles even harder. Children can recover from the divorce when their parents allow them to heal. Regrettably, some parents continue to argue and fight after the separation and divorce. The children become the focal point for their arguments and bitterness. Parental hostility often escalates and never ends. For some children there is no relief from parental conflict throughout their entire childhood. When these children grow up many of them carry unhappy memories of this experience into adulthood, and this can ruin their lives.

"In an age of much violence and harshness throughout the world, there are small inroads being made toward humanizing life for children. In some birth centers and hospitals newborns are being placed in a warm bath to soothe their entrance to the world. There is much talk and action being taken to protect children from physical and sexual abuse. One very important inroad is divorce counseling and mediation for parents as a measure for protecting children from the abuse of divorce."

*   *   *

BIERMAN, Stanley M(elvin)   1935-

PERSONAL: Born March 26, 1935, in Los Angeles, Calif.; son of Maurice L. (a pharmacist) and Bella (a pharmacist; maiden name, Koran) Bierman; married Marlene Ceazan, November 26, 1957; children: Wendy, Robert, Jeffrey. *Education:* University of California, Los Angeles, B.A., 1956, M.D., 1960. *Home:* 1078 Maybrook, Beverly Hills, Calif. 90210. *Office:* 2080 Century Park E., Los Angeles, Calif. 90067.

CAREER: University of California, Los Angeles, intern, 1960-61, resident in dermatology, 1961-64; private practice of dermatology in Los Angeles, Calif., 1964—. University of California, Los Angeles, instructor, 1964-69, assistant professor, 1970-76, associate professor of dermatology, 1977—. *Member:* American College of Physicians (fellow), California Medical Association (member of scientific advisory committee).

WRITINGS: The World's Greatest Stamp Collectors, Fell, 1981. Contributor of more than thirty articles to medical and philatelic journals.

WORK IN PROGRESS: The Virus of Love, a book for lay people on genital herpes simplex, completion expected in 1985.

SIDELIGHTS: Bierman told *CA:* "Our journey through life can be considered complete if we have raised a family, planted a tree, and written a book. As author-biographers, we have responsibilities to capture for posterity the personal reveries and reminiscences lying fallow (and unwritten) in the minds of our graying colleagues."

AVOCATIONAL INTERESTS: Philately, "the finest private philatelic library in the world."

*   *   *

BIERS, William Richard   1938-

PERSONAL: Born October 29, 1938, in Brussels, Belgium; American citizen born abroad; son of Howard (an engineer) and Constance (Britain) Biers; married Jane Carol Chitty (a museum curator), 1966; children: Katherine Laura. *Education:* Brown University, A.B., 1961; University of Pennsylvania, Ph.D., 1968. *Home:* 2310 Fairmont, Columbia, Mo. 65201. *Office:* Department of Art History and Archaeology, University of Missouri, Pickard Hall, Columbia, Mo. 65211.

CAREER: American School of Classical Studies, Athens, Greece, secretary, 1964-68; University of Missouri, Columbia, assistant professor, 1968-72, associate professor, 1972-81, professor of classical archaeology, 1981—, chairman of department, 1973-75, 1977-80. Member of managing committee of American School of Classical Studies, Athens. *Member:* Archaeological Institute of America, University Club (New York), Athenaeum (London).

WRITINGS: The Archaeology of Greece: An Introduction, Cornell University Press, 1980. Contributor to archaeology journals.

WORK IN PROGRESS: Archaeological projects in Greece and Portugal; studies of ancient Greek ceramics.

*   *   *

BILOW, Pat   1941-

PERSONAL: Surname is pronounced *By*-low; born December 17, 1941, in Toledo, Ohio; daughter of Robert Helmuth and Mildred (Hoffman) Foels; married Earl Bilow (an operating engineer), May 27, 1961; children: Mark, Matthew. *Education:* Attended University of Toledo, 1959-60, 1972-74. *Religion:* Lutheran. *Home:* J-640 Road 10, Malinta, Ohio 43535. *Office:* United Way of Henry County, 611 North Perry St., Napolean, Ohio 43545.

CAREER: Owens-Illinois, Inc., Toledo, Ohio, administrative assistant, 1960-63, 1969-76; free-lance writer, 1976-78; United Way, Toledo, assistant communications director, 1978-82; United Way of Henry County, Napoleon, Ohio, executive director, 1982—. Distributor for Wilderness Log Homes. Guest on radio and television programs. *Member:* Women in Communications (vice-president, 1979), Ohio Historical Society, Toledo Press Club, Malinta Historical Society.

WRITINGS: And Now We Are Four, Logos International, 1980. Contributor to management journals and popular magazines, including *Today's Secretary, Home Life, Country Living,* and *Decision.* Newsletter editor for Gladieux Corp. and Sight Center.

WORK IN PROGRESS: Research for a book on coping with the elderly.

SIDELIGHTS: Pat Bilow commented: "My book on coping with the elderly is based on personal experiences with my eighty-year-old grandmother, who is senile. It will incorporate interviews with professionals in the field and others who cope with the same problem." *Avocational interests:* Travel.

BIOGRAPHICAL/CRITICAL SOURCES: Toledo Blade, May 2, 1980; *West Toledo Herald,* January 21, 1981; *Northwest Signal,* February 10, 1981; *Northwest Courier,* February 11, 1981; *Defiance Crescent-News,* February 16, 1981; *Marketeer,* February 17, 1981; *School Library Journal,* March, 1981; *Library Journal,* March 15, 1981.

*   *   *

BINGHAM, (George) Barry, Jr.   1933-

PERSONAL: Born September 23, 1933, in Louisville, Ky.; son of George Barry (an editor) and Mary Clifford (a newspaper executive; maiden name, Caperton) Bingham; married Edith Wharton Stenhouse, November 30, 1963; children: Emily Simms, Mary Caperton, Philip John (adopted), Charles Wharton (adopted). *Education:* Harvard University, A.B., 1956. *Home:* 4309 Glenview Ave., Glenview, Ky. 40025. *Office:* Louisville Courier-Journal, 525 West Broadway, Louisville, Ky. 40202.

CAREER/WRITINGS: Columbia Broadcasting Systems, Inc. (CBS), New York City, management trainee, 1958-59; National Broadcasting Co. (NBC), New York City, researcher, 1960-61, field producer of documentaries in Washington, D.C., 1961-62; *Louisville Courier-Journal* and *Louisville Times,* Louisville, Ky., 1962—, editor and publisher, beginning in 1971; Standard Gravure Corp. (printing company), Louisville,

1962—, vice-chairman of board of directors, beginning in 1971; WHAS, Inc., Louisville, 1962—, president, beginning in 1971. President of Actors Theatre Louisville, 1965-66, Louisville Orchestra, 1971-74, and Isaac W. Bernheim Forest Foundation. Member of board of directors of Advocates for the Arts, Berea College, Bingham Child Guidance Clinic, Council of Better Business Bureaus, Regional Cancer Center Corp., and African Wildlife Leadership Foundation; secretary of executive committee of Louisville Fund for Arts, 1979—. *Military service:* U.S. Marine Corps, 1956-58; became captain. *Member:* American Society of Newspaper Editors (member of ethics committee), National Advertising Bureau, Sigma Delta Chi, Harvard Club (New York City), Louisville Country Club, River Valley Club.

SIDELIGHTS: Consistently ranked among the nation's top ten newspapers, the *Louisville Courier-Journal* and *Louisville Times* have been Bingham family enterprises since Robert Worth Bingham, a lawyer, judge, diplomat, and former mayor of Louisville, purchased them in 1918. When Louisville's only other newspaper, the *Herald-Post,* folded in 1936, the Bingham papers became a Louisville press monopoly, which they remain to this day. Upon his death in 1937, Judge Bingham was succeeded by his son Barry Bingham, Sr., who, during his more than thirty years as editor and publisher of the *Louisville Courier-Journal* and *Louisville Times,* set the ethical standards and liberal editorial policies with which the Louisville newspapers are still identified. In the book *Makers of Modern Journalism* Bingham, Sr., is quoted as saying, ''Monopoly forces a newspaper's management to think over its course of action with painful care, to generate within itself ever-rising goals of public service.'' Maintaining this philosophy after the *Herald-Post* closed, the Binghams waived exclusive rights to local United Press (UP) and Associated Press (AP) franchises—in the event that someday someone else might wish to start a competing paper.

When Barry Bingham, Sr., retired in 1971, direction of the newspapers passed on to his son Barry, Jr. At first, the papers' staffs were concerned about the new leadership. *Wall Street Journal* reporter David P. Garino explained: ''Barry Jr.'s older brother, Worth, who died in a 1966 auto accident, had been groomed for the newspaper posts, while Barry was to have taken over the family's broadcasting interests, including Louisville radio and television stations WHAS.'' As it was, Bingham became editor and publisher of the newspapers in the same year that he was made president of WHAS, Inc., which includes WHAS-AM, WAMZ-FM, and WHAS-TV. Additionally, within six months of his appointment the new young editor had to undergo serious medical treatment, having discovered that he had Hodgkin's disease, a cancer of the lymph system.

After apparently successful treatment, Bingham, Jr., returned to his post as editor-publisher and immediately began to dispel suspicions about his ability to run the newspapers. By 1974 *Time* magazine mentioned him in their cover story ''Leadership in America,'' spotlighting him in their list of two hundred young American leaders for the future. ''Clearly, the 40-year-old Mr. Bingham is no ordinary publisher, just as the papers his family has headed for three generations are no ordinary newspapers,'' commented Garino in the same year. ''Moreover,'' he continued, ''the Bingham papers are the acknowledged Messrs. Clean of the newspaper industry. This is no small distinction at a time when the ethics and credibility of the American press are undergoing their closest scrutiny in recent memory.''

Under Barry Bingham, Jr.'s, leadership the Louisville papers have maintained rigid policies established to ensure journalistic integrity. Gifts or junkets from news sources are strictly prohibited. All tickets for performances attended by critics, including film, theatre, musical, and sports events are paid for by the newspapers. Rent is paid for space used in government buildings during news coverage, and the papers insist on paying for copies of all books they review. Newspaper executives with the Bingham papers are not allowed to own an interest in any business that advertises in the *Louisville Times* or *Courier-Journal,* and a special office was established by the Binghams to evaluate and monitor the papers' advertising ethics. The Louisville papers strictly avoid commercialism in news stories, including sports events sponsored by large companies. For example, much to the sponsor's chagrin, the Buick Open Golf tournament is referred to by the Bingham papers as the Flint Open, after the city in which it is played.

In addition, the Louisville newspapers were among the first in the nation to hire an ombudsman to be responsible for investigating complaints and for watchdogging the publications, noting any errors, and seeing to it that corrections are printed where warranted. In 1974 the *Louisville Times* hired a news critic to monitor the performance of both papers and the broadcasting media as well. Such staunch commitment to responsible journalism was explained in a quotation which appeared in the *Wall Street Journal.* Repeating a sentiment originally voiced by his father, Barry Bingham, Jr., stated: ''Newspapers have a responsibility to be fair and neutral and I think that goes double for papers that are in a monopoly situation like we are.''

AVOCATIONAL INTERESTS: Hunting, photography, environmental preservation, music, theatre.

CA INTERVIEW

CA interviewed Barry Bingham, Jr., at his *Louisville Courier-Journal* office on September 30, 1980.

CA: The Courier-Journal *has somewhat of a left-wing reputation among the local population, doesn't it?*

BINGHAM: They probably call it the *Communist-Journal.* I even got a letter—I nearly died laughing—addressed to ''Communist Headquarters, 6th and Broadway,'' and it came right to my office. I said: ''The Federal Building is right across the street; that may be the Communist Headquarters for all I know. How come it comes to my office?'' But, we are more liberal than the community, there's no doubt about it. The newspapers, editorially and politically, are more liberal than the state. Richard Nixon carried this state twice, but not with our help.

CA: I noted with interest that you spent a year with CBS, then moved to NBC. Were you dissatisfied at CBS-TV?

BINGHAM: I got out of the Marine Corps in 1958, and I was very interested in broadcasting. I remember when I was in college I went by the common room one day, and there were people in there watching television in the daytime, which was just unheard of at that time. I wandered in to see what was going on and sat down because I had ten minutes until class. I found myself still there about four hours later; I literally just lost track of everything. I was watching the Army-McCarthy hearings, and I said to myself, ''If that little black box has the power I see in it, I want to get into that line of work.'' Well, at the same time we were building a television station here, and I wanted to get involved.

My family has had a tradition of sending the children away somewhere else to learn. I don't mean school, although we went to boarding school, too. My brother Worth, who was going into the newspaper business, went to Minneapolis and worked on the *Tribune* and then went to San Francisco and worked on the *Chronicle*. The theory being that if you're a Bingham and working on the *Courier-Journal* and *Louisville Times*, nobody is going to say, "You're crazy" or run the risk of saying, "That's the stupidest thing I ever heard." Whereas in Minneapolis they'd tell Worth, "Kid, if you don't shape up, we're going to fire your ass." And CBS would certainly do the same thing for me in New York.

So I went into CBS's training program. There were three trainees: two other guys, who happened to be lawyers, and me. The training program got a terrible reputation from the very beginning. Every week—we went from department to department, never staying in one department more than a week or two—we had to write a report, and it was fairly well known that we were writing reports. It was remarkable the number of people who were fired shortly after a trainee had gone through the department. We weren't writing anything like that; we were writing about what our experiences had been, but for some reason we coincided with a sort of housecleaning. It got to the point where at the end of the training program, nobody would talk to us. I went into one department and they said: "There's a desk over there. Sit at it and shut up. You can open the mail if you want." So I was somewhat disillusioned with the training program.

Also, just as I was reaching the end of the training program, WHAS-Radio decided to disaffiliate with CBS Network. At that time radio was a lot more important than it is today, and the people at CBS were furious. They probably were thinking: "Here they sent the kid up to learn, and then they disaffiliate the radio station." So when the training program ended, and I had always made it clear I was interested in going into either news or public affairs, they said there was no room there, but that I could go into station relations, which was, I thought, a beautiful twist, because that's the department that signs up new affiliates. I said I didn't have any interest in that area, and they said, "Well, that's it, draw your check on Friday," and that was the end.

So I went over to NBC. My father knew Julian Goodman, who was then president of the news division. He's from Glasgow, Kentucky, and Julian said, "Hmm, a person who's just been through the CBS training program, I think I can find you a job," and he hired me as a researcher for seventy-five dollars a week. I worked for a couple of years in New York and a couple of years in Washington—I was moved down there to work with a documentary group—and, frankly, I loved it. I guess I would have stayed at NBC for another ten years if my father hadn't said, "Now it's time to come home and put into practice in Louisville some of what you've learned up there."

CA: Did you like working on documentaries?

BINGHAM: I worked on two documentaries that were my heart and soul. I was working with a producer named Lou Hazam, a wonderful madman. He'd roll around on the floor and scream when he couldn't get the money he wanted—marvelous guy to work for. It was at a time when NBC had gotten a lot of criticism from the FCC (Federal Communications Commission) over the rigging of quiz shows and was under a lot of pressure to clean up its act. Hazam had been doing medical documentaries, about a half-dozen a year, and they said, "Lou, we need you to do bigger stuff than that." He started doing art documentaries. He'd done one on Vincent Van Gogh, when he asked me for ten show ideas, and I gave him one on the Nile. The Alan Moorehead books, *The Blue Nile* and *The White Nile,* had just come out, and I gave him an idea about the

White Nile—how you could film from its origin in Burundi and go all the way down to the Mediterranean—and he bought it. I then spent six to eight weeks doing research on every segment of what he would film; what the important things were. Then he said, "How about going on it?," and I said, "You've gotta be kidding!"

Well, we spent eighteen weeks going down the Nile with a film crew, and I'll live a long time before I have another experience like that. It was hair-raising. Burundi was in the middle of a revolution, and we literally saw villages in flames. When I got back, they spent a year editing the film and putting the sound and the narration and the music with it, and it was one of the few times in my life where I've been in from the very genesis all the way to the time they put the show on the air. It was more than two years, and although I hadn't done all the writing, I'd done the research, I'd been with the film crew, I'd been involved with the editing, I'd been involved with the writing, the narration, the music, the script, and everything else; and being a part of the world I was very interested in, and a subject that I was interested in, was like shooting heroin into an addict.

Later on, Lou Hazam also asked me to do a show on Shakespeare, and we worked twenty-one weeks on that one, filming in Stratford, in England, all over Wales, Scotland, and France. Again we brought back about twenty-five hours of film that they cut back to fifty-six minutes. The editing was the heartbreak.

It was a little bit bizarre, though, my family owning a CBS-affiliated TV station and me working at NBC. People still shake their heads about that.

CA: Have you been able to apply your training on documentaries to the work here at WHAS-TV?

BINGHAM: Documentary work is a very rarified experience, and to some extent coming back to an affiliate is a heartbreak. The NBC budgets must have been $100,000 a show, and back then $100,000 went a long way. We could hire Lee J. Cobb to do narration, for instance. When an affiliate starts a documentary, they've got a budget of maybe twenty-five hundred dollars. There are no outtakes. In a way it was like coming from the champagne diet to the beer budget. I think I learned some management techniques at CBS/NBC that were useful to me, but actually learning how to put a documentary together ended up as a contribution to my artistic background more than anything I was able to transport back here, because no local station can amortize on one station the cost of a documentary the way a network can.

CA: WHAS-TV has done at least one investigative documentary, hasn't it, a film on Louisville bookies, involving hidden hand-held cameras?

BINGHAM: Yes. I was very much involved in that, although not shooting it or editing it or anything. It was called "Open City." It was about 1971, and this town was wide open. At that point I was with the newspapers, although not yet publisher, and the newspapers were utterly disinterested in the story. I remember talking to the managing editor, and he said, "Well, yeah, there are some whore houses and some pimps and some bookie joints, but nothing important." Well, shortly before that CBS had done a documentary called "Biography of a Bookie Joint," and it was spectacular.

So I thought, if the newspapers aren't interested, we've got another way of getting at this story. We hired an investigative reporter, because the station didn't have one, and he came into town under the guise of being a computer expert who was going to work with the census bureau that had a big office across the river. No association with our companies at all; it was a deep dark secret. We just wanted to find out what was going on and, once we knew, to get the film crews to go out and film it. The reporter dug up the stuff, and we put on two one-hour documentaries on two successive nights—one about the city and one about the county surrounding the city—and it was tough stuff. He [the reporter] put the camera in a lunch pail, an old CBS trick, and put it down on the table, and you could hear people betting on the horses. The newspapers got a black eye out of it. At first they pooh-poohed it, said it wasn't really important, but it got a lot of local attention. The mayor was just out of his tree. "What the hell are you doing blowing this town up like that?" he said. The county judge was laughing behind his hand, and then the second night we did the one about the county, and the judge was saying, "What the hell are you doing tearing up the county like that?" But, my experience, making a documentary on the Nile, didn't help here. With the Nile film, we were more worried about color quality than anything else. You wanted good footage, but you weren't out after tough political stuff. This was tough stuff.

CA: What do you think are the long-term results of something like that? It may lead to change in the short run, but does it lead to change or reform in the long run?

BINGHAM: It's hard to say, but I'd be inclined to say it depends on how well you follow it up. You can't drop a bomb such as "Open City" and then not go back six months later and say, "Is that bookie joint still operating?" or "Are the prostitutes still on the corner?" If you don't follow it up, you can't expect to have very much effect, but once the law enforcement people discover that you're not going to let this die, that you're going to keep coming back, then they decide something has to be done.

A good example is the series the *Courier-Journal* did a couple of months ago on nursing homes and the tragic mess they're in. We had one guy die of bed sores, *die* of bed sores! There were maggots in his scrotum when they took him to the hospital; the examining doctor vomited. The newspaper did a six-part series on nursing homes and their problems, and they've followed up on it. About every month there will be a story about what the Department of Health and Welfare [now Department of Health and Human Services] is doing to try to clean up the nursing home problem. The process continues, and that's what makes successful investigative reporting. But, if you do it once and then forget it, everyone else is going to say it's a twenty-four-hour wonder.

CA: Two reporters for the Louisville newspapers were arrested while apparently eavesdropping on a police union meeting in 1974. At the time you attempted to balance the possible immorality in that situation with the reporters' right to seek news. How did you manage to balance those two?

BINGHAM: Well, the reporters had not entered the room but were in an adjoining room where they could hear through a door which was partly open, or under the door or something like that, and they had a tape recorder. My feeling is that it is kind of disreputable, and I wouldn't want to do it. If somebody had come to me and said, "These guys have a chance to do this, should they do it?" I would have said, "I don't think we ought to do that." On the other hand, I don't fire somebody for doing it. There's no violation of the law. It's not wiretapping, and there's some question as to whether it's bugging or not. We got all kinds of legal opinions on it, and our lawyer

said it was a very grey area. It's a moral issue more than anything else. Well, my answer was, morally you shouldn't do that sort of thing, and that's what I said; but also I said, "We're not going to fire these guys for doing it." There was a real split in my family over it. My mother said, "What you're saying is that the ends justify the means," and Clayton Fritchey, who happened to be visiting at the time, said, "If the ends don't justify the means, what does?" which I thought was a funny way of turning it around. It was a tough issue, a tough issue, and one on which the newspapers got quite a bit of flack. My feeling after that was that we've really got to be a little more careful about this sort of thing. I mean, we land on the FBI like a ton of bricks every time they do something like bugging Martin Luther King's room to get material they can use to embarrass him, and it makes me feel uneasy if we're doing the same thing.

Now we did have another case, the Tim McCall case, in which a woman alleged that McCall, a famous trial attorney here, had said that he could fix a trial. This woman was going to be charged with, I think, narcotics possession, and she had a pretty long record and was facing a serious penalty if convicted. She told two of our reporters that McCall had said that he could fix the judge. The reporters gave her a tape recorder, which she put in her purse, and she went to McCall's office and said, "Now tell me about how you're going to fix the judge." He said, "No! No! No fix. But I'll give you a guarantee that if you give me ten thousand dollars, I'll get you off, or I'll give you the money back," which of course is a contingency fee, which is not allowed in a criminal case. Well, we came out with a story about it, and McCall's still suing us. That's going on, I guess, into its fifth year, but the different issue here is that the woman was taping a conversation to which she was a party, and there's no legal problem with that. It's not the same as creeping up to the door and trying to record somebody else's conversation. I think we were justified in the McCall case. It made a hell of a story, because he ended the conversation by saying that he wasn't going to fix the case, but he was going fishing with the judge that weekend, and he would make sure that the judge understood that he had a big stake in this coming out right. The tape is just incredible.

CA: You publish, or try to publish, every letter to the editor you receive, and you run a large number of columns, some of them in conflict with your editorial viewpoint. Is that in any way a reaction to the monopoly status of your newspapers in Louisville?

BINGHAM: Oh, sure. If we weren't a monopoly, if we had daily competition here in Louisville, let's say the *Herald-Post*, which went out of business in 1936, was still operating, would we still do all these things? I don't think so. When competition exists you can appeal more to people who believe in your point of view, and you don't have an obligation to represent all points of view. If you're the only daily newspaper in town, you've got a responsibility to publish the letters that say, "The publisher's a fink." The only thing we screen out is libel or really bad taste, but we publish at least 95 percent of what we get. Although, you can only get one letter published a month, and if you write us a letter a day, we're not going to publish all of them.

CA: I was interested to learn that your newspapers had the first newspaper ombudsman. Do ombudsmen at other newspapers respond to the public as much as he does?

BINGHAM: It depends on where you are. Charlie Seib at the *Washington Post* did some internal responding, but at a very high level. I don't know to whom he gave his report, but it wasn't widely disseminated, and I think it was a source of suspicion. Our ombudsman writes a report that goes everywhere; it's posted on the bulletin board in the news department. It's a very widely disseminated criticism of the daily newspaper. Other ombudsmen write columns, and Charlie Seib did that. Our ombudsman doesn't, but we have a news critic [Bud Schulman] on the *Louisville Times* who does. [Note: Bud Schulman left the *Times* to produce television programs for "Inside Story." He has since returned to Louisville to do press commentary for WHAS-TV.]

CA: You publish a column of media criticism, as you just mentioned. Is that in part because you believe that the public distrusts the media?

BINGHAM: My feeling is that the media is pretty shoddy in this country. Once you get by the *New York Times* and the *Washington Post*—and they do some pretty fishy things—you get into some pretty marginal ethical issues. And the question is, "Who can speak on those issues?" Now I can lambaste Orion or WAVE, the Louisville TV stations the Binghams don't own, or I could even lambaste WHAS if I wanted to, but it's a little bit difficult on the part of ownership and management. The best thing, in my opinion, is to get somebody who is independent, who has had experience in broadcasting as well as newspapers, who has an ethical bent and is attuned to ethical problems, and let him do it. Give him independence. Bud Schulman has been writing his column for the *Louisville Times* now for five years, and I have never once told him, "I don't want that in the paper." I see it on the proof page in the morning when it comes out, and I have never told him to change anything. As a matter of fact, as he can tell you, the only time I wrote him a note was when I thought he was being too obscure. Once he wrote, "Maybe the publisher should have thought a second time before doing this," and I wrote him a note that said, "Come out and say it. If the publisher's wrong, just say 'I think the publisher is wrong. The publisher shouldn't have done this,' or whatever." He has never been bridled by me, and I've never muzzled him, and I think that's important.

CA: One of the other things your newspapers did first was shift from eight columns to six columns. Was that done as an experiment?

BINGHAM: That was done in my father's time, before I was here, in the 1950's. They did two things at the same time. They went to a six-column layout, not just on page one but throughout the paper, which was revolutionary. Nobody was doing it. The other thing was that they jumped the page-one stories to the back page of the first section. Even today, that's very rare. The reason most papers don't do it is that they can sell the back page of the first section for a premium as an advertising page. We bumped a lot of advertisers to clear the back page for the jumps of page-one stories. So, you don't have to go leafing through the middle of the paper. We don't, as some newspapers do, jump an A-1 story to B-6 or D-9 or wherever it happens to land, which makes reading some papers very difficult. We get letters from people saying, "I don't agree with your editorial policies, but I think the *Courier-Journal* and the *Louisville Times* are easy to read." It's easy to find your way through the papers because they're well-organized, and the wider column is easier to read than the narrow eight-column makeup. There are some newspapers now that have a six-column page one and an eight-column inside, and it's kind of a bastard-looking mess. Both the *Courier-Journal* and the *Times* have been six-column papers for fifteen years or more.

CA: The Miami Herald *is experimenting now with the delivery of newspapers on TV screens. Are you doing anything like that?*

BINGHAM: We're on the verge of an experiment, but what the *Miami Herald* is doing in Coral Gables is a very expensive experiment. I expect it's going to cost three or four million dollars before they're finished, maybe even more. What we're doing is going to be much simpler and much less expensive. We're going to go to the cable-head end, and we'll have somebody who keyboards into part of their computer the information from the newspaper. They'll put that on a dedicated cable channel, which will be for the newspaper, for news, and maybe promotion. You'll have a sort of headline service. If you want to see the whole story, you'll be told, "Read tomorrow morning's *Louisville Courier-Journal* or this afternoon's *Louisville Times*." We'll probably also get a separate channel for classified advertising. But at first we're not going to do anything like what the *Herald* is doing. They have an interactive system that works through the telephone. You can make inquiries of a computer and get information back. Ours is not going to be anything like that. Eventually we may get there. Starting off, they've got the Cadillac, and we've got a dinky little Moped by comparison.

CA: Is this a big enough market area to support an elaborate system?

BINGHAM: I'm not sure I'd want to invest in what the *Miami Herald* is doing until I knew where the industry is going. I don't want to bet on the wrong technology, but this area is big enough by all means to eventually support electronic delivery. I've been giving a speech for five years now about how newspapers are going to have to go to electronic delivery. Our energy consumption is phenomenal. We consume more than a million gallons of gasoline a year just to deliver the product. That's not reporters and photographers, that's just for circulation. Also, our energy consumption for our pressroom is monumental, and newsprint is very expensive. All of our costs are going up because all of them are energy related. Someday if we can beam delivery out over the air or over a channel on cable, if we can go out sixty miles without it costing us any more to go the second mile than the first, that's going to be a tremendous efficiency, and that's the efficiency broadcasters now have over newspapers. You could jam into a computer in your home the whole contents of the *Louisville Courier-Journal* and *Times* and maybe the *Wall Street Journal* and the *New York Times* as well, and then you could fish around and select among that material what you actually want to read. We could never deliver those four newspapers to your doorstep forty miles from Louisville and do it without losing money.

The thing is, I'm kind of on a kick about this because in the early part of this century the government was very rurally oriented. We were very interested in things like TVA, rural electrification. We had to do something for those poor folks on the farm, who otherwise would not have any of the amenities of civilized life. Well, the whole thing is turned around, and now every decision from the FCC is to do something for a metropolitan area. People have forgotten about the poor folks out on the farm. Well, this state is a very rural state; you get twenty miles outside of Louisville and you see a lot more cows than you see people. I don't think we can let this opportunity go by, because I think this state is built for that kind of communication, much more than it is for wired-up, cable-type communication.

CA: Speaking of broadcasting, one of your companies still owns a radio station here, doesn't it?

BINGHAM: We have AM, FM, and TV. Channel eleven is the television station; 840, WHAS-AM, is the AM radio station. Actually, that station bears out what I was just saying about rural areas. My grandfather got the license for that station in 1922. It was the first radio station in the state, licensed by the old Radio Commission before the FCC came into existence. He put it on the air, because his theory was—and it was a good theory—that there are parts of the state where you couldn't get a newspaper. The roads were so bad that, although you could print a newspaper in Louisville and ship it by train to Bowling Green, if you had to go forty miles from Bowling Green up some valleys and hollows, you just couldn't get there. So his concept was that if you got a clear-channel signal, which this was, you could then electronically take to those people out in the boondocks the information you couldn't get to them on paper. Well, that's a 1980's idea, for God's sake, and that was his idea back in 1922. He was a man way ahead of his time.

CA: Doesn't one of your stations broadcast only classical music?

BINGHAM: Now you're really going to hurt me, but that's all right. When I worked for NBC in Washington, D.C., I listened to WGMS, an excellent, top-flight, well-operated classical music station. I'm interested in music, and when I moved back to Louisville, I thought that the city needed a classical music service. So we put WHAS-FM on the air as a classical music station and ran it for about nine years and lost our shirts. I mean we lost about a million dollars in nine years, and there was no prospect. I think we could have run it another eighteen years and still would have had no prospect of ever breaking even, much less of making a profit. So at that point NBC came along with an all-news network, and I said, "Well, if you can't make it in classical music, maybe all news will work," and we went into that for two years and lost another million. I mean that was a hemorrhage compared with the other loss. Finally, the station manager said, "We can't do this anymore. Either we turn in the license or we do something else." We're now playing country music, but we busted our hump for eleven years trying to do what I thought we ought to do, and it just didn't pay out.

CA: There was some commercial support, wasn't there?

BINGHAM: Oh yeah, but it was peanuts. So finally the time came, and we just looked at the numbers. If I could have seen that in three more years we would have finally broken even, I would have said let's run it for three more years, but there were just no prospects. I had lots of people who told me they listened to it all of the time and loved the station, but they weren't going to advertise on it. Finally I think we made the best out of a bad situation. We gave all our tapes and records to the university, and they now have a classical music radio station which is still playing much of what we gave them. So the service is still here, and we haven't lost it completely. It's a sore subject, because my wife and I are both very interested in classical music, and when we had to take classical music off the air, it was a sad day for both of us. It was a sad day for the town, too.

CA: During the 1976 disturbances over busing here, the newspapers were pro-busing, weren't they?

BINGHAM: Well, we said that people ought to abide by the court order. I can't remember that our newspapers have ever told people to break the law or not to abide by a court order. And yes, it's inconvenient; and yes, it's time-consuming, and some children are going to be frightened, and some parents are going to be frightened, but the schools are going to work. We were the only institution in this town—and I mean the only institution, including the mayor, the county judge, and the chamber of commerce—standing with the federal judge. We all got a lot of grief. It was a very hard time. Of all the times since I've been publisher here, that was the worst, bar none; even when we had a strike of photoengravers, and we had a hard time putting out the newspaper, and there was a picket line out there, and you didn't know when you started your car if it would start or go blewy! That wasn't half as bad as busing. The phone calls at three in the morning. . . .

CA: What are you proudest of doing?

BINGHAM: I'm proudest of the prizes we've won. The last Pulitzer Prize we won was for international reporting, which has never been won in this town by these newspapers, for a series on Cambodia and the problems there. I just came out of my cave! Winning a Pulitzer Prize is something everybody celebrates, and we've won a good collection, including one for public service, for our stories on strip mining, and one for the Beverly Hills, Kentucky, fire—Richard Whitt did a fantastic investigative job on that. But the one for international reporting, for a newspaper in Louisville, Kentucky, to win for international reporting, well I just couldn't believe it! I was absolutely overjoyed. I'm not saying there haven't been a lot of other things I was proud of, but that one, because it was so unexpected and so unusual, just gave me goose bumps.

CA: I'm amazed you keep your standards so high without anyone breathing down your neck, without any competition.

BINGHAM: I think we breathe down our own necks. I know what kind of newspapers I want to run, and my father knew what kind of newspapers he wanted to run. The world is full of really rotten, corrupt publishers, and I don't want to be like that. We have a family that is willing to take a lower profit margin than even Kay Graham takes out of the *Washington Post*, about half of what Kay Graham takes, and if the family is willing to plow that kind of money back into the operation, if the people who work here see the publisher come to work early in the morning and stay late at night, so there's a commitment, then they say, "This is the kind of place I want to work." It isn't like being owned in say, New York, and they tell the local publisher you've got to get your bottom line in better shape and to hell with the news product, that's your problem. We don't run it that way. I send notes upstairs all the time about stories I like or don't like, and if I owned a newspaper in Denver, I wouldn't be sending notes to anybody, because if I saw the story I wouldn't know if it was right or not, because I don't live there.

CA: I presume you're not thinking of buying newspapers in other towns.

BINGHAM: No, but it's a very touchy issue with the management, because we've been offered newspapers elsewhere. When people have wanted to sell, instead of selling to Scripps-Howard they'd rather have sold to the Binghams. We've had offers of good newspapers at attractive prices, and my answer's been no. We've got enough on our plate here in Louisville.

BIOGRAPHICAL/CRITICAL SOURCES: Fortune, August, 1950; Kenneth Stewart and John Tebbel, *Makers of Modern Journalism,* Prentice-Hall, 1952; *Wall Street Journal,* July, 1974; *Time,* July 15, 1974.

—*Interview by Peter Benjaminson*

BINKLEY, Anne
  See RAND, Ann (Binkley)

* * *

BIRCH, Lionel   ?-1982(?)

OBITUARY NOTICE: Journalist and author. Birch was associated with both *Picture Post* and the *Sunday Telegram.* Among his writings are a collection of poems, *Between Sunset and Dawn,* an analysis of industrialization, *The Waggoner on the Footplate,* and novels, including *The System* and *The Pyramid.* Obituaries and other sources: *London Times,* February 20, 1982.

* * *

BIRD, Junius Bouton   1907-1982

OBITUARY NOTICE: Born September 21, 1907, in Rye, N.Y.; died April 2, 1982, in New York, N.Y. Curator, educator, and author of works in the field of natural history. Bird was associated with the American Museum of Natural History for fifty-four years, during which time he organized numerous expeditions into South America. In Chile during the 1930's, Bird unearthed what were then the oldest-known human remains. He also discovered textile fragments in Peru that dated from the third millenium B.C. Among the many exhibits he developed at the American Museum of Natural History were "Art and Life in Old Peru" and "Gold of the Americas." Obituaries and other sources: *American Men and Women of Science,* 13th edition, Bowker, 1976; *New York Times,* April 2, 1982.

* * *

BISHOP, Ian Benjamin   1927-

PERSONAL: Born April 18, 1927, in Gillingham, Kent, England; son of Arthur John and Edith (Smart) Bishop; married Pamela Haddacks (a nurse), December 14, 1968; children: Lucy, Gillian. *Education:* Attended Worcester College for the Blind, 1939-45; Queen's College, Oxford, M.A., 1954, M.Litt., 1954. *Office:* Department of English, University of Bristol BS8 1TH, England.

CAREER: University of Bristol, Bristol, England, assistant lecturer, 1953-56, lecturer, 1956-77; senior lecturer in English, 1977—.

WRITINGS: *"Pearl" in Its Setting: A Critical Study of the Middle English Poem,* Basil Blackwell, 1968; *Chaucer's "Troilus and Criseyde": A Critical Study,* University of Bristol, 1981. Contributor to *Encyclopaedia Britannica.* Contributor to scholarly journals.

WORK IN PROGRESS: Research on medieval English literature.

SIDELIGHTS: Bishop told *CA:* "The reign of Richard II, 1377 to 1399, is one of the periods of greatest poetic achievement in the whole history of English literature. Everyone has heard of Chaucer, but he is only the most outstanding of a number of major poets writing in English at that time. At least one of the others—the author of *Pearl* and *Sir Gawain and the Green Knight*—is no less significant for being anonymous. The effort involved in mastering the older form of English in which these poets wrote is richly rewarded by the experience of reading them in the original."

BISZTRAY, George   1938-

PERSONAL: Born October 2, 1938, in Budapest, Hungary; came to the United States in 1966, naturalized citizen, 1974; son of Gyula (a professor) and Margit (a teacher; maiden name, Borbely) Bisztray. *Education:* Eoetvoes University, Diploma in Hungarian and English, 1962; University of Minnesota, Ph.D., 1972. *Religion:* Roman Catholic. *Residence:* Toronto, Ontario, Canada. *Office:* Department of Slavic Languages and Literatures, University of Toronto, 21 Sussex Ave., Toronto, Ontario, Canada M5S 1A1.

CAREER: Professional translator in Budapest, Hungary, 1962-65; University of Chicago, Chicago, Ill., assistant professor of Scandinavian, 1972-75; University of Alberta, Edmonton, visiting assistant professor of Scandinavian, comparative literature, and German, 1976-78; University of Toronto, Toronto, Ontario, associate professor of Hungarian, 1978—. *Member:* International Comparative Literature Association, American Comparative Literature Association, American Hungarian Educators Association, Canadian Comparative Literature Association, Society for the Advancement of Scandinavian Study.

WRITINGS: Humanities in the Modern World: The Nineteenth Century, University of Minnesota Press, 1976; *Marxist Models of Literary Realism,* Columbia University Press, 1978; *Humanities in the Modern World: The Twentieth Century,* University of Minnesota Press, 1980. Contributor to language and literature journals.

WORK IN PROGRESS: A survey of the methods and tendencies of literary sociology, completion expected in 1985; radio plays.

SIDELIGHTS: Bisztray told *CA:* "As a native of Hungary, citizen of the United States, and resident in Canada, with a working knowledge of some eight languages, I should have a slight feeling of multiple split identity. Actually, I have managed so far to integrate all cosmopolitan impressions of the world. This cosmopolitanism is already reflected in the variety of my scholarly preoccupations and publications, and I may try to put my experiences in the form of a novel as well. It would be mostly for my own entertainment, but others are also welcome to join in—especially if the miracle happens that it is printed at all. The leitmotif is the life-lies of intellectuals."

* * *

BLADEN, Ashby   1929-

PERSONAL: Surname is pronounced *Blay*-den; born May 3, 1929, in Hartford, Conn. *Education:* Amherst College, B.A., 1950; Columbia University, M.A., 1952. *Office:* Phoenix Mutual Life Insurance Co., 1 American Row, Hartford, Conn. 06115.

CAREER: Connecticut Mutual Life Insurance Co., Hartford, research analyst, 1958-62; Cornell University, Ithaca, N.Y., assistant to the treasurer, 1962-65; Salomon Brothers, New York City, head of convertible securities research, 1965-68; manager of corporate investments for American Standard, Inc., 1968-71; Guardian Life Insurance Company of America, New York City, senior vice-president in investments, 1971-81; Phoenix Mutual Life Insurance Co., Hartford, senior vice-president in investments, 1981—.

WRITINGS: How to Cope With the Developing Financial Crisis, McGraw, 1979. Author of column, "Money and Investments," in *Forbes.*

BLAINE, Thomas R(obert) 1895-
(Tom R. Blaine)

PERSONAL: Born September 26, 1895, in Enid, Okla.; son of George A. (a farmer) and Frances (Smith) Blaine; married Athalie Williams, June 16, 1928; children: Kent R. *Education:* Attended University of Oklahoma, 1914-17. *Religion:* Presbyterian. *Home:* 1316 Indian Dr., Enid, Okla. 73701. *Agent:* Alex Jackinson, 55 West 42nd St., New York, N.Y. 10036. *Office:* Court House, Enid, Okla. 73701.

CAREER: State of Oklahoma, state judge in Enid, 1943—.

WRITINGS—Under name Tom R. Blaine: *Goodbye Allergies,* Citadel, 1965; *Mental Health Through Nutrition,* Citadel, 1974; *The Easy Natural Way to Reduce,* Keats Publishing, 1978; *Nutrition and Your Heart,* Keats Publishing, 1979. Also author of *Prevent That Heart Attack,* Citadel.

*   *   *

BLAINE, Tom R.
See BLAINE, Thomas R(obert)

*   *   *

BLAIR, Thomas (Lucien Vincent) 1926-

PERSONAL: Born June 9, 1926, in New York, N.Y.; son of Thomas and Lucy (Gage) Blair; married Myrtle Desmond (an artist and illustrator), 1952; children: Lucille, Katharine, Gage, Ellen. *Education:* Northwestern University, B.A., 1950; Boston University, M.A., 1951; attended Columbia University, 1952-53; Michigan State University, Ph.D., 1956. *Agent:* Hilary Rubinstein, A. P. Watt Ltd., 26/28 Bedford Row, London WC1R 4HL, England. *Office:* Urban Habitat Forum, Department of Social and Environmental Planning, Polytechnic of Central London, 309 Regent St., London W1R 8AL, England.

CAREER: State University of New York College at New Paltz, assistant professor of sociology, 1956-60; Ford Foundation fellow in African urban studies, 1960-62; conducted independent sociological research on urbanization and social change in Nigeria and Algeria, 1962-64; Architectural Association School of Architecture, London, England, consulting sociologist in department of tropical studies, 1964-67; Polytechnic of Central London, senior lecturer, 1967, professor of social and environmental planning, 1973—, head of department of planning, 1970—, director of Urban Habitat Forum, 1975—. Consultant to United Nations Centre for Human Settlements, 1976-79. Member of international school committee of the Royal Town Planning Institute. *Member:* World Society of Ekistics, Royal Society of Arts, Zoological Society, American Planning Association. *Awards, honors:* John Hay Whitney Foundation fellowship in Brazilian Studies, 1953-54.

WRITINGS: Africa: A Market Profile, Praeger, 1965; *The Land to Those Who Work It: Algeria's Experiment in Workers Management,* Doubleday, 1969; *The Poverty of Planning,* Macdonald & Co., 1973; *The International Urban Crisis,* Hill & Wang, 1974; *Retreat to the Ghetto: The End of a Dream?,* Hill & Wang, 1977.

Editor; published by Habitat Forum Publications: *Action for Habitat in a Third World Perspective: People, Shelter, Environment, Politics,* 1975-76; *Habitat United Kingdom: A Shift of Vision,* 1977; *Aspects of the British Planning Experience,* 1977; *Inner Cities: A Condition of England Question?,* 1978; *Human Settlements in the Eighties: Implications of New In-*

ternational Development Strategy, 1980; *Problem Cities in Search of Solutions: Nairobi, Delhi, Lusaka,* 1981.

Contributor: *Proceedings of the Town and Country Planning Summer School,* University of Keele, 1966; R. Mateles and S. Tannenbaum, editors, *Single-Cell Protein,* M.I.T. Press, 1968; Max Milner, editor, *Protein-Enriched Cereal Foods for World Needs,* American Association of Cereal Chemists, 1969; Paul Oliver, editor, *Shelter in Africa,* Barrie and Jenkins, 1971; *Collier's Year Book 1976,* Macmillan Educational, 1976; *New Society Social Studies Reader: Race and Ethnicity,* 3rd edition, New Society Journal, 1982. Also contributor to *Proceedings of the Nutrition Society,* 1970. Contributor to architecture and urban/regional planning journals, including *Architectural Association Quarterly, Architectural Design, Built Environment, Habitat Journal,* and *Official Architecture and Planning.*

WORK IN PROGRESS: An appraisal of the achievements, failures, and prospects for urban management and plan implementation in contrasting world situations, tentatively titled *Problem Cities in Search of Solutions,* publication by Plenum, expected in 1983; *Urban Habitat: A Human Settlements Approach to Urban Management and Planning in Third World Cities,* completion expected in 1984; an article, "Urbanisation, Housing, and Human Settlement Planning in Africa," for *The International Encyclopedia of Architecture, Engineering, and Urban Planning,* for Garland Publishing.

SIDELIGHTS: Blair told *CA:* "My writing career began out of professional necessity—to make one's mark, so to speak, as a sociologist/planner, researcher, public policy analyst, and professor. But there has always been an underlying motivating factor, a concern with understanding 'the human condition.' This has led me to many different places and cultures, studying, for example, changing social patterns in Brazilian rural towns, modernization in Kano, the capital of an ancient African kingdom, and the challenges to economic and political change in postliberation Algeria.

"In the 1970's I tured my attention to the failures of modern urban planning to solve the crises of housing and social welfare. *The Poverty of Planning* highlighted the plight of beleaguered urban communities and helped me to understand how urban design, wrongly used, can inhibit balanced city development.

"*The International Urban Crisis* examined in a broad perspective the most urgent problems facing urban man in an age of chaotic growth, predatory technology, and exploitive economic development. I tried to show that urban problems are truly regional and international and drew upon examples from New York, Moscow, Paris, London, Tokyo, and other great metropolitan centers. Though I did not attempt to offer any panaceas, I did discuss current ameliorative efforts and suggested that solutions must be found in new modes of private and public action to redirect basic social, economic, cultural, and political forces.

"*Retreat to the Ghetto: The End of a Dream?,* which completes my 1970's published work, took a close look at the results of the vigorous black American protest of the sixties against segregation and discrimination. I traveled many Southern roads and Northern city pavements seeking answers to important questions about the black struggle whose volatile quality gave it the appellation 'Black Revolution.' What were its origins? What leaders, ideas, and social groups sustained it? What is its legacy, in terms of images of cultural unity, the quest for economic equity, and the political and planning aspects of black urbanization?

"In regard to my professional development and long-term interests: I have been associated with the built environment professions over the past seventeen years, and have developed teaching skills, expertise, and research interests in the social and cultural aspects of urban and regional planning, the politics of planning and social policy formulation, inner cities and urban renewal and design, new towns, the sociology of housing, and the ethics of planning education, theory, and practice.

"Cross-cultural interests include the emergent region in eastern, western, and northern Africa, Malaysia, and Brazil, in European countries at intermediate stages of development such as Greece, Yugoslavia, Portugal, Spain, and Turkey, as well as developed countries like the United States, the United Kingdom, and the countries of Western Europe.

"Broadly, my long-term interests are in the application of academic experience, professional perspectives and personal concern to the investigation of the concept and methods of human settlements planning, and the search for new insights into social, political, and institutional processes, technologies, and values, which further our understanding and ability to resolve human settlement problems.

"In *The International Urban Crisis* I wrote of the problems and solutions evident in world metropolitan centers, with examples drawn mainly from Western and developed countries. I am now engaged in research which seeks to explore the situation in Third World cities from a fresh perspective, based on my recent five years' experience as director of the Urban Habitat Forum for urban administrators from developing countries.

"The massive problems of urbanization and city poverty in Third World cities are well-known—chronic lack of basic services, including housing for the urban poor, unemployment, chaotic land-use patterns, general environmental deterioration, and critical problems of city finance and management—but how well have these problems been dealt with by urban planners, administrators, and international aid agencies? And what are the requirements for a new human settlements policy for guiding and managing urban settlement planning and development, with special reference to the improvement of the poorest communities, the slums and squatters that house the majority of urban dwellers?

"My work seeks to enhance our knowledge of the complexity and interrelated nature of urban planning, management, and implementation and to demonstrate the need for and utility of an integrated trans-sectoral human settlements approach to policy-making and planning actions. When completed, the work will provide an appraisal of the achievements, failures, and prospects of management and plan implementation in Third World cities.

"The International Centre for Human Settlement Studies and Urban Development, which I am actively engaged in formulating, is conceived as an academic, research, and teaching center within an established school, directly concerned with the interdisciplinary study of development planning and implementation problems faced by human settlements, in a national and international perspective, and the education and training of specially qualified personnel to deal with these problems.

"The center's activities would be conducted within an overall perspective of human settlement development, namely an integrated approach to the implementation of settlement planning. The subject areas of research and teaching would include global review of human settlements, national settlement policies and strategies, land, shelter, infra-structure and services, institutions, finance, management, public participation, aid and the role of multilateral agencies, the upgrading of slums and squatter areas, planning, design, and development of human settlements.''

*   *   *

BLANCH, Stuart Yarworth   1918-

PERSONAL: Born February 2, 1918, in Blakeney, Gloucestershire, England; son of William Edwin (a farmer) and Elizabeth Blanch; married Brenda Coyte; children: Susan, Hilary, Angela Blanch Ambrose, Timothy, Alison. *Education:* Attended Alleyns School, London, England; St. Catherine's College and Wycliffe Hall, Oxford, B.A. (with first class honors), 1948, M.A., 1952. *Home:* Bishopthorpe, York YO2 1QE, England.

CAREER: Ordained priest in the Church of England, 1950; associated with Law Fire Insurance Society Ltd., London, England, 1936-40; curate in Diocese of Oxford, England, 1949-52; vicar of Eynsham in Diocese of Oxford, 1952-57; vice-principal of Wycliffe Hall, Oxford, 1957-60; oriel canon of Rochester Cathedral and warden of Rochester Theological College, Rochester, England, 1960-66; bishop of Liverpool, England, 1966-75; archbishop of York, England, and primate of England and Metropolitan, 1975—. Member of House of Lords, 1972—, member of Privy Council, 1975. Member of council of University of Liverpool, 1966-75; prochancellor of University of Hull, 1975—; member of council of University of York, 1967—, prochancellor, 1977—; chairman of Wycliffe Hall Theological College, Oxford. *Military service:* Royal Air Force, navigator, 1940-46. *Member:* Royal Commonwealth Society. *Awards, honors:* LL.D. from University of Liverpool, 1975; D.D. from University of Hull, 1977, and Wycliffe College, Toronto, Ontario, 1979; honorary doctorate from University of York, 1979.

WRITINGS: The World Our Orphanage, Epworth, 1972; *For All Mankind,* J. Murray, 1976; *The Christian Militant,* Society for Promoting Christian Knowledge, 1978; *The Burning Bush,* Lutterworth, 1978; *The Trumpet in the Morning,* Hodder & Stoughton, 1979; *The Ten Commandments,* Hodder & Stoughton, 1981; *Living by Faith,* Darton, Longman & Todd, 1983.

*   *   *

BLAND, Alexander
See GOSLING, Nigel

*   *   *

BLAND, Jeffrey   1946-

PERSONAL: Born March 21, 1946, in Peoria, Ill.; son of Stewart B. (a controller) and Marjorie (Morsman) Bland; married Pamela Manley (a company president), June 17, 1967; children: Kelly (son), Kyle. *Education:* University of California, Irvine, B.S., 1967; University of Oregon, Ph.D., 1971. *Agent:* Mary Batterson, 15613 Bellevue-Redmond Rd., Bellevue, Wash. 98008. *Office:* Department of Chemistry, University of Puget Sound, Tacoma, Wash. 98416.

CAREER: University of Puget Sound, Tacoma, Wash., assistant professor, 1971-75, associate professor, 1975-79, professor of biochemistry, 1979—. Director of Bellevue Redmond Medical Laboratory, Seattle, Wash., 1975—; president of Northwest Diagnostic Services, 1979—. *Member:* International Academy of Preventive Medicine, American Chemical Society, American Association for Clinical Chemistry, American Academy for Clinical Biochemistry, Northwest Academy of Preventive Medicine (president).

WRITINGS: *Recent Progress in Human Nutrition,* Mosby, 1981; *Nutritional Elements of Clinical Biochemistry,* Plenum, 1981; *Your Health Under Siege: Using Nutrition to Fight Back,* Stephen Green, 1981.

WORK IN PROGRESS: *Environmental Ethics,* publication by Stephen Green; *Preventive Medicine and the Western Health Care Delivery System.*

SIDELIGHTS: Bland wrote: "Ten years of teaching environmental science, biochemistry, ethics, and nutrition and a year of lecturing nationally have allowed me a broad-based interest in health, lifestyle, and social design."

*   *   *

BLATHWAYT, Jean 1918-

PERSONAL: Born in 1918 in Melbury Osmund, Dorset, England. *Education:* Attended St. Mary's School, Caine, Wiltshire, England, and Welgarth Nursery Training College. *Home:* 9 East Terrace, Budleigh Salterton, Devonshire, England.

CAREER: Children's nurse and nursery school teacher in Gloucestershire, England, 1939-70; co-owner of small residential nursery home, 1939-50; author of children's books.

WRITINGS—Juveniles: *Uncle Paul's House,* Lutterworth, 1957; *The Well Cabin,* Lutterworth, 1957; *Jenny Leads the Way,* Lutterworth, 1958; *Jo's Neighbours,* Lutterworth, 1958; *The Beach People,* Lutterworth, 1960; *The Mushroom Girl* (illustrated by Lilian Buchanan), Warne, 1960; *The Fisherman's Little Girl,* Lutterworth, 1961; *Peter's Adventure,* Lutterworth, 1961; *On the Run for Home* (illustrated by Philip Gough), Macdonald & Co., 1965; *House of Shadows* (illustrated by Laszlo Acs), Macdonald & Co., 1967; *Lucy's Brownie Road* (illustrated by Lynette Hemmant), Brockhampton Press, 1970; *River in the Hills* (illustrated by Hemmant), Epworth, 1971; *Lucy's Last Brownie Challenge* (illustrated by Hemmant), Brockhampton Press, 1972.

Also contributor of articles to Girl Guide publications.

AVOCATIONAL INTERESTS: Youth work, music, natural history.

BIOGRAPHICAL/CRITICAL SOURCES: *Times Literary Supplement,* December 9, 1965, May 25, 1967; *Punch,* December 15, 1965.*

*   *   *

BLAU, Francine D(ee) 1946-

PERSONAL: Born August 29, 1946, in New York, N.Y.; daughter of Harold (an educator) and Sylvia (Goldberg) Blau; married Richard Weisskoff, August, 1969 (divorced, June, 1972); married Lawrence Kahn (a college professor), January 1, 1979; children: (second marriage) Daniel Blau, Lisa Blau. *Education:* Cornell University, B.S., 1966; Harvard University, M.A., 1969, Ph.D., 1975. *Residence:* Urbana, Ill. *Office:* Institute of Labor and Industrial Relations, University of Illinois, 504 East Armory Ave., Champaign, Ill. 61820.

CAREER: Yale University, New Haven, Conn., visiting lecturer in economics, spring, 1971; Trinity College, Hartford, Conn., instructor in economics, 1971-74; Ohio State University, Columbus, research associate at Center for Human Resource Research, 1974-75; University of Illinois, Champaign-Urbana, assistant professor, 1975-78, associate professor of economics and labor and industrial relations, 1978—. Testified before New York City Human Rights Commission; consultant to U.S. Commission on Civil Rights, Equal Employment Op-

portunity Commission, and Agency for International Development. *Member:* American Economic Association, Phi Kappa Phi, Pi Gamma Mu, Pi Delta Epsilon. *Awards, honors:* Grants from U.S. Department of Labor's Employment and Training Administration, 1977-78, 1979-80.

WRITINGS: (With Adele Simmons, Ann Freedman, and Margaret Dunkle) *Exploitation From Nine to Five: Report of the Twentieth Century Fund Task Force on Women and Employment,* Lexington Books, 1975; *Pay Differentials and Differences in the Distribution of Employment of Male and Female Office Workers,* Manpower Administration, U.S. Department of Labor, 1975; *Equal Pay in the Office,* Lexington Books, 1977; (with husband, Lawrence Kahn) *Race and Sex Differences in the Probability and Consequences of Turnover,* Employment and Training Administration, U.S. Department of Labor, 1979.

Contributor: H. Jon Rosenbaum and William Tyler, editors, *Contemporary Brazil: Issues in Economic and Political Development,* Praeger, 1972; Richard C. Edwards, Michael Reich, and David M. Gordon, editors, *Labor Market Segmentation,* Lexington Books, 1975; Herbert S. Parnes and other editors, *Dual Careers: A Longitudinal Study of the Labor Market Experience of Women,* Volume IV, U.S. Government Printing Office, 1976; Nona Glazer and Helen Youngelson Waehrer, editors, *Woman in a Man-Made World: A Socioeconomic Reader,* 2nd edition (Blau was not included in 1st edition), Rand McNally, 1977; Naomi Berger Davidson, editor, *Supplementary Papers From the Conference on Youth Unemployment: Its Measurement and Meaning,* Employment and Training Administration, U.S. Department of Labor, 1978; Isabel Sawhill, editor, *Women's Changing Roles at Home and on the Job,* National Commission on Manpower Policy, 1978; Ann Stromberg and Shirley Harkness, editors, *Women and Their Work,* Mayfield, 1978; Joe Freeman, editor, *Women: A Feminist Perspective,* 2nd edition, Mayfield, 1979.

Contributor of more than a dozen articles and reviews to economic and women's studies journals. Member of editorial board of *Social Science Quarterly,* 1978—, and *Signs: Journal of Women in Culture and Society,* 1979—.

WORK IN PROGRESS: Research on the economic impact of immigration, the economic consequences of the growth of the "two-earner" family, job turnover, and the impact of shifting participation patterns on consumption.

SIDELIGHTS: Blau told *CA:* "An important motivating factor in much of my research has been a desire to better understand the causes of sex and race inequalities in the economy. Such an understanding is crucial to the formulation of social policies that can lessen these inequities."

*   *   *

BLEVINS, James Lowell 1936-

PERSONAL: Born August 25, 1936, in Hot Coal, W.Va.; son of James Franklin (a carpenter) and Lona Marie (a secretary; maiden name, Maxie) Blevins; married Maxine Ruth Benson (a secretary), August 26, 1961; children: Jennifer, Cynthia, James. *Education:* Duke University, A.B., 1958; Eastern Baptist Seminary, B.D., 1961; Southeastern Baptist Seminary, Th.M., 1962; Southern Baptist Seminary, Ph.D., 1965; also attended University of Hamburg, University of Tuebingen, University of Marburg, and University of Goettingen. *Home:* 4412 Deepwood Dr., Louisville, Ky. 40222. *Office:* Department of New Testament, Southern Baptist Theological Seminary, 2825 Lexington Rd., Louisville, Ky. 40206.

CAREER: Ordained Southern Baptist minister, 1961; Southern Baptist Theological Seminary, Louisville, Ky., instructor in New Testament, 1963-68; pastor of Southern Baptist church in Arlington, Va., 1968-69; Mars Hill College, Mars Hill, N.C., associate professor, 1969-73, professor of religion, 1973-76; Southern Baptist Theological Seminary, professor of New Testament, 1976—. *Member:* Society of Biblical Literature, Association of Baptist Professors of Religion.

WRITINGS: (Translator) Eckhardt Otto and Tim Schramm, *Festival and Joy,* Abingdon, 1980; (translator) Siegfried Hermann, *Time and History,* Abingdon, 1981; *The Messianic Secret in Markan Research, 1901-1976,* University Press of America, 1981. Writer for Baptist Sunday School Board. Member of board of editors of *Perspectives in Religious Studies,* 1974—, and *Review and Expositor.*

WORK IN PROGRESS: A commentary on the book of Revelation, publication by Broadman expected in 1983.

SIDELIGHTS: Blevins leads annual study tours to the Middle East, visiting Egypt, Jordan, Israel, Turkey, and Greece. He plans to dramatize the book of Revelation on location in Ephesus.

*   *   *

BLINDER, Elliot 1949-
(Asa Elliot)

PERSONAL: Born April 2, 1949, in New York; married Catherine Marriott, June 2, 1974 (divorced, 1977); married wife, Ellen Michelle (a real estate broker), June 12, 1978; children: Amos, Lolita. *Education:* Boston University, B.A., 1969. *Religion:* Jewish (Orthodox).

CAREER: Le Cronique, Boston, Mass., editor in chief, 1969-70; Tree Frog Workshop, Guilford, Vt., writer-in-residence, 1970-72; proprietor of Home Comfort Restaurant, 1972-75; real estate broker in Palm Springs, Calif., 1975—.

WRITINGS: (Under pseudonym Asa Elliot; with Peter Simon) *Bloom Highway* (photography), Delacorte, 1973; *Home Comfort,* Simon & Schuster, 1974; *More Home Comfort,* Simon & Schuster, 1975; *Waitress From Home Comfort,* Delacorte, 1975.

*   *   *

BLOCH, Barbara 1925-
(Phoebe Edwards)

PERSONAL: Born May 26, 1925, in New York, N.Y.; daughter of Emil William (a stockbroker) and Dorothy (a bacteriologist and executive administrator; maiden name, Lowengrund) Bloch; married Joseph Bennet Sanders, August 3, 1944 (divorced January 4, 1961); married Theodore Simon Benjamin (a publisher), September 20, 1964; children: (first marriage) Elizabeth Sanders-Hines, Ellen; (stepchildren from second marriage) Phyllis, Jill. *Education:* Attended New York University and New School for Social Research; courses with American Symphony Orchestra League. *Politics:* Democrat. *Religion:* "Jewish/Humanist by affiliation." *Home and office:* International Cookbook Services, 21 Dupont Ave., White Plains, N.Y. 10605.

CAREER: Westchester Democratic County Committee, White Plains, N.Y., office manager, 1955-56; Westchester Symphony Orchestra, Scarsdale, N.Y., manager, 1957-62; P. K. Halstead Associates, Larchmont, N.Y., assistant to president, 1962-63; Active Employment Service, White Plains, office manager, 1963-65; free-lance editorial assignments, Rutledge

Books, New York, N.Y., 1965-78; International Cookbook Services, White Plains, president, 1978—.

WRITINGS: (Under pseudonym Phoebe Edwards) *Anyone Can Quilt,* Benjamin Co., 1975; *The Meat Board Meat Book,* introduction by Julia Child, McGraw, 1977; *If It Doesn't Pan Out: How to Cope With Cooking Disasters* (selection of Book-of-the-Month Cooking and Craft Club), Dembner, 1981.

Editor: (And contributor) *The All Beef Cookbook,* Scribner, 1973; (and contributor) Anne Borella, *In Glass Naturally,* Benjamin Co., 1974; *Microwave Miracles,* Rutledge/Benjamin, 1974; (and contributor) *Fresh Ideas With Mushrooms,* Benjamin Co., 1977; *Good Food Ideas Cheese Cookbook,* Benjamin Co., 1977; *Polly-O Cooking With Cheese,* Polly-O Cheese Co., 1977; *Cook's Choice,* Benjamin Co., 1979; *Yesterday and Today, From the Kitchens of Stokely,* Benjamin, 1980; *The Sun Maid Cookbook,* Benjamin Co., 1980; *The Any Oven Cookbook,* Benjamin Co., 1981; *Ovenware of the Future Cookbook,* Benjamin Co., 1981; *Twelve Cookbooks,* Octopus, 1980; *Favorite Family Baking,* Meredith Corp., 1982-83; *Any Way You Make It,* Benjamin Co., 1982.

WORK IN PROGRESS: "Americanizing" a second baking book for Better Homes and Gardens, ten cookbooks for Octopus, and a cookbook series for Marshall Cavendish; a French cookbook for Larousse.

SIDELIGHTS: Bloch told *CA:* "Outside of my family and career, my main interests have been classical music, liberal politics, and young people. My interest in travel did not develop until I could afford it, and my interest in food did not develop until my second marriage, when I found I had a husband who enjoyed eating good food.

"I became a full-time writer, editor, and teacher about ten years ago when I decided I could not sit through another meeting, or listen to the reading of the minutes of the previous meeting. It was also the time at which I concluded my four daughters no longer needed a full-time mother, a concept from which very few of us had been liberated at that time.

"Although I have always specialized in cookbooks, in recent years I have added another specialty—that of Americanizing cookbooks. Both English and American publishers are finally coming to the realization that, although we speak the same language over the dinner table, we do not speak the same language in the kitchen. It is a specialty that has developed into a surprisingly successful business.

"I have been a guest on several radio and television programs, and I lecture periodically. I have also taught cooking classes and love teaching, although I no longer have the time to include it in my schedule.

"The number of poorly written cookbooks published every year distresses me. Too often, books are written by people who seem to be good cooks, but do not understand the demands of proper cookbook writing—and evidently there are not enough good cookbook editors around to make proper judgments. Cookbooks should be written carefully and clearly, and the recipes should be completely reliable—both food and time are too expensive to waste on improperly written recipes. However, in spite of the fact that I take the writing of a cookbook very seriously, my advice for most people who cook is 'relax.' People who make a fetish of food and cooking make me uncomfortable.

"I have always had an enormous urge to be creative. Having finally acknowledged that I could not act, paint, or make music, I have found a satisfying creative outlet in the combination of cooking and writing."

BLOCK, Julian 1934-

PERSONAL: Born July 8, 1934, in Chicago, Ill.; son of Nathan (a grocer) and Ruth (a grocer; maiden name, Rubinstein) Block; married Zelda Miller, August 23, 1964; children: Robert Jeremy, Nadine Ellen. *Education:* Attended Theodore Herzl Junior College, 1952-53; Roosevelt University, B.S.C., 1956; DePaul University, J.D., 1962; New York University, LL.M., 1969. *Politics:* Democrat. *Religion:* Jewish. *Office:* Research Institute of America, 589 Fifth Ave., New York, N.Y. 10017.

CAREER: Formerly associated with Internal Revenue Service, Washington, D.C.; Research Institute of America, New York, N.Y., managing editor of *Recommendations,* 1973—. *Military service:* U.S. Army, 1956-57. *Member:* American Society of Journalists and Authors, New York State Bar Association.

WRITINGS: Tax Saving: A Year-Round Guide, Chilton, 1981, revised edition, 1982. Author of columns "Taxes," in *Vogue,* 1977, "Taxes and You," in *Electrical Contractor,* 1978, "Taxes," in *American Bookseller,* 1979 and "Tax Q & A," in *Dental Economics,* 1980.

SIDELIGHTS: Block told *CA:* "I started out as an IRS agent but switched sides to show people legal ways to avoid taxes. When I'm not doing that, I cope with my own tax problems and opportunities, which center on three dependents and a home."

BIOGRAPHICAL/CRITICAL SOURCES: U.S. News and World Report, June 1, 1981.

*   *   *

BLOCK, Marvin Avram 1903-

PERSONAL: Born January 11, 1903, in Buffalo, N.Y.; son of Robert and Sarah (Sernoffsky) Block; married Lillian Kevitt, November 29, 1933 (died, 1981). *Education:* State University of New York at Buffalo, B.S., 1923, M.D., 1925; postdoctoral study at University of London, University of Paris, University of Berlin, and University of Vienna. *Religion:* Jewish. *Home:* 371 Linwood Ave., Buffalo, N.Y. 14209. *Agent:* McIntosh & Otis, Inc., 475 Fifth Ave., New York, N.Y. 10017.

CAREER: Associated with Buffalo General Hospital, 1924-25, and Buffalo City Hospital, 1925-26; State University of New York at Buffalo, instructor, 1927-29, assistant professor, 1929, associate professor of clinical medicine, 1949-73, professor emeritus, 1973—. Adjunct professor at Clifford Furnas College, 1975-80. Past vice-president of National Council on Alcoholism, and member of board of directors; founder and past president of New York State Council of Committees on Alcoholism; past president of Buffalo Area Council on Alcoholism, and member of board of directors. Member of board of directors of Harmony Foundation, Buffalo Council on World Affairs, E. M. Jellinek Memorial Fund, International Institute on Alcohol and Alcoholism, Meyer Memorial Hospital, Rosa Coplon Jewish Home and Infirmary, Travelers' Aid Society, Buffalo and Erie County Library, Buffalo and Erie County Community Chest, Jewish Federation for Social Service, and Erie County Community Welfare Council. Member of advisory board of New York State Department of Health advisory committee on narcotics, New York State Interagency Council, and National Institute on Alcoholism and Alcohol Abuse. Member of American Jewish Physicians Committee, American Jewish Committee, American Red Mogen David for Israel, Zionist Organization of America, American National Red Cross, American Education Foundation, Buffalo Fine Arts Academy,

Buffalo Philharmonic Orchestra Society, and Buffalo Chamber Music Society. Consultant to National Institute of Mental Health and National Congress of Parents and Teachers.

MEMBER: International Platform Association, International Narcotics Enforcement Officers Association, World Medical Association, North American Association of Alcoholism Programs, American Medical Association (chairman of committee on alcoholism, 1954-64), American Medical Society on Alcoholism (past president; member of board of directors), Academy of Psychosomatic Medicine (fellow), American Association for the Advancement of Science, American Academy of Political and Social Science, Association of American Medical Colleges, American Public Health Association, American Geriatrics Society, Wisdom Society, British Society for the Study of Addiction, Medical Society of the State of New York (chairman of committee on alcoholism and drug abuse, 1959-68; chairman of physicians committee), New York State Public Health Association, New York State Society for Medical Research, New York State Association of the Professions, Erie County Medical Society (past chairman of committee on alcoholism), Erie County Mental Health Association, Erie County Society for the Prevention of Cruelty to Animals, Buffalo Academy of Medicine, Maimonides Medical Society, Salvation Army Association, B'nai B'rith, Montefiore Club of Buffalo, Westwood Country Club, Automobile Club of Buffalo, Alumni Association of the University of Buffalo.

AWARDS, HONORS: M & R National Award from American Academy of General Practice, 1953; outstanding citizen award from *Buffalo Evening News,* 1955; Lane Bryant citation, 1958, for outstanding community service; citation of merit from Malvern Institute, 1964, for service to problems of alcoholism; Wisdom Award of Honor from Wisdom Society, 1966, for service to alcoholics; medal of achievement from American Medical Society on Alcoholism, 1972, for outstanding achievement on alcoholism; fellow of Clifford C. Furnas College, 1973.

WRITINGS: Alcoholism: Its Facets and Phases, John Day, 1965; *Alcohol and Alcoholism: Modern Treatment,* Harper, 1966; *Alcohol and Alcoholism: Drinking and Dependence,* Wadsworth, 1970; *Modern Treatment of Alcoholism,* Harcourt, 1972; *Motivating the Alcoholic Patient,* Grune, 1980. Contributor to medical journals. Member of editorial board of *Group Medicine* and *Encyclopedia of Problems of Alcohol.*

WORK IN PROGRESS: Alcoholism Is a Disease—Do You Believe It?

SIDELIGHTS: Block told *CA:* "During the early years of my medical practice I encountered innumerable cases of what were called 'geographic abdomens.' They were so named because of the number of surgical procedures perpetrated upon patients whose abdominal scars resembled roadmaps. Upon exhaustive questioning and investigation, I found that all too many of these patients had focused their emotional and psychological problems on their abdominal organs. Before the days of utilization and tissue committees, such repeated surgical procedures were not uncommon.

"Throughout my entire medical career I have been fascinated by the relationship of the body and mind—psychosomatic problems. After several years of practicing internal medicine, I was challenged by a colleague, who had recovered from alcoholism through Alcoholics Anonymous, to look into the matter of alcoholism—a much neglected area. Upon his urging, we formed the first committee on alcoholism of a medical society. This was in Erie County of New York State. In the 1940's, as its first chairman, I undertook to interest physicians in this problem. After a few years I urged the New York State Medical Society to form a similar committee. In 1953 I was able to convince the American Medical Association that a committee on alcoholism would help bring to the attention of the country's physicians the necessity for treating a large neglected segment of the population afflicted with this illness. As a result, I was appointed chairman of a subcommittee on alcoholism of the Committee of Mental Health. Later, when the Mental Health Committee was raised to council status, we became a full committee on alcoholism, on which I served as chairman for the following ten years.

"In 1956, as a result of our committee's work, the American Medical Association specifically designated alcoholism as a disease which properly falls within the purview of medical practice. This was the first time that any illness had to be so designated. It marked a milestone as far as alcoholism was concerned. The progress of the work of our committee was not without resistance. With this in mind, I began to write on the subject of alcoholism in an effort to educate not only the medical profession but lay people as well. The vast majority of alcoholics in our population were unaware that they were suffering from this disease and would deny it if so advised. In my opinion, this situation still prevails.

"Although there were many physicians in the past who had interested themselves in the problem of alcoholism, the 1950's were the first time that the organized profession as a whole lent its prestige and energy to convincing everyone that alcoholism was indeed a tremendous health problem and should be the physicians' concern. Since then, of course, physicians as well as other professionals have engaged in efforts to help alcoholic patients. Much in the way of funds, both private and public, have been made available for helping in this effort. From the sparse writings on the subject in the 1950's, there is now a plethora of literature on the subject.

"A great deal, however, has yet to be done. The answer to the problem will not only lie in treating such patients. The eradication of the problem will succeed only if extensive preventive measures are instituted. This will necessitate a change of basic attitudes and environment, so that it will not be necessary for so many to depend upon outside vectors for stabilizing their lives. The education of young people on how to expect and encounter the realities of living in a more mature way will help accomplish this goal."

*   *   *

BLOND, Anthony 1928-

PERSONAL: Born March 20, 1928, in Sale, England; son of Neville Blond Laski (a philanthropist) and Reba (a decorator; maiden name, Nahum) Blond; married Laura Hesketh (a diarist), March 1, 1981; children: Aaron Angelo Lindsay. *Education:* New College, Oxford, M.A. (with honors), 1951. *Politics:* Radical. *Religion:* Jewish. *Home:* 36 Chester Row, London, S.W.1, England; and 622 Greenwich St., Apt. 3C, New York, N.Y. 10014. *Agent:* Curtis Brown Ltd., 575 Madison Ave., New York, N.Y. 10022. *Office:* Blond & Briggs Ltd., 8 Alexandra Rd., London SW19 7JU, England.

CAREER: Worked as literary agent, 1951-57; associated with Anthony Blond Ltd., 1957-71; Blond & Briggs Ltd. (publisher), London, England, director, 1971—. Member of board of directors of *Pressdram* (title means "Private Eye"), 1969—, GMIR-Picadilly Radio, 1971—, and Frederick Muller (publisher), 1979—. Sponsor and member of board of trustees of Cobden Trust (for civil liberties). *Military service:* British Army, Royal Artillery, 1948; became second lieutenant. *Member:* Coffee House Club (New York City), Reform Club (London).

WRITINGS: The Publishing Game, J. Cape, 1971; *Family Business* (novel), Harper, 1978; *The Lord My Light* (novel), Deutsch, 1982; *A Book on Books* (nonfiction), J. Cape, 1983. Contributor to London newspapers and journals, including *Spectator.*

WORK IN PROGRESS: "Paul in Rome," a play.

AVOCATIONAL INTERESTS: Travel (including Sri Lanka and Jerusalem), talking, walking, eating, drinking, publishing, converting Christians.

*   *   *

BLOTNICK, Elihu 1939-

PERSONAL: Born December 2, 1939, in New York, N.Y.; son of Hyman and Eva (Stein) Blotnick; married Esther Blank (marriage ended); married Nancy Sue Graham, January, 1976 (marriage ended); *Education:* City College of the City University of New York, B.A., 1962; also attended Brooklyn College of the City University of New York, New York University, New School for Social Research, San Francisco State University, and University of California, Berkeley. *Residence:* Berkeley, Calif. *Office:* 723 Dwight Way, Berkeley, Calif. 94710.

CAREER: BBM Associates (photography agency, publishing company, and production group), Berkeley, Calif., director, 1969-75. Staff photographer for *Ramparts,* 1971; project photographer for Field Educational Publications, 1972, and Addison-Wesley Publishing Co., Inc., 1974-75. Work exhibited in international traveling exhibit, "People's Park." *Awards, honors:* Awards of excellence for learning material from American Institute of Graphic Arts, 1972, for Field Math Series; awards from Bookbuilder's West, *Communication Arts,* and Art Direction/Creativity '75, 1975, all for *Saltwater Flats.*

WRITINGS—With own photographs: *Saltwater Flats,* BBM Associates, 1975; (with Barbara Robinson) *The Flag Book: Fireworks,* BBM Associates, 1976; *Never Distrust an Asparagus,* California Street, 1977; *Mysterious Mr. Blot,* California Street, 1979; *Chants of the Hokapot Clan,* California Street, 1980; *California Street Number One,* California Street, 1980; *Blue Turtle Moon Queen,* California Street, 1980. Contributor of articles, poems, and photographs to magazines, including *Minnesota Review* and *Esquire.*

WORK IN PROGRESS: A novel, *The Ghost of Teac Nos Pos;* A journal, *Rio Arriba;* an art book, *Artista: Art-Gang-Art.*

SIDELIGHTS: Blotnick commented: "I like subtlety, perhaps to distraction. In *Saltwater Flats,* I tried to create the emotional backbone of a novel, with only seven pages of words and not a plot in sight. There were fifty-two photographs, however, in counterpoint. In *The Flag Book,* I tried to reach a new integration, personally, politically, aesthetically. Putting photographs together is like stringing beads in a straight line. Ultimately, they web. Words, too, have visual form. If I had a choice, I'd be a different typeface every year. Now I'm at a turning point, wanting to define art before I continue writing articles for the local press, trying to discipline and purify my writing before I make the larger leap into noveldom, if indeed magically there is such a place."

AVOCATIONAL INTERESTS: Travel (Norway, Thailand, India, Mexico, Japan).

*   *   *

BLUMENTHAL, Sidney 1909-

PERSONAL: Born June 24, 1909, in New York, N.Y.; son of

Jacob and Lena (Uhran) Blumenthal; married Elaine Levy, April 4, 1953; children: Patricia (Mrs. Gilbert Schedler), Peggy. *Education:* University of Iowa, B.S., 1930, M.D., 1933. *Home:* 50 East 89th St., No. 20A, New York, N.Y. 10028. *Office:* School of Medicine, University of Miami, Coral Gables, Fla. 33152.

CAREER: Milwaukee Children's Hospital, Milwaukee, Wis., intern, 1933-34; Mount Sinai Hospital, New York City, resident, 1934-36; private practice of pediatrics in New York City, 1936-50; Mount Sinai Hospital, director of pediatric cardiology, 1950-58; Babies Hospital, New York City, director of pediatric cardiology, 1955-70; University of Miami, Coral Gables, Fla., professor of pediatric cardiology and dean of postgraduate medical education, 1970-75; associated with National Institutes of Health, beginning in 1975. Diplomate of American Board of Pediatrics. Professor at Columbia University, 1959-70; visiting professor at National Taiwan University, 1964. *Military service:* U.S. Army, Medical Corps, 1942-45; became lieutenant colonel; received Bronze Star. *Member:* Alpha Omega Alpha.

WRITINGS: The Permanent Campaign, Beacon Press, 1980.

*   *   *

BLUMING, Mildred G. 1919-

PERSONAL: Born March 29, 1919, in New York, N.Y.; daughter of Abraham H. Goodblatt (a rabbi); married Hy C. Bluming (an investment counselor), November 27, 1937; children: Avrum Z., Rebecca Bluming Sobol. *Education:* Columbia University, B.S., 1957; University of Southern California, M.S., 1969; graduate study at University of California at Los Angeles, 1973. *Religion:* "Hebrew." *Home:* 3416 Ione Dr., Hollywood, Calif. 90068.

CAREER: Los Angeles City Unified Schools, Los Angeles, Calif., teacher, consultant, adviser, and psychologist, beginning in 1961. *Member:* Association of Women in Education (honorary member).

WRITINGS: (With Myron Dembo) *Solving Teaching Problems,* Goodyear Publishing, 1973; *Individualizing Early Childhood Education,* Career-Aids, 1975. Author of filmstrip, "A Day in a Children's Center." Contributor of articles to educational journals.

*   *   *

BLUTH, B(etty) J(ean) 1934-

PERSONAL: Born December 5, 1934, in Philadelphia, Pa.; daughter of Robert Thomas (a realtor) and Catherine (a model; maiden name, Boxman) Gowland; married Thomas Del Bluth, August 20, 1960 (deceased); children: Robert, Richard. *Education:* Bucknell University, B.A. (cum laude), 1957; Fordham University, M.A., 1960; University of California, Los Angeles, Ph.D., 1970. *Residence:* Granada Hills, Calif. *Office:* Department of Sociology, California State University, Northridge, Calif. 91321.

CAREER: Reading Laboratory, Philadelphia, Pa., instructor, 1958-59; high school teacher of history, civics, and English in San Diego, Calif., 1959-60; Immaculate Heart College, Los Angeles, Calif., instructor, 1960-63; assistant professor of sociology, 1963-65; California State University, Northridge, assistant professor, 1965-75, associate professor, 1975-79, professor of sociology, 1979—, fellow at Institute for the Advancement of Teaching and Learning, 1974. Member of United Nations team on the relevance of space activities to

economic and social development; member of Citizens Advisory Council on National Space Policy; member of board of directors of Space Cadets of America and World Space Federation; public speaker.

MEMBER: International Academy of Astronautics, American Sociological Association, American Institution of Aeronautics and Astronautics, American Astronautical Society, American Society for Aerospace Education, Institute for the Social Science Study of Space (member of academic advisory board), Space Studies Institute, Air Force Association, L-5 Society, British Interplanetary Society, Phi Beta Kappa. *Awards, honors:* Teaching award from Alpha Omega, 1966, 1974; certificate of appreciation from American Astronautical Society, 1978, for "The SMD III and Spacelab Simulation: A Critical Look"; grants from Rockwell International Corp., TRW, Inc., and Lockheed Corp., 1978-80; certificate of appreciation from Society of American Military Engineers, 1980, for presentation "Social and Psychological Aspects of Long Duration Space Flight"; special program award from Los Angeles section of American Institution of Aeronautics and Astronautics, 1980, for "An Evening With Krafft Ehricke."

WRITINGS: (Editor with Robert Chianese, James Kellenberger, and others) *Search for Identity Reader,* Xerox College Publishing, 1973; (with John Irving, Sherry May, and Dick Smith) *Search for Community Reader,* Xerox College Publishing, 1977; (contributor) Richard Johnson and other editors, *The Future of the U.S. Space Program: Advances in the Astronautical Sciences,* Univelt, Volume XXXVI, Part II, 1979, Volume XXXVIII, Part II, 1979; (contributor) Stan Kent, editor, *Remember the Future: The Apollo Legacy,* Univelt, 1979; (editor with S. R. McNeal) *Update on Space,* Behavior Systems, Volume I, 1981, Volume II, 1982; (contributor) Stephen Cheston, editor, *NASA Guide for Teaching and Student Research,* Georgetown University, 1981. Contributor to scientific and sociology journals.

WORK IN PROGRESS: Research on Soviet and U.S. social and psychological aspects of long-duration space flight, techniques of stress reduction, and women in space.

SIDELIGHTS: Bluth commented: "Being involved with mankind's evolution into space is a distinctly exciting and challenging enterprise—worth a life. Unlike those at the departure of Columbus, we are able to participate in the momentous changes to come as a result of the exploration and habitation of space, because we can anticipate their importance. By moving off-planet, humanity will probably grow and change far beyond our present imagination, and I hope to do all I can to be part of and help others be part of that change."

*   *   *

BOASE, Wendy 1944-

PERSONAL: Surname rhymes with "rose"; born October 14, 1944, in Melbourne, Australia; daughter of Cecil Branwell (a store manager) and Daisy (Devine) Boase; married John Vigurs (a book designer), May 25, 1979. *Education:* University of New South Wales, B.A. (with honors), 1965. *Home:* 56 Southwold Mansions, Widley Road, London W. 9, England. *Office:* Walker Books, Hanway House, Hanway St., London W. 1, England.

CAREER: Teacher in Wollongong, New South Wales, Australia, 1966-67; London city schools, London, England, teacher, 1968-69; *Reader's Digest,* London, 1970-76, began as secretary, became assistant editor; Marshall Cavendish Ltd., London, editor, 1976-78; Walker Books, London, free-lance children's book editor, 1978—. *Member:* Folklore Society.

WRITINGS: The Folklore of Hampshire and the Isle of Wight, Rowman & Littlefield, 1976; *A Closer Look at Ancient Egypt* (juvenile), illustrations by Angus McBride and Eric Thomas, Hamish Hamilton, 1977, published as *Ancient Egypt,* F. Watts, 1978; *A Closer Look at Early China* (juvenile), illustrations by McBride and Terry Dalley, Hamish Hamilton, 1977, published as *Early China,* F. Watts, 1978; *Grow It for Fun* (juvenile), illustrations by Donald Myall and Gary Hincks, Hamish Hamilton, 1978, published as *Growing Plants and Flowers,* F. Watts, 1980; *The Sky's the Limit: Women Pioneers in Aviation,* Macmillan, 1979.

WORK IN PROGRESS: A series of books for very young children (up to eight years old) dealing with early concepts, both visual and aural.

SIDELIGHTS: Boase told *CA:* "When I was only three years old, my parents left Melbourne, where I was born, to run a general store in a backwoods farming area in northern New South Wales. The store, with a house attached, was a huge, rambling place—ideal for imaginative adventures. It had dark rooms full of molasses, grain, bags of sugar and flour, pickaxes, and shovels. Outside, planted in the dusty, bare earth, two petrol pumps stood like sentinels guarding our weatherboard establishment.

"Ours was the only store for miles around, and although a lot of people came to do business there, my early childhood was a solitary one. With no regular playmates, I invented a 'friend' called Sally. She was so real to me that I would invite her home to supper, insisting to my bewildered mother that another place be set and an extra meal served on such occasions. I made up many stories about our adventures together.

"When I was five, my father attempted to curb my daydreaming by giving me a responsible job. I was to help him with the paper run. He had a motorbike with a sidecar, which made a terrific row and leaked a lot of oil. As we tore by the various farms, I would hurl a paper from the sidecar as hard as I could. Very often it fell in the road. This particular activity was so exciting that it only served as material for further story-making on my part. My mother used to read to me, but the adventures in books never seemed as worthwhile as my own.

"Once I had learned to read for myself, though, I found other people's stories gripping, tantalizing, fascinating. I particularly liked tales that were set in far-off places. I think my love of traveling stemmed from the kinds of stories I read at that young age. Much later, when I had grown up and left home, I traveled right 'round the world, and I still travel whenever I have the chance.

"My own writing is in the nonfiction field, and history is my particular interest. I have always enjoyed reading about the lives people lived in times other than my own. But however familiar I am with a topic I tackle, I still have to research it thoroughly. This means a lot of reading and visits to museums. Sometimes I interview scholars, or, if the period is a recent one, people who have lived at the time of which I wish to write. It is refreshing that so many people are willing to help an author get the facts right. Having had teaching experience helps me a great deal in knowing what kind of approach to use and how to express myself. Working now as an editor of children's books also gives me some insight into the kinds of books children enjoy, the language they appreciate, and the illustrations they like.

"As I write in my 'spare' time, I have to work to a strict and disciplined schedule. When I begin a book, I estimate the time I need for research and then calculate carefully the time I need for writing. Sometimes I have to take a 'holiday' so I can research full time, and thereafter I read on the train going to and from work, in the evening, on the weekends—any free moment I can find. I may spend months researching and thinking—much more time than it takes to write the book. When I finally sit at my typewriter, I have the approach and ideas clearly in my head. I type one draft fairly quickly. This means coming home from work and writing most evenings as well as on the weekends. Then I sit back and rest for a week or so. Next, I correct the first draft, checking the facts as I go and trying to make sure that the prose is interesting and meaningful, but exact. Then retyping begins, and again in text receives my undivided attention until it is complete. I always need another holiday when I finish a book!''

*   *   *

BODART, Joni 1947-

PERSONAL: Surname is pronounced Bo-dar; born December 16, 1947, in Winchester, Va.; daughter of Albin J.J. (an income tax consultant) and Frances (a high school English teacher; maiden name, Higginbotham) Bodart. *Education:* Texas Woman's University, B.A. and B.S.., both 1969, M.L.S., 1971, M.A., 1982, Ph.D., 1983. *Politics:* Democrat. *Religion:* Presbyterian. *Home:* 713 Woodland, Denton, Tex. 76201.

CAREER: Albuquerque Public Library, Albuquerque, N.M., children's librarian and assistant branch head, 1969-70; Santa Rosa-Sonoma County Public Library, Santa Rosa, Calif., young adult and reference librarian, 1971-73; Alameda County Public Library, Fremont Main Library, Fremont, Calif., young adult librarian, 1973-78; Stanislaus County Free Library, Modesto, Calif., young adult librarian, 1978-79; writer, 1979—, Pergamon Press, Elmsford, N.Y., library consultant, 1981—. Teaching assistant. Gives workshops and lectures. *Member:* American Library Association (chairperson of Young Adult Services Division best books committee, 1980-81), Bay Area Young Adult Librarians (past president).

WRITINGS: Booktalk!: Booktalking and School Visiting for Young Adults, H. W. Wilson, 1980. Author of "Adult Books for Young Adults," a column in *School Library Journal,* 1971-76. Contributor to library journals.

WORK IN PROGRESS: Revising *Booktalk!,* completion expected in 1983; research on a systems theory approach to libraries and organizational development for libraries; research on bibliotherapy with adolescents and families.

SIDELIGHTS: Joni Bodart wrote: "Being a teenager was not easy for me, and I want to use my talents as a librarian and therapist to help others work through their problems as successfully as possible. I would suggest that novices get involved. Don't hestitate to work for your professional organizations, to ask questions, take risks, and care about the people you work with. If you are open with teenagers, they will open up to you—the rewards are worth the work and the risk!

AVOCATIONAL INTERESTS: Reading (especially mystery and science fiction), writing, traveling, movies, music, Oriental cuisine, sport cars, "autocrossing" and rallying, waterskiing, "plus anything else that sounds like it might be fun."

*   *   *

BOK, Derek Curtis 1930-

PERSONAL: Born March 22, 1930, in Bryn Mawr, Pa.; son of Curtis and Margaret Adams (Plummer) Bok; married Sissela Ann Myrdal (a lecturer in medical ethics), 1955; children: Hilary, Victoria, Tomas. *Education:* Stanford University, A.B.,

1951; Harvard University, J.D., 1954; attended University of Paris, 1954-55; George Washington University, A.M., 1958. *Home:* 33 Elmwood Ave., Cambridge, Mass. 02138. *Office:* Office of the President, Harvard University, Massachusetts Hall, Cambridge, Mass. 02138.

CAREER: Harvard University, Cambridge, Mass., assistant professor, 1958-61, professor of law, 1961—, dean of Harvard Law School, 1968-71, president of university, 1971—. Chairman of American Council on Education, 1981-82; member of Commission on Federal Paperwork. *Military service:* U.S. Army, 1956-58; became first lieutenant. *Member:* American Academy of Arts and Sciences, National Endowment for the Humanities, Committee for Economic Development, Consortium on Financing Higher Education, Institute of Medicine. *Awards, honors:* Fulbright scholar in France, 1954-55; A.B. from Harvard University, 1971; LL.D. from University of Illinois, Princeton University, and Yale University, all 1971.

WRITINGS: The First Three Years of the Schuman Plan, Princeton University, 1955; (editor with Archibald Cox) *Cases and Materials on Labor Law,* Foundation Press, 1962; (with John Dunlop) *Labor and the American Community,* Simon & Schuster, 1970; *The Ivory Tower,* Harvard University Press, 1982. Contributor to law journals and *Daedalus.*

SIDELIGHTS: Derek Bok was named the twenty-fifth president of Harvard University in 1971. Chosen after a detailed eleven-month search, he became one of Harvard's youngest presidents and the first head of the University in three hundred years to have earned his undergraduate degree elsewhere. Before his appointment, Bok taught labor and antitrust law at the Harvard Law School for a decade, ascending to the deanship of that school in 1968.

As dean of the law school he distinguished himself as a peacemaker in the turbulent years of student unrest. At one point, first-year law students staged a sit-in demanding that they be graded on a pass/fail system. Supplied with coffee and doughnuts, Bok talked with the demonstrators until early in the morning, when they reached a compromise in which the pass/fail system could be elected by students on an optional basis. Some of Bok's colleagues complimented him on his role as mediator. One professor asserted, "As a dean, he has made our life very good indeed. He is excellent at handling confrontation." Another agreed that Bok "is flexible, imaginative and good at anticipating problems." The dean also instituted a number of other reforms: he revitalized the largely corporate law curriculum offered by Harvard by adding classes on environmental and criminal law; he encouraged recruitment of more black and female students; and he created joint degree programs with the John F. Kennedy School of Government and the Harvard Business School.

Bok's appointment to the Harvard University presidency was due, however, to his reputation, *Newsweek* noted, as "a pragmatic problem solver." In 1969 and 1970 Harvard was racked by student protests. In one demonstration in April, 1969, approximately fifty students gained control of the main administration building on campus, mistreating some deans and rifling through files. Nathan Pusey, the university's president at the time, had police clear the building of the trespassers. The confrontation, called the "Harvard bust," ended in forty-five injuries and almost two hundred arrests. Pusey was criticized for his handling of the affair and soon afterwards announced his early retirement.

The Harvard Corporation, which was responsible for finding a new president, looked for a man who could deal with the particular problems of the late 1960's and early 1970's. Their

search was the most democratic and widespread in Harvard's history. The corporation queried more than two hundred thousand alumni and interviewed faculty members to come up with a list of names of people from a wide range of backgrounds. The corporation finally settled on Bok. After the new president's appointment, a Harvard faculty member explained that the corporation "wanted complete openness and it only makes sense in light of the current scene. But no Harvard president will be again selected like this."

BIOGRAPHICAL/CRITICAL SOURCES: Washington Post, April 29, 1970; *Time,* January 18, 1971, January 25, 1971, July 15, 1974; *Newsweek,* January 18, 1971; *Life,* January 22, 1971; *New York Times Book Review,* May 23, 1982, June 6, 1982.

*   *   *

BONATTI, Walter   1930-

PERSONAL: Born June 22, 1930, in Bergamo, Italy; son of Angelo and Agostina (Appiani) Bonatti; married (separated). *Religion:* Christian. *Home:* Via Gentilino 9/A, Milan, Italy 20136. *Agent:* Agenzia Letteraria Internazionale Milano, via Manzoni 41, Milan, Italy 20121.

CAREER: Epoca (weekly magazine), Milan, Italy, journalist and correspondent, 1965-79; writer, 1979—. *Military service:* Corpo Militare Alpini, 1951-52. *Awards, honors:* Gold, silver, and bronze medals from the Italian Republic for civil valor; French Legion of Honor; gold medal from the Consiglio d'Europa; grand prize from the Sports Academy of Paris; gold medal for sports valor; Argosy Giant of Adventure Award, 1971.

WRITINGS: (Also photographer) *Le mie montagne,* Zanichelli, 1961, translation by Lovett F. Edwards published as *On the Heights,* Hart-Davis, 1964; *I giorni grandi,* preface by Dino Buzzati, A. Mondadori, 1971, Zanichelli, 1978, translation by Geoffrey Sutton published as *The Great Days,* Gollancz, 1974; *Ho vissuto tra gli animali selvaggi,* Zanichelli, 1980.

BIOGRAPHICAL/CRITICAL SOURCES: Reader's Digest, September, 1965; *Esquire,* November, 1965; *Guardian Weekly,* December 21, 1974; *Times Literary Supplement,* March 28, 1975.

*   *   *

BONAVIA, David Michael   1940-

PERSONAL: Surname is pronounced Bonna-*vee*-ya; born March 4, 1940, in Aberdeen, Scotland; son of Michael Robert (a transport economist) and Catriona Annie (a librarian; maiden name, Begg) Bonavia; married Judith Eileen Watt (a researcher), December 15, 1967. *Education:* Corpus Christi College, Cambridge, M.A., 1961. *Politics:* "Liberal conservative." *Religion:* "Episcopalian Church of Scotland (lapsed)." *Residence:* Hong Kong, Hong Kong. *Agent:* Robert Ducas, 610 Fifth Ave., New York, N.Y. *Office address:* Far Eastern Economic Review, P.O. Box 160, Hong Kong, Hong Kong.

CAREER: Writer. Reuters News Agency, London, England, correspondent in central Africa, 1961-63; *London Times,* London, correspondent in Hong Kong, Hong Kong, 1967, in Saigon, Vietnam, 1967-68, in Moscow, U.S.S.R., 1969-72, and in Peking, China, 1972—. *Member:* Hong Kong Foreign Correspondents Club, Hong Kong Journalists Association.

WRITINGS—Nonfiction: Fat Sasha and the Urban Guerilla: Protest and Conformism in the Soviet Union, Atheneum, 1973; *Peking,* Time-Life, 1977; *The Chinese,* Harper, 1980; (author of introduction and co-photographer) *Tibet,* Shangri-La Press,

1981; *Verdict in Peking,* Putnam, 1983. Contributor to periodicals, including *London Times* and *Far Eastern Economic Review.*

SIDELIGHTS: Bonavia's first book, *Fat Sasha and the Urban Guerilla,* recounts his experiences as a *London Times* correspondent in Moscow, U.S.S.R. He concentrates on the development of the protest movement in the Soviet Union during the early 1970's. Many of the characters' names are changed to prevent retaliation from the Russian secret police (KGB). In *Times Literary Supplement* a reviewer noted, "Mr. Bonavia wisely refrains from forecasting the future of those diverse elements that make up the human rights movement in Russia, beyond saying that the KGB deals with it by a series of expedients."

The Chinese is culled from Bonavia's service as a correspondent in Peking, China. The book deals with several contemporary topics, including birth control, industrialization, and medicine. *New York Times Book Review*'s Robert Elegant declared that Bonavia's "sense—and knowledge—of history permeates his book." Elegant called the book "always sound—and frequently brilliant."

Bonavia told *CA:* "*Fat Sasha* was a personal account of the Soviet dissident movement and life in the Soviet Union. *Peking* was an evocative description of life in the Chinese capital. *The Chinese* is a general reader's book on modern China. *Tibet* is a coffee-tabler for which I wrote the introduction and took some of the pictures. *Verdict in Peking* will be a more scholarly piece of work drawing on many sources."

Bonavia is fluent in French, German, Russian, and Chinese, and "can read several other languages."

BIOGRAPHICAL/CRITICAL SOURCES: Times Literary Supplement, October 19, 1973, June 19, 1981; *Economist,* December 1, 1973; *New York Times Book Review,* November 23, 1980; *Washington Post Book World,* November 30, 1980.

* * *

BOND, Jean Carey

PERSONAL: Born in New York, N.Y.; married Max Bond. *Education:* Graduate of Sarah Lawrence College.

CAREER: Author of books for young people. Worked for a state senator following college graduation.

WRITINGS: A Is for Africa (juvenile), F. Watts, 1969; *Brown Is a Beautiful Color* (juvenile), illustrated by Barbara Zuber, F. Watts, 1969; *Time to Stir: A Personal Collection of Home-Made Recipes,* illustrated by John A. Rushton, Hendon, 1977. Contributor of articles and reviews to periodicals such as *Freedomways.**

* * *

BOOTH, Philip 1907-1981

PERSONAL: Born June 30, 1907, in Virginia, Minn.; died in November, 1981; son of Morris B. (a cantor) and Jennie (Kanter) Booth; married Mary Markowitz (a social worker), August 30, 1931; children: Michael D., Paul Robert. *Education:* University of Arizona, B.A., 1930; graduate study at University of Chicago, 1931-35. *Politics:* Democrat. *Religion:* Jewish. *Home:* 808 Mount Vernon, Ann Arbor, Mich. 48103. *Office:* Institute for Labor and Industrial Relations, University of Michigan, 401 South Fourth St., Ann Arbor, Mich. 48103.

CAREER: U.S. Department of Labor, Social Security Administration, Washington, D.C., 1937-62, became director of Office of Program Policy and Legislation; University of Michigan, Ann Arbor, professor of social work, 1962-73, professor emeritus, 1973-81. Lecturer at London School of Economics and Political Science, London, 1974; principal member of Social Security Division of International Labor Office, Geneva, Switzerland, 1957-59; consultant to W. E. Upjohn Institute for Employment Research. *Member:* Industrial Relations Research Association, American Public Welfare Association, National Conference on Social Welfare, American Civil Liberties Union.

WRITINGS: (Editor) *Income Maintenance and the Social Security System,* Institute for Labor and Industrial Relations, University of Michigan, 1969; (editor) *Social Security: Policy for the Seventies,* Institute for Labor and Industrial Relations, University of Michigan, 1973; *Social Security in America,* Institute for Labor and Industrial Relations, University of Michigan, 1973; *Available Light,* Viking, 1976; *Before Sleep,* Viking, 1980. Contributor of articles and reviews to professional journals.

SIDELIGHTS: Booth commented: "I see government as capable of playing a constructive role in helping to equalize opportunity, especially for the benefit of people who are handicapped in 'making it' in the private enterprise economy. I see my experience enabling me to help improve public understanding of mechanisms such as social security, that can contribute to these ends. Retirement from government service and the university has given me the freedom to engage in writing and expressing my own views in these important areas of public social policy. My experience (in government and teaching) has also added spice to frequent foreign travel."

* * *

BOREK, Ernest 1911-

PERSONAL: Born May 25, 1911, in Hungary; naturalized U.S. citizen; married, 1938 (marriage ended); married, 1951; children: two. *Education:* City College (now of City University of New York), B.S., 1933; Columbia University, A.M., 1934, Ph.D., 1938. *Office:* Department of Microbiology, University of Colorado School of Medicine, Denver, Colo. 80220.

CAREER: City College (now of the City University of New York), New York, N.Y., 1938-69, began as instructor, became professor of chemistry; University of Colorado School of Medicine, Denver, professor of microbiology, 1969—. Visiting scholar at Pasteur Institute, 1951; associated with Columbia University, 1955. *Member:* American Chemical Society, American Society of Biological Chemists, British Biochemical Society. *Awards, honors:* Guggenheim fellowship, 1951-58.

WRITINGS—Nonfiction; published by Columbia University Press: *Man, the Chemical Machine,* 1952; *The Atoms Within Us,* 1961; *The Code of Life,* 1965, revised edition, 1969; (editor with Jacques Monod) *Of Microbes and Life,* 1971; *The Sculpture of Life,* 1973.

Contributor to periodicals and journals, including *Science Digest, Science, Cancer Research,* and *Journal of Biological Chemistry.**

* * *

BORING, Mel 1939-

PERSONAL: Born September 12, 1939, in St. Clair Shores, Mich.; son of Harold Truman (an electrician) and Helen Irene (Hatfield) Boring; married Carol Lynne Trettin (a registered nurse), June 21, 1975; children: Joshua Scott, Jeremy Davies. *Education:* Sterling College, B.A., 1961; Princeton Theological Seminary, M.Div., 1965. *Home and office address:* 1343 Chaney Ave., Carpinteria, Calif. 93013. *Agent:* Carol Mann, Carol Mann Literary Agency, 168 Pacific St., Brooklyn, N.Y. 11201.

CAREER: Elementary school teacher in Meriden, Kan., 1961-62; Chi Alpha Student Center, Berkeley, Calif., assistant director, 1965-67; ordained Interdenominational minister, 1966; Inter-Church Team Ministries, Newhall, Calif., director of student conferences and seminars, 1967-69; elementary school teacher in Monroe Center, Mich., 1969-71; junior high school teacher of mathematics in Palmdale, Calif., 1971-76; worked as a radio announcer, 1976-80; high school teacher of social studies in Vergennes, Vt., 1978-80. Writer and editor for Hoffman Information Systems, 1972-74; member of Green Valley, Calif., Volunteer Fire Department, 1972-76. *Member:* Society of Children's Book Writers.

WRITINGS—For children: *Sealth: The Story of an American Indian,* Dillon, 1978; *The Rainmaker,* Random House, 1980; *Clowns: The Fun Makers,* Messner, 1980; *Wovoka: The Story of an American Indian,* Dillon, 1980. Contributor to magazines, including *Highlights for Children, Young World,* and *Children's Playmate.*

WORK IN PROGRESS: Winning: The Story of Jill Kinmont, a biography of the former ski star now a paraplegic; *The Flim-flam Flivver,* a fiction work.

SIDELIGHTS: Mel Boring told *CA:* "A young friend of my son's once asked me if I had 'made' the book *Clowns: The Fun Makers.* I started to correct him, saying that I had 'written' it. Then I realized that *making* a book is more correct. Publishing a book is more than writing. It's the revision, the publisher-seeking, the chaptering, the artwork, the meeting of deadlines. *And* the unparalleled thrill of holding in your hands the result of a creative idea once inside your head and heart.

"My work day goes from 7:00 A.M. to 4:00 P.M., five days a week. I compose sentences for at least six of those eight hours each day, and I revise each sentence an average ten times. That's down from twenty a few years ago, because I have found that with experience I've learned not only to spot something wrong, but also how to fix it.

"I had always had an unfocused interest in writing. It came into focus as I was reading to my students in a one-room school in Michigan in 1970. I saw such enjoyment in their eyes that it made me want to give that enjoyment myself. So I began writing magazine stories and articles in order to gain the experience that would teach me how to write.

"At first I thought of children's books as a stepping stone to writing 'serious' books for adults. But stepping along the stones, I found my imagination being captured by a world of literature that I had never taken seriously. I've been a willing captive of children's books ever since.

"What I discovered is that children's books *are* serious literature. They are roads that children travel as they develop into adults. Hopefully, the ideas they feed on along the way in books will be included in their adult selves and not surrendered to the demands of a falsely-sophisticated adult world in which imagination is often undernourished.

"There is much in adult media that fails to exercise imagination and thus threatens to 'obsolesce' it. Imaginative children's books can deliver a child's imagination intact into their adult self. For me, this has made writing children's books a pretty serious business. But fortunately, humor is one of the tools I have found most useful. It keeps us from the opposite extreme that also smothers imagination—taking life too seriously."

"I take neither rejections nor acceptances too seriously. For the rejection of a manuscript can be the road to its revision and acceptance, and continual acceptance can be the road to unimaginative books. Long live rejection and acceptance, and *longer* live imaginative children's books!"

* * *

BOROWSKI, Tadeusz 1922-1951

BRIEF ENTRY: Born November 12, 1922, in Zytomierz, Poland; died July 3, 1951, in Warsaw, Poland. Polish author. Borowski's incarceration at Auschwitz and Dachau concentration camps during World War II formed the basis for his poems of desperation, collected in *Imiona nurtu* (1945), and his nihilist stories, such as those in *Pozegnanie z Maria* (1948) and *This Way for the Gas, Ladies and Gentlemen, and Other Stories* (1967). Borowski's fiction, harsh to the point of brutality, was presented from the viewpoint of a moralist and a cynic.

* * *

BOSSE, Malcolm J(oseph) 1933-

PERSONAL: Born May 6, 1933, in Detroit, Mich.; son of Malcolm Clifford and Thelma (Malone) Bosse; married Marie-Claude Aullas (a translator), July 4, 1969; children: Malcolm-Scott. *Education:* Yale University, B.A., 1950; University of Michigan, M.A., 1956; New York University, Ph.D., 1969. *Home:* 40 East Tenth St., New York, N.Y. 10003. *Office:* Department of English, City College of the City University of New York, New York, N.Y. 10031.

CAREER: Barron's Financial Weekly, New York City, editorial writer, 1950-52; free-lance writer, 1957-66; City College of the City University of New York, New York City, professor of English, 1969—; novelist, 1959—. Lecturer in India, Bangladesh, Burma, Thailand, Malaysia, Singapore, Taiwan, and China. *Military service:* U.S. Navy, 1950-54; received two Bronze Stars. Also served in U.S. Army and U.S. Merchant Marines. *Member:* Authors Guild, Society of Eighteenth Century Studies and Scholars (England), Modern Language Association of America, Yale Club, Andiron Club, Fulbright-Hays Alumni Association, Phi Gamma Delta, Phi Beta Kappa.

AWARDS, HONORS: Masefield Award from Yale University, 1949, for poetry and fiction; Hopwood Awards from University of Michigan, 1956, for poetry and fiction; *The Journey of Tao Kim Nam* was selected by *Saturday Review of Literature* as one of the best novels of the year, 1960; University Scholar Award from New York University, 1969.

The Incident at Naha was nominated for Edgar Allan Poe Award, 1974, for best first mystery of the year; *The Man Who Loved Zoos* was nominated for Edgar Allan Poe Award, 1975, for best mystery of the year; certificate of merit from Society of the *Dictionary of International Biography,* 1976, for distinguished service to the community; certificate of merit from Society of *Who's Who in America,* 1977; creative writing fellowship from National Endowment for the Arts, 1977-78; Fulbright-Hays lectureship grants for India, 1978 and 1980; *The Seventy-nine Squares* was named notable book for 1979 by American Library Association, was selected as one of the best books of the year by Library of Congress, 1979, and was named to the master list for Dorothy Canfield Fisher Award, 1981.

Special commendation from International Communication Agency, 1980, for work in India; *Cave Beyond Time* received award from National Council of Social Studies Teachers, 1981, as notable book in the field of social studies; *Ganesh* was named notable children's trade book in the field of social studies.

WRITINGS—Novels: *Journey of Tao Kim Nam*, Doubleday, 1959; *The Incident at Naha*, Simon & Schuster, 1972; *The Man Who Loved Zoos*, Putnam, 1974; *The Seventy-nine Squares* (juvenile), Crowell, 1979; *Cave Beyond Time* (juvenile), Crowell, 1980; *Ganesh* (juvenile), Crowell, 1981; *The Barracuda Gang* (juvenile), Dutton, 1982.

Co-editor: *Flowering of the Novel*, Garland Publishing, 1975 (also see below). Also co-editor of *Foundations of the Novel*, Garland Publishing, reissued with *Flowering of the Novel* as *The Novel in England: 1700-1775*.

Contributor of major critical essay to Charles Johnstone's *Chrysal: 1760-1765*, Garland Publishing. Also contributor of articles to periodicals, including *Literary Criterion, Remington Review, Voyages, California Quarterly, North American Review, Michigan Quarterly, Artesian*, and *Massachusetts Review*. Work included in Mississippi Valley Writers Collection.

WORK IN PROGRESS: A novel, publication by Simon & Schuster expected in 1982.

SIDELIGHTS: Malcolm Bosse's first novel met with much critical success as did the endeavors that followed it. A witness to the plight of the Vietnamese, Bosse illustrates the politics and culture of that people in the *Journey of Tao Kim Nam*. The story of a Vietnamese farmer, the book records the many trials and perils he experiences as a refugee who leaves his home in the north in order to escape the communism of the Vietminh. "This novel," wrote a *Christian Century* reviewer, "comes very close to being a minor classic." It "is absorbing all the way," remarked Henry Cavendish of the *New Yok Times Book Review*.

"A very satisfyingly different tale" followed *Journey of Tao Kim Nam*. *The Incident at Naha*, Bosse's second novel, was the author's first attempt at mystery writing. In this book, the war buddy of a Vietnam veteran is murdered, so the vet and his girlfriend set out to find the killer, uncovering an age-old racial conflict. Critically, the novel was recognized for its linking of separate elements such as Vietnam, drugs, Admiral Matthew Perry's trip to Japan in 1852, and racism.

Another mystery, *The Man Who Loved Zoos*, tells the story of a psychologically disturbed Vietnam veteran, Warren Shore, who happens on a busload of dead tourists and rifles through their pockets, keeping whatever seems of value. Unaware of the import of what he has taken, Shore is hunted and killed by a ruthless government agent, Alexander Boyle, who has been assigned to find the thief. The crimes are solved by Shore's Aunt Victoria, a character who, according to the *New York Times Book Review*, proves little old librarians make "immortal" and "indestructible" heroines. "Mr. Bosse," a critic stated in the *New Yorker*, "has put together a very strong plot, and his characterizations are too convincing to be discounted, and much too real to be easily forgotten." Optioned by Paramount Pictures as well as a French film director and producer, *The Man Who Loved Zoos* was featured on the "Today Show."

After *The Man Who Loved Zoos*, Bosse produced his first novel for young adults, *The Seventy-nine Squares*. In this book, Eric Fisher, a fourteen-year-old vandal on probation for pelting rocks through his school's windows, discovers the meaning of life. The child of a couple more interested in social status than in him, Eric is just a lonely gang member until he meets Mr. Beck.

Years earlier, Mr. Beck was convicted of killing his wife in a crime of passion, an act for which he served forty years in prison. Because he is dying of cancer, the eighty-two-year-old Beck is released from prison to live out his few remaining months in his garden. He instructs Eric, who befriended the old man after considerable hesitation, to divide the garden into seventy-nine squares and then to spend time in each plot studying the life there. In this way, Eric learns to "see."

This novel, heralded as a work that "shows the value of human commitment," was widely reviewed and praised by critics. As Anne G. Toensmeier of the *Interracial Books for Children Bulletin* noted: "The story is so compelling and the imagery so visual that the reader seems to see it all happening. This is only appropriate because the story is about learning to see." Other critics, such as Jack Forman of the *New York Times Book Review*, called the novel "a very moving, very private story." *The Seventy-nine Squares*, said *Best Sellers*'s Mary Columba, is "exquisite."

For his second young-adult novel, Bosse wrote the bildungsroman *Cave Beyond Time*. With a "fascinating blend of fact and legend," the author, observed Patricia Anne Reilly of *Best Sellers*, created "a real winner." A disillusioned and bored fifteen-year-old orphan, Ben, is bitten by rattlesnakes while on an archaeological dig in Arizona. While unconscious, he dreams he is a nomad and a hunter in a prehistoric tribe, learning from various father figures and battling wild animals. "The extraordinarily vivid re-creation of primitive life," commented A. A. Flowers in *Horn Book*, "make a strong, often touching novel filled with absorbing detail, head-long action, and echoes of the past."

Ganesh, another novel for young adults, uses some of the insights Bosse gained as a lecturer in India for two years. "Ganesh," the name of the elephant-headed Hindu god of strength and wisdom, is the nickname of Jeffrey Moore, an American born and raised in India. While residing in that country, Jeffrey spends his fourteen years in a happy enough lifestyle, studying yoga and playing ball. Orphaned, he is sent to live with his understanding Aunt Betty in the American Midwest, where, because of his foreign mannerisms, he is not easily accepted by his peers. Jeffrey's place in the community, however, is secured when he battles the government, which is planning to route a highway over Aunt Betty's home, by using the peaceful resistence theories of the *Satyagraha*.

Again, Bosse's novel was applauded by reviewers. "'Ganesh' is not a book to be read by children looking only for light entertainment," maintained Bryna J. Fireside of the *New York Times Book Review*. "It is, rather, a shining little jewel to be savored and treasured by those who already know the merits of fine literature." Summing up the comments of many reviewers, Martha Cruse of the *Voice of Youth Advocates* exclaimed: "What a refreshing book!"

Bosse told *CA:* "I consider any reader above ten or twelve years old (depending on the rate of maturation) to be an adult. I write for a young person as I would for someone my own age, leaving out perhaps the worst of my philosophical reflections or distortions, which, of course, is all for the best."

AVOCATIONAL INTERESTS: Tai-Chi Chuan, yoga, Oriental mythology, archaeology, myrmecology, Asian history, art (especially sculpture), music (especially jazz), watching football on television, classical ballet, Chinese cooking, jogging, swimming.

BIOGRAPHICAL/CRITICAL SOURCES: New York Times Book Review, March 22, 1959, August 25, 1974, December 9, 1979, August 9, 1981; *Chicago Sunday Tribune*, April 5, 1959; *New York Herald Tribune*, April 12, 1959; *Christian Century*, April 8, 1959; *Booklist*, May 1, 1959, October 1, 1974, October 1, 1979, November 1, 1980, April 15, 1981; *Publishers Weekly*, February 28, 1972; *Observer*, October 15, 1972, February 2,

1975; *Times Literary Supplement,* February 2, 1973; *Washington Post Book World,* August 18, 1974; *New Yorker,* September 9, 1974.

Daily Peoples View (Bangladesh), July 7, 1979; *School Library Journal,* September, 1979, November, 1980, May, 1981; *Children's Book Review Service,* November, 1979, December, 1980, June, 1981; *Interracial Books for Children Bulletin,* Volume 11, Numbers 3 and 4, 1980; *Bulletin of the Center for Children's Books,* January, 1980, December, 1980, July/August, 1981; *Best Sellers,* February, 1980, January, 1981; *Childhood Education,* April, 1980; *English Journal,* May, 1980; *Voice of Youth Advocate,* June, 1980, December, 1980, June, 1981; *Ms.,* August, 1980; *China News,* August 7, 1980; *Horn Book,* February, 1981; *Language Arts,* September, 1981.

—*Sketch by Charity Anne Dorgan*

* * *

BOSTWICK, Burdette Edwards 1908-

PERSONAL: Born March 31, 1908, in Washington, D.C.; son of John Wilson and Harriet Caroline (Edwards) Bostwick; married Betty Bannister Brown, September 19, 1936; children: Burdette E., Sherry B. *Education:* Rutgers University, J.D., 1935. *Politics:* Republican. *Religion:* Episcopalian. *Home:* 292 Short Hills Ave., Springfield, N.J. 07081.

CAREER: J. Wiss & Sons, Inc., Newark, N.J., began as salesman, became vice-president, 1927-70; B. E. Bostwick Co., Inc., president, 1970—. Member of board of directors of 228 Burnett Avenue Corp., 1960-67; member of board of trustees of Hospital Center at Orange; past member of board of trustees of St. Barnabas Hospital. *Member:* Short Hills Club. *Awards, honors:* Merchandising awards.

WRITINGS: Resume Writing: A Comprehensive How-to-Do-It Guide, Wiley, 1976, revised edition, 1980; *How to Find the Job You've Always Wanted,* Wiley, 1977, revised edition, 1980; *One Hundred Eleven Proven Techniques and Strategies for Getting the Job Interview,* Wiley, 1981. Contributor to business journals.

WORK IN PROGRESS: How to Conduct Recruitment Interviews; Stepping Ahead in Management.

SIDELIGHTS: Bostwick told *CA:* "My writing started as a result of personal dissatisfaction with the approach taken in books and other advisories on job seeking. There are two ways to get a job or enter into a new, more satisfying career. One is to know someone who can open doors for you; the second is to bring yourself to the attention of companies by writing or by using other means of communication. If one knows the right people no other assistance is necessary. Most people do not have this advantage and need help in communicating. In my experience, writing—in the form of resumes, letters, or proposals—is the best approach. The better the writing, the greater the possibilities of success. Since writing about oneself is among the most difficult forms of expression, guidance is needed on getting to know yourself.

"Having been exposed to hundreds of resumes, most poorly written, and believing that most people who tell others how to write resumes have had little experience themselves, I decided to write my own book on the subject. To those who will study it, it provides a key to self-expression that will multiply any job seeker's chances of getting interviews. I have used the principles many times. They work!

"Following this first attempt at writing a book it was natural to move into other areas affecting the job search; hence the

two additional volumes. They are characterized by comprehensive advice in contrast to books that espouse one or two tricky superficial techniques.

"As a successful manager, I have naturally accumulated many ideas on management processes. I have outlined a book to deal with these methods. There is currently a plethora of writing on management subjects, although my direction will be somewhat different, that is, helping middle managers climb the corporate ladder.'

* * *

BOSWELL, Jeanetta 1922-

PERSONAL: Born July 7, 1922, in Emory, Tex.; daughter of John W. (an oil driller) and Mary Ethel (Knight) Tarbutton; married Fred P. Boswell, June 7, 1957 (died, 1978). *Education:* East Texas University, B.A., 1950, M.A., 1953; Stephen F. Austin State University, M.S., 1956; further study at University of Oklahoma. *Politics:* Liberal Democrat. *Religion:* "Christian tradition." *Home:* 625 South Fielder, Arlington, Tex. 76013.

CAREER: Worked as public school teacher in Texas, c. 1945; University of Texas, Arlington, 1956-77, began as instructor, became professor of American literature; writer.

WRITINGS: Ralph Waldo Emerson and the Critics, Scarecrow, 1979; *Walt Whitman and the Critics,* Scarecrow, 1980; *Henry David Thoreau and the Critics,* Scarecrow, 1981; *Herman Melville and the Critics,* Scarecrow, 1981; *Nathaniel Hawthorne and the Critics,* Scarecrow, 1981; *What Men or Gods?: A Study of Genealogy in Greco-Roman Mythology,* Scarecrow, 1981; *Past Ruin'd Ilion,* Scarecrow, 1982.

SIDELIGHTS: Jeanetta Boswell commented: "After thirty-five years of teaching American literature, I believed it was a kind of responsibility to write what I could in my retirement, and leave it for the students of the future."

* * *

BOSWORTH, R(ichard) J(ames) B(oon) 1943-

PERSONAL: Born December 7, 1943, in Sydney, Australia; son of Richard C.L. (a professor of chemistry) and Thelma H.E. (Boon) Bosworth; married Michal Twyn Newell (a writer), September 23, 1965; children: Edmund R.F., Mary F. *Education:* University of Sydney, B.A. (with honors), 1965, M.A. (with honors), 1967; Cambridge University, Ph.D., 1971. *Politics:* Australian Labor Party. *Religion:* None. *Home:* 118 Albion St., Annandale, New South Wales 2038, Australia. *Office:* Department of History, University of Sydney, Sydney, New South Wales 2006, Australia.

CAREER: University of Sydney, Sydney, Australia, lecturer, 1969-73, senior lecturer, 1974-81, associate professor of history, 1981—. Deputy director of F. May Foundation for Italian Studies. *Member:* Australasian Association for European History (president), Australian Historical Association.

WRITINGS: Benito Mussolini and the Fascist Destruction of Liberal Italy, Rigby (Adelaide, Australia), 1973; *Italy, the Least of the Great Powers: Italian Foreign Policy Before the First World War,* Cambridge University Press, 1979; (with J. K. Wilton) *Italy and the Approach of the First World War,* Macmillan, 1982; *Old Worlds and New Australia: A History of European Migration to Australia Since 1945,* Penguin, in press.

Editor: (With Gianfranco Cresciani) *Altro Polo: A Volume of Italian Studies,* F. May Foundation (Sydney, Australia), 1979;

(with Cresciani) *Italian Emigration and Australia,* F. Angeli, in press. Editor of *Teaching History,* 1971-79.

Contributor: Marian Kent, editor, *The Great Powers and the Downfall of the Ottoman Empire,* Allen & Unwin, 1982; M. M. Guidetti, editor, *Corso di storia d'Italia e d'Europa: Communita e popoli* (title means "Introductory Textbook to the History of Italy and Europe: Community and People"), Volume VII, Jaca Books, 1982. Australian correspondent for *Risorgimento.*

SIDELIGHTS: Bosworth told *CA:* "My interest in Italian history is accidental; my being an Australian is accidental. I would like to be an enemy of all nationalisms, but once committed to Italy (or Australia), I don't see how one can change. This means that my critical interpretation of Italian foreign policy as managed by its ruling elite from 1860 to 1945, or of Australian immigration policy since the Second World War, tends to place me on the left politically. At the same time I remain enough of a liberal to be almost as skeptical of the ideologizing of some Marxist or other radical historians. But, safely enclosed in the cozy nook of Australia, beyond what one Australian novelist has called 'the rage of history,' one can afford the luxury of being soft-centered."

* * *

BOTHMER, Dietrich Felix von
See von BOTHMER, Dietrich Felix

* * *

BOUGH, Lee
See HUSER, (La)Verne (Carl)

* * *

BOWDEN, Roland Heywood 1916-

PERSONAL: Born December 19, 1916, in Lincoln, England; son of Reginald (an engineer) and Marjorie (Heywood) Bowden; married Riki Rainer (a clerical assistant), January 2, 1946; children: Katherine Bowden Bradley, Mark. *Education:* University of Liverpool, B.Arch., 1939. *Politics:* "Left-wing radical." *Religion:* Agnostic. *Home:* 2 Roughmere Cottage, Lavant, Chichester, Sussex, England.

CAREER: Teacher at grammar school in Harrow, England, 1948-49, and comprehensive school in Harrow (also head of department), 1949-55; Manhood High School, Selsey, England, art teacher and head of department, 1956-79; writer, 1979—. *Military service:* British Army, Royal Army Medical Corps, 1939-45. *Member:* National Poetry Secretariat. *Awards, honors:* Arts Council grant, 1976.

WRITINGS: Poems From Italy, Chatto & Windus, 1970.

Plays: "And" (one-act), first produced in London at Questors Theatre, October, 1971; "The Last Analysis" (two-act), first produced in London at Questors Theatre, June 10, 1974; "The Death of Pasolini" (three-act), first produced in Edinburgh, Scotland, at Heriot-Watt Theatre, August 15, 1980. Contributor to *Arts Review.*

WORK IN PROGRESS: "Voices in Exile," a three-act play based on the life and work of Russian dissident poet Osip Mandelstam.

SIDELIGHTS: Bowden wrote: "Drama should disturb and disrupt. At present the media are drowning us with opiates, brainwashing us with consumerist values. As Ernest Fischer com-

mented, 'Art is the irreconcilable, the resistance of the human being to its vanishing in the established order and systems.'

"Drama is the ideal medium through which to expose the conflict between the artist's search for increased sensibility, greater individuation, and the destructive, dehumanizing forces of the society in which he lives. The artist is the ideal protagonist: so often in him is brought into focus the creative essence and potential of the period in which he lives. Hence my last three plays deal with the death of Pablo Neruda in Chili, of Pier Paolo Pasolini in Italy, and of Osip Mandelstam in Stalinist Russia.

"Poetry, on the other hand (and the short story, which is very much an extension of poetry), I regard as the most direct and concise method of both expressing and continually reintegrating the flux of one's own personal awareness.

"In the drama my main influences have been Georg Buechner, John Arden, Edward Albee, Samuel Beckett; in poetry, influences so numerous as to be beyond listing."

* * *

BOWE, (Paul Thomas) Patrick 1945-

PERSONAL: Born December 6, 1945, in Waterford, Ireland; son of Thomas Christopher (a company director) and Breda (a teacher; maiden name, Gahan) Bowe; married Nicola Gordon (an art historian), September 15, 1973. *Education:* University College, Dublin, National University of Ireland, B.Arch., 1968. *Home:* Parsley Cottage, 11 Ashfield Ave., Ranelagh, Dublin 6, Ireland.

CAREER: C. F. Murphy & Associates (architectural firm), Chicago, Ill., architect, 1968-69; architect with Michael Scott & Partners, 1969-71; O'Neill Flanagan & Partners (architectural firm), Dublin, Ireland, director, 1971—. Member of National Institute of Physical Planning and Research's committee for national inventory of gardens and parks; garden designer and consultant. *Member:* National Trust of Ireland, Royal Institute of Architects of Ireland, Landscape Institute, An Taisce, Heritage Gardens Committee, Kildare Street and University Club.

WRITINGS: (With Edward Malins) *Irish Gardens and Demesnes From 1830,* Barrie & Jenkins, 1980; (co-editor) *Gardens of Outstanding Historic Interest in the Republic of Ireland,* An Taisce, 1980; (contributor) Gervase Jackson-Stops, editor, *National Trust Studies, 1981,* Sotheby, Parke, Bernet, 1980. Contributor to *Cultural Encyclopaedia of Ireland* and *Oxford Companion to Gardens.* Contributor to magazines, including *Garden History, Country Life,* and *Ireland Today.* Garden editor of *Image.*

WORK IN PROGRESS: The Gardeners of Ireland, with J.C.D. Lamb, publication by Gill & Macmillan expected in 1984; research on the history of the small garden.

SIDELIGHTS: Bowe led tours to gardens of the French Riviera in 1981 and gardens of Tuscany and Normandy in 1982.

He wrote: "My motivation in writing about and designing gardens is to help put modern man, living as he does in an increasingly artificial environment, in touch in a creative and practical way with the natural world around him."

* * *

BOWLES, John 1938-

PERSONAL: Born June 28, 1938, in Springfield, Mass.; son of Sherman H. (a publisher) and Esther (Johnson) Bowles;

married Patricia Dixon (a treasurer and secretary), December 29, 1962; children: Tiffany, John, Matthew, Amy. *Education:* Brown University, B.A., 1958; Wharton School of Finance, M.B.A., 1963. *Politics:* Democrat. *Home:* 54 Beverly Dr., Somers, Conn. 06071. *Office:* Public Policy Analysis, Inc., Box 639, Somers, Conn. 06071.

CAREER: Investment banker. Kidder Peabody & Co., Inc., New York City, vice-president and stockholder, 1982—; Public Policy Analysis, Inc., Somers, Conn., president, 1982—. *Military service:* U.S. Marine Corps, 1958-61.

WRITINGS: (With Richard Bolling) *America's Competitive Edge: How to Get Our Country Moving Again*, McGraw, 1981.

WORK IN PROGRESS: Maybe!: America Fighting Back, publication expected in 1984.

SIDELIGHTS: Bowles told *CA:* "*America's Competitive Edge* was the best widely-unread book of 1981. My second book will undoubtedly not be as well written, but Ronald Reagan's disastrous presidency will make it a best-seller. I ought to share the royalties with him."

*   *   *

BOYER, William H(arrison)   1924-

PERSONAL: Born October 12, 1924, in Newberg, Ore.; son of William Francis (in grocery business) and Lucy (Schatz) Boyer; married Ann M. Lahr, August 18, 1949; children: David, Jeffrey. *Education:* University of Oregon, B.A., 1948; graduate study at Stanford University, 1950-51, 1960-61; University of Colorado, M.Ed., 1952; Arizona State University, Ed.D., 1956. *Home:* 17575 Jordan Rd., Star Route, Redmond, Ore. 97756.

CAREER: Stockton College, Stockton, Calif., instructor in English and social studies, 1952-54; Milwaukee-Downer College, Milwaukee, Wis., assistant professor of education and psychology, 1956; Chico State University, Chico, Calif., assistant professor of education, 1958-60; University of Hawaii, Honolulu, professor of philosophy of education, environmental education, and world order education, 1961-82, professor of educational foundations and chairman of department, 1978-80. Educational adviser to U.S. military government in Germany, 1948-50. *Military service:* U.S. Army Air Forces, 1943-46.

WRITINGS: Education for Annihilation, Hogarth Press (Honolulu, Hawaii), 1972; *Alternative Futures: Designing Social Change,* Kendall/Hunt, 1975. Contributor to professional journals and popular magazines.

WORK IN PROGRESS: Transition to the Twenty-first Century, publication expected in 1983.

SIDELIGHTS: Boyer told *CA:* "I left my tenured position at the University of Hawaii because of the dangers of nuclear war. Hawaii is a strategic target.

"I am active in anti-nuclear war work through media and lecture. My focus is on public policy and planning toward transformation of the war system and ecocide system to a peacekeeping system, sustainable environmental economics, and full employment opportunity. My current book in progress proposes long-range planning and identifies current transition steps toward these goals as a basis for the redirection of American politics."

*   *   *

BRADLEY, C. Paul   1918-

PERSONAL: Born July 20, 1918, in Eaton Rapids, Mich.; son

of James B. (a physician) and Pearl (Parshall) Bradley; married Anna Yanbrick (a college instructor), August 9, 1958; children: James O., Mark P. *Education:* Attended University of Michigan, 1938-41; Yale University, A.B., 1947; Columbia University, M.A., 1949, Ph.D., 1955. *Home:* 915 East Court St., No. 403, Flint, Mich. 48503. *Office:* Department of Political Science, University of Michigan, 1321 Court St., Flint, Mich. 48503.

CAREER: University of Puerto Rico, San Juan, lecturer in political science, 1952-54; Northern Iowa State College (now University of Northern Iowa), Cedar Falls, instructor in political science, 1954-55; Oberlin College, Oberlin, Ohio, visiting professor of political science, 1955-56; University of Michigan, Flint, 1956—, began as assistant professor, became professor of political science. *Military service:* U.S. Army Air Forces, 1941-46; became captain. *Member:* Association for Asian Studies, Middle East Institute.

WRITINGS: The Camp David Peace Process, Shoe String, 1981; *Electoral Politics in Israel,* Shoe String, 1981; *U.S. Policy in the Persian Gulf, 1977-82,* Shoe String, 1982. Contributor to political science journals.

SIDELIGHTS: Bradley, who has conducted field studies on comparative politics in Jamaica, Guyana, Trinidad, Malaysia, Singapore, Borneo, and Israel, told *CA:* "I regard the future of the Camp David peace accord as bleak. The major negative factors are, in my opinion, Israeli intransigence and the uncertainty of President Mubarak's future alignments in the Arab world. Since the advent of the Reagan administration Camp David has been pushed into the background by U.S. policymakers, as the preoccupation with Soviet expansion has become more pronounced.

"The most striking feature of U.S. policy in the Persian Gulf has been the increasingly heavy reliance on U.S. military power to effectuate American goals there since 1971. In my opinion the policy is a near-failure, or prospectively so, because of our reliance on very unstable regimes as in Saudi Arabia and the Gulf sheikdoms.

"The single most memorable aspect of my field research in the Third World countries since 1957 has been my largely futile efforts to disentangle my independent research from CIA (Central Intelligence Agency) associations in these various countries. I deplore the widespread evidence of government financing of scholarly research overseas, surreptitiously arranged. This is a real setback for American scholarship that will require years to overcome."

*   *   *

BRADY, Mary Lou   1937-

PERSONAL: Born March 14, 1937, in Newark, N.J.; daughter of Thomas (a tailor) and Anne (Scarano) Zegarelli; married Richard J. Brady (a trombonist), June 28, 1958 (divorced December 18, 1969). *Education:* Attended Monmouth Junior College and Katharine Gibbs School. *Home:* 1242 North Crescent Heights, Los Angeles, Calif. 90046. *Office:* J. P. Tarcher, Inc., 9110 Sunset Blvd., Suite 212, Los Angeles, Calif. 90069.

CAREER: Arthur P. Jacobs Co., Inc., New York City, secretary in television department and publicist, 1960-61; Tarcher Productions, Inc., New York City, assistant to producer of "The Shari Lewis Show" and personal assistant to Mr. Tarcher, 1961-67; Buddy Clarke Associates, New York City, publicist, 1967-70; Allan, Ingersoll & Weber, New York City, publicist, 1970-72; free-lance publicist, 1972; Las Vegas Television Productions, Las Vegas, Nev., administrative assistant and researcher, 1973-76; J. P. Tarcher, Inc., Los Angeles, Calif., administrative assistant, 1976-79, director of publicity, advertising, and marketing, 1979—. *Member:* Women's National Book Association, Southern California Booksellers, Southern California Book Publicists.

WRITINGS: (With Lucinda Dyer and Sara Parriott) *Woman Power!: A Woman's Guide to Making It on Top,* J. P. Tarcher, 1981.

* * *

BRADY, Terence 1939-

PERSONAL: Born March 13, 1939, in London, England; son of Arthur Noel and Elizabeth Mary (Moore) Brady; married Charlotte Bingham (a writer), January 15, 1964; children: Candida, Matthew. *Education:* Trinity College, Dublin, moderatorship in history and political science, 1961. *Agent:* A. D. Peters & Co., 10 Buckingham St., London W. C. 2, England.

CAREER: Actor, 1957—; writer, 1961—. Actor in plays, including "Jim Dandy," 1957, "Glory Be," 1961, "Would Anyone Who Saw the Accident," 1962, "Beyond the Fringe," 1962, "A Quick One 'Ere," 1966, "In the Picture," 1967, "A Present From the Corporation," 1967, "The Dock Brief," and "The Long the Short and the Tall." Actor in films, including "Baby Love," 1968. Also actor in over two hundred episodes of television programs, including "Pig in the Middle." Broadcaster. *Member:* British Academy of Film and Television Arts, Roehampton Club, Stage Golfing Society. *Awards, honors:* Named best writer of radio light entertainment by Writers Guild, c. 1964.

WRITINGS—All with wife, Charlotte Bingham, except as noted: *Rose's Story,* Sphere Books, 1972; *Victoria,* W. H. Allen, 1972; (sole author) *Rehearsal* (novel), W. H. Allen, 1973; *Victoria and Company,* W. H. Allen, 1974; *No, Honestly,* Penguin, 1974; (with Evan Jones) *The Fight Against Slavery* (nonfiction), BBC Publications, 1975, Norton, 1977; *Yes, Honestly,* Sphere Books, 1977.

Revues: (With Michael Bogdanov) "Would Anyone Who Saw the Accident," first produced in London, England, at Stratford Theatre, January, 1962; (with Bogdanov) "A Quick One 'Ere," first produced in Dublin, Ireland, at Eblana Theatre, October, 1966; "Three to One On," first produced in London at Playhouse Theatre, 1968.

Scripts for television series; with Bingham: "Take Three Girls," British Broadcasting Corp. (BBC-TV), 1970; "Upstairs, Downstairs," LWTV, 1972; "No, Honestly," LWTV, 1974; "Yes, Honestly," LWTV, 1975; "Plays for Today," BBC-TV, 1977; "Pig in the Middle," LWTV, 1980; "Nanny," BBC-TV, 1981-83. Also co-author with Bingham of "One of the Family," Thames-TV.

Also author of radio programs, including "Hear Hear," "Thank Goodness It's Saturday," and "Lines From My Grandfather's Forehead."

WORK IN PROGRESS: Another series of "Nanny" for the British Broadcasting Corp. and of "Pig in the Middle" for LWTV; a dramatization of *The Hills Is Lonely* for LWTV; "Take Three Women," "a new drama series for BBC based on the highly successful 'Take Three Girls.'"

SIDELIGHTS: Many of Terence Brady's books are based on scripts for television series. For instance, *Rose's Story* is the biography of the parlor maid from "Upstairs, Downstairs," and *The Fight Against Slavery* comes from the British Broadcasting Corporation's series of the same name. Stressing the

economic aspects of the slave trade, the latter book illustrates that the wealth slavery accrued for entrepreneurs was a stumbling block to abolition.

Unlike Brady's other books, *Rehearsal* has been found to be largely autobiographical. Covering the author's life as a student and as an actor, the novel, said a *Books and Bookmen* reviewer, "is well written in a neat, sharp prose."

Brady told *CA:* "I have always been attracted to writing for television because, as a dramatist and humorist, it affords splendidly flexible facilities for the writer as well as, if the proper controls are imposed upon the production, the best chance for a writer's work to be seen by the largest possible audience. To those considering a career in the medium, the secret is to fight for the elevation, not the depression, of standards. Television is the most exciting creative innovation of our lifetimes and should be cherished and respected accordingly instead of allowing it to become the broadcaster of mediocrity."

BIOGRAPHICAL/CRITICAL SOURCES: Observer, June 18, 1972, June 30, 1974; *Listener,* January 25, 1973; *Times Literary Supplement,* February 9, 1973; *Books and Bookmen,* June, 1973, October, 1973; *Time,* April 18, 1975.

* * *

BRAITHWAITE, (Eustace) E(dward) R(icardo) 1920-

PERSONAL: Born June 27, 1920 (some sources cite 1912), in Georgetown, British Guiana (now Guyana); son of Charles Edwardo and Elizabeth Martha (Greene) Braithwaite. *Education:* Attended Queen's College, British Guiana; City College (now of the City University of New York), B.Sc., 1940; Gonville and Caius College, Cambridge, M.Sc., 1949; further study at Institute of Education, London. *Home:* Parker 40, Apt. 16K, 305 East 40th St., New York, N.Y. 10017.

CAREER: Writer. Schoolmaster in London, England, 1950-57; London County Council, Department of Child Welfare, London, welfare officer and consultant on affairs of blacks, 1958-60; World Veterans' Foundation, Paris, France, human rights officer, 1960-63; UNESCO, Paris, educational consultant and lecturer, 1963-66; United Nations, New York, N.Y., permanent representative from Guyana, 1967-68; ambassador of Guyana to Venezuela, 1968-69. *Military service:* Royal Air Force, 1941-45, served as fighter pilot. *Member:* International P.E.N. Club. *Awards, honors:* Anisfield-Wolf Award from *Saturday Review,* 1960, for *To Sir, With Love;* Cholmondeley Award for poets from the Society of Authors, 1970.

WRITINGS: To Sir, With Love (autobiography), Bodley Head, 1959, Prentice-Hall, 1960, new edition in large print, Chivers, 1980; *A Kind of Homecoming,* Prentice-Hall, 1962; *Paid Servant* (autobiography), Bodley Head, 1962, McGraw, 1968; *Choice of Straws* (novel), Bodley Head, 1965, Bobbs-Merrill, 1967; *The Arrivants: A New World Trilogy* (poems), Oxford University Press, Volume I: *Rites of Passage,* 1967 (also see below), Volume II: *Masks,* 1968 (also see below), Volume III: *Islands,* 1970; *Reluctant Neighbors* (autobiography), McGraw, 1972; *Honorary White: A Visit to South Africa,* McGraw, 1975.

Recordings: "Rites of Passage" (poems read by the author), Argo, 1969; "Masks" (poems read by the author) Argo, 1972.

Contributor of articles to *Time.*

SIDELIGHTS: Braithwaite's experiences as a teacher and social worker in London provided much material for his writing. His first publication, *To Sir, With Love,* recounts the eight years he spent in the East End working-class district of London teaching black children. The poignant tale was adapted into a motion picture of the same title, starring Sidney Poitier, by Columbia Pictures in 1966.

AVOCATIONAL INTERESTS: Tennis, dancing.

BIOGRAPHICAL/CRITICAL SOURCES: New York Herald Tribune Weekly Book Review, February 28, 1960, April 29, 1962; *Chicago Sunday Tribune,* April 3, 1960, August 5, 1962; *New York Times Book Review,* May 1, 1960, August 5, 1962, May 19, 1968, September 17, 1972, July 13, 1975; *Saturday Review,* June 16, 1962, May 11, 1968; *Newsweek,* April 1, 1968; *America,* April 13, 1968.*

*   *   *

BRAMESCO, Norton J.   1924-
(Daedalus, Bram Norton)

PERSONAL: Born March 2, 1924, in New York, N.Y.; son of Alfred and Rose (Tepper) Bramesco; married Pearl Stark, June 19, 1948 (divorced May 1, 1979); married Ronnie Zolondek (a theatre producer), May 12, 1979; children: Erica Bramesco Stull, Clinton. *Education:* Columbia University, B.S., 1949. *Home:* 120 East 34th St., New York, N.Y. 10016. *Agent:* John Boswell Associates, 45 East 51st St., Suite 301, New York, N.Y. 10022. *Office:* Healthmark Communications, Inc., 1633 Broadway, New York, N.Y. 10019.

CAREER: Star Drug, Bronx, N.Y., registered pharmacist, 1950-54; A. H. Robins Co., Inc., Richmond, Va., medical service representative, 1954-56; L. W. Frohlich & Co., Inc., New York City, creative director, 1956-72; Grey Medical Advertising, Inc., New York City, creative director, 1972-75; Healthmark Communications, Inc., New York City, creative director, 1975—. Member of board of trustees of Murray Hill Committee, 1982. *Military service:* U.S. Army, aviation cadet, 1943-45. *Member:* Medical Writers of America, American Institute of the History of Pharmacy, Pharmaceutical Advertising Club.

WRITINGS: (With Jordan Lasher) *The Crossword Puzzle Compendium,* Publications International, 1980; (with Martin Ecker) *Radiation: All You Need to Know to Stop Worrying, or to Start,* Random House, 1981; (with Michael Donner) *The Crossword Encyclopedia,* Workman Publishing, 1982. Author of "Wit's End," a monthly column (under pseudonym Daedalus) in *Diversion.* Contributor of stories to mystery magazines, under pseudonym Bram Norton.

WORK IN PROGRESS: The Safety Parade, a novel.

SIDELIGHTS: Bramesco commented: "I had always wanted to be a writer, but found myself trapped in pharmacy by an uncle who had suggested we would go into business together after I graduated from pharmacy school. He reneged and I had to write my way out of the drugstore, first with short mystery fiction, and then with medical advertising work. I have been doing this since 1956. Health and medicine are therefore major areas of interest, as are words.

"The subject of radiation, however, is of particular interest. I think that while we as a nation lost our nuclear virginity at Three Mile Island, most of the concern was generated out of emotion rather than knowledge. And statements issued by the government were of no help since their ambiguity put the burden of doubt right back on the shoulders of a public already worried about radiation absorbed from medical and dental X rays, microwave ovens, radar communications, etc. *Radiation: All You Need to Know to Stop Worrying, or to Start* was written to provide easily digestible information so that the reader could

make decisions affecting his or her family's welfare on a foundation of fact rather than the utterances of the Chicken Littles or the Pollyannas.''

AVOCATIONAL INTERESTS: Foreign travel.

*   *   *

BRANDT, Catharine   1905-

PERSONAL: Born January 23, 1905, in Jacksonville, Ill.; daughter of Jerome E. (a business executive) and Charlotte (Halstead) Gates; married Russell L. Brandt (a chain store manager, superintendent, and buyer), June 2, 1927 (died January 21, 1966); children: Russell L., Jr., Barbara (Mrs. Philip Weiler). *Education:* Bethel College, St. Paul, Minn., 1951-56; University of Minnesota, 1953-54. *Religion:* Protestant. *Home:* 5800 St. Croix Ave., Apt. 404, Minneapolis, Minn. 55422.

CAREER: Writer, 1953—. Member of faculty at North Central Bible College, Minneapolis, Minn., and Decision School of Christian Writing. Also worked as private secretary. Volunteer worker at nursing home. *Member:* American Bell Association, National League of American Pen Women, Minnesota Christian Writers Guild (past president).

WRITINGS: A Woman's Money: How to Protect and Increase It in the Stock Market, Parker Publishing, 1970; *The Story of Christmas for Children,* Augsburg, 1974; *Praise God for This New Day: Second Thoughts for Busy Women,* Augsburg, 1975; *You're Only Old Once,* Augsburg, 1977; *Flowers for the Living,* Augsburg, 1977; *God Bless Grandparents: The Adventures of Being a Grandparent,* Augsburg, 1978; *Forgotten People,* Moody, 1978; *Still Time to Sing: Prayers and Praise for Late in Life,* Augsburg, 1980.

Author of "Talking With Teens," a weekly column for teenagers in Union Gospel Press's *My Delight,* 1969-73. Contributor of more than seven hundred articles and stories to magazines.

WORK IN PROGRESS: A juvenile novel; a devotional book for people on the verge of retirement; a story of World War II, as told by a participant.

SIDELIGHTS: Brandt told *CA:* "As a young person I was unable to go to college. In 1952, with my son in college and my daughter in high school, I began a series of college and university courses with a view toward writing. I write a great deal on the subject of old age. An editor of a Baptist Sunday school take-home paper, for whom I once wrote, suggested that I do an article on how young people can help the elderly. I've been writing on that subject ever since.

"Most of my writing, but not all, has been for religious markets. While not top-paying, they represent a wide readership. My articles and prayers printed in *Decision* magazine reach a potential three million readers. I write because I'd rather be writing than doing anything else. Also, I can explain to readers what it means to me to be a Christian and how I feel about God.

"A small critique group met monthly at my home for eleven years. So far we have had published numerous articles and thirty-five books. The group is still going strong.

"I support young people today in every way I can. The ones I know are bright and knowledgeable, eager to accomplish what the older generation has sometimes failed to do. All of us, including teens, are living under a great stress today and all of us need encouragement. I see my writing as that—encouragement wherever possible.''

BRANSCOMB, (Bennett) Harvie 1894-

PERSONAL: Born December 25, 1894, in Huntsville, Ala.; son of Lewis C. and Nancy (McAdory) Branscomb; married Margaret Vaughan; children: Harvie, Ben, Lewis. *Education:* Birmingham Southern College, B.A.; Oxford University, M.A.; Columbia University, Ph.D. *Home:* 1620 Chickering Rd., Nashville, Tenn. 37215.

CAREER: Southern Methodist University, Dallas, Tex., adjunct professor, 1919-20, associate professor, 1920-21, professor of New Testament, 1921-25; Duke University, Durham, N.C., professor of New Testament, 1925-45, director of libraries, 1931-41, chairman of Division of Ancient Languages and Literatures, 1937-44, dean of university, 1945-46; Vanderbilt University, Nashville, Tenn., chancellor, 1946-63, chancellor emeritus and member of board of trustees, 1963—. Chairman of U.S. National Commission for United Nations Educational, Scientific and Cultural Organization, 1962-65; past member of board of trustees of Tennessee Botanical Gardens and Fine Arts Center and Nashville's Urban League and Planned Parenthood; past member of board of directors of New York General Education Board, Carnegie Endowment for Teaching, Colonial Williamsburg, and Cordell Hull Foundation.

WRITINGS: The Message of Jesus: A Survey of the Teaching of Jesus Contained in the Synoptic Gospels, Cokesbury Press, 1926, revised edition, Abingdon, 1960; *Jesus and the Law of Moses,* R. R. Smith, 1930; *The Teachings of Jesus: A Textbook for College and Individual Use,* Cokesbury Press, 1931, reprinted, Abingdon, 1959; *The Gospel of Mark,* Hodder & Stoughton, 1937; *Teaching With Books: A Study of College Libraries,* American Library Association, 1940, reprinted, Shoe String, 1964; *Purely Academic: An Autobiography,* Vanderbilt University, 1978.

* * *

BRECHT, George 1924-

PERSONAL: Born March 7, 1924 (some sources say 1925), in Blomkest, Minn.; married Marceline Allemand, 1951 (divorced); children: Eric. *Education:* Philadelphia College of Pharmacy and Science, B.Sc., 1950; attended New York School for Social Research, 1958-59. *Home:* Wildenburgstrasse 9, 5 Cologne-Sulz 41, West Germany. *Agent:* Arturo Schwarz, via Gesu 17, Milan 20121, Italy.

CAREER: Artist. Analytical chemist and quality control supervisor with Charles Pfizer & Co., Brooklyn, N.Y.; quality control supervisor, research chemist, engineer, and inventor with Johnson & Johnson, New Brunswick, N.J.; research inventor, chemist, and engineer with Mobil Chemicals, New Brunswick; James Waring Dance Co., New York City, composer and designer of sets, 1962; instructor in art history at Rutgers University, New Brunswick; Leeds College of Art, England, instructor, 1968-69; Leicester University, England, instructor in art, 1969-70.

Exhibited work in one-man shows, including those at Reuben Gallery, New York City, 1959; Cafe au Go Go, New York City, 1964; Fischbach Gallery, New York City, 1965; Galleria Schwarz, Milan, Italy, 1967 and 1969; Galerie Hansjorg Mayer, Stuttgart, West Germany, 1969; Galerie Rudolf Zwirner, Cologne, West Germany, 1969; and Los Angeles County Museum of Art, Los Angeles, Calif., 1969. Exhibited work in group shows, including those at Reuben Gallery, 1960; Moderna Mu-

seet, Stockholm, Sweden, 1961; Museum of Modern Art, New York City, 1961; Washington Gallery of Modern Art, Washington, D.C., 1963; Cordier & Ekstrom Gallery, New York City, 1964; Guggenheim Museum, New York City, 1965; Fischbach Gallery, 1966; Museum of Contemporary Art, Chicago, Ill., 1967; Stadtisches Museum, Monchengladbach, Germany, 1969; Tate Gallery, London, England, 1969; and Gallery House, London, 1972. Work represented in permanent collections, including those at Museum of Modern Art; Stadtisches Museum; Archiv Sohm, Markgroningen, Germany; and Fluxus West Collection, San Diego, Calif. *Military service:* U.S. Army, 1943-45.

WRITINGS: (With Robert Filliou) *Games at the Cedilla; or, The Cedilla Takes Off,* Something Else Press, 1967; (with Patrick Hughes) *Vicious Circles and Infinity: A Panoply of Paradoxes,* Doubleday, 1975, reprinted as *Vicious Circles and Infinity: An Anthology of Paradoxes,* Penguin, 1979; *Present Projects,* Ed. Leger, 1976.

BIOGRAPHICAL/CRITICAL SOURCES: Art News, September, 1961; *Artforum,* August, 1967; *Studio International,* March, 1968; *Art in America,* July, 1974; *Economist,* April 3, 1976; *New Statesman,* May 7, 1976; *Studio,* November, 1976.*

* * *

BREEDEN, Stanley 1938-

PERSONAL: Born May 2, 1938, in Soest, Netherlands; married Kay Carter (an author and photographer). *Home:* 35 Stoneleigh St., Albion, Brisbane, Queensland 4010, Australia.

CAREER: Queensland Museum, Fortitude Valley, Australia, photographer, 1958-66; free-lance writer and photographer, 1967—. *Member:* Australian Society of Authors. *Awards, honors:* (Co-recipient) second prize, Captain Cook Bicentenary Literary Competition, 1970.

WRITINGS—With wife, Kay Breeden: *The Life of the Kangaroo,* Angus & Robertson, 1966, Taplinger, 1967; *Animals of Eastern Australia,* Harrap, 1967; (with Peter Slater) *Birds of Australia,* Taplinger, 1968; *Living Marsupials,* Collins (Sydney), 1970; *A Natural History of Australia,* Volume I: *Tropical Queensland,* Volume II: *Australia's South East,* Collins, 1970, Taplinger, 1971, abridged edition published as *Wildlife of Eastern Australia,* Collins, 1973, Taplinger, 1974; *Australia's North,* Collins, 1980.

Contributor to periodicals, including *National Geographic, Natural History,* and *National Audubon.* Editor of *Quarterly Wildlife in Australia,* 1966.

AVOCATIONAL INTERESTS: Reading, attending movies.*

* * *

BRENNAN, Matthew J. 1917-

PERSONAL: Born July 12, 1917, in Litchfield, Conn.; son of Patrick S. and Jane (Bannon) Brennan; married Muriel Trebay, September 3, 1943; children: Patti Jo. *Education:* Brown University, A.B., 1939; Columbia University, A.M., 1946, Ed.D., 1949; graduate study at Massachusetts Institute of Technology, 1943. *Home:* Brentree Farms, Milford, Pa. 18337.

CAREER: Manhattan College, Bronx, N.Y., instructor in biology, 1946-49; Jersey City State College, Jersey City, N.J., assistant professor of biology, 1949-55; Fitchburg State College, Fitchburg, Mass., professor of biology, 1955-57; Ellsworth Station, Antarctica, chief scientist, 1957-59; specialist scientist with U.S. Office of Education, 1959-60; chief of conservation education with U.S. Forest Service, 1960-63; director of Pinchot Institute for Conservation Studies, 1963-70; Brentree Environmental Center, Pennsylvania, director, 1970—. Director of National Science Foundation Summer Institutes, Rutgers University, 1957 and 1959; director of UNESCO Conservation Curriculum Project for Venezuela, 1970—; visiting professor of environmental studies at Pennsylvania State University, 1974. Member of national board of directors of Girl Scouts of the U.S.A. *Member:* American Forestry Association (honorary vice-president, 1964; director, 1968-70). *Awards, honors:* Antarctica's Mount Brennan is named in his honor.

WRITINGS: (With Paul F. Brandwein and others) *The World of Living Things,* Harcourt, 1964; (editor) *People and Their Environment: Teacher's Curriculum Guide to Conservation Education,* Ferguson, 1969; (with Brandwein and others) *The Earth: Its Living Things,* Harcourt, 1970; *The Environment and You* (juvenile; illustrated by Anthony Tallarico), Grosset, 1973. Contributor of articles to periodicals such as *National Wildlife* and *Education Digest.**

* * *

BRENNAN, Nicholas (Stephen) 1948-

PERSONAL: Born in 1948 in Coventry, England. *Education:* Attended Coventry College of Art.

CAREER: Author and illustrator of books for young people.

WRITINGS—All juvenile; self-illustrated: *Jasper and the Giant,* Holt, 1970; *The Wonderful Potion, and Other Stories,* Longman Young Books, 1970; *Olaf's Incredible Machine,* Longman Young Books, 1973, Windmill Books, 1975; *The Blundles' Bad Day,* Kestrel Books, 1974; *The Magic Jacket,* Kestrel Books, 1976.

Illustrator: Ruth Jennings, *In the Bin,* Kestrel Books, 1979.*

* * *

BRIGGS, Shirley Ann 1918-

PERSONAL: Born May 12, 1918, in Iowa City, Iowa; daughter of John Ely and Nellie (Upham) Briggs. *Education:* University of Iowa, B.A. (with highest distinction), 1939, M.A., 1940. *Religion:* Presbyterian. *Home:* 7605 Honeywell Lane, Bethesda, Md. 20014. *Office:* Rachel Carson Trust for the Living Environment, Inc., 8940 Jones Mill Rd., Washington, D.C. 20015.

CAREER: North Dakota State College, Fargo, instructor in art, 1941-43; Glen Martin Co., Baltimore, Md., illustrator, 1943-45; U.S. Fish and Wildlife Service, Washington, D.C., information specialist, 1945-47; chief of graphics section of Bureau of Reclamation of Department of Interior, 1948-54; Smithsonian Institute, Washington, D.C., painter of habitat group backgrounds, 1954-55; associated with diorama productions of National Park Service, 1956-57; teacher of natural history field studies at graduate school of U.S. Department of Agriculture, 1962—; Rachel Carson Trust for the Living Environment, Inc., Washington, D.C., secretary, 1966-70, executive director, 1970—. Member of advisory commission on pesticide policy of Environmental Protection Agency (EPA), 1975-77; member of executive committee of Natural Resources Council of America, 1977—; member of advisory panel on monitoring environmental contaminants for Office of Technical Assessment of U.S. Congress, 1978-79.

MEMBER: American Ornithologists Union, American Association of University Women (art chairman of Washington, D.C., chapter, 1956-57), Ecological Society of America, So-

ciety for Occupational and Environmental Health, Wilson Ornithological Society, Audubon Naturalist Society of the Central Atlantic States (director, 1948-49; vice-president of publications, 1956-69; honorary vice-president, 1975), Phi Beta Kappa, Pi Beta Phi. *Awards, honors:* Paul Bartsch Award from Audubon Naturalist Society of the Central Atlantic States, 1972.

WRITINGS—Illustrator: Arthur S. Einarsen, *The Pronghorn Antelope and Its Management,* Wildlife Management Institute, 1948; (with Bob Hines; and editor with Chandler S. Robbins) *Where Birds Live: Habitats in the Middle Atlantic States,* Audubon Society of the District of Columbia, 1951; Alfred Stefferud, *The Wonders of Seeds* (juvenile), Harcourt, 1956; (and editor) *The Trumpeter Swan: Its History, Habitats, and Population in the United States,* U.S. Fish and Wildlife Service, 1960; Elizabeth Keyser Cooper, *Insects and Plants* (juvenile), Harcourt, 1963; (and editor with Irston R. Barnes and others) *Landscaping for Birds,* Audubon Naturalist Society of the Central Atlantic States, 1973. Also illustrator and editor, with others, of Audubon Naturalist Society of the Central Atlantic States's field guides, including *A Field List of Birds of the District of Columbia Region,* 1961, revised edition, 1968.

Contributor of articles to magazines, including *American Forests.* Editor of *Atlantic Naturalist,* 1947-69.*

* * *

BRILES, Judith 1946-

PERSONAL: Born February 20, 1946, in Pasadena, Calif.; daughter of James and Mary Tuthill; married John Maling (a professor), December 18, 1973; children: Shelley Briles, Frank Briles, Sheryl Briles. *Education:* College of Financial Planning, Denver, Colo., C.F.P., 1978; Pepperdine University, M.B.A., 1980. *Politics:* Republican. *Home:* 1790 Holly Ave., Menlo Park, Calif. 94025. *Agent:* Jacques de Spoelberch, South Norwalk, Conn. 06854. *Office:* Briles & Associates, 2345 Yale St., Palo Alto, Calif. 94025.

CAREER: Bateman, Eicher, Hill, Richards (stockbrokers), Torrance, Calif., broker's assistant, 1970-72; E. F. Hutton (stockbroker), Palo Alto, Calif., stockbroker, 1972-78; Briles-Lefourt Co., Palo Alto, president and principal, 1978-79; Briles & Associates, Palo Alto, president and principal, 1979—. Instructor at Foothill College, Los Altos Hills, Calif., and De Anza College, Cupertino, Calif., both 1976—. Past director and past president of advisory board of Ws Women's Bank. Secretary, treasurer, vice-president, president, and member of executive committee of Foothill-De Anza Colleges Foundation, 1979-82. Director of Scholar Opera. *Member:* International Association of Financial Planners, Network, Professional Women's Alliance (president, 1977-78), Commonwealth Club, Women's Forum West, Bay Area Executive Women's Forum, Beta Sigma Phi.

WRITINGS: The Woman's Guide to Financial Savvy, St. Martin's, 1981; *Minding Your Own Money,* Simon & Schuster, 1983. Editor of monthly *More Money.* Contributing editor of National Association of Female Executives.

WORK IN PROGRESS: "A study on female relations versus male relations in business."

SIDELIGHTS: In *The Woman's Guide to Financial Savvy,* Judith Briles advises single wage earners on long-range financial planning. In short, the work is a guide for fighting taxes and inflation as well as a handbook with instructions for building a nest egg. Besides stocks and bonds, the financial planner discusses real estate plus money market and mutual funds. Praising the book and its author, a *Washington Post Book World* critic wrote: "She likes the subject, has worked hard to make sense out of it and she's as lucid a writer as you're likely to find in the literature."

Briles told *CA:* "I find it essential to write in simple jargon versus the complex that so many of my associates produce. I am extremely interested in the differences between men and women in business practices—is it cultural or planned? Very motivated, I want to spend more time writing and less in service-related areas. I am looking forward to newsletter editing."

BIOGRAPHICAL/CRITICAL SOURCES: Washington Post Book World, August 23, 1981.

*　　*　　*

BRING, Mitchell 1951-

PERSONAL: Born November 1, 1951, in Brooklyn, N.Y.; son of Stanley (a businessman) and Gloria (a teacher; maiden name, Freidman) Bring. *Education:* Washington University, St. Louis, Mo., A.B., 1973; attended Kyoto University, 1977-79; University of California, Berkeley, M.Arch., 1981. *Office:* College of Architecture, Georgia Institute of Technology, Atlanta, Ga. 30332.

CAREER: Commercial Design, St. Louis, Mo., designer, 1973; Missouri Machinery and Engineering, St. Louis, designer, 1974-75; University of California, Berkeley, lecturer in architecture, 1981; Montana State University, Bozeman, assistant professor of architecture, 1981-82; Georgia Institute of Technology, Atlanta, assistant professor of architecture, 1982—. *Member:* Society of Architectural Historians. *Awards, honors:* First place award from St. Louis Art Museum competition, 1975; fellow of Japanese Ministry of Education, 1978-79.

WRITINGS: (With Josse Wayembergh) *Japanese Gardens: Design and Meaning,* McGraw, 1981. Contributor to architecture journals.

WORK IN PROGRESS: The Roots of Modern Japanese Architecture; The Beaux Arts Pattern Book.

SIDELIGHTS: Bring commented: "I am deeply moved by the vast panorama of cultural contact and influence, especially as it has been expressed in the meeting of East and West. My own experience in Asia has given me an opportunity to participate as an agent, observer, and interpreter in that process of cultural diffusion.

"While I am studying the Western influence on Japan following the trade treaties secured by Perry in 1854, I'm specifically interested in changes in the Japanese design aesthetic as it applies to architecture and to graphic and product design."

BIOGRAPHICAL/CRITICAL SOURCES: Washington University Alumni News, winter, 1981.

*　　*　　*

BRONAUGH, Robert Brett 1947-

PERSONAL: Surname is pronounced Bra-gnaw; born April 23, 1947, in Washington, D.C.; son of Frank Harwood (a government official) and Mary Eleanor (Brett) Bronaugh. *Education:* North Carolina Wesleyan College, B.A., 1970. *Politics:* Democrat. *Religion:* Episcopalian. *Home:* 7417 Lynnhurst St., Chevy Chase, Md. 20815.

CAREER: Performing arts administrator. *The Performer* (magazine), Washington, D.C., editor and feature writer, 1971-72; Lewis Fields Associates (advertising and public relations agency), Washington, D.C., public relations and advertising account executive, 1971-72; Ford's Theatre Society, Washington, D.C., assistant general manager, 1972-73; Loews L'Enfant Plaza Hotel, Washington, D.C., director of public relations, 1973; American Theatre, Washington, D.C., public relations director and press agent, 1973; free-lance creative communications consultant, promotional manager, and literary agent, Washington, D.C., 1973-75; Harlequin Dinner Theatre, Atlanta, Ga., director of public relations, 1975; Maryland Outdoor Drama Association, Inc., Columbia, company manager, business manager and public relations director, 1975-76; researcher and writer, 1977—. Campaign coordinator at Chelsea Projects Ltd., 1973.

WRITINGS: The Celebrity Birthday Book (Movie/Entertainment Book Club selection), Jonathan David, 1981. Contributor to *The Performer.*

SIDELIGHTS: Bronaugh told *CA:* "The publication of any book represents a great personal and inner gratification for the author, but the challenge of creating and authoring a new and completely different type of book, dissimilar from any book which has ever been previously published, is the ultimate literary high." Bronaugh's reference work, *The Celebrity Birthday Book,* lists the professional and full real names of more than ten thousand celebrities in alphabetical order, supplies the fields of endeavor in which they have achieved their prominence, and provides their birth dates, all of which is supplied in both alphabetical and chronological sections. The book deals primarily with twentieth-century people, representing a comprehensive cross-section of individuals who have received recognition in all walks of life. In addition, the work supplies astrological and numerological information.

Besides Bronaugh's interests in celebrities and the performing arts, the author is an avid genealogist. Bronaugh commented: "As a tenth-generation American, I have traced both my paternal and maternal heritage back to the mid-seventeenth century in the colonies. I believe that a thorough knowledge and understanding of an individual's own personal family history provides one with a deeper appreciation and interest in our country's history. The 'me first principle' continues to flourish, and we often ask ourselves: 'How does this relate to me?' The study of the colonial period, the War of 1812, the Civil War, etc., is often boring, but becomes fascinatingly relevant if you can relate your relatives' whereabouts, lifestyles, and even participations in these and other key eras. Hence, genealogy is the prime prerequisite to American history."

AVOCATIONAL INTERESTS: Collecting political memorabilia (especially campaign buttons of Lyndon Johnson and Jimmy Carter), following the PGA and LPGA golf tours and the NASCAR auto racing circuit, traveling.

*　　*　　*

BROPHY, Ann 1931-

PERSONAL: Born January 14, 1931, in Indianapolis, Ind.; daughter of Harvey Mitchell (a physician and professor) and Ruth (a kindergarten teacher and nurse; maiden name, Leffler) Anthony; married Charles G. Brophy (in public relations), December 9, 1961; children: Anthony, Ruth Ann, Andrew. *Education:* Attended Skidmore College, 1948-49; Western College for Women, B.A., 1952; studied with Katharine Gibbs, 1952-53. *Religion:* Episcopalian. *Home:* 142 Main St., Southport, Conn. 06490. *Agent:* Writers House, Inc., 21 West 26th St., New York, N.Y. 10010.

CAREER: Assistant to playwrights Samson Raphaelson, Robert Sherwood, Sydney Kingsley, and George Kaufman, and to cartoonist Walt Kelly, 1954-61; writer, 1954—. *Member:* National Writers Club, National Academy of Television Arts and Sciences, Society of Children's Book Writers, Authors Guild.

WRITINGS: Flash and the Swan (juvenile), F. Warne, 1981. Author of television script "Flash and the Swan." Contributor to magazines, including *Humpty Dumpty* and *Highlights.*

WORK IN PROGRESS: A juvenile picture book, *A Thing on a String,* publication by F. Warne expected in 1984; a sequel to *Flash and the Swan;* a science fiction fantasy for middle-grade readers; a television script for a teenage (or family) special.

SIDELIGHTS: Brophy told *CA:* "I came into writing for children through the back door—an afternoon class on the subject at a local university. Once I entered the room of children's literature, I had no desire to leave what, I feel, is the most substantial and worthwhile literary location. And it is so much fun!"

BIOGRAPHICAL/CRITICAL SOURCES: Bridgeport Sunday Post, April 12, 1981; *Fairfield Citizen News,* July 8, 1981.

* * *

BROWN, Sanborn C(onner)   1913-1981

OBITUARY NOTICE—See index for *CA* sketch: Born January 19, 1913, in Beirut, Lebanon; died after a long illness, November 28, 1981, in Henniker, N.H. Educator, physicist, editor, and author. Brown taught physics at the Massachusetts Institute of Technology for more than thirty years. He also served as a technical adviser to the U.S. delegation of the United Nations International Conference on Peaceful Uses of Atomic Energy and as a U.S. delegate to the International Atomic Energy Agency Conference on Plasma Physics and Controlled Thermonuclear Fusion. Brown specialized in the behavior and structure of plasmas, high-temperature ionized gases. He wrote a textbook about plasmas titled *Basic Data of Plasma Physics.* Brown's other works include *Count Rumford, Physicist Extraordinary, The Education of a Physicist,* and *Physics Fifty Years Later.* In addition, he edited such works as *Electrons, Ions, and Waves: Selected Works of William Phelps Allis* and *Collected Works of Count Rumford.* Obituaries and other sources: *New York Times,* December 2, 1981.

* * *

BROWNSTEIN, Ronald J.   1958-

PERSONAL: Born April 6, 1958, in New York, N.Y.; son of David (an electrician) and Shirley Brownstein. *Education:* Attended State University of New York at Binghamton, 1979. *Residence:* Washington, D.C. *Office address:* P.O. Box 19367, Washington, D.C. 20036.

CAREER: Staff writer for Ralph Nader, Washington, D.C., 1979—.

WRITINGS: (Editor) *Selecting a President,* Public Citizen, 1980; (editor with Ralph Nader and John Richard) *Who's Poisoning America?,* Sierra Books, 1981; (with Nina Easton) *The Reagan Regime,* Presidential Accountability Group, 1982. Contributor of several dozen articles to magazines, including *Newsday, Reader's Digest, Parade, Nation, Progressive,* and *Washington Monthly,* and to newspapers.

* * *

BRUNING, Nancy P(auline)   1948-

PERSONAL: Born November 7, 1948, in New York; daughter of Nicholas Cornelius and Anne Marie (Liebenberg) Bruning; married Michael Ross (a writer and musician), December 12, 1981. *Education:* Pratt Institute, B.A., 1969. *Home:* 325 First Ave., New York, N.Y. 10003. *Agent:* Susan Ann Protter, 110 West 40th St., New York, N.Y. 10018. *Office:* 100 Fifth Ave., New York, N.Y. 10011.

CAREER: McCall's Needlework and Crafts, New York City, writer and crafts designer, 1971-73; Tree Communications, Inc., New York City, editor and project director, 1974-77; free-lance writer, 1977—. *Member:* Authors Guild.

WRITINGS: (Editor with Robert Levine) *The Cold Weather Catalog: Learning to Love Winter,* Doubleday, 1977; (editor) Sylvia Rosenthal, *Cosmetic Surgery: A Consumer's Guide,* Lippincott, 1977; (contributor) Maggie Oster, editor, *The Green Pages,* Ballantine, 1977; *Lady's Luck Companion* (on gambling), Harper, 1979; *The Beach Book,* Houghton, 1981; (with Jane Katz) *Total Fitness Through Swimming,* Doubleday, 1981; *A Consumer Guide to Contact Lenses,* Dial, 1982. Contributor to *Family Creative Workshop.* Contributor to magazines and newspapers, including *Travel and Leisure.*

SIDELIGHTS: Nancy Bruning told *CA:* "I write and edit illustrated books as an extension of my degree in visual communication. No matter what the subject matter, one of my goals is to combine words and pictures in order to communicate most effectively. I always try to inform entertainingly and entertain informatively.

"The age of video-computer communications will no doubt change the face of publishing. I find this exciting, not frightening. Besides, nothing can ever take the place of curling up under a shady tree with a good book that has real pages to turn."

* * *

BUERO VALLEJO, Antonio   1916-

PERSONAL: Born September 29, 1916, in Guadalajara, Spain; son of Francisco Buero and Cruz Vallejo; married Victoria Rodriguez, 1969; children: two sons. *Education:* Attended Instituto de Segunda Ensenanza de Guadalajara and Escuela de Bellas Artes de Madrid. *Address:* Calle General Diaz Porlier 36, Madrid 1, Spain.

CAREER: Painter and playwright, 1949—. Lecturer at universities in the United States, 1966. *Member:* International Committee of the Theatre of the Nations, Hispanic Society of America, American Association of Teachers of Spanish and Portuguese (honorary fellow), Society of Spanish and Spanish-American Studies (honorary fellow), Modern Language Association (honorary fellow), Deutscher Hispanistenverband (honorary fellow), Sociedad General de Autores de Espana, Real Academia Espanola, Ateneo de Madrid, Circulo de Bellas Artes de Madrid (honorary fellow).

AWARDS, HONORS: Premio Lope de Vega, 1949, for "Historia de una escalera"; Premio Amigos de los Quintero, 1949, for "Las palabras en la arena"; Premio Maria Rolland, 1956, 1958, and 1960; Premio Nacional de Teatro, 1957, 1958, 1959, and 1980; Premio March de Teatro, 1959; Premio de la critica de Barcelona, 1960; Premio Larra, 1962; Medalla de oro del espectador y la critica, 1967, 1970, 1974, 1976, 1977, and 1981; Premio Leopoldo Cano, 1968, 1972, 1974, 1975, and 1977; elected to Royal Spanish Academy, 1971; Premio Mayte, 1974; Premio Foro Teatral, 1974; Medalla de oro "Gaceta illustrada," 1976; Officer des Palmes Academiques de France, 1980.

WRITINGS—Plays; all published by Ediciones Alfil, except as noted: *Historia de una escalera* (three-act drama; title means "Story of a Staircase"; first produced in Madrid, Spain, at Teatro Espanol, October 14, 1949), J. Janes, 1950, Scribner (edited by Jose Sanchez), 1955 (also see below); *En la ardiente oscuridad* (three-act drama; title means "In the Burning Darkness"; first produced in Madrid at Teatro Nacional Maria Guerrero, December 1, 1950), 1951, Scribner (edited by Samuel A. Wofsy; introduction by Juan Rodriguez-Castellano), 1954, 7th edition, Escelicer, 1970 (also see below); *Palabras en la arena* (one-act tragedy; title means "Words in the Sand"; first produced in Madrid at Teatro Espanol, December 19, 1949), [Madrid], 1952 (also see below); *La tejedora de suenos* (three-act drama; title means "The Dream Weaver"; first produced in Madrid at Teatro Espanol, January 11, 1952), 1952, Escelicer, 1970 (also see below); *La Senal que se espera* (three-act dramatic comedy; title means "The Expected Sign"; first produced in Madrid at Teatro de la Infanta Isabel, May 21, 1952), 1952, 3rd edition, 1966.

Casi un cuento de hadas (three-act variation on Perrault; title means "Almost a Fairy Tale"; first produced in Madrid at Teatro Alcazar, January 9, 1953), 1953, 2nd edition, 1965, 3rd edition, Narcea, 1981; *Madrugada* (two-act dramatic episode; title means "Daybreak"; first produced in Madrid at Teatro Alcazar, December 9, 1953), 1953, 3rd edition, 1968, Blaisdell Publishing Co. (edited by Donald W. Bleznick and Martha T. Halsey), 1969 (also see below); *Irene o el tesoro* (three-act; title means "Irene; or, the Treasure"; first produced in Madrid at Teatro Nacional Maria Guerrero, December 14, 1954), 1955, 2nd edition, 1965 (also see below); *Hoy es fiesta* (three-act tragicomedy; title means "Today Is a Holiday"; first produced in Madrid at Teatro Nacional Maria Guerrero, September 20, 1956), 1957, Harrap (edited by J. E. Lejon), 1964, Heath, 1966, Ediciones Alman, 1978 (also see below); *Las cartas boca abajo* (two-part drama; title means "The Cards Face Down"; first produced in Madrid at Teatro de la Reina Victoria, November 5, 1957), 1958, 3rd edition, 1967, Prentice-Hall (edited by Felix G. Ilarraz), 1967 (also see below); *Un sonador para un pueblo* (two-part historical drama; title means "A Dreamer for the People"; first produced in Madrid at Teatro Espanol, December 18, 1958), 1959, Norton (edited by M. Manzanares de Cirre), 1965, 3rd edition, Escelicer, 1973 (also see below).

Las meninas (two-part historical drama; title means "The Ladies-in-Waiting"; first produced Madrid at Teatro Espanol, December 9, 1960), 1961, Scribner (edited by Rodriguez-Castellano), 1963, 6th edition, Escelicer, 1972 (also see below); *El concierto de San Ovidio* (three-act dramatic parable; first produced in Madrid at Teatro Goya, November 16, 1962), prologue by J. P. Borel, Ayma, 1963, Scribner (edited by Pedro N. Trakas; introduction by Rodriguez-Castellano), 1965, translation by Farris Anderson published as *The Concert at Saint Ovide*, Pennsylvania State University Press, 1967, new edition, Escelicer, 1968; *Aventura en lo gris* (two-act drama with one dream; title means "Adventure in Grayness"; first produced in Madrid at Teatro Recoletos, October 1, 1963), 1964 (also see below); *El tragaluz* (two parts; title means "The Skylight"; first produced in Madrid at Teatro Bellas Artes, October 7, 1967), 1968, 4th edition, Escelicer, 1972, Scribner (edited by Anthony M. Pasquariello and Patricia W. O'Connor), 1977 (also see below); *Mito* (book of an opera; title means "Myth"), 1968.

El sueno de la razon (two-act; title means "The Dream of Reason"; first produced in Madrid at Teatro de la Reina Victoria, February 6, 1970), Escelicer, 1970, Center for Curriculum Development (Philadelphia; edited by John Dowling),

1971 (also see below); *La doble historia del Doctor Valmy* (two parts; title means "The Double Case History of Doctor Valmy"; first produced in Chester, England, at Gateway Theatre, 1968 [written in 1964]), prologue and notes by Alfonso M. Gil, illustrated by Michele C. Gil, Center for Curriculum Development, 1970 (also see below); *Llegada de los dioses* (title means "The Gods' Arrival"; first produced in Madrid at Teatro Lara, September 17, 1971), Aguilar, 1973 (also see below); *El terror inmovil* (tragedy in six scenes; title means "Motionless Terror"), Universidad de Murcia, 1979.

Also author of "La fundacion" (two parts; title means "The Foundation"), first produced in Madrid at Teatro Figaro, January 15, 1974 (also see below); "La detonacion" (two parts; title means "The Detonation"), first produced in Madrid at Teatro Bellas Artes, September 20, 1977 (also see below); "Jueces en la noche" (two parts; title means "Judges in the Night"), first produced in Madrid at Teatro Lara, October 2, 1979 (also see below); "Caiman" (two parts title means "Alligator"), first produced in Madrid at Teatro Reina Victoria, September 10, 1981 (also see below).

Omnibus volumes: *Historia de una escalera* [y] *Las palabras en la arena*, Ediciones Alfil, 1952, 12th edition, Escelicer, 1974; *Teatro: En la ardiente oscuridad, Madrugada, Hoy es fiesta, Las cartas boca abajo*, Editorial Losada, 1959; *Teatro: Historia de una escalera, La tejedora de suenos, Irene o el tesoro, un sonador para un pueblo*, Editorial Losada, 1962; *Teatro selecto: Historia de una escalera, Las cartas boca abajo, Un sonador para un pueblo, Las meninas, El concierto de San Ovidio*, Escelicer, 1966, 2nd edition, 1972; *Dos dramas de Buero Vallejo; Aventura en lo gris* [y] *Las palabras en la arena*, edited by Isabel Magana Schevill, Apple-Century-Crofts, 1967; *En la ardiente oscuridad* [y] *Irene o el tesoro*, E.M.E.S.A. (Madrid), 1967, 2nd edition, 1972; *Hoy es fiesta, Las meninas,* [y] *El tragaluz*, Taurus Ediciones, 1968, 4th edition, 1982.

El tragaluz [y] *El sueno de la razon*, Espasa-Calpe, 1970, 7th edition, 1981; *El concierto de San Ovidio* [y] *El tragaluz*, introduction by Ricardo Domenech, Castalia, 1971; *En el ardiente oscuridad* [y] *Un sonador para un pueblo*, Espasa-Calpe, 1972, 3rd edition, 1977; *Historia de una escalera* [y] *Llegada de los dioses*, Salvat, 1973; *Hoy es fiesta* [y] *Aventura en lo gris*, E.M.E.S.A., 1974; *El concierto de San Ovidio* [y] *La fundacion*, Espasa-Calpe, 1974, 4th edition, 1980; *Historia de una escalera* [y] *Las meninas*, prologue by Domenech, Espasa-Calpe, 1975, 5th edition, 1980; *La doble historia del Doctor Valmy* [y] *Mito*, prologue by Francisco Garcia Pavon, Espasa-Calpe, 1976; *La Tejedora de suenos* [y] *Llegada de los dioses*, edited by Luis Iglesias Feijoo, D. L. Catedra, 1976, 5th edition, 1982; *La detonacion* [y] *Las palabras en la arena*, prologue by Luciano Garcia Lorenzo, Espasa-Calpe, 1979; *Jueces en la noche* [y] *Hoy es fiesta*, prologue by Feijoo, Espasa-Calpe, 1981; *Caiman* [y] *Las cartas boca abajo*, Espasa-Calpe, 1981.

Work represented in "Teatro espanol" series; edited by F. C. Sainz de Robles; published by Aguilar: *Teatro espanol, 1949-50*, 1951; . . . , *1950-1951*, 1952; . . . , *1951-52*, 1953; . . . , *1953-1954*, 1955; . . . , *1954-1955*, 1956; . . . , *1956-1957*, 1958; . . . , *1957-1958*, 1959; . . . , *1958-1959*, 1960; . . . , *1962-1963*, 1964; . . . , *1967-1968*, 1969; . . . , *1969-1970*, 1971; . . . , *1971-1972*, 1973; . . . , *1973-1974*, 1975.

Work represented in anthologies, including: *Teatro: Buero Vallejo, Delgado Benavente y Alfonso Sastre*, Ediciones Tawantinsuyu, 1960; *Buero Vallejo: Antologia teatral*, Coculsa, 1966; Robert W. Corrigan, *Masterpieces of the Modern Spanish Theatre*, Collier, 1967; Marion Holt, *The Modern Spanish Stage: Four Plays*, Hill & Wang, 1970; *Spanische Stuecke*, Henschelverlag Berlin, 1976; *Anos dificiles*, Bruguera, 1977; *Las cartas boca abajo por Antonio Buero Vallejo* [y] *Los buenos dias perdidos por Antonio Galau,* edited by Alvaro M. Custodio and Angeles Cardona de Gibert, Tarraco, 1977. Plays also included in *Collection teatro,* Ediciones Alfil.

Other: (Translator) William Shakespeare, *Hamlet,* Ediciones Alfil, 1962; "Me llamo Antonio Buero Vallejo" (recording; title means "My Name Is Antonio Buero Vallejo"), La Palabra, 1964; (with others) *Teatro* (essays), Taurus Ediciones, 1968; *Tres maestros ante el publico* (biographical essays on Ramon del Valle-Inclan, Diego Rodriguez de Silva y Velazquez, and Frederico Garcia Lorca; title means "Three Teachers Before the Public"), Alianza Editorial, 1973; (with others) *Teatro espanol actual* (literary criticism), Fundacion Juan March, 1977. Also author of screenplays and translator of Brecht's *Mutter Courage* and of Ibsen's *Vildanden.*

Contributor: *Informaciones: Extraordinario teatral del sabado de Gloria,* Madrid], 1956; Guillermo Diaz Plaja, editor, *El teatro: Encyclopedia de arte escenico,* [Madrid], 1958. Also contributor of articles and criticisms to periodicals, including *Correo literario, Primer acto, Revista de occidente,* and *Cuadernos de agora.*

WORK IN PROGRESS: "I am preparing a new play, and I am finishing up a Spanish adaptation of Pirandello's 'Come tu mi vuoi.'"

SIDELIGHTS: Initially Antonio Buero Vallejo aspired to be a painter, but he was sidetracked by the Spanish Civil War in 1936. At that time, he left school to become a medical corpsman for the Loyalists, though he had no major role in the war. When the fighting ended in a victory for Franco's government, Buero Vallejo was sentenced to death for his involvement with the Republicans. Although the sentence was commuted, he was imprisoned until 1945. Upon his release, while he continued to paint, Buero Vallejo began writing plays for screen and stage productions, particularly for Spain's Theatre of Commitment.

The Theatre of Commitment, in which Buero Vallejo is the leading figure, is a reaction to the restrained conditions in the Spanish theatre and in Spanish life. A protest against the Spanish establishment, "the Theatre of Commitment," said Francis Donahue in *Books Abroad,* "is characterized by the importance of the dramatist's political view in relation to his art." For his part, Buero Vallejo, angered at the social conditions in his homeland, writes (under censorship) to change the lives of the oppressed members of Spanish society.

Given his political situation, the playwright must promulgate a social message covertly, constructing a social drama that allows his audience to see the problems of men without incurring the wrath of a government unreceptive to criticism. The result, Donahue noticed, is "non-political, political theater" productions with indirect impact so nobody's toes are stepped on. The playwright also presents drama with implicit social messages because, as *Hispania*'s Kessel Schwartz stated, "he realizes the inefficacy of direct action against the resistance of the spectator to change his established ideas." "These, then," suggested Donahue, "are plays of protest and outrage directed to the middle-class theater-going public. There is no direct protest, yet their hoped-for effect—on middle-level people 'who may be vaguely sympathetic to the cause preached but are a little sluggish and sleepy about it'—is one of thoughtful anger."

Buero Vallejo's aim in writing, contended Martha T. Halsey in her book *Antonio Buero Vallejo,* is to move beyond the fanaticism and sectarianism so prevalent in Spain's past. Promoting self-realization through compassion, "Bueroism," in

Sergio Nerva's opinion, is a "search for love, faith, justice, and, in short, peace. Or if one prefers, for truth."

Structurally, his plays are open-ended in that the curtain closes with a question, and "answers to that question belong to life, not necessarily to art," the playwright once remarked. They are all tragedies since that genre allows Buero Vallejo to comprehend "the great miracle of reality," which is his goal. To Buero Vallejo, only tragedy can bring an understanding of man and his universe while advancing social causes, thus making it ideal material for the Theatre of Commitment. As Schwartz noted, "Tragedy helps man understand life's sorrows, face his situation positively, and attempt to overcome it as he seeks meaning in a world whose reality may be sombre and pessimistic in appearance."

At the root of man's tragedy is catharsis, which Buero Vallejo defines as inspired revelation that prompts action. "Catharsis, as Buero views it in nearly almost all his works," Schwartz assessed, "is a sublimation, an improvement rather than a relief. Compassion, terror and anger, once sublimated, must clearly approximate the human condition which tragedy attempts to define for us, but every spectator will react differently to the pathetic, moral, or religious ingredients of the tragedy." It is the sadness of tragedy that abets reflection on social ills. But it is catharsis that transports the evoked emotions, like pity or fear, from a primitive level to a moral one.

For the playwright, tragedy, Halsey indicated, is "a phenomenon which is always positive, which proposes an encounter with the truth which may free man from his spiritual blindness." It occurs whenever an individual questions his destiny or when he is overwhelmed by life. Buero Vallejo's tragic figures fail to realize their true potentials and leave nothing to future generations. The characters search for truth through the realization of their capabilities and by discovering the metaphysical meaning of life.

Accepting the fact that tragedy ennobles men (both his characters and his audience), Buero Vallejo still calls tragedy the result of man's blundering. Said Halsey: "The universe imposes limitations, but it is the individual's own moral blindness—his self-deception or unwillingness to confront the reality of his situation, as well as his innate egoism—which prevent his from overcoming these limitations and which bring down upon him suffering and grief." Buero Vallejo's brand of tragedy, Schwartz submitted, "reveals his preoccupation with man's fate, both metaphysical and social, as reflected in the repeated conflicts one finds in his theater between individuality and collectivity, between necessity [free will] and liberty [human limitations]."

Buero Vallejo's heroes, then, are morally superior individuals, labeled insane or derided as idealists, who attempt to build a better world. "A man's success in life," wrote William Giuliano in *Hispanofila,* "is to be measured by the importance of the contribution he has made to the betterment of society." To help society, the playwright maintained, a man must move beyond his own faults, transcend himself. But his primary obstacle in overcoming himself, his inherent self-deception or his tendency to accept illusion in place of truth, means that he will only achieve happiness through tremendous effort. With so tragic a nature, man must transcend by self-abnegation; that is, man defeats his egoism only through kindness and compassion. So from the playwright's point of view, man is not a victim of his fate because he has the ability to overcome reverses of fortune.

Typically, "the underlying theme of Buero Vallejo's plays," Giuliano observed, "is unquestionably man's efforts to realize his full capacities against the internal and external forces that restrain him.'' But at the center of this tragic fight in nearly every one of Buero Vallejo's creations is hope, for without a background of hope there is no anguish, no despair. ''In the eternal struggle between faith and doubt, the essence of all tragedy, hope helps revitalize faith and aids spiritual development, as part of the living conflict in man's soul,'' Schwartz commented. Hope, therefore, with optimism and achievement, is always evident in Buero Vallejo's work since it contributes to a more complete comprehension of man and his universe.

Of hope there are two types: one being metaphysical—man's hope in a transcendent order; the other being social—man's hope in a remedy for earthly suffering. As Halsey explained: ''Some of Buero's characters search for the understanding or truth which will permit them to find an earthly solution to human problems; others, for the truth which will enable them to find a metaphysical justification for the world.''

As a social dramatist, Buero Vallejo maintains his belief in tragic hope since, Schwartz remarked, he desires ''a better world of peace and brotherhood for which he feels all men are responsible.'' For example, in ''Historia de una escalera,'' the playwright asks for a more fluid social structure in Spain. The play revolves around a stairway that has nothing at the top or at the bottom. A symbol of the Spanish people who have little, if any, social mobility, the stairs illustrate that generation after generation of Spaniards are stuck in a rut from which there is no escape. ''Coursing through the play are sharp scenes of individual conflict which gather like a summer storm and break with lightning rapidity over the staircase,'' said Donahue. ''Simmering there are such words as: *misery, squalor, pettiness, quarrels, anguish, poverty*.'' Like ''Historia de una escalera,'' ''Hoy es fiesta'' continues the criticism of Spanish life by portraying the anguish of those living in the tenements of Madrid.

Sporting too obvious a social message, ''La doble historia del Doctor Valmy'' never was performed in Spain until 1976 because of its political implications. Written in 1964, it contains, said critics, a sense of moral outrage. The play is about man's reluctance to face reality, about ''the deafness—and the guilt—of all men who prefer to remain unaware of the world in which they live,'' explained Halsey. One character, Daniel, a National Security Policeman, becomes impotent after torturing a prisoner. His psychiatrist tells Daniel that his condition is a manifestation of his repressed guilt accompanied by the fact that his wife will not believe that the government tortures people. More acceptable politically, ''El tragaluz'' is a study of the guilt of a son, who during a war leaves his sister to die, and of his father, driven insane with resentment for his son.

Buero Vallejo's historical plays provide an analysis of contemporary issues under the guise of the past. In ''Un sonador para un pueblo,'' the ideological struggles of Esquilache are used to reveal the good and evil aspects of the Spanish class structure. By employing the painter Velazquez as a character in ''Las meninas,'' ''Buero,'' stated Robert L. Nicholas in *Revista de estudios hispanicos,* ''seems to be saying that only he who appreciates artistic beauty can comprehend how intolerable is the suffering of the world. Conversely, only he who is cognizant of human suffering can comprehend the beautiful in art.''

Perhaps his most notable historical play, ''El sueno de la razon'' parallels the playwright's Spain with Goya's *Black Paintings,* illustrations of the evilness of the artist's time exemplified through vile creatures and captions like ''the dream of reason produces monsters.'' The inscription of one painting, the *Capricho,* reads: ''Fantasy without reason produces monstrosities,

but together they beget true artists and wonderful things.'' With this in mind, Buero Vallejo suggests that, rather than viewing Goya's work as a product of his alleged madness, it should be considered ''reasoned fantasy,'' thus it becomes a vehicle for understanding reality. ''We may conclude that he is saying,'' decided Schwartz, ''that when reason sleeps, monsters (Franco) may once again appear and that he is exposing the intolerance and absolutism of his own government which in all good conscience he feels he must continue to oppose.''

In addition, ''El sueno de la razon'' is held to be the first example of the ''total theatre'' in Spain. Always known for his ability to blend several art forms, Buero Vallejo combines visual and auditory effects to produce marked audience involvement in this play. Slides of the *Black Paintings* together with sounds without origins, such as hoots and howls, simulate the dark world of Goya's hallucinations. To communicate the artist's deafness, the playwright has the actors mouth their lines when Goya's character is on stage, so the audience can empathize with his deficiency.

Whether a historical production like ''El sueno de la razon'' or a straight-forward social drama like ''Historia de una escalera,'' Buero Vallejo still writes about the tragic nature of man in order to better society. Said Schwartz: He ''encourages the hope which lies in the human soul, postulating the possibility that one has of gaining over himself, because as long as man fights for faith and against his own evil, humanity and the world will survive.''

Buero Vallejo told *CA:* ''After three years of war and six long years in prison, I had fallen so far behind in my painting studies that I gave them up, and I set out to write for the theatre because, naturally, I had also loved the theatre since I was a child. Under Franco's strict censorship this undertaking proved even more difficult, but a set of favorable circumstances permitted me to continue onward. For me and for others, this censorship was a challenge, not just an obstacle, and I wasn't the only one to accept it. Poets, novelists, essayists, and other dramatists tried to convince the Spanish people (and themselves) that, although frequently very painful, a critical and reformative literature was possible in spite of all the environmental and administrative obstacles.

''In regards to the theatre, the official, unwritten watchwords were patriotism, escapism, moralism, and as much laughter as possible. Therefore, one had to do the opposite: tragedy which revealed instead of concealed the fact that one's destiny is a result of human and social factors instead of fate; a denunciation of injustices and frauds, a defense of liberty. And one had, at the same time, to produce serious experiences. Others will say to what extent each of us has attained these goals; perhaps they'll explain it tomorrow when the biases against this literature, which remain very strong, have been dismantled sociologically. I believe undeniably that, between all of us, something, and perhaps even a lot, has been gained. And because of this, our nation also had more support for resistance, hope and clear thinking.

''The Greek tragedians, Shakespeare, Cervantes, Calderon, Unamuno, Ibsen, Pirandello, Brecht have been, among others, my teachers, and their imprint can be observed in my theatre. Although less frequently noted, but perhaps even more important in some of my works, is the presence of Wells and Kafka. As a poet-friend of mine says about himself, I am also a 'child of well-known parents.' My originality, if I have any, is not based on denying them.''

AVOCATIONAL INTERESTS: Painting.

BIOGRAPHICAL/CRITICAL SOURCES: The Theatre Annual, Volume 19, 1962; Robert W. Corrigan, *Masterpieces of the Modern Spanish Theatre,* Collier Books, 1967; *Hispania,* December, 1968, September, 1969, December, 1969, September, 1971, December, 1972, September, 1974, September, 1978; *Revista de estudios hispanicos,* November, 1969, May, 1978; *Books Abroad,* summer, 1969; Emilio F. Bejel, *Lo moral, lo social y lo metafisico an el teatro de Buero Vallejo,* Florida State University, 1970; Marion Holt, *The Modern Spanish Stage: Four Plays,* Hill & Wang, 1970; *Hispanofila,* May, 1970; Robert L. Nicholas, *Tragic Stages of Antonio Buero Vallejo,* University of North Carolina, 1972; *Modern Language Journal,* February, 1972, January, 1973, December, 1978; Martha T. Halsey, *Antonio Buero Vallejo,* Twayne, 1973; *Modern Drama,* September, 1977; *Contemporary Literary Criticism,* Volume 15, Gale, 1980.

—*Sketch by Charity Anne Dorgan*

* * *

BULLARD, Pamela 1948-

PERSONAL: Born September 14, 1948, in Stoughton, Mass.; daughter of Richard K. (a banker) and Nancy (a clerk; maiden name, Stone) Bullard. *Education:* New York University, B.A., 1970; Yale University, M.S.L., 1979. *Home:* 30 Forest Rd., Acton, Mass. 01720. *Office:* WCVB-TV, 5 TV Pl., Needham, Mass. 01920.

CAREER: WCVB-TV, Needham, Mass., producer and director of national documentaries, 1979-80, senior producer, 1981—. Assistant professor at Boston University.

WRITINGS: (With Judith Stoia) *The Hardest Lesson: Personal Stories of a School Desegregation,* Little, Brown, 1980.

* * *

BULLEN, Keith Edward 1906-1976

OBITUARY NOTICE: Born June 29, 1906, in Auckland, New Zealand; died September 23, 1976. Scientist, educator, and author. Bullen was a professor of mathematics at the University of Sydney from 1946 to 1971. He also presided over the International Association of Seismology and Physics of the Interior of the Earth and was vice-president of the Scientific Committee on Antarctic Research. Bullen's writings include *Seismology, Introduction to the Theory of Mechanics,* and *The Earth's Density.* (Date of death provided by the University of Sydney.)

* * *

BULLOUGH, Geoffrey 1901-1982

OBITUARY NOTICE—See index for *CA* sketch: Born January 27, 1901, in Prestwich, England; died February 12, 1982, in Edinburgh, Scotland. Educator, lecturer, editor, and author. Bullough taught at Manchester, Edinburgh, and Sheffield universities for several years before joining the University of London's King's College as a professor. While at the college, he instituted a number of innovations, including the first baccalaureate degree in American literature at the university. Bullough's writings include *The Trend of Modern Poetry* and *Mirror of Minds: Changing Psychological Beliefs in English Poetry.* He also edited many volumes in the field of English literature, such as *The Oxford Book of Seventeenth Century Verse, Poems and Dramas of Fulke Greville, First Lord Brook,* and *Milton's Dramatic Poems.* The eight-volume *Narrative and Dramatic Sources of Shakespeare,* however, is considered to be the major

work of Bullough's career. Obituaries and other sources: *London Times,* February 23, 1982.

* * *

BURCH, Philip H. 1930-

PERSONAL: Born February 16, 1930, in Trenton, N.J. *Education:* Rutgers University, Ph.D., 1959. *Office:* Rutgers University, New Brunswick, N.J. 08903.

CAREER: Rutgers University, New Brunswick, N.J., 1962—, began as assistant professor, became professor. *Member:* American Political Science Association, Southern Political Science Association.

WRITINGS: Highway Revenue and Expenditure Policy in the United States, Rutgers University Press, 1962; *The Managerial Revolution Reassessed,* Heath, 1972; *Elites in American History,* three volumes, Holmes & Meier, 1980-81.

* * *

BURCHELL, R(obert) A(rthur) 1941-

PERSONAL: Born in 1941, in Plymouth, England; son of Arthur Thomas (an electrician) and Lucy Mary Leonora (Symons) Burchell. *Education:* Oxford University, B.A., 1963, M.A., 1967, B.Litt., 1969; also attended University of California, Berkeley, 1964-65. *Office:* Department of American Studies, Victoria University of Manchester, Manchester M13 9PL, England.

CAREER: Victoria University of Manchester, Manchester, England, assistant lecturer, 1965-68, lecturer, 1968-80, senior lecturer in American history and institutions, 1980—. *Member:* British Association for American Studies (honorary treasurer), Organization of American Historians.

WRITINGS: Westward Expansion, Harrap, 1974; *The San Francisco Irish, 1848-80,* University of California Press, 1980. Member of editorial board of *Journal of American Studies,* 1979—.

WORK IN PROGRESS: A study of the wealthy in northern California in the period after the Gold Rush.

SIDELIGHTS: Burchell told *CA:* "I began with an interest in the immigration history of California, which, in the early sixties, was not much written on. I was studying California in its early period and this led to consideration of the whole frontier theme in American history. I then chose to write about the Irish in San Francisco since preliminary work suggested that their experiences there differed markedly from those of Irish immigrants in the East. Having finished this I veered back toward frontier studies, particularly the evolution of society as the white man came.

"I have become interested in the differential roles played by several social groups in this process, particularly that of the elite. This is a wealthy group and I am presently engaged in a study of northern California in its early American period that concentrates on its role. I hope, at the same time, to discover more about the connection between the frontier and upward socio-economic mobility. Many went West but few appear to have done very well from the move, if by this one means to achieve elite status."

* * *

BURCK, Jacob 1907-1982

OBITUARY NOTICE: Born January 10, 1907 (listed in some

sources as 1904), in Poland; died of injuries suffered in a fire, May 11, 1982, in Chicago, Ill. Painter, sculptor, and cartoonist best known for his prominently featured work in the *Chicago Sun-Times.* Burck's sculpture and paintings have been displayed in many museums, including the Art Institute of Chicago and the Museum of Modern Art in New York City. Burck was awarded a Pulitzer Prize in 1940 for one of his editorial cartoons. Obituaries and other sources: *Who's Who in American Art,* Bowker, 1978; *Who's Who in America,* 41st edition, 1980; *Chicago Tribune,* May 13, 1982; *Newsweek,* May 24, 1982.

*   *   *

BURG, Dale R(onda) 1942-

PERSONAL: Born April 27, 1942, in New York; daughter of Sylvan A. (an attorney) and Miriam (an actress and writer; maiden name, Layn) Burg. *Education:* Brown University, A.B., 1962; Cornell University, M.A., 1964. *Home:* 145 East 84th St., New York, N.Y. 10028.

CAREER: Columbia Pictures Industries, New York, N.Y., manager of corporate communications, 1972—, and director of television writers' workshop. Instructor at New York University, 1980—. *Member:* Writers Guild of America (East), Women in Film.

WRITINGS: (With Abby Hirsch) *The Great Carmen Miranda Look-Alike Contest* (nonfiction), St. Martin's, 1974. Writer for Columbia Broadcasting System (CBS) and National Broadcasting Co. (NBC). Contributor to magazines, including *Working Woman, Cosmopolitan,* and *Glamour.*

WORK IN PROGRESS: Writing nonfiction.

*   *   *

BURGESS, Lorraine Marshall 1913-

PERSONAL: Born May 13, 1913, in Chicago, Ill.; daughter of James Benjamin (an engineer) and Ida B. (an artist; maiden name, Franz) Marshall; married Guy Burgess (a photographer), December 1, 1945; children: Guy Marshall, Jeffrey Marshall. *Education:* Attended Art Institute of Chicago, 1934-35; University of Illinois, B.F.A., 1935; Colorado College, M.F.A., 1949. *Home and office:* 202 Old Broadmoor Rd., Colorado Springs, Colo. 80906. *Agent:* Frances Collin, Marie Rodell-Frances Collin Literary Agency, 110 West 40th St., New York, N.Y. 10022.

CAREER: Commercial artist in Chicago, Ill., 1935-41; designer and editorial scout in Colorado Springs, Colo., 1946-75. Member of advisory board of Pike National Forest; member of Colorado Springs Landmarks Council and of Colorado Springs Historical Advisory Board. *Military service:* Women's Army Corps, 1942-46; special services. *Member:* Garden Writers of America (member of regional board of directors), Colorado Springs Horticultural Society (president), Colorado Springs Art Guild (president), Springs Area Beautiful Association. *Awards, honors:* Award from Springs Area Beautiful Association, 1968, for environmental conservation; award from Colorado Springs Landmarks Council, 1969, for preservation exhibition.

WRITINGS: The Garden Maker's Answer Book, Association Press, 1975; *Garden Art,* Walker & Co., 1981. Author of a monthly gardening feature in *Colorado Springs City,* 1977-80. Contributor to magazines, including *American Home, House and Garden, Newsweek, Woman's Day,* and gardening journals. Garden ideas editor of *Better Homes and Gardens,* 1974-75.

WORK IN PROGRESS: A book on frugal garden practices; a book on containment gardening; a series of large acrylic paintings of flowers, for exhibition in museums and galleries.

SIDELIGHTS: Burgess told *CA:* "I prefer to focus on the positive qualities of gardening, its creative opportunities, its follies and conceits. Too often these pleasures are overlooked in the worrisome pursuit of crabgrass, dandelions, and pesticides. This is foolish. Relax and enjoy. Nature most often heals itself."

*   *   *

BURGOS, Joseph A(gner), Jr. 1945-

PERSONAL: Born May 6, 1945, in San Juan, Puerto Rico; came to the United States in 1950; son of Jose Federico (a poet) and Leonidas (Martinez) Burgos. *Education:* Attended New York City Community College, 1975. *Politics:* Liberal. *Religion:* Roman Catholic. *Home:* 71 Graham Ave., Brooklyn, N.Y. 11206. *Agent:* Antonio Garcia Copado, 605 West 111th St., New York, N.Y. 10025.

CAREER: Artist, printer, and bookbinder. Community volunteer worker. *Member:* Ediciones Puerto Rico de Autores Nuevos, Circulo de Escritores y Poetas Iberoamericanos de Nueva York, Aerial Phenomena Research Organization, Rosicrucians.

WRITINGS: (Contributor) Maria Teresa Babin and Stan Steiner, editors, *Borinquen: An Anthology of Puerto Rican Literature,* Knopf, 1974; (contributor) William C. Duncan, editor, *Cornucopia: An Anthology of Contemporary Poetry,* Contemporary Literature, 1978; (editor) *Burgos Philosophy of Life,* Editorial Parnaso, in press. Contributor to magazines, including *Songwriters Review,* and newspapers.

WORK IN PROGRESS: A collection of watercolor paintings; Spanish and English poems.

SIDELIGHTS: Burgos told *CA:* "I am the nephew of Julia de Burgos, one of the greatest women poets in Latin American literature. Through reading her books, I developed an interest in poetry and art. In my poems, I try to communicate messages that are important not only to me, but to the reader as well, especially in support of human rights in our country and around the world. Philosophy has been my subject through the years."

BIOGRAPHICAL/CRITICAL SOURCES: Playero, June, 1978.

*   *   *

BURKE, Alan Dennis 1949-

PERSONAL: Born November 23, 1949, in Boston, Mass.; son of Albert P. (a copywriter) and Anne (Gartland) Burke; married Catherine Sheffield (a teacher), July 2, 1972; children: Dennis Christopher-Sheffield. *Education:* Attended Quincy Junior College; Boston University, B.S., 1972. *Agent:* John Hawkins, 12 East 41st St., New York, N.Y. 10017.

CAREER: Quincy Patriot Ledger, Quincy, Mass., reporter, 1971-72; worked as substitute teacher in Boston, Mass., 1973-74; writer.

WRITINGS: Fire Watch (novel), Little, Brown, 1980; *Getting Away With Murder* (novel), Little, Brown, 1981.

SIDELIGHTS: Burke's first novel, *Fire Watch,* detailed the violent repercussions of court-ordered busing. The primary character is Peter Lyons, a high-school administrator whose position is jeopardized by racial tensions. In the *New York Times Book Review,* Jonathan Yardley wrote: " 'Fire Watch' is not a nice book. Few of its characters are even remotely likeable, its language is uncompromisingly rough, its depiction of racial hatred is unsparing.''

Getting Away With Murder details a reporter's efforts to vindicate himself from charges of murdering his editor's wife. *Newsweek*'s Walter Clemons claimed that Burke ''induces the ideal condition in the reader of a thriller: the desire to speed ahead balked by an equal desire to pay attention moment by moment.'' He concluded, ''The result is intelligent, goggle-eyed excitement. This is good work.''

BIOGRAPHICAL/CRITICAL SOURCES: New York Times Book Review, May 11, 1980, August 2, 1981; *Chicago Tribune,* July 15, 1981; *Newsweek,* August, 1981.

* * *

BURNETT, W(illiam) R(iley)   1899-1982
(James Updyke)

OBITUARY NOTICE—See index for *CA* sketch: Born in 1899 in Springfield, Ohio; died of heart failure, April 25, 1982, in Santa Monica, Calif. Screenwriter, statistician, and novelist. Best known for his books *Little Caesar, High Sierra,* and *The Asphalt Jungle,* Burnett worked as a statistician for the Ohio Department of Industrial Relations for several years before becoming a writer. He wrote his first novel, *Little Caesar,* after moving to Chicago in 1927. The criminal underworld of that city inspired Burnett's portrayal of the vicious gangster Cesare Bandello. In 1930 the author's screenplay of the novel was filmed, starring Edward G. Robinson as Bandello. The film ''Little Caesar'' made Robinson a star and Burnett one of the highest-paid screenwriters in Hollywood. In the more than forty films he worked on during his career, Burnett often employed the ''tough guy'' role. His screenplays ''High Sierra'' and ''This Gun for Hire'' were filmed with Humphrey Bogart and Alan Ladd portraying such characters. The roles helped both actors attract critical attention. Other Burnett films include ''Scarface'' and ''The Great Escape.'' He also wrote *King Cole* and *The Roar of the Crowd.* The author's screenplay ''Wake Island'' earned him an Academy Award nomination. Obituaries and other sources: *New York Times,* April 29, 1982; *Washington Post,* April 29, 1982; *London Times,* April 30, 1982; *Chicago Tribune,* May 1, 1982; *Newsweek,* May 10, 1982; *Time,* May 10, 1982.

* * *

BURNS, Ruby V(ermillion)   1901-

PERSONAL: Born December 6, 1901, in Arkadelphia, Ark.; daughter of Henry F. (a minister) and Kate (Gray) Vermillion; married Earl S. Burns, June 14, 1953 (deceased); children: Nancy (stepdaughter). *Education:* Baylor University, A.B. (cum laude), 1922; attended Juilliard School of Music, 1923-24. *Religion:* Episcopalian. *Home and office:* 6029 Bel Mar, El Paso, Tex. 79912.

CAREER: Worked as public school teacher, 1925-30; *El Paso Times,* El Paso, Tex., woman's editor and author of column, ''Around El Paso,'' 1948-70. Member of Tri-State Opera Guild, El Paso Symphony Guild, and woman's department of El Paso Chamber of Commerce. *Member:* El Paso County Historical Society, Woman's Club of El Paso (member of board of directors, 1978-79).

WRITINGS: Josephine Clardy Fox, Texas Western Press, 1973.

WORK IN PROGRESS: A history of the Vermillion family; research for biography of Sheriff Pat Garrett's daughter, Elizabeth.

AVOCATIONAL INTERESTS: Travel (Europe, the Caribbean, the Orient).

* * *

BURROUGHS, Raleigh (Simpson)   1901-

PERSONAL: Born October 15, 1901, in Baltimore, Md.; son of W. Dwight (a writer and editor) and Jennie (Simpson) Burroughs; married Jessie Paxton (a Christian Science reader), April 8, 1926; children: Audrey Joan (Mrs. George Fraise). *Education:* Attended high school in Baltimore, Md. *Politics:* Independent. *Religion:* Presbyterian. *Address:* c/o A.S. Barnes & Co., P.O. Box 421, Cranbury, N.J. 08512.

CAREER: Turf and Sport Digest, Baltimore, Md., editor and staff writer, 1941-68; free-lance writer. *Awards, honors:* Walter Haight Award from National Turf Writers Association, 1974.

WRITINGS: American Race Horses, 1962, Thoroughbred Owners and Breeders, 1963; *American Race Horses, 1963,* Thoroughbred Owners and Breeders, 1964; (with Humphrey S. Finney) *Fair Exchange* (autobiography of Finney), Scribner, 1974; *Horses, Burroughs and Other Animals (Mostly Human),* A. S. Barnes, 1977. Also author of *Training Your Dog,* 1933. Contributor to magazines, including *Thoroughbred Record, Chronicle of the Horse, Horsemen's Journal, Blood-Horse,* and *Florida Horse.* Editor of *Maryland Horse,* 1953-58.

* * *

BURT, William Henry   1903-

PERSONAL: Born January 22, 1903, in Haddam, Kan.; son of Frank P. and Hattie (Carlson) Burt; married Leona S. Galutia, September 15, 1928 (died, 1973). *Education:* University of Kansas, A.B., 1926, A.M., 1927; University of California, Berkeley, Ph.D., 1930. *Home:* 4545 Laguna Pl., Boulder, Colo. 80303.

CAREER: California Institute of Technology, Pasadena, research fellow, 1930-35; University of Michigan, Ann Arbor, instructor, 1935-41, professor of zoology, 1941-69, professor emeritus, 1969—, assistant curator of mammals at Museum of Zoology, 1935-38, curator, 1938-69, curator emeritus, 1969—. Visiting lecturer at National Research Council, 1963—, and University of Colorado, 1969—. *Member:* American Society of Mammalogists (member of board of directors; vice-president, 1951-53; president, 1953-55), Izaak Walton League of America (honorary member; president of Michigan division, 1949), Society for Systematic Zoology (member of council, 1957-60), Explorers Club, Wilson Ornithological Society, Cooper Ornithological Society, Phi Beta Kappa, Sigma Xi, Phi Sigma. *Awards, honors:* Jackson Award from American Society of Mammalogists, 1978.

WRITINGS: The Mammals of Michigan, University of Michigan Press, 1946, revised edition, 1948; *A Field Guide to the Mammals,* Houghton, 1951, 3rd edition, 1976; *Mammals of the Great Lakes Area,* University of Michigan Press, 1957. Contributor to scientific journals. Editor of *Journal of Mammalogy,* 1947-52.

AVOCATIONAL INTERESTS: Travel (South America, Mexico, Asia, Africa, Europe).

* * *

BURTON, Mary E(lizabeth)   1900-

PERSONAL: Born October 11, 1900, in St. Louis, Mo.; daughter of Johnston Crutcher and Laura (Froh) Burton. *Education:* University of Louisville, A.B., 1922, A.M., 1925; Cornell University, Ph.D., 1934. *Politics:* Democrat. *Religion:* Methodist. *Home:* 3125 Randolph Ave., Louisville, Ky. 40206.

CAREER: Illinois Woman's College, Macmurray, instructor in English, 1924-25; Randolph-Macon Woman's College, Lynchburg, Va., instructor in English, 1925-29; University of Louisville, Louisville, Ky., 1929—, began as instructor, became professor of English, professor emeritus, 1970—. *Member:* Modern Language Association of America, Modern Humanities Research Association, American Association of University Professors, American Association of University Women, English-Speaking Union, Phi Beta Kappa, Phi Kappa Phi, Pi Lambda Theta, Altrusa Club, Arts Club.

WRITINGS: The One Wordsworth: A Detailed Study of Wordsworth's Revision of the Prelude, University of North Carolina Press, 1942, reprinted, Archon Books, 1972; (editor) *The Letters of Mary Wordsworth,* Clarendon Press, 1958, Greenwood Press, 1979. Contributor of articles and reviews to periodicals, including *Kentucky Poetry Review.*

WORK IN PROGRESS: An autobiography; poems.

AVOCATIONAL INTERESTS: Travel (England), photography.

*   *   *

BUSHMAN, Claudia L(auper)   1934-

PERSONAL: Born June 11, 1934, in Oakland, Calif.; daughter of Serge J. (in sales) and Jean Vernon (Gordon) Lauper; married Richard Lyman Bushman (a professor of history), August 19, 1955; children: Clarissa Bushman Ortel, Richard Lyman, Jr., Karl, Margaret, Serge, Ben. *Education:* Wellesley College, A.B., 1956; Brigham Young University, M.A., 1963; Boston University, Ph.D., 1978. *Politics:* "Liberal conservative." *Religion:* Church of Jesus Christ of Latter-day Saints (Mormons). *Home:* 107 Cheltenham Rd., Newark, Del. 19711. *Office:* University Honors Program, University of Delaware, 186 South College Ave., Newark, Del. 19711.

CAREER: Rhode Island College, Providence, instructor in English, 1964-65; Brigham Young University, Provo, Utah, instructor in English, 1965-66; Boston University, Boston, Mass., instructor in American studies, 1973-75; University of Delaware, Newark, instructor in history and literature, honors program, 1978—. President of Mormon Sisters, Inc., 1974-75, member of board of directors, 1975—; member of board of directors and president-elect of Belmont Music School, 1976-77. Member of board of advisers of Women's Archives at Brigham Young University, 1974—; lecturer. *Member:* Newark Historical Society (president, 1981—).

WRITINGS: (Editor and contributor) *Mormon Sisters: Women in Early Utah,* Emmeline, 1976; *"A Good Poor Man's Wife": Being the Chronicles of Harriet Hanson Robinson and Her Family in Nineteenth-Century New England,* University Press of New England, 1981; (author of introduction to reprint) Harriet H. Robinson, *Loom and Spindle; or, Life Among the Early Mill Girls,* Press Pacifica, 1981; (contributor) Alden Whitman, editor, *Great American Reformers,* H. W. Wilson, in press. Also editor of revision and contributor to *A Beginner's Boston,* 1973. Contributor to *Dialogue: A Journal of Mormon Thought.* Founding editor of *Exponent II,* 1974-76.

WORK IN PROGRESS: Research on historical housewifery, from practical and personal angles.

SIDELIGHTS: Bushman told *CA:* "My abiding interest is the daily life of real people of the past. I love to find details that illuminate repeated activities, to see how things have changed, to find the pride of creation of people in the past. Social history has been the focus for this information. I hope to work toward historically accurate fiction. In the past year I have also made cheese and soap, and hope to write about that, too."

*   *   *

BUSTAD, Leo Kenneth   1920-

PERSONAL: Surname is pronounced *Byou*-sted; born January 10, 1920, in Stanwood, Wash.; son of Rasmus (a logger and farmer) and Thora (Larson) Bustad; married Signe Byrd, June 13, 1942; children: Leo Byrd, Karen Ann, Rebecca Lee. *Education:* Washington State University, B.S., 1941, M.S., 1948, D.V.M., 1949; University of Washington, Seattle, Ph.D., 1960. *Religion:* Lutheran. *Home:* Northeast 1705 Upper Dr., Pullman, Wash. 99163. *Office:* College of Veterinary Medicine, Washington State University, 305 College Hall, Pullman, Wash. 99163.

CAREER: General Electric Co., Hanford Laboratories, Richland, Wash., manager of experimental farm, 1949-64; University of California, Davis, professor of radiation biology and director of radiobiology and comparative oncology laboratories, 1965-73; Washington State University, Pullman, professor of physiology and dean of College of Veterinary Medicine, 1973—, executive dean of Washington-Oregon-Idaho Regional Program in Veterinary Medicine, 1978—. Guest lecturer at Washington State University, 1955-65; John Gunion Rutherford Memorial Lecturer at University of Saskatchewan, 1959; guest member of faculty at University of Washington, Seattle, 1960—, member of national advisory committee of Regional Primate Research Center, 1965—; Wesley Spink Lecturer at University of Minnesota, 1979; J. V. LaCroix Memorial Lecturer of American Animal Hospital Association, 1980. Member of National Council on Radiation Protection and Measurements, 1969-75; member of National Institutes of Health Advisory Research Resources Council, 1975-78; member of National Academy of Sciences-National Research Council committees at Institute of Laboratory Animal Resources, 1966-68, member of advisory council, 1969-73, vice-chairman of executive council, 1972-73, chairman of committee on veterinary medical sciences, 1975-80; member of advisory committee of Los Alamos Scientific Laboratory, 1973-77.

Member of board of regents of California Lutheran College, 1970-73, board of governors of Foundation for Human Ecology, 1970-76, and board of directors of Holden Village, 1970-76, and Sutter Memorial Hospital Medical Research Foundation, 1971-73. Member of Pullman Council on Aging, 1973—; chairman of Holden Village Scientific Advisory Committee, 1975—; co-director of Pullman People-Pet Partnership Program, 1979—. Consultant to U.S. Air Force, Nuclear Regulatory Commission, and Battelle Memorial Institute. *Military service:* U.S. Army, active duty, 1941-45; U.S. Army Reserve, research and development, 1945-73; became colonel.

MEMBER: World Association of Veterinary Physiologists, Pharmacologists, and Biochemists, Radiation Research Society (councilor of medicine, 1969-72), American Cancer Society (member of county board of directors, 1972-73), American Association for the Advancement of Science, American Association for Laboratory Animal Science, American Institute of Biological Sciences (member of advisory committee, 1963—), American Physiological Society, American Society of Veterinary Physiologists and Pharmacologists, American Veterinary Medical Association, Association of American Veterinary Medical Colleges, Gerontological Society, Society of Experimental Biology and Medicine, Institute of Society, Ethics, and the Life Sciences, Washington State Veterinary Medical Association, Pullman Chamber of Commerce, Sigma Xi, Alpha Zeta, Phi Kappa Phi, Cosmos Club, Delta Society (president). *Awards, honors:* National Science Foundation fellow, 1958; named veterinarian of the year for the state of Washington by Washington State Veterinary Medical Association, 1980.

WRITINGS: (Editor and contributor) *Biology of Radioiodine,* Pergamon, 1964; (editor with R.O. McClellan, and contributor) *Swine in Biomedical Research,* Pacific Northwest Laboratory, Battelle Memorial Institute, 1966; (editor with Marvin Goldman, and contributor) *Biomedical Implications of Radiostrontium Exposure,* Office of Information Services, U.S. Atomic Energy Commission, 1972; (with G. A. Hegreberg and G. A. Padgett) *Naturally Occurring Animal Models of Human Disease: A Bibliography,* Institute of Laboratory Animal Resources, National Academy of Sciences, 1976; *Animals, Aging, and the Aged,* University of Minnesota Press, 1980; (with L. H. Hines and C. W. Leathers) *The Human-Companion Animal Bond and the Veterinarian,* Veterinary Clinics of North America, 1981.

Contributor: R. S. Caldecott and L. A. Snyder, editors, *Radioisotopes in the Biosphere,* Center for Continuation Study, University of Minnesota, 1960; R. W. Dougherty, editor, *Physiology of Digestion in the Ruminant,* Butterworth, 1965; *Radioisotopes in Animal Nutrition and Physiology: Proceedings,* International Atomic Energy Agency, 1965; *The Laboratory Animal in Gerontological Research,* National Academy of Sciences, 1968; H. A. Kornberg and W. D. Norwood, editors, *Diagnosis and Treatment of Deposited Radionuclides,* Excerpta Medica Foundation, 1968; C. W. Mays, W.S.S. Jee, R. D. Lloyd, and other editors, *Delayed Effects of Bone-Seeking Radionuclides,* University of Utah Press, 1969; *Radiation-Induced Cancer,* International Atomic Energy Agency, 1969.

Contributor: H. W. Dunne, editor, *Diseases of Swine,* 3rd edition (Bustad was not included in earlier editions), Iowa State University Press, 1970, 4th edition, 1975; *Defining the Laboratory Animal,* National Academy of Sciences, 1971; *Peaceful Uses of Atomic Energy,* Volume II, United Nations, 1972; *Proceedings of the Second International Conference on Strontium Metabolism,* National Technical Information Service, 1972; R. M. Dutcher and L. Chieco-Bianchi, editors, *Unifying Concepts of Leukemia,* S. Karger, 1973; G. Walinder, editor, *Symposium on Tumorigenic and Genetic Effects of Radiation,* National Swedish Environment Protection Board, 1976; J. M. Yuhas, R. W. Tennant, and J. D. Regan, editors, *Biology of Radiation Carcinogenesis,* Raven Press, 1976; *The Future of Animals, Cells, Models, and Systems in Research, Development, Education, and Testing,* National Academy of Sciences, 1977.

Contributor: B. Fogel, editor, *Proceedings of the British Small Animal Veterinary Association Meeting on the Human Companion Animal Bond,* C. C Thomas, 1980; *Abstract Digest Symposium of Mount St. Helens Eruption: Its Atmospheric Effects and Potential Climatic Impact,* Institute for Atmospheric Optics and Remote Sensing, 1980. Contributor of about one hundred fifty articles and reviews to scientific journals and popular magazines, including *Nature* and *Scientific American.* Associate editor of *Laboratory Animal Science,* 1967-77; member of editorial board of *American Journal of Veterinary Research,* 1972-78.

WORK IN PROGRESS: Research on the human/companion animal bond, evaluation of its effects on people and animals, selection of proper animal, and history of bond.

SIDELIGHTS: Bustad commented: "Many elderly and handicapped people have discovered that animal companions satisfy some of their greatest needs. Pets restore order to their lives, provide a more secure grasp of reality, and link their owners to a community of caring, concern, and sacrifice, and intense emotional relationships. When older people withdraw from active participation in daily human affairs, the nonhuman environment in general, and animals in particular, can become increasingly important. Animals have boundless capacity for acceptance, adoration, attention, forgiveness, and unconditional love. The potential for significant benefits to a great variety of people exists through association with companion animals.

"Relative to this association, it seems that the bond between the handicapped and elderly and their animal companions is stronger and more profound than with anyone else. Unfortunately, very little data exists on measurable effects of animal companionship on people, including the elderly, even though people have been associated with animals for thousands of years. I feel strategies for current programs can be developed based on what data is available, as well as on our own experiences and those of many others. I also believe that if properly selected, animals can be utilized by health delivery specialists far more extensively than now with great benefits to patients and with cost savings to both society and the patient. It can also be of great consequence to the young and almost all members of society, including many prisoners."

*   *   *

BUTLER, Christina Violet   1884-1982

OBITUARY NOTICE: Born in January, 1884; died May 19, 1982. Educator and author of *Social Conditions in Oxford.* From 1914 to 1945 Butler was a tutor at the Society of Oxford Home Students. Obituaries and other sources: *London Times,* May 26, 1982.

*   *   *

BUTLER, John Alfred Valentine   1899-1977

OBITUARY NOTICE—See index for *CA* sketch: Born February 14, 1899; died July 16, 1977. Educator, editor, and author. Butler taught chemistry and physical chemistry at the University of Edinburgh and the University of London. He wrote several books in his field, including *Chemical Thermodynamics, Electrically Charged Interfaces,* and *Gene Control in the Living Cell.* Butler also edited the annual publication *Progress in Biophysics and Molecular Biology.* Obituaries and other sources: *Who Was Who,* Volume VII: *1971-1980,* A. & C. Black, 1981.

*   *   *

BUTLER, Rab
See BUTLER, Richard Austen

*   *   *

BUTLER, Richard Austen   1902-1982
(Rab Butler; Lord Butler of Saffron Walden)

OBITUARY NOTICE: Born December 9, 1902, in Attock Serai, India (now Campbellpore, Rawalpindi, Pakistan); died of heart failure, March 8, 1982, in Great Yeldham, Essex, England. Politician, educator, and author. Often called "the best Prime Minister Britain never had," Butler entered British public service in 1928 as a member of the House of Commons. A member of Parliament for nearly thirty-six years, he helped formulate the Government of India Act of 1935 and sponsored the Education Act of 1944. He served in several ministerial posts, including lord privy seal, chancellor of the Exchequer, and leader of the House of Commons. In 1965 Butler left politics to become master of Trinity College of Cambridge University, where he advised Prince Charles, heir to the British throne, from 1967 to 1970. He wrote *The Responsibilities of Education,* published in 1969, and edited *The Conservatives: A History From Their Origins to 1965,* published in 1977. His autobiography, *The Memories of Lord Butler,* appeared in 1971. Obituaries and other sources: *Who's Who in the World,* 4th edition, Marquis, 1978; *The Writers Directory, 1980-82,* St. Martin's, 1979; *London Times,* March 10, 1982; *New York Times,* March 10, 1982; *Washington Post,* March 10, 1982; *Newsweek,* March 22, 1982; *Time,* March 22, 1982.

*   *   *

BUTTERFIELD, Lyman H(enry)   1909-1982

OBITUARY NOTICE: Born August 8, 1909, in Lyndonville, N.Y.; died April 25, 1982, in Boston, Mass. Historian, educator, editor, and author. As a member of the Massachusetts Historical Society, Butterfield spent more than twenty years editing the Adams Papers, preparing twenty volumes of diaries, letters, and documents associated with the family that supplied two U.S. presidents. He served as editor or consultant for many publications and organizations, including the *New England Quarterly,* Harvard University Press, and the Library of Congress. An editor of many historical works, Butterfield also wrote *John Witherspoon Comes to America.* Obituaries and other sources: *American Authors and Books, 1640 to the Present Day,* 3rd revised edition, Crown, 1962; *Directory of American Scholars,* Volume I: *History,* 7th edition, Bowker, 1978; *Who's Who in America,* 41st edition, Marquis, 1980; *Chicago Tribune,* April 27, 1982; *Washington Post,* April 28, 1982; *Newsweek,* May 10, 1982.

C

CABLE, Thomas Monroe 1942-

BRIEF ENTRY: Born June 17, 1942, in Conroe, Tex. American educator and author. Cable has been teaching English at the University of Texas since 1972. He was a fellow of the American Council of Learned Societies in 1976 and 1977. His writings include *The Meter and Melody of Beowulf* (University of Illinois Press, 1974) and *A History of the English Language,* 3rd edition (Prentice-Hall, 1978). *Address:* Department of English, University of Texas, Austin, Tex. 78712. *Biographical/critical sources: Times Literary Supplement,* August 29, 1975; *Directory of American Scholars,* Volume II: *English, Speech, and Drama,* 7th edition, Bowker, 1978.

* * *

CADOGAN, Alexander (George Montagu) 1884-1968

OBITUARY NOTICE: Born November 25, 1884; died July 9, 1968. Diplomat, broadcasting official, and author of *The Diaries of Alexander Cadogan, 1938-1945.* Cadogan entered British public service at age twenty-three, serving in Constantinople (now Istanbul), Vienna, and Paris. In 1928 he became counselor in Britain's Foreign Office, and in 1934 he was a member of the British diplomatic corps in China, becoming ambassador in the newly created embassy in 1935. In 1938 Cadogan was named permanent undersecretary of state for foreign affairs. Immune from party influence, he controlled the Foreign Office staff and British Intelligence. During World War II he participated in high-level Allied and international discussions. Cadogan served as Britain's representative to the United Nations from 1946 to 1950 and as chairman of British Broadcasting Corporation from 1952 to 1957. Cadogan was created a Knight Grand Cross of St. Michael and St. George in 1939 and Knight Commander of the Bath in 1941. His diaries were published posthumously in 1971. Obituaries and other sources: *Current Biography,* Wilson, 1944, September, 1968; *New Republic,* April 22, 1946; *New York Times,* July 10, 1968; *Time,* July 19, 1968; *Newsweek,* July 22, 1968.

* * *

CADOGAN, Mary (Rose) 1928-

PERSONAL: Born May 30, 1928, in London, England; daughter of Thomas Harold (a policeman) and Ivy (a nurse; maiden name, Farrow) Summersby; married Alexander Cadogan (a technical writer), May 27, 1950; children: Teresa Mary. *Education:* Margaret Morris School of Dance and Movement, earned teaching and performance diplomas, 1954. *Politics:* "I swing between idealism and disillusion about the main parties. My present hopes are with the newly formed Social Democrats." *Home:* 46 Overbury Ave., Beckenham, Kent BR3 2PY, England.

CAREER: Associated with British Broadcasting Corp. (BBC), London, England, 1944-47, and 1953-57; worked in London as welfare secretary in infantile paralysis fellowship, 1947-50; Krishnamurti Writings, Inc., London, secretary, 1958-68; Krishnamurti Foundation, Beckenham, England, company secretary, 1968—. Teacher of movement and dance; governor of Brockwood Park International school in Hampshire, England. Appeared on BBC-radio and television programs. *Member:* Ephemera Society, Beatrix Potter Society, Children's Book History Society, Lewis Carroll Society, P.E.N., London Old Boy's Book Club.

WRITINGS: (With Patricia Craig) *You're a Brick, Angela!: A New Look at Girls' Fiction From 1839 to 1975,* Gollancz, 1976; (with John Wernham) *The Greyfriar's Characters,* Museum Press, 1976; (with Craig) *Women and Children First: The Fiction of Two World Wars,* Gollancz, 1978; (with Wernham) *Charles Hamilton Schoolgirls' Album,* Museum Press, 1978; (with Craig) *The Lady Investigates: Women Detectives and Spies in Fiction,* Gollancz, 1981, St. Martin's, 1982; (with Tommy Keen) *The Morcove Companion,* Museum Press, 1981; (author of introduction) Winifred Holtby, *Anderby Wold,* Virago, 1981; (contributor) *Twentieth Century Romance and Gothic Writers,* Gale, 1982.

Contributor of scripts for "BBC Woman's Hour," including "Don't Put Your Daughter on the Stage Mrs. Worthington," 1979, and "The Home Front," 1979.

Contributor to reference books, including *Twentieth Century Children's Writers,* St. Martin's, 1978, and *Dictionary of National Biography,* Cambridge University Press, 1981. Contributor to periodicals, including *Books & Bookmen, Times Literary Supplement, Guardian, Literary Review, Now,* and *Woman Journalist.*

WORK IN PROGRESS: Two ethnic novels, *Passionate Friends* and *Second Chance;* an Anglo-American ghost novel, *The Paradise Walk;* co-editing a detective series with Patricia Craig.

SIDELIGHTS: Cadogan told *CA:* "Although an avid reader all my life, I only began to write in my late forties, beginning with nostalgic articles about the world of books, films, theatre, and radio of my own youth. Suddenly I seemed unable to stop the flow of words and, happily, there were audiences interested in the influence of 'popular culture' of the recent past on our present lives.

"I do quite a lot of book features and reviews on radio, in newspapers and magazines. My literary tastes are wide-ranging, from 'classics' to many contemporary bestsellers—but because I feel that some critics are over-academic and dismissive about 'popular' fiction, I particularly enjoy reviewing this. After all, what matters most in any field of literature is word-magic—something that most popular storytellers have, but certain critics unfortunately do not. Children's fiction especially fascinates me, because it offers extraordinary scope for imaginative writing.

"I think my starting point as a writer was an awareness that many of the books I had loved as a child still appealed to my daughter, who read them two and a half decades later. These books are timeless in their attraction even though they may vividly evoke a particular period, or a specific background. Other children's books which I had enjoyed, however, produced less favorable responses in my daughter because they expressed values that were meaningless or repressive to her generation. This led to my doing research into ways in which past, present, and future children (and girls in particular) might be 'conditioned' by juvenile literature and the social attitudes it so often encapsulates. Inevitably these researches made me extremely conscious of anti-feminist views in many early children's books.

"*You're a Brick, Angela!*, and its resultant publicity, at first had the effect of 'typecasting' me as a writer on 'feminist' and 'children's' topics but now, fortunately, I have managed to depart from this pattern and to write also about subjects of broader relevance."

*   *   *

CALDER, Jason
See DUNMORE, John

*   *   *

CAMPBELL, Edward D(unscomb) C(hristian), Jr. 1946-

PERSONAL: Born October 24, 1946, in Richmond, Va.; son of Edward Dunscomb Christian (a realtor) and Jane (Robertson) Campbell. *Education:* Virginia Polytechnic Institute and State University, B.A., 1970, M.A., 1973; University of South Carolina, Ph.D., 1979. *Residence:* Richmond, Va. *Office:* Museum of the Confederacy, 1201 East Clay St., Richmond, Va. 23219.

CAREER: United Virginia Bank, Richmond, portfolio analyst, 1972-73; University of South Carolina, Columbia, instructor in history, 1975-78; Museum of the Confederacy, Richmond, director, 1978—. Member of adjunct faculty of Virginia Commonwealth University, 1979—. Member of board of advisers of Historic Lexington Foundation and Historic Gordonsville, 1981—. Co-director of film and lecture series, "Images of the South in History, Fiction, and Film," Virginia Foundation for the Humanities and Public Policy, 1980; chairman of attractions committee of Richmond Convention and Visitors Bureau, 1979-80.

MEMBER: American Historical Association, Organization of American Historians, American Association for State and Local History, American Association of Museums, American Film Institute, Association for the Study of Afro-American Life, Victorian Society in America, Southern Historical Association, Virginia Historical Society, Virginia Association of Museums (member of board of directors, 1980—), Phi Alpha Theta.

WRITINGS: The Celluloid South: Hollywood and the Southern Myth, University of Tennessee Press, 1981; (contributor) Walter J. Fraser and Winfred B. Moore, editors, *From the Old South to the New: Essays on the Transitional South,* Greenwood Press, 1981. Contributor of articles and reviews to history journals.

WORK IN PROGRESS: The Youngest Slaves: Black Children on the Eve of Emancipation, on development and transition to adulthood of black children, publication expected in 1985; "Film as Politics: The Virginia Film Censorship Board, 1930-1955"; research on images of American history and society in film, literature as history, Afro-American slavery and its aftermath, and the "old" and "new" South.

*   *   *

CAMPBELL, Keith 1938-

PERSONAL: Born December 19, 1938, in Wellington, New Zealand; son of Ian Drummond (a professor of law) and Emily (a teacher; maiden name, Kennedy) Campbell; married Julianne Joan McKenzie (a college professor), January 30, 1960; children: Helen, Andrew, Kirsten. *Education:* Victoria University of Wellington, B.A., 1959, M.A., 1961; Oxford University, B.Phil., 1963. *Residence:* Sydney, Australia. *Office:* Department of Traditional and Modern Philosophy, University of Sydney, Darlinghurst, Sydney, New South Wales 2006, Australia.

CAREER: University of Melbourne, Melbourne, Australia, lecturer, 1963-64, senior lecturer in philosophy, 1964-65; University of Sydney, Sydney, Australia, senior lecturer, 1966-71, associate professor of philosophy, 1972—. Visiting fellow at Victoria University of Wellington, 1981, and Australian National University, 1982-84. *Member:* Australasian Association of Philosophy (president, 1980-81). *Awards, honors:* Fellow of the Australian Academy of the Humanities, 1978.

WRITINGS: Body and Mind, Doubleday, 1970; *Metaphysics: An Introduction,* Dickenson, 1976. Contributor to philosophy journals. Member of editorial board of *Australasian Journal of Philosophy.*

WORK IN PROGRESS: Modern Stoicism (tentative title).

SIDELIGHTS: Campbell wrote: "*Modern Stoicism* is designed to bring philosophy, especially the moral philosophy of the Stoics, back into the consciousness of contemporary civilization. I am motivated by the conviction that our culture needs a return to old-fashioned virtue without the supernatural machinery of religion."

He added that this conviction leads, on the nonacademic level, to his pursuit of "self-reliance and retreat from the consumer life."

*   *   *

CAMPBELL, Lawrence James 1931-

PERSONAL: Born October 19, 1931, in Wallsend, England; son of James (an engineer) and Laura Woolnough (Dransfield) Campbell; married wife, Catherine Dorothy, December 22, 1960; children: Kathryn Mary. *Education:* University of London, B.Sc., 1953, P.G.C.E., 1954. *Home:* Cruachan, 14 Moor Lane, Brightstone, Newport, Isle of Wight PO30 4DL, England. *Office:* Isle of Wight County Council, Newport, Isle of Wight PO30 14D, England.

CAREER: Assistant master at school in Esher, England, 1957-60, head of science department, 1960-67; Isle of Wight County Educational Administration, Newport, England, assistant county education officer, 1967-80, deputy county education officer, 1980—. Chief scientific adviser to Isle of Wight County Council; consultant to E. S. Perry Ltd. *Military service:* Royal Air Force, technician, 1955-56. *Member:* British Institute of Management, Society of Education Officers, Society of Authors, Association for Science Education.

WRITINGS: Projects: An "A" Level Physics Course, Edward Arnold, 1968; (with R. J. Carlton, E. J. Ewington, D. F. Moore, and others) *Common Core Science,* Routledge & Kegan Paul, 1969.

(Editor with Carlton) *Chemistry,* Routledge & Kegan Paul, 1971, 2nd edition, 1978; (editor with Carlton) *General Plant and Animal Biology,* Routledge & Kegan Paul, 1971; (editor with Carlton) *Human Biology and Hygiene,* Routledge & Kegan Paul, 1971; *A Workguide to "A" Level Physics,* Edward Arnold, 1971; (editor with Carlton) *Matter and Energy,* Routledge & Kegan Paul, 1972, 2nd edition, 1979; (editor with Carlton) *Man and His Environment,* Routledge & Kegan Paul, 1972, 2nd edition, 1979; (with Carlton, Ewington, N. E. Savage, and others) *Foundation Science,* Routledge & Kegan Paul, 1973, 2nd edition, 1978; *Centric Electricity,* Osmiroid Perry, 1974; (with Carlton) *Force and Energy,* Routledge & Kegan Paul, 1974; (with Carlton) *Atoms and Waves,* Routledge & Kegan Paul, 1975; (with Carlton, Ewington, R. H. Stone, and others) *Science: The Basic Skills,* Routledge & Kegan Paul, 1978.

(With Carlton) *Projects in Physics,* Routledge & Kegan Paul, 1981; (editor with Carlton) *Projects in Biology,* Routledge & Kegan Paul, 1981; (editor with Carlton) *Projects in Chemistry,* Routledge & Kegan Paul, 1981; (editor with Carlton) *Projects in General Science,* Routledge & Kegan Paul, 1981. Editor of "C.S.E. Science Series," Routledge & Kegan Paul. Contributor to education journals.

WORK IN PROGRESS: A book or radio/television play on incidents involving hazardous chemicals.

SIDELIGHTS: Campbell told *CA:* "I enjoy writing science books; there is a challenge in finding simple words and phrases, appropriate to the age range, to express complex scientific ideas. The books in the Routledge series try to break away from the idea that physical sciences are mainly a male domain. I first started writing after developing and successfully testing a course of individualized learning for advanced level physics.

"I have designed a number of pieces of science equipment which have been developed and marketed commercially. I am interested in the development of science teaching in other countries, especially where resources are limited.

"As chief scientific adviser for the county I lead a team of scientists, who working with the fire service have the task of dealing with containers of hazardous chemicals which are, from time to time, washed ashore from ships or found in old stores or dumps. Whilst recognizing the need for increased activity in the chemical industry, including the transport of chemicals, I am concerned to see the maximum possible safeguards established for the public. I have assisted in representations made to national government on safety matters, including radio and television interviews.

"I feel that my personal experiences in dealing with hazardous chemicals in a variety of difficult situations could be made into

an interesting and informative radio or television series, and I hope to venture into this new (for me) field of writing in the near future."

AVOCATIONAL INTERESTS: Travel.

*   *   *

CAMPBELL, Margaret   1916-

PERSONAL: Born in 1916 in Birmingham, England; daughter of Frank and Jessie (Gibson) Hill; married Bruce Campbell (an ornithologist), 1938; children: David, Robert, Rona. *Education:* University of Edinburgh, M.A. (with honors), 1938. *Politics:* Liberal. *Religion:* Church of England. *Home:* West End Barn, Wootton, Woodstock, Oxford, England.

CAREER: Age Concern, Oxford, England, chairperson, 1970-78; Community Health Council, Oxford, chairperson, 1977-80; writer, 1980—. Chairperson of Oxfordshire Rural Community Council, 1982.

WRITINGS: Lend a Hand!: An Introduction to Social Welfare Work for Young People, Museum Press, 1965; (editor with husband, Bruce Campbell) *The Countryman Animal Book,* David & Charles, 1973; (editor with B. Campbell) *The Countryman Bird Book,* David & Charles, 1974, (editor) *The Countryman Book of Humour,* David & Charles, 1975.

AVOCATIONAL INTERESTS: Helping with Red Cross Disabled Club, raising money for Age Concern's mobile van for villages too small to support an old people's club.

*   *   *

CAMPBELL, Wilfred
See CAMPBELL, William

*   *   *

CAMPBELL, William   1858(?)-1918
(Wilfred Campbell)

BRIEF ENTRY: Born June 1, 1858 (some sources say 1861), in Berlin (now Kitchener), Ontario, Canada; died January 1, 1918. Canadian civil servant and author. Campbell was ordained as an Anglican minister in 1885. After about six years of service in New England and Canada, he left the ministry to pursue a less restricted way of life. His volumes of poems, including *Lake Lyrics* (1889), and nonfiction, such as *Canada* (1907), reveal the skill with which Campbell depicted Canada's Lake District, the location of his boyhood home. Later poems, collected in *Sagas of Vaster Britain: Poems of the Race, the Empire, and the Divinity of Man* (1914), showed him as an imperialist and an Anglophile. Campbell also wrote plays and historical novels, and edited *The Oxford Book of Canadian Verse* (1914). *Biographical/critical sources: The Reader's Encyclopedia of American Literature,* Crowell, 1962; *The Oxford Companion to Canadian History and Literature,* Oxford University Press, 1967.

*   *   *

CANNAN, Joanna
See PULLEIN-THOMPSON, Joanna Maxwell

*   *   *

CANNELL, Kathleen Biggar (Eaton)   1891-1974

PERSONAL: Born March 6, 1891, in New York, N.Y.; died May 23, 1974; daughter of Frederick and Mary (Wilson) Eaton;

married Skipwith Cannell (a poet; divorced, 1921). *Education:* Attended University of Toronto and Sorbonne, University of Paris. *Home:* 398 Marlborough St., Boston, Mass.

CAREER: Broom, Paris, France, translator, 1921-23; *New York Times,* New York City, fashion editor in Paris, 1931-41, covered German occupation forces' press conferences, c.1940-41; *New Yorker,* New York City, fashion correspondent in Paris, 1939; free-lance writer of reviews of books and fashion, women's feature articles, and editorials for periodicals, c.1944-74; Brooklyn Museum, Brooklyn, N.Y., publicity director for special exhibitions, 1947-48; *Providence Journal,* Providence, R.I., book reviewer, c.1958-74; *Christian Science Monitor,* Boston, Mass., dance critic, c.1964-74. Teacher of "Books and Authors" at Cambridge Center for Adult Education. Editor of French books for G. P. Putnam's Sons. Host of radio program, "Women in France," on Radio Diffusion Nationale. Fashion consultant and lecturer. *Awards, honors:* PEN grant for furthering the cause of literature.

WRITINGS: (Contributor) Peter Neagoe, editor, *Americans Abroad; An Anthology,* Servire, 1932; *Jam Yesterday* (autobiography), Morrow, 1945. Contributor of short stories to *transition.* Scriptwriter for Walter Winchell. Editor of three women's magazines.

SIDELIGHTS: Cannell was living in Paris in 1921, studying French and waiting for a divorce from her husband, poet Skipwith Cannell, when she met author and editor Harold Loeb. Cannell took a job as a translator with Loeb's Paris-based literary magazine, *Broom,* and the pair soon became lovers. Their affair was parodied by Ernest Hemingway in *The Sun Also Rises,* in which Loeb served as the model for the Robert Cohn character and Cannell was cast as the jaded Frances Cline.

Although only a few of Cannell's short stories were published, her donation to the intellectual life of the era is considered significant, especially to a circle of American writers who were living in Paris between the world wars. Appearing in *transition,* "Miss Bliggins" (July, 1927) and "The Money" (May, 1928) are dark tales of society women who are forced by circumstances to deal with women they consider repulsively ugly. The central character in "Miss Bliggins," for example, is so grotesque that her only friend is a tamed rat named Colin. The girl becomes pregnant by a young man keeping a deathwatch over his mother's corpse. Colin dies, the young man abandons the girl, and she dies in childbirth, alone and unwanted.

Cannell's short story "Fantocci" appeared in *Americans Abroad: An Anthology* in 1932. It is the story of a woman marionette builder, beginning to lose touch with reality, who manipulates two men by means of preferential treatment of one over the other. The woman cunningly orchestrates the growing tension between the men until the more pious of the pair murders the other in a jealous rage. With one man dead and the other in jail, the woman, who has now become psychotic, decides that the men were only marionettes to begin with.

Cannell enjoyed a long and successful journalism career, beginning with her assignment to become Paris fashion editor for the *New York Times* in 1931. With the advent of World War II and the Nazi occupation of France, Cannell expanded her duties and also covered German press conferences for news-hungry American readers in the days and months prior to Pearl Harbor and the American entrance into the war. She began free-lancing reviews and articles in 1944 and for years worked as a book reviewer for the *Providence Journal.* Cannell joined the staff of the *Christian Science Monitor* in 1964 as a ballet critic.

BIOGRAPHICAL/CRITICAL SOURCES: Bertram D. Sarason, *Hemingway and* The Sun *Set,* Bruccoli Clark, 1972; *Dictionary of Literary Biography,* Volume 4: *American Writers in Paris, 1920-1939,* Gale, 1980.*

* * *

CAPLAN, Arthur L(eonard) 1950-

PERSONAL: Born March 31, 1950, in Boston, Mass.; son of Sidney D. (a pharmacist) and Natalie Caplan; married Janet Stojak (a professor), June 6, 1971. *Education:* Brandeis University, B.A., 1971; Columbia University, M.A., 1973, Ph.D., 1979. *Home:* 765 North Broadway, Hastings-on-Hudson, N.Y. 10706. *Office:* Institute of Society, Ethics, and the Life Sciences, Hastings Center, 360 Broadway, Hastings-on-Hudson, N.Y. 10706.

CAREER: Institute of Society, Ethics, and the Life Sciences, Hastings-on-Hudson, N.Y., associate for the humanities, 1976—. Instructor at Columbia University, 1977-78; adjunct associate professor at City University of New York, 1981—; consultant to National Endowment for the Humanities, National Science Foundation, and Exxon Foundation. *Member:* American Philosophical Association, Philosophy of Science Association, Society for Health and Human Values.

WRITINGS: (Editor) *The Sociobiology Debate,* Harper, 1978; *Ethics in the Undergraduate Curriculum,* Hastings Center, 1980; (editor with H. Tristram Engelhardt, Jr.) *Concepts of Health and Disease: Interdisciplinary Perspectives,* Addison-Wesley, 1981; (editor with Daniel Callahan) *Ethics and Hard Times,* Plenum, 1981. Contributor to philosophy and scientific journals, and *Commonweal.*

WORK IN PROGRESS: Books on the allocation of scarce resources in health care and on the philosophy of medicine, publication by Prentice-Hall expected in 1984.

* * *

CAPON, Robert Farrar 1925-

BRIEF ENTRY: Born October 26, 1925, in Queens, N.Y. American Episcopal priest and author. Capon has been the vicar of Christ Church, Port Jefferson, N.Y., since 1949. He described his book *The Supper of the Lamb: A Culinary Reflection* (Doubleday, 1969) as "an excursion into meat, metaphysics, and metalware." In a similar way, his later books intertwine serious discussion of philosophy and theology with lively comment on popular subjects. His writings include *Exit 36: A Fictional Chronicle* (Seabury, 1975), *Food for Thought: Resurrecting the Art of Eating* (Harcourt, 1978), *Party Spirit: Some Entertaining Principles* (Morrow, 1979), and *A Second Day: Reflections on Remarriage* (Morrow, 1980). *Address:* P.O. Box 37, Port Jefferson, N.Y. 11777.

* * *

CAPPON, Lester J(esse) 1900-1981

PERSONAL: Born September 18, 1900, in Milwaukee, Wis.; died August 24, 1981; son of Jesse and Mary Elizabeth (Geisinger) Cappon; married Dorothy Elizabeth Bernet, June 25, 1932 (deceased); children: Mary Elizabeth Cappon Yarbrough (deceased); Stanley Bernet. *Education:* Wisconsin Conservatory of Music, earned diploma, 1920; University of Wisconsin (now University of Wisconsin—Madison), B.A., 1922, M.A., 1923; Harvard University, M.A., 1925, Ph.D., 1928. *Politics:* Democrat. *Religion:* Episcopal. *Home:* 416 Griffin Ave., Williamsburg, Va. 23185. *Office:* Newberry Library, 60 West Walton St., Chicago, Ill. 60610.

CAREER: University of Virginia, Charlottesville, assistant professor of history, 1930-45, archivist at library, 1930-45; Institute of Early American History and Culture, Williamsburg, Va., editor of publications, 1945-55, director, 1955-69; Newberry Library, Chicago, Ill., senior fellow, 1969-70, editor-in-chief of *Atlas of Early American History,* 1970-76, distinguished research fellow, 1975-76, emeritus, 1976-81. Director of Colonial Williamsburg, Inc., 1945-52. *Member:* American Historical Association, Organization of American Historians, Society of American Archivists (fellow; president, 1957), American Antiquarian Society, Southern Historical Association (president, 1949), Massachusetts Historical Society, Wisconsin Historical Society, Virginia Historical Society (honorary member), Caxton Club.

WRITINGS: Bibliography of Virginia History Since 1865, Institute for Research in Social Sciences, University of Virginia, 1930; *Virginia Newspapers, 1821-1935: A Bibliography,* Appleton, 1936; *Iron Works at Tuball [of] Alexander Spotswood,* Library, University of Virginia, 1945; *Virginia Gazette Index, 1736-1780,* two volumes, Institute of Early American History and Culture, 1950; (editor) *The Adams-Jefferson Letters,* two volumes, University of North Carolina Press, 1959; *American Genealogical Periodicals: A Bibliography With a Chronological Finding-List,* New York Public Library, 1964; *Atlas of Early American History: The American Revolution, 1760-1790,* Princeton University Press, 1976. Editor of *Papers* of the Albemarle County Historical Society, 1940-45, and *William and Mary Quarterly,* 1955-56, 1961-62.

WORK IN PROGRESS: Editing Jared Sparks's travel journals, at time of death.

AVOCATIONAL INTERESTS: Horseback riding, hiking, river trips in the Far West, European travel, conservation, music (especially piano), collecting books (especially on the West).

BIOGRAPHICAL/CRITICAL SOURCES: William and Mary Quarterly, July, 1969.

OBITUARIES: New York Times, August 27, 1981; *AB Bookman's Weekly,* September 14, 1981.

[Date of death provided by Sandra Hunnicutt of the Newberry Library]

* * *

CARLEN, Claudia   1906-

PERSONAL: Born July 24, 1906, in Detroit, Mich.; daughter of Albert Bernard and Theresa Mary (Ternes) Carlen. *Education:* University of Michigan, A.B.L.S. (with high distinction), 1928, A.M.L.S., 1938. *Home and office:* St. John's Provincial Seminary, 44011 Five Mile Rd., Plymouth, Mich. 48170.

CAREER: Entered order of Sisters, Servants of the Immaculate Heart of Mary (I.H.M.), 1926, became Roman Catholic nun, 1928; Marygrove College, Detroit, Mich., assistant librarian, 1929-44, librarian, 1944-69; Corpus Instrumentorum, Inc., Washington, D.C., vice-president and managing editor of dictionary program, 1969-70; Marygrove College, associate librarian, 1970-71; North American Graduate School, Rome, Italy, library consultant, 1971-72; St. John's Provincial Seminary, Plymouth, Mich., librarian, 1972-79, administrative assistant to rector of seminary, 1979-80, librarian emerita, 1980—, scholar-in-residence, 1982—. Lecturer at University of Michigan, Wayne State University, Villanova University, Catholic University of America, St. John's University, Jamaica, N.Y., Rosary College, and Western Michigan University. Member of advisory board of Corpus Instrumentorum, Inc. and Pierian

Press, 1967—; vice-president of board of trustees of Marygrove College, 1977-79; founder of American Friends of the Vatican Library, 1980—.

MEMBER: International Federation of Library Associations (member of Committee on Liturgical Subject Headings, 1972-75), American Library Association (member of council, 1958-61, 1968-71), Catholic Library Association (life member; president, 1965-67), American Society of Indexers, Society of American Archivists, Society of Indexers (England), Phi Beta Kappa, Phi Kappa Phi, Beta Phi Mu. *Awards, honors:* Award from Marygrove College's Library Guild, 1958, for contributions to the promotion of books and reading; distinguished alumnus award from School of Library Science, University of Michigan, 1974; L.H.D. from Marygrove College, 1981.

WRITINGS: Guide to the Encyclicals of the Roman Pontiffs, H. W. Wilson, 1939; *Guide to the Documents of Pius XII,* Newman Press, 1951; *Dictionary of Papal Pronouncements,* Kenedy, 1958; (editor) *The Papal Encyclicals, 1740-1981,* five volumes, McGrath, 1981.

Author of "Professionally Speaking," a monthly column in *Catholic Library World,* 1952-71. Contributor to *Catholic Bookman's Manual, Translatio Studii,* and *New Catholic Encyclopedia.* Contributor to library journals. Index editor of *New Catholic Encyclopedia,* 1963-67; member of advisory board of *Pope Speaks,* 1963—, *Encyclopedia of World Biography,* 1966-72, and *Way.*

WORK IN PROGRESS: Revising *Dictionary of Papal Pronouncements,* publication expected in 1983; collecting pastoral letters of national conferences of bishops throughout the world.

SIDELIGHTS: Carlen told *CA:* "Time contains the great risk in human existence. It may be on the one hand destructive, flinging everything back into the past, or it may be creative, bringing the future to fulfillment and the past to meaningful integration. Our freedom determines which it will be. If only the passage and weight of time concern us, the spirit will renounce its task, dry up, or even disintegrate. If, on the other hand, we boldly grasp what has been, as well as what is yet to be, we will indeed be masters of the personal significance of our lives, the artists and, in a way, the prophets of our own past."

* * *

CARPENTER, William   1940-

PERSONAL: Born October 31, 1940, in Cambridge, Mass.; son of James (an artist) and Dorothy (Sauer) Carpenter; married JoAnne Laventis (an artist), August 19, 1962; children: Matthew. *Education:* Dartmouth College, B.A., 1962; University of Minnesota, Ph.D., 1967. *Politics:* Socialist. *Religion:* "Transcendentalist." *Home address:* P.O. Box 1297, Stockton Springs, Maine 04981. *Office:* Human Studies Program, College of the Atlantic, Bar Harbor, Maine 04609.

CAREER: University of Minnesota, Minneapolis, instructor in English, 1963-67; University of Chicago, Chicago, Ill., assistant professor of English, 1967-72; College of the Atlantic, Bar Harbor, Maine, faculty member in department of literature, 1972—. Founder and director of Maine Poets' Festival, 1977-79; writer-in-residence at Stonecoast Writers' Workshop, University of Maine, 1982. *Member:* Associated Writing Programs, Modern Language Association of America, Poets and Writers. *Awards, honors:* Pablo Neruda Award in Poetry from *Nimrod,* 1979, for "The Yacht"; poetry award from Associated Writing Programs, 1980, for *The Hours of Morning; Black Warrior Review* award, 1982, for "New York City."

WRITINGS: The Hours of Morning: Poems, 1976-1979, University Press of Virginia, 1981. Contributor of poems to magazines, including *American Poetry Review, Poetry, Black Warrior Review, New England Review, Quarry West,* and *Beloit Poetry Journal.*

WORK IN PROGRESS: Night Fishing, poems.

SIDELIGHTS: Carpenter wrote: "For poets, the most important contributing factor is which other poets' work they read. Now I read Wallace Stevens, William Butler Yeats, Cesar Pavese, Eugenio Montale, and Yannis Ritsos, but when I first saw poetry it was in the late fifties, the heyday of Dylan Thomas and of the energetic and humorous 'beat' poems like Corso's 'Marriage.' My life has very little to do with my poetry, entering only occasionally, and in disguise. My poems seem to be written by someone quite opposite to my daily life, almost a stranger, with perhaps a metaphorical relation to myself.

"I never wrote anything until I moved from Chicago to downeast coastal Maine. The city is no place for a poet; there's too much reality there, which is a distraction. In Maine there is nothing to do, so you're forced upon yourself, and you write out of that encounter."

BIOGRAPHICAL/CRITICAL SOURCES: Stony Hills, No. 12, 1982.

*   *   *

CARRIS, Joan Davenport   1938-

PERSONAL: Born August 18, 1938, in Toledo, Ohio; daughter of Roy (a sales manager) and Elfrid (an artist; maiden name, Nichols) Davenport; married Barr Tupper (in data processing), December 28, 1960; children: Mindy, Leigh Ann, Bradley. *Education:* Iowa State University, B.S., 1960; graduate study at Drake University, 1970-71. *Politics:* "Greek 'Golden Mean' group." *Religion:* Protestant. *Home and office address:* Box 231, 48 Princeton Ave., Rocky Hill, N.J. 08553. *Agent:* Dorothy Markinko, McIntosh & Otis, Inc., 475 Fifth Ave., New York, N.Y. 10017.

CAREER: High school English teacher in Nevada, Iowa, 1960-61; high school teacher of French, speech, and English in Des Moines, Iowa, 1963-65; Franklin Convalescent Center, Princeton, N.J., occupational therapist, 1974; private English tutor in Princeton, 1974—. Member of New Jersey Council for Children's Literature. *Member:* National League of American Pen Women (president of Princeton, N.J., branch, 1980-84), Society of Children's Book Writers, Rocky Hill Community Group (member of executive board, 1974-78).

WRITINGS: The Revolt of 10-X (Junior Literary Guild selection), Harcourt, 1980; *S.A.T. Success,* Peterson's Guides, 1982; *When the Boys Ran the House* (juvenile), Crowell, 1982.

Author of "The Revolution Continues" (one-act play), first produced in Princeton, N.J., at Princeton Unitarian Church, May, 1976. Author of "Tremendous Trifles," a humor column in the *Princeton Spectrum* and the *Trenton Times,* 1977-81. Contributor to magazines, including *Better Homes and Gardens,* and newspapers.

WORK IN PROGRESS: Witch-Cat, a juvenile fantasy; children's books.

SIDELIGHTS: Joan Carris told *CA:* "I discovered the vast number of things I couldn't do pretty early in life. I couldn't do a handstand, jump rope past 'pepper,' skate without bloodying my entire body, or dance. I thought I might have to take my mother to college with me so that she could continue doing my hair—a feat I'd never managed alone.

"Just as I was about to declare myself a washout, I discovered that I could understand literature, really understand it. I could diagram sentences and spell—of all things. Moreover, I could write an analytical essay in English class and some God-sent professor would read it aloud, or even publish it in a literary magazine. What a relief. Even my French was passable, and in a feeble way I can still communicate and read that sonorous language descended from Latin, my all-time favorite.

"Now that I am older, I am still involved with language, and my love for it grows, even though it *is* tricky to work those old spelling medals into a cocktail-party conversation.

"My impetus for writing was the glut of English teachers in the field at the time I wanted to return to teaching. There was no place for me—I'd been gone ten years (whomping up three children) and it was too long. In a snit, I plunked my typewriter on the dining room table and said I'd try my hand at the only other possibility: education through writing for young people. But I didn't want to lure people to reading in the traditional way. I wanted to do it through humor, with as much warmth as I could transfer to paper, with that always-difficult goal of making readers laugh and say 'ah, yes' at the same time.

"Trying to teach young people to love and emulate good English is behind everything I do. For that reason I began teaching Scholastic Aptitude Test (SAT) and American College Testing (ACT) preparation classes. In class we discuss old myths, the fascinating stories behind words, the power words have to take us anywhere we want to go. Out of this class has grown a book. I have a hunch it will be much like a house I would build—full of faults that get discovered only after I take possession.

"Writing children's books is my delight. If I can create even one character who truly comes to life, I'll feel immense satisfaction. And there will never be enough time for all the stories I want to tell about the kids who are like my kids, like the ones next door, like me when I was a kid. It is the hardest work I have ever done, the loneliest, the least rewarding financially, and the most frustrating.

"I wouldn't trade it for anything."

AVOCATIONAL INTERESTS: Walking, playing tennis and bridge.

*   *   *

CARSON, S. M.
See GORSLINE, (Sally) Marie

*   *   *

CARTER, Anne Pitts   1925-

BRIEF ENTRY: Born May 7, 1925, in New York, N.Y. American economist, educator, and author. Carter has been a professor of economics at Brandeis University since 1972. She wrote *Structural Change in the American Economy* (Harvard University Press, 1970), edited *Input-Output Techniques* (North-Holland Publishing, 1972) and *Energy and the Environment: A Structural Analysis* (University Press of New England, 1976), and contributed to *Capital Coefficients and Dynamic Input-Output Models* (Input-Output Publishing, 1975). *Address:* 202 Brattle St., Cambridge, Mass. 02138; and Department of Economics, Brandeis University, 415 S St., Waltham, Mass. 02154.

*   *   *

CARTER, Harry Graham   1901-1982

OBITUARY NOTICE: Born March 27, 1901, in Croydon, England; died March 10, 1982. Typographer, archivist, lecturer, translator, and author. After studying for a career in law, Carter became interested in engraving, punch-cutting, and the design of printed letters. Influenced by the revival of private presses and fine typography that flowered in the 1920's, Carter began, in 1928, to work at the Monotype Corporation. His translation of a classic French work on typography, Fournier's *Manuel*, was published in 1930. While working at the Kynoch Press, Carter wrote, with Herbert Simon, *Printing Explained*, which appeared in 1931. Beginning in 1937 he also worked at Nonesuch Press. Following service in Palestine during World War II, Carter was appointed head of typographic design at the Royal Stationery Office. He served as archivist for the Oxford University Press from 1954 to 1980, during which time he developed several typefaces and wrote *A View of Early Typography* and *History of the Oxford University Press*. He was named officer of the Order of the British Empire in 1951. Obituaries and other sources: *London Times*, March 13, 1982.

* * *

CASDORPH, Paul D(ouglas) 1932-

PERSONAL: Born September 5, 1932, in Charleston, W.Va.; son of Newell D. (an engineer) and Virginia (Miller) Casdorph; married Patricia Ilene Barker, July 22, 1972. *Education:* Victoria College, A.A., 1958; University of Texas, B.A., 1960, M.A., 1961; University of Kentucky, Ed.D., 1970. *Home:* 1413 Alexandria Pl., Charleston, W.Va. 25314. *Office:* Department of History, West Virginia State College, Institute, W.Va. 25112.

CAREER: Union Carbide Chemicals Co., Seadrift, Tex., mail clerk, 1953-57; Texas Department of Public Welfare, Victoria, Tex., social worker, 1962-66; West Virginia State College, Institute, instructor, 1966-71, assistant professor, 1971-72, associate professor, 1972-77, professor of history, 1977—. Instructor at University of Charleston, 1971-73; lecturer at West Virginia University, 1971-72, and West Virginia College of Graduate Studies, 1972-74. *Member:* Southern Historical Association, Phi Delta Kappa (historian and member of executive committee, 1976-78), Phi Alpha Theta, Phi Theta Kappa.

WRITINGS: A History of the Republican Party in Texas, 1865-1965, introduction by Dwight D. Eisenhower, Pemberton Press, 1965; (contributor) Eldon Stephen Branda, editor, *The Handbook of Texas: A Supplement*, Volume III, Texas State Historical Association, 1976; *Republicans, Negroes, and Progressives in the South, 1912-1916*, University of Alabama Press, 1981. Contributor of nearly forty articles and reviews to history journals and newspapers. Member of editorial board of *West Virginia History*.

WORK IN PROGRESS: A study of the southern Republican party in the twentieth century.

SIDELIGHTS: Casdorph told *CA:* "Over the years I have had two loves besides my family: writing southern history and amateur radio (W8HXX). When I am not busy earning the daily bread as a history professor, I am constantly engaged with one or the other. I began pounding the Morse code key in 1949 at age sixteen and writing southern history in 1957 at age twenty-four. Radio operation has proven to be a very refreshing stimulus for my writing, which I try to do every day. My aim is to write southern and political history with as much detail and clarity as possible."

BIOGRAPHICAL/CRITICAL SOURCES: American Historical Review, April, 1967.

CASH, Philip 1931-

PERSONAL: Born January 28, 1931, in Portland, Maine; son of Leonard D. and Margaret (Feury) Cash; married Louise Gadbois (a professor and vocalist), July 7, 1962; children: Adam, Matthew, Ethan. *Education:* Gorham State Teachers College, B.S.Ed., 1953; Boston College, M.A., 1955, Ph.D., 1968; further graduate study at Rice University, 1955-56. *Politics:* Democrat. *Religion:* Roman Catholic. *Home:* 163 Crestwood Dr., Framingham, Mass. 01701. *Office:* Department of History, Emmanuel College, Boston, Mass. 02115.

CAREER: Emmanuel College, Boston, Mass., lecturer, 1958-60, assistant professor, 1960-64, associate professor, 1964-68, professor of history, 1968—, chairman of department, 1963-72. Guest on "House Call," on WCVB-TV. Member of advisory board of Associate Artists Opera Company, 1969-74. *Member:* International Society for the History of Medicine, American Historical Association, American Association of University Professors, American Association for the History of Medicine, American Institute of the History of Pharmacy, Benjamin Waterhouse Medical History Society.

WRITINGS: Medical Men at the Siege of Boston, April 1775-April, 1776: Problems of the Massachusetts and Continental Armies, American Philosophical Society, 1973; (contributor) George Gifford, editor, *Physician Signers of the Declaration of Independence*, Neale Watson, 1976; (editor with Eric H. Christianson and J. Worth Estes, and contributor) *Medicine in Massachusetts, 1630-1860*, Colonial Society of Massachusetts, 1980.

Contributor to journals, including *New England Journal of Medicine* and *Journal of the American Medical Association*.

SIDELIGHTS: Cash told *CA:* "One primary area of research interest is the role of military medicine in the development of the American medical profession during the eighteenth century. Military medicine was second only to the apprenticeship system in the education of American doctors during this era. It provided opportunities to encounter a wide range of diseases and surgical problems, to broaden one's social and medical outlook by coming into contact with more experienced and better-trained medical men, especially those from Europe, and to work in hospitals. During the Revolution probably 40 percent or more of American doctors had some sort of medical experience with either the Patriot or British military forces or on board privateers. The other major area of research interest concerns the development of the medical profession in Boston between 1760 and 1840. Boston medicine of this period was unusual in having a socially and culturally homogeneous medical community and only one hospital, one medical school, and one medical society."

* * *

CASS, Ronald A(ndrew) 1949-

PERSONAL: Born August 12, 1949, in Washington, D.C.; son of Millard (a labor arbitrator) and Ruth (an artist; maiden name, Marx) Cass; married Valerie Swanson, August 24, 1969; children: Laura Rebecca. *Education:* University of Virginia, B.A. (with high distinction), 1970; University of Chicago, J.D. (with honors), 1973. *Home:* 40 Pinewood Rd., Wellesley, Mass. 02181. *Office:* School of Law, Boston University, 765 Commonwealth Ave., Boston, Mass. 02215.

CAREER: Member of Bar of U.S. Supreme Court, Supreme Court of Maryland, Court of Appeals of Maryland, and District of Columbia Court of Appeals. U.S. Court of Appeals for the Third Circuit, Wilmington, Del., law clerk, 1973-74; Arent, Fox, Kintner, Plotkin & Kahn, Washington, D.C., associate, 1974-76; University of Virginia, Charlottesville, assistant professor of law, 1976-81, sesquicentennial associate of Center for Advanced Studies, 1980-81; Boston University, Boston, Mass., associate professor of law, 1981—. Fellow at International Labor Organization, Geneva, Switzerland, 1968; Member of board of directors of Subarea Health Advisory Council of Northwestern Virginia Health Systems Agency, 1978-81, vice-chairman of council, 1979-80, chairman of council, 1980-81, member of board of directors of agency, 1980. Public speaker; consultant to Administrative Conference of the United States. *Military service:* U.S. Naval Reserve, 1966-70. *Member:* American Bar Association, Federal Communications Bar Association, Association of American Law Schools, Order of the Coif, Phi Beta Kappa, Phi Eta Sigma.

WRITINGS: Revolution in the Wasteland: Value and Diversity in Television, University Press of Virginia, 1981. Contributor to law journals.

WORK IN PROGRESS: Research on administrative agency decision-making and freedom of speech.

SIDELIGHTS: Cass wrote: "I am interested in the operation of government, public decision-making, communication, and speech. My book grew out of a paper on new communications media that I wrote for Aspen Institute for Humanistic Studies."

*   *   *

CATHERWOOD, (Henry) Frederick (Ross) 1925-

PERSONAL: Born January 30, 1925, in Castledawson, Northern Ireland; son of Stuart and Jean Catherwood; married Elizabeth Lloyd-Jones, February 27, 1954; children: Christopher Martyn Stuart, Bethan Jane, Jonathan. *Education:* Clare College, Cambridge, B.A., 1946. *Politics:* Conservative. *Home:* 25 Woodville Gardens, London W5 2LL, England. *Office:* 7 Rose Cres., Trinity St., Cambridge CB2 3LL, England.

CAREER: Articled Price, Waterhouse & Co., 1946-51; Law Stores Ltd., Gateshead, England, secretary, 1952-54; Richard Costain Ltd., secretary and controller, 1954-55, chief executive, 1955-60; British Aluminum Co., assistant managing director, 1960-62, managing director, 1962-64; Department of Economic Affairs, chief industrial adviser, 1964-66; National Economic Development Council, director-general, 1966-71; John Laing & Sons Ltd., managing director and chief executive, 1971-74; British Overseas Trade Board, chairman, 1975-79; European Parliament, member of Parliament for Cambridgeshire and Wellingborough, and chairman of its committee on external economic relations, 1979—. Chairman of Wittenborg Automat Ltd.; member of board of directors of Mallinson-Denny Ltd., 1974, chairman, 1976-79; member of board of directors of Goodyear Tyre & Rubber Co. Ltd. (United Kingdom) and John Laing & Sons Ltd., 1975—. Member of council of Northern Ireland Development Council, 1963-64; member of British National Export Council, 1965-70; member of central religious advisory committee to British Broadcasting Corp. and IBA, 1975—. Guest on television and radio programs.

MEMBER: International Fellowship of Evangelical Students, British Institute of Management (fellow; member of council, 1961-66, 1969—; vice-chairman, 1972-74; chairman, 1974-76; vice-president, 1976—; chairman of economic and social committee, 1978), Universities and Colleges Christian Fellowship (chairman of council, 1971-77), Fellowship of Independent Evangelical Christians (vice-president, 1976-77; president, 1977-78), Royal Institute of Chartered Accountants (fellow; member of council, 1964-77), Machine Tool Industry Research Association (president, 1977—), Association of Colleges of Further Education (president, 1979—), United Oxford and Cambridge University Club. *Awards, honors:* Created Knight Bachelor, 1971; D.Sc. from University of Aston in Birmingham, 1972, Queen's University, Belfast, 1973, and University of Surrey, 1979.

WRITINGS: The Christian in Industrial Society, Inter-Varsity Press, 1964, 3rd edition, 1980; *Britain With the Brakes Off,* Hodder & Stoughton, 1966; *The High Risks of Low Growth,* Oxford University Press, 1968; *The Christian Citizen,* Hodder & Stoughton, 1969; *The Christian College,* 1969; *Christian Duty in Ulster Today,* Evangelical Press, 1970.

Government Industry Dialogue: An Aspect of Economic Strategy, Manchester Statistical Society, 1972; *Making Knowledge Useful,* British Association for Commercial and Industrial Education, 1975; *A Better Way: A Case for a Christian Social Order,* Inter-Varsity Press, 1976; *The Difference Between a Reformer and a Progressive,* Shaftesbury Society, 1978; *First Things First: The Practice of Principles in Modern Society,* Lion (Berkhamsted), 1980. Contributor to magazines and newspapers.

WORK IN PROGRESS: Pamphlet on the Christian attitude toward nuclear war; diary of a member of the European Parliament ("which is different from any democratically elected assembly in history and on which there are so far no diaries or memoirs").

SIDELIGHTS: Catherwood told *CA:* "Since I have a very full life as an industrialist, public servant, and now politician, I have little time for writing, so I confine it to those issues on which I have some special knowledge and on which something needs to be said.

"I believe that the influence of good writing is much more enduring than political power. To change the public mind is to establish a new direction. To change public actions without changing minds makes a swing back to the old direction inevitable as soon as your power slips."

*   *   *

CAUGHEY, John Walton 1902-

BRIEF ENTRY: Born July 3, 1902, in Wichita, Kan. American historian, educator, editor, and author. Caughey was a member of the faculty at University of California, Los Angeles, for forty years, and was managing editor of *Pacific Historical Review* and literary editor of *Frontier.* He is a prolific writer of history books, including surveys of American history from colonial days to the present. They include *History of the Pacific Coast of North America* (Prentice-Hall, 1938), *America Since 1763: A Survey of Its History* (1955), and *The American West: Frontier and Region* (Ward Ritchie, 1969). He also wrote *To Kill a Child's Spirit: The Tragedy of School Segregation in Los Angeles* (F. E. Peacock, 1973) and *A Plan to Desegregate the Los Angeles Schools* (1977) and edited *Los Angeles: Biography of a City* (University of California Press, 1976). *Address:* 1897 Mango Way, Los Angeles, Calif. 90049. *Biographical/critical sources: University Bookman,* autumn, 1967; *The Reader's Encyclopedia of the American West,* Crowell, 1977; *Who's Who in America,* 40th edition, Marquis, 1978.

*   *   *

CAUTELA, Joseph R(ichard) 1927-

PERSONAL: Born February 21, 1927; son of Salvatore and

Domenica (D'Amico) Cautela; married Joan T. Gleason, May 6, 1972; children: (from previous marriage) Joseph R., Jr., Richard, Robert, John, Carole, Christopher, Tory; (from present marriage) Salvatore, Mark Anthony. *Education:* Boston College, A.B., 1949, M.A., 1950, Ph.D., 1954. *Home:* 10 Phillips Rd., Sudbury, Mass. 01776. *Office:* Department of Psychology, Boston College, Chestnut Hill, Mass. 02167.

CAREER: Boston College, Chestnut Hill, Mass., instructor, 1951-54, assistant professor, 1954-59, associate professor, 1959-66, professor of psychology, 1966—, past director of guidance at Evening School. Private practice of clinical psychology. Visiting professor at Max Planck Institute of Psychiatry, summer, 1967, and Wesleyan University, Middletown, Conn., 1969. Research assistant at Atomic Energy Commission and Massachusetts Division of the Blind; coordinator of behavior therapy at Medfield State Hospital; consultant to U.S. Veterans Administration, Kennedy Memorial Hospital for Children, and Rhode Island Rehabilitation Center. *Military service:* U.S. Navy, pharmacist, 1945-46.

MEMBER: Pavlovian Society of North America, American Psychological Association, Gerontological Society, Association for the Advancement of Behavior Therapy (member of executive board; New England coordinator; president, 1973-74), Eastern Psychological Association, New England Psychological Association, Massachusetts Psychological Association (fellow), Sigma Xi (past president).

WRITINGS: Behavior Analysis Forms for Clinical Intervention, Research Press, 1977; *Relaxation: A Comprehensive Manual for Adults, Children, and Children With Special Needs*, Research Press, 1978.

Contributor: B. P. Rourke, editor, *Explorations in the Psychology of Stress and Anxiety*, Longmans, Green, 1969; Cyril Maurice Franks, editor, *Behavior Therapy: Appraisal and Status*, McGraw, 1969; Franks and R. Rubin, editors, *Advances in Behavior Therapy, 1969*, Academic Press, 1969; Leonard Hersher, editor, *Four Psychotherapies*, Appleton, 1970; Rubin, editor, *Advances in Behavior Therapy*, Academic Press, 1970; Alfred Jacobs and Louis B. Sachs, editors, *Psychology of Private Events*, Academic Press, 1971; L. Diamant, editor, *Case Studies in Psychopathology*, C. E. Merrill, 1971; Rubin, J. Henderson, and other editors, *Advances in Behavior Therapy*, Academic Press, 1972; Michael Hersen and R. M. Eisler, editors, *Progress in Behavior Therapy*, Academic Press, 1975. Also contributor to *Planning, Research, and Action for the Aged: The Power and Potential of Science*, edited by R. Kastenbaum, D. Kent, and S. Sherwood, 1971. Contributor of more than sixty articles to psychology journals.

*			*			*

CHAFFEE, Steven Henry   1935-

PERSONAL: Born August 21, 1935, in South Gate, Calif.; son of Edwin W. (an attorney) and Nancy M. (Kinghorn) Chaffee; married Sheila McGoldrick (a civic leader), September 20, 1958; children: Laura, Adam, Amy. *Education:* University of Redlands, B.A. (with distinction), 1957; University of California, Los Angeles, M.S., 1962; Stanford University, Ph.D. (with distinction), 1965. *Home:* 183 Creekside Dr., Palo Alto, Calif. 94306. *Office:* Institute for Communication Research, Stanford University, Cypress Hall, Stanford, Calif. 94305.

CAREER: Angeles Mesa News-Advertiser, Los Angeles, Calif., news editor, 1957; *Tribune News-Advertiser*, Los Angeles, news editor, 1957; Southern Counties Gas Co., Los Angeles, publications assistant, 1961; *Export-Import News*, Los Ange-

les, part-time assistant to editor, 1961-62; *Santa Monica Evening Outlook*, Santa Monica, Calif., reporter, 1962; University of Wisconsin—Madison, assistant professor, 1965-68, associate professor, 1968-72, professor of journalism and mass communication, 1972-81, Willard G. Bleyer Professor, 1973-74, Vilas Research Professor, 1974-81, director of School of Journalism and Mass Communication, 1980-81; Stanford University, Stanford, Calif., professor of communication and director of Institute for Communication Research, 1981—. Visiting assistant professor at Stanford University, summer, 1967, visiting associate professor, summer, 1971; lecturer at U.S. Foreign Service Institute, 1972, 1973, and U.S. International Communication Agency, 1978-80; visiting professor at University of California, Los Angeles, 1979. Public opinion analyst for political candidates, 1968-82; consultant to RAND Corp., National Institute of Mental Health, and U.S. International Communication Agency. *Military service:* U.S. Naval Reserve, active duty as public information officer, 1958-61; became lieutenant junior grade.

MEMBER: International Communication Association (president, 1981-82), Association for Education in Journalism (member of executive committee, 1971-72; chairman of standing committee on research, 1971-72; head of Communication Theory and Methodology Division, 1973-74), American Association for Public Opinion Research. *Awards, honors:* Grants from National Science Foundation, 1967-71, 1979-82, and National Institute of Mental Health, 1969-71, 1970-71.

WRITINGS: (With Richard F. Carter) *The Structure and Process of School-Community Relations,* Volume II: *Between Citizens and Schools,* Institute for Communication Research, Stanford University, 1966; (with Michael Petrick) *Using the Mass Media: Communication Problems in American Society,* McGraw, 1975; (editor and contributor) *Political Communication: Issues and Strategies for Research,* Sage Publications, 1975; (with George Comstock, Natan Katzman, Maxwell McCombs, and Donald Roberts) *Television and Human Behavior,* Columbia University Press, 1978.

Contributor: Jack Lyle and Walter Wilcox, editors, *A Community Daily in a Changing Metropolitan Press Environment,* University of California, Los Angeles, 1962; Eli Robinstein, George Comstock, and John Murray, editors, *Television and Social Behavior,* Volume III, U.S. Government Printing Office, 1971; James Tedeschi, editor, *The Social Influence Process,* Aldine, 1972; F. Gerald Kline and Phillip J. Tichenor, editors, *Current Perspectives in Mass Communication Research,* Sage Publications, 1972; Jack S. Dennis, editor, *Socialization to Politics: Selected Readings,* Wiley, 1973; Scott Ward and Thomas Robertson, editors, *Consumer Behavior: Theoretical Sources,* Prentice-Hall, 1973; Kline and Peter Clarke, editors, *Mass Communications and Youth,* Sage Publications, 1975; McCombs, Donald L. Shaw, and David Grey, editors, *Handbook of Reporting Methods,* Houghton, 1976; David Lerner and Lyle Nelson, editors, *Communication Research: A Half-Century Appraisal,* University Press of Hawaii, 1977; Stanley Renshon, editor, *Handbook of Political Communication,* Free Press, 1977; Sidney Kraus, editor, *The Great Debates, 1976: Ford Versus Carter,* Indiana University Press, 1979; Austin Ranney, editor, *The Past and Future of Presidential Debates,* American Enterprise Institute for Public Policy Research, 1979; Gary Gumpert and Robert Cathcart, editors, *Inter-Media: Interpersonal Communication in a Media World,* 2nd edition (Chaffee was not included in 1st edition), Oxford University Press, 1982.

Contributor of nearly fifty articles and reviews to communication journals. Editor of *Journalism Monographs,* October,

1974, *Communication Research,* October, 1974, and *American Politics Quarterly,* October, 1975; member of editorial board of *Journalism Monographs,* 1968—, *Journalism Quarterly,* 1972—, *Communication Research,* 1972—, *Sage Annual Reviews of Communication Research,* 1972—, *Human Communication Research,* 1973-77, 1979—, *Public Opinion Quarterly,* 1976—, and *Sage Yearbook of Communication Research,* 1978—.

WORK IN PROGRESS: "A panel study of the role of mass media in political socialization, funded by the National Science Foundation; history of research in the U.S. on mass media in election campaigns; applications of social research to the study of mass communication processes, with Byron Reeves and Albert Tims."

SIDELIGHTS: Chaffee told *CA:* "My writing is devoted to establishing the identity of human communication as a field of research that is distinct from the more established social sciences such as psychology and sociology, and from technical skills preparation for careers in communication, or from the discursive school of criticism of communication institutions and practices."

*   *   *

CHAMBERLIN, Enid C. S.   1900(?)-1982(?)

OBITUARY NOTICE: Born c. 1900; died c. March, 1982, in Brunswick, Me. Educator, bookseller, and author. Chamberlin and her husband, both teachers, collaborated in compiling an educational survey for the Rockefeller Foundation that resulted in the publication of *Did They Succeed in College?* Upon retirement Chamberlin and her husband operated a doll and book shop. Obituaries and other sources: *AB Bookman's Weekly,* March 29, 1982.

*   *   *

CHANAN, Michael   1946-

PERSONAL: Born August 19, 1946, in London, England; son of Elchanan (in small business) and Miriam (Bromberg) Chanan. *Education:* University of Sussex, B.A. (with honors), 1968; Wolfson College, Oxford, B.Litt., 1970. *Religion:* "Jewish by birth, but as Kafka said, 'I'm an atheist, thank God.'" *Home:* 18 Moreland Court, Finchley Rd., London N.W.2, England.

CAREER: Free-lance music critic and radio broadcaster, 1967—; director of documentary films, 1970—; Polytechnic of Central London, London, England, senior lecturer in film, 1976-80. Director of documentary films for BBC-TV, 1970, 1972. *Member:* Independent Filmmakers Association.

WRITINGS: Labour Power in the British Film Industry, British Film Institute, 1976; (editor) *Chilean Cinema,* British Film Institute, 1976; (translator) Armand Mattelart, *Multinational Corporations and the Control of Culture,* Harvester, 1979; *The Dream That Kicks: The Prehistory and Early Years of Cinema in Britain,* Routledge & Kegan Paul, 1980; (editor) *Santiago Alvarez,* British Film Institute, 1980. Contributor to magazines, including *Media, Culture and Society* and *L'Homme et la Societe.* Music and film critic for *Tribune* (London, England), 1979—.

WORK IN PROGRESS: The Cuban Image, a history of Cuban cinema, publication by Indiana University Press and British Film Institute; a sequel to *The Dream That Kicks;* research for an anthology on film music, publication by British Film Institute.

SIDELIGHTS: Chanan commented: "Since 1973, when I spent six months doing fieldwork in Bolivia with an anthropologist friend, I have become increasingly drawn to Latin America—its cinema, its music, its culture. Most of my activities are now oriented to this interest.

"My first abiding interest, however, is music, especially twentieth-century music, which for me was born with Mahler. Though my tastes are catholic and I bow to no one in my love of the great composers of the past, I am guided by Mahler's dictum that 'tradition is bunk,' above all because our responsibility as artists and intellectuals is to the present.

"I have tried to apply this to my work as a film historian, being always concerned with the implications of the study of history for the understanding of the present. For this reason I have been concerned with analyzing the institution of filmmaking and the intimate relationship between the aesthetics of cinema and its political economy. For me, this gives rise to another principle, one that might be called 'aesthetics from below'—that is, an aesthetics, a critical practice, and a history which grows out of practical concerns and practical knowledge. Most film history and criticism is entirely worthless, not just because of its crass reflection of commercial values, but also because it's written by people who have no practical knowledge of what they're writing about. This is not a problem in the case in writing about music, which suffers, on the other hand, from a peculiar lack of awareness of music as a social activity.

"But aesthetics from below also has two other referents. First, it means an awareness of what arises from beneath consciousness, for full and proper phenomenological attention to the creative process itself reveals not so much an unconscious in the classical Freudian sense as an apparently inchoate structure, which is capable of a much more accurate perception of reality than our frequently rigidified and regimented consciousness. It is this that gives rise to the property of ambiguity and paradox that is inseparable from artistic creation.

"Secondly, aesthetics from below in the sense that the recognized art and learning of any age, which we fondly refer to as culture, rests upon creative receptivity in the anonymous populace and the sensibility of the popular imagination. As John Huston said to Sam Goldwyn when Goldwyn told him to remember they were making films for people with a mental age of twelve, 'Sure, Sam, but twelve-year-olds are a damn sight more intelligent than you think they are.'

"Finally, I consider that the work of the critic and the cultural historian makes no sense if it is not organically linked to a commitment to the defense of contemporary culture. While some of the threats doubtless come from political dogma and sectarianism, the greatest danger by far is the slow murder of the imagination by an internally contradictory economic system which knows only that its survival depends not on the freedom of the individual as a social and economic agent, in which its own origins can be located, but rather upon an unprecedented degree of pre-planning, scientific management, and market control. Cultural creativity depends upon the free play of the imagination, spontaneity, and the play impulse. This economic system is bent upon programming everybody and everything completely. It's the same international economic order that quite happily sanctions the genocide of Brazilian Indians in its own interests, and disregards the human rights in the countries dependent upon it of illiterate peasants and 'dissident' artists and intellectuals alike."

BIOGRAPHICAL/CRITICAL SOURCES: Unomasuno, August 25, 1978.

CHAND, Meira (Angela) 1942-

PERSONAL: Born August 19, 1942, in London, England; daughter of Harbans Lal (a doctor) and Norah (Knobel) Gulati; married Kumar Chand (in business), December 21, 1961; children: Vikram, Anjali. *Education:* Educated in England. *Home:* Obanoyama CHO 3-CHOME 1-7, Shinohara, Nada-Ku, Kobe, Japan.

CAREER: Stella Man's International School, Kobe, Japan, art teacher, 1968-71; writer.

WRITINGS—Novels: *The Gossamer Fly,* John Murray, 1979, Ticknor & Fields, 1980; *Last Quadrant,* John Murray, 1981, Ticknor & Fields, 1982.

WORK IN PROGRESS: A novel of Japanese life; research for fourth novel.

SIDELIGHTS: Chand's *Last Quadrant* concerns a multi-ethnic group trapped in an orphanage by a typhoon. In *Times Literary Supplement,* Louis Allen praised Chand's "poetic quality of prose" and noted, "Some of the description . . . is sensitive and powerful." Allen also noted that Chand adeptly mines her own experiences spanning twenty years in Japan. He declared that "her characters are from the world of expatriates and mixed blood . . . aware of themselves on the fringe of a world which consents to them with difficulty and never takes them into itself."

Chand told *CA:* "Being half Swiss and half Indian, I have lived always with a sense of alienation's lack of belonging to any place or people. My themes through circumstance are those of alienation and the clash of Eastern and Western cultures with a special concern for the outsider or the mixed blood. My material is modern Japan, whose closed and complex society I have lived in for twenty years, a society few Westerners know in detail, and it is a continuing source of frustration and fascination to me."

BIOGRAPHICAL/CRITICAL SOURCES: Times Literary Supplement, September 18, 1981.

*   *   *

CHANDLER, Linda S(mith) 1929-

PERSONAL: Born February 4, 1929, in Wadesboro, N.C.; daughter of Clinton Ashe and Emma (Sikes) Smith; married Gordon Yearby Chandler (a pressman), October 17, 1948; children: Gordon Lee, Judi Chandler Crouse, Linda Ann. *Education:* Attended Croft Secretarial School, 1947-48, and Duke University. *Politics:* Democrat. *Religion:* Southern Baptist. *Home:* 106 Stallings Rd., Durham, N.C. 27703. *Office:* Chapel, Duke University, P.O. Box 4752 D.S., Durham, N.C. 27706.

CAREER: Held part-time secretarial positions in Durham, N.C., 1957-75; Duke University, Durham, hostess at university chapel, 1975—. Taught at Ridgecrest and Glorieta conference centers. Member of Durham County Board of Health, 1972—, Durham County Board of Education, 1976—, North Carolina Interagency Council on Community Schools, 1979—, board of trustees of North Carolina Baptist Homes, 1981—, advisory committee of Child Abuse and Prevention of Parental Stress (CAPPS), Durham Citizens' Safety Council, Durham Democratic Women, and advisory board of Parents Involved in Preschool Education (PIPE). *Member:* Society of Children's Book Writers, National Writers Club, North Carolina Poetry Society, North Carolina Community Education Association, Durham

County Association for Childhood Education, Delta Kappa Gamma.

WRITINGS—For children: *My Family Loves Me,* Convention Press, 1978; *Hello, My Church,* Broadman, 1980; *Uncle Ike,* Broadman, 1981; *David Asks, "Why?,"* Broadman, 1981.

Curriculum writer for Southern Baptist Convention Sunday School Board. Contributor to magazines, including *Christian Advocate, Child Life, Biblical Recorder, Look and Listen, Living With Teenagers,* and *Church Administration.*

WORK IN PROGRESS: A book dealing with prayer and the young child, "to help him understand how he can express himself and talk to God"; a book for young children dealing with the importance of nonsexist lifestyle.

SIDELIGHTS: Linda Chandler commented: "Writing for children has been an important part of my life. I have made two child-study trips abroad, visiting schools in Italy, Israel, Switzerland, and England. I am also involved in conducting book fairs in different parts of the country and enjoy going into classrooms to talk to children about writing, books, and the importance of self-expression. I believe we should do everything we can to help children learn to love books and think of them as friends."

BIOGRAPHICAL/CRITICAL SOURCES: Durham Herald, April 20, 1980, October 11, 1981; *Raleigh News and Observer,* January 31, 1982.

*   *   *

CHAO, Yuen Ren 1892-1982

OBITUARY NOTICE—See index for *CA* sketch: Born November 3, 1892, in Tientsin, China; died February 24, 1982, in Cambridge, Mass. Educator, translator, editor, author, and linguist best known for his creation of a phonetic alphabet used in transliterating Chinese into English. His method was officially adopted in 1928 by the Chinese Government and called the "National Romanization." It was employed until 1950, when the Pinyin system came into use. From 1919 to 1920 Chao taught physics at Cornell University but thereafter devoted his academic career to the study and teaching of linguistics and Chinese and other Oriental languages. He taught at several schools, including Harvard University, National Tsing Hau University in Peking, University of Hawaii, and Yale University. He spent his later years as the Agassiz Professor of Oriental Languages and Literature at the University of California at Berkeley. Among Chao's several books are *Studies in Modern Wu Dialects, Mandarin Primer: An Intensive Course in Spoken Chinese,* and *Readings in Sayable Chinese.* He also translated *Autobiography of a Chinese Woman* and edited the volume *Linguistics in East Asia and South East Asia.* Obituaries and other sources: *Chicago Tribune,* February 27, 1982.

*   *   *

CHAPIAN, Marie 1938-

PERSONAL: Surname is pronounced *Chay*-pian; born October 10, 1938, in Minneapolis, Minn.; daughter of Leo R. and Dorothy (a businesswoman and author; maiden name, Buck) Jordan; married Peter Chapian (an artist), February 5, 1965 (divorced April 18, 1977); children: Christa Deirdre, Liza Dorothy. *Education:* Attended University of Minnesota and Moody Bible Institute; Metropolitan State University, B.A., 1978. *Religion:* Christian. *Address:* Marie Chapian Ministries, P.O. Box 897, La Jolla, Calif. 92038.

CAREER: Elementary school teacher in Minneapolis, Minn.; Creation House (publisher), Carol Stream, Ill., originator of "Mustard Seed Library" books for children, 1974; Center for Christian Psychological Services, Roseville, Minn., psychotherapist, 1978-80; Marie Chapian Ministries, La Jolla, Calif., Christian minister, 1980—. Lecturer and seminar leader, 1972—; originator of television program, "Being a Loved Person." *Member:* Authors Guild, Christian Association for Psychological Studies. *Awards, honors:* Most significant book of the year, poetry category, from *Chicago Church News,* 1973, award of recognition of graphic arts excellence from Consolidated Papers, 1973, Poetry and Fiction Mark of Excellence award from *Campus Life,* 1974, all for *Mind Things;* the San Diego Christian Writers' Guild cited Chapian for having made the most outstanding contribution to Christian literature in 1979.

WRITINGS: City Psalms (poems; illustrated by husband, Peter Chapian), Moody, 1972; *Mind Things* (poems; illustrated by P. Chapian), Creation House, 1973; *I Learn About the Fruit of the Holy Spirit* (juvenile; illustrated by P. Chapian), Creation House, 1974; *I Learn About the Gifts of the Holy Spirit* (juvenile; illustrated by P. Chapian), Creation House, 1974; *The Holy Spirit and Me* (juvenile; illustrated by P. Chapian), Creation House, 1974; "To My Friend" series, twelve books, Successful Living, 1974; *The Emancipation of Robert Sadler* (biography), Bethany Fellowship, 1976; *Of Whom the World Was Not Worthy* (biography), Bethany Fellowship, 1978; *Free To Be Thin,* Bethany Fellowship, 1979; (with Tom Netherton) *In the Morning of My Life* (biography), Tyndale, 1979; (with William Backus) *Telling Yourself the Truth,* Bethany Fellowship, 1980; *At the End of the Rainbow* (biography), Tyndale, 1981.

WORK IN PROGRESS: "Currently writing *Being a Loved Person* which is also the name of my television program. It is a book of five years of research and clinical case histories of lives touched by love"; *Where Do I Find Heaven?,* the life story of evangelist Roger Vann.

* * *

CHAPMAN, Sydney 1888-1970

PERSONAL: Born January 29, 1888, in Eccles, Lancashire, England; died of a heart attack, June 16, 1970, in Boulder, Colo.; son of Joseph and Sarah Louisa (Gray) Chapman; married Katherine Nora Steinthal, March 23, 1922; children: Cecil Hall, Robert Gray, Richard Joseph Ernest, Mary Midnes McAlley. *Education:* Attended Royal Technical Institute; Victoria University of Manchester, B.Sc. (first class honors), 1907, M.Sc. (first class honors), 1908, D.Sc., 1914; Trinity College, Cambridge, M.A., 1914. *Residence:* London, England.

CAREER: Royal Greenwich Observatory, Greenwich, England, chief assistant, 1910-18; Cambridge University, Trinity College, Cambridge, England, lecturer, beginning in 1914; Victoria University of Manchester, Manchester, England, professor of mathematics and natural philosophy, 1919-24; Imperial College of Science and Technology, London, England, professor of mathematics, 1924-46; Oxford University, Queen's College, Oxford, England, Sedleian Professor of Natural Philosophy and professor of mathematics, 1946-53. Head coordinator of the Special Committee for the International Geophysical Year, 1957-58; visiting professor at University of Michigan, New York University, State University of Iowa, Istanbul University (Turkey), and University of Alaska. *Member:* International Association of Meteorology (former president), International Association for Terrestrial Magnetism and Electricity (former president), International Union of Geodesy

and Geophysics (former president), American Physical Society (fellow), Royal Astronomical Society (fellow; former president), Royal Meteorological Society (fellow; former president), Royal Society (fellow), London Mathematical Society (fellow; former president), London Physical Society (fellow; former president), Cambridge Philosophical Society (fellow), national academies of science of Norway, Sweden, and Finland, Athenaeum Club. *Awards, honors:* Smith Prize and Adams Prize, both from Cambridge University, both 1929.

WRITINGS: (Editor) Thomas Watson, *Pioneers of Progress,* S.P.C.K., 1918, W. & R. Holmes, 1950; *The Earth's Magnetism,* Methuen, 1936, 2nd edition, Wiley, 1951; (with T. G. Cowling) *The Mathematical Theory of Non-Uniform Gases: An Account of the Kinetic Theory of Viscosity, Thermal Conduction, and Diffusion in Gases,* Cambridge University Press, 1939, reprinted, 1970; (with Julius Bartels) *Geomagnetism,* two volumes, Clarendon Press, 1940, revised edition, 1962; (author of foreword) *The Histories of the International Polar Years and the Inception and Development of the International Geophysical Year,* Pergamon, 1959.

IGY: Year of Discovery—The Story of the International Geophysical Year, University of Michigan Press, 1959; (with Syun-Ichi Akasofu) *A Study of Magnetic Storms and Auroras,* Geophysical Institute of the University of Alaska, 1961; *Solar Plasma, Geomagnetism, and Aurora,* Gordon & Breach, 1964; (with Richard S. Lindzen) *Atmospheric Tides: Thermal and Gravitational,* Gordon & Breach, 1970; (with Akasofu) *Solar-Terrestrial Physics: An Account of the Wave and Particle Radiations From the Quiet and the Active Sun, and of the Consequent Terrestrial Phenomena,* Clarendon Press, 1972.

Contributor of more than one hundred scientific articles to periodicals, including *Nature, Sky and Telescope, Popular Mechanics, Scientific American, Bulletin of Atomic Science, Geographical Journal, Physical Review, Philosophical Magazine, Science, Quarterly Journal of the Royal Meteorological Society, Journal of the London Mathematical Society,* and *Geographical Supplement of the Royal Astronomical Society.*

SIDELIGHTS: During his lengthy career, Sydney Chapman made several contributions to the study of geophysics. Most notable was his theory explaining connections between sunspot activity, auroras, and terrestrial magnetism.

BIOGRAPHICAL/CRITICAL SOURCES: Nature, December 16, 1939, February 9, 1946, June 18, 1949, May 23, 1953; *Chemical and Metallurgical Engineering,* February, 1940; *Journal of the American Chemical Society,* July, 1940; *Scientific American,* May, 1954, October, 1959; *New York Times Book Review,* January 24, 1960; Syun-Ichi Akasofu, Benson Fogle, and Bernhard Haurwitz, editors, *Sydney Chapman, Eighty: From His Friends,* National Center for Atmospheric Research, 1968; *Saturday Review,* July 6, 1968.

OBITUARIES: New York Times, June 20, 1970; *Newsweek,* June 29, 1970; *Time,* June 29, 1970; *Nature,* August 29, 1979; *Physics Today,* September, 1970.*

* * *

CHAPPELL, William (Evelyn) 1908-

PERSONAL: Born September 27, 1908, in Wolverhampton, England; son of Archibald and Edith Eva Clara (Blair-Staples) Chappell. *Education:* Attended Chelsea School of Art; studied dance with Marie Rambert. *Home:* 40 Thurloe Sq., London S.W.7, England. *Office:* Adza Vincent Ltd., 11a Ivor Pl., London N.W.1, England.

CAREER: Professional ballet dancer, 1929—; designer of scenery and costumes for the stage, 1932—; director and choreographer of stage shows, 1951—. Appeared in film, "The Trial," 1963.

WRITINGS: Studies in Ballet, Lehmann, 1948; *Fonteyn: Impressions of a Ballerina* (self-illustrated), Rockliff, 1951. Also author of *Popular Music of the Olden Time,* two volumes, Peter Smith.

(Author of libretto) Malcolm Williamson, *The Violins of Saint-Jacques* (three-act opera), J. Weinberger, 1966.

AVOCATIONAL INTERESTS: Walking, reading, cinema, painting.

* * *

CHARTHAM, Robert
See SETH, Ronald (Sydney)

* * *

CHASE, Clinton I(rvin) 1927-

PERSONAL: Born August 14, 1927, in Reubens, Idaho; son of Charles Irvin (a farmer) and Agnes (Eikum) Chase; married Patricia L. Cronenberger, August 3, 1957; children: Steven Michael. *Education:* University of Idaho, B.S., 1950, M.S.Ed., 1951; University of California, Berkeley, Ph.D., 1958. *Home:* 405 Meadowbrook, Bloomington, Ind. 47401. *Office:* Department of Education, Indiana University, Bloomington, Ind. 47401.

CAREER: Indiana University, Bloomington, began as assistant professor, 1962, became professor of education. *Military service:* U.S. Navy, 1945-46. U.S. Air Force, 1952-55; became captain. *Member:* American Psychological Association, American Educational Research Association, National Council on Measurement in Education, Phi Beta Kappa.

WRITINGS: (With H. Glenn Wadlow) *Readings in Educational and Psychological Measurement,* Houghton, 1966; *Elementary Statistical Procedures,* McGraw, 1967, 3rd edition, 1983; *Measurement for Educational Evaluation,* Addison-Wesley, 1974, 2nd edition, 1978. Contributor to educational and psychological journals.

WORK IN PROGRESS: Research in sex bias in tests.

* * *

CHASE, Mildred Portney 1921-

PERSONAL: Born February 5, 1921, in Brooklyn, N.Y.; daughter of Marcus (in produce) and Sarah (a chiropractor; maiden name, Pilson) Portney; married William Francis Chase (an accountant and sculptor), February 26, 1942; children: Kenneth H., Sanders J. *Education:* Juilliard School of Music, Diploma, 1942. *Residence:* Los Angeles, Calif. *Office address:* P.O. Box 372, Idyllwild, Calif. 90046.

CAREER: Pianist and piano teacher in Los Angeles, Calif., 1950—.

WRITINGS: Just Being at the Piano (adult nonfiction), Peace Press, 1981.

SIDELIGHTS: Mildred Chase wrote: "The aim of my book and my teaching is to instill a love and joy in making music. The emotional or spiritual quality must accompany and facilitate the acquisition of physical technique. Only by keeping the sensory and emotional experience foremost at all times can an artist communicate effectively with an audience."

CHECK, Otto Premier
See BERMAN, Ed

* * *

CHEEVER, John 1912-1982

OBITUARY NOTICE—See index for *CA* sketch: Born May 27, 1912, in Quincy, Mass.; died of cancer, June 18, 1982, in Ossining, N.Y.; buried in Norwell, Mass. Novelist and short story writer. Best known as a chronicler of suburbia, Cheever won critical acclaim for his humorous, yet compassionate, accounts of privileged communities populated by affluent people living spiritually impoverished lives. A rehabilitated alcoholic and a suburban dweller himself, "Cheever knew," eulogized Peter S. Prescott in *Newsweek,* "that in a world that most people envy there are people who are bravely enduring." Cheever wrote five novels and more than one hundred short stories during his career and was the recipient of America's most prestigious literary awards. His most celebrated work, *The Stories of John Cheever,* earned him a Pulitzer Prize in fiction, the National Book Critics Circle Award, and an American Book Award. He also received the coveted Howells Medal of the American Academy of Arts and Letters for the best work of fiction in a five-year period, *The Wopshot Scandal.* In addition he was awarded the O. Henry Award for "The Country Husband," the National Book Award for *The Wopshot Chronicle,* and the National Medal for Literature for his "distinguished and continuing contribution to American letters." Among his other writing are *Bullet Park, Falconer, Housebreaker of Shady Hill and Other Stories, The Way Some People Live: A Book of Stories,* and *Some People, Places, and Things That Will Not Appear in My Next Novel.* Obituaries and other sources: *New York Times,* June 19, 1982; *Detroit Free Press,* June 20, 1982; *London Times,* June 21, 1982; *Detroit News,* June 27, 1982; *Newsweek,* June 28, 1982; *Time,* June 28, 1982.

* * *

CHEN, Ching-chih 1937-

PERSONAL: Born September 3, 1937, in Foochow, China; came to the United States in 1959, naturalized citizen, 1974; daughter of Han-cha and May-ying Liu; married Sow-Hsin Chen (a professor), 1961; children: Anne, Cathy, John. *Education:* National Taiwan University, B.A., 1959; University of Michigan, A.M.L.S., 1961; Case Western Reserve University, Ph.D., 1974. *Office:* Graduate School of Library and Information Science, Simmons College, 300 The Fenway, Boston, Mass. 02115.

CAREER: Queens Borough Public Library, New York, N.Y., library trainee, 1960; University of Michigan, Ann Arbor, service librarian, 1961-62; Windsor Public Library, Windsor, Ontario, science reference librarian, 1962; McMaster University, Hamilton, Ontario, reference and circulation librarian, 1962-63, head of science library, 1963-64; University of Waterloo, Waterloo, Ontario, senior science librarian, 1964-65, head of Engineering, Mathematics, and Science Library, 1965-68; Massachusetts Institute of Technology, Cambridge, associate science librarian, 1968-71; Simmons College, Boston, Mass., assistant professor, 1971-75, associate professor, 1975-79, professor of library and information science, 1979—, associate dean of Graduate School of Library and Information Science, 1979—. Member of special faculty for Mexican Library Association at University of Guanajuato, 1980; member of U.S. delegation on biomedical information to China, 1980. Member of advisory committee of Continuing Library Education Network and Exchange, 1976-79; witness before U.S. House of Representatives; workshop leader; public speaker in the United States and abroad. Consultant to numerous organizations, including Taiwan's National Science Council, Chung-Shan Institute of Scientific Research, National Library of Medicine, and World Health Organization.

MEMBER: American Library Association (councilor at large, 1981—), American Society for Information Science (chairperson of New England Chapter, 1977-78, Special Interest Group on Education of Information Science, 1979-80, and subcommittee on the People's Republic of China, 1979—; member of board of directors, 1981—), Special Library Association, Medical Library Association (chairperson of surveys and statistics committee, 1980-82), Association of College and Research Libraries, American Association of University Professors (member of executive board, 1975-76), Association of American Library Schools, New England Library Association, Massachusetts Library Association, Beta Phi Mu.

AWARDS, HONORS: Barbour scholar at University of Michigan, 1959-61; grants from Emily Hollowell Research Fund, 1972—, Digital Equipment Corp., 1977, and National Library of Medicine, 1977; fellowship for North Atlantic Treaty Organization's Advanced Study Institute on the Evaluation and Scientific Management of Library and Information Centers, 1975; Marion and Jasper Whiting Foundation travel grant, 1976; U.S. Office of Education fellowships, 1976, 1977, 1978, 1979, 1981, research grants, 1978-1982; first runner-up for best information science book award from American Society for Information Science, 1978, for *Applications of Operations Research Models to Libraries;* Distinguished Alumni Award from University of Michigan School of Library Science, 1980.

WRITINGS: Applications of Operations Research Models to Libraries: A Case Study of the Use of Monographs in the Francis A. Countway Library of Medicine, M.I.T. Press, 1976; *Biomedical, Scientific, and Technical Book Reviewing,* Scarecrow, 1976; *Sourcebook on Health Sciences Librarianship,* Scarecrow, 1971; *Scientific and Technical Information Sciences,* M.I.T. Press, 1977; (editor) *Quantitative Measurement and Dynamic Library Service,* Oryx, 1978; (editor) *Library Management Without Bias,* JAI Press, 1980; (with Susanna Schweizer) *Online Bibliographic Searching: A Manual for Librarians,* Neal-Schuman, 1981; *Zero-Base Budgeting in Library Management: A Manual for Library Administrators,* Oryx, 1981; *Health Sciences Information Sources,* M.I.T. Press, 1981; (with Peter Hernon) *Information-Seeking: Assessing and Anticipating User Needs,* Neal-Schuman, 1982; (co-editor with Stacey Bressler) *Microcomputer Applications in Libraries,* Neal-Schuman, 1982.

General editor of "Applications in Information Management and Technology," a series, Neal-Schuman, 1980—. Contributor to *American Reference Book Annual* and *Encyclopedia of Library and Information Science.* Contributor of more than sixty articles and reviews to library journals in the United States and abroad. Member of advisory board of *Legal Abstracts,* 1977-79; member of editorial board of *Progress in Communication Science,* 1979—.

SIDELIGHTS: Chen told *CA:* "I am active in international consulting work. For example, as consultant to the World Health Organization, I taught management courses in India, China, and many other countries. I travel extensively in all parts of the world, and share my expertise and knowledge with people and professionals in developing countries."

CHEN, Yuan-tsung 1932-

PERSONAL: Born April 15, 1932, in Shanghai, China; came to the United States in 1972; daughter of Shi-cheng (an engineer) and Tung-yin (Chin) Chen; married Jack Chen (an artist and writer), April 26, 1958; children: Jay. *Education:* Empire State College of the State University of New York, B.A., 1975. *Office:* East Asiatic Library, University of California, Berkeley, Berkeley, Calif. 94720.

CAREER: Film Publishing House, Peking, China, translator and editor, 1950-64; Cornell University, Ithaca, N.Y., instructor of Chinese, 1974-77; Chinese Culture Center of San Francisco, San Francisco, Calif., researcher and writer, 1978-79; East Asiatic Library, University of California, Berkeley, librarian's assistant, 1979—. Coordinator of Chinese Film Retrospective at San Francisco International Film Festival, 1981.

WRITINGS: The Dragon's Village (novel), Pantheon, 1980.

WORK IN PROGRESS: A novel about China's Cultural Revolution, tentatively titled *The Unfinished Duet,* for Pantheon.

SIDELIGHTS: Chen's *The Dragon's Village* is an autobiographical novel depicting the revolutionary changes that transformed China when the People's Republic was founded. Events are seen through the eyes of Chen's heroine, Guan Ling-ling, a middle-class teenager who forsakes her comfortable urban life to live and work with the peasants of an impoverished village and help them enforce land reform. Although Ling-ling ardently believes in the redistribution of land from the few wealthy landowners to the mass of landless peasants, she is unprepared for the tragedies she experiences as the revolution gathers momentum: a co-worker is murdered, a landowner's young daughter is raped, and a young man, wrongly accused of being a landowner, is driven to suicide. Ling-ling is unaccustomed not only to the violence, but to the operose labor and meager diet of peasant life. Though raised on Peking Duck, Ling-ling must subsist on a daily ration of thin cornmeal gruel. She survives on her naive vision of future comfort when the peasants will receive their land.

The Dragon's Village is based on actual events that Chen lived through when during high school she left her parents for one year to share the struggles and hunger of the peasants. "We went not because we understood Marxism, but to help the poor," Chen told Judy Stone of the *New York Times Book Review.* "Land reform was a dream of many centuries, especially among the intellectuals."

Few books firsthandedly describe the human cost of the revolution in China; hence Chen's book is considered an eye-opener to the mysteries of China. "In writing about the inner struggle of one such person to embrace the Revolution, Yuan-tsung Chen brings a piece of modern Chinese history to life," wrote Orville Schell of the *New York Times Book Review.* "With both empathy and realism, Mrs. Chen breathes life into the poor but often petty people of Dragon Village. . . . [She has] broken loose from the old and stultifying world of political apologies, and begun to plumb the depths of individuals who participated in the momentous struggles of the last 40 years. . . . If there is anything worth writing about in the modern Chinese experience, it is surely here." W.J.F. Jenner of the *Times Literary Supplement* predicted that "The Dragon's Village will for many Western readers be a much easier way of approaching an otherwise hardly accessible area of history. . . . The vividly conveyed experience contained in it makes it a book well worth having." And the *Los Angeles Times Book Review*'s Beverly

Beyette commented that *The Dragon's Village* ''is perceptive, non-propagandist, and quite enthralling.''

Chen told *CA:* ''I am a Chinese, born and raised in mainland China. After working in Peking for about fifteen years as translator and editor in the Film Publishing House, I came to the United States with my husband and son in 1972. Settled in the new country I adopted, I began writing my first novel, *The Dragon's Village*, dealing with the momentous land-reform movement in China. I am now working on my second novel, in which another important happening—the Cultural Revolution—is described. I prefer to write books which tell the individual stories of people caught up in crucial moments of the Chinese revolution. Both the land reform and Cultural Revolution in different ways brought about fundamental transformations in China's economy and society.

''I follow the Chinese literary tradition of presenting social background and events through individual experiences. For this reason, my writing is different from many books written in the West about China and which have mostly been theoretical, academic studies or reportage. The emotional and spiritual realities of the Chinese people (especially after 1949) are little known in the West. My writing, I hope, helps to fill in this gap by revealing the inner world of its protagonists during those tumultuous, revolutionary times that I experienced.''

BIOGRAPHICAL/CRITICAL SOURCES: New York Times Book Review, May 4, 1980; *Los Angeles Times Book Review,* June 22, 1980; *Times Literary Supplement,* July 3, 1981.

*   *   *

CHESHER, Richard (Harvey)   1940-

PERSONAL: Born in 1940. *Address:* c/o Clarkson N. Potter, Inc., 419 Park Ave., S., New York, N.Y. 10016.

CAREER: Writer. *Awards, honors:* Nomination for The National Book Award for science, 1980, for *Living Corals.*

WRITINGS: The Systematics of Sympatric Species in West Indian Spatangoids, University of Miami Press, 1968; *Acanthaster Planci: Impact on Pacific Coral Reefs,* Research Laboratories, Westinghouse Electric Corp., 1969; *Biological Impact of a Large-Scale Desalination Plant at Key West,* U.S. Government Printing Office, 1971; *Environmental Analysis: Canals and Quarries, Lower Florida Keys,* Marine Research Foundation, 1973; *Canal Survey: Florida Keys,* Marine Research Foundation, 1974; (with Douglas Faulkner) *Living Corals,* photographs by Faulkner, C. N. Potter, 1979.

*   *   *

CHESNUTT, Charles Waddell   1858-1932

BRIEF ENTRY: Born June 20, 1858, in Cleveland, Ohio; died November 15, 1932, in Cleveland, Ohio. American educator, journalist, lawyer, short story writer, and novelist. Sometimes called ''the first Negro novelist,'' Chesnutt's first short story, ''The Goophered Grapevine'' (1887), was also the first work written by a black author to be accepted by the *Atlantic Monthly.* His first full-length book, *The Conjure Women* (1899), a series of stories, centers around a black gardener, Uncle Julius McDoo, a character similar to Joel Chandler Harris's Uncle Remus. Chesnutt's later writings dealt primarily with racial prejudice, and in 1928 he was awarded the Spingarn Medal for his pioneer work in ''depicting the life and struggle of Americans of Negro descent.'' Teaching from the age of sixteen, Chesnutt was the principal of the State Normal School in Fayetteville, North Carolina, when he was only twenty-three. After working as a

journalist in New York City, Chesnutt studied law and was admitted to the Cleveland bar in 1887. In 1958 the city of Cleveland celebrated his centenary. Among his best-known works are *The Wife of His Youth and Other Stories of the Color Line* (1899), *The House Behind the Cedars* (1900), and *The Colonel's Dream* (1905). *Biographical/critical sources:* Helen M. Chesnutt, *Charles Waddell Chesnutt: Pioneer of the Color Line,* University of North Carolina Press, 1952; *Cyclopedia of World Authors,* Harper, 1958; *Reader's Encyclopedia of American Literature,* Crowell, 1962; *Concise Dictionary of American Literature,* Greenwood Press, 1969; *Cassell's Encyclopaedia of World Literature,* revised edition, Morrow, 1973.

*   *   *

CHEVALIER, Paul Eugene George   1925-
(Eugene George)

PERSONAL: Born September 21, 1925, in London, England; son of Alfred Victor (in business) and Frida (Brehm) Chevalier; married Sylvia Senior (a psychologist), March 11, 1956 (divorced); married Toni Blatt (an editor), November 16, 1970; children: (first marriage) Leigh Laura (Mrs. Murray Hunt). *Educatio:* Attended school in London, England. *Politics:* Liberal. *Religion:* None. *Home and office:* Lamanva, Goosey, near Faringdon, Oxfordshire SN7 8PA, England. *Agent:* David Higham Associates Ltd., 5-8 Lower John St., Golden Sq., London W1R 4HA, England.

CAREER: Sub-editor for various newspapers in London, England, 1947-55; Pan Books Ltd., London, director in publicity, advertising, promotion, and merchandising, 1955-77, became executive director; writer, 1977—. *Military service:* British Army, Royal Corps of Signals and Royal Educational Corps, editor of *Burma Star,* 1943-47; became warrant officer. *Member:* Institute of Journalists, Institute of Marketing.

WRITINGS: The Grudge (suspense novel), Hodder & Stoughton, 1980, St. Martin's, 1981; *The Shaft* (suspense novel), Hodder & Stoughton, 1981.

Under name Eugene George: *Estelle,* Consul, 1960; *Stay Away From Benjamin,* Consul, 1963; *I Can See You, But You Can't See Me,* Lippincott, 1966; *The Private Twilight of Jacko Tate,* Pan Books, 1968. Contributor to shipping journals.

WORK IN PROGRESS: The Generals (tentative title), a World War II novel.

SIDELIGHTS: Chevalier wrote: ''Goosey is a tiny hamlet fifteen miles south of Oxford, where I retired to write full-time after twenty-two (pensionable) years in publishing. It has no shops, no school, and more Friesian cattle than people; it is smack in the middle of the Vale of the White Horse, just below the historic iron-age Ridgeway.

''My interests are the British Army—its history, customs, and survivals; World Wars I and II, the War Between the States. I have a substantial library on this latter subject, and a secret—well, not so much secret as suppressed—desire to write a nicely biased history of the war, in favor of the Confederacy.

''*The Shaft* was a necessary diversion from a long-time preoccupation with trying to inject substance and color into the format thriller. I saw a chance to get a different sort of thriller out of a true but much-neglected story (before someone else did it). *The Grudge* is a World War II thriller, yet described by the *Sunday Times* as having a 'true Orwellian tang' and 'shades of Greene' and described by Colin Forbes as 'probably the most original World War II novel yet written,' so perhaps I'm having some success. In *The Generals* I am reverting to my original experiment.''

AVOCATIONAL INTERESTS: Gardening (mostly vegetable), playing chess, visiting historic churches.

*   *   *

CHRIST, John M(ichael)   1934-

PERSONAL: Born February 4, 1934, in Kansas City, Kan.; son of Anthony William (in business) and Genevieve Veronica (Mahaney) Christ; married Peggy Ann Phalen, August 6, 1960; children: Mary Ellen, John Joseph, Joseph Anthony, James Francis. *Education:* Creighton University, A.B., 1960; Rutgers University, M.L.S., 1961; University of Missouri at Kansas City, Ph.D., 1971. *Politics:* Democrat. *Religion:* Roman Catholic. *Home:* 106 South 55th St., Omaha, Neb. 68132. *Office:* University of Nebraska at Omaha, Box 688, Omaha, Neb. 68101.

CAREER: Creighton University, Omaha, Neb., reference librarian, 1961-63; Rockhurst College, Kansas City, Mo., library director, 1963-70; University of Nebraska at Omaha, library director, 1970—. Chairman of Centralized Processing Commission, Kansas City Regional Council on Higher Education, beginning 1964. *Military service:* U.S. Army, 1955-57. *Member:* American Library Association, Catholic Library Association, Mountain Plains Library Association, Nebraska Library Association, Missouri Library Association.

WRITINGS: Concepts and Subject Headings, Scarecrow, 1972; *Toward a Philosophy of Educational Librarianship,* Libraries Unlimited, 1972. Contributor to professional journals. Editor, *Mountain Plains Library Association Quarterly,* 1972-75. Book reviewer, *Library Journal,* 1962—.

*   *   *

CHUIKOV, Vasili Ivanovich   1900-1982

OBITUARY NOTICE: Born February 12, 1900 (some sources say January, 1900), in Serebryanye Prudy, Tula, Russia (now Moscow Oblast, U.S.S.R.); died March 18, 1982, in Moscow, U.S.S.R. Military officer, government administrator, and author. Chuikov fought in the Russian Revolution beginning in 1917, and joined the nascent Soviet Red Army battling in World War I. After his graduation from Fruze Military Academy between the World Wars, Chuikov was sent to China as a military attache at the onset of World War II. As commander of the 62nd Army he successfully defended Stalingrad against the German Army in 1942, and in 1945 he accepted the German surrender in Berlin. The much-decorated Chuikov served as commander in chief of the Soviet occupation forces in East Germany from 1949 to 1953 and later as deputy minister of defense. Among his publications are *The Beginning of the Road,* a 1963 account of the crucial Stalingrad battle, and *Immortal Heroic Deed,* which appeared in 1965. Obituaries and other sources: *Newsweek,* April 11, 1949, March 29, 1982; *The International Who's Who,* Europa, 1975; *Who's Who in Military History: From 1453 to the Present Day,* Morrow, 1976; *Who's Who in the Socialist Countries,* K. G. Saur, 1978; *New York Times,* March 20, 1982; *London Times,* March 20, 1982; *Time,* March 29, 1982.

*   *   *

CHURCHILL, David   1935-

PERSONAL: Born November 6, 1935, in Swindon, Wiltshire, England; son of Ernest Edward and Alice (Embling) Churchill; married Jacqueline Anne Joyce (a nurse), April 18, 1960; children: Alison Jane, Jonathan David. *Education:* St. Paul's College, Cheltenham, England, Certificate of Education, 1958;

University of Bristol, M.Ed., 1974. *Home:* 10 Brixham Ave., Swindon, Wiltshire, England. *Office:* Bradon Forest School, Purton, Wiltshire, England.

CAREER: English teacher at various schools in England, 1958-81; Bradon Forest School, Purton, Wiltshire, head of English department, 1981—. *Military service:* Royal Air Force, 1954-56; senior aircraftsman.

WRITINGS: It, Us, and the Others (juvenile fiction), Heinemann, 1978, Harper, 1979; *The Silbury Triangle* (juvenile fiction), Heinemann, 1979; *Not My World* (juvenile fiction), Heinemann, 1980; *A Focus for Writing* (adult nonfiction), Heinemann Educational, 1980.

WORK IN PROGRESS: "I am rewriting a novel and writing a new novel, when I am able to find time."

SIDELIGHTS: David Churchill told *CA:* "I write with particular enjoyment when places I am fond of are involved—hence the three novels above, all centered on particular landscapes. Writing is difficult while also teaching, which demands much time and energy. I am interested in the problems and the courage of young people who have to make their own identities and lives, despite the problems the adult world has created for them. My English book, *A Focus for Writing,* is a writer's approach to teaching writing and I hope, in its own small way, it will influence teaching methods in England in a rational direction."

AVOCATIONAL INTERESTS: Walking, fishing, gardening, canoeing, squash.

*   *   *

CLANCY, William   1922-1982

OBITUARY NOTICE: Born December 21, 1922, in Detroit, Mich.; died after a long illness, January 6, 1982, in Pittsburgh, Pa. Roman Catholic priest, educator, lecturer, editor, and journalist. He taught at the University of Notre Dame and served as associate editor of *Commonweal* and as religion editor of *Newsweek.* After leaving *Newsweek,* he founded *Worldview,* a magazine published by the Council on Religion and International Affairs. He began preparing for the priesthood in 1961 and was ordained in 1964. A supporter of the liberal reforms brought about by the Second Vatican Council, Clancy participated in several public debates with conservative Catholic writer William F. Buckley, Jr. In 1961 he helped to found the Pittsburgh Oratory, a community of priests that offers chaplaincy services to students and faculty in the Pittsburgh area. Clancy was serving as provost of the oratory at the time of his death. Obituaries and other sources: *New York Times,* January 7, 1982.

*   *   *

CLARK, J(ohn) H(oward)   1929-

PERSONAL: Born June 6, 1929, in Hendon, England; son of Reginald John (a dental surgeon) and Elsie Kate (Ginger) Clark; married Audrey Evelyn Collins (a music teacher), April 2, 1964 (divorced, 1979); children: Vivien Monica Elizabeth, Oliver John. *Education:* Gonville and Caius College, Cambridge, B.Chir., 1955, M.B., 1956, M.A., 1957; Westminster Hospital Medical School, London, D.P.M., 1961; research student at Brasenose College, Oxford, 1966; Oxford University, M.A., 1966. *Office:* Department of Psychology, University of Manchester, Manchester M13 9PL, England.

CAREER: Guy's Hospital, London, England, house physician in department of psychological medicine, 1957-58; R. Gordon

Pask, London, researcher, 1959; Fountain Hospital, London, and Queen Mary's Hospital, Carshalton, England, junior hospital medical officer, 1960-62; Burden Neurological Institute, Bristol, England, member of medical research council (senior fellow), 1962-64; University of Bristol, Bristol, member of medical research council (senior fellow), 1964-65; Oxford University, Institute of Experimental Psychology, Oxford, England, member of scientific staff of Medical Research Council Psycho-Linguistics Research Unit, 1965-66; Victoria University of Manchester, Manchester, England, senior lecturer in psychology, 1967—. Visiting lecturer at University of Iceland, 1973. *Military service:* British Army, Royal Artillery, 1947-49; became second lieutenant. *Member:* Society of European Psychologists of Religion, Royal College of Physicians (licentiate), Royal College of Surgeons, Cybernetic Society, Association for the Study of Medical Education.

WRITINGS: (Contributor) J. Rose, editor, *Survey of Cybernetics,* Iliffe Books, 1969; (with John Cohen) *Medicine, Mind, and Man,* W. H. Freeman, 1977; *A Map of Mental States,* Routledge & Kegan Paul, in press.

Work represented in *England Swings Science Fiction* (anthology), edited by Judith Merrill, Doubleday, 1968. Contributor to *New Worlds* (magazine) and *Foundation* (science fiction review).

WORK IN PROGRESS: People, a collection of character studies; further research on his "map of mental states" and on "argument analysis," a way of displaying patterns of thinking.

SIDELIGHTS: Clark commented: "I am very interested in the analysis of language. My map of mental states is based on an analysis of mystical language. 'Argument analysis' examines the sequences of sentences uttered by people and the way in which such sequences portray their world. Argument analysis pays particular attention to the words or phrases that link such sentences, such as: 'and then,' 'and so,' 'because,' 'but,' and 'therefore.' Several patterns are beginning to emerge, such as arguments that go round in circles, arguments that stop with a 'throw-away' remark, and so on. Such a 'Linnaean' collection of patterns is mentioned as a possibility by R. D. Laing in his book *Knots*.

"I enjoy writing science fiction and, in addition, I have been an influence on writer James Blish. Blish was chairman of a conference at which I read a scientific paper on my map of mental states. He was very interested in the map, and he acknowledged its influence on his novel *Midsummer Century*."

AVOCATIONAL INTERESTS: Potato-print art.

*   *   *

CLARK, J(eff) R(ay) 1947-

PERSONAL: Born November 6, 1947, in Waynesboro, Va.; son of Jefferson Davis and Mildred (Cameron) Clark. *Education:* Attended University of Richmond, 1964-66; Virginia Commonwealth University, B.S., 1968; Virginia Polytechnic Institute and State University, M.A., 1972, Ph.D., 1974. *Home:* 1308 Broad St., Clifton, N.J. 07013. *Office:* J. R. Clark & Associates, Clifton, N.J. 07013.

CAREER: Joint Council on Economic Education, New York, N.Y., director of college and university division, 1974-80; J. R. Clark & Associates (consulting economists), Clifton, N.J., president, 1976—. Professor of economics at Fairleigh Dickinson University; consultant to National Science Foundation, Phillips Petroleum, and U.S. Government. *Member:* American Economic Association, Southern Economic Association, Eastern Economic Association (member of board of directors).

Awards, honors: Presbyterian scholar of Presbyterian Church of North America, 1967.

WRITINGS: A Guide to Teaching Economics, McGraw, 1978; *Strategies for Teaching Economics,* Joint Council on Education, 1981; *Essentials of Economics,* Academic Press, 1982; *Economics: The Science of Cost-Benefit and Choice,* South-Western, 1982. Contributor to periodicals, including *Eastern Economic Journal* and *Journal of Business Education.*

SIDELIGHTS: Clark told *CA:* "My writing career has been devoted to communicating economic theory and practice to laymen and students in the simplest terms possible. I have strived to make the more esoteric aspects of economics clear and understandable. I believe that only a more informed public than we have is capable of making the necessary choices to guide our economy through the next two decades. I strongly believe that individual choice and self interest are the most powerful forces that exist in our economy today and must be protected and encouraged if we are to prosper."

*   *   *

CLARK, Malcolm (Hamilton), Jr. 1917-

PERSONAL: Born April 13, 1917, in Portland, Ore.; son of Malcolm H. (an attorney) and May M. (Clarke) Clark; married Elsie Kimpton, 1943 (divorced, 1974); married Maxine Kirkland, 1974 (divorced, 1980); children: Shelley Clark Daldegan, Leigh Clarkgranville, Thomas J. *Education:* Attended University of Washington, 1935-37. *Home and office:* 3150 Southwest Bertha Blvd., No. 15, Portland, Ore. 97201.

CAREER: Free-lance writer, 1940—; *Oregon Journal,* Portland, columnist, 1981—. *Member:* Oregon Historical Society.

WRITINGS: (With Kenneth W. Porter) *War on the Webfoot Saloon, and Other Tales,* Oregon Historical Society, 1969; (editor) *Pharisee Among Philistines: The Diary of Judge Matthew P. Deady, 1871-1892,* Oregon Historical Society, 1975; (contributor) Thomas Vaughan, editor, *The Western Shore,* Oregon Historical Society, 1975; *Eden Seekers: The Settlement of Oregon, 1818-1862,* Houghton, 1981. Contributor to national and regional periodicals.

WORK IN PROGRESS: Island Story, novel, publication expected in 1983; *The End of Eden,* nonfiction, publication expected in 1984; *The Od Chronicles,* novel, publication expected in 1984.

SIDELIGHTS: Clark told *CA:* "*Eden Seekers* is an attempt to recreate, almost entirely from contemporary sources, an era and an area in American history. The people who appear in it are, so far as I have been able to make them so, real people, and I have drawn them, warts and all.

"A brief excerpt from the book illustrates what I mean: 'The reader . . . will do well to put from his or her mind the pioneer of legend. He is a virtuous afterthought, an idealization in spurious homespun, created by fabulists and romancers and set to music by the minions of Mr. Disney. Consider, instead, Ishmael Bush. Of all Cooper's characters he comes closest to the mark: crude, cross-grained, savage when it serves—and as remote from us as the dim brute that Millet painted in his *Man with the Hoe.* A reminder that each generation is raised up according to its own images; that we and our grandfathers and their fathers are connected by consanguinity, not convention; that every man must be judged within the frame of his time. The westering Americans were a bark-skinned lot—few saints if many martyrs—and all riveted fast to the main chance. No niceties impeded them. It was sweat, not perspiration, and soap did not place high on the list of necessaries. The whole of the corn ear had its uses: husk, kernel, silk and cob. Tongues ran to saw edges; vituperation was a fine art. The richest humour reeked of the hen run. None of this is derogatory nor even, to the judgment of history, important. It illuminates the pioneers' methods and their motivations but it does not touch upon their achievements. That they were crass and coarse-fibered does not mean they were ineffectual.'''

*   *   *

CLARKE, Gillian 1937-

PERSONAL: Born June 8, 1937, in Cardiff, Wales; daughter of Penri and Ceinwen (Evans) Williams. *Education:* University of Wales, University College, Cardiff, B.A. (with honors), 1958. *Home:* 1 Cyncoed Ave., Cyncoed, Cardiff, Wales.

CAREER: British Broadcasting Corp., London, England, news researcher, 1958-60; free-lance lecturer, writer, and broadcaster, 1960-75; Gwent College of Art and Design, Newport, Wales, lecturer in art history, 1975—. *Member:* Yr Academi Gymreig (member of executive committee). *Awards, honors:* Travel grants from Yr Academi Gymreig for Ireland, 1974, the Soviet Union, 1977, Yugoslavia, 1979, and the United States, 1982; poetry prize from Welsh Arts Council, 1979, for *The Sundial.*

WRITINGS—Books of poems: *Snow on the Mountain,* Christopher Davies, 1972; *The Sundial,* Gomer Press, 1978; *Letter From a Far Country,* Carcanet Press, 1982. Also author of radio plays, including "Talking in the Dark," 1977, and "Letter From a Far Country." Contributor to journals in England, Wales, and the United States. Editor of *Anglo-Welsh Review,* 1976—.

WORK IN PROGRESS: Cofiant, poems; *The Poet's Boast: Teaching Poetry in the Secondary School;* adapting *Letter From a Far Country* for television.

SIDELIGHTS: Gillian Clarke told *CA:* "My main occupation here in Wales seems to be the public performance of my own and other people's poetry and teaching creative writing in various ways."

*   *   *

CLAUSEN, Dennis M(onroe) 1943-

PERSONAL: Born November 1, 1943, in Morris, Minn.; son of Lloyd A. (in construction work) and Arlene (Anderson) Clausen; divorced; children: Timothy William, Kristen Suzanne. *Education:* University of Minnesota, Morris, B.A., 1965; University of Minnesota, Minneapolis, M.A., 1967; University of California, Riverside, Ph.D., 1972. *Office:* Department of English, University of San Diego—Alcala Park, San Diego, Calif. 92110.

CAREER: Lecturer at University of California, Riverside, and California State University, Los Angeles, 1970-72; University of San Diego—Alcala Park, San Diego, Calif., assistant professor, 1972-76, associate professor, 1976-82, professor of English, 1982—, director of writing program.

WRITINGS: A Simple Lesson in Grammar, University of San Diego Press, 1979; *Ghost Lover* (suspense novel), Bantam, 1981. Contributor to local newspapers.

WORK IN PROGRESS: A novel set in the Midwest, dealing with a small town and small-town characters; a screenplay based on *Ghost Lover;* two other screenplays.

SIDELIGHTS: Clausen told *CA:* "Ideally, what I try to do in my writings is to blend together art, craftsmanship, and commercial appeal. Thus, I stress a strong, driving storyline that keeps the reader involved in the narrative from beginning to end. I am also concerned, however, with characters that transcend stereotypes, symbolic patterns that blend into and reinforce action and theme, and various prose styles and rhythms that hopefully affect the reader at the subconscious level—much in the way a good poet plays to the ear as well as to the mind.

"I am, and probably always will be, interested in stories set in a midwestern locale. I am firmly convinced that a writer's experiences during the first twenty years of his life soak into the marrow of his bones and become a part of the sum total of his personality. These earlier experiences are thus easier to write about, and I think they have a greater ring of authenticity. I also write about small towns because the characters tend to stand out against such a background, and I find their idiosyncracies are easier to capture. Southern California life, on the other hand, surrounds me with a variety of types but few individuals that stand out in this manner. Perhaps such is true of all metropolitan areas. Or perhaps I am not artistically in tune with the deeper levels of life in larger cities."

*   *   *

CLAY, Patrice 1947-

PERSONAL: Born April 8, 1947, in McKeesport, Pa.; daughter of Jack S. (a builder) and Pat (Gibbons) Clay; married Ron Green (a publishing company vice-president), November 27, 1981. *Education:* University of Connecticut, B.A. (cum laude), 1969. *Residence:* Woodbridge, N.J. *Office:* Bantam Books, Inc., 666 Fifth Ave., New York, N.Y. 10019.

CAREER: G. P. Putnam's Sons, New York City, assistant editor, 1973-75, juvenile editor, 1975-78, promotions manager, 1978-81; Bantam Books, Inc., New York City, advertising and promotions manager, 1981—.

WRITINGS: Your Own Horse, Putnam, 1977; *We Work With Horses,* Putnam, 1980.

WORK IN PROGRESS: A novel about a girl and her horse, a champion show jumper.

SIDELIGHTS: Patrice Clay commented: "I was one of those girls who grew up loving horses, and I never grew out of it! My books are natural extensions of my fascination with horses and are books I wish I'd had when I was younger—a practical guide for first-time horse owners and a look at horse-related careers. I plan to continue to ride and write about my 'first love.'''

*   *   *

CLAYPOOL, Jane
See MINER, Jane Claypool

*   *   *

CLEARY, David Powers 1915-

PERSONAL: Born January 8, 1915, in Grand Rapids, Mich.; son of Leo John (an engineer) and Gertrude (an instructor in speech; maiden name, Powers) Cleary; married Marguerite Paine, January 1, 1937 (died May 28, 1974); married Virginia Glynn, March 17, 1975; children: Michael Paine, Timothy Owen, Shelley Anne, Christopher Leo. *Education:* Michigan State College (now University), B.A., 1936. *Politics:* Republican. *Religion:* Roman Catholic. *Home address:* R.R.2, Box 80, Tavares, Fla. 32778.

CAREER: Buick Magazine, Detroit, Mich., editor, 1936-40; Young & Rubicam (advertising agency), New York, N.Y., copy-contact man in Detroit office, 1940, copy chief, 1945-51, associate copy director in New York City office, 1954-61, vice-president and associate creative director, 1961-67. Freelance writer, 1938—. *Military service:* U.S. Army, 1941-45; became captain; received Bronze Star and two battle stars. *Member:* Marketing Research Association.

WRITINGS: Great American Brands, Fairchild Books, 1981. Contributor to magazines, including *American Legion, Coronet, Forum, Southern Living, Today's Health,* and *Pan American Clipper.*

* * *

CLEMENTS, William M(orris) 1943-

PERSONAL: Born May 21, 1943, in Portsmouth, Va.; son of Ralph Mayo (a physician) and Ima Carl (an educator; maiden name, Turner) Clements; married Betty Hayes (a librarian and editor), June 15, 1968; children: David Stewart. *Education:* University of Alabama, B.A., 1965; Union Theological Seminary, New York, N.Y., M.Div., 1969; University of Southern California, Certificate in Gerontology, 1971; School of Theology, Claremont, Calif., Ph.D., 1972. *Religion:* United Methodist. *Home:* 111 West Fourth St., Riverside, Iowa 52327. *Office:* Department of Family Practice, College of Medicine, University of Iowa, Iowa City, Iowa 52242.

CAREER: Bryce State Hospital, Tuscaloosa, Ala., intern in clinical pastoral education, 1968; Pomona Pastoral Counseling Center, Claremont, Calif., associate director, 1970-71; Birmingham Area Pastoral Care and Counseling, Birmingham, Ala., clinical director, 1972-75; University of Iowa, Iowa City, assistant professor, 1976-80, associate professor of family practice, 1980—, pastoral counselor, 1976—. Associate chaplain and clinical director of pastoral counseling at Baptist Medical Centers, Birmingham, and adjunct clinical assistant professor at Samford University, 1972-75. Clinical director of pastoral care and counselor for the Birmingham Episcopal Area of the United Methodist Church, 1972-75. Visiting professor at Iowa Network of Family Practice Residency Programs, 1975—, and Wartburg Theological Seminary, 1980. Deacon of United Methodist Church, 1966, elder, 1971. Workshop speaker. *Member:* American Association of Pastoral Counselors (diplomate; member of executive committee of Southeastern region, 1974, Central region, 1980), American Association for Marriage and Family Therapy (clinical member), Society for the Scientific Study of Religion, Society for Health and Human Values, Gerontological Society, Society of Teachers of Family Medicine, Omicron Delta Kappa, Pi Tau Chi.

WRITINGS: (Contributor) Robert E. Rakel and Howard F. Conn, *Family Practice,* Saunders, 1978; *Care and Counseling for the Aged,* Fortress, 1979; (contributor) Nicholas Colangelo and Charles Pulvino, editors, *Counseling for the Growing Years: Sixty-Five and Over,* Educational Media Corporation, 1980; (editor and contributor) *Ministry With the Aging: Foundations, Challenges, and Design,* Harper, 1981; (contributor) Woodrow W. Morris and Iva Bader, editors, *Hoffman's Daily Needs and Interests of Older People,* 2nd edition (Clements was not included in 1st edition), C. C Thomas, 1982; (contributor) Michael Teague and Richard MacNeil, editors, *Leisure and Aging,* University of Missouri Press, 1982. Contributor to *Britannica 1980 Medical and Health Annual* and *1981 Medical and Health Annual.* Contributor of more than a dozen articles and reviews to medical and theology journals.

WORK IN PROGRESS: Pastoral Counseling, with Remi J. Cadoret, Harper, 1984; *Cognitive Therapy in Pastoral Per-*

spective, tentative title, publication expected in 1985; research for a book on short-term counseling within a medical practice, for primary-care physicians, medical students, and residents; research on undiagnosed patients, marital turmoil, Wesleyan spirituality for the eighties, human dimensions in medicine, publication characteristics in family practice, and religious factors and bereavement among functionally dependent elderly people.

SIDELIGHTS: Clements wrote: "I am a pastoral counselor working within a clinical department at a medical school. My specialized training has led me to write articles for professionals in the areas of gerontology, religion, and medicine, and future books will be within these broad areas as well.

"My particular areas of interest within psychotherapy, personality development, and religious commitment focus on the second half of life—from thirty-five years of age onward. In contrast to what is already known about the early years, much remains to be discovered about the last decades of life. This is an exciting time to be a religious gerontologist and a pastoral counselor."

* * *

CLEMINSHAW, Clarence Higbee 1902-

BRIEF ENTRY: Born January 15, 1902, in Cleveland, Ohio. American astronomer, educator, and author. Cleminshaw began his career as an attorney. He joined the administrative staff of Griffith Observatory and Planetarium in 1936, became its director in 1959, and was named director emeritus in 1969. His books include *Pictorial Astronomy* (Griffith Observatory, 1948), *Monthly Star Maps* (Griffith Observatory, 1951), *Pictorial Guide to the Moon* (Crowell, 1963), and *The Beginner's Guide to the Skies: A Month-by-Month Handbook for Stargazers and Planet Watchers* (Crowell, 1977). *Address:* 1941 North New Hampshire Ave., Los Angeles, Calif. 90027. *Biographical/critical sources: Who's Who in America,* 40th edition, Marquis, 1978.

* * *

CLIFTON, Jack (Whitney) 1912-

PERSONAL: Born February 3, 1912, in Norfolk, Va.; son of Clyde Orlando (a cashier) and Bessie (Whitney) Clifton; married Patricia Murray (an artist), June 29, 1946; children: Whitney, Deborah (Mrs. Thomas Frank), David, Christopher, Philip. *Education:* Attended Art Institute of Pittsburgh, 1931-32, and Pennsylvania Academy of the Fine Arts, 1933-38. *Home and office:* 1615 Chesapeake Ave., Hampton, Va. 23661.

CAREER: Portrait painter; Palace Theater, Newport News, Va., poster artist, 1926-30; Armour & Co., Chicago, Ill., cartoonist for *Armour Magazine,* 1927-30; Clifton School of Art, Hampton, Va., director, 1932—. Artist-in-residence at Davis and Elkins College, 1946. Postal clerk at Newport News Post Office, 1940-42. *Military service:* U.S. Navy, 1942-45. *Member:* Virginia Museum of Art.

WRITINGS: Manual of Drawing and Painting, Watson-Guptill, 1957; *The Eye of the Artist,* North Light Publications, 1973.

* * *

CLINE, Ray Steiner 1918-

BRIEF ENTRY: Born June 4, 1918, in Anderson, Ill. American educator, government official, and author. Cline worked for the Central Intelligence Agency, off and on, from 1949 to 1966.

Since 1973 he has been director of studies at Georgetown University's Center for Strategic and International Studies. He wrote *Secrets, Spies, and Scholars: Blueprint of the Essential CIA* (Acropolis Books, 1976), *World Power Assessment—1977: A Calculus of Strategic Drift* (Westview, 1977), *Main Trends in World Power* (Center for Strategic and International Studies, Georgetown University, 1978), and *World Power Trends and U.S. Foreign Policy for the 1980's* (Westview, 1980). *Address:* 3027 North Pollard St., Arlington, Va. 22207. *Biographical/critical sources: New York Times Book Review,* January 9, 1977.

*   *   *

CLIPMAN, William   1954-

PERSONAL: Born July 20, 1954, in Bryn Mawr, Pa.; son of William H. III (a lawyer) and Marjorie (a teacher; maiden name, Combs) Clipman. *Education:* Syracuse University, B.A., 1976; University of Arizona, M.F.A., 1980. *Politics:* "No." *Religion:* "Yes." *Home:* 3371 East Silverlake, Tucson, Ariz. 85713.

CAREER: Arizona Commission on the Arts, Tucson, poet in residence and instructor at workshops for inmates of Arizona State Prison Complex and Arizona Correctional Training Facility, 1980—. *Awards, honors:* Whiffen Poetry Prize from Syracuse University, 1975, for "The Muskrat"; Margaret Sterling Memorial Poetry Prize from University of Arizona, 1980, for "The State Legislator Accused of Pederasty Enters Prisons."

WRITINGS—Poetry: *Dog Light,* Wesleyan University Press, 1981; *Salt of the Body, Salt of the Sea,* Wesleyan University Press, 1983.

WORK IN PROGRESS: Bhakti, poems; *The Art of Falling,* tales; *Coming to the Water's Edge,* essays; *Taking Aim,* a novel.

SIDELIGHTS: Clipman told *CA:* "I write every day as a way of surviving in a chaotic and often hostile universe. I run, play drums, and meditate every day for the same reason. The ability to give love in the face of massive indifference and arbitrary violence, spiritual progress amid gross materialism, friendship as the key to life, and celebration of the wilderness—these are vital subjects."

*   *   *

CLOPTON, Beverly Virginia B(eck)

PERSONAL: Born in Salt Lake City, Utah; daughter of Clarence M. (an attorney) and Hazel A. (Cutler) Beck; married James W. Clopton (a design engineer and consultant). *Education:* University of Utah, B.A.; also attended Chouinard Art Institute. *Residence:* Salt Lake City, Utah.

CAREER: Commercial artist and landscape and portrait painter, 1960-80. Work exhibited in one-artist shows in Salt Lake City, Utah, Park City, Utah, and Sun Valley, Idaho.

WRITINGS: Her Honor, the Judge: The Story of Reva Beck Bosone, Iowa State University Press, 1980. Contributor to magazines.

WORK IN PROGRESS: A novel.

SIDELIGHTS: Clopton told *CA:* "At age twelve, when I saw my simple short, short story given life on a newspaper page, I sensed a type of fulfillment that a writer is privileged to experience. Not until much later, when my aunt Judge Reva Beck Bosone, asked me to write her biography, did I realize

what incomparable literary challenges were involved before experiencing that fulfillment. In my estimation, there is no work more intense than writing. Vital to this is the morale support rendered by my husband.

"Judge Bosone's struggle to prominence through dedicated service at a time of suppressed women's opportunities is unique in the annals of feminist career achievements."

*   *   *

COATES, Charles R(obert)   1915-

PERSONAL: Born November 2, 1915, in Fairview, N.C.; son of John Wesley (a carpenter) and Hattie (Price) Coates; married Lucille May Blackman, October 30, 1942; children: Charles R., Jr., John T., Christopher S. *Education:* Lake Forest College, B.A., 1955; College of William and Mary, M.Ed., 1958; University of Virginia, Ed.D., 1965. *Politics:* Democrat. *Religion:* Methodist. *Home address:* P.O. Box 654, Chambersburg, Pa. 17201.

CAREER: Instructor in meteorology for Civilian Pilot Training Program, 1939-40; teacher and instructional supervisor, 1946-50; U.S. Naval Examination Center, Great Lakes, Ill., examination specialist and adviser for Naval Reserve Training Center in Glenview, Ill., 1952-55; U.S. Army Transportation School, Fort Eustis, Va., education specialist for correspondence school and chief of Grading and Instruction Division, 1955-58; guidance coordinator for public school system in Courtland, Va., and assistant superintendent of schools (for guidance), 1958-62; U.S. Army Quartermaster School, Fort Lee, Va., education adviser and director of training, 1962-65; Shippensburg State College, Shippensburg, Pa., professor of teacher and counselor education, beginning in 1965, director of testing and part-time counselor. Private practice as learning psychologist. Instructor at College of William and Mary, 1958-65, and University of Virginia, 1960-65; lecturer on self-improvement. Chairman of Campus Ministries. Member of Register to Improve Communicative Habits (RICH) and Educational Resources Information Center (ERIC); consultant to U.S. Department of Defense and to industry. *Military service:* U.S. Navy, meteorologist, 1941-46, 1950-52. *Member:* National Education Association (life member), American Association for the Advancement of Science, American Personnel and Guidance Association, American Vocational Association, Phi Delta Kappa (life member).

WRITINGS: Increase Your Learning Power, Dorrance, 1964; *Developing a Commanding Personality,* Nelson-Hall, 1980. Contributor to education journals.

*   *   *

COE, Michelle E(ileen)   1917-

PERSONAL: Born August 30, 1917, in Greenfield, Ind.; daughter of Robert Andrew (a minister) and Ruth Pauline (a pianist and artist; maiden name, Holt) Mckinley; married Robert L. Coe, December 5, 1947 (deceased); children: deceased. *Education:* Attended Butler University, Arthur Jordan Conservatory, Max Wiley Workshop, American Academy of Dramatic Art, French Institute, and New York Institute of Advertising. *Religion:* Anglican. *Residence:* New York, N.Y. *Address:* c/o Crown Publishers, Inc., 1 Park Ave., New York, N.Y. 10016.

CAREER: WKBF-Radio, Indianapolis, Ind., writer and commentator, 1932-35; L.S. Ayres & Co., Indianapolis, director of broadcasting, 1942-46; WFBM-Radio, Indianapolis, producer, writer, and commentator, 1942-46; WISH-Radio, Indianapolis, announcer of classical music programs, 1942-46;

WIRE-Radio, Indianapolis, news commentator and commercial spokesperson, 1942-46; teacher at high schools in Indianapolis, 1942-46; Young & Rubicam (advertising agency), New York City, member of staff and fashion editor of *Complete Shopper,* 1946-47; KSD-TV, St. Louis, Mo., producer and writer, 1946-47; KSD-Radio, St. Louis, producer and writer, 1946-47; WSPR-Radio, Springfield, Mass., commentator, 1947; WPIX-TV, New York City, interviewer and commentator, 1948-50; WABD-TV, New York City, interviewer, 1952-55; WFAS-Radio, White Plains, N.Y., commentator on women and religion, 1953; American Broadcasting Co. (ABC), New York City, consultant, 1955-57; F. C. Productions, New York City, producer, writer, and commentator, 1960-67; Young, Smith & Dorian (advertising agency), New York City, vice-president and creative director of women's products advertising, 1964-65; WNEW-TV, New York City, senior writer and interviewer, 1966-68; Ohio University, Athens, instructor in television writing and performance, 1968-73; Shield Productions, New York City, creative director, 1974-78; Harcourt, Brace, Jovanovich, New York City, researcher, interviewer, consultant, and writer, 1978; College for Human Services, New York City, vice-president in public relations, 1980-81; Comcoe (television syndicate company), New York City, founder and president, 1981—. Presentation and script writer for Rhodes Productions—East. Professional actress on stage, television, and radio; appeared in plays, including "King Lear," "Merchant of Venice," "Death of a Salesman," and "The Corn Is Green"; appeared on television programs, including "All My Children," "Valiant Lady," and "Candid Camera." Chairperson of social events for Interdenominational Guild for the Blind. Researcher and writer for Television Bureau of Advertising; seminar coordinator. Writer for Muscular Dystrophy Association telethon, 1979.

MEMBER: International Television Society, American Federation of Television and Radio Artists, Writers Guild of America (East), Screen Actors Guild, Broadcast Pioneers. *Awards, honors:* Photography award from East Ender Photographic Society, 1954.

WRITINGS: The Life of Robert Koch, Greenvale Press, 1926; *How to Sell Television Time,* Crown, 1978; *How to Write for Television,* Crown, 1980.

One-act plays: "The Lion's Den"; "Yesterday Last Year"; "Mary and Martha."

Contributor to magazines, including *Ink Drops.*

WORK IN PROGRESS: A collection of short stories, publication expected in 1983.

SIDELIGHTS: Michelle Coe told *CA:* "It is important to me to delineate accurately emotions and the reasons behind them. My nonfiction is geared to telling the truth about the marketplace where skills are used. In fiction, I try to help people understand themselves and others and communicate their feelings honestly."

*   *   *

COEL, Margaret 1937-

PERSONAL: Born October 11, 1937, in Denver, Colo.; daughter of Samuel F. (a railroad engineer) and Margaret (McCloskey) Speas; married George W. Coel (a dentist), July 22, 1961; children: Bill (deceased), Kristin, Lisa. *Education:* Marquette University, B.A., 1960. *Politics:* Democrat. *Religion:* Roman Catholic. *Home:* 3155 Lafayette Dr., Boulder, Colo. 80303.

CAREER: Westminster Journal, Westminster, Colo., reporter, 1960-61; *Boulder Daily Camera,* Boulder, Colo., feature writer,

1972-75. Member of board of directors of Historic Boulder. *Member:* National Federation of Press Women, Colorado Press Women, Boulder Meadows Club (member of board of directors). *Awards, honors:* Fellow at Bread Loaf Writers' Conference, 1981.

WRITINGS: Chief Left Hand: Southern Arapahoe, University of Oklahoma Press, 1981. Contributor of articles to newspapers and magazines, including *Christian Science Monitor, National Observer,* and *Old West Magazine.* Contributor of book reviews to *Denver Post.*

WORK IN PROGRESS: Locomotives and Kings, on the way of life of early Colorado railroad workers, publication expected in 1983.

SIDELIGHTS: Margaret Coel told *CA:* "In writing history, I am interested in the people who were involved in great events. With *Chief Left Hand,* I hoped to convey to the reader a sense that the inhabitants of the plains before the white man arrived were people with hopes and plans, talents and abilities, just like any other group of people. In my book on railroading, I am interested in people at work under special circumstances and at a special time."

AVOCATIONAL INTERESTS: Travel (Mexico, the British Isles, the Soviet Union).

*   *   *

COGHLAN, Margaret M. 1920-
(Jessica Stirling)

PERSONAL: Born January 26, 1920, in Glasgow, Scotland; daughter of Arthur and Jane (McBrien) Walls; married Eugene O. Coghlan; children: Janice A., Rosemary M. Coghlan Gilchrist. *Religion:* Roman Catholic. *Home:* 109 Mugdock Rd., Milngavie, Dunbartonshire, Scotland.

CAREER: Writer. *Member:* International P.E.N., Association of Scottish Writers (founding member), Glasgow Writers Club (past president).

WRITINGS—Under pseudonym Jessica Stirling: *Spoiled Earth,* Hodder & Stoughton, 1974; *Strathmore,* Delacorte, 1975; *The Dresden Finch,* Delacorte, 1976; *Beloved Sinner,* Pan Books, 1976; *Hiring Fair,* Pan Books, 1976; *Call Home the Heart,* St. Martin's, 1977; *The Dark Pasture,* St. Martin's, 1978; *The Drums of Time,* St. Martin's, 1979; *Deep Well at Noon,* Hodder & Stoughton, 1979; *Blue Evening Gone,* St. Martin's, 1982.

WORK IN PROGRESS: A trilogy of stories, set in Scotland.

*   *   *

COHEN, Harry 1936-

PERSONAL: Born April 8, 1936, in Brooklyn, N.Y.; son of Sol and Dina (Soifer) Cohen. *Education:* City College (now of the City University of New York), B.B.A., 1956, M.A., 1959; University of Illinois, Ph.D., 1962. *Residence:* Ames, Iowa. *Office:* Department of Sociology and Anthropology, Iowa State University, 203B Old East Hall, Ames, Iowa 50011.

CAREER: U.S. Department of Labor, Washington, D.C., employment interviewer, 1956-59; University of Miami, Coral Gables, Fla., assistant professor of sociology, 1962-63; Iowa State University, Ames, assistant professor, 1963-65, associate professor, 1966-74, professor of sociology, 1974—. Visiting assistant professor of labor and industrial relations and sociology, University of Illinois, Champaign-Urbana, 1965-66. *Member:* Association for Humanistic Psychology, Clinical Sociology Association, Humanist Sociology Association (regional representative, 1978-79 and 1982-83), Institute of Advanced Philosophic Research (member of national advisory board, 1979—). *Awards, honors:* First prize from Iowa State University Press, 1964, for *The Demonics of Bureaucracy.*

WRITINGS: (Contributor) Peter M. Blau, *The Dynamics of Bureaucracy,* revised edition (Cohen was not included in first edition), University of Chicago Press, 1963; *The Demonics of Bureaucracy,* Iowa State University Press, 1965; (contributor) George Ritzer, editor, *Issues, Debates, and Controversies: An Introduction to Sociology,* Allyn & Bacon, 1972, 2nd edition, 1980; (contributor) Alfred E. Koenig, editor, *Philosophy of the Humanistic Society,* University Press of America, 1981; *Connections: Understanding Social Relationships,* Iowa State University Press, 1981. Contributor of nearly fifteen articles and forty book reviews to professional journals.

SIDELIGHTS: Cohen told *CA:* "My writing reflects my feeling that academic work (such as sociology) should not be limited to technical esoteric aspects, but should be presented to a broader public to be used for purposes of better living. In my book and teaching I include a clinical or applied aspect, showing people how sociological perspectives can illuminate the meaning and processes of social life and how these can be used as tools for improvement and change.

"A quotation from the cover of my book, *Connections,* summarizes my aims: 'The processes making social life are the same everywhere. Only the content differs. Understand social processes, handle their content, and you will make connections—in love, sex, marriage, work. Social life is fluid and hot too. We must cup and handle it to understand, analyze, and improve it. This book teaches "cups and handles" for holding and savoring the life of social relationships everywhere.'"

*   *   *

COHEN, Miriam   1926-

PERSONAL: Born October 14, 1926, in Brooklyn, N.Y.; daughter of Jacob and Bessie Echelman; married Sid Grossman, 1949 (died, 1955); married Monroe D. Cohen (a professor), May 31, 1959; children: (first marriage) Adam; (second marriage) Gabriel, Jean. *Education:* Attended Antioch College, 1944-45. *Politics:* Independent progressive. *Religion:* Jewish. *Home and office:* 618 Sixth St., Brooklyn, N.Y. 11215.

CAREER: Writer.

WRITINGS—For children; illustrated by Lillian Hoban: *Will I Have a Friend?,* Macmillan, 1967, adapted as filmstrip with cassette, Threshold Filmstrips, 1974; *Best Friends,* Macmillan, 1971; *The New Teacher* (Junior Literary Guild selection), Macmillan, 1972; *Tough Jim,* Macmillan, 1974; *When Will I Read?,* Greenwillow, 1977; *Bee My Valentine!,* Greenwillow, 1978; *Lost in the Museum,* Greenwillow, 1979; *First Grade Takes a Test,* Greenwillow, 1980; *No Good in Art,* Greenwillow, 1980; *Jim Meets the Thing,* Greenwillow, 1981.

WORK IN PROGRESS: A novel on Brazil, for ages nine to eleven.

SIDELIGHTS: An advocate of the emotional rights of children, Cohen tries to portray in her books the sorrows and triumphs of early childhood. Her works are included in the Kerlan Collection at the University of Minnesota. Cohen told *CA:* "I've always been fascinated by the idea of bringing something into being that wasn't there before, like a painting or a play or a story. It wasn't until I met Susan Carr Hirschman (then at Harper, and now children's book editor at Greenwillow) that I began to think I really might try to be a writer. I'd written

a children's story (a very bad one), and I looked in the phone book for the nearest publisher. Harper was closest to my apartment in Manhattan, so I just put my first baby into his buggy with the story and pushed up the ten blocks. Susan looked at my work and said, 'This isn't it. But you *are* a writer. You must read everything that's been written for children, and then write something different, something that comes from you.'

"That gave me the courage to keep trying. It was eight years and two babies later before I had a story accepted by this same editor. The story was *Will I Have a Friend?.* My books are all about the same little kids. I love watching nursery and kindergarten life as my boys went through. *The New Teacher* was written because I was angry and sad at the meanness of a few teachers (not those my boys had; they were wonderful). But I didn't want my story to make little children anxious about school. So I made the new teacher's meanness only a fantasy rumor of how she *might* be. She isn't at all, as it turns out."

*   *   *

COLDWELL, Joan   1936-

PERSONAL: Born November 3, 1936, in Huddersfield, England; daughter of Arthur and Nellie (Johnson) Coldwell. *Education:* University of London, B.A. (with honors), 1958, M.A., 1960; Harvard University, Ph.D., 1967. *Home:* 297 Watson Ave., Oakville, Ontario, Canada. *Office:* Department of English, McMaster University, Hamilton, Ontario, Canada.

CAREER: Victoria University, Victoria, British Columbia, Canada, assistant professor of English, 1963-72; McMaster University, Hamilton, Ontario, Canada, associate professor of English, 1972—. *Awards, honors:* Senior fellow of Canada Council, 1969-70, and 1977-78.

WRITINGS: (Contributor) Robin Skelton and Ann Saddlemyer, editors, *The World of W. B. Yeats,* University of Washington Press, 1965; (editor) *Charles Lamb on Shakespeare,* Barnes & Noble, 1978. Author of a column in *Victoria Daily Times,* 1967-69. Contributor to literature journals. Contributor to *Oxford Companion to Canadian Literature.* Book editor of *Victoria Daily Times,* 1967-69.

WORK IN PROGRESS: A book on Canadian women novelists.

*   *   *

COLE, David Chamberlain   1928-

BRIEF ENTRY: Born May 24, 1928, in Detroit, Mich. American economist, educator, and author. Cole worked for the United Nations Relief and Rehabilitation Administration in China after World War II. He was an economist for the U.S. Agency for International Development from 1962 to 1964 and senior economic adviser for the agency in Korea from 1964 to 1966. Since 1971 he has been a lecturer at Harvard University. Cole wrote *Report on Taxation in the Provinces of South Viet-Nam* (National Institute of Administration, 1956), *Dorean Development: The Interplay of Politics and Economics* (Harvard University Press, 1971), and *The Korean Economy: Issues of Development* (Center for Korean Studies, Institute of East Asian Studies, University of California, Berkeley, 1980). *Address:* Department of Economics, Harvard University, 1737 Cambridge St., Cambridge, Mass. 02138.

*   *   *

COLE, Sonia (Mary)   1918-1982

OBITUARY NOTICE—See index for *CA* sketch: Born in 1918 in London, England; died May 9, 1982. Editor and author best known for her writings on East African archaeology. A student of geology at the University of London, Cole's professional interest in the subject began on her husband's family lands in the Rift Valley of Kenya, Africa. It was there, in 1945, that she met anthropologist Louis Leakey and his wife and began an association with them that lasted thirty years. Participating in the Leakeys' expeditions in search of prehuman fossils, Cole quickly recognized the interrelationship between geology, anthropology, and archaeology and began synthesizing and systematically explaining the progress of Leakeys' findings and excavations of the post-World War II period. When Leakey died in 1972, Cole was the family's natural choice as his biographer. *Leakey's Luck: The Life of Louis Seymour Bazett Leakey, 1903-1972*, was Cole's last book. Her other writings include *The Prehistory of East Africa, An Outline of the Geology of Kenya, The Neolithic Revolution, Races of Man*, and *Counterfeit*, a book about fakes and frauds in the world of art and archaeology. Obituaries and other sources: *London Times*, May 28, 1982.

* * *

COLIE, Rosalie L(ittell)   1924-1972

OBITUARY NOTICE: Born June 18, 1924, in New York, N.Y.; died July 7, 1972; buried in Evergreen Cemetery, Morristown, N.J. Historian, educator, and author. A professor of history and English, Colie taught at Barnard College from 1948 to 1961, then at Wesleyan University, University of Iowa, and University of Toronto. From 1969 until her death Colie was a Nancy Duke Lewis Professor at Brown University. Her books include *Light and Enlightenment: A Study of the Cambridge Platonists and the Dutch Arminians, Paradoxia Epidemica: The Renaissance Tradition of Paradox*, and *"My Echoing Song": Andrew Marvell's Poetry of Criticism*. Some of Colie's books appeared posthumously, including *Atlantic Wall*, a collection of poems, and *Shakespeare's Living Art*, both published in 1974. Obituaries and other sources: *Comparative Literature*, spring, 1969; *Who Was Who in America, With World Notables*, Volume V: *1969-1973*, Marquis, 1973; *American Historical Review*, June 8, 1973; *Who's Who of American Women*, 8th edition, Marquis, 1974.

* * *

COLLINS, Trish   1927-

PERSONAL: Born July 27, 1927, in Janesville, Wis.; daughter of Norman Edgar (a realtor) and Mayme Isabelle (an artist; maiden name, Austin) Simonsen; married Robert Edward Collins (a company vice-president and general counsel), June 23, 1949; children: Judith Patricia, Jane Isabel, Daniel John, David Peter. *Education:* Attended Ward-Belmont Junior College, 1945-47; University of Wisconsin (now University of Wisconsin—Madison), B.S., 1949. *Residence:* Janesville, Wis. 53545.

CAREER: Free-lance writer for children. Mercy Hospital, Janesville, Wis., emergency room receptionist, 1972; WCLO-WJVL-Radio, Janesville, radio copywriter, 1972-73; *Janesville Gazette*, Janesville, reporter for "Woman's Page," 1973-74. *Member:* National League of American Pen Women, Society of Children's Book Writers, Council for Wisconsin Writers, Chicago Children's Reading Round Table.

WRITINGS: Grinkles: A Keen Halloween Story (self-illustrated juvenile), F. Watts, 1981. Contributor of stories and articles to magazines, including *American Girl, Highlights for Children, Jack and Jill, Children's Playmate, Child Life*, and *Wee Wisdom*.

WORK IN PROGRESS: A Box of Book Mystery, a mystery for children; *Balloons and Baboons,* a picture book for pre-schoolers.

SIDELIGHTS: Collins told *CA:* "Children's magazines and books are a child's first experience with reading. If they are entertaining and enticing, they can launch the child on a lifetime of reading. When I'm working at my desk or art table, I keep this responsibility in mind. I take the humor and fantasy emerging from my projects very seriously, always trying to get the best out of myself for the entertainment and expansion of those just starting out in life.

"For me, the creative life arose out of a compelling need to communicate with other human beings. It is sustained by the fun and fulfillment of doing just that.

"Much good material is being produced for children, but the market is vast and needs continual updating and expanding. There is always room for talented writers and artists who can communicate with children. To succeed they need two strengths, confidence and persistence."

* * *

COLQUHOUN, Frank   1909-

PERSONAL: Born October 28, 1909, in Ventnor, Isle of Wight, England; son of Robert Woods and Violet (Walkey) Colquhoun; married Dora G.H. Slater, June 1, 1935; children: David, Mary. *Education:* University of Durham, L.Th., 1932, B.A., 1933, M.A., 1936.

CAREER: Ordained priest of Church of England; vicar of Wallington, England, 1954-61; Southwark Cathedral, London, England, precentor, 1961—. Examining chaplain to Bishop of Southwark and vice-principal of Southwark Ordination Course, 1961—.

WRITINGS—Published by Hodder & Stoughton, except as noted: *Harringay Story: The Official Record of the Billy Graham Greater London Crusade, 1954*, 1954; *The Fellowship of the Gospel: A New Testament Study in the Principles of Christian Cooperation*, Zondervan, 1957; *Your Child's Baptism: A Book for Parents and Godparents Who Are Prepared to Think Seriously About Baptism*, 1961; *The Gospels for the Sundays and the Principal Holy Days of the Church's Year*, 1961; *The Catechism and the Order of Confirmation*, 1963; *Christ's Ambassadors: The Priority of Preaching*, Westminster Press, 1965; *Total Christianity*, Moody, 1965; (editor) *Parish Prayers*, 1967; *Prayers for Every Occasion*, Morehouse, 1974; *Contemporary Parish Prayers*, 1975; (editor) *Hard Questions: A Discussion of Thirty-Eight Basic Christian Problems*, Church Pastoral Aid Society (London, England), 1976, published as *Hard Questions*, Inter-Varsity Press, 1977; *Moral Questions*, Falcon Books, 1977.

Contributor to religious journals, including *Christian*, and newspapers. Editor of *Churchman*, 1946-52, and *Crusade*, 1954-60.

* * *

COLVIN, Elaine Wright   1942-

PERSONAL: Born September 3, 1942, in Chico, Calif.; daughter of Harold S. (a real estate broker) and Paulene Ruth (a merchant and seamstress; maiden name, Cripe) Wright; married Robert Colvin (an adjudication officer for U.S. Veterans Administration), August 22, 1964; children: Catherine Suzanne. *Education:* Western Baptist Bible College, B.A., 1964. *Politics:* Conservative. *Religion:* Protestant. *Home:* 1633

Flowerree, Helena, Mont. 59601. *Office address:* P.O. Box 797, Helena, Mont. 59624.

CAREER: Mount Hermon Christian Writers Conference, Mount Hermon, Calif., associate director, 1978—. Leader of writing conferences and workshop teacher; adult education instructor; consultant. *Member:* Christian Writers Guild, Christian Writers Fellowship, Christian Writers League, Society of Christian Poets. *Awards, honors:* Best writer's helps award from Mount Hermon Christian Writers Conference, 1981, for *The Religious Writers Marketplace.*

WRITINGS: (With William H. Gentz) *The Religious Writers Marketplace,* Running Press, 1980; (contributor) Gentz, Lee Roddy, and others, editors, *Writing to Inspire,* Writer's Digest, 1982. Author of "Market Update," a marketing column in *Christian Writers Newsletter,* 1981—. Contributor of articles and poems to magazines, including *Christian Herald, Decision, Today's Christian Woman, Family Life Today, Herald of Holiness,* and *Pastor's Manual.*

WORK IN PROGRESS: A women's devotional book; a book of poems; a book on moving; and a textbook and workshop leader's guide on creative writing.

SIDELIGHTS: Elaine Colvin commented: "In three months in 1976, I wrote 250 poems out of the desperation and loneliness following my sixth cross-country move. While attending my first writer's conference that same year, I learned that only through the discipline of market research would I be able to place those poems in 'paying' magazines. Thus followed five years of compiling my comprehensive resource files for Christian writers. As a market specialist and authority on Christian writers' resources, I have addressed conferences, club meetings, and creative writing classes nationwide, and have organized both the Idaho Fellowship of Christian Writers and the Montana Christian Writers Fellowship."

*   *   *

COMREY, Andrew Laurence   1923-

BRIEF ENTRY: Born April 14, 1923, in Charleston, W.Va. American psychologist, educator, and author. Comrey began teaching in 1949 and has been a professor of psychology at University of California, Los Angeles, since 1962. He received Guggenheim and Fulbright fellowships for Italy in 1957. Comrey's books include *A First Course in Factor Analysis* (Academic Press, 1973), *A Sourcebook for Mental Health Measures* (Human Interaction Research Institute, 1973), *Elementary Statistics: A Problem Solving Approach* (Dorsey, 1975), and *Handbook of Interpretations for the Comrey Personality Scales* (EDITS, 1980). *Address:* 489 Denslow Ave., Los Angeles, Calif. 90049; and Department of Psychology, University of California, 405 Hilgard Ave., Los Angeles, Calif. 90024. *Biographical/critical sources: American Men and Women of Science: The Social and Behavioral Sciences,* 13th edition, Bowker, 1978.

*   *   *

CONDLIFFE, John B(ell)   1891-1981

OBITUARY NOTICE—See index for *CA* sketch: Born December 23, 1891, in Melbourne, Australia; died December 23, 1981, in Walnut Creek, Calif. Economist, educator, and author. An international monetary policy and trade relations specialist, Condliffe served as professor of economics at several universities, including the University of New Zealand, Canterbury University College (now University of Canterbury), University of Michigan, and University of California, Berke-

ley, before becoming senior economist at the Stanford Institute in 1960. From 1943 to 1948 Condliffe was associate director of the division of history and economics of the Carnegie Endowment for International Peace. In that capacity he played an important role at the Bretton Woods Conference on monetary reform, becoming a spokesman for the conference's agreements that led to the establishment of the World Bank and the International Monetary Fund. He received numerous awards for his work, including the Gold Cross, Order of the Phoenix from Greece, the Henry E. Howland Memorial Prize from Yale University, and the Wendell L. Wilkie Prize from the American Political Science Organization. In 1979 Queen Elizabeth II named him an Honorary Knight Commander of the Order of St. Michael and St. George. His writings include *New Zealand in the Making: A Study of Economic and Social Development, China Today, The Commerce of Nations, Reconstruction of World Trade,* and *Te Rangi Hiroa: The Life of Sir Peter Buck.* Obituaries and other sources: *New York Times,* December 26, 1981.

*   *   *

CONNER, Patrick (Roy Mountifort)   1947-

PERSONAL: Born September 18, 1947, in London, England; son of William Louis Mountifort and Cherisy Doreen (Oram) Conner; married Edwina Jacqueline Bewkey (a publisher), July 6, 1973; children: Anna Bianca. *Education:* Worcester College, Oxford, B.A., 1969; University of Sussex, D.Phil., 1974. *Office:* Royal Pavilion, Art Gallery and Museums, Brighton, Sussex, England.

CAREER: Teacher of Latin at private secondary school in Marlborough, England, 1969-70; Royal Pavilion, Art Gallery and Museums, Brighton, England, keeper of fine art, 1975—. Adjunct professor at Bucknell University, 1978. *Awards, honors:* Grant from National Gallery, 1976; Leverhulme Award, 1981, for research into eighteenth-century watercolors; fellow at Yale University's Center for British Art, 1982.

WRITINGS: Oriental Architecture in the West, Thames & Hudson, 1979; *Savage Ruskin,* Wayne State University Press, 1979; *People at Work,* Wayland Publishers, 1982; *People at Home,* Wayland Publishers, 1982; *Michael "Angelo" Rooker and the Art of Topographical Watercolour,* Batsford, in press. Contributor to periodicals, including *Apollo, Art History, Burlington Magazine,* and *Country Life.*

SIDELIGHTS: Conner told *CA:* "Travelers' reactions (drawn, painted, or written) to other cultures seem to me particularly fascinating—often revealing as much about the traveler's own assumptions and prejudices as about the foreign land itself. The subjects on which I have written are fairly obscure, I suppose, but I have tried to make them accessible and appealing to nonspecialists; my own prejudice is against the massive output of tediously mystificatory and shelf-clogging publications that are written solely to impress small circles of introverted academics."

AVOCATIONAL INTERESTS: The Middle East and Far East, "and early travelers and artists there."

*   *   *

CONNER, Susanna (Whitney) Pflaum
See PFLAUM-CONNER, Susanna (Whitney)

*   *   *

CONNOR, Walter Downing   1942-

PERSONAL: Born April 20, 1942, in Bay Shore, N.Y.; son

of Edward J. and Mary (Downing) Connor; married Eileen M. Donohue (a health planner), October 22, 1966; children: Christine, Elizabeth. *Education:* College of the Holy Cross, A.B., 1963; Princeton University, M.A., 1966, Ph.D., 1969. *Religion:* Roman Catholic. *Home:* 1105 North Rockingham St., Arlington, Va. 22205. *Office:* Foreign Service Institute, U.S. Department of State, 1400 Key Blvd., Arlington, Va. 22209.

CAREER: University of Michigan, Ann Arbor, lecturer, 1968-69, assistant professor of sociology, 1969-76; U.S. Department of State, Foreign Service Institute, Arlington, Va., chairman of Soviet and East European studies, 1976—. Senior fellow at University of Pennsylvania, 1976-79; visiting professor at University of Virginia, 1981—. Consultant to American Council of Learned Societies, International Research and Exchanges Board, and National Council on Foreign Language and International Studies. *Member:* American Association for the Advancement of Science. *Awards, honors:* Fellow of American Council of Learned Societies, 1973, 1975-76.

WRITINGS: Deviance in Soviet Society: Crime, Delinquency, and Alcoholism, Columbia University Press, 1972; (with Zvi Y. Gitelman) *Public Opinion in European Socialist Systems,* Praeger, 1977; *Socialism, Politics, and Equality: Hierarchy and Change in Eastern Europe and the U.S.S.R.,* Columbia University Press, 1979. Contributor to history, sociology, and political science journals.

*   *   *

CONNORS, Joseph 1945-

PERSONAL: Born February 5, 1945, in New York, N.Y.; son of Thomas V. (an electrician) and Margaret (O'Neill) Connors; married Francoise Moison (a banker), July 30, 1969; children: Genevieve, Thomas. *Education:* Boston College, A.B., 1966; Cambridge University, B.A. and M.A., both 1968; Harvard University, M.A., 1972, Ph.D., 1978. *Residence:* New York, N.Y. *Office:* Department of Art History, Columbia University, New York, N.Y. 10027.

CAREER: University of Chicago, Chicago, Ill., instructor, 1975-78, assistant professor of art history, 1978-80; Columbia University, New York, N.Y., associate professor of art history, 1980—. Visiting assistant professor at University of California, Berkeley, spring, 1979.

WRITINGS: Borromini and the Roman Oratory, M.I.T. Press, 1980. Contributor of articles and reviews to architectural history journals.

WORK IN PROGRESS: The Robie House of Frank Lloyd Wright, publication expected in 1982; *The Architecture of Francesco Borromini,* for Zwemmer; *Baroque Rome.*

SIDELIGHTS: Connors told *CA:* "The kind of inspiration that Palladio provided to modern architecture in the postwar period now seems to be coming from architects like Borromini, a seventeenth-century baroque architect. The most interesting response to my book, *Borromini and the Roman Oratory,* has come from skyscraper designers and town planners who have found a case study from baroque Rome unexpectedly relevant."

*   *   *

CONOLLY, L(eonard) W(illiam) 1941-

PERSONAL: Born September 13, 1941, in Walsall, England; married, 1964; children: James, Rebecca. *Education:* University College of Swansea, University of Wales, B.A., 1963, Ph.D., 1970; McMaster University, M.A., 1964. *Office:* De-

partment of Drama, University of Guelph, Guelph, Ontario, Canada N1G 2W1.

CAREER: University of Saskatchewan, Saskatoon, instructor in English, 1965-67; University of Alberta, Edmonton, assistant professor, 1970-74, associate professor, 1974-79, professor of English, 1979-81; University of Guelph, Guelph, Ontario, professor of drama and chairman of department, 1981—. Member of board of governors of Guelph Spring Festival, 1981—. *Member:* International Federation for Theatre Research (executive member, 1980—), Association for Canadian Theatre History (president, 1977-79), American Society for Theatre Research (executive member, 1980—).

WRITINGS: The Censorship of English Drama, 1737-1824, Huntington Library, 1976; (with J. P. Wearing) *English Drama and Theatre, 1800-1900,* Gale, 1978; *A Directory of British Theatre Research Resources in North America,* British Theatre Institute, 1978. Co-editor of *Nineteenth-Century Theatre Research,* 1974-81; advisory editor of *Theatre History in Canada.*

WORK IN PROGRESS: Research on Canadian theatre history.

*   *   *

CONWAY, David 1939-

PERSONAL: Born January 29, 1939, in Aberystwyth, Wales; son of James (in business) and Marjorie (Jones) Thomas. *Education:* Attended University of Strasbourg, 1958, and University of Rennes, 1960; King's College, London, B.A., 1961, M.A., 1963. *Residence:* Munich, West Germany. *Office:* European Patent Office, Erhardstrasse 27, 8000 Munich 80, West Germany.

CAREER: British Civil Service, London, assistant principal, 1963-67, principal, 1967-72; British Diplomatic Service, London, first secretary in Brussels, Belgium, 1972-75; British Civil Service, London, assistant secretary, 1975-77; European Patent Office, Munich, West Germany, principal director of personnel, 1977—. *Member:* Anthroposophical Society, Cymdeithas yr Iaith Gymraeg.

WRITINGS: The Magic of Herbs, Dutton, 1972; *Magic: An Occult Primer,* Dutton, 1974. Contributor to magazines, including *Vogue* and *Destiny.*

WORK IN PROGRESS: A study of Celtic mythology and Druidic beliefs, with emphasis on their survival in the superstitions and folk traditions of rural Wales, Scotland, and Ireland, together with their contemporary significance.

SIDELIGHTS: Conway told *CA:* "The intention of my writings has been to rehabilitate esoteric traditions, their theory and practice, in the twentieth century. By stripping them of all spurious mumbo-jumbo, I have endeavored to show how our modern thinking can be illuminated by them, thereby enabling us to discern man's place and that of the world he occupies within the stream of cosmic evolution. While the standards of proof applied in physical science are often inappropriate to occultism, the latter should nevertheless be made subject to rational enquiry. Discoveries made here will be found to enhance our understanding as science, notably in the field of physics, edges toward the frontier of super-physical reality."

BIOGRAPHICAL/CRITICAL SOURCES: Sunday Times, January 28, 1972; *Y Cymro,* March, 1972; *American Express,* April, 1973.

*   *   *

COOK, Alan Hugh 1922-

PERSONAL: Born December 2, 1922, in Felstead, England;

son of Reginald Thomas (a civil servant) and Ethel (a teacher; maiden name, Saxon) Cook; married Isabell Weir Anderson, January 30, 1948; children: Elspeth Mary Cook James, Alasdair James Alan. *Education:* Cambridge University, B.A., 1943, M.A., 1948, Ph.D., 1950, Sc.D., 1968. *Politics:* None. *Religion:* Church of England. *Home:* 8 Wootton Way, Cambridge CB3 9LX, England. *Office:* Cavendish Laboratory, Cambridge University, Cambridge CBS OHE, England.

CAREER: Admiralty Signal Establishment, Haslemere, England, temporary experimental officer, 1943-46; Cambridge University, Cambridge, England, research assistant in geodesy and geophysics, 1949-52; National Physical Laboratory, Teddington, England, research scientist, 1952-66, superintendent of Division of Quantum Metrology, 1966-69; University of Edinburgh, Edinburgh, Scotland, professor of geophysics, 1969-72; Cambridge University, Jacksonian Professor of Natural Philosophy, 1972—, head of department of physics, 1979—, fellow of King's College, 1972—. Visiting professor at University of California, Los Angeles, 1981, and at University of California, Berkeley, 1982; Green Scholar at Institute of Geophysics and Planetary Physics, University of California, San Diego, 1982. Visiting fellow at Joint Institute of Laboratory Astrophysics, 1965-66; organizer of courses in geophysics for International Centre for Theoretical Physics. Member of Natural Environment Research Council, 1974-80. *Member:* Royal Society (fellow), Institute of Physics (fellow), Royal Astronomical Society (fellow president, 1977-79), Royal Society Edinburgh (fellow), Academia Nazionale dei Lincei, Explorers Club (fellow).

WRITINGS: Gravity and the Earth, Wykeham Press, 1969; (with R. H. Tucker, H. M. Iyer, and F. D. Stacey) *Global Geophysics,* English Universities Press, 1970; *Interference of Electromagnetic Waves,* Oxford University Press, 1971; *Physics of the Earth and Planets,* Macmillan, 1973; *Celestial Masers,* Cambridge University Press, 1977; *Interiors of the Planets,* Cambridge University Press, 1980. Contributor of about one hundred articles to journals.

WORK IN PROGRESS: Research on the physics of the interiors of planets and on theoretical and experimental molecular physics.

SIDELIGHTS: Cook commented: "I have a particular interest in the logical foundations of physics and in the ways in which human existence is influenced by the physical state of the earth." *Avocational interests:* Theatre, travel (including Italy), painting, architecture, history.

*   *   *

COOK, John Lennox   1923-
   (Lennox Cook)

PERSONAL: Born in 1923, in Richmond, England; son of Arthur and Gladys (Lennox) Cook; married Ann Doreen Pryor; children: two daughters. *Education:* Trinity College, Oxford (with honors), 1946. *Politics:* Conservative. *Religion:* Church of England. *Home:* Toll Bar, 75 Barton Rd., Cambridge CB3 9LJ, England. *Agent:* David Higham Associates Ltd., 5-8 Lower John St., Golden Sq., London W1R 4HA, England.

CAREER: Associated with Bell School of Languages, 1955-62, senior tutor, 1962; Lennox Cook School of English, Cambridge, England, director, 1962—; writer.

WRITINGS—Novels; under name Lennox Cook: Dark to the Sun, Fortune Press, 1951; *The World Before Us* (travel book), Collins, 1955; *The Lucky Man,* Collins, 1956; *No Language But a Cry,* Hamish Hamilton, 1958; *A Feeling of Disquiet,*

Hodder & Stoughton, 1972; *The Bridge,* Weidenfeld & Nicolson, 1974; *The Manipulator,* Coward, 1978; *Under Etna,* M. Joseph, 1982.

Also co-author under name John Lennox Cook with Amorey Gethin and Keilt Mitchell of *A New Way to Proficiency in English,* 1967.

WORK IN PROGRESS: A novel tentatively entitled *Journey Into Terror.*

SIDELIGHTS: Cook told *CA:* "For me the novel is first and foremost an entertainment, having that elusive but essential quality of readability. It needs to be about real people, to convey an atmosphere or moral, a time and place, and should pinpoint some aspect of a truth. At the end the reader should be able to say, 'So that's how it was,' and feel his own experience has been extended and himself become not necessarily a sadder but certainly a wiser man."

*   *   *

COOK, Lennox
   See COOK, John Lennox

*   *   *

COOK, Paul H(arlin)   1950-

PERSONAL: Born November 12, 1950, in Tucson, Ariz.; son of Harlin Maurice (a professor) and Patricia (in public relations; maiden name, Cochran) Cook. *Education:* Northern Arizona University, B.A., 1972; Arizona State University, M.A., 1978; University of Utah, Ph.D., 1981. *Politics:* None. *Religion:* "Awakener (Meher Baba)." *Home:* 4400 West Missouri, No. 276, Glendale, Ariz. 85301. *Agent:* Howard Morhaim, 501 Fifth Ave., New York, N.Y. 10017.

CAREER: Arizona State University, Hayden Library, Tempe, Ariz., librarian, 1973-78; instructor in English and novelist, 1981—. *Member:* Modern Language Association of America.

WRITINGS: Casa de Luz (poems; title means "House of Light"), Department of English, Arizona State University, 1979; *Tintagel* (novel), Berkley-Jove, 1981. Editor of *Yellow Brick Road.*

WORK IN PROGRESS: Five novels, *The Fortress of Solitude,* publication expected in 1982, *The Alejandra Variations,* 1983, *Mayberry Agonistes,* 1983, *Just Us Kids,* 1984, and *The Night of the Kachinas,* 1985; three screenplays, "Wise Guys," "The Werewolf Retires," and "Tintagel."

SIDELIGHTS: Cook wrote: "I am trying to incorporate spiritual compensations and visions I've been dealing with all my life into a fictional or meta-fictional framework. I am now a science fiction writer, but, publishing conventions being what they are, I seem to be heading toward film. I wish to become enlightened in this lifetime and live like Han Shan on Cold Mountain—except this time I want to do it right!"

*   *   *

COOK, Stephani   1944-

PERSONAL: Born October 19, 1944, in Chicago, Ill.; divorced; children: Alexandra Siegel, Zachary Siegel. *Education:* Barnard College, B.A., 1966; Columbia University, M.A., 1972. *Residence:* New York, N.Y. *Agent:* Lynn Nesbitt, International Creative Management, 40 West 57th St., New York, N.Y. 10019.

CAREER: Eileen Ford Agency, New York City, model, 1964-70; private practice of psychotherapy and sex therapy in New

York City, 1971-78. Family Counseling host on television talk show, 1976-77; developed and presented self-image seminars for *Glamour,* 1977-78; writer. *Member:* American Psychological Association, Women's Inc., Barnard Business and Professional Women.

WRITINGS: Second Life (autobiography; Literary Guild dual main selection, Young Parents Book Club alternate selection), Simon & Schuster, 1981. Also contributor of articles to periodicals, including *Glamour* and *Journal of Current Social Issues.*

WORK IN PROGRESS: A novel.

SIDELIGHTS: Cook's autobiographical *Second Life,* which describes the author's experience with patronizing doctors who consistently misdiagnosed her life-threatening illness, is "a medical horror story," according to *Newsweek*'s Walter Clemons. When Cook, a former cover girl and model, began to experience sporadic chest pains her doctors dismissed them as postpartum hysteria brought on by the birth of her second child. When the pains persisted, Cook underwent a D&C (a surgical procedure in which tissue is scraped from the wall of the uterus), and she was administered periodic doses of antibiotics. When subsequent tests revealed blood clots in her venal system, Cook was subjected to a radical hysterectomy because her doctors believed that her ovarian veins were producing the dangerous emboli. Following the surgery, however, Cook's pain increased and she began to exhibit new symptoms.

Open-heart surgery came next because her doctors suspected that a tumor on her heart might be causing the clots. Cook underwent the procedure only to find out later that the clots were actually fragments of a rare placental cancer that could have been readily diagnosed two years earlier with a simple urinalysis and that neither the hysterectomy nor the heart surgery had been necessary. Cook eventually recovered after extensive treatment with chemotherapy.

Washington Post critic Laurel Lee praised Cook's account of her ordeal, noting that the author's "skill with the written word . . . makes vivid her physical and mental sufferings. Her language," Lee continued, "is rich with insights and imagery." Clemons, who admitted that he hadn't wanted to read *Second Life,* reported that he "was fascinated and shaken by it," and commended the book as "a salutary manual of hard-earned rage."

Cook told *CA:* "My book is really much more about a woman's search for self than about cancer, which only supplies the overriding metaphor and the narrative trajectory."

Vivian Castleberry of the *Dallas Times Herald* agreed, praising *Second Life* as "the best feminist book of this decade—maybe ever—and it is all the more powerful because it isn't meant to be a feminist book at all. . . . [It] is a feminist book because it portrays in absolute candor the psychology of women, how they feel, what they think, how they perceive, what they dream."

BIOGRAPHICAL/CRITICAL SOURCES: Washington Post, September 12, 1981, November 5, 1981; *Newsweek,* November 2, 1982; *Dallas Times Herald,* November 4, 1981; *People,* December 14, 1981.

*   *   *

COOKE, John D(aniel)   1892-1972

OBITUARY NOTICE: Born May 26, 1892, in Beloit, Kan.; died in June, 1972. Educator, editor, and author. During his forty-year career at the University of Southern California, Cooke held several positions, including professor of English, head of the English department, chairman of the humanities division, dean of summer sessions, and acting dean of the graduate school. He edited *Minor Victorian Poets,* compiled and selected *Essays for the New America,* and wrote, with Lionel Stevenson, *English Literature of the Victorian Period.* Obituaries and other sources: *Who Was Who in America, With World Notables,* Volume V: *1969-1973,* Marquis, 1973.

*   *   *

COOPER, Alice   1948-

PERSONAL: Birth-given name, Vincent Damon Furnier; name legally changed in 1975; born February 4, 1948, in Detroit, Mich.; son of Ether Moroni (a minister) and Ella Mae (McCart) Furnier; married Sheryl Goddard (a singer and dancer), March 20, 1976; children: Calico (daughter). *Education:* Attended school in Phoenix, Ariz. *Home:* Beverly Hills, Calif. *Agent:* Shep Gordon. *Office:* c/o Alive Enterprises, Inc., 8600 Melrose Ave., Los Angeles, Calif. 90069.

CAREER: Songwriter, recording artist, and performer in concerts and on television, 1965—. Also appeared in motion pictures, including "Diary of a Mad Housewife," Universal, 1970; "Good to See You Again Alice Cooper," Alive Enterprises, 1974; "Sergeant Pepper's Lonely Hearts Club Band," Universal, 1978; "Sextette," Briggs & Sullivan, 1978; and "Roadie," Alive Enterprises, 1980. *Member:* Friars Club. *Awards, honors:* Received gold and platinum records for albums, "Love It to Death," "Killer," "School's Out," "Billion Dollar Babies," "Muscle of Love," and "Alice Cooper Goes to Hell."

WRITINGS: (With Steven Gaines) *Me, Alice: The Autobiography of Alice Cooper,* Putnam, 1976.

Recordings; albums except as noted: "Pretties for You," Straight, 1969; "Easy Action," Straight, 1970; "Love It to Death," Warner Brothers, 1970; "Killer," Warner Brothers, 1971; "School's Out," Warner Brothers, 1972; "Billion Dollar Babies," Warner Brothers, 1973; "Muscle of Love," Warner Brothers, 1974; "Welcome to My Nightmare," Atlantic/Anchor, 1975; "Alice Cooper Goes to Hell," Warner Brothers, 1976; "Lace and Whiskey," Warner Brothers, 1977; (with Bernie Taupin) "From the Inside," Warner Brothers, 1979; "Flush the Fashion," Warner Brothers, 1980; "Special Forces," Warner Brothers, 1982; "For Britain Only" (single), WEA Records, 1982.

Compilations: "Schooldays: The Early Recordings" (contains "Pretties for You" and "Easy Action" [see both above]), Warner Brothers, 1973; "Greatest Hits," Warner Brothers, 1974.

WORK IN PROGRESS: An album.

SIDELIGHTS: Cooper became famous during the early 1970's as the lead singer in the flamboyant rock group, Alice Cooper. After first performing in Phoenix under the names Earwigs, Spiders, and Nazz, the band (including Cooper, Glen Buxton, Michael Bruce, Dennis Dunaway, and Neal Smith) moved to Los Angeles. There, billed as Alice Cooper, the group began performing in garish makeup and bizarre dress, and also indulged in a variety of on-stage histrionics that were designed to shock audiences. For example, the band staged mock battles using boxes of detergent as weapons, threw dead chickens at its audiences, decapitated dolls, held mock executions, simulated self-dismemberment, and feigned sexual assaults on department store mannequins. Cooper would also sing while embracing a boa constrictor or while wearing a straitjacket.

Though the group's antics began to draw a lot of attention, some audiences found its behavior so offensive that they walked out during performances of the group. On one occasion members of a motorcycle club charged the stage, threatening the band with murder. Critics also were unimpressed with the band, finding its music fairly undistinguished. In 1970, however, with the release of "Love It to Death," the group's fortunes changed. Critics began to write favorable reviews of their albums, and by 1972 Alice Cooper concerts were major box office attractions. Though their artistic credibility escalated rapidly, they continued to feature chaotic stage productions. "Cooper did not purport to present music as an end in itself but as a part of theatre," wrote Noel Coppage in *Stereo Review*.

After producing seven albums the group broke up, but Cooper continued to perform and record albums using the Alice Cooper name, which he legally assumed in 1975. His first solo album, "Welcome to My Nightmare," was released in 1975. His autobiography, *Me, Alice*, described by Michael Lyden of the *New York Times Book Review* as "a funny, lively book," was published the following year. Cooper continues to make recordings and concert tours.

BIOGRAPHICAL/CRITICAL SOURCES: Newsweek, May 28, 1973, January 13, 1975, April 5, 1976, March 28, 1977; Bob Greene, *Billion Dollar Baby*, Atheneum, 1974; *Miami Herald*, January 13, 1974; *Biography News*, February, 1974; Alice Cooper and Steven Gaines, *Me, Alice: The Autobiography of Alice Cooper*, Putnam, 1976; *New York Times Book Review*, May 23, 1976; *Rolling Stone*, September 8, 1977; *People*, September 4, 1978, June 30, 1980; *Stereo Review*, April, 1979, September, 1980; *Detroit Free Press*, July 10, 1981.

* * *

COPELAND, James Isaac   1910-

PERSONAL: Born May 5, 1910, in Clinton, S.C.; son of William David (a hardware merchant) and Laura (Vance) Copeland. *Education:* Presbyterian College, A.B., 1931; George Peabody College for Teachers, B.S., 1932, M.A., 1934; further graduate study at University of Chicago, 1936-40; University of North Carolina, Ph.D., 1957. *Politics:* Democrat. *Religion:* Presbyterian. *Home:* 7 Davie Circle, Chapel Hill, N.C. 27514. *Office:* Wilson Library, University of North Carolina, Chapel Hill, N.C. 27514.

CAREER: George Peabody College for Teachers, Nashville, Tenn., assistant reference and periodicals librarian, 1932-35; Furman University, Greenville, S.C., librarian, 1936-42; Presbyterian College, Clinton, S.C., librarian, 1942-45; University of North Carolina, Chapel Hill, documents librarian, 1947-50; George Peabody College for Teachers, professor of history and librarian, 1952-67; University of North Carolina, professor of history and director of Southern Historical Collection at library, 1967-75. Member of board of directors of Nashville Council on Human Relations, 1961-63.

MEMBER: American Library Association (member of council, 1962-65), American Historical Association, Organization of American Historians, Southeastern Library Association, Southern Historical Association, North Carolina Library Association, Literary and Historical Association of North Carolina, Historical Society of North Carolina, South Carolina Historical Association, Kiwanis Club of Chapel Hill. *Awards, honors:* Award of merit from American Association for State and Local History, 1971, for *Democracy in the Old South and Other Essays*.

WRITINGS: (Contributor) Arthur Link and Rembert Patrick, editors, *Writing Southern History: Essays in Historiography in Honor of Fletcher M. Green*, Louisiana State University Press, 1965, revised edition, 1967; (editor) Fletcher M. Green, *Democracy in the Old South and Other Essays*, Vanderbilt University Press, 1969; (editor with Green) *The Old South*, AHM Publishing, 1980.

BIOGRAPHICAL/CRITICAL SOURCES: Presbyterian College, spring, 1971; *Peabody Journal of Education*, November, 1966.

* * *

CORDIER, Andrew W(ellington)   1901-1975

OBITUARY NOTICE: Born March 3, 1901, in Canton, Ohio; died of cirrhosis of the liver, July 11, 1975, in Manhasset, Long Island, N.Y. Diplomat, educator, and author. Cordier taught history and political science at Manchester College from 1927 to 1944, traveled extensively throughout the world, and lectured for the Republican Committee in Indiana. After serving as expert on international security for the U.S. State Department from 1944 to 1946, during which time he helped organize the United Nations (U.N.), he began a sixteen-year association with the U.N. Cordier served as both adviser to the president of the United Nations General Assembly and as executive assistant to the United Nations secretary general. He was known for his ability to recall precise rules of parliamentary procedure and for his calm management in crisis situations. He was often able to persuade adversaries to meet and reach a settlement. In 1962 Cordier left the U.N. to become head of the School of International Affairs at Columbia University. When campus discord paralyzed the university in 1968, Cordier was asked to assume the presidency of Columbia. In this capacity he served for two years, confirming his reputation for cooly resolving crises; he even joined with student activists in speaking out against American military involvement in Indochina. Cordier retired as dean of Columbia's School of International Affairs in 1972. Following his death the school created a scholarship fund in his name. Obituaries and other sources: *Current Biography*, Wilson, 1950, September, 1975; *Time*, August 30, 1968, August 29, 1969; *Newsweek*, September 2, 1968, September 1, 1969, July 21, 1975; *Who's Who*, 126th edition, St. Martin's, 1974; *Who's Who in America*, 38th edition, Marquis, 1974; *International Who's Who*, Europa, 1975; *Who's Who in the United Nations and Related Agencies*, Arno, 1975; *New York Times*, July 13, 1975; *Who Was Who in America, With World Notables*, Volume VI: *1974-1976*, Marquis, 1976.

* * *

CORN, Ira George, Jr.   1921-1982

OBITUARY NOTICE—See index for *CA* sketch: Born August 22, 1921, in Little Rock, Ark.; died of a heart attack, April 28, 1982, in Dallas, Tex. Industrialist, educator, and author best known for originating and financing the first full-time professional bridge team in America, the Aces. A championship tournament bridge player, Corn organized the Aces in 1968 with the intent of bringing the world team-bridge championship back to the United States. Under his leadership, as nonplaying team captain, the aces won the World Championship Bermuda Cup five times, in addition to capturing the Vanderbilt Cup and the Springfield trophy in the United States. Corn was director of the American Contract Bridge League from 1971 to 1981, serving as president in 1980. Also a highly enterprising businessman, Corn founded or co-founded twenty-four companies. At the time of his death he was chairman of the board and chief executive officer of Michigan General

Corporation, a Dallas-based conglomerate with eleven subsidiaries. He also served as a trustee of the American Economic Foundation and vice-chairman of the Graduate School of Business at the University of Chicago. His writings include *Play Bridge With the Aces, A Businessman Answers Questions by College Students, The Story of the Declaration of Independence,* and a syndicated newspaper column "Aces on Bridge." Obituaries and other sources: *New York Times,* April 29, 1982; *Newsweek,* May 10, 1982.

*   *   *

CORNELL, Douglas B.   1906(?)-1982

OBITUARY NOTICE: Born c. 1906; died February 20, 1982, in Detroit, Mich. Journalist. Known for his skillfully written lead sentences, Cornell wrote for the Associated Press for nearly forty years. His articles from the White House and the nation's capital covered many major events. During World War II he accompanied President Franklin D. Roosevelt on all his overseas trips, both secret and publicized. He rarely used a typewriter, preferring to dictate over the telephone. Obituaries and other sources: *New York Times,* February 22, 1982.

*   *   *

COSLOW, Sam   1905-1982

OBITUARY NOTICE—See index for *CA* sketch: Born December 12, 1905, in New York, N.Y.; died April 2, 1982, in Bronxville, N.Y. Composer, lyricist, investment analyst, publisher, and author. Coslow began his songwriting career in the early 1920's, composing songs for Al Jolson and for Broadway productions, including "Artists and Models." After moving to Hollywood, California, he spent several years as a contract songwriter for Paramount Pictures before going to Metro-Goldwyn-Mayer, where he produced musical film shorts. In 1943 Coslow won an Academy Award for producing the year's best musical short, "Heavenly Music." He was elected into the Songwriters Hall of Fame in 1974. Among his best-known songs are "Cocktails for Two," "Just One More Chance," "Sing You Sinners," and "Moon Song." Changing careers in 1961, Coslow became a stockmarket analyst and founded the *Indicator Digest,* an investment-advisory newsletter. He wrote his autobiography, *Cocktails for Two: The Many Lives of Giant Songwriter Sam Coslow,* in 1977. He also wrote *Make Money on the Interest Rate Roller Coaster,* which is to be published posthumously by Coward, McCann & Geoghegan. Obituaries and oher sources: *New York Times,* April 6, 1982.

*   *   *

COUNSELMAN, Mary Elizabeth   1911-
(Charles Dubois, Sanders McCrorey, John Starr)

PERSONAL: Born November 19, 1911, in Birmingham, Ala.; daughter of John Sanders (a professor) and Netti Young (an art teacher; maiden name, McCrorey) Counselman; married Horace Benton Vinyard, November 13, 1941 (died, 1978); children: William Sanders. *Education:* Attended Alabama College and University of Alabama. *Politics:* "Citizen of the world." *Religion:* "Universalist (inherited Methodist)." *Home:* 239 East Cherry St., Gadsden, Ala. 35903. *Agent:* Kirby Mac-Cauley, 220 East 26th St., New York, N.Y. 10010.

CAREER: Reporter for *Birmingham News,* Birmingham, Ala.; instructor in creative writing at Gadsden State Junior College, Gadsden, Ala.; instructor in creative writing at University of Alabama; founder, publisher, and editor of Verity Publishing Co., Gadsden, beginning in 1976. Lecturer at writer's con-

claves and colonies throughout southern United States, including Venice Writer's Colony, Birmingham Penwomen, and Biloxi Writer's Colony. *Member:* American Penwomen (Birmingham chapter), National Fantasy Fan Federation, Chi Delta Phi, Dinosaurs. *Awards, honors:* National Endowment for the Arts fellow, 1976-77; award from the National Fantasy Fan Federation, for short story, "Overture."

WRITINGS: African Yesterdays (young adult short stories), Verity Publishing, 1975, revised and enlarged edition, 1977; *Move Over—It's Only Me* (poetry), Verity Publishing, 1976; *Half in Shadow* (young adult short stories), Arkham, 1978; *The Fifth Door* (a textbook on the subgenre of science fiction), Strange Books, 1982; *The Face of Fear,* Depot Press, 1982. Also author of *Everything You Want To Know About the Supernatural,* Verity Publishing, and *The Eye and the Hand* (poetry), Verity Publishing.

Editor, *Year at the Spring* magazine, 1977-80. Short stories have appeared in anthologies, including *Ghostly Gentlewomen, Far Below and Other Horrors,* and *The Roots of Evil,* and in school textbook anthologies. Contributor (sometimes under pseudonyms Charles Dubois, Sanders McCrorey, and John Starr) of short stories and poetry to periodicals, including *Collier's, Saturday Evening Post,* and *Ladies' Home Journal.*

WORK IN PROGRESS: Several young adult science fiction, fantasy, and suspense novels; *The Tempters,* a novel of Appalachian life among the snake handlers; a factual novel of river life based on the author's experiences on the steamboat *Leota* during World War II, entitled *Steamboat 'Round the OPA.*

SIDELIGHTS: Mary Elizabeth Counselman told *CA:* "I have always been interested in the parable as an oblique method of 'counseling' the readers who object to 'stuffy preaching.' The symbol has been used from the Greek, Egyptian, and Mesopotamian myths through current fantasies to explore the subconscious drives and rationales of mankind—as groups and as individuals. I feel that our basic sense of values can be regained through the in-depth study of old myths and legends, as well as modern fiction based on these. Judging from reader response to my stories (which have been translated into languages I do not even know) this use of symbol has universal appeal."

Television adaptations of Counselman's short stories have appeared on "G.E. Theatre" and other programs, and have been televised in fifteen different countries. Her televised stories include "The Three Marked Pennies," "Parasite Mansion," and "Gleason's Calendar."

*   *   *

COURT, Margaret Smith   1942-

BRIEF ENTRY: Born July 16, 1942, in Albury, Australia. Australian professional tennis player and author. When she was seventeen years old, Court became the youngest person to win the Australian Senior Invitational tennis championship. In 1970 she became the second woman to win the series of U.S., British, French, and Australian championships commonly known as the "Grand Slam." She wrote *The Margaret Smith Story* (Stanley Paul, 1965) and *Court on Court: A Life in Tennis* (Dodd, 1975). *Address:* 65 The Esplanade, Perth, Australia.

*   *   *

COUTARD, Wanda Lundy Hale   1902(?)-1982
(Wanda Hale)

OBITUARY NOTICE: Born c. 1902; died May 24, 1982, in

Burbank, Calif.; buried in Forest Lawn Cemetery, Hollywood Hills, Calif. Film critic. The principal film critic for the *New York Daily News* for over forty years, Coutard, under the name Wanda Hale, was also known for her interviews with celebrities. She was one of the founders of the New York Film Critics organization and headed the group in 1949. Retiring in 1973, Coutard conferred her highest rating on the controversial subject of her final film review, "Last Tango in Paris." Obituaries and other sources: *Chicago Tribune,* May 28, 1982.

*   *   *

COWLES, Kathleen
See KRULL, Kathleen

*   *   *

COWLEY, Joseph (Gilbert) 1923-

PERSONAL: Born October 9, 1923, in Yonkers, N.Y.; son of Joseph Gilbert (in police work) and Gertrude Claire (Hersey) Cowley; married Ruth Muriel Wilson, February 28, 1948; children: Barbara Claire Cowley Durst, Charles Abraham, Jennifer Jo, Joseph Gilbert, Jr. *Education:* Columbia University, B.A. (with honors), 1947, M.A., 1948. *Home:* 12 Andover Pl., Huntington, N.Y. 11743. *Agent:* Charlotte Sheedy Literary Agency, Inc., 145 West 86th St., New York, N.Y. 10024. *Office:* Research Institute of America, 589 Fifth Ave., New York, N.Y. 10017.

CAREER: Partner of Writing-Editing Services, Inc., 1946; managing editor of *Stateside,* 1947; Cornell University, Ithaca, N.Y., instructor in English, 1948-49; Allyn & Bacon, Inc., New York City, sales representative, 1949-52; sales representative of National Cash Register Co., 1952-53; J. K. Smit & Sons (manufacturers of industrial diamond products), Murray Hill, N.J., sales representative, 1953-54; Home Life Insurance Co., New York City, assistant to vice-president of sales promotion, 1954-56; Research Institute of America, New York City, editor, 1956-65. managing editor of sales and marketing division, 1965-75, senior editor, 1975-82; free-lance writer, 1983—. Past member of Long Island Council for Great Books; past chairman of Huntington Commitee for Great Books. *Military service:* U.S. Army Air Forces, 1943-45; became second lieutenant. *Awards, honors:* Award of excellence for group promotion from Life Insurance Advertisers Association, 1955.

WRITINGS: (Editor of revision with Albert H. Morehead, William Birmingham, and others) *Illustrated World Encyclopedia,* Bobley, 1965; (with Robert Weisselberg) *The Executive Strategist: An Armchair Guide to Scientific Decision-Making,* McGraw, 1969; *The Chrysanthemum Garden* (novel), Simon & Schuster, 1981.

WORK IN PROGRESS: A novel, *Home by Seven.*

*   *   *

COX, William E(dwin), Jr. 1930-

PERSONAL: Born February 20, 1930, in Miami, Fla.; son of William Edwin (a painter) and Bessie M. Cox; married Barbara Belknap (a speech therapist), May 15, 1955; children: W. Lyle, Brian G. *Education:* University of Florida, B.S.B.A., 1952; University of Michigan, M.B.A., 1957, Ph.D., 1963. *Home:* 448 Bentleyville Rd., Chagrin Falls, Ohio 44022.

CAREER: Procter & Gamble Co., Cincinnati, Ohio, management trainee, 1954-56; Case Western Reserve University, Cleveland, Ohio, began as assistant professor, 1958, became

professor of marketing, 1967, served as department chairman, beginning in 1968. Consultant to industry, commerce, and government. *Military service:* U.S. Army, 1952-54; became first lieutenant. *Member:* American Marketing Association, American Economic Association, American Statistical Association, Institute of Management Sciences.

WRITINGS: Industrial Marketing Research, Wiley, 1979. Contributor to business and marketing journals.

AVOCATIONAL INTERESTS: Sports (especially golf and tennis), European travel.

*   *   *

CRAFTS, Roger Conant 1911-

PERSONAL: Born January 26, 1911, in Lewiston, Me.; married Margaret Findley, August 10, 1938; children: Roger C., Susan Dean. *Education:* Received B.S. from Bates College and Ph.D. from Columbia University. *Home:* 3230 Daytona Ave., Cincinnati, Ohio 45211.

CAREER: Bates College, Lewiston, Me., teaching assistant in biology department, 1931-33; Columbia University College of Medicine, New York, N.Y., research assistant in department of anatomy, 1934-39, instructor in gross anatomy, 1939-40, university research fellow, 1940-41; Boston University School of Medicine, Boston, Mass., instructor, 1941-43, assistant professor, 1943-49, associate professor of anatomy, 1949-50; University of Cincinnati College of Medicine, Cincinnati, Ohio, Francis Brunning Professor of Anatomy, 1950-81, director of anatomy department, 1950-79, Francis Brunning Professor Emeritus of Anatomy, 1981—. Delegate to Ohio State House Conference on Education, 1960. Fellow of graduate school of University of Cincinnati, 1961. Member of board of management of Western Hills branch of Young Men's Christian Association, 1955-59; member of board of trustees of Cincinnati School Foundation, 1957-63, WCET, 1968—, and St. James Day Care Center, 1972-76; member of Citizens School Committee, 1967-77. Speaker at University of Dayton, University of Tennessee, Ohio State Medical Association, American Rhinological Association, American Association of Anatomists, Indiana University School of Medicine, University of North Dakota, and Medical College of Virginia. Consultant to National Institutes of Health and East Tennessee State University.

MEMBER: American Association of Anatomists (chairman of nominating committee, 1965-66, member of nominating committee, 1979), American Association for the Advancement of Science (fellow), Association of American Medical Colleges, Midwest Anatomist Association (treasurer, 1966), Midwest-Great Plains Association of the American Medical Colleges (representative to council of faculties, 1969-72; vice-chairman, 1969; chairman, 1970), Association of Anatomy Chairmen (chairman of nominating committee, 1977), Westwood Civic Association (chairman of education committee, 1978-81), Cincinnatus Association (member of education panel, 1969—; chairman, 1972-74; executive committee, 1975-77). *Awards, honors:* Silver medallion from Columbia University College of Physicians and Surgeons, 1967, in recognition of achievements that have contributed to the status of the university.

WRITINGS: (With James G. Wilson) *A Guide to Regional Dissection: Study of the Human Body,* J. W. Edwards, 1954, 4th edition (with Robert T. Binhammer) published as *A Guide to a Regional Dissection and Study of the Human Body,* Wiley, 1979; (contributor) L.J.A. DiDio, editor, *Synopsis of Anatomy,* C. V. Macky, 1970; *A Textbook of Human Anatomy,* Ronald, 1966, 2nd edition, Wiley, 1979; (contributor) David Danforth, editor, *A Textbook of Obstetrics and Gynecology*, Lippincott, 1982. Contributor to journals, including *Journal of Medical Education, Cincinnati Journal of Medicine, Endocrinology, American Journal of Physiology, Journal of Laboratory and Clinical Medicine, American Journal of Anatomy, Anatomical Record,* and *American Journal of Clinical Nutrition.* Associate editor of *American Journal of Anatomy,* 1968-69.

WORK IN PROGRESS: A book tentatively titled *The Anatomy of Your Ailments.*

SIDELIGHTS: Crafts told *CA:* ''I have devoted my life to teaching the gross anatomy of the human body to medical students and to contributing to our knowledge of anatomy, mainly in the relation between the endocrine glands and blood cell development. My goal has always been to help students learn anatomy in a fashion that would allow them to remember it for a lifetime of curing the ailments of their patients. My writing has this same goal. My textbook and guide actually teach the subject rather than serving as mere compilations of facts. My work in progress will endeavor to provide patients an understanding of their ailments. The task is great; it is difficult to describe the body in terms comprehensible to a lay person without insulting his or her intelligence.''

*   *   *

CRAIK, Thomas Wallace   1927-

PERSONAL: Born April 17, 1927, in Warrington, England; son of Thomas (a licensee) and Ada (a teacher; maiden name, Atherton) Craik; married Wendy Ann Sowter, August 25, 1955 (divorced, 1975); children: Roger James. *Education:* Christ's College, Cambridge, B.A., 1948, M.A., 1952, Ph.D., 1952. *Residence:* Durham, England. *Office:* Department of English, University of Durham, Elvet Riverside, New Elvet, Durham DH1, 3JT, England.

CAREER: University of Leicester, Leicester, England, assistant lecturer, 1953-55, lecturer in English, 1955-65; University of Aberdeen, Aberdeen, Scotland, lecturer, 1965-67, senior lecturer in English, 1967-73; University of Dundee, Dundee, Scotland, professor of English, 1973-77; University of Durham, Durham, England, professor of English, 1977—. Visiting lecturer at Queens College of the City of New York (now of the City University of New York), 1958-59; British Academy Shakespeare Lecturer, 1979. *Member:* International Shakespeare Association, International Association of University Professors of English.

WRITINGS: The Tudor Interlude: Stage, Costume, and Acting, Leicester University Press, 1958, 3rd edition, 1967; *The Comic Tales of Chaucer,* Methuen, 1963.

Editor: Philip Massinger, *The City Madam,* Benn, 1964; Massinger, *A New Way to Pay Old Debts,* Benn, 1964, 2nd edition, 1981; *Selected Poetry and Prose of Sir Philip Sidney,* Methuen, 1965; Christopher Marlowe, *The Jew of Malta,* Benn, 1966, 2nd edition, 1978; *Minor Elizabethan Tragedies,* Dent, 1974; (with J. M. Lothian) William Shakespeare, *Twelfth Night,* Methuen, 1975, 2nd edition, 1977.

General editor of *Revels History of Drama in English,* Methuen, Volume II (and contributor): *1500-1576,* 1980, Volume III: *1576-1613,* 1975; Volume V: *1660-1750,* 1976; Volume VI: *1750-1880,* 1975; Volume VII: *1880 to the Present,* 1978; Volume VIII: *American Drama,* 1978.

Contributor to *Stratford-upon-Avon-Studies* (collected essays) Volume IX: *Elizabethan Theatre,* 1966, and Volume XVI: *Medieval Drama,* 1973.

Contributor to academic periodicals, including *Modern Language Review, Notes and Queries, Renaissance Drama, Review of English Studies, Scrutiny,* and *Times Literary Supplement.*

WORK IN PROGRESS: Editing Francis Beaumont's and John Fletcher's *The Maid's Tragedy,* publication by Manchester University Press expected in 1984; editing Shakespeare's *The Merry Wives of Windsor,* publication by Clarendon Press expected in 1988.

SIDELIGHTS: Craik told *CA:* ''In *The Tudor Interlude* I sought to recreate for modern readers the effect that these sixteenth-century plays must have had when they were performed, and most of my later work on dramatic literature has been concerned with this practical aspect. I have had nearly thirty years' experience of acting and directing with academic groups, and have found this useful. I am also interested in textual emendation: most plays contain plenty of errors, not all of which have yet been corrected by editors. I expect that any future work I do will be in the editing of Tudor and Stuart drama.''

BIOGRAPHICAL/CRITICAL SOURCES: Times Literary Supplement, January 12, 1967, September 11, 1981.

*   *   *

CRASE, Douglas   1944-

PERSONAL: Born July 5, 1944, in Battle Creek, Mich.; son of Norman Ward (a farmer) and Margaret (Walmsley) Crase; divorced, 1971. *Education:* Princeton University, A.B., 1966; graduate study at University of Michigan, 1966-69. *Residence:* New York, N.Y. *Address:* c/o Little, Brown & Co., 34 Beacon St., Boston, Mass. 02106.

CAREER: Levin-for-Governor Committee, Detroit, Mich., speechwriter, 1970; W. B. Doner (advertising agency), Detroit, copywriter, 1971; free-lance speechwriter and scriptwriter, 1972—. Visiting lecturer in English at University of Rochester, 1976-77. *Awards, honors:* Newcomers Prize from *Poetry Now* (magazine), 1978, for poetry; Ingram Merrill Foundation Award, 1979; *The Revisionist* was nominated for a National Book Critics Circle Award in poetry, 1981.

WRITINGS: The Revisionist (poems), Little, Brown, 1981.

Other writings: (Contributor) David Lehman, editor, *Beyond Amazement: New Essays on John Ashbery,* Cornell University Press, 1980.

WORK IN PROGRESS: Poems.

SIDELIGHTS: In his review of *The Revisionist,* Christopher Cox held that Douglas Crase ''may be the most important poet of his generation.'' Cox was joined by other critics and writers, among them poets John Ashbery and David Lehman, who considered the book a remarkable debut. Ashbery, winner of the Pulitzer Prize in poetry, asserted that ''*The Revisionist* is a first book of poetry (that) rivals any produced by a younger American poet in the last decade,'' and Lehman contended, ''Crase is that rarest of young poets, he who seems able to give us tomorrow's poetry today.'' According to these and other reviewers, the success and importance of the book can be found in its subject, its richness of style, and its deft execution.

The subject of *The Revisionist* is America, particularly its history and how the imagination might restore the country to its native beauty. Phoebe Pettingell wrote in the *New Leader* about the kind of restoration Crase envisions: ''In one section of the long title poem, he catalogues his methods for righting sundry wrongs: Asphalt parking lots will be torn up to restore lost buildings, interstates scribbled across the plains will be erased, foreign trees (and their blights, like Dutch elm disease) will be deported, and European art treasures will be sold to buy back American paintings in museums abroad.'' In his *Soho News* review, Cox commented on the motive behind such a project: ''Revisionism for [Crase] is restoring the world in a way that makes affirmation possible. . . . As Crase says, 'Everything allows itself to be seen again in the focus of its possibilities.'''

Among the landscapes and cities Crase visits in his poems is a place of special meaning to the poet: Rochester, New York. Before his arrival in the city in 1971, Crase was intent on a political career. ''I wanted to change American history,'' he told Stephen Wigler of the *Rochester Democrat and Chronicle*. In 1969 he dropped out of law school to write speeches for state Senator Sander Levin, a Democratic candidate for Michigan governor. After the campaign failed and his marriage ended in divorce, however, Crase moved to Rochester and went to work as a speechwriter for the Eastman Kodak Company. ''I've often thought that writing poetry now represents what I wasn't able to do as a politician,'' he related to Cox. ''I guess that's one of the imports of *The Revisionist*. When you're writing a poem, you can make the world any way you want to.''

Crase's three years in Rochester were crucial to his development as a poet. Prior to 1971 he had written only occasional verse, what he called ''sappy stuff filled with falling leaves and lost love you put in a drawer.'' Then he met Rochester-born John Ashbery. Crase commented: ''Ashbery is my inspiration. I feel about him the way Dante felt about Virgil. . . . It wasn't until then that I felt I could write poetry. Here was this real live person who actually did it. And he didn't have horns.'' He adopted Ashbery's longer, prosier line and began incorporating the formal language he was using as a speechwriter at Kodak. Although critics perceive in Crase's poems the influence of many American poets, Crase likes to say that ''one of the main influences on my poetry has been the Kodak Co.''

In his review of *The Revisionist*, Lehman focused on the strength of Crase's poetic talent. ''What distinguishes Crase's initial volume from nearly all competitors,'' he wrote, ''is its (and his) enormous intelligence—a virtue which, among contemporary poets and critics, is more honored in the breach than the observance. Add to this Crase's splendid powers of rhetoric, his oratory rich in syllables that roll off the tongue in grape-like clusters. The result is mastery: of voice, of tone, and of a subject worthy of a poet's ambition.''

Charles Molesworth of the *New York Times Book Review* also found much to praise in Crase's poetry: ''Mr. Crase has what it usually takes several books to achieve: an important subject; a consistent and supple attitude toward it; and a style rich enough to answer to it. . . . His attitude is probing, tenacious, and he conveys it without too much cynicism or weariness and with an occasional sprightliness. Stylistically, his work uses a free loose verse that comes close to musical prose. Like Merrill's and Ashbery's, his writing argues sinuously. . . . He has written on a large scale, and with considerable authority.''

Crase told *CA:* ''For me, right now, the liveliest poetry is an act of citizenship. Not in the 'good citizen' sense, because a poem is by nature seditious or seductive in its argument. It was said by a poet, who was known for putting us on, that poetry makes nothing happen. Of course, poetry settles nothing, but this is precisely okay; it's the great accomplishment

of a poem to keep even one possibility intact. There are enough vandals in the world.''

BIOGRAPHICAL/CRITICAL SOURCES: Rochester Democrat and Chronicle, May 10, 1981; *New Leader,* June 1, 1981; *Washington Post Book World,* June 7, 1981; *Soho News,* July 1, 1981; *New York Times Book Review,* August 23, 1981; *Newsday,* December 13, 1981.

—Sketch by B. Hal May

*   *   *

CRAWFORD, Jerry L(eroy) 1934-

PERSONAL: Born August 20, 1934, in Whittemore, Iowa; son of Roy B. and Elizabeth (Riebhoff) Crawford; married Patricia L. Bunn, June 7, 1956; children: Mitchell L., Vali E., Keli A. *Education:* Drake University, B.F.A., 1956; Stanford University, M.A., 1957; University of Iowa, Ph.D., 1964. *Politics:* Democrat. *Religion:* Protestant. *Home:* 1916 Bonita Ave., Las Vegas, Nev. 89104. *Agent:* Robert A. Freedman, Harold Freedman, Brandt & Brandt Literary Agents, Inc., 1501 Broadway, New York, N.Y. 10036. *Office:* Department of Theatre Arts, University of Nevada, Las Vegas, Nev. 89154.

CAREER: University of Nevada, Las Vegas, instructor, 1962-64, assistant professor, 1964-65, associate professor, 1965, professor of theatre arts, 1965—, dean of faculty, 1965-68, chairman of department of speech and drama, 1968-70 and 1980-81. Actor and director. *Military service:* U.S. Army, 1957-59. *Member:* American Theatre Association, Phi Kappa Phi. *Awards, honors:* Best new play award from Southeastern Theatre Conference, 1974, for ''The Auction Tomorrow''; gold medallion from American Oil Co., 1977 and 1979, for outstanding service to the American College Theatre Festival; Governor's Award for outstanding arts educator in Nevada, 1982.

WRITINGS: (With Joan Snyder) *Acting: In Person and in Style,* W. C. Brown, 1976, 3rd edition (sole author), 1983.

Plays: ''The Dark Roots'' (three-act), first produced in Iowa City, Iowa, at University of Iowa Theatre, spring, 1961; ''Half a Pound of Tea'' (three-act), first produced in Iowa City at University of Iowa Theatre, December, 1963; ''The Look of Eagles'' (three-act), first produced in Burlington, Vt., at University of Vermont Theatre, spring, 1965; ''The Auction Tomorrow'' (two-act), first produced in Las Vegas, Nev., at Judy Bayley Summer Repertory Theater, July, 1976; ''The Passing of Corky Brewster'' (one-act), first produced in New York City at Circle Repertory Company, February, 1977; ''Halftime at the Superbowl'' (one-act), first produced in New York City at Actors Studio, January, 1977; ''Those Were the Days They Gave Babies Away With Half a Pound of Tea'' (three-act), first produced in Las Vegas at Meadows Playhouse, April, 1978; ''The Last President'' (two-act), first produced as a staged professional reading in New York City at St. Clement's Theatre, 1978, produced in Las Vegas at University of Nevada, fall, 1982; ''Dance for Rain, Redmen, That Was Number Ninety-Nine'' (one-act; first produced in Fullerton, Calif., at California State University, fall, 1982), published in *Dramatics,* April/May, 1982. Also author of one-act plays ''Revelation at the 'Y,''' ''Facelifting at St. Viators,'' and ''The Palomino Caper.''

Contributor to theatre journals.

WORK IN PROGRESS: A book, *Indirecting: Directing for Actor Creativity,* for Allyn & Bacon; a two-act play, ''The Third Desire.''

SIDELIGHTS: Crawford told *CA:* "The forms of my plays are usually a rich mix of the comic with the serious and in usually realistic styles. My subjects and themes tend to focus on family unity, professional sports and athletics, and the conflicts of passion versus public responsibility. A rural childhood in Iowa with a close-knit family and a solid marriage spanning over a quarter century dominately influenced my writing. A deep love for baseball and sports also influenced my life and work. A major heart attack in 1981 resulted in new directions and insights into human relations and the conflicts between private and public responsibilities. Fatherhood and the influences of three children also focus my latter work. An unusual and abiding love for the professional baseball team the Cleveland Indians marks much of my work with a unique quality. Conflicts of sexual power, political power, career drive, and religious search also figure, as does satire bearing on the factor of innocence, particularly the innocence of children or young people of school and college age prior to their subjugation to worldly experience and disillusionment. I am a very 'American' author with particular strength in balancing the serious with the comic."

* * *

CRAWFORD, John Richard 1932-
(J. Walker)

PERSONAL: Born August 21, 1932, in Karuizawa, Japan; U.S. citizen born abroad; son of Vernon Allen and Matsu (Wofford) Crawford; married Sylvia Jean Peresenyi, May 27, 1956; children: Jean Lee, John Allen, Mark Farel, Ellen Dee. *Education:* King College, B.A., 1953; Union Theological Seminary, Richmond, Va., M.Div., 1956; University of Aberdeen, Ph.D., 1958; postdoctoral study at University of Marburg, University of Neuchatel, and University of South Carolina. *Politics:* "Republican-leaning independent." *Home:* 100 Sunrise Ter., Black Mountain, N.C. 28711. *Office:* Division of Social Sciences, Montreat-Anderson College, Montreat, N.C. 28757.

CAREER: Ordained Presbyterian minister, 1956; Austin College, Sherman, Tex., assistant professor of religion and assistant dean of chapel, 1958-60; Universite Libre du Congo (now Universite Nationale du Zaire), Kinshasa, professor of ecclesiastical history and vice-dean of faculty of theology, 1960-69; Montreat-Anderson College, Montreat, N.C., professor of history and chairman of division of social sciences, 1970—. Founding partner of calendar publisher, MEDCOR. Visiting professor; frequent interim pastor. *Member:* International Primitive, Odd, and Curious Money Club, Southern Historical Association, Southern Association of Africanists, Blue Ridge Numismatic Association, Asheville Coin Club (president), Alston Wilkes Society. *Awards, honors:* Cited by American Numismatic Association, 1968, for contributions to numismatic studies; named outstanding educator of America, 1971 and 1972; two educational awards from American Numismatic Association.

WRITINGS: (Under pseudonym J. Walker) *Only by Thumb* (autobiography), Vantage, 1964; *A Christian and His Money,* Abingdon, 1967; *Protestant Missions in Congo, 1878-1969,* Centre d'Editions et Diffusions, 1970; *Dieu et votre argent,* Centre d'Editions et Diffusions, 1973, translation published as *God and Your Money,* Central Tanganyika Press, 1974. Contributor of more than eighty articles to magazines, including *Coin World, Eternity, Christian Life, Missiology, Journal of Presbyterian History, Numismatist, Home Life,* and *Christian Century.*

WORK IN PROGRESS: Research on the life and work of Guillaume Farel, French-born leader of the Reformation in France and Switzerland.

SIDELIGHTS: "I write either for fun," Crawford commented, "or when I feel there is something which needs saying. My life is full and rich as a professor in the United States and abroad, a sometime-pastor, tree farmer, landlord, and businessman. God has given me certain gifts and talents—not great, but usable—and it is my privilege to use them. I have traveled fairly extensively, living in Japan for seven years as a child, in Europe for more than three years, and in Zaire for six years."

BIOGRAPHICAL/CRITICAL SOURCES: Sandlapper, August, 1970; *World Coins,* November, 1970.

* * *

CRAWFORD, John S(herman) 1928-

PERSONAL: Born January 24, 1928, in Sunnyside, Wash.; son of Arthur Forbes (a grape grower) and Maud Ethel (Crawford) Crawford. *Education:* University of Washington, Seattle, B.A., 1954. *Politics:* "Essentially independent, but lean toward Democratic party." *Religion:* United Methodist. *Home:* 15824 75th Pl. W., Edmonds, Wash. 98020.

CAREER: U.S. Fish and Wildlife Service, Seattle, Wash., assisted on study of Columbia River system, 1955-56, field supervisor of research crews and river surveys in Alaska, 1957-58; photojournalist, outdoorsman, and writer, 1959—. Photographs have been exhibited in "The Athapaskan Peoples: Strangers of the North," a joint production of National Museum of Canada and Royal Scottish Museum, 1974. *Military service:* U.S. Marine Corps, 1946-47. U.S. Army, survival instructor with Field Medicine and Surgery Committee, 1954-55. *Member:* Cousteau Society, Sierra Club, Defenders of Wildlife, Phi Kappa Psi. *Awards, honors:* Alberta Achievement Award from provincial government of Alberta, 1978, for services to Canadian Red Cross.

WRITINGS—With own photographs: *At Home With the High Ones: Comparative Observations of North American Mountain Sheep and the Rocky Mountain Goat,* Alaska Northwest Publishing, 1974; *Wolves, Bears, and Bighorns: Wilderness Observations and Experiences of a Professional Outdoorsman,* Alaska Northwest Publishing, 1980. Contributor of articles and photographs to magazines, including *Outdoor Life, Alaska, Sunset, True, Field and Stream, National Wildlife,* and *National Geographic.*

WORK IN PROGRESS: A book of pictorial essays on the theme of wildlife adjusting to changing seasons in northern latitudes of northwestern North America, publication by Alaska Northwest Publishing expected in 1983.

SIDELIGHTS: Crawford told *CA:* "During summers as an undergraduate student, and following my military service, I worked on Pacific salmon research in Alaska, studying racial identification of salmon and their migration routes, and later worked in Washington, Oregon, and Idaho on the Columbia River system. In 1959 I made the decision to go on my own as a wildlife researcher and nature photojournalist, an endeavor which I have continued.

"My major professional concern is the preservation of wildlife and its habitat. I have a deep sense of gratitude to my parents, and feel fortunate for having had the experience of the particular time, place, and circumstances in which I grew up. Among those circumstances was the near proximity of open and unspoiled land, even semiwilderness pockets of sagebrush, native bunch grass, and canyons of basalt rock in the Horse Heaven and Rattlesnake Hills flanking the Yakima Valley. As I wrote in *Wolves, Bears, and Bighorns,* 'The motivation for the work I do now is rooted in a bone-deep love for wild country I've had since I was a small boy—and not just for northern forests and mountains, but for every natural landscape I've ever seen.'

"Another positive factor early in my life was the good fortune of having sympathetic and dedicated teachers at the three-room country school where I completed the first eight grades. Later inspirational influence came from the writings of the late great Texan J. Frank Dobie, educator, philosopher, western historian, and outdoorsman—more than from the work of any other author. I rate Walter Van Tilburg Clark's marvelously wrought story *The Indian Well* as one of the finest fictional pieces ever done on the American West. And I feel that every environmentalist—indeed, every citizen—owes a debt of gratitude to Joseph Wood Krutch for his profoundly eloquent, though inaccurately titled, essay 'Wilderness: America's Unique Possession,' from *Grand Canyon: Today and All Its Yesterdays*.

"My personal philosophy as an outdoor writer can perhaps best be summed up by quoting the last paragraph from the foreword of *Wolves, Bears, and Bighorns:* 'The overall theme of this book is, I would like to think, the appreciation of wilderness country and the wildlife that inhabits it. Of the chapters that follow, several deal with predator-prey relationships in western Canada and Alaska. More than once I've been accused of having an emotional bias in favor of predatory animals. Well, perhaps I'm guilty as charged. But I think not. To me, both the northern carnivores and their ungulate prey species are beautiful and vastly interesting animals. I went afield on these predator—prey studies and photo projects taking nothing for granted, determined to set aside preconceived notions, and to witness for myself the drama of predator-prey interaction. Rather than carrying a particular bias for predatory animals, I have the deepest sympathy for all wildlife and for the preservation of wilderness country. And I hope that is apparent in the chapters that follow.'"

Wolves, Bears, and Bighorns is an oversized book of photographs and prose descriptions of animal life in the wilderness. Robert E. Shotwell wrote in the *Broadside:* "With the author as a guide, we are allowed to share in everything from the smallest animal yawn to the most powerful battles for survival. There are very few of us who will ever witness the dramatic, sensitive encounters about which Crawford writes, but just to know that they exist, and that they can be shared so vividly through his writing is enough to start a flow of adrenalin." In her review for *Canadian Geographic* Lyn Hancock held that "Anyone with an interest in the wildlife of Alberta, British Columbia, Yukon and Alaska should read this book."

A number of reviewers focused especially on the author's approach to his subject. Anne Ruggles-Black commented in the *Journal:* "Crawford seldom allows his opinions to intrude upon the narrative; rather he describes situations and encounters. He judges no animal and leaves the firm impression that to do so would be to demean them." Similarly, Stew Lang observed in the *Victoria Times-Colonist:* "The many photos, both black-and-white and color, and the incredibly-concise text reflect the author's deep feelings and understanding of the subject. He doesn't view the wilderness and its inhabitants through Disney-like blinkers, but sees the underlying principles and harmony through clear, unbiased eyes." And in Hancock's opinion, Crawford "combines the prose of the scientist's accurate and detailed observations with the poetry of the imaginative nature writer. He paints, in vivid words and superb pictures, both the look and the feeling of animal interactions."

BIOGRAPHICAL/CRITICAL SOURCES: Victoria Times-Colonist (Victoria, B.C.), December 5, 1980; *Canadian Geographic,* February-March, 1981; *Broadside,* March 18, 1981; *Journal* (North American Wolf Society), spring, 1981.

CRAWFORD, William P(atrick) 1922-

PERSONAL: Born October 4, 1922, in San Francisco, Calif.; son of Lorcan Felim (a shipmaster) and Hannah (Sullivan) Crawford; married Jane Crawford, June 21, 1949 (died January 30, 1963); married Dorothy Donoghue, July 3, 1965; children: Patricia, Thomas, John, Christine, Andrew, Daniel, Joseph, Robert, Timothy, James, Margaret, Catherine, William. *Education:* Attended University of Santa Clara, 1939-41; University of Southern California, B.A., 1949, J.D., 1949. *Politics:* Democrat. *Religion:* Roman Catholic. *Home:* 1557 White Oak Way, San Carlos, Calif. 94070. *Office:* Crawford Nautical Center, Agriculture Building, San Francisco, Calif. 94109.

CAREER: Associated with Weyerhaeuser Steamship Co., San Francisco, Calif., Mississippi Shipping Co., New Orleans, La., and U.S. Maritime Service, Washington, D.C., 1941-46, and with Crawford Nautical School, Los Angeles, Calif.; attorney in private law practice in Long Beach, Calif.; Crawford Nautical Center, San Francisco, Calif., director, 1958—. Member of National Transportation Board, 1979—. *Member:* Authors Guild, Institute of Navigation, Institute of Navigation (England).

WRITINGS: Mariner's Rules of the Road (pictorial display), Mariner Publications, 1960; *Mariner's Notebook,* CBS Publications, 1960, 5th edition, Norton, 1971; *Mariner's Celestial Navigation,* Norton, 1972; *Sea Marine Atlas,* CBS Publications, 1972, 2nd edition, Norton, 1979; *Boatowner's Legal Guide,* CBS Publications, 1975; *Mariner's Weather,* Norton, 1979.

WORK IN PROGRESS: A textbook tentatively titled *Mariner's Rules of the Road,* publication by Norton expected in 1982.

SIDELIGHTS: Crawford wrote: "My major activity is preparing maritime works, emphasizing navigation, marine electronics, and meteorology, 'rules of the road,' and related subjects that are relevant to the operation of all vessels of all sizes on any waters.

"Crawford Nautical Center is a family enterprise, founded in 1923 by my uncle, Captain John T. Sullivan, in New Orleans. It was carried forward by my father to the point where I took over. Seafaring has been our family affair for an unbroken five or so generations. Of my mother's seven brothers, all but two followed the sea. The wayward ones entered politics and real estate. I also temperarily interrupted the chain for ten years of admiralty law practice. Of my nine sons, two are now senior deck officers and another two are going to sea between bouts of education. The remaining five must age some before heeding the call.

"In the United Kingdom of my parents' day, a ship's officer followed a high calling. We seem to want to perpetuate that view. Certainly, I found it a most rewarding occupation. It combines the need for expertise with extreme variety and a highly effective means to withdraw into one's thoughts while still a part of a society. My present occupation, teaching aspiring deck officers, brings vicarious enjoyment of those benefits. And I couldn't find a better student body. In our classes there is sufficient immersion in technical matters to discourage pomposity, yet such an atmosphere of literally worldwide experience as to prevent much tunnel vision. A city such as San Francisco is considered cosmopolitan because it brings together so many cultures. I like to feel that my seafaring students are each even more so since within each I can see the influence of a wider kaleidoscope. I very much love my work with these people and consider myself a sort of conduit to channel their experience into technical works and, soon, I hope, on broader tracks.

"As far as technical writing is concerned, I have one conscious aim. The technical material must approach validity, of course, but sea lore must also be preserved. No matter how many electrons go aboard and in no matter how many modules, nature will see to it that the adventure remains. My aim is to try to give nature a hand."

* * *

CRAWLEY, Gerard M(arcus)   1938-

PERSONAL: Born April 10, 1938, in Airdrie, Scotland; came to the United States in 1961; son of Patrick and Elizabeth (Drummond) Crawley; married Margaret McInerney (a child care specialist), May 20, 1961; children: Janine, Kathryn, Peter, Anne. *Education:* University of Melbourne, B.Sc., 1959, M.Sc., 1961; Princeton University, Ph.D., 1965. *Home:* 157 Kedzie Dr., East Lansing, Mich. 48823. *Office:* Department of Physics, Michigan State University, East Lansing, Mich. 48823.

CAREER: Michigan State University, East Lansing, assistant professor, 1968-70, associate professor, 1970-74, professor of physics, 1974—. Visiting fellow at Australian National University, 1974-75; program officer for National Science Foundation, 1975-76. *Member:* American Physical Society. *Awards, honors:* Fulbright scholarship, 1961-66; Ford Foundation fellowship, 1961-62; James Queen fellowship for Princeton University, 1964-65; Queen Elizabeth II fellowship, 1966-68.

WRITINGS: (Editor with S. M. Austin) *The Two Body Force in Nuclei,* Plenum, 1969; *Energy,* Macmillan, 1975. Contributor of about sixty articles to physics journals.

* * *

CREMER, Robert Wyndham Ketton
See KETTON-CREMER, Robert Wyndham

* * *

CROSS, Ira Brown   1880-1977

OBITUARY NOTICE: Born December 1, 1880, in Decatur, Ill.; died March 24, 1977. Economist, educator, editor, and author. Cross taught economics at Stanford University from 1909 to 1914 and at the University of California from 1914 to his retirement in 1951. In addition he wrote book reviews for the *San Francisco Bulletin* for two years and served for one year as assistant editor of *Coast Banker.* He was vice-president of the American Economic Association in 1926. An enthusiast of horticultural hybridizing, Cross won the highest award of the National Chrysanthemum Society in 1963. Among his publications are *A History of the Labor Movement in California* and *Money and Banking.* He edited *Frank Roney: An Autobiography,* which was reprinted in 1976. Obituaries and other sources: *Time,* June 25, 1951; *Who Was Who Among North American Authors, 1921-1939,* Gale, 1976; *International Who's Who,* Europa, 1978.

* * *

CROUCH, Tom D.   1944-

PERSONAL: Born February 28, 1944, in Dayton, Ohio; son of Harald Day (an electrician) and Joan (Dragoo) Crouch; married Anne Gochenouer (a clerk), November 12, 1963; children:

Bruce, Abigail, Nathan. *Education:* Ohio University, B.A., 1966; Miami University, M.A., 1968; Ohio State University, Ph.D., 1976. *Home:* 9555 Blake Ln., Fairfax, Va. 20331. *Office:* Department of Aeronautics, National Air and Space Museum, Smithsonian Institution, Washington, D.C. 20560.

CAREER: National Air and Space Museum, Smithsonian Institution, Washington, D.C., curator of aeronautics, 1974—; University of Maryland at College Park, lecturer on the history of technology, 1976—. *Member:* American Institute of Aeronautics and Astronautics (member of history committee), American Astronautical Society (member of history committee). *Awards, honors:* American Institute of Aeronautics and Astronautics book award for history, 1976, for *A Dream of Wings: Americans and the Airplane, 1875-1905;* Aerospace Writers Association literary award, 1980, for *Apollo: Ten Years Since Tranquility Base.*

WRITINGS: The Giant Leap: A Chronology of Ohio Aerospace Events and Personalities, Ohio Historical Society, 1970; *Charles A. Lindbergh: An American Life,* Smithsonian Institution Press, 1977; (with Richard Hallion) *Apollo: Ten Years Since Tranquility Base,* Smithsonian Institution Press, 1979; *A Dream of Wings: Americans and the Airplane, 1875-1905,* Norton, 1981.

WORK IN PROGRESS: The Eagle Aloft: Two Centuries of Ballooning in America, publication by the Smithsonian Institution Press expected in 1984.

SIDELIGHTS: Crouch's *A Dream of Wings* is about the American pioneers of flight. Realizing that the subject of early aviation often conjures up only visions of Orville and Wilbur Wright at Kitty Hawk, Crouch focuses his attention on the pioneers of aeronautics—the men whose engineering and experience, failures and triumphs, allowed the Wrights to accomplish the first successful flight of a motor-powered vehicle.

Among those Crouch credits as pioneers of aviation is Samuel Pierpont Langley, after whom Langley Air Force Base is named. In the late 1800's Langley, then head of the Smithsonian Institution, was diligently working on his unmanned, steam-powered aircraft called the "aerodrome," which could fly three-fourths of a mile. Langley hoped that one day the aircraft would be a multi-passenger means of locomotion. Although that particular dream was not realized, Langley nevertheless persevered, and was the first aviator to seek government funding of his project.

Another early aeronaut was Octave Chanute, a railroad builder who flew gliders at his test sight over sand dunes near Lake Michigan. According to Crouch, Chanute proposed the addition of a propeller and motor to gliders in 1894. And Augustus Moore Herring, a glider pilot, created hang gliders powered by stabilizing tails. But it was the Wright brothers who jointly won the race to build and fly the first true airplane.

Robert Buckhorn of the *Washington Post* called *Dream Wings* "a fast-moving blend of scholarship and trivia about a group of colorful characters."

Crouch told *CA:* "Most of my work is derived from a basic attempt to understand the way in which technology has interacted with other social forces to shape society. For me, the history of flight is a means of studying deeper questions involving the response of man to machines."

BIOGRAPHICAL/CRITICAL SOURCES: Washington Post, January 31, 1981.

CROUCH, Winston Winford 1907-

BRIEF ENTRY: Born July 4, 1907, in Vandalia, Ill. American political scientist, educator, and author. Crouch taught at the University of California, Los Angeles, from 1936 to 1975; since 1975 he has been emeritus professor of political science. He was a Fulbright fellow in India in 1954. Crouch wrote *State and Local Government in California* (University of California Press, 1952), *Agricultural Cities: Paradoxes in Politics of a Metropolis* (Department of Political Science, University of California, Los Angeles, 1964), *Employer-Employee Relations in Council-Manager Cities* (International City Managers' Association, 1968), *Guide for Modern Personnel Commissions* (International Personnel Management Association, 1972), and *Organized Civil Servants: Public Employer-Employee Relations in California* (University of California Press, 1978). He also edited *Local Government Personnel Administration* (International City Management Association, 1976). *Address:* 1035 Anoka Pl., Pacific Palisades, Calif. 90272. *Biographical/critical sources: Who's Who in America,* 40th edition, Marquis, 1978; *Los Angeles Times,* April 2, 1979.

* * *

CROWLEY, Raymond 1895-1982

OBITUARY NOTICE: Born in 1895; died after a long illness, April 6, 1982, in St. Louis, Mo. Journalist and editor. After working for a time as a reporter for the *Minneapolis Journal,* Crowley became a copy editor for the *St. Louis Post-Dispatch* in 1922. During his forty-year career at that newspaper, he held several positions, serving as city editor from 1938 to 1951 and as managing editor from 1951 to his retirement in 1962. During Crowley's tenure as city editor, the *St. Louis Post-Dispatch* won three Pulitzer Prizes for reports on mining hazards, on a scandal involving state payoffs to press leaders in Illinois, and on corruption in the Internal Revenue Bureau (now the Internal Revenue Service). Obituaries and other sources: *New York Times,* April 10, 1982.

* * *

CRUD
See CRUMB, R(obert)

* * *

CRUMARUMS
See CRUMB, R(obert)

* * *

CRUMB, R(obert) 1943-
(Crud, Crumarums, Crumbum, Crumski, Crum the Bum, Crunk, Crustt, R. Cum, Steve Ditcum, El Crummo, Grubb, Grunge, Krumb, Krumwitz, Scum, Little Bobby Scumbag, R. Scrum)

PERSONAL: Born August 30, 1943, in Philadelphia, Pa.; son of a career marine; married wife, Dana, 1964; children: Jesse. *Education:* Attended schools in Philadelphia, Pa., and Milford, Del. *Residence:* Winters, Calif.

CAREER: American Greeting Card Co., Cleveland, Ohio, artist, 1962-68; artist for Topps Co., New York, N.Y.; cartoonist. Free-lance portrait artist in Atlantic City, N.J.

WRITINGS—Cartoons; self-illustrated: *R. Crumb's 'The Yum Yum Book'* (cartoon novel), c. 1963, Scrimshaw Press, 1975;

(under pseudonyms Crumarums, R. Cum, and R. Scrum; with others) *Snatch,* three issues, Apex Novelty Co., 1968; *Head Comix,* Viking, 1968; *Fritz the Cat,* Ballantine, 1968, reprinted as *Fritz the Cat: Three Big Stories,* 1969; *Despair,* Print Mint, 1969; (with S. Clay Wilson) *Jiz Comics,* Apex Novelty Co., 1970; *Uneeda,* Print Mint, 1970; *Uneeda Comix: The Artistic Comic!,* Frank H. Fleer, 1970; *XYZ Comics,* Krupp Comic Works, 1972; *Crumbland et autres pecadilles,* Kesselring, 1975; *R. Crumb's Carloads o' Comics: An Anthology of Choice Strips and Stories, 1968 to 1976—and Including a Brand-New Fourteen Page Story,* introduction by Harvey Kurtzman, Belier, 1976; *The Complete Fritz the Cat,* Belier, 1978; *R. Crumb's Sketchbook: November 1974 to January 1978,* Zweitausendeeins, 1978.

Cartoon series: (With others) "Zap Comix" series; published by Print Mint, except as noted: *Zap No. 0,* 1967; . . . *No. 1,* Apex Novelty Co., 1967; . . . *No. 2,* Moe Moskowitz; . . . *No. 3;* . . . *No. 4,* 1969; . . . *No. 5;* . . . *No. 6;* . . . *No. 7.*

Contributor: *Bijou Funnies No. 3,* Bijou Publishing Empire, 1969; *Hydrogen Bomb and Biochemical Warfare Funnies,* Ripp Off Press, 1970. Also contributor to comic books, magazines, and newspapers, including *Motor City Comics, Home Grown Funnies, Help!, Yarrowstalk, East Village Other, Big Ass, Cavalier, Us, Playboy,* and *Los Angeles Free Press* (contributions to these and other publications have appeared under various pseudonyms, including Crumarums, Crumbum, Crumski, Crud, Crum the Bum, Crunk, Crustt, R. Cum, Steve Ditcum, El Crummo, Grubb, Grunge, Krumb, Krumwitz, Scum, Little Bobby Scumbag, R. Scrum).

Performer and lyricist of songs for record album "R. Crumb and His Cheap Suit Serenaders," Blue Goose, 1974.

SIDELIGHTS: Robert Crumb first started as a cartoonist at the age of six when he began drawing comic books with his older brother Charles. Since then he has produced some of the most controversial works in the history of comic-book art, and his cartoons have been condemned as obscene as well as hailed as works of genius. Noted for ridiculing the inhibitions and priorities of middle-class America, Crumb's cartoons are often sexually explicit and graphic in their depiction of violence. In the early 1970's his *Zap Comix No. 4* and his "Snatch" series were the subject of obscenity trials and were removed from circulation on both the East and West coasts. But, defends editor Susan Goodrick in *The Apex Treasury of Underground Comics,* "the violence and sexual fantasies in his work are not pornography; they are an attack on the 'straight' culture's dictum that sex and anger are to be kept in tight rein at all costs." Cartoonist Foolbert Sturgeon, quoted in Mark James Estren's *A History of Underground Comics,* shares Goodrick's view. He contends: "Crumb is important as an artist who makes current pressures and feelings expressible. . . . That's bound to be important—probably more important really than . . . the hotshot respectable novelists as an influence." According to *New York Times Magazine* reporter Thomas Maremaa, "Whatever the verdict, Crumb's work has nevertheless established him as the most important underground cartoonist—and, by extension, social satirist—in America today."

Settling in San Francisco's Haight-Ashbury district in 1966, then considered the center of the "hippie" movement in America, Crumb found publication easily in the underground newspapers flourishing in the area. His early works, including the "Zap Comix" series, published beginning in 1967, have been credited with rejuvenating "the American comic avant-garde by returning the art to its roots," commented Maremaa. "Original American comic strips . . . were daring and innovative, the 'head' comics of their day. In these comics, social satire and even vulgarity were accepted as givens; cartoonists reveled in the outrageous." Sparing no feelings, Crumb revived the genre, and his creations "have become recognized as archetypal American grotesques," Maremaa opined. In the process "Crumb's work has had a revolutionary effect on the comic-book industry as a whole by inspiring 'straight' comics to become more relevant."

Although many Crumb characters such as Angelfood McSpade, a super sex symbol who represents the hidden desires of white civilization, and Whiteman, a stereotypical uptight bourgeois businessman, are parodies of repressed middle-class thinking and hangups, the cartoonist's barbs have not been limited to the establishment. Crumb's work also targets the absurdities of the counterculture he represents. Among Crumb's most celebrated characters are Mr. Natural, a capitalistic guru, and his bumbling disciple, Flakey Foont. Loosely based on Master Subramuniya of San Francisco's Himalayan Academy, by whom Crumb believed many of his friends were being duped, Mr. Natural is essentially a con-man. "A horny old man with a bald head and long flowing whiskers," Mr. Natural, explains Arthur Asa Berger in his book *The Comic-Stripped American,* "is a fake and his disciple Flakey is a fool." "In fact," Berger continues, "Mr. Natural seems to have contempt for Flakey and all that he stands for." And Foont is characterized as a hopelessly repressed city-dweller seeking easy solutions to the world's most complex problems. Although he is repeatedly used and abused by Mr. Natural, Foont is never disillusioned.

In 1968 Crumb became the first underground cartoonist to have his work published in what the hippie counterculture referred to as the "straight" publishing world. A collection of the cartoonist's early comic strips plus an original story, "Fritz the Cat," were brought out in book form as *Head Comix* by the Viking Press. In publishing *Head Comix* Viking exercised only moderate censorship, but after contracting Crumb for a second book based on his Fritz the Cat character, the publishing company "became so uptight about some mild sex scenes in the book that they rejected it," claimed Estren in his *A History of Underground Comics.* Even so, *Fritz the Cat* was picked up and published by Ballantine Books. "Unfortunately, the Crumb stories for the Ballantine Book weren't up to his usual work," Estren assessed, adding also that "*R. Crumb's Fritz the Cat* had poorer writing and much poorer art than almost anything else produced by Crumb." Nonetheless, the book, with its swinging, feline hero, remains one of Crumb's best-known and most popular creations.

Much of the credit for the notoriety and popularity of Crumb's "hep-cat" Fritz belongs to director-animator Ralph Bakshi and producer Steve Krantz, who brought the character to life in the movie "Fritz the Cat," the first feature-length, x-rated, animated cartoon in the history of motion pictures. The film, which was critically acclaimed and financially successful, was produced after Warner Brothers bought the rights to make movies based on the Crumb character. However, when the movie was completed, Crumb was not pleased with the finished product. "They put words into his [Fritz's] mouth that I never would have had him say," Crumb told Maremaa. "It was *not* my movie," he insisted. "I had nothing to do with it. They just used a couple of my stories. But a lot of people seem to think I was involved. That bothers me." Shortly after the film's national release in 1972, Crumb issued a statement denying any connection with the movie, and within three months he won a legal battle to have his name removed from the list of credits. "For his part," wrote Maremaa, "Bakshi was quoted as saying: 'I did it out of my love for animation, my love for Robert. . . . It's tough working with an idol. You touch a line of his stuff and it hurts a lot of people.'"

In spite of Crumb's personal disappointment in "Fritz the Cat," the fact that the movie was made at all was clearly an indication of the cartoonist's growing influence on the so-called "straight" media. Beginning with the earliest "Zap Comix," Crumb's work has had a pervasive impact on changing American mores. His revival, in the "Zap" series, of an old blues phrase from the 1930's, "Keep on truckin'," accompanied by a "series of screwball cartoon characters with tiny heads, funky old clothes and huge clodhoppers, strutting on down the street," observed Maremaa, "has become as ingrained in the collective American psyche as 'Kilroy was here.' Needless to say, it is more than a way of walking. For the generation that came of age in the middle sixties, it is a ritual affirmation, a slogan of goodwill." In Maremaa's words, "Crumb brought 'trash' art into the cultural mainstream and made it respectable."

BIOGRAPHICAL/CRITICAL SOURCES: Washington Post Book World, November 9, 1969; *New York Times,* December 19, 1969; *Journal of Popular Culture,* spring, 1970; *Playboy,* December, 1970; *New York Times Magazine,* October 1, 1972; Arthur Asa Berger, *The Comic-Stripped American,* Walker & Co., 1973; *Crawdaddy,* November, 1974; Susan Goodrick and Don Donahue, editors, *The Apex Treasury of Underground Comics,* Links Books, 1974; Mark James Estren, *A History of Underground Comics,* Straight Arrow Books, 1974; *Kirkus Reviews,* October 1, 1975; *Rolling Stone,* May 6, 1976.*

—*Sketch by Lillian S. Sims*

* * *

CRUMBUM
See CRUMB, R(obert)

* * *

CRUMSKI
See CRUMB, R(obert)

* * *

CRUM THE BUM
See CRUMB, R(obert)

* * *

CRUNK
See CRUMB, R(obert)

* * *

CRUSTT
See CRUMB, R(obert)

* * *

CULLINGFORD, Guy
See TAYLOR, Constance Lindsay

* * *

CULLMANN, Oscar 1902-

PERSONAL: Born February 25, 1902, in Strasbourg, France; son of Georges and Frederique (Mandel) Cullmann. *Education:* University of Strasbourg, D.Th., 1930; also attended Sorbonne, University of Paris. *Religion:* Protestant. *Home:* Birmannsgass 10A, Basel, Switzerland CH-4055; and rue Ravignan 20, F-75018 Paris, France.

CAREER: University of Strasbourg, Strasbourg, France, professor, 1927-38; University of Basel, Basel, Switzerland, professor of New Testament study and church history, 1938-72, alumni director, 1941-72, rector, 1968; writer, 1972—. Professor of Protestant theology at Sorbonne, University of Paris, 1951-72. Co-founder of Ecumenical Institute of Jerusalem; observer at Vatican II Council. *Member:* Institut de France (Academy Paris), British Academy, Royal Dutch Academy, Academy of Literature and Sciences (Germany). *Awards, honors:* Commander of Palmes Academiques; commander of Legion d'Honneur; cross of Romanian Pabria; Dr. Theol. from University of Lausanne, 1944, University of Manchester, 1948, University of Edinburgh, 1952, and University of Lund, 1953; Dr. Phil. from University of Basel, 1972.

WRITINGS—In English translation: *Die ersten christlichen Glaubensbekenntnisse, aus dem Franzoesischen uebersetzt,* Evangelischer Verlag, 1943, translation by J.K.S. Reid published as *The Earliest Christian Confessions,* Allenson, 1949; *Christus und de Zeit: Die urchristliche Zeit und Geschichtsauffassung,* Evangelischer Verlag, 1946, 3rd edition, EVZ Verlag, 1962, translation by Floyd V. Filson published as *Christ and Time: The Primitive Christian Conception of Time and History,* Westminster, 1950, 3rd edition, S.C.M. Press, 1962, Westminster, 1964; *Die Tauflehre des Neuen Testaments: Erwachsenen und Kindertaufe,* Zwingli-Verlag, 1948, 2nd edition, 1958, translation by Reid published as *Baptism in the New Testament,* Regnery, 1950, reprinted, Westminster, 1978.

Petrus, Juenger, Apostel, Maertyrer: Das historische und das theologische Petrusproblem, Zwingli-Verlag, 1952, 2nd edition, 1960, translation by Filson published as *Peter, Disciple, Apostle, Martyr: A Historical and Theological Study,* Westminster, 1952, 2nd edition, 1962; *Urchristentum und Gottesdienst,* 4th edition, Zwingli-Verlag, 1962, translation by A. Stewart Todd and James B. Torrance published as *Early Christian Worship,* Westminster, 1953, reprinted, 1978; *Der Staat im Neuen Testament,* Mohr, 1956, 2nd edition, 1961, translation published as *The State in the New Testament,* Scribner, 1956, revised edition, S.C.M. Press, 1963; *Immortalite de l'ame ou resurrection des morts?: Le Temoignage du Nouveau Testament,* Delachaux & Niestle, 1956, 2nd edition, 1959, translation published as *Immortality of the Soul or Resurrection of the Dead?: The Witness of the New Testament,* Epworth, 1956, Macmillan, 1958; *Die Christologie des Neuen Testaments,* Mohr, 1957, 4th edition, 1966, translation by Shirley C. Guthrie and Charles A. M. Hall published as *The Christology of the New Testament,* Westminster, 1959, revised edition, 1963; *Katholiken und Protestanten: Ein Vorschlag zur Verwirklichung christlicher Solidaritaet,* Reinhardt, 1958, translation by Joseph A. Burgess published as *Message to Catholics and Protestants,* Eerdmans, 1959 (published in England as *Catholics and Protestants: A Proposal for Realizing Christian Solidarity,* Lutterworth, 1960).

Heil als Geschichte: Heilsgeschichtliche Existenz im Neuen Testament, Mohr, 1965, 2nd edition, 1967, translation by Sidney G. Sowers published as *Salvation in History,* Harper, 1967; *Le Nouveau Testament,* Presses Universitaires de France, 1966, translation by Dennis Pardee published as *The New Testament: An Introduction for the General Reader,* Westminster, 1968; *Vatican Council II: The New Direction* (edited by James D. Hester; translated from German by Hester and others), Harper, 1968; *Jesus und die Revolutionaeren seiner Zeit: Gottesdienst, Gesellschaft, Politik,* Mohr, 1970, translation by Gareth Putnam published as *Jesus and the Revolutionaries,* Harper, 1970.

Also author of *The Early Church* (edited by A.J.B. Higgins; translated by Higgins and Stanley Godman), Westminster Press,

1956, abridged edition published as *The Early Church: Studies in Early Christian History,* 1966 (published in England as *The Early Church: Five Essays,* S.C.M. Press, 1966), and *Der johanniesche Kreis,* translation by John Bowden published as *The Johannine Circle,* Westminster Press, 1976 (published in England as *The Johannine Circle: Its Place in Judaism Among the Disciples of Jesus and in Early Christianity—A Study in the Origin of the Gospel of John,* S.C.M. Press, 1976). Co-author of *Essays on the Lord's Supper* (translated by J. G. Davies), John Knox Press, 1958.

In French: *Le Probleme litteraire et historique du roman pseudo-Clementin: Etude sur le rapport entre le gnosticisme et le judeo-christianisme,* F. Alcan, 1930; *Les Sacrements dans l'Evangile Johannique: La Vie de Jesus et le culte de l'eglise primitive,* Presses Universitaires de France, 1951; *Dieu et Cesar: Le Proces de Jesus, Saint Paul et l'autorite, l'Apocalypse et l'etat totalitaire,* Delachaux & Niestle, 1956; *La Foi et le culte de l'eglise primitive,* Delachaux & Niestle, 1963; *Etudes de theologie biblique,* Delachaux & Niestle, 1968; *Des Sources de l'Evangile a la formation de la theologie chretienne,* Delachaux & Niestle, 1969; *Royaute du Christ et Eglise, selon le Nouveau Testament,* Delachaux & Niestle, 1971.

In German: *Koenigsherrschaft Christi und Kirche im Neue Testament,* Evangelischer Verlag, 1941; *Die Tradition: Als exegetisches, historisches und theologisches Problem,* Zwingli-Verlag, 1954; *Beitraege zur Geschichte der biblischen Exegese,* Mohr, 1955; *Einheit in Christus: Evangelische und katholische Bekenntnisse,* Zwingli-Verlag, 1960; (with Lukas Vischer) *Zwischen zwei Konzilssessionen: Rueckblick und Ausschau zweier protestantischer Beobachter,* EVZ-Verlag, 1963; *Unsterblichkeit der Seele oder Auferstehung der Toten?: Antwort des Neuen Testaments,* Kreuz-Verlag, 1963; *Einheit in Christus II,* Zwingli-Verlag, 1964; *Einheit in Christus III,* Zwingli-Verlag, 1966; (with Karl Rahner and Heinrich Fries) *Sind die Erwartungen erfullt?: Ueberlegungen nach dem Konzil,* Hueber, 1966; *Was bedeutet das Zweite Vatikanische Konzil fuer uns?* (edited by Werner Schatz), Reinhardt, 1966; (editor with Otto Karrer) *Das moderne Menschenbild und das Evangelium,* Benziger Verlag, 1969. Also author of *Beitraege zur Geschichte der biblischen Hermeneutik,* 1959. Co-author of appendix of *Begegnung der Christen,* by Otto Karrer, 1959.

In English: (Contributor) Krister O. Stendahl, editor, *Immortality and Resurrection: Four Essays,* Macmillan, 1965. Co-author of *Christianity Divided,* 1962.

In Italian: (Contributor) *Il primato di Pietro nel pensiero critiano contemporaneo,* Il Mulino, 1965.

WORK IN PROGRESS: Prayer According to the New Testament.

BIOGRAPHICAL/CRITICAL SOURCES: Luigi Bini, *L'intervento di Oscar Cullmann nella discussione Bultanianniana,* Analecta Gregoriana, 1961; Otto Karrer, *Peter and the Church: An Examination of Cullmann's Thesis,* Herder & Herder, 1963; Felix Christ, editor, *Oikonomia: Heilsgeschichte als Thema der Theologie: Oscar Cullmann zum funfundsechsigste Geburtstag gewidmet,* Reich, 1967; Heinrich Baltensweiler and Bo Ivar Reicke, editors, *Neues Testament und Geschichte: Historisches Geschehen und Deutung im Neuen Testament—Oscar Cullmann zum siebenzigste Geburtstag,* Mohr, 1972.

*   *   *

CUM, R.
   See CRUMB, R(obert)

CUMBERLAND, John Hammett 1924-

BRIEF ENTRY: Born May 29, 1924, in Yosemite, Calif. American economist, educator, and author. Cumberland has been a professor of economics at University of Maryland since 1953, specializing in regional and urban economics. His writings include *Methods of Regional Analysis* (1960), *Regional Economic Planning* (European Productivity Agency, Organization for European Economic Cooperation, 1961), *Regional Development: Experiences and Prospects in the United States of America*, 2nd edition (Mouton, 1973), and *Effects on Economic Development Upon Water Resources* (Bureau of Business and Economic Research, University of Maryland, 1973). *Address:* 4200 Cloyt Rd., College Heights, Md. 20740; and Department of Economics, University of Maryland, College Park, Md. 20742. *Biographical/critical sources: American Men and Women of Science: The Social and Behavioral Sciences,* 13th edition, Bowker, 1978.

*   *   *

CUMMING, Robert 1945-

PERSONAL: Born May 31, 1945, in Yorkshire, England; son of Alexander Ian (in business) and Beryl Mary (Stevenson) Cumming; married Carolyn Alison Jenkins (a modern picture appraiser), June 7, 1975. *Education:* Trinity Hall, Cambridge, M.A., 1969. *Home:* The Old Mill House, Maids Moreton, Buckingham, England. *Office:* Christie's, 63 Old Brompton Rd., London SW7, England.

CAREER: Tate Gallery, London, England, lecturer, 1974-77; Christie's Fine Arts Course, London, principal, 1978—.

WRITINGS: (Contributor) Trewin Copplestone and Bernard S. Myers, editors, *Encyclopaedia of Art,* Macmillan (London), 1979; *Just Look . . . A Book About Paintings,* Scribner, 1980. Contributor of articles and reviews to periodicals, including *Times Literary Supplement, Times Educational Supplement, Country Life,* and *Burlington Magazine.*

WORK IN PROGRESS: Just Imagine, a sequel to *Just Look;* art books and art games.

SIDELIGHTS: Cumming's *Just Look* is designed to introduce young people (ages nine and up) to the vast world of art. A collection of more than fifty photographs of famous paintings, *Just Look* contains examples of the work of artists from seven hundred years past to the present time, and offers definitions of a number of art terms.

Just Look has been warmly received by critics, such as Barbara Karlin of the *Los Angeles Times Book Review.* "The concept is marvelous and could certainly stimulate an early interest in art," Karlin opined. *Times Literary Supplement*'s Lucy Micklethwait wrote that Cumming "guides the reader around the paintings as if he were in an art gallery. . . . If the reader is left unsatisfied, and feeling that he ought to have been told more, both about the paintings and the artists, perhaps that is just the sort of curiosity that Mr. Cumming intended to stimulate."

Cumming told *CA:* "I am excited by all areas of the fine and decorative arts although my main interest is modern and contemporary art. I believe we live in one of the great artistic centuries, and I am fascinated by our present-day view of our historical and cultural inheritance. My writings, teaching, and lecturing are aimed at making our art and our history accessible and exciting. I believe profoundly in the humanizing influence of great art."

BIOGRAPHICAL/CRITICAL SOURCES: Times Literary Supplement, March 28, 1980; *Los Angeles Times Book Review,* August 24, 1980.

*   *   *

CURRIE, David P. 1936-

BRIEF ENTRY: Born May 29, 1936, in Macon, Ga. American lawyer, educator, and author. Currie began teaching at University of Chicago in 1962 and became a professor of law in 1968. He served as chairman of the Illinois Pollution Control Board from 1970 to 1972. Currie wrote *Conflict of Laws: Cases, Comments, Questions* (West Publishing, 1968), *Federal Courts: Cases and Materials* (West Publishing, 1968), *Pollution: Cases and Materials* (West Publishing, 1975), and *Federal Jurisdiction in a Nutshell* (West Publishing, 1976). Curried edited *Federalism and the New Nations of Africa* (University of Chicago Press, 1964). *Address:* School of Law, University of Chicago, Chicago, Ill. 60637.

*   *   *

CURTIS, Richard (Alan) 1937-
(Ray Lilly, Morton Stultifer, Melanie Ward)

PERSONAL: Born June 23, 1937, in New York, N.Y.; son of Charles (a manufacturer) and Betty Curtis; married Joanne Stone, August 17, 1966; married second wife, Leslie Tonner (an author), June 21, 1981. *Education:* Received B.A., Syracuse University; received M.A., University of Wyoming. *Agent:* Richard Curtis Associates, Inc., 340 East 66th St., New York, N.Y. 10021.

CAREER: Free-lance writer; literary agent.

WRITINGS: (Compiler) *Future Tense* (short stories), Dell, 1968; *The Genial Idiots: The American Saga as Seen by Our Humorists* (juvenile), Crowell-Collier Press, 1968; (with Althea Gibson) *So Much to Live For* (juvenile autobiography), Putnam, 1968; *Chiang Kai-Shek* (juvenile biography), Hawthorn, 1969; (with Elizabeth Hogan) *Perils of the Peaceful Atom: The Myth of Safe Nuclear Power Plants,* Doubleday, 1969.

(Under pseudonym Morton Stultifer) *The Case for Extinction: An Answer to Conservationists,* illustrated by Robert Powell, Dial, 1970; *The Life of Malcolm X* (juvenile biography), Macrae Smith, 1971; (with Maggie Wells) *Not Exactly a Crime: Our Vice-Presidents From Adams to Agnew,* Dial, 1972; (with Irwin Touster) *The Perez Arson Mystery* (juvenile), illustrations by Richard Cuffari, Dial, 1972; *Ralph Nader's Crusade* (juvenile biography), Macrae Smith, 1972; (with Touster) *The Runaway Bus Mystery* (juvenile), Dial, 1972; *The Berrigan Brothers: The Story of Daniel and Philip Berrigan,* Hawthorn, 1974; (under pseudonym Ray Lilly) *The Sunday Alibi,* Manor, 1977; (under pseudonym Melanie Ward) *Dreams to Come,* BJ Publishing Group, 1978; (with Hogan) *Nuclear Lessons,* Stackpole, 1980; *How to Prosper in the Coming Apocalypse,* St. Martin's, 1981; *How to Be Your Own Literary Agent,* Houghton, 1982.

Contributor of articles to periodicals, including *Esquire, Gentleman's Quarterly, Natural History, News Front,* and *American Legion,* and of crime fiction to mystery magazines, including *Ellery Queen's Mystery Magazine.*

BIOGRAPHICAL/CRITICAL SOURCES: Natural History, March, 1969.

*   *   *

CURTIS, Tony 1946-

PERSONAL: Born December 26, 1946, in Carmarthen, Wales;

son of Leslie Thomas (a mechanic) and Doris Elizabeth (Williams) Curtis; married Margaret Blundell (a teacher), March 30, 1971; children: Gareth, Bronwen. *Education:* University College of Swansea, University of Wales, B.A. (with honors), 1969; Goddard College, M.F.A., 1980. *Home:* 47 Glen Mavis Way, Barry CF6 8DN, Wales.

CAREER: Assistant teacher at grammar school in Wilmslow, England, 1969-71; second in charge of English at grammar school in Maltby, England, 1971-74; Polytechnic of Wales, Pontypridd, senior lecturer in English, 1974—. Founder of Edge Press, 1977. *Member:* Yr Academi Gymreig (executive member, 1977-82). *Awards, honors:* Eric Gregory Award from Society of Authors, 1972, for poetry; Young Poet's Prize from Welsh Arts Council, 1974; poetry prize from Stroud Festival, 1980, for ''Jack Watts,'' and 1981, for ''Affairs.''

WRITINGS—Poetry, except as noted: *Walk Down a Welsh Wind,* Phoenix Pamphlet Poets Press, 1972; *Album,* Christopher Davies, 1974; (with Duncan Bush and Nigel Jenkins) *Three Young Anglo-Welsh Poets,* Welsh Arts Council, 1974; (editor) *Pembrokeshire Poems,* Pembrokeshire Handbooks, 1975; *Out of the Dark Woods* (stories), Edge Press, 1977; *Carnival,* Alun, 1978; *Preparations,* Gomer Press, 1980; (editor) *The Art of Seamus Heaney,* Poetry Wales Press, 1982.

Author of ''Islands'' (one-act play), first broadcast by British Broadcasting Corp. (BBC-Radio Wales), March 26, 1975. Editor of *Madog Arts,* 1977-81.

WORK IN PROGRESS: An anthology of Welsh poets, publication by Bellevue Press expected in 1982; ''Occupied Territory,'' a one-act play for stage and radio; *Throwing the Punch,* a book of selected stories.

SIDELIGHTS: Curtis told *CA:* ''I believe that one can be taught to write. We in the United Kingdom have lagged behind the United States in this respect. However, one has to keep returning to one's own feelings and needs, and weighing one's work against those criteria despite critical or commercial pressures. A really serious writer ought to be able to go into areas of experience without restraint and to explore his or her reaction to those experiences in the most suitable medium.''

*   *   *

CUTTING, Edith E(lsie) 1918-

PERSONAL: Born March 31, 1918, in Lewis, N.Y.; daughter of Leon O. (a farmer) and Amy (a teacher; maiden name, White) Cutting. *Education:* New York College for Teachers (now State University of New York at Albany), B.S., 1938; Cornell University, M.A., 1946. *Religion:* Protestant. *Home:* 86 Allen St., Johnson City, N.Y. 13790.

CAREER: English teacher and librarian at public school in Ellenburg, N.Y., 1938-41; Larson Junior College, New Haven, Conn., librarian, 1941-43; English teacher and librarian at public school in DeRuyter, N.Y., 1943-47; librarian at public school in Dryden, N.Y., 1947-49; Johnson City Central School, Johnson City, N.Y., English teacher and department coordinator, 1949-75; free-lance writer, 1975—. *Member:* Society of Children's Book Writers, National Retired Teachers Association, New York State Retired Teachers Association, Society International, Delta Kappa Gamma.

WRITINGS: Lore of an Adirondack County, Cornell University Press, 1944; *Whistling Girls and Jumping Sheep* (folklore), Farmers' Museum, 1951; (assistant editor with Harold W. Thompson) *A Pioneer Songster,* Cornell University Press, 1958; *A Quilt for Bermuda* (juvenile), Scholastic Book Services, 1978. Contributor of poems, stories, and articles to adult and children's magazines, including *New York Folklore Quarterly.*

WORK IN PROGRESS: Several short stories and poems; two stories for picture books; a teenage romance.

SIDELIGHTS: ''Listen!'' Cutting wrote. ''That has been one of my keys to writing style. I first consciously realized the importance of listening in Dr. Harold W. Thompson's college class on American folklore. There my assignment for the term was the recording (by hand, not by tape) of tall tales and anecdotes, proverbs and songs from the Adirondacks. The specific word, the idiomatic phrase, the natural humor, the speech rhythms made all the difference between a dry reference report and a live retelling, which led to my first book. Then as I began teaching, I listened to teenagers in the cafeteria, at a school dance—wherever they were. Dialogue in teenage fiction should not be concerned with the latest slang—that is outdated too quickly—but again with the natural rhythms, the mature and immature insights, the music of speech. So, too, with children's stories. As I listened to my little nieces and nephews, I have been alert to the simple beauty and reality of their speech, from one whose new red boots could 'walk through the ocean' to one who objected to 'used oatmeal.' Listen!''

AVOCATIONAL INTERESTS: Travel (including Europe).

D

DABROWSKA, Maria (Szumska)   1889-1965

PERSONAL: Born October 6, 1889 (some sources say 1882), in Russow, Poland; died of heart and kidney disease, May 19, 1965, in Warsaw, Poland; buried in Warsaw Catholic Cemetery; married a social worker. *Education:* Attended University of Lausanne.

CAREER: Writer. Worked as journalist, translator, critic, and social worker.

WRITINGS—In English translation: *A Village Wedding and Other Stories* (contains "A Pilgrimage to Warsaw" [see below], "The Winter Coat," "The Child," "A Morning at the Zoo," "Night Encounter," "Madame Sophie," "A Change Came O'er the Scenes of My Dream," "The Third Autumn" [see below], and "A Village Wedding" [see below]), Polonia, 1957.

In Polish: *O wykonaniu reformy rolnej* (nonfiction), skl. gl. w ksieg. Rolniczej, 1921; *Galaz czeresni,* [Poland], 1922; *Ludzie stamtad* (collection of short stories; title means "The People From Yonder"), [Poland], 1927, reprinted, Czytelnik, 1971; *Noce i dnie* (novels; title means "Nights and Days"), Volume I: *Bogumil i Barbara* (title means "Bogumil and Barbara"), Volume II: *Wieszne zmartwienie* (title means "Eternal Worry"), Volume II: *Milosc* (title means "Love"), Volume IV: *Wiatr w oczy* (title means "Wind in the Eyes"), [Poland], 1932-34, 11th edition (two volumes), Czytelnik, 1955, 12th edition (five volumes), 1959, 17th edition, edited by Ewa Korzeniewska, 1972, 18th edition (three volumes), 1972, 21st abridged edition (two volumes), edited by Ryszarda Matuszewskiego, 1978; *Rozdroze* (title means "The Crossroads"), [Poland], 1937; *Znaki zycia* (collection of short stories; title means "Signs of Life"), [Poland], 1938, 6th edition, Czytelnik, 1962; *Rece w uscikku* (title means "Hand in Hand"), [Poland], 1939.

Marcin Kozera (fiction), Bibljoteka wolnej Polski, 1942, 6th edition published as *Marcin Kozera; Wilczeta z czarnego podworza,* Nasza Ksiegarnia, 1972 (see below); *Zolnierze Koscuiszki,* J. Mortkowicz, 1946; *Gwiazda zaranna* (novel; title means "Morning Star"), Czytelnik, 1955, 5th edition, 1970; *Usmiech dziecinstwa,* Iskry, 1956, reprinted, Czytelnik, 1979; *Pisma wybrane* (three volumes; stories and plays), Czytelnik, 1956; *Zdarzenia* (stories), Nasza Ksiegarnia, 1956; *Szkice z podrozy* (addresses, essays, and lectures), Czytelnik, 1956; *Opowiadania,* Wydawniczy Literackie, 1956; *Czyste serca,* Nasza Ksiegarnia, 1956; *Mysli o sprawach i ludziach* (addresses, essays, and lectures), Czytelnik, 1956.

Na wsi wesele (title means "A Village Wedding"), [Poland], c. 1957, reprinted under same title with stories "Szklane konie," "Pocieszenie," "Jesionka," and "Trzecia jesien," Nasza Ksiegarnia, 1965 (see below); *Dramaty: Geniusz sierocy; Stanislaw i Bogumil* (plays; former title means "The Orphan Genius"; latter title means "Stanley and Bogumil"), Panstwowy Instytut Wydawniczy, 1957; *Szkice o Konradzie* (addresses, essays, and lectures), Panstwowy Instytut Wydawniczy, 1959, enlarged edition, Czytelnik, 1974; *Wybor opowiadan* (title means "Selected Stories"), Czytelnik, 1960, 3rd edition, 1969; *Przyjazn; Marcin Kozera; Wilczeta z czarnego podworza,* Nasza Ksiegarnia, 1962, 3rd edition, 1965; *Maria Dabrowska,* edited by Zdzislaw Libera, Panstwowe Zaklady Wydawniczy Szkolnych, 1963, 2nd edition, 1965; *Pisma rozproszone* (two volumes), Wydawniczy Literackie, 1964.

Lucia z Pokucic; Zegar z kukulka (fiction), Panstwowy Instytut Wydawniczy, 1966 (see below); *Tu zaszla zmiana; Pielgrzymka do Warszawy,* Czytelnik, 1967 (see below); *Trzecia jesien; Na wsi wesele* (former title means "The Third Autumn"), Czytelnik, 1967; (with others) *O Tadeuszu Sulkowshim,* edited by Kazimierz Sowinski and Tymon Terlecki, Oficyna Poetow i Malarzy, 1967; *Najdalsza droga; Lucja z Pokucic; Tryumf Dionizego* (first title means "The Longest Road"), Ksiazka i Wiedza, 1968; *Pielgrzymak do Warszawy* (title means "A Pilgrimage to Warsaw"; contains "Najdalsza droga," "Pielgrzymka do Warszawy," "Nocne spotkanie," and "Tu zaszla zmiana"), Czytelnik, 1969, 2nd edition, 1972; *Domowe progi* (novel), Czytelnik, 1969; (editor) *Pamietniki mlodziezy wiejskiej, 1918-1939,* Panstwowe Zaklady Wydawnictw Szkolnych, 1969; *Przygody czlowieka myslacego* (autobiographical novel; title means "Adventures of a Thinking Man"), edited by Korzeniewska, Czytelnik, 1970, 3rd edition, two volumes, 1975.

Translator of works, including *Niels Lyhne* by Jens Peter Jacobsen. Contributor of stories to periodicals, including *Gazeta Kaliska, Kobieta wspolczesna* (title means "The Modern Woman"), and *Gazeta Zachodnia* (title means "Western Gazette").

SIDELIGHTS: Called "Poland's *grande dame* of letters" by *Time,* Dabrowska was a widely respected author who maintained her integrity in the face of governmental censorship and control. Critic Zbigniew Folejewski described her in *Books Abroad* as a "great, independent artist, who, even under the most difficult conditions of strict political controls, continued to remain faithful to her moral and artistic ideals." In 1964

Dabrowska signed a letter protesting censorship with thirty-three other writers and scholars. It was sent to Jozef Cyrankiewicz, the Polish premier at that time. Whereas many of her colleagues abandoned their criticism of government policy with that gesture, the author continued hers. Later the same year Dabrowska spoke out against the lack of freedom for authors at a meeting of the Polish Writers Union. She received a standing ovation for her speech from the five hundred writers in attendance. Despite her outspokenness, Dabrowska remained one of Poland's major literary figures. After her death in 1965 she was given a state funeral and the press declared that "Polish Literature has been cast into mourning. There is not in Poland a man who can read who will not be deeply touched by this news."

Perhaps the best known of Dabrowska's works is the four-volume *Nights and Days.* Set between 1860 and the beginning of World War I, *Nights and Days* tells the story of a family of landed gentry attempting to resettle. Using her training as a sociologist, Dabrowska accurately chronicles the social and historical changes that took place during those years. "Thanks to its historical 'authenticity' and artistic truth," commented Manfred Kridl in his book, *A Survey of Polish Literature and Culture,* "[Nights and Days] . . . is a document of no mean value, eloquently portraying the life of plain, average people." Folejewski noted that the "emphasis" of the work "is . . . on the problem of creating new values for the landless and hard-working former landowning class." Reviewers have remarked that the tetralogy is epic in scope. "The author's narrative is . . . of the simplist kind," revealed Kirdl; "it flows slowly, in a broad stream in true epic manner." The *Polish Review*'s Maria Kuncewicz agreed and pronounced Dabrowska "a born epic writer."

BIOGRAPHICAL/CRITICAL SOURCES: Manfred Kridl, *A Survey of Polish Literature and Culture,* Mouton, 1956; *Books Abroad,* winter, 1964; *Polish Review,* autumn, 1965; Zbigniew Folejewski, *Maria Dabrowska,* Twayne, 1967; *Contemporary Literary Criticism,* Volume 15, Gale, 1980.

OBITUARIES: New York Times, May 21, 1965; *Time,* May 28, 1965.*

*   *   *

DACE, Letitia (Skinner)   1941-
(Tish Dace)

PERSONAL: Born September 13, 1941, in Washington, D.C.; daughter of Edward Durnford (a food broker) and Marshall (a writer; maiden name, Russell) Skinner; married Wallace Dace (divorced); married Michael Lookretis (divorced); children: (first marriage) Hal, Teddy. *Education:* Sweet Briar College, A.B., 1963; Kansas State University, M.A., 1967, Ph.D., 1971. *Residence:* Buzzards Bay, Mass. *Office:* College of Arts and Sciences, Southeastern Massachusetts University, North Dartmouth, Mass. 02747.

CAREER: Kansas State University, Manhattan, instructor in speech and associate director of university theatre, 1967-71; John Jay College of Criminal Justice of the City University of New York, New York, N.Y., assistant professor, 1971-74, associate professor of speech, drama, and English, 1975-80, chairman of department of speech and theatre, 1979-80; Southeastern Massachusetts University, North Dartmouth, professor of English and dean of College of Arts and Sciences, 1980—. Judge of theatre awards competitions. *Member:* American Theatre Critics Association, American Society for Theatre Research, Modern Language Association of America, Theatre Library Association, New Drama Forum, Outer Critics Circle

(member of executive committee, 1980—), British Theatre Institute, Phi Beta Kappa (president of Alpha chapter of Kansas, 1969-70). *Awards, honors:* City University of New York faculty research award, 1972, 1973.

WRITINGS: LeRoi Jones (Imamu Amiri Baraka): A Checklist of Works by and About Him, Nether Press, 1971; (with Wallace Dace) *The Theater Student: Modern Theater and Drama,* Richards Rosen, 1973; *The Osborne Generation: A Bibliography of Works by and About and a List of Production Data on Twenty Contemporary English and Irish Dramatists,* Garland Publishing, Volume I, 1983. Contributor, sometimes under name Tish Dace, to magazines, including *New York, Vogue, Playbill,* and *Harper's and Queen,* and newspapers. Theatre editor of *Greenwich Village News,* 1976-77, *Soho Weekly News,* 1977-82, *Other Stages,* 1978-82, and *Villager* and *Advocate,* both 1982—; associate editor of *Shakespearean Research and Opportunities,* 1971-75.

WORK IN PROGRESS: Additional volumes of *The Osborne Generation: A Bibliography of Works by and About and a List of Production Data on Twenty Contemporary English and Irish Dramatists,* for Garland Publishing; *Langston Hughes: The Critical Tradition,* for B. Franklin.

SIDELIGHTS: Dace commented: "I am particularly interested in experimental theatre (such as Mabou Mines, the Wooster Group, and the Ridiculous Theatrical Company), contemporary English and American drama, and drama viewed from a feminist perspective."

*   *   *

DACE, Tish
See DACE, Letitia (Skinner)

*   *   *

DAEDALUS
See BRAMESCO, Norton J.

*   *   *

D'AGOSTINO, Dennis John   1957-

PERSONAL: Born July 31, 1957, in Brooklyn, N.Y.; son of Angelo (a teacher) and Florence (Del Casino) D'Agostino. *Education:* Fordham University, B.A., 1978. *Home:* 38 Independence St., Tarrytown, N.Y. 10591. *Office:* Associated Press, 50 Rockefeller Plaza, New York, N.Y. 10020.

CAREER: Associated Press, New York, N.Y., sportswriter and statistician, 1978—. Member of Museum of Broadcasting, 1978—. *Member:* Society for American Baseball Research, Sigma Delta Chi.

WRITINGS: This Date in New York Mets History, Stein & Day, 1982.

WORK IN PROGRESS: A sequel to *This Date in New York Mets History,* with material on the 1981 and 1982 seasons.

SIDELIGHTS: D'Agostino told *CA:* "In my writing, I strive for the offbeat, writing about things that haven't been written about before. When writing sports books, you run the risk of being mundane if you're not careful. There are only so many ways you can write about how Enos Slaughter scored from first base to win a World Series, or how Reggie Jackson hit three homers in one game to win another one. Luckily for me, the Mets, a team with an unusual and colorful history, provided a subject that lent itself to the offbeat. For example, Jimmy Piersall running backwards around the bases after hitting a home run. That's the kind of thing I enjoy writing about more than anything else.

"I hope I can continue to break new ground in future writing. I would like to do books on the history of baseball broadcasting, a look at the New York Mets of 1969, then and now, and a history of baseball's League Championship series."

*   *   *

DAHOOD, Mitchell 1922-1982

OBITUARY NOTICE: See index for *CA* sketch: Born February 2, 1922, in Anaconda, Mont. (some sources say Lebanon); died March 8, 1982, in Rome, Italy. Clergyman, educator, translator, and author. A well-known authority on the Hebrew language and the Bible, Dahood was a Jesuit priest and professor of Ugaritic language and literature at the Pontifical Biblical Institute in Rome. Closely involved in the work of interpreting the Cuneiform tablet discovered in 1975 at Ebla, he traveled extensively lecturing on this and other subjects. He wrote hundreds of scholarly articles as well as a three-volume study of the Psalms, which he also translated. At the time of his death he was planning a book on Ebla and the Bible. Obituaries and other sources: *Chicago Tribune,* March 10, 1982; *London Times,* March 16, 1982.

*   *   *

DAKIN, Arthur Hazard 1905-

BRIEF ENTRY: Born January 25, 1905, in Boston, Mass. American philosopher and author. A writer since the 1930's, Dakin served as a commander in the U.S. Naval Reserve, with active duty during World War II as executive officer of the U.S. Naval Training School in Hampton, Va. His writings include *Man the Measure: An Essay on Humanism as Religion* (Princeton University Press, 1939), *Von Huegel and the Supernatural* (S.P.C.K., 1934), *Paul Elmer More* (Princeton University Press, 1960), and *A Scotch Paisano in Old Los Angeles.* *Address:* 305 South Pleasant St., Amherst, Mass. 01002. *Biographical/critical sources: Directory of American Scholars,* Volume IV: *Philosophy, Religion, and Law,* 7th edition, Bowker, 1978; *Who's Who in the East,* 17th edition, Marquis, 1979.

*   *   *

DALSASS, Diana 1947-

PERSONAL: Born October 8, 1947, in Boston, Mass.; daughter of Daniel (a mathematician) and Helen (a writer; maiden name, Brav) Gorenstein; married Mario Dalsass (a neurophysiologist), November 14, 1978. *Education:* University of Chicago, B.A., 1969; University of Connecticut, M.A., 1971; further graduate study at Rutgers University, 1971-76. *Residence:* Teaneck, N.J. *Office:* Robert Marston & Associates, 485 Madison Ave., New York, N.Y. 10022.

CAREER: Harvard University, Cambridge, Mass., research assistant, 1970; University of California, Los Angeles, staff research associate at Brain Research Institute, 1972-74; freelance writer, 1976-79; Dudley-Anderson-Yutzey Public Relations, New York City, copy chief, 1979-81; Robert Marston & Associates (public relations firm), New York City, account supervisor, 1981—. Member of faculty at New School for Social Research, 1981. *Awards, honors:* Grant from National Institutes of Health, 1975-76; award from Texas Medical Association, 1978, for article on health-food fads.

WRITINGS: Cashews and Lentils, Apples and Oats (alternate selection of Book-of-the-Month Cooking and Craft Club), Con-

temporary Books, 1981. Author of "The Fresh Cook," a column in the *Princeton Spectrum,* 1976, and "Home Cooked," a column in the *Trenton Times,* 1977-80. Contributor to psychology journals, popular magazines, and newspapers, including *Vegetarian Times, D, Texas Woman,* and *Nutrition Action.*

WORK IN PROGRESS: Another cookbook.

SIDELIGHTS: Diana Dalsass wrote: "When I decided to leave graduate school, I knew that I liked to write and to cook. I started writing a weekly column on foods for a local newspaper in Princeton, New Jersey, and later began writing for the *Trenton Times.* It was during this time that I wrote my cookbook, although it took some time before it was actually published. I also undertook a number of free-lance writing assignments and then obtained a job in public relations, writing releases for a variety of food and non-food accounts. After one-and-a-half years of this, I went into the actual account work and now handle a champagne account and a medical account. Cooking and writing continue to be both a satisfying hobby, as well as a means of earning a living."

*   *   *

DALTON, George 1926-

BRIEF ENTRY: Born August 2, 1926, in Brooklyn, N.Y. American economist, educator, and author. Dalton began teaching in 1953 and has been a professor of economics at Northwestern University since 1976. His publications include *Tribal and Peasant Economies: Readings in Economic Anthropology* (Natural History Press, 1967), *Studies in Economic Anthropology* (American Anthropological Association, 1971), *Economic Anthropology and Development: Essays on Tribal and Peasant Economies* (Basic Books, 1971), and *Economic Systems and Society: Capitalism, Communism, and the Third World* (Penguin, 1974). Since 1978 Dalton has edited the annual publication of *Research in Economic Anthropology* (Jai Press). *Address:* Department of Economics, Northwestern University, Evanston, Ill. 60201.

*   *   *

DANEFF, Stephen Constantine 1931-

PERSONAL: Born December 9, 1931, in Sofia, Bulgaria; son of Vladimir (a diplomat) and Teofana (a concert pianist; maiden name, Kalcheva) Daneff; married Diana Rosemary Cleaver, October 19, 1957; children: Tiffany Clare Constantia. *Education:* St. John's College, Cambridge, B.A. (with honors), 1953. *Politics:* "Anti-totalitarian." *Religion:* Christian. *Home:* 44 Limerston St., London S.W.10, England. *Agent:* Ewan MacNaughton, Peterborough Literary Agency, 135 Fleet St., London EC4P 4BL, England.

CAREER: Daily Telegraph, London, England, special correspondent, 1953-55; associated with United Press of America, London, 1955-56; *Daily Express,* London, special correspondent, 1956-61; *Daily Telegraph,* special correspondent, 1961-73; British Broadcasting Corp., London, broadcaster, 1973—. *Member:* Society of Authors. *Awards, honors:* Nominated for National Book Award from Arts Council of Great Britain, 1980, for *Foxy Ferdinand.*

WRITINGS: Foxy Ferdinand: Tsar of Bulgaria, Sidgwick & Jackson, 1979. Contributor to *London Telegraph.*

WORK IN PROGRESS: Biographical research.

*   *   *

DANIELS, Norman 1942-

PERSONAL: Born June 30, 1942, in New York, N.Y.; son of

Manus and Evelyn Daniels; married Anne L. Hooker (a learning disability teacher); children: Noah. *Education:* Wesleyan University, Middletown, Conn., A.B. (summa cum laude), 1964; Balliol College, Oxford, B.A. (with first class honors), 1966; Harvard University, Ph.D., 1970. *Home:* 103 Sagamore Ave., Medford, Mass. 02155. *Office:* Department of Philosophy, Tufts University, Medford, Mass. 02155.

CAREER: Tufts University, Medford, Mass., lecturer, 1969-70, assistant professor, 1970-76, associate professor of philosophy, 1976—. Harvard University, teaching fellow, 1968-69, lecturer in health policy and management, fall, 1979, and member of extension faculty, 1976—; visiting associate professor of bioethics at Brown University, spring, 1979. *Member:* American Philosophical Association, American Association for the Advancement of Science, Philosophy of Science Association, Hastings Center Insitute for Society, Ethics, and Life Sciences, Phi Beta Kappa. *Awards, honors:* National Endowment for the Humanities grant, 1975, and fellowship, 1977-78; National Center for Health Services research grant, 1978-81; Woodrow Wilson Career Development Award, 1980.

WRITINGS: Thomas Reid's Inquiry: The Geometry of Visibles and the Case for Realism, B. Franklin, 1974; (editor and contributor) *Reading Rawls: Critical Studies of John Rawls' "A Theory of Justice,"* Basic Books, 1975; (contributor) Stephen Barker and Thomas Beauchamp, editors, *Essays on Thomas Reid,* University City Science Center, 1977; (contributor) John Arthur and William Shaw, editors, *Justice and Economic Distribution,* Prentice-Hall, 1978; (contributor) M. Basson, editor, *Ethics, Humanism, and Medicine,* Alan R. Liss, 1981; *Justice and Health Care Delivery,* Cambridge University Press, 1982; (editor with Ron Bayer and Arthur Caplan) *Essays on Just Health Care Policy,* Pergamon, 1982; (contributor) P. Brown and others, editors, *Income Support: Conceptual and Ethical Issues,* Rowman & Littlefield, 1982. Contributor to philosophy journals. Member of editorial boards of *Australasian Journal of Philosophy, Ethics,* and *Human Rights Quarterly.*

WORK IN PROGRESS: Theory Acceptance in Ethics.

*   *   *

DANTZIG, George Bernard 1914-

BRIEF ENTRY: Born November 8, 1914, in Portland, Ore. American computer scientist, educator, and author. Dantzig began teaching after spending eight years as a staff research mathematician at Rand Corp. Since 1966 he has been a professor of operations research and computer science at Stanford University. He was awarded the National Medal of Science in 1975. In addition to more than one hundred scientific and technical books and articles, he wrote *Compact City: A Plan for a Liveable Urban Environment* (W. H. Freeman, 1973). *Address:* 821 Tolman Dr., Stanford, Calif. 94305; and Department of Operations Research, Stanford University, Stanford, Calif. 94305. *Biographical/critical sources: Who's Who in America,* 40th edition, Marquis, 1978.

*   *   *

DARRACOTT, Joseph C(orbould) 1934-

PERSONAL: Born February 22, 1934, in Aldershot, England; son of Joseph Stuart and Henrietta (Hoey) Darracott; married Britt-Marie Holm (a jeweler); children: Ingrid, Thomas, Jonathan. *Education:* Lincoln College, Oxford, M.A., 1957; attended Institut d'Art et d'Archaeologie, 1957-58; University of London, B.A., 1965. *Home:* 18 Fitzwarren Gardens, London N19 3TP, England. *Office:* Imperial War Museum, Lambeth Rd., London SE1 6H2, England.

CAREER: Thames & Hudson Ltd. (publisher), London, England, research and editorial assistant, 1959-61; City Art Gallery, Manchester, England, keeper of Rutherston Collection, 1961-63; Hornsey College of Art, London, lecturer in art history, 1963-68; Imperial War Museum, London, keeper of department of art, 1969-81, keeper of art and design history, 1981—. *Military service:* Royal Naval Volunteer Reserve, 1952-54; became sub-lieutenant. *Member:* Museums Association (associate and fellow; member of advisory committee), National Heritage (member of advisory committee).

WRITINGS: The First World War in Posters, Dover, 1974; *The World of Charles Ricketts,* Methuen, 1980; (with John Keegan) *The Nature of War,* Holt, 1981.

WORK IN PROGRESS: Museum publications, including a book on cartoons from World War I and World War II.

AVOCATIONAL INTERESTS: Twentieth-century graphic arts.

*   *   *

DAUGHERTY, Sarah Bowyer 1949-

PERSONAL: Born March 22, 1949, in Cleveland, Ohio; daughter of Albert Lee (a teacher) and Lucy (a teacher; maiden name, Bowyer) Daugherty. *Education:* College of Wooster, B.A., 1969; University of Pennsylvania, M.A., 1970, Ph.D., 1973. *Home:* 1008 Morgan St., Apt. 8, Normal, Ill. 61761. *Office:* Department of English, Illinois State University, Normal, Ill. 61761.

CAREER: University of Notre Dame, Notre Dame, Ind., assistant professor of English, 1973-80; Illinois State University, Normal, assistant professor of English, 1980—. *Member:* Modern Language Association of America, Phi Beta Kappa.

WRITINGS: The Literary Criticism of Henry James, Ohio University Press, 1981. Contributor to literature journals.

WORK IN PROGRESS: A study of the criticism of William Dean Howells.

SIDELIGHTS: Daugherty told *CA:* "My book on James is a comprehensive study of the author's criticism, with a special focus on his effort to harmonize romance and realism. The works of Hawthorne and Balzac were of particular importance to this synthesis. My research on Howells has just begun, but I believe that he was less doctrinaire a realist than some scholars have supposed."

*   *   *

DAVIDSON, Cathy Notari 1949-

PERSONAL: Born June 21, 1949, in Chicago, Ill.; daughter of Paul C. (an executive in solar energy) and Leeann (a caseworker; maiden name, Behnke) Notari; married Arnold E. Davidson (a college teacher); children: Charles R. *Education:* Elmhurst College, B.A., 1970; State University of New York at Binghamton, M.A., 1973, Ph.D., 1974; postdoctoral study at University of Chicago, 1975-76. *Office:* Department of English, Morrill Hall, Michigan State University, East Lansing, Mich. 48824.

CAREER: Elmhurst College, Elmhurst, Ill., instructor in English, 1973-74; St. Bonaventure University, St. Bonaventure, N.Y., instructor in English, 1974-75; Michigan State University, East Lansing, assistant professor, 1976-82, associate professor of English, 1982—. Visiting professor at Kobe College, 1980-81. *Member:* Modern Language Association of America, Women's Caucus on Modern Languages, College English Association, Women's Studies Association, Midwest Modern

Language Association (chairperson of Late Nineteenth-Century American Literature Division, 1982). *Awards, honors:* Irving J. Lee Memorial Award from International Society for General Semantics, 1974, for dissertation, "The Poetics of Perception: A Semantic Analysis of the Fiction of Ambrose Bierce"; fellow at Newberry Library, 1976; Michigan State University Teacher-Scholar Award, 1979; grant from National Endowment for the Humanities, 1980.

WRITINGS: (Editor with E. M. Broner) *The Lost Tradition: Mothers and Daughters in Literature,* Ungar, 1980; (editor with husband, Arnold E. Davidson) *The Art of Margaret Atwood: Essays in Criticism,* House of Anansi Press, 1981; (editor) *Critical Essays on Ambrose Bierce,* G. K. Hall, 1982. Contributor to literature journals. Contributing editor of *Women's Studies Newsletter.*

WORK IN PROGRESS: The Origins of American Fiction; Structuring the Ineffable: A Study of the Short Fiction of Ambrose Bierce.

SIDELIGHTS: Cathy Davidson commented: "I am very interested in relationships between social and political activities and the creative arts, particularly fiction. Right now my principal obsession is the relationship between what happened after the American Revolution (the various radical and reactionary stances) and the first novels written in America. It's a 'pure' way to study the impact of society on literature, and literature on society, since both American culture and American fiction were being defined as 'American' for the first time. Part of my concern with this question arises from my work with Canadian literature, because I can see there the differences between Canadian and American culture and Canadian and American literature. My recent year of teaching in Japan also increased my interest in cultural and literary phenomena."

*　　*　　*

DAVIDSON, Michael   1944-

PERSONAL: Born December 18, 1944, in Oakland, Calif.; son of Robert F. (a banker) and Mildred (a teacher; maiden name, Harrison) Davidson; married Carol Wikarska, July, 1970 (divorced, 1974). *Education:* San Francisco State University, B.A., 1967; State University of New York at Buffalo, Ph.D., 1971. *Home:* 1220 Hygeia, Leucadia, Calif. 92024. *Office:* D-007, Department of Literature, University of California, San Diego, La Jolla, Calif. 92093.

CAREER: San Diego State University, San Diego, Calif., visiting lecturer in English literature, 1973-75; University of California, San Diego, La Jolla, research historian and assistant professor, 1976-81, associate professor of literature, 1981—, director of Archive for New Poetry. *Awards, honors:* Grant from National Endowment for the Arts, 1975.

WRITINGS: Exchanges (poems), Prose and Verses, 1972; *Two Views of Pears* (poems), Sandollar Press, 1973; *The Mutabilities, and The Foul Papers* (poems and prose), Sandollar Press, 1976; *Summer Letters* (poems), Black Sparrow Press, 1976; *The Prose of Fact* (poems and prose), Figures, 1980; *The San Francisco Renaissance and Postmodern Poetics,* Cambridge University Press, 1983. Co-editor of *Credences;* editor of *Documents for New Poetry* and *Archieve Newsletter.*

SIDELIGHTS: Davidson told *CA:* "Writing is a form of recognition in which language is encountered not in its communicational function but as the major element in producing meaning. One understands what is happening is writing *by* the act of writing. What the poet anticipates as 'correct' or 'right' will always legislate against what the poet's language wants to do,

and the poet must be ready to accept the latter's instructions, even when the direction seems spurious. In this sense, 'craft' implies the ability to respond, not the maintenance of a will to power over form."

*　　*　　*

DAVIES, Margaret Lloyd   1935-

PERSONAL: Born December 8, 1935, in Rhondda, South Wales; married Trefor Lloyd Davies (a mechanical and electrical engineer), July 15, 1961; children: Geoffrey Lloyd. *Education:* University of Wales, University College, Aberystwyth, (with honors), 1957. *Home:* 129 Warren Rd., Orpington, Kent BR6 6JE, England.

CAREER: Cowbridge High School, Glamorgan, South Wales, head of geography department, 1958-67; tutor in geography for private tutoring business in Sevenoaks, Kent, England, 1968-69; Babington House School, London, England, geography mistress, 1979—.

WRITINGS—For children: The Coast (illustrated by Angela Lewer), Muller, 1977; *Lowlands* (illustrated by Lewer), Muller, 1977; *Mountains and Hills* (illustrated by Lewer), Muller, 1977. Contributor of articles on physical geography to *Junior Education.*

WORK IN PROGRESS: Rocks, Fossils, and *The Ever-Moving Earth,* a set of educational books for children; *The Sleepy Spook,* a children's novel.

SIDELIGHTS: "I have always been fascinated by geomorphology," Davies told *CA,* "and feel that many children would be interested if they could start reading about it in the junior school."

*　　*　　*

DAVIES, P.C.W.
See DAVIES, Paul (Charles William)

*　　*　　*

DAVIES, Paul (Charles William)   1946-
(P.C.W. Davies)

PERSONAL: Born April 22, 1946, in London, England; son of Hugh and Pearl (Birrel) Davies; married Susan Woodcock, July 27, 1972; children: Caroline, Victoria, Annabel, Charles. *Education:* University College, London, B.Sc. (with first class honors), 1967, Ph.D., 1970. *Home:* 16 Elgy Rd., Gosforth, Newcastle upon Tyne, England. *Office:* Department of Theoretical Physics, University of Newcastle upon Tyne, Newcastle upon Tyne, England.

CAREER: Cambridge University, Cambridge, England, fellow of Institute of Theoretical Astronomy, 1970-72; University of London, King's College, London, England, lecturer in mathematics, 1972-80; University of Newcastle upon Tyne, Newcastle upon Tyne, England, professor of theoretical physics, 1980—.

WRITINGS—Under name P.C.W. Davies, except as noted: The Physics of Time Asymmetry, University of California Press, 1974, second edition, 1977; *Space and Time in the Modern Universe,* Cambridge University Press, 1977; (under name Paul Davies) *The Runaway Universe,* Harper, 1978 (published in England as *Stardoom: A Scientific Account of the Beginning and End of the Universe,* Fontana, 1979); *The Forces of Nature,* Cambridge University Press, 1979; *The Search for Gravity Waves,* Cambridge University Press, 1980; (under name

Paul Davies) *Other Worlds,* Dent, 1980, published as *Other Worlds: A Portrait of Nature in Rebellion, Space, Superspace, and the Quantum Universe,* Simon & Schuster, 1980, published as *Other Worlds: Space, Superspace, and the Quantum Universe,* Simon & Schuster, 1981; (under name Paul Davies) *The Edge of Infinity: Beyond Black Holes to the End of the Universe,* Dent, 1981, published as *The Edge of Infinity: Where the Universe Came From and How It Will End,* Simon & Schuster, 1982; (with N. D. Birrell) *Quantum Fields in Curved Space,* Cambridge University Press, 1982; *The Accidental Universe,* Cambridge University Press, 1982.

Member of editorial board of *Journal of Physics.*

SIDELIGHTS: Davies has sought in his books to bring the realms of space, time, and physics to the lay public. In *The Runaway Universe* the author examines cosmology—the science of the universe as a whole—and explores how the universe, space, time, and existence came into being. He introduces the reader to some basic scientific ideas, including relativity and the concept of entropy, and contemplates the fate of an ever-expanding, energy-losing universe. Calling the book "one of the most readable surveys to date," Malcolm Browne of the *New York Times* noted that Davies "suggests some ingenious and mind-boggling ways in which man might prolong his existence a billion billion years after most of the universe has become cold and dead." Davies proposes, for example, that future man might be able to control the energy in black holes, releasing it when other sources of energy have been depleted. "This is a book whose horizons are as distant as man can imagine," Browne claimed.

Although Browne commended Davies for introducing his readers to "both the proven and the speculative aspects of the subject," Gerald Jonas of the *New York Times Book Review* objected to "the impression that certain issues have been settled to everyone's satisfaction." The reviewer remained unconvinced that the calculations underlying current scientific cosmology were firmly based and expressed skepticism when calling to mind those existing mysteries of space and physics that could not be explained by current theories. Jonas wrote: "[Davies] is at pains to distinguish fact from speculation. . . . By the very nature of his exposition, however, he cannot do justice to the possibility that current scientific cosmology may be, like the cosmologies of the past, a conceptual house of cards. . . . There is still room for doubt, and humility, in our confrontation with the universe."

In *Other Worlds* Davies describes the revolution in physics and philosophy precipitated by the quantum theory and the theories of relativity. As Richard Dyott noted in his review for the *Chicago Tribune,* these theories subverted the Newtonian concept of man as a cog in a clockwork universe, subject to the same laws of cause and effect that govern all other natural objects. Quantum theory in particular disputes this viewpoint, he explained, because it asserts that the laws of chance control all events. In philosophical terms, the theory returns man to the center of things and suggests that reality is a perception of the human mind, as are past, present, and future. Walter Sullivan observed in the *New York Times* that *Other Worlds* was "almost as much philosophy as science. Like any treatment of subjects so alien to our daily experiences, it is not easy to read, but it opens the mind to vistas normally reserved to those who lean on arcane mathematics to formulate their ideas." And Dyott held that Davies "manages to cope lucidly with such concepts as super space, the beginning of the world, and black holes—all without mathematical formula. . . . This is surely a book to be read not only for information's sake, but also for the sense of achievement of man's attempts to understand the universe."

Another critic, Timothy Ferris of the *New York Review of Books,* faulted Davies for using words like "amazing," "mindboggling," and "profound" in *Other Worlds* when discussing scientific concepts, but admitted that such a style does "keep things lively." Readers prepared for Davies's popular approach to science, he concluded, "will find informative descriptions of how the principles of quantum mechanics have affected the scientific world view."

Davies told *CA:* "In my books I try to communicate to the layperson the sense of excitement and awe which I myself feel when confronted by the challenge of modern physics. Though I may entertain, startle, provoke and perhaps baffle the reader, my primary aim is to share with them some glimpses of nature's dazzling secrets revealed by the power of scientific analysis."

BIOGRAPHICAL/CRITICAL SOURCES: New York Times Book Review, November 26, 1978, May 3, 1981, April 25, 1982; *New York Times,* January 9, 1979, April 7, 1981; *Chicago Tribune,* June 19, 1980.

* * *

DAVIS, Allison 1902-

BRIEF ENTRY: Born October 14 (some sources say October 10), 1902, in Washington, D.C. American anthropologist, psychologist, educator, and author. Davis joined the faculty at University of Chicago in 1939; in 1970 he was named John Dewey Distinguished Service Professor of Education. He was a member of the President's Commission on Civil Rights in 1966 and 1967. Davis's books include *Children of Bondage: The Personality Development of Negro Youth in the Urban South* (American Council on Education, 1940), *Deep South: A Social Anthropological Study of Caste and Class* (University of Chicago Press, 1941), *The Psychology of the Child in the Middle Class* (University of Pittsburgh Press, 1960), *Compensatory Education for Cultural Deprivation* (Holt, 1965), *The Crisis of the Negro Intellectual* (Morrow, 1967), and *Rebellion or Revolution* (Morrow, 1968). *Address:* 5801 South Dorchester Ave., Apt. 9A, Chicago, Ill. 60637; and Judd Hall, University of Chicago, Chicago, Ill. 60637. *Biographical/critical sources: Journal of Negro History,* April, 1970; *Who's Who in America,* 40th edition, Marquis, 1978.

* * *

DAVIS, Eleanor Harmon 1909-

PERSONAL: Born October 12, 1909, in Seattle, Wash.; daughter of Albert (a house painter) and Josephine (Carlson) Harmon; married Edward Thomas White (divorced, 1947); married Carl DeVore Davis (died, 1978). *Education:* University of Washington, Seattle, B.L.S. (cum laude), 1932, Certificate in Library Work With Children, 1933. *Politics:* Independent. *Religion:* Unitarian-Universalist. *Home:* 312 Ehilani St., Pukalani, Hawaii 96788.

CAREER: Seattle Public Library, Seattle, Wash., children's librarian, 1933-38; Maui County Free Library, Wailuku, Hawaii, children's librarian, 1938-39; Kauai Public Library, Lihue, Hawaii, children's librarian and cataloger, 1939-46; New York Public Library, New York, N.Y., young adult and reference librarian, 1946-47; Prince George's County Library, Hyattsville, Md., children's librarian, 1947-48; Maui County Free Library, children's librarian, 1948-49, acting chief librarian, 1949-50; Hawaii County Library, Hilo, children's librarian, 1950-51; Maui County Free Library, chief librarian, 1951-52; Library of Hawaii, Honolulu, assistant chief librarian, 1952-65; Hawaii State Library, Honolulu, state coordinator of adult book selection, 1965-66; University of Hawaii, East-West Center, Honolulu, administrator and part-time teacher of library technology, 1967-71.

MEMBER: American Library Association, American Manchester Terrier Club, Hawaii Library Association (honorary life member; vice-president, 1955; president, 1956), Hawaiian Historical Society (member of board of directors, 1972, 1973), Historic Hawaii Foundation, Maui Obedience Training Club, Maui Historical Society, Phi Beta Kappa. *Awards, honors:* Bicentennial Medal of Merit from King Carl Gustaf XVI of Sweden, 1981, for *Abraham Fornander: A Biography.*

WRITINGS: Norwegian Labor in Hawaii: The Norse Immigrants (monograph), Industrial Relations Center, University of Hawaii, 1962; *Abraham Fornander: A Biography,* University Press of Hawaii, 1979. Contributor to library journals, historical journals, and dog magazines.

WORK IN PROGRESS: Biographical research on Hawaiian women for three articles for *Notable Women of Hawaii, 1778-1978.*

SIDELIGHTS: Davis told *CA:* "My Swedish parentage led to my interest in Fornander, a Swede and champion of the Hawaiian people who played an important and varied role in the life of their kingdom from the 1840's through the 1880's. I have traveled in Denmark and Sweden, as well as England and Ireland. For many years I bred, exhibited, and obedience-trained Toy Manchester Terriers."

*   *   *

DAVIS, Gary A(lan)   1938-

PERSONAL: Born July 28, 1938, in Salt Lake City, Utah; son of L. O. (a cement mason) and E. Pearl (a waitress; maiden name, Westwood) Davis; married Frances Clemmer, December 19, 1961; children: Kirsten Kay, Ingrid Marie, Sonja Cathrine. *Education:* University of Utah, B.A., 1962; University of Wisconsin—Madison, M.S., 1963, Ph.D., 1965. *Home:* 7919 Deer Run Rd., Cross Plains, Wis. 53528. *Office:* Department of Educational Psychology, University of Wisconsin—Madison, Madison, Wis. 53706.

CAREER: University of Wisconsin—Madison, assistant professor, 1965-68, associate professor, 1968-71, professor of educational psychology, 1971—. Member of Wisconsin State Superintendent's advisory committee on the gifted and talented, 1980-83. *Member:* American Psychological Association, American Educational Research Association, Creative Education Foundation. *Awards, honors:* Wilhelm Wandt Award from Twenty-second International Congress of Psychology, 1981.

WRITINGS: (With J. A. Scott) *Training Creative Thinking,* Holt, 1971; *Psychology of Problem Solving,* Basic Books, 1973; (with T. F. Warren) *Psychology of Education,* Heath, 1974; (with M. A. Jacobson) *Stock Option Strategies,* Badger Press, 1976; *Creativity Is Forever,* Badger Press, 1981; *Educational Psychology: Theory and Practice,* Addison-Wesley, 1983. Contributor to psychology journals.

WORK IN PROGRESS: Tomorrow's Promise: Education of the Gifted and Talented, publication by Prentice-Hall expected in 1984; research on characteristics of creatively gifted students.

SIDELIGHTS: Davis told *CA:* "The majority of my writing and research interests relate to creative thinking. I see creativity as a personality characteristic and a lifestyle. We can take a creative, flexible, innovative approach to all aspects of life,

hopefully achieving what psychologists call 'self-actualization'—the mentally healthy tendency to be a forward-growing person who is using his/her capabilities to become what he/she is capable of becoming. It's important.

"Creative development is especially important in the education of gifted and talented children, since these students have the capability to make creative contributions to society."

*   *   *

DAVIS, Jack Leonard   1917-

PERSONAL: Born November 3, 1917, in Perth, Australia; son of William (a laborer) and Alice (McPhee) Davis. *Education:* Educated in Australia. *Home and office:* 22 Knutsford Ave., Rivervale, Perth, Western Australia.

CAREER: Worked in Australia as editor of Aboriginal Publications Foundation, 1942-79; writer, 1979—. Director of Aboriginal Advancement Council, 1967-72; member of Aboriginal Arts Board. Lecturer on aboriginal issues; gives poetry readings. *Member:* Australian Institute of Aboriginal Studies. *Awards, honors:* British Empire Medal, 1977.

WRITINGS: The First Born (poems), Angus & Robertson, 1970; *Poems From Aboriginal Australia,* Methuen of Australia, 1978. Author of play *Kullark,* 1981.

Unpublished plays: "The Dreamer," 1981. Contributor to *Identity.*

WORK IN PROGRESS: What Happened at School Today?, a novel; *A Pot-Pourri of Poems.*

SIDELIGHTS: Davis wrote: "Because my aboriginal people are unable to compete successfully with non-aboriginal Australians, all my writing is aimed at improving race relations, not only in this country, but worldwide. I have traveled to the United States to give poetry readings and lectures, spent four weeks in Nigeria, and have traveled extensively in my own country."

*   *   *

DAVIS, James Kotsilibas
See KOTSILIBAS-DAVIS, James

*   *   *

DAVIS, Judith   1925-

PERSONAL: Born July 6, 1925, in Jersey City, N.J.; daughter of Abraham (a surgeon) and Harriet (a psychotherapist; maiden name, Wolf) Strachstein; married Jack C. Davis, July 19, 1944 (divorced September 11, 1981); children: Rebecca, Timothy, Matthew. *Education:* University of California, Berkeley, B.A. (cum laude), 1947; Temple University, M.A., 1968. *Residence:* New York, N.Y. *Agent:* Diane Cleaver, Sanford J. Greenburger Associates, Inc., 825 Third Ave., New York, N.Y. 10022. *Office:* Department of Psychology, Pennsylvania State University, University Park, Pa. 16802.

CAREER: Philadelphia Board of Education, Philadelphia, Pa., psychology consultant, 1968-69; Philadelphia Community College, Philadelphia, instructor in psychology, 1969-70; Pennsylvania State University, University Park, assistant professor of psychology, 1970—. *Member:* American Psychological Association, Authors League of America, Dramatists Guild, Society for the Psychological Study of Social Issues (member of council, 1971-73), League of Women Voters (president, 1961-64), Eastern Psychological Association, New York Zoological Society.

WRITINGS: Amazing Grace (novel), New American Library, 1981. Work represented in anthologies, including *The Best American Short Stories of 1951*. Contributor of articles and stories to magazines.

WORK IN PROGRESS: The Marriage Counselors, a novel; *A World Without Elephants,* a novel about vigilante mobs; a musical comedy.

SIDELIGHTS: Judith Davis wrote: "In my memory, it seems that my first novel, completed at age six, was a joy to write. Now, like many other authors, I brood about confronting the next day's writing stint, am surprisingly content when actually at the typewriter, then depressed when finished and faced with the prospect of having to do this again tomorrow.

"Why do we do this? Possibly to decipher, through writing, the meaning of our individual experience of life, and to transmit this discovery not only to others, but to ourselves. I think, through one's characters, it is sometimes possible to find the courage and sense of personal responsibility one would like to possess in real life."

*   *   *

DAVIS, Norman 1913-

BRIEF ENTRY: Born May 16, 1913, in Dunedin, New Zealand. Educator and author. Davis, who was a Rhodes scholar in 1934; taught in Lithuania and Bulgaria in the 1930's, then in England and Scotland. Since 1959 he has been Merton Professor of English Language and Literature at Oxford University. Davis edited *English and Medieval Studies: Presented to J.R.R. Tolkien on the Occasion of His Seventieth Birthday* (Allen & Unwin, 1962), *The Paston Letters: A Selection in Modern Spelling* (Oxford University Press, 1963), *Non-Cycle Plays and Fragments* (Oxford University Press, 1970), *Paston Letters and Papers of the Fifteenth Century* (Clarendon Press, 1971-76), *A Chaucer Glossary* (Oxford University Press, 1979), and *Non-Cycle Plays and the Winchester Dialogues* (School of English, University of Leeds, 1979). *Address:* Merton College, Oxford University, Oxford, England. *Biographical/critical sources: Who's Who,* 126th edition, St. Martin's, 1974.

*   *   *

DAVIS, William Virgil 1940-

PERSONAL: Born May 26, 1940, in Canton, Ohio; son of Virgil Sanor (a skilled factory worker) and Anna Bertha (Orth) Davis; married Carol Ann Demske (an English teacher), July 17, 1971; children: William Lawrence. *Education:* Ohio University, A.B., 1962, M.A., 1965, Ph.D., 1967; Pittsburgh Theological Seminary, M.Div., 1965. *Home:* 2633 Lake Oaks Rd., Waco, Tex. 76710. *Office:* Department of English, Baylor University, Waco, Tex. 76798.

CAREER: Ordained Presbyterian minister, 1970; Ohio University, Athens, assistant professor of English, 1967-68; Central Connecticut State College, New Britain, assistant professor of English, 1968-71; Tunxis Community College, Farmington, Conn., assistant professor of English, 1971-72; University of Illinois at Chicago Circle, Chicago, assistant professor of English, 1972-77; Baylor University, Waco, Tex., associate professor, 1977-79, professor of English and writer-in-residence, 1979—. Guest professor of English and American literature at the University of Vienna, 1979-80. Gives poetry readings. *Member:* Modern Language Association of America, Poetry Society of America, Phi Kappa Phi, Tau Kappa Alpha. *Awards, honors:* Bread Loaf Writers' Conference scholar in poetry, 1970, and fellow in poetry, 1980; graduate faculty fellow in

creative writing at the University of Illinois, 1974; faculty fellow in poetry at Baylor University, 1979; Yale Series of Younger Poets award, 1979, for *One Way to Reconstruct the Scene;* Fulbright grant for guest professorship at University of Vienna, 1979-80; Lilly Foundation grant, 1979-80.

WRITINGS: (Author of introduction) *George Whitefield's Journals, 1737-1741,* Scholars' Facsimiles & Reprints, 1969; (contributor) James Richard McLeod, editor, *Theodore Roethke: A Bibliography,* Kent State University Press, 1973; *One Way to Reconstruct the Scene* (poems), Yale University Press, 1980.

Contributor of more than fifty articles to journals, including *James Joyce Quarterly, Studies in Short Fiction,* and *Modern Poetry;* of more than five hundred poems to more than one hundred journals, including *Poetry, Atlantic Monthly, North American Review,* and *Poetry Northwest;* and of short stories to *Northeast, U.S. Catholic,* and *Confrontation.* Also author of numerous reviews of poetry, fiction, and scholarly books, and of entry on Edward Lewis Wallant in *Encyclopedia of World Literature in the Twentieth Century,* Ungar, 1975.

WORK IN PROGRESS: A chapbook of poems, *The Dark Hours;* a second collection of poems; several articles on contemporary American poetry.

AVOCATIONAL INTERESTS: Painting, travel.

*   *   *

de BOISSIERE, Ralph (Anthony) 1907-

PERSONAL: Surname is pronounced Bwa-see-*air;* born October 6, 1907, in Trinidad; son of Armand (an attorney) and Maud (Harper) de Boissiere; married Ivy Alcantara, June 17, 1935; children: Jacqueline, Marcelle Drinkwater. *Education:* Attended Queen's Royal College (Port-of-Spain), 1916-22. *Home:* 10 Vega St., North Balwyn (Melbourne), Victoria, Australia 3104. *Agent:* R. W. Sander, Bayreuth University, 8580 Bayreuth, West Germany.

CAREER: Chartered Accountants, Trinidad, clerk, 1927-28; Standard Brands, Inc., salesman, 1929-39; Trinidad Clay Products, Trinidad, clerk, 1940-47; General Motors-Holden, Australia, auto assembler, 1948; cost clerk in car repair shops in Australia, 1949-55; writer, 1955-60; Gas & Fuel Corp., Victoria, Australia, statistical clerk, 1960-80. *Member:* Australian Society of Authors.

WRITINGS: Crown Jewel (novel), Australasian Book Society, 1952, reprinted, Allison & Busby, 1981; "Calypso Isle" (musical play), first performed in 1955; *Rum and Coca-Cola* (novel), Australasian Book Society, 1957; *No Saddles for Kangaroos* (novel), Australasian Book Society, 1964.

WORK IN PROGRESS: Tales of My Past, an autobiography, for Allison & Busby; *Homeless in Paradise,* a novel.

SIDELIGHTS: De Boissiere's novel *Crown Jewel* describes how poverty, dissatisfaction with colonial rule, and the emergence of the labor movement in Trinidad contributed to the political awakening of that former British colony during the 1930's. Following its initial publication by an Australian book club in 1952, the book was published in eight different languages by various foreign firms, and soon became a cult favorite in many parts of the world. It was not, however, published in Trinidad or Great Britain until 1981.

This was described as "neglect" by some reviewers, including *Spectator*'s Caroline Moorehead, who argued, "*Crown Jewel* belongs in the mainstream of colonial independence novels, and," she insisted, "Ralph de Boissiere does for Trinidad's recent political history much what Paul Scott did for India and Yambo Ouologuem for Africa.'' Salman Rushdie of *Times Literary Supplement* concurred, adding "For a political novel to seem as relevant today as it was three decades ago is a triumph; yet *Crown Jewel . . .* manages the trick without seeming to strain for universality.''

Listener critic John Mellors was also impressed with the novel and praised its ''strength, its celebration of human dignity in squalid circumstances and its ability to make the reader care about what happens to the people in the story.''

De Boissiere told *CA:* "The motivation of all my work comes from the political and social developments in society, their effect on characters, and the influence of characters on events.

''My first novel, *Crown Jewel,* covers very important events in Trinidad from 1935-37, when the island was a British colony. The second, *Rum and Coca-Cola,* is about the war years, 1940-45, when the U.S. armed forces were in control of the island and many bases were being built there. The disruption to life and the influence of different ideas brought in by the 'new masters,' numbering tens of thousands, was considerable. What interested me was the illusions that arose, the disillusionment that followed, and the concept of nationhood that emerged strongly in that period. The third novel, *No Saddles for Kangaroos,* is set in Australia at the time of the Korean war, when the government tried unsuccessfully to ban the Communist Party. It was a time of much inner searching and conflict when people had to make important decisions. *Homeless in Paradise,* my fourth novel [awaiting publication], deals with a Trinidad that has become an independent nation plagued by corruption. It is also set partly in Australia. On the one hand, a native Trinidad girl is driven out of the island because her ideas do not suit the authorities. On the other, Hungarian refugees who have made their home in Australia, but want to return to Hungary, are not permitted to do so because, ironically, their ideas also do not suit the authorities.

''In the former colonial countries everything is in turmoil for a long time, life changes, or fails to change to meet the desires of various social forces, and big conflicts are always latent if they have not already broken out into the open. I am looking forward to writing another novel about Trinidad, to be set in the 1970's and 1980's.''

BIOGRAPHICAL/CRITICAL SOURCES: Observer, June 14, 1981; *Listener,* June 18, 1981; *Spectator,* July 18, 1981; *Times Literary Supplement,* August 7, 1981.

* * *

DeFRANCIS, John 1911-

BRIEF ENTRY: Born August 31, 1911, in Bridgeport, Conn. American educator and author. DeFrancis was professor of Chinese at University of Hawaii from 1966 to 1976, when he was named professor emeritus. His writings include *Nationalism and Language Reform in China* (Princeton University Press, 1950), *Things Japanese in Hawaii* (University Press of Hawaii, 1973), *Annotated Quotations From Chairman Mao* (Yale University Press, 1975), and *Colonialism and Language Policy in Vietnam* (Mouton, 1977). He edited *Supplementary Readers for Intermediate Chinese Reader,* Volume I: *The White Haired Girl by Chi-Yu Ho,* Volume II: *The Red Detachment of Women by Chi-Yu Ho,* Volume III: *Episodes From the Dream of the Red Chamber by Louise H. Li,* Volume IV: *Sun Yat-sen by Yung Teng Chia-Yee,* Volume V: *Wu Sung Kills a Tiger by Yung Teng Chia-Yee* (Far Eastern Publications, Yale University, 1976). *Address:* Department of East Asian Languages,

370 Moore Hall, University of Hawaii at Manoa, 1890 East West Rd., Honolulu, Hawaii 96822. *Biographical/critical sources: Directory of American Scholars,* Volume III: *Foreign Languages, Linguistics, and Philology,* 7th edition, Bowker, 1978.

* * *

DEGENHARDT, Henry W(illiam) 1910-

PERSONAL: Born March 24, 1910, in Osnabrueck, Germany; son of August (a high school teacher) and Jane B.T. (a teacher; maiden name, Macdonald) Degenhardt; married Almuth Brecht, May 28, 1943; children: Donald W. *Education:* Attended University of Freiburg, 1928-29, University of Munich, 1929, University of Berlin, 1929-30, and University of Marburg, 1930-33. *Home:* 3 Horsecombe Brow, Bath BA2 5QY, England.

CAREER: Free-lance teacher and translator, 1933-51; College of Careers (Pty.) Ltd. (publisher of study aids), Cape Town, South Africa, managing director, 1951-62; writer for *Keesing's Contemporary Archives,* 1962-81.

WRITINGS: Treaties and Alliances of the World, Keesing's, 1968, 3rd edition, Longman, 1981; (with Alan J. Day) *Political Parties of the World,* Longman, 1980; (contributor) Alan J. Day, editor, *Border and Territorial Disputes,* Longman, 1982.

* * *

DEHQANI-TAFTI, H. B. 1920-

PERSONAL: Born May 14, 1920, in Yezd, Iran; son of Muhammad and Sakinneh Dehqani; married Margaret Isabel Thompson; children: Shirin Rachel, Sussanne Margaret Dehqani-Tafti Lock, Bahram William (deceased), Gulnar Eleanor. *Education:* Attended University of Tehran, 1940-42; Radley Hall, 1947-49; General Ordination Examination, 1949; also attended Virginia Theological Seminary. *Home:* Sohrab, 1 Camberry Close, Basingstoke, Hampshire RG21 3AG, England. *Office:* St. Mary's Church, Goat Lane, Basingstoke, Hampshire RG21 1PZ, England.

CAREER: Ordained Anglican priest, 1950; pastor of Anglican churches in Iran, 1950-61; Anglican bishop in Iran, 1961-76; president–bishop of the Episcopal Church in Jerusalem and the Middle East, 1976-82; assistant bishop of Winchester, England, 1982—. *Military service:* Iranian Imperial Army, 1943-44; became second lieutenant. *Awards, honors:* D. D. from Virginia Theological Seminary, 1981.

WRITINGS: Design for My World, Lutterworth, 1959; *The Hard Awakening,* Seabury, 1981.

In Persian; all published by Nuri Jahan Publications: *Ejal-i-Enhetat-i-Massihieyat dar Mashriq Zamin* (title means ''The Decline of Christianity in Asia''), 1950; *Baqieh Vafa dar,* (title means ''The Faithful Remnant''), 1952; *Yad dasht hay-i-Safar-i-Farang,* (title means ''Notes on a Journey to Europe''), 1953; *Choon Mahzoon Vali Shademan,* (poems; title means ''As Sorrowful, Yet Always Rejoicing''), 1955; (translator from English into Persian) Stephen Neill, *Christian Character,* translation published as *Seerat-i-Kamel* (title means ''The Character of a Perfect Man''), 1957; (translator from English to Persian) William Temple, *From Palm Sunday to Easter,* translation published as *Sokhanan-i-Akhar* (title means ''The Last Words''), 1957; *Ranj-i-Elahi* (poems; title means ''Divine Suffering''), 1958; *Mardan-i-Khoda* (title means ''Men of God''), 1961; *Alaj* (poems; title means ''Cure''), 1972.

WORK IN PROGRESS: Safar-i-Umr, an adaptation and translation into Persian of George Appleton's "Journey for a Soul."

SIDELIGHTS: Dehqani-Tafti wrote: "My books in English describe events experienced by the church in Iran and myself; my books in Persian were written because of the pastoral and educational needs of the church in Iran." *Avocational interests:* Persian poetry (primarily mystical), painting in water colors.

* * *

DELANEY, William A(nthony) 1926-

PERSONAL: Born September 8, 1926, in Lawrence, Mass.; son of Thomas L. and Esther (Hennessey) Delaney; married Helena Crowley, June 29, 1957; children: Catherine, William A., Jr., Mary. *Education:* Boston College, Chestnut Hill, Mass., B.S., 1949, M.B.A., 1966. *Home:* 30 Hathaway Rd., Lexington, Mass. 02173. *Office:* Analysis & Computer Systems, Inc., 54 Middlesex Turnpike, Bedford, Mass. 01730.

CAREER: Naval Research Lab, Washington, D.C., chief of computer system, 1952-58; Hanscom Air Force Base, Bedford, Mass., chief of computer system, 1958-60; RCA Corp., Burlington, Mass., technical project director, 1960-63; Raytheon Co., Sudbury, Mass., manager of software department, 1963-66; Analysis & Computer Systems, Inc. (ACSI), Bedford, president, 1966—. Public speaker. *Military service:* U.S. Naval Reserve, active duty, 1944-46. *Member:* Mensa, Presidents Association. *Awards, honors:* Small business of the year award (for New England) from Small Business Administration, 1975.

WRITINGS: Micromanagement, American Management Association, 1981; *Thirty Common Management Problems,* American Management Association, 1982. Contributor of more than thirty articles to management and computer science journals and newspapers.

SIDELIGHTS: Delaney wrote: "I am interested in entrepreneurial management as opposed to bureaucratic management—they are not the same. One important reason for failures of small businesses to survive is management failures. Some managers try to use bureaucratic management techniques, learned from working in large organizations, in small businesses in which entrepreneurial management is called for—at least until the companies grow to moderate size.

"My books are mainly directed at the differences in management techniques that exist between the large and very small business. The management principles are the same, but how and when they are applied vary significantly between large and small companies."

AVOCATIONAL INTERESTS: Foreign travel.

* * *

DELEHANTY, Randolph 1944-

PERSONAL: Born July 5, 1944, in Memphis, Tenn. *Education:* Georgetown University, A.B., 1966; University of Chicago, M.A. (social science), 1968; Harvard University, M.A. (arts and science), 1970. *Home:* 1427 Larkin St., No. 4, San Francisco, Calif. 94109.

CAREER: Foundation for San Francisco's Architectural Heritage, San Francisco, Calif., historian, 1973-78; writer, 1978—.

WRITINGS: San Francisco: Walks and Tours in the Golden Gate City, Dial, 1980.

WORK IN PROGRESS: An "intelligent interpretive guide to California"; poems.

SIDELIGHTS: Delehanty wrote: "I am a writer, lecturer, and architectural restoration and city planning consultant. I am interested in the snail and the shell, in society and architecture (the so-called 'built environment'). I am interested in how the life of the snail *is* the shell, how buildings and landscapes witness to the histories of individuals, groups, and civilizations."

* * *

DeLONG, Thomas A(nderton) 1935-

PERSONAL: Born June 26, 1935, in Freeport, N.Y.; son of Howard Anderton (a sales executive) and Sara M. (Sprague) DeLong; married Katharine Robert Clark, September 7, 1968; children: Sarah Ramsen, Elizabeth Clark. *Education:* Williams College, B.A., 1957; Columbia University, M.A., 1959; New York University, M.B.A., 1969. *Politics:* Republican. *Religion:* Episcopalian. *Home:* 51 Mill Hill Lane, Southport, Conn. 06490.

CAREER: Olin Corp., New York City and New Haven, Conn., editor and public relations writer, 1966-75; Pfizer Inc., New York City, in corporate communications, 1975—. Producer and host of radio series on American popular music for WVOF-FM, Fairfield, Conn.; originator and producer of exhibit "Golden Age of Musical Radio," at Henry Flagler Museum, Songwriters Hall of Fame, Yonkers Public Library, and Pequot Library, 1980. President of the Hong Kong True Light School Foundation, 1974-79; member of Board of Directors of Westport School of Music. *Military service:* U.S. Army, 1959-61. *Member:* International Radio & Television Society, St. Nicholas Society, Acorn Society, Sons of the Revolution, Military Society of the War of 1812, Military Order of the Loyal Legion, Racquet & Tennis Club. *Awards, honors:* Deems Taylor Award for outstanding book on music from American Society of Composers, Authors, and Publishers, 1981, for *The Mighty Music Box;* Learned Research Journal award from Brandeis University, 1981.

WRITINGS: The DeLongs of New York and Brooklyn: A Huguenot Family Portrait, Sasco Associates, 1972; *The Mighty Music Box: The Golden Age of Musical Radio* (Nostalgia Book Club Selection), Amber Crest, 1980. Contributor of articles and stories to magazines and newspapers, including *New York Times, Los Angeles Times, Music Journal, FM Guide,* and *Country Music.*

WORK IN PROGRESS: A book on early television.

SIDELIGHTS: DeLong wrote: "The naval career of Lieutenant Commander George Washington DeLong, polar explorer and leader of the Jeannette Arctic Expedition in 1879, sparked my interest in family biography, an endeavor that took nine years of research and travel from the two hundred-year-old DeLong farm at Bowers, Pennsylvania, to the polar museums of Norway.

"Music was, and is, the keystone of radio, beginning in the era of the crystal set and continuing on today's stereo receiver. The golden age of musical radio, which lasted from the 1920's to the mid-1950's, was a period of 'live' network music emanating from 'radio cities' throughout the country. Much has been written on comedians, newscasters, sports announcers, war correspondents, and daytime serials, but little on music on the air. I wrote *The Mighty Music Box* to fill that void. This story covers the wide choice of music available at the twist of a dial—dance bands, symphonies, crooners, country and western, operettas, musical quizzes, ballad singers, choral concerts, organ interludes, operas, nursery rhymes, and even singing canaries."

AVOCATIONAL INTERESTS: Travel, music, tennis, sixteen-millimeter photography.

* * *

DELTON, Jina 1961-

PERSONAL: Born August 25, 1961, in St. Paul, Minn.; daughter of Jeffrey (a school psychologist) and Judy (a writer; maiden name, Jaschke) Delton. *Education:* Attended high school in Hudson, Wis. *Politics:* Social Democrat. *Religion:* Roman Catholic. *Home:* 1367 Breda Ave., St. Paul, Minn. 55108. *Office:* J. J. Hill Reference Library, 80 West Fourth St., St. Paul, Minn. 55102.

CAREER: J. J. Hill Reference Library, St. Paul, Minn., head of interlibrary loan, 1979—.

WRITINGS: Two Blocks Down (novel), Harper, 1981.

WORK IN PROGRESS: Night Without Tears (tentative title), a novel about leaving home.

SIDELIGHTS: "For me," Jina Delton told *CA*, "writing began as a sort of antidote to the falseness I felt in day-by-day social interchanges. As I have concentrated on perceiving the forces behind the falseness, whole exciting vistas of emotional evolution have opened up for me, and I'm impatient to get them onto paper."

BIOGRAPHICAL/CRITICAL SOURCES: St. Paul Pioneer Press, May 31, 1981.

* * *

De MICHAEL, Don(ald Anthony) 1928-1982

OBITUARY NOTICE: Born May 12, 1928, in Louisville Ky.; died February 4, 1982, in Skokie, Ill. Jazz musician, publisher, critic, editor, and author. A jazz vibraphonist and drummer, De Michael began playing professionally in 1944 and led his own band from 1951 to 1960. He was a member of two jazz ensembles at the time of his death. Success as a jazz critic led him to join the staff of *Downbeat* magazine in 1960, where he served as editor in chief from 1961 to 1967. De Michael served as president of the Jazz Institute of Chicago from 1974 to 1978. He edited several trade magazines and was editor and publisher of *Plate World* at the time of his death. The co-author of a book on drums, De Michael was also editor and compiler of *Jazz Record Review,* Volumes 5 through 8, which appeared from 1961 to 1964. Obituaries and other sources: *Who's Who in America,* 42nd edition, Marquis, 1982; *Washington Post,* February 6, 1982.

* * *

DEMONG, Phyllis 1920-

PERSONAL: Born March 3, 1920, in Washington, D.C.; daughter of Frank (a carpenter) and Minnie (White) Hickman; married Francis Demong, March 24, 1941 (died August 3, 1981); children: Peter, Geoffrey, Thomas, Sarah. *Education:* Syracuse University, B.F.A., 1940. *Politics:* Democrat. *Religion:* Episcopalian. *Home and office address:* Box 70, Middlebury, Vt. 05753; and Box 818, East Orleans, Mass. 02643.

CAREER: Painter, 1968—; writer, 1979—. Work exhibited in over twenty one-woman shows. *Member:* Southern Vermont Artists, Northern Vermont Artists, Provincetown Art Association. *Awards, honors:* George Arents Medal from Syracuse University, 1974, for outstanding achievement in the arts.

WRITINGS—Self-illustrated; published by Paul Eriksson: *Celebearities and Other Bears,* 1979; *It's a Pig World Out There,* 1980; *Rare and Undone Saints,* 1981.

WORK IN PROGRESS: Several more books of word plays; "one serious book about my personal relationship with my environments—the mountains and the ocean."

SIDELIGHTS: Both *Celebearities and Other Bears* and *It's a Pig World Out There* contain scratchboard illustrations and puns about their respective animals. For example, in *It's a Pig World Out There* Phyllis Demong introduces "imporktant" personalities like Cary Grunt, Bert Porks, Pigasso, and Dorothy Porker. She includes "geohography" lessons, focusing on such places as Central Pork in the Pig Apple, and "spigetti" and pig-up trucks are among the common objects the artist presents to her readers. Cliches, namely, "hogs and kisses" or "all snout-hearted men and true," are also incorporated into the book.

BIOGRAPHICAL/CRITICAL SOURCES: New York Times Book Review, November 9, 1980, May 10, 1981.

* * *

DEMPSTER, Chris 1943-

PERSONAL: Born October 3, 1943, in Simla, India; son of George (a soldier) and Yvonne (a nurse) Dempster; married Mary (an accountant), September 24, 1967. *Education:* Attended Guildford Technical College, 1958-62. *Politics:* Conservative. *Religion:* Church of England. *Residence:* Surrey, England.

CAREER: Mercenary soldier in Africa, Lebanon, Israel, Cambodia, and Jordan, 1969—. Also works as pipefitter and welder, radio announcer, and merchant seaman. *Military service:* British Army, Parachute Brigade, 1962-67.

WRITINGS: (With David Tomkins) *Firepower* (novel), Bantam, 1977; *Hit* (novel), Corgi, 1982; *Krsko Option* (novel), Corgi, in press.

SIDELIGHTS: Dempster commented: "I started to write after being involved in the Angolan civil war. I personally received some bad press and my only redress was to tell my side of the story. That produced my first book, *Firepower,* which I wrote with another mercenary.

"The plots for all my books are based upon mercenary activities in which I have been involved. A lot of jobs are aborted for one reason or another at different stages and it is these 'jobs' that I use, fictionalizing characters and sometimes places.

"I speak a smattering of Spanish, Cantonese Chinese, Lingala (an African dialect), and am reasonably fluent in French, German, Portuguese, and Arabic, although I am not very competent in their written word."

AVOCATIONAL INTERESTS: Motorbikes, horseback riding.

* * *

DENBIGH, Kenneth George 1911-

PERSONAL: Born May 30, 1911, in Luton, England; son of George James (a chemist) and Emily (Higgins) Denbigh; married Kathleen Beatrice Enoch (a writer), September 14, 1935; children: Jonathan Stafford, Philip Noel. *Education:* Attended University of Leeds, 1929-34. *Home:* 19 Sheridan Rd., London SW19 3HW, England.

CAREER: Imperial Chemical Industries Ltd., Billingham, Durham, England, chemist, 1934-48; Cambridge University, Cambridge, England, lecturer in chemical engineering, 1948-55; University of Edinburgh, Edinburgh, Scotland, professor of chemical engineering, 1955-60; University of London, London, England, professor of chemical engineering at Imperial College of Science and Technology, 1960-66, principal of Queen Elizabeth College, 1966-77; Council for Science and Society, London, England, director, 1977—. *Member:* Royal Society (fellow), National Academy of Engineering (foreign associate).

WRITINGS: The Thermodynamics of the Steady State, Methuen, 1951; *The Principles of Chemical Equilibrium,* Cambridge University Press, 1955; *Science, Industry, and Social Policy,* Oliver & Boyd, 1963; *Chemical Reactor Theory,* Cambridge University Press, 1966; *An Inventive Universe,* Hutchinson, 1975; *Three Concepts of Time,* Springer-Verlag, 1981.

WORK IN PROGRESS: Research on thermodynamics, time, and objectivity and/or subjectivity in science.

SIDELIGHTS: Denbigh told *CA:* "I write science books in order to advance my own understanding of the natural world through the effort to achieve the utmost clarity, so far as lies in my powers. All of my books are the result of four or more successive drafts, each taking a year. There have been translations into ten languages.

"My *Three Concepts of Time* views 'time' as being neither a purely physical nor a purely mental concept, but rather as being a composite notion having different sources. Accordingly, the book analyzes the distinctive features of (1) the 'time' of theoretical physics, (2) the 'time' of thermodynamics and the evolutionary sciences such as biology, and (3) the 'time' of conscious awareness.

"At present I am working on the concept of entropy in thermodynamics; in particular whether it is fully objective or whether it contains subjective aspects."

* * *

DERBER, Milton 1915-

BRIEF ENTRY: Born June 19, 1915, in Providence, R.I. American labor economist, educator, editor, and author. Derber worked as a U.S. Government economist during World War II. He has been a professor of labor and industrial relations at University of Illinois since 1949. He was a Fulbright scholar in Australia from 1975 to 1976. Derber's publications include *The Aged and Society* (Industrial Relations Research Association, 1960), *Labor and the New Deal* (University of Wisconsin Press, 1957), *Plant Union-Management Relations: From Practice to Theory* (Institute of Labor and Industrial Relations, University of Illinois, 1965), *The American Idea of Industrial Democracy, 1865-1965* (University of Illinois Press, 1970), *Collective Bargaining by State Governments in the Twelve Midwestern States* (1974), and *The Metalworking Industry* (International Institute for Labour Studies, 1976). *Address:* 1103 Brighton Dr., Urbana, Ill. 61801; and Institute of Labor and Industrial Relations, University of Illinois, Champaign, Ill. 61820. *Biographical/critical sources: Who's Who in America,* 40th edition, Marquis, 1978.

* * *

DERRIMAN, James Parkyns 1922-

PERSONAL: Born February 19, 1922, in London, England; son of Arthur Parkins (a bank manager) and Constance Lilian (Cronk) Derriman; married Iris Ada Hogben (a justice of the peace and municipal official), April 17, 1948; children: Jane Mary (Mrs. H.J.R. Meesters). *Education:* Communication,

Advertising, and Marketing Educational Foundation, diploma, 1975. *Home:* 34 Mossville Gardens, Morden, Surrey SM4 4DG, England.

CAREER: Called to the Bar at Lincoln's Inn, 1947; *Marylebone Record,* London, England, reporter, 1938-39; *Hampshire Observer,* Winchester, England, reporter, 1939-41; *Daily Herald,* London, reporter, 1946-47; Reuters News Agency, London, sub-editor, 1947-50; *News Chronicle,* London, deputy political and parliamentary correspondent, 1954-55; J. Walter Thompson Co. Ltd. (advertising agency), London, senior executive in public relations department, 1955-61, associate director, 1961-62; Charles Barker & Sons Ltd. (now Charles Barker Group Ltd.), London, founded public relations department, 1962-64, associate director, 1964-68, joint managing director of Charles Barker City Ltd., 1968-73, joint vice-chairman, 1973-74, company secretary, 1975-82, group general manager and personnel director, 1978-82; writer, 1982—. Lecturer at College for the Distributive Trades until 1971, and at City of London Polytechnic, 1971-72. Member of board of directors of Charles Barker City Ltd., 1968-76, and Charles Barker Lyons Ltd., 1976-82; member of board of trustees of Thomas Carpenter Trust, 1971-81; vice-chairman of St. John Fisher's parish advisory council. *Military service:* British Merchant Navy, radio officer, 1941-45.

MEMBER: Confederation Europeenne des Relations Publiques (member of council, 1976-81; president of working group of European national professional bodies for public relations, 1977-80; member of executive committee, 1978-81; vice-president of confederation, 1979-81; honorary vice-president, 1981—), Institute of Public Relations (fellow; chairman of professional practices committee, 1968-71; member of council, 1968-75; chairman of board of management, 1971-72; president, 1973-74), Society of Genealogists, Selden Society, Devon and Cornwall Record Society, Somerset and Dorset Family History Society, Cornwall Family History Society, Bread Street Ward Club (chairman, 1970-71), Keys. *Awards, honors:* Named Freeman of the City of London, 1963; president's medal from Institute of Public Relations, 1978.

WRITINGS: Pageantry of the Law, Eyre & Spottiswoode, 1955; *Discovering the Law,* University of London Press, 1962; *Public Relations in Business Management,* University of London Press, 1964; *Company-Investor Relations,* University of London Press, 1969; (editor with George Pulay) *The Bridge Builders: Public Relations Today,* Associated Business Press, 1980.

WORK IN PROGRESS: A detailed study of the history of Talland, West Looe, and Polperro, in Cornwall.

SIDELIGHTS: Derriman told *CA:* "A curiosity about people, along with the ability to ask the right questions, to research a mass of detail and reduce it to essentials, and to present material accurately, clearly, and with integrity and feeling for the subject matter: These are the essential qualities of a reporter, my first career. They are equally necessary to the practice of law, for which I qualified, and to that of public relations, my second and longest career.

"Now, in my pension years, I am fortunate enough to have the chance to apply them, if I can, to another challenging field—the writing of history, which I have long wanted to do. Whether I succeed, my readers will judge."

AVOCATIONAL INTERESTS: Local history, genealogy.

* * *

de SCHANSCHIEFF, Juliet Dymoke 1919-
(Juliet Dymoke)

PERSONAL: Born June 28, 1919, in Enfield, Middlesex, England; daughter of Edward Dymoke (in business) and Juliet Cora Siddons (an actress; maiden name, Holloway) Pennington; married Hugo de Schanschieff, May 9, 1942; children: Patricia Juliet Fitzroy. *Education:* Studied at a private school in England. *Religion:* Roman Catholic. *Home:* 89 Westwood Green, Cookham, Berkshire SL6 9DE, England.

CAREER: Associated with Bank of England, 1938-42; film script reader and historical researcher at Paramount Pictures Corp., Ealing Studios, South Bronston Productions, London, England; free-lance writer, 1956—. *Wartime service:* Canadian Army; served with medical records section.

WRITINGS—All under name Juliet Dymoke: *The Sons of the Tribune: An Adventure on the Roman Wall* (juvenile), illustrated by John Harris, Edward Arnold, 1956; *The Orange Sash,* Jarrolds, 1958; *London in the Eighteenth Century,* illustrated by G. Fry, Longmans, Green, 1958; *Born for Victory,* Jarrolds, 1960; *Treason in November,* Jarrolds, 1961; *Bend Sinister,* Jarrolds, 1962; *The Cloisterman,* Dobson, 1969.

Of the Ring of Earls, Dobson, 1970; *Henry of the High Rock,* Dobson, 1971; *Serpent in Eden,* Wingate, 1973; *The Lion's Legacy,* Dobson, 1974; *Prisoner of Rome,* illustrated by Frances Phillips, Dobson, 1975; *Shadows on a Throne,* Wingate, 1976; *A Pride of Kings,* Dobson, 1978; *The Royal Griffin,* Dobson, 1978; *The Lion of Mortimer,* Dobson, 1979; *Lady of the Garter,* Dobson, 1979; *The White Cockade,* Dobson, 1979; *The Lord of Greenwich,* Dobson, 1980; *The Sun in Splendour,* Dobson, 1980; *A Kind of Warfare,* Dobson, 1981.

Contributor of articles to periodicals, including *Lady,* and to encyclopedias, including *Virtue Encyclopedia* and *Collins'.*

WORK IN PROGRESS: A novel on the French Revolution.

SIDELIGHTS: Juliet de Schanschieff told *CA* her historical books are based on intensive research. She often collects material, she said, by visiting such historical sites as battlefields, castles, and abbeys. "My most recent book, *A Kind of Warfare,* was written specifically for Lord and Lady Camoys," she commented. "It deals with the happenings at the Stonor home during the years 1580 and 1581. During this time, St. Edmund Campion visited the house and there printed on a secret press his famous book *Ten Reasons.* My book was published in 1981, the 400th anniversary of Campion's death."

AVOCATIONAL INTERESTS: Gardening.

*   *   *

DESSAU, Joanna 1921-

PERSONAL: Surname is pronounced Dess-so; born June 11, 1921, in London, England; daughter of George William Darling (an educator) and Hilda (Ledward-Wallers) Thomsett; married Walter Saloman, June 3, 1949 (divorced, 1959); married Henry Montague Dessau-Greene (an accountant), August 27, 1971; children: (first marriage) Nicholas. *Education:* Studied at Royal Academy of Music, 1927-37; Rachel McMillan Training College, qualified teacher, 1938-41, nursery school diploma, 1941. *Religion:* Church of England. *Home:* 12 Wavertree Rd., South Woodford, London E18 1BL, England.

CAREER: Teacher at nursery school at Glyndebourne Opera House, Sussex, England, 1941-45; nursery school teacher in London, England, 1946-49; headmistress of nursery school in London, 1949-53; teacher of general subjects at infant school in London, 1958-66; Avondale Park School, London, teacher of remedial subjects, 1966-70, music specialist, 1970-77; full-time writer, 1977—. Guest on radio programs. *Awards, hon-*

ors: First prize in a national poetry competition, 1965, for "Neptune."

WRITINGS—Novels: *The Red-Haired Brat* (first volume of a trilogy), R. Hale, 1978, St. Martin's, 1979; *Absolute Elizabeth* (second volume of trilogy), R. Hale, 1978, St. Martin's, 1979; *Fantastic Marvellous Queen* (third volume of trilogy), R. Hale, 1979; *The Grey Goose,* R. Hale, 1979; *Cock Robin,* R. Hale, 1980; *Amazing Grace,* R. Hale, 1980; *Lord of the Ladies,* R. Hale, 1981; *The Constant Lover,* R. Hale, 1982; *The Loveliest Girl in London,* R. Hale, in press.

Children's plays: "Long Ago on Christmas Eve," published in *Child Education,* 1952. Also author of "Virtue Victorious," "Virus Victrix," "The Misadventures of Miss," "Never Say Die," and "Press on Regardless."

WORK IN PROGRESS: Three children's plays.

SIDELIGHTS: Joanna Dessau told *CA:* "I have written all my life, but not for publication. In 1959 my marriage broke down and my husband and I divorced. The next ten years were very difficult indeed and I had a great struggle with tough circumstances and declining health, but I never stopped writing. I wrote plays, stories, and music for children, all of which were used and/or performed in the schools in which I taught.

"One of my pupils was the pop music star Adam Ant, with whom I never lost touch, for he was one of my son's greatest friends; he still writes to me and telephones me.

"In 1971 I remarried and at once my life became less pressured. I found myself able to relax enough to collect my thoughts, to have time to sit and work on a project that had been dear to my heart for a very long time—a historical novel on the subject of my favorite lady, Queen Elizabeth I. History is a passion with me and was one of the subjects I taught.

"I did not hurry over this project, for my new husband owned a large-ish Victorian house on the edge of Essex which was in dire and urgent need of decoration and restoration. Regretfully, I gave up my beloved flat in St. John's Wood, and turned many of my energies to the herculean task of the house. We did it all ourselves and, in the main, it was great, for I love interior decorating. I made enormous curtains, covered furniture, brought the garden back to life, and discovered a talent for wallpapering and plastering!

"During this time I was working in a deprived area in West London, driving myself right across London every day. I had also become a music specialist, working in the mornings only, on doctor's orders.

"In 1976 my book was ready to send to a publisher. Six weeks later the manuscript was accepted, with an option for two more novels. I have not stopped writing since then, and all my work has been published.

"*The Red-Haired Brat* and *Absolute Elizabeth* are the first two books of my trilogy on Queen Elizabeth I; they deal with the childhood and teenage years of the great queen and the early years of her reign. *Fantastical Marvellous Queen* is the story of Elizabeth until the end of her life—her sorrows, triumphs, her canny politics, and her death in 1603. These three books may be read on their own as separate works.

"*The Grey Goose* is the tale of Lady Jane Grey's (the Nine Days Queen) sister, Lady Catherine Grey, whose life was one of great misfortune and sadness. An heiress to the throne, she made a secret and what was considered an unsuitable marriage, was parted from her husband and children, and kept under house arrest in various great mansions, eventually dying of sorrow at the early age of twenty-seven.

"*Cock Robin* tells the story of Robert Dudley, Earl of Leicester, the handsome, dashing favorite of Queen Elizabeth I, of his family's disgrace, his own eventual rise to fame and fortune, and his lonely death.

"*Lord of the Ladies* is the life story of the poet Lord Byron. It describes his childhood as a cripple, his great beauty and genius, and his myriad love affairs (one probably with his half-sister). This scandal and his mountainous debts caused him to leave England for the Continent, where his wild lifestyle is still recalled today. He died, the victim of that lifestyle and his doctors, and was hailed as the Savior of Greece in that country's struggle for independence.

"*The Constant Lover* is about the Prince Regent who eventually became King George IV. He lived from 1762 to 1830 and was possessed of a wild, wayward, excitable, dramatic temperament that longed for love. The book tells of his amours and the great, though erratic, love he bore for Maria Fitzherbert, the beautiful widow he married in secret. It was said of him that he 'was not constant in love, but constantly a lover.' I had great fun writing this.

"My mother was descended from Sir John Dowdall, a courtier at the court of Queen Elizabeth I. His daughter, Elizabeth, married the Cromwellian general Sir Hardress Waller, the Wolf of Cornwall. He was Oliver Cromwell's aide-de-camp and cousin to Edmund Waller, the Restoration poet-laureate under King Charles II. My mother was also descended from Sir Josiah Wedgwood of pottery fame, and from Charles Darwin, the naturalist.

"My father is descended from a farming family in Scotland, a son of which left for England in the eighteenth century and became a lighthouse keeper at Bamburgh, a remote village on the coast of Northumberland. His name was Robert Darling. His son, William, succeeded him as lighthouse keeper and William's youngest daughter was the famous Grace Darling. William's elder brother, Robert, left for London in 1797, and my father is descended from this branch of the family.

"*Amazing Grace* is the story of the life and death of Grace Darling, England's first national heroine, who, with her father, rowed out in a terrible storm to rescue shipwrecked survivors stranded on a rock far out to sea. She lived with her parents in the lonely lighthouse and was very shy; her resultant fame was really the cause of her death.

"I retired early from teaching, after a mastectomy, and now wonder how I ever found time to go to work! I collect antique china, rare books, and Victorian children's books, but I also own some enjoyable heirlooms, some of which were Grace Darling's, sent by her to our branch of the family.

"I have traveled to Venice for my book on Lord Byron, and all over England for my other books. I am very lucky in that my publisher allows me my own way over the book jackets. I choose what I want, get permission to use pictures or works of art that I like, and a wonderful artist reproduces these most beautifully. I enjoy this very much.

"As far as other travels and expeditions go, I have been behind the Iron Curtain, in Czechoslovakia and Hungary, and found it very depressing. I have been to Amsterdam and other parts of the Netherlands, which I love, and to the Loire Valley, the Haute Auvergne, to Paris and to Brussels. I hope to visit glorious Venice again, purely for pleasure this time. It is the most marvelous place I have ever seen. I feel that I belong there.

"As for my writings, I should add that one of my children's musical plays was published in an educational periodical in 1952, and the songs from it were later published in an album of songs for infants, ''Songs for the School Assembly,'' released by Evans Brothers Ltd. in 1957, which, I believe, is still going strong.''

AVOCATIONAL INTERESTS: "I draw and paint, knit and sew, play the piano and write music, and am a very keen photographer. I am greatly interested in architecture and archaeology and social history. I am a voracious reader with an extremely catholic taste. I model in clay and sing to professional standard. I have, in addition, a great attraction to psychology and psychiatry, finding people and their motivations utterly fascinating. I am an astrologer and draw up birth charts; although I was not trained to do this, I come from a very psychic family.''

* * *

DEUTSCH, Helene (Rosenbach)   1884-1982

OBITUARY NOTICE: Born October 9, 1884, in Przemysl, Austro-Hungarian Empire (now Poland); died March 29, 1982, in Cambridge, Mass. Psychoanalyst, educator, social activist, and author. Deutsch was the first female analyst to be psychoanalyzed by Sigmund Freud, the founder of psychoanalysis, who appointed her director of the Vienna Psychoanalytic Institute in 1923. Deutsch later immigrated to the United States, where she established a private practice. Politically active all her life, Deutsch marched against the war in Vietnam and worked for women's rights. Yet her psychoanalytic theories, which follow those of Freud, have been attacked by feminists who discredit Deutsch's two-volume study, *The Psychology of Women.* In this work, Deutsch contends that three essential female traits are passivity, masochism, and narcissism. Deutsch is also known for her identification and description of a dependent personality type called the ''as if'' personality. Her other publications include *Selected Problems of Adolescence* and *Confrontations With Myself: An Epilogue.* Obituaries and other sources: *New York Times,* July 30, 1978, April 1, 1982; *Washington Post,* April 1, 1982; *Newsweek,* April 5, 1982; *Time,* April 12, 1982.

* * *

DEVERAUX, Jude
See WHITE, Jude Gilliam

* * *

DEW, Donald   1928-

PERSONAL: Born March 26, 1928, in Baltimore, Md.; son of Edgar Homer (a watchmaker) and Henrietta (an art teacher; maiden name, Castler) Dew; married Norma Wright, August 16, 1952 (divorced, April, 1968); married Myra Ellen Westman (an X-ray technologist), June 21, 1968; children: Elizabeth, Edward Donald, John Frederick. *Education:* University of Maryland, B.A., 1950; University of Iowa, M.A., 1956, Ph.D., 1958. *Politics:* Democrat. *Religion:* Episcopalian. *Home:* 2139 Northwest 29th Ave., Gainesville, Fla. 32605. *Office:* Department of Speech, University of Florida, Gainesville, Fla. 32611.

CAREER: University of Maryland, College Park, instructor, 1957-58, assistant professor of speech, 1958-61; University of Alabama, University, assistant professor of speech, 1961-63; University of Florida, Gainesville, assistant professor, 1963-69, associate professor, 1970-77, professor of speech, 1977—. Visiting assistant professor at University of Washington, Seattle, 1969-70. *Military service:* U.S. Navy, 1945-46.

MEMBER: International Society for Phonetic Sciences, Acoustical Society of America, American Speech and Hearing

Association (fellow), American Association for the Advancement of Science, Speech Communication Association, Society for the Preservation and Encouragement of Barber Shop Quartet Singing in America (president, 1978), Sigma Xi.

WRITINGS: (With Alfred D. Jenson) *Phonetic Transcription: An Audio Tutorial Program,* C. E. Merrill, 1974, 2nd edition, 1979; (with Paul J. Jenson) *Phonetic Processing: The Dynamics of Speech,* C. E. Merrill, 1977. Assistant editor of *Journal of Speech and Hearing Research;* associate editor of *Speech Monographs* and *Quarterly Journal of Speech;* ad hoc editor of *Phonetica.*

SIDELIGHTS: Dew wrote: "Although speaking is basic to human societies, little is known of the process involved. Phonetics, the study of the production, transmission, and perception of speech, offers the brightest prospects for scientific investigation. Moreover, this study of normal processes is basic to an understanding of misarticulations—the most common speech disorder. Thus, my efforts have been devoted to understanding phonetics and relating that understanding to others."

* * *

DICK, Philip K(indred)   1928-1982
(Richard Phillips)

OBITUARY NOTICE—See index for *CA* sketch: Born December 16, 1928, in Chicago, Ill.; died of heart failure following a stroke, March 2, 1982, in Santa Ana, Calif. Author. Best known for his science-fiction novels, Dick wrote thirty-five books and six collections of short stories, most dealing with the nature of reality. Dick's writings, in which ordinary protagonists confront bizarre, frightening, or extraordinary circumstances, are linked by recurring themes involving drugs, precognition, androids, and subworlds. *The Man in the High Castle,* his 1962 fantasy novel about Hitler winning World War II, received the Hugo Award for best science fiction novel of the year, and in 1974 Dick won the Campbell Memorial Award for an anti-drug novel, *Flow My Tears, the Policeman Said.* His last novel, *The Transmigration of Timothy Archer,* was published posthumously by Timescape. "Blade Runner," a motion picture based on Dick's book *Do Androids Dream of Electric Sheep,* was released shortly after the author's death. Obituaries and other sources: *New York Times,* March 3, 1982; *Chicago Tribune,* March 4, 1982; *Los Angeles Times,* March 8, 1982; *Newsweek,* March 15, 1982; *London Times,* March 15, 1982; *Time,* March 15, 1982; *Publishers Weekly,* March 19, 1982.

* * *

DICK, Trevor J.O.   1934-

BRIEF ENTRY: Born in 1934 in Toronto, Ontario, Canada. Canadian economist, educator, and author. Dick lectured at the Royal Military College of Canada from 1963 to 1965, and then spent two years as a statistician for the Canadian Government. In 1970 he began teaching economics at the University of Western Ontario. Dick compiled *Economic History of Canada: A Guide to Information Sources* (Gale, 1978) and wrote *An Economic Theory of Technological Change: The Case of Patents and the United States Railroads, 1871-1950* (Arno, 1978). *Address:* Department of Economics, University of Lethbridge, 4401 University Dr., Lethbridge, Alberta, Canada T1K 3M4.

DICKERSON, Oliver M(orton)   1875-1966

OBITUARY NOTICE: Born September 8, 1875, in Jasper County, Ill.; died November 26, 1966. Historian, educator, and author. A teacher of history, political science, and social science, Dickerson was an expert on colonial America and the American Revolution. He taught at schools and colleges in Illinois, Minnesota, and Colorado. His many publications include *American Colonial Government, Boston Under Military Rule, 1768-1769, The Navigation Acts and the American Revolution,* and *Use Made of the Revenue From the Tax on Tea.* Obituaries and other sources: *Who Was Who in America, With World Notables,* Volume IV: *1961-1968,* Marquis, 1968.

* * *

DICKERSON, Robert B(radford), Jr.   1955-

PERSONAL: Born August 22, 1955, in Detroit, Mich.; son of Robert Bradford and Anna J. (Marlow) Dickerson. *Education:* Attended Wayne State University, 1971-72; University of Hawaii, 1972-73; Escuela Nacional de Idiomas, Spanish Teaching Certificate, 1977. *Religion:* "Heavily influenced by a Jewish grandparent." *Home:* 7941 Vernier Lane, Fair Haven, Mich. 48023.

CAREER: Associated with Ford Espana (Spanish division of Ford Motor Co.), 1975-78; flight coordinator with Bard Air, 1978-79; associated with B. Dalton Bookseller, 1981-82. Has worked as a teacher and as a translator.

WRITINGS: Final Placement: A Guide to the Deaths, Funerals, and Burials of Famous Americans, Reference Publications, 1982.

WORK IN PROGRESS: Child's Play: A Guide to Using Play as Therapy.

SIDELIGHTS: Dickerson commented: "I feel most at home in Western Europe, preferably in the south of France or the Levante coast of Spain. Although I speak Spanish fluently, my real love is Catalan, and I would very much like to do some writing in that language.

"I began to write seriously while living in Europe. Although I composed reams of material, I lacked the guidance and feedback of an experienced editor. Shortly after returning to the United States I met Keith Irvine, who was to become something of a mentor to me. Keith suggested the concept for my book, *Final Placement,* and guided that project from the intial outline stage to finished book.

"My writing habits tend to be sporadic and nocturnal. I find that I work best from midnight until eight o'clock in the morning. Unfortunately, I was unable to work on *Final Placement* on that schedule. Few libraries, if any, are open to accommodate such hours. Perhaps meeting the right woman (something my life very much needs) would change my schedule.

"The writers that have most influenced me are Keith Irvine and Henry Miller. Keith has such dedication to intense and thorough research. Truth and integrity are very important parts of his life. If only a small amount of his philosophies have rubbed off on me then I consider myself to be quite privileged. As for Henry Miller, I am not sure whether he loved Europe or beautiful women more. In that way I consider myself to be very much like him. I very much wanted to meet him but was not able to.

"James Michener has also influenced me to a great extent. He is able to paint a very true and total picture of so many far-off places that I developed an intense wanderlust that cannot be tamed.

"There is also a group of English, French, and Spanish authors who have influenced me. Among them are D. H. Lawrence, Albert Camus, Paul Nizan, Miguel de Unamuno, Ortega y Gasset, Ramon Sender, and Buero Vallejo.

"My advice to anyone who seriously desires to be published is to somehow begin a friendship or correspondence with an established writer. The feedback, advice, experience, and ideas to be garnered will be invaluable."

*   *   *

DIETRICH, Noah   1889-1982

OBITUARY NOTICE—See index for *CA* sketch: Born February 28, 1889, in Batavia, Wis.; died February 15, 1982, in Palm Springs, Calif. Accountant, financial adviser, and author. As chief business adviser to the late Howard Hughes for more than thirty years, Dietrich directed most of the billionaire's business interests, including the Hughes Tool Company, defense contracting, hotel investments, and motion-picture dealings. In 1957, after a bitter dispute with Hughes over money, Dietrich was fired. He wrote the controversial biography *Howard: The Amazing Mr. Hughes,* in which he questioned the sanity of his former employer. Obituaries and other sources: *Time,* March 1, 1982; *Newsweek,* March 1, 1982.

*   *   *

DIGGS, Bernard James   1916-

BRIEF ENTRY: Born July 11, 1916, in Norfolk, Va. American philosopher, educator, and author. Diggs joined the faculty at University of Illinois in 1946 and became a professor of philosophy in 1963. He wrote *Love and Being: An Investigation Into the Metaphysics of St. Thomas Aquinas* (S. F. Vanni, 1974)and edited *The State, Justice, and the Common Good: An Introduction to Social and Political Philosophy* (Scott, Foresman, 1974). *Address:* Department of Philosophy, University of Illinois, 105 Gregory Hall, Urbana, Ill. 61801. *Biographical/critical sources: Directory of American Scholars,* Volume IV: *Philosophy, Religion, and Law,* 7th edition, Bowker, 1978.

*   *   *

di GUISA, Giano
See PRAZ, Mario

*   *   *

DIRKS, Raymond L(ouis)   1934-

PERSONAL: Born in 1934 in Fort Wayne, Ind.; son of Raymond (an army officer) and Virginia Dirks; divorced. *Education:* Received degree from DePauw University, 1955. *Residence:* New York, N.Y.

CAREER: Associated with Bankers Trust, 1959-63, became chief insurance analyst; senior insurance analyst with Goldman, Sachs & Co., 1963-64; worked at G. A. Saxton & Co., New York City, 1964-69; Dirks Brothers Ltd. (now division of Delafield Childs, Inc.), New York City, co-founder, 1969; Delafield Childs, Inc., New York City, senior vice-president until 1973; associated with John Muir & Co., New York City. Producer of plays during 1960's.

WRITINGS: (With Leonard Gross) *The Great Wall Street Scandal,* McGraw, 1974; *Heads, You Win, Tails, You Win: The Dirks Investment Formula,* Stein & Day, 1979.

SIDELIGHTS: Stock market analyst Raymond Dirks is often described as a hardworking individualist who relishes any chance to uncover corporate wrongdoings. It was largely because of this reputation that a discontented ex-employee of Equity Funding Corporation of America approached Dirks with evidence that officials of the corporation were engaged in a scheme that involved falsified records, counterfeit insurance policies, and millions of dollars in fraudulent assets. In his effort to discover whether the accusations against the insurance firm were true, Dirks met secretly with other disgruntled Equity Funding executives. As soon as they had confirmed their former co-worker's allegations, Dirks alerted institutions holding large blocks of Equity stock. They reacted to the tip-off by selling their stock, and in a short time the once-thriving insurance firm was bankrupt.

In his book *The Great Wall Street Scandal* Dirks illustrates his role in the downfall of Equity Funding. When he first learned of the potential scandal, he decided not to go to the regulatory authorities because, he claims, an investigation through normal channels would have taken too long. Had Equity Funding officials learned of an impending investigation by the New York Stock Exchange (NYSE) or the Securities and Exchange Commission (SEC), they would have had time to effect a cover-up. "I felt my job was to check out the information given to me and expose the fraud," Dirks explained to *Newsweek.* "I had to act quickly, and the only way to do it was to make it public." As a result of Dirks's swift actions, Equity stock (once considered highly desirable) rapidly lost its market value. Investors who were incurring vast losses began to pressure the regulators, and the resulting confusion eliminated the possibility of a cover-up.

Though Dirks did succeed in "blowing the whistle" on Equity Funding, he did not win friends in the NYSE or the SEC. Both accused him of fraud and of spreading rumors for personal profit. (Several of Dirks's clients had been Equity shareholders.) Although defending himself against those charges has cost Dirks thousands of dollars, he insisted that he would do the same thing again. "I feel a lot of satisfaction from the notoriety; I enjoy being recognized as a well-known individual," he told *Newsweek.* "Sure, I feel bitter against the SEC. And yet, I feel I've accomplished something."

BIOGRAPHICAL/CRITICAL SOURCES: New York Times, April 21, 1973; *Biography News,* Volume 1, Gale, 1974; *Philadelphia Bulletin,* June 25, 1974; *Newsweek,* February 14, 1977.*

*   *   *

DIRKS, Rudolph   1877-1968

OBITUARY NOTICE: Born in 1877 in Heinde, Germany; died April 20, 1968, in New York, N.Y. Painter, engraver, and cartoonist. Considered one of the founding fathers of American comics, Dirks created the successful "Katzenjammer Kids" strip in 1897 at the age of twenty. "The Katzenjammer Kids" originally appeared in the *New York Journal,* a newspaper owned by William Randolph Hearst. When Dirks decided in 1912 to devote himself to a life of painting in Europe, Hearst took the comic strip away from its creator. The ensuing court battle set legal precedents that affect current comic strip jurisprudence. In 1914 Dirks won the right to draw his characters for another newspaper under a different title, "Hans and Fritz," later changed to "The Captain and the Kids." A painter and engraver associated with various artistic movements, Dirks co-founded the Ogunquit, Maine, artists' colony. His cartoons were published in collections, including *The Katzenjammer Kids: Early Strips in Full Color,* which appeared in 1974.

Obituaries and other sources: *Time,* March 4, 1957, May 3, 1968; *New York Times,* April 22, 1968; *Newsweek,* May 6, 1968; *The World Encyclopedia of Comics,* Chelsea House, 1976; *Who's Who in American Art,* Bowker, 1978.

*   *   *

DITCUM, Steve
   See CRUMB, R(obert)

*   *   *

DIXON, Franklin W.
   See ADAMS, Harriet S(tratemeyer)

*   *   *

DOBIE, Ann B(rewster)   1935-

PERSONAL: Born December 20, 1935, in El Dorado, Ark.; daughter of O.T. and Lila (Krebs) Brewster; married C. Walter Dobie (a petroleum geologist), July 14, 1956; children: David Brewster, Charles A. *Education:* University of Oklahoma, B.Mus., 1956; University of Southwestern Louisiana, M.A. (education), 1963, M.A. (English), 1966; Columbia University, Ed.D., 1981. *Politics:* Republican. *Religion:* Episcopalian. *Home:* 7 Oak Glen, Lafayette, La. 70503. *Office:* Department of English, University of Southwestern Louisiana, Lafayette, La. 70504-4691.

CAREER: University of Southwestern Louisiana, Lafayette, instructor, 1963-72, assistant professor of English, 1973—. Gives workshops. *Member:* American Association of University Professors, American Association of University Women, Conference on College Composition and Communication, South Central Modern Language Association, Louisiana Teachers Association.

WRITINGS: Comprehension and Composition: An Introduction to the Essay, Macmillan, 1980; *Using Words, Sentences, Paragraphs,* Macmillan, 1982. Contributor of more than twenty-five articles and reviews to language and speech journals and newspapers.

WORK IN PROGRESS: A revised edition of *Comprehension and Composition.*

SIDELIGHTS: Ann Dobie wrote: "Because of my varied academic background, including as it does degrees in music, education, and English, I find myself interested in more than one form of human expression. I am concerned with all forms of the humanities and the arts because I feel it increasingly important for man to pursue the creation and study of those artifacts which help him to understand himself. They may take shape in language, paint and canvas, or body movement, but their value lies in their power to show us ourselves and our possibilities."

*   *   *

DOBSON, Julia   1941-

PERSONAL: Born September 23, 1941, in Tanzania, East Africa; daughter of Kenneth (a civil servant) and Barbara (Phillips) Dobson; married Christopher Tugendhat (a politician), April 8, 1967; children: James, Angus. *Education:* Lady Margaret Hall, Oxford, B.A., 1963. *Politics:* Conservative. *Religion:* Church of England. *Home:* 1 Caroline Ter., London S.W.1, England. *Agent:* Pat White, 11 Mortimer St., London W1N 7RH, England.

CAREER: Grey Coat School for Girls, London, England, history teacher, 1963-64; Peckham Manor School for Boys, Peckham, England, history teacher, 1964-65; *Time,* New York City, secretary, 1965-66; *Town,* London, general writer, 1966-67; Glendower Primary School, London, teacher, 1967-71; writer, 1971—. Member of committee for Salvation Army's children's home; member of Waterloo Committee; member of Board of Management of British Schools in Brussels. Patron of British and Commonwealth Women's Club. *Member:* Westminster Children's Society.

WRITINGS—Juveniles; published by Heinemann: *The Children of Charles I* (illustrated by David Walker), 1975; *The Smallest Man in England* (illustrated by Joanna Troughton), 1977; *Children of the Tower* (illustrated by Jeroo Roy), 1978; *They Were at Waterloo* (illustrated by Roy), 1979.

Adventure series for Magnet Books: *The Ivory Poachers,* 1981; *The Tomb Robbers,* 1981; *Animals in Danger,* 1982; *The Wreak Finders,* 1982.

WORK IN PROGRESS: "I am in the process of writing two more books for the adventure series."

SIDELIGHTS: "My writing arose out of my teaching experience," Dobson told *CA.* "I found that children read too little and too unwillingly about 'boring' subjects like history, so I set out to write educational books that were exciting as well as informative. In so doing, I may have dealt with my historical material too selectively, but I may have succeeded in livening up history.

"My father wrote some novels when he was young, and my great grandfather, Austin Dobson, was a famous biographer and poet. So I guess I have inherited some literary urge from the Dobsons. My chief problem as a writer married to a public figure is finding time for creative thought in a life in which public and social duties play a large part."

AVOCATIONAL INTERESTS: "My avocational interests are largely centered round children."

*   *   *

DOGG, Professor R. L.
   See BERMAN, Ed

*   *   *

DOLAN, John Patrick   1923-1982(?)

OBITUARY NOTICE—See index for *CA* sketch: Born March 11, 1923, in Waterloo, Iowa; died c. 1982 in Columbia, S.C. Educator, translator, editor, and author. Best known as the editor of the ten-volume work *History of the Church,* Dolan was a professor of history at the University of South Carolina before becoming professor of public health in 1976. He also served as the "Cold War Chaplain" with the U.S. High Commission in Germany from 1952 until 1957. Among the works he edited are *The Essential Thomas More* and *The Church in the Age of Feudalism.* His writings include *Erasmus, Erasmian Influences in the Cleve Church Ordinances, History of the Reformation,* and *Catholicism: An Historical Survey.* He also translated the work of Desiderus Erasmus, which he published as *The Essential Erasmus.* Obituaries and other sources: *AB Bookman's Weekly,* February 22, 1982.

*   *   *

DOLLAR, Jimmy
   See SHAGINYAN, Marietta Sergeyevna

DONNER, Fred McGraw 1945-

PERSONAL: Born September 30, 1945, in Washington, D.C.; son of George Robert, Sr. (an insurance executive) and Myrtilla (McGraw) Donner. *Education:* Princeton University, B.A., 1968, Ph.D., 1975; attended University of Erlangen, 1970-71. *Office:* Oriental Institute, University of Chicago, 1155 East 58th St., Chicago, Ill. 60637.

CAREER: Yale University, New Haven, Conn., assistant professor, 1975-81, associate professor of Middle Eastern history, 1981-82; University of Chicago, Chicago, Ill., associate professor of near Eastern languages, 1982—. *Military service:* U.S. Army, 1968-70. *Member:* Middle East Studies Association of North America, Middle East Institute, American Oriental Society.

WRITINGS: The Early Islamic Conquests, Princeton University Press, 1981. Contributor of articles and reviews to scholarly journals.

WORK IN PROGRESS: Early Arabic Historiography, a monograph.

SIDELIGHTS: Donner lived in Lebanon, 1966-67, and has conducted research in England, Ireland, Germany, Turkey, Iran, Syria, Lebanon, India, and Egypt. He told *CA:* ''Despite the subject of my current research, I am really most interested in various topics of social history, particularly in how social structures in various societies support power structures; what I like to call the 'social foundations of power.' Eastern context this has involved me in an examination of the 'tribal' organization of some groups, and into examining the role of nomadic groups in Middle Eastern history.''

*   *   *

DONNISON, David Vernon 1926-

PERSONAL: Born January 19, 1926, in Yenangyaung, Burma; son of F.S.V. and Ruth (Singer) Donnison; married Jean Elizabeth Kidger, 1950; children: Rachel, Christopher, Polly, Harry. *Education:* Magdalen College, Oxford, B.A., 1950. *Home:* 12 Holyrood Cres., Glasgow G20 6HJ, Scotland. *Office:* Department of Town and Regional Planning, University of Glasgow, Glasgow, Scotland.

CAREER: University of Manchester, Manchester, England, assistant lecturer in social administration, 1950-53; University of Toronto, Toronto, Ontario, lecturer in social work, 1953-55; University of London, London School of Economics and Political Science, London, England, reader, 1956-61, professor of social administration, 1961-69; chairman of Public Schools Commission, 1968-70; director of Centre for Environmental Studies, 1969-75; chairman of Supplementary Benefits Commission, 1975-80; University of Glasgow, Glasgow, Scotland, professor of town and regional planning, 1980—.

WRITINGS: The Neglected Child and the Social Services, Manchester University Press, 1954; *Welfare Services in a Canadian Community,* University of Toronto Press, 1958; *The Government of Housing,* Penguin, 1965; *Social Policy and Administration,* Allen & Unwin, 1967; (editor with D. Eversley) *London: Urban Patterns, Problems, and Policies,* Heinemann, 1973; *Social Policy and Administration Revisited,* Allen & Unwin, 1975; (with Paul Soto) *The Good City: A Study of Urban Development and Policy in Britain,* Heinemann, 1979; *The Politics of Poverty,* Martin Robertson, 1982; (with Clare Ungerson) *Housing Policy,* Penguin, 1982.

DONOVAN, Josephine 1941-

PERSONAL: Born March 10, 1941, in Manila, Philippines; American citizen born abroad; daughter of William N. (a physician) and Josephine (Devigne) Donovan. *Education:* Bryn Mawr College, A.B. (cum laude), 1962; University of Wisconsin—Madison (formerly University of Wisconsin), M.A., 1967, Ph.D., 1971. *Home:* 294 Dennett St., Portsmouth, N.H. 03801.

CAREER: University of Kentucky, Lexington, assistant professor in honors program, 1971-76; University of New Hampshire, Durham, coordinator of women's studies program, 1977-80; University of Tulsa, Tulsa, Okla., visiting scholar, 1982—. Consultant to National Endowment for the Humanities. *Member:* Modern Language Association of America, Women's Caucus for the Modern Languages.

WRITINGS: (Contributor) Susan Koppelman-Cornillon, editor, *Images of Women in Fiction,* Bowling Green Popular Press, 1972; (editor and contributor) *Feminist Literary Criticism: Explorations in Theory,* University Press of Kentucky, 1975; (contributor) Lina Mainiero, editor, *American Women Writers: A Critical Reference Guide From Colonial Times to the Present,* Ungar, 1979; (contributor) Ruth Borker, Nelly Furman, and Sally McConnell-Ginet, editors, *Women and Language in Literature and Society,* Praeger, 1980; *Sarah Orne Jewett,* Ungar, 1980; (contributor) *Feminist Literary Criticism,* National Humanities Center, 1981; *The New England Local Color School: Women's Literary Realism From Stowe to Freeman,* Unger, 1982; *Feminist Theory: A Historical Survey,* Ungar, in press. Contributor of articles and reviews to literature journals.

SIDELIGHTS: Donovan told *CA:* ''Feminist literary criticism assumes that there is a moral dimension to literature, that literature functions as part of the cultural propaganda of society, that it does affect people's lives, their ways of thinking, their behavior. In much of Western literature the moral being of women has been denied or repressed. Feminist literary criticism points this out and looks for works (often by women) in which women characters seek to achieve fullness of being.

''In this feminist critical process numerous lost and important works by women have been (and are being) recovered. Feminist literary historians are now beginning to chart the traditions of this lost women's literature. I hope to continue to participate in this work of retrieval and revision: recovering and reanalyzing women's works and rewriting literary history.''

*   *   *

DORMAN, N. B. 1927-

PERSONAL: Born July 12, 1927, in Iowa; daughter of a mail carrier and a dietitian; divorced, 1973; children: two sons. *Education:* California State University, Chico, B.A., 1963. *Residence:* Chico, Calif. *Office address:* Box 775, Chico, Calif. 95927.

CAREER: Worked in clerical and sales positions; assistant county librarian; writer, 1972—. Volunteer in alcohol recovery programs.

WRITINGS: Laughter in the Background (juvenile fiction), Elsevier/North Holland, 1980. Contributor of stories to magazines.

WORK IN PROGRESS: Daddy's Sick and *What Daddy Can Do,* primers on parental alcoholism; *Petey and Miss Magic,* a book on family rejection; *The Mystery of the Red Hen,* a juvenile mystery dealing with child abuse; *The Secret Summer,* a juvenile adventure; *The Day of the Great Apple Sale,* a juvenile set during the Depression and dealing with a death in the family; *The Smallest Farm,* with Morgan H. Mussel, a juvenile on urban homesteading; *Sister to Sheauna,* a juvenile on mental retardation; *What's Wrong?,* a book on parental alcoholism; *Mad Olga* and *The Beekeeper's Tale,* both essays for adults on urban homesteading.

SIDELIGHTS: Dorman told *CA:* "I began to write from a sense of my own inadequacy, inferiority, and ignorance—and I still do. My fiction concerns legitimate problems and the struggles necessary to begin finding solutions or coming to terms with the situations. Usually the subjects are alcoholism, retardation, death, or loneliness. My main theme is probably personal responsibility.

"I know several small farmers or workers with poor people, such as teachers and monks, in impoverished sections of the world—Africa, South America, and areas of the Pacific. I feel strongly (and try to live so) that if you have even a scrap of land, you have perhaps a moral obligation to raise at least some part of your own food. I grow fruit, vegetables, and nuts, and have chickens, ducks, and rabbits on a city-sized lot."

*   *   *

DORSON, Richard M(ercer)   1916-1981

PERSONAL: Born March 12, 1916, in New York, N.Y.; died September 11, 1981, in Bloomington, Ind.; son of Louis Jasper (in business) and Gertrude (Lester) Dorson; married Dorothy Diamond, 1940 (divorced, 1948); married Gloria Irene Gluski (an actress), August 8, 1953; children: (first marriage) Ronald; (second marriage) Roland, Jeffrey, Linda. *Education:* Harvard University, A.B., 1937, M.A., 1940, Ph.D., 1943. *Home:* 1223 Southdowns Dr., Bloomington, Ind. 47401. *Office:* 504 North Fess St., Bloomington, Ind. 47401.

CAREER: Harvard University, Cambridge, Mass., instructor in history, 1943-44; Michigan State University, East Lansing, instructor, 1944-46, assistant professor, 1946-48, associate professor, 1948-56, professor of history, 1956-57; University of Tokyo, Tokyo, Japan, Fulbright visiting professor of American studies, 1956-57; Indiana University, Bloomington, professor of history and folklore, 1957-71, distinguished professor, 1971-81, director of Folklore Institute, 1963-81. Visiting professor at University of Minnesota, summer, 1947, Harvard University, summer, 1952, University of California, Berkeley, spring, 1968, and University of Pennsylvania, fall, 1980. Referee on folklore, 1955-81, and member of educational advisory board, 1971-81, for John Simon Guggenheim Memorial Foundation. Member of National Endowment for the Humanities research grants selection committee, 1972-75; member of Smithsonian Institution Folklife Council, 1977-81; chairman of Conference on Folklore and Literary Anthropology, Calcutta, India, 1978.

MEMBER: American Council of Learned Societies, American Folklore Society (member of executive board, 1962-66; president, 1966-68; secretary, vice-president, and president of Society of Fellows, 1969-72) American Historical Association, Organization of American Historians, English Folklore Society, American Studies Association, International Society for Folk Narrative Research (vice-president, 1959-64), International Society of Ethnology and Folklore (vice-president, 1964-71), Cosmos Club.

AWARDS, HONORS: Library of Congress fellowship, 1946; Chicago Folklore Prizes, 1947, for *Jonathan Draws the Long*

Bow, 1965, for *Buying the Wind,* 1969, for *The British Folklorists* and *Peasant Customs and Savage Myths;* Guggenheim fellowships, 1949-50, 1964-65, 1971-72; American Council of Learned Societies fellowships, 1952, 1961-62; National Humanities Center fellowship, 1978-79; recipient of research grants from National Endowment for the Humanities, American Philosophical Society, Olds Foundation, Japan Foundation, Ditchley Foundation, Smithsonian Institution, and Department of Justice.

WRITINGS: Jonathan Draws the Long Bow: New England Popular Tales and Legends, Harvard University Press, 1946, reprinted, Russell, 1970; *Bloodstoppers and Bearwalkers: Folk Traditions of the Upper Peninsula,* Harvard University Press, 1952, reprinted, 1972; *American Folklore,* University of Chicago Press, 1959, revised edition, 1977; *Folk Legends of Japan* (illustrated by Yoshie Noguchi), Tuttle, 1961; *Buying the Wind: Regional Folklore in the United States,* University of Chicago Press, 1964; *The British Folklorists: A History,* Routledge & Kegan Paul, 1968, University of Chicago Press, 1969; *American Folklore and the Historian,* University of Chicago Press, 1971; *Folklore: Selected Essays,* Indiana University Press, 1972; *America in Legend: Folklore From the Colonial Period to the Present* (Book-of-the-Month Club selection), Pantheon, 1973; *Folklore and Fakelore: Essays Toward a Discipline of Folk Studies,* Harvard University Press, 1976.

Editor: Davy Crockett, American Comic Legend, Spiral Press, 1939, reprinted, Arno, 1980; *America Begins: Early American Writing,* Pantheon, 1950, reprinted, Books for Libraries, 1972; *America Rebels: Narratives of the Patriots* (American History Publication Society selection), Pantheon, 1953, reprinted, Greenwood Press, 1973; *Negro Folktales in Michigan,* Harvard University Press, 1956, reprinted, Greenwood Press, 1974; *Negro Tales From Pine Bluff, Arkansas, and Calvin, Michigan,* Indiana University Press, 1958; *Folklore Research Around the World: A North American Point of View,* Indiana University Press, 1961; (with Toichi Mabuchi and Tokihiko Oto) *Studies in Japanese Folklore,* Indiana University Press, 1963; *American Negro Folktales,* Fawcett Publications, 1967, hardcover edition, Peter Smith, 1969; *Peasant Customs and Savage Myths: Selections From the British Folklorists,* two volumes, University of Chicago Press, 1968; *African Folklore,* Doubleday, 1972; *Folklore and Folklife: An Introduction,* University of Chicago Press, 1972; *Folklore and Traditional History,* Mouton, 1973; *Folktales Told Around the World,* University of Chicago Press, 1975; *Folklore in the Modern World,* Mouton, 1978.

Series editor: (General editor) *Folktales of the World,* University of Chicago Press, 1963-73; (advisory editor) *International Folklore,* forty-eight volumes, Arno, 1977; *Folklore of the World,* thirty-eight volumes, Arno, 1980. Also editor of volumes 12-32 of Indiana University Folklore Institute's monograph series, 1957-81.

Contributor: R. B. Browne and others, editors, *Frontiers of American Culture,* Purdue University Press, 1968; T. P. Coffin, editor, *Our Living Traditions,* Basic Books, 1968; Wayland D. Hand, editor, *American Folk Legend: A Symposium,* University of California Press, 1971; Bernard J. Siegel, editor, *Annual Review of Anthropology,* two volumes, Annual Reviews, 1973; *We Americans,* National Geographic Society, 1975.

Contributor to periodicals, including *American Scholar, Saturday Review of Literature, Science Digest, American Heritage, Atlantic, Times Literary Supplement, New Republic, American Folklore, New American Mercury, Folklore Forum,* and *Current Anthropology.* Contributor to encyclopedias, including *Encyclopaedia Britannica* and *Encyclopedia Universalis*. Book review editor of *Southern Folklore Quarterly,* 1945-49; book review editor, 1952-56, and editor, 1957-62, of *Journal of American Folklore Society;* founder and editor of *Journal of Folklore Institute,* 1963-81.

SIDELIGHTS: Richard Dorson, said Ann Chowning in the *American Anthropologist,* was influential in "presenting the study of folklore as something approaching an exact science." As a collector, the folklorist accumulated examples of magic, marchen, music, nursery rhymes, and other folk literature and art from all areas of the world, particularly from the United States.

His *Jonathan Draws the Long Bow* exemplifies the folktales of New England while *Bloodstoppers and Bearwalkers* preserves the folk traditions of Michigan's Upper Peninsula. He has anthologized the lore of early American writers, including that which was inspired by their voyages, their perceptions of witchcraft, and their relationships with Indians. What emerges from his *America Begins,* noted a writer in the *New York Herald Tribune Book Review,* is "a remarkable sense of what that new continent was like to the eyes that first saw it, and how it struck them, and what they believed about it or wanted to make others believe." In *America Rebels* Dorson compiled the popular narratives of Revolutionary War veterans, producing "a veritable epitome of the War for Independence," remarked C. E. Carter in the *American Historical Review.*

With writings such as these, Dorson, wrote John McElroy of the *New York Times Book Review,* "tried to establish American folklore as a well-defined branch of our cultural history." "He must surely be," McElroy praised, "one of the great collectors."

BIOGRAPHICAL/CRITICAL SOURCES: Christian Science Monitor, July 25, 1946, July 9, 1964, January 22, 1975; *New York Times,* August 4, 1946, July 5, 1953; *Weekly Book Review,* August 4, 1946; *Springfield Republican,* August 18, 1946, August 16, 1953; *U.S. Quarterly Book List,* December, 1946; *San Francisco Chronicle,* December 29, 1946; *Chicago Sunday Tribune,* July 9, 1950, December 13, 1953; *New York Herald Tribune Book Review,* July 18, 1950, October 12, 1953, September, 4, 1960; *New Yorker,* October 14, 1950, August 1, 1953; *Saturday Review,* July 18, 1953; *New England Quarterly,* September, 1953; *Atlantic,* September, 1953; *American Historical Review,* October, 1953, July, 1960; *Bookmark,* November, 1953.

Times Literary Supplement, March 4, 1960, September 18, 1969; *New York Times Book Review,* January 3, 1960, January 6, 1974, October 13, 1974; *American Anthropologist,* December, 1960, March, 1978, September, 1979; *Spectator,* April 18, 1969; *Journal of American Folklore,* April, 1973, July, 1973, January, 1974, April, 1975, July, 1975, July, 1978, April, 1979; *Washington Post Book World,* December 30, 1973, March 10, 1974; *Saturday Review/World,* February 9, 1974; *Pacific Historical Review,* May, 1974; *Virginia Quarterly Review,* summer, 1974; *Journal of American History,* March, 1975; *America,* March 1, 1975; *Progressive,* June, 1976; *Scientific American,* October, 1976; *Criticism,* spring, 1977.

* * *

DOUDS, Charles Tucker 1898-1982

OBITUARY NOTICE: Born April 11, 1898, in Plumville, Pa.; died January 13, 1982, in Camp Hill, Pa. Government official and author. A regional director for the National Labor Relations Board for nearly twenty years, Douds also served as director

of mediation for the State of Pennsylvania and as an arbitrator in numerous labor disputes. He wrote many articles for professional journals as well as a book of verse, *I Remember Another April.* Obituaries and other sources: *Who's Who in Labor,* Arno, 1976; *Who's Who in America,* 41st edition, Marquis, 1980; *New York Times,* January 15, 1982.

* * *

DOUGHERTY, James (Patrick) 1937-

PERSONAL: Born March 20, 1937, in Wichita, Kan.; son of James P. (in oil business) and Cora (Smyth) Dougherty; married Jacqueline Centunzi, August 18, 1962; children: three. *Education:* St. Louis University, B.A., 1959; University of Pennsylvania, M.A., 1960, Ph.D., 1962. *Religion:* Roman Catholic. *Office:* Department of English, University of Notre Dame, 356 O'Shaughnessy Hall, Notre Dame, Ind. 46556.

CAREER: University of Calgary, Calgary, Alberta, assistant professor of English, 1962-66; University of Notre Dame, Notre Dame, Ind., assistant professor, 1966-69, associate professor, 1969-81, professor of English, 1981—. Vice-president of low-income housing agency, Renew, Inc., 1980—. *Member:* American Studies Association, Conference on Christianity and Literature. *Awards, honors:* Book of the year award from Conference on Christianity and Literature, 1980, for *The Fivesquare City.*

WRITINGS: The Fivesquare City: The City in the Religious Imagination, University of Notre Dame Press, 1980. Contributor to academic journals.

WORK IN PROGRESS: Essays on American visions of city life.

SIDELIGHTS: Dougherty told *CA:* "To me, the city is neither just a sum of social facts, nor just an imaginative construction or 'symbol.' The divorce of imagination from the use of facts has given us the kind of cities we have today. What I look for in literature, and seek in my own life, is an interrelationship of fact with imagination and an awareness of the values that our imaginations seek to express."

* * *

DOUVAN, Elizabeth (Ann Malcolm) 1926-

PERSONAL: Surname is pronounced *Dow*-van; born November 3, 1926, in South Bend, Ind.; daughter of John (an engineer) and Janet (Powers) Malcolm; married Eugene Douvan (an attorney), December 27, 1947; children: Thomas, Catherine. *Education:* Vassar College, A.B., 1946; University of Michigan, M.A., 1948, Ph.D., 1951. *Home:* 2014 Devolson, Ann Arbor, Mich. 48104. *Office:* Department of Psychology, University of Michigan, 580 Union Dr., Ann Arbor, Mich. 48109.

CAREER: University of Michigan, Ann Arbor, study director for social science research at Survey Research Center, 1950-59, lecturer, 1959-63, associate professor, 1963-64, professor, 1964-70, Kellogg professor of psychology, 1965—, program director at Institute for Social Research, 1974—. Member of Ann Arbor Board of Health. *Member:* Women's International League for Peace and Freedom, American Psychological Association (division president), American Sociological Association, American Association of University Women, Democratic Women's Club.

WRITINGS: (With Joseph Adelson) *The Adolescent Experience,* Wiley, 1966; (with Judith M. Bardwick and T. Horner) *Feminine Personality and Conflict,* Brooks/Cole, 1970; (editor with Martin Gold) *Adolescent Development,* Allyn & Bacon, 1971; (with Joseph Veroff and R. Kulka) *The Inner American,* Basic Books, 1981; (with Veroff and Kulka) *Mental Health in America,* Basic Books, 1981. Contributor to psychology and women's studies journals.

WORK IN PROGRESS: A study of American stories, especially historical changes in the structure and content of fantasy.

SIDELIGHTS: Elizabeth Douvan commented: "I seek to encourage, inspire, and instruct the young in all that I do and write."

BIOGRAPHICAL/CRITICAL SOURCES: New York Times Book Review, November 8, 1981.

*   *   *

DOWNIE, Freda (Christina)   1929-

PERSONAL: Born October 20, 1929, in London, England; daughter of Cecil Christian (an engineer) and Rose (Dobinson) Downie; married David Charles James Turner (a civil servant), March, 1957. *Education:* Educated in England and Australia. *Home:* 32 Kings Rd., Berkhamsted, Hertforshire HP4 3BD, England.

CAREER: Worked as music publisher, art agent, commercial librarian, and in bookshop; writer. *Member:* Chopin Society. *Awards, honors:* First prize for poetry from Stroud Festival, 1970, for "Shell" and "A Plain Girl"; poetry award from Arts Council and Provincial Booksellers Fairs Association, 1977, for *A Stranger Here.*

WRITINGS—All Poetry: *Night Music,* Mandeville Press, 1974; *Night Sucks Me In,* Mandeville Press, 1976; *A Stranger Here,* Secker & Warburg, 1977; *Man Dancing With the Moon,* Mandeville Press, 1979; *Plainsong,* Secker & Warburg, 1981. Also author of *A Sensation,* 1975, and co-author with Fred Sedgwick and John Cotton of *A Berkhamsted Three,* 1978.

SIDELIGHTS: Freda Downie wrote: "I have been obsessed with music and painting all my life—I am even spasmodically interested in literature—so I suppose I can only say the poetry, when it's around, is just a condition of my life. I must add that an early discovery of poetry written in America in the 1940's, or thereabouts, was no mean affair."

*   *   *

DRAKE, Paul Winter   1944-

PERSONAL: Born January 23, 1944, in Northfield, Minn.; son of Lyle F. and Mary (Winter) Drake; married Susan Bryant (a lawyer), December 21, 1966; children: Joshua, Elizabeth, Katherine. *Education:* Miami University, Oxford, Ohio, B.A., 1966; Stanford University, Ph.D., 1971. *Office:* Department of History, University of Illinois, 309 Gregory Hall, Urbana, Ill. 61801.

CAREER: University of Illinois, Urbana, assistant professor, 1971-76, associate professor of history, 1976—, director of Center for Latin American and Caribbean Studies. *Member:* Conference on Latin American History, Latin American Studies Association. *Awards, honors:* Bolton Prize from Conference on Latin American History, 1979, for *Socialism and Populism in Chile.*

WRITINGS: (Contributor) Frederic Cople Jaher, editor, *The Rich, the Well-Born, and the Powerful: Elites and Upper Classes in History,* University of Illinois Press, 1973; *Socialism and Populism in Chile, 1932-52,* University of Illinois Press, 1978. Contributor to history journals.

WORK IN PROGRESS: Research on U.S. economic missions to Latin America.

*   *   *

DREISER, Theodore (Herman Albert)   1871-1945

BRIEF ENTRY: Born August 27, 1871, in Terre Haute, Ind.; died of a heart attack, December 28, 1945, in Hollywood, Calif. American journalist and author. Although Dreiser's writing has often been criticized for its clumsiness and sentimentality, he is considered a major contributor to modern American realistic fiction. Dreiser first achieved success with his 1911 novel, *Jennie Gerhardt.* His previous novel, *Sister Carrie* (1900), had been withdrawn from circulation on grounds of immorality when it was first published. The major complaint against the book was not that Dreiser wrote about an unvirtuous woman, but that he justified her behavior as necessary for her survival. Perceiving life as permeated by accident and chance, Dreiser believed that, in the long run, man can do little to shape his own destiny. This Darwinistic point of view is evident in all his major works. In his trilogy of novels, *The Financier* (1910), and *The Titan* (1914), and *The Stoic* (1947), Dreiser also dealt with the chasm between the individual's desire for personal fulfillment and the repressiveness of society, and with the effect of a man's financial situation on his moral behavior. Dreiser's *An American Tragedy* (1925) was an instant success and is considered by many to be the author's masterpiece. Based on a 1906 murder trial, the novel emphasized the conflict between morality and the pursuit of the American Dream. In 1951 it was adapted as a motion picture entitled "A Place in the Sun." *Biographical/critical sources:* Theodore Dreiser, *Theodore Dreiser: A Book About Myself,* Boni & Liveright, 1922; *Webster's New World Companion to English and American Literature,* World Publishing, 1973; *The McGraw-Hill Encyclopedia of World Biography,* McGraw, 1973.

*   *   *

DRESCHER, Joan E(lizabeth)   1939-

PERSONAL: Born March 6, 1939, in New York, N.Y.; daughter of Joseph (an artist) and Elizabeth (an artist; maiden name, Straub) McIntosh; married Kenneth Drescher (a printer), June 11, 1960; children: Lisa, Kim, Ken. *Education:* Attended Rochester Institute of Technology, 1957-58, Parsons School of Design, 1958-60, and Art Students League, 1961-62. *Home and office:* 23 Cedar St., Hingham, Mass. 02043.

CAREER: Writer and illustrator. Former member of faculty at Cambridge Center for Adult Education, Cambridge Art Association, Massachusetts College of Art, Art Institute of Boston, and Lesley College. Artist; works included in solo shows and special exhibits for children. *Member:* Graphic Artists Guild, Authors Guild, Society of Children's Book Writers, New York Society of Illustrators, Boston Society of Illustrators. *Awards, honors:* Honorable mention from New York Academy of Sciences, 1979, for illustrating *Bubbles and Soap Films;* National Council for the Social Studies Award from National Children's Book Council, 1981, for *Your Family, My Family.*

WRITINGS—Self-illustrated children's books: *What Are Daisies For?,* Rand McNally, 1975; *The Marvelous Mess,* Houghton, 1980; *Your Family, My Family,* Walker & Co., 1980; *I'm in Charge,* Little, Brown, 1981; *Max and Rufus,* Houghton, 1982.

Illustrator: K. W. Moseley, *Only Birds Have Feathers,* Harvey House, 1973; Elisabeth Yates, *Skeezer: Dog With a Mission,*

Harvey House, 1973; Jennifer Bartoli, *Nonna*, Harvey House, 1975; Bernice Chesler, *In and Out of Boston With (or Without) Children*, Crown, 1975; Chesler and Evelyn Kaye, *The Family Guide to Cape Cod*, Crown, 1976; Nancy Robison, *The Other Place* (science fiction), Walker & Co., 1978; Bernie Zubrowski, *Bubbles and Soap Films*, Little, Brown, 1979; Shirlee Newman, *Tell Me Grandma, Tell Me Grandpa*, Houghton, 1979; Dale Fife, *Follow That Ghost*, Dutton, 1979; Barbara Bottner, *Horrible Hannah*, Crown, 1980.

WORK IN PROGRESS: A book about a single mother and her daughter, for Houghton.

SIDELIGHTS: Joan Drescher commented: ''Ever since I was a small child, I wanted to write and illustrate books. Lying on my stomach, I would draw until I was cross-eyed. I never stopped making little books and still have many I did when I was a child. Because I feel it is very important to encourage young authors and illustrators, I spend a portion of my time sharing my knowledge of picture books.

''Everyday problems are important to me and appear in many of my books. These problems include what to do when your mother is not home, which I dealt with in *I'm in Charge*, and how to get a boy to clean his room, the subject of *The Marvelous Mess*. I am also concerned with social issues, as in *Your Family, My Family*, and with just plain fun: *Max and Rufus* is about a boy and a dog who swap roles. All of these give a young reader plenty to think about.''

BIOGRAPHICAL/CRITICAL SOURCES: Ms., March, 1981.

* * *

DRESSMAN, Dennis L(ee) 1945-
(Denny Dressman)

PERSONAL: Born August 10, 1945, in Fort Mitchell, Ky.; son of Charles Bernard (a press operator) and Marie (Koelker) Dressman; married Melanie Foltz (a teacher), July 2, 1966; children: Melissa. *Education:* Attended University of Kentucky, 1964-66. *Religion:* Roman Catholic. *Home:* 810 Indian Trace Court, Cincinnati, Ohio 45230. *Office: Rocky Mountain News*, 400 West Colfax, Denver, Colo. 80204.

CAREER: Dixie News, Erlanger, Ky., reporter and photographer, 1964; *Kentucky Post*, Covington, reporter and makeup editor, 1965-66; *Louisville Courier-Journal*, Louisville, Ky., sports reporter, 1966-68; *Louisville Times*, Louisville, Indiana sports editor, 1968-69; *Cincinnati Enquirer*, Cincinnati, Ohio, sports reporter, 1969-76, assistant city editor, 1976, city editor, 1976-79, assistant managing editor, 1979-82; *Rocky Mountain News*, Denver, Colo., executive sports editor, 1982—. Writer, editor, and host of ''This Week in High School Sports,'' on WLW-TV, 1974-75; managing editor of *Sports Digest*, 1974; stringer for Reuters News Service; editor of *Oakland Tribune*, summer, 1979. *Awards, honors:* Journalism awards include Ohio Prep sports writer of the year award from Ohio Preps Sports Writers Association, 1972, for excellence in writing; best column award from Ohio Associated Press Sports Editors Association, 1974, for ''Private Triumph of Captain Hare''; award from Dolly Cohen Chapter of National Football Foundation for contribution to amateur football.

WRITINGS—Under name Denny Dressman: *Gerry Faust: Notre Dame's Man in Motion*, A. S. Barnes, 1981.

SIDELIGHTS: Dressman told *CA:* ''I feel the strength of my writing lies in my understanding of human nature, my appreciation for and fascination with people as individuals, and my ability to personalize stories.''

DRESSMAN, Denny
See DRESSMAN, Dennis L(ee)

* * *

DRUCKER, H(enry) M(atthew) 1942-

PERSONAL: Born April 29, 1942, in Paterson, N.J.; son of Arthur (a merchant) and Frances (Katz) Drucker; married Nancy Newman (a lecturer), March 29, 1975. *Education:* Allegheny College, B.A., 1964; London School of Economics and Political Science, London, Ph.D., 1967. *Politics:* Labour. *Home:* 1 Hatton Pl., Edinburgh, Scotland. *Office:* Department of Politics, University of Edinburgh, 31 Buccleuch Pl., Edinburgh 8, Scotland.

CAREER: University of Edinburgh, Edinburgh, Scotland, assistant lecturer, 1967, lecturer, 1967-78, senior lecturer in politics, 1978—.

WRITINGS: The Political Uses of Ideology, Macmillan, 1974; *The Scottish Government Yearbook*, six volumes, Rowman, 1976-82; *Breakaway: The Scottish Labour Party*, EUSPB, 1978; *Doctrine and Ethos in the Labour Party*, Allen & Unwin, 1979; *Multi-Party Britain*, Macmillan, 1980; (with Gordon Brown) *The Politics of Nationalism and Devolution*, Longman, 1980. Contributor to *Parliamentary Affairs*.

WORK IN PROGRESS: Local Organisation of the SDP, completion expected about 1985.

SIDELIGHTS: Drucker told *CA:* ''My writing is very much a part of my teaching. Most of the things I have written about first came to my attention as part of some course or other I was teaching; conversely, much that I have written has influenced my subsequent teaching. This has reached something of a new peak in the past few months. With a group of a dozen undergraduates, I have been studying the parliamentary by-elections at which the new Social Democratic Party is establishing its creditibility. We have been spending as much as two weeks in the seat during the campaign and then writing up our observations. Our observations of the Crosby (November, 1981) and Hillhead (March, 1982) have been published by *Parliamentary Affairs*. I will be applying these studies to my forthcoming book on the Social Democrats. The Social Democrats have been strongly influenced by the ideas their leaders have formed of American politics. They are best understood by Americans by thinking of them as like the Eugene McCarthy, McGovern, Anderson campaigns. On the other hand they have to compete against best-organized and more durable opponents than those campaigns and are trying to create an organization capable of doing so. Their popular appeal to a public, much of which is frightened by the rigidly monetarist Conservative government and the left-wing Labour party of Mr. Tony Benn, is considerable. Their chance of forming part of the next government is real.''

* * *

DRUMMOND, John 1900-1982
(Lord Strange)

OBITUARY NOTICE: Born May 6, 1900; died April 13, 1982. Fifteenth baron of Megginch and author of several books, including such murder mysteries as *The Bride Wore Black* and *Proof Positive*, nonfiction accounts of farming on his estate, and a novel, *The Naughty Mrs. Thornton*. Obituaries and other sources: *Who's Who*, 125th edition, St. Martin's, 1973; *London Times*, April 21, 1982.

DRURY, Alan 1949-

PERSONAL: Born May 22, 1949, in Hull, Yorkshire, England; son of Harold (an insurance inspector) and Patricia (a teacher; maiden name, Tait) Drury. *Education:* Queens' College, Cambridge, B.A., 1971. *Agent:* John Rush, David Higham Associates, 5-8 Lower John St., Golden Square, London W.1, England.

CAREER: London borough of Camden, London, England, clerk in department of architecture, 1972-74; York Theatre Royal, York, England, resident dramatist, 1976-78; Royal Court Theatre, London, resident dramatist, 1979. *Member:* Theatre Writers' Union.

WRITINGS—Translator: Claude Duneton, *The Hills* (two-act play; first produced in London at King's Head Theatre, 1974), Fringescripts, 1973; Moliere, *The Miser* (two-act play; first produced in York, England, at York Theatre Royal, 1978) and *The Hypochondriac* (one-act play; first produced by National Theatre Co. in London at Olivier Theatre, 1981), both in *Moliere: Five Plays,* Methuen, 1982.

Plays: "Evening and Morning" (one-act), first produced in Cambridge, England, at Pembroke College, 1971; "Shoreline" (two-act), first produced at Edinburgh International Festival of Music and Drama in Edinburgh, Scotland, at University Union, 1971; "You Know Me" (one-act), first produced in London at Little Theatre, 1972; "And How Are You This Bright and Early Morning?" (two-act), first produced at Edinburgh Festival at Tollcoons Theatre, 1972; "Fall" (one-act), first produced in London at Little Theatre, 1973; "Glynis" (one-act), first produced in London at Oval House, 1974; "Asides" (one-act), first produced in London at Bush Theatre, 1974; "The Railway Game" (one-act), first produced in York, England, at York Theatre Royal, 1975; "Antonio" (one-act), first produced in York at York Theatre Royal, 1975; "Spotty Hilda" (one-act), first produced in York at York Theatre Royal, 1975; "The Man Himself" (one-act), first produced by National Theatre Co. in London at ICA Theatre, 1975.

"Sparrowfall" (two-act), music by Brian Eno, first produced in London at Hampstead Theatre Club, July 5, 1976; "Sense of Loss" (one-act), first produced in London at Open Space Theatre, 1976; "Black Dog" (two-act), first produced in Saarbruecken, West Germany, at University Theatre, 1976; "Communion" (one-act), first produced in London at Soho Poly, 1976; "Dick Turpin" (one-act), first produced in York at York Theatre Royal, 1976; "Under the Skin" (one-act), first produced in Farnham, England, at Redgrave Theatre, 1977; "Margaret Clitherow" (two-act), first produced in York at York Theatre Royal, 1977; "A Change of Mind" (one-act), first produced by National Theatre Co. in London at Lyttleton Theatre, 1977; "Simple Simon" (one-act), first produced in York at York Theatre Royal, 1978; "Looking Back" (two-act), first produced at Edinburgh Festival at Masonic Hall, 1978; "An Empty Desk" (two-act), first produced in London at Theatre Upstairs, June 5, 1979.

Musical plays: "Silver" (one-act), music by Nic Rowley, first produced in Cambridge, England, at Arts Theatre, 1973; "King David" (one-act), music by Humphrey Stewart, first produced in London at All Hallows by the Tower, 1975; "Up and Away" (two-act), music by Rowley, first produced in York at York Theatre Royal, 1976; "Mother Goose" (two-act; traditional English pantomime), music by Simon Webb, first produced in York at York Theatre Royal, 1980.

Adaptations: "Godot Has Come" (two-act play; adapted from play "Godo je dosao" by Miodrag Bulatovic), first produced at Edinburgh Festival at University Union, 1971; "The Ancient Mariner" (one-act ballet scenario; adapted from poem "The Rime of the Ancient Mariner" by Samuel Taylor Coleridge), first produced in London at Questor's Theatre, 1972; "Diary of a Madman" (one-act play; adapted from short story with same title by Nikolai Vasilievich Gogol), first produced in York at York Arts Centre, 1977; "A Shorter Faustus" (two-act play; adapted from play "The Tragedy of Dr. Faustus" by Christopher Marlow), first produced in York at York Arts Centre, 1977.

Other: (With theatre company; and director) "Soap Opera" (two-act improvisation), first produced in York by York Theatre Royal, 1977; (with theatre company; and director) "The Training" (one-act improvisation), first produced in London at ICA Theatre, 1978; "Mr. Jones" (radio play), first broadcast by British Broadcasting Corp. (BBC-Radio), 1979; "Winding Up" (television play), first televised on Associated Television Ltd. (ATV), 1981; "Keeping in Touch" (television play), first televised by BBC-TV, 1982.

Also drama critic for *Listener,* 1979-81.

WORK IN PROGRESS: "Singles," a television play awaiting production on BBC-TV; "The Sword of Heaven," a four-act epic drama; "Maven," a one-act play for the National Theatre Co.

SIDELIGHTS: Drury told *CA:* "I am not related to the writer, with a similar name, of very long, middle-brow novels."

* * *

DUBOIS, Charles
See COUNSELMAN, Mary Elizabeth

* * *

DUBOS, Rene (Jules) 1901-1982

OBITUARY NOTICE—See index for *CA* sketch: Born February 20, 1901, in Saint Brice, France; died of heart failure, February 20, 1982, in New York, N.Y. Microbiologist, environmentalist, and Pulitzer Prize-winning author who first earned recognition with his 1939 research that led to the commercial production of antibiotics. Dubos wrote more than twenty books on science and the environment. *So Human an Animal* received the 1969 Pulitzer Prize for nonfiction, and *Only One Earth: The Care and Maintenance of a Small Planet* served as the platform for the United Nations Conference on the Human Environment in 1972. Obituaries and other sources: *Washington Post,* February 21, 1982; *Time,* March 1, 1982; *Publishers Weekly,* March 5, 1982.

* * *

DUELAND, Joy V(ivian)

PERSONAL: Surname is pronounced *Doo*-land; born in Brooklyn, N.Y.; daughter of Carl (a sea captain) and Clara (Hansen) Dueland. *Education:* Barnard College, A.B., 1950; Columbia University, communications materials certificate, 1962. *Religion:* Christian Scientist. *Home:* The Old Mill, Scribner Rd., Raymond, N.H. 03077. *Office:* Millstream Press, Route 3, Raymond, N.H. 03077.

CAREER: Christian Science Monitor, Boston, Mass., writer, 1958-78; author and illustrator of children's books, 1968—; Millstream Press, Raymond, N.H., owner and publisher, 1976—.

Play reader for Broadway producer, 1962—; producer and scriptwriter of children's public television programs, 1979—.

WRITINGS—Self-illustrated; all for children, except as noted: *The Beaver Boy,* Ginn, 1968; *The Pine Tree That Went to Sea,* Ginn, 1968; *My Best Friend,* Christian Science Publishing Society, 1970; *The Book of the Lobster* (adult recipe book), New Hampshire Publishing, 1973; *Filled Up Full,* Christian Science Publishing Society, 1973; *Who's Afraid? Not You!,* Christian Science Publishing Society, 1973; *Barn Kitten, House Kitten,* Millstream Press, 1977; *The Blessings of Jesus,* Millstream Press, 1979; *God's Great Adventure,* Millstream Press, 1980.

Author of column in *New Hampshire Profiles* (magazine), 1969-75.

WORK IN PROGRESS: The Day of the Falcon.

SIDELIGHTS: Joy Dueland told *CA:* "Much of my time these days is involved with the children's educational programs I am producing and writing. With my art, photography, and writing, I feel I am essentially a 'communicator' rather than strictly an author. Since children today are living stressful lives in a complicated world, I am trying, through books and television, to lead them to the old simple values, to help them live with a deeper conviction of the Ten Commandments, the Golden Rule, and all that spells real happiness.

"I am particularly interested in helping children find their niche in life and in fulfilling their creative potential. Rather than encouraging a child to 'go with the herd,' I feel he should be comfortable going out on his own, walking alone, thinking quietly, and cherishing his creativity. Much of my writing has also aimed at developing a child's love of wildlife and compassion for animals."

* * *

DUKORE, Margaret Mitchell 1950-

PERSONAL: Born September 27, 1950, in Honolulu, Hawaii; daughter of Donald D. (a teacher) and Winifred (a social worker; maiden name, Murfin) Mitchell; married Bernard F. Dukore (a professor), November 13, 1973 (separated); children: Joan. *Education:* Lewis and Clark College, B.S., 1972. *Residence:* Honolulu, Hawaii. *Agent:* Bobbe Siegel, 41 West 83rd St., New York, N.Y. 10024.

CAREER: Worked in retailing in Honolulu, Hawaii, 1972-74; actress in Honolulu, 1972-81; writer. *Member:* Screen Actors Guild. *Awards, honors:* Maxwell Perkins Award from Scribner, 1982, for *A Novel Called Heritage.*

WRITINGS: "Move" (two-act play), first produced in Richmond, Va., at Virginia Museum Theatre, 1981; *A Novel Called Heritage,* Scribner, 1982. Also author of the play "Family Weekend" and the screenplay "Jane Doe."

WORK IN PROGRESS: An untitled novel; a screenplay, "Dream Man"; a play, "Survival of the Fittest."

SIDELIGHTS: Dukore told *CA:* "I was always a raconteur, so I wrote because it was a shame to waste all those good stories on people who would just laugh and then forget them. The writer who has influenced me the most is J. D. Salinger. The writer I most admire is Vladimir Nabokov. I believe a writer should read *everything*—Nabokov, Jacqueline Susann, *New Republic, National Review, Cosmopolitan.* I believe every 'serious' thing I write should have something funny in it, and I believe that every funny thing I write should have something serious in it. If not . . . well, then it wouldn't be at all like life."

BIOGRAPHICAL/CRITICAL SOURCES: Library Journal, February 1, 1982; *Chicago Tribune Book World,* April 25, 1982.

* * *

du MAS, Frank (Maurice) 1918-

PERSONAL: Surname is pronounced du-*Mah;* born September 16, 1918, in Edenwold, Tenn.; son of George Nicholas (in business) and Bessie Lee (Hartsook) du Mas; married Dorothy Mae Jones (a bank officer), November 20, 1941; children: Donald, Michael, Mark, Douglas, Dorothy Sue. *Education:* University of Virginia, B.S., 1940, M.A., 1941; University of Texas, Ph.D., 1953. *Politics:* Independent.

CAREER: University of Denver, Denver, Colo., instructor in psychology, 1945-47; University of Iowa, Iowa City, research assistant, 1947-48; Florida State University, Tallahassee, associate professor of psychology, 1948-49; American Council on Education, director of Office of Naval Research project, 1949-50; Louisiana State University, Baton Rouge, assistant professor of psychology, 1951-53; Michigan State University, East Lansing, assistant professor of psychology, 1953-54; University of Montana, Missoula, 1954-63, began as assistant professor, became professor of psychology; New Mexico State University, Las Cruces, professor of psychology and head of department, 1963-65; Augusta College, Augusta, Ga., professor of psychology, 1966-71, head of department; private practice of psychology, 1971-72; Altoona Hospital, Community Mental Health Center, chief psychologist in department of consultation, education, and research, 1972-73; private practice of psychology, 1973—. *Military service:* U.S. Army Air Forces, clinical psychologist, 1944-45. *Member:* American Psychological Association, Southeastern Psychological Association. *Awards, honors:* Award from Rocky Mountain Psychological Association, 1964, for article, "Some Mathematical Models in Theoretical Management."

WRITINGS: Manifest Structure Analysis, University of Montana Press, 1955; *Gay Is Not Good,* Thomas Nelson, 1979. Contributor of about forty articles to psychology, psychiatry, and banking journals. Member of editorial staff of *Excerpta Medica,* 1952-59; associate editor of *Psychological Reports,* 1958-62; member of board of editors of *Rocky Mountain Psychologist,* 1964-66.

SIDELIGHTS: Du Mas wrote: "For the first part of my life my writings were scientific, mathematical, and theoretical. War, violence, perversion, corruption, mental illness, pollution, and other symptoms of cultural disintegration and social sickness led me to become interested in developing a new science of deranged societies which I call 'sociatry.' I believe that America today is at least unsane, at most insane. The most critical events that led to my work were the rape of a state (Montana) by a giant corporation (Anaconda), the defense of my children as my four boys were taken for service in Vietnam, my firing from Augusta College for dissenting, the rise of perversion, Nixon and Watergate, and the continuation of corruption by the election of Jimmy Carter as president."

* * *

DUNCAN, Robert L(ipscomb) 1927-
(James Hall Roberts; W. R. Duncan, a joint pseudonym)

PERSONAL: Born September 9, 1927, in Oklahoma City, Okla.; son of Norman (an attorney) and Eva Pearl (Hall) Duncan; married Wanda Scott (a writer), April 14, 1949; children: Mary

Carole, Christopher Scott. *Education:* University of Oklahoma, B.A., 1950, M.A., 1972. *Home address:* Box I, Tuttle, Okla. 73089. *Agent:* Paul R. Reynolds, Inc., 12 East 41st Street, New York, N.Y. 10017.

CAREER: Writer, 1952—. University of California, Irvine, lecturer in television writing, 1967-68, coordinator of Business Aspects of the Arts Seminar, 1969-70; Chapman College, Orange, Calif., writer-in-residence, 1969-70; University of Oklahoma School of Professional Writing, Norman, associate professor of journalism, 1972-80.

WRITINGS: The Dicky Bird Was Singing: Men, Women, and Black Gold (short stories), Rinehart, 1952, (with Irene Castle and wife, Wanda Duncan) *Castles in the Air: The Memoirs of Irene Castle* (biography), Doubleday, 1958; *Buffalo Country* (short stories; self-illustrated), Dutton, 1959; *The Voice of Strangers* (novel), Doubleday, 1961; *If It Moves Salute It* (novel), Doubleday, 1961; *Reluctant General: The Life and Times of Albert Pike* (biography), Dutton, 1961; *The General and the Coed* (novel), Doubleday, 1962; "Black Gold" (screenplay), Warner Bros., 1962; *The Day the Sun Fell* (novel), Morrow, 1970; *Dragons at the Gate* (novel), Morrow, 1975; *Temple Dogs* (novel), Morrow, 1977; *Firestorm* (novel), Morrow, 1978; *Brimstone* (novel), Morrow, 1979.

Novels; under pseudonym James Hall Roberts: *The Q Document,* Morrow, 1964; *The Burning Sky,* Morrow, 1966; *The February Plan,* Morrow, 1967.

With wife, Wanda Duncan, under joint pseudonym W. R. Duncan: *The Queen's Messenger* (novel), Delacorte, 1982.

Television scripts; under name Robert L. Duncan: More than one hundred television dramas broadcast between 1956 and 1970, including "To Die Alone" and "Windfall" for the *U.S. Steel Hour,* "The Gardenia Bush," "A House With Golden Streets," and "A Long Way Home" for the *NBC Matinee Theatre,* "Homecoming" and "Frederick" for *G. E. Theatre,* and "Chinese Finale," "The Last Flight Out," and "Minister Accused" for *Alcoa-Goodyear Theatre.* Also author of episodes for television series, including "Riverboat," "Barbara Stanwyck Theatre," "One Step Beyond," "The Man From Blackhawk," "Two Faces West," "Checkmate," "Bonanza," "Have Gun, Will Travel," "Custer," "Dr. Kildare," "The Virginian," "Iron Horse," "Slattery's People," "Time Tunnel," "Lost in Space," "Land of the Giants," "The Immortal," "The Young Lawyers," and "The Professionals."

Contributor of articles to periodicals.

SIDELIGHTS: Creative in many genres, Duncan is best known for his suspense novels. Duncan's modern thrillers, often set in the Far East, characteristically concern a lone man's struggle against a large, powerful, and corrupt organization. In the 1967 novel *The February Plan,* for example, protagonist Phillip Corman is in Tokyo investigating the mysterious death of his soldier son. There the American discovers a U.S. military plot to launch the H-bomb from Japan to Red China, and with this discovery, Corman's own life is in danger. "Our hair is kept constantly on end as searches, captures, escapes, hunts, follow in rapid series with corpses beginning to accumulate and an inevtiable World War III but days away," commented reviewer Pamela Marsh in the *Christian Science Monitor.* Although Anthony Boucher of the *New York Times Book Review* claimed that *The February Plan* "manages to elude both entertainment and significance," Marsh found that the author "stretches the tension nail-bitingly tight and throws in some convincing Japanese backgrounds."

In Duncan's 1977 novel, *Temple Dogs,* an American ex-general plots to protect his corporate interests in the Far East through a program of assassination, blackmail, terrorism, and even full-scale war. *Temple Dogs* details the efforts of William Corbett, who has learned of the ex-general's scheme, to expose and halt the corrupt corporate machinery. Similarly, in Duncan's 1978 novel, *Firestorm,* an American shipbuilding executive mistakenly witnesses the deliberate incineration of a Japanese port and uncovers a plot that could lead to international disaster. The American finds himself battling corrupt Japanese officials and his murderous former associates in an attempt to forestall the plan and bring the criminals to justice.

"Robert L. Duncan does the one man against an omnipotent organization plot very well indeed," wrote *Times Literary Supplement* reviewer T. J. Binyon about Duncan's 1979 novel, *Brimstone.* Set in Washington, D.C., *Brimstone* offers the story of a computer technician in the General Accounting Office whose computer terminal suddenly emits maps of Russian towns. The technician soon discovers project Brimstone, a secret operation connected with the missing eighteen-minute segment of President Nixon's White House tapes. "This is adventure writing at its best," noted Newgate Callendar in the *New York Times Book Review,* "with its usual down-to-the-line maneuverings where a few seonds will make all the difference. . . . It certainly has all the ingredients for a major thriller."

Duncan told *CA:* "From the time that I was twelve years old, I knew I wanted to be a novelist and nothing else. I consider myself fortunate to have been able to realize that dream, to indulge my curiousity about the world and to satisfy the urge to travel extensively. I think I am more an international writer than an American one although I am keenly interested in what is happening to my country and use my writings as a way of affirming the conviction that individual belief, translated into action, can be effective in solving some of the problems of the world which, on first glance, seem beyond solution. My books deal with the clash of cultures, which I find exciting, and they are regularly published in England, France, Norway, Sweden, Finland, Holland, Denmark, West Germany, Italy, Spain, Portugal, and the South American countries as well as an occasional translation into Japanese.

"In the past three years, I have made a book promotion tour in New Zealand and Australia, explored the South Pacific, researched in such places as Denpasar, Jakarta, and Bangkok, and have spent months in Europe gathering material as far east as Moscow. My next book will probably explore the relationship between the Soviet Union and the United States although I find that the gestation period for a novel, during which time I sort out my research material and impressions, occupies a good bit of my time. The characters and the situations are already beginning to form in my mind; I have glimpses of scenes and little flashes of dialogue; I know that if I wait long enough, all of these rather nebulous elements will form into something solid, and the basic story will be there.

"I have taught professional writing in various universities over the years on a part-time basis, attempting to pass on the practical aspects of the craft and marketing which I have learned during my career. (I distinguish, by the way, between 'creative writing' and 'professional writing' in that the former is a definition of a fuzzy university course designed for esoteric hobbyists, and the latter directs a student toward publication.) I have pretty much come to the conclusion that 'writing' as such cannot be taught, that my students who have become successful television writers or novelists would have done so without my help, and that the teaching process, properly done, merely shortens the time of apprenticeship. The beginning writer already has the fire within him which cannot be dampened, a wide ranging curiosity which is always asking 'why?,' a love of language, a basic urge to restructure a highly imperfect world into a more orderly fictional one, and above all, a compulsion to put words on paper despite continual early discouragement and rejection.''

BIOGRAPHICAL/CRITICAL SOURCES: New York Times Book Review, February 12, 1967, November 23, 1975, May 9, 1976, September 11, 1977, November 23, 1980; *Christian Science Monitor,* February 23, 1967; *New Republic,* November 26, 1977, July 22, 1978; *Times Literary Supplement,* April 7, 1978, December 26, 1980; *Chicago Tribune Book World,* June 8, 1980.

*   *   *

DUNCAN, W. R.
See DUNCAN, Robert L(ipscomb)

*   *   *

DUNMORE, John   1923-
(Jason Calder)

PERSONAL: Born August 6, 1923, in Trouville, France; son of William Ernest (a businessman) and Marguerite (Martin) Dunmore; married Joyce Langley (a city councillor); children: Paul Vincent, Patricia Margaret. *Education:* University of London, B.A., 1950; University of New Zealand, Ph.D., 1961. *Politics:* Labour Party. *Religion:* Roman Catholic. *Home:* 46 Epsom Rd., Palmerston North, New Zealand. *Office:* Massey University, Palmerston North, New Zealand.

CAREER: Worked as school teacher, 1951-57; Massey University, Palmerston North, New Zealand, senior lecturer, 1961-66, professor of French, 1966—. Chairman of Dunmore Press Ltd.; director of Palmerston North Newspapers Ltd. *Member:* P.E.N., New Zealand Playwrights' Association (executive member), Australasian Language and Literature Association (president, 1980-82). *Awards, honors:* Sir James Wattie Book of the Year Award, 1969, for *The Fateful Voyage of the St. Jean-Baptiste;* named *chevalier* of French Legion of Honour, 1977.

WRITINGS: French Explorers in the Pacific, Volume 1, Oxford University Press, 1965; *Le Mystere d'Omboula,* Longmans, Paul, 1966; (editor) R. R. Milligan, *The Map Drawn by the Chief Tuki-tahua,* Reeds, 1966; *Aventures dans le Pacifique,* Reeds, 1967; *Success at University,* Whitcoulls, 1968; *French Explorers in the Pacific,* Volume 2, Oxford University Press, 1969; *Success at School,* Whitcoulls, 1969, reprinted as *Step by Step Exam Success,* Cavanaun Books, 1979; *The Fateful Voyage of the St. Jean-Baptiste,* Pegasus Press, 1969; (editor) Norman Kirk, *Towards Nationhood,* New Zealand Books, 1969.

Meurtre a Tahiti (title means ''Murder in Tahiti''), Longmans, Paul, 1971; *Norman Kirk: A Portrait,* New Zealand Books, 1972; (editor) *An Anthology of French Scientific Prose,* Hutchinson, 1973; (translator) Gabriel Linge, *In Search of the Maori,* New Zealand Books, 1974; (translator) Georges Pisier, *Kunie; or, The Isle of Pines,* Noumea, 1978; *The Expedition of the St. Jean-Baptiste,* Hakluyt Society [Cambridge], 1981.

Under pseudonym Jason Calder: *The Man Who Shot Rob Muldoon,* Dunmore Press, 1976; *A Wreath for the Springboks,* Dunmore Press, 1978; *The O'Rourke Affair,* Dunmore Press, 1979; *Target Margaret Thatcher,* Robert Hale, 1981.

WORK IN PROGRESS: A biography of French explorer La Perouse, publication expected in 1984; editing La Perouse's journals, publication expected in 1985.

SIDELIGHTS: Dunmore told *CA:* ''I have always moved freely from scholarly work to the theatre or the adventure thriller. My special field is the Pacific in the eighteenth century, in particular the work of explorers and especially the French. As an academic, I have published what academics are expected to publish; but like many academics, I have found relaxation and useful outlets in drama, thrillers, and politics (but then these three may well be synonymous).''

*   *   *

DUTTON, Richard Edward   1929-

BRIEF ENTRY: Born May 28, 1929, in Titusville, Pa. American behavioral scientist, educator, and author. Before he began teaching in 1963, Dutton worked as a personnel technician and business analyst. Since 1969 he has been a professor of behavioral sciences and management at University of South Florida. He wrote *The Behavior Laboratory: A Manual* (Goodyear Publishing, 1975). *Address:* College of Business Administration, University of South Florida, 4202 Fowler Ave., Tampa, Fla. 33620. *Biographical/critical sources: Who's Who in Consulting,* 2nd edition, Gale, 1973.

*   *   *

DWARAKI, Leela   1942-

PERSONAL: Born November 7, 1942, in Tiptur, India; daughter of Honavalli (an official) and Susheelamma Nagappa; married Bangalore Ramanna Dwaraki (a university teacher), October 26, 1975. *Education:* Bangalore University, M.A., 1967; National Institute of Mental Health and Neuro-Sciences, diploma in psychiatric social work, 1972. *Religion:* Hindu. *Home:* 37th ''A'' Cross, No. 248, Jayanagar, Bangalore, Karnataka 560 069, India. *Office:* Department of Sociology, Gandhigram Rural University, Gandhigram, Madurai Dt., Tamil Nadu 624 302, India.

CAREER: University of Erlangen-Nuernberg, Erlangen, West Germany, visiting scholar and research assistant in sociology, 1969-70; S.V.P. Junior College, Bangalore, India, lecturer in sociology, 1970-72; Gandhigram Rural University, Gandhigram, India, lecturer in sociology and psychology, 1976—.

WRITINGS: (With Rhoda Blumberg) *India's Educated Women: Options and Constraints,* Hindustan Publishing, 1980. Contributor to sociology journals.

WORK IN PROGRESS: Research on the roles of women in change and development in rural India.

SIDELIGHTS: Leela Dwaraki commented: ''I came from a Hindu, orthodox, high caste family, and took up higher academic achievement as a challenge because, until then, no girl in the family or kin-group circles had even reached the graduation level.

''It is Rhoda, the senior author of my book, and my husband who are mainly responsible for my research. I am also interested in counseling the emotionally disturbed.

''How does an average-educated woman in modern India contribute to the problem of the emancipation of women? She seems content enough either conducting or participating in seminars concerning women, conferences, and the like, but not quite ready to 'soil' her hands through joining hands with her rural counterparts, with whom much of the work needs to be done! Paradoxically, even the better-educated women of the villages choose to run away from the problems rather than attempt to work for improving the situation.

"The modern, educated youth in India—men and women alike—do not generally offer much to solve the social problems. For instance, it is not uncommon to see such a youth slip away from the scene of dowry through shifting the responsibility to the parents.

"How many educated and modern husbands in India treat their wives as individuals? An urban housewife gets her liberties as an individual, if offered her at all, well within the framework of the chauvinistic outlook of her husband! I thank my stars that my husband isn't a male chauvinist!"

AVOCATIONAL INTERESTS: Gardening, interior decoration, crafts, reading, learning languages.

*   *   *

DYMOKE, Juliet
   See de SCHANSCHIEFF, Juliet Dymoke

E

EAKIN, Mary Mulford 1914-

BRIEF ENTRY: Born May 17, 1914, in Ithaca, N.Y. American minister and author. Mary Eakin was ordained a minister of the United Church of Christ in 1966 and has served since then as associate minister of the First Congregational Church of Berkeley, Calif. She wrote *Baptism: By Water and the Spirit* (United Church Board for Homeland Ministries, 1966) and *The Ministering Congregation* (United Church Press, 1972). *Address:* 1627 Spruce St., Berkeley, Calif. 94709; and 2345 Channing Way, Berkeley, Calif. 94704. *Biographical/critical sources: Who's Who in Religion,* Marquis, 1977.

*　　*　　*

EASTAUGH, Kenneth 1929-

PERSONAL: Surname is pronounced *East*-oh; born January 30, 1929, in Preston, England; son of Herbert (a teacher of the blind) and Mabel (Farrell) Eastaugh; married Eileen Sarah Mooney, May 1, 1956 (divorced, 1972); married Susan Joy Ellis, June 17, 1972; children: John Paul, Andrew, Helen Susan. *Education:* Attended secondary school in Preston, England. *Politics:* "Skeptical of most politicians, but veer toward Social Democrat." *Religion:* "My own." *Agent:* David Bolt, Bolt & Watson Ltd., Cedar House, High St., Ripley, Surrey GU23 6AE, England. *Office:* Daily Star, Express Newspapers, Fleet St., London E.C.4, England.

CAREER: Morecambe Guardian, Morecambe, England, reporter, 1952-53; *Morecambe Visitor,* Morecambe, senior reporter, 1953; *Leyonstone Independent,* London, England, chief sub-editor, 1953; *Chigwell Times,* Essex, England, editor, 1953-54; *Lincolnshire Evening Echo,* Lincoln, England, feature writer, 1954; *Star,* Sheffield, England, feature writer, 1954; associated with *Daily Express,* Manchester, England, 1954-56, and *Daily Mirror,* Manchester, 1956-57; *Daily Mirror,* London, television critic, 1957-67; free-lance writer, 1967-69; *Daily Mirror,* London, show business writer, 1969-70; *Sun,* London, chief show business writer, 1970-73; free-lance writer, 1973-78; *Daily Star,* London, television editor, 1978—, show business editor, 1981—. Film critic for *Prima,* 1976-77. *Military service:* British Army, chief clerk in Scots Guards, 1946-48, in Royal Medical Corps, 1948-52; became sergeant. *Member:* Writers Guild of Great Britain (member of executive council, 1975), National Union of Journalists.

WRITINGS: Havergal Brian: The Making of a Composer, Harrap, 1976; *The Carry On Book,* David & Charles, 1978.

Plays: "The Event" (two-act), first broadcast by Associated Television (ATV), February 21, 1968; "Better Than a Man" (two-act), first broadcast by BBC1-TV, 1970; "Awkward Cuss" (two-act), first produced in Stoke on Trent, England, at Victoria Theatre, September 8, 1976.

Author of "Havergal Who?," a television documentary, first broadcast by ATV, March 4, 1980. Creator of "Dapple Downs," a serial, broadcast by Capital Radio, 1973-74. Writer for television series, "Coronation Street," 1976. Author of a television and criticism column in the *London Times,* 1976-78. Editor of *Guild,* 1975. Contributor to magazines, including *Classical Music, Weekend,* and *Reveille.*

WORK IN PROGRESS: A biography of entertainer Frankie Vaughan, publication by Granada expected in 1982; a biography of entertaner Terry Thomas, publication by New English Library expected in 1983; *Soloists,* interviews with musicians, with Julian Lloyd-Webber, publication by Macdonald & Co. expected in 1984; *Intacta,* a novel; *Mountain,* a novel.

SIDELIGHTS: Eastaugh commented: "I write because I have no alternative. I get restless and irritable when I'm not writing, and the need nags me until I have to start again. I'm glad about that—I suppose it's normal to kick against something that has a hold on you. It doesn't matter what I write—pulp journalism or serious books and plays. The need is satisifed, though to varying degrees.

"I am basically a man of the times in which I live. History is not my subject, nor science fiction of the future. I am interested in how people live and think today, and in their fears, motivations, joys. I like the way the human race, despite its appalling drawbacks, keeps trying, keeps going on—like a fly determined to get to the top of a window.

"What worries me? Compromise. I see the need of it sometimes, but I am always suspicious of it.

"I read a lot, and whatever else I am reading, I always have a Dickens novel on the go. I read them over and over—year after year amid other books. I think Arthur Miller's 'Death of a Salesman' is still the best play of the century about twentieth-century life, and despite changes in fashion I still get a lot out of Hemingway, Thomas Wolfe, Arthur Hugh Clough, Genet, and Voltaire.

"My book on Havergal Brian was the result of my skepticism over many statements made about his life, his personality, and his motivation by musicians and by Brian himself—some of these statements were made to me personally when I interviewed Brian for the *Daily Mirror* in 1969, three years before his death at the age of ninety-six. Research, some of it obstructed by Brian supporters, revealed my skepticism to be well-founded. I wrote the book because I wanted to clear away the lies, and I wanted to do something to try to help Brian gain the recognition his music deserves but which, until recently, had been denied him. My long letter in *Books and Bookmen* (February, 1977), in reply to their review (December, 1976) accusing me of making Brian's life too colorful, is a summing up of this matter.

"Other reviewers appreciated my research. The *London Times* (September 23, 1976) included these comments in their review: 'But why was Brian for so long neglected? The reason, it has often been suggested, lay in the change of fashion against Brian's sort of large-scale romanticism, in the spurning of a man of working-class origin, or in his own failure to push himself. Kenneth Eastaugh suggests another cause. In 1913 Brian left his wife and young family to live with a girl who had been a maid in his house, and who had recently borne him a child. Immediately, silently, the assistance and acknowledgement bestowed by musical society were for the most part withdrawn. In exposing this scandal . . . Mr. Eastaugh has made Brian's descent into obscurity more comprehensible, and he has also dealt a blow to his subject's current image of steadfast rectitude in the face of adversity. Many of the other new details he reveals do the same.'"

"The *Birmingham Post*, among others, also noted the new facts: 'The life is brilliantly illuminated by Kenneth Eastaugh's biography. It is a colourful and dramatic account. . . . Eastaugh unravels the tangle of Brian's personal relationships and throws new light on his fall from the grace of the musical establishment of the day. . . . The book goes into absorbing detail. . . . It can be recommended even to the reader with not the slightest interest in music. . . . It would make a splendid film.'"

AVOCATIONAL INTERESTS: Walking with his Irish terrier, weeds ("I like their stamina and stickability as well as the beauty of many of them. I like weeds second only to sunflowers.")

BIOGRAPHICAL/CRITICAL SOURCES: London Guardian, February 22, 1968; *London Evening Standard,* January 28, 1976; *Staffordshire Evening Sentinel,* August 30, 1976, September 9, 1976; *London Daily Telegraph,* September 4, 1976, September 9, 1976; *Birmingham Post,* September 4, 1976, November 13, 1976; *London Times,* September 9, 1976, September 23, 1976; *London Daily Mail,* September 24, 1976, January 19, 1977; *Lancashire Evening Post,* October 4, 1976; *Books and Bookmen,* December, 1976, February, 1977.

*   *   *

EASTAWAY, Edward
See THOMAS, (Philip) Edward

*   *   *

EASTLICK, John Taylor   1912-

PERSONAL: Born April 28, 1912, in Norris, Mont.; son of Jack T. and Stella Mae (Tate) Taylor. *Education:* Arizona State Teachers College, A.B., 1934; Colorado State College, M.A., 1939; University of Denver, B.L.S., 1940; graduate study at University of Colorado, 1949-54. *Home:* 3914 East Evans Ave., Denver, Colo. 80210. *Office:* Graduate School of Librarianship, University of Denver, Denver, Colo. 80210.

CAREER: Teacher in high school in Yuma, Ariz., 1934-38; librarian in high school in Madison, Wis., 1940-42; Veterans Administration, Denver, Colo., chief of library division, 1946-48; Denver Public Library, Denver, assistant librarian, 1948-51, city librarian, 1951-69; University of Denver, Denver, Colo., professor of librarianship, 1969-76, associate dean, 1976—. *Military service:* U.S. Army Air Forces, 1942-46; became captain. *Member:* American Library Association (president of public libraries division, 1956-57, vice-president, 1959-60), Colorado Library Association, Alpha Psi Omega, Phi Delta Kappa, City Club (Denver).

WRITINGS: (With Ernest F. Miller) *The Chattanooga Public Library: A Survey,* American Library Association, 1958; (with Willard O. Youngs) *A Survey of the Pikes Peak Regional District Library, Colorado Springs, Colorado,* American Library Association, 1967; (editor) *The Changing Environment of Libraries,* American Library Association, 1971; (with Robert D. Stueart) *Library Management,* Libraries Unlimited, 1977, 2nd edition, 1980. Contributor to *Encyclopedia of Library and Information Science.* Contributor to library journals.

*   *   *

EAYRS, James George   1926-

BRIEF ENTRY: Born in 1926 in London, England. Canadian journalist, broadcaster, and editor. Eayrs has been co-editor of *International Journal* since 1957. He has also worked as a broadcaster on Canadian radio and television programs and as a columnist for *Family Herald.* Among his awards are a 1967 Guggenheim fellowship and a Governor General's Award for Volume II of *In Defence of Canada,* which is entitled *Appeasement and Rearmament* (University of Toronto Press, 1965). He also wrote *The Art of the Possible: Government and Foreign Policy in Canada* (University of Toronto Press, 1961), *Northern Approaches: Canada and the Search for Peace* (Macmillan, 1961), *Minutes of the Sixties* (Macmillan, 1968), *Diplomacy and Its Discontents* (University of Toronto Press, 1971), and *Greenpeace and Her Enemies* (House of Anansi Press, 1973). *Address:* Department of Political Science, University of Toronto, Toronto, Ontario, Canada M5S 1A8. *Biographical/critical sources: Supplement to the Oxford Companion to Canadian History and Literature,* Oxford University Press, 1973.

*   *   *

EBERT, John E(dward)   1922-

PERSONAL: Born September 16, 1922, in New York, N.Y.; son of Charles F. (in sales) and Katherine (Heinecke) Ebert; married Katherine Schaefer (an antiques dealer and writer), July 21, 1946; children: Carol (Mrs. Edward Franklin Perry III), Ellen. *Education:* Polytechnic Institute of Brooklyn, B.E.E., 1947. *Religion:* Protestant. *Home:* 21 Wachusett Rd., Wellesley Hills, Mass. 02181.

CAREER: Polytechnic Institute of Brooklyn, Brooklyn, N.Y., research assistant at Microwave Research Institute, 1942-46, senior instructor in electrical engineering, 1943-53, section head for P.R.D., Inc., 1946-53; FXR, Inc., New York, N.Y., vice-president and member of board of directors, 1953-62; Weinschel Engineering Co., Inc., Gaithersburg, Md., executive vice-president, chief engineer, and member of board of directors, 1962-66; Microwave Associates, Inc., Burlington Mass., corporate vice-president and manager of circuits division, 1966-73; engineering consultant, antiques dealer, and free-lance writer, 1973—. *Member:* Institute of Electrical and Electronic Engineers (senior member), Institute of Radio Engineers (senior member), Sigma Xi, Tau Beta Pi, Eta Kappa Nu.

WRITINGS: (With wife, Katherine Ebert) *Old American Prints for Collectors,* Scribner, 1974; (with K. Ebert) *American Folk Painters,* Scribner, 1975. Contributor to *Handbook of Microwave Measurements.* Contributor to technical journals.

*   *   *

ECHEVARRIA, Roberto Gonzalez
See GONZALEZ-ECHEVARRIA, Roberto

*   *   *

ECHOLS, Barbara E(llen)   1934-

PERSONAL: Born September 29, 1934, in Atlanta, Ga.; daughter of Harold T. and Ellen E. (Lyon); children: Barbara Ellen Bucci, Laura Marie Bucci. *Education:* Wake Forest University, M.B.A., 1978; attending North Carolina Central University Law School, 1981—. *Office:* Medical Center, Duke University, Durham, N.C. 27710.

CAREER: Johns Hopkins Hospital, Baltimore, Md., electroencephalography technician, 1952-54, chief of Electroencephalography Laboratory, 1954-66, research assistant in medical care and hospitals, 1967-68; Association of American Medical Colleges, Washington, D.C., administrative assistant to president, 1969-71; Duke University, Medical Center, Durham, N.C., director of Office of Grants and Contracts, 1971—, executive secretary of committee for clinical investigations, 1972-75, and biosafety committee, 1977—, co-chairperson of committee for clinical investigations, 1975—. Member of board of examiners of American Board of Registration of Electroencephalographic Technologists, 1964-66; consultant to International Business Machines Corp.

MEMBER: International Union for Health Education, American Bar Association, American Society of Electroencephalographic Technicians (vice-president, 1961-62; president, 1962-64; member of executive council, 1964-65), Authors Guild.

WRITINGS: (Contributor) *Preventive Medicine U.S.A.* (task force reports), Prodist, 1976; (with Jay M. Arena) *The Commonsense Guide to Good Eating,* Barron's, 1978; *Vegetarian Delights,* Barron's, 1981. Author of a column in *Duke Alumni Newsletter,* 1975-79. Contributor to technical journals.

WORK IN PROGRESS: A satire about overachievers.

SIDELIGHTS: Echols told *CA:* "I read everything I can get my hands on, including cereal box labels. Books have been my constant companions since childhood. I would like to return to the world, through my writing, a little of the pleasure that I have taken from the printed word."

*   *   *

EDEN, Dorothy (Enid)   1912-1982

OBITUARY NOTICE:—See index for *CA* sketch: Born April 3, 1912, in Canterbury Plains, New Zealand; died of cancer, March 4, 1982, in London, England. Author of more than thirty novels in the historical, suspense, and Gothic genres. Her books include *The Vines of Yarrabee, Time of the Dragon,* and *The Millionaire's Daughter.* For the last eighteen years of her life Eden suffered from severe rheumatoid arthritis, yet she continued to write. Obituaries and other sources: *London Times,* March 8, 1982; *New York Times,* March 11, 1982; *Publishers Weekly,* March 19, 1982; *Time,* March 22, 1982; *AB Bookman's Weekly,* April 12, 1982.

EDMUNDS, H(enry) Tudor   1897-

PERSONAL: Born July 13, 1897, in Buenos Aires, Argentina; son of Gwilym Saunders (a bank manager) and Frances Mary (a teacher; maiden name, Philippe) Edmunds; married Grace Ida Jones (a teacher), June 1, 1929; children: Maureen (Mrs. Hugh Haig), Janice (Mrs. Reginald Uphill). *Education:* Kings College Hospital, London, M.R.C.S. and L.R.C.P., 1923, M.B. and B.S., 1924. *Politics:* None. *Religion:* Christian. *Residence:* Oxford, England. *Agent:* Theosophical Publishing House Ltd., 68 Great Russel St., London WC1B 3BU, England.

CAREER: Registered general medical practitioner in England, 1924-62. Author and editor of medical textbooks. *Military service:* British Army, infantry, 1916-18, medical officer, 1939-45; became major. Theosophical Society in England (chairman of Science Research Group).

WRITINGS: (With others) *The Mystery of Healing,* Theosophical Publishing (London), 1968; (editor) Lawrence J. Bendit and others, *Psychism and the Unconscious Mind,* Theosophical Publishing, 1968; (contributor) E. Lester Smith, editor, *Intelligence Came First,* Theosophical Publishing (London), 1975; (editor with others) *Some Unrecognized Factors in Medicine,* Theosophical Publishing, 1976.

*   *   *

EDWARDS, Michael   1938-

PERSONAL: Born April 29, 1938, in Surrey, England; son of Frank (a garage manager) and Irene (Dalliston) Edwards; married Danielle Bourdin (a lecturer in science), July 7, 1964; children: Paul, Catherine. *Education:* Cambridge University, B.A., 1960, M.A., 1964, Ph.D., 1965. *Religion:* Christian. *Home:* 30 Alma St., Wivenhoe, Essex CO7 9DL, England. *Office:* Department of Literature, University of Essex, Colchester, England.

CAREER: University of Warwick, Coventry, England, lecturer in French, 1965-73; University of Essex, Colchester, England, senior lecturer, 1973-77, reader in literature, 1977—. *Member:* Cambridge Union Club (life member).

WRITINGS: La Thebaide de Racine (title means "The *Thebais* of Racine"), Nizet, 1965; *Commonplace* (poem), Adam, 1971; *La Tragedie racinienne* (criticism; title means "Racinian Tragedy"), Pensee Universelle, 1972; *To Kindle the Starling* (poems), Aquila, 1972; *Where* (poems), Aquila, 1975; (editor) *French Poetry Now,* Aquila, 1975; *Eliot/Language,* Aquila, 1975; (editor with Guiliano Dego) *Directions in Italian Poetry,* Aquila, 1976; *The Ballad of Mobb Conroy* (poems), Aquila, 1977; (editor) *Raymond Queneau,* Aquila, 1978; (editor) *Words/Music,* Aquila, 1979.

Author of "Commonplace" (verse play based on own poem), first broadcast by BBC-Radio, July 3, 1971. Co-editor of *Prospice Review,* 1973—.

WORK IN PROGRESS: The Magic, Unquiet Body, poems; *Another Art of Poetry,* poems; *The Possibility of Literature,* nonfiction.

SIDELIGHTS: Edwards told *CA:* "I aim to write Christian poetry, and by doing so, to find out what it is; and, as a critic, to understand language, literature, and other arts, in a Christian perspective."

EDWARDS, Phoebe
 See BLOCH, Barbara

*   *   *

EGEJURU, Phanuel Akubueze

PERSONAL: Born in Avu-Owerri, Nigeria; daughter of Daniel and Margaret Egejuru; married Samuel Jarvis Hunt (a pilot), September 13, 1975; children: Emezuem Wema. *Education:* University of Ibadan, B.Ed., 1966; University of Abidjan, Diploma in French Studies, 1967; University of Minnesota, B.A. (magna cum laude), 1968; University of California, Los Angeles, M.A. (French), 1971, Ph.D., 1972, M.A. (public health), 1983. *Residence:* Avu-Owerri, Imo State, Nigeria. *Office:* School of Humanities, Imo State University, Box 2000, Owerri, Imo State, Nigeria.

CAREER: California State University, Los Angeles, assistant professor of African studies, 1972-74; University of Dar es Salaam, Dar es Salaam, Tanzania, lecturer in literature, 1974-76; University of California, Riverside, assistant professor of literature, 1976-77; State University of New York College at Brockport, associate professor of literature, 1977-80; Imo State University, Owerri, Nigeria, senior lecturer in literature and English, 1981—. Coordinator of Cultural Revival Mezie Avu Age Group Association. *Member:* Modern Language Association of America, African Literature Association, Literary Society of Nigeria. *Awards, honors:* Poetry awards from Catholic Mission of Nigeria, 1963, for ''High Life Music,'' 1963, for ''The Dry Season,'' and 1964, for ''A Look at the Village''; nominated for the Herskovits Award for distinguished scholarly work on Africa, 1979, for *Black Writers, White Audience: A Critical Approach to African Literature.*

WRITINGS: Black Writers, White Audiences: A Critical Approach to African Literature, Exposition Press, 1978; *Towards African Literary Independence,* Greenwood Press, 1980; *Continuity of African Oral Tradition in the New World,* Flame International, 1981. Contributor to journals, including *Obsidian, Callaloo, Research in African Literature,* and *Umoja.*

WORK IN PROGRESS: The Vanished Culture of Owerri People; Folktales and Moonlight Games Among Owerri People: Their Social Significance; research on the knowledge, attitudes, and practice of family planning in Nigeria.

SIDELIGHTS: ''My main interest is literary criticism,'' Egejuru told *CA,* ''especially criticism in African literature. But I am also studying population, the family, and international health. I was motivated to embark on this venture by the poor health services given to children and pregnant women in rural areas of Nigeria, especially in Imo State. I intend to run a maternity and well-baby clinic to serve the rural community in my local government area. My research in family planning is to help me when advising couples. I am also helping to establish the School of Humanities at the new Imo State University at Etiti campus.

''I have traveled extensively in Europe, including England, Germany, France, and Iceland. I have also traveled and studied in many different parts of Africa. Igbo is my mother tongue, and I speak English, French, German, and KiSwahili as well.''

*   *   *

EISENACH, Eldon J(ohn) 1938-

PERSONAL: Born January 19, 1938, in Sheboygan, Wis.; son of George John (a professor) and Olga (a teacher; maiden name, Grauman) Eisenach; married Valerie White (a secretary), Sep-

tember 2, 1961; children: Emlyn, Gretchen. *Education:* Harvard University, A.B. (magna cum laude), 1960; University of California, Berkeley, M.A., 1962, Ph.D., 1970. *Politics:* Democrat. *Religion:* Protestant. *Home:* 1701 Arch St., Little Rock, Ark. 72206. *Office:* Department of Political Science, University of Arkansas, Little Rock, Ark. 72204.

CAREER: Cornell University, Ithaca, N.Y., assistant professor of government, 1970-79; University of Arkansas, Little Rock, associate professor of political science, 1979—. *Member:* American Political Science Association, Conference for the Study of Political Thought.

WRITINGS: Two Worlds of Liberalism: Religion and Politics in Hobbes, Locke and Mill, University of Chicago Press, 1981. Contributor to political science and American studies journals.

WORK IN PROGRESS: A book on John Stuart Mill and religion; continuing research on legal culture and religion in America.

SIDELIGHTS: Eisenach told *CA:* ''As is the case with most who teach in the humanities, the problems I address in my writing arise from trying to make sense to my students. From a number of different directions I have addressed the issue of how and why a political doctrine of self-interest and individual liberty could arise and gain power in a historical world dominated by collective and intergenerational duty sanctioned by religious belief. Who would die for others in order to establish a regime based on the primacy of material interest? What kinds of cultural and historical and religious assumptions might be required to sanction such a regime?

''The answers I have tendered suggest that liberalism involves two separate theories of man and history. One theory of liberalism, involving legal logic, economic rationality, individual consent, and negative liberty, is so well known and so thoroughly criticized and defended that contemporary discussion has attained the status of a ritual. I have sought to recover and articulate the other world of liberalism first found in the religious writings of Hobbes and Locke and later in the cultural and historical theories of John Stuart Mill. By making past theories of liberalism look markedly different with the addition of these elements, I think that contemporary liberalism, its strengths and weaknesses, will appear in a new light.''

*   *   *

EISLER, Georg 1928-

BRIEF ENTRY: Born April 20, 1928, in Vienna, Austria. Austrian artist and editor. Eisler received his art training in England, including studies with Oskar Kokoschka from 1944 to 1946. His work has been exhibited in solo shows throughout Europe, and is included in the permanent collection of museums, including the Victoria and Albert Museum in London, England. He received the Austrian Cross of Honor and the Austrian State Prize. Eisler edited *Ver sacrum: Neue Hefte fuer Kunst und Literatur* (Verlag Jugend & Volk, 1969) and *From Naked to Nude: Life Drawing in the Twentieth Century* (Morrow, 1977). *Address:* Bechardgasse 17, A-1030 Vienna, Austria.

*   *   *

EL CRUMMO
 See CRUMB, R(obert)

ELLERBECK, Rosemary (Anne L'Estrange) (Anna L'Estrange, Nicola Thorne, Katherine Yorke)

PERSONAL: Born in Cape Town, South Africa. *Home:* 96 Townshend Court, Mackennal St., London N.W.8, England.

CAREER: Editor, until 1976; writer, 1976—.

WRITINGS—Novels; under name Rosemary Ellerbeck: *Hammersleigh,* McKay, 1976; *Rose, Rose, Where Are You?,* Coward, 1978.

Novels; under pseudonym Anna L'Estrange: *Return to Wuthering Heights* (historical novel), Pinnacle Books, 1977.

Novels; under pseudonym Nicola Thorne: *The Girls,* Random House, 1967; *Bridie Climbing,* Ace Books, 1974; *In Love,* Quartet, 1974; *A Woman Like Us,* St. Martin's, 1979; *The Perfect Wife and Mother,* St. Martin's, 1981; *Sisters and Lovers* (historical novel), Doubleday, 1982; *Cashmere* (historical novel), Doubleday, in press (to be published in England as *Where the Rivers Meet,* Granada, in press).

Novels; under pseudonym Katherine Yorke: *The Enchantress,* Pocket Books, 1979; *Lady of the Lakes,* Futura, 1982; *Falcon Gold,* Pinnacle Books.

SIDELIGHTS: Rosemary Ellerbeck told *CA:* "I became a full-time novelist in 1976. My first historical enterprise was *Return to Wuthering Heights.* I discovered I love research and became interested in historical novels. *The Enchantress* trilogy followed (though not all volumes have been published in the United States) and *Sisters and Lovers,* which is set in the middle of the nineteenth century, ending with the Crimean War.

"I have not abandoned the modern novel, but I write only on commission, after discussion with my publishers. This makes sense at a time when the cost of books means that many publishers are pruning their lists. Sometimes the publishers suggest a subject, as in *Cashmere,* the story of a Scottish family involved in the woolen industry from 1919 to 1951. It is a rewarding, creative process for both writer and publisher."

*   *   *

ELLIOT, Asa
See BLINDER, Elliot

*   *   *

ELLIOT, Jeffrey M.   1947-

PERSONAL: Born June 14, 1947, in Los Angeles, Calif.; son of Gene (a corporation executive) and Harriet (an interior decorator; maiden name, Sobsey) Elliot; *Education:* University of Southern California, B.A. (with high honors), 1969, M.A., 1970; attended Carnegie-Mellon University (A.B.D.), 1973-74, California State University, Long Beach, 1975, and Old Dominion University, 1979; Claremont Graduate School, D.A., 1978. *Home:* 1420 Wyldewood Rd., No. B-1, Durham, N.C. 27704. *Office:* Department of Political Science, North Carolina Central University, Durham, N.C. 27707.

CAREER: Glendale College, Glendale, Calif., instructor in political science, 1969-72; Cerritos College, Norwalk, Calif., instructor in political science, 1970-72; University of Alaska-Anchorage Community College, Anchorage, assistant professor of history and political science, 1972-74; Miami-Dade Community College, Miami, Fla., assistant dean of academic affairs and assistant professor of social science, 1974-76; freelance newspaper and magazine journalist, 1976-78; Virginia Wesleyan College, Norfolk, assistant professor of political science, 1978-79; Education Development Center, Newton, Mass., senior curriculum specialist in political science and history, 1979-81; North Carolina Central University, Durham, assistant professor of political science, 1981—. Political speechwriter and campaign strategist for U.S. Senator Howard W. Cannon, 1969—; co-founder and historian of the People's Lobby, 1970-72; host of "Commentary," a weekly program on KPFK-Radio, 1971-72; member of Dade County Social Studies Instructional Materials Council and Miami Community Services Advisory Council, both 1975; member of national advisory board of *Community College Frontiers,* 1975—; vice-chairman of Florida Committee for Educational Stability, 1976; contributing editor of *Negro History Bulletin,* 1976-79; election commentator for WGH-Radio, 1978; contributing editor, *West Coast Writer's Conspiracy,* 1978-79; chairman of board of directors of Crispus Attucks Theater for the Arts Foundation, 1978-79; contributing editor of *Questar* magazine, 1979-80; assistant editor of Borgo Press, 1978—, contributing editor of *American Fantasy,* 1982—; assistant editor of *The Year's Scholarship in Science Fiction, Fantasy, and Horror Literature,* 1982—.

MEMBER: International Visual Literacy Association, American Association of University Professors, American Historical Association, American Political Science Association, National Council for the Social Studies, Association for the Study of Afro-American Life and History, Association for Supervision and Curriculum Development, Community College Social Science Association (member of board of directors, 1973-77; president, 1975-77), Southern Political Science Association, Western Political Science Association, Western College Reading Association, Phi Delta Kappa, Pi Sigma Alpha.

AWARDS, HONORS: Excellence in Teaching Citation from Cerritos College, 1971; Outstanding Educator Citation from U.S. Senator Mike Gravel, 1973; Distinguished Service Through Community Effort award from Florida Association of Community Colleges, 1976; Outstanding Educator of Florida award from Florida Committee for Educational Stability, 1976; Balrog Award finalist for outstanding science fiction and fantasy author, 1981; Distinguished Literary Achievement award for books, articles and interviews from American Biographical Institute, 1981; Small Press Writers and Artists Organization finalist for best writer in nonfiction, 1982.

WRITINGS: (With Francis Shieh) *Keys to Economic Understanding,* Kendall/Hunt, 1976; *The Middle East Crisis: A Confederative Solution?,* Society for Middle East Confederation, 1977; *Science Fiction Voices,* Borgo, Volume II (Elliot was not associated with Volume I), 1979, Volume III, 1980, Volume V (Elliot was not associated with Volume IV), 1982, Volume VI, 1983.

Literary Voices, Volume I, Borgo, 1980; *The Future of the U.S. Space Program,* Borgo, 1981; (with Steven E. Miller and Lawrence H. Fuchs) *Political Ideals, Policy Dilemmas,* Education Development Center, 1981; (with Miller and Fuchs) *Treaty Rights and Dual Status: Who Owes What to Native Americans,* Education Development Center, 1981; (with Miller and Fuchs) *Making a Living: Equal Opportunity and Affirmative Action,* Education Development Center, 1981; (with Miller and Fuchs) *Educational Opportunity: Equal for Everyone?,* Education Development Center, 1981; (with Miller and Fuchs) *Immigration and Public Policy: Who Can Become an American?,* Education Development Center, 1981; (with Miller and Fuchs) *Getting and Using Power: Political Access Without Discrimination,* Education Development Center, 1981; (with

Catherine Cobb Morocco and Marilyn Clayton Felt) *The American Experiment: E Pluribus Unum,* Education Development Center, 1981; (with Robert Reginald) *The Analytical Congressional Directory,* Borgo, 1981; *Black Voices,* Borgo, Volume I, 1981, Volume II, 1982; *Political Voices,* Borgo, Volume I, 1981, Volume II, 1983; (with Reginald) *If Kennedy Had Lived,* Borgo, 1981; *Fantasy Voices,* Borgo, Volume I, 1981, Volume II, 1983; *Pulp Voices,* Volume I, Borgo, 1981; *Literary Masters: Science Fiction,* Borgo, 1981; (with Reginald) *Directory of Minority Leaders,* Borgo, 1981; *Stanton A. Coblentz: Adventures of a Freelancer,* Borgo, 1982; *Philip Brasfield: Freedom in Darkness,* Borgo, 1982; *Voices of Imaginative Fiction,* Arno, 1982; *A. E. van Vogt: A Reader's Guide,* Starmount House, 1982; *A Conversation With Robert A. W. "Doc" Lowndes,* Borgo, 1982; *George Zebrowski: Perfecting Visions, Slaying Cynics,* Borgo, 1982; *Masters of "Hard" Science Fiction: A Primary and Secondary Bibliography,* G. K. Hall, 1983; *Great Issues: The Battle for Congressional Reform,* Borgo, 1983; (with Joseph R. Aicher, Jr.), *American Government: One Hundred Classroom Games,* Borgo, 1983.

Contributor of nearly four hundred articles to magazines and newspapers. Contributing editor of *Negro History Bulletin,* 1976-79, and *West Coast Writer's Conspiracy,* 1978-80. Associate editor of *Community College Social Science Journal,* 1972-75.

WORK IN PROGRESS—Publication of all titles expected by Borgo in 1984: (With Sheikh R. Ali) *The Trilemma of World Oil Politics; The N.C.C.U. Eagle: No Common, Ordinary Barnyard Foul; Raymond Z. Gallun: Magician of Dream Valley; American Federalism: Problems and Prospects; Chicano Voices,* Volume I; *Radical Voices,* Volume I.

SIDELIGHTS: Elliot told *CA:* "I view myself as a multigenre writer, having authored academic treatises, empirical research, reference works, textbooks, anthologies, interviews, essays, book reviews, biographies, novels, film reviews, bibliographies, editorials, popular articles, etc. In recent years, however, I have concentrated on 'celebrity' interviews, writing more than forty such pieces a year. My subjects include political leaders, authors, sports figures, entertainers, business leaders, poets, scientists, philosophers, newsmakers, artists, and countless others.

"Before I interview a person—let's say, a writer—I invest heavily in preparation: An investment of time and energy. I scour myriad bookshops and libraries to find everything I can by the author. I read not only that person's works, but everything I can find that has been written *about* the author. I also try to track down people who know the author and who are willing to share their perceptions of the writer and his work.

"Before I ever make my call on the author, I think through the direction, the *shape* of the interview, and prepare anywhere from fifty to one hundred questions. Once the session begins, I ask these questions and others as the interview develops, often departing significantly from my original list of questions. Usually, I tape anywhere from several hours to several days of conversation with the person.

"Typically, I arrive at the author's home early in the morning—just after breakfast—armed with a tape recorder, a pad of ammunition, and an arsenal of tapes. We work all through the morning—and it is work, although by no means unpleasant. We break for lunch, often in the company of my photographer, but although the tape recorder is left behind, the questioning will not cease. And after dessert and coffee, it is back to the person's home and back to work until very nearly dinner time.

"Now, with the interview completed, my work really begins. First, I transcribe all of the tapes, leaving me with anywhere from forty to two hundred pages of text. From there I edit the interview to the required length, usually about thirty-five typed pages. This is a herculean undertaking, as I must pare down the transcript to the specified length. This is no simple feat. At this point, I take my cut-down version and begin the process of editing it for consistency, flow, lucidity, and language. This phase will often require three to five separate edits, until I reach the point where I am satisfied with the finished product. Now, I am ready to write my introduction, the aim of which is to put the interview into proper perspective, providing the reader with a behind-the-scenes account of what it was like to interview the person. The introduction will run anywhere from two to ten pages, depending on the length of the article.

"At this point, I think up an appropriate title, which is often more difficult than one might surmise. And finally, I select anywhere from five to ten photographs to accompany the piece. At the end, I am left with the least pleasant task—namely, typing up the finished article, during which time I also make some slight editorial changes. Then, it is off to the publisher, not to be seen again until the galleys are sent or the piece is published."

*   *   *

ELSHTAIN, Jean Bethke 1941-

PERSONAL: Born January 1, 1941, in Windsor, Colo.; daughter of Paul George (an educator) and Helen (a community activist; maiden name, Lind) Bethke; married Errol L. Elshtain (a public health official), September 5, 1965; children: Sheri, Heidi, Jenny, Eric. *Education:* Colorado State University, B.A., 1963; attended University of Wisconsin (now University of Wisconsin—Madison), 1963-64; University of Colorado, M.A., 1965; Brandeis University, Ph.D., 1973. *Residence:* Amherst, Mass. *Office:* Department of Political Science, University of Massachusetts, 228 Thompson, Amherst, Mass. 01002.

CAREER: Colorado State University, Fort Collins, instructor in history, 1964-65; Northeastern University, Boston, Mass., lecturer in political science, 1972-73; University of Massachusetts, Amherst, instructor, 1973, assistant professor, 1973-76, associate professor, 1976-80, professor of political science, 1980—. Member of Institute for Advanced Study, Princeton, N.J., 1981-82.

MEMBER: International Political Science Association, International Association for Philosophy of Law and Social Philosophy, American Political Science Association, Caucus for a New Political Science, Conference for the Study of Political Thought, Women's Caucus for Political Science, Northeastern-New England Political Science Association (chairperson of committee on the status of women, 1975). *Awards, honors:* Woodrow Wilson fellowship, 1963-64; MacDowell Colony fellowship, summer, 1981.

WRITINGS: (Contributor) Theodore M. Norton and Bertell Ollman, editors, *Studies in Socialist Pedagogy,* Monthly Review Press, 1978; (contributor) Michael J. Gargas McGrath, editor, *Liberalism and the Modern Policy,* Dekker, 1978; (contributor) Julia Sherman and Evelyn T. Beck, editors, *The Prism of Sex: Toward an Equitable Pursuit of Knowledge,* University of Wisconsin Press, 1980; *Public Man, Private Woman: Women in Social and Political Thought,* Princeton University Press, 1981; (editor and contributor) *The Family in Political Thought,* University of Massachusetts Press, 1982; (contributor) Irene Diamond, editor, *Women and Public Policy,* Longman, 1982. Also author of *Intimacy and Cultural Form,* 1983. Contributor to *Great American Reformers.* Contributor of about seventy articles and reviews to political science journals and popular magazines, including *Commonweal, Dissent, Quest, Nation, Newsday,* and *Progressive.* Member of editorial board of *Women and Politics.*

WORK IN PROGRESS: Women, War, and Feminism, publication expected in 1984.

SIDELIGHTS: Jean Elshtain wrote: "My work is iconoclastic, challenging received 'truths' from the history of political thought and within contemporary political and social thought, including feminism. I am concerned with the way innovative ideas become hardened into deadening dogmas. One of my chief concerns is children, the way they are viewed and the way they are treated. It seems to me that much of the political ferment of our recent past concentrated almost exclusively on promoting a certain kind of 'individual liberation' that rapidly turned into self-serving individualism. Within this frame of reference, concern for others gets derogatively labeled 'self-abnegation.' We have lost a sense of community and of the dignity of caring and being of service. I would restore this without, at the same time, restoring the unjust constraints that previously prevented persons, especially women, from expressing their own sense of self. This is a complex task, but one that is worthwhile and important. I attribute this ethical and moral dimension of my work to having been reared in a family in which such imperatives were central and in which responsibility for self *and* others was seen as necessarily intertwined.

"All this heavy moral concern leads me to be (alas) uplifting and demanding. Thankfully, I am spared, at least most of the time, from moralistic heavy-handedness by a deeply rooted sense of irony and a recognition that there is much to laugh about and at—most often oneself."

*   *   *

EMMENS, Carol Ann   1944-

PERSONAL: Born October 12, 1944, in Newark, N.J.; daughter of Carmine John and Antoinette (Rosano) Rossi; married Christopher Emmens, June 26, 1966; children: Scott Christopher. *Education:* Fairleigh Dickinson University, B.S., 1966; Rutgers University, M.L.S., 1970. *Religion:* Society of Friends (Quakers). *Home:* 213 Highfield Lane, Nutley, N.J. 07110.

CAREER: New York Public Library, Donnell Library Center, New York City, young adult librarian, 1966-70; Belleville Public Library, Belleville, N.J., librarian, 1970-71, part-time reference librarian, 1971-73; Educational Film Library Association, New York City, film reference librarian, 1974-77; freelance writer, 1977—. High school English teacher in Rutherford, N.J., 1966-69. Writer, host, and producer of "TV Tips and Thoughts," a television program for United Artists and Columbia cable television. *Member:* Society of Children's Book Writers.

WRITINGS: Short Stories on Film, Libraries Unlimited, 1979; *An Album of Television* (juvenile), F. Watts, 1980; *An Album of the Sixties* (juvenile), F. Watts, 1981; *Stunts and Stunt People* (juvenile), F. Watts, 1982. Contributor of articles and reviews to magazines. Assistant editor of *Sightlines,* 1971-77; television editor of *Children's World.*

WORK IN PROGRESS: Stunt Men and Women, publication expected in 1982; a biography of John Lennon, publication by F. Watts expected in 1982.

SIDELIGHTS: Emmens told *CA:* "It is important for parents and educators to discuss television with children and to note its effects on them. But let's not lose sight of the fact that in homes where love, honesty, and humanistic values are in evidence every day, TV will not harm our children. Let's work on creating an atmosphere of caring and sharing so we will not have to worry so much about television."

AVOCATIONAL INTERESTS: European travel, collecting camels, silk, antique jewelry, indoor plants, watching television.

*   *   *

EMMERSON, Richard Kenneth   1948-

PERSONAL: Born May 11, 1948, in Montemorellos, Mexico; came to the United States in 1959; son of Kenneth Harvey (in business and mission work) and Dorothy (a secretary; maiden name, Ayars) Emmerson; married Sharon Page, May 3, 1970 (divorced January 5, 1975); married Sandra Clayton (a teacher), September 12, 1976; children: Ariel Elisabeth Rebecca. *Education:* Columbia Union College, B.A., 1970; Andrews University, M.A., 1971; Stanford University, Ph.D., 1977. *Office:* Department of English, Walla Walla College, College Place, Wash. 99324.

CAREER: Walla Walla College, College Place, Wash., instructor, 1971-74, assistant professor, 1974-78, associate professor, 1978-82, professor of English, 1982—. *Member:* Modern Language Association of America, Medieval Academy of America, Medieval and Renaissance Drama Society, Medieval Association of the Pacific. *Awards, honors:* Woodrow Wilson fellow, 1970-71; National Endowment for the Humanities fellow, 1978-79; American Philosophical Society grant, 1982.

WRITINGS: Antichrist in the Middle Ages: A Study of Medieval Apocalypticism, Art, and Literature, University of Washington Press, 1981. Contributor to church and literary history journals. Executive editor of *Spectrum: A Quarterly Journal of the Adventist Forums,* 1977-82.

WORK IN PROGRESS: A study of the relationship between late medieval and Renaissance apocalypticism and the visual and literary arts.

SIDELIGHTS: Emmerson commented: "I have been fascinated with the apocalyptic outlook, with both the religious and the psychological motivations leading people to believe that the end of the world is imminent. Particularly, I am interested in how this outlook is reflected culturally in literature and the visual arts.

"After publication of my book on the medieval Antichrist I received a letter asking if I thought the world would last until the year 2000. I'm no prophet, but I do predict that with the approaching end of the millenium expectations, both religious and secular, as to the end of time will multiply. It will be interesting to see how these contemporary expectations are reflected in modern culture, from evangelical preachers to Hollywood films."

Emmerson's languages include Old and Middle English, Old and modern French, German, Italian, Spanish, and Latin.

*   *   *

ENDERLE, Judith (Ann)   1941-

PERSONAL: Surname is pronounced *En*-der-lee; born November 26, 1941, in Detroit, Mich.; daughter of Theodore P. (an engineer) and Ellenore (a teacher; maiden name, Tanner) Ross; married Dennis Joseph Enderle (a vice-president and controller), August 18, 1962; children: Kevin Dennis, Brian Peter, Monica Ann. *Education:* University of Detroit, Certificate in

Secretarial Business, 1962; also attended University of California, Los Angeles. *Residence:* Malibu, Calif. *Agent:* Andrea Brown, 240 East 48th St., New York, N.Y. 10017.

CAREER: Ford Motor Co., Wixom, Mich., secretary, 1963-65; Santa Monica Emeritus College, Santa Monica, Calif., teacher of writing for children, 1981-82. *Member:* Society of Children's Book Writers, Authors Guild, Southern California Council on Literature for Children and Young People.

WRITINGS: Good Junk (juvenile), Elsevier-Nelson, 1981; *Karyn and Steve* (juvenile), Tempo Books, 1982; *Someone for Sara* (juvenile), Tempo Books, 1982; *Sealed With a Kiss* (romance), Tempo Books, 1983; *Computer Cupid* (romance), Tempo Books, 1983. Contributor to *Highlights for Children.*

SIDELIGHTS: Enderle told *CA:* "Teaching the craft of writing has made the most amazing impact on my own work. There is something about saying the rules out loud that reinforces them in my mind, so that I look at my manuscripts with a different eye. One cannot be an absolute judge of one's own work, however. The final judgment comes from the reader. A writer of children's books hopes the reader will find some small tidbit of recognition in the books he creates—a feeling of 'that's exactly how I feel,' or 'that person has my problem and acted,' or 'that person is like someone I know; now I understand.'' Two of my favorite themes are friendship and the importance of communication. Growing up in today's world is often difficult. If I can sympathize a lot, help a little, and make a few people smile, I'll feel I have been a successful writer. Writing is draining, demanding, giving, and very, very satisfying.''

AVOCATIONAL INTERESTS: Reading, gardening.

*   *   *

ENGELMANN, Ruth   1919-

PERSONAL: Born November 6, 1919, in Hurley, Wis.; daughter of John E. (a farmer) and Hulda (Harper) Gould; married Hugo Engelmann (a university professor), October 4, 1941; children: John. *Education:* University of Wisconsin (now University of Wisconsin—Madison), B.A., 1943, M.A., 1944. *Home:* 421 West Hillcrest Dr., DeKalb, Ill. 60115.

CAREER: Michigan State University, East Lansing, instructor in English, 1945-47; private tutor, 1947-49; University of Wisconsin—Milwaukee, extension instructor in English, 1949-51; Neighborhood House, Milwaukee, recreation leader, 1951-52; editor, private tutor, and free-lance writer, 1952-59; Shorewood Public Library, Shorewood, Wis., assistant librarian, 1959-60; editor, private tutor, and teacher associated with inner-city schools, 1960-65; University of Wisconsin—Milwaukee, instructor in creative writing, 1965-66; writer, 1966—. *Member:* Wisconsin Academy of Sciences, Arts, and Letters, Art Institute of Chicago, Friends of Northern Illinois University.

WRITINGS: Leaf House: Days of Remembering (memoir), Harper, 1982. Contributor of stories to magazines, including *Partisan Review* and *Saturday Review.*

WORK IN PROGRESS: Ties of Birth (tentative title), a novel about a group of people at a rundown hotel in the Austrian Alps, publication by Harper expected in 1984; *Elton Winter* (tentative title), a novel about a group of academicians whose lives become involved in the deterioration of one of their own, completion expected in 1984.

SIDELIGHTS: Ruth Engelmann wrote: "I speak and read Finnish and German; I learned Finnish before I learned English. I travel to Europe every year, and spend a month in Vienna, where my husband and I have an apartment. Perhaps because

I grew up bilingual and became trilingual, the nuances of language intrigue me. Thus, I am less concerned with action and spend most of my time creating a voice that suits the tale I wish to tell. Then I explore the details of the characters' lives. My goals are to make the reader live the life within the story, to make him regret, at the end, that the tale is done, and to make him wish to go back to reread the book. I am concerned about style and craftsmanship. I am intrigued by the complexities of ordinary people who have little say in solving the problems facing mankind."

BIOGRAPHICAL/CRITICAL SOURCES: Milwaukee Journal, February 17, 1982.

*   *   *

ENOCH, Kurt   1895-1982

OBITUARY NOTICE: Born November 22, 1895, in Hamburg, Germany (now West Germany); died of heart failure, February 15, 1982, in Puerto Rico. Publisher. Enoch is best known as a co-founder of New American Library. He began his publishing career in Germany with the Albatross Modern Continental Library, an English language paperback reprint series. He fled the Nazis in 1936 and came to New York in 1940, where he became vice-president of Penguin Books. In 1947 Enoch and Victor Weybright founded New American Library, which soon became one of the pioneers of the "paperback revolution." Obituaries and other sources: *Who's Who in the East,* 17th edition, Marquis, 1979; *New York Times,* February 17, 1982; *Publishers Weekly,* February 26, 1982.

*   *   *

EPPERLY, Elizabeth Rollins   1951-

PERSONAL: Born April 23, 1951, in Martinsville, Va.; daughter of John David (a lawyer) and Elizabeth (Rollins) Epperly. *Education:* University of Prince Edward Island, B.A., 1973; Dalhousie University, M.A., 1974; University of London, Ph.D., 1978. *Office:* Department of English, University of Prince Edward Island, Charlottetown, Prince Edward Island, Canada C1A 4P3.

CAREER: University of Prince Edward Island, Charlottetown, assistant professor of English, 1977—. *Member:* Association of Canadian University Teachers of English, Canadian Council of Teachers of English, University of Prince Edward Island Alumni Association (member of executive committee).

WRITINGS: (With F.W.P. Bolger) *My Dear Mr. M: Letters to G. B. Macmillan From L. M. Montgomery,* McGraw, 1980. Contributor to magazines.

WORK IN PROGRESS: Trollope and Austin Dobson; research on L. M. Montgomery's poems and novels in manuscript.

SIDELIGHTS: Elizabeth Epperly commented: "I came to Prince Edward Island from Virginia because of a long-time fascination with L. M. Montgomery's 'Anne' and 'Emily' books. My enthusiasm for her writing and for the island itself have led to research and a change of citizenship. My other enduring interest is Anthony Trollope and the Victorian novel.

"I love travel and have found joy in England, Scotland, and Greece."

*   *   *

ERAZMUS, Edward T.   1920-

BRIEF ENTRY: Born April 22, 1920, in Grand Rapids, Mich.

American linguist, educator, and author. Erazmus has been linguistics teacher and director of the Intensive English Center at University of Kansas since 1964. He wrote *English as a Second Language: A Reader* (W. C. Brown, 1970). *Address:* Intensive English Center, University of Kansas, 1200 Louisiana St., Lawrence, Kan. 66044.

*   *   *

ERDT, Terrence 1942-

PERSONAL: Born October 11, 1942, in Albany, N.Y.; son of Frederick T. (in sales) and Helen M. Erdt; married Torborg Lundell, February 6, 1972 (divorced January, 1976). *Education:* Siena College, B.A., 1965; University of Connecticut, M.A., 1966; University of California, Santa Barbara, Ph.D., 1977; University of California, Berkeley, M.L.I.S., 1981. *Home:* 1723 Greenwood St., Evanston, Ill. 60201. *Office:* Reference Department, Library, Northwestern University, Evanston, Ill. 60201.

CAREER: U.S. Peace Corps, Washington, D.C., English teacher at University of Tehran, 1966-68; University of California, Santa Barbara, English teacher, 1968-72; worked as bicycle mechanic, 1972-74; University of California, Santa Barbara, English teacher, 1974-80; University of California, Berkeley, library assistant, 1980-81; Northwestern University, Evanston, Ill., reference librarian, 1981—. *Member:* Modern Language Association of America, American Library Association.

WRITINGS: Jonathan Edwards: Art and the Sense of the Heart, University of Massachusetts Press, 1980. Contributor to literature journals. Editor of *Channels.*

WORK IN PROGRESS: Research on the influence, or continuation, of certain Puritan beliefs, particularly those of an aesthetic nature, in nineteenth- and twentieth-century American thought.

SIDELIGHTS: Erdt told *CA* that his writing has been motivated by "the potential benefits of new technologies and new library resources to humanists, and the presentation of scholarly research to non-scholarly readers."

*   *   *

ERICKSON, Milton H(yland) 1901-1980

PERSONAL: Born December 5, 1901, in Aurum, Nev.; died following a brief illness, March 25, 1980, in Phoenix, Ariz.; married wife, Elizabeth; children: Albert, Lance, Allan, Robert, Kristina, Carol Erickson Deerington, Betty Alice Erickson Elliot, Roxanna Erickson Klein. *Education:* University of Wisconsin (now University of Wisconsin—Madison), B.A., 1927, M.A., 1928, M.D., 1928. *Address:* 1201 East Hayward Ave., Phoenix, Ariz. 85020.

CAREER: Licensed to practice medicine in Colorado, Massachusetts, Rhode Island, Michigan, and Arizona. Colorado General Hospital, Denver, intern, 1928-29; Colorado Psychopathic Hospital, Denver, psychiatric intern, 1929; Massachusetts State Hospital, Worcester, director of psychiatric training, 1932-34; Wayne County General Hospital, Eloise, Mich., director of psychiatric training, 1934-48; Wayne State University, Detroit, Mich., assistant professor, 1940-44, associate professor of psychiatry, 1944-48, professor at graduate school, 1943-48; Michigan State University, East Lansing, professor at graduate school, 1948; private practice of psychiatry in Phoenix, Ariz., 1949-80. *Member:* International Congress for Hypnosis and Psychosomatic Medicine, International Society for Hypnosis, American Society of Clinical Hypnosis (founder,

1957; president, 1957-59), American Psychological Association, American Psychopathological Association, American Psychiatric Association, American Association for the Advancement of Science. *Awards, honors:* Benjamin Franklin Gold Medal for outstanding achievement from International Society for Hypnosis.

WRITINGS: (With Linn F. Cooper) *Time Distortion in Hypnosis: An Experimental and Clinical Investigation,* foreword by Harold Rosen, Williams & Wilkins, 1954; (with Seymour Hershman and Irving I. Secter) *The Practical Application of Medical and Dental Hypnosis,* Julian Press, 1961; *Advanced Techniques of Hypnosis and Therapy: Selected Papers of Milton H. Erickson,* edited by Jay Haley, Grune, 1967; (with Ernest L. Rossi and Shiela I. Rossi) *Hypnotic Realities: The Induction of Clinical Hypnosis and Forms of Indirect Suggestion,* foreword by Andre M. Weitzenhoffer, Irvington, 1976; (with E. Rossi) *Hypnotherapy: An Exploratory Casebook,* foreword by Sidney Rosen, Irvington, 1979; (editor with E. Rossi) *Collected Papers of Milton H. Erickson on Hypnosis,* Halsted, 1979, Volume I: *The Nature of Hypnosis and Suggestion,* Volume II: *Hypnotic Alteration of Sensory, Perceptual, and Psychophysical Processes,* Volume III: *Hypnotic Investigation of Psychodynamic Processes,* Volume IV: *Innovative Hypnotherapy.* Contributor of more than one hundred forty articles on hypnosis to professional journals. Associate editor of *Diseases of the Nervous System,* 1940-55; editor of *The American Journal of Clinical Hypnosis,* 1958-68.

SIDELIGHTS: Erickson rose to prominence during the 1940's and 1950's as a pioneer in the medical, dental, and psychotherapeutic uses of hypnosis. He was considered the world's leading authority on the subject of hypnotherapy and was instrumental in establishing worldwide recognition and acceptance of hypnosis as a valid and effective therapeutic technique. He was frequently consulted by doctors and scientists, including anthropologist Margaret Mead, and during the 1950's he collaborated with author Aldous Huxley on research on hypnosis and other states of consciousness.

Erickson practiced psychiatry in Massachusetts and Michigan before moving to Arizona in the late 1940's. He was confined to a wheelchair following a bout with polio but continued to conduct teaching seminars from his Phoenix home. Erickson's teaching style was similar to his psychotherapeutic method— distraction by verbal communication and other forms of indirection disrupted the conscious set, providing access to the subject's unconscious mind. His orientation was eclectic, drawing on the widest range of schools of personality theory for the most useful elements of each. Erickson's books on the subject of hypnotherapy are geared toward health professionals and are, according to a *Psychology Today* reviewer, "written in a style . . . as original and personal as [Erickson's] technique."

BIOGRAPHICAL/CRITICAL SOURCES: Jeffery K. Zeig, editor, *Teaching Seminar With Milton H. Erickson, M.D.,* foreword by Richard Van Dyck, Brunner, 1980; *Choice,* March, 1980; *Psychology Today,* December, 1980; *Science Books and Films,* September/October, 1981.

OBITUARIES: New York Times, March 29, 1980.*

*   *   *

ESOHG, Lama
See GHOSE, Amal

ESTY, John Cushing, Jr. 1928-

BRIEF ENTRY: Born August 9, 1928, in White Plains, N.Y. American educator and author. Esty taught mathematics and held administrative positions at Amherst College. Later he was headmaster of a private school in Watertown, Conn., and in 1973 he became senior staff associate at the Education Development Center in Newton, Mass. Since 1978 Esty has been president of the National Association of Independent Schools. He wrote *Choosing a Private School* (Dodd, 1974). *Address:* 25 Everett St., Concord, Mass. 01742. *Biographical/critical sources: Who's Who in America,* 42nd edition, Marquis, 1982.

*   *   *

ETCHEMENDY, Nancy 1952-

PERSONAL: Born February 19, 1952, in Reno, Nev.; daughter of Frederick Lewis (a public school teacher) and Barbara Fay (Nelson) Howell; married John William Etchemendy (a professor of philosophy), April 14, 1973. *Education:* University of Nevada, B.A., 1974. *Home and office:* 34 Lake Lane, Princeton, N.J. 08540. *Agent:* Carol Mann Literary Agency, 168 Pacific St., Brooklyn, N.Y. 11201.

CAREER: Western Industrial Parts, Reno, Nev., lithographer, 1970-75; Sutherland Printing, Reno, worked in art, stripping, and camera, 1975-76; Menlo Graphics and Lithography, Menlo Park, Calif., art director, 1976-78; Etchemendy Commercial Graphics, Palo Alto, Calif., sole proprietor, 1978-81; writer, 1981—.

WRITINGS: *The Watchers of Space* (juvenile science fiction), Avon, 1980; *Stranger From the Stars* (juvenile science fiction), Avon, 1982.

WORK IN PROGRESS: *Skywheel* (tentative title), a novel for young readers, about children living in an orbital space colony; research on methods of radioactive waste storage, with a short story expected to result.

SIDELIGHTS: Etchemendy told *CA:* "From the time my sister and I were four or five years old until we were teenagers, my dad used to read to us on a regular basis. He always had a passion for science fiction, so we heard a lot of it during our evening story time. Tom Swift, the Tom Corbett series, and even judicious amounts of Jules Verne and Ray Bradbury all found places on Dad's reading list. By the time I was eight years old, I *knew* that I was going to live in space when I grew up. Other little girls talked about becoming nurses or stewardesses or mommies when they grew up. But *I* wanted to be an astronaut, or a brave settler on some far-flung and mysterious world.

"At the same time, I was rapidly discovering a second love— the love of words, and the thrill of making them leap and dance to a tune of my own. I learned the alphabet; I discovered the miraculous connection between marks on a sheet of paper and the thoughts inside my head; and I began to write stories and poems. All of that happened to me at once in Miss Elcano's first grade class.

"For a long time I hoped I could be a writer *and* an astronaut. It didn't seem too farfetched. Surely they were going to need somebody to chronicle all those adventures we were going to have. But then several things happened. John Kennedy died. We found ourselves in a seemingly endless war in Southeast Asia. And our social priorities began to change. People started saying things like, 'Why are we spending all this money on the moon when the masses are starving right here on Earth?' and 'Look at the mess we've made of this planet. Do you want the same thing to happen to the other planets?' and 'Why don't we solve the problems of this world before we worry about solving the problems of space travel?'

"Feeling very bleak indeed, I watched the space program fizzle to a smoldering stump, like a big Roman candle that turned out to be a dud. To make matters worse, I was getting old. And I knew that sooner or later I was going to have to find a way to pay the rent and keep potatoes in the pot. Writing was fun, but you couldn't rely on the income. So basically I chickened out. I went to work in a printshop, and that's how I came to be a graphic designer writing science fiction novels on my lunch hours.

"Eventually it became clear to me that no matter what happened, I was going to be dead or too old to make the trip by the time the call went out for space colonists. But I was never able to shake the conviction that mankind belongs in space; that it is in fact our best hope for civilized survival in a dangerous age. As I recently explained to a young fan, 'Why do I write science fiction? It's a lot of fun to consider scientific possibilities. It's important for people to think about all the different things science means to us, and how it might affect our lives. That's partly because scientific inventions can be very dangerous if we use them without thinking about them. I believe it's especially important for today's kids to think about science, particularly space science, because I think that space is the future home of mankind and that we should start exploring it as soon and as fast as possible. People your age will probably be able to live in space if we just hurry up a little.'

"It's a joy to write for kids. As a group they're more sincere and concise about things than any other people I can think of. If you've missed the mark, they'll tell you so—plainly and candidly, without any intention of either sparing you or hurting you. But if you're on target, and a child somewhere begins to think about what you've said, then in a small way you've really affected eternity."

AVOCATIONAL INTERESTS: "I'm a dedicated dabbler—these days particularly in anthropology, archaeology, and paleontology. In addition, I like to spend time in the deserts of the North American West."

*   *   *

ETCHISON, Birdie L(ee) 1937-
(Leigh Hunter, Catherine Wood)

PERSONAL: Born June 22, 1937, in San Diego, Calif.; daughter of Leland H. (an aircraft inspector) and Naomi E. (an artist; maiden name, Brumwell) Leighton; married William R. Tucker, May 28, 1955 (divorced March 25, 1971); married Vernon L. Etchison (a cashier), August 14, 1971; children: (first marriage) William R., Jr., Tamela Cia, Naomi Leanne, Barbara Tucker Kowalski; (second marriage) Matthew, Sarah. *Education:* Attended University of Oklahoma. *Politics:* Democrat. *Religion:* Church of God. *Home:* 6306 Southeast 19th Ave., Portland, Ore. 97202.

CAREER: Burke Marketing Research, Portland, Ore., supervisor, 1973-78; *Oregonian-Oregon Journal,* Portland, typist-salesperson in classified advertisements, 1978-79; free-lance writer, 1979—. Member of staff of Warner Pacific Christian Writers Conference, 1978-82, Mount Herman Christian Writers Conference, and Willamette Writers Conference. *Member:* Oregon Association of Christian Writers (president). *Awards, honors:* Writer of the Year award in juvenile fiction, 1982, from Warner Pacific Writer's Conference.

WRITINGS: Me and Greenley (juvenile novel), Herald Press, 1981; *Strawberry Mountain* (juvenile novel), Herald Press, 1982; *Don't Drop the Sugar Bowl in the Sink* (devotions), Standard Publishing, 1983; (with Diane Nason) *The Celebration of Family,* Thomas Nelson, 1983.

Author, under pseudonyms Catherine Wood and Leigh Hunter, of personal experience articles.

Contributor of more than three hundred fifty articles and stories to magazines.

WORK IN PROGRESS: Cassie's Choice, for teenagers, publication expected in 1983; a romance novel, under pseudonym Leigh Hunter, tentatively titled *Cane Hill.*

SIDELIGHTS: Birdie Etchison told *CA:* "I began writing in May, 1963. Over the next several years I sold fifty confession stories to various magazines, and in 1974 turned almost exclusively to the Christian writing field. My articles, fillers, and stories have now been published in approximately sixty-five different publications.

"In order to stay at home and make it as a full-time free-lance writer, I must keep about two hundred pieces circulating at all times, and still work on my fiction books for young teens. Speaking at writers conferences has been a means of support, as has the inspiration and fellowship of other writers and editors."

*   *   *

EVANS, Luther H.   1902-1981

OBITUARY NOTICE—See index for *CA* sketch: Born October 13, 1902, in Sayers, Tex.; died December 23, 1981, in San Antonio, Tex. Librarian and author. Evans directed the legislative reference department of the Library of Congress for six years before his appointment as librarian of Congress in 1945. He became known for his efforts to prevent censorship of the library's collections. In 1953 Evans became director-general of UNESCO, an organization he helped found in 1945. He later directed the international and legal collections of the Columbia University Library. His writings include *The Virgin Islands From Naval Base to New Deal.* Obituaries and other sources: *New York Times,* December 24, 1981; *AB Bookman's Weekly,* February 22, 1982; *Library Journal,* May 15, 1982.

*   *   *

EVANS, Paul Richer   1925-

BRIEF ENTRY: Born August 31, 1925, in Dunmore, Pa. American music historian, educator, and author. Evans taught at Oberlin College from 1960 to 1964 and at the University of Pennsylvania from 1964 to 1969. He then became a professor of music history at Smith College. Evans wrote *The Early Trope Repertory of Saint Martial de Limoges* (Princeton University Press, 1970). *Address:* 210 Elm St., Northampton, Mass. 01060.

EVANS, Richard   1939-

PERSONAL: Born February 10, 1939, in Paris, France; son of Charles Henry (a chartered accountant) and Mary (Laurens) Evans. *Education:* Attended private boys' school in Wimborne, England. *Office: Tennis Week,* 1107 Broadway, 7a, New York, N.Y. 10010.

CAREER: Evening Standard, London, England, tennis and rugby correspondent, 1960-65; *Evening News,* London, U.S. correspondent, 1966-69, Paris correspondent, 1969-70; writer. Commentator for the British Broadcasting Corp. (BBC-TV) at Wimbledon, England, 1981. Broadcaster on "Radio Sports," American Broadcasting Co., "Worldwide Sports," Columbia Broadcasting System, and "Sound of Sports," Canadian Broadcasting Corp. *Military service:* British Army, 1958-60; became acting captain.

WRITINGS: Whineray's All Blacks, Pelham Books, 1964; (with Marty Riessen) *Match Point,* Prentice-Hall, 1974; *Nasty: Ilie Nastase Versus Tennis,* Stein & Day, 1979; (with Allen Fox) *If I'm the Better Player, Why Can't I Win?,* Tennis Magazine Books, 1980; *McEnroe: A Rage for Perfection,* Sidgewick & Jackson, 1982. Contributor to periodicals, including *Tennis Week* and *World Tennis.*

SIDELIGHTS: Evans told *CA:* "*If I'm the Better Player* proved to be the most interesting and taxing piece of authorship I have ever done. Unlike the regular ghosted book, such as the one I did with Marty Riessen, it required a great deal more effort than getting someone to talk into a tape recorder and retiring to one's own typewriter. Allen Fox, a doctor of psychology from U.C.L.A., is a meticulous but snail-like writer. Apart from adding some anecdotes to what was essentially a psychology of competition, my job was to ensure that we produced a book in approximately the time it would normally have taken Allen to write one article. We worked together at the same table, virtually writing each paragraph together. Progress would frequently be interrupted as we argued over the merits and exact meaning of particular words. There were moments when both of us thought the task impossible, but, in the end, it worked out well and it was, in a strange way, immensely satisfying.

"In comparison, writing my own biography of John McEnroe —although far from easy—is like being released from a set of literary chains. I only have myself to argue with! Time is my biggest enemy as I have to meet a deadline so that the book can be on sale at Wimbledon in 1982. McEnroe is cooperating as far as his schedule will allow, and will, I hope, emerge from the book as a very different person from the one he puts before the public."

F

FAELTEN, Sharon 1950-

PERSONAL: Born March 16, 1950, in Wilson Borough, Pa.; daughter of Joseph Edward (an engineer) and Marie (a music teacher; maiden name, Sabatine) Policelli; married John Faelten (a pipeline records keeper), April 13, 1974. *Education:* Grove City College, B.A., 1972; attended Cedar Crest College, 1979-81. *Office:* Rodale Press, Inc., 33 East Minor St., Emmaus, Pa. 18049.

CAREER: Worked in sales, restaurants, and a health-care agency on Cape Cod, Mass., 1972-77; Rodale Press, Inc., Emmaus, Pa., associate editor, 1977—.

WRITINGS—All published by Rodale Press: *Recipes for Natural Slenderness,* 1979; (with Rebecca Christian, Jim Nechas, and Emrika Padus) *The Prevention Guide to Surgery and Its Alternatives,* 1980; *The Complete Book of Minerals for Health,* 1981; *No More Headaches,* 1982; *Pep Up Naturally,* 1982; *Ten Ways to Live Longer,* 1982; *Vitamins for Better Health,* 1982; *The Complete Book of Natural Allergy Relief,* in press. Contributor to *Prevention.*

SIDELIGHTS: Sharon Faelten told *CA:* "Health journalism presents quite a challenge. For every person who exercises and eats whole wheat bread, there are two who smoke and guzzle soda. Yet sermonizing won't reach people. I try to write in a compelling yet friendly and humorous manner. Health journalism must be lively as well as clear and accurate, or the reader never goes beyond the first paragraph. I regard my books as links between people in the medical profession and the reading public."

*   *   *

FAESSLER, Shirley 1921(?)-

PERSONAL: Born c. December 3, 1921, in Toronto, Ontario, Canada; daughter of Avrom Mendl and Becci (Popescu) Rotstein; married Haeckel Faessler (divorced); married James Edmond (a writer), 1958; children: Bernice Hines. *Education:* Attended public schools in Toronto. *Religion:* Jewish. *Home:* 576 Sherbourne St., Toronto, Ontario M4X IL3, Canada. *Agent:* Julie Fallowfield, McIntosh & Otis, 475 Fifth Ave., New York, N.Y. 10017.

CAREER: Daily Herald, London, England, feature writer, 1939-48; Myer Dress (a dressmaking company), Toronto, Ontario, bookkeeper, 1948-60; writer, 1960—.

WRITINGS: Everything in the Window (novel), McClelland & Stewart, 1979, Atlantic/Little, Brown, 1980. Contributor of short stories to *Atlantic Monthly* and *Tamarack Review.*

WORK IN PROGRESS: A collection of short stories, tentatively titled *A Basket of Apples,* publication by McClelland & Stewart expected in 1982.

SIDELIGHTS: Faessler's novel, *Everything in the Window,* tells the story of a family of Rumanian Jews in Toronto during the 1930's and of their daughter's marriage to a young gentile. The setting and atmosphere of the book were based on the author's own background. Sondra Lowell of the *Los Angeles Times Book Review* wrote that "Faessler's story is too simple at times but her instincts are clear, her writing deft." The *New Yorker* called Faessler a skilled storyteller and deemed *Everything in the Window* "a striking first novel."

Faessler told *CA:* "I had a two-year hiatus after completing my novel, the result of an edema and open-heart surgery. Now I am back at work full time and grateful for it. I feel a need to make up for the lost time, especially since I came late to the writing scene."

BIOGRAPHICAL/CRITICAL SOURCES: Library Journal, June 15, 1980; *New Yorker,* July 28, 1980; *Los Angeles Times Book Review,* September 21, 1980.

*   *   *

FAIRBANK, Alfred John 1895-1982

OBITUARY NOTICE—See index for *CA* sketch: Born July 12, 1895, in Great Ginsby, England; died March 14, 1982, in Hove, England. Calligrapher, type designer, and author of books on fine hand writing. Fairbank designed the elegant, compact italic type, Narrow Bembo, and italic script. His publications include *A Book of Scripts* and *Renaissance Handwriting.* Obituaries and other sources: *London Times,* March 20, 1982; *AB Bookman's Weekly,* April 12, 1982.

*   *   *

FALLON, Peter 1951-

BRIEF ENTRY: Born February 26, 1951, in Osnabrueck, West Germany. Editor, publisher, and poet. Fallon became editor and publisher of Gallery Press in 1970. His poems have been collected in *Among the Walls* (Tara Telephone Publications, 1971), *The Speaking Stones* (Gallery Press, 1978), and *Finding the Dead* (Deerfield Press, 1978). Fallon edited *The First Ten Years: Dublin Arts Festival Poetry* (Dublin Arts Festival, 1979), *Soft Day: A Miscellany of Contemporary Irish Writing* (University of Notre Dame Press, 1980), and *The Writers: A Sense of Ireland* (Braziller, 1980). *Address:* Garden Lodge, Loughcrew, County Meath, Ireland; and 19 Oakdown Rd., Dublin 14, Ireland. *Biographical/critical sources: International Who's Who in Poetry,* 5th edition, Melrose Press, 1977.

* * *

FARAH, Nuruddin 1945-

PERSONAL: Born in 1945, in Baidoa, Somalia; son of Hassan (a merchant) and Aleeli (a poet; maiden name, Faduma) Farah; divorced; children: Koschin Nuruddin (son). *Education:* Attended Panjab University, University of London, and University of Essex. *Religion:* "Born Muslim." *Home address:* P.O. Box 95, Mogadiscio, Somalia. *Agent:* A. D. Peters & Co. Ltd., 10 Buckingham St., London WC2N 6BU, England.

CAREER: Clerk-typist for Ministry of Education in Somalia, 1964-66; teacher at secondary school in Mogadiscio, Somalia, 1969-71; lecturer in comparative literature at Afgoi College of Education, 1971-74; free-lance writer, translator, and broadcaster; University of Ibadan, Jos Campus, Jos, Nigeria, associate professor. *Member:* Union of Writers of the African Peoples. *Awards, honors:* Fellow of United Nations Educational, Scientific and Cultural Organization, 1974-76; literary award from English-Speaking Union, 1980, for *Sweet and Sour Milk.*

WRITINGS: From a Crooked Rib (novel), Heinemann, 1970; *A Naked Needle,* Heinemann, 1976; *Sweet and Sour Milk,* Allison & Busby, 1979; *Sardines,* Allison & Busby, 1981; *Close Sesame,* Allison & Busby, 1982.

Author of "A Dagger in Vacuum" (two-act play), first produced in 1969. Contributor to newspapers.

WORK IN PROGRESS: What If . . .? (tentative title), a novel; a collection of plays for radio and/or the stage; "The Dark Knob of a Potato," a two-act play; "Crooked Rib," a filmscript.

SIDELIGHTS: Farah speaks Somali, Arabic, English, Italian, and French. He commented: "I write in Somali and English, and have collaborated with others in writing in Italian and Arabic. I hope to move eventually into filmmaking. I also plan to write a comprehensive history of the Ogaden, once my novel-writing commitments are dealt with."

BIOGRAPHICAL/CRITICAL SOURCES: Kenneth Little, *Women and Urbanization in African Literature,* Macmillan, 1981; *Bananas,* March-April, 1981; *Index,* May, 1981; *Ariel,* summer, 1981; *Neue Zuricher Zertung,* July 3, 1981.

* * *

FARBER, Susan L. 1945-

PERSONAL: Born July 12, 1945, in Ontario, Ore.; daughter of Jack Russell (a physician) and Amelia (Bozich) Farber; married Richard Gottlieb, March 16, 1969 (divorced, 1972). *Education:* University of Chicago, B.A., 1967; Teachers College, Columbia University, Ph.D., 1973. *Office:* Department of Clinical Psychology, New York University, 6 Washington Pl., New York, N.Y. 10003.

CAREER: Catalyst for Youth, Chicago, Ill., counselor, 1967-68; Child Development Center, New York City, researcher, 1970-77; New York University, New York City, assistant pro-

fessor of clinical psychology, 1977—. *Member:* American Psychological Association, American Association for the Advancement of Science, New York Academy of Sciences.

WRITINGS: Identical Twins Reared Apart: A Reanalysis, Basic Books, 1981. Contributor to periodicals, including *Psychology Today.*

WORK IN PROGRESS: Research on the offspring of bipolar parents.

SIDELIGHTS: Susan Farber's *Identical Twins Reared Apart* studies the similarities and difference of twins raised in separate environments. In compiling the book, Farber reviewed 121 case studies of identical twins. Three sets did not know of their twins until the time of the study. The rest knew of their identical siblings, and most of the pairs had met their twins at least once.

Farber found that in many cases, the twins who had had the least amount of contact with each other shared the most similarities. Many had chosen the same vocation, enjoyed the same interests, and exhibited like habits and mannerisms, such as a particular handshake, tilt of head, or laugh. According to Farber, "twinning," a process whereby twins consciously make themselves different from each other to establish separate identities, may be the reason that twins who were raised together or had met are less alike than those raised apart. She cites genetic factors as the reason that separated monozygotic twins are often remarkably similar in personality.

Farber's analysis of IQ test scores, however, indicated that the twins were less alike than previously thought. Farber told *CA:* "The mutual influence of the twins on each other and the broad similarities in background, despite having different families, had been overlooked by previous investigators and had been acting to make them appear more similar. There is no evidence to support the idea that IQ is predominantly determined by genes. I suggest that the type of evaluation that has been done on the nature-nurture issue in the past is incorrect. A more fruitful approach is to study how genes influence the blueprint of development and, hence, the unfolding of personality and cognitive traits."

Farber's book has been hailed as a refreshing study of twins. In a *Los Angeles Times* review, Arthur Lerner wrote: "[*Identical Twins Reared Apart*] is a vital contribution to a field that had long been waiting for such a study." And Howard E. Gruber of the *New York Times Book Review* admired Farber's "thoughtful appraisal" and "rare and valuable point of view," noting that Farber opens the door for future research by providing a novel approach to her subject. "Dr. Farber's book has the great merit of giving a powerful new impetus to this way of thinking."

BIOGRAPHICAL/CRITICAL SOURCES: Psychology Today, January, 1981; *New York Times Book Review,* March 1, 1981; *Los Angeles Times,* May 15, 1981.

* * *

FARISH, Donald J(ames) 1942-

PERSONAL: Born December 7, 1942, in Winnipeg, Manitoba, Canada; came to the United States in 1963; son of James A. and Alice (Williams) Farish; married Diane Barriere, December 28, 1964; children: Lincoln, Alexander, Kenneth. *Education:* University of British Columbia, B.Sc. (with honors), 1963; North Carolina State University, M.S., 1965; Harvard University, Ph.D., 1968; University of Missouri, J.D., 1976. *Home address:* Laurel Lane, West Kingston, R.I. 02892. *Of-*

fice: Office of the Dean, College of Arts and Science, University of Rhode Island, Kingston, R.I. 02881.

CAREER: University of Missouri, Columbia, instructor, 1968-69, assistant professor, 1969-74, associate professor of biological sciences, 1975-79; University of Rhode Island, Kingston, adjunct professor of zoology and assistant dean of College of Arts and Science, 1979—. Soccer coach. *Awards, honors:* Award from British Columbia Entomological Society, 1963.

WRITINGS: Biology: The Human Perspective, Harper, 1978.

WORK IN PROGRESS: Introduction to Biology, publication by Willard Grant Press expected in 1984; *Biological Imperatives: Inherent Limits on Human Freedoms.*

SIDELIGHTS: Farish commented: "I believe strongly in the need for professional scientists to communicate directly with the public. Lectures and public speaking pale in importance next to the impact of books, and it is in that arena that I am directing my present efforts."

* * *

FARR, John
See WEBB, Jack (Randolph)

* * *

FARR, Walter Greene, Jr. 1925-

BRIEF ENTRY: Born February 24, 1925, in Wenonah, N.J. American attorney and author. Farr has been a lawyer since 1951. He has worked for the U.S. Agency for International Development and U.S. Department of Housing and Urban Development. Before becoming chief counsel for the Economic Development Administration of the U.S. Department of Commerce, Farr was a professor of law at New York University from 1969 to 1977. In 1981 he was appointed executive director of the California Housing Finance Agency. Farr edited *Economic Development: Problems and Materials* (1969) and wrote *Decentralizing City Government: A Practical Study of a Radical Proposal for New York City* (Irvington, 1972). *Address:* 460 Cragmont Ave., Berkeley, Calif. 94708.

* * *

FASSBINDER, Rainer Werner 1946-1982

*OBITUARY NOTICE—*See index for *CA* sketch: Born May 31, 1946, in Bad Woerishofen, Germany (now West Germany); died June 10, 1982, in Munich, West Germany. Director of plays and motion pictures, actor, screenwriter, and playwright. Fassbinder's untimely death at age thirty-six dealt a severe blow to the German cinema he had helped revive in the 1970's. Critics such as Vincent Canby and Andrew Sarris considered him among the most profound and most prolific filmmakers. His forty-one films, made within a fifteen-year period, indicated both a satiric perception of suffering and cruelty and a consistent urgency in expressing that perception. Most of Fassbinder's attention was devoted to the anguish of life's outcasts—foreigners, homosexuals, and the poor—in a world where happiness is measured by success and social class. In "Katzelmacher" he depicts a group of aimless individuals united only in their efforts to thwart the happiness of a foreigner. Similarly, in "Ali: Fear Eats the Soul," a romance between an elderly woman and a youthful Moroccan is viciously undermined by the woman's family and co-workers. In films such as "Fox and His Friends" and "In a Year of Thirteen Moons," Fassbinder chronicles the demise of trusting and naive homosexuals in the hands of opportunistic and ultimately uncaring

acquaintances. In the late 1970's Fassbinder achieved modest commercial success with "The Marriage of Maria Braun," his film of a woman destroyed by one careless act after years of struggling while awaiting her husband's release from prison. Maria's rise to social and financial prominence is intended as a parallel to West Germany's own "economic miracle" within a decade of that country's defeat in World War II. Obituaries and other sources: Ruth McCormick, editor, *Fassbinder,* Tanam Press, 1982; *Detroit Free Press,* June 11, 1982; *New York Times,* June 11, 1982; *Chicago Tribune,* June 11, 1982; *London Times,* June 11, 1982; *Washington Post,* June 11, 1982; *Los Angeles Times,* June 11, 1982; *Newsweek,* June 21, 1982; *Time,* June 21, 1982.

* * *

FAUROT, Jeannette 1943-

PERSONAL: Born March 1, 1943, in Lambert, Quebec, Canada; American citizen born abroad; daughter of Jean Hiatt (a professor) and Louise (a nurse; maiden name, Johnson) Faurot. *Education:* Harvard University, B.A., 1964; University of California, Berkeley, M.A., 1967, Ph.D., 1972. *Office:* Department of Oriental and African Languages, University of Texas, Austin, Tex. 78712.

CAREER: University of Texas, Austin, instructor, 1971-73, assistant professor, 1973-77, associate professor of Chinese, 1977—. *Member:* Association for Asian Studies, Chinese Language Teachers Association, South Central Modern Language Association, Southwest Conference on Asian Studies.

WRITINGS: Chinese Fiction From Taiwan, Indiana University Press, 1980.

WORK IN PROGRESS: Research on contemporary Chinese fiction and the cultural history of the city of Chengdu.

* * *

FEDOROV, Yevgeny Konstantinovich 1910-1981
(Yevgeny Konstantinovich Fyodorov)

OBITUARY NOTICE: Born April 10, 1910, in Bendery, Moldavia (now part of the U.S.S.R.); died December 30, 1981, in the U.S.S.R. Geophysicist and author. One of the Soviet Union's most prominent scientists, Fedorov was the director of Moscow's Institute for Applied Geophysics and was associated with the Soviet space program. He also headed the Soviet weather service for several years and, as an expert on the problems of detecting underground nuclear explosions, participated in nuclear test ban treaty talks with the United States in the late 1950's. Fedorov was the author of several scientific works, including *The Influence of Atomic Blasts on Meteorological Processes* and *Physical Methods of Influence on Weather.* He was awarded the Order of Lenin five times and was named a Hero of the Soviet Union. Obituaries and other sources: *The International Who's Who,* Europa, 1978; *New York Times,* January 3, 1982.

* * *

FEELY, Terence John 1928-

PERSONAL: Born July 20, 1928, in Liverpool, England; son of Edward (a sales director) and Mary (Glancy) Feely; married Elizabeth Adams (an interior designer). *Education:* University of Liverpool, B.A. (first-class honors), 1950. *Politics:* Conservative. *Religion:* Roman Catholic. *Home:* 21 Drayton Gardens, London SW10 9RY, England. *Agent:* Douglas Rae, 28 Charing Cross Rd., London WC2H 0DB, England.

CAREER: Evening Gazette, Middlesborough, Yorkshire, England, columnist, 1950-52; *Evening Press,* York, Yorkshire, England, columnist, 1952-53; *Sunday Graphic,* London, England, deputy editor, 1953-60; London International Press Ltd., London, editorial director, 1960-62; Thames Television, London, producer, 1962-67; Paramount Films, London, European story chief, 1967-69; Warner Brothers, London, European story chief, 1969-71; playwright, screenwriter, and novelist. Member of the council of the People's Dispensary for Sick Animals, 1973—. *Member:* British Legion, Carlton Club, 1900 Club.

WRITINGS—Plays: "Shout for Life" (two-act; originally titled "Sergeant Dower Must Die"), first produced on the West End at the Vaudeville Theatre, 1963; "Don't Let Summer Come" (two-act), first produced in London at the Mermaid Theatre, 1964; "Adam's Apple" (two-act), first produced in London at the Golders Green Theatre, 1966; *Who Killed Santa Claus?* (two-act; first produced in Windsor, England, at the Theatre Royal, October 16, 1969, produced on the West End at the Piccadilly Theatre, April 2, 1970), Samuel French, 1971; (with Brian Clemens) "The Avengers" (two-act), first produced in Birmingham, England, at the Birmingham Theatre, July 15, 1971, produced on the West End at Prince of Wales Theatre, August 2, 1971; "Dear Hearts" (two-act), first produced in London at the Mountview Theatre, September, 1974; "Murder in Mind" (two-act), first produced in Windsor at the Theatre Royal, June 26, 1979, first produced on the West End at Strand Theatre, February 3, 1982; "The Team" (two-act), first produced Off-Broadway, 1982.

Screenplays: "Written in the Sand," Parador, 1969; "Quest for Love," Viacom, 1970; "Our Miss Fred," E.M.I., 1971; "Comment fais-tu l'amour, Cerise?," Film Sonar, 1972.

Television plays; broadcast by Independent Television (ITV), except as noted: "The Duel," January 16, 1973; "Country Wedding," May 26, 1973; "Spell of Evil," June 6, 1973; "The Eyes Have It," June 9, 1973; "The Marriage Feast," October 17, 1973; "The Gift of Life," December, 1973; "The Girl From Rome," 1973; "The Swordsman," 1973; "The Pupil," 1973; "Rolf the Penitent," 1973; "The Treaty," 1973; "The Preacher," 1973; "The Challenge," 1973; "Only a Scream Away," January 26, 1974; "The Group," February 8, 1974; "Kiss Me and Die," February 9, 1974; "Ring Once for Death," 1974; "The Horns of Pentecost," 1974.

"Going Home," 1975; "The Next Voice You See," 1975; "Affairs of the Heart" (thirteen-part series based on the works of Henry James), 1975; "Mother's Girl," 1976; "Miss Tita," 1976; "Kate," 1976; "Maisie," 1976; "Elizabeth," 1976; "Leonie," 1976; "Bessie," 1976; "The Bringers of Wonder," 1977; "The Heavy Mob (series), 1979; "A Hiding to Nothing," 1979; "Shoestring," first broadcast by British Broadcasting Corp. (BBC-TV), 1980; "Company & Co.," first broadcast by BBC-TV, 1980; "Melody," 1980; "Decoy," 1980; "Break-In," 1980; "Gifts," October, 1980; "The Hit," November, 1980; "Number Ten" (series), October, 1982.

Also author of scripts for numerous television series, including "The Return of the Saint," "Within These Walls," "The New Avengers," "The Scarlet Pimpernel," "This Racing Game," and "The Man."

Other writings: (With Frederick E. Smith, Val Guest, and Brian Clemens) *The Persuaders* (fiction), Book 3, Pan, 1973, also published as *The Persuaders at Large,* Henry Publications, 1977; *Arthur of the Britons* (fiction), HTV, 1974; (with Graham Weaver and John Kruse) *Leslie Charteris' The Saint in Trouble* (fiction), Doubleday, 1978; *Rich Little Poor Girl* (novel), Hamlyn, 1981, Pocket Books, 1982; *The Gentle Touch* (novel), Sphere, 1981.

WORK IN PROGRESS: A book, based on the television series "Number Ten," about the private lives of British prime ministers, for Sidgwick & Jackson; a play about a British prime minister.

SIDELIGHTS: Feely told *CA:* "My motivation is . . . what is the triplicate form of schizophrenia called? I love the one-to-one confrontation of writer and reader in the novel; I adore the flesh and blood warmth of a thousand real people in the theatre responding to my lines in the mouths of flesh-and-blood actors; I'm coolly exhilarated by the thought of twenty million people all watching a television play at the same time. However, I would still write if I had never had a word published, acted, or filmed. It's like an itch in the center of oneself, which can only be appeased or scratched by writing. I've been writing since I was five; I was publishing a school magazine when I was seven. If I'm unhappy, I write. If I'm happy, I write. I'll use any excuse to put words on paper. People praise my construction, but I have no constructional ability. I let it all come out, see how it's shaped itself, and then fine-tune it; that's all.

"I'm interested in positive characters like the heroine of *Rich Little Poor Girl.* The first thing I ever sold commercially, to Alfred Hitchcock, was a story about a man with a heart condition who lived a whole glorious life in one day. It was adapted for television by a superb American professional, Ernest Kinnoy. I learned a great deal from reading his adaptation. "Heartbeat," it was called, and it was a life-affirming story. I'm not very good at depicting the defeated or despairing, much as I admire those who can depict them. I like life enhancers.

"The future is already with us. The world as a whole—and within national boundaries—is being polarized into the makers and the takers. The only way it can work is for the makers to give thanks for the privilege of having their gift by supporting the takers. By 'makers' I don't just mean writers; I mean anyone to whom it has been given to do something and to enjoy what he's doing. We can't keep the pleasure and the prizes to ourselves any more; we have to spread them around as kids are taught to do with their candies. How we do it is up to us.

"I speak fluent French, less fluent German, and have had plays staged in both countries. I have had psychic abilities and experiences since childhood, but I never use them in my writing—something tells me it would be wrong. I can sometimes, in a very minor way, heal."

BIOGRAPHICAL/CRITICAL SOURCES: Variety, April 8, 1970; *Spectator,* April 11, 1970; *Punch,* April 15, 1970; *Plays and Players,* May, 1970.

*   *   *

FEHR, Howard Franklin   1901-1982

OBITUARY NOTICE: Born December 4, 1901, in Bethlehem, Pa.; died May 6, 1982, in New York, N.Y. Educator and author. A professor of mathematics education, Fehr helped to introduce the teaching approach known as "new math" that radically changed the teaching of mathematics in the 1960's. He was the editor and principal author of the influential 1961 report *New Thinking in School Mathematics* and served as a consultant to UNESCO on advancing education in many parts of the world. He wrote hundreds of articles for professional journals as well as several books. Obituaries and other sources: *Who's Who in America,* 39th edition, Marquis, 1976; *New York Times,* May 7, 1982.

*   *   *

FEINBERG, Barbara Jane   1938-

PERSONAL: Born June 1, 1938, in New York, N.Y.; daughter

of Norman (an accountant) and Harriet (Scheldon) Silberdick; married Gerald Feinberg (a professor of physics), August 9, 1968; children: Jeremy Russell, Douglas Loren. *Education:* Wellesley College, B.A., 1959; Yale University, M.A., 1960, Ph.D., 1963. *Home and office:* 535 East 86th St., New York, N.Y. 10028.

CAREER: City College of the City University of New York, New York City, lecturer, 1963-64, instructor in political science, 1964-67; Brooklyn College of the City University of New York, Brooklyn, N.Y., visiting lecturer in political science, 1967-68; Seton Hall University, South Orange, N.J., assistant professor of political science, 1968-70; Hunter College of the City University of New York, New York City, adjunct assistant professor of political science, 1970-73; freelance writer and editor, 1973—. *Member:* American Political Science Association, American Society of Political and Legal Philosophy, Editorial Freelancers Association, Phi Beta Kappa. *Awards, honors:* Woodrow Wilson Prize from Wellesley College, 1959, for essay on modern politics.

WRITINGS: Franklin D. Roosevelt: Gallant President (juvenile), Lothrop, 1981. Contributor to political science journals.

WORK IN PROGRESS: Editorial and writing assignments.

SIDELIGHTS: Barbara Feinberg wrote: "Initially, my book was a family project. My sons asked me to do it because there was nothing suitable for them to read at the time. I would like to write other children's biographies on political figures.

"Presently I am writing supplements to college textbooks in the social sciences. I enjoy the work; it is a constant challenge to review or adapt new material on subjects I once studied or taught.

"Recently I tried something new—editing and rewriting portions of a children's textbook on American history. I found the assignment so enjoyable that I hope others of a similar nature will come my way. There is so much about our past as a nation and as a people that can be interesting to young readers."

*   *   *

FEINGOLD, Ben(jamin) F(ranklin)   1900-1982

OBITUARY NOTICE—See index for *CA* sketch: Born June 15, 1900, in Pittsburgh, Pa.; died after a brief illness, March 23, 1982, in San Francisco, Calif. Pediatric allergist, physician, and author. Best known as the developer of the Feingold diet for hyperactive children, Feingold determined that the behavior of hyperactive children could be modified by eliminating additives in food and favored dietary control as a natural alternative to behavior-controlling drugs. He wrote about his dietary studies in numerous articles and in two books, *Why Your Child Is Hyperactive* and *The Feingold Cookbook for Hyperactive Children.* Obituaries and other sources: *New York Times,* March 24, 1982; *Los Angeles Times,* March 29, 1982; *Time,* April 5, 1982; *Newsweek,* April 5, 1982.

*   *   *

FELDMAN, Ruth   1911-

PERSONAL: Born May 21, 1911, in East Liverpool, Ohio; daughter of Mendel (in business) and May (a musician; maiden name, Rosenthal) Wasby; married Moses D. Feldman (a lawyer), May 3, 1934 (died March 4, 1963). *Education:* Attended Western Reserve University (now Case Western Reserve University), 1927-29; Wellesley College, B.A., 1931. *Home and office:* 221 Mount Auburn St., Cambridge, Mass. 02138.

CAREER: Painter; work exhibited in shows. Translator. *Member:* American Translators Association, American Literary Translators Association, Poetry Society of America, New England Poetry Club. *Awards, honors:* Devil's Advocate award from Poetry Society of America, 1971, for "Delos"; John Florio Award from Translators Association, 1976, for translating *Shema: Collected Poems of Primo Levi;* Members' Prize from New England Poetry Club, 1977.

WRITINGS—Poems: *The Ambition of Ghosts,* Green River Press, 1979; *Poesie di Ruth Feldman,* La Giuntina, 1981.

Editor and translator with Brian Swann: *Collected Poems of Lucio Piccolo,* Princeton University Press, 1972; *Selected Poetry of Andrea Zanzotto,* Princeton University Press, 1975; *Shema: Collected Poems of Primo Levi,* Menard, 1976; *Italian Poetry Today,* New Rivers Press, 1979; *The Dawn Is Always New: Selected Poetry of Rocco Scotellaro,* Princeton University Press, 1980; *The Hands of the South: Selected Poetry of Vittorio Bodini,* Charioteer, 1981; *The Dry Air of The Fire: Selected Poetry of Bartolo Cattafi,* Ardis, 1982.

Work represented in anthologies, including *Penguin Book of Women Poets,* Penguin, 1978; *A Book of Women Poets,* Schocken, 1980; *Anthology of Magazine Verse,* Monitor, 1981; *Affinities I,* Latitudes Press; *Border Crossings,* Latitudes Press; *New York Times Book of Verse.* Contributor of poems and translations to numerous magazines and newspapers, including *Nation, Commonweal, Yankee, Malahat Review, Yale Review, New York Times,* and *Prairie Schooner.* Co-editor of *Modern Poetry in Translation,* 1975.

WORK IN PROGRESS: Another book of poems; translations of short stories by Primo Levi; translations of poems by Margherita Guidacci.

SIDELIGHTS: Ruth Feldman wrote: "I have loved Italy since my first trip there in 1936. I have worked with and visited many of Italy's leading poets. I find translating a constant and fascinating challenge. It is too often poorly done. My original motivation remains the same: to make things I like and admire accessible to people who do not know Italian, while preserving the language's spirit and style. I started writing my own poetry when my husband died."

*   *   *

FENDERSON, Lewis H.   1907-

PERSONAL: Born July 24, 1907, in Baltimore, Md.; married in 1965. *Education:* University of Pittsburgh, B.A., 1941, M.Litt., 1942, Ph.D., 1948; Oxford University, certificate, 1950. *Office address:* Box 914, College of Liberal Arts, Howard University, Washington, D.C. 20001.

CAREER: Pittsburgh Courier, Pittsburgh, Pa., correspondent, 1935-45; Soho Community House, Pittsburgh, educational and vocational counselor, 1940-42; associated with Urban League, Pittsburgh, 1941-42; West Virginia State College, Institute, W.Va., associate professor of English, 1948-49; Howard University, Washington, D.C., began as assistant professor, professor of English, 1967—. Visiting professor, Texas Southern University, summers, 1956-67, and District of Columbia Teachers College, 1962—; member of evaluation team for Mid-Atlantic States Association of Colleges and Secondary Schools, 1966—; consultant to colleges for curriculum design and evaluation. *Military service:* U.S. Army Air Forces, 1942-45; became second lieutenant. *Member:* Modern Language Association of America. *Awards, honors:* Grant from *Washington Evening Star* to develop a book-length epic poem on the American Negro, 1965.

WRITINGS: (Contributor) Siegfried Mandel, editor, *Modern Journalism*, Pitman, 1962; (with Charles G. Hurst) *Effective Expression: A New Approach to Better Speaking*, C. E. Merrill, 1965; (editor with Stanton L. Wormley) *Many Shades of Black* (nonfiction), Morrow, 1969; *Thurgood Marshall: Fighter for Justice* (juvenile biography; illustrated by Dave Hodges), McGraw, 1969; (editor with Lettie J. Austin and Sophia P. Nelson) *The Black Man and the Promise of America* (nonfiction), Scott, Foresman, 1970; *Daniel Hale Williams: Open-Heart Doctor* (juvenile biography; illustrated by Don Miller), McGraw, 1971.

Editorial adviser of *Howard University Liberal Arts Bulletin*, 1960-65. Contributor of articles to *Howard University Magazine*.

*   *   *

FENNER, Phyllis R(eid)   1899-1982

OBITUARY NOTICE—See index for *CA* sketch: Born October 24, 1899, in Almond, N.Y.; died February 26, 1982, in Manchester, Vt. Librarian, anthologist of books for children, and author. For thirty-two years Fenner served as librarian at the Plandome Road School in Manhasset, N.Y. She told of her efforts to develop a centralized library service at the elementary school level in her first book, *Our Library: Story of a School That Works*. Her anthologies include *Ghost, Ghost, Ghosts, Giggle Box*, and *Midnight Prowlers: Stories of Cats and Their Enslaved Owners*. Obituaries and other sources: *Publishers Weekly*, April 2, 1982; *School Library Journal*, April 15, 1982.

*   *   *

FENTON, Clyde   1901-1982

OBITUARY NOTICE: Born in 1901 in Warrnambool, Victoria, Australia; died in 1982. Physician and author. Fenton, one of Australia's first "flying doctors," was known for both aerial and medical exploits. Appointed to the Northern Territory Medical Service in 1935, he flew his own open-cockpit biplane on house calls in remote parts of the outback. His willingness to take off in any weather to treat a patient made him a folk hero, though his penchant for flamboyant stunts often brought him into conflict with civil aviation authorities. Fenton wrote a memoir, *Flying Doctor*. He was awarded the Order of the British Empire in 1940. Obituaries and other sources: *London Times*, April 2, 1982.

*   *   *

FENVESSY, Stanley J(ohn)   1918-

PERSONAL: Born October 30, 1918, in Rochester, N.Y.; son of John H. W. (a theatre owner) and Bessie Ruth (Weber) Fenvessy; married Doris Goodman, July 10, 1943; children: Alice Fenvessy Healy and Barbara Fenvessy Young (twins). *Education:* University of Pennsylvania, B.S., 1940; Georgetown University, LL.B., 1943. *Politics:* Republican. *Home:* 205 East 63rd St., New York, N.Y. 10021. *Office:* Fenvessy Associates, Inc., 745 Fifth Ave., New York, N.Y. 10151.

CAREER: Aldens, Inc., Chicago, Ill., methods engineer, 1945-49; Cresap, McCormick & Paget, New York City, principal, 1949-55; Rapid American Corp., New York City, executive vice-president of American Merchandising Division, 1955-60; Ethan Allen, Inc., Danbury, Conn., administrative vice-president, 1960-65; Fenvessy Associates, Inc. (management consultants), New York City, president, 1965—. Member of board of directors of Present Company. Presents lectures and seminars on direct marketing in the United States, Europe, and Mexico. *Military service:* U.S. Naval Reserve, active duty in Intelligence Corps, 1941-45; became lieutenant senior grade.

MEMBER: American Arbitration Association, Institute of Management Consultants (past vice-president; past member of board of directors; chairman of professional conduct committee), Associaton of Consulting Management Engineers (past treasurer and member of board of directors), Direct Mail/Marketing Association (vice-chairman of Ethics Committee), Chicago Bar Association, New York City University Club.

WRITINGS: Keep Your Customers and Keep Them Happy, Dow Jones-Irwin, 1976; (contributor) Joseph R. Rowen, editor, *Direct Mail Advertising and Selling for Retailers*, National Retail Merchants Association, 1978; (contributor) Janet N. Field, editor, *Graphic Arts Guide*, Arno, 1980; (contributor) Edward L. Nash, editor, *Direct Marketing Handbook*, McGraw, 1983; *Managing for Fulfillment Excellence*, Direct Marketing News, 1983. Author of "Questions and Answers on Mail Order Fulfillments," a column in *Direct Marketing News*. Contributor to professional journals. Contributing editor of *Direct Marketing News*.

SIDELIGHTS: Fenvessy told *CA:* "My education and career in law and accounting was interrupted by World War II. During my service as a naval officer in intelligence, I was responsible for devising systems and training people to process hundreds of thousands of communications (our own and enemy intercepted) and then returning 'information' to our ships and shore stations. In this connection we used machinery that was the forerunner of today's computers. After the war and ever since, I have employed the skills obtained in the navy to help companies with large volumes of paper process orders, correspondence, mail, checks, etc. Two of the largest industries processing paper are mail order and publishing. Hence, my concentration in those two areas.

"I have written, spoken, and instructed extensively in my specialty because I feel it is my obligation to pass on to others the extensive exposure I have obtained over the years. I have assisted over two hundred companies, over one hundred in the mail order and publishing fields. Further, I have personally visited and studied the fulfillment operations of an additional one hundred-plus direct marketers."

*   *   *

FERMAN, Edward L(ewis)   1937-

PERSONAL: Born March 6, 1937, in New York, N.Y.; son of Joseph W. (a publisher) and Ruth (Eisen) Ferman; married Audrey Bonchak, May 25, 1964; children: Emily Allison. *Education:* Middlebury College, B.A., 1958. *Home and office address:* P.O. Box 56, Cornwall, Conn. 06753.

CAREER: The Magazine of Fantasy and Science Fiction, Cornwall, Conn., editorial assistant, 1958-59; Prentice-Hall, Inc., Englewood, N.J., assistant editor, 1959-60; Dunn & Bradstreet, New York, N.Y., financial writer, 1960-62; *The Magazine of Fantasy and Science Fiction*, managing editor, 1962-65, editor, 1966—, publisher, 1970—. Director of Housatonic Valley Association; member of Cornwall Planning and Zoning Commission; member of Northwestern Connecticut Regional Planning Association. *Awards, honors:* Hugo Award from World Science Fiction Convention, 1968, 1969, 1970, 1971, and 1972, all for *The Magazine of Fantasy and Science Fiction*.

WRITINGS—Editor: *The Best From Fantasy and Science Fiction*, Doubleday, 15th series, 1966, 16th series, 1967, 17th series, 1968, 18th series, 1969, 19th series, 1971, 20th series, 1973, 21st series (subtitled *A Special 25th Anniversary An-*

thology), 1974, 22nd series, 1977, 23rd series, 1980; *Once and Future Tales From the Magazine of Fantasy and Science Fiction*, Delphi Press (Jacksonville, Ill.), 1968; (with Robert P. Mills) *Twenty Years of the Magazine of Fantasy and Science Fiction*, Putnam, 1970; (with Barry N. Malzberg) *Final Stage: The Ultimate Science Fiction Anthology*, Charterhouse, 1974; (with Malzberg) *Arena*, Doubleday, 1976; (with Malzberg) *Graven Images*, Nelson, 1977; *Magazine of Fantasy and Science Fiction: A Thirty Year Retrospective*, Doubleday, 1980; *Fantasy and Science Fiction, April Nineteen Sixty-Five*, Southern Illinois University Press, 1981; *The Best From Fantasy and Science Fiction*, 24th edition, Scribner's, 1982.

* * *

FERNANDEZ, Gladys Craven 1939-
(Happy Craven Fernandez)

PERSONAL: Born March 3, 1939, in Scranton, Pa.; daughter of Orvin William (in business) and Florence (Waite) Craven; married Richard Ritter Fernandez (a minister), June 10, 1961; children: John Ritter, David Craven, Richard William. *Education:* Wellesley College, B.A., 1961; Harvard University, M.A. (teaching), 1962; University of Pennsylvania, M.A. (history), 1970. *Politics:* Democrat. *Religion:* United Church of Christ. *Home:* 3400 Baring St., Philadelphia, Pa. 19104. *Office:* Child Care Dept., School of Social Administration, Temple University, Philadelphia, Pa. 19122.

CAREER: Junior high school social studies teacher in Newton, Mass., 1962; United Church of Christ Work Camp, Wadley, Ala., co-director, summer, 1962; social studies teacher at public schools in Albany, Ohio, 1962-63; Brooklyn Council of Churches, Brooklyn, N.Y., co-director of urban intern program, summer, 1963; high school social studies teacher in Hingham, Mass., 1963-64; Science Research Associates, Palo Alto, Calif., staff consultant, 1965-69; National Committee for Citizens in Education, Columbia, Md., field staff consultant for eastern region of Parents Network, 1975-76; Temple University, Philadelphia, Pa., assistant professor of child care, 1976-80; Parents Union for Public Schools, Philadelphia, executive coordinator, 1980-82; Temple University, assistant professor of child care, 1982—. Member of numerous peace organizations, including Women Strike for Peace, 1966-71. Founder of Mantua-Powelton Children's School, 1967-70; founder and co-chairperson of Powelton-Mantua Educational Fund, 1968-72, and Parents Union for Public Schools, 1972-75, 1977-79; member of board of directors of Citizens Committee on Public Education, 1973-78, and Philadelphia Citizens for Children and Youth, 1980—; member of advisory panel of Women's Educational Equity Project, 1979-80. *Member:* American Orthopsychiatric Association, Americans for Democratic Action (member of board of directors, 1974—), National Coalition of Advocates for Students (member of board of directors).

WRITINGS—Under name Happy Craven Fernandez: *Parents Organizing to Improve Schools*, National Committee for Citizens in Education, 1975; (contributor) Robert Doherty, editor, *Public Access: Citizens and Collective Bargaining in the Public Schools*, New York State School of Industrial and Labor Relations, Cornell University, 1979; *The Child Advocacy Handbook*, Pilgrim Press (New York City), 1981. Contributor to education and urban studies journals.

SIDELIGHTS: Fernandez commented: "My writing grows out of community-based experience, especially with public school parents in large urban systems." *Avocational interests:* Tennis (past girls and junior girls divisional champion).

FERNANDEZ, Happy Craven
See FERNANDEZ, Gladys Craven

* * *

FERULLO, Dan 1948-

PERSONAL: Born July 31, 1948, in Lowell, Mass.; son of Daniel Charles and Frances (Haley) Ferullo; married Diane M. Buzzotta, May 26, 1974. *Education:* Attended Leland Powers School of Radio, Television, and Theatre, 1968-70, Boston Conservatory of Music, 1970-71, and Northeastern University, 1973. *Residence:* Woburn, Mass. *Office: Woburn Daily Times*, Woburn, Mass. 01801.

CAREER: Colony Communications, Providence, R.I., broadcaster, 1971-81. *Member:* Woburn Chamber of Commerce (assistant executive director), North Suburban Chamber of Commerce (assistant executive director). *Awards, honors:* "Best feature writer award" from New England Press Association, 1979, for a series of articles on teenage alcoholism.

WRITINGS: (With Harold Russell) *The Best Years of My Life*, Paul Eriksson, 1981. Author of a column in *Woburn Daily Times* and a column syndicated by Middlesex East Publications to twelve newspapers, both 1976—. Contributing editor of *Nightfall*.

WORK IN PROGRESS: A suspense novel set in Boston.

* * *

FETTER, Frank Whitson 1899-

PERSONAL: Born May 22, 1899, in San Francisco, Calif.; son of Frank A. (a teacher) and Martha (Whitson) Fetter; married Elizabeth G. Pollard, January 14, 1929; children: Robert Pollard, Thomas Whitson, Ellen Cole (Mrs. John C. Gille). *Education:* Swarthmore College, B.A., 1920; Princeton University, M.A., 1922, Ph.D., 1926; Harvard University, M.A., 1924. *Home:* 8 Smith Rd., Hanover, N.H. 03755.

CAREER: Princeton University, Princeton, N.J., assistant professor of economics, 1928-34; Haverford College, Haverford, Pa., associate professor, 1934-36, professor of economics, 1936-48; Northwestern University, Evanston, Ill., professor of economics, 1948-67; Dartmouth College, Hanover, N.H., visiting professor of economics, 1967-68. Lecturer. *Military service:* U.S. Army, 1918. *Member:* American Economic Association (member of executive committee, 1944-46), Midwest Economic Association (president, 1952), Phi Beta Kappa. *Awards, honors:* Guggenheim fellowship, 1937-38.

WRITINGS: Monetary Inflation in Chile, Princeton University Press, 1931; *The Irish Pound*, Allen & Unwin, 1955; (editor) *The Economic Writings of Francis Horner in the Edinburgh Review*, Augustus Kelley, 1957; (editor) *Selected Economic Writings of Thomas Attwood*, London School of Economics and Political Science, London, 1964; *The Development of British Economic Orthodoxy, 1797-1875*, Harvard University Press, 1965; *The Economist in Parliament, 1780 to 1868*, Duke University Press, 1980. Contributor to economic journals.

* * *

FICKLE, James Edward 1939-

PERSONAL: Born May 21, 1939, in Royal Centre, Ind.; son of Dale Matthew (in small business) and Virginia (a teacher; maiden name, Olsen) Fickle; married Marian L. Woodruff (in business), January, 1958; children: Valerie, Steven, Edward. *Education:* Purdue University, B.S., 1961; Louisiana State University, M.A., 1963, Ph.D., 1970. *Religion:* Presbyterian. *Home:* 1076 South Perkins Rd., Memphis, Tenn. 38117. *Office:* Department of History, Memphis State University, Memphis, Tenn. 38152.

CAREER: Louisiana State University, New Orleans, special lecturer, 1965-67, lecturer in history, 1967-68; Memphis State University, Memphis, Tenn., instructor, 1968-70, assistant professor, 1970-75, associate professor, 1975-81, professor of history, 1981—. *Member:* Organization of American Historians, Southern Historical Association. *Awards, honors:* Theodore C. Blegen Award from Forest History Society, 1974, for article, "Management Looks at the Labor 'Problem.'"

WRITINGS: (Contributor) John L. Loos, editor, *Great Events in American History,* Salem Press, 1974; *The New South and the "New Competition,"* University of Illinois Press, 1980; (contributor) Joseph R. Conlin, editor, *At the Point of Production,* Greenwood Press, 1981; (author of introduction) Charles A. Heavron, *Baskets, Barrels, and Boards: Anderson-Tully Company,* Memphis State University Press, 1981. Contributor to history journals.

WORK IN PROGRESS: A History of Nineteenth-Century Indiana Transporation; A History of the Llano Cooperative Society.

*　　*　　*

FIEG, Victor P. 1924-

PERSONAL: Born April 23, 1924, in Oneonta, N.Y.; son of Lothar (a builder) and Florence (Shields) Fieg; married Jean Davie, September 2, 1950; children: Judith Fieg Kestner, Diana Fieg Monaco, Phyllis. *Education:* Attended Syracuse University, 1946-50. *Religion:* None. *Home:* 1405 Knightwood Dr., Greensboro, N.C. 27410. *Office:* Ciba-Geigy Corp., P.O. Box 18300, Greensboro, N.C. 27419.

CAREER: Oneonta Star, Oneonta, N.Y., reporter, 1951-52; Agway, Syracuse, N.Y., 1964-68, began as copywriter, became editor; Ciba-Geigy Corp., Greensboro, N.C., specialist in visual aids and merchandising, 1968-72, manager of advertising and promotion, 1972—. *Military service:* U.S. Army Air Forces, transport pilot, 1941-46.

WRITINGS: Why There Aren't Many Witches (juvenile stories), Houghton, 1979. Contributor to *Boating.*

*　　*　　*

FIELD, Adelaide (Anderson) 1916-

PERSONAL: Born June 6, 1916, in Memphis, Tenn.; daughter of Harry Bennett and Patty (Crook) Anderson; married Donald T. Field, October 7, 1939 (divorced September, 1958); married W. Leverett Cummings, October 2, 1959; children: (first marriage) Deborah, Martha, Hartry. *Education:* Radcliffe College, A.B., 1934. *Home:* 8 Warren Terr., Newton Center, Mass. 02159. *Office:* 21 Shug Harbor Lane, West Falmouth, Mass. 02574.

CAREER: Staff member of *Life,* 1937-38; author of children's books and free-lance writer, 1938—; *Junior League,* Boston, Mass., editor, 1947-50; editor-in-chief of *Child Life,* 1951-64; vice-president of Review Publishing Co., 1964—; feature writer for *National Observer,* 1974—. Secretary and director of Wilevco Corp., 1963-66. *Member:* Junior League, Longwood Cricket Club.

WRITINGS—Juveniles: (Editor) *The Second "Child Life" Story Book,* Winston, 1953; *Adventures on the Cloud 9* (illustrated by Walter Buehr), Putnam, 1968; *Auguste Piccard: Captain of Space, Admiral of the Abyss* (biography), Houghton, 1969; *The Challenge of the Seafloor* (nonfiction), Houghton, 1970.*

*　　*　　*

FIELDS, Wilmer Clemont 1922-

BRIEF ENTRY: Born March 16, 1922, in Saline, La. American minister and author. An ordained Baptist minister since 1940, Fields has served congregations in Louisiana, Kentucky, and Mississippi. He has been the public relations secretary and a member of the executive committee of the Southern Baptist Convention since 1959 as well as a director of the Baptist Press. Fields wrote *The Chains Are Strong* (1963) and *Trumpets in Dixie* (Home Missions Board, Southern Baptist Convention, 1967). He also edited the *Religious Public Relations Handbook* (1976). *Address:* 2223 Woodmont Blvd., Nashville, Tenn. 37215; and 460 James Robertson Parkway, Nashville, Tenn. 37219; and Department of Religious Education, Golden Gate Baptist Theological Seminary, Mill Valley, Calif. 94941. *Biographical/critical sources: Who's Who in America,* 40th edition, Marquis, 1978.

*　　*　　*

FINNIN, (Olive) Mary
(John Hogarth, Lawrence Vigil)

PERSONAL: Born near Geelong, Victoria, Australia; daughter of William and Mary Finnin; married John Joseph Connellan, April 19, 1949; children: Catherine Mary. *Education:* Attended Melbourne University, 1932; received master's diploma from Gordon Institute of Technology, Geelong, Victoria; further graduate studies, 1933-35; attended Bell Store School, 1935. *Home and office:* 105 Mathoura Rd., Toorak, Victoria 3142, Australia.

CAREER: Geelong Church of England Grammar School, Corio, Victoria, Australia, art mistress, 1928-41; research officer in industrial relations department of Commonwealth Department of Labour and National Service, 1944-46; *Advocate,* Melbourne, Victoria, art critic, 1957-59; Melbourne Printer Propriety Ltd., Victoria, owner and managing director, 1973—; poet, 1938—. Founder and fellow of International Academy of Poets, Cambridge, England, 1977. *Wartime service:* Australian Red Cross, 1941-43; became rehabilitation officer. *Member:* International P.E.N. (treasurer, 1951-54), British Society of Authors, Fellowship of Australian Writers (secretary, 1947-48), Contemporary Art Society (founding member), National Council of Women, Australian Letters Society (founding member), Lyceum Club.

AWARDS, HONORS: Australian Literature Society Award, 1945, for poetry; Commonwealth Literary Fund fellowship, 1957, for *The Shield of Place;* received special notice from Society of the *Dictionary of International Biography* (Cambridge, England), 1977-81, for contributions to art and literature; elected to Academia Internationale Leonardo da Vinci (Rome, Italy), 1980; received diploma of merit from university in Salsomaggiore, Italy, 1981; received diploma of honor from Academia Internationale Leonardo da Vinci, 1982, for "The Glory."

WRITINGS—Poetry; all published by W. A. Hamer, except as noted: *A Beggar's Opera,* 1938; *Look Down, Olympians,* 1939; *Royal,* 1941; *Book of Bauble* (self-illustrated), 1945; *Alms for Oblivion,* 1947; *The Shield of Place,* Angus & Robertson, 1957; *Off-Shears, 1958-1978,* Hawthorn Press, 1979.

Poetry represented in over fifty international and Australian anthologies, including *A Book of Australian Verse,* Oxford University Press, 1956; *Songs for All Seasons,* Angus & Robertson, 1967; and *This Land,* Pergamon, 1968. Work also represented in Russian anthology of Australian poetry.

Contributor of poetry to periodicals, including *Twentieth Century, Sydney Bulletin,* and *Quadrant.* Contributor during the 1950's, under pseudonym John Hogarth, of picture articles on historical subjects to *Australian Journal.* Contributor of philosophic writings, under pseudonym Lawrence Vigil. Also contributor of historical and scientific articles to periodicals, including *Reader's Digest* and *World Digest.*

WORK IN PROGRESS: Guest writer for special features in *Tales of Old Geelong,* for Neptune Press; "various" projects.

* * *

FIORENZA, Elisabeth Schuessler 1938-

PERSONAL: Born April 17, 1938, in Tschanad, Germany; came to the United States in 1970; daughter of Peter and Magdalena Schuessler; married Francis Schuessler Fiorenza (a professor of theology), December 17, 1967; children: Christina Schuessler. *Education:* University of Wuerzburg, M.Div., 1962, Lic.Theol., 1963; University of Muenster, Dr.Theol., 1970. *Religion:* Roman Catholic. *Home:* 1223 North Lawrence St., South Bend, Ind. 46617. *Office:* Department of Theology, University of Notre Dame, Notre Dame, Ind. 46556.

CAREER: University of Muenster, Muenster, West Germany, instructor in theology, 1976-77; University of Notre Dame, Notre Dame, Ind., assistant professor, 1970-75, associate professor, 1975-80, professor of theology, 1980—. Harry Emerson Fosdick visiting professor at Union Theological Seminary, New York, N.Y., 1974-75. *Member:* Catholic Biblical Association, Society of Biblical Literature, Studiorum Novi Testamenti Societas, American Academy of Religion, College Theology Society.

WRITINGS—In English: The Apocalypse, Franciscan Herald, 1976; (editor) *Aspects of Religious Propaganda in Judaism and Early Christianity,* University of Notre Dame Press, 1976; *Invitation to the Book of Revelation,* Doubleday, 1981; (contributor) Brian Mahon and Gail Richesin, editors, *The Challenge of Liberation Theology,* Orbis, 1981; *In Memory of Her,* Crossroads, 1982.

In German: *Der Vergessene Partner: Grundlagen, Tatsachen, und Moeglichkeiten der Mitarbeit der Frau in der Kirche* (title means "On Ministries of Women in the Church"), Patmos Verlag, 1964; *Priester fuer Gott Zum Herrschafts: Und Priestermotiv in der Apocalypse* (title means "Priesthood in the New Testament: Especially in the Book of Revelations"), Aschendorff Verlag, 1972. Associate editor of monograph series for Society of Biblical Literature. Associate editor of *Concilium, Cross Currents,* and *Horizons.*

WORK IN PROGRESS: Commentary on the Book of Revelation, for Fortress; "Interpreting the Apocalypse," an article for inclusion in *The New Testament and Its Modern Interpretors* (tentative title).

SIDELIGHTS: Elisabeth Fiorenza wrote: "My major research interests are focused on New Testament exegesis, the history of early Christianity, and biblical theology as well as feminist theology, women's studies in religion, and women in church and society. I am actively involved within the women's movement in religion and church."

FIRMIN, Charlotte 1954-

PERSONAL: Born May 2, 1954, in London, England; daughter of Peter (a writer and illustrator) and Joan (a bookbinder; maiden name, Clapham) Firmin. *Education:* Attended Hornsey School of Art, 1972-73; Brighton Polytechnic, B.A. (with honors), 1976. *Politics:* Socialist. *Religion:* Agnostic. *Home:* 4, Vale Cottages, Chapel St., Ryarsh, Maidstone, Kent, England.

CAREER: Author and illustrator of books for young people. Assistant at London Society of Genealogists, 1980—.

WRITINGS—Juveniles; self-illustrated: Hannah's Great Decision, Macmillan (London), 1978; *Claire's Secret Ambition,* Macmillan, 1979; *Eggbert's Balloon,* Collins, 1979; *The Eggham Pot of Gold,* Collins, 1979; *Egglantine's Party,* Collins, 1979; *The Giant Egg Plant,* Collins, 1979.

Illustrator: Annabel Farjeon, *The Cock of Round Hill,* Kaye & Ward, 1977; Terence Deary, *The Custard Kid,* A. & C. Black, 1978; H. Rice, *The Remarkable Feat of King Caboodle,* A. & C. Black, 1979; Birthe Alton, *The Magic of Ah,* Kaye & Ward, 1980; Deary, *Calamity Kate,* A. & C. Black, 1980; Mary Dickinson, *Alex's Bed,* Deutsch, 1980; Dickinson, *Alex and Roy,* Deutsch, 1981; Deary, *The Lambton Worm,* A. & C. Black, 1981.

WORK IN PROGRESS: Further books in the "Alex" series, for Deutsch.

SIDELIGHTS: Charlotte Firmin told *CA* that her work "is all a matter of luck, observation, persistence, and optimism. And, it's no good sitting down to a typewriter when you can only think of where the next month's rent is going to come from— you just can't write good stories in this mood."

* * *

FISCH, Richard 1926-

BRIEF ENTRY: Born December 15, 1926, in New York, N.Y. American psychiatrist, educator, and author. Fisch, in addition to maintaining a private practice of psychiatry, serves as clinical director of the Brief Therapy Center at Palo Alto's Mental Research Institute. He is also a psychiatrist at San Mateo County Juvenile Hall and a member of the faculty at Stanford University. He wrote *Change: Principles of Problem Formation and Problem Resolution* (Norton, 1974). *Address:* 467 Hamilton Ave., Palo Alto, Calif. 94301.

* * *

FISHER, Neal F(loyd) 1936-

PERSONAL: Born April 14, 1936, in Washington, Ind.; son of Floyd R. and Florence (Williams) Fisher; married Ila Alexander (a teacher), August 18, 1957; children: Edwin Kirk, Julia Bryn. *Education:* DePauw University, A.B., 1957; Boston University, M.Div., 1960, Ph.D., 1966. *Religion:* United Methodist. *Home:* 2426 Lincolnwood Dr., Evanston, Ill. 60201. *Office:* Office of the President, Garrett-Evangelical Theological Seminary, 2121 Sheridan Rd., Evanston, Ill. 60201.

CAREER: Ordained United Methodist minister, 1958; Board of Global Ministries, National Division, New York, N.Y., director of planning, 1968-77; Boston University, Boston, Mass., assistant professor of theology and associate dean of School of Theology, 1977-80; Garrett-Evangelical Theological Seminary, Evanston, Ill., president of seminary and professor of theology and society, 1980—. Member of advisory panel on the future, United Methodist Church General Council on Ministries; member of executive committee of North Central Jurisdiction Board of Ministry. *Member:* Association of United Methodist Theological Schools (secretary).

WRITINGS: From Slavery to Nationhood, United Methodist Publishing House, 1977; *The Parables of Jesus: Glimpses of the New Age,* United Methodist Women, 1979; *Context for Discovery,* Abingdon, 1981.

*   *   *

FITCH, Donald S(heldon)   1949-

PERSONAL: Born June 10, 1949, in Medford, Ore.; son of Chester and Jessie (Tangren) Fitch. *Education:* Southern Oregon State College, B.A., 1972; U.S. International University, M.A., 1974. *Home and office:* 3420 Southwest Marigold, Portland, Ore. 97219.

CAREER: Well-Being Skills, Portland, Ore., president, 1976—. Member of adjunct faculty at Marylhurst College, 1981—. *Member:* Association for the Advancement of Behavior Therapy.

WRITINGS: Increasing Productivity in the Microcomputer Age, Addison-Wesley, 1981.

WORK IN PROGRESS: Well-Being 2001, on preventive health and self-help; *The Tlaloc Eclipse,* a science fiction novel set on a solar power satellite in the twenty-first century.

SIDELIGHTS: Fitch wrote: "The microcomputer in its many forms is a revolutionary new tool for boosting human productivity and well-being. Most of my work and writing focuses on how this powerful technology can be put to good use. It is personally rewarding to have a tool as potent as a microcomputer programmed as a word processor helping me in all my work and writing. This technology offers by far the most effective method for getting thoughts from one's head out onto paper.

"I am very grateful for the opportunity to write *Increasing Productivity.* Up until contracting the book I had written little and published virtually nothing. The book is giving me the power to be much more effective in my work to help boost the productivity of the country. Without such an increase, we will as a country face dismal decline. With renewed productive vigor, the U.S.A. can resume its leadership as a beacon of prosperity and security in a dangerous world. I am grateful to be working in an area of such importance."

*   *   *

FITTON, James   1899-1982

OBITUARY NOTICE: Born in 1899 in Oldham, Lancashire, England; died May 2, 1982. Painter. Fitton had his first one-man show in 1933 and first attracted the attention of art critics two years later. His work has been exhibited in the United States and Great Britain and is included in the permanent collections of several major museums, including London's Tate Gallery, the Victoria and Albert Museum, and the National Museum of Wales. He published a book of humorous drawings, *The First Six Months Are the Worst.* Obituaries and other sources: *Who's Who,* 125th edition, St. Martin's, 1973; *London Times,* May 4, 1982.

*   *   *

FLACK, Audrey   1931-

PERSONAL: Born May 30, 1931, in Brooklyn, N.Y.; daughter of Morris and Jeanette Flack; married H. Robert Marcus, June 7, 1970; children: Melissa, Hannah. *Education:* Cooper Union, graduated, 1951; Yale University, B.F.A., 1952. *Agent:* Louis K. Meisel Gallery, 141 Prince St., New York, N.Y. 10012.

CAREER: New York University, New York City, instructor in anatomy, 1960-68; Pratt Institute, Brooklyn, N.Y., instructor in drawing and painting, 1960-68; School of Visual Arts, New York City, instructor in drawing and painting, 1970-74; University of Bridgeport, Bridgeport, Conn., Albert Dorne Professorship, 1975. Work exhibited in solo shows at Roko Gallery and Louis K. Meisel Gallery, in group exhibitions at Whitney Museum of American Art, Wadsworth Athenaeum, and Tokyo Metropolitan Art Museum, and in permanent collections at Museum of Modern Art, Guggenheim Museum, and National Gallery of Australia. Member of advisory board of Women's Caucus for Art and of Visual Artists and Galleries Association (VAGA). Visiting professor and lecturer at national and international universities and museums. *Awards, honors:* Second prize from national exhibit of paintings at Butler Institute of American Art, 1974; honorary doctorate from Cooper Union, 1977.

WRITINGS: Audrey Flack on Painting, self-illustrated, Abrams, 1981. Contributor of illustrations to magazines, including *Time, Art News,* and *Arts,* and to newspapers.

WORK IN PROGRESS: A book, *The Artist's Book of Notes.*

BIOGRAPHICAL/CRITICAL SOURCES: Van Deren Coke, *The Painter and the Photograph,* University of New Mexico Press, 1972; Udo Kultermann, *New Realism,* New Yale Graphic Society, 1972; Cindy Nemser, *Art Talk,* Scribner, 1975; Louis K. Meisel, *Photorealism,* Abrams, 1980.

*   *   *

FLANNERY, Sean
See HAGBERG, David J(ames)

*   *   *

FLETCHER, Marilyn P(endleton)   1940-

PERSONAL: Born August 3, 1940, in El Dorado, Ark.; daughter of James C. (an automobile dealer) and Helen (Spires) Pendleton; married Tom C. Fletcher (an architect), December 28, 1971; children: Elizabeth, Catherine. *Education:* Gulf Park College, A.A., 1960; Centenary College of Louisiana, B.S., 1962; Louisiana State University, M.S., 1965. *Politics:* Democrat. *Religion:* Episcopalian. *Home:* 10429 Karen Ave. N.E., Albuquerque, N.M. 87111. *Office:* Serials Department, General Library, University of New Mexico, Albuquerque, N.M. 87131.

CAREER: University of New Mexico, Albuquerque, assistant acquisitions librarian, 1965-66, acquisitions librarian, 1966-68; Sandia Laboratories, Technical Library, Albuquerque, cataloger, 1968-70; University of New Mexico, assistant professor of library science and serials librarian, 1970-73, serials cataloger, 1973-77; University of Southwestern Louisiana, Lafayette, serials cataloger, 1977-79; University of New Mexico, serials cataloger, 1980-81, assistant professor of library science and serials acquisitions librarian, 1981—. Workshop organizer. *Member:* American Library Association, Southwestern Library Association, New Mexico Library Association (chairperson of College, University, and Special Libraries Division, 1970), Beta Phi Mu.

WRITINGS: Science Fiction Story Index, 1950-1979, American Library Association, 1981. Contributor of articles and reviews to library journals.

WORK IN PROGRESS: "Science Fiction Magazines and Annual Anthologies: An Annotated Checklist," for publication in *The Serials Librarian.*

SIDELIGHTS: Fletcher told *CA:* "Reading science fiction has long been a favorite pastime of mine. I was pleased to be able to work on the index to science fiction short stories. It was also frustrating, seeing all those collections of short stories and not being able to read every one of them. I became well acquainted with used paperback book dealers (so much science fiction is only available in paperback), and I was a regular customer. I hope to continue to strengthen my interest in science fiction by taking courses at the University of New Mexico."

* * *

FLOOD, Robert 1935-

PERSONAL: Born March 1, 1935, in San Jose, Calif.; son of George R. (a grocer) and Evelyn (Fretwell) Flood; married Lorelei Callaway, October 6, 1962; children: David Scott. *Education:* California State Polytechnic College (now California Polytechnic State University, San Luis Obispo), B.S., 1958; graduate study at Moody Bible Institute, 1959-60. *Politics:* Republican. *Religion:* Evangelical Christian. *Home and office:* 20712 Greenwood Dr., Olympia Fields, Ill. 60461.

CAREER: U.S. Department of Agriculture, Atlanta, Ga., market reporter, 1957; Moody Bible Institute, Chicago, Ill., editorial assistant for *Moody Monthly,* 1960-64, assistant editor, 1964-69, managing editor, 1969-72, administrative director, 1972-78, director of editorial and production departments of Moody Press, 1979-80; free-lance writer, 1980—. *Member:* Evangelical Press Association (member of board of directors).

WRITINGS: America, God Shed His Grace on Thee, Moody, 1976; *Men Who Shaped America,* Moody, 1976; *Graduation: A New Start,* Moody, 1981; *The Christian's Vacation and Travel Guide,* Tyndale, 1982. Contributor to magazines.

SIDELIGHTS: Flood spent the later part of his childhood on a grain ranch in a semiarid part of California. He was interested in agriculture, and orginally considered combining that interest with his journalistic skill by editing a farm journal.

While studying agricultural journalism in college, Flood joined a Bible study group and changed the direction of his writing. His first two books looked at American history from the perspective of an evangelical Christian.

Flood told *CA:* "During my time as administrative director of *Moody Monthly,* in which I coordinated all phases of operation, magazine circulation rose from one hundred thousand to three hundred thousand readers. It won numerous awards from the Evangelical Press Association and was the fastest-growing religious periodical within the nationally recognized Magazine Publishers Association.

"Evangelical convictions still motivate my free-lance writing, which is almost entirely for the religious press. I have a special interest in creating new kinds of book and magazine products, especially products that are heavily graphic. I don't believe the evangelical publishing world as a whole has yet grasped the great potential in this arena."

BIOGRAPHICAL/CRITICAL SOURCES: Bookstore Journal, July-August, 1976.

FLORENCE, Philip Sargant 1890-1982

OBITUARY NOTICE: Born June 25, 1890, in Nutley, N.J.; died January 29, 1982, in England. Economist, educator, and author. An American citizen, Florence spent most of his life in England, teaching at Cambridge University and the University of Birmingham. A specialist in applied economics, he was noted for his studies of the economics of urban and regional planning: *County Town, English County,* and *Conurbation.* Obituaries and other sources: *Who's Who,* 126th edition, St. Martin's, 1974; *London Times,* February 3, 1982.

* * *

FLOWERS, John V(ictor) 1938-

PERSONAL: Born August 20, 1938, in Baltimore, Md.; son of Jack (a mathematician) and Maryon F. (a nurse; maiden name, Herndon) Flowers. *Education:* California State University, Fullerton, B.A., 1963; University of Southern California, Ph.D., 1971. *Home:* 2545 Westminster, Costa Mesa, Calif. 92626. *Office:* Department of Psychology, Chapman College, 333 North Glassell, Orange, Calif. 92666.

CAREER: University of California, Irvine, assistant professor of social ecology, 1972-80; Chapman College, Orange, Calif., associate professor of psychology, 1981—. Psychologist with Booraem, Flowers & Associates, 1972—. *Military service:* U.S. Navy, 1955-59. *Member:* American Psychological Association, American Group Psychotherapy Association, Association for the Advancement of Behavior Therapy, Sierra Club, Western Psychological Association, Phi Beta Kappa. *Awards, honors:* Woodrow Wilson fellowship, 1963.

WRITINGS: (Editor with J.M. Whiteley) *Approaches to Assertion Training,* Brooks/Cole, 1978; (with Curtis Booraem and Bernard Schwartz) *Help Your Children Be Self-Confident,* Prentice-Hall, 1978; (with Schwartz and Jennifer Horsman) *Raising Your Child to Be a Sexually Healthy Adult,* Prentice-Hall, 1982; *How to Raise a Gifted Child,* Prentice-Hall, 1983. Contributor to psychology journals.

WORK IN PROGRESS: Research for a book on boredom and a book that will be a spoof on self-help books.

SIDELIGHTS: Flowers wrote: "As a psychologist I am interested in techniques that help people live happier and more productive lives. I like to include humor in my writing in order not to take myself, my profession, and my ideas too seriously. As a scholar I want to write a longer work that will combine philosophy, literature, and psychology."

* * *

FOGLE, Bruce 1944-

PERSONAL: Born February 17, 1944, in Toronto, Ontario, Canada; married Julia Foster (an actress), April 13, 1973; children: Emily, Ben, Tamara. *Education:* University of Guelph, D.V.M., 1970. *Agent:* Gill Coleridge, 2/3 Morwell St., London W.C.1, England. *Office:* 22 Seymour St., London W.1, England.

CAREER: Zoological Society of London, London, England, veterinarian at Regent's Park Zoo, 1970; assistant in small animal veterinary practice, 1971-72; veterinarian in private practice in London, 1973—. Vice-chairman of Royal National Institute for the Deaf's "Hearing Dogs for the Deaf Scheme." *Member:* Royal College of Veterinary Surgeons, British Veterinary Association, British Small Animal Veterinary Association (metropolitan chairman, 1973), British Veterinary Dermatology Study Group (founding member), Society of Practicing Veterinary Surgeons, Society for Companion Animal Studies (founding member), Veterinary Cardiovascular Club (founding member).

WRITINGS: (Editor and contributor) *Interrelations Between People and Pets,* C. C Thomas, 1981; *Pets and Their People,* Collins, 1983. Contributor to veterinary journals.

SIDELIGHTS: Fogle told *CA:* "I edited my first textbook because I felt that the subject would be of interest both to veterinarians and to health professionals who might be presented with situations involving the relationship between their clients and the clients' pets. I wrote my second book because I thought that it would be fun to do so. The illustrator is very pretty, and that was as good an excuse as any to spend three weeks in Siesta Keys."

*   *   *

FOLLIS, Anne Bowen   1947-

PERSONAL: Born August 22, 1947, in Albany, N.Y.; daughter of Donald Coleman (an engineer) and Leona (Hotaling) Bowen; married D. Dean Follis (a Methodist minister), August 24, 1968; children: Troy Daniel, Ryan Donn, Megan Jean. *Education:* Attended Houghton College. *Politics:* Independent ("former Republican"). *Religion:* United Methodist. *Home address:* P.O. Box 157, Dunlap, Ill. 61525.

CAREER: Worked as homemaker, 1964-65, and as executive secretary, 1968-72; public speaker and writer, 1978—. *Member:* Homemakers' Equal Rights Association (founding member, past president, and president emerita).

WRITINGS: *"I'm Not a Women's Libber, But . . ."* and Other Confessions of a Christian Feminist,* Abington, 1981. Contributor of articles to magazines and newspapers, including *Ladies' Home Journal, Christian Science Monitor, The Daughters of Sarah,* and *Interpreter.*

WORK IN PROGRESS: *The First Stone,* on women in the Bible.

SIDELIGHTS: Anne Bowen Follis has been called "one of the best advocates for the ERA"; she calls herself "a homemaker . . . a Christian . . . [and] a very traditional person." As an activist and as a writer, she has sought a middle ground between "the Christians who claim that God is an anti-feminist and the feminists who insist Christianity is anti-woman." Her arguments in favor of the Equal Rights Amendment are based on traditional values, especially on the importance of women's roles as wives and mothers. Discriminatory laws, she argues, penalize women for choosing traditional roles and degrade those roles by failing to recognize the value of a housewife's contribution to her family. Follis told *Family Circle,* "No one stands to gain more from the ERA than the American homemaker."

Follis considers her activism and her writing as sidelines to her career as a wife and mother. "My ambition was always to have children and stay home and take care of them," she told *Woman's Day.* "This distinction between housewives and working women makes me laugh. What's the idea—that housewives don't *work*? . . . There will be more respect for the role of housewife when this is seen as a matter of choice, not as an inferior position women have had to accept."

As a housewife, Follis at first thought that the ERA had nothing to do with her. But she soon changed her mind: "The biggest shock of my life was to discover the number of rights women lose when they get married." She cites state laws that deny married women control over their own property, burden widows with higher inheritance taxes than widowers, and assume that a homemaker's contribution to her family is without financial value. Follis insists that such laws, rather than strengthening the family, weaken it. "The family survives now in spite of the laws we have right now, not because of them," she told the *New York Times.* And she told the *Fort Lauderdale Sun-Sentinel:* "The contributions of the homemaker are just as important as the contributions of the wage earner. But what you do doesn't count with some laws in some states. These laws encourage women to leave the home. These laws break up families."

Follis's book, *"I'm Not a Women's Libber, But . . . ,"* was praised by Martha Bayles of the *New York Times Book Review* as "earnest and thoughtful . . . a good case for the compatibility of Scripture and equality," though Bayles found the book's treatment of many political and philosophical questions superficial. *Nation* reviewer Carol Flake made similar objections, writing that Follis's book "begs too many questions to become a substantive addition to the literature of evangelical feminism." But Bayles pointed out that in spite of the book's weaknesses as a political argument, as a personal statement it is "peculiarly affecting . . . and reassuring because it suggests that even in the most polarized situations, there are ordinary American citizens who, in spite of the fanatics on both sides, continue to think for themselves."

Follis told *CA:* "My writing has evolved out of my work for women's rights. As the women's movement emerged, I began to discover that as a homemaker I not only was denied social status and recognition, but many legal rights as well. I got involved to change things. My involvement raised questions about my Christian faith—and strengthened it."

BIOGRAPHICAL/CRITICAL SOURCES: *Woman's Day,* July, 1976; *New York Times,* January 7, 1979; *Ms.,* May, 1979; *Family Circle,* November 20, 1979; *Richmond News-Leader,* January 9, 1980; *Richmond Times-Dispatch,* January 10, 1980; *Fort Lauderdale Sun-Sentinel,* April 25, 1980; *Miami Herald,* April 29, 1980; *New York Times Book Review,* September 6, 1981; *Nation,* December 12, 1981.

*   *   *

FONTENELLE, Don H(arris)   1946-

PERSONAL: Born March 11, 1946, in New Orleans, La.; son of J. Irvin (an accountant) and Olga (an office manager; maiden name, Thoele) Fontenelle; married Carla M. Leto (a secretary), August 26, 1967; children: Jason, Alan. *Education:* Attended Southeastern Louisiana University, 1963-64; Louisiana State University, B.A., 1967; Northwestern State University of Louisiana, M.S., 1969; attended University of Southern Mississippi, 1969, and University of Arkansas Medical Center, 1971-72; Oklahoma State University, Ph.D., 1972. *Home:* 2009 Aycock St., Arabi, La. 70032. *Office:* St. Bernard Developmental Center, 3114 Paris Rd., Chalmette, La. 70043.

CAREER: Central Louisiana State Hopsital, Pineville, psychology trainee, 1969; Payne County Mental Health Center, Stillwater, Okla., staff psychologist, 1970-71; Bi-State Mental Health Center, Stillwater, staff psychologist, 1971; University of Arkansas Medical Center, Little Rock, clinical psychology intern, 1971-72; Tulane Medical Center, New Orleans, La., instructor in psychiatry and neurology, 1972-73; Orleans Clinics of Psychology, New Orleans, private practice of psychology, 1973-78; St. Bernard Developmental Center, Chalmette, La., director, 1979—. Guest lecturer at Tulane University;

instructor at Louisiana State University Medical Center, 1972, and St. Bernard Community College, 1975-76. Member of advisory board of St. Bernard Mental Health Center; gives workshops on positive parent training.

MEMBER: American Psychological Association, Association for the Advancement of Behavior Therapy, Southeastern Psychological Association, Southwestern Psychological Association, Louisiana Psychological Association, New Orleans Association for Children With Learning Disabilities, New Orleans Behavior Therapy Society, Phi Kappa Phi, Psi Chi.

WRITINGS: How to Live With Your Children: A Guide for Parents, Almar, 1981; (with Mallary Collins) *Changing Student Behavior,* Schenkman, 1982; *Understanding and Managing Overactive Children: A Guide for Parents,* Prentice-Hall, 1983.

WORK IN PROGRESS: Building Confidence in Children, publication expected in 1983; *Developing Responsible Behaviors in Children,* 1984.

SIDELIGHTS: Fontenelle told *CA:* "I find that far too often mental health material written for parents is very confusing and difficult to understand. Therefore in all of my works the main purpose is to convey information in a very practical, informal, and commonsense manner. Complex concepts and terms are presented in everyday language, and jargon and excessive terminology are avoided. Most of the material is aimed at giving parents and lay people a better understanding of the possible causes of children's behavior and, more importantly, how to effectively manage them."

*   *   *

FORDHAM, Peta   1905-

PERSONAL: Born October 12, 1905, in Birmingham, England; daughter of William (an attorney) and Florence Jane (Crisp) Marshall-Freeman; married Wilfrid Gurney Fordham (a judge), December 20, 1930; children: Colin. *Education:* Attended Sorbonne, University of Paris, 1921; Girton College, Cambridge, B.A. (with honors), 1928. *Politics:* Liberal. *Religion:* Church of England. *Home:* 4 Paper Buildings, Temple, London E.C.4, England. *Office:* 9 King's Bench Walk, Temple, London E.C.4, England.

CAREER: Association of British Chambers of Commerce, London, England, legal secretary, 1928-30; free-lance journalist, 1930—; *British Survey,* assistant director and editor, 1939-45; Consumers Association, London, director, 1955-56; *Which?,* London, editor, 1955-56; *Illustrated London News,* London, wine correspondent, 1960—; *Sunday Times,* London, crime consultant, 1965-72; *Law Guardian Gazette,* London, leisure editor, 1972—. *Member:* Circle of Wine Writers (honorary secretary, 1974-80), London Press Club. *Awards, honors:* Glenfiddich awards, 1973 (silver medal) and 1976 (gold medal).

WRITINGS: The Robbers' Tale: The Real Story of the Great Train Robbery, Popular Library, 1965; *The Villains: Inside the London Underworld,* Harper, 1972 (published in England as *Inside the Underworld,* Allen & Unwin, 1972). Author of "Dionysus," a column on wine, food, and restaurants, in *Law Guardian Gazette,* 1972—. Contributor of articles on travel, wine, and crime to newspapers, journals, magazines, and legal books.

SIDELIGHTS: The daughter of a barrister, Peta Fordham was introduced to London's criminal underworld when, as a child, she met some of the children of her father's clients. She developed an interest in the subject of crime that was encouraged by her father, and since that time has become an expert on the

structure and workings of that underworld society. As depicted by Fordham in *The Villains,* Britain's criminal class is a microcosm of the larger society, with generations of families engaged in criminal careers, building family reputations, and owing allegiance and obedience to a code of conduct as strict as the larger society's law, a code that until recently viewed the use of violence in the commission of a crime as a mark of incompetence.

Fordham's book also reveals a system of subclasses within the underworld based, to a large extent, on heredity and skill, with jewel thieves occupying the highest rung on the ladder. Rather than engaging in crimes of opportunity, these aristocrats of crime plan thefts with military-like precision and care for months, using specialists (often "disposable" small-time villains) to circumvent alarm systems, drive getaway cars, or to perform any of the tasks required to engineer a major theft.

The Villains presents a view of criminality unfamiliar to most Americans, who have become, according to some critics, numbingly accustomed to crime accompanied by violence and savagery. Fordham's portrait of English crime, in the view of one *New York Times Book Review* critic, "make[s] it seem quaint and oddly appealing."

Nearly nine years after that *New York Times Book Review* article was written Fordham told *CA:* "This deduction cannot now be made. Although the professional and skilled criminal is still considerably less violent than his American counterpart, crime has been invaded by (especially *young*) free-lance operators, often working only occasionally, who consider violence to be a routine precaution against capture. Mugging—often exaggerated—is another facet of this. The true underworld is currently in a state of some turmoil and there is a definite growth in 'grassing.' How much of this is due to social conditioning is anyone's guess."

MEDIA ADAPTATIONS: The Robbers' Tale was made into the British motion picture "Robbery," a 1967 Avco-Embassy film directed by Peter Yates.

BIOGRAPHICAL/CRITICAL SOURCES: Best Sellers, July 15, 1973; *New York Times Book Review,* September 2, 1973.

*   *   *

FORRESTER, Marian
See SCHACHTEL, Roger (Bernard)

*   *   *

FORTAS, Abe   1910-1982

OBITUARY NOTICE: Born June 19, 1910, in Memphis, Tenn.; died of a ruptured aorta, April 5, 1982, in Washington, D.C. Attorney, Supreme Court justice, and author. A founding partner in one of Washington's most influential law firms, Fortas was a friend and adviser to President Lyndon Johnson from Johnson's first term in the Senate. When Johnson offered Fortas the Supreme Court seat vacated by Arthur Goldberg in 1965, Fortas at first refused, but accepted the nomination a week later when the president urged him to reconsider. During his tenure on the Supreme Court, Fortas wrote a number of important opinions on civil liberties for the Court's liberal majority, and in 1968 he was nominated to succeed Earl Warren as chief justice. Senate Republicans blocked his confirmation, however, and in 1969 it was revealed that Fortas had accepted $20,000 from a foundation that was under investigation by the Securities and Exchange Commission. Fortas returned the money and denied any conflict of interest or other impropriety, but in May, 1969, he resigned amid calls for his impeachment. Fortas was the author of a book-length essay, *Concerning Dissent and Civil Disobedience,* as well as numerous articles for professional journals. Obituaries and other sources: *Current Biography,* Wilson, 1966, May, 1982; *Time,* May 23, 1969, April 19, 1982; *Britannica Book of the Year,* Encyclopaedia Britannica International, 1970; *New York Times,* August 1, 1971; *Newsweek,* April 19, 1982.

* * *

FOSTER, Elizabeth Read   1912-

PERSONAL: Born June 26, 1912, in Chicago, Ill.; daughter of Conyers (a historian) and Edith C. (Kirk) Read; married Richard W. Foster (a bookstore owner), December 31, 1938; children: Richard C., Timothy, Benjamin R., Daniel W. *Education:* Vassar College, A.B., 1933; Columbia University, A.M., 1934; Yale University, Ph.D., 1938. *Home:* 205 Strafford Ave., Wayne, Pa.

CAREER: Ursinus College, Collegeville, Pa., instructor, 1939-40, and 1953-65, became assistant professor, then associate professor; Bryn Mawr College, Bryn Mawr, Pa., professor of history, 1966-81, dean of Graduate School of Arts and Sciences, 1966-72; writer, 1981—. Visiting professor at University of Delaware, 1962-63; acting director of Yale Parliamentary Diaries Project, 1965-66. *Member:* American Historical Association, Conference of British Studies (member of executive council), Royal Historical Society.

WRITINGS: (Editor) *Proceedings in Parliament, 1610,* two volumes, Yale University Press, 1966; *The Painful Labor of Mr. Elsying,* American Philosophical Society, 1972; *The House of Lords, 1603-1649,* University of North Carolina Press, 1983. Member of editorial board of *American Historical Review,* 1979-81.

* * *

FOSTER, John Burt, Jr.   1945-

PERSONAL: Born December 19, 1945, in Chicago, Ill.; son of John Burt (a professor) and Jane (a social security administrator; maiden name, Armour) Foster; married Andrea Dimino (a teacher), March 27, 1970. *Education:* Harvard University, A.B., 1967; Yale University, M.Phil., 1970, Ph.D., 1974; also attended University of Konstanz, 1971-72. *Office:* Department of Comparative Literature, 401 Boylston Hall, Harvard University, Cambridge, Mass. 02138.

CAREER: Stanford University, Stanford, Calif., assistant professor of English and comparative literature, 1972-81; Harvard University, Cambridge, Mass., Mellon Faculty Fellow in comparative literature, 1982-83. *Member:* Modern Language Association of America, American Comparative Literature Association, American Association for the Advancement of Slavic Studies, English Institute. *Awards, honors:* Mellon fellow in Italy, 1975-76; American Council of Learned Societies fellow, 1981-82.

WRITINGS: Heirs to Dionysus: A Nietzschean Current in Literary Modernism, Princeton University Press, 1981.

WORK IN PROGRESS: A cultural biography of Vladimir Nabokov, focusing on the European side of his career.

SIDELIGHTS: Foster commented: "My two great interests as a writer are the phenomenon of modernism in twentieth-century artistic and intellectual life and the contributions of western Europe and England to American culture. Both tend to be neglected as too difficult or too remote in contemporary America, especially when one steps outside the colleges and uni-

versities. We need to remember that art and literature can be a great challenge to our capacities, and not simply a way of filling our leisure time."

* * *

FOSTER, Mark Stewart   1939-

PERSONAL: Born May 2, 1939, in Evanston, Ill.; son of Winfield (in business) and Jeannette (Lamb) Foster; married Judith Marie Buck, June 17, 1967 (divorced January 3, 1979); married Rickey Lynn Hendricks, 1982. *Education:* Brown University, A.B., 1961; University of Southern California, M.A., 1968, Ph.D., 1971. *Home:* 757 Williams, Denver, Colo. 80218. *Office:* Department of History, University of Colorado, Denver, 1100 14th St., Denver, Colo. 80202.

CAREER: History teacher at school in Claremont, Calif., 1964-66; University of Missouri, St. Louis, visiting assistant professor of history, 1971-72; University of Colorado, Denver, assistant professor, 1972-76, associate professor, 1976-81, professor of history, 1981—, director of urban studies, 1975-77, chairman of department, 1976-77. *Military service:* Air National Guard Reserves, 1961-67. *Member:* American Historical Association, Organization of American Historians, American Society of Baseball Researchers, Phi Alpha Theta. *Awards, honors:* Grants from Ford Motor Company Fund, 1977-78, Eleanor Roosevelt Institute, 1979, and Harry S. Truman Library, 1982.

WRITINGS: (With Frederick S. Allen, Ernest Andrade, Jr., and others) *The University of Colorado, 1876-1976,* Harcourt, 1976; *From Streetcar to Superhighway: American City Planners and Urban Transportation, 1900-1940,* Temple University Press, 1981; *The Denver Bears: Minor League Baseball in the Mile High Metropolis, 1885-1983,* Pruett, 1983. Co-editor of "Technology and Urban Growth" series, Temple University Press, 1979—. Contributor of about thirty articles and reviews to history magazines.

WORK IN PROGRESS: A biography of American industrialist Henry J. Kaiser.

SIDELIGHTS: Foster wrote: "Having partly repaid my dues to the historical profession in the form of numerous scholarly books and articles, I am now concentrating more on the general field of popular or literary history. The more enjoyable a book is to research and write, the more enjoyable it will be for the reader."

AVOCATIONAL INTERESTS: Marathon running.

* * *

FOWKES, Robert Allen   1913-

BRIEF ENTRY: Born April 7, 1913, in Harrison, N.Y. American educator and author. Fowkes joined the faculty at New York University in 1936 and became a professor of German in 1959. He also lectured in Sanskrit at Columbia University from 1947 to 1960 and was a Guggenheim fellow in 1950. Fowkes wrote *The German Lied and Its Poetry* (New York University Press, 1971). He edited *Studies in Germanic Languages and Literature* (Hutzler, 1967) and *Das Marmorbild* (Blaisdell, 1969). *Address:* 632 Van Cortlandt Park Ave., Yonkers, N.Y. 10705; and Department of German, New York University, Washington Sq., New York, N.Y. 10003. *Biographical/critical sources: Who's Who in America,* 41st edition, Marquis, 1980.

FOWLER, Sandra (Lynn) 1937-

PERSONAL: Born February 4, 1937, in West Columbia, W.Va.; daughter of Okey Donley (a welder) and Romona Jean (Roach) Fowler. *Education:* Palmer Institute of Authorship, diploma, 1966. *Politics:* Democrat. *Religion:* Protestant-Fundamentalist. *Residence:* West Columbia, W.Va. 25287.

CAREER: Writer and poet; *Ocarina: Journal of Poetry and Aesthetics,* Madras, India, contributing editor, 1972-78, associate editor, 1978—. *Member:* World Poetry Society (representative-at-large, 1969—), Avalon, United Poets, Centro Studi e Scambi Internazionali-Accademia Leonardo da Vinci (honorary representative). *Awards, honors:* Received citations of merit from Avalon international poetry contests, 1963, for "The Stag-King," and 1964, for "Elegy for a Tiger"; medal of honor, 1967, for contributions to world peace through poetry, certificate of merit, 1979, for poem "In the Shape of Sun," and diploma of honor for contributions to development of letters, arts, sciences, and international brotherhood, 1982, all from Centro Studi e Scambi Internazionali-Accademia Leonardo da Vinci; award, 1976, and citation, 1981, both from American Biographical Institute; selected poet of the month by *Mondo,* 1980; distinguished service citation from World Poetry Society, 1981; cultural doctorate in literature from World University Roundtable, 1981.

WRITINGS: In the Shape of Sun (poems), edited by W. M. Barzelay, Shalom Publications, 1973; (guest editor) *Friendship Bridge,* Ocarina, 1979; (editor with Amal Ghose) *The Album* (anthology), Tagore Institute of Creative Writing International, 1981; (editor with Ghose) *Eve's Eden* (anthology), Tagore Institute of Creative Writing International, in press.

SIDELIGHTS: Fowler told *CA:* "God called me to write poetry while I was sweeping the floor of a church. I asked him to make me a voice in the world. Since then, although the poet has remained in West Virginia, the poetry itself has built many strong bridges across the countries of the mind. Perhaps, as I recently wrote Menke Katz, my Yiddish poet-friend, 'thoughts can make short journeys out of time.'

"The Ohio Valley is a good place for a poet. One can pluck poetic thoughts like wildflowers out of its landscape on almost any given day. Music used to make the words come easier, but now I find that cricket and crow sounds or even no sounds at all will do quite as well.

"The editorial work I have been doing with Amal Ghose of India since 1972 has been an inspiration. It has given me an opportunity, via letter, to communicate my love, compassion, and understanding to the poets of the world without regard to race, culture, or creed. In so doing, it has strengthened my belief that a letter is indeed the language of the soul.

"For me the creative process has always been an involuntary one. Words, images, voices, and colors must come to me and make themselves into a poem. If the Light does not find me then I walk in darkness. I know no other way."

BIOGRAPHICAL/CRITICAL SOURCES: North American Mentor, summer, 1974; *ken,* March 3, 1975; *Hindu* (India), December 8, 1981; *Politika* (Yugoslavia), January 29, 1982.

* * *

FOX, Edward Whiting 1911-

BRIEF ENTRY: Born June 28, 1911, in Seattle, Wash. American historian, educator, and author. Fox taught modern European history at Cornell University from 1946 to 1977 when he was named professor emeritus. He wrote *History in Geographic Perspective: The Other France* (Norton, 1971) and edited the "Development of Western Civilization" series (Cornell University Press, 1950), *Atlas of European History* (Oxford University Press, 1957), *Ancient Israel* (Cornell University Press, 1958), and *Atlas of American History* (Oxford University Press, 1964). *Address:* 507 Triphammer Rd., Ithaca, N.Y. 14850; and Department of History, Cornell University, Ithaca, N.Y. 14850.

* * *

FOX, Jack Vernon 1918-1982

OBITUARY NOTICE: Born November 28, 1918, in St. Joseph, Mo.; died of cancer, January 15, 1982, in Oxnard, Calif. As a roving correspondent for United Press International (UPI) for forty years, Fox earned a reputation as a fine reporter and writer. He covered World War II, the deaths of Stalin and Churchill, the Hungarian revolt of 1956, the assassination of John F. Kennedy, and many other front-page stories. Obituaries and other sources: *Who's Who in America,* 40th edition, Marquis, 1978; *New York Times,* January 16, 1982.

* * *

FOX, Joseph M(ichael) 1934-

PERSONAL: Born August 19, 1934, in Brooklyn, N.Y.; son of Patrick J. and Mona (Keegan) Fox; married Carole Scharf, May 10, 1958; children: John, William, Daniel, Mary, Lucy, Paul. *Education:* St. John's College (now University), Jamaica, N.Y., B.S., 1956. *Home:* 7000 Tilden Lane, Rockville, Md. 20852.

CAREER: International Business Machines Corp. (IBM), New York City, 1969-77, worked in sales positions and product marketing, and as division vice-president; Software Architecture and Engineering, Washington, D.C., chairman, 1978—. Member of board of directors of Montgomery General Hospital, Olney, Md.

WRITINGS: Executive Qualities, Addison-Wesley, 1977; *What If. . .?,* Price, Stern, 1979; *Trapped in the Organization,* Price, Stern, 1980; *Software and Its Development,* Prentice-Hall, 1982.

WORK IN PROGRESS: What Do You Do at Work, Daddy?, a story about IBM and air traffic controllers.

SIDELIGHTS: Fox told *CA:* "My books are based on real life experiences at IBM, with the United States government as chairman of computer review committees, and as chairman of my own firm."

* * *

FOX, Larry

PERSONAL—Education: Attended University of North Carolina and Columbia University. *Home:* 51 Choate Lane, Pleasantville, N.Y. 10570.

CAREER: Author and sportswriter. Associated with *New York Daily News* and *New York World Telegram. Awards, honors:* Grantland Rice fellowship, 1951.

WRITINGS: (With Zander Hollander) *The Home Run Story* (juvenile biography), Norton, 1966; *Little Men in Sports* (juvenile biography), Norton, 1968; *Broadway Joe and His Super Jets,* Coward, 1969; *Last to First: The Story of the Mets,* Harper, 1970; *Willis Reed: Take-Charge Man of the Knicks,*

Grosset, 1970; *Willis Reed: The Knicks' Comeback Captain*, Grosset, 1973; *The Giant Killers* (juvenile), Grosset, 1974; *The Illustrated History of Basketball*, Grosset, 1974; *The O. J. Simpson Story: Born to Run* (juvenile), Dodd, 1974; *Mean Joe Green and the Steelers' Front Four*, Dodd, 1975; *Bert Jones and the Battling Colts*, Dodd, 1977; *The New England Patriots*, Atheneum, 1979.*

* * *

FRANCE, Anatole
See THIBAULT, Jacques Anatole Francois

* * *

FRANCISCO, Clyde Taylor 1916-

BRIEF ENTRY: Born June 2, 1916, in Virgilina, Va. American biblical scholar, educator, and author. Francisco has been an ordained Baptist minister since 1940. After serving congregations in Virginia, Kentucky, and West Virginia, he joined the faculty of the Southern Baptist Theological Seminary. Francisco was named John R. Sampey Professor of Old Testament Interpretation in 1951. His publications include *Introducing the Old Testament: Based Upon John R. Sampey's Syllabus* (Broadman, 1950), *Studies in Jeremiah* (Convention Press, 1961), and *The Book of Deuteronomy: A Study Manual* (Baker Book, 1964). *Address:* 640 Upland Rd., Louisville, Ky. 40206; and Department of Old Testament, Southern Baptist Theological Seminary, 2825 Lexington Rd., Louisville, Ky. 40206. *Biographical/critical sources: Directory of American Scholars*, Volume IV: *Philosophy, Religion, and Law*, 7th edition, Bowker, 1978.

* * *

FRANK, Adolph F(rederick) 1918-

PERSONAL: Born September 1, 1918, in McKeesport, Pa.; son of William R., Sr. (a metal patternmaker) and Wilhelmina (Boss) Frank; married Virginia M. Houserman, February 2, 1944; children: Carol L. Frank Couchenour, Donald G. *Education:* Attended high school in McKeesport, Pa. *Religion:* Protestant. *Home:* 906 Franklin St., McKeesport, Pa. 15132.

CAREER: Bell Telephone Co. of Pennsylvania, Pittsburgh, in repair, 1939-57, foreman, 1957-61, staff associate, 1961-81; writer, 1981—. *Military service:* U.S. Army Air Forces, 1942-45; served in China-Burma-India theater; became master sergeant. *Member:* National Model Railroad Association, American Association of Retired Persons. *Awards, honors:* Silver Beaver award from Boy Scouts of America, 1958; good neighbor award from Bell Telephone Co. of Pennsylvania, 1963.

WRITINGS: Animated Scale Models Handbook (self-illustrated), Arco, 1981.

SIDELIGHTS: Frank commented: "I have had a lifetime interest in model railroading. I was not satisfied just with trains operating, so my father and I elected to animate parts of our layout. As the years passed and my father died, I developed my own animated model railroad. I am not sure what prompted me to do this—a frustration with seeing a model railroad in a dead setting, or an inborn mechanical nature to watch things operate and in turn satisfy this mechanical hunger. It may have been both. My first HO scale layout was sold after the advent of N scale, since N scale is about half the size of HO scale, and I could have about twice as much animation in half the space.

"As time went on, my model railroad friends would ask how this or that piece of animation operated, and I would try to

explain the operation while they viewed it. For some time I mulled over in my mind the idea of writing a book on this subject. I never could find one in a library or book store. I started gathering my notes together. I felt this had to be more than a book on mechanical parts: it had to be a complete book on modeling from A to Z. I did the drawings and illustrations, using my high school education in engineering drafting. Once these were completed, I wrote the text.

"Seven years later, the book was published. I received satisfaction from this, and if one other person receives pleasure from using the book, then the whole effort has been worthwhile.

"I am still in the process of adding new animation to my own layout, and with it, of course, I am using new mechanical movements and new technology. I am ever striving to build better, simpler, and more reliable animation, and continuing to compile and add to my notes and my own satisfaction."

* * *

FRANK, William L(uke) 1929-

PERSONAL: Born August 16, 1929, in New York, N.Y.; son of Henry J. (an attorney) and Helen (Luff) Frank; married Angeline Webb (a teacher), December 19, 1960; children: William L., Jr., Catherine Ellen, Tracey Elizabeth. *Education:* University of Southern Mississippi, B.A., 1955, M.A. (education), 1956; Northwestern University M.A. (English), 1958, Ph.D., 1964. *Politics:* Independent. *Religion:* Roman Catholic. *Home:* 26 G Fox Hill Rd., Rice, Va. 23966. *Office:* Division of Language, Literature, and Philosophy, Longwood College, Farmville, Va. 23901.

CAREER: Bloomingdale's (department store), New Rochelle, N.Y., department manager, 1952-53; Delta State University, Cleveland, Miss., assistant professor of English, 1958-63; University of Southeast Missouri, Cape Girardeau, assistant professor, 1963-65, associate professor, 1965-68, professor of English, 1968; Longwood College, Farmville, Va., professor of English, 1968—, chairman of department of English and philosophy, 1968-78, chairman of Division of Language, Literature, and Philosophy, 1975-79, coordinator of institutional grants, 1979—. *Military service:* U.S. Air Force, instructor at Radio Operating School, 1948-52.

MEMBER: Modern Language Association of America, Association of Departments of English, National Council of Teachers of English, Conference on College Composition and Communication, South Atlantic Modern Language Association, South Central Modern Language Association, South Atlantic Association of Departments of English (member of executive committee, 1968-70; executive secretary, 1970—), Pi Kappa Pi, Phi Kappa Phi, Omicron Delta Kappa, Farmville Rotary Club (member of board of directors; president, 1973-74), Wedgewood Country Club (member of board of directors; president, 1973-74).

WRITINGS: A Critical Introduction to Sherwood Bonner, G. K. Hall, 1976; (contributor) *Collected Stories of Sherwood Bonner*, College and University Press, 1982. Contributor to literature journals.

WORK IN PROGRESS: An Introduction to the Novels of William Hoffman; a monograph on Whitman's "Out of the Cradle Endlessly Rocking."

SIDELIGHTS: Frank commented: "The two most interesting aspects of my life are that I'm a native New Yorker who married a Mississippi gal, and I started out in the retail trade with Gimbel's and Bloomingdale's and switched to college teaching. At times I have been able to view situations, problems, and people from an unusual perspective, and have discovered that basic problems about which people worry are the same in and outside of academe. I continue to believe that teaching, especially college teaching, offers one a rewarding and relatively good life. Perhaps it's a matter of a new beginning with each semester and each year, perhaps it's being surrounded by the eternally young—the reality of Keats's urn—but for whatever reason or reasons, those of us who teach and write on college campuses do for the most part live, lead, and contribute to the good life.''

* * *

FRANKEL, William 1917-

PERSONAL: Born February 3, 1917, in London, England; son of Isaac (a merchant) and Anna (Lecker) Frankel; married Gertrude Freda Reed, 1939 (divorced, 1971); married Claire Schwab Neuman (a sculptor), December 16, 1973; children: (first marriage) one son, one daughter. *Education:* University of London, LL.B. (with honors), 1943. *Religion:* Jewish. *Home:* 5 Pump Court, Temple, London E.C. 4, England.

CAREER: Called to the Bar at Middle Temple, England, 1944; private practice of law on South-Eastern Circuit, England, 1944-55; *Jewish Chronicle,* London, England, general manager, 1955-58, editor, 1958-77; *London Times,* London, England, special adviser, 1977-81. Chairman of Mental Health Review Tribunal and of Supplementary Benefits Appeal Tribunal. Governor of Oxford Center for Postgraduate Hebrew Studies. Trustee of Oxford House in Bethnal Green and of Jewish Youth Fund. *Member:* Athenaeum Club, Marleybone Cricket Club. *Awards, honors:* Commander of Order of the British Empire, 1970.

WRITINGS: (Editor) *Friday Nights,* Valentine, Mitchell, 1973; *Israel Observed: An Anatomy of the State,* Thames & Hudson, 1981. Author of weekly column in *The Statesman* (Calcutta and Delhi). Contributor of articles to periodicals, including *London Times, Jewish Chronicle,* and *Asian Wall Street Journal.*

SIDELIGHTS: "As a Jew committed to the support of Israel I am not impartial,'' wrote William Frankel in *Israel Observed: An Anatomy of the State.* Yet, he went on to produce what *Booklist* called a "wide-angle, objective look at the state" by relying on his insight and his observations gained as the former editor of a Jewish periodical, as a frequent visitor to that country, and as an acquaintance of Israel's leaders.

In *Israel Observed,* Frankel endeavors "to describe the structure and workings of the main political and social institutions of Israel which determine national policies and influence the way people live.'' Besides showing Israel's political organizations, her judicial system, and the mechanics of her government, the author also illustrates the important roles of religious leaders. He presents both the attractive and unappealing features of Israel, often showing, to use David Pryce-Jones's words, a "very ordinary and uninspiring" country. As other critics noted, Frankel captures the heroic nature of the Israeli people, most of whom are the survivors of Nazi and Soviet persecutions. Frankel's Israel, continued Pryce-Jones in a *Times Literary Supplement,* is "an extended ghetto to be subjected to all manner of particular discriminations.''

Heralded as a timely book, *Israel Observed* appeared at a time when Israel's concerns were world issues. A build-up of arms in the states around Israel caused her to boost her allowances for defense spending until it absorbed two-thirds of her budget. Then, in 1981, an international incident resulted in a United

Nations' censure against Israel when the Israeli Air Force destroyed a nuclear reactor in Baghdad, Iraq. In his review of the book, the *Listener*'s David Steel cited the question of sovereignty for Palestine as "the central dilemma facing the peace-seekers'' in the Middle East. He added that the lack of communication and the acts of violence between Israel and the Palestine Liberation Organization (PLO) are stumbling blocks to negotiations for liberation.

Highly praised by reviewers, *Israel Observed* was labeled such things as "objective" and "critical." Brian W. Beely of the *British Book News* applauded the work for being "a clear, informative and incisive account of a national political system,'' while a *Choice* critic complimented Frankel on his "unusually lucid and readable style." "It is the best introduction to the organization of Israel's internal government and society that I have read,'' commented Harry Schwartz of the *New York Times Book Review.*

Israel Observed, said Steel, "is an admirably readable account of the institutions and personalities which make up that fascinating and complex state. . . . It is more than just a useful factual handbook, including as it does some fascinating thumbnail sketches such as the one of Begin's progress from terrorist through fundamentalist politician to flexible statesman.''

Frankel told *CA:* "Considering that twenty years of newspaper editorship was an ample relationship for both parties, I decided it was time for a change. Since then, I have enjoyed writing (for which, as a working editor, I had little time) and have undertaken a wide variety of activities: literary, legal, public service, and teaching.''

BIOGRAPHICAL/CRITICAL SOURCES: Times Literary Supplement, November 7, 1980; *Contemporary Review,* December, 1980; *Listener,* December 4, 1980; *Observer,* December 14, 1980; *British Book News,* February, 1981; *Booklist,* June 1, 1981; *New York Times Book Review,* July 26, 1981; *Choice,* November, 1981.

* * *

FRANKLIN, Jimmie Lewis 1939-

BRIEF ENTRY: Born April 10, 1939, in Moscow, Miss. American historian, educator, and author. Franklin has been a member of the faculty at the University of Wisconsin—Stevens Point and the University of Washington, Seattle. In 1970 he began teaching history at Eastern Illinois University. Franklin wrote *Born Sober: Prohibition in Oklahoma, 1907-1959* (University of Oklahoma Press, 1971) and *The Blacks in Oklahoma* (University of Oklahoma Press, 1980). *Address:* Department of History, Eastern Illinois University, Charleston, Ill. 61920.

* * *

FRANTZ, Harry Warner 1891-1982

OBITUARY NOTICE: Born November 4, 1891, in Cerro Gordo, Ill.; died April 26, 1982, in Ithaca, N.Y. Frantz covered international news for United Press International (UPI) for forty-four years, specializing in Latin American events. He covered Herbert Hoover's 1928 tour of Central and South America, border disputes between Chile and Peru in 1925 and between Costa Rica and Nicaragua in 1948, and the Dominican revolution in 1930. He was awarded the Maria Moors Cabot Gold Medal for Journalism by Columbia University in 1957. Obituaries and other sources: *Who's Who in America,* 39th edition, Marquis, 1976; *Chicago Tribune,* May 1, 1982.

FRASER, Kathleen 1937-

PERSONAL: Born in 1937; married Jack Marshall; children: one son. *Education:* Attended Occidental College. *Home:* 554 Jersey St., San Francisco, Calif. 94114.

CAREER: Poet.

WRITINGS—All poetry, except as noted: *Change of Address and Other Poems* (adult), Kayak, 1966; *Stilts, Somersaults, and Headstands* (juvenile), Atheneum, 1968; *In Defiance of the Rains* (adult; illustrated by Judy Starbuck), Kayak, 1969; (with Miriam F. Levy) *Adam's World: San Francisco* (juvenile fiction; illustrated by Helen D. Hipshman), Albert Whitman, 1971; *Little Notes to You, From Lucas Street*, Penumbra Press, 1972; *What I Want* (adult), Harper, 1974; *Magritte Series* (adult), chapbook edition, Tuumba, 1977; *New Shoes* (adult), Harper, 1978.

Work represented in anthology *Young American Poets,* edited by P. Carroll, Follet, 1968. Contributor of poems to *Mademoiselle, New Yorker, Harper's Bazaar, Poetry,* and *Rolling Stone.**

* * *

FREDDI, Cris 1955-

PERSONAL: Born January 30, 1955, in Reading, England; son of Luigi (a charge nurse) and Rosalba (Canciani) Freddi. *Education:* Oxford University, B.A. (with honors), 1977. *Agent:* Gloria Safier, 667 Madison Ave., New York, N.Y. 10021. *Office:* J. Walter Thompson Company Ltd., 40 Berkeley Sq., London W1X 6AD, England.

CAREER: J. Walter Thompson Company Ltd. (advertising), London, England, copywriter, 1977—.

WRITINGS: Pork (short stories), Knopf, 1981.

WORK IN PROGRESS: A novel.

SIDELIGHTS: Fantasy and grim reality counterpoint one another in *Pork,* Freddi's stories of struggle and survival in the animal world. Walter Wangerin, Jr., of the *Washington Post* called *Pork* ''a very good book'' and went on to say: ''So careful is Freddi's eye in surveying his northern swatch of nature; so particular his words in describing its forest, soils, mountains, streams, river, ocean coastline, all conditions of weather and seasons, all sensate responses to growth, color, odors and decay; so content his mood with the laws that cause both life and death that I am reminded of a book neither fiction nor fantasy: Aldo Leopold's 'A Sand County Almanac.''' Wangerin admired the cohesiveness of the stories within the book and marvelled at Freddi's ability to deal with death ''again and again until it emerges as a fixed ordinance'' while avoiding morbidity.

BIOGRAPHICAL/CRITICAL SOURCES: Washington Post, September 18, 1981.

* * *

FREDMAN, Ruth Gruber 1934-

PERSONAL: Born December 16, 1934, in Philadelphia, Pa.; daughter of Julius Joseph (a pharmacist) and Mary (Boxman) Gruber; married Irwin Jay Fredman, April 3, 1955; children: Jonathan, Andrew, Lauren. *Education:* Temple University, B.A., 1956, M.A., 1975, Ph.D., 1982; attended University of Kansas

City, 1958. *Religion:* Jewish. *Home:* 11910 Tildenwood Dr., Rockville, Md. 20852.

CAREER: Temple University, Philadelphia, Pa., instructor in anthropology, 1975-77; writer, 1977—. *Member:* American Anthropological Association, American Folklore Society, American Civil Liberties Union, Washington Association of Professional Anthropologists, Anthropological Society of Washington, Society for Medical Anthropology.

WRITINGS: The Passover Seder: Afikoman in Exile, University of Pennsylvania Press, 1981. Contributor of articles and reviews to magazines and newspapers.

WORK IN PROGRESS: Research on the Sephardi Jews of Washington, D.C.

SIDELIGHTS: Ruth Fredman wrote: ''For me, anthropology is the study of how societies impose meaning on existence. As social constructions akin to art forms, ritual and myth act as texts for the analyst; they reveal the unique way a society employs common forms to express the particular configuration of meanings that is its culture.

''I am interested in bringing home the insights gained from cross-cultural study. Not only can anthropology make the exotic intelligible, and so reduce its capacity to threaten, but it can also illuminate common experience in America. I would like to see the focus of cross-cultural study in children's education shifted from what people do (costumes, foods, dances, and so on) to what these items mean to their users. Too much is made of exotica; even children tire of talk of wooden shoes and know that tacos are eaten by many non-Mexicans. What they need to know is what the Mexican, Chinese, Arab, or Israeli view of reality is, and this can be explained on any level of complexity. This change of emphasis is needed in religious as well as secular education. It is crucial that Americans learn early to understand the bonds we have in common with others, and make sense of the differences, if we are ever to have peace and, more immediately, if our national goals and programs are to be effective. If this makes anthropology missionary, so be it.''

* * *

FREEMAN, Leslie J(ane) 1944-

PERSONAL: Born January 26, 1944, in New York, N.Y.; daughter of Lionel J. (a lawyer) and Eve (Chalson) Freeman. *Education:* City College of the City University of New York, B.A., 1964; University of California, Berkeley, M.A., 1960; Columbia University, Ph.D., 1970, M.A., 1977. *Home:* 338 West 84th St., New York, N.Y. 10024. *Agent:* John Brockman Associates, Inc., 200 West 57th St., New York, N.Y. 10019. *Office:* New York Institute of Technology, 1855 Broadway, New York, N.Y. 10023.

CAREER: Miles College, Birmingham, Ala., instructor in English, 1966; City College of New York (now of the City University of New York), New York City, instructor in English composition, 1966-67; New School for Social Research, New York City, instructor in humanities, 1966-68; Columbia University, New York City, assistant professor of English, 1970-77; New York Institute of Technology, New York City, director of English-as-second-language program, 1977—. Instructor at City College of the City University of New York, 1967-68; supervisor at Columbia University's Teachers College. *Awards, honors:* Woodrow Wilson fellow, 1964; MacDowell Colony writing fellow, 1972.

WRITINGS: (With Mary Reinbold Jerome, Gail Fingado, and Catherine Summers) *The English Connection,* Little, Brown, 1981; *Nuclear Witnesses: Insiders Speak Out,* Norton, 1981.

WORK IN PROGRESS: Research on radioactive waste, transport, nuclear medicine, deregulation, toxic waste, radiation and human waste, worker compensation, and nuclear power connected to nuclear weapons.

SIDELIGHTS: Leslie Freeman commented: "*Nuclear Witnesses* was written because there is no issue of greater urgency in the world today than that involving the commitment of our resources and politics to a suicidal energy and military policy."

BIOGRAPHICAL/CRITICAL SOURCES: Los Angeles Times Book Review, September 13, 1981; *New York Times Book Review,* January 31, 1982.

* * *

FREEMAN, Mary Eleanor Wilkins 1852-1930
(Mary Wilkins)

BRIEF ENTRY: Born October 31, 1852, in Randolph, Mass.; died of a heart attack, March 13, 1930, in Metuchen, N.J.; buried in Hillside Cemetery, Plainfield, N.J. American author. Freeman is best remembered for her short stories, collected in *A Humble Romance* (1887) and *A New England Nun and Other Stories* (1891), though she also wrote novels, including *Jane Field* (1893) and *Pembroke* (1894). She was a popular writer in her day because of her dispassionate skill in describing small-town life in New England. Her characters were the people who had chosen to remain in their quiet towns rather than seek more adventurous lives elsewhere, people whose lives often culminated in alienation from their repressed societies and eventually from themselves. Freeman wrote of the pride that sustained these stubborn survivors through poverty and defeat and of the personal cost of such strong-willed pride. But Freeman's lack of bitterness, her avoidance of excessive sentimentality, and her narrative skill, brightened at times by dry, New England humor, contributed to a body of stories that remain realistic portrayals of the human character. *Biographical/critical sources: Twentieth Century Authors: A Biographical Dictionary of Modern Literature,* H. W. Wilson, 1942; *Notable American Women, 1607-1950: A Biographical Dictionary,* Belknap Press, 1971.

* * *

FRIEDLAND, Ronnie 1945-

PERSONAL: Born February 2, 1945, in Jersey City, N.J.; daughter of Abner M. (a manufacturer) and Adele (Gottlieb) Friedland; married Daniel E. Little (a professor of philosophy), September 12, 1976; children: Joshua Michael Friedland-Little, Rebecca Aviva Friedland-Little. *Education:* Attended Northwestern University, 1963-65; Barnard College, B.A., 1967; New York University, M.A., 1970, doctoral study, 1970-72. *Politics:* Liberal. *Religion:* Jewish. *Residence:* Belmont, Mass. *Agent:* Emily Jacobson, Curtis Brown Ltd., 575 Madison Ave., New York, N.Y. 10022.

CAREER: Manhattan Community College of the City University of New York, New York, N.Y., assistant professor of English, 1971-72; North Shore Community College, Beverly, Mass., instructor in English, 1972-74; Bentley College, Waltham, Mass., instructor in English, 1974-76; University of Wisconsin, Parkside, instructor in English, 1977; free-lance writer, 1977—.

WRITINGS: (Editor with Carol Kort) *The Mothers' Book: Shared Experiences,* Houghton, 1981. Contributor to *Barnard Alumnae News* and *Family Journal.*

WORK IN PROGRESS: Editing *The Fathers' Book: Shared Experiences,* with Carol Kort.

SIDELIGHTS: Ronnie Friedland wrote: "The two factors which have most influenced my career and present life are feminism and motherhood. I am currently trying to combine both interests in a creative and literary way."

BIOGRAPHICAL/CRITICAL SOURCES: Los Angeles Times Book Review, May 24, 1981.

* * *

FRIEDMANN, Herbert 1900-

PERSONAL: Born April 22, 1900, in New York, N.Y.; son of Uriah M. and Mary (Behrmann) Friedmann; married Karen Juul Vejlo (an economist), May 7, 1937; children: Karen Alice (Mrs. John N. Beall). *Education:* City College (now of the City University of New York), B.Sc., 1920; Cornell University, Ph.D., 1923; postdoctoral study at Harvard University, 1923-26. *Home:* 350 South Fuller Ave., Apt. 12H, Los Angeles, Calif. 90036.

CAREER: Brown University, Providence, R.I., instructor in biology, 1926-27; Amherst College, Amherst, Mass., instructor in biology, 1927-29; Smithsonian Institution, U.S. National Museum, Washington, D.C., curator of ornithology, 1929-58, head curator of zoology, 1958-61; Los Angeles County Museum of Natural History, Los Angeles, Calif., director, 1961-70; University of California, Los Angeles, professor of zoology, 1963-67, professor of history of art, 1966. *Military service:* U.S. Army, Infantry, 1918.

MEMBER: National Academy of Sciences, American Association for the Advancement of Science (president of zoology section, 1953), American Ornithologists Union (president, 1939), Cooper Ornithological Society, Deutsche Ornithologisch Gesellschaft (honorary member), South African Ornithological Society (honorary member). *Awards, honors:* Leidy Medal from Academy of Natural Sciences of Philadelphia, 1955, and Elliott Medal from National Academy of Sciences, 1959, both for *The Honey Guides;* Brewster Medal from American Ornithologists Union, 1964, for *Host Relations of the Parasitic Cowbirds.*

WRITINGS: The Cowbirds: A Study in the Biology of Social Parasitism, C. C Thomas, 1929; *The Symbolic Goldfinch: Its History and Significance in European Devotional Art,* Bollingen Foundation, 1946; *The Parasitic Cuckoos of Africa,* Washington Academy of Sciences, 1948; *The Honey Guides,* Smithsonian Institution Press, 1955; *The Parasitic Weaverbirds,* U.S. National Museum, 1960; *Host Relations of the Parasitic Cowbirds,* Smithsonian Institution Press, 1963; *Results of the 1964 Cheney Tanganyikan Expedition: Ornithology,* Los Angeles County Museum of Natural History, 1964; *Evolutionary Trends in the Avian Genus* Clamator, Smithsonian Institution Press, 1964; *A Contribution to the Ornithology of Uganda: Scientitic Results of the 1963 Knudsen-Marchris Expedition to Kenya and Uganda,* Los Angeles County Museum of Natural History, 1966; *The Evolutionary History of the Avian Genus* Chrysococcyx, Smithsonian Institution Press, 1968; (with John G. Williams) *The Birds of the Lowlands of Bwamba, Toro Province, Uganda,* Los Angeles County Museum of Natural History, 1971; (with Lloyd F. Kiff and Stephen I. Rothstein) *A Further Contribution of Knowledge of the Host Relations of the Parasitic Cowbirds,* Smithsonian Institution Press, 1977; *A Bestiary for Saint Jerome: Animal Symbolism in European Religious Art,* Smithsonian Institution Press, 1980.

Contributor to proceedings of the U.S. National Museum. Contributor of about three hundred fifty articles to zoology and art history journals.

WORK IN PROGRESS: Manuscripts on art history, chiefly on animal symbolism in European religious art from the Middle Ages to the baroque period, and on ornithology.

*   *   *

FRIES, Robert Francis 1911-

PERSONAL: Born December 16, 1911, in La Crosse, Wis.; son of William James and Laura (Olsen) Fries; married Frances K. Clements, January 2, 1936; children: Mary Ann, Margaret Frances. *Education:* Wisconsin State College, La Crosse (now University of Wisconsin—La Crosse), B.E., 1933; University of Wisconsin—Madison, Ph.M., 1936, Ph.D., 1939. *Home:* 7410 South Paxton Ave., Chicago, Ill. 60649. *Office:* Department of History, DePaul University, 25 East Jackson Blvd., Chicago, Ill. 60604.

CAREER: DePaul University, Chicago, Ill., assistant professor, 1939-43, associate professor, 1943-45, professor of history, 1945—, chairman of department, 1945-56, dean of University College, 1955-80. *Member:* American Historical Association, Organization of American Historians, American Association of University Professors, Association of University Evening Colleges, State Historical Society of Wisconsin, Kappa Delta Pi, Delta Epsilon Sigma. *Awards, honors:* David Clark Everest Prize for *Empire in Pine.*

WRITINGS: Empire in Pine, State Historical Society of Wisconsin, 1951; (editor with Paul L. Hughes) *Documents of Western Civilization,* Littlefield, 1956; (with Hughes) *Crown and Parliament in Tudor-Stuart England,* Putnam, 1959; *Basic Historical Documents of European Civilization,* Littlefield, 1972. Contributor to history journals.

*   *   *

FROMME, Babbette Brandt 1925-

PERSONAL: Born December 25, 1925, in New York, N.Y.; daughter of Harry N. (a theatre owner) and Helen (Satenstein) Brandt; married Allan Fromme (a clinical psychologist and writer), December 26, 1943; children: Pamela Fromme Formato, Lewis Steven. *Education:* Attended Sarah Lawrence College, 1943. *Home:* 4234 Gulf of Mexico Dr., Longboat Key, Fla. 33548.

CAREER: Museum of the City of New York, New York, N.Y., tour conductor for education department, 1969-76. Worked in public information department of Metropolitan Museum of Art, 1969-74.

WRITINGS: Curators' Choice: An Introduction to the Art Museums of the United States, four volumes *(Northeastern Edition, Southern Edition, Midwestern Edition,* and *Western Edition),* Crown, 1981.

SIDELIGHTS: Babbette Fromme wrote: "My interest in art and museums promotes considerable travel—an extra dividend in my life. I feel strongly about increasing people's appreciation of the arts, and personally I welcome additional ways of involving myself in such projects. I am now contemplating writing a series of introductions to the decorative arts."

*   *   *

FURNIER, Vincent Damon
See COOPER, Alice

*   *   *

FURNISH, Dorothy Jean 1921-

PERSONAL: Born August 25, 1921, in Plano, Ill.; daughter of Reuben McKinley (a minister) and Mildred L. (Feller) Furnish. *Education:* Cornell College, Mount Vernon, Iowa, B.A., 1943; Northwestern University, M.A., 1945, Ph.D., 1968. *Religion:* United Methodist. *Office:* Department of Christian Education, Garrett-Evangelical Theological Seminary, 2121 Sheridan Rd., Evanston, Ill. 60201.

CAREER: Director of Christian education at United Methodist churches in Hutchinson, Kan., 1945-52, and Lincoln, Neb., 1952-65; Garrett-Evangelical Theological Seminary, Evanston, Ill., instructor, 1968-70, assistant professor, 1970-73, associate professor, 1973-77, professor of Christian education, 1977—. *Member:* Association of Professors and Researchers in Religious Education, United Methodist Association of Professors of Christian Education, Association for Supervision and Curriculum Development, Christian Educators Fellowship, Religious Education Association.

WRITINGS: Exploring the Bible With Children, Abingdon, 1975; *DRE/DCE: History of a Profession,* Christian Educators Fellowship, 1976; *Living the Bible With Children,* Abingdon, 1979.

*   *   *

FYODOROV, Yevgeny Konstantinovich
See FEDOROV, Yevgeny Konstantinovich

G

GABEL, (W.) Creighton 1931-

BRIEF ENTRY: Born April 5, 1931, in Muskegon, Mich. American anthropologist, educator, and author. Gabel joined the faculty of Boston University in 1963 and became a professor of anthropology in 1969. He has conducted research in northern Rhodesia and Kenya and was a senior Fulbright fellow in Liberia in 1973. His writings include *Man Before History* (Prentice-Hall, 1964), *Stone Age Hunters of the Kafue: The Gwisho A Site* (Boston University Press, 1965), *Analysis of Prehistoric Economic Patterns* (Holt, 1967), and *Reconstructing African Culture History* (Boston University Press, 1967). *Address:* African Studies Center, Boston University, 10 Lenox St., Brookline, Mass. 02146. *Biographical/critical sources: American Anthropologist,* August, 1965; *American Historical Review,* June, 1968; *Directory of American Scholars,* Volume I: *History,* 7th edition, Bowker, 1978.

*   *   *

GALIANO, Juan Valera y Alcala
See VALERA y ALCALA-GALIANO, Juan

*   *   *

GALLAGHER, Tess 1943-

PERSONAL: Born July 21, 1943, in Port Angeles, Wash.; daughter of Leslie O. (a logger and longshoreman) and Georgia Marie (a logger; maiden name, Morris) Bond; married Lawrence Gallagher (a sculptor), June, 1963 (divorced, 1968); married Michael Burkard (a poet), May, 1973 (divorced, 1977); living with Raymond Carver (an author and teacher), 1979—. *Education:* University of Washington, B.A., 1963, M.A., 1970; University of Iowa, M.F.A., 1974. *Address:* 932 Maryland Ave., Syracuse, N.Y. 13210. *Office:* Department of English, Syracuse University, Syracuse, N.Y. 13210.

CAREER: St. Lawrence University, Canton, N.Y., instructor in English, 1974-75; Kirkland College, Clinton, N.Y., assistant professor of creative writing, 1975-77; University of Montana, Missoula, visiting lecturer of creative writing, 1977-78; University of Arizona, Tucson, assistant professor of creative writing, 1979-80; Syracuse University, Syracuse, N.Y., associate professor of English and coordinator of creative writing program, 1980-82; poet. Instructor at Willamette University, 1981. *Member:* P.E.N., National Organization for Women.

AWARDS, HONORS: Award from National Endowment for the Arts, 1976 and 1981; CAPS grant from New York State Arts Council, 1976; Elliston Award for "best book of poetry published by a small press," 1976, for *Instructions to the Double;* Governor's Award from State of Washington, 1977; Voertman Award, 1978; fellowship from Guggenheim Foundation, 1978-79; award from *American Poetry Review* for "best poems of 1980," 1981, for "Some With Wings, Some With Manes" and others.

WRITINGS—Poetry: *Stepping Outside,* Penumbra Press, 1974; *Instructions to the Double,* Graywolf Press, 1976; *Under Stars,* Graywolf Press, 1978; *Portable Kisses,* Sea Pen, 1978.

Author of television play "The Wheel," 1970, and screenplay "The Night Belongs to the Police," 1982. Work anthologized in *Influences,* Harper, 1982. Columnist for *American Poetry Review.* Contributor of poems, short stories, and essays to periodicals, including *Parnassus, Ironwood, New Yorker, American Poetry Review, Antaeus, Missouri Review,* and *North American Review.*

WORK IN PROGRESS: Other Women, a collection of short stories; a third collection of poetry; a screenplay with Raymond Carver.

SIDELIGHTS: Gallagher is ranked among America's finest contemporary poets. Her first collection, *Stepping Outside,* was compared by *Prairie Schooner's* Robert Ross to "the accomplished stripper, who has vanished from the stage by the time the yokels realized that it is her sequined G-string that is spinning toward them through the smoky air." Ross added, "This is a beautiful and also a refreshing book."

Instructions to the Double is probably Gallagher's best-known work. Many of these poems focus on the conflicting values of the family, and on departure and return. But Gallagher's main interest seems to be with comparisons of the self. As Valerie Trueblood noted in *American Poetry Review,* "The poems are full of doubles: shadows, reflections in eyes and water and mirrors, resemblances . . . , photographs, a body's impression burnt onto bedsprings in a fire." Trueblood contended, however, that "the buried excitement of family life produces the strongest poems in the book."

Gallagher continued to impress readers with her next collection, *Under Stars.* Fellow poet Hayden Carruth was especially pleased with the "feminine" quality of the poems. He declared that "Gallagher's poems, beyond their delicacy of language, have a delicacy of perception that I . . . associate with women: the capacity to see oneself objectively as another person doing the things one really does, but without the hard philosophical intrusions most men resort to; instead with clear affection and natural concern.'' Carruth concluded, ''Delicacy and light and the feminine strength of a clear view—these are the qualities that give me much pleasure in Gallagher' s work.'' Also complimentary of *Under Stars,* Peter Davison noted in *Atlantic* that ''Gallagher has undertaken one of the most daunting of poetic adventures: utilizing all the resources of language to explore the nuances of feeling, the nature of the passage of time, and most intricately, the nature of language itself.'' Critic Stanley Kunitz told a Greywolf Press editor that Gallagher ''is outstanding among her contemporaries in the naturalness of her inflection, the fine excess of her spirit, and the energy of her dramatic imagination.''

Gallagher told *CA:* ''I sing traditional Irish dirge and have traveled and lived in Northern Ireland and also near Sligo in the Republic for months at a time since 1968. I feel very close to the poets in Northern Ireland, who have become my friends. My interest in filmmaking has now led me to the writing of scripts with Raymond Carver, the short-story writer I live and work with.

''My main obsession in the poems of late has been with how memory works or doesn't work in the creating of 'what matters' in our lives. The nature of Time is of continual interest. I have been reading a great deal on this subject in the hopes of bringing more of such thought to my poems. J. T. Fraser and Henri Bergson have been recent valuable sources.''

BIOGRAPHICAL/CRITICAL SOURCES: Prairie Schooner, winter, 1975-76; *Antioch Review,* spring-summer, 1977; *American Poetry Review,* July-August, 1978; *Harper's,* May, 1979; *Atlantic,* June, 1979; *Open Places,* spring, 1980; *Ontario Review,* spring-summer, 1980; *Contemporary Literary Criticism,* Volume 18, Gale, 1981.

*   *   *

GALLANT, Christine C. 1940-

BRIEF ENTRY: Born July 25, 1940, in Toledo, Ohio. American educator and author. Gallant joined the faculty of the English department at Virginia Commonwealth University in 1977. She wrote *Blake and the Assimilation of Chaos* (Princeton University Press, 1978). *Address:* Department of English, Virginia Commonwealth University, 901 West Franklin St., Richmond, Va. 23284.

*   *   *

GANDEVIA, Bryan Harle 1925-

PERSONAL: Born April 5, 1925, in Melbourne, Australia; son of Eric Harle (a physician) and Vera (a nurse; maiden name, Hannah) Gandevia; married Dorothy Murphy (a medical practitioner), August 25, 1950; children: Simon Charles, Robin Harle. *Education:* University of Melbourne, M.B., B.S., 1948, M.D., 1953. *Home:* 109 Darling Point Rd., Darling Point, Sydney, New South Wales 2027, Australia. *Office:* Prince Henry Hospital, Sydney, New South Wales 2036, Australia.

CAREER: Served in various postgraduate appointments in Melbourne, Australia, 1950-54; served in postgraduate positions at Postgraduate Medical School, Hammersmith, England, and Institute for Diseases of the Chest, Brompton, England, and fellowship to Royal Australian College of Physicians, 1954-57; University of Melbourne, Parkville, Australia, senior fellow in occupational health, 1958-62; University of New South

Wales, Sydney, Australia, associate professor of thoracic medicine, 1963—. Member of council of Australian War Memorial, 1968—. *Military service:* Australian Army, Royal Australian Army Medical Corps, 1949-50; served with British Commonwealth Occupation Force in Japan and Korea; became major. *Member:* Royal Australasian College of Physicians (fellow), Faculty of the History and Philosophy of Medicine (fellow), Society of Apothecaries (London), Royal Society of Medicine (London; fellow), Naval and Military Club (Melbourne), Melbourne Cricket Club, Sydney Cricket Club.

WRITINGS: The Melbourne Medical Students, 1862-1942, Melbourne Medical Students Society, 1948; *An Annotated Bibliography of the History of Medicine in Australia,* Australasian Medical Publishing, 1957; *Tears Often Shed: Child Health and Welfare in Australia Since 1788,* Pergamon, 1978. Contributor to scientific journals and history magazines.

WORK IN PROGRESS: A medico-social history of Australia.

SIDELIGHTS: Gandevia told *CA:* ''I maintain a fervent belief in medical, epidemiological, and demographic data as the factual basis of social history. I advise medical students to meditate on the fourth phrase of the first Hippocratic aphorism (experience fallacious) in the hope that they do not discover its significance until after their need for didactic teaching is past.''

AVOCATIONAL INTERESTS: Collecting books; wine and food.

*   *   *

GARDINER, Mary Summerfield 1896-1982

OBITUARY NOTICE: Born September 28, 1896, in Garden City, N.Y.; died of congestive heart failure, April 1, 1982, in Washington, D.C. Biologist, educator, and author. A specialist in invertebrate biology, Gardiner taught at Bryn Mawr College for more than thirty-five years. She was the author of two textbooks, *The Principles of General Biology* and *The Biology of Invertebrates.* Obituaries and other sources: *Who's Who of American Women,* 5th edition, Marquis, 1968; *Washington Post,* April 3, 1982.

*   *   *

GARGAN, William Dennis 1905-1979

OBITUARY NOTICE: Born July 17, 1905, in Brooklyn, N.Y.; died of a heart attack on an airplane flight between New York City and San Diego, Calif., February 16, 1979. Actor and author. Gargan made his Broadway debut in 1925 and appeared in his first film in 1932. He was nominated for an Oscar in 1940 for his performance in the film ''They Knew What They Wanted.'' Gargan, who often played ''tough guy'' roles in war films and thrillers, was best known for his starring role in the television series ''Martin Kane, Private Eye.'' In 1960 Gargan contracted cancer of the larynx. Although the surgery he underwent was successful, it resulted in the loss of his ability to speak normally and so ended his acting career. But Gargan mastered esophageal speech—a ''controlled belch'' that enables people without larynxes to produce sounds—and devoted much of the next two decades to raising money for the American Cancer Society and working with laryngectomees. He wrote an autobiography, *Why Me?,* in 1969. Obituaries and other sources: William Gargan, *Why Me?,* Doubleday, 1969; *Current Biography,* Wilson, 1969, April, 1979; *Hollywood Players,* Volume I: *The Thirties,* Arlington House, 1976; *Los Angeles Times,* February 19, 1979; *Newsweek,* March 5, 1979.

GARRET, Maxwell R. 1917-

PERSONAL: Born April 18, 1917, in New York, N.Y.; son of Harry and Esther (Lieber) Goldstein; married Diana Rosen, April 3, 1943; children: Roger, Roberta, Esther, Bruce. *Education:* City College of New York (now of the City University of New York), B.Ed., 1939; University of Illinois, M.S., 1942; further study at Washington and Lee University, 1943 and 1945; accredited fencing master by the National Fencing Coaches Association of America. *Home:* 1261 University Dr., State College, Pa. 16801. *Office:* Pennsylvania State University, 267 Recreation Building, University Park, Pa. 16802.

CAREER: Teacher of health education at public schools in New York, N.Y., 1939-41 and 1946; University of Illinois, Urbana, instructor, 1947-53, assistant professor, 1953-58, associate professor of recreation, 1958-72, fencing coach, 1940-42 and 1946-72; Pennsylvania State University, University Park, associate professor of recreation and parks, 1972—, varsity fencing coach, 1972—. Director, Camp Illini, 1954-68, and Israel Academy for Fencing Teachers, 1969-70. U.S. fencing coach, World University Games, Torino, Italy, 1970, World Fencing Championships, Ankara, Turkey, 1970, Junior World Championships, South Bend, Ind., 1971, and Maccabiah Games, 1981. *Military service:* U.S. Army Air Forces, 1942-46.

MEMBER: National Recreation and Park Association, National Education Association, National Fencing Coaches Association of America (former president), U.S. Fencing Association, U.S. Academy of Arms, American Society of Testing and Materials, American Camping Association, American Youth Hostels, Pennsylvania Recreation and Park Association, B'nai B'rith, Alpha Epsilon Pi, Chi Gamma Iota, Phi Delta Kappa, Phi Epsilon Kappa. *Awards, honors:* Certificate of merit from the Amateur Fencers League of America, 1952; Fred K. Moskowitz Award from Central Illinois Council of B'nai B'rith, 1958; named B'nai B'rith man of the year, 1959; named fencing coach of the year, 1962 and 1965; named National Fencing Coach of Israel, 1969-70; inducted into City College of New York Athletic Hall of Fame, 1975; elected to Helm's Hall of Fame for Fencing.

WRITINGS: (Consultant) *How to Improve Your Fencing,* Athletic Institute, 1960; (with Mary F. Heinecke) *Fencing,* Sterling, 1961, revised edition, Allyn & Bacon, 1971; *Science-Hobby Book of Boating* (juvenile), Pastimes (Morton Grove, Ill.), 1967, revised edition, Lerner, 1968; (with Mary Heinecke Poulson) *Foil Fencing: Skills, Safety, Operations, and Responsibilities,* Pennsylvania State University, 1981.

Contributor of articles to journals, including *Parks and Recreation, Physical Educator, Illinois Parks, Pennsylvania Recreation and Parks.* Contributing editor, *American Fencing,* 1950-52; member of editorial board, *Physical Educator,* 1958-61, and *Mentor,* 1958-68.

SIDELIGHTS: Garret told *CA:* "Fencing, camping, and all forms of physical and cultural recreational activities should be considered lifelong pursuits. They can provide enjoyment, improved health, and well-being for all participants. I have always had a keen interest in helping young people to develop their utmost potential through such activities."

AVOCATIONAL INTERESTS: Athletics, carpentry, camping, dancing, reading, writing, music.

* * *

GASCOIGNE, Marguerite
See Lazarus, Marguerite

GASSET, Jose Ortega y
See ORTEGA y GASSET, Jose

* * *

GEHLBACH, Frederick Renner 1935-

PERSONAL: Born July 5, 1935, in Steubenville, Ohio; son of Wilbur A. and Dorothy Evelyn (Renner) Gehlbach; married Nancy Young, 1960; children: Gretchen, Mark. *Education:* Cornell University, A.B., 1957, M.S., 1959; University of Michigan, Ph.D., 1963. *Office:* Department of Biology, Baylor University, Waco, Tex. 76703.

CAREER: University of Michigan, Ann Arbor, lecturer in conservation, 1963; Baylor University, Waco, Tex., assistant professor, 1963-68, associate professor, 1968-79, professor of biology, 1979—. Vice-chairman of Texas Natural Areas Survey; fellow of Texas Citizens Committee on Natural Resources; consultant to National Park Service, Girl Scouts of America, and U.S. Fish and Wildlife Service.

MEMBER: American Society of Ichthyologists and Herpetologists, Ecological Society of America, American Ornithologist's Union, Herpetologists League (fellow; member of executive council, 1963-65), American Association for the Advancement of Science (fellow), Nature Conservancy (member of board of trustees), Southwestern Association of Naturalists (member of board of governors, 1971-74), Texas Academy of Science (fellow; vice-president for environmental sciences, 1967; member of board of directors, 1976-77), Texas Organization for Endangered Species (past president), Sigma Xi, Beta Beta Beta, Phi Sigma. *Awards, honors:* Grants from Sigma Xi, 1958, National Park Service, 1960, American Philosophical Society, 1966 and 1968, National Science Foundation, 1969, and National Geographic Society, 1971; Guggenheim fellowship, 1970-71.

WRITINGS: Mountain Islands and Desert Seas: A Natural History of the U.S.–Mexican Borderlands, Texas A & M University Press, 1981. Contributor of more than sixty articles to scientific journals and popular magazines. Member of editorial board of Herpetologists League, 1980-82.

WORK IN PROGRESS: A book on the natural history and cultural alterations of a wild ravine in the midst of suburban central Texas, based on Gehlbach's residence there since 1964.

SIDELIGHTS: Gehlbach told *CA:* "My operational philosophy is to combine logical and intuitive (left-and right-brained) approaches to the study of nature, to use modern quantitative techniques to verify repeated patterns, and to contrast the principals of natural history with those of culture so as to better understand man's role on his home planet."

* * *

GENAUER, Emily 1911-

PERSONAL: Born in 1911 in New York, N.Y.; daughter of Joseph and Rose (Milch) Genauer; married Frederick Gash (a broker), 1935; children: Constance Lee. *Education:* Attended Hunter College, 1926-29; Columbia School of Journalism, B.Lit., 1930. *Home:* 243 East 49th St., New York, N.Y. 10017.

CAREER: New York World, New York City, staff writer and art feature writer, 1929-31; *New York World-Telegram,* New York City, art critic and editor, 1932-49; *New York Herald*

Tribune, New York City, art critic, 1949-66; *New York World Journal Tribune,* New York City, editor and art critic, 1966-67; Newsday Syndicate, Long Island, N.Y., art critic and columnist, 1967-78; National Educational Television (NET), New York City, art commentator on program "City Edition," 1967-80. Lecturer. Member (appointed by President Johnson) of First National Council on the Humanities and National Foundation on Arts and Humanities, 1966-70. Member of executive board of Connecticut College School of Dance; member of board of directors of Martha Graham School of Contemporary Dance; member of advisory board of Columbia University School of Journalism. *Member:* International Association of Art Critics, New York Newspaper Women's Club. *Awards, honors:* New York Newspaper Women's Club award, 1937, for outstanding writing in a specialized field, 1949, 1956, 1958, 1960, and 1969, all for outstanding column in any field; journalism alumni award from Columbia University, 1960; Pulitzer Prize for distinguished criticism, 1974; numerous awards from universities and the Venice International Exhibition.

WRITINGS: (Author of introduction) Max Kalish, *Labor Sculpture,* M. Kalish, 1938; *Modern Interiors Today and Tomorrow: A Critical Analysis of Trends in Contemporary Decoration as Seen at the New York World's Fair,* Illustrated Editions Co., 1939; *Best of Art,* Doubleday, 1948; *Marc Chagall* (biography), Abrams, 1956; (author of introduction) Ed McCarthy, editor, *Hommage a l'ecole de Paris* (in English and French), Graphophile, 1962, revised edition, with text by Genauer, published as *Arbit Blatas' School of Paris,* Bresler & Small, 1964; *Charles Demuth of Lancaster* (exhibition catalogue), William Penn Memorial Museum, 1966; *Chagall at the Met,* Tudor, 1971; *Rufino Tamayo* (biography), Abrams, 1974; (editor and author of introduction) *American Ballet Theatre,* International Exhibitions Foundation, 1976. Contributor of articles to periodicals, including *Horizon, Geo, Harper's,* and *Art in America.*

WORK IN PROGRESS: A book of memoirs, publication expected in 1983.

CA INTERVIEW

CA interviewed Emily Genauer in her Manhattan townhouse on January 5, 1981.

Emily Genauer has the singular honor of being the only individual ever to win the Pulitzer Prize for distinguished art criticism. Her career as an art journalist and critic spans half of a century: "Longer than any critic now writing in *any* area," she proudly asserts. During this time she garnered many other awards commenting, reviewing, and reporting on an exciting sequence of events in the American and European art world ranging from Picasso's early fame and the Works Progress Administration's (WPA) art projects to abstract expressionism and subsequent art movements. She has witnessed profound innovations as well as revivals of earlier styles while modernist art flowered. She has formed friendships with many of the great artists involved in these developments, such as Henry Moore, Marc Chagall, Rufino Tamayo, David Smith, and Louise Nevelson. The works of these artists adorn Genauer's home as striking remembrances of her associations.

Despite her success, Genauer did not anticipate art criticism as her primary career, but journalism. With her father an amateur sculptor and half her family owners of an art gallery, she originally intended to become a "Sunday" sculptor. After studies in art history and sculpture, she decided she "was not good enough." She turned instead to journalism and attended the Columbia University Graduate School of Journalism. She had

thought to write about politics but, before long, her background steered her towards writing about art.

From 1929, when Genauer's first free-lance pieces appeared in the *New York Times,* her career—although punctuated by the sales, mergers, and deaths of New York's various newspapers over the past five decades—has never missed a beat. In the early 1930's she wrote articles on art for the Sunday morning *New York World.* These articles were also syndicated by the North American Newspaper Alliance. Forbes Watson, art editor of the *World,* also had her interview artists such as Edward Hopper and John Marin, among others, thus iniating what was to be one of the staples of her career.

When, in 1931, the *World* was sold to the *Telegram,* "which at the time was popular and primarily a sports sheet," the newly created *World Telegram* hired her, "because," according to Genauer, "they felt that to gain circulation and advertising they needed some class." What the paper wanted at the beginning were columns on collectors' homes, but after one week she began to do a full weekly page of art reviews. "The first one was on a show of the sculptor Isamu Noguchi's work," she remembers. Within six months she was writing regular reviews of all shows and continued to do so as an editor/art critic for the next seventeen years, until she resigned in 1949, when the newspaper's publisher, Roy Howard, became convinced by some academic illustrator friends that all modern art was Communist. Howard referred to her 1949 review of the Picasso retrospective at the Museum of Modern Art (Picasso was a member of the Communist party), and asked, "Why do you write about these paintings?" She recalls answering: "I just review them; I don't paint them." After turning down placating offers by the *World Telegram* to take on tasks other than art reviewing, such as writing editorials, she resigned to accept a long-standing offer from the *New York Herald Tribune* to serve as its chief art critic in the post occupied by the renowned Royal Cortissoz until his death.

The break was a difficult one. Genauer had worked at the *World Telegram* for seventeen years, acquiring much power in that time and gaining control over the arts and leisure page and a voice in all cultural departments: to illustrate how prominent her position was, Genauer showed *CA* some carefully folded, tattered papers, which she had placed in her files many years ago. They were enormous promotional banners featuring a photograph of Genauer wearing a broad-brimmed hat. Her name accompanied her portrait in huge block letters placed above the name of the newspaper itself, set in noticeably smaller print. "They were pasted on the sides of city buses and delivery trucks for years," the journalist recalls with wry amusement. But Genauer was extremely pleased to be working for the *New York Herald Tribune.* In retrospect, her only regret at leaving the *World Telegram* was that, in anger, she left so hastily. She didn't take time to clean out her desk and files, thereby abandoning many valuable and historically important letters from well-known artists with whom she had corresponded.

For another seventeen-year stint, Genauer was the art critic and editorialist on other cultural subjects at the *Herald Tribune.* In 1966 the paper was merged with the *World Telegram,* creating the *New York World Journal Tribune.* "I found myself in the absurd position of returning to the very same office I had worked in thirty-four years earlier." She remained there, however, until the newspaper folded in 1967, and then accepted an offer from Harry Guggenheim, owner of the Newsday Syndicate (also owner of *Newsday* newspaper), to write a column of art criticism that touched on the other arts—especially dance and theatre—to make for the first interdisciplinary column to be published in the country.

Her column ran in the *New York Post* during these years despite the fact, Genauer explained, that the *Post* normally did not publish Newsday Syndicate material because Newsday felt anything appearing within fifty miles of its own area of circulation represented competition. The *Post* avoided the snag by calculating the trip via a circuitous route. When Rupert Murdoch became owner of the newspaper in 1977, Genauer refused to appear in the *Post* and then decided to stop writing the column altogether.

After Genauer quit the Newsday Syndicate in 1978, the *New York Times* offered her a position. Arthur Gelb, then the managing editor, asked her to write a column on the houses of famous art collectors for the home section of the paper as well as write criticism. As such, Genauer felt the column would represent a return to what she had done over forty years before and so refused the assignment. Nevertheless, the veteran journalist misses what she terms "the excitement of each day being different," when regularly reviewing and writing for a newspaper.

When asked to name some art writers who have influenced her, Genauer cites Watson, her first editor at the *New York World*. Other writers who have had an impact on her work include such nineteenth-century historian-critics as Crowe and Cavalcaselle, John Ruskin, Baudelaire, and Jacob Burckhardt, in addition to the twentieth-century writers Bernard Berenson and R. H. Wilenski. She also named Sheldon Cheney, John Dewey, and especially Edgar Wind with great enthusiasm, mentioning in particular his Reith lectures at Oxford, which were published as *Art and Anarchy* in 1963.

What about her influence on others as an art writer? Genauer is always gratified to learn from readers of her columns that she had helped them to look really closely and see things for pleasure and with knowledge. "Newspapers have that impact. Working on a paper meant I could regularly speak my piece. I miss that." As a critic Genauer has concerned herself with architecture as well as painting and sculpture. She feels she was able to create in this area a climate in which new things could function and prosper. For example, she admired the new Guggenheim Museum designed by Frank Lloyd Wright, which so many people objected to at the time it was built. "I wrote a front-page column lauding it," Genauer remarked. She wanted to force people to see how effective it was as a working museum and "to be able to go with something new." On the other hand, she also campaigned in a first-page column against Marcel Breuer's design for a building to be erected on top of Grand Central Station. She feels her opposition to the proposal, together with that of Ada Louise Huxtable's in the *New York Times,* effectively helped kill the project.

Genauer takes special pleasure in recalling the impact she had in unexpected quarters, which she sometimes discovered long after the fact. She told of an incident involving the well-known sculptor Tony Smith. Reviewing a show of his early abstract work which featured blocks that looked like pedestals, she quipped, "Here are the pedestals, but where is the sculpture?" The sculptor chided her for the review at a party some time later, but also revealed that he owed her a great debt. Smith explained that years before, Genauer wrote an article on the role of detail in contemporary architecture in which she used as an example a home she had rented for the summer. Unknown to her, the dwelling had been designed by Smith. "I was an obscure architect at that time," Smith asserted. "No one had singled me out, but you did. You knew me without a name."

In the field of present-day art criticism, Genauer is reluctant to discuss the work of specific writers. She objects strongly to those critics who address their comments to artist, telling them what to do, wanting to improve on their work. Rather, she contends, the art consumer, the general public, not the artist, should be addressed. "The critic's duty is to look carefully at a picture, describe and assess all the objective evidence, which might include the historical background, so that people can make up their own minds." She regrets that so many younger critics are ignorant of the past. "One trouble with too much recent art criticism is that it makes great new discoveries of people we have known all our lives." She cited the great praise lavished by young critics on Arshile Gorky's work for its originality, without recognition or acknowledgement of his great debt to surrealists such as Joan Miro and Matta.

Commenting on her own volumes of art criticism, Genauer dismissed her first endeavor, the introduction to her former teacher Max Kalish's book, *Labor Sculpture,* as being about academic art. *Modern Interiors Today and Tomorrow* examines the contemporary trend in interior decoration, or Art Deco, as it is known today, as it was reflected at the Paris Exposition of 1925 and the 1939 New York World's Fair. With the mention of the heavily illustrated book, Genauer recalled a television interview she once conducted with pop artist Roy Lichtenstein. On camera, Lichtenstein informed the surprised critic that she had been the greatest influence on him. He singled out *Modern Interiors* and its discussion of the new style of modern design. The artist maintained that her volume and art deco have had an enormous and lasting impact on his work.

Asked to reconcile the title of her 1949 volume, *Best of Art,* with its contents, which includes several extensive references to artists whose work has not endured beyond that time period, Genauer explained that the original conception of the book was modeled after the annual publication of Burns Mantle's selection of *Ten Best Plays*. "The idea was to do that for art, with an analysis of each picture, rather than to present the artists as all-time 'bests.'" But Doubleday decided yearly publication was impractical because of the cost of color reproductions and changed the title without consulting her, so that it suggests a more long-term assessment of art. Genauer refers readers to the introduction, which accurately describes the book's original intention and to the text accompanying each selection, which presents a cross section of the artists' thinking at the time, as well as their relationship to the recent past and their ideas about future possibilities.

Genauer's monographs on Charles Demuth, Marc Chagall, and Rufino Tamayo had been requested by the publishers who knew of her friendships with each of the artists. Taking a worn, creased photograph from a drawer, Genauer identified Rufino Tamayo, his wife Olga, herself, and her husband Frederick Gash on vacation together in Mexico forty years ago. "We all started out together," she reflected. "We married in 1935 and have remained friendly throughout the years." Critics claim her book on Tamayo is one of the best introductions to the artist's work in print in English.

There have been many other book offers that she has turned down. Discussing the distinction between art journalism and art history, Genauer noted that "a publisher wanted me to do a book on Turner on the basis of an article of mine that he admired." "I turned it down, because I would have had to spend at least a year researching and writing it," she explained. "Sometimes publishers don't have a clue about the work or expertise involved when they suggest that someone do a book. They mistakenly think that because you can write a good column about someone, you can just as easily turn out a book on them."

Genauer works in her high-ceilinged study, which is lined from top to bottom with art books, requiring a tall stepladder to reach the upper shelves. Her collection of art books spills over into the adjacent room, also covering entire walls there. She notes that she has given quantities of them to the Smith College Library and to the Memorial Museum of the University of Rochester, as well as to others. The author is currently at work on her memoirs, which will be ''about people I have known— artists like David Smith, Brancusi, Giacometti, Jacques Lipchitz, and Henry Moore—during the past fifty years, rather than about myself.'' She admits that she gets easily diverted from her project by lucrative offers to lecture and write magazine articles. Genauer insists on always looking forward. After a recent bout with illness, she has happily resumed her energetic gallery hopping to keep abreast of new developments.

—*Interview by Barbara Braun*

* * *

GENTLE, Mary 1956-

PERSONAL: Born March 29, 1956, in Eastbourne, East Sussex, England; daughter of George William (a cinema manager) and Amy Mary (Champion) Gentle. *Education:* Attended high school in Hastings, East Sussex, England. *Politics:* ''Feminist.'' *Home:* Flat No. 1, 11 Alumhurst Rd., Westbourne, Bournemouth, Dorset, England.

CAREER: Author. Has worked as assistant movie projectionist, clerk for a wholesale bookseller, and civil servant. *Member:* Bournemouth Writers Circle (secretary, 1979-80).

WRITINGS: A Hawk in Silver (young adult novel), Gollancz, 1977. Contributor of reviews and articles to *Vector*.

WORK IN PROGRESS: A science fiction novel for young adults, tentatively entitled *Star of Africa*.

SIDELIGHTS: Mary Gentle told *CA:* ''I was writing for a good long while before I realized it was a serious occupation. Since then it has taken up progressively larger amounts of my time, though I am a lazy writer and should be chained forcibly to a typewriter. In short, I hate writing, but love having written. One of my avocational interests is gainful employment!''

* * *

GEORGE, Eugene
See CHEVALIER, Paul Eugene George

* * *

GERGELY, Tibor 1900-1978

OBITUARY NOTICE: Born August 3, 1900, in Budapest, Hungary; died January 13, 1978, in New York, N.Y. Painter, graphic artist, and illustrator of children's books. Gergely was a successful artist, illustrator, and cartoonist in Europe before coming to the United States in 1939. Thereafter, he worked mainly as a commercial artist and as an illustrator of children's books, including Margaret Wise Brown's *Wheel on the Chimney*, a runner-up for the Caldecott Medal in 1955. Obituaries and other sources: *Illustrators of Children's Books, 1744-1945,* Horn Book, 1945, reprinted, 1970; *Illustrators of Children's Books, 1946-1956,* Horn Book, 1958; *Illustrators of Books for Young People,* 2nd edition, Scarecrow, 1975; *Publishers Weekly,* January 30, 1978.

* * *

GHOSE, Amal 1929-
(Lama Esohg)

PERSONAL: Born May 19, 1929, in Undivided Old Bengal (now Bangladesh); son of Manmatha Nath and Sarala Devi Ghose; married Prity Chakraborty (a dance and music academy principal), 1956; children: Dipankar, Nabarun. *Religion:* ''Universalism.'' *Home and office:* Diparun, T-29 Seventh Ave., Besant Nagar, Madras 600 090, India; and *Ocarina* and Tagore Institute of Creative Writing International (TICWI), T-29B Seventh Ave., Besant Nagar, Madras 600 090, India. *Agent:* Laser Services, National Biographical Centre, India-Asia.

CAREER: Special correspondent for *Jungantar* and *Amarita Bazar Patrika,* newspapers in Calcutta, India, 1950-74. Founder and director of Laser Services. Consultant. *Member:* Leonardo da Vinci Academy, Cinq Ports Poets (England). *Awards, honors:* D. Litt. from World Academy of Languages and Literature, 1972, for *Ruby and Rouge* and *So Many Roses;* Ph.D. from Academy of Philosophy (U.S.A.).

WRITINGS—All in English, except as noted: *Ruby and Rouge* (poems), Diparun, 1969; *Pebbles and Pearls* (novel), Diparun, 1971; *So Many Roses* (poems), Diparun, 1972; *Flames of Agonies* (poems), Diparun, 1973; *Art: I Adore* (art book), Diparun, 1973; *The Depth* (five-act drama), Diparun, 1974; *Bouquet of Amaranths* (poems), Diparun, 1976; *Living-Loving-Green* (poems), Tagore Institute of Creative Writing International (TICWI), 1981; (with Sri Lankan) *Beauty That Never Fades* (travel), Rajesh Publications, 1981; (in Bengali) *Debabhumi Dahshin* (travel), A. Mukherj, 1981.

Editor: *Motoring Guide of India,* Automobile Association of Eastern India, 1970; *Who's Who of Indian Women, International,* National Biographical Centre, 1977; (with Sandra Fowler) *The Album of International Poets* (anthology), TICWI, 1981; (with Fowler and Stella Browning) *Eve's Eden* (anthology), TICWI, in press. Also editor of ''Friendship Bridge'' anthology series, including *Friendship Bridge, The Japonica Sings, The Eastern Sun Is So Inviting,* and *Flowers of Great Southland.*

Author of poems and reviews under pseudonym Lama Esohg.

Editor of *Ocarina: English Poetry Journal of International Poems,* 1969—.

WORK IN PROGRESS: The Birth of the Album, publication by TICWI expected in 1984; two research projects involving Indian history and Indo-American basic commitment to democracy and democratic living.

SIDELIGHTS: Ghose, who is conversant in four languages, told *CA* that his ''entire motivation is aimed at universal manhood and inspiring others to give their best to bring reality to intellectual friendship, to remove (as far as is practicable) pettiness from creative minds, and to flood the world with a beacon of the heart's greatness, not merely in words but in creative action.

''To serve humanity and mankind without any reservation or bias has been the most important factor in my career. From a tender age I have had the feeling that nothing equals creativity in the subtlest sense of the word. Men and women may earn riches and wealth and employ them to grab power, but creativity alone stands above all for all time. This prompted me to begin writing, not for making money, but for superb ecstacy.

''I write like passing through nature's wonders at ease, without any routine or plan. Anytime is good for my writing, either by day or by night. Sometimes, when I begin writing a novel or essay, I feel restless until I bring the piece to a satisfactory conclusion.

''I have been influenced by Shakespeare, Rabindranath Tagore, Dostoevski, and a few French authors, but I have always been interested in going ahead in exploring the depth and magnitude, mysteries and majestic traits, and feeling and potentiality of the human mind. No doubt, epic authors' unbounded love for humanity and the ever-living presence of their concepts inspire me to add a little more to the treasure of civilization's store.

"Nowadays most of our contemporary writers try to fool the readers in general and intellectuals in particular by mere superlatives and tall talk. Very few are truly keen about developing international understanding and wiping out narrowness of so-called educated and power-mad minds that always exploit the mean tendencies dwelling in ordinary human beings. Many things go marching on in the name of world organizations, but very few keep their aim fixed at unspoiled universalism. Creative quality is the first victim, closely followed by the slaughter of real humanism and pure compassion. I wish that writers would search their own hearts and seek feelings rather than parade pollutions purchased from trash as best-sellers."

*   *   *

GIAMATTI, Valentine   1911-1982

OBITUARY NOTICE: Born February 9, 1911, in New Haven, Conn.; died March 17, 1982, in Bonita Springs, Fla. Educator and author. A professor of Italian at Mount Holyoke College for more than thirty years, Giamatti was an expert on the life and works of Dante. His books include *A Panoramic View of Dante's Inferno, A Panoramic View of Dante's Purgatory,* and *A Panoramic View of Dante's Paradise.* Obituaries and other sources: *Who's Who in America,* 38th edition, Marquis, 1974; *Directory of American Scholars,* Volume III: *Foreign Languages, Linguistics, and Philology,* 7th edition, Bowker, 1978; *New York Times,* March 19, 1982.

*   *   *

GIAUQUE, William Francis   1895-1982

OBITUARY NOTICE: Born May 12, 1895, in Niagara Falls, Ontario, Canada; died after a brief illness, March 28, 1982, in Oakland, Calif. Chemist, educator, and author. Giauque won the Nobel Prize in chemistry in 1949 for his research on the properties of chemicals at extremely low temperatures. His findings have had many important industrial applications, leading to improvements in gasoline, steel, rubber, and glass. Giauque was the author of *Low Temperature, Chemical, and Magneto Thermodynamics.* Obituaries and other sources: *Newsweek,* November 14, 1949; *Saturday Evening Post,* December 10, 1949; *Current Biography,* Wilson, 1950; May, 1982; *Chicago Tribune,* March 31, 1982.

*   *   *

GIBLIN, James Cross   1933-

PERSONAL: Surname is pronounced with a hard "g"; born July 8, 1933, in Cleveland, Ohio; son of Edward Kelley (a lawyer) and Anna (a teacher; maiden name, Cross) Giblin. *Education:* Case Western Reserve University, B.A., 1954; Columbia University, M.F.A., 1955. *Home:* 200 East 24th St., Apt. 1410, New York, N.Y. 10010. *Office:* Clarion Books, 52 Vanderbilt Ave., New York, N.Y. 10017.

CAREER: Criterion Books, Inc., New York City, assistant editor, 1959-62; Lothrop, Lee & Shepard Co., New York City, associate editor, 1962-65, editor, 1965-67; Seabury Press, Inc., New York City, editor-in-chief of Clarion Books (for children), 1967-79, vice-president, 1975-79; Ticknor & Fields, New York City, editor and publisher of Clarion Books, 1979—. Adjunct professor at Graduate Center of the City University of New

York, 1979—. *Member:* Society of Children's Book Writers (member of board of directors), Children's Book Council (president, 1976), U.S.-China People's Friendship Association. *Awards, honors: The Scarecrow Book* and *The Skyscraper Book* were each named "notable children's book" by American Library Association in 1981 and 1982, respectively.

WRITINGS—For children: *The Scarecrow Book,* Crown, 1980; *The Skyscraper Book,* Crowell, 1981; *Chimney Sweeps, Yesterday and Today,* Crowell, 1982; *Fireworks, Picnics, and Flags,* Clarion Books, 1983; *Walls: Defenses Throughout History,* Crowell, 1983.

For adults: *My Bus Is Always Late* (one-act play; first produced in Cleveland, Ohio, at Western Reserve University, December 14, 1953), Dramatic Publishing, 1955. Contributor to magazines, including *Writer's Digest, Cricket, School Library Journal, Horn Book,* and *Publishers Weekly.* Member of editorial board of *Children's Literature in Education.*

SIDELIGHTS: Giblin commented: "Nonfiction books for children aged eight to twelve give me the opportunity to pursue my research interests, meet interesting and stimulating experts in various fields, and share my enthusiasms with a young audience. I try to write books that I would have enjoyed reading when I was the age of my readers.

"In college I trained as an actor and playwright, which might seem a far cry from the work I'm doing now. But when, as an editor, I suggest to an author that she give a character a stronger entrance in a novel, or when, as an author, I inject authentic dialogue into a nonfiction text, I realize that I'm utilizing dramatic techniques I learned long ago. The job of an editor isn't really so far removed from that of a theatrical director. And authors of books have much in common with playwrights. Of course they don't have actors to help them get across their points—they have to do it all by themselves. But having written books as well as plays, I think that's more often a blessing than a handicap."

BIOGRAPHICAL/CRITICAL SOURCES: Chicago Tribune Book World, April 11, 1982.

*   *   *

GIFFORD, Terry   1946-

PERSONAL: Born June 28, 1946, in Cambridge, England; son of Dennis (a gardener) and Edna (White) Gifford; married Judith Hickling (a teacher), August, 1968; children: Tom, Ruth. *Education:* Sheffield City College of Education, Certificate of Education, 1967; University of Lancaster, B. Ed. (with honors), 1973; University of Sheffield, M.A., 1978. *Politics:* Labour. *Home:* 66 St. Quentin Dr., Sheffield S17 4PP, Yorkshire, England.

CAREER: Teacher in grammar school in Sheffield, England, 1967; British Broadcasting Corporation (BBC-Radio), Sheffield, seconded teacher, 1970-71; Yewlands Comprehensive School, Sheffield, head of English department, 1979—. Chairman of Sheffield English 'A' level syllabus of Joint Matriculation Board.

WRITINGS: (Contributor) John Macbeath, editor, *A Question of Schooling,* Hodder & Stoughton, 1976; (with Neil Roberts) *Ted Hughes: A Critical Study,* Faber, 1981; (contributor) Keith Sagar, editor, *The Achievement of Ted Hughes,* Manchester University Press, 1983.

Contributor of articles on Brecht, teenage literature, social education, and Thomas Hardy to journals.

WORK IN PROGRESS: Poems; an edition of John Donne's love poems.

BIOGRAPHICAL/CRITICAL SOURCES: Times Literary Supplement, July 24, 1981.

*   *   *

GILBAR, Steven 1941-

PERSONAL: Born August 7, 1941, in Detroit, Mich.; son of A. Marvin (an optometrist) and Sylvia (Broudy) Gilbar; married Deborah Weiner (a social worker), August 26, 1974; children: Sky Marin. *Education:* University of Michigan, B.A., 1963; Wayne State University, J.D., 1966. *Agent:* Maria Carvainis Agency, 235 West End Ave., New York, N.Y. 10023.

CAREER: Practicing lawyer, 1967-72; Matthew Mender & Co. (in publishing), San Francisco, Calif., senior managing editor, 1973-77; writer. *Member:* California Bar Association.

WRITINGS: The Book Blue (nonfiction), St. Martin's, 1981.

WORK IN PROGRESS: An annotated book guide, publication by Ticknor & Fields expected in 1982.

SIDELIGHTS: Gilbar's *The Book Blue* is a collection of literary anecdotes and trivia. A *Washington Post Book World* reviewer called it ''good fun and games for bibliophagists.''

Gilbar told *CA:* ''I have constructively combined what were formerly aberrations—bibliophilia and list-making—into a career as an antiquarian and popular bibliographer. I desire to save books that have been unjustly ignored or forgotten and bring them to the attention of a new generation of readers. I see myself as a 'recycler' of literature who believes too many of the niagara of books published each year are superfluous when there are already so many fine books begging for readers.''

BIOGRAPHICAL/CRITICAL SOURCES: Washington Post Book World, September 27, 1981.

*   *   *

GILBERT, Anna
See Lazarus, Marguerite

*   *   *

GILBERT, David T(hompson) 1953-

PERSONAL: Born April 5, 1953, in New Haven, Conn.; son of Alfred C., Jr., and Jean (Tibbetts) Gilbert. *Education:* University of Virginia, B.A., 1975. *Home address:* Route 3, Box 514, Harpers Ferry, W.Va. 25425. *Office:* River and Trail Outfitters, Box 246, Valley Rd., Knoxville, Md. 21758.

CAREER: American Youth Hostels, Washington, D.C., trip leader, summers, 1974-75, executive director of Potomac Area Council, 1975-77, trip leader, summer, 1978; River and Trail Outfitters, Knoxville, Md., head river guide, 1978—, cross-country ski instructor, 1979—. Director of Kiwanis Hostel, 1977-81. *Member:* Phi Beta Kappa.

WRITINGS: (Editor) *Greater Washington Area Bicycle Atlas,* Potomac Area Council of American Youth Hostels, 2nd edition (Gilbert was not associated with 1st edition), 1977; *Rivers and Trails,* Outdoor Press, 1978; *Exploring Potomac Water Gap,* Outdoor Press, 1979; *American Bicycle Atlas,* Dutton, 1980; (contributor) *Bicycling's Best Tours,* Rodale Press, 1980. Contributor to *Country.*

WORK IN PROGRESS: Walker's Guide to Harpers Ferry; Gristmills of the Potomac River Valley.

SIDELIGHTS: Gilbert wrote: ''My professional involvement in outdoor recreation and experiential education has presented to me a profusion of people and places, which I enjoy rendering into written form. By so doing, I make it possible for other people to enjoy outdoor sports, either actively or vicariously—such sports as bicycling, hiking, or general outdoor exploring.

''I also want to present topics of history and nature in such a way that people can discover these things by getting out of doors and seeing them firsthand.''

*   *   *

GILBERT, Felix 1905-

BRIEF ENTRY: Born May 21, 1905, in Baden-Baden, Germany (now West Germany). American historian, educator, and author. Gilbert worked as a research analyst for the Office of Strategic Services and the U.S. Department of State for about fifteen years. He was a professor at the School of Historical Studies at the Institute for Advanced Study in Princeton, N.J., from 1962 to 1975. His books include the *Dictionary of the History of Ideas* (Scribner, 1973), *The Historical Essays of Otto Hintze* (Oxford University Press, 1975), *History: Choice and Commitment* (Belknap Press, 1977), and *The Pope, His Banker, and Venice* (Harvard University Press, 1980). *Address:* 266 Mercer St., Princeton, N.J. 08540; and School of Historical Studies, Institute for Advanced Study, Princeton, N.J. 08540. *Biographical/critical sources: Directory of American Scholars,* Volume I: *History,* 7th edition, Bowker, 1978; *Who's Who in America,* 40th edition, Marquis, 1978.

*   *   *

GILBERT, Harry 1946-

PERSONAL: Born January 18, 1946, in Pembroke, Ontario, Canada; son of Charles (a physicist) and Irene (a teacher of French; maiden name, Gunn) Gilbert; married Supasri Chantra, May 19, 1979. *Education:* University of Sussex, B.A., 1967. *Residence:* London, England. *Agent:* Strathmore Literary Agency, 145 Park Rd., St. John's Wood, London N.W. 8, England.

CAREER: Teacher of English at grammar school in Lewes, Sussex, England, 1967-68; lifeguard, 1970; driver, 1970; security guard, 1971; teacher of English as a foreign language at a private school in Pescara, Italy, 1971-72; railway ticket clerk, 1973-74; Westminster College, London, England, teacher of English as a foreign language, 1976—.

WRITINGS: Sarah's Nest (science fiction), Faber, 1981.

WORK IN PROGRESS: Kissing Cousins, a science fiction novel; *The Pod,* a science fiction novel; *So-What and What-If,* a juvenile science fiction novel; *Ghost Twin,* a juvenile; *The Man in the Height of Fashion,* a suspense novel.

SIDELIGHTS: Sarah's Nest, Gilbert's 1981 science fiction novel, tells the story of a fourteen-year-old girl with family problems who enters an ant colony in the body of an ant with her human thought processes intact. The *London Sunday Times* observed that in *Sarah's Nest* ''the analogy between ants and humans works, not in scientific terms but as an insistent metaphor for the sanctions and drives which exist in family relationships.''

Gilbert told *CA:* ''Early reading of science fiction (such as *Astounding Science Fiction*) stimulated me to write stories. I kept writing until *Sarah's Nest* was published. Now I devote half my day to writing and half to teaching. When it becomes financially possible, I will become a professional writer. My dream would be to live half the year in Thailand (my wife's country of origin) and the other half in England.''

BIOGRAPHICAL/CRITICAL SOURCES: London Sunday Times, April 19, 1981.

* * *

GILBERT, Manu
See WEST, Joyce (Tarlton)

* * *

GILES, C(harles) W(ilfred) Scott
See SCOTT-GILES, C(harles) W(ilfred)

* * *

GILKYSON, Bernice Kenyon   1898(?)-1982
(Bernice Kenyon)

OBITUARY NOTICE: Born c. 1898 in Oakside, N.Y.; died May 12, 1982, in Winsted, Conn. Editor and poet. Gilkyson, who wrote under the name Bernice Kenyon, was ranked as one of America's best young women poets in the 1920's and 1930's. She published four volumes of verse, *Songs of Unrest, Meridian, Night Sky,* and *Mortal Music,* the last finished just before her death. She also wrote the libretto for Efrem Zimbalist's opera ''Landara.'' Gilkyson worked as a story editor for *Scribner's* magazine and, as an editorial assistant to Maxwell Perkins of Scribner's book division, worked with such authors as Ernest Hemingway and F. Scott Fitzgerald. Obituaries and other sources: *New York Times,* May 15, 1982.

* * *

GILL, Dominic   1941-

PERSONAL: Born June 8, 1941, in London, England; son of Donald Lee (an economist) and Joyce E. (Fagan) Gill; married Elizabeth Landau (a historian), December 9, 1967; children: Benjamin, Ayala. *Education:* Attended Oxford University, 1961; Royal Academy of Music, L.R.A.M., 1966. *Residence:* London, England. *Agent:* David Higham Associates Ltd., 5/8 Lower John St., Golden Sq., London W1R 4HA, England.

CAREER: Free-lance music critic, 1967-69; *Financial Times,* London, England, music critic, 1969—. Visiting professor at City University, 1978—; broadcaster for British Broadcasting Corp.

WRITINGS: (Editor) *The Book of the Piano,* Cornell University Press, 1980. Contributor to music journals.

* * *

GILL, John Edward   1938-

PERSONAL: Born August 31, 1938, in Trenton, N.J.; son of John Goodner (an educator) and Verna (Lindert) Gill; married Ann Pinson Clarke, July 29, 1967 (divorced October 8, 1976); children: Alison Lindert. *Education:* University of Virginia, B.A., 1961; San Francisco State University, M.A., 1971. *Politics:* Democrat. *Religion:* Protestant. *Home:* 19 Maple Ave., Stony Brook, N.Y. 11290. *Office:* Department of English, Suffolk College, 533 College Rd., Selden, N.Y. 11284.

CAREER: Paterson Call, Paterson, N.J., reporter, 1967; University of California, Berkeley, director of publications, 1968; free-lance writer and speechwriter, San Francisco, Calif., 1968-

71; Suffolk College, Selden, N.Y., instructor, 1971-74, assistant professor, 1974-78, associate professor of English, 1978—. President of Children's Rights of New York, 1977—. *Military service:* U.S. Marine Corps, 1961-64; became first lieutenant. *Member:* Authors Guild.

WRITINGS: Stolen Children: How and Why Parents Kidnap Their Kids—And What to Do About It, Seaview, 1981.

SIDELIGHTS: Gill's book grew out of a personal experience in 1975, which led him to establish Children's Rights of New York.

BIOGRAPHICAL/CRITICAL SOURCES: Newsday, March 7, 1977, September 18, 1980; *New York Daily News,* April 3, 1977; *New York Post,* June 17, 1977; *New York Times,* October 17, 1977.

* * *

GILLIS, Daniel   1935-

PERSONAL: Born September 25, 1935, in New Bedford, Mass.; son of Angus Dan (a cable splicer) and Mary Margaret (a nurse; maiden name, Campbell) Gillis. *Education:* Harvard University, B.A., 1957; attended Free University of Berlin, 1957-58; Cornell University, M.A., 1959, Ph.D., 1963; postdoctoral study at University of Munich, 1963-64. *Politics:* Democrat. *Religion:* Roman Catholic. *Home:* 4141 Terrace St., Philadelphia, Pa. 19128. *Office:* Department of Classics, Haverford College, Haverford, Pa. 19041.

CAREER: Brown University, Providence, R.I., instructor in classics, 1959-60; University of Texas at Austin, assistant professor of classics, 1964-65; Swarthmore College, Swarthmore, Pa., visiting assistant professor, 1965-66; Haverford College, Haverford, Pa., assistant professor, 1966-70, associate professor, 1970-76, professor of classics, 1976—. *Member:* American Philological Association, American Association of University Professors.

WRITINGS: (Editor) *Furtwaengler Recalled,* John DeGraff, 1966; *Furtwaengler and America,* Manyland Books, 1970; *Collaboration With the Persians,* Franz Steiner, 1979; *Vita,* Ramparts, 1979; *Furtwaengler,* Iona Foundation, 1982; *Eros and Death in the Aeneid,* Bretschneider, 1982; *Measure of a Man,* Iona Foundation, 1982. Contributor of about fifteen articles to classical journals.

WORK IN PROGRESS: The Pity of Power.

SIDELIGHTS: Gillis commented: ''There is a Greco-Roman-Germanic-Celtic blend in my literary interests, with Scottish-Gaelic deepening.''

* * *

GILMAN, Charlotte (Anna) Perkins (Stetson)   1860-1935

BRIEF ENTRY: Born July 3, 1860, in Hartford, Conn.; committed suicide, August 17, 1935, in Pasadena, Calif.; cremated and ashes scattered. American lecturer and author. Gilman's feminist views became apparent with the publication of her first major book, *Women and Economics* (1898), the work upon which her literary reputation is most solidly based. Popular throughout the world, the book, an appeal for the financial independence of women, came at a time when women were just beginning to venture from their traditional places at home. Gilman was a co-founder of the Women's Peace Party in 1915 and leaned toward socialism, though active social and political involvement was always secondary to her writing and public speaking activities. She supported women's suffrage but wrote about issues she felt were more vital. In *Concerning Children* (1900), for example, Gilman set forth her theory that children should be cared for collectively by women well-suited for the job, not necessarily their own mothers. *Human Work* (1904) was her glorification of work as an end in itself, and in *Man-Made World* (1911) she asserted her view of the social and intellectual superiority of women. Gilman's outspoken books and lectures earned her a firm place in American literature and a dominant position in the early development of American feminism. *Biographical/critical sources:* Charlotte Perkins Gilman, *The Living of Charlotte Perkins Gilman: An Autobiography,* Appleton, 1935; *Notable American Women, 1607-1950: A Biographical Dictionary,* Belknap Press, 1971.

*   *   *

GIPPIUS, Zinaida (Nikolayevna)   1869-1945
(Zinaida Hippius, Zinaida Merezhkovsky)

BRIEF ENTRY: Born in 1869 in Belevo, Russia (now U.S.S.R.); died in 1945 in Paris, France. Russian poet, novelist, and essayist. Gippius was noted for her sharp-tongued criticisms, which often alienated her contemporaries. One of her best-known books, *Zhivye litsa* (1925), contained vignettes about the Russian poets Gippius had known. Although some critics thought the essays spiteful, others regarded them as insightful commentaries about the poets' lives. Gippius wrote poems about the harshness of daily life, the mysticism she shared with her husband, poet Dmitri Merezhkovsky, and the eventual victory of justice and love over man's miserable temporal existence. Her intellectual and technical skills, evident in such verse collections as *Sobranniye stikhov* (1904) and *Siyaniya* (1938), have earned her a reputation as one of Russia's finest female poets. *Biographical/critical sources: Cassell's Encyclopaedia of World Literature,* revised edition, Morrow, 1973; *Who's Who in Twentieth Century Literature,* Holt, 1976.

*   *   *

GIRLING, John L(awrence) S(cott)   1926-

PERSONAL: Born May 21, 1926, in Farnborough, England; son of Lawrence H.G. (a civil servant) and Mary M.A.M. (Scott) Girling; married Nina Ludmila Simansky (a mixed-media sculptor), April 12, 1953. *Education:* Queen's College, Oxford, B.A., 1950. *Politics:* Social Democrat. *Home:* 9 Patey St., Campbell, Australian Capital Territory 2601, Australia. *Office:* Department of International Relations, Australian National University, P.O. Box 4, Canberra, Australian Capital Territory 2600, Australia.

CAREER: Foreign Office, London, England, member of research staff in London, 1951-57, Thailand, 1958-63, and London, 1963-66; Australian National University, Canberra, senior research fellow, 1966-69, fellow in international relations, 1969-78, senior fellow, 1978—, researcher at Research School of Pacific Studies, 1966—. *Military service:* Royal Navy, coder, 1947-50. *Member:* Association of Asian Studies, Asian Studies Association of Australia, Australian Institute of International Affairs (president of Canberra branch, 1970-71).

WRITINGS: People's War: Conditions and Consequences in China and Southeast Asia, Praeger, 1969; *America and the Third World: Revolution and Intervention,* Routledge & Kegan Paul, 1980; *Thailand: Society and Politics,* Cornell University Press, 1981; *The Bureaucratic Polity in Modernizing Societies,* Institute of Southeast Asian Studies (Singapore), 1981; *The State in the Third World,* Allen & Unwin (Australia), 1982.

Contributor to international studies and Australian studies journals.

WORK IN PROGRESS: Research on U.S. foreign policy.

SIDELIGHTS: Girling wrote: "I am interested in political scenarios, but have recently written a piece of 'faction.' In a scenario the form is real—it is a projection of real, current events—but the substance is imaginary; it represents various possibilities, options, or 'surprises,' most of which are unlikely or even highly improbable, but which may just happen. Thus the scenario writer prepares himself, and his readers, for eventualities. He hopes, in this way, that he will not be taken by surprise. My idea, in writing a political 'faction,' is the reverse. The substance is real, but the form is imaginary. A world-political faction may provide insights which are lacking in more 'serious' conventional studies. Whether this is so or not, I found it fun to write."

*   *   *

GLEN, Frank Grenfell   1933-

PERSONAL: Born September 20, 1933, in Invercargill, New Zealand; son of Eric Ross Alexander Livingston and Muriel (Keast) Glen; married Margret Hamilton (an accounts clerk), January 21, 1958. *Education:* Trinity Theological College, Diploma in Theology, 1957; University of Newcastle, Diploma in Social Work, 1973. *Home address:* Golden Hills Rd., R.D.1, Richmond, Nelson, New Zealand.

CAREER: Minister in Otautau-Riverton area of New Zealand, 1958-60; ordained to Methodist ministry, 1960; Manapouri Hydro, Ohai-Nightcaps area, New Zealand, industrial minister, 1960-62; Shirley Methodist Church, Christchurch, New Zealand, minister and part-time chaplain at Kingslea Girls Centre, 1963-66; Moree Methodist Church, New South Wales, Australia, minister, 1967; Far West Mission, Cobar, New South Wales, Australia, superintendent of mission and chief pilot, 1968-70; New Zealand Department of Justice, probation officer at Invercargill, 1976-79, and at Nelson, 1979—. Appointed self-supporting minister of the Methodist church, 1979—. *Military service:* New Zealand Territorial Army, chaplain, 1962-70, served in Fiji, 1967; Australian Citizens Military Forces, chaplain, 1966-70; Royal Australian Air Force, senior chaplain, 1970-76. *Member:* Missionary Aviation Fellowship, Imperial Officers Club, Returned Servicemans Association, Wesley Historical Society, New Zealand Military History Society, Cobar Aero Club (president, 1968), Institute of Australian Welfare Officers.

WRITINGS: Methodism in Southland, Wesley Historical Society, 1956; *Methodism in Auckland During the Maori Wars,* Wesley Historical Society, 1958; *Methodism in the Coal Fields of Southland,* Wesley Historical Society, 1961; *John Luxford, C.M.G.,* Wesley Historical Society, 1965; *Journal: Fiordland,* privately printed, 1966; (editor) *Journal: Walter Harris,* privately printed, 1966; *Holy Joe's People,* A. H. & A. W. Reed, 1968, 2nd edition, 1969; *Fly High, Reach Far,* A. H. & A. W. Reed, 1971; *Religion and Welfare in the R.A.A.F.,* Royal Australian Air Force, 1973; *For Glory and a Farm,* Australian National War Memorial, 1979; *Bush in Our Yard,* A. H. & A. W. Reed, 1981.

WORK IN PROGRESS: A novel dealing with a national crisis caused by the effect of international events on New Zealand, publication expected in 1984.

SIDELIGHTS: "One must have the determination to write," Glen commented, "not just the desire. The beginning of writing is writing, and having a series of notebooks, or a collectible pile of this and that. Writing it down is the raw material of the future.

"My own writing has come to a crossroads. As a clergyman I'm known as a special kind of writer, either of religious history in New Zealand or biographical material about my various ministries. This boxes me up and limits me. If I am to move forward as a real writer, then I have to produce something quite real, different, and challenging. My novel in progress, the first such effort on my part, cannot be published under my own name. To do so would in some way fail to do the book justice.

"It is not what you have written in the past that makes you a writer; it's what you can produce for the contemporary scene. In the past I have sought to share the fun and humor of Christian living in my writing, certainly with plenty of earthy events. Above all, I have tried to show that God has a sense of humor, and that being a Christian adds a dimension to life and is not a subtractive influence. This kind of writing, of a personal nature, has seldom been of a high literary quality, though in a creative way there have been some high spots. Experience inspires reality in writing, and when experience is exhausted, as it is now in my case, real and perhaps less encumbered writing can begin. That is part of one's growth toward becoming a real writer, rather than just an author.

"For me, this attempt at a novel might make or break me as a writer. I feel like the soldier who, preparing his gear before the patrol, knows full well he may not return. He hopes he will and is prepared to do his best to make that possible. So it is with a writer, and it is an exceptional individual who can continue to grow and improve through the 'patrol' of his career."

BIOGRAPHICAL/CRITICAL SOURCES: Southland Times, January 25, 1958, June 8, 1968, August 21, 1971; *Southland News,* November 5, 1960, April 14, 1961; *Christchurch Star,* August 21, 1963; George Howard, *The Heart of Fiordland,* Whitcombe & Tombs, 1966; *Australian Shooter Journal,* July, 1973; J. S. Thompson, *Pasture, Coal Seam, and Settlement,* Times Publishing (Invercargill), 1980; V. G. Boyle, *Ohai-Nightcaps District 1880-1980,* Times Publishing (Invercargill), 1981.

*   *   *

GLENN, Frank 1901-1982

OBITUARY NOTICE: Born August 7, 1901, in Marissa, Ill., died after a short illness, January 12, 1982, in New York, N.Y. Surgeon, educator, and author. As chief surgeon of the Cornell University Medical Center, Glenn treated several prominent patients, including Oscar Hammerstein and the shah of Iran, whose appendix Glenn removed in 1951. Glenn served as an editorial consultant to Macmillan and as consulting editor to *Surgery, Gynecology and Obstetrics.* Glenn wrote more than three hundred fifty papers on various aspects of surgery and was the author, co-author, or editor of a number of books, including *Problems in Surgery* and *Surgery in the Aged.* Obituaries and other sources: *Who's Who in America,* 38th edition, Marquis, 1974; *The International Who's Who,* Europa, 1976; *New York Times,* January 14, 1982.

*   *   *

GLOVER, Judith 1943-

PERSONAL: Born March 31, 1943, in Penn Fields, England; daughter of John Thomas and Gwendoline (Fowler) Glover; married Anthony Rowley (divorced, 1971); children: Sonja Judith, Isobel Antonia. *Education:* Attended girls' secondary

school in Wolverhampton, England. *Politics:* None. *Religion:* Roman Catholic. *Home and office:* 45 Mount Sion, Royal Tunbridge Wells, Kent TN1 1TN, England. *Agent:* London Management, 235/241 Regent St., London W1A 2JT, England.

CAREER: Wolverhampton Express and Star, Wolverhampton, England, reporter, 1960-62; free-lance writer, 1962—. *Member:* Romantic Novelists Association.

WRITINGS: The Place Names of Sussex, Batsford, 1974; *The Place Names of Kent,* Batsford, 1975; *Colour Book of Sussex,* Batsford, 1975; *Colour Book of Kent,* Batsford, 1976; (with Anthony Kersting) *Sussex in Photographs,* Batsford, 1976; *Drink Your Own Garden,* Batsford, 1979; *The Stallion Man* (novel), Hodder & Stoughton, 1982. Author of review column in *Sussex Express.*

WORK IN PROGRESS: A second novel in the trilogy begun with *The Stallion Man,* set in Sussex in the 1870's, publication by Hodder & Stoughton expected in 1984.

SIDELIGHTS: "My only motivation," Judith Glover commented, "is that I enjoy writing so much. It's the only thing I want to do. If I can share my enjoyment with my readers, so much the better. History fascinates me, especially English rural history, and to be able to bring it alive through my writing is the most satsifying thing I know."

*   *   *

GODMAN, Arthur 1916-

PERSONAL: Born October 10, 1916, in Hereford, England; son of Arthur Andrew (a schoolmaster) and Mary (Newman) Godman; married Jean Barr Morton, June 24, 1950; children: Ian Barr, Diana Barr Godman Allan, Brian Barr. *Education:* University of London, B.Sc. (with honors), 1937, B.Sc. (with honors), 1938; Institute of Education, London, Diploma in Education, 1939. *Politics:* None. *Religion:* "Nominally Church of England." *Home:* Sondes House, Patrixbourne, Canterbury, Kent, England.

CAREER: Overseas Civil Service, London, England, assistant director of education in Federation of Malaya, 1946-58; Cambridge University, Local Examinations Syndicate, Cambridge, England, examiner, 1952-70, chief examiner, 1970—. With Overseas Civil Service in Hong Kong, 1978—; honorary fellow of Eliot College, University of Kent at Canterbury; member of board of directors of Educational Publishing Services, Singapore. *Military service:* British Army, Royal Artillery, 1939-46; became captain. *Member:* Royal Chemical Society, Royal Asiatic Society, Society of Authors, Royal Overseas League, Association for Science Education.

WRITINGS—Published by Longmans, Green, except as noted: (With Walter Vivian Hobson) *Everyday Science for the Tropics,* Book I, 1956, Book II, 1957, Book III, 1959, Book IV, 1962, Book V, 1964; *Health Science for the Tropics,* 1962, revised edition, 1967, new edition with Anne C. Gutteridge published as *A New Health Science for Africa,* 1979; (with J. Copeland) *Upper Primary Arithmetic,* 1964; (editor) *The Attainment and Ability of Hong Kong Primary IV Pupils,* Oxford University Press, 1964; (with Hobson) *Everyday Science for Malaysia,* 1965; (with J. F. Talbert) *Malaysian General Mathematics,* 1965; (with H. Lau) *Remove Mathematics,* 1967; (with A. Johnson and D. Chua) *General Science Certificate Course,* 1968; (with N. Muraguri) *Practical Certificate Chemistry,* 1969; (with Sam 'Tunde Bajah) *Chemistry: A New Certificate Approach,* 1969, revised edition, 1978; (with Johnson) *Junior Tropical Biology,* 1970; *Health Science,* 1970.

Published by Longman: (With Talbert) *Additional Mathematics: Pure and Applied,* 1971, revised edition, 1976; *Physical Science,* Book I, 1973, revised edition, 1976, Book II, 1973, revised edition, 1978; (with C. J. Webb) *Certificate Human and Social Biology,* 1974; (with Louis Ekue Folivi) *New Certificate Physics,* 1974, new edition, 1977; *Human and Social Biology,* 1978; (with E.M.F. Payne) *Longman Dictionary of Scientific Usage,* 1979; (editor) *Longman Illustrated Science Dictionary,* 1981; (with Gutteridge) *Objective Tests,* 1981; (with Gutteridge) *Certificate Notes,* 1981.

WORK IN PROGRESS: English Usage in Science; What Can a Microcomputer Do?; revising a chemistry book.

SIDELIGHTS: Godman told *CA:* "My army service in the Far East led to an interest in Oriental languages, and it increased when I was in government service in Malaya. Teaching and examining science in both English and Malay showed me cross-cultural difficulties in translating scientific and technical books. This led to my present research on problems of nonnative speakers of English when they read technical literature."

*　　*　　*

GOLDMAN, Shifra M(eyerowitz) 1926-

PERSONAL: Born July 18, 1926, in New York, N.Y.; daughter of Abraham (a waiter) and Sylvia (a seamstress; maiden name, Kadish) Meyerowitz; divorced; children: Eric Garcia. *Education:* University of California, Los Angeles, B.A., 1963, Ph.D., 1977; California State University, Los Angeles, M.A., 1966. *Residence:* Los Angeles, Calif. *Office:* Department of Art, Santa Ana College, 17th at Bristol Sts., Santa Ana, Calif. 92706.

CAREER: Citrus College, Azusa, Calif., instructor in art history, 1966-70; East Los Angeles College, Monterey Park, Calif., instructor in art history, 1970-71; Santa Ana College, Santa Ana, Calif., instructor in art history, 1971—. Member of faculty at California State University, Los Angeles, summer, 1979, and University of California, Los Angeles, spring, 1980 and 1981; guest lecturer at University of Southern California, University of Texas at Austin, Laredo State University, San Diego State University, Academy of San Carlo of University of Mexico, Detroit Institute of Arts, and Stanford University; appeared on radio and television programs in the United States and Mexico. *Member:* College Art Association of America, Latin American Studies Association, Pacific Coast Council of Latin American Studies.

WRITINGS: Contemporary Mexican Painting in a Time of Change, University of Texas Press, 1981. Art critic for newspaper *La Opinion* and for *Artweek.* Contributor of about twenty articles to art, Latin American, and Chicano journals in the United States, Mexico, and Europe. Member of editorial board of *Studies in Latin American Popular Culture.*

WORK IN PROGRESS: Chicano Art in Social Perspective, 1965-1980, an interpretive essay with an annotated bibliography, with Tomas Ubarra-Frausto, publication by University of California, Los Angeles, Chicano Studies Research Center expected in 1982 or 1983; "Images of Mexican/Chicano Workers in the Visual Arts" for *Das Andere Amerika: Kunst und Kultur Der Amerikanischen Arbeiterbewegung seit 1700 in Stichen, Grafik, Fotografie, Malerei, Film, und Dokumenten,* publication expected in 1983.

SIDELIGHTS: Shifra Goldman's current interests include "nationalism and Latin American art, contemporary Chicano art, contemporary Latin American photography, all aspects of public art, realist art of the twentieth century, and theoretical problems in modern art."

*　　*　　*

GOLDSTEIN, Abraham 1903(?)-1982

OBITUARY NOTICE: Born c. 1903; died May 24, 1982, in Queens, N.Y. Expert on contract bridge and author. An avid and accomplished contract bridge player, Abraham Goldstein was the winner of the Eastern States Master Pairs in 1943 and 1949. He wrote *Commonsense Bridge for the Intermediate Player.* Obituaries and other sources: *New York Times,* May 26, 1982.

*　　*　　*

GOLDSTEIN-JACKSON, Kevin 1946-

PERSONAL: Born November 2, 1946, in Windsor, England; son of Harold (an engineer) and Winifred (Fellows) Jackson; married Jenny Mei Leng Ng, September, 1975; children: Jenkev Samantha Sing Yu. *Education:* University of Reading, B.A., 1970; University of Southampton, M. Phil., 1976. *Politics:* "Utilitarian." *Office:* Television South West Ltd. (TSW-TV), Derry's Cross, Plymouth, Devonshire, England.

CAREER: Southern Television, Southampton, England, program organizer, 1970-73; free-lance writer and television producer in England and Hong Kong, 1973-75; Dhofar Region Television Service, Salalah, Oman, head of film, 1975-76; Anglia Television, London, England, assistant to head of drama department, 1977-81; TSW-TV, Plymouth, England, founder, 1981, joint managing director and program controller, 1981—. Member of board of directors of Television South West Music Ltd. and Independent Television Publications Ltd. *Member:* Royal Society of Arts (fellow), British Institute of Management (fellow), Writers Guild of Great Britain, Crime Writers Association.

WRITINGS: The Right Joke for the Right Occasion, Elliot Right Way Books, 1973; *Ridiculous Facts,* Leslie Frewin, 1974; *Encyclopaedia of Ridiculous Facts,* Leslie Frewin, 1975; *Experiments With Everyday Objects,* Souvenir Press, 1976; *Joke After Joke After Joke,* Elliot Right Way Books, 1977; *Things to Make With Everyday Objects,* Souvenir Press, 1978, Atheneum, 1980; *Magic With Everyday Objects,* Souvenir Press, 1979; *Activities With Everyday Objects,* Souvenir Press, 1980.

Numerous television scripts, including "Man From the South," first telecast on ITV in 1979, and "Mr. Botibol's First Love," first telecast in England in 1980.

WORK IN PROGRESS: A nonfiction book; a novel set in the Middle East.

SIDELIGHTS: Goldstein-Jackson told *CA:* "The trouble with me is that when I see an interesting alleyway I go down it. The result is that I end up doing far too much in too many areas of activity—whether they be business, academic, or writing. If it looks interesting, I find it difficult to say 'no.' Except that now, pressures of work at TSW, a commercial TV station in the southwest of England, mean that I have relatively little time to write or do much other than work! However, I do get job satisfaction from TSW but still wish I had time to write more. My eventual aim is to leave the United Kingdom in about five years and then generally travel and write."

AVOCATIONAL INTERESTS: Gardening, walking, cinema, theatre, television, reading.

GOLLEY, Frank Benjamin 1930-

BRIEF ENTRY: Born September 24, 1930, in Chicago, Ill. American ecologist, educator, and author. Golley taught zoology at the University of North Carolina and North Carolina College until 1959. In that year he joined the faculty at the University of Georgia, and he became a professor of zoology there in 1968. He is also director of the university's Institute of Ecology. Golley wrote *Ecological Principles as a Basis for a Quality Life* (International Scientific Publications, 1975). He edited *Fragile Ecosystems: Evaluation of Research and Applications in the Neotropics* (Springer-Verlag, 1974), *Small Mammals: Their Productivity and Population Dynamics* (Cambridge University Press, 1975), *Tropical Ecological Systems: Trends in Terrestrial and Aquatic Research* (Springer-Verlag, 1975), *Ecological Succession* (Dowden, 1977), and *A World Census of Tropical Ecologists* (Institute of Ecology, University of Georgia, 1977). *Address:* Institute of Ecology, University of Georgia, Athens, Ga. 30601.

*   *   *

GONZALEZ-ECHEVARRIA, Roberto 1943-

PERSONAL: Born November 18, 1943, in Sagua la Grande, Cuba; came to the United States in 1959, naturalized citizen, 1978; son of Roberto M. (a lawyer) and Zenaida (a professor; maiden name, Echevarria) Gonzalez; married Isabel Gomez; children: Roberto, Isabel, Carlos. *Education:* University of South Florida, B.A., 1964; Indiana University, M.A., 1966; Yale University, M.Phil., 1968, Ph.D., 1970. *Home:* 47 Mather St., Hamden, Conn. 06514. *Office:* Latin American Studies Program, Yale University, P.O. Box 1881, Yale Station, New Haven, Conn. 06520.

CAREER: Yale University, New Haven, Conn., instructor, 1969-70, assistant professor of Latin American studies, 1970-71; Cornell University, Ithaca, N.Y., assistant professor, 1971-75, associate professor of Latin American studies, 1975-77; Yale University, associate professor, 1977-80, professor of Latin American studies, 1980—, chairman of Latin American studies program, 1981—. Visiting assistant professor at Trinity College, Hartford, Conn., summers, 1969-70, and Wesleyan University, Middletown, Conn., autumn, 1970; lecturer at colleges and universities, including Stanford University, 1974, New School for Social Research, 1975, Brown University, 1978, and Universidad Simon Bolivar, University of Ottawa, and Johns Hopkins University, 1980. Member of University of Mississippi's Center for Southern Culture, 1979—; director of National Endowment for the Humanities seminar on the narrative of America, 1981-82.

MEMBER: Instituto Internacional de Literature Iberoamericana, Modern Language Association of America (member of executive committee of Division of Latin American Literature to 1900, 1980-84), American Association of Teachers of Spanish and Portuguese, Latin American Studies Association, Cervantes Society of America. *Awards, honors:* Grants from Yale University, for France and Spain, 1969, Cornell University, for Venezuela, 1972, and France, 1973, Social Science Research Council, 1979, and National Endowment for the Humanities, 1979 and 1982-83; Berkowitz grants from Cornell University, for France, 1971 and 1975, and for Spain, 1977.

WRITINGS: (With Manuel Duran) *Calderon ante la critica: Historia y antologia* (title means "Calderon and the Critics: History and Anthology"), two volumes, Gredoes, 1976; *Relecturas: Estudios de literature cubana* (title means "Reread-

ings: Studies in Cuban Literature"), Monte Avila, 1976; *Alejo Carpentier: The Pilgrim at Home,* Cornell University Press, 1977. Editor of *Historia y ficcion en la narrativa hispanoamericana: Coloquio de Yale* (title means "History and Fiction in Latin American Literature: A Symposium"), Monte Avila.

Translator: *Triple Cross,* Dutton, 1972; (contributor) *All Fires the Fire and Other Stories* by Julio Cortazar, Pantheon, 1973. Also translator, with Jill Levine, of Severo Sarduy's *Cobra,* Dutton.

Contributor: Klaus Mueller-Bergh, editor, *Asedios a Carpentier: Once ensayos criticos sobre el novelista cubano* (title means "Approaches to Carpentier: Eleven Critical Essays About the Cuban Novelist"), Editorial Universitaria, 1972; Andrew P. Debicki and Enrique Pupo-Walker, editors, *Estudios de literatura hispanoamericana en honor a Jose J. Arrom* (title means "Studies of Latin American Literature in Honor of Jose J. Arrom"), Studies in Romance Languages and Literatures, University of North Carolina, 1974; *Modern Latin American Literature,* Ungar, 1975; Donald A. Yates, editor, *Otros mundos, otros fuegos: Fantasia y realismo magico en Iberoamericana* (title means "Other Worlds, Other Fires: Fantasy and Realism in Iberoamerica"), Latin American Studies Center, Michigan State University, 1975; Julian Rios, editor, *Severo Sarduy,* Editorial Fundamentos, 1976; Joaquin Roy, editor, *Narrativa y critica de nuestra America* (title means "Narrative and Criticism in Our America"), Editorial Castalia, 1978. Also contributor to *Carlos Fuentes,* edited by Robert Brody, University of Texas Press.

Associate editor of "Monographs in Romance Languages," Purdue University, 1978—. Contributor to *Academic American Encyclopedia.* Contributor of about seventy-five articles and reviews to literature and Latin American studies journals. Member of editorial board of *Diacritics,* 1971-77, editor, 1974; member of editorial board of *Revista Iberoamericana,* 1973-77, and *Modern Language Studies,* 1980—; member of editorial advisory board of *Journal of Spanish Studies: Twentieth Century,* 1977-80, and *Studies in Twentieth-Century Literature,* 1978—; contributing editor of *Handbook of Latin American Studies,* 1974—; editor of *Latin American Literary Review* and *Review* (of Center for Inter-American Relations).

WORK IN PROGRESS: A book on the relationship between culture and literature in Latin America; a book on Cuban exile author Severo Sarduy; a study of the relationship of the novel to nonliterary texts.

*   *   *

GOODCHILD, Peter 1939-

PERSONAL: Born August 18, 1939, in Windsor, England; son of Douglas Richard A. (a senior manager of a chemical firm) and Lottie May (Ager) Goodchild; married Penelope Jane Pointon-Dick (a teacher), July 20, 1968; children: Abigail, Hannah. *Education:* St. John's College, Oxford, B.A. (with honors), 1963, M.A., 1974. *Home:* White Hall Cottage, White Hall Lane, Checkendon, Oxfordshire, England. *Agent:* Bolt & Watson Ltd., 8-12 Old Queen St., Storey's Gate, London, SW1H 9HP, England. *Office:* British Broadcasting Corp., Kensington House, Richmond Way, London, W.14, England.

CAREER: British Broadcasting Corp. (BBC-TV), London, England, trainee, 1963-65, producer, 1965-69, editor of television series "Horizon," 1969-76, producer of television series "Marie Curie," 1976-78, editor of special drama projects, 1978-80, head of science and features department, 1980—. *Member:* Royal Society of Chemistry (fellow). *Awards, hon-*

ors: Best factual series award from British Academy of Film and Television Arts, 1973 and 1975, for "Horizon"; best drama series award from British Academy of Film and Television Arts, 1977, for "Marie Curie," and 1980, for "J. Robert Oppenheimer: Shatterer of Worlds."

WRITINGS: J. Robert Oppenheimer: Shatterer of Worlds, Houghton, 1981. Author of numerous television scripts, including "Marie Curie," BBC-TV, 1977, and "J. Robert Oppenheimer: Shatterer of Worlds," BBC-TV, 1980. Also author of television documentaries on cancer and smoking, the testing of ethical drugs, the future of space exploration after the Apollo missions, the activities of scientists during the Second World War, and a biography of Lord Charewell. Contributor of articles to magazines, including *Listener* and *New Scientist.*

SIDELIGHTS: Goodchild told *CA:* "For much of my working career I have specialized in biographies in one form or another, ranging from television dramatization through books and articles to television documentaries. I find nothing more intriguing than the building of an internal model of a person that you can never meet. All the people that I have worked on exist in my mind as strongly as most of the people I know well in real life. It is building those pictures which gives me my greatest satisfaction."

BIOGRAPHICAL/CRITICAL SOURCES: Vogue, October, 1978; *New York Times Book Review,* July 12, 1981.

*   *   *

GOODWIN, Geoffrey (Lawrence)   1916-

PERSONAL: Born June 14, 1916, in London, England; son of John Howard (an Anglican priest) and Ellen (a nurse; maiden name, Meany) Goodwin; married Janet Audrey Sewell (a secretary), January 6, 1951; children: Lorna Goodwin Attwell, Nigel Howard, Frances. *Education:* Attended Royal Military College, Sandhurst, 1934-35, and London School of Economics and Political Science, London, B.Sc., 1945. *Politics:* Social Democrat. *Religion:* Anglican. *Home:* Webbs Farm, Church Lane, Headley, Surrey, England.

CAREER: Associated with Foreign Office, London, England, 1945-48; University of London, London School of Economics and Political Science, London, lecturer in international relations, 1948-62, Montague Burton Professor of International Relations, 1962-78, professor emeritus, 1978—. Principal of King George VI and Queen Elizabeth Foundation of St. Catharines, Cumberland Lodge, Windsor, 1971-72. Member of World Council of Churches Commission on International Affairs, 1968-75; honorary resident of British International Studies Association, 1977-80. *Military service:* British Army, 1936-43; became major. *Member:* International Institute for Strategic Studies, Royal Institute of International Affairs (member of council, 1968-77), Royal Society of Arts (fellow).

WRITINGS: (Editor) *The University Teaching of International Relations,* Basil Blackwell, 1951; *Britain and the United Nations,* Oxford University Press, 1958; (editor) *New Dimensions of World Politics,* St. Martin's, 1975; (editor) *A New International Commodity Regime,* St. Martin's, 1979; (editor) *Ethics and Nuclear Deterrence,* St. Martin's, 1982.

WORK IN PROGRESS: An introduction to international relationships, publication by Hutchinson expected in 1983.

SIDELIGHTS: Goodwin commented: "My main efforts have been aimed at helping young people to understand better the world in which they live, particularly the international issues which closely affect all our lives—to understand and appreciate the realities, political and economic, which determine choices,

but also to appreciate the moral dimension in most issues, and in particular the bearing of the Christian faith on world problems. In addition, I am convinced of the need to bring together people from different walks of life: politicians, diplomats, business people, academics, to explore together how the perennial problems of peace and poverty can best be tackled in a nuclear age. No one has a monopoly on wisdom, and we have a lot to learn from each other. People also like to pose as 'realists' and to stress the power aspects of international life; Reinhold Niebuhr pointed a way of appreciating its moral dimension. His work needs to be carried further."

AVOCATIONAL INTERESTS: Painting, singing.

*   *   *

GORMAN, George H.   1916-1982

OBITUARY NOTICE: Born in 1916; died February 20, 1982, in Sicily. General secretary of England's Friends Home Service Committee (now Quaker Home Service) and author. An active and well-known member of the Society of Friends, Gorman served for thirty years as general secretary of the Friends Home Service Committee. Held in high regard by his fellow Quakers in both Europe and the United States, he was a popular speaker at Quaker meetings and conferences. Gorman was the author of *Introducing Quakers* and *The Amazing Fact of Quaker Worship.* Obituaries and other sources: *London Times,* February 24, 1982.

*   *   *

GORSLINE, (Sally) Marie   1928-
(S. M. Carson, S. M. Gorsline)

PERSONAL: Born October 3, 1928, in Winchester, Mass.; daughter of James Reed (a power engineer) and Marie (a pianist and painter; maiden name, Tice) Carson; married Joseph R. Cox, June 10, 1950 (divorced, 1964); married Douglas Warner Gorsline (an artist), December 24, 1968. *Education:* Attended Smith College, 1946-49, and Pennsylvania Academy of Fine Art, 1949-50. *Home:* Bussy Le Grand, 21150 Les Laumes, France.

CAREER: Little Studio (art gallery), New York City, director, 1952-56; free-lance artist's representative, New York City, 1956—. *Member:* Authors Guild.

WRITINGS—Juveniles: (With husband, Douglas Gorsline) *North American Indians* (illustrated by D. Gorsline), Random House, 1977; (compiler) *Nursery Rhymes* (illustrated by D. Gorsline), Random House, 1977; (with D. Gorsline) *Cowboys* (illustrated by D. Gorsline), Random House, 1978; *The Pioneers,* Random House, 1979.

Contributor, under name S. M. Gorsline, of articles to professional journals; contributor, under name S. M. Carson, to *Eastern Horizon.*

WORK IN PROGRESS: Research and writing in the field of cognitive psychology from a psychoanalytic point of view.

SIDELIGHTS: Marie Gorsline told *CA:* "The children's books were written at the request of my husband's editor. We were asked to create accounts of complex historical situations in a way that would interest young children in history. We did a great deal of research before we started each book. The emphasis, of course, was on the pictures: given the many-faceted subject matter of each book, we often had to combine several variants, recognizing that a book of this type could not be academically definitive, but could be an honest portrayal of a subject—hopefully without errors. We tried to choose scenes that would allow us to present a clear and balanced sequence of pictures and narrative, hoping to stimulate a child's interest and imagination so that he or she would ask questions and take in more detail when ready for it. (A parent recently complained that we were not pictorially exact in portraying a setting that changed three times during the period the book covered; the problem could only have been solved with an intricate footnote.)''

AVOCATIONAL INTERESTS: The fine arts, amateur theatre, poetry, reading aloud, nineteenth- and twentieth-century novels, mythology, history, travel (especially in France, England, Italy, and China).

* * *

GORSLINE, S. M.
See GORSLINE, (Sally) Marie

* * *

GOSLING, Nigel 1909-1982
(Alexander Bland)

OBITUARY NOTICE: Born January 29, 1909, in London, England; died of cancer, May 21, 1982, in London, England. Painter, art and dance critic, and editor. Gosling became interested in dance after meeting dancer Maude Lloyd, whom he later married. He studied dance himself for a time and in 1948 began writing dance criticism under the pseudonym Alexander Bland. From 1955 to 1975 he served as dance critic for the *Observer.* He edited dancer Rudolph Nureyev's autobiography as well as a book entitled *The Nureyev Image.* Obituaries and other sources: *London Times,* May 22, 1982.

* * *

GOULDING, Peter Geoffrey 1920-
(Guy Villiers)

PERSONAL: Born in 1920 in Hampstead, London, England. *Education:* Attended Acton Technical College, 1935-36, and Buckinghamshire Agricultural College. *Home:* 14 Bradshaw Close, Steeple Aston, Oxford, England. *Office: Shooting Times & Country Magazine,* 10 Sheet St., Windsor, Berkshire, England.

CAREER: Free-lance technical writer, 1941-70; Northwood Publishers, London, England, subeditor and technical writer, 1970-72; Hulton's Technical Publishers, London, associate editor, 1972-73; Burlington Publishing Co., Maidenhead, England, senior assistant editor and photographer, 1973—. Hunt supporter of the Heythrop Foxhounds Hunt, Chipping Norton, Oxford, England. *Military service:* Royal Air Force, 1940-45. *Member:* British Field Sports Society, British Association for Shooting and Conservation.

WRITINGS: (Under pseudonym Guy Villiers) *The British Heavy Horse,* Barrie & Jenkins, 1976; *Sporting Hotels and Inns,* Argus Books, 1980. Contributor of articles on field sports and the countryside to magazines, including *This England, Horse & Hound,* and *The Field;* reviewer of nonfiction books for magazines, including *Shooting Times & Country Magazine.*

WORK IN PROGRESS: Research for a book on specialized shooting and a book on country matters.

SIDELIGHTS: Goulding told *CA:* ''In addition to field sports and country matters, I also have an interest in and knowledge of some aspects of agriculture, cricket as a game, and the special requirements of inns and hotels that cater to visitors who wish to shoot, fish, or ride/hunt, etc.''

GRADY, Tex
See WEBB, Jack (Randolph)

* * *

GRANT, Gwen(doline Ellen) 1940-

PERSONAL: Born May 5, 1940, in Worksop, Nottinghamshire, England; daughter of George Arthur (a miner) and Alice (Hall) Rewston; married Ian Grant (a tree feller and lecturer in computer science), April 13, 1963; children: Andrew and Ian (twins). *Education:* Open University, B.A., 1977. *Home:* 95 Watson Rd., Worksop, Nottinghamshire, England.

CAREER: Worked as a shop assistant and secretary, 1955-74; former lecturer in creative writing at North Nottinghamshire College of Further Education, Nottinghamshire, England. *Member:* International P.E.N. Club. Writers' Guild of Great Britain, International Poetry Society, Poetry Society (London), Nottingham Poetry Society. *Awards, honors:* Fourth place, Lake Aske Memorial Award, 1975; second place, Queenie Lee Memorial Prize, 1981.

WRITINGS: Matthew and His Magic Kite, Andersen Press, 1977; *Private: Keep Out,* Heinemann, 1978; *Knock and Wait,* Heinemann, 1979; *Enemies Are Dangerous,* Heinemann, 1980; *The Lily Pickle Band Book,* Heinemann, 1982. Work represented in anthologies, including *All the Year Round,* Evans Brothers, 1980, and *The Second Methuen Book of Strange Tales,* Methuen, 1982. Contributor of short stories and poems to the British Broadcasting Corp. and to periodicals, including *Tracks, Scrip, Expression One,* and *Manuscript.*

WORK IN PROGRESS: A radio play, a children's novel, and an adult novel; children's poetry.

SIDELIGHTS: Gwen Grant commented: ''Although I read a lot when I was a child, I didn't want to be a writer when I grew up simply because the thought never occurred to me. I didn't realize real people wrote books—I thought they had to be dead! Now, of course, I know differently, and writing for children is one of my particular joys.

''One of the nicest things about writing for children is that I go out to schools and libraries to meet them and talk about my books. I particularly like it when children identify with either the characters or the problems faced by the characters in my books. I very much enjoy making children laugh through my work.

''My future writing plans include more writing for adults, probably a novel, and radio work. One of my great interests at the moment is children's poetry; I am hoping to work more in that field.''

* * *

GRANT, Joanne B(enzel) 1940-

PERSONAL: Born December 2, 1940, in Grand Junction, Colo.; daughter of Alex (a rancher) and Gertrude (Barnett) Benzel; married C. H. Grant, June 16, 1959 (divorced March 10, 1975); children: Gina Ann. *Education:* Attended Texas Christian University, 1958-59, Tarrant Community College, 1968-75, and Dallas Community College, 1968-75. *Politics:* Republican. *Religion:* Methodist. *Home:* 7615 Dentcrest, Dallas, Tex. 75240. *Office:* 12820 Hillcrest, Suite 218, Dallas, Tex. 75230.

CAREER: Kim Dawson Agency, Dallas, Tex., model, 1975—. Sales representative of Dallas Market Center, 1977—. Announcer for North Texas Radio, 1977-78. *Member:* Authors Guild, Women in Communication, National Organization for Women.

WRITINGS: (With Melvyn A. Berke) *Games Divorced People Play,* Prentice-Hall, 1980. Author with Berke of "After Divorce," a column distributed by Register and Tribune Syndicate, 1976-81, and "On Marriage and Divorce," Register and Tribune Syndicate, 1981—.

WORK IN PROGRESS: Another book, with Melvyn A. Berke, publication by Prentice-Hall expected in 1984; "Just Between Us," a syndicated radio program, with Berke.

SIDELIGHTS: Grant told *CA:* "Ours was the first syndicated column on divorce. From that we went on and began giving divorce workshops. Then came our first book—an exciting experience!"

* * *

GRAYSON C(harles) Jackson, Jr. 1923-

PERSONAL: Born October 8, 1923, at Fort Necessity, La.; son of Charles Jackson Grayson; children: Christopher Jackson, Michael Wiley, Randall Charles, Daniel Jackson. *Education:* Tulane University, B.B.A., 1944; University of Pennsylvania, M.B.A., 1947; Harvard University, D.B.A., 1959. *Office:* American Productivity Center, 123 North Post Oak Lane, Houston, Tex. 77024.

CAREER: Tulane University, New Orleans, La., instructor, 1947-49; *New Orleans Item,* New Orleans, reporter, 1949-50; Federal Bureau of Investigation (FBI), Washington, D.C., special agent, 1950-52; James E. O'Neill & Associates, New Orleans, partner, 1952-53; Tulane University, assistant professor and assistant to vice-president, 1953-55; Harvard University, Cambridge Mass., assistant professor, 1958-59; Tulane University, associate professor, 1959-63, professor, 1963-68, associate dean, 1961-63, dean of School of Business Administration, 1963-68; Southern Methodist University, Dallas, Tex., professor and dean of School of Business Administration, 1968-75; founder and head of American Productivity Center, Inc., 1975—. Certified Public Accountant, 1948—. Professor at IMEDE, Switzerland, 1963-64; visiting professor at Stanford University, 1967; visiting professor at INSEAD, Fontainbleu, France, 1972, 1973, 1975; instructor for various management programs.

Chairman of Price Commission, Washington, D.C., 1971-73; counselor to chairman of Cost of Living Council, 1973; councillor for Conference Board, 1975; member of President's Commission for a National Agenda for the Eighties, 1980; consultant to comptroller general of the United States. Member of board of directors of various companies, including Lever Brothers. Manager of C. J. Grayson Farm. *Military service:* U.S. Navy, 1943-46; became lieutenant junior grade. *Member:* World Future Society, American Accounting Association, American Finance Association, Operations Research Society of Certified Public Accountants of Louisiana, Beta Gamma Sigma (honorary member).

WRITINGS: Decisions Under Uncertainty: Drilling Decisions by Oil and Gas Operators, Harvard Business School, Division of Research, 1960; (contributor) *Financial Research and Management Decisions,* Wiley, 1967; (contributor) *Professional School and World Affairs,* Education and World Affairs, 1967; *Confessions of a Price Controller,* Dow Jones-Irwin, 1974. Contributor of numerous articles and monographs to publications, including *Fortune, Nation's Business, Wharton Magazine, Time, U.S. News & World Report, Dun's Review, Busi-*

ness Week, New York Times, Chicago Sun-Times, Wall Street Journal, and *Reader's Digest.*

SIDELIGHTS: Productivity, which is "a key measure of economic health," as Philip Shabecoff of the *New York Times* readily admits, "is now the ruling passion of [C. Jackson] Grayson's life." "Improving national productivity must be an important part of the nation's agenda in the 1980's," Grayson told the *New York Times.* "Instead of yelling about a sinking ship we ought to be asking what positively we can do about our economy."

Grayson resigned his academic post and formed the American Productivity Center, Inc., which, in addition to research in its field, also sponsors seminars and other educational efforts. "To increase productivity is the best way to fight unemployment," Grayson reasons. "We have the statistics to show that higher productivity produces more jobs. The higher the growth of productivity the more resources there are for health services, education and fighting pollution."

BIOGRAPHICAL/CRITICAL SOURCES: New York Times, February 17, 1980.

* * *

GREER, Francesca
See JANAS, Frankie-Lee

* * *

GREGORY, Horace (Victor) 1898-1982

OBITUARY NOTICE—See index for *CA* sketch: Born April 10, 1898, in Milwaukee, Wis.; died March 11, 1982, in Shelburne Falls, Mass. Professor, poet, critic, translator, and biographer. Considered one of the most prominent American poets, Gregory received the Bollingen Prize for *Collected Poems,* one of his eight books of poetry. Gregory began to receive critical acclaim in the early 1930's and continued to be popular throughout his career. He was often praised for the emotional range and rhythm he achieved in poetry, and his writing is characterized by classical echoes in what are otherwise contemporary lyrics. Gregory was also well-known for his translations of the poems of Catullus and Ovid and for his biographies of James McNeill Whistler and Amy Lowell. He taught at Sarah Lawrence College from 1934 until 1960, when he was named professor emeritus. Obituaries and other sources: *New York Times,* March 13, 1982; *Publishers Weekly,* April 9, 1982.

* * *

GRIFFITH, Francis 1906-

PERSONAL: Born March 12, 1906, in Omagh, County Tyrone, Ireland; came to the United States in 1913, naturalized citizen, 1916; son of Paul G. and Jane (Duggan) Griffith. *Education:* St. John's University, Jamaica, N.Y., B.A. (summa cum laude), 1927, M.A., 1929; Columbia University, Ed.D., 1958. *Politics:* "Conservative, Right to Life." *Religion:* Roman Catholic. *Home:* 49 Amherst Rd., Port Washington, N.Y. 11050.

CAREER: Teacher in public schools in New York, N.Y., 1929-39, chairman, 1939-46, high school principal, 1946-60, assistant superintendent, 1960-64; St. John's University, Jamaica, N.Y., associate professor of educational administration, 1964-67; Hofstra University, Hempstead, N.Y., professor of educational administration, 1967-74; writer, 1964—. Visiting professor at York College of the City University of New York, 1974-75. *Military service:* U.S. Army Air Forces, 1942-46;

served in Pacific theater; became major; received four battle stars. *Member:* Emerald Society of New York City Board of Education (historian, 1978-82). *Awards, honors:* L.H.D. from St. John's University, Jamaica, N.Y., 1954; Fulbright grant, 1962.

WRITINGS: (With Catherine Nelson and Edward Stasheff) *Your Speech,* Harcourt, 1955, 3rd edition, 1979; (with John Warriner) *English Grammar and Composition,* Harcourt, 1958, 6th edition, 1979; *Handbook for the Observation of Teaching and Learning,* Pendell, 1973; (with Joseph Mersand) *Eight American Ethnic Plays,* Scribner, 1974; *Administrative Theory in Education,* Pendell, 1979; (with Mersand) *Spelling Your Way to Success,* Barron's, 1980; (with Mersand) *Spelling Made Easy,* Barron's, 1982.

Editor: (With Mersand) *One-Act Plays for Today,* Globe Book Co., 1945; (with Mersand) *Modern One-Act Plays,* Harcourt, 1950; William Shakespeare, *Macbeth,* Dell, 1968; Walt Whitman, *Leaves of Grass,* Avon, 1969; Henry Wadsworth Longfellow, *Evangeline,* Avon, 1971.

Contributor to magazines, including *Commonweal, Catholic World, America, English Record, Medicin Heute,* and *Newsday,* and newspapers.

WORK IN PROGRESS: A book on twentieth-century Irish speakers, such as Timothy Healy, DeValera, Padriac Pearse, Ian Paisley, and Bernadette Devlin, tentatively titled *Modern Irish Orators.*

SIDELIGHTS: Griffith told *CA:* "I dread writing because it is drudgery, but I'm driven to it by an urge to communicate my ideas, especially on matters about which I feel strongly. I try to write clearly and simply. I do not always succeed, but I continue to try."

*   *   *

GRIFFITHS, (Edith) Grace (Chalmers)   1921-

PERSONAL: Born February 9, 1921, in Bow, Devonshire, England; daughter of George Chalmers (an accountant) and Edith Louise (Riddaway) Lane; married Gordon Douglas Griffiths (a writer), October 14, 1948 (died July, 1973). *Education:* Attended public schools in England. *Politics:* None. *Religion:* Agnostic. *Home:* 3 Winterbourne Rd., Teignmouth, Devonshire, TQ14 8JT, England. *Office:* Public Library, Teignmouth, Devonshire, TQ14 8JT, England.

CAREER: Devon Library Services, Teignmouth, Devonshire, England, librarian, 1946-74, area children's librarian, 1974-81. *Military service:* Auxiliary Territorial Service, 1942.

WRITINGS: (With husband, Gordon Douglas Griffiths) *History of Teignmouth,* Brunswick Press, 1965; *The Days of My Freedom* (illustrated by David Knight), World's Work, 1978. Also collaborator on books for children by G. D. Griffiths: *Mattie: The Story of a Hedgehog,* World's Work, 1967, *Silver Blue,* World's Work, 1971, and *Abandoned,* World's Work, 1973.

WORK IN PROGRESS: A local history; a story of a lost dachshund.

SIDELIGHTS: "I was a lonely child and spent much of my time telling stories to my pet cats," Grace Griffiths told *CA.* "Later, I wrote these stories down, but made no attempt at publication."

"My husband suffered from congenital heart disease," Griffiths continued, "and was often unable to work. He felt aggrieved because I had a full-time job. I wrote *Mattie* in rough, about the hedgehogs I fed in our garden. He edited it and typed

the manuscript, and it was published under his initials. This gave him an interest and a feeling of usefulness. After his death in 1973, I wrote and published *The Days of My Freedom* under my own name, and shall continue now to write as 'Grace Griffiths.'"

*   *   *

GRIFFITHS, John Gwyn   1911-

PERSONAL: Born December 7, 1911, in Porth, Wales; son of Robert (a Baptist minister) and Mimah (Davies) Griffiths; married Kate Bosse (an archaeologist), September 13, 1939; children: Robert Paul, Gwilym Heini. *Education:* University College, University of Wales, B.A., 1932, D.D., 1980; University of Liverpool, M.A., 1936; Queen's College, Oxford, D.Phil., 1949, D.Litt., 1973. *Politics:* "Welsh Nationalist." *Religion:* Baptist. *Home:* 3 Long Oaks Ave., Abertawe, Swansea, Wales.

CAREER: Y Eflam (literary journal), Bala, Wales, co-editor, 1941-47; University of Wales, University College, Swansea, lecturer, 1946-58, senior lecturer, 1958-66, reader, 1966-72, professor of classics and Egyptology, 1973-79; writer, 1979—. Lady Wallis Budge Research Lecturer at Oxford University, 1957-58, visiting fellow at All Souls College, 1976-77; guest professor at University of Cairo, 1965-66. *Member:* Plaid Cymru. *Awards, honors:* Prize from Welsh Arts Council, 1971, for *Songs of Cairo.*

WRITINGS: The Conflict of Horus and Seth, University of Liverpool Press, 1960; *Dragon's Nostrils,* Gomer Press, 1961; *The Origins of Osiris,* Hessling, 1966; *Songs of Cairo,* Lolfa Press, 1970; (editor) *Plutarch's de Iside et Osiride,* University of Wales Press, 1970; (editor) *The Isis-Book of Apuleius,* E. J. Brill, 1975; *Aristotle's Poetics,* University of Wales Press, 1978; *The Origins of Osiris and His Cult,* E. J. Brill, 1980; *Triads and Trinity* (a history of religions), Gottingen University Press, 1983. Editor of *Welsh Nation,* 1964-65, and *Journal of Egyptian Archaeology,* 1970-78.

*   *   *

GRIMES, Orville F(rank), Jr.   1943-

PERSONAL: Born March 1, 1943, in San Francisco, Calif.; son of Orville F. and June (Levelle) Grimes; married Elizabeth J. Conerty, February 8, 1971; children: Alan, Laura. *Education:* University of California, Berkeley, A.B., 1964; University of Chicago, M.A., 1968, Ph.D., 1971. *Office:* World Bank, 1818 H St. N.W., Washington, D.C. 20433.

CAREER: Associated with World Bank, Washington, D.C., beginning in 1971, senior economist in eastern African projects, 1981—.

WRITINGS: Housing for Low-Income Urban Families, Johns Hopkins Press, 1976. Contributor to land and housing journals.

*   *   *

GROSSMAN, Manuel Lester   1939-

BRIEF ENTRY: Born September 8, 1939, in Brockton, Mass. American educator and author. Grossman has taught speech at Queens College of the City University of New York since 1969. He wrote *Dada: Paradox, Mystification and Ambiguity in European Literature* (Pegasus, 1971). *Address:* Department of Communication Arts and Sciences, Queens College of the City University of New York, Flushing, N.Y. 11367. *Biographical/ critical sources: Directory of American Scholars,* Volume II: *English, Speech, and Drama,* 7th edition, Bowker, 1978.

GROSVENOR, Melville Bell   1901-1982

OBITUARY NOTICE—See index for *CA* sketch: Born November 26, 1901, in Washington, D.C.; died of cardiac arrest, April 22, 1982, in Miami, Fla. President of the National Geographic Society, editor of *National Geographic* magazine from 1957 to 1967, and author. Grosvenor's great-grandfather, Gardiner Greene Hubbard, founded the society in 1888, his grandfather, Alexander Graham Bell, was its second president, and his father, Gilbert Hovey Grosvenor, was editor of National Geographic from 1899 to 1954. Grosvenor's career with the National Geographic Society spanned nearly sixty years. He began as an apprentice writer-editor on *National Geographic* in 1924 and progressed to chairman and editor emeritus. His ten years as editor were marked by innovation and growth for the society. Under Grosvenor's leadership, the society expanded publication of books, undertook television and film productions, increased grants for research and exploration (sponsoring the work of anthropologist Louis S. B. Leakey, oceanographer Jacques-Yves Cousteau, and others), and modernized the magazine's photographic and cover styles. Membership in the society rose by nearly three million during his years as editor and has since doubled to a current membership of 10.7 million. Grosvenor's writings include *The National Geographic Society Book of Dogs, Wonderous World of Fishes,* and *John Fitzgerald Kennedy: The Last Full Measure.* Obituaries and other sources: *Washington Post,* April 24, 1982; *New York Times,* April 24, 1982; *Chicago Tribune,* April 25, 1982; *Newsweek,* May 3, 1982; *Time,* May 3, 1982.

*   *   *

GROUNDWATER, William   1906(?)-1982

OBITUARY NOTICE: Educator, naturalist, editor, and poet. Groundwater, who served for twenty-one years as rector of Stromness Academy in the Orkney Islands, was co-editor of *The New Orkney Book.* He also wrote a book entitled *Birds and Mammals of Orkney.* Obituaries and other sources: *London Times,* April 21, 1982.

*   *   *

GROVES, Don(ald) George

PERSONAL: Born in Syracuse, N.Y.; son of Perry Edward (an engineer) and Margarite (Grass) Groves; married Barbara L. Matticks, March 19, 1949. *Education:* Syracuse University, B.Sc., 1939, M.Sc., 1949, doctoral study, 1951-52; also attended Universidad de Santo Domingo and University of Puerto Rico. *Home:* Columbia Plaza, No. C-623, 2400 Virginia Ave. N.W., Washington, D.C. 20037. *Office:* National Academy of Sciences-National Research Council, 2101 Constitution Ave. N.W., Washington, D.C. 20418.

CAREER: Crucible Steel Co., Syracuse, N.Y., engineer, 1940; Easy Washer Corp., Syracuse, mechanical design engineer, 1940-41; Hudson Motor Car Co., Detroit, Mich., mechanical design engineer, 1941-43; General Electric Co., Fort Wayne, Ind., electrical design engineer and materials scientist, 1954-58; General Electric Co., Syracuse, systems specialist in advanced missile detection and oceanography, 1958-62; National Academy of Sciences-National Research Council, Washington, D.C., senior member of scientific staff in materials and engineering, 1962—, staff member of committee on advanced design criteria and committee on ceramic materials, 1962, committee on design with brittle materials, 1963-64, committee on protective materials for aerospace vehicles, 1964-65, committee on atomic characterization materials, 1964-67, committee on ceramic processing studies, 1965-68, committee on fundamentals of amorphous materials for ballistic missile defense hardening, 1970-71, committee for studies in infrared and laser-glass, and committee for glass.

Professional and semi-professional baseball player; batting practice pitcher for American League baseball teams playing in Washington, D.C.; commissioned baseball scout for such teams as Chicago White Sox, 1961, New York Mets, 1962, and Pittsburgh Pirates, 1971-75; instructor at Howsers Baseball School, 1963. Member of International Oceanographic Foundation. Chairman of Syracuse Chamber of Commerce Economic Discussion Groups, 1959-60; president of Industrial Baseball League of Washington, D.C., 1965-66, and Industrial Baseball League of Maryland, 1967; member of board of management of Young Men's Christian Association, Washington, D.C., 1969-75; member of cultural affairs committee of Washington Board of Trade. *Military service:* U.S. Naval Reserve, 1943-70, active duty, 1943-46, 1951-54.

MEMBER: American Society of Naval Engineers, U.S. Naval Institute, National Academy of Sciences-National Research Council Academies' Recreational Activities Association (president, 1973), Washington Academy of Sciences (fellow), Washington Independent Writers Association, Washington Athletic Club (member of board of governors, 1967—; president, 1969-70), Military Order of the World Wars, Pentagon Officers Athletic Club, Fort Myers Officers Athletic Club. *Awards, honors:* Fellowship from U.S. Government for Latin America, 1950; named honorary citizen of Key West and Florida Keys, 1967; George Washington Honor Medal from Freedoms Foundation, 1970, for article "Freedom: Privilege or Obligation?," national awards, 1974, for article "The Old Man," and 1974, for article "A Freedoms Foundation."

WRITINGS: (With Lee M. Hunt) *A Glossary of Ocean Science and Underseas Technology Terms,* Compass Publications, 1965; (contributor) James Young and Robert Shane, editors, *Materials and Processes,* 3rd edition (Groves was not included in earlier editions), Dekker, 1979; (with Hunt) *The Ocean World Encyclopedia,* McGraw, 1980.

Contributor of more than two hundred articles to technical journals, popular magazines, and newspapers, including *Oceans, Our Navy, Sea Frontiers,* and *Skin Diver.* Member of editorial boards of technical journals, 1962-65.

WORK IN PROGRESS: Articles for various magazines and scientific journals.

SIDELIGHTS: Groves told *CA:* "I personally view writing for publication as a delightful challenge. It is most gratifying to have one's brainchild 'born' in print and even more important to find that, in some cases, one's ideas expressed in articles were translated into practice by readers. Of course, any professional writer must be responsible for the things he writes about; he should know the subject firsthand and present it in a persuasive and interesting manner. On this latter point, I, along with thousands of other writers, have at times regretted the publication of some of my articles after viewing them in retrospect. But we learn by doing; and also as Miguel de Cervantes Saavedra once said, 'You may depend upon my bare word, reader, without further security, that I wish this offspring of my brain were as ingenious, sprightly, and accomplished as yourself could desire; but the mischief of it is, nature will have its course: every production must resemble its author. . . .'"

GRUBB
See CRUMB, R(obert)

* * *

GRUMMER, Arnold E(dward) 1923-

PERSONAL: Born August 19, 1923, in Spencer, Iowa; son of Edward H. and Anna (Christiansen) Grummer; married Mabel Emmel (a teacher), August 11, 1948; children: Mark, Gregory, Kimberly Grummer Schiedermayer. *Education:* Iowa State Teachers College (now University of Northern Iowa), B.A., 1949; Iowa State University, M.A., 1952. *Religion:* Lutheran. *Home and office:* 63 Bellaire Court, Appleton, Wis. 54911.

CAREER: Iowa State Teachers College (now University of Northern Iowa), Cedar Falls, member of radio and television staff, 1949-51; Armstrong Cork Co., Lancaster, Pa., in advertising, 1952-53; high school teacher of English and speech in Osage, Iowa, 1954-57; Aid Association for Lutherans, Appleton, Wis., in advertising and public relations, 1957-59; Institute of Paper Chemistry, Appleton, assistant professor of general studies, 1960-70, editor of general publications, 1960-76, curator of Dard Hunter Paper Museum, 1970-76; writer, lecturer, and consultant, 1976—. *Military service:* U.S. Coast Guard, 1942-45; served in the South Pacific and Australia. *Member:* Society of Children's Book Writers.

WRITINGS: Paper by Kids, Dillon, 1980.

Author of "Aspects of the Commercial Handmade Paper Industry of Taiwan," a film released by Institute of Paper Chemistry in 1964. Contributor to *Collier's Encyclopedia* and *Dictionary of American History.* Contributor to trade journals and newspapers in the United States and abroad.

WORK IN PROGRESS: Balloon Game Book; Not Even Uncle Sam Wants You, a humorous novel; research on cloning trees and on paper history.

SIDELIGHTS: Grummer told *CA:* "Paper is an amazing subject. It sends its tendrils into every facet of life. As a technical process, it depends entirely on a natural bond between fibers that are so small it is difficult to see them as individuals without the aid of magnification. As a manufacturing process, the bond between these small items is acquired by an industry that is capital-intensive, including papermaking machines that are a block long and can turn out paper up to sixty miles an hour at a width of over thirty feet. Run one of those a month without stopping and you've produced a lot of product. It's a natural product, mostly parts of trees these days. And so the paper you touch stems from the forests and drinks heavily of mighty rivers and lakes because the natural bond will not occur unless there is water around the fibers.

"In its borning, paper invades forests, streams, sounds, and bays, cotton fields, bamboo patches, sugar cane fields, and, more recently, kenaf fields. From each of these forests, fields, and patches, paper bleeds the cellulose fibers that form a part of each growing plant. And each year, paper devours a goodly bit of Georgia (kaolin clay) to give itself a modified surface or optical properties.

"But paper's most heavy touch is in people's lives. It has been the main medium for one generation to speak to another. It has been the world's memory, recorder, and reporter. It has been man's immortality in language—thought, music, and art. Sometime during the tenth century it dealt the fatal blow to Egypt's papyrus, a product that had reigned supreme or at a significant level as the world's writing and communicating material for four thousand years. Today, it has achieved as-

cendency. Paper used in the United States averages to each man, woman, and child more than six hundred pounds.

"A voracious eater with a never-sated appetite, paper spawned research on cloning trees that did indeed produce the world's first cloned tree with the hope of being able to produce a master race of forests that would forever and adequately produce the fiber needed for papers multiplication. The tree still grows on the campus of The Institute of Paper Chemistry in Appleton, Wisconsin. But, alas, for that particular tree and others cloned at the same time, a part is missing, a key needs to be found, for the clone does not stand proud, tall, and well-formed as did its tissue donor. So very likely there is much being said these days about this paper-spawned tree and why it didn't do what was expected and how the genetic directions can be stabilized for future clones.

"Thus, as a receptacle for a million minds, as the wrapper for a million products, trod on by millions of feet as a component of millions of shoe soles, held high and sacredly uplifted as Bible or Koran, paper, a most common product, is a most unusual substance. A small, almost microscopic fiber, is a world colossus. So while other people might write of medicine, psychology, philosophy, spirituality, sexuality, history, poetry, or fiction, it is likely to be many reams before I exhaust the possibilities of writing on paper . . . about paper."

Grummer is the designer and manufacturer of "The Great American Paper Machine, Jr.," a hand papermaking device and kit.

* * *

GRUNGE
See CRUMB, R(obert)

* * *

GUILD, Vera Palmer 1906-

BRIEF ENTRY: Born May 25, 1906, in Stamford, Neb. American magazine editor. Guild has been the sewing and needlepoint editor of *Good Housekeeping* since 1955. Her books include *Creative Use of Stitches* (Davis Publications, 1964), *Good Housekeeping New Complete Book of Needlecraft* (Good Housekeeping Books, 1971), *Painting With Stitches: A Guide to Embroidery, Needlepoint, Crochet, and Macrame* (Davis Publications, 1976), and *Good Housekeeping Book of Quilt Making* (Hearst Books, 1976). *Address:* 90 Chestnut St., Millburn, N.J. 07041; and *Good Housekeeping,* 959 Eighth Ave., New York, N.Y. 10019.

* * *

GUSTAFSON, Paula Catherine 1941-

PERSONAL: Born February 25, 1941, in Abbotsford, British Columbia, Canada; daughter of Ernest and Lois Alberta (MacPherson) Eaton; married John Gustafson (divorced); children: Monica Lee Schmutz, Nisse Elizabeth. *Education:* Attended public schools in British Columbia. *Home:* 34909 Old Yale Rd., No. 623, Abbotsford, British Columbia, Canada V2S 5W4.

CAREER: Legal secretary in Vancouver, British Columbia, 1960-65; Bahamian Pottery Ltd., Nassau, Bahamas, manager, 1965-66; operated pottery business in Yarrow, British Columbia, 1971-75; legal secretary to attorney in Chilliwack, British Columbia, 1976-78; City of Chilliwack, deputy clerk, 1979; District of Abbotsford, Abbotsford, British Columbia, executive secretary to mayor and council, 1980; District of Matsqui,

Clearbrook, British Columbia, assistant municipal clerk, 1981—. Co-founder of Traverse City Arts Council; coordinator of Bluegrass Festival; administrative assistant for Vancouver's Habitat Crafts Festival. Lecturer at Pacific Northwest Anthropology Conference, Eugene, Ore.; National Museums of Canada, Langley, British Columbia; and Simon Fraser University, Burnaby, British Columbia. Pottery and weavings exhibited at festivals and museums. Consultant to British Columbia Department of Economic Development. *Member:* British Columbia Potters Guild, Craftsmen's Association of British Columbia. *Awards, honors:* Canada Council grants, 1978, 1979; nomination for British Columbia Book Award from T. Eaton Co., 1981, for *Salish Weaving.*

WRITINGS: (Editor) *Handbook for Craftspeople in British Columbia,* British Columbia Department of Economic Development, 1977; *Salish Weaving,* University of Washington Press, 1980. Contributor to magazines, including *Canadian Living* and *Western Living.* Editor of *Craft Contacts;* contributing editor of *Harrowsmith,* 1977—.

WORK IN PROGRESS: Research on the various types of Pacific Northwest Coast Indian textiles, including Chilkat blankets, Makah birdskin blankets, and Bella Coola and Salish weaving.

SIDELIGHTS: Paula Gustafson conducted research in southeast Alaska, Copenhagen, Helsinki, Leningrad, Dublin, New York, Chicago, and Washington, where she examined artifacts of the Pacific Northwest coast in museums and private collections.

Gustafson told *CA:* "I never planned to be an author. Writing a book is simply the best way I know to compress all my research notes and my thoughts into a neat, tidy package. In much the same way that a poem crystallizes a moment in time, a book encompasses a level of understanding. When it's done, it can be put aside and I'm free (finally!) to go on."

*   *   *

GUTHRIE, John 1908-

PERSONAL: Born January 8, 1908, in Antwerp, Belgium; son of James Denton (an engineer) and Christine (McLellan) Guthrie; married Phyllis Mary Hole; children: Diana Hilary, Valerie Claire Guthrie Rowell. *Education:* Attended Royal Technical College, Glasgow, Scotland, 1926-30. *Religion:* Church of England. *Home:* 15 Edensor Rd., Meads, Eastbourne, Sussex BN20 7XR, England.

CAREER: Marine engineer with various shipping companies, 1930-38; Lloyd's Register of Shipping, London, England, marine surveyor in Cardiff, Wales, Belfast, Northern Ireland, Nottingham, England, Lisbon and Oporto, Portugal, and London, 1938-72; writer, 1972—. *Member:* Institute of Marine Engineers (fellow), Institute of Mechanical Engineers (fellow).

WRITINGS: Bizarre Ships of the Nineteenth Century, Hutchinson, 1970; *A History of Marine Engineering,* Hutchinson, 1971. Contributor to marine engineering and mechanical engineering journals.

WORK IN PROGRESS: Research on the S.S. *Great Britain.*

SIDELIGHTS: Guthrie commented: "I am motivated to attempt to raise the status of engineer in Great Britain to that position held by American and European engineers."

*   *   *

GUTHRIE, Russell Dale 1936-

BRIEF ENTRY: Born October 27, 1936, in Nebo, Ill. American

zoologist, educator, and author. Guthrie joined the faculty at the University of Alaska in 1963 and has been a professor of zoology since 1974. He wrote *Body Hot Spots: The Anatomy of Human Social Organs and Behavior* (Van Nostrand, 1976). *Address:* Department of Biological Science, University of Alaska, Fairbanks, Alaska 99701. *Biographical/critical sources: American Men and Women of Science: The Physical and Biological Sciences,* 14th edition, Bowker, 1979.

*   *   *

GWENDOLYN
See BENNETT, (Enoch) Arnold

*   *   *

GZOWSKI, Peter 1934-

PERSONAL: Surname is pronounced *Zah*-ski; born July 13, 1934, in Toronto, Ontario, Canada; son of Harold E. and Margaret McGregor (Young) Gzowski; married wife, A. Jeanette (an interior designer), February 15, 1958; children: Peter, Alison, Maria, John, Mickey. *Education:* Attended University of Toronto. *Home:* Old Quarry Rd., Rockwood, Ontario N0B 2K0.

CAREER: Journalist. Associated with *Timmins Press, Chatham Daily News, Moose Jaw Times-Herald, Toronto Telegram,* and *Toronto Star; Maclean's* (magazine), Toronto, Ontario, staff writer, 1958-64; *Toronto Star Weekly,* Toronto, editor, 1966; *Maclean's,* editor, 1968; Canadian Broadcasting Corp. (CBC), Toronto, host of daily radio program, "This Country in the Morning," and host of television program, "90 Minutes Live"; currently free-lance writer. Director of Key Publishers and *Toronto Life* (magazine). *Awards, honors:* President's Medal, 1964, for magazine writing.

WRITINGS—All nonfiction: (With Trent Frayne) *Great Canadian Sports Stories: A Century of Competition,* Canadian Centennial Publishing Co., 1965; (with Nancy Greene and Jack Batten) *Nancy,* Star Reader Service, 1968; *Peter Gzowski's Book About This Country in the Morning,* Hurtig, 1974; *Peter Gzowski's Spring Tonic,* Hurtig, 1979; *The Sacrament,* McClelland & Stewart, 1980. Contributor of articles to newspapers and magazines, including *Toronto Life* and *Saturday Night.*

WORK IN PROGRESS: A book about hockey.

SIDELIGHTS: Early in his career as a newsman, Peter Gzowski was known as Canada's "boy wonder of journalism." By age twenty-three he had progressed from the small *Timmins Press* to city editor of the *Chatham Daily News,* and from there to positions with *Maclean's* and Toronto's major dailies, the *Star* and *Telegram.* The articles he wrote during his years at *Maclean's* are still regarded as among the best ever published by the magazine. Gzowski stayed with *Maclean's* until 1964, when he and several other writers and editors quit over the issue of editorial freedom. During the next several years he held editing jobs at the *Star Weekly* and *Saturday Night,* wrote books and newspaper columns, and tried to launch his own magazine, *This City,* which failed. By the early seventies he had all but left newspaper and magazine writing to work in radio and television.

Gzowski's radio and television commentaries began in the late 1960's, when he also started hosting a weekly radio show on Friday nights. Then he was chosen by the Canadian Broadcasting Corporation (CBC) to host a new radio program called "This Country in the Morning," patterned largely on the talk-show format. Within a year Gzowski was nationally famous and the star of what many called "the best radio program in the world." "This Country in the Morning" became the most successful radio venture in the CBC's corporate history, and Gzowski, who was winning critical praise as an interviewer, soon found himself hosting a television show as well, called "90 Minutes Live."

When the entertainment needs of his shows began to interfere with his professionalism as a journalist, Gzowski resigned from his broadcasting duties. He turned to writing books, instead, including a personal review of "This Country in the Morning," an oral history, and a detailed account of a plane crash and its two survivors. In the latter book, called *The Sacrament*, Gzowski reconstructs the story of Brent Dyer and Donna Johnson, whose chartered Cessna crashed into a snow-bound Idaho mountainside on May 5, 1979, killing the pilot and Johnson's father. As their ordeal worsened they were forced to choose between starvation and cannibalism.

"It's a gripping, gruesome story touched with compassion," wrote Marty Gervais in his review for the *Windsor Star*. "[Gzowski] got into the souls of Brent Dyer and Donna Johnson. . . . He brings you into the blizzard-ravaged canyon with Brent and Donna. He makes you experience the pain and the hunger. He leads you through the anguish, the euphoric highs as the two anticipated rescue, the agonizing depression of dying. . . . The result is an exceptional account that leaves nothing unturned. It is also one that makes it quite clear that this isn't the story of cannibalism, but a story of faith, of two young people who find God."

CA INTERVIEW

CA interviewed Peter Gzowski at his home in Rockwood, Ontario, on August 30, 1980.

CA: Is the book you're working on, your hockey book, a "writing book," something you're writing, or is it an "oral" history kind of thing, like Spring Tonic?

GZOWSKI: It's very much a "writing book," very much. It's not at all an interview book. I wish it were. It would be a lot easier. I think people are bored with that oral history stuff, you know. I know there are those who disagree with me. I actually did look at an oral-history approach to this book, because there is a beautiful book I like very much called *The Glory of Their Time*. And I think I would like to see somebody do that. I have some stuff on tape, as a matter of fact, but it's source material.

CA: You told me earlier this book on hockey would be the first "serious" book on hockey ever written.

GZOWSKI: I'm not sure whether that's fair to other people who've written about hockey. In a way I'd call it the first "adult" book about hockey, but then that's not fair to them either, you see, because I think that most people who have written about hockey have assumed that their audience is fourteen years old. There's a wonderful literature of baseball in the United States and no comparable literature of hockey. It's been argued that baseball is a much more writerly sport, and I guess that's true. One of the things I find difficult to do is to capture a hockey game on a page. In fact, I don't think anybody can do it, because the game is so much faster than your typewriter, faster than your reading eye, so you have to slow the game down. It's the most interesting writing I've ever done. Of course, you're supposed to say that about anything new you're working on, but it's quite a different thing for me. It keeps me awake, and I live it.

CA: Why do you think people are bored with oral history?

GZOWSKI: Maybe it's just that I am, having done one book (*Spring Tonic*) which I'm not very proud of—an easy book. I'm very anti easy books, and oral histories can be an easy way out, an easy way of handling a subject. But that doesn't make them less pleasant to read.

CA: Tell me about your latest book, The Sacrament. *It's a book about survivors of a plane crash and cannibalism. How did you get to do this?*

GZOWSKI: I was in Jack McClelland's (publisher of Mc-Clelland and Stewart) one day doing a little editing, and he said, "Come on down and we'll talk about a story." It turned out that I'd read about it in *Maclean's,* and I had thought that somebody would probably do a book on this. So I went down to Jack's office, and he told me much of the story, a little more than what was in *Maclean's.* It turned out he'd had a call from their lawyer—the lawyer of the survivors, Brent Dyer and Donna Johnston. And there was something in the way he told the story that really interested me. So I was going out to Winnipeg the following week to host the folk festival there, and I said I'd go down to Estevan to meet these two young people. I just wanted to check them out and let them check me out. They had decided to tell their story in book form, but they didn't know anything about writers. So I went to talk to them.

I spent a couple of days on that first trip, and my first impressions were quite favorable. I wrote Jack a letter saying I thought there was a hell of a book in it, but it depended on a lot of things—it was a real reporter's book. It needed other dimensions to it; it couldn't be a first-person book. There were a lot of negotiations back and forth, and they agreed and I agreed, and I went and spent most of the summer with them. I went down to Idaho with Brent and went over the route that they had walked out. I had a researcher who did much of the work on putting together the search process. And I wrote a book.

CA: So it's not a book about the survivors as told to Peter Gzowski?

GZOWSKI: No, not at all. It's a book about them, about a part of the world they come from, about the search; it's about a lot of things. I don't want to say anything about it. I'd rather other people say something about it. I'm very proud of it, I'm very happy about it. I think people who just hear about it will be surprised. It's not a book about cannibalism.

CA: You see yourself as a journalist, but what kind of journalist? Like Truman Capote, who says he's raised journalism to a high art in his book Music For Chameleons?

GZOWSKI: I'm not much in favor of people who put labels on their own stuff, and I'm too much an admirer of Capote to try to talk about my work on the same level, but whether a word like "the new journalism" means anything, I don't know. I think it does. There's a wonderful collection of stuff called "new journalism" that Tom Wolfe and another guy did which has work by Wolfe, Jimmy Breslin, Talese, Capote, Hunter Thompson, a whole bunch of people who write in that style. I could ramble on for hours about that. I've thought about and worked with it a lot.

I think the major figure of that revolution was Wolfe, not Capote, and an awful lot of people in this country tried to imitate his style. I saw writers when I was editing *Maclean's* —it was right at the peak of Wolfe's fashionability—and writer after writer would try to capture his style. I always thought that the fundamentally important thing that Wolfe had done was to raise the level of reportage. And so did Capote. There are people who argue with that, too, and say that Wolfe is a very sloppy reporter—he's always being caught in factual errors—but he says the truth is greater than the sum of the facts. I know of stories that he's written, of which I have personal knowledge, and to me they ring dead-on true, and yet the facts in them are demonstratively wrong. But in Wolfe's early work what he was doing then changed a lot of perceptions of what journalism and writing were all about. When Capote published *In Cold Blood* in the *New Yorker*—he called it a "nonfiction novel"—there was some question about his ability. I mean, could anyone have absorbed that much dialogue, that much information? How was he able to recreate the dialogue when in fact he wasn't there?

In *The Sacrament* I used exactly that same technique. There are long passages in *The Sacrament* that are dialogue between Brent and Donna that I obviously couldn't have heard. I'll vouch for its accuracy because it's all been read by them, and I made very few changes in it. What happened was that I spent so much time with them, got so far inside their heads, that when I came to do the writing, which was here, a couple of thousand miles away from them, those two people existed for me in the way that I've heard novelists talk about their characters existing. They really did get a life of their own, so that the dialogue was written or spoken, for my purposes, by two people whom I had gotten to know.

CA: What is your method of working? Do you take notes, or do you rely strictly on a typewriter?

GZOWSKI: Well, I do take notes, but I am a terrible handwriter. My handwriting is virtually illegible, to me as well. I am not one of those neat, methodical note takers. I envy people who are, and I wish to hell I was because I ought to be. I will read my notes over before I do anything. Work for me means reading three or four hours before I ever start writing. I'll read over my notes. I'll read my original sources over. I'll then take notes with a pencil, or I'll pin things up on the wall, or I'll write little outlines or skeletal notes, and after that, when it's back in my head—it's sort of been through my head and on to a piece of paper and then back in my head—*then* I write.

I write compulsively and at great length. In my magazine days I was regarded as a tremendously fast writer. I still write quickly, and I rewrite a lot. If it's possible, I'll leave some time between the first draft and the second and the third, but that's the process for me. I've been twenty-six years in journalism, from the *Timmins Press* to whatever I'm doing now. The funny thing, though, is that I lost a lot of those muscles, those writing muscles, when I left *Maclean's* to go into radio and television. This process of writing a book—what the musicians call sustaining a longer line—is quite a new act for me. So if I'm sounding wise and certain and sure of myself, in fact, I'm groping toward techniques. I learned an awful lot by doing *The Sacrament*, about my own habits. And I was very fortunate in having a book which had a defined beginning, middle, and end. The process I'm in now, in writing this hockey book, has none of those things. I have to impose structure, but I know I'm doing this book better because of *The Sacrament*.

BIOGRAPHICAL/CRITICAL SOURCES: Windsor Star, November 21, 1972, September 27, 1980; *Canadian Forum*, June, 1975; *Books in Canada*, April, 1979.

—*Interview by C. H. Gervais*

H

HAAVIKKO, Paavo Juhani 1931-
(Anders Lieksman)

PERSONAL: Born January 25, 1931, in Helsinki, Finland; son of Heikki Adrian (a businessman) and Rauha (Pyykonen) Haavikko; married Marja-liisa Vartio Sairanen (a poet and novelist), June 7, 1955 (died, 1966); married Ritva Rainio Hanhineva (a university lecturer), March 6, 1971; children: (first marriage) Johanna, Heikki. *Home:* Tamminiementie 15, 02940 Espoo 94, Finland. *Office:* c/o Otava Publishing Co., P.O. Box 134, SF-00120 Helsinki 12, Finland.

CAREER: Worked in real estate, 1951-67; writer, 1951—; Otava Publishing Co., Hensinki, Finland, literary director, 1967—, member of board of directors, 1968—. Member of the State Committee for Literature, 1966-67. Member of the board of Great Finnish Book Club, 1969, Yhtyneet Kuvalehdet Magazine Co., 1970-82, and Kalevala Society, 1976—. *Military service:* Finnish Army, 1951-52; became sergeant. *Member:* Finnish Writers Union (member of board, 1962-67).

AWARDS, HONORS: Aleksis Kivi Prize from Finnish Literature Society, 1966, for literary merits; Pro Finlandia medal, 1967, and Knight First Class of the White Rose of Finland, 1978, both from Orders of Finland for literary merits; honorary doctorate from the University of Helsinki, 1969; eight literary prizes from the State.

WRITINGS—All published by Otava, except as noted, in English: *Talvipalatsi* (poems), 1959, translation by Anselm Hollo published as ''The Winter Palace,'' in *Chelsea 17,* [Gibraltar], 1961; *Lasi Claudius Civiliksen salaliittolaisten poydalla* (stories; title means ''A Glass on the Table of Julius Civilis''; contains ''Lumeton aika,'' translation by Philip Binham published as ''Before History Begins,'' in *The Story Today,* Simon & Schuster, 1967, a new translation by Herbert Lomas published as ''Snowless Time,'' in *Territorial Song: Contemporary Writing From Finland,* London Magazine, 1981), 1964; *Selected Poems* (contains ''The Winter Palace'' [also see above] and fifteen short poems), edited and translated by Hollo, Grossman, 1968, also in *Selected Poems by Paavo Haavikko and Tomas Transtromer,* Penguin, 1974; (author of libretto) *Ratsumies/The Horseman* (three-act opera; first produced at Savonlinna Opera Festival, Savonlinna, Finland, 1975), music composed by Aulis Sallinen, translation of bilingual edition by Binham privately printed, 1974; (lyricist) ''Four Dream Songs,'' music by Sallinen, translation by Binham published by Edition Fazer, 1975; ''Ylilaakari'' (television play; title

means ''The Superintendent''; first broadcast by Finnish Television, 1966), translation by Binham published in *Snow in May: An Anthology of Finnish Writing, 1945-1972,* edited by Richard Dauenhauer and Binham, Associated University Press, 1978.

Novels: *Yksityisia asioita* (title means ''Private Affairs''), 1960; *Toinen taivas ja maa* (title means ''Another Heaven and Earth''), 1961; *Vuodet* (title means ''The Years''), 1962; (under pseudonym Anders Lieksman) *Barr-niminen mies* (title means ''A Man Called Barr''), 1976.

Poems: *Tiet etaisyyksiin* (title means ''The Ways to Faraway''), Werner Soderstrom, 1951; *Tuulioina* (title means ''On Windy Nights''), 1953; *Synnyinmaa* (title means ''Native Land''), 1955; *Lehdet lehtia* (title means ''Leaves, Leaves''), 1958; *Runot, 1951-1961* (title means ''Poems, 1951-1961''), 1962; *Puut, kaikki heidan vihreytensa* (title means ''Trees in All Their Verdure''), 1966; *Neljatoista hallitsijaa* (title means ''Fourteen Rulers''), 1970; *Runoja matkalta salmen ylitse* (title means ''Poems From a Voyage Across the Sound''), 1973; *Kaksikymmenta ja yksi* (title means ''Twenty and One''), 1974; *Viinia, kirjoitusta* (title means ''Wine, Writing''), 1976.

Plays: ''Munchhausen'' (three-act), first produced in Helsinki, Finland at Finnish National Theatre, 1958; ''Nuket'' (three-act; title means ''The Dolls''), first produced in Helsinki at Finnish National Theatre, 1960; ''Agricola ja kettu'' (seven scenes; title means ''Agricola and the Fox''), first produced in Helsinki at Helsinki City Theatre, 1968; ''Brotteruksen perhe'' (three-act; title means ''The Brotterus Family''), first produced in Helsinki at Finnish National Theatre, 1969; *Sulka* (fourteen scenes; title means ''The Feather''; first produced in Helsinki at Finnish National Theatre, 1973), privately printed, 1973; ''Ne vahvimmat miehet ei ehjiksi jaa'' (three-act; title means ''The Strongest Men Don't Stay Unscathed''), first produced in Turku, Finland, at Turku City Theatre, 1976; ''Kaisa ja Otto'' (three-act; title means ''Kaisa and Otto''), first produced in Helsinki at Helsinki City Theatre, 1977.

Published radio plays: ''Audun ja jaakarhu'' (title means ''Audun and the Polar Bear''; first broadcast by Finnish Broadcasting Corp., 1967), published in *Kahden vuoden aanet,* 1969; ''Kilpikonna'' (title means ''The Turtle''; first broadcast by Finnish Broadcasting Corp., 1968), published in *Aanet myohassa,* 1970; *Kuningas lahtee Ranskaan* (title means ''The King Leaves for France''; first broadcast by Finnish Broadcasting Corp., 1975), 1974; *Harald Pitkaikainen* (title means

"Harald the Long-Lived"; first broadcast by Finnish Broadcasting Corp., 1974), 1974, translation by Diana Tullberg first broadcast by British Broadcasting Corp., 1977; *Soitannollinen ilta Viipurissa 1918* (title means "Soiree in Viipuri 1918"; first broadcast by Finnish Broadcasting Corp., 1978), 1978.

Unpublished radio plays: "Lyhytaikai-set lainat" (title means "Short-Term Loans"), first broadcast by Finnish Broadcasting Corp., 1966; "Freyan pelto" (title means "Freya's Field"), first broadcast by Finnish Broadcasting Corp., 1967; "Kuningas Haraldin pitka reissu" (title means "King Harald's Long Trip"), first broadcast by Finnish Broadcasting Corp., 1975; "Kertomus siita miten kuningas Harald kasitteli eraita hankalia kysymyksia" (title means "The Story of How King Harald Dealt With Some Tough Problems"), first broadcast by Finnish Broadcasting Corp., 1976; "Kuningas Harald, jaahyvaiset" (title means "King Harald's Farewell"), first broadcast by Finnish Broadcasting Corp., 1976; "Kuninkaat, veljekset" (title means "Kings, Brothers"), first broadcast by Finnish Broadcasting Corp., 1979; "Herra Ostanskog" (title means "Mr. Ostanskog"), first broadcast by Finnish Broadcasting Corp., 1981; "Viinin karsimykset Venajalla" (title means "The Afflictions of Wine in Russia"), first broadcast by Finnish Broadcasting Corp., 1981.

Omnibus volumes: *Munchhausen* [and] *Nuket,* 1960; *Runot, 1951-1961* (title means "Poems, 1951-1961"; contains "Tiet etaisyyksiin" [also see above], "Juhlat" [title means "Festivities"], "Tuulioina" [also see above], "Synnyinmaa" [also see above], "Lehdet lehtia" [also see above], "Talvipalatsi" [also see above], "Joulukuun runot" [title means "December Poems"], and "Viisi runoa klassillisesta aiheesta" [title means "Five Poems About Classical Subjects"]), 1962; *Ylilaakari* (contains "Ylilaakari" [also see above] and "Agricola ja kettu" [also see above]), 1968; *Runot, 1949-1974* (title means "Poems, 1949-1974"; contains "Sillat" [title means "Bridges"], "Tiet etaisyyksiin" [also see above], "Maanosa" [title means "Continent"], "Tuulioina" [also see above], "Synnyinma" [also see above], "Lehdet lehtia" [also see above], "Talvipalatsi" [also see above], "Viisi runoa klassillisesta aiheesta" [also see above], "Puut, kaikki heidan vihreytensa" [also see above], "Kymmenen runoa vuodelta 1966" [title means "Ten Poems From 1966], "Runoja matkalta salmen ylitse" [also see above], and "Maailmassa" [title means "In the World"]), 1975; *Runoelmat* (title means "Longer Poems"; contains "Roomalaisia iltoja" [title means "Roman Evenings"], "Juhlat" [also see above], "Suomalainen sarja" [title means "Finnish Series"], "Ministerin talvisota" [title means "The Minister's Winter War"], "Selva johdatus myohempaan historiaan" [title means "A Plain Introduction to Later History"], "Neljatoista hallitsijaa" [also see above], "Kaytannollisia toimia" [title means "Practical Deeds"], "Puhua, vastata, opettaa" [also see below], "Ammatti" [title means "Profession"], "Viimeinen versio myohemmasta historiasta" [title means "The Final Version of Later History"], and "Kaksikymmenta ja yksi" [also see above]), 1975.

Naytelmat (title means "Plays"; contains "Munchhausen," "Ylilaakari," "Agricola ja kettu," "Audun ja jaakarhu," "Kilpikonna," "Sulka," "Ratsumies," "Kuningas lahtee Ranskaan," "Ne vahvimmat miehet ei ehjiksi jaa," "Kaisa ja Otto," "Harold Pitkaikainen," and "Harald, jaahyvaiset" [see all above]), 1978; *Viisi pienta draamallista tekstia* (title means "Five Small Dramatic Pieces"; contains "Kuninkaat, veljekset" [also see above], "Naismetsa" [title means "Woman's Forest"], "Herra Ostanskog" [also see above], and "Viinin karsimykset Venajalla" [also see above], and "Tilintarkastus Viini-Yhtiossa" [title means "Audit in the Wine Company"]), 1981. Works also collected in *Romaanit ja novellit* (title means

"Novels and Short Stories"; contains "Yksityisia asioita" [also see above], "Toinen taivas ja maa" [also see above], "Vuodet" [also see above], "Barr-niminen mies" [also see above], "Lasi Claudius Civiliksen salaliittolaisten poydalla" [also see above], "3.s (III) Suomen Teollisuuden Harjoittajain Ambulanssi Venajalla" [title means "The Third Finnish Industrialists' Ambulance in Russia"]).

Other: *Puhua, vastata, opettaa* (aphorisms; title means "Speak, Answer, Teach"), 1972, enlarged edition, 1973; *Kansakunnan linja* (essay; title means "The National Line"), 1977; *Ihmisen aani* (essay; title means "The Human Voice"), Werner Soderstrom Oy, 1977; *Ikuisen rauhan aika* (aphorisms; title means "Eternal Peacetime"), 1981; *Rauta-aika* (four-part television play; title means "Iron Age"; first broadcast by Finnish Television Corp., 1982), 1982.

SIDELIGHTS: In *Suomalaisia nykykirjailijoita,* critic Pekka Tarkka noted that Haavikko has become a sort of Finnish "oracle," who is able to write in a variety of genres, including fiction, poetry, and essays. A major contributor to the post-World War II modernist revival in Finland, Haavikko is recognized as one of his homeland's most talented and innovative writers. Though he was not the first Finnish poet to break with tradition, Haavikko was the only one of the postwar revivalists, said *Books Abroad* critic Kai Laitinen, "who did not seem to need any preparatory stage or to go through any five-finger exercises to find his own style . . . [for] he was born complete into Finnish poetry." Haavikko's first collection of verse, *Tiet etaisyyksiin,* Laitinen continued, "[introduces] the aims of the poet," which are "to get Finnish poetry stylistically up-to-date, and . . . to give expression to the voice of the young postwar generation." Richard Dauenhauer, also writing in *Books Abroad,* concurred, describing Haavikko's poetry as "a two-pronged attack on the style and content of Finnish poetry before 1950." Published in 1951 when Haavikko was just twenty, *Tiet etaisyyksiin* "has been called a manifesto of the new poetry," according to Laitinen.

One of Haavikko's best known works is *Talvipalatsi,* a nine-cycle poem that was published in the United States as "The Winter Palace." The volume, which contains many references to the old Russian capital of St. Petersburg, became "one of the landmarks of modern Finnish literature," reported Dauenhauer, "and firmly established Haavikko as the most original voice in postwar Finnish poetry." The book's significance, he continued, lay in its impact on younger poets who were forced "to redefine their conception of lyric poetry."

Haavikko is unusual among modern lyric poets in that he often draws upon events from ancient Rome, the Middle Ages, and Russian and Finnish history for his poems. When questioned about his frequent use of historical subjects, Haavikko declared, "Everything is history." He then disclosed that as a youth he had found poetry unintelligible because it was comprised entirely of "generalizations." "I thought," he recalled, "that if I should write poetry myself I would start from reality, from real events."

Reality, though, is constantly in a state of flux, according to Haavikko. "The concept of impermanence is one of the common denominators in Haavikko's imagery," observed Dauenhauer, adding that "for Haavikko, permanence is an illusion." Laitinen concurred but pointed out that Haavikko also suggests that "[man's] fundamental situation is essentially the same," for in the poet's works "past periods are implicitly present today, men are different, but their actions, passions, dreams, errors are identical." It has been said, wrote Philip Binham in *Books Abroad,* that "in Haavikko's philosophy the unpredictability of history and the future forms the uniqueness of each situation, and this gives man his small freedom." But, wrote Haavikko in *Puut, kaikki heidan vihreytensa,* though "full of free will / [man] is completely dependent on everything." This paradox, he implies, contributes to man's difficulty in understanding his world. But Haavikko's view, according to Laitinen, is that "the world is a cruel place" where "irony and paradox are the language of reality." The only way to cope with this dilemma, insists Haavikko, is "to know almost everything yourself."

Haavikko's poems, with their allusions to little known historical events, challenge the reader to learn as much as possible about the past. Some critics have commented that these references tend to limit access to Haavikko's poetry to well-educated readers. Binham, for example, remarked, "The poet can hardly expect all his readers to study eleventh-century Byzantium in order to appreciate 'Fourteen Rulers.'" Insight into Haavikko's verse is also hampered by the poet's reluctance to provide titles for his individual poems. However, Binham pointed out, "there are signs in the comparatively clear, aphoristic wisdom of 'Speak, Answer, Teach' that [Haavikko] is looking for a more direct form of communication." "Haavikko's treatment of historic motifs has with time become clearer and clearer," agreed Jaakko A. Ahokas of *Books Abroad,* but insisted "he has still managed occasionally to leave his readers in doubt about his intentions." "Despite this difficulty," argued Laitinen, "[Haavikko's] texts can have an immediate impact on the reader. The atmosphere, the images, the ironic undertones are enough to guide him in the right direction at least."

During the early 1960's Haavikko began writing prose works, including four novels, a collection of short stories, and an opera libretto. He also became known as an innovative playwright. Haavikko, for example, introduced the theatre of the absurd to Finland. His first play, an absurdist drama entitled "Munchhausen," concerns the political machinations surrounding an attempt to partition Poland by Russia's empress Catherine the Great and Austria's emissary Baron von Munchhausen. In its portrayal of man's attempt to acquire power, the play reflects the same view of the preposterousness of human existence that its author reveals in his poetry.

Binham wrote in *World Literature Today* that "the motifs of *Munchausen* [sic] appear more richly and profoundly in . . . Haavikko's best play, *Agricola ja kettu.*" Both "Agricola" and Haavikko's later work, "Ratsumies," resemble "Munchhausen" in that they feature the actions of public leaders who are involved in a similar situation, the potential dismemberment of Finland by Russia and Sweden. These works are, however, more realistically drawn than his earlier "Munchhausen." In Haavikko's later dramas, Binham also noted, "women characters are more common, more important and less dumb" than in his early plays. Furthermore, "Haavikko's women remind their men that for all their strutting and their big talk they are still at the mercy of forces beyond their powers."

According to Haavikko, Tarkka commented, "Haavikko's dramatical works are temporally diverse, the scene can be in any period, from the time of the Old Icelandic sagas to the present. The stage setting can just as well be on land or on sea, in a primitive woodman's hut or in a king's court. His characters can be gods, heroes of epic poems, kings, bishops, businessmen or intellectuals. His characters reflect the hard realities of life both gloomily and bitingly, but often characterised by shrewd comedy."

After publishing only works of prose for several years, Haavikko wrote a new volume of poetry entitled *Puut, kaikko heidan vihreytensa,* which is regarded by many critics as the author's finest work. All of Haavikko's writings, though, are executed "with ease and assurance," asserted Binham, who argued that they would be translated more often if it "were not so difficult to render the subtlety of Haavikko's rhythms and use of language satisfactorily."

BIOGRAPHICAL/CRITICAL SOURCES: *Books Abroad,* winter, 1969, winter, 1970, spring, 1970, winter, 1972, spring, 1976; *Nation,* February 17, 1969; *Poetry,* July, 1969; *World Literature Today,* spring, 1977, spring, 1979; Pekka Tarkka, *Suomalaisia nykykirjailijoita* (title means "Modern Finnish Writers"), Tammi Publishers, 1980; *Contemporary Literary Criticism,* Volume XVIII, Gale, 1981.

—*Sketch by Susan M. Trosky*

*   *   *

HABERLY, David T(ristram)   1942-

PERSONAL: Born December 11, 1942, in Tucson, Ariz.; son of Loyd (a poet and professor) and Virginia (Dean) Haberly; married Carol E. Lindblom (a technical writer), June 9, 1963; children: Duncan Charles, Anne Sills. *Education:* Harvard University, A.B., 1963, A.M., 1964, Ph.D., 1966. *Residence:* Charlottesville, Va. *Office:* Department of Spanish, Italian, and Portuguese, University of Virginia, Charlottesville, Va. 22901.

CAREER: Harvard University, Cambridge, Mass., assistant professor of Portuguese, 1966-73; University of Virginia, Charlottesville, associate professor of Portuguese, 1973—, chairman of dpeartment of Spanish, Italian, and Portuguese, 1973-78. *Member:* Modern Language Association of America (member of executive committee of Portuguese-Brazilian Division, 1974-80, chairman of division, 1979-80), Partners of the Americas. *Awards, honors:* Grants from Gulbenkian Foundation, 1972, Ford Foundation (for Brazil), 1972, and Partners of the Americas, 1978.

WRITINGS: (With F. M. Rogers) *Brazil, Portugal, and Other Portuguese-Speaking Lands: A List of Books Primarily in English,* Harvard University Press, 1968; *The Three Sad Races: Racial Identity and National Consciousness in Brazilian Literature,* Cambridge University Press, 1982. Contributor to scholarly journals.

WORK IN PROGRESS: Editing *Joao da Cruz e Sousa: The Black Swan,* an English translation with critical introduction; research on nineteenth-century literature in the United States, Latin America, and Australia; research on Brazilian literature.

SIDELIGHTS: Haberly told *CA:* "Brazil, for most Americans, is a strange and exotic land of palm trees and coffee plantations, beaches and jungles, Carnival and Carmen Miranda—'where the nuts come from,' to quote *Charley's Aunt.* Obviously these stereotypical and somewhat patronizing impressions do not accurately reflect Brazil's vastness and diversity; nor do they prepare us to deal with a dynamic and ambitious nation that is our most important neighbor—and our only potential rival—in this hemisphere.

"My own interest in Brazil has relatively little to do with these geopolitical considerations. What fascinates me is Brazil's literature—the only national literature of the Americas which is comparable, in quantity and in quality, to that of the United States. Brazilian literature is worthy of study for its own sake, but it is particularly interesting because it provides a vital counterpoint to the literary history of the United States. Specialists in American literature have long tended to consider it either in isolation or within the context of European influence. At least as fruitful as these approaches is the comparative study of Brazilian and American literature—two rich traditions which began at almost the same time and which endeavored, particularly in the nineteenth century, to deal with problems to which European culture offered few if any answers: the representation of the Indian and African, the role of the nonwhite writer, the literary utilization of the rapid expansion into vast new lands and the assimilation of hundreds of thousands of European immigrants, to give but a few examples. This, for me at least, is exciting and absorbing material which can teach us a great deal—not only about Brazil and its culture, but about ourselves.''

*   *   *

HACKLEMAN, Michael A(lan)   1946-

PERSONAL: Born April 22, 1946, in Atkinson, Neb.; son of Robert John (in U.S. Air Force) and Ruth (Kubitschek) Hackleman; married Vanessa Naumann (a research assistant), June 22, 1977; children: Brett Robert, Glenn Charles. *Education:* Attended Western State College, Gunnison, Colo., 1964-65, and San Diego City College, 1970-72. *Home and office:* Earthmind, 4844 Hirsch Rd., Mariposa, Calif. 95338. *Agent:* Harold Moskovitz, The Associates, 8961 Sunset Blvd., Suite B, Los Angeles, Calif. 90069.

CAREER: Scripps Institute of Oceanography, La Jolla, Calif., technician, 1970-73; Earthmind, Mariposa, Calif., founder, president of board of directors, and research director, 1974—. Seminar instructor at Merced College. *Military service:* U.S. Navy, electronics technician, 1964-69; served in Vietnam.

WRITINGS: Wind and Windspinners: A Nuts and Bolts Approach to Wind Systems, Peace Press, 1974; *The Homebuilt Wind-Generated Electricity Handbook,* Peace Press, 1975; *Electric Vehicles: Design and Build Your Own,* Peace Press, 1977, 2nd edition, 1980; *At Home With Alternative Energy,* Peace Press, 1980; *Better Use of . . . Utility-Supplied Electricity and Low-Voltage DC in Home and Shop,* Peace Press, 1981; *Waterworks: An Owner-Builder Guide to Rural Water Systems,* Doubleday, 1980; *Hybrid Electric Vehicles,* Peace Press, 1983.

WORK IN PROGRESS: Solar Welding; Tower Houses; Silent Weaponry; The Great Pyramid as an Irrigation Pump; City Run, on surviving national and man-made disasters in the city.

SIDELIGHTS: Hackleman commented: "I'm devoted to allowing people to take more control of their lives. I believe that my books are written in a manner which is easy to read, study, and apply because they are *not* theoretical, and they are not as dry as most technical publications. I don't believe in writing books on material which has already been published, and I always try to write for the layperson. I also believe that any book should sell on its own merit (such as a table of contents) and not on any kind of advertising hype. I'm proud that I've never spent one dollar on advertising my books (though my publisher sometimes does).''

In 1972, Hackleman created Earthmind, "a public nonprofit education and research corporation, a small organization working with natural energy sources, organic gardening, and other aspects of a more self-reliant living, funded exclusively through the sale of our publications.

"We are extensively involved in research with wind-electric machines, electric vehicles, and means whereby alternate energy users may make better use of the energy they tap. We are building a four-level, solar-heated, wind-electrified shop to better house our library, offices, and projects and to demonstrate more dramatically the effectiveness of alternate energy in meeting everyday power needs in the home and shop.

"We are only a few people. Between corporation projects and some semblance of a personal life, there's not much time left. So, our valiant efforts to answer all-hours phone calls or 'surprise' visits have taken their toll. We continue to be a resource, but since it *is* finite, we've had to strike a balance; at the present time, we can only be reached by mail.

"We are hopeful that our work contributes to a greener, cleaner, less abused environment and to a wider range of alternatives from which people may choose.''

*   *   *

HADDEN, Jeffrey K(eith)   1936-

PERSONAL: Born August 22, 1936, in Salina, Kan.; son of Roy Keith (a businessman) and Marjoie (Pike) Hadden; married Joy Dugan, June 3, 1955 (divorced, 1968); married Elaine D. McQueen (an editor), March 21, 1969; children: Nora (Mrs. Charles Sperry), Donna. *Education:* University of Kansas, B.A., 1959, and M.A., 1960; graduate study at Cornell University, 1960-61; University of Wisconsin (now University of Wisconsin—Madison), Ph.D., 1963. *Home:* 103 Vicar Ct., Charlottesville, Va. 22901. *Office:* Department of Sociology, University of Virginia, Charlottesville, Va. 22903.

CAREER: Purdue University, Lafayette, Ind., assistant professor of sociology, 1964-66; Case Western Reserve University, Cleveland, Ohio, associate professor of sociology, 1966-69; Tulane University, New Orleans, La., professor of sociology and urban studies, 1969-72; University of Virginia, Charlottesville, professor of sociology, 1972—, chairman of department, 1982—. Associate director of Civil Violence Research Center, 1968-69; visiting professor at Baylor College of Medicine, 1980-81. *Member:* American Association for the Advancement of Science (fellow), American Sociological Association (chairman of committee on publications, 1977-79), Southern Sociological Society (vice-president, 1980-81), Association for the Sociology of Religion (president, 1978-79), Society for the Scientific Study of Religion (vice-president, 1981-83).

WRITINGS: (With Edgar F. Borgatta) *American Cities: Their Social Characteristics,* Rand McNally, 1965; (with E. F. Borgatta) *A Study of the Demography of Nuclear War* (research monograph), Human Sciences Research, 1966; (with E. F. Borgatta and W. W. Pendleton) *A Second Study of the Demography of Nuclear War* (research monograph), Human Sciences Research, 1967; (editor with Louis H. Masotti and Calvin J. Larson) *Metropolis in Crisis: Social and Political Perspectives,* F. E. Peacock, 1967, 2nd edition, 1971; *The Gathering Storm in the Churches: The Widening Gap Between Clergy and Laymen,* Doubleday, 1969; (with Masotti, Kenneth F. Seminatore, and Jerome Corsi) *A Time to Burn?: An Evaluation of the Present Crisis in Race Relations,* Rand McNally, 1969; (editor with Marie L. Borgatta) *Marriage and the Family: A Comprehensive Reader,* F. E. Peacock, 1969.

(Editor) *Religion in Radical Transition,* Aldine, 1971; (with Masotti) *Suburbs, Suburbia, and Suburbanization: A Bibliography,* Center for Urban Affairs, Northwestern University, 1972; (editor with Masotti) *The Urbanization of the Suburbs,* Sage Publications, 1973; (with C. F. Longino, Jr.) *Gideon's Gang: A Case Study of the Church in Social Action,* United Church Press, 1974; (compiler, editor, and author of introduction with Masotti) *Suburbia in Transition,* New Viewpoints, 1974; (with E. E. Erickson) *Charlottesville: What We Say, What We Do, What We Hope For* (research monograph), Central Piedmont Urban Observatory, 1976; *The Emergence of Secular Faith* (sound recording), Thesis Theological Cassettes, 1978; (with Charles E. Swann) *Prime Time Preachers: The Rising Power of Televangelism,* Addison-Wesley, 1981; *The New Relevance of Religion* (festschrift), Continuum Books, 1982.

Contributor of articles and reviews to newspapers, magazines, and periodicals, including *Urban Affairs Quarterly, Sociological Quarterly, Social Science Quarterly, Christian Herald, Commonweal, Psychology Today,* and *Careers Today.* Member of editorial board of *Ministry Studies Monographs,* 1966-69, and *Sociological Focus,* 1968-69; faculty advisory editor of *Case Western Reserve University Journal of Sociology,* 1967-68; senior research editor of *Careers Today,* 1968-69; contributing editor of *Christian Ministry,* 1969-70; associate editor of *Sociological Analysis,* 1971-76, and *Social Forces,* 1975-78; book review editor of *Journal for the Scientific Study of Religion,* 1973-79; guest editor of *Sociological Analysis,* winter, 1979, and summer, 1980.

WORK IN PROGRESS: The Salvation Business, a sequel to *Prime Time Preachers: The Rising Power of Televangelism;* a research monograph on medical students.

SIDELIGHTS: Among Hadden's interests as a sociologist is the sociology of religion, particularly the relationship between organized religion and social change, civil rights, and political power. Religion has been the topic of many of his publications, including *The Gathering Storm in the Churches: The Widening Gap Between Clergy and Laymen* and *Prime Time Preachers: The Rising Power of Televangelism.*

The Gathering Storm in the Churches is an interpretation of the relationship between political and religious attitudes of both clergy and laity. Referring to a 1965 poll of Protestant clergy, Hadden discovers a correlation between the religious attitudes of the clergy and their political views, especially concerning civil rights. He also discovers that the same correlation is nonexistent in the attitudes of the laity. The disparity between and within Protestant churches leads Hadden to assess the implied consequences for organized religion. Using his own case studies of ministers in Chicago and Cleveland, Hadden demonstrates how the laity sometimes pressures the clergy into conformist behavior. The result of such pressure, according to Hadden, is that Protestant seminarians are avoiding the parish ministry, thus jeopardizing the survival of Protestant churches.

Prime Time Preachers consists of short, journalistic perspectives on America's television preachers. Written in conjunction with Charles Swann, a Presbyterian minister and radio broadcaster, the book covers the major televangelists, their fundraising techniques, their role in the emergence of the "moral majority," and the opposition to the "moral majority" by mainline Protestant leaders and liberal concerns. The authors try to establish the true size of the televangelic audience by examining the causes for the gross discrepancies between televangelist Jerry Falwell's claim of 25 million viewers and Arbitron figures showing 1.5 million viewers. Using demographic data, the authors attempt to determine the scope and effects of televangelic influence. They demonstrate, for example, reasons for believing that the "moral majority" may be a fourth to a sixth smaller than Jerry Falwell claims, and they identify an error in pollster Louis Harris's calculation that the "moral majority" was responsible for a conservative victory in the 1980 elections. As part of their analysis Hadden and Swann interpret the arguments in favor of televangelism posed by conservative voices as well as the opposition arguments from liberal concerns.

In each of the above books Hadden demonstrates the sociologist's ability for demographic analysis. *Prime Time Preachers*

was praised by Frances Taliaferro of the *New York Times Book Review* for its well-documented data, and *Christian Century* reviewer Richard L. Means declared that *The Gathering Storm in the Churches* meets the criteria for a "classic" of sociological writing. In his opinion the book contains "both a great deal of hard data and a modicum of relevance to 'sociological theory'" and "may be destined to rank among the best of its research genre. Its greatest value lies in author Hadden's ability to transcend the limits of data and search out meaning."

BIOGRAPHICAL/CRITICAL SOURCES: New York Times Book Review, March 16, 1969, March 15, 1970, July 26, 1981; *Christian Century,* April 23, 1969, March 1, 1972, December 4, 1974, October 14, 1981; *American Sociological Review,* December, 1969, August, 1970, October, 1970; *American Academy of Political and Social Science Annals,* January, 1970, January, 1975; *Social Science Quarterly,* March, 1976; *Washington Post Book World,* July 25, 1981; *Columbia Journalism Review,* November, 1981.

*   *   *

HADFIELD, Miles H(eywood)   1903-1982

OBITUARY NOTICE—See index for *CA* sketch: Born October 15, 1903, in Birmingham, England; died March 31, 1982, in England. Author and illustrator of numerous books on gardening, including *The Gardener's Companion, Everyman's Wild Flowers and Trees,* and *British Trees.* Hadfield was a regular contributor to *Country Life* and *The Gardener's Chronicle.* Obituaries and other sources: *London Times,* April 1, 1982.

*   *   *

HADFIELD, Vic(tor Edward)   1940-

BRIEF ENTRY: Born October 4, 1940, in Oakville, Ontario, Canada. Canadian professional hockey player. Hadfield joined the New York Rangers, a professional hockey team, in 1961. He wrote *Vic Hadfield's Diary: From Moscow to the Play-Offs* (Doubleday, 1974). *Address:* c/o New York Rangers, Madison Square Garden, 4 Pennsylvania Plaza, New York, N.Y. 10001.

*   *   *

HAGBERG, David J(ames)   1942-
(Sean Flannery, David James, Robert Pell, Eric Ramsey)

PERSONAL: Born October 9, 1942, in Duluth, Minn.; son of Conrad D. (a meatcutter) and Katherine (Doucette) Hagberg; married Stephanie Bullock (a legal secretary), April, 1960 (divorced, 1960); married Janet Zimmer, September, 1962 (divorced, April, 1967); married Laurie Morgan (a writer and librarian), May, 1968; children: (second marriage) Travis Peyton; (third marriage) Tammy Kraus, Kevin, Justin, Gina. *Education:* Attended University of Maryland, 1962-65, and University of Wisconsin, Madison, 1965-66. *Politics:* Republican. *Religion:* Agnostic. *Residence:* Cambridge, Wis. *Agent:* Peekner Literary Agency, 3210 South 7th St., Milwaukee, Wis. 53215.

CAREER: Duluth Herald and News-Tribune, Duluth, Minn., reporter, 1968-70; Associated Press, New York, N.Y., news desk editor in Sioux Falls, S.D., 1970-72; worked as janitor, bricklayer, factory worker, and tree trimmer, 1972-74; freelance writer. Founder of Editorial Services Enterprises in Wisconsin, 1972-73. Municipal court judge in Oakland Township, Wis., 1981-82. *Military service:* U.S. Air Force, 1960-67; in electronics. *Member:* Mystery Writers of America, Raconteurs. *Awards, honors:* Bronze Porgy from *West Coast Review of Books*, 1978, for *The Kummersdorf Connection;* nomination for American Book Award and for Edgar Allan Poe Award from Mystery Writers of America, both 1979, both for *The Kremlin Conspiracy.*

WRITINGS: Twister, Dell, 1975; *The Capsule,* Dell, 1976; *Last Come the Children,* Pinnacle Books, 1982.

"Nick Carter" series; published by Charter Books, except as noted: *The Sign of the Prayer Shawl,* Award Books, 1976; *Race of Death,* 1978; *The Ouster Conspiracy,* 1981; *The Strontium Code,* 1981; *The Puppet Master,* 1982; *The Damocles Threat,* 1982; *The Hunter,* 1982; *Operation: McMurdo Sound,* 1982; *Appointment in Haiphong,* 1982; *Retreat for Death,* 1982.

"Flash Gordon" series; published by Tempo Books: *Massacre in the 22nd Century,* 1980; *War of the Citadels,* 1980; *Crises on Citadel II,* 1980; *Forces From the Federation,* 1981; *Citadels Under Attack,* 1981; *Citadels on Earth,* 1981.

Under pseudonym Sean Flannery; published by Ace Books/ Charter Books: *The Kremlin Conspiracy,* 1979; *Eagles Fly,* 1980; *The Trinity Factor,* 1981; *The Hollow Men,* 1982.

Under pseudonym David James; *Blizzard,* Belmont-Tower, 1975; *Forest Fire,* Tower, 1975; *Croc',* Tower, 1976.

Under pseudonym Robert Pell: *That Winslow Woman,* Playboy Press, 1977.

Under pseudonym Eric Ramsey: *The Kummersdorf Connection,* Playboy Press, 1978.

WORK IN PROGRESS: The Valley of the Dying Stars (tentative title), for TOR Books; an occult novel for TOR Books; four more "Nick Carter" adventures; *False Prophets,* under pseudonym Sean Flannery.

SIDELIGHTS: Hagberg told *CA:* "A few years ago I told a writers' group that elegance in writing is not so dependent upon the fine turn of phrase or accomplished use of the language as beginning writers often suspect. Instead, elegance (which is what most of us are after) depends in a large measure on the elegance of the idea. Anne Frank's poetic diary and Ernest Hemingway's old fisherman in dire battle with the sea are perfect examples. But when that rare artist comes along who can combine elegant ideas with a supreme mastery of the craft, well then, that writer is a definite winner.

"I guess from the beginning I've struggled to do nothing more than write the very best I could. I've worked for the truest sentences, the most nearly real characters and the most believable situations, so that my readers could have the vicarious experience of living my story.

"It's not easy. It's never been easy. John Steinbeck said that a writer is like a donkey with the carrot dangling in front of his nose. We *know* what we want to do. We know that somewhere out there is the perfect sentence, the perfect paragraph. And every now and then, we hit one. The goal, of course, is to write a complete novel containing nothing but perfection. In the end, however, that is impossible. So, like the donkey with the carrot, we may be getting somewhere, but we are bound to fail. (It's why many writers have problems with booze. After beating our brains out at the typewriter, we often seek solace in oblivion.)

"When I started writing, I often dreamed of the Pulitzer Prize, the Nobel Prize and all the accolades that are commonly associated with success in this business. In fact I dreamed so hard and so often about these things that my writing suffered.

One day, however, I woke up to the fact that here I was, an honest-to-God novelist. I was making my living doing what I loved most: writing books—good books—to the best of my abilities at that moment. What else is there?

"I woke up to another fact about that same time. For years I had been paying lip service to the phrase: Write for your readers. Finally I understood what it was to be a novelist. I was an entertainer. After all, we're doing nothing more than taking our readers away from their daily cares for a few hours at a time. If, slipped between lines, there is a message or an education, than so be it. But primarily we are entertainers who take life as we see it, pass it through our own particular set of experiences, and spit it out the other side.

"If all that seems complicated, or perhaps artificial, it is. A writer (contrary to what many instructors of writing may say) does nothing more or less than sit down and write about what moves him or her most. Simple. I've been trying to do nothing more than that.

"Speaking strictly for myself, I cannot work in a vacuum. My life must provide the impetus for my novels. I write adventure novels, so I must adventure. When I was a newspaper reporter in Minnesota, I interviewed a medical doctor who had gone on an expedition to the north pole, and who had spent a lifetime of adventure. 'Do it,' he told me, as I listened wide-eyed. 'Do it now if it's in your blood, because if you don't, you'll wake up one day to the fact that your life has passed, and now it's too late.'

"My wife and I have learned to sail. It's our goal to circumnavigate the globe aboard a thirty-three foot cutter-rigged sailboat. Just the two of us. Free. Going wherever the wind may blow. Settling in for a week or a month or a year in each port, however the mood strikes, being cold or hot and frightened and worried, but most of all being alive! Isn't that what life is all about? Novelists, I think, should not play it safe. We should live at the edge. Those who survive write about it.

"I was asked, at a recent mystery fan convention, where I came up with my ideas. I gave some flip answer, I think, but in truth the answer is: It beats the hell out of me. Imagination is nothing more than a muscle. Not used, it atrophies. Exercised, however, it grows strong. J.R.R. Tolkien spent a life of imagination. So did, I think, William Shakespeare, who had the gratification of seeing his musings up on a stage in front of a live audience."

AVOCATIONAL INTERESTS: Sailing, flying, scuba diving.

*   *   *

HAGERMAN, Paul Stirling   1949-

PERSONAL: Born January 1, 1949, in Glen Cove, N.Y.; son of George (a personnel director) and Barbara (Briggs) Hagerman. *Education:* Hamilton College, B.A., 1971. *Office:* 400 West 43rd St., 36R, New York, N.Y. 10036.

CAREER: Editorial supervisor, writer, and researcher for network game shows, 1971-75; free-lance editor and writer, 1975—. Consultant and public relationist for cable television companies. Judge for the National Academy of Television Arts and Sciences community service awards, National Emmy Awards, New York Emmy Awards, and Writers Guild documentary awards. *Member:* National Academy of Television Arts and Sciences, American Mensa Ltd., Writers Guild of America. *Awards, honors:* Received New York local Emmy Award nomination for research and national Emmy Award for writing, both 1981, and more than thirty awards, including Melbourne International Film Festival grand prize, Black Orca Film Festival grand prize, and San Francisco International Film Festival grand prize, all for "Manimals"; Congressional Citation for "Inflation: A Few Answers."

WRITINGS: (Contributor) *Historical Guide to the Old West,* McKay, 1976; (contributor) David Wallechinsky and Irving Wallace, *The Book of Lists,* Morrow, 1977; *It's a Odd World* (humor), Sterling, 1977; (contributor) I. Wallace, D. Wallechinsky, and Amy Wallace, *The Book of Lists II,* Morrow, 1978; (contributor) *The New York Kid's Book,* Doubleday, 1978; *It's a Mad, Mad World* (humor), Sterling, 1978.

Screenplays: "Manimals," Opus Films, 1978; "The Magic Tree House," Opus Films, 1981. Also creator of industrial films for Jim Sant'Andrea Productions, and films and video projects for the U.S. pavilion at the 1982 World's Fair in Knoxville, Tenn.

Teleplays: "Inflation: A Few Answers," RKO; creator of more than thirty-five network game show pilots, including "Showdown," American Broadcasting Company (ABC-TV), "Three On a Match," Columbia Broadcasting System (CBS-TV), "Who, What, Where," National Broadcasting Company (NBC-TV), and "Dilemma," British Broadcasting Corporation (BBC-TV).

Associate editor of *Mensa Bulletin,* 1972-74; editor of *Mphasis* (New York Mensa newsletter), 1973-74; editor of *Manhattan Plaza News* (performing arts newspaper); contributing editor and writer for *Fodor's Modern Guides,* and *Houghton Mifflin Travel Guides;* contributor of articles to periodicals, including *Reader's Digest* and *New York Times Magazine.*

SIDELIGHTS: In 1982 Hagerman was chosen by the National Academy of Television Arts and Sciences, Writers Guild, and New York mayor's office to participate in a television writing seminar for promising young writers. *Avocational interests:* Designing and building furniture, gymnastics, swimming, scuba diving, horseback riding.

*   *   *

HAINES, Pamela Mary   1929-

PERSONAL: Born November 4, 1929, in Harrogate, England; daughter of Harry Beeley (a lawyer) and Muriel (Armstrong) Burrows; married Anthony Haines (a physician), June 24, 1955; children: Charlotte Haines Brignall, Lucy, Nicholas, Hal, Emily. *Education:* Newnham College, Cambridge, M.A., 1952. *Home:* 57 Middle Lane, London N. 8, England. *Agent:* A. D. Peters & Co. Ltd., 10 Buckingham St., London WC2N 6BU, England.

CAREER: Writer, 1971—. *Member:* International P.E.N., Society of Authors. *Awards, honors:* New writing prize from *Spectator,* 1971, for story, "Foxy's Not at Home"; young writers award from Yorkshire Arts Society, 1975, for *Tea at Gunter's.*

WRITINGS—Novels: *Tea at Gunter's,* Heinemann, 1974; *A Kind of War,* Heinemann, 1976; *Men on White Horses,* Collins, 1978; *The Kissing Gate* (Book-of-the-Month Club alternate selection), Doubleday, 1981. Contributor to magazines, including *Nova.*

WORK IN PROGRESS: A novel (family saga), publication by Doubleday expected in 1983.

BIOGRAPHICAL/CRITICAL SOURCES: Washington Post, May 16, 1981.

HALE, Wanda
See COUTARD, Wanda Lundy Hale

*   *   *

HALES, Edward John   1927-

PERSONAL: Born October 1, 1927, in Pennsauken, N.J.; son of James Alfred (in drafting) and Elsa Alexandria (Almquist) Hales; married Frances June Moberg (a nurse), August 18, 1951; children: David, Deborah, Darlene, Diane, Donna, Daniel. *Education:* Attended Moody Bible Institute, 1945-47; Gordon College, Boston, Mass., B.A., 1951; Wheaton College, Wheaton, Ill., M.A., 1976. *Home:* 113 Woodfield Rd., Portland, Maine 04102. *Office:* First Baptist Church, 353 Congress St., Portland, Maine 04101.

CAREER: Ordained Baptist minister, 1951; pastor of Baptist churches in New Britain, Conn., 1951-54, and New Bedford, Mass., 1954-59; Baptist General Conference of New England, Brockton, Mass., director of church extension, 1959-62; pastor of Baptist church in Kingsford, Mich., 1962-63; Baptist General Conference, Chicago, Ill., director of stewardship, 1963-71; National Association of Evangelicals, Wheaton, Ill., director of field services, 1971-77; First Baptist Church, Wheaton, pastor, 1977-81; First Baptist Church, Portland, Maine, pastor, 1982—. Chairman of Christian Stewardship Council, 1971-78; member of standards committee of Evangelical Council for Financial Accountability (ECFA). Conducts seminars and workshops. *Member:* National Association of Evangelicals. *Awards, honors:* Distinguished service award from New Bedford Junior Chamber of Commerce, 1958.

WRITINGS: Building the Budget for the Local Church, Neibauer Press, 1968; *Let Love Guide You: Stewardship Program,* Neibauer Press, 1969; (with Alan Youngren) *Your Money, Their Ministry: A Guide to Responsible Giving,* Eerdmans, 1981. Contributor to *Eternity, United Evangelical Action,* and *Standard.*

WORK IN PROGRESS: A book on Biblical standards for fund raising; research on local churches and missionary support.

SIDELIGHTS: Hales wrote: "For a number of years I have had a great interest in the entire field of stewardship and fund raising. I have had a considerable amount of personal campaign experience and have served as consultant for a number of churches, religious organizations, and denominations. I have conducted more than one hundred fifty seminars and workshops in that field in nearly every state of the union.

"I have also had a continuing interest in religious radio, beginning with my master's thesis, 'Local Church Use of Radio and Television.' The proliferation of religious broadcasting and the subsequent need for funds poses the potential for fund raising abuses. Our book on responsible giving and our service with the Evangelical Council for Financial Accountability put us in contact with the problem areas. I am hopeful that future writing will be useful as a stimulus to corrective actions."

*   *   *

HALL, Adrian   1927-

PERSONAL: Born December 3, 1927, in Van, Tex.; son of Lennie and Mattie Hall. *Education:* East Texas State University, B.S., 1948; Pasadena Playhouse, M.A., 1950. *Politics:* None. *Religion:* None. *Home:* 176 Pleasant St., Providence, R.I. 02906. *Office:* Trinity Square Repertory Co., 201 Washington St., Providence, R.I. 02903.

CAREER: Stage director of numerous Off-Broadway plays, 1955-64; Trinity Square Repertory Co., Providence, R.I., founder and artistic director, 1964—. Member of theatre arts and policy panels of National Endowment for the Arts, 1978, 1979, and 1980; member of board of directors of Theatre Communications Group, 1981—. *Military service:* U.S. Army; served with Special Services in Korean War. *Member:* Writers Guild of America, Directors Guild of America, Actors' Equity Association. *Awards, honors:* Margo Jones Award, 1969, for production of new American plays; Doctor of Fine Arts from Brown University, 1972, and Rhode Island College, 1976; government arts award, 1975, for contributions to cultural life in Rhode Island; New England Theatre Conference Award, 1976, for outstanding contributions to theatre in New England; Elliott Norton Award, 1980, for personal contributions to American theatre; Antoinette Perry Award, 1981, for best American repertory company.

WRITINGS: (With Richard Cumming) "Feasting With Panthers" (play), first produced in Providence, R.I., at Trinity Square Repertory Co., 1973, televised by Public Broadcasting Service (PBS), 1974; "Brother to Dragons" (play), first produced in Providence at Trinity Square Repertory Co., 1975, televised by PBS, 1975; "Life Among the Lowly" (television script for "Vision" series), televised by PBS, 1976; (with Cumming) "House of Mirth" (television script), televised by PBS, 1981.

WORK IN PROGRESS: A stage adaptation of James Reston, Jr.'s, book *Our Father Who Art in Hell,* production expected in 1982.

SIDELIGHTS: Hall told *CA:* "I am deeply committed to the repertory theatre movement in America. Only there can we hope to find and live a life in art. I am more interested in the *process* of the theatre than the *product* of the theatre. Important influences on my thinking include Margo Jones, Gilmore Brown, and Stella Holt. The most important impact on the success of the repertory theatre movement has been the National Endowment for the Arts. Fifteen years ago there was no place that a professional artist could find continuous employment except in the commercial centers. For the playwright the field was very narrow. Today it is much better—more opportunities and easier to get produced."

* * *

HALL, B. K. 1932-

PERSONAL: Born February 29, 1932, in Wyandotte, Mich.; son of Bernard (a plumber and director of a burial-at-sea company) and Kayla (a hydrologist; maiden name, Rivers) Hall; married Janet Lake (a motion picture actress), January 13, 1954 (died, 1956); married Laura Falles (a vocalist), April 30, 1962; children: (first marriage) Marina; (second marriage) B. K., Jr., Kate, Laurence. *Education:* University of Windsor, Windsor, Ontario, B.A., 1960. *Politics:* "Utopian." *Religion:* Unitarian Universalist. *Home and office:* 221 Lewiston Rd., Grosse Pointe Farms, Mich. 48236.

CAREER: Jazz trombonist in various dance bands, 1952-57; leader of "B. K. and the Dancehalls," riverboat band for Bob-Lo Co., Detroit, Mich., summers, 1953-57; Henry Ford Museum, Dearborn, Mich., assistant curator of musical instruments, 1960-69; Psychedelic Hall of Planets, Inc. (planetarium), Ann Arbor, Mich., founder and spiritual leader, 1969-71; Music of the Spheres, Ltd. (music psychotherapy consultants), West Bloomfield, Mich., founder, director, and therapist, 1971-78; Media Hall, Inc., Troy, Mich., founder and president, 1978—. Owner of Treasure Hall and Treasure Hall

East, arts and antiques galleries, 1975—. Guest lecturer, on the history of musical instruments, at Cornell University, Wayne State University, Oakland University, University of Michigan, University of Windsor, Western Michigan University, and Kalamazoo College. Director of Lake Erie Memorial, Inc., family burial-at-sea business, 1965—. *Military service:* U.S. Coast Guard, 1950-52; served in Alaska.

MEMBER: American Society of Composers, Authors, and Publishers, American Society of Ancient Instruments, American Federation of Musicians of the United States and Canada, National Association for Music Therapy, Astronomical League, Detroit Video Brethren, Grosse Pointe Yacht Club. *Awards, honors:* Stowe Poetry Award from Kalamazoo College, 1970, for *Star Feast;* Man of the Year award from Troy (Mich.) Business Council, 1979; grant from Great Lakes Maritime Consortium to study funeral practices on the Great Lakes, 1982.

WRITINGS: Steamin' Along: Life in a Riverboat Band (autobiography), Euridice Books, 1955; *From Sackbut to Superbone: A History of the Trombone* (nonfiction), Archive, 1965; *Zen and the Art of Jazz Arranging* (essays), Scat Karma Publishing, 1969; *Star Feast* (poems), Phopi Parchments, 1969; *Be Your Own Symphony Orchestra: A Personality Enhancement Guide* (self-help), Music Lab Publications, 1977; *The Media Wedding* (nonfiction), Rivers, 1979; *Hall of Mirrors: The Art of Media Memorabilia* (nonfiction), Rivers, 1982. Contributor of articles to journals and magazines. Composer of music and lyrics for radio and television commercials.

WORK IN PROGRESS: Great Lakes Memorials, a chronicle of funeral practices on the Great Lakes, publication by Gale expected in 1985; *Tape Worm,* a thriller set in Detroit about a psychotic news cameraman.

SIDELIGHTS: Hall's experiences as leader of a dance band that performed on a Detroit River steamboat formed the basis for his 1955 memoirs, *Steamin' Along: Life in a Riverboat Band.* A trombonist, Hall became an expert on the development of the trombone from the medieval sackbut to the combination slide and valve trombone, called the Superbone, created by jazz figure Maynard Ferguson. Hall wrote *From Sackbut to Superbone: A History of the Trombone* while serving as a museum curator of musical instruments. He left his museum post in 1969 to found a planetarium for adherents to an Eastern astrology-oriented religion. The writings from this period of Hall's life reflect a new focus on spirituality and the cosmos. *Zen and the Art of Jazz Arranging,* published in 1969, discusses the discipline of jazz arranging as a catalyst for philosophical reflection. *Star Feast,* a volume of poetry appearing in the same year, uses metaphors drawn from astrology and health food to underscore the drawbacks of Western urban mindsets and to promote Oriental concepts of reality.

Astronomy and music both played a part in Hall's formation of a music psychotherapy consulting firm in 1971. Hall's success in the field of psychotherapy led to a self-help best-seller, *Be Your Own Symphony Orchestra: A Personality Enhancement Guide,* published in 1977. Continued experimentation with sound resulted in Hall's interest in media production. Hall founded Media Hall, Inc., in 1978, to provide various specialized and customized media services to a wide range of clients. Concentrating mainly on videotape production, Hall's service captures and preserves events such as weddings, graduations, funerals, and recitals. Hall wrote about his media techniques in *The Media Wedding* and *Hall of Mirrors: The Art of Media Memorabilia.* The *Detroit Free Press* deemed Hall's service "invaluable to those who seek to make family keepsakes with professional quality videotaping. . . . Hall has become progenitor of the future's heirlooms."

Hall told *CA:* "Video is the wave of the future, and I'm just glad to be on the crest of that wave."

BIOGRAPHICAL/CRITICAL SOURCES: *Consumer Reports,* October, 1975; *Detroit Free Press,* September 14, 1980.

*   *   *

HALL, Linda B(iesele)   1939-

PERSONAL: Born August 2, 1939, in Cleveland, Ohio; daughter of Rudolph Leopold (an engineer) and Peggy (a writer; maiden name, Soule) Biesele; married James Q. Hall, August 4, 1960 (divorced October, 1975); children: Leslie Elena, Douglas Winfield. *Education:* University of Texas, B.A., 1960; Southern Methodist University, M.A., 1970; Columbia University, M.Phil., 1975, Ph.D., 1976. *Politics:* Democrat. *Religion:* Unitarian-Universalist. *Home:* 535 Nottingham, San Antonio, Tex. 78209. *Office:* Department of History, Trinity University, 1715 Stadium Dr., San Antonio, Tex. 78284.

CAREER: Universidad del Valle, Cali, Colombia, instructor in English, 1962-63; Universidad de los Andes, Bogota, Colombia, instructor in English, 1964-68; Trinity University, San Antonio, Tex., assistant professor, 1976-80, associate professor of history, 1980—, and chairperson of inter-American studies. Member of steering committee of National Task Force on Mexico-U.S. Relations and Migration of the Undocumented, 1979-80. *Member:* Latin American Studies Association, Association of Borderlands Scholars, Western Historical Association. *Awards, honors:* Kent fellow of Danforth Association, 1974-76; Danforth associate, 1977-83; National Endowment for the Humanities grant, 1977, fellow, 1981-82.

WRITINGS: *Alvaro Obregon: Power and Revolution in Mexico, 1911-1920,* Texas A & M University Press, 1981. Contributor to history journals and *Southwest Review.*

WORK IN PROGRESS: *Revolution on the Border: The United States and Mexico, 1910-1920,* with Don M. Coerver, publication expected in 1983.

SIDELIGHTS: Linda Hall told *CA:* "I am interested in the revolutionary process and its effects on individual lives as well as on social institutions. My book on Obregon was particularly directed toward the effect that one man had on bringing the violence of an especially bloody revolution to a close and to the reestablishment of institutional government. My work on the U.S.-Mexican border addressed the social and economic effects of that same revolution. I have done extensive oral history work with survivors, and find that a fruitful method of historical inquiry. My literary criticism is quite different from my historical writing, and my choice of subjects reflects my enthusiasm for the universal insights of contemporary Latin American authors. All my writing is profoundly influenced by the seven years, 1961 to 1968, that I spent in Colombia."

*   *   *

HALLIDAY, F(rank) E(rnest)   1903-1982

OBITUARY NOTICE—See index for *CA* sketch: Born February 10, 1903, in Bradford, Yorkshire, England; died March 26, 1982. Shakespearean critic, historian, and author. Halliday wrote and edited more than twenty-five works of literary research and history, including *A Shakespeare Companion, The Cult of Shakespeare,* and *A Cultural History of England.* Obituaries and other sources: *London Times,* March 29, 1982.

*   *   *

HALLINAN, Hazel Hunkins   1891(?)-1982

OBITUARY NOTICE: Born c. 1891 in Billings, Mont.; died of respiratory failure, May 17, 1982, in London, England. Feminist, journalist, and author. Initially trained as a chemist, Hallinan joined the suffrage movement when prospective employers informed her that they did not hire women. In 1916 she went to Washington, D.C., and become a member of the National Women's party. The next year, along with several other suffragists, she was arrested and jailed for setting fire to the White House lawn and for chaining herself to the mansion's gates in a demonstration for women's rights. In 1920, following the passage of the Nineteenth Amendment (which gave women the right to vote), she moved to London, where she continued to work actively for women's rights. Hallinan wrote a column for the *Chicago Tribune* entitled "London Letter," and she published *In Her Own Right,* a collection of her essays. Obituaries and other sources: *New York Times,* May 19, 1982; *Newsweek,* May 31, 1982.

*   *   *

HALLSTEIN, Walter   1901-1982

OBITUARY NOTICE: Born November 17, 1901, in Mainz, Germany (now West Germany); died March 29, 1982, in Stuttgart, West Germany. Educator, president of the European Common Market, and author. Prior to World War II, Hallstein served as a professor of civil, commercial, and economic law at Rostock University in Germany and as chairman of the law department at the University of Frankfort-on-Main. A lieutenant in the German army during the war, Hallstein was captured by American soldiers in 1944 and interned in Mississippi. After the war he was invited to the United States to lecture on foreign policy and law at Georgetown University. From 1951 to 1958 he served as secretary of state for the reformed German Foreign Office. A central figure in the movement for European unity, Hallstein helped bring about the formation of the Common Market. He served as president of the Commission of the European Economic Community for nine years, during which time he "successfully created the *elan* and the apparatus for Western Europe's most ambitious move towards economic unity," noted the *London Times.* His 1969 book, *Die Unvollendete Bundesstaat,* was published in the United States as *Europe in the Making.* Earlier works include *Wissenschaft und Politik, Der Schuman-Plan,* and *United Europe: Challenge and Opportunity.* Obituaries and other sources: *Current Biography,* Wilson, 1953, May, 1982; *Who's Who,* 126th edition, St. Martin's, 1974; *The International Who's Who,* Europa, 1978; *Who's Who in the World,* 4th edition, Marquis, 1978; *London Times,* March 31, 1982; *Newsweek,* April 5, 1982.

*   *   *

HALPERN, Barbara Strachey   1912-
   (Barbara Strachey)

PERSONAL: Born July 17, 1912, in Arundel, England; daughter of Oliver (a cryptographer) and Rachel (a writer; maiden name, Costelloe) Strachey; married Olav Hultin, January 17, 1934 (divorced, 1937); married Wolf Halpern, September 17, 1937 (died, 1943); children: (second marriage) Roger. *Education:* Received B.A. in 1933. *Residence:* Oxford, England.

CAREER: British Broadcasting Corp., radio director for BBC-Radio, 1950-62, planner for international world service, 1962-74; writer.

WRITINGS—Under name Barbara Strachey: *Remarkable Relations: The Story of the Pearsall Smith Family* (nonfiction), Gollancz, 1980; *Journeys of Frodo,* Ballantine, 1981.

WORK IN PROGRESS: Editing, with Jayne Samuels, the letters and diaries of Mary Berenson.

SIDELIGHTS: Strachey told *CA:* "I started writing upon retiring from thirty-three years with the BBC (too busy before that). My first book was a family history based on some twenty thousand letters inherited. I was brought up among 'Bloomsbury' uncles and aunts (my uncle is Lytton Strachey; my mother's sister married Virginia Woolf's brother). Virtually all my relatives on both sides were writers, but I was daunted by this and could not start writing till all were dead. (Material relatives: great aunt was Bertrand Russell's first wife; grandmother ran away from grandfather with Bernard Berenson and later married him; great grandparents—originally Quakers from Philadelphia—became celebrated Revivalist preachers both in United States and Europe.)

"My father worked as a cryptologist in two world wars and my brother, Christopher Strachey, was one of the first British computer experts and first professor of computer science at Oxford. I have always found all this a bit oppressive, and have tried (but not too successfully) to revolt. After Oxford I went to Australia in a windjammer. My second husband was a Jew and was killed in the Royal Air Force during World War II. His family became Israelis, and we have remained close friends.

"I joined the BBC during the war and greatly enjoyed working there, particularly in World Service, which encouraged my greatest pleasure: worldwide travel, particularly to offbeat places.

"*Journeys of Frodo,* the atlas for J.R.R. Tolkien's *Lord of the Rings,* was not constructed for publication but for my own pleasure. A friend told Rayner Unwin, who originally published Tolkien, about it, and he asked me to bring it in and then decided to publish it.

"I have always been fascinated by history and biography, and any further books I write will probably pursue this line."

AVOCATIONAL INTERESTS: Reading and collecting science fiction; crossword and jigsaw puzzles.

*   *   *

HAMILTON, (Robert) Ian   1938-

PERSONAL: Born March 24, 1938, in King's Lynn, Norfolk, England; son of Robert Tough and Daisy (Mckay) Hamilton; married Gisela Dietzel, 1963; children: one son. *Education:* Keble College, Oxford, B.A., 1962.

CAREER: Tomorrow, Oxford, England, founder and editor, 1959-60; *Review* (now *New Review*), London, England, founder and editor, beginning in 1962. Assistant editor of *Times Literary Supplement,* 1965-73; lecturer in poetry, University of Hull, 1971-72. *Awards, honors:* E. C. Gregory Award, 1963; Malta Cultural Award, 1974.

WRITINGS: Pretending Not to Sleep: Poems (pamphlet), Review, 1964; (contributor) *Poetry: Introduction One,* Faber, 1969; *The Visit: Poems,* Faber, 1970; *Anniversary and Vigil* (poems), Poem-of-the-Month Club, 1971; *A Poetry Chronicle: Essays and Reviews,* Barnes & Noble, 1973; *The Little Magazines: A Study of Six Editors,* Weidenfeld & Nicolson, 1976.

Editor: *The Poetry of War, 1939-45,* Alan Ross, 1965; Alun Lewis, *Selected Poetry and Prose,* Allen & Unwin, 1966; *The Modern Poet: Essays From "The Review,"* Macdonald & Co., 1968, Horizon Press, 1969; *Eight Poets,* Poetry Book Society, 1968; (and author of introduction) Robert Frost, *The Poetry of Robert Frost,* J. Cape, 1971, published as *Selected Poems,* Penguin, 1973; (with Colin Falck) *Poems Since 1900: An Anthology of British and American Verse in the Twentieth Century,* Macdonald & Jane's, 1974, published as *Poems Since 1900: An Anthology,* Beekman, 1975.

Poetry reviewer for *London Magazine,* 1962-64; poetry critic for *Observer,* 1965-70.

SIDELIGHTS: Hamilton has published several volumes of poetry, but he is best known as a poetry critic. A representative sampling of his critical style, consisting of miscellaneous articles and reviews that he has written for *Observer, Times Literary Supplement,* and *London Magazine,* is collected in his book *A Poetry Chronicle.* Upon reviewing that collection Derek Stanford of *Books and Bookmen* concluded that Hamilton "is the best critic of modern verse we have had since G S Fraser."

Among the poets and poems discussed are William Carlos Williams and T. S. Eliot's *The Waste Land.* Hamilton argues that *The Waste Land* is blanketed in an aura of allusiveness resulting from Eliot's inability to explore his own personal despair in the context of his poetry. According to Hamilton, Eliot would have written "more complex and affecting work" had he been as willing to pass judgment on his own "crippling refinement" as he was to judge the "crippling vulgarity" of others. As Stanford points out, Hamilton does not allow reverence to oppress his criticism of Eliot, or any other poet. In fact, one of Hamilton's best critiques, Stanford observes, is his "demolition" of the Williams cult. In his Williams criticism, Hamilton concentrates on the poet's "open syntax" technique, its drawbacks, and what Hamilton perceives as its utter failure as practiced by Williams's disciples, especially Robert Creely.

Hamilton's criticism, says Stanford, "by the operation of discrimination and intellectual scorn, proceeds to question, scaledown or explode current and fashionable reputations which lack an adequate validity." Some critics of Hamilton have, however, objected to his critical and editorial methods. Auberon Waugh, for example, takes exception to the "dismal" poetry Hamilton prints in the *New Review,* commenting in *Books and Bookmen,* "Perhaps there are simply not the writers and poets in Britain to produce a good magazine of this sort, but that is no reason for producing a bad one." Waugh further contends that the *New Review* contains journalism "marred by a conscious effort to be weighty" and displays an "apparent lack of any clear will to discriminate between good writing and bad." Even though Waugh is critical of the *New Review,* he recognizes a talent in Ian Hamilton. Waugh comments that Hamilton's book *The Little Magazines: A Study of Six Editors* is "intelligently written, well informed, and even highly entertaining."

As the *New Review* editor, Hamilton nurtured an interest in periodical publications which prompted his writing *The Little Magazines.* His own periodical is committed to raising the general level of English poetry, both by criticizing that which is less than adequate and by helping to establish foundling poets producing quality work. The *New Review* belongs in the history of "little magazines," periodicals dedicated to the advancement of literary excellence and aimed at an elite minority of poets and critics challenging established, heavy reviews and similar literature. These publications are often doomed to economic failure because as they reject establishment reviews they reject establishment funding. Hamilton has, however, avoided that economic disaster, and something of a furor surrounds the large subsidies he has been awarded by the British Arts Council.

Hamilton's *The Little Magazines* does not draw directly from his personal experiences as an editor, but is largely an anecdotal account of the experiences of other editors, as well as an evaluation of their magazines. Of the publications he discusses, three are American—*Little Review, Poetry,* and *Partisan Re-*

view—and three are British—*Criterion, New Verse,* and *Horizon. Little Review* and *Poetry* both bore the influence of Ezra Pound and are important to literary history as early publishers of T. S. Eliot and W. B. Yeats. Likewise, *New Verse,* edited by Geoffrey Grigson, introduced many new talents, including W. H. Auden. *Criterion,* interesting because it was edited by T. S. Eliot, was not as effective and, like *Horizon,* was much more conservative about introducing new writers.

Besides criticizing and reviewing poetry, Hamilton writes poetry of his own. Robert Lowell and Sylvia Plath are apparent influences upon his work, poems which Hamilton describes as "dramatic lyrics." They focus on a single, intense, emotional moment, leaving the detail of surrounding circumstance to the reader's imagination. They are usually devoid of any personal voice, and many of these lyrics are only six or seven lines long and extremely refined.

BIOGRAPHICAL/CRITICAL SOURCES: Poetry, June, 1961; *Times Literary Supplement,* January 30, 1969, February 7, 1970, August 11, 1972, March 23, 1973, October 19, 1973; *Poetry Review,* autumn, 1970; *London Observer,* January 14, 1973; *Encounter,* May, 1973; *Books and Bookmen,* June, 1973, August, 1976; *New Statesman,* August 27, 1976; *Spectator,* September 4, 1976; *Modern Language Review,* October, 1979.*

* * *

HAMMOND, Charles Montgomery, Jr. 1922-

PERSONAL: Born April 18, 1922, in Auburn, N.Y.; son of Charles M. (a manufacturer) and Ida (Overhiser) Hammond; married Rita Semmel, 1947 (marriage ended); married Mary Klysa (a teacher), 1976; children: Edward M., Deborah S. *Education:* Syracuse University, B.A., 1947, M.A., 1965. *Home:* 59 Lincklaen St., Cazenovia, N.Y. 13035. *Office:* Department of Journalism, State University of New York Agricultural and Technical College, Morrisville, N.Y. 13408.

CAREER: Radio and television announcer, 1947-57; public relations director at Barlow Advertising Agency, 1957-60; principal, Charles Hammond & Associates, 1960-65; Cazenovia College, Cazenovia, N.Y., instructor in American literature, 1962-68; assistant majority press secretary to New York State Assembly, 1968-70; State University of New York Agricultural and Technical College, Morrisville, associate professor of journalism, 1970—. Visiting associate professor at Washington State University, 1975-76. *Military service:* U.S. Army Air Forces, Control Net System operator, 1943-46. *Member:* Public Relations Society of America, Sigma Delta Chi, Alpha Delta Sigma.

WRITINGS: The Image Decade: Television Documentary, 1965-1975, Hastings House, 1981.

* * *

HAMMOND, John (Henry, Jr.) 1910-
(Henry Johnson)

PERSONAL: Born December 15, 1910, in New York, N.Y.; son of John Henry (an attorney) and Emily Vanderbilt (Sloane) Hammond; married Jemison McBride, March 13, 1941 (divorced, 1948); married Esme O'Brien Sarnoff, September 8, 1949; children: (first marriage) John Paul, Jason. *Education:* Attended Yale University, 1929-31. *Home:* 444 East 57th St., New York, N.Y. 10022. *Office:* Hammond Music Enterprises, Inc., 311 West 57th St., New York, N.Y. 10019.

CAREER: Violist in string quartets, 1928-39; record producer for Columbia, Parlophone, Victor, Okeh, Brunswick, Voca-

lion, and other labels, 1932-39; American recording director for English Columbia and Parlophone Co., Ltd., 1933-36; producer of plays and concerts, 1933-39; Columbia Records, New York City, associate recording director, 1939-42, 1946; Keynote Records, New York City, member of board, 1946, president, 1947; Majestic Records, New York City, recording director, 1947; Mercury Records, New York City, vice-president, 1947-52; Vanguard Records, New York City, producer, 1953-58; CBS Records, New York City, producer and director of talent acquisition, became vice-president, 1958-76; independent record producer, 1976—; Hammond Music Enterprises, New York City, chairman of board, 1982—. Producer of plays "Little Old Boy," 1933, and "Jayhawker," 1935; producer of concerts, including "Spirituals to Swing" series, 1938, 1939, and 1967; casting director of Broadway production of opera "Carmen Jones," 1943; lecturer at New York University, 1953-56; member of board of Newport Jazz Festival, 1956-70; consultant to CBS Records, 1976—. Member of executive board of National Association for the Advancement of Colored People (NAACP), 1935-67. *Military service:* U.S. Army, 1943-46.

WRITINGS: (With Irving Townsend) *John Hammond on Record* (autobiography), Ridge Press/Summit Books, 1977. American correspondent for *Gramophone,* 1930-32, *Melody Maker,* and *Rhythm,* 1932-39; music critic for the *Brooklyn Eagle,* 1933-35. Contributor of numerous articles and reviews to *Down Beat, Metronome,* the *New York Times, Nation,* and (under pseudonym Henry Johnson) *New Masses.* Associate editor of *Melody News,* 1934; co-editor of *Music and Rhythm,* 1942-43.

SIDELIGHTS: John Hammond has long been known as one of the most astute listeners and record producers in the music business. He discovered some of jazz's most influential musicians, produced several of the most important records in the history of jazz, and was instrumental in breaking down the barriers between black and white musicians. Nat Hentoff wrote in the *Village Voice:* "No non-musician has had anywhere near as fundamental an effect on jazz as Hammond, with his big, quick ears and his stubborn zeal in proselytizing his discoveries. Nor has his musical legacy been limited to jazz. Hammond, for example, first recorded Bob Dylan and, later, Bruce Springsteen. In both cases he somehow heard what his colleagues at Columbia records could not. 'No player can be taught to swing,' says Hammond. And no layman can be taught how to listen like Hammond.''

Hammond began learning to listen before he was ten years old: to classical music on his family's Victrola and to popular music, including early jazz and blues, on the servants' phonograph. By the time he was twelve, he was spending most of his allowance on records and was soon seeking out live jazz in vaudeville theatres and nightclubs. His enthusiasm for jazz soon led to an awareness of the discrimination faced by the black people who had originated the music he loved and ignited his lifelong commitment to racial equality. For Hammond, black music and black rights have always been inextricably linked, and both have been central in his life and work. Hammond joined the executive board of the NAACP in 1935 and remained one of its most active members until he resigned from the organization in 1967 to protest its support for the Vietnam War.

Hammond entered the music business as the American jazz correspondent for the British magazines *Gramophone* and *Melody Maker.* In 1931 he produced his first record—at his own expense—with pianist Garland Wilson. The record was never released, but it gave Hammond his start. His sessions with Wilson and with the Fletcher Henderson Orchestra, the next year, were released by Columbia, and in 1933 English Columbia offered him a contract to record several important American artists. They included Henderson, Coleman Hawkins, Benny Carter, Joe Venuti, and Benny Goodman, who was a little-known sideman at the time. The first record Hammond made with Goodman ("Ain'tcha Glad" and "I Gotta Right to Sing the Blues") became a hit. Hammond was established as a producer, and the stage was set for his first two great discoveries: Teddy Wilson and Billie Holiday.

Hammond found the seventeen-year-old Holiday singing in a Harlem speakeasy in early 1933. "I decided that night that she was the best jazz singer I had ever heard," he writes in his autobiography. Hammond brought everyone he knew to hear Holiday sing, and he wrote about her in *Melody Maker,* but it was not until that November that he was able to record her singing with Goodman's band. Holiday soon became a major star, with Hammond producing some of her most memorable records, including "Miss Brown to You," "A Fine Romance," and "I'll Get By."

Hammond first heard Teddy Wilson playing piano on a Chicago radio show. Wilson's style, Hammond writes, "was absolutely unique, . . . never flashy, but swinging and with an excellent left hand." Hammond brought Wilson to New York, where he won acclaim as a soloist, a bandleader, and as Billie Holiday's accompanist. In 1936, Wilson joined the Goodman Orchestra, becoming the first black musician to join a white band and shattering the musical color bar that Hammond had worked against for years.

Throughout the thirties and early forties, Hammond continued to produce for Columbia and other labels, and also to seek out new talent. He discovered the Count Basie Band and its featured soloist, Lester Young, in 1936, but Basie signed with Decca Records and Hammond did not get to produce Basie's records until 1939. Basie has remained Hammond's favorite jazz musician because of his energy and his "extraordinary economy of style." Hammond also discovered Charlie Christian, a pioneer of the electric guitar and one of the most influential guitarists in the history of jazz.

Hammond publicized his discoveries in articles for *Melody Maker* and *Down Beat*. He also wrote articles publicizing the exploitation of musicians and other workers in the music industry for *New Masses* and his own short-lived magazine, *Music and Rhythm.* His exposes were sometimes quite effective: a 1937 article on conditions in American Record's (then the parent company of Columbia) pressing plant helped force the company's unionization, and a 1942 article on discrimination against black musicians at NBC resulted in at least a temporary change in that company's hiring policies.

After World War II, Hammond became less involved with current jazz. He was not enthusiastic about the musical trends of the late forties and early fifties, considering bebop and progressive jazz a dead end. "Bop lacked the swing I believe essential to great jazz playing, lacked the humor and the free-flowing invention of the best jazz creators," he wrote. "In their place it offered a new self-consciousness, an excessive emphasis on harmonic and rhythmic revolt, a concentration on technique at the expense of musical emotion. It defied the jazz verities without improving on them." Consequently, Hammond concentrated on classical music during much of his tenure with Mercury Records. When he joined Vanguard Records in 1953, it was to produce the first high fidelity jazz records with some of the artists he had worked with in previous decades.

Returning to Columbia in 1958, Hammond found himself drawn into folk music and rhythm and blues as well as jazz. Among his first discoveries of the sixties was Aretha Franklin, with whom he produced two gospel-influenced albums. Hammond found her "the most dynamic jazz voice I'd encountered since Billie [Holiday]," though Franklin achieved her greatest success as a rhythm and blues singer on Atlantic Records a few years later. Hammond's other great discovery was Bob Dylan, whom he discovered playing in folksinger Carolyn Hester's backup group. For several months Columbia executives referred to Dylan as "Hammond's folly," and Hammond had to fight to keep Dylan on the label. But when Dylan's song "Blowing in the Wind" became a hit for Peter, Paul, and Mary in 1963, the songwriter became a star and Hammond's judgment was vindicated once again. Hammond produced albums by other folksingers, including Pete Seeger, Leonard Cohen, and Malvina Reynolds, during the sixties and seventies, as well as records by jazz artists like George Benson, Don Ellis, Paul Winter, and Eubie Blake. He was the first Columbia executive to hear and appreciate rock singer Bruce Springsteen, though he did not produce Springsteen's records.

Hammond retired from Columbia in 1976, but he has continued to serve as a consultant and to produce records for blues singer Alberta Hunter. He has also formed his own record label, Hammond Music Enterprises. In his autobiography, which Roland Gelatt of *Saturday Review* pronounced "engaging and informative," Hammond concludes: "I still expect to hear, if not today then tomorrow, a voice or sound I have never heard, with something to say which has never been said before."

BIOGRAPHICAL/CRITICAL SOURCES: New Yorker, December 5, 1959; *Newsweek,* March 29, 1971; *High Fidelity,* June, 1976; John Hammond, *John Hammond on Record,* Ridge Press/Summit Books, 1977; *Saturday Review,* November 12, 1977; *New York Times Book Review,* November 20, 1977; *New Times,* November 25, 1977; *Village Voice,* December 12, 1977; *New York,* January 9, 1978; *Down Beat,* January 12, 1978.

—*Sketch by Tim Connor*

* * *

HAMNER, Robert Daniel 1941-

PERSONAL: Born January 16, 1941, in Tuscaloosa, Ala.; son of Robert Felix (a fire fighter) and Margaret Louise (Atkins) Hamner; married Carol Ann Elmore (a librarian), August 24, 1963; children: Jared Robert, Ryan Fernando. *Education:* Wayland Baptist College, B.A., 1964; University of Texas, M.A., 1966, Ph.D., 1971. *Office:* Department of English, Hardin-Simmons University, Box 1195, Abilene, Tex. 79698.

CAREER: Wayland Baptist College, Plainview, Tex., instructor in English, 1968-70; Hardin-Simmons University, Abilene, Tex., assistant professor, 1971-74, associate professor, 1974-79, professor of English, 1979—, and humanities, 1980—. Fulbright professor at University of Guyana, 1975-76. *Member:* Modern Language Association of America, Joseph Conrad Society of America (member of executive committee), African Literature Association, Association of Caribbean Studies, Association of Commonwealth Literature and Language Studies, Conference of College Teachers of English, South Central Modern Language Association. *Awards, honors:* Fulbright-Hays grant, 1975-76.

WRITINGS: V. S. Naipaul, Twayne, 1973; (editor) *Critical Perspectives on V. S. Naipaul,* Three Continents Press, 1977; *Derek Walcott,* Twayne, 1981; (author of introduction) Walcott, *Another Life,* 2nd edition, Three Continents Press, 1982. Contributor to academic journals.

WORK IN PROGRESS: Third World Perspectives on Joseph Conrad, publication by Three Continents Press expected in

1984; research on Derek Walcott, Earl Lovelace, Joseph Conrad, and V. S. Naipaul.

SIDELIGHTS: Hamner commented: "My primary focus for research and writing has been the Third World and colonial writing. There are substantial writers in nearly all of the nations that have emerged since World War II; the unique difficulties that these creative writers face in newly independent countries are intriguing.

"What is remarkable is not that societies in turmoil produce fine writers, but that some of the writers have converted their adversities into art that speaks profoundly to man at large. This is one of my sustaining motivations. A second factor which keeps up my interest is the vitality which exists among artists and scholars in this area of study. In my travels to the Pacific Islands (Fiji in 1980) and the Caribbean basin (1975-76, 1981, and 1982), and in my correspondence from around the world, I have sensed the living concerns of people engaged in the processes of formulating their indigenous literature, languages, and critical theories. Specialized bibliographies are especially needed; therefore, I have compiled several to date.

"For many of these countries, the evolution of a nation is far more complex than it was historically for the American colonies and for Ireland. In most cases, there is a confluence of cultures—Western, Eastern, African—and the rapidity of modern communications does not allow time for smooth transitions.

"At the same time, modern technology has made it possible for national writers to address a vast international audience. The best of these have earned a place among the great writers. V. S. Naipaul and Derek Walcott have acquired particular significance. Through their references to Joseph Conrad and my concerns with Conrad as a man who pioneered in the subject matter and settings of the British colonial empire, I have turned my attention to Conrad's influences on other Third World writers."

AVOCATIONAL INTERESTS: "I grew up with a love for the sea and for islands. Whenever time permits, I still enjoy sailing and visiting tropical countries. My study of fiction, poetry, and drama has extended in recent years to include painting, sculpture, architecture, and cultural expression in general."

*　　*　　*

HAMSA, Bobbie   1944-

PERSONAL: Born June 14, 1944, in Ord, Neb.; daughter of R. A. (a dentist) and Doris (a writer; maiden name, Sanborn) Hamsa; married Mike Eisenhart, September 20, 1967 (divorced, 1976); married Dick Sullivan (an advertising executive), June 18, 1977; children: (first marriage) John; (stepchildren from second marriage) Kenton, Tracy. *Education:* University of Nebraska, B.A., 1966. *Religion:* None. *Home:* 2302 South 102nd St., Omaha, Neb. 68124. *Office:* Bozell & Jacobs, Inc., 10250 Regency Circle, Omaha, Neb. 68114.

CAREER: First National Bank of Omaha, Omaha, Neb., management trainee, 1966-67; United Airlines, Omaha, reservation agent, 1967-68; Freeman-Thompson Insurance Agency, Omaha, secretary and junior underwriter, 1968-69; Bozell & Jacobs, Inc. (advertising agency), Omaha, copywriter, 1975—. *Member:* Kappa Kappa Gamma (member of alumnae executive board, 1973-75), Junior League of Omaha, Planned Parenthood. *Awards, honors:* Advertising awards include three Cornhusker Addy Awards between 1977 and 1981.

WRITINGS—Juveniles; "Far-Fetched Pets" series; published by Childrens Press: *Your Pet Bear,* 1980; *Your Pet Beaver,* 1980; *Your Pet Elephant,* 1980; *Your Pet Kangaroo,* 1980;

Your Pet Camel, 1980; *Your Pet Penguin,* 1980; *Your Pet Gorilla,* 1981; *Your Pet Lion,* 1981; *Your Pet Sea Lion,* 1982; *Your Pet Giraffe,* 1982.

WORK IN PROGRESS: Children's books; parodies and other short pieces.

SIDELIGHTS: Bobbie Hamsa told *CA:* "The idea for my series began when my son asked for a pet lizard. 'If you're going to have a pet, at least choose something that's useful around the house,' I answered, 'like an elephant. At least he could clean your aquarium.' In the series, children learn many otherwise dry vital statistics about animals by imagining what it's like to have them around the house. Needless to say, this leads to some pretty funny stuff!

"'Fools rush in . . .' and that I did, busting brazenly 'over the transom' via the U.S. Mails, with three manuscripts for 'Far-Fetched Pets.' I was not afraid of the word 'no' and had even made plans for papering a wall with rejection slips, an idea I thought delightfully camp! This aspect of my career began in 1980 as an extension of—and diversion from—writing advertising copy for a variety of clients, including Mutual of Omaha's 'Wild Kingdom,' sometime source of factual material for the 'Far-Fetched Pets' series.

"If there's any philosophy behind my writings, it's the same philosophy that lies behind my life. . . . I enjoy making light of the world around me, turning the commonplace into the unexpected, observing things in a fresh light. Tongue-in-cheek humor is my forte and, to me, it is not work.

"I stand as proof to aspiring writers that anyone can do it provided they have (1) desire, (2) luck, and (3) talent, named last because it alone is no guarantee of success. You can't lose more than a few bucks postage by trying, by forging ahead, by taking that first awful chance. And if you aren't by nature genuinely self-confident, at least pretend you are until your manuscript is in the mail."

*　　*　　*

HANAN, Patrick Dewes   1927-

PERSONAL: Born January 4, 1927, in Morrinsville, New Zealand; came to the United States in 1963; son of Frederick Arthur (a farmer) and Ida Helen (Dewes) Hanan; married Anneliese Drube, July 27, 1951; children: Rupert Guy. *Education:* University of New Zealand, B.A., 1948, M.A., 1949; University of London, B.A., 1953, Ph.D., 1960. *Home:* 43 Langdon St., Cambridge, Mass. 02138. *Office:* Department of East Asian Languages and Civilizations, Harvard University, 2 Divinity Ave., Cambridge, Mass. 02138.

CAREER: University of London, School of Oriental and African Languages, London, England, lecturer in Chinese, 1954-63; Stanford University, Stanford, Calif., associate professor, 1963-66, professor of Chinese literature, 1966-68; Harvard University, Cambridge, Mass., professor of Chinese literature, 1968—. *Member:* American Oriental Society, American Academy of Arts and Sciences, Association for Asian Studies. *Awards, honors:* Grant from American Council of Learned Societies, 1970; Guggenheim fellow, 1977.

WRITINGS: The Chinese Short Story, Harvard University Press, 1973; *The Chinese Vernacular Story,* Harvard University Press, 1981.

WORK IN PROGRESS: The Old Man of the Lake (tentative title), a study of Chinese writer Li Yu, 1611-1680.

SIDELIGHTS: Hanan commented that his specialties are "Chinese traditional fiction, the modern Chinese writer's use of foreign literature, and literary theory, especially as it applies to fiction."

* * *

HANSON, Isabel 1929-

PERSONAL: Born September 3, 1929, in Los Angeles, Calif.; daughter of Meyer (an electrical contractor) and Vera (a medical social worker; maiden name, Keylin) Baylin; married Lewis S. Hanson (separated); children: Paul, Christopher, Jonathan. *Education:* University of California, Berkeley, B.A., 1951. *Home:* 1141 Colusa Ave., Berkeley, Calif. 94707.

CAREER: Free-lance writer and editor, 1961—. Piano accompanist.

WRITINGS: Outwitting Arthritis, Creative Arts, 1980.

SIDELIGHTS: Isabel Hanson wrote: "My personal frustrations and bewilderment engendered by the severe rheumatoid arthritis I was beginning to encounter led me to other arthritics. I had an intense curiosity about how they felt, what experiences they'd gone through, both in treatment and daily life, what approaches they'd settled on. From these came *Outwitting Arthritis,* in-depth interviews combined with my own story and the overall observations I formed."

* * *

HARDING, Lee 1937-

PERSONAL: Born February 19, 1937, in Colac, Victoria, Australia; married; children: three. *Education:* Educated in Victoria, Australia. *Home and office:* 19 Kia-Ora Parade, Ferntree Gully, Victoria 3156, Australia. *Agent:* Virginia Kidd, Literary Agent, 538 East Harford St., Milford, Pa. 18337.

CAREER: Writer and editor of science fiction for adults and young people. *Member:* Science Fiction Writers of America, Australian Society of Authors, Fellowship of Australian Writers. *Awards, honors:* Ditmar Trophy for best Australian science fiction story of the year, 1970, for "Dancing Gerontius," and 1972, for "The Fallen Spaceman"; Australian Children's Book of the Year award, 1980, for *Displaced Person.*

WRITINGS—All science fiction: *The Fallen Spaceman* (juvenile), Cassell, 1973, Harper, 1980, revised edition, illustrated by John Schoenherr and Ian Schoenherr, Bantam, 1982; *A World of Shadows* (novel), R. Hale, 1975; (editor) Ursula K. Le Guin and others, *The Altered I: An Encounter With Science Fiction* (anthology), Nostrilia Press, 1976, Berkley Publishing, 1978; (editor) *Beyond Tomorrow: An Anthology of Modern Science Fiction,* foreword by Isaac Asimov, Wren, 1976; *The Frozen Sky* (juvenile), Cassell, 1976; *Future Sanctuary* (novel), Laser, 1976; *The Children of Atlantis* (juvenile), Cassell, 1976; *Return to Tomorrow* (juvenile), Cassell, 1977; *The Weeping Sky* (novel), Cassell, 1977; *Displaced Person* (juvenile), Hyland House, 1979, published as *Misplaced Persons,* Harper, 1979; (editor) *Rooms of Paradise* (anthology), foreword by Roger Zelazny, St. Martin's, 1979. Also author of *The Web of Time,* 1980.

Contributor of stories to periodicals, including *New Writings in Science Fiction* and *If.*

WORK IN PROGRESS: Several novels, including a novel for young adults tentatively titled *Waiting for the End of the World.*

SIDELIGHTS: Harding told *CA:* "I began writing in the science fiction genre more than twenty years ago. I now find that today's young people are living in a world I merely wrote about. That perhaps explains my deep commitment to writing for this audience. I have three teenage children by a former marriage, and it honestly terrifies me sometimes to imagine what it must be like for them in today's world. *Displaced Person* was the first of my novels to approach this theme. Nowadays, with technological change being so rapid, I am no longer attracted to writing standard science fiction. Nor does far-future fantasy—so popular at the moment—attract my interest. I guess that for the next few years I'll be concentrating on what I call 'urban fantasy'—finding new metaphors for today's readers.

"For many years I worked as a photographer before I decided that I would rather work from inside of people rather than concern myself with surfaces. Only writing can do that well. I also worked for a while as a bookshop manager, but five years of that was quite enough, thank you. I was losing my love of books, and for a writer that can be disastrous. But I value the years I spent 'in the trade' for the insight I was given into how books are merchandised."

Harding's short stories and novels have been translated into nine languages.

AVOCATIONAL INTERESTS: Travel, cooking, music, cinema, gardening, reading.

* * *

HARMAN, Fred 1902(?)-1982

OBITUARY NOTICE: Born c. 1902; died after a stroke, January 2, 1982, in Phoenix, Ariz. Cowboy, illustrator, and cartoonist. After working as a cowboy for much of his youth and early adulthood, Harman joined the Kansas City Film Ad Company, where he worked as an illustrator with Walt Disney. Harman's first comic strip, "Bronc Peeler," was followed by "Red Ryder," which, at the height of its popularity, appeared in more than seven hundred newspapers. Harman, who founded the Cowboy Artists Association, also helped create the "Red Ryder" movies during the 1940's and 1950's. Obituaries and other sources: *New York Times,* January 5, 1982.

* * *

HARMSEL, Henrietta Ten
See TEN HARMSEL, Henrietta

* * *

HARNWELL, Gaylord Probasco 1903-1982

OBITUARY NOTICE: Born September 29, 1903, in Evanston, Ill.; died of a stroke, April 18, 1982, in Haverford, Pa. Physicist, educator, business executive, and author. In his thirty-two year association with the University of Pennsylvania, Harnwell held a number of posts, including associate professor, professor of physics, chairman of the physics department, researcher, and director of the Randal Morgan Laboratory of Physics. In 1953 he became the university's president, a position he held until 1970. His office was the scene of a 1967 sit-in by students who were protesting research on chemical and biological warfare that was being conducted in the university's laboratories. Harnwell responded to the protests by convincing university trustees to discontinue the research project. During his career he served as director of a number of corporations, including the Pennsylvania Railroad. In addition to several textbooks, Harnwell also wrote *Russian Diary* and *Educational Voyaging in Iran.* Obituaries and other sources:

Current Biography, Wilson, 1956; *Who's Who in America,* 40th edition, Marquis, 1978; *American Men and Women of Science: The Physical and Biological Sciences,* 14th edition, Bowker, 1979; *New York Times,* April 20, 1982; *Time,* May 3, 1982.

*   *   *

HARRELL, (Clyde) Stevan   1947-

PERSONAL: Born August 15, 1947, in Los Angeles, Calif.; son of Clyde P. (an attorney) and Frances (an elementary school teacher; maiden name, Dull) Harrell; married Barbara Blain (a physician), December 20, 1968; children: Cynthia, Deborah. *Education:* Stanford University, A.B., 1968, M.A., 1971, Ph.D., 1974. *Residence:* Seattle, Wash. *Office:* Department of Anthropology, University of Washington, Seattle, Wash. 98195.

CAREER: University of Washington, Seattle, assistant professor, 1974-81, associate professor of anthropology and international studies, 1981—.

WRITINGS: (Editor with Pamela T. Amoss) *Other Ways of Growing Old,* Stanford University Press, 1981; *Ploughshare Village: Culture and Context in Taiwan,* University of Washington Press, 1982.

Contributor: Arthur P. Wolf, editor, *Religion and Ritual in Chinese Society,* Stanford University Press, 1974; William H. Newell, editor, *Ancestors,* Mouton, 1976; Wolf and S. B. Hanley, editors, *Social Demography and Family History in East Asia,* Stanford University Press, in press. Contributor to Asian studies journals.

WORK IN PROGRESS: A book on the history of the family, publication expected in 1984; research on Chinese historical demography and history of the Chinese in Seattle.

SIDELIGHTS: Harrell wrote: "I like to do a lot of public and community speaking, to bring specialized knowledge to the general public. I enjoy teaching at any age level, from small children to advanced graduate students. I think anthropology has an important perspective to contribute, a way of appreciating other cultures and other ways of dealing with the world. Unfortunately, a lot of outsiders to the field are put off by our unnecessary jargon and our turgid writing style. I thus try, and encourage others to try, to write in plain English. I will take a group of ten- to thirteen-year-olds to China soon, and I speak Mandarin Chinese and Taiwanese."

AVOCATIONAL INTERESTS: Travel, gardening, swimming.

*   *   *

HART, Allan H(untley)   1935-

PERSONAL: Born December 7, 1935, in New Haven, Conn.; son of Ernest H. (an artist and writer) and Louise (Rielly) Hart; married wife, Sandra, June 29, 1957 (divorced, October, 1980); married Julie Trembly (a veterinarian), November 29, 1980; children: April, Stephanie, Matthew. *Education:* Attended University of Pennsylvania, 1954-57; University of Sydney, B.V.Sc., 1962. *Home address:* Turnbuckle Lane, Guilford, Conn. *Agent:* Raines & Raines, 475 Fifth Ave., New York, N.Y. 10017. *Office:* Veterinary Associates, Route 80, North Branford, Conn.

CAREER: Veterinary Associates, North Branford, Conn., Veterinarian, 1962—. *Member:* Connecticut Veterinary Medical Association, Rotary International.

WRITINGS: The Dog Owner's Encyclopedia of Veterinary Medicine, T.F.H. Publications, 1970; (with Ernest H. Hart)

The Complete Guide to All Cats, Scribner, 1980. Contributor to veterinary magazines, including *Modern Veterinary Practice.*

*   *   *

HART, Gavin   1939-

PERSONAL: Born May 17, 1939, in Yorketown, Australia; son of Keith (a farmer) and Freda (Gericke) Hart; married Astrid Heyne, July 13, 1963; children: Justin, Quentin, Sharelle. *Education:* Attended Adelaide Teachers College, 1957-60; University of Adelaide, B.Sc. (with honors), 1960, M.B., B.S., 1968, M.D., 1974; Harvard University, M.P.H., 1977. *Home:* 4 Ellis Ave., Eden Hills, South Australia 5050. *Office:* South Australia Health Commission, 52 Pirie St., Adelaide, South Australia 5000.

CAREER: University of Adelaide, Adelaide, Australia, research chemist in organic chemistry, 1960; teacher of chemistry at boys' high school in Adelaide, 1961; Department of Native Affairs, Port Moresby, Papua New Guinea, agricultural chemist, 1963-64; Queen Elizabeth Hospital, Adelaide, South Australia, resident, 1969; First Australian Field Hospital, Vung Tau, South Vietnam, registrar, 1970; Taurama Medical Centre, Port Moresby, commanding officer, 1972-73; South Australia Venereal Disease Control Centre, Adelaide, clinical assistant, 1974; U.S. Center for Disease Control, Atlanta, Ga., visiting scientist, 1974-76; Community and Child Health Services, Trigg, Australia, senior medical officer in education and community health, 1977-80; South Australia Health Commission, Information Services Division, epidemiologist, 1981—. Anesthetist at Port Moresby Hospital, 1972-73; consultant to World Health Organization and Government of Australia; member of World Health Organization Expert Advisory Panel on Venereal Diseases, Treponematoses, and Neisseria Infections. *Military service:* Australian Army, 1969-70; served in Vietnam; became major. *Member:* American Venereal Disease Association, Australian and New Zealand Society for Epidemiology and Research in Community Health. *Awards, honors:* Leadership award from Australian Medical Association, 1969; certificate of appreciation from U.S. Center for Disease Control, 1976.

WRITINGS: Nutritional Studies of "Coffea arabica" in Papua New Guinea, Papua New Guinea Department of Agriculture, 1969; *Chancroid, Donovanosis, Lymphogranuloma Venereum,* U.S. Public Health Service, 1975; *Sexually Transmitted Diseases,* Carolina Biological, 1976; *Human Sexual Behavior,* Carolina Biological, 1977; *Sexual Maladjustment and Disease,* Nelson-Hall, 1977.

Contributor: G. L. Mandell, R. G. Douglas, and J. E. Bennett, editors, *Principles and Practices of Infectious Diseases,* Wiley, 1978; J. Y. Shen, editor, *Clinical Practice of Adolescent Medicine,* Mosby, 1978; H. F. Conn, editor, *Current Therapy,* Saunders, 1979; A. S. Evans and H. A. Feldman, editors, *Bacterial Infections of Humans,* Plenum, 1982; K. K. Holmes, P. March, P. F. Sparling, and P. J. Wiesner, editors, *Sexually Transmitted Diseases,* McGraw, 1982. Also contributor to *Top's Communicable and Infectious Diseases,* 8th edition, 1976. Contributor to medical and chemistry journals.

WORK IN PROGRESS: Developing curricula and training aids for training physicians, nurses, and health assistants in epidemiology and such social issues as sexuality and drugs.

SIDELIGHTS: Hart told *CA:* "The underlying direct force in my career has been a longstanding interest in anthropology. When I joined the Anthropological Society of South Australia in 1957 I was strongly influenced by Norman Tindale and C. P.

Mountford. After I completed my university programs and worked as a research chemist and school teacher, this force took me to New Guinea as a patrol officer, with the ultimate goal a career in anthropology. Political instability in New Guinea suggested an alternative plan, and I returned to Adelaide to study medicine, with a view to practicing in developing communities.

"War service in Vietnam opened a new area of interest—venereology. Although venereal disease was epidemic in the Australian troops, the social and psychological aspects of sexual behavior producing this problem were of greatest interest. This led to a doctoral thesis, 'The Impact of Prostitution on Australian Troops at War.'

"After Vietnam, I returned to New Guinea, where I was in charge of a fifty-bed hospital and the training of military medical personnel. I continued to develop further my experience and training in problems related to sexual behavior. Since then my major efforts have been directed to propagating two major philosophies.

"The first philosophy is that unwanted *sequelae* of sexual behavior, such as sexually transmitted diseases or unwanted pregnancy, are only symptoms of sexual maladjustment, and this underlying maladjustment must be addressed if the outcome of treatment is to be successful. This also led to the realization of the inadequacies of the medical profession in dealing with the types of sexual problems which are so common in most communities. Much of my work in New Guinea, the United States, and Australia has been directed toward alleviating these deficiencies.

"My second professional philosophy is that the lack of control of venereal disease is much less related to sexual behavior than most people believe. The health-seeking behavior of infected people is probably more important, but the real problem resides with the behavior of community leaders, health administrators, and clinicians who determine the funds and treatment facilities provided, who are responsible for developing appropriate vacancies in health departments and for the training of clinical personnel. The real reason for the perpetuation of these infectious diseases is the preference of these groups to talk about the issues, form committees, and undertake other token approaches without facing the reality that action, hard work, and implementation of our present adequate knowledge is a prerequisite for any impact."

AVOCATIONAL INTERESTS: "Copper beating of traditional New Guinea artifacts," weaving *ojo de dios*.

*   *   *

HART, Roderick P(atrick) 1945-

PERSONAL: Born February 17, 1945, in Fall River, Mass.; son of R. P. (a manager) and Claire (Sullivan) Hart; married Margaret McVey (a computer scientist), August 27, 1966; children: Christopher David, Kathleen Mary. *Education:* University of Massachusetts, B.A. 1966; Pennsylvania State University, M.A., 1968, Ph.D., 1970. *Politics:* Democrat. *Religion:* Unitarian-Universalist. *Home:* 2916 Kassarine Pass, Austin, Tex. 78704. *Office:* Department of Speech Communication, University of Texas, Austin, Tex. 78712.

CAREER: Purdue University, West Lafayette, Ind., assistant professor, 1970-74, associate professor of communication, 1974-79; University of Texas, Austin, professor of speech communication, 1979—. *Member:* International Communication Association, International Society of Political Psychology, Speech Communication Association of America (chairman of

research board), Center for the Study of the Presidency. *Awards, honors:* Woodrow Wilson fellow, 1969; monograph award from Speech Communication Association of America, 1972, for *Rhetoric of True Believer*, 1974, for *Rhetoric of Goodbye*, and 1980, for *Attitudes Toward Communication*.

WRITINGS: (With Gustav Friedrich) *Public Communication*, Harper, 1975, 2nd edition, 1982; *The Political Pulpit*, Purdue University Press, 1979. Editor of "Modcom Series," for Science Research Associates, and "Procom Series," Scott, Foresman. Contributing associate editor of *Communication Monographs* and *Human Communication Research*.

WORK IN PROGRESS: Persuasion and the Presidency, publication expected in 1985.

SIDELIGHTS: Hart commented: "My writing is dedicated to pointing up the distinctive light shed upon contemporary public affairs by one who looks at how and why humans talk as they do."

*   *   *

HARTLEY, Fred Allan III 1953-

PERSONAL: Born March 22, 1953, in Morristown, N.J.; son of H. Allan (an artist and writer) and Hermine (Peppinger) Hartley; married Sherry Dykstra, June 14, 1974; children: Fred Allan IV, Andrea Joy. *Education:* Wheaton College, Wheaton, Ill., B.A., 1975; Gordon-Conwell Theological Seminary, M.Div., 1979. *Home:* 1736 Northwest Eighth Terr., Homestead, Fla. 33030. *Office:* South Dade Alliance Church, 29501 Southwest 152nd Ave., Leisure City, Fla. 33033.

CAREER: Ordained Christian & Missionary Alliance minister, 1980; associate pastor of village church in Fort Myers, Fla., 1976-78; South Dade Alliance Church, Leisure City, Fla., senior pastor, 1979—. Lecturer and conference speaker.

WRITINGS: Update: A New Perspective on Christian Dating (young adult), Revell, 1977; *Dare to Be Different*, Revell, 1979; *Growing Pains: First-Aid for Teenagers*, Revell, 1981; *One Hundred Per Cent Discipleship* (young adult), Revell, 1983.

SIDELIGHTS: Hartley told *CA:* "When I was nineteen years of age, I accompanied my father to an editorial conference at the Fleming H. Revell Co. (publishers). There, conversation obviously centered on books—particularly my father's work. Over dessert they turned to me and asked, 'What have you ever published?' I chuckled and replied, 'A term paper for college.' They responded that they were always looking for new authors and would be glad to have me submit some material. I had just finished writing a short story on a dating relationship I had had, so I sent it to them.

"Soon after, they sent me a contract for a book that was to become my first publication, *Update: A New Perspective on Christian Dating*. I have since been impressed with the powerful medium of printed copy and am currently working on my fourth manuscript. As a Christian writer, I work from the philosophical base of absolute truth and the conviction that God has spoken in history through his son, Jesus Christ . . . the Incarnate Word. In my publications I have sought to transcribe eternal truths into concrete realities that are livable for today's adolescents. I trust I have been at least partially successful."

*   *   *

HARVEY, Anthony Peter 1940-

PERSONAL: Born May 21, 1940, in Andover, England; son

of Frederick William Henry and Fanny Evelyn (Dixon) Harvey; married Margaret Hayward, January 16, 1963; children: Terence David, Iain Michael, Joanne Louise, Kevin John. *Home:* Ragstones, Broad Oak, Heathfield, East Sussex TN21 8UD, England. *Office:* British Museum (Natural History), London SW7 5BD, England.

CAREER: British Museum and British Museum (Natural History), London, England, worked in various positions, 1961-81, head of department of library services (Natural History), 1981—. Chairman of committee for International Conference on Geological Information. Member of Heathfield and Waldren Parish Council. *Member:* International Federation for Documentation, European Association of Earth Science Editors, Bibliographical Society, Museums Association, Printing Historical Society, Royal Geographical Society, Aslib, Library Association, Institute of Information Scientists, Geological Society of London (chairman of geological information group committee, 1976-78; chairman of library committee), Society for the Bibliography of Natural History, Association of Earth Science Editors. *Awards, honors: Directory of Scientific Directories* was named an outstanding reference book of the year by *Library Journal,* 1969.

WRITINGS: (Editor) *Secrets of the Earth,* Hamlyn, 1967; *Directory of Scientific Directories,* Hodgson, 1969, 4th edition, Longman, 1983.

(Contributor) *Ocean Research Index,* Hodgson, 1970, 2nd edition, 1976; (contributor) T. F. Williams, editor, *Industrial Research in Britain,* Hodgson, 1972; *Prehistoric Man,* Hamlyn, 1972; (contributor) D. N. Wood, editor, *The Use of Earth Sciences Literature,* Butterworth, 1973; *Guide to World Science,* Volume I, Hodgson, 1974; *Prehistoric Animals* (juvenile), Macmillan, 1976; *Early Man* (juvenile), Macmillan, 1976; (editor) *The Hamlyn Book of Early Man* (juvenile), Hamlyn, 1976; (with D. Tills) *Joy of Knowledge: Man and Society,* Mitchell Beazley, 1977; (with Tills) *Physical Earth,* Mitchell Beazley, 1978; (contributor) *The Future of Publishing by Scientific and Learned Societies,* Commission of the European Communities, 1978; (editor and contributor) *Encyclopaedia of Prehistoric Life,* Mitchell Beazley, 1979; (editor with J. A. Diment) *Geoscience Information: An International State-of-the-Art Review,* Broad Oak Press, 1979.

(With A. J. Walford) *Walford's Guide to Reference Material,* Volume I: *Science and Technology,* 4th edition (Harvey was not associated with earlier editions), Library Association, 1980; (with G.D.R. Bridson and V. Phillips) *Natural History Manuscript Resources in the British Isles,* Mansell, 1980; (with A. Pernet) *Guide to European Sources of Scientific and Technical Information,* 5th edition (Harvey was not associated with earlier editions), Longman, 1981; *Guide to United Kingdom Science and Technology,* 2nd edition, Longman, 1982.

Contributor to *Encyclopaedia of Library and Information Science, Children's Wonderful World Encyclopaedia,* and *Hamlyn Children's Encyclopaedia.* Contributor to scientific journals.

WORK IN PROGRESS: Research on history of geology, especially evolution of paleontology, and history of publishing by museums.

SIDELIGHTS: Harvey told *CA:* "An interest in geology led to the writing and editing of books for juniors, in the hope that they would come to appreciate better the natural wonders of the Earth and to also realize how fragile such seemingly permanent features are, in reality. Writing for juniors developed into texts for interested adults and especially to writing the short (one thousand-word) texts, accompanied by vivid illus-

trations, that characterize the *Joy of Knowledge: Man and Society.*

"By complete contrast the compilation of reference works stems from my professional work in a major national library and having an intense interest in reference librarianship and in serving library users. The challenges that such works present are most stimulating—rather like undertaking a giant crossword puzzle in which one first has to locate the clues. Further, if successful, such works become major sources of information of value to a broad spectrum of enquirers on an international scale."

* * *

HASLER, Eveline 1937-

PERSONAL: Born March 22, 1937, in Glarus, Switzerland; daughter of Walter (in business) and Lili (Bircher) Schubiger; married Paul Hasler (a professor), October 5, 1962; children: Regula, Paul, Isabel. *Education:* Attended University of Paris and University of Fribourg. *Home:* Lehnhaldenstrasse 46, 9014 St. Gallen, Switzerland.

CAREER: College instructor in French. *Member:* Schweizer Schriftstellerverein. *Awards, honors:* Diploma of Merit, 1968; Hans Christian Andersen award from the International Board on Books, 1976; Schweizerischer Jugendbuchpreis, 1978; Preis der Schillerstiftung, 1980, for *Novemberinsel.*

WRITINGS—In English translation: *Miranda's Magic,* translated by Elizabeth Shub, Macmillan, 1975.

Other: *Stop, Daniela! Sowie, die Eidechse mit den Similisteinen, und andere Erzaehlungen,* Rex-Verlag (Lucerne, Switzerland), 1962; *Ferdi und die Angelrute,* Rex-Verlag, 1963; *Komm wieder, Pepino!,* Benziger (Zurich, Switzerland), 1967; *Adieu Paris, Adieu Catherine,* Benziger, 1969; *Die seltsamen Freunde,* Benziger, 1970; *Ein Baum fuer Filippo,* Atlantis, 1973; *Der Sonntagsvater,* Otto Maier, 1973; *Unterm Neonmond,* George Bitter, 1974; *Denk an mich Mauro,* Benziger, 1976; *Der Buchstabenkoenig und die Hexe Lakritze,* Benziger, 1977; *Novemberinsel,* Arche, 1979. Also author of *Die Insei des blauen Arturo,* Benziger; *Der Zauberelefant,* Benziger; *Dann kroch Martin durch den Zaun,* Benziger; *Denk an den Trick, Nelly,* Benziger; *Jahre mit Fluegeln,* Arena.

BIOGRAPHICAL/CRITICAL SOURCES: Vaterland, December 15, 1979.

* * *

HATHAWAY, Bo 1942-

PERSONAL: Born December 14, 1942, in Biloxi, Miss.; son of William Thomas Schuster and Carolyn Daugherty Hathaway; married Nancy Berman (a writer), August 26, 1973. *Education:* Attended Columbia University, 1969-71; University of Washington, Seattle, B.A., 1974, M.A., 1977. *Home:* 36 Breeze Ave., Venice, Calif. 90291. *Agent:* Berenice Hoffman Literary Agency, 215 West 75th St., New York, N.Y. 10023.

CAREER: Crafton Hills College, Yucaipa, Calif., instructor in English, 1977-78; Rosebud Books, Los Angeles, Calif., editor, 1979—. Teacher of Transcendental Meditation, 1971—. *Military service:* U.S. Army, Special Forces, 1964-67; served in Vietnam; became sergeant; received Bronze Star. *Awards, honors:* Award from Mary Roberts Rinehart Foundation, 1975, for *A World of Hurt.*

WRITINGS: A World of Hurt (novel), Taplinger, 1981.

WORK IN PROGRESS: A nonfantasy novel on "the evolution of consciousness toward enlightenment."

SIDELIGHTS: Hathaway told *CA:* "*A World of Hurt* portrays the blocked sexuality and internalized paternal structures that seem to me to be the psychological roots of war. It shows the primary function of war to be the mass purgation of psychic stress, a periodic convulsion that will apparently keep occurring until we reach a higher stage of development. I tried to write this within the bounds of a strict realism, in order to avoid the prevalent distortions caused by journalistic capsulizing and by the creation of composite characters and situations to hype the melodrama. I wanted to present the war as it was, but also to show its deeper significance, both of which I found to be far different from the commonly held views."

* * *

HATLEY, George B(erton) 1924-

PERSONAL: Born July 18, 1924, in Pullman, Wash.; son of Ray E. (a rancher) and Neva (Dole) Hatley; married Iola Golden (a computer operator), June 21, 1947; children: John Craig. *Education:* University of Idaho, B.S., 1950. *Home:* 820 East First, Moscow, Idaho 83843. *Office:* Appaloosa Horse Club, Inc., P.O. Box 8403, Moscow, Idaho 83843.

CAREER: Appaloosa Horse Club, Inc., Moscow, Idaho, executive secretary, 1947-78, administrative consultant, 1978—. Director of Idaho Trail Council, 1977-79. *Military service:* U.S. Navy, 1944-45. *Awards, honors:* "Pat on the Back" trophy from *Sports Illustrated,* 1961, for work in saving the Appaloosa breed from extinction; elected to Washington State University's Lariat Hall of Fame, 1963; distinguished equine award from Agriservice, 1971, for service to the light horse industry; named all-time great horseman, 1981.

WRITINGS: The Appaloosa Horse, R. G. Bailey, 1950; *Horse Camping,* Dial, 1981. Editor of *Appaloosa News,* 1946-66.

SIDELIGHTS: Hatley told *CA:* "My grandfather had come to the Palouse country by wagon train in 1876 and my family has owned Appaloosas since then. My father thoroughly enjoyed pack trips into the mountains so I learned packing and horse camping at an early age. It is exciting to see new country from the back of a horse and relive the horse camping experience of the mountain men (fur trappers), prospectors, and cowboys.

"I have used Appaloosas for ranch work, hunting, racing (I bred two stakes winners), and endurance (I completed the one-hundred-mile Tevis Ride in one day) in addition to trail riding and horse camping. Appaloosas are an important part of my life.

"I began writing articles about Appaloosas in 1946, the year I started *Appaloosa News.* I felt the Appaloosa played an important role in the history of the Northwest and was a colorful, useful horse that should have the opportunity to take its rightful place among the other breeds."

* * *

HATMON, Paul W. 1921-

PERSONAL: Born June 23, 1921, in Cabool, Mo.; son of Herbert Howard (a carpenter) and Bessie Odessa (Hunter) Hatmon; married Margaret L. Barrett, August 14, 1942. *Education:* Attended Miami Junior College, Miami, Okla. *Home and office:* 11306 Thompson, Independence, Mo. 64054.

CAREER: Truck driver, 1945-55; U.S. Post Office, station superintendent in Independence and Kansas City, Mo., 1955-72; writer, 1972—. *Military service:* U.S. Army, 1942-45.

WRITINGS: Yesterday's Fire Engines, Lerner, 1980; *Yesterday's Motorcycles,* Lerner, 1981. Also author of *Auto Bright-*

work for Lerner. Author of "Car Talk," a weekly column in *Independence Examiner,* 1966-70. Contributor of more than three hundred articles to magazines, including *Motor Trend, Road Rides, VFW,* and *Old Cars.*

WORK IN PROGRESS: Research on blacksmithing and on the postal history of Independence, Mo.

SIDELIGHTS: "A veteran of World War II," Hatmon commented, "I was badly bitten by the old car bug while stationed in England in the pre-D-Day lull. The vintage cars on the streets at that time opened up possibilities that I had never dreamed of. Upon my release from the army, I purchased a 1914 Ford touring car, restored it to mint condition, and drove it more than five thousand trouble-free miles to meets and tours. From this springboard a genuine raving addict was launched.

"My job at that time was transporting new cars, enabling me to scout far and wide for the rare and unusual. I unearthed many cars, among them a whole gaggle of rare types, including a 1913 Imp Cycle car, a Model 10 Buick White Streak, a two-cylinder Maxwell, and a 1907 Brush. I became acquainted with James Melton, purchasing from him a 1908 Brush chassis that had been displayed in his museum, and restoring the little blue one-lunger to perfection. From my interest in Bugattis, I met many of the famous collectors of the day.

"Due to a chance encounter with Ken Purdy at a vintage race car meet, I became interested in vintage sport cars, progressing through MGs, Healys, Jaguars, Alfas, Ferraris, the 300 SLS, Bugattis, Rolls Royces, and Bentleys, and the ensuing years have been spent happily restoring and gathering up the rarest of these cars that finances would permit.

"Blessed with an understanding *hausfrau* who enjoys tours and meets, I trek to any event that can be fitted into my schedule. I have one of the largest automotive nameplate collections in the country, now complemented by an extensive porcelain sign collection. I am driving a 1972 240 Z Datsun, with over one hundred thousand miles on it, that still screams and goes. I have a four-wheel drive IHC Travelall, and for Sunday driving a 1973 Series II Excalibur phaeton.

"Out of financial necessity, I do all my own restoration work and maintenance in my well-equipped basement shop, built especially to accommodate four to six cars at any given time. For this reason, it is necessary to dispose of one car before another can be added to the stable. The last crop, a 1956 SI Bentley, a 1966 Cadillac pickup truck, and a 1931 Reo Speed-wagon fire truck, went the route recently.

"There is a Delahaye, the 135 MS-type engine like the one that set records at Brooklands in 1938, that maybe, with a great deal of dollar-squeezing, can be my newest project; its condition would be classified as pitiful. Or even a chain gang Fraser Nash has been offered, if it can be worked out without having to go on food stamps."

* * *

HAWES, Lynne Salop 1931-
(Lynne Salop)

PERSONAL: Born February 17, 1931, in New York, N.Y.; daughter of Isadore (a musician) and Alice (an optometrist; maiden name, Pallant) Gusikoff; married Arnold Salop, September 24, 1950 (divorced, June, 1979); married Gene R. Hawes (a writer), September 6, 1980. children: (first marriage) Andrea Salop Terdiman, Holly, Evan. *Education:* New York University, B.A., 1950; State University of New York College at New Paltz, Teaching Certificate, 1973; Fairfield University,

M.A., 1973. *Home and office:* 34 Aldridge, Chappaqua, N.Y. 10514.

CAREER: Panas High School, Peekskill, N.Y., English teacher, 1973-76. *Member:* Hudson Group.

WRITINGS: (With husband, Gene R. Hawes) *Hawes Guide to Successful Study Skills,* New American Library, 1981; *Concise Dictionary of Education,* Van Nostrand, 1982.

Under name Lynne Salop: *Suisong* (literary study of Sylvia Plath), Vantage, 1978.

WORK IN PROGRESS: A musical guide book.

*   *   *

HAWKINS, John C(harles) 1948-

PERSONAL: Born May 14, 1948, in Sewickley, Pa.; son of Frank N. (a college professor) and Lottie (Norton) Hawkins; married Dorothy Szura, June 5, 1971; children: Mary Julia. *Education:* Princeton University, B.A., 1970. *Politics:* Independent. *Religion:* Roman Catholic. *Home:* 309 Windsor Dr., Coraopolis, Pa. 15108. *Office:* Gulf Oil Corp., P.O. Box 1166, Pittsburgh, Pa. 15230.

CAREER: Allegheny County Health Department, Pittsburgh, Pa., public information officer, 1970-72; *Harrisburg Patriot-News,* Harrisburg, Pa., reporter, 1972-75; National Wildlife Federation, Washington, D.C., assistant information director, 1975-76; McIlhenny-Humphrey Inc., Pittsburgh, account executive, 1976-79; E.I. du Pont de Nemours & Co., Wilmington, Del., public affairs representative, 1979-81; Gulf Oil Corp., Pittsburgh, public communications representative, 1981—. Adviser to Pittsburgh Pirates. *Military service:* U.S. Naval Reserve, 1966-70. *Member:* Society for American Baseball Research, Harvard-Yale-Princeton Club of Pittsburgh (member of board of directors), Pittsburgh Pirates Captains Club.

WRITINGS: This Date in Detroit Tigers History, Stein & Day, 1981; *This Date in Baltimore Orioles History,* Stein & Day, 1982.

WORK IN PROGRESS: Research for a book on corporate and judicial corruption in western Pennsylvania.

SIDELIGHTS: Hawkins told *CA:* "My love for and interest in baseball has grown from a hobby into an almost full-time occupation. My association with the Pittsburgh Pirates and subsequent research involving other teams has proved a fascinating look at how large metropolitan areas have developed intricate and intimate links with professional baseball. Understanding baseball history helps me toward a greater understanding of human nature and the tribal links we all seek in our society."

*   *   *

HAYES, Alfred 1911-

PERSONAL: Born April 17, 1911, in London, England; came to United States, c. 1913; son of Michael (a barber) and Rachel (Topper) Hayes; married wife, Marietta; children: Alan, Alfred Eliot, and a daughter. *Education:* Attended City College of New York (now of the City University of New York). *Politics:* None. *Religion:* Jewish. *Home:* 5060 Gloria St., Encino, Calif. 91316.

CAREER: Worked as reporter for *Daily Mirror* and *New York American,* 1932-35; free-lance writer, 1935-39; associated with Warner Bros., RKO, and Twentieth Century-Fox, 1945-50; writer. *Military service:* U.S. Army, 1943-45. *Member:* American Society of Composers, Authors, and Publishers (ASCAP),

Writers Guild. *Awards, honors:* Eunice Tietjens Prize for poetry, 1950.

WRITINGS: The Big Time (poetry), Howell, Sosken, 1944; *All Thy Conquests* (novel), Howell, Sosken, 1946; *Shadow of Heaven* (novel), Howell, Sosken, 1947; (with Trudi Rittman) *Jewish Holiday Dances* (songs; music by Rittman, lyrics by Hayes), Behrman House, 1948; *The Girl on the Via Flaminia* (novel), Harper, 1949; *Welcome to the Castle* (poetry), Harper, 1950; *In Love* (novel), Harper, 1953; *My Face for the World to See* (novel), Harper, 1958; *The Temptation of Don Volpi* (short stories), Atheneum, 1960; *Just Before the Divorce* (poetry), Atheneum, 1968; *The End of Me* (novel), Atheneum, 1968; *The Stockbroker, the Bitter Young Man, and the Beautiful Girl* (novel), Gollancz, 1973.

Screenplays: (With Federico Fellini, Sergio Amidei, Marcello Pagliero, and Roberto Rossellini) "Paisan," [Italy], 1949; "Clash by Night" (adapted from the play by Clifford Odets), RKO, 1952; "Human Desire" (adapted from the novel by Emile Zola, *The Human Beast*), Columbia, 1954; "Island in the Sun" (adapted from the novel by Alex Waugh), Twentieth Century-Fox, 1957; (with Michael Vincente Gazzo) "A Hatful of Rain" (adapted from the play by Gazzo), 1957; "The Left Hand of God" (adapted from the novel by William E. Barrett), Warner Bros., 1958; "These Thousand Hills" (adapted from the novel by A. B. Guthrie, Jr.), Twentieth Century-Fox, 1959; "The Mountain Road" (adapted from the novel by Theodore White), Columbia, 1960; (with Sally Benson and Norman Lessing) "Joy in the Morning" (adapted from the novel by Betty Smith), Metro-Goldwyn-Mayer (MGM), 1965; (with Frank Tarloff) "The Double Man" (adapted from the novel by Henry S. Maxfield, *Legacy of a Spy*), Warner Bros., 1968; (with Edward Anhalt) "In Enemy Country" (adapted from the novel by Sy Bartlett), Universal, 1969.

Co-author of "Journeyman," 1938, and "Tis of Thee," 1940. Writer for television series, including "Mannix." Film critic for *Friday* magazine. Contributor to periodicals.

SIDELIGHTS: Hayes's writings are often compared to those of Ernest Hemingway, for both feature clipped and direct sentences that emphasize realistic content. Hayes's first novel, *All Thy Conquests,* is a war story dealing with the liberation of Rome by American troops during World War II. "Here are excellent portrait sketches, haunting suggestions of the fetid atmosphere of Rome," summarized Orville Prescott, "where hunger and poverty were less serious than hysteria and corruption." Malcolm Cowley also noted a similarity to Hemingway's style in Hayes's *The Girl on the Via Flaminia.* "There are passages that come a little too close to Hemingway," Cowley wrote, "although this fault appears less in the dialogue than in the expository writing." And Siegfried Mandel declared in 1949 that "with more substance and intensity, *The Girl on the Via Flaminia* conceivably could have been this war's *A Farewell to Arms.*" Hayes's later novels, though not as popular as the first few, were nonetheless well received in some critical quarters. Some critics detected the influence of Henry James, especially in love stories such as *In Love* and *My Face for the World to See.*

Critics have also generously praised Hayes's poetry. Oscar Williams called *The Big Time* "an American document of importance." Alfred Kreymborg wrote, "*Welcome to the Castle* is harsh and tender, clear and profound, beautifully composed." And William Rose Benet said Hayes's "work has drama, sophistication, and bite. It is fully of irony."

CA INTERVIEW

Alfred Hayes was interviewed by *CA* on August 18, 1980, in Encino, Calif.

CA: You were born in London. How old were you when you came to America?

HAYES: Two years old. I grew up in New York. I'm really a New Yorker.

CA: And you became a journalist?

HAYES: I always wanted to be a newspaperman. That was my first ambition. I liked that kind of life. I worked on the papers for about three years and then when the Depression came, they started to lay off everybody. I got laid off and I drifted away.

CA: What kind of news did you cover?

HAYES: I was a crime reporter down at the old Federal Building in New York. I worked on the *New York American* and the *Daily Mirror,* then I floated around in New York. I did some magazine writing and wrote for some of the radio variety shows. I wrote the stuff for the singer to say in between his songs. I wrote for a magazine called *Friday.* It was the first pictorial magazine, and I was the movie critic. It folded after a year. Then I went into the army in 1943.

CA: When did you write your first book?

HAYES: When I came out of the army in 1945. William Soskin gave me a little money and I sat down and I wrote a novel.

CA: Just like that?

HAYES: Well, it took me about four months, but just like that— do or die. The novel went well and I came out to Hollywood to work for Warner Brothers. After a year I went back to New York and wrote two more novels. Then I came back to Hollywood and went back to Warner Brothers, then RKO and Twentieth Century-Fox.

CA: What did you do at the studios?

HAYES: I was under contract. I did adaptations of novels. You did whatever the job was that they assigned you to do. It was just like it is today, except you sat in an office then; now you work at home. But it was the same stuff—same story conferences, the same nonsense. Nothing changes; it was a little dull, but it was a job. I built a house out here in the valley in 1960 and I stayed here.

CA: What was life like in Hollywood then?

HAYES: When I came here, Hollywood was a small town; it was very nice. There were good people. We used to meet at a kind of theatre restaurant Preston Sturges had—the old Player's Restaurant—it's not there anymore. Most of the writers used to come there. William Faulkner used to eat there at night. It was a kind of off-shoot of New York. But all that has kind of vanished now. It was a place to go to meet people who were more or less like yourself. I don't think any great ideas were exchanged, just a lot of gripes and a lot of drinking. I don't even know if that exists here anymore.

CA: Your last novel was published in 1973. Have you retired?

HAYES: It was difficult to get published after that. My last novel was not even published here. It was published in England and it didn't do well at all. I got a little discouraged.

CA: Which did you like better, being a reporter or a novelist?

HAYES: It's more fun, I think, in journalism than it is in novel writing. It's a very solitary occupation, sitting home for a year trying to write a novel that you're not even sure anybody's going to read or care about. If you have succeeded in convincing some publisher to finance you, fine, but I have very little contact now at any of the publishers. You know everything has changed within the last ten years. People who were in publishing are out. My generation is dying off every day.

CA: Was there more caring for the art of writing in your day?

HAYES: It's hard to remember now. About all that I write now is poems. They satisfy me and I like them. I don't publish them, but I write them. And whatever jobs are around, you know, when you need money, you get a television job or some other kind of job. I have long ceased to be ambitious.

CA: How has publishing changed? Are publishers less concerned with literature and more concerned with a money-making proposition?

HAYES: They always were concerned with a money-making proposition, but different things made money in different times. The older movies, the more traditional movies were more connected to literature, but that is no longer true. I don't know what it's connected with now, whether it's comic strips or what. Half the stuff looks like it's made up at the Hasty Pudding Club, or extensions of the scripts for skits up in the Catskills. That's what becomes movies today.

CA: Do people read anymore, or are they getting their literature from television and films?

HAYES: I don't know if they read. They seem to buy books. But I don't read the best-sellers, so I don't know what they're like. I think I read a couple of Harold Robbins's books, and once I tried to read an Irving Wallace book and threw that away. There are some good books still being published. *Sophie's Choice* was a kind of a nice novel, no great world-shaking event, but a nice novel. But that's about all. I don't think I've read anything that I cared about. I didn't like *The World According to Garp.* I didn't know what all the huzzahs were about. I thought it was a bore and I thought it was flat. Maybe I'm looking at it with different eyes. There's a great line by Bernard Shaw. He says, "The trouble with me is that I have twenty-twenty vision, and everybody else is a little bit cockeyed."

CA: Are there any films today that you like?

HAYES: The new Italian sex movies that they've been making with Laura Antonelli have been very good, very sharp, very funny, and very accurate about women and love. But we don't make that kind of movie. Sex with us has to be erotic and shabby, or it's sentimental.

CA: But you don't write anymore. Is there anything you're burning to say?

HAYES: Nothing burns anymore. I write for whatever somebody pays me to write. It's no sweat; I can do it. I've always had a certain amount of knowledge and professional skill, and

I do it, that's all. I still can't get them bad enough when I write for television. There are still elements in me that make the stuff too good, and that's too bad.

CA: Looking back, which work are you most pleased with?

HAYES: I think my novels are still pretty good. I've reread them and they're very good. They're very different from everybody else's. I think they're very commercial, although only one of them ever sold very well and that was *The Girl on the Via Flaminia.* I always had a much better literary reputation in England than I did here, for some strange reason. Perhaps they read more there and admire quality more. I also think their critical standards are a lot more understanding of literature. I don't think our critics know what they're talking about.

CA: Which novel is your favorite?

HAYES: *The End of Me* and *My Face for the World to See.* They read true when I read them. What's said in the books seems to me still true. They don't ring any false notes or clinkers.

CA: Your novels remain as you wrote them. What happens to your screenplays? Are they altered during the filming?

HAYES: Well, ''Island in the Sun,'' for example, was a pretty good script, but it wasn't the script that they finally did. It was rewritten by Darryl Zanuck down in Jamaica when they went down to shoot it. Same thing that happens all the time. Harry Belafonte wouldn't play a certain kind of character. They don't tell me what's going on; I'm back here and they're down in Jamaica. Belafonte says, ''I don't want to play a sharpie,'' so they rewrite the part. Well, you learn not to suffer. You're manufacturing a product and they tailor it for all the different customers, and the star is as much a customer as the audience. But the result is they flatten out the movie, they flatten out the story, they flatten out the character, everything.

CA: What do you write for television?

HAYES: I have a few friends left who are in my age bracket who have survived and who still work; they're producers and directors. So, when they get jobs, they hand me something to do. I don't go out and look for anything anymore. I wait for them to go out and look. When they work, I work. It's as simple as that.

CA: Who are they?

HAYES: Well, I have two really good friends, Ben Roberts and Ivan Goff. They've been very successful for a very long time. They did ''Charlie's Angels'' and loads of other television series. So whenever they get a series, either I work for them rewriting scripts that they have, or they assign me a segment and that makes me enough money to get by on. I must have rewritten about thirty ''Mannix'' scripts. Now they have a new ''Nero Wolf'' series and I've done one of those. It's the line of least resistance.

CA: Perhaps you're entitled to take it easy since you've been quite prolific?

HAYES: Not as much as I should have been. There were usually four or five years between novels. I could have done much more than that, but I was never a driver or self-driven either. But, the issues of life are never settled in novels or screenplays. They are, at best, a diversion.

BIOGRAPHICAL/CRITICAL SOURCES: New Republic, April 24, 1944; *Saturday Review,* April 29, 1944, April 2, 1949, May 20, 1950; *Yale Review,* winter, 1947; *New York Times,* March 20, 1949, April 16, 1950; *New York Times Book Review,* March 17, 1968; *New Yorker,* March 30, 1968; *Punch,* August 3, 1968.

—*Interview by Judith Spiegelman*

* * *

HAYES, Sheila 1937-

PERSONAL: Born June 16, 1937, in New York, N.Y.; daughter of Michael (a carpenter) and Mary (Flaherty) Hagan; married Michael Hayes (an attorney), May 26, 1962; children: Laura, Allison, Susannah. *Education:* Attended Marymount College (now Marymount Manhattan College), 1955-57, and Columbia University, 1957-58. *Politics:* Independent. *Religion:* Roman Catholic. *Home address:* Deer Hill Lane, Briarcliff Manor, N.Y. 10510.

CAREER: Ted Deglin & Associates (public relations firm), New York City, receptionist and public relations assistant, 1957-59; *Simplicity Pattern Book,* New York City, beauty editor, 1959; Peck & Peck (retail store chain), New York City, assistant to director of public relations, 1960-62; writer, 1969—. *Member:* Authors Guild.

WRITINGS—Juveniles: *Where Did the Baby Go?,* Golden Press, 1974; *The Carousel Horse,* Thomas Nelson, 1978; *Me and My Mona Lisa Smile,* Elsevier/Nelson, 1981. Contributor to *Friend.*

WORK IN PROGRESS: The Enchanted T-Shirt, a juvenile novel dealing with single parenthood and old age.

SIDELIGHTS: Sheila Hayes wrote: ''I feel very fortunate that, for me, creativity is fueled in a very direct way by my personal life. To write for children you must *be* a child, remembering how it feels to be low man on the totem pole in this adult world. Keeping these feelings fresh adds an extra dimension to parenthood. Parent and writer don't just co-exist; they give essential nourishment to each other.''

MEDIA ADAPTATIONS: The Carousel Horse was adapted into a segment of ''Afterschool Special,'' by American Broadcasting Co. (ABC-TV), 1982-83.

AVOCATIONAL INTERESTS: Gardening, paddle tennis, tennis, theatre, books.

* * *

HEADINGTON, Christopher John Magenis 1930-

BRIEF ENTRY: Born April 28, 1930, in London, England. British composer, pianist, and author. Headington has been a tutor in music at Oxford University since 1965. He worked for the British Broadcasting Corporation (BBC) and served as a record critic for magazines. He wrote *The Orchestra and Its Instruments* (Bodley Head, 1965), *The Bodley Head History of Western Music* (Bodley Head, 1974), *Illustrated Dictionary of Musical Terms* (Bodley Head, 1980), and *Listener's Guide to Chamber Music* (Facts on File, 1982). *Address:* Old Quarry House, 1 Beckley Court, Beckley, Oxfordshire OX3 9UB, England. *Biographical/critical sources: The International Who's Who,* Europa, 1978; *London Times,* July 2, 1981.

* * *

HEATH, Roy A(ubrey) K(elvin) 1926-

PERSONAL: Born August 13, 1926, in Georgetown, Guyana;

son of Melrose A. (a teacher) and Jessie R. (a teacher) Heath; married Aemilia Oberli; children: three. *Education:* University of London, B.A. *Agent:* A. M. Heath & Co. Ltd., 40-42 William IV St., London WC2N 4DD, England.

CAREER: Worked in civil service in Guyana, 1942-50; held various clerical jobs in London, England, 1951-58; teacher of French and German in London, 1959—. Called to the Bar, Lincoln's Inn. *Awards, honors:* Drama Award from Theatre Guild of Guyana, 1971, for "Inez Combray"; fiction prize from *London Guardian*, 1978, for *The Murderer*.

WRITINGS—Novels: A Man Come Home, Longman, 1974; *The Murderer*, Allison & Busby, 1978; *From the Heat of the Day*, Allison & Busby, 1979; *One Generation*, Allison & Busby, 1980; *Kwaku*, Allison & Busby, 1982. Also author of *Genetha*, Allison & Busby.

Plays: "Inez Combray."

WORK IN PROGRESS: A novel.

SIDELIGHTS: Heath told *CA:* "My work is intended to be a dramatic chronicle of twentieth-century Guyana."

*   *   *

HEBERT, F(elix) Edward   1901-1979

OBITUARY NOTICE: Born October 12, 1901, in New Orleans, La.; died of a heart attack, December 29, 1979, in New Orleans, La. Politician, journalist, and author. Hebert, a long-time democratic congressman from Louisiana, began his career in 1919 as a sportswriter for the *New Orleans Times-Picayune*. He went on to serve as that paper's assistant sports editor, leaving in 1925 to serve in the same capacity for the *New Orleans States*. He later became a political editor and columnist for the *States*, and in 1937 he was promoted to city editor. In 1939 the paper began reporting on the "Louisiana scandals," which centered on the political machine that had been headed by political boss Huey Long prior to his assasination in 1935. The series of articles, written under Hebert's direction, exposed ongoing corruption in Louisiana government and resulted in the jailing of many of Long's former associates. In 1940 Hebert successfully campaigned for a seat in the U.S. Congress, a position he held for the next thirty-six years. Described by the *New York Times* as "a hard-line conservative," the democratic congressman from Louisiana "established a virtually unblemished voting record in support of a strong military and against civil rights legislation, welfare programs and other issues he saw as evils of a permissive society." Upon his return from an inspection tour of Europe in 1945, Hebert wrote *I Went, I Saw, I Heard: Being the European Diary of F. Edward Hebert.* His autobiography, *Last of the Titans: The Life and Times of F. Edward Hebert*, was published in 1976. Obituaries and other sources: *Current Biography*, Wilson, 1951, February, 1980; *Who's Who in America*, 40th edition, Marquis, 1978; *New York Times*, December 30, 1979.

*   *   *

HEGINBOTHAM, Stanley J.   1938-

BRIEF ENTRY: Born May 22, 1938, in Salt Lake City, Utah. American political scientist, educator, and author. Heginbotham has taught political science at Columbia University since 1970. He wrote *The Prince and the Peasant: Social Organization and Traditional Politics in Cambodia* (M.I.T. Press, 1965), *India and Japan: The Emerging Balance of Power in Asia and Opportunities for Arms Control, 1970-1975* (Southern Asian Institute and East Asian Institute, Columbia University, 1971), *Between Community and City Bureaucracy: New York's District Manager Experiment* (Bureau of Applied Social Research, Columbia University, 1973), and *Cultures in Conflict: The Four Faces of Indian Bureaucracy* (Columbia University Press, 1975). *Address:* 430 West 116th St., New York, N.Y. 10027; and Department of Political Science, Columbia University, New York, N.Y. 10027. *Biographical/critical sources: American Men and Women of Science: The Social and Behavioral Sciences,* 13th edition, Bowker, 1978.

*   *   *

HELFGOTT, Daniel   1952-

PERSONAL: Born March 16, 1952, in New York, N.Y.; son of Roy B. (a professor and writer) and Gloria (an artist; maiden name, Wolfe) Helfgott; married Janet Turner (a television producer). *Education:* Oberlin College, A.B., 1972; graduate study at Temple University. *Residence:* Los Angeles, Calif. *Agent:* Joan Stewart, William Morris Agency, 1350 Avenue of the Americas, New York, N.Y. 10019.

CAREER: Television producer in Los Angeles, Calif. *Member:* Directors Guild of America, Writers Guild of America, Academy of Television Arts and Sciences. *Awards, honors:* Emmy Award for writing from Academy of Television Arts and Sciences, 1981, for "The Emergency Blues."

WRITINGS: Enter the Conglomerates, Temple University Press, 1974; *The Buried* (novel), Avon, 1981; *The Golden Hour* (novel), Doubleday, 1983.

Scripts: "Carey Farm" (short film; also producer), released by Warner Brothers in 1971; "Fire and Ice" (television documentary; also producer and director), first broadcast by Public Broadcasting Service (PBS-TV), 1977; "The Uncertain T" (television documentary; also producer and director), released by Group W Productions, 1978; "John Wayne: The Duke Lives On" (television documentary; also producer), released by RKO-Nederlander Productions, 1980; "Monsters, Madmen, and Machines" (television special; also producer), released by RKO-Nederlander Productions, 1980; "The Emergency Blues" (television documentary; also director), first broadcast by National Broadcasting Co. (NBC-TV), 1980; "Tracy and Hepburn" (television special; also producer), released by RKO-Nederlander Productions, 1981; "Fifty Years of Hollywood" (television special; also producer), released by RKO-Nederlander Productions, 1981; "Treasure" (television film; also producer), first broadcast by American Broadcasting Co. (ABC-TV), 1982. Writer, producer, and director of television series, "Economically Speaking," for Public Broadcasting Service, 1977-78.

SIDELIGHTS: Helfgott produced the films "Lindbergh," "Rockefellers," and "Grambling's White Tiger," the television special "Hollywood Musicals," and the series "Television Inside Out" and "People" (both of which he also directed) and "The New Candid Camera Show."

*   *   *

HELLMANN, Ellen   1908-

PERSONAL: Born August 25, 1908, in Johannesburg, South Africa; daughter of Bernard and Clotilda Kaumheimer; married J. M. Hellmann, 1932 (deceased); married Bodo Koch (a physician), March 17, 1948; children: Ruth Hellmann Runciman. *Education:* University of the Witwatersrand, B.A., 1930, B.A. (with honors), 1932, M.A., 1936, D.Phil., 1940. *Politics:* Progressive Federal. *Religion:* Jewish. *Home:* 14 First Ave., Lower Houghton, Johannesburg, 2196, South Africa.

CAREER: Associated with South African Institute of Race Relations, 1932-80, began as honorary secretary, became chairman of Joint Council of Africans and Europeans, 1932-44, member of executive council and general purposes committee, 1936-80, treasurer, 1938-48, president, 1954-56, chairman of general purposes committee, 1967-73, and research committee, 1966-67; writer, 1980—. Chairman of Isaacson Foundation Bursary Fund for Africans. Head of colored and Indian section of Govenor General's National War Fund, 1939-44. Member of Jewish Board of Deputies, 1940-80, executive, 1940-50. Honorary treasurer of Entokozweni Early Learning Centre. Member of executive board of Legal Aid Bureau, Witwatersrand Branch of South African Institute of International Affairs, Women for Peace, and Women's Legal Status Committee. Trustee of Treason Trial Defence Fund, 1956-60. Part-time lecturer in sociology at Jan Hofmeyr School of Social Work, 1937-44. Foundation member of Progressive Party (now Progressive Federal Party), member of national executive committee, 1959-71, chairman of Houghton constituency. *Member:* Johannesburg Soroptimist Club (past chairman). *Awards, honors:* Bronze medal from Royal African Society, 1970; LL.D. from University of the Witwatersrand, 1978.

WRITINGS: Problems of Urban Bantu Youth, South African Institute of Race Relations, 1940; *Rooiyard: A Sociological Survey of an Urban Native Slum Yard,* Oxford University Press, 1948; (editor) *Handbook on Race Relations in South Africa,* Oxford University Press, 1949, Octogon, 1975; *Sellgoods: A Sociological Survey of an African Commercial Labour Force,* South African Institute of Race Relations, 1953; *Soweto: Johannesburg's African City,* South African Institute of Race Relations, 1969; (contributor) Kenneth Kirkwood, editor, *African Affairs,* Chatto & Windus, 1961; (contributor) Heribert Adams, editor, *South Africa: Sociological Perspectives,* Oxford University Press, 1971; (contributor) N. H. Rhoodie, editor, *South African Dialogue,* McGraw (Johannesburg, South Africa), 1972; (editor) *Conflict and Progress,* Macmillan (South Africa), 1979. Contributor to journals, including *Journal of Race Relations, Race Relations News,* and *Journal of the International Institute of African Affairs.*

SIDELIGHTS: Hellmann told *CA:* "I do not understand how I came to be included in *Contemporary Authors,* since I have always regarded authors as creative artists. On the other hand, I regard myself and my colleagues, our main contributions being the writing up of our research materials, as writers. But, of course, I'm pleased to be in such distinguished company.

"Way back in 1934 when I first started my research on Rooiyard, an urban native (then a respectable word) slum yard, I was the first anthropologist to embark on urban work in South Africa. I emerged with two main, somewhat mundane, conclusions: Urban natives were people, and their chief problem was their great poverty. At that time the South African public in general was hardly aware of the existence of urban Africans. Except in their ever-present role of laborer and domestic, the urban Africans vanished from public consciousness. So, I was invited to give talks on my strange subject and startling discoveries.

"I suppose that one of the encouraging things that has happened in South Africa is the realization at long last that Africans are a permanent part of the urban population. I have been saying this loud and clear since the 1930's, along with my colleagues at the South African Institute of Race Relations, on the Joint Council, and on many other committees and bodies. In 1948, just before the election which returned the National party to power, the Prime Minister, General Smuts, made it clear that when he was returned to power he would greatly improve the

position and status of black townsmen. But, the National party adopted precisely the contrary policy, believing that with the strict application of apartheid the tide of urban migration would be turned and all urban Africans would be returned to their original 'homelands' by 1984. This was, of course, unrealism of a nightmare quality. The harm it caused the country was—and is, in its effects and still remaining laws—enormous.

"We have a long way to go yet in South Africa. The constitutional issue presents the knottiet problems, but at least the need for change is being increasingly recognized, not, of course, by the whole white population, but by growing sections of all language groups. A number of the heresies of the 1930's and 1940's have become the commonplaces of the 1980's.

"The course of my work and general experience has compelled me, most reluctantly, to abandon my early Rooiyard belief that acculturation takes place in one generation among the urban-born. Increasingly I have come to realize how important early beliefs and a home environment molded largely in accord with tribal beliefs are, and how strongly they influence the adjustment of the adult. The whole process of adaptability to a modern industrial environment takes longer. How long, I don't know. These generalizations are of course subject to a number of exceptions—no attempted generalizations about human behavior can be other than subject to exceptions. After all, the exceptional thing about people is how exceptional they are in their infinite diversity."

* * *

HENDERSON, (Alan) Keith 1883-1982

OBITUARY NOTICE: Born in 1883; died February 24, 1982, in South Africa. Painter, illustrator, poet, playwright, and author. A highly regarded painter in the Victorian tradition, Henderson exhibited his works in many of the leading art galleries in England and Europe. Numbered among the books he illustrated are *The Romaunt of the Rose, Green Mansions,* and *No Second Spring.* He was the author of books, including *Letters to Helen, Palm Groves and Hummingbirds, Prehistoric Man,* and *Till Twenty-one,* his autobiography. Obituaries and other sources: *Who's Who,* 126th edition, St. Martin's, 1974; *The Dictionary of British Book Illustrators and Caricaturists, 1800-1914,* Baron, 1978; *London Times,* February 27, 1982.

* * *

HENDERSON, Robert 1906-

PERSONAL: Born March 19, 1906, in Chicago, Ill.; son of James Robert (in business) and Catherine (Springer) Henderson; married Margaret Knapp (a professor), February 23, 1942. *Education:* University of Illinois, A.B., 1928, A.M., 1930. *Politics:* Democrat. *Home:* 22 Gramercy Park, New York, N.Y. 10003. *Office: New Yorker,* 25 West 43rd St., New York, N.Y. 10036.

CAREER: University of Illinois, Urbana, instructor, 1928-36; *New Yorker,* New York, N.Y., member of editorial staff, 1937-47, associate editor, 1947-76. *Military service:* U.S. Army Air Forces, 1942-46; became captain. *Member:* The Century Association. *Awards, honors:* O. Henry Award from Doubleday & Co., Inc., 1960, for "Immortality"; "Into the Wind" was selected one of the best short stories of 1979 by Houghton Mifflin.

WRITINGS: (Translator with Paul Nissley Landis) Pierre Corneille and Jean Baptiste Racine, *Six Plays by Corneille and Racine,* introduced and edited by Landis, Modern Library, 1931; *Whether There Be Knowledge* (novel), Lippincott, 1935;

The Enameled Wishbone, and Other Touchstones (essays), Macmillan, 1963; *Into the Wind* (short stories), University of Illinois Press, 1981.

Also contributor of articles and stories to periodicals, including *Esquire, Saturday Evening Post,* and *New Yorker.*

WORK IN PROGRESS: Short stories.

SIDELIGHTS: Henderson told *CA:* "I have always moved toward writing, even in childhood. Though making a living has sometimes intervened (along with indolence), writing has been a basic preoccupation and still is. It is a very slow process, and the results have been fairly small. Aside from some early efforts, I have published chiefly in the *New Yorker*—essays, paragraphs for the 'Notes and Comments' section, and a number of short stories."

*   *   *

HENDRY, Allan 1950-

PERSONAL: Born March 26, 1950, in Detroit, Mich.; son of James Alexander (in industrial heating) and Elizabeth (a waitress; maiden name, Aitken) Hendry; married Elaine Gugula (an astronomer), June 23, 1973. *Education:* University of Michigan, B.A., 1972. *Residence:* Stone Mountain, Ga. *Agent:* Ron Bernstein Agency, 200 West 58th St., No. 10-C, New York, N.Y. 10019.

CAREER: Quasar Electronics Corp., Franklin Park, Ill., commercial artist, 1973-76; *International UFO Reporter,* Evanston, Ill., writer, researcher, and editor, 1976-81; free-lance science writer, 1981—. *Awards, honors:* Award for investigation of best unidentified flying object case of 1979 from *National Enquirer,* 1980.

WRITINGS: The UFO Handbook, Doubleday, 1979. Contributing editor to *Probe,* 1980, and *Frontiers of Science,* 1980-81.

SIDELIGHTS: Hendry commented: "If there had to be only one reason why I think my UFO handbook received strong critical acclaim both in the United States and abroad, it would be that I endeavored to weigh the facts objectively—pro and con—rather than to adopt a 'position' to defend. That's a strong temptation when writing about inherently emotive subjects like UFOs, but it served me well to avoid it."

BIOGRAPHICAL/CRITICAL SOURCES: Akron Beacon Journal, October 13, 1978; *Atlanta Journal and Constitution,* November 18, 1976; *UFO Report,* June, 1980.

*   *   *

HENLEY, Nancy Eloise Main 1934-

BRIEF ENTRY: Born October 27, 1934, in Palatka, Fla. American psychologist, educator, and author. Henley began teaching at the University of Lowell in 1974 and is now a professor of psychology. She wrote *Sex Differences in Language, Speech, and Nonverbal Communication: An Annotated Bibliography* (revised edition, 1974), *Language and Sex: Difference and Dominance* (Newbury House, 1975), *She Said/He Said: An Annotated Bibliography* (Know, Inc., 1975), and *Body Politics: Power, Sex, and Nonverbal Communication* (Prentice-Hall, 1977). *Address:* Department of Psychology, University of Lowell, Lowell, Mass. 01854. *Biographical/critical sources: Who's Who of American Women,* 11th edition, Marquis, 1979.

HENNESSEY, David James George 1932-
(Lord Windlesham)

PERSONAL: Born January 28, 1932, in London, England; son of Lord Windlesham and Angela Mary Duggan; married Prudence Glynn (a journalist), 1965; children: one son, one daughter. *Education:* Trinity College, Oxford, M.A. *Office:* House of Lords, London S.W.1, England.

CAREER: Member of Westminster City Council, Westminster, England, 1958-62; Rediffusion Television, head of features and chief program director, 1962-65, director, 1965-67; managing director of Grampian Television, 1967-70; minister of state at Home Office, 1970-72, minister of state for Northern Ireland, 1972-73; leader of House of Lords and Lord Privy Seal, 1973-74; Associated Television Ltd. (A-TV), joint managing director, 1974-75, managing director, 1975-81, chairman, 1981. Chairman of Bow Group, 1959-60, 1962-63; member of board of directors of Gateway Building Society and *Observer;* member of board of trustees of British Museum, Community Service Volunteers, and Oxford Preservation Trust (also chairman). *Member:* International Institute of Communications (member of board of trustees), Royal Television Society (vice-president).

WRITINGS: Communication and Political Power, J. Cape, 1966; *Politics in Practice,* J. Cape, 1975; *Broadcasting in a Free Society,* Basil Blackwell, 1980.

*   *   *

HENRY, David Dodds 1905-

PERSONAL: Born October 21, 1905, in East McKeesport, Pa.; son of Ferdinand William and Myrtle (Byerly) Henry; married Sara Emily Koerper, 1927; children: David Byerly. *Education:* Pennsylvania State College (now University), A.B., 1926, A.M., 1927, Ph.D., 1931. *Home:* 311 West University Ave., Champaign, Ill. 61820. *Office:* 333 Education Building W., University of Illinois, 1310 South Sixth St., Champaign, Ill. 61820.

CAREER: Instructor at Pennsylvania State College (now University), University Park; Battle Creek College, Battle Creek, Mich., professor of English and head of department, 1929-33, dean of men, 1930-31, director of School of Liberal Arts, 1931-33; State of Michigan, Lansing, assistant superintendent of public instruction, 1933-35; Wayne University (now Wayne State University), Detroit, Michigan, professor of English, 1935-52, executive vice-president of university, 1939-45, president, 1945-52; New York University, New York, N.Y., executive vice-chancellor, 1952-55; University of Illinois, Urbana, president, 1955-71, president emeritus and distinguished professor of higher education, 1971-74, consultant in higher education, 1974—. Member of President's Committee on Employment of the Handicapped, 1956-62; president of National Commission on Accrediting, 1956-58; vice-chairman of President's Committee on Education Beyond the High School, 1956-57; member of board of directors of Council for Financial Aid to Education, 1958-65, American Council on Education, 1961-64, and Illinois Bell Telephone Co., 1964-75; member of advisory council of National Fund for Medical Education, 1959-65; member of board of trustees of Carnegie Foundation for the Advancement of Teaching, 1960-1970 (chairman, 1969-70), Museum of Science and Industry, 1964-72, and Institute of International Education, 1965-68; member of Commission on Federal Relations (chairman, 1961-64); member of Carnegie Commission on Higher Education, 1967-75; chairman of National Board on Graduate Education, 1971-75. Consultant to

The International Encyclopedia of Higher Education, 1977; consulting editor of *Change* (magazine), 1980—.

MEMBER: National Society for Crippled Children and Adults (sponsor), American Association of State Universities and Land-Grant Colleges (president, 1964-65, chairman of executive committee, 1965-66), Association of American Universities (president, 1967-69), Association of Urban Universities (president, 1945-46), Council on Foreign Relations, Phi Beta Kappa, Delta Sigma Rho, Phi Kappa Phi, Phi Delta Kappa, Pi Delta Epsilon, Omicron Delta Kappa, Beta Gamma Sigma, Alpha Omega Alpha, Kappa Delta Pi, Alpha Kappa Psi, Chi Gamma Iota, Phi Eta Sigma, Phi Kappa Psi, Scabbard and Blade, Executives Club, University Club, Rotary International, Torch Club of America.

AWARDS, HONORS: LL.D. from University of Toledo, 1946, University of Louisville, 1951, University of Miami, and Millikin University, both 1957, University of Rhode Island, 1958, Knox College, 1959, Butler University, 1962, Roosevelt University, 1963, University of Notre Dame, 1964, Eastern Michigan University, 1966, Indiana Central College, 1968, Shimer College, 1968, St. Louis University, 1969, and University of Illinois, 1976; HH.D. from Wayne University, 1953; Litt.D. from Albion College, 1954, University of Pittsburgh, 1961, Monmouth College, 1962, DePaul University, 1963, and Lincoln College, 1963; L.H.D. from New York University, 1955, Rockford College, 1957, Southern Illinois University, 1969, Loyola University, 1970, and Spertus College of Judaica, 1974; D.Sc.Ed. from University of Akron, 1956; Pd.D. from Bradley University, 1957; D.C.L. from University of Sierra Leone, 1969; D.Sc. from Govind Ballabh Pant University, 1974. Distinguished Alumnus Award from Pennsylvania State University, 1955; Northern Illinois University Foundation Humanitarian Award, 1977.

WRITINGS: William Vaughn Moody: A Study, Bruce Humphries, 1934, reprinted, Arden, 1978; *What Priority for Education?: The American People Must Soon Decide,* University of Illinois Press, 1961; *Challenges Past, Challenges Present: An Analysis of American Higher Education Since 1930,* Jossey-Bass, 1975. Contributor of over three hundred fifty articles to education journals.

WORK IN PROGRESS: Editing, reviewing, and writing essays.

SIDELIGHTS: David Henry told *CA:* "Nearly all of my writing has been related to my professional work, a tool of my professional assignments. Early in my career, I had some aspiration to do creative writing, but as I became caught up in administrative work, as well as teaching, I discovered that the administrative tasks were consuming. Early on, I was responsible for official reports and I conducted an extensive correspondence. Public speaking became a necessity and some of the speeches were transformed into essays and published. They were all directed to educational welfare, or in exposition of educational problems and issues.

"I was also involved in contributing to group writing—that is, reports of assignments. Particularly important was the work of the Carnegie Commission on Higher Education that sponsored over one hundred volumes in the approximately seven years of its existence. The report of the Carnegie Commission on Public Television was important in the legislative establishment of the national television system.

"As you know, professional writing is quite different in style and purpose from creative writing. It is a vital force on the current scene in many fields of endeavor. It requires the basic skills of all effective writing, but it deals with analysis and exposition, not entertainment."

HENRY, Francoise   1902-1982

OBITUARY NOTICE: Born in June, 1902, in Paris, France; died February 10, 1982, in France. Art expert, archaeologist, educator, and author. An authority on the subject of early Irish Christian art, Henry had been inspired to study that subject during a visit to Ireland in 1926. Her first published work, *La Sculpture irlandaise,* appeared in 1933. Later works include the three-volume *L'Art irlandais, Irish Art,* and *The Book of Kells and Its Decoration.* In 1932 Henry began a forty-two-year teaching career with University College, Dublin, serving first in the French department and later in the departments of archaeology and history. She was the recipient of numerous honors and awards, including honorary doctorates from Dublin University and the National University of Ireland and the Legion of Honor from France. Obituaries and other sources: *London Times,* February 19, 1982; *AB Bookman's Weekly,* April 12, 1982.

*   *   *

HENSON, James Maury   1936-
(Jim Henson)

BRIEF ENTRY: Born September 24, 1936, in Greenville, Miss. American puppeteer, television producer, and author best known as the creator of the Muppets. Henson's popular puppets, which first appeared on television commercials in the 1950's, became featured characters on the acclaimed children's series "Sesame Street" when it debuted in 1969. The Muppets are also the stars of their own television program, "The Muppet Show," a variety show that is popular with both adults and children. Henson has earned Emmy Awards and an entertainer-of-the-year award from the American Guild of Variety Artists. His experimental film, "Time Piece" (Pathe, 1965), was nominated for an Academy Award by the Motion Picture Academy of Arts and Sciences. *Biographical/critical sources: Current Biography,* Wilson, 1977.

*   *   *

HENSON, Jim
See HENSON, James Maury

*   *   *

HERZBERGER, Maximillian Jacob   1899-1982

OBITUARY NOTICE: Born March 7, 1899, in Charlottenburg (now West Berlin), Germany; died April 9, 1982, in New Orleans, La. Educator, optical physicist, and author. Herzberger, founder of the Optical Institute in Zurich, Switzerland, studied under Albert Einstein at the University of Berlin. In 1934 he immigrated to the United States, where he began a thirty-year career with the Eastman Kodak Company in Rochester, N.Y. Herzberger was the developer of the Superachromat lens, which continues to be used today in aerial color photography. A former physics professor at the University of New Orleans, Herzberger wrote more than three hundred books and scientific papers, including the reference work *Modern Geometrical Optics.* Obituaries and other sources: *Who's Who in World Jewry: A Biographical Dictionary of Outstanding Jews,* Pitman, 1972; *Who's Who in America,* 39th edition, Marquis, 1976; *American Men and Women of Science: The Physical and Biological Sciences,* 14th edition, Bowker, 1979; *Chicago Tribune,* April 12, 1982; *New York Times,* April 12, 1982.

HEY, John D(enis) 1944-

PERSONAL: Born September 26, 1944, in Tynemouth, England; son of George Brian (an actuary) and Elizabeth (a teacher; maiden name, Burns) Hey; married Margaret Robertson Bissett, November 18, 1968; children: Elizabeth Clare Hamilton, Thomas Marshall. *Education:* Cambridge University, B.A., 1965; University of Edinburgh, M.Sc., 1968. *Religion:* Church of England. *Office:* Department of Economics and Related Studies, University of York, Heslington, Yorkshire Y01 5DD, England.

CAREER: Mathematics and physics teacher and department head at high school in Dormaa Ahenkro, Ghana, 1965-66; Hoare & Co. (stockbrokers), London, England, econometrician, 1968-69; University of Durham, Durham, England, lecturer in economics, 1969-73; University of St. Andrews, St. Andrews, Scotland, lecturer in economics, 1974-75; University of York, Heslington, England, lecturer, 1975-81, senior lecturer in social and economic statistics, 1981—. Guest on radio programs; consultant to Wise Speke & Co. *Member:* Royal Economic Society, American Economic Association.

WRITINGS: Statistics in Economics, Martin Robertson, 1974, revised edition, Praeger, 1977; *Uncertainty in Microeconomics,* New York University Press, 1979; *Britain in Context,* Basil Blackwell, 1979; *Economics in Disequilibrium,* Martin Robertson, 1981; *Data in Doubt,* Martin Robertson, 1983.

Contributor: R. M. Grant and G. K. Shaw, editors, *Current Issues in Economic Policy,* Philip Alan, 1974, 2nd edition, 1980; D. A. Currie and Will Peters, editors, *Contemporary Economic Analysis,* Volume II, Croom Helm, 1980; Currie and other editors, *Microeconomic Analysis,* Croom Helm, 1981. Contributor of articles and reviews to economic journals.

SIDELIGHTS: Hey's current research areas include the general field of uncertainty in economics, "how the existence of uncertainty, and imperfect knowledge, affects the decisions of economic agents, how information is obtained and used in decision-making processes, and how economic agents react to disequilibrium situations; the development of price adjustment theories (closely linked with the above), which represents an important step toward the formulation of a dynamic macro theory in a quantity-constrained world; and behavioral economics and experimental investigation, the 'laboratory' investigation into 'actual' economic behavior, the exploration of whether economic agents actually use optimal rules of behavior, or whether 'rules of thumb' are used."

Other areas of interest are "monetary theory—the identification of the peculiar properties of money, particularly those which derive from the existence of uncertainty, and their incorporation in an appropriate general equilibrium framework; expectations and the demand for money; the effect of measurement errors on macroeconometric models; the pattern of, and the effect of, revisions to published economic data; inflation and the sectoral distribution of unemployment; and various simulation studies."

* * *

HEYM, Georg (Theodor Franz Arthur) 1887-1912

BRIEF ENTRY: Born October 30, 1887, in Hirschberg, Silesia (now Jelenia Gora, Poland); drowned, January 16, 1912, in Berlin, Germany. German poet. Heym's lyric poems display an aggression and heightened sense of color that identify him as one of the earliest German expressionists. His contempt and fear of urbanization was expressed in the traditional lyric form, but the subject matter, infused with his own pessimism and sense of personal discomfort, marked a new era in German poetry. The tension Heym experienced from the decay and nihilism he saw around him and the terrifying isolation he felt among the masses in the cities drove him to write some of the most striking, brilliant poetry of his day, which was collected in *Der ewige Tag* (1911) and *Umbra vitae* (1912). Heym died at the age of twenty-five when he fell through the ice while skating on the Havel River. *Biographical/critical sources: Encyclopedia of World Literature in the Twentieth Century,* updated edition, Ungar, 1967.

* * *

HIBBETT, Howard (Scott) 1920-

PERSONAL: Born July 27, 1920, in Akron, Ohio; son of Howard Scott (in business) and Florence (an auditor; maiden name, Line) Hibbett; married Akiko Yamagawa, January 25, 1960; children: Mariko, Reiko, David. *Education:* Harvard University, A.B. (summa cum laude), 1947, Ph.D., 1950; postdoctoral study at Tokyo University, 1950-51, 1964-65, and Kyoto University, 1955-57. *Home:* 220 Pleasant St., Arlington, Mass. 02174. *Office:* Department of East Asian Languages and Civilizations, Harvard University, 2 Divinity Ave., Cambridge, Mass. 02138.

CAREER: University of California, Los Angeles, instructor, 1952-54, assistant professor of Oriental languages, 1954-58; Harvard University, Cambridge, Mass., associate professor, 1958-63, professor of Japanese literature, 1963—, chairman of department of Far Eastern languages, 1965-70, associate director of East Asian Research Center, 1975—. Member of board of syndics of Harvard University Press, 1974-78. *Member:* American Academy of Arts and Sciences (fellow). *Awards, honors:* Fulbright grant for Japan, 1955-57, 1964-65; Rockefeller Foundation grant, 1958; Guggenheim fellowship, 1964-65; National Endowment for the Humanities fellowship, 1979-80.

WRITINGS: The Floating World in Japanese Fiction, Oxford University Press, 1959; (with Gen Itasaka) *Modern Japanese: A Basic Reader,* Harvard University Press, 1965; (editor and translator) *Contemporary Japanese Literature: An Anthology of Fiction, Film, and Other Writing Since 1945,* Knopf, 1977.

Translator: Tankzaki Jun'ichiro, *The Key* (novel), Knopf, 1961; *Seven Japanese Tales,* Knopf, 1963; Tanizaki, *Diary of a Mad Old Man,* Knopf, 1965; Takeyama Michio, *The Harp of Burma* (novel), Tuttle, 1966; Kawabata Yasumari, *Beauty and Sadness* (novel), Knopf, 1974.

Contributor: Horst Frenz, editor, *Asia and the Humanities,* Indiana University Press, 1959; Albert Craig and Donald H. Shively, editors, *Personality in Japanese Culture,* University of California Press, 1970; *Studies on Japanese Culture,* Volume I, Japan P.E.N. Club, 1973. Also contributor to *Tradition and Modernization in Japanese Culture,* edited by Shively, 1971. Contributor to Asian studies journals.

WORK IN PROGRESS: A study of Japanese humor.

* * *

HIGGINS, Paul C. 1950-

PERSONAL: Born September 1, 1950, in Washington, D.C.; son of Francis C. (a professor) and Catherine (a teacher; maiden name, Bronson) Higgins; married Leigh C. Goode (a teacher), July 6, 1974; children: Samantha. *Education:* University of

Maryland, B.A., 1972; Northwestern University, M.A., 1974, Ph.D., 1977. *Office:* Department of Sociology, University of South Carolina, Columbia, S.C. 29208.

CAREER: Teacher at state school for the deaf in Falmouth, Me., 1972-73; University of South Carolina, Columbia, assistant professor, 1977-81, associate professor of sociology, 1981—. *Member:* American Sociological Association, Society for the Study of Social Problems.

WRITINGS: (Editor with Gary L. Albrecht) *Health, Illness, and Medicine: A Reader in Medical Sociology,* Rand McNally, 1979; *Outsiders in a Hearing World: A Sociology of Deafness,* Sage Publications, 1980; (with Richard R. Butler) *Understanding Deviance,* McGraw, 1982.

SIDELIGHTS: Higgins commented: "Sociologists should use their personal lives to inform their professional work; in turn, their professional work can inform their personal lives."

* * *

HIGGS, Gerald B. 1921-

PERSONAL: Born December 31, 1921, in American Fork, Utah; son of Gerald H. (in business) and Theresa (Ball) Higgs; married Betty Jeanne Price, August 30, 1941 (divorced December 24, 1964); married Cathrine Powell (in business), December 25, 1964; children: (first marriage) Terry Jeanne. *Education:* Attended University of Utah, 1940, and University of Cairo (Egypt), 1943-44. *Politics:* "Rock-ribbed Republican." *Religion:* Church of Jesus Christ of Latter-day Saints. *Home and office:* 1904 Terrace Dr., Sandy, Utah 84092.

CAREER: Pilot for Aaxico Airlines, Hill Air Force Base, Utah, and pilot and founder, Liner Aero Transporte de National (airline), Ascunsion, Paraguay, 1947-59; writer, 1947—; independent real estate economist and appraiser, 1960—. Owner and operator of Vegas Sky Corral. Consultant for Interstate Farms. *Military service:* U.S. Army Air Forces, 1942-47, attached to Free French Air Force as bomber pilot; became major; named chevalier of French Legion of Honor; received Croix de Guerre with palms, Medale les Ils Grandiront, Air Medal, Purple Heart, and Distinguished Flying Cross.

MEMBER: American Society of Farm Managers and Rural Appraisers, American Society of Appraisers (member of board of directors, 1963—; president, 1972; state director, 1973), Aircraft Owners and Pilots Association, Air Force Association, OX-5 Club, Confederate Air Force, Order of Daedalians (flight commander, 1981), Western Writers of America, League of Utah Writers.

AWARDS, HONORS: Story "Ghost With a Gun" selected as best published article of the year by Western States Writing Conference, 1952; outstanding pilot award from National Pilots Association, 1970; safe flying award from state of Utah, 1976; Quill award from League of Utah Writers, 1976, for *Lost Legends of the Silver State;* gold medal for best pioneer story from Sons of Utah Pioneers, 1977, for "Up the Irish, Murphy Came to Leeds"; honorary rank of captain in Israeli Air Force Intelligence; thirty writing awards.

WRITINGS: Lost Legends of the Silver State, Western Epics, 1976. Author of "Massacre at Palisade," published in *People's Almanac #2,* edited by Irving Wallace and David Wallenchinsky, 1978. Also author of more than eighty other short stories, published in periodicals, including *People on Parade, Stag, Saga, True,* and *Argosy.*

WORK IN PROGRESS: The Trail of Many Guns, based upon a true story about the theft of six Gatling guns, publication expected in 1983; *Winters Day at Burning Water,* based upon a true story about the theft of five hundred horses, for Western Epics.

SIDELIGHTS: Higgs told *CA:* "I am primarily motivated by my love of Western history which was passed on to me by my father who was the last and youngest (thirteen years old) stage driver to Gold Hill, Utah. He was not only a good father but was a friend and companion to his three sons and one daughter. A fighter pilot in World War I and an airmail pilot after, he was a founding member of the Order of Daedalians in 1934, and he indoctrinated me into flying at a very early age. He encouraged me to find historical events and bring them to life by fictionalizing them, and he supplied many of the stories of Nevada that appeared in my first book.

"I have had a love affair with the West for as long as I can remember. In 1925 I can remember it took seven days for my dad to drive his Peerless nine-passenger touring sedan from Salt Lake City to Los Angeles, California. We were on dirt roads for 99 percent of the trip, and Las Vegas was just a Union Pacific train depot. During the period that I was researching my book, I drove nearly fifteen thousand miles in Nevada and Utah, all of it on paved roads. This was just forty years later. At the time I marveled that any old towns had survived the 'time shock.' I'm afraid that if I returned now I would find nothing—and that would break my heart. It is my desire to give the reader a breath of the air that existed in the wonderful, wacky period from 1859 to 1903 in Nevada.

"I believe that Will Henry and Clay Fisher have had the most influence on my writing style. Their historical fiction and cryptic writing style still turns me on. Of course, Clay Fisher and Will Henry are one and the same. They are both noms de plume of Henry W. Allen, also an active member of the Western Writers of America."

BIOGRAPHICAL/CRITICAL SOURCES: Nevada State Journal, November 7, 1976; *Deseret News,* December 4, 1976; *Utah Holiday,* March 29, 1977.

* * *

HILL, Denise 1919-

PERSONAL: Born August 1, 1919, in London, England; daughter of Harry (a company secretary) and Marie-Louise (Arrault) Dixon; married Patrick John Hill (a scientific assistant), May 17, 1946; children: Peter Nicholas, Frances Elisabeth. *Education:* Attended secondary school in England, 1932-35. *Home:* Anchorage, Avenue Rd., North Hayling Island, Hampshire, England.

CAREER: Writer. Home Office, London, England, civil servant, 1939-47; Hampshire County, Hayling Island, Hampshire, England, librarian, 1956-64; Hampshire County Council, school secretary in Havant, Hampshire, 1964-72, social worker for the blind in Portsmouth, Hampshire, 1974-79.

WRITINGS—Juveniles: The Clever Car (illustrated by Robert Hales), Methuen, 1965; *A Pony for Two,* Collins, 1965; *Coco the Gift Horse,* Collins, 1966; *The Helicopter Children* (illustrated by Ferelith Eccles-Williams), Methuen, 1967; *The Witch at Lundy Cottage* (illustrated by Paul Wright), Hamish Hamilton, 1975; *The Castle Grey Pony* (illustrated by Trevor Ridley), Hamish Hamilton, 1976; *No Friends for Simon* (illustrated by Doreen Caldwell), Hamish Hamilton, 1977; *William and the Mutt* (illustrated by Jane Paton), Hamish Hamilton, 1977; *The Birthday Surprise* (illustrated by Maureen Bradley), Hamish Hamilton, 1978; *The Wrong Side of the Bed* (illustrated by Caldwell), Hamish Hamilton, 1981.

WORK IN PROGRESS: Two Boys and a Donkey, a story for young readers about two boys during Jesus' time; *Misti,* a story for young readers about the adventures of eleven-year-old twins in the wilds of Wales.

SIDELIGHTS: Hill told *CA:* "I was born in 1919, so I have become what is known as a senior citizen. I started writing with adult short stories. I had some success with these in magazines, and three of them were broadcast on the 'BBC Morning Story' around 1960. I turned to writing for children in the early 1960's and was lucky enough to have two books about horses accepted. I must say that in my teens I was madly horsey, and was able to transfer some of this enthusiasm onto paper."

Hill says that her positions as a librarian and school secretary were useful and of "tremendous value in writing for children, particularly the one as a school secretary. It is a unique position in that a school secretary can be approached and yet has no responsibility for discipline—the pupils tended to talk among themselves as if I were invisible, and dialogue was presented to me on a plate!"

Her position as a social worker has contributed to her book *Misti.* "For the last five years before retiring I worked as a social worker with special responsibility for blind welfare. Some of this experience is written into *Misti,* which has been submitted to the Welsh Arts Council for a children's fiction competition. I might add that 'retirement' is a laughable word— it just means that I have given up the job for which I was paid! I shall continue to write, and write, and write, and hope publishers will appreciate my efforts. I would very much like to feel that children in America will read my books."

* * *

HILLER, Catherine 1946-

PERSONAL: Born November 16, 1946, in White Plains, N.Y.; daughter of Joseph (a psychologist) and Glynne (a writer; maiden name, Mishan) Nahem; married Stan Warnow (a film editor), December 21, 1969; children: Alexander, Zachary. *Education:* Attended University of Sussex, 1965-66; Brooklyn College of the City University of New York, B.A. (summa cum laude), 1967; Brown University, Ph.D., 1972. *Politics:* Liberal. *Religion:* Jewish. *Residence:* New York, N.Y., and Roxbury, N.Y. *Agent:* Julia Coopersmith Literary Agency, 10 West 15th St., New York, N.Y. 10011.

CAREER: New York City Community College of the City University of New York, Brooklyn, N.Y., instructor in English, 1971-72; Brooklyn College of the City University of New York, Brooklyn, instructor in English, 1972-73; Togg Films, New York City, script writer, 1973; writer, 1973—. *Member:* Poets and Writers, Writers' Community.

WRITINGS: An Old Friend From High School (novel), Pocket Books, 1978; *Argentaybee and the Boonie* (juvenile), Coward, 1979; *Abracatabby* (juvenile), Coward, 1981. Also author of screenplays. Contributor of essays, satires and stories to magazines and newspapers, including *Penthouse, Redbook, Viva,* and *New York Times.*

WORK IN PROGRESS: Blood Sugar, a novel about a diabetic; *Daughter,* a novel about parents and step-parents.

SIDELIGHTS: Hiller told *CA:* "I have always enjoyed school writing assignments, and I spent a happy year writing my doctoral dissertation on John Updike's fiction. But it was only when I found myself pregnant and jobless that I considered making writing a career. I was encouraged by the publication, in 1974, of the first short story I had tried since college—but it was years before I sold a second. During this time, I wrote

several screenplays, all unproduced. One of these became an 'outline' for my first novel: all I had to do was fill in and expand. (I recommend the method, especially for beginners.) My second novel, *Blood Sugar,* a jaunty book about housework, diabetes, and adultery, began as a short story that proved untamable. Each of my books for children appeared to me as wholes: I felt I wrote down what was 'there' already. *Daughter,* the novel I am presently writing, is the most personal piece of fiction I have ever attempted.

"In all of my fiction, I attempt to explore new aspects of everyday life. I feel that ordinary happiness and its quest is my particular territory—yet I am often drawn to the exotic emotion, the paradoxical passion, and the experience that generates profound ambivalence. I feel driven to communicate what isn't clear."

AVOCATIONAL INTERESTS: Songwriting, tennis.

* * *

HILLGRUBER, Andreas 1925-

PERSONAL: Born January 18, 1925, in Angerburg, Germany (now Wegorzewo, Poland); son of Andreas (a high school teacher) and Irmgard (Schilling) Hillgruber; married Karin Zierau, January 11, 1960; children: Michael, Christian, Gabriele. *Education:* University of Goettingen, D.Phil., 1952. *Religion:* Evangelical. *Home:* Franzstrasse II, 5000 Cologne 41, West Germany. *Office:* Department of History, University of Cologne, Albertus-Magnus-Platz, D-5000 Cologne 41, West Germany.

CAREER: High school history teacher in Wiesbaden, West Germany, 1954-58, Darmstadt, West Germany, 1958-61, and Marburg/Lahn, West Germany, 1961-64; University of Marburg/Lahn, Marburg/Lahn, instructor, 1965-67, professor of modern history, 1967-68; University of Freiberg/Breisgau, Freiburg/Breisgau, West Germany, professor of modern and contemporary history, 1968-72; University of Cologne, Cologne, West Germany, professor of modern and contemporary history, 1972—. *Military service:* German Army, 1943-45, prisoner of war in France, 1945-48.

WRITINGS: Hitler, King Carol, and Marshall Antonescu, Franz Steiner Verlag, 1954, 2nd edition, 1965; *Hitler's Strategy, Politics, and War, 1940-1941,* Bernard & Graefe, 1965, 2nd edition, 1982; *The Role of Germany in the History Preceding the Two World Wars,* Vandenhoeck & Ruprecht, 1967, 2nd edition, 1979; *Continuity and Discontinuity in German Foreign Politics From Bismarck to Hitler,* Droste Verlag, 1969, 3rd edition, 1971; *Bismarck's Foreign Policy,* Verlag Rombach, 1972, 2nd edition, 1981; *German History, 1945-1972,* Ullstein, 1974, 3rd edition, 1980; *Germany and the Two World Wars,* Harvard University Press, 1981; *Der Zweite Weltkrieg, Kriegsziele und Strategie der grossen Maechte,* W. Kohlhammer Verlag, 1982. Contributor to history journals.

SIDELIGHTS: Hillgruber told *CA:* "My specialty is research into the history of Germany as a great power in international politics between 1871 and 1945, from Bismarck to Hitler. My particular focus is on the problem of continuity and discontinuity in the major trends in German foreign policy during Bismarck's epoch, the Wilhelmine era, the First World War, the Weimar Republic, the Third Reich, and the Second World War. I consider the result of my research 'political history' in a modern sense: the emphasis is on understanding the sequence of great decisions by working out the alternatives. Intellectual and social history supplement my study of political outcomes, but are not central points."

HILLS, C(harles) A(lbert) R(eis) 1955-

PERSONAL: Born August 21, 1955, in London, England; son of Arthur Ernest and Maria Jose (Reis) Hills. *Education:* Hertford College, Oxford, B.A., 1976; University of Sussex, M.A., 1977; doctoral research at St. Antony's College, Oxford, 1977-78. *Politics:* Conservative. *Home:* 3 Lucas House, Albion Ave., London S.W.8, England. *Office:* IPC Business Press, Quadrant House, The Quadrant, Sutton, Surrey, England.

CAREER: Stonehart Publications, London, England, editorial/production assistant, 1978-79; free-lance writer and editor, 1979-81; IPC Business Press, Sutton, England, news reporter for *Electrical and Radio Trading,* 1981—.

WRITINGS: The Rhine (juvenile), Wayland, 1979; *The Danube* (juvenile), Wayland, 1979; *The Fascist Dictatorships* (textbook), Batsford, 1979; *The Hitler File* (textbook), Batsford, 1980; *World Trade* (textbook), Batsford, 1981; *The Seine* (juvenile), Wayland, 1981; *Modern Industry* (textbook), Batsford, 1982; *Growing Up in the 1950's,* Batsford, 1983; *Law and Order,* Batsford, 1983.

Contributor: John Gaisford, editor, *Atlas of Man,* Marshall Cavendish, 1978; J. P. Kenyon, editor, *A Dictionary of British History,* Secker & Warburg, 1981; *Guide to Historic Britain,* Nicholson Guides, 1982.

SIDELIGHTS: Hills commented: "Since I work as a full-time journalist, my writing books is only an interesting and rewarding hobby. The books are largely intended to be used in schools, although I have also written reference material for adults. My degrees are in geography and modern history, so I have written mainly in these fields.

"I began doing educational and reference writing while still at university. For two years I was writing full time, and during that time I worked regular hours, usually in the afternoon and early evening and took my books rather more earnestly than I do now. These days, I have to squeeze in time for them in the evenings and on holidays. But my view of what is important in educational writing has not changed. When you are writing for children or students, you should not try to simplify insights to the point of falsehood or to 'write down.' You should tell the truth exactly as you would have wished to put it, only in simplified language, etc.

"I would eventually like to branch out into other types of writing, possibly novels, but I will not be ready to do that for some years. When I do, I will give up this sort of writing to leave my time and mind free."

*   *   *

HIM, George 1900-1982

OBITUARY NOTICE: Born August 8, 1900, in Lodz, Poland; died April 4, 1982, in London, England. Graphic designer, illustrator, and author of children's fiction. George Him, renowned graphic designer and partner of Jan Lewitt, was the chief designer of the Israel pavilion at Expo 67 in Montreal. He illustrated numerous children's books as well as works by George Bernard Shaw, Max Beerbohm, and Cervantes. Him wrote *Israel: The Story of a Nation* and was the co-author of *Polish Panorama* and *The Football's Revolt.* Obituaries and other sources: *Who's Who in Graphic Art,* Amstutz & Herdeg Graphis, 1962; *Who's Who in World Jewry: A Biographical Dictionary of Outstanding Jews,* Pitman, 1972; *Who's Who,* 126th edition, St. Martin's, 1974; *The Writers Directory, 1980-82,* St. Martin's, 1979; *London Times,* April 8, 1982.

HIPPIUS, Zinaida
See GIPPIUS, Zinaida (Nikolayevna)

*   *   *

HIRSCH, Miriam F. 1927-

PERSONAL: Born June 5, 1927, in New York, N.Y.; daughter of Gus (a tailor) and Gussie (Kotler) Freeman; married Lester M. Hirsch (a professor of English), June 19, 1949; children: George R., Diane E. *Education:* Brooklyn College (now of the City University of New York), B.A., 1944; Columbia University, M.S., 1950; University of Massachusetts, Ed.D., 1971. *Religion:* Jewish. *Home:* 281 Newton Rd., Springfield, Mass. 01118. *Office:* Department of Sociology, Springfield College, Springfield, Mass. 01109.

CAREER: Brooklyn Bureau of Social Services, Brooklyn, N.Y., psychiatric social worker, 1948-49; Mount Sinai Hospital of New York, New York, N.Y., psychiatric social worker in Child Psychiatry Division, 1949-53; Auburn University, Auburn, Ala., instructor in sociology, summer, 1954; Springfield Jewish Community Center, Springfield, Mass., member of professional staff, 1957; Bay Path Junior College, Longmeadow, Mass., assistant professor of behavioral sciences, 1961-66; Springfield College, Springfield, associate professor, 1966-79, professor of sociology, 1979—, field work director, 1966-68, director of Community Tensions Center, 1967-69, chairperson of department of community leadership and development, 1971-75. Day camp counselor for East Bronx Young Men's-Young Women's Christian Association, summer, 1948, and Stuyvesant House, summer, 1949; psychiatric social worker at Springfield Mental Health Center, 1960-64; founder and director of local Hotline (telephone counseling and referral service), 1970—. Coordinator of local Police Institute, 1968; incorporator of Hilltop Children's Service, 1968, vice-president of board of directors, 1968, president, 1969-72; member of Springfield Action Commission, 1969-71. *Member:* Academy of Certified Social Workers (charter member), Hampton County Civil Liberites Union (member of board of directors, 1974—), Alpha Kappa Delta.

WRITINGS: Women and Violence, Van Nostrand, 1981.

WORK IN PROGRESS: Aspects of Violence.

SIDELIGHTS: Miriam Hirsch told *CA:* "As a woman, I have felt that I am the object of violence, emotional rather than physical violence. Women are directly and indirectly given the message that they are second-class citizens and legitimate objects of violence. It is only fairly recently that battering and rape have aroused indignation. Would there not have been an earlier reaction if men had been the victims?

"I have become increasingly aware of the violence that appears to be increasing in our society, and I have become involved in researching in order to better understand and to write about why this violence exists. It is important for me to write about characteristics of our society that either allow or encourage the abuse that people perpetrate on others. Understanding is the first step to taking action."

*   *   *

HIRSCHMANN, Linda (Ann) 1941-

PERSONAL: Born September 14, 1941, in Charleston, S.C.; daughter of L. A. (an accountant) and J. (Berkman) Hirschmann. *Education:* University of South Carolina, B.A., 1962;

Columbia University, M.A., 1965; also attended Harvard University and San Carlos Universidad. *Home and office:* 1610 Peace, Durham, N.C. 27701.

CAREER: Elementary school teacher in Charleston, S.C., 1962-64; teacher of emotionally disturbed and mentally retarded in Spring Valley, N.Y., 1965-66; *Scholastic* (magazine), New York City, editor and staff writer, 1966-67; editor at publishers Thomas Y. Crowell Co., Scranton, Pa., Collier, Inc., New York, and Macmillan Publishing Co., New York City, 1967-68; teacher of emotionally disturbed and mentally retarded in San Francisco, Calif., 1968-69; Model Cities of U.S. Department of Housing and Urban Development, Atlanta, Ga., public affairs and information officer, 1970-71; art gallery hostess in Cambridge, Mass., private detective trainee in Boston, Mass., apartment rental agent in New York, and bookkeeper in California, 1971-75; tour leader and assistant manager of pension in Guatemala City, Guatemala, 1975-76; Durham Technical Institute, Durham, N.C., teacher of intellectual stimulation courses at rest homes and of writing courses at Arts Council, 1977-78; Continuing Education Division of Duke University, Durham, teacher of writing for children, 1981—. Producer of television scripts.

WRITINGS—Juveniles; nonfiction: *Adventures in South Carolina,* Sandlapper Magazine Press, 1970; *In a Lick of a Flick of a Tongue,* Dodd, 1980.

Author of four television scripts. Also author of short stories (fiction and biographies) for five basal readers, published by Macmillan and by Allyn & Bacon, c. 1970-78. Author of pamphlets for Model Cities Atlanta, 1970-71, and of teaching guides for Croft-Nei, 1975-76. Founder of and writer for newsletter. Contributor of articles and book reviews to newspapers and periodicals, including *Boston Globe* and *Durham Herald.* Editor of U.S. Department of Housing and Urban Development (HUD) submittals.

WORK IN PROGRESS: *Heart of the Jaguars,* a juvenile quest novel based on Guatemalan experiences; picture books, both fiction and nonfiction.

SIDELIGHTS: Linda Hirschmann told *CA:* "Writing was neither a dream nor a faint interest of mine. After I left teaching, I stumbled by happenstance into a variety of jobs that demanded writing skills. Forced to develop mine, I fell in love with the challenge and now am addicted to the profession, especially writing for children.

"My travels include a six-month hitchhike through the United States and Canada and numerous extensive trips through Europe and Central and South America. The catastrophic Guate earthquake of 1976 guided me into a wonder-filled awareness of our interconnectedness with each other and with the universe. Writing has become one avenue for sharing and expanding this realization.

"To live even an exciting life without being fully aware/awake is, for me, sloppily easy. Writing is a path—one way to focus both the details and patterns. . . . Writing/living, it's the Zen gestault."

*   *   *

HOBBS, Robert   1946-

PERSONAL: Born December 6, 1946, in Brookings, S.D.; son of Charles Seright (a college professor) and Corinne (a teacher; maiden name, Clay) Hobbs. *Education:* University of Tennessee, A.B., 1969; University of North Carolina, Ph.D., 1975. *Residence:* Lansing, N.Y. *Office:* Department of History of

Art, Goldwin Smith Hall, Cornell University, Ithaca, N.Y. 14850.

CAREER: Yale University, New Haven, Conn., instructor in art history, 1975-76; Cornell University, Ithaca, N.Y., assistant professor of art history and curator, 1976—. Chief curator at Tehran Museum of Contemporary Art, 1978. *Military service:* U.S. Army Reserve, 1968-74. *Member:* College Art Association of America. *Awards, honors:* Kress fellowship from University of North Carolina at Chapel Hill, 1974; Helena Rubenstein fellowship from Whitney Museum of American Art, 1975.

WRITINGS: *Abstract Expressionism: The Formative Years,* Cornell University Press, 1981; *Robert Smithson: Sculpture,* Cornell University Press, 1981. Guest editor of *College Art Journal,* autumn, 1982.

WORK IN PROGRESS: *History of Post-1940 American Art;* a monograph on the art of Helen and Newton Harrison.

SIDELIGHTS: Hobbs wrote: "My great concern is with the qualitative endeavor of our time. I am a contextual art historian who wishes to see how art functions in our society."

BIOGRAPHICAL/CRITICAL SOURCES: *Art in America,* October, 1981.

*   *   *

HOBSON, Mary   1926-

PERSONAL: Born July 24, 1926, in Wimbledon, London, England; daughter of Ernest Joseph (a research chemist) and Adelaide (an import/export agent; maiden name, Bradley) Lush; married Neil Hobson (a music therapist), October 30, 1954; children: Matthew Edward, Emma Victoria, Sarah Elizabeth, Lucy Jane. *Education:* Attended Royal Academy of Music, 1947-51. *Home:* 63 Horniman Dr., Forest Hill, London S.E.23, England. *Agent:* A. M. Heath & Co. Ltd., 4042 William IV St., London WC2N 4DD, England.

CAREER: Piano teacher, manager of antique shop, and model maker for stage design, London, England, 1951-61; writer, 1980—. *Awards, honors:* Grant from the Arts Council of Great Britain to write *Poor Tom.*

WRITINGS: *This Place Is a Madhouse* (novel), Heinemann, 1980; *Oh Lily* (novel), Heinemann, 1981; *Poor Tom* (novel), Heinemann, 1982.

WORK IN PROGRESS: A novel, publication expected in 1983.

SIDELIGHTS: Mary Hobson's novel *This Place Is a Madhouse* concerns Ruth, a devoted housewife and mother who suddenly shirks her duties and indulges in selfish irresponsibility. The shame she feels for rejecting her family and her life, however, sends her to a psychiatric hospital, where Ruth shares her problems with the other patients. As she draws close to them, bonds form, and Ruth's inborn selflessness emerges, causing her to develop a new set of responsibilities. According to Craig Brown of *Times Literary Supplement,* "Mary Hobson has written a carefully constructed, bizarre and tender book, producing many fresh ideas from a setting usually befuddled by banality and cliche."

Hobson's second novel, *Oh Lily,* is the story of the relationship between Lily, a domineering mother, and Charlotte, her sheltered, twenty-eight-year-old daughter. When Charlotte marries she finds she knows little about living her own life, a result of Lily's smothering care. But with the birth of her own daughter and the death of Lily, Charlotte, despite the damage she suffered from her mother's overprotective love, realizes that

Lily lived for her, just as she will devote her life to her baby, Laura.

Hobson told *CA:* "The ordinary pressures of living made writing first impossible, then a necessity—a means of discharging accumulated experience, a way of thinking more clearly, of using everything. I hate waste. I was forty-eight when I finished my first novel, fifty by the time it was published. It's a good age for getting down to work."

BIOGRAPHICAL/CRITICAL SOURCES: Times Literary Supplement, March 7, 1980, April 24, 1981.

* * *

HOEKSEMA, Gertrude 1921-

PERSONAL: Born October 6, 1921, in Sibley, Iowa; daughter of Dick (a minister) and Marie (Flokstra) Jonker; married Homer C. Hoeksema (a minister and professor of theology), December 19, 1947; children: Mark, Eunice, Lois, Candace. *Education:* Calvin College, A.B., 1967; Michigan State University, Teaching Certificate, 1969. *Religion:* Protestant Reformed. *Home:* 4975 Ivanrest S.W., Grand Rapids, Mich. 49418. *Office:* Protestant Reformed Christian School, 1150 Adams St., Grand Rapids, Mich. 49507.

CAREER: Protestant Reformed Christian School, Grand Rapids, Mich., teacher of first grade, 1961—.

WRITINGS: Therefore Have I Spoken (biography), Kregel, 1969; *Peaceable Fruit,* Kregel, 1974; (editor) *God's Covenant Faithfulness,* Kregel, 1975; *Suffer Little Children* (juvenile), Reformed Free Publishing Association, Book I, 1977, Book II, 1978, Book III, 1979.

WORK IN PROGRESS: A story book for young children.

SIDELIGHTS: Gertrude Hoeksema wrote: "In my early years I lived in a manse, was brought up in the Calvinist tradition of the Reformation, and was educated through high school in private, parent-controlled Christian schools. My fields of interest in college were English studies and music, including organ. Then I discovered that I would rather teach than perform, and that my first love was young children, those of primary age. Because of my interest in young children, I geared my graduate work toward their needs and took courses in speech problems and remedial reading.

"For most of my teaching career I have taught beginning reading, developing my own approach. Alongside my primary work, I have taught music classes and conducted choirs each year.

"I married the second son of a recognized and controversial theologian, Herman Hoeksema, and it was my father-in-law's life which sparked my writing career. One of my most admired college professors offered his help in writing Herman Hoeksema's biography, and I accepted and wrote *Therefore Have I Spoken.* In my next work, *Peaceable Fruit,* I put down my ideas about training children. Soon after its publication, I was asked to edit *God's Covenant Faithfulness,* a commemoration of the fifty-year history of the Protestant Reformed Church in America. In 1973 the Federation of Protestant Reformed School Boards, under which I teach, asked me to take a year off and begin work on a Bible textbook for young children, *Suffer Little Children.*"

* * *

HOEY, Joanne Nobes 1936-

PERSONAL: Born December 8, 1936, in Rochester, N.Y.; daughter of Joseph James (an antiques dealer) and Dolores (a court clerk; maiden name, Balsam) Nobes; married Charles Hoey (a research and development manager), August 25, 1956; children: Stephen, Leslie Ann, David, Matthew, Jennifer, Nancy. *Education:* Glassboro State College, B.A. (cum laude), 1981. *Home address:* East Centennial Dr., Marlton, N.J. 08053.

CAREER: Writer, 1978—. Also worked as secretary, substitute teacher, and in real estate sales. Gives weekly poetry readings.

WRITINGS—Poetry: *Listen to My Touch,* Blackbird Press, 1981; *May I Touch You Now . . . ,* Blackbird Press, 1983.

Contributor to magazines, including *Asphodel, Jersey Woman, Dragonfly,* and *Avant.*

SIDELIGHTS: Joanne Hoey commented: "My motivation has come from my professors and from within. I like challenge, and it has been quite a challenge to work toward a college degree and publish while raising six children. The people of the world are in great need of beauty at this time—beauty through nature, art, music, and poetry. Through my poetry I hope to share the beauty I feel.

"I have felt a great need to do something concrete. *Listen to My Touch* was the answer. Through my poetry I hope to touch people warmly. Most often, I write when the spirit moves me, which is usually in the early hours of the morning. I collect favored words and phrases in my notebooks and in the back of my head and somehow they manage to jell into a poem. The poems in *Listen to My Touch* were selected by the publisher from poems I have written over the past four years. I find writing to be very rewarding hard work. The ego suffering involved in publishing was most difficult for me. It took a while for me to accept the fact that a lot of people wouldn't like what I wrote. The poem "Fortitude" was added to the book at the last minute. It gave me strength to go on.

"A. C. Libro (my publisher) wrote: 'In this, her first collection of poems, you will find Joanne's sensitive response to nature, her poignant childhood memories, her tender glimpses of love. Here you will experience and enjoy Joanne's sure and steady voice as she builds an unforgettable moment for you in language vivid and deft. Her vision helps us to realize ever more fully this gift we call life.'"

AVOCATIONAL INTERESTS: Playing Appalachian dulcimer, long walks in the woods.

* * *

HOFFELD, Laura 1946(?)-1982

OBITUARY NOTICE: Born c. 1946 in Brooklyn, N.Y.; died of cancer, March 12, 1982, in New York, N.Y. Editor and author of numerous poems and short stories. Hoffeld was the fiction editor of *Women's World* magazine. Obituaries and other sources: *New York Times,* March 14, 1982.

* * *

HOFFMAN, Abraham 1938-

PERSONAL: Born September 25, 1938, in Los Angeles, Calif.; son of Harry (in business) and Hilda (Sofian) Hoffman; married Judith Luboviski, December 26, 1966 (divorced May 8, 1973); married Susan Levine, November 11, 1973; children: Heather, Joshua, Gregory. *Education:* California State University, Los Angeles, B.A., 1960, M.A., 1962; University of California, Los Angeles, Ph.D., 1970. *Politics:* Democrat. *Religion:* Jewish. *Home:* 19211-1 Haynes St., Reseda, Calif. 91335. *Office:* Department of History, Los Angeles Valley College, 5800 Fulton Ave., Van Nuys, Calif. 91401.

CAREER: Teacher of social studies at public schools in Los Angeles, Calif., 1962-70; University of Oklahoma, Norman, assistant professor of history, 1970-73; Los Angeles Valley College, Van Nuys, Calif., instructor in history, 1974—. Adjunct instructor at University of Southern California. *Member:* American Historical Association, Organization of American Historians, Immigration History Society, Academy of Magical Arts (life associate member), Western History Association, Historical Society of Southern California, Los Angeles Westerners Corral. *Awards, honors:* National Endowment for the Humanities fellowships, 1973-74, 1977; grant from San Jose State University, for Sourisseau Academy, 1974-76; second place Philip A. Danielson Award from Westerners International, 1977, for best 1976 Westerners program.

WRITINGS: Unwanted Mexican Americans in the Great Depression: Repatriation Pressures, 1929-1939, University of Arizona Press, 1974; (contributor) Norris Hundley, Jr., editor, *The Chicano,* Clio Books, 1975; (contributor) Judson Grenier, editor, *A Guide to Historic Places in Los Angeles County,* Kendall/Hunt, 1978; (contributor) Arthur F. Corwin, editor, *Immigrants—and Immigrants: Perspectives on Mexican Labor Migration to the United States,* Greenwood Press, 1978; *Vision or Villainy: Origins of the Owens Valley-Los Angeles Water Controversy,* Texas A & M University Press, 1981; (contributor) Donald R. Whitnah, editor, *Government Agencies,* Greenwood Press, 1983. Contributor of more than eighty articles and reviews to history journals. Editor of newsletter of Historical Society of Southern California, 1979—.

WORK IN PROGRESS: An evaluation of predictions for the future of science to be found in the comic strip, "Our New Age," with Athelstan Spilhaus, publication expected in 1986; a biography of William Mulholland, chief engineer of the Los Angeles Department of Water and Power, "a major figure in Los Angeles history," publication expected in 1987.

SIDELIGHTS: "I look upon the study of history as a search for truth," Hoffman wrote. "This point of view was gradually acquired when, as a graduate student at University of California, Los Angeles, I came across the conventional accounts of the long-standing controversy between the city of Los Angeles and Inyo County over the Owens Valley-Los Angeles Aqueduct, which supplies the city with 80 per cent of its water. After I received my Ph.D., I began to make an in-depth study of the water controversy. I became aware that to a very disturbing degree much of what purported to be the historical record was actually based on hearsay, poor judgment, and insufficient data. If this was the case with the water dispute, how superficial must be the acceptance level of the general public to popular versions of history? I try to educate my students in the importance of context, perspective, objectivity in evaluating evidence, and the need to search out all sources of information whether or not the material gathered contradicts the thesis the student is attempting to validate.

"My teaching interests include courses in the history of California, the American West, the United States, Latin America, as well as the history of immigration to America and of ethnic minorities in America, especially the experiences of Jews and Mexican Americans. In 1981, as an adjunct instructor at the University of Southern California, I developed a course on the history of sports in America. My research interests parallel my teaching of history to some degree. I find California a rich source for studies on water resource development, minority history, and topics in local history."

AVOCATIONAL INTERESTS: "I enjoy hiking in the nearby San Gabriel mountains when time permits, building model airplanes and HO and N gauge train layouts. Although I have little aptitude in prestidigitation, I enjoy magic shows. Cats are preferable to dogs; our cat, Spooky, feels the same way."

*   *   *

HOFFMAN, Edward

PERSONAL: Born in Bronx, N.Y.; son of Irwin L. (an English teacher) and Roslyn (a music teacher; maiden name, Lipitz) Hoffman; married Laurel Brainin (a clinical social worker), August 31, 1976. *Education:* Cornell University, B.A., 1971; University of Michigan, M.A., 1974, Ph.D., 1976. *Residence:* Pembroke Pines, Fla. *Agent:* John White, 60 Pound Ridge Rd., Cheshire, Conn. 06410. *Office:* Hollywood Pavilion Psychiatric Hospital, 1201 N. 37th Ave., Hollywood, Fla. 33021.

CAREER: Psychologist. Clinical psychologist at South Florida State Hospital, 1979-1981; Hollywood Pavilion Psychiatric Hospital, Hollywood, Fla., clinical director, 1981—. Clinical psychologist for mental health programs; consultant to educational and mental health agencies, including Head Start, Association for Retarded Citizens, and Jewish Federation. Assistant professor of psychology at Keuka College, Keuka Park, N.Y.; instructor in psychology at University of Michigan; adjunct professor at Nova University, Fort Lauderdale, Fla. 1979—. *Awards, honors:* Fellowship from U.S. Office of Education, 1971-72.

WRITINGS: (With W. Edward Mann) *The Man Who Dreamed of Tomorrow: A Conceptual Biography of Wilhelm Reich,* J. P. Tarcher, 1980; *The Way of Splendor: Jewish Mysticism and Modern Psychology,* Shambhala, 1981. Contributor of articles to professional journals, including *American Journal of Psychiatry, Journal of Humanistic Psychology,* and *Journal of Clinical Psychology.*

WORK IN PROGRESS: Several research projects on topics such as "the evolution of modern psychology, the relationship of Judaism to scientific interest in the mind, and the future of family and community in this socially chaotic period."

SIDELIGHTS: Edward Hoffman's *The Man Who Dreamed of Tomorrow* was described by Madeline Gray of the *Washington Post* as "both timely and provocative." A *Choice* reviewer called the work "a fascinating book."

Like *The Man Who Dreamed of Tomorrow,* Hoffman's second book, *The Way of Splendor,* received favorable reviews. This book introduces the general reader to the psychological insights of Jewish mysticism, especially the mysticism of the Kabbalists who delve into the phenomena that lacks rational explanations. In *The Way of Splendor,* wrote the *Jewish Advocate*'s Sylvia Rothchild, "Edward Hoffman . . . opens a Pandora's box of possibilities for thought and study for those wishing to create some harmony between spiritual and scientific paths to knowledge." It is a "beautifully clear and precise work," remarked Norma Feld in the *Library Journal.*

Hoffman told *CA:* "Much of my impetus in writing has come from my desire to make accessible for people today aspects of psychology usually ignored in mainstream accounts. Educated men and women are certainly aware that standard approaches have proved wanting, yet alternatives are often not easily visible. Hence, my first two books—one on the ideas of Wilhelm Reich, the other on the powerful insights of Jewish mysticism. I also feel that few 'experts' in the field are able to clearly describe their findings and the larger implications related to their work.

"I am intrigued by the intensity with which much of the intellectual and cultural establishment embraces such a gloomy and negative picture of our inner nature and potential. One of the most needed tasks for our times, I am convinced, is for writers and other creative persons to offer an antidote to this 'no future,' despairing, hand-wringing posture.

"Personally, my own attitudes have been shaped in part by events I experienced in the late 1960's like so many others of my generation. I think large numbers of us are still struggling to make sense of the tremendous energy generated in those few, short years. Travels to England, the Greek islands, Israel, and other locales have also sparked a variety of interests."

BIOGRAPHICAL/CRITICAL SOURCES: Los Angeles Times, November 27, 1980; *Washington Post,* January 29, 1981; *Choice,* March, 1981; *Library Journal,* November 15, 1981; *Jewish Advocate,* December 10, 1981.

* * *

HOFFMAN, Marshall 1942-

PERSONAL: Born October 9, 1942, in Boston, Mass.; son of Nathan (a Hebrew teacher) and Lillian (a secretary; maiden name, Cohen) Hoffman; married Birgitta Ulla Svensson (a surgical nurse), February 15, 1969; children: Nils, Peter. *Education:* Boston College, B.S. (cum laude), 1964; graduate study at Iowa State University, 1964-65. *Religion:* Jewish. *Home:* 8019 Lewinsville Rd., McLean, Va. 22102.

CAREER: Central Intelligence Agency (CIA), Washington, D.C., economist, 1966-69; *U.S. News and World Report,* Washington, D.C., economist/writer, 1969-77; New York Times Syndicate, New York, N.Y., columnist, 1977—; Patrick Productions, McLean, Va., executive producer, 1980—.

WRITINGS: (With Gabe Mirkin) *The Sportsmedicine Book* (Literary Guild alternate selection), Little, Brown, 1978; (with William Southmayd) *Sports Health: The Complete Book of Athletic Injuries,* Quick Fox, 1981.

WORK IN PROGRESS: Producing television programs on sports and fitness.

SIDELIGHTS: "For 16.5 million Americans, the pursuit of happiness is being carried out in track shoes," commented *New York Times* critic Anatole Broyard. One result of this "American romance with running" is a marked increase in athletic injuries. Hoffman's first book, *The Sportsmedicine Book,* co-written with Gabe Mirkin, a physician and marathoner, is a "clearly and expertly written layman's guide to athletic medicine," remarked a reviewer in *People.* Sportsmedicine, as defined by the authors, "deals with the physiological, anatomical, psychological and biochemical effects of exercise, and includes such diverse concerns as training methods, the prevention and treatment of injuries, nutrition and the effect of weather on the athlete." In addition to addressing these concerns, the book also devotes a chapter to dispelling widely-held misconceptions about athletic exercise, training, and diet. The authors point out that training hard daily is not desirable, vitamins do not improve performance, cold air is not harmful to the lungs, salt tablets are not beneficial, and that an ordinary electrocardiogram is insufficient as a guarantee of a normal heart.

Hoffman's second book, *Sports Health,* co-authored by William Southmayd, a twelve-year practitioner of sportsmedicine, offers an in-depth look at common sports injuries, exploring causes, symptoms, diagnosis, and treatment.

AVOCATIONAL INTERESTS: Running, reading.

BIOGRAPHICAL/CRITICAL SOURCES: New York Times, December 30, 1978; *People,* January 29, 1979; *U.S. News and World Report,* December 21, 1981.

HOFFMAN, Michael Allen 1944-

PERSONAL: Born October 14, 1944, in Washington, D.C.; son of Donald B. (an architectural engineer) and Mary (Neason) Hoffman. *Education:* University of Kentucky, B.A., 1966; University of Wisconsin—Madison, M.A., 1968, Ph.D., 1970. *Home:* 216 Colonial Ave., Colonial Beach, Va. 22443.

CAREER: University of Virginia, Charlottesville, assistant professor of anthropology, 1972-77, assistant professor of architecture, 1977-79; Virginia Museum of Fine Arts, Richmond, adviser to Egyptian Gallery, 1979-81; Western Illinois University, Macomb, associate professor of anthropology, 1981—. *Member:* International Platform Association, American Anthropological Association, Society for American Archaeology, American Research Center in Egypt, Egypt Exploration Society, Egyptian Studies Association (director), Earth Sciences and Resources Institute at the University of South Carolina, Illinois Archaeological Survey, Council of Virginia Archeologists, Archeological Society of Virginia.

WRITINGS: (With James H. Cleland) *The Lithic Industry at Allahdino—A Metric and Quantitative Analysis of an Harappan Activity System* (monograph), Papers of the Allahdino Expedition, No. 2 (New York, N.Y.), 1977; *Egypt Before the Pharaohs: The Prehistoric Foundations of Egyptian Civilization,* Knopf, 1979; (editor and contributor) *The Predynastics of Hierakonpolis* (monograph), Alden Press Ltd., 1981. Contributor of articles and reviews to numerous periodicals, including *Anthropological Quarterly, American Antiquity, Journal of the American Research Center in Egypt, American Anthropologist, East and West, Expedition, Journal of Near Eastern Studies, Anthropology, Archaeometry,* and *Arts in Virginia Magazine.* Also author of publications for the U.S. National Park Service and Kentucky Department of Highways.

WORK IN PROGRESS: Directing an expedition to Hierakonpolis, Egypt, to study the origins of Egyptian civilization, complex societies, human ecology, long-range international planning and development, and interdisciplinary research techniques; research on human ecology and cultural history at Shenandoah National Park in the Blue Ridge Mountains of Virginia.

SIDELIGHTS: Hoffman told *CA:* "I decided on a career in archaeology as a young boy and have done fieldwork in Egypt, Afghanistan, Turkey, Pakistan, Cyprus, Norway, Germany, Kentucky, Illinois, and Virginia. My book *Egypt Before the Pharaohs* was written to share the often technical findings of prehistorians with the educated public. I am involved in ongoing research in Egypt as director of the Hierakonpolis Expedition. My projects both overseas and in the United States emphasize an interdisciplinary approach to cultural and environmental problems and the development of a new and more responsive approach to solving world problems."

BIOGRAPHICAL/CRITICAL SOURCES: Christian Science Monitor, February 27, 1980; *Times Literary Supplement,* April 25, 1980.

* * *

HOFFMANN, Charles 1921-

PERSONAL: Born January 10, 1921, in New York, N.Y.; son of William and Regine (Jonkler) Hoffmann; married July 26, 1953; children: Richard, Brian. *Education:* Queens College (now of the City University of New York), B.A., 1942; Columbia University, M.A., 1947, Ph.D., 1954. *Home:* 270 Fairhaven Blvd., Woodbury, N.Y. 11797. *Office:* Department of

Social Services, Queens College of the City University of New York, Flushing, N.Y. 11367.

CAREER: Office of Price Administration, Washington, D.C., economist, 1942 and 1946; Queens College (now of the City University of New York), Flushing, N.Y., associated with department of economics, 1947-63; State University of New York at Stony Brook, professor of economics, 1965—; Queens College, dean of department of social services, 1979—. Lecturer and consultant. *Military service:* U.S. Naval Reserve, active duty as executive officer and personnel officer with Bureau of Naval Personnel, 1942-46.

MEMBER: American Economic Association, Economic History Association, Association for Asian Studies, American Association for the Advancement of Science, American Association of University Professors, Association for Evolutionary Economics, New York Civil Liberties Union (member of county board of directors, 1965-74; chairman, 1972), Metropolitan Economic Association, Phi Beta Kappa. *Awards, honors:* Fellowship from Social Science Research Council and American Council of Learned Societies, 1961-62.

WRITINGS: (With Alfred Oxenfeldt) *Economic Principles and Public Issues,* Rinehart, 1959; *Work Incentive Practices and Policies in the People's Republic of China, 1953-1965,* State University of New York Press, 1967; *Depression of the Nineties,* Greenwood Press, 1970; *The Chinese Worker,* State University of New York Press, 1974. Contributor to economic and Asian studies journals.

WORK IN PROGRESS: Articles on employment and unemployment in China, for *Asian Thought and Society.*

* * *

HOFFMANN, Frank W(illiam) 1949-

PERSONAL: Born May 2, 1949, in Geneva, N.Y.; son of Frank Anton (a professor of English) and Lydia (an assistant library director; maiden name, Mayer) Hoffmann; married Lee Ann Black (a slide librarian), January 5, 1980. *Education:* Indiana University, B.A., 1971, M.L.S., 1972; University of Pittsburgh, Ph.D., 1977. *Home:* 2322 South Park, Huntsville, Tex. 77340. *Office:* School of Library Science, Sam Houston State University, Huntsville, Tex. 77341.

CAREER: Bloomington Courier-Journal, Bloomington, Ind., staff reporter and interviewer, 1971-72; Indiana University, Bloomington, library assistant, 1972; Memphis Public Library, Memphis, Tenn., librarian, 1972-74; WLYX-FM Radio, Memphis, disc jockey, 1974; Carlow College, Pittsburgh, Pa., reference librarian at Grace Library, 1974-76; Woodville State Hospital, Carnegie, Pa., librarian at Patient Library, 1976-78; Sam Houston State University, Huntsville, Tex., assistant professor of library science, 1979—. Reference librarian at Northland Public Library, Pittsburgh, 1976-78; visiting professor at Louisiana State University, summer, 1980. *Member:* American Library Association, American Association of Library Schools (member of membership committee and program planning committee, both 1981-83), Special Libraries Association (member of executive board, 1981—), Popular Culture Association, Beta Phi Mu. *Awards, honors: Choice* named *The Literature of Rock, 1954-1978* one of the outstanding books of 1981-82; nomination for outstanding young man of America, 1982.

WRITINGS: The Development of Library Collections of Sound Recordings, Dekker, 1979; *The Literature of Rock, 1954-1978,* Scarecrow, 1981; *Popular Culture as a Learning Tool in Libraries,* Shoe String, 1983; *The Cash Box Pop Singles Charts,*

1950-1981, Scarecrow, 1983. Editor of "Occasional Papers Series," School of Library Science, Sam Houston State University, 1981—. Contributor to *Encyclopedia of Library and Information Science.* Contributor of articles and reviews to academic journals and newspapers. Member of editorial board of *Journal of Educational Studies,* 1980—.

WORK IN PROGRESS: The Cash Box Pop Music Sourcebook, publication expected in 1984.

SIDELIGHTS: Hoffmann wrote: "I consider it vital that aesthetic and cultural elitism with respect to education and library activities be vigorously opposed. All learning experiences should be judged in relation to their own intrinsic merits. My research, publishing, and teaching is a testament to this belief."

* * *

HOFMANNSTHAL, Hugo von 1874-1929
(Loris, Loris Melikow, Theophil Morren)

BRIEF ENTRY: Born Feburary 1, 1874, in Vienna, Austria, died of a heart attack, July 15, 1929, in Rodaun, Austria. Austrian author. Hofmannsthal was described as a prodigy and a genius, because he was just sixteen years old when the first of his highly regarded works were published. The early poems and fragmentary verse plays, such as *Der Tod des Tizian* (1892; translated as *The Death of Titian,* 1913-15) and *Der Tor und der Tod* (1894; translated as *Death and the Fool,* 1913), were almost magical, combining rich language with nearly perfect form, mature vision, and the philosophy of art for art's sake. Hofmannsthal has often been commended for his skill and extraordinary versatility. In his later, most popular writing, he revealed a concern with social responsibility and humanity, adapting classics such as the medieval morality play *Jedermann* (1911; translated as *Everyman,* 1917). He established a long and successful collaboration with composer Richard Strauss, which resulted in *Der Rosenkavalier* (1911; translated as *The Cavalier and the Rose,* 1912) and several other operas. Near the end of his career, Hofmannsthal returned to a theme he had pursued earlier: the preservation of European values. One of his major dramas of this period, *Der Turm* (1925; translated as *The Tower,* 1966), dealt with the problem of might versus right. The play expressed Hofmannsthal's concern over Austria's fate in the coming years. His apprehensions proved to be well-founded, as the country was occupied by Nazi Germany only nine years after Hofmannsthal's death. *Biographical/critical sources: Encyclopedia of World Literature in the Twentieth Century,* updated edition, Ungar, 1967.

* * *

HOGARTH, John
See FINNIN, (Olive) Mary

* * *

HOLDEN, George S(cott) 1926-

PERSONAL: Born January 29, 1926, in Yonkers, N.Y.; son of George Alvin and Maude (Scott) Holden; married Janice Miner (a teacher), August 12, 1978; children: Bruce, David, Kent, Robert, Susan. *Education:* State Teachers College (now State University of New York College at Fredonia), B.S., 1949; Alfred University, M.S., 1954; State University of New York at Buffalo, Ed.D., 1966; postdoctoral study at Indiana State University, 1972. *Home:* 1108 Glidden Ave., DeKalb, Ill. 60115. *Office:* Department of Leadership and Educational Policy Studies, Northern Illinois University, DeKalb, Ill. 60115.

CAREER: Music teacher at public school in Andover, N.Y., 1949-54; high school band director in Clarence, N.Y., 1954-56, guidance counselor, 1956-59, principal of summer school, 1959; University of Buffalo (now State University of New York at Buffalo), Buffalo, N.Y., director of placement, 1959-60; guidance counselor at public school in Clarence, 1960-63; director of guidance and Pupil Personnel Services at public school in Hamburg, N.Y., 1963-66; Northern Illinois University, DeKalb, assistant professor, 1966-69, associate professor, 1969-77, professor of counselor education, 1977—. Visiting professor at New Mexico State University, summer, 1969. Private practice of psychotherapy; consultant on staff development and human relations. *Military service:* U.S. Marine Corps, 1944-46.

MEMBER: American Psychological Association, American Personnel and Guidance Association, American Association of Sex Educators, Counselors, and Therapists, American School Counselor Association, North Central Association for Counselor Education and Supervision, Illinois Guidance and Personnel Association, Illinois Elementary School Counselor Association, Phi Delta Kappa, Kiwanis.

WRITINGS: (Contributor) Maurie Hillson and Ronald Hyman, editors, *Change and Innovation in Elementary and Secondary Organization*, Holt, 1971; *On Loving*, Richards Rosen, 1975; (contributor) Harold Collins, John Johansen, and James Johnson, editors, *Educational Measurement and Evaluation*, Scott, Foresman, 1975. Contributor to education and guidance journals.

WORK IN PROGRESS: (With wife, Janice Miner-Holden) *Sex Counseling and Therapy*.

SIDELIGHTS: Holden commented: "As a humanist, I devote much of my time to helping people discover meaning and fulfillment in their lives. I work with individuals and couples as a psychotherapist, a marriage counselor and sex therapist, and with groups as an educator and facilitator of intrapersonal and interpersonal relations. I enjoy people, but more importantly, I enjoy life, and seek ways of experiencing new adventures. My joy is to lead a full life and help others do the same."

AVOCATIONAL INTERESTS: Travel, camping, music, painting, water skiing, riding sand buggies, snowmobiling, horseback riding.

*　　*　　*

HOLDEN, Matthew
    See PARKINSON, Roger

*　　*　　*

HOLLING, Holling C(lancy)　1900-1973

OBITUARY NOTICE: Born August 2, 1900, in Holling Corners, Mich.; died September 7, 1973. Naturalist, illustrator, and author. Holling, who was best known for his geo-historical-fiction volumes for children, believed that children's literature should be both entertaining and instructive and therefore filled his adventuresome tales with well-researched historical and scientific data. Two film adaptations of his *Paddle to the Sea* have been released since the book's publication in 1941. His other titles include *Claws of the Thunderbird: A Tale of Three Lost Indians*, *The Twins Who Flew Round the World*, and *Seabird*. Obituaries and other sources: *Twentieth Century Children's Writers*, St. Martin's, 1978.

HOLLOWAY, Stanley　1890-1982

OBITUARY NOTICE: Born October 1, 1890, in London, England; died January 30, 1982, in Littlehampton, Sussex, England. Actor and author of an autobiography. Best known in the United States for his portrayal of Alfred P. Doolittle in the movie version of Lerner and Lowe's popular musical "My Fair Lady," Stanley Holloway enjoyed his first major success as an actor in 1921. That year, he performed in "The Co-optimists," a long-running stage event that the *London Times* described as "essentially a concert party with two pianists to play the tunes." Later stage roles included appearances in "Savoy Follies," "Three Sisters," "A Midsummer Night's Dream," "The Pleasure of His Company," and, beginning in 1956, "My Fair Lady." Holloway also appeared in a number of films, including "Major Barbara," "Brief Encounter," "Hamlet," and "The Lavender Hill Mob." His autobiography, *Wiv a Little Bit o' Luck*, was published in 1967. Obituaries and other sources: *Current Biography*, Wilson, 1963, March, 1982; *International Motion Picture Almanac*, Quigley, 1979; *Who's Who*, 134th edition, St. Martin's, 1982; *New York Times*, January 31, 1982; *London Times*, February 1, 1982; *Newsweek*, February 8, 1982; *Time*, February 8, 1982.

*　　*　　*

HOLLOWAY, Thomas H(alsey)　1944-

PERSONAL: Born June 24, 1944, in Enterprise, Ore.; son of Merritt L. (a cowboy) and Winona (a teacher; maiden name, Johnson) Holloway; married Judith Brown, June 15, 1963; children: Timothy Steven, Susana Erin. *Education:* University of California, Santa Barbara, B.A., 1968; University of Wisconsin—Madison, Ph.D., 1974. *Office:* Department of History, Cornell University, Ithaca, N.Y. 14853.

CAREER: Cornell University, Ithaca, N.Y., assistant professor, 1974-80, associate professor of history, 1980—. *Military service:* U.S. Army, 1962-65. *Member:* Latin American Studies Association, Conference on Latin American History, Phi Beta Kappa.

WRITINGS: The Brazilian Coffee Valorization of 1906, Wisconsin State Historical Society, 1975; *Immigrants on the Land: Coffee in Sao Paulo, 1886-1934*, University of North Carolina Press, 1980.

WORK IN PROGRESS: Continuing research on Latin American agrarian history and Brazilian social history.

*　　*　　*

HOLMES, Richard　1946-

PERSONAL: Born March 29, 1946, in Aldridge, Staffordshire, England; son of William (an engineer) and Helen (Jacques) Holmes; married Elizabeth Saxton (a theatre designer), August 2, 1975; children: Jessica Helen. *Education:* Emmanuel College, Cambridge, B.A., 1968, M.A., 1973; attended Northern Illinois University, 1968-69; Reading University, Ph.D., 1975. *Home:* 10 High St., Alton, Hampshire GU34 1BN, England. *Office:* Department of War Studies, Royal Military Academy Sandhurst, Camberley, Surrey, England.

CAREER: Department of War Studies and International Affairs, Royal Military Academy Sandhurst, Camberley, Surrey, England, senior lecturer, 1969—. *Military service:* Territorial Army, 1965—; became major. *Member:* Royal United Services Institute for Defence Studies, Writers Guild. *Awards, honors:*

History Scholar, Emmanuel College, Cambridge, 1965-67; bronze award for documentary from the New York International Film and Television Festival, 1980, for "Comrades in Arms? Dunkirk 1940."

WRITINGS: Borodino 1812, Charles Knight, 1972; *Bir Hacheim,* Ballantine, 1972; (with Brig Peter Young) *The English Civil War,* Methuen, 1974; (contributor) John Keegan, editor, *World Armies,* Macmillan, 1979; *The Little Field-Marshal: Sir John French,* J. Cape, 1981; (with Anthony Kemp) *The Bitter End,* Antony Bird, 1982; *The Road to Sedan: The French Army, 1866-70,* Royal Historical Society, 1982.

Teleplays: "Tanks," Southern Television, 1977; "Comrades in Arms? Dunkirk 1940," Southern Television, 1980. Also served as military adviser for "The Duellists," 1976.

WORK IN PROGRESS: War and the Soldier, completion expected in 1984.

SIDELIGHTS: Holmes's *The Little Field-Marshal: Sir John French* is a biography of John Denton Pinkstone French, a noted British military figure. According to Brian Bond of the *Times Literary Supplement,* "Holmes has been reasonably successful in overcoming the military biographer's chief difficulty; namely how to provide a convincing portrait of a man of action without digressing into detailed narratives of the operations in which he took part. A biographer less interested in military history would doubtless have devoted more space to his subject's philandering and its repercussions on his family, but Holmes is circumspect."

Holmes told *CA:* "I was initially interested in the broad spread of military history, but have recently become increasingly concerned with the role of the individual on the battlefield. My current research is devoted to exploring questions of morale, motivation, and loyalty."

BIOGRAPHICAL/CRITICAL SOURCES: Times Literary Supplement, November 13, 1981.

* * *

HOMBERGER, Eric (Ross) 1942-

PERSONAL: Born May 30, 1942, in Philadelphia, Pa.; son of Alexander and Marilyn (Glick) Homberger; married Judy Jones, June 2, 1967; children: Martin Joshua, Margaret Alissa, Charles Michael. *Education:* University of California, Berkeley, B.A., 1964; University of Chicago, M.A., 1965; Cambridge University, Ph.D., 1972. *Politics:* Socialist. *Religion:* None. *Home:* 74 Clarendon Rd., Norwich NR2 2PN, England.

CAREER: University of Exeter, Exeter, England, temporary lecturer in American literature, 1969-70; University of East Anglia, Norwich, England, lecturer in American literature, 1970—. Visiting member of faculty at University of Minnesota, 1977-78. *Member:* British Association for American Studies. *Awards, honors:* Leverhulme fellowship in European studies, 1978-79.

WRITINGS: (Editor with William Janeway and Simon Schama) *The Cambridge Mind: Ninety Years of the "Cambridge Review," 1879-1969,* Little, Brown, 1970; (editor) *Ezra Pound: The Critical Heritage,* Routledge & Kegan Paul, 1972; *The Art of the Real: Poetry in England and America Since 1939,* Rowman & Littlefield, 1977; (co-author) *The Novel and the Second World War,* Macmillan, 1983. Contributor to magazines and newspapers, including *Times Literary Supplement, Nation, Economist,* and *Journal of American Studies.*

WORK IN PROGRESS: A study of culture and American radicalism, publication by Routledge & Kegan Paul expected in 1984; a study of Jewish writers in America, publication by Weidenfeld & Nicolson expected in 1984.

SIDELIGHTS: Homberger wrote: "Living in England since 1965 has enabled me to confront the historical experience of my family (as emigrants, within living memory, from Europe) and of America itself. It has been hard to wave the flag; and I haven't really tried to do so. In partial consequence, I have become interested in fugitive areas of experience, of alienated sensibilities, whether ethnic or political, whose experience may in some way stand for the larger tendency of a society and a way of life.

"I would like to write the kind of literary criticism which is on the brink of becoming history, with its confident and unthinking grasp of the real. Criticism now has almost wholly surrendered that ambition, to its impoverishment, I think; it has the willingness to address a non-specialist reading public. In England fifteen years ago critics still hoped to speak to such an audience. But that has mostly gone and has been replaced by a more vigorous hunger for theorization. The end result: critics only able to speak to each other, inmates, really, in a crumbling and neglected ward, trying to persuade each other that the discipline advances. I want to write a stronger, more political sort of thing. Maybe the form ought to be different. I can imagine writing, quite consciously, to reach a wider audience; the only problem is that the audience may no longer exist."

* * *

HOOPER, Meredith (Jean) 1939-

PERSONAL: Born October 21, 1939, in Adelaide, Australia; daughter of Clifford (an educationist) and Jean (Hosking) Rooney; married Richard Hooper, March, 1964; children: Rachel, Thomas, Benjamin. *Education:* University of Adelaide, B.A., 1960; Lady Margaret Hall and Nuffield College, Oxford, M.Phil., 1964. *Home:* 4 Western Rd., London N2 9HX, England.

CAREER: University of Adelaide, Adelaide, Australia, tutor in history, 1961; Voluntary Service Overseas, London, administrator, 1964-65; free-lance writer, 1968—. *Awards, honors:* Beit Prize from University of Oxford, 1966; Children's Book of the Year Award commendation from Children's Book Council of Australia, 1973, for *Everyday Inventions.*

WRITINGS—All juveniles: *Land of the Free: The United States of America,* Blond Educational, 1968; *Gold Rush in Australia,* Hulton Educational Publications, 1969; *Everyday Inventions,* Angus & Robertson, 1972, Taplinger, 1976; *The Story of Australia* (illustrated by Elaine Haxton), Angus & Robertson, 1974, Taplinger, 1976; *More Everyday Inventions,* Angus & Robertson, 1976; *Dr. Hunger and Captain Thirst: Stories of Australian Explorers,* Methuen, 1982.

* * *

HOOVER, Herbert Theodore 1930-

PERSONAL: Born March 9, 1930, in Millville, Minn.; son of Clyde A. and Bessie M. (Olin) Hoover; married Karolyn Joyce Kruger (a registered nurse), 1957; children: Carmen, Christopher. *Education:* New Mexico State University, B.A., 1960, M.A., 1961; University of Oklahoma, Ph.D., 1966. *Home address:* Route 2, Vermillion, S.D. 57069. *Office:* Department of History, University of South Dakota, Vermillion, S.D. 57069.

CAREER: East Texas State University, Commerce, assistant professor of history, 1965-66; University of South Dakota,

Vermillion, associate professor, 1967-74, professor of history, 1974—. Acting director of Newberry Library's Center for the History of the American Indian; director of South Dakota Oral History Center, 1977-78. *Member:* Organization of American Historians, Western History Association. *Awards, honors:* Newberry Library fellowship, 1977; grant from National Endowment for the Humanities, 1978-81.

WRITINGS: To Be an Indian, Holt, 1971; *The Chitimacha People,* Phoenix Indian Tribal Series, 1975; *The Practice of Oral History,* Microfilming Corp., 1975; *The Sioux,* Indiana University Press, 1979; *Bibliography of the Sioux,* Scarecrow, 1980.

Contributor: Michael Kammen, editor, *The Past Before Us,* Cornell University Press, 1979; Ron Lora, editor, *The American West,* University of Toledo Press, 1980; R. David Edmunds, editor, *American Indian Leaders,* University of Nebraska Press, 1980; Richard A. Bartlett, *Rolling Rivers: An Encyclopedia of America's Rivers,* McGraw-Hill, 1982; Roger J. Spiller, editor, *Dictionary of American Military Biography,* Greenwood Press, 1982; Michael Malone, editor, *Western Historiography,* University of Nebraska Press, 1982. Also contributor to *Encyclopedia Americana* and *Worldmark Encyclopedia of the States,* and to history journals, including *Western Historical Quarterly.*

WORK IN PROGRESS: A general history of contact between the Sioux federation and non-Indians since 1640, five volumes, completion expected in 1984.

SIDELIGHTS: Hoover told *CA:* "The chapter I prepared for Mike Malone's book on Western historiography for the University of Nebraska Press begins: 'Few if any noteworthy groups in the society of the United States have received as little attention by historians as have American Indians. Before the 1930's, their historic plight was described mainly by amateurs and professional writers in disciplines other than history, and the few reliable publications to appear treated them mainly as obstacles to the progress of Anglo-American civilization, or as antiquarian curiosities. During the past half century or so, small groups of professional historians and ethnologists finally have assumed responsibility for the Indian's presence in history, and have begun to recognize them as a cultural force deserving treatment in a separate field of interest. Unfortunately these groups have not been large enough to keep pace with other bodies of professionals who have been engaged in the improvement of historiography. . . . So few bona fide scholars have been attracted to native Americans that unwary readers still are supplied as much semi-fictional literature as soundly written history. So few have been engaged in the work that the consuming public has yet to receive elementary guidance by qualified authors on the complexities of the field as a whole, or of its several sub-divisions in particular.'

"But with growing interest (I go on to explain), the identification of sub-divisions has taken place: the histories of the internal affairs of all the tribes; the history of policies devised and enforced by federal officials; and the history of contact from the arrival of European colonials to the present time. And gradually scholars—of both Indian and non-Indian extraction—have begun to prepare themselves to work in these sub-fields. Gradually, scholarship on 'Indian history' has begun to mature to take its place among the major areas of interest that make up the whole of American history."

*   *   *

HOPE, Christopher (David Tully) 1944-

PERSONAL: Born February 26, 1944, in Johannesburg, South

Africa; son of Dudley Mitford and Kathleen Margaret (McKenna) Hope; married Eleanor Marilyn Margaret Klein (a music administrator), February 18, 1967; children: Jasper Antony, Daniel Clement. *Education:* University of Witwatersrand, B.A., 1965, M.A., 1971; University of Natal, B.A. (with honors), 1970. *Residence:* London, England. *Agent:* Maia Gregory, 311 East 72nd St., New York, N.Y. 10021.

CAREER: Writer. *Military service:* South African Navy, 1962. *Awards, honors:* Pringle Award from the English Academy of Southern Africa, 1972, for creative writing; Cholmondeley Award for poetry from British Society of Authors, 1977; Professor Alexander Petrie Award from Convocation of the University of Natal, 1981, for "outstanding contribution to the arts and humanities"; David Higham Prize for fiction from National Book League of Great Britain, 1981, for *A Separate Development.*

WRITINGS: (With Mike Kirkwood) *Whitewashes,* privately printed, 1971; *Cape Drives* (poetry), London Magazine Editions, 1974; *A Separate Development* (novel), Ravan Press, 1980, Scribner, 1981; *In the Country of the Black Pig* (poetry), London Magazine Editions, 1981; *Private Parts* (short stories), Bateleur Press, 1981; (with Yehudi Menuhin) *The King, the Cat, and the Fiddle* (juvenile), Benn, 1983.

Author of plays "Ducktails," "Bye-Bye Booysens," and "An Entirely New Concept in Packaging" for South African television. Work anthologized in *On the Edge of the World,* Ad. Donker, 1974; *A World of Their Own,* Ad. Donker, 1976; *A New Book of South African Verse in English,* Oxford University Press, 1979; *Modern South African Stories,* Ad. Donker, 1980; and *Theatre Two,* Ad. Donker, 1981. Contributor to *London Magazine, Times Literary Supplement, Poetry Review, New Yorker, Transatlantic Review,* and *New Statesman.*

WORK IN PROGRESS: A novel, publication expected in 1983.

SIDELIGHTS: Hope's *A Separate Development* concerns a dark Caucasian's experiences with apartheid in South Africa. *Newsweek*'s Walter Clemons called it "another odd, funny adult novel" and noted its "bitterly hilarious results."

Hope told *CA:* "Most of my work, I think, has been an attempt to explore the effects of discrimination, particularly racial discrimination, as exemplified by apartheid in South Africa, the injustice of which and the misery it causes are widely known; less well understood, perhaps, is the richly bizarre existence of the various population groups who must live under enforced segregation in a society obsessed with skin color. A tiny minority operate a system of racial separation everyone knows to be crazy. My novel *A Separate Development* (the official euphemism for apartheid) is a kind of joke-book, because if apartheid is cruel it is also ridiculous, and the most cheering thing about its victims is their well-nourished sense of the ridiculous. It is something the guardians of racial purity find more disconcerting than earnest moralizing. I try to convey the eerie comedy of South African life."

BIOGRAPHICAL/CRITICAL SOURCES: Newsweek, December 7, 1981; *New Yorker,* December 14, 1981; *New York Times Book Review,* December 20, 1981; *Los Angeles Times Book Review,* December 20, 1981; *Washington Post Book World,* January 3, 1982.

*   *   *

HOPE, Laura Lee
See ADAMS, Harriet S(tratemeyer)

HOPKINS, Lightnin'
See HOPKINS, Sam

*   *   *

HOPKINS, Sam   1912-1982
(Lightnin' Hopkins)

OBITUARY NOTICE: Born March 15, 1912, in Centerville, Tex.; died of cancer, January 30, 1982, in Houston, Tex. Singer and songwriter. Blues singer Sam Hopkins, contemporary of such other blues artists as Muddy Waters, B.B. King, and John Lee Hooker, was recognized for his distinct improvisational style of bass guitar playing. He adopted the nickname "Lightnin'" following an early association with pianist "Thunder" Smith. The approximately six hundred songs that Hopkins wrote were characterized by what *Newsweek* called "frequently bitter and brooding lyrics." *Lightnin' Hopkins, Blues in My Bottle, Smokes Like Lightnin',* and *Country Blues* are among the many albums he recorded. Obituaries and other sources: *Biographical Dictionary of American Music,* Parker Publishing, 1973; *The Illustrated Encyclopedia of Jazz,* Harmony Books, 1978; *Blues Who's Who: A Biographical Dictionary of Blues Singers,* Arlington House, 1979; *New York Times,* February 1, 1982; *Newsweek,* February 15, 1982; *Time,* February 15, 1982.

*   *   *

HORCHOW, (Samuel) Roger   1928-

PERSONAL: Born July 3, 1928, in Cincinnati, Ohio; son of Reuben (an attorney) and Beatrice (Schwartz) Horchow; married Carolyn Pfeifer (a business executive), December 29, 1960; children: Regen, Elizabeth, Sally. *Education:* Yale University, B.A., 1950. *Home:* 5722 Chatham Rd., Dallas, Tex. 75225. *Office:* 4435 Simonton Rd., Dallas, Tex. 75240.

CAREER: Mail-order executive. Foley's (department store), Houston, Tex., buyer, 1953-60; Neiman-Marcus (department store), Dallas, Tex., vice-president, 1960-68 and 1969-71; Design Research (home furnishings company), Cambridge, Mass., president, 1968-69; Kenton Collection (mail-order house), Dallas, president, 1971-73; Horchow Collection (mail-order house), Dallas, president, 1973—. Chairman of Georg Jensen, Inc., 1971-73; member of board of directors of Dallas Museum of Fine Arts, 1975—, American Institute of Public Service, 1976—, American Heart Association, 1977-81, National Trust for Historic Preservation, 1978—, World Wildlife Fund, Hockaday School, and Asthma and Allergy Foundation. *Military service:* U.S. Army, 1950-53; became first lieutenant. *Member:* Direct Mail/Marketing Association, Yale Club of New York City, Nantucket Yacht Club.

WRITINGS: Elephants in Your Mailbox: How I Learned the Secrets of Mail-Order Marketing Despite Having Made Twenty-five Horrendous Mistakes (autobiography), edited by A. C. Greene, Times Books, 1980; (with Patricia Linden) *Living in Style: In a Time When Taste Means More Than Money,* Rawson, Wade, 1981.

SIDELIGHTS: Besides publishing *The Horchow Collection,* a catalog that offers elegant and expensive goods to buyers around the world, Roger Horchow has produced two books, *Elephants in Your Mailbox: How I Learned the Secrets of Mail-Order Marketing Despite Having Made Twenty-five Horrendous Mistakes* and *Living in Style: In a Time When Taste Means More Than Money.* In the first book, an autobiography, Horchow recounts his business career from his beginnings as a door-to-door salesman to his present position as president of the Hor-

chow Collection, a mail-order firm specializing in luxury items. The author discusses the business lessons and disasters, anecdotes and experiences that he has encountered in his rise to success.

Christopher Lehmann-Haupt commented in *Books of the Times* that although the reader won't really learn any "tricks of the trade" while digesting the secrets and "genial ramble" that Horchow presents in *Elephants,* he will learn that there is a lot more to the mail-order business than one might think. If the book does have a flaw, the reviewer continued, it is in the author's "slight tendency toward self-importance. He looks back upon his life as if it were a pre-ordained passage to success, and finds radiant significance even in the Burpee seeds and Christmas seals he sold as a child in Columbus, Ohio." Still, Lehmann-Haupt concluded that Horchow's autobiography does contain enough curious tales to remain intriguing.

Horchow's second publication, *Living in Style,* is a primer to gracious living. In the book the author gives advice on how to develop a satisfying style, a characteristic that he believes depends more on individuality than on money. Offering glimpses of his own well-to-do lifestyle, Horchow counsels on such subjects as entertaining, home and office decorating, collecting, gift-giving, traveling, and creating more free time.

BIOGRAPHICAL/CRITICAL SOURCES: Forbes, October 30, 1978; *Books of the Times,* September, 1980.

*   *   *

HORNBY, William H(arry)   1923-

PERSONAL: Born July 14, 1923, in Kalispell, Mont.; son of Lloyd G. and Margaret E. (Miller) Hornby; married Rosemary Cross, 1947 (divorced); married Helen Schnitzler Sullivan, 1957; children: (first marriage) Margaret (deceased), Megan, Melinda; (second marriage) John, Mary, Catherine. *Education:* Stanford University, A.B., 1944, M.A., 1947; postgraduate work at University of London, 1949-50. *Politics:* Republican. *Religion:* Episcopalian. *Home:* 5300 East Mansfield, Denver, Colo. 80237. *Office:* Denver Post, 650 15th St., Denver, Colo. 80201.

CAREER/WRITINGS: San Francisco News, San Francisco, Calif., reporter and copyreader, 1947-48; Associated Press, San Francisco, reporter, 1949; Economic Cooperation Administration, Paris, France, and The Hague, Netherlands, information officer, 1950-52; Kalispell Lumber Co., Kalispell, Mont., assistant general manager, 1953-56, partner, 1955-62; *Great Falls Tribune,* Great Falls, Mont., reporter, 1957; *Denver Post,* Denver, Colo., copy-desk chief and editorial writer, 1957-60, managing editor, 1960-70, executive editor and vice-president, 1970-77, editor and vice-president, 1977—. Vice-president of Yellowstone Newspapers, Inc.; director of Schnitzler Corp., Froid, Mont., and First State Bank of Newcastle, Wyo. *Member:* American Society of Newspaper Editors (served as president), Colorado Historical Society (served as president, and on board of directors), Buffalo Bill Memorial Association (member of board of directors), Sigma Delta Chi, Sigma Nu, Denver Country Club, Elks Club.

*   *   *

HORNE, R(alph) A(lbert)   1929-

PERSONAL: Born March 10, 1929, in Haverhill, Mass.; son of Ralph L. and Flora T. (Kelly) Horne. *Education:* Massachusetts Institute of Technology, S.B., 1950; University of Vermont, M.S., 1952; Boston University, M.A., 1953; Columbia University, Ph.D., 1955; Suffolk University, J.D., 1979.

Home address: R.F.D. 3, Raymond, N.H. 03077. *Office:* Free Speech Foundation, Inc., 9 Wellington St., Boston, Mass. 02118.

CAREER: University of Vermont, Burlington, teaching assistant, 1950-52; Columbia University, New York, N.Y., teaching assistant, 1953; Brookhaven National Laboratory, Upton, N.Y., research assistant, 1953-55, postdoctoral fellow, 1955; Massachusetts Institute of Technology, Cambridge, Mass., postdoctoral fellow, 1955-57; Radio Corporation of America, Needham, Mass., senior scientist, 1957-58; Joseph Kave & Co., Cambridge, senior scientist, 1958-60; Arthur D. Little, Inc., Cambridge, member of scientific staff, 1960-69; Woods Hole Oceanographic Institution, Woods Hole, Mass., associate scientist, 1970-71; faculty member of Woods Hole Oceanographic Institution and Massachusetts Institute of Technology joint program, 1970-71; JBP Scientific Corp., Burlington, Mass., principle scientist, 1971-72; Arthur D. Little, Inc., member of scientific staff, 1972-78; GCA Corp., Bedford, Mass., senior scientist in Technology Division, 1978-80; admitted to the Bar of Massachusetts, 1979; Free Speech Foundation, Inc., Boston, Mass., founder and president, 1980—; Energy & Environmental Engineering, Inc., Cambridge, senior scientist, 1980—. Consultant to U.S. Environmental Protection Agency and U.S. Army Corps of Engineers. Lectured on the environment, energy resources, and chemistry in Japan, Canada, Israel, Puerto Rico, Hungary, and Yugoslavia.

WRITINGS: Marine Chemistry, Wiley, 1969; (editor) *Water and Aqueous Solutions,* Wiley, 1972; *The Chemistry of Our Environment,* Wiley, 1978. Contributor of about one hundred articles to scientific journals.

WORK IN PROGRESS: Subject Index to the Dialogues of Plato; The Quest for Truth in Ancient Greece; A History of the Atomic Theory; Black War, a short novel about a black overthrow of the government; *The Pool of Poison,* about a hazardous waste dump; *Solar Energy; Energy, Environment, and Resources in Developing Nations; Costly Free Speech; The Death of the Great Love Experiment;* essays about his life in Haight-Ashbury during the 1960's.

SIDELIGHTS: Horne told *CA:* "My interests are science, law (constitutional and civil rights), art (I am a painter who studied at Boston's Museum of Fine Arts School, San Francisco Art Institute, and in Florence, Italy), architecture (I design and build Victorian follies), antiques and decoration, history (ancient and nineteenth-century American), and philosophy (ancient Greek)."

Horne also told *CA* that, through his own experience as a victim of political oppression, he became committed to the defense of the First Amendment. After becoming a lawyer, at age fifty, he founded Free Speech Foundation, Inc. "The purpose of the Free Speech Foundation is to make speech truly free in our country. Our First Amendment rights will only be secure when would-be censors are afraid to ban a book or seize a film, when would-be stonewallers are afraid to file a libel suit."

*   *   *

HORNMAN, Wim   1920-

BRIEF ENTRY: Born June 21, 1920, in Tilburg, Netherlands. Dutch author. Hornman's translated works include *The Stones Cry Out: A Novel of Camilo Torres* (Lippincott, 1971). *Address:* Heereweg 132, Schoorl, Netherlands.

*   *   *

HORNSTEIN, Reuben Aaron   1912-

PERSONAL: Born December 18, 1912, in London, Ontario,

Canada; son of Morris (a contractor) and Sophia (Rosenthal) Hornstein; married Flora Burt Montgomery, October 6, 1941 (divorced); married Helen Christina MacDonald, February 11, 1956. *Education:* University of Western Ontario, B.A., 1934, M.A. (physics; with honors), 1936; University of Toronto, M.A. (meteorology), 1938. *Politics:* Independent. *Religion:* Roman Catholic. *Home:* 1074 Wellington St., Apt. 301, Halifax, Nova Scotia, Canada B3H 2Z8.

CAREER: Department of Transport, Meteorological Branch, Toronto, Ontario, meteorological forecaster at St. Hubert Airport, 1938-40, and at Malton Airport, 1939; Eastern Air Command Weather Office, Halifax, Nova Scotia, meteorologist in charge, 1940-46; Halifax Atlantic Weather Central, Halifax, meteorologist in charge, 1946-72; Canadian Broadcasting Corp. (CBC), Halifax, free-lance performer, 1972-81. Broadcaster on CBC-Radio, Halifax, 1946-60; weather reporter on CBC-TV, Halifax, 1954-81.

MEMBER: Canadian Association of Physicists, Canadian Meteorological and Oceanographic Society, Association of Canadian Television and Radio Artists, American Association for the Advancement of Science, Royal Meteorological Society (fellow), Nova Scotia Institute of Science, Ashburn Golf and Country Club, Saraguay Club. *Awards, honors:* Member of Order of the British Empire, 1946; Patterson Medal from Canadian Meteorological and Oceanographic Society, 1962; named honorary Big Brother by Big Brothers of Dartmouth-Halifax, 1976-77; special merit award from Federal Institute of Management, 1977.

WRITINGS: Weather Facts and Fancies, Queen's Printer, 1949; *It's in the Wind,* Queen's Printer, 1950; *Weather and Why,* Queen's Printer, 1954; *The Weather Book,* Harper, 1980; *Apres la pluie, le beau temps* (title means "After the Rain, Fine Weather"), Environnement Canada, 1981. Contributor of about twenty-five articles to scientific journals.

SIDELIGHTS: Hornstein commented: "My desire to inform the public, in popular terminology, about the science of meteorology led to the initiation of radio talks in 1946. They were carried for thirteen years as a weekly series on a regional network of the Canadian Broadcasting Corporation, with a separate series running for ten years on the national network. This led naturally into a television career as a meteorologist, then host and interviewer, beginning in 1954. I do the very best I possibly can at whatever activity I undertake and hope it will be of benefit to the greatest possible number of citizens.

"Regarding my work in progress in 1982: I plan to reassess my future activities and may devote myself almost exclusively to writing. If so, it will be a solitary effort with no co-authors and may be directed more specifically at journalism rather than book publication, although some vague ideas regarding the latter are also germinating."

*   *   *

HORTON, Paul Chester   1942-

PERSONAL: Born January 29, 1942, in Cincinnati, Ohio; son of Paul Chester, Sr. (a teacher) and Elizabeth Pauline (Rice) Horton; married Mary Kathryn Kuphal, September 11, 1965; children: Paul Andrey, Alexander Robert. *Education:* University of Minnesota, B.A. (magna cum laude), 1964, M.D., 1968. *Home:* 570 Redstone Dr., Cheshire, Conn. 06410. *Office:* 234 Hobart St., Meriden, Conn. 06450.

CAREER: Cincinnati General Hospital, Cincinnati, Ohio, intern, 1968-69; University of Michigan, Ann Arbor, resident in psychiatry, 1969-71; Yale University, Psychiatric Institute,

New Haven, Conn., resident in psychiatry, 1971-72; private practice of psychiatry, 1974—. Studied and served as clinical associate at Western New England Institute for Psychoanalysis, 1974-78; assistant clinical professor at Yale University, 1974-76; member of faculty at University of Connecticut, 1978-79. Consulting psychiatrist at Meriden Family and Child Guidance Clinic, 1980—. *Military service:* U.S. Navy, 1972-74; served as staff psychiatrist; became lieutenant commander. *Member:* American Psychiatric Association, Authors Guild. *Awards, honors:* Seymour Lustman Prize from Yale University School of Medicine Department of Psychiatry, 1972, for paper, "The Mystical Experience as a Transitional Phenomenon."

WRITINGS: Solace: The Missing Dimension in Psychiatry, University of Chicago Press, 1981. Contributor to psychiatry journals.

WORK IN PROGRESS: A book on the politics of solace, publication expected in 1983; a formal study of successor transitional objects from ages three to seventeen.

SIDELIGHTS: Horton told *CA:* "Undergraduate studies in philosophy sensitized me to the issues that became an integral part of my book, *Solace,* as did specific studies of solacing objects begun during my psychiatric residence at Yale University and carried on as a staff psychiatrist in the Navy.

"The need for psychological comfort is the most basic, most important human need. Paradoxically, it is also the need most neglected by the mental health professions. I should like to help psychiatry, in particular, to recognize the need for solace and to accord it the importance it requires in meeting the needs of people in distress."

* * *

HOTHEM, Lar(ry Lee) 1938-

PERSONAL: Born July 26, 1938, in Fresno, Ohio; son of Luther Clark and Edith Irene (Maurer) Hothem; married Caroline Della Morte, 1964 (divorced, 1972); married Sue McClurg (a media specialist), June 25, 1976. *Education:* Attended College of Wooster, 1956-59; Ohio State University, B.S., 1962. *Politics:* Independent. *Religion:* Agnostic. *Home and office:* 65 Oberle, Carroll, Ohio 43112.

CAREER: Social worker, 1962-64; owner of sporting goods business, 1964-73. *Military service:* Ohio Army National Guard, 1959-65. *Member:* Artifact Society, Central States Archaeological Society, Ohio Archaeological Society, Ohio Historical Society.

WRITINGS: Collector's Guide to Indian Artifacts, Books Americana, 1978, 2nd edition, 1980; *Collector's Guide to Antiques,* Books Americana, 1980; *Farm Collectibles (Antiques),* Books Americana, 1982. Author of introduction to *American Indian Pottery,* by Jack Barry, 1980. Contributor to *Encyclopedia of Collectibles.* Contributor of more than five hundred articles to national and regional magazines. Contributing editor of *Antiques Journal.*

WORK IN PROGRESS: A book on finding and collecting prehistoric artifacts.

SIDELIGHTS: Hothem commented: "As a writer and photographer I have traveled in fifty-four countries, including all of Europe, the Middle East, and Central and South America. My interests include pre-Columbian and prehistoric cultures, antiques and collectibles of all kinds, and collecting most associated objects. A main preoccupation is with the past and how it determines the present, and the process of change, both positive and negative aspects. I want to convey in print im-

portant, but little-known, glimpses of other times, other things. We can learn from all this. Also, I would like to see writers—myself included—use fewer big words and more great ideas."

* * *

HOUBLON, Doreen (Lindsay) Archer
See ARCHER HOUBLON, Doreen (Lindsay)

* * *

HOUSE, John William 1919-

PERSONAL: Born September 15, 1919, in Bradford, England; son of John Albert and Eveline (Brunton) House; married Eva Timm, February 21, 1942; children: Katherine Ann Brunton House Carmody, John Richard Brunton, Elizabeth Mary House Harrison, Edward Mayland. *Education:* Jesus College, Oxford, B.A., 1940, M.A., 1946, D.Litt., 1980. *Religion:* Anglican. *Home:* 38 North St., Islip, Oxfordshire OX5 2SQ, England. *Office:* St. Peter's College, Oxford University, Oxford OX1 2DL, England.

CAREER: University of Durham, Durham, England, lecturer, 1946-58, senior lecturer, 1958-61, reader in applied geography, 1961-63; University of Newcastle upon Tyne, Newcastle upon Tyne, England, professor of geography, 1964-74; Oxford University, St. Peter's College, Oxford, England, Halford Mackinder Professor of Geography, 1974—. Member of Northern Economic Planning Council, 1966-75, and Northern Pennines Rural Development Board, 1967-70. *Military service:* British Army, Intelligence Corps, 1940-46; became major; received Medaille de la Reconnaissance Francaise. *Member:* Royal Geographical Society (fellow), Institute of British Geographers (vice-president, 1982-83; president, 1983-84). *Awards, honors:* Murchison Award from Royal Geographical Society, 1970.

WRITINGS: (With Brian Fullerton) *Teesside at Mid-Century,* Macmillan, 1960; (editor and contributor) *Northern Geographical Essays,* Oriel, 1966; *Industrial Britain: The North East,* David & Charles, 1969; (editor and contributor) *The United Kingdom Space: Resources, Environment, and the Future,* Weidenfeld & Nicolson, 1974, 3rd edition, 1982; *France: An Applied Geography,* Methuen, 1978; *Frontier on the Rio Grande,* Oxford University Press, 1982; (editor and contributor) *The Geography of U.S. Policies,* Oxford University Press, 1983.

WORK IN PROGRESS: Political Geography of the Indian Ocean; The TransNational Frontier Region.

SIDELIGHTS: House wrote: "I am interested in the application of geographical analysis, in an operational sense, to the study of contemporary economic, social, and political problems. From a local/regional focus this has developed into national, international, and global perspectives. The belief is that the geographer as social scientist must be both scholar and man of action. My own career has included extensive travel and residence abroad, including Texas, 1977-78, Illinois, 1970, Nebraska, 1962-63, and Australia, 1976."

* * *

HOUSMAN, Laurence 1865-1959

BRIEF ENTRY: Born July 18, 1865, in Bromsgrove, England; died February 20, 1959, in Shepton Mallet, England. British novelist, playwright, and illustrator. Housman wrote over one hundred plays, more than thirty of which were banned by the British censor for their treatment of Biblical characters or British royalty. His concern for religious subjects ran through most of his work, from "Bethlehem" (1902) to "Palestine Plays" (1943). Among his most popular works were "Victoria Regina" (1935), which contained ten short plays about Queen Victoria, and "The Little Plays of St. Francis" (1922). In the latter critics found the best examples of Housman's humor, cynicism, and intense individualism. Housman also wrote more than one hundred novels, fairy tales, and books of verse, many self-illustrated. His short poems, though often considered "erotic metaphors," were popular as simple, romantic verses, saved from sentimentality by his talent for the pointed epigram. *Biographical/critical sources: Twentieth Century Authors: A Biographical Dictionary of Modern Literature,* H. W. Wilson, 1942; *Who's Who in Twentieth Century Literature,* Holt, 1976.

* * *

HOWARD, Don (Marcel) 1940-

PERSONAL: Born July 19, 1940, in Mountain View, Mo.; son of John Whalen (a mechanic) and Fannie (a writer and artist; maiden name, Yankee) Howard; married Kazuko Washio, January, 1961 (divorced, 1980); married Susan Wheeler (a secretary), October 3, 1980; children: (first marriage) John Kenichi; (second marriage) Andrew Lawrence, Sarah Dianne. *Education:* Attended Roman Catholic high school in Pomona, Calif. *Politics:* "Independent conservative." *Religion:* "Nonaffiliated Christian." *Home:* 7404 Archibald Ave., Rancho Cucamonga, Calif. 91730. *Agent:* Heacock Literary Agency, 1121 Lake St., Venice, Calif. 90291. *Office:* Fleet Analysis Center, Corona, Calif.

CAREER: U.S. Postal Service, Ontario, Calif., postal clerk, 1966-68; construction worker in southern California, 1968-75; Fleet Analysis Center, Corona, painter, 1975-79, illustrator, 1978—. Little League manager. *Military service:* U.S. Air Force, radio traffic analyst, 1957-65.

WRITINGS: Moving Dirt (juvenile novel), Scholastic Book Services, 1978. Contributor to magazines, including *True Experience.*

WORK IN PROGRESS: The Boy Who Wouldn't Quit (tentative title), a juvenile adventure novel; adult suspense novels.

SIDELIGHTS: Howard told *CA:* "I've been a writer since I was a child in elementary school, but didn't become serious about writing until 1975, when *True Experience* purchased one of the short stories I'd written to amuse myself during a period of unemployment. Lydia Paglio, former editor of the magazine, provided the inspiration and motivation for writing professionally. She bought several dozen short stories over the ensuing five years and taught me how to work with an editor and under a monthly deadline.

"During those years of writing for the confession markets, I was also working on full-length novels, and when *Moving Dirt* was published in 1978, I realized I was weary of writing to the confession formula. I wanted to write suspense novels, a genre in which I could let my imagination soar and in which the rewards could be much greater and more satisfying.

"Perhaps because I am an artist and illustrator as well as a writer, I write in a very visual manner, literally 'seeing' the scenes and characters as I write about them. My stories are filled with action and movement, with few long, expository passages either from author or characters, and are aimed at the sort of reader who enjoys John D. McDonald, Stephen King, R. Lance Hill, Justin Scott, and other writers of their ilk. My goal is to entertain the reader for a few hours with suspenseful, action-packed, fast-paced yarns of terror and danger, peopled by likable, believable, recognizable characters. Greater writers

than I will produce the literature of these times; I simply want to entertain."

BIOGRAPHICAL/CRITICAL SOURCES: Weaponeer, December, 1980.

* * *

HOWARD-WILLIAMS, Jeremy (Napier) 1922-

PERSONAL: Born March 13, 1922, in Cowes, Isle of Wight, England; married in 1951; children: two sons, one daughter. *Education:* Attended Institut de Touraine, 1939, and Royal Air Force Staff College, 1952. *Home:* Rassendyll, Havelock Rd., Warsash, Southampton, Hampshire, England.

CAREER: Royal Air Force, career officer (pilot), 1940-58, served in Nightfighter squadron, 1942-43, Central Fighter's Establishment 1943-47, Auxiliary Air Force, 1947-49, stationed at Air Headquarters Singapore 1949-53, served in Germany, 1953-55, air attache in Paris, 1955-58, leaving service as squadron leader; Ratsey & Lapthorn (sailmakers), Cowes, Isle of Wight, England, manager, 1959-65; Cheverton Workboats (boat builders), Cowes, sales director, 1965-66; Morgan Giles Ltd. (motorboat builders), Warsash, England, sales director, 1967-70; Langston Marine (yacht builders), Havant, England, sales director, 1970-73; Adlard Coles Ltd. (publisher), St. Albans, England, managing editor, 1974-82, consulting editor, 1982—. Proprietor of Water-Wise, 1964—. Lecturer on sails, sailmaking, yacht racing, and military history. Member of Mosquito Museum. *Member:* Royal Yachting Association, Royal Air Force Sailing Association (life member), Royal Air Force Club, Island Sailing Club. *Awards, honors—*Military: Distinguished Flying Cross.

WRITINGS: Teach Your Child About Sailing, Arthur Pearson, 1963; *Sails,* Adlard Coles, 1967, De Fraff, 1968, 5th edition, 1983; *Dinghy Sails,* Adlard Coles, 1971, 2nd edition, 1978, Dodd, 1979; *Offshore Crew,* Adlard Coles, 1973, 2nd edition, 1979, Dodd, 1979; *Night Intruder,* David & Charles, 1975; *Care and Repair of Sails,* Sail Books, 1976; *Practical Pilotage for Yachtsmen,* Adlard Coles, 1977, 2nd edition, 1981. Contributor to sailing magazines in the United States, England, Europe, and Japan, and to *Aeroplane Monthly;* ghost writer of two books on sailing.

WORK IN PROGRESS: Research on new kinds of sailcloth.

SIDELIGHTS: Howard-Williams's books have been translated into Dutch, German, Italian, Russian, Japanese, Spanish, and Swedish. He told *CA:* "For some years *Sails* was the only work on the subject in the English language, and I like to think it led the awakening to the importance of the subject among racing yachtsmen. I like to do my creative writing starting at four o'clock in the morning—the mind is fresh then and there are no distractions."

* * *

HOWER, Edward 1941-

PERSONAL: Born January 10, 1941, in New York, N.Y.; son of Virgil Allen and Dorothy (Condit) Hower; children: Daniel Pablo, Jenifer Yolanda. *Education:* Cornell University, B.A., 1963; University of California, Los Angeles, M.A., 1971. *Home:* 1409 Hanshaw Rd., Ithaca, N.Y. 14850. *Agent:* Liz Darhansoff, 70 East 91st St., New York, N.Y. 10028. *Office:* Gannet Center, Ithaca College, Ithaca, N.Y. 14850.

CAREER: Kenyatta College, Nairobi, Kenya, education officer, 1964-66; youth counselor for New York State Division for Youth, 1967-68 and 1971-75; Ithaca College, Ithaca, N.Y., instructor, 1975—. Instructor at Cornell University, summer, 1981. Television entertainer in Nairobi. Member of Amnesty International. *Awards, honors:* Writing grants from National Endowment for the Arts, 1976-77, and New York State Council of the Arts, 1981; residency fellowship from Fine Arts Work Center of Provincetown, Mass., 1980-81.

WRITINGS: Kikuyu Woman (short fiction), Coalition of Publishers for Employment, 1979; *The New Life Hotel,* Avon, 1980. Contributor of stories, poetry, and articles to periodicals, including *Epoch, Atlantic Monthly, Cornell Review, Transatlantic Review, Transition,* and *East Africa Review.*

WORK IN PROGRESS: A novel.

SIDELIGHTS: Hower's first novel, *The New Life Hotel,* is the tale of two African women living amid the political and social turmoil in modern East Africa. The book, according to *New York Times Book Review* critic Todd Watson, ''is a beautifully rendered story about the terrifying and complex world they discover.''

BIOGRAPHICAL/CRITICAL SOURCES: New York Times Book Review, January 14, 1980.

* * *

HOYT, Erich 1950-

PERSONAL: Born Spetember 28, 1950, in Akron, Ohio; son of Robert Emmett (a writer and television producer) and Betty Jane (an editor and public relations representative; maiden name, Shutrump) Hoyt. *Education:* Attended high school in Prairie du Chien, Wis. *Agent:* Katinka Matson, John Brockman Associates, Inc., 2307 Broadway, New York, N.Y. 10024. *Office:* 6400 rue De Gaspe, Montreal, Quebec, Canada H2S 2X7.

CAREER: Studio, outdoor, and nature photographer in Toronto, Ontario, and Victoria, British Columbia, 1968-70; farmer near Nelson, British Columbia, 1970-73; documentary filmmaker in Vancouver, British Columbia, 1973-75; writer and photographer in Vancouver and Montreal, Quebec, 1975—. Owner and operator of a record store in Victoria, 1969-70; film score composer in Vancouver, 1973-78.

WRITINGS: The Whale Called Killer (nonfiction), Dutton, 1981.

Co-author of ''Cries and Whistles'' (radio play), first broadcast by Canadian Broadcasting Corp., 1981. Contributing editor to *Equinox* (Magazine), 1982—. Contributor to magazines, including *National Wildlife, Oceans, Defenders, Diver, Pacific Discovery,* and *Canadian Geographic,* and newspapers.

WORK IN PROGRESS: Research for a book on natural history and expeditions in British Columbia, and a book about a hyperkinetic child.

SIDELIGHTS: Hoyt commented: ''To really get inside an idea or subject I live with it for months, sometimes years, before writing anything. It helps me to play with the material, to rephrase it in many forms. While I was living some eight summers with three family groups (or pods) of killer whales off northern Vancouver Island, I wrote about them, photographed them, made films, and recorded their eerie underwater sounds, which were then incorporated into electronic musical compositions. Killer whales are extraordinary creatures, possessing massive complex brains and equally complex social systems; they are also fearsome pack predators with no enemies in the sea. For me, they become a metaphor for humans and our own supreme yet precarious position on the planet. We are all threatened by food and habitat shortages, and global pollution. My future work will be about exploring and expeditions

to the forgotten or the undiscovered, whether these are people, places, or ideas.''

BIOGRAPHICAL/CRITICAL SOURCES: Publishers Weekly, June 26, 1981; *Discover,* September, 1981; *Westworld,* September, 1981; *Montreal Gazette,* October 17, 1981; *Akron Beacon Journal,* October 25, 1981; *Detroit Free Press,* November 6, 1981; *Toronto Globe and Mail,* January 16, 1982; *Seattle Times,* March 7, 1982.

* * *

HRABAL, Bohumil 1914-

PERSONAL: Born March 28, 1914, in Brno, Czechoslovakia. *Education:* Attended Charles University (Prague). *Home:* Na Hrazi 24, Prague 8-Liben, Czechoslovakia.

CAREER: Employed as lawyer's clerk, railway worker, insurance agent, salesman, foundry worker, paper salvage worker, stage hand, and stage extra, 1939-62; writer, 1962—. *Awards, honors:* Klement Gottwald State Prize, 1968; Academy Award for best foreign language film from Academy of Motion Picture Arts and Sciences, 1967, for ''Closely Watched Trains.''

WRITINGS—In English: *Ostre sledovane vlaky* (novella), Ceskoslovensky Spisovatel, 1965, translation by Edith Pargeter published as *Closely Watched Trains,* Grove, 1968 (published in England as *A Close Watch on the Trains,* Cape, 1968); *Automat svet* (stories; contains ''Romance,'' ''Palaverers,'' ''Angel Eyes,'' ''A Dull Afternoon,'' ''Evening Course,'' ''The Funeral,'' ''The Notary,'' ''At the Sign of the Greentree,'' ''Diamond Eyes,'' ''A Prague Nativity,'' ''Little Eman,'' ''The Death of Mr. Baltisberger,'' ''The World Cafeteria,'' and ''Want to See Golden Prague?''), Mlada Fronta, 1966, translation by Michael Henry Heim published as *The Death of Mr. Baltisberger,* introduction translated by Kaca Polackova, Doubleday, 1975; ''The World Cafeteria'' (short story; also see above), published in *Czech and Slovak Short Stories,* edited by Jeanne Nemcova, Oxford University Press, 1968.

(With Jiri Menzel) ''Ostre sledovane vlaky'' (film adapted from his novella with the same title; see above), Barrandov Film Studio, 1967, released in the United States as ''Closely Watched Trains,'' Sigma III, 1968 (released in England as ''Closely Observed Trains,'' 1968), translation of film script by Joseph Holzbecher published as *Closely Watched Trains,* Simon & Schuster, 1971 (published in England as *Closely Observed Trains,* Lorrimer, 1971).

Fiction: *Perlicka na dne* (stories; title means ''Pearl at the Bottom''; includes ''Baron Prasil'' and ''Krtiny 1947'' [title means ''Christening 1947'']), Ceskoslovensky Spisovatel, 1964; *Pabitete* (title means ''Palaverers''), Mlada Fronta, 1964, also published in *Automat svet* (see above); *Tanecni hodiny pro starsi a pokrocile* (novella; title means ''Dancing Lessons for Adults and Advanced''), Ceskoslovensky Spisovatel, 1964, *Inzerat na dum, ve kterem uz nechci bydlet* (stories; title means ''An Advertisement for a House in Which I Don't Want to Live Anymore''), Mlada Fronta, 1965; *Morytaty a legendy* (novella; title means ''These Premises Are in the Joint Care of Citizens''), Ceskoslovensky Spisovatel, 1968; *Postriziny* (title means ''Shortcut''), Ceskoslovensky Spisovatel, 1976.

Films: (With Ivan Passer) ''Fadni odpoledne'' (adapted from his short story, ''A Dull Afternoon''; also see above), Barrandov Film Studio, 1965, released in the United States as ''A Boring Afternoon,'' 1968; ''Postriziny'' (adapted from his work with the same title; also see above).

Other: (Editor) *Vybor z ceske prczy* (anthology), Mlada Fronta, 1967; *Toto mesto je ve spoleane peci obyvatel; montaz* (nonfiction), photographs by Miroslav Peterka, Ceskoslovensky Spisovatel, 1967; *Slavnosti snezenek,* Ceskoslovensky Spisovatel, 1978.

SIDELIGHTS: After training for a career in law, Bohumil Hrabal was unable to practice his profession during the Nazi occupation of his homeland. Forced to work at a variety of odd jobs, Hrabal was forty-eight before he began his career as a writer. His stories, though written in a colloquial, rambling style, are complex and sophisticated tales of ordinary individuals compelled to cope with forces that are essentially beyond their control. While confronting the vagaries of human existence, Hrabal's characters reveal warmly human qualities that contrast with the cold indifference of the world in which they live. What is more, observed Kvetoslav Chvatik in *Orientace,* "Hrabal's people . . . are able to see new, hitherto unsuspected, aspects of reality, allowing them to marvel at the inexhaustible miracles of a world that has been thrown off its bearings." In Hrabal's introduction to his first collection of short stories, *Perlicka na dne* ("Pearl at the Bottom"), "he attests that he has glimpsed at the bottom of these figures a pearl, that is, something pure and rare that gives us pleasure," wrote Milan Jungmann in *Oblehani Troje.*

Czech authorities, however, found Hrabal's characters too "unconstructive," theorized Jungmann, for in the wake of the invasion of Czechoslovakia by the Soviet Union and the Warsaw Pact allies in 1968, all of Hrabal's existing books were destroyed and his subsequent writings were suppressed. Hrabal was not rehabilitated by the government until 1976. Consequently, for about eight years Czechs had no access to Hrabal's works except in underground editions.

Hrabal became known in the United States in 1967 when an Academy Award for best foreign language film was conferred upon the motion picture adaptation of his novella, *Closely Watched Trains.* The book, set in Nazi-occupied Czechoslovakia, tells the story of a young railroad employee who becomes anxious to prove his manhood, especially when inexperience and youthful nervousness cause him to fail during a romantic encounter with a pretty young woman. Though known for its wit and humor, the book also contains an underlying sense of violence and impending tragedy that finally erupts when the young man is killed while attempting to blow up a German ammunition train. A *Times Literary Supplement* writer explained, "The blend of stoic and epicurean remains consistent to the conclusion of this witty, comprehensive tale, seeing the necessary murders of warfare through the eyes of Falstaff and Hotspur at once."

The internationally successful film adaptation of the novella, written by Hrabal and director Jiri Menzel, was praised by several critics, including *New York Times* reviewer Bosley Crowther, *Punch* writer Richard Mallett, and *Movies Into Film* author John Simon. "The charm of [this] film," said Crowther, "in in the quietness and slyness of [its] earthy comedy, the wonderful finesse of understatements, the wise and humorous understanding of primal sex." Mallett also applauded the film's humor, adding that the "wittily written" motion picture "is as gay as a character comedy and very much funnier than most." Impressed with the "fine screenplay" by Hrabal and Menzel, Simon maintained that "the best thing about 'Closely Watched Trains' is that it impresses one as unique, indebted only to its individual genius."

Hrabal collaborated also with director Ivan Passer on the screen adaptation of his short story, "A Boring Afternoon" (also translated as "A Dull Afternoon"). The film is set in a tavern where some older patrons reveal their resentment of the indif-

ference of the young. The picture was released in the United States in 1968.

Another of Hrabal's works that has become available to American readers is *The Death of Mr. Baltisberger,* a collection of fourteen short stories based upon tales told in the beer halls of Prague. "In these stories," wrote Igor Hajek of *Times Literary Supplement,* "Hrabal is as strong, sparkling and invigorating as Pilsner Urquell." Commenting on the author's method, Thomas Lask of the *New York Times Book Review* observed that Hrabal writes "with a splendid ear for the trivia, the ephemera that make up so much of our discourse." "The key to Hrabal," he added, "is that though the details are always realistic, the uses he puts them to are not." According to Hajek, "Hrabal has his own particular way of looking at or reading the world, of exposing aspects of character or reality one hadn't thought of. It is a quasi-surrealist method, in which everything depends on an extraordinary angle of perception." Though admitting that weaknesses occasionally appear in Hrabal's work, Hajek insisted that in *The Death of Mr. Baltisberger,* they "are avoided with bravura."

In 1976, after assuring the government of his support, Hrabal was granted permission to publish *Postriziny,* a semi-fictional work based upon his parents' lives. The first printing of twenty thousand copies sold out in less than two hours. Since his rehabilitation Hrabal has also published *Slavnosti snezenek.*

BIOGRAPHICAL/CRITICAL SOURCES: Jiri Hajek, *Lidska situace,* Ceskoslovensky Spisovatel, 1966; *Orientace,* No. 6, 1966; *Punch,* May 15, 1968; *Listener,* July 11, 1968; *Times Literary Supplement,* July 25, 1968, May 20, 1977; Milan Jungmann, *Oblehani Troje,* Ceskoslovensky Spisovatel, 1969; *Observer,* December 21, 1969; Milada Souckova, *A Literary Satellite,* University of Chicago Press, 1970; John Simon, *Movies Into Film: Film Criticism, 1967-1970,* Dial, 1971; *Atlantic Monthly,* February, 1975; *Virginia Quarterly Review,* autumn, 1975; *New York Times Book Review,* October 5, 1975; *Contemporary Literary Criticism,* Volume 13, Gale, 1980.*

—*Sketch by Susan M. Trosky*

*   *   *

HUCKABY, Elizabeth (Paisley)   1905-

PERSONAL: Born April 14, 1905, in Hamburg, Ariz.; daughter of Henry Lewis (a Presbyterian minister) and Elizabeth (Merrell) Paisley; married Glendon T. Huckaby (a junior high school principal), August 16, 1933 (deceased). *Education:* University of Arkansas, B.A., 1926, M.A., 1930. *Home:* 307 Fairfax Ave., Little Rock, Ark. 72205.

CAREER: High school English teacher in Fort Smith, Ark., 1926-28, junior high school English teacher and department chairman, 1928-29; Little Rock Central High School, Little Rock, Ark., English teacher, 1930-47, girls' vice-principal, 1947-69; writer, 1969—. Member of Little Rock Family Service Board in the 1950's. *Member:* National Education Association (life member), National Retired Teachers Association, National Wildlife Federation, Arkansas Council of Parents and Teachers (life member), Arkansas Retired Teachers Association (life member). *Awards, honors:* Arkansiana Award from Arkansas Library Association, 1981, for *Crisis at Central High, 1957-1958.*

WRITINGS: Crisis at Central High, 1957-1958, Louisiana State University Press, 1980.

WORK IN PROGRESS: A sequel to *Crisis at Central High, 1957-1958,* covering the years 1958-59.

SIDELIGHTS: Elizabeth Huckaby wrote: "*Crisis at Central High* was written during the years immediately following the initial desegregation of Central High School at Little Rock, Arkansas, from notes made during that crisis. I had recorded the events because I realized that they were recognized as historic: a part of the explosive sociological changes in the South. The confrontation of state and federal authorities that caused President Eisenhower to send the 101st Airborne unit to enforce the rulings of the federal courts was unprecedented. *Crisis at Central High* is the 'inside the school' account of events that accompanied the well-documented public happenings.

"I did not try to find a publisher immediately, for feelings were too high in Little Rock; the city was too divided on the issue for me to continue teaching if I had published such an account at the time. Only after I was ready to retire did I try—unsuccessfully—to find a publisher. All thought my story came 'too late.'

"But one person who had read the book as it was being rejected mentioned it to an executive of Time-Life Films. Eventually it was produced as a 'docu-drama' for television. The film, with Joanne Woodward playing Elizabeth Huckaby, was broadcast by CBS-TV, February 4, 1981. While the film was being made, the book was published. One great pleasure for me has been the response of many former students, by mail and telephone, to both book and film.

"Now I have begun assembling material for a report of the 1958-59 school year at Central High, a year in which all secondary public schools in Little Rock were closed as the result of the continuing effort of the state administration to avoid desegregation. That year, since no children attended Central (though teachers, under contract, attended daily) may not be interesting enough to draw a reading audience, but I feel it should be chronicled at least for local history. Parents, deprived of an education for their children, and businessmen, who found that their community was being ruined economically, organized the next year to reopen the schools—desegregated."

AVOCATIONAL INTERESTS: The outdoors and the woods, New York theatre and its music, volunteer work teaching illiterate people to read, travel (including Europe, the Soviet Union, and China).

* * *

HUEY, F. B., Jr. 1925-

PERSONAL: Born January 12, 1925, in Denton, Tex.; son of F. B. (in insurance) and Gwendolyn (Chambers) Huey; married Nonna Turner, December 22, 1950; children: Mary Anne, Linda Kaye, William David. *Education:* University of Texas, B.B.A., 1945; Southwestern Baptist Theological Seminary, M.Div., 1958, Th.D., 1961; Ph.D., 1979. *Home:* 6128 Whitman, Fort Worth, Tex. 76133. *Office:* Department of Old Testament, Southwestern Baptist Theological Seminary, 2001 West Seminary, Fort Worth, Tex. 76122.

CAREER: Ordained Baptist minister, 1956; Security National Life Insurance Co., Denton, Tex., accountant, 1947-55; pastor of Baptist churches in Bolivar, Texas, 1956-61; Southern Baptist Convention, Foreign Mission Board, Richmond, Va., missionary in Rio de Janeiro, Brazil, 1961-66; professor of Old Testament at South Brazil Baptist Theological Seminary, 1961-66; Southwestern Baptist Theological Seminary, Fort Worth, Tex., professor of Old Testament, 1965—. *Member:* National Association of Baptist Professors of Religion, Society of Biblical Studies, Theta Xi, Delta Sigma Pi, Beta Gamma Sigma.

WRITINGS: (Contributor) C. W. Scudder, editor, *Crises in Morality,* Broadman, 1964; *Exodus: A Study Guide Commentary,* Zondervan, 1977; *Yesterday's Prophets for Today's World,* Broadman, 1980; *Jeremiah: Bible Study Commentary,* Zondervan, 1981; *Numbers: Bible Study Commentary,* Zondervan, 1981. Co-translator of *New American Standard Bible.* Contributor to *Pictorial Encyclopedia of the Bible.* Contributor to theology journals.

WORK IN PROGRESS: Commentaries on Ruth and Esther for *The Expositor's Bible Commentary,* for Zondervan.

* * *

HUGHES, Dean 1943-

PERSONAL: Born August 24, 1943, in Ogden, Utah; son of Emery T. (a government worker) and Lorraine (Pierce) Hughes; married Kathleen Hurst (a teacher and business manager), November 23, 1966; children: Tom, Amy, Robert. *Education:* Weber State College, B.A. (cum laude), 1967; University of Washington, M.A., 1968, Ph.D., 1972; postdoctoral study at Stanford University, summer, 1975, and Yale University, summer, 1978. *Politics:* "Lean towards Democrats." *Religion:* Mormon. *Home and office:* 1466 West 1100 N., Provo, Utah 84604.

CAREER: Roosevelt Hotel, Seattle, Wash., bellman, 1967-72; Central Missouri State University, Warrensburg, associate professor of English, 1972-80; Brigham Young University, Provo, Utah, part-time visiting professor, 1980—; writer, part-time editor, and consultant, 1980—. Consultant to Shipley Associates (technical writing company). Guest author, speaker, and workshop leader at writing conferences. *Member:* Children's Literature Association, Society of Children's Book Writers, Authors Guild. *Awards, honors:* National Endowment for the Humanities summer seminar stipend, 1975 and 1978; Outstanding Faculty Achievement Award from Central Missouri State University, 1980; Children's Book Award nomination for *Nutty for President.*

WRITINGS: *Under the Same Stars* (historical novel), Deseret, 1979; *As Wide as the River* (historical novel), Deseret, 1980; *Romance and Psychological Realism in William Godwin's Novels,* Arno, 1981; *Nutty for President* (juvenile novel), illustrated by Blanche Sims, Atheneum, 1981; *Hooper Haller* (novel), Deseret, 1981; *Honestly, Myron* (juvenile novel; illustrated by Martha Westory), Atheneum, 1982; *Switching Tracks* (novel), Atheneum, 1982; *Millie Willenheimer and the Chestnut Corporation* (juvenile novel), Atheneum, 1983. Contributor of articles, reviews, and poems to numerous periodicals, including *Dickens Studies Newsletter, Blackwater Review, Dialogue, English Journal,* and *Averett Journal.*

WORK IN PROGRESS: A sequel to *As Wide as the River;* a historical novel on Nauvoo, Illinois; *Jenny Haller,* a sequel to *Hooper Haller;* a novel for teenagers "based on my experience as a bellman."

SIDELIGHTS: A native of Utah, Dean Hughes often profiles Mormons in his novels. His first two books, *Under the Same Stars* and *As Wide as the River,* trace the life of the fictitious Williams family, early Mormons driven out of Jackson County, Missouri, because of their religious practices. A Mormon baseball player is featured in *Hooper Haller.*

Also the author of novels for children, Hughes wrote *Nutty for President,* dealing with William Bilks, a fifth-grader who persuades the class "goof off," "Nutty" Nutsell, to run for school president. During the campaign William discovers Nutty's hidden talents, transforming Nutty from a bumbler into a confident leader. Another novel, *Honestly, Myron,* concerns a fifth-grader who wants to be a great man, such as Abraham Lincoln. The boy begins telling the truth at *all* times, soon finding himself in many sticky situations. *Switching Tracks,* unlike Hughes's other juvenile novels, is written in a serious tone and describes the anguish of a young teen as he deals with the suicide of his father and the comfort he finds from an older gentleman in his neighborhood.

Hughes told *CA:* "In 1980 I took a leave of absence from teaching and wrote full time. I wrote and sold five books in that year. I extended my leave, and now I plan to stay with full-time writing, although I do some editing and teach technical writing. I try to raise serious questions for young readers, often in the context of a humorous book. How does America elect its leaders? Is honesty really possible? Can you avoid greed in business? These are some of the kinds of questions I have tried to get young people thinking about. Some of my books are about Mormons, but I don't think they are only *for* Mormons."

BIOGRAPHICAL/CRITICAL SOURCES: Standard-Examiner (Ogden, Utah), May 25, 1981.

*   *   *

HULL, Cary Schuler   1946-

PERSONAL: Born September 23, 1946, in Greenwich, Conn.; daughter of Stanley Carter (a writer) and Elizabeth (a writer; maiden name, Meriwether) Schuler; married Charles L. Hull (a sales engineer), September 19, 1970; children: Katherine, David. *Education:* Centenary College for Women, A.A., 1966; University of Louisville, B.A., 1968. *Politics:* Republican. *Religion:* Protestant. *Home and office:* 10 East Liberty St., Chester, Conn. 06412.

CAREER: Redbook, New York City, first reader and secretary, 1968-70, assistant editor in fiction department, 1970-71, associate editor, 1971, first reader in "Young Mother's Story" department, 1973—; associate editor of *Handy Andy,* 1977-81.

WRITINGS: (With father, Stanley C. Schuler) *Coal Heat,* Schiffer, 1980. Contributor of articles and reviews to magazines and newspapers.

WORK IN PROGRESS: A book on decoy carving, with William Veasey, publication by Schiffer expected in 1982.

SIDELIGHTS: Hull told *CA:* "Coal heat may be the answer to rising fuel bills."

BIOGRAPHICAL/CRITICAL SOURCES: Parents' Magazine, May, 1980.

*   *   *

HULSE, Clark   1947-

PERSONAL: Born January 1, 1947, in Pittsburgh, Pa.; son of Shirley C., Jr. (an electrical engineer) and Jane (Graham) Hulse; married Carolyn Winters (a journalist), September 5, 1969; children: Benjamin Winters, Daniel Joseph. *Education:* Williams College, B.A., 1969; Claremont Graduate School, M.A., 1970, Ph.D., 1974. *Residence:* Oak Park, Ill. *Office:* Department of English, University of Illinois, P.O. Box 4348, Chicago, Ill. 60680.

CAREER: University of Illinois at Chicago Circle, Chicago, instructor, 1972-74, assistant professor, 1974-80, associate professor of English, 1980—. *Member:* Modern Language Association of America, Renaissance Society of America. *Awards,*

honors: Fellowship from Newberry Library and National Endowment for the Humanities, 1979.

WRITINGS: Metamorphic Verse, Princeton University Press, 1981. Contributor to literature journals.

WORK IN PROGRESS: A book on poetry and painting in the English Renaissance; a monograph on the theory of inter-art analogies.

SIDELIGHTS: Hulse told *CA:* "While writing primarily for an academic audience, I keep my style as unacademic as possible. There is no need to discourage readers."

*   *   *

HUME, John Robert   1939-

PERSONAL: Born February 26, 1939, in Glasgow, Scotland; son of William (a solicitor) and Ruth (Westcott) Hume; married Hope Macnab, September 24, 1965; children: Matthew James, Kenneth John, Peter David William, Colin Angus. *Education:* University of Glasgow, B.Sc., 1961. *Office:* Department of History, University of Strathclyde, Glasgow G.1, Scotland.

CAREER: University of Strathclyde, Glasgow, Scotland, lecturer in history, 1964—. Member of Inland Waterways Amenity Advisory Council, 1975—; chairman of Seagull Trust, 1979—; member of Ancient Monuments Board of Scotland, 1981—. *Member:* Scottish Railway Preservation Society (chairman, 1966-75), Scottish Society for Industrial Archaeology, Society of Antiquaries in Scotland, Economic History Society, Newcomen Society. *Awards, honors:* Book prize from Andre Simon Memorial Fund, 1982, for *The Making of Scotch Whisky.*

WRITINGS: (With John Butt and I. L. Donnachie) *Industrial History in Pictures: Scotland,* David & Charles, 1967; (with Baron F. Duckham) *Steam Entertainment,* David & Charles, 1974; *The Industrial Archaeology of Scotland,* Blackie & Son, 1974; (with Michael Moss) *Glasgow as It Was,* Hendon Publishing, Volume I: *City Life,* 1975, Volume II: *Sports and Pastimes,* 1975, Volume III: *Glasgow at Work,* 1976; *Clyde Shipbuilding From Old Photographs,* Batsford, 1975; (with Moss) *A Plumber's Pastime,* Turner & Earnshaw, 1975; *The Industrial Archaeology of Scotland: The Lowlands and the Borders,* Batsford, 1976; *The Industrial Archaeology of Scotland: The Highlands and Islands,* Batsford, 1977; (with Moss) *The Workshop of the British Empire,* Heinemann, 1977; (with Moss) *Glasgow at War,* Volume I, Hendon Publishing, 1977; (with Moss and Donnachie) *Historic Industrial Scenes: Scotland,* Moorland Press, 1977; (with Colin Johnston) *Glasgow Railway Stations,* David & Charles, 1979; (with Moss) *Beardmore: History of a Scottish Industrial Giant,* Heinemann, 1979; (editor) *Early Days in a Dundee Mill: Extracts From the Diary of William Brown, an Early Dundee Spinner,* Abertay Historical Society, 1980; (with Moss) *Old Photographs From Scottish Country Houses,* Hendon Publishing, 1980; (with Moss) *The Making of Scotch Whisky,* James & James, 1981. Co-editor of *Transport History,* 1968-75.

WORK IN PROGRESS: A survey of Scottish industrial archaeology and history, especially engineering and the brick and tile industry.

SIDELIGHTS: Hume wrote: "Since my appointment to the staff at Strathcylde I have been actively engaged in studying the industrial history and archaeology of Scotland. I am most concerned with the importance of techniques, including their embodiment in physical remains, to a proper understanding of historical change. I also believe firmly that academics should endeavor to make their work accessible to the non-specialist, and that historians have a particular responsibility to do this.''

* * *

HUNT, Joyce 1927-

PERSONAL: Born October 31, 1927, in New York, N.Y.; daughter of Victor and Anne Wiscotch; married Irwin Hunt (in paper industry), June 25, 1950; children: Gregory, Ethan. *Education:* Brooklyn College (now of the City University of New York), B.A., 1949; Hunter College (now of the City University of New York), M.A., 1958. *Home:* 131 Riverside Dr., New York, N.Y. 10024.

CAREER: New York City public schools, teacher of children with learning and behavioral problems, 1968—.

WRITINGS—Juveniles; ''A First Look At'' series; published by Walker & Co.; all with Millicent Ellis Selsam and illustrated by Harriet Springer: *A First Look at Fish,* 1972; . . . *Leaves,* 1972; . . . *Birds,* 1973; . . . *Mammals,* 1973; . . . *Insects,* 1974; . . . *Snakes, Lizards, and Other Reptiles,* 1975; . . . *Animals Without Backbones,* 1976; . . . *Flowers,* 1976; . . . *Frogs, Toads, and Salamanders,* 1976; . . . *Animals With Backbones,* 1978; . . . *the World of Plants,* 1978; . . . *Monkeys and Apes,* 1979; . . . *Sharks,* 1979; . . . *Whales,* 1980; . . . *Cats,* 1981; . . . *Dogs,* 1981; . . . *Horses,* 1981; . . . *Dinosaurs,* 1982.

WORK IN PROGRESS: A First Look at Spiders, to be published by Walker & Co.

SIDELIGHTS: Hunt told *CA:* ''I am disgustingly enthusiastic about all aspects of life. Somehow in this world of impending doom, threatening destruction, and crumbling civilization, I manage to remain sanguine and optimistic—the result of a happy childhood and volatile marriage.

''I love kids, nature, travel, and my *Roget's Thesaurus.* I hope to indulge all to the hilt while working with my husband on a new series of nature-travel books for young children.''

* * *

HUNT, Linda 1940-

PERSONAL: Born September 3, 1940, in Spokane, Wash.; daughter of Harold and Evelyn (Roth) Christensen; married James Barton Hunt (a professor of history), February 21, 1968; children: Susan Noelle, Jefferson Kim (adopted), Krista Kimberly. *Education:* University of Washington, Seattle, B.A., 1962, graduate study, 1968; Whitworth College, M.A.T., 1978. *Residence:* Spokane, Wash. *Office:* Department of English, Whitworth College, Spokane, Wash. 99218.

CAREER: Junior high school teacher of English and social studies in Glendora, Calif., 1962-64; high school teacher of English and social studies in Edmunds, Wash., 1967-69; Young Women's Christian Association, Spokane, Wash., director of public relations and coordinator of volunteers, 1975-77; Spokane Community College, Spokane, instructor in communications, 1978-81; Whitworth College, Spokane, coordinator of freshman writing program, 1981—. Member of board of directors of Spokane Cooperative Health Plan, 1975-77. *Awards, honors:* Danforth associate, 1980.

WRITINGS: (With Marianne Frase and Doris Liebert) *Loaves and Fishes* (nonfiction), Herald Press, 1980; (with Frase and Liebert) *Celebrate the Seasons* (a children's gardening book), Herald Press, 1981. Contributor to regional and national magazines. Contributing editor of *Spokane.*

WORK IN PROGRESS: Christina's World, an inspirational account of a family and its efforts to adopt a battered foster child, with Twyla Lubben, publication expected in 1983 or 1984; *Meaning Making: A Journey Inward With Working Women,* based on in-depth interviews.

* * *

HUNT, Mabel Leigh 1892-1971

OBITUARY NOTICE—See index for *CA* sketch: Born November 1, 1892, in Coatesville, Ind.; died September 3, 1971. Author of more than thirty books for children. Most of Hunt's books focus on family relationships, although she also wrote several biographies. *Have You Seen Tom Thumb?* and *Better Known as Johnny Appleseed* were nominated for Newbery Medals. Obituaries and other sources: *Who Was Who in America, With World Notables,* Volume V: *1969-1973,* Marquis, 1973.

* * *

HUNTER, Gordon C. 1924-

PERSONAL: Born February 8, 1924, in North Bay, Ontario, Canada; son of Ernest Crossley (a minister) and Mabel Margaret (Dunbar) Hunter; married Anne Lena Olson (an artist), July 4, 1947; children: John, Jane, Stanley, Marjorie, Angela. *Education:* University of Winnipeg, B.A., 1945; University of Victoria, B.D., 1948. *Home:* 241 Avenue Rd., Richmond Hill, Ontario, Canada. *Office:* Christian Discovery, Inc., Box 535, Thornhill, Ontario, Canada.

CAREER: Ordained minister of United Church of Canada, 1948; missionary in Cariboo District, Williams Lake, British Columbia, 1948-50; pastor of United Churches of Canada in Schomberg, Ontario, 1950-53, Toronto, Ontario, 1953-67, and Willowdale, Ontario, 1972; Christian Discovery, Inc., Thornhill, Ontario, founder and president, 1973—. Executive director of Faith at Work, 1967-72; chairman of the National Project of Evangelism. *Member:* World Ashram Movement.

WRITINGS: Sing a New Tune (nonfiction), privately printed, 1958; *When the Walls Come Tumblin' Down* (nonfiction), Word Publishing, 1970; *Grace Abounding* (nonfiction), Abingdon, 1978.

WORK IN PROGRESS: Married and Free, a book on marriage.

SIDELIGHTS: Hunter told *CA:* ''My main thrust and concern is for evangelism and renewal in the local church.''

* * *

HUNTER, Leigh
See ETCHISON, Birdie L(ee)

* * *

HURD, Thacher 1949-

PERSONAL: Born March 6, 1949, in Burlington, Vt.; son of Clement G. (an illustrator of children's books) and Edith (an author of children's books; maiden name, Thacher) Hurd; married Olivia Scott (a counselor), June 12, 1976; children: Manton. *Education:* Attended University of California, Berkeley, 1967-68; California College of Arts and Crafts, B.F.A., 1972. *Home:* 2954 Hillegass, Berkeley, Calif. 94705. *Agent:* Marilyn Marlow, Curtis Brown Ltd., 575 Madison Ave., New York, N.Y. 10022.

CAREER: Grabhorn-Hoyem Press (now Arion Press), San Francisco, Calif., apprentice printer, 1967 and 1969; self-employed builder, designer, and cabinetmaker, 1972-78; California College of Arts and Crafts, Oakland, and Dominican College, San Rafael, Calif., teacher of writing and illustrating children's books; writer and illustrator of children's books, 1974—. Artist with group shows at California College of Arts and Crafts, 1972, and San Francisco World Plan Center, 1976; one-man show in Monkton, Vt., 1973. Lecturer and guest speaker at seminars and conferences.

WRITINGS—Juveniles: (With mother, Edith Thacher Hurd) *Little Dog Dreaming,* Harper, 1965; (self-illustrated) *The Old Chair,* Greenwillow, 1978; (self-illustrated) *The Quiet Evening,* Greenwillow, 1978; (self-illustrated) *Hobo Dog,* Scholastic Book Services, 1980; (self-illustrated) *Axle the Freeway Cat,* Harper, 1981.

WORK IN PROGRESS: The Mystery on the Docks, for Harper; *A Christmas Tree for Hobo Dog,* a sequel to *Hobo Dog;* a picture book based on the jazz song ''Mama Don't Allow.''

SIDELIGHTS: Speaking about writing children's literature, Thacher Hurd told Mary Ann Hogan of the *Oakland Tribune:* ''I live in the city, a lot of kids live in the city. I try to take an approach that has some kind of relevance. To do that, you try to avoid the little bunny rabbit living in the woods.''

Hurd's book *Axle the Freeway Cat* is a far cry from the ''bunny in the woods'' story. Axle is a cat who lives in an old abandoned car under a freeway overpass. By day he collects trash along the highway, and by night he plays a harmonica, serenading the passing motorists, who zip by without acknowledging the cat's musical skills. Despite his lack of recognition, however, Axle is content with his life, and he finds ultimate fulfillment when he comes to the rescue of a female cat whose sportscar malfunctions. Axle discovers his new friend is also musically inclined—she plays the car horn—and the two become close friends.

Hurd told *CA:* ''My parents worked on a number of books with Margaret Wise Brown. My mother co-authored *Five Little Firemen, Two Little Miners,* and *Two Little Gardeners,* among others. My father illustrated *Goodnight Moon, The Runaway Bunny, My World,* and a number of others that Margaret wrote. And of course my parents have done many books with each other, books that my mother wrote and my father illustrated. I think by now they have published more than one hundred books.

''I was always aware that they did books, and I have always been proud of them. There was an air of creativity around the house, and I think I always knew that I would end up doing something in the creative arts, though while I was growing up it ranged from playing in a rock band to being an English major at Berkeley, to building houses. I majored in painting at California College of Arts and Crafts, and that was the field I graduated in. I thought of myself as a painter, a 'fine artist,' and I would have rebelled at the idea of being called an illustrator, but as I look back on the paintings I did at art school, I recall people saying things to me like: 'What's the story behind this?' or 'It has a narrative quality to it.' So perhaps there were the seeds of later children's books in those pictures.

''I wasn't pushed into doing children's books by my parents. A few years after I graduated from school I just started to think in that vein. I became fascinated with the idea of telling a story in pictures, of making pictures in series that were bound together by a common thread. My parents encouraged me and gave me thoughts and ideas, but always in a very unobtrusive way.

''I'm not particularly proud of my first book efforts, which were rejected by a number of publishers. My first attempts at children's books were stiff, pale fairy tales with watery morals and dangling plots. Slowly, though, I began to think 'closer to home,' so to speak. I became aware of my own childhood memories and childlike feelings within myself. I began to realize that stories could come out of the feelings that were closest to me. My book *The Old Chair* came in this way, very simply and directly out of my own childhood feelings for the comfortable chair we had in our house when I was growing up.

''Now I find that lots of ideas come and go, and I say to myself as they come: 'Oh, I must write that down, that would be a terrific story,' but then they have gone again almost as quickly as they came, and I can't for the life of me remember what they were. Or if I do write them down, I will look at them a few months later and wonder what could have possessed me to write down such an idea. Perhaps this is because all too often they have that quality of being ideas rather than something more. These ideas have a surface quality, a contrived quality, a quality of being forced or of being too obvious. Often they are simply not true to one's feelings.

''Then there are the other kinds of ideas, the ones that spring from real feelings, that rise up as intuitions, without plot, characters, or action. Just a feeling, welling up, bubbling into consciousness from some broader field than one's limited ordinary consciousness. These are the feelings that hang around, that cling to one and won't go away. Slowly they gestate in one's mind, until they are ready to be born. Then they cry out: 'Write me! Draw me!' Six months or a year may go by before they start to come out, but when the book is ready, it seems to come of itself.''

BIOGRAPHICAL/CRITICAL SOURCES: Oakland Tribune, November 26, 1981.

*   *   *

HURM, Ken 1934-

PERSONAL: Born October 19, 1934, in Owensboro, Ky.; son of Edward J. (a factory worker) and Mary O. (a factory worker; maiden name, Price) Hurm; married Mary Therese Fraize (an art teacher), February 6, 1978. *Education:* Brescia College, B.S., 1959; Xavier University, Cincinnati, Ohio, M.Ed., 1965. *Home address:* Route 4, Box 256, Morganfield, Ky. 42437.

CAREER: Teacher at public and private schools, school administrator, and counselor in Cincinnati, Ohio, 1962-71; Brescia College, Owensboro, Ky., dean of students, 1971-75; underground supervisor at coal mines in western Kentucky, 1975—. Photographer, with exhibits of prints. *Military service:* U.S. Air Force, 1951-55. *Awards, honors:* Award from *Career Journal,* 1979, for nature photography.

WRITINGS: Breakthrough (poetry), Abbey Press, 1974. Contributor of articles and poems to magazines and newspapers.

WORK IN PROGRESS: Two books of poems; *Grey Labyrinths,* based on the author's experiences in underground coal mines.

SIDELIGHTS: Hurm wrote: ''I dropped out of high school in 1951 to join the Air Force during the final months of the Korean conflict. I later attended college on the G.I. Bill. After a two-year stint in the business world, I turned to my first love, teaching, and for fourteen years taught in public and private schools from junior high through college. At the age of forty I decided to change careers, and since 1975 have been employed underground in the western Kentucky coal fields.

''I believe most people can achieve almost anything, provided they manage their time, set clear goals, and have patience, perseverance, determination, and flexibility. The key to staying young, I think, is holding on to the ability to wonder, to discover, and the willingness to grow through new challenges and interests.

"As for my writing, I have learned to write for myself. If now and then a small newspaper or magazine finds a poem worth publishing, that's certainly frosting on the cake. My greatest thrill is having someone I've never met write to tell me he was moved by something I wrote. It's communication of spirit."

*   *   *

HURT, Henry 1942-

PERSONAL: Born July 17, 1942, in Chatham, Va.; son of Henry C. (a banker) and Frances (Hallam) Hurt; married Margaret Nolting Williams, 1968; children: Robert, Charles, Elizabeth. *Education:* Attended Randolph-Macon College, 1961-64 (expelled for "journalistic activities"); University of Mississippi, B.A., 1966. *Religion:* Presbyterian. *Residence:* Chatham, Va. *Office: Reader's Digest,* Pleasantville, N.Y., 10570.

CAREER: Reporter for *Richmond News Leader, Roanoke World-News,* and *Jackson Daily News,* early 1960's; Shawmut Inn, Kennebunkport, Me., bartender, 1967-68; *City News,* New York, editor, 1968-71; *Reader's Digest,* Pleasantville, N.Y., editor, 1971-77, roving editor and writer, 1977—. *Awards, honors:* Winner of Southern Literary Festival, 1965; grant from Rockefeller Foundation, 1966.

WRITINGS: Shadrin: The Spy Who Never Came Back, Reader's Digest Press, 1981. Contributor of articles and fiction to magazines, including *Southern Review.*

SIDELIGHTS: Henry Hurt's *Shadrin: The Spy Who Never Came Back* recounts the events leading up to the disappearance and probable death of Nikolai Fedorovich Artamonov, a Soviet defector and spy for the United States. A destroyer commander in the Soviet Navy, Artamonov defected to the United States in 1959, adopting the name of Nicholas Shadrin. The defector, anxious to share his knowledge of the Soviet Navy, went to work as a consultant for the Office of Naval Intelligence (ONI) and later for the American Defense Intelligence Agency (DIA). In 1966 the Central Intelligence Agency (CIA) and the Federal Bureau of Investigation (FBI) persuaded Shadrin to go to work against the Soviets as a double agent. According to Hurt, the FBI and the CIA used Shadrin as bait when another Soviet, known as Igor, wanted to defect. On December 20, 1975, Shadrin unwillingly met with the Soviets in Vienna, but he never returned from the meeting. In fact, he was never heard from again.

Of the book, Robert G. Kaiser of the *Washington Post Book World* said: "It is a fantastic yarn that deserves not only a wide readership, but a full-blown congressional investigation as well." The reviewer continued: "Henry Hurt has done an impressive job of finding out all he could about the Artamonov/Shadrin case, and an even better job of putting it into an exciting, readable narrative."

BIOGRAPHICAL/CRITICAL SOURCES: Washington Post Book World, November 24, 1981.

*   *   *

HURVITZ, Leon Nahum 1923-

PERSONAL: Born August 4, 1923, in Boston, Mass.; son of Benjamin and Rose (Marcus) Hurvitz; married Reiko Kobayashi, July 22, 1958; children: Hannah, Nathaniel, Philip. *Education:* University of Chicago, B.A., 1949; Columbia University, M.A., 1952, Ph.D., 1959. *Office:* Department of Asian Languages, University of British Columbia, Vancouver, British Columbia, Canada V6T 1W5.

CAREER: University of Washington, Seattle, acting assistant professor, 1955-57, assistant professor, 1957-62, associate professor, 1962-68, professor of Far Eastern languages, 1968-71; University of British Columbia, Vancouver, professor of Asian languages, 1971—. Visiting research scholar at Kyoto University, 1952-55. *Military service:* U.S. Army, 1943-48; became first lieutenant. *Member:* International Association for Buddhist Studies, American Oriental Society, Canadian Society for the Study of Religion, Association for Asian Studies, Philological Association of the Pacific Coast. *Awards, honors:* Rockefeller Foundation grant, 1960; American Council of Learned Societies grant, 1969-70; Canada Council grant, 1976-77.

WRITINGS: Chih-h (538-597): An Introduction to the Life and Ideas of a Chinese Buddhist Monk, Institut Belge Hautes Etudes Chinoises, 1963; (with Nicholas Poppe and Hidehiro Okada) *Catalogue of the Manchu-Mongol Section of the Toyo Bunko,* University of Washington Press, 1964; *Scripture of the Lotus Blossom of the Fine Dharma: The Lotus Sutra,* Columbia University Press, 1976. Contributor to learned journals.

*   *   *

HUSER, (La)Verne (Carl) 1931-
(Lee Bough)

PERSONAL: Surname is pronounced Who-zer; born March 2, 1931, in Schulenburg, Tex.; son of Carl Martin (in dairy business) and Emily (a teacher; maiden name, Liebau) Huser; married Jean Hurlbert (divorced November 12, 1969); married Willa Runyon (a psychologist), March 17, 1972; children: (first marriage) Heidi Louise, Paul Martin. *Education:* University of Texas, B.S., 1953; Hardin-Simmons University, M.Ed., 1958. *Home:* 23020 Southeast Sixth Pl., Redmond, Wash. 98052. *Office:* 3318 Queen Anne Ave. N., Seattle, Wash. 98109.

CAREER: English teacher at high schools in California, 1958-68, and Utah, Wyoming, and Oregon, 1971-72; Utah Environment Center, Salt Lake City, executive director, 1972-73; Kennecott Copper Corp., Salt Lake City, in public relations, 1974-77; Institute for Environmental Mediation, Seattle, Wash., mediator, 1977—. River guide, 1957—. Adjunct instructor at University of Utah, 1973-75; research associate at University of Washington, Seattle, 1977-80. *Military service:* U.S. Army, 1953-55; served in England. *Member:* Outdoor Writers Association of America, Northwest Outdoor Writers Association, Western River Guides Association (safety chairman).

WRITINGS: Snake River Guide, Westwater, 1972; *River Running,* Regnery, 1975; *Canyon Country Paddles,* Wasatch, 1978; *River Camping,* North Country Press, 1981. Contributor to magazines (sometimes under pseudonym Lee Bough), including *Audubon, Dynamic Years, National Parks, American Forests, Adventure Travel,* and *Alaskafest.*

WORK IN PROGRESS: A book on Washington's rivers, completion expected in 1984; an anthology of river writing, 1987.

SIDELIGHTS: Huser wrote: "The outdoors and my activities in the outdoors—river running, hiking, ski touring, climbing, and natural history study—have been the major inspiration for my writing and for my interest in and concern about the environment. Presently I make my living as an environmental mediator, trying to help settle specific disputes over environmental matters. My writing is an avocation at present, but when I retire it will become a full-time occupation.

"My views on the outdoors—I consider myself a Thoreauback, a devotee of Henry David Thoreau, who sought simplicity in his life and who believed that 'in wildness is the preservation of the world.' That statement can be construed in many ways, but to me it means we can find order in the natural world and in ourselves as part of that natural world, that we can learn from nature. As Wallace Stegner wrote, 'We need to demonstrate our acceptance of the natural world, including ourselves; we need the spiritual refreshment that being natural can produce.'

"I am a westerner. My heroes include Lewis and Clark, John Wesley Powell and Gustavas Doane, Stegner and his mentor Bernard DeVoto, J. Frank Dobie and Aldo Leopold, Adolph and Olaus Murie, Edward Abbey (at times), and John McPhee. My heroines include Willa Cather and Mari Sandoz, Sally Carrighar and Rachael Carson, Mardy Murie and Ann Zwinger. I share with Stegner the feeling that all too often, 'in gaining the lovely and the usable, we have given up the incomparable': Glen Canyon, Hells Canyon, Hetch Hetchy. I would that we live Aldo Leopold's ethic and see the land as a community to which we belong as we begin to use it with love and respect.

"With Antoine de Saint-Exuperey, I believe that 'what is essential is invisible to the eye,' that 'one sees truly only with the heart.' Homer and Shakespeare, Thomas Wolfe (the earlier) and Kazantzakis, Paul Gallico and Michael Frome have all provided me with inspiration at times as have all of the wild places I have experienced in Greece, in England, in the American West. Turning again to Stegner, I believe that 'an American, insofar as he is new and different at all, is a civilized man who has renewed himself in the wild.'

"My views on environmental mediation—Mediation techniques, properly applied in appropriate situations, can be useful decision-making tools in environmental disputes. They will not resolve conflicts based on values, which are not likely to be changed by mediation or any other conflict-resolution technique, but mediation can help to settle specific disputes in the environmental arena when a balance of power exists. Only when all of the parties have some sanction on others and everyone is willing to seek a solution rather than to continue to delay or attempt to build power bases is mediation appropriate. It must be totally voluntary, and all parties at interest must be involved in some manner. Vital to the process is the independence of the mediator, and critical to that independence is, 'Who pays the mediator?' Only a mediator operating from an independent base can effectively mediate environmental disputes.''

*   *   *

HUTCHINSON, Mary Jane   1924-

PERSONAL: Born Feburary 8, 1924, in Tulsa, Okla.; daughter of William Henry (a geologist) and Carrie Annette (Berry) Foster; married William George Hutchinson (a physicist), October 30, 1954 (deceased); children: Mary, Margaret, William, George. *Education:* Wellesley College, B.A., 1945; Columbia University, M.A., 1947; also attended University of Oslo, 1947. *Religion:* Episcopalian. *Home:* 5709 Katydid Lane, Austin, Tex. 78744.

CAREER: Bishop College, Dallas, Tex., instructor in English, 1970-71; Dallas Community College District, Dallas, instructor in English, 1972-75; English teacher at public schools in Richardson, Tex., 1975-79; Texas Conservation Foundation,

Austin, Tex., administrator, 1980—. Figure and freestyle judge for U.S. Figure Skating Association. *Member:* U.S. Figure Skating Association, Northcross Figure Skating Club.

WRITINGS: A Newcomers' Guide to the Wonderful World of Ice, privately printed, 1974, revised edition, 1981; *Red Ice* (novel), Avon, 1981; *Doomsday Festival* (novel), Avon, 1983. Contributor of poems to magazines.

SIDELIGHTS: Mary Hutchinson wrote: "After a lifetime of writing, mostly poetry (some published) and newspaper articles, I am still a little surprised to find myself a published novelist at age fifty-eight. *Red Ice* was born of my fascination with the lives of world-class athletes whom I met for the first time when I became involved with figure skating about ten years ago. Through my son, who trained for four years at the Broadmoor World Arena in Colorado Springs, and my own activities in the U.S. Figure Skating Association, I entered a world which is utterly unlike any I had ever known before: the all-or-nothing world of Olympic sport. Like the very rich, super-skaters are different from the rest of us. And so—the book, *Red Ice.*"

*   *   *

HUTH, Marta   1898-

BRIEF ENTRY: Born December 25, 1898, in Munich, Germany (now West Germany). American painter, photographer, and author. Huth's work has been exhibited in Germany and the United States. She wrote *Baroness von Riedesel and the American Revolution* (University of North Carolina Press, 1965). *Address:* P.O. Box 4414, Carmel, Calif. 93921. *Biographical/critical sources: Who's Who in American Art,* Bowker, 1978.

*   *   *

HUTSON, Jan   1932-

PERSONAL: Born April 23, 1932, in Lincoln, Neb.; daughter of John L. and Dora (Dienert) Ninneman; married Jean Hutson (in U.S. Air Force), June 6, 1959; children: Robin Burbach, Kim Burbach Cuddy, Jon Massey. *Education:* Attended University of Nebraska, 1948-51. *Home:* 8028 Acton Dr., Austin, Tex. 78736.

CAREER: Woodman Accident and Life Insurance Co., Lincoln, Neb., statistical analyst, 1953-55; Continental Trailways, Lincoln, assistant to treasurer, 1956-58; administrative supervisor of Noncommissioned Officers Club at Grissom Air Force Base, 1959-61; J. W. Winkley Enterprises (independent oil producer), Austin, Tex., administrative manager, 1961-63; Wendell Mayes Stations (commercial radio broadcasting and cable television holding company), Austin, Tex., administrative executive, 1963-81. Producer and hostess of "About Books," a syndicated radio program. *Member:* Women in Communications, Altrusa International, American Women in Radio and Television, Austin Writers' League.

WRITINGS: The Chicken Ranch: The True Story of the Best Little Whorehouse in Texas, A. S. Barnes, 1980. Editor of *Grapevine,* 1974-81.

WORK IN PROGRESS: Research for *Tejas* (tentative title), a historical novel set in Texas, completion expected in 1986; a contemporary novel about the relationship between politicians and journalists and the influence of organized labor on both camps.

SIDELIGHTS: Jan Hutson commented: "I write to clear up misconceptions about Texas. Its history did *not* begin at the Alamo! The two hundred years prior to events at the Alamo are more interesting and more important. The Alamo heroes, Crockett and Boone, weren't even Texans, but visitors who happened to get caught in the cross fire. My current projects concentrate on neglected areas of Texas history and its neglected heroes. *Tejas* also deals with the innate 'maverick' character of native Texans.

"I want anything I write on any subject to be, first and foremost, entertaining. But my primary objective is to disseminate information. (If my work does not appeal to intellectuals, fine. It's not directed toward those who *have* the answers.) My goal is to reach the largest audience possible—and with that goal in mind, entertainment serves as the vehicle to deliver the message. Library stacks are filled with specimens of literary excellence, but books about lovers, witches, spies, aliens, dead cats, killer whales, killer dogs, and killer sharks are the ones checked out at the libraries and supermarkets.

"A writer's worth should not be judged by prizes and awards received, but rather by the number of people who have read and retained 'the message.'"

I

IBELE, Oscar Herman 1917-

BRIEF ENTRY: Born February 5, 1917. American political scientist, educator, and author. Ibele began teaching at Kent State University in 1946 and became a professor of political science in 1967. In 1961 he was awarded a George Washington Medal by the Freedoms Foundation. Ibele wrote *Introduction to Political Science* (American Press, 1964), *British Police Administration* (C.C Thomas, 1965), *Bibliography of Political Science, Public Safety, and Criminology* (C.C Thomas, 1967), and *Political Science: An Introduction* (Chandler, 1971). *Address:* Department of Political Science, Kent State University, Kent, Ohio 44242.

* * *

ILICH, John 1933-

PERSONAL: Born December 16, 1933, in Omaha, Neb.; son of John and Katherine Ilich; married Marjorie Jennings (a schoolteacher); children: Susan, Mark. *Education:* University of Omaha, B.S., 1959; University of Nebraska, LL.B., 1962. *Home and office:* 1885 Spaulding, Grand Rapids, Mich. 49501.

CAREER: Admitted to the American Bar, 1962, the Bar of Illinois, 1962, and the Bar of Nebraska, 1962; Internal Revenue Service agent for U.S. Treasury Department, 1963; business consultant. *Military service:* U.S. Army, 1953-55. *Member:* American Bar Association, Illinois Bar Association, Nebraska Bar Association.

WRITINGS: *The Art and Skill of Successful Negotiation*, Prentice-Hall, 1973; *Restaurant Finance: A Handbook for Successful Management and Operation*, Chain Store, 1975; (with Barbara S. Jones) *Successful Negotiating Skills for Women*, A & W Pubs., 1980; *Power Negotiating: Strategies for Winning in Life and Business*, A & W Pubs., 1980; *The Happiest One*, Bengal Press, 1981.

WORK IN PROGRESS: *Seventy Times Seven;* a mystery.

SIDELIGHTS: John Ilich commented: "As a lawyer, I find writing to be a natural extension of my professional tools—the written and spoken word. In addition to my four 'professional' books, I anticipate writing a number of books of fiction, books that I hope will be enjoyed by the readers as much as I enjoy writing them. When I write, I use Hemingway's advice, namely, long periods of thinking and short periods of writing, and to try to polish my work until I am completely satisfied that I am expressing myself in a clear and concise way in order to communicate more effectively.

"I am particularly pleased to have co-authored *Successful Negotiating Skills for Women* as a small contribution to the long overdue advancement of women in society. The book has received excellent reviews by virtually every women's magazine that has received a review copy. I am also particularly pleased with *The Happiest One* as an inspirational contribution."

* * *

ILOWITE, Sheldon A. 1931-

PERSONAL: Surname is pronounced Ill-o-white; born February 19, 1931, in Brooklyn, N.Y.; son of Arthur (a real estate broker) and Mae (Terdiman) Ilowite; married Rosa Weinstein (a professor of nursing), August 23, 1954; children: Robert, Leslie, Lynne. *Education:* Attended University of Laval, summers, 1951, 1952; Champlain College, Plattsburg, N.Y., B.A., 1953; State Teachers College (now of the State University of New York College at New Paltz), M.S., 1956. *Home:* 16 Montgomery Pl., Jericho, N.Y. 11753.

CAREER: Old Bethpage Central School District, Plainview, N.Y., elementary school teacher, 1954-80. Statistician for New York Islanders of National Hockey League, 1972—. *Member:* American Federation of Teachers.

WRITINGS—Juveniles: *Fury on Ice: A Canadian-American Hockey Story*, Hastings House, 1970; *Hockey Defenseman*, Hastings House, 1971; *Centerman From Quebec*, Hastings House, 1972; *Penalty Killer: A Hockey Story*, Hastings House, 1974; *On the Wing: Rod Gilbert*, Raintree Publications, 1976.

AVOCATIONAL INTERESTS: Collecting art nouveau and art deco posters.

* * *

IMPERATO, Pascal James 1937-

BRIEF ENTRY: Born January 13, 1937, in New York, N.Y. American physician, educator, and author. Imperato gained experience in epidemiology through fellowships in Kenya, Uganda, Tanzania, Colombia, and Mali. He directed the New York City Bureau of Infectious Disease Control from 1972 to 1974 and has taught medicine at Cornell University and State University of New York Downstate Medical Center since the early 1970's. Imperato was named New York City commissioner of health in 1977, and he is also chairman of the board of directors of New York City Health and Hospitals Corporation and chairman of the executive committee of New York City Health Systems Agency. His books include *A Wind in Africa: A Story of Modern Medicine in Mali* (Warren Green, 1975), *What to Do About the Flu* (Dutton, 1976), *Historical Dictionary of Mali* (Scarecrow, 1977), *African Folk Medicine: Practices and Beliefs of the Bambara and Other Peoples* (York Press, 1977), *Dogon Cliff Dwellers: The Art of Mali's Mountain People* (African Arts, 1978), and *Medical Detective* (Richard Marek, 1979). *Address:* 125 Worth St., New York, N.Y. 10013; and Department of Preventive Medicine, State University of New York Downstate Medical Center, 450 Clarkson Ave., Brooklyn, N.Y. 11203. *Biographical/critical sources: American Men and Women of Science: The Physical and Biological Sciences,* 14th edition, Bowker, 1979.

*   *   *

INCLAN, Ramon (Maria) del Valle
See VALLE-INCLAN, Ramon (Maria) del

*   *   *

ING, Dean 1931-

PERSONAL: Born June 17, 1931, in Austin, Tex.; son of Dean Emory (a personnel specialist) and Louise (a linotype operator; maiden name, Hardin) Ing; married Geneva Baker (a broadcaster), August 21, 1959; children: Diana Capri, Laura Victoire, Dina Valerie, Dana Christie. *Education:* Fresno State University, B.A., 1956; San Jose State University, M.A., 1970; University of Oregon, Ph.D., 1974. *Agent:* Joseph Elder Agency, 150 West 87th St., 6D, New York, N.Y. 10024.

CAREER: Aerojet-General, Sacramento, Calif., engineer, 1957-62; Lockhead & United Technologies, San Jose, Calif., senior engineer, 1962-70; Missouri State University, Maryville, assistant professor of speech, psycholinguistics, and media, 1974-77; full-time writer, 1977—. *Military service:* U.S. Air Force, 1951-55; became airman first class. *Member:* Science Fiction Writers of America.

WRITINGS:—Science fiction novels: *Soft Targets,* Ace Books, 1979; *Anasazi,* Ace Books, 1980; *Systemic Shock,* Ace Books, 1981; *High Tension,* Ace Books, 1982; *Pulling Through,* Ace Books, 1982; *Single Combat,* TOR Books, in press; *Wild Country,* TOR Books, in press. Contributor of stories to magazines.

WORK IN PROGRESS: Continuing research on urban survival.

SIDELIGHTS: Ing wrote: "Since I deplore the voracious appetite of the public for entertainment-for-entertainment's sake, most of my work has a clear didactic element. You may expect ninety percent entertainment and ten percent message from me. I believe that Jefferson's ideal of the independent yeoman farmer should be familiar to every generation because I mistrust a technological society in which most members are thoroughly incompetent to maintain the hardware or the software."

*   *   *

INGLEBY, Terry 1901-

PERSONAL: Born May 7, 1901, in Frankfurt am Main, Hesse, West Germany; daughter of Joseph and Teresa (Gause) Ingleby. *Education:* Attended Froebel College, 1918-19; Mather Training College, Teacher's Certificate, 1922. *Home and office:* 34 Norwich Rd., Chichester, Sussex PO19 4DG, England.

CAREER: Mulberry Street Infants School, Manchester, Lancashire, England, teacher, 1922-49, head assistant, 1949-66; free-lance writer, 1958—.

WRITINGS—All with Jenny Taylor; juveniles: "Round and About Books" series, four books, Oliver & Boyd, 1958; "Town Books" series, four books, Oliver & Boyd, 1958; "Let's Learn to Read" series, eight books, Blackie & Son, 1960; "Reading With Rhythm" series (illustrated by Derek Crowe), five books, Longmans, Green, 1961; "Infant Book Shelf" series, four books, Blackie & Son, 1962, reprinted as *Blackie's Infant Bookshelf,* 1967; "What Would You Like to Be?" series (illustrated by Sam Fair), Blackie & Son, 1962, Book I: *Kennel Maid?,* Book II: *Air Stewardess?,* Book III: *Postman?,* Book IV: *Policeman,* Book V: *Footballer?,* Book VI: *Nurse?;* "A Lot of Things" series, four books, Oliver & Boyd, 1963; *Measuring and Recording* (illustrated by Alan Jessett), Longmans, Green, 1963; *Number Words* (illustrated by Jessett), Longmans, Green, 1963; "Read by Reading" series, three books, Longmans, Green, 1964; "Stories Around Us" series, eight books, Longmans, Green, 1964.

"The Baxter Family" series (illustrated by Will Nickless), six books, Blackie & Son, 1965; "Numbers" series (illustrated by Jessett), two books, Longmans, Green, 1965; "Shapes" series, six books, Longmans, Green, 1965; "This Is the Way I Go" series (illustrated by Jessett), six books, Longmans, Green, 1965; *Picture Dictionary,* Longmans, Green, 1969; "A Set of Things to See" series, four books, Oliver & Boyd, 1970; *Messy Malcolm,* World's Work, 1972; *Maps for Mandy and Mark,* Longman, 1974; *The Scope Storybook* (illustrated by Andrew Sier, Joanna Troughton, and Barry Wilkinson), Longman, 1974; "Seven Silly Stories" series, Longman, 1974, Book I: *The Fox and Stork,* Book II: *Brer Rabbit and the Honey Pot,* Book III: *Noisy Neville,* Book IV: *Mr. Stupid,* Book V: *The Foolish Tortoise,* Book VI: *The Well Diggers,* Book VII: *The Miller and His Donkey;* "Whizz Bang" series, two books, Longman, 1976; "Can You Do This" series (illustrated by David Frankland), Longman, 1978, Set I: four books, Set II: four books; *Messy Malcolm's Birthday* (illustrated by Lynette Hemmant), World's Work, 1978; *Messy Malcolm's Dream,* World's Work, 1982.

WORK IN PROGRESS: The Talking Cat.

SIDELIGHTS: Terry Ingleby said Jenny Taylor's "highly infectious enthusiasm for writing books especially suited to children from deprived homes" led to their writing partnership. "Since 1956," she said, "we have worked together and all our books are published under our joint names.

"Having taught in a very deprived area," Ingleby said, "we felt the great need for a wide range of simple books, with plenty of repetition and rhythm, to create an interest in reading. Most of our books are written for the teacher and teaching parent to use, and all for the young child to enjoy."

AVOCATIONAL INTERESTS: Nature expeditions, gardening, wildlife, music, travel.

*   *   *

INGLIS, John K(enneth) 1933-

PERSONAL: Surname is pronounced *In*-guls; born March 1, 1933, in Kent, England; son of Frank Kenneth (a radiologist) and Lorna (French) Inglis; married Annelies Ulrike Seifert (a translator, secretary, and teacher), April 3, 1965. *Education:* University of Nottingham, B.Sc. (with honors), 1957, B.A. (with honors), 1960; University of Birmingham, Diploma in Education, 1958. *Politics:* "Variable expediency?!" *Religion:*

None. *Home:* 14 Hosker Close, Headington, Oxford, England. *Office:* College of Further Education, Oxford, England.

CAREER: College of Further Education, Oxford, England, 1961—, began as lecturer, became section leader in life sciences. Exchange professor of anatomy, physiology, and health at College of Lake County, Ill., 1976-77, and of anatomy, physiology, and biology in Canada, 1982-83. *Member:* Institute of Biology, Oxford International Students Society (founding member and secretary).

WRITINGS: (With C. M. Lee) *Science for Hairdressing Students,* Pergamon, 1964, 3rd edition, 1982; *A Textbook of Human Biology,* Pergamon, 1968, 2nd edition, 1974, revised edition, 1982; *Introduction to Laboratory Animal Technology,* Pergamon, 1980.

WORK IN PROGRESS: Laboratory Techniques in the Life Sciences; A Textbook of Social Biology; Survival: USA.

SIDELIGHTS: Inglis told *CA:* "It seems to me that writers are people with overactive brains and thinking, who talk to themselves. They put their thoughts onto paper because nobody seems to listen to them. This outlet is very time-consuming, frustrating and, in the main, financially unrewarding. It is thought by many to be time-wasting and self-indulgent. It is, in truth, a form of self-punishment requiring a self-discipline not often found outside of closed religious orders! Heaven knows why we do it, because it very often hurts, especially since most of us have a day job.

"Original thought is the spearhead of our human condition. As writers our main concern must be to produce something that outlives us and produces change—change in thought, change in behavior. Science-textbook authors can only claim to be guides to new thought. Fiction writers are the creators of new thought, and they deservedly attract a recognition that is denied the former. Oh, to be a successful novelist—a creative and satisfying task attempted by many, achieved by few."

*   *   *

INGOLD, Gerard (Antoine Hubert)   1922-

PERSONAL: Born September 22, 1922, in Agadir, Morocco; son of Francois Joseph Jean (a general and author) and Marie-Antoinette (Didierjean) Ingold; married Jacqueline Valentin, June 28, 1946; children: Francois-Rodolphe, Charles. *Education:* University of Paris, degree in law, 1946. *Religion:* Catholic. *Home:* 40 boulevard Suchet, Paris, France 75016. *Office:* 30 rue Paradis, Paris, France 75010.

CAREER: Worked in colonial administration in Brazzaville, Middle Congo (now People's Republic of the Congo), 1946-48; Cristalleries de Saint-Louis, Paris, France, head of commercial department, 1949-51, office director, 1951-57, sales manager, 1957—. Sales consultant, 1961—. *Military service:* Second French Armored Division, 1939-45; received Croix de Guerre; Order of Merit; chevalier of Legion of Honor. *Member:* Sons of the American Revolution (France). *Awards, honors:* History prize from Academie d'Alsace, 1969, for *Un Matin bien rempli.*

WRITINGS—In English: The Art of the Paperweight: Saint Louis, Paperweight Press, 1981.

In French: *St. Louis* (history of the Saint Louis Co.), Synergic, 1957; *Un Matin bien rempli; ou, La Vie d'un pilote de chasse de la France libre, 1921-1941,* preface by Charles de Gaulle, Charles-Lavauzelle, 1969.

WORK IN PROGRESS: Researching the history of glass and crystal in Europe and the United States.

SIDELIGHTS: Ingold told *CA:* "I came to write a book about paperweights because of requests from American friends and collectors and because I work in a glass company (one of the most ancient in France). Since the mid-nineteenth century my mother's family has headed the St. Louis Crystal Company. I speak and write English and German."

*   *   *

IRANI, Merwan S.
   See BABA, Meher

*   *   *

IRVINE, Sidney H(erbert)   1931-

BRIEF ENTRY: Born September 26, 1931, in Aberdeen, Scotland. Educator and author. Irvine has taught in Rhodesia, Zambia, and England, and was a member of the education faculty at University of Western Ontario. In 1971 he became a professor of education and dean of the College of Education at Brock University. He wrote *The Northern Rhodesia Mental Ability Survey, 1963* (Rhodes-Livingstone Institute, 1964). Irvine edited *Human Behaviour in Africa: A Bibliography of Psychological and Related Writings* (1970), and *Cultural Adaptation Within Modern Africa* (Teachers College Press, Columbia University, 1972). *Address:* 12 Oak Lane, Fonthill, Ontario, Canada L0S 1EO; and College of Education, Brock University, St. Catharines, Ontario, Canada L2S 3A1. *Biographical/critical sources: Leaders in Education,* 5th edition, Bowker, 1974.

*   *   *

IRVINE, William   1906-1964

OBITUARY NOTICE: Born June 9, 1906, in Carson Hill, Calif.; died October 8, 1964; buried in San Francisco, Calif. Educator, literary historian, and author. Irvine joined the faculty of Stanford University in 1935 and became a professor of English in 1948, a position he held until his death. A member of the Modern Language Association, World Federalists, and Phi Beta Kappa, Irvine was best known for his writings on nineteenth-century figures who influenced the development of social thought. His books include *Walter Bagehot,* a study of the nineteenth-century economist and journalist; *The Universe of G.B.S.,* a view of George Bernard Shaw within the context of his times; *The Book, the Ring, and the Poet,* a biography of Robert Browning; and *Apes, Angels, and Victorians,* the story of Charles Darwin, T. H. Huxley, and evolution. Obituaries and other sources: *Twentieth-Century Authors: A Biographical Dictionary of Modern Literature,* 1st supplement, H. W. Wilson, 1955; *American Authors and Books, 1640 to the Present Day,* 3rd revised edition, Crown, 1962; *The Reader's Encyclopedia of American Literature,* Crowell, 1962; *Who Was Who in America, With World Notables,* Volume IV: *1961-1968,* Marquis, 1968.

*   *   *

IVERSON, Peter James   1944-

PERSONAL: Born April 4, 1944, in Whittier, Calif.; son of William James (a teacher) and Adelaide (a teacher; maiden name, Schmitt) Iverson; married Katherine Jensen (a teacher), August 18, 1968 (divorced November, 1981); children: Erika, Jens. *Education:* Carleton College, B.A., 1967; University of Wisconsin—Madison, M.A., 1969, Ph.D., 1975. *Politics:* Democrat. *Religion:* Unitarian-Universalist. *Home:* 104 South

Eighth St., Laramie, Wyo. 82070. *Office:* Department of History, University of Wyoming, Laramie, Wyo. 82071.

CAREER: Navajo Community College, Many Farms (Navajo Nation), Ariz., instructor in history, 1969-72; Arizona State University, Tempe, assistant professor of history, 1975-76; University of Wyoming, Laramie, assistant professor, 1976-81, associate professor of history, 1981—. Member of public advisory council of KUWR-FM Radio, 1980-83; chairman of Wyoming Council for the Humanities, 1981-82; member of board of directors of Laramie Plains Museum, 1981-82. *Member:* American Historical Association, Organization of American Historians, Western History Association, Western Social Science Association (member of executive council, 1982-85), Albany County Historical Society (president, 1981-82), Laramie Westerners (president, 1979-81). *Awards, honors:* Grants from American Philosophical Society, 1979, and National Endowment for the Humanities, 1980; fellowship from National Endowment for the Humanities, 1982-83; Kellogg National Fellow, 1982-85.

WRITINGS: (Contributor) George Carter and Bruce Mouser, editors, *Identity and Awareness in the Minority Experience,* University of Wisconsin—La Crosse, 1975; *The Navajos: A Critical Bibliography,* Indiana University Press, 1976; (contributor) R. David Edmunds, editor, *American Indian Leaders,* University of Nebraska Press, 1980; *The Navajo Nation,* Greenwood Press, 1981; *Carlos Montezuma and the Changing World of American Indians,* University of New Mexico Press, 1982; (with John Wunder and Rita Napier) *The Plains Indians: A History,* University of Oklahoma Press, in press. Contributor to *Handbook of North American Indians.* Contributor to history and ethnic studies journals.

WORK IN PROGRESS: Cowboys and Indians in the Post-Frontier West, publication expected in 1984.

SIDELIGHTS: Iverson told *CA:* "As a child growing up in California, I listened to my grandfather tell stories about the Southwest. He talked especially about the Navajos, whom he had taught in several schools. I realized very early on that American Indians were enduring, continuing peoples, and I became fascinated with their histories and their cultures. In addition, I became interested in the rural West that existed beyond the urban confines of coastal California. Years later I had the opportunity to teach at a new college established by the Navajo nation. My residence there and my subsequent residence in Wyoming have affected my work in a most direct way.

"Unlike most historians of the West, I write about the region during the era since the close of the frontier. My first book, a critical bibliography of the extensive literature about the Navajos, emphasized recent and Navajo perspectives on our country's largest Indian tribe. Then, *The Navajo Nation* stressed the experiences of the 1960's and 1970's. My book on Carlos Montezuma explores issues faced by Indians in the early twentieth-century West through a review of a colorful and important life. Montezuma's life and career, I believe, illustrate important dimensions of modern Indian identity.

"Now I am shifting more of my attention to the Northern Plains. I am contributing five chapters on the Plains Indian experience in the twentieth century to one volume and am writing another book about modern 'cowboys and Indians.' With the latter, I hope to show commonalities and differences between ranchers who are white and Indians who may be ranchers, too. In my future work I want to examine more fully basic questions that we all face in the West. In particular, I wish to review the choices we have made, are making, and will make about our land.''

J

JACKSON, Kevin Goldstein
See GOLDSTEIN-JACKSON, Kevin

* * *

JACKSON, Sara
See THOMAS, Sara (Sally)

* * *

JACOBS, Sheldon 1931-

PERSONAL: Born January 29, 1931, in Milwaukee, Wis.; son of Berthald (a clothier) and Ruth Jacobs; married Lisbeth Schwalb (in marketing), February 29, 1964; children: Roy, Julie. *Education:* University of Nebraska, B.Sc., 1952; New York University, M.Sc., 1955. *Home:* 80 Circle Dr., Hastings-on-Hudson, N.Y. 10706.

CAREER: American Broadcasting Corp. (ABC-TV), New York City, in research, 1957-70; National Broadcasting Corp. (NBC-TV), New York City, in research, 1970—. *Military service:* U.S. Army, 1952-54; became captain.

WRITINGS: Put Money in Your Pocket, Simon & Schuster, 1974; *Handbook for No-Load Fund Investors: 1981 Edition,* No-Load Fund Investor, 1981. Contributor to magazines.

WORK IN PROGRESS: Handbook for No-Load Fund Investors: 1982 Edition.

* * *

JACOBS, Sophia Yarnall 1902-
(Sophia Yarnall)

PERSONAL: Born June 23, 1902, in Haverford, Pa.; daughter of Charlton (in business) and Anna (Coxe) Yarnall; married Reginald Robert Jacobs, October 14, 1921 (divorced, 1937); children: Denholm Muir, Charlton Yarnall (Mrs. Stowe Catlin Phelps). *Education:* Attended Bryn Mawr College, 1920-21. *Politics:* Democrat. *Religion:* Protestant. *Home:* 11 East 73rd St., New York, N.Y. 10021.

CAREER: Philadelphia Orchestra Club, Philadelphia, Pa., secretary, 1936-40, promotion adviser, 1940-42, promotion manager, 1942-45; writer, 1930-45, 1970-81. Past secretary of United Nations Council; past member of board of trustees of National Urban League and Howard University; past president and chairman of board of directors of New York Urban League;

past president of National Council of Women of the United States. Member of board of directors of American Committee on Africa, American Symphony Orchestra, Planned Parenthood-World Population, and Rachel Carson Trust for the Living Environment. *Member:* American Civil Liberties Union (past member of board of directors), Cosmopolitan Club.

WRITINGS: (Under name Sophia Yarnall) *The Clark Inheritance* (historical novel), Walker & Co., 1981. Contributor to magazines, including *Country Life, Good Housekeeping, Harper's Bazaar, Parents' Magazine, Country Gentleman,* and *Reader's Digest,* and to newspapers.

SIDELIGHTS: Jacobs has spent much of her adult life in volunteer work and civic activities. Her first effort was to provide music for soldiers in the Philadelphia area during World War II. She has worked for peace, for recognition of the United Nations in its early days, and for civil rights and improved race relations. Such work has taken her to India, France, and Italy.

The Clark Inheritance is based on the history of her mother's family, coal mine owners and operators of eastern Pennsylvania. Jacobs's own story has appeared in part in the writings of Emily Kimbrough, as one of Kimbrough's characters.

BIOGRAPHICAL/CRITICAL SOURCES: Library Journal, June 15, 1981.

* * *

JACQUET, Constant Herbert, Jr. 1925-

PERSONAL: Born December 3, 1925, in Bridgeport, Conn.; son of Constant Herbert and Hazel Elizabeth (Herthal) Jacquet; married Sally Graham, June 18, 1949; children: Timothy John. *Education:* Columbia University, B.S., 1949, A.M., 1951, M.Phil., 1973. *Religion:* Episcopalian. *Home:* 150 East 93rd St., New York, N.Y. 10028. *Office:* National Council of Churches of Christ in the United States of America, 475 Riverside Dr., New York, N.Y. 10115.

CAREER: Union Theological Seminary, New York City, research associate, 1953-56; National Council of Churches of Christ in the United States of America, New York City, research associate and staff writer for *Information Service* in Bureau of Research and Survey, 1956-64, director of research library of Office of Planning and Program, 1964-73, staff associate for Information Services, 1974—. *Member:* American Political Science Association, Religious Research Association, Association of Statisticians of American Religious Bodies.

WRITINGS—Editor; published by Abingdon, except as noted: *Yearbook of American Churches, 1967: Information on All Faiths in the U.S.A.*, National Council of Churches of Christ, 1967, 1972 edition published as *Yearbook of American Churches, 1972: With Information on Religious Bodies in Canada*, 1973 edition published as *Yearbook of American and Canadian Churches, 1973*, 1981 edition, 1981. Contributing editor of *Review of Religious Research*, 1973—.

WORK IN PROGRESS: Another edition of the *Yearbook of American and Canadian Churches;* a pamphlet titled "Church Financial Statistics and Related Data."

SIDELIGHTS: Jacquet told *CA:* "My writing has been the lens through which to communicate research results in the social sciences, particularly in the sociology of religion, to a variety of audiences. It is more expository than artistic (although one always has hopes) and has the goal of simplifying and interpreting complex research materials for the nonspecialist as clearly and succinctly as possible. Much of what I produce is unique as to subject matter. Fortunately, I am in a good position to learn what kinds of information are needed in organized religion and to choose a few topics I can deal with successfully given the resources I have and the contacts with people across the nation."

*   *   *

JAFFE, Nora Crow   1944-

PERSONAL: Born February 12, 1944, in Los Angeles, Calif.; daughter of Thomas J. (a script editor of feature films) and Helen E. (a commercial artist) Crow; married Arthur M. Jaffe (a professor of mathematics and physics), July 24, 1971. *Education:* Stanford University, A.B., 1965; Harvard University, M.A., 1968, Ph.D., 1972. *Politics:* "Liberal; all other attitudes conservative." *Religion:* None. *Home:* 27 Lancaster St., Cambridge, Mass. 02140. *Office:* Department of English, Smith College, Northampton, Mass. 01063.

CAREER: Smith College, Northampton, Mass., assistant professor, 1971-79, associate professor of English, 1979—. *Member:* Modern Language Association of America, American Society for Eighteenth-Century Studies, Northeast Society for Eighteenth-Century Studies, Phi Beta Kappa.

WRITINGS: *The Poet Swift*, University Press of New England, 1977; (contributor) John Irwin Fischer and Donald C. Mell, Jr., editors, *Contemporary Studies of Swift's Poetry*, University of Delaware Press, 1981; *The Evil Image: Two Centuries of Gothic Short Fiction and Poetry*, New American Library, 1981. Contributor to language and literature journals.

WORK IN PROGRESS: A study of William Jensen's novel, *Gradiva*, and Freud's commentary on it, *Delusion and Dream in Gradiva*, "describing differences between the scientist's and the literary artist's views of delusion, illusion, and fiction."

SIDELIGHTS: Nora Jaffe wrote: "I am motivated, primarily, by my father's explicit wish that I become a lawyer, and by the desire he indicated indirectly that I become a writer instead.

"I have traveled throughout the world—to England, Ireland, Scotland, France, Switzerland, Mexico, Russia, Rumania, Hungary, Germany, Austria, Denmark, Italy, Greece, and so on. But I take little pride in this accomplishment, since I have always wished more than anything to be able to stay at home."

*   *   *

JAHSMANN, Allan Hart   1916-

PERSONAL: Born November 3, 1916, in Wausau, Wis.; son of Fred W. (a cattle buyer) and Helen (Herrmann) Jahsmann; married Lois Herbert (a mental health center director), January 29, 1945; children: Lucia Marie, Hila Ann, Alicia Jean. *Education:* Received diploma from Concordia Teachers College, River Forest, Ill., 1937; St. Louis University, B.S., 1939, A.M., 1952, Ph.D., 1956; Concordia Seminary, M. Div., 1945; Menninger School of Psychiatry, postdoctoral certificate, 1961. *Home:* 3904 Landes Rd., Collegeville, Pa. 19426. *Office:* Lutheran Church in America, 2900 Queen Lane, Philadelphia, Pa. 19129.

CAREER: Teacher at Lutheran schools in St. Louis, Mo., and Chicago, Ill., 1937-42; ordained minister of Lutheran Church, Missouri Synod, 1945; Trinity Lutheran Church, Warren, Ohio, pastor, 1945-48; Lutheran Church, Missouri Synod, St. Louis, assistant editor of Sunday school literature, 1948-56, associate editor, 1956-59, general secretary of Sunday schools, 1959-68, executive editor of educational publications for the Missouri Synod board of education, 1968-73; Lutheran Church in America, Philadelphia, Pa., senior editor of children's program resources, 1974-81, senior editor for leadership resources, 1981—. Visiting professor of education at Concordia Teachers College, River Forest, Ill., 1958, and Concordia Seminary, St. Louis, Mo., 1954, 1957, 1964, and 1973; member Collegeville-Trappe Municipal Authority, 1974-81. *Member:* Association for Supervision and Curriculum Development, Religious Education Association, Lutheran Education Association, Lutheran Society for Worship, Music, and the Arts, Academy for Scholarship. *Awards, honors:* D.Litt., Concordia Teachers College, River Forest, Ill., 1971.

WRITINGS—Published by Concordia; for children: (With Martin P. Simon) *Little Visits With God: Devotions for Families With Small Children*, illustrated by Frances Hook, 1956; (compiler) *Words of Joy: A Collection of Christmas Poems and Recitations*, 1958; *Little Folded Hands*, illustrated by Hook, 1959; (with Arthur W. Gross) *Little Children Sing to God*, 1960; (with Simon) *More Little Visits With God: Devotions for Families With Young Children*, illustrated by Hook, 1961; *My Favorite Bible Stories*, selected by Lillian Brune, 1967; *It's All About Jesus: A Book of Devotional Readings*, illustrated by Art Kirchhoff, 1975; *The Holy Bible for Children: A Simplified Version of the Old and New Testaments*, illustrated by Don Kueker, 1977; *I Wonder . . . Answers to Religious Questions Children Ask*, 1980.

For adults; published by Concordia: *Teaching Little Amalee Jane*, 1954, revised edition published as *The Church Teaching Her Young*, 1967; *What's Lutheran in Education?*, 1960; *How You Too Can Teach: Reading Text of a Basic Training Course for Church School Teachers*, 1963; *Ministering Through Administering: A Guide for Workers in the Church School*, 1965; *Power Beyond Words: Communication Systems of the Spirit and Ways of Teaching Religion*, 1969; *What We'd All Better Do (or Do Better) to Help Others Learn the Word and Ways of God*, 1972.

Editor of *Interaction*, 1956-66, and *My Devotions*, 1956-68.

WORK IN PROGRESS: *Images of Angels: From Byzantine Times to the Present; Bible Stories About Angels; Member of the Council: A Church Council Guidebook.*

SIDELIGHTS: Jahsmann told *CA:* "The need for artful writing for children is especially evident in areas of religious subjects and life. Because adult Christians tend to assume a responsibility to transmit their biblical heritage and faith by direct didactic means and methods, Christian religious writings for children too often are adult, inappropriate for children, unimaginative, and dull. This is one of the reasons I have devoted much of my life to communicating *with* children in reference to the Christian faith. My purpose has been the nurturing of that faith in them through the involvement of their interest.

"A second concern of mine, and the reason for much of my writing for adults has been the need that Christian parents and teachers have of knowing the faith they hope to foster in their children. Equally important is knowing ways of nurturing children in the Christian faith and way of life. This is why most of my writing for adults has been in the service of Christian education through both the home and the local church.

"My rich, long, wonderful life, I have no doubt, has been a gift of God. I had a mother who cared about me and also about my Christian faith and religious life; a father who liked me and related to me through a mutual love of animals, particularly horses. Of almost equal importance to my life was the company of great teachers I have had from kindergarten to the present day. The list is almost entirely four-star generals—from Robert Frost and Karl Menninger all the way down to teachers in Lutheran elementary grades.

"I learned to know and love children first as a teacher in Lutheran elementary schools in St. Louis and Chicago. As a pastor of a church in Warren, Ohio, I taught the kindergarten. I'll never forget the snowpants and rubber boots that had to be put on at the end of a snowy day. To keep in touch with children while developing and editing Sunday church-school materials, I produced and conducted a weekly radio program on KFUO in St. Louis. It involved a group of five-year-olds in a variety of learning activities and was called 'Uncle Allan's Kindergarten.'

"I think I'm primarily an educator. I am the only person I know who has taught an experimental nursery school, a kindergarten, all elementary grades, all high school grades, college courses, graduate school classes, seminary classes, and non-professional adult groups of all ages, including retirees.

"Three months after retiring as an executive editor at the age of fifty-seven, I accepted a position that moved us from St. Louis to Philadelphia, where my wife and I have enjoyed the culture of the East Coast. At sixty-five we moved into a one-hundred-fifty-year-old, ten-room farmhouse, and vocationally I moved from editing children's educational materials to church leadership resources. My wife, who directs a county-wide program of mental health centers, has a more demanding life than I have, so we both get away often by traveling. It's the surest way and always interesting and educational.

"When do I plan to retire again? Putting on new tires can be done every day."

*   *   *

JAMES, David
   See HAGBERG, David J(ames)

*   *   *

JANAS, Frankie-Lee   1908-
   (Zachary Ball, a joint pseudonym; Francesca
   Greer; Saliee O'Brien)

PERSONAL: Born November 19, 1908, in Appleton City, Mo.; daughter of Benjamin Franklin (a rural mail carrier) and Lillian (Bremer) Griggs; married third husband, Eugene Janas, January 22, 1950; children: (from previous marriage) Thurlow Benjamin Weed. *Education:* Attended Iola Junior College and University of Texas. *Religion:* Protestant. *Residence:* Holly-

wood, Fla. *Agent:* Jay Garon, Jay Garon-Brooke Associates, Inc., 415 Central Park W., New York, N.Y. 10025.

CAREER: Proofreader and writer. Active in amateur dramatics and radio work.

WRITINGS—With Kelly R. Masters, under joint pseudonym Zachary Ball: *Pull Down to New Orleans,* Crown, 1946; *Keelboat Journey,* Dutton, 1958.

Under pseudonym Saliee O'Brien: *Farewell the Stranger,* Morrow, 1956; *Too Swift the Tide,* Morrow, 1960; *Beelfontaine,* Berkley Publishing, 1974; *Heiress to Evil,* Ballantine, 1974; *Shadow of the Caravan,* Berkley Publishing, 1974; *The Bride of Gaylord Hall,* Pocket Books, 1978; *Bayou,* Bantam, 1979; *So Wild the Woman,* Bantam, 1979; *Captain's Woman,* Pocket Books, 1979; *Black Ivory,* Bantam, 1980; *Blood West,* Pocket Books, 1980; *Night of the Scorpion,* Berkley Publishing.

Under pseudonym Francesca Greer: *First Fire,* Warner Books, 1979; *Second Sunrise,* Warner Books, 1981.

Contributor of hundreds of short stories to magazines.

*   *   *

JANOS, Andrew C(saba)   1934-

PERSONAL: Born February 9, 1934, in Budapest, Hungary; came to the United States in 1956, naturalized citizen, 1962. *Education:* University of Budapest, A.B., 1955; Princeton University, M.A., 1959, Ph.D., 1961. *Office:* Department of Political Science, University of California, Berkeley, Calif. 94720.

CAREER: Princeton University, Princeton, N.J., lecturer in political science, 1961-63; University of California, Berkeley, assistant professor, 1963-69, associate professor, 1970-77, professor of political science, 1977—, past director of Center for Slavic and East European studies. Visiting associate professor at Harvard University, 1969-70. *Member:* American Association for the Advancement of Slavic Studies.

WRITINGS: (With William B. Slottman) *Revolution in Perspective,* University of California Press, 1971; *Authoritarian Politics in Communist Europe,* Institute of International Studies, University of California, Berkeley, 1976; *The Politics of Backwardness in Hungary,* Princeton University Press, 1981.

AVOCATIONAL INTERESTS: Travel (eastern and western Europe, Latin America).

*   *   *

JANOWITZ, Tama   1957-

PERSONAL: Born April 12, 1957, in San Francisco, Calif.; daughter of Julian Frederick (a psychiatrist) and Phyllis (a poet and professor; maiden name, Winer) Janowitz. *Education:* Barnard College, B.A., 1977; Hollins College, M.A., 1979; postgraduate studies at Yale University, 1980-81. *Home:* Lansing 17 2B, 700 Warren Rd., Ithaca, N.Y. 08540. *Agent:* Jonathan Dolger, 49 East 96th St., New York, N.Y. 10028. *Office:* Fine Arts Work Center, 24 Pearl St., Provincetown, Mass. 02657.

CAREER: Model with Vidal Sassoon (international hair salon) in London, England, and New York, N.Y., 1975-77; Kenyon & Eckhardt, Boston, Mass., assistant art director, 1977-78; Fine Arts Work Center, Provincetown, Mass., writer in residence, 1981-82. Member of Barnard College Arts and Literature Committee (member of board of directors, 1974-75). *Member:* Poets and Writers, Writers' Community (fellow, 1976), Associated Writing Program. *Awards, honors:* Breadloaf Writers' Conference, 1975; Elizabeth Janeway Fiction Prize, 1976 and 1977; Amy Loveman Prize for poetry, 1977; fellowship from Hollins College, 1978; award from National Endowment for the Arts, 1982.

WRITINGS: American Dad (novel), Putnam, 1981. Guest editor of *Mademoiselle* (magazine), 1977.

Contributor of short stories to magazines and periodicals, including *Paris Review, Mississippi Review,* and *Pawn Review.* Contributor of articles to magazines, including *Rolling Stone* and *Mademoiselle.*

WORK IN PROGRESS: A Cannibal in Manhattan, a novel; another novel.

SIDELIGHTS: Earl Przepasniak, the protagonist and narrator of Tama Janowitz's *American Dad,* is eleven years old when his parents divorce. Earl's father, a psychiatrist, is an amiable, self-absorbed, pot-smoking philanderer whose unrepressed behavior upsets and embarrasses his family. His mother, a poet, is killed halfway through the novel during a fight with her ex-husband over alimony payments. Earl's father is convicted of involuntary manslaughter (Earl testifies against him at the trial) and he is sentenced to ten to fifteen years in prison. With his mother dead and his father in jail, Earl decides to travel abroad. He goes to London, where he pursues women and indulges in various other misadventures. Upon his return from Europe, Earl is, as some reviewers of *American Dad* observed, predictably wiser, and his greater understanding of himself leads to improved relations with his father.

Like Earl, Tama Janowitz is the product of a broken marriage between a psychiatrist and a poet. Her father is the head of the mental health department at the University of Massachusetts, and her mother (who, unlike Earl's mother, is still alive) is a professor of poetry at Cornell University. Janowitz shares with Earl the experience of having had to seek unusual ways to rebel against exceptionally permissive parents, and her book examines some of the ordeals that accompany such an upbringing. Critics generally agreed that the first half of the book, drawn as it is from Janowitz's own experience, is the stronger half. The story flounders, some thought, after Earl embarks on what one reviewer called his European rite-of-passage trip. "Earl's adventures are mostly filler," wrote the *New Republic*'s Garrett Epps, "[and they mar] what is otherwise one of the most impressive first novels I've read in a long time."

Although Arnold Klein of the *Soho News* found *American Dad* "episodic and trivial," he felt that it had the "considerable virtue of being funny." He was also delighted with Janowitz's depiction of Earl's psychiatrist father, which he called "an uncannily acute portrayal of a distinct social type." Epps concurred, saying: "There is not a false note in the presentation of this engaging villain." David Quammen, writing for the *New York Times Book Review,* lamented the untimely death of Earl's mother, who he thought was the novel's most well-drawn and endearing character. Echoing the reaction of several other reviewers, he declared: "Tama Janowitz has a fine comedic inventiveness, especially as applied in light dabs to character." According to Epps, Janowitz also has "a sharp eye for the things of this world . . . and her sensuous writing enlivens the book."

Tama Janowitz told *CA:* "Daily it is a struggle for me to rise from bed. But generally the need to go to the bathroom and the desire for Wheat Chex forces me to get up. Then too there is the floor to be swept, and the thought that perchance on this day some mail will come. Though as it happens, I rarely receive mail, no matter how many letters I write. This is not to say that I despise life. On the contrary, life is an overwhelming experience for me, so much so that getting out of bed becomes

an Everest of Olympian proportions for me to climb. The glory of eating Wheat Chex is quite beyond belief. And then if I can actually drag myself to the typewriter and get some words down on paper, what joy I experience! For me, writing is overwhelmingly difficult, yet not so difficult, it seems, as actually having to go out and get a job. That is something I am not capable of.

"Once I did have a job, as an assistant art director. I was hired for mysterious reasons, but when they discovered shortly thereafter that I could not draw, I was sent to my office for six months. I felt it would be better for me to go back to school; luckily I applied to Hollins and was awarded enough financial aid to enable me to attend a short time before the advertising agency laid me off due to cutbacks in the Underwood Deviled Ham account. Some people, sadly, are not meant to work, but I have learned this about myself at an early age.

"Certain people (though whom I cannot say) might feel that as a writer I should be working in order to collect experience; but it was Flannery O'Connor who said that each person has had enough experiences by the age of twenty to write for the rest of his or her life. Or something to that effect.

"I write about myself by pretending to be others. In my first novel I am a young boy trying to win his father's approval; in my second I am an elderly 'primitive' cannibal visiting 'civilized' New York City for the first time; and in my work in progress I am a young painter who is burdened with the weight of all of history, and is preoccupied with death and immortality. When I have actually managed to get a few words down on the paper, how happy I feel! And there is no one in the room to tell me I have done poorly or well, only I am left with my own transmutable angst and joy."

BIOGRAPHICAL/CRITICAL SOURCES: Houston Chronicle, April 4, 1981; *Soho News,* April 15, 1981; *Newark Star-Ledger,* April 26, 1981; *Boston Phoenix,* May 12, 1981; *New York Times Book Review,* May 17, 1981; *New York Daily News,* May 21, 1981; *Baltimore News-American,* May 24, 1981; *Horizon,* June, 1981; *New Republic,* June 6, 1981; *Baltimore Sun,* June 7, 1981; *West Coast Review of Books,* July, 1981; *Pittsburgh Press,* July 20, 1981; *Interview,* August, 1981; *Springfield Republican,* August 30, 1981.

*   *   *

JANSON, Dora Jane (Heineberg) 1916-

PERSONAL: Married Horst Woldemar Janson (an educator and writer), 1941; children: Anthony, Peter, Josephine, Charles. *Education:* Received degree from Radcliffe College; graduate study at New York University. *Residence:* New Rochelle, N.Y.

CAREER: Lectured at St. Louis City Museum, St. Louis, Mo., and at the Metropolitan Museum, New York, N.Y.

WRITINGS—With husband, Horst Woldemar Janson: *The Story of Painting for Young People: From Cave Painting to Modern Times* (juvenile), Abrams, 1952, reprinted as *The Story of Painting: From Cave Painting to Modern Times,* 1966; *The Picture History of Painting: From Cave Painting to Modern Times* (juvenile), Abrams, 1957; *Key Monuments of the History of Art: A Visual Survey,* Prentice-Hall, 1959.

Standard Treasury of the World's Great Paintings, Abrams, 1960; *History of Art: A Survey of the Major Visual Arts From the Dawn of History to the Present Day,* Prentice-Hall, 1962, revised edition, 1969; *A History of Art and Music,* Prentice-Hall, 1968; *A History of Art for Young People,* Abrams, 1971.

SIDELIGHTS: A *New York Times* reviewer commented that in *The Story of Painting for Young People,* "generalizations are discarded in favor of concrete discussion of admirably selected pictures. The book represents a heroic job of esthetics made easy without vulgarization.'' *History of Art,* a more extensive work, has also been applauded for its comprehensive yet entertaining account of the history of architecture, sculpture, and painting in Western civilization. As the *Christian Science Monitor* stated: ''Each forthcoming history of art aims for a fresher approach and a more captivating presentation of its encyclopedic data. . . . Janson has fulfilled this staggering assignment with distinction and readability.''

BIOGRAPHICAL/CRITICAL SOURCES: New York Times, November 16, 1952; *Christian Science Monitor,* November 29, 1962.*

* * *

JAWIEN, Andrzej
  See JOHN PAUL II, Pope

* * *

JAY, Robert Ravenelle   1925-

BRIEF ENTRY: Born March 22, 1925, in New York, N.Y. American social anthropologist, educator, and author. Jay has been a professor of anthropology at Brown University since 1970. He wrote *Religion and Politics in Rural Central Java* (Southeast Asia Studies, Yale University, 1963) and *Javanese Villagers: Social Relations in Rural Modjokuto* (M.I.T. Press, 1969). *Address:* Department of Anthropology, Brown University, 79 Waterman St., Providence, R.I. 02912. *Biographical/critical sources: American Men and Women of Science: The Social and Behavioral Sciences,* 13th edition, Bowker, 1978.

* * *

JENKINS, Iredell   1909-

PERSONAL: Born August 12, 1909, in Blue Ridge Summit, Md.; son of James Iredell (a manufacturer) and Mary Louise (Dobie) Jenkins; married Isabel Lawson Cook, December 27, 1934; children: Anne (Mrs. William F. Bridgers), Armistead Dobie. *Education:* University of Virginia, B.A., 1933, M.A., 1934, Ph.D., 1937; attended University of Paris, 1935-36. *Politics:* Democrat. *Religion:* Episcopalian (''high church''). *Home:* 90 Brookhaven, Tuscaloosa, Ala. 35401.

CAREER: Tulane University, New Orleans, La., instructor, 1937-40, assistant professor, 1940-43, associate professor of philosophy, 1943-46; Yale University, New Haven, Conn., assistant professor of philosophy, 1946-49; University of Alabama, Tuscaloosa, professor of philosophy, 1949—, chairman of department, 1949-78, philosopher-in-residence at School of Medicine, 1971. Hill Family Foundation lecturer at Macalester College and Hamline University, 1955; senior fellow in law and behavioral science at University of Chicago, 1959-60; visiting professor at Northwestern University, 1964-65; lecturer at University of Notre Dame, 1973.

MEMBER: International Association for Philosophy of Law and Social Philosophy (president of American section, 1969-72), American Philosophical Association, Metaphysical Society of America, American Society of Aesthetics, American Society of Political and Legal Philosophy, Phi Beta Kappa. *Awards, honors:* Grants from Social Science Research Council, 1940, American Council of Learned Societies, 1952-53, and National Science Foundation, 1975-76; fellow of Rockefeller Foundation, 1957-58, and Ford Foundation, 1959-60.

WRITINGS: Art and the Human Enterprise, Harvard University Press, 1958; *Social Order and the Limits of Law: A Theoretical Essay,* Princeton University Press, 1980.

Contributor: Irwin C. Lieb, editor, *Experience, Existence, and the Good: Essays in Honor of Paul Weiss,* Southern Illinois University Press, 1961; Paul G. Kuntz, editor, *The Concept of Order,* University of Washington Press, 1968; Ralph A. Smith, editor, *Aesthetic Concepts and Education,* University of Illinois Press, 1970; Ervin Pollack, editor, *Human Rights,* William S. Hein, 1971; Ralph A. Smith, editor, *Art as Performance,* University of Illinois Press, 1972.

Contributor of more than fifty articles to law and philosophy journals. Member of editorial board of *American Journal of Jurisprudence,* 1959—, *Law and Society Review,* and *Southern Journal of Philosophy,* 1961—.

WORK IN PROGRESS: A book on human or status rights; a long essay on the ''open'' society and how open it can or should be; a book on the dissolution of our culture and its basic institutions.

AVOCATIONAL INTERESTS: Golf, sailing, riding, plant taxonomy, English history of the fifteenth and sixteenth centuries.

* * *

JENKINS, Patricia   1927-1982

PERSONAL: Born November 5, 1927, in Chicago, Ill.; died January 18, 1982; daughter of Paul Ronald and Helen (Dunnom) Jenkins. *Education:* Knox College, B.A. (cum laude), 1950. *Office:* American Association of University Women, 2401 Virginia Ave. N.W., Washington, D.C. 20037.

CAREER: American Medical Association, Chicago, Ill., member of editorial staff of *Today's Health,* 1947-57; *Consumer Reports,* Mount Vernon, N.Y., member of editorial staff, 1958-67; free-lance publications consultant, 1967-78; American Association of University Women, Washington, D.C., manager of publications and editor of *Graduate Woman,* 1978-82.

WRITINGS: For to Forget the Pain, Libra, 1975.

[Date of death provided by Rosalie Kent of American Association of University Women]

* * *

JENSEN, Gordon Duff   1926-

BRIEF ENTRY: Born January 28, 1926, in Seattle, Wash. American pediatrician, psychiatrist, educator, and author. Jensen has been a professor of pediatrics and psychiatry at University of California, Davis, since 1969. He has been a physician since 1952. He wrote *A Guide to the Physician's Care of the Healthy Child: Birth to Five Years* (School of Medicine, University of Washington, Seattle, 1959), *The Well Child's Problems: Management in the First Six Years* (Year Book Medical Publishers, 1962), and *Youth and Sex: Pleasure and Responsibility* (Nelson-Hall, 1973). *Address:* Division of Mental Health, School of Medicine, University of California, Davis, Calif. 95616. *Biographical/critical sources: Biographical Directory of the Fellows and Members of the American Psychiatric Association,* Bowker, 1977.

* * *

JENSEN, Larry Cyril   1938-

PERSONAL: Born March 31, 1938, in Logan, Utah; married; children: seven. *Education:* Brigham Young University, B.S.,

1960, M.S., 1961; Michigan State University, Ph.D., 1966. *Office:* Department of Psychology, Brigham Young University, Provo, Utah 84601.

CAREER: State University of New York College at Potsdam, instructor in psychology, 1962-64; Michigan State University, East Lansing, assistant instructor in educational psychology, 1964-65; Brigham Young University, Provo, Utah, assistant professor, 1965-69, associate professor, 1969-73, professor of psychology, 1973-78; Utah State University, Logan, professor of family and human development, 1978-80; Brigham Young University, professor of psychology, 1980—, member of executive committee of Family Research Center. *Member:* American Psychological Association, American Educational Research Association. *Awards, honors:* Grants from U.S. Department of Health, Education and Welfare, 1970, Lilly Foundation, 1973, 1975, and Thrasher Foundation, 1979.

WRITINGS: What's Right; What's Wrong, Public Affairs Press, 1975; (with Kenneth L. Higbee) *Understanding and Using Social Influence Techniques*, Brigham Young University Press, 1976; *That's Not Fair!*, Brigham Young University Press, 1977; (with William D. Boyce) *Moral Reasoning: A Psychological-Philosophical Integration*, University of Nebraska Press, 1978; (with Higbee) *Influence: What It Is and How to Use It*, Brigham Young University Press, 1978; (with Karen M. Hughston) *Responsibility and Morality*, Brigham Young University Press, 1979; (with M. Gawain Wells) *Feelings: Helping Children Understand Emotions*, Brigham Young University Press, 1979; (with Janet M. Jensen) *Stepping Into Stepparenting*, R & E Research Associates, 1981; (with Richard S. Knight) *Moral Education: Historical Perspectives*, University Press of America, 1982.

Contributor: R. A. Hill and J. D. Wallace, editors, *Selected Readings in Moral Education*, Research for Better Schools, 1976; *College-Education Proceedings Mid-Year Educational Conference*, Brigham Young University Press, 1978; *The Pro-Social Theorists' Approach to Moral Citizenship Education*, Research for Better Schools, 1978. Contributor of more than thirty-five articles to periodicals, including *Journal of Educational Psychology, Journal of Developmental Psychology, Journal of Experimental Psychology, Journal of Genetic Psychology, British Journal of Social and Clinical Psychology, Journal of Moral Education*, and *Salt Lake Tribune*.

WORK IN PROGRESS: Parenting.

*   *   *

JENSEN, Vernon H(ortin)   1907-

PERSONAL: Born July 10, 1907, in Salt Lake City, Utah; son of Joseph E. (a carpenter and builder) and Grace E. (Hortin) Jensen; married Esther Chapman, June 3, 1931; children: Karen Jensen Harvey, Vernon H., Margaret Jensen Gasch, Linda Jensen Hamlet. *Education:* Attended University of Utah, 1926-27; Brigham Young University, B.S., 1933; University of California, Berkeley, Ph.D., 1939. *Home:* 326 Fall Creek Dr., Ithaca, N.Y. 14850. *Office:* New York State School of Industrial and Labor Relations, Cornell University, Ithaca, N.Y. 14850.

CAREER: University of Colorado, Boulder, professor of economics, 1937-45; Cornell University, Ithaca, N.Y., professor of industrial and labor relations, 1946-73, professor emeritus, 1973—, associate dean of New York State School of Industrial and Labor Relations, 1965-71. Montague Burton Professor at University of Leeds, 1959-60. Arbitrator, director of stabilization, and member of public board of War Labor Board, 1942-

45; member of Presidential Board of Inquiry, East Coast Longshore Dispute, 1962; Presidential R.R. Marine Workers Commission, 1962; member of New York advisory council of Labor and Management Improper Practices Act, 1967-73 (chairman, 1969); consultant to National Defense Mediation Board. Arbitrator for various companies and unions. *Member:* International Industrial Relations Association, Industrial Relations Research Association, National Academy of Arbitration. *Awards, honors:* Guggenheim fellowship, 1959-60; Wertheim fellowship, 1960; grants from Social Science Research Council.

WRITINGS: Lumber and Labor, Farrar & Rinehart, 1945, reprinted, Arno, 1971; *Heritage of Conflict: Labor Relations in the Nonferrous Metals Industry up to 1930*, New York State School of Industrial and Labor Relations, Cornell University, 1950, *Nonferrous Metals Industry Unionism, 1932-1954: A Story of Leadership Controversy*, Cornell University, 1954; (with Harold G. Ross) *Bibliography of Dispute Settlement by Third Parties*, New York State School of Industrial and Labor Relations, Cornell University, 1955; *Collective Bargaining in the Nonferrous Metals Industry*, Institute of Industrial Relations, University of California, 1955; *Hiring of Dock Workers and Employment Practices in the Ports of New York, Liverpool, London, Rotterdam, and Marseilles*, Harvard University Press, 1964; *Decasualization and Modernization of Dock Work in London*, New York State School of Industrial and Labor Relations, Cornell University, 1971; *Strife on the Waterfront: The Port of New York Since 1945*, Cornell University Press, 1974; *Argumentation*, Van Nostrand, 1980. Contributor of articles to periodicals, including *Industrial and Labor Relations Review.**

*   *   *

JOHN PAUL II, Pope   1920-
(Karol Wojtyla; Andrzej Jawien, pseudonym)

BRIEF ENTRY: Born May 18, 1920, in Wadowice, Poland. Polish church official and author. Pope John Paul II, whose birth-given name is Karol Wojtyla, served as Archbiship of Krakow and as a Roman Catholic cardinal before his election as pope in 1978. He has also been a professor of moral theology at University of Krakow and University of Lublin. Writing for many years under the pseudonym Andrzej Jawien, John Paul II published several volumes of poetry and a play entitled "Przed sklepem jubilers" (*Znak*, December, 1960; translated as *The Jeweler's Shop*, Random House, 1980). The prelate's writings also include *Fruitful and Responsible Love* (Seabury, 1979), *Easter Vigil and Other Poems* (Random House, 1979), *The Acting Person* (Kluwer, 1979), *Sign of Contradiction* (St. Paul Publications, 1979), and *You Are My Favorites* (Daughters of St. Paul, 1980). *Address:* Apostolic Palace, Vatican City, Italy. *Biographical/critical sources: New York Times*, March 15, 1979; *Washington Post*, October 2, 1979; *Chicago Tribune*, February 21, 1980.

*   *   *

JOHNSON, Brian (Martin)   1925-

PERSONAL: Born December 5, 1925, in Liverpool, England; son of Reginald (an engineer) and Gladys (Johnson) Johnson; married Sybil Temperton, February 1, 1949; children: Christine, Hilary, Caroline Barbara. *Education:* Attended high school in Birkenhead, England. *Home:* 10 California Lane, Bushey Heath, Watford, Hertfordshire WD2 1EY, England. *Agent:* Bolt & Watson Ltd., Suite 8, 26 Charing Cross Rd., London WC2H ODG, England. *Office:* BBC-TV, Television Centre, Wood Lane, Shepherds Bush, London W. 14, England.

CAREER: British Broadcasting Corp. (BBC), London, England, radio engineer, 1942-44, studio manager in radio drama department, 1947-51, sound technician for Television Service film unit, 1951-56, camera operator for film unit, 1956-58, assistant producer of documentaries, 1958-63, producer of remote broadcasts on music and sports, 1963-73, producer of science features and editor of weekly science television program, "Tomorrow's World," 1973-76, senior producer of science television documentaries, 1976—. *Military service:* British Army, Royal Electrical and Mechanical Engineers, 1944-47; served in the Middle East; became sergeant.

WRITINGS: *The Secret War* (nonfiction; based on six-part television series of the same name), Methuen, 1978; *Fly Navy: A History of Maritime Aviation,* Morrow, 1981.

Documentary scripts; all for BBC-TV: "The Crowded Sky," first broadcast April 11, 1978; "Bombers," first broadcast June 12, 1979; "The Flying Machines of Ken Wallis," first broadcast May 13, 1980; "Sir Frank Whittle, Jet Pioneer," first broadcast May 12, 1981; "Jump Jet," first broadcast July 7, 1981.

Writer for BBC-TV series, "Tomorrow's World" and "The Secret War." Contributor to magazines, including *Aeroplane Monthly, Shortwave,* and *Radio Times.*

WORK IN PROGRESS: *A Most Secret Place,* on the Aircraft and Armaments Research Establishment at Boscombe Down during World War II, with Terry Heffernan; *Night Bomber,* an account of the wartime attacks on Germany by Royal Air Force (RAF) Bomber Command with Air Commander Cozeur, who was an operational bomber pilot and later the station commander of the RAF Heurswell night bomber base, publication expected in 1982.

SIDELIGHTS: Johnson told *CA:* "After many years in BBC-TV, writing, producing, and directing programs as diverse as sports and music, I became fascinated by the archives of the Imperial War Museum, in particular a very large quantity of captured German footage dealing mainly with the experimental work on V2 rockets at Peenemunde, Germany. This material—it was the equivalent of about eighty full-length feature films—was uncataloged and had been released as a consequence of the 'Thirty Year Rule,' which was making available a very large amount of classified material pertaining to World War II.

"The quality of the archive film enabled me to produce six fifty-minute television documentary programs under the general title of 'The Secret War.' The series was very successful in TV terms, and I was asked to write a book on the subject. This book, I am pleased to say, became a best-seller; it has since been reprinted and translated into Dutch and German. The success of the book led me to write others, so that now my leisure time is almost totally taken up with writing. Thus, largely by accident, I have become involved in the history of World War II—a war in which I played a distinctly minor role.

"I try, whenever possible, to work from primary sources: it is pleasing to discover some hitherto overlooked fact of history, however small, and, I must confess, to handle and read the documents that once were closely guarded state secrets is a unique experience. There is a strong sense of anticipation when a folder of such documents is before one for the first time: what will it contain? Seldom is there a feeling of disappointment. Archives like the Public Record Office in London might seem to the uninitiated to be dull, dry places. I have not found them so.

"It seems to me that the task of a historian writing for the general reader is to try to convey the excitement of the affairs of the recent past in a way that retains the feeling of being present at, for example, a tense meeting of the war cabinet under Winston Churchill, who was considering intelligence reports of German long-range rockets or the meaning of mysterious radio signals thought to be guiding Luftwaffe night bombers to targets in England and reading the reports of eminent scientists as they considered countermeasures. One mistake by them and over a thousand people could die in a single air raid (as indeed happened on the night of the German attack on Coventry).

"Henry Ford is reported once to have said, 'History is bunk.' Not so!"

*   *   *

JOHNSON, Christopher Howard   1937-

BRIEF ENTRY: Born November 22, 1937, in Washington, Ind. American historian, educator, and author. Johnson began teaching European social history at Wayne State University in 1966. He wrote *Utopian Communism in France: Cabet and the Icarians, 1838-1851* (Cornell University Press, 1974). *Address:* Department of History, Wayne State University, Detroit, Mich. 48202. *Biographical/critical sources: Directory of American Scholars,* Volume I: *History,* 7th edition, Bowker, 1978.

*   *   *

JOHNSON, Donna Kay   1935-

PERSONAL: Born February 27, 1935, in Oakland, Calif.; daughter of Walter H. (a carpenter) and Esther (Carpenter) Eral; married Jack Lloyd Johnson (an auto dealer), November 27, 1967. *Education:* Attended Bible Institute of Los Angeles, 1956-57; later studied portrait painting. *Religion:* Protestant. *Home:* 1930 Pool Rd., Felton, Calif. 95018.

CAREER: Worked as telephone operator and at various sales jobs in California, 1952-58; Disneyland, Anaheim, Calif., portrait artist, 1958-62; United Advertising (billboard company), Oakland, Calif., art department, 1963-67; free-lance artist and author, 1967—. *Member:* American Wildlife Reserve Service, National Wildlife Federation, African Wildlife Leadership Foundation, San Francisco Zoo, Oakland Zoo, School Jungle Safari.

WRITINGS: *Brighteyes* (juvenile; self-illustrated), Holt, 1978.

WORK IN PROGRESS: More books for children, including *Notch,* a lion story, and *Tigers Seven.*

SIDELIGHTS: Donna Kay Johnson told *CA:* "From the time I was old enough to comprehend the world, I gravitated toward colors, flowers, and animals. As soon as I could transmit my feelings about such things, they were expressed in art. We spent many summers at Lake Tahoe, a beautiful area almost unknown then, and its beauty inspired more artwork. I hiked all over the mountains, taking in the scenery and wildlife.

"As the result of a vacation visit to Disneyland I became a portrait artist there for about four years. To be associated with Disney in any way was an inspiration. Disneyland was an education in living as well as an artistic experience. It greatly influenced my character development by exposure to all kinds of people and activities.

"I later married, and due to the combination of moving to our lovely Felton home and my husband's encouragement, I got into my art full force. He suggested that animals should be the main focus of my work because I love them so much. There began the real magic, as the animals inspired my creativeness as nothing else could. The desire to be near animals of all varieties led me to Marine World Africa, U.S.A., where I have enjoyed many hours of photographing and playing with the animals. Lion, tiger, and cougar cubs are the most adorable playmates in the world. I also have had young wolves, skunks, chipmunks, raccoons, a fawn, and other assorted animals as friends. All this has resulted in my pen and ink, oil, and stained glass interpretations of them.

"Now a new dimension has been added—that of author. It's a truly wonderful and satisfying form of expression. The furthest thing from my mind was becoming an author, though I love to read. To be published is really a wonderful surprise."

Johnson was inspired to write the story *Brighteyes* after she helped a blind raccoon, which had been attracted to Johnson's backyard feeding station, raise a litter of four kits. Johnson and Brighteyes have been featured on local television programs, and the book was shown and given to talk show host Merv Griffin on his television show by actor Ed Asner.

AVOCATIONAL INTERESTS: Swimming, biking, hiking, travel, including Europe, Mexico, and Japan.

* * *

JOHNSON, Forrest B(ryant) 1935-
(Frosty Johnson)

PERSONAL: Born December 14, 1935, in Louisville, Ky.; son of William Forrest and Martha (a teacher; maiden name, Shelnutt) Johnson; married second wife, Patricia Enriquez (an accountant), October 3, 1971. *Education:* University of Louisville, B.A., 1957. *Politics:* Independent ("Right-wing conservative"). *Religion:* Roman Catholic. *Residence:* Las Vegas, Nev.

CAREER: Worked as an assistant chemist in Louisville, Ky., 1957-59, industrial paint salesman in Cedar Rapids, Iowa, 1962-67, and sales manager in Chicago, Ill., 1967-81; writer, 1982—. *Military service:* U.S. Army Reserve, Medical Service Corps, 1960-68; became captain.

WRITINGS: The Ancient History of the Basenji (nonfiction), Merrell, 1967; *Basenji: Dog From the Past* (nonfiction), Merrell, 1972; (under name Frosty Johnson) *The Strange Case of Big Harry* (novel), Exposition Press, 1972; *Hour of Redemption,* Manor, 1978. Also author of unpublished novels *What Are You Doing Derby Day?* and *Tektite.*

WORK IN PROGRESS: Revising *What Are You Doing Derby Day?*

SIDELIGHTS: Johnson told CA: "I consider myself a 'storyteller' rather than a complex writer using mind-straining words. I attempt to create a fast-paced story with a surface which is easy to understand. But, for those who wish to dig into the characters, I incorporate a more involved meaning, sprinkled with a message. My explorations serve as a catalyst for much of my work. For example, in 1970 I organized and led an expedition into the wilderness of northern Minnesota for the *Chicago Tribune* in order to prove that reports of 'ape men' in the area were pure fiction. The *Tribune's* coverage of the story produced such an interest in the subject that I wrote *The Strange Case of Big Harry* so that people could get a look (and a laugh) at themselves."

* * *

JOHNSON, Frosty
See JOHNSON, Forrest B(ryant)

JOHNSON, Henry
See HAMMOND, John (Henry, Jr.)

* * *

JOHNSON, Jann
See JOHNSON, Paula Janice

* * *

JOHNSON, Joan D. 1929-

BRIEF ENTRY: Born October 10, 1929, in Wyandotte, Mich. American educator and author. Johnson began teaching at California State University, Los Angeles, in 1955 and became a professor of physical education in 1970. She coached the U.S. women's tennis team in the World University Games in 1977. Johnson wrote *Tennis* (W. C. Brown, 1967) and *A Workbook for Tests and Measurements in Physical Education* (Peek Publications, 1967). *Address:* 3341 Balzac St., Alhambra, Calif. 91803; and Department of Physical Education, California State University, 5151 State University Dr., Los Angeles, Calif. 90032.

* * *

JOHNSON, John Bockover, Jr. 1912-1972

OBITUARY NOTICE: Born September 21, 1912, in Chicago, Ill.; died April 6, 1972; buried in Norfolk, Va. Educator and author. A member and past president of the Association of Wisconsin Presidents and Deans, and the Greater Milwaukee Association of Phi Beta Kappa, Johnson served as president of Milwaukee Downer College from 1951 to 1964 and as provost of Old Dominion College from 1964 until his death. He was co-author, with Graves T. Wilson, of the two-volume work *History of World War II Research and Development of Medical Field Equipment,* for which he received a U.S. Army commendation award in 1946. He also co-wrote *Registration for Voting in the United States* with Irving Lewis. Obituaries and other sources: *Who Was Who in America, With World Notables,* Volume V: *1969-1973,* Marquis, 1973.

* * *

JOHNSON, Nora 1933-

PERSONAL: Born in 1933, in Hollywood, Calif.; daughter of Nunnally (a screenwriter, producer, and director) and Marion Johnson; married Leonard Siweck (separated); children: two daughters. *Education:* Smith College, B.A. *Home:* 215 East 80th St., New York, N.Y. 10021. *Agent:* Curtis Brown Ltd., 575 Madison Ave., New York, N.Y. 10022.

CAREER: Free-lance writer, 1958—. *Awards, honors:* Nomination for award from Writers Guild, for film "The World of Henry Orient."

WRITINGS: The World of Henry Orient (novel), Little, Brown, 1958 (and co-author with father, Nunnally Johnson, of screenplay with same name, United Artists, 1964); *A Step Beyond Innocence* (novel), Little, Brown, 1961; *Loveletter in the Dead-Letter Office,* Delacorte, 1966; (co-author with Pat Loud) *Pat Loud: A Woman's Story,* Coward, 1974; *Flashback: Nora Johnson on Nunnally Johnson,* Doubleday, 1979.

Contributor of articles and stories to periodicals, including *New Yorker, McCall's, Mademoiselle, Sports Illustrated,* and *Atlantic Monthly.*

SIDELIGHTS: Nora Johnson is best known as the daughter of screenwriter Nunnally Johnson, and as author of *The World of Henry Orient,* a novel about two teenage girls who develop a crush on a middle-aged piano player. Judith Crist wrote in the *New York Herald Tribune Book Review* that Johnson reveals in *Henry Orient* ''a very special gift for recalling—and re-creating—the poignant bittersweet of late childhood.'' The book was adapted as a motion picture by Johnson and her father, and it starred Peter Sellers. In 1967, a Broadway musical entitled ''Henry, Sweet Henry'' was adapted from the novel and starred Don Ameche.

Following her father's death in 1977, Nora Johnson wrote *Flashback: Nora Johnson on Nunnally Johnson,* a biography that includes the author's personal reminiscences of her famous father, excerpts from his letters, descriptions of his many films, and quotations from his family and friends. The best part of the book, reported Mel Watkins in the *New York Times,* is where Johnson describes her relationship with her father. ''Here the author . . . penetrates the superficial glitter of the lives of Hollywood's rich and famous to engage those personal aspects of relating and surviving that finally mold one's life, no matter how charismatic the public image.'' In the words of *New York Times Book Review* critic Caroline Seebohm, *Flashback* is ''a wonderful book—a primer for the would-be screenwriter, a personal memoir of a marvelous man, and a painfully honest examination of that timeless subject, the relationship between fathers and daughters.''

BIOGRAPHICAL/CRITICAL SOURCES: New York Times, August 10, 1958, October 24, 1967, October 12, 1979; *New York Herald Tribune Book Review,* August 10, 1958; *Commonweal,* September 5, 1958; *New York Times Book Review,* October 21, 1979.*

*   *   *

JOHNSON, Paula Janice   1946-
(Jann Johnson)

PERSONAL: Born September 12, 1946, in Biloxi, Miss.; daughter of Willie T. (a meteorologist and Air Force pilot) and Vivian M. (an aeronautical tool designer; maiden name, McBeth) Johnson; married Jerald Wigdortz (an investment banker), December 12, 1975. *Education:* Attended San Jose State College (now San Jose State University), 1964-66; Parsons School of Design, Certificate, 1969. *Home:* 6 West 77th St., New York, N.Y. 10024. *Office:* 133 West 72nd St., New York, N.Y. 10023.

CAREER: Mr. Mort (women's wear), New York City, designer, 1969-71; Super Shoe Biz, New York City, designer, 1972-75; Moc Co., Tokyo, Japan, designer, 1972-75; McCall's Pattern Co., New York City, licensed designer, 1980—.

WRITINGS—Under name Jann Johnson: *The Jeans Book,* Ballantine, 1972; *Jann Johnson's Discovery Book of Crafts,* Reader's Digest Press, 1975. Contributor of articles to magazines, including *Self* and *Mademoiselle.*

WORK IN PROGRESS: Continued work in adult and children's crafts, including such areas as embroidery and knitting.

SIDELIGHTS: Johnson told *CA:* ''I am first a designer, then an author. My writing revolves around my designs for clothes, shoes, quilts, patterns, plates, and other items. Obvious career influences were my mother, grandmother, and father. The cultures of many countries left their mark as well. My father's Air Force career took us to Japan, Puerto Rico, Guam, Louisiana, Texas, and California. Later I visited Peru, Greece, Egypt, Israel, Turkey, Spain, France, Scotland, Ireland, Italy,

Hong Kong, and England—sometimes for business, oftentimes for fun. Each visit offered a lesson in color or design, particularly in Japan, where even mundane items are beautifully designed and functional, and illustrate a resourceful use of raw materials. Mother's influence was strongly mathematical and classically artistic. Grandmother quilted, canned, painted, and ran a farm. She taught my brother and me crafts when we went for visits. Writing started with Leonore Fleischer, my editor for *The Jeans Book*—I'd talk, she'd type, then we'd review. After a while I was on my own. I shall continue, grateful to many teachers, official and unofficial.''

*   *   *

JOHNSON, Philip Cortelyou   1906-

BRIEF ENTRY: Born July 8, 1906, in Cleveland, Ohio. American architect and author. In 1932 Johnson became chairman of the department of architecture at Musuem of Modern Art; his designs include the museum's annex and sculpture garden. He also designed New York City's Seagram Building in 1956, with Mies Van Der Rohe. Johnson's books include *Machine Art* (1934), *Mies Van Der Rohe* (1947), *Architecture, 1949-1965* (Holt, 1966), and *Writings* (Oxford University Press, 1979). *Address:* Ponus St., New Canaan, Conn. 06840; and 375 Park Ave., New York, N.Y. 10022. *Biographical/critical sources: Webster's American Biographies,* Merriam, 1974.

*   *   *

JOHNSON, Sabina Thorne
See THORNE, Sabina

*   *   *

JOHNSON, Siddie Joe   1905-1977

OBITUARY NOTICE: Born August 20, 1905, in Dallas, Tex.; died July 27, 1977, in Corpus Christi, Tex. Librarian, educator, and author of children's books. A graduate of Texas Christian University at Fort Worth, Johnson taught school before earning a degree in library science from Louisiana State University. Head of the children's department of the Dallas Public Library for many years, she became coordinator of children's services. In 1954 Johnson received the first Grolier Award for her library work, and in 1964 she was named Texas Librarian of the Year. A children's book reviewer for the *Dallas Morning News* for thirty years, Johnson's own juvenile titles include *Cat Hotel, New Town in Texas, Texas,* and *A Month of Christmases.* Obituaries and other sources: *The Junior Book of Authors,* 2nd edition, revised, H. W. Wilson, 1951; *A Biographical Directory of Librarians in the United States and Canada,* 5th edition, American Library Association, 1970; *Authors of Books for Young People,* 2nd edition, Scarecrow, 1971; *Texas Writers of Today,* Gryphon Books, 1971; *School Library Journal,* January, 1978.

*   *   *

JONES, D(avid) Gareth   1940-

PERSONAL: Born August 28, 1940, in Cardiff, Wales; son of Thomas Brynwyn (a bank manager) and Gladys (a teacher; maiden name, Phillips) Jones; married Beryl Watson (a lecturer), July 30, 1966; children: Kathryn Ann, Martyn Hywel, Carolyn Heather. *Education:* University of London, B.Sc. (with honors), 1961, M.B.B.S., 1965; University of Western Australia, D.Sc., 1976. *Religion:* Christian. *Home:* 3 Sabina St., Woodlands, Western Australia 6018. *Office:* Department of

Anatomy and Human Biology, University of Western Australia, Nedlands, Western Australia 6009.

CAREER: University of London, London, England, lecturer in anatomy, 1965-70; University of Western Australia, Nedlands, Australia, senior lecturer, 1970-76, associate professor of anatomy and human biology and head of department, 1977—. *Member:* Australian Neuroscience Society, Human Genetics Society of Australia, Institute of Biology, Institute of Society, Ethics, and Life Sciences, Anatomical Society of the United Kingdom and Australia, Australian and New Zealand Association for the Advancement of Science, American Scientific Affiliation, Victoria Institute, Sigma Xi. *Awards, honors:* W. E. Adams grant from Anatomical Society of Australia, 1975.

WRITINGS: Teilhard de Chardin: An Analysis and Assessment, Inter-Varsity Press, 1969; *Synapses and Synaptosomes: Morphological Aspects,* Chapman & Hall, 1975; *Some Current Concepts of Synaptic Organization,* Springer-Verlag, 1978; *Genetic Engineering,* Grove, 1978; *Our Fragile Brains,* Inter-Varsity Press, 1981; *Neurons and Synapses,* Edward Arnold, 1981; *Biology and the Human Predicament,* Inter-Varsity Press, 1983.

Contributor: G. H. Bourne, editor, *Structure and Function of Nervous Tissue,* Volume 6, Academic Press, 1972; M. A. Hayat, editor, *Principles and Techniques of Electron Microscopy,* Volume 7, Van Nostrand, 1976; C.F.H. Henry, editor, *Horizons of Science,* Harper, 1978; D. L. Willis, editor, *Origins and Change,* American Scientific Affiliation, 1978; R. L. Herrmann, editor, *Making Whole Persons: Ethical Issues in Biology and Medicine,* American Scientific Affiliation, 1980; E. Acosta Vidrio and S. Fedoroff, editors, *Eleventh International Congress of Anatomy, Part A: Glial and Neuronal Cell Biology,* Alan R. Liss, 1981; H. Parvez, T. Nagatsu, and S. Parvez, editors, *Methods in Biogenic Amino Research,* Elsevier-North Holland, 1982; Fedoroff and L. Hertz, editors, *Advances in Cellular Neurobiology,* Volume 4, Academic Press, in press.

Editor-in-chief of "Current Topics in Research on Synapses," a series published by Alan R. Liss. Contributor to scientific journals. Editor of *Journal of the American Scientific Affiliation* and *Interchange.*

SIDELIGHTS: Jones commented: "I study a diverse range of topics that may appear daunting to some people. They are my professional concern of neurobiology, in particular the synaptic connections between nerve cells of the brain, and my interests in more general scientific, ethical, and theological issues. This is not an eclectic assortment of topics, though, because they all tend to revolve around biology, especially human biology. As a life-scientist I am motivated to relate the area of my speciality to human issues and to view human beings in terms of our contemporary understanding of neurobiology and genetics. Hence, while my activities at first glance may appear to be a motley assortment of unconnected bits and pieces, this is far from the case.

"As a scientist I feel strongly that the scientific endeavor cannot be understood as if it were morally neutral. Science is carried out by human beings, all of whom have their biases, predilections, social concerns, and political affiliations. While these may not explicitly intrude into the way in which scientific analyses are carried out, they obviously have a part to play in the selection of research projects, in the way in which finances are channeled into certain specialties and not others, and in the application of the results of research.

"My own writings tend to be at a number of different levels—technical (for neurobiologists), semi-technical (for other bi-

ologists and scientists) and, hopefully, relatively nontechnical (for the general public). It is not easy to move between these levels, and I am sure I do not please all my readers all the time. Perhaps the major difficulty I experience at the nontechnical level is imparting information, which by its very nature is difficult to understand by the 'uninitiated,' in a manner that will be understood and yet will retain its inherent subtleties, contradictions, and ethical dilemmas."

*   *   *

JONES, Elwyn   1923-1982

OBITUARY NOTICE—See index for *CA* sketch: Born May 4, 1923, in Aberdare, Wales; died May 19, 1982, in Wales. Author and television scriptwriter best known for his police series "Z Cars" and "Softly Softly," both broadcast by the British Broadcasting Corporation (BBC-TV). Jones studied real crimes and visited police stations to gather background information and assure the authenticity of his scripts. He also wrote several books, including *The Ripper File, Dick Barton—Special Agent,* and *The Last Two to Hang,* which received the Edgar Allen Poe Award for best crime-fact novel from the Mystery Writers of America. Obituaries and other sources: *London Times,* May 20, 1982.

*   *   *

JONES, J. Faragut
See STREIB, Dan(iel Thomas)

*   *   *

JONES, Judith Paterson   1938-
(Judith Paterson, Judith Paterson-Jones)

PERSONAL: Born September 28, 1938, in Montgomery, Ala.; daughter of Julius Porter (a florist) and Emily (Hillman) Paterson; married Charles William Jones, Jr., September 4, 1958 (divorced May, 1978); children: Beth, Charles. *Education:* Hollins College, B.A., 1958; Auburn University, M.A., 1972, Ph.D., 1975. *Home:* 4577 MacArthur Blvd., Washington, D.C. 20007. *Office:* Department of English, Auburn University, Montgomery, Ala. 36109.

CAREER: Political campaign worker and free-lance editor and writer, 1958-68; Headstart teacher and coordinator in Montgomery, Ala., 1968; Auburn University, Montgomery, instructor, 1972-75, assistant professor, 1975-77, associate professor of English and women's studies, 1978-81; Network News, Inc., executive editor, 1981—. Managing editor of *Washington Book Review,* 1981—. Adjunct professor at University of Maryland, George Washington University, and U.S. Government Graduate School, 1980—. *Member:* Renaissance Society of America, Modern Language Association of America, National Council of Teachers of English, National Organization for Women, Amici Thomae Mori, Washington Independent Writers. *Awards, honors:* Fellowships for Newberry Library, 1974, and from National Endowment for the Humanities, 1979.

WRITINGS: Thomas More, Twayne, 1979; *Philip Roth,* Ungar, 1981. Contributor to literature journals and poetry magazines (with poems under name Judith Paterson-Jones) and to newspapers (under name Judith Paterson).

WORK IN PROGRESS: A book of poetry; a collection of interviews of women writers.

SIDELIGHTS: Jones told *CA:* "My career as a reader and writer began, I believe, one day in the hot, dusty little library of my elementary school in Montgomery, Alabama. The whole fourth grade had been taken to the library to check out books. As I sat there in my first library, reading the first book of my own choosing, I realized that I had found the most enjoyable way for a human being to live. From that day, I was a compulsive reader and lover of the language. I write because writing is an extension of reading and because it is the most enjoyable way I have ever found to make a living. It is not a lucrative way and usually not an easy one, but it is challenging—ultimately always fun.''

*   *   *

JONES, Raymond F.   1915-

BRIEF ENTRY: Born in 1915 in Salt Lake City, Utah. American science fiction author. Jones began writing stories for science fiction magazines in the 1940's. His novel *This Island Earth* (Shasta Publishers, 1952) was adapted as a feature film by Universal-International in 1955. Jones's other books include *Planet of Light* (Winston, 1953), *The Secret People* (Avalon, 1956), *Moonbase One* (Criterian, 1971), *Radar: How It Works* (Putnam, 1972), and *Renegades of Time* (Harlequin Enterprises, 1975).

*   *   *

JONES, Rebecca C(astaldi)   1947-

PERSONAL: Born September 10, 1947, in Evergreen Park, Ill.; daughter of Lawrence J. (an accountant) and Ruth (Speitel) Castaldi; married Christopher Jones (a research manager), August 8, 1970; children: Amanda, David. *Education:* Northwestern University, B.S., 1969, M.S., 1970. *Religion:* Roman Catholic. *Office:* University College, University of Maryland, College Park, Md. 20742.

CAREER: Warsaw Times-Union, Warsaw, Ind., reporter, 1965-66; Illinois Children's Home and Aide Society, Chicago, public relations aide, 1967; *Cue,* New York City, staff intern, 1968; *Ingenue,* New York City, staff intern, 1968; *Newark Advocate,* Newark, Ohio, reporter, 1970-71; WBNS-TV, Columbus, Ohio, assignment editor and reporter, 1971-72; Ohio State University, Columbus, instructor in journalism, 1972-75; University of Maryland at College Park, associate professor of journalism, 1975—. Public relations consultant.

WRITINGS: Angie and Me (juvenile), Macmillan, 1981; *The Biggest, Meanest, Ugliest Dog in the Whole Wide World* (juvenile), Macmillan, 1982. Author of "A Woman's Words," a weekly column in *Catholic Times,* 1970-72. Contributor of about thirty articles to magazines and newspapers, including *Young Miss, Army, Young World,* and *Washington Post.*

WORK IN PROGRESS: A juvenile novel tentatively titled *Old Lady Who;* a picture book.

SIDELIGHTS: Rebecca Jones wrote: "I was sick a great deal as a child, and our parish priest used to warn me of the dangers of 'playing with yourself' when alone in bed. I wasn't sure what that meant but interpreted it to be the same as 'playing *by* yourself.' I avoided the evil by creating great imaginary characters to keep me company in the sickroom. Today many of those imaginary characters sit down with me at the typewriter to tell their stories."

*   *   *

JONES, Russell   1918-1979

PERSONAL: Born January 5, 1918, in Minneapolis, Minn.; died June 9, 1979, in Vienna, Austria; son of Lewis (a newspaper editor) and Elizabeth J. (a journalist; maiden name,

McLeod) Russell; married Marta Sennyey von Kissenye, July 29, 1955; children: Jozsef Karolyi von Nagykaroly, Erzseber Karoli von Nagykaroly (stepchildren). *Education:* Attended high school in Stillwater, Minn. *Politics:* Independent. *Residence:* Vienna, Austria.

CAREER/WRITINGS: Stillwater Post Messenger, Stillwater, Minn. reporter, c. 1935-37; *St. Paul Dispatch,* St. Paul, Minn., reporter and radio columnist, c. 1937-41; *Stars and Stripes,* co-founder of European edition, 1942, combat reporter in England, North Africa, France, Belgium, and Germany, 1942-45, civilian reporter in New York and Europe, 1946-48; *Weekend* (magazine), Paris, France, co-owner and editor, 1948-49; United Press International (UPI), foreign correspondent in London, Prague, Vienna, and Frankfurt, 1949-56, chief Eastern European correspondent, 1956-57; Middle East correspondent for Columbia Broadcasting System (CBS-TV) and bureau chief in Beirut, Tel Aviv, and Moscow for American Broadcasting Co. (ABC-TV), 1957-77. *Military service:* U.S. Army, 1941-45, served in infantry and as combat reporter for *Stars and Stripes;* became technical sergeant. *Member:* Overseas Press Club. *Awards, honors:* Received Pultizer Prize, Overseas Press Club George Polk Memorial Award, and Sigma Delta Chi award, 1957, for coverage of 1956 Hungarian Revolt.

SIDELIGHTS: Russell Jones was the only newspaperman ever to win all three of journalism's most prestigious awards—a Pultizer Prize, a George Polk Memorial Award, and a Sigma Delta Chi award. The honors were presented to Jones for his United Press coverage of the Hungarian Revolt in 1956, when he was the only American correspondent to remain in Budapest as Russian troops stormed the city to crush the revolutionaries. When Jones arrived in the Hungarian capital on October 29, 1956, about a week after the insurrection began, telephone and cable lines were down and train and plane service suspended. Jones, however, managed to dispatch briefs on one teletype circuit to Vienna and send carbon copies of his longer reports out with acquaintances and passersby. He remained in his shell-riddled, unheated hotel room for the next month, reporting on the Soviet takeover until the communists expelled him. Jones was the first member of the United Press to win the Pultizer Prize, which cited him "for his excellent and sustained coverage of the Hungarian revolt against communist domination, during which he worked at great personal risk within Russian-held Budapest and gave frontline eyewitness reports of the ruthless Soviet repression of the Hungarian people."

OBITUARIES: New York Times, June, 11, 1979; *Washington Post,* June 11, 1979; *Current Biography,* Wilson, August, 1979.*

*   *   *

JOSPE, Alfred   1909-

PERSONAL: Surname is pronounced Yos-*pay;* born March 31, 1909, in Berlin, Germany; came to the United States in 1939, naturalized citizen, 1945; son of Josef (a cantor) and Rosa (Cerini) Jospe; married Eva Scheyer (a university lecturer), January 27, 1935; children: Susanne Jospe Greenberg, Naomi Jospe Pisetzky, Raphael R. *Education:* University of Breslau, Ph.D., 1932; Jewish Theological Seminary, Breslau, Germany, Rabbi, 1935. *Home:* 2949 Upton St. N.W., Washington, D.C. 20008.

CAREER: Rabbi of Jewish congregations in Schneidemuehl, Germany (now Poland), 1934-36, and Berlin, Germany, 1936-39; B'nai B'rith Hillel Foundations (an international agency serving the religious, cultural, and counseling needs of Jewish students), director of units at West Virginia University, Morgantown, 1940-44, and Indiana University, Bloomington, 1944-

49, national director of program and resources at colleges and universities, 1949-71, international director, 1971-74; writer and researcher, 1974—. Visiting lecturer at University of Maryland, 1977; adjunct professor at American University, 1979-81. Member of board of directors of Leo Baeck Institute, 1974—; member of B'nai B'rith Hillel Commission, 1977—. *Member:* Zionist Organization of America, Central Conference of American Rabbis, Washington Board of Rabbis, B'nai B'rith. *Awards, honors:* D.D. from Hebrew Union College-Jewish Institute of Religion, 1971.

WRITINGS: *Die Unterscheidung von Religion und Mythos bei Herman Cohen und Ernst Cassirer in ihrer Bedeutung fuer die juedische Religionsphilosophie* (title means "The Distinction Between Religion and Myth in the Systems of Hermann Cohen and Ernst Cassirer and Its Significance for the Jewish Philosophy of Religion"), Reuther & Reichart, 1932; *Judaism on the Campus: Essays on Jewish Education in the University Community,* B'nai B'rith Hillel Foundations, 1953; *A Handbook for Student Leaders,* B'nai B'rith Hillel Foundations, 1954, 5th edition, 1968; (with S. Norman Feingold) *College Guide for Jewish Youth,* B'nai B'rith Hillel Foundations, 1955, 5th edition, 1968; (contributor) Simon Noveck, editor, *Great Jewish Personalities in Modern Times,* B'nai B'rith Adult Education, 1960; (editor with Daniel Thursz) *Israel as Idea and Reality: A Sourcebook for Study and Discussion,* B'nai B'rith Hillel Foundations, 1962; (editor and translator) H. S. Bergmann, *Faith and Reason: An Introduction to Modern Jewish Thought,* Schocken, 1963.

(Editor and author of introduction) *The Legacy of Maurice Pekarsky,* Quadrangle, 1965; (editor) *Dimensions of Jewish Existence Today,* B'nai B'rith Hillel Foundations, 1965; (editor) *Hanukkah in the Hillel Foundation: A Guide to Hanukkah Programs and Resources,* B'nai B'rith Hillel Foundations, 1965; (editor and contributor) *Campus 1966: Change and Challenge,* B'nai B'rith Hillel Foundations, 1966; (editor and contributor) *New Frontiers for Jewish Life on the Campus,* B'nai B'rith Hillel Foundations, 1968; (editor and translator) *Jerusalem and Other Writings by Moses Mendelssohn,* Schocken, 1969; *The Campus: Conflict or Challenge?,* B'nai B'rith Hillel Foundations, 1969; *Issues of Faith: Two Letters on Theological Concerns,* B'nai B'rith Hillel Foundations, 1969; (editor) *Tradition and Contemporary Experience: Essays in Jewish Thought and Life,* Schocken, 1970; (editor) *Jewish Studies in American Colleges and Universities: A Catalogue,* B'nai B'rith Hillel Foundations, 1972; (editor with Richard N. Levy) *Bridges to a Holy Time: New Worship for the Sabbath and Minor Festivals,* Ktav, 1973; (editor and author of introduction) *Studies in Jewish Thought: An Anthology of German Jewish Scholarship,* Wayne State University Press, 1981; (contributor) *Yearbook of the Leo Baeck Institute,* [London, England], 1982.

General editor of "Hillel Library Series," 1950-68, and "Hillel Little Books," 1954—. Contributor to *Encyclopedia Judaica* and *American Jewish Yearbook.* Contributor to magazines. Editor of *Clearing House,* 1949-71.

SIDELIGHTS: Jospe wrote: "My primary personal and scholarly interest has always been in the area of religious thought and philosophy (as well as theology), especially Jewish religious and philosophical thought since the Emancipation, leading to the study of the social, political, and intellectual factors influencing the making of the modern Jew. Professional travels have taken me to Europe, Israel, Australia, New Zealand, and Latin America."

BIOGRAPHICAL/CRITICAL SOURCES: Raphael Jospe and Samuel Z. Fishman, *Go and Study: Essays and Studies in Honor of Alfred Jospe,* Ktav, 1980.

JOYCE, Brian T(homas) 1938-

PERSONAL: Born January 8, 1938, in Oakland, Calif.; son of Thomas (a saloon owner) and Margaret (Sweehey) Joyce. *Education:* St. Patrick's Seminary, Menlo Park, Calif., B.S., 1963; Manhattan College, Riverdale, N.Y., M.A., 1970. *Home:* 1007 Larch Ave., Moraga, Calif. 94556.

CAREER: Ordained Roman Catholic priest, 1963; associate pastor of Roman Catholic churches in Oakland, Calif., 1963-67; Diocese of Oakland, director of adult education, 1967-70, chancellor, 1970-79; St. Monica's Church, Moraga, Calif., pastor, 1979—. Regional president of Conference of Priest Senates for the western states, 1978, 1979; president of Oakland Diocese's Priests Senate, 1981—; consultant to National Conference of Catholic Bishops.

WRITINGS: *Religion, Parent, and Child,* Sadlier, 1970; *Communion, Parent, and Child,* Sadlier, 1971; *Penance, Parent, and Child,* Sadlier, 1971, revised edition, 1974.

*   *   *

JOYNT, Robert R(ichard) 1915-

PERSONAL: Born December 29, 1915, in East Jordan, Mich.; son of Thomas (a carpenter) and Alice (a teacher; maiden name, Morrow) Joynt; married Mary Carolyn Harger (a realtor), June 21, 1941; children: Patricia Joynt Williams, Suzanne Joynt Roggenkamp, Thomas, Robert. *Education:* Central Michigan University, B.S., 1940; Wayne State University, M.S., 1962; University of Northern Colorado, Ed.D., 1967. *Politics:* Republican. *Religion:* Brethren. *Home:* 257 State, Bowling Green, Ohio 43402. *Office:* Department of Special Education, Bowling Green State University, Bowling Green, Ohio 43403.

CAREER: Detroit Tap and Tool Co., Detroit, Mich., personnel director, 1940-47; special education teacher at public schools in Mount Clemens, Mich., 1958-65, school psychologist, 1965-66; Bowling Green State University, Bowling Green, Ohio, began as assistant professor, became associate professor of special education, 1967-82. Educational psychologist, Wood County Mental Health Clinic, 1967—. *Member:* National Education Association, Council for Exceptional Children.

WRITINGS: *The Planner,* four volumes, Mafex, 1970; (editor with Robert B. Blackwell) *Learning Disabilities Handbook for Teachers,* C. C Thomas, 1976; (with Blackwell) *Mainstreaming: What to Expect . . . What to Do,* Mafex, 1980.

*   *   *

JUEL-NIELSEN, Niels 1920-

PERSONAL: Born March 24, 1920, in Holbaek, Denmark; son of Carl (a business manager) Nielsen and Karen Christine Laura Juel; married Lis Moeller, August 10, 1947; children: Ulla, Nina. *Education:* University of Copenhagen, M.D., 1948; University of Aarhus, Ph.D., 1965. *Home:* 12 Overgade, 5000 Odense, Denmark. *Agent:* International Universities Press, New York, N.Y. *Office:* Institute of Psychiatry, Odense University, Odense, Denmark.

CAREER: Worked as specialist in psychiatry, 1955; University of Aarhus, Aarhus, Denmark, principal research psychiatrist, 1959-67; Odense University, Odense, Denmark, head of psychiatry department, 1967—, professor of psychiatry, 1970—. Member of Danish Medical Research Council, 1972-79. *Member:* Danish Psychiatric Association, Finnish Psychiatric Association. *Awards, honors:* Antonius Prize from Danish Mental Health Assocation, 1966.

WRITINGS: Individual and Environment: Monozygotic Twins Reared Apart, Munksgaard, 1965, revised edition, International Universities Press, 1980.

WORK IN PROGRESS: Epidemiological and clinical research on suicidal behavior in the Nordic countries.

SIDELIGHTS: Juel-Nielsen's *Individual and Environment* documents his study of twelve sets of separated twins. Juel-Nielsen determined during his research that the relations between genetic and environmental impact on human development are far from easy summarization. As *New York Times Book Review*'s Howard E. Gruber noted, "The task is not to squeeze the data for some answer to the well-nigh meaningless question of 'how much' heredity and environment influence development. The task . . . is to understand the manifold interactions through which individual development comes about."

Juel-Nielsen told *CA:* "The interplay between nature and nurture in the development of the human individual has been the object of most of my research activity and thinking."

BIOGRAPHICAL/CRITICAL SOURCES: New York Times Book Review, March 1, 1981.

K

KADISH, Mortimer Raymond 1916-

BRIEF ENTRY: Born December 2, 1916, in New York, N.Y. American philosopher, educator, and author. Kadish began teaching at Case Western Reserve University in 1948 and became a professor of philosophy in 1961. He was a Guggenheim fellow, 1954-55, and an American Council of Learned Societies fellow, 1967-68. His writings include *Point of Honor* (Random House, 1952), *Reason and Controversy in the Arts* (Press of Case Western Reserve University, 1968), and *Discretion to Disobey: A Study of Lawful Departures From Legal Rules* (Stanford University Press, 1973). *Address:* 13906 Larchmere Rd., Cleveland, Ohio 44120; and Department of Philosophy, Case Western Reserve University, Cleveland, Ohio 44106. *Biographical/critical sources: Annals of the American Academy of Political and Social Science*, September, 1974; *Directory of American Scholars*, Volume IV: *Philosophy, Religion, and Law*, 7th edition, Bowker, 1978.

* * *

KAHN, Samuel 1897-1981

OBITUARY NOTICE: Born June 16, 1897, in Latvia (now Latvian Soviet Socialist Republic; some sources list birthplace as Atlanta, Ga.); died December 24, 1981, in White Plains, N.Y. Psychiatrist, educator, and author. A graduate of Emory University, where he also received a medical degree, Kahn studied with Freud in Vienna and interned at several New York hospitals before serving as a psychiatrist at Sing Sing State Prison from 1929 to 1931. In addition to having a private practice in psychoanalysis, Kahn worked as a clinical psychiatrist at Mt. Sinai Hospital and as an associate professor at Long Island University. He also founded and directed the Quakerbridge School, a youth camp in Ossining, N.Y. The author of more than thirty books on psychotherapy, Kahn wrote *Master Your Mind, Psychodrama Explained, An Introduction to Parapsychology, Anxieties, Phobias, and Fears, Thanks for a Better Memory*, and *Practical Child Guidance and Mental Hygiene*. Obituaries and other sources: *Who's Who in the East*, 18th edition, Marquis, 1981; *New York Times*, December 28, 1981.

* * *

KAHN, Sandra S(utker) 1942-

PERSONAL: Born June 24, 1942, in Chicago, Ill.; daughter of Chester (in sales) and Ruth (Goldblatt) Sutker; married Jack Kahn (a steel company president), June 1, 1965; children: Erick, Jennifer. *Education:* University of Miami, Coral Gables, Fla., B.A., 1964; Roosevelt University, M.A., 1976. *Religion:* Jewish. *Residence:* Highland Park, Ill. *Office:* 2970 Maria Ave., Northbrook, Ill. 60062.

CAREER: High school English teacher, 1965-67; therapist at Elgin State Hospital, 1972-73; private practice of psychotherapy in Northbrook, Ill., 1976—. Lecturer. *Member:* Illinois Psychological Association, Chicago Psychological Association.

WRITINGS: The Kahn Report on Sexual Preferences, St. Martin's, 1981.

WORK IN PROGRESS: A book on parenthood, publication by Avon expected in 1984.

SIDELIGHTS: Sandra Kahn wrote: "The research for my first book was motivated by my clinical work and the lack of baseline data on male and female sexual preferences. The book was written as an aid to professionals and the general public.

"*The Kahn Report* has been printed in nine different countries. It is a book which attempts to explain why men and women have trouble telling one another what sexual activities they enjoy. Sexuality is our adult way of communicating intimately with each other and an important part of a meaningful relationship. I have attempted to deal with the problems that exist between couples in a language that is both readable and enjoyable.

"My second book deals with the negative aspects of parenthood that we all feel and with the guilt experienced in having and sharing these feelings. I also do a lot of public speaking on a variety of psycho-social issues."

* * *

KAISER, Georg 1878-1945

BRIEF ENTRY: Born November 25, 1878, in Magdeburg, Germany; died June 4, 1945, in Ascona, Switzerland. German playwright. With about seventy plays to his credit, Kaiser was not only one of Germany's most prolific and popular playwrights, but was perhaps the most solid representative of the German expressionist writers. His greatest popularity came from *Die Buerger von Calais* (1914), an appeal for peace and a rebirth of morality, *Von Morgans bis Mittennachts* (1916;

translated as *From Morn to Midnight*, 1920), and *"Gas I"* (1918; translated as *Gas,* 1924), which depicted the dehumanization of man by an industrial complex. These themes run through much of Kaiser's work, along with his hopes for man's salvation through self-sacrifice and love. His work is almost purely expressionistic: the dramas were plays of ideas, at the expense of form; language was minimized, even truncated, in favor of action; characters were merely types, not individuals. Because of the technical perfection of his expressionism, some claim that Kaiser contributed more than almost anyone else to the transformation of twentieth-century German drama. In a departure from his usual style, Kaiser wrote a mythological trilogy, *Griechische Dramen* (1948), which was produced after his death. Written during the playwright's self-imposed exile from Nazi Germany, the work expressed a passionate love for the world and its beauty, coupled with undying hatred for those who would destroy it. Except for during the Nazi period, when his plays were banned and burned, Kaiser remained popular in his homeland. He still holds a prominent place in German letters. *Biographical/critical sources: Encyclopedia of World Literature in the Twentieth Century,* updated edition, Ungar, 1967; *McGraw-Hill Encyclopedia of World Drama,* McGraw, 1972.

* * *

KALICH, Robert 1947-

PERSONAL: Born March 18, 1947, in Brooklyn, N.Y.; son of Kalmen (a cantor) and Beatrice (a professor of psychology; maiden name, Block) Kalich. *Education:* New York University, B.S., 1968; Columbia University, M.A., 1971. *Home:* 240 Central Park S., New York, N.Y. 10019. *Office:* Kalich Organization, 65 Central Park W., New York, N.Y. 10023.

CAREER: Associated with *New York Mirror,* New York City, 1968—; Kalich Organization, New York City, film producer, 1968—. Social worker with Department of Social Services in ghettos of New York City; film producer with Sid Bernstein Enterprises, New York City.

WRITINGS: The Basketball Rating Handbook, A. S. Barnes, 1969; *The Baseball Rating Handbook,* A. S. Barnes, 1969; *The Negro Manifesto,* Sayer Ross, 1970; *The Vitalis Man of the Year Football Handbook,* Vitalis, 1973; *The Great Three Hundred,* Bert Sugar, 1975; *The Handicapper* (novel), Crown, 1981.

Scripts: "The Tutor" (screenplay), produced by Margolies & Paleck, in 1974; "Allen" (one-act play), first produced in Long Beach, Calif., at Long Beach Memorial Church, 1978.

WORK IN PROGRESS: The Tissue Man, a novel, completion expected in 1983.

SIDELIGHTS: Kalich told *CA:* "In all my work, my motivation has always been a woman. Most of my work has been inspired by the experiences I have had and know most intimately. I have worked in many and varied positions, from Harlem ghettos to the fantasy world of Hollywood, from handicapping horses for the *New York Mirror* to working with Winchell and Mortimer, to covering basketball, baseball, and football as a journalist and free-lance writer.

"Insight to young writers: Do not knock your head against the wall thinking in terms of art. The publishing industry is interested in the 'big' book. They are interested in reaching markets, not publishing literature. Robbins, Clavell, and Krantz are the household words and the 'successes' of this industry. Join 'em, don't fight 'em."

KANTZER, Kenneth S(ealer) 1917-

PERSONAL: Born March 29, 1917, in Detroit, Mich.; son of Edwin Frederick (a factory worker) and Clara (Sealer) Kantzer; married Ruth Forbes, September 21, 1939; children: Mary Ruth Kantzer Wilkinson, Richard Forbes. *Education:* Ashland College, A.B., 1938; Ohio State University, M.A., 1939; Faith Theological Seminary, B.D., 1942, S.T.M., 1943; Harvard University, Ph.D., 1950; postdoctoral study at University of Goettingen and University of Basel, 1954-55. *Politics:* Republican. *Home:* 1752 Spruce, Highland Park, Ill. 60035. *Office: Christianity Today,* 465 Gundersen Dr., Carol Stream, Ill. 60187.

CAREER: Ordained minister of Evangelical Free Church of America, 1948; King's College, New Castle, Del., instructor in Bible, 1941-43; Gordon College, Wenham, Mass., instructor in Old Testament, 1944-46; Wheaton College, Wheaton, Ill., instructor, 1946-49, assistant professor, 1949-52, associate professor, 1952-57, Deal Professor of Theology, 1957-63, chairman of department of Bible and philosophy, 1952-63; Trinity Evangelical Divinity School, Deerfield, Ill., dean, 1963-78, vice-president of graduate studies, 1969-78, dean emeritus, 1979—; *Christianity Today,* Carol Stream, Ill., editor, 1978—. Pastor of Pidgeon Cove Chapel, Rockport, Mass., 1945-46. Dean and vice-president of Winona Summer Seminary, 1958-65. Member of board of directors of Columbia Bible College of Evangelical Alliance Mission, of China Graduate School of Theology, and of Ministers Life Insurance Co. *Member:* Evangelical Theological Society (past president), Evangelical Philosophical Society, American Association of Religious Instructors.

WRITINGS: Evangelical Roots, Thomas Nelson, 1978; *Perspectives on Evangelical Theology,* Baker Book, 1980.

Contributor: Howard Vos, editor, *Religions in a Changing World,* Moody, 1966; John Walvoord, editor, *Inspiration and Interpretation,* Eerdmans, 1966; Carl F.H. Henry, editor, *Jesus of Nazareth: Savior and Lord,* Eerdmans, 1968. Contributor to theology journals.

BIOGRAPHICAL/CRITICAL SOURCES: Time, August 29, 1977; *Christianity Today,* September 9, 1977, April 7, 1978.

* * *

KAPPAUF, William Emil (Jr.) 1913-

PERSONAL: Born October 2, 1913, in New York, N.Y.; son of William Emil and Juliet Theodora (Bonnlander) Kappauf; married Catharine Anne Hamilton, June 16, 1945; children: Barbara Kappauf Andreassen, Charles, Katharine Kappauf Johnson, William F. *Education:* Columbia University, A.B., 1934; Brown University, M.A., 1935; University of Rochester, Ph.D., 1937. *Religion:* Episcopalian. *Home:* 1401 Waverly Dr., Champaign, Ill. 61820. *Office:* Department of Psychology, University of Illinois, 713 Psychology Bldg., Champaign, Ill. 61820.

CAREER/WRITINGS: University of Rochester, Rochester, N.Y., instructor in psychology, 1937-41; participant in research projects under National Defense Research Committee and Office of Scientific Research and Development, 1941-46; Princeton University, Princeton, N.J., associate professor of psychology, 1946-51; University of Illinois, Champaign, professor of psychology, 1951-80, associate head of department of psychology, 1976-78. Editor of *American Journal of Psychology,* 1971—. Consultant to Bell Telephone Laboratory, National Institutes of Health, National Science Foundation, and military agencies. *Member:* American Psychological Association, American Association of University Professors, American Association for the Advancement of Science, Midwestern Psychological Association, Society of Experimental Psychologists (secretary-treasurer, 1967-70), Phi Beta Kappa, Sigma Xi. *Awards, honors:* Presidential Certificate of Merit, 1948.

SIDELIGHTS: Kappauf told *CA* that his "publications include journal articles in areas of comparative psychology, vision, audition, perception, human engineering, and quantitative methods."

* * *

KARPEL, Bernard 1911-

PERSONAL: Born February 10, 1911, in Brooklyn, N.Y.; son of Abraham and Tilly (Barach) Karpel; married Raye Spitz (a secretarial collaborator); children: George, Kenneth, Mara. *Education:* City College (now of the City University of New York), B.A., 1932; Pratt Institute, B.L.S., 1937; graduate study at Columbia University, 1940-41. *Home:* 3 Wilbur Blvd., Poughkeepsie, N.Y. 12603.

CAREER: City College (now of the City University of New York), New York City, reader in art, 1934-36; New York Public Library, New York City, art librarian at branch library, 1937-41; Museum of Modern Art, New York City, chief librarian and bibliographer, 1942-73, executive director of International Council's overseas library program, 1967-73; Smithsonain Institution, Washington, D.C., director of Bicentennial Bibliography of American Art, 1973-78; writer and consultant, 1978—. Instructor at Columbia University, 1967-69; lecturer at Pratt Institute, 1969; associate professor at Queens College of the City University of New York, 1970. Member of advisory board of Archives of American Art; member of Burchfield Center. *Military service:* Signal Corps, Astoria, N.Y., 1941-42; worked in film research department. *Member:* Art Librarians of North America, College Art Association of America, Archons of Colophon. *Awards, honors:* Grants from Rockefeller Foundation, 1952-53, and John D. Rockefeller III Fund, 1966-67; award of merit from Philadelphia College of Art, 1969; D.H.L. from Maryland Institute, 1976.

WRITINGS; (Contributor of bibliography) Carola Gledion-Welcker, *Contemporary Sculpture: An Evolution in Volume and Space*, Wittenborn, 1955, revised edition, Faber, 1961; (author of introduction) *The Armory Show: An International Exhibition of Modern Art*, Volume I: *Catalogues*, Volume II: *Pamphlets*, Volume III: *Contemporary and Retrospective Documents*, Arno, 1972; Jurg Spiller, editor, *Notebooks of Paul Klee*, Volume II: *The Nature of Nature*, Wittenborn, 1973; (editor) *Arts in America: A Bibliography*, Volume I: *Art of the Native Americans, Architecture, Decorative Arts, Design, Sculptures, Art of the West*, Volume II: *Painting and Graphic Arts*, Volume III: *Photography, Film, Theater, Dance, Music, Serials and Periodicals, Dissertations and Theses, Visual Resources*, Volume IV: *General Index*, Smithsonian Institution Press, 1979; *The Dada Painters and Poets*, revised edition, Hall, 1981. Associate editor of "Documents of Modern Art," a series, Wittenborn, 1962-66; of "Contemporary Art," a series, Arno, 1968-72; and of "Documents of 20th-Century Art," a series, Viking, 1971-78.

WORK IN PROGRESS: An updated edition, with Robert Motherwell and Ad Reinhardt, of *Modern Artists in America*, to cover 1951 to 1981.

SIDELIGHTS: Karpel told *CA:* "My work in documentation, libraries, research in art and teaching was directed by the con-

cepts of earlier decades. Insofar as they related to those areas, the data was largely literary and concentrated in comparatively few centers seriously devoted to art.

"With the passing of time, providing greater opportunities for thinking and feeling, and a growing sense for sharing specialized resources that increase in intensity and cost, there are other changes. The net of need embraces both the verbal and the visual which, like lovers, are enriched by the joining of hands.

"To this primary insight, a reborn professional has to add a fresh perception: to disperse rather than to concentrate the relevant and varied materials, to distrust a luxury of resource in five cities and comparative poverty in fifty towns (worldwide). Every reasonable device should be employed in this explosion, not merely bibliographic but electronic, provided it is a shared experience. Albers said it to me, using the enigma, as usual, to clarify the esthetic truth: 'We own only what we give away.'"

BIOGRAPHICAL/CRITICAL SOURCES: Museum of Modern Art Bulletin, Volume XI, number 3, 1943-44, Volume XXI, number 2, 1953-54; *Pratt Alumnus*, spring, 1969.

* * *

KATZ, Judith Milstein 1943-

PERSONAL: Born March 16, 1943, in New York, N.Y.; daughter of Paul (a lawyer) and Sylvia (a teacher; maiden name, Vogel) Milstein. *Education:* Connecticut College for Women, A.B., 1964; Boston University, A.M., 1966; Harvard University, Ed.D., 1970. *Agent:* Richard A. Balkin, Balkin Agency, 403 West 115th St., New York, N.Y. 10025. *Office:* Department of Psychology, Atkinson College, York University, Toronto, Ontario, Canada.

CAREER: Lecturer at Ontario Institute for Studies in Education, 1967-70; York University, Toronto, Ontario, assistant professor, 1970-74, associate professor of psychology, 1975—. Visiting scholar at University of California, Berkeley, 1976-77. *Member:* Phi Beta Kappa.

WRITINGS: Why Don't You Listen to What I'm Not Saying?, Doubleday, 1981.

* * *

KAY, Jane Holtz 1938-

PERSONAL: Born July 7, 1938, in Boston, Mass.; daughter of Jackson J. (a lawyer) and Edith (Weinstein) Holtz; divorced; children: Jacqueline, Julie. *Education:* Radcliffe College, B.A. (magna cum laude), 1960. *Agent:* Lois Wallace, Wallace & Sheil Agency, Inc., 170 East 70th St., New York, N.Y. 10021. *Office:* 102 South St., Boston, Mass. 02111.

CAREER: Patriot Ledger, Quincy, Mass., reporter and arts critic, 1960-69; *Boston Globe*, Boston, Mass., architecture and urban design critic, 1969-73; *Nation*, New York, N.Y., architecture and urban design critic, 1973—. Art critic for *Christian Science Monitor*, 1965-70, architecture and urban design critic, 1981—; U.S. correspondent for *Building Design*, 1972-79; New England correspondent for *Art News*, 1975—. Member of faculty at Boston University; lecturer at Harvard University, museums, art institutes and meetings, and on television. *Awards, honors:* National Endowment for the Arts fellowship, 1982.

WRITINGS: (Contributor) David Godine, editor, *A Book for Boston*, David R. Godine, 1979; *Lost Boston*, Houghton, 1980. Contributing columnist for New York Times Feature Syndicate. Contributor to *Annual of American Architecture.* Contributor to library and architecture journals, popular and regional magazines, and newspapers, including *Americas, Change, Craft Horizon, Ms., Saturday Review,* and *Smithsonian.* Contributing editor of *Inland Architect* and *American Preservation.*

WORK IN PROGRESS: Preserving America: New England, publication by Pantheon expected in 1984.

SIDELIGHTS: Kay told *CA:* "My field—the built environment—is both awesomely inclusive and chimerical. In some senses it is a fabrication to cover an interest in the human-made world from architecture (the Taj Mahal) to its substructure (the New York sewage system). And in some senses it is the essence of civilized life. Either way it is challenging and frustrating to communicate the demands of shaping and supporting our surroundings."

* * *

KEELE, Reba Lou 1941-

BRIEF ENTRY: Born October 28, 1941, in Emery, Utah. American educator, academic administrator, and author. Keele has taught educational psychology at Brigham Young University since 1967. She wrote *Let's Talk: Adults and Children Sharing Feelings* (Brigham Young University Press, 1977). *Address:* 459 East 800 North, Orem, Utah 84057; and Department of Education, Brigham Young University, Provo, Utah 84602. *Biographical/critical sources: Who's Who of American Women,* 11th edition, Marquis, 1979.

* * *

KEENE, Carolyn
See ADAMS, Harriet S(tratemeyer)

* * *

KELLERMAN, Jonathan 1949-

PERSONAL: Born August 9, 1949, in New York, N.Y.; son of David (an electrical engineer) and Sylvia (Fiacre) Kellerman; married Faye Marilyn Marder (a dentist), July, 1972; children: Jesse, Rachel. *Education:* University of California, Los Angeles, B.A., 1971; University of Southern California, M.A., 1973, Ph.D., 1974. *Agent:* John Schaffner Literary Agency, 425 East 51st St., New York, N.Y. 10022. *Office:* Psychosocial Program, Children's Hospital, Los Angeles, Calif. 90054; and 14755 Ventura Blvd., St. 102, Sherman Oaks, Calif. 91403.

CAREER: University of California, Los Angeles, *Daily Bruin,* editorial cartoonist and political satirist, 1967-71; free-lance illustrator, 1966-72; Children's Hospital, Los Angeles, Calif., director of psychosocial program, 1976-81. Assistant clinical professor at University of Southern California, 1978-80, associate clinical professor, 1980—. *Awards, honors:* Samuel Goldwyn literary award from University of California, Los Angeles/Metro-Goldwyn-Mayer, 1971, for *Poor Lieber.*

WRITINGS: Psychological Aspects of Childhood Cancer, C. C Thomas, 1980; *Helping the Fearful Child,* Norton, 1981. Also author of *Poor Lieber,* a novel, as yet unpublished.

SIDELIGHTS: Kellerman told *CA:* "I've always enjoyed writing, and this has made it easy for me to pursue an academic career. Writing *Helping the Fearful Child* was especially pleasurable, because it enabled me to escape the narrow confines of technical and scientific writing and to address myself to the lay audience. I wrote the book after seeing how useful parents could be in helping their children overcome problematic fears.

My intention was to be informative and readable without being condescending and to avoid the major pitfalls of many books in the 'pop psych' genre: ambiguity that borders on meaninglessness and endless exposition of the obvious.

"While I have written a bit of fiction (satire, mystery story, etc.), my goal is to write a first class detective novel in the tradition of Chandler, MacDonald, etc.—a work in which I can put my psychological training to use in creating something suspenseful, entertaining, and insightful."

AVOCATIONAL INTERESTS: Collecting vintage stringed instruments and mystery fiction.

* * *

KELLY, Joyce 1933-

PERSONAL: Born November 30, 1933, in New Orleans, La.; daughter of Ernest Joseph (a construction superintendent) and Anna (Pflieger) Babin; married Thomas Gerald Kelly (a hobby shop owner and operator), November 27, 1954. *Education:* Attended University of Southwest Louisiana, 1951-54, and Instituto Allende, summers, 1972-75; John McCrady Art School of New Orleans, graduated, 1964. *Politics:* "No particular party affiliation." *Religion:* Roman Catholic. *Home and office:* 713 North Murat St., New Orleans, La. 70119.

CAREER: Tulane University, New Orleans, La., medical research technician at School of Medicine, 1954-56; Louisiana State University, New Orleans, medical research technician at School of Medicine, 1956-61; John McCrady Art School of New Orleans, New Orleans, instructor in fine art, 1964—. Photographer. *Member:* American Institute of Archaeology, Louisiana Crafts Council, New Orleans Art Association, New Orleans Museum of Art Association.

WRITINGS: The Poetic Realism of Alan Flattmann, privately printed, 1980; *The Complete Visitor's Guide to Mesoamerican Ruins,* University of Oklahoma Press, 1982. Contributor to *American Artist, Art Voice,* and newspapers.

WORK IN PROGRESS: Yaxchilan and Bonampak, thorough coverage of the Maya sites.

SIDELIGHTS: Joyce Kelly told *CA:* "I wrote *The Poetic Realism of Alan Flattmann* on assignment to promote the career of a talented young artist. I felt he deserved all the promotion he could get.

"*The Complete Visitor's Guide to Mesoamerican Ruins* was written simply because there was nothing like it on the market and I felt there should be. There are a number of archaeological guides to this area, but generally they only cover about twenty sites—the major ones, of course. It is very difficult for the prospective visitor to get information—especially reliable information—about the smaller sites and those in remote areas. My guide covers one hundred nineteen sites and forty-one archaeological museums in Mexico, Guatemala, Belize, Honduras, and El Salvador. My husband (who took most of the more than three hundred black and white photographs in the guide) and I have visited all these sites, many on several occasions, and our guide includes *detailed* information on reaching the sites.

"We have made eighteen trips to Mexico and/or Central America since 1957, and parts of some of these trips were indeed expeditions, although not in the sense that we received any sort of funding. We have reached sites by car, jeep, privately chartered light aircraft, dugout canoe, on foot over muddy trails, and, in recent years, in a van with four-wheel drive, purchased for this purpose. We have slept in hammocks inside ruins and under open-sided thatch shelters, and have winched out of two-and-a-half-foot-deep mud more times than I care to remember. These minor inconveniences, as well as cutting back dozens of trees blocking back roads, are necessarily a part of gathering information to write an accurate guide, and we do not regret any of our experiences.

"As a photographer, I took many thousands of photographs (mostly color transparencies) of the ruins and monuments in Mesoamerica, and some of these are used as illustrations in my guide. I also made the drawings and maps therein.

"On my first trip to Mexico, I became intrigued with Mesoamerican archaeology and have studied this subject continuously since then. I took one formal course on high civilizations of Middle America at Tulane University. I feel that my past experiences in science, art, and photography, and my interest in travel and Mesoamerican archaeology all came together in my book. This was very satisfying.

"Although I am not fluent in Spanish, I can speak and understand enough to travel comfortably in those parts of Mesoamerica where it is the only Western language spoken.

"To travel writers, I would say that it is vital for you to gather first-hand information in detail. What you have been told by others, more often than not, will be at least inaccurate and sometimes totally incorrect. This advice, which seems obvious, sometimes goes unheeded.

"I have exhibited as a professional artist since 1964, although in the last few years I have devoted more time to writing than painting."

BIOGRAPHICAL/CRITICAL SOURCES: Los Angeles Times Book Review, April 18, 1982.

* * *

KEMPTON, Richard 1935-

PERSONAL: Born January 27, 1935, in Los Angeles, Calif.; son of Albert and Elizabeth Kempton; married Suzanne Gerson (a computer programmer), September 9, 1963; children: Madeleine, Alexander. *Education:* University of California, Berkeley, B.A., 1960, M.L.S., 1969. *Politics:* "None of the above." *Religion:* "None of the above." *Home:* 1227 San Miguel Ave., Santa Barbara, Calif. 93109. *Office:* Library, University of California, Santa Barbara, Calif. 93106.

CAREER: University of California, Berkeley, library clerk, 1964-67; University of California, Santa Barbara, librarian, 1970-80. *Military service:* U.S. Army, 1955-57.

WRITINGS: Detumescence: A Moral Tale, Suppository Press, 1976; *Art Nouveau: An Annotated Bibliography,* Volume I, Hennessey & Ingalls, 1977; *French Literature: An Annotated Guide to Selected Bibliographies,* Modern Language Association of America, 1981.

* * *

KENNY, Kathryn
See KRULL, Kathleen

* * *

KENNY, Kevin
See KRULL, Kathleen

KENT, Fortune
See TOOMBS, John

* * *

KENYON, Bernice
See GILKYSON, Bernice Kenyon

* * *

KENYON, Karen 1938-

PERSONAL: Born September 4, 1938, in Oklahoma City, Okla.; daughter of Claude E. (a lawyer) and Evelyn (a pianist; maiden name, Brown) Smith; married Richard B. Kenyon, February 14, 1963 (died, 1978); children: Richard L., Johanna (deceased). *Education:* Attended University of New Mexico, 1959-63; San Diego State University, B.A., 1977. *Home:* 3440 Dorchester Dr., San Diego, Calif. 92123. *Agent:* Jane Jordan Browne, Multimedia Product Development, Inc., 410 South Michigan Ave., Room 828, Chicago, Ill. 60605.

CAREER: Secretary, 1963-66; That Gallery (art gallery), San Diego, Calif., co-owner, 1969-72; free-lance writer, 1972—. Member of faculty at University of California, San Diego and Mira Costa College. *Member:* International P.E.N., San Diego Press Club. *Awards, honors:* Recognition award from San Diego Institute for Creativity, 1974; certificate of merit for poetry from *Atlantic Monthly,* 1975.

WRITINGS: (With Margaret Birch, Josie Rodriguez, and Nancy Schaffroth) *Many Faces* (poems), Calendula, 1972; *Sunshower* (autobiographical novel with poetry), Richard Marek, 1981. Contributor to magazines and newspapers, including *Newsweek, Redbook, Ladies' Home Journal,* and *Life and Health.*

WORK IN PROGRESS: Raindance, nonfiction, for Richard Marek; an autobiographical novel.

SIDELIGHTS: Karen Kenyon told *CA:* "I always wrote poetry. Later other longer writing grew from deep personal experience. All forms of writing, if they are close to the heart, are healing, and I feel that writing causes us to appreciate life and the human experience. Writing deepens our awareness, and our conscious experience deepens our writing."

AVOCATIONAL INTERESTS: Art (painting watercolors), batik.

BIOGRAPHICAL/CRITICAL SOURCES: San Diego Evening Tribune, September 2, 1981.

* * *

KEOHANE, Nannerl O(verholser) 1940-

PERSONAL: Surname is pronounced *Ko*-han; born September 18, 1940, in Blytheville, Ark.; daughter of James A. (a minister) and Grace (a journalist; maiden name, McSpadden) Overholser; married Patrick Henry (divorced); married Robert O. Keohane (a professor); children: Sarah, Stephan, Jonathan, Nathaniel. *Education:* Wellesley College, B.A., 1961; St. Anne's College, Oxford, B.A., M.A. (with first class honors), 1963; Yale University, Ph.D., 1967. *Home:* 735 Washington St., Wellesley, Mass. 02181. *Office:* Office of the President, Wellesley College, Wellesley, Mass. 02181.

CAREER: Swarthmore College, Swarthmore, Pa., lecturer, 1967-68, assistant professor of political science, 1969-73; Stanford University, Stanford, Calif., assistant professor, 1973-76, associate professor of political science, 1977-81; Wellesley College, Wellesley, Mass., professor of political science and president of college, 1981—. Visiting lecturer at University of Pennsylvania, 1970-72. Fellow of Center for Advanced Studies in the Behavioral Sciences, Palo Alto, Calif., 1978-79. Member of Rockefeller Commission on the Humanities, 1978-80; member of board of trustees of WGBH Educational Television Foundation; consultant to National Endowment for the Humanities and California Council for the Humanities in Public Policy. *Member:* American Political Science Association, Conference for the Study of Political Thought (vice-chairperson, 1978-81), Phi Beta Kappa. *Awards, honors:* Woodrow Wilson fellowship; younger humanist grant from National Endowment for the Humanities, 1971.

WRITINGS: Philosophy and the State in France: The Renaissance to the Enlightenment, Princeton University Press, 1980. Contributor to political science journals. Member of editorial board of *American Political Science Review,* 1971-73 and 1977-81, and *Ethics,* 1979-83; associate editor of *Signs,* 1980-85.

*   *   *

KERTZER, David I(srael)   1948-

PERSONAL: Born February 20, 1948, in New York, N.Y.; son of Morris Norman (a rabbi and writer) and Julia (Hoffman) Kertzer; married Susan Dana (an attorney), May 24, 1970; children: Molly, Seth. *Education:* Brown University, A.B. (magna cum laude), 1969; Brandeis University, Ph.D., 1974. *Politics:* Socialist. *Religion:* Jewish. *Home:* 291 Maine St., Brunswick, Me. 04011. *Office:* Department of Sociology and Anthropology, Bowdoin College, Brunswick, Me. 04011.

CAREER: Bowdoin College, Brunswick, Me., assistant professor, 1973-79, associate professor, 1979—, chairman of department of sociology and anthropology, 1978-81. *Member:* International Union for the Scientific Study of Population, American Anthropological Association, Social Science History Association, Society for the Scientific Study of Religion, Conference Group on Italian Politics, Phi Beta Kappa. *Awards, honors:* Woodrow Wilson Dissertation fellow, 1972-73; Fulbright senior lecturer in Catania, Italy, 1978; fellow of Center for Advanced Study in the Behavioral Sciences, 1982-83.

WRITINGS: Comrades and Christians: Religion and Political Struggle in Communist Italy, Cambridge University Press, 1980; *Famiglia Contadina e Urbanizzazione,* Il Mulino (Bologna, Italy), 1981; (editor with Michael Kenny) *Urban Life in Mediterranean Europe: Anthropological Perspectives,* University of Illinois Press, 1982.

Contributor: George L. Hicks and Philip E. Leis, editors, *Ethnic Encounters,* Duxbury, 1977; George Appell, editor, *Ethical Dilemmas in Anthropological Inquiry,* Cross Roads, 1978; Matilda White Riley, editor, *Aging From Birth to Death,* Westview, 1979; Christine Fry, editor, *Dimensions: Aging, Culture, and Health,* Praeger, 1981; Myron J. Aronoff, editor, *Political Anthropology Yearbook II,* Transaction Press, 1982; Riley, editor, *Aging From Birth to Death: Sociotemporal Perspectives,* Westview, 1982. Contributor of dozens of articles to periodicals, including *American Journal of Sociology, American Ethnologist,* and *Journal for the Scientific Study of Religion.*

WORK IN PROGRESS: Editing *Age and Anthropological Theory* with Jennie Keith, publication expected in 1983; *Living With Kin: Family Life in Sharecropping Italy,* publication expected in 1983; editing *European Population Registers* with Andrea Schiaffino, publication expected in 1984; *Politics Through Ritual,* publication expected in 1984.

SIDELIGHTS: Kertzer told *CA:* "Since 1971 I have been spending as much time as possible in Italy and am in the midst of a multiyear historical family study with Andrea Schiaffino, a professor of demography at the University of Bologna. I am fluent in Italian and read French."

Kertzer's book *Comrades and Christians* studies the relationship between communism and Catholicism in Bologna, Italy, during the 1970's. Percy Allum related in the *Times Literary Supplement* that Kertzer "gives us plenty of information about, and some insights into, the life of a working-class district in the city which is the administrative capital of Italian Communism, Bologna being the largest Italian city to have been administered continuously by the Communist Party since 1946." Despite the critic's complaint that Kertzer failed to deal with several weighty problems mentioned in the work, Allum called the book "a lively and interesting study." Another critic, Robert H. Evans of the *American Political Science Review,* noted that Kertzer "offers an interesting study, supported by much information, well-penned vignettes, attentive description, careful analysis and discussion of theoretical issues." Evans added that *Comrades and Christians* provides "a solid study which helps fathom the complexities of Italian voting behavior while illustrating how the PCI [Communist party] operates at the grass-root level."

BIOGRAPHICAL/CRITICAL SOURCES: Times Literary Supplement, January 23, 1981; *American Political Science Review,* March, 1981; *Sociological Analysis,* Volume 42, 1981; *Journal of Politics,* Volume 43, 1981.

*   *   *

KETCHAM, Howard   1902-1982

OBITUARY NOTICE: Born September 4, 1902, in New York, N.Y.; died May 4, 1982, in West Palm Beach, Fla. Color engineer and author of books in his field. The founder of a color design and illuminating firm, which he headed for thirty-five years, Ketcham is credited with originating the profession of color engineering. Pioneering in the use of nationwide consumer surveys to determine color, texture, and design preferences for manufactured products, Ketcham's company colorstyled, created lighting, or designed more than five hundred products, establishments, and packages for American businesses. His clients included all U.S. automobile manufacturers, Pan American World Airways, General Electric, Cities Service Oil Company, Bell Telephone, Lionel Corporation, and the New York Central Railroad. Ketcham also initiated the transmission of color by cable in 1936 with the development of a color viewing apparatus he called a Colorcode. His writings include *How to Use Color and Design in the Home* (a Book-of-the-Month Club selection), *Color: Its Theory and Application, Paint It Yourself,* and *Color Planning for Business and Industry.* Obituaries and other sources: *Who's Who in America,* 42nd edition, Marquis, 1982; *New York Times,* May 7, 1982.

*   *   *

KETTERMAN, Grace H(orst)   1926-

PERSONAL: Born September 11, 1926, in Newton, Kan.; daughter of Titus Frank (a farmer) and Elizabeth (Winey) Horst; married Herbert L. Ketterman (a physician), September 2, 1950; children: Kathleen Ketterman Simpson, Lyndon, Wendy. *Education:* University of Kansas, B.A., 1948, M.D., 1952. *Politics:* Republican. *Religion:* Protestant. *Home:* 9231 Belinder, Leawood, Kan. 66206. *Office:* Florence Crittenton Center, 10918 Elm, Kansas City, Mo. 64134.

CAREER: Menorah Medical Center, Kansas City, Mo., intern, 1952-53; Wyandotte County Public Health Clinic, Kansas City, clinical director, 1953-55; Kansas City General Hospital, Kansas City, resident in pediatrics, 1955-57; private practice of pediatrics in Hickman Mills, Mo., 1957-63; Western Missouri Mental Health Center, Kansas City, child psychiatry fellow, 1963-65, organizer and director of in-patient service for children, 1965-67; Florence Crittenton Center, Kansas City, executive director, 1967-72, medical director, 1972—. Private practice of psychiatry, 1970-79; worked with Jackson County Juvenile Court; conducts workshops; lecturer. Member of Missouri governor's committee on the education of the young child and parents, 1975-76. *Member:* American Medical Association, American Psychiatric Association, American Medical Women's Society, American Association of University Women, Kansas State Medical Society, Missouri State Medical Society.

WRITINGS: (With Truman Dollar) *Teenage Rebellion,* Revell, 1979; *How to Teach Your Child About Sex,* Revell, 1981; *Complete Book of Baby and Child Care for Christian Parents,* Revell, 1981.

WORK IN PROGRESS: Helping a Troubled Child, publication expected in 1982; *Rearing a Confident Child,* publication expected in 1983.

SIDELIGHTS: Grace Ketterman told *CA:* "In my public health work, I was clinical director of a venereal disease clinic. I worked with all contagious and infectious disease control in a populous city-county area. We served the indigent people as well as more affluent people.

"My pediatrics practice was in an area of Kansas City that had never had a woman doctor. Although I was initially faced with problems that reflected considerable prejudice against me as a woman, by the end of six months I was enjoying a rapidly growing practice. This was a gratifying experience, and I still find warm friends in my former patients.

"In my experiences as a psychiatrist, I have found endless needs and rewarding areas of service. I was a major facilitator in the transition of a small private maternity home (thirty-five-person capacity) to a fairly large, totally accredited psychiatric hospital serving some one hundred twenty-five children and adolescents. I was a major influence in the development of a center for unmarried mothers in the Kansas City, Missouri, school district. This has grown steadily over ten years and serves about one-third of the teenage mothers there with excellent counseling, medical supervision, and practical educational opportunities. We have recently added a nursery for the babies of these young mothers.

"I have had a number of opportunities to conduct workshops in communications skills and interdepartmental collaboration for some large business firms. I have also conducted countless seminars, workshops, and lectures for churches, schools, and service clubs on family issues, teenage suicide, alcholism, and drug addiction.

"For five years I have worked in a school district that contained eleven elementary schools, and five junior and senior high schools. My work consists of leading a series of classes for teachers to help them understand themselves and their students as whole people, to work more effectively with the parents, and to promote a healthy climate socially and personally that will be conducive to better learning, success, and growth. I have also evaluated children and adolescents with special problems, discussed the recommendations with their parents and teachers, and set up plans to correct those problems. In addition, I have been able to help set up support groups among the teachers and principals and have conducted many classes on child-rearing for parents in the elementary schools.

"As you can see, I have worked with people of all races and from all economic levels. They represent an amazing array of problems—abuse, incest, murder, rape, prostitution, and other crimes, as well as physical, mental, social, emotional, and spiritual issues. I try to avoid hurting anyone needlessly and do everything I can, a day at a time, to help make all those whose lives I touch be a bit more whole, more productive, and happier than they were when I found them. My writing is one more opportunity to do this job."

*　　　*　　　*

KETTON-CREMER, Robert Wyndham　1906-1969

OBITUARY NOTICE: Born May 2, 1906, in Plymouth, Devonshire, England; died December 12, 1969. Civil servant, educator, and author. A justice of the peace in Norfolk, England, from 1935 to 1969, Ketton-Cremer also served as Rede Lecturer at Cambridge University, Warton Lecturer at the British Academy, Lamont Lecturer at Yale University, and as a trustee of the National Portrait Gallery in London. Best known for his biographical writings, the author received the James Tait Black Memorial Prize and the W.H. Heinemann Foundation award for best biography for his book *Thomas Gray.* His other works include *The Early Life and Diaries of William Windham, Horace Walpole, Norfolk Portraits,* and *Forty Norfolk Essays.* Obituaries and other sources: *Who Was Who in America, With World Notables,* Volume V: *1969-1973,* Marquis, 1973; *Who Was Who Among English and European Authors, 1931-1949,* Gale, 1978.

*　　　*　　　*

KEYSER, Samuel Jay　1935-

PERSONAL: Born July 7, 1935, in Philadelphia, Pa.; son of Abraham (an accountant) and Sabina (Shaplen) Keyser; married Margaret Joan Horridge (a teacher), March 18, 1959; children: Rachel Suzanne, Beth Rebecca, Benjamin Jay Kendall. *Education:* George Washington University, B.A., 1956; Merton College, Oxford, B.A., 1958, M.A., 1960; Yale University, M.A., 1960, Ph.D., 1962. *Home:* M.I.T. Senior House, 4 Ames St., Cambridge, Mass. 02139. *Office:* Department of Linguistics and Philosophy, Massachusetts Institute of Technology (M.I.T.), Cambridge, Mass. 02139.

CAREER: Brandeis University, Waltham, Mass., assistant professor, 1965-69, associate professor, 1969-71, professor of linguistics, 1971-72; University of London, University College, London, England, Fulbright professor of linguistics, 1971-72; University of Massachusetts, Amherst, head of department and professor of linguistics, 1972-77; Massachusetts Institute of Technology, Cambridge, head of department of linguistics and philosophy, 1977—, and director of Center for Cognitive Science, 1979—. *Military service:* U.S. Air Force, 1962-65; became captain. *Member:* Linguistic Society of America, Linguistic Society of Great Britain, British Philological Society, American Association of University Professors, Phi Beta Kappa. *Awards, honors:* Fulbright scholar, 1956-58; senior Fulbright lecturer, 1971-72.

WRITINGS: (With Morris Halle) *English Stress: Its Form, Its Growth, and Its Role in Verse,* Harper, 1971; (with Paul Postal) *Beginning English Grammar* (textbook), Harper, 1975. Editor of *Linguistic Inquiry,* 1970—, *Current Studies in Linguistics,* 1972—, *Linguistic Inquiry* (monograph series), 1975—, and *Cognitive Theory and Mental Representation,* 1980—.

WORK IN PROGRESS: A monograph with G. N. Clements entitled "A Three-Tiered Theory of the Syllable"; a monograph with Wayne O'Neil entitled "A Phonology of Old and Middle English"; a study of the form and structure of advertisements.

SIDELIGHTS: Keyser told *CA:* "In my opinion the intellectual historians of the twentieth century will mark this period as the beginning of the study of human cognition as a natural science. Work in linguistics, psychology, electrical engineering, computer science, and in artificial intelligence is beginning to converge on a common methodology designed to answer the fundamental question in the study of human cognition; namely, how is knowledge represented mentally. The bulk of my own research is intended to help shed light on this question. The remainder of my research time is spent in questions relating to the theory of poetic structure and, in particular, the poetry of Wallace Stevens. My work in advertising, for example, is an outgrowth of this interest, treating modern American advertisements as examples of work which shares a great many properties with works of poetry."

AVOCATIONAL INTERESTS: Jazz trombone.

*   *   *

KIM, Hee-Jin 1927-

PERSONAL: Born April 8, 1927, in Masan, Korea; came to the United States in 1952, naturalized citizen, 1969; son of Young-Ho (a custom tailor) and Um-Chon Kim; married Jung-Sun, February 7, 1965; children: Sun-Chul, Hae-Sil, Yeong-Jue. *Education:* University of California, Berkeley, B.A., 1957, M.A., 1958; Claremont Graduate School, Ph.D., 1966. *Office:* Department of Religious Studies, University of Oregon, Eugene, Ore. 97403.

CAREER: University of Vermont, Burlington, assistant professor of philosophy and religion, 1965-67; Wright State University, Dayton, Ohio, assistant professor of religion, 1967-70; Claremont Graduate School, Claremont, Calif., visiting assistant professor of religion, 1970-72; University of Oregon, Eugene, assistant professor of religious studies, 1973—. Fellow at Blaisdell Institute, 1970-72. *Member:* Association for Asian Studies, Society for Asian and Comparative Philosophy, Society for the Scientific Study of Religion, American Academy of Religion, American Humanist Association, Fellowship of Religious Humanists, American Philosophical Association.

WRITINGS: Dogen Kigen, Mystical Realist, University of Arizona Press, 1975.

WORK IN PROGRESS: The Flowers of Emptiness: Selections From Dogen's "Shobogenzo," "a translation, with extensive annotations, of selections from the entire ninety-two fascicles of the *Shobogenzo,* in three parts."

SIDELIGHTS: Kim told *CA:* "What fascinates me most about Dogen, a Zen master of thirteenth-century Japan, is that his thought is a rare combination of vision and analysis. Among other things, Dogen was an exquisite alchemist of language who knew it inside and out, realizing that the interior and exterior of language were the very fabric of existence. His understanding of and compassion for words and letters *(monji)* is one of the most remarkable aspects of his Zen. My research at the moment revolves around this thinker in relation to such broader issues as philosophy and religion, language and symbols, mysticism and culture, and others."

*   *   *

KIMBALL, Robert Eric 1939-

BRIEF ENTRY: Born August 23, 1939, in New York, N.Y.

American author. Kimball's varied career includes teaching American studies at Yale University, serving as a Congressman's legislative assistant, and working as curator of Yale University's collection of literature on American musical theatre. He has reviewed dance and music for the *New York Post* since 1973 and for the National Broadcasting Company since 1975. Kimball wrote *Reminiscing With Sissle and Blake* (Viking, 1973) and *The Gershwins* (Atheneum, 1973). He edited *Cole* (Holt, 1971) and *The Unpublished Cole Porter* (Simon & Schuster, 1975). *Address:* 180 West 58th St., New York, N.Y. 10019. *Biographical/critical sources: Newsweek,* December 20, 1971.

*   *   *

KIMMICH, Flora (Graham Horne) 1939-

PERSONAL: Born February 3, 1939, in Raleigh, N.C.; daughter of William Henry (an engineer) and Katharine Morrison (Denny) Horne; married Christoph M. Kimmich (a professor of history), July 10, 1965. *Education:* Duke University, B.A. (magna cum laude), 1959; attended Free University of Berlin, 1960-61; Yale University, M.A., 1961, Ph.D., 1969; University of Pennsylvania, J.D., 1982. *Home address:* Route 2, Plainsboro Rd., Cranbury, N.J. 08512.

CAREER: Queens College of City University of New York, Flushing, N.Y., lecturer, 1967-70, assistant professor of German, 1970-72; Princeton University, Princeton, N.J., assistant professor of German, 1972-79. *Member:* Phi Beta Kappa. *Awards, honors:* Woodrow Wilson fellow, 1959-60; Fulbright grant, 1960-61; fellow of American Association of University Women, 1965-66; fellow of Alexander von Humboldt Foundation and American Council of Learned Societies, both 1971-72.

WRITINGS: Sonnets of Catharina von Greiffenberg: Methods of Composition, University of North Carolina Press, 1975. Contributor to language journals.

*   *   *

KINCL, (Gladys) Kay Owens 1955-

PERSONAL: Surname rhymes with "tinsel"; born June 23, 1955, in Wills Point, Tex.; daughter of Troy H. (a merchant) and Gladys (an artist; maiden name, Kinney) Owens; married Richard Louis Kincl (a minister), May 14, 1978. *Education:* University of Texas, B.J., 1977; University of Arkansas, teacher certification, 1979. *Religion:* Baptist. *Home:* 502 East Madison, Berryville, Ark. 72616.

CAREER: Austin Aqua Festival, Austin, Tex., public relations director, 1977; free-lance writer, 1978—; Dollarway School District, Pine Bluff, Ark., teacher, 1979-80.

WRITINGS: Mandy's Laughing Book (juvenile; self-illustrated), Shoal Creek Pubs., 1978.

WORK IN PROGRESS: A book about "the riches in the life of a senior citizen."

SIDELIGHTS: Kay Kincl told *CA:* "I believe my talents not only come from God, but are tapped to the fullest by him alone. Anything I write will always be to share a truth, to teach a moral, to point one to a full and meaningful life, to bring joy and good things into a world laden with much depression and sorrow. I want the things I write to cause the reader to make a change for the better in his life."

*   *   *

KINDERLEHRER, Jane 1913-

PERSONAL: Born March 4, 1913, in Fall River, Mass.; daughter of Samuel (a philosopher) and Sophie (Loeff) Sapadin; married Harry Charles Kinderlehrer (an accountant), April 13, 1938; children: David, Robert, Ruth Kinderlehrer Henteleff. *Education:* Attended Bryant-Stratton College, 1931-32, and Columbia University, 1935-36. *Religion:* Jewish. *Home:* 27 South West St., Allentown, Pa. 18102. *Office:* Rodale Press, Inc., 33 East Minor St., Emmaus, Pa. 18049.

CAREER: New York Times, New York, N.Y., in advertising, 1932-38; Allentown Hospital, Allentown, Pa., in public relations and publications, 1964-67; Rodale Press, *Prevention* (magazine), Emmaus, Pa., food editor, 1967—. Guest speaker on radio and television, for women's organizations, and at universities, including University of Ohio and Cornell University. Actress in summer stock and Little Theatre productions.

WRITINGS: Confessions of a Sneaky Organic Cook, Rodale Press, 1971; *How to Feel Younger Longer,* Rodale Press, 1974; *The Art of Cooking with Love and Wheat Germ,* Rodale Press, 1977; *Cooking Kosher the Natural Way,* Jonathan David, 1980. Editor of *Center News* of the Jewish Community Center, Allentown, Pa., 1950-69.

WORK IN PROGRESS: A total health book for the Jewish community, for Jonathan David.

SIDELIGHTS: A frequent guest lecturer, Kinderlehrer speaks on subjects such as health, family life and relationships, and cooking. The titles of her lectures include "How to Make Your Family Healthy When They're not Looking," "How to Change Your Sex Life Without Changing Your Partner," "The Fountain of Youth Is Your Kitchen," "Cooking Kosher the Natural Way," and "Darling, Your Deficiencies Are Showing."

*   *   *

KING, Leslie John 1934-

BRIEF ENTRY: Born November 10, 1934, in Christchurch, New Zealand. Geographer, educator, and author. King was a professor of geography at Ohio State University from 1964 to 1970. Since then he has been a professor at McMaster University, where he became dean of the School of Graduate Studies in 1973. He was a Fulbright fellow in 1957. King wrote *Statistical Analysis in Geography* (Prentice-Hall, 1969), *Models of Urban Land-Use Development* (Battelle Memorial Institute, 1969), and *Cities, Space, and Behavior: The Elements of Urban Geography* (Prentice-Hall, 1978). He edited *Readings in Economic Geography: The Location of Economic Activity* (Rand McNally, 1968). *Address:* 117 Mansfield Dr., Ancaster, Ontario, Canada L9G 1M6; and Department of Geography, McMaster University, Hamilton, Ontario, Canada. *Biographical/critical sources: American Men and Women of Science: The Social and Behavioral Sciences,* 12th edition, Bowker, 1973; *Who's Who in Canada,* International Press, 1977.

*   *   *

KINNEY, Francis S(herwood) 1915-

PERSONAL: Born November 2, 1915, in New York, N.Y.; son of Warren and Genevieve Amy Kinney; married Mary Fowler, June 1, 1940; children: Anne (Mrs. John P. Duffy), Christopher, Jeremy, Beatrice (Mrs. Douglas Broadwater). *Education:* Attended Princeton University, 1934-38. *Politics:* Republican. *Religion:* Roman Catholic. *Home:* 331 Southtown Rd., Lloyd Harbor, Huntington, N.Y. 11743. *Office:* Sparkman & Stephens, Inc., 79 Madison Ave., New York, N.Y. 10016.

CAREER: Jakobson Shipyard, Oyster Bay, N.Y., shipfitter, 1940-45; worked for Philip L. Rhodes (naval architects), New York City, 1945-53; Sparkman & Stephens, Inc. (naval architects), New York City, 1945-53; Sparkman & Stephens, Inc. (naval architects), New York City, senior designer, 1953—. Fellow and member of library steering committee of Mystic Seaport Museum, Mystic, Conn. Member of board of consultants to Portsmouth (R.I.) Abbey School. *Member:* Society of Naval Architects and Marine Engineers, Cruising Club of America (New York station historian), New York Yacht Club, Edgartown Yacht Club, Cold Spring Harbor Beach Club, Huntington Country Club.

WRITINGS: Skene's Elements of Yacht Design, Dodd, 1962, 8th edition, 1982; *You Are First: The Story of Olin and Rod Stephens of Sparkman & Stephens,* Dodd, 1978.

SIDELIGHTS: Kinney designed two of the eight sailboats he has owned. His design for a pipe dream sloop is being built in Maine.

*   *   *

KINZER, Nora Scott 1936-

BRIEF ENTRY: Born December 30, 1936, in Toronto, Ontario, Canada. American sociologist, educator, and author. Kinzer has been a senior research scientist for the U.S. Army Research Institute for Behavioral Sciences. In 1978 she became a professor of human resource management at National Defense University. Kinzer wrote *Report of the Admission of Women to the U.S. Military Academy: Project Athena* (Department of Behavioral Sciences and Leadership, U.S. Military Academy, 1977), *Put Down and Ripped Off: The American Woman and the Beauty Cult* (Crowell, 1977), and *Stress and the American Woman* (Doubleday, 1979). She edited *Urbanization in the Americas: From Its Beginnings to the Present* (Mouton, 1978). *Address:* Industrial College of the Armed Forces, National Defense University, Fort McNair, Washington, D.C. 20315.

*   *   *

KITAO, T(imothy) Kaori 1933-

PERSONAL: Born January 30, 1933, in Tokyo, Japan; came to the United States in 1952, naturalized citizen, 1971; daughter of Harumichi (an architect and author) and Aiko (Yoshida) Kitao. *Education:* University of California, Berkeley, A.B., 1958, M.A., 1961; Harvard University, Ph.D., 1966. *Office:* Department of Art, Swarthmore College, Swarthmore, Pa. 19081.

CAREER: Rhode Island School of Design, Providence, assistant professor of history of architecture, 1963-66; Swarthmore College, Swarthmore, Pa., assistant professor, 1966-68, associate professor, 1968-75, professor of art history and chairman of department of art, both 1975—. Lecturer, 1965—. *Member:* International Society for the Comparative Study of Civilizations (vice-president, 1980—), National Trust for Historic Preservation, College Art Association of America, American Film Institute, Semiotic Society of America, Victorian Society of America, Society of Architectural Historians, Society for Cinema Studies, Japan Society. *Awards, honors:* Old Dominion grant from Swarthmore College, 1969-70; Younger humanist fellow of National Endowment for the Humanities, 1973-74; Andrew Mellon grant from Swarthmore College, 1977-78, for faculty development.

WRITINGS: (Contributor) *The American Peoples Encyclopedia,* Grolier, 1969; *Circle and Oval in the Square of St. Peter's: Bernini's Art of Planning* (monograph), New York University

Press, 1974; (contributor) *La Prospettiva rinascimentale-codificazioni e trasgressioni,* [Florence, Italy], 1980. Contributor to art history and cultural history journals, including *Journal of the Society of Architectural Historians, Art Bulletin,* and *Comparative Civilizations Review.*

WORK IN PROGRESS: Encounters and Parallels: Cross-Cultural Semiotics, Studies in Art and Architecture East and West, completion expected in 1984; *Bernini, Architect; Row House Phenomenon: Design, Taste, and Economics;* "Philadelphia and Europe: Studies in Architecture and Urbanism," a series of articles.

SIDELIGHTS: Kitao told *CA:* "I always find myself at a loss for an answer when I am asked what my interests are. I am often tempted to say 'almost anything,' but refrain from doing so because I think it sounds pretentious or flippant. But the fact is, there are so few things that fail to interest me that it is far easier to list my 'disinterests' than my interests, which I don't do because those 'disinterests' of mine might turn into interests if I started to pay attention to them.

"I started out as an art historian, which is what I trained to be. While I was teaching, it became apparent to me that works of art constitute only a very small part of the world of artifacts that surrounds us or that fills up our life and history. I became interested in studying all of the visible things around us—streets and terrains, buildings and people, pictures in magazines and on billboards, images on the screen, clothes we wear, furnishings, utensils, machinery, and all kinds of objects, including those things we call works of art. It is a marvel how civilizations accumulate objects and how they almost define themselves by the objects they have accumulated. It is not the objects in themselves that interest me, but what they tell us about various civilizations. If I must, then, I concede to state my interest as the 'History of Material Culture as History of Ideas.'

"My friends and colleagues sometimes express concern that I am spreading myself too thin. I don't believe so, and I have several reasons for saying so. First, I don't think it is either right or called for to curb the curiosity to know—to wonder, inquire, think. Second, knowledge is indivisible; colleges today overemphasize specialization, purportedly necessary for developing systematic understanding of things; but academic division of labor is, after all, only one way of sorting out a mass of information, and there are obviously any number of other ways. Finally, inasmuch as I make my living mostly by teaching, I want to insist that what we teach is not information but learning to use information in thinking. Nothing is more stimulating for that kind of education than the example of the unbounded curiosity to know, and nothing is so misleading as knowledge hampered by arbitrary selectivity disguised as specialized knowledge.

"I spent the last decade talking about these matters; I hope to devote the next decade to writing them down."

*   *   *

KLAWANS, Harold L(eo)   1937-

PERSONAL: Born November 1, 1937, in Chicago, Ill.; son of Harold L. (a physician) and Blanche (a nurse; maiden name, Rosenberg) Klawans; married Paula Barkan (a teacher of Hebrew), August 23, 1959; children: Deborah, Rebecca, Jonathan. *Education:* Attended University of Michigan, 1955-58; University of Illinois, M.D., 1962. *Religion:* Jewish. *Office:* 1725 West Harrison, Chicago, Ill. 60612.

CAREER: Presbyterian-St. Luke's Hospital, Chicago, Ill., intern, 1962-63; University of Minnesota, Minneapolis, resident

in neurology, 1963-64; Presbyterian-St. Luke's Hospital, resident in neurology, 1966-68; University of Illinois Medical School, Chicago, assistant professor of neurology, 1968-71; Rush Medical College, Chicago, associate professor of neurology, 1971-73; University of Chicago, Chicago, professor of medicine, 1974-77; Rush Medical College, professor of neurology and pharmacology and associate chairman of department of neurological sciences, 1977—. Chairman of medical advisory board of United Parkinson Foundation and scientific advisory board of Tourette Syndrome Association; member of World Federation of Neurology research group on Huntington's Chorea. *Military service:* U.S. Army, 1964-66; became captain. *Member:* International College of Neuropharmacology, American Academy of Neurology (fellow), American Neurological Society, Society for Neurosciences, Society for Biological Psychiatry, Society for Neurochemistry, Royal Numismatic Society (fellow), Phi Beta Kappa, Alpha Omega Alpha. *Awards, honors:* Grants from United Parkinson Foundation, 1968—, Boothroyd Fund, 1974—, and State of Illinois, 1978-82.

WRITINGS: The Pharmacology of Extrapyramidal Movement Disorders, S. Karger, 1973; (with William J. Weiner) *Textbook of Clinical Neuropharmacology,* Raven Press, 1981; *The Medicine of History,* Raven Press, 1982; *Sins of Commission* (novel), Contemporary Books, 1982; *The Third Temple* (novel), Raven Press, 1983. Contributor of more than two hundred articles to scientific journals. Editor-in-chief of *Clinical Neuropharmacology;* past associate editor of *Handbook of Clinical Neurology.*

WORK IN PROGRESS: A collection of medical historical essays.

SIDELIGHTS: Klawans wrote: "I am presently conducting research on various disease states and new drugs for treatment of Parkinson's disease. I plan to continue to balance my career as an academic neurologist by encompassing teaching, research, and patient care with fiction writing.

"It was Conan Doyle who first noted the direct analogy between medicine and classic detective work, and my first two novels are based on this analogy.

"My other major interest is history, which has resulted in one set of essays on the interaction of medicine and history, with a second set to follow."

*   *   *

KLENICKI, Leon   1930-

PERSONAL: Born September 7, 1930, in Buenos Aires, Argentina; came to the United States in 1973, naturalized citizen, 1980; son of Isaias and Inda (Kuzewika) Klenicki; married Ana Raquel Dimsitz (a lawyer), August 16, 1959; children: Ruth Sharon, Daniel Raphael. *Education:* Colegio Nacional Nicolas Avellaneda, B.A., 1958; University of Cincinnati, B.A., 1963; Hebrew Union College-Jewish Institute of Religion, M.H.L. and Rabbi, 1967. *Home:* 13 Stonicker Dr., Lawrenceville, N.J. 08648. *Office:* Anti-Defamation League of B'nai B'rith, 823 United Nations Plaza, New York, N.Y. 10017.

CAREER: World Union for Progressive Judaism, Latin American Office, Buenos Aires, Argentina, director, 1967-73; Anti-Defamation League of B'nai B'rith, New York, N.Y., codirector of department of interfaith affairs, 1973—. Served as rabbi of Congregacion Emanu-El, Buenos Aires, 1970-73. Professor at Immaculate Conception Seminary, 1978—. *Member:* Central Conference of American Rabbis, New York Board of Rabbis.

WRITINGS: Libro de Oraciones (title means "Book of Prayers"), Congregacion Emanu-El, 1973; (editor with Helga Croner) *Issues in the Jewish-Christian Dialogue*, Paulist Press, 1979; *Biblical Studies: Meeting Ground of Jews and Christians*, Paulist Press, 1980; *The Passover Celebration*, Archdiocese of Chicago, 1980; (editor with Mary Maher) *Preaching the Christian-Jewish Dialogue*, Liturgical Conference, 1980; *La Hagada de Pesaj* (title means "Passover Haggadah"), Bloch Publishing, 1981; (editor with Eugene J. Fisher) *Liturgy for the Holocaust*, Archdiocese of Chicago, in press. Co-editor of *Face to Face: An Interreligious Bulletin*, 1977—, and *Nuestro Encuentro*, 1979—.

WORK IN PROGRESS: Editing a book on Jewish and Christian spirituality, with Gabe Huck, publication by Paulist Press expected in 1982; editing *Contemporary Jewish Views on Christianity*, completion expected in 1983.

SIDELIGHTS: Klenicki told *CA:* "I consider interreligious dialogue the greatest challenge of religious commitment—God's call after total exile for my people, the death of Auschwitz and return, the State of Israel for the Jewish community, Vatican II and Christian reckoning of the soul." *Avocational interests:* "I love chamber music, like to walk miles and miles, love to talk to friends, share prayer, and silence. I believe fanatically in friendship."

*   *   *

KLIBAN, B(ernard)   1935-

PERSONAL: Surname is pronounced "*Klee*-ban"; born January 1, 1935, in Norwalk, Conn.; divorced; children: one. *Education:* Attended Pratt Institute and Cooper Union. *Address:* c/o Workman Publishing Co., Inc., 1 West 39th St., New York, N.Y. 10018. *Residence:* Marin County, Calif.

CAREER: Cartoonist and painter. Piggy bank painter in Brooklyn, N.Y., 1954-55; worked for U.S. Post Office.

WRITINGS—Cartoons; all published by Workman Publishing, except as noted: *Cat*, 1975, revised edition, 1976; *Never Eat Anything Bigger Than Your Head, and Other Drawings*, 1976; *Whack Your Porcupine, and Other Drawings*, 1977; *B. Kliban's Cat Posters*, 1977; *Tiny Footprints, and Other Drawings*, 1978; *Playboy's Kliban*, Wideview, 1979; *Playboy's New Kliban*, Wideview, 1980; *Catcalendar Cats*, 1981; *Two Guys Fooling Around With the Moon*, 1982.

Omnibus volumes: *Kliban in a Box*, Workman Publishing, 1977; *Kliban in a Bigger Box*, Workman Publishing, 1979.

Contributor of cartoons and drawings to magazines, including *Playboy*.

SIDELIGHTS: Undoubtedly best known for his cat cartoons, Kliban defines a cat as "one hell of a nice animal, frequently mistaken for a meat loaf." Among the more popular of his striped mousers are "Momcat," a cat with her kitten in a kangaroo-type pouch, cats wearing oversized red tennis shoes, the roller-skate endowed "skatey cat," and a folk cat singing "Love to eat them mousies / Mousies what I love to eat / Bite they little heads off / Nibble on they tiny feet."

Cat, Kliban's first book, has sold more than 800,000 copies, and various items sporting the creatures have made the felines a $50 million industry. The cats, which appear on calendars, greeting cards, clothing, teapots, bed sheets, towels, clocks, pillows, umbrellas, and countless other products, have swept the nation and made their way around the world. New York's Bloomingdale's department store had a Kliban cat worth $1,500, and Harrods of London created a special department for Kliban imports.

After *Cat*, Kliban produced *Never Eat Anything Bigger Than Your Head*, a collection of captioned drawings that comment on the ironies, absurdities, grotesqueries, and mysteries of human beings and human society, past and present. Charles M. Young of *Rolling Stone* declared that *Never Eat Anything Bigger Than Your Head* is "the only book I've read in years that made me howl. I mean thigh-slapping, roll-on-the-ground, can't-catch-my-breath howling." The *New York Times Book Review* noted that Kliban "displayed a rare artist's talent for puns, fantasies, and long thoughts," and that he "illustrates the surrealistic and often raunchy fantasies the most innocent expressions can conjure up in a lively male's mind."

Never Eat Anything Bigger Than Your Head, Whack Your Porcupine, and *Tiny Footprints* are similar in content, all chock full of the cliches, puns, and subtle wit that make Kliban's humor and art unique. Kliban offers characters like Robert, a pimply-faced boy with glasses who "lived in Vermont, where he ate only the heads off chocolate bunnies," and Lucille, who "was secretly thrilled when Norman sucked on her toaster." Some of Kliban's drawings are accompanied by rhyming verse, such as the picture of a man seated before a plate of bird claws, some of them in his left nostril. The caption: "Dirty scaly chicken toes / Harry puts them up his nose."

Before becoming a professional artist, Kliban was a postal employee dragging bags of mail around a post office basement. Since *Cat* brought him fame, however, Kliban has led a quiet life in affluent Marin County, California, where, when not cartooning, he paints watercolors of the San Francisco Bay. He worries little about his future and marvels at his success. "I find it amazing to be making money at what I like doing," he told Young. "I never tried to make money in my life. . . . If the cartoon thing ended tomorrow, I would have a craft [his painting] to fall back on and not have to work for some corporation. I could just take one of these and trade it to some farmer for a chicken. . . . All I want is enough to pay the bills and stay here. I don't want to live with cockroaches anymore."

BIOGRAPHICAL/CRITICAL SOURCES: New York Times Book Review, July 3, 1977, May 21, 1978, August 28, 1981, September 20, 1981; *Publishers Weekly*, August 1, 1977; *New York Times*, February 12, 1978; *Rolling Stone*, September 21, 1978; *People*, November 17, 1980; *Time*, December 7, 1981; *Chicago Tribune Book World*, May 16, 1982.*

*   *   *

KNOPF, Alfred A.   1892-

PERSONAL: Born September 12, 1892, in New York, N.Y.; son of Samuel (an advertising executive and financial consultant) and Ida (Japhe) Knopf; married Blanche Wolf (an editor and publisher), April 4, 1916 (died June 4, 1966); married Helen Norcross Hedrick, April 20, 1967; children: (first marriage) Alfred A., Jr. *Education:* Columbia University, A.B., 1912. *Home:* 63 Purchase St., Purchase, N.Y. 10577. *Office:* Alfred A. Knopf, Inc., 201 East 50th St., New York, N.Y. 10022.

CAREER: Doubleday, Page & Co., New York City, clerk, 1912-13; Mitchell Kennerley (publisher), New York City, assistant, 1914; Alfred A. Knopf, Inc., New York City, founder and president, 1915-57, chairman of the board, 1957-72, chairman of the board emeritus, 1972—. *Member:* American Academy of Arts and Sciences (fellow), American Historical Association, Colonial Society of Massachusetts, Massachusetts

Historical Society, Typophiles, Cosmos Club (Washington, D.C.), Lotos Club (New York City), Century Country Club (Harrison, N.Y.).

AWARDS, HONORS: Gold medal from American Institute of Graphic Arts, 1950; C. A. Pugsley Gold Medal for conservation and preservation, 1960; Alexander Hamilton Medal from Columbia University, 1966; Francis Parkman Silver Medal from Society of American Historians, 1974; distinguished service award from Association of American University Presses, 1975; distinguished achievement award from Drexel University Library School Alumni Association, 1975; distinguished achievement award from National Book Awards Committee, 1975; notable achievement award from Brandeis University, 1977. L.H.D. from Yale University, 1958, Columbia University and Bucknell University, both 1959, Lehigh University and College of William and Mary, both 1960, University of Michigan, 1969, and Bates College, 1971; LL.D. from Brandeis University, 1963; D.Litt. from Adelphi University and University of Chattanooga, both 1966, and Long Island University, 1973.

WRITINGS: (With James Gibbons Huneker) *Joseph Conrad,* Doubleday, Page, 1913, reprinted, Folcroft, 1977; (contributor) *The New Colophon,* [New York], 1949; *Some Random Recollections,* Typophiles, 1949; *Publishing Then and Now,* New York Public Library, 1964; *Portrait of a Publisher,* Typophiles, 1965; *Blanche W. Knopf, July 30, 1894-June 4, 1966,* [New York], 1966; *Sixty Photographs,* Knopf, 1975.

WORK IN PROGRESS: An autobiography to be published, Knopf has said, "posthumously" by Houghton.

SIDELIGHTS: H. L. Mencken called Knopf "the perfect publisher." Herbert Wissel of *W* described him as "the publisher best known to the public, not because he had produced strings of best sellers but because he set and maintained the highest standards in American publishing." In the more than half a century he headed the company that bears his name, Knopf was among the most consistent publishers of well-written and well-designed books in the United States. Amid sweeping changes in the industry, both the house and its founder have, in the words of John Tebbel of *Saturday Review,* kept "one well-shod foot planted in the nineteenth century and the other somewhat reluctantly in the present."

Knopf's interest in publishing dates from his senior year at Columbia University, when he began a correspondence with author John Galsworthy. Knopf gave up his plans for a law career, visited the author in England, and on returning, as he told Israel Shenker of the *New York Times,* "I thought the woods were full of publishers who'd be glad to have me, which was not the case." Nonetheless, he got a job in the accounting department at Doubleday, where he later worked in manufacturing, advertising, sales, and publicity.

"I learned how to publish from Doubleday," Knopf told Shenker, "and how not to publish from my next employer, Mitchell Kennerley." It was while working for Kennerley that Knopf began to think of starting his own publishing house. When Kennerley found out about his plans, Knopf was fired. He then raised $5,000 and with his fiancee, Blanche Wolf, founded Alfred A. Knopf, Inc.

The company initially emphasized European, especially Russian, literature, hence the choice of the borzoi (a Russian wolfhound) as a colophon. Though the list of Borzoi Books became more American in content after 1917 when Knopf published its first American novel, *The Three Black Pennys* by Joseph Hergesheimer, the strong interest in European authors continued. Knopf published Thomas Mann, Albert Camus, Jean-Paul Sartre, Simone de Beauvoir, Andre Gide, and

Knut Hamsun, among others, and introduced many now-prominent European writers to American readers. Since World War II, Knopf has published several important Latin American authors, including Jorge Amado and German Arciniegas.

Among Knopf's first American authors was H. L. Mencken, who was the publisher's close friend and also editor of the *American Mercury,* Knopf's one venture into magazine publishing. The *American Mercury* was known as "the intellectual's bible" during its eleven-year lifespan, and many Knopf authors were first published in its pages. These included Ruth Suckow, Harvey Fergusson, Julia Peterkin, Herbert Asbury, Logan Clendening, and, perhaps most notably, James M. Cain, who, with Dashiell Hammett and Raymond Chandler, produced some of the most famous books in the "Borzoi Mystery Series."

Knopf's stable has also included Clarence Day, Robert Nathan, John Updike, Elizabeth Bowen, Ross Macdonald, Shirley Ann Grau, and Knopf's own favorite, Willa Cather. Cather came to Knopf from Houghton Mifflin, appearing at Knopf's office one day in 1920 and offering him her book of short stories, *Youth and the Bright Medusa.* She remained with Knopf until her death, bringing him *Death Comes for the Archbishop* and *Shadows on the Rock,* among other books. Knopf admired her integrity as well as her writing: "She never made any compromise for money," he observed. She disapproved of book clubs, and she refused, after one unsatisfying experience with Hollywood, to allow films to be made of her books. Nor would she have her books published in inexpensive school and college editions, because "she did not want boys and girls to grow up to hate her because they had been forced to read her books when they were students."

Knopf has also been one of the foremost publishers of historical works, including Oswald Spengler's *The Decline of the West* and Robert R. Palmer's *A History of the Modern World,* as well as books by Samuel Eliot Morison, Arthur Schlesinger, Sr., and Kenneth Stampp. "History has remained my greatest interest," Knopf told Linda Kuehl of the *New York Times Book Review.* "Arthur Schlesinger called me 'Clio's boyfriend'—Clio, you know, is the muse of history." And Julian P. Boyd, former president of the American Historical Association, cited Knopf's constant support and encouragement of historical writing and told him, "You have done more for the cause of history than any other publisher."

The most successful book ever published by Knopf is Kahlil Gibran's *The Prophet,* of which several million copies are in print. Knopf has said he doesn't understand the book's success, and Bennett Cerf has suggested that Knopf doesn't like the book and is embarrassed by its popularity: "When someone mentions *The Prophet,* Alfred merely grumbles." But Knopf remembers its author fondly: "When . . . I would meet Kahlil Gibran and tell him how well *The Prophet* was doing, he would say, 'What did I tell you!' He had always believed in it. He was such a charming little man with a bushy mustache and a gentle voice." *The Prophet* achieved its success on the strength of little more than word of mouth. "We advertised the book only once," Knopf comments, "and believe it or not, the sale seemed to slow down. We stopped the advertising in a hurry."

Knopf frowns on publishers who sacrifice editorial standards for commercial success, but he claims no special purity in that regard: "To publish what you don't like because you think a lot of readers will disagree with you is, I think, a mistake. Of course, I have published many, many such books, but if you select from our list only those titles that have sold more than 100,000 copies in the original edition, you might well conclude that virtue *is* rewarded." Knopf published the early novels of both Irving Wallace ("he was writing serious books then," Knopf notes) and Harold Robbins, who are now among the world's most popular authors. But Bennett Cerf, in his autobiography *At Random,* quotes Knopf as saying: "Two of the things I'm happiest about is that I'm rid of those two hacks. The stuff they're writing now I wouldn't publish." And he told Herbert Mitgang of the *New York Times,* "I think that best seller lists ought to be abolished by law. They're just another example of running with the crowd." Willa Cather said of him: "He has of course published books he thought very second-rate, and he has successfully done business with people who were not congenial to him. But in his own mind he kept the two sets of values apart, clear and distinct."

Knopf cares deeply about the appearance as well as the content of books, and from the beginning the Borzoi device on the spine of a Knopf book was a mark of good design. "In a time when most trade books were drab in appearance," *Publishers Weekly* noted, "the early Knopf editions were issued attired in bright cloth or gay boards, wrapped in jackets of arresting design and printed on high-quality paper in unusual and eye-pleasing type faces." Knopf designed some of the early books himself, and many distinguished designers have been associated with his imprint, including Elmer Adler, Claude Bragdon, W. A. Dwiggins, and Guy Fleming. An indication of the importance accorded to appearance, "A Note on the Type" appears on the last page of every Knopf book, giving information on the typeface, its designers, and the composition and printing of the volume.

When Knopf's son left the company in 1959 to found Atheneum Publications, Alfred and Blanche became concerned about the eventual fate of Alfred A. Knopf, Inc., which had always been very much a family business. The problem was solved in 1960; Knopf merged with Random House, which was owned by the Knopfs' close friends Bennett Cerf and Donald Klopfer. Knopf retained complete editorial control for five years, and then gave up only his right to veto other editors' manuscript selections. The editorial departments of the two companies remain separate, and Knopf, Inc., retains its distinctive character. Knopf has called the merger "a perfect marriage."

Since 1972 Knopf has taken little active part in running the firm, but he remains an influence, a symbol of integrity, and a link with a distinguished past. He has little enthusiasm for most of the changes that have taken place in the publishing industry. Too many books are published, he says, and they are overpriced; these are things "about which all publishers agree, and about which no publisher does anything." The most fundamental change, he observes, is the increased importance of the editor. "In the early days, things were quite simple," he told *Saturday Review.* "The books came in; we published them as written. . . . A publisher was regarded—and so, in turn, was the writer—as a pro. A writer's job was to write a book and give it to you." And he remarked to Shenker: "I guess business became more complicated and publishers less literate. It ceased to be the fact that publishers publish and authors write. Today authors submit manuscripts and editors write books." The editor is hired largely to acquire books, "and if he can't get good books, he usually takes what he *can* get— books that are not so good. And then he sometimes wrecks himself trying to make a silk purse out of what can never become anything but a sow's ear."

"The ideal relationship between publisher and author," Knopf told Tebbel, "is when you know what he's doing and he knows what you're doing, and you both go ahead and do it with trust in each other." Knopf is disturbed by the deterioration of that relationship, which he blames in part on the expanded roles of

editors and agents. An agent, he remarks, is often expected to be "the alibi for anything unpleasant the author wants to do, and he will very seldom refuse that assignment." The editor, under constant pressure to acquire new manuscripts and authors, often just "picks an author on somebody else's list and buys him." Knopf has frequently been the victim of such "author stealing," though his relations with authors, especially in the early days, were cordial and informal, often marked by a high degree of personal loyalty and trust. "In those days you could do something verbally," he has remarked. "I never had an option with Willa Cather or H. L. Mencken or Clarence Day. It never occurred to us to discuss such things." Knopf's own sense of loyalty and of the proper relationship between authors and publishers could extend well beyond contractual obligations, as it did in the case of Knopf's first best-seller, W. H. Hudson's *Green Mansions.* The book had been published in 1904 and because of the peculiarities of American copyright law was in the public domain. Although not legally required to do so, Knopf paid royalties to the author, a precedent he followed in the case of Thomas Mann's novel *Buddenbrooks* several years later.

Knopf deplores the profusion of large advances, often paid for books that are as yet unwritten. He recalls that Cather "didn't even know publishers gave advances and might have left us if she had known *we* did." Kahlil Gibran once demanded an advance of $2,000, which was paid, but he would not accept a similar advance on his next book. "I was just testing your confidence in me," he told Knopf. Knopf has written: "Today a writer who publishes a short story in the *New Yorker* has within the week offers of a substantial advance . . . for a novel. No one—including the author much of the time—even knows whether he *could* write a novel."

Knopf is generally unimpressed with current literature, though he admires John Hersey, John Updike, Jorge Amado, and a few other contemporary authors. In *Publishing Then and Now* he said: "Frequently . . . our American author, whatever his age, experience in life, and technical knowledge, simply can't write. I don't mean that he is not the master of a prose style of elegance and distinction; I mean that he can't write simple straightforward and correct English. And here, only an exceptional editor will really help him." American authors are not very durable, he said in 1964, and "there are no giants in Europe now." And though twelve Knopf authors have won Nobel Prizes, Knopf acknowledges that "some Nobel Prize books aren't very good," calling *Doctor Zhivago,* for example, "incredibly tedious. . . . If Krushchev had banned it for dullness instead of its political implications, he might have been in the clear."

Knopf also laments the "shockingly bad taste" that characterizes much modern fiction, and has warned of the danger of a "legal backlash" against pornography, a possible revival of censorship. He speaks from firsthand experience. In his first year as a publisher, the New York Society for the Suppression of Vice brought suit against him for publishing *Homo Sapiens,* a novel by Polish author Stanislaw Przybyszewski. As Knopf told Kuehl: "The prosecuting assistant D.A. argued in all seriousness that our entire list was pornographic. I countered that a book of short stories by Maupassant which we had published . . . could hardly be regarded as obscene. . . . He turned to me and said, 'Don't you know that Maupassant was the greatest master of pornography that ever lived?'" Knopf settled out of court, agreeing to withdraw the book. "I have always felt," he writes, "that a civilized person could take only one position with regard to censorship—to be against it in every known form. Who is fit to be the censor? You censor my book today and next year I will censor yours. . . . You can only philosophically grin and bear it and take comfort in the fact that time will dispose of the worthless books.''

BIOGRAPHICAL/CRITICAL SOURCES: New Yorker, November 20, 1948, November 27, 1948, December 4, 1948; Alfred A. Knopf, *Some Random Recollections,* Typophiles, 1949; *Saturday Review,* August 29, 1964, November 29, 1975; Knopf, *Publishing Then and Now,* New York Public Library, 1964; Knopf, *Portrait of a Publisher,* Typophiles, 1965; *Publishers Weekly,* January 25, 1965, February 1, 1965, May 19, 1975; *Current Biography,* Wilson, 1966; *New York Times,* September 12, 1972, September 12, 1977; *New York Times Book Review,* February 24, 1974; *Saturday Review/World,* August 10, 1974; *W,* October 31-November 7, 1975; John Tebbel, *A History of Book Publishing in the United States,* Bowker, Volume II: *The Creation of an Industry, 1865-1919,* 1975, Volume III: *The Golden Age Between Two Wars, 1920-1940,* 1978; Bennett Cerf, *At Random,* Random House, 1977.*

—Sketch by Tim Connor

* * *

KOCH, James Harold 1926-

PERSONAL: Born March 5, 1926, in Milwaukee, Wis.; son of Harold E. (an executive and engineer) and Margaret (Thomas) Koch; married Anne-Marie Beledin Sautour (a writer), February 6, 1954. *Education:* Carleton College, B.A., 1949; attended Princeton University, 1949-52. *Home:* 397A Heritage Village, Southbury, Conn. 06488. *Agent:* Scott Meredith Literary Agency, Inc., 845 Third Ave., New York, N.Y. 10022. *Office:* Aquarian Advertising Associates, Inc., 397A Heritage Village, Southbury, Conn. 06488.

CAREER: Dun & Bradstreet, Inc., New York City, credit reporter, 1952-56, copywriter, 1957-61, direct mail marketing manager, 1962-65; Aquarian Advertising Associates, Inc., New York City, senior partner, 1964-72, president, 1972—. *Military service:* U.S. Naval Reserve, active duty, 1944-46. *Member:* Poetry Society of America, Mensa, Direct Marketing Writers Guild, Men's Gallery, Parliament of Women. *Awards, honors:* Woodrow Wilson fellowship, 1949-50.

WRITINGS: How Banks Can Use Direct Mail as an Effective Marketing Tool, American Bankers Association, 1972; *Pitfalls in Issuing Municipal Bonds,* Moody's Investors Service, 1962, 2nd edition, 1975; *Profits From Country Property: How to Select, Buy, Maintain, and Improve Country Property,* McGraw, 1981; *How to Get the Most Profit From Your Collectibles,* Arco, 1982; *Profits From Small Town Property,* Van Nostrand, 1983. Also author of *A Selected, Annotated Bank Marketing Bibliography,* 1st edition, 1969, 2nd edition, 1971. Author of "Profits From Country Real Estate," a column in *Country Living.* Contributor of articles and poems to magazines. Editor of *Country Property News,* 1971—.

WORK IN PROGRESS: 101 Aquarian Concepts, essays, publication expected in 1985.

SIDELIGHTS: Koch wrote: ''Ever since I was a toddler I enjoyed hearing and then reading the stuff of literature. For my twelfth birthday I received a portable typewriter, and, ever since, thinking and feeling through my fingers has been my most natural and effective way of communicating with relatives, friends, and strangers. During recent years I have been fascinated by facets of change as Western, industrialized countries move into the electronic or Aquarian Age.''

* * *

KOENKER, Ernest Benjamin 1920-

BRIEF ENTRY: Born August 8, 1920, in Regent, N.D. American historian, educator, and author. Koenker has been a professor of history at University of Southern California since 1967, specializing in the history of Christian thought. He wrote *The Liturgical Renaissance in the Roman Catholic Church* (University of Chicago Press, 1954), *Worship in Word and Sacrament* (Concordia, 1959), *Great Dialecticians in Modern Christian Thought* (Augsburg, 1971), and a translation of *Ancient Christianity* by Rudolf Sohm (1964). *Address:* Department of History, University of Southern California, University Park, Los Angeles, Calif. 90007.

* * *

KOERTGE, Noretta 1935-

PERSONAL: Born October 7, 1935, in Olney, Ill., daughter of Forrest (a farmer) and Carmen (a teacher; maiden name, Paddick) Koertge. *Education:* University of Illinois, B.S., 1955, M.S., 1956; University of London, Ph.D., 1969. *Politics:* ''No party affiliation.'' *Religion:* None. *Office:* Department of History and Philosophy of Science, Indiana University, 130 Goodbody Hall, Bloomington, Ind. 47401.

CAREER: Elmhurst College, Elmhurst, Ill., instructor in chemistry, 1960-63; American College for Girls, Istanbul, Turkey, teacher of chemistry and head of chemistry section, 1963-64; Ontario Institute for Studies in Education, Toronto, Canada, lecturer in philosophy of science, 1968-69; Indiana University, Bloomington, assistant professor, 1970-73, associate professor, 1973-80, professor of history and philosophy of science, 1980—. *Member:* Philosophy of Science Association, British Society for Philosophy of Science (American representative).

WRITINGS: (Editor) *Nature and Causes of Homosexuality: A Philosophic and Scientific Inquiry,* Haworth Press, 1981; *Who Was That Masked Woman?* (novel), St. Martin's, 1981. Work appears in anthologies. Contributor to numerous scholarly journals. Book review editor of *Erkenntnis.*

WORK IN PROGRESS: A novel about the gay community, tentatively titled *Valley of the Amazons,* publication expected in 1983; continuing research on theories of scientific method.

SIDELIGHTS: Koertge told *CA:* ''Readers may be curious as to why a professional philosopher of science who was totally innocent of any fictional aspirations would write a novel. My reasons can be roughly sorted out into three categories—political, personal, and philosophical. In April, 1976, I became a tenured professor at Indiana University. According to the faculty handbook, tenured faculty can only be dismissed for incompetence, serious personal or professional misconduct, or extraordinary financial exigencies of the university. The tenure system does not offer perfect security to the teacher who adopts unpopular political or academic positions, but it is an enormous help. Before tenure one is constantly competing for one's job, and the more well-qualified unemployed people there are, the more likely it is that the holding of unorthodox views will count against you.

''Thanks to lots of hard work and my good fortune in having extraordinarily fair-minded colleagues, I was finally dubbed a 'trusty.' But my rejoicing and relief had hardly begun before I was besieged by a crisis of personal autonomy: All through college, graduate school, and a six-year pre-tenure probation period, I had always put my career first. Did the NAACP (National Association for the Advancement of Colored People), AFT (American Federation of Teachers), or Bloomington Gay Alliance need me for a special committee? Sorry, I had a paper due. Did my lover need me at home? Sorry, I had to go do research in London. I think my mother was even a little surprised that I came back for my father's funeral.

"Not only had my political and personal duties taken a backseat to my drive to make it in the academic world, it was arguable that my philosophical development had been warped in the process. Published books are a necessary condition for tenure and some projects are more apt to lead to publication than others. For example, a friend asked me to read a paper on Galileo at a workshop. I'm no expert on Galileo's theory of method, but the proceedings of the conference were to be published, and unless my paper was a total disaster it would be published. It would have been dumb to refuse. In this case, the paper I wrote turned out to be a good one, but one still feels a little like a prostitute who happended to enjoy a trick—one lucks out occasionally, but it's a hell of an inefficient way to look for real satisfaction.

"And so I had this big tripartite question on my plate: Now that you're a big girl and have tenure, what do you *really* want to do personally, politically, philosophically? (No pragmatic cop-outs allowed this time.) I still haven't answered that question to my own satisfaction, but writing *Who Was That Masked Woman?* was one way to work towards an answer.

"My advice to authors is: Write about something important to you; write to an audience; write on a schedule—every day at the same time, even if its just for an hour; write first—criticize and edit later."

*   *   *

KOHLS, Richard Louis   1921-

BRIEF ENTRY: Born April 19, 1921, in Kentland, Ind. American agricultural economist, educator, and author. Kohls has been teaching since 1946. He has been a professor of agricultural economics at Purdue University since 1954 and dean of the School of Agriculture since 1968. Kohls wrote *Marketing of Agricultural Products* (Macmillan, 1955). *Address:* 1520 Woodland St., West Lafayette, Ind. 47906; and School of Agriculture, Purdue University, West Lafayette, Ind. 47907. *Biographical/critical sources: Leaders in Education,* 5th edition, Bowker, 1974; *Who's Who in America,* 42nd edition, Marquis, 1982.

*   *   *

KONOVALOV, Sergey   1899-1982

OBITUARY NOTICE: Born August 31, 1899, in Moscow, Russia (now U.S.S.R.); died February 12, 1982. Educator, editor, and author. Konovalov began his career as a professor of Russian language and literature at Birmingham University in 1929, remaining there until 1945 when he moved to Oxford University as its first professor of Russian. At the time of his death he was professor emeritus and emeritus fellow of New College, Oxford. From 1950 to 1967 Konovalov was the editor of and a regular contributor to the *Oxford Slavonic Papers,* which he founded. For many years he was also editor of *Blackwell's Russian Texts* and of the Oxford University Press "Russian Readers" series. His publications include *Anthology of Contemporary Russian Literature.* Obituaries and other sources: *The Author's and Writer's Who's Who,* 6th edition, Burke's Peerage, 1971; *International Who's Who,* Europa, 1980; *Who's Who,* 132nd edition, St. Martin's, 1980; *London Times,* February 16, 1982.

*   *   *

KORDEL, Lelord   1904-

PERSONAL: Born December 16, 1904, in Warsaw, Poland; children: Lelord Jan, Gayelord Michael, Lordeen. *Education:*
University of Krakow, Ph.D., 1930. *Religion:* Catholic. *Office:* 17255 Redford Ave., Detroit, Mich. 49219.

CAREER: University of Krakow, Krakow, Poland, instructor in biochemical sciences, 1930-31; assistant to medical nutritionist Sir Arbuthnot Lane, 1931-32; California Nutrition Center, Beverly Hills, director, 1933-39; nutrition researcher and consultant to private industry, 1940-42; conductor and supervisor of nutrition seminars and consultant to the Food and Nutrition for Victory programs, 1942-45; independent researcher, lecturer, and writer on nutrition, 1946—.

WRITINGS—Published by World Publishing, except as noted: *Health the Easy Way,* Fell, 1946; (editor) *Health Through Nutrition,* 1950, 4th edition, Manor, 1975; *Eat and Grow Younger,* 1952, 11th edition, Manor, 1977; *Lady, Be Loved!,* 1953; *Eat Your Troubles Away,* 1955; *Live to Enjoy the Money You Make,* 1956; *Stay Alive Longer,* 1957, 2nd edition, Manor, 1977; *How to Make People Like You,* 1959; *Eat and Grow Slender: The Sure Way to Get Slim—and Stay Slim,* 1962, 9th edition, Manor, 1977.

Published by Putnam: *Cook Right—Live Longer,* 1962; *How to Keep Your Youthful Vitality After Forty,* 1969; *Secrets for Staying Slim,* 1969; *Natural Folk Remedies,* 1972; *You're Younger Than You Think: The Mature Person's Guide to Vibrant Health,* 1976; *The Easy, Low-Cost Way to Total Beauty,* 1978.

WORK IN PROGRESS: Two books, one on the subject of healthy eyes and the other on the effect of nutrition on personality.

SIDELIGHTS: "The whole idea of eating for health was [once] considered crackpot," Kordel has said, "but nowadays this is far from being the case." His basic plan calls for plenty of fruits and vegetables, whole grain bread, and fish and fatless meats. He also advocates exercise and the use of Vitamin C, and he cautions against prescription medicines and white sugar. "White sugar," he says, "is public enemy number one. It is very hard to digest and disturbs the balance of the body." Despite such restrictions, Kordel maintains that his "policy is to put fun back in life and not take it out."

Kordel has written nearly twenty books and boasts of sales of more than twelve million; his most popular book, *Eat and Grow Younger,* has sold more than four million copies. People from various segments of society, including such film stars as Zsa Zsa and Eva Gabor, Gloria Swanson, and Raquel Welch have sought Kordel's advice on staying healthy and looking young. Perhaps the best evidence of his success, however, is Kordel himself. "He looks at least 20 years younger than what he calls 'my calendar age' and physically is 30 years his own junior," reported Ann Kent in her 1975 *London Daily Mail* feature. "He cycles and walks ten miles a day, positively bounds up long staircases and claims he has never had a day's illness in his life. Even his teeth are his own."

BIOGRAPHICAL/CRITICAL SOURCES: *London Daily Mail,* March 31, 1975; *Port Elizabeth Evening Post,* (South Africa), October 12, 1975; *Sydney Daily Mirror* (Australia), May 17, 1977; *Healthy Living Magazine* (London), December 19, 1977.

*   *   *

KORNBLATT, Joyce (Reiser)   1944-

PERSONAL: Born May 29, 1944, in Boston, Mass.; daughter of Morris (in sales) and Shirley (in sales; maiden name, Nathansen) Reiser; children: Sara. *Education:* Carnegie-Mellon University, B.A., 1966; Western Reserve University (now Case Western Reserve University), M.A., 1969. *Home:* 8101 Custer

Rd., Bethesda, Md. 20814. *Agent:* Ellen Levine, 370 Lexington Ave., New York, N.Y. 10017. *Office:* Department of English, University of Maryland, College Park, Md. 20742.

CAREER: University of Maryland, College Park, assistant professor of English, 1975—. Member of board of directors of Glen Echo Park Writer's Center. *Awards, honors:* Fellowship from Maryland Arts Council, 1980; creative arts performance award from University of Maryland, 1981.

WRITINGS: Nothing to Do With Love, Viking, 1981.

WORK IN PROGRESS: Down to Earth, a novel.

SIDELIGHTS: Kornblatt told *CA:* "During the 1960's and early 1970's I worked as a community organizer and technical writer for the city of Cleveland. I wrote speeches and campaign materials for Carl Stokes, Eugene McCarthy, and Harold Hughes. After this immersion in the 'real world' I returned to literary pursuits more conscious of how human beings live in this culture. I am concerned with the ways humans break out of the isolation imposed on them by culture and by historical circumstance. What moves me are the extremes to which people will go in order to experience love. Hate comes easily, indifference comes easily. I am no sentimentalist. Still, I watch my fellows risk intimacy over and over again, and I am trying in my fiction to record, as an anthropologist might, those courageous gestures of affection, those sorties into devotion."

BIOGRAPHICAL/CRITICAL SOURCES: Los Angeles Times, May 14, 1981; *Chicago Tribune Book World,* August 23, 1981.

* * *

KORT, Carol 1945-

PERSONAL: Born July 25, 1945, in Jersey City, N.J.; daughter of Jack and Florence (Tunkel) Chvat; married Michael Kort (a professor), August 30, 1968; children: Eleza Natasha. *Education:* Attended Washington University, St. Louis, Mo., 1963-65, and Sorbonne, University of Paris, 1965-66; New York University, B.A., 1968. *Politics:* Liberal. *Religion:* Jewish. *Home:* 20 Abbottsford Rd., Brookline, Mass. 02146. *Agent:* Stephen Axelrod, Curtis Brown Ltd., 575 Madison Ave., New York, N.Y. 10022. *Office:* Graduate School of Design, Harvard University, Cambridge, Mass. 02138.

CAREER: Schenkman Publishing Co., Inc., Cambridge, Mass., director of advertising, 1970-72; Harvard University, Cambridge, Mass., editor of newsletter of Fogg Art Museum, 1972-73; Lesley College, Cambridge, director of public relations, 1973-78; Harvard University, director of public relations of special programs at Graduate School of Design, 1978—. Member of board of directors of Wider Opportunities for Women. *Member:* Women in Communications, Authors Guild. *Awards, honors:* Award from Council for Advancement and Support of Education, 1977, for article "Do One Thing and Do It Well."

WRITINGS: (Editor with Ronnie Friedlander) *The Mothers' Book: Shared Experiences,* Houghton, 1981. Contributor of articles and poems to magazines and newspapers, including *Sojourner, Genesis, Gnosis,* and *Tufts Literary Review.* Co-editor of local newsletter of Women in Communications. Contributor of weekly and monthly columns to the *Boston Herald American.*

WORK IN PROGRESS: Editing *The Fathers' Book: Shared Experiences,* with Ronnie Friendland, publication expected in 1982.

SIDELIGHTS: Carol Kort told *CA:* "The combination of being a free-lance writer and editor, mother, and author of free-lance travel articles makes for an unstable but captivating life."

KORTY, John Van Cleave 1936-

PERSONAL: Born June 22, 1936, in Lafayette, Ind.; son of Richard Marshall (a salesman) and Mary Elizabeth (Van Cleave) Korty; married Beulah Chang (an interior decorator), January 16, 1966; children: Jonathan, David. *Education:* Antioch College, B.A., 1959. *Agent:* William Morris Agency, 151 El Camino Dr., Beverly Hills, Calif. 90213.

CAREER: American Friends Service Committee, Philadelphia, Pa., and New York, N.Y., audiovisual coordinator, 1959-62; Korty Films, Inc., Mill Valley, Calif., president, 1963—. Animator of "Breaking the Habit," 1964, "A Scrap of Paper, a Piece of String," 1965, "The Owl and the Pussycat," 1970, "The Dragon's Tears," 1971, and numerous sequences for television shows "Sesame Street," "Vegetable Soup," and "The Electric Company." Director of motion pictures, including "The Language of Faces," 1961, "The Crazy Quilt," 1966, "Funnyman," 1967, "riverrun," 1970, "Imogen Cunningham, Photographer" 1970, "Alex and the Gypsy," Twentieth Century-Fox, 1976, "Oliver's Story," 1978, and animated feature "Twice Upon a Time," 1982; director of television programs, including "The People," American Broadcasting Co. (ABC-TV), 1973, "The Autobiography of Miss Jane Pittman," Columbia Broadcasting System (CBS-TV), 1973, "The Music School," 1976, "Farewell to Manzanar," 1976, "Forever," CBS-TV, 1977, "Who Are the Debolts? And Where Did They Get Nineteen Kids?," ABC-TV, 1978, "A Christmas Without Snow," 1980. Cinematographer of motion pictures, including "The Language of Faces," 1961, " The Crazy Quilt," 1966, "riverrun," 1970, "Imogen Cunningham, Photographer," 1970. Producer of "The Crazy Quilt," 1966, "Who Are the DeBolts? And Where Did They Get Nineteen Kids?" and "The Rushers of Din," 1982; executive producer of television documentaries, including "Stepping Out: The Debolts Grow Up," Home Box Office (HBO), 1980, and "Can't It Be Anyone Else?," ABC-TV, 1980. *Member:* Directors Guild of America (West), Writers Guild of America (West).

AWARDS, HONORS: Emmy Award for outstanding special from National Academy of Television Arts and Sciences, 1973-74, and award from Directors Guild of America, 1974, both for "The Autobiography of Miss Jane Pittman"; Humanitas Award from National Association for Humanities Education, 1976, and Christopher Award from the Christophers, 1976, both for "Farewell to Manzanar"; award from Directors Guild of America, 1977, Academy Award ("Oscar") from Academy of Motion Picture Arts and Sciences, 1977, Emmy Award from National Academy of Television Arts and Sciences, 1978-79, and Humanitas Award, 1979, all for "Who Are the DeBolts? And Where Did They Get Nineteen Kids?"

WRITINGS: "The Music School" (television play; adaptation of story by John Updike; first broadcast by Public Broadcasting Service [PBS-TV], 1976), published in *The American Short Story,* Dell, 1977.

Screenplays: "The Language of Faces" (documentary about nuclear war), 1961; "The Crazy Quilt," (adaptation of Allen Wheelis's short story "The Illusionless Man and the Visionary Maid"), Continental, 1966; (with Peter Bonerz) "Funnyman," New Yorker Films, 1967, rereleased, 1971; "riverrun," Columbia, 1970; "Imogen Cunningham, Photographer," 1970; (with James Houston and Jeanne Wakatsuki Houston) "Farewell to Manzanar" (television play), National Broadcasting Co. (NBC-TV), 1976; (with Erich Segal) "Oliver's Story," Paramount, 1978; (with Richard William Beban and Judith

Anne Nielsen) "A Christmas Without Snow" (television play), CBS-TV, 1980; (with Charles Swenson, Suella Kennedy, and Bill Couturie) "Twice Upon A Time," Ladd Co., 1982.

SIDELIGHTS: "Being a young man of taste, intelligence and high aspirations, John Korty refuses to make conventional films," noted *New York Times* critic Vincent Canby in 1967. Korty's first feature-length film, "The Crazy Quilt," prompted Canby to assert that "it's not only a happy achievement in its own right, but as an example of the vitality of some of our independent filmmakers who spin dreams from shoestrings outside the Hollywood Establishment." The film depicts the fifty-year marriage of two very different people. Lorabelle is an incurable dreamer while her husband Henry remains a determined pessimist. The tale of their union is a "wonderfully funny—yet curiously fey—comedy," declared the reviewer. In the film, which Korty produced, photographed, directed, and edited, voiced-over narration is combined with conventional color photography and black-and-white sketches. The mixture enables Korty to "tell a very full story in just 75 minutes," according to Canby.

Korty's second feature film, "Funnyman," concerns an actor working with the Committee, an improvisational comedy group in San Francisco, California. The comedian dreams of performing socially-significant material on the stage. But when he finally gets his break in his own one-man show, the actor, according to Canby, is regarded only as "charming." Like "The Crazy Quilt," "Funnyman" utilizes a narrator, but it is filmed in color and black-and-white. As an added dimension, nearly all the movie's dialogue is improvised. The result, observed Canby, is that "charming, unfortunately, may also be the most appropriate word to describe 'Funnyman,' at least its best moments. Over all, the film is so loosely structured and blandly played that it packs little or no emotional or intellectual punch,"

Expressing similar reservations about the filmmaker's third endeavor, "riverrun," Canby contended that "it is a movie so without tension that it's more descriptive than narrative." "riverrun" chronicles the pastoral life of Sarah and Dan, two vegetarians living on a sheep ranch. The two characters "have the earnest humorlessness of people to whom the truth has been revealed," explained the reviewer. Canby continued: "It seems apparent from the sweet solemnity of much of the film that Korty agrees that it has. . . . [But] about halfway through 'riverrun,' one realizes—with real relief—that Korty does understand the kind of muted desperation . . . that has shaped their lives. . . . Being a polite filmmaker (unfortunately), he never stresses the fact." Canby suggested that if Korty filmed a screenplay not his own, his movies might be better. "Left to his own devices, . . . [Korty] leans toward the sort of affectation that asks that his title be set in humble lowercase."

These very aspects of Korty's style, however, proved to be assets in filming for television. As director of the television movie "The Autobiography of Miss Jane Pittman," Korty was credited by several reviewers, including Pauline Kael in the *New Yorker,* with helping to create "quite possibly the finest movie ever made for American television." The film outlines the life of the one hundred-and-ten-year-old Miss Jane Pittman. Her story is illustrated within the framework of an interview sprinkled liberally with flashbacks. Born into slavery, Miss Jane lived through the Civil War, Reconstruction, both world wars, and the beginnings of the civil rights movement in the early 1960's. As such, her experiences become a general composite of the experiences of blacks in America. Thus, although "The Autobiography of Miss Jane Pittman" is a fictional work, it takes on the quality of a documentary. The movie, reflected

Richard A. Blake in *America,* presents "a documentary history of the alternating forms of liberation and repression that white Americans, through malice or oversight, managed to contrive, almost at whim, for their black-skinned fellow Americans." Joseph Kanon agreed in *Atlantic.* The film, "The Autobiography of Miss Jane Pittman," he stated, is "as moving and powerful a study of black life in this country as has yet been produced."

Given the emotional nature of the subject, critics praised Korty for his objectivity. In this respect, surmised Blake, "the director, John Korty, was the perfect choice for this dramatic-documentary venture." The writer explained: Korty's "own documentary, *Language of Faces,* was much more successful than either of his full length dramas, *riverrun* and *Crazy Quilt.* . . . He deals precisely and with restraint in areas of controversy more noted for rhetoric than intelligence." Blake's colleagues concurred with his opinion. *Time*'s Richard Schinckel noted that "Korty, a director whose feature films . . . have lacked emotional fire, here employs his unobstrusive and objective camera to excellent effect. Violence is seen as a constant element rather than a shocking intrusion on a black's existence. As such, its impact is all the more terrible." Kael called Korty's restraint a "principled unwillingness to push for dramatic effect." "This makes him the ideal director for 'The Autobiography of Miss Jane Pittman,'" she reasoned. "One shove and we would say , 'Oh, here it comes—more guilt piled high on us.' . . . The full force of 'The Autobiography of Miss Jane Pittman' is that no defense is possible, so none is called for."

In 1976 Korty wrote and directed another television movie entitled "Farewell to Manzanar." Set in America during World War II, the film is concerned with the confinement of more than one hundred thousand Japanese-Americans in concentration camps after the Japanese attack on Pearl Harbor. While exploring the plight of these dispossessed people, "Farewell to Manzanar" focuses on the experiences of the Wakatsuki family in Camp Manzanar in the California desert. Harry F. Waters explained in *Newsweek* that the drama traces the Wakatsukis' four years behind barbed wire—and their forced psychic march from resentment to resignation to a kind of atrophy of the soul." The critic also noted that " in a spare, austere style, the film movingly captures one Japanese-American generation's shame and humiliation and their children's efforts to atone for crimes they never committed."

Korty's return to the cinema with "Alex and the Gypsy," which starred Jack Lemmon and Genevieve Bujold, was not met with enthusiasm. The film is about Alexander Main, a troubled middle-aged bail bondsman who becomes involved with the free-spirited, earthy gypsy, Maritza. "There is something almost disarming about the banality of *Alex and the Gypsy,*" contended Jay Cocks in *Time.* "It looks like detritus from the last decade, all full of soured good vibes and oafish notions about freedom of the spirit. Maritza is supposed to represent the wildness that Main longs for, the last chance of his life. From everything . . . [shown us], she is as liberating as Lucrezia Borgia." Kael was also disappointed with the motion picture. She wondered, "Has . . . [Korty] picked up such bad habits from working in TV that he thinks making movies means cutting to a close shot each time a person has a line of dialogue? In the cramped, ugly-looking 'Alex & the Gypsy,' Korty does the things that he seemed promising for not doing."

"Oliver's Story" did not fare any better when it was released in 1978. Picking up where the movie "Love Story" left off, the film begins with the burial of Oliver's wife Jenny. After the funeral, the grieving Oliver (played by Ryan O'Neal) immerses himself in his work as a reformer and attorney. He shuns socializing until he meets Marcie Bonwit (Candace Bergen). They have an unsuccessful affair at the end of which Oliver reconciles with his father and joins the family business. *Newsweek*'s David Ansen described "Oliver's Story" as "a curiosity piece." "Audiences expecting a heavy dose of romance," he elucidated, "may be startled to find themselves confronted with the problems of tenant groups and absentee landlords in New York, working conditions in Hong Kong factories and New England textile mills."

BIOGRAPHICAL/CRITICAL SOURCES: *New York Times,* October 4, 1966, September 25, 1967, April 28, 1970, September 28, 1971; June 30, 1972; *New Yorker,* January 28, 1974, October 18, 1976; *Time,* February 4, 1974, November 1, 1976, January 8, 1979; *America,* March 4, 1974, October 30, 1976; *Atlantic,* April, 1974; *Newsweek,* March 15, 1976, January 8, 1979; *Macleans,* December 25, 1978; *New York,* January 15, 1979.

—*Sketch by Anne M. Guerrini*

* * *

KOS, Erih 1913-
(Erich Kosch)

BRIEF ENTRY: Born April 15, 1913, in Sarajevo, Yugoslavia. Yugoslav author. Kos was an attorney until World War II. Since then he has worked as a journalist and novelist. Kos's translated works include *The Strange Story of the Great Whale, Also Known as Big Mac* (Harcourt, 1962) and *Names* (Harcourt, 1966). *Address:* Jovanova 32b, Belgrade, Yugoslavia.

* * *

KOSCH, Erich
See KOS, Erih

* * *

KOTSILIBAS-DAVIS, James 1940-

PERSONAL: Surname is pronounced Cot-syllabus; born June 21, 1940, in Worcester, Mass.; son of Harry (a restauranteur) and Georgia (Kentros) Kotsilibas-Davis. *Education:* Attended Bard College, 1958-59, Mitchell College, 1959-61, and Hunter College, 1961-62. *Politics:* "Drugstore Liberal." *Religion:* Greek Orthodox. *Home:* 31 Old Wharf Rd., Harwichport, Mass. 02646. *Agent:* Helen Barrett, William Morris Agency, 1350 Sixth Ave., New York, N.Y. 10036. *Office:* 420 West 46th St., New York, N.Y. 10019.

CAREER: *Time,* New York City, writer for "Milestones" section, 1966; *Life,* New York City, reporter and writer at large and for "Newsfronts" section, 1966-70; *Penthouse,* New York City, film critic, 1970-71; *Firehouse,* New York City, managing editor, 1977-79; writer, 1977—. Consultant for MMA Productions's television mini-series, "The Barrymores," 1982—. *Military service:* U.S. Army, 1963-65. *Member:* Time-Life Alumni Association.

WRITINGS: *Great Times, Good Times: The Odyssey of Maurice Barrymore,* Doubleday, 1977; *The Barrymores: The Royal Family in Hollywood,* Crown, 1981.

WORK IN PROGRESS: *At Long Last Loy: Myrna Loy's Own Story,* for Coward-McCann.

SIDELIGHTS: Kotsilibas-Davis's first book, *Great Times, Good Times,* a biographical portrait of Maurice Barrymore, patriarch of the noted acting family, is, according to a *New Yorker* critic, "Like a nineteenth-century theatrical program, it has a bit of

everything—action, adventure, comedy, farce, melodrama, romance, sex, and tragedy." The author's second book, *The Barrymores,* continues the family saga, focusing on the second generation of the Drew-Barrymore clan, beginning with the earliest motion picture appearances of Lionel, John, and Ethyl. In a review for the *Los Angeles Times Book Review,* Lary May called the book "the pinnacle of the biography genre."

Kotsilibas-Davis told *CA:* "I try to remain true to my interests—if not passions—while attempting to make a living in a publishing marketplace where, God help us, quality is no longer considered even a viable commodity. Avocations that have helped maintain my balance while enhancing my books are collecting victoriana and theatre and movie memorabilia, particularly commemorative mugs, Barrymore material, and movie ads."

BIOGRAPHICAL/CRITICAL SOURCES: *New Yorker,* March 7, 1977; *Los Angeles Times Book Review,* May 10, 1981.

* * *

KRASOVSKAYA, Vera 1915-

BRIEF ENTRY: Born September 11, 1915, in Petrograd, Russia (now Leningrad, U.S.S.R.). Russian ballet dancer, historian, and author. Krasovskaya danced with Kirov's State Theatre of Opera and Ballet from 1933 to 1941 and taught ballet during World War II. She has worked at Leningrad's Institute of Theatre, Music, and Cinematography since 1945. Krasovskaya wrote several books in Russian. Her translated works include *Marius Petipa and "The Sleeping Beauty"* (Dance Perspectives Foundation, 1972) and *Nijinsky* (Schirmer Books, 1979). *Address:* Institute of Theatre, Music, and Cinematography, Isaakievskaya Pl., Sadavaya 14, Apt. 14, Leningrad 191011, U.S.S.R. *Biographical/critical sources: Who's Who of American Women,* 8th edition, Marquis, 1974.

* * *

KRULL, Kathleen 1952-
(Kathleen Cowles, Kathryn Kenny, Kevin Kenny)

PERSONAL: Born July 29, 1952, in Fort Leonard Wood, Mo.; daughter of Kenneth (an artist's representative) and Helen (a counselor) Krull. *Education:* Lawrence University, B.A., 1974. *Office:* Raintree Publishers Ltd., 205 West Highland, Milwaukee, Wis. 53203.

CAREER: Harper & Row Publishers, Inc., Evanston, Ill., editorial assistant, 1973-74; Western Publishing, Inc., Racine, Wis., associate editor, 1974-79; Raintree Publishers Ltd., Milwaukee, Wis., managing editor, 1979—. Speaker at writers and librarians conferences and workshops; teacher at University of Wisconsin—Milwaukee. *Member:* Society of Children's Book Writers, Allied Authors of Wisconsin, Chicago Children's Reading Roundtable. *Awards, honors: Sometimes My Mom Drinks Too Much* was named outstanding social studies trade book by Children's Book Council/National Council for Social Studies, 1980; Chicago Book Clinic award, 1980, for *Beginning to Learn About Colors;* New York Art Directors Club award, 1980, for *Beginning to Learn About Shapes.*

WRITINGS—For children; under name Kathleen Krull: "Beginning to Learn About" series; published by Raintree: *Beginning to Learn About Colors,* 1979; . . . *Shapes,* 1979; . . . *Numbers,* 1979; . . . *Opposites,* 1979 . . . *Hearing,* 1980; . . . *Looking,* 1980; . . . *Tasting,* 1980; . . . *Smelling,* 1980; . . . *Feelings,* 1980; . . . *Touching,* 1980; . . . *Thinking,* 1981; . . . *Writing,* 1981; . . . *Reading,* 1981; . . . *Talking,* 1981; . . . *Spring,* 1981; . . . *Summer,* 1981; . . . *Winter,* 1981; . . .

Autumn, 1981; . . . *Letters*, 1982; . . . *Words*, 1982; . . . *Stories*, 1982; . . . *Science*, 1982; . . . *Time*, 1982; . . . *Measuring*, 1982.

Under pseudonym Kathleen Cowles: *The Bugs Bunny Book*, Western Publishing, 1975; *The Seven Wishes*, Western Publishing, 1976; *Golden Everything Workbook Series*, Western Publishing, 1979; *What Will I Be?/A Wish Book*, Western Publishing, 1979.

Under pseudonym Kathryn Kenny: *Trixie Belden and the Hudson River Mystery*, Western Publishing, 1979.

Under pseudonym Kevin Kenny: *Sometimes My Mom Drinks Too Much*, Raintree, 1980.

Contributor, under name Kathleen Krull, to *Word Guild*.

WORK IN PROGRESS: A book on child abuse.

BIOGRAPHICAL/CRITICAL SOURCES: Milwaukee Sentinel, November 14, 1980; *Follett Library Book Newsletter*, winter, 1981.

*   *   *

KRUMB
See CRUMB, R(obert)

*   *   *

KRUMMEL, Donald William   1929-

PERSONAL: Born July 12, 1929, in Sioux City, Iowa; son of William (a minister) and Leta Margarete (a teacher; maiden name, Fischer) Krummel; married Marilyn Darlene Frederick (a musician), June 19, 1956; children: Karen Elisabeth, Matthew Frederick. *Education:* University of Michigan, Mus.B., 1951, Mus.M., 1953, M.A. in L.S., 1955, Ph.D., 1958. *Home:* 702 West Delaware Ave., Urbana, Ill. 61801. *Office:* Graduate School of Library and Information Science, 432 David Kinley Hall, University of Illinois, 1407 West Gregory St., Urbana, Ill. 61801.

CAREER: University of Michigan, Ann Arbor, instructor in music literature, 1952-56; Library of Congress, Washington, D.C., reference librarian, 1956-61; Newberry Library, Chicago, Ill., head of reference department and associate librarian, 1962-69; University of Illinois, Urbana, associate professor, 1970-71, professor of library science and music, 1971—, associate of Center for Advanced Study, 1974. Middle management intern of U.S. Civil Service, 1960.

MEMBER: International Association of Music Libraries, American Library Association, Bibliographical Society of America, American Musicological Society, Music Library Association (president, 1981-83), Bibliographical Society (England), Sonneck Society, Caxton Club, Dial Club. *Awards, honors:* Grants from Huntington Library, 1965, American Council of Learned Societies, 1966-77, Council for Library Resources, 1967, American Philosophical Society, 1969, and National Endowment for the Humanities, 1976-79; scholar in residence at Aspen Institute, 1969; fellow of Newberry Library, 1969-70; honorary research fellow at University College, London, 1974-75; Guggenheim fellow, 1976-77.

WRITINGS: Bibliotheca Bolduaniana, Information Coordinators, 1972; *Guide for Dating Early Published Music*, Boonin, 1974; *English Music Printing, 1553-1700*, Bibliographical Society, 1975; *Bibliographical Inventory of the Early Music in the Newberry Library*, G. K. Hall, 1977; *Organizing the Library's Support*, Allerton Institute, 1980; (with Jean Geil, Doris

Dyen, and Deane Root) *Resources of American Music History: A Directory of Source Materials for the Study of Music in the United States From the Beginnings to World War II*, University of Illinois Press, 1981. Contributor of articles and reviews to library and music journals. Special issue editor of *Library Trends*, 1977.

WORK IN PROGRESS: Research on enumerative, historical, and music bibliography and library history.

SIDELIGHTS: Krummel told *CA:* "Work in the contrasting disciplines of bibliography and music—the first essentially practical and the other aesthetic, the one groping for identity in a changing world and the other encumbered by a profound tradition—is inevitably a great joy and a beneficial stimulation. It is also unsettling; it demands keeping up with two burgeoning scholarly literatures, defining topics very narrowly when specifics are involved, and juggling professional commitments. Ultimately, it confirms J.B.S. Haldane's suggestion that our fields of research deal not with 'statements of ultimate fact, but . . . art forms.'"

BIOGRAPHICAL/CRITICAL SOURCES: Champaign-Urbana Courier, March 12, 1978; *Champaign-Urbana News-Gazette*, March 12, 1978.

*   *   *

KRUMWITZ
See CRUMB, R(obert)

*   *   *

KUNDSIN, Ruth Blumfeld   1916-

PERSONAL: Born July 30, 1916, in New York, N.Y.; daughter of John David (a carpenter) and Emily (a dressmaker; maiden name, Krumin) Blumfeld; married Edwin Stanley Kundsin (a lawyer), June 17, 1935; children: Andrea Kundsin Dupree, Dennis E. *Education:* Hunter College (now of the City University of New York), B.S., 1936; Boston University, M.A., 1949; Harvard University, Sc.D., 1958. *Politics:* Independent. *Religion:* None. *Home:* 71 Pratt Rd., Squantum, Mass. 02171. *Office:* Brigham and Women's Hospital, 75 Francis St., Boston, Mass. 02115.

CAREER: Research microbiologist at Harvard School of Public Health and University of Pennsylvania, 1936-38; Springfield School Department, Springfield, Mass., developed course "Building Health Through the Strategic Years," 1939-41; Peter Bent Brigham Hospital (now Brigham and Women's Hospital), Boston, Mass., research microbiologist, 1951-58, assistant in surgery, 1958-64, member of associate bacteriology staff in surgery, 1964-70, hospital epidemiologist, 1970-81, director of Environmental Sepsis Laboratory, Surgical Bacteriology Laboratory, and Specialty Microbiology Laboratory, 1970—, chairperson of infection control committee, 1974-78. Diplomate of American Board of Microbiology. President of Kundsin Laboratory, Inc., 1981—. Research associate in surgery, 1961-69, principal associate in microbiology and molecular genetics, 1969-76, and associate professor, 1976—, all at Harvard University. Lecturer for Foundation for Microbiology, 1974-75; lecturer at Latvian Academy of Sciences. Member of Federal Drug Administration subcommittee on end product testing of national coordinating committee on large volume parenterals, 1974-76; member of U.S. Pharmacopeia and National Formulary microbiology advisory panel, 1981—.

MEMBER: International Congress for Microbiology, International Organization of Mycoplasmologists, American Society for Microbiology (president of northeast branch, 1968-69),

American Association for the Advancement of Science, American Academy of Microbiology (fellow), American Venereal Disease Association, Surgical Infection Society (charter member), Institute of Environmental Sciences, New York Academy of Sciences (fellow), Phi Beta Kappa. *Awards, honors:* Sc.D. from University of Lowell, 1975; grant from National Institutes of Health, 1978-82.

WRITINGS—Editor: *Unusual Isolates From Clinical Material,* New York Academy of Sciences, 1970; *Successful Women in the Sciences: An Analysis of Determinants,* New York Academy of Sciences, 1973; *Women and Success: The Anatomy of Achievement,* Morrow, 1974; *Airborne Contagion,* New York Academy of Sciences, 1980. Contributor of more than a hundred articles and reviews to medical and scientific journals.

WORK IN PROGRESS: Research on mycoplasmas, ureaplasmas, and chlamydia as related to genitourinary tract infection and infertility; research on epidemology, including nosocomial infections and airborne infections; research on sterilization, disinfection, and ultraviolet irradiation of occupied spaces.

SIDELIGHTS: Ruth Kundsin wrote: "I have a deep concern for the problems of achieving women. I am a microbiologist, specializing in ureaplasmas and mycoplasmas as etiologic agents of infertility and perinatal mortality and morbidity, and in chlamydia as agents of neonatal conjunctivitis and pneumonia, with additional research in epidemiology, environmental microbiology, and disinfection and sterilization. My research has concentrated on these newly recognized human pathogens (ureaplasmas, mycoplasmas, chlamydia) and their effects upon women and their children.

"The sexually transmitted diseases have been a concern primarily in the male patient. One infection, currently the most common sexually transmitted disease, is nongonococcal urethritis (NGU), and it is the name of the male infection; the female counterpart does not even have a name. The sequelae of this infection in the female and her fetus must be evaluated. Current research, sponsored by the National Institute of Health (NIH), has resulted in documentation that the presence of one of these microorganisms, the ureaplasmas, in the placenta is associated with adverse effects on the fetus. My personal philosophy is that the quality of life is our greatest asset. Consequently, all factors adversely affecting our children and their potential must be intensely explored.

"I speak Latvian fluently and travel frequently to lecture at the Latvian Academy of Sciences."

*   *   *

KUPFER, Fern   1946-

PERSONAL: Born October 17, 1946, in Bronx, N.Y.; daughter of Milton (a furrier) and Ruth (a real estate agent; maiden name, Wiener) Yasser; married Joseph Harris Kupfer (a professor of philosophy), May 3, 1968; children: Gabi Elizabeth, Zachariah Abraham. *Education:* State University of New York College at Cortland, B.S., 1968; Iowa State University, M.A., 1973. *Religion:* Jewish. *Home:* 607 Lynn Ave., Ames, Iowa 50010. *Agent:* Benderoff/Geltman, 1120 Park Ave., New York, N.Y. 10028.

CAREER: Des Moines Area Community College, Ankeny, Iowa, part-time instructor in composition, 1977-81; writer, 1981—. *Member:* Association for Retarded Citizens.

WRITINGS: Before and After Zachariah (nonfiction), Delacorte, 1982. Contributor to *Redbook.*

WORK IN PROGRESS: Other Stories to Tell, dealing with the birth of a handicapped child and its effect on a marriage.

SIDELIGHTS: Fern Kupfer wrote: "I'm proud of my book. It is a personal narrative about what happens to a family, and to a marriage, when a damaged child is born. I would like my book to make a significant political statement about the rights of true *families* into which a handicapped child is born.

"I don't know that I'm a writer, though, and I don't know that I will write another book. Writing is hard and lonely work. I like 'having written,' but I'd rather *do* anything else—even wash dishes."

*   *   *

KUSTOW, Michael (David)   1939-

BRIEF ENTRY: Born November 18, 1939, in London, England. British actor, director, and author. Kustow has been an acting member of Theatre Nationale Populaire and Royal Shakespeare Company. He founded the mobile theatre unit, Theatregoround, in the early 1960's. Kustow was director of London's Institute of Contemporary Arts from 1967 to 1971. In 1973 he became associate director of the National Theatre of Great Britain. Kustow's publications include *Punch and Judas* (1964), *Tell Me Lies* (Bobbs-Merrill, 1968), *Tank: An Autobiographical Fiction* (J. Cape, 1975), and *Roger Planchon and People's Theatre* (1975). Kustow translated *The Night of the Assassins* (1968). *Address:* 84 Etheldene Ave., London N.10, England; and National Theatre of Great Britain, South Bank, London SE1 9PX, England. *Biographical/critical sources: Who's Who in the Theatre: A Biographical Record of the Contemporary Stage,* 17th edition, Gale, 1981.

*   *   *

KUZMA, Kay   1941-

PERSONAL: Born April 25, 1941, in Ogallala, Neb.; daughter of Willard J. (in real estate) and Irene (a manager; maiden name, Helm) Humpal; married Jan W. Kuzma (a biostatistician), September 1, 1963; children: Kimberly Kay, Karlene Michelle, Kevin Clark. *Education:* Loma Linda University, B.S., 1962; Michigan State University, M.A., 1963; University of California, Los Angeles, Ed.D., 1970. *Office:* School of Health, Loma Linda University, Loma Linda, Calif. 92350.

CAREER: Loma Linda University, Loma Linda, Calif., assistant professor, 1967-73, associate professor of health sciences, 1973—. Director of Parenting Seminars.

WRITINGS: Understanding Children, with study guide, Pacific Press, 1978; *Child Study Through Observation and Participation,* R & E Research Associates, 1978; *Guidelines for Child Care Centers,* Education Department, Seventh-Day Adventist General Conference, 1978; *My Unforgettable Parents,* Pacific Press, 1978; (with Clare Cherry and Barbara Harkness) *Nursery School and Day Care Center Management Guide,* Fearon, 1978; *The Kim, Kari, and Kevin Storybook* (juvenile), Pacific Press, 1979; (with husband, Jan W. Kuzma) *Building Character,* Pacific Press, 1979; *Don't Step on the Pansies* (poetry), Review & Herald, 1979; *Prime Time Parenting,* Rawson Wade, 1980; *Working Mothers: How You Can Have a Career and Be a Good Parent, Too,* Stratford Press, 1981. Editor of *Parent Scene Newsletter,* Loma Linda University.

WORK IN PROGRESS: Two books, *Christian-Style Parenting* and *The Energized Marriage.*

SIDELIGHTS: Kuzma told *CA:* "I never planned to be a working mother. I only wanted to be a good parent. But before I knew it, I was doing both and liking it.

"I believe rearing healthy, happy, competent children is the most important task anyone can be called on to perform. And I feel blessed to have had the opportunity to receive academic training in child development which has allowed me to put good theory into successful practice. How can I share this expertise with other parents who are not as fortunate as I? Teaching and presenting seminars is one way, and I have continued to do this, but it does take time away from home. Writing has provided a wider audience while the children can be playing next to me in my own living room.

"I believe God has a special work for each of us to do, and ne can find ways and means of preparing us for that work. That's what he has done for me. I didn't start out a good writer. But with my husband's ideas, critiques, encouragement, and editing and with Esther Glaser's creative writing classes, my skills have developed. Writing has allowed me to have my career and be a good parent, too."

*　　*　　*

KYDD, Sam(uel) 1917-1982

OBITUARY NOTICE: Born in 1917 in Belfast, Ireland; died March 26, 1982, in London, England. Actor and author. Best known for his comic character roles, Kydd began his film career in 1945, acting in more than two hundred movies before his death. Among his screen credits are "The Captive Heart," "Treasure Island," "I'm All Right Jack," "Too Late the Hero," and "Law and Disorder." Taken prisoner in 1940 during the war in Europe, Kydd spent several years in a prison camp, where he directed theatrical activities for the inmates. In recognition of this service the Red Cross presented him with a pair of barbed wire drama masks. This experience and others are recounted in his book For You the War Is Over. Obituaries and other sources: Halliwell's Filmgoer's Companion, 7th edition, Granada, 1980; The Writers Directory, 1982-84, St. Martin's, 1981; London Times, April 6, 1982.

*　　*　　*

KYNETT, Harold Havelock 1889-1973

OBITUARY NOTICE: Born September 13, 1889, in Philadelphia, Pa.; died September 20, 1973, in Nantucket, Mass. Journalist, advertising executive, educator, and author. Kynett worked as a reporter for several years before beginning his career in advertising in 1914. He joined the Philadelphia advertising agency of Dippy & Aitkin in 1919, becoming a partner in 1921 when the firm reorganized as Aitkin-Kynett Company. In 1958 the company incorporated, and Kynett was elected chairman of the board of directors, a position he retained until his death. A lecturer in marketing at the Wharton School of Finance and Commerce at the University of Pennsylvania, Kynett also was an active member in the councils of the Audit Bureau of Circulations, a cooperative association of U.S. and Canadian advertisers, advertising agencies, newspapers, and magazine publishers. As director of the bureau, and subsequently as bureau president and chairman of the board, Kynett was influential in establishing standards for the advertising field. In 1962 he received the Printer's Ink Award of the Advertising Federation of America. Also a prolific writer, Kynett published more than thirty books, including Amiable Vice, Harbor Ahoy, All the Forms Are Fugitive, The Folly of Abuse, We Crawl Before We Walk, Travels With Trivia, The Pervasive Spirit, and Fountains of Memory. Obituaries and other sources: Who's Who in Advertising, 2nd edition, Redfield, 1972; Who Was Who in America, With World Notables, Volume VI: 1974-1976, Marquis, 1976; The National Cyclopaedia of American Biography, Volume 58, James T. White, 1979.

*　　*　　*

KYSELKA, Will 1921-

PERSONAL: Born June 7, 1921, in Detroit, Mich.; son of Edward and Addie Kyselka; married Leila Ford, December 29, 1967. Education: Attended Olivet College, 1941, and Alma College, 1943; University of Michigan, B.S., 1947, M.S., 1949, M.A., 1951. Home: 124 Forest Ridge Way, Honolulu, Hawaii 96822. Office: Department of Education, University of Hawaii at Manoa, Honolulu, Hawaii 96822.

CAREER: University of Hawaii at Manoa, Honolulu, associate professor, 1959-81, professor of education, 1981—. Lecturer at Bishop Museum Planetarium. Military service: U.S. Navy, 1942-46.

WRITINGS: (With Gordon A. Macdonald) Anatomy of an Island, Bishop Museum Press, 1967; (with George W. Bunton) Polynesian Stars and Men, Bishop Museum Press, 1969; (with Ray Lanterman) North Star to Southern Cross (astronomy guide), University Press of Hawaii, 1976; (with Lanterman) Maui: How It Came to Be, University Press of Hawaii, 1980; (with wife, Lee Kyselka) Stars in Mind, Pacific Press—Hawaii, 1981; An Ocean in Mind, University Press of Hawaii, 1982; Kauai: First Over the Hot Spot, University Press of Hawaii, in press. Also author of The Hawaiian Sky, 1971, and of Twelve Sky Maps, with Lanterman, 1974.

WORK IN PROGRESS: Hawaii: The Abode of Pele.

SIDELIGHTS: In An Ocean in Mind, Kyselka documented Nainoa Thompson's round-trip voyage from Hawaii to Tahiti. Relying only on his mind, his senses, and the stars, Thompson sailed the Hokule'a, a canoe provided by the Polynesian Voyaging Society, in the same manner as ancient Polynesians— without the aid of scientific instruments. "What we have gained from our work in the Planetarium and from the voyage of Hokule'a will have effective results," explained Will Kyselka in the Congressional Record. "We have documented our understanding of noninstrument navigation. It is rational, efficient, and explicit in thought. Nainoa's methods are based on a set of principles that governs the relationship between various phenomena. These principles can be learned and used by others." Kyselka is now engaged in another project on noninstrument sailing for the Polynesian Voyaging Society.

He wrote: "I am interested in presenting the findings of science, particularly astronomy and geology, in a form that can be understood easily by the general reader."

BIOGRAPHICAL/CRITICAL SOURCES: Congressional Record, September 17, 1980.

L

LaCROIX, Mary 1937-

PERSONAL: Surname rhymes with joy; born July 22, 1937, in Minnesota; daughter of David E. (a farmer) and Jaunda I. (Carlisle) Froman; married Ronald LaCroix (a farmer), June 9, 1956; children: Cheryl, Terrence, Lori, Kris. *Education:* Completed correspondence course in fiction writing. *Religion:* Catholic. *Residence:* Minnesota. *Agent:* Richard I. Abrams, 10 East End Ave., New York, N.Y. 10021.

CAREER: Farmer. Writer, 1981—.

WRITINGS: The Remnant, Avon, 1981.

WORK IN PROGRESS: "I am currently working on a novel set against the background of the first century of the Christian church. I'm interested in any material concerning this time period."

SIDELIGHTS: Mary LaCroix's first novel, *The Remnant,* is a fictional account of the life of Christ expressed through the views of four women: Judith, his spiritual counselor; Ruth, his sister; Sarah, the innkeeper's daughter who witnessed his birth; and Mary, his mother. Critically, the book has been praised by a *Chicago Tribune Book World* reviewer for its very human characters and for capturing the atmosphere of the historical time.

LaCroix told *CA:* "I always wanted to write a book, but I never knew what to write about. When I finally did, it was not planned, but evolved and grew out of my avid interest in the Dead Sea Scrolls and the meaning of Christianity. Voila!"

BIOGRAPHICAL/CRITICAL SOURCES: Chicago Tribune Book World, May 3, 1981.

*   *   *

LADD, Veronica
See MINER, Jane Claypool

*   *   *

LAING, Jennifer 1948-

PERSONAL: Born March 30, 1948, in Halifax, England; daughter of Gordon (a clerk in holy orders) and Stella (a teacher; maiden name, Dix) Johnson; married Lloyd Robert Laing (a university lecturer in archaeology), January 5, 1972; children: Angus James Fortune. *Education:* University of Liverpool, B.A. (with honors), 1970. *Home:* 23 Kingswalk, West Kirby, Wirral, Merseyside L48 8AF, England.

CAREER: Free-lance archaeologist and lecturer; free-lance writer. Conducted archaeological excavations at medieval, Roman, and Dark Age sites in England. Guest on radio and television shows.

WRITINGS: (With husband, Lloyd Laing) *The Young Archaeologist's Handbook* (juvenile), Pan Books, 1976; *Finding Roman Britain,* David & Charles, 1977; (with L. Laing) *All About Archaeology,* W. H. Allen, 1977; *Buried Treasure,* Pan Books, 1978; (with L. Laing) *Anglo-Saxon England* (Ancient History Book Club selection), Scribner, 1979; (with L. Laing) *Celtic Britain* (Ancient History Book Club selection), Scribner, 1979; *Traders and Warriors,* Macmillan, 1979; (with L. Laing) *Origins of Britain* (Ancient History Book Club selection), Scribner, 1980. Also author of *Britain's Mysterious Past,* David & Charles, and *A Guide to the Dark Age Remains in Britain,* with L. Laing, Constable. Contributor to *Shell Touring Atlas of Great Britain.* Contributor to *Britain.*

WORK IN PROGRESS: A book on Greek and Roman gods.

SIDELIGHTS: Jennifer Laing wrote: "I am motivated by the need to disseminate technical information on archaeology to the layman in a way that is intelligible and stimulates interest." *Avocational interests:* Travel.

*   *   *

LAL, Gobind Behari 1890(?)-1982

OBITUARY NOTICE: Born c. 1890, in Delhi, India; died of cancer, April 1, 1982. Educator, editor, and journalist. Educated at the University of Punjab, Lal taught school in India before coming to the United States in 1912 as a research fellow at University of California, Berkeley. He joined the *San Francisco Examiner* in 1925 and subsequently worked as a reporter for other Hearst newspapers in New York and Los Angeles. During his career Lal interviewed some of the most illustrious figures of the twentieth century, including Albert Einstein, Edna St. Vincent Millay, Enrico Fermi, Mohandas Gandhi, H. L. Mencken, and Sinclair Lewis. In 1937 Lal won the Pulitzer Prize for distinguished reporting, sharing the award with four other journalists. Among other honors he received were the George Westinghouse Award from the American Association for the Advancement of Science, a Guggenheim fellowship, and a distinguished service award from the American

Medical Society. At the time of his death Lal was science editor emeritus of the Hearst newspapers. *Obituaries and other sources: New York Times,* April 3, 1982; *Chicago Tribune,* April 3, 1982.

* * *

LAMBERT, Saul 1928-

PERSONAL: Born March 12, 1928, in New York, N.Y.; son of Abraham (a vendor) and Esther (a garment worker; maiden name, Nistel) Lambert; married Emily Whitty, May 27, 1955 (divorced); children: Jonathan Whitty, Katherine Aviva. *Education:* Brooklyn College, B.A., 1949. *Home:* 153 Carter Rd., Princeton, N.J. 08540. *Agent:* Leslie Korda, 34 West 65th St., New York N.Y.

CAREER: Artist and free-lance illustrator. Worked as an advertising assistant in New York City, 1955-57. Work exhibited at Art Directors Club, New York City and Chicago, Ill., Communication Arts Exhibition, Artists Guild of Chicago, Bolles Gallery, New York City, City Center Gallery, New York City, and at annual exhibitions at Society of Illustrators, New York City. *Military service:* U.S. Army, 1951-53; became corporal. *Awards, honors:* Award of distinctive merit from Art Directors Club, New York City, 1960 and 1961, and Chicago, 1963; award for excellence from Society of Illustrators, 1961 and 1964; best category award from Artists Guild, 1967; award for excellence from Communication Arts Exhibition, 1968; twenty-five certificates of merit from Society of Illustrators.

WRITINGS—Self-illustrated: Mrs. Poggi's Holiday (juvenile), Random House, 1969.

Illustrator: Charles Perrault, *Fairy Tales,* Macmillan, 1963; James P. Wood, *The Lantern Bearer: A Life of Robert Louis Stevenson,* Pantheon, 1965; Robert Arthur, *Mystery and More Mystery,* Random House, 1966; Arthur, editor, *Spies and More Spies,* Random House, 1967; Emily Lambert, *The Man Who Drew Cats,* Harper, 1967; Arthur, *Thrillers and More Thrillers,* Random House, 1968; *The Usurping Ghost,* Pantheon, 1969; Leon Garfield, *The Restless Ghost: Three Stories,* Pantheon, 1969; Paula Fox, *Portrait of Ivan,* Bradbury, 1969; *Haiku,* Houghton, 1971; *Diary of a Madman,* Houghton, 1971; Joyce Harrington, *Five Profiles,* Houghton, 1971; Anne Frank, *The Diary of Anne Frank,* Houghton, 1972; *Miss Mandlebaum Came Back,* Houghton, 1972; Suzanne Ryer, *Transcripts H4,* Houghton, 1973; Linda Mancini, *Songs IV,* Houghton, 1973; Florence Fisher, *Search for Anna Fisher,* Reader's Digest, 1973; *Lady in Black of Boston Harbor,* Houghton, 1974; Thomas Rockwell, *Tin Cans,* Bradbury, 1975. Also supplied illustrations for "The Magic Word" series for Macmillan Reading Program.

WORK IN PROGRESS: A series of posters concerning spiritual values; "my own paintings."

SIDELIGHTS: Lambert told *CA:* "My basic concern in illustration is communicating. I use the medium which, I feel, best suits the point of view I have taken for that illustration. Therefore, I will use watercolors, pencil, oils, or whatever."

* * *

LAMPKIN, William R(obert) 1932-

PERSONAL: Born April 22, 1932, in Baldwyn, Miss.; son of Andrew J. and Etna Lavonia (Harralson) Lampkin; married Johnnie Marie Swindull (a church secretary), August 22, 1958; children: Jennifer, Eric, Julie. *Education:* Millsaps College, B.A., 1960; Emory University, B.D., 1962; Methodist Theo-logical School, Delaware, Ohio, D.Min., 1977. *Home:* 815 Pinecrest, Macon, Miss. 39341. *Office:* First United Methodist Church, Macon, Miss. 39341.

CAREER: Ordained United Methodist minister, 1962; student pastor at United Methodist churches in Learned, Miss., 1959-60, and Griffin, Ga., 1960-62; program counselor and member of conference council at United Methodist church in Grenada, Miss., 1966-70; pastor of United Methodist churches in Verona, Miss., 1970-76, and Lee Acres, Miss., 1976-77; First United Methodist Church, Tupelo, Miss., staff member, 1977-79; First United Methodist Church, Macon, Miss., pastor, 1979—. Founder of Society of Wounded Healers (an "auxiliary lay pastoral grief ministry group"), member of staff of North Mississippi Conference Council on Ministries, 1966-70; chairman of Lee County Family Life Education Committee, 1977-79. *Military service:* U.S. Air Force, 1953-56; became staff sergeant. *Member:* Macon Rotary Club (president, 1981).

WRITINGS: One Minute With God, Abingdon, 1978; *Palm Leaves and Peanuts,* Abingdon, 1981. Contributor to *Mississippi United Methodist Advocate.*

WORK IN PROGRESS: Workbook for training paraprofessional counselors in stress; a theology for youth; a book of brief devotions; a book on questions ministers ask about death and grief.

SIDELIGHTS: Lampkin leads seminars on death and grief, on marriage and divorce, on human sexuality, on counseling, and on publishing church newsletters. He is a hypnotist, certified by the Associate Trainers of Clinical Hypnosis. He designs church building and renovation plans and has conducted devotions through radio broadcasts for ten years and through television broadcasts for three years.

* * *

LANE, John (Richard) 1932-

PERSONAL: Born August 12, 1932, in Jefferson, Mo.; son of Ralph (a cartoonist) and Florence (a fashion illustrator; maiden name, Naegelin) Lane; married Jane Callinan (a writer), May 30, 1964; children: Matthew John. *Education:* Attended Cleveland Institute of Art, 1950-52. *Office:* Newspaper Enterprise Association, 230 Park Ave., New York, N.Y. 10017.

CAREER: Worked as art director of printing firm in Cleveland, Ohio, and free-lance illustrator, 1954-56; Newspaper Enterprise Association, New York City, staff artist, 1956-70, art director, 1970-75, chief editorial cartoonist, 1976—; United Feature Service, New York City, art director, 1978—. Scientific and medical cartoonist for Enterprise Science News, a division of Newspaper Enterprise Association; editorial cartoons distributed to more than seven hundred fifty daily newspapers in North America; most notable assignments include coverage of presidential elections, national political conventions, races at Daytona, and several major criminal trials. Lane's paintings have been exhibited at galleries in northern Ohio. *Military service:* U.S. Navy, 1952-54.

WRITINGS: (With wife, Jane Lane) *How to Make Play Places and Secret Hidy Holes,* Doubleday, 1979.

Illustrator; published by Doubleday: Bill McCormick, *The Complete Beginner's Guide to Golf,* 1974; Brian Lindsay Denyer, *Basic Soccer Strategy: An Introduction for Young Players,* 1976; Edward F. Dolan, *Basic Football Strategy: An Introduction for Young Players,* 1976; Richard B. Lyttle, *Basic Hockey Strategy: An Introduction for Young Players,* 1976; Dolan, *The Complete Beginner's Guide to Making and Flying Kites,* 1977; Aaron E. Klein, *You and Your Body: A Book of*

Experiments to Perform on Yourself, 1977; Howard Everett Smith, *Giant Animals,* 1977; Lee Ann Williams, *Basic Field Hockey Strategy,* 1978; Smith, *The Animal Olympics,* 1979; Henry E. Flanagan, Jr. and Robert Gardner, *Basic Lacrosse Strategy: An Introduction for Young Players,* 1979.

Contributor of illustrations to magazines, including *Business Week, Homelife,* and *Golf.*

* * *

LANG, David 1913-

PERSONAL: Born November 30, 1913, in New York, N.Y.; son of Albert (a salesman) and Rosa (Epstin) Lang; married Babette Greenbaum (a psychologist), October 5, 1939; children: Toni, Sherman. *Education:* Attended public schools in New York, N.Y., and Los Angeles, Calif. *Agent:* Jo Stewart, 201 East 66th St., Suite 18G, New York, N.Y. 10021.

CAREER: U.S. Merchant Marine, 1936; Charles Mintz Productions, Hollywood, Calif., cartoonist, 1930's; Metro-Goldwyn-Mayer, Hollywood, cartoonist, 1938-40, junior screenwriter, beginning 1941; free-lance screenwriter, beginning mid-1940's.

WRITINGS—Screenplays: (with Gordon Kahn and Hugo Butler) "A Yank on the Burma Road," Metro-Goldwyn-Mayer, 1942; (with Kahn) "Northwest Rangers," Metro-Goldwyn-Mayer, 1942; "One Exciting Night," Paramount, 1945; "Midnight Manhunt," Paramount, 1945; "People Are Funny," Paramount, 1946; "Traffic in Crime," Republic, 1946; "Queen of Burlesque," Producers Releasing Corp., 1946; "Jungle Flight," Paramount, 1947; "Web of Danger," Republic, 1947; "Caged Fury," Paramount, 1948; "Flaxy Martin," Warner Brothers, 1949; "The Last Outpost," Paramount, 1951; "Chain of Circumstance," Columbia, 1951; "Ambush at Tomahawk Gap," Columbia, 1953; "The Nebraskan," Columbia, 1953; "Massacre Canyon," Columbia, 1954; "The Outlaw Stallion," Columbia, 1954; "Black Horse Canyon," Universal, 1954; "Wyoming Renegades," Columbia, 1955; "Apache Ambush," Columbia, 1955; "Fury at Gunsight Pass," Columbia, 1956; "Secret of Treasure Mountain," Columbia, 1956; "Screaming Eagles," Allied Artists, 1956; "Hellcats of the Navy," Columbia, 1957; "The Phantom Stagecoach," Columbia, 1957; "The Buckskin Lady," United Artists, 1957; "The Hired Gun," Metro-Goldwyn-Mayer, 1957.

Novels: *Oedipus Burning,* Stein & Day, 1981.

Also author of over two hundred scripts for television series, including "Cheyenne," "Have Gun, Will Travel," "Wanted, Dead or Alive," and "The Rifleman."

WORK IN PROGRESS: Consenting Adults, a novel, completion expection in 1982; another novel; "The Broxton Woman," a play.

BIOGRAPHICAL/CRITICAL SOURCES: Los Angeles Times, March 31, 1982.

* * *

LANG, Mabel Louise 1917-

BRIEF ENTRY: Born November 12, 1917, in Utica, N.Y. American philosopher, educator, and author. Lang has been a member of the faculty at Bryn Mawr College since 1943, becoming a professor of Greek in 1959. She was a Guggenheim fellow in 1953 and a Fulbright fellow in Greece in 1959. Lang wrote *Weights, Measures, and Tokens* (American School of Classical Studies at Athens, 1964), *The Palace of Nestor at*

Pylos in Western Messenia: The Frescoes (Princeton University Press, 1969), and *Graffiti and Dipinti* (American School of Classical Studies at Athens, 1976). *Address:* 905 New Gulph Rd., Bryn Mawr, Pa. 19010; and Department of Greek, Bryn Mawr College, Bryn Mawr, Pa. 19010. *Biographical/critical sources: Directory of American Scholars,* Volume III: *Foreign Languages, Linguistics, and Philology,* 7th edition, Bowker, 1978; *Who's Who in America,* 42nd edition, Marquis, 1982.

* * *

LANG-SIMS, Lois Dorothy 1917-

PERSONAL: Born February 9, 1917, in Herne Bay, Kent, England; daughter of John Henry (a colonel) and Dorothy (Wake) Lang-Sims. *Education:* Attended girls' high school in Tunbridge Wells, England. *Religion:* Roman Catholic. *Home:* 78 Kings Hall Rd., Beckenham, Kent, England.

CAREER: Writer.

WRITINGS: The Presence of Tibet (nonfiction), Cress Press, 1963; *The Contrite Heart* (novel), Deutsch, 1968; *A Time to Be Born* (autobiography), Deutsch, 1971; *Flower in a Teacup* (autobiography), Deutsch, 1973; *Canterbury Cathedral* (nonfiction), Cassell, 1979; *The Christian Mystery* (nonfiction), Allen & Unwin, 1980.

WORK IN PROGRESS: The Stray Camel, publication expected by Wildwood House.

SIDELIGHTS: Lang-Sims told *CA:* "The advice I would give to aspiring writers is: love and revere the English language; mean what you say and *say what you mean;* never write a sentence that does not fall pleasantly on the ear; never write three words where two will do; study punctuation and paragraphing; prune your adjectives; acquire detachment."

* * *

LANTERMAN, Ray(mond E.) 1916-

PERSONAL: Born May 20, 1916, in Kokomo, Ind.; son of Harry W. (a tool designer) and Minnie (Brown) Lanterman. *Education:* Chicago Academy of Fine Arts, certificate, 1936. *Politics:* Independent. *Residence:* Honolulu, Hawaii. *Office:* 850 Kapiolani Blvd., Honolulu, Hawaii 96813.

CAREER: Free-lance artist and illustrator in Chicago, Ill., 1937-40, and in Honolulu, Hawaii, 1947—; Weiss Decalcomana, Chicago, art director, 1945-47. *Military service:* U.S. Army, 1940-45; became first lieutenant; received Distinguished Service Cross. *Member:* Smithsonian Associates, Hawaiian Astronomical Society (president, 1964), Polynesian Voyaging Society (member of board of directors), Honolulu Academy of Arts, Bishop Museum Association.

WRITINGS: (With Terence Barrow) *Incredible Hawaii,* Tuttle, 1974; (with Will Kyselka) *North Star to Southern Cross,* University Press of Hawaii, 1976; (with Kyselka) *Maui: How It Came to Be,* University Press of Hawaii, 1980. Also author of *Twelve Sky Maps,* with Kyselka, 1974.

WORK IN PROGRESS: A sequel to *Incredible Hawaii,* with Terence Barrow, publication by Tuttle expected in 1982.

SIDELIGHTS: Lanterman told *CA:* "An incorrigible buff about the Pacific since childhood, I fell in love with it through the writings of Robert Louis Stevenson and others who had experiences in the western ocean to write about, and it has been a requited love. In the forty-odd years since I first came to Hawaii, there have been many drastic changes—social, political, and physical, particularly with the advent of statehood in 1959—yet the charm and the aura remain. We call it *Aloha.*

"Before the English navigator Captain James Cook stumbled upon Hawaii in 1778 and until the appearance of American missionaries in the 1820's, there was no written Hawaiian language; history was passed from generation to generation via chants, stories, geneologies, and legends. My approach to the legends has usually been lighthearted but never derogatory or bluenose, for these legends have come down to us from a people who have a world view that is not hostile to man and from whom we can learn much.

"For example, once while I was delving into Fijian culture I noticed a tall pole from which fluttered some brightly colored fabric. Assuming this had some ritual significance, I asked the chief what it symbolized. He laughed and said, 'It rained last night and the dancers have hung their costumes up there to dry in the breeze.'

"Since the 1970's there has been a notable renaissance of interest in the Hawaiian culture, which for more than a hundred years has been suppressed and virtually buried under the onslaught of Western culture. An example of this renaissance is the interest in ancient Polynesian navigation methods and in the performance of the double-hulled vessels used in colonization. The adventuresome Polynesians, who discovered and settled Hawaii many centuries ago, were intimately acquainted with the stars, the sea, the sky, and the winds; they were a people who, with no scientific instruments of any sort to aid them, made successful landfalls after sailing over thousands of kilometers of trackless ocean.

"Today the *Hokule'a,* a 'performance-accurate' replica of those early colonizing double-hulled canoes, exists; it has made two round trips from Hawaii to Tahiti (in 1976 and 1980) using noninstrumental navigation—the first of such voyages in at least seven hundred years. It has been my privilege to assist in the documentation of how a modern Hawaiian man has reconstructed and successfully used such navigational knowledge.

"The Polynesian Voyaging Society, who conceived and built the *Hokule'a,* plans other trips in the future for the purposes of keeping the noninstrumental navigation knowledge fresh and passing it on to other interested minds. Meanwhile, the vessel is in use as a teaching aid and is moved from island to island for this purpose, reaching thousands of school children and adults.

"Painting trips to Tahiti and Micronesia were extensions of my love for the Pacific and its people. Poking about and talking with inhabitants, one soon discovers that beneath the veneer of our various cultures man is indeed a brother to every other man, and women are our sisters the world over. One finds long noses, short noses, skinny, fat, short, and tall people in every location and, behind the physical facades, great minds, good minds, small minds, and common concerns.''

AVOCATIONAL INTERESTS: Writing limericks.

* * *

LAPHAM, Samuel, Jr.   1892-1972

OBITUARY NOTICE: Born September 23, 1892, in Charleston, S.C.; died October 2, 1972; buried in Magnolia Cemetery, Charleston, S. C. Architect, editor, and author. A partner in the architectural firm of Simons, Lapham, Mitchell & Small from 1920 until his death, Lapham served as the company's president from 1964. He was the editor, with Albert Simons, of *The Early Architecture of Charleston* and *Plantations of the*

Carolina Low Country. Lapham also contributed articles to architectural and historical publications. Obituaries and other sources: *American Architects Directory,* 3rd edition, Bowker, 1970; *Who Was Who in America, With World Notables,* Volume V: *1969-1973,* Marquis, 1973.

* * *

LARBAUD, Valery (Nicolas)   1881-1957

BRIEF ENTRY: Born August 29, 1881, in Vichy, France; died February 2, 1957, in Vichy, France. French author. Larbaud's reputation as a novelist was established by *A. O. Barnabooth: Ses oeuvres completes* (1913; translated as *A. O. Barnabooth: His Diary,* 1924), the semi-autobiographical adventures of a wealthy young South American. Larbaud's lasting contribution to French letters is his adept translations of the works of such literary giants as Walt Whitman, Samuel Butler, and, most notably, James Joyce. He also helped introduce to the English-speaking world several important French writers, including Jean Giradoux, Arthur Rimbaud, and Paul Claudel. *Biographical/critical sources: Twentieth Century Authors: A Biographical Dictionary of Modern Literature,* H. W. Wilson, 1942; *Columbia Dictionary of Modern European Literature,* Columbia University Press, 1947.

* * *

LARSEN, Ernest   1946-

PERSONAL: Born January 17, 1946, in Chicago, Ill.; son of Ernest (a house painter) and Rita (Guihan) Larsen. *Education:* New York University, B.A., 1975; Columbia University, M.A., 1977. *Home:* 4831½ Saratoga Ave., San Diego, Calif. 92107. *Agent:* Amanda Urban, I.C.M., 40 West 57th St., New York, N.Y.

CAREER: Worked as cab driver, janitor, and house painter. *Sociological Abstracts,* San Diego, Calif., editor, 1980; University of California at San Diego, La Jolla, Calif., visiting lecturer in department of literature, 1981-82. *Member:* National Writers Union (member of organizing committee), Associated Writing Programs, Poets and Writers. *Awards, honors:* Fellow of Macdowell Colony.

WRITINGS: Not a Through Street (mystery), Random House, 1981. Contributor of short stories and of movie and book reviews to periodicals, including *Village Voice, Jump Cut, Number, Mulch, Box 749, Contemporary Literary Criticism,* and *TRA.* Editor of *Jump Cut.*

WORK IN PROGRESS: Ravachol, a novel about the French anarchist who terrorized western Europe with his ''dynamite outrages'' during 1891 and was executed that same year, completion expected in 1983.

SIDELIGHTS: Ernest Larsen's novel, *Not a Through Street,* is one of the first detective novels to feature a woman in the starring role. In this case, a female cab driver, Emma Hobart, solves the mystery of her murdered lover. In writing the novel, Larsen hoped to produce a book that people, particularly women, ''could and would read in buses and subways as an antidote to or weapon against the muffled bombardment of working for a living.'' Critically, Larsen has been praised for being ''a marvelous, inventive writer.''

Larsen told *CA:* ''Like *Not a Through Street,* my novel in progress, *Ravachol,* shares many of my concerns with working people, but it is written in a more difficult, perhaps more experimental, style. Both books, as well as my other writings, share a concern with the need to create an oppositional culture.''

BIOGRAPHICAL/CRITICAL SOURCES: *Library Journal*, June 15, 1981; *Publishers Weekly*, July 10, 1981; *Chicago Tribune Book World*, August 2, 1981; *Washington Post Book World*, August 23, 1981.

* * *

LASAGNA, Louis (Cesare) 1923-

BRIEF ENTRY: Born February 22, 1923, in New York, N.Y. American physician, educator, and author. Lasagna taught medicine at Johns Hopkins University from 1950 to 1970. Since then he has been a professor of pharmacology, toxicolgy, and medicine at University of Rochester. Lasagna wrote *Life, Death, and the Doctor* (Knopf, 1968), *Regulation and Drug Development* (American Enterprise Institute for Public Policy Research, 1975), *The VD Epidemic: How It Started, Where It's Going, and What to Do About It* (Temple University Press, 1975), and *Postmarketing Surveillance of Drugs* (Medicine in the Public Interest, 1977). He edited *Patient Compliance* (Futura Publishing, 1976) and *Controversies in Therapeutics* (Saunders, 1980). *Address:* Department of Pharmacology, School of Medicine, University of Rochester, Rochester, N.Y. 14642. *Biographical/critical sources: Newsweek*, June 17, 1968; *Washington Post*, July 9, 1968; *New Republic*, August 3, 1968; *New York Times Book Review*, November 10, 1968; *American Men and Women of Science: The Physical and Biological Sciences*, 14th edition, Bowker, 1979.

* * *

LATNER, Helen (Stambler) 1918-
(Helen Stambler)

PERSONAL: Born October 14, 1918, in New York, N.Y., daughter of Harry (a manufacturer) and Pauline (Spiro) Hudesman; married Benedict Stambler, November 17, 1940 (died July 4, 1967); married David Latner, June 22, 1969; children: Zipporah S. Bennett, Morris J., Sarah-Elizabeth, Abigail S. Bordeleau. *Education:* Hunter College (now of the City University of New York), B.A. (cum laude), 1939; Columbia University, M.A. (with honors), 1972. *Religion:* Jewish. *Residence:* Becket, Mass. 01223. *Agent:* Max Gartenberg, 331 Madison Ave., New York, N.Y. 10017.

CAREER: Worked as teacher of English in high schools in New York City, 1950-70; Theodore Roosevelt High School, Bronx, N.Y., assistant principal and head of English department, 1970-77; writer. Coordinator of College Bound Program in Brooklyn, N.Y., 1967-70; producer and director of recordings of Jewish music for Record Collectors Guild in New York City. *Member:* Retired School Supervisors Association, Authors Guild, Hadassah, Phi Beta Kappa. *Awards, honors:* Award for best educational film strip from Union of American Hebrew Congregations Media Department, 1962, for "Song of the Ba'al Shem."

WRITINGS: (Under name Helen Stambler) *Round-the-World Jewish Cookbook*, Ktav, 1964; *The Book of Modern Jewish Etiquette*, Schocken, 1981. Author of weekly column, "Ask Helen Latner," in *Jewish Week*. Contributor of articles to periodical *Jewish Life* and to Record Collectors Guild album covers.

WORK IN PROGRESS: Research for nonfiction works on mixed marriage and Jewish world travel; short stories; a novel on American Jewish life tentatively entitled *A Matter of Business*.

SIDELIGHTS: Latner's *The Book of Modern Jewish Etiquette* was praised in *Library Journal* as "a useful and authoritative reference work for the entire American Jewish community."

A reviewer for *Los Angeles Times* declared, "The author's voice is one of authoritative ethnic wisdom." Latner acknowledged: "This book is the fruition of an interest that goes back more than twenty-five years to a time when I was overseeing the details of a very large Orthodox wedding. Researching the subject in standard etiquette books, I found that our lifestyle was just a footnote to the description of another culture. I was put off by the underlying assumption that the only 'correct' way was the majority, non-Jewish way. I felt that someone ought to record truly Jewish customs and lifeways in all their unique vitality and gather up in one sourcebook all the modern applications of our centuries-old traditions.

"My book is the first modern treatment in English, written for people not scholars, and the only book in print that gives the *Jewish* answer to questions of etiquette, social usage, and custom in every area of life. It is concerned not merely with the use of the 'right fork' and the protocol of formal social events, but with the larger aspects of human relations, of personal interaction in a Jewish context."

She told *CA:* "I divide my time between an apartment in New York City, a country home in the Berkshires (where I have surrendered to the battalions of woodchucks and raccoons that have ruined my organic garden year after year—I took a vow to raise nothing but flowers from now on!), and assorted warm, dry places for part of the winter. If I didn't love my garden so, I think I'd be happy to spend most of my time gypsying around the world."

AVOCATIONAL INTERESTS: Opera, theatre, travel, lapswimming, cross-country skiing, stitchery, houseplants.

BIOGRAPHICAL/CRITICAL SOURCES: Library Journal, May 1, 1981; *Los Angeles Times*, October 11, 1981; *Jewish News*, December 12, 1981.

* * *

LATTIMER, John Kingsley 1914-

PERSONAL: Born October 14, 1914, in Mount Clemens, Mich.; son of Eugene (a telephone company engineer and inventor) and Gladys Soulier (Lenfestey) Lattimer; married Jamie Elizabeth Hill (a fashion artist), January, 1948; children: Evan, Jon, Gary. *Education:* Columbia University, A.B., 1935, M.D., 1938, Sc.D., 1943; attended Balliol College, Oxford, 1944, and Medical Field Service School, Paris, France, 1946. *Office:* Department of Urology, College of Physicians and Surgeons, Columbia University, 630 West 168th St., New York, N.Y. 10032.

CAREER: Methodist-Episcopal Hospital, New York City, intern in surgery, 1938-40; Columbia University, New York City, instructor, 1940-53, assistant professor, 1953-55, professor of urology and chairman of department, 1955—. Urology resident at Presbyterian Hospital, 1940-43, director of urology service and Squier Urology Clinic, 1955—, director of urology at School of Nursing; chief of urology at Babies Hospital, Vanderbilt Clinic, and Frances Delafield Hospital, 1955. Richard Chute Lecturer at Boston University Medical School, 1973; Stoneburner Lecturer at Medical College of Virginia, 1973; visiting professor at Mayo Clinic, 1977; guest lecturer at Akron City Hospital and Reno Surgical Society, both 1977, and Loma Linda Medical School, 1982. Member of board of directors of Fort Ticonderoga Museum. Member of World Health Organization expert advisory panel on biology of human reproduction; member of New York Supreme Court Medical Arbitration Panel, 1975; member of board of trustees of Presbyterian Hospital, 1974—, and New York Academy of

Medicine, 1980—. Guest on television programs, including "Good Morning, America," "David Susskind Show," "In Search of . . ." and "Frank Field's Medical Research Show"; consultant to Veterans Administration and U.S. Public Health Service. *Military service:* U.S. Army, Medical Corps, 1943-46; served in Europe; became major.

MEMBER: International Societe d'Urology (president, 1973—), American College of Surgeons (chairman of advisory committee on urology, 1962-64; member of board of governors, 1966—), American Medical Association, Association for Pediatric Urology (president, 1961), American Academy of Pediatrics (president of urology section, 1973—), American Association of Clinical Urologists, Association of American Medical Colleges, American Association of Genito-Urinary Surgeons (president, 1982), American Association for the Advancement of Science, American Urological Association (president, 1975-76; chairman of committee on pediatric urology; president of New York section, 1966; president of executive committee, 1967—; chairman of committee to gather information about urology and coordinating council for urology, 1976-77), Clinical Society of Genito-Urinary Surgeons, American Thoracic Society, American Association of University Professors, National Tuberculosis Association, Society of University Urologists (president, 1969—), National Institute of Social Sciences, Manuscript Society, Association of Military Surgeons, Society for Pediatric Urology (president, 1961-62), Sons of the American Revolution, Military Order of Foreign Wars of the United States, Order of Founders and Patriots, Association of Military Historians, Society of the War of 1812, Society of Colonial Wars, British Association of Urological Surgeons (corresponding member), Arms and Armour Society (England), Guernsey Society, New York Society of Surgeons, New York Society of Professions, New York Academy of Medicine (chairman of genito-urinary surgical section, 1956-57; member of board of trustees), New York Academy of Sciences, New York State Pediatric Society, New York Medical Society, Arms and Armour Society of New York, Revolutionary War Round Table of New York, New York County Medical Society, Alumni Association of Presbyterian Hospital (president, 1967-68), St. Nicholas Society, Harvey Society, Metropolitan Club.

AWARDS, HONORS: Joseph Mather Smith Prize from Columbia University, 1943, for research on kidney disease; first prize from American Urological Association, 1950, for research on kidney tuberculosis, 1960, for best medical motion picture of the year; prize from American Medical Association, 1953, for kidney research; honor award from American Association of Tuberculosis Physicians, 1965, for eradication of renal tuberculosis; gold medal from Alumni Association of Columbia University's College of Physicians and Surgeons, 1971, for excellence as an educator, researcher, and clinician; Hugh Young Medal from American Urological Association, 1973; Belfield Medal from Chicago Urological Society, 1975, for contributions to American urology; Burpeau Medal from New Jersey Academy of Medicine, 1976; Edward Henderson Gold Medal from American Geriatrics Society, 1978, for studies of the aging patient; medal from city of Paris, France, 1979, for contributions to international medical cooperation.

WRITINGS: Kennedy and Lincoln: Medical and Ballistic Comparisons of Their Assassinations, Harcourt, 1980.

Contributor of more than three hundred articles to medical and scientific journals. Member of editorial board of *Journal of Urology,* 1965—.

WORK IN PROGRESS: Research on prostate cancer, bladder cancer, exstrophy, cryptorchidism, and kidney tuberculosis.

SIDELIGHTS: Lattimer told *CA:* "My wartime experience with gunshot wounds made me wonder why there was so much confusion over John F. Kennedy's wounds. Because of the facilities at the medical school I was able to do proper tests to find out what really happened. I applied the same techniques to questions about Abraham Lincoln's assassination. One thing led to another and now I am on the lecture circuit much of the time speaking on this subject."

BIOGRAPHICAL/CRITICAL SOURCES: New York, July 21, 1980.

*   *   *

LAURENTIN, Rene   1917-

PERSONAL: Born October 19, 1917, in Tours, France; son of Maurice (an architect) and Marie (Jactel) Laurentin. *Education:* Institut Catholique de Paris, licence es lettres, 1934, Doctor of Theology, 1953; Sorbonne, University of Paris, Doctor of Letters, 1952. *Religion:* Roman Catholic. *Home:* Rue San Martin, 91001 Evry Cedex, France. *Agent:* Georges Borchardt, Inc., 136 East 5th St., New York, N.Y. 10022.

CAREER: Ordained Roman Catholic priest, December 8, 1946; Universite Catholique d'Angers, Angers, France, professor of theology, 1953—; Universite Catholique de l'Ouest, Angers, professor of theology, 1953—; Institut Catholique de Paris, Paris, France, professor of theology, 1975—. Visiting professor at universities in cities including Dayton, Montreal, Florence, Milan, and Rome. Member of l'Academie Mariale Internationale de Rome, 1955; vice-president of Societe Francaise d'Etudes Mariales, 1962. Consultant to the preparatory commissions, 1960-61, and expert for the Council Vatican II, 1962-65. Editorialist for *Le Figaro;* radio and television broadcaster; lecturer. *Military service:* French Army Reserves, 1939-45; became captain; taken prisoner in Belgium, held for five years in German prison camp; awarded Croix de Guerre (two citations), Chevalier of French Legion of Honor.

MEMBER: National Center of Scientific Research (elector member). *Awards, honors:* Marian Award from University of Dayton, 1965; Wlodzimierz Pietrzak literary prize for book translated into Polish, 1974; several prizes from the Academie Francaise, including Prix Cardinal Grente, 1979, and Prix Montyon, 1981.

WRITINGS: Le Titre de Coredemptrice: Etude historique (title means "The Title of Coredemptrix: Historical Study"), Lethielleux, 1952; *Marie, l'Eglise, et le sacerdoce* (title means "Mary, Church and Priesthood"), Nouvelles Editions Latines, 1953; *Notre Dame et la messe au service de la paix du Christ,* Desclee De Brouwer, 1954, translation by Francis McHenry published as *Our Lady and the Mass, in the Service of the Peace of Christ,* Macmillan, 1960; *Court Traite de theologie mariale,* Lethielleux, 1954, fourth enlarged, revised edition, 1959, fifth edition revised after the Vatican Council, 1968, translation by Gordon Smith of first edition published as *Queen of Heaven: A Short Treatise on Marian Theology,* Clonmore & Reynolds, 1956, Macmillan, 1961; *Sens de Lourdes,* preface by P. M. Theas, Lethielleux, 1955, translation published as *Meaning of Lourdes,* Clonmore & Reynolds, 1959; (editor) *Lourdes: Dossier des documents authentiques* (title means "Authentic Documents on Lourdes"), seven volumes (Volumes III and IV edited with Bernard Billet, Volume VI edited with Billet and Paul Galland, Volume VII edited solely by Billet), Lethielleux, 1957-66; *Structure et theologie de Luc I-II* (title means "Structure and Theology of Luke I-II"), Gabalda, 1957; *Message de Lourdes* (title means "Message of Lourdes"), Bonne Presse, 1958; (editor) *Les Apparitions re-*

contees par Bernadette (title means "The Apparitions According to the Accounts of Bernadette"), Lethielleux, 1958.

Lourdes: Histoire authentique des apparitions (title means "Lourdes: Authentic History of the Apparitions"), six volumes, Lethielleux, 1961-64, Volumes II, IV, V and VI reprinted in *Les Apparitions de Lourdes: Recit authentique* (title means "The Apparitions of Lourdes: Authentic Account"), 1966; *L'Enjeu du Concile* (title means "Stake of the Council") Editions du Seuil, 1962-65; *La question mariale,* Editions du Seuil, 1963, translation by I. G. Pidoux with preface by Hilda Graef published as *The Question of Mary,* Holt, Rinehart & Winston, 1965 (published in England as *Mary's Place in the Church,* Burns & Oates, 1965); *Bilan de la troisieme session,* Editions du Seuil, 1965, also published in *L'Enjeu du concile* (see above) and in *Bilan du Concile Vatican II: Histoire, textes, commentaires* (see below); *La Vierge au Concile: Presentation, texte et traduction du chapitre VIII de la Constitution dogmatique Lumen gentium consacre a la Bienheureuse Vierge Marie, Mere de Dieu dans le mystere de l'Eglise* (title means "The virgin Mary at the Council Vatican II"), Lethielleux, 1965; *Bilan du Concile: Histoire, textes, commentaires avec une chronique de la quatrieme session,* Editions du Seuil, 1966, also published in *Bilan du Concile Vatican II: Histoire, textes, commentaires* (see below); (commentator with Joseph Neuner) *The Declaration on the Relation of the Church to Non-Christian Religions, Promulgated by Pope Paul VI, October 28, 1965,* Paulist Press, 1966; *Jesus au temple: Mystere de Paques et foi de Marie, en Luc 2, 48-50* (title means "Jesus at the Temple: Mystery of Easter and Mary's Faith"), Librairie Lecoffre, 1966, Gabalda, 1966.

L'Enjeu du Synode: Suite de Concile (title means "The Stake of the Synod"), Editions du Seuil, 1967; *L'Eglise et les Juifs a Vatican II* (title means "Church and Jews at Vatican II"), Casterman, 1967, reprinted from *The Declaration on the Relation of the Church to Non-Christian Religions, Promulgated by Pope Paul VI, October 28, 1965* (see above); *Bilan du Concile Vatican II: Histoire, textes, commentaires* (contains condensed versions of *L'Enjeu du Concile,* "Bilan de la premiere session," "Bilan de la deuxieme session," *Bilan de la troisieme session,* and *Bilan du Concile: Histoire, textes, commentaries avec une chronique de la quatrieme session*), Editions du Seuil, 1967.

Le Premier Synode: Histoire et bilan (title means "The First Synod: History and Balance"), Editions du Seuil, 1968; *Dieu: Est-Il mort?* Apostolat des Editions, 1968, translation by Sister Mary Dominic published as *Has Our Faith Changed?: Reflections on the Faith for Today's Adult Christian,* Alba House, 1972; *Flashes sur l'Amerique latine, suivis de documents* (title means "Flashes on Latin America"), supplementary material by Jose De Broucker, Editions du Seuil, 1968; *L'Amerique latine a l'heure de l'enfantement* (title means "Latin America at the Hour of Birth"), Editions du Seuil, 1969; *Developpement et Salut,* Editions du Seuil, 1969, translation by Charles Underhill Quinn published as *Liberation, Development, and Salvation,* Orbis Books, 1972; *Enjeu du deuxieme Synode et contestation dans l'Eglise* (title means "Stake of the Second Synod and Contestation in the Church"), Editions du Seuil, 1969.

Le Synode permanent: Naissance et avenir (title means "The Permanent Synod: Birth and Future"), Editions du Seuil, 1970; (with Albert Durand) *Pontmain: Histoire authentique* (title means "Pontmain: Authentic Story"), Lethielleux, 1970; *Nouvelles Dimensions de la charite* (title means "New Dimensions of Charity"), Apostolat des Editions, 1970; *Crise et promesse de l'Englise aux U.S.A.* (title means "Crisis and Promises of the Church in the United States"), Apostolat des Editions, 1971;

Flashes sur l'Extreme-Orient (title means "Flashes on the Far East"), Editions du Seuil, 1971; (with Marie-Therese Bourgeade) *Logia de Bernadette: Etude critique de ses paroles de 1866 a 1870* (title means "Logia of Bernadette: Critical History of Her Words"), Apostolat des Editions, 1971; *Nouveaux Ministeres et fin du clerge devant le IIIe Synode* (title means "New Ministries and the End of the Clergy"), Editions du Seuil, 1971.

Bernadette vous parle . . . (title means "Bernadette Speaks to You"), Lethielleux, 1972; *Nouvelles Dimensions de l'esperence* (title means "New Dimensions of Hope"), Editions du Cerf, 1972; *Reorientation de l'Eglise apres le IIIe Synode* (title means "New Directions of the Church After Vatican II"), Editions du Seuil, 1972; *Therese de Lisieux: Mythes et realite* (title means "Therese of Lisieux: Myths and Reality"), Beauchesne, 1972; *Renaissance des eglises locales: Israel* (title means "Revival of the Local Churches: Israel"), Editions du Seuil, 1973; (with Jean-Francois Six) *Therese de Lisieux: Dialogue entre Rene Laurentin et Jean-Francois Six* (title means "Therese de Lisieux: Dialogue Between Rene Laurentin and Jean-Francois Six"), Beauchesne, 1973; *Pentecotisme chez les catholiques: Risques et avenir,* Beauchesne, 1974, translation by Matthew J. O'Connell published as *Catholic Pentecostalism,* Doubleday, 1977; (with Jean Fourastie) *L'Eglise a-t-elle trahi?: Dialogue entre Jean Fourastie et Rene Laurentin* (title means "Did the Church Fail?: Dialogue Between Jean Fourastie and Rene Laurentin"), Beauchesne, 1974.

L'Evangelisation apres le IVe Synode (title means "Evangelization After the Fourth Synod"), Editions du Seuil, 1975; (with P. Roche) *Catherine Laboure et la medaille miraculeuse: Documents authentiques, 1830-1876* (title means "Catherine Laboure and the Miraculous Medal: Authentic Documents, 1830-1876"), Lazarists, 1976; *Chine et christianisme: Apres les occasions manquees* (title means "China and Christianity: After Missed Opportunities"), Desclee De Brouwer, 1977; *Lourdes: Pelerinage pour notre temps* (title means "Lourdes: Pilgrimage for Our Time"), Chalet, 1977; *Vie de Bernadette,* Desclee de Brouwer, 1978, translation by John Drury published as *Bernadette of Lourdes: A Life Based on Authenticated Documents,* Winston Press, 1979; (with others) *L'Esprit Saint* (title means "The Holy Spirit"), Facultes Universitaires Saint-Louis, 1978.

Also author of *Visage de Bernadette* (title means "The Face of Bernadette"), two volumes, 1979. Editorial director for Desclee de Brouwer of the collection "Sanctuaires, Pelerinages, Apparitions," 1980—.

WORK IN PROGRESS: The Birth Gospels, an exegetical study; theological work on Mary; a study of miracles, healings, and apparitions; a Christian history.

SIDELIGHTS: Laurentin told *CA:* "I began my career with long years of obscure research. I became ecumenical without knowing it, because my 'Catholic' works were biblical, and well-received by Protestants, and this is a difficult era. I wish to reconcile rigorous scientific research with faith, which is a profound and discreet light. Theology does not have to be pure abstraction, but the evaluation of the impact of God in the life of men. I consider journalism and contemporary history as dimensions of my theological work."

*   *   *

LAURIN, Anne
See McLAURIN, Anne

LAVIN, Marilyn Aronberg 1925-

PERSONAL: Born October 27, 1925, in St. Louis, Mo.; daughter of Charles and Blanch (Silverstone) Aronberg; married Irving Lavin (a professor), August 31, 1952; children: Amelia, Sylvia. Education: Washington University, St. Louis, Mo., B.A., 1947, M.A., 1949; Free University of Brussels, Certificate, 1949; New York University, Ph.D., 1973. Home: 56 Maxwell Lane, Princeton, N.J. 08540. Office: Department of Art and Archaeology, Princeton University, Princeton, N.J. 08544.

CAREER: Washington University, St. Louis, Mo., instructor in art history, 1949-50; Robbins Print Collection, Arlington, Mass., curator, 1953-55; Metropolitan Museum of Art, New York, N.Y., staff writer, 1957-59; writer and researcher, 1959-75; Princeton University, Princeton, N.J., visiting professor of art history, 1975—. Visiting professor at Yale University, 1977, and University of Maryland, 1979. Consultant for Time, Inc., 1965-66. Member: College Art Association of America (member of board of directors), Renaissance Society of America. Awards, honors: Fulbright fellowship for Rome, Italy, 1955-57; Charles Rufus Morey Award from College Art Association of America, 1977, for Seventeenth-Century Barberini Documents and Inventories of Art.

WRITINGS: (Editor and author of introduction) Giorgio Vasari, Lives of the Most Eminent Painters, two volumes (Heritage Book Club selection), Limited Edition Book Club, 1967; Piero della Francesca: The Flagellation, Penguin, 1972; Seventeenth-Century Barberini Documents and Inventories of Art, New York University Press, 1975; (contributor) M. Barach, L. E. Sandler, and P. Egan, editors, Art, the Ape of Nature: Studies in Honor of H. W. Janson, Abrams, 1980; Piero della Francesca's "Baptism of Christ," Yale University Press, 1981. Contributor of more than fifteen articles to art journals.

WORK IN PROGRESS: Narrative Art of the Italian Renaissance, Volume I dealing with fresco cycles in fourteenth- and fifteenth-century Italy, and Volume II on the emergence of narrative theme as the subject of devotional altarpieces in the second part of the fifteenth century in Italy.

SIDELIGHTS: Marilyn Lavin wrote: "Study with great art historians of the earlier generation (Panofsky, Lehmann, Mylonas, Janson, Friedlaender, and Smyth), plus many years of living in Italy, shaped my interests. Most of my research has been the result of inner need, rather than a need for employment. Research and direct experience with works of art supply my greatest rewards and pleasure."

*   *   *

LAW, Carol Russell

PERSONAL: Born in Minneapolis, Minn.; daughter of Arthur DeRussy (an accountant) and Wilhelmina (a dressmaker; maiden name, Moberg) Russell; married Warner Law, October 14, 1972 (died January 10, 1979). Education: Attended University of Minnesota. Politics: Democrat. Religion: Episcopalian. Home address: P.O. Box 41184, Los Angeles, Calif. 90041. Agent: H. N. Swanson, Inc., 8523 Sunset Blvd., Los Angeles, Calif. 90069.

CAREER: KSTP-Radio and Televison, Minneapolis, Minn., secretary, 1951-61; Ziv-United Artists, New York City, secretary, 1961-62; Vinti Advertising, New York City, secretary, 1962-65; J. C. Penney & Co., Inc., New York City, copywriter, 1966; Scholastic Magazines and Books, New York City,

copywriter, 1967-68; May Co. (department stores), Los Angeles, Calif., copywriter, 1968-69; Barker Brothers (department stores), Los Angeles, copywriter, 1969; Walt Disney Educational Media Co., Burbank, Calif., promotion director and copy chief, 1970-75; Carol R. Law Creative Advertising, Los Angeles, owner and copywriter, 1976—. Member of board of directors of Imagina School of Art.

MEMBER: International P.E.N., Authors Guild, Women's National Book Association, Mystery Writers of America (member of board of directors), Malibran Society (chief administrator), Pacific Music Association, Los Angeles Advertising Women. Awards, honors: Certificate of merit in retail advertising copy from Los Angeles Advertising Women, 1969, for May Company carpeting advertisement "Social Security."

WRITINGS: The Case of the Weird Street Firebug (juvenile), Knopf, 1980; Overture to Love (historical novel), Pinnacle Books, 1981; Dave's Double Mystery (juvenile), Scholastic Book Services, 1981; The Silken Cord, Harlequin Books, 1983. Contributor of stories to Alfred Hitchcock's Mystery Magazine.

WORK IN PROGRESS: A historical novel continuing the story of nineteenth-century opera star Maria Malibran.

SIDELIGHTS: Law told CA: "Music has always been an abiding interest of mine. When I left my last full-time job to devote myself to writing fiction, I found a way to combine my love of music and my wish to tell good stories. The answer was a historical novel based on the life of Maria Malibran, the first superstar of opera. I researched her life and times meticulously for two years before beginning to write the book. As I ran out of pages before she ran out of life (in Overture to Love), I will write another novel about her, and after that I would like to fictionalize the life stories of other illustrious nineteenth-century musicians. The study of great historical characters has illuminated my life, and I hope telling their stories will do the same for my readers. I feel that historical novels can give a truer picture of past times than nonfiction books, as the reader experiences the times along with the characters."

*   *   *

LAW, Marie Hamilton 1884-1981

OBITUARY NOTICE: Born in 1884; died October 6, 1981. Educator, librarian, and author. Director of the Drexel Library from 1937 to 1949, Law was also a former dean of the Drexel University Library School. Her writings include The English Familiar Essay in the Early Nineteenth Century and How to Read German. Obituaries and other sources: Library Journal, February 15, 1982.

*   *   *

LAWRENSON, Helen 1907-1982
(Helen Brown Norden)

OBITUARY NOTICE: Born in 1907 in LaFargeville, N.Y.; died of coronary artery disease and diabetes, April 5, 1982, in New York, N.Y. Journalist, editor, critic, and author. A Vanity Fair film critic and editor during the 1920's, Lawrenson achieved her greatest notoriety in 1936 when she became the first woman contributor to Esquire magazine with the article "Latins Are Lousy Lovers." Considered sensational at the time, the Esquire piece ridiculed the Latin lover mystique, calling it a matter of "quantity, not quality." Lawrenson published two collections of memoirs, Stranger at the Party and Whistling Girl, and was working on her first novel, Dance of Scorpions, at the time of her death. Obituaries and other sources: Who's Who of American Women, 6th edition, Marquis, 1970; New York Times,

April 8, 1982; *Washington Post,* April 9, 1982; *Time,* April 19, 1982; *Newsweek,* April 19, 1982; *Publishers Weekly,* April 30, 1982.

*   *   *

LAWRENSON, Thomas Edward   1918-1982

OBITUARY NOTICE: Born September 19, 1918, in Middlewich, Cheshire, England; died after a short illness, April 4, 1982. Educator, editor, and author. A graduate of Manchester University, Lawrenson held academic positions at various universities, including Manchester University, Glasgow University, Aberdeen University, and University College of the Gold Coast, before becoming one of Lancaster University's foundation professors as head of the department of French studies. He remained with the department from 1964 until 1979, at which time he became a professor of theatre studies. A chevalier de l'Ordre National du Merite, Lawrenson was also secretary-general of the International Federation for Theatre Research. Publications edited by Lawrenson include *Turcaret, Crispin Rival de son Maitre,* and *Modern Miscellany: Studies in Honour of Eugene Vinaver.* His best-known writing is *The French Stage in the Seventeenth Century.* Obituaries and other sources: *The Author's and Writer's Who's Who,* 6th edition, Burke's Peerage, 1971; *The Writers Directory, 1982-84,* Gale, 1981; *London Times,* April 10, 1982.

*   *   *

LAYTON, Wilbur L.   1922-

BRIEF ENTRY: Born March 26, 1922, in Atlantic, Iowa. American psychologist, educator, editor, and author. Layton has been a professor of psychology at Iowa State University since 1960, where he also served for ten years as vice-president for academic affairs. His publications include *The Strong Vocational Interest Blank: Research and Uses* (University of Minnesota Press, 1960) and *Testing in Guidance and Counseling* (McGraw, 1963). *Address:* Department of Psychology, Iowa State University, 152 Quad, Ames, Iowa 50011. *Biographical/ critical sources: American Men and Women of Science: The Social and Behavioral Sciences,* 13th edition, Bowker, 1978.

*   *   *

LAZARUS, Marguerite   1916-
(Marguerite Gascoigne; Anna Gilbert)

PERSONAL: Born May 1, 1916, in Durham, England; daughter of John Jackson (an inspector of schools) and Hannah (Keers) Gascoigne; married Jack Lazarus (an architect), April 3, 1956. *Education:* Durham University, B.A. (with honors), 1937, M.A., 1945. *Religion:* Nonconformist. *Home:* Oakley Cottage, Swainsea Lane, Pickering, North Yorkshire, England. *Agent:* Bolt & Watson, 26 Charing Cross Rd., London WC2H 0DG England.

CAREER: Grammar school teacher in England, 1941-73; writer, 1956—. *Awards, honors:* Romantic Novelists Association award, 1976, for *The Look of Innocence.*

WRITINGS—Novels; under pseudonym Anna Gilbert, except as noted: (Under name Marguerite Gasgoigne) *The Song of the Gipsy,* F. Warne, 1956; *Images of Rose,* Delacourt, 1973; *The Look of Innocence,* St. Martin's, 1975; *A Family Likeness,* St. Martin's, 1977; *Remembering Louise,* St. Martin's, 1978; *The Leavetaking,* St. Martin's, 1979; *Flowers for Lilian,* St. Martin's, 1980; *Miss Bede Is Staying,* Piatkus Books, 1982.

Contributor of stories to *Good Housekeeping* and *Woman.*

WORK IN PROGRESS: A novel.

SIDELIGHTS: Lazarus told *CA:* "What motivates me? The compulsion to tell a story: a feeling of candlelight, the fireside, wind in the chimney, and someone listening. What kind of story? I accept Thomas Hardy's advice that a story should be unusual enough to justify the telling, close enough to normal life to be convincing.

"For me the germ of a story often lies in an imagined or remembered scene; a visual experience rather than an abstract idea; a place that haunts me with its intimations of the people who might have lived there. My favorite setting is the English countryside: remote hamlets and villages, woods and moors, small market towns, a country in itself beautiful and menacing and, for me, interfused with the promise, or presence, of more than can be apprehended by the usual five senses.

"My stories revolve around close-knit, claustrophobic relationships. Their tension arises from some element of mystery: secrecy, deception, and illusion, and the gradual accumulation of detail leading to its disclosure. The central character progresses from ignorance to knowledge, from innocence to maturity. In *The Look of Innocence,* for instance, Cassie moves from childhood memories of the family tragedy to her discovery of the complex interplay of characters involved in it and so to acceptance and forgiveness. I am interested in the contrast between the surface of civilized society and the more primitive impulses it conceals, and in the exploitation of gentle and generous people by their opposites.

"There's no end to what one learns in writing. Fiction is a form of myth making. One finds a pattern of images emerging, and similar themes recur in stories which seemed in their inception quite different. The thrill lies in trying to strike the right balance between being in control as the mastermind and listening to the inner prompting which tells one what really happened. It isn't so much a matter of creating another world as of being admitted to it. The story is there. One finds it. For instance in *Flowers for Lilian* my original intention was to reverse the situation of the usual whodunnit, which begins with a death and continues with an exploration of possible motives. I thought it would make for more interesting characterization to start with the motives which might cause several people to wish for Lilian's death. However, on getting to know the people, I found that only one of them would actually have wanted Lilian to die or have been capable of killing her. Similarly, in *A Family Likeness* I was astonished and angry to discover that the grandmother had known the truth all the time.

"Most of my novels have been set in Victorian England, a society near enough in time to be well documented, far enough away to offer escape from the complications of contemporary life. Through television we are forced to confront immediate problems of previously unimagined magnitude. Imaginative escape is essential and can only be brief. Stories of course are composed of problems, but they are other people's, and the author's role is to present them in manageable form and in most cases to resolve them. (One of the pleasures of escape is vicarious sadness.) By placing one's characters in a society that seems through the passage of time more fixed than our own, one can concentrate on the timeless human preoccupations: love, loss, and illusion.

"I have always loved writing, but it was a long time before I was free to devote most of my time to it. After the publication of one youthful novel I had to give my mind to other things, such as teaching. Fortunately there can be few better places than a school for getting to know about people of all ages— less spectacular, perhaps, than sailing single-handed around the world, but equally demanding of endurance and discipline, not to mention resourcefulness and cunning. Most of the ingredients of the human situation are there, and when school closes there is plenty of time to look for the rest elsewhere. At the moment I feel that, like Othello, I have done the state some service and can now enjoy the self-indulgence of writing without guilt. If only he could have done the same!

"My advice to aspiring writers would be to do lots of other things besides writing and to secure their bread and butter by other means. And I do feel most strongly that a writer should respect his readers—if any. Readers deserve no less than one's best. Writers have a lonely life without them. To please the reader whose attention he solicits is the best reward a writer can hope to have."

BIOGRAPHICAL/CRITICAL SOURCES: New Republic, March 23, 1974; *New York Times Book Review,* July 21, 1974; *West Coast Review of Books,* September, 1978.

*　　　*　　　*

LEA, Sydney Wright 1942-

PERSONAL: Born December 22, 1942, in Philadelphia, Pa.; son of Sydney L.W. (in business) and Jane (Jordan) Lea; married, 1966 (marriage ended); children: Creston, Erika. *Education:* Yale University, B.A., 1964, M.A., 1968, Ph.D., 1972. *Office: New England Review,* P.O. Box 170, Lyme, N.H. 03755.

CAREER: Dartmouth College, Hanover, N.H., assistant professor, 1970-78, adjunct professor of English, 1978-80, editor of *New England Review,* 1978—. Adjunct professor at Yale University and Middlebury College, both 1980—. *Member:* Modern Language Association of America, Committee of Small Magazine Editors and Publishers, Poets and Writers. *Awards, honors:* Scholar at Bread Loaf Writer's Conference, 1977, fellow, 1979; Lamont Award nomination, 1982, for *The Floating Candles.*

WRITINGS: Searching the Drowned Man (poems), University of Illinois Press, 1980; *Gothic to Fantastic* (critical study), Arno, 1981; *The Floating Candles* (poems), University of Illinois Press, 1982. Contributor to magazines, including *New Republic, New Yorker, Nation,* and *Studies in Romanticism.*

WORK IN PROGRESS: A book of poems, completion expected in 1984; editing an anthology of American nature poetry since 1960, with John Elder.

SIDELIGHTS: Lea commented: "My chief interests are in the out of doors and in 'outdoorsy' people, especially oldtimers whose ilk is vanishing. I turned to poetry as the most suitable mode of recording not only natural facts (as a poet I'm as much interested in facts as anything), but also the cadences and locutions of the oldtimer. Having gotten that far with *Searching the Drowned Man,* I have tried to apply what I learned about fact and eloquence (and fact *as* eloquence) to a wider range of places and concerns."

*　　　*　　　*

LEANDER, Ed
See RICHELSON, Geraldine

*　　　*　　　*

LEBOYER, Frederick 1918-

PERSONAL: Born November 1, 1918, in Paris, France; son of Henry-Rene and Judith Leboyer. *Education:* University of

Paris, M.D. *Home:* 98 Rue Lepic, Paris 18, France. *Agent:* Georges Borchardt, Inc., 136 East 57th St., New York, N.Y. 10022.

CAREER: In private practice of obstetrics. Served as chef de clinique at University of Paris, Paris, France.

WRITINGS: Pour une naissance sans violence, Editions du Seuil, 1974, published as *Birth Without Violence,* Knopf, 1975; *Loving Hands,* Knopf, 1976; *Inner Beauty, Inner Light: Yoga for Pregnant Women,* foreword by B.K.S. Iyengar, Knopf, 1978. Also author of *Heart or Head.* Films: "Birth" and "Loving Hands."

SIDELIGHTS: A newborn's first cries—typically met with relief from parents and attending medical staff—are expressions of agonizing fear and pain, obstetrician Frederick Leboyer maintains. Being born is a traumatic event, he says in his book *Birth Without Violence,* and traditional delivery-room procedure prolongs and intensifies the baby's discomfort. Changes in obstetrical practices have tended to benefit the mother, making it possible for her to enjoy increasingly "natural" childbirth. But, as *Ms.* reviewer Susan Lydon noted, the baby's own experience is often far from natural. Recalling the birth of her daughter, Lydon wrote: "The second she was born, she was yanked up by her feet, slapped on the bottom, weighed, eyedropped, braceletted, cleaned, dressed, handed briefly to me for inspection, whisked away for 24 hours, and then put on a rigid four-hour feeding schedule. She never howled again the way she did in the hospital."

Such treatment of new babies, though typical, is needlessly harsh, and prospective parents and obstetricians would do well, Leboyer admonishes, to empathize with the child being born. He asks readers of *Birth Without Violence* to reflect, for example, on the contrast between the infant's dark, quiet, warm pre-natal surroundings and the bright, noisy, sterile delivery-room environment. At best, he says, the contrast between the two worlds startles the baby; at worst, it terrifies. Equally unsettling to the child, Leboyer asserts, is the common practice of cutting the umbilical cord—the pre-natal oxygen source—immediately after delivery. If left intact, the cord would continue to supply oxygen for several minutes, giving the child time to adjust to using its lungs. Severing it immediately, an act that forces the child to draw its first independent breath, is unnecessarily abrupt, Leboyer protests. Abrupt, too, is the accompanying practice of holding the child upside-down to hasten breathing. Inverting the child must provide it with a frightening sensation of falling, Leboyer reasons; he also claims this practice is harmful to the child's spine.

Leboyer hopes that greater awareness of the newborn's birth experience will lead to more humane treatment in the delivery room. To that end, *Birth Without Violence* focuses almost entirely on the baby and provides simple suggestions designed to minimize birth trauma. In a brief text supplemented by numerous photographs, Leboyer illustrates the contrast between conventional delivery methods and his own method, which he developed in the course of delivering more than ten thousand babies. In a Leboyer delivery, the baby's introduction into the world is accompanied by almost total silence and dim lighting. The newborn is placed on its mother's stomach, where it receives a gentle massage that encourages it to begin breathing on its own. The umbilical cord, left intact until it stops beating, provides the infant with a supplementary source of oxygen. The baby is handled firmly but gently, and its spine is allowed to straighten gradually. Finally, to eliminate any remaining tension, the baby is given a bath in water similar in temperature to the amniotic fluid that surrounded it before birth.

Leboyer's proposals ask only that the infant be given time to adjust to its new surroundings gradually; he condemns the established medical practice of employing emergency measures for normal deliveries. His views have angered many. Opponents of Leboyer's method protest that it is old-fashioned and unsafe for the baby, whose immediate condition cannot be determined until some time after birth. They also take issue with Leboyer's apparent lack of concern to maintain a sterile field on the mother's stomach and his scorn for the surgical gloves that place a barrier between the obstetrician's hands and the baby's skin. Discussing the opposition to *Birth Without Violence* in the *New York Times Book Review,* Jane Wilson wrote: "So now we have reached a point, in the sterile, no-risk scheme of American obstetrics, where simple procedure, requiring only human hands, sensitivity and time, cannot be found acceptable." In a similar discussion in *Newsweek,* Shana Alexander observed that "at a Leboyer delivery, all the sophisticated equipment of modern medicine is at hand. But the prime concern of the attending adults is not for apparatus and procedure but for the comfort and serenity of the newborn. Leboyer does not discard science. He merely puts it in its place."

Leboyer's dedication to his method of childbirth is based on his belief that the quality of a person's birth experience has a profound effect on the quality of his or her entire life. He also believes that we are conscious from the moment of birth—if not before—and that our memories of birth are stored deep within us. Whether his assumptions are true or not—and Wilson suggests that there is some evidence that they are—"the most eloquent argument for Leboyer's method comes," attested Susan Lydon, "from the babies he has delivered. What is most moving and astonishing in the book are the photographs of newborns. Wide-open and innocent eyes peer out of radiant, smooth-skinned faces. Gone are the scrunched-up face, shriveled skin, and fists tightly clenched around eyes or ears."

In a follow-up study of children delivered by the Leboyer method, psychologist Danielle Rapoport discovered that, although they learned to speak at approximately the same age as children delivered by traditional methods, they walked earlier and did better on tests for psychomotor functioning. Leboyer children also had considerably less difficulty with toilet training or with learning to feed themselves. Michael Odent, a doctor who uses Leboyer's method, noted also that "children born in a serene and peaceful way seem to be secure, in their first months, from such psychosomatic symptoms as colic, as well as the paroxysmic crying associated with a neonate." Though controversy continues over both the short- and long-term benefits of Leboyer's method, Shana Alexander expects that, "very soon, . . . the 'radical' Leboyer technique will be the accepted way of childbirth in our so-called civilized world, as it always has been elsewhere, before the technocrats of medicine got their hooks, so to speak, into the baby business."

BIOGRAPHICAL/CRITICAL SOURCES: Newsweek, March 31, 1975; *Village Voice,* April 14, 1975; *New York Times Book Review,* June 22, 1975; *Ms.,* September, 1975; *New York Review of Books,* October 2, 1975; *Psychology Today,* March, 1977.

—*Sketch by Mary Sullivan*

*   *   *

LEE, Betsy 1949-

PERSONAL: Born June 4, 1949, in Bayshore, N.Y.; daughter of James Weir (an educational administrator) and Betty (a teacher; maiden name, Crowder) Colmey; married Lawrence Lee (an assistant city manager), December 31, 1972; children: Brenna Elizabeth. *Education:* Attended University of New Mexico, 1967-68, and Chapman College's World Campus Afloat, 1969; University of Wyoming, B.A., 1971. *Politics:* Democrat. *Religion:* Christian. *Home and office:* 8 East Minnehaha Parkway, Minneapolis, Minn. 55419.

CAREER: Chapman College, Orange, Calif., publications adviser for World Campus Afloat, 1972; free-lance photographer and consultant, 1973; Open University, Milton Keynes, England, assistant publications and information officer, 1974-76; consultant, 1976-77; free-lance writer and photographer, 1978—. *Member:* Authors Guild.

WRITINGS: No Man to Himself (poems and photographs), Post Press, 1971; (editor) *This Place Has Its Ups and Downs* (juvenile), People's Press, 1977; *Charles A. Eastman: The Story of an American Indian* (juvenile biography), Dillon, 1979; *Mother Teresa: Caring for All God's Children* (juvenile biography), Dillon, 1980; *Judy Blume's Story,* Dillon, 1981; *Seasons of Love,* Augsburg, 1983.

Contributor of articles and photographs (including covers) to magazines and newspapers, including *Easy Living, Carte Blanche, Cross-Country, New York Times, St. Louis Post-Dispatch, Republic Scene, Living Trends, Corporate Report, Nuestro, Minnesota Monthly, Alaska, Scope,* and *Maryknoll.*

SIDELIGHTS: Betsy Lee wrote: "I am amazed by the number of would-be writers I meet at autograph parties. 'How did you get your lucky break?' they ask. I tell them it wasn't luck, and offer this advice: believe in yourself and don't take rejection slips personally. Most writers survive years of rejections before they have anything accepted.

"A writer's life is not easy. You spend years having your ego battered by rejection slips; when you have some success, you gain the privilege of having your ego battered by reviews! But I wouldn't trade the writing life for any other. The setbacks all seem worth it when you see your name on a glossy cover in the bookstore.

"People ask me if I'm lonely working at home by myself. No, I can honestly say I love it. Solitude is the womb of creativity: all original thoughts are planted and nurtured there. The mystery of giving birth is a profoundly private experience. It draws you inward to a deeper knowledge of yourself. There is something sacred about it that can't be shared. The fruit of your labors can be shared, but not the life-giving process itself.

"I've always wanted to do two things with my writing: say something meaningful and move people. When I was in high school, I remember reading John Steinbeck's *The Grapes of Wrath,* and thinking, Wow! Steinbeck described the death of a dog with such acute detail that I could actually feel the impact of the speeding car smashing into the animal. I was so shaken that I dropped the book. Writing should have that power.

"Robert Frost said: 'Every philosopher has one big metaphor in him. That is all he has.' I think writers basically have one big theme to explore. They spend their careers trying to express it more eloquently, more profoundly, more conclusively. I'm intrigued with human relationships, particularly between parents and children. I'm writing a book now about the spiritual dimension of the parent-child relationship as it develops during the first year of life. I feel it's only the beginning."

*   *   *

LEED, Theodore William 1927-

BRIEF ENTRY: Born February 11, 1927, in Canton, Ohio.

American agricultural economist, educator, and author. Since 1957 Leeds has been a professor of agricultural economics at University of Massachusetts. He wrote *Research Papers in Food Distribution* (Department of Agricultural and Food Economics, University of Massachusetts, 1965), *An Economic Analysis of Competitive Strategy and Sales in the Supermarket Industry* (Department of Agricultural and Food Economics, University of Massachusetts, 1966), and *Food Merchandising: Principles and Practices* (Chain Store Age Books, 1973). *Address:* Department of Agricultural and Food Economics, University of Massachusetts, 328 Draper Hall, Amherst, Mass. 01002.

*   *   *

Le FONTAINE, Joseph (Raymond) 1927-
(Joseph H. Raymond)

PERSONAL: Born April 6, 1927, in Buffalo, N.Y.; son of Joseph Romeo (a real estate broker) and Charlotte (a pianist; maiden name, Bertrand) Le Fontaine; married June Aldred, July 22, 1944 (divorced); children: Stephen, Bruce, David, Suzanne Le Fontaine Conley. *Education:* Rochester Institute of Technology, B.S.M.E., 1949. *Politics:* Republican. *Religion:* Episcopalian. *Home:* 17018 Magnolia Blvd., Encino, Calif. 91316. *Agent:* Mayorga & Co., P.O. Box 868, Santa Barbara, Calif. 93102. *Office:* 13624 Sherman Way, Suite 604, Van Nuys, Calif. 91405.

CAREER: National Engineering Co., Los Angeles, Calif., design engineer, 1950-52; Houston Fearless Corp., Los Angeles, design engineer, 1952-54; Koehler Aircraft Products Co., Los Angeles, chief engineer, 1955-58; Skyvalve, Inc., Los Angeles, chief engineer, 1959-65; Snap Tite, Inc., Erie, Pa., director of research and development, 1965-67; Scoville Fluid Products, Wake Forest, N.C., director of research and development, 1967-69; Western Precipitation Co., Los Angeles, national sales manager, 1969-72; rare book dealer in Los Angeles and New York City, 1972-76; writer and publisher, 1976—. Conducts writing seminars. *Military service:* U.S. Army, 1944-46, served in European theater; became sergeant. *Member:* Committee of Small Magazine Editors and Publishers, National Writers Club, Independent Consultants of America.

WRITINGS: A Directory of Buyers: Old Books and Paper Americana, InvestArt Publishers, 1978; *Turning Paper to Gold: The Paper Miners Manual*, Pegasus, 1982.

Under pseudonym Joseph H. Raymond: *The Investors Guide to Rare Books*, InvestArt Publishers, 1978; *You Can Write Yourself a Fortune*, InvestArt Publishers, 1979. Editor and publisher of *The InvestArt Almanac, Graphic Arts Collector*, and *Information Marketers Newsletter*.

WORK IN PROGRESS: Research for a book (and seminar series) on writing, self-publishing, and marketing how-to books by mail order.

SIDELIGHTS: Le Fontaine told *CA:* "On writing: I think it is one of our great national tragedies that our colleges and universities produce such a preponderance of graduates who are very nearly illiterate when it comes to written communication. It almost seems that they are taught that jargon, slang, and obfuscation are a desireable antidote to clarity—as if clarity and brevity were somehow shameful.

"On book collecting: It gives me a great sense of happiness and well-being to know that I have surrounded myself with the printed manifestation of the original thoughts, dreams, and accomplishments of all the great minds who have preceded us.

"On self-publishing: It is one of the few means available to many writers who have something to offer the world by way of information, or valid but divergent opinion. Too often the publishable work of authors never sees the light of day, or sees it in a very limited way simply because it does not offer the possibility of becoming a so-called best-seller for a major publisher.

"I am sure most people would be quite surprised to know that many of the biggest selling books of recent years have never appeared on any 'Best Seller' list, simply because they have been self-published and marketed by direct mail rather than through the traditional publisher-to-bookstore route. I can name at least one title which has sold over a million copies in the past eight years and in the process created a very wealthy author-publisher.

"There are also hundreds of newsletters which have emerged in the past two decades—all founded by a single individual conveying information that found a ready market in a wide variety of fields. Without these imaginative and enterprising individuals, a tremendous body of information would never emerge to help improve every aspect of our lives, careers, and general well-being."

AVOCATIONAL INTERESTS: Collecting rare books, travel, playing golf and tennis, wildlife conservation.

*   *   *

LEIBENGUTH, Charla Ann
See BANNER, Charla Ann Leibenguth

*   *   *

LEKACHMAN, Robert 1920-

BRIEF ENTRY: Born May 12, 1920, in New York, N.Y. American economist, educator, and author. In 1973 Lekachman was named distinguished professor of economics at Herbert H. Lehman College of the City University of New York. He has served as adviser to the Fund for the Republic, the Twentieth Century Fund, and the Committee for Economic Development. His publications include *A History of Economic Ideas* (Harper, 1959), *The Age of Keynes* (Random House, 1966), *National Income and the Public Welfare* (Random House, 1972), *Inflation: The Permanent Problem of Boom and Bust* (Random House, 1973), *Economists at Bay: Why the Experts Will Never Solve Your Problems* (McGraw, 1976), and a pamphlet, *The Great Tax Debate* (Public Affairs Committee, 1980). Lekachman's most recent book, *Greed Is Not Enough: Reaganomics* (Pantheon, 1982), is an indictment of President Reagan's supply-side economic policies. *Address:* 600 West 115th St., New York, N.Y. 10025. *Biographical/critical sources: Punch*, May 10, 1967; *American Men and Women of Science: The Social and Behavioral Sciences*, 13th edition, Bowker, 1978; *New York Times*, February 22, 1982; *Newsweek*, March 1, 1982.

*   *   *

LeMON, Lynn
See WERT, Lynette L(emon)

*   *   *

LENGLE, James I(rvin) 1949-

PERSONAL: Born July 18, 1949, in Reading, Pa.; son of Irvin J. (a railroad conductor) and Margaret (Zebertavage) Lengle; married Patricia Moczydlowski, September 4, 1971; children: Michael, Christopher. *Education:* Kutztown State College, B.A., 1971; University of California, Berkeley, M.A., 1972, Ph.D., 1978. *Office:* Department of Government, Georgetown University, Washington, D.C. 20057.

CAREER: University of California, Berkeley, director of American History and Institutions Office, 1974-77; Georgetown University, Washington, D.C., assistant professor, 1977-81, associate professor of American government, 1981—. Visiting lecturer at California State University, Hayward, 1976; guest speaker at Meridian House International, 1979—, and Washington Workshop, 1980—. Presidential election campaign commentator on WDVM-TV, 1980. *Member:* American Political Science Association, National Capital Area Political Science Association (member of council, 1981-82). *Awards, honors:* Russell Sage Foundation fellowship, 1978-79.

WRITINGS: (Editor with Byron Shafer, and contributor) *Presidential Politics: Readings on Nominations and Elections,* St. Martin's 1980; *Representation and Presidential Primaries: The Democratic Party in the Post-Reform Era,* Greenwood Press, 1981; (contributor) Bernard Grofmen, Arend Lijphart, and other editors, *Representation and Apportionment Issues in the 1980's,* Lexington Books, 1981. Contributor of articles and reviews to political science journals, *Commonsense,* and *America.* Editorial intern for *American Political Science Review,* 1975-77.

WORK IN PROGRESS: A book on the dynamics, strategies, and politics of presidential nominating campaigns, publication expected in 1984.

*   *   *

LENTNER, Howard H(enry)   1931-

PERSONAL: Born September 8, 1931, in Detroit, Mich.; son of Frank R. and Millicent (Kelley) Lentner; married M. Nancy Taylor, August 23, 1958 (separated, January 2, 1982); children: Tarah, J. Talar, Leseh. *Education:* Miami University, Oxford, Ohio, B.S., 1958; Syracuse University, M.A., 1959, Ph.D., 1964. *Residence:* Pelham, N.Y. *Office:* Department of Political Science, Bernard M. Baruch College of the City University of New York, 17 Lexington Ave., New York, N.Y. 10010.

CAREER: Western Reserve University (now Case Western Reserve University), Cleveland, Ohio, instructor, 1962-63, assistant professor of political science, 1963-68; McMaster University, Hamilton, Ontario, associate professor of political science and chairman of department, 1968-72; Bernard M. Baruch College of the City University of New York, New York, N.Y., associate professor and chairman of department of political science, 1973-76, professor of political science, 1976—. Member of board of trustees of Shaker Heights Public Library, 1965-68. *Military service:* U.S. Army, 1953-55; became sergeant. *Member:* International Studies Association, American Political Science Association, Northeastern Political Science Association.

WRITINGS: Foreign Policy Analysis: A Comparative and Conceptual Approach, C. E. Merrill, 1974; (contributor) Charles F. Hermann, editor, *International Crises: Insights From Behavioral Research,* Free Press, 1972. Contributor to scholarly journals, *Highlights for Children,* and newspapers.

*   *   *

LERNER, Sharon (Ruth)   1938-1982

OBITUARY NOTICE—See index for *CA* sketch: Born November 9, 1938, in Chicago, Ill.; died of cancer, March 8, 1982.

Publisher and author. In 1961 Lerner joined the newly formed Lerner Publications Company as vice-president and art director. Eight years later she and her husband, Harry J. Lerner, founded Carolrhoda Books. Lerner also wrote and illustrated children's books, including *I Like Vegetables, Who Will Wake Up Spring,* and *Orange Is a Color.* Obituaries and other sources: *Publishers Weekly,* April 2, 1982.

*   *   *

Le ROY, Bruce Murdock   1920-

BRIEF ENTRY: Born June 9, 1920, in Hornell, N.Y. American historian and author. Le Roy has been director of the Washington State Historical Society since 1959. He was a visiting lecturer at University of Puget Sound in 1967 and 1971. Le Roy's writings include *Lairds, Bards, and Mariners: The Scot in Northwest America* (Washington State Historical Society and Center for Northwest Folklore, 1978). He edited *H. M. Chittenden: A Western Epic; Being a Selection From His Unpublished Journals, Diaries, and Reports* (Washington State Historical Society, 1961). *Address:* 10511 Sunnybrook Lane, Tacoma, Wash. 98498; and 315 North Stadium Way, Tacoma, Wash. 98403.

*   *   *

L'ESTRANGE, Anna
   See ELLERBECK, Rosemary (Anne L'Estrange)

*   *   *

LEVENSTEIN, Harvey A(llan)   1938-

PERSONAL: Born June 29, 1938, in Toronto, Ontario, Canada; son of Sam and Fanny Levenstein; married Mona Croatti (an art educator), March 21, 1969; children: Lisa, Monica. *Education:* University of Toronto, B.A., 1960; University of Wisconsin—Madison, M.S., 1962, Ph.D., 1966. *Home:* 28 Dromore Cres., Hamilton, Ontario, Canada L8S 4A6. *Office:* Department of History, McMaster University, Hamilton, Ontario, Canada L8S 4L9.

CAREER: Brooklyn College of the City University of New York, Brooklyn, N.Y., instructor in history, 1965-66; Columbia University, Teachers College, New York, N.Y., assistant professor, 1966, associate professor of history, 1966-72; McMaster University, Hamilton, Ontario, assistant professor, 1972-73, associate professor, 1973-80, professor of history, 1980—. Visiting senior lecturer at University of Warwick, 1977-78. *Member:* American Historical Association, Organization of American Historians. *Awards, honors:* Grants from Canada Council, 1973—, and Social Science Research Council, 1977 and 1979; award from *American Quarterly,* 1981, for article "The New England Kitchen and the Origins of American Eating Habits."

WRITINGS: Labor Organizations in the United States and Mexico, Greenwood Press, 1971; (contributor) Joseph Conlin, editor, *The American Radical Press, 1880-1960,* Greenwood Press, 1974; *Communism, Anti-Communism, and the CIO,* Greenwood Press, 1981. Contributor to history journals.

WORK IN PROGRESS: A Social History of American Food, 1880-1930.

SIDELIGHTS: Labor Organizations in the United States and Mexico has been translated into Spanish.

*   *   *

LEVI, Julian (Edwin)   1900-1982

OBITUARY NOTICE: Born June 20, 1900, in New York, N.Y.;

died of a heart attack, February 28, 1982, in New York, N.Y. Artist, educator, and author of *Modern Art: An Introduction.* Best known for his paintings of seascapes, Levi's work is represented in permanent collections at several museums, including the Metropolitan Museum of Art, the Museum of Modern Art, the Whitney Museum, the Toledo Museum, the Chicago Art Institute, and the Pennsylvania Academy of Fine Arts. Painter-in-residence at the American Academy in Rome from 1967 to 1968, Levi also directed workshops at the New School for Social Research and was an instructor in painting at the Art Students League in New York City. Numbered among his most famous paintings are "Shrimp Scow on Barnegat Bay," "Shipbottom Fishery," "Driftwood," and "Boots on the Beach." Obituaries and other sources: *Current Biography,* Wilson, 1943, April, 1982; *Who's Who in America,* 40th edition, Marquis, 1978; *New York Times,* March 2, 1982; *Time,* March 15, 1982.

* * *

LEVIN, Jane Whitbread 1914-
(Jane Whitbread)

BRIEF ENTRY: Born November 15, 1914, in Larchmont, N.Y. American author. Levin has been a free-lance writer since 1937. She also worked as a publicity and research director and as an advertising copywriter for the film industry. Levin wrote *The Intelligent Man's Guide to Women* (Schuman, 1951), *Bringing Up Puppies: A Child's Book of Dog Breeding and Care* (Harcourt, 1958), *How to Help Your Child Get the Most Out of School* (Doubleday, 1974), and *Daughters: From Infancy to Independence* (Doubleday, 1978). *Address:* 25 East End Ave., New York, N.Y. 10028.

* * *

LEVINE, Lois (Elaine) L. 1931-

PERSONAL: Born April 20, 1931, in Waterbury, Conn.; daughter of Harry (a merchant) and Selma (Levin) Liebeskind; married Paul B. Levine (a business executive in manufacturing), June 7, 1953; children: Andrew, Betsy. *Education:* Wellesley College, B.A., 1952. *Home:* 72 Spring Glen Ter., Hamden, Conn. 06517.

CAREER: Hamden Chronicle, Hamden, Conn., food columnist, 1960-70; Day Prospect Hill School, New Haven, Conn., cooking teacher, 1970-73; in free-lance public relations, 1970—; writer and lecturer. Member of board of directors of International Student Center, New Haven, 1974-80. *Awards, honors:* Tastemaker award from R. T. French Co., 1973, for *The Summertime Cookbook.*

WRITINGS: (With Marion Burros) *The Elegant But Easy Cookbook,* Macmillan, 1960; (with Burros) *Freeze With Ease,* Macmillan, 1965; *The Kids in the Kitchen Cookbook,* Macmillan, 1968; (with Burros) *Come for Cocktails, Stay for Supper,* Macmillan, 1970; (with Burros) *The Summertime Cookbook,* Macmillan, 1972; *Delicious Diet Cookbook,* Macmillan, 1974; (with Mary A. Frankenberger) *The Fine Restaurants of Connecticut,* Pequot Press, 1978; *Lois Levine's Vegetable Favorites,* Western Publishing, 1980.

WORK IN PROGRESS: Another cookbook.

* * *

LEVY, Joseph V(ictor) 1928-

PERSONAL: Surname is pronounced *Lee-vee;* born April 7, 1928, in Los Angeles, Calif.; married, 1954; children: two.

Education: Stanford University, B.A., 1950; University of California, Los Angeles, M.S., 1956; University of Washington, Seattle, Ph.D., 1959. *Office address:* P.O. Box 7999, San Francisco, Calif. 94120.

CAREER: Stanford University, Palo Alto, Calif., assistant physiologist, 1951-53, assistant pharmacologist, 1954-56; University of Washington, Seattle, assistant, 1956-57; pharmacologist at Western Laboratories Resources Research, 1960; senior resident pharmacologist at Presby Medical Center Research Laboratories, 1960-65; Institutes of Medical Sciences, San Francisco, Calif., director of Pharmacology Laboratories, 1960—; associate professor at School of Medical Science, 1969-77; clinical associate professor at University of the Pacific, 1972—; associate director of Kuzell Institute for Arthritis Research, 1981—; member of National Heart and Blood Institute hypertension task force; consultant to World Health Organization and Academy of Traditional Chinese Medicine.

MEMBER: American Society of Pharmacology and Experimental Therapeutics, American Society of Clinical Pharmacology, Society of Experimental Biology and Medicine, American Chemical Society, American Heart Association (member of basic science council), American Pharmaceutical Association (member of drug interactions task force), Western Pharmacology Society. *Awards, honors:* Fellowships from National Heart Institute, 1965-70, career development award; advanced research fellowship from American Heart Association, 1959-60; career development awards from National Institutes of Health, 1958-59, and U.S. Public Health Service; travel fellowship from International Union of Pharmacology for Sweden, Finland, and France.

WRITINGS: (With Paul Bach-y-Rita) *Vitamins: Their Use and Abuse,* Liveright, 1976.

Contributor of more than one hundred articles to scientific journals. Member of editorial board of *Proceedings of the Society of Experimental Biology and Medicine.*

WORK IN PROGRESS: Research on pharmacology, therapeutics, physiology, and medicine.

* * *

LEVY, Sidney Jay 1921-

BRIEF ENTRY: Born May 29, 1921, in St. Louis, Mo. American psychologist, educator, and author. Levy has been director of psychological research at Social Research, Inc., since 1952 and a professor of behavioral science in management at Northwestern University since 1970. His writings include *Living With Television* (Aldine, 1962), *Promotion: A Behavioral View* (Prentice-Hall, 1967), *Promotional Behavior* (Scott, Foresman, 1971), *Man's Interface With the Money Machine* (Bank Marketing Association, 1972), *Marketing, Society, and Conflict* (Prentice-Hall, 1975), and *Marketplace Behavior: Its Meaning for Management* (American Management Association, 1978). *Address:* 945 Sheridan Rd., Evanston, Ill. 60202.

* * *

LEWIS, Eils Moorhouse 1919-

PERSONAL: First name rhymes with "miles"; born December 15, 1919, in Springhill, Nova Scotia, Canada; daughter of Gordon S. and Christine (McAloney) Moorhouse; married Joseph F. Lewis, August 17, 1946; children: Barbara Ellen Lotz. *Education:* Attended school in Brooklyn, N.Y. *Politics:* Republican. *Religion:* Episcopalian. *Home:* 156 Trenton Rd., Fairless Hills, Pa. 19030.

CAREER: L. A. Mathey & Co. (broker), New York City, assistant cashier, 1941-45; G. H. Walker & Co. (investment banking firm), New York City, executive secretary in research department, 1955-60; associated with Fulton Surgical Supply Co., 1970-73; writer.

WRITINGS: The Snug Little House (juvenile), Atheneum, 1981.

WORK IN PROGRESS: A novelette set before World War I; an adventure fantasy about two boys and a girl set in mythical India; several children's stories.

SIDELIGHTS: Lewis told *CA:* "Writing for publication came to me late in life, and although my stories are usually about simple things, I find writing hard work. Not being a teacher, psychologist, or psychiatrist, I do not feel qualified to solve the weighty problems that often beset children. My stories are 'fun' tales, and I do not set out to give a 'message.' But, if something in a story helps a child along the way then I've accomplished more than I aimed for, and that's all to the good.

"The most difficult thing the older novice such as myself has to face is, I think, the public attitude. While I was discussing my work with an intelligent, well-educated nun, she remarked, 'My, it's really great that you have such a nice hobby.' I gritted my teeth, bit my tongue, and said nothing."

AVOCATIONAL INTERESTS: Quilting, piano, water colors.

*   *   *

LEWIS, G(ranville) Douglass   1934-

PERSONAL: Born August 2, 1934, in Bolivar, Tenn; son of Hollis and Alton Lewis; married Shirley Savage (a teacher at an alternative high school), children: Laura, G. Douglass, Jr. *Education:* University of Tennessee, B.A. (with highest honors), 1957; Vanderbilt University, B.D. (with honors), 1960; attended University of Hamburg, 1960-61; Duke University, Ph.D., 1964; Case Method Institute, Certificate in Teaching Methodology, 1979; Harvard University, Certificate in Educational Management, 1981. *Home:* 77 Sherman St., Hartford, Conn. 06105. *Office:* Field Program, Hartford Seminary Foundation, Hartford, Conn.

CAREER: Ordained United Methodist minister, 1964; Tennessee Wesleyan College, Athens, chaplain and associate professor of religion and philosophy, 1964-67; National Council of Churches, Chicago, Ill., director of "Ministry in the Seventies" enlistment project, 1967-70, project director, 1970-71; Institute for Ministry Development, Chicago, Ill., director, 1971-74; Hartford Seminary Foundation, Hartford, Conn., director of field program and services and doctor of ministry program, 1974—. Visiting professor at Fuller Theological Seminary, 1976, Case Method Institute, 1980, and Evangelical Seminary of Puerto Rico, 1980; member of faculty at McCormick Theological Seminary, 1972-74. President of Greater Hartford Social Club (halfway-house program for persons recovering from emotional problems); President of Wesley Theological Seminary, Washington, D.C., 1982—. Vice-president of New England Committee on Holistic Health. Member of board of directors of Center for Parish Development and department of professional church leadership of National Council of Churches; member of Institute for Ministry Development. *Member:* American Academy of Religion, Association of Case Teachers (member of board of directors), Religious Research Association (president, 1980-81), Phi Delta Kappa.

WRITINGS: The Church Reaching Out: Interpreting Ministry as a Career, I.D.O.C., 1970; (editor) *Explorations in Ministry,* I.D.O.C., 1971; (contributor) John Biersdorf, editor, *Creating an Intentional Ministry,* Abingdon, 1976; (with Rhea Gray,

Norman Shawchuck, and Robert Worley) *Experiences in Activating Congregations: A Cross-Denominational Study,* Institute for Ministry Development, 1978; *Resolving Church Conflicts: A Case Method Approach,* Harper, 1981. Contributor to magazines, including *Christian Century, Pastoral Psychology, Religion in Life, Encounter,* and *Christian Advocate.*

*   *   *

LEWIS, Grover Virgil   1934-

PERSONAL: Born November 8, 1934, in San Antonio, Tex.; son of Grover Virgil (a tenant farmer) and Opal Lee (Bailey) Lewis; married Raona Ence (an executive secretary), July 4, 1973. *Education:* North Texas State University, B.A., 1959; graduate study at Texas Tech University, 1960-63. *Home:* 960 Third St., No. 403, Santa Monica, Calif. 90403. *Agent:* Natalia Murray, 785 Park Ave., New York, N.Y. 10021. *Office: New West,* 9665 Wilshire Blvd., Beverly Hills, Calif. 90212.

CAREER: Fort Worth Star Telegram, Fort Worth, Tex., copy editor, 1963-66; *Houston Chronicle,* Houston, Tex., reporter, 1967-69; *Village Voice,* New York, N.Y., reporter, 1969-70; *Rolling Stone,* San Francisco, Calif., associate editor, 1970-73; *New West,* Beverly Hills, Calif., editor, 1976-80; writer, 1980—. *Awards, honors:* Samuel French Playwriting Award, 1958, for "Wait for Morning, Child"; nominee for National Magazine Award, 1979, for article "Buried Alive in Hype."

WRITINGS: Wait for Morning, Child (one-act play; first produced in Denton, Tex., at North Texas State University Theatre, fall, 1958), Samuel French, 1958; *I'll Be There in the Morning If I Live* (poetry), Straight Arrow, 1973; *Academy All the Way* (reportage), Straight Arrow, 1974. Editor of *Cafe Solo 9* (magazine), 1975.

WORK IN PROGRESS: A novel set in Hollywood, publication by Atheneum expected in 1984.

SIDELIGHTS: Grover Lewis commented: "All I know about writing is encompassed in the observation of the late Red Smith: 'Hell, writing's easy. All you do is sit down at the typewriter and wait for little drops of blood to appear on your forehead.' I might add that I learned early to pay attention to my elders and betters."

*   *   *

LI, Yao-wen   1924-

PERSONAL: Born May 7, 1924, in Canton, China; daughter of Sung-ling (a professor) and Sum-oi (a doctor; maiden name, Yang) Kwang; married Chu-tsing Li (a professor of art history), June 18, 1948; children: B li, Amy. *Education:* Ginling College, Nanking, China, B.S., 1947; University of Iowa, M.S., 1951. *Home:* 1108 Avalon Rd., Lawrence, Kan. 66044.

CAREER: University of Iowa, Iowa City, department of surgery research assistant, 1953-59; writer, 1975—.

WRITINGS: (With Carol Kendall) *Sweet and Sour: Tales From China* (juvenile), Bodley Head, 1978, Seabury, 1979; (contributor) *Three Folktales,* Houghton, 1981. Contributor to periodicals, including *Asia.*

WORK IN PROGRESS: Cinnamon Moon, a book of Chinese folktales, with Carol Kendall.

SIDELIGHTS: Li told *CA:* "In my early years I never thought of becoming a writer. After many years of working as a scientist, a housewife, a mother, and at other jobs, I finally began writing and translating. To my great surprise, I got tremendous satisfaction from it. I feel that there is some kind of predestination in this. It just happened, and I found myself a writer.

"Born and raised in China in the pre-Communist years, I attended college before coming to the United States. Now, having lived for more than thirty years in my adopted country, I have gained a perspective in my understanding of these two cultures. I would like to take the fullest advantage of this perspective in presenting China to my English readers."

*   *   *

LIEBERMAN, Mendel Halliday 1913-

PERSONAL: Born August 3, 1913, in Denver, Colo.; son of Jacob Julius (an attorney) and Minnie (Morris) Lieberman; married Inez Liffman, February 6, 1942 (divorced, 1969); married Marion Hardie (a counselor and teacher), June 3, 1973; children: Peter C., Lynn Lieberman Williams. *Education:* University of California, Los Angeles, A.B., 1935; University of Southern California, J.D., 1938. *Home and office:* 13393 Sousa Lane, Saratoga, Calif. 95070.

CAREER: Admitted to the State Bar of California; teacher of current social, economic, and political problems at night school in Los Angeles, Calif., and teacher of English and social living for juvenile prisoners, Sheriff's Forestry Camp, Los Angeles, 1939-44; Lieberman, Weisz & Lieberman (law firm), Los Angeles, associate, 1944-50, partner, 1950-63; University of California, Berkeley, legal researcher and editor for Continuing Education of the Bar, 1963-71; marriage, family, and child counselor in Los Gatos, Calif., 1971-81; writer, 1981—. Director of adult education at Japanese relocation center in Arizona, 1942-43; teacher of adult education classes in Los Gatos and San Jose, Calif., 1972-80. *Military service:* U.S. Army, 1942. *Member:* California Association of Marriage, Family, and Child Counselors.

WRITINGS: (Editor with Robin Foster and William A. Carroll) *California Will Drafting,* University of California Press, 1965; (editor with Irving Slater and Herbert Gross) *California Real Estate Sales Transactions,* University of California Press, 1967; *California Real Estate Syndicates,* University of California Press, 1969; (editor) *Ground Lease Practice,* 1970; (with wife Marion Hardie) *Resolving Family (and Other) Conflicts So That Everybody Wins,* Unity Press, 1981.

Also author of two mini-dramas for the "Kate Smith Radio Hour" (one was performed by the Group Theatre of New York, the other was read by Orson Welles), 1941.

WORK IN PROGRESS: Robin Hood: Hero in Hiding, a novel, publication expected in 1984; articles on stepparents, relationships, family meetings, counseling, and aging.

SIDELIGHTS: Lieberman told *CA:* "An element growing steadily more important in my writing (*writing* the verb, more than *writing* the noun) is the race with death—my death—as I confront age sixty-eight, sixty-nine, seventy. Should I forget about the novel because I may not have time to finish it, only to find out, as my life continues to lengthen, that I probably could have finished it after all? Then, even as I write the words, I become aware (again) that I confronted the same question when I enrolled in law school, when I contracted marriage, when I fathered two children, when I made a career change at great risk, and when I remarried. What I have done has been to act as if my life would continue indefinitely, and as if it would end today."

LIEKSMAN, Anders
   See HAAVIKKO, Paavo Juhani

*   *   *

LILLY, Ray
   See CURTIS, Richard (Alan)

*   *   *

LINDBLOM, Steven (Winther) 1946-

PERSONAL: Born March 29, 1946, in Minneapolis, Minn.; son of Charles Edward (a professor of political science and writer) and Rose Catherine Lindblom; married True A. Kelley (a writer and illustrator). *Education:* Attended St. John's College, Annapolis, Md., 1964-65; Rhode Island School of Design, B.F.A., 1972. *Residence:* Warner, N.H.

CAREER: Free-lance illustrator and writer.

WRITINGS—Juveniles: *The Mouse's Terrible Christmas,* Lothrop, 1978; *The Fantastic Bicycles Book,* Houghton, 1979; *The Mouse's Terrible Halloween,* Lothrop, 1980; *Let's Give Kitty a Bath,* Addison-Wesley, 1982.

WORK IN PROGRESS: A juvenile book about robots, publication expected in 1983; juvenile books about croquet and machine tools.

SIDELIGHTS: Lindblom told *CA:* "While I have written more fiction than nonfiction at this point, nonfiction writing is my first love.

"I think there are two very negative forces at work on our children today. One is television, which is turning children into drones who are only observers, and who have been convinced that experiences seen on television are somehow as valid as the real thing. (I think a child who neither read nor watched television might be happier and more constructive than one who did both!) The other is that modern technology has become so complex and remote that we begin to see ourselves as its victims rather than its masters and cease accepting any responsibility for the future.

"There are two things good children's nonfiction can do about this: encourage kids to get out and do things for themselves and reduce the world that surrounds them to manageable terms, restoring to them the feeling that they can comprehend it, and therefore control it.

"It's important that kids realize that whenever someone tells them, 'It's too complicated for you to understand,' the person probably is just covering up his own lack of understanding."

AVOCATIONAL INTERESTS: Old bicycles and machinery, designing and building his "solar-gothik" home.

*   *   *

LINDENFELD, David Frank 1944-

PERSONAL: Born January 25, 1944, in Bethlehem, Pa. *Education:* Princeton University, A.B., 1965; Harvard University, M.A.T., 1966; University of Chicago, Ph.D., 1973. *Office:* Department of History, Louisiana State University, Baton Rouge, La. 70803.

CAREER: University of Chicago, Chicago, Ill., lecturer in history, 1969; Ohio State University, Columbus, assistant professor of history, 1972-74; Louisiana State University, Baton Rouge, assistant professor of history, 1974—. *Member:* Society for the History of Sociology and the Behavioral Sciences.

WRITINGS: *The Transformation of Positivism: Alexius Meinong and European Thought, 1880-1920,* University of California Press, 1981. Contributor to journals in the behavioral sciences.

WORK IN PROGRESS: *A History of the Social Sciences in Germany;* research on the historical materialism of Ferdinand Tonnies.

SIDELIGHTS: Lindenfeld wrote: "I am aiming at a comprehensive intellectual and cultural history of Europe at the turn of the century—a period which has shaped the assumptions of contemporary culture in so many ways. I am approaching it through a series of studies of different disciplines and areas of cultural expression. My first book concentrated on philosophy and psychology; my current project deals with the social sciences—then I am on to literature, the arts, natural science, and finally a synthesis, if I live that long!"

*   *   *

LINDLEY, Denver   1904-1982

OBITUARY NOTICE: Born in 1904 in New York, N.Y.; died after a long illness, February 11, 1982, in Tucson, Ariz. Editor and translator. A graduate of Princeton University, Lindley began his editing career as an article and fiction editor for *Collier's* magazine in 1928, remaining there until 1944. Subsequently he served as an editor with Appleton-Century, Henry Holt & Company, Harcourt Brace, and Viking Press. Among the authors whose writings he edited were Robert Frost, Saul Bellow, Thomas Mann, and Herman Hesse. In addition to editing, Lindley translated books, including Mann's *Confessions of Felix Krull, Confidence Man,* Erich Maria Remarque's *Arch of Triumph* and *A Time to Live and a Time to Die,* and Andre Maurois's *Memoirs, 1885-1967.* Obituaries and other sources: *Who's Who in America,* 40th edition, Marquis, 1978; *New York Times,* February 13, 1982, February 15, 1982; *Chicago Tribune,* February 16, 1982.

*   *   *

LINDSAY, Jeanne Warren   1929-

PERSONAL: Born December 13, 1929, in Garnett, Kan.; daughter of William W. (a farmer) and Hazel (a teacher and farmer; maiden name, Donaldson) Warren; married Robert E. Lindsay (a contracts administrator), March 23, 1951; children: Michael, Steven, Pati, Eric, Erin. *Education:* Kansas State University, B.S., 1951; California State University, Long Beach, M.A. (home economics), 1966, M.A. (anthropology), 1970. *Politics:* Democrat. *Home:* 6595 San Haroldo Way, Buena Park, Calif. 90620. *Office:* Teen Mother Program, ABC Unified School District, 12222 Cuesta, Cerritos, Calif. 90701.

CAREER: Teen Mother Program, Cerritos, Calif., coordinating teacher, 1972—. *Member:* California Alliance Concerned With School Age Parents.

WRITINGS: *They'll Read If It Matters: Study Guides for Books About Pregnancy and Parenting,* Morning Glory, 1977; *You'll Read If It Matters,* Morning Glory, 1977; *Parenting Preschoolers: Study Guides for Child Care Books,* Morning Glory, 1978; *Pregnant Too Soon: Adoption Is an Option,* EMC Corp., 1980; *Teens Parenting: The Challenge of Babies and Toddlers,* Morning Glory, 1981; *Do I Have a Daddy?* (juvenile), Morning Glory, 1982. Editor of *CACSAP Newsletter,* 1976—, and *Tracy News,* 1978—.

WORK IN PROGRESS: A followup study of school-age mothers, with the aim of identifying a culture of school-age parenthood.

SIDELIGHTS: Jeanne Lindsay commented: "At this time, my writing is primarily concerned with school-age parents. One-fifth of the babies born in the United States are born to teenagers, yet this segment of our population has only recently begun to be noticed by the general public, and that notice is often negative. Teenage parents often have greater need for community support than do older parents. If very young parents receive this help (for example, infant centers on school campuses so they can continue their education), they often will not have the expensive problems (expensive in terms of tax dollars and of human suffering) they will have if they must cope alone. Most of my writing is based on observation of and interviews with pregnant adolescents and school-age parents."

*   *   *

LINK, Martin   1934-

PERSONAL: Born September 26, 1934, in Madison, Wis.; son of Lucian A. (a postman) and Lucille (Davis) Link. *Education:* University of Arizona, B.A., 1958. *Politics:* Republican. *Religion:* Roman Catholic. *Home:* 2302 Mariyana Dr., Gallup, N.M. 87301. *Agent:* Hera Associates, 18 Village Lane, Middletown, N.J. 07748. *Office address:* Red Rock Park, P.O. Box 328, Church Rock, N.M. 87311.

CAREER: Archaeologist. Navajo Tribal Museum, Window Rock, Ariz., director, 1960-77; Red Rock State Park, Church Rock, N.M., manager, 1977—. Chairman, Navajo Centennial Committee, 1968, and Gallup Centennial, 1980. *Military service:* U.S. Army, 1959. *Member:* National Audubon Society, Plateau Sciences Society, New Mexico Archaeological Society, Knights of Columbus, Lions Clubs International.

WRITINGS: *Navajo: A Century of Progress,* K.C. Publications, 1968; (with Charles L. Blood) *The Goat in the Rug* (juvenile), Parents Magazine Press, 1976.

WORK IN PROGRESS: *The Indian Givers,* a book about all the foods, names, medicines, etc., that the American Indian has given to our culture.

SIDELIGHTS: "With my background in archaeology and history," Link told *CA,* "I constantly find a lot of adult material, but very little published for young people's enjoyment." One of his goals, therefore, is "to do good historical books for children."

*   *   *

LIPP, Frederick (John)   1916-

PERSONAL: Born July 23, 1916, in Toledo, Ohio; son of Frederick John (a realtor) and Lulu (a music teacher; maiden name, Hasenpflug) Lipp; married Marian Ruth Bechstein, September 7, 1946. *Education:* University of Toledo, B.Phil., 1939; University of Iowa, M.A., 1941. *Politics:* "Independent, but a strong Democratic bias." *Religion:* Episcopalian. *Home:* 3223 Rocky River Dr., No. 20, Cleveland, Ohio 44111. *Agent:* McIntosh & Otis, Inc., 475 Fifth Ave., New York, N.Y. 10017.

CAREER: National Broadcasting Co. (NBC), Chicago, Ill., continuity writer, 1945-48; *Ottawa County Exponent,* Oak Harbor, Ohio, editor, 1948-53; associated with Storycraft, Inc. (writing organization for business and industry), Cleveland, Ohio, 1953-61; Cleveland Electric Illuminating Co., Cleveland, executive writer, 1961-81; free-lance writer, 1981—. *Military service:* U.S. Navy, Correspondent Unit, 1943-46. *Awards, honors:* Award from Friends of American Writers, 1967, and literary award from Cleveland Arts Prize, 1968, both for *Rulers of Darkness.*

WRITINGS: Rulers of Darkness (novel), World Publishing, 1966; *Some Lose Their Way* (juvenile), Atheneum, 1980.

Also author of radio and television plays, 1941-60. Work represented in anthologies, including *American Writing, 1943,* edited by Alan Swallow for Bruce Humphreys. Contributor of stories to literary magazines.

WORK IN PROGRESS: A novel; a biography of the medieval poet Thomas Hoccleve.

SIDELIGHTS: "For me," Lipp told *CA,* "much about the profession of writing is summed up in a clipping which, for many years, was clamped by a small magnet to the metal wall of my office. The clipping was a xerox of those lines from T. S. Eliot's 'East Coker,' in which Eliot looked back over his long years of writing. He spoke of them as years of trying to learn to use words, with every attempt being a wholly new start and a different kind of failure. Each venture, as he described it, was a new beginning, a raid on the inarticulate with shabby equipment that was always deteriorating.

"I kept the clipping on the wall because it said something, not only *to* me, but *for* me, better than I could hope to say it. What it did not say, however, and what is for me an equally valid statement, is that this never-ending raid on the inarticulate with the equipment one has left is precisely what constitutes the zest, the challenge, and those occasional moments of glory in writing. I have had the good fortune to practice this trade, craft, art—it is all of these—for the greater part of my life. Like most writers, I expect to go on practicing it. And here again, for me, at least, Eliot has the last word: 'For us there is only the trying. The rest is not our business.'"

* * *

LIPP, Martin R(obert) 1940-

PERSONAL: Born May 30, 1940, in Kimball, Neb.; son of Frank E. (a physician) and Lucy (an executive secretary of an eye bank; maiden name, Krutchkoff) Lipp; married Jane Phillips, 1970 (marriage ended, 1977); married Suzanne Quick, 1980 (marriage ended, 1981). *Education:* Attended University of Michigan, 1958-61; University of Nebraska, B.S., 1963, M.D., 1966. *Home:* 117 Fountain Ave., Pacific Grove, Calif. 93950. *Office:* P.O. Box 26393, San Francisco, Calif. 94126.

CAREER: University of Nebraska, Omaha, instructor in physiology and pharmacology, 1963-66; University of Pennsylvania, Philadelphia, rotating intern, 1966-67; Stanford University, Stanford, Calif., resident in psychiatry, 1969-72; Veterans Administration Hospital, San Francisco, Calif., staff psychiatrist and chief of Psychiatric Consultation Service, 1972-75; Kaiser Permanente Medical Group, Hayward, Calif., emergency room physician, 1975—. Assistant clinical professor at University of California, San Francisco, 1973—. Emergency room physician at Williamsburg Community Hospital, 1967, and Alexian Brothers Hospital, 1969-70; physician and surgeon at Agnews State Hospital, 1970-71; visiting fellow at Royal Edinburgh Hospital, 1971; physician at Presbyterian Hospital and Pacific Medical Center, 1973-75. *Military service:* U.S. Public Health Service, physician with U.S. Coast Guard, 1967-69; served in the Arctic and western Pacific; became lieutenant commander. *Member:* American Psychiatric Association, Authors Guild, Authors League of America, Physicians for Social Responsibility, American Civil Liberties Union, Sierra Club, Northern California Psychiatric Society (chairman of committee on well-being, 1979-80).

WRITINGS: Respectful Treatment: The Human Side of Medical Care, Harper, 1977; *The Bitter Pill: Doctors, Patients, and*

Failed Expectations, Harper, 1980. Contributor of more than twenty articles and reviews to medical journals.

WORK IN PROGRESS: A nonfiction book, publication expected in 1984; short stories.

SIDELIGHTS: Lipp described his specialties as "personality and decision making in health professionals, clinical teaching, professional and nonprofessional writing, social and political trends in medicine and psychiatry, physician and patient roles and their interaction, social regulatory functions of physicians, the role of the prescription in the doctor-patient relationship, and deregulation of medical practice."

* * *

LIPSON, Leslie (Michel) 1912-

PERSONAL: Born November 14, 1912, in London, England; son of Alexander Mia (in business) and Caroline Rachel (Goodman) Lipson; married Sara Davida Bogan, June 13, 1937 (died, 1971); married Elizabeth Monroe Drews, November 3, 1972 (died, November, 1976); married Helen Morgenstern (a public relations consultant), October 2, 1980; children: David Roger. *Education:* Balliol College, Oxford, B.A., 1935, M.A., 1945; University of Chicago, Ph.D., 1938. *Politics:* Independent Democrat. *Religion:* "Humanist." *Home:* 25 Stoddard Way, Berkeley, Calif. 94708.

CAREER: Victoria University of Wellington, Wellington, New Zealand, 1939-46, became professor of political science; Swarthmore College, Swarthmore, Pa., associate professor of political science, 1947-50; University of California, Berkeley, professor of political science, 1950-80, professor emeritus, 1980—. Guest lecturer at more than twenty-five schools, including National War College and Air War College; member of board of directors of KQED-TV. *Military service:* Served with New Zealand Home Guard. *Member:* National Organization for Women, World Affairs Council of Northern California (member of board of trustees).

WRITINGS: The American Governor: From Figurehead to Leader, University of Chicago Press, 1939, reprinted, Greenwood Press, 1968; *The Politics of Equality: New Zealand's Adventures in Democracy,* University of Chicago Press, 1948; *The Great Issues of Politics,* Prentice-Hall, 1954, 6th edition, 1981; *The Democratic Civilization,* Oxford University Press, 1964; (with Elizabeth M. Drews) *Values and Humanity,* St. Martin's, 1971. Contributor to *Encyclopaedia Britannica.*

WORK IN PROGRESS: On the Ethics of Civilization; a collection of nonsense verse.

SIDELIGHTS: Lipson commented: "I am a humanist who specializes in the study of the political aspect of society. Hence, I ask of every system and every theory, 'Are the results, in practice, good or bad?' I am inquiring now into the progress, or lack of it, which civilization has recorded thus far in its ethical standards."

AVOCATIONAL INTERESTS: Travel (including Western Europe).

* * *

LITTLE, Nina Fletcher 1903-

BRIEF ENTRY: Born January 25, 1903, in Brookline, Mass. American art collector, historian, and author. Little is chairman of the curatorial committee at Old Sturbridge Village. Her books include *American Decorative Wall Painting, 1700-1850* (Studio Publications, 1952), *The Abby Aldrich Rockefeller Folk*

Art Collection: A Descriptive Catalogue (Colonial Williamsburg, 1975), *Country Arts in Early American Homes* (Dutton, 1975), *Paintings by New England Provincial Artists, 1775-1800* (Museum of Fine Arts, Boston, Mass., 1976), and *Neat and Tidy: Boxes and Their Contents Used in Early American Households* (Dutton, 1980). *Address:* 305 Warren St., Brookline, Mass. 02146. *Biographical/critical sources: Who's Who in American Art,* Bowker, 1978.

*   *   *

LITTLE, Royal 1896-

PERSONAL: Born March 1, 1896, in Wakefield, Mass.; married Augusta Willoughby Ellis, September 10, 1932 (divorced, 1959); children: Augusta Willoughby, Arthur Dehon. *Education:* Attended Harvard University, 1919. *Residence:* Narragansett, R.I. *Office:* 40 Westminster St., Providence, R.I. 12903.

CAREER: Board chairman of Lonsdale Enterprises, Inc. (financial consultants); partner in Little & Casler (financial consultants); board chairman and director of Amtel, Inc.; board chairman of Indian Head Mills, Inc.; founder and board chairman of Textron Inc. Director of Litwin France, Galileo Electric-Optics Corp., Cleveland Metal Abrasive, Inc., Greenville Tube Co., MD Pneumatics, Inc., Old Fox Chemical Co., Wood Flong Corp., SW Tube Co., Fuqua Industries, Inc., Orba Corp., Span International Ltd., and Span Holdings Ltd.; trustee and vice-president of Music Science. *Awards, honors:* Inducted into the Business Hall of Fame.

WRITINGS: How to Lose One Hundred Million Dollars and Other Valuable Advice (nonfiction), Little, Brown, 1979.

SIDELIGHTS: Little's *How to Lose One Hundred Million Dollars and Other Valuable Advice* is a humorous reminiscence in which the author describes his long career as a financial consultant.

BIOGRAPHICAL/CRITICAL SOURCES: Forbes, March 1, 1966, *Fortune,* January, 1975, July 16, 1979, August 27, 1979; *Human Events,* August 11, 1979; *Wall Street Journal,* September 19, 1979; *Saturday Review,* September 29, 1979; *Changing Times,* December, 1979.*

*   *   *

LO, Ruth Earnshaw 1910-

PERSONAL: Born October 12, 1910, in Philadelphia, Pa.; daughter of Arthur C. (an educator) and Ethel (an educator; maiden name, Kirk) Earnshaw; married John C.F. Lo, August 5, 1937 (deceased); children: Catherine T., Kirk M. *Education:* University of Chicago, Ph.B., 1931; also attended Columbia University, 1935-36. *Residence:* Boulder, Colo. *Agent:* Timothy Seldes, Russell & Volkening, Inc., 551 Fifth Ave., New York, N.Y. 10176.

CAREER: University of Chicago, Chicago, Ill., associate editor of university magazine, 1931-35; Institute of Pacific Relations, New York, N.Y., research assistant, 1935-37; Huachun University, Wuhan, China, instructor in English, 1937-53; Zhongshan University, Guangzhou, China, professor of English, 1953-78; writer, 1978—. *Member:* American Association of University Women, Phi Beta Kappa.

WRITINGS: (With Katherine S. Kinderman) *In the Eye of the Typhoon* (memoir), Harcourt, 1978.

WORK IN PROGRESS: Writing about her experiences in Chinese universities.

SIDELIGHTS: Lo told *CA:* "Having made my home in China from 1937 to 1978, I have witnessed and shared a good deal

of history. My own peculiar place has been that of a Chinese teacher, and a member of a Chinese family, while retaining my American identity. I have never been a missionary, an 'imperialist,' a 'fellow-traveler,' or a professional China-watcher or sinologist. I have just lived in China and watched what happened to most of the people there. I think it worth recording."

*   *   *

LOCHAK, Michele 1936-

PERSONAL: Born June 6, 1936, in Nancy, France; daughter of Daniel (a certified public accountant) and Rose (Ditlea) Papo; married Georges Lochak (a physicist), December 22, 1956; children: Pierre, Catherine, Ivan. *Education:* Sorbonne, University of Paris, M.A., 1958. *Home:* 67 Boulevard de Picpus, 75012 Paris, France. *Office:* Gautier-Languereau, 18 rue Jacob, 75006 Paris, France.

CAREER: Chatenay-Malabry High School, Paris, France, history teacher, 1958-1970; writer, 1970—. *Awards, honors:* Loisirs-jeunes from French Specialized Press for Children's Literature, 1973, for *Les histories d'Ivan.*

WRITINGS:—Juveniles: *Les histoire's d'Ivan* (title means "The Stories of Ivan"), Fleurus, 1973; *Vingt-watts, la petite ampoule* (title means "Twenty Watts, the Little Bulb"), illustrations by Noelle Herrenschmidt, Flammarion, 1975; *Le pain des autres* (title means "The Bread of Each and Everybody"), Flammarion, 1980; (with M. F. Mangin) *Suzette et Nicolas et le cirque des enfants,* Languereau, 1980, published as *Suzette and Nicholas and the Sunijudi Circus,* Philomel, 1981; *Ivan, Mourka et le moineau* (title means "Ivan, Mourka, and the Sparrow"), Flammarion, 1982; *Louis XIII enfant* (title means "Louis XIII as a Child"), Magnard, 1982.

"Si tu vas" series of children's travel guides; published by Languereau: *Si tu vas en Bretagne* (title means "If You Go to Brittany"), 1982; *. . . dans les Alpes* (title means "If You Go to the Alps"), 1982; *. . . en Provence* (title means "If You Go to Provence"), 1982; *. . . en Auvergne* (title means "If You Go to Auvergne"), 1982; *. . . a Paris* (title means "If You Go to Paris"), 1983; *. . . en Alsace* (title means "If You Go to Alsace"), 1983; *. . . au pays basque* (title means "If You Go to Basque Country"), 1983.

WORK IN PROGRESS: Four editions for the "Si tu vas" series, publication by Languereau expected in 1984: *Si tu vas en Corse* (title means "If You Go to Corsica"); *. . . en Belgique* (title means "If You Go to Belgium"); *. . . en Suisse* (title means "If You Go to Switzerland"); *. . . au Quebec* (title means "If You Go to Quebec").

SIDELIGHTS: Lochak told *CA:* "From history to stories for children, it is the same travel of human memory and its sensibilities through space and time. Here is my interest. To grow harmoniously, children need roots in the family and in the country they are from. I begin with France, but, in my collection of travel guides for children, I hope to be able to make them love foreign people and countries."

*   *   *

LOCKE, Alain LeRoy 1886-1954

BRIEF ENTRY: Born September 13, 1886, in Philadelphia, Pa.; died June 9, 1954, in New York, N.Y. American philosopher, educator, and author. Locke was a professor at Harvard University and a former Rhodes scholar who worked to increase the respect and recognition afforded black artists and writers in America. He believed that black nationalism was compatible with the pursuit of the American dream and that the artist held the key to better race relations. In such works as *The Negro in America* (1933) and *The Negro in Art* (1940), he urged black artists and musicians to look to their African heritage for inspiration. He also called upon black writers to search for their subjects and themes in the contemporary black community. Locke edited an anthology, *The New Negro: An Interpretation* (1925), which was hailed as an important stimulus to black achievement and a lasting contribution to the Harlem Renaissance of the 1920's. *Biographical/critical sources: Webster's American Biographies,* Merriam, 1974; *Black American Writers Past and Present: A Biographical and Bibliographical Dictionary,* Scarecrow, 1975.

*   *   *

LODRICK, Deryck O(scar)   1942-

PERSONAL: Born February 25, 1942, in Rajasthan, India; came to the United States in 1965; son of Oscar Clifford (a civil servant) and Cora (Benbow) Lodrick; married Carol Wallisch, June 30, 1979 (divorced, 1980). *Education:* University of St. Andrews, M.A. (with honors), 1965; attended University of Texas, 1968-69; University of Wisconsin—Madison, M.Sc., 1969; University of California, Davis, Ph.D., 1977. *Residence:* San Francisco, Calif.

CAREER: University of Wisconsin Center System, Masinette, lecturer in geography, 1966-67; San Francisco State University, San Francisco, Calif., lecturer in geography, 1969-73 and 1976-77; Humboldt State University, Arcata, Calif., lecturer in geography, 1977-79; University of California, Davis, research associate in geography, 1979-80; American Institute of Indian Studies, Chicago, Ill., senior research fellow, 1980-81.

WRITINGS: Sacred Cows, Sacred Places: Origins and Survivals of Animal Homes in India, University of California Press, 1981. Contributor to anthropology journals.

SIDELIGHTS: Lodrick wrote: "In Rajasthan, India, I have been working on a research project focusing on the ecology of cattle-keeping in villages. For over a decade, a debate has been underway in academic circles, both in India and the West, concerning the nature of the so-called 'sacred cow' of India. Recent interpretations of this phenomenon have attempted to explain attitudes toward cattle in India in terms of techno-environmental factors, arguing that cow-worship, beef-avoidance, anti-slaughter legislation, and so on, reflect ecological pressures rather than the influence of religious ideologies. My research in Hindu and Moslem villages attempts to isolate and identify religious, ecological, or economic factors that influence attitudes and behavior toward cattle in India. I see an understanding of this to be significant in terms of economic development and resource utilization in a country facing tremendous problems of overpopulation, poverty, and pressures on the environment. This work should result in a book or monograph, and represents a logical extension of the research presented in *Sacred Cows, Sacred Places.*

"As a cultural geographer concerned with the relationships between society on the one hand and the environment on the other, I am particularly interested in the way ideologies influence the way peoples view and utilize the world around them. Much of my work relates to ways in which Indian philosophies affect the way society has perceived and made use of the environment in South Asia. I am currently working on an article about the Bishnoi, a Hindu sect that worships trees and animals. The article explains how Bishnoi attitudes have served to preserve the environment at a time of extreme environmental deg-

radation. Such indigenous conservationism may hold lessons for other parts of the Third World that are in the throes of development.

"Development, the panacea of the postcolonial era, has itself led to serious problems in much of the world; while we in the West have been exposed to these problems through the media, it is another thing to 'experience' them firsthand. An understanding of foreign cultures and an awareness of their problems is essential for the student of today, for, perhaps now more than ever, their problems are our problems."

AVOCATIONAL INTERESTS: Travel (South Asia, Southeast Asia, Europe, the Pacific).

*   *   *

LOEB, Harold A(lbert)   1891-1974

PERSONAL: Born October 18, 1891, in New York, N.Y.; died January 20, 1974; buried in Marrakesh, Morocco; son of Albert (a banker) and Rose (Guggenheim) Loeb; married Marjorie Content, April, 1914 (divorced, 1923); married Vera B. Currie, 1933 (died July 14, 1961); married Barbara McKenzie, July 26, 1963; children: (first marriage) Susan Loeb Sandburg; (second marriage) Anah Loeb Pytte. *Education:* Princeton University, B.A., 1913. *Residence:* Weston, Conn.

CAREER: Worked as cement contractor and cattle rancher in Empress, Alberta, Canada, 1913-17, then held various odd jobs in New York City; American Smelting and Lead Co., California, supply purchaser, 1917; Sunwise Turn (bookstore), New York City, proprietor, 1918-20; *Broom: An International Magazine of the Arts,* Paris, France, founder and chief editor, 1921-24; writer, 1924-29; worked as economist and government administrator for Office of Price Administration and War Production Board in Washington, D.C., 1929-54. *Military service:* U.S. Army, 1917.

WRITINGS—Novels: Doodab, Boni & Liveright, 1925; *The Professors Like Vodka,* Boni & Liveright, 1927, reprinted (with afterword by author), Southern Illinois University Press, 1974; *Tumbling Mustard,* Liveright, 1929.

Other: (With Felix Frazer, Walter Polakov, Graham Montgomery, William Smith, and Montgomery Schuyler) *The Chart of Plenty: A Study of America's Product Capacity Based on Findings of the National Survey of Potential Product Capacity,* foreword by Stuart Chase, Viking, 1933; *Life in a Technocracy: What It Might Be Like,* Viking, 1933; *Production For Use,* Basic Books, 1936; *Full Production Without War,* Princeton University Press, 1946; *The Way It Was* (autobiography), Criterion, 1959; (editor) *The Broom Anthology,* Milford House, 1969; (with Dorothea Maier) *Training and Work Experience of Former Apprentices, New York State,* Division of Research and Statistics, Department of Labor, State of New York, 1975. Contributor of articles to *New Republic, Opinion, Southern Review,* and other publications.

WORK IN PROGRESS: The Arabs Come on Friday, a novel, unpublished at time of death.

SIDELIGHTS: Harold Loeb was founder and chief editor of *Broom: An International Magazine of the Arts* from 1921 to 1924. It was one of the first English-language reviews of the arts in Europe, and one of several "little magazines" that expressed the flippancy of the post-World War I "lost generation." It was a showcase for new expressions in literature and art, and the avant-garde experiments found within its pages did much to expand artistic form and scope in following decades. Contributors to these issues included such luminaries as Hart Crane, Gertrude Stein, Sherwood Anderson, John Dos Passos, William Carlos Williams, and E. E. Cummings.

Loeb initially familiarized himself with writers and writings in 1918, when he abandoned his business enterprises and bought a partnership in The Sunwise Turn, a bookshop in Greenwich Village. There he became acquainted with a number of writers and artists, including Georgia O'Keefe, Alfred Kreymborg, and F. Scott Fitzgerald. The associations that Loeb developed during this time assisted him when he went to Europe in 1921 to establish *Broom.*

It was during Loeb's expatriation, when he was living among his contributors, that he met Ernest Hemingway in 1923. The two shared many interests, did much together, and it appeared to Loeb that he and Hemingway had formed a firm friendship. Yet the author painted a ruthless picture of Loeb in *The Sun Also Rises,* published in 1926. Loeb served as the prototype for the character Robert Cohn, a rich Jewish toady and status seeker.

In 1924 Loeb essentially relinquished his editorship to devote his next five years in Paris to writing fiction. His first novel, *Doodab,* is the semi-autobiographical story of a defeated man who escapes a reality of business and marriage failures by living in an imaginary world in which he is powerful and successful. Experimental in form, the novel contains many surreal dream episodes. A reviewer for the *Boston Transcript* observed that while the mechanics of the novel show the author's inexperience, the story "carries an emotional thrill, a delicate satire, and abundance of pointed episodes and expressions furnishing food for thought, all reminding us of melodrama in the highest sense of the word." Malcolm Cowley reiterated these observations in his review for the *New York Tribune.* He noted that while much of the writing was uninspired, "there are realistic passages written with a gusto, an excess of animal spirits, which make them something far better than realism. Writing imaginatively . . . requires a different sort of talent. So does the creation of living characters. Both elements are present in this first novel."

Loeb's second novel, *The Professors Like Vodka,* relates the adventures of two American university professors on a post-World War I vacation in Paris. The two men fall in love with a pair of Russian refugees, and the emotional demands of these relationships restir in them feelings that have all but atrophied in the intellectual climate of their university lives. The novel received many favorable reviews, including these comments by H. H. Brown in the *Saturday Review of Literature:* "Mr. Loeb . . . can register both the comic and the tragic effect. His style, like his characters, like his theme, can be gay, sombre, poetic, or dryly realistic at will. If he has written a melodrama, it is a melodrama of the mind; and like the Russians, he has the gift of making melodrama convincing." *The Professors Like Vodka* was reprinted in 1974 in a Lost American Fiction series, with an afterword by Loeb that recalls autobiographical details of both that period and his life following.

In *Tumbling Mustard,* Loeb's third novel, the author presents a psychological study of a man trapped in an unhappy marriage to a sullen, mentally unbalanced woman. Although the book was largely ignored by critics, one reviewer for the *New York Times* remarked: "Here are all the elements of strong drama: love, hate, fear, and, above all, suspense. . . . Attention is held until the last, and is at the last, almost breathless." Loeb also wrote an unpublished fourth novel, *The Arabs Come on Friday,* about an American expatriate who is inspired by the Zionist movement, travels to the Middle East, and eventually lives on a kibbutz, where his lover is killed by an Arab. The novel followed Loeb's own trip to Palestine, where he developed an intense concern for Zionist issues.

After 1929 Loeb wrote no more fiction, but published four books on economics while he worked as an economist and government administrator for the next twenty-five years. He did publish an autobiography in 1959, *The Way It Was,* which focused particularly on his expatriate years. W. T. Scott stated in the *New York Herald Tribune Book Review:* "It is an important contribution to what many of us of a younger and more staid generation find the endlessly fascinating chronicles of post-World War I expatriatism. From New York to Paris to Rome to London, it touches on just about all facets of that era. . . . On his own he has recaptured—with a lot of humble, unmitigated frankness about himself—the heady wine of those days."

BIOGRAPHICAL/CRITICAL SOURCES—Books: Alfred Kreymborg, *Troubadour,* Liveright, 1925; Harold Loeb, *The Way It Was* (autobiography), Criterion, 1959; Bertram D. Sarason, *Hemingway and the Sun Set,* Bruccoli Clark/NCR Microcard Editions, 1972; *Dictionary of Literary Biography,* Volume 4: *American Writers in Paris, 1920-1939,* Gale, 1980.

Periodicals: *New York Times,* August 30, 1925, June 12, 1927, June 2, 1929, May 24, 1959; *Boston Transcript,* September 23, 1925, July 3, 1929; *New York Tribune,* November 22, 1925; *Literary Review,* April 23, 1927; *New York Herald Tribune Books,* May 15, 1927, April 21, 1929; *Saturday Review of Literature,* May 21, 1927; *New York Evening Post,* June 15, 1929; *Saturday Review,* May 16, 1959; *New York Herald Tribune Book Review,* May 17, 1959; *Nation,* June 6, 1959; *Time,* June 22, 1959; *San Francisco Chronicle,* July 5, 1959.

OBITUARIES: *New York Times,* January 23, 1974, January 25, 1974; *Washington Post,* January 26, 1974; *Newsweek,* February 4, 1974; *Publishers Weekly,* February 18, 1974.*

—*Sketch by Nancy Pear*

*   *   *

LONGSWORTH, Polly   1933-

PERSONAL: Born October 21, 1933, in Buffalo, N.Y.; daughter of Charles C. (an architect and engineer) and Katharine (Van Keuren) Ormsby; married Charles R. Longsworth (a foundation president), June 30, 1956; children: Amy, Elizabeth, Laura, Anne. *Education:* Smith College, B.A., 1955. *Home:* Coke-Garrett House, Williamsburg, Va. 23185.

CAREER: Thomas Y. Crowell Co. (publisher), Scranton, Pa., assistant in juvenile department, 1955-56; J. B. Lippincott Co. (publisher), Philadelphia, Pa., coordinator of children's books, 1956-58; Virginia Research Center for Archaeology, editor, 1978—. *Awards, honors: Emily Dickinson: Her Letter to the World* was a *New York Herald Tribune* Spring Book Festival honor book, 1965.

WRITINGS: *Exploring Caves* (juvenile), Crowell, 1958; *Emily Dickinson: Her Letter to the World* (juvenile), Crowell, 1965; *I, Charlotte Forten, Black and Free* (juvenile), Crowell, 1970.

WORK IN PROGRESS: An edition of letters of Austin Dickinson and Mabel Loomis Todd, for adults, publication expected by Farrar, Straus in 1982.

SIDELIGHTS: Longsworth told *CA:* "While growing up I didn't realize how much of the time I lived in fantasy. It is only looking back, and comparing my experiences with others, that I realize that when I couldn't do something I wanted to do, I would go inside my head and do it.

"I grew up in Waterford, New York, an old manufacturing town on the Hudson River north of Albany. With my four brothers I played along the river bank and near the locks of the Champlain Canal. We lived in my grandmother's house, where several generations of family had lived, and their pictures on the wall, their clothes and possessions in the attic, their books on the shelves, and their old diaries and letters in desk drawers inspired me with a dramatic sense of the past. I always wanted to write, and did so through school and college, and was editor of the newspaper my last year at Smith.

"After marrying, my husband and I lived for sixteen years in Amherst, Massachusetts, where I fell in love with Emily Dickinson and the nineteenth century. I have explored that town's nineteenth century thoroughly by way of town records, newspapers, letters, and objects at the historical society.

"Now we live in a restored eighteenth-century Virginia town, and I've become interested in the seventeenth century as well by getting involved in archaeology. So many traces of the past are still in the ground.

"A writer interested in biography, as I am, spends a lot of time thinking about the behavior of the people he or she is trying to recreate, attempting to explain from evidence in letters, diaries, and other documents how the living human being who wrote them perceived life. Archaeology and the reading of books on psychology (the two are closely related) have helped me enormously in my writing and continue to fascinate me. Since I've discovered that almost no experience one has in life is irrelevant to one's creative life (although sometimes the relationship seems obscure), the following up of whatever interests one intensely sooner or later proves useful to one's work."

*   *   *

LORD, Gabrielle 1946-

PERSONAL: Born February 26, 1946, in Sydney, Australia; daughter of John Ferdinand (a physician) and Gwen (Craig) Butler; children: Madeleine. *Education:* University of New England, B.A. (with honors), 1975. *Politics:* "Moderately left-wing." *Religion:* None. *Home:* 10B Reading St., Glenbrook, New South Wales 2773, Australia. *Agent:* Tim Curnow, Curtis Brown Ltd., 86 William St., Paddington, New South Wales, Australia.

CAREER: Australian Public Service, Penrith, New South Wales, Australia, employment officer, 1975—. *Member:* Australian Society of Authors. *Awards, honors:* New writer's fellowship from Australia Council for the Arts, 1978.

WRITINGS: Fortress (novel), Aurora Press, 1980, St. Martin's, 1981; *Tooth and Claw* (novel), Bodley Head, 1982.

WORK IN PROGRESS: Surviving the Ice Age; a thriller, tentatively titled *Where Are You?*, completion expected in 1982.

SIDELIGHTS: Gabrielle Lord wrote: "Like Byron, I think writing is mostly habit. I don't know what I would do with myself if I didn't write.

"I'm concerned about the ugly old men who run the world but am not sure what can be done about them. It seems to me that political action of some sort *must* be undertaken by the serious, moral adult if this world is to become less insane and unbalanced. Now that there is no real conviction concerning another 'life' in the religious sense, it is imperative that the one we do have be taken seriously. Otherwise, life *is* pointless, not just for the millions of people who are forced to live like beasts but for the comfortable, well-educated, and privileged people

like myself. I would want to see a Mother Teresa of the living, not the dying."

*   *   *

LORD BUTLER OF SAFFRON WALDEN
See BUTLER, Richard Austen

*   *   *

LORD STRANGE
See DRUMMOND, John

*   *   *

LORD WINDLESHAM
See HENNESSEY, David James George

*   *   *

LORIS
See HOFMANNSTHAL, Hugo von

*   *   *

LOUIS, Arthur M(urray) 1938-

PERSONAL: Born January 21, 1938, in Toledo, Ohio; son of Elmer (a professional fundraiser) and Ida Sylvia (Abrams) Louis; married Frances Ellen Deutsch, June 12, 1960 (divorced September 4, 1970); children: Matthew Gordon, Richard Henry. *Education:* Columbia University, A.B., 1959, M.S., 1960. *Home:* 333 East 49th St., New York, N.Y. 10017. *Agent:* Meredith Bernstein, 33 Riverside Dr., New York, N.Y. 10023. *Office:* Time, Inc., 1271 Avenue of the Americas, New York, N.Y. 10020.

CAREER: Philadelphia Inquirer, Philadelphia, Pa., rewriter, 1960-64; McGraw-Hill Inc., New York City, associate editor, 1964-66; Time, Inc., New York City, associate editor, 1966-81; member of board of editors of *Fortune,* 1981—. *Member:* Manhattan Chess Club (member of board of directors, 1978—). *Awards, honors:* Financial news award from Sigma Delta Chi, 1978, for "Lessons From the Firestone Fraes."

WRITINGS: The Tycoons (nonfiction), Simon & Schuster, 1981. Contributor to magazines, including *Nation, Saturday Review, New York, Harper's,* and *Psychology Today.*

WORK IN PROGRESS: A book about the Bloomingdale family, publication by Putnam expected in 1984; a mystery story.

SIDELIGHTS: Louis commented: "I became a writer because, as a teenager, I considered writing to be the most glamorous profession. I still think so, though it's not as glamorous as I had hoped. Writing is hard, and anyone who doesn't think so doesn't know how to write. Frankly, I would rather read what I've written than write it."

*   *   *

LOWENFISH, Lee (Elihu) 1942-

PERSONAL: Born June 27, 1942, in New York, N.Y.; son of Felix Philip (a physician) and Evelyn (a singer; maiden name, Schiff) Lowenfish; married Greta Minsky (a stage manager), April 30, 1979. *Education:* Columbia University, B.A., 1963; University of Wisconsin—Madison, M.A., 1965, Ph.D., 1968. *Politics:* "Left-wing conservative." *Religion:* Jewish. *Home:* 308 West 104th St., New York, N.Y. 10025.

CAREER: Goucher College, Towson, Md., assistant professor of history and American studies, 1968-69; Rutgers University,

New Brunswick, N.J., assistant professor of history and American studies, 1969-71; Maryland Institute and College of Art and Harford Community College, Bel Air, Md., part-time instructor of history, 1971-73; University of Maryland—Baltimore County, assistant professor of history and American studies, 1973-75; University of Maryland—College Park, instructor, 1975-76; John Jay College of Criminal Justice, New York City, adjunct lecturer, 1977; free-lance writer, 1976—. *Member:* North American Society for Sport History, Society for American Baseball Research, Authors Guild, Authors League of America, Organization of American Historians, American Studies Association. *Awards, honors:* Ford Foundation Fellow in urban studies, 1964-65.

WRITINGS: (With Tony Lupien) *The Imperfect Diamond: The Story of Baseball's Reserve System and the Men Who Fought to Change It,* Stein & Day, 1980. Contributor to history journals and newspapers, including *Minnesota Review, Columbia Library Columns, Arena Review, Journal of the West, Journal of Sport History,* and *New York Times.*

WORK IN PROGRESS: A study of the changing relationships between managers, owners, players, and performers in contemporary sports and the entertainment arts, publication expected in 1983 or 1984.

SIDELIGHTS: Lowenfish wrote: "I am interested in studying the world of sport in the general context of American business and culture. I want to portray the changing patterns of growth and maturation of the American athlete and entertainer. I want to probe the process of glorification of the athlete which paradoxically often infantilizes him or at least encourages him to become a perpetual adolescent.

"I am also interested in the myths by which societies live. The 'game is never over until the last man is out' and the 'superstar-athlete-as-savior' I see as healthy myths. The craving to be number one, the foolish reiteration of the cliche 'nice guys finish last,' and the branding of competitors and people as 'losers,' on the other hand, I feel are destructive ideas in our society, encouraged by the false analogy between sport competition and social life. I want to capture the feel and sweat of the sporting life in my writing and to bring to the reader's attention the fascinating and often troubling aspects of life behind-the-scenes in the business and industry of sports."

* * *

LUFT, David Sheers 1944-

PERSONAL: Born May 6, 1944, in Youngstown, Ohio; son of John Mayhugh (an architect) and Martha (a teacher; maiden name, Sheers) Luft; married Sarah McCarley (a television producer), August 26, 1967; children: Catherine Morrow. *Education:* Wesleyan University, Middletown, Conn., B.A., 1966; Harvard University, M.A., 1967, Ph.D., 1972. *Office:* Department of History, University of California, San Diego, B-007, La Jolla, Calif. 92093.

CAREER: University of California, San Diego, La Jolla, assistant professor, 1972-79, associate professor of modern European history, 1979—.

WRITINGS: Robert Musil and the Crisis of European Culture, 1880-1942, University of California Press, 1980.

WORK IN PROGRESS: Research on modern intellectual history, "particularly the distinctive character of Austrian intellectual traditions and contributions to contemporary thought."

BIOGRAPHICAL/CRITICAL SOURCES: Times Literary Supplement, October 9, 1981.

LUHR, William 1946-

PERSONAL: Born March 31, 1946, in Brooklyn, N.Y.; son of Walter C. (a banker) and Eillien (Kealy) Luhr; married Judith Challop (a neuropsychologist), August 16, 1981. *Education:* Fordham University, B.A., 1967; graduate study at Queens College of the City University of New York, 1968-69; New York University, M.A., 1969, Ph.D., 1978. *Home:* 180 West Poplar St., Floral Park, N.Y. 11001. *Office:* Department of English, St. Peter's College, Kennedy Blvd., Jersey City, N.J. 07306.

CAREER: Teacher of English, film, and remedial reading at public junior high school in Flushing, N.Y., 1968-76, chairperson of film department, 1970-76, acting assistant principal, 1971; St. Peter's College, Jersey City, N.J., associate professor of English, 1976—. Adjunct lecturer at Queens College of the City University of New York, 1970-73, guest lecturer, 1976; guest lecturer at Mercy College, White Plains, N.Y., 1976; lecturer at Hudson County Community College, 1977. Judge at Athens International Film Festival and American Film Festival, 1976-81; consultant to Films, Inc. *Member:* Modern Language Association of America, American Film Institute, College English Association, Media Educators Association, University Film Association, Society for Cinema Studies.

WRITINGS: (With Peter Lehman) *Authorship and Narrative in the Cinema: Issues in Contemporary Aesthetics and Criticism,* Putnam, 1977; (with Lehman) *Blake Edwards,* Ohio University Press, 1981; (contributor) Michael Klein and Gillian Parker, editors, *The English Novel in Film,* Ungar, 1981; *Raymond Chandler and Film,* Ungar, 1982. Member of editorial advisory board of film series, Ohio University Press, 1979—. Contributor of about fifteen articles and reviews to magazines, including *Wide Angle.*

WORK IN PROGRESS: Victorian Novels on Film; a second volume on *Blake Edwards,* with Peter Lehman.

* * *

LUPUL, Manoly Robert 1927-

BRIEF ENTRY: Born August 14, 1927, in Willingdon, Alberta, Canada. Canadian educator and author. Lupul began teaching in 1957. He has been a professor of history and philosophy of education at University of Alberta since 1970. Lupul's books include *Minorities, Schools, and Politics: Essays* (University of Toronto Press, 1969), *Ukrainian Canadians, Multiculturalism, and Separation: An Assessment* (University of Alberta Press, 1978), and *The Roman Catholic Church and the North-West School Question* (University of Toronto Press, 1974). *Address:* Department of Educational Foundations, University of Alberta, Edmonton, Alberta, Canada T6G 2G2.

* * *

LYDECKER, Beatrice 1938-

PERSONAL: Born July 12, 1938, in Long Island, N.Y.; daughter of John (a carpenter) and Cornelia Lydecker. *Education:* Columbia Bible College, Columbia, S.C., B.B.E., 1960; graduate study at California State Polytechnic University. *Home:* 3007 Durfee Ave., El Monte, Calif. 91732.

CAREER: Worked as substitute teacher and cosmetics salesperson; animal psychologist, 1969—; writer and lecturer, 1977—. Guest on television programs in the United States, Canada, and England, including "That's Incredible," "The Tonight Show," and "Good Morning, America."

WRITINGS: What the Animals Tell Me, Harper, 1977; *Stories the Animals Tell Me,* Harper, 1979.

WORK IN PROGRESS: A children's record album about animals; a book on holistic animal care.

SIDELIGHTS: Beatrice Lydecker calls herself a specialist in non-verbal communication and an animal psychologist. Her diagnostic skill has brought her national recognition among veterinarians, animal trainers, the media, and the pet owners who have come to her for consultations in her private practice. Her talent for non-verbal communication extends to work with autistic children and individuals suffering from strokes and other diseases.

She has worked with the head animal trainer at Marineworld and Africa U.S.A., and with the horse trainer for Kodax and Turlingua.

Lydecker lectures on "Visualization: A New Dimension in Communication," and conducts a course for branches of the University of California.

She also works as a soprano vocalist and has studied saxophone and clarinet. She has given semi-classical and sacred music concerts for religious organizations.

*   *   *

LYNCH, Marietta 1947-

PERSONAL: Born December 21, 1947. *Education:* Vassar College, A.B. (cum laude), 1969; Wheelock College, M.Ed., 1973. *Home:* 240 Atlantic Rd., Gloucester, Mass. 01930.

CAREER: Belmont Hill School, Belmont, Mass., teacher, 1966-69; David Ellis School, Roxbury, Mass., teacher, 1969-72; North Shore Nursery School, Beverly, Mass., teacher, 1973-76, director, 1976—. North Shore Education Center, Beverly, education director, 1977. Trustee of North Shore Middle School, Cape Ann Symphony Orchestra, and Ravenswood Park.

WRITINGS: (With Patricia Perry) *Mommy and Daddy Are Divorced* (juvenile), Dial, 1978.

*   *   *

LYON, Bryce Dale 1920-

BRIEF ENTRY: Born April 22, 1920, in Bellevue, Ohio. American historian, educator, and author. Lyon has been Keeney Professor of History at Brown University since 1965. He was a Guggenheim fellow in 1954 and 1972. Lyon's writings on medieval history include *A Constitutional and Legal History of Medieval England* (Harper, 1960), *The Origins of the Middle Ages,* Norton, 1972, and *Studies of West European Medieval Institutions* (Variorum, 1978). He also wrote *Henri Pirenne: A Biographical and Intellectual Study* (E. Story-Scientia, 1974) and edited *The Journal de Guerre of Henri Pirenne* (North-Holland Publishing, 1976). *Address:* 41 Laurel Ave., Providence, R.I. 02906; and Department of History, Brown University, Providence, R.I. 02912.

*   *   *

LYON, Eugene 1929-

PERSONAL: Born April 9, 1929, in Miami, Fla.; son of Homer B. (an airline executive) and Katharine (Garner) Lyon; married Dorothy Mathews (a librarian), June 15, 1952; children: Margaret Sue Lyon Stewart, Kenneth Eugene, Katharine Vinelle, Mary Beth. *Education:* University of Florida, B.A. (with honors), 1951, Ph.D., 1973; University of Denver, M.S.,

1953. *Religion:* Methodist. *Home and office:* 1597 Pelican Lane, P.O. Box 3621, Beach Station, Vero Beach, Fla. 32960. *Agent:* Maximilian Becker, 115 East 82nd St., New York, N.Y. 10028.

CAREER: City of Vero Beach, Fla., city manager, 1958-62; Congo Polytechnique Institute, Leopoldville, Congo (now Kinshasa, Zaire), business manager, 1961-62; Indian River Community College, Fort Pierce, Fla., 1964-72, began as instructor, became associate professor of history; consulting historian and writer in Vero Beach, 1972—. Member of board of directors of Treasure Salvors, Inc.; member of steering committee of Maritime Heritage Trust. *Military service:* U.S. Naval Reserve, active duty as quartermaster on destroyer-mine sweeper, "U.S.S. Hobson," 1951-52. *Member:* Florida Historical Society (member of board of directors), Historical Association of South Florida, St. Augustine Historical Society. *Awards, honors:* Arthur Thompson Award, 1972, for article "Captives of Florida," and Rembert Patrick Award, 1977, for *The Enterprise of Florida,* both from Florida Historical Society.

WRITINGS: The Enterprise of Florida, University Presses of Florida, 1976; *The Search for the Atocha,* Harper, 1977. Contributor to *National Geographic.*

SIDELIGHTS: In 1980, using information uncovered by Lyon, Treasure Salvors was able to locate the sunken Spanish galleon *Santa Margarita.* Value of the gold recovered from the wrecked ship is expected to approach $20 million.

Lyon wrote: "My interest in marine archaeology and in the location and identification of colonial ships arose accidentally out of archival research performed for broader academic projects. These include essentially work on the Spanish presence in North America, the cultural impact of Hispanic folkways on American Indians, and specific work with archaeologists on the material culture arising from Hispanic sources. In turn, this has led to travel and seven years' work in Spanish archives, and has increased my language skills in both modern and archaic Spanish."

BIOGRAPHICAL/CRITICAL SOURCES: National Geographic, February, 1982.

*   *   *

LYONS, Louis M. 1897-1982

OBITUARY NOTICE: Born September 1, 1897, in Dorchester, Mass.; died of malignant lymphoma, April 11, 1982, in Cambridge, Mass. Administrator, radio and television commentator, and journalist. While still an undergraduate student at Harvard University in 1919, Lyon began his career as a reporter for the *Boston Globe,* eventually becoming an editorial writer. In 1938 he was among the first nine journalists selected to spend a year at Harvard studying in the field of their choice under the newly established Nieman Foundation fellowship program for journalists. After his year of study, Lyons remained with the foundation as an assistant curator, succeeding poet Archibald MacLeish as curator in 1946. Upon Lyons's retirement in 1964, Harvard University awarded him an honorary degree, describing him as the "conscience of his profession." Also a commentator on WGBH public television and radio stations, Lyons received the George Foster Peabody Award for his news broadcasts. Other honors he received include the Richard Lauterback Civil Liberties Award, the Freedoms Foundation Medal, the Overseas Press Club Citation, and the Alfred I. duPont Award. Obituaries and other sources: *New York Times,* April 13, 1982; *Washington Post,* April 13, 1982; *Newsweek,* April 26, 1982; *Time,* April 26, 1982.

M

MAAR, Leonard (Frank, Jr.) 1927-

PERSONAL: Born April 27, 1927, in Poughkeepsie, N.Y.; son of Leonard F. (a writer) and Lillian (an administrative assistant; maiden name, Hibbert) Maar; married Stella Gudnidottir, October 18, 1947 (divorced, 1969); married Nancy Toensmeier (a writer), February 18, 1972; children: Peter, Liza Maar Esposito, Michael, Heidi, Virginia. *Education:* Attended Columbia University, 1947-49, and 1950-51. *Politics:* Independent. *Religion:* Unitarian Universalist. *Home and office:* 1924 Long Ridge Rd., Stamford, Conn. 06903. *Agent:* Ned Brown Associates, 407 North Maple Dr., Box 5020, Beverly Hills, Calif. 90210.

CAREER: Free-lance journalist and photographer in New York, N.Y., 1950-60; Pitney-Bowes, Inc., Stamford, Conn., public relations manager, 1960-69; communications consultant to corporations, including Allied Corp., Monsanto, and St. Regis, 1970-78; Long Ridge Communications, Stamford, president, 1978—. Chairman of education and public relations for Citizens Energy Committee, 1980—. Member of board of Industrial Communications Council and International Association of Industrial Communicators; founding officer of Public Relations Group of Fairfield County. *Military service:* U.S. Naval Reserve, 1944-46; served on submarines. *Member:* New York Association of Industrial Communicators (president).

WRITINGS—All with Roy Doty, except as noted; juveniles; published by Doubleday: *Where Are You Going With That Oil?,* 1976; *Where Are You Going With That Tree?,* 1976; *Where Are You Going With That Coal?,* 1977; *Where Are You Going With That Energy?,* 1977; *How Much Does America Cost?,* 1979; (with wife, Nancy Maar) *Out-of-Sight Games* (illustrated by John Lane), 1980.

WORK IN PROGRESS: A novel.

SIDELIGHTS: Maar told *CA:* "The study of human communication dominates my work. My company creates communication programs for industry, associations, and governmental groups. Long Ridge Communications is also involved in graphic design in order to produce total-concept communication materials. My current work includes creating corporate identification designs for two new firms and adapting our programs to an audiovisual format."

MacCORMACK, Sabine G(abriele) 1941-
(Sabine Oswalt)

PERSONAL: Born February 24, 1941, in Frankfurt on the Main, Germany (now West Germany); came to the United States in 1979; daughter of Alfred (an architect) and Gabriele (Buhl) Oswalt; married Geoffrey MacCormack (a university professor), June 22, 1965; children: Catherine. *Education:* Attended University of Frankfurt, 1960-61; Lady Margaret Hall, Oxford, B.A. (with second class honors), 1964, D.Phil., 1974; University of Liverpool, diploma in archives, 1965. *Home:* 2102 Townes Lane, Austin, Tex. 78703. *Office:* Department of History, University of Texas, Austin, Tex. 78712.

CAREER: William Collins Sons & Co. Ltd. (publisher), Glasgow, Scotland, editor, 1968-69; free lance in publishing and researcher, 1969-71; Oxford University, Oxford, England, tutor of late antique and early medieval history, 1971-75; Phaidon Press Ltd., Oxford, librarian and archivist, 1975-76; independent researcher, 1976-79; University of Texas, Austin, assistant professor of history, 1979—. Visiting fellow at Dumbarton Oaks, 1977-78; broadcaster in the United States and Spain. Member of American Academy in Rome. *Member:* American Academy of Religion, Byzantine Studies Association. *Awards, honors:* Maude Royden traveling scholarship from Lady Margaret Hall, Oxford, for Italy, 1962; Thomas Greene scholarship from Craven Committee at Oxford University, 1969 (for British School, Rome, Italy), 1970—; grant from Anglo-Spanish Society, for Spain, 1977; Canada Blanch Senior Award from University of London, for Spain, 1978-79; grant from American Philosophical Society, 1981.

WRITINGS: (Under name Sabine Oswalt) *Concise Encyclopedia of Greek and Roman Mythology,* Collins, 1969; (translator) W. H. Schuchhardt, *Greek Art,* Weidenfeld & Nicolson, 1971; (translator and author of updated notes) Johannes Geffcken *The Last Days of Greco-Roman Paganism,* North-Holland Publishing, 1978; (editor of abridgement and pictures, and author of notes) J. G. Fraser, *The Illustrated Golden Bough,* Macmillan, 1978; (translator) Jakob Leuschner, *Germany in the Later Middle Ages,* North-Holland Publishing, 1980; *Art and Ceremony in Late Antiquity,* University of California Press, 1981. Contributor to scholarly journals.

WORK IN PROGRESS: Between the Two Worlds: The Intellectual Horizons of a Seventeenth-Century Historian of the Viceroyalty of Peru, publication expected in 1985; a book on the interplay between rational thought and the miraculous in antiquity and late antiquity, publication expected in 1987.

SIDELIGHTS: MacCormack wrote: "The mainspring of my writing is an interest in change and continuity in the Western cultural and religious tradition, beginning in the ancient world, and the cultural and religious conflicts which tend to arise when that tradition encounters other cultures (such as the conflicts in seventeenth-century Peru).

"My principal nonacademic interests are painting in watercolors and sketching in pen and ink." MacCormack's work was exhibited in Oxford, England.

*   *   *

MacDERMOTT, Mercia   1927-

PERSONAL: Born April 7, 1927, in Plymouth, England; daughter of Geoffrey Palmer (a naval surgeon) and Olive (a teacher; maiden name, Orme) Adshead; divorced; children: Alexandra. *Education:* St. Anne's College, Oxford, B.A., 1948, and M.A.; London School of Slavonic and East European Studies, London, diploma in Bulgarian regional studies, 1950; Sofia University, D.Historical Sciences, 1979. *Residence:* Sofia, Bulgaria. *Office:* Department of History, Sofia University "Kliment Ohridsky," Sofia, Bulgaria 1000.

CAREER: Society for Cultural Relations With U.S.S.R., London, England, information officer, 1956-63; English Language School, Sofia, Bulgaria, teacher, 1963-64; private teacher of English at various embassies in London, 1964-73; English Language School, teacher, 1973-79; Sofia University, Sofia, Bulgaria, lecturer in history, 1979—. *Member:* British-Bulgarian Friendship Society (chairman, 1958-73). *Awards, honors:* Order of Cyril and Methodius (first class) from Praesidium and State Council of the People's Republic of Bulgaria, 1963, for *The History of Bulgaria*, and 1970, for *The Apostle of Freedom;* Order of the Rose (golden) from State Council of People's Republic of Bulgaria, 1977; Paisi Hilendarsky Prize from Sofia University and Bulgaria Academy of Sciences, 1980, for *Freedom or Death.*

WRITINGS: The History of Bulgaria, 1393-1885, Allen & Unwin, 1962; *The Apostle of Freedom,* Allen & Unwin, 1968; *Freedom or Death,* Journeyman Press, 1978.

WORK IN PROGRESS: A biography of Bulgarian revolutionary Yane Sandansky (1872-1915).

SIDELIGHTS: Mercia MacDermott wrote: "My interest in Bulgaria dates from 1947, when I went to Yugoslavia with a youth brigade to participate in the construction of the Samac-Sarajevo railway line. There, I met members of a Bulgarian youth brigade similarly employed, who so impressed me with their energy and enthusiasm that, in the following year, I went to Bulgaria and helped to build the Georgi Dimitrov Dam.

"My sympathies lie with revolutionary movements throughout the world, and one of the reasons I chose to write about the history of the Bulgarian National Liberation Movement is that there is much, both in its ideology and experience, that could be valuable and instructive for present-day fighters for freedom and social justice.

"My books usually take the form of biographies of Bulgarian national heroes who lived and worked in the nineteenth and early twentieth centuries, such as Vasil Levsky, Gotse Delchev, and, currently, Yane Sandansky. I endeavor to observe strict academic standards regarding accuracy and source material, even to the point of visiting the scenes of events in order to observe the flora and fauna. At the same time, I try to employ

a style which will make my books accessible and interesting to the lay reader with little or no previous knowledge of Bulgarian history.

"Because of the amount of local research involved in my books, I have for some years sought appointments which will permit me to live in Bulgaria and devote my spare time to the collection of material and writing. I am a very slow writer and usually take at least five years to complete a book."

*   *   *

MACDONALD, David W(hyte)   1951-

PERSONAL: Born September 30, 1951, in Oxford, England; son of William Alexandre Fraser (a doctor) and Williamina (Whyte) Macdonald; married Jennifer Mary Wells (a teacher), August 2, 1975. *Education:* Wadham College, Oxford, B.A. (with honors), 1972, M.A., 1975, D.Phil., 1977. *Residence:* The Old Bakery, Longworth, Oxfordshire OX1 5EP, England. *Office:* Department of Zoology, Oxford University, South Parks Rd., Oxford OX1 3PS, England.

CAREER: Oxford University, Oxford, England, biological science research fellow of Balliol College, 1976-79, Ernest Cook research fellow in animal behavior, 1980—. Broadcaster, British Broadcasting Corp. (BBC), 1976—; director, Wildlife Consultants Ltd., 1977—; advisor on fox behavior and rabies, World Health Organization, 1980—. *Member:* International Union for the Conservation of Nature, British Ecological Society, Royal Geographical Society (fellow), British Ornithologists Union, Mammal Society (council member), Fauna and Flora Preservation Society (council member), Association for the Study of Animal Behaviour. *Awards, honors:* Winston Churchill Memorial fellowship, 1976; Thomas Henry Huxley Award from Zoological Society of London, 1978, for contributions to zoology.

WRITINGS: Vulpina: The Story of a Fox (juvenile), Collins, 1977; (with C. J. Amlaner) *A Handbook on Biotelemetry and Radio Tracking,* Pergamon, 1980; *Rabies and Wildlife: A Biologist's Perspective,* Oxford University Press for Earth Resources Research, 1980; *The Red Fox,* Oxford University Press, 1982; *Olfactory Communication in Mammals,* Oxford University Press, 1982; *A Naturalist in Borneo,* Dent, 1982; *An Encyclopedia of Mammals of the World,* Equinox, 1983. Author of three dozen television documentaries, including "The Night of the Fox" and "The Curious Cat," all aired on BBC-TV; contributor of more than thirty articles to professional journals, including *New Scientist, Nature,* and *Journal of Zoological Society of London.*

SIDELIGHTS: David Macdonald told *CA:* "Since childhood, I have had a fascination with words and a desire to write things down. As an adult, I have been preoccupied with the belief that the intriguing ideas of biology and the problems of conservation could and should be written down in an accurate and yet good humored form that captures the layman's imagination. My children's book carries out this notion since it is the story of research into foxes, explained in simple but accurate terms." Macdonald has traveled widely in his capacity as a naturalist to such areas as Southeast Asia, India, Europe, North and South America, and China.

*   *   *

MacDONALD, George   1824-1905

BRIEF ENTRY: Born December 10, 1824, in Huntly, Scotland; died September 18, 1905, in Ashstead, England. Scottish minister and author. MacDonald's novels, including *Phantastes:*

A Faerie Romance (1858) and *Lilith* (1895) are moving testaments to country life in Scotland and to the dignity of rural work. Though he served in the Congregational ministry for only a brief time, his poems reveal the power and depth of his religious convictions. His poems, often written in dialect, were collected in *Poetical Works* (1893). His fairy tales and allegories, *At the Back of the North Wind* (1870), *The Princess and the Goblin* (1871), and *The Princess and Curdie* (1882), are still popular today, and are considered by some critics to be MacDonald's most worthwhile achievements. *Biographical/critical sources:* R. L. Wolff, *The Golden Key: A Study of the Fiction of George MacDonald,* Yale University Press, 1961; *Cassell's Encyclopaedia of World Literature,* revised edition, Morrow, 1973.

*   *   *

MacDOUGALL, (George) Donald (Alastair)   1912-

PERSONAL: Born October 26, 1912, in Glasgow, Scotland; son of Daniel Douglas (a china merchant) and Beatrice Amy (Miller) MacDougall; married Bridget Christabel Bartrum, July 14, 1937 (divorced, 1977); married Laura Margaret Linfoot Hall (an economist), 1977; children: John Douglas, Mary Jean. *Education:* Balliol College, Oxford, M.A., 1936. *Home:* 86a Denbigh St., London S.W.1, England. *Office:* Confederation of British Industry, Centre Point, 103 New Oxford St., London W.C.1, England.

CAREER: University of Leeds, Leeds, England, assistant lecturer in economics, 1936-39; Oxford University, Oxford, England, official fellow of Wadham College, 1946-48, faculty fellow of Nuffield College, 1947-50, professorial fellow, 1951-52, official fellow, 1952-64, first bursar, 1958-64; Department of Economic Affairs, London, England, director-general, 1964-68; Government Economic Service, London, head of service and chief economic adviser to Treasury, 1969-73; Confederation of British Industry, London, chief economic adviser, 1973—. Economic director of Organization for European Economic Cooperation, 1948-49, and National Economic Development Council, 1962-64; member of European Economic Commission Study Group on Economic and Monetary Union, 1974-75, chairman of Study Group on the Role of Public Finance, 1975-77. *Wartime service:* Served in First Lord of the Admiralty's (Sir Winston Churchill's) Statistical Branch, England, 1939-40, and Prime Minister's Statistical Branch, England, 1940-45.

MEMBER: Royal Economic Society (president, 1972-74), Society of Long Range Planning (president, 1977—), Society of Business Economists (vice-president, 1978—), National Institute of Economic and Social Research (chairman of executive committee, 1974—), British Academy (fellow, 1968—). *Awards, honors:* Officer of Order of the British Empire, 1942, commander, 1945, knight, 1953; LL.D. from University of Strathclyde, 1968; Litt.D. from University of Leeds, 1971; D.Sc. from University of Aston in Birmingham, 1979.

WRITINGS: (With others) *Measures for International Economic Stability,* United Nations, 1951; *The World Dollar Problem,* St. Martin's, 1957; (with others) *The Fiscal System of Venezuela,* Johns Hopkins University Press, 1959; *The Dollar Problem: A Reappraisal,* Princeton Essays in International Finance, 1960; *Studies in Political Economy,* Macmillan, 1975, Volume I: *The Interwar Years and the 1940's,* Volume II: *International Trade and Domestic Economic Policy.*

MACK, John E(dward)   1929-

PERSONAL: Born October 4, 1929, in New York, N.Y.; son of Edward Clarence (a professor) and Ruth (an economist; maiden name, Prince) Mack; married Sally Stahl (a psychiatric social worker), July 12, 1959; children: Daniel, Kenneth, David Anthony (Tony). *Education:* Oberlin College, A.B., 1951; Harvard University, M.D., 1955. *Residence:* Chestnut Hill, Mass. *Agent:* Russell & Volkening, Inc., 551 Fifth Avenue, New York, N.Y. 10176. *Office:* Cambridge Hospital, Harvard University, 1493 Cambridge St., Cambridge, Mass. 02139.

CAREER: Massachusetts General Hospital, Boston, intern, 1955-56; Massachusetts Mental Health Center, Boston, resident in psychiatry, 1956-59, chief resident of day and night hospitals, 1957-59; Harvard University Medical School, Cambridge, Mass., began as teaching fellow, became research fellow, 1956-59; practiced medicine specializing in psychiatry, in Cambridge and Brookline, Mass., 1961; Boston Psychoanalytic Society and Institute, Boston, Mass., candidate in training, 1961-67; Massachusetts Mental Health Center, senior physician, 1961, fellow in child psychiatry of the children's unit, 1961-63, staff psychiatrist, 1963-67, staff visit, 1963-65, principle psychiatrist, 1965, associate director of psychiatry, 1965-67, director of research in children's unit, 1967-70, coordinator of Harvard University Medical School teaching, children's unit, 1968-70; Roxbury Court Clinic, Roxbury, Mass., member of legal medicine division, 1962-63; Harvard University Medical School, assistant in psychiatry, 1963-64, faculty member, 1964—, professor of psychiatry, 1972—, department head, 1973-77; Cambridge City Hospital, Cambridge, Mass., junior visiting physician, 1967, senior visiting physician, 1968-69, chief of department of psychiatry, 1969-77; Cambridge Hospital at Harvard University, Cambridge, Mass., head of department of psychiatry, 1967-77, professor of psychiatry, 1972—, consultant to University Health Services, 1972-75, chairman of executive committee of Harvard departments of psychiatry, 1980—; Cambridge-Somerville Mental Health and Retardation Center, Cambridge and Somerville, Mass., director of education, 1975—; Boston Psychoanalytic Society and Institute, faculty member, 1969—, education committee member, 1975—. Member of editorial board of the Journal of the American Psychoanalytic Association. Lecturer on psychological aspects of the Arab-Israeli conflict. *Military service:* U.S. Air Force, 1959-61; became captain.

MEMBER: American Board of Psychology (diplomate), American Psychiatric Association (fellow), American Group Psychotherapy Association, American Academy of Child Psychiatry, Association for the Psychophysiological Study of Sleep, Group for the Advancement of Psychiatry, New England Council of Child Psychiatry, Massachusetts Medical Society, Norfolk County Medical Society, Boylston Society, Alpha Omega Alpha. *Awards, honors:* Felix and Helene Deutsch Science Prize from the Boston Psychoanalytic Society and Institute, 1964, for *Heterosexual Impass in the Precipitation of Schizophrenia;* Harry S. Solomon award from the Massachusetts Mental Health Center, 1967; Pulitzer Prize in biography, 1976, for *A Prince of Our Disorder: The Life of T. E. Lawrence.*

WRITINGS: Nightmares and Human Conflict, Little, Brown, 1970; (editor) *Borderline States in Psychiatry,* Grune, 1975; *A Prince of Our Disorder: The Life of T. E. Lawrence,* Little, Brown, 1976; *Vivienne: The Life and Suicide of an Adolescent Girl,* Little, Brown, 1981; (editor, with Steven Ablon) *Development and Sustenance of Self-Esteem in Childhood,* International Universities Press, in press. Also author of unpublished work, *Heterosexual Impass in the Precipitation of Schizophrenia,* with William Katz. Contributor of articles to psychiatric journals.

WORK IN PROGRESS: "A work concerned with the psychology of nationalism—how people become identified with a nation, and how they behave as part of a nation as compared to how they act in personal interactions."

SIDELIGHTS: Mack is the author of several medical textbooks and two biographies. His first biography, *Prince of Our Disorder: The Life of T. E. Lawrence,* analyzes the life of the World War I hero commonly known as "Lawrence of Arabia." Lawrence was a member of the British army's intelligence section in Egypt before joining the Arab revolt against Turkey in 1916. During the battle he was captured, tortured, and allegedly raped by Turkish soldiers, but was nevertheless responsible for helping the small Arab army halt the Turks. Following the war, Lawrence continued contending for Arab independence as a delegate to the Paris Peace Conference and as a Middle East adviser in England, becoming a legendary figure as a result of his Arab loyalty. His reputation for valor was marred later in his career, however, by accounts of his alleged homosexual and sadomasochistic tendencies.

Mack's Pulitzer Prize-winning biography of Lawrence has been applauded for not dwelling on the popular stories of Lawrence's supposed perversities. The author focuses instead on the qualities that made Lawrence a respected fighter and diplomat. *New Statesman*'s Phillip Knightley declared that Mack "has dealt with the personal and private side of Lawrence's life so comprehensively that it should now be possible to shut the pathetic part of the man away forever, and weigh him in the one role that really counted—that of the Imperial Hero, an agent of his time and class." Jan Morris of *Spectator* called *A Prince of Our Disorder* "beyond all doubt the best, fairest and sincerest biography of the hero ever published." And Paul Zweig of the *New York Times Book Review* concluded: "The virtue of Mack's low-key approach is to have moved debate on Lawrence away from polemical slogans about his supposed homosexuality, sadism and masochism, and brought it closer to an appreciation of the gifts and flaws of an extraordinarily complex human being."

Another of Mack's books, *Vivienne: The Life and Suicide of an Adolescent Girl,* deals not with a legendary hero, but with a fourteen-year-old who found life an unconquerable battle. The volume is a retrospective look at Vivienne Loomis, a seemingly typical teenager who hung herself from the ceiling of her mother's silverworks shop, leaving only a diary of sensitive, intense poems and letters from which her family could learn of her silent suffering and despair. No one suspected Vivienne was inclined to suicide; she was outwardly energetic and outgoing. But often she was tormented within, as when she wrote: "And then / There are times / When I have nothing / To look forward to / In life / At all / Like now."

Mack and co-author Holly Hickler, Vivienne's creative-writing instructor, attempt in their book to identify the reasons why thousands of teenagers are compelled to end their lives, but they find no pat answer. Mack and Hickler indicate, however, that there is "an extensive set of determining forces—biological, psychological, interpersonal, familial and social—that build, not necessarily in a regular . . . or orderly fashion, toward the final outcome." And though they recognize that there is no specific treatment to prevent suicide, the authors note: "The balance is often so delicate that a harsh word or a supportive talk with a friend, teacher or therapist may make, at least for a brief time, the difference between death and life."

CA INTERVIEW

CA interviewed John Mack in January, 1981, at his home in Chestnut Hill, Mass.

"Someone once said we live the uncompleted lives of our parents. This is particularly true in my case," says John E. Mack, M.D., psychiatrist, professor, editor and biographer. "My father, Edward Mack, wrote biographies, and I believe he always wanted to incorporate psychology into his books. As a psychiatrist who writes biographies, I'm doing just that. I also look to my father as having been a major influence on my writing career. He was a professor of English at City College in New York and always stressed the importance of developing a literate writing style."

Mack confesses that he doesn't perceive of himself as a "true" imaginative writer because his books are the stuff of facts and real-life events. "I think every writer in his heart of hearts would like to be an imaginative writer—a novelist or a poet. In some ways, I fear writing because I don't know if I have the talent or freedom of imagination required. Perhaps I am afraid of finding out."

But in his own defense as a nonfiction author he notes that his strong suit is an ability to integrate a large body of material into a coherent, readable whole. "I have a way of finding relationships between ideas so that the synthesis is greater than the parts. In addition, I think I've used psychology in a new way to relate the motivations of historical figures and private individuals to the larger picture."

Mack's biographies are of a genre sometimes referred to as "psychohistory," a genre that combines history with psychoanalysis to achieve an understanding of a subject's life with regard to his psyche. But this classification bothers Mack. In the introduction to his book on Lawrence of Arabia, the author says the term implies a causality between psychology and history that is too simplistic. "The value of psychology in biography is that it deepens our appreciation of the inner life of public figures, and illuminates some of the motivating determinants of action. But psychology is only useful in a greater context that includes the political, social, and economic factors that form the weave of history."

For his subjects, Mack must necessarily choose individuals who combine deep introspection and the ability to act forcefully in the outside world. They should also be the kind of people who write insightful letters and keep journals of their inner thoughts. If they write novels, essays, or poetry, all the better.

What in Mack's estimation distinguishes the good "psychological" biography from the mediocre? One factor is a conscientious use of documentary material that holds interpretations within the bounds of the data at hand. Another, he believes, is a use of creative imagination, what he calls "playing with the material in an interesting fashion that gives us a new way of looking at something without distorting the facts."

The author he most admires in this respect is Walt Whitman's biographer Justin Kaplan. "He synthesizes Whitman's poetry and daily life in a way that is smooth and understated," according to Mack. "Kaplan's voice as a writer is present, yet he handles his subject matter with a light touch."

In addition to perfecting his craft as a biographer, Mack's biggest challenge as a writer is finding the time to write. It's easy to fill our time with activities imposed on us from the outside, he notes, but writing time does not come about unless time is made for it. One time-saver he appreciates is the photocopying machine. "Instead of the unduly laborious process of writing several drafts, I now work from a basic copy that is cut, pasted, and photocopied. All this allows me to treat my manuscript like a piece of clay.''

BIOGRAPHICAL/CRITICAL SOURCES: Village Voice, September 15, 1975; *Saturday Review,* February 21, 1976; *New York Times Book Review,* March 21, 1976, October 25, 1981; *New York Review of Books,* April 1, 1976; *Newsweek,* April 12, 1976; *Time,* April 12, 1976; *Christian Science Monitor,* May 5, 1976; *Nation,* May 8, 1976; *Economist,* May 15, 1976; *New Statesman,* May 21, 1976; *Spectator,* June 5, 1976; *National Review,* June 25, 1976; *Books and Bookmen,* July, 1976; *New Republic,* September 4, 1976; *Virginia Quarterly Review,* Autumn, 1976; *Commonweal,* July 22, 1977; *Washington Post Book World,* November 8, 1981.

—Interview by Trisha Gorman

* * *

MACKOWSKI, Richard M(artin) 1929-

PERSONAL: Born May 19, 1929, in Detroit, Mich.; son of Martin Jerome (in business) and Helen Virginia (Borowski) Mackowski. *Education:* Attended Xavier University, Cincinnati, Ohio, 1950-52; Loyola University, Chicago, Ill., B.A., 1953, M.A., 1956; West Baden College, Ph.L., 1955, S.T.B., 1962, S.T.L., 1962; Citta Universitaria di Roma, Certificate of Scholarity, 1966; Hebrew University of Jerusalem, Ph.D., 1970. *Home:* 7303 West Seven Mile Rd., Detroit, Mich. 48221.

CAREER: Entered Society of Jesus (Jesuits; S.J.), 1948, ordained Roman Catholic priest, 1961; teacher of Latin, Greek, French, and theology at high schools in Chicago and Wilmette, Ill., and Cleveland, Ohio, 1955-63; Pontifical Biblical Institute, Jerusalem, Israel, professor of biblical languages and exegesis and biblical geography and archaeology, 1966-73; Birzeit University, Birzeit on West Bank, Israel, lecturer in Near Eastern literature, 1974-75; Loyola University, Chicago, Ill., assistant professor of sacred scripture and languages and director of biblical study tours, 1975-80; Pontifical Gregorian University, Rome, Italy, adjunct professor of biblical languages and exegesis, 1982—. Professor and scholar-in-residence at North American College, Vatican City, 1980-81. Director of biblical study tours for Biblical Institute of Rome and Jerusalem, 1966-73; research scholar and special Roman Catholic adviser to rector of Ecumenical Institute for Advanced Theological Research, Tantur, Israel, 1975. *Member:* Catholic Biblical Association of America, Archaeological Association of America, Israel Exploration Society, Oriental Institute of Chicago.

WRITINGS: Jerusalem, City of Jesus: An Exploration of the Traditions, Writings, and Remains of the Holy City From the Time of Christ, Eerdmans, 1981; *Insight Into New Testament Greek,* Gregorian University Press, 1982; (in Latin) *Introductio in Linguam Latinam,* Gregorian University Press, 1982. Contributor to theology and classical studies journals.

WORK IN PROGRESS: Editing *Canticles in the New Testament,* publication by Gregorian University Press expected in 1982 or 1983; a lexicon of Latinisms in Greek.

SIDELIGHTS: Mackowski wrote: ''My motivation is to share my research and study with others, to promote interest and understanding of various areas of biblical studies, especially biblical languages and archaeology. Biblical or classical Latin, Greek, and Hebrew should be revived, since they are so important, not only in the training of students, but also in the understanding of our spiritual and cultural heritage. The study of languages is important for a fuller, more balanced education. In addition to these classical languages, I also speak and/or

read Italian, Polish, French, German, modern Israeli Hebrew, and some Arabic, modern Greek, and Turkish.''

* * *

MacLAREN, A. Allan 1938-

PERSONAL: Born in 1938, in Brechin, Scotland; son of William (a locomotive engineer) and Jane (Ritchie) MacLaren; married Margaret Marr (divorced); married Marcia Nott (a psychologist); children: Fiona Hope, Jane, William John Nott. *Education:* University of Aberdeen, M.A., 1964, Ph.D., 1971. *Politics:* Labour. *Religion:* None. *Office:* Department of Sociology, University of Strathclyde, Glasgow 1, Scotland.

CAREER: University of Aberdeen, Aberdeen, Scotland, lecturer in political economy, 1965-68; University of Strathclyde, Glasgow, Scotland, senior lecturer in sociology. Member of faculty at Open University. *Member:* British Sociological Association.

WRITINGS: Religion and Social Class: The Disruption Years in Aberdeen, Routledge & Kegan Paul, 1974; (editor) *Social Class in Scotland,* J. Donald, 1976. Contributor to history and sociology journals.

* * *

MacLEISH, Archibald 1892-1982

OBITUARY NOTICE—See index for *CA* sketch: Born May 7, 1892, in Glencoe, Ill.; died after a short illness, April 20, 1982, in Boston, Mass. Statesman, educator, librarian of Congress, playwright, and poet. MacLeish, one of America's most prominent poets and public statesmen, won three Pulitzer Prizes for his poetry and drama. Though he graduated first in his class from Harvard Law School and was a practicing attorney for several years, MacLeish gave up his practice in 1923 to join fellow writers T. S. Eliot, Ezra Pound, Thornton Wilder, and F. Scott Fitzgerald in Paris. A major poem of his expatriate years, ''The Hamlet of A. MacLeish,'' is sometimes compared with Eliot's ''The Waste Land.'' After a journey through Mexico by pack mule, MacLeish wrote *Conquistador,* an epic about Cortez that won a Pulitzer Prize in 1932. He then began to write impassioned objections to Hoover and the spread of Nazism. MacLeish supported President Roosevelt's New Deal and joined his administration as librarian of Congress in 1939, becoming assistant director of the newly formed Office of War Information in 1942 and assistant secretary of state in 1944. Although MacLeish continued to be politically outspoken, actively objecting to McCarthyism and the Vietnam War in his later years, the public phase of his career ended when he accepted a professorship at Harvard in 1949. He won a Pulitzer Prize in 1953 for *Collected Poems: 1917-1952* and one in 1959 for his major postwar work, the play ''J.B.,'' a twentieth-century rendition of the story of Job that ran for ten months on Broadway. His screenplay for ''The Eleanor Roosevelt Story'' won an Academy Award in 1966. Other well-known titles by MacLeish include ''Ars Poetica,'' ''You, Andrew Marvell,'' and ''The Black Day.'' Obituaries and other sources: *Chicago Tribune,* April 22, 1982; *London Times,* April 22, 1982; *New York Times,* April 22, 1982; *Washington Post,* April 22, 1982; *Time,* May 3, 1982; *Newsweek,* May 3, 1982; *Publishers Weekly,* May 7, 1982; *Library Journal,* June 1, 1982.

* * *

MACRAE, Norman 1923-

PERSONAL: Born September 10, 1923, in Koenigsberg, Germany; son of Russell Duncan (a British diplomat) and Dorothy

(Clayton) Macrae; married Jannet Kemp; children: Christopher, Gillian Macrae Morgan. *Education:* Cambridge University, M.A. (with first class honors), 1947, post graduate studies, 1947-49. *Religion:* Christian. *Home:* 20a Arterberry Rd., Wimbledon, London SW20 8AJ, England. *Office:* The Economist, 25 St. James's St., London SW1A 1HG, England.

CAREER: The Economist, London, England, began as journalist, became assistant editor, 1949-65, deputy editor, 1965—. Lecturer and business consultant. *Military service:* Royal Air Force, navigator, 1942-45; became flight lieutenant. *Awards, honors:* Wincott Prize from Wincott Foundation, 1973, for British financial journalist of the year.

WRITINGS: London Capital Market, Staples, 1952; *Consider Japan,* Duckworth, 1963; *Sunshades in October,* Allen & Unwin, 1963; *The Neurotic Trillionaire* (on Nixon's America), Harcourt, 1969; *America's Third Century,* Harcourt, 1976; (with John Hackett and others) *The Third World War,* Sidgwick & Jackson, 1979. Contributor of more than three thousand articles to journals.

WORK IN PROGRESS: The Third World War: The Untold Story, with John Hackett and others, publication expected in 1982; research on public affairs, economics, modern methods of management and entrepreneurship, and future studies.

SIDELIGHTS: Macrae commented: "As deputy editor of the The Economist, most of my work appears anonymously in that newspaper. Usually, however, I take one or two months off each year to write at length on some topic of interest. Recent ones have included Japan, Reagan's America, China, or new modes of entrepreneurship. Since the early 1960's I have been an advocate of the sort of economic policy followed by Japan—which means (contrary to general belief in the West) low government expenditure, very competitive internal economic policies with lots of subcontracting to small firms and small profit centers, but generally expansive fiscal policies."

*   *   *

MADSEN, Truman Grant   1926-

BRIEF ENTRY: Born December 13, 1926, in Salt Lake City, Utah. American philosopher, educator, and author. Madsen began teaching at Brigham Young University in 1957. He was Richard L. Evans Professor of Christian Understanding from 1971 to 1977, when he was named director of the Judeo-Christian Studies Center. Madsen wrote *Eternal Man* (Deseret, 1966), *Four Essays on Love* (1971), *Christ and the Inner Life* (Provo Community Workshop, 1973), *The Highest in Us* (Bookcraft, 1978), and *Defender of the Faith: The B. H. Roberts Story* (Bookcraft, 1981). He edited *Nibley on the Timely and the Timeless* (Religious Studies Center, Brigham Young University, 1978). *Address:* Judeo-Christian Studies Center, Brigham Young University, 165 Joseph Smith Building, Provo, Utah 84602.

*   *   *

MAGNUSON, Paul Budd   1884-1968

OBITUARY NOTICE: Born June 14, 1884, in St. Paul, Minn.; died November 5, 1968, in Washington, D.C. Surgeon, government administrator, educator, and author. Chief medical director of the Veterans Administration (VA) from 1948 to 1951, Magnuson is credited with improving the quality of care in VA hospitals by devising a recruitment program that attracted the best young doctors and medical professors in the country. In 1952 he served as chairman of President Harry Truman's Commission on Health Needs of the Country and

wound up combatting American Medical Association charges that the commission slanted its five-volume report to favor compulsory national health insurance and socialized medicine. A leading orthopedic surgeon, Magnuson pioneered in bone and joint surgery and founded the Rehabilitation Institute of Chicago. He was also professor emeritus of surgery and chairman of the department of bone and joint surgery at Northwestern University Medical School. Magnuson's writings include a textbook, *Fractures,* and an autobiography, *Ring the Night Bell.* Obituaries and other sources: *Current Biography,* Wilson, 1948, January, 1969; *New York Times,* November 6, 1968; *The National Cyclopaedia of American Biography,* Volume 54, James T. White, 1973.

*   *   *

MAGWOOD, John McLean   1912-

PERSONAL: Born August 26, 1912, in Toronto, Ontario, Canada; son of S.J.N. (a doctor) and Susannah Maud (McLean) Magwood; married Doris Johnston (a dietitian); children: Dawn Magwood Jamieson, Charles. *Education:* Earned B.A., 1933, M.A., 1937, LL.B., 1938, and D.Jur., 1981. *Home:* 10 Avoca Ave., Toronto, Ontario, Canada M4T 2B7. *Office:* 1 St. Clair Ave. W., Suite 1201, Toronto, Ontario, Canada M4V 1K6.

CAREER: Worked as lawyer in Toronto, Ontario, 1936-50; Magwood, Frith, Pocock, Rogers, O'Callaghan (law firm), Toronto, 1950-80, began as partner, became senior partner. Named Queen's Counsel, 1956; chairman of Canadian Executive Service Overseas. Director of City Home Ltd., and Toronto Symphony. *Military service:* Canadian Army, 1942-45; became major. *Member:* Canadian Council for International Cooperation (past president), Young Men's Christian Association of Canada (past president of national council), York County Law Association. *Awards, honors:* Canada Centennial Medal, 1967; Jubilee Medal from Queen Elizabeth II, 1977.

WRITINGS: Competition Law of Canada, Carswell, 1981.

*   *   *

MANN, (Luiz) Heinrich   1871-1950

BRIEF ENTRY: Born March 27, 1871, in Luebeck, Germany; died of a heart attack, March 12, 1950, in Santa Monica, Calif. German social critic and novelist. In his early novel, *Im Schlaraffenland* (1900; translated as *In the Land of Cockaigne,* 1929), Mann satirized the decadence of high society. Some of his later novels contained even more bitter attacks on the upper classes of Germany. *Der Untertan* (1918; translated as *The Patrioteer,* 1921), for example, was a scorching indictment of the rules of Wilhelmian Germany. Mann also wrote political essays in collections such as *Macht und Mensch* (1919), which voiced his plea for a natural order and a rational civilization. His ambition was to someday see a blended European culture to which everyone could contribute, a humanistic society enriched by intellectual and political freedom. Mann's historical novels, *Die Jugend des Koenigs Henri Quatre,* (1935; translated as *Young Henry of Navarre,* 1937) and *Die Vollendung des Koenigs Henri Quatre,* (1937; translated as *Henry, King of France,* 1939), revealed his ideal of humane, enlightened leadership and are generally considered to be his best works. One of Mann's novels, *Professor Unrat, oder: Dad Ende eines Tyrannen* (1904), was made into the classic 1930 film "The Blue Angel," starring Marlene Dietrich. *Biographical/critical sources: Columbia Dictionary of Modern European Literature,* Columbia University Press, 1947; *The Oxford Companion to German Literature,* Clarendon Press, 1976.

MANNERS, David X. 1912-

PERSONAL: Born February 23, 1912, in Zanesville, Ohio; son of Harris (a rabbi) and Bertha (Schildhaus) Rosenberg; married Ruth Ann Bauer (a writer), February 22, 1945; children: Paul, Jonathan, Michael, Timothy. *Education:* University of Cincinnati, B.A., 1933; Hebrew Union College, B.H.L., 1933. *Home and office:* David X. Manners Co., Inc., 237 East Rocks Rd., Norwalk, Conn. 06851.

CAREER: Free-lance writer, 1933-35; Popular Publications, Inc., New York City, editor, 1935-39; free-lance writer, 1939-41; RKO Pictures, New York City, story editor, 1941-44; Standard Magazines, Inc., New York City, editorial director, 1944-52; Universal Publishing Co., New York City, editorial director, 1952-53; free-lance writer, 1953-60; *House Beautiful,* New York City, building editor, 1960-66; David X. Manners Co., Inc. (public relations firm), Norwalk, Conn., president, 1966—. Consultant to Water Quality Research Council. *Member:* Authors Guild.

WRITINGS—Novels: *Memory of a Scream,* Mystery House, 1946; *Dead to the World,* McKay, 1947.

Nonfiction: (With Tedd Cott and William Manners) *Isn't It a Crime?,* Arco, 1947; *How to Plan and Build Your Workshop,* Arco, 1955; (with John H. Battison, Harry Campbell, and Ralph J. Wolf) *How to Make Plumbing Repairs,* Fawcett, 1956; (with Joseph Piazza) *The Handyman's Concrete and Masonry Handbook,* Fawcett, 1956; (with Bill Baker, Louis Hochman, Paul Corey, and Darrell Huff) *How to Build Outdoor Fireplaces and Furniture,* Fawcett, 1957; (with Campbell) *How to Repair Appliances,* Arco, 1957; (with T. H. Everett and others) *Manual of Home Repairs,* Grosset, 1958; *The Handyman's Concrete and Masonry Guide,* Fawcett, 1958; *The Handyman's Handbook,* Fawcett, 1958; *Home Improvements You Can Do,* Fawcett, 1959.

Projects You Can Make for Outdoor Living, Fawcett, 1960; *Plumbing and Heating Handbook,* Fawcett, 1960; *The Complete Book of Home Workshops,* Harper, 1969; *Hand Tools for the Home Workshop,* Audel, 1969; *Home Workshop Work Centers,* Audel, 1969; (editor) *Water: Its Effects on Life Quality,* Water Quality Research Council, 1976; *The Great Tool Emporium,* Dutton, 1979.

Other: "Conflict" (screenplay), Warner Bros., 1943; "Ah, Sweet Mystery" (three-act play), 1948; "Father and the Angels" (three-act teleplay), first broadcast by Studio One for Columbia Broadcasting Systems (CBS), 1949.

Also author of more than three hundred fifty short stories, two hundred articles, numerous booklets, and many scripts for broadcast media. Contributor to periodicals, including *Reader's Digest, Popular Science, Science Digest, Better Homes and Gardens, House Beautiful, American Legion, Ellery Queen's Mystery Magazine, Alfred Hitchcock's Mystery Magazine,* and *Treasury of Great Western Stories.*

WORK IN PROGRESS: A vegetarian cookbook, with wife, Ruth Ann Manners, publication expected in 1982.

SIDELIGHTS: Manners told *CA:* "I began writing fiction after graduating from college. After I built my own house in Connecticut, I switched to writing nonfiction based on my own experiences.

"I have always been torn between writing what I like and writing, editing, or doing related jobs to make money. In 1966, an article I wrote for the *Reader's Digest* attracted the attention

of manufacturers and led to my founding my own public relations firm with them as my clients. My writing background fitted me ideally for helping them with their communication problems and for offering such services as preparing brochures, newsletters, press releases, public service announcements, speeches, wire service stories, and advertising copy. When my son Tim joined the firm, aware that most writers did not receive the promotion their books deserved, we established a special department to place authors on television and radio shows. This service has since been expanded to include anyone with a cause to promote or a product to sell.

"Tim has always been interested in politics. Aware of the power of the written word, he'd like, through counseling and promotion, to turn a capable local or state candidate into a national figure. We know it can be done. But he has to be someone with an acceptable philosophy.

"How about more books? We're a writing family. Tim is just finishing his first book. My wife, Ruth Ann, is on her fourth. My brother William has written twenty-three. His wife, Ande, wrote two. I'm now aiming for number nineteen. After thirty years of nonfiction, I am again beckoned by fiction. It means less money, but it's more exciting. I have folders full of data. All I have to do now is find about three thousand extra hours."

* * *

MANNERS, John (Errol) 1914-

PERSONAL: Born September 25, 1914, in Exeter, England; married in October, 1940; children: one son, two daughters. *Home:* Laurel House, Great Cheverell, Devizes, Wiltshire, England.

CAREER: Writer.

WRITINGS: Country Crafts Today, Gale, 1974; *Country Crafts in Pictures,* David & Charles, 1976; *Crafts of the Highlands and Islands,* David & Charles, 1978. Contributor to magazines, including *Country Life, Countryman,* and *Lady.*

* * *

MANZONI, Pablo Michelangelo 1939-

BRIEF ENTRY: Born in 1939 in Bologna (some sources say Romagna), Italy. Makeup artist and author. Manzoni began working in Elizabeth Arden salons in the early 1960's and became creative director of the Arden salon in New York City. In 1965 he received a Coty Fashion Award for facial design through cosmetics. He wrote *Instant Beauty: The Complete Way to Perfect Makeup* (Simon & Schuster, 1979). *Biographical/critical sources: New York Times,* January 30, 1976.

* * *

MARATH, Laurie
See ROBERTS, Suzanne

* * *

MARATH, Sparrow
See ROBERTS, Suzanne

* * *

MARBLE, Samuel D(avey) 1915-

PERSONAL: Born November 15, 1915, in Mitchel, S.D.; son of Samuel W. and Elsie Naomi (Davey) Marble; married Rebecca Sturtevant (marriage ended); married Gladys Theison;

children: (first marriage) Peggy, Anne Davey, Rebecca Constance. *Education:* University of New Mexico, A.B., 1937; Syracuse University, M.A., 1939, Ph.D., 1941. *Religion:* Society of Friends (Quakers). *Home:* 4152 Quaker Hill Dr., Port Huron, Mich. 48060. *Office:* 305 Bard St., Port Huron, Mich. 48060.

CAREER: Associate secretary for American Friends Service Committee, 1941-47; Wilmington College, Wilmington, Ohio, president, 1947-59; Delta College, University Center, Mich., president, 1959-61; Saginaw Valley College, University Center, president, 1961-72; John Wesley College, Owosso, Mich., president, 1973-77; executive director of Family Service Agency, Port Huron, Mich., 1977-81. Executive director of Sound Mind Foundation, 1981—. *Awards, honors:* LL.D. from Cedarville College, 1957; L.H.D. from Wilmington College, 1967.

WRITINGS: Guide to Public Affairs Organizations, Public Affairs Press, 1947; *Glimpses of Africa,* Saginaw Valley College Press, 1975; *Before Columbus,* A. S. Barnes, 1981; *The Discovery of America: Passages From the East,* A. S. Barnes, 1983. Contributor of about forty articles to magazines.

WORK IN PROGRESS: An educational television series on pre-Columbian America.

* * *

MARCELIN, Pierre 1908-

PERSONAL: Born August 6, 1908, in Port-au-Prince, Haiti; son of Emile (a politician, novelist, and literary critic) and Eva (Thoby) Marcelin. *Education:* Attended private Catholic schools in Haiti. *Residence:* Haiti.

CAREER: Novelist. *Awards, honors:* Second Latin American Literary Prize Competition award from John Dos Passos, Ernesto Montenegro, and Blair Niles, 1943, for *Canape-Vert;* Guggenheim fellowship, 1951.

WRITINGS—All with brother, Philippe Thoby-Marcelin: *Canape-Vert* (novel), Editions de la Maison Francaise (New York), 1944, translation by Edward Larocque Tinker, Farrar & Rinehart, 1944; *La Bete de Musseau* (novel), Editions de la Maison Francaise, 1946, translation by Peter C. Rhodes published as *The Beast of the Haitian Hills,* Rinehart, 1946, new edition, introduction by Philippe Thoby-Marcelin, Time Inc., 1964; *Le Crayon de Dieu* (novel), La Table Ronde (Paris), 1952, translation by Leonard Thomas published as *The Pencil of God,* introduction by Edmund Wilson, Houghton, 1951; *Contes et legendes d'Haiti* (juvenile), illustrations by Philippe Degrave, F. Nathan, 1967, translation by Eva Thoby-Marcelin published as *The Singing Turtle, and Other Tales From Haiti,* illustrations by George Ford, Farrar, Straus, 1971; *Tous les hommes son fous* (novel), 1970, translation by Eva Thoby-Marcelin published as *All Men Are Mad,* introduction by Wilson, Farrar, Straus, 1970.

SIDELIGHTS: Pierre Marcelin, in collaboration with his brother Philippe, has written many novels centered around Haitian peasant life. Their first novel, *Canape-Vert,* presented in standard Haitian French rather than Creole patois, was the first piece of Haitian literature to be translated into English and Spanish. The book, which describes the unique voodoo-filled culture of the Haitian Negro population, is considered a classic among novels representative of life on the Caribbean islands.

Pierre Marcelin grew up in a family of distinguished Haitian literary and political figures, making it no surprise that he chose writing as his own career. As a child, he was surrounded by such notables as his grandfather Armand Thoby, a popular Haitian politician and writer, his cousin Frederic Marcelin, the

creator of the Haitian realistic novel, and his own father, Emile Marcelin, a popular novelist and literary critic who also served as the Haitian Minister of Finance.

Following the literary tradition that they fell heir to, the Marcelin brothers created novels which critics lauded for their clear, precise prose and full, detailed descriptions. Although their work is laced with social comment, it is usually implied and appears in the form of unemphasized irony and tongue-in-cheek prose.

BIOGRAPHICAL/CRITICAL SOURCES: New York Times, February 20, 1944, November 24, 1946, February 4, 1951; *Book Week,* November 17, 1946; *San Francisco Chronicle,* February 20, 1951.*

* * *

MARCHANT, Herbert S(tanley)

PERSONAL: Born in Cambridge, England; son of Ernest Joseph and Gertrude Selina Marchant; married Diana Selway in 1937; children: Timothy Jolyon. *Education:* Cambridge University, degree in modern languages (first class honors), 1928. *Home:* Flat 1, 5 Kensington Park Gardens, London W. 11, England.

CAREER: Modern languages master at Harrow School, 1928-39; associated with Intelligence Service, 1939-45; served in United States, France, Rumania, Germany, and Yugoslavia with Foreign Service, 1946-66; served as ambassador to Cuba, 1960-63, and Tunisia, 1963-66; deputy director of the Institute of Race Relations, 1966-68; British delegate at United Nations, 1969-73; member of Civil Service Selection Board, 1971-76. *Awards, honors:* Fellow of Woodrow Wilson Foundation, 1970-76; Officer of the Order of the British Empire; Knight Commander of St. Michael and St. George.

WRITINGS: Scratch a Russian, Lindsay Drummond, 1938; *Castro's Cuba,* Atlantic Education Trust, 1969; *His Excellency Regrets,* William Kimber, 1980. Contributor to newspapers.

WORK IN PROGRESS: Not Mentioned in Dispatches, memoirs.

* * *

MARCUS, Sheldon 1937-

BRIEF ENTRY: Born August 4, 1937, in New York, N.Y. American educational administrator, educator, and author. Marcus taught social studies in the public schools of New York City until 1968. He then joined the faculty at Fordham University in 1968 and was chairman of the Division of Urban Education from 1970 to 1976. Marcus is a member of the board of directors of Encampment for Citizenship, Inc. He wrote *Father Coughlin: The Tumultuous Life of the Priest of the Little Flower* (Little, Brown, 1973), which received a Pulitzer Prize nomination, and *The Urban In-Service Education Experience* (1977). Marcus also edited *Conflicts in Urban Education* (Basic Books, 1970) and *Urban Education: Crisis or Opportunity?* (Scarecrow, 1972). *Address:* 410 Benedict Ave., Tarrytown, N.Y. 10591; and School of Education, Fordham University, Lincoln Center Campus, New York, N.Y. 10023.

* * *

MARINO, John J. 1948-

PERSONAL: Born November 26, 1948, in Burbank, Calif.; son of John B. and Josephine (a financial executive; maiden name, Inglima) Marino; married Joan M. Trudeau (a registered nurse), August 8, 1980. *Education:* San Diego State University, B.A., 1971; United States International University, teaching certificate, 1972. *Residence:* Irvine, Calif. *Agent:* Jerrold Kushnick, 9100 Wilshire Blvd., W 1070, Beverly Hills, Calif. 90212.

CAREER: John H. Francis Polytechnic High School, Los Angeles, Calif., teacher, 1974-77; Huffy Corporation, Dayton, Ohio, cyclist, 1980—; writer, 1978—. *Awards, honors:* Set world records for transcontinental bicycling, 1978 and 1980.

WRITINGS: Wheels of Health, privately printed, 1978; (with Lawrence May and Hall Bennett) *John Marino's Bicycling Book,* J. P. Tarcher, 1981; "Psychling" (documentary film), CRM/McGraw-Hill, 1980.

WORK IN PROGRESS: Preparing for the annual Great American Bike Race from Los Angeles to New York, which will take place during June, 1982, and which features four cyclists.

SIDELIGHTS: In 1969 John Marino was a university student who, although already drafted by the Los Angeles Dodgers, was completing his bachelor's degree in physical education before fulfilling his desire to be a professional baseball player. His ambition was shattered, however, when he suffered a severe back injury while lifting weights. His doctors predicted Marino would never walk without difficulties and advised him against arduous movement. But a sedentary life was not acceptable to Marino, an athlete since childhood. For the next seven years he sought to "find himself" and to establish some goals. His job as a high school teacher did not satiate his yearning to accomplish something spectacular.

Marino's outlook on life brightened in 1976 when he found that holistic medicine, diet modification, and massage eased his chronic back pain and improved his overall health. As he grew increasingly stronger and able to endure strenuous activity, Marino set a goal for himself: He decided to surpass the transcontinental bicycling world record. Cycling, he found, did not worsen his condition.

Marino realized his dream in August, 1978, when he completed his cross-country trek from Santa Monica, Calif., to New York City in thirteen days, one hour, and twenty minutes, setting a new world's record. Not satisfied with accomplishing the feat only once, Marino made the trip again, beating his own record in 1980 by an entire day, averaging 240 miles per day.

In training for his transcontinental events, Marino discovered the importance of rebuilding his body and his mind through positive thinking, goal-setting, and motivation. He told *CA:* "My success as a cyclist/writer is attributed to Gordon W. Smith, Jr., whose auto-generational acquisition theory dealing with learning and motivation has motivated me to reach beyond what I once considered to be impossible."

*   *   *

MARKS, Rita   1938-

PERSONAL: Born August 14, 1938, in Akron, Ohio; daughter of Ben and Esther (Jacobs) Weiss; married Burton Marks (a writer), August 28, 1960; children: Craig, Wayne. *Education:* Western Reserve University (now Case Western Reserve University), B.A., 1959; University of Akron, J.D., 1981. *Residence:* Akron, Ohio. *Address:* c/o Lothrop, Lee & Shepard Co., 105 Madison Ave., New York, N.Y. 10016.

CAREER: Teacher at public schools in Akron and Cleveland, Ohio, 1959-60; Public Defender's Office, Akron, Ohio, attorney, 1981—.

WRITINGS—Juveniles; with husband, Burton Marks: *Give a Magic Show,* Lothrop, 1977; *Kites for Kids,* Lothrop, 1980; *The Spook Book,* Lothrop, 1981.

WORK IN PROGRESS: With husband, Burton Marks, a book on puppet plays.

SIDELIGHTS: Give a Magic Show and *The Spook Book* have been translated into French for distribution in Canada and Europe.

*   *   *

MARLOT, Raymond
See ANGREMY, Jean-Pierre

*   *   *

MARPLE, Allen Clark   1901(?)-1968

OBITUARY NOTICE: Born c. 1901; died March 24, 1968, in Ft. Lauderdale, Fla. Editor and author. Marple served the literary field in a number of capacities during his career, including East Coast story editor for Metro-Goldwyn-Mayer, book reviewer for the *New York Times,* editor of *Collier's,* and literary columnist for *Writer.* He also wrote fiction for such magazines as *Saturday Evening Post* and *Esquire.* Marple's books include the novel *Best Seller* and a collection of his *Writer* columns, *Write It and Sell It.* Obituaries and other sources: *New York Times,* March 27, 1968; *Publishers Weekly,* April 1, 1968.

*   *   *

MARRIS, Ruth   1948-

PERSONAL: Born April 29, 1948, in Hertford, England; daughter of John Geoffrey (a civil engineer) and Joan Doreen (Ward) Marris; married David Alexander Macaulay (an author and illustrator), August 18, 1978. *Education:* University of Leeds, B.A. (with honors), 1970. *Residence:* Providence, R.I. *Agent:* Laura Cecil, 10 Exeter Mansions, 106 Shaftesbury Ave., London W.1, England.

CAREER: Austicks University Bookshop, Leeds, England, salesperson, 1970; Dillons University Bookshop, London, England, children's book buyer, 1971-72; World's Work Ltd., Kingswood, England, children's editor, 1972-73; William Collins Sons & Co. Ltd., London, children's editor, 1973-77; A. & C. Black Ltd., London, commissioning editor of children's and educational books, 1977-78. *Member:* National Union of Journalists, Society of Young Publishers.

WRITINGS—Juveniles: *The Singing Swans* (illustrated by Miles Thistlethwaite), Heinemann, 1975, enlarged edition, Fontana, 1978; *The Cornerstone* (illustrated by Eliza Trimby), Heinemann, 1976; *The Virgin and the Angel* (illustrated by Anne Dalton), Heinemann, 1977; (editor) Palle Petersen, *The Vikings,* A. & C. Black, 1980.

WORK IN PROGRESS: Juvenile novel and picture book.

SIDELIGHTS: Ruth Marris told *CA:* "I feel my books should speak for themselves, and personal anecdotes say little or nothing about why I write. No vision on the road to Damascus set me off—I just decided to get going one day. Places are significant in my books so far—Ireland, Dorset, and Florence—but I am now much more preoccupied with the people in my books. People in life are quite different; thus my life and my books are separate. My books are public, my life quite private."

MARSH, Margaret Sammartino 1945-

PERSONAL: Born November 30, 1945, in Roanoke, Va.; daughter of Frank and Mildred (Hansbrough) Sammartino; married Robert H. Marsh (a financial analyst), March 21, 1970. *Education:* Rutgers University, B.A., 1967, M.A., 1969, Ph.D., 1974. *Office:* Historical Studies Program, Richard Stockton State College, Pomona, N.J. 08240.

CAREER: College of Staten Island of the City University of New York, New York City, visiting instructor in American studies, 1973-74; Bergen Community College, Paramus, N.J., assistant professor of social science, 1974-75; Richard Stockton State College, Pomona, N.J., assistant professor of history, 1975-80, associate professor of history, 1980—. *Member:* Amnesty International, American Historical Association, American Studies Association, Organization of American Historians, National Organization for Women, South Jersey Adoption Group, Coordinating Committee for Women in the Historical Profession, Fellowship of Reconciliation. *Awards, honors:* National Endowment for the Humanities Fellowship for College Teachers, 1982.

WRITINGS: (Contributor) Philip Dolce, editor, *Suburbia: The American Dream and Dilemma,* Doubleday, 1976; (contributor) Howard Gillette and William Cutler, editors, *The Divided Metropolis,* Greenwood Press, 1978; *Anarchist Women, 1870-1920,* Temple University Press, 1981; (contributor) Alden Whitman, editor, *Great American Reformers,* H. W. Wilson, in press.

WORK IN PROGRESS: A book on suburbanization and the family in the United States from 1865 to 1930.

SIDELIGHTS: Marsh's book, *Anarchist Women,* examines the ways in which the American women who espoused anarchism at the turn of the century reacted to the social issues and conflicts of their time. While some of the women were pacifists, others were aggressive, using violent tactics in order to spread their political doctrine.

One of the most well known of anarchists was Emma Goldman, an activist who was jailed in 1893 for inciting to riot, in 1916 for publicly advocating birth control, and in 1917 for obstructing the draft, before being deported to her Russian homeland in 1919. Goldman and seven other leading anarchists are profiled in Marsh's volume, which the *Los Angeles Times Book Review*'s Lynne Bronstein called "must reading for those interested in feminist issues."

Marsh told *CA:* "When I was involved in research for *Anarchist Women* I wrote to one of them, Mollie Steimer, who was then in her eighties and living in Mexico. She had spent most of her life in trouble with authorities because of her uncompromising beliefs: she had been deported from the United States for leafleting against this country's anti-Bolshevik stance during World War I; she was later deported from Russia because of her criticism of Communist repression; and during World War II she spent time in a concentration camp. Her life was a remarkable example of fidelity to principle. Yet when I solicited biographical information from her, she demurred, saying that she was simply an ordinary person who had tried to live in accordance with her most deeply-held beliefs. She seemed not to know that a life of principle is truly remarkable. Although I never came to share her faith in anarchism, her integrity as a human being continues to evoke my admiration.

"It may seem odd that after studying some of the most determined convention-breakers as the anarchists, I'm turning my attention to middle-class housewives. But what I'm really interested in, as a feminist and as a human being trying to understand cultural change, is the idea of gender. What does it mean, ultimately, to be male or female? And how does that meaning vary from society to society, from era to era? I believe that if we are ever to create an egalitarian society, differences in roles—whether in sexual relationships, childrearing, work, or political life—must be based on capacity or preference, not on gender. In studying the past, I hope that I can help us understand how to get to a future based on equality."

BIOGRAPHICAL/CRITICAL SOURCES: Los Angeles Times Book Review, March 15, 1981.

* * *

MARSHALL, Muriel

PERSONAL: Born in Nara Visa, N.M.; daughter of Eber Robert and Leta (Chamberlain) Edwards; married Walter Raymond Marshall; children: Halbert, Linda, Crystal. *Home address:* P.O. Box 139, Delta, Colo. 81416.

CAREER: Free-lance writer, photographer, and painter. Newspaper feature editor and part-time teacher of creative writing.

WRITINGS: Lovely Rebel (novel; Fiction Book Club selection), Rinehart, 1950; *Uncompahgre* (nonfiction), Caxton, 1981. Contributor of articles, stories, and poems to magazines, including *Collier's, Woman's Day, Sunset, Empire, Yankee,* and *Reader's Digest.*

WORK IN PROGRESS: Escalante, Ghost Canyon, nonfiction; *They Dig Sunlight,* nonfiction about coal mining.

SIDELIGHTS: Murial Marshall commented: "*Lovely Rebel,* a novel about the Irish Fenian revolt in 1866, was described by the *New York Herald Tribune* as follows: 'The book has depth as the study of inherited hates.' The *Boston Post* uncategorized it as 'neither historical nor "romantic" but instead both timeless and contemporary.' It was, however, a comment in the *Saturday Review of Literature* that touched on the dilemma of working through an agent—the agency's need to lean a book toward what it conceives will be heavy sales, and the trepidation of a new writer that any disagreement with the contract in hand will result in its withdrawal or in the published book's failure. 'Lovely Rebel is written in clipped, colorful prose,' *Saturday Review* commented, 'and deserves a less banal title.' The publication history of *Lovely Rebel* did not solve the dilemma in this instance, because, whether owing to title or content, it was also published by Frederick Muller in London and, after translation, by De Leo in Genoa.

"*Uncompahgre* was described by Alice Wright, *Sentinel* reviewer, as a 'mix of geology, geography, paleontology, legend, folklore and history of the vast plateau.' She ended by touching on the dilemma those who write about the pleasant places of this earth must face with their consciences—whether to share or hoard these delights. She continued in her review, 'So far the Uncompahgre Plateau has been spared the overuse that has spoiled so much of the western country. Let's hope Marshall's book won't hasten the time when it too will be strewn with beer cans and scarred by motorcycles.'"

* * *

MARSHBURN, Joseph Hancock 1890-1975

OBITUARY NOTICE: Born January 11, 1890, in Josselyn, Ga.; died April 13, 1975. Educator and author. Marshburn began his teaching career in 1912 at the University of Georgia, later becoming a professor of English at Georgia Military College, where he served as department head, vice-president, and president. He spent his next fifty-five years at the University of Oklahoma as a professor of English. He was also a reader at the Folger Shakespeare Library and the British Museum. Marshburn produced two books, *Witchcraft in England, 1550-1640* and, with Alan R. Velie, *Blood and Knavery: A Collection of English Renaissance Pamphlets and Ballads of Crime and Sin.* Obituaries and other sources: *Who Was Who in America, With World Notables,* Volume VI, *1974-1976,* Marquis, 1976.

* * *

MARTIN, Graham Dunstan 1932-

PERSONAL: Born October 21, 1932, in Leeds, England; son of Edward Dunstan (a schoolmaster) and Margaret (Lightbody) Martin; married Ryllis Daniel, August 21, 1954 (divorced); married Anne Moone Crombie (a social worker), June 14, 1969; children: Jonathan, Stefan, Juliet, Lewis, Aidan. *Education:* Oriel College, Oxford, B.A., 1954; Victoria University of Manchester, graduate certificate, 1955; Linacre House, Oxford, B. Litt., 1965. *Office:* Department of French, University of Edinburgh, 4 Buccleuch Pl., Edinburgh 8, Scotland.

CAREER: Writer. Worked as teacher of French and English in secondary schools in England, 1956-65; University of Edinburgh, Edinburgh, Scotland, lecturer in French, 1965—. Lecturer in English at University of Paris, 1976-77. *Member:* British Society of Aesthetics.

WRITINGS: Language, Truth, and Poetry: Notes Towards a Philosophy of Literature, Edinburgh University Press, 1975; *Giftwish* (novel), Allen & Unwin, 1980, Houghton, 1981; *The Architecture of Experience: The Role of Language and Literature in the Construction of the World,* Edinburgh University Press, 1981; *Catchfire* (novel), Allen & Unwin, 1981.

Editor and translator, except as noted: (Translator only; with John H. Scott) *In the Year of the Strike* (poetry), Rapp & Whiting, 1968; Paul Valery, *Le Cimetiere marin,* Edinburgh University Press, 1971; (translator only; with Scott) *Love & Protest* (poetry), Harper, 1972; *Anthology of Contemporary French Poetry,* Edinburgh University Press, 1972; (translator only) Peter Sharrett, editor, Louise Labe, *Sonnets,* Edinburgh University Press, 1973; (translator with others) Jean-Claude Renard, *Selected Poems,* Oasis Press, 1978.

WORK IN PROGRESS: A fairy tale for adults; a work of philosophy.

SIDELIGHTS: Martin told *CA:* "My academic work is based on a love of poetry, a love of teaching, a detestation of 'conventional wisdom,' and a belief in the relevance of literature to life. Nor is anything more relevant than fantasy; my essays in this genre having arisen out of reading fairy tales to my small sons. I have on two occasions spent a year working in France (my favorite place, along with Scotland), and of course speak French (a physical pleasure, like food or folksinging)."

* * *

MARTINEAU, Robert Arnold Schurhoff 1913-

PERSONAL: Born August 22, 1913, in Solihull, England; son of Charles Edward and Ellen Martineau; married Elinor Gertrude Ap-Thomas, June 20, 1941; children: Elizabeth Anne (Mrs. Ronald Wayne Williams), Robert Patrick, Susan Barbara (Mrs. Mark Andrew Rice-Oxley). *Education:* Trinity Hall, Cambridge, B.A., 1935, M.A., 1939. *Home:* Gwenallt, Park St., Denbigh, Wales.

CAREER: Ordained priest of Church of England, 1939; curate in Melksham, England, 1938-41; vicar of Ovenden in Halifax, England, 1946-52, and of Allerton in Liverpool, England, 1952-66, honorary canon of Liverpool, 1961, rural dean of Childwall, England, 1964, proctor in convocation, 1964, suffragan bishop of Huntingdon, England and residentiary-canon of Ely Cathedral, 1966-72, bishop of Blackburn, England, 1972-81; writer, 1981—. Exchange vicar in San Lorenzo, Calif., 1961-62. *Military service:* Royal Air Force Voluntary Reserve, chaplain, 1941-46. Royal Auxiliary Air Force, chaplain, 1947-52.

WRITINGS: (Editor with Walter Kagerah) *The Church in Germany in Prayer,* Mowbray, 1937; *Rhodesian Wild Flowers,* Longmans, Green, 1953; *The Office and Work of a Reader,* Mowbray, 1970, revised edition, 1980; *The Office and Work of a Priest,* Mowbray, 1972, revised edition, 1981; *Moments That Matter,* S.P.C.K., 1975; *Preaching Through the Christian Year,* Mowbray, 1978; *Travelling With Christ,* S.P.C.K., 1981; *Preaching Through the Christian Year,* Mowbray, 1983.

* * *

MARTINEZ, Jacinto Benavente y
See BENAVENTE (y MARTINEZ), Jacinto

* * *

MARWICK, Lawrence 1909-1981

OBITUARY NOTICE: Born September 16, 1909, in Sopockinie, Poland; died October 17, 1981. Librarian, educator, and author. Marwick headed the Hebraic section of the Library of Congress for many years, beginning in 1948. Under his supervision, the library acquired the largest collection of Hebraic, Judaic, and Semitic materials ever compiled under government sponsorship. Marwick also taught Arabic and Islamic studies at Dropsie College and New York University. His writings include *A Handbook of Diplomatic Hebrew* and articles for professional journals. Obituaries and other sources: *A Biographical Directory of Librarians in the United States and Canada,* 5th edition, American Library Association, 1970; *Who's Who in World Jewry: A Biographical Dictionary of Outstanding Jews,* Olive Press, 1978; *Library Journal,* February 15, 1982.

* * *

MATHESON, John Ross 1917-

PERSONAL: Born November 14, 1917, in Arundel, Quebec, Canada; son of Alexander Dawson (a minister) and Gertrude (McCuaig) Matheson; married Edith May Bickley, August 4, 1945; children: Duncan, Wendy (Mrs. Michael Douglas Simpson), Jill (Mrs. Robert Brent Perry), Donald, Roderick, Murdoch. *Education:* Queen's University, Kingston, Ontario, B.A., 1940; Osgoode Hall Law School, Barrister-at-Law, 1948; University of Western Ontario, LL.M., 1954; Mount Allison University, M.A., 1975. *Religion:* United Church of Canada. *Residence:* Rideau Ferry, Ontario, Canada KOG 1WO. *Office:* Court House, Perth, Ontario, Canada K7H 1G1.

CAREER: Called to the Bar of Ontario, 1948; Matheson, Henderson & Hart (law firm), Brockville, Ontario, attorney, 1949-68; created Queen's Counsel, 1967; Judicial District of Ottawa-Carleton, Ontario, judge, 1968-78; County Court of Lanark, Ontario, judge, 1978—. Local judge of Supreme Court of Ontario, 1968—. Member of Canadian House of Commons for Leeds, 1961-68, chairman of standing committee on external affairs, 1963-65, parliamentary secretary to prime minister, 1966-68. Life member of council of Queen's University,

Kingston, Ontario. Member of United Services Institute of Canada. *Military service:* Canadian Army, Royal Canadian Horse Artillery, 1940-44; received Canadian Forces Decoration, 1975; appointed honorary colonel, 1977.

MEMBER: United Empire Loyalists Association of Canada (honorary vice-president, 1974—), Canadian Amateur Boxing Association (honorary secretary, 1972—), Canadian Bible Society (life governor), Canadian Bar Association (life member), Canadian Economic Association (life member), Canadian Olympic Association, Royal Canadian Artillery Association (life member), Heraldry Society of Canada (fellow), Royal Economic Association (fellow), Society of Antiquaries of Scotland (fellow), National Trust for Scotland (life member), Royal Order of Scotland, Order of St. John (genealogist of Priory of Canada), Phi Delta Phi, Masons (Scottish Rite 33), Rotary International. *Awards, honors:* Armigerous by Lyon Court, 1959, and College of Arms, 1972; knight of justice of Order of St. John, 1974; knight commander of merit of Order of St. Lazarus, 1975; companion of Most Honourable Order of Meritorious Heritage, 1976; distinguished service award from Queen's University, 1977; essay prize from Commonwealth Heraldry Board, 1980, for "The Beley Lecture"; Montreal Medal from Queen's University Alumni, 1981.

WRITINGS: Canada's Flag: A Search for a Country, G. K. Hall, 1980. Contributor to *Encyclopedia Canadiana.*

WORK IN PROGRESS: The Order of Canada: The Search for Merit; a book of poems.

SIDELIGHTS: "In 1943," Matheson told *CA,* "when I was a forward observation officer of artillery with the British Eighth Army in Italy, a German shell burst over my head and put fragments of steel through my helmet into my skull. I changed from a young athlete to a traumatic epileptic, an amnesiac, a partial paraplegic, and partial hemiplegic. There was a long period of recovery, a happy marriage, six great children, and now grandchildren. My ambitions have always exceeded my real ability. I believe I recognize my limitations now, and am discovering new avenues for challenge. While I serve daily as a judge, I hope and pray I am growing wiser and am by no means through."

Matheson's books were motivated, at least in part, by his own involvement in the research and development that led to Canada's flag and the establishment of the Order of Canada.

*   *   *

MATHEWSON, William (Glen, Jr.)   1940-

PERSONAL: Born March 8, 1940, in Yonkers, N.Y.; son of William Glen (a retailer) and Mary Virginia (Bosworth) Mathewson; married Sally Aiken Olhausen, March 6, 1976; children: Christina. *Education:* Yale University, B.A., 1961; Harvard University, M.B.A., 1965. *Home:* 1111 Park Ave., New York, N.Y. 10028. *Agent:* Robbins & Covey, 2 Dag Hammarskjold Plaza, New York, N.Y. 10017. *Office: Wall Street Journal,* 22 Cortlandt St., New York, N.Y. 10007.

CAREER: Look, New York City, in advertising sales, 1965-68; *Suffolk Sun,* Deer Park, N.Y., reporter, 1969; *Wall Street Journal,* New York City, reporter, 1969-71, rewrite editor, 1971-75, reporter in London, England, 1975-77, rewrite editor, 1977—. *Military service:* U.S. Army, 1961-65; became first lieutenant.

WRITINGS: Immediate Release (novel), Simon & Schuster, 1982.

WORK IN PROGRESS: Another novel.

SIDELIGHTS: Mathewson told *CA:* "My writing of fiction is confined to odd hours in the evening and on weekends. Therefore, it has to be something that I truly want to do, but I cannot honestly say that the process is one of unalloyed enjoyment. Most difficult of all for me is the moment that I get up from the dinner table and head for the typewriter; but once there, and once the words start to flow, I know I'm home free—for one more day."

BIOGRAPHICAL/CRITICAL SOURCES: Los Angeles Times, February 26, 1982.

*   *   *

MATTIL, Edward La Marr   1918-

BRIEF ENTRY: Born November 25, 1918, in Williamsport, Pa. American educator and author. Mattil began teaching art in the 1940's. He has been chairman of the art department at North Texas State University since 1971. Mattil has also produced films and children's television series. He received a distinguished service medal from the National Gallery of Art in 1966. Mattil wrote *Meaning in Crafts* (Prentice-Hall, 1959) and *Meaning in Children's Art: Projects for Teachers* (Prentice-Hall, 1981). He has edited *Everyday Art* since 1957. *Address:* 600 Roberts Ave., Denton, Tex. 76201; and Department of Art, North Texas State University, Denton, Tex. 76203. *Biographical/critical sources: Who's Who in American Art,* Bowker, 1978.

*   *   *

MAURICIO, Victoria Courtney   1928-

PERSONAL: Born February 6, 1928, in Bridgend, Glamorgan, South Wales; came to the United States in 1952; daughter of Phillip Douglas and Mary (a restaurateur; maiden name, Howells) Skinner; married Paul Mauricio (deceased); children: Paul C. *Education:* Educated privately in Europe. *Politics:* "Labour in England." *Religion:* "Spiritualist." *Home:* 253 Raintree Rd., Virginia Beach, Va. 23452. *Office:* Light of Truth Church of Divine Healing, 1809 East Bay View Blvd., Norfolk, Va. 23505.

CAREER: Light of Truth Church of Divine Healing, Norfolk, Va., minister, 1979—. Spiritualist; gives readings and lectures; healer; clairvoyant. Guest on television and radio programs. Past adjutant and commander of Disabled American Veterans Auxiliary.

WRITINGS: The Return of Chief Black Foot, Donning, 1981.

WORK IN PROGRESS: Chief Black Foot and the Medicine Woman, publication expected in 1983; spiritual poems.

SIDELIGHTS: Victoria Mauricio commented: "Due to my parents' early divorce, I was raised primarily by my uncle, a contractor in London, England. I was educated in England and Europe, and earned cups and medals for swimming in elementary school, and diplomas for biblical knowledge in preparatory school. My psychic ability and healing gift is a family trait, handed down for many generations. I have traveled extensively in Europe, North Africa, and Canada, and think America is the greatest country in the world. The opportunities here are boundless."

Commenting on her first book, Mauricio added: "It has been said that *The Return of Chief Black Foot* is fifty years ahead of its time. It is absolute proof of communication between the so-called dead and the living. It is incredible when one realizes that a spirit came to me and told me that he wanted to be brought back to his own tribe. This great Indian chief cannot be researched, for as great as he was, there is nothing written about him. He was a white man's chief, a believer that his white friends would honor all they promised him, then he was betrayed at every step. His people (the Crow Indians) were led to his burial place through visions and dreams he brought to me. The story is even more incredible when one realizes that the search for this man was directed by me to the Crow Indians by telephone, over two thousand miles away. This is also recognized by the Indian Shaman as the great prophesy that came true; a prophesy of more than two hundred years that a great chief would be brought back to his tribe, that an outsider would bring him back and that the outsider would have healing powers.

"The Crows had searched for this man for more than fifty years when he contacted me, and I told the Indians of Chief Black Foot's wishes. He was found within thirty-one days. The burial place he picked was astonishing, for in over several million acres of land, the chief selected the only place on the map that had never been surveyed. This was not discovered until after the burial. The small plot does not belong to the government or the Crow Indians.

"Through the powers of Chief Black Foot, I speak to the Crow Indians in their own language, though I cannot understand the Crow dialect. It is the Crow tongue of over one hundred years ago, however.

"Many miracles are attributed to the chief since his return to his people. The necklace he wore (made only for the great chiefs of the Plains Indians in the State of Washington) was found in the cave, and the few remaining beads were sent to me on his instructions. Since his return to the Crow Tribe, the Eagle is back on the reservation. He was known to be an Eagle Shaman who worked his medicine through the tribe. He was also known as a coyote, which howls whenever help is asked from the chief.

"In the television media, Chief Black Foot has become a name because he refused to allow a program to be filmed for ''P.M. Magazine.'' When the producer and cameraman came to film the show, cameras would not work on two separate occasions. Extra cameras were brought in, but they also would not work. Then Chief told me that he would not allow the filming to take place because the 'Yellowhair Custer was there.' (It is on the Crow reservation that the Battle of the Little Bighorn took place.) I told the producer what the chief had said, and learned that the cameraman was a direct descendant of General Custer. He was a dead ringer for the general. A follow up was done on the show to explain the phenomena. Life with Chief Black Foot is never dull.''

AVOCATIONAL INTEREST: Ballet, opera, reading, travel, animals, swimming, solitude, mountains.

BIOGRAPHICAL/CRITICAL SOURCES: Gazette (Billings, Mont.), September 10, 1978, October 4, 1978, October 5, 1978, March 17, 1979, May 6, 1979, September 7, 1979, September 14, 1979; *National Enquirer,* December 19, 1978; *Psychic News,* March 3, 1979; *Norfolk Virginian-Pilot,* April 1, 1979; *Fate,* March, 1980; *Norfolk Ledger-Star,* March 24, 1980, May 28, 1980; *Richmond Times-Dispatch,* March 30, 1980; *Holistic Living News,* April-May, 1981; Wendy Jeffries, *That's Incredible,* Volume II, Jove, 1981.

*   *   *

MAUSER, Patricia Rhoads 1943-

PERSONAL: Surname is pronounced *Mah*-zer; born January 14, 1943, in Sacramento, Calif.; daughter of Kenneth C. (a

real estate broker) and Betty Jane (Arnold) Rhoads; married Richard Lewis Mauser (a national account manager for American Telephone and Telegraph), June 5, 1965; children: Laura Elaine, Peter Brent. *Education:* Attended Washington State University, 1961-63 and 1964-65, and University of Oregon, 1963-64. *Home and office:* 5111 26th St. N.W., Puyallup, Wash. 98371. *Agent:* Amy Berkower, Writer's House, Inc., 21 West 26th St., New York, N.Y. 10010.

CAREER: Writer, 1955—. *Member:* Pacific Northwest Writer's Conference.

WRITINGS: How I Found Myself at the Fair (juvenile novel), Atheneum, 1980; *A Bundle of Sticks* (juvenile novel), Atheneum, 1982. Author of ''Broadview,'' a weekly column in *Federal Way.* Contributor to local magazines.

WORK IN PROGRESS: Rip-Off (tentative title), a novel for junior high school students, about a girl involved in shoplifting; another novel, about a girl and her horse, for high school students.

SIDELIGHTS: Mauser told *CA:* ''In today's society I see the good kids finishing last. At my son's junior high school, for instance, it is the 'stoners' (kids on drugs) and the bullies who are looked up to and hold positions of leadership and popularity. The kind, gentle kids who work for good grades often find themselves isolated and miserable, at conflict with the values their parents have taught them. Without having planned to do so, I seem to write for that group, the decent kids who need to know they are not alone. In my books the 'good guys' emerge victorious over difficult odds. I don't waste type feeling sorry for the 'bad guys.' They are disposed of neatly and fairly.''

BIOGRAPHICAL/CRITICAL SOURCES: Pierce County Herald, September 16, 1980; *WSU Hilltops,* October, 1981.

*   *   *

MAVIN, John
See RICKWORD, (John) Edgell

*   *   *

MAXMEN, Jerrold S(amuel) 1942-

PERSONAL: Born June 27, 1942, in Detroit, Mich.; son of Harold A. (a dentist) and Ethel (Tucker) Maxmen; married Mary Elizabeth Berman (a costume designer), December 18, 1966. *Education:* Wayne State University, B.A., 1963, M.D., 1967. *Politics:* ''Progressive-Libertarian.'' *Religion:* Jewish. *Home and office:* 30 Fifth Ave., No. 6E, New York, N.Y. 10011. *Agent:* Carl Brandt, Brandt & Brandt Literary Agents, Inc., 1501 Broadway, New York, N.Y. 10036.

CAREER: Mount Zion Hospital, San Francisco, Calif., intern, 1967-68; Yale University, New Haven, Conn., resident in psychiatry, 1968-71; Dartmouth College, Hanover, N.H., assistant professor of psychiatry, 1971-74; Albert Einstein College of Medicine, Bronx, N.Y., assistant professor of psychiatry, 1974-77; Columbia University, New York, N.Y., associate professor of clinical psychology, 1977—, director of medical student training in psychiatry at College of Physicians and Surgeons, 1977-80. Private practice of psychiatry, 1980—. Director of inpatient unit at Dartmouth-Hitchcock Mental Health Center, 1971-74; director of hospital services at Soundview Throgs-Neck Community Mental Health Center, 1975. *Member:* American Civil Liberties Union, American Psychiatric Association, Hastings Center, Hemlock. *Awards, honors:* Fellow of National Fund for Medical Education, 1973-74; distinguished psychiatrist lecturer of American Psychiatric Association, 1979.

WRITINGS: (With G. J. Tucker and M. D. LeBow) *Rational Hospital Psychiatry*, Brunner, 1974; *The Post-Physician Era: Medicine in the Twenty-first Century*, Wiley, 1976; *A Good Night's Sleep*, Norton, 1981. Contributor of more than thirty articles to medical journals, *Social Policy*, and *Self*.

WORK IN PROGRESS: Two nonfiction books.

* * *

MAY, Lawrence Alan 1948-

PERSONAL: Born July 5, 1948, in Brooklyn, N.Y.; son of Harry I. (an optometrist) and Edith (an attorney; maiden name, Nachamkin) May; married Sarita Gilbert, September 1, 1973; children: Corey Gilbert, Lindsay Rachel. *Education:* Harvard University, A.B., 1970, M.D., 1974. *Residence:* Encino, Calif. *Office:* 16260 Ventura Blvd., Encino, Calif. 91436.

CAREER: Massachusetts General Hospital, Boston, intern, 1974-75, resident, 1975-77; University of California, Los Angeles, assistant professor of medicine, 1977-79; private practice of medicine in Encino, Calif., 1979—. Director of medical education at Encino Hospital; consultant to Bureau of Medical Quality Assurance. *Member:* American Medical Association, American College of Physicians, Boylston Society, Phi Beta Kappa.

WRITINGS: (With Joel Levine) *Getting In: A Guide to Acceptance at the College of Your Choice*, Random House, 1972; (editor) *Classic Descriptions of Disease*, Dabor Science, 1977; (editor) *Classic Descriptions of Physical Signs in Medicine*, Dabor Science, 1977; *Getting the Most Out of Your Doctor*, Basic Books, 1978; (with Alan Goroll and Albert Mulley) *Primary Care Medicine*, Lippincott, 1981; (with John Marino and Hal Bennet) *John Marino's Bicycling Book*, J. P. Tarcher, 1981. Managing editor of *Geriatric Medicine Alert*; editor of *Infectious Disease Alert*; consulting editor of *Eye Care Digest*.

WORK IN PROGRESS: Patients' Desk Reference (tentative title), for the lay person.

SIDELIGHTS: May told *CA:* "Writing has been a rewarding diversion from the predictability of daily medical practice. My published works have given me access to the print and broadcast media with the attendant glamour and opportunity to communicate with large numbers of people. In writing *Getting the Most Out of Your Doctor* I aspired to change the public's attitudes and physicians's modes of practice. When the book's impact fell short of this goal, I realized that the process of writing, being published, and reflecting on the work was a sufficient end in itself."

BIOGRAPHICAL/CRITICAL SOURCES: New England Journal of Medicine, October 8, 1981; *Journal of the American Medical Association*, October 16, 1981; *British Medical Journal*, January 2, 1982; *Annals of Internal Medicine*, March, 1982.

* * *

MAYER, Gerda (Kamilla) 1927-

PERSONAL: Born June 9, 1927, in Carlsbad, Czechoslovakia; came to England March 14, 1939, became English citizen, 1949; daughter of Arnold (a shopkeeper) and Erna (Eisenberger) Stein; married Adolf Mayer (a businessman), September 3, 1949. *Education:* Bedford College, London, B.A., 1963. *Religion:* Jewish. *Home:* 12 Margaret Ave., Chingford, London E4 7NP, England.

CAREER: Poet. Worked on a farm, 1945-46, and as a secretary, 1946-52. *Awards, honors: Monkey on the Analyst's Couch* was given a recommendation by Poetry Book Society, 1980.

WRITINGS—Poetry: *Oddments*, privately printed, 1970; *Gerda Mayer's Library Folder* (illustrated by Deirdre Farrell), All-In, 1972; (editor) *Poet Tree Centaur*, Oddments, 1973; (with Florence Elon and Daniel Halpern) *Treble Poets 2*, Chatto & Windus, 1975; *The Knockabout Show* (juvenile), Chatto & Windus, 1978; *Monkey on the Analyst's Couch*, Ceolfrith Press, 1980. Contributor of poetry to magazines and anthologies.

WORK IN PROGRESS: An autobiography.

SIDELIGHTS: Gerda Mayer told *CA:* "*The Knockabout Show*, my book for children, contains only a few poems written deliberately for young people. I don't think I myself had realized before quite how frequently I had made use of childhood material." She added: "Most were written for adults but were considered suitable for young people by the publisher."

Critics have noted this tendency in Mayer's work. Laurence Lerner reflected in *Encounter* that her poetry is "cool, witty, sometimes on the edge of nursery rhymes . . . and often on very big subjects." *London Observer* reviewer Peter Porter commented, "Her short wry poems of the dislocation of human life have lent distinction to little magazines. . . . She is a genuine aphorist and far truer to the human spirit than most manufacturers of haiku . . . but her poems of everyday disenchantment are deepened by a powerful bitterness. . . . Like Stevie Smith she writes children's rhymes for grown-ups." Andrew Motion speculated in *New Statesman* that in Mayer's poetry "forms are broken, nursery rhyme rhythms adapted, and fairy story emblems redeployed in order to project—and protect—her vulnerability."

BIOGRAPHICAL/CRITICAL SOURCES: Listener, June 3, 1976, January 29, 1981; *London Sunday Times*, February 26, 1978; *London Times*, March 8, 1978; *London Times Educational Supplement*, March 10, 1978; *Birmingham Post*, August 3, 1978; *New Statesman*, February, 1981; *London Observer*, March 15, 1981; *Quarto*, May, 1981; *Encounter*, September, 1981.

* * *

MAYHEW, Christopher Paget 1915-

BRIEF ENTRY: Born June 12, 1915, in London, England. British government official and author. Mayhew was a Labour member of Parliament from 1945 to 1974, under-secretary of state for foreign affairs from 1946 to 1950; and minister of defense to the Royal Navy from 1964 to 1966. He has also served as editor in chief of *Middle East International*. Mayhew wrote *Coexistence Plus: A Positive Approach to World Peace* (Bodley Head, 1962), *Britain's Role Tomorrow* (Hutchinson, 1967), *Party Games* (Hutchinson, 1969), *Publish It Not: The Middle East Coverup* (Longman, 1975), and *The Disillusioned Voter's Guide to Electoral Reform* (Arrow Books, 1976). *Address:* 39 Wool Rd., Wimbledon, London S.W.20, England. *Biographical/critical sources: Times Literary Supplement*, February 2, 1967; *Punch*, October 1, 1969; *Spectator*, October 4, 1969; *The International Who's Who*, Europa, 1980.

* * *

McBAIN, Gordon D(uncan) III 1946-

PERSONAL: Born August 21, 1946, in Loma Linda, Calif.; son of Gordon D., Jr. (in U.S. Air Force) and Virginia (a writer; maiden name, Scharber) McBain. *Education:* San Bernardino Valley College, A.A., 1966; California State College,

San Bernardino, B.A., 1968; California State University, Northridge, Teaching Credential, 1970; California Lutheran College, M.S., 1978. *Home:* 3415 McLaughlin Ave., Los Angeles, Calif. 90066. *Office:* Palms Junior High School, 10860 Woodbine, Los Angeles, Calif. 90034.

CAREER: Los Angeles Unified Schools, Los Angeles, Calif., teacher, 1970-75, counselor, 1975-80, head counselor and administrator at Palms Junior High School, 1980—. *Member:* Authors Guild, California School Administrators, Association of Administrators of Los Angeles.

WRITINGS: The Path of Exoterra (science fiction novel), Avon, 1981; *Quest of the Dawnstar* (science fiction novel), Avon, 1982; *The Forsaken Fleet* (science fiction novel), Avon, 1983.

WORK IN PROGRESS: Twin Moons of Verdana, a science fiction novel, publication by Avon expected in 1984; research for a historical novel set in ancient Greece and for a contemporary novel.

SIDELIGHTS: McBain wrote: "My father taught me early about the stars; many years later my sister, Laurie McBain, urged me to write. My family moved often when I was a child. To amuse ourselves during summer break from school, my brother, sister, and I called on our imaginations. Those childhood games have surfaced in the space adventure of my novels and in the swashbuckling adventures my sister, Laurie, writes.

"People ask why I chose teenagers as the main characters in *The Path of Exoterra*—it just seemed natural after working twelve years in junior and senior high schools. My work in education has increased my understanding of people and helps in the creation of interesting characters regardless of setting—ancient or future. Recently I was asked what I thought was a problem facing urban teenagers today. Beyond the more obvious concerns that hit the headlines, I feel the failure to use the imagination—to dream—is a serious concern. So many of the beautiful things in our lives were the result of dreaming and imagination.

"In Los Angeles today children grow up under a blurred, starless sky; I treasure memories of a crisp, clear sky flooded with the starlight of countless suns. Once, on a trip to Peru, I found that beauty again—in the skies above Machu Picchu. This led me to use that locale in a scene of *Quest of the Dawnstar*. If I had to pick one all-time favorite novel it would be Richard Adams's *Watership Down*. The struggle of the rabbits to find a new future seems to parallel the fate of humankind in the years ahead. I like to think of humankind spreading into the stars, with colonies flourishing around distant stars."

AVOCATIONAL INTERESTS: Travel (including Europe, Egypt, South America, and Mexico).

* * *

McCALL, Dorothy Lawson 1889(?)-1982

OBITUARY NOTICE: Born c. 1889 in Boston, Mass.; died April 2, 1982, in Portland, Ore. Humanitarian and author. Daughter of copper baron Thomas W. Lawson and mother of former Oregon Governor Tom McCall, Dorothy McCall was known for her outspoken political comments, often in opposition to her son. She was also noted for her charitable activities, earning the title of outstanding mother of America in 1976. Among McCall's books are *Ranch Under the Rimrock,* an autobiography about life on her Oregon ranch, and *The Copper King's Daughter,* a tribute to her father. Obituaries and other sources: *Chicago Tribune,* April 5, 1982.

McCARR, Ken(neth George) 1903-1977

OBITUARY NOTICE: Born September 25, 1903, in Neillsville, Wis.; died May 6, 1977. Horseman and author. McCarr served as registrar of the United Trotting Horse Association for sixteen years and also as editor of *Horseman and Fair World. The Kentucky Harness Horse* is among his publications. (Date of death provided by wife, Mrs. Kenneth McCarr.)

* * *

McCLANE, Albert Jules 1922-

BRIEF ENTRY: Born January 26, 1922, in New York, N.Y. American editor and author. McClane, a registered fisheries research technician, began working as fishing editor of *Field and Stream* in 1942. In 1972 he became executive editor and has been editor-at-large since 1977. In that year he also became chairman of the board of directors of McClane Fishing Schools. He wrote *Fishing With McClane: Thirty Years of Angling With America's Foremost Fisherman* (Prentice-Hall, 1975), *The Encyclopedia of Fish Cookery* (Holt, 1977), and *McClane's Secrets of Successful Fishing* (Holt, 1980). He edited *McClane's Field Guide to Saltwater Fishes of North America: A Project of the Gamefish Research Association* (Holt, 1978) and *McClane's Field Guide to Freshwater Fishes of North America* (Holt, 1978). *Address:* 200 Queens Lane, Palm Beach, Fla. 33480; and 383 Madison Ave., New York, N.Y. 10017.

* * *

McCONNELL, Malcolm 1939-

PERSONAL: Born September 18, 1939, in Elmhurst, Ill.; son of Charles Fremont (an engineer) and Mary Edna (Mitchell) McConnell; married Carol Lynn Emery (an editor), June 10, 1981. *Education:* University of Wisconsin (now University of Wisconsin—Madison), B.A. (with honors), 1962; attended Alliance Francaise, 1957, and Foreign Service Institute. *Politics:* "Apolitical." *Religion:* Roman Catholic. *Home:* 350 Thunderbird Dr., No. 46, El Paso, Tex. 79912. *Office:* Department of English, University of Texas, El Paso, Tex. 79968.

CAREER: U.S. Foreign Service, Washington, D.C., stationed at American embassies in Rabat, Morocco, 1963-64, Leopoldville, Congo, 1965-66, Kigali, Rwanda, 1966-67, and Tangier, Morocco, 1967-69; free-lance writer in Lindos, Rhodes, Greece, 1969-77; Purdue University, West Lafayette, Ind., writer-in-residence, 1977-79; University of Texas, El Paso, visiting distinguished writer, 1980—. Visiting writer at St. Lawrence University, 1978-79. *Military service:* U.S. Army, 1957-58. *Awards, honors:* Fellow of National Endowment for the Arts, 1975.

WRITINGS: Matata (novel), Viking, 1971; *Clinton Is Assigned* (novel), Pocket Books, 1978; *Just Causes* (novel), Viking, 1981.

Contributor to magazines, including *Vogue, Sail, Yachting,* and *Cruising World,* and to newspapers.

WORK IN PROGRESS: Stepping Over, "novelistic nonfiction" about contemporary extremism.

SIDELIGHTS: McConnell told *CA:* "I draw on my experience as a foreign service officer and overseas journalist to write realistic action fiction concerned with the role of the individual and his morality in a world of rapid and confusing change.

"To me, the world of contemporary social and political turmoil as exemplified by the phenomenon of European terrorism and

American street crime—both 'irrational' manifestations of extremism—offers a valid and interesting area of investigation for the novelist. I find the array of confusing moral choices—often colored by extremist dogma—which young people are facing today to be a rich and varied subject for my novels. In *Matata* and *Just Causes,* I tried to portray young people caught up in the morally confusing and personally negating complexity of contemporary geopolitical struggles: the Third World and the underworld of European terrorism. I believe that the psychological extremes produced in these struggles, the hard choices between personal loyalties and group identities, to be both a compelling and important area for literary exploration: as valid now as they were for previous writers like Hemingway, Faulkner, and Fitzgerald. I think writers like Pynchon, V. S. Naipaul, and Robert Stone are exploring this new turmoil, and I'd like to follow suit.''

BIOGRAPHICAL/CRITICAL SOURCES: New York Times Book Review, September 21, 1971; *Washington Post,* September 29, 1971.

* * *

McCONNOR, Vincent

PERSONAL—Agent: Jane Jordan Browne, Multimedia Development, Inc., 410 South Michigan Ave., Room 828, Chicago, Ill. 60605.

CAREER: Writer, editor, and producer in New York, N.Y.; worked in radio, 1935-49, and in television, 1949-63; novelist, 1965—.

WRITINGS—Novels: The French Doll, Hill & Wang, 1965; *The Provence Puzzle: An Inspector Damiot Mystery,* Macmillan, 1980; *The Riviera Puzzle: An Inspector Damiot Mystery,* Macmillan, 1981; *The Paris Puzzle: An Inspector Damiot Mystery,* Macmillan, 1982.

Contributor of more than thirty short stories to periodicals, including *Esquire, MD, Alfred Hitchcock Mystery Magazine,* and *Ellery Queen Mystery Magazine.*

WORK IN PROGRESS: Another novel and two original screenplays.

* * *

McCRORY, Sanders
See COUNSELMAN, Mary Elizabeth

* * *

McCULLIN, Donald 1935-

BRIEF ENTRY: Born October 9, 1935, in London, England. British photojournalist. McCullin has been an award-winning photographer for the *Sunday Times* since 1967. He has covered war and famine in Vietnam, Cambodia, Biafra, the Congo, Israel, Cyprus, and Chad. McCullin wrote *The Destruction Business* (Open Gate Books, 1971) and *Homecoming* (St. Martin's, 1979). *Address:* Hill Farm, Levels Green, Farnham, Essex, England.

* * *

McGAW, Charles James 1910-1978

OBITUARY NOTICE: Born August 30, 1910, in Grand Rapids, Mich.; died April 8, 1978. Educator, theatre director, and author. Beginning in 1940 McGaw taught theatre at a number of American colleges, including Ohio State University, the University of Chicago, and the Art Institute of Chicago's Goodman Theatre and School of Drama, where he served as dean from 1966 to 1977. McGaw also acted as visiting professor and guest director at other universities and theatre organizations throughout his career. He wrote two books, *Acting Is Believing* and *Working a Scene.* Obituaries and other sources: *The Biographical Encyclopaedia and Who's Who of the American Theatre,* James Heineman, 1966; *Dictionary of American Scholars,* Volume II: *English, Speech, and Drama,* 6th edition, Bowker, 1974; *Notable Names in American Theatre,* James T. White, 1976; *Who Was Who in America, With World Notables,* Volume VII: *1977-1981,* Marquis, 1981.

* * *

McGINN, Matt 1928-1977

PERSONAL: Born January 17, 1928, in Glasgow, Scotland; died January 6, 1977; son of John (a laborer) and Helen (Havalan) McGinn; married Janette Gallacher (organizer of a citizens' advice bureau), July 7, 1950; children: Anna, Matt, Eleanor, Shonagh. *Education:* Ruskin College, Oxford, Diploma in Economic and Political History, 1960; Huddersfield Polytechnic, Teaching Certificate, 1961. *Politics:* Left-wing socialist. *Religion:* None.

CAREER: Writer, 1958-77. Singer and songwriter, teacher, and actor. Worked at a shipyard, 1958. *Military service:* British Army, 1948.

WRITINGS—Books of poems: Poems for Working Men, 1958; *Scottish Songs of Today,* 1964; *Once Again Matt McGinn,* 1972; *Fry the Little Fishes,* Calder & Boyars, 1975.

*WORK IN PROGRESS—At time of death: An autobiography; plays; stories and songs.

SIDELIGHTS: McGinn's wife, Janette, told *CA* that her husband's motivation for writing was ''to eliminate political and religious bigotry—a socialist system of society!''

* * *

McGOWAN, John J. 1936(?)-1982

OBITUARY NOTICE: Born c. 1936; died after a long illness, April 7, 1982, in Concord, Mass. Educator and economist. From 1965 to 1972 McGowan served as associate professor of economics at Yale University, leaving to become vice-president of Charles River Associates of Boston. He co-authored *Economic Aspects of Television Regulation* with Merton J. Peck. Obituaries and other sources: *New York Times,* April 11, 1982.

* * *

McGRORY, Mary 1918-

PERSONAL: Born August 22, 1918, in Boston, Mass.; daughter of Edward Patrick and Mary (Jacobs) McGrory. *Education:* Emmanuel College, A.B., 1939. *Residence:* Washington, D.C. *Office:* Washington Post, 1150 15th St. N.W., Washington, D.C. 20071; and Universal Press Syndicate, 4400 Johnson Dr., Fairway, Kan. 66205.

CAREER: Journalist. Houghton Mifflin Co., Boston, Mass., picture cropper, 1939-42; *Boston Herald Traveler,* Mass., 1942-47, began as secretary, became book reviewer; *Washington Evening Star,* Washington, D.C., book reviewer, 1947-54, feature writer, 1954-81; *Washington Post,* Washington, D.C., columnist, 1981—; Universal Press Syndicate, Fairway, Kan., syndicated columnist, 1981—. Volunteer at St. Ann's Infant

Home. *Awards, honors:* George Polk Memorial Award, 1962, for coverage of Richard Nixon's "farewell" press conference; Pulitzer Prize, 1975, for commentary.

WRITINGS: In Memorium: John Fitzgerald Kennedy, Evening Star Newspaper Co., 1963; "Talks at the National Press Club Luncheon" (recording), first broadcast by National Public Radio, November 5, 1976. Formerly contributor of articles on Washington front to *America.*

WORK IN PROGRESS: "Three columns a week."

SIDELIGHTS: Until 1954, Mary McGrory had been writing book reviews, stories about dogs, and profiles—things to which, in her eyes at least, "no one seemed to pay the slightest attention." Her "great breakthrough" came on April 23 of that year, when *Washington Star* editor Newbold Noyes, Jr., asked her to cover the Army-McCarthy hearings for the paper. Terrified, she was nevertheless delighted with the assignment. "I was *petrified!*," she recalled for Sara Sanborn of *Ms.* magazine. "I was paralyzed with fear! I didn't know anything, hadn't read anything." She wrote the story just as a news reporter would, but it fell short of everyone's expectations. So Noyes advised her to "write it like a letter to your favorite aunt," which McGrory did. Then "all of a sudden," she remembered, "people wanted to adopt me, marry me, poison me, run me out of town."

With her coverage of the hearings, McGrory developed a unique style, a "technique," wrote a *Time* reporter, "[that] is all her own." According to Duncan Spencer, who wrote for the *Washington Star* before it dissolved in 1981, McGrory's writing transmits to her readers her hunches, the mental pictures she forms in her observations. Relying on her instincts, the journalist searches the faces of common people and records their words, too. "They call her a columnist," Spencer pointed out, "but this is not quite it: She's a reporter. She has never been known not to leg a story. She doesn't write tips, scoops, rumors: She writes what she sees, what she hears, sometimes what people tell her; she writes what is on their faces, what their clothes or their pace shows—knowing with the sureness of good nerves what clues are given by the surface." With few opinions, McGrory only records her "powerful impressions." As she explained to *Time,* "I'm poor at summary, significance, relating—all I can do is respond."

In her reactions, the journalist communicates through what James Reston of the *New York Times* termed a "poet's gift of analogy" or the ability to make acute assessments with verbal illustrations. For example, one impression from the Army-McCarthy hearings described Robert Stevens, the Secretary of the Army, as "about as dangerous as an eagle scout leading his first patrol." In 1958 she portrayed a participant in the Adams-Goldfine hearing, stating: "Better you should ask a bear to dance than Mr. Goldfine to unravel personally this business of misbranded fabrics." She drew vice-president Nixon as one who "still stalks the light touch with all the grimness that the butterfly collectors bring to pursuit of a rare specimen." At his "farewell" press conference in 1962, Nixon, suggested McGrory, "was like a kamikaze pilot who keeps apologizing for the attack."

Not unexpectedly, McGrory's columns often rankled officials. As a self-proclaimed "Watergate junkie," her "daily hate Nixon articles" earned her the twentieth position on John Dean's enemies list, an honor McGrory holds to be the "nicest thing that ever happened" to her. Obsessed with the issue of Vietnam, McGrory wrote against her paper's editorial policy, producing perhaps her most angry, bitter columns. Sanborn, writing in *Ms.,* considered McGrory's "style of denunciation" to

be "the more deadly for its perfect decorum and control." She is "so gentle," Robert Kennedy once remarked, "so gentle—until she gets to the typewriter." McGrory agreed, admitting, "I can only be mean in writing."

Though a noted opinion maker, the journalist also has troubles. Uncooperative politicians will not talk to her, seldom returning her phone calls; some, she hinted in *Ms.,* push her off because she does not tote a television camera. McGrory often recounts an incident in which Senator John Stennis of Mississippi "said to me, 'Well now, Little Lady, I don't think I'd want to comment on that, Miss Mary.' Then he went down the hall and said to Roger Mudd, 'I'd like to tell you what we were talking about.'"

Perhaps McGrory's greatest difficulty is that she does not like to write. "[S]he hates to write and . . . it's hard for her," Spencer reported, "a fact that never shows for an instant on the surface of the graceful, spare prose, the one fair copy that didn't end in the wastebasket." A diligent writer, McGrory produces approximately four columns in five days, averaging 3400 words per week. But the constant demand for her writing makes her "anxious." "I'm always one step ahead of the sheriff," the writer found, though she told *CA:* "It's gotten better since I came to the *Post* and work under an earlier deadline."

McGrory's struggle with writing is not evident in the result, often characterized as "perceptive, pungent copy." "Mary is the tops—the best I've seen," said Lyle Wilson, formerly the United Press International (UPI) bureau chief for the *Washington Star.* "Her stuff stands up next day; it has survival value." Sanborn credited McGrory with "writing [that] is fully logical, but the logic is ethical and emotional, an acute comprehensive sense of what events mean to human beings." Then, when McGrory won the Pulitzer Prize in 1975, Noyes, one of the first to recognize the journalist's talents, questioned "why it took so long for her to win it."

In the face of public attention, McGrory guards her privacy. "I want to be read," she explained to a *Newsweek* reporter, "but I don't want to be a personality." "I'm a very private person," she continued in the *Ms.* interview. "If people want to know about me—well, I write in the paper four times every week."

AVOCATIONAL INTERESTS: Words, faces, cooking, gardening.

CA INTERVIEW

CA interviewed Mary McGrory, a syndicated political columnist, in the cafeteria at the *Washington Star* in the early afternoon on November 21, 1980.

CA: You began your career with the Boston Herald Traveler. *Why did you leave to join the staff of the* Washington Star?

McGRORY: I was stymied in Boston. I would have liked to do some reporting or feature writing, but it was out of the question. Blank wall. A friend of mine was driving to Washington about that time, and it so happened that I had written a letter to a great friend of mine, John Hutchens, who was then the book editor of the *New York Times* and who had been wonderful and encouraging and kind. I told him that I just wasn't happy, that I didn't like my situation. So he said that he had a great friend in Washington named Jay Carmody, who was the drama editor of the *Star,* and maybe there was something doing there. So he wrote to Jay Carmody; and we drove down; and I came to the *Star.* I met him and the Sunday editor.

They were looking for a book reviewer, it turned out. So they said, "Would you like?"

CA: What was holding you back in Boston?

McGRORY: Well, the book editor was a woman older than myself, and we didn't get on all that well. Then the managing editor just would not give me a chance. When I was syndicated, I understand that the *Boston Herald Traveler* made quite a bid for my column—one of life's meaner, smaller satisfactions.

CA: I'm assuming that being a book reviewer was not something you dreamed about as a little girl.

McGRORY: I loved to read, and I read all the time. I'm sure some people really want to be book reviewers. I'm sure they think of it as "book critic" or something like that, something a little more elegant. But that's what was available, so I was one for thirteen years.

CA: You said once that you were writing away on your book reviews or book criticisms or whatever, but no one paid any attention. Did you feel frustrated at the thought of no one noticing your work?

McGRORY: No, not particularly. I didn't mind. I didn't think I was a particularly good book reviewer. I was not offended or oppressed by it, but there's no question, when you get out into the news columns, the response is altogether different. People feel involved and feel they have to reproach you if you do wrong. There's much more connection with the reader.

CA: You progressed from a book reviewer to a feature writer before you became a columnist. How did that come about?

McGRORY: It wasn't even my idea. I really never wanted to be a columnist, either. I wanted to be a certain kind of reporter. I mean a reporter with a lot of latitude, allowed to laugh at things and all that.

CA: In some sense, you're doing that now. Aren't you?

McGRORY: It's still more in the legs than in the head. I like to see it and hear it. That's what I really like to do. I would like to write overnight features; that would be my ideal. But it didn't work out that way.

CA: Is there enough of a similarity between book reviewing and column writing so that generating reviews helped you write columns?

McGRORY: I don't think so. I think writing is hard—pick and shovel. And it doesn't get easier. That's the thing I really regret. For me, anyway, it doesn't get easier. Whatever form it's in, it turns out to be hard. The only think that isn't hard is writing letters.

CA: It's funny you should say that. When you were assigned to cover the Army-McCarthy hearings, didn't your editor suggest that you write the story as if you were writing a letter to your favorite aunt? That worked out, didn't it?

McGRORY: It did. It did. I used to write a lot to a favorite aunt, my Aunt Sarah, who was elderly and sick. I used to write to her all the time. Everybody likes to get mail, you know? Nobody's going to get mad at you for writing a letter. And it was very liberating when he said that.

CA: Did he know about Aunt Sarah?

McGRORY: No, but he was the kind of guy you didn't have to tell anything because he had the little man on the shoulder. He was an editor, just wonderful. Newbold Noyes—such an editor! A real St. Bernard, right with you all the time, rescuing you. Wonderful, wonderful.

CA: Could you name another person who was helpful to you?

McGRORY: When I met Walter Lippman, he said, "My dear, I hear you are to be syndicated." I said, "That's what they tell me." He said, "May I give you a word of advice? Ignore it. They will send you lists of papers that printed you but only used half the copy. They will send you lists of newspapers that have dropped you or newspapers that have picked you up or newspapers that have only printed one out of four. It will take all of your time. You will read those lists and think, 'Why did they drop me?' Pay no attention to it." I took his advice. I literally never saw any of those lists. To this day, it's up to them [the syndicate].

CA: Did politics ever start to bore you?

McGRORY: Never. It's awful, isn't it? It should by now. But it doesn't bore me at all. It really doesn't. It's the most entertaining thing possible. It involves high risk and excitement and suspense, human nature and comedy and tragedy. What more do you want?

CA: You've covered a number of campaigns. Do you prefer writing about campaigns to writing about other subjects?

McGRORY: Sure. The only thing worse than doing it is not doing it. It's absolute hell, war. Wasn't it Robert E. Lee who said, "It's lucky war is so dreadful because men love it so?"

CA: What do you particularly like about covering campaigns?

McGRORY: I don't know. Maybe I'm just a junkie. Well, there's always a chance that something will happen. Someone will say something absolutely irretrievable or idiotic or get mad or cry. Or he might say something interesting. Who knows? It's that endless possibility. When I was covering John Anderson, for instance, I would listen to him. I was interested in his ideas, not the big, set-piece ideas like the fifty cents gas tax. But when you'd ask him about a situation, just to see that intelligence gather itself together, to focus on it, to articulate it, that was very interesting to me.

CA: In your judgment, which of your columns have been your best?

McGRORY: I've written God knows how many, but I think two are OK, only two. One was the story of John Fitzgerald Kennedy's funeral, and the other was the account of a press conference with McGovern and Eagleton, when Eagleton finally got off the ticket in 1972. The rest of them can always be better. You know, Chaucer: "The life's so short, the craft's so long to lerne."

CA: What made those columns better than the others?

McGRORY: I guess because they were technically OK. I made a very important discovery when I was writing the Kennedy funeral story. I was working that whole weekend. I just kept moving all the time. Everybody here at the *Star* was wonderful. Everybody behaved just the way you'd like them to behave. You'd hear conversations between people on the desk: "You go home. You must be tired." "Oh, no. I came in after you.

Why don't you go home?'' ''I'm fine.'' Lots of kindness, helpfulness. Anyway, I just kept moving that whole time; I didn't stop. I guess a lot of people just sat and cried all weekend. I thought I was very lucky because I had something to do. I went to the funeral. I was with Bill Walton, who was a great friend of Kennedy. We were talking about Kennedy, and I think we forgot for a minute that he was dead. Then I said, ''Do you know I've got to go now and write his funeral?'' ''All right,'' he said. ''I'll tell you one thing, just one thing: No crap. OK?'' I said, ''That seems fair enough. I'll try.''

So I got back, and I couldn't do it, just couldn't do it. So soggy, so weighty, what do you say? It was so heavy it fell of its own weight. Victorian black crepe hanging, it was awful. Then I made a discovery. If you write short sentences, you can do it. It won't sink to the bottom, and it won't drag. So all the sentences were simple, declarative sentences. And then I got it moving. And once I got it moving, I could get through it.

The other one I like is good for the same reason. You know, all writing is movement. You read Mark Twain, and you notice that every single sentence advances the action, every paragraph. It's just movement, movement, movement, all the time. And that's the trick, I guess. But that's not the hard part. Not to be stodgy, not to be static, not to be toiling, that's the hard part. And transitions are very hard. The McGovern-Eagleton column worked because it had a fair amount of information in it, and it sort of moved around in the whole story of that unfortunate occurrence.

The rest, I never read them in the paper. I know if I do I will say, ''You idiot, why did you do that?'' I also still have trouble with the order of things, little things. I write the whole story, write the tag, and then say: ''Oh, that's the lead.'' You would think that I would be well beyond these troubles. The whole thing is to start it in the right place, isn't it? And I still don't do that.

CA: Have you noticed significant changes in your writing style over the years?

McGRORY: Oh, I think during the Vietnam period the tone was much angrier. It became more opinionated, less reporting, more opinion.

CA: One of your readers wrote you during that period and accused you of being nagging and bitter.

McGRORY: Oh, that's one of the milder ones. I was really angry in those years.

CA: You're less angry now?

McGRORY: Yes. There isn't that absolute daily outrage: people are dying; bombs are dropping. You have your feelings absolutely excoriated. You take the Christmas bombing [of Vietnam], for instance. I feel the same way today as I did then. I just couldn't handle it.

And the letters we used to get. From ''You communist bitch'' to ''You are saving my sanity. I thought I was the only person who felt this way, and I never heard anyone say it until you wrote it. At least I know I have not lost my mind.'' That kind of thing. So there was a much greater sense of urgency then.

Now you point out the ironies and the contradictions; you're amused and bemused by it. There are grave injustices, terrible injustices, and there probably will be more. I daresay I will become more and more excited as I see that we're spending all this money for MX missiles while people are going hungry.

CA: In your earlier columns, more often than now, you sought out someone, say, in a campaign crowd, to comment on what was going on. And then you used that comment as a peg for a story. You don't seem to do that as much anymore.

McGRORY: Well, I talk to voters all the time. Political headquarters are by and large a waste of time. There may be one really shrewd person there who knows what's going on and has the plan in mind, but you hear things on the street you wouldn't hear at the Woodrow Wilson Center or the Library of Congress or the United States Senate. People have really doped things out and can express them very cogently.

The minute a speech begins, I am right out into the crowd, asking: ''What do you think?'' and ''How do you like him?'' In the New Hampshire primary, the first thing I did was go out with a Kennedy canvasser, a very polite, well-groomed, nonthreatening, nonprovocative kind of person. We went to blue-collar houses to see the reactions to Kennedy there, without any provocation from the young man. He didn't have long hair. He didn't hassle them. You could see that there were some very deep feelings about the senator. It was only when I got on the street that I got some idea about the emotional part of the problem.

In New York and Massachusetts, I like to talk to the politicians because they're very sharp and astute, and they follow it. Most of them are a little detached, and they enjoy it very much and like to talk about it the way some people like to talk about baseball, the fine points, the faults. In other states, they can be a little more ideological, a little more committed. They take it a little more seriously. But in those two states it's fun.

CA: Why did you turn down the job offers from James ''Scotty'' Reston of the New York Times?

McGRORY: Well, the famous one was the one where I was to come on sort of a trial basis and spend part of my time working on the switchboard.

CA: What would you do if you got a decent offer from the New York Times?

McGRORY: Well, to be honest about the *Times,* I always thought they got a kick out of reading [my column] in another paper. But if it came over the wire from their Washington bureau, someone would say, ''We can't print this.'' My kind of irreverent approach wouldn't work there.

CA: What happened when your columns and the Star's *editorials disagreed? Or did that ever happen?*

McGRORY: Yes, it did. At the time of the invasion of Cambodia, which we supported editorially, I was in a screaming, slashing state. So I went to the editor and said, ''I think I ought to resign.'' And he said, ''Sit down. Don't be ridiculous. I don't care what you write, just write it for us.'' That was Newby [Newbold] Noyes—never interfered, never. They believed in freedom of speech at the *Star.*

CA: You haven't mentioned it, but I get the impression you may have had to face some discrimination being a woman in what was at that time largely a male profession.

McGRORY: It wasn't that tough. I'm sorry. I'm a traitor to my sex, but it really wasn't that bad—once I got out there. And there are advantages. I guess all wrong by today's standards. You'd be the only woman, and you were treated very nicely: doors were held; baggage was carried; jokes were made.

It was very pleasant. I was patronized a great deal, condescended to. It was part of it. I thought, "Well, OK. Go ahead. Be my guest. I'll show you." But I was never confrontational. I always waited until I got to the typewriter.

It was always maddening, particularly with the Southerners. I would go up to [Senator] John Stennis after a closed budget hearing and ask him something, and he'd say, "Now, Miss Mary, little lady." (Pat me on the shoulder.) "I couldn't talk about that; it's an executive matter." Then he'd go down the hall; and Roger Mudd would be there with a microphone and camera; and he'd tell him everything that happened.

I think a lot of politicians still have trouble with a woman reporter. When I first started out, they thought I was related to the candidate, that I must be Kennedy's cousin. I went to a meeting with Averill Harriman years and years ago, and the press aide was trying to figure it out. "You're one of the volunteers from Westchester?" I said no. "You're on the governor's staff?" I said, "No. I'm a reporter." Well, of course he accepted it, but reluctantly. But it really didn't bother me that much. It really didn't. There are pluses and minuses. Not so much now, but then the politician, whoever he was, would sort of play to you. We could have a little badinage and banter and so forth. You were sort of used to create a slightly more social climate in order to try to keep you off the hot stuff. There was a lot of that.

CA: What do you think of your fellow columnists?

McGRORY: I read 'em.

CA: What do you think of the state of column writing these days?

McGRORY: That's a subject I never think about. That isn't arrogance. It's just that, when you write for a living, you don't do nothin' else. I mean the sheriff is ever at your heels. You always have to fill up that space.

We have [Jack] Germond and [Jules] Witcover who are immensely informative. David Broder, who used to sit behind me at the *Star*—I find his writing very graceful and illuminating, although he's a little bit in love with structure. He likes political parties more than I do, but he has an admirable tone to what he writes, always reasonable but not smarmy or bland. George Will, of course, is very literate. [William] Safire is much more of an investigative reporter. He did some really showy stuff on Billy [Carter] and Bert Lance. I like him best on the attack.

CA: Does the fact that he came from the Nixon administration bother you?

McGRORY: It did for a long time, and I made a very mean crack. Somebody from *Time*, when Safire started out, called me up and asked me what I thought. I said, "Oh, I hate to criticize a colleague, but then I don't think of him as one," which was mean, very low. But I did think that he was embarking on a very dubious crusade—to prove that all politicians were as rotten as Richard Nixon—which I didn't think was a very worthy enterprise. But I think he seems to have earned a place for himself.

We [the *Star*] now have Rod McLeish, very light, very good. But I think the pendulum is maybe swinging the other way a little bit. [James J.] Kilpatrick's nature columns I enjoy, but the politics I do not. Bill Buckley's tireless defense of the fascists in South America just wears me out. I'm sorry to say we've added an ex-CIA official to our list of columnists, Cord

Meyer, which drives me crazy. [Rowland] Evans and [Robert] Novak are finding [President] Reagan insufficiently conservative. They do some excellent political reporting but tend to be a little bit melodramatic, and the metaphors really do get mangled. Their writing's a bit lurid, and they really do get excited about weaponry and tactics.

CA: At one point you said you wanted to be read, but you didn't want to become a public personality. Why not?

McGRORY: I don't like to make speeches because I really don't know anything. I know little specific things, like how to write a sad story and make it bearable by writing short sentences. I know that. I really have spent my life in the trees, and I don't know what the forest looks like. I don't have much of a grasp on abstractions. That's why I don't make speeches. I don't know what it all means. Don't ask me. And I think you're so vulnerable if you write. Out of twenty-four columns, maybe two have some validity or have a shelf life of more than twelve hours. And if you're going to make speeches, you have to have a general idea.

I really like it [writing columns] very much. It's what I want to do and what I like to do, even though I find it difficult. But on the big picture, I'm very poor. The trick is to relate one thing to another: what happened before and how it effects the present. The fascination, of course, is the challenge. In the first place, it could always be better, and in the second place, no matter how much research you do, there's always one more thing you could have found out or tried to.

BIOGRAPHICAL/CRITICAL SOURCES: Time, November 10, 1958; *Newsweek,* March 21, 1960, April 1, 1968; *New York Times,* March 13, 1971, January 3, 1973, June 18, 1973, June 28, 1973, February 11, 1974, May 2, 1974, May 6, 1975, May 7, 1975, May 8, 1975, February 16, 1976, May 25, 1980; *Ms.,* May, 1975; *Biography News,* May, 1975; *Washington Star,* May 6, 1975; *Authors in the News,* Volume II, Gale, 1976; *Field and Stream,* October, 1980.

—Sketch by Charity Anne Dorgan

—Interview by Peter Benjaminson

*   *   *

McHALE, Tom   1942(?)-1982

OBITUARY NOTICE—See index for *CA* sketch: Born c. 1942 in Scranton, Pa.; died of a heart attack (some sources say suicide), March 30, 1982, in Pembroke Pines, Fla. Novelist. McHale wrote black comedies about the conflicts between middle-class Irish and Italian Catholics. His books received enthusiastic reviews, and in 1976 McHale won the Thomas More Medal for his fourth novel, *School Spirit.* His other publications include *Principato, Farragan's Retreat,* and *The Lady From Boston.* Obituaries and other sources: *Time,* April 26, 1982; *Publishers Weekly,* April 30, 1982.

*   *   *

McKAY, George Frederick   1899-1970

OBITUARY NOTICE: Born June 11, 1899, in Harrington, Wash.; died October 4, 1970, in Stateline, Nev. Composer, educator, and author. McKay served as professor of music at the University of Washington from 1941 until his retirement in 1968. He was a prolific composer, producing symphonies, chamber music, and works for band and chorus. His works include "Seattle Centennial Symphony," "Fantasy on a Western Folk Song," and "Organ Sonata," which won first prize from the

American Guild of Organists. McKay also wrote two books, *The Technic of Modern Harmony* and *Creative Orchestration.* Obituaries and other sources: *Biographical Dictionary of American Music,* Parker Publishing, 1973; *Baker's Biographical Dictionary of Musicians,* 6th edition, Schirmer Books, 1978; *The ASCAP Biographical Dictionary of Composers, Authors, and Publishers,* 4th edition, Cattell, 1980.

*   *   *

McKNIGHT, Brian Emerson   1938-

PERSONAL: Born June 10, 1938, in Philadelphia, Pa.; son of Donald G. and Isobel K. (Allison) McKnight; married Patricia Ann Morrow, April 26, 1962; children: Jennifer, Ian, Matthew. *Education:* University of Chicago, A.B., 1960, M.A., 1964, Ph.D., 1968. *Office:* Department of History, University of Hawaii—Manoa, Honolulu, Hawaii 96822.

CAREER: North Park College, Chicago, Ill., lecturer in history and political science, 1964-65; University of Nebraska, Lincoln, assistant professor of history, 1965-70; University of Hawaii—Manoa, Honolulu, associate professor, 1970-75, professor of history, 1975—, chairman of department, 1981—, member of board of directors of Center for Asian and Pacific Studies. *Member:* Association for Asian Studies. *Awards, honors:* Younger humanist fellow of National Endowment for the Humanities, 1974-75.

WRITINGS: Village and Bureaucracy in Southern Sung China, University of Chicago Press, 1972; (contributor) John W. Haeger, editor, *Crisis and Prosperity in Sung China,* University of Arizona Press, 1975; *T'sung-shu So-yin Sung-wen Tzu-mu* (title means "Works by Sung Dynasty Authors Extant in Collectanea"), Chinese Materials Center (Taipei, Taiwan), 1977; *The Quality of Mercy: Amnesties in Traditional Chinese Justice,* University Press of Hawaii, 1981; *The Washing Away of Wrongs: Forensic Medicine in Thirteenth-Century China,* Center for Chinese Studies (Ann Arbor, Mich.), 1981; (editor) *Law and the State in Traditional East Asia: Six Studies on the Sources of East Asian Law,* University Press of Hawaii, in press. Contributor to Asian studies journals. Editor of *Asian Studies.*

WORK IN PROGRESS: "Law in Sung China," a chapter in Denis Turtchett's *The Cambridge History of China* for Cambridge University Press.

*   *   *

McLAREN, Colin Andrew   1940-

PERSONAL: Born December 14, 1940, in Eastcote, Middlesex, England; son of Kenneth George (a meteorologist) and Elizabeth Maxwell (a teacher; maiden name, Raisbeck) McLaren; married Janice Patricia Foale (a medical sociologist), March 25, 1964; children: Judith Rebecca, Justin Benedict. *Education:* University of London, B.A., 1963, M.Phil., 1973. *Residence:* Aberdeen, Scotland. *Office:* The Library, King's College, University of Aberdeen, Aberdeen, Scotland.

CAREER: London County Council, London, England, assistant archivist, 1963-65; University of London, London, research assistant, 1965-67; London Borough of Hammersmith, London, archivist, 1967-69; University of Aberdeen, Aberdeen, Scotland, archivist and keeper of manuscripts, 1969—. *Awards, honors:* Festival Fringe First Award from Edinburgh Festival, 1976.

WRITINGS—Adult fiction; published by Rex Collins: *Rattus Rex,* 1978; *Crows in a Winter Landscape,* 1979; *Mother of the*

Free, 1980; *A Twister Over the Thames,* 1981; *The Warriors Under the Stone,* 1982.

Plays; first produced in Edinburgh, Scotland, at Edinburgh Festival: (With W.J.S. Kirton) "STG 75" (revue), 1975; "An Exotic in Edinburgh" (one-act), 1976; (with Kirton) "STG 76" (revue), 1976; "The Anatomy Lesson" (one-act), 1977; (with Kirton) "ARC 1" (revue), 1977.

Radio plays; first broadcast by British Broadcasting Corp. (BBC-Radio): "An Exotic in Edinburgh" (based on own one-act play), 1977; "Round Tower Tales," 1980; "Thirty-nine and Counting," 1981; "Six From South Kensington," 1982.

Contributor of stories and articles to *Look and Listen.*

SIDELIGHTS: McLaren told *CA:* "When I was young I quickly picked up my parents' enthusiasm for historical fiction and cannot now remember a time when I did not intend to write it. By the age of ten, however, I realized that a writer's life was a lot more comfortable if he had a profession to support him and discovered, to my astonishment, that if I became an archivist, people would actually pay me a salary for doing what I most enjoyed—reading and deciphering historical documents. I therefore did what was necessary at school and university to enter that profession. Once I was established in it, I served the usual apprenticeship of writing for magazines and the stage and published my first novel when I was thirty-seven, two years later than I had intended. I have no other interests or occupations beyond reading the (*London*) *Times* and watching a decent game of rugby or cricket."

*   *   *

McLAREN, Ian Francis   1912-

PERSONAL: Born March 30, 1912, in Launceston, Australia; son of Alexander Morrison (a draper) and Elsie Elizabeth (Gibbins) McLaren; married Eileen Adele Porter, April 16, 1941; children: Andrew Forbes, Ailsa Louise McLaren McLeary, Neil Stuart, Ian Hugh. *Education:* University of Melbourne, Dip.Com., 1954. *Home:* 237 Waverley Rd., East Malvern, Victoria 3145, Australia.

CAREER: Chartered accountant, 1930-36; associated with Argus & Australasian Ltd., 1936-38; secretary of Davies Coop. N.S.W. Ltd., 1939-41; Victorian Legislative Assembly, Independent member of assembly for Glen Iris, 1945-47; chartered accountant, 1947-65; Victorian Legislative Assembly, Liberal member of assembly for Caulfield, 1965-67, and for Bennettswood, 1967-79, deputy speaker, 1973-79, chairman of Parliamentary Liberal Federal Affairs Committee, delegate to Australian Constitutional Convention, 1973-79; director of Nicholas Kiwi Ltd., 1981—. Writer, 1954—. President of Caulfield Technical College, 1951-52. Chairman of Victoria Federation of Co-operative Housing Societies, 1946-49, Wyperfeld National Park, 1946-57, Australian Institute of Political Science, 1953-54, Good Neighbour Council of Victoria, 1955-58, Estate Agents Committee, 1956-65, and Australian Wool Testing Authority, 1964-65. Member of board of directors of Kiwi International Co. Ltd., 1952-81, Gas and Fuel Corp. of Victoria, 1958-65, Power Corp. Australia Ltd., and Victoria Portland Cement Co.; member of Commission for Taking Declarations and Affadavits, 1946—; member of Malvern City Council, 1951-53, council of University of Melbourne, 1977-79, National Fitness Council of Victoria, and Youth Advisory Council of Victoria. *Military service:* Royal Australian Naval Volunteer Reserve, active duty, 1940-45; served in Papua New Guinea, Dutch New Guinea, and the Philippines; became lieutenant.

MEMBER: World Council of Young Men's Christian Associations (vice-president, 1961-69), International Association of Y's Men's Clubs (director-at-large, 1938-39; vice-president, 1952-54), Royal Institute of Public Administration (fellow), Bibliographical Society of Australia and New Zealand, Institute of Chartered Accountants (fellow), Chartered Institute of Secretaries (associate), Private Libraries Association, Australian Young Men's Christian Association (national president, 1948-65; member of national council, 1958-62; member of board of governors, 1978), Royal Historical Society of Victoria (fellow; president, 1956-59), Book Collectors' Society of Victoria (president, 1965), Former Victorian Parliamentary Executive Members Association, Youth Hostels Association of Victoria (president, 1947-48). *Awards, honors:* Officer of Order of the British Empire, 1959; honorary bibliographer of library at University of Melbourne, 1975.

WRITINGS: Local History in Australia, R.H.S.V. (Melbourne), 1954; *History of Latrobe Valley,* R.H.S.V., 1957; *Como,* R.H.S.V., 1957; *Australian Aviation: A Bibliographical Survey,* Ballarat, 1958; (author of introduction) Henry H. Lawson, *The Ghosts of Many Christmases,* Hawthorn Press, 1958; *All Saints, St. Kilda* [Melbourne], 1958; *The Burke and Wills Tragedy,* R.H.S.V., 1960; *McEvoy Mine Disaster,* R.H.S.V., 1962; *William Wills,* R.H.S.V., 1963; *Edward Edgar Pescott, 1872-1954,* R.H.S.V., 1965; *How Victoria Began,* R.H.S.V., 1968; *In the Wake of Flinders,* R.H.S.V., 1974; *C. J. Dennis: A Comprehensive Bibliography Based on the Collection of the Compiler,* Libraries Board of South Australia, 1979; *C. J. Dennis in the Herald,* Dalriade Press, 1981; *Marcus Clarke,* State Library of Victoria, 1981; *C. J. Dennis Contributions to Literary Magazines,* State Library of South Australia, 1976; *Talking About C. J. Dennis,* Monash University Press, 1982; *Annotated Bibliography of Marcus Clarke,* State Library of Victoria, 1982; *Rolf Boldrewood, A. L. Gordon, Henry Lawson: State Bibliography,* Dalriade Press, 1983.

WORK IN PROGRESS: Research on Irish rebellions that resulted in transportation to Australia.

SIDELIGHTS: McLaren's forty-thousand-volume library, now housed at the University of Melbourne, was begun in 1943, and grew rapidly during the collector's years in political office. McLaren's collection focuses on Australian history, particularly events such as the industrial revolution, and riots and rebellions that led to transportation or immigration to Australia.

BIOGRAPHICAL/CRITICAL SOURCES: Age, January 26, 1963; *The Library of Ian F. McLaren,* Hawthorn Press, 1974.

* * *

McLAURIN, Anne 1953-
(Anne Laurin)

PERSONAL: Born September 29, 1953, in St. Louis, Mo.; daughter of John Robert (a businessman) and Carol Jean (a businesswoman; maiden name, Tripp) McLaurin. *Education:* University of California, Los Angeles, B.S., 1977; attended University of Edinburgh, 1977-78. *Religion:* Baptist. *Home:* 2346 31st St., Santa Monica, Calif. 90405.

CAREER: Curtis Brown Ltd., London, England, assistant literary agent, 1978-79; free-lance writer, 1978—; G. K. Hall & Co., Boston, Mass., assistant editor, 1979-80. *Awards, honors: Little Things* was named a notable book by the American Library Association, 1978.

WRITINGS—Under pseudonym Anne Laurin: *Little Things* (juvenile; illustrated by Marcia Sewall), Atheneum, 1978; *Perfect Crane,* Harper, 1980.

WORK IN PROGRESS: Saying Goodbye to the Moon, a novel for young readers; *Circus,* a novel for adults.

* * *

McLEAN, Susan 1937-

PERSONAL: Surname is pronounced Mc-*Lane;* born March 26, 1937, in Hibbing, Minn.; daughter of Louis Hamilton (an accountant) and Hildur (a teacher; maiden name, Bertel) Hunter; married Austin Jersey McLean (a librarian), September 3, 1960; children: Sara Gillian (deceased). *Education:* Hanover College, B.A., 1959. *Residence:* Minneapolis, Minn. *Agent:* Dorothy Pittman, Illington Rd., Ossining, N.Y. 10562.

CAREER: Encyclopaedia Britannica, Inc., Chicago, Ill., library research specialist, 1959-60; Michigan State University Press, East Lansing, editorial assistant and production manager, 1960-62, book indexer, 1962-68; writer, 1972—.

WRITINGS: Pennies for the Piper (juvenile), Farrar, Straus, 1981.

WORK IN PROGRESS: The Silver Butterfly, a myth; *Echoes,* a first-person narrative beginning in the early 1930's.

SIDELIGHTS: Susan McLean wrote: "In 1976, on a rainy afternoon shortly after Memorial Day, I was walking past St. Mary's Cemetery in south Minneapolis. I saw a coffee can filled with wilted lilacs on a grave near the fence, and speculated about who might have placed them there. In *Pennies for the Piper,* I tried to explain, for a child's viewpoint, what sorrow is—how it feels to lose someone you love.

"My muse is a very large, ersatz Siamese cat, with white feet, an apple face, and big blue eyes, who *must* sit to my left whenever I'm working."

* * *

McLENDON, James (Nelson) 1942-1982

OBITUARY NOTICE—See index for *CA* sketch: Born March 7, 1942, in Gainsville, Fla.; died of cancer, March 12 (some sources say March 11), 1982, in Charlotte, N.C. Author of *Deathwork* and *Eddie Macon's Run,* the first two in a planned series of four novels concerning human freedom. The third novel of the series, *Swagman,* was unpublished at the time of McLendon's death, but movie rights to all three books have been sold. Obituaries and other sources: *Chicago Tribune,* March 14, 1982; *Publishers Weekly,* April 9, 1982.

* * *

McMURRY, Linda O. 1945-

PERSONAL: Born October 24, 1945, in Montgomery, Ala.; daughter of William B. (an accountant) and Tressie (a dental assistant; maiden name, James) Ott; married James W. Hines, January 22, 1967 (divorced December, 1978); married Richard M. McMurry (a historian), July 12, 1980; children: Parie Lynn Hines; stepsons: Brian, Jonathan. *Education:* Emory University, A.A., 1964; Auburn University, B.A., 1968, M.A., 1972, Ph.D., 1976. *Politics:* Democrat. *Home:* 3212 Caldwell Dr., Raleigh, N.C. 27607. *Office:* Department of History, North Carolina State University, Raleigh, N.C. 27650.

CAREER: Auburn University at Montgomery, Montgomery, Ala., adjunct instructor, 1976; Valdosta State College, Valdosta, Ga., assistant professor, 1976-79, associate professor of history, 1979-81; North Carolina State University, Raleigh, N.C., associate professor of history, 1981—. *Member:* Organization of American Historians, Southern Historical Association, Association for the Study of Afro-American Life and History, Phi Kappa Phi, Phi Alpha Theta. *Awards, honors:* Ambassador of Honor award from Books-Across-the-Sea, 1982, for *George Washington Carver: Scientist and Symbol.*

WRITINGS: George Washington Carver: Scientist and Symbol, Oxford University Press, 1981. Contributor to articles to periodicals, including *Journal of Negro History, Agricultural History,* and *Phylon.*

WORK IN PROGRESS: A biography of Monroe Nathan Work, publication by Louisiana State University Press expected in 1983.

SIDELIGHTS: In her first book, Linda O. McMurry writes of the famous black agriculturist, George Washington Carver, who was born to Missouri slaves, but raised by the Carver family. A gifted student, Carver sought a college education, studying agriculture at Iowa State College. In the midst of racial discrimination and segregation, Carver had to struggle to receive his education. But the Jim Crow laws did not make Carver bitter. Instead of fighting the system, he joined it, making friends among the white students. He went on to join the faculty of Tuskegee Institute, becoming the nation's first black manager of an agricultural experiment station. During his tenure at Tuskegee, Carver sought to improve the life of black sharecroppers and to promote the peanut for industrial uses.

McMurry's volume on Carver captures both the legends of the man and the lesser-known facts about him, telling of his devotion to God, his love of art, and his failure at romantic pursuits. James H. Jones of the *New York Times Book Review* applauded McMurry's effort. "Without being blind to his faults, she has managed to leave us with the portrait of a gifted teacher, a gentle spirit, a keen intelligence and a loving friend. The Carver who emerges in these pages is not enough to sustain the myth, but more than enough to touch our hearts."

McMurry told *CA:* "Growing up and going to school in a white suburb of Atlanta, I met few blacks and read about even fewer in my textbooks. One black always mentioned, however, was George Washington Carver. By the time I entered college, the civil rights movement had enhanced my childhood interest in the role of blacks in American society. When I arrived in Auburn, I soon learned that Tuskegee Institute was only a half-hour's drive away and visited the campus. My general interest in black history soon became focused on that famous black school when I entered graduate school, largely due to its proximity. Carver was a natural subject to explore, and I became fascinated with the complexity of his personality and endeavors. His vision is inspiring to a world struggling to face the fact of diminishing resources, and his life story reflects the great tragedy of racism."

BIOGRAPHICAL/CRITICAL SOURCES: New York Times Book Review, November 8, 1981.

*   *   *

McNAUGHT, Harry

PERSONAL: Born in Scotland; children: four. *Education:* Attended Philadelphia Museum School of Art. *Address:* c/o Random House, Inc., 201 East 50th St., New York, N.Y. 10022.

CAREER: Writer and illustrator of books for young people.

*WRITINGS—*Self-illustrated; juveniles: *Five Hundred Words to Grow On,* Random House, 1973; *Baby Animals,* Random House, 1976; *Trucks,* Random House, 1976; *Animal Babies,*

Random House, 1977; *Muppets in My Neighborhood,* Random House, 1977; *The Truck Book,* Random House, 1978.

Illustrator: (With Herschel Wartik) Herbert Zim and others, *Photography,* Golden Press, 1964; Hedy Baklin-Landman and Edna Shapiro, *The Story of Porcelain,* Odyssey, 1965; Adelaide Holl and Seymour Reit, *Time and Measuring,* Golden Book Educational Services, 1966; Melvin Keene, *Beginners' Story of Minerals and Rocks,* Harper, 1966; Peter Farb, *Land, Wildlife, and Peoples of the Bible,* Harper, 1967; (with Charles J. Berger) Norman Lloyd, *Golden Encyclopedia of Music,* Golden Press, 1968; Eugene Rachlis and Katherine Rachlis, *Our Fifty United States,* Golden Press, 1974; Sarah Riedman, *Heart,* Golden Press, 1974; B. G. Ford, *Do You Know?,* Random House, 1979.*

*   *   *

McQUOWN, Norman Anthony   1914-

BRIEF ENTRY: Born January 30, 1914, in Peoria, Ill. American anthropologist, educator, and author. McQuown joined the faculty at University of Chicago in 1946 and became a professor of anthropology in 1958. He has taught at universities in Spain, South America, Mexico, and West Germany, and conducted anthropological research in Mexico. His books include *Spoken Turkish: Basic Course,* two volumes (Linguistic Society of America, 1944-45), *Ensayos de antropologia en la Zona Central de Chiapas* (Instituto Nacional Indigenista, 1970), *The Natural History of an Interview,* four volumes (Library, University of Chicago, 1971), *American Indian Linguistics in New Spain* (Humanities, 1976), and *Language, Culture, and Education: Essays* (Stanford University Press, 1981). *Address:* 5708 South Drexel Ave., Chicago, Ill. 60637; and Department of Anthropology, University of Chicago, 1126 East 59th St., Chicago, Ill. 60637. *Biographical/critical sources: Directory of American Scholars,* Volume III: *Foreign Languages, Linguistics, and Philology,* 7th edition, Bowker, 1978.

*   *   *

McRAE, William John   1933-

PERSONAL: Born April 8, 1933, in Toronto, Ontario, Canada; son of William B. (a wholesaler) and Jean (a teacher; maiden name, Anderson) McRae; married Marilyn Eve Lockridge; children: Mary-Lynn, Elisabeth, Janice, Mark. *Education:* Toronto Teachers College, graduated, 1956; Queen's University, B.A., 1966; Dallas Theological Seminary, Th.M., 1970, doctoral study. *Home:* 71 Killarney Rd., London, Ontario, Canada N5X 2A6. *Office:* North Park Community Chapel, 1470 Glendra Dr., London, Ontario, Canada N5Y 1V2.

CAREER: Ordained minister; teacher at public schools in Renfrew, Ontario, 1956-58; director at Camp Mini-Yo-We; itinerant teacher, minister, and leader of Camp Galilee in the Ottaway Valley area of Ontario, 1958-64; minister at gospel chapel in Kingston, Ontario, 1964-66, and chapel in Dallas, Tex., 1966-75; pastor at North Park Community Chapel, London, Ontario. Public speaker; conducts camps, conferences, youth seminars, and workshops, and tours to the Holy Land.

WRITINGS: Dynamics of Spiritual Gifts, Zondervan, 1976; *Preparing for Your Marriage,* Zondervan, 1980. Contributor to magazines, including *Focus.*

WORK IN PROGRESS: The Birth of the Bible.

SIDELIGHTS: McRae commented: "The primary direction of my ministry is the building of strong, healthy, well-balanced lives and homes." *Avocational interests:* Athletics (especially football and tennis).

McROBERTS, Agnesann
See MEEK, Pauline Palmer

* * *

McVICKAR, Elinor Guthrie 1902(?)-1982

OBITUARY NOTICE: Born c. 1902 in New Orleans, La.; died after a short illness, April 15, 1982, in New York, N.Y. Executive and fashion editor. McVickar began her fashion career in 1926 as an editor for *Harper's Bazaar,* where she worked intermittently until 1969. She was also the first editor of *Modern Bride* magazine, from 1950 to 1954, and served in an executive capacity for such firms as Saks Fifth Avenue, Dorothy Gray, and Helena Rubenstein. Obituaries and other sources: *New York Times,* April 17, 1982.

* * *

MEAD, Sidney Moko 1927-

PERSONAL: Born January 8, 1927, in Wairoa, New Zealand; son of Sidney Montague (a contractor) and Paranihia Mead; married June Te Rina (a teacher), October 22, 1950. *Education:* University of Auckland, B.A., 1964, M.A., 1965; University of Southern Illinois, Ph.D., 1968. *Politics:* Mana Motuhake (Independence Party). *Religion:* Anglican. *Home:* 10 Spiers St., Karori, Wellington N.2, New Zealand. *Office:* Department of Maori, Victoria University of Wellington, Private Bag, Wellington, New Zealand.

CAREER: Art and craft specialist, 1947-51; head teacher at schools in New Zealand, 1951-70; University of Auckland, Auckland, New Zealand, senior lecturer in Maori studies, 1970-71; McMaster University, Hamilton, Ontario, Canada, associate professor of anthropology, 1971-72 and 1973-77; Victoria University of Wellington, Wellington, New Zealand, professor of Maori, 1977—. Chairman of Horouta-Ki-Poneke Marae Society; member of board of directors of Ngati Awa Trust and council of National Art Gallery; member of New Zealand Council for Educational Research. *Member:* Pacific Arts Association, Polynesian Society. *Awards, honors:* Canadian Commonwealth research fellowship for University of British Columbia, Vancouver, Canada, 1972-73.

*WRITINGS—*Published by A. H. & A. W. Reed (Wellington, New Zealand), except as noted: *Taniko Weaving,* 1952; *We Speak Maori,* 1959; (editor with Bruce Biggs and Patrick Hohepa) *Selected Readings in Maori,* 1959, revised edition, University of Auckland, 1963, revised edition with illustrations by Mead, 1967; *The Art of Taniko Weaving: A Study of Its Context, Technique, Style, and Developments,* 1968; *Traditional Maori Clothing: A Study of Technological and Functional Change,* 1969; (translator into modern text with G. C. Petersen) *Portraits of the New Zealand Maori Painted in 1844 by George French Angas,* 1972.

Material Culture and Art in the Star Harbour Region, Eastern Solomons (monograph), Royal Ontario Museum, 1973; (with L. Birks, H. Birks, and E. Shaw) *The Lapita Pottery Style of Fiji and Its Associations,* Polynesian Society, 1975; *Exploring the Visual Art of Oceania,* University Press of Hawaii, 1979. Also author of *The Art of Maori Carving,* 1961; *The Costume Styles of Classical Maori in New Zealand,* 1969.

In Maori: *Ko Te Tahae Nei ko Tawhaki* (title means "This Fellow Tawhaki"), 1960; (editor with Biggs) *He Kohikohinga Aronui* (title means "A Collection of Valuable Texts"), 1964;

Nga Taonga Tuki Iho a Ngati Awa: The Writings of Hamiora Tumutara Te Tihi-o-te-whenua Pio, 1885-87, 1981.

WORK IN PROGRESS: A history of the Ngati Awa tribe, publication expected in 1983; a biography of a Ngati Awa chief, 1984; editing books on Maori art, 1984 and 1985.

SIDELIGHTS: Mead wrote: "I am concerned with Maori rights in New Zealand and with the right of home rule; also, the plight of my own Ngati Awa tribe, of the North Island's Bay of Plenty."

* * *

MEDDAUGH, Susan 1944-

PERSONAL: Surname is pronounced Med-aw; born October 4, 1944, in Montclair, N.J.; daughter of John Stuart (a naval captain) and Justine (Leach) Meddaugh. *Education:* Wheaton College, Norton, Mass., B.A., 1966. *Home and office:* 46 Monument Sq., Charlestown, Mass. 02129.

CAREER: Houghton Mifflin, Co., Boston, Mass., trade division of children's book department, designer and art director, 1968-78; writer and illustrator of children's books, 1978—.

WRITINGS: Too Short Fred (juvenile; self-illustrated), Houghton, 1978; *Maude and Claude Go Abroad* (juvenile; self-illustrated), Houghton, 1980; *Beast* (juvenile; self-illustrated), Houghton, 1981; *Too Many Monsters* (juvenile; self-illustrated), Houghton, 1982.

Illustrator: Anne Epstein, *Good Stones,* Houghton, 1977; Carol-Lynn Roessel Waugh, *My Friend Bear,* Little, Brown, 1982.

SIDELIGHTS: Susan Meddaugh confesses that she feels "massive adult confusion about what makes a book work for children." Meddaugh told *CA:* "I cannot comfortably speculate on my motivations and theories of writing children's books. I'll have to make it up as I go along, using rationalization via hindsight (and astigmatic hindsight at that). I do love the whole process of putting a book together, from idea to finished art. I enjoy telling stories to myself through words and pictures. It's what I did when I was ten years old, and it's still good for me now."

* * *

MEEK, Pauline Palmer 1917-
(Agnesann McRoberts)

PERSONAL: Born March 10, 1917, in Miltonvale, Kan.; daughter of George Henry (a banker) and Frances (Smith) Palmer; married Milo A. Meek (a farmer), November 6, 1940; children: Margaret Meek Meredith, Palmer Frank, Milo Ben, Thomas Emry. *Education:* Attended Miltonvale Wesleyan College, 1935-36, and Kansas State College, 1936. *Politics:* Republican. *Religion:* United Presbyterian. *Residence:* Idana, Kan. 67453.

CAREER: Ottawa County (Kan.) public schools, teacher, 1937-39; free-lance author, 1945—. Has been active within government of Presbyterian church and has conducted training sessions for church school teachers throughout the southern United States.

*WRITINGS—*All for children: *All Day Long,* John Knox, 1965; *Hop-Skip-Hop,* John Knox, 1965; *Who Is Debbie?,* John Knox, 1965; *Knock! Knock!,* John Knox, 1965; *The Broken Vase,* John Knox, 1965; *God Sent His Son,* John Knox, 1965; *Just-Alike Princes,* Whitman Publishing, 1966; (with Kathryn Johnson Hardie) *The Book of God's People,* John Knox, 1966; (under pseudonym Agnesann McRoberts) *Two New Babies,*

Whitman Publishing, 1967; *Backyard Giant,* Whitman Publishing, 1968; *Where's Harry!,* Western Publishing, 1969; *The Hiding Place,* Western Publishing, 1971; *When Joy Came,* Western Publishing, 1971; *Noah and the Ark,* Hallmark, 1973; *Everyone—Rejoice!,* General Assembly Mission Board of Presbyterian Church, 1982; *God's Wide World,* General Assembly Mission Board of Presbyterian Church, 1983.

Author of religious resource materials for preschool children and their teachers, and contributor of articles to periodicals, including *Parents' Magazine.*

SIDELIGHTS: Pauline Meek told *CA:* "When I was fifteen years old, I submitted a story to a Sunday school paper. They bought it, and I was hooked for life! But writing has remained more of a hobby than a vocation, and for the most part it has related to my interest in and commitment to church work. Between 1945 and 1965, my sporadic efforts at writing were mostly directed toward articles on family life, which were printed in various church periodicals.

"Since 1965 I have rarely been without an assignment for church school curriculum materials. I provide stories, songs, games, art, and science activities for children and Bible background, 'how to' skills, and session plans for their teachers. The whole of experience is grist for this mill. Honest emotions, genuine conflicts, and universal human needs can become religious subject matter when they are placed in the context of the deepest truths a writer knows. Religious belief is sometimes, but not always, expressed in Biblical terms, sometimes, but not always, expressed in church vocabulary.

"Children need to be introduced to the traditions of their family and of their family's faith. They need also to sense that this faith has a bearing on their here-and-now experiences.

"My little book *The Broken Vase* tells about a child's impulsive misbehavior and the resulting alienation and reconciliation. It has been a favorite with children. To my surprise, it has also been widely used in adult study groups. Perhaps even a child's story can convey something that is profoundly true and, therefore, religious.

"I've done all the typical things farm housewives do in the process of bringing up four children. I raise a garden, can and freeze produce, bake, sew, knit, and crochet. Our nine grandchildren now keep me current with the world of the very young and supply me with ideas for children's stories. When I am writing, other activities wait while I keep office hours at the typewriter. Like other working housewives, I can manage the cooking, cleaning, and laundry on Saturdays."

*   *   *

MEEN, Victor Ben   1910-1971

OBITUARY NOTICE: Born July 1, 1910, in Toronto, Ontario, Canada; died after a two-month illness, January 7, 1971. Geologist, mineralogist, and author. As mineralogist for the Royal Ontario Museum, Meen's career encompassed writing, teaching, field studies, and executive activities. In 1950 he headed the first of many scientific expeditions to Chubb Crater (now New Quebec Crater), and in 1966 the scientist led a team to Iran to investigate the world's most valuable crown jewels. Meen produced a number of writings on gem deposits and collections, including *Quetico Geology* and, with H. D. Tushingham, *Crown Jewels of Iran.* Obituaries and other sources: *Toronto Telegraph,* January 11, 1971. (Date of death provided by Mrs. M. L. Scheffel, secretary to the chief mineralogist, Royal Ontario Museum, Toronto.)

MEGILL, Kenneth Alden   1939-

BRIEF ENTRY: Born November 9, 1939, in Esbon, Kan. American philosopher, educator, and author. Megill has taught philosophy at University of Florida since 1966. He wrote *The New Democratic Theory* (Free Press, 1970). *Address:* Department of Philosophy, University of Florida, Gainesville, Fla. 32601.

*   *   *

MEHTA, Shahnaz

PERSONAL: Born in Lucknow, India; came to the United States in 1977; daughter of Ahmed Nazir (an administrator in Indian Civil Service) and Birjees (Abdullah) Kidwai; married Vijay K. Mehta (a financial consultant), July 25, 1971; children: Devika, Nayantara. *Education:* University of North Bengal, A.B. (with honors); University of British Columbia, M.S.W., 1967. *Religion:* Buddhist. *Home and office:* 7336 Eldorado St., McLean, Va. 22102.

CAREER: Children's Aid Society, Calgary, Alberta, social worker, 1960-67; Ford Foundation, Calcutta, India, research assistant in family planning, 1970-71; Balkunj (welfare organization), Delhi, India, member of advisory board, 1971-73; instructor in classical Indian dance in Washington, D.C., 1979—. Exhibited driftwood sculpture and floral arrangements, 1968-78.

WRITINGS: (With Joan Korenblit) *Good Cooking From India,* Rodale Press, 1981.

WORK IN PROGRESS: Indian Folk Tales and Legends, publication expected in 1983; *Five Women,* short stories, publication expected in 1983; *The Glorious Cuisine of the Mughals.*

SIDELIGHTS: Shahnaz Mehta wrote: "I am very interested in the women's movement, but as a *part* of human development. I consider it equally crucial to educate and 'liberate' men, for unless that is done (especially in a country like India) women have an almost impossible task in achieving self-realization.

"A great source of my inspiration is India's religious literature, as well as devotional dance and song. These provide an added dimension to contemporary 'western' life, whether in the United States or in Indian cities."

*   *   *

MEISELAS, Susan   1948-

PERSONAL: Surname is pronounced my-*sell*-us; born June 21, 1948, in Baltimore, Md.; daughter of Leonard (a physician) and Murrayl (a teacher; maiden name, Groh) Meiselas. *Education:* Sarah Lawrence College, B.A., 1970; Harvard University, Ed. M., 1971. *Office:* Magnum Photos, 251 Park Ave. S., New York, N.Y. 10010.

CAREER: Community Resources Institute, New York, N.Y., photographic adviser in public schools, 1972-74; South Carolina State Arts Commission, Columbia, photographic adviser in public schools, 1975; Magnum Photos, New York, N.Y., free-lance photographer, 1976—. Assistant film editor for Fred Wiseman on film "Basic Training," 1971. *Awards, honors:* Robert Capa Gold Medal from Overseas Press Club, 1979, for work done during the Nicaraguan insurrection.

WRITINGS: (Editor) *Learning to See* (teaching projects using photography), Polaroid Corp., 1975; *Carnival Strippers* (oral history and photographs), Farrar, Straus, 1976; *Nicaragua: June 1978 to July 1979* (photo-documentary), Pantheon, 1981. Contributor to magazines and newspapers, including *Geo, Time, Life, Mother Jones,* and *New York Times.*

SIDELIGHTS: *Nicaragua,* Meiselas's photo-documentary of the 1978-79 Nicaraguan revolt, was described by Andy Grundberg in the *New York Times Book Review* as "often intensely beautiful" and "haunting." Grundberg also noted: "If one needed visual confirmation of what Yeats meant by 'a terrible beauty' being born of insurrection, 'Nicaragua' supplies it in spades. Not since Vietnam and the original incarnation of Life magazine has there been war photography this graphic and wrenching." *Washington Post Book World*'s Richard E. Feinberg commented, "Susan Meiselas explores with considerable sensitivity and technical skill, the emotions of ordinary combatants and civilians as the struggle builds from spontaneous insurrection to full-scale civil war leading to popular victory."

BIOGRAPHICAL/CRITICAL SOURCES: *New York Times,* June 2, 1981; *New York Times Book Review,* June 14, 1981; *Washington Post Book World,* September 27, 1981.

* * *

MELBY, John Fremont 1913-

BRIEF ENTRY: Born July 1, 1913, in Portland, Ore. American political scientist, educator, and author. Melby was a foreign service officer of the U.S. Department of State from 1937 to 1953. Some of his experiences abroad were reported in his *Mandate of Heaven: Record of a Civil War—China, 1945-49* (University of Toronto Press, 1968). Melby was executive vice-president of the National Council on Asian Affairs from 1955 to 1958 and lecturer at University of Pennsylvania from 1958 to 1964. In 1966 he became a professor of political studies at University of Guelph and was made a member of the university's board of governors in 1971. Melby's other books include *The Rising Demand for International Education* (American Academy of Political and Social Science, 1961), *Looking Glass for Americans: A Study of the Foreign Students at the University of Pennsylvania* (1961), and *China and Japan* (Canadian Institute of International Affairs, 1971). *Address:* 134 Dublin N., Guelph, Ontario, Canada; and Department of Political Studies, University of Guelph, Guelph, Ontario, Canada N1G 2W1. *Biographical/critical sources: New York Times Book Review,* February 2, 1969; *American Men and Women of Science: The Social and Behavioral Sciences,* 13th edition, Bowker, 1978.

* * *

MELICK, Arden Davis 1940-

PERSONAL: Born December 31, 1940, in Irvington, N.J.; daughter of Arthur L. (an electrical engineer) and Bernice (a teacher; maiden name, Spies) Davis; divorced; children: Randolph, David, Douglas. *Education:* Centenary College, A.A. (cum laude), 1960; Seton Hall University, B.A. (magna cum laude), 1973; Syracuse University, M.A., 1977. *Religion:* Protestant. *Home:* 11 Kendal Ave., Maplewood, N.J. 07040. *Office:* Suburban Propane Gas Corp., Madison, N.J. 07960.

CAREER: Director of public relations, 1974-75, public relations officer, 1975-78, and second vice-president, 1978, of Fidelity Union Trust Co.; Suburban Propane Gas Corp., Madison, N.J., manager of corporate communications, 1979—. Member of board of trustees of Centenary College. *Member:* Executive Women of New Jersey (co-founder; charter member), Advertising Club of New Jersey (senior vice-president).

WRITINGS: *Dolley Madison, First Lady* (juvenile biography), Putnam, 1970; *Wives of the Presidents* (collective biography), Hammond, Inc., 1972, 4th edition, 1981; *A Taste of White House Cooking,* Hammond Inc., 1974; (with Syd Frank) *The Presidents: Tidbits and Trivia,* Hammond, Inc., 1980. Social editor and columnist for *Catham Courier,* 1962-64; contributing editor of *Suburban Life Magazine,* 1964-66; editor of *Mobile Travel Guide,* 1966-74.

SIDELIGHTS: Arden Davis Melick has traveled throughout the United States to investigate oil and gas exploration and production, petroleum refining, and liquefied petroleum gas distribution.

* * *

MELIKOW, Loris
See HOFMANNSTHAL, Hugo von

* * *

MERCOURI, Melina 1925-

BRIEF ENTRY: Born October 18, 1925, in Greece. Greek film actress and author. Mercouri has made more than fifteen films, but is best-known for her performance in "Never on Sunday." She left Greece in the late 1960's in protest against the government then in power. After a decade of voluntary exile and political activity intended to restore democracy in her homeland, Mercouri became a member of the Greek Parliament in 1977. She wrote a critically successful autobiography, *I Was Born Greek* (Doubleday, 1971). *Address:* c/o William Morris Agency, 1350 Avenue of the Americas, New York, N.Y. 10019. *Biographical/critical sources: Washington Post,* October 2, 1971; *Detroit News,* November 21, 1971; *Book World,* November 28, 1971.

* * *

MEREDITH, Char(lotte) 1921-

PERSONAL: Born November 26, 1921, in Petersburg, Mich.; daughter of Ralph A. (a Baptist minister) and Florence (Cole) Brown; married John Finley Meredith (a photographer and filmmaker), April 14, 1944 (died November 13, 1961); married Lawrence Wesley Hartzell (a journalist), August 4, 1979; children: (first marriage) Richard Finley. *Education:* Wheaton College, Wheaton, Ill., B.A., 1943. *Religion:* Christian. *Home and office:* 87 King Henry Court, Palatine, Ill. 60067.

CAREER: Wheaton College News Bureau, Wheaton, Ill., assistant, 1943-44; general assistant and script girl with John Finley Meredith Photography, 1944-61; Cavalcade Productions, Chicago, Ill., script girl, writer, and vice-president, 1961-64; Russ Reid Co., Park Ridge, Ill., staff writer, 1964-65; free-lance writer and editor in Chicago, Ill., 1965-67; Tom Morris, Inc., Park Ridge, writer and vice-president of creative services, 1967-77; Young Life International, Colorado Springs, Colo., senior editor and associate director of communications, 1977-79; free-lance writer in Palatine, Ill., 1979—. Member of board of directors of Faith at Work; member of Young Life International Core Group. *Member:* Smithsonian Institution.

WRITINGS: (With John Giminez) *Uptight* (biography), Word, Inc., 1967; (with Bill Milliken) *Tough Love* (biography), Revell, 1968; *It's a Sin to Bore a Kid* (nonfiction), Word, Inc., 1978; (with James Oraker) *Almost Grown* (nonfiction), Harper, 1980; (with Bill Starr) *His Quiet Splendor* (nonfiction), Word, Inc., 1982. Also author of book of poems *Early Portrait of a Marriage,* 1981.

Author of television script "Bridge of Love," for Project Concern, 1976. Contributor to magazines, including *Today's Christian Woman* and *Faith at Work*. Editor of *Young Life* and *Focus on Youth*.

WORK IN PROGRESS: Never Too Late to Love, with husband, Wesley Hartzell, publication expected in 1983.

SIDELIGHTS: Charlotte Meredith wrote: "The death of my first husband thrust me into writing for a living—and opened many doors of learning for me. His effect on my life has been beautiful. We met in a college journalism class and edited the college newspaper together before committing ourselves to marriage. Being a mother and helping to shape a child is an irreplaceable joy that has continued to hone my perceptions in many areas of understanding and endeavor.

"Travel on assignment has also been important and enjoyable, including work in Japan, Korea, the Philippines, Guatemala, Ecuador, Peru, Costa Rica, Venezuela, Honduras, Nicaragua, Mexico, and Haiti; England and the Channel Islands have been a personal retreat.

"Friends have occupied much of my time, and have also opened many doors. I believe we have been created to relate interdependently to each other, and that our effect on others is permanent. My religious faith is the unifying force of my life, and most of what I write seeks to demonstrate that."

*　　*　　*

MEREZHKOVSKY, Zinaida
See GIPPIUS, Zinaida (Nikolayevna)

*　　*　　*

MERRITT, Don 1945-

PERSONAL: Born February 18, 1945, in Little Rock, Ark.; son of Henry Donigan (in business) and Wilma (a beautician; maiden name, Seagers) Merritt; married Barbara Parks, October 10, 1964 (divorced, 1970); married Pamela Farnham (an assistant vice-president in banking), July 3, 1971; children: Andrea, Kymberly. *Education:* Simpson College, B.A., 1975; Claremont Graduate School, M.A., 1977; University of Iowa, M.F.A., 1981. *Religion:* None. *Residence:* Indianola, Iowa. *Agent:* Molly Friedrich, Aaron M. Priest Literary Agency, 150 East 35th St., New York, N.Y. 10016.

CAREER: South Haven Daily Tribune, South Haven, Mich., reporter, 1968-69; Captain Bean's Cruises, Kailua-Kona, Hawaii, deckhand and diver, 1969-70; Dancing Dolphin, Inc. (charter fishing boat), Kailua-Kona, captain, 1970-71; Simpson College, Indianola, Iowa, conference coordinator, 1971-80; teacher at College of St. Francis, 1980. *Military service:* U.S. Army, Airborne Infantry, 1962-64. *Awards, honors:* Prairie Playwright Award from Iowa Arts Council, 1980, for "Candles in the Wind."

WRITINGS: Miguel de Unamuno (monograph), Simpson College Press, 1975; "Candles in the Wind" (one-act play), first produced in Indianola, Iowa, at Carousel Theatre, 1980; *One Easy Piece* (novel), Coward, 1981; *My Sister's Keeper* (novel), Coward, 1983.

SIDELIGHTS: Merritt told *CA:* "I grew up in a small oil-and-gas town called Magnolia, in southern Arkansas, a town where the principal ambition of most children was to figure out a way to live in Dallas, Texas. Try to imagine a place where a city like Dallas can seem a Mecca. My mother graduated from high school; my father stopped some years short. Neither were readers. In fact, the only books in our house were the few in my bedroom. Those of my friends who had even minimal creative impulses wanted to be singers or musicians in a rock and roll band, and a couple of them had some success. I can't remember wanting to do anything.

"Then I met a girl and fell in love, or at least in lust. I was not a sports star, a good student, or particularly gregarious, so to get her attention I wrote poems to her. They were wildly successful. I was fourteen years old. I lost the girl within a month, but writing became an addiction. Becoming a writer begins as an act of imagination, or rather, a reimagining of oneself, but it has great sticking power. I believe I became a writer the moment I wrote that first ten-line poem to seduce Mary Evelyn. I ended up seducing myself.

"Writing became my principal tool; it became my personality. I had stumbled onto something I could do fairly well, certainly better than any of my friends. And it wasn't even all that hard to do—sort of like talking with a pencil. I used that ability for everything, not only to seduce girls, but to get jobs, to improve my grades without studying, to be noticed. The song my sirens sang was literature.

"During my last teenage year, my first poem and first short story were published in a now-defunct Arkansas literary magazine. Within a year, two other poems and another short story were published. And then, for reasons I still do not understand, I stopped writing and began to travel. I wandered through Mexico, circumnavigated the Pacific Basin in a small sailboat, and worked as a diver and fisherman in Hawaii. I kept a daily journal, but did not write with the intent to publish. That period lasted three or four years. Looking back, I can only assume that there was nothing in my life to write about. Or, more likely, that writing had become much harder as my intent became more serious.

"Then in 1971, at the age of twenty-six, I began to write again. It was ten years later that my first novel was published. During those ten years, many of which were spent as a student of some sort, I completed three novels, some dozen short stories, three one-act plays, and a handful of poems. None of them were much good, although I did try to sell one of the novels. It gathered a dozen or so rejection slips before I became discouraged and put it away. I suppose I was paying a few long-overdue dues.

"I have no explanation of why *One Easy Piece* sold. I do not think it is appreciably better than any of the three others that preceded it and did not sell. A central theme in all my work is that the world is a capricious, undependable place; that I sold a novel at all is, I believe, capricious, not something I should depend on ever doing again. Maybe I will, maybe I won't, but I don't feel that I control it. But believing this has no effect on whether or not I continue to write novels. I write fairly quickly and tend to work out my ideas by writing them, not by thinking them out beforehand. It does not particularly bother me that I may continue to write three or four novels for each one I publish. You see, I couldn't stop doing it anyway, and I'm not sure it matters. Writing is my heroin, and since that first dose at the age of fourteen, I've been addicted.

"Sometimes people who want to be writers ask me for advice. What can be said to them? If one has to write, nothing can be said that will kill that need. If one doesn't, nothing can create it. Of course, given the dismal state of book publishing these days, I do advise people with some verbal skills to try their hand at category or genre fiction, which is three full steps below advertising copywriting. It can be a pretty good job, certainly easier and more lucrative than washing cars or pumping gas. But that's all it is—a job. Literature is a calling.

"In order to keep writing from becoming 'just my job,' I have chosen to live in a quiet, inexpensive farming community so I can devote my energies to writing rather than surviving. Even that wouldn't be enough, except that my wife, Pam, believes so strongly in me as a writer that she has for a long time been willing to give me the financial freedom to write what I please. If anyone wonders what has happened to the patronage system in this country, I suggest they look to the spouses of writers for their answer."

AVOCATIONAL INTERESTS: Hot-air ballooning, fishing.

BIOGRAPHICAL/CRITICAL SOURCES: Grinnell Herald-Register, October 5, 1981; *Library Journal,* October 11, 1981; *Magnolia Banner-News,* December 22, 1981; *Record-Herald and Indianola Tribune,* December 31, 1981; *Houston Chronicle,* January 17, 1982.

* * *

MESSENT, Peter Ronald 1949-

PERSONAL: Born April 22, 1949, in Surrey, England; son of Cyril Edwin (a solicitor) and Eileen (Thomas) Messent; married Mary June Boyd, September 20, 1975 (divorced October 1, 1981). *Education:* Pembroke College, Cambridge, M.A., 1970; University of Sussex, D.Phil., 1973. *Home:* White Lodge Stables, Main St., Whissendine, Rutland, Leicestershire, England. *Office:* Pedigree Petfoods, Waltham-on-the-Wolds, Melton Mowbray, Leicestershire, England.

CAREER: University of Keele, Keele, England, research assistant in psychology, 1973-74; Pedigree Petfoods, Melton Mowbray, England, animal behaviorist, 1974—. Volunteer warden at Rutland Water Nature Reserve. *Member:* Association for the Study of Animal Behaviour, British Ornithologists Union, Society for Companion Animal Studies, Society for Veterinary Ethology.

WRITINGS: Understanding Your Dog, Quarto, 1980; (contributor) Bruce Fogle, editor, *Interrelations Between People and Pets,* C. C Thomas, 1981; (contributor) Richard Marples, editor, *Encyclopedia of the Dog,* Octopus, 1981. Author of "Pets Insight," a column in *Our Dogs.* Contributor to magazines. Editor of newsletter of Group for the Study of the Human-Companion Animal Bond, 1980—.

WORK IN PROGRESS: Editing a book on companion animals; research on cage birds, with publication expected to result.

SIDELIGHTS: Messent commented: "I have always been interested in animals and involve myself with those living in the wild as well as those in the home. Many people view them as two different kinds of animals, but I believe our pets provide a close link to the other creatures with whom we share the earth. Pets certainly provide great benefit to many people, and I think we will see growing interest in the relationship of pets to society in general."

* * *

MESSER, Thomas M. 1920-

BRIEF ENTRY: Born February 9, 1920, in Bratislava, Czechoslovakia. American museum director, art historian, and author. Messer has been director of the Solomon R. Guggenheim Museum since 1961. Before that, he worked for the American Federation of Arts and the Boston Institute of Contemporary Art. Messer has also taught at Harvard University and Barnard College, and he is chairman of the International Council of Museums' international committee for museums and collections of modern art. Messer's books include *Modern Art: An*

Introductory Commentary (Solomon R. Guggenheim Foundation, 1962), *The Emergent Decade: Latin American Painters and Painting in the 1960's* (Cornell University Press, 1966), and *Edvard Munch* (Abrams, 1971). Messer has also prepared several catalogues of exhibitions, including *Contemporary Painters of Japanese Origin in America* (1958) and *Marc Chagall: Work on Paper* (International Exhibit Foundation, 1975). *Address:* 1105 Park Ave., New York, N.Y. 10028; and Solomon R. Guggenheim Museum, 1071 Fifth Ave., New York, N.Y. 10028. *Biographical/critical sources: Current Biography,* Wilson, 1961; *Who's Who in American Art,* Bowker, 1978.

* * *

MICKOLUS, Edward F(rancis) 1950-

PERSONAL: Born December 28, 1950, in Cincinnati, Ohio; son of Edward Francis, Sr. (an automobile engineer) and Catherine (Lawlor) Mickolus; married Linda Kay Florence, August 24, 1973 (divorced October 2, 1980). *Education:* Georgetown University, A.B. (magna cum laude), 1973; Yale University, M.A., 1974, M.Phil., 1975, Ph.D., 1981. *Politics:* "Small 'd' democrat." *Religion:* Roman Catholic. *Office:* Central Intelligence Agency, Washington, D.C. 20505.

CAREER: Central Intelligence Agency, Washington, D.C., intelligence officer, 1975—. *Member:* International Studies Association, American Academy of Political and Social Science, American Political Science Association, American Society for International Law, Mensa, Academy of Political Science, Society for Basic Irreproducible Research, Phi Beta Kappa, Delta Tau Kappa, Pi Sigma Alpha.

WRITINGS: (With Christopher M. Rocca, Robert F. Simmons, and Julie Christiano) *Preparing a Delegation for a High School Model United Nations: A Bibliography,* National Collegiate Conference Association, 1974; *ITERATE: International Terrorism, Attributes of Terrorist Events, Data Codebook,* Inter-University Consortium for Political and Social Research (Ann Arbor, Mich.), 1976, revised edition, 1981; *Annotated Bibliography on International and Transnational Terrorism,* Central Intelligence Agency, 1976; *The Literature of Terrorism: A Selectively Annotated Bibliography,* Greenwood Press, 1980; *Transnational Terrorism: A Chronology of Events, 1968-1979,* Greenwood Press, 1980; (with Edward Heyman) *Who's Who in International Terrorism: A Directory of the World's Revolutionaries,* Greenwood Press, 1983; *Combatting International Terrorism: A Quantitative Analysis,* Greenwood Press, 1983.

Contributor: Seymour Maxwell Finger and Yonah Alexander, editors, *Terrorism: Interdisciplinary Perspectives,* John Jay, 1977; John D. Elliott and Lesley Gibson, editors, *Contemporary Terrorism: Selected Readings,* International Association of Chiefs of Police, 1978; Marius Livingston, editor, *Terrorism in the Contemporary World,* Greenwood Press, 1978; Richards J. Heuer, editor, *Quantitative Approaches to Political Intelligence: The CIA Experience,* Westview, 1978; Y. Alexander and Robert A. Kilmarx, editors, *Political Terrorism and Business: The Threat and Response,* Praeger, 1979; Michael Stohl, editor, *The Politics of Terrorism,* Dekker, 1979, revised edition, 1982; Stephen Sloan and Richard Schultz, editors, *Responding to the Terrorist Threat: Security and Crisis Management,* Pergamon, 1980; Y. Alexander and John Gleason, editors, *Behavioral Approaches to the Study of Terrorism,* Pergamon, 1981; George S. Roukis and Patrick J. Montana, editors, *Managing Terrorism: Strategies for the Corporate Executive,* Greenwood Press, 1982. Contributor of articles and reviews to scholarly journals.

AVOCATIONAL INTERESTS: Travel (especially Europe and Africa), coaching women's softball, teaching dance, photography.

*   *   *

MIDLER, Bette 1945-

PERSONAL: Born December 1, 1945, in Honolulu, Hawaii; daughter of Fred (a house painter) and Ruth (Schindel) Midler. *Education:* Attended University of Hawaii, 1965, and Hunter College. *Residence:* Beverly Hills, Calif. *Agent:* Paul Bloch, Rogers & Cowan, Inc., 9665 Wilshire Blvd., Beverly Hills, Calif. 90212.

CAREER: Performer, recording artist, and actress. Singer and entertainer alone or with group, the Harlettes, in nightclubs and concert halls; made tour around the world, 1978; recordings as singer include "The Divine Miss M," Atlantic, 1972, "Bette Midler," 1973, "Songs for the New Depression," Atlantic, 1975, "Broken Blossom," 1977, "Thighs and Whispers," Atlantic, 1979, and "In Concert," Atlantic. Actress in motion pictures, including "Hawaii," United Artists, 1966, "The Detective," Twentieth Century-Fox, 1968, "Goodbye Columbus," Paramount, 1969, "The Rose," Twentieth Century-Fox, 1979, "Divine Madness," Ladd Company, 1980, and "Jinxed," United Artists; actress in plays, including "Fiddler on the Roof," 1966-69, "Salvation," 1970, "Tommy," 1971, "Clams on the Half-Shell Revue," 1975, and "Bette! Divine Madness," 1979; actress in television special "Bette Midler: Ol' Red Hair Is Back," 1977, and guest on television talk shows, including "The David Frost Show," "The Tonight Show Starring Johnny Carson," and "The Merv Griffin Show." Also worked as canner in pineapple factory, secretary at radio station, salesperson, typist, and chorus girl.

AWARDS, HONORS: Grammy Award from National Academy of Recording Artists, 1973; Emmy Award from National Academy of Television Arts and Sciences, 1973; special Antoinette Perry ("Tony") Award, 1973; Ruby Award from *After Dark,* 1973, for performer of the year; named woman of the year by Harvard Hasty Pudding Club, 1976; gold record award from Recording Industry Association of America, Inc. for album "The Divine Miss M," and for single "Show and Tell," both 1973; platinum album award from Recording Industry Association of America, Inc.; Academy Award nomination from Academy of Motion Picture Arts and Sciences, 1980, for best actress in "The Rose"; Golden Globe Award, 1980, for "The Rose."

WRITINGS: A View From a Broad, Simon & Schuster, 1980.

WORK IN PROGRESS: Baby Divine, a children's book.

SIDELIGHTS: Presenting "trash with flash" and "sleaze with ease," Bette Midler captivates audiences with her amazing energy, bawdy, irreverent jokes, ribald stories, and racy skits. "When she strides onto a concert stage, something of a metaphysical marvel occurs," declared Warren Hoge of the *New York Times Magazine.* "Her small engine begins turning out an impossible number of thermal energy units. She is large and loud, shaking her head with a vigor that sends the curls dancing around her temples like poppies in a high wind." Dressed in campy costumes ranging from a feathered, sequined dress with a matching green parrot hat to rhinestone girdles and peddle pushers, the on-stage Midler embodies uncouthness. "I use vulgarity because it amuses me, but I don't abuse it," she explained. "It's a very fine line that I walk. I am a consummately vulgar performer, but at the same time, I'm just on the other side of it. My use of it is extremely classy, I think. It's in a tradition that people don't have anymore."

Midler developed her earthy style while appearing at Manhattan's Continental Baths ("the tubs") in the late 1960's and early 1970's. Singing before a predominantly homosexual crowd, Midler established her stage persona. "Me and those boys, we just went somewhere else," Midler assessed. "I had the best time. It was something I just had to do, and I did it for them, and I did it all." She later disclosed: "They gave me the confidence to be tacky, cheesy, to take risks. They encouraged my spur-of-the-moment improvisations." "The more outrageous I was, the more they liked it," she added. "It loosened me up."

It was while entertaining at the baths that Midler and her newly created "Divine Miss M" character began to attract attention. Mixed audiences were allowed in the establishment to view the energetic performer, and invitations came from talk show hosts Johnny Carson, David Frost, and Merv Griffin. "I became this freak who sings in the tubs," Midler recounted. At this time, she and her group the Harlettes, which then included Melissa Manchester, teamed up with pianist Barry Manilow. Midler's resulting 1972 debut album, "The Divine Miss M," scored an impressive success, selling more than one hundred thousand copies in the first month of its release. Moreover, "her reviews could have been written by her mother," quipped Chris Chase in the *New York Times.* The critic listed a few: "Cashbox: 'A really great star'; Rolling Stone, 'one hell of a talent'; Record World, 'a superstar of superstars, she is not to be believed.'" By the end of 1972 Midler was performing at the Lincoln Center's Philharmonic Hall. At a special New Year's Eve event, she entertained two sell-out crowds. With her customary liveliness, the "Divine Miss M" brought in the new year dressed in a diaper and bedecked with a banner that read "1973."

Midler, who seven years after her arrival in New York had become a celebrity, grew up in Honolulu as a member of the only Jewish family in a largely Samoan neighborhood. "My family was the only white family on the block, and we were not wanted," she confessed. "White was weird, but Jewish, which we were, was the weirdest." Midler had a lonely childhood and has "a lot of old . . . scars. Kids are the cruelest of creatures, and the scars take a long time to heal. I know mine did."

Named after her mother's screen favorite, Bette Davis, Midler often escaped into the imaginary world of show business. The future entertainer mimicked the stars and "used to call people 'dahling'" and exclaim "'Oh, my deah.'" In *Woman's Journal,* Margaret Morley described what Midler was like as a student at the University of Hawaii: "Bette was a rather hyperactive undergraduate given to singing virtually non-stop, sometimes in the company of a girlfriend and sometimes by herself. She sang in the classroom, she sang at lunch, she sang in the corridors, she jumped out from behind trees and sang—very loudly."

In 1965 Midler got her first acting job as an extra on the set of the motion picture "Hawaii." She played the part of a continuously seasick missionary wife. When the company moved to Hollywood to finish filming, she went along. Midler saved her wages and after the shooting was concluded, she traveled to New York City. The singer sold gloves for a brief time before joining the chorus of the Broadway play "Fiddler on the Roof." Soon she graduated to the role of Tzeitel, Tevye's oldest daughter in the show.

One of Midler's fellow performers in the play collected music and allowed her to listen to his records. Thus during her stint on Broadway she was exposed to the music of such singers as Helen Morgan, Billie Holliday, Aretha Franklin, Ethel Waters, and the Ronettes. It was also at this point in the late 1960's that Midler learned of the singing job at the Continental Baths. She auditioned and was hired to sing at midnight each night after finishing her part in "Fiddler on the Roof." When she had achieved national recognition with her appearances on the talk shows of Johnny Carson, Merv Griffin, and David Frost, Midler began to perform on the nightclub circuit.

In her acts, the singer made use of the rich musical history with which she had become familiar. She sang songs from a wide variety of sources, prompting critics to comment on her musical scope. Chase maintained that "there's nothing she can't sing. Rock. Blues. Songs from the 40's, the 50's, the 60's, songs which once belonged to the Shangri Las, the Dixie Cups, the Andrew Sisters." Richard Poirier in the *New Republic* likewise noted that "she has the vocal resources to sing in the style of any woman vocalist of the past 30 years." He further ventured: "Midler doesn't imitate or parody a specific singer through an entire song, however. Rather, like a person truly haunted, Midler in the phrasing of a song will suddenly veer off from one coloration into another. It sometimes happens with an air of true discovery. As with most great jazz singers, she therefore never does a song exactly the same way twice. The avenue of experimentation is always left open."

In 1972 the performer met Aaron Russo, who became her longtime manager. She told him to "make me a legend!" and, to this end, he took charge of her career with what some writers have called the dominance of Svengali. Their collaboration was a rocky one. "We got to a point where we didn't see eye-to-eye on anything," Midler reflected. "At times, the relationship was extremely violent, physically violent." She later stated that Russo "made my personal life so miserable that I became nonfunctional from 1973 on." They ended their partnership in 1979, but Midler admitted he was a good manager.

Russo acquired "The Rose" for Midler's first starring motion picture role, and her performance won her an Academy Award nomination. In his search for "a role that only Bette Midler could play," he turned down parts in such films as "The Fortune," "Foul Play," "Rocky," "King Kong," "Nashville," and "Won Ton Ton, the Dog Who Saved Hollywood." Midler received glowing compliments for her acting in the picture. Mark Rydell, director of "The Rose," praised her as "one of those people who come along once every 100 years." He continued: "There's some odd thing about her . . . some strange and wonderful combination of genetic factors that has produced someone with instincts that are so free, so full and so deep. . . . She's an American natural resource, and I feel very responsible recording her for history."

Midler has also extended her pursuits to include writing. Her largely tongue-in-cheek account of her 1978 worldwide tour entitled *A View From a Broad* was published in 1980. Susan Wood of the *Washington Post* observed that "the book is, like Midler herself, a curious mixture of the ridiculous and the sublime—moving from rapid-fire jokes that appear to be verbatim transcripts of the opening of her concert act . . . to serious reflections about how she felt to be a Jew performing in Germany or on the fragile existence of life in Thailand." Although Wood claimed the work "enjoyable enough," she concluded that Midler "doesn't translate to the printed page extremely well."

Bette Midler remains most popular as a stage personality. Advanced ticket sales for her "Clams on the Half-Shell Revue" broke Broadway box office records by bringing in more than $200,000 in a single day, and the revue grossed more money than any other show in a ten-week run. Meanwhile, reviewers continually wonder at her stage presence. Stephen M. Silver-

man of *American Film* asserted that "she is a deft monologuist, with a breathtaking range of cultural references, from fifties' high school slang to Samuel Johnson." Her raunchy jibes poke fun at everyone and everything. Among her targets number "Filthydelphia," Princess Anne ("she loves nature in spite of what it did to her"), Cher, Barbara Streisand, "Ratso" Rizzo, and the queen of England, Elizabeth II ("the whitest woman in the world . . . she makes all the rest of us look like the Third World"). Her concerts are riddled with the unsavory antics of "Delores DeLago, the toast of Chicago" and off-color Sophie Tucker jokes. It is also not unusual for Midler to introduce a song by declaring, "Now here's another blasto from the pasto! You're gonna like this one 'cuz I shake my tits a lot!"

This "last of the real tacky ladies" openly parodies herself, her audience, and the wealth of nostalgia she employs in her shows. Poirier pointed out, though, that Midler's "parodistic predelictions shouldn't be mistaken, as they almost invariably are—for camp." He explained: "Behind them is a vulnerability that is the reverse of camp; many of her jokes derive from earlier sentiments that are nearly embarrassing in their self-exposure. It is this quality that softens her toughness. She has been completely open, as only a strong and loving person can be, to the half trashy, half beautiful, and always totemized world of the recent past."

BIOGRAPHICAL/CRITICAL SOURCES: New York Times, January 14, 1973, November 11, 1979; *Time,* September 10, 1973, December 31, 1979; *Philadelphia Magazine,* January, 1974; *Newsweek,* April 28, 1975; *Biography News,* Volume II, Gale, 1975; *New Republic,* August 2, 1975; *American Film,* September, 1978; *New York Times Magazine,* December 10, 1978; *Woman's Journal,* February, 1979; *Contra Costa Times,* September 14, 1979; *Detroit Free Press,* September 16, 1979, September 28, 1979; *Los Angeles Times,* September 16, 1979, September 19, 1979; *Los Angeles Herald Examiner,* September 19, 1979; *People,* January 7, 1980; *Washington Post,* March 6, 1980; *New York Times Book Review,* June 29, 1980, April 5, 1981.*

—Sketch by Anne M. Guerrini

*   *   *

MILLER, Barbara D(iane)   1948-

PERSONAL: Born September 18, 1948, in Geneva, N.Y.; daughter of Donald E. (in business) and Genevieve A. (a bookkeeper) Miller; married Christopher A. Heaton, August 4, 1973; children: Jack Ernest. *Education:* Syracuse University, B.A., 1971, M.A., 1976, Ph.D. (with distinction), 1978. *Home:* 644 Fellows Ave., Syracuse, N.Y. 13210. *Office:* Local Revenue Administration Project, Syracuse University, 409 Maxwell Hall, Syracuse, N.Y. 13210.

CAREER: Syracuse University, Syracuse, N.Y., senior research associate in local revenue administration at Maxwell School of Citizenship and Public Affairs, 1979—. *Awards, honors:* Woodrow Wilson fellowship in Women's studies, 1976; Rockefeller-Ford Foundation grant in population and development policy, 1977-78.

WRITINGS: The Endangered Sex: Neglect of Female Children in Rural North India, Cornell University Press, 1981. Contributor to academic journals.

WORK IN PROGRESS: Editing *Local Government Finance in the Third World: A Case Study of the Philippines,* with Roy Bahl; research on local government finance in Bangladesh and on sociocultural aspects of local revenue administration in Third World countries.

SIDELIGHTS: Barbara Miller told *CA:* "I was trained as an anthropologist, which can mean a lot of things. To me, anthropology must be useful; therefore I have tried consistently in the past few years to bring the expertise of anthropology to fields as diverse as demography and public finance. I have tried to think, speak, and write in a way that is interdisciplinary, that can be understood by people who work in different fields and in different areas of the world. Asia is the part of the world where I have lived and studied, but I am now hoping to bring some of my experience and perspective to bear on problems here in the United States."

*   *   *

MILLER, Bernard S.   1920-

PERSONAL: Born October 21, 1920, in New York, N.Y.; son of Samuel and Sophie (Klonsky) Miller; married Betty C. Cottin (a teacher), June 20, 1946; children: Steven, Donald, Jeffrey, Cyral. *Education:* Queens College (now of the City University of New York), B.A., 1942; University of Nancy, certificate of excellence, 1946; Columbia University, M.A., 1948, Ed.D., 1957. *Home:* 60 Cooper Lane, Larchmont, N.Y. 10538. *Office:* Department of Curriculum, Hunter College of the City University of New York, 695 Park Ave., New York, N.Y. 10021.

CAREER: History teacher at high school in Highland Falls, N.Y., 1948-50, and high school in Peekskill, N.Y., 1950-54; director of adult education in Peekskill, 1954-56, principal, 1958-60; John Hay Fellowships Program, associate director of humanities, 1960-65; Hunter College of the City University of New York, New York, N.Y., professor of education, 1965—, director of campus schools, 1970—. Executive associate of James B. Conant with Carnegie Corp., 1956-58; director of Bennington College summer institute in humanities, 1973; consultant to National Endowment for the Humanities and Swedish Ministry of Education. *Military service:* U.S. Army, Antiaircraft Battalion, 1942-46; became captain; received five battle stars. *Member:* National Association for Humanities Education (member of board of directors, 1968—), American Association for Gifted Children (vice-president), National Network of Complementary Schools (member of board of directors). *Awards, honors:* Ford Foundation grant, 1957; John Hay summer grant, 1959; Rockefeller Foundation grant, 1965-67.

WRITINGS: The Humanities Approach to the Modern School Curriculum, Prentice-Hall, 1972; *The Gifted Child, the Family, and the Community,* Walker & Co., 1981. Contributor to *Macmillan Encyclopedia of Education.* Contributor to academic journals, including *College Board Review.*

SIDELIGHTS: Miller wrote: "I have always felt that education was a Jacob's Ladder that had to be climbed if life was to have meaning. I am profoundly concerned that not enough of our nation's bright, committed people see teaching as a purposeful career. A reverence for learning and a desire to be part of the learning process must become a more common denominator in our society."

*   *   *

MILLER, Donald Eugene   1929-

PERSONAL: Born December 2, 1929, in Dayton, Ohio; son of Daniel L. (a farmer) and Eliza Myrtle (Coning) Miller; married Phyllis Louise Gibbel, August 19, 1956; children: Bryan Daniel, Lisa Kathleen, Bruce David. *Education:* Attended Manchester College, 1947-49; University of Chicago, M.A., 1952; graduate study at United Theological Seminary, Dayton,

Ohio, 1955-56; Bethany Theological Seminary, Oak Brook, Ill., B.D., 1958; Harvard University, Ph.D., 1962; postdoctoral study at Yale University, 1968-69, and Cambridge University, 1975-76. *Office:* Department of Christian Education and Ethics, Bethany Theological Seminary, Meyers and Butterfield Rds., Oak Brook, Ill. 60521.

CAREER: Ordained minister of Church of the Brethren, 1958; Brethren Service Commission, Elgin, Ill., church service worker in Europe, 1952-54; high school teacher of social studies in Trotwood, Ohio, 1954-55, and junior high school teacher in Chicago, Ill., 1957-58; Bethany Theological Seminary, Oak Brook, Ill., associate professor, 1961-70, professor of Christian education and ethics, 1970—, director of graduate studies, 1976—. Director of self-study for Chicago Cluster of Theological Schools, 1980-81. *Member:* Association of Professors and Researchers in Religious Education (president, 1968), Association for Professional Education for the Ministry (president, 1976—). *Awards, honors:* Fellow of American Association of Theological Schools, 1968-69, and the association's Case Study Institute, 1972.

WRITINGS: (With Warren F. Groff) *The Shaping of Modern Christian Thought,* World Publishing, 1968; (with Graydon F. Snyder and Robert W. Neff) *Using Biblical Simulations,* Judson, Volume I, 1973, 2nd edition, 1974, Volume II, 1975; *A Self-Instruction Guide Through Brethren History,* Brethren Press, 1976; *The Wing-Footed Wanderer: Conscience and Transcendence,* Abingdon, 1977; *Contemporary Approaches to Christian Education,* Abingdon, 1982. Editor of *Yearbook of Association for Professional Education for the Ministry,* 1972.

*   *   *

MILLER, Edna (Anita)   1920-

PERSONAL: Born March 8, 1920, in Weehawken, N. J.; daughter of Curt (an engineer) and Jean (Johansen) Freyschmidt; married Theodore R. Miller (a cartographer), July 18, 1946 (divorced, 1971), married Leslie Lovett, December 31, 1971 (deceased); children: Theodore R., Jr. *Education:* Attended Traphagen School of Fashion and Design, 1938-40. *Religion:* Protestant. *Residence:* North Hero, Vt. *Address:* c/o Prentice-Hall, Inc., Englewood Cliffs, N.J. 07632.

CAREER: B. H. Wragge, New York, N.Y., designer of sportswear, 1940-50. Trustee, North Hero Public Library, 1974—.

*WRITINGS—*For children; all self-illustrated; all published by Prentice-Hall, unless otherwise indicated: *Mousekin's Golden House,* 1964; *Mousekin's Christmas Eve,* 1965; *Mousekin Finds a Friend,* 1967; *Mousekin's Family,* 1969; *Mousekin's Woodland Sleepers,* 1970; *Duck Duck,* Holiday House, 1971; *Mousekin's ABC,* 1972; *Mousekin's Woodland Birthday,* 1974; *Mousekin Takes a Trip,* 1976; *Pebbles, a Pack Rat,* 1976; *Mousekin's Close Call,* 1978; *Jumping Bean,* 1979.

Illustrator: Michael Rheta Martin, *Graphic Guide to World History,* Holt, 1959; Phyllis Powell Sarasy, *Winter Sleepers,* Prentice-Hall, 1962; Agnes McCarthy, *Creatures of the Deep,* Prentice-Hall, 1963; Natalie Friendly, *Wildlife Teams,* Prentice-Hall, 1963; Gladys Sakon, *Secrets in Animal Names,* Prentice-Hall, 1964; Dorothy Wisbeski, *Picaro, a Pet Otter,* Hawthorn, 1971.

WORK IN PROGRESS: A new Mousekin book.

SIDELIGHTS: Edna Miller told *CA:* "I was born in New Jersey but grew up in New York City. I lived with my parents and older sister in an apartment overlooking Central Park and next to the American Museum of Natural History. As a child I developed a great love of animals mainly because, as an apartment dweller, I was not permitted to have what I wanted most—a dog. There were tidier substitutes, however: two thoroughbred turtles, a white mouse, a rabbit, and a small alligator. At the zoo in Central Park I made childish sketches of my favorite animals. The Museum of Natural History was my second home.

"For ten years I worked as a designer for a leading sportswear manufacturer. During this period I married Ted Miller, an architect and cartographer. In the Ramapo hills north of New York City we built a house overlooking untouched woodland with enough animals to satisfy the most ardent naturalist. We divided our time between the city and country, and traveled extensively in Europe, North Africa, Mexico, and the United States. When our son Teddy was born we made the Ramapos our year-round home, and I turned to illustrating as a second career. I did illustrations for high school textbooks and assisted my husband in his work as a historical cartographer.

"As our son grew I found it little effort to invent stories of the creatures who shared the land with us. When Teddy entered school I began illustrating children's books. The idea for my first book, *Mousekin's Golden House,* came to me shortly after Halloween when I had put the family pumpkin outside. One evening I noticed a small white-footed mouse exploring the jack-o'-lantern for the few seeds it contained. I watched with great amusement as it scrambled in one entrance and out another. As the weeks passed the pumpkin rolled to the base of a tree, and I watched its expression change, day by day, from blank joviality to sweet serenity as it closed its eyes and pressed its smiling mouth shut in the cold wind. I thought what a fine house it would make for a white-footed mouse who forever discards one home and searches for another.

"Mousekin has found many homes and has had many adventures since my first story of this charming creature. I have found a new home in Vermont, on an island in Lake Champlain. There are white-footed mice in the woodland for future stories of Mousekin. And I have a new audience in our grandchildren. I hope they shall learn, as I did, that nature writes its own stories—there need only be an interested observer."

* * *

MILLER, Judi 1941-

PERSONAL: Born September 8, 1941, in Warren, Pa. *Education:* Attended Ohio University; attended Juilliard School of Music, 1961-62. *Agent:* David Cogan, Cogan Management, 350 Fifth Ave., New York, N.Y.

CAREER: Worked as advertising copywriter in New York, N.Y.; actress, singer, dancer, and writer. *Member:* Mystery Writers of America, Authors Guild, Screen Actors Guild, Actors Equity Association.

WRITINGS: Women Who Changed America (biographies), Manor Books, 1977; *How to Ask a Man,* Dell, 1979; *Boys Talk About Girls/Girls Talk About Boys,* Scholastic Books, 1981; *Save the Last Dance for Me* (suspense novel), Pocket Books, 1981; *Hush Little Baby* (suspense novel), Pocket Books, 1982; *Figuring Out Boys,* Scholastic Books, 1982. Contributor of stories to confession magazines.

SIDELIGHTS: Judi Miller commented: "I write psychological thrillers about plausible people in implausible situations."

BIOGRAPHICAL/CRITICAL SOURCES: Los Angeles Times Book Review, May 24, 1981.

* * *

MILLER, Ruth 1921-

BRIEF ENTRY: Born April 5, 1921, in Chicago, Ill. American

educator and author. Miller has been a professor of English and comparative literature at State University of New York at Stony Brook since 1969. She was a Fulbright fellow in India in 1965 and taught at Hebrew University of Jerusalem from 1970 to 1972. Miller wrote *Floating Island: Poems* (Human & Rousseau, 1965), *The City Rose* (McGraw, 1977), and *Poetry: An Introduction* (St. Martin's, 1981). She edited *Race Awareness: The Nightmare and the Vision* (Oxford University Press, 1971), *Blackamerican Literature, 1760 to the Present* (Glencoe, 1971), and *Backgrounds in Blackamerican Literature* (Chandler, 1971). *Address:* 6 Dogwood Dr., Stony Brook, N.Y. 11790; and Department of English, State University of New York at Stony Brook, Stony Brook, N.Y. 11794. *Biographical/critical sources: Criticism,* winter, 1969.

* * *

MILLSTEAD, Thomas E.

PERSONAL: Born in Milwaukee, Wis.; son of Edward C. (an army officer) and Crystal (a nurse; maiden name, Rasmussen) Millstead; married Judith Kresl, December 28, 1968. *Education:* Marquette University, Ph.B., 1951. *Home:* 1750 North Wells St., Chicago, Ill. 60614. *Office:* Continental National American Financial Corp., CNA Plaza, Chicago, Ill. 60685.

CAREER: Racine Journal Times, Racine, Wis., newspaperman, 1953-68; Continental National America Financial Corp., Chicago, Ill., manager of public information, 1971—. *Military service:* U.S. Army, 1951-53; editor of weekly Army newspaper. *Member:* Dramatists Guild, Mystery Writers of America.

WRITINGS: Comanche Stallion, Bouregy, 1957; *Cave of the Moving Shadows* (juvenile novel), Dial, 1979. Contributor of short stories to mystery magazines; contributor of articles to various periodicals, including *Fate, Chicago Tribune Sunday Magazine, Westways,* and *Coronet.*

WORK IN PROGRESS: A suspense novel entitled *Behind You.*

* * *

MILTON, Joyce 1946-

PERSONAL: Born January 12, 1946, in McKeesport, Pa.; daughter of Joseph Kent (a steelworker) and Elsie (a librarian; maiden name, Wilson) Milton. *Education:* Swarthmore College, B.A., 1967; Pratt Institute of Technology, M.L.S., 1969. *Home:* 60 Plaza St., Brooklyn, N.Y. 11238.

CAREER: New York Public Library, New York City, librarian, 1967-69; librarian at private school in New York City, 1969-71; *Kirkus Review,* New York City, young adult editor, 1971-77; free-lance writer, 1977—.

WRITINGS: Sunrise of Power, Harcourt, 1979; (with Rafael Steinberg and Sarah Lewis) *Religion at the Crossroads: Byzantium and the Turks,* Harcourt, 1979; *Controversy: Science in Conflict,* Messner, 1980; *A Friend of China* (biography of Agnes Smedley), Hastings House, 1980; *Here Come the Robots* (juvenile), Hastings House, 1981. Contributor to poetry magazines, including *Southern Review, New York Quarterly,* and *Beloit Poetry Journal.*

WORK IN PROGRESS: The Hidden Rosenberg Case (tentative title), with Ronald Radosh, for Holt.

SIDELIGHTS: Joyce Milton wrote: "I am basically a writer of popular/journalistic historical works; my primary fields of interest are history of science and technology, Eastern Europe, and history of U.S. politics, especially left-wing movements.

The book on the Rosenberg case is definitely my most important project to date, as it will be the first thorough historical study of the subject to be based on recently released government documents as well as extensive interviews with principals who have never before spoken for publication.''

*   *   *

MINEKA, Francis Edward   1907-

BRIEF ENTRY: Born July 26, 1907, in Caneadea, N.Y. American educator, editor, and author. Mineka taught English literature at Cornell University from 1946 to 1973 and has been a professor emeritus since 1973. He was a Guggenheim fellow and Fulbright fellow, 1962-63. He wrote *The Dissidence of Dissent: The Monthly Repository, 1806-1838, Under the Editorship of Robert Aspland, W.J. Fox, R. H. Horne, and Leigh Hunt* (University of North Carolina Press, 1944), and edited *The Earlier Letters of John Stuart Mill* (University of Toronto Press, 1963) and *The Later Letters of John Stuart Mill* (University of Toronto Press, 1972). *Address:* 110 Irving Pl., Ithaca, N.Y. 14850.

*   *   *

MINER, Jane Claypool   1933-
(Jane Claypool; Veronica Ladd, a pseudonym)

PERSONAL: Born April 22, 1933, in McAllen, Tex.; married and widowed twice; children: Kathryn Du Vivier. *Education:* California State University, Long Beach, B.A., 1956; graduate study at University of California, Los Angeles, and California State University, Los Angeles. *Home:* 103 Dawes Ave., Pittsfield, Mass. 01201. *Agent:* Writer's House, Inc., 21 West 26th St., New York, N.Y. 10010.

CAREER: Teacher at public schools in Long Beach, Calif., 1956-58, Torrance, Calif., 1959-62 and 1964-69, Trenton, Calif., 1963-64, and Los Angeles, Calif., 1969-71; junior high school teacher in Pittsfield, Mass., 1978-81; Taconic High School, Pittsfield, teacher, ending 1981; writer, 1981—. Public speaker on romance novels. *Member:* Society of Children's Book Writers, Authors League of America, American Society of Journalists and Authors.

WRITINGS—Young adult novels; under name Jane Claypool Miner; published by Scholastic Book Services, except as noted: *Choices,* 1978; *Why Did You Leave Me?,* 1978; *Dreams Can Come True,* 1981; *Senior Class,* 1982; *No Place to Go,* 1982; *Maggie,* 1982; *To Pursue a Dream,* Grosset, 1982; *I'll Love You Forever,* 1983; *Teenage Models,* 1983.

Young adult novels; under name Jane Claypool; published by Crestwood, except as noted: *A Day at a Time,* 1982; *A Man's Pride,* 1982; *Navajo Victory,* 1982; *Split Decision,* 1982; *A New Beginning,* 1982; *Miracle of Time,* 1982; *This Day Is Mine,* 1982; *The Tough Guy,* 1982; *A Love for Violet,* Westminster, 1982; *Jasmine Finds Love,* Westminster, 1982.

Young adult nonfiction; under name Jane Claypool: *Alcohol and You,* F. Watts, 1981; *How to Get a Good Job,* F. Watts, 1982; *Working in a Hospital,* Messner, 1983; *Alcohol and Teens,* Messner, 1983; *Unemployment,* F. Watts, 1983; *Eating Disorders,* F. Watts, 1983; *Why Are Some People Fat?,* Creative Education.

Young adult novels; under pseudonym Veronica Ladd: *Flowers for Lisa,* Simon & Schuster, 1982; *Promised Kiss,* Simon & Schuster, 1982; *For Love of Lori,* Simon & Schuster, 1982; *Wildest Heart,* Simon & Schuster, 1983.

Author of reading lessons and educational filmstrips. Contributor of more than one hundred stories and articles to magazines and newspapers.

WORK IN PROGRESS: Three young adult novels, under pseudonym Veronica Ladd, for Simon & Schuster; nonfiction, tentatively titled *Second Husbands: A Better Choice,* publication by Warner Press expected in 1983.

AVOCATIONAL INTERESTS: Reading, attending plays, music (including blues and jazz), weaving, making pottery, sewing, bicycling, painting.

BIOGRAPHICAL/CRITICAL SOURCES: Berkshire Eagle, April 14, 1981.

*   *   *

MINER, Joshua L.   1920-

PERSONAL: Born July 11, 1920, in Plainsfield, N.J.; son of Joshua L. Miner and Louise Matlock Miner Houghton; married Phebe Ten Broeck Stevens; children: Phebe T. Miner Goldman, Louise M. Miner Morrow, Joshua L. IV, John S., Daniel G. *Education:* Princeton University, B.A. (cum laude), 1943. *Politics:* Independent. *Religion:* Protestant. *Home:* 42 School Street, Andover, Mass. 01810. *Office:* Phillips Academy, Andover, Mass. 01810.

CAREER: The Hun School, Princeton, N.J., assistant headmaster and instructor in physics, 1948-50; Gordonstoun School, Scotland, director of activities and instructor in math, 1950-52; Phillips Academy, Andover, Mass., physics instructor, house master, and athletics coach, 1952-64; Outward Bound, Inc., Greenwich, Conn., founding president of local branch, founding trustee, and chairman of board of directors, 1964-72; Phillips Academy, dean of admissions, 1972—.

Director of Colorado Outward Bound School; trustee of Lawrence General Hospital, Thompson Academy, Hurricane Island Outward Bound School, Colorado Outward Bound School, and Judge Baker Clinic; member of advisory board of Reading is Fundamental, Hampshire College, and National Service Secretariat; consultant on urban affairs to Peace Corps and Ford Foundation; vice-chairman of White House Conference on Youth; member of state advisory committee of U.S. Commission on Civil Rights; member of long range planning committee of Secondary School Admissions Test Board; member of national board of directors of the Congressional Award; overseer of Boys' Club of Boston; sponsor of St. John's College. *Military service:* U.S. Army; became battery commander; received Purple Heart, Bronze Star, and five combat stars.

MEMBER: Kettering Foundation (lecturer in IDEA series), Atlantic Foundation (trustee), Andover YMCA (trustee). *Awards, honors:* American Academy of Achievement award, 1970, for educator of the year; elected to Woolrich Hall of Fame, 1981; Council for the Advancement of Experiential Education award, 1981.

WRITINGS: (With Joe Boldt) *Outward Bound, U.S.A.: A Learning Through Experience in Adventure Based Education,* Morrow, 1981.

SIDELIGHTS: The objective of the Outward Bound program is to train its participants to realize their capabilities and self-reliance by presenting them with increasingly difficult challenges to survival in the wilderness. Included in the course, which runs from four to twenty-six days, is training in mountain climbing, sailing, life saving and first aid, and search and rescue. Outward Bound, which has seven schools in the United

States and branches in sixteen foreign countries, was founded by Dr. Kurt Hahn in Wales in 1941.

* * *

MITCHAM, Samuel W(ayne), Jr. 1949-

PERSONAL: Born January 2, 1949, in Mer Rouge, La.; son of Samuel Wayne (in business) and Addye Mae (a newspaper editor; maiden name, McGough) Mitcham. *Education:* Northeast Louisiana University, B.A., 1971, M.S., 1976; doctoral study at University of Tennessee, 1978-81. *Home:* 501 Van Frank Ave., Bastrop, La. 71220.

CAREER: Northeast Louisiana University, Monroe, geographer and cartographer at Pure and Applied Science Research Institute, 1977-78; Heartfield, Price & Greene (environmental consultants), Monroe, geographer and cartographer, 1978; Oak Ridge National Laboratory, Oak Ridge, Tenn., geographer, 1980-81; writer, 1981—. *Military service:* U.S. Army, Infantry, helicopter pilot, 1971-73. U.S. Army Reserve, 1973—; present rank, captain. *Member:* Association of American Geographers, Agricultural History Society, Gamma Theta Epsilon.

WRITINGS: Rommel's Desert War, Stein & Day, 1982. Contributor to professional journals.

WORK IN PROGRESS: Rommel's Last Campaign (tentative title), on the Normandy campaign of 1944, publication expected in 1983.

SIDELIGHTS: Mitcham wrote: "Military history has been a hobby with me since I was a child. I plan to write some more solid, substantial works dealing with World War II over the next few years."

* * *

MITCHELL, Cynthia 1922-

PERSONAL: Born August 10, 1922, in Sharlston, Yorkshire, England; daughter of Claude (a colliery accountant) and Lillian (a teacher; maiden name, Berry) Moverlay; married Dennis Hardie Mitchell (a secondary school teacher of mathematics and physics), March 22, 1951; children: Jeannette Louise, Caroline Jane. *Education:* Balls Park College of Education, Teaching Certificate, 1949. *Religion:* Religious Society of Friends. *Home:* 32 Barnsley Rd., Ackworth, West Yorkshire WF7 7NB, England. *Office:* Howard School, Low Ackworth, Pontefract, Yorkshire, England.

CAREER: Wakefield Food Office, Wakefield, Yorkshire, England, civil servant, 1939-45; schoolteacher in Yorkshire and Hertfordshire, 1945-52; Wakefield Metropolitan Education Authority, Wakefield, Yorkshire, deputy head and teacher, 1964—. Secretary of local freedom from hunger campaign, 1961-63. *Member:* National Union of Teachers (British), Campaign for Nuclear Disarmament.

WRITINGS: Time for School: A Practical Guide for Parents of Young Children, Penguin, 1973; *Halloweena Hecatee and Other Rhymes to Skip To* (juvenile; illustrated by Eileen Browne), Heinemann, 1978, Crowell, 1979; *Playtime* (juvenile; illustrated by Satomi Ichikawa), Heinemann, 1978, Collins & World, 1979; *Hop-Along Happily and Other Rhymes for the Playground* (juvenile; illustrated by Browne), Heinemann, 1979; (compiler) *Under the Cherry Tree* (juvenile; illustrated by Ichikawa), Collins & World, 1979; (contributor) Frank Muirs and Polly Muirs, *Big Dipper,* Heinemann, 1981. Contributor to journals and BBC Schools Programs.

WORK IN PROGRESS: Granny in the Kitchen (tentative title), publication by Heinemann expected in 1983; *Big and Beastly,*

a collection of verse about big animals; verse for young children; a book for older children; a long story in rhyme.

SIDELIGHTS: Cynthia Mitchell told *CA:* "I had never written anything for publication before *Time for School,* which was the result of years of discussing children's progress with parents, and being constantly told, in effect, 'We have access to a lot of advice about the health care of babies and young children, but the only thing we ever seem to be told about preparing them for school is to teach them to tie their shoelaces.' Tying laces is an extremely difficult skill for the average preschooler to acquire, and there is so much more of far greater value that young children need to experience. So I decided to write, in nonjargon language for the benefit of the local parents, about the more profitable activities they might encourage and why. I envisaged a school leaflet for distribution at the local playgroup. The 'leaflet' finished up, three years later, as a 246-page Penguin paperback. So I became an author by accident, discovering a need that I had the experience to meet, as, of course, have thousands of other infant teachers.

"Contact with publishers and 'book people' led to the publication of the children's books. Not able to find enough vigorous, worthwhile, vocabulary-extending rhyme to bridge the gap between nursery rhymes and more sophisticated poetry, I had written some verse of my own for class use. I have attempted to harness the young child's ready response to rhyme and rhythm in order for them to practice control of bodily movement. Children need to extend usable vocabulary in a way that doesn't present poetry as something to be received passively because grownups think it's good for them, like medicine or a haircut. It seems to me that too often when children come to school they quickly lose their spontaneous delight in chanting nursery rhymes and begin to think of poems as small doses of description to be swallowed in relation to a topic. For instance: 'We're doing hibernation, so here's a poem about a hedgehog. . . .'

"Poetry should stimulate a feel for language; poetry should be a way of pithily expressing thought and emotion; poetry should be a means of stretching the imagination to help it work in a wide variety of subjects. These points are missed by young children unless they continue to experience delight in the feel of the words, the emotions, and the new ideas opened up. My class hears poems about hedgehogs, of course, but they also hop, skip, clap, and jump to rhymes, as to music, just for the fun of wrapping the words around their tongues and the sparkle that chanting to movement brings to their eyes.

"My day-by-day classroom work is a continuing research into how young children learn, and how they respond to varied efforts to teach them specific skills. I am particularly interested in teaching reading, in increasing vocabulary, in encouraging articulate response, and in settling children happily in school."

AVOCATIONAL INTERESTS: Nuclear disarmament and environmental protection, gardening, reading (especially the science fiction of Ursula LeGuin and J.R.R. Tolkien), travel, and "conversation that explores ideas."

* * *

MITCHELL, Lionel H. 1942-

PERSONAL: Born September 7, 1942, in New York, N.Y.; son of Alexander John (a jazz drummer) and Ethyl (Burgfierdt) Mitchell. *Education:* Attended Louisiana State University, New Orleans, 1961-63. *Politics:* Democrat. *Religion:* Buddhist. *Home:* 245 East 11th St., New York, N.Y. 10003. *Agent:* Ned Leavitt, William Morris Agency, 1350 Avenue of the Americas, New York, N.Y. 10019.

CAREER: Free-lance writer prior to 1977; *New York Amsterdam News,* New York, N.Y., drama critic, 1977—. *Awards, honors:* American Book Award from Before Columbus Foundation, 1981, for literary excellence.

WRITINGS: (Contributor) Jesse Kornbluth, editor, *Notes From the New Underground,* Viking, 1968; *Traveling Light* (novel), Seaview, 1980.

WORK IN PROGRESS: Noble Ruins, a sequel to *Traveling Light.*

SIDELIGHTS: Mitchell told *CA:* "Since roughly 1966 I have been interested in Eastern mysticism and have been initiated into the Shakti yoga system. In the early 1970's, according to predictions made to me by various yogis and adepts, I further followed my 'dharma' into studies of Tibetan Buddhism. H. H. Dudjom Rimpoche gave me the name 'Kunsang Wangchuk,' which means 'he who will subdue countless thousands of lower natures and will always be giving.'

"It is because of my deep-seated conviction that we owe so much to our basic American background that I have refrained from declaring myself through any Eastern titles, refrained from taking monastic vows, and have insisted upon living a secular American way of life. This has brought me into conflict with many Eastern sects that I have found deceptive to the extent that they do not honor the timeless etiquette of informing the initiate in advance of the ascetical aim of the initiations they give out. Though a practitioner of various Eastern techniques, I insist upon honoring my black, Southern Christianity because of the debt that I feel I owe to the importance placed upon the individual's worth by the Judeo-Christian tradition. I also insist upon a nonsectarian, universal approach that embraces all universal spiritualities, such as African, Islamic, and other anthropological cultures.

"I read my first book on Lao Tzu in high school, and so I am resistant to any religious or cultural reverse imperialism, which I feel is all too often perpetrated against American culture by various advocates of foreign spirituality. I believe and support all studies and even practical application of various useful wisdoms as long as they recognize the peculiar situation and the value of American life as it is. Anything that seeks by subterfuge to disorient, disrupt, or ride roughly over the requirements of decent American existence meets with my opposition."

BIOGRAPHICAL/CRITICAL SOURCES: National Review, July 30, 1968; *New York Times,* February 27, 1975; *Village Voice,* March 10, 1975; *Kirkus Reviews,* May 5, 1980; *Los Angeles Times,* August 3, 1980; *Cleveland Plain Dealer,* August 3, 1980; *New York Times Book Review,* August 17, 1980; *New York Amsterdam News,* August 23, 1980.

*   *   *

MOHAMMED RIZA PAHLEVI
See PAHLEVI, Mohammed Riza

*   *   *

MOHN, Peter B(urnet) 1934-

PERSONAL: Surname rhymes with "loan"; born May 17, 1934, in New York, N.Y.; son of George Liddle (a pathologist) and Margaret Louise (a medical technician; maiden name, Burnet) Fite; legally adopted by stepfather, Willard A. Mohn (a dentist); married Janet Athlene Young, September 8, 1958 (divorced, February, 1969); children: Steven Leigh, Kathryn Gail, Thomas Peter, Andrew Scott. *Education:* Attended University of Minnesota, 1955-59. *Politics:* "Liberal to wishy-washy." *Religion:* Episcopalian. *Home address:* P.O. Box 313, Inverness, Calif. 94937.

CAREER: Worked as a radio and television reporter, 1957-69, newspaper reporter and photographer, 1959-65, newspaper editor, 1965-68, advertising account executive, 1968-71, and commercial and multimedia photographer, 1971-76, in association with KSTP, St. Paul, Minn., *Redwood Gazette,* Redwood Falls, Minn., *Daily Journal,* New Ulm, Minn., *Reflector,* Norwalk, Ohio, *Evening News,* Cadillac, Mich., *Free Press,* Mankato, Minn.; free-lance writer, 1976—. Lecturer at Southwest Florida Writers' Conference, 1980; public relations adviser to nonprofit groups, Lee County, Fla.; actor and technical worker in community theatre. *Military service:* U.S. Navy, sonarman, 1952-55.

WRITINGS—All for children: *Bicycle Touring,* Crestwood, 1975; *Hiking,* Crestwood, 1975; *Hot Air Ballooning,* Crestwood, 1975; *Scuba Diving and Snorkeling,* Crestwood, 1975; *Trailbiking,* Crestwood, 1975; *Whitewater Challenge,* Crestwood, 1975; *The Blue Angels,* Children's Press, 1977; *The Golden Knights,* Children's Press, 1977; *The Silver Eagles,* Children's Press, 1978; *The Thunderbirds,* Children's Press, 1980; *The Confederate Air Force,* Children's Press, 1981; *Naval Special Warfare Teams,* Children's Press, 1981.

WORK IN PROGRESS: The Snowbirds, for Children's Press; books for children about experimental aircraft, Florida history and natural history, and two adventure novels, entitled *Ghost of the Porkchop* and *Steer Clear of Bocamo; Celebration,* a novel for young adults; an adult novel, *Revival.*

SIDELIGHTS: Mohn told *CA:* "I have learned the hard way, even though I knew all along that one does not become a successful author overnight. Were it not for other activities, I'd have given up writing rather early. During the leaner years I had other ways of supporting myself. I now find myself addicted to seeing my name in print on the spines of more and more books, and I'm not limiting myself to children's books either. And even if I should become the author of a bestselling novel in time, I doubt that I'd drop the writing for children entirely.

"One of my principal reasons for continuing to write is simply that I seem to get better with every book I get into print. If I look through some of the first books I wrote, I sometimes cringe because I see things that could have been written better. Young people, I think, have a large appetite for exciting, quality nonfiction. It has been a privilege to be able to do the first-ever series of books in print on America's military flight demonstration teams, and an ever rarer privilege to have known these people.

"When the words don't flow, I'm likely to go fishing or, perhaps, tie a knot. To the best of my knowledge, I'm one of only a handful of people in the country who know how to tie a large number of different ornamental knots. I've decorated whole restaurants with these knots, but once I get started on a large project, I'm right back to writing because working with my hands tends to free my mind.

"When I go places, I prefer them to be primitive. I enjoyed travel in Europe late in the sixties, but seeing and staying for three weeks in the Galapagos Islands was a thrill, an education and an inspiration. One of these next years, I've promised myself Australia.

AVOCATIONAL INTERESTS: Mohn occasionally serves as a boatswain's mate.

MOHRENSCHILDT, Dimitri Sergius Von
See Von MOHRENSCHILDT, Dimitri Sergius

*   *   *

MOLHO, Anthony 1939-

BRIEF ENTRY: Born July 12, 1939, in Thessaloniki, Greece. American historian, educator, and author. Molho has been teaching since 1959. He joined the faculty at Brown University in 1966 and became a professor of history in 1974. He was a Fulbright fellow in 1969. Molho wrote *Florentine Public Finances in the Early Renaissance, 1400-1433* (Harvard University Press, 1971) and edited *Social and Economic Foundations of the Italian Renaissance* (Wiley, 1969) and *Renaissance: Studies in Honor of Hans Baron* (G. C. Sansoni, 1970). *Address:* Department of History, Brown University, 79 Waterman St., Providence, R.I. 02912.

*   *   *

MOLLER, Richard Jay 1952-

PERSONAL: Surname is pronounced Muller; born September 29, 1952, in Summit, N.J.; son of Richard William (a businessman) and Elizabeth Ruth (a piano teacher; maiden name, Jones) Moller; married Kathryn Marie Holtermann, March 29, 1981; children: Andrew. *Education:* Trinity College, Hartford, Conn., B.A., 1974; University of California, Berkeley, J.D., 1980. *Politics:* Democrat (liberal). *Religion:* Hindu. *Home:* 255 Stanford Ave., Berkeley, Calif. 94708. *Office address:* U.S. Court of Appeals, Box 547, San Francisco, Calif. 94101.

CAREER: Admitted to the Bar of California; Environmental Defense Fund, Berkeley, Calif., law clerk, 1979; California Supreme Court, San Francisco, student extern, 1979; State Public Defender's Office, San Francisco, law clerk, 1980; U.S. Court of Appeals, San Francisco, staff attorney, 1980—. *Member:* American Bar Association, California Bar Association.

WRITINGS: *Marijuana: Your Legal Rights,* Addison-Wesley, 1981. Associate editor of *Ecology Law Quarterly,* 1979-80.

WORK IN PROGRESS: *The Wishing Room* (tentative title), an allegorical fantasy for children and adults, publication expected in 1984.

SIDELIGHTS: Moller told *CA:* ''In trying to understand the reasons for the human condition and my existence, I traveled around the world visiting twenty countries; studied religion, philosophy, and mysticism; joined various religious groups; experimented with most hallucinogenic and mind-altering drugs; and lived in a countercultural community in rural, northern California. I finally gave up the search and went to law school. During that time, however, I had spiritual experiences with Swami Muktananda that answered many of my questions about life.

''Although I had stopped using mind-altering drugs, I wrote *Marijuana: Your Legal Rights* to explain to those who prefer illicit drugs to legal, addictive drugs how best to protect their constitutional rights.'' Moller contends in his book that marijuana should be legalized. To support his position, he investigates case histories, describes the criminal justice system's treatment of drug violators, and argues that the enforcement of drug laws has encroached upon the Fourth and Fifth amendments to the Constitution. He focuses specifically on what constitutes a legal search and advises users of marijuana on what indiscretions to avoid.

MOLLINGER, Robert N. 1945-

PERSONAL: Born April 25, 1945, in Philadelphia, Pa.; son of Owen S. (a merchant) and Florence (Devensky) Mollinger; married Shernaz Mehta (a professor), August, 1969. *Education:* Oberlin College, B.A., 1967; Indiana University, M.A., 1971, Ph.D., 1973; National Psychological Association for Psychoanalysis, certificate in psychoanalysis, 1979. *Office:* Department of English, Nassau Community College, Garden City, N.Y. 11530.

CAREER: Nassau Community College, Garden City, N.Y., instructor, 1971-73, assistant professor, 1973-77, associate professor of English, 1977—. Member of faculty, control analyst, and training analyst at Training Institute of National Psychological Association for Psychoanalysis, New York Center for Psychoanalytic Training, and New Jersey Institute for Training in Psychoanalysis. *Member:* National Psychological Association for Psychoanalysis, Society for Psychoanalytic Training, American Personnel and Guidance Association.

WRITINGS: *Psychoanalysis and Literature,* Nelson-Hall, 1981. Contributor to psychology and library journals, and *American Imago.* Fiction editor of *Psychoanalytic Review.*

WORK IN PROGRESS: *Interdisciplinary Psychoanalysis.*

AVOCATIONAL INTERESTS: Travel (Europe, Mexico, Latin America, the Middle East, India).

*   *   *

MORLEY, Felix M. 1894-1982

OBITUARY NOTICE: Born in 1894 in Haverford, Pa.; died of cancer, March 13, 1982, in Baltimore, Md. Scholar, journalist, and author. Morley began his distinguished career as a Rhodes scholar at Oxford, a research fellow at the London School of Economics and Political Science, and a Guggenheim fellow at the League of Nations. In 1922 he joined the *Baltimore Sun,* becoming that newspaper's first correspondent in China. Morley arrived at the *Washington Post* in 1933 and served as its editorial page editor for seven years, receiving the Pulitzer Prize in 1936 for his distinctive commentaries. He left the newspaper in 1940 to become president of Haverford College. Following World War II, Morley resumed writing, working as a Washington correspondent for *Barron's* and contributing to *Nation's Business* magazine and the National Broadcasting Company. He was also co-founder and editor of the newsletter *Human Events.* During his career Morley produced seven books on economics and politics, including *The Power in the People, The Foreign Policy of the United States,* and *Freedom and Federalism.* In addition, he wrote an autobiography, *For the Record.* Obituaries and other sources: *American Authors and Books, 1640 to the Present Day,* 3rd revised edition, Crown, 1962; *American Men and Women of Science: The Social and Behavioral Sciences,* 12th edition, Bowker, 1973; *Who Was Who Among North American Authors, 1921-1939,* Gale, 1976; *Who's Who in America,* 40th edition, Marquis, 1978; *Washington Post,* March 15, 1982; *New York Times,* March 16, 1982; *Newsweek,* March 29, 1982; *Time,* March 29, 1982.

*   *   *

MORREN, Theophil
See HOFMANNSTHAL, Hugo von

*   *   *

MORRIS, Phyllis 1894-1982

OBITUARY NOTICE: Born July 18, 1894, in London, England; died February 6, 1982, in Northwood, England. Actress and playwright. Although originally trained in journalism, Morris began a theatrical career in 1926 with the production of her first stageplay, "The Rescue Party," in London. By the mid-1930's the writer was appearing on stage herself in a number of successful character roles. Morris secured her first part in British films in 1935, and she was seen frequently on British television as well. The actress also performed in Hollywood movies from 1946 to 1951. In addition to a small number of stageplays, including "Made in Heaven" and "A-Hunting We Will Go," Morris produced several children's books and showed her paintings in many London galleries. Obituaries and other sources: *Who's Who in the Theatre: A Biographical Record of the Contemporary Stage*, 17th edition, Gale, 1981; *London Times*, February 12, 1982.

*   *   *

MORRISON, Philip 1915-

BRIEF ENTRY: Born November 7, 1915, in Somerville, N.J. American physicist, educator, and author. Morrison was a physicist at Los Alamos Scientific Laboratory during World War II. Since 1965 he has been a professor of physics at Massachusetts Institute of Technology. He wrote *Cosmic Rays* (Springer, 1961) and *My Father's Watch: Aspects of the Physical World* (Prentice-Hall, 1969). He edited *The Search for Extraterrestrial Intelligence, SETI* (National Aeronautics and Space Administration Scientific and Technical Information Office, 1977). *Address:* Department of Physics, Massachusetts Institute of Technology, Cambridge, Mass. 02139.

*   *   *

MORROW, Mable 1892-1977

OBITUARY NOTICE: Born July 15, 1892, in Zanesville, Ohio; died June 9, 1977. Civil servant and author. Morrow worked for the Bureau of Indian Affairs for almost thirty years. During much of that time she served as arts and crafts supervisor, living and working on Indian reservations throughout the United States. She wrote *Indian Rawhide: An American Folk Art.* (Date of death provided by sister, Helen M. Cahusac.)

*   *   *

MORSE, Flo 1921-

PERSONAL: Born June 21, 1921, in Yonkers, N.Y.; married Joseph Morse (a banker and lawyer), October 1, 1943; children: Joel, Jonathan. *Education:* Barnard College, B.A., 1943. *Residence:* Lyme, N.H. 03768. *Agent:* Marilyn Marlow, Curtis Brown, Ltd., 575 Madison Ave., New York, N.Y. 10022.

CAREER: Writer, 1935—; *Patent Trader*, Mt. Kisco, N.Y., free-lance writer, 1951-1964; *Reporter Dispatch;* White Plains, N.Y., reporter, feature writer, and columnist, 1964-65; *New York Herald Tribune*, New York, N.Y., Westchester correspondent and feature writer, 1965-66. Also writer and publicist for WINS-Radio. Lecturer on Shakerism. Supporter of Shaker-related museums and groups. *Member:* Authors Guild, National Association of Historic Communal Societies, New Hampshire Historical Society, and many local organizations. *Awards, honors: Commonweal* cited *Yankee Communes: Another American Way* as one of best books for children of 1971.

WRITINGS: Yankee Communes: Another American Way (young adult), Harcourt, 1971; *How Does It Feel to Be a Tree?* (juvenile poetry) illustrations by Clyde Watson, Parents' Magazine Press, 1976; *The Shakers and the World's People* (adult non-fiction), Dodd, 1981. Contributor of book reviews to *New*

York Times, Shaker Quarterly, World of Shaker, and *Shaker Messenger*. Verse published in periodicals, including *Look*.

WORK IN PROGRESS: A novel.

SIDELIGHTS: Flo Morse told *CA:* "I enjoy book reviewing, feature writing, and making new gardens for my hillside home. I have been a historian and have written poetry and verse for children. I have lectured on the Shakers in New England and elsewhere. I seek serenity in my special interest, the Shakers."

*   *   *

MORTON, Lynne 1952-

PERSONAL: Born August 18, 1952, in New York, N.Y.; daughter of Leonard Ira (a professor) and Barbara (a teacher) Morton. *Education:* Vassar College, B.A. (with honors), 1974; Georgetown University, M.A., 1975. *Office:* Korn/Ferry International, 277 Park Ave., New York, N.Y. 10172.

CAREER: Delacorte Press, New York City, publicity manager, 1976-78; Mayflower Books, Inc., New York City, director of publicity, 1978-79; American Management Association, New York City, public relations associate, 1979-81; Korn/Ferry International, New York City, public relations associate, 1981—.

WRITINGS: (With Stephen H. Schneider) *The Primordial Bond*, Plenum, 1981.

WORK IN PROGRESS: A novel.

SIDELIGHTS: Acclaimed by critics, Lynne Morton's book deals with the manner in which man identifies nature and his relationship to it. "*The Primordial Bond*," wrote David Burns of the *Washington Post Book World*, "is a provocative and highly readable discussion of the limitations of both science and humanism in confronting such issues" as environmental and technological problems.

Exploring both the views of humanists and the theories of scientists, Morton and her co-author, Stephen H. Schneider, "feel that it is not enough to look at the environment from either a purely technical view, or through the eyes of nostalgia for the nonindustrial past," noted Richard Severo of the *New York Times*. So part of their book attempts to define science in terms of natural biological and chemical cycles while illustrating the ramifications of man's interference in the natural order. On the other hand, the humanist's point of view is given through examples of art, legend, mythology, and astrology.

Juxtaposed in this fashion, the two schools of thought exemplify the age-old historical and ethical dilemma of whether man should preserve or master nature. "It takes scientific information to estimate both risks and benefits," the authors commented, "and it takes elucidation of our feelings and values to translate these estimates into acceptable action. Providing data is a specialty of scientists. Interpretation of our feelings and values is a pursuit of artists and other humanists."

AVOCATIONAL INTERESTS: Literature, dance, fine arts.

BIOGRAPHICAL/CRITICAL SOURCES: Washington Post Book World, July 18, 1981; *New York Times*, September 1, 1981.

*   *   *

MOSER, Don(ald Bruce) 1932-

PERSONAL: Born October 19, 1932, in Cleveland, Ohio; son of Donald Lyman and Kathryn (McHugh) Moser; married Penny Lee Ward (a journalist), December 20, 1975. *Education:* Ohio University, B.A., 1957; graduate study at Stanford University, 1957-58, and University of Sydney, 1959-60. *Home:* 2220 40th

St. N.W., Washington, D.C. 20007. *Agent:* Curtis Brown Ltd., 575 Madison Ave., New York, N.Y. 10022. *Office:* Smithsonian Magazine, 900 Jefferson Dr., Washington, D.C. 20007.

CAREER: Life, New York, N.Y., reporter and assistant editor, 1961-64, West Coast bureau chief, 1964-65, Far East bureau chief, 1966-69, assistant managing editor, 1970-72; *Smithsonian,* Washington, D.C., managing editor, 1978-80, editor, 1981—. *Military service:* U.S. Army, 1953-55. *Member:* Phi Beta Kappa. *Awards, honors:* Stegner fellowship, 1957; Fulbright scholarship, 1958.

WRITINGS: The Peninsula: A Story of the Olympic Country in Words and Photographs, Sierra Books, 1962; (with Jerry Cohen) *The Pied Piper of Tucson,* New American Library, 1968; (with the editors of Time-Life Books) *The Snake River Country,* Time-Life, 1974; (with the editors of Time-Life Books) *Central American Jungles,* photographs by C. Rentmeester, Time-Life, 1975; *A Heart to the Hawks* (juvenile novel), Atheneum, 1975; *China-Burma-India Theater,* Time-Life, 1977.

Contributor of articles to periodicals, such as *Life, National Geographic, Smithsonian, Audubon, Harper's, Sports Illustrated,* and *American Heritage.*

BIOGRAPHICAL/CRITICAL SOURCES: Life, November 8, 1963, January 22, 1971; *Audubon,* September, 1974.

*   *   *

MOSLEY, Diana 1910-

PERSONAL: Born June 17, 1910, in London, England; daughter of David Bertram Ogilvy (second baron of Redesdale) and Sydney (Bowles) Mitford; married Bryan Walter Guinness, January 30, 1929 (divorced, 1934); married Oswald Mosley (a politician and writer), October 6, 1936 (died, 1980); children: (first marriage) Jonathan, Desmond; (second marriage) Alexander, Max. *Education:* Educated privately. *Home:* Temple de la Gloire, Orsay 91400, France.

CAREER: Writer.

WRITINGS: A Life of Contrasts, Hamish Hamilton, 1977, New York Times, 1978; (translator) Nicki Lauda, *My Years With Ferrari,* William Kimber, 1979; *The Duchess of Windsor,* Stein & Day, 1980. Editor of *European,* 1953-59.

SIDELIGHTS: Diana Mosley was born into an aristocartic English family, and numbered among her siblings novelist Nancy Mitford and journalist Jessica Mitford. When Diana married Oswald Mosley, leader of the British Union of Fascists, in Berlin, the wedding guests included Adolf Hitler and Joseph Goebbels. Because of Oswald Mosley's opposition to war against Germany, Diana Mosley was imprisoned without charge or trial for three and a half years. "I was arrested in June, 1940, when our youngest son was eleven weeks old, and released in November, 1943, owing to my husband's illness," she told *CA.*

Diana Mosley writes of her imprisonment as well as of her family, friends, and acquaintances, including Lytton Strachey, Evelyn Waugh, and Hitler, whom she found "exceptionally charming, clever, and original," in her autobiography, *A Life of Contrasts.* Anne Duchene of the *Times Literary Supplement* noted: "Lady Mosley is capable of arguing that what happened to the Jews under Hitler was largely the fault of world Jewry, in not giving them somewhere else to go. Everything else may be read in this appalling light." But Duchene also found Mosley's memoirs "suffused and strengthened by the family virtues of intense love and loyalty, courage, enjoyment of friends and approval of laughter . . . and by a saving honesty." Alice

Gilmore Vines, in the *Historian,* wrote: "[Mosley's] autobiography's most interesting chapter is the one in which she professes to find many similarities between Der Fuhrer and Winston Churchill. Her sense of proportion (or lack of it) is shown in her equation of 'evil things' done in Germany with England's prewar slums!. . . A British Bourbon to the end, she has unfortunately forgotten nothing and learned nothing. Her life's story is an exercise in persistent wrong-headedness."

The *Listener*'s Mary Warnock found the book "fascinating," remarking: "As one would expect of a Mitford, [Diana Mosley] emerges as always sharp, beautiful, prone to 'laughs,' not as irreverent as she might like to think, and above all a loyal member of her famous family." That loyalty to and absorption in her family seemed to dominate Mosley's autobiography, in Warnock's view. Even the political chapters are informed by her "pervasive domesticity": Mosley's defense of her husband's views, of her sister Unity's attachment to Hitler, and of Hitler himself, "seems in these pages to be just an aspect of defence of the family. . . . It is this which gives the central chapters of this book an odd naivety, a sort of frivolity which some may find deeply unattractive."

Mosley said that she wrote *The Duchess of Windsor* to counter the "many unkind and untrue books" about the duchess and her husband, the former King Edward VIII. In the *Listener,* E. S. Turner wrote: "It is in an impeccably kindly spirit that this book is written, . . . [but it does] not add much to the over-familiar story. . . . Much of the description of life with the Windsors is women's magazine stuff." A reviewer for the *Economist* noted that "Lady Mosley has nothing new to tell in her unpretentious summary. . . . The story is reasonably realistic. Its burden is that the pair did live happily ever after; that the Duke was neither sad nor bitter . . . ; that Mrs. Simpson really did not know what she was doing until the abdication, and was really ready to withdraw." Alistair Forbes of the *Spectator* found *The Duchess of Windsor* an "un-Mitfordishly bland book."

BIOGRAPHICAL/CRITICAL SOURCES: Jessica Mitford, *Daughters and Rebels,* Houghton, 1960 (published in England as *Hons and Rebels,* Gollancz, 1960); Michael Holroyd, *Lytton Strachey: A Critical Biography,* Holt, 1968; Dora de Houghton Carrington, *Carrington: Letters and Extracts From Her Diaries,* Holt, 1971; Harold Acton, *Nancy Mitford: A Memoir,* Harper, 1975; Diana Mosley, *A Life of Contrasts,* Hamish Hamilton, 1977, New York Times, 1978; *Listener,* April 14, 1977, July 3, 1980; *Times Literary Supplement,* April 15, 1977; *Spectator,* April 16, 1977, August 2, 1980; *Historian,* November, 1979; Mark Amory, editor, *Letters of Evelyn Waugh,* Ticknor & Fields, 1980; *Economist,* July 12, 1980.

*   *   *

MOTA, Avelino Teixeira da
See TEIXEIRA da MOTA, Avelino

*   *   *

MOTLEY, Willard Francis 1912-1965

OBITUARY NOTICE: Born July 14, 1912, in Chicago, Ill.; died of gangrene, March 4, 1965, in Mexico City, Mexico. Author. Motley's diverse career included working as a migratory laborer, ranch hand, cook, shipping clerk, photographer, radio scriptwriter, and interviewer. His transitory life-style gave him an intimate knowledge of life's darker side, which he encountered in the nation's slums and flophouses. When Motley decided to become a writer, he settled in Chicago's toughest section to study its skid-row inhabitants. A "naturalistic" writer,

Motley presented the theme of tragic human existence in his works. Among his novels are *Knock on Any Door,* which was made into a movie with Humphrey Bogart, *We Fished All Night,* and *Let No Man Write My Epitaph.* Obituaries and other sources: *American Authors and Books, 1640 to the Present Day,* 3rd revised edition, Crown, 1962; *New York Times,* March 5, 1965; *Time,* March 12, 1965; *Newsweek,* March 15, 1965; *Publishers Weekly,* March 15, 1965; *Who Was Who in America, With World Notables,* Volume IV: *1961-1968,* Marquis, 1968.

* * *

MUIR, Richard 1943-

PERSONAL: Born June 18, 1943, in Harrogate, England; son of Kenneth (a hotelier) and Edna (Hugall) Muir; married Nina Rajpal (an academic editor), October 13, 1978. *Education:* University of Aberdeen, M.A. (with first class honors), 1967, Ph.D., 1970. *Politics:* "Liberal/Social Democrat." *Home and office:* Gardener's Cottage, 175 Hinton Way, Great Shelford, Cambridgeshire CB5 2AN, England.

CAREER: University of Dublin, Trinity College, Dublin, Ireland, lecturer in geography, 1970-71; Cambridgeshire College of Arts and Technology, Cambridge, England, senior lecturer in geography, 1971-80; free-lance writer and landscape photographer, 1980—. *Member:* Institute of British Geographers, Society for Landscape Studies, Medieval Village Research Group.

WRITINGS: Modern Political Geography, Macmillan, 1975; (and photographer) *The English Village,* Thames & Hudson, 1980; (with R. Paddison) *Geography, Politics, and Behaviour,* Methuen, 1981; *Riddles in the British Landscape,* Thames & Hudson, 1981; (and photographer) *The Shell Guide to Reading the Landscape,* M. Joseph, 1981; (and photographer) *Lost Villages of Britain,* M. Joseph, 1982; (and photographer) *Stone in the Landscape,* Collins, 1982; *Britain From the Air,* Collins, 1983; (with C. C. Taylor, and photographer) *Visions of the Past,* Dent, 1983. Contributor to *Shell Book of Villages; The English World.* Contributor to magazines and newspapers, including *London Sunday Times, Observer, Geographical,* and *House and Garden.*

WORK IN PROGRESS: Travelers in Time, with own photographs, publication by M. Joseph expected in 1982 or 1983.

SIDELIGHTS: Muir wrote: "In 1980 I resigned my senior lectureship in geography in order to write for the general reader on different aspects of the history of the British landscape. I had established a position as a leading authority on political geography, but thought I could do more service to the cause of conservation and return to my geographical grassroots by this change of career. *The English Village* was a bestseller in the United Kingdom. *The Shell Guide to Reading the Landscape* is equally successful. I also specialize in landscape, historical, and archaeological photography.

"As a free-lance landscape historian and photographer, I spend much of my time visiting monuments and archaeological sites, all within the setting of the wonderful British and Irish landscapes I love. If I have a mission, it is to alert public opinion to the forces which threaten this incomparable heritage and to explain the evolution of the scenery. I have recently done radio broadcasts on the lost villages of England."

Commenting on Muir's landscape studies, Ronald Blythe of the *London Sunday Times* noted that the author "has managed" to write his books "only by touring in every direction, reading every (it seems) relevant authority, taking all his own pictures

and spurning the usual picture-banks, and generally letting his own philosophical, trenchant and always lively pen pour out facts with such verve, that no one without his zeal for the subject could possibly keep up." Blythe continued: Muir "is a missionary, not just a well-informed escort, and his aim is to produce followers in his steps, readers who will have absorbed enough of the deeper understanding of the landscape to be aware of the many dangers which now threaten it."

BIOGRAPHICAL/CRITICAL SOURCES: London Sunday Times, May 24, 1981.

* * *

MULLER, H(erman) J(oseph) 1890-1967

OBITUARY NOTICE: Born December 21, 1890, in New York, N.Y.; died of a heart ailment, April 5, 1967, in Indianapolis, Ind. Geneticist, biologist, educator, and author. Interested in science and evolution since his childhood, Muller, it is believed, helped found the first science club in a secondary school when he was a student at Morris High School. While at Columbia University, where he earned a B.A. in 1910, an M.A. in 1912, and a Ph.D. in 1916, the scientist concentrated his studies in the field of genetics. Viewing biological problems in the light of the chromosome theory of heredity, to which he was introduced by his teacher Edmund B. Wilson, Muller experimented with mutations and radiation, finding that X rays break apart and rearrange genes and thereby artificially accelerate the evolutionary process. Working as a graduate student under the famous Thomas Hunt Morgan, the geneticist established the law of linear linking and discovered "M," the fruit fly's fourth chromosome. Thus Muller's most important theory, that the components of a cell are produced by "naked genes," evolved. Hoping to improve the genetic composition of mankind and to bring about "the control of the evolution of man by man himself," Muller espoused "germinal choice," that is, storing the semen of extraordinarily gifted men in sperm banks for future use. For his work the geneticist received a Guggenheim fellowship and the 1946 Nobel Prize in physiology and medicine. An instructor and researcher in the United States, Germany, the Soviet Union, and Scotland, Muller campaigned against the abuse of radiation in medicine, industry, and the military. In particular, he was opposed to testing nuclear weapons because of the possibility of creating mutations from the radiation. Muller's writings include *Out of the Night* and *The Mechanism of Mendelian Heredity.* Obituaries and other sources: *Current Biography,* Wilson, 1947, June, 1967; *New York Times,* April 6, 1967; *Time,* April 14, 1967; *Newsweek,* April 17, 1967; *Dictionary of Scientific Biography,* Scribner, 1970-1976; *McGraw-Hill Encyclopedia of World Biography,* McGraw, 1973.

* * *

MUNROW, David John 1942-1976

OBITUARY NOTICE—See index for *CA* sketch: Born August 12, 1942, in Birmingham, England; died in May, 1976. Educator, researcher, musician, composer, and author. After associations with Cambridge University and the University of Birmingham, Munrow founded the Early Music Consort of London in 1967. During the 1970's he scored several motion pictures, including "The Devils" and "Zardoz," and a radio series, "The Pied Piper of Hamlyn." Munrow wrote *Instruments of the Middle Ages and Renaissance.* Obituaries and other sources: *Who's Who,* 126th edition, St. Martin's, 1974; *Who Was Who,* Volume VII: *1971-1980,* A. & C. Black, 1981.

MURDIN, Paul 1942-

PERSONAL: Born January 5, 1942, in Croydon, England; son of Robert (a draftsman) and Ethel (a clerk; maiden name, Chubb) Murdin; married Lesley Milburn (a lecturer), August 8, 1964; children: Benedict, Alexander, Louisa. *Education:* Oxford University, B.A., 1963; University of Rochester, Ph.D., 1970. *Home:* 15 Woodbrook Rd., Hastings, Sussex TN34 2DQ, England. *Office:* Royal Greenwich Observatory, Hailsham, Sussex BN27 1RP, England.

CAREER: Royal Greenwich Observatory, Hailsham, England, principal, 1971-75; Anglo Australian Observatory, Epping, Australia, research scientist, 1975-78; Royal Greenwich Observatory, senior principal, 1978—. *Member:* International Astronomical Union, Royal Astronomical Society (fellow).

WRITINGS: (With Patrick Moore) *The Astronomer's Telescope*, Brockhampton Press, 1964; *Radio Waves From Space*, Brockhampton Press, 1965; (with wife, Lesley Murdin) *New Astronomy*, Crowell, 1975; (with David Allen and David Malin) *Catalog of the Universe*, Crown, 1979. Contributor of more than one hundred articles to scientific journals.

WORK IN PROGRESS: Continuing astronomical research.

SIDELIGHTS: Murdin wrote: "My books are attempts to communicate my excitement about astronomy."

*   *   *

MURRAH, David Joe 1941-

PERSONAL: Born September 13, 1941, in Shattuck, Okla.; son of LeRoy (a farmer) and Leila (a secretary; maiden name, Montgomery) Murrah; married Sherry Edwards, 1962 (divorced, 1966); married Anne Sanders (a teacher), December 29, 1973; children: Jerel Dwain. *Education:* Hardin-Simmons University, B.A., 1964; attended Southwestern Baptist Theological Seminary, 1965-66; Texas Tech University, M.A., 1971, Ph.D., 1979. *Religion:* Baptist. *Home:* 5542 18th, Lubbock, Tex. 79416. *Office:* Southwest Collection, Texas Tech University, Lubbock, Tex. 79409.

CAREER: Teacher at public schools in Springtown, Tex., 1966-67, and Morton, Tex., 1967-71; Texas Tech University, Lubbock, assistant archivist of Southwest Collection, 1971-76, assistant director, 1976-77, director, 1977—. *Member:* Society of American Archivists, Westerners International, Society of Southwest Archivists, Texas State Historical Association, West Texas Historical Association, Lubbock Heritage Society (president, 1981-82). *Awards, honors:* Best article award from West Texas Historical Association, 1975, for "From Corset Stays to Cattle Ranching: Charles K. Warren's Muleshoe Ranch."

WRITINGS: (Editor) V. W. Peterman, *Pioneer Days*, Friends of the Library, Texas Tech University, 1978; *C. C. Slaughter: Rancher, Banker, Baptist*, University of Texas Press, 1981. Contributor to history journals.

WORK IN PROGRESS: A history of the Pitchfork Land and Cattle Company, publication expected in 1983.

SIDELIGHTS: David Murrah told *CA:* "As a native west Texan, I am very interested in the production of quality local history. As director of a regional historical research center, I am in the position to encourage the collecting and preservation of our region's history; as a historian, I am also in the position to write and to encourage the writing of regional history.

"As director of the Southwest Collection, I now give much of my attention to the production of our series of symposia on the American Southwest, held in September of each year. I also teach a nine-hour graduate history program in archival administration at Texas Tech University.

"My interest in ranch history is not easily explained. I have always been fascinated with institutional history—business, railroads, etc.—and my view of ranch history is from a business approach. Otherwise it stems from an interest in the west Texas region, whose early history is a ranching story."

*   *   *

MURRAY, Dick 1924-

PERSONAL: Born April 4, 1924, in Des Moines, Iowa; son of Wallace R. and Caroline M. Murray; married Joyce Martin (a secretary), September 28, 1944; children: Ruth Murray Alexander, Martin. *Education:* Attended Drake University, 1942; Southern Methodist University, B.A., 1948; Union Theological Seminary, New York, N.Y., M.Div., 1951. *Religion:* United Methodist. *Office:* Department of Christian Education, Perkins School of Theology, Southern Methodist University, Dallas, Tex. 75275.

CAREER: United Methodist Church, Hyde Park, N.Y., pastor, 1951-53; National Missionary in Paducah, Ky., 1953-54; Union Avenue Methodist Church, Memphis, Tenn., youth minister, 1954; United Methodist Church, Hooks, Tex., pastor, 1955; United Methodist Church, Palestine, Tex., director of adult work for Texas Conference, 1956-61; First United Methodist Church, Houston, Tex., minister of education, 1961-65; Southern Methodist University, Dallas, Tex., assistant professor, 1965-69, associate professor, 1969-81, professor of Christian education, 1981—. *Military service:* U.S. Army, 1943-46.

WRITINGS: *Strengthening the Adult Sunday School Class*, Abingdon, 1981.

WORK IN PROGRESS: *Teaching the Bible to Adults*, publication expected in 1983; *Adult Church*.

SIDELIGHTS: Murray told *CA:* "I am interested in encouraging a balance between subjective and objective bible study."

*   *   *

MURRAY, John Courtney 1904-1967

OBITUARY NOTICE: Born September 12, 1904, in New York, N.Y.; died August 16, 1967, in New York, N.Y.; buried in Woodstock, Md. Theologian, clergyman, and author. Though he was considered an expert on the Trinity, Murray, a Jesuit, wrote primarily on the problem of religious pluralism and on the relationship between the Catholic church and governments in modern culture. Disagreeing with the age-old view particularly prevalent in Europe that the Catholic church should administer both the spiritual and civic rights of states, the priest concluded that, through reason, the authorities of church and state could achieve consensus. Religion, he contended, has power *in* government through the virtuous examples set by believers, but religion has no power *over* government. Because of his views, Murray was subjected to an order of silence, which he obeyed until the drafting of the Second Vatican Council's Declaration on Religious Liberty, of which he was one of the chief writers. Ordained a Jesuit in 1933, the theologian earned his bachelor's degree in 1926 and his master's degree in 1927, both from Boston College. In 1934 he received another degree from Woodstock College, and three years later he completed his doctoral study at the Gregorian University in Rome. Murray taught Latin and English in the Philippines for three years and later served as a professor of theology at Woodstock

College. The Jesuit received many awards, including the Order of Merit of the Government of Chile and several honorary degrees. Murray edited *Theological Studies* and contributed to *Thought,* a scholarly journal. His writings include *The Problem of God: Yesterday and Today, We Hold These Truths: Catholic Reflections on the American Proposition, Morality and Man,* and *The Crippled Giant: American Foreign Policy and Its Domestic Consequences.* Obituaries and other sources: *Current Biography,* Wilson, 1961; *Who Was Who in America, With World Notables,* Volume IV: *1961-1968,* Marquis, 1968; *Dictionary of American Religious Biography,* Greenwood Press, 1977; *Webster's American Biographies,* Merriam, 1979.

*   *   *

MUSTO, Barry 1930-
(Robert Simon)

PERSONAL: Born January 18, 1930, in Birmingham, England; son of Cyril (an actor) and Kathleen (an actress; maiden name, Hughes) Musto; married Jean McKie, April 29, 1954; children: Simon Robert. *Education:* Attended secondary school in Llandrindod Wells, Wales. *Religion:* Protestant. *Home:* Thistles, Little Addington, Kettering, Northamptonshire, England. *Agent:* J. F. Gibson, P.O. Box 173, London S.W.3, England.

CAREER: Worked in technical sales, advertising, and public relations, 1951-74; Harper & Tunstall Ltd., Wellingborough, England, export manager, 1974—. *Member:* Institute of Advanced Motorists.

WRITINGS: The Lawrence Barclay File, R. Hale, 1969; *The Fatal Flaw,* R. Hale, 1970; *Storm Centre,* R. Hale, 1970; *Codename—Bastille,* R. Hale, 1972; *No Way Out,* R. Hale, 1973; *The Weighted Scales,* R. Hale, 1973.

Under pseudonym Robert Simon: *The Sunless Land,* R. Hale,

1972. Writer for British Broadcasting Corp. Contributor of stories to magazines.

WORK IN PROGRESS: Two crime novels; a book on the death of Mussolini.

AVOCATIONAL INTERESTS: Travel, music.

*   *   *

MYERS, David G. 1942-

PERSONAL: Born September 20, 1942, in Seattle, Wash.; son of Kenneth G. (in business) and Luella (Nelson) Myers; married Carol Peterkin, August 24, 1963; children: Peter, Andrew, Laura. *Education:* Whitworth College, B.A., 1964; University of Iowa, M.A., 1966, Ph.D., 1967. *Religion:* Christian. *Residence:* Holland, Mich. *Office:* Department of Psychology, Hope College, Holland, Mich. 49423.

CAREER: Hope College, Holland, Mich., assistant professor, 1967-70, associate professor, 1970-75, professor of psychology, 1975—. *Member:* American Psychological Association, American Association for the Advancement of Science, Society of Experimental Social Psychology, American Scientific Affiliation, Sigma Xi. *Awards, honors:* Gordon Allport Prize from American Psychological Association, 1978, for research on group polarization.

WRITINGS: The Human Puzzle: Psychological Research and Christian Belief, Harper, 1978; *The Inflated Self: Human Illusions and the Biblical Call to Hope,* Seabury, 1980; (with Thomas Ludwig, Merold Westphal, and Robin Klay) *Inflation, Poortalk, and the Gospel,* Judson, 1981; *Social Psychology,* McGraw, 1983. Contributor to scientific journals and popular magazines, including *Saturday Review, Psychology Today, Science Digest, Christianity Today,* and *Christian Century.*

N

NAAMANI, Israel Tarkow   1913(?)-

BRIEF ENTRY: Born November 3, 1913 (some sources say 1912) in Zhitomir, Russia (now U.S.S.R.). American social scientist, educator, and author. Naamani joined the faculty at University of Louisville in 1949. He was named professor of political science in 1964 and professor emeritus in 1975. Naamani has edited *Hebrew Studies* since 1971. Naamani's books include *Israel Through the Eyes of Its Leaders: An Annotated Reader* (Meorot, 1971, published as *Israel: Its Politics and Philosophy: An Annotated Reader,* Behrman, 1974), *Israel: A Profile* (Praeger, 1972), and *The State of Israel* (Behrman, 1980). *Address:* 2804 Lime Kiln Lane, Louisville, Ky. 40222. *Biographical/critical sources: Who's Who in World Jewry,* Pitman, 1972.

*   *   *

NADEL, Norman (Sanford)   1915-

PERSONAL: Born June 19, 1915, in Newark, N.J.; son of Louis David (an engineer) and Sara (Fiverson) Nadel; married Martha Jane Smith, February 8, 1941; children: David William, Arlene Judith Nadel Hammer, Mark Alan. *Education:* Denison University, A.B., 1938; attended University of Chicago, 1943. *Politics:* Democrat. *Religion:* Jewish. *Home:* 234 College Ave., Staten Island, N.Y. 10314.

CAREER: Urban Newspapers, Inc., Cleveland, Ohio, editor of two weekly newspapers, *Garfield Heights Record* and *Euclid Observer,* 1938-39; *Columbus Citizen-Journal* (formerly *Columbus Citizen*), Columbus, Ohio, make-up editor, 1939-40, radio editor, 1940-42, music, film, and drama critic, 1946-61, theatre editor, 1946-61; *New York World-Telegram and Sun,* New York City, drama critic, 1961-66, theatre editor, 1963-64; *New York World Journal Tribune,* New York City, drama critic, 1966-67; Scripps-Howard Newspaper Alliance, New York City, cultural affairs writer, 1967-80; critic-at-large of Newspapers Enterprise Association (NEA), 1976-80; contributing editor for *Horizon* and arts writer for Independent News Alliance, 1980—. Founder, 1940, and board member and trombonist of Columbus Philharmonic Orchestra, 1940-49; co-founder and faculty member of National Critics Institute. Arbiter for Actors Equity and League of New York Theatres and Producers, 1968; adjudicator for theatre competitions; judge of Stanley Playwriting Award, 1977-78. Visiting professor at Kansas State University, 1982, and Florida State University, 1981-83; lecturer and critic-in-residence at colleges and universities, including Ohio State University, Florida State University, Kansas State University, Oklahoma University, Oklahoma State University, University of New Mexico, University of Oregon, Mount Holyoke College, Wagner College, and University of Calgary. Guest critic for regional community and college theatre festivals. Conductor of theatre tours to New York City and Europe.

Member of board of directors of Snug Harbor Cultural Center, Staten Island, N.Y., American Community Theatre Association, Four Winds Theatre, Columbus Boychoir School, New York City Cultural Council, Station WNYC. Consultant to Theatre Guild, 1967-70. *Military service:* U.S. Army, 1942-45; became sergeant and bandleader. *Member:* American Theatre Critics Association, American Community Theatre Association, New York Drama Critics Circle (president, 1966-67), White's Point Yacht Club, Richmond County Yacht Club, Phi Mu Alpha Sinfonia (music). *Awards, honors:* Spotlight Award from *Variety,* 1956, for service to American theatre; citation from National Federation of Music Clubs, 1957, for music criticism; alumni citation, 1963, and Doctor of Humane Letters degree, 1967, both from Denison University; four Scripps-Howard story-of-the-month prizes.

WRITINGS: (Contributor) Otis L. Guernsey, Jr., editor, *The Best Plays of 1966-67: The Burns Mantle Yearbook,* Dodd, 1967; *A Pictorial History of the Theatre Guild,* Crown, 1970. Contributor of articles to periodicals, including *New York Times, Saturday Review, Bravo, Theatre Arts, Yachting, Boating, Rudder, Cue, Together, Minutes.* Editor of *Critic's Choice* magazine.

WORK IN PROGRESS: Book projects on memory and on the "arts and the aging."

SIDELIGHTS: Nadel told *CA:* "As a professional critic and writer on the arts, I have been and am able to function as liaison among people in the arts and everyone else who might be touched by them. I believe that the arts, along with philosophy of one sort or another and religion, are essential to the life of the spirit. And that my function as one who evaluates, explains, enlightens (I hope), opens doors, and in other ways serves as a catalyst, helping bring about reactions among people and the various arts, is a valid and useful function."

In his book, *A Pictorial History of the Theatre Guild,* Nadel chronicles the first fifty years of the Theatre Guild, beginning with its inception in 1919. In that time, the guild produced 230 plays, which Nadel describes in detail. A comprehensive work, the book illustrates the importance of the Theatre Guild to the development of entertainment in New York. "Since The Theatre Guild has been so active an organization for more than half a century," noted writer Paul Meyers, "the book is almost a history of the theatre in New York during this period." Lewis Nichols added in the *New York Times Book Review* that this "was a period in which the American theatre changed its way of life, and in this the Guild was the leader." Nichols commented that *A Pictorial History of the Theatre Guild* "prove[s] . . . the theatre was a wonderful thing."

AVOCATIONAL INTERESTS: The arts, "as participant as well as consumer," sailing, canoeing, kayaking, photography, outdoor living, travel in the United States and abroad.

BIOGRAPHICAL/CRITICAL SOURCES: Library Journal, January 15, 1970; *New York Times Book Review,* February 22, 1970; *Wilson Library Bulletin,* April, 1970.

*   *   *

NAGEL, Otto   1894-1967

OBITUARY NOTICE: Born in 1894 in Berlin, Germany (now East Germany); died in 1967 in Berlin, East Germany. Painter and author. Associated with the Berlin Academy of Arts, Nagel devoted the greater part of his career to depicting the poor and suffering lower classes of his country. His works attracted the attention of fellow artist and noted humanitarian Kathe Kollwitz. In 1963 Nagel produced a biography of this friend, recounting her life and examining her art in *Kathe Kollwitz.* Obituaries and other sources: *Gazette de Beaux-Arts,* January, 1968.

*   *   *

NAKASHIMA, George Katsutoshi   1905-
(Sundarananda)

PERSONAL: Born May 24, 1905, in Spokane, Wash.; son of Katsuharu and Suzu (Thoma) Nakashima; married Marion Sumire Okajima, February 14, 1941; children: Mira Shizu Nakashima Amagasu, Kevin Katsuya. *Education:* Ecole Americaine des Beaux Arts, Diploma, 1928; University of Washington, Seattle, B.Arch., 1929; Massachusetts Institute of Technology, M.Arch., 1930. *Religion:* "Hindu Catholic." *Home and office:* 293 Aquetong Rd., New Hope, Pa. 18938.

CAREER: Private practice of architecture and furniture design in the United States, France, Japan, and India, 1930—. Independent designer and manufacturer of furniture in New Hope, Pa., 1943—. *Member:* American Crafts Council (fellow). *Awards, honors:* Named Sundarananda ("one who delights in beauty," a Sanskrit name of renunciation) by Sri Aurobindo, 1938; gold craftsmanship medal from American Institute of Architects, 1952, award for craftsmanship, 1959, honor award for inspired creativity and outstanding sensitivity in design, 1980; annual award for design in hardwoods from the Fine Hardwoods Association, 1956; silver medal of honor in design and craftsmanship from Architectural League of New York, 1960; medal from Catholic Art Association, 1969; award from American Crafts Council, 1979; silver plaque from Central Bucks Chamber of Commerce, 1980; gold medal and title of Japanese American of the Biennium in the Field of Arts, from the Japanese American Citizens League, 1980.

WRITINGS: The Soul of a Tree: A Woodworker's Reflections, Kodansha, 1981.

SIDELIGHTS: Nakashima commented: "Early in my life I began a search for what I would call a 'reason for doing.' This

took me to Paris in the early 1930's, when modern art and architecture were in deep creation, but I found it lacking. Then I went on to Japan, the country of my forebears, to experience the rich traditions and the intrinsic spirit of the Japanese people, and from Japan went to Pondicherry, India, to become one of the early disciples of the great Sri Aurobindo, who is by far the most important seer and prophet of the twentieth century.

"During these times I developed a feeling for being a citizen of the world. I have a fair fluency in English, Japanese, and French, can speak bad Russian, and have an almost complete illiteracy in Bengali—a language in which, at one time, I did a fair amount of reading.

"Finally I settled in New Hope, Pennsylvania, to develop an integrated small craft industry, very much as an expression of intermediate technology and meta-industry. This was started and developed long before Schumacher and others had written about it. It has been a quest for excellence and beauty, which is so often shunned in our society.

"Although the earlier days were full of trials and isolation, people are finally beginning to listen."

*   *   *

NANCE, Guinevera Ann   1939-

PERSONAL: Born February 27, 1939, in Rhome, Tex.; daughter of Elmer (a farmer) and Esther L. Splawn; married J. Larry Nance, June 4, 1960 (divorced, 1966). *Education:* Texas Christian University, B.A., 1967; University of Virginia, M.A., 1968, Ph.D., 1971. *Home:* 1206 Edgeworth Dr., Montgomery, Ala. 36109. *Office:* Office of the Chancellor, Auburn University, Montgomery, Ala. 36193.

CAREER: Auburn University, Montgomery, Ala., assistant professor, 1971-72, associate professor of English, 1975—, coordinator of department, 1972-73, chairman of Division of Liberal Arts, 1974-75, dean of School of Liberal Arts, 1975-81, vice-chancellor for academic affairs, 1981—. *Member:* Modern Language Association of America, Byron Society, South Atlantic Modern Language Association. *Awards, honors:* Woodrow Wilson fellowship, 1967.

WRITINGS: (With Judith P. Jones) *Philip Roth,* Ungar, 1981. Contributor to literature journals.

WORK IN PROGRESS: Aldous Huxley, publication by Ungar expected in 1984.

SIDELIGHTS: Guinevera Nance wrote: "When Aldous Huxley was questioned in an interview about the motivation for his art and his way of life, he responded, 'Well, I always had a feeling that I wanted to learn, to explore.' I suppose that the people I admire most are those who make it their life's work to learn, and when I am my 'best self'—the one I like most—I am engaged in learning and discovering. I have always preferred the idea of 'becoming' to that of 'being' and like to think of my teaching and writing as activities in progress. I am almost always certain that today's aesthetic views will be shaped and modified tomorrow as I learn and discover more.

"It seems to me that in general we Americans place a high value on the firmly fixed and unchangeable, and at least in the realm of intellectual pursuits, I think that is unfortunate. Openness to ideas is likely to precipitate changes in views, and I think both are healthy."

*   *   *

NASH, Ray   1905-1982

OBITUARY NOTICE: Born February 27, 1905, in Milwaukie,

Ore.; died May 21, 1982, in Royalton, Vt. Educator, graphic arts historian, and author. Nash began teaching at Dartmouth College in 1937, becoming a professor in 1949 and professor emeritus in 1970. An authority on handwriting, calligraphy, and printing, Nash lectured widely on graphic arts and acted as an adviser and consultant to businesses and organizations. In 1956 Nash received the American Institute of Graphic Arts Gold Medal for his outstanding contribution to his field, becoming the first professor from a liberal arts college ever to receive the medal. Nash contributed to many professional journals throughout his career and served on the editorial boards of *Print, Printing and Graphic Arts,* and *Renaissance News.* Among his books are *Calligraphy and Printing in the Sixteenth Century, Printing as an Art,* and *American Penmanship, 1800-1850.* Obituaries and other sources: *Publishers Weekly,* July 2, 1956; *American Authors and Books, 1640 to the Present Day,* 3rd revised edition, Crown, 1962; *Who's Who in American Art,* Bowker, 1973; *Directory of American Scholars,* Volume I: *History,* 7th edition, Bowker, 1978.

* * *

NAVARRO (GERASSI), Marysa 1934-

PERSONAL: Born October 12, 1934, in Pamplona, Spain; naturalized U.S. citizen; divorced; children: one. *Education:* Instituto Jose Batlle y Ordonez, B.A., 1955; attended Rutgers University, 1956-57; Columbia University, M.A., 1960, Ph.D., 1964. *Home:* 3 Sargent St., Hanover, N.H. 03755. *Office:* Department of History, Dartmouth College, Hanover, N.H. 03755.

CAREER: High school teacher of Latin American history in Montevideo, Uruguay, 1958; Rutgers University, New Brunswick, N.J., lecturer in Latin American history and economics, 1963-64; Yeshiva University, New York, N.Y., guest lecturer in Latin American history, 1964-65; Newark State College, Union, N.J., associate professor of history, 1965-67; Dartmouth College, Hanover, N.H., assistant professor, 1968-72, associate professor, 1972-77, professor of history, 1978—, vice-chairperson of department and chairperson of women's studies program, 1979-81, member of governing board of Student Center, 1979—, member of World Affairs Seminar, Feminist Inquiry Seminar, and Latin American Seminar. Lecturer at Hunter College of the City University of New York, 1963-64; visiting associate professor at Long Island University, 1966-67; lecturer at Yale University and University of Wisconsin, 1973, Columbia University and University of Connecticut, 1976, Princeton University and Northwestern University, 1977, University of Minnesota, 1978, Indiana University, 1979, and Brandeis University, University of Connecticut, and Smith College, 1980; visiting associate researcher at Centro de Estudios de Poblacion in Buenos Aires, Argentina, 1977; distinguished woman scholar at University of New Hampshire, spring, 1981; member of *Ms.* advisory board on research, scholarship, and education.

MEMBER: American Historical Association, Latin American Studies Association, Conference on Latin American History, New England Council for Latin American Studies (vice-president, 1980-81; president, 1981-82), Phi Beta Kappa. *Awards, honors:* Study and research grants from Institute of International Education, 1956-57, Organization of American States, 1961-62, Social Science Research Council, 1967-68 and 1977, and American Philosophical Society, 1970.

WRITINGS: Argentine Nationalism of the Right: The History of an Ideological Development, 1930-1946, Social Science Institute, Washington University (St. Louis, Mo.), 1965; (con-

tributor) *Perspectivas femenina en America Latina,* Sep-Setentas, 1976; (contributor) *Women and National Development: The Complexities of Change,* University of Chicago Press, 1977; (with Catalina H. Wainerman) *El trabajo de la mujer en la Argentina: Un analisis preliminar de las ideas dominantes en las primeras decades del siglo XX,* Centro de Estudios de Poblacion, 1979; (contributor) *Latin American Populism in Comparative Perspective,* University of New Mexico Press, 1981; (with Nicholas Fraser) *Eva Peron,* Norton, 1981. Also author of *The Tupamaros: Uruguay's Urban Guerrillas,* Latin American Working Group.

Contributor of articles and reviews to Latin American studies journals and popular magazines, including *Nation* and *New Left Review.* Member of editorial board of *Signs.*

* * *

NAZZARO, Anthony M. 1927-

BRIEF ENTRY: Born June 8, 1927, in Dover, N.J. American educator and author. Nazzaro taught at Oberlin College from 1955 to 1956 and at Russell Sage College from 1957 to 1962. He joined the faculty at Skidmore College in 1962 and became a professor of French in 1972. Nazzaro edited collections of work by Georges Simenon: *Trois nouvelles* (Appleton, 1966) and *Choix de Simenon* (Appleton, 1972). He also edited *Realite et fantaisie: Neuf nouvelles modernes* (Xerox College Publishing, 1971). *Address:* Department of Modern Languages, Skidmore College, Saratoga Springs, N.Y. 12866.

* * *

NEAGLEY, Ross Linn 1907-

PERSONAL: Born July 16, 1907, in Fallsington, Pa.; son of Henry Clinton and Minnie (Grosh) Neagley; married Isabel Steever (a teacher), December 27, 1931; children: Lynn, Elaine (Mrs. Charles F. Parvin), Sylvia (Mrs. Joseph Gallagher). *Education:* Shippensburg State College, B.S., 1929; Columbia University, M.A., 1933; Temple University, Ed.D., 1938. *Religion:* Methodist. *Home:* 524 School Lane, Rehoboth Beach, Del. 19971.

CAREER: Teacher of science and instrumental music at public schools in Darby, Pa., 1929-31, and Media, Pa., 1931-41; supervising principal of schools in Newtown Boro, Pa., 1941-44; superintendent of schools in Wilmington, Del., 1944-49; Temple University, Philadelphia, Pa., professor of educational administration, 1949-73, professor emeritus, 1973—, department head, 1958-65, director of evening school, 1949-58.

MEMBER: American Association of University Professors, American Association of School Administrators, National Education Association, National Association of Elementary School Principals, Council of Educational Facility Planners, Pennsylvania Department of Elementary School Principals, Phi Delta Kappa. *Awards, honors:* Educator of the year award from Pennsylvania Department of Elementary School Principals, 1971; distinguished alumnus award from Shippensburg State College, 1976.

WRITINGS: Planning Facilities for Higher Education, National Council on Schoolhouse Construction, 1960; (with James Burr, William Coffield, and Theodore Jenson) *Elementary School Admininstration,* Allyn & Bacon, 1963, 2nd edition, 1967; (with N. Dean Evans) *Handbook for Effective Supervision of Instruction,* Prentice-Hall, 1964, 3rd edition, 1980; (with Evans) *Handbook for Effective Curriculum Development,* Prentice-Hall, 1967; (with Evans and Clarence Lynn, Jr.) *The Administrator and Learning Resources,* Prentice-Hall, 1969;

Planning and Developing Innovative Community Colleges, Prentice-Hall, 1972. Contributor to music and education journals.

WORK IN PROGRESS: Research on death and dying.

SIDELIGHTS: Neagley commented: "I have devoted my life to the improvement of our schools by improving instruction and learning, as well as school administration. I have visited schools in England, France, Italy, Germany, Spain, Portugal, Greece, Norway, Sweden, Denmark, Japan, Australia, and New Zealand."

* * *

NEALE-SILVA, Eduardo 1905-

BRIEF ENTRY: Born December 10, 1905, in Talca, Chile. American educator and author. Neale-Silva was a professor of Spanish at University of Wisconsin—Madison from 1941 to 1976; in 1976 he became an emeritus professor. His writings include *Lecturas amenas* (Harper, 1972), *Cesar Vallejo en su fase trilcica* (University of Wisconsin Press, 1975), *Adelante!: A Cultural Approach to Intermediate Spanish* (Scott, Foresman, 1977), and *En Camino!: A Cultural Approach to Beginning Spanish* (Scott, Foresman, 1977). *Address:* 5302 Fairway Dr., Madison, Wis. 53711. *Biographical/critical sources: Directory of American Scholars,* Volume III: *Foreign Languages, Linguistics, and Philology,* 7th edition, Bowker, 1978.

* * *

NEEDLE, Jan 1943-

PERSONAL: Born February 8, 1943, in Holybourne, England; son of Bernard Lionel and Dorothy (Brice) Needle. *Education:* Received drama degree, with first class honors, from Victoria University of Manchester, 1971. *Home:* 4 Springbank, Uppermill, Oldham, Lancashire, England. *Agent:* Curtis Brown Ltd., 1 Craven Hill, London W2 3EP, England.

CAREER: Portsmouth Evening News, Portsmouth, England, reporter, 1960-64; reporter and sub-editor for *Daily Herald and Sun,* 1964-68; free-lance writer, 1971—.

WRITINGS: Albeson and the Germans (juvenile novel), Deutsch, 1977; *My Mate Shofiq* (juvenile novel), Deutsch, 1978; *A Fine Boy for Killing* (adult novel), Deutsch, 1979; *Rottenteeth* (picture book), Deutsch, 1979; *The Size Spies* (juvenile novel), Deutsch, 1980; *The Bee Rustlers* (juvenile novel), Collins, 1980; *A Sense of Shame* (short stories), Deutsch, 1980; *Wild Wood* (adult novel), Deutsch, 1981; (with Peter Thomson) *Brecht* (criticism), University of Chicago Press, 1981; *Losers Weepers* (juvenile novel), Methuen, 1981; *Piggy in the Middle* (novel), Deutsch, 1982. Also author of *Another Fine Mess* (juvenile novel), 1981.

Author of more than ten radio plays broadcast in England and New Zealand between 1971 and 1980.

WORK IN PROGRESS: A book of ghost stories, publication expected in 1983.

SIDELIGHTS: Needle wrote: "I am not aware of when, or why, I started to write. It came naturally. I was first published when I was eight years old, in a small local newspaper, and I have never looked back.

"Although most of my books are published as children's stories, they are equally intended for adults. Many of them have problematical themes and explore difficult social problems. Even the comedy books are intended to amuse adults as well as children. I like each book to be different—and they do seem to defy critical categorization. I think I would be very bored to write the same kind of book over and over again."

AVOCATIONAL INTERESTS: Drama, European travel (especially France).

BIOGRAPHICAL/CRITICAL SOURCES: Times Literary Supplement, September 29, 1978, November 20, 1981; *Punch,* December 10, 1980; *Spectator,* February 28, 1981; *New Statesman,* March 13, 1981.

* * *

NEELY, Mark Edward, Jr. 1944-

PERSONAL: Born November 10, 1944, in Amarillo, Tex.; son of Mark Edward (a businessman) and Lottie (Wright) Neely; married: Sylvia Eakes (a college professor), June 15, 1966. *Education:* Yale University, B.A., 1966, Ph.D., 1973. *Politics:* Democrat. *Home:* 1425 West Wildwood, Fort Wayne, Ind. 46807. *Office:* Louis A. Warren Lincoln Library and Museum, 1300 South Clinton St., Fort Wayne, Ind. 46807.

CAREER: Iowa State University, Ames, visiting instructor in American history, 1971-72; Louis A. Warren Lincoln Library and Museum, Fort Wayne, Ind., director, 1972—. Member of advisory board of Indiana Historical Bureau, 1980—. *Member:* Abraham Lincoln Association (member of board of directors, 1981—), Society of Indiana Archivists (president, 1980-81). *Awards, honors:* D.H.L. from Lincoln College, 1981.

WRITINGS: The Abraham Lincoln Encyclopedia, McGraw, 1981. Contributor to history journals and newspapers. Editor of "Lincoln Lore," 1973—. Member of editorial advisory committee of *Indiana Magazine of History,* 1981—; member of editorial board of Ulysses S. Grant Association, 1981—.

WORK IN PROGRESS: The Insanity File: The Case of Mary Todd Lincoln, with R. Gerald McMurtry, publication expected in 1983; research on Lincoln and the U.S. Constitution.

SIDELIGHTS: Hailed by the *Chicago Tribune* as "extraordinary," "remarkable," and "a major achievement," Neely's *The Abraham Lincoln Encyclopedia* includes facts on virtually every aspect of the life and death of the sixteenth U.S. president. The book's several hundred entries, arranged alphabetically, are accompanied by three hundred illustrations and extensive bibliographical references. *Chicago Tribune* reviewer Harold Holzer praised *The Abraham Lincoln Encyclopedia's* "especially fine brief essays on such key Lincoln subjects as slavery, the debates with Stephen A. Douglas, the rise and fall of the Whig Party, and the assassination conspiracy. . . . Alongside these 'big subject' entries," Holzer continued, "come 'small,' anecdotal revelations that refresh, amuse and astound. . . . Deserving of mention, too, are Neely's biographical sketches of all Lincoln's contemporaries, his leading biographers (their works expertly analyzed), and even the top Lincoln collectors."

Director of the Louis A. Warren Lincoln Library and Museum since 1972 and editor of the monthly "Lincoln Lore" since 1973, Neely approached the writing of *The Abraham Lincoln Encyclopedia* with the authority of an acknowledged expert. "Neely has a point of view," observed critic Holzer, "knows how to express it forcefully but subtly, and this transforms what might have become a stodgy almanac into a surprisingly complete and consistently readable biography-by-minisubject." Holzer concluded that *The Abraham Lincoln Encyclopedia* "is a priceless addition to the Lincoln shelf. Painstakingly indexed and footnoted, it will take its place among the chief Lincoln references."

Neely told *CA:* "When I took a job at a Lincoln institution ten years ago, my only hesitation stemmed from the fear of entering a field in which there were already some seven thousand titles. Now I am wondering which of the subjects that I'd like to treat in the future must be dropped for want of time in a normal life span. To be sure, I got an unusual break in being able to write a book on Mrs. Lincoln's insanity trial, based on documents no historian had ever seen before. (Robert Lincoln Beckwith gave my co-author and me exclusive access to the Lincoln family's extensive file on the case.) For the most part, those of us who work on Lincoln use documents read by hundreds of scholars before us. Even so, Lincoln was so complex (and personally secretive) and so intertwined with the important events of his era that opportunities for research still abound. For example, there is no book on the Emancipation Proclamation that uses the Abraham Lincoln Papers at the Library of Congress, and there is no work on the Lincoln-Douglas Debates (and the senatorial election of which they were a part), which uses the modern statistical tools for voting analysis.

"My work thus far has two distinguishing traits. Because there is already a great body of literature on Lincoln, I feel that any new work must do two things: (1) Say what's wrong with our previous understanding of the particular aspect of Lincoln's life and (2) say *why* those who looked at the problem before did not get the answer right. I am always looking at two historical layers. The first is the stratum laid by Lincoln's era itself. The second is the layer (or layers) above it left by historians who interpreted the original stratum of evidence. In other words, I believe there are two answers to every Lincoln question: What really happened and why are we only just now figuring out what really happened.

"The second distinguishing trait stems from my belief that the vast Lincoln literature takes so long to read that historians have too often been weak on the context of Lincoln's life. The modern era's ability to speed up research (photocopying instead of writing notes, microfilm instead of long and uncomfortable research trips, and reliable published editions of the central documents) allows us—and, I think, requires us—to look outside the strictly Lincoln literature to appreciate the era in which he lived. Most of the advances in the modern literature on Lincoln have come about this way. For example, we have an altogether more sympathetic understanding of his racial views than we did in the 1960's because we are now able to place them in the context of the commonly-held racial assumptions of his day. I am always trying to put Lincoln's life in its proper context, to measure him against the men of his era."

AVOCATIONAL INTERESTS: Literature of World War I, tennis, movies, birdwatching.

BIOGRAPHICAL/CRITICAL SOURCES: Chicago Tribune Book World, January 3, 1982; *Civil War Times Illustrated,* April, 1982.

* * *

NEFF, Robert W(ilbur) 1936-

PERSONAL: Born June 16, 1936, in Lancaster, Pa.; son of Wilbur H. (an executive) and Hazel (a teacher; maiden name, Martin) Neff; married Dorothy Rosewarne (a teacher), August 16, 1959; children: Scott, Heather. *Education:* Pennsylvania State University, B.S., 1958; Yale University, B.D., 1961, M.A., 1964, Ph.D., 1969. *Religion:* Church of the Brethren. *Home:* 509 North Melrose Ave., Elgin, Ill. 60120. *Office:* 1451 Dundee Rd., Elgin, Ill. 60120.

CAREER: Ordained minister, 1959; Bridgewater College, Bridgewater, Va., assistant professor of biblical studies, 1964-

65; Bethany Theological Seminary, Oak Brook, Ill., assistant professor, 1965-70, associate professor, 1970-73, professor of biblical studies, 1973-77; Church of the Brethren, Elgin, Ill., general secretary of General Board, 1977—. *Ex officio* member of board of directors of Bethany Theological Seminary; member of executive committee and governing board of National Council of Churches of Christ of the United States of America, member of special Mid-East panel, and member of delegation to China; member of board of directors of York Center Cooperative, 1972-74, 1975-76.

MEMBER: Society for Religion in Higher Education, Society of Biblical Literature, Catholic Biblical Association of America, Society of Old Testament Study, Chicago Society of Biblical Research, Omicron Delta Kappa. *Awards, honors:* Danforth fellow, 1958, Two Brothers' fellow of Yale University in Germany and Israel, 1962; D.D. from Juniata College, 1978, and Manchester College, 1979; D.H.L. from Bridgewater College, 1979.

WRITINGS: The Announcement in Old Testament Birth Stories, Yale University Press, 1969; (with Graydon Snyder and Donald E. Miller) *Using Biblical Simulations,* Judson, Volume I, 1973, Volume II, 1975. Contributor to theology journals and church magazines. Co-editor of *Guide to Biblical Studies,* 1971-74.

WORK IN PROGRESS: The Use of the Old Testament in the Church of the Brethren, for Brethren Press; research on Pentateuchal narratives.

* * *

NESSEN, Ron(ald Harold) 1934-

BRIEF ENTRY: Born May 25, 1934, in Rockville, Md. American journalist. Nessen was a Washington correspondent for National Broadcasting Company in 1962, then covered the Vietnam war and other foreign news. In 1974 he became White House correspondent and, later that year, was appointed press secretary to President Gerald Ford, a position he held throughout Ford's presidency. Since 1977 Nessen has returned to journalism. His books are *It Sure Looks Different From the Inside* (Playboy Press, 1978) and *The First Lady: A Novel* (Playboy Press, 1979). *Biographical/critical sources: Current Biography,* Wilson, 1976; *Washington Post,* August 21, 1978; *Political Profiles: The Nixon/Ford Years,* Facts on File, 1979.

* * *

NEUBERT, Christopher J. 1948-

PERSONAL: Born October 9, 1948, in Rochester, N.Y.; son of Paul Neubert. *Education:* University of Notre Dame, B.B.A., 1970; New York Law School, J.D., 1974; attended University of Pennsylvania, 1980. *Politics:* Democrat. *Religion:* Roman Catholic. *Home:* 29 Rutland Sq., Boston, Mass. 02118. *Office:* Mutual of New York, 15 New Chardon St., Boston, Mass. 02114; Gerren & Neubert, Prudential Center, Boston, Mass. 02199; and Moneco, Inc., Prudential Center, Boston, Mass. 02199.

CAREER: Mutual of New York, Boston, Mass., senior advanced consultant, 1976-80, associate manager, 1980—; Gerren & Neubert, Boston, attorney and partner, 1980—. Member of board of directors of Moneco, Inc., and Franklin & Lasoff; consultant to Moneco, Inc., and New England Montessori Children's Center. *Member:* American Bar Association, National Life Underwriters Association, New Lawyers Tax Group, Boston Bar Association, Boston Life Underwriters Association.

WRITINGS: How to Handle Your Own Contracts, Sterling, 1975; *The Law School Game,* Sterling, 1976.

WORK IN PROGRESS: Books on estate planning and financing a small business.

AVOCATIONAL INTERESTS: Skiing, golf, squash, foreign travel.

*   *   *

NEWCOMBE, Park Judson   1930-

PERSONAL: Born in 1930, in Grand Rapids, Mich.; son of Park Hunt and Frances Lucelia (Clark) Newcombe. *Education:* Western Michigan University, B.A., 1953; Northwestern University, M.A., 1957, Ph.D., 1963. *Home:* 314 Deer Park, Temple Terrace, Fla. 33617. *Office:* Department of Communication, University of South Florida, 432 LET, Tampa, Fla. 33620.

CAREER: Fort Knox, Kentucky, instructor and section chief for U.S. Army personnel school, 1955-56; Boys Club, Muncie, Ind., program director, 1955-56; high school teacher in Michigan, 1957-61; Chaminade College of Hawaii, 1962-65, began as instructor, became assistant professor; Northwestern University, Evanston, Ill., assistant professor of speech education, 1965-70, chairman of department, 1967-70; University of South Florida, Tampa, associate professor, 1970-76, professor of speech education, 1976—. *Member:* International Council on Education for Teaching, Rare Fruit Council International (chapter president), Teachers of English to Speakers of Other Languages, Speech Communication Association, American Theatre Association, American Association of University Professors, American Horticultural Society, Communication Association of the Pacific, Florida Speech Communication Association (vice-president, 1981-82), Phi Delta Kappa.

WRITINGS: New Horizons for Teacher Education in Speech Communication, National Textbook, 1974; *Teaching Speech Communication,* McKay, 1975; *Communicating Message and Meaning,* Ginn, 1982. Associate editor of *Communication Education,* 1981-84.

WORK IN PROGRESS: Research on international programs in the preparation of teachers of speech communication, English as an international spoken language, and elements of articulation or diction that have been standardized in national settings.

SIDELIGHTS: Newcombe wrote: "I have completed a sabbatical leave, during which I visited East Africa, Morocco, and Yugoslavia via two commercial freighters. My vocational interests are spoken English or speech communication and the preparation of secondary school teachers.

"Most of my writing has been devoted to the speaking and listening process called 'speech.' In writing about this topic, I realize the difficulty of describing a process that involves many variables which are not obvious to most participants at the moment of speaking and listening. Words are not the total experience of a spoken message. Of equal, or more importance are the inflections, volume, voice quality, gestures, facial responses, movement, physical distance, intensity, pitch, fluency, eye contact, and other vocal and nonverbal components of oral communication used by the speaker. My constant challenge is to be able to write about an occurrence that involves words without making it appear to be totally dependent upon words."

AVOCATIONAL INTERESTS: Horticulture, poetry.

*   *   *

NEWMAN, Elmer S(imon)   1919-

PERSONAL: Born March 19, 1919, in Cleveland, Ohio; son of Emanuel B. (in sales) and Rizell (Cohn) Newman; married Mary Kratt (a library assistant), November 20, 1943; children: Dave R., Joyce Newman Norman. *Education:* Western Reserve University (now Case Western Reserve University), B.A., 1941, M.L.S., 1965. *Politics:* Independent. *Home:* 8 South Green Rd., Cleveland, Ohio 44121. *Office:* Freiberger Library, Case Western Reserve University, Cleveland, Ohio 44106.

CAREER: Worked as a credit manager for an auto parts manufacturer and pricing supervisor for a building supply company, 1946-63; Cuyahoga County Public Library, Cleveland, Ohio, adult services librarian, 1965-67; Cleveland State University, Cleveland, acquisitions librarian, 1967-69; Case Western Reserve University, Cleveland, assistant head of reference department at Freiberger Library, 1970—. *Military service:* U.S. Army, 1941-45; became first lieutenant. *Member:* American Civil Liberties Union, Academic Library Association of Ohio, Phi Beta Kappa.

WRITINGS: Lewis Mumford: A Bibliography, 1914-1970, Harcourt, 1971; (compiler) *The Best of Our Lives* (prose and poems), Hallmark, 1975. Contributor of essays to the *Cleveland Plain Dealer* and a script to the National Public Radio program "All Things Considered."

WORK IN PROGRESS: An anthology for retired people.

SIDELIGHTS: Newman wrote: "My work on the Mumford bibliography convinced me that Lewis Mumford has yet to be fully recognized in this country for the original and distinguished works he has written for a period of more than half a century."

*   *   *

NEWMAN, George   1936-

PERSONAL: Born August 26, 1936, in Vienna, Austria; came to the United States in 1938; naturalized U.S. citizen, 1943; son of Paul (a haberdasher) and Gerda (a fashion designer; maiden name, Kuschnitzky) Newman; married in 1963 (divorced, 1967); children: Richard. *Education:* College of San Mateo, A.A., 1971; San Jose State University, B.A., 1972; University of Wisconsin—Milwaukee, M.S., 1973. *Home:* 26873-A Moody Rd., Los Altos Hills, Calif. 94022. *Agent:* Norm Bowman, 935 Thornton Way, San Jose, Calif. 95128. *Office address:* P.O. Box 4044, Blossom Valley Station, Mountain View, Calif. 94040.

CAREER: Miami News, Miami, Fla., reporter, 1961-64; Miami Department of Publicity and Tourism, Miami, in public relations, 1964-67; Peninsula Newspapers, Inc., Palo Alto, Calif., reporter on newspapers in Burlingame, Calif., and Redwood City, Calif., 1967-71; *San Jose Mercury News,* San Jose, Calif., staff writer specializing in legal affairs, 1973—. Part-time faculty member of West Valley College, Saratoga, Calif., 1973—. Volunteer in Big Brothers of the San Francisco Bay Area, 1968-71. *Military service:* U.S. Coast Guard, 1955-57. *Member:* Sierra Club.

AWARDS, HONORS: Award for distinguished reporting of public affairs from American Political Science Association, 1968; award for best news story from San Francisco Press Club, 1969, for coverage of a vice-presidential candidate's day of campaigning; award for best feature story from South Bay Press Club and award for best feature story from Associated Press News Executives Conference, both 1976, both for feature on a professional child stealer; State Bar of California's Golden Medallion Media Award for outstanding reporting on the administration of justice, 1980.

WRITINGS: 101 Ways to Be a Long-Distance Super-Dad, Blossom Valley Press, 1981.

SIDELIGHTS: Newman and his wife were divorced in 1967, when his son, Rick, was eighteen months old. Newman moved to California, but was determined to maintain a strong emotional bond with Rick, who remained with his mother in Florida, and to be an influential force in his young son's life. The inherent difficulty in the situation prompted Newman to develop creative means of effective long-distance parenting. That endeavor was so successful that Newman's friends encouraged him to write a book sharing his ideas with other long-distance fathers and mothers. The resulting book is entitled *101 Ways to Be a Long-Distance Super-Dad.*

Although many long-distance parents spend some amount of vacation time with their children each year, those vacations can be a strain if there is not sufficient contact throughout the year, Newman cautions. He stresses the importance of regular contact, be it by telephone, or mail, or by one of the more unusual methods he suggests in his book. Frequent contact will make parent and child more familiar with one another, and will therefore increase the quality of time they actually spend together, he says.

Newman's book contains numerous practical tips for making written correspondence exciting for the child. He suggests, for example, that long-distance parents use brightly colored stationery and unusual stamps in order to make their letters distinctive. He also advises keeping children supplied with stationery and stamps of their own. To make the letters themselves interesting, Newman advises sending snapshots and newspaper and magazine clippings. In addition, he suggests sending telegrams for special occasions such as opening night of a school play in which the youngster is involved. He also tells parents that children enjoy receiving greeting cards on such lesser holidays as Halloween and Valentine's Day as well as on their birthdays and other major holidays.

Long-distance "phone visits" should be regularly scheduled events, says Newman. He recommends that parents keep an on-going list of things to discuss with their children. Parents should also try to find out what their children's favorite television programs are, and make an effort to watch them occasionally. They can then discuss recent episodes with their children, either by phone or mail. Playing games such as "Twenty Questions," and telling jokes and riddles, will also make telephone visits fun for children.

Newman advises long-distance parents to keep informed of their child's progress in school. The child should be encouraged to send samples of school work to the "non-custodial" parent. The parent can praise the work, offer constructive criticism, and even help the child with problems he or she is having in school. The parent should also attempt to meet his child's teacher if at all possible, says Newman.

These tips, and numerous others, are included in *101 Ways to Be a Long-Distance Super-Dad.* Newman told a writer for the *San Jose Mercury News* that he sees the book as a primer. "It's like a how-to book on remodeling a house. The book gives you the steps, but you have to add the effort. I just wanted to let men who find themselves in this situation [fewer than 6 percent of the divorced fathers in America have custody of their children, Newman reports] know that there is no need for despair—only for a little creativity."

AVOCATIONAL INTERESTS: Gardening, sports, hiking, coaching Little League, chamber music, opera, and travel.

BIOGRAPHICAL/CRITICAL SOURCES: San Jose Mercury News, June 21, 1981; *Detroit Free Press,* November 23, 1981.

NEWMAN, Parley Wright 1923-

BRIEF ENTRY: Born October 27, 1923, in Ogden, Utah. American speech pathologist, educator, and author. Newman has been a professor of speech pathology at Brigham Young University since 1966. He wrote *Opportunities in Speech Pathology* (Educational Books Division, Universal Publishing & Distributing, 1968). *Address:* 581 East 3460 N., Provo, Utah 84601; and Department of Speech, Brigham Young University, Provo, Utah 84602.

*   *   *

NEWMAN, Sharan 1949-

PERSONAL: Born April 15, 1949, in Ann Arbor, Mich.; daughter of Charles William (a U.S. Air Force captain) and Betty (a psychologist; maiden name, Martin) Hill; married Paul Richard Newman (a physicist), June 12, 1971; children: Allison. *Education:* Antioch College, B.A., 1971; Michigan State University M.A., 1973, further graduate study, 1973-75. *Residence:* Newbury Park, Calif. *Agent:* Don Congdon, c/o Harold Matson Co., 276 Fifth Ave., New York, N.Y. 10001.

CAREER: Temple University, Philadelphia, Pa., instructor in English as a second language and director of evening program, 1976; Oxnard College, Oxnard, Calif., instructor in English as a second language, 1977-79; Asian Refugee Committee, Thousand Oaks, Calif., director of and teacher in English school, 1980—. *Member:* Authors Guild, Leo Baeck Institute, Medieval Academy of the Pacific, Medieval Academy of America. *Awards, honors:* Philadelphia Children's Reading Round Table Award, 1976, for *The Dagda's Harp.*

WRITINGS: The Dagda's Harp (juvenile), St. Martin's, 1977; *Guinevere* (novel), St. Martin's, 1981.

WORK IN PROGRESS: A sequel to *Guinevere.*

SIDELIGHTS: Sharan Newman told CA: "I write when I have time free, and the rest of the time I do housewife drudge work and genealogy, work with Asian refugees, love my family, and read (not necessarily in that order). I am a polyglot and love language study. I am moderately good in French and German, and have studied Chinese, Latin, Anglo-Saxon, Russian, and Japanese with varying success. Although I have never gotten farther than Canada, I intend to start traveling when my daughter is slightly older. I write because I love to, drawing on my six years of medieval study for background. I am a medievalist by choice and a teacher of English as a second language by training. There are no jobs for medievalists in the area where I live, so I teach and write in my spare time. I have strong points of view on many subjects but feel that they should be expressed through my writing or at the dining room table."

BIOGRAPHICAL/CRITICAL SOURCES: Los Angeles Times Book Review, May 24, 1981.

*   *   *

NICHOLS, Lewis 1903-1982

OBITUARY NOTICE: Born September 1, 1903, in Lock Haven, Pa.; died after a long illness, April 29, 1982, in Greenfield, Mass. Journalist and drama critic. Nichols became known during the 1940's for his accurate appraisals of the success potential of plays he critiqued for the *New York Times.* Productions reviewed by Nichols include "Oklahoma," "The Corn Is Green," "Carmen Jones," and "Born Yesterday." He also wrote a column, "In and Out of Books," for the *New York*

Times Book Review. Obituaries and other sources: *Who Was Who in the Theatre, 1912-1976,* Gale, 1978; *New York Times,* May 1, 1982; *Publishers Weekly,* May 28, 1982.

* * *

NICHOLSON, (Edward) Max   1904-

BRIEF ENTRY: British environmentalist and author. Nicholson was director-general of England's Nature Conservancy from 1952 to 1966. Since then he has served as chairman of Land Use Consultants. Nicholson has also been managing editor of Environmental Data Services Ltd. since 1978. In 1963 he was awarded the John C. Phillips Medal from the International Union for the Conservation of Nature and Natural Resources. He wrote *How Birds Live* (1927), *Birds and Men* (1951), *Britain's Nature Reserves* (Country Life, 1957), *The System* (Hodder & Stoughton, 1967), *The Environmental Revolution* (McGraw, 1970), and *The Big Change: After the Environmental Revolution* (McGraw, 1973). *Address:* 13 Upper Cheyne Row, London S.W.3, England. *Biographical/critical sources: Book World,* April 27, 1969; *Observer,* January 11, 1970; *New Statesman,* January 16, 1970; *Washington Post,* June 19, 1970.

* * *

NIELSEN, Knut Schmidt
   See SCHMIDT-NIELSEN, Knut

* * *

NIELSEN, Niels Juel
   See JUEL-NIELSEN, Niels

* * *

NILAND, Deborah   1951-

PERSONAL: Born September 16, 1951, in Auckland, New Zealand; daughter of Ruth Park (a writer). *Education:* Attended Julian Ashton Art School.

CAREER: Writer and illustrator of books for children. *Awards, honors:* Australian Books of the Year Award from the Australian Children's Book Council, 1974, for *Mulga Bill's Bicycle,* and 1977, for *ABC of Monsters;* Commonwealth Visual Arts Award for best book illustration, 1974.

*WRITINGS—*Self-illustrated: (With sister, Kilmeny Niland) *Birds on a Bough: A Counting Book,* Hodder & Stoughton, 1975; *ABC of Monsters,* Hodder & Stoughton, 1976, McGraw, 1978.

Illustrator: *Animal Tales,* Angus & Robertson, 1974; Michael Dugan, compiler, *Stuff and Nonsense,* Collins, 1974; Barbara Ireson, *Tumbling Jack, and Other Rhymes,* Transworld, 1976; Jean Chapman, compiler, *The Sugar-Plum Christmas Book,* Hodder & Stoughton, 1977; Eric C. Rolls, *Miss Strawberry Verses,* Kestrel Books, 1978; *The Drover's Dream* (poetry), Collins, 1979; Chapman, compiler, *Velvet Paws and Whiskers,* Hodder & Stoughton, 1979.

Illustrator; all with sister, Kilmeny Niland: Elizabeth Fletcher, *The Little Goat,* Transworld, 1971; Elizabeth M. Wilton, *Riverview Kids,* Angus & Robertson, 1972; Fletcher, *The Farm Alphabet,* Transworld, 1973; Andrew Barton Paterson, *Mulga Bill's Bicycle* (poem), Collins, 1973, Parents' Magazine Press, 1975; Fletcher, *What Am I?,* Transworld, 1974; Ruth Park, *The Gigantic Balloon,* Collins, 1975, Parents' Magazine Press, 1976; Jean Chapman, *Tell Me Another Tale: Stories, Verses,*

Songs, and Things to Do, Hodder & Stoughton, 1976; *Park, Roger Bandy,* Rigby, 1977.

* * *

NIWA, Tamako   1922-

BRIEF ENTRY: Born November 6, 1922, in Berkeley, Calif. American linguist, educator, and author. After working as a linguist at the American embassy in Tokyo, Japan, Niwa began teaching at University of Washington, Seattle, and became a professor of Japanese language in 1977. Niwa's publications include *Basic Japanese for College Students* (University of Washington Press, 1964), *Kabuki Plays* (Samuel French, 1966), *Introduction to Hirangana and Characters: A Self-Study Workbook* (University of Washington Press, 1969), and *First Course in Japanese* (University of Washington Press, 1971). *Address:* 3363 West Commodore Way, Seattle, Wash. 98199; and Department of Asian Language and Literature, University of Washington, Seattle, Wash. 98105.

* * *

NORDEN, Helen Brown
   See LAWRENSON, Helen

* * *

NORDHAM, George Washington   1929-

PERSONAL: Born February 22, 1929, in Waldwick, N.J.; son of George (an architect) and Florence (Rockett) Nordham; married Jean Andrews, April 7, 1956 (died October 13, 1969); children: John Andrews. *Education:* George Washington University, B.A., 1949; University of Pennsylvania Law School, LL.B., 1952. *Home:* 67 East Prospect St., Waldwick, N.J. 07463. *Office:* Prentice-Hall, Inc., Englewood Cliffs, N.J. 07632.

CAREER: Admitted to the Bar of New York State, 1959; Morgan Guaranty Trust Co., New York City, trust administrator, 1955-60; Richardson-Vicks, Inc., New York City, assistant treasurer, 1960-66; Binney & Smith, Inc., New York City, corporate secretary, 1966-71; Prentice-Hall, Inc., Englewood Cliffs, N.J., legal editor, 1971-73; legal administrator for private law firms in New Jersey, 1973-77; Prentice-Hall, Inc., Englewood Cliffs, legal editor, 1977—. *Military service:* U.S. Army, Finance Corps, 1952-55; became second lieutenant. *Member:* American Bar Association, American Society of Corporate Secretaries, New York State Bar Association, Legal Administrators Association.

WRITINGS: George Washington: Vignettes and Memorabilia, Dorrance, 1977; *George Washington's Women: Mary, Martha, Sally, and 146 Others,* Dorrance, 1977; *George Washington and Money,* University Press of America, 1982; *George Washington and the Law,* Adams Press, 1982; *George Washington: A Treasury* (short stories), Adams Press, 1982. Contributor of articles to magazines, including *Daughters of the American Revolution.*

WORK IN PROGRESS: George Washington in Perspective, a major biography, publication expected in 1983.

SIDELIGHTS: Sharing both birthday and moniker with the first president of the United States, Nordham has built a lifelong avocation around his namesake. A collector of Washington memorabilia, he was encouraged in his hobby by his father, who, in 1932, purchased the first item for his son's collection—a replica of Jean-Antoine Houdon's life-sized bust of George Washington, finished in gold and weighing forty pounds. Since that time Nordham's collection has grown to include more than twenty-five busts, one hundred paintings, prints, and wall plates, hundreds of commemorative coins and stamps, paper currency, and a library of more than three hundred books on the founding father. Some of the items Nordham has acquired date back to the early 1800's, but although many of the objects in the collection are limited editions or rare, others are still readily available at little cost.

Since the publication of his books on Washington, Nordham has been amazed at the generosity of his readers, who have sent him all sorts of items—cups, thimbles, ashtrays, etc.—for his collection. In addition, his expertise has been sought out by historical societies, and he has exhibited his Washington paraphernalia in several New Jersey cities.

BIOGRAPHICAL/CRITICAL SOURCES: New York, February 25, 1980; GW Times, February, 1982.

* * *

NORODOM SIHANOUK (VARMAN), Samdech Preah 1922-
(Norodom Sihanouk)

BRIEF ENTRY: Born October 31, 1922. Cambodian ruler and author. Sihanouk was elected king of Cambodia in 1941 while the country was under French rule. When the country gained independence in 1955 he abdicated the throne in favor of his father, but five years later was elected head of state following his father's death. In 1970 Sihanouk was deposed. He fled to Peking, China, and remained there until 1975, when he was restored as ruler of Cambodia for a third time. He resigned from that position in 1976 to become a member of the People's Representative Assembly. In the 1970's, Sihanouk came to believe he was being plotted against by U.S. intelligence agents. He described the alleged plot in My War With the C.I.A.: The Memoirs of Prince Norodom Sihanouk (Pantheon, 1973). Later he wrote Chroniques de guerre et d'espoir (Hachette/Stock, 1979; translated as War and Hope: The Case for Cambodia, Pantheon, 1980). Biographical/critical sources: The McGraw-Hill Encyclopedia of World Biography, McGraw, 1973; New York Times, July 31, 1973, August 12, 1973, January 9, 1979.

* * *

NORRIE, Ian 1927-

PERSONAL: Born August 3, 1927, in Southborough, England; son of James Shepherd (a chemist) and Elsie (Tapley) Norrie; married Mavis Kathleen Matthews (a teacher), April 2, 1955; children: two daughters. Politics: "Pragmatist." Religion: None. Residence: Barnet, England. Agent: Giles Gordon, Anthony Sheil Associates Ltd., 2-3 Morwell St., London WC1B 3AR, England. Office: High Hill Bookshops Ltd., 6-7 High St., Hampstead, London N.W.3, England.

CAREER: High Hill Bookshops, London, England, manager, 1956-64, managing director, 1964—. Director of High Hill Press, 1968—. Member: National Book League, Society of Bookmen (chairman, 1971-73), Garrick Club.

WRITINGS—Novels: Hackles Rise and Fall, Dobson, 1962; Quentin and the Bogomils, Dobson, 1966; Plum's Grand Tour, Macdonald & Co., 1978.

Nonfiction: (With Frank Arthur Mumby) Publishing and Bookselling, J. Cape, 1974; Hampstead, Highgate Village, and Kenwood: A Short Guide, With Suggested Walks, photographs by Philip Greenall, drawings by Ronald Saxby, High Hill Press, 1977; Hampstead: London Hill Town, High Hill Press, 1981;

Publishing and Bookselling in the Twentieth Century, Bell & Hyman, 1982.

Editor; published by High Hill Press; illustrated with photographs by Edwin Smith and drawings by Ronald Saxby, except as noted: The Book of Hampstead, drawings by Moy Keightley, 1960, second revised edition, photographs by Christopher Oxford, Colin Penn, L. H. Reader, and Smith, 1968; The Book of the City, 1961; The Hearthside Book of Hampstead and Highgate, 1962; The Book of Westminster, 1964. Also a guest editor of A Celebration of Books, National Book League, 1975.

Contributor to Bookseller and Hampstead and Highgate Express.

SIDELIGHTS: Norrie told CA: "My critical source has not been diagnosed; my critical sauce, however, is said to be highly spiced and verging on the astringent. When I was young there were articles about me in bookish and book trade journals; now what appears is autobiographical."

* * *

NORTON, Bram
See BRAMESCO, Norton J.

* * *

NUMEROFF, Laura Joffe 1953-

PERSONAL: Born July 14, 1953, in Brooklyn, N.Y.; daughter of William (an artist) and Florence (a teacher; maiden name, Joffe) Numeroff. Education: Pratt Institute, B.F.A. (with honors), 1975; further study at Parsons College, 1975. Religion: Jewish. Residence: San Francisco, Calif.

CAREER: Author and illustrator of books for young people. Lecturer.

WRITINGS—All juveniles; all self-illustrated: Amy for Short, Macmillan, 1976; Phoebe Dexter Has Harriet Peterson's Sniffles, Greenwillow, 1977; Walter, Macmillan, 1978; (with sister, Alice Numeroff Richter) Emily's Bunch, Macmillan, 1978; (with Richter) You Can't Put Braces on Spaces, Greenwillow, 1979; Does Grandma Have an Elmo Elephant Jungle Kit?, Greenwillow, 1980; The Ugliest Sweater, F. Watts, 1980; Beatrice Doesn't Want To, F. Watts, 1981. Also author of Digger, Dutton.

WORK IN PROGRESS: Say Hello to the Statue of Liberty, a novel for young people; a screenplay; several children's books; a script for a television situation comedy.

SIDELIGHTS: Numeroff told CA: "I grew up in a world of books, music, and art. I was a voracious reader and read six books every week. I've also been drawing pictures since I was old enough to hold a crayon, and writing came soon after. Doing children's books combines the two things I love the most. At Pratt Institute, I took a class taught by Barbara Bottner called 'Writing and Illustrating for Children's Books.' Amy for Short was a homework assignment!

"I am an avid reader and was from the start. I prefer biographies, nonfiction, and stories dealing with 'real-life' dramas—never did like fairy tales all that much. I guess that's why my children's stories tend to be based on things kids actually go through, like wearing braces, being too tall for your age, being a daydreamer, having to wear something your grandmother gave you even though you think it's hideous. The best reviews come from kids who write to me—that makes it all worth it! On October 16, 1980, the Sierra Oaks School in Sacramento held 'Laura Joffe Numeroff Day.' I lectured, and several of the students came dressed as some of the characters in my books. It was quite a treat!

"I collect children's books and can usually be found in the library or bookstore. I'm also a film freak; last year I saw seventy-two movies. I enjoy exploring California and get a thrill from just driving through the country and watching cows (I spent twenty-five years in New York City). To supplement my income, I've had such odd jobs as running a merry-go-round and doing private investigation.

"My work is my life. I can draw no distinction between the words 'work' and 'spare time.' I love what I'm doing and the only time it becomes work is when there's rewriting. I'd eventually like to write screenplays and adult fiction, but I'll always have a first love for children's books. I hope to be writing until my last days."

Numeroff's *Emily's Bunch* has appeared in school textbooks published by Ginn and by Scott, Foresman. *You Can't Put Braces on Spaces* and *The Ugliest Sweater* have been made into educational filmstrips.

*　　*　　*

NYE, Loyal 1921-

PERSONAL: Born March 27, 1921, in Ogden, Utah; daughter of Alfred (a merchant) and Elizabeth (Kline) Christenson; married Delbert L. Nye (a U.S. Public Health Service officer), November 16, 1943; children: M. Christian, Miles, Elizabeth, Kevin. *Education:* Weber State College, A.A., 1941; attended University of Utah, 1948. *Politics:* Republican. *Religion:* Presbyterian. *Home:* 4525 Clearbrook Lane, Kensington, Md. 20895.

CAREER: Mountain States Telephone Co., Ogden, Utah, service representative, 1941-45; Neighborhood House, Salt Lake City, Utah, teacher, 1947-48; adult education teacher in Fresno, Calif., 1956; Warner Memorial Presbyterian Church, Kensington, Md., preschool teacher, 1962-77.

WRITINGS: What Color Am I? (juvenile), Abingdon, 1977. Contributor to *Presbyterian Journal.*

WORK IN PROGRESS: Church Rabbit, a juvenile; *A Most-Fun Valentine Day,* a juvenile.

SIDELIGHTS: Loyal Nye wrote: "*What Color Am I?* was written to answer a parent's question—'What do I tell my child?'

"*The Church Rabbit* is an autobiography. I don't like 'cutesy' stories for children. The real church rabbit had dignity. He was housebroken and enjoyed his freedom in the classroom. He provided an opportunity for children to question and voice their concerns about or interest in many subjects, including death. Pets do not live as long as people, so we should love them and enjoy them as long as we can. We did, until summer came and the rabbit moved back with his family. The book is his story.

"Although adults are divided about the merits of anthropomorphic literature for children, when one teaches young children it becomes apparent how much they enjoy pretending that animals can talk and how much they enjoy hearing stories about them.

"*A Most-Fun Valentine Day* came from the frustration I experienced trying to find suitable material for young children about the origin of this holiday. The story takes place partly in the classroom and could be adapted easily into a play with a class full of characters.

"I tend to write for children to fill what I consider to be a void, dealing with such subjects as human color, death, or the origin of Valentine customs. I enjoy children and have a special fondness for exuberant four-year-old boys."

O

OAKLEY, Graham 1929-

PERSONAL: Born August 27, 1929, in Shrewsbury, England; son of Thomas (a shop manager) and Flora (Madeley) Oakley. *Education:* Attended Warrington Art School, 1950. *Residence:* Chippenham, Wiltshire, England.

CAREER: Free-lance artist and book illustrator. Worked as scenic artist for British repertory companies, 1950-55; designer's assistant for Royal Opera House, Covent Garden, London, England, 1955-57; worked for Crawford Advertising Agency, 1960-62; British Broadcasting Corporation, London, television set designer for motion pictures and series, including "How Green Was My Valley," "Nicholas Nickleby," "Treasure Island," and "Softly, Softly," 1962-77. *Military service:* Served in the British Army, 1945-47. *Awards, honors: The Church Mice Adrift* was nominated for a Kate Greenaway Medal, 1976, and was selected as one of the best illustrated children's books of the year by the *New York Times,* 1977.

WRITINGS—All for children; all self-illustrated: *The Church Mouse,* Atheneum, 1972; *The Church Cat Abroad,* Atheneum, 1973; *The Church Mice and the Moon,* Atheneum, 1974; *The Church Mice Spread Their Wings,* Macmillan (London), 1975, Atheneum, 1976; *The Church Mice Adrift,* Macmillan, 1976, Atheneum, 1977; *The Church Mice at Bay,* Macmillan, 1978, Atheneum, 1979; *The Church Mice at Christmas,* Atheneum, 1980; *Graham Oakley's Magical Changes,* Atheneum, 1980; *Hetty and Harriet,* Atheneum, 1982; *Church Mice in Action,* 1982.

Illustrator: John Ruskin, *The King of the Golden River,* or; *The Black Brothers,* Hutchinson, 1958; Hugh Popham, *Fabulous Voyage of the Pegasus,* Criterion, 1959; Robert Louis Stevenson, *Kidnapped,* Dutton, 1960; Charles Kervern, *White Horizons,* University of London Press, 1962; Mollie Clarke, adapter, *The Three Feathers: A German Folk Tale Retold,* Hart-Davis, 1963, Follett, 1968; Richard Garnett, *The White Dragon,* Hart-Davis, 1963; Garnett, *Jack of Dover,* Vanguard, 1966; Brian Read, *The Water Wheel,* World's Work, 1970; Tanith Lee, *Dragon Hoard,* Farrar, Straus, 1971; Elizabeth MacDonald, *The Two Sisters,* World's Work, 1975.

SIDELIGHTS: The success of Graham Oakley's "Church Mouse" stories for children is credited to his illustrations as well as to his text. A *New York Times Book Review* writer, who calls the author/artist "brilliant," says he "draws like an angel, whether his brush is outlining an almost invisible quivering whisker or washing in the green shimmer of a lush riverscape." Another reviewer for the same publication refers to one of Oakley's tales as "irresistible."

In an interview for *Publishers Weekly,* Oakley commented on the engaging creatures that populate these books: "I try not to let anything human creep into my portrayal of Sampson," Oakley explained, "to keep him looking like a cat at all times. He does just what a cat would do in any situation, when he is frightened, happy, puzzled. . . . The church mice, on the other hand, are easy to anthropomorphize, and I think it's no great affront to nature to do so."

In each of the highly popular tales, the author places the mice in a dire situation that must be resolved, often through the bungling efforts of Sampson, a self-proclaimed "Friend to Mice." "I try to think," Oakley told his interviewer, "'How could a little creature get rid of a man?' The devices have to be contrived. I suppose what I'm trying to do is create a James Bond-type story on the mice level."

AVOCATIONAL INTERESTS: Motoring.

BIOGRAPHICAL/CRITICAL SOURCES: Times Literary Supplement, November 3, 1972; *New York Times Book Review,* December 10, 1972, May 8, 1977; *Time,* November 21, 1977; *Publishers Weekly,* February 26, 1979; *Punch,* January 16, 1980.*

*   *   *

OBACH, Robert 1939-

PERSONAL: Born May 16, 1939, in Brooklyn, N.Y.; son of George Robert and Violet (a social director; maiden name, St. Eve) Obach; married Rose Mary Clark (an artist and liturgist), November 25, 1967; children: Noel, Jennifer, Rebecca, Sarah. *Education:* Loyola University, Chicago, Ill., B.A., 1963; Catholic University of America, M.A., 1968; attended Syracuse University, 1970-72, and University of Strasbourg, 1972-73; Syracuse University, Ph.D., 1981. *Office:* Office of Religious Education—Dayton Region, Archdiocese of Cincinnati, 266 Bainbridge St., Dayton, Ohio 45402.

CAREER: Daemen College, Buffalo, N.Y., instructor, 1967-70, assistant professor of theology, 1970; Diocese of Memphis, Memphis, Tenn., coordinator of adult education, 1973-74, director of religious education for parishes within the diocese, 1974-77, member of theological task force, 1976-80, adult education consultant, 1978-80; Archdiocese of Cincinnati,

Dayton, Ohio, assistant to director of Office of Religious Education, 1981—.

WRITINGS: (With Al Kirk) *Commentary on the Gospel According to Matthew,* Paulist Press, 1979; (with Kirk) *Commentary on the Gospel According to John,* Paulist Press, 1981. Author of church school curriculum material. Contributor to magazines and newspapers, including *Living Light* and *Common Sense.*

WORK IN PROGRESS: Commentary on the Gospel according to Luke.

SIDELIGHTS: Obach told *CA:* "I think that on the global scale the most important moral issue facing Christian believers is the nuclear arms race. Most people do not seem to be able to make the connections between what technology can do and their responsibilities for controlling and directing our technology to build a truly human world. However, to be serious about being a disciple of Jesus is to be willing to see things anew and act upon them. Adult religious education offers many possibilities for seeing the implications of discipleship—one of them being a resistance to the current ideological world view that insists on protecting the United States from external enemies by building larger and more complex weapons systems. The monies, manpower, and national treasure and resources that go into building weapons that can't be used (without destroying our civilization) can be said to be monies, etc., that are stolen from the hungry, the sick, the homeless, and the uneducated."

*　　*　　*

OBREGON, Mauricio   1921-

PERSONAL: Born January 24, 1921, in Barcelona, Spain; son of Mauricio (an engineer) and Madronita (Andreu) Obregon; married Cristina Martinez-Irujo, August 26, 1952; children: Sancho, Javier, Santiago, Ines, Ana Maria, Beltran. *Education:* Attended Oxford University, 1939-40, and Massachusetts Institute of Technology, 1940-41; Harvard University, B.A., 1943. *Religion:* Roman Catholic. *Agent:* Aaron Priest, Aaron M. Priest Literary Agency, Inc., 150 East 35th St., New York, N.Y. 10016. *Office:* Apartado Aereo 3529, Bogota 1, Colombia.

CAREER: Grumman Aircraft Corp., Bethpage, N.Y., engineer and test flight captain, 1944-45; Lansa Airlines, Barranquilla, Colombia, founder and technical vice-president, 1945-47; Government of Colombia, Bogota, director-general of civil aviation, 1947-48; *Semana* (news magazine), Bogota, Colombia, editor, 1948-51; Government of Colombia, coordinator of economic planning, 1951-55, ambassador to Venezuela, 1955-58, ambassador to the Organization of American States in Washington, D.C., 1958-63; Colombian Educational Radio and Publishing Network, Bogota, president, 1963-64; Choco Development and Interoceanic Canal Corp., Bogota, president, 1969-71; chairman of Avianca International Airlines, 1975; University of the Andes, Bogota, professor of history of discovery, 1979—, president of university, 1979—, chancellor, 1981—. Visiting lecturer at Harvard University, 1976, member of board of overseers, 1980—. Member of founding council of United Nations Aviation Organization, 1947; member of board of directors of Energy Fund, 1968, now adviser; member of board of directors of Colombian Aircraft Industry, 1974—; vice-chairman of Colombian Oceanographic Commission and Colombia delegate to Caribbean Oceanographic Commission, 1981—. Lecturer in the United States, Brazil, Spain, Venezuela, Argentina, the Philippines, Yugoslavia, and Austria. *Military service:* Colombian Air Force,

1948—; became flight lieutenant. Served with British Army. *Member:* Federation Aeronautique Internationale (past president; honorary president).

WRITINGS: (With Samuel Eliot Morison) *The Caribbean as Columbus Saw It,* Little, Brown, 1964; *Ulysses Airborne,* Harper, 1971; *De los argonautas a los astronautas,* Argos Vergara, 1977, translation published as *Argonauts to Astronauts,* Harper, 1980. Contributor to magazines.

WORK IN PROGRESS: Juan Sebastian de Elcano; The Polynesians; Early Chinese Navigators.

SIDELIGHTS: In 1965 Obregon established a world light airplane speed record. In light planes and under sail, he has followed the routes of the Argonauts, Odysseus, the Vikings, Columbus, Ojeda, Amerigo Vespucci, Pinzon, Lepe, Cabral, Magellan, Cabot, Cartier, and Cabeza de Vaca. Obregan told *CA:* "I believe history should be researched afloat and aloft as well as in archives. In any case, it is a wonderful excuse for bumming around the pleasant seas of the world."

*　　*　　*

O'BRIEN, Geoffrey   1948-

PERSONAL: Born May 4, 1948, in New York, N.Y.; son of Joseph A. (a radio show host) and Margaret (an actress; maiden name, Owens) O'Brien; married Kaalii Francis (a consultant), March 18, 1977. *Education:* Attended Yale University, 1966-67, and State University of New York at Stony Brook, 1968-70; Nichibei Kaiwa Gaku-in, Tokyo, Japan, intermediate diploma, 1979. *Home:* 200 East 15th St., New York, N.Y. 10003.

CAREER: Dale System Detective Agency, New York City, clerical worker, 1970-71; Robinson & Watkins Ltd., London, England, mail order clerk, 1973-74; Cambridge Graphics, New York City, computer typesetter, 1974-78, 1979-80; free-lance writer and translator of French, 1980—. *Member:* Haiku Society of America.

WRITINGS: Hard-Boiled America: The Lurid Years of Paperbacks, Van Nostrand, 1981. Work represented in anthologies, including *Open Poetry,* Simon & Schuster, 1973, *Active Anthology,* Sumac Press, 1974, and *Selected Poetry of Vincente Huidobro,* New Directions, 1981. Contributor to journals and periodicals, including *Stony Brook, Chicago Review, Soho News, Village Voice, On Film, Res Gestae, Airplane, Wind Chimes,* and *Dyslexia.* Co-editor, with Eliot Weinberger, of *Pony Tail,* 1968-70, and *Montemora,* 1975-76; editor of *Frogpond,* 1981.

WORK IN PROGRESS: Research on the roots, ramifications, and repercussions, in fact and in media fiction, of American psychedelic culture of the late 1960's; research on "two little-known novelists, Jim Thompson and David Goodis."

SIDELIGHTS: O'Brien's *Hard-Boiled America* chronicles a period in American publishing, primarily the 1940's and '50's, when a popular taste for sensationalism spawned countless examples of the tough-detective novel. Leading authors included Mickey Spillane, Dwight V. Babcock, and Richard Ellington. Algis Budrys of the *Chicago Sun-Times* called O'Brien's volume an "engaging, often deadly appraisal of the evolution and devolution of the American paperback novel. . . . O'Brien's text lends lucid perspectives to the paperback phenomenon without descending to either sneers or the tinhorn sincerity of ordinary 'popular culture' studies." Herbert Gold of the *Los Angeles Times Book Review* also applauded O'Brien's effort. "His book is balanced, intelligent, and sings like a saxophone for a lost time of comfort in the lower depths." Patricia Craig of the *Times Literary Supplement,* however, noted that the genre displays a ''distrust of understatement,'' and that ''artists and writers share an attachment to the overblown.'' This extreme treatment includes people depicted on the book covers, of whom Craig remarked, ''Whatever they're doing, they do it inadequately clothed.'' Craig added that O'Brien's ''study provides a satisfactory guide to the themes and the embellishments of popular literature, but he often gives in to the temptation of taking his material too seriously.''

O'Brien told *CA:* ''In poetry or prose I aim to make a unity out of as many disparate elements as possible: a kind of harmonious collage. Those elements have included (beyond the circumstances of daily life and those more horrid ones of the daily paper) such American artifacts as movies, private-eye novels, comic books, and all the various musics, as well as the literature and culture of Japan, and of England and France (my wife being English and my sometime livelihood that of French translator). Roughly, my poetry is dedicated to imagination and my prose to history, but I like best the uncertain area between those poles. I am particularly interested in the way fanciful or delusory ideas can function as historical phenomena.''

BIOGRAPHICAL/CRITICAL SOURCES: Chicago Sun-Times, August 30, 1981; *Los Angeles Times Book Review,* September 20, 1981; *Times Literary Supplement,* December 25, 1981.

* * *

O'BRIEN, Saliee
See JANAS, Frankie-Lee

* * *

O'BRIEN, Thomas C(lement) 1938-

PERSONAL: Born July 10, 1938, in New York, N.Y.; son of Thomas C. (an accountant) and Dorothy (Beers) O'Brien; married Gail Marshall (a researcher), July 1, 1961; children: Thomas C. III., Ellen Marie, Virginia Ann. *Education:* Iona College, B.S., 1959; Columbia University, M.A., 1960; New York University, Ph.D., 1967. *Home:* 7050 Washington Ave., University City, Mo. 63130. *Office:* Southern Illinois University, Edwardsville, Ill. 62026.

CAREER: Iona College, New Rochelle, N.Y., instructor in mathematics, 1960-61; Macmillan Publishing Company, New York, N.Y., senior editor of school mathematics department, 1961-63; Educational Research Council, Greater Cleveland Mathematics Program, Cleveland, Ohio, research associate and co-author of program materials, 1963-68; Boston University, Boston, Mass., assistant professor of mathematics, 1968-70; Southern Illinois University, Edwardsville, Ill., associate professor of mathematics, 1970-75, professor of mathematics, 1975—. Consultant to Eastern Regional Institute for Education, 1968; mathematics test evaluator, Exploratory Committee for the Assessment of Progress in Education, 1968; originator of Boston University videotape child watching series and videotape interview series in mathematics, 1968-70; instructor at seminars and conferences, including Froebel Institute, Jean Piaget Society, and Association of Teachers of Mathematics, beginning 1971; founder, Belleville Area Teachers' Center, 1972, River Bluffs Teachers' Center, 1975; chairman, First American Conference on Teachers' Centers in Mathematics Education, 1974, Teachers' Center Project, Southern Illinois University, 1976; American representative to International Day on Mathematics Education, Netherlands, 1976; participated in forty-eight five-minute radio programs for public radio station WSIE-FM, 1978. *Member:* American Educational Research Association, Association of Teachers of Mathematics, National Council of Teachers of Mathematics. *Awards, honors:* Senior research fellowship in science from North Atlantic Treaty Organization, 1978; A. A. Loftus Award from Iona College, 1979.

WRITINGS: Odds and Evens, Crowell, 1971; ''Solve It!'' series, five books, Educational Teaching Aids, 1977; *Wollygoggles and Other Creatures,* Cuisenaire Co., 1980; *Puzzle Tables,* Cuisenaire Co., 1980; ''Mathematical Brain Teasers'' series, five books, Educational Teaching Aids, 1980; *Mathematical Problem Solving,* Cuisenaire Co., Book 1, 1980, Book 2, 1980.

Contributor of articles to periodicals, including *Arithmetic Teacher, School Science and Mathematics, Elementary School Journal, Childhood Education, American Education Research Journal, Child Development,* and *Journal of Research in Mathematics Education.* Editor, *Seedbed* (quarterly teaching journal), 1979—.

WORK IN PROGRESS: Research on children's concepts of numbers; manuscript for children's problem solving.

SIDELIGHTS: The contemporary approach to education is outmoded, according to Thomas O'Brien. ''My work and research are done from the Piagetian constructivist point of view. That is, the child (or the adult) is not a passive receptor of knowledge but an active constructor of reality tending toward coherence, stability, economy, and generalizability.'' O'Brien feels American education must adopt this point of view in order to better serve students. ''Today's children will spend most of their lives in the twenty-first century, yet present approaches provide them with a nineteenth-century education.''

* * *

ODEGAARD, Charles Edwin 1911-

BRIEF ENTRY: Born January 10, 1911, in Chicago Heights, Ill. American educator and author. Odegaard is a professor of biomedical history at University of Washington, Seattle. From 1958 to 1973 he was also president of the university. He served as executive director of the American Council of Learned Societies from 1948 to 1952. Odegaard's books include *Man and Learning in Modern Society* (University of Washington Press, 1959), *Minorities in Medicine: From Receptive Passivity to Positive Action, 1966-76* (Josiah Macy, Jr., Foundation, 1977), *Area Health Education Centers: The Pioneering Years, 1972-1978* (Carnegie Council on Policy Studies in Higher Education, 1979), and *Eleven Area Health Education Centers: The View From the Grass Roots* (Carnegie Council on Policy Studies in Higher Education, 1980). *Address:* 6333 Sand Point Way N.E., Seattle, Wash. 98115; and College of Education, 222 Miller Hall, DQ12, University of Washington, Seattle, Wash. 98195. *Biographical/critical sources: Who's Who in America,* 41st edition, Marquis, 1980.

* * *

O'DONNELL, Kevin, Jr. 1950-

PERSONAL: Born November 29, 1950, in Cleveland, Ohio; son of Kevin (a company president) and Ellen (Blydenburgh) O'Donnell; married Lillian Tchang (a sales representative), September 7, 1974. *Education:* Yale University, B.A., 1972. *Home and office:* 35 Sherman Court, New Haven, Conn. 06511. *Agent:* Cherry Weiner, 1734 Church St., Rahway, N.J. 07065.

CAREER: Hong Kong Baptist College, Hong Kong, lecturer in English, 1972-73; American English Language Institute, Taipei, Taiwan, instructor in English, 1973-74; free-lance writer,

1976—; *Empire* (quarterly magazine for science fiction writers), New Haven, Conn., managing editor, 1979-81, publisher, 1981—. Member of board of directors of Sherman Court Condominium Association, 1979-84, chairman, 1979-82. *Awards, honors:* Second prize from *Galileo*, 1977, for short-short story, "Do Not Go Gentle."

WRITINGS—Science fiction: *Bander Snatch,* Bantam, 1979; *Mayflies,* Berkley Books, 1979; *Caverns,* Berkley Books, 1981; *Reefs,* Berkley Books, 1981; *War of Omission,* Bantam, 1982; *Lava,* Berkley Books, 1982. Contributor of more than forty stories and articles to science fiction and mystery magazines.

WORK IN PROGRESS: ORA:CLE, a novel focusing on life in a fully computerized but stagnant society of the future, publication expected in 1983.

SIDELIGHTS: O'Donnell commented: "I have traveled widely through eastern Asia, where I lived for four years (in Seoul, South Korea, 1966-68, in Hong Kong, 1972-73, and in Taipei, Taiwan, 1973-74). My linguistic competency—now sadly atrophied—once included French, Korean, Mandarin Chinese, and survival Japanese. The major motivating forces behind my choice of career are love of language, laziness, and the desire to be my own boss. The short commute-time helped, too."

AVOCATIONAL INTERESTS: Horticulture, microcomputers.

*   *   *

OEKSENHOLT, Svein   1925-

BRIEF ENTRY: Born January 12, 1925, in Larvik, Norway. Educator and author. Oeksenholt was a high school teacher in the 1950's. He has been a professor of German at Eastern Montana College since 1967. Oeksenholt was awarded a Fulbright grant for Germany in 1960. He edited *Deutsch der Gegenwart: Readings in the Social and Natural Sciences* (Prentice-Hall, 1971). He translated *To Everyone It May Concern* (1978). *Address:* 3014 Laredo Pl., Billings, Mont. 59102; and Department of German, East Montana College, Billings, Mont. 59101.

*   *   *

OKSENHOLT, Svein
See OEKSENHOLT, Svein

*   *   *

OLCOTT, Anthony   1950-

PERSONAL: Born April 10, 1950, in Red Lodge, Mont.; son of Harry J. (a dealer in farm equipment) and Alison (a social worker; maiden name, Ball) Olcott; married Martha Brill (a college professor), July 5, 1975; children: Alison, Andrew. *Education:* Stanford University, B.A., 1971, M.A., 1973, Ph.D., 1976. *Residence:* Andover, Mass. *Office:* Phillips Academy, Andover, Mass. 01810.

CAREER: University of Virginia, Charlottesville, assistant professor of Slavic, 1975-76; Chenango Inn, Norwich, N.Y., beverage manager, 1977; Colgate University Bookstore, Hamilton, N.Y., manager of book department, 1978-81; Phillips Academy, Andover, Mass., instructor in English, 1981—. Instructor at Colgate University, 1979-81. *Member:* Associated Writing Programs, Poets and Writers.

WRITINGS: (Translator) Andrei Platonov, *Chevengur* (novel), Ardis, 1978; (editor) *Complete Works of Boris Poplavsky,* Berkeley Slavic Specialists, 1980; *Murder at the Red October* (novel), Academy Chicago, 1981.

Work represented in anthologies, including *Recent Russian Fiction,* Random House, and *Bitter Air of Exile: Russian Writers in the West, 1922-72,* revised edition, University of California Press, 1977. Contributor to magazines, including *TriQuarterly, Country Life, Yale Literary Review,* and *Russian Literature Triquarterly.*

WORK IN PROGRESS: A sequel to *Murder at the Red October,* publication expected in 1982; a book about Montana, completion expected in 1983; a novel set in the Russia of Catherine the Great.

SIDELIGHTS: Olcott commented: "Writing has always been a goal, but one assiduously avoided for years while I did other (mostly academic) things. It seems that writing requires a certain stock of experience, maturity, or perhaps simply age. For whatever reasons, skills have converged over the past few years, and I now generate projects faster than I can execute them."

Jean White of the *Washington Post Book World* said that Olcott's *Murder at the Red October* "is an exceptional novel, offering penetrating glimpses of life in contemporary Russian society while telling the tense story of a murder investigation within the Soviet bureaucracy." White added that Olcott's novel "can stand side by side" with Martin Cruz Smith's bestseller *Gorky Park,* "which is high praise."

BIOGRAPHICAL/CRITICAL SOURCES: Washington Post Book World, December 20, 1981.

*   *   *

OLIN, William   1929-

PERSONAL: Born January 23, 1929, in Akron, Ohio; son of F. R. (in sales) and Sarah (Guinter) Olin; married Phyllis R. Kwalwasser (an exporter), March 23, 1967; children: Ruth, Elizabeth, Adam, Gabriel. *Education:* Attended University of Akron, 1947-49; Ohio State University, B.Arch., 1954; attended Starr King School for the Ministry, 1963-64. *Politics:* Democrat. *Home and office:* 1204 Neilson St., Berkeley, Calif. 94706.

CAREER: Architect in private practice in Ohio, Illinois, Missouri, Texas, and California. *Military service:* U.S. Army, 1955-57.

WRITINGS: Escape From Utopia: My Ten Years in Synanon, Unity Press, 1981.

SIDELIGHTS: Olin joined Synanon, not as a drug user in need of rehabilitation, but in search of a new lifestyle. When he left the cult, he was disillusioned by changes he observed in Synanon's practices and the philosophy of its leader, Chuck Dederich. Olin's book has been described overall as a fair and generally positive account.

Olin told *CA:* "When my wife and I first stumbled onto Synanon, the fledgling organization had just opened its doors to 'squares,' that is, those of us who lack some life-crippling disorder. Immediately we were dazzled by the 'Game'—a communication/education tool so powerful that regular usage transformed drug addicts, muggers, and murderers into exemplary human beings. After three years of increasing involvement as nonresident members, both of us were convinced that here was an unprecedented utopian experiment, one which bridged the antihuman gaps of race, sex, age, and education, demonstrating that true brotherhood is achievable. Forthwith, we sold our house, donated all our worldly goods, grabbed our infant son, and moved into what Synanon's feisty founder, Chuck Dederich, called 'the nuthouse staffed by the nuts.'

"The best one-liner I've come up with to describe our life 'inside' is that the Olins had simply moved to another planet. Every aspect of our existence was affected, from physical appearance and diet to child-rearing and personal relationships. Within our extended family of two thousand (most of whom were society's worst rejects) no one smoked, drank, used drugs, fought, stole, or even littered. Members worked hard, enthusiastically assumed community responsibilities, and laughed a lot. Professionals of every description, business tycoons, and little old ladies dwelt happily and securely among their ex-felon brothers and sisters in Synanon houses, where doors had no locks. Everyone, from youngest to oldest, was continually involved in radical new learning situations, hell-bent on improving themselves and their home. Change was the deliberate goal sought, as Synanites found themselves caught up in an unending series of social experiments dreamed up by Dederich. The lifestyle was both exhausting and exhilarating—what we called 'accelerated evolutions.'

"Unfortunately, with the passage of time, my wife and I detected trends in Synanon which bothered us. More and more, new directions emanating from the leadership smacked of the very middle-class consumerist goals we had renounced. Cooperation and trust gave way to greed and paranoia about the world outside. Finally, the almighty Game itself degenerated from a tool of communication to one of manipulation—a psychic cattle prod to keep the troops in line. After seven years of residency we had lost the vision. And so, we left utopia, sad of heart and empty of pocket, yet grateful for an adventure so rich that it seemed to have condensed the experience of several lifetimes.

"Consider but one example of a truism about the human animal convincingly demonstrated in Synanon: When a person is *enabled to verbalize his or her fears, anger, and hostility, the pressure to act out against self or others disappears.* Think of the implications of this truism for our violence-ravaged society, within our nuclear-nightmarish world.''

BIOGRAPHICAL/CRITICAL SOURCES: Los Angeles Times Book Review, December 7, 1980.

*　　*　　*

OLIVER, Carl Russell 1941-

PERSONAL: Born February 23, 1941, in Fort Lewis, Wash.; son of Ralph Lorimer and Dorothy (Fodrea) Oliver; married Dianne Larson; children: Carol. *Education:* Stanford University, A.B., 1962, graduate study, 1968-70. *Home address:* Box 4647, APO Miami, Fla. 34001.

WRITINGS: Plane Talk: Aviators' and Astronauts' Own Stories (juvenile), Houghton, 1980.

*　　*　　*

OLIVER, James A(rthur) 1914-1981

OBITUARY NOTICE: Born January 1, 1914, in Caruthersville, Mo.; died of cardiac arrest, December 2, 1981, in New York, N.Y. Herpetologist, zoo and museum director, and author of books on reptiles and amphibians. While serving as director of the Bronx Zoo, Oliver helped design and supervise the innovative renovation of the zoo's reptile house, which has been described as the most attractive in the world. Oliver, who was the first herpetologist to induce king cobras to mate in captivity, also served as director of the New York Aquarium and was director emeritus of the American Museum of Natural History and the New York Zoological Society. His books include *Prevention and Treatment of Snake Bite, The Natural*

History of North American Amphibians and Reptiles, and *Snakes in Fact and Fiction.* Obituaries and other sources: *New Yorker,* July 18, 1953; *Natural History,* August, 1959; *Current Biography,* Wilson, 1966, May, 1982; *New York Times,* December 4, 1981.

*　　*　　*

OLSEN, Hans Christian, Jr. 1929-

BRIEF ENTRY: Born April 20, 1929, in Kearney, Neb. American educator, editor, and author. Olsen has been a professor of elementary education at University of Missouri, St. Louis, since 1968. His publications include *The Psycholinguistic Nature of the Reading Process* (Wayne State University Press, 1968), *Choosing Materials to Teach Reading* (Wayne State University Press, 1966), *Partnership in Teacher Education* (Association for Student Teaching and Association of Colleges for Teacher Education, 1968), *A Guide to Professional Excellence in Clinical Experiences in Teacher Education* (Association for Student Teaching and Association of Colleges for Teacher Education, 1970), and *The Teaching Clinic: A Team Approach to the Improvement of Teaching* (Association of Teacher Educators, 1971). *Address:* Department of Childhood Education, University of Missouri, 8001 Natural Bridge, St. Louis, Mo. 63121.

*　　*　　*

OLSON, Gene 1922-

PERSONAL: Born in 1922 in Montevideo, Minn. *Education:* Attended University of Oregon; Pacific University, M.A. *Home:* 780 Oxyoke Rd., Grants Pass, Ore. 97526.

CAREER: Author of novels and histories for young people. Has worked as a teacher, newspaper editor, and television scriptwriter. *Military service:* Served in U.S. Army during World War II.

WRITINGS—For young people: Stampede at Blue Springs, Dodd, 1956, adaptation published as *Between Me and the Marshal,* Dodd, 1964; *The Tall One: A Basketball Story,* Dodd, 1956; *Last Night at Black Hammer,* Dodd, 1957; *The Bucket of Thunderbolts,* Dodd, 1959; *The Ballhawks,* Westminster, 1960; *Sacramento Gold,* Macrae, 1961; *The Red, Red Roadster,* Macrae, 1962; *The Roaring Road,* Dodd, 1962; *The Tin Goose,* Westminster, 1962; *Bonus Boy: The Story of a Southpaw Pitcher,* Dodd, 1963; *Bailey and the Bearcat* (Junior Literary Guild selection), Westminster, 1964; *Fullback Fury,* Dodd, 1964; (with Joan Olson) *Oregon Times and Trails,* Windyridge, 1965; *Three Men on Third,* Westminster, 1965; *Cross-Country Chaos,* Westminster, 1966; *Pistons and Powderpuffs,* Westminster, 1967; *The Iron Foxhole,* Westminster, 1968; *The Most Beautiful Girl in the World,* Westminster, 1968; *Drop into Hell,* Westminster, 1969; (with J. Olson) *Washington Times and Trails,* Windyridge, 1970; (with J. Olson) *California Times and Trails,* Windyridge, 1971; *Sweet Agony: A Writing Manual of Sorts,* Windyridge, 1972; (with J. Olson) *Silver Dust and Spanish Wine: A Bilingual History of Mexico,* Windyridge, 1978.*

*　　*　　*

ONEAL, Elizabeth 1934-
(Zibby Oneal)

PERSONAL: Born March 17, 1934, in Omaha, Neb.; daughter of James D. (a thoracic surgeon) and Mary Elizabeth (Dowling) Bisgard; married Robert Moore Oneal (a plastic surgeon), December 27, 1955; children: Elizabeth, Michael. *Education:*

Attended Stanford University, 1952-55; University of Michigan, B.A., 1970. *Politics:* Democrat. *Religion:* Episcopalian. *Home:* 501 Onondaga St., Ann Arbor, Mich. 48104. *Agent:* Marilyn Marlow, Curtis Brown Ltd., 575 Madison Ave., New York, N.Y. 10022. *Office:* 1609 Haven Hall, University of Michigan, Ann Arbor, Mich. 48105.

CAREER: University of Michigan, Ann Arbor, lecturer in English, 1976—. Member of board of trustees, Greenhills School, 1975-79. *Awards, honors:* Friends of American Writers Award, 1972, for *War Work.*

WRITINGS—All for children, except as noted; all under name Zibby Oneal: *War Work* (illustrated by George Porter), Viking, 1971; *The Improbable Adventures of Marvelous O'Hara Soapstone* (illustrated by Paul Galdone), Viking, 1972; *Turtle and Snail* (illustrated by Margot Tomes), Lippincott, 1979; *The Language of Goldfish* (young adult novel), Viking, 1980.

WORK IN PROGRESS: Two juvenile novels to be completed in 1982.

*   *   *

ONEAL, Zibby
See ONEAL, Elizabeth

*   *   *

O'NEIL, Robert M(archant) 1934-

PERSONAL: Born October 16, 1934, in Boston, Mass.; son of Walter G. and Isabel S. (Marchant) O'Neil; married Karen Elson, June 18, 1967; children: Elizabeth, Peter, David, Benjamin. *Education:* Harvard University, A.B., 1956, A.M., 1957, LL.B., 1961. *Home:* 6021 South Highlands Ave., Madison, Wis. 53705. *Office:* University of Wisconsin System, 1220 Linden Dr., Madison, Wis. 53706.

CAREER: Tufts University, Medford, Mass., instructor in speech, 1956-61; San Francisco State College, San Francisco, Calif., visiting instructor in speech, 1962; U.S. Supreme Court, Washington, D.C., law clerk, 1962-63; University of California, Berkeley, acting associate professor, 1963-66, professor of law, 1966-67; State University of New York at Buffalo, professor of law and executive assistant to president of the university, 1967-69; University of California, Berkeley, professor of law, 1969-71; University of Cincinnati, Cincinnati, Ohio, professor of law, 1972-75, vice-president and provost for academic affairs, 1972-73, executive vice-president for academic affairs, 1973-75; Indiana University, Bloomington, professor of law and vice-president of Bloomington campus, 1975-80; University of Wisconsin System, Madison, president and professor of law at University of Wisconsin—Madison, 1980—. Counsel to Assembly on University Goals and Governance, 1969-71; chairman of Council on Legal Education Opportunity, 1972-74; member of National Commission on Higher Education for Police Officers, 1976-78; member of Carnegie Council on Policy Studies in Higher Education, 1977-79; member of executive committee of Committee on Institutional Cooperation, 1978-80; member of board of trustees of Carnegie Foundation for the Advancement of Teaching, 1978—.

MEMBER: American Council on Education (member of Commission on Academic Affairs, 1971-73), American Bar Association (chairman of committee on educational policy of section on legal education and admission to the bar, 1978-79), American Association of University Professors (general counsel, 1970-72; member of governing board of Academic Freedom Fund, 1977—), Association of American Colleges (member of Commission on Institutional Affairs, 1973-75), National

Association of State Universities and Land-Grant Colleges, American Association for Higher Education (chairman of cooperative program advisory committee, 1974-75), Association of American Law Schools (past chairman of committee on teaching law outside of law schools).

WRITINGS: Civil Liberties: Case Studies and the Law, Houghton, 1965; *Free Speech: Responsible Communication Under Law,* Bobbs-Merrill, 1966, 2nd edition, 1972; *The Price of Dependency: Civil Liberties in the Welfare State,* Dutton, 1970; (with others) *No Heroes, No Villains,* Jossey-Bass, 1972; (with Anthony D'Amato) *The Judiciary and Vietnam,* St. Martin's, 1972; *The Courts, Government, and Higher Education,* Committee for Economic Development, 1972; (with Donald Parker, Nicholas Econopoly, and Karen E. O'Neil) *Civil Liberties Today,* Houghton, 1974; *Discrimination Against Discrimination,* Indiana University Press, 1976; *Handbook of the Law of Public Employment,* Avon, 1978; *Classrooms in the Crossfire,* Indiana University Press, 1981. Also author of, with John A. Lynch, *Eight Special Analyses on Current Problems for High School and College Debates,* American Enterprise Institute for Public Policy Research, and, with Russel Widnes and J. Weston-Walch, *A Guide to Debate,* 1964.

Contributor: Warren Todd Furniss, editor, *Higher Education for Everybody: Issues and Implications,* American Council on Education, 1971; G. Kerry Smith and others, editors, *New Teaching, New Learning: Current Issues in Higher Education,* Jossey-Bass, 1971; Bardwell L. Smith, editor, *The Tenure Debate,* Jossey-Bass, 1973; Furniss and Patricia Albjerg Graham, editors, *Women in Higher Education,* American Council on Education, 1974; Barry Gross, editor, *Reverse Discrimination,* Prometheus Books, 1977. Contributor of more than thirty articles to law journals. Member of editorial board of *Journal of Higher Education,* 1973-79.

SIDELIGHTS: Paul Chevigny of *Nation* called Robert O'Neil's *The Price of Dependency* a "superb book." He said: "This book is a balanced study of the problem of dependence in our welfare state, and the growth of legal rules to combat some of its evils. It is the best sort of book about the law—through the concrete facts of the cases, it tells us about the rules of law, as well as the underlying problems. Better than most lawyers, O'Neil knows how to use his cases as though they were stories of human conflict (which, of course, they are). And yet, by some magic, he manages to use all the important cases."

BIOGRAPHICAL/CRITICAL SOURCES: Nation, June 29, 1970.

*   *   *

O'NEILL, Daniel Joseph 1905-

BRIEF ENTRY: Born March 19, 1905, in Pawtucket, R.I. American educator, academic administrator, and author. O'Neill was a professor of education at St. Louis University from 1957 to 1970, when he was named emeritus professor. In the same year he became historian at Providence College. His books include *Latinity, a College Textbook: A Scientific Approach to Classical Composition Through Grammar, Style, Rhetoric* (Oxford Press, 1935), *A Book About Books* (Oxford Press, 1936), *The Science of English Grammar* (Oxford Press, 1943), *The Science of English Rhetoric* (Oxford Press, 1943), *Speeches by Black Americans* (Dickenson, 1971), and *Concepts in Communication* (Allyn & Bacon, 1973). *Address:* Archives, Phillips Memorial Library, Providence College, Providence, R.I. 02918.

OPIE, Peter (Mason) 1918-1982

OBITUARY NOTICE—See index for *CA* sketch: Born November 25, 1918, in Cairo, Egypt; died February 5, 1982, in West Liss, Hampshire, England. Folklorist and author. Opie is best known as an authority on the folklore of childhood and on children's books. His "peerless" collection of literature for children was used to study patterns and traditions in the genre. With his wife, Iona, Opie published studies of rhymes, games, and customs of childhood, the most notable of which is the *Oxford Dictionary of Nursery Rhymes*. In 1953 the folklorist was awarded the Silver Medal of the Royal Society of Arts. He was president of both the anthropology section of the British Association and the Folklore Society. Opie's writings include *The Puffin Book of Nursery Rhymes, The Lore and Language of School Children, The Oxford Book of Children's Verse, The Classic Fairy Tales,* and *A Nursery Companion*. At the time of his death, Opie was writing the *Oxford Book of Narrative Verse*. Obituaries and other sources: *London Times,* February 8, 1982; *Chicago Tribune,* February 9, 1982.

*   *   *

OPLAND, Jeff 1943-

PERSONAL: Born July 26, 1943, in Cape Town, South Africa; son of Marcus (an accountant) and Annie (a store owner; maiden name, Charlaff) Opland; married Cynthia Vivian Classen (a registered nurse), December 12, 1964; children: Russell Martin, Daniel Joseph, Janine Suzanne, Samantha Ann. *Education:* University of Cape Town, B.A. and B.Sc., both 1963, B.A. (with honors), 1964, M.A., 1968, Ph.D., 1973; Cape Technical College, National Teachers' Certificate, 1967. *Home:* 4 Constitution St., Grahamstown 6140, South Africa. *Office:* Institute of Social and Economic Research, Rhodes University, Grahamstown 6140, South Africa.

CAREER: Assistant teacher at high school in Cape Town, South Africa, 1965; University of Cape Town, Cape Town, temporary lecturer, 1966-67, junior lecturer, 1967-68, lecturer in English, 1968-72; University of Durban—Westville, Durban, South Africa, associate professor of English and head of department, 1972-74; Pontifical Institute of Mediaeval Studies, Toronto, Ontario, visiting professor of English, 1974-75; Rhodes University, Grahamstown, South Africa, fellow of Institute of Social and Economic Research, 1976, director of institute and professor of social and economic research, 1977—. Visiting professor and fellow at Yale University, 1980-81; Alexander von Humboldt Foundation research fellow in West Germany, 1981; guest lecturer at universities in the United States, Australia, and Canada, including Stanford University, University of California, Berkeley, Harvard University, University of Toronto, Australian National University, and State University of New York at Stony Brook.

MEMBER: Medieval Society of Southern Africa (founding member; chairman, 1972-74, 1976-78; member of council, 1974-76), English Academy of Southern Africa, African Literature Association, African Language Association of Southern Africa, Mediaeval Academy of America, Modern Language Association of America, American Folklore Society, Connecticut Academy of Arts and Sciences. *Awards, honors:* Pringle Award from English Academy of Southern Africa, 1971, for article "*Scop* and *Imbongi*: Anglo-Saxon and Bantu Oral Poets"; grant from Human Sciences Research Council, 1975; fellowships from Medieval Society of Southern Africa and Alexander von Humboldt Foundation, both 1981.

WRITINGS: (Contributor) Christopher Saunders and Robin Derricourt, editors, *Beyond the Cape Frontier: Studies in the History of Transkei and Ciskei,* Longman, 1974; *Notes on J. D. Salinger's "The Catcher in the Rye,"* Methuen, 1976; *Notes on John Steinbeck's "Grapes of Wrath,"* Methuen, 1977; *Notes on Ernest Hemingway's "A Farewell to Arms" and "For Whom the Bell Tolls,"* Methuen, 1978.

(Contributor) John D. Niles, editor, *Old English Literature in Context: Ten Essays,* Rowman & Littlefield, 1980; *Anglo-Saxon Oral Poetry: A Study of the Traditions,* Yale University Press, 1980; (editor with F. van Zyl Slabbert) *South Africa: Dilemmas of Evolutionary Change,* Institute of Social and Economic Research, Rhodes University, 1980; (editor with Gillian P. Cook) *Mdantsane: Transitional City,* Institute of Social and Economic Research, Rhodes University, 1980; *Xhosa Oral Poetry: Aspects of a Black South African Tradition,* Cambridge University Press, 1983.

General editor of "ISER Xhosa Texts," a series, Institute of Social and Economic Research, Rhodes University, 1977-80. Contributor of more than twenty articles and reviews to scholarly journals.

WORK IN PROGRESS: An essay, "The Isolation of the Xhosa Oral Poet," for a volume of essays on South African literature edited by Landeg White and T. J. Couzens, publication by Longman expected in 1983.

SIDELIGHTS: Opland wrote: "Because I resist the tendency of academics to specialize, my work is essentially comparative and interdisciplinary. Because I believe that fresh ideas and insights are more important than the vapid trappings of academic scholarship, I tend to resist compendious footnotes and documentation. Because I suppose I could write fiction, I approach my academic writing creatively, always trying to provoke thought and suggest ideas even if I do not express them explicitly. I am always open to new ideas: it thrills me to catch myself in the process of changing my mind. Hence (I suppose) travel is important to me. I have lived my life in South Africa but have spent extended periods in Canada, the United States, Germany, and England, and can stumble through a conversation in Afrikaans (and hence, Dutch), Xhosa, and German."

*   *   *

ORAM, Hiawyn 1946-

PERSONAL: Born September 28, 1946, in Johannesburg, South Africa; daughter of John Woolerton (in business) and Eileen (Hargraves) Shilling; married Gavin T. Oram (a stockbroker), April 7, 1973; children: Maximilian, Felix. *Education:* University of Natal, B.A., 1966. *Religion:* None. *Home:* 41 Crestway, London SW15 5DB, England.

CAREER: Natal Performing Arts Council, Durban, South Africa, actress, 1966; Young Advertising, Johannesburg, South Africa, copywriter, 1967-68; De Beers/Charter Consolidated, London, England, public affairs assistant, 1968-69; J. Walter Thompson (advertising agency), Johannesburg, copywriter, 1970-72; Leo Burnett (advertising agency), London, copywriter, 1972-74; free-lance writer, 1974—.

WRITINGS:—For children: *Skittlewonder and the Wizard,* Dial, 1980; *Angry Arthur,* Harcourt, 1982.

Scripts: "Enemies Within" (stage play); "A Working Woman" (television situation comedy); "The Woman and the Idol" (screenplay); "The Lucifer Match" (screenplay).

WORK IN PROGRESS: A novel; children's books; a screenplay; a television drama series.

SIDELIGHTS: Hiawyn Oram commented: "An early sense of loss, plus early indignation at the widespread injustice in the universe (both man-made and natural) drew me toward the empires of the imagination, where I could rearrange and control the component parts. Writing is an extension of that process. The vital subject for me is the interface between fact and fiction, between the conscious and subconscious worlds, and the human animal's seeming dependence on fictions (ideologies, religions, dreams, and images) for his motivation and fulfillment.

"Works that have had formative effects include Walt Disney's 'Snow White,' as my first film, F. H. Burnett's *The Secret Garden*, the poetry of T. S. Eliot and William Blake, Henry James's *Portrait of a Lady*, Dostoevski's *Crime and Punishment*, Romain Gary's *Dance of Genghis Cohen*, Oriana Falaci's *A Man*, R. W. Fassbinder's films, especially 'Saturn's Brew,' Robert Bresson's 'Pickpocket' and 'A Gentle Creature,' and Nellie Kaplan's *A Very Curious Woman* and *Nea*."

*   *   *

O'REILLY, Timothy   1954-

PERSONAL: Born June 6, 1954, in Cork, Ireland; came to the United States in 1954, naturalized citizen, 1971; son of Sean (a neurologist) and Anne (Hillam) O'Reilly; married Christina Feldmann (a writer and dancer), June 28, 1975; children: Arwen Kathryn. *Education:* Harvard University, A.B. (cum laude), 1975. *Home:* 171 Jackson St., Newton, Mass. 02159.

CAREER: Brajer, O'Reilly & Associates (management and systems consultants), partner, 1978-81; O'Reilly & Associates (technical writing consultants), Newton, principal, 1981—. *Member:* Science Fiction Writers of America (affiliate member), Community for Conscious Evolution (member of board of directors 1981), L-5 Society.

WRITINGS: (Editor of abridgement and author of commentary) *George Simon: Notebooks, 1965-1973*, Community for Conscious Evolution, 1976; *Frank Herbert*, Ungar, 1981; (editor with Martin Cohen) *Fragments of an Evolving Language*, Community for Conscious Evolution, 1981. Author of technical manuals. Contributor to *Survey of Science Fiction Literature*.

WORK IN PROGRESS: Editing a collection of essays by Frank Herbert, publication by Putnam expected in 1983; *The Mad Philosophers*, translations of humorous anecdotes about the ancient Greek philosophers; *The Gift of Fire*, a biography and "philosophical apology" for the work of George Simon, pioneer researcher on consciousness, completion expected in 1985.

SIDELIGHTS: O'Reilly commented: "In my writing, I want to communicate a sense of the experiential dimensions of ideas—to show truly original thought as a kind of perception, not a rehearsal of what is already known, but a participation in the unknown. I do not wish only to *talk* about such a dimension of thought, but to awaken it as I write.

"This approach is very much a product of my studies with George Simon. Watching Simon in his attempts to develop a 'language for consciousness' by distinguishing inner experiences and then finding the relationships between them, I became convinced that original thought does not come from the manipulation of other thoughts, but from grasping afresh at the nature of reality. (This is obviously true in the physical sciences, but less understood in literature and philosophy.) Simon himself has said 'perception and philosophy are one.' In my undergraduate work in classics, I studied Plato from this point of view and believe I uncovered many of the same dynamics in his work as I had seen in Simon's.

"As a literary critic, I have also been influenced by Colin Wilson, Stewart Brand, and John Cowper Powys. Each of these men in his own way appreciates books for the ideas they contain, and for the use those ideas have in enriching the life and awareness of the reader."

*   *   *

ORFF, Carl   1895-1982

OBITUARY NOTICE: Born July 10, 1895, in Munich, Germany (now West Germany); died of cancer, March 29, 1982, in Munich, West Germany. Composer, educator, and author. Rebelling against the intricacies of modern musical styles, Orff used simple folk songs and primitive themes as models for his musical compositions. His most famous work, "Carmina Burana," for example, is based on a collection of medieval songs celebrating food, drink, love, sex, and life. The work was awarded the New York Music Critics' Prize in 1954. Other compositions by Orff include "Oedipus der Tyrann," "Antigonae," "Prometheus," and "Der Mond." Orff was also known for creating an unusual method of teaching musical concepts to children through a combination of rhythmic and gymnastic participation. He introduced his method at the Guentherschule, which he founded in 1924 with Dorothee Guenther. Orff later adapted the technique for a series of radio broadcasts in the 1940's. The Orff method of music education is described in the composer's five-volume textbook, *Das Schulwerk* (translation published as *Music for Children*). Obituaries and other sources: Andreas Liess, *Carl Orff*, Atlantis Verlag, 1955, St. Martin's, 1966; *New Encyclopedia of the Opera*, Hill & Wang, 1971; *Current Biography*, Wilson, 1976, May, 1982; *Baker's Biographical Dictionary of Musicians*, 6th edition, Schirmer Books, 1978; *New York Times*, March 31, 1982; *Chicago Tribune*, March 31, 1982; *Newsweek*, April 5, 1982; *Time*, April 12, 1982.

*   *   *

ORTEGA y GASSET, Jose   1883-1955

BRIEF ENTRY: Born May 9, 1883, in Madrid, Spain; died October 18, 1955, in Madrid, Spain. Spanish philosopher and author. Ortega was one of Spain's best-known philosophers and a solid representative of twentieth-century Spanish thought. He believed that man's life consisted only of the present, and since he saw no spiritual purpose in existence, he argued that it should be regarded as sport. This theme ran through most of Ortega's writing, including *Meditaciones del Quijote* (1914; translated as *Meditations on Quixote*, 1961) and *El tema de nuestro tiempo* (1923; translated as *The Modern Theme*, 1931). In the earlier book, he also expressed the need for a more European atmosphere in Spain, one more supportive of philosophical inquiry and systematic thought. Ortega's writings covered an extraordinary range of subject matter, all presented in eloquent style. His humanistic approach and wide circulation in journals and newspapers made him extremely popular, especially in Latin America. His most famous book is *La rebelion de las masas* (1930; translated as *The Revolt of the Masses*, 1932). In it Ortega described the existence of a weakened nobility, unfit to rule, and the growth of "mass man," who was taking over the functions of government and society. He saw this trend as a threat to all the traditional values of civilization, and called for an intellectual, enlightened minority to come forth and govern in a refined spirit of liberalism and freedom. *Biographical/critical sources: Twentieth Century Authors: A Biographical Dictionary of Modern Literature*, H. W. Wilson, 1942; *Columbia Dictionary of Modern European Literature*, Columbia University Press, 1947; *Encyclopedia of*

World Literature in the Twentieth Century, updated edition, Ungar, 1967, supplement, Ungar, 1975.

*   *   *

ORTLUND, Anne   1923-

PERSONAL: Born December 3, 1923, in Wichita, Kan.; daughter of Joseph B. (a brigadier general in the U.S. Army) and Mary (Weible) Sweet; married Raymond C. Ortlund (a minister), April 27, 1946; children: Sherrill Anne (Mrs. Walter S. Harrah), Margot Jeanne (Mrs. John C. McClure III), Raymond C., Jr., Nels Robert. *Education:* University of Redlands, B.Mus. (with honors), 1945. *Home:* 32 Whitewater Dr., Corona del Mar, Calif. 92625.

CAREER: Songwriter under contract with SESAC, Inc., 1964-81; speaker at Christian conferences, worldwide, 1970—; Bible teacher and organist. *Awards, honors:* Woman of the year award from Pasadena Business and Professional Women, 1975; Humanist Award from SESAC, Inc., 1978.

WRITINGS: Up With Worship, Regal Books, 1975; *Disciplines of the Beautiful Woman,* Word, Inc., 1977; *Love Me With Tough Love, Life: Disciplines for Living Together in the Body of Christ,* Word, Inc., 1979; *Children Are Wet Cement: Make the Right Impression in Their Lives,* Revell, 1981. Also author of *The Acts of Joanna,* Word, Inc., and, with husband, Raymond C. Ortland, *The Best Half of Life,* Word, Inc.

WORK IN PROGRESS: Two books.

SIDELIGHTS: Ortlund told *CA:* ''As far as I can see, the only things in life that are important are God and people, and connecting the latter with the former. Part of my life's purpose is to leave a mark on others contemporary to me and following me, through my life and my talents, which will point them to God.

''I seek to affect my contemporaries to this end through speaking at perhaps two conferences a month across the United States and overseas. My music and book writing can also affect my contemporaries, and can go on changing lives long after I'm gone.

''God has been so good! My husband and I do most of our speaking together, side by side, and we've ministered on every continent and stay booked about four years in advance. We've each authored five books, co-authored one, and between us we've had three best-sellers. Our love for God in Jesus Christ, and secondly, for each other, makes life wonderfully full and rewarding.''

*   *   *

OSBORN, Alex(ander) F(aickney)   1888-1966

OBITUARY NOTICE: Born May 24, 1888, in New York, N.Y.; died of cancer, May 4 (some sources say May 5), 1966, in Buffalo, N.Y. Advertising executive and author of *A Short*

Course in Advertising, How to Think Up, Your Creative Power, Wake Up Your Mind, Applied Imagination: The Principles and Procedures of Creative Thinking, and *How to Become More Creative.* Obituaries and other sources: *New York Times,* May 6, 1966; *Newsweek,* May 16, 1966; *Publishers Weekly,* May 16, 1966; *Who Was Who in America, With World Notables,* Volume IV: *1961-1968,* Marquis, 1968.

*   *   *

OSTERWEIS, Rollin G(ustav)   1907-1982(?)

OBITUARY NOTICE—See index for *CA* sketch: Born August 15, 1907, in West Haven, Conn.; died c. 1982 in Branford, Conn. Educator, historian, and author. Osterweis began his career as an instructor at Yale University in 1943. In 1948 he was named director of public speaking and debate at the institution, and twenty years later he became a professor of history, specializing in urban history. His interest in the antebellum South led to several books on the topic, among them *Romanticism and Nationalism in the Old South.* His other writings include *Rebecca Gratz, Three Centuries of New Haven: 1638-1938, Santarem, Charter Number Two: The Centennial History of the First New Haven National Bank,* and *The New Haven Green and the American Bicentennial.* Obituaries and other sources: *AB Bookman's Weekly,* March 29, 1982.

*   *   *

OSWALT, Sabine
See MacCORMACK, Sabine G(abriele)

*   *   *

OTTESON, Schuyler Franklin   1917-

BRIEF ENTRY: Born July 17, 1917, in Mondovi, Wis. American educator, academic administrator, and author. After working for several years in business, Otteson joined the faculty at Indiana University in 1946. He has been a professor of marketing at that school since 1952, director of its Bureau of Business Research from 1954 to 1960, dean of its Graduate School of Business since 1971, and director of its International Business Research Institute. His books include *Marketing: Current Problems and Theories* (School of Business, Indiana University, 1952), *An Introduction to the Field of Marketing Research* (School of Business, Indiana University, 1954), *Orientation to Business Research* (School of Business, Indiana University, 1955), *Marketing: The Firm's Viewpoint* (Macmillan, 1964), and *Internationalizing the Traditional Business Research Curriculum in Accounting, Business Policy, Finance, and Marketing* (Bureau of Business Research, Indiana University, 1968). *Address:* 512 South Jordan Ave., Bloomington, Ind. 47401; and Graduate School of Business, Indiana University, Bloomington, Ind. 47401. *Biographical/critical sources: Who's Who in America,* 41st edition, Marquis, 1980.

P

PAAK, Carl Erich 1922-

PERSONAL: Born February 17, 1922, in Milwaukee, Wis.; son of Karl Erich and Ella (Risse) Paak; married Elizabeth Brueggemann (an elementary school principal), March 18, 1951; children: Lissa Ellen, Erick Joseph. *Education:* Chicago Art Institute, B.A., 1950; Ohio State University, M.A., 1953; attended State University of New York College of Ceramics, Alfred, 1955. *Politics:* Democrat. *Religion:* Unitarian-Universalist. *Home:* 1719 Notre Dame Dr. N.E., Albuquerque, N.M. 87106. *Office:* Department of Art, University of New Mexico, Albuquerque, N.M. 87131.

CAREER: Cornell College, Mount Vernon, Iowa, instructor in art, 1953-56; University of New Mexico, Albuquerque, assistant professor, 1956-60, associate professor, 1961-65; professor of art, 1966—. Ceramic artist; work exhibited in numerous shows. *Member:* World Craft Council, American Craft Council, National Council for Ceramic Arts Education, American Association of University Professors.

WRITINGS: The Decorative Touch, Prentice-Hall, 1981.

SIDELIGHTS: Paak wrote: "When Prentice-Hall requested I write a book on ceramics, I had to think carefully about why it should be written. Having taught ceramics for thirty years and having been a productive ceramic artist at the same time, I understood well the problems of a student trying to create ideas in clay.

"Many ceramic books tell 'how-to-do,' but few try to alleviate problems before they happen. With a profusion of illustrations, I discuss various methods of decoration, glazing, firing, and studio needs, trying at the same time to eliminate technical problems and decrease some of the frustrations of doing the wrong thing at the wrong time!

"My interest in clay as a form of personal expression has always been a vocational and avocational interest, one which has taken me to Sweden, Finland, Denmark, Ecuador, Peru, Portugal, Spain, and Italy to view and photograph ceramic works of the past and present. This personal enrichment is extended to my students in the form of slides."

*   *   *

PACKARD, Jerrold M(ichael) 1943-

PERSONAL: Born May 14, 1943, in Orange, Calif.; son of Lee R. (a printer) and Elizabeth (Miller) Packard. *Education:* Portland State University, B.A., 1967. *Residence:* San Francisco, Calif. *Agent:* William Reiss, Paul R. Reynolds, Inc., 12 East 41st St., New York, N.Y. 10017.

CAREER: Blue Cross of Oregon, Portland, health administrator and manager of Medicare claims dept., 1969-73; Blue Cross of Northern California, Oakland, health administrator and utilization review manager, 1973-76; independent rare-book dealer in San Francisco, Calif., 1976-80; writer, 1980—. *Military service:* U.S. Air Force, 1961-65; became sergeant.

WRITINGS: The Queen and Her Court: A Guide to the British Monarchy Today (alternate selection of Book-of-the-Month Club), Scribner, 1981; *American Monarchy: A Social Guide to the Presidency,* Delacorte, 1982.

*   *   *

PAGE, Emma
See TIRBUTT, Honoria

*   *   *

PAHLAVI, Mohammed Riza
See PAHLEVI, Mohammed Riza

*   *   *

PAHLEVI, Mohammed Riza 1919-1980
(Shah of Iran)

OBITUARY NOTICE: Born October 26, 1919, in Tehran, Persia (now Iran); died of cancer, July 27, 1980, near Cairo, Egypt; buried at al-Rifai Mosque, in Egypt. Emperor of Iran and author. Pahlevi ruled over Iran from 1941 until 1979, when he was deposed by the revolutionary forces of Ayatollah Ruhollah Khomeini. Though Pahlevi has been credited with modernizing his feudal nation, he has also been accused of brutally suppressing those who opposed his rule. Following his deposition, Pahlevi was granted permission by President Jimmy Carter to seek medical treatment in the United States for his cancerous condition. The shah's arrival in the United States precipitated an assault on the U.S. embassy in Tehran on November 4, 1979, by Iranian students who demanded the return of the shah. The Americans who were taken hostage at that time were not released until six months after the exiled shah's death in Egypt. In addition to several books on Iran's foreign and domestic affairs, Pahlevi wrote an autobiography, *Mission for My Country.* His last book, *Answer to History,* was published in 1980. Obituaries and other sources: Mohammed Riza Pahlevi, *Mission for My Country,* McGraw, 1961; *Current Biography,* Wilson, 1977, September, 1980; Margaret Irene Laing, *The Shah,* Sidgwick & Jackson, 1977; *The International Who's Who,* Europa, 1980; *The Middle East and North Africa,* 27th edition, Europa, 1980; *New York Times,* July 28, 1980; *Newsweek,* August 4, 1980; *Maclean's Magazine,* August 4, 1980; *Time,* August 4, 1980; *New Republic,* August 16, 1980; *National Review,* August 22, 1980.

* * *

PALM, John Daniel 1924-

BRIEF ENTRY: Born September 5, 1924, in Missoula, Mont. American geneticist, educator, and author. Palm has taught biology at St. Olaf College since 1962. He worked as a biologist at General Mills from 1953 to 1956. He wrote *Diet Away Your Stress, Tension, and Anxiety: The Fructose Diet Book* (Doubleday, 1976). *Address:* Department of Biology, St. Olaf College, Northfield, Minn. 55057. *Biographical/critical sources: American Men and Women of Science: The Physical and Biological Sciences,* 14th edition, Bowker, 1979.

* * *

PANITT, Merrill 1917-

PERSONAL: Born September 11, 1917, in Hartford, Conn.; son of Irving and Anna (Shear) Panitt; married Marjorie Hoover, April 2, 1942; children: Jeffrey. *Education:* Attended University of Missouri, 1933-37; received B.J., 1977. *Home address:* R.D. 3, Box 62, Malvern, Pa. 19355. *Office:* TV Guide Bldg., Radnor, Pa. 19088; and *Seventeen,* 850 3rd Ave., New York, N.Y. 10022.

CAREER: United Press, Jefferson City, Mo., reporter, 1937-39; public relations official for Missouri Public Expenditure Survey, 1939-41; Triangle Publications, Inc., Philadelphia, Pa., reporter and editor, 1946-48, administrative assistant to president, 1948-53, managing editor of *TV Guide,* 1953-59, editor of *TV Guide,* 1959-73, and editorial director of Triangle Magazines, 1973—. Trustee of Annenberg School of Communications, 1967—. *Military service:* U.S. Army, 1941-46; became major. *Member:* Sigma Delta Chi. *Awards, honors:* Journalism award from University of California, 1972; journalism honor medal from University of Missouri, 1980.

WRITINGS: (With E. Ernest Dupuy and Herbert Bregstein) *Soldier's Album,* Houghton, 1946. Editorial director of *TV Digest* and *TV Factbook,* 1959-61; editor of *TV Guide Roundup,* 1960.

* * *

PARASURAM, T(attamangalam) V(iswanatha Iyer) 1923-

PERSONAL: Born April 1, 1923, in Tattamangalam, Kerala, India; son of K. P. Viswanatha Iyer (a tube well drill supervisor) and Visalaksai Ammal; married Anantham Narayana Iyer (an interior designer), April 30, 1950; children: Ashok, Anita. *Education:* Attended Laxmi Technical Institute, Bombay, India, and Harvard University. *Politics:* Independent. *Office: Indian Express* Newspapers, 3723 Emily St., Kensington, Md. 20895.

CAREER: Worked for Associated Press of India, 1940-48; Press Trust of India, chief parliamentary and defense correspondent in New Delhi, India, 1949-58, United Nations correspondent in New York, N.Y., 1959-62; *Indian Express,* Washington, D.C., and Kensington, Md., Washington correspondent, 1962—. Notable assignments include coverage of Mahatma Gandhi's campaign, 1945, Bandung Conference, 1955, and Prime Minister Jawaharlal Nehru's European tours, 1956 and 1957. President of P.T.I. journalist trade union in India, 1956; member of executive bodies of several unions in India. Lecturer at universities in India and the United States. *Military service:* Indian Army, 1948; became major. *Member:* United Nations Correspondents Association, Foreign Press Association (New York), National Sports Club of India (life member), Sigma Delta Chi. *Awards, honors:* Chaman Lal Award, 1974, for excellence in reporting; Nieman fellow at Harvard University, 1958-59.

WRITINGS: *Defending Kashmir,* Publications Division, Government of India, 1949; *A Medal for Kashmir,* S. Chand, 1958; *India's Jewish Heritage,* Sagar, 1982. Author of weekly column "Letter From America," in *Indian Express,* 1962—.

SIDELIGHTS: Parasuram told *CA:* "I am interested mainly in politics, economics, and social welfare with a view to rectifying injustices both within and between nations. Furthermore, I am committed to political and economic justice without sacrificing personal freedom, individual rights, and the rule of law."

* * *

PARKER, Watson 1924-

PERSONAL: Born June 15, 1924, in Chicago, Ill.; son of Troy L. and Janet S. Parker; married Olga Glassman, 1950; children: James, David, Rebecca. *Education:* University of Chicago, A.B., 1948; Cornell University, B.S., 1951; University of Oklahoma, M.A., 1962, Ph.D., 1965. *Politics:* "Millsian Liberal." *Religion:* Protestant. *Home:* 727 Wright St., Oshkosh, Wis. 54901. *Office:* Department of History, University of Wisconsin—Oshkosh, Oshkosh, Wis. 54901.

CAREER: Palmer Gulch Lodge, Hill City, S.D., manager, 1948-60; University of Wisconsin—Oshkosh (formerly Wisconsin State University—Oshkosh), 1965—, became professor of history, 1973. *Military service:* U.S. Army, Medical Department, 1943-46; served in European and Pacific theaters; became staff sergeant. U.S. Army Reserve, 1946-51. *Member:* Western History Association, South Dakota State Historical Society, Black Hills Corral of Westerners, Chicago Corral of Westerners. *Awards, honors:* Woodrow Wilson fellowship, 1962-63.

WRITINGS: *Palmer Gulch Lodge Guide to the Black Hills,* privately printed, 1954; *Black Hills Ghost Towns and Others,* privately printed, 1964; *Gold in the Black Hills,* University of Oklahoma Press, 1966; (with Hugh K. Lambert) *Black Hills Ghost Towns,* Swallow Press, 1974; *Deadwood: The Golden Years,* University of Nebraska Press, 1981. Contributor to history journals.

WORK IN PROGRESS: A guide book to the Black Hills; a supplement to *Black Hills Ghost Towns.*

SIDELIGHTS: Parker wrote: "I was raised up in the Black Hills of South Dakota, a westerner by adoption, and I have loved the West ever since. It is, in my opinion, the most American part of the American nation, the part of our lives which is distinctive, and gives us distinction. I came late to the profession of scholarship, just as our family came late (in 1927) to the West, and in both cases the time of arrival added zest to pursuit of the activity. Certainly being raised up in the Black Hills gave a sense of immediacy and intimacy to everything which I have since learned about the frontier in American history, and I have always thought it fortunate that I was thus an actual participant in what was probably one of the last of the western frontiers as the gold rush of the 1930's reactivated the mining prospects all around us.''

* * *

PARKIN, G(eorge) Raleigh   1896-1977(?)

OBITUARY NOTICE: Born in 1896 in Toronto, Ontario, Canada; died c. 1977. Investment supervisor and author of *India Today: An Introduction to Indian Politics.* Obituaries and other sources: *The Author's and Writer's Who's Who,* 6th edition, Burke's Peerage, 1971. (Notice of death provided by wife, Louise Margaret Parkin.)

* * *

PARKINSON, Roger   1939-1978
(Matthew Holden)

PERSONAL: Born July 8, 1939, in Skipton, England; died April, 1978; married Betty Sheppard; children: one son, one daughter. *Education:* King's College, London, M.A. *Agent:* Campbell, Thomson & McLaughlin, Smeer Hall, Roeburndale E., Lancaster, England.

CAREER: Writer.

WRITINGS: The Origins of World War I, Putnam, 1970; *The Origins of World War II,* Putnam, 1970; *Clausewitz: A Biography,* Stein & Day, 1970; *The American Revolution,* Putnam, 1971; *Peace for Our Time: Munich to Dunkirk—The Inside Story,* Hart-Davis, 1971, McKay, 1972; *Attack on Pearl Harbor,* Putnam, 1973; *Blood, Toil, Tears, and Sweat: The War History From Dunkirk to Alamein, Based on the War Cabinet Papers of 1940 to 1942,* McKay, 1973; *The Peninsular War,* Hart-Davis, 1973; *A Day's March Nearer Home: The War History From Alamein to VE Day Based on the War Cabinet Papers of 1942 to 1945,* McKay, 1974; *The Hussar General: The Life of Bluecher, Man of Waterloo,* P. Davies, 1975; *Zapata: A Biography,* Stein & Day, 1975; *Moore of Corunna,* Hart-Davis, 1976; *The War in the Desert,* Hart-Davis, 1976; *The Fox of the North: The Life of Kutuzov, General of "War and Peace,"* McKay, 1976; *The Auk: Auchinleck, Victor at Alamein,* Hart-Davis, 1977; *Dawn on Our Darkness: The Summer of 1940,* Granada, 1977; *Encyclopedia of Modern War,* Stein & Day, 1977; *Tormented Warrior: Ludendorff and the Supreme Command,* Hodder & Stoughton, 1978, Stein & Day, 1979.

Under pseudonym Matthew Holden: *The British Soldier,* Wayland, 1974; *The Desert Rats,* Wayland, 1974; *Hitler,* Wayland, 1974; *Napoleon in Russia,* Wayland, 1975; *Squadron Two: The Sun Climbs Slowly,* Sphere Books, 1978; *Sons of the Morning,* Sphere Books, 1978; *Desert Spitfire,* Sphere Books, 1980; *Squadron Three: Scramble Dieppe,* Sphere Books, 1980; *Whirlwind at Arromanches,* Sphere Books, 1981. Contributor to magazines and newspapers, including *Scotsman.*

* * *

PATERSON, Judith
See JONES, Judith Paterson

* * *

PATERSON-JONES, Judith
See JONES, Judith Paterson

PATTERSON, Carolyn Bennett   1921-

PERSONAL: Born April 12, 1921, in Laurel, Miss.; daughter of James Hamric and Nola (Lansdale) Bennett; married Frederick Gillis Patterson; children: Frederick Gillis, Jr., Lansdale Martyn. *Education:* Attended Blue Mountain College, 1938-39, Mississippi State College for Women, 1939-40, and University of Missouri, 1940-41; Louisiana State University, B.A., 1942. *Home:* 3607 Newark St. N.W., Washington, D.C. 20016. *Office: National Geographic,* 17 and M Sts. N.W., Washington, D.C. 20036.

CAREER/WRITINGS: National Geographic, Washington, D.C., member of staff, 1949, news service writer, 1950-53, caption and magazine writer, 1953-65, assistant legend editor, 1960-63, member of senior editorial staff, 1960—, legend editor, 1964—, senior assistant editor, 1973—. Notable assignments include articles on the Mardi Gras in New Orleans, the Seattle and New York World's Fairs, Churchill's funeral, the United Nations, Haiti, New Zealand, and Mississippi's Neshoba County Fair. Chairman of the board of Wally Byam Foundation, 1962-78.

AWARDS, HONORS: Certificate of distinguished service from U.S. Travel Service, 1967, for promotion of tourism in U.S.; presidential citation from President Richard Nixon, 1971, for work with Caravan America and Rediscover America programs; award for excellence from Pacific Area Travel Association, 1979, for article "New Zealand's Milford Track: Walk of a Lifetime"; inducted into journalism Hall of Fame at Louisiana State University, 1981.

* * *

PATTERSON, Gardner   1916-

BRIEF ENTRY: Born May 13, 1916, in Burt, Iowa. American economist and author. Patterson was a professor of economics at Princeton University from 1949 to 1969, and dean of Woodrow Wilson School of Public and International Affairs from 1958 to 1964. He was assistant director of General Agreement on Tariffs and Trade (GATT), 1966-67 and 1969-73, and has been its deputy director general for trade policy since 1973. He wrote *Survey of United States International Finance, 1949* (Princeton University Press, 1950), *A Critique of the Randall Commission Report on United States Foreign Economic Policy* (International Finance Section, Princeton University, 1954), *NATO: A Critical Appraisal* (Princeton University, 1957), and *Discrimination in International Trade: The Policy Issues, 1945-1965* (Princeton University Press, 1966). *Address:* 32 Chemin du Pommier, 1218 Grand Saconnex, Geneva, Switzerland; and General Agreement on Tariffs and Trade, CH-1211, Geneva 10, Switzerland. *Biographical/critical sources: The International Who's Who,* Europa, 1981.

* * *

PATTI, Archimedes L(eonida) A(ttilio)   1913-

PERSONAL: Born July 21, 1913, in New York, N.Y.; son of John (in investments) and Marianna Patti; married Margaret K. Telford (a genealogical researcher), September 22, 1944; children: Alexandra L. Patti Eldridge, Giuliana F. *Education:* University of Maryland, B.S., 1951. *Politics:* Independent. *Religion:* Roman Catholic. *Home and office:* 50 Loudon Court, Maitland, Fla. 32751. *Agent:* Sterling Lord Agency, Inc., 660 Madison Ave., New York, N.Y. 10021.

CAREER: U.S. Army, career officer, 1936-57, special military adviser to Turkish high command in Ankara, 1951-52, assistant chief of staff for intelligence in the states, 1952-57, retiring as lieutenant colonel; Executive Office of the President, Washington, D.C., political analyst, 1959-71, consultant on national security affairs, 1971-75; writer, 1975—. *Awards, honors—* Military: Two Bronze Stars with oak leaf cluster.

WRITINGS: Why Viet Nam?: Prelude to America's Albatross, University of California Press, 1980.

WORK IN PROGRESS: A biography, tentatively titled *Who Was Ho Chi Minh?: Profile of a Vietnamese Patriot,* completion expected in 1983.

SIDELIGHTS: Patti told *CA:* "I came upon the international scene as an intelligence officer in the early years of World War II amid the complexities and cabals of the French power struggle between Darlan, Giraud, and de Gaulle. From 1942 until 1971 I was actively engaged in national security affairs, concerned with American interests in North Africa, Italy, Indochina, Trieste, Turkey, and with the North Atlantic Treaty Organization.

"I was reared in a milieu of political reformism, during the thirties, and was among the first Americans to volunteer for overseas service after Pearl Harbor.

"In May, 1942, I was invited to participate in planning a program of Allied propaganda by the British Ministry of Information against the Axis partners in Europe. This was the prelude to a career in political warfare and clandestine activities with the British and American intelligence services.

"My association with the ultra-secret British officers of Political Warfare Executive and Special Operations Executive, counterparts to the American Office of Strategic Services, placed me in a unique position to observe at first hand the development and making of American-British war policy and, on occasion, to influence its direction.

"Moving across the North African scene to Sicily and Italy, where I planned and directed a series of political warfare operations involving the French and Italian resistance movements, I was tapped for a particularly sensitive assignment. In mid-1944 General William J. Donovan, director of the wartime OSS, personally selected me to head a special mission to French Indochina. At a time when our Asian operations were being readied for the global decisions which would follow war's end, President Roosevelt was very much concerned for his policy in that area of the world to be faithfully carried out.

"Thrust between the French obsession to retrieve its full colonial eminence and my own certain knowledge that the Vietnamese would pursue their aspirations for national independence to the bitter end, I participated in the critical period, 1944-45, when the die was finally cast for the futile war in Viet Nam.

"After the death of President Roosevelt, I was never able to convince our government of the depth of Vietnamese perseverance for freedom, a blind spot which dogged the French and our own presidents, ambassadors, and military leaders throughout the hostilities. My book is a first-person account of the gestation of the first war we ever lost.

"Even before Ho Chi Minh and his fledgling government had reached Hanoi and while the Japanese were still in full control of Southeast Asia, I led the first American mission into the future capital of Viet Nam to demand the surrender of the Japanese. The dramatic events of those first months in Indochina which, in a larger sense, influenced American policy from 1945 to date is also revealed for the first time in my book.

"It contains my personal observations of the emergence of Viet Nam's first provisional government from the deep jungles of Tonkin to the westernized city of Hanoi, the brutal occupation of the country by rag-tag Chinese warlords under the aegis of Chiang Kai-shek, aided and abetted by the insensitive Allied powers, Ho Chi Minh's struggle to maintain his government in power in the face of combined French-British determination to salvage their crumbling empires, and Chinese covetousness to 'pick the bones.'

"Paris and London, quick to sense the threat posed by the American presence in Hanoi to their Far Eastern colonial holdings, convinced Washington to withdraw me and my mission from Indochina and return the area to the *status quo ante.* Three months after the capitulation of Japan, from my Washington office on Constitution Avenue, I witnessed our nation's foreign intelligence apparatus being fragmented and emasculated, President Truman's persuasion by the 'red-baiters' to ignore Mao's new China in favor of Chiang's dying regime, and the sanctioning of an American-supported military reign of terror in Viet Nam by the French colonialists.

"Returning to Italy in 1946, I headed an American-British observation team in Trieste during the United Nations debate on the partitioning of the city between the Yugoslavs and the Italians. In the spring and summer of 1948 I was once more in Washington to monitor, from the Pentagon, Soviet political-military maneuvers for control of the Berlin Allied sectors during the Berlin Blockade. In 1952 my expertise in politico-military affairs was put to use in Turkey.

"Turning to a different career in the Executive Office of the President in 1959, I addressed myself to the pressing problems of crisis management in the event of a nuclear war, national catastrophe, or terrorist attack. In collaboration with the staff of the National Security Council, the departments of State and Defense, I spearheaded the development of highly sensitive plans for national emergency preparedness, continuity of government, economic management, and international cooperation. In the last field, I represented the United States as delegate to the NATO Civil Emergency Preparedness Committee.

"Yielding to the insistent demand from the media and scholars of Asian studies for factual information about what happened in Viet Nam as World War II ended, I left full-time government service to write my book. It took me several years to locate my original reports and diaries and get them declassified to use in preparing this picture of how we lost sight of our American dream and our own national best interests, and paved the way to heartbreak in Viet Nam.

"My aim in writing this book, about a subject that is still troubling our national conscience, is to focus on the abominable practice of policymakers to predetermine national policy despite our best interests and the evaluated advice of our field officials. I believe that policy formulated in ignorance generally leads to disaster; similarly an uninformed constituency soon becomes the victim of that policy. Such was the case of America's misadventures in Southeast Asia, and such is the case of our current meddling in Latin America and elsewhere in the world."

AVOCATIONAL INTERESTS: Photography, boating, national politics.

BIOGRAPHICAL/CRITICAL SOURCES: New York Times Book Review, January 11, 1981; *Los Angeles Times,* May 15, 1981.

PAUL, Raymond 1940-

PERSONAL: Born in January, 1940, in Weehawken, N.J.; son of R. V. (an executive) and Elsie (McKee) Paul; divorced. *Education:* Princeton University, A.B., 1961; Columbia University, M.A., 1964. *Residence:* Troy Hills, N.J. 07054. *Office:* Department of English, Montclair State College, Upper Montclair, N.J. 07043.

CAREER: Bloomfield College, Bloomfield, N.J., instructor in English, 1962-66; Montclair State College, Upper Montclair, N.J., instructor, 1966-70, assistant professor, 1970-75, associate professor, 1975-81, professor of English, 1981—, director of basic skills program, 1969-81. *Member:* Mystery Writers of America, New York Historical Society, New Jersey Historical Society.

WRITINGS: Who Murdered Mary Rogers?: Including the Fully Annotated Text of "The Mystery of Marie Roget" by Edgar Allan Poe—the Story Based on the True Crime, Prentice-Hall, 1971; (with Pellegrino W. Goione) *Perception and Persuasion: A New Approach to Effective Writing,* Harper, 1973; *The Thomas Street Horror: An Historical Novel of Murder* (Literary Guild selection), Viking, 1982.

Co-author with Goione of "Mock Trial: An Exercise in Perception and Logic" (film/slide kit for students), Crowell, 1973. Contributor to *Exceptional Children.*

WORK IN PROGRESS: The Marlowe Murder Mystery; or, Who Murdered Christopher Marlowe?; a writing textbook with Pellegrino W. Goione and James Nash, for Boynton-Cook; a sequel to *The Thomas Street Horror,* for Viking.

SIDELIGHTS: Paul commented: "I would rather speak of my books than of myself. I suspect that any individual, especially a writer, is better off listening than talking, observing than posturing. In a nation where celebrity-worship is a major industry it is easy to forget that the people we deal with on a regular basis—our friends and enemies—are just as unique and interesting as the people interviewed by Barbara Walters or splashed across the front page of the *National Enquirer.*

"Briefly, however, in my checkered career I have been a sports writer, bartender, and lifeguard. I have sold ice cream from a truck and haberdashery over a counter. I have been a credit officer, lyricist, playwright, and I have slung slabs of sheet metal in the bowels of an aluminum factory. I became a college teacher because of my love of intellectual inquiry, my devotion to the education of the young, and my preference for civilian life over the army.

"I collect old murders—trial transcripts, broadsides, et cetera—primarily from nineteenth-century America. I believe that an excellent way to discover the prevailing attitudes of any era—social, moral, political—is to study its major public trials. Thus the format of the historical whodunit novel, *The Thomas Street Horror,* can be used to illuminate the social history of our national past, and parallels can be suggested to increase our understanding of contemporary issues, attitudes, biases. This has always been a major purpose of historical fiction in general, but it seems to me the marriage of historical fiction to the detective mystery formula can provide a unique, effective method for conducting such an investigation.

"I make no grandiose claims for my book, however. If it is a good story about interesting people, then probably it will be read, and if it isn't, then whatever else it purports to be won't matter very much. Above all, *The Thomas Street Horror* is a whodunit, a genre both honorable and, for the most part, unpretentious.

"There is an old story which pertains to, among other things, the publishing business. It is the one about the guy who jumped off the Chrysler Building and, every time he passed a floor, he said, 'So far, so good.' I have published nonfiction, an academic textbook, and now a novel, and if I've learned anything, it is that publishing is playing Russian roulette with a Gatling gun. There hangs in my study a quotation from Joseph Conrad: 'What you say is rather profound, and probably erroneous.'"

AVOCATIONAL INTERESTS: Swimming, "season tickets for watching the New Jersey Nets basketball team, playing good poker and bad golf."

BIOGRAPHICAL/CRITICAL SOURCES: Library Journal, February 1, 1982; *Atlantic,* March, 1982; *People,* March 29, 1982.

*   *   *

PAULEY, (Margaret) Jane 1950-

PERSONAL: Born October 31, 1950, in Indianapolis, Ind.; daughter of Richard (a food products distributor) and Mary (an office clerk) Pauley; married Garry Trudeau (a cartoonist), June 14, 1980. *Education:* Indiana University at Bloomington, B.A., 1971. *Residence:* New York, N.Y. *Office:* National Broadcasting Co., 30 Rockefeller Plaza, New York, N.Y. 10020.

CAREER/WRITINGS: WISH, Indianapolis, Ind., reporter, 1972-73, co-anchor of midday newscasts and anchor of weekend evening newscasts, 1973-75; WMAQ-TV, Chicago, Ill., co-anchor of evening newscasts, 1975-76; National Broadcasting Co. (NBC-TV), co-host of "Today" show, 1976—, reader on news briefs, 1977—, anchor of Sunday evening news, 1980—; National Broadcasting Co. (NBC-Radio), anchor of morning news broadcast, 1981—. Worked for Indiana Democratic Central Committee, 1972.

AWARDS, HONORS: D.Jour. from DePauw University, 1978; media award for television news from the American Association of University Women, 1980-81; Rita V. Tishman Award from the women's division of the Anti-Defamation League, Spirit of Achievement Award from the national women's division of Albert Einstein College of Medicine, and communicator of the year award from New York chapter of Business/Professional Advertising Association, all 1982.

SIDELIGHTS: In 1976, less than five years after Jane Pauley graduated from Indiana University, the National Broadcasting Company (NBC) invited her to join the on-air staff of its long-running morning program, the "Today" show. She was chosen after a five-month search for a successor to Barbara Walters, who left "Today" in a much-publicized defection to the American Broadcasting Company (ABC). NBC's choice of Pauley over more seasoned journalists surprised some, but "Today" show host Tom Brokaw was pleased: "She's bright and enterprising and engaging," he said of the newest member of the "Today" cast. Viewer response was promising, also; within two weeks of Pauley's arrival, the show enjoyed its highest ratings in six months.

Pauley's rapid rise in broadcast journalism can be partially attributed, said a *Forbes* writer, to her knack for "being in the right place at the right time." When she applied for a job as a news reporter at Indianpolis's WISH-TV after graduating from college, she had neither training nor experience. Although Lee Giles, the station's news director, was reluctant to grant her an audition, he eventually agreed—in part because the station needed a female reporter in order to comply with Federal Communications Commission (FCC) regulations. His skepticism vanished, he confessed to *Crawdaddy*'s Steven Levy, "the minute I saw her on camera. I knew she was something special. You can look at thousands of auditions and not see sparkle like that. . . . She just lights up, responds to the people in the studio and beyond the camera. It's a gift that few people have." Hired as a cub reporter, Pauley was soon directing a film crew, doing on-camera reporting, and, Levy related, "writing news so well that station personnel would come to her to provide catchy leads for their stories." Within fifteen months, she was co-anchoring midday newscasts and anchoring weekend evening newscasts.

One of her newscasts was observed by an NBC official who urged her to apply for a co-anchor position with the network affiliate in Chicago, WMAQ-TV. After a successful audition, she was hired to join with Floyd Kalber in anchoring two newscasts per day. The move, which earned her the distinction of being Chicago's first evening news anchorwoman, evoked harsh criticism from some who believed she had been hired for her looks rather than her experience. Once described by *Time* as resembling a "corn-fed Catherine Deneuve," Pauley dismissed such criticism. "I won't argue if people say I'm pretty, and I'm certainly young, but I don't think young and pretty is all I'm about," she told *Newsday*. "Young and pretty is easy to come by in Chicago. If that's all they were looking for, why did they have to go all the way to Indiana?" Despite Pauley's optimism, the network's news ratings fell, and the Kalber-Pauley team was disbanded. Kalber transferred to New York while Pauley remained in Chicago, appearing on one newscast per day and contributing special reports to another.

When Barbara Walters left the "Today" show in the spring of 1976 to co-anchor the ABC evening news with Harry Reasoner, Pauley was asked to audition for the vacant position. Her guest appearances on the show drew overwhelming viewer approval. She was chosen to succeed Walters from a field of over two thousand applicants that included consumer affairs reporter Betty Furness and congressional correspondent Catherine Mackin. According to then NBC news division president Dick Wald, Pauley was selected for the coveted spot because "she was better on the air." Five months after Pauley became a "Today" regular, a *Time* reviewer commented: "Pauley has demonstrated precocious poise in her *Today* interviews and ad libs."

When Pauley signed on with "Today"—television's early morning institution since its inception in 1956—the show's long-held lead in the ratings had already begun to be seriously challenged by "Good Morning America." Hosted by former actor David Hartman, "Good Morning America" is, according to *Newsweek*, "ABC's flashy, feature-packed alternative." NBC executives, attempting to lure viewers back to "Today," made several changes in the show's format and cast. They hired Willard Scott, the jovial, folksy weather forecaster, and began featuring syndicated talk show host Phil Donahue in short interview segments. For a time, there was speculation that NBC intended to replace Pauley with actress Mariette Hartley, but that rumor was quelled in 1980, when Pauley's contract was extended for three years. An additional change in the "Today" cast occurred in late 1981, when Tom Brokaw left to co-anchor the "NBC Nightly News" with Roger Mudd. In January, 1982, former sportscaster Bryant Gumbel became Pauley's new co-host.

In an article entitled "Battle for the Morning," *Time*'s Gerald Clarke discussed the early morning programs and their various hosts. He noted that Pauley sometimes seems "flustered if an interview goes in a direction different from the one she had prepared for. She is slow at shifting gears, an essential ability for anyone who must appear live on-camera." Yet no one, he admitted, "can anticipate everything, especially at that hour." The "5 million people who watch Jane Pauley every morning are not likely to switch channels," predicted Levy. Hailed by *Mademoiselle* as "the woman America loves to wake up to," she provides, Levy reflected, "what television viewers want. . . . [She] is more digestible than the morning newspaper, an easier pill to swallow than any rush-hour radiocast."

AVOCATIONAL INTERESTS: Swimming, travel, reading nonfiction.

BIOGRAPHICAL/CRITICAL SOURCES: Time, October 11, 1976, March 21, 1977, December 1, 1980; *Newsday,* November 9, 1976; *Saturday Evening Post,* February, 1977; *Crawdaddy,* April, 1977; *Forbes,* October 1, 1977; *Mademoiselle,* March, 1979; *Quest/80,* September, 1980; *Newsweek,* September 1, 1980; *New York Sunday News Magazine,* November 30, 1980; *Vogue,* December, 1980; *New York Times,* January 25, 1981; *Indianapolis Monthly,* October, 1981; *Woman's Life,* November, 1981; *Redbook,* April, 1982.

—*Sketch by Mary Sullivan*

*   *   *

PEARCE, J. Winston 1907-

BRIEF ENTRY: Born September 2, 1907, in Franklin County, N.C. American minister, educator, and author. Pearce has been a Baptist minister since 1937, and a professor of homiletics at Baptist seminaries since 1961. In 1971, he became writer-in-residence at Campbell College. His books include *The Light on the Lord's Face* (Broadman, 1970), *Campbell College* (Broadman, 1976), *Big Miracle: Little Buies Creek* (Broadman, 1976), and *Planning Your Preaching* (Broadman, 1979). *Address:* Win-Knoll, Buies Creek, N.C. 27506.

*   *   *

PEARSALL, William Harold 1891-1964

OBITUARY NOTICE: Born July 23, 1891, in Stourbridge, England; died October 14, 1964. Educator, botanist, and author of books on natural history. Pearsall wrote *The Lake District* and *Mountains and Moorlands* and was editor of the periodical *Annals of Botany.* Obituaries and other sources: *Nature,* February 16, 1957, January 2, 1965; *Annals of Botany,* January, 1965; *Who Was Who,* Volume VI, *1961-1970,* A. & C. Black, 1972; *Who Was Who Among English and European Authors, 1931-1949,* Gale, 1978.

*   *   *

PEASE, Howard 1894-1974

OBITUARY NOTICE—See index for *CA* sketch: Born September 6, 1894, in Stockton, Calif.; died April 14, 1974, in Mill Valley, Calif. Merchant seaman, educator, and author. As a young man, Pease taught at schools in California and at Vassar College. Later he became a sailor whose interest in the sea was manifested in his many writings. His seafaring experiences are preserved in the "Tod Moran" mystery series, which includes such titles as *The Tattooed Man, The Jinx Ship, Foghorns,* and *Mystery on Telegraph Hill.* Among his other works are *The Gypsy Caravan, Wind in the Rigging, Captain Binnacle, The Long Wharf,* and *Shipwreck.* Obituaries and other sources: *Elementary English,* September, 1974; *Twentieth-Century Children's Writers,* St. Martin's, 1978.

PEET, Creighton B.   1899-1977

PERSONAL: Born in 1899 in New York, N.Y.; died May 16, 1977, in Manhattan, N.Y.; married Bertha A. Hauck; children: Creighton. *Education:* Received undergraduate degree from University of Pennsylvania and graduate degree from Columbia University. *Residence:* New York, N.Y.

CAREER: Writer. Reporter for *Philadelphia Evening Bulletin* and drama reviewer for a West Coast newspaper.

WRITINGS—All juveniles; all as photographer, except as indicated: *Mike the Cat,* Loring & Mussey, 1934; *Captain Teddy and Sailor Chips,* Loring & Mussey, 1935; *Dude Ranch: The Story of a Modern Cowboy,* Albert Whitman, 1939; *This Is the Way We Build a House,* Holt, 1940; *Defending America* (illustrated by Fritz Kredel), Harper & Brothers (London), 1941; *How Things Work,* Holt, 1941; *All About Broadcasting,* Knopf, 1942; *The Runaway Train,* Holt, 1943; *The First Book of Bridges* (illustrated by Deane Cate), F. Watts, 1953, revised edition, 1966; *The First Book of Skyscrapers,* F. Watts, 1964; *Eye on the Sky: How Aircraft Controllers Work,* Macrae, 1970; *Man in Flight: How Airlines Operate,* Macrae, 1972.

Contributor of articles to periodicals, including *New Yorker, Life, Science Digest, New York Times Book Review,* and *New York Times Magazine.*

SIDELIGHTS: Creighton Peet's books for young readers have been praised for quality of text and illustration. Many of his books are informative works designed to explain such things as the way a house is built or how a radio station is run.

All About Broadcasting takes the young reader on a photographic tour of network radio stations, explains the daily routine at a radio station, and discusses developments in radio technology. *Dude Ranch: The Story of a Modern Cowboy* describes the workings of a ranch and the life of the modern cowboy through words and pictures.

Peet's *First Book of Bridges* and *First Book of Skyscrapers* — for readers in grades five through eight—are illustrated with photographs and include glossaries of relevant terms. *How Things Work* is a book of elementary physics that discusses not only theory but mechanical application as well.

Mike the Cat and *Captain Teddy and Sailor Chips* are fictional stories written and photographed by Peet for younger children. Both have been praised for their engaging photography as well as for story content.

OBITUARIES: New York Times, May 17, 1977.*

*   *   *

PEGIS, Anton Charles   1905-

BRIEF ENTRY: Born August 24, 1905, in Milwaukee, Wis. American educator and author. Pegis began teaching at Marquette University in 1931 and also taught at Fordham University. He has been a professor of the history of philosophy at Pontifical Institute of Medieval Studies and at University of Toronto since 1944. Pegis's books include *At the Origins of the Thomistic Notion of Man* (Macmillan, 1963), *Saint Thomas and Philosophy* (Marquette University Press, 1964), and *The Middle Ages and Philosophy* (Regnery, 1963). He also edited *Introduction to Saint Thomas Aquinas* (Modern Library, 1948) and *The Wisdom of Catholicism* (M. Joseph, 1950) and translated *Summa Contra Gentiles,* by Saint Thomas Aquinas, Book I: *God* (University of Notre Dame Press, 1975). *Address:* 36

Castle Frank Rd., Toronto, Ontario, Canada; Pontifical Institute of Medieval Studies, 59 Queen's Park, Toronto, Ontario, Canada M5S 2C4; and Faculty of Arts and Sciences, St. Michael's College, University of Toronto, Toronto, Ontario, Canada M5S 1A1. *Biographical/critical sources: Catholic Authors: Contemporary Biographical Sketches,* Volume I: *1930-1947,* St. Mary's Abbey, 1948; *The Canadian Who's Who,* Volume XI, Who's Who Canadian Publications, 1970; *Directory of American Scholars,* Volume IV: *Philosophy, Religion, and Law,* 6th edition, Bowker, 1974.

*   *   *

PELAVIN, Cheryl   1946-

PERSONAL: Born March 14, 1946, in Brooklyn, N.Y.; daughter of Joseph Yale (a luggage manufacturer) and Alice (an artist; maiden name, Droutman) Pelavin; married Oliver Albert Rosengart, January 11, 1970 (divorced January, 1972). *Education:* Cornell University, B.F.A., 1966; further study at Pratt Institute. *Residence:* London, England. *Studio:* 27 Clerkenwell Close, London E.C.1, England.

CAREER: Free-lance book illustrator and writer, 1968-73; World's Work Ltd., London, England, book illustrator, 1972-75; free-lance animation designer and instructor in graphic arts, both in London. Producer and director for "Electric Company." *Member:* Association of Illustrators, Cornell Club (both London).

WRITINGS—For children; all self-illustrated: *There Once Was a Cat,* Dial, 1969; *The Little Brown Bear,* Putnam, 1972; *Ruby's Revenge,* Putnam, 1972.

Illustrator; for children: Gloria D. Miklowitz, *The Marshmallow Caper,* Putnam, 1971; Victor Keller, *The Scary Woods,* Four Winds Press, 1971; Rita Golden Gelman, *Dumb Joey,* Holt, 1973; Vivienne Mann, *Harry the Hedgehog,* World's Work, 1978; E. N. Stevens, *Mr. Fox,* World's Work, 1978; Jo Shepherd, *Enormouse,* World's Work, 1979.

WORK IN PROGRESS: The Animal's Circus, a self-illustrated children's book.

SIDELIGHTS: Pelavin told *CA:* "I am an artist but often feel the need to create a 'whole,' or illustrated manuscript." With her etchings and illustrations, she loves "to create an alternative world of dancing hippos and laughing crocodiles—who are actually friends and acquaintances!"

"I live in London," Pelavin continued, "where I feel there is less of a constant commercial pressure. I have my own studio where I print and teach etching to art history students, collectors, and artists." The studio, which boasts a press she claims is the largest in London, is fully equipped for practical instruction. Pelavin's course in the theory and techniques of etching is designed, as she told *Arts Review,* to "give students a deeper appreciation of the medium, heighten the pleasure of collecting, and develop a clearer understanding of the beauty and investment potential of etchings."

In her own etchings, Pelavin uses aquatint in black and white or soft-toned colors. The *London Times* called some of her black and white scenes "stylistically reminiscent of Goya and of similar intensity," and said her etchings are "some of the best humanized animal illustrations since Beatrix Potter."

BIOGRAPHICAL/CRITICAL SOURCES: London Times, August 19, 1978; *Arts Review,* January 30, 1981.

PELL, Robert
See HAGBERG, David J(ames)

* * *

PENA, Ramon del Valle y
See VALLE-INCLAN, Ramon (Maria) del

* * *

PERHAM, Margery (Freda) 1895-1982

OBITUARY NOTICE—See index for CA sketch: Born September 6, 1895, in Bury, Lancashire, England; died February 19, 1982, in Burcot, Oxford, England. Authority on Africa, educator, and author. Perham's 1922 visit to Somaliland inspired her interest in British policy in African colonies, the topic of most of her writing. As her opinions gained credence, more and more officials sought her advice. Native Administration in Nigeria, Perham's most influential book, "was . . . the first scholarly study of what is meant by indirect rule," noted a London Times reporter. This book introduced innovative theories which elicited the respect of British Secretary of State Creech-Jones, who thought the author equal to an "oracle." Perham was instrumental in founding the school of colonial studies at Oxford, and she won the first official fellowship at Nuffield College. Her awards were numerous, among them three honorary degrees, commander of the Order of the British Empire, and honorary fellow of St. Hugh's College. Her writings include Africans and British Rule, The Government of Ethiopia, The Life of Lord Lugard, The Colonial Sequence, and East African Journey, the source of the British Broadcasting Corporation (BBC) productions titled "The Time of My Life." Obituaries and other sources: London Times, February 22, 1982; Chicago Tribune, February 24, 1982.

* * *

PERINO, Joseph 1946-

PERSONAL: Born November 17, 1946, in New York, N.Y.; son of Anthony (a truck driver) and Fannie (a factory worker; maiden name, Cuccia) Perino; married Sheila Ancona (a psychologist), September 29, 1971; children: Steven Lawrence. Education: St. John's University, Jamaica, N.Y., B.A., 1968; Hofstra University, M.A., 1970, Ph.D., 1973. Office: 12 Four Winds Rd., Setauket, N.Y. 11733.

CAREER: Psychologist for public schools in Brentwood, N.Y. 1970-71; Nassau Boces, Jericho, N.Y., psychologist and educational researcher, 1972-73; Half Hollow Hills Schools, Melville, N.Y., school psychologist, 1973—. Private practice of psychology, working with adults and with children who have learning and emotional difficulties. Member: American Psychological Association, Nassau County Psychological Association, Suffolk County Psychological Association (member of executive board), Council for the National Register of Health Service Providers in Psychology.

WRITINGS: (With wife, Sheila C. Perino) Parenting the Gifted: Developing the Promise, Bowker, 1981. Contributor to education journals.

WORK IN PROGRESS: Research on gifted children and on a preschool gifted-screening measure.

SIDELIGHTS: Perino commented: "Although I find many frustrations in the educational profession, I believe it is the best approach to helping mankind advance and develop a better world. My hope is that educators believe in themselves and in what they do, not allowing themselves to give in to outside forces and criticisms which lead them to compromise themselves and the profession.

"Educators are notorious, however, for being wary of innovation. They tend to teach children to be convergent and conforming thinkers. The youngsters who are most conforming and convergent in their thinking go to the head of the class, and many of them find a career in education attractive. The cycle continues.

"Schools require a balance of teaching children to be self-disciplined rote-learners as well as divergent-thinking risktakers. In order for this to happen, we need educators who are not afraid to question the existing establishment and who are flexible and creative models to their students. Otherwise schools will continue to be sterile, uninspiring places where the teaching profession has lost respect from those inside as well as those outside the profession."

* * *

PERINO, Sheila C. 1948-

PERSONAL: Born April 26, 1948, in Bay Shore, N.Y.; daughter of Joseph Francis (an artist) and Elizabeth (a bookkeeper; maiden name, North) Ancona; married Joseph Perino (a psychologist), September 29, 1971; children: Steven Lawrence. Education: Hofstra University, B.A., 1970, M.A., 1972, Ph.D., 1975. Office: 12 Four Winds Rd., Setauket, N.Y. 11733.

CAREER: Sachem Central Schools, Holbrook, N.Y., school psychologist, 1973—. Instructor at Hofstra University, 1973, Southampton College, 1976, and Adelphi University (Dowling extension), 1980, 1981. Private practice of psychology, specializing in the gifted and handicapped. Member of Suffolk County Coordinating Council for the Education of the Gifted/Talented (member of board of trustees, 1980-81), Member: National Association for Gifted Children, American Association on Mental Deficiency.

WRITINGS: (With husband, Joseph Perino) Parenting the Gifted: Developing the Promise, Bowker, 1981. Author of column in Purebred Dogs, 1965-67.

WORK IN PROGRESS: A preschool screening measure to identify gifted children more adequately.

SIDELIGHTS: Sheila Perino wrote: "Too often we fail to view our children as individuals whose school performance is not determined by a single causal factor. Educators become mired in stereotypes and cannot make shifts in their thinking to accommodate a child who is gifted and handicapped. They cannot accept that the immaturity of the preschooler may have little relationship to his or her ability to think or analyze problems. In the same manner parents are generally relegated to a caretaker position and are discouraged from active participation in instructing their children. These circumstances comprised our chief reasons for writing a handbook.

"While the material for the book was being prepared, it also became apparent that too many people insist on applying adult standards to bright young children. Because their life experiences are as yet so limited, it is often unrealistic to expect the type of interest focusing exhibited by adults. This is not to imply that motivation is trivial, but rather that we are dealing with potential, not finished product. We should not ignore those who have not yet discovered their own talents."

* * *

PERKINS, Edwin Judson 1939-

PERSONAL: Born May 16, 1939, in Charlottesville, Va.; son

of I. Paul (in sales) and Elizabeth (Cabaniss) Perkins; divorced; children: Julia, Braxton. *Education:* College of William and Mary, A.B., 1961; University of Virginia, M.B.A., 1963; Johns Hopkins University, M.A., 1970, Ph.D., 1972. *Home:* 1480 Lorain Rd., San Marino, Calif. 91108. *Office:* Department of History, University of Southern California, University Park, Los Angeles, Calif. 90007.

CAREER: Chase Manhattan Bank, New York, N.Y., member of executive training program, 1963-64; Virginia Polytechnic Institute and State University, Blacksburg, instructor in accounting 1966-68; University of Southern California, Los Angeles, assistant professor, 1973-77, associate professor of history, 1977—. *Member:* American Historical Association, Organization of American Historians, Economic History Association, Economic and Business History Society (president, 1979), Business History Conference.

WRITINGS: Financing Anglo-American Trade: The House of Brown, 1800-1880, Harvard University Press, 1975; (editor) *Men and Organizations: The American Economy in the Twentieth Century,* Putnam, 1977; *The Economy of Colonial America,* Columbia University Press, 1980; *The World Economy in the Twentieth Century,* Schenkman, 1982. Contributor to business, economic, and history journals. Associate editor of *Pacific Historical Review,* 1979—.

WORK IN PROGRESS: A biography of J. P. Morgan; a textbook on American business and labor history; research on American banking and finance.

AVOCATIONAL INTERESTS: Playing tennis, camping, collecting U.S. postage stamps, whitewater canoeing.

*   *   *

PERKINS, Van L.   1930-

BRIEF ENTRY: Born May 22, 1930, in Standardville, Utah. American historian, educator, and author. Perkins began teaching at University of California, Riverside, in 1964. He has been a professor of history and vice-chancellor of academic affairs since 1973. Perkins wrote *Crisis in Agriculture: The Agricultural Adjustment Administration and the New Deal, 1933* (University of California Press, 1969). *Address:*Department of History, University of California, Box 112, Riverside, Calif. 92502. *Biographical/critical sources: Directory of American Scholars,* Volume I: *History,* 7th edition, Bowker, 1978.

*   *   *

PERKINS, Whitney Trow   1921-

PERSONAL: Born February 28, 1921, in Boston, Mass.; son of Wesley Trow (a Young Men's Christian Association officer) and Hazel A. (Mason) Perkins; married Kathryn A. Sylvester, June 28, 1947; children: Rebecca Perkins Sedat, Mason, Wesley, Rachel. *Education:* Tufts University, A.B. (summa cum laude), 1942; Fletcher School of Law and Diplomacy, Ph.D., 1948. *Politics:* Democrat. *Home:* 11 Catalpa Rd., Providence, R.I. 02906. *Office:* Department of Political Science, Brown University, Brown Station, Providence, R.I. 02912.

CAREER: University of Denver, Denver, Colo., assistant professor of international relations, 1948-53; Brown University, Providence, R.I., associate professor, 1953-62, professor of political science, 1962—, chairman of concentration in international relations, 1955—. Vice-president of World Affairs Council of Rhode Island, 1981-82; consultant to U.S.-Puerto Rican Commission on the Status of Puerto Rico. *Military service:* U.S. Army Air Forces, statistical officer, 1942-45; served

in New Guinea, the Philippines, and Okinawa; became captain. *Member:* International Studies Association, American Political Science Association. *Awards, honors:* Fulbright grant for the Netherlands, 1952-53.

WRITINGS: Denial of Empire: The United States and Its Dependencies, Nijhoff, 1962; *Constraint of Empire: The United States and Caribbean Interventions,* Greenwood Press, 1981.

WORK IN PROGRESS: Balance of Politics, a discussion of the relationship between domestic and international politics.

SIDELIGHTS: Perkins commented: "My basic concern is to see how the experiment in democracy in the United States adapts its myths, its values, its policies, and its institutions in situations where apparent domination intermixes with uncertainty, ineffectiveness, and repudiation.

"I have examined situations of formal dependency in *Denial of Empire* and situations of intervention and occupation in *Constraint of Empire.* My purpose in further work is to see and explain the linkages between stability or instability in international power relations and the capacity for stable politics within states."

*   *   *

PERRY, Patricia   1949-

PERSONAL: Born September 21, 1949. *Education:* Wheelock College, B.S., 1971; Antioch College, M.Ed., 1974. *Home:* 40 Clarke St., Lexington, Mass. 02173.

CAREER: Federal Reserve Bank of Boston, Boston, Mass., analyst, 1971; teacher at private schools in Roxbury, Mass., 1971-74; Roger Wellington School, Belmont, Mass., teacher, 1974-78.

WRITINGS: (With Marietta Lynch) *Mommy and Daddy Are Divorced* (juvenile), Dial, 1978.*

*   *   *

PERSKE, Robert   1927-

PERSONAL: Born October 16, 1927, in Denver, Colo.; son of Paul Frederick (a municipal and state government official) and Elva (Laveck) Perske; married Martha Packard (an artist), 1970; children: Richard, Ann, Dawn, Lee, Marc. *Education:* Attended University of Colorado, 1946-48; Westmar College, B.A., 1950; Garrett-Evangelical Seminary, B.D., 1955. *Home and office:* 159 Hollow Tree Ridge Rd., Darien, Conn. 06820.

CAREER: Ordained United Methodist minister, 1955; pastor of United Methodist churches in Genoa, Colo., 1952-55, Sterling, Colo., 1955-59, and Espanola, N.M., 1959-60; Kansas Neurological Institute, Topeka, psychiatric chaplain, 1960-70; Greater Omaha Association for Retarded Citizens, Omaha, Neb., executive director, 1970-74; Accreditation Council for Services for the Mentally Retarded and Other Disabled, Chicago, Ill., accreditation surveyor, 1974-76; Random House, Inc., New York, N.Y., director of joint project (with U.S. Department of Health, Education & Welfare) on persons with handicaps, 1976-78; free-lance writer, 1978—. Fellow at Menninger Foundation, 1963-64, staff affiliate in department of education, 1964-70; writer for and consultant to President's Committee on Mental Retardation. *Member:* American Association on Mental Deficiency (fellow), Association for Retarded Citizens, Association for the Severely Handicapped, Connecticut Association for Retarded Citizens (president, 1980-81).

AWARDS, HONORS: Distinguished service awards from Sterling Junior Chamber of Commerce, 1958, and Greater Omaha

Association for Retarded Citizens, 1975; Rosemary Dybwad International Award from Association for Retarded Citizens, for research in Sweden and Denmark, 1968; book award from Printing Industries of America, 1974, for *New Directions for Parents of Persons Who Are Retarded;* book award from American Medical Writers Association, 1978, for editing *Mealtimes for Severely and Profoundly Handicapped Persons;* National Media Award from One to One, 1981, for *New Life in the Neighborhood.*

WRITINGS: (Contributor) Robert Noland, editor, *Counselling Parents of the Mentally Retarded,* C. C Thomas, 1968; (contributor) Wolf Wolfensburger, editor, *The Principle of Normalization in Human Services,* National Institute on Mental Retardation, 1972; *New Directions for Parents of Persons Who Are Retarded,* Abingdon, 1973; (contributor) Carolyn Cherington and Gunnar Dybwad, editors, *New Neighbors: The Retarded Citizen in Search of a Home,* President's Committee on Mental Retardation, 1974; (contributor) Ray Nathan and Henry Cobb, editors, *Mental Retardation: The Century of Decision,* President's Committee on Mental Retardation, 1976; (chief editor) *Mealtimes for Severely and Profoundly Handicapped Persons,* University Park Press, 1977; *Listen Please,* Canadian Association for the Mentally Retarded, 1978; *Mental Retardation, the Leading Edge: Service Programs That Work,* President's Committee on Mental Retardation, 1978; *New Life in the Neighborhood,* Abingdon, 1980; *Hope for the Families,* Abingdon, 1981.

Contributor of articles to professional journals.

WORK IN PROGRESS: A novel, "focusing on the limits, longings, and heroics of an eighteen-year-old boy with Down's Syndrome."

SIDELIGHTS: Perske wrote: "I try to build bridges between ordinary citizens and persons with handicaps. I try to chase myths about handicapping conditions, cast fresh light on awkward human situations with these people, and inspire my audience to value and make healthy connections with them.

"My writing career, which began at age forty-six, draws on better than twenty years of personal experiences with persons who have handicaps—as a pastor, a professional in institutions, a director of a community agency, and an accreditation surveyor.

"I believe that the more a civilization understands, values, and relates healthily with its members who have severe handicapping conditions, the more advanced that civilization can become."

*   *   *

PETRIDES, George Athan 1916-

BRIEF ENTRY: Born August 1, 1916, in New York, N.Y. American ecologist, educator, and author. Petrides, who worked as a naturalist at U.S. national parks, has been a professor of wildlife management, zoology, and African studies at Michigan State University since 1958. He has participated in expeditions to the Antarctic, Afghanistan, and Malaya and has been a Fulbright fellow in Kenya and Uganda. Petrides wrote *A Field Guide to Trees and Shrubs: Field Marks of All Trees, Shrubs, and Woody Vines That Grow Wild in the Northeastern and North-Central United States and in Southeastern and South-Central Canada* (Houghton, 1958) and *The Black Bear in Michigan* (Agricultural Experiment Station, Michigan State University, 1964). *Address:* 4895 Barton Rd., Williamston, Mich. 48895; and Department of Fisheries and Wildlife, Michigan State University, East Lansing, Mich. 48824. *Biographical/*

critical sources: American Men and Women of Science: The Physical and Biological Sciences, 14th edition, Bowker, 1979.

*   *   *

PETROSKI, Catherine (Ann Groom) 1939-

PERSONAL: Born September 7, 1939, in St. Louis, Mo.; daughter of Robert John and Mary Louise (Sterling) Groom; married Henry Petroski (an engineer, professor, and writer), July 15, 1966; children: Karen Beth, Stephen James. *Education:* MacMurray College, B.A., 1961; graduate study at Bread Loaf School of English, Middlebury College, 1961; University of Illinois, M.A., 1962, further graduate study, 1965-67. *Home and office:* 2501 Perkins Rd., Durham, N.C. 27706.

CAREER: Junior college and high school teacher of English in Belleville, Ill., 1962-65; University of Illinois, Urbana, instructor in rhetoric, 1965-67; National Council of Teachers of English, Champaign, Ill., staff writer and editor, 1967-68; freelance writer and book critic, 1968—. Writer-in-residence of Illinois Arts Council, 1976-78. *Awards, honors:* John Crowe Ransom Fiction Prize from *Sou'wester,* 1974, for "You and Me, Claude"; Bridgman scholar at Bread Loaf Writers Conference, 1974; short fiction prize from Texas Institute of Letters, 1976, for "Beautiful My Mane in the Wind"; National Endowment for the Arts writing fellow for fiction, 1977-78; Yaddo fellow, 1980.

WRITINGS: Gravity and Other Stories, Fiction International, 1981; *Lady's Day,* Night Eye Press, 1982.

Work represented in anthologies, including *Having Been There,* edited by Allan Luks, Scribner, 1979. Contributor to magazines, including *Ms., Playgirl, North American Review, Virginia Quarterly Review, Gallimaufry, Prairie Schooner, Fiddlehead,* and *Descant.*

WORK IN PROGRESS: A novel; short stories; a children's book based on "Beautiful My Mane in the Wind," publication by Houghton expected in 1983.

*   *   *

PETRY, Carl Forbes 1943-

PERSONAL: Born June 29, 1943, in Camden, N.J.; son of Eduard Carl and Jean (Hamill) Petry. *Education:* Carleton College, B.A., 1965; University of Michigan, M.A., 1966, Ph.D., 1974. *Office:* Department of History, Northwestern University, Evanston, Ill. 60201.

CAREER: University of Michigan, Ann Arbor, lecturer in history, 1973-74; Northwestern University, Evanston, Ill., assistant professor, 1974-80, associate professor of Middle East history, 1980—. *Member:* Middle East Studies Association of North America, Mediaeval Academy of America, American Research Center in Egypt, Phi Beta Kappa. *Awards, honors:* Senior of National Endowment for the Humanities, 1980-81.

WRITINGS: The Civilian Elite of Cairo in the Later Middle Ages, Princeton University Press, 1982. Contributor to scholarly journals.

WORK IN PROGRESS: The Political Economy of Egypt Preceding the Ottoman Conquest; Medieval Egypt; research on biographical history and computerized data retrieval.

SIDELIGHTS: Petry has made three research trips to Egypt since 1968, and one to Iran in 1976.

Petry told *CA:* "My interest in Egypt began with a child's fascination with ancient monuments and deities. But I was motivated to explore Egypt's medieval past by questions that emerged when I reflected on how a former great power became an economic dependency in the modern period. I also sought to prove that various procedures developed by social scientists could be applied to the analysis of a premodern, non-Western society of great antiquity. My studies of several thousand learned Cairenes who flourished in the Middle Ages have revealed a world of scholarship and intrigue which was remarkable for its richness and diversity. Since this world no longer exists, I have enjoyed the excitement and the challenge of its rediscovery.''

*   *   *

PFLAUM, Susanna Whitney
See PFLAUM-CONNOR, Susanna (Whitney)

*   *   *

PFLAUM-CONNOR, Susanna (Whitney)   1937-
(Susanna Whitney Pflaum)

BRIEF ENTRY: Born December 7, 1937, in Boston, Mass. American educator and author. Pflaum-Connor began teaching in 1959, at the elementary school level. Since 1971 she has taught reading at University of Illinois at Chicago Circle. She wrote *The Development of Language and Reading in the Young Child* (C. E. Merrill, 1974) and *Aspects of Reading Education* (McCutchan, 1978). *Address:* College of Education, University of Illinois at Chicago Circle, P.O. Box 4348, Chicago, Ill. 60680.

*   *   *

PHELPS, Ethel Johnston   1914-

PERSONAL: Born March 8, 1914, in Long Island City, N.Y.; daughter of John Alexander (an engineer) and Frances (a teacher; maiden name, Curran) Johnston; married Richard J. Phelps (in computer data), October 31, 1937; children: John H., Richard M., Kevin T. *Education:* Adelphi University, B.A., 1934, M.A., 1972. *Residence:* Rockville Centre, N.Y.

CAREER: The Feminist Press, Old Westbury, N.Y., marketing manager, 1973-79. Consultant to Nassau Library System's storytelling pilot project; member of board of trustees of Friends of Rockville Centre Library, 1980-82; judge for Rockville Centre Storytelling Contests, 1980-82. *Member:* Society of Children's Book Writers. *Awards, honors: Maid of the North* was named ''notable book'' by the Children's Book Council. 1981.

WRITINGS—For children: (Editor) *Tatterhood and Other Tales* (Book-of-the-Month Club selection), illustrated by Pamela Baldwin Ford, Feminist Press, 1978; *Maid of the North: Feminist Folk Tales From Around the World,* illustrated by Lloyd Bloom, Holt, 1981.

For adults; one-act plays: ''The Fall of Pride,'' first produced by the Fortnightly Players in Long Island, N.Y., 1958; ''The Pardoner's Tale,'' first produced by Universal Players in Long Island, N.Y., 1969. Author of a one-act Christmas play, first produced by Adelphi College Theatre in Garden City, N.Y., 1934.

Author of column, ''Southside School News,'' in *News-Owl* (Rockville Centre, N.Y.), 1928-30. Author of a series of thirteen half-hour radio plays broadcast by WGBB, Freeport, N.Y., c. 1937. Co-editor of and contributor of articles to *Ricardian* (journal of the Richard III Society).

WORK IN PROGRESS: A juvenile historical novel set in the eleventh century; an adult novel set in the Regency period; a collection of new northern British tales of King Arthur.

SIDELIGHTS: Phelps, seeking to provide alternate role models in children's literature, researched thousands of folk and fairy tales to select those that featured clever, courageous, likable heroines. The author presented her selections in two collections, *Tatterhood and Other Tales,* published in 1978, and *Maid of the North,* which appeared in 1981. ''She has found a marvelous selection from a wide variety of cultures,'' declared *Los Angeles Times* reviewer Elaine Kendall, who praised Phelps's ''diligent research'' and called *Maid of the North* ''altogether delightful.'' Critics agreed that Phelps's collections offer children positive female role models. ''Girls who read [*Maid of the North*] will grow up expecting to slay their own dragons. . . . Best of all, they won't grow up to be lazy, greedy or vain,'' asserted Kendall. She continued, ''Small boys should also have the benefit of this collection. . . . [They] will learn respect.'' Carolyn Heilbrun of the *New York Times Book Review* concurred: ''The child hearing these stories will know that girls, like boys, can be active rather than passive, and grow up to be productive people. . . . If one is going to read any modern version of the old tales . . . this collection has the great advantage of featuring plucky women.''

While reviewers admired Phelps's heroines, some felt that the tales were not completely effective. Heilbrun noted that, with one exception, all heroines in *The Maid of the North* were eventually married. ''In these tales,'' concluded Heilbrun, ''as in the most conservative societies, women are not allowed, as males would be, to treat marriage as only one event in a life of many events. *The Maid of the North* has the right intentions. But it dilutes the magic without rescuing the heroine from the persistent fate of being the object of male desire.'' On the other hand, a *Times* critic asserted that ''Phelps' updated dialogue offers a feminist case against marriage: 'A wife is like a house dog tied with a rope. Why should I be a servant and wait upon a husband?' ''

Although *Time* lauded Phelps for achieving her feminist aims in her collections, the review judged the author's tales psychologically ineffective. ''Though Phelps celebrates females who have brains and energy,'' observed the *Time* critic, ''her feminist lens at times distorts the drama beneath the surface of folk tales.'' Citing the theories of psychologists like Bruno Bettelheim, the *Time* review asserted that ''the real business of fairy tales is not propaganda. It is to help the young deal with anger, sibling rivalry, fear of separation and death and the eerie omnipotence of the adult world.'' *Time* concluded that, given children's need for reassurance in a world where they feel helpless, they might better identify ''with the bewildered, prefeminist likes of Cinderella and Snow White.'' Kendall, however, hailed Phelps's characters as satisfying literary creations: ''They may be role models for the next generation but that's hardly noticeable. Every one of these young women is lovable for herself alone and not her feminist ideology.''

Phelps told *CA:* ''The publisher's subtitle of *Feminist Folk Tales* on one of my books may have encouraged some critics to regard the tales as 'propaganda.' Actually, they are traditional tales selected for the collection because they contain examples of heroines—and heroes—in nonstereotyped roles. (The critic who claimed dialogue was 'updated to present a feminist case against marriage' was mistaken. The Maid of the North's sharp remarks were taken from Kirby's 1907 translation of *The Kalevala,* the source of the tale.)

''Of course, 'the real business of folktales is not propaganda,' as someone has said. Their business is simply to entertain. Folk and fairy tales developed several thousands of years ago (earliest recorded in c. 4000 B.C.) purely as social entertainment for adults. Because they are relatively simple and unsophisticated, illustrating older (and more idealistic) moral values (such as the good and virtuous are rewarded, evildoers punished), they have, in recent centuries, been regarded as suitable for entertaining children. I cannot agree with Bettelheim that their real business 'is to help the young deal with anger, sibling rivalry,' etc. and etc., although he may have found certain tales useful in his case treatment of emotionally disturbed children.

"Folk and fairy tales are adventure stories with a moral—oral literature from an earlier point in time. For the average young reader today one would hope that the tales add to his knowledge of a past oral heritage, that they are fun to read, and that the supernatural elements of fantasy stretch the child's imagination.

"I think of 'feminist literature' as a term more applicable to adult literature and the literary concerns of the feminist movement. Applied to children's books it might mean a greater number of books available depicting the widely varied roles and accomplishments of females in history and in the world of today. For children's books I prefer the terms 'nonsexist' and 'nonracist'—i.e., free from narrow or demeaning stereotypes that encourage unconscious prejudice. Young readers absorb both attitudes and role models from books. To absorb, for example, that females are generally meek, silly, or helpless, that mothers belong in the kitchen, that only males can tinker with machinery or accomplish important deeds, can only be harmful to their perceptions of themselves and each other. Fortunately, the past ten years have brought considerable changes in children's books, and the older male/female/race stereotypes are less common.''

In response to a question about Phelps's new career goals in later life, the author responded, "As you can see, my earlier 'credits' are exceedingly sketchy. Writing was an occasional thing, a hobby. It was not until after I returned for a post-graduate degree later in life that time and circumstances gave me the opportunity to embark on the research project that led to the publication of two books. I wish now I had had the confidence—and time!—to apply myself much earlier to the discipline of writing fiction as a professional goal."

BIOGRAPHICAL/CRITICAL SOURCES: New York Times Book Review, April 26, 1981; *Los Angeles Times,* April 30, 1981; *Time,* July 20, 1981.

* * *

PHILIPPATOS, George Crito 1938-

BRIEF ENTRY: Born November 2, 1938, in Patras, Greece. American educator and author. Philippatos taught finance at Pennsylvania State University from 1969 to 1975. He wrote *Financial Management: Theory and Techniques* (Holden-Day, 1973), *Essentials of Financial Management: Text and Cases* (Holden-Day, 1974), and *Case Studies in Basic Finance* (Saunders, 1978). *Address:* 487 Sierra Lane, State College, Pa. 16801; and 701 Business Administration Building, Pennsylvania State University, University Park, Pa. 16802. *Biographical/critical sources: Who's Who in Consulting,* 2nd edition, Gale, 1973; *Who's Who in the East,* 15th edition, Marquis, 1975; *American Men and Women of Science: The Social and Behavioral Sciences,* 13th edition, Bowker, 1978.

* * *

PHILLIPS, J(ohn) B(ertram) 1906-

PERSONAL: Born in 1906, in London, England; son of Philip William (a civil servant) and Emily (Maud) Phillips; married Vera May Jones (a secretary), April 19, 1939; children: Jen-

nifer (Mrs. R. A. Croft). *Education:* Emmanuel College, Cambridge, M.A. (with second class honors); also attended Ridley Hall, Cambridge. *Home:* Golden Cap, 17 Gannetts Park, Swanage, Dorsetshire BH19 1PF, England.

CAREER: Ordained minister of Church of England; prebendary of cathedral in Chichester, England, 1957-60; Salisbury Cathedral, Salisbury, England, 1964—, began as canon, became canon emeritus. *Awards, honors:* D.Litt. from University of Exeter, 1970.

WRITINGS: Your God Is Too Small, Macmillan, 1952; *Making Men Whole,* Word, Inc., 1952; *When God Was Man,* Abingdon, 1954; *Appointment With God,* Macmillan, 1954; *Plain Christianity,* Macmillan, 1954; *St. Luke's Life of Christ,* Collins, 1956; *New Testament Christianity,* Hodder & Stoughton, 1956; *The Church Under the Cross,* Macmillan, 1956; *Is God at Home?,* Abingdon, 1957; *The New Testament in Modern English: Four Prophets,* Macmillan, 1958; *A Man Called Jesus* (plays), Macmillan, 1959.

God Our Contemporary, Macmillan, 1960; *Good News,* Macmillan, 1963; *Four Prophets,* Macmillan, 1963; *Ring of Truth,* Macmillan, 1967; *For This Day: Three-Hundred-Sixty-Five Meditations* (edited by Denis Duncan), Word, Inc., 1974 (published in England as *Through the Year With J. B. Phillips,* Hodder & Stoughton, 1974); *Peter's Portrait of Jesus,* Collins, 1976; *The Newborn Christian,* Macmillan, 1978.

WORK IN PROGRESS: An autobiography.

SIDELIGHTS: Phillips's books have been translated into German, Swedish, Dutch, Portuguese, Finnish, Japanese, Chinese, and French.

Phillips wrote: "*Is God at Home* is a collection of tracts printed together. *The Church Under the Cross,* written for the Church Missionary Society, explains some of the difficulties of spreading the Gospel throughout the world. *Appointment With God* is about Holy Communion, largely a reproduction of a Lenten series of lectures. *When God Was Man* is based on a series of broadcasts on the significance of God becoming Man in Jesus Christ. *Your God Is Too Small* I especially recommend: it attempts to get rid of outworn or outgrown concepts of the Almighty, and *New Testament Christianity* tries to explain the message of the New Testament in today's language. *God Our Contemporary* was an attempt made, after a good deal of research and consultation, to re-establish a sense of the living God in the modern world. *Ring of Truth* is my personal testimony to the historic reliability of the New Testament, and in particular of the resurrection of Jesus. *A Man Called Jesus* is a series of plays written for the British Broadcasting Corp., but used fairly widely in schools and youth groups.''

* * *

PHILLIPS, James M(cJunkin) 1929-

PERSONAL: Born March 21, 1929, in Pittsburgh, Pa.; son of Harry P. (a bank clerk) and Ruth (a nurse; maiden name, McJunkin) Phillips; married Ruth Joyce Henning, June 29, 1957; children: Catherine, Marjorie. *Education:* Princeton University, B.A., 1946, M.A., 1957, Ph.D., 1959; Yale University, B.D., 1955. *Politics:* Independent. *Home:* 118 Bolinas Ave., San Anselmo, Calif. 94960. *Office:* Department of Church History, San Francisco Theological Seminary, San Anselmo, Calif. 94960.

CAREER: Ordained United Presbyterian minister, 1955; Yonsei University, Seoul, Korea (now South Korea), instructor in politics and history, 1944-52; Tokyo Union Theological Seminary, Tokyo, Japan, assistant professor, 1960-66, professor of church history, 1966-75; San Francisco Theological Seminary, San Anselmo, Calif., visiting professor of church history, 1975—. Visiting professor at Graduate Theological Union, 1975—. Field representative of United Presbyterian Commission in Japan, 1965-70; pastor of West Tokyo Union Church, 1966-67. North American director of Pacific Basin Theological Network. *Member:* International Association of Mission Studies, American Society of Church History, American Society of Missiology, American Association of University Professors, Pacific Coast Theological Society, American Academy of Religion.

WRITINGS: Between Conscience and the Law: The Ethics of Richard Baxter (1615-1691), University Microfilms, 1959; *From the Rising of the Sun: Christians and Society in Contemporary Japan,* Orbis, 1981. Contributor of about thirty articles to Asian studies journals. Editor of *Northeast Asian Journal of Theology,* 1968-75, and Pacific Basin's Theological Network's *Network Newsletter,* 1977—.

WORK IN PROGRESS: International Issues in Religious Perspectives.

SIDELIGHTS: Phillips commented: "As an American with service in both Korea and Japan, I've been trying to share cross-cultural viewpoints between Asians and Westerners, particularly among Christians and other religious groups in both areas. The Pacific Basin has been the scene of three major international wars during my lifetime, and my hope is that efforts for peace by all concerned peoples in this area can be better advanced by mutual understanding."

*　*　*

PHILLIPS, Richard
 See DICK, Philip K(indred)

*　*　*

PICKEN, Stuart D(onald) B(lair) 1942-

PERSONAL: Born May 12, 1942, in Glasgow, Scotland; son of William Blair and Janet (Stewart) Picken; married Hiroyo Fujino, July 6, 1976. *Education:* University of Glasgow, M.A. (with honors), 1973, B.D., 1976, Ph.D., 1971. *Home:* International Christian University, Town House W-107, Mitaka City, Osawa 3-10-5, Tokyo 181, Japan.

CAREER: Ordained Presbyterian minister; pastor of Churches of Scotland in South Ronaldsay and Burray, 1966-72; International Christian University, Tokyo, Japan, 1972—, assistant professor, 1974-80, associate professor of philosophy and comparative ethics, 1980—. Consultant to Asahi Shimbun Culture Center and Mitsui Engineering Co. *Member:* Japan-British Philosophical Association, Japan Society for Comparative Thought, Royal Society for Asian Affairs, Royal Asiatic Society (fellow), American Oriental Society, Mind Society, Society for Health and Human Values, St. Andrew Society of Tokyo and Yokohama (chieftain, 1982-83).

WRITINGS: Shinto: Japan's Spiritual Roots, Kodansha, 1980; *Buddhism: Japan's Cultural Identity,* Kodansha, 1982. Also co-author and editor of *Pivotal Christian Personalities,* in press.

In Japanese: *Nihongin no Jisatust: Seiyo to no Hikaku* (title means "Suicide: Japan and the West"), Simul International, 1979; *Wakamonotachi yo, Jiritsu o Mezase* (title means "Younger Generation, Be Independent"), Daiwa Shobo, 1981. Also co-author, with Yokochi Fukushima, of a book on environmental ethics in Eastern and Western societies, in press.

Contributor of about thirty-five articles to journals in the humanities.

WORK IN PROGRESS: Death and the Japanese, a book on the cultural background of Japanese business practices; a work on Buddhist mountain asceticism and the life sciences.

SIDELIGHTS: Picken commented: "Although I spread my interests widely, I am deeply interested in human values, especially shown in attitudes toward aspects of life (sex, love, marriage, friendship) and death (suicidology and thanatology in general) and the influence of traditional religion on the formation and transmission of these values. I was in Japan when novelist Yukio Mishima commited *hara-kiri* in 1970, and I began my comparative research with that event. Japan and the West sometimes differ only in degree, while on other matters they present startling contrasts. I wish my writing to reflect the mutual penetration of cultures that has become a feature of the present age. I am committed to working on the interfaces between cultures and between disciplines to achieve that goal. This kind of writing comes from a commitment to civilization itself."

*　*　*

PIERCE, Milton Plotz 1933-

PERSONAL: Born March 21, 1933, in New York, N.Y.; son of Louis Plotz (a real estate broker) and Dinah (a nurse; maiden name, Press) Pierce; married Deborah Ritter (a teacher), December 25, 1964; children: Samuel, Esther. *Education:* Bernard M. Baruch College of the City University of New York, B.B.A., 1959; City College of the City University of New York, M.S., 1967. *Politics:* Democrat. *Religion:* Jewish. *Home and office:* Pierce & Associates, 162 West 54th St., New York, N.Y. 10019.

CAREER: Hearst Magazines, New York City, associate copy chief, 1962-65; Vos & Reichberg, New York City, account executive, 1956-58; *New York Times,* New York City, assistant promotion director, 1958-59; New York Institute of Technology, Old Westbury, dean of Evening College, 1959-63; Pierce & Associates, New York City, president, 1964—. Associate professor at New York Institute of Technology, 1970—. Member of New York City Planning Board, 1973—, and New York City mayor's Committee to Clean Up Times Square, 1977-78. *Member:* Direct Mail Marketing Association, Direct Mail Writers Guild, Hundred Million Club, B'nai B'rith. *Awards, honors:* Awards from Direct Mail Marketing Association, 1963, 1965, 1970, and 1972.

WRITINGS: (With Shawn Robbins) *Ahead of Myself: Confessions of a Professional Psychic,* Prentice-Hall, 1980; (with John Lee) *Hour Power,* Dow Jones, 1981; *How to Collect Your Overdue Bills,* Dow Jones, 1981; *Money Matters,* Quick Fox Publishers, 1982; *The Five Golden Treasures of Alan Shawn Feinstein,* Prentice-Hall, 1982. Contributor to magazines, including *Direct Marketing, Zip,* and *Adult Education.*

SIDELIGHTS: Pierce wrote: "I recently met a brain surgeon at a cocktail party. 'You're a writer,' he said. 'I'm going to take up writing when I retire.' 'Funny,' I answered, 'I'm planning to take up brain surgery when I retire.' All too many people treat writing as a casual activity. The reverse is true. Writing requires the most intense training and professional preparation."

*　*　*

PIFER, Ellen 1942-

PERSONAL: Born June 26, 1942, in New York, N.Y.; daughter of Carl (in business) and Mae (Stein) Rosenberg; married Drury L. Pifer (a writer), December 30, 1962; children: Rebecca Anne. *Education:* University of California, Berkeley, B.A., 1964, M.A., 1969, Ph.D., 1976. *Office:* Department of English, University of Delaware, 204 Memorial Hall, Newark, Del. 19711.

CAREER: University of California, Berkeley, acting instructor in comparative literature, 1974-76; University of Delaware, Newark, assistant professor, 1977-81, associate professor of English and comparative literature, 1981—. Member of planning board of Delaware Theatre Company, 1980-81. *Member:* Modern Language Association of America, American Association of Teachers of Slavic and East European Languages, Northeast Modern Language Association.

WRITINGS: Nabokov and the Novel, Harvard University Press, 1980. Co-author of "New West Magazine Competition," a column in *New West,* 1976-77. Contributor of articles and reviews to literature and Slavic studies journals and newspapers.

WORK IN PROGRESS: A book tentatively titled *Mystery and Knowledge in Contemporary Fiction: Bellow, West, and O'Connor.*

SIDELIGHTS: Ellen Pifer commented: "I am committed to studying literature in a comparative context. Even when I am writing on American literature exclusively, as I am right now, I find cross-cultural issues and influences most compelling. Current indifference in this country to the study of foreign languages and literatures, as well as to the humanities in general, is something that every literary critic, scholar, and teacher must oppose. The health, intelligence, and vitality of our own cultural life is at stake."

AVOCATIONAL INTERESTS: "Theatre and the other arts."

*   *   *

PINSENT, Gordon (Edward)   1930-

PERSONAL: Born July 12, 1930, in Grand Falls, Newfoundland, Canada; son of Stephen Arthur (a papermill worker) and Flossie (Cooper) Pinsent; married second wife, Charmion King, November 2, 1962; children: Leah King. *Education:* University of Prince Edward Island, LL.D., 1975. *Religion:* Anglican. *Residence:* Toronto, Ontario, Canada.

CAREER: Writer and actor. Performed with repertory companies at Winnipeg Repertory Theatre, Winnipeg, Manitoba, at Manhattan Theatre Centre, New York, N.Y., 1954-60, with Straw Hat Players, Toronto, Ontario, with New Play Society, at Crest Theatre, 1960-69, and at Shakespearean Festival, Stratford, Ontario, 1962 and 1975; featured in radio and television series, including "The Forest Ranger," Canadian Broadcasting Corp. (CBC), 1962-64, "Quentin Durgens, M.P.," CBC-TV, 1965-68, and "A Gift to Last," CBC; appeared in television films "Fifteen Miles of Broken Glass," CBC-TV, 1966, and "Quarantined," 1969; host of "People Talking Back," CBC. Also appeared in motion pictures, including "The Thomas Crown Affair," United Artists, 1968, "The Forbin Project," Universal, 1969, "Chandler," Metro-Goldwyn-Mayer, 1972, "Blacula," American-International, 1972, "The Rowdy Man," 1972, and "Newman's Law," Universal, 1974. *Military service:* Royal Canadian Regiment, infantry and paratroopers, 1948-51.

WRITINGS—Novels: The Rowdyman (adapted from own screenplay; see below), McGraw, 1973; *John and the Missus,* McGraw, 1974; (with Grahame Woods) *A Gift to Last* (based on own television series; see below), Seal Books, 1978.

Also author of "The Rowdyman" (screenplay), 1971; "John and the Missus" (unproduced screenplay; author's stage adaptation produced in Halifax, Nova Scotia, at Neptune Theatre, 1976), 1974; "A Gift to Last," CBC-TV.

AVOCATIONAL INTERESTS: Hiking, painting, swimming.

BIOGRAPHICAL/CRITICAL SOURCES: Best Sellers, March 15, 1975; *Christian Science Monitor,* April 30, 1975; *Maclean's,* May 15, 1978; *Books in Canada,* April, 1979.*

*   *   *

PLAYFAIR, Guy Lyon   1935-

PERSONAL: Born April 5, 1935, in Quetta, India; son of I.S.O. (a military officer) and Jocelyn (Malan) Playfair. *Education:* Pembroke College, Cambridge, B.A. (with honors), 1959. *Agent:* Bolt & Watson Ltd., 8-12 Old Queen St., London SW1, England. *Office:* 7 Earls Court Sq., London SW5, England.

CAREER: Free-lance writer and photographer in Brazil, 1961-75; U.S. Agency for International Development, Information Office, Rio de Janeiro, Brazil, writer, 1967-71. *Member:* Society for Psychical Research, Society of Authors, College of Psychic Studies.

WRITINGS—Nonfiction: The Unknown Power, Pocket Books, 1975; *The Indefinite Boundary,* St. Martin's, 1977; (with Scott Hill) *The Cycles of Heaven,* St. Martin's, 1978; *This House Is Haunted: The True Story of a Poltergeist,* Stein & Day, 1980. Contributor to *The Unexplained,* Orbis, 1980-82.

SIDELIGHTS: Guy Playfair told *CA:* "I am interested in border areas of human experience and in anomalous phenomena of all kinds. I find the influence of sunspots as interesting as the behavior of poltergeists or psychic surgeons, and I strongly object to finding my books classified as 'occult.' I am not concerned with the 'supernatural' but with unexplored areas of nature that are by definition natural."

Playfair is an amateur musician who has played trombone in several orchestras and jazz groups. He admits to having almost become a professional jazz musician, "but the life was too hectic." Now he owns a concert harpsichord, "which I keep meaning to learn to play properly. But however badly I play, it's better than watching television, which I gave up several years ago after reading Jerry Mander's *Four Arguments for the Elimination of Television.*"

*   *   *

PLUMPTRE, Arthur Fitzwalter Wynne   1907-1977

OBITUARY NOTICE: Born June 5, 1907, in Montreal, Quebec, Canada; died June, 1977. Economist, educator, administrator, and author of books on economics. Plumptre, who served for many years as assistant deputy minister in Canada's Department of Finance, wrote *Central Banking in the British Dominions, Mobilizing Canada's Resources for War,* and *Three Decades of Decision: Canada and the World Monetary System, 1944-75.* Obituaries and other sources: *The Canadian Who's Who,* Volume 12, Who's Who Canadian Publications, 1972; *Who's Who in Canada,* International Press, 1977; *The International Who's Who,* Europa, 1977; *Canadian Journal of Economics,* November, 1978. (Date of death provided by wife, Beryl Plumptre.)

*   *   *

POLIAKOFF, Stephen   1952-

PERSONAL: Born in 1952 in London, England. *Agent:* Margaret Ramsey Ltd., 14A Goodwin's Ct., St. Martin's Lane, London W.C.2, England.

CAREER: Playwright. Writer-in-residence at the British National Theatre, 1976—. *Awards, honors:* Designated one of London's most promising new talents by *London Evening Standard,* 1976.

WRITINGS—Published and produced plays: *Hitting Town* [and] *City Sugar,* Methuen, 1976 (also see below); *Hitting Town* (produced in New York at South Street Theatre, January 6, 1979), Samuel French, 1977, also published with *City Sugar* (see above); *City Sugar* (first produced on the West End at Comedy Theatre, March 4, 1976; produced Off-Broadway at Phoenix Marymount Theatre, June 5, 1978), Samuel French, 1977, also published with *Hitting Town* (see above); *Strawberry Fields* (first produced in London at Young Vic Theatre, August 19, 1976; produced Off-Broadway at Manhattan Theatre Club, June 4, 1978), Methuen, 1977; *Shout Across the River* (first produced in London at The Warehouse, September 19, 1978; produced Off-Broadway at Phoenix Marymount Theatre, January 2, 1980), Methuen, 1979; *American Days* (first produced in London at ICA Theatre, June 14, 1979; produced Off-Broadway at Manhattan Theatre Club, December, 1980), Methuen, 1980.

Unpublished plays: "Granny," first produced in London, 1969; "Bambi Ramm," first produced in London at Abbey Community Centre, September 7, 1970; "A Day With My Sister," first produced in Edinburgh, Scotland, 1971; "Pretty Boy," first produced in London, 1972; "Theatre Outside," first produced in London, 1973; "Berlin Days," first produced in London, 1973; "The Carnation Gang," first produced in London, 1973; "Clever Soldiers," first produced in London, 1974; "Heroes," first produced in London, 1975; "Join the Dance," first produced in New York, 1975; "The Summer Party," first produced in Sheffield, England, at Crucible Theatre, 1980.

Also author of the screenplay "Bloody Kids."

SIDELIGHTS: Poliakoff was only sixteen when his short play, "Granny," was first performed in Britain and just seventeen when his full-length drama, "Bambi Ramm," was also produced. Both plays were praised by Oleg Kerensky, who wrote in *Stage and Television Today* that Poliakoff's work contains "sufficient . . . psychological interest to prove him a worthy disciple of [Harold] Pinter." Poliakoff later became known as one of Britain's new-left playwrights who view the stage as a forum for social and political commentary.

Poliakoff's dramas, which explore the ills of contemporary society, appeared frequently on the British stage during the early 1970's, but they were not introduced to American audiences until 1978 when "Strawberry Fields" and "City Sugar" made their Off-Broadway debuts. Both plays "precisely [catch] the creeping horrors of urban life," wrote Michael Billington in the *New York Times.* Richard Eder concurred, adding that Poliakoff's work contains "bleak accounts of the lives of working class youth."

"Strawberry Fields" is about two right-wing radicals, Charlotte and Kevin, who travel throughout Britain distributing pamphlets and collecting money for a fascist organization. When Charlotte shoots a policeman who questions her about a robbery, she and her companion become convinced that they have precipitated a new civil war and that they will be its first heroes. The pair illustrates the "threat of the extreme right," wrote Eder in the *New York Times,* for, however pathetic and absurd the couple may seem, their obsession with traditional values, their bigotry, and their naivety make them dangerous.

"Strawberry Fields" received favorable reviews from critics, including *New Republic*'s Stanley Kauffmann, who pronounced the play "a good piece of work," and *New York Post*'s Clive Barnes, who described the drama as "a strange, blood-red play" that demonstrates the "unusual talent and original voice" of its author.

The principle character in Poliakoff's "City Sugar" is Leonard Brazil, a successful disc jockey who abhors his work. Longing for the era of the Beatles, Leonard detests the contemporary music that he must play, as well as the social values that it reflects. But "in no sense," noted Eder, "does Leonard stand against what he hates." Instead, in an attempt to satisfy his sense of rage and frustration, Leonard vindictively bullies his assistant and insults his listeners. His cruelty becomes most conspicuous when he encourages the aspirations of a drab young woman by manipulating a pop-music contest so that she becomes a finalist and then sadistically rigging the last match so that she cannot possibly win.

"Mr. Poliakoff, of course, is playing with several notions," remarked John Corry of the *New York Times:* "the decline of popular taste; the emptiness of success . . . , and the vacancy of the public mind." Eder described "City Sugar" as "a bleak but beautifully precise look at tawdriness and microscopic expectations." *America*'s Catherine Hughes agreed, adding "Poliakoff . . . tells his tale of futility with scathing wit and just the right amount of poignance."

In "Hitting Town" Poliakoff is again concerned with the emptiness of modern life. The play focuses on Ralph and Clare, a pair of siblings who attempt to relieve their boredom by announcing on a radio call-in show that they are sleeping together. According to Eder, Poliakoff is saying that "British society . . . is so routinized and anti-human that . . . conventional protest . . . has nothing to get hold of." Eder agreed with a *Drama* critic that the play contains little plot development, but he observed that "the dialogue is sharp and accurate, and the energy of outrage is neatly focused by the author's precise characterizations."

Critics were less favorably impressed with Poliakoff's "Shout Across the River," which describes the bizarre relationship between an agorophobic mother and her oppressive daughter. Mel Gussow wrote in the *New York Times* that "Shout Across the River" fails to arouse the "empathy" of its audience. He said that the characters' actions were "inexplicable" and that the play was "abrasive without being especially revealing." *New Yorker*'s Brendan Gill concurred, pronouncing the work "an incoherent little play."

Poliakoff's continuing interest in "the bleak moral landscape of present-day England" is revealed in his provocative comedy, "American Days." The play, which explores the pop-music industry, features an insensitive recording tycoon who brutally ridicules the abilities of three young rock singers who audition before him. Their talent, it soon appears, matters less to him than their willingness to submit to unlimited humiliation. As Frank Rich pointed out in the *New York Times,* a contract will be offered only to "that singer who, like [the tycoon], is willing to prostitute his real identity to the disposable, lucrative fashions of America's record charts."

Poliakoff, said Rich, "has created a play that is at once a nasty lampoon of contemporary show business, a broadside about the Americanization of English culture, and an aching portrait of proletarian kids who are so lost that they hardly exist." A *New York* reviewer found the "texture of the play absorbing," but commented that the playwright's "plotting is not nearly so good as his dialogue or atmosphere." But, he concluded, "even if the play is finally a little less than the sum of its parts, those parts are mostly good.''

New York Times critic Janet Maslin similarly appraised ''Bloody Kids,'' Poliakoff's screenplay about two boys who scheme to get inside police headquarters by pretending that one of them has been stabbed by the other boy. The film, said Maslin, fails to reach a ''true conclusion,'' but it ''moves gracefully and economically through a cool, forbidding world of the urban young.''

BIOGRAPHICAL/CRITICAL SOURCES: Stage and Television Today, September 17, 1970; *Drama,* autumn, 1976, January, 1980; *New York Times,* June 5, 1978, June 6, 1978, January 9, 1979, March 18, 1979, January 3, 1980, August 4, 1980, September 23, 1980, January 2, 1981; *New York Post,* June 5, 1978, June 6, 1978, January 3, 1980; *Daily News,* June 5, 1978, June 6, 1978; *Village Voice,* June 12, 1978, June 19, 1978; *New Yorker,* June 19, 1978, January 14, 1980; *America,* June 24, 1978; *New Republic,* July 8, 1978; *New Statesman,* March 21, 1980; *New York,* January 19, 1981.*

—*Sketch by Susan M. Trosky*

* * *

POORMAN, Paul Arthur 1930-

PERSONAL: Born August 29, 1930, in Lock Haven, Pa.; son of Wilson Paul and Margaret (Heylmun) Poorman; married Sylvia Elizabeth Powers, November 22, 1952; children: Pamela (Mrs. Robert Phillips), Cynthia (Mrs. Donald Paul), Peter, Stephen, Thomas, Andrew, Robert, William. *Education:* Pennsylvania State University, B.A., 1952. *Home:* 827 Wallwood Dr., Copley, Ohio 44321. *Office: Akron Beacon Journal,* 44 East Exchange St., Akron, Ohio 44328.

CAREER/WRITINGS: Centre Daily Times, State College, Pa., reporter, 1953-57, news editor, 1957-62; *Harrisburg Patriot,* Harrisburg, Pa., news editor, 1962-63; *Philadelphia Bulletin,* Philadelphia, Pa., news editor, 1963-66; *Detroit News,* Detroit, Mich., managing editor, 1966-69; Northwestern University, Evanston, Ill., visiting professor of journalism, 1975-76; *Akron Beacon Journal,* Akron, Ohio, editor, 1976—, vice-president, 1976—. *Military service:* U.S. Air Force, 1951-53. *Member:* American Society of Newspaper Editors, Associated Press Managing Editors Association.

* * *

POPHAM, Margaret Evelyn 1895(?)-1982

OBITUARY NOTICE: Born c. 1895; died April 25, 1982. Educator, school administrator, and author of an autobiography entitled *Boring—Never!* Popham was made a commander of the Order of the British Empire in 1953. Obituaries and other sources: *Who's Who in America,* 38th edition, Marquis, 1974; *London Times,* April 27, 1982.

* * *

PORTER, Burton F(rederick) 1936-

PERSONAL: Born June 22, 1936, in New York; son of John (in business administration) and Doris (Neloway) Porter; married Barbara Taylor Metcalf; children: Anastasia. *Education:* University of Maryland, B.A. (cum laude), 1959; University of St. Andrews, Ph.D., 1961; Oxford University, Ph.D., 1962. *Home:* 90 First St., Troy, N.Y. 12180. *Office:* Department of Philosophy, Russell Sage College, Troy, N.Y. 12180.

CAREER: University of Maryland, College Park, assistant professor of philosophy, 1966-69; King's College, Wilkes-Barre,

Pa., associate professor of philosophy, 1969-71; Russell Sage College, Troy, N.Y., professor of philosophy and chairman of department, 1971—.

WRITINGS: Deity and Morality: With Regard to the Naturalistic Fallacy, Allen & Unwin, 1968; *Philosophy: A Literary and Conceptual Approach,* Harcourt, 1974, revised edition, 1980; *Personal Philosophy: Perspectives on Living,* Harcourt, 1976; *The Good Life: Alternatives in Ethics,* Macmillan, 1980.

WORK IN PROGRESS: The Moebius Strip, a philosophical novel; *Reflections From the Nursery,* children's poems.

SIDELIGHTS: Porter commented: ''Throughout my writing career I have been preoccupied with several recurrent themes: the validity of ethical principles in a purely physical universe (devoid of God), the self-creating character of human existence, and the autonomies of thought that render rational choice impossible.''

* * *

POSNER, David Louis 1938-

PERSONAL: Born July 23, 1938, in New York; son of Louis S. and Nell (a dog breeder; maiden name, Nathan) Posner; married Olivia Germaine Wedgwood, 1965; children: Piers, Dominic. *Education:* Kenyon College, B.A.; Harvard University, M.A.; also attended Wadham College, Oxford. *Politics:* Democrat. *Home:* 4425 Fairview, Orlando, Fla. 32804.

CAREER: State University of New York at Buffalo, 1958-69, began as lecturer, became assistant professor of English and curator of poetry collection at Lockwood Library; University of California, Northridge, assistant professor of English, 1970-73; associated with Florida Technological University, Orlando, 1973-78. Member of faculty at University of California, Los Angeles, 1970-73. Host of radio program in Paris, France. Worked at British Museum's excavation at Leptis Magna, in Crete. *Member:* Phi Beta Kappa. *Awards, honors:* Awards from Florida Fine Arts Council for *The Sandpipers* and for *Geographies.*

WRITINGS: Poems: In Single Key, Faulconer Press, 1943; *The Deserted Alter* (poems), Harcourt, 1957; *A Rake's Progress: A Poem in Five Sections,* Lion & Unicorn, 1962; *The Dialogues,* Black Sparrow Press, 1969; *Visit to the East,* Academy Editions, 1971; *The Sandpipers: Selected Poems (1965-1975),* University Presses of Florida, 1976. Also author of *Geographies,* Bellevue Press, and *The May-Game,* 1946. Author of ''Philoctetes Eoperatu'' (verse play), published in *Charioteer.*

Work represented in anthologies, including *New Directions Fourteen.* Contributor of poetry to magazines, including *New Yorker, Kenyon Review, Evergreen Review, Kayak, Encounter,* and *London.*

WORK IN PROGRESS: Three book-length poems, *Labrador, Variations on a Tinamou,* and *Bone.*

SIDELIGHTS: Posner told *CA:* ''Writing is simply the first compulsion of life, without which one couldn't survive. Moments of understanding where and how one is are infrequent, but such as they are, come only after a poem is done.'' *Avocational interests:* Travel (France, Italy, Greece), collecting first editions, china, and British drawings and caricatures.

* * *

POWELL, Dorothy M. 1914-

PERSONAL: Born May 31, 1914, in Toronto, Ontario, Canada; daughter of John Thomas (a blacksmith) and Hannah Elizabeth

(Austin) Adams; married George I. Powell, April 10, 1936; children: Peter, Wendy, Nancy. *Education:* Attended business school in Toronto, Ontario, Canada. *Home:* 110-1680 Poplar St., Victoria, British Columbia, Canada V8P 4K7.

CAREER: Worked as a secretary and model in Toronto, Ontario, in the 1950's; creative writing instructor at Camosun College, 1975—. *Member:* Canadian Society of Children's Authors, Illustrators, and Publishers, Writer's Union of Canada, Canadian Author's Association (national membership secretary, 1967-74). *Awards, honors:* Allan Sangster Memorial Award from Canadian Authors Association, 1975, for distinguished service.

WRITINGS—Juvenile: *Summer of Satan's Gorge,* Scholastic Book Services, 1974; *Captives in Cauldron Cave,* Scholastic Book Services, 1977.

Contributor of numerous short stories and articles to magazines, including *Saturday Evening Post, Chatelaine,* and *Family Herald.* Author of eight stories broadcast on the Canadian Broadcasting Corporation's radio programs "Stories with John Drainie" and "Canadian Short Stories."

WORK IN PROGRESS: The Haunting of Kerri Maureen, about an island lighthouse, and *Noah's Bark,* a story of two boys and a supernatural dog.

SIDELIGHTS: Dorothy Powell is dedicated to writing for the "in-between" reader, ages eleven to sixteen. She told *CA:* "If books for the younger reader are not given the importance of adult books, how can we expect avid adult readers in the future? It's up to writers and publishers, in particular, to correct this."

* * *

POWELL, Shirley 1931-

PERSONAL: Born May 5, 1931, in Ohio; daughter of Harold W. (a mechanic) and Elsie B. (a bookkeeper; maiden name, Elton) Powell. *Education:* Miami University, Oxford, Ohio, B.S.Ed., 1954; New York University, M.A., 1976. *Home:* 501 Cedar Dr., R.R.2, Kerhonkson, N.Y. 12446. *Agent:* Jane Rotrosen Agency, 318 East 51st St., New York, N.Y. 10022. *Office:* Village Poetry Workshop, 69 First Ave., New York, N.Y. 10003.

CAREER: High school English teacher in DeGraff, Ohio, 1954-55; junior high school teacher in Decoto, Calif., 1955-56; elementary school teacher in Okeana, Ohio, 1956-57, Hamilton, Ohio, 1957-71, and New York, N.Y., 1972-77; Rye Neck High School, Rye Neck, N.Y., high school English teacher, 1979. *Member:* Village Poetry Workshop (director), Stone Ridge Poetry Society (co-director). *Awards, honors:* Poetry prizes include first prize from *Calliope,* 1979, for "There Is a Sphinx."

WRITINGS: Running Wild (novel), Avon, 1981. Contributor of stories and poems to magazines, including *For Now, Stone Soup, Small Pond, Home Planet News, Ball State University Forum,* and *Coldspring Journal.*

WORK IN PROGRESS: The Last Disciple, a novel; *Dance of the Ancestors,* poems; *Rooms,* stories.

SIDELIGHTS: Shirley Powell commented: "For the last ten years or so, since coming to New York, I've been associating with other writers, directing workshops, and doing public readings. Now that I'm in the Catskills, I continue the readings and workshops. Though I write a lot of prose now, my interest in poetry continues. I'd also like to write a book about survival in the Atomic Age.

"For me, writing seemed to progress from lyric poems to narratives, and from narratives to short stories, and finally to the novel form. My work has always attempted—or I attempted through it—an emotional appeal. My prose writing has dealt mostly with suspense, sometimes melodrama."

BIOGRAPHICAL/CRITICAL SOURCES: Woodstock Times, April 8, 1982, April 15, 1982.

* * *

POWYS, T(heodore) F(rancis) 1875-1953

BRIEF ENTRY: Born December 20, 1875, in Shirley, England; died November 27, 1953, in Sturminster Newton (some sources say Mappowder), England. British author. Powys's novels and stories are noted for their simple, haunting narratives. His allegorical novel, *Mr. Weston's Good Wine* (1927), and his short stories, particularly those collected in *Fables* (1929), illustrate Powys's tragic view of life, and have been cited as examples of the author's best work. Though his writings evoked an animistic view of nature, Powys, who wrote from a deeply religious, though unorthodox, point of view, focused his attention on the "demon within." The fatalism present in much of his work was presented with irony and humor, as in the novel, *Kindness in a Corner* (1930), though even the humor was laced with a tragic quality and a bitter tone. Powys also described his views of life and nature in essays, which were published in *An Interpretation of Genesis* (1908) and *The Soliloquy of a Hermit* (1916). They revealed him as a perceptive and original writer, mired in a conflict between Christian values and personal vision, who ultimately was unable to abandon a small vestige of hope for mankind. *Biographical/critical sources: Twentieth Century Authors: A Biographical Dictionary of Modern Literature,* H. W. Wilson, 1942, 1st supplement, 1955; *Encyclopedia of World Literature in the Twentieth Century,* updated edition, Ungar, 1967.

* * *

PRADOS, John 1951-

PERSONAL: Born January 9, 1951, in New York, N.Y.; son of Jose (in public relations) and Betty-Lou (a teacher of English as a second language; maiden name, McGuire) Prados-Herrero. *Education:* Columbia University, B.A., 1973, M.A., 1975, M.Phil., 1977, Ph.D., 1982. *Residence:* Washington, D.C.

CAREER: Free-lance writer, 1972—, and designer of games, including "Year of the Rat," Simulations Publications, 1972, "The Rise and Decline of the Third Reich," Avalon Hill Game Co., 1974, "Vicksburg: The War for the West, 1862-1863," Rand Game Associates, 1975, "Von Manstein: Battles for the Ukraine, 1941-1944," Rand Game Associates, 1975, "Last Days at Saigon," 1975, "Pearl Harbor: The War Against Japan, 1941-1945," Game Designers Workshop, 1977, "Panzerkrieg: Von Manstein in the Ukraine, 1941-1944," Operational Studies Group, 1978, "The Battle of Cassino: Assaulting the Gustav Line, 1944," Simulations Publications, 1978, "Campaigns of Napoleon: Bonaparte Against Europe, 1800-1815," West End Games, 1980, "Kanev: Parachutes Across the Dnepr," People's War Games, 1981, "Spies," Simulations Publications, 1981, "Objective Ruhr," West End Game Co., and "Suez," Avalon Hill Game Co. *Member:* International Institute of Strategic Studies, Society of Historians of American Foreign Relations, U.S. Naval Institute, Game Designers' Guild (founding member), Awards Academy of Adventure Gaming, Inter-University Seminar on the Armed Forces and Society. *Awards, honors:* Charles R. Roberts Award from Awards Academy of Adventure Gaming, 1975, best game of the year award from *Campaign,* 1976, and best game of all time awards, 1977 and 1978, all for ''The Rise and Decline of the Third Reich.''

WRITINGS: (Contributor) *U.S. Military Involvement in Southern Africa,* South End Press, 1978; *The Soviet Estimate,* Dial, 1982. Author of ''Simulation Corner,'' a monthly column in *Dragon,* 1980-82, and ''Boardgame Talk,'' a monthly column in *Adventure Gaming,* 1981—. Contributor to magazines, including *Strategy and Tactics, Indochina Chronicle, Bridge, Little Wars,* and *Moves.* Contributing editor of *Battle Plan,* 1975-76, *Fire and Movement,* 1976—, and *Wargamer,* 1980—.

WORK IN PROGRESS: A book on a major foreign policy crisis of the Eisenhower administration; ''C.I.A.,'' a party game; a Civil War simulation game.

SIDELIGHTS: Prados told *CA:* ''I enjoy writing and designing games; both kinds of work involve analysis and research, but are completely different as forms of expression. Being able to change from one to the other has helped me to avoid becoming too tired of either.''

BIOGRAPHICAL/CRITICAL SOURCES: Moves, December, 1979; *Toy and Hobby World,* September, 1980.

*   *   *

PRATT, Dallas 1914-

PERSONAL: Born August 21, 1914, in Islip, N.Y.; son of Alexander D.B. (a stockbroker) and Beatrice (Benjamin) Pratt. *Education:* Yale University, B.A., 1936; Columbia University, M.D., 1941. *Residence:* Garrison, N.Y. *Office:* 228 East 49th St., New York, N.Y. 10017.

CAREER: Bellevue Hospital, New York City, psychiatric intern, 1941-42; National Mental Health Foundation, Philadelphia, Pa., staff psychiatrist, 1946-51; Columbia University, New York City, attending psychiatrist, 1947-50; New York University, New York City, lecturer in psychiatry, 1951-52; private practice of psychiatry in New York City, 1952-62; Columbia University, attending psychiatrist, 1957-67; Argus Archives (library on animal protection and welfare), New York City, president, 1969—. Co-founder and member of board of trustees of American Museum in Britain, Bath, England, 1959—; founder and member of board of trustees of John Judkyn Memorial, Bath, 1964—. Chairman of Halcyon Foundation, 1956—. *Military service:* U.S. Army, Medical Corps, 1941-46; became major.

MEMBER: Friends of Columbia University Libraries (member of council, 1951—). *Awards, honors:* Presidential citation from Columbia University, 1976, for services to university libraries; annual award from New York Humane Society, and Albert Schweitzer Award from Animal Welfare Institute, both 1981, for humanity to animals.

WRITINGS: (Contributor) Paul B. Maves, editor, *The Church and Mental Health,* Scribner, 1953; *Painful Experiments on Animals,* Argus Archives, 1976; (with Jack Neher and others) *The Family Guide to Good Living,* Bobley, 1977; *Alternatives to Pain in Experiments on Animals,* Argus Archives, 1980. Editor of ''Columbia Library Columns'' (magazine of the Friends of Columbia University Libraries), 1951-80. Contributor to psychiatry, museum, library, and animal welfare journals.

SIDELIGHTS: Pratt told *CA:* ''My writing naturally reflects my vocational and avocational interests. These have included, first, psychiatry and work with mental health organizations; secondly, the collecting of art, books, early maps, and a long involvement with the Columbia University Library, the American Museum in Britain and its affiliate, the John Judkyn Mem-

orial; and, more recently, an interest in the protection and welfare of animals and in humane education.''

*   *   *

PRAZ, Mario 1896-1982
(Alcibiade, Giano di Guisa)

OBITUARY NOTICE—See index for *CA* sketch: Born September 6, 1896, in Rome, Italy; died March 23, 1982, in Rome, Italy. Scholar, collector, educator, critic, translator, and author. Praz is best known as an authority on the literature of the baroque and romantic periods. His pioneer study, *The Romantic Agony,* explored the tradition of sadism in literature, art, and music. ''He was one of the last humanists,'' commented critic Masolini d'Amico, ''a member of an ideal academy that transcended the confines of nations, correspondent of many of the most prestigious literary figures of every country.'' Also an educator, Praz taught Italian literature at the University of Manchester and English literature at the University of Rome for thirty-two years. His translations include works by Charles Lamb, Ben Jonson, Jane Austen, Walter Pater, and T. S. Eliot. In addition, Praz translated some of Shakespeare's plays as well as edited an Italian translation of his works. The recipient of numerous awards, such as the Italian Gold Medal for cultural merits and the Premio Marzotto, Praz was presented with a Golden Pen Award by Italy's President Sandro Pertini in January, 1982. Writings by Praz include *Conversation Pieces: A Study of the Informal Group Portrait in Europe and America, The Flaming Heart, Mnemosyne: The Parallel Between Literature and the Visual Arts,* and *Voce dietro la scena* (title means ''Voices Backstage''). Obituaries and other sources: Mario Praz, *The House of Life* (autobiography), Oxford University Press, 1964; *Time,* April 5, 1982; *New York Times,* April 8, 1982; *Newsweek,* April 19, 1982.

*   *   *

PREGEL, Boris 1893-1976

OBITUARY NOTICE: Born January 24, 1893, in Odessa, Russia (now U.S.S.R.); died December 7, 1976, in New York, N.Y. Scientist, business executive, editor, and author of scientific articles published in the *Encyclopedia of Chemical Technology.* Pregel was a businessman who became known for developing practical uses for radioactive substances for medicine and industry. In the 1940's he also supplied scientists working on the Manhattan Project with uranium necessary for the development of the atomic bomb. Among Pregel's many honors were gold medals from the city of Athens, the French Professional Engineers, and the French Association of Inventors, as well as membership in the Legion of Honor of France. Pregel edited *World Priorities.* Obituaries and other sources: *New York Times,* December 9, 1976; *Who's Who in America,* 40th edition, Marquis, 1978; *The National Cyclopaedia of American Biography,* Volume 59, James T. White, 1980.

*   *   *

PRESLAN, Kristina 1945-

PERSONAL: Born February 15, 1945, in Dresden, Germany. *Education:* University of Wisconsin, Madison, B.A., 1970, M.L.S., 1973. *Home:* 259 Sherwood Pl., Pomona, Calif. 91768. *Office:* Colton Public Library, 380 North La Cadena, Colton, Calif. 92324.

CAREER: Worked as children's librarian of Madison Public Library, Madison, Wis.; head children's librarian of Decatur Public Library, Decatur, Ill.; supervisor of children's services of Pomona Public Library, Pomona, Calif.; library supervisor in children's department of Colton Public Library, Colton, Calif. Chairperson of children's services committee of Inland Library System, 1977-78, chairperson of public relations committee, 1977-79. *Member:* National Association of Business and Professional Women's Clubs, California Library Association.

WRITINGS: Group Crafts for Teachers and Librarians on Limited Budgets, Libraries Unlimited, 1980.

*   *   *

PRICE, Beverley Joan   1931-
(Beverley Randell)

PERSONAL: Born in 1931 in Wellington, New Zealand; daughter of William Harding and Gwendolyn Louise (Ryall) Randell; married Hugh Price (a book publisher), October 17, 1959; children: Susan. *Education:* Victoria University of Wellington, B.A., 1952; Wellington Teachers College, Diploma of Teaching, 1953. *Home:* 24 Glasgow St., Kelburn, Wellington, New Zealand. *Office:* Price Milburn & Co. Ltd., P.O. Box 2919, Wellington, New Zealand.

CAREER: Teacher of junior classes at schools in Wellington, Raumati, and Marlborough, New Zealand, 1953-59, and London, England, 1957-58; Price Milburn & Co. Ltd., Wellington, editor, 1962—. *Member:* International P.E.N., New Zealand Women Writers Society, Australian Society of Authors.

WRITINGS—Juveniles; all under name Beverley Randell: *Tiny Tales,* sixteen volumes, Wheaton, 1965; *PM Commonwealth Readers,* sixteen volumes, A. H. & A. W. Reed, 1965; *John, the Mouse Who Learned to Read,* Collins, 1966; *Methuen Number Story Caption Books,* sixteen volumes, Methuen, 1967; (with Conrad Frieboe) *Methuen Caption Books,* Volumes I-IV: *Blue Set,* Volumes V-VIII: *Green Set,* Volumes IX-XII: *Orange Set,* Volumes XIII-XVI: *Purple Set,* Volumes XVII-XX: *Red Set,* Volumes XX-XXIV: *Yellow Set,* Methuen, 1967, 2nd edition, 1974; (editor) *Red Car Books,* six volumes, Methuen, 1967; *Instant Readers,* sixteen volumes, Price Milburn, 1969-70; (with Olive Harvey and Joy Cowley) *Bowmar Primary Reading Series: Supplementary to All Basic Reading Series,* sixty-six volumes, Bowmar, 1969.

Listening Skillbuilders, twenty-four volumes, Price Milburn, 1971; (with Susanne Emanuel) *Mark and Meg Books,* nine volumes, Methuen, 1971; *Guide to the Ready to Read Series, and Supporting Books,* Price Milburn, 1972; *Methuen Story Readers,* one hundred two volumes, Methuen, 1972-76; *First Phonics,* twenty-four volumes, Methuen, 1973; *PM Creative Workbooks,* nine volumes, Price Milburn, 1973; (with Robin Robilliard) *Country Readers,* eighteen volumes, Price Milburn, 1974; (with Robilliard) *Methuen Country Books,* four volumes, Methuen, 1974; (editor) *People at Work,* fourteen volumes, Price Milburn, 1974; (editor) *Everyday Stories,* twenty-eight volumes, Price Milburn, 1976; (with Clive Harper) *Animal Books,* sixteen volumes, Thomas Nelson, 1978; (with James K. Baxter) *Readalongs,* eighteen volumes, Price Milburn, 1979-81; *Phonic Blends,* twenty-four volumes, Methuen, 1979; *Singing Games,* Price Milburn, 1981.

Editor of series: "PM Instant Readers," Price Milburn, 1969-70; "PM Town Readers," Price Milburn, 1971; "Dinghy Stories," Methuen, 1973; "PM Everyday Stories," Price Milburn, 1973-80; "PM Science Concept Books," Price Milburn, 1974; "People at Work," Price Milburn, 1974; "PM Seagulls," Price Milburn, 1980; "Early Days," Price Milburn, 1982.

WORK IN PROGRESS: Eighteen "Readalong" books, for Price Milburn.

SIDELIGHTS: Beverley Price wrote: "In 1972 I traveled to England to lecture on reading at teachers' centers, and I have several times lectured in Australia, particularly in 1980. My interests are reading schemes, understanding how children learn to read, and writing the sort of books that can help them. The school books I dislike most are all those that are narrow and restricting—mere reading exercises (often 'based on linguistic principles'). But I like those that strike a spark—that are exciting, memorable, splendid.''

Price's books have been translated into several languages, including Chinese and Welsh, and aboriginal languages.

BIOGRAPHICAL/CRITICAL SOURCES: Reading Is Everybody's Business, International Reading Association, 1972.

*   *   *

PRICE, Sally   1943-

PERSONAL: Born September 16, 1943, in Boston, Mass.; daughter of Arthur T. (a librarian) and Pauline (a director of a college scholarship foundation; maiden name, Randolph) Hamlin; married Richard Price (an anthropologist), June 21, 1963; children: Niko, Leah. *Education:* Radcliffe College, A.B., 1965; Johns Hopkins University, Ph.D., 1981; also attended Sorbonne, University of Paris, 1963-64. *Home:* 215 Overhill Rd., Baltimore, Md. 21210. *Office:* Department of Anthropology, Johns Hopkins University, Baltimore, Md. 21218.

CAREER: Johns Hopkins University, Baltimore, Md., associated with department of anthropology, 1982—.

WRITINGS—Books: (With husband, Richard Price) *Afro-American Arts of the Suriname Rain Forest* (nonfiction), University of California Press, 1980.

Other: (With R. Price) "Music From Saramaka" (sound recording), Folkways, 1977. Contributor of articles to magazines, including *American Anthropologist, Caribbean Review, Ethnology, Man,* and *Natural History.* Book review editor, *Nieuwe West-Indische Gids,* 1982—.

WORK IN PROGRESS: Cowives and Calabashes, completion expected in 1982.

SIDELIGHTS: Price's *Afro-American Arts of the Suriname Rain Forest* catalogues an exhibition of artifacts made by the Maroons (Bush Negroes) of Suriname that was presented by the Museum of Cultural History at the University of California, Los Angeles, the Dallas Museum of Fine Arts, the Walters Art Gallery in Baltimore, and the American Museum of Natural History in New York City. In the *Times Literary Supplement,* anthropologist Philip Dark wrote that the book is "an outstanding study in the relatively new field of 'ethno-aesthetics.'"

BIOGRAPHICAL/CRITICAL SOURCES: Times Literary Supplement, January 15, 1982.

*   *   *

PRIMROSE, William   1904-1982

OBITUARY NOTICE: Born August 23, 1904, in Glasgow, Scotland; died of cancer, May 1, 1982, in Provo, Utah. Violist, educator, and author of *Walk on the North Side,* an autobiography. Primrose began his musical career as a student of the violin, studying first with his father, musician John Primrose, and later with Belgian violininst Eugene Ysaye. It was Ysaye who convinced John Primrose that his son should give up the violin and pursue a career as a violist. Primrose, who performed with the NBC Orchestra under Arturo Toscanini, with several small ensembles, and as a concert soloist, became known as the world's foremost violist. In later years, Primrose joined the music faculty of the University of Indiana. He became a commander of the Order of the British Empire in 1953. Obituaries and other sources: *Current Biography*, Wilson, 1946; *Who's Who in Music and Musicians' International Directory*, 6th edition, Hafner, 1972; *Musicians Since 1900: Performers in Concert and Opera*, H. W. Wilson, 1978; *Who's Who*, 134th edition, St. Martin's, 1982; *London Times*, May 4, 1982; *Time*, May 17, 1982; *Newsweek*, May 17, 1982.

* * *

PROBST, Leonard   1921-1982

OBITUARY NOTICE—See index for *CA* sketch: Born June 10, 1921, in Brooklyn, N.Y.; died of cancer, March 19, 1982, in Brooklyn Heights, N.Y. Critic, broadcaster, producer, journalist, and author. Probst was one of the first drama critics to broadcast opening night reviews on television. He began reading drama reviews on WNBC-TV's "Eleventh Hour News" during New York's newspaper strike in 1962. Because of this innovation, Jack Gould of the *New York Times* dubbed Probst the "dean of the new breed" of television critics. For his reviews, the radio and television broadcaster was designated the "best critic of Off-Broadway theater" by *Show Business*. Probst worked for the United Press International (UPI), the *Los Angeles Mirror*, the Cooperative for American Relief Everywhere (CARE), and the United Nations High Commissioner for Refugees before joining the National Broadcasting Company (NBC) in 1958. A skilled athlete, Probst had a tennis stroke, the Probstian hoist, named after him. It is, in his words, "a lob of lofty proportions." In 1976 Probst wrote *Off Camera*, a book about actors and directors. Obituaries and other sources: *New York Times*, March 21, 1982.

* * *

PROGER, Samuel (Herschel)   1906-

BRIEF ENTRY: Born January 21, 1906. American physician and author. Proger has been a member of the medical staff of New England Medical Center at Tufts University since 1931, and was a professor of medicine at the university from 1948 to 1971. He was named president of the medical center in 1971. Proger edited *The Medicated Society* (Macmillan, 1968) and wrote *A Career in Primary Care* (Ballinger, 1976). *Address:* 45 Willow Cres., Brookline, Mass. 02146; and New England Medical Center, Tufts University, 171 Harrison Ave., Boston, Mass. 02111. *Biographical/critical sources: New York Times Book Review*, November 10, 1968; *American Men and Women of Science: The Physical and Biological Sciences*, 14th edition, Bowker, 1979.

* * *

PULLEIN-THOMPSON, Joanna Maxwell   1898-1961
   (Joanna Cannan)

PERSONAL: Born in 1898 in Oxford, England; died April, 1961, in England; daughter of Charles Cannan (secretary to the delegates of the Oxford University Press); married H. J. Pullein-Thompson (an army officer and businessman), 1918; children: Dennis, Josephine, and twins Christine (Mrs. Julian J.H. Popescu) and Diana (Mrs. Dennis L.A. Farr). *Education:* Educated in Oxford, England, and Paris, France. *Residence:* Oxford, England.

CAREER: Writer of fiction, mysteries, and children's books.

WRITINGS—All under name Joanna Cannan; novels: *The Misty Valley*, [London], 1922, George H. Doran, 1924; *Wild Berry Wine*, Frederick A. Stokes, 1925; *The Lady of the Heights*, T. Fisher Unwin, 1926; *Sheila Both-Ways*, Benn, 1928, Frederick A. Stokes, 1929; *The Simple Pass On*, Benn, 1929, published as *Orphan of Mars*, Bobbs-Merrill, 1930; *No Walls of Jasper* (mystery), Benn, 1930, Doubleday, 1931; *High Table*, Doubleday, 1931; *Ithuriel's Hour*, Hodder & Stoughton, 1931, Doubleday, 1932; *Snow in Harvest*, Hodder & Stoughton, 1932; *North Wall*, Hodder & Stoughton, 1933; *Under Proof* (mystery), Hodder & Stoughton, 1934; *The Hills Sleep On*, Hodder & Stoughton, 1935; *Frightened Angels*, Harper & Brothers, 1936; *A Hand to Burn* (mystery), Hodder & Stoughton, 1936; *Pray Do Not Venture*, Gollancz, 1937; *Princes in the Land*, Gollancz, 1938; *London Pride* (illustrated by Anne Bullen), Collins, 1939; *They Rang Up the Police* (mystery), Gollancz, 1939.

Death at the Dog (mystery), Gollancz, 1940, Reynal & Hitchcock, 1941; *Idle Apprentice*, Gollancz, 1940; *Blind Messenger*, Gollancz, 1941; *Little I Understood*, Gollancz, 1948, reprinted, Lythway Press, 1973; *The Hour of the Angel: Ithuriel's Hour*, Pan Books, 1949; *Poisonous Relations*, Morrow, 1950 (published in England as *Murder Included*, Gollancz, 1950); *And All I Learned*, Gollancz, 1951; *Body in the Beck*, Gollancz, 1952; *Oxfordshire*, R. Hale, 1952; *Long Shadows*, Gollancz, 1955; *People to be Found*, Gollancz, 1956.

Juveniles: *A Pony for Jean* (illustrated by Bullen), John Lane, 1936, Scribner, 1937, reprinted, Brockhampton Press, 1970; *We Met Our Cousins* (illustrated by Bullen), Collins, 1937; *Another Pony for Jean* (illustrated by Bullen), Collins, 1938, reprinted, Brockhampton Press, 1973; *More Ponies for Jean* (illustrated by Bullen), Collins, 1943, reprinted, Hodder & Stoughton, 1976; *Hamish: The Story of a Shetland Pony* (illustrated by Bullen), Penguin, 1944; *They Bought Her a Pony* (illustrated by Rosemary Robertson), Collins, 1944; *I Wrote a Pony Book* (illustrated by Sheila Rose), Collins, 1950, reprinted, Hodder & Stoughton, 1977; *Gaze at the Moon* (illustrated by Rose), Collins, 1957.

Contributor of stories to periodicals, including *Good Housekeeping*, *Fortune*, and *Woman's Journal*.

AVOCATIONAL INTERESTS: Fox hunting, mountain climbing, horses.

BIOGRAPHICAL/CRITICAL SOURCES: New York Times Book Review, April 20, 1924, April 5, 1925, March 23, 1930, March 22, 1931, November 1, 1931, April 10, 1932, March 22, 1936, January 15, 1939; *Literary Review of the New York Evening Post*, April 26, 1924, April 25, 1925; *New York Herald and Tribune*, June 15, 1924; *Boston Transcript*, July 19, 1924, June 6, 1925, May 18, 1929, November 4, 1931, May 21, 1932; *Saturday Review of Literature*, April 6, 1929; *Times Literary Supplement*, October 31, 1929, May 1, 1930, July 16, 1931, July 25, 1936; *New York World*, May 18, 1930; *Spectator*, February 7, 1931; *New York Herald Tribune Books*, November 8, 1931.

OBITUARIES: London Times, April 24, 1961.*

* * *

PUTNAM, John Fay   1924(?)-1982

OBITUARY NOTICE: Born c. 1924; died of cancer, May 9, 1982, in Silver Spring, Md. Educator, composer of sacred music, and author of a book on folk music. Obituaries and other sources: *Washington Post*, May 15, 1982.

PYNE, Stephen J(oseph) 1949-

PERSONAL: Born March 6, 1949, in San Francisco, Calif.; son of Joseph R. (a special agent of the Federal Bureau of Investigation) and Barbara (Boles) Pyne; married Sonja Sandberg, May 14, 1977; children: Lydia Virginia. *Education:* Stanford University, B.A., 1971; University of Texas, M.A., 1974, Ph.D., 1976. *Home:* 1227 Second Ave., Iowa City, Iowa 52240. *Office:* Department of History, University of Iowa, Iowa City, Iowa 52242.

CAREER: Grand Canyon National Park, Grand Canyon, Ariz., fire control aid at North Rim, summers, 1967-69, foreman of fire crew at North Rim, summers, 1970-81, park ranger at Desert View, winter, 1976-77; University of Iowa, Iowa City, assistant professor of history, 1981—. Research coordinator at U.S. Forest Service's History Office, winters, 1977-81. *Member:* History of Science Society, American Association for the Advancement of Science, American Historical Association, Forest History Society. *Awards, honors:* Fellow of Smithsonian Institution, 1974, National Humanities Center, 1979-80, and National Endowment for the Humanities (in Antarctica), 1981-82.

WRITINGS: Grove Karl Gilbert, Unversity of Texas Press, 1980; *Fire in America: A Cultural History of Wildland and Rural Fire,* Princeton University Press, 1982; *Dutton's Point: An Intellectual History of the Grand Canyon* (monograph), Grand Canyon Natural History Association, 1982; *Introduction to Wildland Fires* (textbook), Wiley, 1983. Also contributor of articles to periodicals.

WORK IN PROGRESS: Earth and Ice: Essays on the History of Antarctica.

SIDELIGHTS: Pyne commented: ''I am basically interested in nature, and in the ways in which people do things with the natural world and how they understand that world. This has led to special interests in the history of exploration and science. My current work on fire combines this general curiosity with some personal experience, including fifteen summers working on a forest fire crew at Grand Canyon. My projected work on Antarctica includes a three-month tour of 'the ice' by plane, motor toboggan, helicopter, and icebreaker. It is like traveling to another planet.

Q-R

QUADE, Quentin Lon 1933-

BRIEF ENTRY: Born January 28, 1933, in Fort Dodge, Iowa. American political scientist, educator, and author. Quade has been a member of the political science faculty at Marquette University since 1961. He became a professor and dean of the graduate school in 1968, and in 1974 he was named executive vice-president of the university. Quade wrote *The United States and Wars of National Liberation* (Council on Religion and International Affairs, 1966) and *American Politics: Effective and Responsible?* (American Book Co., 1969). *Address:* 7326 Maple Ter., Wauwatosa, Wis. 53213; and 615 North 11th St., Milwaukee, Wis. 53233; and Department of Political Science, Marquette University, Milwaukee, Wis. 53233.

* * *

RAAT, W(illiam) Dirk 1939-

PERSONAL: Born July 1, 1939, in Ogden, Utah; son of Elmer W. (a plumber) and Iris (Calkins) Raat; married Carole Hayes, 1971 (divorced, 1980); children: Kelly, Michael. *Education:* University of Utah, B.S., 1961, Ph.D., 1967; also attended National University of Mexico and Center for Intercultural Documentation, Cuernavaca, Mexico. *Home:* 39 Forest Pl., Fredonia, N.Y. 14063. *Office:* Department of History, State University of New York College at Fredonia, Fredonia, N.Y. 14063.

CAREER: Moorhead State College, Moorhead, Minn., assistant professor, 1966-68, associate professor of history, 1968-70; State University of New York College at Fredonia, associate professor, 1970-77, professor of history, 1977—, chairman of department, 1973-74. Member of local community theatre; consultant to National Endowment for the Humanities. *Military service:* Utah National Guard, 1956-64. *Member:* American Historical Association, Conference on Latin American History, Latin American Studies Association. *Awards, honors:* James A. Robertson Award from Conference on Latin American History, 1968, for article "Leopoldo Zea and Mexican Positivism"; American Council of Learned Societies fellowship, 1976-77.

WRITINGS: *El positivismo durante el Porfiriato* (title means "Positivism During the Porifiriato"), SepSetentas, 1975; *Revoltosos: Mexico's Rebels in the United States, 1903-23,* Texas A & M University Press, 1981; *Mexico: From Independence to Revolution, 1810-1910,* University of Nebraska Press, 1982;

The Mexican Revolution: Historiography and Bibliography, G. K. Hall, 1982. Contributor of nearly twenty articles and essays to history journals and books.

WORK IN PROGRESS: *Copper Canyon Country: An Adventure in Time and Space,* a photohistory of Chihuahua's canyon country; a videotape series on Mexican history.

SIDELIGHTS: Raat told *CA:* "Anyone desiring to be a historian should like to travel, have an excellent command of foreign languages, and be independently wealthy. As for myself, I do like to travel.

"More seriously, I believe that the historian has a special task to perform. Like the philosopher, he is analytical; unlike the great philosophers, he is seldom speculative. Like the social scientist, he is a researcher; unlike the sociologist, the historian has a story to tell. The telling of history is both a craft and an art. To create and publish a historical work is to engage in craftsmanship. To write well and effectively is the task of the artist."

Many of Raat's own works were written in Spanish and Japanese.

* * *

RABINOWICH, Ellen 1946-

PERSONAL: Born October 21, 1946, in Brooklyn, N.Y.; daughter of Paul (a psychologist) and Miriam (a piano teacher; maiden name, Feldman) Rabinowich; married G. Richardson Cook (a film producer), July 15, 1975. *Education:* University of Wisconsin (now University of Wisconsin—Madison), B.A., 1969. *Home:* 2830 Lambert Dr., Los Angeles, Calif. 90068.

CAREER: Plenum Publishing Corp., New York City, copywriter 1969-70; Courier Production Co., New York City, co-producer, 1975; Mallory Factor Assoc., New York City, account executive, writer, producer, 1975-77; Martin Erlichman Productions, Los Angeles, Calif., story editor, 1980—. *Member:* Society of Children's Book Writers, Women in Film. *Awards, honors:* Children's Book Council named *Seals, Sea Lions, and Walruses* an outstanding science book for children in 1980.

WRITINGS—Juveniles: *Queen Minna,* Macmillan, 1973; *Kangaroos, Koalas, and Other Marsupials,* F. Watts, 1978; *Horses and Foals,* F. Watts, 1979; *The Loch Ness Monster,* F. Watts, 1979; *Rock Fever,* F. Watts, 1979; *Toni's Crowd,* F. Watts,

1979; *Seals, Sea Lions, and Walruses,* F. Watts, 1980; *Rock Fever, Number 4,* Bantam, 1981; *Underneath I'm Different,* Delacorte, 1983.

Contributor of articles on health and beauty, television personalities, and film to various periodicals; writer of press and promotional materials for New York State Council on the Arts, Association for Retarded Children, and Association of Independent Filmmakers.

WORK IN PROGRESS: Research for a film project about two step-brothers.

SIDELIGHTS: "Some people are much more connected with a certain phase of their lives than with others," Ellen Rabinowich commented. "I'm more connected to the time I was a teenager than to my college days." This affinity for adolescence is evident throughout Rabinowich's fiction, which is geared to attract the interest of a low-reading-level group. Her novels deal with the typical problems of middle-class teenagers, such as peer pressure, drugs and alcohol, and divorced parents, yet are written in simple language and are heavily illustrated with photographs.

BIOGRAPHICAL/CRITICAL SOURCES: New York Times, December 10, 1978.

*   *   *

RADLAUER, David 1952-

PERSONAL: Surname is pronounced "Rad-lower"; born January 3, 1952, in Los Angeles, Calif.; son of Edward (an author of children's books) and Ruth (an author of children's books; maiden name, Shaw) Radlauer. *Education:* San Francisco State University, 1977—. *Politics:* Progressive. *Home:* 546 Alameda, San Carlos, Calif. 94070.

CAREER: San Mateo County Bookmobile, Belmont, Calif., bookmobile operator, 1972-76; Radlauer Productions, Inc., San Mateo County, Calif., research consultant and public relations representative, 1974—; Great American Bookfairs, Santa Clara, Calif., sales representative, 1979-80; currently archives clerk in San Mateo, Calif. Shop steward; delegate to Central Labor Council of San Mateo County, Calif., 1975. Publisher of *Record Footnotes,* a newsletter for record collectors, 1977-78.

WRITINGS—Juveniles; with father, Edward Radlauer: *Model Airplanes,* Childrens Press, 1976; *Skateboard Mania,* Childrens Press, 1976; *Model Trains,* Childrens Press, 1979.

Editor of *Record Footnotes,* 1977-78; managing editor of *New Labor Review,* 1981-82.

WORK IN PROGRESS: Research on American history since 1870, particularly on labor, social history, music, and Indian education.

AVOCATIONAL INTERESTS: Collecting music, history.

*   *   *

RADZINOWICZ, Leon 1906-

PERSONAL: Surname is pronounced "Ra-jin-o-vitch"; born August 15, 1906, in Lodz, Poland; came to England in 1936; naturalized British subject, 1947; son of David (a physician) and Maria (Braude) Radzinowicz; married third wife, Isolde (Doernenburg) Klarmann, 1979; children: (second marriage) Ann Stacy, William Francis Henry. *Education:* In Cracow, Geneva, Paris, Rome, and Cambridge. M.A., Geneva; LL.D., Cracow; LL.D., Rome (cum laude); Diploma of the Criminological Institute, Rome; M.A., Cambridge; LL.D., Cam-

bridge—Fellow of Trinity College, Cambridge, 1948—. Pupil of Enrico Ferri, the leader of the positivist school. Studied penal systems in Europe and elsewhere. *Home:* 21 Cranmer Rd., Cambridge CB3 9BL, England. *Office:* Trinity College, Cambridge University, Cambridge, England.

CAREER: Assistant professor at the University of Geneva and the Free University of Warsaw; lectured at several other European universities, including Paris, Brussels, and Strasbourg; came to England in 1936 on behalf of the Polish Ministry of Justice to report on the English penal system; invited to Cambridge University in 1937 to help establish criminological study there; became assistant director of research in criminal sciences at Cambridge University in 1946; helped establish the Department of Criminal Science and became its director in 1949; became the first Wolfson Professor of Criminology and director of the newly-established Institute of Criminology in 1959. He remained in this position until his retirement in 1973.

Walter E. Meyer Visiting Professor at Yale Law School, 1962-63; adjunct professor of criminal law and criminology at Columbia Law School, 1966-77; distinguished visiting professor at Rutgers University, 1968-72, 1979-81; visiting professor at the University of Virginia Law School, 1968-69, 1970-74; visiting fellow at the Princeton Institute of Advanced Studies and at the Rockefeller Foundation Center at Belagio, 1975; Law Alumni Chair for Distinguished Professors at the University of Minnesota Law School, 1977; distinguished visiting professor of criminology at Wichita State University, 1977, 1980; distinguished visiting professor at the Pennsylvania State University, 1977, 1979, 1981; distinguished visiting professor of law at the Benjamin N. Cardozo Law School, Yeshiva University, New York, 1978-79; distinguished visiting professor of criminal justice at John Jay College of Criminal Justice, City University of New York 1978-79; overseer of the University of Pennsylvania Law School and associate trustee of the University, 1979—.

Member of the Royal Commission on Capital Punishment, 1949-68; member of the Home Office Advisory Council on the Treatment of Offenders, 1950-68, and chairman of its subcommittee on maximum security in prisons, 1967-68; member of the Royal Commission on the Penal System in England and Wales, 1964-66.

Head of the social defense section of the United Nations, 1947; joint vice-president of the Second United Nations International Congress on Crime, 1955; general rapporteur of the Fourth United Nations Congress on Crime; 1970; honorary vice-chairman of the Fifth Congress, 1975; first chairman of the Criminological Council of the Council of Europe, 1963-70. Consultant to the Bar Association of the City of New York and the Ford Foundation on the promotion of criminological research and teaching, 1965, to President Johnson's Commission of the Causes and Prevention of Violence, 1968-69, to the United States Law Enforcement Assistance Administration, 1976-77, to the Ministry of Justice of New South Wales, Australia, and to the National Institute of Criminology in Canberra, Australia, 1973. Visiting lecturer in consultation with criminological centers in Denmark and Norway, 1963, and Yugoslavia, 1964; Carpentier Lecturer, Columbia Law School, 1965; visiting lecturer at Bundeskriminalamt, Wiesbaden, West Germany, 1968, in Buenos Aires and Mendoza, Argentina, 1969-70, and in South Africa, 1972; rapporteur, penal systems, at International Mental Association Congress, Vancouver, British Columbia, Canada, 1968; Lionel Cohen Lecturer in Israel, 1969; visiting lecturer at Criminological Center, Toronto University, 1982.

AWARDS, HONORS: James Barr Ames Prize and medal of the Harvard Law School, 1950; first president of the British Academy of Forensic Sciences, 1960-61; honorary LL.D. from the University of Leicester, 1965; associate fellow of Silliman College, Yale University, 1966; honorary fellow of the Police College at Bramshill, 1968; honorary foreign member of the Australian Academy of Forensic Sciences, 1973; honorary foreign member of the American Academy of Forensic Sciences, 1973; fellow of the British Academy, 1973; Bruce Smith, Sr., Award for outstanding contributions to criminal justice science in the United States, 1976; Sellin-Glueck Award of the American Society of Criminology, 1976; and the Joseph L. Andrews Award of the American Association of Law Libraries.

Chevalier de l'Ordre de Leopold of Belgium, 1930; Coronation Medal, 1953; knighted by Queen Elizabeth II, 1970.

WRITINGS: (Editor with J.W.C. Turner, and contributor) *The Modern Approach to Criminal Law,* Macmillan, 1945; *A History of English Criminal Law and Its Administration From 1750,* Stevens, Volume I: *The Movement for Reform,* 1948, Volume II: *The Clash Between Private Initiative and Public Interest in the Enforcement of the Law,* 1956, Volume III: *Cross-Currents in the Movement for the Reform of the Police,* 1956, Volume IV: *Grappling for Control,* 1968; (contributor) *Studi in memoria de Arturo Rocco,* Juffre, 1952; *Sir James Fitzjames Stephen, 1829-1894, and His Contribution to the Development of Criminal Law,* Quaritch, 1957; (editor with Marc Ancel) *Introduction au droit criminel de l'Angleterre,* Editions de l'Epargne, 1959.

In Search of Criminology, Harvard University Press, 1962; (author of introduction) Sidney Webb and Beatrice Webb, *English Prisons Under Local Government,* Cass, 1963; (contributor) *Estratto dagli atti del Convegno Internazionale su Cesare Beccaria,* Vincenzo Bona, 1964; *Criminology and the Climate of Social Responsibility,* Heffer, 1964; *The Need for Criminology,* Heinemann, 1965; *Ideology and Crime,* Columbia University Press, 1966; (contributor) Marvin E. Wolfgang, editor, *Crime and Culture: Essays in Honor of Thorsten Sellin,* Wiley, 1968; (contributor) J. P. Buhl and other editors, *Liber Amicorum in Honour of Professor Stephen Hurwitz, LL.D.,* Juristforbundets Forlag, 1971; (editor with Wolfgang) *Crime and Justice,* Volume I: *The Criminal and Society,* Volume II: *The Criminal in the Arms of the Law,* Volume III: *The Criminal in Confinement,* Basic Books, 1971, revised edition, 1977; (with Roger Hood) *Criminology and the Administration of Criminal Justice: A Bibliography,* Mansell, 1976; (with Joan F. S. King) *The Growth of Crime: The International Experience,* Basic Books, 1977.

Co-editor of "English Studies in Criminal Science," Macmillan; editor of "Cambridge Studies in Criminology," Macmillan, Heinemann. Contributor of articles to law and social science journals, newspapers, and other periodicals.

WORK IN PROGRESS: Volume V of *A History of English Criminal Law and Its Administration From 1750.*

SIDELIGHTS: One of the world's most distinguished criminologists, Radzinowicz has long emphasized the interdependence of all aspects of the study of crime: the legal, sociological, psychiatric, and biological, as well as questions of enforcement and penal policy. He is particularly concerned about criminology's role in the analysis of public policy, noting that "to rob it of this practical function is to divorce criminology from reality and render it sterile." In seeking to realize his conception of the role of criminology, Radzinowicz has been active in public life as well as in academic affairs, lending his expertise to governments and international bodies such as the United Nations and the Council of Europe. He was the first director of the Institute of Criminology at Cambridge University, where his leadership helped to establish criminology as an academic discipline in England and elsewhere.

Radzinowicz developed his interdisciplinary approach to criminal science early, taking four doctorates by the age of twenty-three, studying sociology, political theory, and history as well as law and criminology. Under the influence of Enrico Ferri of the University of Rome, Radzinowicz became a proponent of the positivist school of criminology, which stressed both economic inequality and innate personality as causes of crime and advocated indeterminate sentences and other then-innovative approaches to punishment and rehabilitation.

Radzinowicz traveled widely in Europe, observing the penal systems of several countries. He became less doctrinaire in his positivism, stressing an empirical, historical attitude toward the study of crime rather than an ideological one. When he traveled to England, in 1936, he was impressed with the "humane and rational" character of the English prison system, which was then having considerable success with a liberal, reformative approach that stressed probation and aftercare rather than confinement for most offenders. Radzinowicz endorsed the principle that imprisonment is to be avoided, except for violent and dangerous criminals. This is a belief to which he still adheres: "The best prison reform is to send as few people there as possible," he told *People* magazine in 1979.

When World War II broke out, Radzinowicz remained in England, living in Cambridge and pursuing his research and writing. After the war, he joined the faculty of Cambridge University and began his major work, *A History of English Criminal Law and Its Administration From 1750.* This four-volume work explored its subject more comprehensively than had ever been attempted, drawing on vast, untapped archives of British government records. The first volume, which focused on the role of capital punishment, "compels a kind of awed admiration," wrote Norman Birkett in *Spectator.* "If further volumes equal this one . . . an outstanding contribution of the highest permanent value will have been made to the history of law and the history of thought." The subsequent volumes examined the development of government's role in peacekeeping and law enforcement and the ideas of various reformers, and were well received. The work as a whole is considered a classic in its field, an exceptionally well-written analysis of the complex relationships between social movements, intellectual history, legislative action, and penal policy and practice.

Radzinowicz's views have evolved considerably over the years; he is less optimistic than he once was about the effectiveness of criminology in preventing crime. He wrote in 1961 that crime is an integral part of society, not a narrow problem to be solved by the application of scientific expertise, and suggested that criminology's role should be to provide "descriptive analytic accounts . . . of all the matters which come within the orbit of penal policy and penology." He noted further that "public morality, social expediency," and "the subtle but vital balance between the rights of the individual and the protection of the community" are as important in formulating policy as are the findings of scientists. Radzinowicz attributes the worldwide increase in crime in recent years to several factors, including increased availability of goods and the breakdown of such institutions as religion and the family, but he has expressed skepticism about the value of searching for the ultimate causes of crime. Nor does he believe that harsher punishments are likely to prove an effective solution: he is opposed to capital punishment.

BIOGRAPHICAL/CRITICAL SOURCES: *Spectator,* January 7, 1949; *Manchester Guardian,* March 1, 1957; *Times Literary Supplement,* November 10, 1961; Leon Radzinowicz, *In Search of Criminology,* Harvard University Press, 1962; *New Statesman,* July 8, 1966; Roger Hood, editor, *Crime, Criminology, and Public Policy: Essays in Honor of Sir Leon Radzinowicz,* Free Press, 1975; *People,* March 12, 1979.

*   *   *

RAEL, Leyla 1948-

PERSONAL: Born November 9, 1948, in Miami, Fla.; daughter of M. J. (a retailer) and Frieda (Offenberg) Schachter; married Dane Rudhyar (a writer and composer), March 31, 1977. *Education:* Attended Michigan State University, 1966-67. *Home and office:* 3635 Lupine Ave., Palo Alto, Calif. 94303.

CAREER: Lecturer and consultant in Miami, Fla., 1971-75, and Palo Alto, Calif., 1975—. Director of Rudhyar Institute for Transpersonal Activity, 1981—. *Member:* National Astrological Society, National Council for Geocosmic Research, American Federation of Astrologers, Association for Transpersonal Psychology.

WRITINGS: *The Lunation Process in Astrological Guidance,* ASI Publishers, 1979; (with husband, Dane Rudhyar) *Astrological Aspects,* ASI Publishers, 1980; *Shambhala Astrological Calendar,* Shambhala, 1981.

SIDELIGHTS: Leyla Rael commented: "My writing has developed spontaneously out of my deep interest in the work of my husband, Dane Rudhyar (which began long before we met personally). My main aim is to convey, in terms understandable to members of my generation, what his basic direction, scope, and quality of point of view can mean to them as they (we) meet the increasingly crucial challenges of our chaotic society and times."

*   *   *

RAFAEL, Gideon 1913-

BRIEF ENTRY: Born March 5, 1913, in Berlin, Germany. Israeli diplomat and author. Rafael was an ambassador and Israel's representative to the European Economic Community from 1957 to 1960. He was director-general of the Ministry of Foreign Affairs from 1967 to 1972 and served as ambassador-at-large and senior political adviser until his retirement in 1978. Rafael wrote *Destination Peace: Three Deca'les of Israeli Foreign Policy—A Personal Memoir* (Stein & Day, 1981). *Address:* 36 Hantke St., Jerusalem, Israel; and Ministry of Foreign Affairs, Tel Aviv, Israel. *Biographical/critical sources: International Who's Who,* Europa, 1978; *The International Yearbook and Statesmen's Who's Who,* Kelly's Directories, 1979; *The Middle East and North Africa,* 26th edition, Europa, 1979.

*   *   *

RAINSBERGER, Todd J(effrey) 1951-

PERSONAL: Born August 6, 1951, in Fort Wayne, Ind.; son of Richard Edwin and Barbara (Mader) Rainsberger; married Brenda Gresham, June 3, 1972; children: Mason, Melissa. *Education:* University of Florida, B.A., 1973, M.A., 1974; University of Southern California, M.F.A., 1977, Ph.D., 1979. *Home:* 2621 Northwest 37th Ter., Gainesville, Fla. 32605.

CAREER: University of Florida, Gainesville, instructor in English and film studies, 1973-74, film producer at Institute of

Food and Agricultural Sciences, 1977-79; GOAL Productions, Pasadena, Calif., writer, director, and cinematographer, 1979-80; Creative Services & Marketing, Inc., Gainesville, account executive and director of broadcast media, 1980-81; WCJB-TV, Gainsville, director of creative services, 1981—. Instructor at University of Southern California, 1980. Part-time writer, director, and cinematographer for GOAL Productions, 1980—; free-lance still photographer and news camera operator; co-camera operator for Los Angeles Lakers Basketball Team, 1975-76. Television, film, and theatre critic for WCJB-TV, also producer, writer, and editor. *Member:* American Film Institute, Phi Beta Kappa, Phi Kappa Phi. *Awards, honors:* First prize from National Agricultural Communications in Education, 1979, for filming and directing "Beginning Beekeeping."

WRITINGS: *James Wong Howe, Cinematographer,* A. S. Barnes, 1981.

Films: "Eternal Water," University of Florida, 1978; "The Law of the Land," University of Florida, 1979; "Aetna Driver Training Series" (eleven films), Goal Productions, 1979—; "The Urban Forest," Florida Department of Forestry, 1980; "Pouring Profits," Goal Productions, 1981.

Creator of more than one hundred television commercials. Film critic for *Gainesville Sun,* 1978—.

WORK IN PROGRESS: A film on recombinant DNA; a film on van safety.

*   *   *

RAKOWSKI, John 1922-

PERSONAL: Born July 22, 1922, in Brooklyn, N.Y.; son of Stanley (a cobbler) and Anna (Byczek) Rakowski; married Pauline LeDuc, May 27, 1944; children: Michael, David, Stephen. *Education:* Cleveland College, B.A. (cum laude), 1951; Rutgers University, M.Ed., 1961. *Home:* 3 Karyn Ter. E., Middletown, N.J. 07748.

CAREER: Cadillac Motor Car, Cleveland Tank Plant Division, Cleveland, Ohio, editor in public relations, 1951-55; Fort Monmouth, Fort Monmouth, N.J., civilian engineering psychologist, 1955-73; writer, 1973—. *Military service:* U.S. Army Air Forces, 1941-45. *Member:* Phi Beta Kappa (Phi Society).

WRITINGS: *Cooking on the Road,* Anderson-World, 1980; *Adventure Cycling in Europe: A Practical Guide to Low-Cost Bicycle Touring in Twenty-seven Countries,* Rodale Press, 1981; *Adventure Cycling in North America,* Rodale Press, in press. Contributor to *Bicycling* and *Bike World.*

SIDELIGHTS: Rakowski told *CA:* "I took an early retirement in 1973. Six months later I began a fourteen-month, sixteen thousand-mile bicycle tour around the world. As an encore I rode more than thirteen thousand miles around the perimeter of the United States. I've been riding ever since, in all parts of the world. In between, I write about bicycle touring, emphasizing both the practical aspects and the health, adventures, and joys inherent in that mode of travel.

"'But why by bicycle?' people often ask. 'Surely, relaxing in a train, bus, or plane would be faster and more pleasant.' Not in my book. For me the heart of traveling is the going, not the arriving; motorized tourists have it backwards. I say use your own foot power at a pace slow enough to see, hear, touch, and smell your surroundings. That's the way to immerse yourself in a country, not by dozing in a bus or by watching the landscape flash by.

"Bicycling encourages a more relaxed life-style. Material gain loses its importance, tensions lessen, the basics are newly appreciated—a shower, a dry place to tent down, some hot food, and someone to share it all. Interacting with local people at their own level is also improved. Plain folk everywhere relate more easily to a bicycling tourist.

"On India's Grand Trunk Road a native fell in beside me. He rode a large, antiquated one-speed bike. We chatted, and then he asked if I would come to his home for tea: 'It may mean little to you to lose an hour, but for me it would be a memorable experience,' he said. And it was for me too. I met his extended family and spent a few hours wandering about his small village, which was some miles off the highway. This experience would be nearly impossible for the usual tourist.

"In Poland, Rumania, and other East European countries I traveled byways and country lanes not reached by public transport, and I talked to peasants, who had never before seen a foreigner. I learned something of their way of life firsthand, not through a screen of officialdom.

"It hasn't all been roses of course. I've been hungry and thirsty, I had stones thrown at me in the Khyber Pass, border officials tried to shake me down in Guatemala, and I suffered hypothermia in northern Norway in mid-summer. But no one has ever physically threatened me; I have never felt real danger. I learned to trust and to endure.

"Even with a companion, one rides mostly in silence. The solitary hours encourage contemplation. I muse on my state, recall and evaluate events of the day, and compose an entry for my notes. My writing technique is simple. I record notes as things happen. Lately I've used a micro-cassette recorder, right on the bike, and transcribe my thoughts to paper later."

*   *   *

RALPHS, Sheila 1923-

PERSONAL: Born February 16, 1923, in Abergavenny, Wales. *Education:* Bedford College, London, B.A. (with honors), 1946, diploma in theology, 1948. *Office:* Victoria University of Manchester, Manchester M13 9PL, England.

CAREER: Nurse, 1943-44; teacher, 1944-45; teacher of religion at girls' grammar school in Ashford, England, 1947-50; senior lecturer at Victoria University of Manchester, Manchester, England, 1964—.

WRITINGS: Etterno Spiro: A Study in the Nature of Dante's Paradise, Manchester University Press, 1959; *Dante's Journey to the Centre: Some Patterns in His Allegory,* Manchester University Press, 1972. Contributor to *Encyclopaedia Britannica* and *Dictionary of Christian Ethics.* Contributor to theology journals.

*   *   *

RAMA RAU, Dhanvanthi (Handoo) 1893-

BRIEF ENTRY: Born May 10, 1893, in Hubli, India. Indian social worker and author. Beginning in the 1920's, Rama Rau helped bring about important political and social changes for the women of India. After attending college at a time when, in India, only men pursued an education, she went on to become a university lecturer. Later, as a social worker, Rama Rau strove to attain improved educational opportunities, legal rights, and social conditions for Indian women. She helped form and later presided over the All India Women's Conference, and in 1949 she founded the Family Planning Association of India. She served as chairman of the Indian government's Social and Moral Hygiene Enquiry Committee in 1955 and as a member of the Central Social Welfare Board from 1956 to 1961. Her

honors include the Kaiser-I-Hind Gold Medal and the Lasker Award. Rama Rau wrote *Report of the Advisory Committee on Social and Moral Hygiene* (Central Social Welfare Board, Government of India, 1958) and *An Inheritance: The Memoirs of Dhanvanthi Rama Rau* (Harper, 1977). *Address:* D/10, Mafatlal Park, Bhulabhai Desai Rd., Bombay 26, India. *Biographical/critical sources: Current Biography,* Wilson, 1954; *New York Times,* October 12, 1977; *Washington Post,* November 11, 1977.

*   *   *

RAMSEY, Eric
See HAGBERG, David J(ames)

*   *   *

RAND, Ann (Binkley)
(Anne Binkley)

PERSONAL: Born in Chicago, Ill.; daughter of Roy G. (a company president) and Helen (a painter and photographer; maiden name, Clarke) Binkley; married Paul Rand (a graphic artist), April 3, 1949 (divorced); married Hasan Ozbekhan (a professor), December 30, 1960; children: (first marriage) Catherine. *Education:* Attended University of Chicago, 1938-39; University of California, Berkeley, 1941-43, Cranbrook Academy of Art, and Institute of Design (Chicago); Illinois Institute of Technology, B.S., 1945. *Home:* 237 Monroe St., Philadelphia, Pa. 19147.

CAREER: Architect, author of novels and books for children, and artist. Teacher of art in the Head Start program and in a community center in Los Angeles, Calif., 1968-69. Art works exhibited in group shows in Wellfleet, Mass., Truro, Mass., Provincetown, Mass., and New York, N.Y. *Awards, honors:* House designed with husband Paul Rand selected as one of *Interiors* magazine's ten best houses for 1953; *New York Times* chose *I Know a Lot of Things,* 1956, *Sparkle and Spin,* 1957, and *Umbrellas, Hats, and Wheels,* 1961, as best illustrated children's books of the year.

WRITINGS—Juveniles, except as noted: *I Know a Lot of Things,* illustrations by husband Paul Rand, Harcourt, 1956; *Sparkle and Spin,* illustrations by P. Rand, Harcourt, 1957; *Little River,* illustrations by Feodor Rojankovsky, Harcourt, 1959; (with Olle Eksell) *Edward and the Horse,* Harcourt, 1961; *Umbrellas, Hats, and Wheels,* illustrations by Jerome Snyder, Harcourt, 1961; *Little One,* illustrations by P. Rand, Harcourt, 1962; *So Small,* illustrations by Rojankovsky, Harcourt, 1962; *Did a Bear Just Walk There?,* illustrations by A. Birnbaum, Harcourt, 1966; (under name Anne Binkley) *What Shall I Cry* (adult novel), Harcourt, 1968; *Listen! Listen!,* illustrations by P. Rand, Harcourt, 1970.

WORK IN PROGRESS: A romantic historical novel set in Turkey during 1789-1808.

SIDELIGHTS: Rand told *CA:* "I began writing for children during my daughter's childhood. By watching her explore and learn about the world, I came to see the world—at least to some extent—through a child's view of it. This experience continued when, in the late 1960's, I worked in the Head Start program and taught art to children in a community center in east Los Angeles. The rediscovery of the world around me through the eyes of children was exciting and stimulating—an added dimension to the way my peers and I looked and felt about things.

"*What Shall I Cry* was largely inspired by Los Angeles—its cool, casual, tough, money/celebrity orientation. I wanted to dramatize the problems and pain that living in such an environment could cause a person—in this case a warm, generous-hearted woman—who held different values and therefore could not accept or adapt to life in Los Angeles.''

*   *   *

RANDALL, Bob 1937-

PERSONAL: Birth-given name, Stanley B. Goldstein; born August 20, 1937, in New York, N.Y.; son of Jerome (in sales) and Bessie (Chiz) Goldstein; married Ruth Gordon, March 11, 1962; children: one daughter, one son. *Education:* New York University, A.B., 1958. *Agent:* Bret Adams, 36 East 61st St., New York, N.Y. 10022.

CAREER: Marschalk Advertising Agency, New York City, copywriter, 1963-73; actor, 1959-62; playwright, television writer, and novelist, 1972—. *Member:* Writers Guild of America, Dramatists Guild. *Awards, honors:* Drama Desk most promising playwright award, 1972, for *6 Rms Riv Vu;* Writers Guild of America award, 1974, for ''Annie and the Seven Hoods''; Emmy nomination from National Academy of Television Arts and Sciences, 1974, for *6 Rms Riv Vu;* Edgar Allan Poe Award, 1977, for *The Fan.*

WRITINGS: The Fan (novel; Literary Guild selection), Random House, 1977; *The Next* (novel), Warner Books, 1981; *The Calling* (novel), Simon & Schuster, 1981.

Stageplays: ''Brief Sublet'' (two-act), 1970, rewritten as *6 Rms Riv Vu* (first produced in New York City at the Helen Hayes Theatre, October 17, 1972), Doubleday, 1973, French, 1973; ''The Magic Show'' (musical), first produced in New York City at the Cort Theatre, May 28, 1974. Also author of ''Annie and the Seven Hoods'' (comedy revue).

Creator of teleplays, including ''Mo and Joe,'' for Columbia Broadcasting System (CBS-TV), 1974, and ''On Our Own,'' for CBS-TV, 1977.

WORK IN PROGRESS: Kahn's Tapes, a novel; ''Dear Ex,'' a sixty-minute pilot, and ''The Television Hour,'' a thirty-minute pilot, both for CBS-TV; ''People Don't Do Things Like That,'' a comedy-thriller stageplay.

SIDELIGHTS: In his first novel, *The Fan,* Randall unfolds his plot through a series of letters written by Sally Ross, an actress, Jake, her ex-husband, Douglas Breen, a demented fan of Miss Ross's, and investigators of Breen's bizarre letters. As the story progresses, the correspondence between Sally and Jake becomes more loving and intense, while the fan letters from Breen to Sally become increasingly personal and threatening.

A best-seller, *The Fan* was critically acclaimed by reviewers, such as *National Review's* David Brudnoy, who wrote: ''The book is a quick read; an intelligent treatment of an unusual subject; an alarming story; and, as everybody's grandmother used to say, it's a caution.'' Nora Johnson of the *New York Times Book Review* described *The Fan* as ''a riveting tale of love, fear and urban woe.'' And an *Atlantic* critic, commenting on Randall's use of letters to tell his story, felt that the device resulted in ''a certain loss of credibility in small matters, such as the need for police officers to communicate through notes. But Randall is more deserving of credit for overcoming his form than of criticism for succumbing to it, because he has contrived a genuine thriller in an unpromising format.''

Randall's subsequent works, *The Next* and *The Calling,* are also suspense novels. *The Next* involves two middle-aged sisters, Molly and Kate. When Molly is injured in an automobile accident, her ten-year-old son, Charles, moves in with Kate.

Several weeks after his arrival, Charles mysteriously transforms into a virile adult who seduces Kate and takes her on a passionate journey. Molly, questioning the whereabouts of the two, sets out in pursuit of them. It is later discovered that Charles is the reincarnation of a molested child who was killed by Kate and Molly's mother.

Satan is the antagonist of *The Calling.* This novel deals with a seemingly average wife and mother, Susan, who begins receiving phone calls from Hell. Although her family, friends, and even Susan think she is losing her mind, the tormented woman is convinced that demons are chasing her when people who try to help her are ''accidentally'' killed. As the drama intensifies, Susan must either cooperate with the spirits or risk losing her husband and daughter.

Randall told *CA:* ''My main interest is human behavior. At the moment my main goal is to return to the theatre. A walloping hit TV series should give me the time and income to do it—there are several in the works. I'll always write books. They're my vacations from the world of directors, actors, and TV executives, all of whom I love but need occasionally to get away from.''

MEDIA ADAPTATIONS: The Fan was adapted as a motion picture, starring Lauren Bacall, James Garner, and Maureen Stapleton, by Paramount in 1981.

BIOGRAPHICAL/CRITICAL SOURCES: Atlantic, May, 1977; *New York Times Book Review,* May 8, 1977; *National Review,* July 22, 1977; *Times Literary Supplement,* September 2, 1977.

*   *   *

RANDELL, Beverley
See PRICE, Beverley Joan

*   *   *

RANDELL, John Bulmer 1918-1982

OBITUARY NOTICE: Born August 25, 1918; died April 30, 1982. Psychiatrist and author of *Sexual Variations.* Obituaries and other sources: *Who's Who,* 134th edition, St. Martin's, 1982; *London Times,* May 11, 1982.

*   *   *

RATCLIFF, John Drury 1903-1973

OBITUARY NOTICE: Born May 4, 1903, in Huntington, W.Va.; died of an apparent heart attack, October 24, 1973, in New York, N.Y.; cremated. Journalist and author of books and more than seven hundred articles on science and medicine. Ratcliff was on the editorial staffs of *Time* and *Fortune* magazines, a member of the organizing group of *Newsweek,* and a founder of the Famous Writers School. His books include *Modern Miracle Men, Lives and Dollars: The Story of Today's Research,* and *Yellow Magic: The Story of Penicillin.* Obituaries and other sources: *American Authors and Books, 1640 to the Present Day,* 3rd revised edition, Crown, 1962; *New York Times,* October 25, 1973; *Who's Who in America,* 38th edition, Marquis, 1974.

*   *   *

RAU, Dhanvanthi Rama
See RAMA RAU, Dhanvanthi (Handoo)

RAYMOND, Joseph H.
    See Le FONTAINE, Joseph (Raymond)

*   *   *

RAYNOR, Dorka

PERSONAL: Born in Warsaw, Poland; daughter of Lazar (in real estate) and Salka (Lindner) Funt; married Severin Raynor (a professor); children: John. *Education:* Educated in Poland. *Politics:* Progressive. *Home and office:* 1063 Ash St., Winnetka, Ill. 60093.

CAREER: Photographer. Former owner of studios in Chicago, Ill., and Winnetka, Ill. Work is represented in permanent collections of the Chicago Art Institute and the Metropolitan Museum of Art (New York). *Member:* American Society of Magazine Photographers. *Awards, honors:* Photographs named best of the summer by *Le Figaro* (Paris), 1967, 1968, 1970, 1971.

WRITINGS—For children; photographs: *This Is My Father and Me,* Albert Whitman, 1973; *Grandparents Around the World,* edited by Caroline Rubin, Albert Whitman, 1977; *My Friends Live in Many Places,* edited by Kathleen Tucker, Albert Whitman, 1980.

Contributor of photographs to foreign language books.

WORK IN PROGRESS: A book on mothers of the world; a book on families of the world; a book tentatively titled *Life Is But a Dream,* including photographs "from cradle to grave around the world."

SIDELIGHTS: One of Dorka Raynor's books is *My Friends Live in Many Places,* and indeed hers do. In her extensive travels to collect photographs of people, Raynor has made friends in all corners of the world. "I like and have a great interest in people. Many of the people I have encountered on trips, for an hour or a moment," she told *CA,* "have remained my friends forever. We meet again."

An intense interest in the human condition directs Raynor's career and thus her travels. "The poignancy of the meaning of life has a profound effect on me. I try to express it in my photographs, and I seem to be reaching people this way." Raynor said she travels at least six months of every year. She has taken two trips around the world and has traveled in Europe and the Americas.

*   *   *

RAYSON, Steven 1932-

PERSONAL: Born in 1932. *Agent:* Sheila Watson, Bolt & Watson Ltd., 8-12 Old Queen St., Storey's Gate, London, SW1H 9HP, England.

CAREER: Physician in general practice, 1964—; author of historical fiction for young people.

WRITINGS: The Crows of War: A Novel of Maiden Castle (juvenile novel), Gollancz, 1974, Atheneum, 1975.*

*   *   *

READER, Dennis Joel 1939-

PERSONAL: Born September 4, 1939, in Santa Cruz, Calif.; son of Dale Ray (a farmer and investor) and Margaret (a bookkeeper; maiden name, Jacob) Reader; married Karen Theriot (a librarian), June 13, 1964; children: Nicole, Erica, Joel. *Education:* California State University, Fresno, B.A., 1962; California State University, San Francisco, M.A., 1967; Univer-

sity of California, San Diego, Ph.D., 1971. *Home:* 2045 Green Valley Rd., Watsonville, Calif. 95076. *Agent:* William Morris Agency, 1350 Avenue of the Americas, New York, N.Y. 10019.

CAREER: Elementary school teacher in Lafayette, Calif., 1963-67; Western Illinois University, Macomb, instructor, 1967-68, assistant professor, 1971-76, associate professor of English, 1976-79, director of Center for Regional Authors, 1974-79; writer, 1979—. *Military service:* U.S. Army, 1957-58.

WRITINGS: (Editor with John E. Hallwas) *The Vision of This Land: Studies of Vachel Lindsay, Edgar Lee Masters, and Carl Sandburg,* Western Illinois University Press, 1976; *Coming Back Alive* (novel), Random House, 1981. Contributor of poems and stories to literary magazines, including *Virginia Quarterly Review, Colorado Quarterly,* and *New Letters.* Associate editor of *Essays in Literature,* 1973-79; member of editorial board of *Western Illinois Regional Studies,* 1977-79.

WORK IN PROGRESS: A novel set in central California during the 1950's, publication expected in 1983; a sequel to this, carrying the story backward about ten years.

SIDELIGHTS: Reader told *CA:* "I often find myself reminded of Thoreau's little couplet with its sizable implication: 'My life has been the poem I would have writ, / But I could not both live and utter it.' What I envy is that Thoreau, it seems, did do both.

"My writing strategy, at the moment, is to put together what my training and taste tell me is an honest book, and then to hide it in the sheep's clothing of a commercial one."

AVOCATIONAL INTERESTS: "These include, besides predictable literary and musical ones, old machines that still work, such as pre-electric radios and vintage tractors and cars. There is a stubborn streak of the antiquarian in me. I also plant redwood trees (*Sequoia sempervirens*) on our ridgetop property as an apology to history (we live in a redwood house) and, of course, for their beauty, too."

*   *   *

RECTOR, Frank

PERSONAL—Residence: New York, N.Y. *Agent:* Scott Meredith Literary Agency, Inc., 845 Third Ave., New York, N.Y. 10022. *Education:* Attended Denver University, 1950-51, New York University, 1961-62, and University of South Florida, 1963-64.

CAREER: Guideposts (magazine), New York City, assistant editor, 1965-67; *Sales and Marketing Management* (magazine), New York City, copy editor, 1967-68; *Sword and Dagger* (trade newsletter for military dealers and collectors), New York City, production administrator, editor, and writer, 1968-69; *Sexology* (magazine), New York City, production administrator, editor, and writer, 1969-73; free-lance writer and editor for businesses, including Alexander Hamilton Institute, New York City, and Bill Communications, New York City, 1973-78; writer, 1978—. *Military service:* U.S. Army, 1951-54; served in Korea; became sergeant; received Korean Service Medal with three bronze service stars and National Defense Service Medal.

WRITINGS: (Editor) *How to Motivate Your Sales Force,* Alexander Hamilton Institute, 1977; *The Nazi Extermination of Homosexuals,* Stein & Day, 1981. Contributor to business journals.

WORK IN PROGRESS: A book about the Third Reich.

REDLICH, Frederick Carl 1910-

BRIEF ENTRY: Born June 2, 1910, in Vienna, Austria. American psychiatrist, educator, and author. Redlich began teaching at Yale University in 1942. He became a professor of psychiatry in 1950, was dean of the School of Medicine from 1967 to 1972, and served as director of the Behavioral Sciences Study Center from 1973 to 1977. Since then Redlich has been a professor of psychiatry and behavioral sciences at University of California, Los Angeles, and chief of staff at Brentwood Veterans Administration Hospital. His publications include *Psychotherapy With Schizophrenics* (International Universities Press, 1952), *Social Class and Mental Illness: A Community Study* (Wiley, 1958), *The Theory and Practice of Psychiatry* (Basic Books, 1966), and *Social Psychiatry* (Williams & Wilkins, 1969). *Address:* 1529 Bel Air Rd., Los Angeles, Calif. 90024; and Veterans Administration Medical Center, Brentwood, Wilshire and Sarvtelle Blvds., Los Angeles, Calif. 90073. *Biographical/critical sources: New York Times,* March 15, 1967; *American Men and Women of Science: The Physical and Biological Sciences,* 14th edition, Bowker, 1979.

*   *   *

REED, Don C(harles) 1945-

PERSONAL: Born August 19, 1945, in Berkeley, Calif.; son of Charles and Christine (Snyder) Reed; married wife, G. Jean, August 23, 1969; children: Desiree Don, Roman Jason Patrick. *Education:* Attended York College, 1967-69; Ohlone College, A.A., 1979; attended California State University, Hayward, 1980-81. *Politics:* "One-world democrat." *Residence:* Fremont, Calif. *Office:* Marine World/Africa USA, Redwood City, Calif. 94065.

CAREER: Strength and Health, York, Pa., assistant editor, 1967-69; Marine World/Africa U.S.A., Redwood City, Calif., diver, 1972—. *Military service:* U.S. Army, 1963-66.

WRITINGS: Notes From an Underwater Zoo, Dial, 1981. Author of "Darts 'n' Dashes," a column in *Fremont News Register,* 1971. Contributor to magazines, including *Oceans* and *Highlights for Children.*

WORK IN PROGRESS: A novel tentatively titled *Jeannie, Me, and the Giant People,* based on Reed's years in competitive weightlifting, for Dial; screenplays.

SIDELIGHTS: Reed told *CA:* "I want to help the world. I want to simplify giant issues and present them as entertainment: I wrote my first book to bring to readers my view on ocean farming, which is a way we can feed the world. If a fish normally lays ten thousand eggs, of which one or two survive to maturity, the fish population remains stable and the harvest from the sea cannot be increased. But if man steps in and protects the thousands of eggs, so that millions of fish can survive, we can exponentially increase the amount of food available to mankind. Marine protein concentrate (MPC) is an odorless, tasteless powder made from 'trash' fish, species generally considered useless. A pinch of this added to pancake flour can give a pancake the nutritional value of a steak—so why are we not developing it?

"I believe in Buckminster Fuller's one-world philosophy and his nonviolent approach to problem solving through improved technology. Fuller claims he can build a house, using his geodesic structure, for one per cent of the cost of a conventional home. Since nobody with an average income can now afford to buy a house, I think we ought to look into this man's ideas.

"I write each day at three o'clock in the morning and live for the day when I can write full time. I want my writing to be a positive force. I will not write empty entertainment. I want my stuff to have food value, like See's candy, which contains milk and eggs and nuts—not just chemical tongue stimulation. I am sick of all this trash that is thrown before the public. People want value, not just killing and endless reproductive fantasies.''

*   *   *

REED, John (Silas) 1887-1920

BRIEF ENTRY: Born October 22, 1887, near Portland, Ore.; died of typhus, October 19, 1920, in Moscow, U.S.S.R.; buried in the Kremlin, in Moscow, U.S.S.R. American journalist and author. Reed was known both for his radical political views and for the fine quality of his journalism. One of his first successful books was *Insurgent Mexico* (1914), based on his experiences with Mexican revolutionary leader, Pancho Villa. Later Reed was in Russia and witnessed the October Revolution of 1917, an event which became the subject of Reed's *Ten Days That Shook the World* (1919). The book is not considered to be a completely accurate document, but it is widely regarded as the finest eyewitness account of the Russian Revolution. Upon returning to the United States, Reed formed the Communist Labor party, in opposition to the Communist party, and escalated his radical activities. When charged with sedition, he fled to Moscow, where he remained until his death at age thirty-three. Though Reed's communist views did not include approval of dictatorial regimes such as that of V. I. Lenin, the flamboyant journalist maintained a friendship with the Russian leader. Reed was given a state funeral by the Bolshevik government. The 1981 motion picture "Reds" was based on Reed's life. *Biographical/critical sources: Twentieth Century Authors: A Biographical Dictionary of Modern Literature,* H. W. Wilson, 1942; *The McGraw-Hill Encyclopedia of World Biography,* McGraw, 1973.

*   *   *

REES, Alan M(axwell) 1929-

PERSONAL: Born May 14, 1929, in London, England; came to the United States in 1952, naturalized citizen, 1959; married June M. Litt (a psychiatrist), September 7, 1952; children: Carolyn, Penelope, Cynthia, Christopher. *Education:* University of London, B.A., 1950; Oxford University, M.Litt., 1952; graduate study at Ohio State University, 1952-55; Western Reserve University (now Case Western Reserve University), M.S. in L.S., 1957. *Home:* 2677 Derbyshire Rd., Cleveland Heights, Ohio 44106. *Office:* School of Library Science, Case Western Reserve University, Cleveland, Ohio 44106.

CAREER: Western Reserve University (now Case Western Reserve University), Cleveland, Ohio, library assistant, 1956-57, research associate in documentation and communication research, 1957-60, assistant director of research, 1964—, assistant professor, 1963-68, associate professor, 1968-71, professor of library science, 1971—, associate dean of School of Library Science, 1972-75. Lecturer at University of Melbourne, 1969. Project manager for American Society for Metals Documentation Service, 1960-62; consultant to National Library of Medicine, U.S. Department of the Army, and U.S. Department of the Navy. Director of Infohealth Project of the consumer health information services of the State Library of Ohio. *Member:* Medical Library Association. *Awards, honors:* Fulbright grant, 1952-55; grants from State Library of Ohio and National Library of Medicine, both 1980-82; *Directory of Health Sciences Libraries in the United States: 1979* was named outstanding reference book by *Choice* and outstanding reference source by *Library Journal* and American Library Association.

WRITINGS: (With Susan Crawford) *Directory of Health Sciences Libraries in the United States: 1979,* Medical Library Association, 1980; (with Blanche A. Young) *The Consumer Health Information Source Book,* Bowker, 1981; (editor) *Developing Consumer Health Information Services,* Bowker, 1982. General editor of *Consumer Health Information Service,* a microform publication of Microfilm Inc. of America.

WORK IN PROGRESS: The Money Management Information Book, publication expected in 1983.

SIDELIGHTS: Rees told *CA:* "My prime focus is on the information needs of consumers in terms of survival and coping information."

*   *   *

REESE, Thomas J(oseph) 1945-

PERSONAL: Born January 11, 1945, in Altadena, Calif.; son of James Bernard (a lawyer) and Gwendolyn M. (a teacher; maiden name, McNeal) Reese. *Education:* St. Louis University, B.A. and M.A., both 1968; Jesuit School of Theology, M.Div., 1974; University of California, Berkeley, Ph.D., 1976. *Home and office: America,* 106 West 56th St., New York, N.Y. 10019.

CAREER: Entered Society of Jesus (Jesuits; S.J.), 1962, ordained Roman Catholic priest, 1974; University of San Francisco, San Francisco, Calif., instructor in political science, 1969; University of Santa Clara, Santa Clara, Calif., assistant to president, 1970-71; Taxation With Representation, Washington, D.C., legislative director, 1975-78; *America,* New York, N.Y., associate editor, 1978—.

WRITINGS: The Politics of Taxation, Greenwood Press, 1980. Reporter for *Tax Notes,* 1975-78.

WORK IN PROGRESS: Research on American politics, and on the decision-making process in the Roman Catholic church.

SIDELIGHTS: Reese told *CA:* "Although the politics of the budgetary process has been given a great deal of attention by political scientists, the politics surrounding the tax-making process has received little attention. It is a difficult area of research because of the complexity of the economic and legal issues, which the writer must have some familiarity with before tackling the political issues. In addition, social scientists are missing an unusual opportunity to examine the Roman Catholic Church—the longest-lived complex organization in history— at a period when it is undergoing radical institutional change. The church and taxes are two wide-open fields ready for any writer foolish enough to go where angels fear to tread."

*   *   *

REGAN, Donald Thomas 1918-

BRIEF ENTRY: Born December 21, 1918, in Cambridge, Mass. American securities executive, cabinet member, and author. Regan joined the investment firm that is now Merrill Lynch, Pierce, Fenner & Smith, Inc., in 1946 and became a partner in 1953. He was president of the company from 1968 to 1971 and chairman of the board of directors from 1971 to 1980. He has been chairman of the board of directors of Merrill Lynch since 1973. Regan served for several years as director of the Securities Investor Protection Corp. and vice-chairman of the board of directors of the New York Stock Exchange. He be-

came a trustee of the Committee for Economic Development in 1978. In 1981 President Reagan appointed him secretary of the Department of the Treasury. Regan wrote *A View From the Street* (New American Library, 1972) and *Utilitarianism and Cooperation* (Oxford University Press, 1980). *Address:* 1 Liberty Plaza, 165 Broadway, New York, N.Y. 10006. *Biographical/critical sources: Who's Who in Finance and Industry,* 22nd edition, Marquis, 1981.

*   *   *

REID, Hilda (Stewart) 1898-1982

OBITUARY NOTICE: Born in 1898; died April 24, 1982. Author of novels, including *Phillida: or, The Reluctant Adventurer, Emily,* and *Ashley Hamel.* Reid also co-edited *Pavements at Anderby,* a collection of Winifred Holtby's works. Obituaries and other sources: *London Times,* May 11, 1982.

*   *   *

REISS, John J.

PERSONAL: Born in Milwaukee, Wis. *Education:* Received degree from a teachers college in Milwaukee, Wis.; graduate study at Black Mountain College, N.C. *Address:* c/o Bradbury Press, 2 Overhill Rd., Scarsdale, N.Y. 10583.

CAREER: Writer, artist, designer, and illustrator. *Awards, honors:* Co-recipient of the Milwaukee Art Directors Club gold medal, 1967; *Shapes* was named a notable book by the American Library Association.

WRITINGS—Juveniles; self-illustrated: *Colors,* Bradbury, 1969; *Numbers,* Bradbury, 1971; (illustrator only) Jane Jonas Srivastava, *Statistics,* Crowell, 1973; *Shapes,* Bradbury 1974.

SIDELIGHTS: Reiss is widely recognized for his advertising art. Examples of his graphic art and designs have been exhibited through *Graphis* magazine in Europe, Africa, and Asia.

Reiss's books for children have been greeted with enthusiasm. A *Publishers Weekly* writer praised *Numbers,* commenting that by "using the same vibrant colors and simplicity of design that made his *Colors* such a successful color identification book, John Reiss has now created an equally dazzling counting and number recognition book." *Shapes* also received a favorable review. A critic for the *Center for Children's Books Bulletin* proclaimed: "Absolutely luscious in its spectrum of vivid colors, this is one of the most attractive of the several books that present to young children examples of such shapes as oval, circle, triangle, rectangle, and square. Reiss carries it a bit farther, showing how squares form a cube, or circles a sphere, and he tosses in a few more complex shapes at the close of the book to intrigue the audience: a hexagon, an octagon, a pentagon."

BIOGRAPHICAL/CRITICAL SOURCES: Publishers Weekly, December 6, 1971; *Center for Children's Books Bulletin,* December, 1974.

*   *   *

REMY, Pierre-Jean
See ANGREMY, Jean-Pierre

*   *   *

RHODE, Irma 1900-1982

OBITUARY NOTICE: Born in 1900 in Berlin, Germany (now East Germany); died February 15, 1982. Food expert and author of cookbooks. Rhode and her brother, Bill Rhode, joined gourmet James Beard in establishing a successful catering business during the 1930's. Rhode and Beard also founded a cooking school in the 1950's. Her books include *The Viennese Cookbook, Cookbook for Fridays and Lent,* and *Cool Entertaining.* Rhode also collaborated with her brother on *Of Cabbages and Kings.* Obituaries and other sources: *New York Times,* February 17, 1982.

* * *

RICE, Edmund C. 1910(?)-1982

OBITUARY NOTICE: Born c. 1910; died of cancer, March 28, 1982. Producer and author of radio and television programs. Rice wrote radio scripts for "The Chase and Sanborn Hour," "The Kraft Music Hall," and "Shell Chateau," among others. He moved to television as the head writer of "The Kraft Television Theatre," a post he held for eleven years. Obituaries and other sources: *New York Times,* March 30, 1982.

* * *

RICHARD, Betty Byrd 1922-

PERSONAL: Born August 30, 1922, in Charleston, W.Va.; daughter of Ernest O'Farrell and Blanche Elizabeth (Davenport); married Samuel J. Richard, Jr. (in business), June 12, 1943; children: Caroline Richard Rossman, Samuel J. III. *Education:* University of Charleston, B.A., 1977. *Religion:* Protestant. *Home:* 321 Mountain View Dr., Charleston, W.Va. 25314. *Agent:* Julian Bach Literary Agency, 747 Third Ave., New York, N.Y. 10017. *Office:* West Virginia Commission on Aging, State Capitol, Charleston, W.Va. 25305.

CAREER: Lawrence Frankel Foundation, associate administrator, 1970-79; holds "gerokinetics" workshops throughout the United States. Lecturer and panelist at the Institute on Man and Science, 1973, Pennsylvania State University, 1978, University of Pittsburgh, 1978, and National Council on Aging, 1979. Consultant for the state of West Virginia, 1979—.

WRITINGS: Age and Mobility: Exercises for the Homebound and Chairbound, Preventicare Publications, 1977; (contributor) Raymond Harris and Lawrence J. Frankel, editors, *Guide to Fitness After Fifty,* Plenum, 1977; (with Frankel) *Be Alive as Long as You Live: The Older Person's Complete Guide to Exercise for Joyful Living,* Lippincott, 1980. Contributor of articles on geriatric fitness to *Modern Maturity, Prevention,* and *Nursing.*

SIDELIGHTS: Richard told *CA:* "There is no cure for aging, but there is a way to slow it down. Though medical care plays an important part, the single biggest influence that inhibits the aging process is regular exercise. There are nearly twenty-five million elderly Americans, many living in senior citizens housing centers and nursing homes, drifting into obsolescence. We must initiate a mass crusade toward mass motivation involving the principles of preventive health care if we are to inhibit the gradual, insidious physical and mental problems associated with aging.

"Gerokinetics is a word which I coined to denote a program of low mobility exercises to prevent and/or manage the physical problems associated with aging. These exercises are designed to strengthen and tone muscles, improve joint flexibility, stimulate circulation and prevent bone deterioration. The program is based upon the Preventicare concept which is outlined in detail in *Be Alive as Long as You Live.*"

BIOGRAPHICAL/CRITICAL SOURCES: Los Angeles Times, November 13, 1980.

RICHARD, John 1954-

PERSONAL: Born February 16, 1954, in Binghamton, N.Y. *Education:* Attended State University of New York at Binghamton, 1976. *Office:* New York Public Interest Research Group, 5 Beekman St., New York, N.Y. 10038.

CAREER: Associated with New York Public Interest Research Group in New York, N.Y.

WRITINGS: (With Ralph Nader and Ron Brownstein) *Who's Poisoning America?,* Sierra Books, 1981.

* * *

RICHARDSON, Dorothy Lee 1900-

PERSONAL: Born August 13, 1900, in Philadelphia, Pa.; daughter of Francis Herbert (a teacher) and Helen (Stavers) Lee; married Arthur H. Richardson (an Episcopal missionary), June 2, 1930 (deceased); children: Francis Lee, Jonathan Lynde, Sarah Appleton Richardson Allan. *Education:* Attended University of Pennsylvania, 1928, Harvard University, 1968-69, and Radcliffe College, 1971-72, 1973-74. *Politics:* "Not committed." *Religion:* Episcopal. *Home and office:* 1437 A Manor House Lane, Lancaster, Pa. 17603.

CAREER: Physician's secretary in Philadelphia, Pa., 1923-28; writer. Staff member of Cape Cod Writers Conference, 1965, and Harvard University's Polyarts Conference, 1974; judge at poetry contests; gives readings at colleges and on public television programs. *Member:* Poetry Society of America (member of board of directors, 1971-73, 1974-75), Academy of American Poets, New England Poetry Club, Pennsylvania Poetry Society, Poetry Society of Massachusetts. *Awards, honors:* Alabama State Poetry Society award, 1971; Clement Hoyt Ballad Award from Texas Poetry Society, 1972; Evans Spencer Wall Memorial Award from National Federation of State Poetry Societies, 1973; Joseph Martin Long Award from Texas Poetry Society, 1973. Also received awards from *Lyric,* Massachusetts Poetry Society, New England Poetry Club, and New York Forum.

WRITINGS: Signs at My Finger-Ends, American Weave Press, 1961; *The Half-Seen Face,* William L. Bauhan, 1979. Contributor of poems to magazines, including *American Scholar, Atlantic Monthly, American Mercury, Christian Century, Saturday Review,* and *Yankee,* and newspapers.

WORK IN PROGRESS: The Invisible Chant, poems; an autobiographical account of her years in the Philippines, 1930-35.

SIDELIGHTS: Dorothy Richardson commented: "At the age of twenty-nine, I married a missionary to the wild tribes of the Philippines, including the Tinguian tribe. Except for the war years, I lived in the Philippines from 1930 to 1960. I also visited Europe and Asia and was in Africa with an ecological expedition."

BIOGRAPHICAL/CRITICAL SOURCES: Lancaster Intelligencer Journal, February 1, 1980; *Quincy Herald Whig,* October 14, 1980.

* * *

RICHELSON, Geraldine 1922-
(Ed Leander)

PERSONAL: Born August 20, 1922, in New York, N.Y.;

daughter of Michael (a lawyer) and Frieda (Wolf) Popper; married Sigmund Richelson, July 10, 1943 (died, July 25, 1961); children: Andrew, Eric. *Education:* Hunter College, B.A., 1943. *Home:* 205 West End Ave., New York, N.Y. 10023. *Agent:* Carol Mann Literary Agency, 168 Pacific St., Brooklyn, N.Y. 11201.

CAREER: Advertising creative director.

WRITINGS—All for children, except as noted: *What Is a Child?*, illustrations by John E. Johnson, Quist, 1966; *What Is a Grownup?*, illustrations by Johnson, Quist, 1967; *From Bad to Worse*, illustrations by Claude Lapoint, Quist, 1973; *What Is a Baby?*, illustrations by Johnson, Quist, 1973; (under pseudonym Ed Leander), *Here's Looking at You!*, illustrations by Monique Gaudriault and others, Dial, 1973; *The Good of It All*, illustrations by Lapointe, Quist, 1975; (under Leander pseudonym) *What's the Big Idea?*, Quist, 1975; *Q Is for Crazy*, illustrations by Josef Sumichrast, Quist, 1977; *Come Out, Come Out, Whoever You Are!*, Quist, 1980; (with Herbert J. Freudenberger), *Burn Out: The High Cost of High Achievement* (adult nonfiction), Anchor Press, 1980.

Adaptations: (Under Leander pseudonym) *Crazy Days* (adapted from a French verse by Alain Diot), illustrations by Keleck, Quist, 1975; *The Piano Man* (adapted from a French fantasy by Diot), illustrations by Henri Galeron, Quist, 1975; *The Star Wars Story Book* (adapted from the film "Star Wars" by George Lucas), Random House, 1978.

*   *   *

RICHMOND, John C(hristopher) B(lake)   1909-

BRIEF ENTRY: Born September 7, 1909, in Hitcham, England. British diplomat and author. Richmond joined England's Foreign Service in 1947, later serving as ambassador to Kuwait from 1961 to 1963, and Sudan from 1965 to 1966. He taught modern Near East history at the University of Durham from 1966 to 1974. He wrote *Egypt, 1798-1952: Her Advance Toward Modern Identity* (Columbia University Press, 1977). *Address:* 20 The Avenue, Durham, England. *Biographical/critical sources: The International Who's Who*, Europa, 1981.

*   *   *

RICKARD, Bob
See RICKARD, Robert J(ohn) M(oberley)

*   *   *

RICKARD, Robert J(ohn) M(oberley)   1945-
(Bob Rickard)

PERSONAL: Born February 17, 1945, in Deolali, India; son of Robert Moberley (a clerk) and Rita Mary (a secretary; maiden name, Cowell) Rickard; married Swee-Lan Sam (a nurse), February 16, 1978; children: Jonathan. *Education:* Birmingham College of Art and Design, M.A., 1966, Higher Diploma in Design, 1968. *Politics:* "I have political feelings but wish no affiliation to parties." *Religion:* "I have religious feelings but wish no affiliation to churches." *Home:* 483 Barking Rd., London E6 2LN, England. *Office: Fortean Times*, BM-Fortean Times, London WC1N 3XX, England.

CAREER: Willey-Rickard Design (industrial designers), Birmingham, England, product designer, director, 1968-76; Fastness Ltd. (housing designers), and Tayelm, Ltd. (design developers), Birmingham, product designer, director, 1970-76; *Fortean Times* (quarterly journal of strange phenomena), Lon-

don, founder, editor, 1973—. *Member:* Society of Authors, London Library, Friends of the National Libraries.

WRITINGS: (With John F. Mitchell) *Phenomena: A Book of Wonders*, Pantheon, 1977; (under name Bob Rickard) *UFOs*, Gloucester Press, 1979; (with Richard Kelly) *Photographs of the Unknown*, New English Library, 1980; *Living Wonders: Mysteries and Curiosities of the Natural World*, Thames & Hudson, 1982.

WORK IN PROGRESS: An Encyclopedia of Visions and Apparitions, completion expected in 1983; *Visions and Contemporary Shamanism*, completion expected in 1984; editing an illustrated edition of *The Books of Charles Fort*, completion expected in 1985.

SIDELIGHTS: Rickard told *CA:* "I am working towards a knowledge, if not an understanding of the human experience of 'reality' and its phenomena. This necessitates developing a nonexclusive, interdisciplinary science and a spirit of untrammeled inquiry and eclectic philosophy." He added, "The main influences on my career are C. G. Jung, Charles Fort, Chuang Tzu, and W. C. Fields."

BIOGRAPHICAL/CRITICAL SOURCES: Time Out, August 24-30, 1979; *Fate*, May, 1979; *New Musical Express*, October 25, 1980.

*   *   *

RICKWORD, (John) Edgell   1898-1982
(John Mavin, a joint pseudonym)

OBITUARY NOTICE—See index for *CA* sketch: Born October 22, 1898, in Colchester, Essex, England; died March 15, 1982. Poet, editor, critic, and author. Rickword began his career as a poet in 1921 with the publication of *Between the Eyes*, a collection of verse. A second volume of poetry, *Invocations to Angels and the Happy New Year*, followed in 1928, and the satiric verse of *Twittingpan and Some Others* was published three years after that. A reviewer of English and French literature, Rickword contributed to the English reading public's appreciation of French writer Arthur Rimbaud with *Rimbaud: The Boy and the Poet*, written in the interim between his poetry collections. The author wrote numerous short stories as well as translated the works of Francoise Porche, Marcel Coulon, and Ronald Firbank. Rickword also served as the editor of the *Left Review* and *Our Time*. In addition to an Arts Council prize and an honorary degree from Essex University, he received the Military Cross for his service with the Royal Berkshire Regiment. Rickword's writings include *Milton: The Revolutionary Intellectual, Collected Poems, William Wordsworth, 1770-1850, Essays and Opinions, 1921-31*, and *Further Studies in a Dying Culture*. Obituaries and other sources: *London Times*, March 16, 1982.

*   *   *

RIDGEWAY, James Fowler   1936-

PERSONAL: Born November 1, 1936, in Auburn, N.Y.; son of George L. and Florence (Fowler) Ridgeway; married Patricia Carol Dodge, November, 1966; children: David Andrew. *Education:* Princeton University, A.B., 1959. *Home:* 3103 Macomb St. N.W., Washington, D.C. 20008. *Office:* c/o *Village Voice*, 842 Broadway, New York, N.Y. 10003.

CAREER: Journalist. Junior reporter in New York office of *Wall Street Journal; New Republic*, Washington, D.C., associate editor, 1962-68; *Hard Times*, Washington, D.C., founder and editor, 1968-70; *Ramparts*, Berkeley, Calif., associate editor, 1970-75; *Village Voice,* New York City, staff writer and political columnist, 1974—, notable assignments include coverage of 1980 presidential election. Founder of *Mayday.* Associate fellow at Institute for Policy Studies, 1973-77. Member of Public Resource Center, 1977—. *Military service:* Army National Guard, 1959.

WRITINGS: The Closed Corporation: American Universities in Crisis, Random House, 1968; *The Politics of Ecology,* Dutton, 1970; (with Andrew Kopkin) *Decade of Crisis: America in the Sixties,* World Publishing, 1972; *The Last Play: The Struggle to Monopolize the World's Energy Resources,* Dutton, 1973; (with Bettina Connor) *New Energy: Understanding the Crisis and a Guide to an Alternative Energy System,* Beacon Press, 1975; (with Alexander Cockburn) *Smoke: Another Jimmy Carter Adventure* (novel), Time Books, 1978; (with Cockburn) *Political Ecology: An Activist's Reader on Energy, Land, Food, Technology, Health, and the Economics and Politics of Social Change* (anthology), Time Books, 1979; (with Carol S. Projansky) *Energy-Efficient Community Planning: A Guide to Saving Energy and Producing Power at the Local Level,* JG Press, 1979; *Who Owns the Earth?,* Macmillan, 1980. Author, with Cockburn, of column "The Moving Target" in *Village Voice.* Writer for Pacific News Service. Contributor of articles on 1980 presidential election to *Rolling Stone;* also contributor to *Parade* and *Economist.* Contributing editor of *New Republic,* 1968-70. Editor of *The Elements,* 1974—.

WORK IN PROGRESS: A long anthology on energy, edited by Thom Englehardt, publication by Pantheon expected in 1982; a book on the public domain of the United States, edited by Elisabeth Scharlatt, publication by Ticknor & Fields expected in 1983; a second volume of *Energy-Efficient Community Planning,* publication expected in 1983.

SIDELIGHTS: Once called "a radical leftist intellectual," James Ridgeway is an investigative journalist who wants to "take a point of view that is unreported and provide people with that different perspective." In short, he is, said an aide of the Federal Power Commission, "a responsible muckraker."

Gathering his information from industry and from reading rather than interviewing, Ridgeway began exposing irregularities in education, industry, and especially the government while gaining prominence as an investigative reporter for the *New Republic.* Two of his earliest successes as a muckraker came at this time. One of Ridgeway's articles on water pollution resulted in the creation of the Water Pollution Control Administration in 1965, and because of his exposes on deceptive practices in the tire industry the Senate Commerce Committee considered the journalist an expert adviser on the matter. In addition, during the 1960's Ridgeway began writing about the ramifications of the energy crisis which emerged in 1973 as a major issue in American society.

While enjoying success at the *New Republic,* Ridgeway launched his own vehicle for criticizing industry and the government, the newsletter *Hard Times,* in 1968. "As a rule," he told *Time* magazine, "these guys [in Washington] don't like to argue. Everyone in Washington takes himself so seriously. They're all very pompous. I try not to take myself too seriously, but I am trying to engage people in arguments about our civilization."

One of the first major arguments that Ridgeway brought to the public's attention concerned institutions of higher learning. In *The Closed Corporation: American Universities in Crisis,* Ridgeway explained that "the idea that the university is a community of scholars is a myth. . . . The university has in large part been reduced to serving as banker-broker for the professors' outside interests. The charming elitism of the professors has long since given way to the greed of the social and political scientists whose manipulative theories aim only at political power."

The crux of the matter, in Ridgeway's opinion, is that universities absorb tax dollars but are not accountable to taxpayers while professors are more interested in outside business ventures than in teaching. According to the journalist, universities have become industries pursuing wealth by acting as research and testing centers subservient to external forces such as federal and local governments and corporations. In Ridgeway's eyes, universities evolved into military and industrial establishments instead of educational institutions. Or, as James H. Bellington of *Life* noted: Ridgeway "sees the university as an arrogant, secret corporation, over-occupied with the concerns of industry and government and largely indifferent to its own students and its poor neighbors."

Financial dependence on the government transformed communities of education into industrial testing grounds, even defense laboratories. When Ridgeway wrote *The Closed Corporation* in 1968, universities were involved in various areas of governmental research as well as in enterprises of "wheeling and dealing," including the development of weapons for use in Vietnam, real estate investments, lobbying, the auto industry, drug prices, espionage, cigarette filters, and poisons. For example, Ridgeway found that Johns Hopkins University and the Massachusetts Instititute of Technology (MIT) designed missiles and that Cornell developed bombs. The University of Michigan was involved in photo reconnaissance operations while Princeton was working on codes for the Central Intelligence Agency.

Professors, on the other hand, are criticized by Ridgeway for using public funds for self-aggrandizement. Looking at the relationship of professors to the rest of society, the author sees that they are entrepreneurs, innovators, lobbyists, and propagandists—businessmen amassing wealth and power at the expense of their teaching careers. According to Ridgeway, professors have become preoccupied with making money through research and consulting jobs, and they, like trustees of universities, "are involved in conflicts of interest between their business and university commitments," observed a critic in the *New York Review of Books.* They are, commented a *Playboy* reviewer, "a community of moneygrubbing, power-grabbing professors who, with big business and Big Government, preside over the national destiny."

As solutions, Ridgeway suggests public scrutiny and "democratizing academic power." Since universities are public institutions which receive public funds and tax exemptions, he feels they should be accountable to and examined by the general public. Ridgeway calls for open universities regenerated through social services. He asks that students and teachers have more control over universities and that trustees be selected through a more democratic process.

For *The Closed Corporation,* Ridgeway received acclaim as a "first-rate muckraker" and a "first-rate journalist." A *Village Voice* reviewer noted that the book "is a useful expose, full of juicy scandals and outrageous incidents, of the near-total subjection of the university to the exigencies of the CIA, the Defense Department, the federal bureaucracy, and the chemical, electronics, computors [sic], and other industries. A muckraking work, *a la* Vance Packard and Fred Cook, it aims at 'arousing public indignation' by presenting the workings of a new and vital capitalist industry as if it were a sex-scandal."

Agreeing, John William Ward of *New York* said: "James Ridgeway's *The Closed Corporation: American Universities in Crisis* is, for the historian of American culture, an intensely valuable book, a palimpsest of styles congenial to the appalled American innocent. Its outraged voice is an echo of Mark Twain, less the capacity for sardonic humor; its stolid march of fact, fact, fact, Dreiser at his plodding best; its blunt directness, the moral certitude of the muckraker. But most of all, there is the apocalyptic vision of utter depravity which sees a world of black and white.''

Moving from universities, Ridgeway investigates the economic causes and cures of pollution in *The Politics of Ecology*. In this work, he reveals the adverse effects of water pollution, of certain environmental policies, and of petroleum trusts. Since World War II, technology and industry have been committing ''ecocide,'' the destruction of natural resources. Ridgeway illustrates how important it is for private enterprises to be ecologically safe and responsible.

Industry is the largest polluter, says Ridgeway, though it escapes any punishment because politicians and tax laws provide no sanctions. In fact, they encourage polluters. For instance, petroleum companies exploit natural resources, but enjoy tax breaks and political influence. ''''The Politics of Ecology,''' remarked John Leonard of the *New York Times*, ''sets out to prove that the principal polluters of our environment—the industrial burners of coal, gas and oil—have taken over the ecology movement in order to control our natural resources and dominate 'the world energy markets.''''

With *The Politics of Ecology*, Ridgeway also proves that environmental concerns serve as public relations issues for politicians, but they are not of genuine interest to officials. ''*The Politics of Ecology*,'' wrote Henry Beetle Hough of the *American Scholar*, ''gives a history of political shenanigans—evasions, failures and high-sounding legislation tapering off in dilution or obstruction.'' Yet, according to Ridgeway, only strict government regulation of fuel and mining resources can control pollution. For as Hough observed, ''Business is unlikely to forego profits merely on a showing of planetary peril.''

Applauded by critics, *The Politics of Ecology* was named ''a fine, tough and indispensible book'' by Leonard. And Bryce Nelson of the *New York Times Book Review* praised Ridgeway for being ''a journalist so earnest and straightforward that he can make a lengthy explanation of sewage interesting.''

Like *The Politics of Ecology*, *The Last Play* and *Who Owns the Earth?* deal with resources. The latter discussed the development of energy from renewable sources. It is a survey of basic materials, resources, and foreign markets surrounding Americans. *The Last Play*, however, concentrates on pork barreling in the oil industry. Ridgeway cites oil cartels, such as Gulf, Mobil, Shell, and Texaco, for monopolizing energy sources. ''The energy companies,'' he revealed, ''plan to exhaust one fossil fuel after another, assuring the highest possible profits as fuels grow scarcer.'' Again, government agencies, Ridgeway claimed, sympathize with the oil companies rather than the consumer.

In order to check the cartel of oil companies, Ridgeway suggests instituting a national energy commission as well as independent government agencies. After reading *The Last Play*, James P. Degnan of the *Hudson Review* stated: ''I am sure, however, . . . that new and drastic plans, quickly implemented, are necessary if we are to achieve anything resembling a sane control and use of the energy sources that remain and the new ones that may be developed.''

Less drastic, though just as effective, methods of energy conservation are given in *Energy-Efficient Community Planning*. This book is a guide for concerned citizens and city planners

looking for ways to make their communities fuel efficient. Besides agricultural experiments or housing and water conservation projects, Ridgeway presents less extravagant endeavors like the city council of Davis, California, allowing the use of clotheslines, to reduce its population's fuel consumption. *Choice* called this work an ''innovative book by an expert in the field of energy.''

Since 1974 Ridgeway has edited a periodical, *The Elements*. ''The purpose and function of *The Elements*,'' Ridgeway once wrote, ''. . . [is to] explore the factors that influence, use and control the world's resources.'' Nineteen seventy-four also marks the year when Ridgeway began writing political columns in conjunction with Alexander Cockburn for the *Village Voice*. One of their more notable series of columns analyzed the issues and happenings of the 1980 presidential election from the pre-convention activities to the days following President Reagan's inauguration.

BIOGRAPHICAL/CRITICAL SOURCES: Time, January 28, 1966; *New York Times,* October 11, 1968, December 16, 1968, October 20, 1970; *Saturday Review,* October 19, 1968; *New York Times Book Review,* October 20, 1968, September 14, 1969, June 8, 1970; April 25, 1971, February 25, 1973; *Atlantic,* November, 1968; *Village Voice,* November 7, 1968; *Life,* November 8, 1968, November 20, 1970; *Best Sellers,* November 15, 1968; *Playboy,* December, 1968; *Christian Science Monitor,* December 26, 1968, January 16, 1971; *Progressive,* January, 1969; *New York Review of Books,* January 30, 1969; *Commonweal,* January 31, 1969, August 10, 1973; *Washington Post Book World,* February 2, 1969, October 25, 1970, February 11, 1973, February 24, 1974; *New York,* February 3, 1969; *Science,* February 14, 1969, December 18, 1970; *Journal of Higher Education,* April, 1969; *Bulletin of the Atomic Scientists,* April, 1969; *Christian Century,* April 16, 1969, October 28, 1970; *Ramparts,* May, 1969; *American Sociological Review,* October, 1969.

Social Education, January, 1970; *Quarterly Journal of Speech,* April, 1970; *Nation,* November 30, 1970; *Science Books and Films,* December, 1970, May, 1973, March, 1981; *American Libraries,* January, 1971; *American Forest,* February, 1971; *Natural History,* February, 1971; *Choice,* February, 1971, December, 1973, March, 1976, June, 1980; *America,* February 27, 1971, May 22, 1971; *Living Wilderness,* autumn, 1971, autumn, 1973; *New Republic,* February 10, 1973; *Hudson Review,* autumn, 1973; *American Scholar,* winter, 1973-74; James H. Dygert, *The Investigative Journalist,* Prentice-Hall, 1976; *The Elements,* June, 1977.

—*Sketch by Charity Anne Dorgan*

*   *   *

RILEY, Glenda 1938-

PERSONAL: Born September 6, 1938, in Cleveland, Ohio; daughter of George F. (a railroad employee) and Lillian (Knafels) Gates; children: Sean. *Education:* Case Western Reserve University, B.A., 1960; Miami University, Oxford, Ohio, M.A., 1963; Ohio State University, Ph.D., 1967. *Home:* 718 Orchard Dr., Cedar Falls, Iowa 50613. *Office:* Department of History, University of Northern Iowa, Cedar Falls, Iowa 50613.

CAREER: Teacher at public schools in Westlake, Ohio, 1960-62; Denison University, Granville, Ohio, instructor in history, 1967-68; Ohio State University, Columbus, visiting assistant professor of history, 1968-69; University of Northern Iowa, Cedar Falls, 1969-77, began as assistant professor, became associate professor, professor of history, 1977—. Member of National Records Advisory Board, 1976-79. *Member:* American Historical Association, Organization of American Historians, Society for Historians of the Early American Republic, American Association for State and Local History, Coordinating Commission on Women in the Historical Profession, Conference Group in Women's History, National Organization for Women, National Women's Studies Association, National Council on Public History, Western History Association, Women Historians of the Midwest.

WRITINGS: Frontierswomen: Iowa as a Test Case, 1830-1870, Iowa State University Press, 1981. Contributor to scholarly journals.

WORK IN PROGRESS: Beyond Myth and Media: Women's Views of Indians in the Trans-Mississippi West.

SIDELIGHTS: Glenda Riley told *CA:* "*Frontierswomen* grew out of my work in women's and Iowa history. Since I have long been active in the feminist movement as well as the women's studies program at the University of Northern Iowa, I was concerned about the dearth of materials regarding frontierswomen. During the past five years, my own personal crusade has been to remedy that lack."

AVOCATIONAL INTERESTS: Travel, jogging, reading in human relations, nutrition, and folk medicine.

*   *   *

RIORDAN, Mary Marguerite 1931-

PERSONAL: Surname is pronounced *Rear*-dan; born September 13, 1931, in Bakersfield, Calif.; daughter of John Jeremiah and Genevieve (McNulty) Riordan. *Education:* San Francisco College for Women (now Lone Mountain College), A.B., 1953; University of San Francisco, General Secondary Credential, 1955; California State University, San Francisco, M.A., 1961. *Politics:* Democrat. *Religion:* Roman Catholic. *Home:* 215 Corbett, Apt. 2, San Francisco, Calif. 94114. *Office:* City College of San Francisco, 50 Phelan Ave., San Francisco, Calif. 94112.

CAREER: High school teacher of English, economics, and history in San Francisco, Calif., 1953-63, counselor, 1959-63; teacher of English at City College of San Francisco, San Francisco, 1963—. Summer workshop instructor at Emmanuel College, Boston, Mass., 1977-81; member of board of trustees of Presentation High School, 1981—.

MEMBER: Modern Language Association of America, American Association of University Women, American Federation of Teachers, Asian Society, Hopkins Society, National Society for Preservation and Trust, Council for Civic Unity, Irish-American Cultural Institute, California Association of Teachers of English, California Classical Association, Heritage Society of San Francisco, Teachers Association of San Francisco, Faculty Association of City College of San Francisco, Lone Mountain Alumni Council, de Young Museum Society, John Hay Fellows Alumni, Common Cause. *Awards, honors:* National Endowment for the Humanities fellowship.

WRITINGS: Lillian Hellman: A Bibliography, 1926-1978, Scarecrow, 1980. Contributor of articles and reviews to education journals and *Choice.*

WORK IN PROGRESS: Editing letters of Gertrude Atherton.

SIDELIGHTS: Mary Riordan told *CA:* "When I began the Hellman bibliography, I hoped to have her cooperation. It struck me as odd that someone had not already compiled such a work for an artist of Hellman's stature."

RIORDAN, Michael 1946-

PERSONAL: Born December 3, 1946, in Springfield, Mass.; son of Edward John (a postal clerk) and Evelyn (a secretary; maiden name, Hnizdo) Riordan; married Linda Michelle Goodman (an artist), April 8, 1979. *Education:* Massachusetts Institute of Technology, S.B., 1968, Ph.D., 1973. *Home address:* P.O. Box 130, La Honda, Calif. 94020. *Office:* Cheshire Books, 514 Bryant St., Palo Alto, Calif. 94301.

CAREER: Massachusetts Institute of Technology, Cambridge, postdoctoral research associate in physics, 1973-75; Cheshire Books, Palo Alto, Calif., editor and publisher, 1976—. Instructor at Cabrillo College, 1978-80. *Member:* International Solar Energy Society, American Association for the advancement of Science, Northern California Solar Energy Association (member of board of directors, 1980-81; vice-president, 1982), Sigma Xi.

WRITINGS: (With Bruce Anderson) *The Solar Home Book,* Brick House, 1976; (editor with Tom Gage and Richard Merrill) *Energy Primer,* Delta Books, 1978; (editor) *No Winners: The Effects of Nuclear War,* Cheshire, 1982. Contributor to *Technology Review.*

WORK IN PROGRESS: The Hunting of the Quark, an illustrated history; research for a series of illustrated science books for a general audience.

SIDELIGHTS: Riordan commented: "From my experience in high-energy physics, I have derived an intense interest in bringing the discoveries of modern science and technology to an educated lay audience. I am particularly concerned that the philosophical underpinnings and assumptions behind modern science be made explicit in my works."

*   *   *

RITCHIE, Donald Arthur 1945-

BRIEF ENTRY: Born December 23, 1945, in New York, N.Y. American historian and author. Ritchie has been associate historian at the U.S. Senate Historical Office since 1976. He wrote *James M. Landis: Dean of the Regulators* (Harvard University Press, 1980). *Address:* Office of the Secretary, U.S. Senate Historical Office, Washington, D.C. 20510. *Biographical/critical sources: Directory of American Scholars,* Volume I: *History,* 7th edition, Bowker, 1978.

*   *   *

RIZZUTO, Anthony 1937-

PERSONAL: Born March 25, 1937, in Brooklyn, N.Y.; son of Carlo (a fur dresser) and Anna (La Rosa) Rizzuto; married Dora Alessandro (a production supervisor), June 8, 1966; children: Carlo, Anthony. *Education:* Columbia University, B.A., 1958, M.A., 1960, Ph.D., 1966. *Home address:* P.O. Box 48, Miller Place, N.Y. 11764. *Office:* Department of French and Italian, State University of New York at Stony Brook, Stony Brook, N.Y. 11794.

CAREER: Columbia University, New York, N.Y., instructor in French, 1962-66; Tufts University, Medford, Mass., assistant professor of French, 1966-68; State University of New York at Stony Brook, assistant professor, 1968-71, associate professor of French, 1971—. *Member:* International Association of Philosophy and Literature, Modern Language Association of America, American Association of Teachers of French. *Awards, honors:* Fulbright fellowship for France, 1960-61;

National Endowment for the Humanities grant, 1970; summer stipend from State University of New York.

WRITINGS: Style and Theme in Pierre Reverdy's "Les Ardoises du Toit," University of Alabama Press, 1971; Camus' Imperial Vision, Southern Illinois University Press, 1981. Contributor to language journals. French area studies editor of Gradiva: Journal of Contemporary Theory and Practice.

WORK IN PROGRESS: The Politics of Sterility: From Symbolism to Sartre, publication expected in 1984.

SIDELIGHTS: Rizzuto told CA: "My first book, on Reverdy, treated the text as a closed linguistic system. Since its publication I have changed my orientation. My book on Camus examines the written work in relationship to its author and his culture, and also to its reader. In other words, I treat the text as 'open' and conditioned by history."

BIOGRAPHICAL/CRITICAL SOURCES: New York Times, October 11, 1981.

*   *   *

ROBERTS, Carey   1935-

PERSONAL: Born April 25, 1935, in Charlotte, N.C.; daughter of Charles L. (an engineer) and Frances C. Cansler; married William C. Roberts (a physician), August 20, 1955; children: Clifford, Charles, Carey, John. Education: Attended Agnes Scott College, 1953-55, and Emory University, 1955-58. Politics: Republican. Religion: Episcopalian. Home: 10508 Scarboro Lane, Potomac, Md. 20854.

CAREER: Montgomery County Bicentennial Commission, Montgomery County, Md., executive director, 1974-76; Bank of Bethesda, Bethesda, Md., director of marketing, 1977-78; writer, 1981—; Suburban Hospital, Bethesda, director of marketing and public relations, 1982—. Lecturer on speed reading and time management.

WRITINGS: (With Rebecca Seely) Tidewater Dynasty: The Lees of Stratford Hall (novelized biography), Harcourt, 1981. Contributor of articles to newspapers and magazines.

WORK IN PROGRESS: A mystery; a second book with Rebecca Seely on Virginia.

SIDELIGHTS: Carey Roberts's Tidewater Dynasty is a fictionalized account of the famous Lee family of Virginia. Called "solidly researched and illuminating" by Publishers Weekly, the book presents factual information about the dynasty and the family that produced General Robert E. Lee, commander-in-chief of the Confederate army. In Tidewater Dynasty, Roberts and Rebecca Seely, the former a southerner and the latter a northerner, summarize political landmarks in American history. "By providing a framework, both physical and chronological," said a Washington Post Book World reviewer, "the authors give the informed but nonspecialist reader a sense of continuity and relationship which his other reading may not have supplied." The reviewer also noted that Roberts and Seely reveal the personal liberation of the Lee women.

Roberts told CA that she has "always loved history" and the "sense of past lives."

BIOGRAPHICAL/CRITICAL SOURCES: Library Journal, February 1, 1981; Publishers Weekly, April 17, 1981; Washington Post Book World, May 30, 1981; Best Sellers, July, 1981.

ROBERTS, James Hall
See DUNCAN, Robert L(ipscomb)

*   *   *

ROBERTS, Suzanne   1931-
(Laurie Marath, Sparrow Marath)

PERSONAL: Born December 13, 1931, in Connersville, Ind.; daughter of Jack (a professional musician) and Mildreth (a poet; maiden name, Mills) Reeder; children: Randolph, Richard and Angele (twins), Marisa, Darren. Education: Attended New School of Social Research, New York, N.Y., 1945; Indiana University, B.S., 1949. Residence: Bloomington, Indiana. Agent: John K. Payne, Lenniger Literary Agency, Inc., 104 East 40th St., New York, N.Y. 10016.

CAREER: Writer, 1956—. Awards, honors: Winner of Writer's Digest contest, 1965, with "Blackberry Summer."

WRITINGS—Novels: Holly Andrews: Nurse in Alaska (juvenile), Messner, 1967; Danger in Paradise (juvenile), Bouregy, 1967; The Loveliest Librarian (juvenile), Avalon, 1967; Penny (juvenile), Avalon, 1968; Terror at Tansey Hill, Dell, 1975; House of Cain, Dell, 1975; The Searching Heart, Dell, 1978; Precious Moments, Dell, 1978; Love's Sweet Illusion, Dell, 1979; Morning in Paris, Dell, 1979; Farewell to Alexandria, Dell, 1980; Love in the Wilds, Dell, 1980; Bittersweet Waltz, Dell, 1982.

Under pseudonym Laurie Marath: Winds of Morning, Jove, 1981.

Under pseudonym Sparrow Marath: Gracie (juvenile), Doubleday, 1965.

WORK IN PROGRESS: When Summer Has Gone, a book with a Paris background; Where the Heart Is, a story about a middle-aged woman who decides to become a single parent and return home to a small town.

SIDELIGHTS: Roberts told CA: "I never tell lies in my books. I really feel innocently romantic about life. I grew up in a household where my parents were romantically in love, so it's not difficult for me to imagine people in love." Avocational interests: Travel (including Ireland), country-style cooking, antique furniture.

*   *   *

ROBERTSON, James Oliver   1932-

BRIEF ENTRY: Born December 22, 1932, in Fargo, N.D. American historian, educator, and author. Robertson has taught American history at the University of Connecticut since 1971. He wrote American Myth, American Reality (Hill & Wang, 1980). Address: Department of History, University of Connecticut, Storrs, Conn. 06268. Biographical/critical sources: Los Angeles Times, November 26, 1980.

*   *   *

ROBINSON, Maurice R(ichard)   1895-1982

OBITUARY NOTICE: Born December 24, 1895,in Wilkinsburg, Pa.; died February 2, 1982, in Pelham, N.Y. Founder, publisher, and editor of Scholastic Magazines, Inc. Robinson's popular Scholastic magazine developed a nationwide circulation within two years of its first appearance as a local newspaper for schoolchildren in western Pennsylvania. Scholastic now produces more than thirty magazines in addition to its major publications, Senior and Junior Scholastic. The corporation also operates five book clubs and is involved in various technological fields. Robinson earned a reputation for encouraging budding artists and writers, primarily through the Scholastic Awards Program in Art, Photography, and Writing, which he established in the 1920's. Past winners of writing awards include Gladys Schmitt, Maureen Daly, and Winfield Townley Scott. Obituaries and other sources: *Current Biography,* Wilson, 1956, May, 1982; *Nation's Business,* December, 1970; *Who's Who in America,* 42nd edition, Marquis, 1982; *New York Times,* February 10, 1982.

*   *   *

ROBINSON, Nancy K(onheim) 1942-

PERSONAL: Born August 12, 1942, in New York, N.Y.; daughter of Norris David (in advertising) and Natalie (Barnett) Konheim; married Peter Beverley Robinson, May 6, 1966; children: Kenneth Beverley, Alice Natalie. *Eduction:* Vassar College, A.B., 1964. *Residence:* New York, N.Y.

CAREER: Free-lance writer, researcher, 1972—. *Member:* Authors Guild, Writers Guild of America, East, PEN American Center, American Society of Picture Professionals, Industrial Photographers Association of New York, Vassar Club of New York. *Awards, honors:* U.S. Customs Award, 1978, for historical article; Four Leaf Clover Award from Scholastic Book Services, 1981.

WRITINGS—All juveniles: Jungle Laboratory: The Story of Ray Carpenter and the Howling Monkeys (nonfiction; illustrated by Bill Tinker), Hastings House, 1973; *Firefighters!* (nonfiction), Scholastic Book Services, 1979; *Wendy and the Bullies* (fiction; illustrated by Ingrid Fetz), Hastings House, 1980; *Just Plain Cat* (fiction), Scholastic Book Services, 1981; *Mom, You're Fired* (fiction; illustrated by Ed Arno), Scholastic Book Services, 1981; *Veronica the Show-Off* (illustrated by Sheila Greenwald), Scholastic Book Services, 1982. Writer of "Men of Bronze," PBS-TV documentary broadcast in February, 1978.

WORK IN PROGRESS: (With Marvin Miller) *T*A*C*K to the Rescue,* "the first in a series of Solve-It-Yourself Adventures," publication expected in 1982.

SIDELIGHTS: Robinson told *CA:* "When I write for children I always pick a subject that has puzzled me for a long time. I do not write any differently for children than for adults, but writing for children has become my first love. Children write letters. They ask very difficult questions. They put me on the spot. They do not let me get away with anything!"

*   *   *

ROCHE, Thomas P(atrick), Jr. 1931-

PERSONAL: Born April 19, 1931, in New Haven, Conn.; son of Thomas P. (in business) and Katherine (Walsh) Roche; married Lyn Vamvakis. *Education:* Yale University, B.A., 1953; attended Cambridge University, 1954; Princeton University, Ph.D., 1958. *Politics:* Democrat. *Religion:* Roman Catholic. *Office:* Department of English, Princeton University, Princeton, N.J. 08544.

CAREER: Latin teacher at private day school, 1953-54; Williams College, Williamstown, Mass., instructor in English, 1958-60; Princeton University, Princeton, N.J., began as instructor, became associate professor, 1960-72, professor of English, 1972—. Member of executive committee of Folger Shakespeare Library's Institute for Renaissance and Eighteenth-Century Studies. *Member:* Renaissance Society of

America, Spenser Society (president), Modern Language Association of America. *Awards, honors:* Henry fellowship for Pembroke College, Oxford, 1954-55; visiting fellow at Brasenose College, Oxford, 1970; National Endowment for the Humanities fellowship, 1974; American Council of Learned Societies fellowship, 1978.

WRITINGS: The Kindly Flame: A Study of the Third and Fourth Books of Spenser's Faerie Queene, Princeton University Press, 1964; (editor) Rosemund Tuve, *Allegorical Imagery: Some Medieval Books and Their Posterity,* Princeton University Press, 1966; (editor) Tuve, *Essays: Spenser, Herbert, Milton,* Princeton University Press, 1970; (editor) Edmund Spenser, *The Faerie Queene,* Penguin, 1978; (editor) D. W. Robertson, Jr., *Essays in Medieval Culture,* Princeton University Press, 1980. Coeditor of *Spenser Studies: A Renaissance Poetry Annual;* member of editorial board of *Studies in English Literature, Duquesne Studies in English, University of Mississippi Studies in English,* and *Spenser Encyclopedia.*

WORK IN PROGRESS: Petrarch and the English Sonnet Sequences; research on English Renaissance poetry and allegory, on Spenser's *Faerie Queene,* and on Italian Renaissance poetry.

BIOGRAPHICAL/CRITICAL SOURCES: Times Literary Supplement, June 18, 1982.

*   *   *

ROCHER, Ludo 1926-

BRIEF ENTRY: Born April 25, 1926, in Hemiksem, Belgium. Belgian educator, Sanskrit scholar, and author. Rocher was director of the Center for the Study of South and Southeast Asia at University of Brussels from 1961 to 1967. He has been professor of Sanskrit at the University of Pennsylvania since 1966. Rocher wrote *Manual of Modern Hindi: For the Use of Colleges* (1958) and *Le probleme linguistique en Inde* (Academie royale des sciences d'outre-mer, 1968). He was editor of *Smrticintamani of Gangaditya* (Oriental Institute, Maharaja Sayajirao University of Baroda, 1976). Rocher also translated *Dissertation on the Sanskrit Language* (Benjamins, 1977). *Address:* 226 Rittenhouse Sq., Philadelphia, Pa. 19013; and Department of Oriental Studies, University of Pennsylvania, Philadelphia, Pa. 19104. *Biographical/critical sources: Directory of American Scholars,* Volume III: *Foreign Languages, Linguistics, and Philology,* 7th edition, Bowker, 1978.

*   *   *

RODGER, Alec
See RODGER, Thomas Alexander

*   *   *

RODGER, Thomas Alexander 1907-1982
(Alec Rodger)

OBITUARY NOTICE: Born November 22, 1907, in Sanquhar, Dumfriesshire, England; died February 15, 1982. Psychologist, educator, and author. Rodger was a pioneer in the field of occupational psychology, serving as head of the vocational guidance department of the National Institute of Industrial Psychology (NIIP) from 1936 to 1947. During World War II Rodger was a psychologist with the British War Office and served as Senior Psychologist to the Admiralty. In his final year with the Admiralty, Rodger was named senior principal psychologist. He joined the faculty of Birkbeck College, London, in 1948 and in 1960 became the first person to be named professor of occupational psychology. In 1961 he became head of the world's first department of occupational psychology. Rodger was the editor of *Occupational Psychology* for twenty years beginning in 1948 and was a frequent contributor to professional journals and encyclopedias. He was the author of *A Borstal Experiment in Vocational Guidance* and *Occupational Versatility and Planned Procrastination.* Obituaries and other sources: *Who's Who,* 126th edition, St. Martin's, 1974; *London Times,* February 24, 1982.

* * *

RODGERS, Stanley 1928-1977

OBITUARY NOTICE: Born in 1928 in Cambridge, Mass.; died of a heart attack, December 11, 1977, in San Francisco, Calif. Clergyman and author. Rodgers was dean of Grace Cathedral in San Francisco. He was the co-author, with David A. Schultz, of both editions of *Marriage, the Family, and Personal Fulfillment.* Obituaries and other sources: *New York Times,* December 13, 1977.

* * *

ROESCH, Ronald 1947-

PERSONAL: Born May 25, 1947, in Montclair, N.J.; son of Irene (a realtor; maiden name, O'Donnell) Roesch; married Kathleen Mitchell Karlberg, November 13, 1976; children: David, Jeremy. *Education:* Arizona State University, B.S., 1971; University of Illinois, Ph.D., 1977. *Office:* Criminology Research Center, Simon Fraser University, Burnaby, British Columbia, Canada V5A 1S6.

CAREER: Simon Fraser University, Burnaby, British Columbia, assistant professor, 1977-80, associate professor of psychology and criminology, 1980—, director of Criminology Research Center, 1979—, director of clinical psychology graduate program, 1981—. *Member:* American Psychological Association. *Awards, honors:* Award from American Psychological Association, 1977, for best psychological dissertation concerned with social issues.

WRITINGS: (With Steve L. Golding) *Competency to Stand Trial,* University of Illinois Press, 1980; (with R.R. Corrado) *Evaluation and Criminal Justice Policy,* Sage Publications, 1981; (contributor with Corrado) E. Seidman, editor, *Handbook of Social and Community Interventions,* Sage Publications, 1983. Contributor of more than a dozen articles to professional journals.

WORK IN PROGRESS: Two chapters, "Competency to Stand Trial" and "Psychology and the Law," to be included in *Wiley Encyclopedia of Psychology,* edited by R. J. Corsini, publication expected in 1984.

SIDELIGHTS: Roesch told *CA:* "An explicit assumption apparent in my research on competency to stand trial is that the interaction of legal and mental health professionals has been less than satisfactory. In our book on competency, Golding and I developed a model for improving this interaction by involving lawyers with mental health professionals in a collaborative assessment of a defendant's competency. In the past these assessments have been completed independently by mental health professionals, who have often simply ignored or misunderstood relevant legal issues. Our research has also been directed at changes in the process of evaluating and treating incompetent defendants. These changes are designed to minimize the loss of liberty, through unnecessary confinement in mental hospitals, suffered by defendants evaluated for incompetency or found incompetent."

ROFES, Eric Edward 1954-

PERSONAL: Surname is pronounced "*Roe*-fess"; born August 31, 1954, in Manhasset, N.Y.; son of William Lopatin (an archivist) and Paula Ruth (a business manager; maiden name, Weinstein) Rofes; lives with David Richard Hocker (an architect). *Education:* Harvard University, B.A. (cum laude), 1976. *Religion:* Jewish. *Agent:* Helen Rees, 655 Boylston St., Boston, Mass. 02116. *Office:* Fayerweather Street School, 74 Fayerweather St., Cambridge, Mass. 02138.

CAREER: Fayerweather Street School, Cambridge, Mass., teacher, administrator, and co-director, 1978—. Delegate to the White House Conference on Families, 1980; area board member of Massachusetts Department of Social Services, 1980-81; member of the Massachusetts Committee for Children and Youth (member of board of directors of Project Assist, chairman of board of directors of Project Aware); member of board of directors of *Gay Community News. Member:* Gay Men's Professional Group of Boston, Boston Area Gay and Lesbian Schoolworkers (founder), Gay Harvard Alumni (director).

WRITINGS: The Kids' Book of Divorce: By, For, and About Kids, Lewis Publishing, 1981; "*I Thought People Like That Killed Themselves*": *Lesbians, Gay Men, and Suicide,* Grey Fox, 1982; *The Kids' Book of Death and Dying,* Little, Brown, 1983. Contributor of articles to periodicals, including *Gay Community News* and *Guardian.*

WORK IN PROGRESS: Research on the New Right, feminism and men, sexuality in the eighties, and urban street crime; an autobiographical book on being a gay school teacher.

SIDELIGHTS: Rofes told *CA:* "I am engaged in two major areas of writing: books for children, which I write in collaboration with children, and books about a broad range of political issues, including social service issues, gay liberation, feminism, and progressive politics. I am a gay man very much involved in youth advocacy work and expect to continue this work for many years."

BIOGRAPHICAL/CRITICAL SOURCES: Newsweek, June 8, 1981.

* * *

ROLLINS, Kelly [a pseudonym] 1924-

PERSONAL: Born April 13, 1924, in Grenada, Miss.; children: Matthew. *Education:* Mississippi State University, B.S., 1948; graduate study at Purdue University, 1951, and Shippensburg State College, 1967-69; Rivier College, M.A., 1973. *Politics:* Independent. *Religion:* Roman Catholic. *Address:* c/o Little, Brown & Co., 34 Beacon St., Boston, Mass. 02114.

CAREER: U.S. Air Force, career officer, 1943-45 and 1948-73, retiring as colonel; writer, 1973—.

WRITINGS: Fighter Pilots (novel), Little, Brown, 1981. Contributor to *Road and Track.*

SIDELIGHTS: Rollins told *CA:* "I never think of myself as a writer; rather, I am someone who wrote a single novel and, decades ago, a few magazine articles, supposedly humorous. I am a reader, an inveterate reader, who likes books that had to be written, full of humor and irony.

"When I retired from the Air Force in 1973, after twenty-eight years of service, half in fighter squadrons, I held a brand-new M.A. in English and thought I might begin a second career as an English teacher. When my applications were ignored, I moved to the woods of New Hampshire and bought a 1785 colonial farmhouse in need of renovation. Simultaneously, I began writing a novel about the more colorful and eccentric fighter pilots I had known over the years. My working title was *Clowns and Birds,* birds being aircraft, and I enjoyed the challenge of heightening and ennobling these clowns. Each morning I would write, and each afternoon I would play carpenter. In time, both projects got completely out of control, so I decided to declare them finished.

"A friend and former pilot liked the manuscript well enough to recommend it to his editor at Little, Brown. After being cut and revised slightly, the book went to press as *Fighter Pilots.* Generally, it was ignored. A few reviews praised its authenticity but discredited it as fiction with the charge of autobiography. Even though the protagonist is a composite of pilots I had known, including myself, I expected this charge because I employed a first-person narrator; and that point of view, coupled with the use of the present tense throughout, provided both the immediacy I sought and its penalty."

*   *   *

ROMBERGER, Judy   1940-

PERSONAL: Born April 26, 1940, in Long Beach, Calif.; daughter of Donald Roger (a business executive) and Jeanne (a decorator and artist; maiden name, Law) Jacobson; married Warren D. Romberger, July 23, 1960 (divorced); married James W. Hoopes (an oil refiner and rancher), February 27, 1978; children: (first marriage) Andrea, Alison; (second marriage—stepchildren) Susie, John. *Education:* University of California, Los Angeles, B.A., 1962; graduate study at California State University, Los Angeles. *Politics:* "I love William F. Buckley." *Religion:* "Catholic in a past life." *Home and office:* Hoopes Ranch, 34090 Briggs Rd., Winchester, Calif. 92396. *Agent:* Lynn Pleshette, 2700 North Beachwood Dr., Los Angeles, Calif. 90068.

CAREER: Part-time teacher of creative writing and drama.

WRITINGS: Lolly (novel), Doubleday, 1981; *The California-Look Book,* Doubleday, 1983.

Plays: "The Waiting Room" (one-act), first produced in Louisville, Ky., at Actors Theatre Louisville, November, 1980; "The Saint of the Day" (one-act), first produced at Actors Theatre Louisville, November, 1981; "The Semi-Finalist" (one-act), first produced at Actors Theatre Louisville, April, 1982. Contributor of about twenty-five stories to magazines, including *Transatlantic Review, Smith,* and *Teen.*

WORK IN PROGRESS: A novel, publication by Doubleday expected in 1985; "Camp Beverly Hills," a two-act play to be produced at Actors Theatre Louisville.

SIDELIGHTS: Lolly, Romberger's first novel, is the fast-paced, often humorous story of a recently divorced mother of two who remarries and moves from the suburbs of southern California to a rural ranch with her new husband, Reg, and his two children. When Lolly fears her husband is attracted to their beautiful Dutch neighbor and when Reg's ex-wife arrives to claim their two children, Lolly winds up in court, fighting to keep her stepchildren and discovering her own strengths in the battle.

Romberger told *CA:* "After living in Pasadena for thirty-seven years, I've moved to a ranch west of Palm Springs, where it is beautiful, serene, and perfect for writing. However, there is no action here, so I travel a lot. I love New York, Paris, and London and want to die in France."

AVOCATIONAL INTERESTS: Cooking, eating, skiing.

*   *   *

ROMNEY, George W(ilcken)   1907-

BRIEF ENTRY: Born July 8, 1907, in Chihuahua, Mexico. American automobile manufacturer, government official, and author. Romney was a Mormon missionary in England and Scotland in the late 1920's. In the 1940's he was general manager of the Automobile Manufacturers Association. Romney was president, chairman of the board of directors, and general manager of American Motors Corp. from 1954 to 1962. He then served as governor of Michigan for six years and as U.S. Secretary of Housing and Urban Development from 1969 to 1972. Since 1979 Romney has been chairman of the National Center for Citizen Involvement. He wrote *Concerns of a Citizen* (Putnam, 1968). *Address:* East Valley Rd., Bloomfield Hills, Mich. 48013. *Biographical/critical sources: Current Biography,* Wilson, 1958; *Who's Who in America,* 41st edition, Marquis, 1980.

*   *   *

ROOSEVELT, Nicholas   1893-1982

OBITUARY NOTICE: Born June 12, 1893, in New York, N.Y.; died February 16, 1982, in Monterey, Calif. Journalist, diplomat, conservationalist, and author. Roosevelt, a cousin of President Theodore Roosevelt, entered the diplomatic service following his graduation from Harvard University in 1914. He served as an infantry captain in France during World War I and was detailed as one of President Woodrow Wilson's aides for the peace talks that concluded the war. In 1920 he began a career in journalism with the *New York Herald Tribune* and remained there until 1923, when he joined the staff of the *New York Times* as a special correspondent covering Asia and the western Pacific. He wrote two books based on his experiences as a correspondent during the 1920's, *The Philippines: A Treasure and a Problem* and *The Restless Pacific.* President Hoover named Roosevelt vice-governor of the Philippines, but Roosevelt declined the appointment in the face of protests from Filipino politicians who felt Roosevelt's writings were an insult to the Filipino national character. During World War II Roosevelt contributed to the war effort by accepting a post with the Office of War Information. Obituaries and other sources: *Who's Who in the West,* 14th edition, Marquis, 1974; *New York Times,* February 18, 1982.

*   *   *

ROSEN, Robert C(harles)   1947-

PERSONAL: Born December 29, 1947, in Brooklyn, N.Y.; son of Morris (a hardware store owner) and Beatrice (an elementary school librarian and preschool teacher; maiden name, Greenberg) Rosen. *Education:* Massachusetts Institute of Technology, B.S. (mathematics) and B.S. (humanities and science), both 1970; Rutgers University, M.A., 1975, Ph.D., 1978. *Office:* Department of English, William Paterson College, 300 Pompton Rd., Wayne, N.Y. 07470.

CAREER: Massachusetts Institute of Technology, Cambridge, mathematician and computer programmer at Draper Laboratory, 1969-70, summers, 1970-71; William Paterson College, Wayne, N.J., assistant professor of English, 1978—. *Member:* Modern Language Association of America, National Council of Teachers of English. *Awards, honors:* National Endowment for the Humanities fellowship, 1980.

WRITINGS: John Dos Passos: Politics and the Writer, University of Nebraska Press, 1981. Contributor to journals.

WORK IN PROGRESS: Research on politics and literature and on the teaching of writing.

SIDELIGHTS: Rosen told *CA:* "In his fiction Dos Passos grappled with the major political issues of his time and sought to lay bare the operations of an increasingly complex social system. So ambitious an undertaking was bound to succeed only partially, but more than any other American novelist of his generation, he did succeed—brilliantly in *U.S.A.*—in dramatizing the ways, subtle as well as brutal, in which history shapes the lives of individuals. His work as a whole remains an enormously valuable and fascinating chronicle of a turbulent age and of the sensibility of a passionate, decent, immensely curious man trying to understand and to survive it."

* * *

ROSENBAUM, Alan Shelby 1941-

BRIEF ENTRY: Born August 27, 1941, in Rochester, N.Y. American philosopher, educator, and author. Rosenbaum has taught philosophy at Cleveland State University since 1975. He edited *The Philosophy of Human Rights* (Greenwood Press, 1980). *Address:* Department of Philosophy, Cleveland State University, Euclid Ave. at East 24th St., Cleveland, Ohio 44115.

* * *

ROSENMAN, John B(rown) 1941-

PERSONAL: Born April 16, 1941, in Cleveland, Ohio; son of Isidor (a lawyer) and Mona (a lawyer; maiden name, Brown) Rosenman; married Jane Palmer, September 7, 1967; children: Lori March, David Gerald. *Education:* Hiram College, B.A., 1963; Kent State University, M.A., 1966, Ph.D., 1970. *Religion:* Jewish. *Home:* 111 Pine Lake Dr., Elizabeth City, N.C. 27909. *Agent:* Victor Chapin, John Schaffner Literary Agency, 425 East 51st St., New York, N.Y. 10022. *Office:* Department of Modern Languages, Elizabeth City State University, 1001 Parkview Dr., Elizabeth City, N.C. 27909.

CAREER: Lakehead University, Thunder Bay, Ontario, assistant professor of English, 1970-74; Claflin College, Orangeburg, S.C., associate professor of English, 1974-81; Elizabeth City State University, Elizabeth City, N.C., assistant professor of English, 1981—. *Member:* Modern Language Association of America, College English Association, South Atlantic Modern Language Association. *Awards, honors:* Grant from Consortium on Research Training, 1979-80.

WRITINGS: The Best Laugh Last (novel), Treacle Press, 1981; *The Merry-Go-Round Man,* Treacle Press, in press. Contributor of articles, stories, and poems to magazines, including *New York Quarterly, Iowa Review, Massachusetts Review, Southern Poetry Review, Southern Humanities Review,* and *Poet Lore.*

WORK IN PROGRESS: Alienated Consciousness in American Literature.

SIDELIGHTS: Rosenman told *CA: "The Best Laugh Last* explores a subject which I believe has never been dealt with before in fiction. In my book, Ashland College is a small black college in South Carolina with backward, apathetic students, poor teachers, and most of all, an incompetent, corrupt administration. As an English professor, I have firsthand knowledge of several such schools, and I have tried here to establish that those in charge have little interest in educating their students.

Instead, they seek higher enrollments, more federal money, and most of all, more power. The result is that southern blacks are denied a last chance at a decent education and are 'ripped off' once again by a society that cares little about their needs.

"Until recently, to criticize minority education at all was to expose oneself to charges of racism. As I expected, therefore, initial publishers rejected the book. Some also saw it as too literary and symbolically complex: qualities ill-suited to a paperback culture where best-sellers fit narrow formats and pigeonholes and 'Harlequin Romances' are sealed in cellophane and sold with Ivory Liquid.

"One reviewer of the book was troubled by the fact that my hero, David Newman, is a 'showoff' who likes sex. Apparently, idealistic rebels who challenge a corrupt Establishment should be pure as snow. However, I wanted to create an antihero with feet of clay, a character recognizably human with internal conflicts who is something more than a stereotype. To me, the soul of literature is people who are complex, imperfect, and involved in the process of change.

"Change, by the way, is important to my poetry and fiction, particularly as it relates to man's capacity or lack of it to shape his destiny by changing his character. Are our characters rigid and frozen early in life, or can we change? Are we mere automatons, products of our genes and environments, or potential masters of our fates? To what extent are we malleable, and are there such things as fate and free will? Such questions play a large part in *The Best Laugh Last,* where David Newman reaches maturity without having yet made the all-important choice that will determine his character and future, and they are important too in my second novel, *The Merry-Go-Round Man,* which portrays three boys growing up. Are some of us born winners, 'merry-go-round men' destined to be on top all our lives, or is the human condition more complex and mysterious than that? Can we achieve success and fulfillment by will and effort, or is everything spelled out, perhaps long before we are born, in the stars? In short, why do we end up the way we do? This is the question that perhaps more than any other, absorbs me in my writing and in life as well."

* * *

ROSS, Bette M. 1932-

PERSONAL: Born June 23, 1932, in Pomona, Calif.; daughter of Harry K. (a businessman) and Alice Marie (Shade) Horn; married Robert Steele Ross (a physical therapist), December 4, 1952; children: James Stuart, Michael Steele, Laurie Beth. *Education:* Mount San Antonio College, A.A., 1952; University of California, Los Angeles, B.A. (cum laude), 1958; graduate study at California Polytechnic State University, Pomona. *Religion:* Protestant. *Residence:* West Covina, Calif. *Address:* c/o Walker & Co., 720 Fifth Ave., New York, N.Y. 10019.

CAREER: Elementary school teacher in Los Angeles, Calif., 1958-60; free-lance writer, c. 1962—. Teacher of creative writing at Mount San Antonio College. Founder and president of Parents Acting for the Handicapped (PATH). Member of board of directors of San Gabriel Valley Regional Center; deacon of First Presbyterian Church. Community volunteer. *Member:* American Association of University Women, Writers Club of Whittier, Junior Women's Club of West Covina (president, 1964-65). *Awards, honors:* Henrietta Mears Award for excellence in fiction, 1975; gold and bronze medals from Los Angeles County Fair, for color photography.

WRITINGS: Song of Deborah (novel), Revell, 1981; *Our Special Child: A Guide to Successful Parenting of Handicapped*

Children (nonfiction), Walker & Co., 1981. Contributor of articles and photography to periodicals, including *California Regional Center Journal, Journal for California Teachers of English, Reeves Journal, Horse and Horseman, Horse of Course, Comment, Lady's Circle, Popular Science, Los Angeles Times, San Gabriel Valley Tribune,* and *Covina Sentinel,* and to Highlander Publications.

WORK IN PROGRESS: A book about a band of Confederate soldiers living in Brazil, publication expected in 1983; a series of American historical novels for Revell.

SIDELIGHTS: Ross's first published book, *Song of Deborah,* is based on the Old Testament character Deborah who successfully led the Israelite army in war against the Canaanites. After her victory, Deborah became Israel's first prophetess and judge. Ross explained in a *San Gabriel Valley Tribune* interview that Deborah's strength appealed to her. "Deborah was chosen because she was an exciting woman in her time. If she were alive today she'd be stumping for the Equal Rights Amendment; she'd be politically aware. I am interested in characters who have to stand against their time because of what they believe in."

The author's second book, *Our Special Child,* tells of experiences she and her husband encountered as the parents of a mentally retarded child. "So much that is published in the field is not very realistic," Ross noted. She observed that parents, not professionals, are best equipped to know what is best for their handicapped child. "Doctors tell parents to put children in an institution, but that's not always the best thing for them." Ross elaborated in an *Oregonian* interview that "even the doctors couldn't agree on our child's potential, whether we should bring him home, or institutionalize him." She asserted that parents must decide: "Painstakingly, you, the parent, must discover for yourself what is available, particularly in the educational system (the Rosses insisted on training for the educable mentally retarded for . . . [their son], and today he can read and write), and be willing to fight for it. Who is your child's most caring, most experienced professional? You are."

The author acknowledged that such responsibility is a "burden, although beloved." She continued that it "is overwhelming at the beginning, and is one you think will always be there." But Ross offered hope in her book: "Parents have an overwhelming sense that they have to take care of that child for the rest of their life with no let up. They don't realize that they have the right to become a couple again once their child is grown."

BIOGRAPHICAL/CRITICAL SOURCES: San Gabriel Valley Tribune, June 7, 1981; *Oregonian,* October 10, 1981.

*   *   *

ROSS, Corinne Madden   1931-

PERSONAL: Born May 17, 1931, in Newton, Mass.; daughter of Alphonsus L. (a captain in U.S. Naval Reserve) and Corinne (Bodwell) Madden; married Charles Kenneth Ross, April 13, 1957 (divorced, 1960). *Education:* Mount Ida Junior College, A.B., 1951. *Home:* 67 Auburn Street Extension, Framingham, Mass. 01701.

CAREER: Charles D. Spencer & Associates, Chicago, Ill., editor, 1953-63; Childrens Press, Inc., Chicago, promotion director, 1964-66; Mid-American Publishing Co., Chicago, managing director, 1965-66; New Horizons Publishers, Chicago, promotion director, 1967—; free-lance writer.

WRITINGS: Christmas in Mexico, World Book, 1976; *Christmas in Scandinavia,* World Book, 1977; *Christmas in Britain,* World Book, 1978; *Christmas in Italy,* World Book, 1979;

The New England Guest House Book, East Woods Press, 1979, revised edition, 1982; *Christmas in France,* World Book, 1980; *To Market, to Market!: Six Walking Tours of the Old and the New Boston,* Charles River, 1980; (with Ralph C. Woodward) *New England: Off the Beaten Path,* East Woods Press, 1981; *The Southern Guest House Book,* East Woods Press, 1981; *The Middle Atlantic States Guest Book,* East Woods Press, 1983.

Work represented in anthologies, including *Bible Stories From the Old and New Testaments.* Contributor to *Young Students Encyclopedia.* Contributor to magazines, including *Mobil Motorist, Sphere, New Hampshire Profile,* and *Barbie.*

WORK IN PROGRESS: Travel writing.

*   *   *

ROSS, Robert Horace

PERSONAL: Born in Philadelphia, Pa.; son of Howard and Helen (Gebauer) Ross. *Education:* Received B.Arch. from University of Pennsylvania; received M.Arch. from University of Michigan. *Home:* East 71st St., New York, N.Y. 10021.

CAREER: Architectural and interior designer of hotels and restaurants; custom carpet stylist.

WRITINGS: Treasures of Tutankhamun in Needlepoint, Morrow, 1978; *Ancient Persian Designs in Needlepoint,* St. Martin's, 1982.

*   *   *

ROSS, Sheila Muriel   1925-

PERSONAL: Born January 23, 1925, in Seremban, Malaya; daughter of George (a rubber planter) and Winifred Mary (an artist; maiden name, Johnson) Wiseman; married Graham Ross (in army and colonial service), November 8, 1947; children: Christina. *Education:* Attended school in England and Cameron Highlands, Malaya. *Politics:* Conservative. *Religion:* Church of Scotland. *Home:* Apartado 138, Altea (Alicante), Spain.

CAREER: Mansfield & Co. Ltd., Kuala Lumpur, Malaysia, travel agent, 1952-55; part-time teacher in Anglican and Lutheran mission schools and Red Cross representative in Malaya and Sabah, 1955-70; novelist and playwright, 1960—. *Military service:* Women's Royal Air Force, 1942-49; became flying officer.

WRITINGS: A Log Across the Road (novel), Collins, 1971; *The Perfect Carrier* (novel), Collins, 1972; *Five Days Till Noon* (novel), Collins, 1973; *The Tower of Monte Rado* (novel), Collins, 1974; *The Foam on the River* (novel), Collins, 1975.

Radio plays: "Monkeys Can't Tell the Date," first broadcast by British Broadcasting Corp. (BBC-Radio), May 5, 1970; "One Man's Island," first broadcast by BBC-Radio, May 22, 1971; "Madonna of the Billabong," first broadcast by BBC-Radio, June 4, 1978. Contributor to *Nation Review.*

WORK IN PROGRESS: The Snuff Box, a four-volume historical novel set in the Far East from 1746 to 1942; *The Costa del Con,* a novel/television serial set in Spain; *Sulu Sound,* a novel set in Borneo and the Philippines.

SIDELIGHTS: Ross told *CA:* "As one of the fifth generation of my family born in the Far East, I remain passionately interested in South East Asia, its history, peoples, and politics. For my books, I tend to draw on my personal experiences in Malaya and Borneo, where I have spent the greater part of my life, and from my time in the Air Force in wartime England

and Italy. I think all my novels have beem prompted by some actual event and will continue to be so.''

* * *

ROSSIE, Jonathan Gregory 1935-

BRIEF ENTRY: Born May 10, 1935, in Binghamton, N.Y. American historian, educator, and author. Rossie has been a member of the faculty at St. Lawrence University since 1965 and a professor of history and department chairman since 1974. He wrote *The Politics of Command in the American Revolution* (Syracuse University Press, 1975). *Address:* Department of History, St. Lawrence University, Canton, N.Y. 13617. *Biographical/critical sources: Directory of American Scholars,* Volume I: *History,* 7th edition, Bowker, 1978.

* * *

ROTCHSTEIN, Janice 1944-

PERSONAL: Born September 2, 1944, in Coronado, Calif.; daughter of Morris (a U.S. Navy commander) and Elizabeth (Wolke) Rotchstein. *Education:* San Diego State College (now University), B.A., 1966; Northwestern University, M.S.J., 1967. *Religion:* Roman Catholic. *Residence:* New York, N.Y. *Agent:* Kathy Robbins, Robbins & Covey, 866 Second Ave., New York, N.Y. 10017.

CAREER: Alexander Co., New York City, media director, 1967-68; Pierce Promotions, Inc., New York City, vice-president, 1968-72; Peter Martin Associates, New York City, creative director, 1972-76; Minnesota, Mining & Manufacturing (3M), New York City, senior public relations representative, 1977-81; free-lance writer. *Member:* American Society of Journalists and Authors.

WRITINGS: (With Alan Ebert) *Traditions* (novel), Crown, 1981; *The Money Diet* (nonfiction), Crown, 1982. Contributor to periodicals, including *Playbill, Us, Mademoiselle, Good Housekeeping, Redbook,* and *Essence.*

WORK IN PROGRESS: A sequel to *Traditions,* publication by Crown expected in 1983.

SIDELIGHTS: Rotchstein described *Traditions* as a book ''about people's contemporary feelings and experiences. It's about the range of strength and the wonderful sense of humor people have and about how special the family can be in our society.''

BIOGRAPHICAL/CRITICAL SOURCES: Library Journal, June 15, 1981.

* * *

ROTH, David 1940-

PERSONAL: Born October 27, 1940, in New York, N.Y.; son of Julius (an engineer) and Clara (a dealer in used books; maiden name, Wenson) Roth; married Lucy Bickford, December 17, 1960 (divorced May, 1973); married Cilla Sheehan (a psychologist), June 17, 1978; children: Katherine Laura, Sheila Louise. *Education:* Attended high school in Acton, Mass. *Politics:* ''Principally Democrat.'' *Home and office address:* P.O. Box 204, Bristol, N.H. 03222. *Agent:* Scott Meredith Literary Agency, Inc., 845 Third Ave., New York, N.Y. 10022.

CAREER: Lobster fisherman in Vinalhaven, Maine, 1963-65; pulp wood cutter and sanitation engineer, 1965-68; Andrew Carnegie Public Library, Vinalhaven, librarian, 1968-70; Aavid Engineering, Laconia, N.H., shift foreman in plating room, 1971-78; house renovator and writer, 1978—.

WRITINGS—Juvenile novels: The Winds of Summer, Abelard, 1972; *The Hermit of Fog Hollow Station,* Beaufort Book Co., 1980; *A World for Joey Carr,* Beaufort Book Co., 1981; *River Runaways,* Houghton, 1981; *The Girl in the Grass,* Beaufort Book Co., 1982.

WORK IN PROGRESS: Secrets, The Best of Friends, and *The Boy From Nowhere.*

SIDELIGHTS: Roth told *CA:* ''I write novels for children because that's the way my writing comes out. I think this is because I like to tell stories, I like to write narratives that are very accessible on the surface, and I keep my books short. Children are close to the sense of life as a journey; this is something I have never been able to lose. I no longer want to lose it, for I've come to believe that it is a most important insight into life—perhaps the only one I'll ever have.''

BIOGRAPHICAL/CRITICAL SOURCES: New York Times Book Review, April 25, 1982.

* * *

ROTH, (Hyam) Leon 1896-1963

OBITUARY NOTICE: Born March 31, 1896, in London, England; died April 1, 1963, in New Zealand. Philosopher, educator, and author best known for his translations of classical works of philosophy into modern Hebrew. Roth was honored as the outstanding philosophy student of the year upon his graduation from Oxford University in 1920. From 1928 to 1953 he was professor of philosophy at Hebrew University. During his tenure at the university he served as rector and as dean of the faculty of humanities. Roth was critical of extreme nationalism and of rigidity in religious thought and emphasized reason and tolerance in his teaching. He was the author of books on philosophy and on the interpretation of Judaism, including *Spinoza, Descartes' Discourse on Method, Illustrations of Post-Biblical Jewish Ethical and Religious Thought, Ex Ore Altissimi: An Anthology of the Hebrew Scriptures,* and *Judaism, a Portrait.* Obituaries and other sources: *Who's Who, 1962,* St. Martin's, 1962; *New York Times,* April 5, 1963.

* * *

ROTHSCHILD, Fritz A(lexander) 1919-

BRIEF ENTRY: Born October 4, 1919, in Hamburg, Germany (now West Germany). American religious scholar, philosopher, educator, and author. Rothschild has been an ordained rabbi since 1955. He has taught philosophy of religion at the Jewish Theological Seminary of America since 1960. Rothschild wrote *The Concept of God in Jewish Education* (1965) and *Teaching the Torah: An Essay on Interpretation* (1966). He edited *Between God and Man: An Interpretation of Judaism* (Harper, 1959). *Address:* 12 Dongan Pl., New York, N.Y. 10040; and Department of Philosophy of Religion, Jewish Theological Seminary of America, 3080 Broadway, New York, N.Y. 10027. *Biographical/critical sources: Directory of American Scholars,* Volume IV: *Philosophy, Religion, and Law,* 7th edition, Bowker, 1978.

* * *

ROY, Robert L(ouis) 1947-

PERSONAL: Born February 17, 1947, in Webster, Mass.; son of Emil Joseph and Lillian (Berthiaume) Roy; married Jacqueline Bates (a registered nurse), November 18, 1972; children: Rohan. *Education:* Attended high school in Farmington, Conn. *Home address:* Murtagh Hill Rd., West Chazy, N.Y. 12992.

CAREER: Rob Roy Ski School, Inc. (water ski school), Webster, Mass., owner and operator, 1965-68; geometry teacher at private school in Webster, 1968; research, writing, and lecturing on alternative building methods, 1977-81; Earth-Shelter/Cordwood Masonry Workshops (became Earthwood Building School), West Chazy, N.Y., owner and operator, 1981—. *Member:* American Underground Space Association.

WRITINGS—Published by Sterling: *How to Build Log-End Houses,* 1977; *Underground Houses: How to Build a Low-Cost Home,* 1979, revised edition, 1980; *Cordwood Masonry Houses: A Practical Guide for the Owner-Builder,* 1980; *Money-Saving Strategies for the Owner-Builder,* 1981; *Earthwood: Integrative Design Concepts,* in press.

WORK IN PROGRESS: Building the Masonry Stove, publication expected in 1983.

SIDELIGHTS: Roy commented: "I toured the world with a backpack for two years, 1967-69, visiting more than forty countries. I settled in Dingwall, Scotland, in 1970, where I renovated a one hundred-year-old cottage and met my wife. We moved to West Chazy in 1975, after looking for land all over the United States. I wanted to pursue a self-reliant lifestyle, which was difficult in Britain because of strict building and planning codes. After building Log End Cottage and Log End Cave, I wrote books about house construction from the point of view of the owner-builder who desires a mortgage-free home. Now I am working on Earthwood, a cordwood/earth-sheltered home integrating all the life support systems (food, fuel, recreation, home industry, and so on), not just shelter."

*   *   *

RUBIN, Amy Kateman 1945-

PERSONAL: Born April 27, 1945, in Cambridge, Mass.; daughter of Abraham Eugene (a physician) and Jeannette (Greenblatt) Kateman; married Michael Rubin (a professor and importer), January 31, 1965; children: Adam, Jennifer. *Education:* Simmons College, B.A., 1966; Goddard College, M.A. 1973; doctoral study at Boston College, 1973-75. *Home:* 42 Nobscot Rd., Newton, Mass. 02159. *Agent:* Carol Mann Literary Agency, 168 Pacific St., Brooklyn, N.Y. 11201.

CAREER: Open House Nursery School, Marlboro, Mass.; co-founder and co-director, 1971-73; Tree House (retailers of children's books and toys), Newton, Mass., owner and operator, 1975-77; writer, 1977—. *Member:* Authors Guild.

WRITINGS—Juvenile novels: *Children of the Seventh Prophecy* (first volume in trilogy), Warne, 1981; *The Timekeepers* (second volume in trilogy), Macmillan, in press.

WORK IN PROGRESS: Independent research exploring the bonds between classical myths, fairy tales, and science fiction.

SIDELIGHTS: Amy Rubin told *CA:* "My maternal grandfather encouraged me in and nurtured my love for stories and books. I was permitted to handle very beautiful editions of special books from an early age and held them in awe as if they were magically formed. Now that I have written the first one of my own, I am still convinced that there is something magical in the formation. I write as an attempt to interpret experience and believe that all art is an attempt to interpret the world around us to ourselves and to others.

"The World War II legacy of the atomic bomb and the Nazi horrors has demonstrated the worst aspects of civilized technological man. We have yet to prove ourselves capable of harnessing our most creative impulses collectively. Continuing

to tell stories and to confront who we are may free us to move toward more promising possibilities.

"My daily reading and writing time ranges from four to six hours. The rest of the day is devoted to my husband, children, and friends, among whom are two dogs who have a distinct taste for digesting literature whole."

*   *   *

RUBIN, James Henry 1944-

PERSONAL: Born May 4, 1944, in Cambridge, Mass.; son of David L. (a manufacturer) and Charlotte (Tarlow) Rubin; married Liliane Braesch (a teacher of French), December 27, 1969; children: Henry, Delphine. *Education:* Yale University, B.A., 1965; University of Paris, Licence es Lettres, 1967; Harvard University, Ph.D., 1972. *Home:* 5 Yorktown Rd., Setauket, N.Y. 11733. *Office:* Department of Art, State University of New York at Stony Brook, 4213 Fine Arts Building, Stony Brook, N.Y. 11794.

CAREER: Boston University, Boston, Mass., assistant professor of humanities, 1972-73; Princeton University, Princeton, N.J., assistant professor of art and archaeology, 1973-79; State University of New York at Stony Brook, associate professor of art, 1979—. Adjunct associate professor at Cooper Union for the Advancement of Art and Science.

WRITINGS: Eighteenth-Century French Life-Drawing, Princeton University Press, 1977; *Realism and Social Vision in Courbet and Proudhon,* Princeton University Press, 1981. Contributor to art history journals.

WORK IN PROGRESS: A book on art and politics in France, c. 1800-1850.

*   *   *

RUBINSTEIN, Robert E(dward) 1943-

PERSONAL: Born November 12, 1943, in Boston, Mass.; son of Jack S. (a broker) and Augusta F. (a teacher; maiden name, Borenstein) Rubinstein; married Pearl Elizabeth Geschmay (a teacher of violin), April 30, 1972; children: Joshua, Seth, Shoshanna. *Education:* Queens College of the City University of New York, B.A., 1965; Northeastern University, M.A., 1967; University of Oregon, M.S., 1979. *Politics:* Democrat. *Religion:* Jewish. *Home:* 90 East 49th Ave., Eugene, Ore. 97405.

CAREER: Volunteers in Service to America (VISTA), Washington, D.C., volunteer worker in Eugene, Ore., 1968-69; Roosevelt Junior High School, Eugene, teacher of language arts, 1969—. Professional storyteller. Guest lecturer and performer at Cabrillo College and conventions. *Member:* American Storytelling Resource Center, National Association for the Preservation and Perpetuation of Storytelling, National Story League, National Education Association, Authors Guild, Society of Children's Book Writers, Kappa Tau Alpha.

WRITINGS—Young adult novels: *Who Wants to Be a Hero!,* Dodd, 1979; *When Sirens Scream,* Dodd, 1981.

Contributor of more than eighty articles to education journals and popular magazines, including *Northwest, World Over, Child Life, Learning,* and *California Today.*

WORK IN PROGRESS: Death of the Prince, a young adult novel; *Learnin',* a nonfiction book on junior high school students' experiences.

SIDELIGHTS: Rubinstein wrote: "After serving as a VISTA volunteer, I began teaching and helped to develop the unique, totally elective program at Roosevelt Junior High School. During my year there, I have created and taught a wide variety of language arts and social studies classes, including storytelling, monsters, short story writing, Jewish culture, Arthur and Merlyn, sports history, playwriting, medieval history, basic communications, children's literature, and mystery stories.

"Since 1965 I have performed professionally as a storyteller, having learned the art as a children's librarian for the Boston Public Library. I have performed and given workshops for various organizations in Oregon and other states. For the past twelve years I have directed the Roosevelt Troupe of Tellers, performing troupes of seventh-, eighth-, and ninth-grade students who travel statewide. These troupes, which I originated, entertain elementary school students in their classrooms. They have appeared on state and local television, and were featured in three national magazine articles. According to the National Storytelling Resource Center in Tennessee, this is the only troupe of its kind in the nation.

"Each of my novels focuses on contemporary themes. *Who Wants to Be a Hero!*, which has been translated into Danish, deals with the responsibilities of being a hero. *When Sirens Scream* concerns the benefits and questions involved with nuclear power plants."

MEDIA ADAPTATIONS: Who Wants to Be a Hero! was made into a film for the cable television program "Showtime," released by Learning Corp. of America, 1981.

* * *

RUDLEY, Stephen 1946-

PERSONAL: Born April 29, 1946, in Los Angeles, Calif.; son of Herbert and Ann (Loring) Rudley. *Education:* Brooklyn College of the City University of New York, B.A., 1966; further study at New York University, 1974-76. *Office:* 90 Eighth Ave., Brooklyn, N.Y. 11215.

CAREER: Worked as science teacher, 1973-76; writer and photographer, 1975—.

WRITINGS—For young people: Construction Industry Careers, F. Watts, 1977; *The Abominable Snow Creature,* F. Watts, 1978; *Psychic Detectives,* F. Watts, 1979; *Marijuana,* F. Watts, 1981.

WORK IN PROGRESS: A novel.

AVOCATIONAL INTERESTS: Science, history, arts, nature, and vocational trades.

* * *

RUSCH, John J(ay) 1942-

PERSONAL: Born April 8, 1942, in Manitowoc, Wis.; son of Norbert John (a farmer) and Viola (Pleuss) Rusch; married Carole Rae Vasey (a teacher), August 15, 1965; children: Karl Phillip, Hans Christoph. *Education:* Carroll College, Waukesha, Wis., B.S., 1963; Indiana University, M.A.T., 1968, Ed.D., 1970. *Politics:* Democrat. *Religion:* Lutheran. *Home:* 3 Maple Ave., Superior, Wis. 54880. *Office:* Center for the Advancement of Science, University of Wisconsin—Superior, Superior, Wis. 54880.

CAREER: Science teacher at public schools in Waukesha, Wis., 1965-67; University of Oklahoma, Norman, assistant professor of earth science, 1970-74; University of Wisconsin—Superior, associate professor of science education, 1974—. Past member of board of directors of Duluth-Superior Goodwill Industries. *Member:* American Association for the Advancement of Science, National Science Teachers Association, National Association of Geology Teachers, Wisconsin Society of Science Teachers, Phi Delta Kappa. *Awards, honors:* Gustav Ohaus Award from National Science Teachers Association, 1977, for article "Bioethics: A Rationale and a Model," and 1981, for article "Science Days: Better Experiences for Preservice Elementary Teachers."

WRITINGS: (With John W. Renner, Don G. Stafford, and Donald H. Kellogg) *The Physical Sciences: Inquiry and Investigation,* Glencoe, 1977; (with Robert Karplus and others) *Teaching Science and the Development of Reasoning,* Regents, University of California, Berkeley, 1977; (with Charles R. Barman and Myron O. Schneiderwent) *Physical Science,* Silver Burdett, 1979; (with Barman and Timothy Cooney) *Science and Societal Issues: A Guide for Science Teachers,* Iowa State University Press, 1981; (with Barman, Michael Leyden, and Virginia Johnson) *Teaching Science: Grades Five to Nine,* Silver Burdett, 1982. Contributor to science and education journals.

WORK IN PROGRESS: Research on reasoning abilities of incoming college freshmen in the University of Wisconsin System.

SIDELIGHTS: Rusch commented: "My involvement in science education writing grows out of my beliefs that science is an exciting and human endeavor, allowing for real creative expression, and that children and adolescents deserve the opportunity to explore this area. At this time science education in America is generally ignored by teachers, the general public, and the government, but we all hope that the harvest of scientific inquiry will continue to enrich our lives. We must raise awareness of the reality that depriving the next generation of a knowledge and appreciation of science will be disastrous."

* * *

RUSS, Martin 1931-

PERSONAL: Born February 14, 1931, in Newark, N.J.; son of Carroll Dunn (a learning specialist) and Lavinia (a writer; maiden name, Faxon) Russ; married Lucy Blaisdell, January 2, 1962; children: Phoebe, Luke, Molly. *Education:* Attended St. Lawrence University. *Address:* Box 38, Oakville, Calif. 94562. *Agent:* Peter Matson, Literistic Ltd., 32 West Fortieth St., New York, N.Y. 10018.

CAREER: Free-lance journalist covering Vietnam, 1966; Charles Scribner's Sons, New York, N.Y., editorial consultant, 1968-71; Carnegie-Mellon University, Pittsburgh, Pa., professor of writing, 1972-79. Visiting writer at Juniata College and Pennsylvania State University, 1971-72. *Military service:* United States Marine Corps; fought in Korean conflict; became sergeant; received Purple Heart. *Member:* Associated Writing Programs.

WRITINGS: The Last Parallel, Holt, 1957 (Book-of-the-Month Club selection); *Half Moon Haven,* Holt, 1959; *War Memorial,* Atheneum, 1967; *Happy Hunting Ground: An Ex-Marine's Odyssey in Vietnam,* Atheneum, 1968; *Line of Departure: Tarawa* (Military Book Club selection), Doubleday, 1975; *Showdown Semester: Advice From a Writing Professor,* Crown, 1980; *Truckstop* (novel), Crown, 1982.

Also author of television scripts, including "Chosin Breakout," 1962, "The Illegals," 1962, "Anatahan," 1963, "Black Winter," 1975, and "King's Mountain," 1975.

SIDELIGHTS: Russ draws upon his experiences as a former Marine and as an instructor in creative writing to produce both his fiction and nonfiction works. His 1967 novel, *War Me-*

morial, presents a Marine veteran of World War II, who, in the early 1950's, seeks to recapture the glory and camaraderie of battle, eventually deciding to join the fighting in Korea. David Williams of *Punch* called *War Memorial* "a funny and horrifying book." "Its flashback scenes are abrupt, macabre, and gruesomely humorous," observed Brian Garfield in *Saturday Review.* *Listener* critic Mary Sullivan declared, "The comedy of earnest stupidity amid horrors is written poker-faced, is very funny, and clothes a message of loathing and despair." *War Memorial's* message, however, was obscured for some critics: "While the reader can admire Russ's wry wit, and grimace appropriately at the pungent puns," noted Garfield, "he will have great difficulty pressing past the stark, arid shorthand of the narrative in order to find the bleak realities meant to underscore the story."

Preparing his 1968 book, *Happy Hunting Ground: An Ex-Marine's Odyssey in Vietnam,* Russ spent six months in Vietnam with front-line American, Australian, and South Vietnamese troops. The book's diary form provides a day-by-day account of the military action and human reactions Russ observed and shared. A *New Yorker* critic hailed the book as "a rational account of irrationality, made the more persuasive and comprehensible by [Russ's] literary control." Russ explored another military situation in his 1974 book, *Line of Departure: Tarawa,* recreating a 1943 battle in the South Pacific. Reviewers found that his personal military experience brought a vividness to the book that ensured its success.

Russ's academic life provided the basis for his 1980 book, *Showdown Semester: Advice From a Writing Professor.* The book consists of journal entries addressed to a potential teacher of creative writing, providing both practical teaching advice and a discussion of the university politics connected with the author's battle for tenure. "As a manual for teachers," wrote *Los Angeles Times* critic Gerald Huckaby, *Showdown Semester* "founders, for it puts Russ in the awkward position of being his own role model." *Washington Post* reviewer Evelyn Wilde Mayerson was more impressed with Russ's teaching ideas and recommended *Showdown Semester* as a teaching guide, asserting that "what comes through in this book is great feeling for the student and an appreciation of the art and philosophy of teaching."

BIOGRAPHICAL/CRITICAL SOURCES: Saturday Review, February 4, 1967; *New Yorker,* April 13, 1968; *Punch,* June 5, 1968; *Listener,* July 18, 1968; *Washington Post Book World,* November 25, 1980; *Los Angeles Times,* December 26, 1980.

*   *   *

RUSSO, Susan   1947-

PERSONAL: Born December 21, 1947, in Chicago, Ill.; daughter of Edwin D. (a state building supervisor) and Nancy (a professor; maiden name, Bixby) Stackhouse; married John B. Russo (a professor of labor studies), September 7, 1968; children: Alexander T. *Education:* Michigan State University, B.F.A., 1969; Rochester Institute of Technology, M.F.A., 1972. *Home:* 1723 Ford Ave., Youngstown, Ohio 44504; and 1 Locks Pond Rd., Shutesbury, Mass. 01072 (summer).

CAREER: Teacher at public schools in Henrietta, N.Y., 1969-70, 1973-74; teacher of art at public schools in Northampton, Mass., 1974-77; free-lance illustrator and graphic designer, 1977—; Youngstown State University, Youngstown, Ohio, adjunct professor of art, 1981—.

WRITINGS—Juveniles; all self-illustrated: (Compiler) *The Moon's the North Wind's Cooky,* Lothrop, 1978; *Joe's Junk,* Holt, 1982; (compiler) *The Ice Cream Ocean: Humorous Sea Poems,* Lothrop, 1983.

Illustrator: Arnold Adoff, *Eats: Poems* (juvenile), Lothrop, 1979; Shirley Murphy and Pat Murphy, *Mrs. Tortino's Return to the Sun* (juvenile), Lothrop, 1980. Contributor of illustrations to Houghton Mifflin Co. textbooks.

SIDELIGHTS: Susan Russo told *CA:* "Working in the realm of children's literature makes it possible to synthesize what I am most interested in—images both verbal and visual. I have always been an avid reader and drawer. Why the idea of making books did not occur to me until I had finished two degrees and five years of teaching, I will never know! Now that I am doing what I love best, I can't imagine another kind of life!"

*   *   *

RUTSTRUM, Calvin   1895-1982

OBITUARY NOTICE—See index for *CA* sketch: Born October 26, 1895, in Hobart, Ind.; died February 5, 1982, in Osceola, Wis. Outdoorsman and author. Prior to becoming a full-time writer, Rutstrum worked as a cowboy, a salesman, a real estate agent, a car dealer, and a conservationist. Beginning in 1945, the adventurer researched survival techniques and equipment for wilderness living as well as organized canoe expeditions. His *The Way of Wilderness* "is considered," said a *New York Times* reporter, "the bible of serious canoeists." Likewise, most of Rutstrum's books describe his wilderness adventures or serve as instruction manuals for those preparing canoe trips. His other writings include *The Wilderness Cabin, The Wilderness Route Finder, Once Upon a Wilderness, The Wilderness Life, Greenhorns in the Southwest,* and *Here's Cal Rutstrum.* Obituaries and other sources: *New York Times,* February 21, 1982.

S

SABKI, Hisham M. 1934-

BRIEF ENTRY: Born November 27, 1934, in Damascus, Syria. Political scientist, educator, and author. Sabki has taught political science at Eastern Michigan University since 1969. He wrote *The United Nations and the Pacific Settlement Disputes: A Case Study of Libya* (Dar El-Mashreq, 1970). *Address:* Department of History and Social Sciences, Eastern Michigan University, Ypsilanti, Mich. 48197. *Biographical/critical sources: American Men and Women of Science: The Social and Behavioral Sciences,* 12th edition, Bowker, 1973.

*　　*　　*

SACKETT, Susan 1943-

PERSONAL: Born December 18, 1943, in New York, N.Y.; daughter of Maxwell (an accountant) and Gertrude (a teacher; maiden name, Kugel) Sackett. *Education:* University of Florida, B.A.E., 1964, M.Ed., 1965. *Residence:* North Hollywood, Calif. *Office:* Paramount Pictures, 5555 Melrose Ave., Hollywood, Calif. 90038.

CAREER: Elementary school teacher in Miami, Fla., 1966-68, and Pacific Palisades, Calif., 1968-69; "NBC and Disney on Parade" (arena show), Burbank, Calif., assistant in publicity, 1970-73; Mission-Argyle Productions, Los Angeles, Calif., director of promotions, 1973-74; personal assistant to the creator and executive producer of "Star Trek," Gene Roddenberry, 1974—; Paramount Pictures, Hollywood, Calif., consultant on "Star Trek" literature, 1977—. Assistant to producer of "Star Trek: The Motion Picture," 1979; guest speaker at "Star Trek" conventions in the United States, England, and Australia. *Member:* American Civil Liberties Union, Academy of Science Fiction, Fantasy, and Horror Films, Federation of Professional Writers, Greenpeace, Greater Los Angeles Zoo Association, Wildlife Waystation.

WRITINGS: (Editor) *Letters to Star Trek,* Ballantine, 1977; (with Fred Goldstein and Stan Goldstein) *Star Trek Speaks!,* Pocket Books, 1979; (with Gene Roddenberry) *The Making of "Star Trek: The Motion Picture,"* Pocket Books, 1980; (with Cheryl Blythe) *You Can Be a Game Show Contestant—and Win!,* Dell, 1982. Author of "Star Trek Report," a column in *Starlog,* 1977-80.

WORK IN PROGRESS: Research for books that tie in with television programs.

SIDELIGHTS: Sackett told *CA:* "As a lifetime science fiction fan, I saw my own fantasies come true when, in 1974, I began working with the creator of my favorite SF program, 'Star Trek.' While working with Gene Roddenberry, I have been able to function as both a professional and an insider/fan. As such, I established a personal rapport with key fans around the world and have maintained correspondence with fandom leaders in Australia, Great Britain, Japan, Italy, Germany, Brazil, New Zealand, Canada, and nearly every state in the United States. I have been invited to speak at fan conventions around the world, and since 1976 I have addressed tens of thousands of the adherents of this phenomenal television show.

"My professional growth has been encouraged by Gene Roddenberry, and although I have ample time to pursue the pleasures afforded me by a writing career, I still enjoy a fine professional relationship (as well as a personal friendship) with this creative and talented person whom I consider to be one of the most gifted, profound thinkers of this or any century. I feel privileged to be associated with this twentieth-century philosopher. Perhaps this is why I prefer to balance a writing career with what some would consider somewhat more mundane, routine work involved with being a personal assistant. But writing, like all work, should be pleasurable. This is why it is not a full-time job for me. I can write when and what I wish, without the worry of writing as my only source of income.

"My main concern is the rather doubtful future of our biological cousin species on this planet, and I feel that the importance of such organizations as Greenpeace, the Cousteau Society, the National Geographic Society, and many others cannot be stressed highly enough. Certainly this planet of ours is large enough to be shared by all species, no matter how powerful we humans have become. Yet we seem determined to extinguish not only our own kind, but other living things who might happen to be in our way as well. Can we really afford to wipe out the whales, dolphins, leopards, harp seals, timber wolves, sea otters, elephants, and countless other species? Can the race of man, which has come so close to destroying itself, show compassion for those who cannot verbally communicate their plight to us?

"What a sterile place Earth would be without the vast variety of animal life it bears. I am reminded of the film 'Silent Running,' in which the character played by Bruce Dern desperately tries to describe to his fellow space travelers the Earth of the past—a time when there were trees growing all over its surface. The other astronauts thought he was just a nostalgic nut, but the point was made, chillingly. Imagining an Earth devoid of trees is not such a remote fantasy, as the Brazilian jungles are opened up just a bit more each day. But an Earth without animals? It's not too difficult to imagine some future grandfather telling his twenty-first-century grandchildren about the time when the seas were filled with living things and the land bore huge herds of creatures with four legs. I prefer my animals live, not in picture books. Unless others feel this way, the fate of our planet's wildlife is going to be a dismal one.''

AVOCATIONAL INTERESTS: Films, television production, travel, animal preservation, anthropology, archaeology, astronomy, natural history.

*   *   *

SAGE, Robert   1899-1962

PERSONAL: Born in 1899 in Detroit, Mich.; died of a heart attack, October 27, 1962, in Paris, France; married wife, Maeve. *Education:* Received degree from University of Michigan, 1922.

CAREER: Journalist. Affiliated with *Detroit Times,* Detroit, Mich., 1922-23; *Chicago Tribune,* Chicago, Ill., literary reviewer, foreign correspondent, and rewriter for European edition (Paris, France), 1923-34; *New York Herald,* New York, N.Y., member of editorial staff, beginning 1934, rejoined staff as travel editor, c. 1945.

WRITINGS: (Editor with Eugene Jolas) *Transition Stories: Twenty-three Stories From "Transition,"* W. V. McKee, 1929, reprinted, Books for Libraries, 1972; (editor) *Symposium of Essays on James Joyce,* Sylvia Beach, 1929; (contributor) Peter Neague, editor, *Americans Abroad: An Anthology,* Servire, 1932; (contributor) Jolas, editor, *Transition Workshop,* Vanguard, 1949; (editor and translator) Stendhal, *The Private Diaries of Stendhal,* Doubleday, 1954. Associate editor of *transition* (literary magazine), 1927-28, co-editor, 1928-29. Contributor of reviews, short stories, and essays to newspapers and magazines, including *transition, Pagany,* and *Modern Quarterly.*

SIDELIGHTS: Sage was best known for his association with *transition,* a literary magazine of the 1920's and 1930's. From 1927 to 1929 he was associate editor and then co-editor of the publication and helped establish it as a leading journal of experimental literature. While on the staff of the Paris edition of the *Chicago Tribune,* Sage met Eugene Jolas and Eliot Paul, fellow Americans working for the *Tribune* and the eventual founders of *transition.* Sage was impressed with their ''creative editorship'' of the magazine and for most of the next twenty issues he contributed reviews, short stories, and essays. With *transition 6* Sage became associate editor and took over the critical section.

Tensions developed between the magazine's founders, and as their relationship deteriorated Sage's editorial responsibilities increased. Eventually Paul left *transition* and Jolas and Sage were co-editors. Under their direction the magazine provided an outlet for almost every new literary movement in the United States and western Europe. Jolas and Sage shared their devotion to experimental literature, and, like most of *transition*'s contributors, were following James Joyce in his revolt against realism in literature. In *transition 14* Sage reviewed the fragments of Joyce's *Work in Progress* (later published as *Finnegans Wake*) and heaped critical praise on the ''miracles'' of Joycean writing. He hoped that American writing would follow Joyce's example and ''reassemble itself into a new form more nearly in tune with the rhythm of the century.'' He believed that *transition* would ''revivify'' American literature and that

under the influence of *transition* ''american literature will be a little different just as all literature has been a little different since the publication of [Joyce's] *Ulysses.*''

In 1929 Sage's job with the *Tribune* took him from Paris to London. He became less involved with *transition,* and in June, 1930, publication temporarily ended. Although Jolas was able to revive the magazine in 1932, Sage was never again involved with its publication.

BIOGRAPHICAL/CRITICAL SOURCES: Eric Hawkins and Robert N. Sturdevant, *Hawkins of the Paris Herald,* Simon & Schuster, 1963; Dougald McMillan, *transition: The History of a Literary Era, 1927-1938,* Braziller, 1976; *Dictionary of Literary Biography,* Volume 4: *American Writers in Paris, 1920-1939,* Gale, 1980.*

*   *   *

SAIDY, Fareed Milhem   1907-1982
(Fred M. Saidy)

OBITUARY NOTICE: Born February 11, 1907, in Los Angeles, Calif.; died May 14, 1982, in Los Angeles, Calif. Librettist best known for his collaborative work with E. Y. (Yip) Harburg on the books for the Broadway hit musicals ''Finian's Rainbow,'' ''Jamaica,'' and ''Bloomer Girl.'' Saidy also wrote screenplays for ''I Dood It'' and for the film version of ''Finian's Rainbow.'' Obituaries and other sources: *New Complete Book of the American Musical Theatre,* Holt, 1970; *Contemporary Dramatists,* St. Martin's, 1973, second edition, 1977; *Notable Names in the American Theatre,* James T. White, 1976; *Encyclopaedia of the Musical Theatre,* Dodd, 1976; *New York Times,* May 18, 1982.

*   *   *

SAIDY, Fred M.
See SAIDY, Fareed Milhem

*   *   *

ST. AUBYN, Fiona   1952-

PERSONAL: Born July 11, 1952, in Hassocks, England; daughter of Oliver Piers (a stockbroker) and Mary Baily (Southwell) St. Aubyn. *Education:* Attended Le Fleuron College, Florence, Italy, 1969-70. *Home:* Woodside House, Barcome, Sussex, England.

CAREER: Royal Opera House, Covent Garden, London, England, secretary, 1971-72; Winston Churchill Memorial Trust, London, press officer, 1974-76; New Zealand Consulate General, New York, N.Y., secretary, 1977-79; writer. *Member:* Army and Navy Club (London).

WRITINGS: (With Stanley Ager) *Ager's Way to Easy Elegance,* Bobbs-Merrill, 1980, published as *The Butler's Guide,* Fireside Books, 1981; (contributor) James Wagenvoord, editor, *The Doubleday Wine Annual,* Doubleday, 1982.

WORK IN PROGRESS: The Mount, an autobiographical work; an article on gentlemen's London clubs for *Best* magazine, publication expected in 1981.

SIDELIGHTS: A granddaughter of the third Lord St. Levan, St. Aubyn wrote *Ager's Way to Easy Elegance* with Stanley Ager, the man who served as her grandfather's butler for twenty-eight years. *Avocational interests:* Travel, ballet, antique porcelain, riding, gymnastics.

BIOGRAPHICAL/CRITICAL SOURCES: People, August 31, 1981.

ST. CLAIR, Clovis
See SKARDA, Patricia Lyn

* * *

SALANT, Nathan N(athaniel) 1955-

PERSONAL: Born June 25, 1955, in Bronx, N.Y.; son of Benjamin B. (an employee of New York City's Transit Authority) and Marilyn (in social services; maiden name, Balterman) Salant. Education: State University of New York at Albany, B.A., 1976; Boston University, J.D., 1979. Home: 42 Sandy Brook Dr., Spring Valley, N.Y. 10977. Agent: Dominick Abel Literary Agency, 498 West End Ave., New York, N.Y. 10024. Office: Department of Athletics, St. Francis College, Remsen St., Brooklyn, N.Y. 11201.

CAREER: Rockland Journal-News, Nyack, N.Y., staff writer, 1974-76; State University of New York at Albany, assistant athletic director, 1979-80; Rockland Community College, Suffern, N.Y., supervisor of family recreation and assistant baseball coach, 1980-82. Director of sports information at St. Francis College; manager of Spring Valley Pirates (baseball team), 1973—; commissioner of Rockland County Big League, 1981—.

WRITINGS: This Date in New York Yankees History, Stein & Day, 1979; Superstars, Stars, and Just Plain Heroes, Stein & Day, 1982. Contributor to Action Sports Hockey and the New York Yankees Magazine.

WORK IN PROGRESS: A baseball encyclopedia; a book about the Philadelphia Flyers hockey team.

SIDELIGHTS: Salant commented: "I would like to host a sports talk show in or near a major city, and couple that with some play-by-play work in hockey and/or baseball. I am always interested in writing in those fields. I am committed to working with youths, particularly high school and college kids. These people are the ones who need a concerned party more than anyone else in our society. As a coach, I try to do more than just give signs and teach the sport—I try to teach the game called LIFE."

AVOCATIONAL INTERESTS: Youth work, collecting stamps, coins, sports memorobilia, and antique and classic editions of books and magazines.

* * *

SALASSI, Otto R(ussell) 1939-

PERSONAL: Born October 2, 1939, in Vicksburg, Miss.; son of Walter Washington (a railroad mechanic) and Ruby (Russell) Salassi; married Margaret Buchanan (a college administrator), 1963; children: Adam, Max. Education: Memphis State University, B.S., 1967; Vanderbilt University, M.L.S., 1968; University of Arkansas, M.F.A., 1978. Politics: Democrat. Home and office: 312 East Maple St., Fayetteville, Ark. 72701. Agent: Lois Wallace, Wallace & Sheil Agency, Inc., 177 East 70th St., New York, N.Y. 10021.

CAREER: Douglas Aircraft Co., Vandenburg Air Force Base, Calif., mathematician with data engineering group at Pacific Missile Range, 1963-66; Bemidji State College, Bemidji, Minn., assistant librarian in charge of technical processing, 1968-69; Motlow State Community College, Tullahoma, Tenn., librarian, 1969-70; Hobart and William Smith Colleges, Geneva, N.Y., head of public services, 1970-74; University of Arkansas, Fayetteville, orientation librarian, 1978-79; writer, 1979—. Military service: U.S. Air Force, 1957-61.

WRITINGS: (Contributor) Miller Williams and James Alan McPherson, editors, Railroads, Trains, and Train People in American Culture, Random House, 1976; On the Ropes (young adult novel), Greenwillow, 1981; Nobody Knew They Were There (young adult novel), Greenwillow, 1982. Author of "Sports," a weekly column in Grapevine, 1977-78, and "Page Two," a feature column, 1980. Contributor of stories to adult and children's magazines, including Boys' Life, Southern Humanities Review, and New Orleans Review.

WORK IN PROGRESS: Sidewinder's Will, a young adult sequel to On the Ropes.

SIDELIGHTS: Salassi commented: "I've always liked telling and writing stories—telling more than writing, of course, because it's easier and doesn't take as long—and I've always been rather good at it, ever since I learned how as a kid in Mississippi. Everybody in Mississippi told stories. It took forever to get through a grocery line because the old geezer at the cash register told stories to everybody who came through. Many's the time I thought I was going to starve to death before my mother got off the phone.

"I was always a lazy child, and not very bright, but one of the things I learned was, if you could keep somebody listening long enough, or laughing long enough, you could get away with murder. If you didn't know something, you could make it up. That got me through school and college. If you could tell a good joke you could usually get out of cleaning the latrine. That got me through the Air Force.

"But eventually I grew up and got married, had a couple of lazy kids of my own, and faced, as we all surely must, the problem of getting money. My useless and misspent youth had prepared me for nothing except telling stories, and so I found myself forced into the world of academics, where people such as myself are paid for telling stories, but no one, alas, is paid to listen.

"After thirteen years of semi-successful storytelling on the college level, I decided that my stories, which had served me so well for so long, were as good as or better than my colleagues' and ought to be preserved for future generations. Thus I have begun to commit them to print.

"Since I've had to draw heavily from my own experiences, the reader of On the Ropes may expect to find the novel peopled with pool sharks, con men, bull slingers, preachers, and other ambitious and worthy types.

"My advice to young writers? Never do anything you don't have to do."

BIOGRAPHICAL/CRITICAL SOURCES: Arkansas Gazette, May 4, 1981.

* * *

SALOP, Lynne
See HAWES, Lynne Salop

* * *

SAMPSON, R. Neil 1938-

PERSONAL: Born November 29, 1938, in Spokane, Wash.; son of Robert J. (an electrician) and Juanita (an artist; maiden name, Hickman) Sampson; married Jeanne L. Stokes (a teacher), June 7, 1960; children: Robert, Eric, Christopher, Heidi. Education: University of Idaho, B.S., 1960; Harvard University, M.P.A., 1974. Religion: Presbyterian. Home: 5209 York Rd., Alexandria, Va. 22310. Office: National Association of Conservation Districts, 1025 Vermont N.W., Suite 730, Washington, D.C. 20005.

CAREER: U.S. Soil Conservation Service, Boise, Idaho, soil conservationist, 1960-72; State of Idaho, Boise, director of land use, 1971-73; U.S. Soil Conservation Service, Washington, D.C., land use specialist, 1974-78; National Association of Conservation Districts, Washington, executive vice-president, 1978—. *Member:* Soil Conservation Society of America fellow, 1979, American Society of Association Executives, Outdoor Writers Association of America, Society for the Preservation of Barbershop Quartet Singing in America (chapter president, 1970-72), Clearwater [Idaho] Sheriffs Posse (president, 1964-65), Orofino [Idaho] Golf Association (president, 1966). *Awards, honors:* Boise Federal Civil Servant of the Year, 1972; president's citation from the Soil Conservation Society of America, 1978.

WRITINGS: "Look to the Land" (documentary film), Idaho Department of Planning and Community Affairs, 1973; (contributor) *The American Land,* Smithsonian Institution Press, 1979; (contributor) Max Schnepf, editor, *Farmland, Food and the Future,* Soil Conservation Society of America, 1979; *Farmland or Wasteland: A Time to Choose,* Rodale Press, 1981; *Stewards of the Land,* Rodale Press, 1983. Also contributor of short stories and articles to periodicals, including *Boise Business, Soil Conservation, Scouting, All Outdoors, Environmental Comment, Snowmobiling, Incredible Idaho,* and *Journal of Soil and Water Conservation.*

SIDELIGHTS: Sampson's book *Farmland or Wasteland: A Time to Choose* deals with land erosion and the possible threat it poses to farming. Noting that the United States grain export market has grown into a $40 billion per year industry, Sampson writes that farmers are tending to grow cash crops, such as soybeans, which leave the land depleted of material to hold the soil after a harvest, hence causing erosion. Sampson also examines land damage due to surface mining and irrigating, predicting that ruined farmland will lead to resource scarcity and exorbitant food prices. According to Ken Cook of the *Washington Post,* Sampson "provides an especially lucid discussion of the powerful economic forces working against soil and water conservation down on the farm."

Sampson told *CA:* "My writings have attempted to illuminate the relationships between people and the environment. Whether short stories on outdoor subjects, how-to pieces on conservation, or essays on ethics, I have tried to convey a feeling for the bond between modern humans and the natural world around them. In addition to writing, I give between ten and twenty paid lectures per year, along with dozens of speeches on soil and water conservation, land use, and other environmental issues. My main goal is to help people see that stewardship of the natural environment is, at its roots, the most humanitarian and civilized manner in which any society can behave."

BIOGRAPHICAL/CRITICAL SOURCES: Des Moines Register, November 8, 1981; *Christian Science Monitor,* January 15, 1982; *Minneapolis Tribune,* January 17, 1982; *New York Tribune,* February 2, 1982; *Washington Post,* February 2, 1982; *Oregon Journal,* March 6, 1982.

*   *   *

SAMUELS, Charles   1902-1982

OBITUARY NOTICE—See index for *CA* sketch: Born September 15, 1902; died April 27, 1982, in Cuernavaca, Mexico. Journalist and author best remembered for his biographies of celebrities, including *The Magnificent Rube: The Life and Gaudy*

Times of Tex Rickard, The Golden Ham: A Candid Biography of Jackie Gleason, and *The King: A Biography of Clark Gable.* He was also the co-author of several famous personalities' autobiographies, namely, Ethel Waters's *His Eye Is on the Sparrow,* Buster Keaton's *My Wonderful World of Slapstick,* and Boris Morros's *My Ten Years as a Counterspy.* In 1960 Morros's book was adapted into a motion picture, "Man on a String," starring Ernest Borgnine and Kerwin Mathews. A journalist as well, Samuels began his career as a sports and feature writer for the *Brooklyn Daily Eagle.* Later he served as a reporter or editor for the *Brooklyn Times, Miami Tribune,* Standard News Service, the King Features Syndicate, and *Paramount News.* A screenwriter and press agent, he also wrote novels, such as *The Frantic Young Man* and *A Rather Simple Fellow,* and nonfiction. The author received an Edgar Allan Poe Award for *Night Fell on Georgia,* the true story of a 1913 lynching. Obituaries and other sources: *New York Times,* May 8, 1982.

*   *   *

SANDLE, Floyd Leslie   1913-

BRIEF ENTRY: Born July 4, 1913, in Magnolia, Miss. American educator and author. Sandle joined the faculty at Grambling State University in 1951 and is now a professor of speech, department chairman, and dean of the Division of General Studies. He wrote *The Negro in the American Educational Theatre: An Organizational Development, 1911-1964* (1964) and *Orientation: An Image of the College, With Emphasis on Books and Libraries* (W. C. Brown, 1967). *Address:* 102 Richmond Dr., Grambling, La. 71245; and Division of General Studies, Grambling State University, Grambling, La. 71245. *Biographical/critical sources: Notable Names in the American Theatre,* James T. White, 1976; *Directory of American Scholars,* Volume II: *English, Speech, and Drama,* 7th edition, Bowker, 1978.

*   *   *

SARAT, Austin Dean   1947-

PERSONAL: Born November 2, 1947, in Fall River, Mass.; son of George Joseph (in business) and Lillian (Sock) Sarat; children: Lauren, Emily. *Education:* Providence College, B.A., 1969; University of Wisconsin—Madison, M.A., 1970, Ph.D., 1973. *Home:* 17 Walnut St., Amherst, Mass. 01002. *Office:* Department of Political Science, Amherst College, Amherst, Mass. 01002.

CAREER: Amherst College, Amherst, Mass., associate professor of political science, 1973—. Research associate at Yale University, 1976—, member of faculty, 1976-78; research associate at University of Wisconsin—Madison, 1981—. Member of staff of U.S. Department of Justice Office for Improvement in the Administration of Justice, 1978-79. Member of National Advisory Commission on Small Claims Courts, 1976-77; research director of Council on the Role of Courts, 1978-79; testified before the U.S. House of Representatives; consultant to RAND Corp., Law Enforcement Assistance Administration, and National Center for State Courts.

MEMBER: American Political Science Association, Law and Society Association (member of board of trustees, 1978-81), American Judicature Society. *Awards, honors:* Woodrow Wilson fellow, 1969-70; Russell Sage Foundation fellow, 1973-74, grant, 1975-76; National Endowment for the Humanities grant, 1978; Social Science Research Council grant, 1978-79.

WRITINGS: (Editor with Sheldon Goldman, and contributor) *American Court Systems,* W. H. Freeman, 1978; (with Malcolm Feeley) *The Policy Dilemma: Federal Crime Policy and the Law Enforcement Assistance Administration, 1968-1978,* University of Minnesota Press, 1980; *The Rule of Law and the American Legal System,* Duxbury, 1982.

Contributor: Hugo A. Bedau and Chester M. Pierce, editors, *Capital Punishment in the United States,* AMS Press, 1976; John A. Gardiner, editor, *Public Law and Public Policy,* Praeger, 1977; Theodore Fetter, editor, *State Courts: A Blueprint for the Future,* National Center for State Courts, 1978; Peter Nardulli, editor, *New Perspectives on Criminal Courts,* Ballinger, 1979. Contributor of more than twenty-five articles and reviews to political science and law journals. Member of editorial board of *Law and Society Review,* 1977-78.

WORK IN PROGRESS: Thinking About Courts, with Ralph Cavanagh; *Sentencing White Collar Criminals,* a monograph on equal justice in criminal sentencing, with Kenneth Mann and Stanton Wheeler, for Yale University Press; *Lawyers and the Transformation of Disputes,* with William Felstiner; research on the relationship of social change and legal policy making, on the relation of legal to social equality, on the cost of civil dispute processing, and on public attitudes toward law and justice.

*   *   *

SARGENT, Jean Vieth   1918-

PERSONAL: Born February 10, 1918, in Oakland, Iowa; daughter of Chester Charles (a merchant) and Mary (Haight) Vieth; married John Hall Klas, August 18, 1940 (divorced, 1969); married Warren Bert Sargent (a contractor and engineer), June 10, 1970; children: (first marriage) Mary Klas Nelson, Caroline, Jacqueline Klas Lacey. *Education:* Iowa State University, B.S., 1939, M.S., 1971. *Religion:* Protestant. *Home and office:* 1101 Murray Dr., Ames, Iowa 50010.

CAREER: Gas Service Co., Kansas City, Mo., home service director, 1939-40; Iowa State University, Ames, instructor in household equipment, 1943-44; free-lance instructor in cooking and freezing methods, 1944-53; Seattle City Light, Seattle, Wash., home service director, 1953-55; free-lance home economist in Salt Lake City, Utah, 1955-60; University of Utah, Salt Lake City, instructor in home economics, 1960-69; author of weekly column, "An Easier Way," in *Ames Tribune,* 1973—, and *Cedar Rapids Gazette,* 1976—. Volunteer worker with young people and the elderly. *Member:* PEO Sisterhood, American Association of University Women, American Home Economics Association, Phi Delta Gamma, Phi Upsilon Omicron, Kappa Delta.

WRITINGS: An Easier Way: Handbook for the Elderly and Handicapped, Iowa State University Press, 1981.

SIDELIGHTS: Jean Sargent wrote: "The enormous amount of mail generated by my weekly columns prompted me to seek publication of the handbook. The elderly and disabled are often homebound and the opportunity to order items by mail is a great help to their independent living."

AVOCATIONAL INTERESTS: Travel (England, Italy, Spain, the Soviet Union, Finland, Norway, Denmark, Hong Kong, Thailand, Singapore, Mexico, Peru), music, golf, cooking.

*   *   *

SARGENT, Sarah   1937-

PERSONAL: Born March 15, 1937, in Roanoke, Va.; daughter of Francis Atwell (a civil engineer) and Mary (a teacher; maiden name, DuPuy) Davis; married Seymour Sargent (a college

teacher), August 25, 1962; children: Edgar, Alice. *Education:* Randolph-Macon Woman's College, B.A., 1959; Yale University, M.A., 1961. *Politics:* Democrat. *Religion:* None. *Home:* 627 Ceape Ave., Oshkosh, Wis. 54901. *Agent:* Dorothy Markinko, McIntosh & Otis, Inc., 475 Fifth Ave., New York, N.Y. 10017.

CAREER: Teacher of English at University of North Dakota, 1961-62, University of Vermont, 1963-67, University of Minnesota, 1967-68, University of Wisconsin—Oshkosh, 1968-72, 1975-78. *Awards, honors:* First place citation from Wisconsin Writers Council, 1978, for *Edward Troy and the Witch Cat; Weird Henry Berg* was listed among the best books of 1980 by *School Library Journal;* juvenile merit award from Friends of American Writers and citation from Library of Congress, both 1980, for *Weird Henry Berg; Secret Lies* was named notable children's book by American Library Association, 1981.

WRITINGS—Juvenile: *Edward Troy and the Witch Cat,* Follett, 1978; *Weird Henry Berg,* Crown, 1980; *Secret Lies,* Crown, 1981; *Edge of Darkness,* Crown, 1982.

WORK IN PROGRESS: The Solstice Son (tentative title), publication by Crown expected in 1983; *The Seeds of Change* (tentative title), dealing with animal-human transformation in a swamp in the southern United States, publication by Crown expected in 1983.

SIDELIGHTS: Sarah Sargent wrote: "I am very interested in myth and in the various ways people add dimension to their lives by their participation in myths of one kind or another. *Secret Lies* is about a girl who shapes her reality by her commitment to soap operas and romance novels. More recent books examine the relevance of older myths to our times—*Edge of Darkness* is about Norse myth and *Solstice Son* is about Celtic myth.

"For me, writing fiction is not something that is under complete conscious control. It involves a dialogue between the conscious, order-producing side of my mind and the unconscious, image-producing side. Working this way, trying to open myself up to the possibilities of meaning that lie just below the surface in my material and in my mind, leads me automatically to work with myth because that is what myths are—attempts to dramatize and personify hidden forces in the world. I think the most important thing about my writing is the way it leads me to explore possibilities. Once words are typed onto a page, they start to be alive, to make suggestions, and to nudge me in directions I hadn't necessarily expected to move in. I am very interested in the way styles create worlds—in the power of language to shape realities."

*   *   *

SARGENT, (Francis) William (Jr.)   1946-

PERSONAL: Born June 1, 1946, in Boston, Mass.; son of Francis William (a governor) and Jessie Fay Sargent; married Claudia F. Praeger (an architect), December 26, 1975; children: Benjamin. *Education:* Harvard University, B.A., 1969; Fletcher School, M.A., 1971; attended Tufts University. *Politics:* Independent. *Religion:* Unitarian Universalist. *Home:* 15 Holly Ave., Cambridge, Mass. 02138. *Office:* Francis W. Sargent Productions, 70 Coolidge Hill Rd., Watertown, Mass. 02172. *Agent:* Steve Axelrod, Curtis Brown, Ltd., 575 Madison Ave., New York, N.Y. 10022.

CAREER: Marine ecologist and biologist. Baltimore Aquarium, Baltimore, Md., director, 1974-75; Francis W. Sargent Productions, Watertown, Mass., president, 1977-81; writer, 1981—. Caucus representative at Sierra Club's Land of the

Seas Conference, 1974. Consultant to television program "NOVA," WGBH-TV, Boston, Mass., 1979; science reporter for television program "OMNI." Research assistant at Woods Hole Oceanographic Institution. Lecturer. *Member:* International Oceanographic Foundation, American Association for the Advancement of Science, Littoral Society.

WRITINGS: Shallow Waters: A Year on Cape Cod's Pleasant Bay, Houghton, 1981. Contributor of articles to periodicals, including *Smithsonian* and *Boston Globe.*

WORK IN PROGRESS: Georges Bank, stories of fishermen and scientists; "Project Jacqueline," a project to raise a Soviet submarine; research on spring waters.

SIDELIGHTS: While serving as a consultant for the television series "NOVA," William Sargent spent one year studying wildlife in Pleasant Bay, the largest estuatary of Cape Cod. After his work for the program was complete, the scientist recorded his observations in *Shallow Waters: A Year on Cape Cod's Pleasant Bay.*

In this book, Sargent follows sea creatures, land animals, and shore birds through the four seasons, beginning with spring and ending with winter. He adheres to a scientific approach to prove that all of life participates i the continuing process of evolution. According to Steve Cady of the *New York Times Book Review, Shallow Waters* "is straight-ahead evolutionary biology, with Darwin as the guide."

The book has been praised for its fine descriptions and explanations. "This book is such a fine mix of reflection, anecdote and quote, so nicely paced and salted, one wishes foolishly to begin again—with a new spring, another glimpse of seal and tern, a whole new series of excursions in fog and flat calm and starry night," wrote the *Washington Post*'s Peggy Thompson. Thompson also applauds Sargent's tenacity as a photographer: he "thinks nothing of lying about for months in six inches of creek water to catch with his handheld camera just the animal behavior he wants."

Sargent told *CA:* "I worked for a year as a research assistant on an oceanographic cruise to Africa, South America, and the Baltic. That and an abiding interest in biology led me to science writing."

BIOGRAPHICAL/CRITICAL SOURCES: New York Times Book Review, August 2, 1981; *Washington Post,* September 24, 1981.

* * *

SARGESON, Frank 1903-1982

OBITUARY NOTICE—See index for *CA* sketch: Born March 23, 1903, in Hamilton, New Zealand; died March 1, 1982. Solicitor and author. Sargeson, one of New Zealand's best-known writers, preferred to remain in his native country instead of becoming an expatriate like many of his peers. "At the time of his death," wrote a *London Times* reporter, "he was the unquestioned doyen of New Zealand letters." Sargeson is also remembered for encouraging the talents of Janet Frame and Maurice Duggan. Showing the influence of Mark Twain and Sherwood Anderson, Sargeson's writings include novels such as *I Saw in My Dream,* collections of plays, notably *Wrestling With the Angel,* and several volumes of memoirs. Obituaries and other sources: Frank Sargeson, *Memoirs of a Peon* (autobiography), MacGibbon & Kee, 1965; Sargeson, *Once Is Enough: A Memoir,* Martin Brian & O'Keefe, 1972; Sargeson, *More Than Enough: A Memoir,* Martin Brian & O'Keefe, 1975; *London Times,* March 11, 1982.

SARNO, Arthur D. 1921(?)-1982

OBITUARY NOTICE: Born c. 1921, in Springfield, Mass.; died after a lengthy illness, April 5, 1982, in Culver City, Calif. Film publicist and screenwriter best known for his work in publicizing the Academy Award ceremonies since the early 1960's. He also served as a unit publicist for films such as "Stalag 17," "Vertigo," and "High Anxiety." In addition, Sarno wrote screenplays for motion pictures and television shows. Obituaries and other sources: *Chicago Tribune,* April 17, 1982.

* * *

SAUNDERS, Jason Lewis 1922-

BRIEF ENTRY: Born April 21, 1922, in Boston, Mass. American philosopher, educator, and author. Saunders began teaching in 1954. Since 1969 he has been a professor of philosophy at City University of New York. He wrote *Justus Lipsius: The Philosophy of Renaissance Stoicism* (Liberal Arts Press, 1955) and *Early Stoic Philosophy.* Saunders edited *Greek and Roman Philosophy After Aristotle* (Free Press, 1966). *Address:* 110 Jones Rd., Englewood, N.J. 07631; and Department of Philosophy, City College of the City University of New York, 33 West 42nd St., New York, N.Y. 10036. *Biographical/critical sources: Directory of American Scholars,* Volume IV: *Philosophy, Religion, and Law,* 7th edition, Bowker, 1978.

* * *

SAUNDERS, Susan 1945-

PERSONAL: Born April 14, 1945, in San Antonio, Tex.; daughter of George S. (a rancher) and Brooksie (Hughes) Saunders; married John J. Cirigliano, September 7, 1969 (divorced, 1976). *Education:* Barnard College, B.A., 1966. *Home and office address:* P.O. Box 736, Westhampton, N.Y. 11977. *Agent:* Amy Berkower, Writer's House, Inc., 21 West 26th St., New York, N.Y. 10010.

CAREER: John Wiley, New York City, copy editor, 1966-67; CBS/Columbia House, New York City, 1967-70, began as proofreader and assistant to production manager, became copy editor, then staff writer; Greystone Press, New York City, copy editor, 1970-72; *Lighting Design and Application* (trade magazine), New York City, associate editor, 1972-76; Visual Information Systems (producer of radio programs and videotapes), New York City, editor, 1976-77; Random House (publisher), New York City, editor for Miller-Brody Productions, Inc., subsidiary, 1977-80; free-lance writer, scriptwriter, editor, copy editor, proofreader, and researcher for Harcourt Brace Jovanovich, *Psychology Today,* Random House, and the Rockefeller Foundation.

WRITINGS—Juveniles: *Wales' Tale,* Viking, 1980; *A Sniff in Time,* Atheneum, 1982; *Fish Fry,* Viking, 1982; *The Green Slime: Choose Your Own Adventure,* Bantam, 1982; *The Creature From Miller's Pond: Choose Your Own Adventure,* Bantam, 1983.

WORK IN PROGRESS: A fantasy for older children, tentatively titled *The Weathermakers.*

SIDELIGHTS: Susan Saunders wrote: "I was an only child for a long time and books were my favorite entertainment, especially fairy tales from other lands, preferably with wizards, elves, dark forests, and rushing rivers. South Texas is semi-arid, so forests and rivers were as wonderful to me as elves.

"Animals were and are an important part of my life. I grew up with horses, lots of dogs, tame deer, tame—more or less—jackrabbits, and once an armadillo who really didn't work out as a pet. Since I've lived in Manhattan I've had to cut back, but I do have two cats and a cairn terrier.

"I have always loved children's books. There is a magic to them, especially picture books, that I think doesn't exist anywhere else in literature. I write in spurts: I can have an idea for a long time, but will only commit it to paper when it's almost all written in my head, or when the suspense is killing me."

*   *   *

SAVIN, Marc   1948-

PERSONAL: Born May 31, 1948, in New York, N.Y.; son of Lee Savin (an attorney for the motion picture industry) and Harriette Smith (in public relations); married Kati Galateo, 1976 (divorced, 1981). *Education:* Attended Santa Monica College, 1967, University of California, Los Angeles, 1967, and Casper College, 1968. *Agent:* Martin Caan, William Morris Agency, 151 El Camino, Beverly Hills, Calif. 90212.

CAREER: Writer, 1964—.

WRITINGS: Coyote (novel), Pinnacle Books, 1980. "Mahalia" (screenplay), Richard St. Johns, 1976; "Whatever Happened to the Class of '65?" (for television), NBC-TV, 1979.

WORK IN PROGRESS: Oil Whore, a novel, completion expected in 1982; screenplay based on own novel *Coyote* for Gaylord Productions and Producers Circle Co., completion of film expected in 1982.

SIDELIGHTS: Savin told *CA:* "The two most fortunate experiences I've had in writing were: First, not being able to afford going to college and learning to write on my own, because colleges are like old age homes, except that more people die in college than in old age homes. Second, selling the screenplay of *Coyote* to Robert Redford, who, for noncreative reasons, ultimately decided not to do the picture, but showed me the way to take chances and make them work."

*   *   *

SCHAAF, Peter   1942-

PERSONAL: Born November 27, 1942, in New York, N.Y.; married Marilyn Brooke Goffstein (a writer), 1965. *Education:* Juilliard School of Music, B.M., 1963, M.S., 1965. *Agent:* Georges Borchardt, 136 East 57th St., New York, N.Y. 10022. *Office:* 697 West End Ave., New York, N.Y. 10025.

CAREER: Pianist, 1965-72; photographer, 1973—; writer. *Member:* American Society of Magazine Photographers.

WRITINGS—And photographer: The Violin Close Up, Four Winds Press, 1980; *An Apartment House Close Up,* Four Winds Press, 1980.

WORK IN PROGRESS: The Piano Close Up.

SIDELIGHTS: Schaaf told *CA:* "I am interested in a variation of the photo essay: strong and beautiful photos arranged in an intelligent sequence that, together with words when necessary, shows you something you can't normally see, or haven't yet seen."

AVOCATIONAL INTERESTS: Bicycle racing, studying French.

BIOGRAPHICAL/CRITICAL SOURCES: New York Times Book Review, November 9, 1980.

SCHACHTEL, Roger (Bernard)   1949-
(Marian Forrester)

PERSONAL: Born November 21, 1949, in New York, N.Y.; son of Irving Ira (a lawyer) and Elinor (a social worker for alcoholics; maiden name, Weiler) Schachtel. *Education:* Yale University, B.A., 1971; studied at Herbert Berghof Studio, 1981-82. *Residence:* New York, N.Y. *Office:* Schachtel Productions, 165 East 72nd St., New York, N.Y. 10021.

CAREER: Teacher at preschool day-care centers in New York City, 1973-75; free-lance film editor, 1975-78; Dalton School, New York City, teacher of English, 1979-80; Schachtel Productions, New York City, story editor in development of film projects, 1981—.

WRITINGS: (Under pseudonym Marian Forrester) *Farewell to Thee* (historical novel), Belmont-Tower, 1978; *Fantastic Flight to Freedom* (juvenile novel), Raintree, 1980; *Caught on a Cliff-Face* (juvenile novel), Raintree, 1980.

WORK IN PROGRESS: A television script with a high school setting.

SIDELIGHTS: Schachtel wrote: "In the beginning, I wrote for the transcendent thrills of, first, discovering my mind and talent and, second, getting published. Now, frankly, my primary motivation is to remain self-employed as I regard the devastating consequences of nine-to-five breadwinning on the lives of friends who are forced to work for institutions or corporations on a full-time basis. A writer's life, however penurious, is preferable to such a fate."

*   *   *

SCHAEFER, Walter Erich   1901-1982(?)

OBITUARY NOTICE: Born March 16 (some sources say March 13) 1901, in Memmingen, Germany (now West Germany); died c. 1982 in Stuttgart, West Germany. Theatrical director, playwright, and author credited with bringing the Wuerttemberg State Theatres to a position of eminence considered by many to be unsurpassed in the world. He headed the Stuttgart and Mannheim state theatres during the 1930's and led the Kassel State Theatre from 1938 to 1948 despite his disfavor with Nazi officials. He was Generalintendant of the Wuerttemberg State Theatre, which produced opera, ballet, and drama performances, from 1949 to 1972. Obituaries and other sources: *The Concise Encyclopedia of Modern Drama,* Horizon Press, 1964; *The International Who's Who,* Europa, 1978; *London Times,* February 10, 1982.

*   *   *

SCHEER, Robert   1936-

PERSONAL: Born April 14, 1936, in New York, N.Y.; married Anne Weills (marriage ended). *Education:* Received degree from City College (now of the City University of New York), 1958; graduate study at Syracuse University, 1958-61, and University of California, Berkeley, beginning 1961. *Office: Los Angeles Times,* Times Mirror Sq., Los Angeles, Calif. 90053.

CAREER: Free-lance writer and journalist, beginning early 1960's; City Lights Bookstore, San Francisco, Calif., sales clerk, to 1964; *Ramparts,* San Francisco, managing editor, 1964-68, editor-in-chief, 1969; *New Times,* New York, N.Y., West Coast editor, 1975-76; *Los Angeles Times,* Los Angeles, Calif., reporter, 1976—.

WRITINGS: (With Maurice Zeitlin) *Cuba: A Tragedy in Our Hemisphere,* Grove, 1963, published in England as *Cuba: An American Tragedy,* Penguin, 1964; *How the United States Got Involved in Vietnam,* Center for the Study of Democratic Institutions, 1965; (editor) *The Diary of Che Guevara, Bolivia: November 7, 1966-October 7, 1967,* Bantam, 1968; (editor) *Eldridge Cleaver: Post-Prison Writings and Speeches,* Random House, 1969; *America After Nixon: The Age of the Multinationals,* McGraw, 1975, also published as *America After Nixon: The Politics of the New World Order; What Happened? The Story of Election 1980,* Random House, 1981.

Author of "The Ruling Class," a column in *New Times,* 1975-76. Contributor of articles to numerous magazines, including *Playboy, Ramparts, New Times,* and *Esquire.*

SIDELIGHTS: During the 1960's, Scheer was among the foremost practitioners of what he calls "counter-journalism," an aggressive, iconoclastic, and controversial style of reporting that grew out of the radical political movements of the period. "I got into journalism doing that Vietnam stuff in 1962, '63," Scheer told *More* interviewer Ken Auletta. "We were kind of guerila-kamikaze journalists." Counter-journalism was closely linked to political activism, and Scheer was deeply involved in both. In 1965 he was an antiwar candidate for Congress from California's seventh district, and in 1970 he ran for the U.S. Senate on the Peace and Freedom party ticket. Scheer is a Marxist and has been called an ideologue rather than a journalist, but he rejects the suggestion that the two roles are incompatible. "Is James Reston an ideologue or a journalist?" Scheer asked Auletta. "Just because you embrace the establishment's dominant ideology doesn't make you any less of an ideologue."

Because of their opposition to the Vietnam War and other government policies, Scheer and other counter-journalists were denied access to information channels used by mainstream reporters. "Politicians try to prevent you from knowing what's going on because that's how they survive," Scheer said at a panel discussion in 1976. "The journalist's job is to get that story by breaking into their offices, by bribing, by seducing people, by lying, by anything else." He later qualified that statement, telling Auletta that such tactics are justifiable only in "extreme situations where there was something important that the public had a right to know . . . that was important to the formulation of public policy. . . . If something is important, your highest obligation is to print it." Scheer has rarely had to use such extreme means, but he admits that when he was editor of *Ramparts* he ventured into "a gray area of activity" to obtain documents proving that the CIA was funding the National Student Association.

Scheer's association with *Ramparts* began when his second book, *How the U.S. Got Involved in Vietnam,* which told how a group of powerful men had worked to bring about the American intervention, was adapted for the magazine's first major expose. *Ramparts,* which had begun as a liberal Catholic journal, soon became one of the most successful and flamboyant radical publications of the decade, and Scheer was one of its most influential editors. Besides the National Student Association story, he was involved in *Ramparts*'s revelation of Michigan State University's links with CIA operations in Vietnam and in former Green Beret Donald Duncan's denunciation of the war. In 1969 Scheer became editor in chief of the magazine, which was by then bankrupt. Though *Ramparts* continued to publish into the mid-1970's, it never regained its former prominence, and Scheer soon left to return to freelancing.

In the 1970's Scheer earned a reputation as a tough and demanding interviewer of political figures, including Nelson Rockefeller, Jerry Brown, radicals Bill and Emily Harris, and presidential candidate Jimmy Carter. At the end of the Carter interview, which was published in *Playboy* in 1976, Scheer asked Carter about his views on sexual morality. Carter responded by confessing that he had "looked on a lot of women with lust," thereby making sexual fantasy a political issue for the first time in American history. Scheer regretted the controversy over that remark, noting that he had not sought a "sexy, *Playboy* kind of interview" and had not wanted to embarrass Carter.

BIOGRAPHICAL/CRITICAL SOURCES: Village Voice, March 6, 1969; *New York Times,* April 10, 1969; *New York Review of Books,* March 20, 1975; *Newsweek,* October 4, 1976, April 4, 1977; *More,* March, 1977.*

*   *   *

SCHERMAN, Thomas K(ielty)   1917-1979

OBITUARY NOTICE: Born February 12, 1917, in New York, N.Y.; died of heart failure, May 14, 1979, in New York, N.Y. Composer and editor of *The Beethoven Companion.* Scherman became an assistant to conductor Otto Klemperer at the New School for Social Research in New York City in 1939. Following service in the Army during World War II, he began conducting radio concerts. In 1947 Scherman used his own funds to organize the Little Orchestra Society, which was dedicated to performing neglected or little-known classical music pieces and also to presenting deserving new compositions by unknown artists. He led the Little Orchestra Society until 1975. Obituaries and other sources: *Current Biography,* Wilson, 1954, July, 1979; *Who's Who in the World,* 2nd edition, Marquis, 1973; *Baker's Biographical Dictionary of Musicians,* 6th edition, Schirmer Books, 1978; *Time,* May 28, 1979.

*   *   *

SCHERMER, Judith (Denise)   1941-

PERSONAL: Born February 19, 1941, in Detroit, Mich.; daughter of George (a consultant in human relations) and Bernice (in real estate sales and a teacher; maiden name, Augdahl) Schermer; married T. Truxtun Hare III, April 27, 1963 (divorced July, 1970); children: Abigail C., Katharine S. *Education:* Attended Radcliffe College, 1959-61, University of Colorado, 1964, University of Pennsylvania, 1964, 1970-72, and University of Chicago, 1965-67. *Politics:* Liberal. *Home:* 402 South 22nd St., Philadelphia, Pa. 19146. *Agents:* Keith Korman, Raines & Raines, 475 Fifth Ave., New York, N.Y. 10017; Jacques de Spoelberch, Woodland Rd., Wilson Point, South Norwalk, Conn. 06584.

CAREER: Painter, illustrator, and author of children's books. *Member:* Philadelphia Art Alliance. *Awards, honors:* Second prize from Regional Council of Community Art Centers, 1973, for painting "Students."

WRITINGS: Mouse in House (juvenile; self-illustrated), Houghton, 1979.

Illustrator: Ovide F. Pomerleau and Cynthia S. Pomerleau, *Break the Smoking Habit,* Research Press, 1977.

WORK IN PROGRESS: Four self-illustrated children's books.

SIDELIGHTS: Judith Schermer told *CA:* "I spend most of my working time painting and some time writing and illustrating. I started out to be an illustrator and became interested in the writing along the way. My books so far, therefore, are for young children and are heavily illustrated." Schermer is a self-taught artist, painting in oils and acrylics. *Avocational interests:* "Playing the recorder, which I do regularly in a quartet."

* * *

SCHIFFER, Michael 1948-

PERSONAL: Born July 6, 1948, in Philadelphia, Pa.; son of Ralph (in personnel) and Dorothy (a teacher; maiden name, Wilson) Schiffer. *Education:* Harvard University, A.B., 1970; attended University of California, Berkeley, 1971-72. *Home:* 907 Bent Lane, Philadelphia, Pa. 19118. *Agent:* Joan Raines, 475 Fifth Ave., New York, N.Y. 10017.

CAREER: Worked as a silversmith and goldsmith in Boston, Mass., San Francisco, Calif., and France, 1971-79; writer, 1980—. *Member:* Philadelphia Writers' Organization, Phi Beta Kappa.

WRITINGS: Lessons of the Road (autobiography), Kenan Press, 1980; *Ballpark* (novel), Simon & Schuster, 1982. Also author of a two unproduced plays, "Titusville, Pa." and "The Gravedigger," a screenplay about the life of Walt Whitman, and an unpublished novel, "Jeweler's Row."

SIDELIGHTS: Schiffer's first book, *Lessons of the Road,* is an account of his overland journey from France to Nepal. In the book Schiffer explains his motivations for the journey: "To those coming up through hard times, the middle class is a dream, a goal, but much of our effort in the late Sixties was devoted to finding our way out of its comforts. . . . We too had been protected, and in an effort to unprotect ourselves and get down to those truths which had eluded us, we hit the streets, let our hair grow, and took on risks we never thought existed." Schiffer writes of his encounters with the cultures of the Aegean, the eastern Mediterranean, southwestern Asia, and India, and of the youth subculture that subsisted along that route in the late sixties and early seventies.

William Hogan of the *San Francisco Chronicle* called *Lessons of the Road* "an ingratiating, intelligent travel log." Sarah Ferrell, in the *New York Times* travel section, wrote that *Lessons of the Road* "is almost continuously interesting and an exception to the rule that what must, for want of a better term, be called hippie memoirs are dumb and boring. . . . Mr. Schiffer is a clear-eyed journalist—unlike many others who followed the overland route, he was never too stoned to know where he was. . . . Two things distinguish Mr. Schiffer's book. . . . He is able to look back at his experiences with some wryness . . . and he can turn a phrase. . . . Lyric evocations of peoples and landscapes are punctuated by little Abbie Hoffmanesque jokes—one waits to see what Mr. Schiffer will give us now that he is grown up."

Ingrid Bengis of the *New York Times Book Review* observed that Schiffer "has an eye for revealing details and an ear for the rhythm of the road. . . . Despite the fact that Mr. Schiffer's 'lessons' turn out to be primarily anecdotal, there are moments . . . that do open up some dark layer of experience. . . . [At times] his journal, which is almost never introspective, becomes genuinely moving, providing a glimmer of an internal life." But Bengis found a lack of psychological depth in the book, noting that *Lessons of the Road* "rarely proceeds beyond mere observation. . . . [Schiffer] leaves out what only a traveler like himself could adequately provide: in depth portraits of his fellow travelers and the complexities of their various states of mind."

Other reviewers made similar objections. Don Strachan of the *Los Angeles Times,* for example, praised Schiffer's writing and observation but remarked that "his people are pencil sketches that leave us longing for a few languourusly-realized oil-portraits." But Schiffer commented to *CA:* "*Lessons of the Road* is a travel journal. It is a record of the overland road through Asia that is no longer open. It is a cultural record of the countries and people of a region that has been violently and perhaps permanently altered through force and political intervention. It is a last look at a way of life, not only overseas, as it was lived by young people in the aftermath of the 1960's. It was never intended to be a psychological treatise."

Schiffer's first novel, *Ballpark,* is about Darryl Pardee, a third baseman in Ballpark, Ohio, a huge amusement park that has its own big league baseball team. The book tells of Pardee's relationship with Pauline, a sports reporter, and Phil Raneer, the megalomaniacal owner of Ballpark. Glenn Dickey, in the *San Francisco Chronicle,* observed that Schiffer "obviously knows and loves the game. He has captured the way the players talk and act as few authors have previously, and he gets the feel and the sounds of the game down in a credible manner. Nonetheless, the action itself is used more as a backdrop for the primary theme, an unusual love story between a star third baseman on the team and a woman reporter. . . . Altogether, it is a well-crafted book, one which should be enjoyable even to those who are not devout baseball fans."

Paul Hagen of the *Dallas Times Herald* also praised *Ballpark:* "On its simplest level, this is nothing more or less than a baseball story. . . . But there's more. . . . Schiffer, by putting his magnifying glass on baseball, is also examining the country. Pardee would like to live a simple, uncomplicated life. Meanwhile, the world around him gets more twisted every day. . . . This is a meticulously written work that draws a clean parallel. A simple baseball player trying to survive baseball—and the logical extension, a simple human being trying to survive the world. Schiffer has spun a modern legend."

Schiffer told *CA:* "My background was in theatre as an undergraduate director at Harvard, a career that got short-circuited by the politics and chaos of the late sixties. Afterward, I traveled around the United States, spent eight months as an apprentice to a silversmith/goldsmith, then put myself through a year of law school by making jewelry at night and selling it on the streets of San Francisco each weekend. I was invited to France to teach a young Frenchwoman the trade, worked the wine harvest there, and spent a year and a half there before taking off with three friends on the overland road to Nepal. Length of trip: seven months. Cost: approximately seven hundred dollars. Upon returning from Asia, I began to play some serious fast-pitch softball with friends in Boston, a passion that ultimately resulted in *Ballpark.*"

AVOCATIONAL INTERESTS: Softball, basketball, blues harmonica, and guitar.

BIOGRAPHICAL/CRITICAL SOURCES: Michael Schiffer, *Lessons of the Road,* Kenan Press, 1980; *San Francisco Chronicle,* October 17, 1980, April 4, 1982; *Los Angeles Times,* October 30, 1980; *New York Times,* November 2, 1980; *Hollywood Reporter,* November 14, 1980; *Washington Post Book World,* January 4, 1981; *New York Times Book Review,* January 11, 1981; *Dallas Times Herald,* April 4, 1982; *Los Angeles Times Book Review,* April 25, 1982.

* * *

SCHILER, Marc (Eugene) 1951-

PERSONAL: Surname is pronounced *Schill*-er; born January 28, 1951, in Mansfield, Ohio; son of Eugene (a machinist) and Elisabeth (a nurse; maiden name, Leimgruber) Schiler; married

Dianne Irene Kinkel, January 29, 1972; children: Karen Elisabeth, Jonathan David, Marianne Renee. *Education:* Attended California Institute of Technology, 1969-71; University of Southern California, B.S., 1974; Cornell University, M.S., 1978. *Home:* 108 Landmark Dr., Ithaca, N.Y. 14850. *Agent:* John Brockman Associates, Inc., 200 West 57th St., New York, N.Y. 10019. *Office:* Department of Architecture, Cornell University, Ithaca, N.Y. 14853.

CAREER: Associated with Ranier Metal Manufacturing, 1972-73; staff member with Raymond Ziegler Partnership (architects), 1974-75; City of Los Angeles, Bureau of Public Buildings, Los Angeles, Calif., member of staff in Design Division, 1975-76; Cornell University, Ithaca, N.Y., assistant professor of architecture, 1978—. Lecturer at colleges and universities; public speaker. *Member:* International Solar Energy Society, American Association of University Professors, American Forestry Association, American Institute of Architects, American Underground-Space Association, Association for Computing Machinery, Consortium for Environmental Forestry Research.

WRITINGS: (With Anne Moffat) *Landscape Design That Saves Energy,* Morrow, 1981. Contributor to magazines and newspapers.

WORK IN PROGRESS: Research on passive solar design, microclimate and landscaping, and earth-sheltered housing.

SIDELIGHTS: Schiler wrote: "The misuse, or inappropriate use, of technology is a central thread in my writing and research. Technological change is not evil, but neither is it always true that the most complex tool is the best solution. A prime example is the case of using landscape or microclimate design to save energy in buildings. When properly positioned, landscape elements may be aesthetic, psychologically beneficial, and economically preferable sources of energy savings. Similarly, although state of the art computer techniques may be used to evaluate solutions, they may indicate that, indeed, the simplest solution was the best solution after all.

"There are two sources of my interest in examining these topics. The first is a strong feeling of stewardship, or the sense that man is abusing his planet, and that is neither moral nor elegant. Secondly, I have always been interested in the question 'what if?' This has led to a great deal of reading both in science and science fiction.

"I believe that books for academicians only are basically wasteful. Books can and should be for the people who are in a position to create or influence results. Furthermore, there are many ways to convey information; not all of them are boring. Information should be accurate, but learning can be interesting. I intend to continue writing on microclimate design and research, earth-sheltered housing and its history, and semifictional accounts of our possible futures."

AVOCATIONAL INTERESTS: Travel (Europe, Mexico, the Caribbean).

*   *   *

SCHILLING, Betty 1925-

PERSONAL: Born April 3, 1925, in El Paso, Tex.; daughter of Wade H. (a farmer) and Carrie (Capt) Miller; divorced; children: Eric, Ronald. *Education:* Mary Hardin-Baylor College, B.A., 1946; graduate study at Cranbrook Academy of Art, 1947-48. *Home and office:* 6201 East Quartz Mountain Rd., Scottsdale, Ariz. 85253.

MEMBER: American Association of University Women.

WRITINGS—For children: (Illustrator) Erene Cheki Haney and Ruth Richards, *Yoga for Children,* Bobbs-Merrill, 1973; *Two Kittens Are Born* (also photographer), Holt, 1980.

WORK IN PROGRESS: Children's books; poems; travel writing.

AVOCATIONAL INTERESTS: Yoga.

*   *   *

SCHINDLER, Marvin Samuel 1932-

BRIEF ENTRY: Born January 2, 1932, in Boston, Mass. American educator and author. Schindler has been a university teacher since 1955. In 1974 he became a professor of German at Wayne State University and chairman of the Department of Romance and German Languages and Literatures. He has been associate editor of *German Quarterly* since 1970. In addition to scholarly articles and contributions to books, Schindler wrote *The Sonnets of Andreas Gryphius: The Use of the Poetic Word in the Seventeenth Century* (University Presses of Florida, 1971). *Address:* Department of Romance and German Languages and Literatures, Wayne State University, 5950 Cass Ave., Detroit, Mich. 48202.

*   *   *

SCHMIDT-NIELSEN, Knut 1915-

PERSONAL: Born September 24, 1915, in Trondheim, Norway; came to the United States in 1946, naturalized citizen, 1950; son of Sigval (a professor of chemistry) and Signe Torborg (a physicist; maiden name, Sturzen-Becker) Schmidt-Nielsen. *Education:* Attended University of Oslo, 1933-37; University of Copenhagen, M.S., 1941, D.Phil., 1946. *Office:* Department of Zoology, Duke University, Durham, N.C. 27706.

CAREER: Carlsberg Laboratory, Copenhagen, Denmark, research fellow, 1941-44; Swarthmore College, Swarthmore, Pa., research associate, 1946-48; Stanford University, Stanford, Calif., research associate, 1948-49; University of Cincinnati, Cincinnati, Ohio, assistant professor of physiology, 1949-52; Duke University, Durham, N.C., professor, 1952-63, James B. Duke Professor of Physiology, 1963—. Brody Memorial Lecturer at University of Missouri, 1962; regents' lecturer at University of California, Davis, 1963; Hans Gadow Lecturer at Cambridge University, 1971; visiting Agassiz Professor at Harvard University, 1972. Organizer and member of scientific expeditions to North Africa, Asia, Australia, South Africa, South America, and Israel; member of board of trustees of Mount Desert Island Biological Laboratory, 1958-60; member of scientific advisory committee of New England Regional Primate Center, 1962-66; member of U.S. National Committee for International Biological Programme's subcommittee on environmental physiology, 1965-67; member of national advisory board of physiological laboratory at Scripps Institute of Oceanography, 1963-69, chairman of board, 1968-69; member of advisory board of Bio-Medical Science, Inc., 1973-74; chairman of Inter-Union Commission on Comparative Physiology, 1976-80; member of National Institutes of Health and National Academy of Sciences committees.

MEMBER: International Union of Physiological Sciences (member of U.S. national committee, 1966—; vice-chairman of committee, 1969—; president of union, 1980—), American Association for the Advancement of Science (fellow), American Physiological Society, American Society of Zoologists (chairman of Division of Comparative Physiology, 1964), American Academy of Arts and Sciences (fellow), National Academy of Sciences, Society of Experimental Biology (England), Royal Norwegian Society of Arts and Science, Royal Danish Academy, French Academy of Sciences (foreign associate), Harvey Society (honorary member), New York Academy of Sciences (fellow), Sigma Xi. *Awards, honors:* Guggenheim fellowship for Algeria, 1953-54; Poteat Award from North Carolina Academy of Sciences, 1957; grant from National Institutes of Health, 1964.

WRITINGS: Animal Physiology, Prentice-Hall, 1960, 3rd edition, 1970; *Desert Animals: Physiological Problems of Heat and Water,* Clarendon Press, 1964; *How Animals Work,* Cambridge University Press, 1972; (editor with Liana Bolis and S.H.P Maddrell) *Comparative Physiology: Locomotion, Respiration, Transport, and Blood,* North-Holland Publishing, 1973; *Animal Physiology: Adaptation and Environment,* Cambridge University Press, 1975, 2nd edition, 1979; (editor with Bolis and Maddrell) *Comparative Physiology: Functional Aspects of Structural Materials,* North-Holland Publishing, 1975.

Contributor of more than two hundred articles to scientific journals. Section editor of *American Journal of Physiology* and *Journal of Applied Physiology,* both 1961-64; member of editorial board of *Physiological Zoology,* 1959-70, *Journal of Cellular and Comparative Physiology,* 1961-66, *American Journal of Physiology,* 1964—, *Journal of Applied Physiology,* 1964—, and *Journal of Experimental Biology,* 1975—; honorary member of editorial advisory board of *Comparative Biochemistry and Physiology,* 1962-63.

WORK IN PROGRESS: Research on respiration, circulation, and heat regulation in exercise.

*   *   *

SCHOEPS, Hans-Joachim   1909-

BRIEF ENTRY: Born January 30, 1909, in Berlin, Germany. German educator and author. Schoeps has been a professor of religion and the history of ideas at University of Erlangen since 1948. He also has been editor of the *Journal of the History of Religion and Ideas* for more than thirty years. His country honored him with the Bavarian Distinguished Service Cross. Some English translations of Schoeps's several dozen books include *Paul: The Theology of the Apostle in the Light of Jewish Religious History* (Westminster, 1961), *The Jewish-Christian Argument: A History of Theologies in Conflict* (Holt, 1963), *The Religions of Mankind* (Doubleday, 1966), and *Jewish Christianity: Factional Disputes in the Early Church* (Fortress, 1969). *Address:* 11 Ebrardstrasse, D852 Erlangen, West Germany; and University of Erlangen, 4 Kochstrasse, D852 Erlangen, West Germany.

*   *   *

SCHOFIELD, Jonathan
See STREIB, Dan(iel Thomas)

*   *   *

SCHOLEM, Gershom (Gerhard)   1897-1982

OBITUARY NOTICE—See index for *CA* sketch: Born December 5, 1897, in Berlin, Germany (now East Germany); died February 20, 1982, in Jerusalem, Israel. Authority on Jewish mysticism and author. Scholem brought the system of Kabbalah, the use of metaphysics and mathematics to understand Scripture, to a respectable position in Jewish thought. This study of mysticism ran counter to Rabbinic Judaism, but Scholem raised the Kabbalah to ''a position of central importance,'' said a writer in the *London Times.* In addition to writing on the mystical interpretation of Scripture, Scholem, a faculty member of the Hebrew University in Palestine (now Israel), wrote on Jewish Messianism. His books include *Major Trends in Jewish Mysticism, The Messianic Idea in Judaism and Other Studies in Jewish Spirituality, On the Kabbalah and Its Symbolism, The Beginnings of Kabbalism,* and *Jewish Mysticism in the Middle Ages.* Obituaries and other sources: Gershom Scholem, *From Berlin to Jerusalem: Memories of My Youth* (autobiography), Schocken, 1980; *London Times,* February 23, 1982; *Time,* March 8, 1982; *Newsweek,* March 8, 1982; *Publishers Weekly,* March 12, 1982; *AB Bookman's Weekly,* April 12, 1982.

*   *   *

SCHOONOVER, Frank (Earle)   1877-1972

PERSONAL: Born August 19, 1877, in Oxford, N.J.; died September 1, 1972, in Wilmington, Del.; buried in Old St. Anne's Cemetery, Middletown, Del.; son of John (a supervisor of a blast furnace operation) and Elizabeth (LeBar) Schoonover; married Martha Culbertson, January 18, 1911; children: Cortlandt, Elizabeth Louise. *Education:* Studied art under Howard Pyle at Drexel Institute, Philadelphia, Pa., and also at his schools in Chadds Ford, Pa., and Wilmington, Del. *Residence:* Wilmington, Del.

CAREER: Muralist, portrait painter, illustrator, and writer. Work exhibited at Wilmington Society of the Fine Arts (now the Delaware Art Museum), one-man show, 1962, and at the Brandywine River Museum of the Brandywine Conservancy, 1979; work is represented in the permanent collections at the Brandywine River Musuem and at the Delaware Art Musuem. *Member:* Society of Illustrators, Franklin Inn Club, Racquet Club (Philadelphia), Wilmington Sketch Club, Lincoln Club (Delaware), Salmugundi Club, Players Club. *Awards, honors:* Honorary M.A. degree from University of Delaware, 1963; Edgar Rice Burroughs Bibliophile's National Award, 1970.

WRITINGS: The Edge of the Wilderness: A Portrait of the Canadian North, self-illustrated, edited by son, Cortlandt Schoonover, Methuen, 1974. Also author and illustrator of ''In the Haunts of Jean LaFitte.''

Illustrator of books, including: E. T. Tomlinson, *Jersey Boy in the Revolution,* Houghton, 1899; Tomlinson, *In the Hands of the Redcoats,* Houghton, 1900; J. M. McIlwraith, *The Curious Career of Roderick Campbell,* Houghton, 1901; Robert W. Chambers, *Cardigan,* Harper, 1901; Gilbert Parker, *The Land That Had No Turning,* Doubleday, Page, 1902; Earnest C. Poole, *Waifs of the Streets,* McClurg, 1903; W. A. Fraser, *The Blood Lilies,* William Biggs, 1903; Ellen Glasgow, *The Deliverance,* Doubleday, Page, 1904; Henry Wadsworth Longfellow, *Evangeline,* Houghton, 1908; Randall Parrish, *The Maid of the Forest,* McClurg, 1913; Dillon Wallace, *Bobby of the Labrador,* McClurg, 1916; Edgar Rice Burroughs, *A Princess of Mars,* McClurg, 1917; D. Wallace, *Arctic Stowaways,* McClurg, 1917; Lucy F. Madison, *Joan of Arc,* Penn, 1918; McKay, c. 1940.

L. F. Madison, *Lafayette,* Penn, 1921; Clarence E. Mulford, *The Bar-20 Three,* McClurg, 1921; George Marsh, *The Whelps of the Wolf,* Penn, 1922; Sir Walter Scott, *Ivanhoe,* Harper, 1922; Kirk Munroe, *Flamingo Feather,* Harper, 1923; James W. Schultz, *Questers of the Desert,* Houghton, 1925; L. F. Madison, *Lincoln,* Penn, 1928; Mary P. W. Smith, *Boy Captive of Old Deerfield,* Little, Brown, 1929; Mary Johnson, *To Have and to Hold,* Houghton, 1931; Rupert S. Holland, *Yankee Ships in Private Waters,* M. Smith, 1931; Henry Frith, *King Arthur and His Knights,* Garden City Publishing, 1932;

Russell G. Carter, *The Crimson Cutlass,* Penn, 1933; Virginia M. Collier and Jeanette Eaton, *Roland the Warrior,* Harcourt, 1934; Katherine Grey, *Rolling Wheels,* Little, Brown, 1937.

Illustrator of frontispieces and cover illustrations, including: Charles and Mary Lamb, *Tales from Shakespeare,* Harper, 1918; Daniel Defoe, *Robinson Crusoe,* Harper, 1921; *Robin Hood,* Harper, 1921; Thomas Hughes, *Tom Brown's School Days,* Harper, 1921; Robert Louis Stevenson, *Kidnapped,* Harper, 1921; *Grimm's Fairy Tales,* Harper, 1921; Johann Spyri, *Heidi,* Harper, 1924.

Illustrator of *Children of the Coal Shadows, Rifles for Washington,* Henry Van Dyke's *The Broken Soldier and the Maid of France,* 1919, and books by Mary Raymond Shipman Andrews, Rex Beach, and Zane Grey.

Contributor of illustrations and stories to magazines, including *American Boy, Century, Collier's, Harper's, McClure's, Outing, Saturday Evening Post,* and *Scribner's Magazine.*

SIDELIGHTS: Schoonover began doing illustrations in 1899 while he was a student at Howard Pyle's summer art school in Chadds Ford, Pennsylvania. After several successful years illustrating books and magazines, he began to have doubts about the artistic validity of his work, which he expressed to Pyle: "I just don't feel right about the work I am doing now for I am having to project to the public too much that is really not out of my experience. You have given me the skill. To progress the way you say you can have faith that I can, I feel that I must pick a field in which I can develop a relationship with the public that will say, 'This rings true; he knows because he has been there.'"

Encouraged by Pyle, Schoonover made a mid-winter expedition to Canada's Northwest Territories in 1903, traveling over twelve hundred miles by dogsled and snowshoe to sketch the wilderness and its Indian inhabitants. He was forced to sketch with colored crayons because the cold made it impossible to work with oils. The sketching was done from a small tent Schoonover devised; its stove and folding glass window permitted him to work in relative comfort despite the sub-zero temperatures. Schoonover's illustrations and written accounts appeared in *Scribner's Magazine* and *Outing.*

Following his Canadian expeditions, Schoonover regularly traveled in order to capture the ambience of assignments. In 1906 he went to Denver, Colorado, to get the story of Judge Ben B. Lindsay and his youth court. From there Schoonover traveled to Butte, Montana, to cover the fight over the Minnie Healy, a copper mine. In 1910 *Harper's* assigned him to Scranton, Pennsylvania, to do a feature on the young women and girls working in the silk mills there. Schoonover traveled to the Mississippi River's bayou region in 1911 to research a piece on Jean LaFitte, a colorful pirate from the early 1800's.

Schoonover continued to illustrate books and magazines through the 1920's, and during the 1930's he also began to paint landscapes and to design stained glass windows. He began his own art school in Wilmington, Delaware, in 1942 and remained active in the school until 1968 when he was debilitated by the first of a series of strokes.

BIOGRAPHICAL/CRITICAL SOURCES: American Artist, November, 1964; Cortlandt Schoonover, *Frank Schoonover: Illustrator of the North American Frontier,* Watson-Guptill, 1976.*

*   *   *

SCHUELER, Donald G(ustave)   1929-

PERSONAL: Born August 6, 1929, in New York, N.Y. Ed-

ucation: University of Georgia, B.A., 1951; Louisiana State University, M.A., 1960, Ph.D., 1962. *Home:* 1311 Pleasant St., New Orleans, La. 70115. *Agent:* Frances Collin, Marie Rodell-Frances Collin Literary Agency, 156 East 52nd St., Suite 601, New York, N.Y. 10022. *Office:* Department of English, University of New Orleans, New Orleans, La. 70122.

CAREER: University of New Orleans, New Orleans, La., began as instructor, 1960, became professor of English, 1969—. *Member:* Modern Language Association of America, South Central Modern Language Association.

WRITINGS: Problems in English Grammar, C. E. Merrill, 1965; *Incident at Eagle Ranch,* Sierra Books, 1980; *Preserving the Pascagoula,* University of Mississippi Press, 1980. Contributor to language journals and national magazines, including *Smithsonian* and *Audubon.*

WORK IN PROGRESS: A futuristic novel.

*   *   *

SCHULER, Carol Ann   1946-

PERSONAL: Born January 29, 1946, in Bethlehem, Pa.; daughter of Walter William (in New Jersey state police) and Essie (a teacher; maiden name, Hess) Schuler. *Education:* Muhlenberg College, B.A., 1968. *Home:* 405 East 51st St., New York, N.Y. 10022.

CAREER: U.S. Department of Housing and Urban Development, New York City, economist, 1968-69; Muriel Siebert & Co., Inc., New York City, administrative assistant, 1969; Hutchins, Mixter & Parkinson, Inc., New York City, administrative assistant, 1970-71; Margaret Larson Public Relations, New York City, assistant to president, 1971-72; General Motors Corp., New York City, computer programmer, 1972-74; Sterling Drug, Inc., New York City, programmer analyst, 1975-79, training coordinator, 1979-81; Henco Research, Inc., New York City, programmer analyst, 1981.

WRITINGS: (With Ellin Dodge Young) *The Vibes Book: A Game of Self-Analysis,* Samuel Weiser, 1979; (with Sandra Stein) *Love Numbers,* Putnam, 1980. Editor of departmental newsletter for Sterling Drug, Inc., 1979-80.

WORK IN PROGRESS: Guide Numbers, with Sandra Stein.

SIDELIGHTS: Carol Schuler wrote: "My motivation is a desire to spread wisdom. Knowledge is food for the soul; it enriches lives. Although numerology may not be as popular as astrology yet, it is by far more suitable for the general public to study, since one does not need the extensive library that astrology requires, nor the time and place of birth. Only the subject's name and birthday are needed. Understanding your numbers is not only fun, it's therapy.

"Whereas *The Vibes Book* is mostly a how-to-do-it book, explaining how to set up a chart and giving a general description of each category, *Love Numbers* is mostly interpretation. There is a chapter on each of the ninety-nine possible combinations for the three major numbers derived from the numerical values of the letters in your name. We did extensive research, and in my opinion the funniest and most poignant anecdotes are from real life. Although it may be impossible for 100 percent of a chapter to fit everyone of that combination, great pains were taken to make it as accurate as possible.

"The first two books I worked on during weekends—every weekend; the third, *Guide Numbers,* I had the luxury of working on during the day or night, on my own schedule, since I was between jobs. For the last book I set a goal for each day and stuck to it, even if it entailed working from midnight until 4:00 A.M. Inspiration and discipline go hand in hand.

"It would be ideal to pursue a career dedicated to world peace, world communication, and helping humanity evolve into a better species. But the rent must be paid, and for this and other mundane requirements of the physical plane, I've joined the job market working with computers. At least as a fringe benefit I got to computerize numerology!"

AVOCATIONAL INTERESTS: "I've been studying the occult sciences for nine years, taught tarot for three and numerology for three. Vacations are anxiously awaited, as travel to foreign lands has always been a longed-for adventure. I enjoy good food, good music, movies, theatre, bicycle riding, and visiting with close friends. I endeavor to enjoy something beautiful each day."

*   *   *

SCHUYLER, Pamela R. 1948-

PERSONAL: Surname is pronounced Sky-ler; born October 26, 1948, in Brooklyn, N.Y.; daughter of Frank (a shoe salesman) and Clare R. Schuyler; married John Wayne Cowens (a physician), August 27, 1977. *Education:* Boston University, B.A., 1970; graduate study at Massachusetts Institute of Technology, 1969-71; Rochester Institute of Technology, M.F.A., 1980. *Office:* 54 Irving Pl., Buffalo, N.Y. 14201.

CAREER: Rivers Country Day School, Weston, Mass., instructor, 1973-76; Boston Celtics, Boston, Mass., team photographer, 1974-76; Associated Press, Boston, Mass., and Buffalo, N.Y., staff photographer, 1976-79; free-lance photographer, printmaker, and artist, 1980—.

WRITINGS: Through the Hoop: A Season With the Celtics (juvenile), Houghton, 1974.

Photographic illustrator: Tom Beer and George Kimball, *Sunday's Fools,* Houghton, 1974; Bob Ryan, *Celtics Pride: The Rebuilding of Boston's World Championship Basketball Team,* Little, Brown, 1975.

WORK IN PROGRESS: Fowl Beasts, a large-format chicken cookbook illustrated with intaglio prints.

SIDELIGHTS: "Currently, I am more interested in the illustration of books than in writing them," Pamela Schuyler told *CA.* "This interest developed from courses taken as part of the M.F.A. program at Rochester Institute of Technology."

*   *   *

SCHWARTZ, Bernard (Sherman) 1945-

PERSONAL: Born October 30, 1945, in Los Angeles, Calif.; son of Hyman and Muriel (Finkelson) Schwartz. *Education:* University of California, Los Angeles, B.A., 1968; California Lutheran College, M.A., 1972. *Residence:* Laguna Beach, Calif. *Office:* Department of Child Development, Santa Ana College, 17th and Bristol St., Santa Ana, Calif. 92706.

CAREER: Head teacher for "Head Start" program in Los Angeles, Calif., 1963-68; Camarillo State Hospital, Camarillo, Calif., counselor, teacher, and foster parent, 1970-72; Santa Ana College, Santa Ana, Calif., instructor in child development, 1971—. Educational therapist at West Los Angeles Center for Educational Therapy, 1972-73; co-director of Brief Family Intervention Training Institute, Newport Beach, Calif.; speaker at colleges and universities; guest on radio and television programs. *Member:* National Association for the Edu-

cation of Young Children, American Federation of Television and Radio Artists.

WRITINGS—Published by Prentice-Hall: (With Paul Wood) *How to Get Your Children to Do What You Want Them to Do,* 1977; (with John V. Flowers and Curtis Booraem) *Help Your Children Be Self-Confident,* 1978; (with James Pugh) *How to Get Your Children to Be Good Students: How to Get Your Students to Be Good Children,* 1981; (with Flowers and Jennifer Horsman) *You and Your Gifted Child,* 1982; (with Flowers and Horsman) *The Sex Life of Your Child,* in press.

Scripts: "Mainstreaming in the Head Start Program" (filmstrip), Orange County Head Start, 1979; "How to Get Your Children to Do What You Want Them to Do" (film), American Personnel and Guidance Association, 1980; "Careers in Early Childhood Education (filmstrip), Santa Ana College, 1981.

Author of "How to Get Your Child to Do What You Want," a column distributed by King Features Syndicate to eighty newspapers, 1979. Contributor to psychology and education journals.

WORK IN PROGRESS: A Parent's Survival Kit, for high school and adult education parenting classes.

SIDELIGHTS: Schwartz told *CA:* "All of my books are the result of the overemphasis on 'mental illness' as an explanation of inappropriate behavior in children. My approach stresses the role of parental communication, modeling, and coaching as shapers of a child's positive and negative actions. Simply put, my view is that parents have tremendous power if they carefully construct their values and then clearly communicate these values to their children. The successful parent doesn't say: "Please *try* to be home on time"; "Why can't you be home on time?"; "If you're not home on time you'll be grounded," etc. Instead the child and parent come to an agreement as to the allowed time to come home and then the parent clearly states: "Remember you are to be home at the time we decided on." Children do well in homes where the rules are known, where they have a part in their formation, and where the child has plenty of areas in which he is not governed by rules."

BIOGRAPHICAL/CRITICAL SOURCES: Psychology Today, October, 1977; *Harper's Bazaar,* October, 1978.

*   *   *

SCHWEID, Richard M. 1946-

PERSONAL: Born July 2, 1946, in Nashville, Tenn. *Politics:* "Idiosyncratic."

CAREER: Writer.

WRITINGS: Hot Peppers: Cajun and Capsicum in New Iberia, Louisiana, Madrona, 1980. Associate editor of *Smoke Signals.*

WORK IN PROGRESS: A novel; research on "detail men" who sell pharmaceutical products.

*   *   *

SCICLUNA, Hannibal Publius 1880-1981(?)

OBITUARY NOTICE: Born February 15, 1880; died c. 1981 in Malta. Museum director, historian, and author of historical studies, including *The French Occupation of Malta, 1798-1900, The Book of Deliberations of the Venerable Tongue of England,* and *The Church of St. John in Valletta.* Scicluna was knighted in 1955 for his years of service to Malta. Obituaries and other sources: *Who's Who,* 126th edition, St. Martin's, 1974; *AB Bookman's Weekly,* February 22, 1982.

SCOFIELD, Jonathan
   See TOOMBS, John

*   *   *

SCOTT, Geoffrey   1952-

PERSONAL: Born July 27, 1952, in Minneapolis, Minn.; son of Clayton M. (an attorney) and Charlotte (Sideris) Scott; married Kathleen Trenter, September 22, 1978; children: Emily. *Education:* University of Minnesota, B.S., 1974. *Home address:* R.R. 1, Box 193, Wheeler, Wis. *Office:* Cray Research, Inc., Hwy. No. 178, Chippewa Falls, Wis. 54729.

CAREER: Teacher in Minneapolis, Minn., 1974-75; free-lance writer, 1976; associated with Honeywell Avionics, 1977-78, and Rosemount, Inc., 1978-82; Cray Research, Inc., Chippewa Falls, Wis., technical writer, 1982—. Professional drummer, 1978—. *Member:* American Federation of Musicians, Society for Technical Communication (vice-president of Twin Cities chapter, 1980), Humanities and Technology Association.

WRITINGS: Egyptian Boats, illustrations by Nancy L. Carlson, Carolrhoda, 1981; *Labor Day,* illustrated by Cherie R. Wyman, Carolrhoda, 1982; *Memorial Day,* Carolrhoda, 1983. Contributor to *Technical Communication* (magazine).

SIDELIGHTS: Scott told *CA:* "I relish the unexpected similarities between writing technical manuals and nonfiction children's books. Writing for two disparate audiences throws new and useful light on the techniques required to write both kinds of books."

*   *   *

SCOTT, Robert Ian   1931-

PERSONAL: Born April 23, 1931, in Berkeley, Calif.; son of Robert Vere (in real estate and photography) and Francis (Gray) Scott; married Karen Lund, June 13, 1953; children: Dana Gray, Ian Andrew (died, 1979), Sam Alexander. *Education:* Reed College, B.A., 1953; Claremont Graduate School, M.A., 1955; State University of New York at Buffalo, Ph.D., 1964. *Office:* Department of English, University of Saskatchewan, Saskatoon, Saskatchewan, Canada S7N OWO.

CAREER: University of Western Australia, Nedlands, Australia, lecturer in English, 1956; State University of New York at Buffalo, instructor in English, 1957-63; Southern Oregon State College, Ashland, assistant professor of English, 1963-66; University of Saskatchewan, Saskatoon, assistant professor, 1966-68, special lecturer, 1968-69, associate professor, 1969-75, professor of English, 1975—. *Member:* Canadian Linguistic Association, Canadian Association for American Studies, Association of Canadian University Teachers of English.

WRITINGS: The Writer's Self-Starter: A Transformational Rhetoric, P. Collier, 1972; (editor) *"What Odd Expedients" and Other Poems by Robinson Jeffers,* Shoe String, 1981. Contributor to language and linguistic journals and popular magazines, including *Harper's* and *North American Review.*

WORK IN PROGRESS: Research on grammar, semantics, Robinson Jeffers, and such forms of modern poetry as imagism.

SIDELIGHTS: Scott told *CA:* "Two sorts of subjects concern me most: how language and the rest of our behavior affect each other, and how the world and we affect each other."

SCOTT, Ronald Bodley   1906-1982

OBITUARY NOTICE: Born September 10, 1906, in Bournemouth, England; died in an automobile accident, May 12, 1982, in Italy. Physician, editor, and author. Scott earned his medical degree from Oxford University in 1937 and began specializing in clinical hematology. He served with the Royal Army Medical Corps in the Middle East during World War II, and in 1949 he was appointed physician to King George VI. In 1952 Scott became physician to Queen Elizabeth II. Scott edited medical textbooks and wrote *Cancer: The Facts.* Obituaries and other sources: *Who's Who,* 126th edition, St. Martin's, 1974; *London Times,* May 13, 1982.

*   *   *

SCOTT-GILES, C(harles) W(ilfred)   1893-1982(?)

OITUARY NOTICE: Born in 1893 in Southampton, England; died c. 1982. Engineer, historian, and author best known as a scholar of heraldry. Scott-Giles was appointed an extraordinary pursuivant in 1957 and was also an officer of the Order of the British Empire. He wrote *The Romance of Heraldry, Civic Heraldry of England and Wales,* and *Shakespeare's Heraldry.* Obituaries and other sources: *The Author's and Writer's Who's Who,* 6th edition, Burke's Peerage, 1971; *Who Was Who Among English and European Authors, 1931-1949,* Gale, 1976; *London Times,* March 12, 1982.

*   *   *

SCRUM, R.
   See CRUMB, R(obert)

*   *   *

SCUDDER, Thayer   1930-

BRIEF ENTRY: Born August 4, 1930, in New Haven, Conn. American anthropologist, educator, and author. Scudder began teaching at California Institute of Technology in 1964 and became a professor of anthropology in 1969. In 1976 he became director of the Institute for Development Anthropology. Scudder was a Guggenheim fellow in 1975. He wrote *The Ecology of the Gwembe Tonga* (Manchester University Press, 1962), *Gathering Among African Woodland Savannah Cultivators: A Case Study—the Gwembe Tonga* (Manchester University Press, 1971), *The Anthropology of Rural Development in the Sahel: Proposals for Research* (Institute for Development Anthropology, 1977), and *Secondary Education and the Formation of an Elite: The Impact of Education on Gwembe District, Zambia* (Academic Press, 1980). *Address:* P.O. Box 45, Westview Station, Binghamton, N.Y. 13905. *Biographical/critical sources: American Men and Women of Science: The Social and Behavioral Sciences,* 13th edition, Bowker, 1978.

*   *   *

SCUM
   See CRUMB, R(obert)

*   *   *

SCUMBAG, Little Bobby
   See CRUMB, R(obert)

*   *   *

SEARLE, Humphrey   1915-1982

OBITUARY NOTICE—See index for *CA* sketch: Born August

26, 1915, in Oxford, England; died May 12, 1982, in London, England. Composer and author. Searle was one of London's foremost proponents of serial music composition, a technique devised by Arnold Shoenberg whereby a composer uses all twelve tones from the chromatic scale. Octave positions and alterations may change as well. In honor of Schoenberg, Searle wrote the "Passacaglietta in nomine Arnold Schoenberg" for the composer's seventy-fifth birthday. The influence of Anton Webern, a pupil of Schoenberg, is also evident in Searle's compositions, particularly in his "Night Music." The composer modeled several of his works after the fashion of Franz Liszt, though he tempered the style with the twelve-tone technique. Searle composed several operas, notably "The Diary of a Madman" and "The Photo of the Colonel," as well as three ballets, "Noctambules," "The Great Peacock," and "Dualities." His books include *Twentieth Century Counterpoint: A Guide for Students, The Music of Liszt, Compositions With Twelve Notes Related Only to One Another, Structural Functions of Harmony,* and *Ballet: An Introduction.* Obituaries and other sources: *London Times,* May 13, 1982.

*   *   *

SEGALMAN, Ralph   1916-

PERSONAL: Born July 15, 1916, in New York, N.Y.; son of Samuel (a truck driver) and Celia (Lasky) Segalman; married Anita Cohen (an artist), August 25, 1940; children: Robert Z., Ruth Segalman Ancheta, Daniel J. *Education:* University of Michigan, B.A., 1937, M.S.W., 1944; New York University, Ph.D., 1967. *Politics:* Independent. *Religion:* Jewish (Reform). *Home:* 18723 Sunburst St., Northridge, Calif. 91324. *Office:* Department of Sociology, California State University, 1811 Nordhoff St., Northridge, Calif. 91330.

CAREER: Child and Family Service, Peoria, Ill., Jewish case worker, 1939-42; worked for United Service Organization in Arizona, 1942-43; Springfield Jewish Federation, Springfield, Ill., executive director, 1943-45; American Joint Distribution Committee, New York, N.Y., director for Vienna, Austria, area and displaced persons program adviser to U.S. forces in Austria, 1945-47; Jewish Federation, Sioux City, Iowa, executive director, 1947-53; Morningside College, Sioux City, part-time visiting lecturer in sociology, 1949-52; Jewish Federation, Waterbury, Conn., executive director, 1953-61; Jewish Community Council, El Paso, Tex., executive director, 1961-65; University of Texas, El Paso, assistant professor of sociology, 1965-67; University of Texas at Austin, associate professor of social work and director of undergraduate social welfare studies program, 1967-68; University of Wisconsin—Madison, visiting professor of social work, 1969-70; California State University, Northridge, associate professor, 1970-74, professor of sociology, 1974—, coordinator of social welfare program, 1972-76.

Member of professional evaluation team of United Jewish Appeal in France, Austria, Israel, and Morocco, 1956; past member of professional advisory board for manpower development project, Texas State Department of Public Welfare; organizer of clinics for parents of crippled children. Testified as expert witness before U.S. Congress; consultant to Office of Economic Opportunity, White Sands Missile Range, and Educational Projects, Inc.

MEMBER: American Association for the Advancement of Science (fellow; member of Pacific Division executive council, 1978; president of social sciences section, 1978), American Sociological Association, American Psychological Association, American Association of Social Workers (charter mem-

ber), Society for the Study of Symbolic Interaction (charter member), Academy of Certified Social Workers (charter member), Society for the Study of Social Problems, Alpha Kappa Delta. *Awards, honors:* Medal from State of Israel, 1963; Harry Lurie fellowship from Council of Jewish Federations and Welfare Funds, 1964; fellowship from National Jewish Cultural Foundation, 1965.

WRITINGS: Crippled Children in Israel: Report of a Survey Conducted for Government Agencies (monograph), Jewish Agency of Israel, 1959; *Theories of Personality: A Schema of Nine Personality Systems* (monograph), privately printed, 1964; *Project Bravo: Building Resources and Vocational Opportunities* (monograph), Community Action Program (El Paso, Tex.), 1965; (contributor) Louis J. Luzbetak, editor, *The Church in the Changing City,* Divine Word Publishers, 1966; *An Army of Despair: The Migrant Worker Stream* (monograph), Educational Systems Corp., 1968; *Some Considerations in the Structuring of an Undergraduate Social Welfare Program: Rationale, Departmental Location on Campus, Objectives, Foundation Courses, and Course Outlines* (monograph), Texas State Welfare Department, 1969; *A Compilation With Annotations of Some of the Texts and References for Social Welfare Programs* (monograph), Texas State Welfare Department, 1969; *The Development of Manpower Resources for Public Welfare Through Recruitment Activities and Undergraduate Social Work Education Programs* (monograph), Texas State Department of Public Welfare, 1969.

(Contributor) Russell N. Cassel and Robert L. Heichelberger, editors, *Leadership Development: Theory and Practice,* Christopher, 1975; *Conflicting Rights: Social Legislation and Policy,* University Press of America, Volume I: *Social Insurance and Public Assistance,* 1977, Volume II: *The Deviant, the Society, and the Law,* 1978; *Dynamics of Social Behavior and Development: A Symbolic Interactionist Integration of Theories,* University Press of America, 1978; (with Asoke Basu) *Poverty in America: The Welfare Dilemma,* Greenwood Press, 1981.

Contributor to *Encyclopedia Judaica.* Contributor of about fifty articles and reviews to scholarly journals, popular magazines, and newspapers, including *Harper's* and *Reconstructionist.* Editor of *Journal of Sociology and Social Welfare,* 1973-76, associate editor, 1976—; associate editor of *Journal of Applied Behavioral Science,* 1978—.

WORK IN PROGRESS: Switzerland as Welfare State, a comparison of American and Western European welfare and social insurance systems with that of Switzerland, "the only industrialized nation without dysfunctional service systems."

SIDELIGHTS: Segalman wrote: "One of my concerns is the dynamics of self-sufficiency versus personal and institutional dependency; thus, I follow research and theory in such fields as the social psychology of welfare dependency, of health care, mental health, family life, and social development and behavior. I am also interested in the success or failure of helping services: some day I'll write *The Helping Hand Strikes Again.*

"The more I study the theories of human behavior and development (Freud, Jung, Adler, Horney, Sullivan, Berne, and others) the more I realize that each theory is like the expression of each of the blind men who studied an elephant—they are all using different terms for the same dynamics. They really need a realistic sociologist to help them find their common meanings.

"The problem of psychotherapy is that each school of therapy is related to a different level of social development in patients. Thus therapy, to be effective, must be based on the level of development and of the dynamic problems of the patient—not the therapist and the theories he may be most comfortable with.

"The problem of helping people (whether in psychotherapy, welfare, employment placement, etc.) is that if you help the client too much, you make him dependent. If you help him too little, then you are prolonging his pain and perhaps his condition. All clients are not the same in their threshold of readiness of dependency, and so the degree of help which will aid one patient may harm another. Help is like drugs (narcotics). It can help or harm, depending upon the skill and knowledge of the practitioner."

*   *   *

SEKORA, John   1939-

BRIEF ENTRY: Born November 18, 1939, in Granite City, Ill. American educator and author. Sekora began teaching at Western Illinois University in 1970 and became a professor of English in 1978. He has also taught Afro-American studies. Sekora wrote *Luxury: The Concept in Western Thought, Eden to Smollett* (Johns Hopkins University Press, 1978). *Address:* Department of English, Western Illinois University, 900 West Adams St., Macomb, Ill. 61455.

*   *   *

SELDEN, Neil R(oy)   1931-

PERSONAL: Born March 20, 1931, in New York, N.Y.; son of Joseph and Ann (Sirota) Selden; married Lee Imbrie, July 21, 1960; children: Michael. *Education:* New York University, B.A., 1952. *Home:* 21 Pine Dr., Roosevelt, N.J. 08555. *Agent:* William Morris Agency, 1350 Avenue of the Americas, New York, N.Y. 10019.

CAREER: Writer. Member of board of directors of Encounter, Inc. (drug rehabilitation organization); consultant to New York City Addiction Services Agency. *Military service:* U.S. Army, Military Police, 1954-56. *Member:* Dramatists Guild. *Awards, honors:* Poetry award from Wisconsin Library, 1953, for poem "Cassandra's Eye"; Audrey Wood Award, 1972, for play "CAR."

WRITINGS—Juveniles: Flood, Scholastic Book Services, 1973; *Night Driver,* Scholastic Book Services, 1978; *The Great Lakeside High Experiment,* Scholastic Book Services, 1982.

Plays: (With brother-in-law, McCrea Imbrie) "Someone's Comin' Hungry" (three-act), first produced Off-Broadway at Pocket Theater, March 31, 1969; (with Imbrie) "Mr. Shandy" (one-act), first produced Off-Broadway at Roundabout Theatre, 1972; (with Imbrie) "CAR" (one-act), first produced in Berlin, West Germany, at Berlin Festival, 1973; "Ocean in a Teacup" (musical), first produced in New York, N.Y., at Rainy Night House, 1975. Also author with Imbrie of plays "Raincheck," first produced in Berlin at Berlin Festival; "The Feeling Shop," first produced in New York, N.Y., at Actor's Studio; "Clearing," first produced at Huntington Theatre Workshop; and "Gino," first produced in New York, N.Y., at Journey Theatre. Also author with Imbrie of screenplays "Someone's Comin' Hungry," "Roll, China, Roll," "Finders Keepers," and "A Girl Like Norman Mailer."

WORK IN PROGRESS: "Sam Dead," a three-act play; collaborating on "The Day the War Went Away," a screenplay.

SIDELIGHTS: Selden told *CA:* "My major effort has been directed toward creating plays, none of which have been specifically for children. I have also continued to write poems for the past twenty-seven years as acts of love and meditation and

hope to persist in such divine madness even into the last moment of my departure.

"I write for the joy and I write for the money, in that order. Of joy there has been more than I dreamed possible; of money far, far less. I love actors and I love theatres, especially when they are bare, transfixed perhaps by one bright light, awaiting a word or a gesture or a note of music to make love alive in its many disguises."

Selden's play "Someone's Comin' Hungry" is about the floundering marriage of a black man and a white woman. Harold Clurman commented in *Nation* that "Someone's Comin' Hungry" "is an honest attempt to reveal the accumulated bitterness of a young black Vietnamese War veteran who experiences the greatest difficulty in returning the love of his white wife. His spirit wounded by the experience of his life as a black and as a soldier, he has become incapable." *New York Times* critic Clive Barnes noted that "well-meaning is the precise word for 'Someone's Comin' Hungry.'" "The authors," he explained, "have taken a completely possible mixed marriage and . . . tried to use it, with tactful unobtrusiveness, as a parable for our troubled times." The *Record*'s Emory Lewis named the drama "one of the most engrossing, passionate, and profound plays of the season."

BIOGRAPHICAL/CRITICAL SOURCES: Record, April 1, 1969; *New York Times,* April 1, 1969; *Village Voice,* April 3, 1969; *Nation,* April 14, 1969.

*   *   *

SENELICK, Laurence P(hilip)   1942-

PERSONAL: Born October 12, 1942, in Chicago, Ill.; son of Theodore (a purchasing agent) and Evelyn (Marder) Senelick. *Education:* Northwestern University, B.A., 1964; Harvard University, A.M., 1968, Ph.D., 1972. *Home:* 117 Mystic St., West Medford, Mass. 02155. *Office:* Department of Drama, Tufts University, Medford, Mass. 02155.

CAREER: Emerson College, Boston, Mass., assistant professor of English, 1968-72; Tufts University, Medford, Mass., assistant professor, 1972-76, associate professor of drama, 1976—. Professional actor and director, 1963—; director of Proposition Cabaret, 1968-69, and Summer School Theatre Workshop at Harvard University, 1974-75. Member of Russian Research Center at Harvard University. *Member:* International Federation for Theatre Research, American Society for Theatre Research, Actors' Equity Association, Society for Cultural Relations With the U.S.S.R., British Music Hall Society, British Theatre Institute. *Awards, honors:* Woodrow Wilson fellow, 1964 and 1965; grant from National Endowment for the Humanities, 1977; Guggenheim fellow, 1979.

WRITINGS: (Editor and translator) Anton Chekhov, *The Seagull and The Cherry Orchard,* AHM Publishing, 1977; (with David Brownell) *Tchaikovsky's Sleeping Beauty,* Bellerophon Books, 1978; *A Cavalcade of Clowns,* Bellerophon Books, 1978; *Russian Dramatic Theory From Pushkin to the Symbolists: An Anthology,* University of Texas Press, 1981; (with D. F. Cheshire and Ulrich Schneider) *British Music-Hall, 1840-1923,* Shoe String, 1981; *Gordon Craig's Moscow Hamlet,* Greenwood Press, 1982; "Dead Souls" (two-act play; adapted from the novel by Nikolay Gogol), first produced in Medford, Mass., at Tufts University, May, 1982; *Serf Actor: A Biography of Mikhail Shchepkin,* Greenwood Press, in press. Contributor to *McGraw-Hill Encyclopedia of World Drama, Oxford Companion to the Theatre,* and *Academic American Encyclopedia.* Contributor to periodicals, including *New Bos-*

ton Review, Call Boy, After Dark, History of Photography, and *Cuisine.* Editor of *Dickens Studies,* 1965-69.

WORK IN PROGRESS: A Biography of George L. Fox, publication by Archon Books expected in 1984; "Russia, 1880-1971," to be included in *Sources and Documents of European Theatre,* edited by Claude Schumacher, Cambridge University Press, 1984.

SIDELIGHTS: Senelick commented: "It is immensely important to inform one's scholarship and research by practical experience in the field studies. I maintain an active life as an actor, director, and playwright as an adjunct to my investigations of the theatre of the past. The traffic works both ways: the practical experience illuminates the historical study."

AVOCATIONAL INTERESTS: Cooking, collecting.

*   *   *

SESSIONS, Kyle Cutler   1934-

BRIEF ENTRY: Born July 6, 1934, in Malad, Idaho. American historian, educator, editor of books, and author. Sessions has taught history at Illinois State University since 1967. He edited *Reformation and Authority: The Meaning of the Peasants' Revolt* (Heath, 1968). *Address:* Department of History, Illinois State University, Normal, Ill. 61761.

*   *   *

SETH, Ronald (Sydney)   1911-
(Robert Chartham)

PERSONAL: Born 1911, in Ely, Cambridgeshire, England; married Josephine Franklin (deceased); married Barbara Pearce Geering; children: one son, one daughter. *Education:* Attended Peterhouse, Cambridge.

CAREER: Writer, 1950—. Former instructor in English language and literature, University of Tallinn, Estonia; British Broadcasting Corp. (BBC), founder and chief of Monitoring Intelligence Bureau. *Military service:* Royal Air Force; served in World War II; became flight lieutenant.

WRITINGS: (Adapter) John Drinkwater, *Abraham Lincoln,* Oxford University Press, 1947; *A Spy Has No Friends,* Deutsch, 1952, Library Publishers, 1954; (translator) Publius Ovidius Naso, *Art of Love* (illustrated by Guy Nicholls), Spearman & Arco, 1953; *Grant of the Secret Service in Operation Lama,* Muller, 1953; *Operation Retriever* (juvenile), Muller, 1953, published as *Operation Getaway,* John Day, 1954; *The True Book About the Secret Service* (illustrated by David H. Walsh), Muller, 1953; *The Patriot,* P. Owen, 1954; *Spies at Work: A History of Espionage,* Philosophical Library, 1954; *Lion with Blue Wings: The Story of the Glider Pilot Regiment, 1942-45,* Gollancz, 1955; *Operation Ormer,* Bles, 1956; *The Undaunted: The Story of Resistance in Western Europe,* Philosophical Library, 1956; *The Art of Spying,* Philosophical Library, 1957; *How Spies Work* (juvenile), Bles, 1957; *Secret Servants: A History of Japanese Espionage,* Farrar, Straus, 1957 (published in England as *Secret Servants: The Story of Japanese Espionage,* Gollancz, 1957), reprinted, Greenwood Press, 1975; *The Spy and the Atom-Gun* (juvenile), Bles, 1957, Farrar, Straus, 1958; *For My Name's Sake,* Bles, 1958; *Rockets on Moon Island,* Bles, 1959; *Smoke Without Fire,* Bles, 1959; *Stalingrad, Point of No Return: The Story of the Battle, August 1942-February 1943,* Coward, 1959.

K.G.B.: The Story of Soviet Espionage, Young Asia Publications, c. 1960; *Robert Gordon Menzies,* Cassell, 1960; *Two Fleets Surprised: The Story of the Battle of Cape Matapan,*

Mediterranean, March, 1941, Bles, 1960; *Anatomy of Spying,* Arthur Barker, 1961, Dutton, 1963; (adapter) *Fairy Tales of Greece* (juvenile; illustrated by George Miller), Dutton, 1961; *The Fiercest Battle: The Story of North Atlantic Convoy ONS 5, 22nd April-7th May 1943,* Hutchinson, 1961, Norton, 1962; *How the Resistance Worked,* Bles, 1961; *Montgomery of Alamein,* Cassell, 1961; *The Specials: The Story of the Special Constabulary in England, Wales and Scotland,* Gollancz, 1961; *Sir Archibald McIndoe,* Cassell, 1962; *Spy in the Nude,* R. Hale, 1962; *The Day War Broke Out: The Story of the 3rd September, 1939,* Neville Spearman, 1963; *Petiot, Victim of Chance,* Hutchinson, 1963; *Operation Barbarossa: The Battle for Moscow,* Anthony Blond, 1964.

Caporetto, the Scapegoat Battle, MacDonald & Co., 1965; *The First Time It Happened: Fifty Memorable Occasions in the Story of Man,* Odhams, 1965; *Forty Years of Soviet Spying,* Cassell, 1965; *Unmasked! The Story of Soviet Espionage,* Hawthorn, 1965; *The Noble Saboteurs,* Hawthorn, 1966; *Russell Pasha,* Kimber, 1966; *The Russian Terrorists: The Story of the Narodniki,* Barrie & Rockliff, 1966; *The Spy Who Wasn't Caught: The Story of Julius Silber,* R. Hale, 1966, published as *The Spy Who Was Never Caught,* Hawthorn, 1967; *The Executioners: The Story of SMERSH,* Cassell, 1967, Hawthorn, 1968; *Lev Davidovich Trotsky: The Eternal Rebel,* Dobson, 1967; *Stories of Great Witch Trials,* Arthur Barker, 1967; *Witches and Their Craft,* Odhams, 1967, Taplinger, 1968.

Milestones in Russian History (juvenile), Chilton, 1968; *The Sleeping Truth: The Hiss-Chambers Affair Reappraised,* Hart Publishing, 1968 (published in England as *The Sleeping Truth: The Hiss-Chambers Affair: The Spy Case That Split a Nation,* Frewin, 1968); *Some of My Favorite Spies,* Chilton, 1968; *The Spy in Silk Breeches,* Frewin, 1968; *Children Against Witches,* Taplinger, 1969; *In the Name of the Devil: Great Scottish Witchcraft Cases,* Jarrolds, 1969, published as *In the Name of the Devil,* Walker & Co., 1970; *Milestones in African History* (juvenile), Chilton, 1969; *Milestones in Japanese History* (juvenile), Chilton, 1969; *The Truth-Benders: Psychological Warfare in the Second World War,* Frewin, 1969; *Encyclopedia of Espionage,* New English Library, 1972, Doubleday, 1974; *Jackals of the Reich: The Story of the British Free Corps,* New English Library, 1972.

Travel books: *Estonian Journey: Travels in a Baltic Corner,* R. M. McBride & Co., 1939 (published in England as *Baltic Corner: Travel in Estonia,* Methuen, 1939); *Let's Visit the Middle East* (juvenile), Burke Publishing, 1968; *Let's Visit Antarctica* (juvenile), Burke Publishing, 1969; *Let's Visit Spain* (juvenile), Burke Publishing, 1973; *Let's Visit the Netherlands* (juvenile), Burke Publishing, 1973; *Let's Visit Portugal* (juvenile), Burke Publishing, 1976; *Let's Visit Malta* (juvenile), Burke Publishing, 1978.

Under pseudonym Robert Chartham: *Mainly for Wives: A Guide to Practical Lovemaking,* Macdonald & Co., 1964, revised edition published as *Mainly for Wives: The Art of Sex for Women,* New American Library, 1969; *Mainly for Women,* Tandem Press, 1966; *Husband and Lover: The Art of Sex for Men,* New American Library, 1967; *Sex Manners for Men,* Frewin, 1967; *Sex Manners for Advanced Lovers,* New English Library, 1969; *Sex and the Over-Fifties,* Frewin, 1970, Brandon Books, 1972; *Sex Manners of the Younger Generation,* New English Library, 1970; *Advice to Men,* Tandem Press, 1971; *Advice to Women,* Tandem Press, 1971; (editor) Ellen Peck, *The Baby Trap,* Geis, 1971; *The Chartham Letters: A Selection of Correspondence Dealing With Sexual Problems Received and Replied To,* New English Library, 1971; *The Sensuous Couple,* Ballantine, 1971; *Sex Manners for Older*

Teenagers, Corgi Books, 1971; *Pictorial Guide to Sexual Fulfillment,* Bruce & Watson, 1972; *S Is for Sex,* Corgi Books, 1972; *Your Sexual Future,* Pinnacle Books, 1972; *Older Teenager's Sex Questions Answered,* Corgi Books, 1973; *You, Your Children and Sex: What to Tell Them, How and When,* Frewin, 1973; *What Turns Women On,* Ballantine, 1974; *You and Sex: Family Guide,* Tandem Press, 1974; *The Forum Guide to Sexual Problems,* Mayflower Books, 1975.

SIDELIGHTS: Seth is a prolific writer of espionage tales. Much of his writing is drawn from his experiences as a secret agent for Britain during World War II. While on a mission in Estonia, Seth was captured by the Germans and tortured. By successfully convincing the Nazis that he could work for them as a spy, Seth found his way back to Britain. The hair-raising tale of adventure and espionage is described in Seth's book, *A Spy Has No Friends.*

BIOGRAPHICAL/CRITICAL SOURCES: New York Times Book Review, April 16, 1939, July 14, 1957; *Chicago Tribune,* July 28, 1957; *New York Herald Tribune Book Review,* August 4, 1957; *New Statesman,* August 22, 1959; *Spectator,* August 28, 1959; *Times Literary Supplement,* September 18, 1959, May 13, 1965, February 23, 1967, June 1, 1967, July 6, 1967, June 8, 1973; *Saturday Review,* May 25, 1963; *Best Sellers,* December 1, 1965, July 15, 1968.

* * *

SHAGINYAN, Marietta Sergeyevna 1888-1982 (Jimmy Dollar)

OBITUARY NOTICE: Born March 21, 1888, in Moscow, Russia (now U.S.S.R.); died in 1982 in Moscow, U.S.S.R. Author. Shaginyan began her literary career at the age of fifteen when she published her first works in journals. As a poet she subscribed to the Symbolist school, but after the Bolshevik Revolution she wrote little verse, concentrating primarily on prose. Shaginyan was a firm supporter of the new Soviet regime. Lending her writing abilities to its purposes, the writer pioneered the Soviet detective novel, merging revolutionary ideology with a mystery plot. In 1951 she was awarded the Stalin Prize for literature, and in 1972 she received the Lenin Prize for her four-volume work on the Vladimir Lenin family. Shaginyan won the Soviet Union's highest award, the Order of Socialist Labor, in 1976. Among her prolific writings are biographies of such notables as William Blake and Sergei Rachmaninov, translations of foreign works, and an autobiography, *The Diary of the Author.* Her novels include *Hydroelectric Station* and *Mess Mend; or, The Yankees in Petrograd.* Obituaries and other sources: *Columbia Dictionary of Modern European Literature,* Columbia University Press, 1947, 2nd revised edition, 1980; *Dictionary of Russian Literature,* Greenwood Press, 1971; *Cassell's Encyclopaedia of World Literature,* revised edition, Morrow, 1973; *The International Who's Who,* Europa, 1974; *New York Times,* March 25, 1982; *London Times,* April 6, 1982.

* * *

SHAHAN, Lynn 1941-

PERSONAL: Born August 16, 1941, in Mesa, Ariz.; daughter of Emory L. (a farmer and rancher) and Lorraine (a postmaster; maiden name, Fluharty) Shahan. *Education:* Arizona State University, B.A., 1963; University of California, Irvine, General Pupil Personnel Services Credential, 1972; Pepperdine University, General Pupil Personnel Services Credential, 1976. *Address:* c/o Stratford Press, Inc., 1880 Century Park E., Suite 1511, Los Angeles, Calif. 90067.

CAREER: Garden Grove Unified School District, Garden Grove, Calif., elementary and junior high school teacher, 1963-71, administrator, 1971-72, guidance counselor, 1972-81. Member of Garden Grove Pupil Personnel Services Association.

WRITINGS: Living Alone and Liking It, Stratford Press, 1981.

WORK IN PROGRESS: A second self-help book.

SIDELIGHTS: Shahan told *CA: "Living Alone and Liking It* is my first book and I am delighted with its success. I felt that it was time to give a positive definition to a burgeoning lifestyle—23 percent of American households are single households—and to develop a guide for people new to living on their own. I have had little time alone since the publication of the book and look forward to renewing the luxuries of my privacy and solitude in the near future."

BIOGRAPHICAL/CRITICAL SOURCES: New York Times Book Review, September 13, 1981; *People,* September 14, 1981.

* * *

SHAH OF IRAN
See PAHLEVI, Mohammed Riza

* * *

SHANKS, Hershel 1930-

BRIEF ENTRY: Born March 8, 1930, in Sharon, Pa. American attorney and author. After beginning his career as a trial attorney with the U.S. Department of Justice, Shanks joined the law firm of Glassie, Pewett, Beebe & Shanks. He has edited *Biblical Archaeology Review* since 1975. His books are *The Art and Craft of Judging: The Decisions of Judge Learned Hand* (Macmillan, 1968), *The City of David: A Guide to Biblical Jerusalem* (Biblical Archaeology Society, 1973-75), and *Judaism in Stone: The Archaeology of Ancient Synagogues* (Harper, 1979). *Address:* 5208 38th St. N.W., Washington, D.C. 20015; and 1737 H St. N.W., Washington, D.C. 20006. *Biographical/critical sources: Directory of American Scholars,* Volume IV: *Philosophy, Religion, and Law,* 7th edition, Bowker, 1978.

* * *

SHANNON, Foster (Houts) 1930-

PERSONAL: Born July 13, 1930, in Chicago, Ill.; son of Homer Houts (a writer) and Florine (a public school teacher; maiden name, Foster) Shannon; married Janis Marie Douglass (a head of a shipping department), June 21, 1952; children: Douglass Foster, Katherine Marie. *Education:* University of California, Berkeley, B.A., 1952; Fuller Theological Seminary, M.Div., 1958; San Francisco Theological Seminary, D.Min., 1975. *Politics:* Democrat. *Home:* 161 Grant St., Campbell, Calif. 95008. *Office:* Immanuel Presbyterian Church, 3675 Payne Ave., San Jose, Calif. 95117.

CAREER: Ordained Presbyterian minister, 1959; pastor of Presbyterian churches in Omaha, Neb., 1958-62, and Ivanhoe, Calif., 1962-68; Immanuel Presbyterian Church, San Jose, Calif., pastor, 1968—. President and chief executive officer of Green Leaf Press. Chairman of executive committee on evangelism of Synod of the Golden Gate, 1969-71; moderator of Presbytery of San Jose, 1972; member of board of directors of Presbyterians United for Biblical Concerns, 1979—. *Military service:* U.S. Army, 1953-55. *Member:* American Schools of Oriental Research, Commonwealth Club of California.

WRITINGS: The Growth Crisis in the American Church, William Carey Library, 1977, revised edition, Green Leaf Press,

1983; *God Is Light,* Green Leaf Press, 1981; *The Green Leaf Bible Series,* Green Leaf Press, 1982. Contributor to church magazines and newspapers, including *Church Growth America, Presbyterian Communique, Presbyterian Outlook, Presbyterian Layman,* and *Monday Morning.*

WORK IN PROGRESS: An exposition of II Timothy; an exposition of Hebrews.

SIDELIGHTS: Shannon wrote: "I am keenly interested in current affairs, archaeology, and ancient history related to the Bible. I have been to the Middle East and Europe four times, visiting Egypt, Jordan, Israel, Syria, Lebanon, Turkey, Greece, Italy, and the Netherlands."

Shannon also told *CA* of another interest. "I believe," he said, "that the percentage growth of small publishing companies will considerably exceed that of the major publishers during the 1980's. Small publishers will provide an increasingly important opening for new talent and new titles in the marketplace."

AVOCATIONAL INTERESTS: Reading, listening to good music, running, swimming, playing tennis.

* * *

SHANNON, George (William Bones) 1952-

PERSONAL: Born February 14, 1952, in Caldwell, Kan.; son of David W. (a professor) and Doris (Bones) Shannon. *Education:* Western Kentucky University, B.S., 1974; University of Kentucky, M.S.L.S., 1976. *Home:* 648 Wisconsin St., No. 3, Eau Claire, Wis. 54701.

CAREER: Librarian at public schools of Muhlenberg County, Ky., 1974-75; Lexington Public Library, Lexington, Ky., librarian, 1976-78; professional storyteller, 1978—. Guest lecturer at University of Kentucky, autumn, 1977. *Member:* National Association for the Preservation and Perpetuation of Storytelling.

WRITINGS: The Gang and Mrs. Higgins (juvenile), Greenwillow, 1981; *Humpty Dumpty: A Pictorial History,* Green Tiger Press, 1981; *The Piney Woods Peddler* (juvenile), Greenwillow, 1981; *Lizard's Song* (juvenile), Greenwillow, 1981; *Folk Literature and Children: An Annotated Bibliography of Secondary Materials,* Greenwood Press, 1981; *Dance Away!* (juvenile), Greenwillow, 1982. Contributor of articles to magazines.

WORK IN PROGRESS: An anthology of worldwide variations of the folktale "Wolf and the Little Kids," including a literary essay and discussion of various interpretations of the tale by writers and psychologists; an anthology of folktales which reflect the soul of the artist and his creative talents.

SIDELIGHTS: Shannon commented: "To date, all my writing has grown from my work as a professional storyteller in the oral tradition, which is itself a form of writing but without ink or paper. I am most fond of brief, intense prose and poetry and am forever working toward distilling my thoughts into tightly formed stories for all ages. Imagery and story form the core of my work rather than character, as they do in the folktales created by all those who lived before us.

"I travel frequently to tell stories, and always at my side is the dog-eared journal filled with dreams, lines, phrases, plot snatches, and impressions that all feed into the next story I tell and the next book I write."

* * *

SHAPIRO, Deborah 1923-

PERSONAL: Born September 1, 1923, in Detroit, Mich.; daughter of Israel Morris (a junk dealer) and Bertha (Lightstone) Shapiro; children: Sharon (adopted). *Education:* Wayne State University, B.A., 1944; University of Chicago, M.A., 1948; Columbia University, D.S.W., 1960. *Politics:* Democrat. *Religion:* Jewish. *Office:* Child Welfare League of America, 67 Irving Pl., New York, N.Y. 10003.

CAREER: New York Medical College, New York City, social worker, 1957-61; Columbia University, New York City, research associate, 1963-73; Child Welfare League of America, New York City, research associate, 1973—. President and member of board of directors of New York Council on Adoptable Children, 1972-73; consultant to Salvation Army and Center for Urban Education. *Member:* National Association of Social Workers (chairman of New York City research council, 1973-74), American Sociological Association.

WRITINGS: (With Lucille J. Grow) *Black Children—White Parents: A Study of Transracial Adoption,* Child Welfare League of America, 1975; (with Grow) *Trans-Racial Adoption Today,* Child Welfare League of America, 1975; *Agencies and Children: A Child Welfare Network's Investment in Its Clients,* Columbia University Press, 1976; *Parents and Protectors: A Study in Child Abuse,* Child Welfare League of America, 1979. Contributor to social work journals.

* * *

SHARP, Francis Michael 1941-

PERSONAL: Born February 10, 1941, in Troy, Kan.; son of Francis Wilson and Shirley (Carlson) Sharp; married Nancy Yukie Nakamura (a teacher), September 20, 1967; children: Lea Christina. *Education:* University of Missouri, B.A., 1964; University of California, Berkeley, M.A., 1969, Ph.D., 1974; further graduate study at Free University of Berlin, 1969-70. *Home:* 2703 Sumac Ave., Stockton, Calif. 95207. *Office:* Department of Modern Language and Literature, University of the Pacific, Stockton, Calif. 95211.

CAREER: Princeton University, Princeton, N.J., assistant professor of German, 1973-79; University of the Pacific, Stockton, Calif., assistant professor of German, 1979—. Public speaker. *Member:* Modern Language Association of America, American Association of Teachers of German, Modern Austrian Literature, Philological Association of the Pacific Coast. *Awards, honors:* Woodrow Wilson fellowship, 1966-67; Fulbright grant for Germany, 1980; Danforth associate, 1981-86; grant from National Endowment for the Humanities, 1981.

WRITINGS: The Poet's Madness: A Reading of George Trakl, Cornell University Press, 1981; (contributor) Bernd Urban and Winfried Kudszus, editors, *Psychoanalytische und Psychopathologische Literaturinterpretation* (title means "Psychoanalytical and Psychopathological Literary Interpretation"), Wissenschaftliche Buchgesellschaft, 1981; (contributor) Gerald Chapple and Hans H. Schulte, *The Turn of the Century: German Literature and Art, 1890-1915,* Bouvier Verlag, 1981; (contributor) Charles Burdick, Hans-Adolf Jacobsen, and Kudszus, editors, *Modern German Culture,* Praeger, 1982. Contributor of about twenty articles and reviews to language and literature journals.

WORK IN PROGRESS: Research on Robert Walser's prose.

SIDELIGHTS: Sharp told *CA:* "As a teacher I regret that today's undergraduates are getting their education in such a regressive and repressive atmosphere. Many are pushed into narrow, vocational studies much too early and miss out entirely on 'education.' I miss the open-ended intellectual search of the 1960's, the politicized tenor of all fields, and I can only hope for their speedy return to the American campus.

"In my own work I've been fascinated by the process of literary creation, particularly in the overlap between creativity and psychopathology. It is the latter interest which first led me to R. D. Laing and then, by the back door, to Freud."

*   *   *

SHAW, Howard 1934-

PERSONAL: Born September 16, 1934, in Bristol, England; son of Cyril Raymond (a test pilot) and Doris Janet (a schoolmistress; maiden name, Saunders) Shaw; married Elizabeth Ann Du Heaume (a schoolmistress), December 26, 1958; children: Rupert Edward, James Francis. *Education:* Queen's College, Oxford, B.A., 1958, M.A., 1963. *Home:* Syon, Harrow Park, Harrow on the Hill, Middlesex, England. *Agent:* Laurence Pollinger Ltd., 18 Maddox St., Mayfair, London W1R 0EU, England.

CAREER: Schoolmaster. King's College School, Cambridge, England, assistant master, 1958-61; Harrow School, Harrow, England, assistant master, 1961-81; writer, 1968—. Elected schoolmaster-fellow of Emmanuel College, Cambridge, 1966. *Military service:* Royal Artillery, 1953-55; became second lieutenant.

WRITINGS: The Levellers, Longmans, Green, 1968, Harper, 1971; *Killing No Murder,* R. Hale, 1972, Scribner, 1981; *Death of a Don,* Scribner, 1981. Also author of broadcast "Puritanism Purified," British Broadcasting Corp. (BBC), 1965. Contributor of articles to periodicals, including *History Today.*

WORK IN PROGRESS: Who Killed Mrs. Pankhurst?, a detective novel.

SIDELIGHTS: Howard Shaw's second novel, *Killing No Murder,* traces Chief Detective Inspector Barnaby's investigation of the murder of a permissive headmaster at Claydon Court School for boys. Besides the murderer, Inspector Barnaby discovers academic rivalries, love affairs, and numerous psychoses at the school.

Shaw told *CA:* "I write for relaxation."

AVOCATIONAL INTERESTS: Music, cricket, butterflies, birds of prey, disused railways.

BIOGRAPHICAL/CRITICAL SOURCES: Washington Post Book World, July 19, 1981; *New York Times Book Review,* July 26, 1981.

*   *   *

SHAW, Linda 1938-

PERSONAL: Born November 28, 1938, in El Dorado, Ark.; married Bennett Shaw (a planning engineer), June 20, 1957; children: Randy, Shelley, Tim. *Education:* North Texas State University, B.Mus., 1977. *Home and office:* 500 Pecan St., Keene, Tex. 76059. *Agent:* Arthur P. Schwartz, 435 Riverside Dr., New York, N.Y. 10025.

CAREER: Professional organist, 1972—. Piano teacher in Gainesville, Tex., 1972-77.

WRITINGS—Novels: Ballad in Blue, Ballantine, 1979; *The Satin Vixen,* Gallen, 1981; *An Innocent Deception,* Gallen, 1981; *December's Wine,* Silhouette Press, 1982; *All She Ever Wanted,* Silhouette Press, 1982; *After The Rain,* Silhouette Press, 1983.

WORK IN PROGRESS: Two historical novels, one tentatively titled *Why the Songbird Sings,* both for Pocket Books.

SIDELIGHTS: Shaw told *CA:* "I would like to see the romance genre develop a fine quality of writing and an experienced authorship that will command respect within the publishing industry. I would also like to see romance novels deal with the contemporary woman in a credible fashion."

*   *   *

SHEAFFER, Robert M(errill) 1949-

PERSONAL: Born May 21, 1949, in Chicago, Ill.; son of Merrill G. (a television technician) and Dorothy (Kaminski) Sheaffer; married Charlene Kellsey (a librarian), June 30, 1973; children: Kenneth. *Education:* Northwestern University, B.A., 1971, M.A., 1972. *Residence:* San Jose, Calif.

CAREER: Teacher of mathematics at high school in Winnetka, Ill.; worked on development of minicomputer telecommunications systems in Arlington, Va., 1972-73, and in Silver Spring and Bethesda, Md., 1973-80, and microprocessor software in San Jose, Calif., 1980—. Guest on television and radio programs; speaker at Smithsonian Institution and at conferences dealing with unidentified flying objects. *Member:* Committee for the Scientific Investigation of Claims of the Paranormal (fellow).

WRITINGS: The UFO Verdict, Prometheus Books, 1981; (contributor) Benjamin Zuckerman and Michael Hart, editors, *Where Are They?: The Implications of Our Failure to Observe Extraterrestrials,* Pergamon, in press. Author of "Psychic Vibrations," a column in *Skeptical Inquirer.* Contributor of articles and reviews to magazines, including *Spaceflight, Astronomy, Humanist, Reason, Fate,* and *Omni.*

SIDELIGHTS: Sheaffer commented: "Unidentified flying objects (UFOs), and other reportedly paranormal phenomena, are what I call 'jealous phenomena,' meaning that they will always continue to slip away before the evidence becomes too convincing. The scientific method is the only reliable path to knowledge, and until such things as UFOs and ghosts hold still long enough to be seen by believers and skeptics alike, they cannot be considered scientifically established.

"I challenge anyone to present convincing and unambiguous evidence of UFOs, extrasensory perception (ESP), or any similar alleged phenomenon. No one ever has, and I suspect that the reason is that these things exist only in the overheated imaginations of those who pursue them. The world today contains so many *real* challenges to human ingenuity and wisdom that it is a shame to waste valuable time and effort on counterfeit ones."

*   *   *

SHEFFIELD, James Rockwell 1936-

BRIEF ENTRY: Born December 15, 1936, in New York, N.Y. American educator and author. Since 1967 Sheffield has taught education at Columbia University. Also director of the university's Center for Education on Africa, Sheffield wrote *Non-Formal Education in African Development* (African-American Institute, 1972), *Education and Rural Development* (Evans Brothers, 1973), *Education in Kenya: An Historical Study* (Teachers College Press, 1973), *Road to the Village: Case Studies in African Community Development* (African-American Institute, 1974), and *Agriculture in African Secondary Schools: Case Studies of Botswana, Kenya, and Tanzania* (African-American Institute, 1976). *Address:* Department of Home and

Family Life, Teachers College, Columbia University, New York, N.Y. 10027.

*   *   *

SHENK, David W(itmer)   1937-

PERSONAL: Born April 18, 1937, in Shirati, Tanzania; son of J. Clyde (an American missionary) and Alta R. (a missionary; maiden name, Barge) Shenk; married K. Grace Witmer (an administrative secretary), June 13, 1959; children: Karen, Doris, Jonathan, Timothy. *Education:* Eastern Mennonite College, B.A., 1959; graduate study at Temple University and University of Pennsylvania, 1961-63; New York University, M.A., 1963, Ph.D., 1972. *Home:* 336 Primrose Lane, Mountville, Pa. 17554. *Office:* Home Ministries, Eastern Mennonite Board of Missions and Charities, Oak Lane and Brandt Blvd., Salunga, Pa. 17538.

CAREER: Ordained Mennonite minister, 1963; Mennonite Voluntary Service, New York, N.Y., youth worker, 1959-61; teacher of history and religion at Mennonite high school in Lancaster, Pa., 1961-63; Somalia Mennonite Mission, Mogadishu, Somali Democratic Republic, history teacher at mission school, 1964-67, headmaster, 1964-67, educational director of mission schools, 1965-72, director of mission, 1969-70; University of Nairobi, Nairobi, Kenya, lecturer in philosophy and religious studies, 1973-79; Eastern Mennonite Board of Missions and Charities, Salunga, Pa., executive secretary of home ministries, 1980—. Chairman of United Nations Educational, Scientific and Cultural Organization's committee on social studies curriculum development in the Somali Democratic Republic, 1968-69; chairman of Kenya's Islam in Africa Panel, 1973-79; administrative secretary of Kenya Mennonite church, 1977-79.

WRITINGS: (Contributor) Paul N. Kraybill, editor, *A Kingdom of Priests: The Church in New Nations,* Herald Press, 1967; *Mennonite Safari,* Herald Press, 1973; (with John P. Kealy) *The Early Church and Africa,* Oxford University Press, 1975; *The People of God,* Evangel Press, 1976; (contributor) Michael Cassidy and Luc Verlinden, editors, *Facing New Challenges: The Message of PACLA,* Evangel Press, 1978; (contributor) Kamuyu Wa Kangethe, editor, *Utumuduni,* Kenyatta University College Press, 1980; *An Introduction to the Holy Book of God,* African Christian Press, 1981; *Peace and Reconciliation in Africa,* Uzima, 1982. Contributor to theology journals.

WORK IN PROGRESS: A comparative study of approaches to community.

SIDELIGHTS: Shenk commented: "My parents were missionaries in Tanzania, so I grew up in East Africa. My adult work began in New York City, where I served as a unit leader of a voluntary service center. After two years of teaching I went to East Africa to serve in church and educational work. From 1963 to 1973 I worked in Islamic Somalia, and from 1973 to 1979 in Nairobi, Kenya.

"I was deeply involved in Christian religious education curriculum development and textbook writing under the auspices of the National Christian Council of Kenya, the Catholic Secretariat, the Ministry of Education, and the Kenya Institute of Education. I was also team leader of an attempt to develop Christian-Muslim dialogical study materials. The four books in that series have been or are being translated into seventeen languages for Asia, Europe, and Africa. My work in Islamic ministries also included serving as director of the Islamic Ministries Office of the Mennonite Area Office.

"I enjoyed the unique experience of living in Eastleigh, Nairobi. Eastleigh is the most congested area of the city, and it is about one quarter Muslim. We lived in a four-apartment complex with a multi-ethnic team of Christians who were attempting to demonstrate Christian community in Eastleigh. Our residence was across the street from the Islamic Qadiriyya mosque. Part of the overall ministry of the center was planned meetings between Christians and Muslims—a most fruitful and interesting experience.

"From both a professional and a religious perspective I found living in East Africa to be exceedingly interesting. We were at the crossroads of much that is happening in religion in Africa today. We faced the dynamism of a Christian church compounded by the anxieties and quest for an African identity. We lived in the throes of Christianity in a mixed culture, and the interaction between Islam and Christianity."

*   *   *

SHERA, Jesse Hauk   1903-1982

OBITUARY NOTICE—See index for *CA* sketch: Born December 8, 1903, in Oxford, Ohio; died March 8, 1982. Librarian, educator, researcher, and author. Shera founded the Center for Documentation and Communication Research at Case Western Reserve University, where he once served as the dean of and as a professor at the School of Library Science. A fellow of the American Association of Science, Shera was elected to the Library Hall of Fame in 1975. He also received a Melvil Dewey Medal from the American Library Association in 1968, and in 1969 he was named librarian of the year. Shera's writings include *Foundations of the Public Library, The Classified Catalogue, Libraries and the Organization of Knowledge, Sociological Foundations of Librarianship, Knowing Books and Men,* and *Introduction to Library Science.* Obituaries and other sources: *School Library Journal,* May, 1982.

*   *   *

SHERMAN, Claire Richter   1930-

PERSONAL: Born February 11, 1930, in Boston, Mass.; daughter of Harry (a grocer) and Fannie (Chaifetz) Richter; married Stanley M. Sherman (an architect and planner), February 21, 1954; children: Daniel James. *Education:* Radcliffe College, B.A., 1951; University of Michigan, M.A., 1958; Johns Hopkins University, Ph.D., 1964. *Home:* 4516 Que Lane N.W., Washington, D.C. 20007.

CAREER: University of Michigan, Ann Arbor, instructor in art history, 1958-59; independent researcher, 1964-66; American University, Washington, D.C., lecturer in art history, 1966-72; independent researcher, 1972-76; University of Virginia, Charlottesville, visiting associate professor of art, 1976; independent researcher and consultant, 1977—. Senior fellow at Center for Advanced Study, National Gallery of Art, Washington, D.C., 1981-82. Consultant to National Endowment for the Humanities. *Member:* Mediaeval Academy of America, College Art Association of America, Women's Caucus for Art (member of advisory board, 1978-80), Women's Equity Action League, Southeastern Medieval Association, Baltimore Bibliophiles. *Awards, honors:* Fulbright scholar, 1951-52; grants from American Philosophical Society, 1968, 1974, and American Council of Learned Societies, 1975.

WRITINGS: The Portraits of Charles V of France, 1338-1380, New York University Press, 1969; (editor with Adele M. Holcomb, and contributor) *Women as Interpreters of the Visual Arts, 1820-1979,* Greenwood Press, 1981. Contributor to art history journals. Member of editorial board of *Women's Art Journal,* 1980—.

WORK IN PROGRESS: A monograph, *Aristotle in Miniatures: The Illustrations of Aristotle's "Nicomachean Ethics" and "Politics" in French Manuscripts of the Fourteenth and Fifteenth Centuries.*

SIDELIGHTS: Claire Sherman commented: "My research has centered on the relationship between art and politics. *The Portraits of Charles V of France* expressed these interests, as have my subsequent publications. My current work on illustrations of Aristotle's work in the French translation of Nicole Oresme carries on these themes in the wider context of cultural history and manuscript studies.

"A second area of my research and writing concerns the roles of women in art history and criticism. I have written biographical essays on prominent women in the field and a history of their professional development."

BIOGRAPHICAL/CRITICAL SOURCES: Burlington Magazine, September, 1971.

* * *

SHEVELOVE, Burt 1915-1982

OBITUARY NOTICE: Born September 19, 1915, in Newark, N.J.; died April 7, 1982, in London, England. Director, producer, lyricist, and playwright best known for co-writing, with Larry Gelbart, "A Funny Thing Happened on the Way to the Forum," for which he won a Tony Award in 1962. Shevelove was involved in the production of numerous television programs and stage plays, including a revival of "No, No Nanette." He was in London working on a new musical at the time of his death. Obituaries and other sources: *Who's Who in the World,* 2nd edition, Marquis, 1973; *Chicago Tribune,* April 10, 1982; *Washington Post,* April 10, 1982; *London Times,* April 12, 1982.

* * *

SHI, David Emory 1951-

PERSONAL: Born August 19, 1951, in Atlanta, Ga.; son of Joseph E.B. (a professor) and Evelyn (Frye) Shi; married Susan Thomson (an assistant principal), June 22, 1974; children: Jason, Jessica. *Education:* Furman University, B.A. (magna cum laude), 1973; University of Virginia, M.A., 1975, Ph.D., 1976. *Home address:* P.O. Box 846, Davidson, N.C. 28036. *Agent:* Gerard McCauley Agency, Inc., P.O. Box AE, Katonah, N.Y. 10536. *Office:* Department of History, Davidson College, Davidson, N.C. 28036.

CAREER: Davidson College, Davidson, N.C., instructor, 1976-77, assistant professor of history, 1977—. *Military service:* U.S. Army Reserve, 1973—; present rank, captain. *Member:* American Studies Association, Organization of American Historians, Popular Culture Association, Southern Historical Association. *Awards, honors:* Member of All-Southern Conference Football Team, 1971, 1972, and All-South Carolina Football Team, 1972.

WRITINGS: Matthew Josephson, Bourgeois Bohemian, Yale University Press, 1981. Contributor to history journals and literary magazines, including *South Atlantic Quarterly, Southern Review,* and *Virginia Quarterly Review.*

WORK IN PROGRESS: The Simple Life: Plain Living and High Thinking in American Culture, publication by Oxford University Press expected in 1984.

SIDELIGHTS: Shi wrote: "My research has been eclectic, ranging across American intellectual and cultural history. Most

of it has been tied together by a value-oriented approach, examining ways in which individuals or groups have struggled to develop and maintain a particular philosophy of living or artistic perspective."

* * *

SHIEL, M(atthew) P(hipps) 1865-1947

BRIEF ENTRY: Born July 21, 1865, in Montserrat, West Indies; died February 17, 1947, in Chichester, England. British novelist. Shiel's fantasy novels excited some readers and confused others, but critics agreed that his flamboyant style and overcharged imagination earned him distinction in British literature. *The Purple Cloud* (1901), a story about the last surviving man on earth, was one of Shiel's most popular books. Many of his novels had been long out of print when an American publisher rediscovered and reprinted them in quick succession. Several critics admired Shiel's extraordinary vocabulary and skillful use of language. Others regarded his style as magically hypnotic; a few considered him mad, but irresistible. Shield produced more than thirty novels, including *The Last Miracle* (1906), *The Isle of Lies* (1909), *The Black Box* (1930), and *Dr. Krasinski's Secret* (1930). *Biographical/critical sources: Twentieth Century Authors: A Biographical Dictionary of Modern Literature,* H. W. Wilson, 1942, 1st supplement, 1955; *London,* September, 1964.

* * *

SHNEERSON, Grigory Mikhailovich 1901-1982

OBITUARY NOTICE: Born March 3, 1901, in Yenisseysk, Siberia, Russia (now U.S.S.R.); died February 5, 1982, in Moscow, U.S.S.R. Musicologist, music critic, pianist, editor, and author. Shneerson was considered one of the leading Soviet authorities on Western and Chinese music. He had served with the Secretariat of the International Music Bureau since 1933 and as head of the music division of the All-Union Society for Cultural Relations with Foreign Countries from 1942 to 1948. Shneerson edited *Sovietsaya muzika* from 1948 to 1961 and wrote essays on contemporary English music. Obituaries and other sources: *London Times,* February 15, 1982.

* * *

SHOUP, Paul Snedden 1929-

PERSONAL: Born July 21, 1929, in New York, N.Y.; son of Carl and Ruth (Snedden) Shoup; married Marija Milandinovic, 1953; children: Lawrence, Carl. *Education:* Swarthmore College, B.A., 1951; Columbia University, Ph.D., 1960. *Office:* Department of Government and Foreign Affairs, University of Virginia, Charlottesville, Va. 22901.

CAREER: Kenyon College, Gambier, Ohio, instructor in political science, 1960-63; University of Virginia, Charlottesville, assistant professor, 1963-67, associate professor, 1967-80, professor of political science, 1980—. *Member:* American Political Science Association, Association for the Advancement of Slavic Studies.

WRITINGS: Communism and the Yugoslav National Question, Columbia University Press, 1968; *The East European and Soviet Data Handbook,* Columbia University Press, 1981. Contributor to political science journals.

* * *

SHULA, Don(ald Francis) 1930-

BRIEF ENTRY: Born January 4, 1930, in Grand River, Ohio.

American professional football coach and author. Shula played football at John Carroll University and with the Cleveland Browns, the Baltimore Colts, and the Washington Redskins. He became head coach and vice-president of the Miami Dolphins in 1970, following a seven-year stint as head coach of the Colts. He wrote *The Winning Edge* (Dutton, 1973). *Address:* 16220 West Prestwick Pl., Miami Lakes, Fla. 33014; and 330 Biscayne Blvd. Building, Miami, Fla. 33132. *Biographical/critical sources: New York Times,* January 14, 1973, January 15, 1973; *Current Biography,* Wilson, 1974; *Biography News,* Volume I, Gale, 1974.

* * *

SHWAYDER, David S(amuel) 1926-

PERSONAL: Born October 21, 1926, in Denver, Colo.; son of Sol (a lawyer) and Ida (Weitz) Shwayder; married Concepcion Viltro Monserrat, April 14, 1954. *Education:* University of California, Berkeley, A.B., 1948; Oxford University, B.A., 1950, M.A., 1950, D.Phil., 1954. *Residence:* Urbana, Ill. *Office:* Department of Philosophy, University of Illinois, Urbana, Ill. 61801.

CAREER: University of Illinois, Urbana, assistant professor of philosophy, 1954-58; University of California, Berkeley, professor of philosophy, 1958-68; University of Illinois, Urbana, professor of philosophy, 1968—, chairman of department, 1969-70. Visiting professor at University of Michigan, 1958, at University of North Carolina, 1964, and at Oberlin College, 1978. Lecturer at American Study Seminar, Kyoto, Japan, summer, 1968. *Military service:* U.S. Naval Reserve, 1944-46. *Member:* American Philosophical Association. *Awards, honors:* Fulbright research fellow in New Zealand, 1961; Guggenheim fellow, 1967.

WRITINGS: Modes of Referring and the Problem of Universals, University of California Press, 1961; *The Stratification of Behavior,* Routledge & Kegan Paul, 1965, text edition, Humanities Press, 1971. Contributor to professional journals.

WORK IN PROGRESS: Statement and Body: An Inquiry Into the Foundations of Our Conceptual Order; A Theory of Practical Reason.

* * *

SIHANOUK, Norodom
See NORODOM SIHANOUK (VARMAN), Samdech Preah

* * *

SILK, Andrew 1953(?)-1981

OBITUARY NOTICE: Born c. 1953 in Neuilly-sur-Seine, France; died of lung cancer, December 12, 1981, in New York, N.Y. Journalist and author. Silk took a year off from his college studies in order to take a job as a visiting reporter in South Africa. Following his graduation from Haverford College, Silk returned to South Africa on a Thomas J. Watson fellowship and investigated living and working conditions of local blacks. Although his notes and tapes had been confiscated by South African police in a raid on a workers' camp, Silk wrote and published his findings in *A South African Shantytown: The Story of Modderdam* upon his return to the United States. Shortly after joining the *Norfolk Virginian-Pilot* in 1979, Silk was stricken with lung cancer. He wrote a piece on his experiences for that newspaper's series on cancer and received an award from the American Cancer Society. Another article on his experiences during the course of his treatment appeared as the cover story of the *New York Times Magazine* in October of 1981. In that account, written while Silk was in temporary remission, he detailed his hopes for a complete recovery and expressed his fears and frustrations. During his brief remission Silk took a job with the *Greenwich Times* as the editorial page editor. *Obituaries and other sources: New York Times Magazine,* October 18, 1981; *New York Times,* December 13, 1981.

* * *

SILVA, Eduardo Neale
See NEALE-SILVA, Eduardo

* * *

SILVER, Philip Warnock 1932-

PERSONAL: Born November 12, 1932, in Bryn Mawr, Pa.; married, 1958; children: two. *Education:* Haverford College, B.A., 1954; Middlebury College, M.A., 1955; Princeton University, M.A., 1960, Ph.D., 1963. *Office:* Department of Spanish and Portuguese, Columbia University, 612 West 116th St., New York, N.Y. 10027.

CAREER: Rutgers University, New Brunswick, N.J., instructor in Spanish, 1961-63; Oberlin College, Oberlin, Ohio, assistant professor, 1963-66, associate professor of Spanish and Portuguese, 1967-71; Columbia University, New York, N.Y., visiting professor, 1971-72, professor of Spanish and Portuguese, 1972—, chairman of department, 1973-76. *Member:* Modern Language Association of America, American Translators Association. *Awards, honors:* Guggenheim fellow, 1966.

WRITINGS: (Translator) *Unamuno: A Philosophy of Tragedy,* University of California Press, 1962; *Et in Arcadia Ego: A Study of the Poetry of Luis Cernuda,* Tamesis Books, 1965; *Sunlight and Crumbs* (poems), Triskelion Press (Oberlin, Ohio), 1969; (translator and author of introduction) Jose Ortega y Gasset, *Phenomenology and Art,* Norton, 1975; *Ortega as Phenomenologist: The Genesis of "Meditations of Quixote,"* Columbia University Press, 1978; (editor and author of prologue) Damaso Alonso, *Antologia poetica,* Alianza, 1979; (translator) Felix Martinez-Bonati, *Fictive Discourse and the Stuctures of Literature: A Phenomenological Approach,* Cornell University Press, 1981.

WORK IN PROGRESS: A History of Hispanic Poetry, 1870-1970.

* * *

SILVERSTEIN, Theodore 1904-

PERSONAL: Born October 11, 1904, in Liverpool, England; came to United States in 1910; naturalized U.S. citizen in 1929; son of David (in business) and Nellie (Dobson) Silverstein; married Mary Elizabeth Poindexter (a historian), December 12, 1945. *Education:* Harvard University, A.B., 1926, A.M., 1927, Ph.D., 1930. *Politics:* Democrat. *Home:* 5811 South Dorchester Ave., Chicago, Ill. 60637. *Office:* Department of English, University of Chicago, 1050 East 59th St., Chicago, Ill. 60637.

CAREER: Harvard University, Cambridge, Mass., instructor in English, 1931-37; University of Kansas City (now University of Missouri), Kansas City, Mo., 1938-42, began as assistant professor, became associate professor; University of Chicago, Chicago, Ill., began as assistant professor, became associate professor, 1947-57, professor of English, 1957-75, professor emeritus, 1975—, chairman of Committee on Ideas and Methods, 1966-72. Lecturer. *Military service:* U.S. Army Air Forces, 1942-45; served in European theater; became major; received Bronze Star and Purple Heart. *Member:* Modern Language Association of America, Mediaeval Academy of America, Chicago Literary Club. *Awards, honors:* Guggenheim fellowship, 1946-47; Fulbright fellowship for Italy, 1952-53; Institute for Advanced Study fellowship, 1955-56.

WRITINGS: Visio Sancti Pauli (title means "The Vision of St. Paul"), Christopher's, 1935; *Liber Hermetis Trismegisti de vi rerum principiis* (title means "The Book of Hermes Trismegisti Concerning the Sex Principles of Things"), J. Vrin, 1956; *Medieval Latin Scientific Writings in the Barberini Collection,* University of Chicago Press, 1957; (editor) *English Lyrics Before 1500,* Northwestern University Press, 1971 (published in England as *Medieval English Lyrics,* Arnold, 1971); *How Arabic Science Reached the West in the Earlier Twelfth Century,* Accademia dei Lincei, 1971; *Sir Gawain and the Green Knight: A Comedy for Christmas,* University of Chicago Press, 1974; *Poeti e filosofi medievali* (title means "Medieval Poets and Philosophers"), Bari, 1975; *Salerno and the Development of Theory,* Accademia dei Lincei, 1978. Contributor to literature, history, and theological journals.

Member of advisory board of *Speculum,* 1940-43, and *Chaucer Studies,* 1966—; member of editorial board of *Modern Philology,* 1959—, acting editor, 1961-62.

WORK IN PROGRESS: Research on the poetics of Dante, on English and French medieval romances, and on poetry and philosophy of the twelfth and thirteenth centuries.

*   *   *

SIMMONS, A(lan) John   1950-

PERSONAL: Born May 4, 1950, in Dover, N.J.; son of Alan G. (an engineer) and Jessie May (a teacher; maiden name, Ahrens) Simmons; married Jean Dreyfus (a skating instructor), March 26, 1969; children: Shawn K. *Education:* Princeton University, A.B., 1972; Cornell University, M.A., 1975, Ph.D., 1977. *Office:* Corcoran Department of Philosophy, University of Virginia, Charlottesville, Va. 22901.

CAREER: University of Virginia, Charlottesville, assistant professor, 1976-80, associate professor of philosophy, 1981—. Visiting assistant professor at Johns Hopkins University, 1981. *Member:* American Philosophical Association, Virginia Philosophical Association. *Awards, honors:* National Endowment for the Humanities fellowship, 1980.

WRITINGS: Moral Principles and Political Obligations, Princeton University Press, 1979. Contributor to philosophy journals. Associate editor of *Philosophy and Public Affairs,* 1982; nominating editor for *Philosopher's Annual,* 1982.

WORK IN PROGRESS: The Lockean Theory of Rights, a book about John Locke's political philosophy and contemporary libertarian works.

SIDELIGHTS: Simmons told *CA:* "My first book was motivated in part by concerns about government authority which arose during the late 1960's. This concern continues to influence my work on rights and individualist theory. I hope to examine critically more of the presuppositions commonly appealed to in American political life."

Simmons's book, *Moral Principles and Political Obligations,* examines basic questions of political obligation, including the role of the individual in the political order and the extent to which he is required to participate in that order. Inspired by questions of duty and patriotism aroused during the Vietnam

War era, Simmons attempts to determine to whom one is obliged, what one is obliged to do, and, ultimately, why one has any obligations at all. According to Robert Booth Fowler in the *Review of Politics,* the thoroughness of Simmons's examination of his topic renders the book "an encyclopedia of arguments about political obligation." Included in his discussion are consent, natural duties, gratitude, and "fair play" or benefit theories. Simmons finds such theories inadequate to justify political obligation. The inherent weaknesses Simmons identifies in each lead him to defend philosophical anarchism as an alternative.

The flaw in all existing theories of obligation, according to Simmons, is an assumption that one is required as a citizen to support the laws and government of one's country of residence. Citizenship alone, he argues, cannot be the foundation for obligation because it does not involve morality. Instead Simmons asserts that one's obligations are determined by the requirements falling under general moral principles rather than official commands. The individual has a duty, he concludes, to obey laws and support governments only when they are morally acceptable and not merely because the individual feels obligated to the voice of authority.

According to Diana Meyers in the *Philosophical Review,* if Simmons is correct in his analysis, "persons everywhere will be morally compelled to decide for themselves whether their respective states are sufficiently just to warrant acknowledging political obligations. Thus, it seems to me that Simmons's determination to emancipate us from mindless political acquiescence is entirely salutary." Simmons's support of philosophical anarchism does not, however, justify disobedience of all law. As William C. Harvard says in the *Journal of Politics,* "Simmons apparently does not really want to accept the larger practical implications of anarchism, so he goes on to adduce (briefly to be sure) some grounds . . . to do what the law requires and to support a government as legitimate. Included are the moral reprehensibility of some legally defined crimes, desirability of consistency in certain rules, and even such illiberal reasons as the general need for public order, the 'quality' of government, and its efficacy in promoting the natural duty of justice."

Robert Booth Fowler observes that Simmons bases his conclusion about philosophical anarchism on the assumption that "the individual and his or her choices are far more important than any other values, very much including the political community." Consequently, he believes that Simmons's views on philosophical anarchism "require much more defense than they get." Even so, Fowler holds that Simmons has written an "excellent book. . . . These detailed and exhaustive arguments again and again forced me to think. Overall I found it very stimulating even though (or perhaps because) I often disagreed with it."

BIOGRAPHICAL/CRITICAL SOURCES: Review of Politics, October, 1980; *American Political Science Review,* December, 1980; *Ethics,* January, 1981; *Journal of Politics,* May, 1981; *Philosophical Review,* July, 1981.

*   *   *

SIMMONS, Ian   1937-

PERSONAL: Born January 22, 1937, in Essex, England; son of Charles F. (an engineer) and Christina (Merrills) Simmons; married Carol Mary Saunders (a counsellor), July 28, 1962; children: Catherine Mary, David John. *Education:* University of London, B.Sc., 1959, Ph.D., 1962. *Politics:* "Pinkish liberal democrat." *Office:* Department of Geography, University of Durham, South Rd., Durham DH1 3LE, England.

CAREER: University of Bristol, Bristol, England, professor of geography, 1978-81; University of Durham, professor of geography, 1981—. Associated with University of California, Berkeley, 1964-65. Minister's member of Yorkshire Dales National Park Planning Committee, 1963-72; chairman of Durham Council for Voluntary Service, 1975-76. *Member:* American Association for the Advancement of Science, Association for Environmental Archaeology, Institute of British Geographers, British Association for American Studies, British Association for Japanese Studies, Society of Antiquaries of London. *Awards, honors:* Fellowship from North Atlantic Treaty Organization, 1968; Churchill Memorial Fellow, 1971.

WRITINGS: *Rural Recreation in the Industrial World,* Arnold, 1975; *Biogeography: Natural and Cultural,* Dixbury, 1979; *The Ecology of Natural Resources,* Halstead, 1981; (co-editor with M. J. Tooley) *The Environment in British Prehistory,* Cornell University Press, 1981.

WORK IN PROGRESS: Scholarly papers on the environmental impact of late hunter-gatherers; a book on the environmental impact of man from African beginnings to present day, for Blackwell.

SIDELIGHTS: Simmons told *CA:* "I get so annoyed with other people's books that I feel I have to have a go myself. I have traveled widely in Europe, North America, and Japan, and have a smattering of several of the relevant languages. I would like to become a poet on early retirement from the academic system but who will feed the kids?

"Professionally, I regard the man-environment relationship as a continuum through time, and what interests me is whether the next phase will be a reversionary one—back to a preindustrial stage—or an evolutionary one to an industrial society in a state of equilibrium."

*   *   *

SIMON, Jo Ann 1946-

PERSONAL: Born November 2, 1946, in Norwalk, Conn.; daughter of Charles Lester (a traffic manager) and Josephine (a hairdresser; maiden name, Berglund) Haessig; married Kenneth W. Campbell, December 27, 1969 (divorced, 1975); married Richard M. Simon, March 6, 1976 (divorced, 1980); children: (first marriage) Kimberly Ann, Kenneth W., Jr. *Education:* Lee Johnson School of Business, Certificate, 1964; attended Norwalk Community College, 1965-66. *Home:* 176 Perry Ave., Norwalk, Conn. 06850. *Agent:* RLR Associates Ltd., 7 West 51st St., New York, N.Y. 10019.

CAREER: Remington Rand Corp., Norwalk, Conn., secretary to sales promotion manager, 1966-68; Riker Information Systems, Norwalk, secretary to vice-president for marketing, 1968-69; Hanson & Orth, Inc. (importers), Darien, Conn., secretary and assistant to vice-president, 1972-81; writer, 1981—. Member of Lockwood Matthews Mansion Museum. *Member:* National Writers Club, Romantic Writers of America (head of local chapter, 1982—), Silvermine Community Association, Norwalk Historical Society.

WRITINGS: *Love Once in Passing* (novel), Avon, 1981; *Hold Fast to Love* (novel), Avon, 1982; *Love Once Again* (novel), Avon, 1983.

WORK IN PROGRESS: *At Last We Love,* set in Nantucket, about a sea captain of the 1840's and a modern woman, who occupied the same house in different eras, publication expected in 1984.

SIDELIGHTS: Simon told *CA:* "When I completed my first novel and sold it, I not only found a true vocation but discovered that hard work, perseverance, and talent *do* have their rewards. A writing career is not one to embark on for easy fame or riches. It requires labor, determination, talent, and good command of the English language (which too many hopeful writers tend to disregard). But if there is success at the end, the sense of accomplishment and the self-satisfaction are worth all the hours of effort."

AVOCATIONAL INTERESTS: History, music, travel, reading, exploring the unknown.

*   *   *

SIMON, Robert
See MUSTO, Barry

*   *   *

SIMONI, John Peter 1911-

BRIEF ENTRY: Born April 12, 1911, in Denver, Colo. American art critic, educator, and author. Simoni was a professor of art history and criticism at Wichita State University until 1978, when he was named professor emeritus. He also wrote newspaper columns, designed murals, and directed art galleries. For his military work in Italy after World War II, Simoni was named knight of the Order of the Crown and knight officer of the Order of Merit. He wrote *The Structure of Form in Painting and Design* (Wichita State University, 1974). *Address:* P.O. Box 1154, Estes Park, Colo. 80517. *Biographical/critical sources: Directory of American Scholars,* Volume I: *History,* 7th edition, Bowker, 1978; *Who's Who in America,* 40th edition, Marquis, 1978.

*   *   *

SIMONS, James Marcus 1939-
(Jim Simons)

PERSONAL: Born May 6, 1939, in Cleburne, Tex.; son of Marcus R. (a painter) and Estelle (Whitworth) Simons; married Helen Read, June 23, 1962 (divorced December 14, 1972); married Nancy Coffey Collins (an illustrator and designer), November 6, 1973; children: (first marriage) Eleanor Estelle. *Education:* Attended Southern Methodist University, 1957-59, and Baylor University, 1958; University of Texas, LL.B., 1965. *Religion:* "No preference." *Home:* 804 Theresa, Austin, Tex. 78703. *Office:* 617 Blanco St., Austin, Tex. 78703.

CAREER: Admitted to the Bar of Texas, 1965; assistant city attorney of Pasadena, Tex., 1965-66; worked in Office of Inspection of U.S. Office of Economic Opportunity, Washington, D.C., 1966-68; private practice of law in Austin, Tex., 1968—. Past chairman of State Bar of Texas Individual Rights Section. *Member:* Federal Bar Association, Travis County Bar Association.

WRITINGS—Under name Jim Simons: (With Myron Moscowitz) *Texas Tenants Handbook,* Addison-Wesley, 1980; (with Jeanine Lehman and Anthony Mancuso) *How to Form Your Own Texas Corporation,* Addison-Wesley, 1980; (with Charles Sherman) *How to Do Your Own Divorce in Texas,* Addison-Wesley, 1980; (with Denis Clifford) *Planning Your Estate With Wills, Probate, and Taxes,* Addison-Wesley, 1981.

*   *   *

SIMONS, Jim
See SIMONS, James Marcus

SIMS, Lois Dorothy Lang
  See LANG-SIMS, Lois Dorothy

*   *   *

SINCLAIR, Bruce A.   **1929-**

BRIEF ENTRY: Born April 30, 1929, in Artesia, N.M. American historian, educator, and author. Sinclair directed the Merrimack Valley Textile Museum from 1959 to 1964 and taught at Kansas State University from 1966 to 1969. Since then he has been a member of the history faculty at University of Toronto. Sinclair wrote *Philadelphia's Philosopher Mechanics: A History of the Franklin Institute, 1824-1865* (Johns Hopkins University Press, 1974) and *A Centennial History of the American Society of Mechanical Engineers, 1880-1980* (University of Toronto Press, 1980). He edited *Let Us Be Honest and Modest: Technology and Society in Canadian History* (Oxford University Press, 1974). *Address:* 550 Spadina Cres., Toronto, Ontario, Canada M5S 2J9. *Biographical/critical sources: Who's Who in America,* 40th edition, Marquis, 1978.

*   *   *

SINCLAIR, Donna   **1943-**

PERSONAL: Born December 24, 1943, in Englehart, Ontario, Canada; daughter of Frank A. (a railroad employee) and Margaret (MacQueen) Knapp; married James Sinclair (a minister), July 1, 1966; children: David, Andrew, Tracy. *Education:* University of Toronto, B.A., 1964. *Religion:* United Church of Canada. *Home and office:* 1400 Pinegrove Cres., North Bay, Ontario, Canada P1B 4B8.

CAREER: Teacher of English, history, and art at collegiate institute in Toronto, Ontario, 1964-67; Knob Lake Protestant School, Schefferville, Quebec, teacher of history and geography, 1967-69; free-lance writer, 1969—. Leader of workshops and seminars, 1975—; creative writing teacher at Canadore College, 1979-81.

WRITINGS: The Pastor's Wife Today, Abingdon, 1981. Author of "A Time to Mourn, a Time to Dance," a film released by United Church of Canada in 1981. Contributor to magazines, including *Financial Post* and *Christian Ministry.* Editor of "Kidspace," in *United Church Observer,* 1975-77, contributing editor, 1979—.

WORK IN PROGRESS: Editing a short personal history of the North Bay area by residents of Castleholme, "Our Golden Past," completion expected in 1982; a book on "writing your own autobiography," publication by Wood Lake Press expected in 1983; research on the children of affluence and their "difficulty in coping."

SIDELIGHTS: Donna Sinclair wrote: "My writing, generally, is informed by my ongoing task of balancing the creative life in writing with the creative life in nurturing children, in working out how to balance the sense of solitude required to write and the sense of otherness required to live in the world and maintain relationships. I am deeply interested in Jungian psychology; and I have a particular interest in both the very young, and the very old, especially in the things they share (a different attitude to productivity than the other generations, perhaps).

"Another 'item to balance' in the struggle to make enough time for real productivity in writing is the part of my life devoted to conducting workshops and seminars on various subjects—usually concerning children and family, or sometimes creative writing. I am also very involved in events for pastors's wives, an interest that comes out of my book, *The Pastor's Wife Today.*"

SINGER, June Flaum   **1933-**

PERSONAL: Born January 17, 1933, in Jersey City, N.J.; daughter of M. and E. (Lamkay) Flaum; married Joe Singer; children: Sharon, Brett, Ian, Valerie. *Education:* Attended Ohio State University. *Home and office:* 22548 Pacific Coast Hwy., Malibu, Calif. 90265. *Agent:* Elaine Markson Literary Agency, Inc., 44 Greenwich Ave., New York, N.Y. 10011.

CAREER: Writer, 1972—.

WRITINGS: The Bluffer's Guide to Interior Decorating, Crown, 1972; *The Bluffer's Guide to Antiques,* Crown, 1972; *What to Do Until the Money Comes,* Drake, 1974; *The Debutantes* (novel), M. Evans, 1982.

WORK IN PROGRESS: Another novel, publication expected in 1983.

SIDELIGHTS: June Singer commented: "Though I started out writing nonfiction, I am in love with fiction, both for reading and writing. I am told that I am a writer of 'women's' books, but only time will tell if that is true. I might decide to write novels from the man's point of view. I do believe, after all, that they too have a right to be heard."

*   *   *

SINGH, Vijai Pratap   **1939-**

BRIEF ENTRY: Born August 7, 1939, in Nibi, India. Sociologist, educator, and author. Singh has taught sociology at University of Pittsburgh since 1971. He has also been a research associate at the university's Center for Urban Research for nearly ten years. He wrote *Caste, Class, and Democracy: Changes in a Stratification System* (Schenkman, 1976). *Address:* Department of Sociology, University of Pittsburgh, Mervis Hall, 4200 Fifth Ave., Pittsburgh, Pa. 15260.

*   *   *

SKARDA, Patricia Lyn   **1946-**
  (Clovis St. Clair)

PERSONAL: Born March 31, 1946, in Clovis, N.M.; daughter of Lynell G. (an attorney) and Kathryn (a nurse; maiden name, Burns) Skarda. *Education:* Attended Sweet Briar College, 1964-68; Texas Tech University, B.A., 1969; University of Texas, Ph.D., 1973. *Religion:* Roman Catholic. *Home:* 8 West St., Northampton, Mass. 01060. *Office:* Department of English, Smith College, Northampton, Mass. 01063.

CAREER: Smith College, Northampton, Mass., assistant professor of English, 1973—, Ace fellow, 1979. Director of New Mexico Girls State, 1973; education director of Girls Nation, 1973-75; member of pastoral team prayer group, 1981—. *Member:* Modern Language Association of America, American Association of University Women, American Association of University Teachers of English, Northeast Victorian Studies Association, League of Women Voters, Phi Beta Kappa (chapter president), Sigma Tau Delta, Phi Kappa Phi. *Awards, honors:* Danforth associate, 1977-83.

WRITINGS: The Evil Image: Two Centuries of Gothic Short Fiction and Poetry, New American Library, 1981. Contributor to literature journals.

WORK IN PROGRESS: Guests of Chance, a novel under pseudonym Clovis St. Clair, publication expected in 1982; a collection of essays and short stories on science and medicine.

SIDELIGHTS: Patricia Skarda told *CA:* "Writing makes me a better teacher and a more interesting human being because it makes my being more intense. Recently I have taken up the study of the Scriptures to inform my interest in Romantic and Victorian poetry. My first sabbatical was spent in Oxford, England, researching the unpublished undergraduate essays of Gerard Manly Hopkins. My second will be spent in Northampton, at the Smith College Library, working on Gothic fiction, Romantic critical theories, and gnosticism. The writing of fiction has made me a more sensitive reader of fiction. In time I may make this new work into more than an avocation."

*   *   *

SKEMP, Joseph Bright   1910-

PERSONAL: Born May 10, 1910, in Bilston, Staffordshire, England; son of Thomas William Widlake and Marion Caroline Alice (Southall) Skemp; married Ruby James, September 6, 1941. *Education:* Attended Gonville and Caius College, Cambridge. *Home:* 10 Highsett, Hills Rd., Cambridge CB2 1NX, England.

CAREER: Gonville and Caius College, Cambridge, Cambridge, England, fellow, 1936-47; Victoria University of Manchester, Manchester, England, lecturer, 1946-49; University of Durham, Durham, England, reader, 1949-50, professor, 1950-73, professor emeritus of Greek, 1973—. Senior friend of Baptist Student Societies in Manchester, Durham, and Cambridge. *Member:* Society for the Protection of Science and Learning.

WRITINGS: The Theory of Motion in Plato's Later Dialogues, Cambridge University Press, 1942, revised and enlarged edition, Hakkert, 1967; *Plato's Stateman,* Routledge & Kegan Paul, 1952; *The Greeks and the Gospel,* Carey Kingsgate Press, 1964; *Plato,* Oxford University Press, 1976. Contributor to scholarly journals. Editor of *Durham University Journal,* 1953-57. Co-editor of *Phronesis,* 1955-64.

WORK IN PROGRESS: Research on Plato's political thought.

AVOCATIONAL INTERESTS: Railway history and time-tabling.

*   *   *

SLEIGH, Barbara   1906-1982

OBITUARY NOTICE—See index for *CA* sketch: Born January 9, 1906, in Worcestershire, England; died February 13, 1982, in Winchester, England. Educator and author. In her career Sleigh worked as an art teacher, a college lecturer, and an assistant on a radio program, though she is best known as the author of children's books. Her contributions to children's literature consist of folktales, anthologies, and original creations. Her writings, which have been published in several languages, include *Carbonel, The Seven Days, North of Nowhere, Pen, Penny, Tuppence, Stirabout Stories,* and *Ninety-nine Dragons.* Obituaries and other sources: *London Times,* February 18, 1982.

*   *   *

SLONE, Dennis   1930-1982

OBITUARY NOTICE: Born January 9, 1930, in Pretoria, South Africa; died after a long illness, May 10, 1982, in Lexington, Mass. Physician and author best known for his research linking the use of birth control pills to heart attacks. Slone was considered one of the world's leading epidemiologists, and his studies into the adverse effects of various drugs helped pioneer techniques to facilitate investigations into the connection be-

tween newly marketed drugs and health risks. He was the author of *Birth Defects and Drugs in Pregnancy.* Obituaries and other sources: *Who's Who in America,* 40th edition, Marquis, 1978; *New York Times,* May 11, 1982; *Newsweek,* May 24, 1982; *Time,* May 24, 1982.

*   *   *

SMITH, Cynthia S.   1924-

PERSONAL: Born December 29, 1924, in New York, N.Y.; daughter of Harry (a flour broker) and Sarah (Cohen) Sharfin; married David Smith (a graphic designer), May 21, 1950; children: Hillary Beth. *Education:* Hunter College (now of City University of New York), B.A., 1944; graduate study at Columbia University, 1944-45. *Home and office address:* C/D Smith Advertising, Inc., Kirby Lane, Rye, N.Y. 10580.

CAREER: Joshua Meier Co., Inc. (manufacturers of plastics for office equipment industry), North Bergen, N.J., advertising director, 1952-62; C/D Smith Advertising, Inc., Rye, N.Y., president, 1963—. Member of faculty at New York University, 1970-73, University of Connecticut, 1974-75, and Pace University, 1976; lecturer for Penton Learning Systems, Inc., 1977—; visiting instructor at colleges and universities; guest on television and radio programs, including "Phil Donahue Show," "Today Show," and "To Tell the Truth." President, editor, and publisher of Hillbart Publications and *Medical/Mrs.,* 1977—. *Member:* Authors Guild.

WRITINGS: How to Get Big Results From a Small Advertising Budget, Hawthorn, 1972; *Doctors' Wives: The Truth About Medical Marriages,* Seaview, 1981.

SIDELIGHTS: Smith told *CA:* "I write, and always have since I was ten years old, about injustices and misconceptions I encounter. The books, I hope, will help people. I know they help me, because the analytical thinking required to develop an observation of behavior patterns to a cognitive conclusion almost always leads me to an ephiphany that is exhilarating and edifying. My first book on advertising was written to support the egos and needs of small-budget advertisers who are regarded by snotty Madison Avenue moguls as noncreative and beneath concern. I point out the multi-faceted ability and ingenuity demanded of individuals who must do magnificent merchandising wonders with limited bucks, who do not have the luxury of departmentalizing problems but must solve them all. And from my long experience in the small-budget advertising field, I tell them how to do it.

"As for my second book, *Doctors' Wives: The Truth About Medical Marriages,* that came from the heavy flow of mail to me as editor/publisher of *Medical/Mrs.* magazine. These letters indicated that, unlike popular perceptions, marriage to a physician was actually the failure of the female American dream. The emotional tone of the letters was then substantiated by my research, which turned up material in medical journals (where it would be supposedly read only by those within the profession) indicating that there were severe behavior and personality problems among doctors that caused them to be less than perfect mates. Apparently the book hit a nerve; it was recommended by Lenore Hershey, editor in chief of *Ladies' Home Journal* and the wife of a physician, with these words: 'They should hand this book to every woman (or man, for that matter) about to enter into a medical marriage. . . . A warm, discerning, insightful, and above all, helpful book.'"

*   *   *

SMITH, Dan Throop   1908-1982

OBITUARY NOTICE: Born November 20, 1908, in Chicago,

Ill.; died May 29, 1982, in Stanford, Calif. Economist, educator, and author best known as the principal architect of the Internal Revenue Code that was adopted in 1954. Smith attended Stanford University, the London School of Economics and Political Science, and Harvard University, where in 1934 he earned his doctorate. He advised both the Eisenhower and the Nixon administrations on economic policies and at one time served as a special assistant to the secretary of the treasury, in charge of tax policy. Smith disagreed with Keynesian economic theory, which favors governmental intervention in the economy in order to achieve social goals. Between stints in government service, Smith taught at several prestigious universities, including Stanford and Harvard. He was the author of books on economic subjects, including *Deficits and Depressions, Federal Tax Reform: The Issues and a Program,* and *Tax Factors in Business Decisions.* Obituaries and other sources: *New York Times,* June 2, 1982; *Newsweek,* June 14, 1982; *Time,* June 14, 1982.

*   *   *

SMITH, Dwight R.   1921-

PERSONAL: Born July 28, 1921, in Sanders, Idaho; son of Andrew Leonard (a lumberjack) and Effie Elizabeth (Simons) Smith; married Carol Elizabeth Breclaw, August 21, 1944; children: Alan Dwight (deceased), Sharon Lee Dequine, Gary Robert, Mark Jonathan (deceased). *Education:* University of Idaho, B.S., 1949, M.S., 1951; Utah State University, Ph.D., 1971. *Politics:* Democrat. *Religion:* Roman Catholic. *Home:* 1119 Stratborough Lane, Fort Collins, Colo. 80525. *Office:* Department of Fishery and Wildlife Biology, Colorado State University, Fort Collins, Colo. 80523.

CAREER: Farmer, 1934-39; Weyerhaeuser Logging Co., Bovill, Idaho, lumberjack, 1940-41; construction worker in Alaska and Idaho, 1942, 1946; Idaho Fish and Game Department, Salmon and Wendell, research biologist studying ecology of bighorn sheep, 1950-52, area manager of big game, 1953-56; Rocky Mountain Forest and Range Experiment Station, Fort Collins, Colo., range scientist studying cattle, 1957-61, wildlife research biologist studying wildlife habitat, 1962-65; Colorado State University, Fort Collins, assistant professor and wildlife extension specialist, 1965-70, associate professor, 1971-75, professor of wildlife biology, 1976—. *Military service:* U.S. Army, Infantry, 1942-45; served in European and Pacific theaters; became second lieutenant; received Bronze Star and three battle stars.

MEMBER: National Wildlife Federation, Wildlife Society, Society for Range Management (past member of council), Wilderness Society, Colorado Wildlife Federation (past member of board of directors; past vice-president; chairman of committees on youth and conservation education), Sigma Xi, Gamma Sigma Delta, Phi Kappa Phi, Phi Sigma Pi. *Awards, honors:* Wildlife Society Terrestrial Publication award runner-up for wildlife literature in North America, 1953 and 1954, for *The Bighorn Sheep in Idaho.*

WRITINGS: The Bighorn Sheep in Idaho, Idaho Fish and Game Department, 1954; *Above Timberline: A Wildlife Biologist's Rocky Mountain Journal,* Knopf, 1981.

Films: "Winter Ecology at Pingree," Office of Instructional Development, Colorado State University, 1973; "Research in the Rockies: A Scientist Explores the Alpine," Office of Instructional Development, Colorado State University, 1973.

Contributor of about twenty-five articles and reviews to scientific journals.

SIDELIGHTS: Smith told *CA:* "Farming, logging, heavy construction work, and being poor during the Depression were forces that taught me about damaging uses of natural resources because of ignorance, greed, and economic necessity. These experiences led me to the strongly held view that society must be willing to make the hard decisions needed to conserve nonrenewable resources and to manage and use renewable resources wisely. To use these resources wisely means neither to exploit needlessly nor to protect mindlessly. Some environmental activists have the attitude: 'Any consumptive use (grazing, logging, hunting) is rape of the environment.' I am dismayed as much by this view as by the economically motivated, exploitive approaches of some industries, Secretary of Interior James Watt, and the Reagan administration. The quality of our future depends, in large part, on our ability to use renewable resources prudently while recognizing that there are finite limits to both productivity and resilience of natural ecosystems.

"I am presently collecting bicycle route maps and detailed information preparatory to taking, then writing about, a 15,600-mile bicycle trip through the thirty-three states forming the 'perimeter' of the 'lower forty-eight.' At 325 miles per week, the trip will take eleven months. Natural resources and beauties will be described and photographically illustrated, as will land uses and abuses. Opinions and the 'humanity' of landholders and users (including urban) will be included. An associated theme will be that older citizens can maintain physical fitness and enthusiasm for new adventures in retirement years. The trip is planned to begin in 1985, when my wife and I will be in our mid-sixties. I'm looking for a publisher and someone to bankroll a year's living expenses!"

*   *   *

SMITH, Thomas Malcolm   1921-

BRIEF ENTRY: Born August 5, 1921, in Dowagiac, Mich. American historian, educator, and author. Smith taught at California Institute of Technology and worked as a science historian for the U.S. Air Force Research and Development Command. In 1959 he joined the faculty at University of Oklahoma, becoming a professor of science in 1968. Smith wrote *Architects of Aviation* (Duell, Sloan & Pearce, 1951) and *Project Whirlwind: The History of a Pioneer Computer* (Digital Press, 1980). He edited *The Challenge of Our Times: Contemporary Trends in Science and Human Affairs* (Burgess, 1953). *Address:* Department of the History of Science, University of Oklahoma, Norman, Okla. 73069.

*   *   *

SMITH, Verla Lee   1927(?)-1982

OBITUARY NOTICE: Born c. 1927 in West Virginia; died of cancer, March 27, 1982. Editor and author. Smith became a correspondent in the school service of the *National Geographic* in 1967 and transferred to the magazine's book service in 1970. She served as editor of J. N. Parry's *Romance of the Sea.* Obituaries and other sources: *Washington Post,* March 31, 1982.

*   *   *

SMUCKER, Barbara (Claassen)   1915-

PERSONAL: Born September 1, 1915, in Newton, Kan.; daughter of Cornelius W. (a banker) and Addie (Lander) Claassen; married Donovan E. Smucker (a minister and professor of sociology and religion), January 21, 1939; children: Timothy, Thomas, Rebecca. *Education:* Kansas State University,

B.S., 1936; further study at Rosary College, River Forest, Ill., 1963-65, and University of Waterloo, 1975-77. *Politics:* Democrat. *Religion:* Mennonite. *Home:* 57 McDougall Rd., Waterloo, Ontario, Canada N2L 2W4. *Office:* Renison College, University of Waterloo, Waterloo, Ontario, Canada N2L 3G2.

CAREER: Public high school teacher of English and journalism in Harper, Kan., 1937-38; *Evening Kansas Republican,* Newton, Kan., reporter, 1939-41; Ferry Hall School, Lake Forest, Ill., teacher, 1960-63; Lake Forest Bookstore, Lake Forest, bookseller, 1963-67; Kitchener Public Library, Kitchener, Ontario, children's librarian, 1969-77; Renison College, Waterloo, Ontario, head librarian, 1977—. Has also worked as an interviewer for Gallup Poll. *Member:* American Association of University Women, Canadian Association of University Women, Canadian Society of Children's Authors, Canadian Writers Union, Illustrators and Performers, Children's Reading Roundtable. *Awards, honors:* Children's Book Center named *Underground to Canada* one of the fifty best books of all time in Canada, 1978; Brotherhood Award from National Conference of Christians and Jews, 1980, for *Underground to Canada;* children's literary award from Canada Council and Ruth Schwartz Foundation Award, both 1980, both for *Days of Terror;* distinguished service award from Kansas State University, 1980, for children's literature.

WRITINGS—Juveniles: Henry's Red Sea, Herald Press, 1955; *Cherokee Run,* Herald Press, 1957; *Wigwam in the City,* Dutton, 1966, reprint published as *Susan,* Scholastic Book Services, 1978; *Underground to Canada,* Clark, Irwin, 1977, published as *Runaway to Freedom: A Story of the Underground Railway,* Harper, 1978; *Days of Terror,* Clarke, Irwin, 1979. Contributor to *American Educator Encyclopedia.*

WORK IN PROGRESS: A children's book with an Amish theme, publication expected in 1982.

SIDELIGHTS: Smucker's juvenile novels bring history to life while educating their readers. To produce historical novels relevant to contemporary social issues, Smucker mixes some of her personal insights with actual past events. For example, *Underground to Canada,* a novel about slavery and the underground railroad, was born out of the author's concern for the civil rights movement, an interest that was previously challenged by a black student who questioned Smucker's ability to empathize with circumstances and feelings she had never experienced. A resident of Mississippi until the 1960's, the author settled in Canada and extended her interest to include Canada's role in the underground railroad and its famous "conductor," Alexander Ross.

Underground to Canada recounts the unhappy lives of fourteen-year-old Julilly and the crippled Liza, two slaves who work over eighteen hours every day and live in small, crowded huts in the Deep South. In the novel, Ross leads the girls and two other slaves to St. Catharine's, Ontario, where they must contend with freedom as it really is, however different than they anticipated it would be. "*All* children should read [*Underground to Canada*]," wrote Virginia Hamilton of the *New York Times Book Review.* "We need scrupulously honest books like this one to inform subsequent generations that a great crime was committed against a people, and that we must always be on guard against victimization and genocide."

Similar to *Underground to Canada,* Smucker's other novels deal with the struggles and triumphs of ethnic or religious groups. *Wigwam in the City* illustrates the plight of Native Americans once they move from reservations to jobs in cities, and several books look at the history of the Mennonites. *Henry's Red Sea,* which is used as an educational tool in Mennonite

schools, describes the perilous movement of wartime refugees from Russia to Germany to Paraguay. Another book, *Days of Terror,* recalls when Mennonites fled to Canada to maintain their religious freedom during the Russian Revolution of 1917. And *Cherokee Run* tells of the institution of Mennonite settlements in Oklahoma.

Smucker's books have been translated into French, German, Japanese, and Danish.

BIOGRAPHICAL/CRITICAL SOURCES: In Review, fall, 1977; *New York Times Book Review,* April 30, 1978; *Saturday Night,* November, 1979; *Mennonite Quarterly Review,* January, 1981.

* * *

SNAITH, Norman Henry   1898-1982

OBITUARY NOTICE: Born April 21, 1898, in Chipping Norton, Oxford, England; died March 3, 1982, in Ipswich, England. Clergyman, scholar, and author. Snaith was ordained a Methodist minister in 1925 and served in the London area until 1936, when he became a tutor in Old Testament languages at Headingley College, where he remained until 1961. He was the author of books on the Old Testament, including *The Distinctive Ideas of the Old Testament* and *The Jewish New Year Festival,* and also edited several versions of the Bible. Obituaries and other sources: *The Author's and Writer's Who's Who,* 6th edition, Burke's Peerage, 1971; *Who's Who,* 126th edition, St. Martin's, 1974; *London Times,* March 6, 1982.

* * *

SNAITH, William Theodore   1908-1974

OBITUARY NOTICE: Born March 26, 1908, in New York, N.Y.; died while undergoing open-heart surgery, February 19, 1974, in New York, N.Y. Designer, architect, and author. Snaith joined the firm of designer Raymond Loewy in 1936, becoming a partner in 1944 and serving as president of Raymond Loewy/William Snaith, Inc., from 1961 until his death. Snaith is credited with planning and designing the modern American department store and numerous logos, including the Coast Guard symbol seen on ships and aircraft. An enthusiastic yachtsman, he raced yachts and wrote two books about his hobby: *Across the Western Ocean* and *On the Wind's Way.* Also an accomplished artist, Snaith wrote *The Irresponsible Arts.* Obituaries and other sources: *Who's Who in the East,* 14th edition, Marquis, 1974; *New York Times,* February 20, 1974.

* * *

SNELL, George Davis   1903-

PERSONAL: Born December 19, 1903, in Bradford, Mass.; son of Cullen Bryant (an inventor) and Katharine (Davis) Snell; married Rhoda Carson, July 28, 1937; children: Thomas Carleton, Roy Carson, Peter Garland. *Education:* Dartmouth College, B.S. 1926; Harvard University, Sc.D., 1930. *Politics:* Independent. *Religion:* Congregationalist. *Home:* 21 Atlantic Ave., Bar Harbor, Me. 04609.

CAREER: Brown University, Providence, R.I., instructor, 1930-31; University of Texas, Austin, researcher, 1931-33; Washington University, St. Louis, Mo., professor, 1933-34; Jackson Laboratory, Bar Harbor, Me., research associate, 1935-37, staff scientific director, 1949-50, senior staff scientist, 1957-68, senior staff scientist emeritus, 1968-73. Member of National Institutes of Health, Allergy and Immunology Study Section, 1958-62. *Member:* British Transplantation Society (honorary), American Academy of Arts and Sciences, National Academy of Sciences, French Academy of Sciences (foreign associate).

AWARDS, HONORS: Fellowship from National Research Council, 1931-33; fellowship from Guggenheim Foundation, 1953-54; Hektoen Silver Medal from American Medical Association, 1955; Griffen Award from Animal Care Panel, 1962; award from Bertner Foundation, 1962; Gregor Mendel Medal from Czechoslovakian Academy of Sciences, 1967; award from Gairdner Foundation, 1976; Wolf Prize in Medicine from Wolf Foundation [Israel], 1978; co-recipient of Nobel Prize in physiology and medicine, 1980.

WRITINGS: (Editor) *Biology of the Laboratory Mouse,* Blakiston, 1941; (with J. Dausset and S. Nathenson) *Histocompatibility,* Academic Press, 1976. Contributor of papers to technical journals, including *Immunological Review.* Editor of *Immunogenetics,* 1947-80.

WORK IN PROGRESS: "A book dealing with some of the broader implications, especially the ethical implications, of biology and genetics."

SIDELIGHTS: Snell told *CA:* "My parents were both New Englanders, though my father was born in Minnesota where his father had moved from Massachusetts to join a frontier community. My father moved East as a young man. Subsequently he invented and worked on the application of a device for winding induction coils used in ignitors for the motorboat engines of that day. My parents moved when I was four to the home built by my great-grandfather in Brookline, Massachusetts, and it was in the excellent Brookline public schools that I received my precollege education.

"Science and mathematics were my favorite subjects. In spare time I read books on astronomy and physics as well as the usual boyhood classics. But I also enjoyed sports, and a group of five or six youngers used to gather at our house to play football or scrub baseball in our yard or a neighboring vacant lot. Imaginative stories and games also were very much a part of my childhood.

"Music was a major interest of the whole family. My mother played the piano and we did a great deal of family singing in which friends often joined. It has been a source of great pleasure that my wife is also a pianist.

"I entered Dartmouth College in 1922 and again found science and mathematics my favorite subjects. A course in genetics taught by Professor John Gerould proved particularly fascinating and it was that course that led me to the choice of a career. When the decision was finally made to enter graduate school, it was on Professor Gerould's advice that I enrolled as a graduate student with Harvard University's Professor Castle, the first American biologist to look for Mendelian inheritance in mammals.

"My thesis on linkage in mice largely determined my future work. Two years spent teaching and two years as a postdoctoral fellow under Herman Muller studying the genetic effect of X rays on mice served to convince me that research was my real love. If it was to be research, mouse genetics was the clear choice and the Jackson Laboratory, founded in 1929 by Dr. Clarence Cook Little, one of Castle's earlier students, almost the inevitable selection as a place to work. The laboratory was a small institution when I joined the staff of seven in 1935, but under the talented leadership of Dr. Little and his successor, Earl Green, it has grown into a world center for studies in mammalian genetics. I owe a great deal to it for providing the ideal home for my subsequent research.

"The area of research on which, after a careful examination of possibilities, I decided to concentrate at the Jackson Laboratory, was the study of histocompatibility genes. These are defined as genes which determine the compatibility or incompatibility of tissue and organ transplants. By one of those serendipitous accidents so common in research, it turned out that one of these presumed genes, histocompatibility-2 (H-2), actually is an intricate complex of closely linked genes, all or nearly all of which play a basic role in the regulation of immune processes. A comparable complex of genes is present in all other mammals, including man. Once this complex was identified, it soon became the object of intensive study in many laboratories. The first application of the findings was to organ transplantation, but applications to a great variety of infectious diseases and possibly to cancer may ultimately become more important.

"Though for twenty-five years I concentrated almost exclusively on studies of histocompatibility genes and especially on the H-2 complex, and for thirty-five years have pursued those subjects to some degree, I also have become involved in other areas. While working under Dr. Castle, I spent parts of two summers at Woods Hole with Dr. Phineas Whiting, an earlier student of Castle's, studying the genetics of the parasitic wasp, *Habrobracon.* An outcome of this work was a paper on 'The Role of Male Parthenogenesis in the Evolution of the Social Hymenoptera.' The problems of social evolution have remained a continuing interest, to which I am now returning in a more active way in retirement.

"The two years with Muller at the University of Texas resulted in the first demonstration of the induction by X rays of chromosomal changes in mammals. My first several years at the Jackson Laboratory were spent in continuation of this work, and especially in the detailed genetic analysis of two of the induced reciprocal translocations. In the late 1930's, I became involved in problems of gene nomenclature in mice, and this, together with problems of strain nomenclature, remained a concern for many years. The efforts of the Committee on Standardized Nomenclature for mice led to the universal acceptance of a well-organized and convenient nomenclature system for this species.

"Some experiments which I carried out at about the same time that I was becoming interested in histocompatibility genetics led to the discovery of immunological enhancement, the curious inversion of the expected growth-inhibition seen with certain tumors when transplanted to preinjected mice. I soon found that I was not the first person to have seen this phenomenon, but the mouse system proved very amenable to further exploitation. I had to drop this topic in favor of the genetic studies, but it has been interesting to see it grow through the work of Dr. Nathan Kaliss and many others into a major area of research with possible implications for organ transplantation in man. A final interest, developed jointly with Dr. Marianna Cherry during my last few years at the Jackson Laboratory, concerned serologically demonstrable alloantigens of lymphocytes.

"Much of the work sketched here was carried out on a collaborative basis. I owe a great debt to the many wonderful people with whom it has been my privilege to work in these studies."

AVOCATIONAL INTERESTS: Gardening, skiing, tennis.

*   *   *

SNOOK, John B.   1927-

PERSONAL: Born October 26, 1927, in Glen Ridge, N.J.; son

of Curtis Pendleton (an engineer) and Helen (Alces) Snook; married Patricia Hartley, 1957; children: John H., Curtis P., Catherine A. *Education:* Harvard University, A.B., 1951; Union Theological Seminary, New York, N.Y., M.Div., 1959; Columbia University, Ph.D., 1967. *Politics:* Democrat. *Religion:* United Church of Christ. *Home:* 100 West 94th St., New York, N.Y. 10025. *Office:* School of Law, Columbia University, 435 West 116th St., New York, N.Y. 10027.

CAREER: Barnard College, New York, N.Y., 1968-74, began as instructor, became assistant professor of religion; Westchester Institute for Training in Counseling and Psychotherapy, Rye, N.Y., professor of psychoanalytic thought, 1971-80, dean of studies, 1974-80; Hudson River Counseling Service, Rye, therapist, 1976-80; associated with Columbia University School of Law; member of board of trustees of Columbia Grammar and Preparatory School. Served as consultant to department of ministry for National Council of Churches, 1967-69. *Military service:* U.S. Army, 1946-47. *Member:* American Association for Marriage and Family Therapy, American Association of Religion, Society for the Scientific Study of Religion.

WRITINGS: Doing Right and Wrong, Association Press, 1966; *The Protestant Clergymen in America,* Social Compass, 1969; *Religious Identification,* University Microfilms, 1970; *Going Further: Life-and-Death Religion in America,* Prentice-Hall, 1973. Associate editor of *Modern Psychotherapy.*

*   *   *

SNOW, Don(ald Merritt) 1943-

PERSONAL: Born June 22, 1943, in Fort Wayne, Ind.; son of C. A. and Dorothea (a writer; maiden name, Johnston) Snow; married Donna Bock (an administrator), May 30, 1969; children: Eric DeVries. *Education:* University of Colorado, B.A., 1965, M.A., 1967; Indiana University, Ph.D., 1969. *Home:* 467 Woodland Hills, Tuscaloosa, Ala. 35405. *Office:* Department of Political Science, University of Alabama, Box I, University, Ala. 35486.

CAREER: University of Alabama, University, assistant professor, 1969-77, associate professor of political science, 1977—, director of international studies, 1972—. Professor at Air Command and Staff College, 1980; guest lecturer at Air War College, Army War College, Naval War College, and U.S. Military Academy. Vice-chairman of Consortium for International Studies Education, 1978—. *Member:* International Studies Association, Academy of Political Science, Air Force Association, Inter-University Seminar on the Armed Forces and Society.

WRITINGS: Introduction to Game Theory, Consortium for International Studies Education, 1978; *Nuclear Strategy in a Dynamic World,* University of Alabama Press, 1981; (editor) *Introduction to World Politics,* University Press of America, 1981; (with Dennis M. Drew) *Introduction to Strategy,* Air Command and Staff College, 1981; *The Nuclear Future,* University of Alabama Press, 1982; (with P. Terrence Hoffman and Timothy King) *Arms and Security in the Global Arena,* Holt, 1983. Contributor to political science and military journals.

WORK IN PROGRESS: Editing *The Future of the International Order;* research for a book on the relationship between political objectives and the physical conduct of war in the American context.

SIDELIGHTS: Snow commented: "In a world of thermonuclear weaponry, an understanding of the dynamics of military force is a matter of national and international survival in a way

more fundamental than at any previous time in history. Trying to make some contribution to that knowledge is my primary motivation. This endeavor, it seems to me, is of particular importance at a time when, in the wake of the Vietnam War, Americans remain uncertain about the continuing relevance and uses of military force. At the same time, the awesome destructive power of modern weapons makes a clear insight absolutely crucial.

AVOCATIONAL INTERESTS: Racquetball, squash, coaching youth sports, candlemaking.

*   *   *

SNOW, Edward Rowe 1902-1982

OBITUARY NOTICE—See index for *CA* sketch: Born August 22, 1902, in Winthrop, Mass.; died of a stroke, April 10, 1982. Adventurer, educator, and author. Known as the "Flying Santa," Snow flew Christmas presents to lighthouse keepers in remote areas of New England beginning in 1936. He did this, he said, to "give some of the profits back to the lighthouse keepers, whose stories provided the material for so much of my writing." In his books, radio programs, and newspaper columns, Snow generated stories of storms, pirates, ghosts, haunted houses, and buried treasure. He wrote ninety-seven books, including *Castle Island, The Story of Minot's Light, True Tales of Buried Treasure, True Tales of Pirates and Their Gold, Ghosts, Gales, and Gold,* and *Pirates, Shipwrecks, and Historical Chronicles.* Obituaries and other sources: *Chicago Tribune,* April 12, 1982.

*   *   *

SNOW, Richard F(olger) 1947-

PERSONAL: Born October 28, 1947, in New York, N.Y.; son of Richard B. (an architect) and Emma (Folger) Snow; married Carol Peckham (a magazine publication manager), August 25, 1979. *Education:* Columbia University, B.A., 1970. *Home:* 490 West End Ave., New York, N.Y. 10024. *Agent:* Brandt & Brandt, 1501 Broadway, New York, N.Y. 10036. *Office:* American Heritage, 10 Rockefeller Plaza, New York, N.Y. 10020.

CAREER: Magazine editor and writer. *American Heritage* (magazine), New York, N.Y., member of staff, 1970-72, associate editor, 1972-77, senior editor in book division, 1977-78, managing editor, 1979—. *Member:* Authors Guild. *Awards, honors: Boston Globe* Hornbook Award, 1979, for *The Iron Road.*

WRITINGS: The Funny Place (poetry), J. Philip O'Hara, 1975; *Freelon Starbird: Being a Narrative of the Extraordinary Hardships Suffered by an Accidental Soldier in a Beaten Army During the Autumn and Winter of 1776* (juvenile), illustrated by Ben F. Stahl, Houghton, 1976; *The Iron Road: A Portrait of American Railroading* (juvenile), photographs by David Plowden, Four Winds Press, 1978; *The Burning* (historical novel), Doubleday, 1981.

WORK IN PROGRESS: A novel set in New York City in the second half of the nineteenth century.

SIDELIGHTS: Richard F. Snow's diverse publications include a novel for teenagers, *Freelon Starbird,* and one for adults, *The Burning.* In the first of these, the author tells the story of Freelon Starbird, a soldier in George Washington's army. While drunk, Starbird unwittingly signs up for a stint in the Revolutionary army and subsequently learns the harsh realities of soldiering—the endless marching, the wretched food, the boredom, the fear in battle. Yet he also comes to know endurance in the face of hardships and courage in the heart of combat. Much to his surprise, Starbird decides to continue with Washington and the freedom fight after his six-month enlistment expires. The *New York Times Book Review* cited *Freelon Starbird* as one of the outstanding juvenile books of 1976.

Olivia Coolidge of *Washington Post Book World* held that although some of the language and stories in *Freelon Starbird* might not be appropriate for younger readers, the book overall "has real vigor. The best parts of it, namely the crossing of the Delaware and the battle of Trenton are splendid, while Freelon Starbird himself is a memorable soldier." Coolidge also found occasional lapses in plot and character development in this first novel, but concluded that these flaws "will probably be of less importance to [Snow's] future than his zest." William M. Wallace, writing in the *New York Times Book Review,* called *Freelon Starbird* "a little gem." He continued: "This is a lively, humorous narrative. Its dialogue often sparkles. Yet there is a passion in this book, if blessedly understated; Freelon and his friends become aware of issues, emotions, and sacrifice. Mr. Snow has a remarkable capacity for sharply delineating character, for telling a story, and for knowing when to stop."

In *The Burning,* Snow creates a fictional account of a historical event—the destruction of Hinckley, Minnesota, by summer fires in 1894. Snow portrays the nineteenth-century lumber town in its final hours and examines the lives of its residents, some fictional, some historical. He follows the course of the raging fire that engulfs the unsuspecting village, stoking it into a site of horror and heroism. Tom Schmidt of the *Saturday Review* remarked that although the author's depiction of the townspeople is not altogether successful and displays "a misplaced nostalgia," "Snow's descriptive powers and his unerring feel for the coming holocaust make *The Burning* an engrossing novel."

On the other hand, Robert W. Smith, writing in the *Cleveland Plain Dealer,* called the novel "the best I've read in years." He remarked: "Among the characters are railroad engineers, telegraphers, traveling salesmen, millers, lumberman and housewives, but, whatever their trade or calling, they speak and act as part and parcel of the place and time, living a realism rare in novels these days. . . . It is superb storytelling . . . without lolling in the nostalgia."

Another critic, Curt Suplee of the *Washington Post,* lauded Snow's skillful evocation of characters in *The Burning.* He stated, "The narrative swells with humorous sketches . . . , wry encounters, romantic interludes and the cheerful vulgarity of the townspeople's dialogue." The reviewer also observed that the story's authenticity is greatly enhanced by abundant, meticulous period details, noting that "such illustrative filigree" never seems gratuitous or impedes the smooth progression of the story. Suplee concluded: "In Snow's eloquently spare prose, astonishing varieties of simple human courage are made moving without melodrama, just as the burning is ghastly without being lurid. . . . Snow is a four-alarm writer."

Snow told *CA:* "The narrator of one of Stephen Vincent Benet's novels, recalling the New York City of his youth, speaks of the horsecars and the tangle of wires on the telegraph poles and the little steam engines that pulled the elevated trains. 'I have seen books since,' he says, 'recalling these things as quaint, and they have made me feel odd. For they assume that I knew I was living in an epoch, and, of course, I did not know.'

"Much of the challenge of writing historical fiction lies, I believe, in successfully avoiding the quaint—in recreating a past where such accessories as starched collars and trolley cars, sad irons and horsebarns are serious working tools, used by real men and women, and not just by extras borrowed for a costume drama from our familiar world of supermarkets and air shuttles. It is a truism, of course, that our forebears were much the same people as we are: they bickered with their landlords, couldn't believe the price of meat, quarrelled, fell in love, wrote bad checks, and lay awake worrying about what the future had in store for them. But looking at the old photographs, peopled with white-faced strangers in their boxy suits and faintly comic hats, it is sometimes hard to really believe this.

"But when the historical novelist succeeds in making us believe, he gives us a good deal more than a tour through a landscape cunningly tricked out with nickel beers and parasols. Watching recognizable people coping as best they can with events whose outcome we know offers a pleasure beyond the story the author is telling. The resource, energy, fear, or fatalism with which people alive a hundred years ago lived through their days can give us comfort in getting through ours."

BIOGRAPHICAL/CRITICAL SOURCES: *Washington Post Book World,* May 2, 1976; *New York Times Book Review,* May 2, 1976, December 10, 1978; *Boston Globe,* August 12, 1976; *San Francisco Chronicle,* July 26, 1981; *Saturday Review,* August, 1981; *Cleveland Plain Dealer,* August 30, 1981; *Washington Post,* September 8, 1981.

*   *   *

SOLAUN, Mauricio   1935-

BRIEF ENTRY: Born September 22, 1935, in Havana, Cuba. American diplomat, sociologist, educator, and author. Solaun has been a professor of sociology at University of Illinois since 1973. He was appointed U.S. ambassador to Nicaragua in 1977. Solaun's books in English include *Discrimination Without Violence: Miscegenation and Racial Conflict in Latin America* (Wiley, 1973), *Sinners and Heretics: The Politics of Military Intervention in Latin America* (University of Illinois Press, 1973), and *Politics of Compromise: Coalition Government in Colombia* (Transaction Books, 1980). *Address:* American Embassy, Managua, Nicaragua, APO New York, N.Y. 09885; and Department of Sociology, University of Illinois, Urbana, Ill. 61801. *Biographical/critical sources:* Who's Who in American Politics, 6th edition, Bowker, 1977; *Who's Who in America,* 40th edition, Marquis, 1978.

*   *   *

SOLERI, Paolo   1919-

PERSONAL: Born June 21, 1919, in Turin, Italy; came to the United States in 1947; son of Emilio (a manufacturer) and Pia (Mastella) Soleri; married Corolyn Woods, September 30, 1949; children: Kristine, Daniela. *Education:* Torino Politecnico, D.Architecture (with highest honors), 1946. *Home:* 6433 Doubletree Ranch Rd., Scottsdale, Ariz. 85253.

CAREER: Apprentice to Frank Lloyd Wright in Taliesin, Ariz., 1947-49; designer and builder with Mark Wills of Domed Desert House in Cave Creek, Ariz., 1951; returned to Italy; commissioned architect of Solimene ceramics factory in Vietri-sul-Mare, Italy, 1953-55; returned to the United States, 1955; architect in Scottsdale, Ariz., 1956—; Cosanti Foundation (working and teaching compound), Scottsdale, founder and architect, 1961—; Arcosanti (project in micro-arcology), Arizona desert, architect, 1970—. Hand sculptor of ceramic wind chimes and designer of dies for bronze bells, 1951—; commissioned sculptor of *Il Donnone* for Phoenix Civic Center, 1972; lecturer on arcology. Major one-man architectural exhibits held at Corcoran Gallery of Art, Washington, D.C., 1970, Whitney Museum of American Art, New York, N.Y., 1970, Museum of Contemporary Art, Chicago, Ill., 1970, National Conference Center, Ottawa, Canada, 1971, University Art Museum, Berkeley, Calif., 1971, and Two Suns Arcology Exhibition, Rochester, N.Y., 1976. *Military service:* Italian Army, 1941-45, served in camouflage corps of engineers. *Awards, honors:* American Institute of Architects Craftsmanship Medal, 1963; grants from Graham Foundation for Advanced Study in the Fine Arts, 1962, and Guggenheim Foundation, 1964 and 1967.

WRITINGS: Arcology: The City in the Image of Man, MIT Press, 1969; *The Sketchbooks of Paolo Soleri*, MIT Press, 1971; *The Bridge Between Matter and Spirit Is Matter Becoming Spirit: The Arcology of Paolo Soleri*, Doubleday, 1973; *Arcology and the Future of Man*, Montgomery Museum of Fine Arts (Montgomery, Ala.), 1975.

SIDELIGHTS: Paolo Soleri has been building a visionary city in the Arizona desert since 1970. Called Arcosanti, the city reflects Soleri's philosophy of "arcology"—a melding of architecture and ecology. The architect envisions a complex of urban structures twenty-five stories high, housing 5,000 people, and self-contained under a huge glass roof. His city would be largely solar-powered, automobile-free, and surrounded by sloped greenhouses that provide food for the community. Soleri visualizes a self-enclosed, self-supporting environment that does not impinge on the surrounding environs. As D. L. Coutu of *Time* was assured by an enthusiastic tour guide, Arcosanti will be "the best of all possible worlds, urban life in a rural setting."

Soleri maintains that since cities shape society, they should be conceived and executed in ways that promote human growth. Robert B. Kaiser summarized Soleri's philosophy in the *Saturday Review:* "He sees man evolving from an exploration of nature to the creation of a neo-nature—one that is daily more complex. Since the energy of such complexity is dissipated unless contained, and since the container for modern man is the city, cities must be designed in as compact and organic a fashion as possible." According to Soleri, urban sprawl is man's undoing. The Soleri solution is to build a metropolis in the country that rises up rather than spreads out, Coutu observed.

Essentially, Arcosanti will be a series of concrete modules slotted into place, but as Kaiser indicated, the number of different forms and their irregular positionings will distinguish the structure's appearance from the grid-like character of other modular creations. As of early 1981, only 2 percent of the complex had been completed. Eight major concrete structures had been finished, one housing a restaurant that serves visitors who sightsee or attend the numerous concerts and arts festivals held at the location. Some apartments had been completed and were housing year-round occupants. The *Saturday Review* reporter revealed that "Soleri would like his community to be an ecological research corporation of some eight hundred employees and their families—people who would not require a city to fuel their activities, people who would prefer his new frontier as the link between their theoretical world and the actual world around them. What Arcosanti will offer them, instead of the variety, chaos, and resultant strain of the city, is an ordered life-work environment surrounded by wide-open land. For although Soleri has 860 acres along the Aqua Fria River, Arcosanti will be constructed on a mere seven of those.''

Eileen Keerdoja and Paul Brinkley-Rogers disclosed in *Newsweek* that the progress of Arcosanti's construction has been hindered not by a shortage of labor, for there has never been a lack of the college students who pay $350 to attend five-week seminars that include nine hours of manual labor a day (the students earn credits toward apartment ownership in the city as they work). Rather, Arcosanti's main problem has been a lack of financial support; Soleri has been unable to attract the resources of government, business, or private foundations. The architect has raised most of the two million dollars spent thus far on the complex himself by selling his books, lecturing, and marketing bronze bells manufactured at the project's site. Soleri predicts that Arcosanti will be completed by the year 2000, and Coutu reported that workers and supporters are undisturbed at the prospect that the project may take from twenty to two hundred years, depending on finances. Coutu quoted one of Soleri's young helpers: "You get tired of people asking you when Arcosanti is going to be completed. We don't think about completion, we don't talk about it. We just work and try not to regret it."

Douglas Davis noted in *Newsweek* that Soleri's design for Arcosanti has altered markedly since the building began: "At first it looked like a flattened Gothic cathedral. Now, on the drawing boards, it slopes in a humbler fashion towards the sun. More radical changes are likely to occur: Soleri seems to be learning the most basic facts of construction as he goes, confirming those who claim he is an architect of ideas rather than reality." It is true that Soleri has never obtained his architect's credentials in the United States. Since the architect's two-year apprenticeship with Frank Lloyd Wright in the late 1940's, only a limited number of his designs have been executed, among them the Domed Desert House (in collaboration with Mark Mills), the Solimene ceramics factory in Vietri-sul-Mare, Italy, and his own molded earth and concrete dwelling in Scottsdale, Arizona. He also designed the structures of his Scottsdale foundation-school, Cosanti.

Soleri has shown an affinity from the beginning for the aesthetic over the technical and the spiritual over the material. "The core of life is esthetic," Soleri has stated. As a youth in Italy, when asked to choose between engineering and architecture, Soleri chose the latter because he believed that art superseded technology. Donald Wall remarked in *Artforum* that Soleri's early designs, like "The Beast," a bridge created for Elizabeth Mock's *The Architecture of Bridges*, reflected a "predilection to transform everything into the esthetically useful." When Soleri set up his own working and teaching compound in Arizona in 1955 he named it Cosanti, which in Italian is a combined word for "object" and "before." The term emphasizes, according to Peter Blake, editor of *Architectural Forum*, "Soleri's overriding concern with the metaphysical structure of man, and therefore, proper architecture." Soleri's one-man architectural exhibits of his chimerical models and plans have drawn record-breaking crowds and comprehensive press coverage. Coutu quoted one Arcosanti worker, "Soleri is the only architect around today better known for what he has not built than for what he has."

Davis examined the appeal of Arcosanti: "[It] is a mystical vision in concrete. This is at once the source of its strength and its weakness. If Soleri's dedication to a single idea attracts believers, it also repels many others. He has gambled . . . that man in the future will want to live in a 3-D city where his neighbors, his libraries, schools and hospitals will be an elevator away. But there is plenty of cussed, contrary evidence in the millions who are fleeing cities for suburban and exurban delights. Arcosanti is doomed to frighten and alienate this public, while it attracts and soothes the rest." And Anne Ferabee, editor of *Design and Environment,* reiterated Davis's skepticism, "We have no idea of the sociological or psychological consequences of populations concentrated to the degree that Soleri's arcologies envision."

Coutu concluded that despite periodic criticism by some discontented workers and the press, Soleri and his followers remain undaunted, their vision of a new way to live together intact. Soleri asserted: "It must be done. As a prototype, it will mean something to people everywhere. It will demonstrate that we can rearrange the structure of our cities and towns in a very different way." And Kaiser concurred: "Most critics, whether they are proponents or opponents of arcologies, agree that the building of Arcosanti may be less important than its conception. For it is Soleri's ideas that have enlarged our notions of the possible in planning future cities. Peter Blake compares Soleri to Antonio Sant' Elia, the visionary architect of the early 1900's, 'who never built anything at all, but whose drawings of ideal cities have profoundly shaped every modern city in the world.'"

BIOGRAPHICAL/CRITICAL SOURCES: Architectural Forum, February, 1961; *Washington Post,* May 8, 1966; *Newsweek,* March 2, 1970, August 16, 1976, March 23, 1981; *Wall Street Journal,* March 11, 1970; *New York Times,* March 15, 1970; *National Observer,* March 23, 1970; *Artforum,* May, 1970; *New York Times Magazine,* July 26, 1970; *Vogue,* August 1, 1970; *American Journal of Sociology,* September, 1971; *Saturday Review,* February 12, 1972; *Architectural Record,* August, 1974; *Journal of Aesthetics and Art Criticism,* fall, 1974; *Time,* August 18, 1980; *Antioch Review,* summer, 1981.

—Sketch by Nancy Pear

*   *   *

SOMMER, Scott 1951-

PERSONAL: Born February 20, 1951, in Orange, N.J.; son of Stan R. (a merchant) and Val (Frankle) Sommer. *Education:* Ohio Wesleyan University, B.A., 1973; Cornell University, M.F.A., 1975. *Home:* 101 West 69th St., New York, N.Y. 10023. *Agent:* Gloria Loomis, 77 Park Ave., New York, N.Y. 10017.

CAREER: Literary Volunteers of New York State, Ithaca, N.Y., coordinator, 1976-78; writer.

WRITINGS: Nearing's Grace (novel), Taplinger, 1979; *Lifetime* (collection; includes "Lifetime," "Entrapped and Abandoned," "Sickness," and "Crisscross"), Random House, 1981; *Last Resort* (novel), Random House, 1981. Also author of screenplays, including "Lifetime" and "Last Resort."

WORK IN PROGRESS: Walled-In, novellas.

SIDELIGHTS: Scott Sommer's first novel, which he wrote while "guarding exhibits in a museum and teaching adult illiterates," took fourteen years to complete, with Sommer writing from nine to noon every day. Thematically, *Nearing's Grace* explores the problems of a teenager with an alcoholic father, a drug-addict brother, a deceased mother (to whom he writes letters), and two love interests. Dwelling on the adolescent's relationships with these individuals, "the novel," Sommer told a *Library Journal* interviewer, "aspires to examine how our almost reflexive affection for the other is so sadly difficult to nurture and maintain and make human."

Relationships, too, figure prominently in the short stories and novellas of *Lifetime.* Here, Sommer writes as a social diagnostician, a reporter composing feature stories on what one critic termed the "transient nightmare" of life. In form, said

the *New York Times Book Review*'s Jonathan Baumbach, he is a post-modern who is romantic in the tradition of J. D. Salinger and F. Scott Fitzgerald. "Sommer's approach," observed Barry Targan in the *Washington Post Book World,* "is to present the texture more than the shape of the consequences of three-quarters of a century of human debasement." He went on to say that, more than just stories, the contents of *Lifetime* are statements that form and clarify a moral vision.

"All relationships in the corrupted world of these fictions are transient," Baumbach assessed. "To survive," the critic continued, "Scott Sommer's characters take refuge in booze, drugs, sex, madness—anything to take the edge off of loneliness and pain." For example, in the title novella, "Lifetime," the alcoholic Mahoney sees the promise of love, and therefore, salvation. But that promise fades when he kills the object of his affection. "The story 'Lifetime' is far richer in ironies and complexities and characters than a brief description can convey," Targan decided. "And it is richer . . . because thematically it . . . reaches up into the possibility and condition of love and the chance for a kind of personal salvation even as it measures the more terrifyingly bleak likelihoods."

In "Entrapped and Abandoned," the narrator, who drives away the woman he loves because he fears the commitment involved in marriage, reveals that "relationships bring to fruitation the worst in all of us." And in "Crisscross," a drug runner, who is also an abandoned, neglected child, reasons: "I bet you'd do the same thing if you were ten and your life was as screwed up as mine."

Meeting with critical acclaim, *Lifetime* earned Sommer the title of "a genuine discovery." "He is a young writer . . . of exceptional resources of language and vision, an ironic chronicler of social depravity among fallen innocents," Baumbach praised. "While these sad dazzling fictions are a legacy of growing up cool in the 60's, they are also—the other side of that sensibility—old-fashionedly romantic, disarming dirges for a world hopelessly lost."

"Truth proceeds by opposites, too, the power of love demonstrated by its absence . . . , togetherness addressed by the revealed pains of loss," noted the *Los Angeles Times*'s art editor, Charles Champlin, after reading *Last Resort,* Sommer's second novel. This work continues the "transient nightmare" theme by centering on a musician whose group just disbanded, sending him home to a crumbling summer resort and an odd family. Only his grandmother has some focus in life. His father is a complainer; his mother is disillusioned as well as emotionally debilitated; and his girl friend is the "perfect woman" who loves him regardless of the fact that he is unprepared for a relationship with her.

The musician's perceptions of life are manifested in the lyrics he writes. For instance: "Sometimes I think the sun and rain / Exist just to traumatize out brain / So we live / From year to year / Age from far to near / Death sticks it in our ear." "What makes 'Last Resort' a novel interesting . . . ," wrote Champlin, "and Sommer a writer to watch for again is a lurking seriousness and a kind of anti-nihilism that insists the lyrics are not the last words."

BIOGRAPHICAL/CRITICAL SOURCES: Library Journal, June 15, 1979; *Times Literary Supplement,* August 22, 1980; *New York Times Book Review,* April 12, 1981, April 25, 1981; *Chicago Tribune Book World,* August 30, 1981; *Washington Post Book World,* August 30, 1981; *Los Angeles Times,* April 2, 1982.

SPEAR, (Thomas George) Percival 1901-

PERSONAL: Born November 2, 1901, in Bath, England; son of Edward Albert (a director) and Lucy (Pearce) Spear; married Dorothy Margaret Gladys Perkins (a writer), July 12, 1933. *Education:* St. Catharine's College, Cambridge, B.A., 1922, M.A., 1926, Ph.D., 1931. *Politics:* Independent. *Religion:* "Non-credal Christian." *Home:* 29 Owlstone Rd., Cambridge CB3 9JH, England. *Office:* Selwyn College, Cambridge University, Grange Rd., Cambridge CB3 9DQ, England.

CAREER: St. Stephen's College, Delhi University, Delhi, India, lecturer in history and vice-president of college, 1924-40; Government of India, worked in War Information Office, 1940-43, served as deputy-secretary, 1943-45; Cambridge University, Cambridge, England, fellow at Selwyn College, 1945—, bursar of College, 1945-63, lecturer in Indian history, 1963-69. Honorary reader at University of Delhi, 1928-40; visiting professor at University of California, Berkeley, 1957-58. Director of Spear Brothers & Clark Ltd., 1951-74. Member of board of management of Cambridge United Hospital; member and past chairman of Cambridge Local Examination Syndicate. *Member:* Royal Asiatic Society (fellow), Centre of South Asian Studies, 1955-69 (chairman, 1965-66), Royal Commonwealth Society (fellow). *Awards, honors:* Leverhulme fellow, 1937-39.

WRITINGS: The Nabobs, Oxford University Press, 1932; *India, Pakistan, and the West,* Home University Library, 1949; *Twilight of the Mughals,* Cambridge University Press, 1951; (editor and contributor) *Oxford History of India,* Oxford University Press, 3rd edition, 1958; *India: A Modern History,* University of Michigan Press, 1961; *Oxford History of Modern India,* Oxford University Press, 1965; *History of India,* Volume II (Spear was not associated with Volume I), Penguin, 1965; *Master of Bengal: Clive and His India,* Thames & Hudson, 1974.

WORK IN PROGRESS: A study of the problem of decline of the Mughal and British Indian empires.

SIDELIGHTS: Spear told *CA:* "My main subject has been Indian history in the Mughal and British periods. The motivation for this arose from my joining St. Stephen's College, a mission college run by the Cambridge Mission to Delhi. I went to teach British and European history and stayed to study Indian history.

"I've been especially interested in the way in which the British and Mughal periods transmuted into each other in the eighteenth and nineteenth centuries, and how India reacted to the impact of western influences in the nineteenth and twentieth centuries. I'm now studying how these two empires worked successfully for two centuries, and why they then both collapsed after two hundred years of dominance.

"The total effect of western influences on India has been my other main interest, along with the study of Indian art and architecture, and world politics, especially in Asia."

AVOCATIONAL INTERESTS: "Trekking in the Himalayan 'hills,' and in the countryside generally."

*   *   *

SPEISER, Stuart Marshall 1923-

BRIEF ENTRY: Born June 4, 1923, in New York, N.Y. American attorney and author. Speiser became a partner in the law firm of Speiser, Shumate, Geoghan & Krause in 1957 and has been a partner in Speiser & Krause since 1971. He is also a member of the faculty at National College of Advocacy. Speiser's writings include *Recovery for Wrongful Death: Economic Handbook* (Lawyers Co-Operative Publishing Co., 1970), *The Negligence Case: Res ipsa loquitur* (Lawyers Co-Operative Publishing Co., 1972), *Attorneys' Fees* (Lawyers Co-Operative Publishing Co., 1973), *A Piece of the Action: A Plan to Provide Every Family With a One Hundred Thousand Dollar Stake in the Economy* (Van Nostrand, 1977), *Aviation Tort Law* (Lawyers Co-Operative Publishing Co., 1978), and *Lawsuit* (Horizon Press, 1980). *Address:* Westover Lane, Stamford, Conn. 06902; Pan Am Building, 200 Park Ave., New York, N.Y. 10017; and 1216 16th St. N.W., Washington, D.C. 20036. *Biographical/critical sources: Who's Who in America,* 40th edition, Marquis, 1978.

*   *   *

SPENCER, Bonnell 1909-

PERSONAL: Born December 31, 1909, in New York, N.Y.; son of Howard Bonnell (an artist) and Viola (Bogart) Spencer. *Education:* Williams College, B.A. (magna cum laude), 1931; Exeter College, Oxford, B.Litt., 1933; attended General Theological Seminary, New York, N.Y., 1933-36. *Politics:* Democrat. *Home:* Holy Cross Monastery, West Park, N.Y. 12493. *Office:* Order of the Holy Cross, West Park, N.Y. 12493.

CAREER: Ordained Episcopal priest, 1937. Member of Order of the Holy Cross (O.H.C.), 1940—, stationed in Kent, Conn., 1940-41; West Park, N.Y., 1941-46, as novice master, 1943-45; St. Andrews, Tenn., at St. Andrew's School, 1946-55, as prior, 1947-55, and headmaster, 1953-55; Santa Barbara, Calif., as prior, 1955-59; West Park, 1959-66, as novice master, 1963-65; St. Andrews at St. Andrew's School, 1966-67; Grapevine, Tex., as father-in-charge of Whitley House, 1967-71; West Park, 1971-75, as assistant superior, 1971-72; Santa Barbara, 1975-77; Nassau, Bahamas, 1977; West Park, 1978—. Participated in more than two hundred preaching and teaching missions in the United States and Canada. Member of Associated Parishes Council, 1961-74 (president, 1971-73), and Standing Liturgical Commission of the Episcopal Church, 1964-76. *Member:* Players Club. *Awards, honors:* Moody scholarship for Oxford University, 1931-33; D.D. from General Theological Seminary, New York, N.Y., 1976.

WRITINGS—Published by Holy Cross Publications, except as noted: *They Saw the Lord,* Morehouse-Gorham, 1947; *Ye Are the Body,* 1950, revised edition, 1965; *The Sin Against the Holy Ghost* (monograph), 1954; *The Church in Christianity* (monograph), 1955; *Dietrich Bonhoeffer: Prophet for Our Time* (monograph), 1961; *Sacrifice of Thanksgiving,* 1965; *Christ in the Old Testament,* 1966; (editor) *A Four Office Breviary,* 1968; (editor) *A Monastic Breviary,* 1976; *God Who Dares to Be Man: Theology for Prayer and Suffering,* Seabury, 1981. Contributor to *Anglican Theological Review.* Editor of *Holy Cross,* 1943-46 and 1960-63.

WORK IN PROGRESS: Doctrine of Atonement, emphasizing the relationship of atonement to Old Testament sin offerings.

SIDELIGHTS: Spencer wrote: "It has always seemed most important to me to maintain a true balance between faith and reason and to integrate theology and biblical studies with the other disciplines of contemporary knowledge. In the face of resurgent fundamentalist literalism and moralism, it is especially necessary today."

BIOGRAPHICAL/CRITICAL SOURCES: Episcopal Church Annual, 1981.

SPERRY, Ralph A(ddison) 1944-

PERSONAL: Born August 19, 1944, in Providence, R.I.; son of Ralph A., Sr. (a jeweler) and Edythe (in advertising; maiden name, Barger) Sperry. *Education:* Attended Purdue University, 1962-65, and Brown University, 1965-67. *Residence:* Portsmouth, N.H. *Address:* c/o Page Cuddy, Senior Editor, Avon Books, 959 Eighth Ave., New York, N.Y. 10019.

CAREER: Filene's (retail store), Boston, Mass., advertising copywriter, 1967-73; Gilchrist (retail store), Boston, advertising manager, 1973-74; Handel and Haydn Society (amateur chorus), Boston, business manager, 1974; free-lance writer, 1974—. *Member:* Mensa. *Awards, honors:* Clio Award, 1971, for copy he wrote for Filene's Christmas television flight.

WRITINGS: The Lieutenant's Indiscretion (satire), National Institute of Creativity Press, 1977; (with Linda Bernbach) *PACE: Civil Service Test Tutor,* Arco, 1980; *Status Quotient: The Carrier* (science fiction novel), Avon, 1981. Author of "Collectibles to Watch For," a column in *Mass Bay Antiques,* 1980—. Contributor of reviews to *Best Sellers* and newspapers.

WORK IN PROGRESS: New volumes in "The Status Quotient" cycle, including *How It Is, Other Foolish Friends, Tales of the Forty-Five, One of Each, The Present Tense, Demet, T'fr'g,* and *The Problem of Conduct;* a novel, *Providence.*

SIDELIGHTS: "I began as a 'mainstream' writer," Sperry commented, "but developed and wrote the science fiction 'Status Quotient' cycle when I discovered that 'mainstream' doesn't sell. *Status Quotient* is the product of ten years' work to date, and of itself has become a profession as dense and demanding as the advertising profession I pursued for seven years.

"I'm a stylist at heart and a Virgo by compulsion (as well as by chart): the rhythm of words conveys meaning for me as much as their connotations do, and I write on as regular a schedule as the income-producing part of my life permits. I cannot afford 'writer's block,' and thus never suffer from it.

"What I consider vital is the development of one's own unique (and hapless) abilities, with the aim of being productive, without the external pressure to be only as good as everyone else. I do not believe in competition, but in the public value of individual effort. I protect my idealism with cynicism. And I'm convinced that writing is just as hard to do as plumbing."

*   *   *

SPIRES, Elizabeth 1952-

PERSONAL: Born May 28, 1952, in Lancaster, Ohio; daughter of Richard C. (in grounds maintenance) and Sue (a real estate broker; maiden name, Wagner) Spires. *Education:* Vassar College, B.A., 1974; Johns Hopkins University, M.A., 1979. *Home:* 3005 Cresmont Ave., Baltimore, Md. 21211.

CAREER: Charles E. Merrill Publishing Co., Columbus, Ohio, assistant editor, 1976-77; free-lance writer, 1977-81; Washington College, Chestertown, Md., visiting assistant professor of English, 1981; Loyola College, Baltimore, Md., adjunct assistant professor of English, 1981—. Teaching fellow at Johns Hopkins University, 1978-79. *Awards, honors:* W. K. Rose Fellowship from Vassar College, 1976; fellowship from National Endowment for the Arts, 1981; Pushcart Prize from Pushcart Press, 1981, for "Blame"; Ingram Merrill Foundation Award, 1982.

WRITINGS: Boardwalk (poems), Bits Press, 1980; *Globe* (poems), Wesleyan University Press, 1981; *The Falling Star*

(juvenile), C. E. Merrill, 1981; *Count With Me* (juvenile), C. E. Merrill, 1981; *The Wheels Go Round* (juvenile), C. E. Merrill, 1981. Contributor of poems to periodicals, including *New Yorker, Mademoiselle, Poetry, American Poetry Review, Yale Review,* and *Partisan Review.*

WORK IN PROGRESS: Letter From Swan's Island, a book of poems, publication expected in 1985.

SIDELIGHTS: Elizabeth Spires wrote: "I've supported myself for the past five years by teaching and free-lance writing. What time I have left I devote to writing poems. They draw on many sources: childhood memories, places, and visual images such as paintings and photographs, illuminated manuscripts, and medieval books of hours. The poet I most admire and who has influenced me most is Elizabeth Bishop."

BIOGRAPHICAL/CRITICAL SOURCES: Baltimore Evening Sun, October 9, 1981.

*   *   *

SPIVACK, Ellen Sue 1937-

PERSONAL: Surname is pronounced *Spee*-vack; born December 2, 1937, in Trenton, N.J.; daughter of David (a mechanic) and Beatrice (Safir) Knopf; married Roger Elliot Spivack (a farmer), May 15, 1960; children: Ira, Eileen, Basha. *Education:* Douglass College, Rutgers University, B.S., 1959. *Religion:* Jewish. *Home and office:* 606 Market St., Lewisberg, Pa. 17837.

CAREER: Elementary school teacher in South Orange, N.J., 1960-63; Deep Roots Trading Co. (natural foods store), Lewisburg, Pa., founder and co-owner, 1976—. Instructor at Bucknell University; lecturer and demonstrator at North American Vegetarian Congress and Pennsylvania Natural Living Convention.

WRITINGS: Beginner's Guide to Meatless Casseroles, privately printed, 1975; *The Whole Food Experience: A Family Guide to Eating Better,* Ross Books, 1982. Author of "Kitchen Nutrition," a column in Union County Journal. Contributor to magazines, including *Herbalist/New Health, Vegetarian Times,* and *Bestways.* Food editor of *Vegetarian World,* 1976-77; editor and publisher of *Family Nutrition Newsletter.*

WORK IN PROGRESS: A children's book, *B Is for Basha,* and a journal, *Bringing Up Beth,* both for Seawing; a children's book with Jan Wolterman, *Soup-to-Nuts Nutrition Workbook.*

SIDELIGHTS: Ellen Spivack commented: "I live to write. My writing is a way of communicating information to others in such areas as sprouting, natural childbirth, whole foods diets, breastfeeding, allergy-free foods, child rearing, holistic health, self-care, economic meatless cooking, baby food and children's diets, eating light to stay lithe, simple ethnic dishes, sound snacking, kitchen transition, natural foods dinner parties, blender foods, and raw foods and salads. I am a people person and try to help others through my writing."

*   *   *

SPIVEY, Robert Atwood 1931-

BRIEF ENTRY: Born May 25, 1931, in Suffolk, Va. American theologian, educator, and author. Spivey has taught religion at Yale University, Williams College, and Florida State University. In 1978 he became president of Randolph-Macon Woman's College. Spivey has been a Woodrow Wilson fellow and a Fulbright scholar. He wrote *Anatomy of the New Testament: A Guide to Its Structure and Meaning* (Macmillan,

1969), *Religious Issues in American Culture* (Addison-Wesley, 1972), *Religious Issues in Western Civilization* (Addison-Wesley, 1973), and *Religious Issues in World Cultures* (Addison-Wesley, 1976). *Address:* 2460 Rivermont Ave., Lynchburg, Va. 24503; and Randolph-Macon Woman's College, Box 448, Lynchburg, Va. 24503. *Biographical/critical sources: Who's Who in America,* 40th edition, Marquis, 1978.

* * *

STAMBLER, Helen
   See LATNER, Helen (Stambler)

* * *

STAPLETON, Marjorie (Winifred) 1932-

PERSONAL: Born February 7, 1932, in Bromborough, Cheshire, England; daughter of George and Lucy Alice Brearley; married Alan Fredrick William Hamilton Chapman, 1953 (died November 13, 1962); married Geoffrey Stapleton (a civil engineer), March 24, 1966; children: Polly Ann Sarah, Johanna Mercedes. *Education:* Leeds College of Art, diploma in design and teacher's certificate, 1953. *Home and office:* Beehive, Halfkey, Malvern, Worcestershire, England. *Agent:* Curtis Brown Ltd., 1 Craven Hill, London W2 3EP, England.

CAREER: Art teacher in Yorkshire, England, 1953-62; Cardiff College of Art, Cardiff, Wales, lecturer in education, 1962-63; antique dealer, 1962-64; illustrator, writer, and lecturer, 1964—. Paintings have been exhibited at the Royal Academy and the Contemporary Art Society. *Awards, honors:* Phil May Book Illustration Prize, 1953.

WRITINGS—Juveniles: Make Things Grandma Made, Taplinger, 1975; *Make Things Sailors Made,* Taplinger, 1975; *Make Things Gypsies Made,* Studio Vista, 1976; *Making Simple Clocks,* Studio Vista, 1976; *Child's Play,* W. H. Allen, 1981.

WORK IN PROGRESS: House Trap; Mum and Me.

SIDELIGHTS: Majorie Stapleton told *CA:* "I'm moving away from craft books to the writing of more general help books for mothers at home with young children." *Avocational interests:* Tap dancing, old toasting forks, megalithic stones.

* * *

STARR, John
   See COUNSELMAN, Mary Elizabeth

* * *

STECHER, Miriam B(rodie) 1917-

PERSONAL: Surname is pronounced *Steck*-er; born July 31, 1917, in Brooklyn, N.Y.; daughter of Isidor (a painter) and Sarah (Levine) Brodie; married Milton Stecher (a professor of physics), June 19, 1943; children: Jody, Janet. *Education:* Brooklyn College (now of the City University of New York), B.A., 1938; Bank Street College of Education, M.Sc., 1957. *Residence:* Brooklyn, N.Y. *Agent:* Carol Mann Literary Agency, 168 Pacific St., Brooklyn, N.Y. 11218.

CAREER: Kindergarten and pre-school teacher in New York City, 1938-43; Bank Street College of Education, New York City, music specialist and classroom teacher, 1950-60; Horace Mann School for Nursery Years, New York City, specialist in music, movement, and dramatics, 1954—. Instructor at Graduate School of Education of City University of New York,

1960-63. *Member:* National Association for the Education of Young Children. *Awards, honors: Max the Music Maker* was named "notable book" by American Library Association and honored by New York Academy of Sciences, both 1980.

WRITINGS: (With Hugh McElheny) *Music and Movement Improvisation,* Macmillan, 1972; (with Alice S. Kandell) *Max the Music Maker* (Junior Literary Guild selection), Lothrop, 1980; (with Kandell) *Daddy and Ben Together* (Junior Literary Guild selection), Lothrop, 1981.

WORK IN PROGRESS: Creative Dramatics With Young Children; children's books on imaginative play.

SIDELIGHTS: Miriam Stecher wrote: "My long experience with young children in a variety of situations and in my roles as classroom teacher, workshop leader for other teachers, and specialist in music, movement, and dramatic improvisation has given me a special insight regarding creativity. I treasure young children's potential for imaginative coping and problem solving. Often I must act as their ombudsman when parents and teachers undervalue the creative process involved. To me, it is fundamental to all learning and the essence of good living. All my books show the child as hero and problem-solver."

* * *

STEEN, Sara Jayne 1949-

PERSONAL: Born December 9, 1949, in Toledo, Ohio; daughter of Forrest Martin (a glass worker) and Opal (a secretary; maiden name, Singleton) Steen; married Joseph Henri Bourque (a professor of English), August 4, 1980. *Education:* Bowling Green State University, B.S., 1970, Ph.D., 1978; Ohio State University, M.A., 1974. *Office:* Department of English, Montana State University, Bozeman, Mont. 59717.

CAREER: English teacher at senior high school in Marion, Ohio, 1970-72; Bluffton College, Bluffton, Ohio, instructor in English, 1972; Bowling Green State University, Bowling Green, Ohio, acting curator of rare books at library, 1977-78; Montana State University, Bozeman, assistant professor of English, 1978—. *Member:* International Council of Shakespeare Bibliographers, Modern Language Association of America, National Council of Teachers of English, Renaissance Society of America, American Association of University Professors, Rocky Mountain Modern Language Association, Montana Association of Teachers of English, Sigma Tau Delta, Kappa Delta Pi.

WRITINGS: (With Thomas L. Wymer, Alice Calderonello, and others) *Intersections: The Elements of Fiction in Science Fiction,* Bowling Green Popular Press, 1978; *Thomas Middleton: A Reference Guide,* G. K. Hall, 1982.

Contributor to *Modern Language Association of America International Bibliography of Books and Articles on the Modern Languages and Literatures.* Contributor of articles and reviews to literature journals. Book review editor of *EANO Bulletin,* 1975-76, editor, 1976-77.

WORK IN PROGRESS: Editing The English Moor, by Richard Brome; editing a collection of articles about Thomas Middleton.

* * *

STEIN, Ben
   See STEIN, Benjamin

STEIN, Benjamin 1944-
(Ben Stein)

PERSONAL: Born November 25, 1944, in Washington, D.C.; son of Herbert (an economist) and Mildred (Fishman) Stein; married Alexandra Denman (a ballerina), September 7, 1977. *Education:* Columbia University, B.A., 1966; Yale University, LL.B., 1970. *Religion:* Jewish. *Residence:* Los Angeles, Calif. *Agent:* Lois Wallace, Wallace & Sheil Agency, Inc., 177 East 70th St., New York, N.Y. 10021.

CAREER: Federal Trade Commission (FTC), Washington, D.C., trial lawyer, 1970-73; speechwriter for President Richard M. Nixon, 1973-74, and President Gerald Ford, 1974; *Wall Street Journal*, New York, N.Y., member of editorial page staff and author of column about popular culture, 1974-76; creative consultant and scriptwriter for Norman Lear, 1976-77; writer, 1977—. Instructor at University of California, Santa Cruz, 1973. *Awards, honors:* Gold medal from Freedoms Foundation, 1979, for a column on work in the *Los Angeles Herald-Examiner*.

WRITINGS: (With father, Herbert Stein) *On the Brink* (novel), Simon & Schuster, 1977; (with William J. McGuiness) *Building Technology: Mechanical and Electrical Systems* (textbook), Wiley, 1977; *Fernwood U.S.A.: An Illustrated Guide From the Folks Who Brought You Mary Hartman, Mary Hartman*, Simon & Schuster, 1977; *The Croesus Conspiracy* (novel), Simon & Schuster, 1978; *Dreemz* (nonfiction), Harper, 1978; (under name Ben Stein) *The View From Sunset Boulevard: America as Brought to You by the People Who Make Television* (nonfiction), Basic Books, 1979; (under name Ben Stein, with H. Stein) *Moneypower: How to Make Inflation Make You Rich*, Harper, 1980; *Bunkhouse Logic: How to Bet on Yourself and Win*, Avon, 1981; *'Ludes: A Ballad of the Drug and the Dreamer* (nonfiction), St. Martin's, 1982.

Also author of television scripts, including "Diary of a Stewardess." Author of columns for *Los Angeles Herald-Examiner*, 1978—, and Kings Feature Syndicate, 1979-80.

WORK IN PROGRESS: The Himmler Gambit, a novel about Nazi conspirators in the United States during World War II, publication by Doubleday expected in 1982 or 1983; *My Only Sin: A Love Story*, a novel for St. Martin's; a nonfiction book on financial planning for Doubleday.

SIDELIGHTS: Stein wrote his first novel, *On the Brink*, in 1977, with technical assistance from his father, Herbert Stein, a former chairman of the President's Council of Economic Advisers. Drawing on recent historical facts and events, the novel combines economics and suspense in a story about the disastrous effects of runaway inflation. The year is 1981, and the head of the Federal Reserve Board, who admits, "I am no economist," nevertheless convinces the president that economic prosperity lies in increasing the money supply to keep up with the rising cost of living. At the same time OPEC (Organization of Petroleum Exporting Countries) raises the price of oil from $20.00 a barrel to $38.00, and inflation skyrockets. Wonder Bread is $2.99 a loaf, bacon sells for $22.00 a pound, the stock market crashes, and anarchy seems imminent. When it becomes necessary for the government to issue megabucks in million dollar denominations the scene is set for a Huey Long-type demagogue to take over America. "Impending Disaster novels with crazy Presidents can grip us because extrapolation of recent reality is all too easy," observed Adam Smith in the *New York Times Book Review*. "So I can say honestly: I could not put down 'On the Brink.' I wanted to see

where those wild characters, the prices, would go.... As plotters and pamphleteers the Steins are brilliant. Their Disaster is truly frightening."

Stein published two books in 1978. *The Croesus Conspiracy*, Stein's second Washington novel, is a political story about a scheme to reestablish the Third Reich. The novel's fictional characters, including a short, stocky, German-born secretary of state, a power-hungry presidential candidate, and their billionaire patron, bear resemblance to certain real-life personages. In the same year *Dreemz* was published. A memoir-diary of Stein's first year of living and working in Los Angeles, the book is, according to the author, his favorite work. In *Dreemz* Stein recounts his escape from the eastern establishment to life in the western sun. *New York Times* critic Christopher Lehmann-Haupt called the book "a stunning little portrait of what life must be like in the city of angels." At the end of his first year in Los Angeles, Stein lived in a Spanish-style house complete with palm tree and drove a Mercedes Benz 450 SLC with a personalized license plate that read "DREEMZ." Nevertheless, he points out, "The cars and the girls and the Spanish house are only the outward appearances of the dreams that have come true in L.A. For me, L.A. means doing and being free."

Among the opportunities that life in Los Angeles provided for Stein was a job as creative consultant to television producer Norman Lear. It was from this occupational vantage point that Stein developed the thesis that forms the basis of his book *The View From Sunset Boulevard*. Exposing the myth that popular culture as represented by television is a mirror of national dreams and nightmares, Stein maintains: "The super-medium of television is spewing out the messages of a few writers and producers (literally in the low hundreds), almost all of whom live in Los Angeles. Television is not necessarily a mirror of anything besides what those few people think."

After conducting long and candid interviews with forty of television's most important writers and producers, Stein concluded: "The fit between the message of the TV shows and the opinions of the people who make the TV shows was excellent. Moreover, the views of these TV people were so highly idiosyncratic and unique that they could not possibly be the dreams of a nation. It was like thinking that a taste for snuff movies or Beluga caviar was the general taste of a nation." Additionally, "In Mr. Stein's view," noted a *New York Times Book Review* critic, "the Hollywood-formed ideas aired on the nation's screens run counter to our traditional folk culture, in which Americans are said to revere small towns, successful businessmen and soldiers, and to have no sympathy for criminals and the poor. The new television culture violates the old-fashioned virtues."

Presenting an "alternate world" juxtaposed to reality, prime-time television, observed Stein, broadcasts daily that businessmen and other high-level people are bad, while workers and rebel cops are "the salt of the earth and smart, too." Also, on television, small towns hide evil beneath their superficial veneer, while big cities are portrayed as basically cheerful, friendly places to raise children. Supporting his contention that television posits an alternate reality, Stein wrote: "In the thousands of hours I have spent watching adventure shows, I have never seen a major crime committed by a poor, teenage, black, Mexican, or Puerto Rican youth, even though they account for a high percentage of all violent crime."

"'The View From Sunset Boulevard' packs a surprisingly strong wallop," opined Lehmann-Haupt in the *New York Times*. "For it puts forth the claim that through the medium of television a handful of people may be altering the most basic assumptions of America's folk culture. And it makes you take that claim just seriously enough to think about it.'' Other critics also reviewed the book favorably. *Washington Post* critic James Lardner commended Stein for asking ''fresh questions about commercial TV and its treatment of crime, wealth, religion, and daily life,'' and M. J. Sobran of the *National Review* applauded Stein's subtlety, remarking: ''He doesn't attack or satirize. He simply objectifies. He says: Look—here is what this little group of people actually thinks. As so often happens, their views are hypnotic only until you notice how they look from outside, and until you notice who holds them.'' Another *National Review* critic, M. Stanton Evans, called the book ''a welcome addition to the growing literature of analysis concerning the bias of the national media.''

Following *The View From Sunset Boulevard*, Stein returned to the subject of inflation in a second collaboration with his father. The result was *Moneypower*, published in 1980. A nonfiction self-help book, *Moneypower* offers advice on investments and financial strategies for use in hyperinflationary periods. According to Lehmann-Haupt the book advises ''in ways that seem entirely practical, and which ought to be clear even to someone who has trouble balancing a checkbook.''

Stein told *CA*: ''I advise all prospective writers to try medicine instead or else try the shoe business. The same qualities that make a writer—sensitivity and awareness—make him vulnerable to torture by publishers and producers.''

CA INTERVIEW

CA interviewed Benjamin Stein by phone on October 2, 1980, at his home in Los Angeles, California.

CA: What kind of cases did you deal with as a lawyer for the Federal Trade Commission?

STEIN: Unfair, false, and deceptive advertising cases—cases in which we believed that the advertising for a product misrepresented it. The main one was a case involving advertising for a very popular fruit-flavored drink called Hi-C. That occupied almost all of my time while I was practicing law.

CA: Did you go directly from that job to being a staff assistant to Nixon and Ford?

STEIN: I taught briefly at the University of California at Santa Cruz. I taught about the political and social content of film, and I also taught about the political and civil rights of the United States. I taught a law course and a course in the art department. Then I became a speech writer for Nixon and then for Ford.

CA: Was speech writing your only staff job for Nixon and Ford?
STEIN: Yes.

CA: Then you went to work for the Wall Street Journal?

STEIN: Yes. I was a member of the editorial page staff—there were six of us. We held meetings to decide what the editorials should be about, and I wrote an occasional editorial; I don't suppose I wrote more than twenty the whole time I was there. I also wrote a column once a week about popular culture, and it was sometimes about television. But I never was like a television reviewer—I didn't just review the new shows—I would try to examine a whole genre of television and explain what it meant and what it revealed about our society. I also wrote about movies and popular phenomena, like Vegas or Disney World or something like that.

CA: How did you get into writing for television?

STEIN: When I was writing at the *Wall Street Journal*, I wrote many very critical columns about Norman Lear's shows. I was extremely critical, and I don't think he had ever seen such negative columns. He asked to meet me. He met me, and we spent the whole day together having a very enjoyable talk. He said, ''You have quite a sense of humor. If you'd ever like to come out and work for me, I'd sure like that.'' I said, ''Well, I don't think I'd like to do that.'' I worked for another year and a half or so for the *Wall Street Journal*, and then I went out to California on business a couple of times and really enjoyed it a lot. In the meantime I had gotten a contract to do two books, so I had some money coming in, and I decided I would live in California. While I was there I started spending a lot of time hanging around with Norman Lear and his friends, and they asked me little by little if I would do work for a show called ''All's Fair,'' which was set in Washington. Since I had lived in Washington, it was easy for me to do. Since I needed the money I said, ''Yes,'' and I started working for Norman Lear on that show. I guess they were fairly happy with my work because they asked me to work on another show called ''Fernwood Tonight.'' I really hated working on *that* show because it didn't seem that funny to me. Then I stopped working for Norman Lear. But I like to think that we're good friends. As a matter of fact, I was at a party at his house last night.

CA: Are you doing any television writing now?

STEIN: I just finished a television movie for CBS called ''Diary of a Stewardess.'' It sounds trashy, but it isn't. We're trying to put together a deal for another one called ''Diary of a Private Secretary.''

CA: Your book Dreemz *describes the process of your settlement—both physical and emotional—in Los Angeles after moving there from the East. Do you miss the East now?*

STEIN: Oh yes, I miss it a lot. I miss the change of seasons and the snow and the scenery. Los Angeles is a beautiful city only by night—it's not really very pretty by day. I miss the architecture in the East, the trees, the mountains. I miss the snow a *lot*.

CA: Do you get back there very much?

STEIN: I used to go back a great deal, but it has gotten so expensive to go back and forth. I made a vow a long time ago that I would either go first class or I wouldn't go at all, and it's gotten to be so expensive to go first class that I hardly ever go anymore.

CA: You wrote On the Brink *and* Moneypower *with your father.*

STEIN: Moneypower was my sixth book, and I did that with him. He's a very brilliant economist.

CA: How did your collaboration with your father develop?

STEIN: I said to him, ''For years you've been telling me there's a way to beat inflation—borrow. I'd like to write that down in a book. Would you be the co-author of it, because people might not believe me. If your name is on it they might believe it.'' He said that would be fine, and that's how we did it.

I wrote almost all of *On the Brink*, but I said, ''I want you to explain to me how such inflation could get going and how it could be stopped.'' Then I wrote all the rest of it. He was the inflation consultant for that book. He is a brilliant man, and I have been after him for at least five years to write a novel himself.

CA: Does he enjoy writing?

STEIN: Yes, he enjoys writing, but he's never written fiction before so he doesn't really understand that it's not that hard. He thinks it's much harder than it is.

CA: With the number of money books already on the market and continuing to come on the market, what did you feel you could offer in Moneypower *to make it of particular value to the reader?*

STEIN: Two things, basically. One, I thought I could make it much clearer than anyone else. I believe that if I have any one extraordinary skill as a writer, it's clarity. I've never had anyone complain that what I wrote wasn't clear. Even if people disagree with me, they say that it's very clearly written. So that, I thought, was helpful. Two, I thought I could offer them some debunking of myths. For instance, *myth:* that mortgage rates were impossibly high. I tried to explain why they are not really that high. *Myth:* that collectibles are a great hedge against inflation; *myth:* that diamonds are a great hedge against inflation; *myth:* that art is a great hedge against inflation. I just tried to debunk a lot of myths. I thought a lot of very famous people had been writing books furthering those myths, and I tried to straighten it out a little.

CA: In The View From Sunset Boulevard *you set forth your thesis that most television programs, though written and directed by a relative handful of people, go against certain basic traditional values of our popular culture. Do you think the viewing public is largely unaware of this?*

STEIN: I think they're aware of it, but they haven't really thought about it that much, just like I think they're aware in a dim way that an extraordinary amount of time on television is devoted to how strong your fingernails should be, but they don't really think about the fact that this is an extremely superficial value in a free society. I tried to take the things that were floating out there in the public consciousness and organize them in a coherent way and say, "This is the method you may have noticed vaguely, but let me just make it clear for you. This is what television is saying to you."

CA: But all those shows continue to get good ratings and they stay on.

STEIN: It's a question of there being a complete lack of any alternative.

CA: You're opposed to any kind of control. Do you think that more representative programming will emerge with the wider availability of cable television?

STEIN: I doubt it, because the same people are going to be writing it. It's all still going to be coming from Hollywood. In a sense, all the religious programming is an alternative.

CA: Isn't that frightening?

STEIN: I think a lot of people find it frightening. I myself am not that frightened by it, but I know many people are.

CA: Do you think a very small group of writers can do anything to bring about a change?

STEIN: Well, the group of writers is so small that, as far as I know, it consists of me and that's all. I think that group is too small.

CA: Did you get a response from the television community in Los Angeles?

STEIN: I got some very angry response from some people and some very positive and encouraging response from others. The head of one of the largest production companies read sections of the book to all of his producers at a meeting and said, "We've all been guilty of this and we've got to stop doing it," but then they all went on and kept doing it.

CA: What difficulties do you encounter in your writing?

STEIN: Well, I'm always struggling to write better. I guess I have the same problems as all writers. I try to write an interesting story, something that's worth reading, try to write in such a way that people won't think I'm writing like a fool. I almost never have writer's block, if that's what you're asking. I do read certain books and feel like I am an extremely poor writer by comparison with those writers. For instance, I'm now reading *The Executioner's Song.* It's so good, it's unbelievable. I don't think I'll ever be able to write as well as Norman Mailer. I guess my problem is that I'm always trying to write as well as someone like Norman Mailer, and I'm never going to succeed.

CA: Have you written any movie scripts?

STEIN: I've written a number of movie scripts but none of them have been produced. The way it works out here—this is kind of interesting—you can sell them [movie scripts], sometimes even for a fairly good price, and yet they will often not get made. But one of the great glories of Hollywood life is that they pay you whether they produce the script or not.

CA: Would you like to be involved in the production of a movie you had written?

STEIN: Not really. I wouldn't really be interested in being a director. I might be interested in being an art director because I'm very interested in the way sets look and the way people are dressed. I'm not that interested in the way actors act. I don't think it would be very much fun to be around actors acting.

CA: Do you miss politics at all?

STEIN: Very much. I enjoyed my work at the White House the best of any work I've ever had. I'd go back there—if I could have those days back again I'd be a very happy man.

CA: Would you want the political conditions to be pretty much the same?

STEIN: Well, I meant working for Nixon. I loved working for Nixon. It wasn't so much that he was such a great guy. I do think he had many, many things to recommend him, but he obviously had many things against him, too. But it was constant excitement and I loved that. It was great!

CA: How many speech writers did he employ at the time you were working for him?

STEIN: He employed eight, and I was by far the most junior. I was the youngest and also had the least seniority. They were always giving me the most complicated speeches to do. If they needed one on international tax policy or something like that, they would always assign it to me because I was a lawyer as well as an economist; so they figured I could understand it. Also, I didn't know until years after I had left that you were allowed to turn down an assignment. I thought that you just had to do everything they told you to do. I didn't learn until 1979 that you could turn down an assignment and ask for something else.

CA: You were there when Nixon left the White House?

STEIN: Yes. It was a wrenching moment.

CA: I gather you did not write that speech.

STEIN: No, I didn't.

CA: Are you in touch with Nixon or Ford at all now?

STEIN: I'm in touch with Nixon very sporadically, and I'm in touch with his wonderful and beautiful daughter Julie and her family fairly often.

CA: You've written quite a variety of books in a short time. Is there one that you enjoyed doing more than the others?

STEIN: If I had to die tomorrow, I would be proud that I had written *Dreemz*. I would feel that my whole life had been justified by having written *Dreemz*.

CA: How have you felt generally about the reviews of your books?

STEIN: My first book got terrible reviews at first, and then the tide turned when I got a rave, super, wonderful review in the *New York Times*. After that, every book I've written has gotten a better and better review in the *New York Times*, so I'm very happy with the reviews I've gotten in the *New York Times*. The *Los Angeles Times* always gives me a bad review because I work for their opposition, the *Herald-Examiner*. So without a second thought—I don't think they even read my books—they just give me a bad review. The newspaper business is a very cutthroat business.

CA: What do you do for the Herald-Examiner?

STEIN: I write a column for them about Hollywood, and I also write one about politics. I used to write two about politics, and they were nationally syndicated until September—I had a year with the national syndicate. It was doing fairly well; I had about forty papers. I was just too extreme in the things I said, so it never got to be the huge success that I hoped it would be.

CA: Is there a book in progress that you'd like to talk about?

STEIN: There are two books in progress. One is called *Bunkhouse Logic: How to Bet on Yourself and Win*. It's a book about how to become successful, and it's really, I think, completely different from any self-help book you've ever read or even heard of. Because most of them say, "Oh, you're perfect as you are, just relax and take it easy, don't worry about things—'I'm OK, You're OK.'" So this book says, "Go out there and work like a maniac and leave no stone unturned until you've gotten what you want." That's already written and has been sold to Avon. Avon has a hard-soft deal on it. Now I'm in the midst of working on a book for Doubleday called *The*

Himmler Gambit, which is a story about Nazi conspirators in the United States during World War II. It's sort of going back to that genre that I used in *The Croesus Conspiracy*.

They're all a slow and agonizing grind because publishers are very hard on authors, and you don't get much money for doing books unless you work very hard at it. But it's also awfully nice to be able to write what's on your mind and have somebody pay you for it. It never ceases to amaze me that I can earn my living writing what's on my mind.

CA: Was writing an early ambition?

STEIN: It was really my earliest occupational ambition. When I was a very small child—like eight years old—I was an enormous fan of Agatha Christie, and my ambition then was to live by the ocean and write books, which is in a sense what I do.

BIOGRAPHICAL/CRITICAL SOURCES: New York Times Book Review, July 3, 1977, February 18, 1979; *National Review,* September 2, 1977, February 16, 1979, July 6, 1979; *New Yorker,* December 19, 1977; *West Coast Review of Books,* May, 1978, November, 1978; *New York Times,* May 17, 1978, January 23, 1979, January 8, 1980; *Los Angeles Times Book Review,* February 18, 1979; *Washington Post,* February 25, 1979; *Nation,* March 10, 1979; *America,* April 7, 1979; *Saturday Review,* May 26, 1979.

—Sketch by Lillian S. Sims

—Interview by Jean W. Ross

*   *   *

STEIN, Herbert 1916-

PERSONAL: Born August 27, 1916, in Detroit, Mich.; son of David (an automotive machinist) and Jessie (Segal) Stein; married Mildred Sylvia Fishman, June 12, 1937; children: Rachel (Mrs. Melvin Epstein), Benjamin. *Education:* Williams College, A.B. (magna cum laude), 1935; University of Chicago, Ph.D., 1958. *Home:* 1704 Yorktown Dr., Charlottesville, Va. 22901. *Office:* Department of Economics, University of Virginia, Charlottesville, Va. 22901.

CAREER: Economist with Federal Deposit Insurance Corp., 1938-40, National Defense Advisory Commission, 1940-41, War Production Board, 1941-44, and Office for War Mobilization and Reconversion, 1945; Committee for Economic Development, economist, 1945-48, associate director of research, 1948-56, director of research, 1956-66, vice-president and chief economist, 1966-67; Brookings Institution, Washington, D.C., senior fellow, 1967-69; President's Council of Economic Advisers, Washington, D.C., member of council, 1969-74, chairman, 1971-74; University of Virginia, Charlottesville, A. Willis Robertson Professor of Economics, 1974—. Fellow at Center for Advanced Study in the Behavioral Sciences, Palo Alto, Calif., 1965-66; adjunct scholar at American Enterprise Institute for Public Policy Research, 1975-77, senior fellow, 1977—. Member of Advisory Committee on National Growth Policy Processes, 1976-77, and Pharmaceutical Reimbursement Advisory Board, 1976-77; member of President's Economic Policy Advisory Board, 1981. Member of board of directors of Reynolds Metals Co. and Ozma Corp.; past member of board of directors of Tax Institute of America. Consultant to Congressional Budget Office. *Military service:* U.S. Naval Reserve, active duty, 1944-45; became lieutenant junior grade.

MEMBER: American Economic Association, National Economists Club (chairman of board of governors, 1969-70), Southern Economic Association, Virginia Economic Association, Phi Beta Kappa, Cosmos Club. *Awards, honors:* Award from Pabst Brewing Co., 1944, for essay on postwar employment problems; LL.D. from Rider College, 1970, University of Hartford, 1972, and Williams College, 1980.

WRITINGS: U.S. Government Price Policy During the World War, Williams College, 1938; (with de Chazeau, Hart, Means, and others) *Jobs and Markets,* McGraw, 1946; (editor) *Policies to Combat Depression,* Princeton University Press, 1956; (with Joseph A. Pechman) *Essays in Federal Taxation,* Committee for Economic Development, 1959.

(Contributor) Kermit Gordon, editor, *Agenda for the Nation: Papers on Domestic and Foreign Policy Issues,* Doubleday, 1969; *The Fiscal Revolution in America,* University of Chicago Press, 1969; (with William J. Fellner and others) *Contemporary Economic Problems,* American Enterprise, 1975, 7th edition, 1981; (with Wassily W. Leontief) *The Economic System in an Age of Discontinuity,* New York University Press, 1976; (with son, Benjamin Stein) *On the Brink* (novel), Simon & Schuster, 1977; (with B. Stein) *Moneypower: How to Make Inflation Make You Rich,* Harper, 1980. Also contributor to *Goals for Americans,* Prentice-Hall.

Author of syndicated column, "The Economy Today," in *Wall Street Journal,* 1974-80. Contributor to *International Encyclopedia of the Social Sciences.* Contributor to magazines, including *Fortune.* Editor of *AEI Economist,* 1977—.

SIDELIGHTS: After being recommended by economist Milton Friedman, Stein was invited to join Richard Nixon's Council of Economic Advisers (CEA) in 1968. In an effort to reduce the 4 percent inflation rate of the time, the three-member council argued for a tightening of credit and a reduction of the money supply, predicting that the unemployment rate would remain low. The council's strategy failed, however, when both the unemployment rate and the inflation rate rose. The administration then eased up on budget and credit controls, expecting that economic recovery would soon follow.

Stein succeeded Paul McCracken as chairman of the CEA in November, 1971, three months after the government had instituted wage and price freezes to control the economy. Stein had been a free-market advocate, but he justified the wage-price controls as a necessary, temporary measure. During fiscal crises in 1973 and 1974, however, Stein returned to his free-market views. He resigned his post as chairman in 1974 to assume the University of Virginia professorship he had been appointed to in 1971.

BIOGRAPHICAL/CRITICAL SOURCES: Washington Post, August 27, 1968; *U.S. News and World Report,* December 30, 1968, December 6, 1971; *New York Times,* February 18, 1969, November 25, 1971; *New York Post,* December 4, 1971; *Business Week,* December 4, 1971, April 20, 1974; *Time,* December 6, 1971; *Newsweek,* December 6, 1971; Leonard Silk, *Nixonomics,* Praeger, 1972.

*   *   *

STEIN, Rita F.   1922-

BRIEF ENTRY: Born July 25, 1922, in Buffalo, N.Y. American nurse, educator, and author. Stein worked as a nurse from 1942 to 1946. In 1959 she began teaching, and she has been a professor of psychiatric nursing at Indiana University since 1968. Stein wrote *Disturbed Youth and Ethnic Family Patterns* (State University of New York Press, 1971). *Address:* 4808

Dorkin Court, Indianapolis, Ind. 46254; and School of Nursing, Indiana University, Indianapolis, Ind. 46202.

*   *   *

STEIN, Sandra Kovacs   1939-

PERSONAL: Born September 30, 1939, in Calcutta, India; came to the United States in 1962, naturalized citizen, 1966; daughter of Alexander (an engineer) and Rose (Batta) Kovacs; married Paul Stein (a teacher), May 29, 1962 (died, 1975); children: Joanne Ellen, Howard Alexander. *Education:* McGill University, B.A., 1960; University of Montreal, M.A., 1962. *Home address:* P.O. Box 921, Woodside, N.Y. 11377.

CAREER: Industrial Home for the Blind, Jamaica, N.Y., speech pathologist and audiologist, 1964-66; Renault/Peugeot, Jackson Heights, N.Y., assistant manager in data processing, 1970-72; writer and free-lance worker, 1972—.

WRITINGS: Instant Numerology, Harper, 1979; (with Carol Ann Schuler) *Love Numbers,* Putnam, 1980. Author of "Numeroscope," a numerology column in Queens Press, 1981—.

WORK IN PROGRESS: Guide Numbers, with Carol Ann Schuler; a self-help book.

SIDELIGHTS: Sandra Stein commented: "I was born in India. At the age of seven we moved to the Dominican Republic and, though my home was based there, I went to high school and college in Canada. I moved to New York after my marriage in 1962. I have tried my hand in many areas, including art, speech pathology, computer programming, and with a home typing service. Now I am deeply involved in writing and the study of numerology.

"I first became interested in numerology and astrology in 1978 as a skeptic trying to disprove their validity, but have done much research since then that has convinced me otherwise. I never had any desire to be a writer, but in 1978 I had a numerology reading by Kevin Quinn Avery, who later became my teacher. He predicted that I would be a writer. When, disbelieving, I asked what I would write about, he said, 'anything you want. It will be published in 1980.' To test the prediction, I picked about fifteen publishers at random and wrote them to see if they would be interested in a numerology handbook. I had not written one and in fact didn't yet know anything about numerology. Three out of the fifteen were interested, and one wanted to see my manuscript right away. Since there was no manuscript, I fudged by telling the editor that it was at the typists', but they were closed for vacation, and I couldn't mail it until they got back. In three to four weeks, I wrote and typed the first draft and sent it in."

*   *   *

STEINBERG, Judah   1861-1908

BRIEF ENTRY: Born in 1861 in Lipcani, Russia (now U.S.S.R.); died in 1908 in Odessa, Russia (now U.S.S.R.). Russian author. Steinberg's gift was for the short story. In collections like *Asher ben Asher* and *Brit Milah,* all written in Hebrew, he described simple people of the Jewish ghetto, focusing on their tribulations in a hostile world and the inner strength with which they triumphed. His most successful novel was *In Those Days,* translated in 1915, a story of Jewish soldiers conscripted during the reign of Czar Nicholas I. *Biographical/critical sources: The Penguin Companion to European Literature,* McGraw, 1969.

STENECK, Nicholas H. 1940-

PERSONAL: Born May 8, 1940, in Jersey City, N.J.; married wife, 1963; children: two sons. *Education:* Rutgers University, B.S., 1962; University of Wisconsin—Madison, M.A., 1969, Ph.D., 1970. *Home:* 127 Grandview Dr., Ann Arbor, Mich. 48103. *Office:* Department of History, University of Michigan, Ann Arbor, Mich. 48103.

CAREER: High school science teacher in New Jersey, 1963-66; University of Michigan, Ann Arbor, assistant professor, 1970-76, associate professor of history, 1976—. Participated in educational television series. Director of Medieval and Renaissance Collegium, 1975-77; executive director of Michigan Consortium for Medieval and Early Modern Studies, 1976-78; co-director of Collegiate Institute for Values and Science, 1977—. *Military service:* U.S. Army Reserve, 1962-68. *Member:* American Historical Society, Mediaeval Academy of America. *Awards, honors:* American Council of Learned Societies fellow, 1973-74; National Science Foundation grants, 1973-76, 1978-79.

WRITINGS: (Contributor) Allen C. Debus, editor, *Science, Medicine, and Society in the Renaissance*, Neale Watson, 1972; (editor) *Science and Society: Past, Present, and Future*, University of Michigan Press, 1975; (editor with Duncan Robertson and Harold Scholler) *Sources for the Study of High Medieval Culture, 1100-1300*, Medieval and Renaissance Collegium Publications, 1976; (editor with William Courtenay) *Sources for the Study of Late Medieval and Renaissance Paleography*, Medieval and Renaissance Collegium Publications, 1976; *Science and Creation in the Middle Ages: Henry of Langenstein (d. 1397) on Genesis*, University of Notre Dame Press, 1976; (editor with Raymond Grew) *Society and History: The Essays of Sylvia Thrupp*, University of Michigan Press, 1977; (contributor) *Albertus Magnus and the Sciences*, Pontifical Institute of Mediaeval Studies, 1980. Contributor to scholarly journals.

WORK IN PROGRESS: A current history of microwave bioeffects research; a project on early critics of science; research on limitations of scientific inquiry and on seventeenth-century London as a scientific center.

*   *   *

STEPHEN, David 1910-

PERSONAL: Born in 1910 in Airdrie, Lanarkshire, Scotland; married Jess Russell; children: one son, one daughter. *Education:* Attended Airdrie Academy.

CAREER: Writer. Worked as correspondent in Spain.

WRITINGS—Juveniles: *String Lug the Fox* (illustrated by Nina Scott Langley), Lutterworth, 1950, Little, Brown, 1952, abridged edition, Collins, 1961; (and photographer) *Days With the Golden Eagle*, A. & J. Donaldson, 1951; *Getting to Know British Wild Animals* (illustrated by Len Fullerton), Collins, 1952; *Six-Pointer Buck*, Lutterworth, 1956, Lippincott, 1957; *Birds and Their Eggs* (illustrated by Fullerton), Collins, 1958; *The Red Stranger* (illustrated by Maurice Wilson), Lutterworth, 1958; *Wild Animals and Their Ways* (illustrated by Langley), Collins, 1959.

David Stephen's Book of the Wild, Collins, 1961; *More About Birds and Their Eggs* (illustrated by Fullerton), Collins, 1961; *Rory the Roebuck* (illustrated by Don Higgins), Bodley Head, 1961, Funk, 1969; *Do You Know About Animals?* (illustrated by G. W. Backhouse), Collins, 1962; *Do You Know About Birds?* (illustrated by Ralston Gudgeon), Collins, 1962; *The*

Living World of Nature, Collins, 1962; *Do You Know About Reptiles and Amphibians?* (illustrated by Fullerton), Collins, 1963; (and photographer) *First Things in Colour Photography*, Collins, 1963; *Timothy's Book of Farming* (illustrated by A. E. Kennedy and T. E. North), Collins, 1963; *Watching Wild Life*, Collins, 1963, revised edition published as *David Stephen's Guide to Watching Wildlife*, 1973; *Scottish Wild Life*, Hutchinson, 1964; (with Jan Hanzak and Zdenek Veselovsky) *Collins Encyclopedia of Animals*, Collins, 1968, published as *Encyclopedia of Animals*, St. Martin's, 1979; (with James Lockie) *Nature's Way: A Look at the Web of Life*, McGraw, 1969.

Animals of the World (illustrated by Takeo Ishida), Collins, 1970, Galahad Books, 1973; *Birds of the World* (illustrated by Ishida), Collins, 1972, Galahad Books, 1973; *Dolphins, Seals, and Other Sea Mammals*, Putnam, 1973; *Highland Animals*, Highlands and Islands Development Board, 1974; *Cats*, Collins, 1976; *Cock Robin's Garden: A Nature Story*, Collins, 1978; *Frog's Pond: A Nature Story*, Collins, 1978; *Squirrel Wood: A Nature Story*, Collins, 1978; *Woodmouse Lane: A Nature Story*, Collins, 1978.

Contributor to periodicals, including *Scotsman*, *Weekly Scotsman*, and *Scottish Field*.*

*   *   *

STEPP, Ann 1935-

PERSONAL: Born July 20, 1935, in Headrick, Okla.; daughter of William W. (a postmaster) and Anna Juanita (a postmaster; maiden name, Ragon) Stepp. *Education:* University of Oklahoma, B.S., 1957; Chapman College, M.A., 1971; also attended Texas Christian University, 1956, University of California, Los Angeles, 1969, California State University, Long Beach, 1969, California State University, Fullerton, 1974-77, and University of Southern California, 1979. *Home:* 12758 Ascot Dr., Garden Grove, Calif. 92640. *Office:* Lampson Junior High School, 10851 East Lampson, Garden Grove, Calif. 92640.

CAREER: Lampson Junior High, Garden Grove, Calif., teacher of life science, 1957—. Member of board of directors of Aguanga Wildlife Reserve Society, 1979—. *Member:* American Cetacean Society, Authors Guild, National Science Teachers' Association, Parent-Teacher Association (honorary member).

WRITINGS—All for children: *Setting Up a Science Project* (illustrated by Polly Bolian), Prentice-Hall, 1966; *The Story of Radioactivity* (illustrated by James E. Barry), Harvey House, 1971; *Grunion: Fish Out of Water* (illustrated by Anne Lewis), Harvey House, 1971; *A Silkworm Is Born*, Sterling, 1972.

WORK IN PROGRESS: Life with Rhoda; The Elm Tree; Bill Cosby: A Comedian Who Educates; Gigi: The California Gray Whale; The Pundits; and *The First Book of Steve Martin.*

*   *   *

STERN, Gerd Jacob 1928-
(USCO)

BRIEF ENTRY: Born October 12, 1928, in Saarbrucken, Germany. American sculptor and poet. Stern is president of Intermedia Systems Corporation. He has taught at Harvard University and University of California, Santa Cruz. His sculpture has been exhibited in the United States and abroad and is part of a collection at the San Francisco Museum of Art. Stern's books include *First Poems and Others* (1952), *Afterimage: Poems* (Maverick, 1965), *Media, Information, and Then?* (State University of New York at Albany, 1975), *Flip-Flop* (International Design Conference in Aspen, 1976), and *Funding of Television Arts: Open Circuits* (M.I.T. Press, 1977). *Address:* 12 Boston Ave., Medford, Mass. 02115; and Intermedia Systems Corp., 711 Massachusetts Ave., Cambridge, Mass. 02139. *Biographical/critical sources:* R. Kostelanetz, *The Theatre of Mixed Means,* Viking, 1968; Douglas Davis, *Art and the Future,* Praeger, 1973; S. Krantz, *Science and Technology in the Arts,* Van Nostrand, 1976; *Who's Who in American Art,* Bowker, 1978.

* * *

STEVENSON, Tom   1899(?)-1982

OBITUARY NOTICE: Born c. 1899 in Marion Station, Md.; died after suffering a heart attack, April 2, 1982, in Baltimore, Md. Journalist and author best known for his articles and books on gardening. Stevenson was a Washington correspondent for numerous American newspapers, including the *Chicago Tribune,* from the thirties until 1951 when he began writing a gardening column for the *Baltimore News-American.* In 1952 Stevenson joined the *Washington Post,* again contributing a column on horticulture, which the *Post's* J. Y. Smith called "one of the most carefully read features in the newspaper." The *Post* carried Stevenson's column until the writer's death. A contributor to *Encyclopaedia Britannica* and the *American Horticultural Society Magazine,* Stevenson also wrote *The Garden Handbook of Maryland, Tom Stevenson's Pruning Guide,* and *The Washington Post Lawn Guide.* Obituaries and other sources: *Washington Post,* April 3, 1982.

* * *

STEWART, Angus (J. M.)   1936-

PERSONAL: Born November 22, 1936, in Adelaide, Australia; son of J.I.M. (a professor) and M. (a physician; maiden name, Hardwick) Stewart. *Education:* Christ Church, Oxford, M.A., 1961. *Agent:* A. P. Watt Ltd., 26/28 Bedford Row, London WC1R 4HL, England.

CAREER: Writer, 1958—. *Member:* Society of Authors. *Awards, honors:* Richard Hillary Award from Oxford University, 1963, for short stories in magazines; grant from Arts Council of Great Britain, 1976.

WRITINGS: Sandel (novel), Hutchinson, 1968; *Snow in Harvest* (novel), Hutchinson, 1969; *Sense and Inconsequence* (verse; foreword by W. H. Auden), Michael de Hartington, 1972; *Tangier: A Writer's Notebook* (nonfiction), Hutchinson, 1977.

Work represented in anthologies, including *Introduction Two* (fiction), Faber, 1964, and *Best Horror Stories 2,* edited by John Keir Cross, Faber, 1965.

Contributor of stories to periodicals, including *London* and *Transatlantic Review.*

WORK IN PROGRESS: A novel.

SIDELIGHTS: Stewart has traveled in the United States, Canada, Mexico, the Caribbean, North Africa, and Europe. He speaks several languages, including Spanish, French, Italian, and Moghrebi (the North African dialect of Arabic).

* * *

STEWART, Michael   1906-

PERSONAL: Born November 6, 1906, in Bromley, England; son of Robert Wallace (a writer) and Eva (a teacher; maiden name, Blaxley) Stewart; married Mary Birkinshaw (Baroness

Stewart of Alvechurch; a member of the House of Lords), July 26, 1941. *Education:* St. John's College, Oxford, B.A., 1929, M.A., 1935. *Politics:* Labour. *Religion:* Methodist. *Home:* 11 Felden St., Fulham, London SW6 5AE, England. *Office:* House of Commons, Westminster, London S.W.1, England.

CAREER: Teacher in London, England, 1940-42; British Parliament, London, member of Parliament, 1945—, undersecretary of state at War Office, 1947-51, Parliamentary secretary at Ministry of Supply, 1951, secretary of state for education and science, 1964-65, secretary of state for foreign affairs, 1965-66, secretary of state for economic affairs, 1966-68, secretary of state for foreign and commonwealth affairs, 1968-70, member of European Assembly, 1975-76. *Military service:* British Army, 1942-45; served in the Middle East; became captain. *Member:* National Union of Teachers, Fabian Society, Reform Club. *Awards, honors:* Companion of Honor; freeman of London borough of Hammersmith; LL.D. from University of Leeds; D.Sc. from University of Benin.

WRITINGS: The British Approach to Politics, Allen & Unwin, 1958, 5th edition, 1965; *Modern Forms of Government,* Allen & Unwin, 1958; *He to Hecuba,* Drama Book, 1968; *Belle,* Macmillan, 1977; *The Jekyll and Hyde Years: Politics and Economic Policy Since 1964,* Rowman & Littlefield, 1977 (published in England as *Politics and Economic Policy in the United Kingdom Since 1964: The Jekyll and Hyde Years,* Pergamon, 1978). Also author of *Life and Labour,* Sidgwick & Jackson. Contributor to magazines and newspapers, including *News of the World.*

SIDELIGHTS: Stewart wrote: "My main interest in life has been politics and all my writing has been derived from this. I am especially concerned with education, housing, and international affairs. As secretary of state for foreign and commonwealth affairs, I have traveled widely."

* * *

STEWART, Phyllis Langton   1933-

BRIEF ENTRY: Born in 1933 in Boston, Mass. American sociologist, educator, and author. Stewart has taught sociology at George Washington University since 1968. She edited *Varieties of Work Experience: The Social Control of Occupational Groups and Roles* (Halsted, 1974). *Address:* Department of Sociology, George Washington University, 2029 G St. N.W., Washington, D.C. 20006.

* * *

STIRLING, Jessica
See COGHLAN, Margaret M.

* * *

STODDARD, George Dinsmore   1897-1981

OBITUARY NOTICE: Born October 8, 1897, in Carbondale, Pa.; died December 28, 1981, in Manhattan, N.Y. Educator and author. Stoddard taught psychology, headed the department of psychology, and was dean of the Graduate College at the University of Iowa from 1925 until 1942 when he accepted the presidency at the University of the State of New York (now State University of New York). He also served as the state's commissioner of education and as a delegate to the first meeting of UNESCO. In 1946 Stoddard was named president of the University of Illinois, where he served for seven years until the board of trustees dismissed him after it discovered that the university was supporting research on a supposed cancer cure.

The American Civil Liberties Union later recognized Stoddard for "resisting political interference in matters of educational policy and administrative discretion—even to the point of discharge from his post." Stoddard joined New York University's School of Education as dean in 1956, becoming chancellor and executive vice-president in 1960. Among his achievments was the establishment of the first Hebrew studies center at a nonsectarian university in the United States. Stoddard subsequently served as chancellor of Long Island University. Among the educator's publications are *A Manual of Child Psychology* and *The Meaning of Intelligence*. Obituaries and other sources: *American Authors and Books, 1640 to the Present Day*, 3rd revised edition, Crown, 1962; *American Men and Women of Science: The Social and Behavioral Sciences*, 12th edition, Bowker, 1973; *Who's Who in the World*, 4th edition, Marquis, 1978; *New York Times*, December 30, 1981.

* * *

STORRY, Richard   1914(?)-1982

OBITUARY NOTICE: Born c. 1914 in Doncaster, England; died February 19, 1982, in Woodeaton, England. Educator, historian, and author best known for his books on Japanese history. On the advice of an instructor at Merton College, Oxford, Storry took a position as lecturer in English at Otaru Higher Commercial School in Hokkaido, Japan, where he remained until 1940. After World War II Storry studied Japan's history full time. His *History of Modern Japan* is recognized as one of the earliest sympathetic postwar profiles of Japan. Because of his devotion to Japanese studies, Storry developed many associations with the Japanese, including acquaintanceships with members of the imperial family. He was one of few Englishmen to receive the Japan Foundation Prize and was the recipient of an *ad hominem* professorship in Japanese studies from St. Antony's College, Oxford. His other writings include *The Double Patriots* and *The Case of Richard Sorge*. Obituaries and other sources: *London Times*, February 25, 1982.

* * *

STOUT, Jeffrey Lee   1950-

PERSONAL: Born September 11, 1950, in Trenton, N.J.; son of Ralph Lewis (a banker) and Betty Ann (Ege) Stout; married Sally Jane Starsky, June 2, 1973; children: Suzannah Elizabeth, Noah Jonathan. *Education:* Brown University, A.B. (magna cum laude), 1972; Princeton University, Ph.D., 1976. *Home:* 8 College Rd., Princeton, N.J. 08540. *Office:* Department of Religion, Princeton University, Princeton, N.J. 08540.

CAREER: Princeton University, Princeton, N.J., instructor, 1975-76, Melancthon Jacobus Instructor, 1976-77, assistant professor of religion, 1977—, John Witherspoon Bicentennial Preceptor, 1981-84. Guest lecturer at University of Illinois, 1976, Amherst College, 1978, and Yale University, 1982. *Member:* American Academy of Religion, Society of Christian Ethics, Phi Beta Kappa. *Awards, honors:* American Council of Learned Societies fellowship, 1979-80.

WRITINGS: The Flight From Authority: Religion, Morality, and the Quest for Autonomy, University of Notre Dame Press, 1981. Contributor of articles and reviews to theology and philosophy journals. Member of editorial board and board of directors of *Journal of Religious Ethics*.

WORK IN PROGRESS: A book on the themes of ethos and tradition.

STOWE, Noel James   1942-

PERSONAL: Born January 16, 1942, in Sacramento, Calif.; son of Harold James (in sales) and Elaine (an educator; maiden name, Hildreth) Stowe; married Gwendolyn Lee (an administrative assistant), November, 1965; children: James Edward. *Education:* Sacramento City College, A.A., 1961; University of Southern California, B.A., 1963, Ph.D., 1970. *Home:* 953 East Driftwood Dr., Tempe, Ariz. 85283. *Office:* Department of History, Arizona State University, Tempe, Ariz. 85287.

CAREER: University of Nevada, Las Vegas, lecturer in history, 1967; Arizona State University, Tempe, assistant professor, 1967-75, associate professor of history, 1975—. *Member:* American Historical Association, Organization of American Historians, American Association for State and Local History, National Council on Public History, Latin American Studies Association, Western History Association, Conference on Latin American History, Oral History Association, Pacific Coast Council on Latin American Studies, Phi Beta Kappa, Phi Kappa Phi.

WRITINGS: California Government: The Challenge of Change, Glencoe, 1975, 2nd edition, 1980.

WORK IN PROGRESS: Research on public history, California and the Southwest, and colonial Mexico.

* * *

STRACHEY, Barbara
See HALPERN, Barbara Strachey

* * *

STRANG, Barbara M(ary) H(ope)   1925-1982

OBITUARY NOTICE—See index for CA sketch: Born April 20, 1925, in Croydon, Surrey, England; died after a brief illness, April 12, 1982. Educator and author. A linguist, Strang studied the historical evolution of the English language and promoted the Tynecide Linguistic Survey. She taught at the University of Newcastle upon Tyne and spoke several languages, including Old English, Gothic, and little-known European languages. Strang wrote two books, *Modern English Structure* and *A History of English*. Obituaries and other sources: *London Times*, April 20, 1982.

* * *

STRASBERG, Lee   1901-1982

OBITUARY NOTICE—See index for CA sketch: Born November 17, 1901, in Budanov, Austria-Hungary (now U.S.S.R.); died of a heart attack, February 17, 1982, in New York, N.Y. Actor, director, educator, and author. Strasberg began his career in 1920 musicals such as "Garrick Gaieties." He went on to direct such theatrical productions as "The House of Connelly," "Clash by Night," and "Men in White," and he appeared in motion pictures beginning in 1974. Though not among the original founders, Strasberg served as the artistic director of the Actors Studio for thirty years. Here he taught "method" acting, a technique of the Russian Konstantin Stanislavsky who expected actors to internalize their roles by relying on their thoughts and feelings. Method acting became renowned for evoking realistic and disciplined performances through physical and emotional exercise. Some of Strasberg's students at the Actors Studio were Marlon Brando, George Peppard, Paul Newman, Marilyn Monroe, Al Pacino, and Jane

Fonda. Strasberg also founded the Group Theatre with Harold Clurman and Cheryl Crawford to inspire a new social consciousness with productions such as "Dead End." In 1969 he founded the Lee Strasberg Theatre Institute with his wife. Strasberg's awards include an Academy Award nomination for best supporting actor in "The Godfather II" and his 1982 election to the Theatre Hall of Fame. "And Justice for All," "Going in Style," and "The Cassandra Crossing" are among his later films. His writings include *Strasberg at the Actors Studio, Lee Strasberg on Acting,* and an autobiography completed just prior to his death. Obituaries and other sources: *Chicago Tribune,* February 18, 1982; *Washington Post,* February 18, 1982, February 21, 1982; *New York Times,* February 18, 1982, March 2, 1982; *London Times,* February 18, 1982; *Time,* March 1, 1982.

* * *

STRAVINSKY, Vera 1889(?)-

PERSONAL: Born c. 1889, in St. Petersburg, Russia (now Leningrad, U.S.S.R.); naturalized U.S. citizen, 1945; married Sergei Sudekine (a painter and set designer; divorced); married Igor Fedorovich Stravinsky (a composer and conductor), March 9, 1940 (died April 6, 1971). *Address:* c/o David R. Godine Publisher, Inc., 306 Dartmouth St., Boston, Mass. 02116.

CAREER: Worked as actress on stage and in films in Russia (now U.S.S.R.); costume designer for opera, ballet, and Sergei Diaghilev in Paris, France; painter.

WRITINGS: (With Robert Craft) *Stravinsky in Pictures and Documents* (biography), Simon & Schuster, 1978; *Fantastic Cities and Other Paintings* (nonfiction), David R. Godine, 1979.

SIDELIGHTS: Vera Stravinsky worked as a costume designer and painter in Paris after emigrating from Russia after the Communist revolution. While a member of the large Russian settlement in the French capital, she met the famous composer and fellow emigre Igor Stravinsky. Beginning a love affair in 1922, the couple married in 1940 after the death of Igor Stravinsky's first wife. While her husband established musical history, Vera pursued a career in painting. On the death of Stravinsky in 1971, his wife inherited a wealth of valuable, mostly unpublished documents and memorabilia. Eight years later, Vera Stravinsky and Robert Craft, Igor's longtime confidant, compiled a large volume marking use of much of this information.

Titled *Stravinsky in Pictures and Documents,* the coffee table book has more than six hundred and fifty pages and numerous plates. Ned Rorem of the *Washington Post Book World* called the work a "gorgeous scrapbook." It contains letters, newspaper clippings, musical compositions, reviews, diaries, and photographs of the composer and his often prominent acquaintances. "The pictures are mostly little-known Kodak shots introducing us into the parlors and cafes and onto the beaches and stages of yore with the awe of utter reality," explained Rorem. "Here sits Debussy, a bourgeois faun, and Rimsky-Korsakov with cigarette, and Ravel with mother, all with the same breathing aliveness as Nijinsky, variously in straw hat and derby, dapper and vulnerable, palpable yet vanished." Michael Steinberg of the *New York Times Book Review* noted that the book "is indispensable as well as entertaining and sometimes moving—a mass of material on Igor Stravinsky . . . put together by the two people who knew him best." *New Statesman*'s Peter Porter complimented the authors on their endeavor: "Robert Craft and Vera Stravinsky draw the portrait of a genius quite without the usual distortions of wasted talent,

and the warts they make no effort to hide are seen for the unimportant specks they are."

BIOGRAPHICAL/CRITICAL SOURCES: Arnold Dobrin, *Igor Stravinsky: His Life and Times,* Crowell, 1970; *New York Times,* November 4, 1971; *Newsweek,* January 8, 1979; *Washington Post Book World,* January 14, 1979; *New York Times Book Review,* January 28, 1979; *New Yorker,* February 5, 1979; *Wall Street Journal,* February 26, 1979, December 13, 1979; *Progressive,* March, 1979; *London Observer,* March 25, 1979; *Economist,* April 14, 1979; *Listener,* April 26, 1979; *Illustrated London News,* May, 1979; *Music Educators Journal,* May, 1979; *New Statesman,* May 4, 1979; *Choice,* June, 1979; *Notes,* September, 1979; *Books in Canada,* November, 1979; *Hudson Review,* winter, 1979-80.*

* * *

STREHLOW, Theodor (George Heinrich) 1908-

BRIEF ENTRY: Born June 6, 1908, in Hermannsburg, Australia. Australian anthropologist, classicist, educator, and author. Strehlow began his career as a patrol officer in Australia's Northern Territory. A professor of aboriginal Australian languages and linguistics at University of Adelaide from 1970 to 1973, Strehlow founded and became director of the Strehlow Research Foundation in 1973. He was awarded a Silver Jubilee Medal by Queen Elizabeth II in 1977. Strehlow's books include *Aranda Traditions* (Melbourne University Press, 1947), *Journey to Horseshoe Bend* (Angus & Robertson, 1969), and *Songs of Central Australia* (Angus & Robertson, 1971). He also produced several films dealing with aboriginal Australian customs and behavior. *Address:* 30 Da Costa Ave., Prospect, South Australia 5082.

* * *

STREHLOW, Theodor George Henry
See STREHLOW, Theodor (George Heinrich)

* * *

STREIB, Dan(iel Thomas) 1928-
(J. Faragut Jones, Jonathan Schofield)

PERSONAL: Born November 8, 1928, in Rockford, Ill.; son of Daniel J. (a merchant) and Nina (Strayer) Streib; married Mary Gray (a teacher), February 10, 1951; children: Dan J., Rebecca V. *Education:* University of Iowa, B.A., 1950; received M.A. from San Diego State University. *Home and office:* 6267 Spruce Lake Ave., San Diego, Calif. 92119. *Agent:* Barbara Lowenstein, 250 West 57th St., New York, N.Y. 10019.

CAREER: Davenport Democrat, Davenport, Iowa, reporter, 1950-51; 3M Co., Chicago, Ill., sales promotion supervisor, 1954-60; Phillips-Ramsey Advertising Agency, San Diego, Calif., account executive, 1961-70; Santana High School, Santee, Calif., teacher of business, 1967-80; writer, 1980—. *Military service:* U.S. Army, Infantry, 1951-53; served in Korea; became first lieutenant; received Silver Star. *Member:* San Diego Writers Workshop.

WRITINGS: Brannon, Pinnacle Books, 1978; *Vengeance Platoon,* Manor, 1979; *Down Under and Dirty,* Jove, 1981; *The Hawaiian Takeover,* Jove, 1981; *The Virgin Stealers,* Jove, 1981.

"Hawk" series; published by Jove, 1981: *Hawk: The Cargo Gods; . . . The Deadly Crusader; . . . The Death Riders; . . . The Enemy Within; . . . The Mind Twisters; . . . The Power*

Barons; . . . The Predators; . . . The Seeds of Evil; . . . The Treasure Divers; . . . The California Shakedown.

Under pseudonym J. Faragut Jones; published by Dell: *Waters Dark and Deep*, 1981; *Tracking the Wolfpack*, 1981; *The Scourge of Scapa Flow*, 1981; *Pearl Harbor Periscopes*, 1981; *Pacific Standoff*, 1982. Also author of *Deepwater Showdown.*

Also author, under pseudonym Jonathan Schofield, of *Tomahawks and Long Rifles, Shellfire on Bay,* and *Volunteers for Glory,* all for Dell.

WORK IN PROGRESS: A six-book series entitled "Counterforce" for Fawcett.

SIDELIGHTS: Streib commented: "I am a world traveler. I have been on six continents, in fifty nations, traveling alone. I research unique locales for the 'Hawk' and 'Counterforce' series, and try to use only locales I have visited when writing contemporary novels."

*   *   *

STRUGATSKII, Arkadii (Natanovich) 1925-

PERSONAL: Surname is pronounced Strew-*gots*-key; born August 28, 1925, in Batumi, Georgia, U.S.S.R.; son of Natan (a bibliographer) and Aleksandra Litvinchova (a teacher) Strugatskii; married Elena Oshanina (a sinologist), 1955; children: Natalia (stepdaughter), Mariia. *Education:* Institute of Foreign Languages, degree, 1949. *Politics:* Marxist. *Religion:* Atheist. *Home:* Moscow, 11751 Prospect Vernadskozo 119, 273, U.S.S.R. *Agent:* Vsesojuznoje Agentstvo Po Avtorskim Pravam (VAAP), Lavrushinskii pereulok, 17 Moscow, U.S.S.R. 109017.

CAREER: Goslitisdat (now Khudozhestvennaia Literatura; publisher), Moscow, U.S.S.R., editor, 1959-61; Detgiz (publisher), Moscow, U.S.S.R., editor, 1961-64; free-lance writer and translator of English and Japanese, 1964—. *Military service:* Served in U.S.S.R., 1943-55; became senior lieutenant. *Member:* Union of Soviet Writers, Union of Soviet Journalists. *Awards, honors:* Second award of Ministry of Education, 1959, for *The Country of the Purple Clouds;* Aelita prize from Union of Soviet Writers, 1981, for *Beetle in the Anthill.*

WRITINGS—All with brother Boris Strugatskii, except as noted; in English translation: *Put' na Amal'teiu* (collection of stories), Molodaia Gvardiia, 1960, title novella published as "Destination: Amaltheia" in anthology *Destination: Amaltheia,* translated by Koesnikov, Central Books, 1962; *Vozvrashchenie (polden', XXII vek)* (collection of short stories), translation by Patrick J. McGuire published as *Noon: Twenty-second Century,* Macmillan, 1978; *Dalekaia raduga,* Molodaia Gvardiia, 1964, translation by A. G. Myers published as *Far Rainbow,* Mir, 1967 (also see below); *Khishchnye veshchi,* Molodaia Gvardiia, 1965, translation by Leonid Renen published as *The Final Circle of Paradise,* DAW Books, 1976; *Ponedel'nik nachinaetsia v subbotu,* Detskaia literatura, 1965, translation by Renen published as *Monday Begins on Saturday,* DAW Books, 1977 (also see below); *Trudno byt' bogom; Ponedel'nik nachinaetsia v subbotu,* Molodaia Gvardiia, 1966, former story translated by Wendayne Ackerman and published as *Hard to Be a God,* Seabury, 1973; *Vtoroe nashestvie Marsian,* [U.S.S.R.], 1968, translation by Matias and Barrett published as "The Second Martian Invasion" in *Vortex: A New Soviet Science Fiction,* edited by C. G. Bearne, MacGibbon & Kee, 1970 (also see below); *Obitaemyi ostrov,* [Moscow, U.S.S.R.], 1969, translation by Helen Saltz Jacobson published as *Prisoners of Power,* Macmillian, 1977.

Gadkie lebedi, [Frankfort, West Germany], 1972, translation by Alice Stone Nakhimovsky and Aleksander Nakhimovshy published as *The Ugly Swans,* Macmillan, 1979; *Ulitka na sklone; Skazka o troike* (former novella first published in magazine in U.S.S.R., 1966-68; latter novella first published in magazine in U.S.S.R., 1968), [Frankfort], 1972, translation of former published as *The Snail on the Slope,* Gollancz, 1980, translation of the latter by Antonina W. Bouis published as *Tale of the Troika* in *Roadside Picnic; Tale of the Troika,* Macmillan, 1977; *Piknik na obochine,* [U.S.S.R.], 1972, published as *Roadside Picnic* in *Roadside Picnic; Tale of the Troika* (see above); "Za milliard let do knotsa sveta" (first published in *Znanie-sila* magazine in U.S.S.R., 1976-77), translation by Bouis published as *Definitely Maybe: A Manuscript Discovered Under Unusual Circumstances,* Macmillan, 1978; *Far Rainbow; The Second Invasion of Mars,* the former translated by Bouis, the latter translated by Gary Kern, Macmillan, 1979; "Zhuck v muraveinike" (first published in *Znanie-sila* magazine in U.S.S.R., 1979-80), translation by Bouis published as *Beetle in the Anthill,* Macmillan, 1980; *Space Apprentice,* Macmillan, 1981.

Work represented in anthologies, including *Path Into the Unknown: The Best of Soviet Science Fiction,* MacGibbon & Kee, 1966.

In Russian: *Izvne,* [U.S.S.R.], 1960; *Strana bagrovykh tuch* (title means "The Country of the Purple Clouds"), Detgiz, 1960; *Shest' spichek* (collection of stories), [U.S.S.R.], 1960; Stazhery (title means "Probationers"; collection of short stories), Molodaia Gvardiia, 1962; *Popytka k begstvu* (title means "Escape Attempt"), [U.S.S.R.], 1962; (sole editor) *Tridtsat' pervoe iiunia,* [Moscow], 1968; "Otel' u pogibshego al'pinista," published in *Yunost* magazine in U.S.S.R., 1970; *Malysh* (title means "The Kid"; novella), [U.S.S.R.], 1971 (also see below); *Polden', XXII vek; Malysh,* Detskaia literatura, 1975; "Paren' iz preispodnei" (title means "The Fellow From Hell"; novella), published in anthology *Nezrimyi most* (title means "Invisible Bridge"), edited by Evgenii Pavlovich Brandis, Detskaia literatura, 1976.

Work represented in anthologies, including *Ellinskii sekret* (title means "The Hellenic Secret"), edited by Evgenii Pavlovich Brandis and Vladimir Ivanovich Dmitrevshii, Lenizdat, 1966.

SIDELIGHTS: Perhaps the best known Soviet science fiction writers outside Russia are the brothers Arkadii and Boris Strugatskii. Virtually undiscovered by Western readers in the early 1970's, the Strugatskii writing team has increased in popularity as its works have been gradually translated into English. Algis Budrys of the *Washington Post Book World* speculated on the reason the Strugatskii brothers have finally gained recognition. They "are among the most Westernized sources of Eastern European SF," he noted, "and normally their work thus rings familiarly upon the ears of the American aficionado." This explanation aside, other critics claim the Strugatskiis exhibit a technical mastery superior to other Soviet authors.

Indeed, reviewers have cited their separate careers as ideal training for a joint effort in writing science fiction. Arkadii edits and translates Japanese and English literature while Boris works as an astronomer, astrophysicist, and computer mathematician. The *Times Literary Supplement*'s C. R. Pike called such experience "a formidable background" conducive to the creation of "high-calibre science fiction." "Since the late 1950's," the critic continued, the Strugatskiis "have fashioned a body of original and enlightened works of speculative literature. Remarkable in their perception of the conflicts between . . . man and the universe which may or may not be his, the

Strugatsky's [*sic*] stories and novels have achieved a unique status within Soviet literature and . . . deserve the attention of Western readers.''

Nevertheless, the Strugatskiis maintain a curious position in the Soviet Union. During the governmental relaxation of censorship in the early and mid-1960's, the brothers began to deal in their writing with topics normally avoided. ''By the early 1960s,'' Patrick L. McGuire explained in *Anatomy of Wonder,* ''they found themes worthy of their skill—in the process moving from fairly hard SF to 'softer' works emphasizing social and moral concerns.'' Two books written in this vein are *Hard to Be a God* and *Prisoners of Power.*

In *Hard to Be a God,* employees from the Institute of Experimental History on Earth must go to an underdeveloped feudal planet to promote class warfare and progress. The novel raises some difficult questions about communism. *New Statesman*'s T. A. Shippey listed some of its themes as ''the difficulty of changing belief systems, the way in which innovations are misunderstood, the obstinate habit slaves have of understanding their masters better than their liberators, [and] the danger that revolutions can turn out to be cyclic rather than spiral.''

Prisoners of Power explores similar ideas. The book is an account of a youth from a futuristic utopian world trapped on a planet ''beset,'' disclosed Tom J. Lewis in *World Literature Today,* ''with nuclear war, pollution of several kinds, totalitarianism and the genetic degeneration of its humanoid population.'' When the youth tries to rid the planet of its ills in an effort to create a better world, many sociopolitical problems are highlighted. Lewis enumerated some: ''Can a society which does not want to be controlled be led to some end against its will; can a single individual, no matter how great an advantage he possesses over others, make any truly significant changes in the social order; can totalitarianism be eradicated by any but totalitarian methods?'' The Strugatskiis, however, offer no easy answers to the questions they pose. They ''are impressive in their refusal to settle for simplistic solutions such as 'liberation,''' complimented a *New Republic* writer. Instead, they acknowledge that such problems are, in the words of Lewis, ''a condition endemic to humankind.''

When the promise of ''the thaw'' on Soviet letters waned, the brothers started to write sharp bureaucratic satires such as *The Snail on the Slope* and *Tale of the Troika.* An incomprehensible bureaucracy named the Directorate is the object of criticism in *The Snail on the Slope.* The Directorate is responsible for both the preservation and the destruction of an unusual forest on a strange planet. Two inhabitants of the forest try to procure a coherent policy regarding it from the Directorate but are unsuccessful. One dweller eventually falls prey to its senseless directives while the other totally alienates himself from the bureaucracy. Likewise, *Tale of the Troika* was described by Gerald Jonas in the *New York Times Book Review* as ''a heated satire of bureaucratic excess, set in a whimsical futuristic society.'' Lewis stated that the book reiterates something ''everyone in the Northern and more people in the Southern Hemisphere by now know[:] what bureaucratic incompetence and mismanagement are and how . . . [they] degrade . . . the lives of us all.''

A crackdown on the Strugatskiis and other writers came in the late 1960's and early 1970's. As the Soviet Government tightened its controls on literature, the works previously allowed were no longer acceptable in the stricter climate. In 1969 the brothers' novel *The Ugly Swans* was rejected by the censor immediately before its scheduled publication. The manuscript was then passed along and read in private circles and was ultimately published by Russian emigres in West Germany in 1972. Arkadii offered *CA* a different version of the affair: ''In 1970 *The Ugly Swans* was ready to be published by the Molodaia Gvardiia publishing house. But just then a manuscript of the novel got abroad and was soon published in an emigre magazine. That was the end of *The Ugly Swans* in the Soviet Union.'' The authors condemned the unauthorized edition, but their position in their native country had changed.

''In the 1970s,'' recounted McGuire, ''the Strugatskiis found themselves in a sort of limbo. Some of their older works have been reissued in book form in the Soviet Union, and new material has come out in magazines and anthologies. Indeed, books composed of this new material have appeared with Soviet consent not only in the United States and elsewhere in the West, but in East European countries such as East Germany. But with the single partial exception of one new novelette, 'The Kid,' . . . published in a combined edition with *Noon: 22nd Century* . . . , none of the new Strugatskii works have been collected into books.'' ''Thus,'' the writer concluded, ''thanks either to division within the leadership or to a calculated decision to administer only a measured punishment, the Strugatskiis have neither been outlawed nor fully accepted as writers.'' Pike concurred that while the brothers ''have been attacked, they have also been defended. They have stimulated an authentic debate on values and the approach of literature to individual and collective life, a debate in which the weight of both [official periodicals] *Pravda* and *Izvestiia* has been felt.''

The Strugatskii books published in the West have been met with enthusiasm. *Roadside Picnic,* printed in an edition with *Tale of the Troika,* was hailed by Alex de Jonge in *Spectator* as ''a very good piece of science fiction.'' In this novella, aliens have briefly camped out in a part of Canada, leaving behind them a number of ''visitation zones'' in which the ordinary earthly territory has been transformed into an alien area. The zones are fraught with dangers such as ''meat grinders,'' ''burning fluff,'' and ''witches jelly,'' a bone-eating substance. Although treacherous, the zones are visited nightly by ''stalkers'' who steal the valuable objects also left behind by the aliens. One stalker, Redrick Schuhart, is the most successful thief because he has cultivated a ''preternatural sensitivity,'' as critic Jonas dubbed it, to the strange environment of the zones. Lewis conjectured that *Roadside Picnic* matches ''the techniques and quality of the best 'encounter'-oriented science fiction.'' It is ''a fascinatingly presented story,'' he added.

A later novel, *Definitely Maybe,* advances the hypothesis that ''the universe can sense attempted reversals of entropy,'' explained reviewer Budrys. The story involves several scientists who are at the point of discovering various important truths about the universe. When they find their research thwarted by odd occurences, they meet to discuss the reasons for such interference. After much discussion the scientists conclude that the universe is angry with them for investigating too closely its workings. Consequently, it has sabotaged their research to render it useless and them foolish. Lewis asserted that despite *Definitely Maybe*'s ''outlandish theory,'' it ''matters little compared to the procedures we become involved in as the novel develops. What we come to see as important is that nothing is as dead as a dead certainty, or that the only certainty is that nothing is certain.''

AVOCATIONAL INTERESTS: History, sociology, literature, Japanese medieval literature.

BIOGRAPHICAL/CRITICAL SOURCES: Renaissance, summer, 1973; *New York Times Book Review,* September 23, 1973, May 22, 1977; *Galaxy,* November, 1973; *Foundation,* January, 1974, September, 1978, May, 1979; *New Statesman,* January

18, 1974; *Futures*, June, 1974; *Locus*, August 20, 1974; *Luna Monthly*, spring, 1975, spring, 1977; *New Scientist*, May 15, 1975; *Times Literary Supplement*, May 23, 1975, June 16, 1978, November 7, 1980; *Science Fiction Commentary*, December, 1975; *Analog: Science Fiction/Science Fact*, March, 1977, September, 1977, May 25, 1981; *Science Fiction Review*, May, 1977; *Best Sellers*, November, 1977, October, 1979; *New Republic*, November 26, 1977; *Vector*, March/April, 1978, May/June, 1978, March/April, 1979; *London Observer*, July 2, 1978, June 24, 1979, August 17, 1980; *Spectator*, August 26, 1978; *Washington Post Book World*, September 3, 1978, January 27, 1980; *Magazine of Fantasy and Science Fiction*, November, 1978, July, 1979, April, 1981; *World Literature Today*, spring, 1979, summer, 1979, winter, 1979, winter, 1980; *Science Fiction and Fantasy Book Review*, August, 1979; *Punch*, June 25, 1980; Neil Barron, editor, *Anatomy of Wonder: A Critical Guide to Science Fiction*, 2nd edition, Bowker, 1981.

—Sketch by Anne M. Guerrini

*   *   *

STRUGATSKII, Boris (Natanovich) 1933-

PERSONAL: Surname is pronounced Strew-*gots*-key; born April 15, 1933, in Leningrad, U.S.S.R.; son of Natan (a bibliographer) and Aleksandra Litvinchova (a teacher) Strugatskii; married Adelaida Karpeliuk (an astronomer), 1957; children: Andrei Borisovich. *Education:* Leningrad University, degree in astronomy, 1956. *Politics:* Marxist. *Religion:* Atheist. *Home:* Leningrad, 196070, ul. Pobedy 4, 186, U.S.S.R. *Agent:* Vsesojuznoje Agentstvo Po Avtorskim Pravam (VAAP), Lavrushinskii pereulok, 17 Moscow, U.S.S.R. 109017.

CAREER: Pulkovskaia Observatory, U.S.S.R., astronomer, astrophysicist, computer mathematician, and associate, 1956-64; free-lance writer, 1964—. *Member:* Union of Soviet Writers. *Awards, honors:* Second award of the Ministry of Education, 1959, for *The Country of the Purple Clouds;* Aelita prize from Union of Soviet Writers, 1981, for *Beetle in the Anthill.*

WRITINGS—All with brother Arkadii Strugatskii; in English translation: *Put' na Amal'teiu* (collection of stories), Molodaia Gvardiia, 1960, title novella published as "Destination: Amaltheia" in anthology *Destination: Amaltheia*, translated by Kolesnikov, Central Books, 1962; *Vozvrashchenie (polden', XXII vek)* (collection of short stories), translation by Patrick J. McGuire published as *Noon: Twenty-second Century*, Macmillan, 1978; *Dalekaia raduga*, Molodaia Gvardiia, 1964, translation by A. G. Myers published as *Far Rainbow*, Mir, 1967 (also see below); *Khishchnye veshchi*, Molodaia Gvardiia, 1965, translation by Leonid Renen published as *The Final Circle of Paradise*, DAW Books, 1976; *Ponedel'nik nachinaetsia v subbotu*, Detskaia literatura, 1965, translation by Renen published as *Monday Begins on Saturday*, DAW Books, 1977 (also see below); *Trudno byt' bogom; Ponedel'nik nachinaetsia v subbotu*, Molodaia Gvardiia, 1966, former story translated by Wendayne Ackerman and published as *Hard to Be a God*, Seabury, 1973; *Vtoroe nashestvie Marsian*, [U.S.S.R.], 1968, translation by Matias and Barrett published as "The Second Martian Invasion" in *Vortex: A New Soviet Science Fiction*, edited by C. G. Bearne, MacGibbon & Kee, 1970 (also see below); *Obitaemyi ostrov*, [Moscow, U.S.S.R.], 1969, translation by Helen Saltz Jacobson published as *Prisoners of Power*, Macmillan, 1977.

Gadkie lebedi [Frankfort, West Germany], 1972, translation by Alice Stone Nakhimovsky and Aleksander Nakhimovshy

published as *The Ugly Swans*, Macmillan, 1979; *Ulitka na sklone; Skazka o troike* (former novella first published in magazine in U.S.S.R., 1966-68; latter novella first published in magazine in U.S.S.R., 1968), [Frankfort], 1972, translation of former published as *The Snail on the Slope*, Gollancz, 1980, translation of the latter by Antonina W. Bouis published as *Tale of the Troika* in *Roadside Picnic; Tale of the Troika*, Macmillan, 1977; *Piknik na obochine*, [U.S.S.R.], 1972, published as *Roadside Picnic* in *Roadside Picnic; Tale of the Troika* (see above); "Za milliard let do kontsa sveta" (first published in *Znanie-sila* magazine in U.S.S.R., 1976-77), translation by Bouis published as *Definitely Maybe: A Manuscript Discovered Under Unusual Circumstances*, Macmillan, 1978; *Far Rainbow; The Second Invasion of Mars*, the former translated by Bouis, the latter translated by Gary Kern, Macmillan, 1979; "Zhuck v muraveinike" (first published in *Znanie-sila* magazine in U.S.S.R., 1979-80), translation by Bouis published as *Beetle in the Anthill*, Macmillan, 1980; *Space Apprentice*, Macmillan, 1981.

Work represented in anthologies, including *Path Into the Unknown: The Best of Soviet Science Fiction*, MacGibbon & Kee, 1966.

In Russian: *Izvne*, [U.S.S.R.], 1960; *Strana Bagrovykh tuch* (title means "The Country of the Purple Clouds"), Detgiz, 1960; *Shest' spicheck* (collection of stories), [U.S.S.R.], 1960; *Stazhery* (title means "Probationers"; collection of short stories), Molodaia Gvardiia, 1962; *Popytka k begstvu* (title means "Escape Attempt"), [U.S.S.R.], 1962; "Otel' u pogibshego al'pinista," published in *Yunost* magazine in U.S.S.R., 1970; *Malysh* (title means "The Kid"; novella), [U.S.S.R.], 1971 (also see below); *Polden', XXII vek; Malysh*, Detskaia literatura, 1975; "Paren' iz preispodnei" (title means "The Fellow From Hell"; novella), published in anthology *Nezrimyi most* (title means "Invisible Bridge"), edited by Evgenii Pavlovich Brandis, Detskaia literatura, 1976.

Work represented in anthologies, including *Ellinskii sekret* (title means "The Hellenic Secret"), edited by Evgenii Pavlovich Brandis and Vladimir Ivanovich Dmitrevshii, Lenizdat, 1966.

SIDELIGHTS: One half of the internationally renowned Russian science fiction team, the Strugatskii brothers, Boris Strugatskii was an astrophysicist, astronomer, and computer mathematician before entering into the successful collaboration that has earned him literary acclaim. Strugatskii's technical background, coupled with his brother Arkaddii's editorial and literary experience, is often cited by critics as a substantive reason for the high quality of the brothers' writings.

Considered to be among the most Westernized of the Eastern European science fiction writers, the brothers Strugatskii have often dealt with subject matter deliberately shunned by other Soviet authors. In books such as *Hard to Be God* and *Prisoner of Power*, the Strugatskiis explore moral and social issues, raising serious questions about communism and totalitarianism. In other books, including *Tale of the Troika* and *The Snail on the Slope*, they acrimoniously satirize bureaucratic bungling, revealing its degrading effect on human life.

After the Soviet Government tightened its controls on literature in the late 1960's, a Strugatskii novel, *The Ugly Swans*, was rejected for publication by the censors. When, in the early 1970's, an unauthorized edition of the same book appeared in an emigre magazine in West Germany, the brothers' literary position within the U.S.S.R. altered abruptly. They "found themselves in a sort of limbo," explained Patrick L. McGuire in *Anatomy of Wonder*, "neither . . . outlawed nor fully accepted as writers.'' Although their older work continues to be reissued and read in their native country and, with Soviet consent, elsewhere throughout the world, their new work has been relegated, in the U.S.S.R., to publication in magazines and anthologies rather than collected into Soviet books. English translations of both their older and more recent works, however, have been enthusiastically received by Western audiences.

See also *STRUGATSKII, Arkadii (Natanovich)*.

AVOCATIONAL INTERESTS: Sociology, some branches of astronomy.

BIOGRAPHICAL/CRITICAL SOURCES: Renaissance, summer, 1973; *New York Times Book Review,* September 23, 1973, May 22, 1977; *Galaxy,* November, 1973; *Foundation,* January, 1974, September, 1978, May, 1979; *New Statesman,* January 18, 1974; *Futures,* June, 1974; *Locus,* August 20, 1974; *Luna Monthly,* spring, 1975, spring, 1977; *New Scientist,* May 15, 1975; *Times Literary Supplement,* May 23, 1975, June 16, 1978, November 7, 1980; *Science Fiction Commentary,* December, 1975; *Analog: Science Fiction/Science Fact,* March, 1977, September, 1977, May 25, 1981; *Science Fiction Review,* May, 1977; *Best Sellers,* November, 1977, October, 1979; *New Republic,* November 26, 1977; *Vector,* March/April, 1978, May/June, 1978, March/April, 1979; *London Observer,* July 2, 1978, June 24, 1979, August 17, 1980; *Spectator,* August 26, 1978; *Washington Post Book World,* September 3, 1978, January 27, 1980; *Magazine of Fantasy and Science Fiction,* November, 1978, July, 1979, April, 1981; *World Literature Today,* spring, 1979, summer, 1979, winter, 1979, winter, 1980; *Science Fiction and Fantasy Book Review,* August, 1979; *Punch,* June 25, 1980; Neil Barron, editor, *Anatomy of Wonder: A Critical Guide to Science Fiction,* 2nd edition, Bowker, 1981.

*   *   *

STUBER, Florian (Cy)   1947-

PERSONAL: Born March 1, 1947, in Buffalo, N.Y.; son of Florian George (a sheet metal worker) and Dorothy (a registered nurse; maiden name, Blatz) Stuber. *Education:* Columbia University, B.A. (cum laude), 1968, M.A. (with highest honors), 1969, Ph.D. (with distinction), 1980. *Residence:* New York, N.Y. *Office:* Department of English, Barnard Hall, Columbia University, Broadway and 116th St., New York, N.Y. 10027.

CAREER: Columbia University, New York, N.Y., instructor in English, 1970-75, 1980—, lecturer at Barnard College, 1979—, administrative coordinator of Conferences on the Humanities and Public Policy Issues, 1977—. Adjunct instructor at Fashion Institute of Technology, 1977—. *Member:* Modern Language Association of America, American Society for Eighteenth-Century Studies (ASECS), Northeast America Society for Eighteenth-Century Studies (NEASECS), Dickens Fellowship of New York (vice-president, 1972-75). *Awards, honors:* Woodrow Wilson fellow, 1968-69.

WRITINGS: Small Comforts for Hard Times: Humanists on Public Policy, Columbia University Press, 1977. Writer for WBAI-FM Radio, 1978-80.

WORK IN PROGRESS: A book, tentatively titled *Clarissa and Her World: The Secular Humanism of Samuel Richardson.* Co-authoring a television series, ''Clarissa.''

STULTIFER, Morton
See CURTIS, Richard (Alan)

*   *   *

SULLIVAN, Vernon
See VIAN, Boris

*   *   *

SUMMERS, JoAn   1943-

PERSONAL: Born August 14, 1943, in Seadrift, Tex.; daughter of Jofred C. and Eva (Darst) Holder; married Robert Andrew Summers (a minister, editor, and author), June 15, 1963; children: Richard Kipling. *Education:* Sam Houston State University, B.A. (cum laude), 1965. *Religion:* ''Born-again Christian.'' *Home:* 631 Grant, Duncanville, Tex. 75137. *Office address:* P.O. Box 210733, Dallas, Tex. 75211.

CAREER: North Shore Junior High School, Houston, Tex., teacher, 1965-68; *Christ for the Nations,* Dallas, Tex., associate editor, 1974-75; Backyard Television Productions, Dallas, producer, scriptwriter, set designer, puppeteer, and hostess of television show ''Backyard,'' 1975—; Tye Preston Memorial Library, Canyon Lake, Tex., secretary, 1977-79. Judge and master of ceremonies, Texas Junior Miss Pageant, 1976-79. *Member:* Women Aglow Fellowship (vice-president).

WRITINGS: God's Little Animals: Easy Illustrations and Bible Parallels (juvenile), Gospel Publishing, 1969; *Happy Faces: Animals Tell Their Favorite Stories* (juvenile), Gospel Publishing, 1971; (editor) *Living Promises,* Logos International, 1973; *Fruitbasket Friends* (juvenile), Logos International, 1975; (with Richard D. Coss) *Wanted,* Beta Book, 1977; *Fruitbasket Fun* (juvenile), privately printed, 1980. Editor with husband, Robert Summers, of the magazine *New Earth.* Contributor of articles to Christian publications, and author of over one hundred-fifty scripts for the children's television program ''Backyard.''

WORK IN PROGRESS: Backyard Fun, a compilation of puppet plays.

SIDELIGHTS: Summers's work centers around her life as a Christian. Her present involvement with her television show, ''Backyard,'' is an offshoot of her attempt to teach children the Gospel. When she was teaching school she used her summer breaks to develop a young people's program for her father-in-law's church, creating her own story-telling and puppet programs. This religious program expanded to include many churches in the Texas area, and she and her husband later developed Bible clubs for children while living in California. But her ability to develop self-sufficient neighborhood programs was limited. As Summers explains: ''We would go to one neighborhood in the morning and hold a club. Then we'd pack up our gear and do another in the afternoon and another at night. But after the summer ended we left, and almost all the clubs folded for lack of someone to carry on. I knew Bob and I couldn't live there and do it ourselves. Yet I began to pray, 'Lord, how can I maintain a contact with children?' Finally the answer came—through television.''

With her husband, she created ''Backyard,'' which premiered on Trinity Broadcasting Network (KTBN-TV) in Los Angeles in November, 1975. With its cast of volunteer actors and puppeteers, it now airs in more than twelve cities, including Chicago, New York, and Los Angeles. Summers told *CA* about her work: ''For the past five years, I have written four thirty-minute scripts per month for the production of 'Backyard.' I strongly believe that what I do to touch others must be positive and uplifting. It must inspire them to reach beyond their everyday limitations to a happier, more fulfilled life through Jesus Christ.''

BIOGRAPHICAL/CRITICAL SOURCES: National Courier, June 25, 1976; *New Braunfels Herald,* July 15, 1976.

* * *

SUNDARANANDA
See NAKASHIMA, George Katsutoshi

* * *

SUNDQUIST, Ralph Roger, Jr. 1922-

BRIEF ENTRY: Born December 9, 1922, in Yakima, Wash. American educator and author. Sundquist was ordained as a Presbyterian minister in 1951, and he has been a professor of religion and education at Hartford Seminary Foundation since 1965. He is also chairman of the Connecticut Commission on United Ministries in Higher Education and of the Church Education Center in Hartford. Sundquist wrote *Consider Your Ministry* (1963) and *Whom God Chooses: The Child in the Church* (Geneva Press, 1964, Westminster, 1973). *Address:* 9 Livingston Rd., Bloomfield, Conn. 06002; and 481 Farmington Ave., Hartford, Conn. 06105.

* * *

SUPER SANTA
See BERMAN, Ed

* * *

SURREY, Peter J. 1928-

PERSONAL: Born June 12, 1928, in Timmins, Ontario, Canada; came to the United States in 1954, naturalized citizen, 1960; son of Herbert and Annie Surrey; children: Margaret Ann. *Education:* University of Toronto, B.A., 1951; Trinity College, S.T.B., 1954; University of Northern Illinois, M.S., 1971. *Politics:* ''Progressive conservative.'' *Home:* 115 North Fourth, Savanna, Ill. 61074.

CAREER: Ordained Episcopal priest, 1955; pastor in Savanna, Ill., 1964—. Member of Savanna's Streets and Alleys Committee and Library Board. *Member:* Savanna Writing Club.

WRITINGS: The Small Town Church, Abingdon, 1981.

WORK IN PROGRESS: An expose of ''left-handed agents'' of the Soviet Union's intelligence network, the KGB; a novel.

SIDELIGHTS: Surrey commented: ''I believe a book should be honest, humorous, and aimed at simple souls.''

* * *

SUTCLIFFE, Anthony (Richard) 1942-

PERSONAL: Born September 28, 1942, in Northampton, England; son of Frederick (a builder and estate agent) and Dora (Shaw) Sutcliffe; married Moyra Elizabeth Gouldsbrough (a city planner), September 9, 1972; children: Isabel Margaret, Edgar Mark. *Education:* Merton College, Oxford, B.A. (with honors), 1963; University of Paris, Dr. de l'Universite (with honors), 1966. *Politics:* Liberal. *Religion:* Methodist. *Home:* 21 Slayleigh Ave., Sheffield S10 3RA, England. *Office:* Department of Economic and Social History, University of Sheffield, Sheffield S10 2TN, England.

CAREER: University of Paris, Paris, France, teacher of scientific English, 1964-66; University of Birmingham, Birmingham, England, research fellow in history, 1966-70; University of Sheffield, Sheffield, England, lecturer, 1970-75, reader in urban history, 1975-81, professor, 1981—, acting head of department of economic and social history, 1978-79 and 1980-82. Visiting tutor at Architectural Association School of Architecture, London, England, 1972-74; visiting professor at University of Ottawa, autumn, 1979. Member of Social Science Research Council's Economic and Social History Committee, 1979—. *Member:* Economic History Society (member of council, 1979—), Planning History Group (cofounder; member of executive committee, 1974—), Urban History Group (chairman of council, 1980—).

WRITINGS: The Autumn of Central Paris: The Defeat of Town Planning, 1850-1970, Edward Arnold, 1970; (editor and contributor) *Multi-Storey Living: The British Working-Class Experience,* Barnes & Noble, 1974; (with R. J. Smith) *Birmingham, 1939-1970,* Oxford University Press, 1974; *The History of Modern Town Planning: A Bibliographic Guide,* Centre for Urban and Regional Studies, University of Birmingham, 1977; (editor and contributor) *The Rise of Modern Urban Planning, 1800-1914,* St. Martin's, 1980; *The History of Urban and Regional Planning: An Annotated Bibliography,* Facts on File, 1981; *Towards the Planned City: Germany, Britain, the United States, and France, 1780-1914,* St. Martin's, 1981; (editor and contributor) *British Town Planning: The Formative Years,* Leicester University Press, 1981.

Contributor: Russell Walden, editor, *The Open Hand: Essays on Le Corbusier,* M.I.T. Press, 1977; G. W. Jones and Alan Norton, editors, *Political Leadership in Local Authorities,* Institute of Local Government Studies, University of Birmingham, 1978; Roberta Martinelli and Lucia Nuti, editors, *Le citta di fondazione* (title means ''Founded Towns''), Marsilio Editori, 1978; Francois Bedarida, Francois Crouzet, and Douglas Johnson, editors, *De Guillaume le conquerant au Marche Commun: Dix siecles d'histoire franco-britannique* (title means ''From William the Conqueror to the Common Market: A Thousand Years of Franco-British History''), Albin Michel, 1979; Ingrid Hammarstroem and Thomas Hall, editors, *Growth and Transformation of the Modern City,* Swedish Council for Building Research, 1979; Gerhard Fehl and Juan Rodriguez-Lores, editors, *Staedtebau um die Jahrhundertwende: Materialien zur Entstehung der Disziplin Staedtebau* (title means ''City Planning at the Turn of the Century: Studies of the Rise of the Science of City Planning''), Deutsche Gemeindeverlag/Verlag W. Kohlhammer, 1980.

Co-editor of ''Studies in History, Planning, and the Environment,'' a series, Mansell, 1976—, and a series of regional economic and social histories of the British Isles, Croom Helm, 1979—. Contributor to *Encyclopedia Americana* and *Urban History Yearbook.* Contributor of articles and reviews to scholarly journals, including *Local Historian, Bulletin of the Society for the Study of Labour History, Architectural Design,* and *Urban History Yearbook.* Member of editorial board of *Urban History Yearbook,* 1974—, and *Journal of Urban History,* 1978—.

WORK IN PROGRESS: Editing proceedings of Planning History Group conference, ''Metropolis, 1890-1940,'' publication by Mansell expected in 1982; editing proceedings of Urban History Group conference, ''The Pursuit of Urban History,'' with Derek Fraser, publication by Edward Arnold expected in 1983.

SIDELIGHTS: Sutcliffe told *CA:* ''I seem to have spent most of my academic career working on various aspects of urban history. In a way, that result is pure accident. I went to Paris in 1963 without very much to do and ended up writing a thesis on the history of the city. But, looking back, I can see that my upbringing and school education marked me out for this type of work. My father's whole business was houses; at school I was captivated by one history teacher, Arnold Fellows, who taught me that the richest historical evidence was all around me.

"I am definitely a frustrated city planner. I relate closely to Haussmann, and I have enjoyed helping the Planning History Group because it brings me closer to people who are actually doing planning. I would like to broaden my interests into world economic development, but perhaps that will have to wait a while. In the meantime, I can indulge my taste for international comparisons by comparing British and North American urban development in the later nineteenth century, my current project."

BIOGRAPHICAL/CRITICAL SOURCES: Journal of Urban History, May, 1981.

* * *

SUTTON, Caroline 1953-

PERSONAL: Born January 10, 1953, in Bryn Mawr, Pa.; daughter of James Anderson (a lawyer) and Caroline Eloise (Chadwick-Collins) Sutton; married Brian Henry Dumaine (a magazine reporter), September 6, 1980. *Education:* Wesleyan University, Middletown, Conn., B.A. (magna cum laude), 1975. *Home:* 136 West 75th St., New York, N.Y. 10023.

CAREER: Charles Scribner's Sons (publisher), New York City, editor, 1976-79; Hilltown Press, New York City, editor, 1980-81.

WRITINGS: How Do They Do That?: Wonders of the Modern World Explained, Morrow, 1981. Contributor to magazines.

* * *

SWEET, Muriel W. 1888-1977

PERSONAL: Born August 13, 1888, in Stamford, Conn.; died March 11, 1977, in Santa Barbara, Calif.; daughter of George A. (an engineer) and Annie (Hoyt) Weber; married Rosen Foote (divorced); married Nathan C. Sweet, March 27, 1915 (died, 1975); children: Virginia F. Haggerty, Nathan C., Jr., Johnn W. (died, 1975).

WRITINGS—For children: Common Edible and Useful Plants of the West (edited by Vinson Brown; illustrated by Emily Reid and others), Naturegraph, 1962; *How Trees Help Your Health* (edited by Brown; illustrated by Jane Judd), Naturegraph, 1965; *Common Edible and Useful Plants of the East and Midwest,* Naturegraph, 1975.

SWINNERTON, A(rnold) R(eber) 1912-

PERSONAL: Born September 28, 1912, in Stoke-on-Trent, England; came to the United States in 1913; naturalized citizen, 1943; son of Bertram John and Elizabeth Camp (a teacher; maiden name, Boerstler) Swinnerton; married Martha Jane Powell; children: Daniel R., Eugene A. *Education:* Dodge Radio School, degree in radio and telegraphy, 1931; Tiffin Business School, secretarial degree, 1934. *Politics:* Democrat. *Religion:* Presbyterian. *Home and office:* 49 Riverlea Park, Tiffin, Ohio 44883.

CAREER: American Standard, Inc., Tiffin, Ohio, plant buyer, 1935-72. *Military service:* U.S. Army, 1943-45.

WRITINGS: Rocky the Cat (juvenile), Addison-Wesley, 1981; *Rocky the Cat, Part II* (juvenile), Addison-Wesley, 1982. Contributor to magazines.

WORK IN PROGRESS: Red Dog, an action adventure story for *Boys Life; The Tumble-Weed Pike Gang,* an action adventure, publication expected in 1982.

SIDELIGHTS: Swinnerton commented: "The ability to put thoughts into words and arranging these words to convey action, reaction, or the simple continuation of a story line is a talent, possibly very small in my case, which has always fascinated me. I expect to be paid when my efforts warrant it, but I have this sneaking feeling that even without pay I would go on writing. For a more compelling reason: Writing is a sitdown job, the best possible position for any steady, prolonged work.

"I am now retired from regular eight-hour duty, and enjoy filling in part of the vacuum with miscellaneous writing, such as short stories, general humor, and forum essays for newspapers. I've been trying to inject humor into book-length stories for children at the eight-to-thirteen age level, an area I feel has been overlooked to a great extent."

* * *

SYRETT, David 1939-

BRIEF ENTRY: Born January 8, 1939, in White Plains, N.Y. American historian, educator, and author. Syrett has taught history at Queens College of the City University of New York since 1966. He wrote *Shipping and the American War, 1775-83: A Study of British Transport Organization* (Athlone Press, 1970) and *The Siege and Capture of Havana, 1762* (Navy Records Society, 1970), and edited *The Lost War: Letters From British Officers During the American Revolution* (Horizon Press, 1975). *Address:* Department of History, Queens College of the City University of New York, 65-30 Kissena Blvd., Flushing, N.Y. 11367.

T

TABER, Julian Ingersoll 1929-

BRIEF ENTRY: Born June 30, 1929, in Detroit, Mich. American psychologist and author. Taber has been a psychologist for the Veterans Administration since 1971. He was a professor of psychology at California State College, California, Pa., from 1969 to 1971. He wrote *Learning and Programmed Instruction* (Addison-Wesley, 1965). *Address:* Psychology Service, Veterans Administration Hospital, Brecksville, Ohio 44141.

* * *

TAEUBER, Irene Barnes 1906-1974

OBITUARY NOTICE: Born December 25, 1906, in Meadville, Mo.; died February 24, 1974, in Hyattsville, Md. Demographer, educator, and author. Taeuber joined the Office of Population Research of Princeton University in 1936, eventually becoming a senior research demographer. She served as president of the Population Association of America and vice-president of the International Union for the Scientific Study of Population. She also headed the social demography section of the American Sociological Association. Taeuber wrote several books in her field, including *The Changing Population of the United States,* which she wrote with her husband, Conrad Taeuber, director of the Population Studies Center of Georgetown University. She also wrote *The Population of Japan,* in which she advised Asian countries to look to Japan for an example of effective population control. Obituaries and other sources: *American Men and Women of Science: The Social and Behavioral Sciences,* 12th edition, Bowker, 1973; *Who's Who of American Women,* 8th edition, Marquis, 1974; *New York Times,* February 26, 1974.

* * *

TAFTI, H. B. Dehqani
See DEHQANI-TAFTI, H. B.

* * *

TANGERMAN, Elmer John 1907-

PERSONAL: Surname is pronounced *Tan*-jer-man; born August 8, 1907, in Hammond, Ind.; son of William John (an inventor and factory superintendent) and Josephine (Karsten) Tangerman; married Mary M. Christopher, September 7, 1929; children: John Tilden (deceased), Mary Tangerman Salerno, Judith Tangerman Hickson. *Education:* Purdue University, B.S.M.E., 1929, M.E., 1937. *Politics:* Republican. *Home:* 111 Ivy Way, Port Washington, N.Y. 11050.

CAREER: *American Machinist,* New York City, assistant editor, 1929-32; *Power,* New York City, assistant editor, 1932-34, associate editor, 1934-36, managing editor, 1937; *American Machinist,* assistant manager, 1938-42; *Power,* business manager, 1942-45; *American Machinist,* managing editor, 1945-50, executive editor, 1950-56; *Product Engineering,* New York City, chief editor, 1957-65, associate publisher, 1965-66; McGraw-Hill Publications, New York City, designer of office of planning and development, 1966-69; writer, 1969—. Technical editor of *Wing* and *McGraw-Hill Digest,* 1942-45; general manager of *Nucleonics,* 1947-49. Woodcarver, with exhibitions of work; public speaker; judge of woodcarving competitions. Past president of local play troupe.

MEMBER: Junior Engineering Technical Society (member of board of directors, 1960-66; president, 1963-64), National Society of Professional Engineers (past chairman of New York Chapter), American Society of Mechanical Engineers, National Wood Carvers Association (vice-chairman, 1975-81), Society of American Value Engineers (honorary member), Tau Beta Pi, Pi Tau Sigma, Sigma Delta Chi, Kappa Phi Sigma, Lambda Chi Alpha, Scabbard and Blade. *Awards, honors:* Medal from Freedom Foundation, 1955, for *Man and His Tools;* Jesse Neal Award of Merit from Associated Business Publications, 1958, for a report on the Soviet Union, 1960, for a report on engineering futures, and 1961, for a report on quality control and redundancy.

WRITINGS: (Editor) *Power Operator's Guide: One Thousand One Practical Helps,* McGraw, 1935; *Whittling and Woodcarving,* McGraw, 1936, reprinted, Dover, 1962; (editor) *Power's Question and Answer Book,* Power, 1938; *Design and Figure Carving,* McGraw, 1940, reprinted, Dover, 1964; (editor) *Power's New Question and Answer Book,* Power, 1944; *Horizons Regained: Seventy Selected Editorial Essays,* Product Engineering, 1964; (editor with Reynold Bennett) *Living Tomorrow, Today: The Magic of New Science and Technology,* J. G. Ferguson, 1969, reprinted as *Living Tomorrow, Today!: Science of the Seventies,* 1972.

The Modern Book of Whittling and Wood-Carving (Better Homes and Gardens Book Club selection), McGraw, 1973; *One Thousand One Designs for Whittling and Woodcarving* (Popular Science Book Club selection), McGraw, 1976; *Build Your Own*

Inexpensive Dollhouse With One Sheet of 4'x8' Plywood and Home Tools (booklet), Dover, 1977; *Carving Wooden Animals,* Sterling, 1979; *Carving Religious Motifs in Wood,* Sterling, 1980; *Carving Faces and Figures in Wood,* Sterling, 1980; *Carving Flora and Fables in Wood,* Sterling, 1981; *Capturing Personality in Wood,* Sterling, 1981; *Relief Woodcarving,* Sterling, 1982; *Carving the Unusual,* Sterling, 1982.

Plays; juveniles: "Jack and the Beanstalk," first produced in Port Washington, N.Y., 1957; "Pinocchio," first produced in Port Washington, 1961; "The Pied Piper of Hamelin," first produced in Port Washington, 1966.

Author of "Tangents," a column in *Chip Chats.* Contributor to technical journals.

WORK IN PROGRESS: A basic book to supplement those written for Sterling Publishing Company; a basic series on whittling for *Woodworking Crafts* magazine; articles for periodicals.

SIDELIGHTS: Tangerman commented: "I began writing for publication as a member of the staff of the *Purdue Exponent,* the daily newspaper of Purdue University (where there is no journalism school) and became chief editor in my senior year. This led me to McGraw-Hill and engineering journalism and away from a strictly engineering career. Early in the Depression, I began to write articles for *Popular Mechanics, Popular Science,* and *Scouting.* About 1935, I suggested changes in the requirements for the Boy Scout merit badge in woodcarving and rewrote the instruction manual. At the same time I prepared a booklet for the Remington Arms Company, then a big manufacturer of pocket knives. 'Things to Do With a Pocket Knife' was distributed free to perhaps seven hundred fifty thousand people. This all led to my first book, *Whittling and Woodcarving,* followed by *Design and Figure Carving.* Both went out of print in 1958, but were reprinted as paperbacks in the early 1960's.

"The great bulge in craft interest in the United States began in the early sixties, and shortly thereafter I began writing again on whittling and woodcarving, but this time for *Chip Chats,* the magazine of the National Wood Carvers Association, and for the bulletin of the International Wood Collectors Society.

"All of my recent books include not only my own work, but also typical examples of folk carving from all over the world, material collected from my own travels over the past forty years. As an engineering editor I traveled widely, then supplemented my business trips with personal travel as well.

"Since I retired in 1969 I have devoted my time to woodcarving and whittling, doing a great many commissioned pieces. I have had a number of shows and exhibits, have won some awards, lectured to woodcarving groups all over the country, judged shows (including the two big ones in Davenport, Iowa, and Toronto, Ontario), and taught locally as well as in Nebraska, Georgia, and North Carolina."

*   *   *

TANNENBAUM, Percy Hyman 1927-

BRIEF ENTRY: Born May 31, 1927, in Montreal, Quebec, Canada. Canadian social psychologist, educator, and author. Tannenbaum has been teaching since 1953. In 1971 he became professor of public policy at University of California, Berkeley. His books include *The Measurement of Meaning* (University of Illinois Press, 1957), *Theories of Cognitive Consistency: A Sourcebook* (Rand McNally, 1968), and *The Entertainment Functions of Television* (L. Erlbaum Associates, 1980). *Address:* 962 Cragmont Ave., Berkeley, Calif. 94708; and De-

partment of Public Policy, University of California, Berkeley, Calif. 94720. *Biographical/critical sources: American Men and Women of Science: The Social and Behavioral Sciences,* 13th edition, Bowker, 1978.

*   *   *

TAYLOR, Constance Lindsay 1907-
(Guy Cullingford)

PERSONAL: Born in 1907 in Dovercourt, England; daughter of S.E. (a chemist) and A.M. (Flowers) Dowdy; married Morris Lindsay Taylor (a town clerk); children: Jennifer Taylor Dixon, Justin Lindsay, John Lindsay. *Education:* Attended private girls' school in Malvern, England. *Religion:* Church of England. *Home:* Moorlands Farm House, Great Tey, Colchester, Essex C06 1AS, England. *Agent:* A.M. Heath & Co. Ltd., 40-42 William IV St., London WC2N 4DD, England; and (plays) Elspeth Cochrane Agency, 1 The Pavement, London SW4 OHY, England.

CAREER: Writer, 1928—. *Member:* Writers Guild of Great Britain, Crime Writers Association, Detection Club. *Awards, honors:* Silver Nymph from Monte Carlo International Festival, 1972-73, for television play, "Sarah."

WRITINGS—Mystery novels, except as noted; all under pseudonym Guy Cullingford: *Murder With Relish,* Hutchinson, 1948; *If Wishes Were Hearses,* Lippincott, 1952; *Post Mortem,* Lippincott, 1953; *Conjuror's Coffin,* Lippincott, 1954; *Framed for Hanging,* Lippincott, 1956; *The Whipping Boys,* Hammond Hammond, 1958; *A Touch of Drama,* Hammond Hammond, 1960; *Third Party Risk,* Bles, 1962; *Brink of Disaster,* Bles, 1964; *The Stylist,* Bles, 1968; *The Bread and Butter Miss* (novel), R. Hale, 1979.

Television plays: "Sarah," first broadcast by ITV Television, January 22, 1973; "Boy Dave," first broadcast by ITV Television, December 30, 1975; "The Winter Ladies," first broadcast by ITV Television, May 15, 1979.

Contributor of articles, stories, and poems to periodicals.

SIDELIGHTS: Constance Taylor commented: "Like all those dubbed 'natural' writers, I don't suppose that I could help it. But at the end of the road, I wish that I had disciplined myself more. Spontaneous writing is fine, and perhaps some things are better left unrevised, but on the whole a long, hard look after the original enthusiasm has abated is a good thing. To produce a few pages every day is, I believe, a stimulus and makes for fluent style and a body of work that can be a useful insurance against the future. A woman may choose to write under a man's name (a whim of my first publisher), but she's still a woman, in my instance a woman with a demanding family. Anyway, it has all been fun."

*   *   *

TAYLOR, Donald Stewart 1924-

BRIEF ENTRY: Born August 8, 1924, in Portland, Ore. American educator and author. Taylor has been a professor of English at University of Oregon since 1968. He was a Guggenheim fellow in 1972. Taylor edited *Story, Poem, Essay: A University Reader* (Holt, 1957), *The Complete Works of Thomas Chatterton: A Bicentenary Edition* (Clarendon Press, 1971) and *Thomas Chatterton's Art: Experiments in Imagined History* (Princeton University Press, 1978). *Address:* Department of English, University of Oregon, Eugene, Ore. 97403.

TEAGUE, Bob
  See TEAGUE, Robert

*   *   *

TEAGUE, Robert   1929-
  (Bob Teague)

PERSONAL: Born in 1929, in Milwaukee, Wis.; divorced, 1974; children: Adam. *Education:* University of Wisconsin, B.S., 1950. *Home:* 400 Central Park W., New York, N.Y. 10025. *Agent:* Goodman Associates, 500 West End Ave., New York, N.Y. 10024.

CAREER: Journalist and author. *Milwaukee Journal,* Milwaukee, Wis., reporter, 1950-56; *New York Times,* New York City, reporter, 1956-63; National Broadcasting Company, Inc., New York City, newscaster, 1963—. *Awards, honors:* Recipient of Amistad Award from American Missionary Association for "his dignity and journalistic skill," 1966.

WRITINGS—All under name Bob Teague: *The Climate of Candor* (novel), Pageant Press, 1962; *Letters to a Black Boy* (biographical civil rights protest), Walker & Co., 1968; *Adam in Blunderland* (juvenile; illustrated by Floyd Sowell), Doubleday, 1971; *Agent K-Thirteen the Super-Spy* (juvenile), Doubleday, 1974; *Super-Spy K-Thirteen in Outer Space* (juvenile), Doubleday, 1980; *Live and Off-Color: News Biz,* A & W Publishers, 1982.

Contributor of articles to periodicals, including *High Fidelity and Musical America, Look, Reader's Digest, Redbook, TV Guide,* and *New York Times Magazine.*

SIDELIGHTS: Bob Teague was a star All-Big Ten halfback for the University of Wisconsin and was the first black newsman ever hired by the NBC television network. His journalism concentration after a few years in the field of sports has been general assignment. He is a twenty-year veteran anchorman and street reporter on WNBC-TV.

BIOGRAPHICAL/CRITICAL SOURCES: Ebony, November, 1955; *Newsweek,* October 14, 1968; *New York Times Book Review,* March 2, 1969.

*   *   *

TEIXEIRA da MOTA, Avelino   ?-1982

OBITUARY NOTICE: Died April 1, 1982. Naval officer and author best known for his six-volume work, *Portugaliae monumenta cartographica,* which he wrote with Armando Cortesao. Teixeira da Mota also published numerous articles and monographs on cartography, anthropology, and nautical science. Obituaries and other sources: *London Times,* April 23, 1982.

*   *   *

TELFER, R(oss)   1937-

PERSONAL: Born September 17, 1937, in Newcastle, Australia; son of Stanley and Irene (Turner) Telfer; married Bronwyn Edwards; children: Julie Telfer Dunn, Joanne, Alison. *Education:* University of New South Wales, B.A., 1964; University of New England, Diploma in Educational Administration, 1967, M.Ed.Admin. (with honors), 1971; University of Newcastle, Ph.D., 1975. *Politics:* "Anti-Conservative." *Religion:* Atheist. *Home:* 20 Macquarie St., Bolton Point, New South Wales 2253, Australia. *Office:* Faculty of Education, University of Newcastle, Newcastle, New South Wales 2308, Australia.

CAREER: Teacher of industrial arts, English, and history at secondary schools in Kurri Kurri, Wallsend, Bankstown, and Coonable, Australia, 1957-72; College of Advanced Education, Newcastle, Australia, lecturer in education, 1972-75; University of Newcastle, Newcastle, senior lecturer in education, 1976—. *Member:* Australian Institute for Educational Research, Australian Association for Research in Education, National Association of Flight Instructors, Royal Lifesaving Society, South Pacific Association for Teacher Education.

WRITINGS: Sailing Small Craft, Readon, 1964, revised edition, 1966; *How to Sail Small Boats,* J. Murray, 1968, 3rd edition, 1976; (with John Rees) *Teacher Tactics,* Symes, 1975; (with Donald R. Cruickshank) *Bibliography of Sources on Simulations and Games,* ERIC, 1980; (with John B. Biggs) *The Process of Learning,* Prentice-Hall, 1981; *Teaching People to Fly,* for flight instructors, Australian Aircrew Publications, in press. New South Wales correspondent for *Australian Seacraft,* 1958-70. Editor of *Newcastle Educational Administration Journal.*

SIDELIGHTS: Telfer commented: "As societal knowledge and technology accumulate, the need for efficiency in transmission and learning increases. There have been advances in teaching and learning, but the gap between theory and practice is wide. I see a need to build bridges over that gap.

"The need for such bridges is most apparent in areas of both skill and knowledge learning, such as learning to fly an aircraft or to sail a boat. Yet, these are the areas where tradition and convention tend to dictate the way we go about teaching. If teachers are seen as facilitators of learning, rather than mere demonstrators or providers of content, then approaches are usually quite different. These differences interest me; and the apparent reluctance of teachers and instructors to be different is even more fascinating."

*   *   *

TEN HARMSEL, Henrietta   1921-

PERSONAL: Born June 1, 1921, in Hull, Iowa; daughter of Antoon (a farmer) and Marie (Ten Brink) Ten Harmsel. *Education:* Calvin College, B.A., 1949; University of Michigan, M.A., 1958, Ph.D., 1962. *Religion:* Protestant. *Home:* 2880 Marshall S.E., Apt. 10, Grand Rapids, Mich. 49508. *Office:* Department of English, Calvin College, 3207 Burton St., Grand Rapids, Mich. 49506.

CAREER: High school teacher in Hull, Iowa, 1950-58; Calvin College, Grand Rapids, Mich., instructor, 1959-60, associate professor, 1962-64, professor of English, 1964—, chairperson of department, 1976-80. *Member:* Modern Language Association of America, Jane Austen Society of America, National Dutch Literary Society, Christianity and Literature. *Awards, honors:* Grant from American Association of University Women, 1965-66.

WRITINGS: Jane Austen: A Study in Fictional Conventions, Mouton, 1964; (translator and author of introduction) Jacobus Revius, *Jacobus Revius: Dutch Metaphysical Poet; Selected Poems,* Wayne State University Press, 1968; *Pink Lemonade* (translations of Dutch children's poems), Eerdmans, 1981; (contributor) *Hooft,* Querido, 1981. Contributor to language and literature journals.

WORK IN PROGRESS: Translating and writing introduction to Dutch baroque poem "Good Friday," to be illustrated with etchings by Rembrandt, publication by Paideia Press expected in 1983.

SIDELIGHTS: Henrietta Ten Harmsel commented: "My Dutch-born parents gave me an early, natural acquaintance with the

Dutch language, which has recently become my major interest in research, translation, and criticism. Meeting Annie M. G. Schmidt—famous Dutch children's poet—has opened up a new and challenging field of translation for me.''

*   *   *

TENNANT, (Charles) Roger 1919-

PERSONAL: Born April 8, 1919, in Tasmania, Australia; son of Charles Graham (a farmer) and Ethel May (Brown) Tennant; married Agnita Myong Hi Hong (a librarian), February 6, 1964; children: Charlotte Myong, Charles Leo. *Education:* Attended Royal Military College, Sandhurst, England, 1942, and Lincoln Theological College, 1949-52; Open University, Ph.D., 1974. *Home:* Bitteswell Vicarage, Lutterworth, Leicestershire, England LE17 4RX. *Agent:* Brandt & Brandt Literary Agents, Inc., 1501 Broadway, New York, N.Y. 10036.

CAREER: Worked as aircraft engineer, 1939-49; priest in Anglican Church, 1952—; writer. *Military service:* British Army, 1941-46; in airborne division. *Awards, honors:* (With wife, Agnita) Translation Prize from *Korea Times*, 1972, for best translation of a Korean short story.

WRITINGS: Born of a Woman: A Short Life of Jesus, S.P.C.K., 1961, published as *Christ Encountered,* Seabury, 1966; *The Litany of St. Charles,* Michael Joseph, 1968, published as *Cast on a Certain Island,* Doubleday, 1970; *Joseph Conrad,* Atheneum, 1981.

WORK IN PROGRESS: The Jesus Mystery, nonfiction.

SIDELIGHTS: Tennant's *Joseph Conrad* was praised by *Time*'s Peter Stoler as a ''concise work.'' Stoler declared that ''none of the recent Conrad books is more manageable—or readable—than Roger Tennant's new study. Tennant examines both the work and the self-manufactured legend, carefully separating rumor, romance and fact.''

Tennant told *CA:* ''I worked in South Korea for the Anglican Church from 1954 to 1962, when I met my wife, and developed a great affection for the country and its people. I revisited South Korea with my family in 1980. We have tried to make our home a welcoming center for Koreans in the Midland area of the United Kingdom.''

BIOGRAPHICAL/CRITICAL SOURCES: Chicago Tribune Book World, July 12, 1981; *Los Angeles Times Book Review,* August 16, 1981; *Time,* August 24, 1981; *New York Times,* September 1, 1981.

*   *   *

TENNISON, Patrick Joseph 1928-

PERSONAL: Born July 16, 1928, in Brisbane, Australia; son of James and Clarice (Ransom) Tennison; married Olga Massey, March 17, 1955; children: Max, Katrina. *Home and office:* 375 High St., Ashburton, Melbourne, Victoria, Australia.

CAREER: Modern Times, Brisbane, Australia, reporter, 1948-50; *Geelong Advertiser,* Geelong, Australia, reporter, 1950-51; *Melbourne Sun,* Melbourne, Australia, reporter, 1951-63; Radio Australia, Melbourne, commentator, 1961-78; commentator for 3AW (radio), 1977—. Commentator for Voice of America, 1973-78. *Member:* Australian Society of Authors, Fellowship of Writers, Sydney Journalists Club, Melbourne Press Club (president, 1971-73).

WRITINGS—All nonfiction: *Meet the Gallery,* Sun Books, 1968; *The Marriage Wilderness,* Angus & Robertson, 1972; *Defence Counsel,* Hill of Content, 1973; *Lucky Country Re-*

born, Hill of Content, 1976; (editor) *Heyday or Doomsday?,* Hill of Content, 1977; *Justice in the Dark,* Drummond Books, 1982. Television writer.

SIDELIGHTS: Tennison commented: ''From a father who was a great raconteur, reciter of poetry, and enthusiast for knowing what was happening in the world, I inherited an appreciation and affection for words and ideas, and for the way they are transmitted. I remain fascinated by the magic of the communication process—how an idea is passed from one mind to another. We live in a bountiful world of people and events. I see the journalist, for newspapers, radio, and television, as the chronicler and interpreter of current history. It is ideal life participation to be involved in that process.

''I write mainly about legal, sociological, political, and psychological topics—since these are what most affect our lives. Although most people are aware of this, they often find them difficult to understand. It is therefore the journalist's job to 'inform and interpret' what they mean, how they operate, how they may best be used.''

*   *   *

TETREAULT, Wilfred F. 1927-

PERSONAL: Born July 31, 1927, in Providence, R.I.; son of Wilfred J. (a contractor) and Mabel (Fisher) Tetreault; married Catherine R. Cavelieri (a corporation secretary), June 2, 1951; children: Theresa Tetreault Freitas, Mike, Elizabeth Tetreault Fleming. *Education:* Rhode Island School of Design, E.M.S.T., 1948; also attended University of Pennsylvania, 1967, and Foothill College, 1968. *Home and office:* c/o American Business Consultants, Inc., 1540 Nuthatch Lane, Sunnyvale, Calif. 94087.

CAREER: Daisy Cup Corp. (manufacturer of paper products), New Bedford, Mass., president, 1958-65; Smith-Tetreault Corp. (manufacturer of paper products), Bristol, R.I., president, 1965-68; American Business Consultants, Inc., Sunnyvale, Calif., president, business consultant, and seminar director, 1979—. Certified business opportunity appraiser; member of Sunnyvale Real Estate Board and California Association of Realtors; expert witness in California Superior Court. *Military service:* U.S. Navy, 1943-46; served in Pacific theater.

WRITINGS—Published by American Business Consultants: *How to Finance a Business!: Little or No Money Down,* 1979; *Business Opportunity Appraiser,* 1979; *Operating and Making My Business Grow,* 1979; *How and Where to Start 195 Businesses at Home,* 1979; *What Should I Pay for a Business,* 1979; *Choosing a Business: Complete Self-Evaluation Charts,* 1979; *Tax Planning and Tax Savings,* 1979; *How to Buy and Sell Business Opportunities,* 1979; *Business Frauds,* in press.

Starting Right in Your New Business, Addison-Wesley, 1981; *Buying and Selling Business Opportunities,* Addison-Wesley, 1981. Author of more than one hundred books, business opportunity contracts, agreements, forms, and pamphlets for appraising, buying, and selling any business.

SIDELIGHTS: Tetreault told *CA:* ''I saw too many people's dreams of business ownership shattered by lack of information, so I decided to do something about it by conducting seminars throughout the United States and by writing books and pamphlets that comprise the first and only definitive guides to legal, ethical, moral, and successful business transactions. They contain agreement forms, contracts, and form letters.''

*   *   *

THATCHER, Joan (Claire) 1934-

PERSONAL: Born June 28, 1934, in Duluth, Minn.; daughter

of Clarence James and Margaret (Hammer) Thatcher. *Education:* Macalester College, B.A., 1955; Andover Newton Theological School, M.A., 1966; American Baptist Seminary of the West, M.Div., 1975. *Home:* 2519 Parker St., Berkeley, Calif. 94704. *Office:* 268 Grand Ave., Oakland, Calif. 94610.

CAREER: Affiliated with American Baptist Board of Education and Publications, New York, N.Y., 1955-62; Andover Newton Theological School, Newton Centre, Mass., director of publicity, 1962-66; Pratt Institute, Brooklyn, N.Y., executive editor of publications, 1966-69; American Baptist Seminary of the West, Berkeley and Covina, Calif., director of communications, 1969-72; Graduate Theological Union, Berkeley, instructor in communications, 1969-72; American Baptist Churches of the West, Oakland, Calif., director of communications, 1973—; American Baptist Film Library, Oakland, western manager, 1973—; ordained Baptist minister, 1974. Member of executive board of Office of Women's Affairs, Graduate Theological Union, 1971-73. *Member:* Public Relations Association (national secretary, 1964-66); Inter Faith Communications Commission. *Awards, honors:* Citation from the American Baptist Convention, 1960.

WRITINGS—Nonfiction: Summoned to Serve: Real-Life Stories of Twelve Persons at Work in the Church Vocations, Judson, 1960; *The Church Responds,* Judson, 1970; (with Paul M. Nagano) *The Asian American Experience,* Fund of Renewal, 1973; (with Joseph O. Bass) *One in Nine Americans Is Black,* Fund of Renewal, 1973; (with Elizabeth L. Walters) *The Trail of Tears: An American Indian Experience,* Fund of Renewal, 1974; (with Wendy S. Pannier) *With a Spanish Heritage,* Fund of Renewal, 1974; *Looking Forward to a Career: Church Vocations* (juvenile), Dillon, 1976.

WORK IN PROGRESS: A travel book.*

*   *   *

THIBAULT, Jacques Anatole Francois 1844-1924
(Anatole France)

BRIEF ENTRY: Born April 16, 1844, in Paris, France; died October 12, 1924 (some sources say October 13), near Tours, France; buried in Paris, France. French critic and novelist. During his lifetime, Anatole France was one of his country's most beloved writers. His near perfection of style, contrasting tenderness with irony and skepticism with sensuality and love of beauty, was first evident in *Le Crime de Sylvestre Bonnard* (1881; translated as *The Crime of Sylvestre Bonnard,* 1890). With the publication of *La Rotisserie de la reine Pedauque* (1893; translated as *At the Sign of the Reine Pedauque,* 1912), his success as a popular novelist was firmly established. During the late 1890's France became noted for writing on themes of political and social irony. *L'Ile des pingouins* (1908; translated as *Penguin Island,* 1909), perhaps his best-known work, was a sharp criticism of contemporary French society. France was considered to be one of his country's foremost journalists and a leading spokesman for liberal humanism in French letters. He was awarded the Nobel Prize for Literature in 1921. *Biographical/critical sources: Cyclopedia of World Authors,* Harper, 1958; *The McGraw-Hill Encyclopedia of World Biography,* McGraw, 1972.

*   *   *

THOMAS, Annabel 1929-

PERSONAL: Born July 28, 1929, in Columbus, Ohio; daughter of George Crawford (an attorney) and Mary (a teacher; maiden name, Byers) Crawford; married William Lawrence Thomas (a veterinarian), September 15, 1951; children: Stephen, Elizabeth Lantz, Katherine, Michael. *Education:* Ohio State University, B.A., 1951; Ohio Wesleyan University, teaching certificate, 1971. *Address:* P.O. Box 88, Ashley, Ohio 43003. *Agent:* Elise Simon Goodman, 500 West End Ave., New York, N.Y. 10024.

CAREER: Columbus Citizen (now *Columbus Citizen-Journal*), Columbus, Ohio, reporter, movie and book reviewer, and feature writer, 1951-54; Ashley Elementary School, Ashley, Ohio, teacher, 1967; writer. *Awards, honors:* Award for short fiction from University of Iowa, 1981, and from PEN American Center, 1982, both for *The Phototropic Woman.*

WRITINGS: The Phototropic Woman (short stories), University of Iowa Press, 1981.

WORK IN PROGRESS: Three short novels, *The Well of Living Water, The Folk Singer,* and *Rachel, Weeping;* two long novels, *Winnie Clemmer* and *The Bell Cow.*

SIDELIGHTS: Thomas's collection of short stories, *The Phototropic Woman,* focuses on life in rural Ohio. Her subjects are primarily women coping with strange situations or circumstances. In the title story, a woman is lost in a cave; other stories detail a woman haunted by horses, two siblings plotting the sale of their farm house, and an old woman coping with an aggressive daughter.

Writing in *Washington Post Book World,* Jonathan Yardley declared, "In these 16 short stories she describes, in a prose notable for its clarity and lack of excess, aspects of life. . . . Her work is surprisingly original, considering that this is her first book, and at its best it is quite powerful." Yardley concluded that Thomas is "a writer to be reckoned with."

Thomas told *CA:* "My parents came out of the Appalachian Hills and settled in the city. Always in the city we were alien. Isolated. As with most people, it took me years to understand the nature of the condition I was born into. I believe the pull of different cultures resulted in a sort of double vision. I stand outside my own time, of it yet apart from it, looking on. Probably because the hill life existed for me in large part in the remembrances of my parents, it assumed the proportion of myth, of symbol for me. The ballads, tales, the very geography of the hill country gathered to themselves deep spiritual significances, and became the basis of my work.

"I now live pretty much the life of a recluse. My little town (1000 people) is surrounded by great fields of wheat, soybeans, corn, sometimes rye or oats that stretch off far as the eye can reach. I walk or bicycle along them. They're there for me constantly, washing the edges of my consciousness like Conrad's sea. These fields, this village, my natal city, the hills are all part of the geography that lies behind my particular vision."

BIOGRAPHICAL/CRITICAL SOURCES: Washington Post Book World, January 13, 1982.

*   *   *

THOMAS, (Philip) Edward 1878-1917
(Edward Eastaway)

BRIEF ENTRY: Born March 3, 1878, in London, England; died April 9, 1917, in Arras, France. British journalist, author, and poet. Though Thomas was known during his lifetime primarily as a hack writer, some of his prose works, like *The Heart of England* (1906) and *The South Country* (1909), expressed a genuine feeling for nature and the British countryside. It was his poetry, however, that revealed his true literary talent. First published in 1916, his simple, delicately rhythmic poetry conveyed Thomas's rather sad look at life and its ultimate futility. His *Poems* (1917) and *Last Poems* (1918) were published after the poet died in battle during World War I, and he was never aware of the respect they were to later earn for him. *Biographical/critical sources:* F. R. Leavis, *New Bearings in English Poetry,* Chatto & Windus, 1932; *Twentieth Century Authors: A Biographical Dictionary of Modern Literature,* H. W. Wilson, 1942.

*   *   *

THOMAS, Jane Resh   1936-

PERSONAL: Born August 15, 1936, in Kalamazoo, Mich.; daughter of Reed Beneval (in sales) and Thelma (a teacher; maiden name, Scott) Resh; married Richard Thomas (a copywriter), November 13, 1961; children: Jason. *Education:* Bronson School of Nursing, R.N., 1957; attended Michigan State University, 1959-60; University of Minnesota, B.A. (summa cum laude), 1967, M.A., 1971. *Residence:* Minneapolis, Minn.

CAREER: Worked as registered nurse, 1957-60; University of Minnesota at Minneapolis, instructor in English composition, 1967-80; free-lance writer, 1972—. *Member:* American Association of University Women, Phi Beta Kappa.

WRITINGS: Elizabeth Catches a Fish (juvenile), illustrated by Joseph Duffy, Seabury, 1977; *The Comeback Dog* (juvenile), illustrated by Troy Howell, Houghton/Clarion, 1981. Also author of "Children's Books," a monthly column in the *Minneapolis Tribune.* Contributor of articles and reviews to periodicals, including *Hornbook Magazine* and *New York Times Book Review.*

WORK IN PROGRESS: How Many Humps Do You Put on Your "M"?; another children's book.

SIDELIGHTS: Thomas's first book, *Elizabeth Catches a Fish,* is a simple story focusing on seven-year-old Elizabeth, who hooks a large bass while on a fishing outing with her father. According to Barbara Karlin of the *New York Times Book Review,* Thomas tells Elizabeth's story with "vivid clarity and precision."

The subject of Thomas's second book is of a more serious nature than her first. Daniel, a nine-year-old, is forced to deal with the death of Captain, his family's dog and the closest friend of Daniel, an only child growing up in the country. When Daniel finds an injured dog, he nurses it to health, but remains coolly aloof, afraid to get emotionally attached. The healed dog runs away, leaving Daniel daunted. But when the dog returns, Daniel resolves to adopt and care for it, despite the risk of being hurt once again. *New York Times Book Review*'s Marjorie N. Allen wrote: "Mrs. Thomas has written a middle reader with substance—a rare achievement."

Thomas told *CA:* "When I was a child in Kalamazoo, Michigan, my father bought an adult English setter named Bill, who flinched at every move we made as if he expected us to kick him. He couldn't be friendly to us until one day he came imploringly to my mother with pronged seeds in his eyes and sat patiently while she removed them with tweezers. After that he forgave us whatever wrongs others had done him and became one of the best dogs we ever had.

"Bill sometimes went with us to our grandparent's farm, a peach orchard and tree nursery near Lake Michigan. A creek, where Mother had hunted snakes when she was a girl, meandered across the meadow. One spring, after a flood had subsided, I found enough blue crayfish claws on the ground to fill a strawberry box. I kept them under our porch for a long time, even though they smelled bad, because they were beautiful.

"We spent weekends at a cottage on Big Cedar Lake, where our parents owned ten acres of land. In the swamp that bordered the lake, wild ladyslippers and rattlesnakes grew among poison sumac and watercress. One oak tree was so big that my brother and I couldn't reach around it, and so old it must have been growing when Indians lived nearby. I often fished with my father, who taught me to see what I looked at—the herons and loons that nested in the reeds, the mist that clung to the water at dawn, the dogwood and cattails, and the deer drinking at the spring at the first morning light that had appeared, it seemed, between one blink and another.

"When we were at home in Kalamazoo, my favorite place was the Washington Square Library, with its stone entryway, its fireplace and leaded windows, and what seemed like miles of books. I wrote to Maud Hart Lovelace once and received an answer. Busy though my mother was, raising four children with little help except financial support from my father, she found time to read to us. I learned to love literature at her side. My family were uncommunicative people, and I relied on books, as I did on nature, not only to entertain but to sustain myself. For a brief, blissful time, we had a membership we could ill afford in the Junior Literary Guild. I remember my utter joy when books like *Big Tree* and *Bonnie's Boy* arrived in the mail.

"I have wanted to be a writer at least since I was seven years old, but was much discouraged by the conventional responses of adults to the things I wrote. The world has always been a wonder and a mystery to me. I write, as I read, in order to understand it and to find out what I think and feel. The dog, Bill, the farm, the crayfish claws, and the dawn-lit lake have come back to me in the stories that are in my head and on paper, even though I now live six hundred miles and twenty-five years from home. And although my father and grandparents died years ago, they have come back too. The oak tree fell in a storm a few years ago, but it lives again in my mind. They are all transformed, mixed with things and people that never happened and never were, and blended with present events, like my son Jason's three-year effort to make friends with Rosie, the standoffish poodle we bought at the pound. Transformed though we are, I recognize all of us and the magical places I love in the stories that make my past present and my present comprehensible.

"Now I am writing about an event in my grandfather's boyhood, when he saw the steamship *Chicora* flounder in heavy seas on Lake Michigan in 1895. His story blends itself with my own life, so that what happens is newly made and happening now to me."

BIOGRAPHICAL/CRITICAL SOURCES: New York Times Book Review, May 1, 1977, May 10, 1981.

*   *   *

THOMAS, Sara (Sally)   1911(?)-1982
(Sara Jackson)

OBITUARY NOTICE: Born c. 1911; died February 22, 1982, in England. Actress, musician, poet, and author. An actress under her maiden name, Sara Jackson, Thomas appeared in numerous Shakespearean productions at England's Stratford-upon-Avon and Birmingham Repertory theatres. The widow of drama director Stephen Thomas, Sara Thomas devoted her later years to giving occasional readings of her poetry. She also wrote a memoir, *Dark With No Sorrow.* Obituaries and other sources: *London Times,* February 26, 1982.

THOMPSON, Brenda 1935-

PERSONAL: Born January 27, 1935, in Manchester, England; daughter of Thomas Barnes (a teacher) and Marjorie (Boddy) Houghton; married Gordon William Thompson (a newspaper executive), January 28, 1956; children: Harry William. *Education:* University of Leeds, B.Sc. (with honors), 1957. *Politics:* None. *Religion:* None. *Home:* Nantdu, Rhandirmwyn, Llandovery, Dyfed SA 20 ONG, South Wales. *Agent:* Murray Pollinger, 4 Garrick St., London WC2 9BH, England. *Office:* Stamford Hill School, Berkeley Rd., London N.15, England.

CAREER: J. Lyons & Co. (food manufacturer), food chemist, 1957; Chelsea Women's Hospital, Chelsea, England, biochemist, 1958-60; teacher at primary schools in London, England, 1964-78; Stamford Hill School, London, head teacher, 1978-81; farmer in South Wales, 1981—. Independent councillor, London borough of Islington, 1968-71; member, Press Council, 1973-76.

WRITINGS: Learning to Read: A Guide for Teachers and Parents, Beekman, 1970; *Learning to Teach,* Beekman, 1973; *The Pre-School Book,* Beekman, 1976; *Reading Success: A Guide for Teachers and Parents,* Sidgwick & Jackson, 1979.

Juveniles: *Under the Sea,* illustrations by Monika Beisner, Sidgwick & Jackson, 1974, (with Cynthia Overbeck) illustrations by Beisner and Rosemary Giesen, Lerner, 1977; *Volcanoes,* illustrations by David Hardy, Sidgwick & Jackson, 1974, (with Overbeck) illustrations by Hardy and L'Enc Matte, Lerner, 1977; *Pirates,* illustrations by Simon Stern, Sidgwick & Jackson, 1974, (with Giesen) illustrations by Stern and Giesen, Lerner, 1977; (editor) *Famous Planes,* illustrations by Andrew Martin, Sidgwick & Jackson, 1974, (with Giesen) illustrations by Martin and Giesen, Lerner, 1977; (editor) *Bones and Skeletons,* illustrations by Carole Viner, Sidgwick & Jackson, 1974, (with Giesen) illustrations by Viner and Giesen, Lerner, 1977; (editor) *The Children's Crusade,* illustrations by Stern, Sidgwick & Jackson, 1974, (with Overbeck) illustrations by Stern and Giesen, Lerner, 1977; (editor) *Monkeys, Gorillas, and Chimpanzees,* illustrations by Bob Williams, Sidgwick & Jackson, 1974, (with Overbeck) illustrations by Williams and Matte, published as *Monkeys and Apes,* Lerner, 1977; (editor) *Where Am I,* Sidgwick & Jackson, 1974.

(With Overbeck) *Animal Attackers,* illustrations by Thomas Houghton and Giesen, Lerner, 1977; (with Giesen) *Flags,* illustrations by David Brogan and Giesen, Lerner, 1977; (with Giesen) *Gold and Jewels,* illustrations by Caroline Austin and Giesen, Lerner, 1977; (with Overbeck) *The Great Wall of China,* illustrations by Barry Mosscrop and Giesen, Lerner, 1977; (with Giesen) *Rockets and Astronauts,* illustrations by Hardy and Matte, Lerner, 1977; (with Overbeck) *Spaceship Earth,* illustrations by Hardy and Giesen, Lerner, 1977; (with Giesen) *The Story of Steel,* illustrations by Terry Furchgott and Giesen, Lerner, 1977; (with Overbeck) *The Winds That Blow,* illustrations by Stern and Giesen, Lerner, 1977.

*   *   *

THOMPSON, Francis George 1931-

PERSONAL: Born March 29, 1931, in Stornoway, Scotland; son of Frank (an engineer) and Georgina (Jappy) Thompson; married Margaret Elaine Pullar (a secretary), April 23, 1960; children: Rona, Ewan, Fay, Eilidh. *Education:* Attended Nicolson Institute, Stornoway, Scotland, 1936-46. *Religion:* Church of Scotland. *Home:* 5 Rathadna Muilne, Stornoway, Isle of Lewis PA87 2TZ, Scotland. *Agent:* Maclean-Dubois Ltd., 3 Rutland Sq., Edinburgh, Scotland.

CAREER: North of Scotland Hydro-Electric Board, Stornoway, Scotland, supply electrician, 1947-57; Associated Electrical Industries, Manchester, England, technical author, 1957-59; Bruce Peebles Ltd.,Edinburgh, Scotland, assistant publicity manager, 1959-63; Inverness Technical College, Inverness, Scotland, lecturer in electrical engineering, 1963-77; Lews Castle College, Stornoway, Scotland, lecturer, 1977—. Managing editor of Club Leabhar Ltd. *Military service:* British Army, Royal Electrical and Mechanical Engineers, 1949-51. *Member:* Institution of Electrical and Electronic Engineers (fellow), Association of Supervisory and Executive Engineers, Society of Antiquaries of Scotland (fellow). *Awards, honors:* Grants from Scottish Arts Council, 1979, 1981.

WRITINGS: Harris Tweed: The Story of a Hebridean Industry, David & Charles, 1968; *Problems in Electrical Installation: Craft, Theory, and Practice,* Longmans, Green, 1968; *Electrical Installation and Workshop Technology,* Longmans, Green, Volume I, 1968, revised edition, 1978, Volume II, 1969, revised edition, 1975, Volume III, 1972; *Harris and Lewis: Outer Hebrides,* David & Charles, 1968, revised edition, 1973; *Our Community at Work,* Longmans, Green, 1969.

St. Kilda and Other Hebridean Outliers, Praeger, 1970; *Highland Smugglers,* Graphis Publications, 1972; *Highland Waterway: The Caledonian Canal,* Graphis Publications, 1972; *The Ghosts, Spirits, and Spectres of Scotland,* Bell, 1973; (editor) *Highland Ways, and Byways,* Club Leabhar, 1973; *The Highlands and Islands,* R. Hale, 1974; *The Uists and Barra,* David & Charles, 1974; *Void—Air Aite Falamh: A Poem Sequence From "The Memory-Books of Donald MacLeod" on the Highland Clearances,* Graphis Publications, 1975; *Victorian and Edwardian Highlands From Old Photographs,* Batsford, 1976; *Supernatural Highlands,* R. Hale, 1976; *Scottish Bestiary: The Lore and Literature of Scottish Beasts,* Molendinar Press, 1978; *Murder and Mystery in the Highlands,* Transatlantic, 1978; *The Highlands and Islands Advisory Panel: A Review of Its Activities and Influence, 1946-1964,* An Comunn Gaidhealach, 1979; *Portrait of the Spey,* R. Hale, 1979; *The National Mod,* Acair Ltd., 1979.

Contributor to *Books in Scotland.* Co-editor of *Sruth Newspaper,* 1966-70; member of editorial board of *Books in Scotland.*

WORK IN PROGRESS: "The Commission," a play based on the Scottish Highland crofters' war; short stories; poems; research on Gaelic folklorist, John Francis Campbell, and on the Highland soldier.

SIDELIGHTS: Thompson told *CA:* "My main area has been socio-economic and cultural aspects of the highlands and islands of Scotland. I have long been involved in Scottish national politics (formerly as a member of the Scottish National party) and the struggle to gain legal status for the Gaelic language in Scotland. I am also involved in aspects of living in the Outer Hebrides and the impact of state impositions on island communities. Writing concentrates the mind wonderfully, in particular the great discipline of poetry."

*   *   *

THOMPSON, Joanna Maxwell Pullein
See PULLEIN-THOMPSON, Joanna Maxwell

*   *   *

THOMPSON, Robert Norman 1914-

PERSONAL: Born May 17, 1914, in Duluth, Minn.; son of

Theodore Olaf (a farmer) and Johanna (a secretary; maiden name, Olufson) Thompson; married Hazel Maxine Kurth (a radiologist), May 4, 1939; children: Grace Arlone Thompson Brunner, Alice Maxine Thompson Miller, George Raymond, David Dale, Lois Marie, Paul Andrew, Robert Makonnen, Stephen James. *Education:* Alberta Normal College, teachers certificate, 1934; Garbutt's Business College, certificate in commercial law, 1935; Palmer College, D.C., 1939; Bob Jones University, B.Sc., 1953; University of British Columbia, degree, 1953. *Politics:* Progressive Conservative. *Religion:* Evangelical Free Church. *Home:* 33133 Bourquin Cres. W., No. 50, Abbotsford, British Columbia, Canada V2S 6B1. *Agent:* Murray Mitchell, 46th A. Ave., Langley, British Columbia, Canada. *Office:* Omega Publications Ltd., No. 218-20226 Fraser Hwy., Langley, British Columbia, Canada V3A 4E6.

CAREER: Teacher in public schools in Red Deer, Alberta, 1934-36; Ethiopian Ministry of Education, Addis Ababa, assistant headmaster of Haile Selassie I secondary school in Addis Ababa, 1945-46, headmaster, 1947-51, superintendent of education for Kaffa Province, 1946, director of provincial education and associate deputy minister, 1947-52; Sudan Interior Mission, Addis Ababa, chairman of educational committee, 1952-58; free-lance lecturer, 1958-62; Canadian Parliament, Ottawa, Ontario, Social Credit party member of Parliament for Red Deer, Alberta, and party chairman, 1960-68, Progressive Conservative member of Parliament, 1968-72, national Conservative party coordinator of organization, 1972; Trinity Western College, Langley, British Columbia, professor of political science, 1972-80, vice-president of college, 1972-80, part-time member of faculty, 1980-82; Omega Publications Ltd., Langley, B.C., president, 1982—. President of consulting firm, Thompson Associates Ltd.; past president of Viking Mines and Petroleums and International Audio Visual, Inc.; past vice-president of Tri-Professional Consultants; member of board of directors of World Concern of Canada, 1982—; past member of board of directors of Great Pacific Management and GreenArctic Consortium; administrator for Nundal, Cherrington, and Easingwood of Fort Law Office. Chairman of board of trustees of Aavengen Foundation; vice-chairman of Renaissance Canada; vice-president of Samaritan's Purse; executive director of Kildonian Foundation; past chairman of board of directors of World Vision International of Canada; past superintendent of Shashemane Leprosarium in Ethiopia, 1953-58. Visiting professor at Sir Wilfrid Laurier University, 1968-72; chairman of board of governors of Trinity Western College, 1968-72; member of board of directors of St. Stephen's University. Past member of Canadian council of Sudan Interior Mission; former head of Canadian government missions to the Congo, Southeast Asia, and Nigeria; past member of Canadian delegations to the United Nations and North Atlantic Treaty Organization (NATO). International coordinator of Gospel Recordings, 1974-79. Consultant to Canada Manpower. *Military service:* Royal Canadian Air Force, 1940-43; commandant of Imperial Ethiopian Air Force, 1944; also served as observer in Vietnam; became lieutenant colonel.

MEMBER: National Geographic Society, National Social Credit Association of Canada (president, 1960-61), Canadian Geographic Society, Canadian Chamber of Commerce (past member of board of directors), Canadian Wildlife Federation, Royal Geographic Society (fellow), Canadian Bible Society (honorary president; past member of board of directors), Association for the Handicapped (past president), Mission Aviation Fellowship (member of board of directors), Evangelical Fellowship of Canada (past president; member of board of directors), Christian Business Men of Canada, Alberta Teachers Association (life member), Langley Chamber of Commerce (pres-

ident), Surrey Chamber of Commerce (member of board of reference), OMS International (member of board of directors), Gideons International of Canada, Heraldry Society, Rotary International.

AWARDS, HONORS: Knight commander of Military and Hospitaller Order of St. Lazarus of Jerusalem, 1965; centennial medal from Queen Elizabeth II, 1967; grand officer of Star of Ethiopia, 1967; honorary colonel of Tiger Division, Republic of Korea Army, 1970; LL.D. from Wheaton College, Wheaton, Ill., 1972; honorary Canadian consul general of Ethiopia, 1974-80; Royal Jubilee Medal from Queen Elizabeth II, 1979; Trinity Western College named the Robert Thompson Centre (for business, aviation, teaching, and administration) in his honor, 1980; medal of honor from Royal Life Saving Society, 1982.

WRITINGS: Canadians: It's Time You Knew, Aavangen Press, 1962; *Canadians: Face Facts,* Aavangen Press, 1963; *Common Sense for Canadians,* McClelland & Stewart, 1965; (with John Redekop) *American Foreign Policy: The Star Spangled Beaver,* P.N.A. Books, 1971; (with Terry Norr) *Social Economics,* Trinity Western College Press, 1978; *A Voice From the Marketplace,* Trinity Western College Press, 1979; *A Model Constitution for Canada,* Omega, 1982; *My Jon Hoy of Ethiopia* (biography of Emperor Haile Selassie), Omega, 1982; *The House of Minorities,* Omega, 1983; *The Horn of Africa,* Omega, 1983. Contributor to magazines. Contributing editor of *Thrust,* 1970—; associate editor of *Encounter,* 1972-79; editor of Vanguard Institute's *Concerns* and *Freemen Report,* 1979—.

BIOGRAPHICAL/CRITICAL SOURCES: In the Heart of the Fraser Valley, September 17, 1980.

         *   *   *

THORNE, Nicola
    See ELLERBECK, Rosemary (Anne L'Estrange)

         *   *   *

THORNE, Sabina   1927-
    (Sabina Thorne Johnson)

PERSONAL: Born January 29, 1927, in Los Angeles, Calif.; daughter of William Joyce (a film director and writer) and Lenore (a writer; maiden name, Coffee) Cowen; married Douglas Storm, February 13, 1950 (divorced); married W. R. Johnson (a professor), March 2, 1962 (divorced); children: Nicholas, Leatrice. *Education:* University of California, Berkeley, B.A. (honors), 1962, M.A., 1970. *Politics:* "Feminist; somewhat radical." *Religion:* Vedantist. *Residence:* Berkeley, Calif. *Agent:* Molly Friedrich, Aaron M. Priest Literary Agency, 334 East 51st St., New York, N.Y. 10022. *Office:* Subject A, University of California, 216 Dwinelle Annex, Berkeley, Calif. 94720.

CAREER: University of California, Berkeley, lecturer in composition. Associated with the theatre and television productions. *Member:* National Council of Teachers of English, Danforth Association.

WRITINGS: Reruns (novel), Viking, 1981; *Of Gravity and Grace* (novella), Janus Press, 1982. Also contributor under name Sabina Thorne Johnson to scholarly journals.

SIDELIGHTS: Thorne told *CA:* "I grew up listening to two typewriters and swore that I would never be a writer, as my parents were. It took a breakdown in my forties for me to realize not only that I had to write but that the interior monologues that had always filled my mind—stories conjured up by strangers I had glimpsed, bits of dialogue, paragraphs of description—were the preoccupations of a writer.

"Since I have started very late, my main concern is that I will not have enough time to write myself into whatever may be my true voice. I read other contemporary women writers a lot. But although I consider myself a feminist, feminist writing holds very little interest for me. I am more drawn to and admiring of women who write about human, rather than feminist, quandries, especially Ella Leffland, Toni Morrison, Joan Didion, and Joyce Carol Oates.

"The day that I do not write is a lost day, and there are far too many of them since I must now teach composition full time to support myself. I enjoy the classroom and student conferences, but writing is what I most care to do."

*   *   *

THORNTON, John W(illiam) 1922-

PERSONAL: Born April 19, 1922, in Philadelphia, Pa.; son of John William, Sr., and Margaret (Pullen) Thornton; married Virginia R. Kauffman; children: John W., Jr., Virginia Joy. *Education:* University of West Florida, B.A., 1974, M.P.A., 1976. *Politics:* Republican. *Religion:* Episcopalian. *Home:* 101 Pintado Dr., Pensacola, Fla. 32503.

CAREER: Tradesman's National Bank, Philadelphia, Pa., bookkeeper, 1940-41; Fleetwings Aircraft, Bristol, Pa., sheet-metal worker, 1941-42; U.S. Navy, Aviation, career officer and aviator, 1942-70, served in World War II, Korea, and Viet Nam, retiring as captain. Lecturer for civic and religious organizations, at universities, and at military activities, including United States Air Force Academy, United States Air Force Special Operations School, Air University, and Naval War College. Guest on radio and television programs, including "This Is Your Life"; interviewed by Edward R. Murrow and Walter Cronkite. Featured on training films and tapes. *Member:* Association of Naval Aviation, Tailhook Association, Navy League Retired Officers Association, Masonic (Blue Lodge, chapter and commandery).

AWARDS, HONORS: Twenty-two citations and campaign ribbons, 1942-1970; Navy Cross for "action against enemy aggressor forces near Wonsan, Korea, on 31 March 1951"; Distinguished Flying Cross, 1951; Bronze Star, 1951; Purple Heart, 1953; Americanism Award from Jewish War Vets (Pittsburgh, Pa.), 1954; received awards from municipal, civic, and service organizations, 1954-82; Air Medal, 1955; Navy-Marine Corps Medal "for heroic conduct in effecting the rescue of the co-pilot of a U.S. Navy helicopter which crashed and burned in a wooded area near Medford, N.J., on 15 August 1960"; Secretary of Defense Identification Badge, 1969; Legion of Merit, 1970, for "exceptionally meritorious service from November, 1968, through April, 1970, as military adviser on prisoner of war affairs to the assistant secretary of defense for international security affairs"; Good Citizenship Award from city of Pensacola, Fla., 1977; honored with city resolution from Pensacola, 1982.

WRITINGS: (With son, John Thornton, Jr.) *Believed to Be Alive,* Paul Eriksson, 1981. Contributor of articles to military magazines.

WORK IN PROGRESS: "A novel based on fact. There are three central characters—a Russian, a Chinese, and an American. The time span is pre-World War II up to and including Viet Nam. The subjects are espionage, counter-insurgency, etc. It begins in three widely separated countries with the central

figures coming together, regardless of their national origins and loyalties, to operate jointly in gallant efforts to assure a people's right to self-determination."

SIDELIGHTS: "I treasured life but living with a conscience I knew would be rabid with guilt of betrayal was not living at all. If dying was the only alternative, I was reconciled to it. I had lived almost thirty years and had drunk deeply the joys and sorrows of this world. I had loved and been loved. I had known freedom and now captivity. I had hated and been hated. I had killed and would now myself be killed. Perhaps a balance had been struck, the circle closed. Alone . . . , enveloped by the darkness of a rainy night, I came to peace with myself. I was ready." But the North Korean firing squad did not end John W. Thornton's life that night. Instead he endured the rest of his two-and-a-half years as a prisoner of war before returning home to his wife and young son as part of "Operation Big Switch." Thornton's was the last name announced on the last day of repatriations in September, 1953.

Nearly twenty-seven years after the firing squad incident, Thornton, the first helicopter pilot to be captured by the enemy during the Korean War, chronicled his time as a POW in *Believed to Be Alive.* Written with his son, John, Jr. (or Jay), the book recalls the elder Thornton's early rescue missions, including the one on March 31, 1951, during which he was shot down while aiding an American intelligence unit that was fleeing from the North Koreans. In the book, the pilot records the ten days he spent in enemy territory before his capture. Then he tells of his harrowing experiences as a prisoner of war, so it is "an often brutal story," said Bill Gordon in the *Pensacola Journal.*

For his part, Jay Thornton edited the book's manuscript and wrote on life on the home front. He conveys his mother's strong faith as well as his own optimism for his father's return. He once told a *Richmond Times-Dispatch* reporter that he had "a childlike faith that my father, someday, would come home. I can't really tell you why, but I always felt that way."

The younger Thornton was brought into the writing of *Believed to Be Alive,* on which his father had been working for nearly two decades, when his infant son died. "My Dad," he explained, "thought it would be a good project, something to keep me busy."

Despite its record of savagery, *Believed to Be Alive* is "above all," remarked an *Henrico Hearsay* reviewer, "uplifting in the realization of what the human spirit can overcome." Selected by President and Mrs. Reagan for inclusion in the Presidential Library Collection, "it is a good book," praised the *Pensacola News-Journal*'s Carlton Proctor, "well-written and full of action, anger, danger and misery and humor. It takes the reader on an emotional roller coaster ride through the heights and depths of human emotion."

Thornton told *CA:* "When I was brought down by enemy fire during a mission behind the lines in Korea, I won the dubious distinction of having become the first helicopter pilot to be shot down and captured. How it happened and what happened to me afterwards is the story I tell in *Believed to Be Alive.*

"The book is a first-hand account of my exploits, in combat and captivity, amid terror, brainwashing, torture, and violent death during the Korean War. In it, I recount my experiences from the time of my captivity to the day, nearly three years later, when I was freed from the nightmare of captivity as the Korean Conflict ended. Sustained by my faith in God, in myself, in my family, and in the cause for which I was fighting, I was one of the 3,508 out of a total of over ten thousand POW's to come out alive."

BIOGRAPHICAL/CRITICAL SOURCES: Pensacola Journal, November 11, 1981; *Richmond Times-Dispatch,* November 12, 1981; *Henrico Hearsay,* December, 1981; *Asian Wall Street Journal,* February 23, 1982; *Pensacola News-Journal,* March 7, 1982.

*   *   *

THORNTON, John W(illiam), Jr.   1948-

PERSONAL: Born May 7, 1948, in Philadelphia, Pa.; son of John W. (a captain in U.S. Navy) and Virginia Kauffman; married Arlie Terry, August 23, 1975; children: Dawn Elisa. *Education:* Pennsylvania State University, B.A., 1970; University of West Florida, M.P.A., 1972. *Religion:* Episcopal. *Residence:* Richmond, Va. *Office:* Henrico County, Virginia, P.O. Box 27032, Richmond, Va. 23273.

CAREER: City of Pensacola, Fla., city clerk, 1972-77, assistant to city manager, 1977-78; County of Henrico, Richmond, Va., assistant to county manager, 1978—. Citizen representative for Action Seventy-six, 1972, and for Goals for Pensacola, 1976; initiator of Panhandle League of Cities, 1973; United Way coordinator; volunteer aerial observer for Henrico police. Also affiliated with Pensacola People-to-People. *Military service:* U.S. Army Reserve, 1970—; staff sergeant; received Army Commendation Medal, Armed Forces Reserve Medal, Army Reserve Components Achievement Medal with oak-leaf cluster.

MEMBER: International Institute of Municipal Clerks, International City Management Association, American Society for Public Administration (member of Gulf Coast Chapter Governing Council; secretary, 1976); Florida Association of City Clerks, Panhandle League of Cities (treasurer and secretary, 1973). *Awards, honors:* Fellowship grant from University of West Florida, 1971; commendatory resolutions from Pensacola, Fla., City Council, 1972, for work as research assistant on Citizens Revenue Study Task Force and, 1982, for *Believed to Be Alive;* received key to city of Pensacola, Fla., 1978, "in appreciation of dedicated service, June, 1972, to September, 1978."

WRITINGS: (With father, John W. Thornton) *Believed to Be Alive,* Paul Eriksson, 1981. Also author of "The Revenue Crunch" and other unpublished reports. Ghostwriter of editorials, speeches, and budget messages for local government officials.

WORK IN PROGRESS: "My wife is working on a 'Gothic' romance, her first such endeavor. I plan to assist her with editing and revising the manuscript when she has completed the first draft. Then, who knows?"

SIDELIGHTS: "I treasured life but living with a conscience I knew would be rabid with guilt of betrayal was not living at all. If dying was the only alternative, I was reconciled to it. I had lived almost thirty years and had drunk deeply the joys and sorrows of this world. I had loved and been loved. I had known freedom and now captivity. I had hated and been hated. I had killed and would now myself be killed. Perhaps a balance had been struck, the circle closed. Alone . . . , enveloped by the darkness of a rainy night, I came to peace with myself. I was ready." But the North Korean firing squad did not end John W. Thornton, Sr.'s life that night. Instead he endured the rest of his two-and-a-half years as a prisoner of war before returning home to his wife and young son as part of "Operation Big Switch." Thornton's was the last name announced on the last day of repatriations in September, 1953.

Nearly twenty-seven years after the firing squad incident, Thornton, the first helicopter pilot to be captured by the enemy during the Korean War, chronicled his time as a POW in *Believed to Be Alive.* Written with his son, John, Jr. (or Jay), the book recalls the elder Thornton's early rescue missions, including the one on March 31, 1951, during which he was shot down while aiding an American intelligence unit that was fleeing from the North Koreans. In the book, the pilot records the ten days he spent wandering in enemy territory before his capture. Then he tells of his harrowing experiences as a prisoner of war, so it is "an often brutal story," said Bill Gordon in the *Pensacola Journal.*

For his part, Jay Thornton edited the book's manuscript and wrote on life on the home front. He conveys his mother's strong faith as well as his own optimism for his father's return. He once told a *Richmond Times-Dispatch* reporter that he had "a childlike faith that my father, someday, would come home. I can't really tell you why, but I always felt that way."

The younger Thornton was brought into the writing of *Believed to Be Alive,* on which his father had been working for nearly two decades, when his infant son died. "My Dad," he explained, "thought it would be a good project, something to keep me busy."

Despite its record of savagery, *Believed to Be Alive* is "above all," remarked an *Henrico Hearsay* reviewer, "uplifting in the realization of what the human spirit can overcome." Selected by President and Mrs. Reagan for inclusion in the Presidential Library Collection, "it is a good book," praised the *Pensacola News-Journal*'s Carlton Proctor, "well-written and full of action, anger, danger and misery and humor. It takes the reader on an emotional roller coaster ride through the heights and depths of human emotion."

Thornton told *CA*: "*Believed to Be Alive* was written to broaden the accounts of the Korean War and to record for posterity the sacrifices of the men who lived and died there as prisoners of war—sacrifices that are too quickly forgotten. It was also designed to show what the enemy faced then, thirty years ago, has not changed anywhere in the world. He is the same. Beyond this, the book is a story of courage, faith, family, and fraternity. The story is told through the eyes and experiences of one POW—my father—and his family. We all felt it was a story that needed to be told and remembered by others."

BIOGRAPHICAL/CRITICAL SOURCES: Pensacola Journal, November 11, 1981; *Richmond Times-Dispatch,* November 12, 1981; *Henrico Hearsay,* December, 1981; *Asian Wall Street Journal,* February 23, 1982; *Pensacola News-Journal,* March 7, 1982.

*   *   *

TIGER, Virginia Marie   1940-

BRIEF ENTRY: Born August 20, 1940, in Montreal, Quebec, Canada. Canadian educator and author. Tiger has taught English at Rutgers University since 1970, and in 1975 she was also named director of women's studies. She worked during the 1960's as a broadcaster and drama critic. Tiger wrote *William Golding: The Dark Fields of Discovery* (Calder & Boyars, 1974) and *Everywoman* (Random House, 1977). *Address:* Department of English, Rutgers University, Newark, N.J. 07102.

*   *   *

TILLEY, Patrick   1928-

PERSONAL: Born July 4, 1928, in Essex, England. *Home:* 27 Coolhurst Rd., London N88ET, England. *Agent:* Peter Matson, Literistic Ltd., 32 West 40th St., 5F, New York, N.Y. 10018;

and A. D. Peters & Co. Ltd., 10 Buckingham St., London WC2N 6BU, England.

CAREER: Graphic designer, illustrator, and consultant art director, 1954-68; scriptwriter and author, 1968—. Production illustrator for film ''Oh What a Lovely War!,'' Paramount, 1969, and historical/technical adviser for film ''A Bridge Too Far,'' Twentieth-Century Fox, 1977.

WRITINGS: Fade-Out, Morrow, 1975; *Mission,* Little, Brown, 1981.

Screenplays: ''Only When I Larf,'' Paramount, 1968; ''Wuthering Heights,'' American-International, 1970; ''The People That Time Forgot,'' American-International, 1977; ''The Legacy,'' Universal, 1977.

Also author, under a pseudonym, of teleplays broadcast in England in the 1950's.

WORK IN PROGRESS: Federation, Cadillac, Hangfire, Clearwater, and *Talisman,* the five volumes in ''The Amtrak Wars,'' a science fiction saga set in a third-millenium, post-nuclear-holocaust U.S.A., for Sphere Books.

SIDELIGHTS: Tilley told *CA:* ''I am one of those unfortunate animals, the cross-category author, and, as such, live for the day when reviewers and booksellers stop judging my work on the basis of what I call 'pigeon-hole criteria' and see it for what it *is:* an attempt to write intelligent, entertaining stories containing, one hopes, intriguing ideas that prompt the reader to review his/her own attitudes, beliefs, and assumptions about both society and the world in general. I enjoy escapist literature but am unable to write it. For me, books have to instruct as well as entertain. The reader should emerge at the end of the book richer than he went in to it. But this didactic element should, ideally, never be obtrusive.

''All my books so far have been set in the United States. As a British writer, I find it more challenging to create characters and locales that ring true for American readers. And also a lot more fun. Names are important. I believe that they reflect the essence of the character. Nothing happens until I get the names right. Once I do, things start to fall into place. But alas, the task becomes more difficult with each book. I look back nostalgically to the days when I was an illustrator. My friends and family were welcome companions who had only to glance over my shoulder to appreciate what I was doing. Instantly. What a painful, lonely business writing is!''

AVOCATIONAL INTERESTS: Raising sheep and poultry, growing fruit and vegetables: ''the first tentative steps towards self-sufficiency on a remote Welsh hill farm.''

BIOGRAPHICAL/CRITICAL SOURCES: Best Sellers, August, 1975; *Christian Science Monitor,* September 3, 1975; *Los Angeles Times,* October 8, 1981; *Sunday Express,* November 1, 1981; *London Times,* November 11, 1981.

* * *

TIRBUTT, Honoria
(Emma Page)

PERSONAL: Born in West Hartlepool, Durham, England; daughter of John (a policeman and farmer) and Mary (a headmistress; maiden name, Sweeney) O'Mahony; married Peter du Sautoy (a government administrator), 1942 (marriage ended); married Eric Tirbutt (a businessman), 1947; children: (first marriage) Christopher, Anthony; (second marriage) Susan. *Education:* St. Anne's College, Oxford, M.A. *Home:* Woodland Lodge, 2 Bank St., Great Malvern, Worcestershire WR14 2JN, England.

CAREER: Worked as English teacher and lecturer in England and Gold Coast (now Ghana), 1944-63; writer.

WRITINGS—Novels; under pseudonym Emma Page: *In Loving Memory,* Collins, 1970; *Family and Friends,* Collins, 1972; *Add a Pinch of Cyanide,* Walker & Co., 1973 (published in England as *A Fortnight by the Sea,* Collins, 1973); *Element of Chance,* Collins, 1975; *Every Second Thursday,* Walker & Co., 1981; *Last Walk Home,* Collins, 1982.

Radio plays; under name Honoria Tirbutt; first broadcast by British Broadcasting Corp. (BBC-Radio): ''The Seeker,'' 1964; ''Years of Discretion,'' 1964; ''You're Only Middleaged Once,'' 1964; ''Prime of Life,'' 1965; ''Face Among the Shadows,'' 1966; ''Spring Comes Once,'' 1966.

Contributor of stories to *Good Housekeeping, Better Homes and Gardens, Woman's Own, Lectures Francaises, Australian Woman's Weekly,* and to other magazines.

SIDELIGHTS: Tirbutt told *CA:* ''I began writing when I was widowed and found it impossible to work outside the home and at the same time bring up my family. I enjoy writing crime novels and consider the genre worthy of serious attention.''

* * *

TOCZEK, Nick 1950-

PERSONAL: Born September 20, 1950, in Shipley, England; son of John (in textile manufacture) and Eileen (a bookshop manager; maiden name, Hayes-Smith) Toczek. *Education:* University of Birmingham, B.Sc. (with honors), 1972. *Politics:* ''Left wing—what else is there?'' *Religion:* ''My own.'' *Home and office:* L.W.M. Publications, 5 Beech Ter., Undercliffe, Bradford, West Yorkshire BD3 0PY, England.

CAREER: Little Word Machine, Bradford, England, founder, editor, and publisher, 1972—. Founder, editor, and publisher of L.W.M. Publications, 1972—; director of School of Living Poetry; conducts writers' workshops and community festivals. Performer and manager of mixed-media group Stereo Graffiti, 1975-77; lyricist and vocalist with rock band Ulterior Motives; radio broadcaster. *Member:* National Poetry Secretariat, London Poetry Secretariat. *Awards, honors:* Literary award from Yorkshire Arts Association, 1975-77.

WRITINGS: Because the Evenings (poems), Aquila, 1972; *The Book of Numbers* (poems and prose), Aquila, 1973; *Evensong* (poems), Sceptre, 1974; *Malignant Humour* (humor), Aquila, 1975; *Autobiography of a Friend* (novella), Aquila, 1975; *God Shave the Queen* (humor), Aquila, 1976; (editor with Philip Nanton and Yann Lovelock) *Melanthika: An Anthology of Pan-Caribbean Writing,* L.W.M. Publications, 1977; *Acts of Violence* (prose), Wayzgoose, 1979; *Complete Strangers Tell You Nothing* (poem), Zenia, 1979; *The Credible Adventures of Nick Toczek* (prose), Kawabata, 1979; *Lies* (poems), Rivelin, 1979; *Rock 'n' Roll Terrorism* (poems, songs, and prose), Aquila, 1981; *Pornograffiti* (humor), Aquila, 1982; (editor) *Melanthika Two,* L.W.M. Publications, 1983.

Author of ''Toczek's Rockcheck,'' a weekly column in *Bradford Star,* and ''Another Stick of Yorkshire Rock,'' a monthly column in *Arts Yorkshire.* Contributor of articles and reviews to magazines. Editor and publisher of *Wool City Rocker,* 1979—.

WORK IN PROGRESS: A collection of writings for Aquila, publication expected in 1982; ''Nick Toczek's Gory Details,'' a record album, release expected in 1983.

SIDELIGHTS: Toczek and his band have recorded ''Another Lover''/''Y'Gotta Shout,'' released by Motive Music in 1979.

He told *CA:* "The aim of my performance and verbal self-presentation is to make creative use of language an accessible and relevant art form for the general public. I want to be seen as a practicing writer rather than a private 'garret' poet, to write on themes of interpersonal, personal, and social politics with humor, verve, freshness, and integrity, to achieve a balance between 'pop' and literature, between ego and commitment, between credo and conscience."

AVOCATIONAL INTERESTS: Underwater diving.

*   *   *

TODD, Virgil H.   1921-

BRIEF ENTRY: Born June 22, 1921, in Jordonia, Tenn. American theologian, educator, and author. Todd was ordained a Presbyterian minister in 1944 and served as a pastor in Tennessee and Kentucky. Since 1954 he has been a professor of Old Testament and Hebrew at Memphis Theological Seminary. Todd wrote *Prophet Without Portfolio: A Study and Interpretation of the Prophecy of Second Isaiah* (Christopher, 1972). *Address:* 3095 East Glengarry Rd., Memphis, Tenn. 38128; and Department of Old Testament, Memphis Theological Seminary, 168 East Parkway S., Memphis, Tenn. 38104. *Biographical/critical sources: Who's Who in Religion,* Marquis, 1977.

*   *   *

TONSON, Jacob
See BENNETT, (Enoch) Arnold

*   *   *

TOOLEY, Michael John   1942-

PERSONAL: Born December 17, 1942, in Barnstaple, England; son of William Alfred (a chartered structural engineer) and Lynda Isis (Bedford) Tooley; married Rosanna Mary Mellor (an artist), September 5, 1973; children: Nicholas William, Anna Catharina Mary. *Education:* University of Birmingham, B.A., 1965; attended Columbia University, 1965-66; University of Lancaster, Ph.D., 1969. *Religion:* Church of England. *Home:* The Old Vicarage, Witton-le-Wear, County Durham DL14 OAN, England. *Office:* Department of Geography, University of Durham, South Rd., Durham DH1 3LE, England.

CAREER: University of Durham, Durham, England, lecturer, 1969-79, tutor at St. Aidan's College, 1973—, senior lecturer in geography, 1979—. British representative to UNESCO's International Geological Correlation Programme Project, 1976—. *Member:* Royal Geographical Society (fellow), British Ecological Society. *Awards, honors:* Fulbright fellow in the United States, 1965-66.

WRITINGS: (Editor with Clarence Kidson) *The Quaternary History of the Irish Sea,* Wiley, 1977; *Sea-Level Changes,* Clarendon Press, 1978; (with I. G. Simmons) *The Environment in British Prehistory,* Cornell University Press, 1981; (with wife, Rosanna M. Tooley) *The Gardens of Gertrude Jekyll in Northern England,* privately published, 1982. Editor of information bulletin of UNESCO's International Geological Correlation Programme Project.

WORK IN PROGRESS: Editing *The Climatic Scene: Essays in Honor of Professor G. Manley,* for Allen & Unwin, completion expected in 1984.

SIDELIGHTS: Tooley told *CA:* "My work, writings, and interests are eclectic. It was perhaps inevitable that I developed an interest in coastal and sea-level changes because I was born and brought up close to the coast of North Devon, England, and went to school on the Lancashire coast at a site only a few meters above sea-level. The coast and the sea have made a strong impression on me, as they have on countless generations of this island people—from Great Tooley of Ipswich onwards. My work on coastal and sea-level changes have both an academic and a practical value: the former to know the position of sea-levels and the dilation and contraction of the seas; the latter to know man's response and adaption to these changes in post-historic, historic, and present times. Human settlements are densely concentrated along estuaries and the world's coastlines: what would the impact be on them of a rise in sea-level of five meters?

"I am interested in the history of landscapes and the impact of prehistoric and historic man on the biosphere. Time and space perspectives have largely been forgotten, and we need to regain a sense of time and place that history, prehistory, and geography teach us. Landscape history can be brought right up to the present century, and the life and work of Gertrude Jekyll has been a continuing inspiration: she was concise and economical in her use of language, inventive and innovative in her craftwork and gardening, and full of wit and a joy for life and living things."

*   *   *

TOOMBS, John   1927-
(Fortune Kent, Jonathan Scofield, Jocelyn Wilde, Lee Davis Willoughby)

PERSONAL: Born March 29, 1927, in Newburgh, N.Y.; son of Wynne (an office supervisor) and Agnes (Hubbard) Toombs; married Betty Brebeck, December 30, 1950 (died January 24, 1968); married Jane Jamison (a writer), March 2, 1972; children: Michael, Leslie. *Education:* Syracuse University, B.A., 1949. *Home:* 4440 Date Ave., La Mesa, Calif. 92041. *Agent:* Jay Garon, Jay Garon-Brooke Associates, Inc., 415 Central Park W., New York, N.Y. 10025.

CAREER: Personnel technician for state of New York, 1950-53, and for state of Arizona, 1953-54; personnel director for Maricopa County, Ariz., 1954-55, and for Santa Cruz County, Calif., 1955-60; personnel analyst-assistant director for city of San Diego, Calif., 1960-66, and for San Diego County, 1966-74; writer, 1975—. *Military service:* U.S. Army, 1945-47. *Member:* Western Writers of America, San Diego Professional Writers. *Awards, honors:* Porgy Gold Medal from *West Coast Review of Books,* 1980, for *Bride of the Baja.*

WRITINGS—All novels: *Flag,* Zebra Books, 1979; *The Forty-Niners,* Dell, 1979; *Birds of War,* Dell, 1982.

Under pseudonym Fortune Kent: *Isle of the Seventh Sentry,* Pocket Books, 1974; *House of Masques,* Ballantine, 1975; *House at Canterbury,* Pocket Books, 1975; *Opal Legacy,* Ballantine, 1975.

Under pseudonym Jocelyn Wilde: *Bride of the Baja,* Pocket Books, 1980.

Under pseudonym Jonathan Scofield: *Storm in the South,* Dell, 1981.

Under pseudonym Lee Davis Willoughby: *The Border Breed,* Dell, 1981; *Flame of Virginia City,* Dell, 1982.

WORK IN PROGRESS: Two novels under Willoughby pseudonym, *The Miners* and *The Southerners,* both for Dell.

TORACK, Richard M(aurice) 1927-

PERSONAL: Born July 23, 1927, in Passaic, N.J.; son of Geza J. and Margaret (Voros) Torack; married Catherine Ann Reagan, April 18, 1953; children: Richard, James, Thomas, Margaret, William. *Education:* Seton Hall University, B.S., 1948; Georgetown University, M.D., 1952. *Home:* 1210 Glenvista Pl., Glendale, Mo. 63122. *Office:* Department of Pathology, Washington University, St. Louis, Mo. 63110.

CAREER: Paterson General Hospital, Paterson, N.J., 1952-53; Montefiore Hospital, Bronx, N.Y., resident, 1955-58, assistant pathologist, 1958-59, assistant neuropathologist, 1959-60; New York Hospital-Cornell Medical Center, New York, N.Y., assistant professor, 1962-65, associate professor of pathology, 1965-68, associate attending pathologist, 1962-68; Washington University, St. Louis, Mo., associate professor, 1968-70, professor of pathology and anatomy, 1970—. Consultant to Sloan-Kettering Memorial Hospital. *Military service:* U.S. Air Force, 1953-55, flight surgeon; became captain. *Member:* American Association for the Advancement of Science, American Association of Neuropathology, American Association of Pathology and Bacteriology, Histochemical Society, American Neurological Association. *Awards, honors:* Fellowships from National Cancer Institute, 1958-59, and National Institutes of Health, 1961-62.

WRITINGS: Pathologic Physiology of Adult Dementia, Springer-Verlag, 1977; *Your Brain Is Younger Than You Think,* Nelson-Hall, 1981.

Contributor: C.W.M. Adams, editor, *Histochemistry and Cytochemistry of the Nervous System,* Elsevier, 1965; Igor Klatzo and Franz Seitelberger, editors, *Brain Edema,* Springer-Verlag, 1967; Charles Wells, editor, *Dementia: The Failing Brain,* F. A. Davis, 1971; H. M. Zimmerman, editor, *Progress in Neuropathology,* Volume II, Grune, 1973; Eli Goldensohn and Stanley Appel, editors, *Scientific Approaches to Clinical Neurology,* Lea & Febiger, 1977. Contributor of more than sixty articles to medical journals.

WORK IN PROGRESS: Working on senility.

SIDELIGHTS: Torack wrote: "After twenty years in a laboratory studying brain diseases, I had a real dilemma on my hands. The brain changes that I used to diagnose senile dementia (senility) were also found to a lesser extent in eighty per cent of the non-demented population over sixty-five years old. Eighty per cent of these 'normal' people also had some type of memory problem, which would suggest that they were semi-senile. Unfortunately the paucity of the medical literature pro or con could afford no conclusion. I decided to make my own survey, to break out of my cloister, to interview old people living in the community and to determine their mental status. After two hundred interviews the conclusion was inescapable: there was no age at which the population at large becomes semi-senile. An unforeseen event occurred during these interviews. I had planned to write a professional monograph on adult dementia, and this news provoked a very consistent reply: 'Doctor, you must also write a book for old people.' My warm experiences during these interviews with the elderly convinced me of their sincerity and their need. As a result, after a hundred scientific publications in journals and books, I wrote *Your Brain Is Younger Than You Think.*

"I am currently working on a program in which I have determined that people with senile dementia have an immune deficiency. I am in the process of vaccinating these people to stimulate their immune responses, in order to arrest or reverse the mental degeneration."

* * *

TOWER, John G(oodwin) 1925-

BRIEF ENTRY: Born September 29, 1925, in Houston, Tex. American senator and author. Tower has been a U.S. senator since 1961, serving since 1973 as chairman of the Republican Policy Committee. Tower was one of several Republican leaders who influenced President Richard M. Nixon to resign his office in the wake of the Watergate scandal. He wrote *A Program for Conservatives* (Macfadden-Bartell, 1962). *Address:* 1609 Sparks St., Wichita Falls, Tex. 76302; and U.S. Senate, 142 Russell, Senate Office Building, Washington, D.C. 20510. *Biographical/critical sources: Current Biography,* Wilson, 1962; *Biographical Directory of the American Congress, 1774-1971,* U.S. Government Printing Office, 1971; *Political Profiles: The Johnson Years,* Facts on File, 1976; *Political Profiles: The Kennedy Years,* Facts on File, 1976; *Political Profiles: The Nixon/Ford Years,* Facts on File, 1979.

* * *

TOWNSEND, William Cameron 1896-1982

OBITUARY NOTICE: Born in 1896; died of leukemia, April 23, 1982, in Lancaster, S.C. Missionary, linguist, and author. As a missionary to Guatemala in 1917, Townsend encountered the Cakchiquel Indians, a tribe that had no written language. He spent the next twelve years learning Cakchiquel, developing an alphabet for the language and ultimately publishing a Cakchiquel translation of the New Testament. In 1935 he helped found Wycliffe Bible Translators, Inc., a nonprofit group that has translated the New Testament into more than one hundred thirty languages. Obituaries and other sources: *Newsweek,* May 10, 1982; *Time,* May 10, 1982.

* * *

TRAHAN, Ronald 1950-

PERSONAL: Surname is pronounced *Tray*-han; born July 22, 1950, in Pawtucket, R.I.; son of Gerard Paul (a steelworker) and Doris (a real estate agent; maiden name, Facteau) Trahan; married Marcia Samways (a sign writer), June 30, 1973; children: Rory Elizabeth. *Education:* Boston University, B.S., 1972; Framingham State College, M.Ed. (summa cum laude), 1977. *Home:* 85 Fairmount St., Marlborough, Mass. 01752. *Office:* Perkins School for the Blind, 175 North Beacon, Watertown, Mass. 02172.

CAREER: High school English teacher in Westford, Mass., 1972-78; free-lance writer and photographer in Marlborough, Mass., 1978-79; Sun Life of Canada, Wellesley Hills, Mass., writer and photographer, 1979-81; Perkins School for the Blind, Watertown, Mass., director of public relations and editor of *Lantern,* 1981—. *Member:* Photographic Society of America, Publicity Club of Boston.

WRITINGS: Careers for Horse Lovers, Houghton, 1981. Contributor of articles and photographs to magazines, including *Yankee, Modern Maturity, Exceptional Child, Horse of Course,* and *Horses for Juniors.*

WORK IN PROGRESS: Heartscars, a novel, publication expected in 1984.

BIOGRAPHICAL/CRITICAL SOURCES: Middlesex News, November 23, 1981; *Acton Independent,* January 17, 1982; *Worcester Telegram,* February 19, 1982.

TRAIN, John 1928-

PERSONAL: Born May 25, 1928, in New York, N.Y.; son of Arthur Cheney (an author and president of the National Institute of Arts and Letters) and Helen (Coster) Train; married Maria Teresa Cini di Pianzano in 1961 (divorced, 1976); married Frances Cheston, July 23, 1977; children: (first marriage) Helen, Nina, Lisa. *Education:* Harvard University, B.A., 1950, M.A., 1951; graduate study at Sorbonne, University of Paris, 1951-52. *Home address:* Box 157, R.D. 2, Bedford, N.Y.

CAREER: Paris Review, Paris, France, co-founder, 1952, managing editor, 1952-54; Train, Smith Counsel, New York, N.Y., president, 1959—. President of Chateau Malcasse, Lamarque-Margaux, Bordeaux, France, 1970—. Trustee of *Harvard Lampoon,* Cambridge, Mass., 1974—. *Military service:* U.S. Army, 1954-56; became first lieutenant. *Member:* Order of Colonial Lords of Manors in America, Pilgrims, Brooks's (London), Travellers (Paris), Century, Racquet and Tennis. *Awards, honors:* Named commendatore of Ordine Della Solidarieta (Italy), 1968, and Ordine del Merito Della Repubblica (Italy), 1977.

WRITINGS: Dance of the Money Bees: A Professional Speaks Frankly on Investing, Harper, 1973; *The Money Masters,* Harper, 1981; *Preserving Capital,* Crown, 1982.

"Remarkable" series; published by C. N. Potter: *Remarkable Names of Real People; or, How to Name Your Baby,* illustrations by Pierre Le Tan, introduction by S. J. Perelman, 1977; *Remarkable Occurrences,* illustrations by Pierre Le Tan, preface by George Plimpton, 1978; *Even More Remarkable Names,* 1979; *Remarkable Words With Astonishing Origins,* 1980; *Remarkable Relatives,* 1981.

Author of column "Financial Strategy" in *Forbes.* Contributor of articles to magazines, including *Reader's Digest, L'Economie* (Paris), and *Harvard.*

SIDELIGHTS: "History enshrines the deeds and dates of the lofty and mighty, but John Train serves as curator of the bizarre," commented *New York Times* critic Lawrence Van Gelder. An investment counselor by profession, Train is also a zealous collector of curiosa, as indicated by the series of books he began publishing in 1977. *Remarkable Names,* the first book in the "Remarkable" series, includes entries such as Dr. E. Z. Filler, a dentist, Mrs. Screech, a singing teacher, and Cardinal Sin, the Archbishop of Manila. The second book in the series, *True Remarkable Occurences,* had its origin in 1952, when Train began collecting accounts of oddities after reading a French newspaper story about a young woman who fell asleep while nursing her baby and awoke to find that she was suckling a snake. After taking the baby's place, the snake, according to the article, waved its tail as a distraction to silence the infant's cries. *Remarkable Words With Astonishing Origins,* the third book in Train's series, is a collection of nearly three hundred word origins, which Mason Buck of the *Los Angeles Times Book Review* called a display of "dedicated etymological sleuthing." It has been followed by *Remarkable Relatives* and *Even More Remarkable Names.*

In addition to the "Remarkable" series, Train has written books in his professional field. The first, *Dance of the Money Bees,* was "one of the more entertaining and informative books on the investment game to appear in the last two decades," assessed Christopher Lehmann-Haupt in the *New York Times. The Money Masters* received equally high praise from *Chicago Tribune Book World* critic Paul E. Erdman, who called the book "the best one in the investment field that I have read in years."

BIOGRAPHICAL/CRITICAL SOURCES: New Statesman, March 31, 1978; *Times Literary Supplement,* November 24, 1978; *New York Times,* December 6, 1978, November 27, 1979, January 8, 1980; *New York Times Book Review,* February 3, 1980, March 8, 1981; *Chicago Tribune Book World,* April 13, 1980; *Los Angeles Times Book Review,* December 7, 1980, March 22, 1981; *Washington Post Book World,* February 8, 1981, March 1, 1981; *London Times,* February 19, 1981.

* * *

TRAVIS, Stephen H(enry) 1944-

PERSONAL: Born March 11, 1944, in Bury, England; son of William (a teacher) and Mildred (Greaves) Travis; married Patricia Eastman (a lecturer), August 29, 1970; children: Emma. *Education:* Corpus Christi College, Cambridge, B.A., 1965, M.A., 1969, Ph.D., 1970. *Religion:* Methodist. *Residence:* Nottingham, England. *Office:* Department of Academic Studies, St. John's College, Bramcote, Nottinghamshire NG9 3DS, England.

CAREER: St. John's College, Bramcote, England, lecturer in biblical studies, 1969—, director of academic studies, 1979—. Visiting lecturer at Union Biblical Seminary, Yavamal, India, summer, 1974. *Member:* Society of New Testament Studies, Tyndale Fellowship for Biblical Research, Fellowship of European Evangelical Theologians.

WRITINGS: The Jesus Hope, Word, 1974, Inter-Varsity Press, 1975, revised edition, 1981; *Christian Hope and the Future,* Inter-Varsity Press, 1980 (published in England as *Christian Hope and the Future of Man,* Inter-Varsity Press, 1980); (with Gerald H. Hughes) *Introducing the Bible,* Lion, 1981; (with William Neil) *More Difficult Sayings of Jesus,* Mowbray, 1982; *I Believe in the Second Coming of Jesus,* Eerdmans, 1982.

WORK IN PROGRESS: Research on the notion of divine retribution in the New Testament.

SIDELIGHTS: Travis wrote: "I have a special interest in developing audiovisual media for Christian communication, and am in charge of the television studio at my college." *Avocational interests:* Sports, music, photography, travel.

* * *

TRESCH, John William, Jr. 1937-

BRIEF ENTRY: Born March 28, 1937, in Nashville, Tenn. American theologian, educator, and author. Tresch has been a professor of evangelism at Southeastern Baptist Theological Seminary since 1978. He was chaplain of the Tennessee General Assembly from 1968 to 1972. He wrote *A Prayer for All Seasons* (Broadman, 1971), *Acorns to Oaks: The Story of Nashville Baptist Association and Its Affiliated Churches* (Nashville Baptist Association, 1972), and *Book Alive!* (Broadman, 1973). *Address:* Department of Evangelism, Southeastern Baptist Theological Seminary, Wake Forest, N.C. 27587. *Biographical/critical sources: Directory of American Scholars,* Volume IV: *Philosophy, Religion, and Law,* 7th edition, Bowker, 1978.

* * *

TRIPP, Wallace Whitney 1940-

PERSONAL: Born June 26, 1940, in Boston, Mass.; children: one son, one daughter. *Education:* Received diploma from Boston Museum School; and B.Ed. from Keene State College;

graduate study at University of New Hampshire. *Home address:* Hancock, N.H. 03449.

CAREER: Free-lance illustrator and author; also illustrator for Pawprints Greeting Cards. *Member:* Authors Guild. *Awards, honors:* Recipient of *Boston Globe-Horn Book* award for illustrations, 1977, for *Granfa' Grig Had a Pig.*

WRITINGS—Self-illustrated; for children: (Adapter) *The Tale of a Pig: A Caucasian Folktale,* McGraw, 1968; (compiler) *A Great Big Ugly Man Came Up and Tied His Horse to Me* (verse), Little, Brown, 1973; *My Uncle Podger: A Picture Book* (based on a passage from *Three Men in a Boat* by Jerome K. Jerome), Little, Brown, 1975; (compiler) *Granfa' Grig Had a Pig* (verse), Little, Brown, 1976; *Sir Toby Jingle's Beastly Journey,* Coward, 1976; *Self-Portrait: Wallace Tripp,* Addison-Wesley, 1979.

Illustrator; all children's fiction, except as noted: Ruth Christoffer Carlsen, *Henrietta Goes West,* Houghton, 1966; Carlsen, *Hildy and the Cuckoo Clock,* Houghton, 1966; Ilse Kleberger, *Grandmother Oma,* Atheneum, 1967; Andrew Lang, editor, *Read Me Another Fairy Tale,* Grosset, 1967; Katherine E. Miller, *Saint George: A Christmas Mummers' Play,* Houghton, 1967; Gerald Dumas, *Rabbits Rafferty,* Houghton, 1968; Carlsen, *Sam Bottleby,* Houghton, 1968; Felice Holman, *The Holiday Rat, and The Utmost Mouse* (short stories), Norton, 1969; John Erwin, *Mrs. Fox,* Simon & Schuster, 1969.

Scott Corbett, *The Baseball Bargain,* Little, Brown, 1970; Tom Paxton, *Jennifer's Rabbit,* Putnam, 1970; Rene Guillot, *Little Dog Lost,* Lothrup, 1970; Betty Brock, *No Flying in the House,* Harper, 1970; F. N. Monjo, *Pirates in Panama,* Simon & Schuster, 1970; Robert Sidney Bigelow, *Stubborn Bear,* Little, Brown, 1970; Julian Bagley, *Candle-Lighting Time in Bodidalee* (folktales), foreword by Alfred V. Frankenstein, American Heritage Publishing Co., 1971; Peggy Parish, *Come, Back, Amelia Bedelia,* Harper, 1971; Victor Sharoff, *The Heart of the Wood,* Coward, 1971; Marguerita Rudolph, adapter, *The Magic Egg, and Other Folk Stories of Rumania,* Little, Brown, 1971; Peter Hallard, *Puppy Lost in Lapland,* F. Watts, 1971; Patricia Thomas, *"Stand Back," Said the Elephant, "I'm Going to Sneeze!,"* Lothrup, 1971; Miriam Anne Bourne, *Tigers in the Woods,* Coward, 1971; Tony Johnston, *The Adventures of Mole and Troll,* Putnam, 1972; Cynthia Jameson, adapter, *Catofy the Clever* (folktale), Coward, 1972; Liesel Moak Skorpen, *Old Arthur,* Harper, 1972; Parish, *Play Ball, Amelia Bedelia,* Harper, 1972; Carolyn Lane, *The Voices of Greenwillow Pond,* Houghton, 1972; Boris Vladimirovich Zakhoder, *The Crocodile's Toothbrush,* McGraw, 1973; Malcolm Hall, *Headlines,* Coward, 1973; Johnston, *Mole and Troll Trim the Tree,* Putnam, 1974, revised edition, 1980; Jan Wahl, *Pleasant Fieldmouse's Halloween Party,* Putnam, 1974; Robert Fremlin, *Three Friends,* Little, Brown, 1975; Ernest Lawrence Thayer, *Casey at the Bat: A Ballad of the Republic, Sung in the Year 1888* (verse), Coward, 1978.

AVOCATIONAL INTERESTS: Classical music, traveling, aviation.

BIOGRAPHICAL/CRITICAL SOURCES: New York Times Book Review, March 5, 1968, May 27, 1973, September 12, 1976; *Times Literary Supplement,* December 5, 1968, December 6, 1974; Wallace Tripp, *Self-Portrait: Wallace Tripp,* Addison-Wesley, 1979.

*   *   *

TRUMAN, Harry S.   1884-1972

PERSONAL: Born May 8, 1884, in Lamar, Mo.; died December 26, 1972, in Kansas City, Mo.; buried on grounds of Truman Library, Independence, Mo.; son of John Anderson (a farmer) and Martha Ellen (Young) Truman; married Elizabeth Virginia (Bess) Wallace, June 18, 1919; children: Mary Margaret (Mrs. Clifton Daniel). *Education:* Attended Kansas City Law School, Kansas City, Mo., 1923-25. *Politics:* Democrat. *Religion:* Baptist. *Residence:* Independence, Mo.

CAREER: Timekeeper for L. J. Smith's railroad construction company, Sheffield, Mo., 1901; *Kansas City Star,* Kansas City, Mo., mail clerk, 1901-c. 1902; National Bank of Commerce, Kansas City, clerk, c. 1902-05; Union National Bank, Kansas City, bookkeeper, 1905-06; manager of Truman family farm at Grandview, Mo., 1906-17; owner of haberdashery with Edward Jacobson, Kansas City, 1919-21; Jackson County Court, Jackson County, Mo., judge, 1922-24, presiding judge, 1927-35; Kansas City Automobile Club, Kansas City, membership salesman, 1925-26; U.S. senator from Missouri, 1935-45; vice-president of the United States, 1945; thirty-third president of the United States, 1945-53. Co-owner and manager of zinc mine in Commerce, Okla., 1915; co-owner and treasurer of Morgan & Co. (oil-drillers), 1916-19; co-owner of Security State Bank, 1926; co-owner and president of Community Savings and Loan Association, 1925-32. Jackson County election clerk, 1906, and road overseer, 1914; postmaster of Grandview, Mo., 1915; organized Jackson County Farm Bureau and first young people's farm club in western Missouri; president of National Old Trails Association and Greater Kansas City Planning Association, 1930; state director of federal reemployment, 1934. *Military service:* Missouri National Guard, 1905-17; U.S. Army, 1917-19, served in artillery; became captain; Field Artillery Reserve, 1919-40; became colonel.

MEMBER: County Judges Association (Missouri), American Legion, Masons (thirty-second degree; former Grand Master of Kansas City Lodge), Kansas City Athletic Club.

WRITINGS: Memoirs, Doubleday, Volume I: *Year of Decisions,* 1955, Volume II: *Years of Trial and Hope,* 1956; *Mr. Citizen,* Random House, 1960, reprinted as *Harry Truman Speaks His Mind,* Popular Library, 1975; *The Autobiography of Harry S. Truman,* edited by Robert H. Ferrell, Colorado Associated University Press, 1980.

Compilations: Cyril Clemens, editor, *Truman Speaks* (speeches), introduction by Andrew J. Higgins, Didier, 1946; M. B. Schnapper, editor, *The Truman Program: Addresses and Messages,* introduction by Francis J. Myers, Public Affairs Press, 1949; William Hillman, editor, *Mr. President: Personal Papers of Harry S. Truman,* Farrar, Straus, 1952; Louis W. Koenig, editor, *The Truman Administration: Its Principles and Practice* (speeches, documents, and press conference discussions), New York University Press, 1956, reprinted, Greenwood Press, 1979; David S. Horton, editor, *Freedom and Equality* (addresses), University of Missouri Press, 1960; George S. Caldwell, editor, *Good Old Harry: The Wit and Wisdom of Harry S. Truman,* Hawthorn Books, 1966; Monty M. Poen, editor, *Strictly Personal and Confidential: The Letters That Harry Truman Never Mailed,* Little, Brown, 1982.

Alex J. Goldman, editor, *The Truman Wit,* Citadel Press, 1966; T. S. Settel and others, editors, *The Quotable Harry S. Truman,* Grosset, 1967; Ted Sheldon, editor, *The Man from Missouri: The Memorable Words of the Thirty-third President,* Hallmark, 1970; Mark Goodman, editor, *Give 'em Hell, Harry!,* Award Books, 1975; Robert L. Polley, editor, *The Truman Years: The Words and Times of Harry S. Truman,* Country Beautiful, 1976; Ferrell, editor, *Off the Record: The Private Papers of Harry S. Truman,* Harper, 1980.

Sound recordings: *Harry Truman,* Mark 56 Records 706, 1975; *World War II Ends,* Mark 56 Records 716, 1976.

SIDELIGHTS: On April 12, 1945, after serving as vice-president for less than three months, Harry S. Truman succeeded Franklin Delano Roosevelt as president of the United States. "With the exception of Abraham Lincoln and perhaps Franklin Roosevelt," wrote political writer Alfred Steinberg, "no President took office in a period of greater crisis than did Harry Truman." During his years as president, Truman was required to make many far-reaching decisions, of which the first, and perhaps most difficult, was his decision to drop atomic bombs on the Japanese cities of Hiroshima and Nagasaki. Truman, who had been advised that the war with Japan would last another year and a half, learned of the atomic project shortly after taking office, and soon became convinced that the powerful weapon could save numerous lives by quickly ending the hostilities. Later disclosing that "it was not an easy decision to make," Truman said, "I did not like the weapon. But I had no qualms if in the long run millions of lives could be saved." Truman never wavered from that conviction nor voiced regret over his decision to drop the bombs, though his action was widely criticized in years to come.

Epitomized by the sign on his White House desk which read, "The buck stops here," Truman became known for his willingness to make difficult decisions and to personally accept full responsibility for them. Describing Truman as "one of the most conscientious, dynamic and . . . clearsighted Presidents we have ever had," historian Allan Nevins wrote in the *New York Times Book Review* that Truman "may well go down in history as The Man of Decision."

Harry S. Truman first ran for public office during the 1920's when political parties were still largely dominated by machine politicians like the Pendergasts of western Missouri. Truman's early campaigns were backed by Tom Pendergast, the Democratic boss of Kansas City, Mo., who also helped elect Truman to the U.S. Senate in 1934. In response to accusations that his role as a senator was to serve as "Boss Tom's mouthpiece in Congress," Truman once declared, "I don't follow his [Pendergast's] advice on legislation. I vote the way I believe Missourians as a whole want me to vote." When Pendergast was later convicted of income tax fraud, Truman remained friendly with the politician even though the relationship nearly cost Truman his Senate seat in the election of 1940. Margaret Truman explained in her biography of the former president that her father was a man of intense party loyalty who "supported the Pendergasts because they were Democrats, and they supported him for the same reason."

From the time Truman arrived in Washington in 1935, he ardently supported Roosevelt's New Deal, and favored such legislation as the Social Security Act, the Wagner Labor Relations Act, and the Tennessee Valley Authority (TVA) Act. Truman was also interested in transportation issues (he had been involved in the construction of $60 million in highways and public buildings while a county judge in Missouri), and presented a bill before the Senate that required operators of motor vehicles used in interstate traffic to be licensed. As chairman of two interstate commerce subcommittees, Truman promoted the passage of the Civil Aeronautics Act, as well as the Railroad Transportation Act of 1940, for which he conducted a thorough investigation of railroad financing. When his probe into the Missouri Pacific Railroad uncovered political malfeasance, Truman resisted pressure from his constituents at home who urged him to abandon the inquiry, and he continued to gather evidence.

Truman began another major enterprise in 1941 when a tour of the nation's defense facilities convinced him of the need for a Senate investigation into waste in the U.S. defense program. The result was the Special Committee to Investigate Contracts Under the National Defense Program, better known as the Truman Committee. Beginning with a study of nine army camps that exposed $100 million waste in construction costs, the committee went on to uncover numerous instances of corruption and wasteful spending within the military establishment. At a cost of only $400,000 the Truman Committee ultimately saved the nation $15 billion. As a result of Truman's work on the committee, reported Steinberg in his biography of Truman, "the *St. Louis Post-Dispatch,* which had been [the senator's] severest critic in the past, called him 'one of the most useful and at the same time one of the most forthright and fearless of the [then] ninety-six senators.'"

Truman's committee work brought him national attention, and he began to be spoken of as a vice-presidential candidate. The ailing Roosevelt, who was not expected to survive a fourth term, at first appeared to favor the incumbent vice-president, Henry A. Wallace, or the director of the Office of War Mobilization, James F. Byrnes, but finally endorsed Truman as the candidate least likely to antagonize voters. Though concerned about the awesome burdens of the presidency, which would devolve upon the vice-president in the event of Roosevelt's death, Truman accepted the nomination and campaigned vigorously for the ticket. As expected, the Roosevelt-Truman slate won easily.

Though similarly energetic when he ran as a presidential candidate against Thomas E. Dewey in 1948, Truman was given little chance of winning. Rejected by major political factions, from Southern segregationists to Northern pacifists, Truman assumed responsibility for his own campaign and went, as he said, "directly to the people in all parts of the country with a personal message." He began with a coast-to-coast railroad trip, giving seventy-six speeches along the way. When the campaign finally drew to a close, he had traveled 31,700 miles and delivered 256 speeches. His plain-talking, fighting spirit gave rise to the popular exclamation, "Give 'em hell, Harry." Even so, as late as election night, Truman was not expected to win; the *Chicago Tribune,* for example, declared Dewey the winner in its early edition. Nevertheless, in an upset that refuted all of the major polls, the pugnacious Missourian won the election.

Truman, said *New York Times Book Review*'s John Herbers, "was . . . the last President to serve when the office was still in human scale, [yet] the crises he confronted both abroad and at home in some ways make today's seem pale." The Cold War, for example, was set in motion when the Soviet Union failed to adhere to the postwar territorial settlement of Europe that had been agreed upon at Yalta and Potsdam in 1945. "The Russians were planning world conquest," wrote Truman in the first volume of his memoirs. "Whereas Roosevelt tended to be flexible in coping with the Russians," observed Alden Whitman in the *New York Times,* "Truman held sterner views." After negotiations with Soviet Foreign Minister Vyacheslav Molotov over installation of a more democratic constitution in Poland proved fruitless, Truman exclaimed, "Force is the only thing the Russians understand." Under Truman tough resistance to Soviet expansion became the essence of U.S. foreign policy.

Viewing the United States as the principal protector of the non-communist (free) world, Truman proposed to Congress in March, 1947, a program of economic and military aid to nations threatened by Soviet invasion or intervention. The first application of the program, known as the Truman Doctrine, occurred when the United States took over support of anti-communist efforts in Greece and Turkey from Great Britain. Truman was later quoted in the *New York Times* as saying that this action "put the world on notice that it would be our policy to support the cause of freedom wherever it was threatened." When the Soviets blockaded the Western sector of Berlin in 1948 in an attempt to undermine American hegemony in Europe, Truman, standing firm, ordered an airlift of food and medicine into the beleaguered city. When the flights were maintained over a period of months, the Soviet Union yielded, withdrawing the blockade.

Truman also supported Secretary of State George Marshall's European Recovery Plan (also known as the Marshall Plan), which encouraged economic cooperation among war-shattered nations of Western Europe and provided for financial support in the recovery efforts from the United States. Moreover, observed Whitman, "Truman's leadership of the non-Communist world was reflected in vigorous support of the United Nations. Through its mechanism he hoped to keep peace by positive actions, as well as by thwarting Soviet power plays and intrigues."

Determined to reinforce America's alliance with Europe, Truman proposed the Point Four program in his inaugural address in 1949. He described the program as "a plan to furnish 'know-how' from our experience in the fabulous development of our own resources," and added that "[Point Four] will be our greatest contribution to world peace." Historian Arnold Toynbee, said Steinberg, "predicted that it would not be the discovery of atomic energy but the solicitude of privileged peoples for the unprivileged as voiced in Truman's Point Four and its implementation that 'will be remembered as the signal achievement of the age.'"

Truman also sought to strengthen American military alliances and so proposed the North Atlantic Treaty Organization (NATO), a mutual security system comprising Western European nations and the United States. Its purpose was to bolster U.S.-supported economic recovery in Europe with American military strength. The treaty was signed in April, 1949, and Dwight D. Eisenhower was selected as NATO's first commander.

Noting Truman's vigorous foreign policy, the *London Times* maintained: "President Truman initiated and to a large extent implemented the great American postwar task of saving Europe, first from economic disaster and then from the threat of Russian military aggression. Faults—some of them serious—in diplomatic timing, tactics, and judgment may mar Truman's record in Europe, but its broad achievement will surely stand the test of history."

Containment of communism, however, proved more elusive in Asia than in Europe. Though Truman was able to limit Russian involvement in the postwar demilitarization and occupation of Japan, according to the terms of the peace treaty which followed the surrender, the Soviets were granted control of Korea north of the thirty-eighth parallel. Truman, moreover, was unable to secure a compromise peace in the Chinese civil war, and in 1949 a communist regime under Mao Tse-Tung took control of mainland China.

The potential for crisis in the Far East became manifest on June 25, 1950, when communist troops from North Korea attacked South Korea. In a move that has been widely heralded, Truman immediately committed American troops to stop the aggression. Though the security of the United States was not in immediate danger, Truman perceived the invasion of South Korea as another Soviet test of Allied strength, and regarded

his own move as an effort to prevent a third world war. Backed by the United Nations Security Council, the operation was described as a "police action." A *London Times* reporter commented: "Truman, in this action, proved himself to be the first world leader to support the principle of collective security with deeds as well as words."

Communist China's entry into the conflict in Korea precipitated a domestic crisis involving General Douglas MacArthur, commander of the United Nations forces and an idolized war hero. In defiance of a presidential mandate restricting the fighting to Korea, MacArthur publicly argued for a military strike against China. In a move that was subsequently praised by historians and politicals scientists as a great victory of civil over military authority, Truman fired MacArthur. At the time, however, the dismissal was widely criticized and seriously threatened Truman's political strength.

Truman consistently met with greater obstacles and lesser successes in domestic matters than in foreign affairs. The core of his domestic policy, dubbed the Fair Deal, consisted of such welfare legislation as a national health program, public housing, federal aid to education, and civil and human rights programs. Truman's "sole Fair Deal victory," reported Steinberg, "came with the passage of his low-cost public housing bill and it passed only because Republican Senator Taft promoted it." Congress was similarly reluctant to approve Truman's economic package which called for full employment, an increased minimum wage, and higher farm prices. He also proposed extending wartime economic controls in an attempt to stem postwar inflation. Though many of these programs eventually became public policy, in most of these goals Truman was considered ahead of his time. When the Medicare bill was finally passed in 1965, it was reported in the *New York Times* that President Lyndon Johnson, who signed the bill in Truman's presence, declared the former president "the real daddy of Medicare."

Truman's resistence to eliminating price controls, his vetoes of the anti-labor Taft-Hartley bill, and a proposed tax cut antagonized the business community and led some observers to regard him as a pro-labor president. However, both labor and industry came to view Truman with distrust as a result of a series of dramatic confrontations with each group. For example, Truman's concern about the impact of rising inflation on the economic stability of the nation led him to break two strikes by coal miners by seizing the mines and fining the United Mine Workers union. He also seized the rail carriers to prevent a strike by railway unions. In each case the union backed down and reduced its demands. In a similar attempt to prevent both a strike and a price increase in the steel industry, Truman seized the nation's steel mills. The industry challenged the seizure before the Supreme Court, which ruled that the president had exceeded his authority; Truman was forced to capitulate and approve a price increase that he believed would stimulate rampant inflation.

Truman was also thwarted on an issue of national security that had emerged from the trial of Alger Hiss, a State Department official who was convicted of perjuring himself when tried for giving classified information to the Soviet Union. In response to subsequent public demands for increased internal security, Congress passed the McCarran bill which called for registering all communist organizations, jailing potential spies and saboteurs, designating communist publications as propaganda, and denying passports and defense plant jobs to communists. Though accused by Senator Joseph McCarthy of being "soft" on communism, Truman vetoed the bill, protesting that it put the government in the business of thought control. "There is," he maintained, "no more fundamental axiom of American freedom than the familiar statement: "In a free country, we punish men for the crimes they commit but never for the opinions they have."" Enacted as the Internal Security Act of 1950, the McCarran bill was passed over Truman's veto.

Puzzled observers have frequently commented upon Truman's difficulties with Congress on domestic issues. Nevins, for example, remarked that "Truman was the greatest 'veto President' since [Grover] Cleveland, and his vetoes were much to his credit. But we are left wondering why a man of his long Senatorial experience was unable to do more to influence legislation in its gestative stages." Truman had some significant domestic successes, however, including unification of the Departments of War and Navy into the Department of Defense and passage of the Atomic Energy Act, under which nuclear research and production of fissionable material came under federal control. "For better or worse," assessed biographer Bert Cochran, "Truman's place in history will be judged not by his lackluster exploits at home, but by his conduct of that complex of matters assigned to foreign affairs. These dominated his administration; they became the forcing house for far-reaching decisions, even in domestic concerns."

Truman's actions as president reflected the complexity and sophistication of the newly emerging atomic age, but "he will probably be remembered," wrote a *London Times* reporter, "as the little man who rose to great places and did great deeds, but who yet remained an ordinary fellow with no aura of power, his fair share of faults and a few endearing idiosyncrasies." The reporter described Truman's strongest political asset as "an enormous earthy relish for the rough and tumble of the hustings; he revelled in attack on a folksy level."

Though sometimes faulted for his short temper, his salty language, and his outspoken criticism of those he disliked, Truman's "single-minded honesty, whatever his limitations," observed Nevins, "gives his career a real loftiness of tone." Also impressive, remarked Nevins, was Truman's "exceptionally high conception of the presidency and his determination to live up to it." What is more, Nevins concluded, "Because of his firm grasp of principle, he . . . raised not only America but the free West to a new level of strength, and placed civilization forever in his debt."

A substantial part of Truman's retirement years was devoted to the Harry S. Truman Library Institute for National and International Affairs, a storehouse of information on the presidency and the Truman administration. In addition to public exhibits, the library houses Truman's public and private papers and a vast collection of books. Truman maintained an office at the library, and frequently addressed students groups who came to visit. Reporters, finding that Truman continued to be feisty and outspoken after his retirement from public office, often accompanied the former president on his morning walks. "Truman's views on public issues were much sought after," it was reported in the *New York Times*, "and he became the master of the walking news conference." He also campaigned on behalf of Democratic presidential candidates Adlai Stevenson, John Kennedy, Lyndon Johnson, and Hubert Humphrey, appeared on a television series on current events, wrote articles for the North American Newspaper Alliance, and prepared a two-volume autobiographical account of his presidency.

The first book of Truman's memoirs, *Year of Decisions*, concerns his realization that with the defeat of Germany the Soviet Union had become the West's major foe, and, observed Nevins, it "is written in precisely the way we would expect: crisp, vigorous, honest, sometimes a bit over-simplified, and with [Truman's] own appealing mixture of modesty and self-con-

fidence." *Social Forces* reporter J. L. Godfrey concurred, asserting that "there is a simplicity and directness in the narrative that bespeak the man himself; there is also a warmth and zest that make the tale amazingly well told." "The former President has no literary style whatever," appraised *Saturday Review*'s Walter Millis, yet the book "is a big one—big in its nearly six hundred pages, big in its grasp of the immense events with which it is concerned, and big in its straightforward, at times almost ingenuous, revelation of the special quality and character of its author."

The second volume, *Years of Trial and Hope,* an account of the many crises that occurred during the final six years of Truman's administration, illustrates the author's characteristic decisiveness and his feisty personality. Though similar to *Year of Decisions* in length, detail, and literary style, *Years of Trial and Hope,* related Millis, is especially notable for Truman's "tart comments upon the men who fought or failed him or savagely attacked policies which to him seemed essential." According to *New Republic* reporter G. W. Johnson, the book "is the most vivid self-portrait ever drawn by a President and it will be indispensable to future historians."

BIOGRAPHICAL/CRITICAL SOURCES—Books: Harry S. Truman, *Memoirs,* Doubleday, Volume I: *Year of Decisions,* 1955, Volume II: *Years of Trial and Hope,* 1956; Alfred Steinberg, *The Man from Missouri: The Life and Times of Harry S. Truman,* Putnam, 1962; Steinberg, *Harry S. Truman,* Putnam, 1963; John W. Spanier, *The Truman-MacArthur Controversy and the Korean War,* Norton, 1965; R. Alton Lee, *Truman and Taft-Hartley: A Question of Mandate,* University of Kentucky Press, 1966; Cabell B.H. Phillips, *The Truman Presidency: The History of Triumphant Succession,* Macmillan, 1966; Joseph Gies, *Harry S. Truman,* Doubleday, 1968; Arthur Frederick McClure, *The Truman Administration and the Problems of Postwar Labor,* Fairleigh Dickinson University Press, 1969.

Howard B. Furer, editor, *Harry S. Truman, 1884- : Chronology-Documents-Biographical Aids,* Oceana, 1970; Susan Meckfessel Hartmann, *Truman and the Eightieth Congress,* University of Missouri Press, 1971; Athan George Theoharis, *Seeds of Repression: Harry S. Truman and the Origins of McCarthyism,* Quadrangle, 1971; Richard M. Freeland, *The Truman Doctrine and the Origins of McCarthyism: Foreign Policy, Domestic Politics, and Internal Security, 1946-1948,* Knopf, 1972; Alonzo L. Hamby, *Beyond the New Deal: Harry S. Truman and American Liberalism,* Columbia University Press, 1973; Bert Cochran, *Harry Truman and the Crisis Presidency,* Funk, 1973; Richard F. Haynes, *The Awesome Power: Harry S. Truman as Commander in Chief,* Louisiana State University Press, 1973; Margaret Truman, *Harry S. Truman,* Morrow, 1973; Hamby, editor, *Harry S. Truman and the Fair Deal,* Heath, 1974.

Philip H. Vaughan, *The Truman Administration's Legacy for Black America,* Mojave Books, 1976; Richard J. Walton, *Henry Wallace, Harry Truman, and the Cold War,* Viking, 1976; Robert J. Donovan, *Conflict and Crisis: The Presidency of Harry S. Truman,* Norton, 1977; Theoharis, *The Truman Presidency: The Origins of the Imperial Presidency and the National Security State,* Earl M. Coleman, 1979; John Hollister Hedley, *Harry S. Truman: The "Little" Man From Missouri,* Barron's, 1979; Harold Foote Gosnell, *Truman's Crises: A Political Biography of Harry S. Truman,* Greenwood Press, 1980; *Autobiography of Harry S. Truman,* edited by Robert H. Ferrell, Colorado Associated University Press, 1980; *Strictly Personal and Confidential: The Letters That Harry Truman Never Mailed,* edited by Monte M. Poen, Little, Brown, 1982.

Periodicals: *Nation,* January 19, 1946, April 21, 1951, December 3, 1955, March 17, 1956; *Saturday Evening Post,* February 2, 1946, April 20, 1946, June 21, 1947, September 25, 1948, October 2, 1948; *New Republic,* April 15, 1946, January 24, 1949, March 19, 1956; *Newsweek,* August 12, 1946, June 23, 1947, October 27, 1947, October 2, 1950, March 24, 1952, November 7, 1955, March 23, 1959, June 13, 1960, March 24, 1975; *Time,* April 7, 1947, April 23, 1951, February 2, 1953, July 2, 1956, February 10, 1958, May 30, 1960, April 12, 1968; *New Statesman & Nation,* June 12, 1948; *New York Times Magazine,* April 10, 1949, October 8, 1950, March 11, 1951, April 22, 1951.

U.S. News & World Report, April 14, 1950, May 2, 1952, May 9, 1952, May 4, 1959, January 2, 1959, September 29, 1975; *Harper's,* May, 1952; *Saturday Review,* November 5, 1955, March 4, 1956; *New York Times Book Review,* November 6, 1955, March 3, 1956, December 7, 1980; *Commonweal,* December 25, 1955; *New Yorker,* May 9, 1959.

Esquire, September, 1969, August, 1971, January, 1976; *Political Science Quarterly,* June, 1972, spring, 1975; *Christian Century,* January 17, 1973; *American Heritage,* April, 1977; *Washington Post Book World,* April 5, 1982.

OBITUARIES: *New York Times,* December 27, 1972; *London Times,* December 27, 1972; *New Republic,* January 6, 1973; *Time,* January 8, 1973; *Newsweek,* January 8, 1973; *National Review,* January 19, 1973; *Christianity Today,* January 19, 1973.*

—*Sketch by Susan M. Trosky*

*   *   *

TUFTE, Virginia J(ames) 1918-

BRIEF ENTRY: Born August 19, 1918, in Meadow Grove, Neb. American educator and author. Tufte began teaching at University of Southern California in 1964. She has been a professor of English there since 1974. She wrote *The Poetry of Marriage: The Epithalamium in Europe and Its Development in England* (Tinnon-Brown, 1970) and *Grammar as Style* (Holt, 1971). She edited *High Wedlock Then Be Honoured: Wedding Poems From Nineteen Countries and Twenty-five Centuries* (Viking, 1970) and *Changing Images of the Family* (Yale University Press, 1979). *Address:* Department of English, University of Southern California, Los Angeles, Calif. 90007. *Biographical/critical sources: Directory of American Scholars,* Volume II: *English, Speech, and Drama,* 7th edition, Bowker, 1978.

*   *   *

TULLETT, James Stuart 1912-

PERSONAL: Born April 24, 1912, in Birmingham, England; son of Arthur Frank (a furniture buyer) and Susan Charlotte (Hamilton) Tullett; married May Isobel Robertson (a school secretary), December 12, 1951; children: John Gordon, Duncan Stuart, Sarah Margaret. *Education:* Attended grammar school in Chipping Campden, England. *Home:* 191 Tukapa St., New Plymouth, New Zealand.

CAREER: *Evesham Journal,* Evesham, Worcestershire, England, indentured apprentice, 1929-35; *Jersey Morning News,* Channel Islands, country correspondent, 1936-38; *Grey River Argus,* New Zealand, subeditor, 1949-51; *Marlborough Express,* New Zealand, subeditor, 1951-62; *Taranaki Herald,* New Zealand, subeditor, features writer, and columnist, 1962-80. Free-lance writer; book reviewer for Radio New Zealand.

Wartime service: Served in Middle East and Germany, 1938-49. *Member:* New Plymouth West Rotary Club (president, 1970).

WRITINGS—Novels: *Tar White,* R. Hale, 1960; *Yellow Streak,* R. Hale, 1963; *Red Abbott,* R. Hale, 1964; *White Pine,* R. Hale, 1965; *Hunting Black,* R. Hale, 1966; *Town of Fear,* R. Hale, 1971.

Nonfiction: (With Graham Alexander) *The Super Men: History of Aerial Topdressing in New Zealand,* A. H. & A. W. Reed, 1967; *Nairn Bus to Baghdad* (history of Nairn Brothers' Transport Service in the Middle East, 1920-50), A. H. & A. W. Reed, 1969; (editor) *Egmont National Park Handbook,* Egmont Park Board, 1980; *The Industrious Heart: A History of New Plymouth, New Zealand, 1841-1980,* New Plymouth City Council, 1981. Also editor of *Family Walks on Egmont,* 1975.

WORK IN PROGRESS: *Skeleton,* a novel about a New Zealander's search for his ancestors, publication expected in 1983.

SIDELIGHTS: Tullett told *CA:* "All my novels have backgrounds of outdoor industries in New Zealand, such as whaling, logging, aerial topdressing, gold mining, and mountain search and rescue." *Avocational interests:* Wood carving, gardening, protection of the environment.

*   *   *

TULLY, Gordon F(rederick) 1935-

PERSONAL: Born September 15, 1935, in Omaha, Neb.; son of Fred E. (a clerk) and Mary J. Tully; married Ellen D.B. Fisher, September 17, 1966; children: Ellen Douglas, David. *Education:* University of California, Berkeley, B.Arch., 1959. *Home:* 112 Lakeview Ave., Cambridge, Mass. 02138. *Office:* Massdesign Architects and Planners, Inc., 146 Mount Auburn St., Cambridge, Mass. 02138.

CAREER: Worked for Kallmann & McKinnell, Boston, Mass., 1962-68, and for Sert, Jackson & Associates, Inc., Cambridge, Mass., 1968-72; Massdesign Architects and Planners, Inc., Cambridge, president, 1972—. Instructor at Harvard University Graduate School of Design. *Member:* American Society of Heating, Refrigerating, and Air-Conditioning Engineers.

WRITINGS: *Sun-Pulse II: Solar Simulation for the TI-59 Hand-Held Calculator,* McGraw, 1979; *Solar Heating Systems: Analysis and Design With the Sun-Pulse Method,* McGraw, 1981. Contributor to technical journals.

WORK IN PROGRESS: Technical papers.

SIDELIGHTS: Tully told *CA:* "Perfectionists like myself should be prohibited by law from writing books. While carefully done and responsible, such jewels of literature become dull glass in the eyes of their supercritical author. My publisher's comment that most writers of technical books have one book inside them, but rarely more, applies especially to perfectionists. Horrified by their flawed child, they divorce the published word and go back to what they feel good about doing."

*   *   *

TURNER, Roland 1943-

PERSONAL: Born March 10, 1943, in Fenstanton, England; came to the United States in 1976; son of James Edward (a machinist) and Emily (Manderfield) Turner; married Carol Brunt (an artist), February, 1981; children: Jeffrey (stepson). *Education:* University of London, B.A., 1964. *Home and office:* 22 St. Mark's Ave., Brooklyn, N.Y. 11217.

CAREER: Royal Shakespeare Co., London, England, manager of Aldwych Theatre, 1965-67; St. James Press, London, editorial director, 1968-76; St. Martin's Press, New York, N.Y., director of Reference Books Division, 1976-81; free-lance writer and publishing consultant, 1981—. Director of St. James Editorial, 1977—.

WRITINGS: (Editor) *The Grants Register,* St. James Press, 1969, 5th edition, St. Martin's, 1977; (editor) *The Annual Obituary 1980,* St. Martin's, 1981; (editor) *Great Engineers,* Volume I, St. Martin's, 1982; (editor) *Notable Historians,* St. Martin's, 1983. Contributor to *Contemporary Poets, Contemporary Novelists, The Annual Obituary,* and *Contemporary Photographers.*

WORK IN PROGRESS: A mystery novel.

* * *

TURNER, Susan 1952-

PERSONAL: Born August 11, 1952, in Palo Alto, Calif.; daughter of John B. (a professor) and Ruth (a teacher; maiden name, Benedict) Turner; married Jon Pohlmann (a musician), May 20, 1978. *Education:* Attended Monterey Peninsula College, 1970-72. *Politics:* Democrat. *Religion:* Protestant. *Home and office:* 210 Riverside Dr., New York, N.Y. 10025.

CAREER: Independent Production Co., New York, N.Y., story editor, 1978—.

WRITINGS: Lost at Sea (juvenile novel), Raintree, 1979.

WORK IN PROGRESS: "The Look of Love," a series of romantic novels, for C/B Concepts.

SIDELIGHTS: Susan Turner commented: "Full-time employment has precluded further writing up to this point, but I am finding time for romantic novels. I aspire to write for the young adult market."

* * *

TURSKA, Krystyna (Zofia) 1933-

PERSONAL: Born August 28, 1933, in Poland; immigrated to England in 1948; daughter of Artur Stanislaw and Maria Witolda (Blanarz) Turska; married Andrzej Voelpel, 1975. *Education:* Graduated from Hammersmith School of Arts and Crafts, 1956. *Home and office:* 35 Tunley Rd., London, S.W.17, England.

CAREER: Illustrator of children's books and adapter of children's tales, folklore, and mythology. *Awards, honors:* Commended for the Kate Greenaway Medal, 1970, for *Pegasus;* Kate Greenaway Medal, 1972, for *Woodcutter's Duck.*

*WRITINGS—*All for children; all retold by Turska: *Pegasus* (Greek mythology), Watts, 1970; *Tamara and the Sea Witch* (folklore), Hamish Hamilton, 1971, Parents' Magazine Press, 1972; *The Woodcutter's Duck* (fairy tale), Macmillan, 1972; *The Magician of Cracow* (folklore), Greenwillow, 1975.

Illustrator: William Mayne, *Book of Heroes,* Dutton, 1966; Jacynth Hope-Simpson, *The Hamish Hamilton Book of Witches* (fiction), Hamish Hamilton, 1966, published as *A Cavalcade of Witches,* Walck, 1967; James Reeves, *The Trojan Horse* (fiction), Hamish Hamilton, 1968, Watts, 1969; Alan Garner, *A Cavalcade of Goblins,* Walck, 1969.

Gillian Avery and others, *Authors' Choice: Stories* (fiction), Hamish Hamilton, 1970, Crowell, 1971; Roger L. Green, *A Cavalcade of Dragons* (stories), Walck, 1970, published as *Hamish Hamilton Book of Dragons,* Hamish Hamilton, 1970;

Geoffrey Trease, *A Masque for the Queen* (fiction), Hamish Hamilton, 1970; Avery, *Ellen and the Queen* (fiction), Hamish Hamilton, 1971, Nelson, 1974; Michael Brown, *The Hamish Hamilton Book of Sea Legends* (folklore), Hamish Hamilton, 1971, published as *A Cavalcade of Sea Legends,* Walck, 1972; Avery, *Red Letter Days,* Hamish Hamilton, 1971; Reeves, *The Path of Gold,* Hamish Hamilton, 1972; Janet McNeill, *The Snow-Clean Pinny,* Hamish Hamilton, 1972; Joan Aiken and others, *Authors' Choice 2: Stories* (fiction), Hamish Hamilton, 1973, Crowell, 1974; Francis Eager, *The Dolphin of the Two Seas,* Hamish Hamilton, 1973, Barbara Willard, compiler, *Happy Families* (prose), Macmillan, 1974.

Elizabeth Jane Coatsworth, *Marra's World* (fiction), Greenwillow, 1975; Kathleen Killip, *Saint Bridget's Night: Stories From the Isle of Man,* Hamish Hamilton, 1975; James Riordan, *Russian Tales* (folklore), Viking Press, 1976; Honor Arundel, *The High House,* Hamish Hamilton, c. 1977; John Ruskin, *The King of the Golden River* (fairy tales), Greenwillow, 1978; Charles Causley, *The Last King of Cornwall,* Hodder & Stoughton, 1978; Helen Cooper, *Great Grandmother Goose,* Greenwillow, 1979; Riordan, *Tales from Central Russia: Russian Tales, Volume I,* Viking, 1979; William Mayne, *The Mouse and the Egg,* Greenwillow, 1981; Ruzena Wood, *The Palace of the Moon and Other Tales From Czechoslovakia,* Deutsch, 1981.

WORK IN PROGRESS: Coppelia, publication by Hodder & Stoughton expected in 1983.

BIOGRAPHICAL/CRITICAL SOURCES: New York Times Book Review, November 16, 1975; *Times Literary Supplement,* December 5, 1975.

* * *

TUVE, Merle Antony 1901-1982

OBITUARY NOTICE: Born June 27, 1901, in Canton, S.D.; died May 20, 1982, in Bethesda, Md. Physicist and author. Tuve's observations of short-pulse radio wave reactions are credited with leading to the development of radar. Among Tuve's other accomplishments were confirmation of the neutron's existence, measurements of bonding forces in atomic nuclei, and construction of the proximity fuse for antiaircraft shells. Tuve taught physics at Johns Hopkins University and Princeton University, and he was a physicist and director at Carnegie Institute's department of terrestrial magnetism. He received numerous awards for his work, including the Presidential Medal of Merit in 1946. Tuve wrote *Velocity Structures in Hydrogen Profiles: A Sky of Neutral Hydrogen Emission* with Soren Lundsager. Obituaries and other sources: *The International Who's Who,* Europa, 1978; *Who's Who in America,* 40th edition, Marquis, 1978; *American Men and Women of Science: The Physical and Biological Sciences,* 14th edition, Bowker, 1979; *Newsweek,* May 31, 1982; *Time,* May 31, 1982.

* * *

TUZIN, Donald F(rancis) 1945-

PERSONAL: Born June 14, 1945, in Chicago, Ill.; son of Constantine Francis (a bakery executive) and Thelma Louis (Smith) Tuzin; married Beverly Chodd (a dietitian), March 7, 1970; children: Gregory Francis, Alexander Hilary. *Education:* Case Western Reserve University, B.A. (cum laude), 1967, M.A., 1968; attended University of London, 1967-69; Australian National University, Ph.D., 1973. *Home:* 1269 Summit Pl., Cardiff-by-the-Sea, Calif. 92007. *Office:* Department of Anthropology, University of California, San Diego, Box 109, La Jolla, Calif. 92037.

CAREER: University of California, San Diego, La Jolla, assistant professor, 1973-77, associate professor, 1977-81, professor of anthropology, 1981—. *Member:* American Anthropological Association, Association for Social Anthropology in Oceania, Society for Political and Legal Anthropology, Royal Anthropological Institute.

WRITINGS: The Ilahita Arapesh: Dimensions of Unity, University of California Press, 1976; *The Voice of the Tambaran,* University of California Press, 1980; (editor) *Ethnography of Cannabalism* (essays; monograph), Society for Psychological Anthropology, 1982. Contributor to anthropology and linguistic journals.

WORK IN PROGRESS: A general theory of symbolism; ethnographic research in Indonesia; an archives in Melanesian studies, with Fitz John Porter Poole.

SIDELIGHTS: Tuzin wrote: ''My attachment to anthropology rests upon its combining the best features of teaching, scholarship, writing, and travel to interesting places. Foreign-language competence includes French, German, Neo-Melanesian, and Arapesh, and I am working on Dutch and Bahasa Indonesia.''

*   *   *

TWINING, Nathan F(arragut)   1897-1982

OBITUARY NOTICE: Born October 11, 1897, in Monroe, Wis.; died of heart failure, March 29, 1982, in San Antonio, Tex.; buried in Arlington National Cemetery. Air Force general and author. A general in World War II, Twining was in command of all air forces in the South Pacific in 1943 until he joined the Fifteenth Air Force and the Mediterranean Allied Strategic Air Forces in Italy. Returning to the Pacific in 1945, Twining commanded the Twentieth Air Force, the squad that dropped the first atomic bomb on Hiroshima. Twining subsequently served as commanding general of the Air Material

Command at Wright Field, commander in chief of the Alaskan Command at Fort Richardson, Air Force chief of staff, and chairman of the Joint Chiefs of Staff under President Eisenhower. He held the latter position from 1957 until his retirement in 1960. In 1966 Twining issued a book, *Neither Liberty Nor Safety: A Hard Look at Military Policy and Strategy.* Obituaries and other sources: *Current Biography,* Wilson, 1953, May, 1982; *Who's Who in the World,* 2nd edition, Marquis, 1973; *Political Profiles: The Eisenhower Years,* Facts on File, 1977; *Who Was Who in World War II,* Arms and Armour Press, 1978; *New York Times,* March 30, 1982; *Chicago Tribune,* March 31, 1982; *Newsweek,* April 5, 1982; *Time,* April 12, 1982.

*   *   *

TWITCHETT, Denis Crispin   1925-

BRIEF ENTRY: Born September 23, 1925. Educator and author. Twitchett taught Far Eastern history at University of London from 1954 to 1956 and classical Chinese at Cambridge University from 1956 to 1960. He was a professor of Chinese at School of Oriental and African Studies, London, during the 1960's and became a professor of Chinese at Cambridge in 1968. Twitchett's books include *Confucian Personalities* (Stanford University Press, 1962), *Financial Administration Under the T'ang Dynasty* (Cambridge University Press, 1970), *Perspectives on the T'ang* (Yale University Press, 1973), *The Times Atlas of China* (Times Books, 1974), and *Printing and Publishing in Medieval China* (Sandstone, 1981). He has also edited volumes on the Sui and Tang dynasties in the ''Cambridge History of China'' series, published by Cambridge University Press. *Address:* St. Catharine's College, Cambridge University, 24 Arbury Rd., Cambridge, England.

U

UDY, Stanley Hart, Jr.   1928-

BRIEF ENTRY: Born September 16, 1928, in Washington, D.C. American sociologist, educator, and author. Udy has been a professor of sociology at Dartmouth College since 1972 and chairman of the department since 1973. His books include *Organization of Work: A Comparative Analysis of Production Among Nonindustrial Peoples* (Human Relations Area File Press, 1959), *Cross-Cultural Analysis: A Case Study* (c.1961), and *Work in Traditional and Modern Societies* (Prentice-Hall, 1970). *Address:* 3 Butternut Lane, Hanover, N.H. 03755; and Department of Sociology, Dartmouth College, Hanover, N.H. 03755. *Biographical/critical sources: Who's Who in the East,* 16th edition, Marquis, 1977.

*   *   *

UHALLEY, Stephen, Jr.   1930-

BRIEF ENTRY: Born September 22, 1930, in Akron, Ohio. American historian, educator, and author. Uhalley began teaching at University of Hawaii in 1971 and has been a professor of contemporary Chinese history and chairman of the department of history since 1972. He has also taught in Taiwan. His writings include *Mao Tse-tung: A Critical Biography* (New Viewpoints, 1975). *Address:* Department of History, University of Hawaii, 2530 Dole St., Honolulu, Hawaii 96822. *Biographical/critical sources: Directory of American Scholars,* Volume I: *History,* 7th edition, Bowker, 1978.

ULLMAN, Allan   1909(?)-1982
   (Sandy Alan)

OBITUARY NOTICE: Born c. 1909; died March 15, 1982, in Southampton, Long Island, New York. Advertising salesman, executive, and author. Ullman was a book advertising salesman for the *New York Times* from 1935 until 1947, leaving that position to become promotion director of Random House, Inc. In 1953 he moved to the Book-of-the-Month Club, where he served as an advertising executive until he was named head of the *New York Times*'s book and education department. Ullman wrote several novels based on screenplays, including Lucille Fletcher's ''Night Man'' and ''Sorry, Wrong Number'' and Rolfe Bloom's ''Naked Spur.'' Under the name Sandy Alan, Ullman wrote a children's book entitled *The Plaid Peacock.* Obituaries and other sources: *New York Times,* March 17, 1982; *Publishers Weekly,* April 2, 1982.

*   *   *

UPDYKE, James
   See BURNETT, W(illiam) R(iley)

*   *   *

USCO
   See STERN, Gerd Jacob

V

VALERA y ALCALA-GALIANO, Juan 1824-1905

BRIEF ENTRY: Born October 18, 1824, in Cabra, Cordoba, Spain; died April 18, 1905, in Madrid, Spain. Spanish diplomat, statesman, and author. Valera has been called one of the best writers of nineteenth-century Spain. He was known for his classical, polished style, similar to that of Cervantes. *Pepita Jimenez* (1874), Valera's most famous novel, and *Dona Luz* (1879), both examined the conflict between passion and divine love, but reached totally different conclusions. They were psychological studies, treating religion as a psychological matter, instead of a spiritual or moral one. His best writing revealed sensitively-drawn images of Andalusian life and custom, as in *Juanita la larga* (1895). Valera also wrote many essays, letters, and short stories and translated several works into Spanish. *Biographical/critical sources: Cyclopedia of World Authors,* Harper, 1958; *The McGraw-Hill Encyclopedia of World Biography,* McGraw, 1973.

*   *   *

VALLE-INCLAN, Ramon (Maria) del 1866-1936 (Ramon del Valle y Pena)

BRIEF ENTRY: Born October 28, 1866, in Villanueva de Arosa, Spain; died January 5, 1936, in Santiago de Compostela, Spain; buried in Santiago de Compostela, Spain. Spanish playwright, novelist, and poet. Valle-Inclan was a member of the "Generation of '98." One of his first successes was the notorious four-volume *Sonatas* (1902-05), describing in French decadent style the amorous adventures of the Marquis de Bradomin, a contemporary Don Juan figure who became a lasting character in Spanish literature. With such sensual writing and his own eccentric, arrogant personality, Valle-Inclan became a popular bohemian figure in the literary circles of Madrid. His style changed after World War I, as he grew disillusioned with and hostile to contemporary society. He created the *esperpento* plays of the 1920's, notably "Los cuernos de Don Friolera" (1925). His characters became increasingly dehumanized, giving his work the flavor of puppet plays; in addition, his plots were deliberately twisted and grotesque. His animosity after being jailed during the dictatorship of Primo de Rivero was expressed in *The Tyrant* (1926), a novel about revolution in Latin America. *El ruedo iberico* (1927-28), his satire of Isabel II and her court, stemmed from his contempt for Alfonso VIII. Valle-Inclan's command of style and language, his distortion of reality, and his use of the discordant note have led critics

to view him as a precursor to the theatre of the absurd movement. *Biographical/critical sources: Twentieth Century Authors: A Biographical Dictionary of Modern Literature,* H. W. Wilson, 1942; Robert Lima, *Ramon del Valle-Inclan,* Columbia University Press, 1972; *Modern World Drama: An Encyclopedia,* Dutton, 1972; *The Oxford Companion to Spanish Literature,* Clarendon Press, 1978.

*   *   *

VALLEJO, Antonio Buero
See BUERO VALLEJO, Antonio

*   *   *

VALLE Y PENA, Ramon del
See VALLE-INCLAN, Ramon (Maria) del

*   *   *

van WITSEN, Leo 1912-

PERSONAL: Born July 12, 1912, in The Hague, Netherlands; came to the United States in 1938, naturalized citizen, 1950; son of Jacques (a merchant) and Rosa (a singer; maiden name, Blok) van Witsen. *Education:* Attended Royal Academy of Fine Arts, The Hague, Netherlands, 1928-29, Schule Reimann, 1930-31, and Academie de la Grande Chaumiere, 1932. *Home:* 115 West 73rd St., Apt. 9D, New York, N.Y. 10023.

CAREER: Bernard & Cie, Paris, France, apprentice fashion designer, 1932; Mason de Vries, Amsterdam, Netherlands, apprentice fashion designer, 1933; Drecoll, Berlin, Germany, fashion designer, 1934; Tarapani, Berlin, fashion designer, 1934; free-lance fashion designer in The Hague, Netherlands, 1935-37; Federal Shipyards, Newark, N.J., office worker, 1942; millinery designer, 1942-44; Goldovsky Grand Opera Co., Boston, Mass., and New York, N.Y., staff costume designer, 1945—. Singer and actor in the 1930's; stage designer at Mercury Theatre, 1939; costume designer for Camp Unity, the summer camp of International Ladies' Garment Workers' Union, 1940. Member of faculty and costume designer at Berkshire Music Center, 1946, and Juilliard School of Music, 1947; member of faculty and costumer at Curtis Institute of Music, 1976—. Head of opera department of Brooks Van Horn Costume Co. of New York, 1958-78. Fashion designs represented in library of Costume Institute of Metropolitan Museum of Art and costume designs represented in theatre collection of Museum of the City of New York.

WRITINGS: (Illustrator) Boris Goldovsky and Arthur Schoep, *Bringing Soprano Arias to Life,* G. Schirmer, 1973; (translator from Dutch) Eline Canter Cremers-van der Does, *The Agony of Fashion,* Blandford, 1980; *Costuming for Opera: Who Wears What and Why,* Indiana University Press, 1981. Contributor to *America Music.*

WORK IN PROGRESS: A Costume Manual for Opera Singers; Opera-Couture; Cut Out to Be a Diva, an opera costume cut-out book.

SIDELIGHTS: Leo van Witsen believes that the Reagan administration, by relegating financial support of the arts to the private sector, is shirking its responsibility to the American people, he told *CA.* Pursuit of the arts is an unalienable right, van Witsen says, and it is the responsibility of the federal government to support the arts and foster their growth.

*   *   *

VERMES, Jean C(ampbell Pattison) 1907-

PERSONAL: Surname is pronounced *Ver*-mez; born November 15, 1907, in Ottawa, Ontario, Canada; daughter of James (an engineer) and Charlotte (Craddock) Pattison; married Hal G. Vermes, November 3, 1941 (died, 1965); stepchildren: Harold J., Roy E. *Education:* Attended New York University, 1972-73. *Religion:* Protestant. *Home:* 15 Washington Pl., New York, N.Y. 10003. *Agent:* Janice Fishbein, Frieda Fishbein Ltd., 353 West 57th St., New York, N.Y. 10019.

CAREER: Bertha Klausner Literary Agency, New York City, secretary, 1965-66; Frieda Fishbein Literary Agency, New York City, manuscript reader, 1966-82. *Member:* Authors League of America, League of Women Voters of the United States, Sierra Club.

WRITINGS: Key to Etiquette for Everyone, Imperial Publishing Co., 1959; *The Girl's Book of Physical Fitness* (young adult), Association Press, 1961, revised edition, 1972; *Etiquette Made Simple,* Doubleday, 1962; (editor with husband, Hal G. Vermes) Jack Finegan, *Step by Step in Theology,* Association Press, 1962; (with H. Vermes) *The Collier Quick and Easy Guide to Bowling,* Collier Books, 1963, published as *Precision Bowling for Higher Scores,* 1972; *The Girl's Book of Personal Development* (young adult), Association Press, 1964; *Secretary's Guide to Dealing with People,* Parker Publishing Co., 1964.

Enjoying Life as a Sportsman's Wife, Stackpole, 1965; *Helping Youth Avoid Four Great Dangers,* Association Press, 1965; *Hobbies for Girls* (young adult), Association Press, 1965; *Secretary's Index to English,* Parker Publishing Co., 1967; (compiler) *The Wilderness Sampler: A Tonic of Great Writings About the Moods of Nature,* Stackpole, 1968; *Pot Is Rot, and Other Horrible Facts About Bad Things* (young adult; illustrated by Art Helfant), Association Press, 1969; *Secretary's Book of Instant Letters,* Parker Publishing Co., 1971; (with Robert H. Loeb) *Male Power: The Young Man's Guide to Good Grooming,* Association Press, 1971; *Complete Book of Business Etiquette,* Parker Publishing Co., 1976; *Secretary's Modern Guide to English Usage,* Parker Publishing Co., 1982.

WORK IN PROGRESS: The Power of Beauty; The Walls, about women's struggle for personal development.

SIDELIGHTS: Jean Vermes told *CA:* "I am particularly interested in women's new roles in society. My interest was first aroused in 1972, when I revised *The Girl's Book of Physical Fitness* from the original 1961 edition, and I was amazed at

the changes I had to make in the expectations a young girl now had, after a lapse of only ten years. Much of the new material in *The Secretary's Modern Guide to English Usage* involves avoiding sexist language and learning to address women in positions of authority, which would not have been considered worth including earlier."

She added, "I like to travel to Europe, Latin America, and the Pacific. I also enjoy quiet vacations on Martha's Vineyard with my dachshund, Mitzi."

*   *   *

VIAN, Boris 1920-1959
(Vernon Sullivan)

BRIEF ENTRY: Born March 10, 1920, in Ville-d'Avray, France; died April 23, 1959 (some sources say June 23), in Paris, France. French engineer, jazz musician, poet, playwright, and novelist. Vian became notorious with the publication of his pseudonymous novel, *J'irai cracher sur vos tombes* (1946; translated as *I Will Spit on Your Graves,* 1971). Its eroticism and violence so shocked the reading public of Vian's day that the novel was officially suppressed. The author's announcement that the book had been written as a hoax and had no literary value angered critics who had favorably reviewed the novel, thus augmenting the scandal. Even in his serious work, Vian was unable to restrain his sense of the comic, his passion for life, and his delight in dream and fantasy. Some critics argue that Vian's writing skill reached it height with his novels, such as the love story *L'Ecume des jours* (1947; translated as *Froth on the Daydream,* 1967). Others insist that Vian's reputation rests on his existential plays. One of the more popular of these is *Les Batisseurs d'empire* (1959; translated as *The Empire Builders,* 1967), a violent attack on middle class society and a testament to the absurdity of life. When Vian died at the age of thirty-nine, his writing credits totaled nearly ten thousand works, including songs, opera librettos, poems, stories, ballet scenarios, translations, articles, and novels. *Biographical/critical sources: Encyclopedia of World Literature in the Twentieth Century,* updated edition, Ungar, 1967; *McGraw-Hill Encyclopedia of World Drama,* McGraw, 1972; *Modern World Drama: An Encyclopedia,* Dutton, 1972.

*   *   *

VICKERS, (Charles) Geoffrey 1894-1982

OBITUARY NOTICE—See index for *CA* sketch: Born October 13, 1894, in Nottingham, England; died March 16, 1982. Solicitor and author. Vickers is best remembered for his heroics in World War I. A member of the Sherwood Foresters and the Robin Hood Battalion, Vickers received the Victoria Cross in 1918 for his valor during the war. For his service in the Lincolnshire Regiment, the author was awarded the Croix de Guerre. After his military service Vickers became a solicitor, working on committees such as the British National Coal Board, the London Transport Board, the Law Society, and the Medical Research Council. This work inspired his writings on the institutional framework of society. For recreation, Vickers enjoyed sailing. His writings include *The Undirected Society, Toward a Sociology of Management, Freedom in a Rocking Boat,* and *Making Institutions Work.* Obituaries and other sources: *London Times,* March 18, 1982.

*   *   *

VIGFUSSON, Robin 1949-

PERSONAL: Born June 4, 1949, in New York, N.Y.; daughter

of Benjamin (an advertising copywriter) and Ann Kluger; married Gudmundur Vigfusson (a mathematician), February 17, 1978; children: Vigfus Christopher. *Education:* Kean College of New Jersey, B.A., 1972; New York University, M.A., 1979. *Agent:* Judith Weber, Nat Sobol Associates, 128 East 56th St., New York, N.Y. 10022.

CAREER: Teacher of English at a private school in Brookline, Mass., 1972-74; New York University, New York, N.Y., secretary, 1974-78; writer, 1978—.

WRITINGS: Expensive Habits (novel), Seaview, 1981.

WORK IN PROGRESS: Another novel.

SIDELIGHTS: In *Expensive Habits,* Robin Vigfusson dealt with what she has referred to as the introduction of corruption (in the form of drug abuse and promiscuity) into respectable middle-class lives. She does not write to shock or offend, and prefers fiction that is real and personal to the reader.

BIOGRAPHICAL/CRITICAL SOURCES: Washington Post Book World, January 3, 1982.

* * *

VIGIL, Lawrence
See FINNIN, (Olive) Mary

* * *

VILA, Bob
See VILA, Robert

* * *

VILA, Robert 1946-
(Bob Vila)

PERSONAL: Born June 20, 1946, in Miami, Fla.; son of Robert (a U.S. Army intelligence officer) and Hope (Robles) Vila; married Diana Barrett (a professor), October 3, 1975; children: Christopher Anthony Vila-Barrett, Monica Patricia Vila-Barrett. *Education:* University of Florida, A.A., 1967, B.S., 1969. *Office:* R. J. Vila, Inc., 263 Beacon St., Boston, Mass. 02116.

CAREER: Independent home improvement contractor, Boston, Mass., 1971-74; R. J. Vila, Inc. (real estate development firm), Boston, president, 1975—; host of "This Old House," for the Public Broadcasting System (PBS-TV), 1979—. Peace Corps volunteer, 1969-70.

WRITINGS: (Under name Bob Vila; with Jane Davison) *This Old House: Restoring, Rehabilitating, and Renovating,* Little, Brown, 1980; (under name Robert Vila; with George Stephen) *Bob Vila's This Old House,* Dutton, 1981.

SIDELIGHTS: In both his books and television show, Vila, using a crew of electricians, plumbers, carpenters, and other specialists, demonstrates how to transform old houses into livable, modern dwellings without destroying the original character of the structure.

Vila told *CA:* "I like to think of myself as a preservationist with common sense. I've seen too many 'rehab purists' with the kind of corseted approach which makes living in a restored home uncomfortable."

* * *

VILLIERS, Guy
See GOULDING, Peter Geoffrey

VOGELMAN, Joyce 1936-

PERSONAL: Born October 3, 1936, in Waterloo, Iowa; daughter of J.M. and Eula Belle Branson; married Henry F. Vogelman (a teacher and coach), April 1, 1961; children: Linda, Henry, June. *Education:* Attended University of Iowa, 1954-55; Gates Business College, junior business certificate, 1956; Iowa State University, B.S., 1960. *Home address:* Route 1, Rockford, Iowa 50468.

CAREER: Copywriter for *Idea Annuals* for *Better Homes and Gardens,* 1960-61; Iowa State University, Ames, copywriter for Information Service, 1961-62; free-lance writer, 1962—. Secretary-treasurer of Rockford Community Volunteer Fire Service.

WRITINGS: Getting It Right (novel), Avon, 1981; "Are You Listening?" (nonfiction), serialized publication in *Campaigns and Elections,* 1982; *The History of Floyd County, 1882-1982,* Floyd County Historical Society, 1983.

WORK IN PROGRESS: The Man Who Wanted It All, a novel, publication expected in 1983.

SIDELIGHTS: Joyce Vogelman told *CA:* "My first book was written after I realized it didn't have to be the best book ever written. The second is a result of wanting to know what it is like to be a woman candidate for a major political office. The third was written because I'd succeeded in placing the first. The fourth is being written because it needs to be written, and the research will provide much material for later fiction.

"*Getting It Right* is a romance set in an authentic rural background. I hoped to entertain readers while at the same time presenting an authentic slice of agricultural American life. There are no windmills or rusty pump handles in *Getting It Right.* The hero and heroine face some of the same problems all contemporary Americans face, in particular, the issue of working versus private lives.

"'Are You Listening?' is a nonfiction work of which I am very proud. It shows how it really is for a woman on the campaign trail. The politician in this instance is Lynn Cutler, candidate for the U.S. House of Representatives. There is the excitement of a race, the tension of a man-woman contest, the poignancy and heartbreak of the death of Cutler's husband two weeks prior to election day. The publisher of *Campaigns and Elections* is planning to make available his galleys to interested publishers so that 'Are You Listening?' can be circulated as a book as well as serialized in his publication.

"The protagonists in my work in progress, *The Man Who Wanted It All,* are a war widow and the owner of a casino. In this work of fiction, I have tried to express a point of view on eternal versus temporal values in an interesting, entertaining, and/or engrossing way.

"*The History of Floyd County, 1882-1982* is a commissioned work. I am fairly rigid about wanting everything I write to have authenticity and a point of view. I want everything I write to be interesting and easy to read. I want to make hard or dull or technical material palatable to ordinary people. To do all this will be the challenge of writing a county history. I think I'll start with the story of Charles Kelly, who hitched his wagon to an elk, thought it humorous when the Indians peered in his windows, but thought it serious business when he visited Indian wigwams and named a town for his son.

"I seem to have fallen into a pattern of alternating fiction and nonfiction work. The nonfiction feeds the fiction. The fiction provides opportunity to comment, a chance to wallow in subjectivity. Writing fiction after years of disciplined free-lance journalism (just the facts, m'am) is like discovering hot water and bathtubs after years of bathing in the creek. What luxury!''

* * *

VOIGT, Cynthia 1942-

PERSONAL: Born February 25, 1942, in Boston, Mass.; daughter of Frederick C. (a corporate executive) and Elise (Keeney) Irving; married September, 1964 (divorced, 1972); married Walter Voigt (a teacher), August 30, 1974; children: Jessica, Peter. *Education:* Smith College, B.A., 1963. *Politics:* Independent. *Residence:* Annapolis, Md. *Agent:* Helen Rees, 655 Boylston St., Boston, Mass. 02116. *Office:* The Key School, 534 Carroll Dr., Annapolis, Md. 21403.

CAREER: Teacher of English at high school in Glen Burnie, Md., 1965-67; The Key School, Annapolis, Md., teacher of English, 1968-69, department chairman, 1971-79, part-time teacher and department chairman, 1981—.

WRITINGS: Homecoming (juvenile), Atheneum, 1981; *Tell Me If the Lovers Are Losers* (young adult), Atheneum, 1982; *Dicey's Song* (juvenile), Atheneum, 1982; *The Callendar Papers* (juvenile), Atheneum, 1983.

BIOGRAPHICAL/CRITICAL SOURCES: New York Times Book Review, May 10, 1981, May 16, 1982.

* * *

von BALTHASAR, Hans Urs 1905-

BRIEF ENTRY: Born August 12, 1905, in Lucerne, Switzerland. Swiss author. Von Balthasar has been a Jesuit priest since 1936. He worked on the staff of *Voice of the Time* from 1938 to 1939 and has been a free-lance writer since 1949. He has written several dozen books on theology, including *Das Herz der Welt* (1946; translated as *Heart of the World,* Ignatius Press, 1979), *Das betrachtende Gebet* (Johannes Verlag, 1955; translated as *Prayer,* Sheed & Ward, 1961), *Erster Blick auf Adrienne von Speyr* (Johannes Verlag, 1968; translated as *A First Glance at Adrienne von Speyr,* Ignatius Press, 1981), *Klarstellungen* (Herder, 1971; translated as *Elucidations,* S.P.C.K., 1975), *In Gottes einsatz leben* (Johannes Verlag, 1971; translated as *Engagement With God,* S.P.C.K., 1975), and *Dante* (Morcelliana, 1973). *Address:* Arnold Boecklinstrasse 42, 4051 Basel, Switzerland. *Biographical/critical sources: Encounter,* summer, 1969; *The Author's and Writer's Who's Who,* 6th edition, Burke's Peerage, 1971.

* * *

von BOTHMER, Dietrich Felix 1918-

PERSONAL: Born October 26, 1918, in Eisenach, Germany (now East Germany); came to the United States in 1939, naturalized citizen, 1944; son of Wilhelm Friedrich Franz Karl and Marie Julie Auguste Karoline (von und zu Egloffstein) von

Bothmer; married Joyce Campbell Blaffer de la Begassiere, May 28, 1966; children: Bernard, Maria; (stepdaughters) Marisol, Jacqueline, Diane. *Education:* Wadham College, Oxford, diploma in classical archaeology, 1939; attended University of Berlin, 1937-38, and University of California, Berkeley, 1940-42; University of Chicago, Ph.D., 1944. *Home:* 401 Centre Island, Oyster Bay, N.Y. 11771. *Office:* Metropolitan Museum of Art, Fifth Ave. and 82nd St., New York, N.Y. 10028.

CAREER: Metropolitan Museum of Art, New York, N.Y., assistant curator, 1946-51, associate curator, 1951-59, curator, 1959-73, chairman of Greek and Roman art, 1973—. Adjunct professor at New York University, 1965—; chairman of U.S. committee of Corpus Vasorum Antiquorum. *Military service:* U.S. Army, 1943-46; received Bronze Star and Purple Heart. *Member:* Archaeological Institute of America (benefactor), Society for the Promotion of Hellenic Studies, Deutsches Archaeologisches Institut, Vereinigung der Freunde Antiker Kunst, Institut de France, Academie des Inscriptions et Belles-Lettres (corresponding member).

WRITINGS—All published by Metropolitan Museum of Art, except as noted: *Amazons in Greek Art,* Clarendon Press, 1957; *Ancient Art From New York Private Collections,* 1961; *Attic Black-Figured Amphorae,* 1963; (with Henri Metzger and J. N. Coldstream) *Les Ceramiques archaiques et classiques de l'acropole lycienne* (title means "The Archaic and Classic Pottery From the Lycian Acropolis"), Klincksieck, 1972; *Greek Vase Painting: An Introduction,* 1972; (with Mary B. Moore) *Attic Black-Figured Neck-Amphorae,* 1976; (with Joan R. Mertens) *Greek Art of the Aegean Islands,* 1979. Book review editor of *American Journal of Archaeology,* 1950-56.

* * *

von HOFMANNSTHAL, Hugo
See HOFMANNSTHAL, Hugo von

* * *

Von MOHRENSCHILDT, Dimitri Sergius 1902-

BRIEF ENTRY: Born April 11, 1902, in St. Petersburg, Russia (now Leningrad, U.S.S.R.). American historian, educator, and author. Von Mohrenschildt was a professor of Russian history and literature at Dartmouth College from 1947 to 1967, when he was named emeritus professor. He was also founder, managing editor, and editor of *Russian Review* from 1941 to 1974. Von Mohrenschildt wrote *Russia in the Intellectual Life of Eighteenth-Century France* (Columbia University Press, 1936) and *Toward a United States of Russia: Plans and Projects of Federal Reconstruction of Russia in the Nineteenth Century* (Fairleigh Dickinson University Press, 1981). He edited *The Russian Revolution of 1917: Contemporary Accounts* (Oxford University Press, 1971). *Address:* Hoover Institution on War, Revolution, and Peace, Stanford, Calif. 94305. *Biographical/critical sources: Who's Who in America,* 39th edition, Marquis, 1976.

W

WACHHORST, Wyn 1938-

PERSONAL: Surname is pronounced *Watch*-horst; born August 18, 1938, in San Francisco, Calif.; son of Newton Edwin (a dentist) and Norma (Harvey) Wachhorst; married Rita Enright, August 16, 1964; children: Brian, Scott. *Education:* Stanford University, A.B., 1960, Ph.D., 1972; San Jose State University, M.A., 1965. *Home:* 298 Park Lane, Atherton, Calif. 94025.

CAREER: San Jose State University, San Jose, Calif., instructor in history, 1978—, executive secretary of Sourisseau Academy for California State and Local History, 1978—, director of academy, 1979-80. Instructor at University of California, Santa Cruz, 1978—. *Military service:* U.S. Coast Guard Reserve, 1960-65, active duty, 1960-61; became lieutenant junior grade. *Member:* American Studies Association, American Historical Association, Popular Culture Association, Phi Kappa Phi.

WRITINGS: Thomas Alva Edison: An American Myth, M.I.T. Press, 1981.

WORK IN PROGRESS: Research on parallel shifts in popular culture genres, from the period 1945-63 to the period 1964 through the seventies, especially in science fiction, musical, sport, and western films; research on the psychocultural debate over the Apollo moonshot and its final significance and symbolism.

SIDELIGHTS: Wachhorst wrote: "My future writing and teaching will focus on American culture and values since 1945. I am particularly interested in popular culture symbolism as a repository of our collective dreams. My central concern is with the need, both individual and collective, for a vision of transcendence, for some context of meaning larger than the ego-self, for awe, wonder, and hope as we experience an increasing sense of limits in postindustrial society."

AVOCATIONAL INTERESTS: Films, music, discussion, tennis, chess, guitar.

*   *   *

WACHSMANN, Klaus Philipp 1907-

BRIEF ENTRY: Born March 8, 1907, in Berlin, Germany. Musicologist, educator, and author. Wachsmann worked as a missionary in Uganda and an ethnologist in England before coming to the United States. He has been a professor of African

studies and music at Northwestern University since 1973. In 1977 he became president of the International Folk Music Council. His writings include *International Catalogue of Published Records of Folk Music* (International Folk Music Council, 1960), *Essays on Music and History in Africa* (Northwestern University Press), and an edited work, *Hornhostel opera omnia* (Nijhoff, 1975). *Address:* 840 Forest Ave., Evanston, Ill. 60202; and Department of Music History, Northwestern University, Evanston, Ill. 60201. *Biographical/critical sources: Essays for a Humanist: An Offering to Klaus Wachsmann,* Town House Press, 1977.

*   *   *

WALKER, J.
See CRAWFORD, John Richard

*   *   *

WALLACH, Janet 1942-

PERSONAL: Born May 4, 1942, in New York, N.Y.; daughter of George (in business) and Sylvia (Feigen) Weil; married second husband, John P. Wallach (a journalist), June 9, 1974; children: David Alan, Michael Adam. *Education:* Attended Syracuse University, 1959-60; New York University, B.A., 1965. *Home:* 2915 Foxhall Rd., Washington, D.C. 20016.

CAREER: Herman Geist, New York, N.Y., designer, 1969-75; Woodward & Lothrop, Washington, D.C., fashion coordinator, 1975-76; Garfinckel's, Washington, D.C., fashion merchandising director, 1976-80; free-lance writer, 1980—. *Member:* National Press Club, Fashion Group.

WRITINGS: Working Wardrobe, Acropolis Books, 1981.

SIDELIGHTS: The "capsule concept"—the idea that twelve basic clothing items in two colors and coordinated shapes and fabrics together yield forty different outfits—"is the basic message of one of the few actually useful books about dressing," claimed fashion editor Mary Peacock. Reviewing Janet Wallach's book, *Working Wardrobe,* in *Ms.* magazine, Peacock admitted, "At first it sounded to me like 'foolproof gourmet' recipes using just three kinds of condensed soup and a package of frozen broccoli." The reviewer conceded that case study interviews in the book clearly indicate how the idea works differently for everyone. "I have to apologize to Janet Wallach," stated Peacock. "Like most great ideas, it just sounded too simple at first. Wallach has moved the goal of a workable personal style from theory into practical reality by providing an organizational key, the 'capsule,' which at least partially codified that great intangible, a 'fashion sense.' And the 'capsule concept' works on any level of budget and sophistication, or at any level of dressiness."

Janet Wallach told *CA:* "It has taken me fifteen years to come full circle to my first love, writing, and I'm grateful that my dream has been fulfilled. Writing about fashion seemed like a natural thing to do as I've spent most of my life in that field. It has been gratifying that my book has helped many women come to terms with their clothes and enabled them to make their wardrobes work for them (rather than the reverse). Clothing is important in the way we present ourselves to the world, and it should also be part of the fun of life."

BIOGRAPHICAL/CRITICAL SOURCES: Ms., September, 1981.

* * *

WALLER, Peter Louis   1935-

PERSONAL: Born February 10, 1935, in Siedlce, Poland; son of Jack and Chaya Waller; married Wendy Poyser (a pharmaceutical chemist), January 11, 1959; children: Anthony, Ian, Eleanor. *Education:* University of Melbourne, LL.B. (with honors), 1955; Oxford University, B.C.L., 1958. *Home:* 2 Hartley Ave., Caulfield, Victoria 3162, Australia. *Office:* Faculty of Law, Monash University, Clayton, Victoria 3168, Australia.

CAREER: University of Melbourne, Parkville, Australia, senior lecturer in law, 1959-65; Monash University, Clayton, Australia, Sir Leo Cussen Professor of Law, 1965—, dean of faculty of law, 1968-70. Victorian Law Reform Commissioner, 1982—. Visiting professor at University of Kent at Canterbury, 1971, and University of Victoria, 1981; consultant to Law Reform Commission of Canada, 1974-75. *Member:* Academy of Social Sciences in Australia (fellow).

WRITINGS: (With Peter Brett) *Cases and Materials in Criminal Law,* Butterworth, 1962, 3rd edition published as *Criminal Law: Text and Cases,* 1971, 4th edition, 1978; (with David Derham and Frank K. H. Maher) *An Introduction to Law,* Law Book Co., 1966, 4th edition, 1983; (with Derham and Maher) K. S. Pose and M.D.H. Smith, editors, *Cases and Materials on the Legal Process,* Law Book Co., 1966, 2nd edition, 1971.

* * *

WALLIG, Gaird (Elizabeth)   1942-

PERSONAL: Born July 1, 1942, in Eau Claire, Wis.; daughter of George B. (a civil engineer) and Haide Arlen (a poet; maiden name, Larson) Griese; married Stephen E. Wallig (a manager of a department store's jewelry division), February 2, 1963; children: Edward Stephen, Joseph George. *Education:* Attended College of the Holy Names, 1960-62, and Oakland City College, 1960-61. *Home and office:* 84 Canal Dr., Shore Acres, West Pittsburg, Calif. 94565.

CAREER: Oakland Recreation Department, Oakland, Calif., counselor in training, 1957-59; telephone solicitor, 1961-67; photographic assistant, 1967-70; House of Wallig (tailors and upholsterers for home and automobile), Pittsburg, Calif., co-owner, 1970—. Tailor for Seminary Cleaners, 1970—; school cook. *Member:* National Writers Club, California Writers Club.

WRITINGS: A Red-Tailed Hawk Named Bucket (nonfiction for young adults), Celestial Arts, 1980.

Work represented in anthologies, including *Dreaming in the Dawn,* edited by Ruth Wildes Schuler; *The Poet,* edited by

Doris Nemeth, 1980, and *As the Leaves Turn Again,* edited by Mary Kentra Ericsson. Contributor of poems, stories, and articles to magazines, including *Driftwood East, Echos, Northwoods Journal, Mother Earth News, Creative Crafts,* and *California Living,* and newspapers.

WORK IN PROGRESS: The Reserves (tentative title), about reserve police officers.

SIDELIGHTS: Gaird Wallig commented: "When I was in the first grade and just learning to read, I got very critical about the book I was supposed to be learning from. A six-year-old me stated firmly, 'It's dumb! I've read it all already, and all it says is two kids and a dog play ball. Dumb!' This was two weeks after school opened, and since the other kids hadn't gone past the first two pages, the teacher didn't know what to do with me. Nothing, it seems, has changed since then. I am a rabid reader. I inhale anything I find interesting, and have been known to trash writing which makes me impatient. All through school, anytime I dared, I'd read.

"My library card was my talisman into any magic world that anyone has ever dreamed of, and away from the sometimes uncomfortable real world. Here was an open door that my mind could close with only me inside a fascinating new place, a place of adventure, life, the might-have-been-real myth worlds, fantasy, and later romance and even science fiction.

"My interest in science fiction began with one of my school readers. It contained a story of strange little men, who reminded me of trolls my Norwegian mother sometimes talked about. They didn't seem to be able to think, but spent their lifetimes dragging around a huge cart, upon which sat the Bumperboom. Everyone else in the story was terrified of that giant cannon. I do not recall the author's name, the actual name of the story (if it wasn't 'Bumperboom'), or the hero's manipulations. I do remember the flavor, the sounds, and the reasons for the story. Fear can be a learned thing, based on no valid premise. It was adventure, away from the real world, that bled over into the real with suggestions of practical help for those who might need it and find the wit to see it.

"In my early teens I was mostly attracted to books for boys. The heroines of girls' books were silly things, most of them, while the boys were doing wonderful things like making friends with wild black stallions, learning to depend on themselves to survive, or being raised by wolves, talking to snakes, and living in cozy jungles.

"Later, of course, I met James Bond and Matt Helm, who had to share mind room with the men and women of stories by Mary Stewart, Dorothy Eden, Mary Roberts Rinehart, and so on to Ursula K. LeGuin, Anne McCaffrey, and James Blish. There are so many there isn't enough space in time to list them, but each and every one helped prod whatever worlds lurk in my own head into being.

"Mine are sleeping worlds, perhaps, as yet, but I'm working on it. A bit of trying soon shows the would-be writer that from that point 'a' to a publishable/published point 'b' isn't quite as easy as it appears. There is the little matter of learning how to transfer the worlds in one's head onto paper accurately, so someone else can see them as clearly and exactly as the author. The only way to learn how, I've now determined, is to sit at the typewriter, writing story after story until one at last proves real enough to be transformed into a long white envelope that arrives with the words 'We will use. . . .'

"For me, it was the ninth science fiction story I'd written, out of twenty or so pieces of work that have made publication so far, all buried in the mountain of unsold work still on my bookshelf.

"When I get discouraged, or one too many rejection slips lands in my mailbox, I go back to that ever-open door of others' worlds. My sadnesses and frustrations get closed outside and I can still be a part of that most special magic, the world of the writers, because I like to read, even more than before."

* * *

WALPOLE, Ronald Noel 1903-

PERSONAL: Born December 24, 1903, in Gwent, Great Britain; came to the United States in 1936; son of George William and Florence M.M. (Blew) Walpole; married Doris Gray Hoyt (a violinist), August 9, 1936; children: Mary Ronald (Mrs. Robert F. Marzke). *Education:* University of Wales, University College, Cardiff, B.A. (with first class honors), 1925; University of Wales, M.A., 1936; University of California, Berkeley, Ph.D., 1939. *Religion:* Anglican. *Home:* 1680 La Loma, Berkeley, Calif. 94709. *Office:* Department of French, University of California, 4217 Dwinelle Hall, Berkeley, Calif. 94720.

CAREER: University of California, Berkeley, instructor, 1939-43, assistant professor, 1943-48, associate professor, 1948-50, professor of French, 1950—, chairman of department, 1957-63. *Member:* Mediaeval Academy of America, American Academy of Arts and Sciences. *Awards, honors:* Guggenheim fellow, 1949-50; chevalier of French Legion of Honor, 1962.

WRITINGS: Charlemagne and Roland: A Study of the Source of Two Middle English Metrical Romances, Roland and Vernagu and Otuel and Roland, University of California Press, 1944; *Philip Mouskes and the Pseudo-Turpin Chronicle,* University of California Press, 1947; (editor and translator) *The Old French Johannes Translation of the Pseudo-Turp in Chronicle: A Critical Edition,* University of California Press, 1976, supplement, 1976; *An Anonymous Old French Translation of the Pseudo-Turpin "Chronicle": A Critical Edition of the Text Contained in Bibliotheque Nationale MSS fr. 2137 and 17203 and Incorporated by Philippe Mouskes in His "Chronique Rimee,"* Mediaeval Academy of America, 1979. Contributor to *Dictionnaire des lettres francaises.* Contributor to journals, including *Speculum* and *Romance Philology.*

WORK IN PROGRESS: Le Turpin Francais dit le Turpin I: Edition Critique, publication expected in 1982.

SIDELIGHTS: Walpole commented: "My Welsh school had a motto, borne all over the school and on our caps, blazers, and prizes—'Nothing is good where better is possible.' That has always been to me a stimulus to my effort and a constant lesson in humility."

* * *

WALSH, Michael J. 1937-

PERSONAL: Born October 30, 1937, in Newcastle, England; son of John Gregory (a banker) and Patricia Elizabeth (Wright) Walsh; married Kathleen Lilly (a teacher), August 30, 1976; children: Clare Elizabeth. *Education:* Heythrope College, Phil.Lic., 1961; Oxford University, B.A., 1964, M.A., 1966; University College, London, Dip.Lib., 1970. *Religion:* Roman Catholic. *Home:* 71 Ambler Rd., London N4 2QS, England. *Office:* Heythrope College, Cavendish Sq., London W1M 0AN, England.

CAREER: Month (magazine), London, England, assistant editor, 1969-74, editor, 1974-76; Heythrope College, London, librarian, 1970—; writer. *Member:* Library Association, Ecclesiastical History Society, Bibliographical Society.

WRITINGS: An Illustrated History of the Popes, St. Martin's, 1980; *From Sword to Ploughshare,* Catholic Institute for International Relations, 1980; (editor) *Religious Bibliography in Serial Liturgy: A Guide,* Mausell, 1981. Review editor of *Heythorpe Journal.*

WORK IN PROGRESS: A Bibliography of the Vatican City State, publication expected in 1982; *The Jesuits, 1814-1975: A History,* completion expected in 1984.

SIDELIGHTS: Walsh told *CA:* "I was, for twenty years, a member of the Society of Jesus (the Jesuits). My Jesuit education gave me a competence in philosophy and history as well as theology, and a working knowledge of German, French, Italian, and Spanish, as well as Latin. My desire is to make much of the scholarly material I see daily as a librarian available to a wider audience."

* * *

WAMBLE, Thelma 1916-

BRIEF ENTRY: Born January 9, 1916, in Fort Smith, Ark. American medical and social work consultant and author. Wamble has been a consultant for Los Angeles County since 1960. She wrote *All in the Family* (New Voices, 1953), *Knight of Courage* (1964), and *Look Over My Shoulder: Letters About President John Fitzgerald Kennedy to John Allen Gould, Grandson of John Fitzherbert Miller* (Vantage, 1969). *Address:* 4319 Santo Thomas Dr., Los Angeles, Calif. 90008. *Biographical/critical sources: Who's Who of American Women,* 7th edition, Marquis, 1972; *Living Black American Authors: A Biographical Dictionary,* Bowker, 1973; *Black American Writers Past and Present: A Biographical and Bibliographical Dictionary,* Scarecrow, 1975.

* * *

WANDRO, Mark 1948-

PERSONAL: Born June 28, 1948, in San Mateo, Calif.; son of Louis George and Louise C. (an aide for disabled children; maiden name, Sillers) Wandro; married Joan E. Blank (a writer and publisher), June 2, 1973; children: Amika. *Education:* St. Joseph's College, Mountain View, Calif., B.A., 1970; University of California, San Francisco, B.S.N., 1977. *Politics:* Liberal Democrat. *Religion:* Unitarian-Universalist. *Home address:* P.O. Box 2086, Burlingame, Calif. 94010.

CAREER: San Francisco General Hospital, San Francisco, Calif., certified emergency nurse, 1980; Peter Bent Brigham and Women's Hospital, Boston, Mass., registered nurse in emergency, 1981; Waltham Hospital, Waltham, Mass., registered nurse in recovery, 1981; Mills Hospital, San Mateo, Calif., rehabilitation nurse, 1982. *Member:* American Nurses' Association, Emergency Department Nurses Association, Red Cross.

WRITINGS: (With wife, Joan Wandro) *My Daddy Is a Nurse* (juvenile), Addison-Wesley, 1981.

SIDELIGHTS: Wandro told *CA:* "My wife and I wrote our book to provide nonsexist alternatives in children's books. We wanted children to see that men can and do work in nontraditional occupations. It's an attempt to break sex-role stereotyping at an early age."

* * *

WARD, Melanie
See CURTIS, Richard (Alan)

WARD, Winfred O('Neil) 1933-

PERSONAL: Born September 28, 1933, in Exmore, Va.; son of Marvin O. and Ruth (Kellam) Ward; married Anne Martin (a research technician), June 21, 1958; children: Anne Elizabeth, Susan Terry. *Education:* College of William and Mary, B.S., 1954; Medical College of Virginia, M.D., 1958. *Religion:* Episcopalian. *Home:* 200 Poplar Lane, Richmond, Va. 23226. *Agent:* Mel Burger, William Morris Agency, 1350 Avenue of the Americas, New York, N.Y. 10019. *Office:* 2004 Bremo Rd., Suite 202, Richmond, Va. 23226.

CAREER: Mercy Hospital, Springfield, Ohio, intern, 1958-59; in private medical practice, 1961-71; preceptor in psychosomatic medicine, 1971-73; in private practice of psychosomatic medicine and medical hypnosis, 1973—. Adjunct professor in department of counseling at College of William and Mary, 1976-78; adjunct professor in department of rehabilitation counseling at Virginia Commonwealth University, 1979—. Affiliated with St. Luke's Hospital, Henrico Doctors Hospital, and St. Mary's Hospital. Chairman of Franklin Republican party and local chamber of commerce. *Military service:* U.S. Navy, physician attached to U.S. Marine Corps, 1959-61. *Member:* International Society for Hypnosis, American Medical Association, American Academy of Family Physicians, American Society for Clinical Hypnosis, Royal Society of Medicine, Society for Clinical and Experimental Hypnosis, Southern Medical Association, Medical Society of Virginia, Washington Independent Writers, Richmond Academy of Medicine. *Awards, honors:* Named outstanding young man by Virginia Jaycees, 1969; Algernon-Sydney Sullivan Award from College of William and Mary.

WRITINGS: (Contributor) Harold J. Wain, editor, *Hypnosis in the Seventies,* Swedish Press, 1975; (contributor) Ilka Shore-Cooper, editor, *Clinical Hypnosis in Medicine,* Year Book Medical Publishers, 1980; (with Lia Farrelli) *The Healing of Lia: A True Account of Multiple Personalities,* Macmillan, 1982. Contributor to medical journals.

WORK IN PROGRESS: A work on the survival of emotional illness by an attorney; research on use of hypnosis to control pain and to improve the quality of life for cancer victims.

SIDELIGHTS: Ward commented: "My goal in writing about Lia was to give encouragement to people with long-standing emotional illness, and to make physicians aware of the dangers of over-medication. My work in progress is being written to draw attention to child abuse and man's insensitivity and inhumanity to others. I was led to my profession from a childhood desire and a view of hypnosis as an expedient vehicle of therapy. Man must be willing to take on new careers if the rewards of life are to be reaped."

*   *   *

WASHBURN, Dorothy K(oster) 1945-

PERSONAL: Born May 17, 1945, in Cleveland, Ohio; daughter of E. Frederick (a pathologist) and Mary Jane (a librarian; maiden name, Miller) Koster; married William N. Washburn (a research chemist), September 20, 1969. *Education:* Oberlin College, B.A., 1967; Columbia University, Ph.D., 1972. *Home:* 1820 Mendon-Ionia Rd., Ionia, N.Y. 14475. *Office:* Department of Anthropology, California Academy of Sciences, Golden Gate Park, San Francisco, Calif. 94118.

CAREER: Harvard University, Cambridge, Mass., research fellow in North American archaeology at Peabody Museum of

Archaeology and Ethnology, 1972-76; University of California, Berkeley, fellow of Miller Institute for Basic Research in Science, 1976-78; California Academy of Sciences, San Francisco, assistant curator, 1978-80, associate curator, 1980—. Assistant director of San Jose State University's Hovenweep expedition, 1975-76. *Member:* American Anthropological Association (fellow), Society for American Archaeology, California Academy of Sciences (fellow).

WRITINGS: A Symmetry Analysis of Upper Gila Area Ceramic Design, Peabody Museum of Archaeology and Ethnology, Harvard University, 1977; (editor) *Hopi Kachina: Spirit of Life,* California Academy of Sciences, 1980; (editor) *The Structure of Art,* Cambridge University Press, in press.

WORK IN PROGRESS: Handbook of Symmetry Analysis, with Donald Crowe, for Princeton University Press.

SIDELIGHTS: Washburn told *CA:* "Originally my major area was the American Southwest, but it has expanded to include analysis of design worldwide. My professional interest lies in problems of classification and systematic analysis. I hope to use a symmetry analysis and geographical models to derive nonmaterial aspects of past cultures from archaeological data."

*   *   *

WATKINS, Keith 1931-

PERSONAL: Born October 31, 1931, in Lancaster, Wash.; son of Harold S. and Lydia S. (Hiukka) Watkins; married Wilhelmina L. Caton, June 16, 1952; children: Sharon, Marilyn, Michael, Carolyn, Kenneth. *Education:* Northwest Christian College, B.Th., 1953; Butler University, B.D., 1956; Pacific School of Religion, Th.D., 1964. *Home:* 5316 North Capitol Ave., Indianapolis, Ind. 46208. *Office:* Christian Theological Seminary, 1000 West 42nd St., Indianapolis, Ind. 46208.

CAREER: Ordained minister of Christian Church (Disciples of Christ), 1953; pastor of Christian church in Sanger, Calif., 1956-59; Christian Theological Seminary, Indianapolis, Ind., assistant professor, 1961-64, associate professor, 1964-68, professor of worship, 1968—, director for advanced professional studies, 1978—. Chairman of Christian Church (Disciples of Christ) Commission on Worship, 1966-72, member of general board, 1976—. *Member:* North American Academy of Liturgy.

WRITINGS: The Breaking of Bread, Bethany Press, 1966; *Liturgies in a Time When Cities Burn,* Abingdon, 1969; *The Feast of Joy,* Bethany Press, 1977; *Faithful and Fair,* Abingdon, 1981.

WORK IN PROGRESS: A history of the eucharist in the United States; prayers and liturgies, "using inclusive language."

SIDELIGHTS: Watkins told *CA:* "I am interested in traditional communities and lifestyles and their import for contemporary American culture. I travel extensively by bicycle and frequently find myself in out-of-the-way places. Sunday preaching in rural churches puts me in touch with older patterns of life."

*   *   *

WATTENBARGER, James L(orenzo) 1922-

PERSONAL: Born May 2, 1922, in Cleveland, Tenn.; son of James Claude (in insurance) and Lura (Hambright) Wattenbarger; married Marion Swanson, June 11, 1947; children: J. Frank, Carl E., Robert D. *Education:* Palm Beach Junior College, A.A., 1941; University of Florida, B.A.E. (high honors), 1943, M.A.E., 1947, Ed.D., 1950. *Religion:* Episcopal.

Home: 8716 Northwest Fourth Pl., Gainesville, Fla. 32601. *Office:* Institute of Higher Education, University of Florida, Gainesville, Fla. 32611.

CAREER: State of Florida, Tallahassee, director of Division of Community and Junior Colleges, 1955-67; University of Florida, Gainesville, professor of education, 1968—, chairman of board of Associated Consultants in Education, 1970—. *Military service:* U.S. Army Air Forces, 1943-46; became captain; received Distinguished Flying Cross with two Oak Leaf Clusters and Air Medal with three Oak Leaf Clusters. *Member:* American Association of Community and Junior Colleges, National Education Association, National Association of Public School Adult Educators, Florida Association of Community Colleges, Order of Constantine, Kappa Delta Pi, Phi Delta Kappa, Phi Kappa Phi.

WRITINGS: A State Plan for Public Junior Colleges, University of Florida Press, 1953; (with Winfred Goodwin) *The Community College in the South,* Southern States Work Conference, 1962; (with Bob Cage) *More Money for More Opportunity,* Jossey-Bass, 1974; (with Louis W. Bender) *Improving Statewide Planning,* Jossey-Bass, 1974. Author of numerous monographs. Contributor to *Community and Junior College Journal, Community College Review,* and *American Encyclopedia of Educational Research.*

WORK IN PROGRESS: Studies of community college finance in the United States.

SIDELIGHTS: Wattenbarger told *CA:* "The progress of the United States and its people is directly related to increased individual growth as educated citizens. In our modern, diverse, and exceedingly complex world, the community college has provided to the largest part of the people an opportunity to learn as members of human society, as persons who work, and as individuals in families who make a contribution to their own well-being as well as to society's. The community college has been the focus of my professional career."

AVOCATIONAL INTERESTS: Philately, reading (science fiction and mythology), jogging.

* * *

WEAVER, Richard L. II 1941-

PERSONAL: Born December 5, 1941, in Hanover, N.H.; son of Richard L. (a professor) and Florence B. (a teacher; maiden name, Grow) Weaver; married Andrea A. Willis, 1965; children: R. Scott, Jacquelynn M., Anthony K., Joanna C. *Education:* University of Michigan, A.B., 1964, M.A., 1965; Indiana University, Ph.D., 1969. *Home:* 9583 Woodleigh Court, Perrysburg, Ohio 43551. *Office:* School of Speech Communication, Bowling Green State University, Bowling Green, Ohio 43403.

CAREER: University of Massachusetts, Amherst, instructor, 1968-69, assistant professor, 1969-74; Bowling Green State University, Bowling Green, Ohio, associate professor, 1974-79, professor of speech, 1979—, director of basic speech communication course, 1974—. Visiting professor at University of Hawaii at Manoa, 1981-82. *Member:* International Communication Association, Speech Communication Association, Central States Speech Association, Midwest Basic Course Director's Conference, Ohio Speech Association.

WRITINGS: (With Saundra Hybels) *Speech/Communication,* 2nd edition, D. Van Nostrand, 1974; *Speech/Communication: A Reader,* 2nd edition, Collegiate Publishing, 1975; *Understanding Interpersonal Communication,* 2nd edition, Scott, Foresman, 1978; (with Raymond K. Tucker and Cynthia Berryman-Fink) *Research in Speech Communication,* Prentice-Hall, 1981; *Speech/Communication: Skills,* Collegiate Publishing; 1982; (editor) *Foundations of Speech Communication: Perspectives of a Discipline,* University of Hawaii, 1982; *Understanding Public Communication,* Prentice-Hall, 1983. Contributor of more than forty articles to education and history journals. Associate editor of *Communication Education,* 1979-81.

WORK IN PROGRESS: Understanding Business Communication, publication by Prentice-Hall expected in 1984; a third edition of *Speech/Communication,* with Saundra Hybels, Wadsworth, 1984; a third edition of *Understanding Interpersonal Communication,* Scott, Foresman, 1984; *Understanding Communication Theory,* completion expected in 1985.

SIDELIGHTS: Weaver told *CA:* "Writing, for me, is an extension of my teaching; I put teaching as my highest priority and commitment. Like teaching, writing is an opportunity to reach out and directly touch college students in a deep and meaningful manner. I write from my teaching experience; I want my writing to be easy to understand, comfortable, and enjoyable. The more students can relate to my writing, identify with my examples, and feel they are being addressed specifically and directly, the more they are likely to comprehend and learn from what they read.

"When I am writing, I put myself in the place of my readers. How are they likely to think? How will they respond? How will they feel? Writing is a personal experience for me, but it is also a fulfilling interpersonal one as well because I feel as if I am having a conversation with my readers. In a sense, when I am writing I am 'in relationship' with them; it is a transactional experience in which I am actually creating an image of them and communicating with that image as I write.

"Writing is also an enjoyable experience for me. I seldom approach it with dread, as a chore, or as something I must get out of the way. Often, I cannot wait to finish other activities so that I can return to writing. It is both cathartic and a way to channel my energies. It is also an escape, because part of writing is an intense, internal experience; you enter the world of the imagination where you can have dialogues with yourself. You can explore and challenge, question and probe. I like to write more than almost anything else.

"When people who read my books say they can really feel me talking to them through my words and ideas, for me that is a valuable, cherished compliment. Although directness, informal style, and specific examples help achieve this, the discipline of speech communication also contributes. I write about a topic that permeates the very core of people's lives. Thus, it is easy to find stimulus for writing from daily encounters, including the acute questions of my students. Much of the substance of my writing comes from the exciting drama and experience of everyday living—something everyone can relate to.

"No matter what career people enter, no matter what profession they pursue, no matter what activity they engage in, speech communication is often a major force in their effectiveness and success. If the concepts and principles I write about help in even the slightest way to make readers' lives more significant, effective, or satisfying, I feel richly rewarded.

"What writing has done for me is to force me out of myself and into the lives of others. It is like the effect that teaching has on my life. It makes me a lover of people, and when you become a lover of people it has an influence on the whole business of living. Once we learn to love people, we learn the true art of living."

AVOCATIONAL INTERESTS: Travel, camping, outdoor activities, hiking, swimming, square dancing, music, reading.

* * *

WEBB, Jack (Randolph) 1920-
(John Farr, Tex Grady)

BRIEF ENTRY: Born April 2, 1920, in Santa Monica, Calif. American radio and television actor, producer, director, and author. Webb's career began in radio in the early 1940's. In 1949 he created the series "Dragnet," which moved to television in 1951. Webb is now the owner of Mark VII Ltd., Mark VII Music, and Pete Kelly Music. His radio and television writing has earned him Edgar Allan Poe Awards from the Mystery Writers of America and an Emmy Award from the Academy of Television Arts and Sciences. Webb's novels include *The Brass Halo* (Rinehart, 1957), *The Deadly Sex* (Rinehart, 1959), *One for My Dame* (Holt, 1961), *The Gilded Witch* (Regency, 1963), and *Make My Bed Soon* (Holt, 1963). He also wrote a nonfiction account of the Los Angeles Police Department, *The Badge* (Prentice-Hall, 1958). *Address:* Mark VII Ltd., Samuel Goldwyn Studio, 1041 North Formosa, Los Angeles, Calif. 90046. *Biographical/critical sources: Current Biography,* Wilson, 1955; *The Oxford Companion to Film,* Oxford University Press, 1976; *International Motion Picture Almanac,* Quigley, 1979.

* * *

WEBB, Peter B(randram) 1941-

PERSONAL: Born May 23, 1941, in Hove, England; son of Francis (an army officer) and Enid (Elliot-Heywood) Webb. *Education:* Cambridge University, B.A. (with honors), 1963, M.A., 1967; Courtauld Institute of Art, London, Academic Diploma in Art History, 1965. *Residence:* London, England. *Office:* Cat Hill, Cockfosters, Barnet, Hertfordshire, England.

CAREER: Coventry College of Art (now Lanchester Polytechnic), Coventry, England, lecturer in art history, 1965-70; Middlesex Polytechnic, London, England, senior lecturer in art history, 1970—. Visiting lecturer at more than sixty schools, including Cambridge University, Oxford University, University of London, University of Hong Kong, Concordia University, and New York University. Guest on British radio and television programs. *Member:* Association of Art Historians.

WRITINGS: (With Grant Lewison and Rosalind Billingham) *Coventry New Architecture,* [Warwickshire, England], 1969; (contributor) Stephen Verney, editor, *Art and the Mind of Man,* University of Birmingham Press, 1970; *The Erotic Arts,* Secker & Warburg, 1975, 3rd edition, 1981, New York Graphic Society, 1976; *The Erotic Drawings of the Marquis von Bayros,* Amorini Press, 1976; (art editor) *The Visual Dictionary of Sex,* A & W Publishers, 1977; (contributor) Maurice Yaffe, editor, *The Influence of Pornography on Behaviour,* Academic Press, 1982; (contributor) Alan Bold, editor, *The Sexual Dimension in Literature,* Barnes & Noble, in press; *Beauty and the Beast: A Study in Iconology and Mythology,* Granada, in press; *David Hockney,* Paul Hamlyn, in press. Contributor to magazines and newspapers, including *Artscribe* and *Scorpio.*

SIDELIGHTS: Webb told *CA:* "My expertise as an art historian is in late nineteenth- and early twentieth-century painting. My writing and lecturing tend to concentrate on the world of erotic art. This is something of a crusade for me. I feel it is of great importance for people to realize the vital role that eroticism has played in the culture of almost every civilization, so that they can have a better understanding of the vital role that sex can and should play in their own lives and in their own society."

AVOCATIONAL INTERESTS: Travel, cinema (attending and making films), collecting books ("an uncontrollable passion, and the reason for continual moves to larger houses").

BIOGRAPHICAL/CRITICAL SOURCES: London Times, February 17, 1971; *Times Literary Supplement,* February 2, 1976; *Washington Post,* December 5, 1976; *Books & Bookmen,* November, 1978.

* * *

WEINBERG, Bernard 1909-1973

OBITUARY NOTICE: Born August 23, 1909, in Chicago, Ill.; died February 13, 1973. Educator and author. A professor of romance languages, Weinberg taught at the University of Chicago, Washington University, and Northwestern University. He wrote numerous books in his field, including *The Art of Jean Racine, French Realism: The Critical Reaction, The Limits of Symbolism: Studies of Five Modern French Poets,* and *A History of Literary Criticism in the Italian Renaissance.* He also edited several volumes, including *Critical Prefaces in the French Renaissance.* Obituaries and other sources: *American Authors and Books, 1640 to the Present Day,* 3rd revised edition, Crown, 1962; *Who's Who in World Jewry: A Biographical Dictionary of Outstanding Jews,* Pitman, 1972; *Who Was Who in America, With World Notables,* Volume V: *1969-73,* Marquis, 1973.

* * *

WEINZWEIG, Helen 1915-

PERSONAL: Born May 21, 1915, in Radom, Poland; immigrated to Canada in 1924; daughter of Joseph and Lily (a hairdresser; maiden name, Wekselman) Tenenbaum; married John Weinzweig (a musical composer), July 19, 1940; children: Paul, Daniel. *Education:* Attended high school in Toronto, Ontario, Canada. *Home:* 107 Manor Rd. E., Toronto, Ontario, Canada M4S 1R3.

CAREER: Worked as a typist, a stenographer, a chaperone for National Youth Orchestra of Canada, and an organizer, teacher, and supervisor of a cooperative nursery school, in Toronto, Ontario, Canada; writer. *Member:* Writers Union of Canada (founding member), Authors Guild. *Awards, honors:* Third prize literary award from Canadian Broadcasting Corp., 1979, for short story "The Homecoming"; fiction award from city of Toronto, Ontario, 1981, for novel *Basic Black with Pearls.*

WRITINGS: Passing Ceremony (novel), House of Anansi Press, 1973; *Basic Black With Pearls* (novel), House of Anansi Press, 1980, Morrow, 1981. Author of short stories.

WORK IN PROGRESS: A novel dealing with memory and loss.

SIDELIGHTS: Helen Weinzweig commented: "By the time I began to write, at age forty-five, I had a fair knowledge of what was called experimental writing. I am still excited by new ways of telling old stories. I believe that many of the conventions of fiction, such as plot and chronology and characterization, now belong to movies and television, and much of our evocative language has been appropriated by advertising. In my fiction, I use dislocation of time, juxtaposition of ideas, and arrangement of words in a manner designed to reach an imagination not now being served by mass print and the camera. My personal preoccupation in writing is to explore the elements of appearance and illusion.

"Writing is desire, I don't know how or why. I hope to achieve self-discovery in the books I write. Personally, I feel the so-called 'mirroring of life' has been taken over completely by movies and television, so that a writer is hard put to be creative. I feel that today the 'experimentalists' have synthesized myth and fact, and the intellect and the emotion. The continental writers, in translation, have influenced me, because their approach to storytelling, I feel, is more subtle, intelligent, and certainly more abstract—a sort of 'what is going on?' Influences, for example, have included Michel Butor, Alain Robbe-Grillet, Claude Simon Pingent, Djuna Barnes, and from South America, Llosa Vargas, Jorge Luis Borges, and Julio Cortazar.''

BIOGRAPHICAL/CRITICAL SOURCES: New Yorker, April 27, 1981.

* * *

WEISS, Peter (Ulrich) 1916-1982

OBITUARY NOTICE—See index for *CA* sketch: Born November 8, 1916, in Nowawes, Germany (now Babelsberg, East Germany); died of a heart attack, May 10, 1982, in Stockholm, Sweden. Artist, filmmaker, playwright, and author. A Marxist, Weiss was a political writer espousing what he termed "humanistic socialism." Much of his viewpoint was shaped by the fact that he escaped the Holocaust during World War II. His father converted from Judaism to the Lutheran religion, the faith of Weiss's mother, and the family fled to Sweden to avoid anti-Semitic sentiments in Germany. "I feel guilty," Weiss remarked once, "because I was not being punished as the others had been for their Jewish blood." An exponent of the Theatre of Cruelty, he designed imagery to shock his audiences because he wanted them to "atone and suffer." The playwright viewed modern society as insane, violent, and chaotic. His most famous work, for example, "The Persecution and Assassination of Jean Paul Marat as Performed by the Inmates of the Asylum of Charenton Under the Direction of the Marquis de Sade," is set in a madhouse and juxtaposes killing for self-aggrandizement (individualism) with killing for the salvation of mankind (collectivism). "Marat-Sade," as the play is referred to, won a Lessing-Preis Award, an Antoinette Perry Award, and a Drama Critics Circle Award. Weiss's other plays include "The Investigation," about the trials of Nazi officials, "Trotsky in Exile," and "The Song of the Lusitanian Bogeyman." Weiss also published two collections of poetry, *Fran O Till O* and *De Besegrade,* as well as novels such as *Point of Escape.* He wrote three autobiographies, *Bodies and Shadows, Leavetaking,* and *Exile,* which won a Charles Veillon Prize. Obituaries and other sources: *Chicago Tribune Book World,* May 12, 1982; *London Times,* May 12, 1982; *Washington Post,* May 13, 1982; *Los Angeles Times,* May 17, 1982; *Time,* May 24, 1982; *Newsweek,* May 24, 1982.

* * *

WELLESLEY, Kenneth 1911-

PERSONAL: Born June 15, 1911, in Weston-super-Mare, England; son of Alfred Arthur (an actor) and Beatrice Lilian (Webb) Wellesley; married Herta Lucija Kossinsky, March 30, 1940; children: Ian K., Inga C. Mantle. *Education:* Peterhouse, Cambridge, B.A., 1934, M.A., 1937. *Home:* 125 Trinity Rd., Edinburgh EH5 3LB, Scotland.

CAREER: Assistant master at Bede School in Sunderland, England, 1934-36; high school teacher of classics in Cambridge, England, 1936-48; University of Edinburgh, Edinburgh, Scotland, lecturer, 1949-63, senior lecturer, 1963-67, reader in

humanity, 1967-81. *Military service:* British Army, Intelligence Corps, 1940-46. *Member:* Classical Association, Society of Roman Studies, Virgilian Society, Classical Association of Scotland.

WRITINGS: Tacitus: The Histories; A New Translation, Penguin, 1964; *Tacitus: The Histories,* Book III: *Text and Commentary,* Sydney University Press, 1972; *The Long Year A. D. 69,* Elek, 1975. Contributor of articles and reviews to scholarly journals.

WORK IN PROGRESS: Editing a standard text of Tacitus, with Istvan Borzsak, publication by Biblioteca Teubneriana expected to begin in 1983.

SIDELIGHTS: Wellesley wrote: "I am equally interested in literature and history; though I specialized in ancient history at university, I consider my involvement in literature to be more profound. I have traveled widely in Europe, especially Italy, France, and Germany."

* * *

WEMPLE, Suzanne Fonay 1927-

PERSONAL: Born August 1, 1927, in Veszprem, Hungary; came to the United States in 1947, naturalized citizen, 1952; daughter of Ernest and Magda (Mihalyfy) Fonay; married George Wemple, 1957; children: Peter, Stephen, Carolyn. *Education:* University of California, Berkeley, B.A., 1953; Columbia University, M.L.S., 1955, Ph.D., 1967. *Office:* Department of History, Barnard College, Columbia University, New York, N.Y. 10027.

CAREER: Columbia University, New York City, reference assistant at libraries, 1955-58; Stern College for Women, New York City, instructor in history, 1962-64; Columbia University, lecturer at Teachers College, 1964-68, instructor at Barnard College, 1966-67, assistant professor, 1967-72, associate professor, 1972-78, professor of history, 1978—. *Member:* Mediaeval Academy of America, American Association of University Professors, American Historical Association.

WRITINGS: Atto of Vercelli: Church, State, and Christian Society in Tenth-Century Italy, Edizioni di Storia e Letteratura, 1979; *Women in Frankish Society: Marriage and the Cloister, 500 to 900,* University of Pennsylvania Press, 1981. Contributor to history and women's studies journals.

WORK IN PROGRESS: Monastic Communities of Women in the Middle Ages.

* * *

WERT, Lynette L(emon) 1938-
(Lynn LeMon)

PERSONAL: Born July 30, 1938, in Dallas, Tex.; daughter of Haskell and Irene (Campbell) Lemon; married Peter K. Wert (an executive), January 31, 1959; children: Andrea, Kenneth, Daniel. *Education:* University of Oklahoma, B.A. (summa cum laude), 1959, M.A., 1960; Central State University, M.A., 1975. *Politics:* "Assorted." *Religion:* Protestant. *Home address:* P.O. Box 20104, Oklahoma City, Okla. 73156. *Agent:* Donald MacCampbell, Inc., 12 East 41st St., New York, N.Y. 10017. *Office:* Department of Creative Studies, Central State University, Edmond, Okla. 73034.

CAREER: Central State University, Edmond, Okla., lecturer in creative studies, 1975—. Volunteer public relations worker for American Red Cross. *Member:* Associated Writing Programs, Phi Beta Kappa, Oklahoma City Panhellenic (president, 1972).

WRITINGS: (With Zella Patterson) *Langston University: A History,* University of Oklahoma Press, 1979; (with Pinky Tomlin) *The Object of My Affection: Biography of Pinky Tomlin,* University of Oklahoma Press, 1981.

Novels; under pseudonym Lynn LeMon: *This Rebel Hunger,* Pocket Books, 1980; *Sunrise Temptation,* Pocket Books, 1982. Contributor of articles and stories to magazines, including *Orbit, Aspects, Motorist, Outdoors,* and *Christian Herald.*

WORK IN PROGRESS: Research for a novel about the diplomatic corps and for a historical novel set in Yorktown, Va.

SIDELIGHTS: Lynette Wert told *CA:* "I began writing when my youngest child finally exited for kindergarten in 1972. A lot of mothers cry when the last chickadee leaves home. I shed tears, too, of joy. Now it was time to crank the typewriter into action! I practically beat my kids to school, returning for a second master's degree in creative studies. My first professional effort—the first thing I sold—was a short humorous sketch of my experiences with 'show-and-tell' time in preschool classes.

"I revise my work completely. Nothing published is ever remotely like its original concept. Three times through the typewriter is about average, although some poems have gone through nearly a hundred variations, and an occasional short article will fall onto the paper in finished form. Nonfiction articles require the least revision.

"I write at the typewriter, hardly ever in longhand. That means I'm stuck at a desk in a study, which used to be the formal dining room in my house. Now it's the study, lined with bookcases, and if we ever eat 'formally,' I clear out the den.

"Apparently I like it quiet, because if the cat purrs too loudly, she's banished to the garage. But sometimes I turn on country and western radio or crank up the stereo for classical music. Usually I forget the music is on. I resent the telephone ringing, the dryer buzzing, and woe to any friend who drops in unexpectedly!

"My first novel, *This Rebel Hunger,* stemmed from a family vacation through the Deep South. While the others looked for cannon balls on the Civil War battlefields, I looked for stories. My second novel, *Sunrise Temptation,* also grew out of a setting first—the four years we lived in Honolulu (when I was a Navy wife) were spent at Pearl Harbor. I began to wonder what the landscape and atmosphere had been like a century before. Soon I had imagined fiery Ariel Cortland longing to leave her almost-paradise for the contrasting wilder landscapes of the mainland.

"Ours is a family of five strong individuals. We support one another strongly and, with the exclusion of the pet cat, dog, and catfish, the five of us take family vacations in a motor home with the motto 'We Suffer Together.' Writing is my personal business, however. My family reads the stories, articles, and books if they happen to be interested in them. My husband and I have an agreement: I won't build roads if he won't write books. The best working arrangement is Elizabeth Hailey's: 'For a marriage to succeed, each partner should be excited by the abilities of the other and not feel threatened by an interest that is not shared.'

"By instinct, I'm a night person, but for the past twenty-three years I've had a family that believes in big breakfasts, usually at the crack of dawn. The family leaves the house at about ten minutes before eight o'clock. I figure that gives me ten minutes

for housework, which is about all the housework I'm interested in doing. I'm at the typewriter at eight and generally work until two. After that, I swim, buy groceries, carpool, and become a 'normal' wife and mother."

*   *   *

WERTIME, Theodore Allen   1919-1982

OBITUARY NOTICE: Born August 31, 1919, in Chambersburg, Pa.; died of cancer, April 8, 1982, in Chambersburg, Pa. Foreign service officer, historian, researcher, and author. Wertime served in China during World War II with the Office of Strategic Services and did further intelligence work with the State Department from 1945 until 1955. He then joined the U.S. Information Agency, for which he was a cultural officer in Iran and Greece. Wertime retired from government service in 1975 and began his association with the Smithsonian Institution, where he was a research associate of the Museum of Natural History. He also led five archaeological expeditions for the Smithsonian and three for the National Geographic Society. A contributor of articles to the *Washington Post,* the *Journal of Communications,* and the *Foreign Service Journal,* Wertime wrote *The Coming of the Age of Iron.* Obituaries and other sources: *Directory of American Scholars,* Volume I: *History,* 7th edition, Bowker, 1978; *Who's Who in America,* 40th edition, Marquis, 1978; *Washington Post,* April 16, 1982.

*   *   *

WEST, Anna   1938-

PERSONAL: Born April 5, 1938, in Crete, Ill.; daughter of A. E. (in sales) and Helen (Janota) Wood; married Paul West (a broadcaster and craftsman), November 28, 1969. *Education:* University of Michigan, B.A., 1959; San Francisco State University, M.A., 1971. *Residence:* Palermo, Calif.

CAREER: Writer. *Awards, honors:* Avery Hopwood Award from University of Michigan, 1955, for a story, "The Revivalists."

WRITINGS: Revenge at the Spycatcher's Picnic (juvenile; Volume I of "The Messina Trilogy"), Addison-Wesley, 1981. Work represented in anthologies, including *Coast to Coast,* Angus & Robertson, 1968.

WORK IN PROGRESS: "The Messina Trilogy," Volume II and Volume III, for Addison-Wesley; a novel for adults.

SIDELIGHTS: West told *CA:* "When I was a child I lived here and there, with mother, with an aunt, and with grandmother. If I wandered in childhood, I continued to do so when I grew up. That peripateticism took me to Alaska, Hawaii, Mexico, England, Morocco, Spain, Greece, and Australia. Now it has brought me to northern California, where my husband is building a home among oak, manzanita, and digger-pine, on a hill that is thistle-dry in summer and mushroom-moist in winter. I love the opposites of this land.

"In order to help us stay here, I took work as a substitute elementary school teacher. As I worked with the children and observed their intrigues, I remembered the games *we* used to play! Those memories compelled me to write a spy novel for children. Then, as I worked, I began to see that Messina's personality is worth more than one book. She is taking me on a new journey—back to some of the old places."

BIOGRAPHICAL/CRITICAL SOURCES: Oroville Mercury Register, December 14, 1981.

WEST, Joyce (Tarlton)
(Manu Gilbert)

PERSONAL: Born in Auckland, New Zealand; daughter of William Edward (a teacher) and Annie Maud W. (a teacher) West. *Education:* Educated in Maori schools in New Zealand and through correspondence courses. *Politics:* Nationalist. *Religion:* Presbyterian. *Home:* 88 Eighteenth Ave., Tauranga, New Zealand.

CAREER: Worked as an accounting clerk in New Zealand; author and illustrator of books for adults and young people.

*WRITINGS—*For young people; all self-illustrated: *Drovers Road,* Dent, 1953; *The Year of the Shining Cuckoo,* Paul's Book Arcade, 1961, Roy, 1964; *Cape Lost,* Dent, 1963; *The Golden Country,* Dent, 1965; *The Sea Islanders,* Roy, 1970; *The Rivei Road,* Dent, 1980.

Adult novels: *Sheep Kings,* Tombs, 1936; (with Mary Scott) *Fatal Lady,* Paul's Book Arcade, 1960; (with Scott) *Such Nice People,* Angus & Robertson, 1962; (with Scott) *The Mangrove Murder,* Angus & Robertson, 1963; (with Scott) *No Red Herrings,* Angus & Robertson, 1963; (with Scott) *Who Put It There?,* Angus & Robertson, 1965; (under pseudonym Manu Gilbert) *Lineman's Ticket,* Blackwood & Janet Paul, 1967.

WORK IN PROGRESS: The Lucky, a children's book set in an old gold mining area of New Zealand.

SIDELIGHTS: Joyce West told *CA:* "I have always been interested in the earlier days of New Zealand. I have set my books in remote country districts because I feel that it is important that the quality of life I experienced as a child should not go unrecorded. There are still happy and isolated regions in this country, but they grow smaller with each passing year." West grew up in remote areas of New Zealand, obtaining her early education from her school-teacher parents, and it is this part of the country she seeks to describe. *The Sea Islanders* is one example of her use of isolated regions as settings in her work. Translated into German, Danish, and Japanese, it was adapted into a five-part serial for BBC-TV, and television rights in America have been purchased by Walt Disney Productions.

*   *   *

WESTBURY, Ian Douglas 1939-

BRIEF ENTRY: Born January 7, 1939, in Melbourne, Australia. Educator and author. Westbury taught in Australia from 1960 to 1964 and in Ontario, Canada, from 1966 to 1968. He has taught secondary education at University of Illinois and served as department chairman since 1973. He edited *Research Into Classroom Processes: Recent Developments and Next Steps* (Teachers College Press, 1971), *The Generalist Program: Description and Evaluation* (School of Social Service Administration, University of Chicago, 1973), and *Science, Curriculum, and Liberal Education: Selected Essays* (University of Chicago Press, 1978). *Address:* Department of Secondary Education, University of Illinois, Urbana, Ill. 61801.

*   *   *

WESTMAN, Paul (Wendell) 1956-

PERSONAL: Born October 27, 1956, in Minneapolis, Minn.; son of Bert Fabian (a laborer; in sales and small business) and Irene Geneva (a cost estimator; maiden name, Taxdahl) Westman. *Education:* University of Minnesota, B.A., 1979; University of North Dakota, J.D., 1984. *Politics:* Democrat. *Religion:* Lutheran. *Home:* 102 Second Ave. S.E., East Grand Forks, Minn. 56721.

CAREER: Free-lance writer, 1978—. *Member:* National Taxpayers Union, University of Minnesota Alumni Association, Phi Beta Kappa, Phi Kappa Phi. *Awards, honors:* Scholastic Writing Award from Scholastic Magazines, 1970, for article "Tornado!," and 1973, for short story "A Christmas Story"; NCTE Achievement Award in Writing from National Council of Teachers of English, 1974.

*WRITINGS—*Juveniles; published by Dillon, except as noted: *Hubert Humphrey: The Politics of Joy,* 1979; *Alan Shepard: First American in Space,* 1979; *Neil Armstrong: Space Pioneer,* Lerner, 1980; *Ray Kroc: Mayor of McDonaldland,* 1980; *Walter Cronkite: The Most Trusted Man in America,* 1980; *John Glenn: Around the World in Ninety Minutes,* 1980; *Jacques Cousteau: Free Flight Undersea,* 1980; *Jesse Jackson: I Am Somebody,* 1980; *Jimmy Carter: From Farm Boy to President,* Lerner, 1981; *Billy Graham: Reaching Out to the World,* 1981; *Frank Borman: To the Moon and Back,* 1981; *John Young,* 1982; *Andrew Young,* 1982; *Thor Heyerdahl,* 1982; *Walter Mondale,* 1983.

WORK IN PROGRESS: Defense and Foreign Policy for a Free Society, "the first in a projected series of books explicating and updating the classical, individualist liberalism of Locke, Montesquieu, Jefferson, Mill, and Gladstone for modern readers."

SIDELIGHTS: Westman told *CA:* "I have written continuously since I was in the sixth grade, everything from poetry and short stories to articles and children's books, and I will undoubtedly continue to write. However, my past work probably gives an imperfect indication at best of the direction my future work is likely to take.

"My writing for children has been especially influenced by the works of Augusta Stevenson, William O. Steele, and some other writers of the 1940's and 1950's. They were born storytellers, with a gift for making history come alive for young readers. It would be nice if the same admirable combination of craftsmanship and sheer creative ability could again become as highly esteemed as it once was.

"I have always been intensely political, and liberal—in the Jeffersonian-Jacksonian sense of that word. As a consequence, I am greatly disturbed by the widespread acceptance of authoritarianism, violence, and totalitarianism in world politics today. In the advanced western nations the major political trends are also anti-liberal: social democracy on the Left and laissez-faire/aristocratic conservatism on the Right. All of these movements have one thing in common: an enmity toward classical democratic liberalism and the humanistic, individualistic values it represents. Democratic liberalism—the philosophy of ordered liberty—is desperately in need of a comprehensive restatement to render its underlying principles consistent and meaningful to a new generation, and to distinguish it sharply as a theoretical system from the twin political juggernauts of socialism and conservatism."

AVOCATIONAL INTERESTS: Reading, motorcycling, boating, swimming, history, philosophy, genealogical research, watching movies.

*   *   *

WEVERS, Richard Franklin 1933-

BRIEF ENTRY: Born March 23, 1933, in Baldwin, Wis. American educator and author. Wevers has taught at Calvin College since 1961. He has been professor of classical languages since 1969 and department chairman since 1975. He wrote *Isaeus: Chronology, Prosoporgraphy, and Social History* (Mouton, 1969). *Address:* Department of Classical Languages, Calvin College, 3207 Burton St., Grand Rapids, Mich. 49506.

*   *   *

WEZEMAN, Frederick Hartog   1915-1981

OBITUARY NOTICE—See index for *CA* sketch: Born May 1, 1915, in Oak Park, Ill.; died November 2, 1981. Librarian, educator, and author. Wezeman was the founding director of the University of Iowa's School of Library Science, where he was employed since 1966. Retiring in 1980, the librarian was a professor emeritus of that institution at the time of his death. He was a life member of both the American Library Association and the Canadian Library Association. Wezeman wrote *The Use of Books and Libraries* with Raymond H. Shove, Blanche E. Moen, and Harold G. Russell, and he contributed to Alfred Stefferud's *Wonderful World of Books*. Obituaries and other sources: *Library Journal*, May 15, 1982.

*   *   *

WHEELER, Raymond Milner   1919-1982

OBITUARY NOTICE: Born September 30, 1919, in Farmville, N.C.; died of an apparent heart attack, February 17, 1982, in Charlotte, N.C. Physician, educator, nutritionist, civil rights leader, and author. Considered one of the most influential figures in the civil rights struggle, Wheeler fought particularly for the rights of blacks and the poor in the South and for the alleviation of hunger throughout the country. An internist and nutritionist in private practice, Wheeler in 1967 conducted a study of hunger in Mississippi. He was appalled to find widespread disease and mental and emotional damage due to hunger. Wheeler presented his revealing statistics to the U.S. Senate, and he later addressed Congress on findings from other areas of the country. He is credited with aiding the establishment of the food stamp program. Obituaries and other sources: *Who's Who in America*, 40th edition, Marquis, 1978; *Chicago Tribune*, February 20, 1982; *New York Times*, February 20, 1982.

*   *   *

WHITBREAD, Jane
See LEVIN, Jane Whitbread

*   *   *

WHITE, Jude Gilliam   1947-
(Jude Deveraux)

PERSONAL: Born September 20, 1947, in Louisville, Ky.; daughter of Harold J. (an electrician) and Virginia (Berry) Gilliam; married Richard G. Sides, February 4, 1967 (divorced, February, 1969); married Claude B. White (a contractor), June 3, 1970. *Education:* Murray State University, B.S., 1970, College of Santa Fe, teaching certificate, 1973; University of New Mexico, remedial reading certificate, 1976. *Home:* 1937 Tijeras Rd., Santa Fe, N.M. 87501.

CAREER: Worked as elementary school teacher in Santa Fe, N.M., 1973-77; writer. *Member:* Romance Writers of America, Costume Society of America.

WRITINGS—Under pseudonym Jude Deveraux: *The Enchanted Land*, Avon, 1978; *The Black Lyon*, Avon, 1980; *Casa Grande*, Avon, 1982.

The "Montgomery Annals" series; under Deveraux pseudonym: *The Velvet Promise*, Gallen/Pocket Books, 1981; *Highland Velvet*, Pocket Books, 1982; *Song of Promise*, Pocket Books, 1983.

WORK IN PROGRESS: One more book in the "Montgomery Annals" series; a series of books set in Virginia in 1795; two books about identical twins in Mexico in 1896.

SIDELIGHTS: Deveraux told *CA:* "I started writing romances because I was tired of reading rape sagas. I was tired of women who hid behind some granite cheeked taciturn man who fought off villains and later threw her on a bed. I'd had enough of women who did little more than stamp their feet and say, 'How dare you?' The heroes also bothered me because they seemed to be cut out of the same mold, afraid to sit down and talk to anyone.

"I wanted to write about women who had some power, who could create things, could make things happen. I consider myself a feminist, a believer in equality between men and women. I don't like being told I must like housecleaning because women are supposed to like that sort of thing. Nor do I believe all men should be expected to be go-getters, hustlers, merely because they are men.

"Although some people say it's a contradiction in terms to be a feminist and a romantic, I am both. I believe in the family, in love between men and women but not in a love where the man gives all the orders and the woman meekly stands by and obeys. It must be a relationship of give and take.

"In starting a book, I take two characters, such as in *The Velvet Promise*, where I had a hero who'd spent most of his life with men, and gave him a heroine who'd been trained to be a nun. In medieval times a nun could become an abbess before she was thirty and as such she learned to rule estates and manage people. The conflict came when the hero, who believed women should be sweet and nice, was married to a woman who ran his business better than he did.

"In another book, tentatively titled *Highland Velvet*, the heroine is the laird of a Scottish clan and she's married to an Englishman who believes he's going to teach the Scots how things should be done. Instead, he learns to compromise, as she does.

"All my books concern people learning to work together, growing and developing. Which brings me to one of my most heartfelt causes. Depending upon the section of the country, romance novels comprise forty-five to fifty-five percent of all sales. In spite of romances being the backbone and most of the muscle of the publishing industry, romance writers are not respected, either by the media or the public. Personally, I've had many people say, 'I thought you were a "real" writer.' The media seems to think romances are easier than other novels, do not require the discipline other novelists must have, or the work. They constantly denigrate romance writers, saying that they are merely frustrated housewives. If a person writes a work of science fiction, or a contemporary novel about insane people, he/she is immediately said to be a writer. A romance writer, even if she has fifty novels in print selling millions of copies, is still called a housewife, and referred to with a smirk.

"I would be the first to admit that romances are fantasies, that they aren't related to our real world, but if they are fantasies, why aren't they treated with respect? Why is a created story about goblins and fairies praised and a story about pirates and beautiful women laughed at?

"All the romance writers I have met are hard-working women, with a firm grasp of what goes into making a good story, and above all, a strong sense of self discipline. In other words, they have all the qualities that go into making a good writer. But even women who call themselves feminists look down on romance writers, seeming to say that all the writers' work means little because they write stories of love.

"The new romances are about strong women, women who fight and travel, women who are restless and want more from life than a sinkful of dishes. Because the heroines also want an interesting, talented man to love does not lessen the story. In the contemporaries, the heroines always have careers. In my proposed contemporary, my heroine is an architect who wins a design contest but because the house is to be built away from a town, the overseeing architect, the hero, says a woman cannot work on the crew. My heroine proves to him that she can hold her own by doing well in her studies as well as in the construction.''

AVOCATIONAL INTERESTS: Body building, costume history.

*   *   *

WHITMARSH, Anne (Mary Gordon)   1933-

PERSONAL: Born July 12, 1933, in Kuala Lumpur, Malaysia; daughter of Benjamin (a civil servant) and Mary Gordon (a teacher; maiden name, Wright) Bunting; married Guy William Whitmarsh (a university lecturer), August 23, 1958; children: Hilary Frances, Sarah Joanna, Kathryn Selina. *Education:* Bedford College, London, B.A. (with first class honors), 1954; University of Warwick, M.A. (with distinction), 1979. *Politics:* Socialist. *Home:* 43 Lansdowne Cres., Leamington Spa, Warwickshire CV32 4PR, England. *Office:* Department of Language Studies, Lanchester Polytechnic, Priory St., Coventry, West Midlands CV1 5FB, England.

CAREER: Writer. Rockliff Publishing Corp., London, England, editorial assistant, 1955-58; Sydenham and Forest Hill Institute, London, part-time lecturer in French, 1961-64; Edgbaston High School, Birmingham, England, teacher, 1968-72; Mid-Warwickshire College of Further Education, England, part-time lecturer in French, 1972-75; Lanchester Polytechnic, Coventry, England, senior lecturer in French, 1975—. Examiner in oral and written French for University of London Board, 1962-75; item writer for University of London French objective tests, 1970-74; oral examiner in French for the Institute of Modern Linguists, 1974-75. *Member:* Association for the Study of Modern and Contemporary France.

WRITINGS: (Translator) J. M. Bulla, *Florentine Sculpture of the Fifteenth Century,* Rockliff, 1956; (translator) Emile Vuillermoz, *Debussy,* Rene Kister, 1959; *Simone de Beauvoir and the Limits of Commitment,* Cambridge University Press, 1981.

WORK IN PROGRESS: A monograph of Simone de Beauvoir's *Les Mandarins,* publication by Grant & Cutler expected in 1983.

SIDELIGHTS: Anne Whitmarsh wrote: "I started my career in higher education rather late in life, having worked only part-time while my children were growing up, so my enthusiasm about teaching, research, and writing has not yet had time to pall. The subject of my first book continues to fascinate me, and I still find it amazing that mine is the first book about Simone de Beauvoir by an English author. I am also interested in contemporary French politics, existentialism, and French left-wing intellectuals."

AVOCATIONAL INTERESTS: Travel, music, theatre.

WHITNEY, John Hay   1904-1982

OBITUARY NOTICE: Born August 17, 1904, in Ellsworth, Me.; died of congestive heart failure, February 8, 1982, in Manhasset, Long Island, New York. Entrepreneur, ambassador, philanthropist, and editor. Born into one of America's wealthiest families, Whitney at his death was worth an estimated $200 million due to inheritance and investments in such enterprises as Minute Maid orange juice and Pan American World Airways. As chairman of the board of Selznick International Pictures during the 1930's, Whitney bought the screen rights to Margaret Mitchell's *Gone With the Wind* for $50,000. The film has grossed more than $75 million since its 1939 release. With the advent of World War II, Whitney became a captain in the Air Force, serving in France where he was captured by the Germans and held prisoner for eighteen days until his daring escape from a train. After the war he resumed his business and philanthropic activities until 1957 when he was asked by President Eisenhower, his personal friend and golf partner, to serve as ambassador to Great Britain. He held that position until 1961. Whitney formed the Whitney Foundation in 1946 to aid disadvantaged groups in bettering themselves and their environments through education and social change. He gave nearly $1 million annually to the fund. He also created Whitney Communications Corporation, through which he had interests in newspapers, radio and television stations, and magazines. He was greatly disappointed when, as editor in chief and publisher of the *New York Herald Tribune,* he could not save the newspaper from dissolving, despite the $40 million he spent trying. Obituaries and other sources: *Current Biography,* Wilson, 1945, April, 1982; *New York Times,* February 9, 1982; *Washington Post,* February 9, 1982; *Chicago Tribune,* February 9, 1982; *Newsweek,* February 22, 1982; *Time,* February 22, 1982.

*   *   *

WHYTE, Mal(colm Kenneth, Jr.)   1933-

PERSONAL: Born February 26, 1933, in Milwaukee, Wis.; son of Malcolm K. (a lawyer) and Bertha K. (a writer and artist) Whyte; married Karen Cross (a writer), December 19, 1959; children: Malcolm K. III, Kirsty, Andrew. *Education:* Cornell University, B.A., 1955. *Residence:* Mill Valley, Calif. *Office:* Troubador Press, 385 Fremont St., San Francisco, Calif. 94105.

CAREER: Troubador Press, San Francisco, Calif., president, 1959—, chairman of board of directors, 1970—. *Military service:* U.S. Navy, 1956-59; became lieutenant junior grade. *Member:* Scott Valley Swim and Tennis Club, Cornell Club of Northern California, San Francisco Symphony Association. *Awards, honors:* Cover award from American Institute of Graphic Arts, 1975, for "Catch the Eye."

WRITINGS: (With Ed Callahan and Bill Shilling) *The Original Old Radio Game,* Pisani Press, 1965; (with John Stanley) *Great Comics Game Book,* Price, Stern, 1966; *Fat Cat Coloring and Limerick Book,* Troubador Press (San Francisco, Calif.), 1967; *Love Bug Coloring and Limerick Book,* Troubador Press (San Francisco), 1968; *The Meaning of Christmas,* Troubador Press (San Francisco), 1973; (with Stanley) *Monster Movie Game,* Troubador Press (San Francisco), 1974; (with Bill Blackbeard) *Great Comic Cats* (Book-of-the-Month Club selection), Troubador Press (San Francisco), 1981.

WORK IN PROGRESS: Bull Terrier, a "pictorial pageant" of the breed; a history of Troubador Press.

SIDELIGHTS: Whyte wrote: "Being a publisher is one of the most satisfying and, perhaps, personal occupations, because all of one's interests are seeds for books. The published work not only shares one's interest with others, but becomes itself a contribution to the field.

"Being a publisher as well as a writer makes it a little easier for me to get published. But my work has to meet the same criteria as any other author's: it must be salable. For Troubador Press, a salable book is a book that is fun and worthwhile to read. No matter who writes and illustrates the book, the purpose behind Troubador books is always the same: to provide educational content in an entertaining medium through the highest quality writing, graphics, paper, and printing, so that the time a reader spends with a Troubador book is always time well spent."

* * *

WHYTE, Robert Orr 1903-

BRIEF ENTRY: Born in 1903 in Dalry, Scotland. Scottish agricultural scientist and author. Whyte wrote *Land, Livestock, and Human Nutrition in India* (Praeger, 1968), *Grasslands of the Monsoon* (Faber, 1968), *Tropical Grazing Lands: Communities and Constituent Species* (Junk, 1974), *Land and Land Appraisal* (Junk, 1976), *The Asian Village as a Basis for Rural Modernization* (Institute of Southeast Asian Studies, 1976), and *Rural Nutrition in Monsoon Asia* (Oxford University Press, 1974). *Address:* Rhydyfirian, Rhydyfelin, Aberystwyth, Cardiganshire, Wales.

* * *

WICKLEIN, John (Frederick) 1924-

PERSONAL: Born July 20, 1924, in Reading, Pa.; son of Raymond Roland (a foundry worker) and Parmilla Catherine (Miller) Wicklein; married Myra Joan Winchester, July 31, 1948; children: Elizabeth Wicklein Hirsh, Peter, Joanna. *Education:* Rutgers University, Litt.B., 1947; Columbia University, M.S. in Journalism, 1948. *Politics:* Democrat. *Home:* 5419 Linden Court, Bethesda, Md. 20814. *Agent:* Frances Goldin, 305 East 11th St., New York, N.Y. 10003. *Office:* Corporation for Public Broadcasting, 1111 16th St. N.W., Washington, D.C. 20036.

CAREER: *Newark Evening News,* Newark, N.J., reporter and feature writer, 1947-51; *Electrical World,* New York City, news managing editor, 1951-54; *Congressional Quarterly,* Washington, D.C., political writer, 1954; *New York Times,* New York City, editor of daily and Sunday drama, television, movie, music, and art reviews, 1954-55, editor on national desk, 1955-59, reporter and national correspondent covering politics and religion, 1959-62; WNET-TV, New York City, news director and producer of "The World at Ten," 1962-64; WABC-TV, New York City, manager of news, public affairs, and documentary staff and producer-writer of local and network documentary programs, 1964-67; National Educational Television, Washington, D.C., Washington bureau chief and executive producer at Public Broadcast Laboratory, 1967-70; WCBS-TV, New York City, manager of news staff in charge of all news and public affairs programs and documentaries, 1970-71; WRVR-Radio, New York City, vice-president and general manager, 1971-74; Boston University, Boston, Mass., professor of journalism and broadcasting and dean of School of Public Communication, 1974-79, fellow of Institute for Democratic Communication, 1975-79; Corporation for Public Broadcasting, Washington, D.C., associate director for news and public affairs programs, 1980—. Danforth lecturer at Bar-

nard College, 1960-61; lecturer at Columbia University, 1966-67; visiting professor of telecommunications at Methodist University of Sao Paulo, 1979; senior associate of Center for International Public Issues, 1979. Member of board of managers of Communication Commission of National Council of Churches; consultant in cable television to United Church of Christ and Children's Television Workshop. *Military service:* U.S. Naval Reserve, active duty, 1943-46; became lieutenant junior grade.

MEMBER: World Future Society, Society of Professional Journalists, Association for Education in Journalism, Phi Beta Kappa, Sigma Delta Chi. *Awards, honors:* Faith and Freedom Award from Religious Heritage of America, 1961, for covering the religious issue in the 1960 Presidential campaign; George Polk Memorial Award from Long Island University, 1963, for news programs on WNET-TV; "best documentary" award from Venice Film Festival, 1968, for "Free at Last"; Armstrong Award from Alfred I. duPont-Columbia University Awards, 1972, for community service programming at WRVR-Radio.

WRITINGS: (With Monroe Price) *Cable Television: A Guide for Citizen Action,* Pilgrim Press (New York), 1972; (editor) *Investigative Reporting: The Lessons of Watergate,* Boston University Press, 1975; *Electronic Nightmare: The New Communications and Freedom,* Viking, 1981.

Television documentary scripts: "Roadblocks to the Reds," first broadcast by American Broadcasting Companies, Inc. (ABC-TV), 1962; (with Joan Ganz Cooney) "Anna Cross's Island," WNET-TV (New York), 1963; "Land of First Asylum," ABC-TV, 1963; "Brand-New U." (three-part series), ABC-TV, 1965; "Vatican II: Council of Reconciliation," ABC-TV, 1966; "The Built-In Blackout," Public Broadcasting Service (PBS-TV), 1969; "Hunger: A National Disgrace" (two-part series), PBS-TV, 1970; "Auto Pollution," PBS-TV, 1970.

Articles and short stories represented in anthologies, including *Stories.* Contributor to *International Encyclopedia of Higher Education.* Contributor to magazines, including *Atlantic Monthly, Sports Illustrated, Progressive, Television Quarterly,* and *Forbes,* and to newspapers. Contributing editor of *Washington Monthly,* 1969-72.

WORK IN PROGRESS: Research for a book on varying concepts of freedom of the press in the Western democracies, publication by Viking expected in 1984; research on the Yucatan Peninsula for a book and television documentary series on pre-Columbian civilizations in Middle America and their impact on present cultures in Middle America and the United States.

SIDELIGHTS: Wicklein commented: "For me, the purpose of writing, whether in books, newspapers, magazines, or documentary films, has been to try to help improve the social condition. As with many writers who grew up in the newspaper tradition, I am interested in trying to reform the world. We can never do it, but maybe I can move my own country an inch toward being more humane, toward putting people ahead of possessions, toward providing a social dividend through private and public enterprise, rather than providing only power and financial gain for the public and private entrepreneurs. I think that my years as a reporter provided excellent training for writing I have done in every field—helping me to know about people: what they believe, what they want, and how their backgrounds and situations influence the way they act. It seems to me that, to be useful in the way I want it to be, writing (and the reporting, research, and thinking that goes into it) has to be based on these human concerns.

"A lot of my efforts, in print, television, radio, and public talks, have gone into supporting freedom of speech and the press. I believe that all other freedoms—certainly our individual liberties—depend upon these.

"I also have a strong interest in pre-Columbian civilizations, and think their contributions have been ignored in our looking almost exclusively to Europe for our cultural heritage. I have been studying these peoples, particularly the Maya, for twenty years. I intend to write a book or produce a television series (or both) that would make Americans take a new look at cultural influences that came to them from the Middle Ages of *this* hemisphere.

"In my reporting, I have visited almost every state in the union. I've also traveled to England, France, Switzerland, Belgium, Luxembourg, West Germany, the Netherlands, Denmark, Sweden, Mexico, Brazil, Canada and the Caribbean."

BIOGRAPHICAL/CRITICAL SOURCES: Los Angeles Times Book Review, September 6, 1981.

*   *   *

WICKSTROM, Lois 1948-

PERSONAL: Born August 14, 1948, in Boston, Mass.; daughter of Robert Louis (a biochemist) and Joan (a counselor; maiden name, Hirsch) Sinsheimer; married Eric Wickstrom (a biochemist), July 1, 1967; children: Erica Lorraine, Eileen Anitra. *Education:* Pasadena City College, A.A., 1968; attended University of California, Berkeley, 1969, and University of Denver, 1974-75; University of Colorado, B.A., 1977. *Politics:* "Left-wing Democrat." *Religion:* Jewish. *Home:* 3721 Barcelona St., Tampa, Fla. 33609.

CAREER: Sewage laboratory technician in Denver, Colo., 1977-78; University of Denver, Denver, laboratory technician, 1979-80; writer, 1980—. *Member:* National Writers Club, Small Press Writers and Artists Organization, Society of Children's Book Writers (director of publicity for Rocky Mountain chapter, 1979). *Awards, honors:* Associate of Rocky Mountain v0Women's Institute, 1979; science fiction short story award from National Fan Fantasy Federation, 1980, for "Order of the Virgin Mothers"; Skellings Poetry Award from *Florida Arts Gazette*, 1981, for "The Mobile."

WRITINGS: The Food Conspiracy Cookbook, 101 Productions, 1974; *Oliver*, Sproing Books, 1978; *Ladybugs for Loretta*, Sproing Books, 1978. Editor of *Pandora*, 1978—.

WORK IN PROGRESS: Race for Love, a teenage romance, with Jean Lorrah; *Visitors of the Dreaming Sun*, science fiction; *The Warehouses*, science fiction.

SIDELIGHTS: Lois Wickstrom told *CA:* "I am very interested in the respect for individual freedom. Sometimes I portray life as I'd like it to be and other times in a satirical and 'if-this-continues' vein. Sometimes I just like to get inside the head of a person who hurts and show others how it feels.

"Since a good fraction of my work is science fiction I am very concerned that the science in stories should be accurate. I even write to authors and publishers of fiction in which the science is inaccurate to offer corrections that have been included in subsequent editions. Also I edit and publish, with Jean Lorrah, a science fiction feminist magazine, *Pandora*, which features role-expanding science fiction and fantasy."

*   *   *

WILBERS, Stephen 1949-

PERSONAL: Born August 13, 1949, in Cincinnati, Ohio; son of Lawrence G. (a metallurgical engineer) and Margaret (Fields)

Wilbers; married Deborah Richards, May 30, 1976; children: Joseph Edward, Kathleen McCoy. *Education:* Vanderbilt University, B.A., 1971; University of Iowa, M.A., 1975, Ph.D., 1978. *Politics:* Independent. *Office:* College of Liberal Arts, University of Minnesota, 106 Johnston Hall, Minneapolis, Minn. 55455.

CAREER: University of Iowa, Iowa City, adjunct assistant professor of continuing education, 1978-80, director of Undergraduate Academic Advising Center, 1979-81; University of Minnesota, Minneapolis, director of Student Academic Support Services, 1981—. Creator and coordinator of Iowa City Creative Reading Series, 1974-79; founding member of board of directors of Iowa City-Johnson County Arts Council, 1975-78. *Member:* American College Personnel Association, National Academic Advising Association. *Awards, honors:* Canaras scholar at St. Lawrence Writers Conference, 1976.

WRITINGS: The Iowa Writers' Workshop: Origins, Emergence, and Growth, University of Iowa Press, 1980. Writer for WSUI-Radio, 1976. Contributor to literature journals and newspapers. Founding editor of *Reading Series Quarterly*, 1974; editor of *prairie grass: a writer's newsletter*, 1976-78.

WORK IN PROGRESS: A symposium on Grant Wood's Iowa City; short stories; research on academic affairs of university administrators.

SIDELIGHTS: Wilbers commented: "Historical perspective and spirit of place influence my writing. Literary regionalism interests me. A sense of community is important. As a university administrator, I would describe myself as a pragmatic humanist. Parenting is the most meaningful and significant endeavor in my life; writing and working follow in that order."

*   *   *

WILDE, Jocelyn
See TOOMBS, John

*   *   *

WILKINS, Mary
See FREEMAN, Mary Eleanor Wilkins

*   *   *

WILLIAMS, Glanville Llewelyn 1911-

PERSONAL: Born February 15, 1911, in Bridgend, Wales; son of B. E. and Gwladys (Llewelyn) Williams; married Lorna Margaret Lawfield, October 19, 1939; children: Rendel. *Education:* University College of Wales, LL.B. (with honors), 1931; St. John's College, Cambridge, B.A., 1933; Cambridge University, Ph.D., 1936. *Office:* Jesus College, Cambridge University, Cambridge, England.

CAREER: Called to the Bar in 1935; Cambridge University, Cambridge, England, fellow of St. John's College, 1936-42; University of London, London, England, reader, 1945-48, professor of public law, 1948-51, Quain Professor of Jurisprudence, 1951-55; Cambridge University, reader, 1957-65, professor of law, 1966-78, Rouse Ball Professor of English Law, 1968-78, fellow of Jesus College, 1955—. Appointed Queen's Counsel, 1968; past member of Criminal Law Revision Committee, Law Commission's Working Party on Codification of the Criminal Law, and Committee on Mentally Abnormal Offenders. *Member:* Abortion Reform Association (president); Eugenics Society (fellow).

AWARDS, HONORS: Council of Legal Education Studentship, 1935; George Long Prize for Jurisprudence, 1935; honorary bencher of Middle Temple, 1966—; James Barr Ames prize from Harvard Law School, 1963; LL.D. from University of Nottingham, 1963, University of Wales, 1974, and University of Glasgow, 1980; Swiney Prize for Jurisprudence from Royal Society of Arts, 1964; honorary fellow of Jesus College, Cambridge, 1978.

WRITINGS: Liability for Animals: An Account of the Development and Present Law of Tortious Liability for Animals, Distress Damage Feasant and the Duty to Fence, in Great Britain, Northern Ireland, and the Common-Law Dominions, Cambridge University Press, 1939.

(Editor and contributor) Roy G. MacElroy, *Impossibility of Performance: A Treatise on the Law of Supervening Impossibility of Performance of Contract, Failure of Consideration, and Frustration,* Cambridge University Press, 1941; *The Law Reform (Frustrated Contracts) Act, 1943: The Text of the Act With an Introduction and Detailed Commentary,* Stevens & Sons, 1944; *Learning the Law: A Book for the Guidance of the Law Student, With a Chapter on Careers,* Stevens & Sons, 1945, 11th edition, 1982; (editor) John W. Salmond, *Jurisprudence,* Sweet & Maxwell, 10th edition (Williams was not associated with earlier editions), 1947, 11th edition, 1957; *Crown Proceedings: An Account of Civil Proceedings by and Against the Crown as Affected by the Crown Proceeding Act, 1947,* Stevens & Sons, 1948; *Joint Obligations: A Treatise on Joint and Joint and Several Liability in Contract, Quasi-Contract, and Trusts in England, Ireland, and the Common-Law Dominions,* Butterworth, 1949.

(Editor) *The Reform of the Law,* Gollancz, 1951; *Joint Torts and Contributory Negligence: A Study of Concurrent Fault in Great Britain, Ireland, and the Common Law Dominions,* Stevens & Sons, 1951; *Speedhand Shorthand,* International Correspondence Schools, 1952, 8th edition, 1980; *Criminal Law: The General Part,* Stevens & Sons, 1953, 2nd edition, 1961; *The Proof of Guilt: A Study of the English Criminal Trial,* Stevens & Sons, 1955, 3rd edition, 1963; *The Sanctity of Life and the Criminal Law: On Contraception, Sterilization, Artificial Insemination, Abortion, Suicide, and Euthanasia,* Knopf, 1957.

The Mental Element in Crime, Magnes Press, 1965; (with Bob Alexander Hepple) *Foundations of the Law of Torts,* Butterworth, 1976; *Textbook of Criminal Law,* Stevens, 1978, supplement, 1980.

WORK IN PROGRESS: (With A.T.H. Smith) *The Protection of Property.*

BIOGRAPHICAL/CRITICAL SOURCES: P. R. Glazebrook, editor, *Reshaping the Criminal Law: Essays in Honour of Glanville Williams,* Stevens & Sons, 1978.

*   *   *

WILLIAMS, Jeremy (Napier) Howard
See HOWARD-WILLIAMS, Jeremy (Napier)

*   *   *

WILLIAMS, Paul O(sborne)   1935-

PERSONAL: Born January 17, 1935, in Chatham, N.J.; son of Naboth Osborne (an electrical engineer) and Helen (Chadwick) Williams; married Nancy Ellis (a teacher), September 2, 1961; children: Anne Chadwick, Evan Osborne. *Education:* Principia College, B.A. (with highest honors), 1956; University of Pennsylvania, M.A., 1958, Ph.D., 1962. *Politics:* Independent. *Home:* 4 Dogwood Lane, Route 1, Elsah, Ill. 62028.

Office: Department of English, Principia College, Elsah, Ill. 62028.

CAREER: University of Pennsylvania, Philadelphia, assistant instructor in English, 1957-60; Duke University, Durham, N.C., instructor, 1961-62, assistant professor of English, 1962-64; Principia College, Elsah, Ill., assistant professor, 1964-68, associate professor, 1968-77, professor of English, 1977-81, Cornelius and Muriel Wood Chair in Humanities, 1981—. Member of board of trustees of village of Elsah, 1969-75; member of Quarry-Elsah Volunteer Firefighters, 1973—, president, 1980-81; director of Elsah Museum, 1978—; founding member of board of directors of Historic Elsah Foundation, 1970-77. Member of board of chancellors of St. Louis Poetry Center, 1974-80, president, 1978-80; member of Illinois Humanities Council, 1977-81. *Member:* Modern Language Association of America, Thoreau Society (president, 1977), Science Fiction Research Association, Midwest Modern Language Association, Illinois Historical Society, Greater St. Louis Historical Association (president, 1975).

WRITINGS: (With Charles B. Hosmer) *Elsah: A Historic Guidebook,* Historic Elsah Foundation, 1967; *The Breaking of Northwall* (science fiction novel), Del Rey Books, 1981; *The Ends of the Circle* (science fiction novel), Del Rey Books, 1981; *The Dome in the Forest* (science fiction novel), Del Rey Books, 1981; *The McNair Family of Elsah, Illinois: Uncommon Common Men* (monograph), Historic Elsah Foundation, 1982; *The Fall of the Shell,* Del Rey Books, 1982.

Work represented in anthologies, including *The Edge of the Woods: Fifty-Five Haiku,* 1968; *Jack, Be Quick: Fifty Poems,* privately printed, 1971; *St. Louis Poetry Center: An Anthology, 1946-1976,* edited by Lucy Hazelton, Sheba Press, 1978. Contributor of more than two hundred articles, poems, and reviews to magazines, including *Sheba Review, Star Line, Webster Review, Thoreau Journal, Arts,* and *Christian Science Sentinel,* and newspapers.

WORK IN PROGRESS: A novel tentatively titled *An Ambush of Shadows,* completion expected 1982.

SIDELIGHTS: Williams commented: "As a scholar, my research specialty has been American transcendentalism, especially the work of Henry Thoreau, but recently I have turned increasingly to writing poetry, essays, and science fiction novels. I have been active in local midwest history for some years, particularly that of the area of Elsah, Illinois, a sleepy Mississippi River town. The first fruits of this, other than a number of articles, has been the setting of my first two novels, which center on a Mississippi River of the future, a millenium after a holocaust."

AVOCATIONAL INTERESTS: Boating, jogging, gardening, photography, beekeeping, numismatics, reading.

BIOGRAPHICAL/CRITICAL SOURCES: Los Angeles Times Book Review, January 31, 1982.

*   *   *

WILLIMON, William H(enry)   1946-

PERSONAL: Born May 15, 1946, in Greenville, S.C.; son of Robert C. and Ruby (Steere) Willimon; married Patricia Parker, June 10, 1969; children: William Parker, Harriet Patricia. *Education:* Wofford College, A.B, 1968; Yale University, M.Div., 1971; Emory University, S.T.D., 1973. *Home:* 5 Ramblewood Lane, Greenville, S. C. 29615. *Office:* Northside United Methodist Church, 435 Summit Dr., Greenville, S.C. 29609.

CAREER: Ordained United Methodist minister, 1971; associate pastor in Clinton, S.C., 1972-74; pastor in North Myrtle Beach, S.C., 1974-76; Duke Divinity School, Durham, N.C., assistant professor of liturgy and worship, 1976-80; Northside United Methodist Church, Greenville, S.C., pastor, 1980—. *Member:* North American Academy of Liturgy. *Awards, honors:* Worship as Pastoral Care was named among the ten most useful books of 1980 by Academy of Parish Clergy, 1980.

WRITINGS: The Gospel for the Person Who Has Everything, Judson, 1977; Saying Yes to Marriage, Judson, 1978; Between Two Advents, C.S.S. Publishing, 1978; Worship as Pastoral Care, Abingdon, 1979; Remember Who You Are, Upper Room, 1979; (with Robert Wilson) Worship and Preaching in the Small Church, Abingdon, 1980; (with John Westerhoff) Liturgy and Learning Through the Life Cycle, Seabury, 1980; Word, Water, Wine, and Bread, Judson, 1980; Integrative Preaching: The Pulpit at the Center, Abingdon, 1981; Family, Friends, and Other Funny People, R. L. Bryan, 1981; Sunday Dinner, Upper Room, 1981; The Bible: A Sustaining Presence in Worship, Judson, 1981.

WORK IN PROGRESS: A book, tentatively titled The Service of God: Christian Worship and Work, publication by Abingdon expected in 1983.

SIDELIGHTS: Willimon told *CA:* "I look upon my writing as an extension of my vocation as a Christian pastor. My books mostly deal with concerns of Christian pastors and Christian laypeople, although some of my work is aimed principally at scholars and students in the field of Christian liturgy. I particularly enjoy interpreting and translating theological concepts into analogies which are understandable to laypeople. My current field of interest is ethics and how a person's participation in worship and ritual influences a person's ethics and behavior."

*   *   *

WILLIS, Ellen Jane 1941-

PERSONAL: Born December 14, 1941, in New York, N.Y.; daughter of Melvin H. (a police lieutenant) and Miriam F. (Weinberger) Willis. *Education:* Barnard College, A.B., 1962; graduate study at University of California, Berkeley, 1962-63. *Residence:* New York, N.Y. *Agent:* Betty Anne Clarke, 28 East 95th St., New York, N.Y. 10028. *Office:* Village Voice, 842 Broadway, New York, N.Y. 10003.

CAREER: Free-lance writer, 1966—; Cheetah (magazine), New York City, associate editor, 1967-68; New Yorker, New York City, rock music critic, 1968-75; Us (magazine), New York City, associate editor, 1969; Ms. (magazine), New York City, contributing editor, 1972-75; Rolling Stone, New York City, contributing editor, 1976-78; Village Voice, New York City, staff writer, 1979—. *Member:* Authors Guild, P.E.N.

WRITINGS: Beginning to See the Light, Knopf, 1981. Contributor of articles to magazines, including New York Review of Books, Commentary, New American Review, and New York Times Book Review.

SIDELIGHTS: The twenty-eight essays that comprise Ellen Willis's Beginning to See the Light present a "sharp, critical, provocative commentary on the last decade," declared the Washington Post's Julia Epstein. Written during the 1970's, the essays originally appeared in such publications as Rolling Stone, New Yorker, Village Voice, and Commentary. They encompass a variety of topics, including rock music and musicians, film, politics, religion, and feminism. Taken together, said Epstein, the essays serve to record and interpret "the

process that brought us from Chicago 1968, LSD and Vietnam to neo-conservatism and the politics of reaction."

The earliest selections in *Beginning to See the Light* concern rock music. Rock 'n' roll, with its messages about rebellion and freedom, "exemplifies for Willis the elemental energy of a generation born between 1940 and 1950," Epstein observed. Willis writes about such musicians as Janis Joplin, Elvis Presley, and Bob Dylan, putting them "into social context, explaining their impact as she discusses their style," reported Elaine Kendall in the *Los Angeles Times.* "She copes similarly," Kendall continued, "with pivotal films like 'Easy Rider,' 'Alice's Restaurant' and 'Deep Throat,' uncovering and analyzing the idea behind the image."

Other selections from the book concern such issues as abortion, pornography, and rape. Willis condemns the anti-abortion movement as "the most dangerous political force in the country." In a piece entitled "The Trial of Arline Hunt," she delivers a "spare and unembellished account of a San Francisco rape case." Reviewers of *Beginning to See the Light* rarely failed to mention this particular piece; they called it impressive, moving, effective, and, in the words of Kendall, "as relevant tomorrow as it was six years ago when she wrote it."

The issue of relevancy is one that any journalist who decides to publish a collection of reviews must confront, maintained Elinor Langer in the *New York Review of Books.* As Langer pointed out, most magazine articles are written hastily about subjects of only temporary interest, and it is a rare article that can withstand close scrutiny years after its initial publication. But the pieces that make up *Beginning to See the Light* avoid the usual obstacles: "Even on transient matters," Langer attested, Willis "finds something durable to say." In addition, the footnotes that Willis provides for some of the articles in the collection allow her the "historical distance to inject humor," said Elizabeth Hess in *Ms.*

Described as a "natural dissident who is always taking unpopular positions," Willis "pushes and pulls relentlessly at theories, attacks the right and the left with insight and an ironic sense of humor." At times, Epstein reflected, Willis is ambivalent, at times she appears self-contradictory, but her book "represents a triumph for the impulse to write it all down, to pursue every last connection." She leaves "no stone unturned," echoed Hess. In a style that Langer called "energetic, provocative, self-conscious, [and] funny," Willis surrounds "even her lesser subjects with the sheer weight of her own thinking, plunging her way through the roughest political and intellectual seas for the sheer joy of riding the waves."

BIOGRAPHICAL/CRITICAL SOURCES: Los Angeles Times, March 3, 1981; New York Times Book Review, March 15, 1981; Washington Post, April 7, 1981; Ms., June, 1981; New Republic, June 20, 1981.

*   *   *

WILLOUGHBY, Lee Davis
See TOOMBS, John

*   *   *

WILSON, David Scofield 1931-

PERSONAL: Born May 26, 1931, in Minneapolis, Minn.; son of Harold Lewis (an artist) and Grace (a writer; maiden name, Scofield) Wilson; married Bonnie Stahler (a writer), August 22, 1960; children: David Scofield, Jr., Deirdre Elizabeth. *Education:* University of Minnesota, B.S., 1953, M.A., 1962, Ph.D., 1968. *Home:* 1109 Radcliffe Dr., Davis, Calif. 95616.

Office: American Studies Program, University of California, Davis, Calif. 95616.

CAREER: University of Minnesota, Minneapolis, instructor in English and humanities, 1962-64; State University of New York College at Cortland, assistant professor of English, 1964-67; University of Minnesota, instructor in English, 1967-68; University of California, Davis, associate professor of American studies, 1968—. Consultant to National American Studies Faculty and California Council for the Humanities. *Member:* American Studies Association, American Federation of Teachers, Popular Culture Association, American Society for Environmental History. *Awards, honors:* Award from *American Quarterly,* 1973, for article, "American Culture Studies: The Discipline and the Curriculum."

WRITINGS: In the Presence of Nature, University of Massachusetts Press, 1978; (illustrator) Jay Mechling and Robert Meredith, *Morning Work: A Trialogue on Issues of Knowledge and Freedom in Doing American Culture Studies,* Connections Press, 1979; (self-illustrated) *Beyond Mediation,* University of California, Davis, 1979; *Signs of Life in the Valley,* University of California, Davis, 1981; (illustrator) June Dwyer, *The Discipline of Crevices: Poems of Yosemite,* Yosemite Natural History Association, 1982. Author of "The Nature Reporter," a column in *Burrowing Owl.*

WORK IN PROGRESS: A book of "readings of places as they interpret themselves," publication expected in 1984; "Highway 50: The Continuing Corridor," an exhibition and catalog.

SIDELIGHTS: Wilson commented: "I am interested in the way supposedly separate things fit together after all: art and science, words and lines, nature and culture, form and content. In my scholarship this takes the form of interdisciplinary writing and teaching, both doing it and thinking about the doing of it (methodology). The gap between objectivity and subjectivity invites bridges between graphic art and verbal art: contour, drawings, gesture sketches, anagrammatic and acrostical verse, and so on. I often find in everyday life and in ordinary places just those phrases or sights that as metaphors (as 'texts') lend shape to my abstract thought. And turning that around, I find that my ideas make sense best when they work out in vernacular speech or turn out well 'in the field.' For me, consulting provides that chance; also, teaching 'outside the walls' for the Yosemite Natural History Association, the Sacramento Science Center's Junior Museum, the Arboretum and Davis Art Center, at University of California, Davis. Designing and illustrating books pull together creative and critical spirit in a similar way, requiring affirmation and then cool appraisal, and then affirmation again."

* * *

WILSON, Dick
See WILSON, Richard Garratt

* * *

WILSON, Gina 1943-

PERSONAL: Born April 1, 1943, in Abergele, North Wales; daughter of Arthur Gordon (a businessman) and Marion (a teacher; maiden name, Herbert) Jones; married Edward Wilson (in education), July 22, 1972; children: Marion, Lewis, Harriet. *Education:* Edinburgh University, M.A. (honors), 1965; attended Mount Holyoke College, 1965-66. *Residence:* Oxford, England. *Office:* c/o Faber & Faber, 3 Queen Sq., London WC1N 3AU, England.

CAREER: Writer. *Awards, honors:* Runner-up for children's book award from Federation of Children's Book Groups, 1980, for *Cora Ravenwing.*

WRITINGS—Juvenile: *Cora Ravenwing,* Atheneum, 1980; *A Friendship of Equals,* Faber & Faber, 1981; *The Whisper,* Faber & Faber, 1982. Work anthologized in *Ducks and Dragons,* edited by Gene Kemp, Faber & Faber, 1980. Assistant editor of *Scottish National Dictionary* and *Dictionary of the Older Scottish Tongue.* Contributor to *Times Literary Supplement.*

WORK IN PROGRESS: A novel.

SIDELIGHTS: Wilson told *CA:* "*Cora Ravenwing* tells of a secret friendship between the narrator, newly arrived to live in an English village, and a solitary girl ostracized by other children. The circumstances of the outcast girl's childhood, and the gossip that circulates about her give a sinister element to the tale.

"*A Friendship of Equals* deals with the relationship between two girls of very different backgrounds. One is the daughter of a village shop keeper, the other the crippled daughter at the manor house. Despite opposition from all sides, and personal problems of their own, they refuse to give up their friendship.

"In addition to juvenile novels, I am interested in writing children's poetry. My writing time is tremendously restricted at present because of my family, but I am working on a new novel."

Reviewing *Cora Ravenwing* for the *Junior Bookshelf,* a critic put forth: "It is certainly a remarkable first novel and Gina Wilson will be hard put to follow it with better." However, following the publication of *A Friendship of Equals,* a second *Junior Bookshelf* reviewer offered this praise: "This is indeed a remarkable story. . . . Wilson shows her observation of human relationships in the school scenes particularly, and puts forth some important truths in a story with humour, excitement and mystery."

BIOGRAPHICAL/CRITICAL SOURCES: Times Literary Supplement, March 28, 1980, July 24, 1981; *Observer,* April 6, 1980; *Kirkus Reviews,* May 1, 1980; *Junior Bookshelf,* August, 1980, October, 1981.

* * *

WILSON, Howard Allan 1927-

BRIEF ENTRY: Born October 11, 1927, in Owen Sound, Ontario, Canada. American philosopher, educator, and author. Wilson began teaching in 1960 and has been a professor of religion at Capital University since 1967. He has taught in Germany, Egypt, and Israel and conducted research in England and Ceylon. Wilson wrote *Invasion From the East* (Augsburg, 1978). *Address:* Department of Religion, Capital University, 2199 East Main St., Columbus, Ohio 43209.

* * *

WILSON, Jussem
See WILSON, Nelly

* * *

WILSON, Nelly 1930-
(Jussem Wilson)

PERSONAL: Born April 2, 1930, in Vienna, Austria; married John Wilson (a lecturer in psychology), March 31, 1956. *Ed-*

ucation: University of Bristol, B.A. (with honors), 1952; University of London, Post-Graduate Certificate in Education, 1954; University of Paris, Doctorat de l'Universite, 1958. *Politics:* Libertarian. *Religion:* ''Jewish agnostic.'' *Home:* 92 Cairns Rd., Bristol BS6 7TQ, England. *Office:* Department of French, University of Bristol, 17-19 Woodland Rd., Bristol 8, England.

CAREER: University of Bristol, Bristol, England, reader in French, 1963—; writer. *Member:* Society of University Teachers of French, Amitie Charles Peguy. *Awards, honors:* Literary award in nonfiction from *Jewish Chronicle,* 1978.

WRITINGS: (Under name Jussem Wilson) *Charles Peguy,* Bowes & Bowes, 1965; *Bernard Lazare: Antisemitism and the Problem of Jewish Identity,* Cambridge University Press, 1978. Also author of a play, ''Shylock.'' Contributor to academic journals (until 1966 under name Jussem Wilson).

WORK IN PROGRESS: Zola and the Scientific Thought of His Age; French Realism: Theory and Practice; research on the myth of Shylock and on anti-semitic myths and symbols in general; research on nineteenth-century anarchist literature.

SIDELIGHTS: Nelly Wilson commented: ''I spent the war years under Nazi occupation, after 1942 in various concentration camps, and this has had a profound influence on my views and attitudes. I hope to write about the concentration camp years one day.''

*   *   *

WILSON, Richard Garratt 1928-
(Dick Wilson)

PERSONAL—Office: c/o *China Quarterly,* Malet St., London WC1E 7HP, England.

CAREER: Editor of *Far Eastern Economic Review,* Hong Kong, beginning 1958; employed by *Financial Times,* London, England; editor of *China Quarterly,* Contemporary China Institute, School of Oriental and African Studies, London. Lecturer at University of London; member of China Conference at University of Chicago.

*WRITINGS—*Under name Dick Wilson: *A Quarter of Mankind: An Anatomy of China Today,* Weidenfeld & Nicolson, 1966, revised edition published as *Anatomy of China: An Introduction to One Quarter of Mankind,* Weybright & Talley, 1968; *Asia Awakes: A Continent in Transition,* Weybright & Talley, 1970; *The Long March, 1935: The Epic of Chinese Communism's Survival,* Viking, 1971, revised edition, Penguin, 1977; *East Meets West: Singapore,* Times Printer, 1971, 2nd revised edition, 1975; *The Future Role of Singapore,* Oxford University Press, 1972; *Solid as a Rock: The First Forty Years of the Oversea-Chinese Banking Corporation,* Oversea-Chinese Banking Corp., 1972; *The Neutralization of Southeast Asia,* Praeger, 1975; (editor) *Mao Tse-tung in the Scales of History,* Cambridge University Press, 1977; *Mao: The People's Emperor,* Hutchinson, 1979, published in the United States as *The People's Emperor, Mao: A Biography of Mao Tse-tung,* Doubleday, 1980.

BIOGRAPHICAL/CRITICAL SOURCES: New Statesman, December 16, 1977, May 18, 1979; *Pacific Affairs,* summer, 1978; *Times Literary Supplement,* November 10, 1978; *American Political Science Review,* December, 1978; *Economist,* May 5, 1979; *New York Times Book Review,* May 25, 1980; *Saturday Review,* July, 1980.*

*   *   *

WILSON, Tom 1931-

PERSONAL: Born August 1, 1931, in Grant Town, W.Va.; son of Charles Albert and Hazel Marie Wilson; married wife, Carol; children: Tom, Ava. *Education:* Received diploma from Art Institute of Pittsburgh, 1955. *Office:* American Greetings Corp., 12120 Elmwood Ave., Cleveland, Ohio 44111.

CAREER: Uniontown Newspapers, Inc., Uniontown, Pa., layout man, 1950-53; American Greetings Corp., Cleveland, Ohio, designer, 1955-56, creative director, 1957-78, vice-president of creative development, 1978—; creator of ''Ziggy'' comic strip, 1971. Faculty member at Cooper Union Art School, 1961-62. *Military service:* U.S. Army, 1953-55.

*WRITINGS—*All self-illustrated; all published by Andrews & McMeel, except as noted: *Life Is Just a Bunch of Ziggys,* Sheed & Ward, 1973; *It's a Ziggy World,* 1974; *Ziggy Coloring Book,* 1974; *Never Get Too Personally Involved With Your Own Life,* Sheed & Ward, 1975; *Promises to Myself: Ziggy's Thirty-Day Ledger of I Owe Me's,* 1975; *Plants Are Some of My Favorite People,* 1976; *Ziggys of the World Unite,* 1976; *Pets Are Friends You Like Who Like You Right Back,* 1977; *The Ziggy Treasury,* 1977; *This Book Is for the Birds,* 1978; *Encore! Encore!,* introduction by Cathy Guisewite, 1979; *Ziggy Love Notes,* 1979; *Ziggy Thinking of You Notebook,* 1979; *Ziggy's Fleeting Thoughts Notebook,* 1979; *A Ziggy Christmas,* 1980; *Ziggy's Door Openers,* 1980.

*   *   *

WILTZ, Chris(tine) 1948-

PERSONAL: Born January 3, 1948, in New Orleans, La.; daughter of Adolphe Michael (an accountant) and Merle (an underwriter; maiden name, Hiers) Wiltz; married Kenneth McElroy, November 25, 1970 (divorced, 1976); married Joseph Pecot (a communications company president), February 13, 1976; children: (second marriage) Marigny Katherine. *Education:* Attended University of Southwestern Louisiana, 1965, Loyola University, New Orleans, La., 1966-67, and University of New Orleans, 1967; San Francisco State College, B.A., 1969. *Residence:* New Orleans, La. *Agent:* Henry William Griffin, Southern Writers, 5120 Prytania, New Orleans, La. 70115.

CAREER: Bowes Co. (advertising firm), Los Angeles, Calif., proofreader, 1969; Tulane University, New Orleans, La., secretary in School of Medicine, 1969-70; Maple Street Bookshop, New Orleans, in sales and orders, 1970-71; Tulane University, grant researcher in School of Medicine, 1971-72; *Dealerscope* (home electronics trade journals), Waltham, Mass., staff writer, 1978; writer, 1978—.

WRITINGS: The Killing Circle (suspense novel), Macmillan, 1981.

WORK IN PROGRESS: A novel about a woman working in New Orleans, ''who becomes obliquely involved and ultimately changed by a pinball trial that took place there in the early 1970's''; *Man Without a Case,* the second volume of the ''Neal Rafferty'' detective series begun with *The Killing Circle.*

SIDELIGHTS: Wiltz told *CA:* ''I think everyone has 'thoughts' which run so deep and yet are so much a part of spontaneous action and reaction that they are nearly nonverbal, very difficult to articulate. I write because of a sense of immediacy I experience when I write that turns these 'thoughts' into a vision.

''I always knew I had to write, but first I had to be able to take the isolation. There came a point when I knew the time was right, and it seemed like the most natural thing in the world. I knew I was more equipped to do this than anything else.

"As to subject matter, I don't choose my subjects, they choose me, and the characters are the only ones with definite views on the subject matter. Most of the time I just feel like a medium, an involved one, to be sure, but without any say so."

BIOGRAPHICAL/CRITICAL SOURCES: Gambit, September 12, 1981; *New Orleans,* January, 1982.

*   *   *

WINN, Albert Curry   1921-

PERSONAL: Born August 16, 1921, in Ocala, Fla.; son of James Anderson (a certified public accountant) and Elizabeth (Curry) Winn; married Grace Neely Walker (an administrator), August 29, 1944; children: Grace Walker (Mrs. Stewart E. Ellis), James Anderson, Albert Bruce Curry, Randolph Axson. *Education:* Davidson College, A.B., 1942; Union Theological Seminary, Richmond, Va., B.D., 1945, Th.D., 1956; Princeton Theological Seminary, Th.M., 1949. *Politics:* Democrat. *Home:* 2425 Harrington Dr., Decatur, Ga. 30033. *Office:* 611 Medlock Rd., Decatur, Ga. 30033.

CAREER: Ordained Presbyterian minister, 1945; Davidson College, Davidson, N.C., assistant professor of Bible, 1946-47; pastor of Presbyterian congregations in Nokesville, Va., 1948-53; Stillman College, Tuscaloosa, Ala., professor of Bible, 1953-60; Louisville Presbyterian Theological Seminary, Louisville, Ky., professor of theology, 1960-73, president of seminary, 1966-73; pastor of Second Presbyterian Church in Richmond, Va., 1974-81; North Decatur Presbyterian Church, Decatur, Ga., pastor, 1981—. Moderator of General Assembly of the Presbyterian Church of the United States, 1979. Chairman of board of trustees of Stillman College, 1965-70. *Military service:* U.S. Naval Reserve, chaplain, 1945-46. *Member:* American Theological Association, Phi Beta Kappa, Beta Theta Pi, Omicron Delta Kappa. *Awards, honors:* LL.D. from Davidson College, 1968, and Stillman College, 1975.

WRITINGS: Layman's Bible Commentary, Volume XX: *The Acts of the Apostles,* John Knox, 1960; *The Wonder and Worry of Being Human,* John Knox, 1966; (with Logan Cockrum) *Where Do I Go From Here?,* Science Research Associates, 1972; *Epiphany,* Fortress, 1980; *A Sense of Mission,* Westminster, 1981; *Christ the Peacemaker,* John Knox, 1982.

SIDELIGHTS: Winn wrote: "Most of my writing has been 'on assignment' for the church. *A Sense of Mission* is the first book 'for me.' My aim is always clarity and simplicity in a field (religion) that is notorious for gobbledygook. I have moved to a smaller parish to find more time for writing. I want to mine the ore of a lifetime of theological thinking and teaching."

*   *   *

WISE, Helen Dickerson   1928-

BRIEF ENTRY: Born September 11, 1928, in Sussex, N.J. American educator, politician, and author. A teacher for twenty-one years, Wise served as president of the Pennsylvania State Education Association and the National Council of State Education Associations before becoming president of the National Association of Education (NEA) in 1973. A trustee of Pennsylvania State University, Wise has also served as a Pennsylvania State representative. In 1961 she was the recipient of the Freedoms Foundation Classroom Teacher Award. Her writings include *What Do We Tell the Children?: Watergate and the Future of Our Country* (Braziller, 1974). *Address:* 1127 South Allen St., State College, Pa. 16801. *Biographical/critical sources: New York Times,* July 7, 1973; *Leaders in Education,* 5th edition, Bowker, 1974; *Who's Who of American Women,*

8th edition, Marquis, 1974; *Who's Who in American Politics,* 6th edition, Bowker, 1977.

*   *   *

WISELY, Rae   1938-

PERSONAL: Born March 27, 1938, in Akron, Ohio; daughter of Ivey and Edith (Smith) Clark; married Robert J. Wisely (in sales), December 24, 1965; children: Samantha Mara. *Education:* Attended Ohio State University, 1959-61; University of California, Los Angeles, B.A., 1971. *Office:* Merle Norman Cosmetics, 9130 Bellanca, Los Angeles, Calif. 90045.

CAREER: Xerox Corp., Columbus, Ohio, instructor in sales, 1963-64; ORMCO Corp., Glendora, Calif., sales manager, 1965-68; developer of first women's dental sales group, 1968-71; Merle Norman Cosmetics, Los Angeles, Calif., director of consumer affairs, 1971—. *Member:* American Women in Radio and Television (member of board of directors), Women in Business, National Association of Women Business Owners.

WRITINGS: The Independent Woman, J. P. Tarcher, 1981. Contributor to professional journals.

SIDELIGHTS: Rae Wisely commented: "I specialize in the areas that deal with the success of women in business. I conduct appearance, management, and career development seminars."

*   *   *

WITT, John (Clermont)   1907-1982

OBITUARY NOTICE: Born November 5, 1907; died April 26, 1982. Lawyer, art collector, and author. An attorney in England beginning in 1935, Witt served on the board of trustees of many art galleries, including the National Gallery and the Tate Gallery. He was also active in many societies for the arts. Among Witt's writings is *William Henry Hunt (1790-1864): Life and Work, With a Catalogue,* a profile of the British watercolor artist. Witt was knighted in 1967. Obituaries and other sources: *Who's Who,* 126th edition, St. Martin's, 1974; *London Times,* April 29, 1982.

*   *   *

WOJTYLA, Karol
See JOHN PAUL II, Pope

*   *   *

WOLFENDEN, John Frederick   1906-

PERSONAL: Born June 26, 1906, in Swindon, England; son of George and Emily Hannah Wolfenden; married Eileen LeMessurier Spilsbury, 1932; children: Priscilla Wolfenden Dainty, Daniel, Deborah Wolfenden Eveleigh. *Education:* Queen's College, Oxford, B.A. (with first class honors), 1928, M.A., 1933; attended Princeton University, 1928-29. *Home:* White House, Guildford Rd., Westcott, Dorking, Surrey, England.

CAREER: Magdalen College, Oxford, Oxford, England, fellow and tutor, 1929-34; headmaster of independent boys' schools in Uppingham, England, 1934-44, and Shrewsbury, England, 1944-50; University of Reading, Reading, England, vice-chancellor, 1950-63, chairman of university grants committee, 1963-68; British Museum, London, England, director and principal librarian, 1969-73; retired. Life member of board of trustees of Carnegie United Kingdom Trust. Chairman of Secondary School Examinations Council, 1951-57, National Council of Social Service, 1953-60, Departmental Committee on Homosexual Offences and Prostitution, 1954-57, and Central Council of Physical Recreation Sports Enquiry, 1957-60. *Member:* Classical Association (president, 1979-80). *Awards, honors:* D.Litt. from University of Reading and University of Warwick; LL.D. from University of Hull, University of Wales, Victoria University of Manchester, and Williams College; L.H.D. from Hamilton College; D.Univ. from University of York; named commander of Order of the British Empire, 1942, knight, 1956, life peer, 1974.

WRITINGS: The Approach to Philosophy, Edward Arnold, 1932; *The Public Schools Today,* University of London Press, 1948; *The Prospect Before Us,* Low, 1948; (contributor) C. H. Dobinson, editor, *Education in a Changing World,* Clarendon Press, 1951; *How to Choose Your School,* Oxford University Press, 1952; *Turning Points* (memoirs), Bodley Head, 1976.

WORK IN PROGRESS: A book on Greek philosophy.

SIDELIGHTS: Lord Wolfenden commented: "People often think that being retired means having unlimited time for reading and writing. In real life it means writing your own letters, doing your own filing, and paying your own postage. The only time for reading is over breakfast or during tedious journeys by train or plane. So my advice is: Get your reading and writing done before you strike seventy."

* * *

WOLLMAN, Nathaniel 1915-

BRIEF ENTRY: Born May 15, 1915, in Philadelphia, Pa. American economist, educator, and author. Wollman has taught at University of New Mexico since 1948. He is now a professor of economics, department chairman, and dean of the College of Arts and Sciences. He has also been an economist for Resources for the Future, Inc., and chairman of the International Environmental Programs Committee. Wollman wrote *An Appraisal of New Mexico Labor Legislation* (Department of Government, University of New Mexico, 1950), *The Value of Water in Alternative Uses, With Special Application to Water Use in the San Juan and Rio Grande Basins of New Mexico* (University of New Mexico Press, 1962), *The Water Resources of Chile: An Economic Method for Analyzing a Key Resource in a Nation's Development* (Johns Hopkins Press, 1968), *The Outlook for Water: Quality, Quantity, and National Growth* (Johns Hopkins Press, 1971), and *Man, Materials, and Environment* (M.I.T. Press, 1973). *Address:* P.O. Box 358, Corrales, N.M. 87048; and College of Arts and Sciences, University of New Mexico, Albuquerque, N.M. 87131. *Biographical/critical sources: American Men and Women of Science: The Social and Behavioral Sciences,* 13th edition, Bowker, 1978.

* * *

WOLTER, Allan B(ernard) 1913-

PERSONAL: Born November 24, 1913, in Peoria, Ill.; son of Bernard Gregory and Marianne Bernadette (Strub) Wolter. *Education:* Attended St. Joseph College, Westmont, Ill., 1931-33; Our Lady of Angels Seminary, Cleveland, Ohio, B.A., 1937; attended St. Joseph Seminary, Teutopolis, Ill., 1937-41; Catholic University of America, M.A., 1942, Ph.D., 1947. *Home and office:* Old Mission, Santa Barbara, Calif. 93105; (autumns) School of Philosophy, Catholic University of America, Washington, D.C. 20064.

CAREER: Entered Ordo Fratrum Minorum (Order of Friars Minor; Observant Franciscans; O.F.M.), 1934, ordained Roman Catholic priest, 1940; Our Lady of Angels Seminary,

Cleveland, Ohio, associate professor of chemistry, biology, and philosophy, 1943-45, associate professor of philosophy, 1946-51; St. Bonaventure University, St. Bonaventure, N.Y., professor of philosophy at Franciscan Institute, 1952-62; Catholic University of America, Washington, D.C., visiting professor, 1962-63, professor of philosophy, 1963—. Editor of Quincy College Publications, 1964—. Research associate at Center for Medieval and Renaissance Studies, University of California, Los Angeles, 1978-82. Visiting associate professor at Franciscan Institute, St. Bonaventure University, 1946-51, *lector generalis,* 1954; visiting lecturer at Princeton University, spring, 1965; visiting professor at University of Michigan, summer, 1967, New York University, spring, 1969, and University of California, Los Angeles, spring, 1978; exchange professor at American University, autumn, 1972.

MEMBER: Societas Internationalis Scotistica, American Philosophica Association, American Catholic Philosophical Association (vice-president, 1956-57; president, 1957-58), Metaphysical Society of America, American Association for the Advancement of Science, Mediaeval Academy of America, Mind Association, Philosophy of Science Association, Society for General Systems Research, Washington Philosophical Club. *Awards, honors:* D.Sc. from Quincy College, 1967; senior fellow of National Endowment for the Humanities, 1973.

WRITINGS: The Transcendentals and Their Function in the Metaphysics of Duns Scotus, Catholic University of America Press, 1946; *Select Problems in the Philosophy of Nature,* Franciscan Institute, St. Bonaventure University, 1952; *The Book of Life: An Explanation of the Rule of the Third Order Regular of St. Francis,* Franciscan Institute, St. Bonaventure University, 1954; *Summula Metaphysicae,* Bruce, 1958; *Life in God's Love,* Franciscan Herald, 1958.

Duns Scotus: Philosophical Writings, Thomas Nelson, 1960; (editor and translator) *John Duns Scotus: A Treatise on God as First Principle,* Forum Books, 1966; (editor with John F. Wippel) *Medieval Philosophy: From St. Augustine to Nicholas of Cusa,* Free Press, 1969; (with Felix Alluntis) *John Duns Scotus: God and Creatures, the Quodlibetal Questions,* Princeton University Press, 1975; *Duns Scotus' Questions on the Metaphysics, Book Nine: Potency and Act,* Catholic University of America Press, 1979; *Duns Scotus: Six Questions on Individuation From the Oxford Lectures,* Catholic University of America Press, 1981.

Contributor: J. K. Ryan, editor, *Philosophical Studies in Honor of the Very Reverend Ignatius Smith, O. P.,* Newman Press, 1952; *Nature: The Mirror of God,* Franciscan Educational Conference, 1955; James Collins, editor, *Readings in Ancient and Medieval Philosophy,* Newman Press, 1960; G. F. McLean, editor, *Philosophy and the Integration of Contemporary Catholic Education,* Catholic University of America Press, 1962; McLean, editor, *Teaching Thomism Today,* Catholic University of American Press, 1963; Herman Shapiro, editor, *Medieval Philosophy,* Modern Library, 1964; Ryan and others editors, *Twentieth-Century Thinkers,* Alba House, 1965; Ryan and B. M. Bonansea, editors, *Studies in Philosophy and the History of Philosophy,* Volume III: *John Duns Scotus, 1265-1965,* Catholic University of America Press, 1965; Ryan, editor, *Studies in Philosophy and the History of Philosophy,* Volume V: *Ancients and Moderns,* Catholic University of America Press, 1970; J. F. Ross, editor, *Inquiries Into Medieval Philosophy,* Greenwood Press, 1971; Damian McElrath editor, *Franciscan Christology,* Franciscan Institute, St. Bonaventure University, 1980; Albert Zimmermann, editor, *Miscellanea Mediaevalia,* Walter de Gruyter, 1981; Parviz Morewedge, editor, *Ancient and Medieval Philosophies of Existence,* Fordham University Press, 1982.

Editor of "Franciscan Institute Publications," a series, St. Bonaventure University, 1946-62. Contributor to *Encyclopaedia Britannica, New Catholic Encyclopedia, Encyclopedia of Philosophy,* and *Catholic Encyclopedia for School and Home.* Contributor of more than thirty articles to philosophy and theology journals. Associate editor of *New Scholasticism,* 1949-51; editor of *Franciscan Studies,* 1949-52.

WORK IN PROGRESS: The Philosophy of John Duns Scotus; The Moral and Political Philosophy of John Duns Scotus; John Duns Scotus: God as First Principle.

*　　　*　　　*

WOLZ, Henry G(eorge)　1905-

PERSONAL: Born September 10, 1905, in Kornwestheim, Germany (now West Germany); came to the United States, 1930, naturalized citizen, 1943; son of Johann M. (a government official) and Kathrine (Pflueger) Wolz; married Barbara L. Dertwinkel, March 20, 1955; children: Ursula. *Education:* Fordham University, B.S., 1936, M.A., 1938, Ph.D., 1946; postdoctoral study at Columbia University, 1946-49. *Home:* 25 Ryan St., Syosett, N.Y. 11791. *Office:* Department of Philosophy, Queens College of the City University of New York, Flushing, N.Y. 11367.

CAREER: Worked in several commercial concerns in Germany, Spain, Venezuela, and the United States, 1926-47; Columbia University, New York, N.Y., tutor of Germanic languages, 1947; Wagner College, Staten Island, N.Y., assistant professor of philosophy, 1947-51; Queens College of the City University of New York, Flushing, N.Y., assistant professor, 1951-56, associate professor, 1956-64, professor of philosophy, 1964—. Member of faculty at Brooklyn College of the City University of New York, 1947, and at Hunter College of the City University of New York, 1947-49. *Military service:* U.S. Army, Finance Department, 1942-45. *Member:* American Philosophical Association, Metaphysical Society of America.

WRITINGS: Plato and Heidegger: In Search of Selfhood, Bucknell University Press, 1980. Contributor of about twenty articles and reviews to philosophy journals.

WORK IN PROGRESS: An Approach to Heidegger's Philosophy Through Literature.

SIDELIGHTS: Wolz told *CA:* "I came late to philosophy. My formal education was seriously interrupted on three occasions. A disastrous inflation after my graduation from high school rendered my attendance at a university financially impossible. After I entered the United States in 1930, the Great Depression made it difficult to find positions lucrative enough to allow sufficient time for studies. Finally, during World War II I served for three years in the U.S. Army. After my discharge, I finished my graduate studies."

AVOCATIONAL INTERESTS: Travel, tennis, jogging, theatre, music, reading.

*　　　*　　　*

WOOD, Catherine
See ETCHISON, Birdie L(ee)

*　　　*　　　*

WOOD, Charles Gerald　1932-

PERSONAL: Born August 6, 1932, in St. Peter Port, Guernsey, Channel Islands; son of John Edward (an actor) and Catherine

Mae (an actress; maiden name, Harris) Wood; married Valerie Elizabeth Newman (an actress), 1954; children: one son, one daughter. *Education:* Attended Birmingham College of Art. *Home:* Manor House, Milton, near Banbury, Oxfordshire, England.

CAREER: Factory worker, 1955-57; stage manager and theatre designer, 1957-59; layout artist, 1959-62; writer, 1962—. Past director of Charles Wood Agency Ltd. *Member:* Dramatists Guild. *Awards, honors:* Most promising playwright award, 1963, for "Cockade," and best comedy award, 1972, for "Veterans," both from *Evening Standard.*

WRITINGS—Plays: *Lines West,* Superior Publishing, 1967; *Dingo* (first produced in Bristol, England, at Bristol Arts Centre, 1967), Grove, 1969; *Veterans* (first produced in Edinburgh, Scotland, at Lyceum), Eyre Methuen, 1972.

Omnibus volumes: *Has "Washington" Legs?* [and] *Dingo* (contains "Has 'Washington' Legs?" [first produced in London by National Theatre Co. at Cottesloe Theatre, November 29, 1978] and "Dingo" [see above]), Eyre Methuen, 1979.

Plays represented in anthologies include "Cockade" (three one-act plays, "Prisoner and Escort," "John Thomas," and "Spare"; first produced in London at New Arts Theatre, 1963) in *New English Dramatists Number Eight,* Penguin, 1965; and "Fill the Stage With Happy Hours" (first produced in Nottingham, England, at Nottingham Playhouse, 1966), in *New English Dramatists Number Eleven,* Penguin, 1967.

Unpublished plays: "Don't Make Me Laugh" (one-act) first produced on West End at Aldwych Theatre, 1965; "Meals on Wheels," first produced on West End at Royal Court Theatre, 1965; "Tie Up the Ballcock," first produced in 1966; "H; or, Monologue at Front of Burning Cities," first produced in 1969; "Labour," first produced in 1971; "Welfare," first produced in Liverpool, England, at Everyman Theatre, 1971; "Collier's Wood," first produced in 1971; "Jingo," first produced on West End by Royal Shakespeare Co. at Aldwych Theatre, 1975; "The Script," first produced in Hampstead, England, at Hampstead Theatre Club, June 20, 1976.

Screenplays: "The Knack . . . and How to Get It," United Artists, 1965; (with Marc Behm) "Help!," United Artists, 1965; "How I Won the War," United Artists, 1967; "The Charge of the Light Brigade," United Artists, 1968; "Cuba," United Artists, 1979.

Author of television scripts, including "Drill Pig," "Drums Along the Avon," "Death or Glory Boys" (trilogy), and "Don't Forget to Write" (series). Also author of radio scripts.*

*　　　*　　　*

WOOD, Lee Blair　1893-1982

OBITUARY NOTICE: Born March 7, 1893, in Corry, Pa.; died of an apparent heart attack, February 7, 1982, in Lakewood, Ohio. Business executive, editor, and journalist. Wood worked as a reporter in Pennsylvania and Ohio before serving in the French and U.S. armies during World War I. Remaining in Paris after his duty, Wood was news editor of the Paris edition of the *Chicago Tribune* until 1921 when he returned to the United States. He worked as an editor of the *Cleveland Press* and as managing editor of the *Oklahoma News* until 1927 when he was appointed news editor of Scripps-Howard's *New York Telegram.* When the paper became the *World-Telegram* (and later the *World-Telegram and Sun*), Wood was named executive editor. Under Wood the paper received four Pulitzer Prizes. Obituaries and other sources: *The International Who's Who,*

Europa, 1978; *Who's Who in America,* 40th edition, Marquis, 1978; *Chicago Tribune,* February 10, 1982.

*   *   *

WOODALL, Corbet   1929(?)-1982

OBITUARY NOTICE: Born c. 1929; died May 19, 1982. Television newscaster and author. Woodall was a newscaster for the British Broadcasting Corporation (BBC-TV and Radio) during the 1960's and hosted the program "Town and Around" for the network. Stricken with rheumatoid arthritis in the late 1960's, Woodall devoted much of the remainder of his life to raising funds to help research and combat the disease. He wrote an autobiography titled *A Disjointed Life.* Obituaries and other sources: *London Times,* May 20, 1982.

*   *   *

WOODREW, Greta   1930-

PERSONAL: Born December 16, 1930, in New York, N.Y.; daughter of David S. (a lawyer) and Hortense (Schlang) Andron; married Richard Smolowe (an executive in manufacturing), November 16, 1952; children: Alan, Jill, Jonathan, Ann. *Education:* University of Florida, B.A., 1951. *Home and office:* 116 Roseville Rd., Westport, Conn. 06880.

CAREER: Grapevine Industries, Inc. (clothing retailer), New York, N.Y., vice-president for merchandising, 1968-75; Woodrew Services (executive search firm), Westport, Conn., president, 1976—. Vice-president of Space Technology and Research Foundation, 1979—. *Awards, honors:* LL.D. from William Penn College, 1979.

WRITINGS: On a Slide of Light (nonfiction), Macmillan, 1981. Editor of *Woodrew Update,* a business newsletter.

SIDELIGHTS: In *On a Slide of Light,* Woodrew describes her experiences and theories of extrasensory perception and other paranormal phenomena. She describes her telepathic contacts with beings from the planet "Ogatta" in another solar system, and the testing she underwent in the laboratory of Dr. Andrija Puharich. The *Planetary Association for Clean Energy Newsletter* praised Woodrew's book, calling it "honest and factual."

Woodrew told *CA:* "I never try to convince anyone of anything. I simply share my own experienced realities, and hope that the reader will listen and contemplate the awesome possibilities—and broaden his or her horizon as a result. I had much to lose and nothing to gain in telling my story. All of the royalties from *On a Slide of Light* go to the S.T.A.R. Foundation for psychic research, as do all of my honorariums from lectures and the subscription fees from the *Woodrew Update.* I really do not care whether people believe or disbelieve, as long as they think . . . and relate."

BIOGRAPHICAL/CRITICAL SOURCES: Andrija Puharich, editor, *The Iceland Papers,* Essentia Research Associates, 1981; *Planetary Association for Clean Energy Newsletter,* June, 1981.

*   *   *

WOODS, Pamela   1938-

PERSONAL: Born January 30, 1938, in Reigate, England; daughter of John (a director) and Nora (a rug designer; maiden name, Cowell) Pearse; married Michael Woods (an artist), August 20, 1960 (divorced, 1975); children: Vanessa, Oliver, Geraldine. *Education:* Attended Nesta Brooking Ballet School, 1955-65, and London Central School of Theatrical Design. *Religion:* Church of England. *Home and office:* 7 Raby Pl.,

Bath, Avon, England. *Agent:* Peter Riva, 207 East 85th St., Suite 212, New York, N.Y. 10028.

CAREER: Pamela Pearse Ballet School, Guildford, England, director, 1955-75; director of Pamela Woods Flowers Ltd., England, 1975-79; Pamela Woods Floral Agency and Design Studio, Bath, England, director, 1979—. Lecturer at colleges; designer for Rayher Hobby; guest on British and American television programs.

WRITINGS—All with Peter Riva: *Paper Flowermaking,* Studio Vista, 1972; *Flowers From Feathers,* David & Charles, 1973; *Flowers From Fabrics,* David & Charles, 1974; *Party Decorations and Crackers,* Blandford, 1974; *Feathercraft,* Search Press, 1974; *Quilling,* Leisure Craft, 1975; *Christmas,* Blandford, 1975; *Creative Flowermaking,* Pan Books, 1975; *Part Works: Victorian Crafts Revived,* Batsford, 1976; *Crafts,* Lutterworth, 1977; *Crafts Encyclopedia,* Marshall Cavendish, 1977; *Papercraft,* Hamlyn, 1979; *Ribbon Flowers,* Rayher, 1980. Contributor to magazines, including *Womancraft* and *Family Circle.*

WORK IN PROGRESS: Ribbon Work, publication by Frech Verlag; *Dried and Pressed Flowers,* for Dryad; *Flowers From Felt,* for Womancraft; *Paperwork,* for Dryad.

*   *   *

WOODS, Randall Bennett   1944-

BRIEF ENTRY: Born October 10, 1944, in Galveston, Tex. American historian, educator, and author. Woods has taught history at University of Arkansas since 1971. He wrote *The Roosevelt Foreign-Policy Establishment and the Good Neighbor: The United States and Argentina, 1941-1945* (Regents Press of Kansas, 1979) and *A Black Odyssey: John Lewis Waller and the Promise of American Life* (Regents Press of Kansas, 1980). *Address:* Department of History, University of Arkansas, Ozark Hall, Fayetteville, Ark. 72701.

*   *   *

WREN, Robert Meriwether   1928-

PERSONAL: Born February 21, 1928, in Washington, D.C.; son of Clark Campbell (a judge) and Mamie (Culpeper) Wren. *Education:* University of Houston, B.A., 1954; Princeton University, M.A., 1956, Ph.D., 1965. *Residence:* Houston, Tex. *Office:* Department of English, University of Houston, Houston, Tex. 77004.

CAREER: Rutgers University, Douglass College, New Brunswick, N.J., instructor in English, 1956-60; State University of New York at Binghamton, instructor in drama, 1960-62; Knox College, Galesburg, Ill., lecturer in English, 1964-65; University of Houston, Houston, Tex., assistant professor, 1965-68, associate professor, 1968-79, professor of English, 1979—. Visiting senior lecturer at University of Lagos, 1972-75. *Member:* International Federation for Theatre Research, Society for Theatre Research, Malone Society, African Studies Association (program director, 1976-77), Western Association of Africanists (president, 1977-79). *Awards, honors:* Fulbright fellowship, 1973-75.

WRITINGS: Achebe's World, Three Continents Press, 1980, revised edition, Longman, 1981; *J. P. Clark,* Twayne, 1982.

Contributor: C. D. Narasimhaiah, editor, *Awakened Conscience: Studies in Commonwealth Literature,* Humanities, 1978; R. V. Weekes, editor, *An Ethnographic Survey of the Muslim World,* Greenwood Press, 1978; C. L. Innes and Bernth Lindfors, editors, *Critical Perspectives on Chinua Achebe,* Three

Continents Press, 1978. Contributor of articles on theatre, literature, African studies, and religion to scholarly journals.

WORK IN PROGRESS: Writers at Ibadan, 1948-1966.

SIDELIGHTS: Wren told *CA:* "In 1968 I changed my dominant research interest from the theatre of northern Europe to African literature. I visit Africa frequently, including spending the academic years from 1972 to 1975 at the University of Lagus, and from 1982 to 1983 at Ibadan. My approach to literature is multidisciplinary, including history and cultural anthropology.

"Contemporary African literature is important not only because of its intrinsic merit but also because of its revelation of diverse cultures. I see our own American life as insular; the mere reading of such masters of English as Achebe, Clark, and Soyinka opens to Americans a hitherto concealed realm of experience. My books are written to augment the cross-cultural understanding that the literature makes possible. I do not write for Americans alone, of course; wherever African literature is read—in New Delhi, Addis Ababa, London—I hope my research will be found useful.

"Travel in Africa awakened my interest in the literature. Rather than jet in just to look at animals and then jet out again, I traveled many thousands of miles in Africa—by foot, by bus, and by train—before returning to Nigeria to live, teach, and study. Teaching an African literature course to Nigerian students from 1973 to 1975 taught me more than any other academic experience of literature in my life. My greatest debt is to those students."

*   *   *

WURMSER, Leon   1931-

PERSONAL: Born January 31, 1931, in Zurich, Switzerland; came to the United States in 1962, naturalized citizen, 1975; son of Alfred (in business) and Lilly (in business; maiden name, Hofmann) Wurmser; married Zdenka Kondelova (a physician), March 27, 1958; children: Daniel W., David W., Yoram. *Education:* Attended University of Zurich, 1949-55; University of Basel, M.D., 1955; postdoctoral study at Baltimore-District of Columbia Institute for Psychoanalysis, 1975. *Religion:* Jewish. *Home:* 904 Crestwick Rd., Towson, Md. 21204. *Office:* Alcohol and Drug Abuse Program, University of Maryland, 721 West Redwood St., Baltimore, Md. 21201.

CAREER: University Hospital, Basel, Switzerland, resident in psychiatry and internal medicine, 1957-61; Sheppart-Enoch Pratt Hospital, Towson, Md., staff psychiatrist, 1962-65; Greater Baltimore Medical Center, Baltimore, Md., intern in internal medicine, 1965-66; Johns Hopkins University, Baltimore, instructor, 1966-69, assistant professor, 1969-71, associate professor of psychiatry, 1971-77, director of Drug Abuse Center at Johns Hopkins Hospital, 1969-71; University of Maryland, School of Medicine, Baltimore, professor of psychiatry and director of alcohol and drug abuse program, 1977—. Intern at Buergerspital, Basel, 1960-61; private practice of psychiatry; director of psychiatric outpatient department at Sinai Hospital, Baltimore, 1966-69. *Military service:* Swiss Army, Medical Corps, 1952-62.

MEMBER: American Association for the Advancement of Science, American Psychoanalytic Association, American Psychiatric Society (fellow), Swiss Medical Association, Swiss Psychiatric Association, Maryland Psychiatric Society, Baltimore-District of Columbia Society and Institute for Psychoanalysis. *Awards, honors:* Lewis B. Hill Award from Baltimore-District of Columbia Society and Institute for Psychoanalysis, 1975, for paper, "A Clinical Study About the

Tragic Character"; award for pioneering excellence and achievement from American Mental Health Foundation, 1979, for *The Hidden Dimension.*

WRITINGS: Raubmorder und Rauber (title means "Murders for Robbery and Robbers"), Kriminalistik, 1959; *The Hidden Dimension: Psychodynamics in Compulsive Drug Use,* Jason Aronson, 1978; (editor with George U. Balis) *Psychiatric Foundations of Medicine* (textbook), six volumes, Butterworth, 1978; *The Mask of Shame* (nonfiction), Johns Hopkins Press, 1981. Contributor of more than two hundred articles to medical and scientific journals.

WORK IN PROGRESS: The Second Shadow, a psychoanalytic novel; research on epistemology of psychoanalysis, psychodynamics of toxicomania, and such literary sources for psychoanalysis as Goethe and Aristotle.

SIDELIGHTS: "I grew up in a small medieval town in Switzerland," Wurmser commented, "a few miles from the German border. My youth was overshadowed by the Nazi threat. The need to master the terror about what was happening, as well as more directly personal experiences, made me decide at the age of sixteen to become a psychoanalyst or psychotherapist. Since my big loves were the humanities (literature and philosophy above all), I hoped to reach this goal through them, but the long and arduous detour through medicine proved to be preferable. All through my late youth I wrote poems, novels, and dramas, none of which I dared submit for review. I learned a number of languages and took courses with some outstanding philosophers—Zurich and Basel were dominant centers of German and European culture at that time. After graduation from medical school in 1955 and a brief stint in Israel, I wrote a book about some of the psychological aspects of murderers, and it was published in Germany. From 1957 through 1961 I wrote a considerable number of aritcles and book reviews. Though the reviews are often dismissed, I saw them as an important piece of work; in my experience this kind of writing served to sharpen the critical faculty *vis-a-vis* scientific, philosophical, historical, and literary books, and the ability to seize and present, succinctly yet comprehensively, the essence of any work to others.

"In 1962 I was certified by the Swiss Specialty Board as a psychiatrist and psychotherapist, but I felt that both my psychoanalytic training and the opportunities to do systematic research in the psychotherapy of severely disturbed patients were insufficient and unsatisfactory in Switzerland. My wife (also a physician) and I decided to emigrate to the United States.

"I began participating some evenings in a research project with narcotics addicts. It was only secondary that I gained a deeper interest in the psychodynamics of these patients. What had really been, at best, a side interest and a moonlighting job quickly turned into a primary expertise—not because I knew so much, but because almost no one else had up to then dealt with these patients with any consistency or sustained psychoanalytic interest. (Actually, the situation even today is not all that different, at least as far as the published literature goes.) After three years as director of the psychiatric out-patient department at Sinai Hospital, I was invited, early in 1969, to build up a comprehensive drug abuse center at Johns Hopkins Hospital. In 1971 I was asked to start a drug abuse treatment program at University of Maryland.

"During this same period of time, 1966-75, I went through another very intensive training as a psychoanalyst. In my scientific work in psychoanalytic technique and theory I was and am most directly influenced by doctors Jenny Walder Hall and Paul Gray, and indirectly by the scientific work of Anna Freud, whose focus on the very detailed and thorough analysis of the defenses is one I share and is work that could have many more practical implications than are generally realized.

"During the last ten years I have continued writing a lot of psychoanalytic papers and more philosophically oriented papers. More and more I have complemented my clinical and administrative work with teaching, mainly in psychotherapy, the history of psychiatry and psychoanalysis, besides my regular work teaching about the psychodynamic aspects of compulsive drug use. A particularly exciting, though very time-consuming, experiment was started in 1977: a course in literature for first-year medical students, which also covered philosophy. Classic works (including Greek tragedies, Shakespeare, Dickens, Ibsen, Dostoevsky, Henry James, and Arthur Miller) were discussed from the viewpoints of history, literature, philosophy, sociology, mythology, biography, and psychoanalysis.

"*The Hidden Dimension* grew out of my work with drug abuse. It is based on my experiences with about fifty patients who I had treated intensively and over long periods of time with about a thousand I had seen only superficially. I tried to order all my observations in a comprehensive theoretical understanding, rooted in the psychoanalytic concept of inner conflict. Much attention was paid to what defenses are used to deal with such conflict and how these defenses are shared with family and culture.

"These observations and conceptualizations required much further development of psychoanalytic theory, so my work is still proceeding, and some of the more arcane discoveries acquire ever more practical importance in treatment technique and prevention. Their relevance for a deeper understanding of some of the other problems of our culture should not be underestimated.

"In 1980 I rewrote papers and drafts of the previous twenty years into a comprehensive book on the spectrum of shame effects, their underlying conflicts, and the characteristic defenses dealing with this much-neglected range of feelings. Its title is *The Mask of Shame*. Connecting lines are drawn to literature, philosophy, and politics. The great influence continuous sensitivity to issues of shame has upon psychoanalytic and psychotherapeutic technique is being detailed.

"My current writing is an outgrowth of the work on the *Mask of Shame*. The problem of the defense against the superego (as shown by 'shamelessness') and its opposite, being crushed by this inner authority, would allow the contraposition of 'anarchic character' and 'tragic character.' Instead of dealing with this fascinating topic scientifically I decided to use much of my own personal experience and to write about it in the form of a novel.

"Besides teaching and administration I spend about twenty-five hours a week seeing individual patients, mainly in psychoanalysis, a few in psychoanalytically oriented, focal, usually brief psychotherapy. This work continues to be my major line of investigation and should be reflected in several new books.

"My scientific goals have been to be as specific as possible, to find the most relevant connections, and not to be trapped by cliches or theoretical constructs and words without imme-diately clear, concrete content. My practical aim has been to see through the facade of the often obnoxious behavior to the hidden suffering, and thus to change both."

*   *   *

WYKSTRA, Ronald A.   1935-

BRIEF ENTRY: Born March 20, 1935, in Plainwell, Mich. American economist, educator, and author. Wykstra has worked as an operations research analyst and financial supervisor. He has been a professor of economics at Colorado State University since 1971. Wykstra wrote *American Labor and Manpower Policy* (Odyssey, 1970). He edited *Nebraska Economic Indicators: A Study of the Timing of Cyclical Fluctuations* (Bureau of Business Research, College of Business Administration, University of Nebraska, 1965), *Human Capital Formation and Manpower Development* (Free Press, 1971), *Readings in Introductory Economics* (Harper, 1971), *Introductory Economics* (Harper, 1971), and *Education and the Economics of Human Capital* (Free Press, 1971). *Address:* Department of Economics, Colorado State University, Fort Collins, Colo. 80521.

*   *   *

WYSS, Max Albert   1908-1977

PERSONAL: Born July 18, 1908, in Kriens, Switzerland; died September 12, 1977; son of Friedrich (a teacher) and Katharine (Theiler) Wyss; married Zita Keller (a professor of music), October 29, 1965. *Education:* Teachers Seminar, Lucerne, Switzerland, Teachers Degree, 1928, Secondary School Teachers Degree, 1931; also attended University of Zurich, University of Paris, and University of Geneva.

CAREER: Private tutor, 1931-32; teacher of history and Germanic and Romantic languages and literature at Lucerne Secondary School in Lucerne, Switzerland, 1933-34; free-lance photojournalist, 1925-77. Editor of C. J. Bucher Publishers, 1965-76; photography theoretician for *Camera*. Secretary of World Exhibition of Photography, 1952. *Military service:* Swiss Army, in News Service, 1939-45.

WRITINGS—And co-illustrator, unless otherwise noted: *Irlande,* Editions Ides et Calendes, 1965; *Lucerne,* Eugen Haag, 1964; *Magic of the Mountains,* Viking, 1966; *Magic of the Woods,* Viking, 1967; *Magic of the Sea,* Viking, 1968; *Zauber des Flusses* (title means "Magic of the River"), C. J. Bucher, 1970; (text only, with Yoshikazi Shirakawa) *The Alps,* Abrams, 1973; *Zurueck zur Natur* (title means "Back to Nature"), C. J. Bucher, 1976. Contributor to magazines and newspapers.

SIDELIGHTS: Zita Wyss told *CA* about her husband: "Max always wanted to be a journalist and writer, and became a teacher only in order to earn his living. He was a self-taught photographer, and he was essentially a visual person—a fact which is also evident in his writing. Although he was an active photographer, he felt photography was really too quick a way to get to the heart of things, and he was also a talented artist (mainly drawings). Before and after the war, he created a number of collages. The main literary influences on his work were James Joyce, Thomas Wolfe, and Ernest Hemingway. A year spent in Africa, from 1931 to 1932, also made a deep impression on him. When he died in 1977, he left behind a considerable number of unpublished poems."

Y

YAFFE, Alan
    See YORINKS, Arthur

*   *   *

YARDLEY, Alice   1913-
    (Angela Young)

BRIEF ENTRY: Born November 14, 1913, in Sheffield, England. British lecturer and author. Yardley's writings (sometimes under the pseudonym Angela Young) include *Learning to Adjust* (Evans Brothers, 1973), *Structure in Early Learning* (Evans Brothers, 1974), and *The Organisation of the Infant School* (Evans Brothers, 1976). *Address:* 2 Crantock Gardens, Keyworth, Nottingham NG12 5FR, England.

*   *   *

YARNALL, Sophia
    See JACOBS, Sophia Yarnall

*   *   *

YARROW, Arnold   1920-

PERSONAL: Born April 17, 1920, in London, England. *Home:* 2 Perry Court Cottages, Brogdale Rd., Faversham, Kent ME13 8ST, England.

CAREER: Writer and actor, 1947—. Script editor for British Broadcasting Corp. (BBC), London, England, 1968-76. *Military service:* British Army, 1940-47. *Member:* Society of Authors, British Actors Equity Association.

WRITINGS: The Greasepaint Jungle (novel), Whiting & Wheaton, 1966; (editor) *Softly Softly Casebook,* Pan Books, 1973; (editor) *Softly Softly Murder Casebook,* Pan Books, 1974; *Death Is a Z* (novel), R. Hale, 1978.

Radio and television scripts: (Contributor) "Softly, Softly" series, British Broadcasting Corp. (BBC-TV), 1966-76; "After Moscow," first broadcast on BBC-Radio, 1980; (adapter) "The Magician of Lublin," first broadcast on BBC-Radio, 1981.

SIDELIGHTS: Yarrow commented: "I started writing because story ideas came unbidden to my mind; having received them there, it seemed the most natural thing to do to set them down. Since I was already an actor, these ideas were predominantly in dramatic form. In my mature years I found, to my delight, that I could get these works performed on radio, on television,

and occasionally in the theatre. My delight was enhanced by the realization that I could make a modest living in the process; writing then became my primary professional activity, with acting taking second place. I know of no more practical reason for becoming a writer, nor, I must admit, is there any less estimable reason. Having come to terms with the concept of myself as a writer, it again seemed a natural process to make the transition from writing plays to writing books.

"The nature of my work has varied. I write of those things which interest me, and my interests are as wide as those of any average theatregoer or book reader. I have written for an award-winning television 'cops' series which was acknowledged as an outstanding example of fictional entertainment wedded to responsible documentary verisimilitude. I have recently had a play performed, 'After Moscow,' which is an impertinent attempt to project what might have happened to Chekhov's 'three sisters' some seventeen years after he wrote them off. My research on that seventeen-year-period of Russian social history, from the date of Chekhov's play to the October Revolution, against which my own play is set, has stirred my interest and provoked sufficient story ideas to keep me busy for the rest of my days. My inclination to start work on these stories will depend to some extent on whether a publisher's advance or a radio/television commission will descend on me from out of the blue skies to coax me away from the garden which now absorbs a considerable portion of my time, interest, and energy."

*   *   *

YAUCH, Wilbur Alden   1904-1982

OBITUARY NOTICE: Born August 4, 1904, in Rochester, N.Y.; died while undergoing surgery, January 18, 1982, in Tucson, Ariz. Educator and author. Yauch wrote eight books on elementary education, among them *How Good Is Your School?* Obituaries and other sources: *Leaders in Education,* 5th edition, Bowker, 1974; *New York Times,* January 28, 1982.

*   *   *

YELTON, Donald Charles   1915-

PERSONAL: Born July 7, 1915, in Pasadena, Calif.; son of Elmer and Bess (Marxmiller) Yelton; married Viola Fortomaroff, November, 1972. *Education:* Hamilton College, A.B., 1935; Georgetown University, M.A. (history), 1950; Columbia

University, M.A. (library science), 1950, Ph.D., 1962. *Home: and office address:* Noonatch Rd., Watch Hill, R.I. 02891.

CAREER: University of Cincinnati, Cincinnati, Ohio, graduate assistant, 1935-36; associated with Central New York School for the Deaf, Rome, 1937-38; National Youth Administration of New York State, Albany, editorial and public relations assistant, 1938-40; University of Vermont, Burlington, instructor in English, 1947-49; City College (now of the City University of New York), New York, N.Y., fellow at library, 1950-52; Lincoln University, Pa., head librarian, 1952-65, lecturer in classics, 1955-56, acting president, 1960-61; State University of New York College at Buffalo, head librarian, 1965-67; State University of New York College at Potsdam, professor of English and director of libraries, 1967-72; University of Rhode Island, Kingston, lecturer in library science, 1972-76; free-lance editorial specialist, 1978—. Member of board of trustees of North Country Reference and Research Resources Council, 1967-72 (president, 1970), and Westerly Public Library, 1980—. *Military service:* U.S. Army, 1941-46; became major. *Member:* Modern Language Association of America, Friends of the Library and Memorial Association of Westerly (member of executive board, 1978—; president, 1980—).

WRITINGS: Mimesis and Metaphor: An Inquiry Into the Genesis and Scope of Conrad's Symbolic Imagery, Mouton, 1968; *Brief American Lives: Four Studies in Collective Biography,* Scarecrow, 1978.

SIDELIGHTS: Yelton told *CA:* "The work of establishing my credentials as a free-lance editor has left me little time to devote to my own writing. Since December, 1978, I have edited thirty-nine books for university presses, indexed a fourth, and served as a consultant for one of R. R. Bowker's publications (Ken Kister's *Encyclopedia Buying Guide*). Within the next year or so I intend to moderate the tempo of my editorial activity and may then find leisure for further writing projects.

"My interest in Conrad, and more generally in literary history and criticism, is perennial, but it would require an immersion in the critical literature of the last fifteen years for me to undertake any new contribution to Conrad studies. However, I am beginning to accumulate a file of notes and quotes that may some day be melded into a book. This is still in the embryonic stage, and all that can be said of it now is that it will, if realized, trace the vicissitudes of a number of selected themes in American civilization."

*   *   *

YEOMAN, John 1934-

PERSONAL: Born in 1934 in Forest Gate, London, England. *Education:* Attended Downing College, Cambridge, and Institute of Education, London. *Office:* c/o A. P. Watt & Son, 26-28 Bedford Row, London W.C.1, England.

CAREER: Writer and translator. Instructor in English at Watford Boys' Grammar School, 1960-62; instructor in English at Lycee Francais de Londres, 1962—, head of English department, 1969.

WRITINGS—Juveniles; all illustrated by Quentin Blake, except as noted: *A Drink of Water, and Other Stories,* Faber, 1960; *The Boy Who Sprouted Antlers,* Faber, 1961, revised edition, Collins, 1977; *The Apple of Youth, and Other Russian Folk Stories,* illustrated by Barbara Swiderska, Oxford University Press, 1967, F. Watts, 1968; *Alphabet Soup* (poems), Faber, 1969, Follett, 1970.

The Bear's Winter House, World Publishing, 1969; *The Bear's Water Picnic,* Macmillan, 1970; *Sixes and Sevens,* Macmillan,

1971; *Mouse Trouble,* Macmillan, 1972; *Beatrice and Vanessa,* Hamish Hamilton, 1974, Macmillan, 1975; (with Blake) *The Puffin Book of Improbable Records,* Puffin, 1975, published as *The Improbable Book of Records,* Atheneum, 1976; *The Young Performing Horse,* Hamish Hamilton, 1977, Parents Magazine Press, 1978; *The Wild Washerwomen: A New Folk Tale,* Greenwillow Books, 1979.

Translator: Vladimir Vietorovich, *Automatic Control and Computer Engineering,* edited by T. Prasad, Pergamon, 1961; Georgy Vasil'evich, *Time Relays,* Pergamon, 1961; Grigory Iosifovich Atabekov, *Linear Network Theory,* edited by P. K. M'Pherson, Pergamon, 1965; Eugene Labiche, *Three Cheers for Paris,* Ginn, 1971.

AVOCATIONAL INTERESTS: Reading, theatre, music.*

*   *   *

YORINKS, Arthur 1953-
(Alan Yaffe)

PERSONAL: Born August 21, 1953, in Roslyn, N.Y.; son of Alexander (a mechanical engineer) and Shirley (Kron) Yorinks. *Education:* Attended New School for Social Research and Hofstra New College, 1971. *Home:* 181 Thompson St., New York, N.Y. 10012. *Agent:* Marian Young, Nat Sobel Associates, 128 East 56th St., New York, N.Y. 10022.

CAREER: Writer. Cornell University, Ithaca, N.Y., instructor in theatre arts, 1972-79. Writer, teacher, and performer at American Mime Theatre, 1972-79. Founder of Moving Theatre, 1979; associate director of New Works Project in New York, N.Y. *Awards, honors:* School Library Journal named *Louis the Fish* one of the best books of 1980.

WRITINGS—Juveniles: Sid and Sol, illustrated by Richard Egielski, Farrar, Straus, 1977; (under pseudonym Alan Yaffe) *The Magic Meatballs,* Dial, 1979; *Louis the Fish,* illustrated by Egielski, Farrar, Straus, 1980; *It Happened in Pinsk,* illustrated by Egielski, Farrar, Straus, 1982.

Plays: "Six" (one-act), first produced in New York City at Hunter College Playhouse, November, 1973; "The Horse" (one-act), first produced in New York City at Cornelia Street Cafe, November, 1978; "Crackers" (one-act), first produced in New York City at Theatre of the Open Eye, June, 1979; "The King" (one-act), first produced in New York City at South Street Theatre, July, 1980; "Kissers" (one-act), first produced in New York City at South Street Theatre, July, 1980; "Piece for a Small Cafe" (one-act), first produced in New York City at Cornelia Street Cafe, February, 1981; "Piece for a Larger Cafe" (one-act), first produced in New York City at Cornelia Street Cafe, April, 1982. Also author of screenplay "Sid and Sol" (adapted from the book by Yorinks), Four Penny Productions, 1982.

WORK IN PROGRESS: Max Strickman, a novel for young adults, completion expected in 1982; a picture book about a singer, publication expected in 1983.

SIDELIGHTS: Yorinks's first book, *Sid and Sol,* is the story of a giant, Sol, who delights in terrorizing the countryside. He meets his match in Sid, a tiny fellow who responds to an advertisement for a giant-killer. Maurice Sendak, reviewing *Sid and Sol* for *New York Times Book Review,* wrote that "Yorinks has the cool audacity to mix purest nonsense with cockeyed fact. . . . It is perfect stand-up comic stuff and gorgeous writing."

The Magic Meatballs concerns a family's youngest sibling, Marvin, who obtains powerful meat that somehow grants the wishes of its owner. By unfortunate accident the meat is fed to his frequently hostile family and they turn into various foods. Marvin uses his prized wish to return them to human form only after procuring promises that they will treat him with more consideration. A critic for *Booklist* declared that "the dialogue is clever and breezy." *Los Angeles Times*'s Barbara Karlin called the book "a splendid moral tale" that is "hilarious."

Louis the Fish, Yorinks's third book, tells of a butcher who turns into a salmon. Most of the book is a flashback account of Louis's life in Flatbush. Selma G. Lanes noted, "Despite a bizarre premise, the story works beautifully."

Yorinks told *CA:* "From an early age I was always involved in some form of the arts. My aunt, a piano teacher in Brooklyn, introduced me to the piano at the age of five during my numerous Sunday visits to her apartment. At six I began formal classical piano training with Robert Bedford, which lasted for seven years. A young perfectionist, Bedford was the earliest professional influence on me. Every Saturday at eleven o'clock I was treated to the exploration of some of the world's greatest music. Through our mutual search (him to impart—I to digest), I learned a great deal of what it means to be an artist—the combination of exacting craft and the miracle of expressing wild and untamed feelings through a medium. If not for his sudden move out of state, I would have been, perhaps, a pianist today.

"Yet other forces were also at work. My brother being six years older than I, my sister nine years older, I was forced to grow up fast and spend a lot of time alone in the house. When I was eleven they were both off and out of the house. So I spent much time with my mother; my dog, Gigi; and by myself. My mother, trained as a fashion illustrator, would pass time painting and drawing at the kitchen table where I watched, copied, and tried my hand. Pictures became very important to me. Paint, paper, pencils, brushes, canvas—it was not only the delight in the magic of art but the tools, the mess, the patient *doing* of it that enthralled me. From those early days on, I have always admired, respected, loved, and envied artists and the visual magic that they indulge in. In sixth grade, with Michael DePaolo, an illustrator friend, I began to travel to New York City to see buildings, subways, visit galleries, museums—a never-satisfied thirst for art began and continues now.

"Spending so much time alone (practicing piano instead of playing football had its share in isolating me), the need to express myself in any form was enormous. Writing poems and stories became a private thread that wove itself through all my experiences, including those of art and music and theatre. The impetus was the intense feelings of childhood—the influences were old movies on afternoon television ('King Kong,' 'Frankenstein,' Fred Astaire, the Marx Brothers, Bette Davis, countless films of the 1930's and 1940's), comic books, classical music, jazz, and in junior high school the initiation into literature. Doyle, Poe, Kafka, Kleist, Gogol, the Brontes—all were my heroes. They were all my teachers.

"Graduating high school a year early and not having any desire to go to college, I explored many roads. I became involved in theatre by studying ballet and acting and ended up at the American Mime Theatre. For ten years I wrote plays, performed, and taught with that theatre company. Paul Curtis, the founder and uncompromising director, had a tremendous impact on me as a model of one who is so dedicated to his craft. Upon leaving that theatre I founded the Moving Theatre (an acting company) in 1979, which still exists today.

"After high school I also attempted to go back to the piano with little success. I could not get past the inevitable torture of struggling to play Chopin pieces that at age nine I was whizzing through.

"So, like it has always been, there was writing. At this time, late high school, I came across children's books, particularly the work of Maurice Sendak. It was a turning point. What I had spent my life cultivating, specific tastes and appreciations—it was all there in the work of Sendak. As a child I had the usual nursery rhymes and fairy tales, but I did not have any real picture books to speak of. Seeing them now, for the first time, was like finding a suit of clothes that seemed to be made for me. They had drama, art, rhythm, music, all rolled into one. I devoured them. Old ones, new ones.

"It was because of the influence of a few major artists of this field that I am a writer of children's books today. Maurice Sendak, William Steig, Tomi Ungerer, Randolph Caldecott, Wilhelm Busch, William Nicholson. I have dedicated myself to this art form in the tradition of those artists who look upon the picture book as a medium where the marriage of words and pictures is all important, and the seam that binds them together is all but invisible. Too many picture books of today have sorry texts used only as vehicles for a set of pictures, like a description attached to a portfolio. That is not what I believe picture books should be. It is a serious art form, most exact. And it is with the responsibility of any artistic pursuit that Richard Egielski (my artist collaborator) and I approach each new work."

BIOGRAPHICAL/CRITICAL SOURCES: New York Times, December 8, 1977; *New York Times Book Review,* December 10, 1978, November 23, 1980; *Booklist,* October 1, 1979; *Los Angeles Times,* October 14, 1979.

* * *

YORKE, Katherine
See ELLERBECK, Rosemary (Anne L'Estrange)

* * *

YOUNG, Angela
See YARDLEY, Alice

* * *

YOUNG, Ellin Dodge 1932-

PERSONAL: Born October 7, 1932, in New York, N.Y.; daughter of William (in retail spirits sales) and Sarah (Roehner) Leibowitz; married James J. Dodge, October 15, 1950 (divorced July, 1959); married John C. Young (a data processing executive), August 1, 1975; children: (first marriage) Ivy, Jeffrey. *Education:* Northeastern University, B.A., 1974. *Home:* 147 Scudder Ave., Northport, N.Y. 11768. *Agent:* Alexandria Hatcher, Alexandria Hatcher Agency, 150 West 55th St., New York, N.Y. 10019. *Office:* Young Design Group, 147 Scudder Ave., Northport, N.Y. 11768.

CAREER: Christian Dior, New York City, mannequin, 1957-60; Coin Fair (automated sundries store), New York City, conceptualizer and owner, 1960-64; Biltmore Liquors, Inc., New York City, owner and manager, 1964-72; Silva Mind Control of New York, New York City, administrative director, 1972-76; Young Design Group (a division of Young Forecasts Ltd.), Northport, N.Y. director, 1977—. Numerologist; director of a publications agency. Associated with New York City Addictions Services Agency and East Harlem Community Corp., 1966-70. Founder and member of Northport Writers Workshop, 1979—.

WRITINGS: (With Carol Schuler) *The Vibes Book: A Game of Self-Analysis,* Samuel Weiser, 1979; *Help Yourself to Understand 1981,* Samuel Weiser, 1980; (with Schuler) *8 in meer dan 1000* (title means "Eight Is More Than One Thousand"), Uitgevery Schors, 1980; (with Schuler) *Il destino nei numeri* (title means "The Destiny in Your Numbers"), La Mediterranee, 1981. Author of "The Number Game," a column in *LIRR-MTA Express,* 1976-79. Editor and publisher of *LIRR-MTA Express,* 1976-79; editor of *Long Island Sound Mariner,* 1979-80, and *Nautical News,* 1979-80.

WORK IN PROGRESS: First Name Numerology Dictionary, publication by Simon & Schuster expected in 1983 or 1984; research for French, Spanish, and Italian versions of her books; research on interpretation of one's age through numerology.

SIDELIGHTS: Ellin Young told *CA:* "Years ago, as an over-the-hill Dior mannequin, I didn't have to be psychic to know that I had to get into the security of the family retail business. It was lucrative but boring. My friends were enthusiastic about a course in Silva Mind Control and convinced me to take four days out of my life to experience the 'wonder' of it. I did find it wondrous and quit financial security for psychic whoopee. I spent four years as an administrative director for Silva Mind Control of New York and also became a professional numerologist. Finally, the numerology won, and once again I left the world of weekly paychecks to begin consulting, teaching, and writing. If labels are in order, I progressed from Marjorie Morningstar to 'the new Dovima' to your friendly-neighborhood-liquor-store-lady to spiritual awakening to now. I hate labels. *Now* is enough for me.

"I write on one subject, numerology, to disprove the beliefs of clients and students that an individual has to have a 'gift' to understand people and predict incoming experiences. I don't believe in 'gifted' readers, witches, or special psychics. Anyone can do this. I write to give people the opportunity to use a simple technique, first used by cave men. If cave men could find deeper meanings for numbers than their cumulative values, then our sophisticated society certainly should be able to as well. We are all psychics. Any form of concentration puts us in touch with the ability and brings it into our daily living experiences. I'm just out to share numerology's easy way to do it.

"The average person who glances at an astrology column will not be able to get personal answers about developing his or her own talents and understand incoming experiences. With numerology, there isn't the complex mathematical research, fraught with human error, that astrology reveals that it is when you try to learn how to get personal information. Anyone can learn numerology's insights and predictions in one sitting and, by completing the chart, increase his or her intuitive ability. After surviving most of my life with the hunt-and-peck method, then living with numerology, I gotta tell ya, I buy a lot less aspirin now!"

Z

ZAJONC, Robert Boleslaw 1923-

BRIEF ENTRY: Born November 23, 1923, in Lodz, Poland. American psychologist, educator, and author. Zajonc has taught at University of Michigan since 1955. He became a professor of psychology in 1961 and was named program director at the Research Center for Group Dynamics in 1960. His writings include *Social Psychology: An Experimental Approach* (Wadsworth, 1966) and *Animal Social Psychology: A Reader of Experimental Studies* (Wiley, 1969). *Address:* Research Center for Group Dynamics, University of Michigan, Ann Arbor, Mich. 48104.

* * *

ZAVARZADEH, Mas'ud 1938-

PERSONAL: Born May 17, 1938, in Tehran, Iran; came to United States, 1966; son of Hossein and Effat (Kaighobady) Zavarzadeh; married Teresa L. Ebert (a literary and art critic), July, 1981. *Education:* Tehran University, B.A., 1963; University of Nottingham, diploma in English studies, 1964; University of Birmingham, M.A., 1966; Indiana University, Ph.D., 1973. *Office:* Department of English, Syracuse University, Syracuse, N.Y. 13210.

CAREER: University of Oregon, Eugene, assistant professor, 1971-76, associate professor, 1976-77; Syracuse University, Syracuse, N.Y., associate professor of English, 1978—. *Member:* Modern Language Association of America, Semiotic Society of America, National Council of Teachers of English, Canadian Semiotic Research Association. *Awards, honors:* Fellowships from National Endowment for the Humanities, 1977-78, and National Humanities Center, 1981-82; *The Mythopoeic Reality* was named an outstanding book of the year by *Choice,* 1977-78.

WRITINGS: The Mythopoeic Reality: The Postwar American Nonfiction Novel, University of Illinois Press, 1977. Contributor to scholarly and literary journals, including *Chicago Review, Poetics Today,* and *Clio.*

WORK IN PROGRESS: Poetics of Innovative Fiction; a book of experimental essays.

SIDELIGHTS: Writing in the *Hudson Review,* Guy Davenport finds Mas'ud Zavarzadeh "a critic of vast talents." Zavarzadeh's book, *The Mythopoeic Reality,* was selected by *Choice* as one of the "outstanding books" of the 1977-78 publishing year because, as the "first sustained analysis of the postwar American 'nonfiction' novel," it sets a "standard all subsequent scholarship will have to meet." It was also evaluated in *American Literary Scholarship* as the "most impressive theoretical criticism of the year." According to *American Literature,* "Zavarzadeh provides a thorough analysis of the epistemological underpinnings of the nonfiction novel, offers a cogent description of its generic identity, and gives illuminating readings of a wide range of texts. . . . Zavarzadeh's book makes a significant contribution to our understanding of the relationship between the documentary novel and contemporary fiction in general, and it boldly challenges a number of widely held beliefs about generic distinctions." Robert Scholes considered *The Mythopoeic Reality* "excellent. . . . It does some hard thinking about the poetics of the form and applies its theory extensively and in the main convincingly." Zavarzadeh's theories for the interpretation of postmodern narrative were demonstrated in an essay titled "Where Do We Go From Here," by Christine Brooke-Rose, who employed his theoretical model in her analysis of contemporary narrative for a symposium on the British novel held by Cambridge University's *Granta.*

Literary theory and narratology, however, are only two of the focuses of Zavarzadeh's writing. He has also been involved in experimenting with the very form and shape of the critical essay in an attempt to develop a mode of critical writing that does not recuperate and naturalize new fiction. The author believes that postmodern fiction is a deconstructive text that refuses to totalize human experience in the logocentric terms of traditional philosophies. Such texts, he argues, require a critical response that is deconstructive not only in its thematics (which is the main concern of American critics who are domesticating continental critical theories), but also in its inventive power to deconstruct its own text. Examples of Zavarzadeh's essays (which he calls "INSCRIPticism") include "The Critic as Riot Police" in the *Chicago Review* and "The Critic as Conservator: Paracriticism and Beyond" in *Poetics Today.* His writing is considered by reviewers to parallel in some ways the later works of Roland Barthes and such texts as *Glas* by Jacques Derrida.

BIOGRAPHICAL/CRITICAL SOURCES: Hudson Review, spring, 1978; *American Literature,* March, 1978; *Choice,* March, 1978; *American Literary Scholarship,* Duke University Press, 1978; *Novel: A Forum on Fiction,* winter, 1978; *Contemporary Literature,* summer, 1979; Manfred Putz, *The Story of Identity:*

American Fiction of the Sixties, Metzler, 1979; *Comparative Literature,* summer, 1980; Ronald Weber, *Literature of Fact,* Ohio University Press, 1980; John Hellmann, *Fables of Facts: New Journalism as Fiction,* Illinois University Press, 1981.

*   *   *

ZEKMAN, Pamela (Lois) 1944-

PERSONAL: Born October 22, 1944, in Chicago, Ill.; daughter of Theodore Nathan and Lois Jane (Bernstein) Zekman; married James B. Zagel, March 8, 1970 (divorced); married Fredric Soll, November 29, 1975. *Education:* University of California, Berkeley, B.A., 1965. *Office:* WBBM-TV, 630 McClurg Ct., Chicago, Ill. 60611.

CAREER: Cook County Department of Public Aid, Chicago, Ill., social worker, 1965-66; City News Bureau, Chicago, reporter, 1966-70; *Chicago Tribune,* Chicago, reporter, 1970-75; *Chicago Sun-Times,* Chicago, reporter, 1975-81; WBBM-TV, Chicago, director of investigative team, 1981—. *Member:* Sigma Delta Chi.

AWARDS, HONORS: Pulitzer Prize, 1972, for series on vote fraud, and 1976, for series on hospital abuses; Illinois Associated Press award, 1971, for series on nursing home abuses, 1973, for series on slum landlords, 1974, for series on police brutality, 1976, for series on baby selling and for the Mirage Bar series, 1977, for series on abuses in a home for retarded children, 1979, for "The Abortion Profiteers," a series on abortion clinics, and 1980, for "The Accident Swindlers," a series on insurance fraud; Community Service award, 1972, for series on vote fraud, Public Service award, 1973, for series on slum landlords, and 1976, for series on currency exchange abuses, all from United Press International; Investigative Reporting or Distinguished Service awards, 1974, 1977, 1979, and 1980, all from Inland Press Association; National Distinguished Service award for the Mirage series and Public Service award for "The Abortion Profiteers," both 1978, both from Sigma Delta Chi; National Public Service Award, 1979, for "The Abortion Profiteers," from the Associated Press Managing Editors Association; Thomas L. Stokes Award, 1980, for "Our Toxic Timebomb," a series on illegal dumping of toxic wastes.

WRITINGS: (With Zay N. Smith) *The Mirage,* illustrated with photographs by Gene Pesek and Jim Frost, Random House, 1979.

SIDELIGHTS: Zekman won a reputation as an investigative reporter in the early 1970's for her role in several undercover investigations carried out by the *Chicago Tribune*'s investigative task force. In the first, Zekman got jobs in four nursing homes to expose the abuses to which patients in the homes were subjected. Subsequent investigations concerned police brutality, vote fraud in Chicago elections, and other scandals.

Zekman's most famous and controversial story came after she had left the *Tribune* for the *Chicago Sun-Times.* In 1977 the *Sun-Times* bought a run-down bar, the Mirage, and had Zekman and fellow reporter Zay Smith pose as a bartender and barmaid to expose the corruption of Chicago liquor-law, building, and health inspectors, many of whom accepted bribes to overlook serious violations. The series attracted national attention and won many awards, but was denied the Pulitzer Prize on ethical grounds. The Pulitzer board felt that the reporters had been guilty of entrapment, encouraging the inspectors to commit crimes they might not have committed otherwise. But L. Edward Mullins, reviewing the book based on the series, noted in *Journalism Quarterly:* "The Mirage makes the claim the

investigation was motivated by the view that deception is justified after traditional methods fail *and* the investigation is *in the public interest,* not just *of interest to the public.* It does so convincingly." The *New Yorker* called *The Mirage* "a shocking and funny story."

CA INTERVIEW

CA interviewed Pam Zekman by telephone at her office in Chicago, December 2, 1981.

CA: You worked as a social worker for the Cook County Department of Public Aid in 1965-66. Had you originally planned to be a social worker?

ZEKMAN: No, I had no life plan. I was an English major and didn't know what to do with my degree, but I knew I didn't want to teach school. I heard about the Public Aid Department, and I wanted to see if I would find social work interesting.

CA: Did you find social work interesting?

ZEKMAN: I was very interested in the aspects of it that are similar to what I do now. I was interested in working with people and trying to help people, but in the context of that agency and that job, and my education, or lack of it, in the social welfare field, I didn't feel it was a good job for me.

A lot of things I'm interested in as a journalist fall roughly into the same category of things I was working on as a social worker, however. The best example I can give you: While I was a social worker interviewing couples who wanted to adopt children, it was general knowledge around the office that certain attorneys were selling babies to some of the couples we were interviewing. But the couples lied to us, and we knew they were lying, about the amount of money they had paid the attorneys. And there was absolutely nothing we could do about it as social workers. We couldn't prove it one way or another. We also knew that the natural mothers were lying to us about what they had been promised by the attorneys, but there was nothing we could do about that either.

Five years later, as an investigative reporter, I did a series on baby selling that exposed the lawyers. Some of them lost their licenses or were indicted. One of the main lawyers involved was one I had known about while doing social work. What I'm saying is that investigative reporting can be a more effective tool for helping people than social work is. I've also done stories involving abuses in homes for retarded children and various ways the sick and elderly are abused, whether it's a nursing home series or stories on fraudulent dance studio operations, mental institutions, hospitals. . . .

CA: How did you make the switch to news reporting?

ZEKMAN: I heard about the City News Bureau and it sounded interesting. And maybe it would be the kind of work, I thought, where my English degree would pay off. So I got a job there and loved it, almost from the first day.

CA: City News Bureau is the organization depicted in the movie "The Front Page" and elsewhere. Does it resemble its fictional depictions?

ZEKMAN: Not really. It's a terrific training ground, and it's a sink-or-swim operation. The City News kid gets the roughest treatment wherever he goes, but he's also getting the best training in the country. You're out there on the street, learning the city and the people and how to put a story together.

CA: Why do the City News kids get treated the worst?

ZEKMAN: I'm talking about the cop in the station, people like that. They have to put up with ever-changing City News kids in their police station or on their beat. So they kid the new City News kids a lot. It's almost an initiation.

City News is like a local Associated Press. People who start there have almost no experience in journalism, but it's actually an operating agency that feeds local news to all the radio and television stations and newspapers in town. They send their stories out to the various outlets that actually use their pieces as leads to go on, or as backup. It's not unusual to hear your story being read over the air on a local radio station—they just rip and read. It's a training ground where there's actual on-the-job training.

CA: You mentioned that some of your ideas for stories came from your experiences at the Department of Public Aid. Where do your other story ideas originate?

ZEKMAN: They come from complaints that come in, or they come from instinct about something you just hear about—you think there might be a story there. Sometimes they're assigned by editors. I've only had a couple of those. And once in a while someone walks in off the street who's had something happen to him that gives you an idea for a possible story.

CA: What was your most satisfying story?

ZEKMAN: I haven't got a "most." I've got a few of them that I'm especially proud of. I was very proud of the series we did [in 1974] on police brutality when I was at the *Tribune*. The subject was very difficult, but we had five people working on it and we documented about forty-five cases of really terrible abuse. The Mirage series, the insurance fraud series, and the abortion clinic abuses series were also very satisfying.

CA: Which story of yours caused the greatest impact, the most actual change in the world?

ZEKMAN: Well, there are a couple there, too. But if you want to talk about clean, clear-cut change, one of the series that I shared a Pulitzer Prize for, the hospital abuses series, exposed medical abuses and fraud at two hospitals. One hospital was closed, and one was taken over by new owners.

As the result of a story on currency exchange abuses [in 1976], a grand jury indicted seventeen currency exchange association officers who also owned currency exchanges, their chief lobbyist and general counsel, and eventually the director of the Department of Financial Institutions. The indictment charged more than ten years of corruption involving a slush fund the association used to manipulate legislators, legislation, and regulation of their industry.

It was a tough subject to make interesting. Currency exchanges are peculiar to Illinois, and there are hundreds of them in the state. The exchanges are mainly check-cashing services. They charge for check cashing, and they make the most money in poor neighborhoods cashing welfare checks. They charge a percentage of whatever they cash; the abuses involve how much they charge for their services and the regulation or lack of regulation of their activities. This was an industry that had long been infamous in Illinois as one of the strongest, toughest, most corrupt lobbying groups in Springfield, but no one had ever done a real story on what that power meant and how it affected people. More than half of the people indicted were convicted; some of them became witnesses for the government. I think we changed the industry's method of operation.

As a result of the Mirage Bar series, numerous people were indicted for income tax evasion, the city created an agency to investigate corruption, and the state of Illinois set up a special unit in the Department of Revenue, which, so far, has found ten million dollars in additional tax liabilities due from small businesses. Assuming they collect that money, we've brought ten million dollars into the state coffers.

CA: What were some of the hospital abuses your series on that subject uncovered?

ZEKMAN: In one hospital they were doing unnecessary surgery on an assembly-line basis, particularly on children. If one kid had a cold, the doctor would haul in all ten kids in the family and take out all their tonsils. He made a lot of money off public aid that way. In the other hospital, they were running an alcoholic treatment program that was nothing but a revolving door. They were making payoffs to the managers of skid-row flophouses to refer tenants to the hospital for what amounted to a five-day drying-out period. The hospital would knock them out and let them sleep for five days, and give them no treatment at all. Some of them had been back many times because it was a place to sleep, the food was better than they were used to, and public aid was footing the bill.

CA: Were there any stories that disappointed you, that didn't work out as well as you had planned?

ZEKMAN: I haven't had any major disappointments, thank goodness. I spend an awful lot of time in preliminary work on a subject before I really commit myself to it. So by the time I'm telling an editor, "Look, this is what I want to look into," I already know pretty well that there's something there to be found. So I haven't had a lot of official failures, but I had a lot of subjects I did unofficial research on that didn't pan out. I'm not going to tell you what they were, because some of them may pan out someday. They're stories that I think are there but on which we just didn't get enough information to be able to work on them full time.

CA: Did receiving the Pulitzer Prizes affect your career at all? Did you get any reaction one way or another from your colleagues?

ZEKMAN: Right or wrong, the Pulitzer gives you stature in this business, although it shouldn't carry any more stature than the other national awards given out by journalistic groups. Sigma Delta Chi [the Society of Professional Journalists] has a national award that is in some ways more prestigious because the entries are judged a little better.

CA: Did it bother you not getting the Pulitzer for the Mirage story?

ZEKMAN: Sure, it bothered me, but I have long been mystified by many of the choices the Pulitzer people make. I have won it for stories that in my wildest dreams I didn't think would win. I never thought the hospital series was going to win a Pulitzer Prize. And we did the police brutality series, one of the best series I ever worked on, which we didn't get a prize for, long before one of the eastern papers did a similar series and got a Pulitzer for it.

CA: The dispute among the Pulitzer people about whether or not to award a Pulitzer to the Mirage story revolved around the issue of entrapment. What do you think of the argument that the Mirage story involved entrapment?

ZEKMAN: It didn't. I don't think they understand what entrapment is. I'd like to hear their definition. Legally, we can't commit entrapment. We're journalists, not cops. But we didn't want to hide behind that. So we took the definition of entrapment that the police use and were even more cautious than cops have to be. The legal definition of entrapment is inducing someone to do something he wouldn't normally be inclined to do, which does not mean you can't set up a bar, or become an Arab sheik, or open a store in skid row and buy stolen goods, or all the other things that the FBI has done. You can create the situation for things to happen, you can open a bar, and then you have to let things happen that would normally happen, and that's what we did. We opened the bar, but we didn't induce those inspectors to do anything they hadn't done before. The fact of the matter is that a lot of inspectors did not ask for money or want money. We never said to them, "Can we give you fifty dollars to forget this [building code violation]?" And even that wouldn't have been entrapment. Under entrapment rules cops can say that, they can go to drug dealers and say, "Can you sell me some of this?" and the convictions of the drug dealers are upheld. We didn't even go that far. We could have, but we didn't.

CA: You and Zay Smith wrote that book about the Mirage Bar. . . .

ZEKMAN: Zay wrote it. I just cheered him along. He took a leave of absence to write the book. I had input, but he's the author.

CA: Did you have any conceptual problems in writing The Mirage?

ZEKMAN: Yes, because the story had been told before. We had done the series, so none of it was new. It was difficult for Zay as a writer not to write the whole series over again, but to write the story of what happened and to reconstruct all of our difficulties in putting the project together. We had to blend the story itself with the story of working on it. It's easy to sit around and tell war stories about what you went through to do a series, but it's another thing to write a book about it.

CA: Did helping to write The Mirage *make you enthusiastic about writing any more books?*

ZEKMAN: Me? No. The reason you see two names on all the stories I do is that I don't write them. I write straight news stories, but I haven't written any of the long projects. I'm not a very good writer. And many terrific investigative stories have fallen on their faces because, although they were terrific investigations, they bored the readers. For some reason investigative reporters tend to be dry writers. I think maybe we get too close to the facts and feel this need to be real factual and official sounding, and can't tell the story in a way that makes it interesting. I have always believed in bringing a strong writer into these projects so all that work won't be wasted.

CA: What was the general reaction to The Mirage?

ZEKMAN: I don't think it sold very well. I think they put a lot of them in the Chicago area on the theory that that's where they would sell, but I think that theory was wrong, because people in Chicago had heard enough about the Mirage already. Some people thought it was delightful, wonderful reading, because Zay's got a wonderful touch. You can't have a light touch for a series about mental health abuses, but with the Mirage there were some very humorous things that happened. It was a unique style of writing for an investigative reporter.

I mean, there was some stuff in it which just made people laugh out loud. And that usually doesn't happen in investigative stories.

CA: Do you think the quality and quantity of investigative reporting in this country is as high as it used to be?

ZEKMAN: Yes. I definitely do. People aren't knocking down presidents every year—you can't do that every year. But I think that the areas they're getting into, especially television. . . . The three-hour broadcast that Pierre Salinger did on the Iranian hostage affair was phenomenal. Tracking the whole history of the fouled-up negotiations.

CA: Why have you moved to television?

ZEKMAN: TV people have been talking to me about moving to television for several years, ever since the Mirage. And I ignored what they were saying. But lately they made the offer a little bit tough to refuse, because they said I could do everything I do at the newspaper, just do it for television. I could have the time I need, the staff I need. I thought it would be a challenge to see if I could do investigative reporting on television, and it offers me something new to learn, a new medium. I think, also, that in a lot of ways television can have a greater impact than newspapers.

CA: Has WBBM-TV done investigative reporting before?

ZEKMAN: It has done some investigative stories. Individuals have done some, but they never had a full-time team, and the other two stations do have teams. So now Chicago has three television stations and two newspapers with full-time investigative teams.

CA: You mentioned you were hiring members of an investigative team for WBBM. You were also in charge of the team that did the series on hospital abuses for the Chicago Sun-Times, *and you were part of the team that did the vote-fraud series for the* Chicago Tribune. *What's your opinion of team reporting?*

ZEKMAN: That's all I do.

CA: What's the advantage of team reporting?

ZEKMAN: You're able to tackle huge subjects from a lot of different angles in a reasonable time period.

CA: A lot of people seem to be critical of team reporting. They think reporters should work alone.

ZEKMAN: You don't see many people doing team reporting because a lot of people in this business have very big egos. That's one of the characteristics that makes them good reporters. They don't like to share stories, and they don't work well with people. It requires a very special ability to be able to work well with other people as a unit and not be in competition with each other. But one reporter could not have done the Mirage Bar series. One reporter could not have done a series of stories on insurance fraud that wound up naming ten lawyers, six hospitals, seven chiropractors, and eight physicians. We had been to all of them and could document it. You can't do things of that breadth on your own. You can do an investigation of one abortion clinic, but one reporter can't do every abortion clinic in the city of Chicago.

CA: Aren't there problems of coordination among team members?

ZEKMAN: That's my job as director of the team: to coordinate. There's some overlap in what they do, of course.

CA: People used to say Chicago produced so many scandals because there were so many people looking for them. Do you think there's any truth to that?

ZEKMAN: No, because I don't think they're made up. And I don't think they're oversold. They're there. I've been doing investigative reporting for twelve years, and there hasn't been that much elapsed time between stories. I've never said, "God, there's nothing to investigate."

BIOGRAPHICAL/CRITICAL SOURCES: New Yorker, April 21, 1980; *Journalism Quarterly,* summer, 1980.

—*Interview by Peter Benjaminson*

*   *   *

ZIFF, Gil 1938-

PERSONAL: Born November 5, 1938, in Bronx, N.Y.; son of Solomon (a waiter) and Sylvia (Deiner) Ziff; married Liel Lowndes, 1969 (divorced); married Sara T. Robinson, September, 1975; children: Zoe Danielle, Stefan Tsriny. *Education:* Attended Utah State University, 1958; Michigan State University, B.A., 1962. *Home and office:* 444 Central Park W., New York, N.Y. 10025. *Agent:* Ron Bernstein Agency, 200 West 58th St., New York, N.Y. 10019.

CAREER: Advertising copywriter with various agencies in New York City and in France, 1964-78; free-lance advertising copywriter in New York City, 1978—. Member of Tibet Center and Gaugues Marchais Tibetan Museum. *Military service:* U.S. Navy, on icebreaker to North and South Poles, 1962-64.

WRITINGS: Tibet, Crown, 1981.

WORK IN PROGRESS: A book on the Chinese invasion of Tibet in 1950.

SIDELIGHTS: Ziff wrote: "My original intention was to write a book from the point of view of a yeti or abominable snowman. This was in reaction to a television show, which, if memory serves (it was more than five years ago) was called 'The Monsters.' I wondered who the 'monsters' really were. The idea of men, weighed down with all sorts of technical equipment going into the Himalayas so they could fingerprint a yeti disturbed me. I guess I'm skeptical of technology.

"In any case, my research (conducted at the 42nd Street Library) led me to Tibet, and I became involved with the struggle of the Tibetan people, but I have never been to Tibet, so I suppose my Tibet is a state of mind.

"In the past, however, I did extensive traveling. I was working as an advertising copywriter in France for four years. Using France as a base, I visited many parts of Western and Eastern Europe, North Africa, and the Ivory Coast and Turkey. My naval experience also took me from the top of the world to the bottom, Antarctica."

AVOCATIONAL INTERESTS: Gourmet cooking, collecting jazz music.

BIOGRAPHICAL/CRITICAL SOURCES: Library Journal, February 1, 1981; *Newsday,* April 26, 1981.

Contemporary Authors

CUMULATIVE INDEX VOLUMES 1-106
Linda Metzger
Index Coordinator

This index includes references to all entries in the series listed below.
References in the index are identified as follows:

Volume number only—*Contemporary Authors* Original Volumes 1-106
R after number—*Contemporary Authors* Revised Volumes 1-44
CANR before number—*Contemporary Authors New Revision Series*, Volumes 1-7
CAP before number—*Contemporary Authors Permanent Series*, Volumes 1-2
CLC before number—*Contemporary Literary Criticism*, Volumes 1-21
SATA before number—*Something About the Author*, Volumes 1-27
AITN before number—*Authors in the News*, Volumes 1-2

INDEX

INDEX

INDEX

INDEX

INDEX

INDEX

INDEX

INDEX

INDEX

INDEX

INDEX

INDEX

INDEX

INDEX

INDEX

INDEX

INDEX

INDEX

INDEX

INDEX

INDEX

INDEX

INDEX

Chein, Isidor 1912- Brief entry 105
Chejne, Anwar G(eorge) 1923- 25-28R
Chekenian, Jane
See Gerard, Jane
Chekhonte, Antosha
See Chekhov, Anton (Pavlovich)
Chekhov, Anton (Pavlovich)
1860-1904 Brief entry 104
Chekhova, Olga 1897-1980 Obituary 97-100
Chekki, Dan(esh) A(yyappa) 1935- CANR-7
Earlier sketch in CA 61-64
Chelf, Carl P. 1937- 37-40R
Chelminski, Rudolph 1934- 93-96
Chelton, John
See Durst, Paul
Chelwood, Tufton Victor Hamilton 1917- 65-68
Chen, Ching-chih 1937- 106
Chen, Chung-Hwan 1906- 45-48
Chen, Jack 1908- 41-44R
Chen, Janey 1922- 73-76
Ch'en, Jerome 1921- 15-16R
Chen, Joseph Tao 1925- 37-40R
Chen, Kan 1928- 49-52
Chen, Kenneth K(uan-) S(heng) 1907- 19-20R
Chen, King C(hing) 1926- CANR-4
Earlier sketch in CA 53-56
Chen, Kuan I. 1926- 41-44R
Chen, Lincoln C(hih-ho) 1942- 49-52
Chen, Nai-Ruenn 1927- 23-24R
Chen, Philip S(tanley) 1903-1978 CANR-5
Earlier sketch in CA 9-10R
Chen, Samuel Shih-Tsai 1915- 41-44R
Chen, Theodore Hsi-En 1902- CANR-1
Earlier sketch in CA 2R
Chen, Tony 1929- 37-40R
See also SATA 6
Chen, Vincent 1917- 37-40R
Chen, Yuan-tsung 1932- 106
Chenault, Lawrence R(oyce) 1897- CAP-2
Earlier sketch in CA 17-18
Chenault, Nell
See Smith, Linell Nash
Chenery, Janet (Dai) 1923- 103
See also SATA 25
Chenery, William Ludlow 1884-1974 97-100
Obituary 53-56
Chenevix Trench, Charles Pocklington
1914- 9-10R
Cheney, Anne 1944- 61-64
Cheney, Brainard (Bartwell) 1900- CAP-2
Earlier sketch in CA 25-28
Cheney, Cora 1916- CANR-4
Earlier sketch in CA 3R
See also SATA 3
Cheney, Frances Neel 1906- 33-36R
Cheney, Lois A. 1931- 29-32R
Cheney, Lynne 1941- 89-92
Cheney, Margaret 1921- 101
Cheney, Roberta Carkeek 1912- 73-76
Cheney, Sheldon Warren
1886-1980 Obituary 102
Cheney, Ted
See Cheney, Theodore Albert
Cheney, Theodore A. Rees
See Cheney, Theodore Albert
Cheney, Theodore Albert 1928- 61-64
See also SATA 11
Cheney, Thomas E. 1901- 41-44R
Cheney-Coker, Syl 1945- 101
Cheng, Chu-yuan 1927- CANR-5
Earlier sketch in CA 15-16R
Cheng, F.T.
See Cheng, Tien-hsi
Cheng, Hang-Sheng 1927- 69-72
Cheng, Hou-Tien 1944- 69-72
Cheng, J(ames) Chester 1926- 9-10R
Cheng, James K(uo) C(hiang) 1936- 25-28R
Cheng, Ronald Ye-lin 1933- 41-44R
Cheng, Tien-hsi 1884-1970 Obituary 104
Cheng, Yi
See Cheng, James K(uo) C(hiang)
Cheng, Ying-wan 41-44R
Chen Hwei
See Stevenson, William
Chen Jo-hsi
See Tuann, Lucy H(siu-mei Chen)
Chennault, Anna (Chan) 1925- 61-64
Chennells, Roy D. 1912(?)-1981 Obituary 105
Chenneviere, Daniel
See Rudhyar, Dane
Chenoweth, Vida S. 1928- 25-28R
Cheraskin, Emanuel 1916- 53-56
Cherim, Stanley M(arshall) 1929- 53-56
Cherington, Paul Whiton 1918-1974 CANR-6
Obituary 53-56
Earlier sketch in CA 4R
Chermayeff, Ivan 1932- 97-100
Chermayeff, Serge 1900- 21-22R
Chernaik, Judith 1934- 61-64
Chernev, Irving 1900-1981 Obituary 105
Cherniavsky, Michael
1923(?)-1973 Obituary 41-44R
Cherniss, Harold 1904- 93-96
Cherniss, Michael D(avid) 1940- 37-40R
Chernoff, Dorothy A.
See Ernst, (Lyman) John
Chernoff, Goldie Taub 1909- 33-36R
See also SATA 10
Chernoff, John Miller 1947- 105
Chernofsky, Jacob L. 1928- 73-76
Chernow, Carol 1934- 57-60
Chernow, Fred B. 1932- 57-60
Chernowitz, Maurice E.
1909-1977 Obituary 73-76
Cherrington, Ernest H(urst), Jr. 1909- 33-36R
Cherrington, Leon G. 1926- 33-36R
Cherry, C. Conrad 1937- 23-24R
Cherry, Caroline L(ockett) 1942- 57-60
Cherry, Charles L(ester) 1942- 57-60
Cherry, Colin 1914-1979 69-72
Obituary 93-96
Cherry, George Loy 1905- 5-6R
Cherry, Kelly CANR-3
Earlier sketch in CA 49-52
See also AITN 1
Cherry, Sheldon H(arold) 1934- 49-52
Cherryh, C(arolyn) J(anice) 1942- 65-68
Cherryholmes, Anne
See Price, Olive
Chervin, Ronda 1937- CANR-6
Earlier sketch in CA 57-60
Cherwinski, Joseph 1915- CANR-5
Earlier sketch in CA 15-16R
Chesbro, George C(lark) 1940- 77-80
Chesen, Eli S. 1944- 37-40R
Chesham, Henry
See Bingley, David Ernest
Chesham, Sallie 29-32R
Chesher, Kim 1955- 102
Chesher, Richard (Harvey) 1940- 106
Cheshire, David 1944- 97-100
Cheshire, Geoffrey Leonard 1917- CAP-1
Earlier sketch in CA 13-14
Cheskin, Louis 1909-1981 CANR-5
Obituary 105
Earlier sketch in CA 5-6R
Chesler, Bernice 1932- 25-28R
Chesler, Phyllis 1940- CANR-4
Earlier sketch in CA 49-52
Cheslock, Louis 1898- CAP-1
Earlier sketch in CA 11-12
Chesney, Inga L. 1928- 45-48
Chesney, Kellow (Robert) 1914- 29-32R
Chesnoff, Richard Z. 1937- 25-28R
Chesnut, J(ames) Stanley 1926- 23-24R
Chesnutt, Charles Waddell
1858-1932 Brief entry 106
Chess, Stella 1914- 85-88
Chesser, Eustace 1902-1973 CANR-4
Obituary 45-48
Earlier sketch in CA 9-10R
Chessex, Jacques 1934- 65-68
Chessman, Caryl (Whittier) 1921-1960 73-76
Chessman, G(eorge) Wallace 1919- 15-16R
Chessman, Ruth (Green) 1910- CAP-2
Earlier sketch in CA 17-18
Chester, Alfred 1929(?)-1971 Obituary 33-36R
Chester, Deborah 1957- 102
Chester, Edward W(illiam) 1935- 23-24R
Chester, Laura 1949- 65-68
Chester, Michael (Arthur) 1928- CANR-1
Earlier sketch in CA 3R
Chester, Peter
See Phillips, D(ennis) J(ohn Andrew)
Chesterton, A(rthur) K(enneth) 1899- CAP-1
Earlier sketch in CA 11-12
Chesterton, G(ilbert) K(eith)
1874-1936 Brief entry 104
Chestor, Rui
See Courtier, S(idney) H(obson)
Chetham-Strode, Warren 1896- CAP-1
Earlier sketch in CA 13-14
Chethimattam, John B(ritto) 1922- 25-28R
Chetin, Helen 1922- 29-32R
See also SATA 6
Chetwode, Penelope 1910- 102
Chetwynd, Berry
See Rayner, Claire
Chetwynd, Tom 1938- 45-48
Chetwynd-Hayes, R(onald Henry Glynn)
1919- 61-64
Cheung, Steven N(g-) S(heong) 1935- 25-28R
Cheuse, Alan 1940- 49-52
Chevalier, Haakon (Maurice) 1902- 61-64
Chevalier, Louis 1911- 85-88
Chevalier, Maurice 1888-1972 Obituary 33-36R
Chevalier, Paul Eugene George 1925- 106
Chevallier, Raymond 1929- 103
Chevigny, Bell Gale 1936- 57-60
Chevigny, Paul G. 1935- 97-100
Cheville, Roy A(rthur) 1897- 97-100
Chew, Allen F. 1924- 33-36R
Chew, Peter 1924- 57-60
Chew, Ruth 1920- 41-44R
See also SATA 7
Cheyette, Irving 1904- 69-72
Cheyney, Arnold B. 1926- 23-24R
Chi, Madeleine 1930- 69-72
Chi, Richard Hu See-Yee 1918- 37-40R
Chi, Wen-shun 1910- 13-14R
Chiang Yee 1903-1977 65-68
Obituary 73-76
Chiara, Piero 1913- 53-56
Chiari, Joseph 1911- CANR-4
Earlier sketch in CA 7-8R
Chiaromonte, Nicola ?-1972 Obituary 104
Chibnall, Marjorie (McCallum) 1915- 29-32R
Chicago, Judy 1939- 85-88
Chichester, Francis (Charles) 1901-1972 CAP-1
Obituary 37-40R
Earlier sketch in CA 13-14
Chichester, Jane
See Longrigg, Jane Chichester
Chick, Edson M(arland) 1924- 23-24R
Chickering, Arthur W. 1927- 29-32R
Chickering, Roger (Philip) 1942- 73-76
Chickos, James Speros 1941- 49-52
Chicorel, Marietta 85-88
Chidsey, Donald Barr 1902-1981 CANR-2
Obituary 103
Earlier sketch in CA 5-6R
See also SATA 3, 27
Chidzero, Bernard Thomas Gibson 1927- 3R
Chielens, Edward E(rnest) 1943- 53-56
Ch'ien, Ts'un-hsun
See Tsien, Tsuen-hsuin
Chiesa, Francesco 1871(?)-1973 Obituary 104
Chignon, Niles
See Lingeman, Richard R(oberts)
Chigounis, Evans 1931- 45-48
Chilcote, Ronald H. 1935- 21-22R
Chilcott, John H(enry) 1924- 41-44R
Child, Heather 1912- 11-12R
Child, Irvin L(ong) 1915- 41-44R
Child, John 1922- 93-96
Child, Julia 1912- 41-44R
Child, Philip 1898-1978 CAP-1
Earlier sketch in CA 13-14
See also CLC 19
Child, Roderick 1949- 25-28R
Childers, Thomas (Allen) 1940- 37-40R
Childress, Alice 1920- CANR-3
Earlier sketch in CA 45-48
See also CLC 12, 15
See also SATA 7
Childress, James Franklin 1940- 65-68
Childress, William 1933- 41-44R
Childs, Barney 1926- 23-24R
Childs, C. Sand
See Childs, Maryanna
Childs, David (Haslam) 1933- 37-40R
Childs, H(alla) Fay (Cochrane) 1890-1971 CAP-1
Earlier sketch in CA 15-16
See also SATA 1, 25
Childs, Harwood Lawrence 1898-1972 CAP-2
Obituary 37-40R
Earlier sketch in CA 25-28
Childs, James Bennett
1896-1977 Obituary 73-76
Childs, Marilyn Grace Carlson 1923- 9-10R
Childs, Marquis W(illiam) 1903- 61-64
Childs, Maryanna 1910- 9-10R
Childs, Timothy 1941- 97-100
Chiles, Robert E(ugene) 1923- 17-18R
Chill, Dan S(amuel) 1945- 69-72
Chilson, Richard William 1943- CANR-6
Earlier sketch in CA 57-60
Chilson, Robert 1945- 69-72
Chilton, Irma 1930- 103
Chilton, John (James) 1932- 61-64
Chilton, Shirley R(ay) 1923- 77-80
Chilver, Peter 1933- 25-28R
Chimaera
See Farjeon, Eleanor
Chin, Chuan
See Chi, Richard Hu See-Yee
Chin, Frank (Chew, Jr.) 1940- 33-36R
Chin, Robert 1918- 61-64
Chinard, Gilbert 1882(?)-1972 Obituary 104
Chinas, Beverly N(ewbold) 1924- 89-92
Chinery, Michael 1938- 103
See also SATA 26
Ching, James C(hristopher) 1926- 37-40R
Ching, Julia (Chia-yi) 1934- 101
Chinitz, Benjamin 1924- 9-10R
Chinmoy, Sri 1931- CANR-2
Earlier sketch in CA 49-52
Chinn, Laurene Chambers 1902-1978 2R
Obituary 103
Chinn, Robert (Edward) 1928- 69-72
Chinn, William G. 1919- 33-36R
Chinoy, Ely 1921-1975 CANR-1
Obituary 57-60
Earlier sketch in CA 3R
Chinoy, Helen Krich 1922- 17-18R
Chinweizu 1943- 103
Chipman, Bruce L(ewis) 1946- 37-40R
Chipman, Donald E(ugene) 1928- 29-32R
Chipman, John S(omerset) 1926- 104
Chipp, Herschel B(rowning) 1913- 25-28R
Chipperfield, Joseph Eugene
1912-1980(?) CANR-6
Earlier sketch in CA 9-10R
See also SATA 2
Chirenje, J. Mutero 1935- 65-68
Chirovsky, Nicholas L. 1919- CANR-4
Earlier sketch in CA 53-56
Chisholm, A(lan) R(owland) 1888- 7-8R
Chisholm, Hugh J., Jr.
1913-1972 Obituary 37-40R
Chisholm, K. Lomneth 1919- 61-64
Chisholm, Mary K(athleen) 1924- 37-40R
Chisholm, Matt
See Watts, Peter Christopher
Chisholm, Michael (Donald Inglis) 1931- 37-40R
Chisholm, R(obert) F(erguson) 1904- CAP-2
Earlier sketch in CA 29-32
Chisholm, Roderick Milton 1916- 102
Chisholm, Roger K. 1937- 33-36R
Chisholm, Sam(uel) Whitten 1919- 5-6R
Chisholm, Shirley (Anita St. Hill) 1924- 29-32R
Chisholm, William S(herman), Jr. 1931- 49-52
Chisolm, Lawrence W(ashington) 1929- 11-12R
Chissell, Joan Olive 61-64
Chitham, Edward (Harry Gordon) 1932- 103
Chitrabhanu, Gurudev Shree 1922- 89-92
Chittenden, Elizabeth F. 1903- 61-64
See also SATA 9
Chittenden, Margaret 1935- CANR-4
Earlier sketch in CA 53-56
Chittick, William O(liver) 1937- 41-44R
Chittum, Ida 1918- 37-40R
See also SATA 7
Chitty, Arthur Benjamin 1914- CANR-4
Earlier sketch in CA 53-56
Chitty, Susan Elspeth 1929- CAP-1
Earlier sketch in CA 9-10
Chitty, Thomas Willes 1926- 7-8R
See also CLC 11
Chitwood, B(illy) J(ames) 1931- 97-100
Chitwood, Marie Downs 1918- 9-10R
Chitwood, Oliver Perry 1874-1971 CAP-1
Earlier sketch in CA 13-14
Chiu, Hong-Yee 1932- 53-56
Chiu, Hungdah 1936- 37-40R
Chi-wei
See Shu, Austin Chi-wei
Chlamyda, Jehudil
See Peshkov, Alexei Maximovich
Chmaj, Betty E. 1930- 97-100
Chmielewski, Edward 1928- 13-14R
Ch'O, Chou
See Shu-Jen, Chou
Cho, Yong Hyo 1934- Brief entry 105
Cho, Yong Sam 1925- 5-6R
Choate, Ernest A(lfred) 1900- 49-52
Choate, Gwen Peterson 1922- 3R
Choate, J(ulian) E(rnest, Jr.) 1916- 33-36R
Choate, Judith (Newkirk) 1940- 105
Choate, R. G.
See Choate, Gwen Peterson
Chochlik
See Radwanski, Pierre A(rthur)
Chodes, John 1939- 61-64
Chodorov, Edward 1904- 102
Chodorov, Jerome 1911- 65-68
Chodorov, Stephan 1934- 17-18R
Chodorow, Nancy (Julia) 1944- 105
Choleric, Brother
See van Zeller, Claud
Chomette, Rene Lucien
1898-1981 Obituary 103
See also CLC 20
Chommie, John C(ampbell) 1914-1974 CAP-2
Earlier sketch in CA 29-32
Chomsky, A(vram) Noam 1928- 17-18R
Chomsky, William 1896-1977 77-80
Obituary 73-76
Chong, Kyona-Jo
See Chung, Kyuna Cho
Chong, Peng-Khuan 25-28R
Choper, Jesse H(erbert) 1935- CANR-5
Earlier sketch in CA 15-16R
Chopin, Kate (O'Flaherty)
1851-1904 Brief entry 104
Chorafas, Dimitris N. 1926- CANR-4
Earlier sketch in CA 7-8R
Chorao, (Ann Mc)Kay (Sproat) 1936- CANR-1
Earlier sketch in CA 49-52
See also SATA 8
Chorny, Merron 1922- 41-44R
Choron, Jacques 1904-1972 CAP-1
Obituary 33-36R
Earlier sketch in CA 9-10
Chothia, Jean 1944- 105
Chotzinoff, Samuel 1889-1964 Obituary 93-96
Chou, Ya-luu 1924- 41-44R
Choucri, Nazli 1943- 81-84
Choudhury, G. W. 1926- 25-28R
Choukas, Michael (Eugene) 1901- CAP-2
Earlier sketch in CA 17-18
Chouraqui, Andre (Nathanael) 1917- 65-68
Chow, Gregory C. 1929- 13-14R
Chow, Yung-Teh 1916- 37-40R
Chowder, Ken 1950- 103
Chowdhary, Savitri Devi (Dumra) 1907- CAP-1
Earlier sketch in CA 11-12
Choy, Bong-youn 1914- 69-72
Chrimes, Stanley Bertram 1907- 7-8R
Chrislock, Carl H(endrick) 1917- 45-48
Chrisman, Harry E. 1906- 4R
Christ, Carl F(inley) 1923- 21-22R
Christ, Carol T(ecla) 1944- 93-96
Christ, Henry I(rvine) 1915- CANR-2
Earlier sketch in CA 7-8R
Christ, John M(ichael) 1934- 106
Christ, Ronald 1936- 25-28R
Christensen, Clyde M. 1905- 53-56
Christensen, David E(mun) 1921- 15-16R
Christensen, Edward L. 1913- 25-28R
Christensen, Eleanor Ingalls 1913- 53-56
Christensen, Erwin O(ttomar) 1890- CAP-1
Earlier sketch in CA 13-14
Christensen, Francis 1902-19(?) CAP-2
Earlier sketch in CA 23-24
Christensen, Gardell Dano 1907- 9-10R
See also SATA 1
Christensen, Harold T(aylor) 1909- 45-48
Christensen, J(ack) A(rden) 1927- 53-56
Christensen, James L(ee) 1922- 97-100
Christensen, Jo Ippolito
See Christensen, Yolanda Maria Ippolito
Christensen, Otto H(enry) 1898- 33-36R
Christensen, Paul 1943- 77-80
Christensen, Yolanda Marie Ippolito 1943- CANR-7
Earlier sketch in CA 57-60
Christenson, Cornelia V(os) 1903- CAP-2
Earlier sketch in CA 33-36
Christenson, Larry 1928- 57-60
Christenson, Reo M. 1918- 37-40R
Christesen, Clement Byrne 1911- 102
Christgau, Alice Erickson 1902- CAP-2
Earlier sketch in CA 17-18
See also SATA 13
Christgau, John (Frederick) 1934- 103
Christgau, Robert (Thomas) 1942- 65-68
Christian, A. B.
See Yabes, Leopoldo Y(abes)
Christian, C(urtis) W(allace) 1927- 21-22R
Christian, Carol (Cathay) 1923- 53-56
Christian, Frederick
See Gehman, Richard (Boyd)
Christian, Garth Hood 1921-1967 CAP-1
Earlier sketch in CA 9-10
Christian, George (Eastland) 1927- 65-68
Christian, Henry A(rthur) 1931- 33-36R
Christian, James L(ee) 1927- 57-60
Christian, Jill
See Dilcock, Noreen
Christian, John
See Dixon, Roger
Christian, Louise
See Grill, Nannette L.
Christian, Marcus Bruce 1900- 73-76

INDEX

INDEX

INDEX

INDEX

D

INDEX

INDEX

INDEX

INDEX

INDEX

INDEX

INDEX

INDEX

INDEX

INDEX

INDEX

INDEX

INDEX

INDEX

INDEX

INDEX

INDEX

INDEX

INDEX

INDEX

INDEX

INDEX

INDEX

INDEX

INDEX

INDEX

INDEX

INDEX

INDEX

INDEX

INDEX

INDEX

INDEX

INDEX

INDEX

INDEX

INDEX

M

INDEX

INDEX

INDEX

INDEX

INDEX

INDEX

INDEX

INDEX

INDEX

INDEX

INDEX

INDEX

INDEX

INDEX

INDEX

INDEX

INDEX

INDEX

INDEX

INDEX

INDEX

Richard, Olga 1914- ... 103
Richards, Alfred (Luther) 1939- ... 45-48
Richards, Allen
See Rosenthal, Richard A.
Richards, Alun 1929- ... 65-68
Richards, Arlene Kramer 1935- ... 65-68
Richards, Audrey I(sabel) 1899- ... 23-24R
Richards, Blair P(atton) 1940- ... 69-72
Richards, Cara E(lizabeth) 1927- ... CANR-1
Earlier sketch in CA 49-52
Richards, Carl Edward, Jr. 1933- ... 45-48
Richards, Caroline 1939- ... 77-80
Richards, Charles
See Marvin, John T.
Richards, Clay
See Crossen, Kendell Foster
Richards, David
See Bickers, Richard Leslie Townshend
Richards, David Adams 1950- ... 93-96
Richards, Denis (George) 1910- ... 11-12R
Richards, Dennis L(ee) 1938- ... 102
Richards, Dorothy B(urney) 1894- ... 85-88
Richards, Duane
See Hurley, Vic
Richards, Frank
See Hamilton, Charles Harold St. John
Richards, Fred
See Richards, Alfred (Luther)
Richards, Guy 1905-1979 ... 61-64
Obituary ... 81-84
Richards, H(arold) M(arshall) S(ylvester)
1894- ... CAP-2
Earlier sketch in CA 23-24
Richards, Hilda
See Hamilton, Charles Harold St. John
Richards, Horace G(ardiner) 1906- ... 5-6R
Richards, I(vor) A(rmstrong) 1893-1979 . 41-44R
Obituary ... 89-92
See also CLC 14
Richards, J(ohn) Howard 1916- ... CANR-2
Earlier sketch in CA 45-48
Richards, J(ames) M(aude) 1907- ... CANR-5
Earlier sketch in CA 5-6R
Richards, Jack W(esley) 1933- ... 33-36R
Richards, James O(lin) 1936- ... 37-40R
Richards, Jane 1934- ... 33-36R
Richards, Jeffrey (Michael) 1945- ... 73-76
Richards, Joe 1909- ... CAP-1
Earlier sketch in CA 9-10
Richards, John 1939- ... 57-60
Richards, John Marvin 1929- ... 15-16R
Richards, Kay
See Baker, Susan (Catherine)
Richards, Kenny
See Broderick, Richard L(awrence)
Richards, Kent David 1938- ... 104
Richards, Larry
See Richards, Lawrence O.
Richards, Lawrence O. 1931- ... 29-32R
Richards, Lewis A(lva) 1925- ... 45-48
Richards, Martin P(aul) M(eredith) 1940- .. 61-64
Richards, Max D(eVoe) 1923- ... 23-24R
Richards, Nat
See Richardson, James Nathaniel
Richards, Peter
See Monger, (Ifor) David
Richards, Phyllis
See Auty, Phyllis
Richards, R(onald) C(harles) W(illiam)
1923- ... 21-22R
Richards, Stanley 1918-1980 ... 25-28R
Obituary ... 101
Richards, Victor 1918- ... 57-60
Richardson, Alan 1923- ... 29-32R
Richardson, Anne
See Roiphe, Anne Richardson
Richardson, Arleta 1923- ... 93-96
Richardson, Beth
See Gutcheon, Beth R(ichardson)
Richardson, Betty 1935- ... 53-56
Richardson, Bradley M. 1928- ... 49-52
Richardson, C.
See Munsey, Cecil (Richard, Jr.)
Richardson, Charles E(verett) 1928- ... 57-60
Richardson, Cyril Charles 1909-1976 ... 37-40R
Obituary ... 69-72
Richardson, Don(ald MacNaughton) 1935- . 65-68
Richardson, Dorothy Lee 1900- ... 106
Richardson, Dorothy Miller
1873-1957 Brief entry ... 104
Richardson, Dorsey 1896-1981 Obituary ... 105
Richardson, Elmo 1930- ... 13-14R
Richardson, Ethel Florence (Lindesay)
1870-1946 Brief entry ... 105
Richardson, Evelyn M(ay Fox) 1902- ... CAP-1
Earlier sketch in CA 13-14
Richardson, Frank Howard
1882-1970 Obituary ... 104
See also SATA 27
Richardson, Frank McLean 1904- ... 103
Richardson, Gayle E(lwin) 1911- ... 11-12R
Richardson, George Barclay 1924- ... 4R
Richardson, Grace Lee
See Dickson, Naida
Richardson, H(arold) Edward 1929- ... 29-32R
Richardson, Harry V(an Buren) 1901- ... 69-72
Richardson, Harry W(ard) 1938- ... 29-32R
Richardson, Henrietta
See Richardson, Ethel Florence (Lindesay)
Richardson, Henry Handel
See Richardson, Ethel Florence (Lindesay)
Richardson, Henry V(okes) M(ackey)
1923- ... 25-28R
Richardson, Howard (Dixon) 1917- ... 41-44R
Richardson, Isla Paschal 1886-1971 ... CAP-1
Earlier sketch in CA 9-10
Richardson, Ivan L(eRoy) 1920- ... 101
Richardson, Ivor Lloyd Morgan 1930- ... 11-12R
Richardson, Jack (Carter) 1935- ... 7-8R
Richardson, James 1950- ... 77-80
Richardson, James F(rancis) 1931- ... 29-32R
Richardson, James L(ongden) 1933- ... 21-22R
Richardson, James Nathaniel 1942- ... 53-56
Richardson, James R. 1911- ... 2R
Richardson, Jeremy John 1942- ... 29-32R
Richardson, Joanna ... 13-14R
Richardson, Joe Martin 1934- ... 45-48
Richardson, John Adkins 1929- ... 57-60
Richardson, John Martin, Jr. 1938- ... 33-36R
Richardson, Justin
1900(?)-1975 Obituary ... 61-64
Richardson, Kenneth Ridley 1934- ... 29-32R
Richardson, Laurence E(aton) 1893- ... CAP-1
Earlier sketch in CA 11-12
Richardson, (Stewart) Lee (Jr.) 1940- ... 21-22R
Richardson, Leopold John Dixon
1893-1979(?) Obituary ... 104
Richardson, Midge Turk 1930- ... 33-36R
Richardson, Miles (Edward) 1932- ... 33-36R
Richardson, Mozelle Groner 1914- ... 33-36R
Richardson, Neil R(yan) 1944- ... 103
Richardson, Nola 1936- ... 57-60
Richardson, Richard C(olby), Jr. 1933- ... 77-80
Richardson, Richard Judson 1935- ... 29-32R
Richardson, Robert (Dale, Jr.) 1934- ... 29-32R
Richardson, Robert Galloway 1926- ... CANR-7
Earlier sketch in CA 15-16R
Richardson, Robert S(hirley) 1902- ... 49-52
See also SATA 8
Richardson, Rupert Norval 1891- ... 19-20R
Richardson, S(tanley) D(ennis) 1925- ... 21-22R
Richardson, Stephen A. 1920- ... 61-64
Richardson, Thomas Dow 1887- ... 7-8R
Richardson, Vokes
See Richardson, Henry V(okes) M(ackey)
Richardson, W(alter) C(ecil) 1902- ... CANR-1
Earlier sketch in CA 2R
Richardson, William John 1920- ... 21-22R
Richason, Benjamin F(ranklin, Jr.) 1922- . 41-44R
Richelieu, Peter
See Robinson, P. W.
Richelson, Geraldine 1922- ... 106
Richette, Lisa Aversa 1928- ... 25-28R
Richey, David 1939- ... 57-60
Richey, Dorothy Hilliard ... CANR-6
Earlier sketch in CA 9-10R
Richey, Elinor 1920- ... 45-48
Richey, Margaret Fitzgerald
1883(?)-1974 Obituary ... 53-56
Richey, Robert W. 1912- ... 25-28R
Richey, Russell Earle 1941- ... 69-72
Richie, Donald (Steiner) 1924- ... 19-20R
Richland, W(ilfred) Bernard 1909- ... 102
Richler, Mordecai 1931- ... 65-68
See also CLC 3, 5, 9, 13, 18
See also SATA 27
See also AITN 1
Richman, Barry M. 1936- ... 23-24R
Richman, Milton 1922- ... 69-72
Richman, Phyllis C. 1939- ... 89-92
Richman, Saul 1917(?)-1979 Obituary ... 85-88
Rich-McCoy, Lois 1941- ... 101
Richmond, Al 1913- ... 41-44R
Richmond, Anthony H(enry) 1925- ... 23-24R
Richmond, Dick 1933- ... 61-64
Richmond, Grace
See Marsh, John
Richmond, H(ugh) M(acrae) 1932- ... CANR-3
Earlier sketch in CA 9-10R
Richmond, John C(hristopher) B(lake)
1909- Brief entry ... 106
Richmond, Julius B(enjamin) 1916- ... 29-32R
Richmond, Lee 1943- ... 49-52
Richmond, Leigh (Tucker) 1911- ... 23-24R
Richmond, Robert P. 1914- ... 21-22R
Richmond, Robert W(illiam) 1927- ... 53-56
Richmond, Rod
See Glut, Donald F(rank)
Richmond, Samuel B(ernard) 1919- ... 41-44R
Richmond, (John) Stanley 1906- ... 45-48
Richmond, Velma E. B(ourgeois) 1931- ... 61-64
Richmond, W(illiam) Kenneth 1910- ... 25-28R
Richmond, Walt(er F.) 1922- ... 23-24R
Richoux, Pat(ricia) 1927- ... 25-28R
See also SATA 7
Richter, Alice 1941- ... 105
Richter, Conrad (Michael) 1890-1968 ... 7-8R
Obituary ... 25-28R
See also SATA 3
Richter, David H. 1945- ... 101
Richter, Derek 1907- ... 101
Richter, Dorothy 1906- ... 29-32R
Richter, Gerard R(ichard) 1905- ... 5-6R
Richter, Gisela M(arie) A(ugusta)
1882-1972 ... CANR-4
Earlier sketch in CA 7-8R
Richter, Hans 1888-1976 ... 73-76
Obituary ... 65-68
Richter, Hans Peter 1925- ... CANR-2
Earlier sketch in CA 45-48
See also SATA 6
Richter, Hans Werner 1908- ... 97-100
Richter, Harvena 1919- ... CANR-3
Earlier sketch in CA 7-8R
Richter, Horst-Eberhard 1923- ... CANR-5
Earlier sketch in CA 53-56
Richter, Irving 1911- ... 57-60
Richter, J. H(ans) 1901- ... CAP-1
Earlier sketch in CA 15-16
Richter, Joan 1930- ... 101
Richter, Lin 1936- ... 73-76
Richter, Maurice N(athaniel), Jr. 1930- ... 49-52
Richter, Valentin
See Pick, Robert
Richter, Vernon
See Hutchcroft, Vera
Rickard, Bob
See Rickard, Robert J(ohn) M(oberley)
Rickard, Robert J(ohn) M(oberley) 1945- ... 106
Rickards, Colin (William) 1937- ... 25-28R
Rickards, Maurice 1919- ... 103
Rickels, Karl 1924- ... CANR-1
Earlier sketch in CA 45-48
Rickels, Milton H. 1920- ... 5-6R
Rickenbacker, Eddie
See Rickenbacker, Edward Vernon
Rickenbacker, Edward Vernon 1890-1973 ... 101
Obituary ... 41-44R
Ricker, George Marvin 1922- ... 89-92
Rickert, Corinne Holt
See Sawyer, Corinne Holt
Rickert, John E. 1923- ... 45-48
Rickett, Harold William 1896- ... 19-20R
Ricketts, C(arl) E(verett) 1906- ... 57-60
Ricketts, Viva Leone (Harris) 1900- ... CAP-1
Earlier sketch in CA 11-12
Rickey, Don, Jr. 1925- ... 7-8R
Rickey, George Warren 1907- ... 65-68
Rickey, Mary Ellen 1929- ... 23-24R
Rickman, Geoffrey (Edwin) 1932- ... 29-32R
Rickman, H(ans) P(eter) 1918- ... 19-20R
Ricks, Christopher (Bruce) 1933- ... CANR-7
Earlier sketch in CA 11-12R
Ricks, David F(rank) 1927- ... 21-22R
Ricks, David Trulock 1936- ... 25-28R
Ricks, Don(ald) M(ax) 1936- ... 25-28R
Ricks, Nadine 1925- ... 77-80
Rickword, (John) Edgell 1898-1982 ... 101
Obituary ... 106
Rico, Don 1917- ... 81-84
Ricoeur, Paul 1913- ... 61-64
Ricou, Laurence (Rodger) 1944- ... 61-64
Riday, George E(mil) 1912- ... 15-16R
Riddel, Frank S(tephen) 1940- ... 85-88
Riddel, Joseph N(eill) 1931- ... CANR-5
Earlier sketch in CA 9-10R
Riddell, Alan 1927- ... 104
Ridder, Marie 1925- ... 73-76
Ridderbos, Herman N(icolaas) 1909- ... 57-60
Riddle, Donald H(usted) 1921- ... 11-12R
Riddle, John M(arion) 1937- ... 45-48
Riddle, Kenneth Wilkinson 1920- ... 3R
Riddle, Maxwell 1907- ... CANR-3
Earlier sketch in CA 7-8R
Riddleberger, Patrick Williams 1915- ... 21-22R
Ridenour, George M(eyer) 1928- ... 93-96
Ridenour, Ron 1939- ... 69-72
Rider, Alice Damon 1895- ... 69-72
Rider, (Arthur) Fremont
1885-1962 Obituary ... 89-92
Rider, John R. 1923- ... 25-28R
Ridge, Antonia (Florence) ?-1981 ... 9-10R
Obituary ... 104
See also SATA 7, 27
Ridge, George Ross 1931- ... 3R
Ridgely, Beverly S(ellman) 1920- ... 25-28R
Ridgely, Joseph Vincent 1921- ... 7-8R
Ridgeway, James Fowler 1936- ... 106
Ridgeway, Jason
See Marlowe, Stephen
Ridgeway, Marian E(lizabeth) 1913- ... 33-36R
Ridgeway, Rick 1949- ... 93-96
Ridgway, Brunilde Sismondo 1929- ... CANR-1
Earlier sketch in CA 45-48
Ridgway, John M. 1938- ... 25-28R
Ridgway, Ronald S(idney) 1923- ... 45-48
Ridgway, Whitman H(awley) 1941- ... 101
Riding, Laura
See Jackson, Laura (Riding)
See also CLC 3, 7
Ridle, Julia Brown 1923- ... 4R
Ridler, Anne Barbara 1912- ... CANR-3
Earlier sketch in CA 5-6R
Ridley, B(rian) K(idd) 1931- ... 104
Ridley, Charles P(rice) 1933- ... 73-76
Ridley, Jasper (Godwin) 1920- ... CANR-6
Earlier sketch in CA 13-14R
Ridley, Nat, Jr. ... CAP-2
Earlier sketch in CA 19-20
Ridlon, Marci
See Balterman, Marcia Ridlon
See also SATA 22
Ridout, Albert K(ilburn) 1905- ... CAP-2
Earlier sketch in CA 19-20
Ridout, Ronald 1916- ... 103
Ridpath, Ian (William) 1947- ... 77-80
Ridruejo, Dionisio 1913(?)-1975 Obituary . 57-60
Rieber, Alfred J(oseph) 1931- ... 11-12R
Rieber, R(obert) W(olff) 1932- ... CANR-3
Earlier sketch in CA 45-48
Riedel, Richard Langham 1908- ... CAP-2
Earlier sketch in CA 29-32
Riedel, Walter E(rwin) 1936- ... 45-48
Riedesel, C(lark) Alan 1930- ... 25-28R
Riedl, John O(rth) 1905- ... CAP-2
Earlier sketch in CA 21-22
Riedman, Sarah R(egal) 1902- ... CANR-1
Earlier sketch in CA 4R
See also SATA 1
Riefe, Alan 1925- ... 61-64
Riefe, Barbara
See Riefe, Alan
Riefenstahl, Leni 1902- ... CLC-16
Rieff, Philip 1922- ... 49-52
Riegel, Robert Edgar 1897- ... 5-6R
Rieger, James H(enry) 1936- ... 93-96
Rieger, Shay 1929- ... 29-32R
Riegert, Eduard Richard 1932- ... 69-72
Riegert, Ray 1947- ... 105
Riemer, George 1920-1973 ... CAP-2
Obituary ... 41-44R
Earlier sketch in CA 25-28
Riemer, Neal 1922- ... 21-22R
Rienits, Rex 1909-1971 ... CAP-1
Obituary ... 29-32R
Earlier sketch in CA 13-14
Rienow, Robert 1909- ... 21-22R
Riepe, Dale (Maurice) 1918- ... 37-40R
Ries, Estelle H. 1896- ... 25-28R
Ries, John C(harles) 1930- ... 15-16R
Ries, Lawrence R(obert) 1940- ... 65-68
Riese, Walther 1890- ... 49-52
Rieseberg, Harry E(arl) 1892- ... 5-6R
Rieselbach, Leroy N(ewman) 1934- ... 23-24R
Riesenberg, Felix, Jr. 1913-1962 ... 101
See also SATA 23
Riesenberg, Saul H(erbert) 1911- ... 49-52
Rieser, Henry
See MacDonald, John D(ann)
Riesman, David 1909- ... 7-8R
Riesman, Evelyn Thompson 1912- ... 21-22R
Riess, Oswald George Lorenz 1896- ... 7-8R
Riess, Walter 1925- ... 19-20R
Riessen, Martin Clare 1941- ... 41-44R
Riessman, Frank 1924- ... CANR-6
Earlier sketch in CA 2R
Riesterer, Berthold P(hillip) 1935- ... 41-44R
Rieu, E(mile) V(ictor) 1887-1972 ... 4R
Obituary ... 103
See also SATA 26
Riewald, J(acobus) G(erhardus) 1910- .. CANR-6
Earlier sketch in CA 57-60
Rife, J(ohn) Merle 1895- ... 61-64
Riffe, Ernest
See Bergman, (Ernst) Ingmar
Rifkin, Shepard 1918- ... CANR-1
Earlier sketch in CA 3R
Rifkind, Carole 1935- ... 85-88
Rift, Valerie
See Bartlett, Marie (Swan)
Riga, Frank P(eter) 1936- ... 89-92
Riga, Peter J(ohn) 1933- ... 5-6R
Rigault, Andre 1922- ... 45-48
Rigby, Andrew 1944- ... 61-64
Rigby, Ida Katherine 1944- ... 65-68
Rigby, Paul H(erbert) 1924- ... 19-20R
Rigby, T(homas) H(enry Richard) 1925- . 19-20R
Rigdon, Raymond M. 1919- ... 29-32R
Rigdon, Walter 1930- ... 15-16R
Rigg, A(rthur) G(eorge) 1937- ... 37-40R
Rigg, H(enry Hemmingway) K(ilburn)
1911-1980 ... 29-32R
Obituary ... 93-96
Rigg, John Linton 1894- ... 7-8R
Rigg, Robinson P(eter) 1918- ... 33-36R
Riggan, William (Edward, Jr.) 1946- ... 103
Riggs, Dionis Coffin 1898- ... CAP-2
Earlier sketch in CA 29-32
Riggs, Fred(erick) W(arren) 1917- ... 25-28R
Riggs, James (Lear) 1929- ... 33-36R
Riggs, Robert E. 1927- ... 15-16R
Riggs, Sidney Noyes 1892-1975 ... 2R
Obituary ... 103
Riggs, William (George) 1938- ... 61-64
Righter, Carroll 1900- ... 93-96
Rigoni, Orlando (Joseph) 1897- ... 15-16R
Rigsby, Howard 1909- ... 11-12R
Riha, Thomas 1929- ... 11-12R
Riker, Tom L. 1936- ... 104
Riker, William H(arrison) 1920- ... 4R
Rikhoff, James C. 1931- ... 13-14R
Rikhoff, Jean 1928- ... 61-64
See also SATA 9
Rikhye, Indar Jit 1920- ... 93-96
Rikki
See Ducornet, Erica
Rikon, Irving 1931- ... 29-32R
Riley, Carroll L(averne) 1923- ... 25-28R
Riley, Clara (Mae Deatherage) 1931- ... 25-28R
Riley, Dick 1946- ... 101
Riley, E(dward) C(alverley) 1923- ... 11-12R
Riley, G. Micheal 1934- ... 45-48
Riley, Glenda 1938- ... 106
Riley, James F. 1912- ... 29-32R
Riley, James Whitcomb 1849-1916 ... SATA-17
Riley, Lawrence 1897(?)-1975 Obituary ... 61-64
Riley, Madeleine 1933- ... 25-28R
Riley, Miles O'Brien 1937- ... 104
Riley, (Thomas) Nord 1914- ... 13-14R
Riley, (Hugh) Ridge(ly, Jr.) 1907-1976 ... 101
Riley, Roy, Jr. 1943(?)-1977 Obituary ... 73-76
Riley, Sandra 1938- ... 104
Riley, Tex
See Creasey, John
Riley, Thomas J. 1901(?)-1977 Obituary .. 73-76
Riley-Smith, Jonathan (Simon Christopher)
1938- ... 23-24R
Riling, Raymond L. J.
1896(?)-1974 Obituary ... 53-56
Rilke, Rainer Maria 1875-1926 Brief entry .. 104
Rilla, Wolf 1925- ... 49-52
Rils
See Bohr, R(ussell) L(eRoi)
Rima, I(ngrid) H(ahne) 1925- ... 23-24R
Rimanoczy, Richard Stanton 1902- ... 73-76
Rimberg, John 1929- ... 57-60
Rimel, Duane (Weldon) 1915- ... 29-32R
Rimington, Critchell 1907-1976 Obituary .. 61-64
Rimland, Bernard 1928- ... CANR-6
Earlier sketch in CA 15-16R
Rimland, Ingrid 1936- ... 61-64
Rimlinger, Gaston V. 1926- ... 37-40R
Rimmer, C(harles) Brandon 1918- ... 61-64
Rimmer, Robert H(enry) 1917- ... CANR-4
Earlier sketch in CA 11-12R
Rimmer, W. J.
See Rowland, D(onald) S(ydney)
Rimmington, Gerald T(horneycroft) 1930- 19-20R
Rinaldi, Nicholas 1934- ... 104
Rinaldini, Angiolo
See Battisti, Eugenio
Rinard, Judith E(llen) 1947- ... 97-100
Rinchen, Byambyn
1905(?)-1977 Obituary ... 69-72
Rinder, Walter Murray 1934- ... 69-72
Rindfleisch, Norval (William) 1930- ... 65-68

INDEX

INDEX

INDEX

INDEX

INDEX

INDEX

INDEX

INDEX

INDEX

INDEX

INDEX

INDEX

INDEX

INDEX

INDEX

INDEX

INDEX

INDEX

INDEX

INDEX

INDEX

INDEX

INDEX

Withers, Sara Cook 1924- 17-18R
Withers, William 1905- 13-14R
Witherspoon, Frances
1887(?)-1973 Obituary 45-48
Witherspoon, Irene Murray 1913- CANR-1
Earlier sketch in CA 4R
Witherspoon, Mary Elizabeth 1919- 77-80
Witherspoon, Naomi Long
See Madgett, Naomi Long
Witherspoon, Thomas E. 1934- 81-84
Withey, J(oseph) A(nthony) 1918- 25-28R
Withington, William Adriance 1924- 41-44R
Withrow, Dorothy E. 1910- 21-22R
Witkacy
See Witkiewicz, Stanislaw Ignacy
Witke, Roxane 1938- 69-72
Witker, Kristi 77-80
Witkiewicz, Stanislaw Ignacy
1885-1939 Brief entry 105
Witkin, Erwin 1926- 37-40R
Witkin, Herman A. 1916-1979 CANR-1
Earlier sketch in CA 2R
Witmer, Helen L(eland) 1898-1979 CAP-2
Obituary 89-92
Earlier sketch in CA 25-28
Witt, Harold (Vernon) 1923- CANR-1
Earlier sketch in CA 3R
Witt, Hubert 1935- 65-68
Witt, James F. 1937- 89-92
Witt, John (Clermont)
1907-1982 Obituary 106
Witt, Reginald Eldred 1907-1980 37-40R
Obituary 97-100
Witt, Shirley Hill 1934- CANR-5
Earlier sketch in CA 53-56
See also SATA 17
Witte, Glenna Finley 1925- 15-16R
See also AITN 1
Witte, John 1948- 93-96
Witten, Herbert F. 1920- 5-6R
Wittenberg, Judith Bryant 1938- 102
Wittenberg, Philip 1895- CAP-2
Earlier sketch in CA 23-24
Wittenberg, Rudolph M. 1906- 69-72
Wittermans, Elizabeth (Pino) 17-18R
Witters, Weldon L. 1929- 93-96
Wittich, Walter A(rno) 1910- 49-52
Wittig, Alice J(osephine) 1929- 101
Witting, Clifford 1907- 4R
Wittke, Carl (Frederick)
1892-1971 Obituary 29-32R
Wittkofski, Joseph Nicholas 1912- 9-10R
Wittkower, Rudolf 1901-1971 Obituary 33-36R
Wittkowski, Wolfgang 1925- 61-64
Wittlin, Alma S(tephanie) 45-48
Wittlin, Jozef 1896-1976 CANR-3
Obituary 65-68
Earlier sketch in CA 49-52
Wittlin, Thaddeus (Andrew) 1909- CANR-2
Earlier sketch in CA 45-48
Wittmer, Joe 1937- 45-48
Wittner, Lawrence S(tephen) 1941- 25-28R
Witton, Dorothy 73-76
Witton-Davies, Carl(yle) 1913- 9-10R
Wittreich, Joseph Anthony, Jr. 1939- 29-32R
Wittrock, M(erlin) C(arl) 1931- CANR-2
Earlier sketch in CA 49-52
Witty, Helen E. S(troop) 1921- 105
Witty, Paul 1898-1976 73-76
Obituary 65-68
Witty, Robert G(ee) 1906- CAP-2
Earlier sketch in CA 23-24
Witucke, Virginia 1937- 37-40R
Witze, Claude 1909(?)-1977 Obituary 73-76
Wizard, Mariann G(arner) 1946- 37-40R
Wobbe, R(oland) A(rthur) 1938- 102
Wodehouse, Lawrence 1934- CANR-4
Earlier sketch in CA 53-56
Wodehouse, P(elham) G(renville)
1881-1975 CANR-3
Obituary 57-60
Earlier sketch in CA 45-48
See also CLC 1, 2, 5, 10
See also SATA 22
See also AITN 2
Woden, George
See Slaney, George Wilson
Wodge, Dreary
See Gorey, Edward (St. John)
Woebcke, Mary-Jane 1933- 25-28R
Woehr, Richard (Arthur) 1942- 57-60
Woehrlin, William F(rederick) 1928- 45-48
Woelfel, James W(arren) 1937- 41-44R
Woelfl, Paul A(loysius) 1913- 17-18R
Woessner, Nina C. 1933- 29-32R
Woessner, Warren (Dexter) 1944- 37-40R
Woestemeyer, Ina Faye
See Van Noppen, Ina (Faye)
W(oestemeyer)
Woetzel, Robert K(urt) 1930- CANR-6
Earlier sketch in CA 5-6R
Wofford, Azile (May) 1896- 5-6R
Wofsey, Marvin M(ilton) 1913- 105
Wogaman, (John) Philip 1932- 25-28R
Wohl, Gerald 1934- 19-20R
Wohl, James P(aul) 1937- 77-80
Wohl, Robert 1936- 104
Wohlgelernter, Maurice 1921- CANR-6
Earlier sketch in CA 15-16R
Wohlrabe, Raymond A. 1900-1977 CANR-3
Earlier sketch in CA 4R
See also SATA 4
Woititz, Janet G. 101
Woiwode, Larry (Alfred) 1941- 73-76
See also CLC 6, 10
Wojciechowska, Maia (Teresa) 1927- CANR-4
Earlier sketch in CA 11-12R
See also SATA 1
Wojtyla, Karol
See John Paul II, Pope
Wolberg, Lewis Robert 1905- CANR-2
Earlier sketch in CA 45-48
Wolcott, Harry F(letcher) 1929- 65-68
Wolcott, Leonard Thompson 13-14R
Wolcott, Patty 1929- 57-60
See also SATA 14
Wold, Allen L. 1943- 105
Wold, Jo Anne 1938- 61-64
Wold, Marguerite Hurrey 1914- 53-56
Wold, Ruth 1923- 37-40R
Woldendorp, R(ichard) 1927- 29-32R
Woldin, Beth Weiner 1955- 102
Wolf, Arnold Jacob 1924- 29-32R
Wolf, Arnold Veryl 1916-1975 Obituary 104
Wolf, Barbara Herrman 1932- 57-60
Wolf, Charlotte (Elizabeth) 1926- 29-32R
Wolf, Christa 1929- 85-88
See also CLC 14
Wolf, Deborah Goleman 1938- 97-100
Wolf, Donald J(oseph) 1929- 13-14R
Wolf, Edwin II 1911- CANR-4
Earlier sketch in CA 2R
Wolf, Eric R(obert) 1923- 19-20R
Wolf, Frank 1940- 57-60
Wolf, Frank L(ouis) 1924- 57-60
Wolf, Frederick
See Dempewolff, Richard F(rederic)
Wolf, George 1890(?)-1980 Obituary 97-100
Wolf, George D(ugan) 1923- 29-32R
Wolf, Harold A. 1923- 15-16R
Wolf, Harvey 1935- 57-60
Wolf, Hazel Catharine 1907- 7-8R
Wolf, Herbert C(hristian) 1923- 15-16R
Wolf, Jack C(lifford) 1922- 57-60
Wolf, John B(aptist) 1907- 11-12R
Wolf, Karl E(verett) 1921- 17-18R
Wolf, Leonard 1923- CANR-3
Earlier sketch in CA 49-52
Wolf, Miriam Bredow 1895- CAP-1
Earlier sketch in CA 9-10
Wolf, Peter (Michael) 1935- 53-56
Wolf, Thomas H(oward) 1916- 69-72
Wolf, William 103
Wolf, William B. 1920- 19-20R
Wolf, William C(harles), Jr. 1933- 41-44R
Wolfbein, Seymour L(ouis) 1915- CANR-6
Earlier sketch in CA 13-14R
Wolfe, Alvin William 1928- 2R
Wolfe, Bernard 1915- CANR-3
Earlier sketch in CA 3R
Wolfe, Bertram D(avid) 1896-1977 7-8R
Obituary 69-72
Wolfe, Burton H. 1932- 25-28R
See also SATA 5
Wolfe, Charles Keith 1943- 77-80
Wolfe, Don Marion 1902-1976 Obituary 65-68
Wolfe, (George) Edgar 1906- CAP-2
Earlier sketch in CA 25-28
Wolfe, Gene (Rodman) 1931- CANR-6
Earlier sketch in CA 57-60
Wolfe, Gerard R(aymond) 1926- 69-72
Wolfe, Harry Deane 1901-1975 41-44R
Wolfe, Harvey 1938- 45-48
Wolfe, Henry C. 1898(?)-1976 Obituary 69-72
Wolfe, Herbert S(now) 1898- CAP-1
Earlier sketch in CA 15-16
Wolfe, James H(astings) 1934- 93-96
Wolfe, John N. 1910(?)-1974 Obituary 53-56
Wolfe, Josephine Brace 1917- 7-8R
Wolfe, Louis 1905- CANR-3
Earlier sketch in CA 5-6R
See also SATA 8
Wolfe, Martin 1920- 37-40R
Wolfe, Michael
See Williams, Gilbert M.
Wolfe, Peter 1933- 21-22R
Wolfe, Randolph 1946- 104
Wolfe, Rinna (Evelyn) 1925- 105
Wolfe, Roy I. 1917- 13-14R
Wolfe, Thomas (Clayton)
1900-1938 Brief entry 104
Wolfe, Thomas Kennerly, Jr. 1931- 15-16R
Wolfe, Thomas W. 1914- 93-96
Wolfe, Tom
See Wolfe, Thomas Kennerly, Jr.
See also CLC 1, 2, 9, 15
See also AITN 2
Wolfe, (William) Willard 1936- 93-96
Wolfe, Winifred 1929-1981 17-18R
Obituary 105
Wolfenden, George
See Beardmore, George
Wolfenden, John Frederick 1906- 106
Wolfenstein, E. Victor 1940- 21-22R
Wolfenstein, Martha
1911(?)-1976 Obituary 69-72
Wolfert, Helen 1904- CAP-2
Earlier sketch in CA 17-18
Wolff, Anthony 1938- 49-52
Wolff, Charlotte 1904- 37-40R
Wolff, Cynthia Griffin 1936- 49-52
Wolff, Diane 1945- 77-80
See also SATA 27
Wolff, Ernst, 1910- 73-76
Wolff, Geoffrey (Ansell) 1937- 29-32R
Wolff, Janet 1943- 77-80
Wolff, Janet L(oeb) 1924- 5-6R
Wolff, John U(lrich) 1932- 102
Wolff, Jurgen M(ichael) 1948- 57-60
Wolff, Konrad (Martin) 1907- 37-40R
Wolff, Kurt H(einrich) 1912- CANR-1
Earlier sketch in CA 49-52
Wolff, Maritta 1918- 17-18R
Wolff, Michael 1930- 25-28R
Wolff, Miles 1945- 73-76
Wolff, Richard D(avid) 1942- 73-76
Wolff, Robert Jay 1905-1977 25-28R
Obituary 73-76
See also SATA 10
Wolff, Robert Lee 1915-1980 Obituary 102
Wolff, Robert Paul 1933- 103
Wolff, Ruth 1909(?)-1972 Obituary 37-40R
Wolfgang, Marvin E(ugene) 1924- 7-8R
Wolfle, Dael (Lee) 1906- 49-52
Wolfman, Augustus
1908(?)-1974 Obituary 53-56
Wolfman, Bernard 1924- 41-44R
Wolf-Phillips, Leslie 1929- 23-24R
Wolfram, Walter A. 1941- 29-32R
Wolfskill, George 1921- CANR-1
Earlier sketch in CA 2R
Wolfson, Harry Austryn 1887-1974 CAP-2
Obituary 53-56
Earlier sketch in CA 19-20
Wolfson, Murray 1927- 17-18R
Wolfson, P(incus) J. 1903- 7-8R
Wolfson, Robert J(oseph) 1925- 93-96
Wolfson, Victor 1910- 33-36R
Wolgensinger, Bernard 1935- 37-40R
Wolitzer, Hilma 1930- 65-68
See also CLC 17
Wolk, Allan 1936- 77-80
Wolkstein, Diane 1942- 37-40R
See also SATA 7
Woll, Peter 1933- 15-16R
Wollaston, Nicholas 1926- 25-28R
Wolle, Muriel Sibell 1898- CAP-1
Earlier sketch in CA 13-14
Wollheim, Donald A(llen) 1914- CANR-1
Earlier sketch in CA 4R
Wollheim, Richard Arthur 1923- 101
Wollman, Nathaniel 1915- Brief entry 106
Wolman, Benjamin B. 1908- 15-16R
Wolman, Harold L. 1942- 37-40R
Wolman, William 1927- 2R
Wolny, P.
See Janeczko, Paul B(ryan)
Woloch, Isser 1937- 29-32R
Woloszynowski, Julian
1898-1978 Obituary 85-88
Wolozin, Harold 1920- 37-40R
Wolpe, Joseph 1915- 17-18R
Wolpert, Stanley A(lbert) 1927- 23-24R
Wolrige Gordon, Anne 1936- 103
Wolsch, Robert Allen 1925- 57-60
Wolseley, Roland E. 1904- CANR-1
Earlier sketch in CA 2R
Wolsk, David 1930- 23-24R
Wolstein, Benjamin 1922- 11-12R
Wolter, Allan B(ernard) 1913- 106
Wolters, O(liver) W(illiam) 1915- 21-22R
Wolters, Raymond 1938- 29-32R
Wolters, Richard A. 1920- CANR-3
Earlier sketch in CA 7-8R
Wolterstorff, Nicholas Paul 1932- 69-72
Woltman, Frederick (Enos)
1905-1970 Obituary 89-92
Wolverton, Robert E(arl) 1925- 37-40R
Wolz, Henry G(eorge) 1905- 106
Womack, David A(lfred) 1933- CANR-7
Earlier sketch in CA 53-56
Womack, Don (L.) 1922- 25-28R
Womack, John, Jr. 1937- 45-48
Womble, Vernon G.
1942(?)-1979 Obituary 89-92
Womer, Frank B(urton) 1921- 45-48
Won, Ko
See Ko, Won
Wonder, Alvin
See Lourie, Dick
Wonder, Stevie 1950- CLC-12
Wonders, Anne
See Passel, Anne W(onders)
Wonders, William C(lare) 1924- 41-44R
Wondriska, William 1931- CANR-4
Earlier sketch in CA 4R
See also SATA 6
Wong, Bing W. 1922- 73-76
Wong, Jade Snow 1922- CLC-17
Wong, Lin Ken 1931- 13-14R
Wong, May 1944- 25-28R
Wong, Molly 1920- 93-96
Wong, Roderick 1932- 65-68
Wonnacott, Paul 1933- 21-22R
Wonnacott, Ronald J(ohnston) 1930- 29-32R
Wonnacott, Thomas H(erbert) 1935- 45-48
Wood, A(rthur) Skevington 1916- CANR-3
Earlier sketch in CA 11-12R
Wood, Allen Tate 1947- 97-100
Wood, Allen W(illiam) 1942- 29-32R
Wood, Barbara 1947- 85-88
Wood, Bari 1936- 81-84
Wood, Barry 1940- 29-32R
Wood, Bruce 1943- 57-60
Wood, Bryce 1909- 2R
Wood, Catherine
See Etchison, Birdie L(ee)
Wood, Charles Gerald 1932- 106
Wood, Charles T(uttle) 1933- 17-18R
Wood, Chauncey 1935- 37-40R
Wood, Christopher (Hovelle) 1935- 29-32R
Wood, Christopher 1941- 103
Wood, Clement Biddle 1925- 21-22R
Wood, David (Bowne) 1945- 93-96
Wood, David 1944- 97-100
Wood, Derek Harold 1930- 93-96
Wood, Donald 1926- 45-48
Wood, Donna (Marie) 1949- 97-100
Wood, Dorothy Adkins 1912-1975 CANR-6
Earlier sketch in CA 13-14R
Wood, E(dward) Rudolf 1907- CANR-3
Earlier sketch in CA 11-12R
Wood, Edgar A(llardyce) 1907- 77-80
See also SATA 14
Wood, Elizabeth A(rmstrong) 1912- 25-28R
Wood, Esther
See Brady, Esther Wood
Wood, Forrest G(len) 1931- 25-28R
Wood, Fred M. 15-16R
Wood, Frederic C(onger), Jr. 1932-1970 CAP-2
Earlier sketch in CA 25-28
Wood, Frederick Thomas 1905- CANR-5
Earlier sketch in CA 7-8R
Wood, G(eorge) R(obert) Harding
1878-1968 CAP-1
Earlier sketch in CA 9-10
Wood, Gordon R(eid) 1913- 77-80
Wood, Gordon S(tewart) 1933- 25-28R
Wood, Harold A(rthur) 1921- 19-20R
Wood, James 1889(?)-1975 Obituary 57-60
Wood, James (Alexander Fraser) 1918- CANR-1
Earlier sketch in CA 2R
Wood, James E(dward), Jr. 1922- 29-32R
Wood, James L(eslie) 1941- 57-60
Wood, James Playsted 1905- CANR-3
Earlier sketch in CA 9-10R
See also SATA 1
Wood, John Thomas 1939- 77-80
Wood, Joyce 1928- 25-28R
Wood, June S(mallwood) 1931- 61-64
Wood, Kenneth 1922- 69-72
Wood, Kerry
See Wood, Edgar A(llardyce)
Wood, Kirk
See Stahl, Le Roy
Wood, Larry
See Wood, Marylaird
Wood, Laura N.
See Roper, Laura Wood
Wood, Lee Blair 1893-1982 Obituary 106
Wood, Leland Foster 1885- 2R
Wood, Leon J. 1918- 29-32R
Wood, Leonard C(lair) 1923- 37-40R
Wood, Leslie A(lfred) 1930- 29-32R
Wood, (James) Lew(is) 1928- 65-68
Wood, Lorna 1913- 69-72
Wood, Margaret (L. E.) 1910- 13-14R
Wood, Margaret I(sabel) 1926- 97-100
Wood, Marion N(ewman) 1909- 61-64
Wood, Mary 1915- 23-24R
Wood, Marylaird 81-84
Wood, Michael 1936- 37-40R
Wood, Nancy 1936- 21-22R
See also SATA 6
Wood, Neal (Norman) 1922- 2R
Wood, Paul W(inthrop) 1922- 61-64
Wood, Peggy 1892-1978 Obituary 77-80
Wood, Peter 1930- 93-96
Wood, Phyllis Anderson 1923- 37-40R
Wood, R(ichard) Coke 1905-1979 CANR-7
Earlier sketch in CA 53-56
Wood, Ramsay 1943- 103
Wood, Raymund F(rancis) 1911- 61-64
Wood, Robert Coldwell 1923- 3R
Wood, Robert L. 1925- 23-24R
Wood, Robert Paul 1931- CANR-5
Earlier sketch in CA 53-56
Wood, Robert S(tephen) 1938- CANR-7
Earlier sketch in CA 57-60
Wood, Robin
See Wood, Robert Paul
Wood, Ruth C. 37-40R
Wood, Serry
See Freeman, G(raydon) L(a Verne)
Wood, Thomas W(esley), Jr. 1920- 81-84
Wood, Ursula
See Vaughan Williams, Ursula Wood
Woodall, Corbet 1929(?)-1982 Obituary 106
Woodall, Ronald 1935- 73-76
Woodard, Bronte 1941(?)-1980 Obituary 101
Woodard, Carol 1929- 73-76
See also SATA 14
Woodard, Christopher R. 1913- 13-14R
Woodard, Gloria (Jean) H(iner) 1937- 45-48
Woodberry, Joan (Merle) 1921- CANR-6
Earlier sketch in CA 11-12R
Woodbridge, Hensley Charles 1923- CANR-3
Earlier sketch in CA 9-10R
Woodburn, John Henry 1914- CANR-4
Earlier sketch in CA 4R
See also SATA 11
Woodbury, Lael J(ay) 1927- 81-84
Woodbury, Marda 1925- 97-100
Woodbury, Mildred Fairchild
1894-1975 Obituary 57-60
Woodcock, George 1912- CANR-1
Earlier sketch in CA 3R
Woodcott, Keith
See Brunner, John (Kilian Houston)
Wooden, Kenneth 1935- 81-84
Woodfield, William Read 1928- 9-10R
Woodford, Arthur M(acKinnon) 1940- CANR-7
Earlier sketch in CA 53-56
Woodford, Bruce P(owers) 1919- 57-60
Woodford, Frank B(ury) 1903-1967 CAP-1
Earlier sketch in CA 15-16
Woodford, Jack
See Woolfolk, Josiah Pitts
Woodford, Peggy 1937- 104
See also SATA 25
Woodforde, John 1925- 25-28R
Woodgate, Mildred Violet 11-12R
Woodham-Smith, Cecil (Blanche Fitzgerald)
1896-1977 77-80
Obituary 69-72
Woodhouse, Barbara Blackburn 1910- 7-8R
Woodhouse, Charles Platten 1915- 105
Woodhouse, Martin 1932- 21-22R
Woodin, Ann Snow 1926- 13-14R
Woodin, Noel 1929- 4R
Wooding, Dan 1940- 102
Woodiwiss, Kathleen E. 89-92
Wood-Legh, Kathleen Louise
1901-1981 Obituary 105

INDEX

INDEX